With this new 1983 edition
of The Answer Book—

- students do better classwork (and *faster* homework)
- parents can answer the 1,001 questions that children ask
- executives can find basic business data quickly
- Crossword fans can solve more difficult puzzles
- *anyone* can answer the little questions of daily living (postage, taxes, metrics, distances, sports, celebrity birthdates)—and the larger questions, too (history, science, statistics, world affairs).

If you need to know, turn to

INFORMATION PLEASE!

READER SURVEY

Could we have some information, please?

We want **Information Please** to be as useful as possible to you. The more we know about our readers and their requirements, the better we, in "The Answer Book," can supply the answers you need.

Would you, therefore, take a moment to give *us* some answers, about yourself and the way you use this Almanac? We'll read your replies carefully, and use them to create an even more helpful book for you in future years.

Please check the sections you find most useful:

____ Special articles
____ Election of 1982
____ Current Events
____ Headline History
____ Business and the Economy
____ Energy
____ Environment
____ World and U.S. Statistics
____ Countries of the World
____ Canada
____ Calendar and Holidays
____ Weights and Measures
____ Weather and Climate
____ Science
____ Astronomy
____ Space
____ Religion
____ Travel
____ Structures
____ United Nations
____ Aviation
____ Military
____ Disasters
____ First Aid
____ Nutrition and Health
____ Where to Find Out More
____ Writer's Guide
____ Crossword Puzzle Guide
____ Geography and Maps
____ U.S. History & Government
____ Postage
____ U.S. Societies
____ Awards
____ People
____ Guide to Growing Older
____ Taxes
____ Media
____ Education
____ Sports
____ Entertainment and Culture

Where do you use **Information Please** the most?

___At home ___At work ___In school ___In college

Your age?

___under 18 ___18–25 ___26–45 ___46–60 ___over 60

Your education?

___now in school ___high school graduate ___some college ___college graduate

Your occupation? ____________________

Have you bought Information Please before? ____________________

How often do you buy an almanac? (every year, every 2 years, etc.)? ____________

We would be very pleased to have you make any other comments you think would be helpful.

Please return this information to the Editor, Information Please Almanac, A&W Publishers, Inc., 95 Madison Avenue, New York, N.Y., 10016.

For convenience, you can remove this page simply by cutting along the dotted line. Or, if you prefer, send us a letter. In either case, we would be grateful for your help.

INFORMATION PLEASE ALMANAC

ATLAS & YEARBOOK

1983

37th EDITION

INFORMATION PLEASE PUBLISHERS
A DIVISION OF
A&W PUBLISHERS, INC.
NEW YORK

Editor
Otto T. Johnson
Associate Editor
Natalie M. Aust
Senior Editors
Vera J. Dailey
George De Gregorio
Arthur Neuhauser
Arthur P. Reed, Jr.
Editors
Konrad J. A. Kundig (Science)
Blanche Ormont (Writer's Guide)
Don Shannon (Countries of the World)
Staff
Editorial Assistants: Lois
Cantor, Ruth Livingston,
and Brent Spencer
Cover Design
Martin S. Moskof and Associates
Maps
Maps copyright © Hammond Incorporated.
Requests for maps should be sent to Hammond Incorporated, Maplewood, New Jersey 07040.

The Information Please Almanac invites comments and suggestions from readers. Because of the many letters received, however, it is not possible to respond personally to every correspondent. Nevertheless, all suggestions are most wlecome, and the editors will consider them carefully. (Information Please Almanac does not rule on bets or wagers.)

Library of Congress Number: 47-845
ISBN (Hardcover): 0-89104-317-9
ISBN (Paperback): 0-89104-316-0

 Published by A&W Publishers, Inc. 95 Madison Avenue, New York, 10016. Manufactured in the United States of America.

Previous editions of INFORMATION PLEASE were published in 1981, 1980, and 1979 by Simon & Schuster, in 1978 and 1977 by Information Please Publishing, Inc., and 1976–1947 by Dan Golenpaul Associates.

INFORMATION PLEASE ALMANAC
Editorial Office
A&W Publishers, Inc.
95 Madison Avenue
New York, N.Y. 10016

CONTENTS

The Comprehensive Index lists in alphabetical order all the important topics, terms, and names covered and gives the page or pages on which they appear • To find a fact, date, or idea, begin by looking under the most specific word. For example, to find the population of Des Moines, start by looking for *Des Moines.* But that city is not listed separately. Therefore, the next step is to look under *Iowa* or *Cities, U.S.* Under *Iowa* the designated page gives the latest population of Des Moines. Under *Cities, U.S.* there is a subhead, *Population figures,* with three alternatives: *Largest* (of which Des Moines is not one), *Largest by state* (which refers back to *Iowa*), and *1970–1980 (table)* (where Des Moines is listed alphabetically). • For President George Washington, look under *Washington,* before checking *President.* Where general headings (such as *Presidents, U.S.*) are given, they refer to a section where the subject is treated at some length.

Cutting the Cost of Higher Education

A Guide to Five Federal Financial Aid Programs

For many years, the federal government has been the major source of direct financial aid for students. The total amount of guaranteed loans rose to a record $8 billion in 1981 and cost the government about $2.5 billion in subsidies. Because of these spiraling costs the Reagan administration, which is committed to lowering the federal budget, proposed changes in the student aid programs. Subsequently, the administration got Congress to pass significent cuts in federal loans and grants, including the requirement that loans be based on need. In addition, Social Security benefits for students are being phased out by 1985.

The federal student aid programs are still the major sources of income to help college students and their parents hold down the cost of higher education. This report outlines the new changes and requirements for student grants and loans, and explains how, when, and where to apply for them.

It is possible that Congress may enact additional changes regarding these federal programs during the year.

GENERAL INFORMATION

The U.S. Department of Education offers five major student financial aid programs: **Pell Grants; Supplemental Educational Opportunity Grants (SEOG); College Work-Study (CW-S); National Direct Student Loans (NDSL); Guaranteed Student Loans (GSL); and PLUS loans.**

Grants are awards of money that the recipient does not have to pay back.

Work-Study gives a student the chance to work and earn the money needed.

Loans are borrowed money that the recipient *must* repay with interest.

Eligibility

A student is generally eligible for aid if:

- He or she is enrolled at least *half-time*[1] as a regular student in an eligible program at one of the more than 7,000 colleges, universities, vocational schools, technical schools, or hospital schools of nursing that take part in Department of Education financial aid programs.
- The student is a U.S. citizen or an eligible noncitizen.
- The student can show need.
- The student is making *satisfactory progress*[2] toward completing the chosen course of study.
- The student is not in default on a National Direct Student Loan, Guaranteed Student Loan, or PLUS Loan at the school attended.
- The student does not owe a refund on a Pell Grant or a Supplemental Educational Opportunity Grant at the school attended.

Undergraduates may apply for any program. Graduate students may apply for any program except Pell Grants and Supplemental Educational Opportunity Grants.

Not all schools take part in all the programs. To check the eligibility of a school and its programs, as well as the availability of financial aid, contact the school's financial aid office.

Need

Federal student aid is awarded on the basis of need. Need is determined by evaluating the information a student fills in on an aid application. Factors such as income, *assets,*[1] and family size are all considered in determining an applicant's need for aid.

Applying

A student may apply by filling out any of these forms:

- The U.S. Department of Education's Application for Federal Student Aid (AFSA).
- The College Scholarship Service's Financial Aid Form (FAF).
- The American College Testing Program's Family Financial Statement (FFS).
- The Pennsylvania Higher Education Assistance Agency (PHEAA) Form.
- The Student Aid Application for California (SAAC).

To find out which form to use, contact the financial aid administrator at each school being considered. There is no charge for applying if the Department of Education's application form is used. If an applicant uses one of the other forms listed above, the organizations that distribute them charge a fee to process the information.

Aid from these programs does not automatically continue from one year to the next. One must reapply every year.

Student Aid Report (SAR)

About four to six weeks after federal student aid has been applied for, an applicant will receive a Student Aid Report (SAR), which reproduces the information given on the student's application.

Based on that information, the SAR shows whether a student is eligible for a Pell Grant. If eligible, the financial aid administrator at the student's school will use the Student Aid index number on the student's SAR to determine the amount of the Grant. Even if one is ineligible for a Pell Grant, one should still check with the financial aid administrator, who may use the SAR to determine whether the applicant is eligible for aid from the Supplemental Educational Opportunity Grant, College Work-Study, and National Direct Student Loan programs. The financial aid administrator may also use the SAR information to determine whether a student is eligible for a Guaranteed Student Loan.

Citizenship

Applicants must meet one of the following citizenship requirements: U.S. citizen; U.S. national; U.S. permanent resident who has an I-151 or I-551 (Alien Registration Receipt Card); Permanent resident of the Trust Territory of the Pacific Islands; Permanent resident of the Northern Mariana Islands.

If the applicant is not in any of these categories, he or she must have one of the following documents from the U.S. Immigration and Naturalization Service:

- I-94 (Arrival-Departure Record) with one of the following endorsements: (a) "adjustment applicant," (b) "refugee," (c) "conditional entrant," or (d) "indefinite parole."
- Official statement that he or she has been granted asylum in the U.S.
- Other proof from the U.S. Immigration and Naturalization Service that the applicant is in the U.S. for other than a temporary purpose. He or she should check with the financial aid administrator at the school attended.

If an applicant is in the U.S. on an F1 or F2 student visa only or a J1 or J2 exchange visitor visa only, he or she cannot get federal student aid. Also, if the student has only an approval notice to apply for permanent residence (I-171 or I-464A), the student cannot get federal student aid.

Transfer Students

If a student transfers from one school to another, financial aid will not automatically go along with the student. To continue receiving financial aid at the new school, students must check with the financial aid administrator at the new school to find out what programs are available and what steps must be taken.

Deadlines

March 15, 1983. Federal student aid applications or Special Condition Applications must be *received* by this date.

May 5, 1983. Corrections to the SAR must be *received* by this date.

May 31, 1983, or a student's last day of enrollment in 1983, whichever comes first. Deadlines for submitting SAR's to a financial aid office—if the student was enrolled *before* May 1.

June 15, 1983. Requests for duplicate SAR's must be *received* by this date.

June 30, 1983, or a student's last day of enrollment in 1983, whichever comes first. Deadlines for submitting the SAR to a financial aid office—if students are enrolled for the first time in the award period (July 1 1982–June 30, 1983) *on or after May 1.*

Addresses

If there are any questions about the application process, one should write to the following addresses for information. Always include full name, correct address, Social Security number, date of birth, and signature in the letter. Students should use their permanent mailing address.

Submit Applications for Federal Student Aid to: Federal Student Aid Programs, P.O. Box 92496, Los Angeles, CA 90009.

Submit Special Condition Applications to: Federal Student Aid Programs, P.O. Box 92499, Los Angeles, CA 90009.

Requests for duplicate copies of SAR's, write to: Federal Student Aid Programs, P.O. Box 92524, Los Angeles, CA 90009.

To make corrections or additions to the information on SAR's, make them on the SAR, sign the Certification on the form, and send to: Federal Student Aid Programs, P.O. Box 92440, Los Angeles, CA 90009.

If an SAR is not received—and it has been more than six weeks since it was applied for, or more than four weeks since an SAR was corrected—write to: Federal Student Aid Programs, P.O. Box 92505, Los Angeles, CA 90009.

FEDERAL AID PROGRAMS

Pell Grants

Description. Pell Grants provide money to help undergraduates pay for their education after high school. The Pell Grant Program is the largest of the federal student aid programs. For many students, these grants provide a "foundation" of financial aid, to which aid from other federal and non-federal sources may be added. Unlike loans, grants do not have to be paid back.

Qualifications

The Department of Education uses a standard formula to evaluate the information supplied on the student aid application. The formula produces a Student Aid Index number. This number appears on the Student Aid Report and will tell whether one is eligible for a Pell Grant.

The formula is too long to appear in this article. However, a pamphlet which describes the formula in detail can be obtained by writing to Federal Student Aid, P.O. Box 84, Washington, D.C. 20044.

Amount

Awards for the 1982–83 academic year (July 1, 1982–June 30, 1983) will depend on program funding. Awards for the 1981–82 academic year ranged from $120 to $1,670. How much a student receives will depend on the information provided on the student aid application, whether the applicant is a full-time or part-time student, how long the student will be enrolled between July 1, 1982 and June 30, 1983, and the *cost of education*[4] at the applicant's school.

Applying

The sooner, the better. The 1982–83 application must be received by March 15, 1983.

Additional Information

If a student's family financial situation has recently changed for the worse because of: death, separation or divorce, loss of job, loss of nontaxable income or benefits such as Social Security, child support, etc., a Special Condition Application can be filed.

The application can be obtained from a high school counselor, from a financial aid office, or by writing to: Pell Grants, P.O. Box 84, Washington, D.C. 20044.

Supplemental Educational Opportunity Grants (SEOG)

Description. A supplemental Educational Opportunity Grant is an award of money to help students pay for their education after high school. It is for undergraduates only, and it does not have to be paid back.

Amount

A student can get up to $2000 a year, depending on need, the availability of SEOG funds at the student's school, and the amount of other aid that a student may be receiving.

Applying

Different schools set different deadlines. Check with the financial aid office at the school. It is a good idea to apply as soon as possible.

Additional Information

There is a major difference between a SEOG and a Pell Grant. A Pell Grant is an entitlement. This means that if a student qualifies for it, the student will get it. The Department of Education guarantees that the school will receive the money it needs to pay the Pell Grants of its students.

An SEOG is not an entitlement. There are no guarantees attached to it. Every year, the Department of Education gives each school a set amount of money to use for SEOG's. When the money is gone, there are no more SEOG's for that year.

College Work-Study (CW-S)

Description. The College Work-Study Program provides jobs for undergraduate and graduate students who need financial aid. CW-S gives students a chance to earn part of their educational expenses.

Amount

The amount of the CW-S award depends on the student's financial need and the amount of money the receipient's school has for this program. The student's pay earned will be at least the current federal minimum wage, but it may also be related to the type of work performed and its difficulty. The total amount of aid received cannot exceed a student's financial need.

Applying

Each school has its own deadlines. However, they usually occur early in each calendar year.

Additional Information

College Work-Study jobs may be performed on-campus or off-campus. However, a CW-S job must always be for a public or private nonprofit agency and be in the public interest.

National Direct Student Loans (NDSL)

Description. National Direct Student Loans are low-interest (5%) loans to help students pay for their education after high school. These loans are made to undergraduate and graduate students through the financial aid office at their schools. These loans must be repaid.

Amount

Recipients may borrow up to a total of:

- $3,000 if they are enrolled in a vocational program, or if they have completed less than two years of a program leading to a Bachelor's degree.
- $6,000 if they are undergraduates who have already completed two years of study toward a Bachelor's degree and have achieved third-year status (this total includes any amount previously borrowed under NDSL for the first two years of study).
- $12,000 for graduate or professional study (this total includes any amount previously borrowed under NDSL for undergraduate study).

Applying

Each school sets its own deadlines. They usually occur early in each calendar year.

Repayment

Repayment begins six months after graduation, or when a reciepient leaves school, or drops below *half-time*[1] status. The amount of payment will depend on the size of one's debt, but usually at least $30 per month must be repaid.

Under certain conditions, such as while serving in the Armed Forces, or The Peace Corps, VISTA, etc., repayment may be deferred up to three years. There are other conditions under which payment may be postponed and also certain conditions under which it may be canceled.

Guaranteed Student Loans (GSL)

Description. A Guaranteed Student Loan is a low-interest loan made to a student by a lender such as a bank, credit union, or savings and loan association to help pay for the student's education after high school. These loans are insured by either the federal government or the guarantee agency[5] in the student's state.

Limitations

A student whose family's adjusted gross income is over $30,000 will have to show financial need, and will qualify for federal interest benefits only up to the amount of need that has not been met by other sources of aid. "Need" is defined as the total cost of attending school minus the amount that, according to a standard formula, the student's family should be able to contribute toward his or her educational expenses. A GSL may not exceed the student's cost of education minus other student financial aid received.

Amount

Undergraduate students can borrow up to $2,500 a year. Graduate students can borrow up to $5,000 a year. (In some states, these amounts may be lower.)

The total GSL debt undergraduate borrowers can have outstanding is $12,500. The total for graduate or professional study is $25,000, including any loans made at the undergraduate level.

Origination Fee

Borrowers must pay an "origination fee" when the money is loaned. Five percent of the amount borrowed ($125 if the undergraduate maximum of $2,500 is borrowed) will be deducted from the loan. This money is passed on to the federal government to help reduce the government's cost of subsidizing these low-interest loans.

An insurance premium of up to 1% of the total loan may also be collected in advance under the guarantee agency program in each state. An insurance premium of one quarter of 1% will be collected for loans insured by the federal government.

Minimum Annual Repayment

Borrowers must repay at least $600 annually, or $50 per month.

Applying

GSL applications may be obtained from a school, a lender, or a state guarantee agency. One should look for a lender as soon as one has been accepted by a school.

After a lender agrees to make the loan, it usually takes four to six weeks to get the loan approved.

Repayment

Loan repayment begins six months after the student leaves school if the interest rate is 9%, and 9 to 12 months after leaving school if the interest rate is 7%. The lender generally must allow the student borrower at least five years to repay the loan, and may allow up to ten years. A student is considered to have left school if he or she falls below *half-time* status.

Under certain conditions, such as while serving in the Armed Forces, or The Peace Corps, Action programs, etc., repayment may be deferred up to three years. The loan can be canceled only if the student borrower becomes totally and permanently disabled or dies.

PLUS Loans

Description. PLUS loans are meant to provide additional funds for educational expenses. The interest rate for these loans is 14%. (Rate may be reduced to 12%. Check with lender). Like GSL's, they are made by a lender such as a bank, credit union, or savings and loan association. In no case can a PLUS loan exceed a student's cost of education minus other aid received.

Amount

- Parents of dependent undergraduate students may borrow up to $3,000 per year, to a total of $15,000, for each child who is at least a half-time dependent undergraduate student.
- Graduate students may borrow up to $3,000 per year, to a total of $15,000. This is in addition to the GSL limits.
- Independent undergraduates may borrow up to $2,500 per year. However, the PLUS loan combined with any GSL the undergraduate may also have cannot exceed the yearly and total GSL undergraduate limits ($2,500 and $12,500).

Applying

This is done the same way that you apply for a GSL, except the PLUS borrowers do not have to show need.

Repayment

Parent borrowers must start repaying these loans within 60 days. Student borrowers, however, may receive a deferment if they are full-time students, but they are responsible for payment of the interest during the deferment. The same deferment conditions available to GSL borrowers are available to PLUS borrowers.

Footnotes

1. **Half-Time:** At schools measuring progress by credit hours and academic terms (semester, trimester, or quarters), "half-time" means at least six semester hours or quarter-hours per term. At schools measuring progress by credit hours but not using academic terms, "half-time" means at least 12 semester hours or 18 quarter hours per year. At schools measuring progress by clock hours, "half-time" means at least 12 hours per week.

2. **Satisfactory Academic Progress:** Each school that takes part in federal student aid programs must establish a written standard of satisfactory academic progress. To receive federal aid, applicants must meet that standard. The Department of Education allows each school to set its own standard, but requires that standard to be uniformly applied to all students who receive federal aid at that school.

3. **Assets:** Savings and checking accounts, home or business value, stocks, bonds, real estate, trust funds, etc. Cars are not considered assets, nor are personal possessions such as stamp collections or musical instruments.

4. **Cost of Education (or Cost of Attendance):** The total amount it will cost a student to go to school. It is usually expressed as a yearly figure. For Pell Grants, it includes tuition and fees; on-campus room and board (or a standard housing and food allowance for off-campus students); and allowances for books, supplies, and miscellaneous. *Campus-based programs* are more flexible and may include other expenses such as travel, child care, and costs related to a handicap.

5. **Guarantee Agency:** The organization that administers the GSL and PLUS programs in each state. The federal government does set loan limits and interest rates, but each state is free to set its own rules within federal guidelines. These agencies are the best source of information on GSL's and PLUS loans.

Sources of Information on GSL's and State Student Aid

ALABAMA
Alabama Commission on Higher Education
1 Court Square, Suite 221
Montgomery, AL 36197
GSL and State Aid:
(205) 832-3790

ALASKA
Alaska Commission on Postsecondary Education
400 Willoughby Ave.
Pouch FP
Juneau, AK 99801
GSL and State Aid:
(907) 465-2962

ARIZONA
GSL: Arizona Educational Loan Program
301 East Virginia Ave.
Phoenix, AZ 85004
(602) 252-5793
State Aid: Arizona Commission for Postsecondary Education
1937 West Jefferson
Phoenix, AZ 85009
(602) 255-3109

ARKANSAS
GSL: Student Loan Guarantee Foundations of Arkansas
1515 West 7th St.—Suite 515
Little Rock, AR 72202
(501) 371-2634
State Aid: Dept. of Higher Education

1301 West 7th St.
Little Rock, AR 72201
(501) 371-1441, Ext. 56

CALIFORNIA
California Student Aid Commission
1410 Fifth St.
Sacramento, CA 95814
GSL: (916) 322-0435
State Aid: (916) 445-0880

COLORADO
GSL: Colorado Guaranteed Student Loan Program
7000 N. Broadway, Suite 100
Denver, CO 80221
(303) 427-0259
State Aid: Colorado Commission on Higher Education
1550 Lincoln St., Rm. 210
Denver, CO 80203
303) 866-2748

CONNECTICUT
GSL: Connecticut Student Loan Foundation
25 Pratt St.
Hartford, CT 06103
203) 547-1510
State Aid: Connecticut Board of Higher Education
1 Woodland St.
Hartford, CT 06105
203) 566-6218

DELAWARE
GSL: Delaware Higher Education Loan Program
c/o Brandywine College
P.O. Box 7139
Wilmington, DE 19803
302) 478-3000 Ext. 201
State Aid: Delaware Postsecondary Education Commission
Carvel State Office Bldg.
820 French St.
Wilmington, DE 19801
302) 571-3240

DISTRICT OF COLUMBIA
GSL: Higher Education Assistance Foundation
Higher Education Loan Program (HELP) of D.C., Inc.
1001 Connecticut Ave., N.W.
Suite 825
Washington, D.C. 20036
202) 861-0701
State Aid: Office of State Education Affairs
1331 H St., N.W.,
th Floor, Rm. 817
Washington, D.C. 20001
202) 727-3688

FLORIDA
Florida Student Financial Assistance Commission
Knott Bldg.
Tallahassee, FL 32301
GSL and State Aid:
904) 487-1800

GEORGIA
Georgia Higher Education Assistance Corporation
9 LaVista Perimeter Park
2187 Northlake Parkway
Suite 110
Tucker, GA 30084
GSL: (404) 393-7241
State Aid: (404) 393-7253

HAWAII
GSL: Hawaii Education Loan Program
1314 South King St., Suite 603
Honolulu, HI 96814
(808) 536-3731
State Aid: State Postsecondary Education Commission
124F Bachman Hall, Univ. of Hawaii
2444 Dole St.
Honolulu, HI 96822
(808) 948-6862

IDAHO
GSL: Student Loan Fund of Idaho, Inc.
Processing Center
Route 2, North Whitley Dr.
Fruitland, ID 83619
(208) 452-4058
State Aid: Office of State Board of Education
650 West State St., Rm. 307
Boise, ID 83720
(208) 334-2270

ILLINOIS
GSL: Illinois Guaranteed Loan Program
102 Wilmot Rd.
Deerfield, IL 60015
(312) 945-7040
State Aid: Illinois State Scholarship Commission
102 Wilmot Rd.
Deerfield, IL 60015
(312) 948-8550

INDIANA
State Student Assistance Commission of Indiana
219 North Senate Ave., 1st Floor
Indianapolis, IN 46202
GSL: (317) 232-2366
State Aid: (317) 232-2351

IOWA
Iowa College Aid Commission
201 Jewett Bldg.
9th and Grand
Des Moines, IA 50309
GSL: (515) 281-8537
State Aid: (515) 281-3501

KANSAS
GSL: Higher Education Assistance Foundation
34 Corporate Woods
10950 Grand View Dr.
Overland Park, KS 66210
(913) 648-4255
State Aid: Board of Regents—State of Kansas
1416 Merchants National Bank
Topeka, KS 66612
(913) 296-3421

KENTUCKY
Kentucky Higher Education Assistance Authority
1050 U.S. 127 South
West Frankfort Office Complex
Frankfort, KY 40601
GSL and State Aid:
(502) 564-7990

LOUISIANA
Governor's Special Commission on Education Services
4637 Jamestown St.
P.O. Box 44127
Baton Rouge, LA 70804
GSL and State Aid:
(504) 925-3630

MAINE
State Dept. of Educational and Cultural Services
Div. of Higher Education Services
State House Station 23
Augusta, ME 04333
GSL and State Aid:
(207) 289-2183

MARYLAND
GSL: Maryland Higher Education Loan Corp.
2100 Guilford Ave.
Baltimore, MD 21218
(301) 659-6555
State Aid: Maryland State Scholarship Board
2100 Guilford Ave.
Baltimore, MD 21218
(301) 659-6420

MASSACHUSETTS
GSL: Massachusetts Higher Education Assistance Corp.
330 Stuart St.
Boston, MA 02116
(617) 426-9796
State Aid: Massachusetts Board of Regents of Higher Education
Scholarship Office
330 Stuart St.
Boston, MA 02116
(617) 727-9420

MICHIGAN
GSL: Michigan Dept. of Education
Guaranteed Student Loan Program
Box 30047
Lansing, MI 48909
(517) 373-0760
State Aid: Michigan Dept. of Education
P.O. Box 30008
Lansing, MI 48909
(517) 373-3394

MINNESOTA
GSL: Higher Education Assistance Foundation
900 American National Bank Bldg.
5th & Minnesota Sts.
St. Paul, MN 55101
(612) 227-7661
State Aid: Minnesota Higher Education Coordinating Board
400 Capitol Square
550 Cedar St.
St. Paul, MN 55101

(612) 296-3974
MISSISSIPPI
GSL: Student Financial Assistance, U.S. Dept. of Education
101 Marietta Tower—Suite 423
Atlanta, GA 30323
(404) 221-5658
State Aid: Mississippi Postsecondary Education Financial Assistance Board
P.O. Box 2336
Jackson, MS 39205
(601) 982-6168
MISSOURI
GSL: Missouri Dept. of Higher Education
P.O. Box 1438
Jefferson City, MO 65102
(314) 751-3940
State Aid: Missouri Dept. of Higher Education
P.O. Box 1437
Jefferson City, MO 65102
(314) 751-3940
MONTANA
GSL and State Aid: Montana University System
33 South Last Chance Gulch
Helena, MT 59601
(406) 449-3024
NEBRASKA
Cornhusker Bank Bldg.
11th & Cornhusker Highway
Suite 304
Lincoln, NE 68521
(402) 476-9129
State Aid: Nebraska Coordinating Commission for Postsecondary Education
301 Centennial Mall South
P.O. Box 95005
Lincoln, NE 68509
(402) 471-2847
NEVADA
GSL: Nevada State Dept. of Education
400 West King St.
Carson City, NV 89710
(702) 885-3107
State Aid: University of Nevada System
405 Marsh Ave.
Reno, NV 89509
(702) 784-4666
NEW HAMPSHIRE
GSL: New Hampshire Higher Education Assistance Foundation
143 North Main St.
P.O. Box 877
Concord, NH 03301
(603) 225-6612
State Aid: New Hampshire Postsecondary Education Commission
61 South Spring St.
Concord, NH 03301
(603) 271-2555
NEW JERSEY
GSL: New Jersey Higher Education Assistance Authority
C. N. 00538
Trenton, NJ 08638
(609) 292-3906
State Aid: Dept. of Higher Education
Office of Student Assistance
No. 4 Quakerbridge Plaza, C. N. 540
Trenton, NJ 08625
(609) 292-4646
NEW MEXICO
GSL: New Mexico Educational Assistance Foundation
2301 Yale S.E., Bldg. F
Albuquerque, NM 87106
(505) 277-6304
State Aid: Board of Education Finance
1068 Cerrillos Rd.
Santa Fe, NM 87503
(505) 827-5017
NEW YORK
New York State Higher Education Services Corp.
99 Washington Ave.
Albany, NY 12255
GSL: (518) 473-1574
State Aid: (518) 474-5642
NORTH CAROLINA
North Carolina State Education Assistance Authority
P.O. Box 2688
Chapel Hill, NC 27514
GSL and State Aid:
(919) 473-1688
NORTH DAKOTA
GSL: Student Financial Assistance Dept. of Education
11037 Federal Office Bldg.
19th & Stout Sts.
Denver, CO 80294
(303) 837-3676
State Aid: North Dakota Student Financial Assistance Program
10th Floor, State Capitol
Bismarck, ND 58505
(701) 224-4114
OHIO
GSL: Ohio Student Loan Commission
P.O. Box 16610
Columbus, OH 43216
(614) 466-3091
State Aid: Ohio Board of Regents
3600 State Office Tower
30 East Broad St.
Columbus, OH 43215
(614) 466-7420
OKLAHOMA
Oklahoma State Regents for Higher Education
500 Education Bldg.
State Capitol Complex
Oklahoma City, OK 73105
GSL and State Aid:
(405) 521-8262
OREGON
Oregon State Scholarship Commission
1445 Willamette St.
Eugene, OR 97401
GSL: (800) 452-8807 (within OR),
(503) 686-3200
State Aid: (503) 686-4166
PENNSYLVANIA
Pennsylvania Higher Education Assistance Agency
660 Boas St.
Harrisburg, PA 17102
GSL: (800) 692-7392 (within PA),
(717) 787-1932
State Aid: (800) 692-7435 (within PA),
(717) 787-1937
RHODE ISLAND
Rhode Island Higher Education Assistance Authority
274 Weybosset St.
Providence, RI 02903
GSL and State Aid:
(401) 277-2050
SOUTH CAROLINA
GSL: South Carolina Student Loan Corp.
Interstate Center, Suite 210
P.O. Box 21337
Columbia, SC 29221
(803) 798-0916
State Aid: Higher Education Tuition Grants Agency
411 Keenan Bldg., Box 11638
Columbia, SC 29211
(803) 758-7070
SOUTH DAKOTA
GSL: South Dakota Education Assistance Corp.
105 First Ave. SW
Aberdeen, SD 57401
(605) 225-6423
State Aid: Dept. of Education and Cultural Affairs
Richard F. Kneip Bldg.
Pierre, SD 57501
(605) 773-3134
TENNESSEE
Tennessee Student Assistance Corp.
B-3 Capitol Towers—Suite 9
Nashville, TN 37219
GSL and State Aid:
(800) 342-1663 (within TN),
(615) 741-1346
TEXAS
GSL: Texas Guaranteed Student Loan Corp.
Champion Tower, Suite 510
Austin, TX 78752
(512) 835-1900
State Aid: Coordinating Board Texas College and University System
P.O. Box 12788, Capitol Station
Austin, TX 78711

(512) 475-8169
UTAH
GSL: Utah Education Loan Service
1800 South West Temple
Suite 101
Salt Lake City, UT 84108
(801) 486-5921
State Aid: Utah State Board of Regents
807 East South Temple
Suite 204
Salt Lake City, UT 84102
(801) 533-5617
VERMONT
Vermont Student Assistance Corp.
5 Burlington Square
Burlington, VT 05401
GSL and State Aid:
(800) 642-3177 (within VT)
(802) 658-4530
VIRGINIA
GSL: Virginia State Education Assistance Authority
6 North Sixth St.
Suite 400
Richmond, VA 23219
(804) 786-2035
State Aid: State Council of Higher Education for Virginia
James Monroe Bldg.
101 N. 14th St.
Richmond, VA 23219
(804) 225-2141
WASHINGTON
GSL: Washington Student Loan Guaranty Association
100 South King St., Suite 560
Westland Bldg.
Seattle, WA 98104
(206) 625-1030
State Aid: Council for Postsecondary Education
908 East Fifth Ave.
Olympia, WA 98504
(206) 753-3571
WEST VIRGINIA
GSL: Higher Education Assistance Foundation
Higher Education Loan Program of West Virginia, Inc.
P.O. Box 591
Union Bldg., Suite 900
723 Kanawha Blvd. East
Charleston, WV 25322
(304) 345-7211
State Aid: West Virginia Board of Regents
950 Kanawha Blvd. East
Charleston, WV 25301
(304) 348-0112
WISCONSIN
GSL: Wisconsin Higher. Education Corp.
137 East Wilson St.
Madison, WI 53702
(608) 266-1653
State Aid: Wisconsin Higher Educational Aids Board
P.O. Box 7858
Madison, WI 53707
(608) 266-2897
WYOMING
GSL: Higher Education Assistance Foundation
American National Bank Bldg.
20 St. at Capitol, Suite 320
Cheyenne, WY 82001
(307) 635-3259
State Aid: Wyoming Community College Commission
1720 Carey Ave.
Boyd Bldg., 5th Floor
Cheyenne, WY 82002
(307) 777-7763

The Un-Professional Professional

What To Do When You Are Treated Dishonestly or Incompetently by a Professional

William L. Wood, Jr., Executive Director, N.Y.S. Office of Professional Discipline

Today, the word "professional" is used in many different ways: We read about the "professional soldier," and television and newspapers are full of the exciting exploits of "professional athletes." In these cases, the word refers to people who do what they do for money—yet are also doing something that many other people do—out of either patriotism or love of sport.

The word "professional" also usually means "highly skilled," and it often suggests great dedication and personal commitment. When the word is used this way, it is used to apply to doctors, nurses, architects—to all those who practice a *profession.*

Professionals like doctors, dentists, pharmacists, and others in the *health professions* safeguard people's health. Others such as accountants and lawyers take responsibility for people's property or money. Architects and engineers may be responsible for the safety or for the quality of a building or for how a machine operates.

These professionals play such an important part in our lives and are so important that they are usually licensed by governments who attest to their education and skill in order to protect the public.

In this very complex world, these professionals have proliferated. In the United States, as another page in the *Information Please Almanac* indicates, there are over 140,000 dentists, 120,000 pharmacists, 400,000 physicians, 1,300,000 nurses, 100,000 psychologists, and over a million engineers, a million accountants, 90,000 architects—an incredibly large number of people who have met certain standards of training and who are expected to display certain very high standards of conscientiousness and seriousness. To use the word again: professionalism.

State Agencies Concerned With Professional Misconduct

ALASKA
Div. of Occupational Licensing
Dept. of Commerce & Economic Development
Pouch D
Juneau, AK 99811
907–465–2535

CALIFORNIA
Dept. of Consumer Affairs
1020 N Street, Room 516
Sacramento, CA 95814
916–445–4465

COLORADO
Dept. of Regulatory Agencies
1525 Sherman St., Rm. 116
Denver, CO 80203
303–839–3304

CONNECTICUT
Div. of Medical Quality Assurance
79 Elm St.
Hartford, CT 06115
203–566–3207

DELAWARE
Div. of Business & Occupational Regulation
O'Neill Bldg.
Dover, DE 19901
302–678–4525

DISTRICT OF COLUMBIA
Dept. of Licenses, Investigations, & Inspections
605 G St., NW
Washington, DC 20001
202–727–6904

FLORIDA
Dept. of Professional Regulation
130 N. Monroe St.
Tallahassee, FL 32301
904–487–2252

GEORGIA
State Examining Boards
166 Pryor St., SW
Atlanta, GA 30334
404–656–3900

HAWAII
Professional & Vocational Licensing
1010 Richards St.
Honolulu, HI 96813
808–548–6520

IDAHO
Bureau of Occupational Licenses
2404 Bank Drive, Rm. 312
Boise, ID 83705
208–384–3233

ILLINOIS
Dept. of Registration & Education
320 W. Washington St.
Springfield, IL 62786
217–785–0800

IOWA
Professional Licensure
Dept. of Health
215 E. 7th St.
Des Moines, IA 50319
515–281–4401

KENTUCKY
Div. of Occupations
Twilight Trail, Bldg. A
Frankfort, KY 40601
502–564–3296

MAINE
Dept. of Business Regulation
Stevens School, State House
Augusta, ME 04333
207–289–2217

MARYLAND
Dept. of Licensing & Regulation
One South Calvert St.
Baltimore, MD 21202
301–659–6200

Dept. of Health & Mental Hygiene
201 West Preston St.
Baltimore, MD 21201
301–383–2709

MASSACHUSETTS
Div. of Registration
Executive Office of Consumer Affairs
100 Cambridge St.
Boston, MA 02202
617–727–3076

MICHIGAN
Dept. of Licensing & Regulation

There are so many professionals in practice today that a few "bad apples" will inevitably turn up. These are the people who treat their patients or clients badly, who are either incompetent or dishonest, and who cause a great deal of trouble for their competent colleagues and for the licensing authorities. Needless to say, they do a great deal of harm.

Most people know that if they have a complaint about an attorney's misbehavior, they should take that complaint to the local bar association. But where do you turn when you believe that you have been treated dishonestly or incompetently by a person with a license to practice another profession?

The procedure in New York State is fairly typical of that across the country as a whole. In New York, a Board of Regents is responsible for the conduct of professionals who are involved with the health and well-being of the public. The Board of Regents, on behalf of the state, licenses physicians, nurses, dentists, pharmacists, psychologists, chiropractors, podiatrists, audiologists, veterinarians, occupational and physical therapists, opticians, certified social workers, and other professions.

The Regents are also concerned with professions that take certain responsibilities for their clients' money or safety, so they also license architects, accountants, land surveyors, and professional engineers.

The State enforces standards of conduct and punishes people and persons guilty of misconduct by fines, by revocation of a license, or by other penalties.

Obviously, *misconduct* has to be defined. It usually includes such things as: practicing fraudulently, negligently, or incompetently; working or practicing while being impaired by alcohol, drugs, or mental disability; being convicted of a crime. These are serious matters and not issues like fee disputes or simple discourtesy. Most state governments are, basically, concerned with actions that imply a violation of the special trust that is part of being "professional."

Some specific examples of this misbehavior are: physically or verbally abusing a patient; not keeping proper patient records or not making them available to a patient upon the proper request; ordering excessive medical laboratory tests; providing treatment or services not authorized; guaranteeing a cure; neglecting a patient in need of immediate care; etc.

You will probably never suffer at the hands of a licensed professional. But if you do, your state probably has an agency to help you. The listing below identifies appropriate agencies in most states. If you live in a state for which no agency is listed, call your nearest consumer protection agency for help.

P.O. Box 30018
Lansing, MI 48909
517-373-1870

MISSOURI
Div. of Professional Registration & Licensing
P.O. Box 1335
Jefferson City, MO 65102
314-751-2334

MONTANA
Dept. of Professional & Occupational Licensing
42½ N. Last Chance Gulch
Helena, MT 59620
406-449-3737

NEW JERSEY
Div. of Consumer Affairs
1100 Raymond Blvd.
Newark, NJ 07102
201-648-3537

NEW YORK
Assistant Commissioner for the Professions
State Education Dept.
Albany, NY 12230
518-474-3862

NORTH CAROLINA
Secretary of State
State Capitol
Raleigh, NC 27611
919-733-3433

NORTH DAKOTA
Office of the Attorney General
Bismarck, ND 58505
701-224-3404

OREGON
Dept. of Commerce
428 Labor & Industries Bldg.
Salem, OR 97310
503-378-4100

Dept. of Human Resources
711 State Office Bldg.
Portland, OR 97201
503-229-5032

PENNSYLVANIA
Bureau of Professional Occupational Affairs
Transportation & Safety Bldg. Rm. 618
Harrisburg, PA 17120
717-787-8503

RHODE ISLAND
Dept. of Business Regulation
100 North Main St.
Providence, RI 02903
401-277-2246

Dept. of Health
75 Davis St.
Providence, RI 02908
401-277-2231

SOUTH DAKOTA
Div. of Professional & Occupational Licensing
State Capitol
Pierre, SD 57501
605-773-3177

TENNESSEE
Regulatory Boards
Dept. of Insurance
444 Doctors Bldg.
Nashville, TN 37203
615-741-3449

Division of Health Related Boards
R.S. Gass State Office Bldg.
Ben Allen Rd., Third Floor
Nashville, TN 37206
615-741-7293

UTAH
Div. of Registration
330 E. Fourth South
Salt Lake City, UT 84111
801-533-5523

VERMONT
Div. of Licensing & Registration
Pavilion Office Bldg.
Montpelier, VT 05602
802-828-2363

VIRGINIA
Dept. of Commerce
2 South Ninth St.
Richmond, VA 23219
804-786-2161

WASHINGTON
Dept. of Licensing
Highways-Licenses Bldg.
Olympia, WA 98504
206-753-6915

Business-Professions Administration
Highways-Licenses Bldg.
Olympia, WA 98504
206-753-1369

WISCONSIN
Dept. of Regulation & Licensing
1400 E. Washington Ave.
Madison, WI 53702
608-266-2112

Choosing a Home Computer

As recently as ten or fifteen years ago, the idea that hundreds of thousands of American families would be seriously considering the purchase of a home computer would have been almost completely unimaginable. After all, computers then were large, complex and very, very expensive. Only the largest corporations, scientific laboratories and the government could afford to buy and maintain a computer, and it almost took an advanced degree in mathematics or electrical engineering to run one. Still, Americans are now buying home computers in record numbers, sometimes with little more hesitation than they would give to the purchase of a new car. Some analysts predict that before the end of this century, the home computer will be as common as the telephone or the color TV set.

Chances are, if you have given any thought to investing in a home computer, you have been struck by the large variety of capabilities and the often confusing array of equipment (hardware) and programs (software) offered by the several dozen computers now on the market. If you haven't already done so, you'll soon find yourself facing the three basic questions that every prospective computer owner has to consider:

1. **Why do I want, or need, a home computer?** This sounds very elementary, but remember that even the largest corporations have to ask themselves a quite similar question whenever they invest in a new, albeit larger, piece of electronics. In one respect, your job is a little harder because a large company probably has some very specific uses in mind and that's that; you may start with a few ideas, but as your knowledge of computers grows, you'll soon be dreaming up - and programming - many new things for your computer to do. This leads us directly to the next important question:

2. **What will I want my computer to do in the future?** Computers are just like any other machine in that they come with certain limited capabilities. (In computer terms, this is a function of their memory, or the amount of information they can handle while performing a given set of instructions.) Unlike, say, a typewriter, a computer's capabilities can often be expanded through the incorporation of additional memory or the attachment of accessories (called peripherals) such as information storage units, printers and interconnections to other computers. If you can be certain that all you will want your computer to do is play video games with the kids (or yourself) and maybe balance your household budget, you can get by with one of the simpler models costing a few hundred dollars. If you are willing to use your existing TV set as a monitor, your initial cost will be very low indeed. But think about it for a minute: do you own stocks or bonds and would you like to analyze their performance periodically? Does your home or apartment have a security system, and would you like to have a way of monitoring it while you're away? Does your job require that you bring a lot of work home, especially of the type that could benefit from a word processor? Do you or your children have an interest in science or mathematics, languages or logic? When you receive one of those "friendly reminders" from the credit card company, do you ever have the urge to answer their computer's letters with one of yours? Do you want to know what your horoscope predicts for next year? All these tasks, and many more, can be performed on today's home computers. But remember, every computer operation requires a minimum amount of computer memory. If your job calls for more memory than your computer has built into it, or which can be added to it, you can't do it. If your intended operation requires a specific piece of peripheral equipment, like a letter-quality printer, for example, you'd better make sure your home computer has, or can accept, that add-on feature. Two things should be kept in mind when considering your computer's future uses. Don't shy away from seemingly complex functions because you fear the programming will go beyond your mathematical abilities. Remember that computers are, above all, excellent teaching devices (even experienced programmers use them to learn new skills, as do fourth graders, for that matter). Much modern software is written with the novice in mind—how else would computer companies find new customers? Also, keep in mind that the most common error new computer owners make is that of buying too little memory. Unless you are certain you'll never want to do anything more than destroy electronic space monsters, make sure you can upgrade your computer's capabilities to suit your changing needs.

3. **How much can (or should) I spend?** This is one of those questions that rates an "it depends" answer. Certainly, the more you spend initially, the more you usually get. Initially. But watch out. The home computer industry is still very young, and manufacturers have their own ideas about what they think the largest share of their potential customers will want, off-the-shelf. Suppose you were buying a car, and the choice was between a Chevrolet and a Cadillac. Stripped-down, the Chevy is thousands of dollars cheaper, but once you add an automatic transmission, power steering, an air conditioner, maybe a stereo, the sticker price will be up in the five-figure range. On the other hand, the price of a "stripped-down" Caddy will likely include many of the less expensive car's options. Or look at your prospective computer purchase from the standpoint of intended function. Compare the Cadillac with a pickup truck.

Both will perform the basic task of moving you from point A to point B, but the truck is built with a specific purpose in mind which, elegant as it is, the Caddy cannot accomplish. In the final analysis, the choice of how much to spend comes down to a three-way compromise among (a) what you can afford, (b) what immediate computer capabilities you need or want, and (c) what you will want or need in the future. Again, if that last question looms large in your thinking, make certain you can add the needed peripherals later on. In terms of actual prices, today's home computers (and we're talking about true computers, not relatively simple video game machines) range from $100 for a basic unit in kit form, which you will have to connect to your color or black and white TV, up to under $10,000, which (usually, but not always) buys you more memory, a built-in TV monitor (sometimes color, sometimes black and white) and various bells and whistles in the form of peripherals or free software.

Finally, remember that being young and competitive, the computer industry's pricing structure is apt to change a lot before the market matures. On the other hand, new suppliers are constantly springing up, offering improvements, or lower prices, compared to "established" brands. Some of these companies will survive and still be able to provide service and upgrading features years from now. Some won't. Conversely, a few of the well-established computer manufacturers have already increased their prices across-the-board. The general trend of home computer prices has been downward (remember when a simple pocket calculator cost $300?), but it is impossible to predict how far they will drop in the future. How long are you willing to wait?

What to Look For

It would obviously be beyond the scope of this article to arm every potential computer buyer with enough information to make a choice among the many models already on the market.

Assuming you are starting completely from scratch, you should prepare yourself for that first visit to the local computer store with perhaps a few weeks of selected reading, plus a few hours spent talking with someone who works with, or services, computers. Several excellent books on the subject of an initial computer purchase are available in book stores or at your library. Most are written with a general and unbiased viewpoint. They're friendly. After you've read through a few of them you will pick up most of the often-baffling jargon that computer types like to speak, and you will be able to understand the product comparisons in terms of your own needs. There are now a number of computer magazines as well. These tend to be a bit more technical, considering their audience, but they often carry features for the novice. They are the best places to look for new-product information, and they are compulsively honest in their analyses, but you have to follow the language. Finally, you should visit several computer stores, if possible. Leave your checkbook at home and don't be afraid to ask basic questions. At the last computer store we visited, the salesman admitted that he was still learning what he could do on the machines he was selling, since he'd only been in the business for six months! Each store will likely be partial to one or more brands, the ones they represent, so shop around. Ask for demonstrations of the things you'd like to do, and pick up some hands-on operating experience, just to get the feel of the different keyboard styles. With the preceding general information, it's time to offer a few of the basic concepts, including explanations of some of the more common terms. We'll keep it simple, because six months ago . . .

What is a computer? It is a machine that manipulates information, in the form of numbers, words, graphics and purely electronic impulses. It differs from the common pocket calculator in that it can be instructed (programmed) to perform a variety of operations, within the limits of its memory, i.e., it can *interact* with its operator.

What does a home computer consist of? First, we have to have a means to *enter* information into the computer. That is accomplished through an *input device,* which on home computers exists in the form of a keyboard. Some keyboards are about the same as those on electric typewriters, with upper and lower case letters and a row of numbers and extra symbols. Some have a separate keypad, just like a pocket calculator. If you expect to be doing a lot of figuring on your computer, perhaps the keypad arrangement will be better for you; if you intend to use your computer as a word processor, the typewriter-style keyboard may be more confortable. Some keyboards have actual buttons, some only have pressure-sensitive pads. The latter are cheaper, but take some getting used to.

Next, the computer must have a place to store the information you enter into it, as well as the information built into it to perform its operations. There are actually two such devices, but they are both concerned with the computer's *memory,* which is nothing more than a measure of the amount of information the machine can handle. Let's back off a minute and consider how a computer receives and uses its information:

Being an electronic device, the only thing a computer can sense is electric current; positive or negative or on or off. Each pulse of "on" current, and each corresponding pulse of "off" current is known as a *bit.* Now, computers operate in a number system that is a little different from the one we're used to. We commonly deal in a *base 10* system; whole numbers range from 0 to 9, after which the next decimal order, from 10 to 99, follows, and so forth. In a *base 2* system, there are only two integers, 0 and 1, in each order. The *binary digits,* or bits, correspond to the on-off states of each computer *register,* the individual units that make up the computer's memory. With proper coding, the computer can "understand" any number, letter, or symbol through an appropriate combination of 0s and 1s. Computers accept instructions in the form of words made up of *binary digits* or bits. Most computers use eight-bit words known as *bytes.* A few combine two eight-bit words to form a 16-bit group, which speeds up calculations somewhat. Computer memories are measured in terms of the number of bytes they can hold. The common terminology uses the letter K, which ordinarily stands for 1000 but in computerese, actually refers to 2^{10}, or 1024. So a 16K memory means the computer can handle 16 X 1024 = 16,384 bytes.

Some of the computer's memory exists in the *microprocessor,* which is often referred to as the "brains" of the machine. The rest of the memory will be on separate *chips,* usually with a 16K capacity. Most home computers use one of the several mass-produced microprocessors now available: the Apple, Commodore PET and Ohio Scientific computers use the MOS Technology 6502 microprocessor; the Radio Shack TRS-80 and Exidy Sorcerer use the Zilog Z-80; Compucolor II, Interact, Processor Technology SOL and Heathkit H-8 use one of the Intel 8080 series microprocessors, and so forth. The microprocessor, its memory and suitable *input/output ports* make up the *central processing unit,* or CPU. Memory is stored in equipment known, appropriately enough, as *mass storage devices,* of which there are several types. The least expensive storage device is nothing more than a small cassette tape recorder, the very same type you would use to record conversations or music. The simplest home computers will, in fact, require you to purchase a cassette recorder separately and plug it in, through an *interface,* to the CPU.

Cassette recorders are cheap, but they are also slow. If the information you are seeking is near the end of a tape, you will have to search, at "fast-forward" or "reverse" speed, through the rest of the cassette before you come to the point you want. Still, at $30 or less for a recorder (you may even own one already) plus a few dollars per cassette, this lack of speed may be justifiable in terms of your initial cash outlay. The common voice/music cassette recorders operate at a speed of $1^{7}/_{8}$ inches per second. The transfer of information to and from the tape is not governed by the tape speed so much as it is by the computer, and the number of bits per second able to be transferred is known as the computer's *baud rate.* Obviously, the higher the baud rate, the faster the operation. Since each eight-bit byte requires one character to signal the onset of information transfer and one more to signal the end, the number of bytes a computer can transfer per second is simply the baud rate divided by ten. Home computers usually have baud rates between 300 and 1500; some offer two speeds for the sake of flexibility.

A faster, but considerably more expensive mass storage device is the *disk.* On large computers, disks are hard, and about the same size as a phonograph record. Home computers use smaller disks, eight or $5^{1}/_{4}$ inches in diameter. Because they are made from flexible plastic, they are commonly called *floppy disks,* or sometimes *diskettes.* Floppies can hold between about 50K and 1.2M (million) bytes, but their main advantage is speed. An often-cited comparison to explain their speed is the phonograph: if you want to hear a selection from one of the middle bands on a record, you simply move the tone arm. A disk drive does just about the same thing, only much faster, so it is able to locate any information stored on the disk in fractions of a second. Some home computers come with built-in disk drives (one or two), and some will accept them as peripherals. There are many suppliers of disk drives to fit the major brands of home computers, and their products are often less expensive. However, the buyer should be careful that the use of such a peripheral does not void provisions of his computer's warranty.

There are two distinct types of computer memory, and the difference between them strongly affects the machines' capabilities. The first type is known as *read-only memory,* or ROM. As its name implies, information can be transferred out of ROM, but it cannot be transferred in. ROM can therefore not be altered by the computer operator; it contains only information placed there by the manufacturer. This information includes instructions that tell the CPU how to operate, how to *fetch* information from storage devices, how to run peripherals, etc. Taken together, this set of general programs is called the *operating system,* or OS. You alert the OS by giving it a simple *system command* and it performs all the electronic gymnastics to carry out your orders. Again, there are a number of operating systems designed for use with the standard CPUs. One popular OS, known as the CP/M Operating System, is written for those computers containing an Intel 800 or a Zilog Z80 CPU. One advantage of buying a home computer using a common OS such as the CP/M is that it will accept a large variety of software (programs) available on the open market. Always remember that software is just as much a part of the computer as the nuts and bolts and, like anything else, it costs money.

The second type of computer memory is called *random access memory,* or RAM. The main difference between ROM and RAM is that you can add to, retrieve from or alter the latter at will. You can enter new data, change and delete information or input entire programs. There is no difference between the ways the CPU treats ROM or RAM; the difference is the way in which you, the operator, can interact with them.

It is common practice to compare home computers on the basis of their total memory capacity; salesmen are very fond of doing this. The catch is that the way a computer handles its memory is as important, or more so, as the total available. Remember that the OS, and self-contained or additional programs such as a *file manager, text editor* or *language translator,* all require specific amounts of memory. Some computers contain their operating systems, translators, etc. in storage devices, disks or cassettes. Before the computer can use the OS, it must be transferred to RAM, decreasing the amount of memory remaining for *user programs.* Such computers contain very little ROM, or none at all. Other models have their OS in ROM, whereby all of the RAM is available to the user. The disadvantage of this system is that it is more difficult, and often impossible, to change the OS. The amount of usable RAM you will need depends entirely on the size of the programs you intend to run, so keep this in mind when making your own comparisons.

So far, we've considered input devices, CPUs, memory and storage. The last component that makes up the basic home computer is the *output device.* This is the component that lets you see what the computer has done. The most common output device is a TV screen. Some computers are equipped with built-in TV displays, others require that you attach the computer to you own set. Also, some models have the capacity to output in color, others will only send out a black and white signal. It isn't just a question of cost; many simple game-type computers allow you to follow the action in color while black and white is used in much more sophisticated machines. You can, incidentally, use an inexpensive (under $100) black and white set to receive the output from a color-equipped computer. For extra money, you can also purchase a TV *monitor,* which is specially designed for use with computers and has much higher resolution.

If you want a permanent record of your computer's output, you will need a *printer.* They come built-in on some models, on others they're added as peripherals purchased separately. If the latter is the case, the computer supplier will either sell you one of his own design, or recommend one from an independent manufacturer. Some computers come with the necessary *printer interface;* others don't in which case it will be an added expense for you.

Most printers for the home computer market are either of the *thermal* or *impact* type. The former make impressions by heating specially treated paper; they can generally accept a wider range of characters, and they are less expensive. However paper costs are a lot higher than for impact printers. Impact printers (much like an electric typewriter, but faster) come in two basic versions *matrix* or *full font.* Matrix printers make up characters out of a series of fine dots. They are cheaper and faster than full font printers, although the clarity of the printing may (but need not necessarily) be lower. Full font printers produce characters much like those on this page. They are best suited for word processor applications (letter writing, reports, etc.). In place of the bars or letter balls used in electric typewriters, full font printers will use a *daisy wheel,* which is much faster. Still, full font printers are the slowest of the lot, and tend to be more expensive. Your best choice of printer, if you have a choice, is the least expensive one that wil produce copy of acceptable clarity for the intended uses, at an acceptable speed.

If you want to output *graphics* (charts, figures, diagrams), you will have to select a printer that has the capability for it. Serious hobbyists, designers, architects or engineers may want to upgrade their home computer with a full-fledged *plotter*, but that's getting a little beyond the scope of this article.

Speaking the language

Finally, a few words about language. We've already said that the "brains" of the computer can only understand bits, Os and ls. This is called *machine language* and it *is* something only mathematicians and computer engineers can understand. You will be concerned with one of the *programming languages*, the choice of which one to use depends once again on the uses you plan for your home computer.

The most popular programming language for home computers by far is called BASIC. It has a broad range of applications, can accept both mathematical formulas and the strings of characters used in word processing, and is especially useful for beginners since it can inform you when you have made a mistake. There are many versions of BASIC, each with its own strengths and limitations. PASCAL is another excellent beginner language. In fact, its first principal purpose was to teach programming. It is also generally applicable to mathematics, business and science, and it is notably easy to understand and debug. Less popular in the home computer field is COBOL, which is mainly used in larger business computers. COBOL programs for home use are consequently rare, but some may appear as people accustomed to using the language in their work environments demand similar software for their own machines.

Decision Time

After you've done your homework, and after you've gained enough knowledge to make an intelligent decision, you'll still have to face the question: buy now, or wait to see what they'll come up with next? You may as well resign yourself to the fact that whatever you buy today, or next year, will be superseded shortly thereafter. Not to worry. The major manufacturers are constantly offering packages that will update their equipment, so there is little danger yours will become obsolete. If you want a home computer now, you'll simply have to byte the bullet.

Konrad J.A. Kundig

ELECTION OF 1982

The Ninety-Eighth Congress

Composition of 97th and 98th Congresses

	97th Congress				98th Congress			
	Dem.	Rep.	Male	Female	Dem.	Rep.	Male	Fem
Senate	46[1]	54	98	2	46	54	98	2
House	241[2]	192[2]	413	20	267[3]	166[3]	412	21

1. Includes one Independent (Byrd of Virginia). 2. There were two vacancies at end of session—in New York and Indiana
Two Georgia districts holding elections Nov. 30. NOTE: There are 20 black members in the House.

The Senate

Senior Senator is listed first. The dates in the first column indicate period of service. The date given in parentheses after Senator's name is year of birth. All terms are for six years and expire in January. Mailing address of Senators: The Sena Washington, D.C. 20510.

ALABAMA
1979–85 Howell T. Heflin, D (1921)
1981–87 Jeremiah A. Denton, Jr., R (1924)
ALASKA
1968–85 Ted Stevens, R (1923)
1981–87 Frank H. Murkowski, R (1933)
ARIZONA
1969–87 Barry Goldwater, R (1909)
1977–89 Dennis DeConcini, D (1937)
ARKANSAS
1975–87 Dale Bumpers, D (1925)
1979–85 David H. Pryor, D (1934)
CALIFORNIA
1969–87 Alan Cranston, D (1914)
1983–89 Pete Wilson, R (1933)
COLORADO
1975–87 Gary Hart, D (1937)
1979–85 William L. Armstrong, R (1937)
CONNECTICUT
1971–89 Lowell P. Weicker, Jr., R (1931)
1981–87 Christopher J. Dodd, D (1944)
DELAWARE
1971–89 William V. Roth, Jr., R (1921)
1973–85 Joseph R. Biden, Jr., D (1942)
FLORIDA
1971–89 Lawton Chiles, D (1930)
1981–87 Paula Hawkins, R (1927)
GEORGIA
1973–85 Sam Nunn, D (1938)
1981–87 Mack Mattingly, R (1931)
HAWAII
1963–87 Daniel K. Inouye, D (1924)
1977–89 Spark M. Matsunaga, D (1916)
IDAHO
1973–85 James A. McClure, R (1924)
1981–87 Steven D. Symms, R (1938)
ILLINOIS
1967–85 Charles H. Percy, R (1919)
1981–87 Alan J. Dixon, D (1927)
INDIANA
1977–89 Richard G. Lugar, R (1932)
1981–87 Dan Quayle, R (1947)
IOWA
1979–85 Roger W. Jepsen, R (1928)
1981–87 Charles E. Grassley, R (1933)
KANSAS
1969–87 Robert J. Dole, R (1923)
1979–85 Nancy Landon Kassebaum, R (1932)
KENTUCKY
1973–85 Walter Huddleston, D (1926)
1975–87 Wendell H. Ford, D (1924)
LOUISIANA
1948–87 Russell B. Long, D (1918)
1973–85 J. Bennett Johnston, D (1932)
MAINE
1979–85 William S. Cohen, R (1940)
1980–89 George J. Mitchell, D (1933)
MARYLAND
1969–87 Charles McC. Mathias, Jr., R (1922)
1977–89 Paul S. Sarbanes, D (1933)
MASSACHUSETTS
1962–89 Edward M. Kennedy, D (1932)
1979–85 Paul E. Tsongas, D (1941)
MICHIGAN
1977–89 Donald W. Riegle, Jr., D (1938)
1979–85 Carl Levin, D (1934)
MINNESOTA
1978–89 David F. Durenberger, R (1934)
1979–85 Rudy Boschwitz, R (1930)
MISSISSIPPI
1947–89 John C. Stennis, D (1901)
1978–85 Thad Cochran, R (1937)
MISSOURI
1968–87 Thomas F. Eagleton, D (1929)
1977–89 John C. Danforth, R (1936)
MONTANA
1977–89 John Melcher, D (1924)
1979–85 Max Baucus, D (1941)
NEBRASKA
1977–89 Edward Zorinsky, D (1928)
1979–85 J. James Exon, D (1921)
NEVADA
1975–87 Paul Laxalt, R (1922)
1983–89 Chic Hecht, R (1928)
NEW HAMPSHIRE
1979–85 Gordon J. Humphrey, R (1940)
1981–87 Warren Rudman, R (1930)
NEW JERSEY
1979–85 Bill Bradley, D (1943)
1983–89 Frank R. Lautenberg, D (1924)
NEW MEXICO
1973–85 Pete V. Domenici, R (1932)
1983–89 Jeff Bingaman, D (1943)
NEW YORK
1977–89 Daniel P. Monynihan, D (1927)
1981–87 Alfonse M. D'Amato, R (1937)

NORTH CAROLINA
1973–85 Jesse Helms, R (1921)
1981–87 John P. East, R (1931)
NORTH DAKOTA
1960–89 Quentin N. Burdick, D (1908)
1981–87 Mark Andrews, R (1926)
OHIO
1975–87 John H. Glenn, Jr., D (1921)
1977–89 Howard M. Metzenbaum, D (1917)
OKLAHOMA
1979–85 David L. Boren, D (1941)
1981–87 Don Nickles, R (1948)
OREGON
1967–85 Mark O. Hatfield, R (1922)
1969–87 Bob Packwood, R (1932)
PENNSYLVANIA
1977–89 John Heinz, R (1938)
1981–87 Arlen Specter, R (1930)
RHODE ISLAND
1961–85 Claiborne Pell, D (1918)
1977–89 John H. Chafee, R (1922)
SOUTH CAROLINA
1956–85 Strom Thurmond, R (1902)
1966–87 Ernest F. Hollings, D (1922)
SOUTH DAKOTA
1979–85 Larry Pressler, R (1942)
1981–87 James Abdnor, R (1923)
TENNESSEE
1967–85 Howard H. Baker, Jr., R (1925)
1977–89 James R. Sasser, D (1936)
TEXAS
1961–85 John G. Tower, R (1925)
1971–89 Lloyd M. Bentsen, D (1921)
UTAH
1975–87 E. J. (Jake) Garn, R (1932)
1977–89 Orrin G. Hatch, R (1934)
VERMONT
1971–89 Robert T. Stafford, R (1913)
1975–87 Patrick J. Leahy, D (1940)
VIRGINIA
1979–85 John W. Warner, R (1927)
1983–89 Paul S. Trible, Jr., D (1946)
WASHINGTON
1953–89 Henry M. Jackson, D (1912)
1981–87 Slade Gorton, R (1928)
WEST VIRGINIA
1958–85 Jennings Randolph, D (1902)
1959–89 Robert C. Byrd, D (1918)
WISCONSIN
1957–89 William Proxmire, D (1915)
1981–87 Robert W. Kasten, Jr., R (1942)
WYOMING
1977–89 Malcolm Wallop, R (1933)
1979–85 Alan K. Simpson, R (1931)

The House of Representatives

The numerals indicate the Congressional Districts of the states; the designation AL means At-Large. All terms end January 1985. Mailing address of Representatives: House of Representatives, Washington, D.C. 20515

ALABAMA
(7 Representatives)
1. Jack Edwards, R
2. William L. Dickinson, R
3. William Nichols, D
4. Tom Bevill, D
5. Ronnie G. Flippo, D
6. Ben Erdreich, D
7. Richard C. Shelby, D

ALASKA
(1 Representative)
AL Don Young, R

ARIZONA
(5 Representatives)
1. John McCain, R
2. Morris K. Udall, D
3. Bob Stump, R
4. Eldon Rudd, R
5. James McNulty, D

ARKANSAS
(4 Representatives)
1. Bill Alexander, D
2. Ed Bethune, R
3. John P. Hammerschmidt, R
4. Beryl F. Anthony, Jr., D

CALIFORNIA
(45 Representatives)
1. Douglas H. Bosco, D
2. Eugene A. Chappie, R
3. Robert T. Matsui, D
4. Vic Fazio, D
5. Phillip Burton, D
6. Barbara Boxer, D
7. George Miller, D
8. Ronald V. Dellums, D
9. Fortney H. Stark, D
10. Don Edwards, D
11. Tom Lantos, D
12. Ed Zschau, R
13. Norman Y. Mineta, D
14. Norman D. Shumway, R
15. Tony Coelho, D
16. Leon E. Panetta, D
17. Charles Pashayan, Jr., R
18. Richard Lehman, D
19. Robert J. Lagomarsino, R
20. William M. Thomas, R
21. Bobbi Fiedler, R
22. Carlos J. Moorhead, R
23. Anthony C. Beilenson, D
24. Henry A. Waxman, D
25. Edward R. Roybal, D
26. Howard L. Berman, D
27. Mel Levine, D
28. Julian C. Dixon, D
29. Augustus F. Hawkins, D
30. Matthew G. Martinez, D
31. Mervyn M. Dymally, D
32. Glenn M. Anderson, D
33. David Dreier, R
34. Estaban Torres, D
35. Jerry Lewis, R
36. George E. Brown, Jr., D
37. Al McCandless, R
38. Jerry M. Patterson, D
39. William E. Dannemeyer, R
40. Robert E. Badham, R
41. William Lowery, R
42. Dan E. Lungren, R
43. Don Packard, R
44. James Bates, D
45. Duncan L. Hunter, R

COLORADO
(6 Representatives)
1. Patricia Schroeder, D
2. Timothy E. Wirth, D
3. Raymond P. Kogovsek, D
4. Hank Brown, R
5. Kenneth B. Kramer, R
6. Jack Swigert, R

CONNECTICUT
(6 Representatives)
1. Barbara B. Kennelly, D
2. Samuel Gejdenson, D
3. Bruce A. Morrison, D
4. Stewart B. McKinney, R
5. William R. Ratchford, D
6. Nancy L. Johnson, R

DELAWARE
(1 Representative)
AL Thomas R. Carper, D

FLORIDA
(19 Representatives)
1. Earl D. Hutto, D
2. Don Fuqua, D
3. Charles E. Bennett, D
4. William V. Chappell, Jr., D
5. Bill McCollum, R
6. Kenneth H. MacKay, D
7. Sam M. Gibbons, D
8. C.W. Bill Young, R
9. Michael Bilirakis, R
10. Andy Ireland, D
11. Bill Nelson, D
12. Tom Lewis, R
13. Connie Mack, R
14. Daniel A. Mica, D

15. Clay Shaw, Jr., R
16. Larry Smith, D
17. William Lehman, D
18. Claude D. Pepper, D
19. Dante B. Fascell, D

GEORGIA
(10 Representatives)
1. Lindsay Thomas, D
2. Charles F. Hatcher, D
3. Richard Ray, D
4. Elliott H. Levitas, D*
4. Richard Winder, R*
5. Wyche Fowler, Jr., D*
5. Douglas Steele, R*
6. Newt Gingrich, R
7. Lawrence P. McDonald, D
8. J. Roy Rowland, D
9. Edgar L. Jenkins, D
10. Doug Barnard, Jr., D

*Election scheduled for Nov. 30, too late to be included.

HAWAII
(2 Representatives)
1. Cecil Heftel, D
2. Daniel K. Akaka, D

IDAHO
(2 Representatives)
1. Larry E. Craig, R
2. George V. Hansen, R

ILLINOIS
(22 Representatives)
1. Harold Washington, D
2. Gus Savage, D
3. Marty Russo, D
4. George M. O'Brien, R
5. William O. Lipinski, D
6. Henry J. Hyde, R
7. Cardiss Collins, D
8. Dan Rostenkowski, D
9. Sidney R. Yates, D
10. John E. Porter, R
11. Frank Annunzio, R
12. Philip M. Crane, R
13. John N. Erlenborn, R
14. Tom Corcoran, R
15. Edward R. Madigan, R
16. Lynn M. Martin, R
17. Lane Evans, D
18. Robert H. Michel, R
19. Daniel B. Crane, R
20. Richard J. Durbin, D
21. Melvin Price, D
22. Paul Simon, D

INDIANA
(10 Representatives)
1. Katie Hall, D
2. Philip R. Sharp, D
3. John P. Hiler, R
4. Daniel R. Coats, R
5. Elwood H. Hillis, R
6. Daniel Burton, R
7. John T. Myers, R
8. Joel Deckard, R
9. Lee H. Hamilton, D
10. Andrew Jacobs, Jr., D

IOWA
(6 Representatives)
1. Jim Leach, R
2. Thomas J. Tauke, R
3. Cooper Evans, R
4. Neal Smith, D
5. Thomas R. Harkin, D
6. Berkley W. Bedell, D

KANSAS
(5 Representatives)
1. Pat Roberts, R
2. James Slattery, D
3. Larry Winn, Jr., R
4. Dan Glickman, D
5. Bob Whittaker, R

KENTUCKY
(7 Representatives)
1. Carroll Hubbard, Jr., D
2. William H. Natcher, D
3. Romano L. Mazzoli, D
4. Gene Snyder, R
5. Harold D. Rogers, R
6. Larry J. Hopkins, R
7. Carl D. Perkins, D

LOUISIANA
(8 Representatives)
1. Robert L. Livingston, Jr., R
2. Corrine C. (Lindy) Boggs, D
3. W. J. (Billy) Tauzin, D
4. Buddy Roemer, D
5. Thomas J. Huckaby, D
6. W. Henson Moore, R
7. John B. Breaux, D
8. Gillis W. Long, D

MAINE
(2 Representatives)
1. John R. McKernan, Jr., R
2. Olympia J. Snowe, R

MARYLAND
(8 Representatives)
1. Roy P. Dyson, D
2. Clarence D. Long, D
3. Barbara A. Mikulski, D
4. Marjorie S. Holt, R
5. Steny H. Hoyer, D
6. Beverly B. Byron, D
7. Parren J. Mitchell, D
8. Michael D. Barnes, D

MASSACHUSETTS
(11 Representatives)
1. Silvio O. Conte, R
2. Edward P. Boland, D
3. Joseph D. Early, D
4. Barney Frank, D
5. James M. Shannon, D
6. Nicholas Mavroules, D
7. Edward J. Markey, D
8. Thomas P. O'Neill, Jr., D
9. John J. Moakley, D
10. Gerry E. Studds, D
11. Brian J. Donnelly, D

MICHIGAN
(18 Representatives)
1. John Conyers, Jr., D
2. Carl D. Pursell, R
3. Howard E. Wolpe, D
4. Mark Siljander, R
5. Harold S. Sawyer, R
6. Jim Dunn, R
7. Dale E. Kildee, D
8. Bob Traxler, D
9. Guy Vander Jagt, R
10. Donald J. Albosta, D
11. Robert W. Davis, R
12. David E. Bonior, D
13. George W. Crockett, Jr., D
14. Dennis M. Hertel, D
15. William D. Ford, D
16. John D. Dingell, D
17. Sander Levin, D
18. William S. Broomfield, R

MINNESOTA
(8 Representatives)
1. Thomas M. Hagedorn, R
2. Vin Weber, R
3. Bill Frenzel, R
4. Bruce F. Vento, D
5. Martin Olav Sabo, D
6. Gerry Sikorski, D
7. Arlan Strangeland, R
8. James L. Oberstar, D

MISSISSIPPI
(5 Representatives)
1. Jamie L. Whitten, D
2. Webb Franklin, R
3. G.V. (Sonny) Montgomery, D
4. Wayne Dowdy, D
5. Trent Lott, R

MISSOURI
(9 Representatives)
1. William L. Clay, D
2. Robert A. Young, D
3. Richard A. Gephardt, D
4. Ike Skelton, D
5. Alan Wheat, D
6. E. Thomas Coleman, R
7. Gene Taylor, R
8. William Emerson, R
9. Harold L. Volkmer, D

MONTANA
(2 Representatives)
1. Pat Williams, D
2. Ron Marlenee, R

NEBRASKA
(3 Representatives)
1. Douglas K. Bereuter, R
2. Hal Daub, R
3. Virginia Smith, R

NEVADA
(2 Representatives)
1. Harry Reid, D
2. Barbara Vucanovich, R

NEW HAMPSHIRE
(2 Representatives)
1. Norman E. D'Amours, D
2. Judd Gregg, R

NEW JERSEY
(14 Representatives)
1. James J. Florio, D
2. William J. Hughes, D
3. James J. Howard, D
4. Christopher H. Smith, R
5. Marge Roukema, R
6. Bernard J. Dwyer, D
7. Matthew J. Rinaldo, R
8. Robert A. Roe, D

9. Robert G. Torricelli, D
10. Peter W. Rodino, Jr., D
11. Joseph G. Minish, D
12. James A. Courter, R
13. Edwin B. Forsythe, R
14. Frank J. Guarini, D

NEW MEXICO
(3 Representatives)
1. Manuel Lujan, Jr., R
2. Joseph R. Skeen, R
3. William Richardson, D

NEW YORK
(34 Representatives)
1. William Carney, R
2. Thomas J. Downey, D
3. Robert J. Mrazek, D
4. Norman F. Lent, R
5. Raymond J. McGrath, R
6. Joseph P. Addabbo, D
7. Benjamin S. Rosenthal, D
8. James H. Scheuer, D
9. Geraldine A. Ferraro, D
10. Charles E. Schumer, D
11. Edolphus Towns, D
12. Major R. Owens, D
13. Stephen J. Solarz, D
14. Guy Molinari, R
15. Bill Green, R
16. Charles B. Rangel, D
17. Ted Weiss, D
18. Robert Garcia, D
19. Mario Biaggi, D
20. Richard L. Ottinger, D
21. Hamilton Fish, Jr., R
22. Benjamin A. Gilman, R
23. Samuel S. Stratton, D
24. Gerald B. Solomon, R
25. Sherwood L. Boehlert, R
26. David O'B. Martin, R
27. George C. Wortley, R
28. Matthew F. McHugh, D
29. Frank Horton, R
30. Barber B. Conable, Jr., R
31. Jack Kemp, R
32. John J. LaFalce, D
33. Henry J. Nowak, D
34. Stanley N. Lundine, D

NORTH CAROLINA
(11 Representatives)
1. Walter B. Jones, D
2. I. T. Valentine, Jr., D
3. Charles O. Whitley, D
4. Ike Andrews, D
5. Stephen L. Neal, D
6. Charles R. Britt, D
7. Charlie Rose, D
8. W. G. Hefner, D
9. James G. Martin, R
10. James T. Broyhill, R
11. Bill Hendon, R*
11. James McC. Clarke, D*

*Outcome subject to possible recount.

NORTH DAKOTA
(1 Representative)
AL Byron L. Dorgan, D

OHIO
(21 Representatives)
1. Thomas A. Luken, D
2. Willis D. Gradison, Jr., R
3. Tony P. Hall, S
4. Michael G. Oxley, R
5. Delbert L. Latta, R
6. Bob McEwen, R
7. Michael DeWine, R
8. Thomas N. Kindness, R
9. Marcy Kaptur, D
10. Clarence E. Miller, R
11. Dennis E. Eckart, D
12. John R. Kasich, R
13. Donald J. Pease, D
14. John F. Seiberling, D
15. Chalmers P. Wylie, R
16. Ralph Regula, R
17. Lyle Williams, R
18. Douglas Applegate, D
19. Edward F. Feighan, D
20. Mary Rose Oakar, D
21. Louis Stokes, D

OKLAHOMA
(6 Representatives)
1. James R. Jones, D
2. Mike Synar, D
3. Wesley W. Watkins, D
4. Dave McCurdy, D
5. Mickey Edwards, R
6. Glenn English, D

OREGON
(5 Representatives)
1. Les AuCoin, D
2. Robert Smith, R
3. Ronald L. Wyden, D
4. Jim Weaver, D
5. Denny Smith, R

PENNSYLVANIA
(23 Representatives)
1. Thomas M. Foglietta, D
2. William H. Gray III, D
3. Robert A. Borski, Jr., D
4. Joseph P. Kolter, D
5. Richard T. Schultze, R
6. Gus Yatron, D
7. Bob Edgar, D
8. Peter H. Kostmayer, D
9. Bud Shuster, R
10. Joseph M. McDade, R
11. Frank Harrison, D
12. John P. Muretha, D
13. Lawrence Coughlin, R
14. William J. Coyne, D
15. Donald L. Ritter, R
16. Robert S. Walker, R
17. George W. Gekas, R
18. Doug Walgren, D
19. William F. Goodling, R
20. Joseph M. Gaydos, D
21. Thomas J. Ridge, R
22. Austin J. Murphy, D
23. William F. Clinger, Jr., R

RHODE ISLAND
(2 Representatives)
1. Fernand J. St. Germain, D
2. Claudine Schneider, R

SOUTH CAROLINA
(6 Representatives)
1. Thomas F. Hartnett, R
2. Floyd D. Spence, R
3. Butler C. Derrick, D
4. Carroll A. Campbell, Jr., R
5. John Spratt, D
6. Robert M. Tallon, Jr., D

SOUTH DAKOTA
(1 Representative)
AL Thomas A. Daschle, D

TENNESSEE
(9 Representatives)
1. James H. Quillen, R
2. John J. Duncan, R
3. Marilyn Lloyd Bouquard, D
4. James Cooper, D
5. William H. Boner, D
6. Albert Gore, Jr., D
7. Don Sundquist, R
8. Ed Jones, D
9. Harold E. Ford, D

TEXAS
(27 Representatives)
1. Sam B. Hall, Jr., D
2. Charles Wilson, D
3. Steven Bartlett, R
4. Ralph M. Hall, D
5. John Bryant, D
6. Phil Gramm, D
7. Bill Archer, R
8. Jack M. Fields, R
9. Jack Brooks, D
10. J. J. (Jake) Pickle, D
11. Marvin Leath, D
12. Jim Wright, D
13. Jack E. Hightower, D
14. William Patman, D
15. E. (Kika) de la Garza, D
16. Ronald Coleman, D
17. Charles W. Stenholm, D
18. George T. (Mickey) Leland, D
19. Kent R. Hance, D
20. Henry B. Gonzalez, D
21. Tom Loeffler, R
22. Ron Paul, R
23. Abraham Kazen, Jr., D
24. Martin Frost, D
25. Mike Andrews, DL
26. Tom Vandergriff, D*
26. James Bradshaw, R*
27. Solomon P. Ortiz, D

*Outcome subject to possible recount.

UTAH
(3 Representatives)
1. James V. Hansen, R
2. David D. Marriott, R
3. Howard C. Nielson, R

VERMONT
(1 Representative)
AL James M. Jeffords, R

VIRGINIA
(10 Representatives)
1. Herbert Bateman, R
2. G. William Whitehurst, R
3. Thomas J. Bliley, Jr., R
4. Norman Sisisky, D
5. Dan Daniel, D
6. James Olin, D
7. J. Kenneth Robinson, R
8. Stan Parris, R

9. Frederick Boucher, D
10. Frank R. Wolf, R

WASHINGTON
(8 Representatives)
1. Joel Pritchard, R
2. Al Swift, D
3. Don L. Bonker, D
4. Sid W. Morrison, D
5. Thomas S. Foley, D
6. Norman D. Dicks, D
7. Mike Lowry, D
8. Rodney Chandler, R

WEST VIRGINIA
(4 Representatives)
1. Alan B. Mollohan, D
2. Harley O. Staggers, Jr., D
3. Robert Wise, D
4. Nick J. Rahall II, R

WISCONSIN
(9 Representatives)
1. Les Aspin, D
2. Robert W. Kastenmeier, D
3. Steven C. Gunderson, R
4. Clement J. Zablocki, D
5. James Moody, D
6. Thomas E. Petri, R
7. David R. Obey, D
8. Toby Roth, D
9. F. James Sensenbrenner, Jr., R

WYOMING
(1 Representative)
AL Dick Cheney, R

The Governors of the Fifty States

State	Governor	Year of birth	Current term[1]	State	Governor	Year of birth	Current term[1]
Ala.	George C. Wallace, D	1919	1983–87	Mont.	Ted Schwinden, D	1925	1981–85
Alaska	William Sheffield, D	1928	1982–86[2]	Neb.	Robert Kerrey	1943	1983–87
Ariz.	Bruce E. Babbitt, D	1938	1983–87	Nev.	Richard H. Bryan, D	1937	1983–87
Ark.	Bill Clinton, R	1946	1983–85	N.H.	John H. Sununu, R	1939	1983–85
Calif.	George Deukmejian, R	1928	1983–87	N.J.	Thomas H. Kean	1935	1982–86
Colo.	Richard D. Lamm, R	1935	1983–87	N.M.	Toney Anaya, D	1941	1983–87
Conn.	William A. O'Neill, D	1930	1983–87	N.Y.	Mario M. Cuomo, D	1932	1983–87
Del.	Pierre S. du Pont, IV, R	1935	1981–85	N.C.	James B. Hunt, Jr., D	1937	1981–85
Fla.	Robert Graham, D	1936	1983–87	N.D.	Allen I. Olson, R	1938	1981–85
Ga.	Joe Frank Harris, D	1936	1983–87	Ohio	Richard F. Celeste, D	1937	1983–87
Hawaii	George R. Ariyoshi, D	1926	1982–86[2]	Okla.	George P. Nigh, D	1927	1983–87
Idaho	John V. Evans, D	1925	1983–87	Ore.	Victor G. Atiyeh, R	1923	1983–87
Ill.	James R. Thompson,[3] R	1936	1983–87	Pa.	Richard L. Thornburgh, R	1932	1983–87
Ind.	Robert D. Orr, R	1917	1981–85	R.I.	J. Joseph Garrahy, D	1931	1983–87
Iowa	Terry E. Branstad, R	1946	1983–87	S.C.	Richard W. Riley, D	1933	1983–87
Kan.	John W. Carlin, D	1940	1983–87	S.D.	William J. Janklow, R	1939	1983–87
Ky.	John Y. Brown, Jr., D	1933	1979–83[2]	Tenn.	Lamar Alexander, R	1940	1983–87
La.	David C. Treen, R	1928	1980–84[4]	Tex.	Mark W. White, Jr., D	1940	1983–87
Me.	Joseph E. Brennan, D	1934	1983–87	Utah	Scott M. Matheson, D	1929	1981–85
Md.	Harry R. Hughes, D	1926	1983–87	Vt.	Richard A. Snelling, R	1928	1983–85
Mass.	Michael S. Dukakis, D	1934	1983–87	Va.	Charles S. Robb, D	1939	1982–86
Mich.	James J. Blanchard, D	1942	1983–87	Wash.	John Spellman, R	1926	1981–85
Minn.	Rudy Perpich, D	1929	1983–87	W.Va.	John D. Rockefeller, IV, D	1937	1981–85
Miss.	William F. Winter	1923	1980–84	Wis.	Anthony S. Earl, D	1936	1983–87
Mo.	Christopher S. Bond, R	1939	1981–85	Wyo.	Ed. C. Herschler, D	1918	1983–87

1. Except where indicated, all terms begin in January. 2. December. 3. Elections subject to possible recount. 4. March.

A Voting Majority Never Elected a President

In the 1964 election, Lyndon B. Johnson became the only President to almost succeed in receiving a majority of votes. He got 43,130,000 votes or 37.8% of those who were eligible to vote. The number of Americans of voting age who did not vote that year was 43,445,000 or 38.1%.

The President who received the smallest share of votes from eligible Americans was Martin Van Buren, who obtained 11.4% of the ballots from voting-age Americans.

Since universal suffrage was enacted, Calvin Coolidge claimed the smallest percentage by receiving only 23.7% of the ballots from voting-age citizens.

CURRENT EVENTS

What Happened in 1981–82

The important events of the year, from September 1981 to August 1982, organized for easy reference:

The Countries of the World section (starting on page 139) covers specific international events, country by country. Special commentaries on Business and the Economy, Energy, Medicine, Religion, Space, and Travel appear in the appropriate sections (*see* Index).

1981–82

Business and the Economy

1981

Tax-Exempt Certificates Go on Sale (Oct. 1): Demand is heavy for highly promoted investment offered by commercial banks, savings banks, and savings and loan associations. They are expected to cause higher tax loss than Government had expected, $10 billion instead of about $3 billion. "All savers" certificates were authorized by 1981 tax law.

Sears, Roebuck Buys Dean Witter Reynolds (Oct. 8): Nation's largest retail store chain announces plan to purchase fifth-largest brokerage house for more than $600 million in cash and stocks.

U.S. Panel Decertifies Air Controller Union (Oct. 22): Federal Labor Relations Authority strips Professional Air Traffic Controllers Organization of status as legal representative of controllers because it called illegal nationwide strike on Aug. 3. **(Oct. 27):** Federal Appeals Court refuses to delay ruling further.

OPEC Nations Freeze Base Oil Price (Oct. 29): Thirteen in Organization of Oil Producing Countries set common level of $34 a barrel for crude until end of 1982. New base due to increase retail fuel and gasoline prices in U.S. principally because agreement calls for Saudi Arabia to increase price from $32.

2 Big Insurance Companies Agree to Merge (Nov. 3): Connecticut General Corporation and INA Corporation plan $4.3-billion transaction for new organization to be called North American General Corporation.

Labor Attacks Reagan's Economic Policies (Nov. 16–17): Delegates at 14th constitutional convention of A.F.L.-C.I.O., in New York, offer own program, including restoration of some assistance in jobs. Also authorize U.S. labor's reaffiliation with the International Confederation of Free Trade Unions.

Free-Trade Banking Zone Opens in New York (Dec. 3): It authorizes new international banking facilities that are expected to draw back billions of dollars from banks overseas and create thousands of jobs.

U.S. Steel Allowed to Buy Marathon Oil (Dec. 24): Federal judge in Ohio approves purchase for $6.3 billion, ending two-month takeover battle with Mobil Corporation, which had offered $6.5 billion but ran afoul of antitrust rulings by the courts. **(Jan. 6):** Chief Justice Warren E. Burger refuses to block U.S. Steel's acquisition of Marathon.

1982

U.S. Settles A.T.&T. and I.B.M. Cases (Jan. 8): American Telephone and Telegraph Company agrees in antitrust action to give up the 22 Bell System companies providing most local telephone service. Settlement, largest in decades, would let Bell System enter data processing, communications between computers, and sale of related equipment. Justice Department drops as "without merit" marathon action to break up International Business Machines Corporation, dominant in computer industry.

British Coal Miners Reject Strike (Jan. 21): Prime Minister Margaret Thatcher scores victory in effort to tame unions when aggressive workers defy leaders and accept pay rise of 9.3%, below inflation rate.

Philadelphia Bulletin Ceases Publication (Jan. 29): City institution for 134 years goes out of business. Five-month drive to cut costs and raise revenues failed, with losses of $10 million in that period. Problems traced to competition from TV, subscriber dispersal, and traffic congestion.

Laker Airways Bankrupt and Halts Flights (Feb. 5): Upstart company founded by Sir Freddie Laker in 1978 had incurred debts amounting to more than $330 million from buying new planes. It is final defeat for colorful entrepreneur whose economy flights transformed pattern of travel across Atlantic. Laker's fleet grounded at airports in England. Plane on way to Canary Islands is called back.

Britain Cuts Price of North Sea Oil by $1.50 (Feb. 8): Level reduced to $35 a barrel, reflecting surplus of oil in world trade. Iran reported cutting price.

Mexico Devalues Peso by 30% (Feb. 18): Government abruptly announces it no longer will intervene on exchange markets to support currency. Move spurred by flight of capital and growing speculation.

Ford Workers Approve Concessions (Feb. 28): Union members accept new contract that for first time in auto industry trades wage and benefit concessions for assured job security. Saving to Ford estimated at $1 billion over 30 months. Company promises to share profits and to guarantee income until retirement for workers with over 15 years of seniority after they are laid off.

Teamsters Union Accepts Wage Freeze (March 1): Members ratify new 37-month contract with Trucking Management Inc., representing 280 companies. It keeps basic levels steady for at least two years.

Britain Cuts North Sea Oil Price $4 a Barrel (March 6): Decrease to $31 is nation's second cut in month and puts downward pressure on world oil prices.

Procter & Gamble Found Negligent (March 19): Federal jury in Denver rules company offered defective product when it put Rely tampons on market. Awards no damages to Colorado teen-ager who sued the company for $25 million, saying she had become ill with toxic shock syndrome several days after using tampons.

G.M. and Auto Workers Agree on New Contract (March 21): Reach accord after 37 hours continuous bargaining on pact giving up raises and paid time off and deferring cost-of-living increases to save estimated $2–3 billion over 30-month life of contract. Company agrees to reopen four plants it planned to close, extend guaranteed income benefits to laid-off workers at two California plants, and extend "lifetime" job guarantees at four plants. Union will share in profits. **(April 9)** Blue-collar workers narrowly approve new contract, 114,468 in favor, 105,000 against.

Procter & Gamble Liable in Death (April 21): Federal jury in Cedar Rapids, Iowa, orders company to pay $300,000 damages to Michael Kehm, husband of Patricia, 25, who died Sept. 6, 1980, of toxic shock syndrome after using its Rely tampons. Trial was second against company involving toxic shock. Product has since been taken off the market.

Braniff Airline Files Petition in Bankruptcy (May 13): International corporation first major airline in U.S. to seek protection under law. Filing comes a few hours after Braniff suspended all domestic and international flights. Airline head says sharp drop in passenger traffic put severe squeeze on airline's cash reserves. Nearly all of Braniff's 9,600 employees are made jobless.

United Press International Sold (June 2): E.W. Scripps Company transfers news service to the Media News Corporation, a new privately owned company.

Service Industries Lead Employment Totals (July 5): Labor Department data show they and consumer and financial sectors exceed production industry for first time in history of U.S. economy. In April they employed 24.3 million, 300,000 above number employed in the goods-producing industries.

British Railway Strike Collapses (July 18): Engineers and firemen, in victory for Thatcher Government, accede to management demands for increased productivity after other unions refuse support **(July 19):** Service nearly normal after 15-day walkout.

Mitsui Subsidiary Pleads Guilty in Fraud (July 20): U.S. jury indicts unit of Japan's largest trading companies and three employees on charges of fraud and false statements in plot to sell imported steel below allowable prices. **(July 21):** American subsidiary agrees to pay $11 million in civil penalties and $210,000 in criminal fines in dumping conspiracy. Settlement largest in Customs Service history.

R.J. Reynolds Acquires Heublein (July 29): Nation's largest cigarette producer agrees with owner of Kentucky fried chicken, top U.S. vodka producer, on merger valued at $1.3 billion in cash and securities.

$2 Million Libel Verdict Against Washington Post (July 30): U.S. jury in Washington finds newspaper company had printed libelous article about president of Mobil Oil Corporation, William P. Tavoulareas. Post had reported he had used Mobil's money and influence to set up son, Peter, in shipping business and to enrich him with millions in Mobil contracts.

Giant German Company Collapses (Aug. 10): Telefunken, electrical and electronics group, announces it has run out of cash and seeks court receiver. Company has lost nearly $800 million since 1978.

Federal Judge Accepts Basic A.T.&T. Pact (Aug. 11): But insists on basic modifications in framework of proposed antitrust settlement between American Telephone & Telegraph Company and Justice Department. Judge Harold H. Greene in Washington says he must review and approve each stage of divestiture. Says A.T.&T must be prohibited from offering electronic information service until the risk of its domination of the field is ended.

Interest Rates Fall, Stocks Spurt (Aug. 17): Market achieves largest one-day gain in history with second largest trading volume on record. Dow-Jones average soars 38.81 points to 831.24. Persistent recession called factor in interest drop.

Manville Corp. Files in Bankruptcy (Aug. 26): Nation's biggest asbestos producer files for reorganization under protection of Federal laws, citing financial drain of more than 10,000 claims against it by persons exposed to injurious effects of asbestos. Mining and manufacturing concern is largest American industrial company ever to seek bankruptcy.

The Courts

1981

Nabisco Inc. to Pay $5 Million in Rights Accord (Sept. 11): Major food and baking concern settles with Equal Employment Opportunity Commission in Federal Court case affecting charges of sex discrimination involving 8,000 women employed in bakeries.

First Woman Justice Joins Supreme Court (Sept. 21): Senate, 99–0, confirms Sandra Day O'Connor, 51-year-old Arizona judge. **(Sept. 25):** The 102nd Justice takes seat. President Reagan attends brief ceremony.

U.S. Judge Dismisses Suit by Hostages (Oct. 26): Los Angeles court rejects action against Iran asking $5 million for each of seven, because of terms of settlement between U.S. and Iran.

Labor Wins Ruling in Supreme Court (Dec. 2): Justices decide unanimously that employees who deal with confidential information are protected by federal labor law in right to join unions, overturning lower court.

Robert H. Bork Named to Appeals Court (Dec. 7): Reagan nominates former Solicitor General, 54, a conservative legal scholar, who carried out President Nixon's order to dismiss Watergate special prosecutor Archibald Cox in "Saturday night massacre."

1982

Arkansas Law on "Creation Science" Overturned (Jan. 5): Federal judge in Little Rock voids as unconstitutional a state law requiring "balanced" teaching of creationism and evolution theories. Court declares creationism has "no scientific merit or educational value" and represents effort to introduce biblical version of creation into curriculum.

Jersey Governor Pardons Newspaper and Reporter (Jan. 18): Brendan T. Byrne clears *New York Times* and its reporter M.A. Farber of criminal contempt charges in refusal to surrender reporter's notes in widely publicized "Dr. X" murder trial in 1978. Farber spent 40 days in jail and paper paid $286,000 fine. **(Jan. 19):** On last day in office, Governor returns to *Times* and the reporter $101,000 imposed for criminal contempt. Case attracted wide attention.

Independent Political Groups Left Unrestricted (Jan. 19): Supreme Court, 4–4, upholds decision approving unlimited spending for Presidential candidates.

Judges Overrule Air Force Verdict (Feb. 22): Federal Court of Military Appeals dismisses court-martial charges against Lieut. Christopher M. Cooke, 26, missile-launch crew member accused of passing information to Soviet Embassy. Civilian judges note Air Force had promised Lieutenant Cooke immunity in exchange for his cooperation in inquiry.

Supreme Court Rebuffs Amish on Social Security (Feb. 23): Rules unanimously that members of Old Order Amish Church who operate businesses must pay Social Security and unemployment taxes required of all employers despite belief that paying taxes is a sin.

Justices Approve Regulation of Drug Equipment (March 6): Supreme Court holds, 8–0, that communities may control sale of such material as pipes, clips, and cigarette papers as long as regulations do not restrict free speech and give "fair warning." **(March 8):** Court refuses to hear challenge to Westchester County, N.Y., law banning sale of "drug paraphernalia." Two shops had brought suit.

Supreme Court Upholds Seniority Systems (April 5): Justices, 5–4, reject challenges to fairness of plans in place since Civil Rights Act of 1964 outlawed job discrimination based on race or sex. Rules plans legal if not adopted for discriminatory purpose.

Justices Clarify School Discrimination Law (May 17): Supreme Court, 6–3, rules ban on sex discrimination in federally aided education programs applies to employees as well as students. Ruling resolves uncertainty about scope of one of more important federal antidiscrimination statutes.

Supreme Court Widens Search Authority (June 1): Justices, 6–3, rule police may search luggage or packages they find inside an automobile if they have "probable cause" to search car without warrant.

High Court Backs Unions' Leaderships (June 14): Decides, 5–4, that unions are legally free to prohibit candidates for union office from accepting campaign contributions from sources outside union.

Justices Uphold Schooling for Aliens (June 15): Supreme Court rules, 5–4, children have constitutional right to free public education. Finds Texas law violates constitutional right to equal protection.

Justices Rule on Civil Rights Suits (June 21): Supreme Court, 7–2, declares Civil Rights Act of 1871 permits individuals to sue state and local officials and agencies directly in federal courts. Overturns Appeals Court ruling requiring exhaustion of state remedies before suing in federal courts.

Supreme Court Upholds Presidential Immunity (June 24): Justices, 5–4, rule no President may be sued for damages for any official action he takes while in office, overturning lower court ruling in case involving Richard M. Nixon. Court refuses, 8–1, to give same immunity to top Presidential aides.

High Court Limits School Book Banning (June 25): Justices, in fragmented decision, rule First Amendment guarantee of freedom of speech curbs discretion of public school officials. In Long Island, N.Y., case, they find that officials sued by pupils may be required to defend actions in federal court. Publishers and civil liberties lawyers hail ruling.

Justices Limit School Aid to Handicapped (June 29): Supreme Court, 6–3, rules federal law entitling children to education does not oblige local school districts to provide service for them to reach full potential. Overturns rulings that Westchester County, N.Y., school district must provide sign-language interpreter for deaf fourth-grader.

Nursing Schools Must Admit Men (July 1): Supreme Court, 5–4, rules state-operated institutions cannot constitutionally exclude them from admission.

Supreme Court Upholds Bar to Child Pornography (July 2): Finds unanimously that New York law barring use of children in sexually explicit material is constitutional, overruling New York court.

Justices Rule for N.A.A.C.P. on Boycott (July 2): Decide, 8–0, that association cannot constitutionally be held liable for seven-year losses to white merchants from action by it and 91 individuals in Mississippi.

Crime and Violence

1981

Racist Convicted in Slaying of 2 Black Joggers (Sept. 19): Salt Lake City jury finds Joseph Paul Franklin, 31, of Alabama, guilty of first-degree murder in sniper killing of two black men jogging with two white women near Liberty Park on Aug. 20, 1980.

People's Temple Case Ends in Mistrial (Sept. 26): Jury in San Francisco Federal Court deadlocked on charges against Larry Layton, 35, former member of People's Temple, growing out of its catastrophic last days in Guyana jungle. Layton was accused of conspiring to murder Rep. Leo J. Ryan, California Democrat, and to attempt to murder Richard Dwyer, chief of U.S. mission to Guyana.

Theft of $2 Million in Rare Books Solved (Oct. 3): Columbia graduate student, John M. Papanastassiou, a 34-year-old Greek citizen, arrested in New York by U.S. customs agents after international hunt, aided by rare-book seller. Volumes valued at $2 million stolen from University College, London, included 1638 edition of Galileo's "Discorsi" and other early treatises.

Life Sentence in Espionage Case (Oct. 16): Former Army code custodian, Joseph George Helmich, 44, sent to prison by federal judge in Jacksonville, Fla., after admitting selling top-secret information to Soviet Union for $131,000 to get out of debt.

Ex-Intelligence Agents Indicted (Nov. 19): Frank E. Terpil, former C.I.A. agent, and associate, George Gregory Korkala, indicted on charges of conspiring to sell guns, ammunition, decoding devices, and instruments of torture in 1979 to Idi Amin, then President of Uganda. Terpil previously indicted with another former agent, Edwin P. Wilson, on charges of shipping explosives to Libya.

Former Green Beret Convicted of Assault (Dec. 4): Eugene Aloys Tafoya, 48, acquitted in Colorado county court of attempted murder in shooting of Libyan student, critic of Libyan Government. Taffoya had contended he was on C.I.A. assignment. **(Jan. 5):** Federal judge sentences Tafoya to two years on the two misdemeanor assault charges.

3 Hijacked Planes Fly From Venezuela to Cuba (Dec. 8): Airliners seized by gunmen with more than 100 hostages aboard. Hijackers' aims called political but varied. By agreement Cuba is obliged to return three planes, hijackers, and all others aboard.

Spy for Poland Gets Life Term (Dec. 14): Marian W. Zacharski sentenced in Los Angeles Federal Court for providing stolen national security information to Polish Government. William Holden Bell, American engineer, gets eight years and $10,000 fine for helping get Hughes Aircraft Company data. He had testified for prosecution.

1982

Coast Truck Driver Guilty of Slaying 10 (Jan. 6): William Benin, 34, convicted by Los Angeles jury of murdering boys and young men and abandoning bodies near freeways. Prosecutor says Benin killed victims after picking them up in homosexual areas, having homosexual relations with them, and robbing them.

Ex-Boxing Promoter Guilty of Embezzlement (Jan. 13): Harold Rossfields Smith, 38, convicted in Los Angeles Federal Court of stealing $21.3 million from Wells Fargo National Bank in one of largest bank embezzlements in U.S. history. Sammie Marshall, business associate, convicted of fraud.

Convict Author Guilty in Slaying (Jan. 21): Jack Henry Abbott, writer of prison memoir "In the Belly of the Beast," convicted of first-degree manslaughter after 14-day trial in New York court in stabbing of East Village waiter. Abbott, who turned 38 on same day, had been sponsored by author Norman Mailer. He had been free six weeks in work-release program.

Senator Harrison A. Williams, Jr., Sentenced (Feb. 16): New Jersey Democrat, 62, given three years in prison and $50,000 fine by Long Island Federal judge on charges of bribery and conspiracy growing out of Justice Department Abscam investigation into political corruption. He faces at least 14 months in prison.

Wayne B. Williams, 23, Guilty in Atlanta Slayings (Feb. 27): Convicted by jury of nine women and three men, eight blacks and four whites, in two killings in wave of 28 that had terrorized Atlanta. Special task force investigating killings has already been virtually disbanded. Mr. Williams, a black, sentenced to two consecutive life terms.

Jury Convicts Claus von Bulow (March 16): Rhode Island panel finds Danish businessman, 55, guilty of twice trying to kill wealthy wife by injecting her with insulin. Wife, 50, called "Sunny" by friends. **(May 7):** Von Bülow sentenced to 30 years in prison. Bail increased to $1,000,000 from $500,000.

Justices Restore Conviction of Ex-Army Doctor (March 31): Supreme Court, 6–3, overturns Appeals Court ruling that Dr. Jeffrey R. MacDonald's constitutional right to speedy trial had been violated. MacDonald convicted in 1979 of murders of his wife and children at Fort Bragg, N.C., nine years earlier.

Conviction Overturned in Fire Deaths (April 14): Judge in Westchester County, N.Y., court frees Luis Marin, 26, Guatemalan, four days after jury had convicted former coffee waiter of arson and murder in starting fire at Stouffer's Inn at Harrison on Dec. 4, 1980, killing 26 businessmen in a conference center. Judge Lawrence N. Martin, Jr., says jury, in six-day deliberation, had gone beyond the facts and that prosecution had not proved case.

Convict-Author Sentenced in Killing (April 15): Jack Henry Abbott, 38, author of prison memoir "In the Belly of the Beast," gets 15 years to life in New York court for slaying waiter in East Village. Abbott has eight years left to serve in prison on convictions for previous crimes.

4 Gunmen Free Airline Hostages in Honduras (May 1): Release 11 remaining captives. Honduras allows hijackers to leave for Cuba by air. They are identified as members of leftist front who sought release of political prisoners and $100,000 ransom. Ten hostages, including eight Americans and pilot, had escaped by breaking out as captors slept.

Rev. Moon Convicted in Income-Tax Case (May 18): Federal jury in New York finds Sun Myung Moon, founder and leader of Unification Church, guilty of conspiracy to defraud Government and filing false returns. One of top aides, Takeru Kamiyama, also convicted of conspiracy, perjury and obstructing investigation. Both men remain free on bail. **(July 16):** Federal judge sentences Moon to 18-month prison term and fines him maximum of $25,000. Codefendant gets six-month sentence and $5,000 fine.

Sirhan B. Sirhan's Parole Date Canceled (May 20): California Board of Prison Terms rescinds 1984 date set in 1975 by panel. Board cites death threats made by Sirhan, assassin of Senator Robert F. Kennedy, in letters he sent from Soledad Prison.

Soldier Sentenced for Murdering Blacks (May 24): Joseph Christopher, 26, given 60 years to life in prison for murdering two black men and a black youth during 26-hour period in 1980. State judge in Buffalo found him guilty of second-degree murder in each of the three slayings in the Buffalo area.

John W. Hinckley Jr. Not Guilty in Reagan Shooting (June 21): Federal jury in Washington finds defendant, 27, innocent by reason of insanity on 13 charges in attack on President and three other men March 30, 1981. Verdict sharply criticized in Congress. Officials call for abolition of insanity defense. **(June 22):** Hinckley ordered to Federal mental hospital for psychiatric examination.

18 Japanese Charged in I.B.M. Theft Plot (June 22): Businessmen accused by U.S. of conspiring to steal confidential computer information from International Business Machines Corporation and transport it to Japan. They are employees of two major electronics companies, Hitachi and Mitsubishi. Undercover F.B.I. agent trapped men through decoy agency. **(June 23):** Hitachi Ltd. admits authorizing $540,000 payment for confidential computer information.

Virginia Executes Killer After Legal Turmoil (Aug. 10): Frank J. Coppola, 38, electrocuted for beating of Newport News housewife in robbery. It is fifth execution in nation since Supreme Court in 1972 forced revision of capital punishment laws.

Suspect Acquitted in Jordan Shooting (Aug. 17): Joseph Paul Franklin, 32, cleared in Federal trial at South Bend, Ind. He had been accused of wounding Vernon E. Jordan, Jr., black civil rights leader outside Fort Wayne, Ind., motel in 1980. Jordan was then director of National Urban League. Franklin serving four life terms in killing of two blacks.

Disasters

1981

Pit Blast Kills 65 Czech Coal Miners (Sept. 4): Rescuers save 40 of 105 in mine in northern Czechoslovakia. Disaster reported country's worst in 20 years.

Chief of Air Force Stunt Team Killed (Sept. 6): Lieut. Col. David L. Smith, 40, leader of Thunderbirds precision flying team, dies in crash of T-38, when it apparently loses power over Cleveland Airport as engine sucks up seagulls on takeoff. Crew chief, Staff Sgt. Dwight Roberts, 31, parachutes to safety.

300 Die as Amazon Riverboat Sinks (Sept. 19): Craft founders in northern Brazil jungle port of Obidos. Officials report 178 of 500 aboard swam to safety.

Crash of Dutch Airliner Kills 17 (Oct. 6): Fokker F-28 *Fellowship* crashes to ground near Rotterdam when sudden turbulence of wind rips off a wing.

Plane Crash Kills 178 Yugoslavs on Corsica (Dec. 1): Chartered Yugoslav Inex Adria DC-9 Super 80 hits mountain while approaching Ajaccio airport, which had been classified as unsafe by International Federation of Airline Pilots Associations. Victims include 172 passengers on one-day holiday and six crew members. Crash listed as 10th worst disaster recorded in aviation.

24 Perish in Coal Mine Disasters (Dec. 9): Deaths in five-day period include 13 killed by methane explosion in Grundy Mine 21 of Tennessee Consolidated Coal Company 20 miles west of Chattanooga, eight dead in blast at Adkins Coal Company's mine 18 at Topmost, Ky., and three crushed to death by falling roof in tunnel under Leatherwood Mountain in north-central West Virginia. Mine-safety partisans charge Reagan Administration's budget slashes are related to nearly 8% increase in mine deaths in 1981 over the total for 1980.

Snow and High Winds Batter British Isles (Dec. 13): Snarl travel and black out large parts of Britain and Ireland in third snowstorm within five days as drifts mount. Temperatures fall to lowest on record for date. At least one dead.

1982

16 Dead in Coast Flood and Mud Slides (Jan. 5): Damage mounts into millions as one of most destructive rain storms in modern times rages across San Francisco Bay area. Three children are among victims.

78 Dead in Washington Jetliner Crash (Jan. 13): Air Florida Boeing 737 crashes into 14th Street bridge and skids into ice on Potomac River shortly after take-off from National Airport in snowstorm. Only five of 79 on plane survive. Four killed in cars as plane hit bridge. Safety experts term ice build-up on jetliner likeliest cause of disaster.

3 Killed in Washington Subway Crash (Jan. 13): Twenty-five injured, some seriously, in derailment at switch near Smithsonian Institution station. It is first fatal accident in six years of operation of capital's Metro subway system. Trains packed with Government workers seeking to avoid snowstorm.

4 Air Force Stunt Fliers Killed (Jan. 18): Team's jets crash one after another into Nevada desert near Indian Springs and explode in flames. It was worst accident in history of Thunderbirds and 15th fatal crash since precision team was formed in 1953.

6 Killed in Oklahoma School Explosion (Jan. 19): Five children and teacher perish in Spencer and 35 are injured as water heater blast rips through kitchen and showers bricks, glass, and metal on cafeteria.

7 Dead in Kentucky Mine Explosion (Jan. 20): Disaster at Floyd County coal field is fourth in Appalachia in less than seven weeks and raises to 14 number killed in first 20 days of 1982. **(Jan. 21):** Demands grow in Washington for Congressional intervention to overcome Reagan Administration's staff reductions in Federal mine safety program.

Two Dead in Boston Harbor Crash (Jan. 23): Unaccounted for after World Airways DC-10 jet skids off end of Logan International Airport runway. Thirty-nine treated for injuries in accident.

Fire Damages Roosevelt's Home (Jan. 23): Destroys much of 75-foot section of roof of F.D.R.'s birthplace at Hyde Park, N.Y., and damages several bedrooms in historic 35-room mansion, 156 years old. Curators rush to save antique furnishings and paintings. **(Jan. 24):** Most of furniture and many art and historical objects reported safe or in condition to be restored. Restoration of house expected in nine months. Centennial tours of house canceled.

Hundreds Perish in Peru Floods (Jan. 27): At least 600, possibly 2,500, dead or missing after Chontayacu River destroys 17 villages along 60-mile stretch.

Fire Kills 23 in Tokyo Hotel (Feb. 8): More than 60 injured as flames rage through top two floors of 10-story luxury Hotel New Japan. Tourists and foreign visitors among 440 registered guests.

84 Perish as Oil Rig Sinks (Feb. 15): All aboard lost when huge craft founders in 50-foot seas off coast of Newfoundland. Rig, the Ocean Ranger, had been described by owners, Ocean Drilling and Exploration Company of New Orleans, as world's largest semisubmersible oil rig. **(Feb. 16):** Planes and ships search in vain for survivors. Sixty miles east of the rig's site, a Soviet freighter, *Mekhanik Tarasov,* with 35 to 40, sinks in heavy seas; seven survivors picked up, 18 bodies recovered.

27 Dead in Illinois Plane Crash (March 19): Air National Guard tanker jet, KC 135 stratotanker, explodes and plummets from night sky into swampy woodlands near Wonder Lake. Plane carried four crew members and 27 Air Force reservists.

4 Army Paratroopers Killed in Airdrop (March 30): High-wind pockets blamed for fatalities in California Mojave Desert as 2,200 soldiers of 82nd Airborne Division parachute from Air Force C-141 and C-130 transports in Pentagon test of quick response to trouble around world. Toll of injured set at 156.

350 Perish in Winter of Rugged Weather (April 1): Losses of at least $7.8 billion set by government meteorologist. For weeks, subfreezing temperatures and paralyzing snow had attacked states from Montana to Maine. As far south as Florida, the citrus crop was damaged. Early spring flooding has plagued Middle West. Storms have hit Far West.

31 Die in Tornadoes and Windstorms (April 3): Worst storms in more than decade cut through 13 states from Ohio to Texas. Arkansas hit worst, with 14 dead, including family of five huddled under mattress.

Collapse of Bridge Kills 12 Workers (April 15): At least 16 of construction crew injured as unfinished structure gives way as workers pour concrete in industrial area at East Chicago, Ind.

Plane Crash Kills 112 in China (April 27): British-made Trident jet operated by Civilian Aviation Administration of China crashes near southern city of Guilin. Two Americans, 50 Chinese residents of Hong Kong, and several Japanese tourists reported aboard airliner on flight from Canton.

7 Dead as Tornadoes Hit Texas and Oklahoma (May 12): Storms crush homes and businesses and cause $200-million damage at Altus Air Force Base in Oklahoma. Heavy rains cause flash floods in some areas.

430 Reported Killed in Major China Flood (May 19): Populous southeastern province of Guangdong recovering from disaster that marooned 450,000 persons. Floods reported worst in province in 30 years.

Tornado Kills 10 in Southern Illinois (May 29): More than 100 injured as storm outs 15-mile swath.

12 Dead in Heavy Connecticut Floods (June 7): Damage in millions over weekend as dams break, bridges and roadways are washed out, and homes and automobiles float away. More than 1,300 flee to emergency centers. Guardsmen assist in rescue efforts.

153 Killed in Crash of Jetliner (July 9): Toll includes 145 aboard and eight on ground when Boeing 727 crashes in residential suburb just after taking off from New Orleans Airport. Two alerts of hazardous wind shifts were broadcast just before accident.

245 Killed in Japanese Floods (July 22): Worst such disaster in 25 years hits Nagasaki. Monsoon rains hamper rescue efforts, with 117 reported missing and feared dead after four days.

Helicopter Crash Kills Vic Morrow (July 23): Actor, 51, dies with two Vietnamese children after explosives hit tail rotor of machine as they make war movie northwest of Los Angeles.

Helicopter Crash Kills 5 in Ireland (July 29): Jack T. Donnell, 53, president of Charter Company, dies with three of his senior executives and their pilot on way to board jetliner for Paris meeting.

53 Dead in France's Worst Road Accident (July 31): Forty-four children perish as two buses carrying 107 children to camp for underprivileged crash and catch fire in 10-vehicle pileup about 200 miles south of Paris. Two camp counselors, driver, relief driver, and five persons in automobiles also killed.

Education

1981

Columbia Dedicates Center for Humanities (Sept. 16): Heyman Center opened as first of its kind on Morningside Heights, New York, as final component in university's $28.7-million residential complex. The $2.5-million interdisciplinary teaching and research center made possible by $700,000 gift from David M. Heyman, 90-year-old New York financier and philanthropist. For the first time it will house several programs in one location.

Wellesley Inaugurates 11th President (Sept. 18): Nannerl O. Keohane, previously professor of political science at Stanford University, in address, defends need of all-women's colleges. She is a 1961 Wellesley graduate.

U. of Pennsylvania Inaugurates 20th President (Oct. 23): Dr. Sheldon Hackney heads 241-year-old university at Philadelphia. In inaugural he refers to "energetic and diverse" institution. Pomp and pageantry, also kite-flying, mark the celebration.

Philadelphia Teachers End 50-Day Strike (Oct. 28): Commonwealth Court averts general city walkout by ordering return to work under previous year's contract provisions. Court orders Federation of Teachers and school officials to resume talks.

M.I.T. Approves Link With Research Institute (Dec. 4): Under controversial agreement, accepts $7.5-million gift from Edwin C. Whitehead, philanthropist, who will spend $120 million to construct and endow Whitehead Institute for Biomedical Research, with staff holding joint appointments with M.I.T.

1982

Gift to Harvard Grows to $77 Million (Jan. 13): Bequest by head of Mallinckrodt Inc. in 1967 of 1.5 million shares increases in value as Avon Products moves to acquire chemical concern, making gift largest single one in history of U.S. education. Washington University in St. Louis also benefits.

Amherst Hires Black Chemistry Professor (Jan. 21): Complies with condition in $1-million gift from a white benefactor, Theodore L. Cross, 57, alumnus. Dr. Richard A. Goldsby, 47, professor at University of Maryland, will be 10th black faculty member.

Columbia College to Accept Women Freshmen (Jan. 22): Last all-male college in Ivy League announces policy change effective in autumn of 1983. Barnard will continue as undergraduate college for women.

Yale and Celanese Sign Research Contract (Feb. 17): University enters three-year, $1.1-million agreement with manufacturer of chemicals and fabrics. Yale will conduct research in composition and synthesis of enzymes. Celanese will fund research. Such subsidies have aroused academic controversy.

Boy, 12, Is College Senior (May 1): Jay Luo about to become youngest university graduate in United States history with a degree in mathematics from Boise, Idaho, State University. Jay is already planning postgraduate work at Stanford University.

Foundation Helps 19 Geniuses (July 13): Eighteen men and a woman to get awards ranging from $24,000 to $60,000 annually for the next five years from John D. and Catherine MacArthur Foundation under program to free creative individuals from economic pressures or other impediments to their careers.

Columbia Honors South African Black Activist (Aug. 3): University President Michael I. Sovern goes to Johannesburg to confer honorary doctorate of sacred theology on Anglican Bishop Desmond M. Tutu, general secretary of South African Council of Churches. He was barred from traveling to New York when passport was withdrawn because of his protests against white government's policy of racial segregation, apartheid. Bishop is 51.

Energy

1981

Start of Coast Nuclear Plant Held Up (Sept. 21): Despite massive protests, with more than a thousand arrests, Nuclear Regulatory Commission gives Pacific Gas and Electric Company preliminary licence to operate first of two reactors at Diablo Canyon Nuclear Power Plant near San Luis Obispo, Calif. **(Sept. 28):** Company delays start-up indefinitely after finding structure of a cooling system does not conform to approved design. Error in use of diagrams blamed. Protesting group ends two-week demonstration and discerns further evidence that reactor is unsafe. It is within 2½ miles of offshore earthquake faultline. **(Oct. 2):** Company notifies commission that construction errors in antiquake supports extended to electrical cabling system. Commission official says these faults were also result of reverse reading of blueprints.

Supreme Court Approves U.S. Oil Leasing Procedures (Dec. 1): Justices rule unanimously that Federal Government is not legally required to aid small companies in competing for offshore petroleum and gas leases. Appeals Court overruled.

1982

France Contracts for Soviet's Natural Gas (Jan. 23): Pact provides for purchase of about 280 billion cubic feet of Siberian natural gas a year for 25 years, starting in 1984. U.S. has objected on grounds Western Europe will be too dependent on Soviet.

$900 Million Damage in Baltic Oil Spill (Jan. 30): Moscow insurance executive discloses loss off Soviet coast on previous Nov. 21. British tanker *Globe Asimi,* with 4.8 million gallons of boiler fuel aboard, ran aground and broke up in storm outside Klaipeda, Lithuania. Spill one of worst on record.

China Opens Offshore Oil to Foreigners (Feb. 16): Declares nearly 58,000 square miles open for eventual exploration and production by outside companies.

Entertainment and Culture

1981

U.S. Art on Exhibit in Peking (Sept. 1): Show is first American-sponsored one since Communist takeover. Opens when hosts back down under threats to close exhibit, and remove ban on 13 modern abstract paintings.

Patron Wills Collection to Washington Museum (Sept. 5): Joseph Hirshhorn, dead at 82, leaves entire private collection of modern works to institution he founded with gift of 6,000 works, the Hirshhorn Museum and Sculpture Garden. Benefactor also leaves $5-million bequest to the museum.

Picasso's "Guernica" Leaves U.S. for Spain (Sept. 9): Monumental antiwar mural goes home after 42 years on loan to New York's Museum of Modern Art.

Ruins of Assyrian Imperial City Uncovered (Oct. 17): Yale scholar finds clue to location of site in modern Syria in cuneiform tablets of itinerary of ancient journey. Dr. Harvey Weiss of Yale reports discovery of site of capital surrounded by massive walls and remains of human occupation dating back 7,000 years.

New York Museum Gets Early Chinese Art (Dec. 11): Gift to Metropolitan Museum of Art of 60 major works of painting and calligraphy valued at $18 million. Works form heart of collection of 200 pieces of John M. Crawford, Jr., bibliophile and patron of arts.

1982

Popular Satirist Published in Moscow (Jan. 17): Soviet authorities for first time authorize publication of collection of songs by late Vladimir Vysotsky, singer and actor. His songs were irreverent and satirical lyrics about life in Soviet Union.

$1-Million Brueghel Stolen in London (Feb. 3): Courtauld Institute reports theft of 1565 picture "Christ and the Woman Taken in Adultery" by Pieter Bruegel the Elder, a Flemish masterpiece.

D'Oyley Carte Company Goes Out of Business (Feb. 27): London opera folds after 106 years as authentic repository of Gilbert and Sullivan tradition. Company had toured world from Sydney to New York.

F.C.C. Opens Way to New Television Stations (March 4): Plans licensing of 3,000–4,000 across nation in next three years. Stations would operate at lower power, and reach viewers within 10–15 mile radius.

Metropolitan Museum Gets $60-Million Gift (March 4): Belle Linsky of New York donates one of greatest private collections in U.S. of European art from Renaissance and later periods. Paintings and objets d'art gathered by Mrs. Linsky and late husband, Jack, stationery industralists, over 40 years.

New Editor for Times of London (March 17): Charles Douglas-Home, 44, deputy editor, appointed after week-long wrangle over management of paper. He succeeds Harold Evans, forced to resign by Rupert Murdoch, owner of *Times* and other papers around world.

Full "Red Badge of Courage" Being Published (April 1): New version of classic Civil War novel by Stephen Crane restores changes, phrases, sentences, paragraphs, and even an entire chapter eliminated for publication in 1895 to popularize it and play down gloominess. Crane's widow had given away manuscript pages that turned up in different archives.

Fire Destroys Wolf Trap Theater (April 5): President Reagan pledges help in restoring $2.2-million performing arts center at National Park near Washington, a 3,500-seat wooden amphitheater in rustic setting in Virginia suburbs.

New Roget Eliminates "Sexism" (April 17): Edition of 130-year-old book of synonyms and antonyms bars categories that woman editor says are biased. "Mankind" becomes "humankind," "countryman" is "country dweller." Category heads as neutral as possible.

1982 World's Fair Opens in Knoxville (May 1): President and Mrs. Reagan attend festival of music, prayers, dancing, speeches, and exhibitions in East Tennessee hills. Also present are diplomats, officials, bankers, and business executives.

Rodin's "Gates of Hell" Displayed in New York (May 26): Workmen erect 21-foot high, 8-ton sculptured relief at Charles Engelhard Court of Metropolitan Museum of Art. Portal incorporates more than 180 figures. It is newest bronze casting of plaster original by Auguste Rodin, the French sculptor.

Monsanto Gives $23.5 Million in Research Pact (June 3): Company signs agreement with Washington University, St. Louis, for five-year collaboration in biomedical study. Contract provisions aimed to minimize possible conflict of interest by professors.

F.C.C. Approves Satellite-Home Transmission (June 23): Approves final rules for enabling consumers to receive 30 or more channels on small disk antennas.

$3.25 Million Paid for Samuel F.B. Morse Painting (July 29): "Gallery of the Louvre," an 1832 work by inventor of telegraph, a celebrated artist, bought by Daniel J. Terra, President Reagan's Ambassador at Large for Cultural Affairs, from Syracuse University. Price highest ever paid for American work of art.

Environment

1981

Pesticide Endangers Birds in 17 States (Sept. 15): High levels of acutely toxic endrin, sprayed on 200,000 acres of wheatland in eastern Montana, found in several species of game birds. Hunting seasons may have to be canceled, Federal officials report. Pesticide also threatens rare endangered whooping crane, peregrine falcon, and bald eagle. **(Sept. 17):** Environmental Protection Agency calls pesticide levels far below danger point for humans.

Nation's 114 Worst Toxic Sites Listed (Oct. 30): Florida leads in numbers, with 16, followed by New Jersey, with 12, and New York and Pennsylvania with 8 each.

1982

Earthquake Jolts New England and Canada (Jan. 9): Coastal area feels first significant temblor in more than a century. No major damage is reported.

Rare Osprey Reappears in New York State (Jan. 15): Bird taken off state's endangered species list after ban on DDT pesticide spurs "tremendous comeback."

U.S. Environment Unit Eliminated (Feb. 27): Department of Transportation drops Office of Environment in reorganization to increase efficiency. Private environmental workers fear danger to moves to prevent destructive effects from new projects.

Quarreling Condors Break Rare Egg (March 5): Parents fighting over care of egg drop only one laid this breeding season off cliff near Ventura, Calif. Specialists seeking to save rare birds watch action.

Birds Make Comeback After DDT Ban (March 10): Bald eagle, brown pelican, peregrine falcon, and others returning to former habitats after being threatened with extinction by insecticide, which the government outlawed 10 years previously, the Department of Interior reports.

Rules on Hazardous Waste Eased (March 14): Environmental Protection Agency suspends requirement that manufacturers report each year on disposition of material. Plans annual survey of 10% of companies.

New Institute to Study Environment (June 3): John D. and Catherine T. MacArthur Foundation to give $15 million over five years for Institute for World Environment and Resources for research and policy planning on such global issues as water resources and modification of atmosphere.

E.P.A. Announces Waste-Dumping Rules (July 13): Says long-deferred regulations for use of land sites will protect nation's drinking water supply and health of citizens. They set design and construction standards for land-disposal facilities.

Love Canal Area Ruled Safe (July 14): Federal Public Health Service declares neighborhood surrounding Niagara Falls, N.Y., section is habitable. At least 21,800 tons of chemical wastes were dumped into canal in 1940s and 1950s. Findings based on a study by the Environmental Protection Agency.

Ban on Commercial Whaling Voted (July 23): International Whaling Commission, meeting in Brighton, England, calls for prohibition starting in 1986. Vote is 25 to 7. Japan and Norway among nations planning to continue whaling.

Health and Medicine

1981

New Drug Blocks Second Heart Attack (Oct. 29): National Heart, Lung, and Blood Institute cuts short clinical tests of propranolol. The drug, already on the market under name of Inderal, has been prescribed for treating hypertension and angina pectoris. Speedy approval by F.D.A. indicated.

Cured Meats Found Relatively Safe (Dec. 10): Committee of experts reports that elimination of nitrites and nitrates as food additives would probably not have major impact on human health. Decides that cured meats account for only small proportion of exposure to cancer-causing nitrosamines. Committee was convened by National Academy of Sciences.

Woman Survives "Elephant Man" Operation (Dec. 10): Philadelphian, 21, recovering well after nine hours of radical surgery to cure severe and unusual form of neurofibromatosis, a rare genetic disease.

Judge Bars Damages for LSD Experiment (Dec. 26): U.S. Court in South Dakota rules Calvin Sweet, former soldier, is not entitled to damages. Sweet had sought $3.9 million, contending he had been made mentally ill by army experiments with drug. Court rules his claim fell outside the statute of limitations.

First Test-Tube Baby Born in U.S. Hospital (Dec. 28): Elizabeth Jordan Carr, 5 pounds 12 ounces and "perfectly healthy," delivered at Norfolk, Va., General Hospital. She was conceived in a laboratory dish. She is 15th born in this manner, the others having been in Britain and Australia.

1982

Final Report Brands Laetrile Useless (Jan. 27): Government-sponsored study published in *New England Journal of Medicine* reports no therapeutic benefit and potentially hazardous effects.

Rule on Teen-Age Contraceptives Issued (Feb. 19): Administration formally requires family planning clinics using federal funds to notify parents whenever children under 18 receive oral contraceptives or prescription birth control devices.

Wet Foam Home Insulation Banned (Feb. 22): U.S. Consumer Product Safety Commission prohibits sale of urea formaldehyde on ground that "it poses an unreasonable risk of injury to consumers." Research links formaldehyde to cancer in animals.

Warning on Cigarette Smoking Broadened (Feb. 22): Surgeon General C. Everett Koop issues sharpest warning since federal report 18 years previously. He finds 30% of all cancer deaths attributed to smoking, not only from cancer in lung, larynx, and esophagus, but also in bladder, kidney, and pancreas.

Panel Raises Doubts Over Marijuana Dangers (Feb. 26): Report released by National Academy of Sciences says smoking has some undesirable short-term effects but finds that reliable evidence is too scanty for conclusions about potential long-range perils.

Laser Helps Avert Blindness in Elderly (May 6): National Eye Institute reports new procedure effective in treating leading cause of new cases of senile macular degeneration. Nonsurgical treatment, which takes 10 minutes, called almost useless if not applied within a few weeks of onset of symptoms.

Cocaine-Related Deaths Quadruple (May 28): Rate up sharply from 1976 to 1981, increasing from 4.5% to 19.1%, Federal Center for Disease Control at Atlanta reports. Hospital treatment up sixfold. Nearly 10 million over 11 years were reported to be using the drug in 1978–79.

Aspirin for Children Called Hazardous (June 4): Government to advise doctors, parents, and chemists against use in treating chicken pox or flu-like symptoms. Studies have linked aspirin to Reye's Syndrome, rare but often fatal disease.

Drug Agency Warns Against Starch-Blockers (July 1): Reports possible danger in diet aids that have swept country and says they must be removed from market.

Distribution of Arthritis Drug Suspended (Aug. 4): Eli Lilly & Co. agrees to remove Oraflex from market. Drug reported to have caused 61 deaths in Britain and nine in U.S., and severe adverse reactions. Britain had temporarily suspended sale of drug.

International Affairs

1981

Iran Gets Prime Minister and Party Leader (Sept. 1): Ayatollah Mohammed Riza Mahdavi-Kani, Interior Minister, provisionally replaces Prime Minister Mohammad Javad Bahonar, victim of bomb explosion. Hojato-lislam Ali Khamenei, Teheran prayer leader, gets Bahonar's post as head of ruling party.

Egyptian President Cracks Down on Critics (Sept. 4): Police use tear gas to break up demonstrations at several Cairo mosques after arrests of at least 1,000 opponents of Anwar el-Sadat. Two-day action is most sweeping conducted by Sadat in 11 years in office. Those arrested include Moslem fundamentalists, Coptic Christian clergymen, politicians, academicians, lawyers, and journalists. **(Sept. 5):** President deposes ~~Coptic~~ Pope, Shenuda III. Addressing Parliament, he denounces religious factionalism, and vows to dissolve Islamic groups that threatened national unity. **(Sept. 7):** In drive against mixing of politics and religion, Egyptian Government will take over supervision of 40,000 mosques. Arrests total 1,536. Sadat says prisoners abetted strife between Moslem majority and Coptic minority.

U.S. and China Sign Cultural Exchange Accord (Sept. 5): Agree in Peking to broaden contacts but leave unresolved complaints that American scholars are denied access to Chinese society and that Chinese government allows only limited view of American society to filter down to ordinary Chinese.

Bomb Kills Another High Iranian Leader (Sept. 9): Revolutionary prosecutor general, Hojatolislam Ali Qoddousi, assassinated in Teheran office. Opponents of regime blamed. Blast knocks balcony off building. Iran's police chief, Col. Houshang Dastgerdi, dies of injuries in previous bomb explosion that killed two other senior Iranian officials.

U.S. and Israel Agree on Strategy (Sept. 9): In Washington talks, President Reagan and Prime Minister Menachem Begin reach accord on need to strengthen strategic ties to counter Soviet threat in Middle East. **(Sept. 10):** Their two days of talks end with agreement on strategic collaboration that is planned to include joint naval maneuvers, stockpiling of American medical supplies in Israel, and joint planning to counter Soviet intervention. **(Sept. 15):** Begin flies home after 10-day visit to U.S. Confers at Kennedy Airport with Secretary of State Alexander M. Haig, Jr.

Independent Polish Union Asks Free Elections (Sept. 10): National convention of Solidarity calls for free ballots for Parliament and local legislative bodies instead of having Communist National Unity Front screen candidates and limit choices.

U.S. Charges Use of Toxin in Asian Conflict (Sept. 13): Secretary of State Alexander M. Haig, Jr., says "physical evidence" shows use of poisonous chemicals in Southeast Asia in apparent violation of international agreements banning use. He notes "continuing reports" of use of "lethal chemical agents" by Soviet Union and allies. Makes comments in West Berlin speech aimed at bolstering West European alliance. **(Sept. 14):** In Moscow, Tass press agency brands Haig statement a "big lie."

Norway's Labor Government Turned Out (Sept. 15): Conservative Party gains almost third of popular vote and with allies takes majority of 175 seats in Parliament. Labor's sway ends after nearly half a century because of discontent with high taxes, 14% inflation, and government intrusion.

Pakistan Accepts U.S. Aid Plan (Sept. 15): Formally agrees to six-year, $3.2-billion military and economic package. Accord follows Reagan Administration plan to speed delivery of F-16 fighter planes that Pakistan is buying in separate deal.

British Liberals Form Alliance with New Party (Sept. 16): Basic ideological realignment foreshadowed as party convention in Wales votes for ties with Social Democrats. Strong popular backing indicated.

1,000 Russians Expelled From Egypt (Sept. 17): Soviets begin flying home diplomats, technicians, and their families. Soviet Ambassador had been accused of being mastermind of plot against President Anwar el-Sadat.

Belize Gains Independence (Sept. 21): Tiny Central American nation, formerly known as British Honduras, celebrates end of more than 300 years of British colonial rule. Inland Belmopan is new capital.

Congress Votes U.S. Citizenship for Swede (Sept. 22): House, 396–2, approves bill passed by Senate to grant honorary citizenship to Raoul Wallenberg, missing diplomat who saved thousands of Jews in Hungary from deportation to death camps in World War II.

4 Armenians Seize Turkish Consulate in Paris (Sept. 24): Nationalist gunmen surrender after threatening to kill 20 persons taken hostage. Turkish security guard slain. Attackers had demanded freedom for Armenian political prisoners held in Turkish jails.

Mexico's Ruling Party Chooses a Moderate (Sept. 25): Institutional Revolutionary Party picks Miguel de la Madrid Hurtado, 46, Planning and Budget Minister, to succeed President José López Portillo in 1982. Nominee viewed as certain to win general election.

British Labor Defeats Left-Wing Challenge (Sept. 27): At Brighton conference, Denis Healey retains deputy leadership of party by narrow margin. Former Chancellor of Exchequer wins, 50.43% to 49.57% for Tony Benn, standard-bearer of left. **(Sept. 28):** Party adopts left-wing program, however, including outlawing of private schools and nationalization of banks. **(Sept. 29):** Right wing takes control of party's National Executive Committee. **(Sept. 30):** Party votes by large majority in favor of unilateral nuclear disarmament, including shutdown of American nuclear bases in Britain. **(Oct. 1):** Parley votes overwhelmingly for British withdrawal from Common Market without referendum.

Canadian Supreme Court Upholds Ottawa Plan (Sept. 28): Rules move to obtain new constitution is legal but "offends the federal principle" because it lacked over-all provincial consent. Eight of 10 provinces object to proposed procedures for terminating the British North America Act of 1867.

Reagan Says U.S. Will Protect Saudi Arabia (Oct. 1): Says he won't permit "another Iran" in broadening American commitment in Persian Gulf to prevent internal or external forces from cutting off oil.

Belfast Prisoners Call Off Hunger Strike (Oct. 3): Irish Nationalists "reluctantly" conclude that families of men now fasting would refuse to let them die. Ten men have perished since May in hunger strike demanding status of political prisoners instead of common criminals. Decision viewed as victory for British Prime Minister Margaret Thatcher. **(Oct. 6):** In conciliatory gesture, British grant prisoners right to wear own clothes all the time.

New President of Iran Proclaimed (Oct. 5): Hojatolislam Ali Khamenei, 42-year-old clergyman, elected as third chief of state in 21 months. Leader of ruling Islamic Republican Party won 95% of votes cast in record Presidential election.

President Anwar el-Sadat of Egypt Assassinated (Oct. 6): Shot dead by four men in uniform who hurl smoke bomb and grenades and rake grandstand with submachine gun fire as he watches Cairo military parade commemorating start of 1973 war against Israel. At least six other spectators also killed and nearly 40 wounded. At least one assassin killed and others captured. Assassins strike as spectators, including President's guards, watch mock fighting by jet planes. The 62-year-old Sadat renowned for innovations in foreign affairs, based on November 1977 journey to Israel to tender peace. News stuns Israel, fearful for peace treaty with Egypt. Public jubilation is reported in most of Arab world. **(Oct. 7):** Official says assassins' leader was army officer with close ties to Moslem fundamentalist group. **(Oct. 9):** Prime Minister Menachem Begin of Israel meets with Vice President Hosni Mubarak, new Egyptian leader, and promises search for peace in Middle East will go on. **(Oct. 10):** Leaders from more than 80 nations attend funeral service. Among them are three former U.S. presidents, Jimmy Carter, Gerald Ford, and Richard M. Nixon, and Mr. Begin. Sadat buried with full military honors in Egypt's Tomb of Unknown Soldier.

Commonwealth Nations End Melbourne Session (Oct. 7): Forty-five states formerly part of British Empire issue communiqué strongly reflecting views of its majority of third-world members, evincing continued rise of anti-Western sentiment.

Irish Bomb Kills Woman in Central London (Oct. 10): Thirty-eight injured as anti-personnel device, apparently planted by Irish Republican Army, explodes outside Chelsea barracks near Victoria Station, spraying nails. It batters military bus carrying 23 members of Irish Guards Regiment returning from duties at Tower of London and shatters shop windows. Eight wounded soldiers undergo major surgery. **(Oct. 13):** Civilian, 18, dies of wounds from bomb.

250,000 Protest U.S. Arms Policy at Bonn Rally (Oct. 10): Denounce NATO plans to modernize nuclear arsenal in Europe. Attack focuses on Reagan's policies and support of them by Chancellor Helmut Schmidt.

Hosni Mubarak Becomes Egypt's President (Oct. 13): National referendum gives Vice President endorsement by 98.63% of electorate to replace slain Anwar el-Sadat. **(Oct. 14):** Former Air Force commander, 53, sworn in. He eulogizes Sadat and pledges to continue fallen leader's policies and to press for a comprehensive Middle East Peace.

Reagan Welcomes Spanish King to White House (Oct. 13): Assures Juan Carlos of U.S. support for "complete integration" of Spain into NATO and Common Market.

Israel Mourns Moshe Dayan, War Hero (Oct. 16): Soldier-statesman dies of heart ailment in Tel Aviv's Sheba Medical Centre at age of 66. He had served as Prime Minister, Chief of Staff, and Defense Minister.

Irish Bomb Wounds Royal Marines Commandant (Oct. 17): Lieut. Gen. Sir Steuart Pringle, 53, severely injured when explosive goes off in car as he drives from home in South London. Right leg amputated. Irish Republican Army takes responsibility for blast. Sir Steuart a former commando leader in Ulster.

Polish Communists Replace Leader (Oct. 18): Central Committee discharges Stanislaw Kania and demands tougher line against Solidarity union. Prime Minister Gen. Wojciech Jaruzelski succeeds Kania.

Greek Socialists Win Sweeping Victory (Oct. 18): Capture 174 of 300 seats in Parliament on platform of radical change in domestic and foreign policy. Get 2,629,870 votes, 48.06% of total, over two other parties. Election ends 35 years of pro-Western conservative rule. **(Oct. 20):** Andreas Papandreou sworn in as Prime Minister, succeeding George Rallis.

150,000 in London March for Nuclear Disarmament (Oct. 24): Peaceful demonstration reflects wide antinuclear feeling spreading in Europe. Campaign for Nuclear Disarmament reports tenfold increase in membership.

Thousands in Europe Protest Nuclear Arming (Oct. 25): Fifty thousand men and women march in Paris, demanding end to East-West armament build-up and spread of atomic weapons. In Brussels, 100,000 join in similar demonstration, largest since World War II. A protest against NATO's nuclear force draws 50,000 in Potsdam, East Germany.

Soviet Submarine Aground Off Sweden (Oct. 27): Swedish government demands apology and explanation of presence in restricted area. **(Oct. 30):** Soviet voices regrets but stalemate develops as Sweden refuses to release submarine until captain is questioned; he refuses. Swedish vessels block Soviet rescue attempt. **(Nov. 2–3):** Captain questioned. Says bad weather and faulty compass caused sub to stray.

New Iranian Prime Minister Named (Oct. 27): Foreign Minister Hojatolislam Hossein Musavi is second choice of President Hojatolislam Ali Khamenei to succeed Ayatollah Mohammed Riza Mahdavi-Kani, who resigned. Parliament had rejected first choice, Ali Akbar Vellayati, pediatrician trained in United States.

U.S. to Help Poland in Economic Crisis (Oct. 27): Announces it will supply $29 million in surplus dairy products to help resolve difficulties peaceably.

Ruling Party Sweeps Tunisia Election (Nov. 3): Government announces no opposition member was elected to new 136-seat National Assembly in first contested elections in 25 years of independence. Opposition had charged irregularities aided government.

Reagan and Hussein Meet in Washington (Nov. 3): President and King of Jordan end two days of talks that they call reassuring. White House emphasizes adherence to Camp David peace plan for Middle East.

India Gets $5.8-Billion Loan (Nov. 9): U.S. abstains as International Monetary Fund approves largest loan it has ever made. Much of the money will be applied to increase India's domestic oil production.

Ulster Turmoil Follows Slaying of Protestant M.P. (Nov. 14 et seq.): Rev. Robert J. Bradford of South Belfast killed by three or four gunmen while meeting constituents in a community center. Bradford, first North Ireland M.P. to be slain in sectarian conflict, was one of most militant Unionists of Ulster's 10 Protestant members of Parliament, and advocated the death penalty. Several Roman Catholics killed in random retaliations during following week. **(Nov. 16):** Rev. Ian Paisley, Unionist leader, says in Parliament that he is dissatisfied with government's handling of Ulster situation. **(Nov. 17):** As Bradford is buried, thousands gather at the funeral and memorial services across Ulster. **(Nov. 18):** Government sends 600 more troops, for a total above 11,000. **(Nov. 23):** Protest strikes shut down much of business and industry on Protestant "day of action." Thousands parade in military formation as Paisley's "third force" to fight enemies. In London, IRA bomb explodes near Royal Artillery Barracks, injuring two women.

Two African Nations Unite (Nov. 14): Senegal and Gambia become Senegambia in formal confederation headed by President Abdou Diouf of Senegal and President Dawda Kairaba Jawara of Gambia. They will integrate security and military forces, form a monetary and economic union, and integrate foreign policy and communications, but each will maintain its own independence and sovereignty.

Reagan Pleads for Arms Control (Nov. 18): In speech televised live to Europe, President proposes that Soviet Union join U.S. in effort to reduce substantially "the dread threat of nuclear war." He proposes a four-point agenda for reducing both sides' arsenals. The key proposal would have the U.S. cancel plans to deploy new medium-range missiles in Europe if Soviet dismantled comparable force.

Huge Peace Rally Held in Amsterdam (Nov. 21): Between 300,000 and 400,000 march in opposition to nuclear weapons. It is biggest demonstration in Dutch history and largest of recent rallies in Europe.

Spanish Parliament Approves Entry Into NATO (Nov. 26): Senate votes for link, previously passed by House. Action opposed by Communists and Socialists. **(Dec. 10:** NATO Foreign ministers sign protocol inviting Spain to become its 16th member.

U.S. and Israel Sign Accord Aimed at Soviet (Nov. 30): Memorandum of understanding provides for military cooperation against threats to Middle East "caused by the Soviet Union or Soviet-controlled forces from outside the region," and is not mutual security pact.

Ciskei Homeland Proclaimed in South Africa (Dec. 4): More than one million Xhosa-speaking blacks cease to be South African citizens. Ciskei is fourth independent black state that South Africa has fashioned from its former "native reserves."

Military Junta Removes Argentina's President (Dec. 11): Decides to oust Roberto Eduardo Viola, 57, who has been recuperating from heart ailment. His successor is one of three-man junta, Gen. Leopoldo Galtieri, 55, who will keep post as army commander.

Dr. Andrei D. Sakharov Ends Hunger Strike (Dec. 11): Sixty-year-old Russian physicist and Nobel Peace Prize winner and his wife recovering from fast at Gorky after Kremlin decides to let Yelizaveta Alekseyeva, 26, emigrate to U.S. to join Dr. Sakharov's stepson, Alexey Semyonov, 25, her husband by proxy, who is a student at Brandeis University. A noted dissident, Sakharov has been a leading campaigner for human rights.

Peruvian Chosen as U.N. Secretary General (Dec. 11): Security Council breaks long deadlock and names Javier Pérez de Cuellar, 61-year-old diplomat and former Under Secretary General for Special Political Affairs. He succeeds Kurt Waldheim, in office 10 years, who failed in bid for third term.

Polish Leaders Impose Martial Law (Dec. 13 et seq.): New military regime issues decree drastically restricting civil rights and suspending operation of Solidarity union. In succeeding days regime tightens grip, taking control of more factories. **Highlights of crisis: (Dec. 17):** Major strikes reported broken by martial law authorities as Roman Catholic Church emerges as powerful opposition voice. **(Dec. 20):** Poland's Ambassador to Washington, Romuald Spasowski, nation's senior diplomat, defects to United States. **(Dec. 21):** Warsaw radio reports more than 2,800 coal miners on strike in Silesia; activists from Solidarity union reported to have barricaded themselves inside Katowice steel mill. **(Dec. 23):** President Reagan announces economic sanctions against Poland. Warns Leonid I. Brezhnev, Soviet leader, of political and economic measures against Moscow for role in Poland. **(Dec. 24):** Zdzislaw Rurarz, Polish Ambassador to Japan, is second diplomat to be granted political asylum in U.S. **(Dec. 29):** Reagan, criticizing Soviet Union, cuts back on Soviet-American trade and scientific exchange and warns of further measures. **(Jan. 7, 1982):** Former Polish party leaders, government officials, and industrial managers reported under indictment for using positions for personal gain. Warsaw radio announces sentences against violators of martial law. **(Jan. 10):** Telephones switched on again in Warsaw 29 days after communications blackout. **(Feb. 9):** House approves the Administration's Jan 31st decision to pay off $71 million owed by Poland to American banks without declaring loans in default. **(Feb. 10):** Senate, 55–39, upholds decision on loans.

Israel Abruptly Annexes Golan Heights (Dec. 14): Prime Minister Menachem Begin pushes measure through Parliament to take strategically sensitive zone along Syrian border, under military occupation since Israel captured it from Syria in 1967. **(Dec. 17):** U.N. Security Council unanimously votes resolution calling action illegal and threatening "appropriate measures" if decision is not reversed. U.S. able to avoid veto since resolution does not condemn Israel. **(Dec. 18):** Because of annexation, President Reagan orders suspension of agreement with Israel for military cooperation to counter Soviet threats to Middle East. **(Dec. 20):** Israel's Prime Minister accuses administration of treating Israel like a "vassal state," refers to "ugly anti-Semitic campaign" for sale of AWACs planes to Saudi Arabia, and says U.S., in view of behavior in Vietnam, has no moral right to punish or preach to Israel. **(Dec. 25):** Israel official says cooperation pact still exists.

Italian Police Free Abducted U.S. General (Dec. 17, 1981, et seq.): Red Brigades, leftist guerrilla group, seize Brig. Gen. James L. Dozier, 50, highest-ranking U.S. officer serving with NATO in Italy, after storming his Verona flat. **(Jan. 28):** Antiterrorist forces raid apartment in Padua and free Gen. Dozier 42 days after abduction. General unhurt and in "excellent health." Five persons, including women, seized in raid. Police say they acted on tip from an undisclosed source within Red Brigades organization. Police capture machine pistols, grenades, other weapons, and ammunition.

Civilian Government of Ghana Overthrown (Dec. 31): Jerry J. Rawlings, former Air Force pilot, seizes power for second time, accusing President Hilla Limann of taking West African nation "down to total economic ruin." Several soldiers die in coup. **(Jan. 4):** President Limann arrested trying to flee country.

1982

Schmidt Supports Reagan on Poland (Jan. 6): West German Chancellor, in Washington, joins President in expressing concern about "serious pressure" brought by Moscow against Polish efforts for change. It is Schmidt's first direct criticism of Soviet involvement.

China Rehabilitates Disgraced Leader (Jan. 10): A book exonerates Liu Shaoqi, former Chief of State, a prime scapegoat in Mae Zedong's Cultural Revolution.

Finns Elect First Leftist President (Jan. 26): Prime Minister Mauno Koivisto gets 167 of 301 votes in electoral college. Koivisto, 58, a Social Democrat, vows to continue his nation's policy of neutrality.

Honduras Gets a Civilian President (Jan. 27): Dr. Roberto Suaze Córdova, a moderate conservative, aged 54, is first civilian leader in decade. Physician succeeds Gen. Policarpo Paz García, third military officer in power since army revolt in 1972.

Presidents of U.S. and Egypt Confer (Feb. 3): Hosni Mubarak tells Reagan solving Palestinian problem is "key to peace" in Middle East. It is Mubarak's first visit to Washington since becoming President. **(Feb. 4):** Presidents conclude talks with pledges to pursue peace efforts through Camp David agreement, but differences over role of Palestinian Liberation Organization continue. **(Feb. 5):** On last of three days in Washington, Mubarak, in speech to National Press Club, pledges to continue to seek "understanding and friendship" with Israel even after Egypt regains Sinai.

U.S. and Morocco Agree on Military Pact (Feb. 11): Will form joint military commission and take other steps leading to transit rights for U.S. military forces. Secretary of State Alexander M. Haig, Jr., discloses developments in news conference at Marrakech, Morocco.

France Begins to Nationalize Industry (Feb. 14): Socialists start $8-billion takeover under national ownership of companies with combined work force of more than 650,000, including five of country's biggest industrial groups, 18 commercial banks, and two leading investment banks with far-flung financial and industrial interests. Cost included interest and government compensation to stockholders.

Woman Elected President of Malta (Feb. 16): Agatha Barbara, 59, former teacher, is first of sex in office.

Joshua Nkomo Ousted in Zimbabwe (Feb. 17): Prime Minister Robert Mugabe dismisses coalition partner from Cabinet and accuses him of scheming to overthrow government by force, ending unity regime.

South Africa Prime Minister Bests Rival (Feb. 27): P.W. Botha rebuffs challenge to leadership of governing National Party by extreme right. Ousts chief rival, Dr. Andries P. Treurnicht, from leadership.

Businessman Named Ireland's Prime Minister (March 9): Charles J. Haughey, Dublin millionaire, chosen by Parliament after inconclusive national election in which his Fianna Fail Party ousted incumbent, Garret Fitzgerald of Fine Gael Party. Five of seven independents vote for Haughey, and now hold balance of power in Parliament of Republic.

Deadlocked Madrid Security Talks Adjourn (March 12): Conference on Security and Cooperation in Europe ends after 16 months, with Soviet Union and U.S. and Allies firing parting charges over Poland, reflecting varying interpretations of 1975 Helsinki accords. NATO nations unanimous in charging Moscow and Warsaw with betraying respect for human rights.

Soviet Freezes Nuclear Missiles in European Russia (March 16): Soviet leader, Leonid I. Brezhnev, announces suspension of deployment and warns of retaliation against U.S. if NATO installs new medium-range missiles in Western Europe. U.S. calls plan "propaganda gesture."

South African Troops Vanquish Guerrillas (March 16): Elite unit, made up mostly of blacks, kills 201 members of South-West Africa People's Organization and wipes out staging post in cross-border raid on southwestern Angola. South Africa rules South-West Africa, known as Namibia, in defiance of U.N.

4 Dutch TV Newsmen Killed in El Salvador (March 18): Slain in rural area where they had gone to film guerrilla group, reportedly in clash between soldiers and rebels. Victims identified as Jacobus Andries Koster, producer; Jan Kuiper, director; Johannes Willemsen, cameraman, and Hans ter Laan, soundman. Men shot at short range from behind. **(March 21):** Dutch government reaffirms doubts about Salvadoran army's account of deaths. Television reporter declares that witnesses said the four were not killed in 40-minute skirmish, as government had maintained, but were killed "in a few minutes of shooting" by government soldiers who had trailed them to interview with guerrillas.

U.S. Reports on Soviet Use of Toxins (March 22): Submits study to Congress and United Nations giving evidence for accusation that Soviet and allies in southeast Asia have used toxins and chemical warfare agents in Laos, Cambodia, and Afghanistan, resulting in 10,000 deaths in nearly 400 attacks.

Army Rebels Seize Power in Guatemala (March 23): Dissident officers oust regime of President Gen. Romeo Lucas Garcia. Denounce Presidential elections earlier in month as fraudulent, and pledge to restore "authentic democracy" to the nation.

Army Chief Seizes Power in Bangladesh (March 24): Lieut. Gen. H.M. Ershad, 52, suspends Constitution, proclaims martial law, and names himself administrator. Deposes President, Abdus Sattar, 75, and pledges to restore democracy, with general election.

Reagan Calls for Heavy Cuts in Nuclear Arms (March 31): In nationally televised news conference, he asks Soviet Union to join U.S. in reducing stocks of weapons. Statement viewed as attempt to counter growing nationwide movement for a nuclear freeze that has gained support of 170 members of Congress. President says, however, that Administration will continue upgrading strategic weapons.

Israeli Soldier Attacks Islam Shrine (April 11): Two Arabs killed and nine wounded as man with automatic rifle shoots way into Dome of the Rock at Jerusalem, spraying inside of mosque with gunfire. Israeli police and border troops capture gunman in 20 minutes. He is identified as Alan Harry Goodman, 37, who moved to Israel from Baltimore in 1977.

U.S. Proceeding With Arms Sale to Taiwan (April 13): Reagan Administration discloses plan to sell $60 million in military spare parts despite Peking's warnings of a "retrogression" in relations.

Egypt Executes 5 Sadat Assassins (April 15): Militant Moslem fundamentalists executed hours after President Hosni Mubarak rejects clemency plea. Two, active in the military, shot by firing squad. Three others, all civilians, are hanged at prison.

Queen Gives Canada Its Constitution (April 16): Elizabeth II flies to Ottawa. (April 17): In ceremony marred by rain, she formally transfers constitutional power to Canada from Britain, ending the British North American Act of 1867, the nation's constitution up to present. Premier René Levesque of Quebec boycotts the ceremony and leads Montreal protest parade. He says new basic law infringes on Quebec's powers.

Dutch Queen Visits U.S. (April 19): President Reagan welcomes Queen Beatrix of Netherlands. Both hail the longtime ties between the two peoples.

Boycott of Russian Cargoes Outlawed (April 20): Supreme Court rules unanimously that International Longshoremen's Association violated federal labor law in 1980 period by refusing to handle Soviet cargo in American ports in protest against Soviet Union's invasion of Afghanistan.

Israeli Jets Bomb Lebanese Villages (April 21): Attack Palestine Liberation Organization guerrilla positions south of Beirut, ending nine-month cease-fire. Lebanese government sources say at least 23 were killed and many were wounded. Air attack came hours after Israeli soldier had been killed by a land mine in southern Lebanon.

Israel Completes Withdrawal From Sinai (April 25): Last of soldiers leaves peninsula, leaving desert wilderness to Egypt under first peace treaty with an Arab country. No joint ceremony is held. Egyptians raise flag at Sharm el Sheik and At Rafa on Mediterranean coast. President Hosni Mubarak of Egypt and Prime Minister Menachem Begin of Israel pledge determination to keep peace.

United Nations Adopts Law of Sea (April 30): Third-world nations approve wide-ranging compact to govern use and exploitation of the seas, by vote of 130 to 4, with U.S. dissenting and 17 nations abstaining. Treaty covers everything from free passage of ships to exploitation of the oceans' wealth of oil, gas, fish, and metals. Treaty will come into force when ratified by 60 nations.

30,000 Poles March in Warsaw Protest (May 1): Crowd demonstrates to show support for suspended Solidarity Union and opposition to military rule in biggest show of resistance since crackdown four and a half months previously. Enthusiams of march contrasts with staid official May Day parade. **(May 3):** Police battle demonstrators in Warsaw and other cities protesting martial law. In Warsaw police charge parade of 10,000 chanting slogans in support of Solidarity. **(May 4):** Military government reintroduces curfews, cuts telephone service, and imposes other restrictions following clashes. **(May 13):** Noon work stoppages and other acts of protest staged to mark five months of martial law. Work disrupted at most of major factories in Warsaw.

Yugoslavia Gets First Woman Prime Minister (May 16): Parliament elects Milka Planino, 58, to succeed Veselin Djuranovic. She had been head of Communist Party in Croatia, nation's second largest republic.

Brezhnev Agrees to Talks on Strategic Arms (May 18): Soviet leader Leonid I. Brezhnev calls Reagan plan for cuts "step in right direction" but one-sided and prejudicial to Moscow's security. He proposes a nuclear freeze as soon as arms talks begin.

Spain Joins NATO as 16th Member (May 30): First new member since West Germany joined in 1955. Depositing of instrument of ratification with U.S. State Department completes formal acceptance of nation by 15 others in Western defense alliance.

Israeli Ambassador Wounded in London (June 4): Shlomo Argov, 52, shot leaving dinner honoring diplomatic corps. Police shoot assailant and arrest three other suspects, all with Arab-nation passports.

Summit Agrees on Trade and Currency (June 4): Leaders of seven industrial nations open economic conference at Versailles, France, on measures to ease recession and rising employment. **(June 6):** U.S., Japan, Britain, France, West Germany, Italy, and Canada reach limited accord on East-West trade and currency fluctuations, with some disagreements.

Israel Invades Lebanon in Attack on P.L.O.—Highlights of campaign: (June 4): Israeli jets strike at Palestinian guerrilla camps in Beirut and southern Lebanon in retaliation for shooting of Israeli ambassador in London. **(June 6):** Israeli forces invade southern Lebanon by land, sea, and air in attempt to destroy main military bases of Palestinian Liberation Organization in retaliation for attacks on Israel. **(June 7):** Tanks and infantrymen seize guerrilla strongholds and sweep northward. Syrian troops begin fighting Israelis. **(June 10):** Israeli planes and gunboats strike outskirts of Beirut. President Reagan calls on Israel to stop fighting and withdraw from Lebanon. **(June 14):** P.L.O. leadership reported trapped in West Beirut. Israelis press to drive Syrian troops back into Bekaa Valley. **(June 21):** Israeli warships and armored units bombard Palestinian refugee camps and civilian areas in West Beirut; Israelis and Syrians exchange gunfire. **(June 22):** Israeli tanks and fighter planes begin major offensive against Palestinians and Syrians. **(July 22):** Philip C. Habib, special American envoy, who has been negotiating for end to fighting, seeks support of Arab nations and agreements to take evacuated Palestinians. **(July 27):** Israeli planes bomb heavily populated area in West Beirut, causing many civilian deaths. **(Aug. 15):** Israeli Cabinet accepts Habib plan for deployment of multinational force in Lebanon. **(Aug. 19):** Cabinet approves proposal for evacuation of upward of 15,000 Palestinians and Syrian fighters, ending 10-week siege of Moslem section of city and opening new chapter in Middle East. **(Aug. 20):** Palestinians return two captured Israelis, first step in American-negotiated peace plans. **(Aug. 21):** First group of guerrillas leaves by ship, beginning two-week withdrawal that will scatter them throughout Arab world. Reagan and Israel Prime Minister Menachem Begin agree that all foreign troops be withdrawn from Lebanon as part of long-term settlement protecting Israel from attacks from Lebanon. French paratroopers land as first contingent of multinational peace-keeping force. Lebanese report thousands of deaths from fighting, mostly of civilians. Israel reports 326 deaths as campaign ends.

Reagans Meet Pope and British Queen (June 7): In 45-minute conference at Vatican, Pontiff repeats appeals against nuclear arms race. President struggles to stay awake. He also confers with Italian leaders. Later in day, Elizabeth II welcomes him in elaborate ceremony at Windsor Castle.

Reagan Bids British Fight for Democracy (June 8): In first speech by an American President to two houses of Parliament, he calls for crusade for democracy, even in Communist countries. Militantly anti-Communist talk pictures Soviet Union as economic failure. **(June 9):** President ends 41-hour visit to Britain with expression of support for British efforts to regain control of Falkland Islands. Visit viewed as strengthening U.S. British alliance.

Reagan Joins Atlantic Alliance Leaders in Bonn (June 9): At conference of 16, he expresses sympathy for antinuclear movement, but differs with tactics. He urges East and West to agree on ceiling of 700,-000 ground troops and 200,000 air force personnel for NATO and Warsaw Pact forces in Europe, which the Allied heads of government approve. **(June 11)**: President visits Berlin at close of European trip and wins applause by reaffirming commitment to Europe's defense. Speeches challenge Soviet to work for safer and freer world and reiterate willingness to negotiate on arms reductions. More than 100,000 anti-American demonstrators parade, with looting and fires. Police disperse them.

King Khalid of Saudi Arabia Dead (June 13): Heart attack fatal to ruler of desert nation. King, 69, succeeded by Crown Prince Fahd, 59, half brother.

Soviet Renounces First Use of Atomic Arms (June 15): U.N. hears pledge by leader, Leonid I. Brezhnev, of the obligation, to be effective immediately.

British Overcome Argentines in Falklands (June 15): Prime Minister Margaret Thatcher announces capitulation after three-week infantry campaign. **Highlights of war: (April 2)**: Several thousand Argentine troops overcome 84 British Royal Marines and seize Falkland Islands in South Atlantic, inhabited by 1,800 residents of British descent who desire to remain under British control. Argentina's claim to islands based on rights inherited from Spain. **(April 3)**: U.N. Security Council votes resolution demanding Argentine withdrawal. **(April 4)**: Buenos Aires announces forces overran last British unit as stringent regulation of inhabitants takes effect. **(April 5)**: Lord Carrington resigns as British Foreign Secretary because of Argentina's "humiliating affront." Francis Pym, leader of House of Commons, succeeds him. **(April 10)**: Ten-nation European Common Market bans imports from Argentina following cutoff of arms sales. (Embargo extended twice with Italy and Ireland dissassociating themselves. Trade embargo lifted June 20 after British reclaim South Atlantic possessions.) **(April 25)**: British recapture principal port on South Georgia Island. **(April 30)**: President Reagan accuses Argentina of "armed aggression" and orders limited sanctions against her. British complete air and sea blockade of Falklands. **(May 3)**: British report sinking of Argentine cruiser *General Belgrano*, hit with two torpedoes from submarine. Dead and missing set at 321. **(May 4)**: British destroyer *Sheffield* sunk after being hit and set on fire by Argentine Exocet missile, with 20 reported killed. British Harrier jet shot down and pilot is lost. **(May 14)**: Flotilla brings British troops back to Falklands in force for first time in six weeks. **(May 21)**: British attack Falklands and establish "firm bridgehead" in fighting with Argentines; five British ships damaged and Harrier jet is lost. **(May 22)**: British pour reinforcements ashore to widen bridgehead, 3,000 of them transported on converted luxury liner, the 67,000-ton *Queen Elizabeth II.* British missile frigate sunk with reported loss of 20 lives. **(May 23)**: Six Argentine aircraft shot down and three others probably drowned in fighting over Falklands. **(May 29)**: British capture Darwin and Goose Green, with victory over well-fortified garrison of 1,000. **(June 14)**: In London, Prime Minister Thatcher announces Argentine troops have begun to throw down weapons in Stanley and show white flags. **(June 15)**: More than 13,000 Argentine troops surrender, bringing total to 15,-000. Mrs. Thatcher bars Argentine role on future of Falklands. **(June 27)**: British death toll in fighting listed at 250 in 10-week war. Sources in Buenos Aires estimate Argentine fatalities at from 700 to 1,000.

Argentine President Resigns Under Pressure (June 17): Gen. Leopoldo Galtieri quits also as Commander in Chief of Army and member of ruling military junta three days after British victory in Falklands. Replaced temporarily by Maj. Gen. Alfredo Oscar St. Jean, Interior Minister. **(June 22)**: Army assumes responsibility for rule and names retired Maj. Gen. Reynaldo Benito Antonio Bignone, 54, as president. **(June 30)**: Bignone names Cabinet of nine civilians and one military officer. **(July 1)**: Air Force head and other military leaders boycott inauguration of Bignone as nation's 43rd president and fourth since military took power six years previously.

U.S. Tightens Curb on Soviet Gas Line (June 18): President Reagan, in rebuff to West Europe allies, retains sanctions on sale of U.S. oil and gas equipment to Soviet Union and extends ban to foreign companies producing such equipment under American licenses. **(June 21)**: Diplomats of 10 Common Market countries, meeting in Luxembourg, contend that decision violates agreements reached at economic summit meeting shortly before at Versailles.

British Prime Minister Meets Reagan (June 23): Margaret Thatcher reports "no difference" between her and President on issue of sovereignty in Falkland Islands and says Britain views matter as closed.

Argentines Free Three Reporters (June 29): Release Britons arrested April 13 in southern Argentina on espionage charges during Falklands war.

Dominican President Dies of a Gunshot (July 4): Antonio Guzmán killed by bullet in head. Government says pistol accidentally discharged, but high officials say President, 71, committed suicide. President-elect Salvador Jorge Blanco, winner in May 16 ballot, took office on schedule Aug. 16.

Mexicans Elect New President (July 4): Miguel de la Madrid Hurtado, candidate of Institutional Revolutionary Party, which has ruled for 53 years, to succeed José López Portillo on Dec. 1.

New Spy Scandal in Britain (July 20): Prime Minister Margaret Thatcher confirms that Geoffrey Arthur Prime, 44, arrested under Official Secrets Act, had been employed for nine years at government's secret electronic eavesdropping center near Cheltenham.

Bombs Kill 10 in 2 London Parks (July 20): Four soldiers killed or fatally injured by car bomb as Queen's Household Cavalry rides to Whitehall ceremony. Six Army musicians killed in Regent's Park in explosion under bandstand during lunch-hour concert. Over-all total of injured reaches 51. Irish Republican Army claims responsibility for both bombings.

Reagan and Mrs. Gandhi Settle Dispute (July 29): Agree that France, instead of U.S., supply uranium fuel for U.S.-built atomic power plant near Bombay. In White House meeting, President and Mrs. Indira Gandhi, Indian's prime Minister, also plan increased scientific, cultural, and economic cooperation.

Peace Protesters End Soviet Rallies (July 29): Three hundred from Nordic countries complete first officially sanctioned antinuclear march by Westerners in Soviet Union. Thirteen-day tour of several cities was closely supervised by the Russian authorities.

Kenya Puts Down Attempted Coup (Aug. 1): President Daniel arap Moi announces police and army crushed attempt to overthrow his government. Eight killed and 50 wounded in looting after first such attempt in East African nation. Air Force blamed for attacks.

Glen Cove, L.I., Causes International Incident (Aug. 5): Ten days after New York town reaffirmed decision to bar Soviet diplomats from golf courses, tennis courts, and beaches, Soviet Union bars American diplomats stationed in Moscow from favorite nearby swimming area along Moskva and Volga Rivers.

Italian Government Collapses (Aug. 7): Cabinet of Prime Minister Giovanni Spadolini resigns after Socialist Party withdraws support. **(Aug. 24):** Spadolini forms nation's 42nd postwar Cabinet with same parties and ministers as previous one.

6 Killed in Attack on Ankara's Airport (Aug. 7): Armed Armenians apparently attempt to take hostages to press for demands on government. Two gunmen killed and a third captured. Three policemen and a passenger also killed. Terrorists said to belong to Asala, Armenian Secret Army for Liberation of Armenia, which has attacked Turks since 1970.

6 Killed in Attacks on Jews in Paris (Aug. 9): Gunmen fire submachine guns and hurl grenade in assault on kosher restaurant and passers-by in Jewish neighborhood at lunchtime. Twenty-two wounded. Anti-Semitism is reported to be motive.

Europe Protests Reagan Ban on Pipeline Sales (Aug. 12): Formal objections to U.S. call it "unacceptable interference" in affairs of European Economic Community. Several nations have planned to defy prohibition on American companies and foreign subsidiaries from selling equipment for 3,600-mile pipeline to deliver natural gas from Siberia.

Polish Police Halt Demonstrations (Aug. 13): Break up march by thousands of Solidarity supporters in Gdansk outside Communist headquarters. Police disperse gatherings to mark eight months of martial law in three other major cities.

Agreement Provides Arms Cut for Taiwan (Aug. 16): U.S. and China sign communiqué to prevent major rift. Peking agrees to seek peaceful reunification with Taiwan. U.S. promises not to exceed current level of arms sales and to reduce them gradually.

U.S. Aids Mexico in Financial Crisis (Aug. 20): Plans multibillion-dollar package of loans and credits to help nation ride out worst financial crisis and make good on her huge debts to foreign banks.

Rightist Named Lebanon President (Aug. 23): Assembly elects Bashir Gemayel, leader of rightist Christian military. Ruthless leader, 34, chosen with at least tacit support of occupying Israeli army.

U.S. Moves Against French Concerns (Aug. 26): Administration acts to penalize major company owned by French Government and French subsidiary of American oil equipment company who had defied U.S. embargo against delivery of equipment for Soviet-Western European natural gas pipeline. Companies prohibited from dealing with U.S.

Yasir Arafat Leaves Beirut by Ship (Aug. 30): Leader of Palestine Liberation Organization vows to fight again. Troops of Syrian army, which has occupied Beirut since 1976, also began leaving.

Polish Police Rout Protesting Crowds (Aug. 31): Riot squads fire tear gas grenades in Warsaw and elsewhere to break up demonstrations called by underground Solidarity Union leaders on anniversary of founding. Clashes reported in Gdansk, Wroclaw, Cracow, and its steel suburb, Nowa Huta.

National Government and Politics

1981

Senate Halts Filibuster on School Busing Curbs (Sept. 12): Votes, 61–36, to end three-month attempt to block passage of severe restrictions on busing of pupils as means of achieving racially balanced schools.

240,000 Protest Reagan Policies at Capital Rally (Sept. 19): Solidarity Day demonstration sponsored by A.F.L.-C.I.O. joins members of organized labor and civil rights groups representing women, blacks, Hispanic Americans, other minorities, and the elderly and disabled. They protest deep cuts in social programs and job safety rules. President at Camp David retreat. White House statement says workers need break from inflation and high taxes.

President Appeals for Budget-Balancing Goals (Sept. 24): Reagan, in fifth TV address to nation, proposes $13 billion in additional spending cuts and $3 billion in increased taxes for fiscal 1982. He makes concessions to flagging Congressional support and raises 1982 deficit target to $43.1 billion. Drops plan to delay cost-of-living rises in Social Security.

Reagan Orders Haitian Refugees Halted (Sept. 29): President authorizes Coast Guard to intercept and turn back ships on high seas suspected of carrying illegal immigrants without the proper documents.

Reagan Rules Out MX "Shell Game" (Oct. 2): President rejects plan for shuttling new intercontinental missile among shelters in Western deserts. Plans to house MX in super-hardened existing silos. Reagan revives controversial B-1 bomber project.

House Votes to Keep Tobacco Price Supports (Oct. 21): Decides, 231–184, not to scrap 48-year-old program allocating acreage. Winning alliance comprises liberals, unions, blacks, and Southern conservatives.

Reagan Victorious in Fight for AWACs (Oct. 28): Senate, 52–46, votes to permit $8.5-billion sale to Saudi Arabia of five Airborne Warning and Control System planes and other air combat equipment. House had voted, 301–111, against the sale, leaving Senate to decide issue. Opponents switch sides following intense lobbying by President and parliamentary maneuvering by Senate Republican leader, Howard H. Baker, Jr., to stave off what had seemed like almost certain defeat. Reagan denies making deals.

Stockman Shocks Capital With Criticisms (Nov. 10): Budget Director David A. Stockman quoted in *Atlantic Monthly* as having said Administration economic program would not work, huge deficits were ahead, and that "supply-side economics" was just a new name for old "trickle-down" policies favoring the rich. **(Nov. 12):** Angry Reagan reprimands Stockman but does not ask resignation. Stockman acknowledges words but affirms faith in Administration's "sound, constructive" course for the economy.

Government Services Curtailed briefly (Nov. 23): Reagan vetoes government spending bill and orders shutdown of all but essential services. Hundreds sent home in crisis atmosphere. Later Congress approves continued current financial levels; Reagan agrees.

Urban League Names Vernon Jordan's Successor (Dec. 7): Board chooses John E. Jacob, 46, executive vice president, as organization's sixth chief executive.

Congress Votes $200 Billion for Military (Dec. 15): Approves compromise measure for current fiscal year.

Congress Votes $11.5 Billion in Foreign Aid (Dec. 16): Sends President two bills allocating funds, first legislation on subject in three years.

Reagan's Security Adviser Exonerated (Dec. 23): Attorney General rules Richard V. Allen did not act illegally in accepting watches from Japanese associates or omitting information in financial disclosure form. Justice Department closes inquiry. Earlier it had cleared Allen of wrongdoing in accepting $1,000 from a Japanese magazine that he had helped.

1982

National Security Adviser Resigns (Jan. 4): Richard V. Allen first senior official in Reagan White House to leave. William P. Clark, Jr., Deputy Secretary of State, succeeds him with more central responsibility, and will report directly to the President.

President to Continue Draft Registration (Jan. 7): Reversing stand in election campaign, he says registration could save as much as six weeks for mobilization.

Reagan Seeks to Transfer Programs to States (Jan. 26): His State of the Union Message reveals plan to shift Federal programs now costing $47 billion to state and local control. U.S. would give up responsibility for food stamps and payments to poor families with dependent children, and relieve states of responsibility for Medicaid. States would be assigned many highway, economic development, urban renewal, education, and social services now administered by the federal government. Democrats immediately present rebuttal on nationwide television, with party leaders speaking, interviews with citizens, and poll results. Basic theme is "unfairness" of Reagan policies.

Franklin D. Roosevelt's 100th Anniversary Marked (Jan. 28): His voice echoes through House chamber as joint session of Congress marks 100th anniversary of birth. **(Jan. 30):** Hundreds of family, friends, neighbors, and officials gather at F.D.R.'s Hyde Park, N.Y., estate in opening year-long observance of centennial of President's birth.

President's Budget Message Reaffirms Policy (Feb. 6): Reagan releases program for continued monetary restraint, brisk reduction of inflation and slow decline of unemployment. Projects 4.5% rise in total spending to $757.6 billion and deficit of $91.5 billion. Reagan calls for rapid growth in military spending and cuts in benefits. Democrats call plan "unfair." Size of deficit shocks many Republicans.

President Reagan's First Economic Report (Feb. 10): It terms curbing of inflation primary objective, in which "private sector is the key engine to growth, employment, and rising living standards." President again opposes pump-priming public works.

Rights Marchers Arrive in Alabama Capital (Feb. 18): Black leaders escorted by black officials and 3,500–5,000 supporters reach Montgomery to call for extension of Voting Rights Act and release of two political activists, ending 13-day, 140-mile pilgrimage from Carrollton courthouse. There the workers had been sentenced on vote fraud charges.

Harrison A. Williams, Jr., Resigns From Senate (March 11): New Jersey Democrat, in Senate 23 years, quits as it prepares to expel him for his conduct in Abscam investigation into corruption. Williams, 62, denies his guilt and offers no apology.

Reagan Tightens Rules on Secret Information (April 2): President signs executive order reversing 25-year trend, to give government officials broader authority to withhold information on ground of national security. Executive Order on National Security Information also makes it more difficult for judges to declassify information sought under the Freedom of Information Act.

U.S. Refuses to Bar Nuclear "First Strike" (April 6): In speech on arms policy, Secretary of State Alexander M. Haig, Jr., also rejects freeze on nuclear weapons at existing levels. Says nuclear deterrent is needed to protect "essential values" of West.

G.O.P. Agreement on Budget Compromise (May 5): White House and Senate Republicans in accord on increase in federal taxes of $95 billion over three years and reduction in Social Security benefits by $40 billion. Plan would carry a deficit of $105 billion for next fiscal year, about $4.5 billion more than is expected in current year. Earlier, Republican-controlled Senate Budget Committee embarrassed Administration by unanimously rejecting President's 1983 budget proposal.

Reagan Asks Cut in Nuclear Warheads (May 9): President, in speech at Eureka College, Illinois, his alma mater, proposes two-step plan for U.S. and Soviet Union to reduce by one third initially their arsenals on land- and sea-based missiles. In second phase of proposal, the two nations would accept an "equal ceiling" on "throw weight", or total payload, of all missiles. President says he has written Leonid I. Brezhnev, Soviet leader, suggesting formal negotiations by governments.

Congress Vetoes Proposed Used-Car Rules (May 26): House, 286–133, joins Senate in rejecting requirement that dealers disclose major defects and state extent of any outstanding warranties. Senate had voted veto by 69–27. Dealers' lobbying assailed.

Congress Votes to Protect Covert Agents (June 11): Senate, 81–4, approves measure making it a crime to disclose names. House voted bill, 315–32. It provides prison terms up to 10 years and $50,000 fines for government agents exposing American spies. Journalists and others outside government face up to four years in prison and $15,000 fines.

Crowds Jam Manhattan in Antinuclear Protest (June 12): Hundreds of thousands fill Central Park and midtown in vast parade and rally uniting pacifists and anarchists, Roman Catholic bishops, Communists, and other disparate groups from across nation. Organizers call demonstration biggest disarmament rally in nation's history. Rally marks United Nations Second Special Session on Disarmament.

Congress Votes Civil Rights Act Extension (June 18): Senate, 85–8, approves renewal of critical section for 25 years, already passed by House. Victory for civil rights movement would make it easier for minority voters to approve racial discrimination. **(June 29):** Reagan signs bill in presence of critics of his rights record. Decries "overblown rhetoric."

Congress Votes Republican Budget (June 22): Democratic House reluctantly approves, 210–208, Republican-sponsored compromise bill. **(June 23):** Senate, 54–45, gives final approval, a victory for President and defeat for Democrats and liberals, who fought a losing battle against cuts in social programs. Final budget provides for federal spending in fiscal 1983 of $769.8 billion while projecting deficit of $103.9 billion.

Haig Resigns as Secretary of State (June 25): In letter to President Reagan, Alexander M. Haig, Jr., says Administration's foreign policy had veered from "careful course" that he and President had laid out. Friction with White House staff over style and policy in Middle East and Soviet called factors in move. Reagan chooses George P. Shultz, former Secretary of Treasury, as successor.

Inquiry Clears Labor Secretary (June 27): Special U.S. prosecutor finds no evidence to justify charging Raymond J. Donovan with criminal activities when Secretary was New Jersey construction executive.

Democratic Conference Attacks Reagan (June 27): National assembly in Philadelphia adopts policy positions including freeze of nuclear arms. Senator Edward M. Kennedy and Walter F. Mondale cheered.

First Indictment Under Draft Registration Law (June 30): Federal grand jury charges Benjamin H. Sasway, 21, a California student, with failing to register.

Equal Rights Amendment Defeated (June 30): Three states short of 38 needed to ratify it as 27th amendment to Constitution. Supporters vow to fight on.

Second Stage of Tax Cut Arrives (July 1): Federal income taxes, reflected in payroll checks, drop 10% in second phase of Reagan three-year "supply side" reductions. Economy still sluggish as Congress seeks new revenue increases. Benefits under Social Security program also increase.

U.S. Won't Sign Law of the Sea Treaty (July 9): President Reagan announces stand because of objections to future sea-bed mining. U.S. had voted against treaty, which was eight years in negotiation.

Congress Overrides Copyright Veto (July 13): In first major rebuff to President, House and Senate vote overwhelmingly to reject veto of copyright legislation intended to preserve jobs in American printing and publishing industries. Measure extends manufacturing clause that requires books and periodicals written in English by authors living in U.S. to be printed and bound in U.S. or Canada to enjoy complete copyright protection in U.S.

Senate Unanimously Confirms Shultz (July 15): By 97–0 vote, it approves George P. Shultz as Secretary of State succeeding Alexander M. Haig, Jr. In hearings, Shultz hints at attempt to modify some key aspects of President Reagan's foreign policy.

House, 204–202, Rejects Nuclear Freeze (Aug. 5): Turns down resolution calling for immediate freeze of Soviet and American weapons, in favor of Administration-backed measure calling for cuts in strategic weapons first. Supporters of freeze movement view narrow margin as showing the strength of their campaign, which has wide public backing.

Reagan Names New Economic Adviser (Aug. 6): Martin Stuart Feldstein, 42, conservative economist, succeeds Murray L. Weidenbaum as council chairman. Feldstein committed to cutting deficit through reductions in spending by the government.

Hinckley Committed for Indefinite Period (Aug. 9): Federal judge in Washington finds John W. Hinckley, Jr., 27, assailant of President Reagan, mentally ill and dangerous on basis of St. Elizabeths Hospital examinations and orders him held in hospital.

Student, 20, First Convicted on Draft Charge (Aug. 17): Enten Eller, student at Bridgewater College, Virginia, found guilty by Federal judge in Roanoke of failing to register. Eller said he followed God's bidding. He is placed on probation and ordered to register.

President Wins Crucial Victory on Tax Bill (Aug. 18); Both houses of Congress set stage for reducing budget deficit by $130 billion in next three years with bipartisan approval of $13.3-billion cut in federal spending. It includes reduction in cost-of-living adjustments for retired federal employees and $1.9-billion cut in food stamps. **(Aug. 19):** House, 226–207, and Senate, 52–47, approve $98.3 billion tax bill after strenuous lobbying by President, who wins support from coalition of Republicans and Democrats, liberals and conservatives. Bill incorporates many tax reforms sought by Democrats and includes higher taxes for business and individuals. It marks reversal of "supply side" tax reductions adopted in 1981.

Draft Opponent Convicted on Coast (Aug. 26): Benjamin H. Sasway, 21, student at Humboldt State University, found guilty in Federal Court in San Diego.

Former Congress Page Recants Charges (Aug. 27): Leroy Williams, 18, says he lied when he said he had had homosexual relations with congressmen. An earlier inquiry by House commission had called charges of sexual misconduct and drug use unfounded.

Reagan Vetoes Spending Measure (Aug. 28): President rejects supplemental appropriations bill to provide $14.1 billion to operate government until Sept. 30. Officials arrange to meet military payrolls.

People, Places, and Things

1981

Vernon E. Jordan, Jr., Quits Urban League Post (Sept. 9): Resigns as president of civil rights group after decade to join Washington law firm. Jordan active in rights groups for previous 21 years.

World's Fastest Train Operates in France (Sept. 23): Bullet-nosed train races quietly through countryside on inaugural run from Paris to Lyons at speeds up to 156 miles an hour, making 300-mile trip in 2 hours 32 minutes, 1 hour and 12 minutes faster than time of regular express service.

Prince Charles Raises His Pay by 50% (Oct. 3): Will get $4,186 more a week, making his yearly stipend $751,350, all tax-free, to offset costs of married life, Buckingham Palace announces.

Reagans Buying More China for White House (Oct. 9): Nancy Reagan herself will pay for new set for family's personal use. Twenty-four place set will be handmade by English studio and will be available to the public for $160 cost a setting. Reagans had been criticized for previous purchase of $209,508 set of china with money donated by Knapp Foundation.

Gold From Sunken Warship Divided (Oct. 9): Soviet and British share $80 million in ingots recovered by divers from Royal Cruiser *H.M.S. Edinburgh,* torpedoed and sunk April 30, 1942, beneath Arctic waters of Barents Sea. Gold destined for U.S. Treasury in payment for war supplies sent to Soviet Union. American claims settled previously from insurance. Haul split between British salvage company and British and Soviet governments.

Woman General of Army Retires (Oct. 30): Maj. Gen. Mary Clarke, 56, honored by parade at Fort McLellam, Ala., and receives Distinguished Service Medal. She entered service as a private in World War II.

Natalie Wood Drowns in Accident (Nov. 29): Death of film actress, 43, off Catalina Island 22 miles from California coast ruled by Medical Examiner "tragic accident while slightly intoxicated."

1982

Male Giraffe First Baby Animal of 1982 at Bronx Zoo (Jan. 1): Calf, 6 feet tall and weighing 125 pounds.

Exiled South African Poet Wins Reprieve (Jan. 14): Dennis Brutus, ruled "deportable" because of an expired visa, wins 20-day stay from U.S. immigration judge in Chicago to seek political asylum. Professor Brutus, a 57-year-old native of Zimbabwe, formerly Rhodesia, is a senior professor of African literature at Northwestern University.

Children Get House in Divorce Pact (Jan. 19): Judge in Traverse City, Mich., gives three adolescent boys custody of parents' home while mother and father alternate month-long visits and pay the bills.

Austria Adopts Rudolf Nureyev (Jan. 19): Dancer, 42, granted citizenship after being stateless for 20 years. He defected from Soviet Union while appearing in Paris with Kirov Ballet of Leningrad in 1961.

Elizabeth II Marks 30th Year as Monarch (Feb. 6): Britain's Queen and Prince Phillip spend day quietly. She succeeded father, George VI, who died in 1952.

Henry Kissinger Has Heart Surgery (Feb. 10): Former Secretary of State in good condition after undergoing triple heart bypass operation to repair blocked and narrowed arteries at Massachusetts General Hospital in Boston. Kissinger is 58.

"Public Citizen" Gets New President (Feb. 16): Joan Claybrook, head of the National Highway Traffic Safety Administration in the Carter Administration, rejoins consumer movement as head of five-group umbrella organization founded by Ralph Nader.

Last of Original Astronauts Retires (Feb. 27): Donald K. Slayton, at 58, only remaining one of Original Seven chosen in 1959 from among 500 skilled test pilots to respond to 1957 Soviet challenge of *Sputnik* satellite in early days of space age.

Harry S. Truman Back in Senate (March 1): Oil painting by John D. Slavin, removed from Reagan White House, hung in office of Democratic leadership.

Lynching Victim Cleared After 69 Years (March 7): Witness gives secret information about disputed trial of Leo Frank, 29-year-old Jewish factory superintendent, his murder conviction in Atlanta, and subsequent mob lynching. In interview, Alonzo Mann, 83, says he saw real killer carrying unconscious body of Mary Phagan, 14, on April 26, 1913. Mann, then 14, says Jim Conley, a factory janitor, killed girl. Frank trial marked rebirth of Ku Klux Klan.

Search for "Jeweled Rabbit" Ends (March 14): Design engineer, 48, finds five-inch gold filigree pendant in park northwest of London after "Masquerade" fable sent thousands from both sides of Atlantic digging holes all over England, following clues given by English artist, Kit Williams, in book.

Ann Landers Has Repeated Material (May 3): Author of column of personal advice read daily by 70 million newspaper readers says about 30 columns in 1982 and 1981 contained letters or answers essentially unchanged from items she wrote 15 years before.

Sophia Loren Goes to Jail in Tax Case (May 19): Begins serving 30-day term in Italy. Actress, 47, convicted in 1980 of evading $180,000 in supplementary taxes for 1963–64. She is confined to jail at Caserta, about 20 miles from Naples, birthplace.

Whooping Crane Dance Succeeds (June 2): Female named Tex hatches chick at International Crane Foundation at Baraboo, Wis., after Dr. George Archibald, foundation head, spent six months performing ritual mating dance to encourage ovulation by rare bird.

Allan M. Bakke Gets Medical Degree (June 3): Center of Supreme Court's 1978 ruling on affirmative action to aid minorities is graduated from University of California School at Davis. Court upheld principle of affirmative action but ordered admission of Bakke, a white, who charged discrimination against him by university.

Deaf and Blind Woman Becomes Ph.D. (June 13): Adeline Becht, 48, of Portland, Ore., graduated from University of Oregon at Eugene with doctoral degrees in clinical and counseling psychology. She credits much of achievement to Beth Schmidt, interpreter.

Princess of Wales Gives Birth to Boy (June 21): First child becomes second in line to British throne, after his father, Prince Charles. Birth at St. Mary's Hospital in London 10 days before expected. **(June 28):** Infant named William Arthur Philip Louis.

Raccoon Kills Tex, a Whooping Crane (June 23): Slays bird that attracted national attention by giving birth after intricate mating rituals with human at International Crane Foundation in Wisconsin.

4,000 "Moonies" Wed in Mass Ceremony (July 1): Rev. Sun Myung Moon marries followers among flags and balloons at Madison Square Garden, New York. Most had been selected for each other by him. Bridegrooms are dressed identically in blue suits and brides in lace and satin gowns made by church.

Intruder Invades Queen's Bedroom (July 9): Sneaks into Buckingham Palace and talks with Elizabeth II for ten minutes before chambermaid leads him away. **(July 13):** Michael Fagan, 31, held at Brixton Prison, charged with entry. Exploit stirs wide furor. **(July 19):** British plan no prosecution of Fagan, since trespassing is not a crime.

Aerialist Achieves First Quadruple Somersault (July 10): Miguel Vazquez, 17, of Flying Vazquez circus team, reaches goal of performers for 123 years in history of trapeze flying. Vazquez performs four back somersaults at Tucson (Ariz.) Community Center before crowd of 7,000. He hurtles at speed of 75 miles an hour to land in hands of brother, Juan, 31.

Nation Mourns Henry Fonda (Aug. 12): Heart disease fatal to actor who for nearly half a century portrayed man of honesty and decency in more than 100 film and stage roles. He dies at 77 in Los Angeles. Last role was in "On Golden Pond," for which he won his first Oscar as best actor.

A Three-Year Round-the-World Voyage (Aug. 29): Two Britons land in Greenwich after journey by way of North and South poles. Sir Ranulph Twisleton-Wykeham Fiennes and Charles Burton return on flagship *Benjamin Bowring*. They were first to cross Antarctic in open snowmobiles.

Ingrid Berman Dead on 67th Birthday (Aug. 30): Cancer fatal at home in London to three-time Academy Award-winning actress. Despite illness for eight years, she played two of most demanding roles.

Religion

1981

U.S. Investigates Chicago Archbishop (Sept. 10): Sifts charges of "improper diversion" of church funds by John Cardinal Cody. Acting U.S. Attorney Dan K. Webb confirms reports that office is examining allegations that 73-year-old cleric used two discretionary funds to divert more than $1 million in tax–exempt church funds to Helen Dolan Wilson of St. Louis, whom he had known for decades. Cardinal denies charges and says Mrs. Wilson, aged 74, is "step-cousin."

Pope Terms Labor Unions "Indispensible" (Sept. 15): In his third encyclical, John Paul II declares them a vehicle "for the struggle for social justice" in modern industrialized society. But he warns unions against "close links" with political parties.

Court Rules Attack on Pope a Conspiracy (Sept. 24): Italian judges find convicted Mehmed Ali Agca, Turkish terrorist, was spearhead of "shadowy" subversive organization in attempt to kill John Paul II.

Vatican Panel Revises Code on Marriage (Oct. 28): New rules for annulments are substantially those used in U.S. for 11 years. Draft of changes in universal church law approved by 74 cardinals and bishops for submission to Pope John Paul II.

Pontiff Defends Right to Protect Freedom (Dec. 21): John Paul II, in annual peace message, says all people should strive to prevent warfare, but "have right and even duty to protect their existence and freedom" against an unjust aggressor.

1982

Pope Moves to End His Rule of Jesuits (Feb. 27): John Paul II announces general congregation of Society later in year to elect new superior general. Pontiff warns worldwide conference of Society of Jesus to give strict obedience to his authority. **(March 3):** Jesuit leaders end week's meeting near Rome with Pope's permission to name own Superior General. Pontiff praises order as "vanguard of renewal" for Roman Catholic Church.

Report on Roman Catholic-Anglican Reunion Issued (March 29): International commission of leading churchmen, in statement after 12-year study, proposes that Pope be "Universal Primate" if two churches are reunited after more than four centuries of separation since the Reformation.

Archbishop of Chicago Dead (April 25): John Cardinal Cody, aged 74, succumbs to heart attack. His most recent controversy was involvement in federal grand jury investigation into allegations that he had diverted church funds to a friend.

Rev. Billy Graham Appears in Moscow (May 9): On visit to Russia, evangelist preaches message of disarmament and Christian rebirth in tightly guarded Baptist church as 250 Russian Christians sing hymns outside behind police barriers. He denounces atomic weapons. **(May 12):** At end of visit, Mr. Graham says he has seen no evidence of religious repression.

Rebel Priest Attacks Pope in Portugal (May 12): Juan Fernández Krohn, 32, Spanish clergyman, wielding bayonet, lunges toward John Paul II after Pontiff gives thanks at Shrine of Fatima for recovery from wounds inflicted by Turkish gunman year previously. Priest identified as follower of anti-Vatican traditionalist French prelate. **(May 14):** Krohn charged with attempted homicide and held for trial. **(May 15):** Pope ends four-day pilgrimage in Portugal. At large meeting of workers he denounces Marxist conception of labor unions.

Pope Makes 6-Day Visit to Britain (May 28): John Paul II first reigning Pontiff in 1,900-year history of papacy to visit nation. He appeals to Britons and Argentines to "put aside weapons of death" in Falklands. Pope celebrates mass in Westminster Cathedral and has audience with Queen Elizabeth II in Buckingham Palace. **(May 29):** At Canterbury Cathedral, birthplace of English Christianity, Pope and Archbishop of Canterbury embrace and pray together. They sign pledge for new effort at reunion of Anglicans and Roman Catholics. **(June 2):** Pope ends historic trip through England, Scotland and Wales with fervent appeal in Cardiff for peace in Falklands, and is serenaded by Welsh choir. He is obviously fatigued. Protestants and Catholics alike judge his visit a success. About two million Britons saw or heard Pontiff. Television coverage was extensive.

Argentina Hails Pope on Arrival (June 11): Hundreds of thousands greet John Paul II in Buenos Aires. Pontiff prays for peace in Falklands and calls on all for measures to heal wounds of war with Britain.

17th Century Monk Becomes Saint (June 20): Pope John Paul II canonizes his first saint, Crispin of Viterbo, 17th century Italian shoemaker who became a monk and worked as nurse, barber, and gardener.

United Presbyterians Name Moderator (June 24): Elect Rev. James H. Costen, 50, dean of John C. Smith Theological Seminary in Atlanta, to succeed Rev. Robert M. Davidson of West Park, N.Y.

U.S. Ends Cardinal Cody Investigation (July 6): Terminates inquiry into allegations that late Chicago Archbishop improperly diverted hundreds of thousands of dollars in church funds for personal use. Inquiry had sharply divided Roman Catholics. **(July 10):** Vatican names Archbishop Joseph L. Bernardin of Cincinnati as successor in largest U.S. see.

New Archbishop of Chicago Installed (Aug. 24): Joseph L. Bernardin, 54, son of immigrant Italian stonecutter, heads nation's largest Roman Catholic archdiocese, with almost 2.4 million members. Pope John Paul II picked him to succeed late John Cardinal Cody.

Science

1981

Genes Changed, Bacteria Make Flu Vaccine (Sept. 1): British journal *Nature* reports use of splicing technique by researchers of Imperial Cancer Research Fund at London. This involves inserting anti-influenza genes into bacteria's genetic material.

Scientists Find Fossil of Unknown Mammal (Sept. 17): Harvard paleontologist reports discovery of jaw of small creature on Navajo reservation in Arizona. Finding among first evidence that mammals were present in North America 180 million years ago. Mammal probably shrew-like, size of a small mouse.

Baby Panda Born at Peking Zoo (Sept. 19): Mother is Juan Juan, who bore first artificially inseminated panda in 1978. Baby's twin dies when dropped to ground. Both also result of artificial insemination.

Voyager 2 Finds Area Hotter Than Sun (Oct. 9): Spacecraft detects cloud of electrified gases circling Saturn 300 times hotter than sun's outer regions and hottest spot ever detected in solar system. This is reported by space-scientist team headed by Dr. S.M. Krimigis of Johns Hopkins laboratory.

Space Shuttle Lands After Second Flight (Nov. 14): *Columbia* down at Edwards Air Force Base in California after mission of 54 hours and 36 orbits of earth instead of planned 124 hours and 83 orbits. Flight cut short because of malfunctioning fuel cell. Two pilots accomplished their major objectives.

1982

More Small Moons of Saturn Discovered (Feb. 2): Four and possibly six revealed by new analysis of *Voyager 2* photographs, scientists at Jet Propulsion Laboratory report, bringing number to 21 or 23.

40-Million-Year-Old Insect Mummy Found (Feb. 26): Specimen from Poland is imbedded in transparent Baltic amber with much of soft tissues intact, and elements within cells apparently visible, scientists at University of California at Berkeley report.

Second Soviet Spacecraft in Week Lands on Venus (March 5): *Venera 14* lander transmits new high-resolution color pictures and chemical assays of planet's cloud-shrouded surface. *Venera 13* sent pictures earlier.

First Land Mammal Fossil Found in Antarctica (March 20): Scientists believe bones, those of small marsupial the size of a rat, are evidence that pouched creatures, now mostly confined to Australia, reached that continent from South America using Antarctica as land bridge before the continents separated.

Space Shuttle Flies Eight-Day Mission (March 22): *Columbia* goes into orbit with two astronauts, Col. Jack R. Lousma of Marine Corps and Col. C. Gordon Fullerton of Air Force. Crowd of 750,000 views launching of 4.5-million-pound vehicle at Cape Canaveral, Fla. **(March 30):** Shuttle lands at White Sands Missile Range, N.M. Flight extended a day because of sandstorm. Third of four missions to test world's first reusable spaceship reported to have accomplished almost all objectives, with some problems.

Frenchman in Orbit on Soviet Rocket (June 24): Air Force Col. Jean-Loup Chrétien, 43, becomes first astronaut who is neither American nor citizen of Communist nation to fly in space. He blasts into space on *Soyuz* T-6 craft with Col. Vladimir A. Dzhanibekov, mission commander, and Aleksandr S. Ivanchenkov, flight engineer. **(July 2):** Charred craft returns safely after nine-day orbital mission to land safely 2,500 miles east of Moscow.

Space Shuttle Columbia Tested Successfully (June 27): Carries first military and commercial payloads for fourth and final test mission to establish ability for regular orbital operation. It is piloted by astronauts Capt. Thomas E. Mattingly 2nd of Navy and Henry W. Hartsfield, Jr. Two rocket boosters, designed to be retrieved, sink off Florida coast after launch at Cape Canaveral. **(July 4):** Crowd cheers landing at Edwards Air Force Base, Calif. NASA announces reusable winged spaceplane, developed over 10 years, could begin cargo runs to and from space. Experimental packages already carried.

Russian Woman Spends 8 Days in Space (Aug. 17): Svetlana Savitskaya, 34, test pilot and parachutist, one of three Russian astronauts to land safely in Soviet Central Asia, breaks 19-year-old endurance record for women in space. Woman is praised for expert performance of research duties, and officials call mission a scientific success. Others on *Soyuz* T-5 capsule when it docked with *Salyut* 7 space station were Lieut. Col. Leonid Popov, commander of spacecraft, and Aleksandr Serebrov, engineer. More women expected to explore space.

Sports

1981

Anti–Apartheid Protest Rages in Auckland (Sept. 12): Demonstrators battle New Zealand police to protest tour by South African rugby team, the Springboks, as tour ends. Arrests put at 148; 45 reported injured. New Zealand wins match, 25–22. Thousands in New Zealand have demonstrated against South Africa.

Springboks Play U.S. Games in Private (Sept. 18): Members of South African rugby team make decision because California and New York have blocked use of public stadiums. Opponents of South Africa's racial segregation have objected to games with the South Africa rugby team, which is integrated. **(Sept. 22):** Courts uphold playing of match in Albany, ruling cancellation would abridge freedom of speech. Rain keeps attendance low at small stadium as visitors defeat Eastern Rugby Union, 41–0. Earlier, bomb damages Rugby Union's Schenectady office. **(Sept. 25):** South Africans defeat American amateur players on private field north of Schenectady, N.Y., 38–7, without demonstrations. Date moved up a day to protect all involved. Earlier in day, explosion destroys building of Indiana team that had voted to play visitors.

Philadelphia Baseball Phillies Sold (Oct. 29): Team bought by group of five investors for record price of $30.175 million from family of Ruly Carpenter. Largest investor in the 1980 World Series winner is Taft Broadcasting Company of Cincinnati.

1982

San Diego Clippers' Owner Fined $10,000 (Jan. 8): Commissioner Larry O'Brien of National Basketball Association imposes penalty on Donald Sterling for "conduct prejudicial and detrimental to the N.B.A." Action follows league inquiry into remarks by Sterling suggesting that losses by Clippers would gain them No. 1 draft choice in spring.

Three Jockeys Indicted for Bribery (Jan. 21): Charged with arranging or receiving payments from New Jersey state police detectives who posed as crooked gamblers in undercover operation at Meadowlands track. State grand jury names Edwin Kelly, 37, of Revere, Mass.; Abad Cabassa, Jr., 22, of East Boston, Mass., and Gilfredo Gonzales, 40, of Queens, N.Y.

Payments to College Basketball Stars Charged (March 25): Richard (Digger) Phelps, head coach at University of Notre Dame, says many colleges are paying standard rate of $10,000 a year to outstanding players in violation of intercollegiate rules.

Record Set for Boston Marathon (April 19): Alberto Salazar, 23, of Massachusetts, runs course in 2 hours 8 minutes 51 seconds, fourth fastest ever in a marathon, in close contest with Dick Beardsley, 26, of Minnesota. Charlotte Teske, 32, West German nurse, wins women's division in 2:29:33.

Timely Writer Misses Kentucky Derby (April 20): Favorite for Kentucky race May 1, 3-year-old colt undergoes emergency surgery for intestinal ailment. **(Oct. 9):** The favorite in Jockey Gold Cup at Belmont Park collapses with broken leg half mile from finish and has to be destroyed, along with Johnny Dance, another horse involved in spill.

Oakland Raiders Win Verdict (May 7): Federal jury in Los Angeles rules National Football League violated Sherman Antitrust Act in forbidding one of 28 teams to move to Los Angeles. Verdict could have deep effect on power of some major sports leagues to control movement of their franchises.

Two-Year Television Agreement for Football (May 26): New United States Football League, with 12 teams, agrees with ABC Sports on two-year network pact. Network to televise 20 games. Two-year payment reported between $20- and $25-million, to be divided evenly among the teams. ABC, CBS, and NBC had recently signed five-year agreement totaling $2 billion with the National Football League.

Indianapolis 500 Automobile Race Is Close (May 30): Gordon Johncock drives Wildcat-Cosworth across finish line 16-hundredths of a second ahead of Rick Mears's Penske PC-10 in closest of 66 contests.

San Francisco U. Drops Varsity Basketball (July 29): University, twice winner of national collegiate championship, moves to preserve school's "integrity and its reputation." University has been penalized by National Collegiate Athletic Association for violation of rules on payments and recruiting.

Auto Crash Kills Boxing Champion (Aug. 12): Salvador Sánchez, 23, of Mexico, World Boxing Council's featherweight titleholder, dies as sports car collides with truck on highway north of Mexico City.

State and Local Governments

1981

Andrew Young Elected Mayor of Atlanta (Oct. 27): Former Congressman and U.N. delegate declared winner of two-man runoff in deep-South capital, with 55.1% of vote. Young, a civil-rights veteran, faces challenge in major city beset by financial problems.

Houston Gets First Woman Mayor (Nov. 17). Kathryn Jean Whitmire, 35, wins 62.5% of vote in runoff election. She had been comptroller four years.

First Black Mayor for Little Rock, Ark. (Nov. 25): Charles Bussey, 62, is first of race to hold post.

1982

Gov. Hugh Carey Bars Third-Term Bid (Jan. 15): New York executive, 62, decides not to seek re-election. He plans to work for "certain, safe course" for state.

San Francisco Bans Most Pistols (June 28): Board of Supervisors makes it first large city to outlaw possession of weapons, with exemptions for police, military personnel, collectors, and others.

Late Events

Bess Truman Dies of Heart Failure (Oct. 18): The 97-year-old widow of President Harry S. Truman dies of congestive heart failure.

Automobile Executive Arrested for Cocaine Dealing (Oct. 19): John Z. DeLorean, chairman of the DeLorean Motor Co., is arrested in Los Angeles and charged with possession of more than 59 pounds of cocaine worth $6.5 million. He is suspected of trying to distribute the drug in order to save his failing company. Earlier, the British government had announced that it was closing his operation in Northern Ireland.

3 Policemen Killed in Northern Ireland (Oct. 27): A 1,000-pound bomb planted in a road in Northern Ireland explodes under a car carrying three policemen, killing all of the occupants. The explosion is heard five miles away. Later, the Irish Republican Army said it was responsible.

U.S. Threatens Nuclear War, Brezhnev Says (Oct. 27): Leonid I. Brezhnev, the Soviet leader, tells a meeting of military leaders in Moscow that the United States is threatening the world with nuclear war. Speaking on the 20th anniversary of the Cuban missile crisis, he charges the U.S. with following a policy of "adventurism and undisguised egotism." He also says the Soviet Union will seek to restore normal relations with China.

China's Population Passes a Billion (Oct. 27): Peking announces that the population of China is 1,008,175,288, according to the 1982 census. The figure represents one-fourth of the world total. More than 5 million canvassers covered the country for four months to obtain the tally. The second most populous country is India, with 700 million.

1982 Nobel Prize Winners

Peace: Alva Myrdal (Swedish), a sociologist, former diplomat and Cabinet minister, and Alfonso Garcia Robles (Mexican), a career diplomat, for their efforts to promote disarmament.

Medicine: Dr. John R. Vane (English), research director of the Wellcome Foundation, Beckenham, England; Dr. Sune K. Bergstrom (Swedish), chairman of the Nobel Foundation in Sweden, and Dr. Bengt I. Samuelsson (Swedish), dean of the medical faculty at the Karolinska Institute in Stockholm, all for their discoveries in controlling prostaglandins.

Physics: Dr. Kenneth G. Wilson (American), a professor at Cornell University, for his theory on "critical phenomena in connection with phase transitions."

Chemistry: Dr. Aaron Klug (South African-born), research scientist at the Medical Research Council's Laboratory of Molecular Biology in Cambridge, England, "for his development of crystallographic electron microscopy and his elucidation of biologically important nucleic acid-protein complexes."

Economics: George J. Stigler (American), a professor at the University of Chicago, for his half century of research on the working of industry and the role of government regulation in the economy.

Literature: Gabriel Garcia Márquez, a Colombian living in Mexico, "for his novels and short stories, in which the fantastic and the realistic are combined in a richly composed world of imagination, reflecting a continent's life and conflicts."

Major Emmy Awards for TV, 1982

Drama series: *Hill Street Blues* (NBC)
- **Actress:** Michael Learned, *Nurse* (CBS)
- **Actor:** Daniel J. Travanti, *Hill Street Blues* (NBC)
- **Supporting actress:** Nancy Marchand, *Lou Grant* (CBS)
- **Supporting actor:** Michael Conrad, *Hill Street Blues* (NBC)

Comedy series: *Barney Miller* (ABC)
- **Actress:** Carol Kane, *Taxi* (ABC)
- **Actor:** Alan Alda, *M*A*S*H* (CBS)
- **Supporting actress:** Loretta Swit, *M*A*S*H* (CBS)
- **Supporting actor:** Christopher Lloyd, *Taxi* (ABC)

Comedy, variety, or music program: *Night of 100 Stars* (ABC)

Limited series or special: *Marco Polo* (NBC)
- **Actress:** Ingrid Bergman, *A Woman Called Golda* (Operation Prime Time)
- **Actor:** Mickey Rooney, *Bill* (CBS)
- **Supporting actress:** Penny Fuller, *The Elephant Man* (ABC)
- **Supporting actor:** Laurence Olivier, *Brideshead Revisited* (PBS)

Drama special: *A Woman Called Golda* (Operation Prime Time)

Animated program: *Grinch Grinches the Cat in the Hat* (ABC)

Information special: *Making of the Raiders of the Lost Ark* (PBS)

Information series: *Creativity With Bill Moyers* (PBS)

Classical program in the performing arts: *La Bohème Live from the Met* (PBS)

Children's program: *The Wave* (ABC)

Network totals: NBC, 20, ABC, 18, CBS, 12, PBS, 5

Deaths in 1981–1982

Ace, Goodman, 83: humorist and writer for radio and TV comedians; appeared with wife, Jane, on radio's *Easy Aces.* March 25, 1982.

Adams, Harriet Stratemeyer, 89: author of Nancy Drew, Hardy Boys, Bobbsey Twins and Tom Swift Jr. children's books under various pseudonyms. March 27, 1982.

Albertson, Jack, 74: actor appeared on Broadway in *The Subject Was Roses* and *The Sunshine Boys* and on TV in *Chico and the Man.* Nov. 25, 1981.

Ashbrook, John M., 53: Republican Representative from Ohio since 1961. April 24, 1982.

Balmain, Pierre, 68: French fashion designer. June 28, 1982.

Banning, Margaret Culkin, 90: novelist and short-story writer. Jan. 4, 1982.

Belushi, John, 33: comedian who starred on *Saturday Night Live* on TV and went on to screen roles in *The Blues Brothers, The National Lampoon's Animal House, 1941,* and *Neighbors.* March 5, 1982.

Benchley, Nathaniel, 66: writer of humorous novels, including *The Russians Are Coming, The Russians Are Coming,* and many children's books. Son of the humorist, Robert; father of the novelist, Peter. Dec. 14, 1981.

Bergman, Ingrid, 67: won Oscars for *Gaslight, Anastasia,* and *Murder on the Orient Express.* Also starred in *Notorious, Spellbound,* and *Casablanca.* Aug. 29, 1982.

Boyer, Ken, 51: former third baseman and manager of St. Louis Cardinals was National League's most valuable player in 1964. Sept. 7, 1982.

Bruce, Virginia, 72: film actress in 1930s and 40s appeared in *The Great Ziegfeld, Born to Dance, Yellow Jack.* Feb. 24, 1982.

Carmichael, Hoagy, 82: composed "Stardust," "Lazy Bones," "Georgia on My Mind," "Old Buttermilk Sky," and other hit songs. Dec. 27, 1981.

Case, Clifford P., 77: liberal Republican U.S. Senator from New Jersey, 1955–79. March 5, 1982.

Chase, Mary C., 74: playwright was author of Pulitzer Prize-winning comedy *Harvey.* Oct. 23, 1981.

Cheever, John, 70: Pulitzer Prize-winning novelist was author of *The Wapshot Chronicle, Bullet Park, The Wapshot Scandal,* and *Falconer.* June 18, 1982.

Cody, John Cardinal, 74: Archbishop of Chicago was elevated to Cardinal in 1967. April 25, 1982.

Conried, Hans, 66: character actor was in *Can-Can* on Broadway and in many films and TV shows. Jan. 5, 1982.

Corcoran, Thomas G., 80: leading adviser to Franklin D. Roosevelt helped shape major New Deal legislation. Dec. 6, 1981.

Curzon, Sir Clifford, 75: concert pianist. Sept. 1, 1982.

Dannay, Frederic, 76: co-author with his late cousin, Manfred Lee, of the Ellery Queen mystery novels. Sept. 3, 1982.

Dayan, Moshe, 66: Israeli military hero and statesman. Oct. 16, 1981.

DiSalle, Michael V., 73: former Governor of Ohio and Director of Price Stabilization in Kennedy Administration. Sept. 15, 1981.

Dubinsky, David, 90: ex-president of the International Ladies Garment Workers Union. Sept. 17, 1982.

Dugan, Jumping Joe, 85: New York Yankees third baseman in 1920s. July 7, 1982.

Durant, Ariel, 83; **Will,** 96: husband-and-wife historians won 1968 Pulitzer Prize for General Non-Fiction for *Rousseau and Revolution,* 10th in their 11-volume *Story of Civilization.* Ariel, Oct. 25; Will, Nov. 7, 1981.

Fassbinder, Rainer Werner, 36: controversial German filmmaker turned out 41 features in 13-year career. June 10, 1982.

Fonda, Henry, 77: stage and screen actor appeared in over 80 films, including *The Grapes of Wrath, the Oxbow Incident, Twelve Angry Men, Mister Roberts,* and *On Golden Pond,* for which he won an Oscar in 1982. Aug. 12, 1982.

Fortas, Abe, 71: Justice of U.S. Supreme Court from 1965 until his resignation in 1969. April 5, 1982.

Gardner, John, 49: poet, novelist, and teacher; wrote *The Sunlight Dialogues, Grendel,* and *October Light.* Sept. 14, 1982.

Garroway, Dave, 69: first host of the NBC *Today* show, which began in 1952. Committed suicide July 21, 1982.

Gemayel, Bashir, 34: President-elect of Lebanon. Killed by bomb, Sept. 14, 1982.

Ghotbzadeh, Sadegh, 46: Foreign Minister of Iran during hostage crisis. Executed in Iran Sept. 15, 1982.

Golden, Harry, 79: North Carolina editor, publisher, and humorist. Oct. 2, 1981.

Goldmann, Nahum, 87: ex-president of World Jewish Congress and a leading Zionist. Aug. 29, 1982.

Gomulka, Wladyslaw, 77: head of Polish Communist Party from 1956 to 1970. Sept. 1, 1982.

Grace, Princess of Monaco, 52: former actress Grace Kelly won Oscar in 1954 for *The Country Girl;* also in *High Noon, Rear Window, High Society,* and *To Catch a Thief.* Sept. 14, 1982.

Grahame, Gloria, 51: actress won Oscar for 1952 film *The Bad and the Beautiful;* also in *It's a Wonderful Life, The Big Heat, The Good Die Young.* Oct. 6, 1981.

Greer, Sonny (William Alexander), 78: drummer in Duke Ellington's first orchestra. March 23, 1982.

Harkness, Rebekah West, 67: patron of dance and medicine. June 17, 1982.

Head, Edith, 82: costume designer won a record eight Academy Awards during 50-year career. Oct. 24, 1981.

Hicks, Granville, 80: novelist, literary critic and leader in the proletariat literature movement of 1930s. June 18, 1982.

Holden, William, 63: actor won Oscar for *Stalag 17;* also in *Golden Boy, Sunset Boulevard, The Bridge on the River Kwai,* and *Network.* Found dead Nov. 16, 1981.

Holloway, Stanley, 91: actor played Alfred Doolittle in *My Fair Lady.* Jan. 30, 1982.

Humes, Helen, 68: singer of ballads and blues appeared with Count Basie's orchestra. Sept. 13, 1981.

Irish, Edward S. (Ned), 76: founder of New York Knickerbockers basketball team. Jan. 21, 1982.

Jensen, Jackie, 55: outfielder with Washington Senators, Yankees, and Red Sox was American League's most valuable player in 1958. July 14, 1982.

Jeritza, Maria, 94: world-famous operatic soprano. July 10, 1982.

Jory, Victor, 79: actor on stage and screen was best known as film villain. Feb. 12, 1982.

Jurgens, Curt, 66: West German actor appeared in many World War II films. June 18, 1982.

Kaufman, Murray, 60: disk jockey known as Murray the K helped introduce the Beatles to U.S. audiences. Feb. 21, 1982.

Kay, Hershy, 62: orchestrator of ballets and Broadway musicals, including *On the Town, Candide, Evita, A Chorus Line, Barnum.* Dec. 2, 1981.

Khalid, King, 68: ruler of Saudi Arabia since 1975. June 13, 1982.

Kieran, John F., 89: former sports columnist of *New York Times;* naturalist and panel member of *Information Please* radio and TV quiz show. Dec. 10, 1981.

Kleinsinger, George, 68: composer of *Tubby the Tuba* and the operas *Archy and Mehitabel* and *Shinbone Alley.* July 28, 1982.

Lenya, Lotte, 83: singer and actress was best known for role in *The Threepenny Opera* by her husband, Kurt Weill, and Bertolt Brecht; in *Cabaret* on Broadway. Nov. 27, 1981.

Lindstrom, Fred, 75: third baseman of New York Giants was member of Baseball Hall of Fame. Oct. 4, 1981.

Lockridge, Richard, 83: author of the Mr. and Mrs. North mystery novels with his wife, Frances. June 19, 1982.

Loeb, William, 75: conservative publisher of *The Manchester Union Leader* and *New Hampshire Sunday News.* Sept. 13, 1981.

Loughran, Tommy, 70: light-heavyweight boxing champion in 1920s. July 7, 1982.

Lynd, Helen M., 85: co-author with husband, Robert, of *Middletown: A Study in American Contemporary Culture.* Jan. 30, 1982.

Lynde, Paul, 55: actor was on TV quiz show *The Hollywood Squares.* Jan. 9, 1982.

MacLeish, Archibald, 89: poet, playwright, and former Librarian of Congress. April 20, 1982.

Markey, Enid, 91: actress played Jane in first Tarzan movie, in 1918; also appeared on Broadway and on TV. Nov. 16, 1981.

McHugh, Frank, 83: popular character in films and on stage over 50 years. Sept. 11, 1981.

Mills, Harry, 68: Member of the Mills Brothers singing quartet (later a trio) for over 55 years. June 28, 1982.

Monk, Thelonious, 64: innovative jazz composer and pianist. Feb. 17, 1982.

Montale, Eugenio, 84: poet won 1975 Nobel Prize for Literature. Sept. 12, 1981.

Montgomery, Robert, 77: actor, director, and producer appeared on screen in *Here Comes Mr. Jordan, The Big House, Petticoat Fever,* and *The Last of Mrs. Cheyney.* Sept. 27, 1981.

Morrow, Vic, 53: actor starred in *Combat* series on TV in 1950s; was in *The Blackboard Jungle* and *The Bad News Bears* on screen. July 23, 1982.

Morton, Thruston B., 74: former United States Senator from Kentucky and national chairman of Republican Party. Aug. 14, 1982.

Nesbitt, Cathleen, 93: British character actress was on stage 70 years; played Mrs. Higgins in *My Fair Lady.* Aug. 2, 1982.

ates, Warren, 52: character actor appeared in *Easy Rider, In the Heat of the Night,* and *The Border.* April 3, 1982.

rff, Carl, 86: German composer was best known for *Carmina Burana.* March 29, 1982.

aige, Leroy (Satchel), 75: pitching star black baseball leagues joined Cleveland Indians at age of 42 and pitched last game in major leagues at 59. June 8, 1982.

elletier, Wilfrid, 85: Canadian conductor. April 9, 1982.

ond, Raymond (Ducky), 80: football coach at Yale and Bates College in 1930s and 40s. Aug. 23, 1982.

ost, Wally, 52: former outfielder with Cincinnati Reds and other major league teams. Jan. 6, 1982.

Powell Eleanor, 69: tap-dancing star of many films was in *Broadway Melody, Rosalie, Born to Dance, Lady Be Good,* and *As Thousands Cheer.* Feb. 11, 1982.

Rafferty, Max L., 65: controversial conservative educator headed California school system in 1960s. June 13, 1982.

Rambert, Dame Marie, 94: leader in development of British ballet. June 12, 1982.

Rand, Ayn, 77: author of *The Fountainhead* and *Atlas Shrugged.* March 6, 1982.

Rawls, Katherine, 64: holder of 33 national swimming and diving titles in 1930s. April 8, 1982.

Rexroth, Kenneth, 76: poet, critic, and author was inspiration for "beat" generation of the 1950's. June 6, 1982.

Sánchez, Salvador, 23: World Boxing Council featherweight champion. Aug. 12, 1982.

Scott, Hazel, 61: jazz pianist appeared on stage and screen. Oct. 2, 1981.

Shevelove, Burt, 66: co-author of Broadway musical *A Funny Thing Happened on the Way to the Forum.* April 4, 1982.

Sillman, Leonard, 72: produced the *New Faces* revues that introduced Henry Fonda, Imogene Coca, Eartha Kitt, and Paul Lynde to Broadway. Jan. 24, 1982.

Simmons, Calvin, 32: music director of Oakland (Calif.) Symphony Orchestra. Drowned, Aug. 21, 1982.

Smith, Red (Walter Wellesley), 76: sports columnist of *New York Times* won 1976 Pulitzer Prize for commentary. Jan. 15, 1982.

Spivak, Charlie, 77: trumpeter led orchestras in the big-band era of the 1940s. March 1, 1982.

Stitt, Sonny, 58: jazz saxophonist worked with Dizzy Gillespie and Zoot Sims, others. July 22, 1982.

Strasberg, Lee, 80: director of the Actors Studio and teacher of Method acting. Feb. 17, 1982.

Thornton, Charles B., 68: a founder of Litton Industries had been president of Ford Motor. Nov. 24, 1981.

Twining, Gen. Nathan F., 84: former commander of Air Force was Chairman of Joint Chiefs of Staff, 1957–60. March 29, 1982.

Uris, Harold, 76: builder of many New York City skyscrapers; donated $10 million to Metropolitan Museum of Art. March 28, 1982.

Von Zell, Harry, 75: announcer for radio shows of Eddie Cantor, Fred Allen, Jack Benny; on TV in *Burns and Allen Show.* Nov. 21, 1981.

Walker, Fred (Dixie), 71: Brooklyn Dodgers outfielder in 1940s led National League in batting in 1944 with .357 average. May 17, 1982.

Waner, Lloyd, 76: Pittsburgh Pirates outfielder in 1920s was known as "Little Poison"; late brother, Paul, was "Big Poison." Both are in Baseball Hall of Fame. July 22, 1982.

Warren, Harry, 87: songwriter turned out "42nd Street," "Lullaby of Broadway," "September in the Rain," and hundreds of others. Sept. 22, 1981.

Whitney, John Hay, 77: sportsman, publisher, and former Ambassador to Britain. Feb. 8, 1982.

Williams, Gluyas, 93: cartoonist for *The New Yorker* magazine satirized suburbia and the upper class. Feb. 13, 1982.

Wilson, Don, 81: announcer and performer on the Jack Benny radio and TV shows for 40 years. April 25, 1982.

Wood, Natalie, 43: film actress 39 years appeared in *Marjorie Morningstar, Rebel Without a Cause, Splendor in the Grass,* and *West Side Story.* Drowned, Nov. 29, 1981.

The Economy in 1982

Monte J. Gordon
Vice President and Director of Research
The Dreyfus Corporation

The year began marked by an increasingly pervasive and sullen recession which relentlessly deepened during the first quarter of 1982 when Gross National Product, adjusted for inflation, declined 3.7% and turned up weakly in the second quarter when Gross National Product, adjusted for inflation, was up 1.3%. Its roots were deep in the past and reflective of the corrosive effects of an inflation pressure which only began to give way late in the year. The marks of the recession were first evident in the steady and severe decline of the automobile markets, the banking industry, and the steel companies but gradually spread throughout the economy. Increasing inroads by foreign competitors also were significant factors in the deterioration of the U.S. economy.

Perhaps one of the most significant and visible signs of the recession was the steady increase of the level of unemployment. In January 1982, unemployment was 8.5% of the labor force and by July the figure had climbed to 9.8%, the highest since May 1941 when unemployment was 10.9%. The main concentration of the unemployed was in the industrial heart of the U.S. and obviously reflective of the declining fortunes of the auto and steel industries which are concentrated there.

Accompanying the rise in unemployment was a pronounced decline in corporate after-tax profits which in current dollars fell from $144.9 billion in the fourth quarter of 1981 to an annual rate of $115.0 billion at the end of the second quarter of 1982. As a result of the decline in corporate profits and the bleak outlook for improvement, capital spending plans for new plant and equipment were cut back substantially. During the second quarter, such business investment fell at an annual rate of $5.6 billion adjusted for inflation. This development was particularly distressing because a rising level of such expenditures was expected to provide a stimulus to the economy and is an important part of the economic recovery program of the Reagan administration.

Perhaps the most encouraging development during the year was the perceptible decline in the rate of inflation to single digit rates by the two measures most watched by observers. The Consumer Price Index fell from an annual rate of increase of 8.9% during 1981 to an annual rate of 7.2% by July 1982. This was prompted mainly by a decline in the cost of energy and a decline in housing costs. The decline in the cost of energy reflected the effects of a developing surplus of oil throughout the world due to the combined effects of conservation and the recession which affected all economies. Prospects favored a continuing reduction in the cost of energy as the Organization of Petroleum Exporting Countries (OPEC) experienced sharply dropping exports and a decline in its rate of production. As a result, Saudi Arabia, the leading producer in OPEC, sharply cut its daily production rate and showed signs of dropping its benchmark price of $34 a barrel. The Producer Price Index, which supplanted the old Wholesale Price Index, also showed signs of a decline with a rise of 0.6% in July, down from a rise of 1% in June following slight declines in the early months. Such action could be interpreted as presaging further declines in prices in the later months of the year. Further pressure toward a lesser inflation was indicated by the reports that industrial production and capacity utilization declined in July for the eleventh time in twelve months.

During the earlier months of the year, interest rates stayed persistently high although they did not again touch record levels. Probably the most widely known surrogate of the interest rate levels is the prime rate which reflects borrowing costs charged by banks to their best customers. The prime rate was at 15.75% in January 1982 and held at 16½% through the middle months of the year. In August the rate broke sharply as monetary policy significantly eased and fell to 14% generally with several banks at 13½%. The high rate of interest was clearly a key factor in extending the recessionary pressures on the economy. It showed its effect in slowing consumer purchases of autos and houses, for example, because of the high interest charges. In the case of housing, it was quite clear that with mortgage rates at around 17%, only a relatively few people could afford to buy homes. These rates declined only slightly as the year turned toward its close. As a consequence, housing starts fell sharply during the early part of the year, falling to below one million units, only rising above that level late in the third quarter. The housing industry was devastated with many builders going out of business.

Another significant effect of the high interest rates was the continued unwillingness of buyers to purchase long-term bonds (maturities exceeding 10 years) and the consequent emphasis on the short-term sector of the debt market (maturities about one year or less). The effect was to keep rates high in the short-term sector particularly as many companies beset by the recession sought to survive and were unable to enter the long-term bond market. This struggle for survival was also evidenced by sharp increases in bank lending and an increasing corporate use of commercial paper (short-term unsecured notes) to finance their activities. All of this kind of activity represented a major disruption of normal financing practices and conditions. Historically, as a recession develops, loan demand declines and interest rates decline, both in the short-term and the long-term. In such an environment, corporations shift their financing emphasis to the longer term sector, easing the burden on the balance sheets and improving their liquidity. Instead, the pattern of using the short-term market because of uncertainties, which began in previous months, continued throughout the early months of 1982 and further severely weakened the balance sheets of U.S. corporations. This, in turn, sharply increased the rate of bankruptcies to levels not seen since the 1930s. Thus, business bankruptcies were 512 in the week ended August 5 compared with 354 in the corresponding period the year earlier. To that date, business failures averaged 454 per week compared with 316 a week in the same period in 1981. The weekly average of bankruptcies was 612 in 1932. These figures do not include the companies which paid their creditors and then went out of business.

A major part of the pattern which contributed to the persistence of high interest rates were the deficits projected by the Reagan administration for fiscal 1983 which began October 1, 1982, to end September 30, 1983. When President Reagan first proposed his budget for fiscal 1983, it called for a deficit of $98.3 billion which was substantially greater than general expectations and caused a major controversy. Forecasts by private economists outside the administration questioned some of the assumptions underlying the projection and raised their forecasts to $140 billion, not only in fiscal 1983 but also in fiscal 1984 and fiscal 1985. The administration subsequently raised its own forecast to about $114 billion. The significance of the deficit figures is that it must be financed by the Treasury borrowing in the financial markets. The pressure of Treasury borrowing at such a level could be severe as it would be competing with business demands for credit. The effect could serve to drive rates upward as the financing absorbs a higher percentage of available funds. For example, in the last two quarters of 1982, the Treasury had projected borrowing needs of $50 billion in each quarter, far above any previous quarter.

Coupled with the concern over the impact of the need for these huge Treasury financings was the official position of the Federal Reserve that it was conducting a restrictive monetary policy designed to combat inflationary pressures. This policy, which seeks to restrict the flow of funds into the economy, acted to add to the pressure maintaining high interest rates. As a result, monetary policy became a center of a major controversy swirling around the concern over the mounting evidence that the recession, coupled with interest rates that were persistently high, was weakening corporate liquidity and corporate balance sheets. Further, not only would the financing of such a deficit be a major problem, but the financial markets were severely depressed and confused. Last, the high interest rates here in the U.S. were causing marked pressures on other countries which were forced to keep their interest rates high to protect their currencies and economies against the magnetic pull of funds into the U.S. economy.

As a result, events leading to a major effort to break this pattern began to develop. First initiated by Republicans in the Senate and then strongly supported by President Reagan, a bill raising taxes by $98.3 billion with additional action to cut spending by about $31 billion in the fiscal years of 1983–1985 was finally passed in late August. The passage of the bill which followed a herculean effort by the administration, encouraged investors and the financial community to believe the administration and the Congress were seeking to mitigate the severe problems raised by the large projected deficits and to deal with the higher interest rates.

Adding to this belief were steps taken by the Federal Reserve which indicated a more accommodative cast to the execution of an essentially restrictive monetary policy. These steps began with a reduction of the discount rate of the Federal Reserve in a series of steps from 12% to 10½%. In response to this action, interest rates fell across a broad front led by 30-day Treasury bills. This led to sharp and decisive rallies in the various debt markets. Perhaps the most dramatic impact was in the stock market which established record levels of advances in prices and trading volume. On August 17, the stock market, in terms of the Dow Jones Average rose a record amount of 38.81 points and, on August 18, the trading volume on the New York Stock Exchange crossed the 100 million share level with 132.7 million shares traded. For the week ended August 20, the stock market rose a record 81.24 points on the Dow Jones Average with total New York Stock Exchange trading volume reaching 455,127,820 shares, also a record high.

The net effect of these series of events and activities was the rise of a new note of optimism as 1982 moved toward its close. Although the prospects for recovery of the economy were still uncertain, the outlook was regarded with more favor.

Consumer Price Indexes
(1967 = 100)

Year	Commodities	Services	Housing	All items	Percent change[1]	Year	Commodities	Services	Housing	All items	Percent change[1]
1940	40.6	43.6	52.4	42.0	1.0	1975	158.4	166.6	166.8	161.2	8.9
1945	56.3	48.2	59.1	53.9	2.3	1976	165.2	180.4	177.2	170.5	5.8
1950	78.8	58.7	72.8	72.1	1.0	1977	174.7	194.3	186.5	181.5	6.5
1955	85.1	70.9	82.3	80.2	−0.4	1978	187.1	210.9	202.8	195.4	7.7
1960	91.5	83.5	90.2	88.7	1.6	1979	208.4	234.2	227.6	217.4	11.3
1965	95.7	92.2	94.9	94.5	1.7	1980	233.9	270.3	263.3	246.8	13.6
1970	113.5	121.6	118.9	116.3	5.9	1981	253.6	305.7	293.5	272.4	10.4

1. Over previous year. *Source:* Department of Labor, Bureau of Labor Statistics.

Consumer Price Index for All Urban Consumers

(1967 = 100)

Group	July 1982	% increase Feb.–July	Group	July 1982	% increase Feb.–July
All items	—	5.7	Fuel oil, coal, bottled gas	659.9	−7.5
Food	287.0	3.9	House operation[1]	234.3	4.6
Alcoholic beverages	209.2	4.5	House furnishings	194.9	4.3
Apparel and upkeep	192.1	3.0	Transportation	293.1	0.8
Men's and boys' apparel	184.6	4.6	Medical care	330.5	11.6
Women's and girls' apparel	158.9	1.7	Personal care	249.4	7.2
Footwear	207.9	3.9	Tobacco products	239.2	10.9
Housing, total	318.4	7.8	Entertainment	236.5	15.6
Rent	224.8	6.5	Personal and educational expenses	302.2	12.0
Gas and electricity	392.3	10.1			

1. Combines house furnishings and operation. *Source:* Department of Labor, Bureau of Labor Statistics.

Consumer Price Index for Urban Wage Earners and Clerical Workers

(1967 = 100)

Effective January 1978, the Consumer Price Index was revised, with two indexes now being produced: A new index for All Urba Consumers covers 80% of the non-institutional population; the other index, the Consumer Price Index for Urban Wage Earner and Clerical Workers, covers about half of those included in the new index and is a major revision of the one that had bee published for many years.

	1982[1]	1981	1980	1975	1970	1965	1960	1955	195
All items	—	272.3	247.0	161.2	116.3	94.5	88.7	80.2	72.
Food total	287.1	274.9	255.3	175.4	114.9	94.4	88.0	81.6	—
Apparel and upkeep	191.0	186.6	177.4	142.3	116.1	93.7	89.6	84.1	79.
Housing total	318.5	293.2	263.2	166.8	118.9	94.9	90.2	82.3	72.
Rent	224.3	207.8	191.3	137.3	110.1	96.9	91.7	84.3	70.
Gas and electricity	391.7	344.8	301.2	169.6	107.3	99.4	98.6	87.5	81.
Fuel oil, coal, bottled gas	662.9	678.9	557.2	253.3	110.1	94.6	89.2	82.3	72.
House operation[2]	231.1	218.0	202.9	158.1	113.4	95.3	93.8	89.9	—
House furnishings	193.1	183.1	172.6	144.4	111.4	97.1	99.3	99.2	95.
Transportation	294.7	281.3	250.5	150.6	112.7	95.9	89.6	77.4	68.
Medical care	328.5	295.1	267.2	168.6	120.6	89.5	79.1	64.8	53.
Personal care	247.5	229.8	212.7	150.7	113.2	95.2	90.1	77.9	68.
Entertainment	233.5	219.0	203.7	144.4	113.4	95.9	87.3	76.7	74.

1. July. 2. Combines house furnishings and operation. *Source:* Department of Labor, Bureau of Labor Statistics.

Per Capita Personal Income

Year	Amount	Year	Amount	Year	Amount	Year	Amount	Year	Amou
1929	$705	1958	$2,074	1964	$2,592	1970	$3,893	1976	$ 6,40
1935	474	1959	2,166	1965	2,773	1971	4,132	1977	7,04
1940	593	1960	2,219	1966	2,987	1972	4,493	1978	7,72
1945	1,223	1961	2,269	1967	3,167	1973	4,980	1979	8,63
1950	1,501	1962	2,373	1968	3,433	1974	5,428	1980	9,51
1955	1,881	1963	2,460	1969	3,667	1975	5,851	1981	10,51

Source: Department of Commerce, Bureau of Economic Analysis.

Foresee Auto Mechanic Shortage

The Automotive Information Council has noted a report indicating that there were 86 cars per mechanic in 1981 compared to 66 cars per mechanic in 1970. The report states that the ratio will rise to 100 cars per mechanic in 1990. In addition, t study states that the new domestic cars alone me that distributors and repairmen must cope wi 30,000 new parts.

Per Capita Personal Income by States

State	1981	1980	1979	1978
Alabama	$ 8,200	$ 7,434	$ 6,815	$ 6,176
Alaska	14,190	12,759	11,320	10,842
Arizona	9,693	8,814	7,945	6,973
Arkansas	8,042	7,185	6,726	6,034
California	12,057	10,929	9,805	8,702
Colorado	11,142	10,033	8,944	7,945
Connecticut	12,995	11,692	10,337	9,110
Delaware	11,279	10,291	9,144	8,217
D.C.	13,487	12,050	10,616	9,418
Florida	10,050	8,993	8,034	7,212
Georgia	8,960	8,041	7,337	6,624
Hawaii	11,096	10,091	9,098	8,288
Idaho	8,906	8,176	7,437	6,835
Illinois	11,479	10,479	9,717	8,751
Indiana	9,656	8,924	8,377	7,552
Iowa	10,149	9,310	8,818	8,054
Kansas	10,870	9,864	9,216	7,972
Kentucky	8,455	7,662	7,103	6,375
Louisiana	9,486	8,456	7,480	6,655
Maine	8,655	7,868	7,025	6,323
Maryland	11,534	10,477	9,430	8,445
Massachusetts	11,158	10,118	8,990	8,000
Michigan	11,009	9,967	9,337	8,426
Minnesota	10,747	9,765	8,925	7,920
Mississippi	7,256	6,557	6,079	5,486
Missouri	9,876	8,865	8,227	7,281
Montana	9,676	8,652	7,787	7,138
Nebraska	10,296	9,086	8,740	7,581
Nevada	11,633	10,723	9,718	8,792
New Hampshire	10,073	9,119	8,137	7,273
New Jersey	12,115	10,935	9,758	8,797
New Mexico	8,654	7,878	7,153	6,448
New York	11,440	10,252	9,157	8,264
North Carolina	8,679	7,832	7,124	6,415
North Dakota	10,525	8,626	8,209	7,484
Ohio	10,371	9,460	8,710	7,824
Oklahoma	10,210	9,066	8,158	7,155
Oregon	9,991	9,276	8,615	7,800
Pennsylvania	10,373	9,427	8,544	7,630
Rhode Island	10,466	9,429	8,371	7,435
South Carolina	8,050	7,265	6,609	5,921
South Dakota	8,793	7,818	7,563	6,629
Tennessee	8,604	7,702	7,104	6,391
Texas	10,743	9,528	8,516	7,058
Utah	8,307	7,681	7,058	6,408
Vermont	8,654	7,810	7,087	6,388
Virginia	10,445	9,406	8,438	7,589
Washington	11,266	10,355	9,428	8,419
West Virginia	8,334	7,814	7,192	6,376
Wisconsin	10,056	9,413	8,657	7,636
Wyoming	11,780	10,875	9,798	8,572
Total	**10,517**	**9,511**	**8,638**	**7,729**

1. Preliminary. *Source:* Department of Commerce, Bureau of Economic Analysis.

Gross National Product or Expenditure
(in billions)

Item	1981	1980	1979	1978	1977	1976	1975	1970	1965	1960	1955	1950	1946	1938	1933	1929
Gross national product	$2,926	$2,626	$2,414	$2,128	$1,900	$1,702	$1,529	$982	$688	$506	$399	$286	$210	$85	$56	$103
GNP in constant (1972) dollars	1,510	1,481	1,483	1,399	1,341	1,273	1,202	1,075	926	737	655	534	477	312	222	315
Personal consumption expenditures	1,858	1,673	1,511	1,351	1,210	1,090	980	619	430	325	254	192	144	64	46	77
Durable goods	232	212	212	200	179	157	133	85	63	43	39	31	16	6	3	9
Nondurable goods	743	676	602	531	481	444	409	265	189	151	123	98	83	34	22	38
Services	883	785	696	620	550	489	438	269	179	131	92	63	45	24	20	30
Gross private domestic investment	451	395	416	352	303	243	189	141	112	76	68	54	31	6	1	16
Residential structures	106	105	119	108	92	68	52	36	31	24	24	20	7	2	1	4
Nonresidential structures	126	109	96	77	63	57	53	38	26	18	14	9	7	2	1	5
Producers' durable equipment	206	190	186	145	127	108	96	64	46	30	24	18	10	3	1	6
Change in business inventories	16	−6	18	22	22	10	−11	4	10	4	6	7	6	−1	−2	2
Net export of goods and services	26	23	13	−10	−10	8	20	4	8	4	2	2	8	1	(1)	1
Government purchases	591	535	474	436	396	361	339	219	138	100	75	38	28	13	8	8
Federal	230	199	168	153	144	130	123	96	67	54	44	19	18	5	2	1
National defense	154	132	111	99	94	86	84	74	49	44	38	14	15	n.a.	n.a.	n.a.
Other	76	67	57	54	50	44	39	22	18	9	6	5	3	n.a.	n.a.	n.a.
State and local	361	336	306	283	252	232	216	123	71	47	31	20	10	8	6	7
Implicit price deflator	194	177	163	150	142	134	127	91	74	69	61	54	44	27	25	33

1. Less than $500 million. NOTE: n.a. = not available. *Source:* Department of Commerce, Bureau of Economic Analysis.

Median Earnings of Full-Time Women Workers
(persons 15 years and over)

Major occupation group	1980 earnings	As percent of men's earnings
Professional and technical workers	$15,285	66.4
Nonfarm managers and administrators	12,936	54.9
Clerical workers	10,997	60.3
Sales workers	9,748	49.0
Operatives (including transport)	9,440	60.1
Service workers (except private household)	7,982	60.9
All occupations	**11,197**	**60.2**

Source: Department of Labor, Women's Bureau.

Median Family Income
(in current dollars)

Year	Income	Percent change	Year	Income	Percent change
1960	$ 5,620	—	1976	$14,958	9.0
1970	9,867	—	1977	16,009	7.0
1972	11,116	—	1978	17,640	10.2
1973	12,051	8.4	1979	19,661	11.5
1974	12,902	7.1	1980	21,023	6.9
1975	13,719	6.3	1981	22,388	6.5

Source: Department of Commerce, Bureau of the Census. NOTE: Figures are latest available.

Farm Indexes
(1977 = 100)

Year	Prices paid by farmers[1]	Prices rec'd by farmers[2]	Ratio
1945	28	45	161
1950	37	56	151
1955	40	51	128
1960	44	52	118
1965	47	54	115
1970	55	60	109
1975	89	101	113
1980	139	134	96
1981	150	138	92

1. Commodities, interest, and taxes, and wage rates. 2. All crops and livestock. *Source:* Department of Agriculture, Economics and Statistics Service.

Life Insurance in Force
(in millions of dollars)

As of Dec. 31	Ordinary	Group	Industrial	Credit	Total
1915	$16,650	$ 100	$ 4,279	—	$ 21,029
1930	78,756	9,801	17,693	73	106,413
1945	101,550	22,172	27,675	365	151,762
1950	149,071	47,793	33,415	3,844	234,168
1955	216,812	101,345	39,682	14,493	373,332
1960	341,881	175,903	39,563	29,101	586,448
1965	499,638	308,078	39,818	53,020	900,554
1970	734,730	551,357	38,644	77,392	1,402,123
1975	1,083,421	904,695	39,423	112,032	2,139,571
1978	1,425,095	1,243,994	38,080	163,081	2,870,250
1979	1,585,878	1,419,418	37,794	179,250	3,222,340
1980	1,760,474	1,579,355	35,994	165,215	3,541,038
1981	1,978,080	1,888,612	34,547	162,356	4,063,595

Source: American Council of Life Insurance.

Producer Price Indexes by Major Commodity Groups
(1967 = 100)

Commodity	1981	1980	1975	1970	1965	1960	1955
All commodities	293.4	268.8	174.9	110.4	96.6	94.9	87.8
Farm products	254.9	249.4	186.7	111.0	98.7	97.2	98.2
Processed foods	248.7	241.2	182.6	112.1	95.5	89.5	85.0
Textile products and apparel	199.6	183.5	137.9	107.1	99.8	99.5	98.7
Hides, skins, and leather products	261.5	248.9	148.5	110.3	94.3	90.8	77.3
Fuels and related products and power	694.4	574.0	245.1	106.2	95.5	96.1	91.2
Chemicals and allied products	287.8	260.3	181.3	102.2	99.0	101.8	98.5
Rubber and plastic products	232.8	217.4	150.2	108.3	95.9	103.1	102.4
Lumber and wood products	292.8	288.9	176.9	113.6	95.9	95.3	97.1
Pulp, paper, and allied products	273.7	249.2	170.4	108.2	96.2	98.1	87.8
Metals and metal products	300.4	286.4	185.6	116.6	96.4	92.4	82.1
Machinery and equipment	263.1	239.8	161.4	111.4	93.9	92.0	75.7
Furniture and household durables	198.4	187.7	139.7	107.5	96.9	99.0	93.3
Nonmetallic mineral products	309.5	283.0	174.0	112.9	97.5	97.2	87.5
Transportation equipment (Dec. 1968 = 100)	235.4	207.0	141.5	104.6	98.5	98.8	—
Miscellaneous products	265.6	258.8	147.7	109.9	95.9	93.0	86.5

Source: Department of Labor, Bureau of Labor Statistics.

Cigarettes Are a Fire Hazard

Fires that result from smoldering cigarettes account for nearly one third of the deaths and injuries in residential fires. The annual toll nationwide is at least 2,300 dead and 5,800 injured. According to Andrew McGuire, executive director of the nonprofit Burn Council in San Francisco, the cigarette is the number one issue in the prevention of fires

Total Family Income
(figures in percent)

Income range	White 1981	White 1980	White 1970	White 1960	Black and other races 1981	Black and other races 1980	Black and other races 1970	Black and other races 1960
Families (thousands)[1]	53,269	52,710	46,535	41,123	7,750	7,599	5,413	4,333
Under $2,500	1.7	1.6	5.6	15.1	4.7	5.0	15.6	39.8
$2,500 to $7,499	7.5	8.6	25.8	52.9	21.2	22.5	41.4	48.9
$7,500 to $12,400	12.3	13.1	33.4	24.6	18.4	18.5	25.6	9.9
$12,500 to $14,999	6.4	6.8	11.5	3.3	6.7	7.4	6.5	0.9
$15,000 to $19,999	12.6	14.1	13.8	2.2	12.3	12.8	7.4	0.3
$20,000 to $24,999	13.0	14.2	4.9	0.9	9.8	10.6	2.1	0.3
$25,000 to $34,999	21.1	20.8	3.2	—	14.2	12.9	1.1	—
$35,000 to $49,999	15.7	13.6	1.2	1.1	9.2	7.6	0.3	—
$50,000 and over	9.7	7.2	0.6	—	3.4	2.8	0.1	—
Median income	$23,517	$21,904	$10,236	$5,835	$14,598	$13,843	$6,516	$3,230

1. As of March 1982. *Source:* Department of Commerce, Bureau of the Census.

National Income by Type
(in billions of dollars)

Type of share	1981	1981 % of total	1980	1979	1975	1970	1965	1960	1950
ational income	$2,347.2	100.0	$2,121.4	$1,963.3	$1,215.0	$800.5	$564.3	$414.5	$241.1
ompensation of employees	1,771.6	75.5	1,596.5	1,460.9	931.1	603.9	393.8	294.2	154.6
Wages and salaries	1,482.8	63.2	1,343.6	1,235.9	805.9	542.0	358.9	270.8	146.8
Supplements to wages and salaries	288.8	12.3	252.9	225.0	125.2	61.9	35.0	23.4	7.8
roprietors' income	134.8	5.7	130.6	131.6	87.0	66.9	57.3	46.2	37.5
Business and professional	112.4	4.8	107.2	100.7	63.5	50.0	42.4	34.2	24.0
Farm	22.4	1.0	23.4	30.8	23.5	16.9	14.8	12.0	13.5
ental income of persons	33.6	1.4	31.8	30.5	22.4	23.9	19.0	15.8	9.4
orporate profits[1]	191.7	8.2	182.7	196.8	95.9	69.4	76.1	49.9	37.7
et interest	215.4	9.2	179.8	143.4	78.6	36.4	18.2	8.4	2.0

Includes inventory valuation adjustment. *Source:* Department of Commerce, Bureau of Economic Analysis.

How Consumers Spend Their Dollar
(in billions)

	1981	1981 % of total	1980	1979	1975	1970	1960	1950	1940	1930
ood	$329.1	17.9	$300.0	$272.2	$185.2	$119.6	$70.5	$46.0	$16.6	$18.0
obacco	23.1	1.3	20.7	19.3	14.8	10.8	6.9	4.3	1.9	1.5
'cohol	46.2	2.5	43.7	39.3	28.4	19.2	10.6	7.9	3.6	n.a.
lothing, accessories, and jewelry	136.4	7.4	124.4	116.3	81.6	55.8	32.2	23.7	8.9	9.7
ersonal care	24.6	1.3	22.9	21.1	14.7	11.0	5.2	2.4	1.0	1.0
ousing	295.3	16.0	266.0	236.1	149.8	93.9	48.1	21.7	9.7	11.1
ousehold operation	256.5	13.9	229.7	207.9	132.9	84.1	46.1	29.1	10.4	9.6
edical care	194.6	10.6	165.2	144.2	87.6	50.4	20.0	9.1	3.0	2.8
rsonal business	99.8	5.4	93.7	83.7	52.2	31.6	14.2	6.6	3.2	3.7
ansportation	260.8	14.1	239.5	219.4	129.4	80.6	42.4	25.4	7.3	6.1
creation	117.2	6.4	106.9	98.9	65.6	41.3	17.9	11.1	3.8	4.0
ivate education and research	29.3	1.6	26.2	23.3	15.8	9.9	3.7	1.7	.6	.7
ligious and welfare activities	25.4	1.4	23.4	20.8	13.9	8.9	4.9	2.3	1.0	1.2
reign travel and other	4.9	0.3	4.8	4.6	4.6	4.5	2.1	.7	.1	.5
tal[1]	**1,843.2**	**100.0**	**1,667.2**	**1,507.2**	**976.4**	**621.7**	**324.9**	**192.0**	**71.0**	**69.9**

Detail may not add to total due to rounding. *Source:* Department of Commerce, Bureau of Economic Analysis.

Annual Budgets for 4-Person Urban Families, Autumn 1981

Item	Lower budget		Intermediate budget		Higher budget	
	Amount	Percent increase 1980–81	Amount	Percent increase 1980–81	Amount	Percent increase 1980–81
Total family consumption	$12,069	7.3	$18,240	7.5	$25,008	7.5
Food	4,545	5.2	5,843	4.9	7,366	4.9
Housing	2,817	8.0	5,546	8.6	8,423	8.7
Transportation	1,311	13.0	2,372	12.1	3,075	11.8
Clothing	937	3.3	1,333	3.2	1,947	3.1
Personal care	379	7.7	508	7.9	719	7.6
Medical care	1,436	10.6	1,443	10.7	1,505	10.7
Other family consumption	644	7.9	1,196	7.8	1,972	7.8
Other items	621	6.5	1,021	6.7	1,718	6.7
Personal income taxes	1,596	19.4	4,443	17.5	9,340	17.9
Social security and disability	1,036	17.6	1,703	19.3	1,993	23.9
Total budget	**15,323**	**9.1**	**25,407**	**9.8**	**38,060**	**10.6**

NOTE: Above budgets illustrate three levels of living based on estimates of costs for goods and services rather than actual expenditures. Totals may not add because of rounding. *Source:* Department of Labor, Bureau of Labor Statistics.

Annual Budgets for a Retired Couple, Autumn 1981

Item	Lower Budget		Intermediate Budget		Higher Budget	
	Amount	Percent increase 1980–81	Amount	Percent increase 1980–81	Amount	Percent increase 1980–81
Total family consumption	$6,914	8.7	$9,611	8.4	$13,960	8.3
Food	2,183	4.9	2,898	4.5	3,642	4.6
Housing	2,377	9.6	3,393	9.2	5,307	9.2
Transportation	553	13.6	1,073	12.9	1,960	12.1
Clothing	244	3.4	409	3.3	629	3.3
Personal care	198	7.6	290	7.8	424	7.6
Medical care[1]	1,085	14.9	1,091	14.8	1,098	14.9
Other consumption	275	7.8	457	7.8	901	7.6
Other items	311	8.7	615	8.3	1,118	7.8
Total budget	**7,226**	**8.8**	**10,226**	**8.4**	**15,078**	**8.3**

1. Contains preliminary estimate for out-of-pocket costs for Medicare. *Source:* Department of Commerce, Bureau of Labor Statistics.

Terms on Conventional First Mortgages: All Major Types of Lenders

Type of homes and year	Contract rate (percent)	Fees and charges (percent)	Effective rate (percent)	Maturity (years)	Loan amount	Purchase price	Loan-to-price ratio (percent)
New homes: 1982[1]	14.74	3.00	15.40	27.4	66.2	89.4	77.0
1981	14.13	2.66	14.70	27.7	65.2	90.3	74.8
1980	12.25	2.09	12.65	28.2	59,200	83,400	73.2
1979	10.48	1.66	10.77	28.5	53,300	74,400	73.9
1978	9.30	1.39	9.54	28.0	45,900	62,600	75.3
1975	8.75	1.54	—	26.8	33,300	44,600	76.1
1970	8.27	1.03	—	25.1	25,200	35,500	71.7
Existing homes: 1982[1]	15.01	2.47	15.56	25.4	49.5	71.2	72.2
1981	14.51	2.27	15.00	25.9	47.7	68.5	72.9
1980	12.58	1.90	12.95	26.8	48,000	68,000	73.3
1979	10.66	1.45	10.92	27.1	46,300	64,600	74.0
1978	9.37	1.26	9.58	26.4	39,400	54,200	75.1
1975	9.01	1.19	—	24.0	27,400	38,200	73.4
1970	8.20	0.92	—	22.8	21,000	30,000	71.1

1. June. *Source:* Federal Home Loan Bank Board.

Interest Rates

Instrument	1982[1]	1981	1980	1979	1978	1977	1976	1975	1974	1973	1970
MONEY MARKET RATES											
Federal funds	14.81	16.38	13.36	11.19	7.94	5.54	5.05	5.82	10.51	8.74	7.17
Prime commercial paper											
3 months	14.71	15.32	12.66	10.97	7.94	5.54	5.24	6.26	10.05	8.20	—
6 months	14.46	14.76	12.29	10.91	7.99	5.60	5.35	6.33	9.87	8.15	7.72
Prime bankers acceptances, 3 months	14.68	15.32	12.78	11.04	8.11	5.59	5.19	6.30	9.92	8.08	7.31
Certificates of deposit, 3 months, secondary market	15.21	15.91	13.07	11.22	8.22	5.64	—	—	—	—	—
U.S. government securities: bills, 6-month yield	13.08	13.80	11.37	10.06	7.58	5.53	5.26	6.11	7.95	7.20	6.51
CAPITAL MARKET RATES											
U.S. Treasury											
Notes and bonds maturing in 3–5 years	—	—	—	9.58	8.30	6.85	6.94	7.55	7.81	6.92	7.37
5 years	14.73	14.24	11.48	9.52	8.32	6.99	7.18	7.77	7.80	—	—
10 years	14.54	13.91	11.46	9.44	8.41	7.42	7.61	7.99	7.56	—	—
State and local											
Moody's series:											
Aaa	11.60	10.43	7.85	5.92	5.52	5.20	5.66	6.42	5.89	—	—
Baa	13.20	11.76	9.01	6.73	6.27	6.12	7.49	7.62	6.53	—	—
Corporate bonds, seasoned issues:											
Aaa	15.07	14.17	11.94	9.63	8.73	8.02	8.43	8.83	8.57	—	—
Aa	15.50	14.75	12.50	9.94	8.92	8.24	8.75	9.17	8.84	—	—
A	16.29	15.29	12.89	10.20	9.12	8.49	9.09	9.65	9.20	—	—
Baa	16.95	16.04	13.67	10.69	9.45	8.97	9.75	10.61	9.50	—	—

1. Week ending July 2. *Source* Federal Reserve Bulletin, July 1982.

Consumer Credit

(non-installment credit; in millions of dollars)

End of year	Service credit	Charge accounts	Single-payment loans	Total credit outstanding	End of year	Service credit	Charge accounts	Single-payment loans	Total credit outstanding
1945	$ 845	$ 2,687	$ 1,491	$ 5,023	1970	9,106	9,156	19,323	37,585
1950	1,638	4,858	3,642	10,138	1975	12,027	11,739	27,378	51,144
1955	2,316	6,761	6,002	15,079	1979	18,619	12,748	39,972	71,339
1960[1]	3,734	7,235	9,084	20,053	1980	19,280	13,135	42,352	74,767
1965	5,545	8,319	15,462	29,326	1981	22,270	14,403	43,496	80,169

1. Beginning with 1960, data include Alaska and Hawaii. *Source:* Federal Reserve Board.

What Americans Pay in Personal Taxes[1] and What They Save

(in billions of current dollars)

Item	1981	1980	1975	1970	1965	1960	1950
Gross personal income	$2,404.1	$2,160.2	$1,255.5	$808.3	$538.9	$401.0	$227.6
Social insurance contributions	104.2	87.9	50.5	28.0	13.4	9.3	2.9
Tax and non-tax payments to governments	388.2	338.5	168.8	116.6	65.7	50.9	20.7
Income available for spending and saving[2]	2,016.0	1,821.7	1,086.7	691.7	473.2	350.0	206.9
Income available per capita (dollars)	8,770.0	8,002	5,088	3,376	2,436	1,937	1,364
Personal saving	107.6	101.3	83.6	56.2	28.4	17.0	13.1
Rate of personal saving	5.3%	5.6%	7.7%	8.1%	6.4%	4.9%	6.3%

1. Personal income basis: direct taxes and payments only; corporate taxes and payments, paid by shareholders or customers, and hidden and consumption taxes not included. 2. Disposable personal income. *Source:* Department of Commerce, Bureau of Economic Analysis.

Federal Reserve Board Indexes of Production

(1967 = 100)

Industry	1982[1]	1980	1975	1970
Total industrial production	138.4	147.1	117.8	106.7
Total manufactures	137.3	146.6	116.3	105.2
Durable manufactures	125.3	136.6	109.3	101.5
Primary metals	70.9	101.6	96.4	106.9
Fabricated metal products	115.0	135.0	109.9	109.4
Machinery	148.4	162.8	125.1	100.3
Transportation equipment	111.4	116.8	97.4	90.4
Instruments and products	164.9	171.0	132.3	110.8
Clay, glass, and stone products	126.8[2]	146.5	117.9	106.4
Lumber and products	108.3[2]	119.3	107.6	106.3
Furniture and fixtures	150.9[2]	150.0	118.2	99.4
Nondurable manufactures	154.6	161.1	126.4	110.6
Textile mill products	125.1[2]	136.8	122.3	106.3
Apparel products	n.a.	128.6	107.6	97.8
Leather products	62.0[2]	70.1	76.5	90.8

Industry	1982[1]	1980	1975	1970
Rubber and plastic products	253.9[2]	255.8	166.7	115.7
Paper and products	144.8	151.0	116.3	113.3
Printing and publishing	142.5	139.6	113.4	104.1
Chemicals and products	195.0[2]	206.7	147.3	120.3
Petroleum products	124.7	134.9	124.1	112.6
Foods	149.4[3]	149.2	123.4	111.7
Tobacco products	116.1[3]	119.8	111.8	100.0
Mining	126.7	132.9	112.8	109.7
Coal	147.7	146.7	113.4	105.7
Oil and gas extraction	129.2	133.8	113.3	109.7
Metal mining	96.8[2]	109.1	115.8	131.3
Stone and earth minerals	116.9[2]	131.7	107.0	98.8
Utilities	168.0	169.9	146.0	128.3

1. June estimate except where otherwise indicated. 2. May preliminary. 3. April. NOTE: n.a. = not available. *Source: Federal Reserve Bulletin,* July 1982.

Value of New Construction Put in Place

(in millions of dollars)

Activity	1981	1980	1970	1960	1950	1940	1933	1929
Total new construction activity	$238,201	$230,749	$95,204	$54,738	$33,575	$8,682	$2,879	$10,793
New private construction activity	185,222	175,699	67,114	38,875	26,709	5,054	1,231	8,307
Residential	86,566	87,261	31,864	22,975	18,126	2,985	470	3,625
New dwelling units	62,664	63,139	24,272	17,279	15,551	2,560	290	3,040
Additions and alterations	20,025	21,125	6,234	4,831	2,400	335	145	340
Nonhousekeeping	3,876	2,997	1,358	865	175	90	35	245
Nonresidential building, except farm and public utility	60,818	52,434	21,412	10,149	3,904	1,025	406	2,694
Industrial	17,030	13,837	6,537	2,851	1,062	442	176	949
Commercial[1]	34,248	29,945	9,753	4,180	1,415	348	130	1,135
Other	9,541	8,652	5,122	3,118	1,427	235	100	610
Public utility	31,231	29,480	11,017	4,621	3,045	771	261	1,578
Railroads	4,080	3,035	304	270	309	217	115	592
Telephone and telegraph	7,074	6,733	2,968	1,088	440	122	45	354
Farm construction	5,341	5,274	1,875	849	1,522	240	49	307
New public construction activity	52,979	55,050	28,090	15,863	6,866	3,628	1,648	2,486
Residential	1,722	1,648	1,106	716	345	200	n.a.	n.a.
Nonresidential building	16,070	16,869	9,550	4,795	2,387	615	230	659
Industrial	1,655	1,441	498	407	224	164	2	n.a.
Educational	6,737	8,050	5,619	2,818	1,133	156	52	389
Hospital and institutional	2,083	1,785	838	401	499	54	49	101
Other	5,595	5,593	2,594	1,169	531	421	127	169
Military facilities	1,964	1,880	717	1,366	177	385	36	19
Highway	13,304	13,807	9,982	5,437	2,134	1,302	847	1,266
Sewer and water	8,939	10,437	2,636	1,487	659	338	95	253
Conservation and development	5,225	5,090	1,907	1,175	942	528	359	115

1. Warehouses, office and loft buildings; stores, restaurants and garages. NOTE: n.a. = not available. *Source:* Department of Commerce, Bureau of the Census.

Gasohol Isn't New

Farmers knew they could make motor fuels long before the current energy crisis. So did Henry Ford. He built his Model T to run on gasoline, alcohol, or any mixture in between.

During the depression, farmers often raised more corn than they could eat, feed to livestock, or haul to markets. By fermenting the grain to get alcohol and feed, they found new ways to use their crops. Some burned the stuff in their "Tin Lizzies," trimming the gas bill at a time when the dollar was hard to come by.

Expenditures for New Plant and Equipment[1]

(in millions of dollars)

Year	Manufacturing and mining	Transportation	All other[2]	Total
1950	$ 8,570	$ 2,380	$ 14,370	$ 25,320
1955	13,810	2,600	20,170	36,580
1960	17,650	3,190	27,800	48,630
1965	26,770	5,460	38,200	70,430
1970	39,010	6,950	59,650	105,610
1974	57,830	8,230	90,920	156,980
1975	61,020	8,680	88,010	157,710
1976	67,390	8,890	95,180	171,450
1977	78,460	9,400	110,230	198,080
1978	89,930	10,680	130,630	231,240
1979	110,060	12,350	148,050	270,460
1980	129,320	12,090	154,220	295,630
1981	143,650	12,050	165,790	321,490

1. Data exclude agriculture. 2. Includes electric and gas utilities, trade, service, communications, construction, and finance. NOTE: This series was revised in October 1980. *Source:* Department of Commerce, Bureau of Economic Analysis.

New Housing Starts[1] and Mobile Homes Shipped

(in thousands)

Year	No. of units started	Year	No. of units started	Year	Mobile homes shipped
1900	189	1965	1,510	1965	217
1910	387	1970	1,469	1970	401
1920	247	1973	2,057	1973	567
1925	937	1974	1,352	1974	329
1930	330	1975	1,171	1975	213
1935	221	1976	1,548	1976	246
1940	603	1977	2,002	1977	277
1945	326	1978	2,036	1978	275
1950	1,952	1979	1,760	1979	277
1955	1,646	1980	1,313	1980	222
1960[1]	1,296	1981	1,100	1981	241

1. Prior to 1960, starts limited to nonfarm housing; from 1960 on, figures include farm housing. *Sources:* Department of Commerce, Housing Construction Statistics, 1900–1965, and Construction Reports, Housing Starts, 1970–80; Manufactured Housing Institute, 1965–76; National Conference of States on Building Codes and Standards.

Shareholders in Public Corporations

Characteristic	1981	1980	1975	1970	1965	1959	1952
Individual shareholders (thousands)	32,260	30,200	25,270	30,850	20,120	12,490	6,490
Owners of shares listed on New York Stock Exchange (thousands)	26,084	23,804	17,950	18,290	12,430	8,510	n.a.
Adult shareowner incidence in population	1 in 5	1 in 5	1 in 6	1 in 4	1 in 6	1 in 8	1 in 16
Median household income	$29,200	$27,750	$19,000	$13,500	$9,500	$7,000	$7,100
Adult shareowners with household income: under $10,000 (thousands)	2,164	1,742	3,420	8,170	10,080	9,340	n.a.
$10,000 and over (thousands)	26,912	25,715	19,970	20,130	8,410	2,740	n.a.
Adult female shareowners (thousands)	14,154	13,696	11,750	14,290	9,430	6,350	3,140
Adult male shareowners (thousands)	15,785	14,196	11,630	14,340	9,060	5,740	3,210
Median age	46	46	53	48	49	49	51

NOTE: n.a. = not available. *Source:* New York Stock Exchange.

50 Most Active Stocks in 1981

Stock	Share volume	Stock	Share volume	Stock	Share volume
nt'l Business Machines	110,720,700	Marathon Oil	56,041,701	Amerada Hess	41,268,700
xxon Corporation	95,733,500	Sears, Roebuck	55,493,854	American Express	41,058,800
ony Corporation	93,245,500	Storage Technology	55,056,600	BankAmerica Corporation	40,015,800
merican Tel. & Tel.	81,790,000	Gulf Oil	54,017,800	Prime Computer	39,472,680
obil Corporation	80,819,600	K mart Corporation	53,403,800	Pennzoil Company	38,940,200
exaco, Inc.	78,107,700	Boeing Company	49,255,700	Bally Manufacturing	38,302,100
eneral Motors	68,181,000	Texas International	49,073,900	RCA Corporation	37,305,000
ities Service	65,662,500	Schlumberger, N.V.	46,510,800	Digital Equipment	37,253,000
iticorp	61,590,800	Ralston Purina	45,966,800	Int'l Tel. & Tel.	37,151,700
tandard Oil (Indiana)	60,111,500	Union Oil	45,756,600	Superior Oil	37,111,700
andy Corporation	59,997,600	Eastman Kodak	45,559,900	United States Steel	37,009,900
hillips Petroleum	57,400,200	American Airlines	45,310,500	Pan American World Airways	37,005,400
. I. du Pont de Nemours	57,124,000	Standard Oil Co. of California	44,147,500	Polaroid Corporation	36,949,300
TV Corporation	56,944,000	Standard Oil (Ohio)	43,814,800	General Electric	36,935,500
onoco, Inc.	56,734,260	Xerox Corporation	43,449,700	Texas Utilities	36,929,300
tlantic Richfield	56,200,100	Dow Chemical	43,183,100	Halliburton Company	36,815,400
		Amax, Inc.	41,987,800		
		Santa Fe Int'l	41,739,000		

ource: New York Stock Exchange.

Business Population

(in thousands of concerns)

Item	1977[1]	1976[1]	1975[1]	1970[1]	1965[1]	1953	1949	1941	1933	1929
Total operating businesses[2]	14,740	14,559	13,979	12,001	11,417	4,188	3,984	3,276	2,782	3,029
Manufacturing	482	467	468	410	408	331	322	230	167	257
Wholesale trade	576	591	587	470	444	283	260	190	142	148
Retail trade	2,459	2,440	2,322	2,210	2,044	1,846	1,783	1,561	1,291	1,327
Service industries	4,043	3,834	3,669	2,964	2,565	750	739	615	575	591
Construction	1,279	1,221	1,144	875	876	405	339	194	185	234
All other[3]	5,901	6,007	5,788	5,072	5,080	573	541	486	422	472
New incorporations	432	376	326	264	204	352	331	290	n.a.	n.a.
Commercial and industrial failures[4]	7.9	9.6	11.4	10.7	13.5	8.9	9.2	11.8	19.9	22.9

1. Data for total operating businesses are now based on tax returns; not comparable with earlier figures. 2. 1929–33, annual average; 1941–53, as of January 1. 3. Includes agriculture, forestry, and fishing; mining; transportation, communication, electric, gas, and sanitary services; finance, insurance, and real estate; wholesale and retail trade not allocable; and nature of business not allocable. 4. Closures resulting in a known loss to creditors. NOTE: New incorporations for 1980 were 534,000; failures, 11,742. n.a. = not available. *Sources:* Departments of Commerce and the Treasury; Dun & Bradstreet. NOTE: Data are latest available.

Largest Businesses, 1981

(in thousands of dollars)

Source: Fortune magazine.

50 LARGEST INDUSTRIAL CORPORATIONS

	Sales	*Assets*
Exxon	$108,107,688	$62,931,055
Mobil	64,488,000	34,776,000
General Motors	62,698,500	38,991,200
Texaco	57,628,000	27,489,000
Standard Oil of California	44,224,000	23,680,000
Ford Motor	38,247,100	23,021,400
Standard Oil (Indiana)	29,947,000	22,916,000
International Business Machines	29,070,000	29,586,000
Gulf Oil	28,252,000	20,429,000
Atlantic Richfield	27,797,436	19,732,539
General Electric	27,240,000	20,942,000
E.I. du Pont de Nemours	22,810,000	23,829,000
Shell Oil	21,629,000	20,118,000
International Telephone & Telegraph	17,306,189	15,052,377
Phillips Petroleum	15,966,000	11,264,000
Tenneco	15,462,000	16,808,000
Sun	15,012,000	11,822,000
Occidental Petroleum	14,707,543	8,074,543
U.S. Steel	13,940,500	13,316,100
United Technologies	13,667,758	7,555,103
Standard Oil (Ohio)	13,457,091	15,743,296
Western Electric	13,008,000	8,338,300
Getty Oil	12,887,360	9,536,356
Dow Chemical	11,873,000	12,496,000
Procter & Gamble	11,416,000	6,961,000
Chrysler	10,821,600	6,270,000
Union Oil of California	10,745,900	7,592,800
Eastman Kodak	10,337,000	9,446,000
Dart & Kraft	10,211,000	5,053,800
Union Carbide	10,168,000	10,423,000
Boeing	9,788,200	6,953,700
R.J. Reynolds Industries	9,765,700	8,096,000
Amerada Hess	9,396,219	6,321,581
Westinghouse Electric	9,367,500	8,316,200
Ashland Oil	9,262,076	4,097,433
Marathon Oil	9,219,991	5,993,623
Caterpillar Tractor	9,154,500	7,284,900
Goodyear Tire & Rubber	9,152,905	5,354,259
Cities Service	8,899,300	6,048,500
LTV	8,822,700	4,332,700
Beatrice Foods	8,772,804	4,236,555
Xerox	8,691,000	7,674,400
Philip Morris	8,306,600	9,245,300
RCA	8,004,800	7,856,700
McDonnell Douglas	7,384,900	4,364,200
International Harvester	7,327,165	5,346,122
Bethlehem Steel	7,298,000	5,282,100
Rockwell International	7,039,700	4,809,000
PepsiCo	7,027,443	4,057,061
Monsanto	6,947,700	6,069,200

50 LARGEST RETAILING COMPANIES

	Sales	*Assets*
Sears Roebuck	$27,357,400	$34,509,400
Safeway Stores	16,580,318	3,690,404
K mart	16,527,012	6,673,004
J.C. Penney	11,860,169	6,216,000
Kroger	11,266,520	2,405,290
F.W. Woolworth	7,223,241	3,141,965
Lucky Stores	7,201,404	1,524,444
American Stores	7,096,590	1,356,328
Federated Department Stores	7,067,673	4,096,877
Great Atlantic & Pacific Tea	6,989,529	1,308,983
Winn-Dixie Stores	6,200,167	924,776
Montgomery Ward	5,742,491	4,116,593
Southland	5,693,636	1,677,791
Jewel Companies	5,107,614	1,379,871
Household Merchandising	5,079,932	1,354,299
Dayton Hudson	4,942,859	2,555,168
Grand Union	3,626,231	781,449
Albertson's	3,480,570	709,847
May Department Stores	3,413,204	2,387,583
Supermarkets General	2,999,379	636,77[illegible]
ARA Services	2,915,876	1,137,778
Carter Hawley Hale Stores	2,870,735	1,741,72[illegible]
Allied Stores	2,760,867	2,179,32[illegible]
Melville	2,760,842	1,134,254
Associated Dry Goods	2,751,200	1,557,47[illegible]
R.H. Macy	2,656,689	1,479,46[illegible]
Dillon Companies	2,494,577	497,58[illegible]
McDonald's	2,477,229	2,899,32[illegible]
Rapid-American	2,457,140	1,567,44[illegible]
Wal-Mart	2,449,997	937,51[illegible]

Stop & Shop Companies	2,168,148	468,578
Marriott	2,000,314	1,454,876
Sigmor	1,835,363	495,216
Zayre	1,797,139	643,444
Jack Eckerd	1,752,550	643,935
Walgreen	1,743,471	521,041
Tandy	1,691,373	936,545
Fisher Foods	1,492,709	222,299
Giant Food	1,483,476	339,542
Waldbaum	1,375,787	240,964
Revco D.S.	1,310,404	447,652
Mercantile Stores	1,269,491	711,370
First National Supermarkets	1,230,173	194,981
Pantry Pride	1,225,263	223,169
Marshall Field	1,193,961	680,758
Pneumo	1,093,611	370,716
U.S. Shoe	1,087,982	519,993
SCOA Industries	1,057,573	373,080
Thrifty	1,054,418	352,774
Service Merchandise	1,027,093	453,555

10 LARGEST COMMERCIAL BANKS

	Assets	*Deposits*
BankAmerica Corp.	$121,158,350	$94,369,453
Citicorp	119,232,000	72,125,000
Chase Manhattan Corp.	77,839,338	55,299,670
Manufacturers Hanover Corp.	59,108,519	42,462,035
J.P. Morgan & Co.	53,522,000	36,024,000
Continental Illinois Corp.	46,971,755	29,594,005
Chemical New York Corp.	44,916,933	29,429,577
First Interstate Bancorp.	36,982,091	27,407,174
Bankers Trust New York Corp.	34,213,010	23,345,022
First Chicago Corp.	33,562,442	25,554,923

10 LARGEST LIFE INSURANCE COMPANIES

	Assets	*Premium and annuity income*
Prudential	$62,498,540	$9,935,180
Metropolitan	51,757,845	5,131,318
Equitable Life Assurance	36,758,160	2,400,771
Aetna Life	25,158,904	4,440,322
New York Life	21,041,380	2,637,020
John Hancock Mutual	19,936,798	2,425,567
Connecticut General Life	15,103,332	2,810,410
Travelers	14,803,168	4,399,880
Northwestern Mutual	12,154,318	1,244,436
Teachers Insurance & Annuity	11,439,344	1,791,958

10 LARGEST TRANSPORTATION COMPANIES

	Operating revenues	*Assets*
CSX	$5,432,200	$8,066,900
Trans World	5,265,468	3,396,758
UAL	5,141,174	3,975,777
Burlington Northern	4,935,823	5,673,536
United Parcel Service	4,748,294	1,755,181
American Airlines	4,108,699	3,738,221
Pan American World Airways	3,797,291	2,963,184
Eastern Air Lines	3,727,093	2,934,519
Delta Air Lines	3,533,326	2,304,327
Santa Fe Industries	3,366,900	4,677,800

10 LARGEST UTILITIES

	Assets	*Operating revenues*
American Telephone & Telegraph	$137,749,500	$58,213,800
General Telephone & Electronics	21,113,299	11,026,296
Southern Company	12,415,034	4,256,237
Pacific Gas & Electric	12,366,659	6,194,575
American Electric Power	11,567,039	4,192,645
Commonwealth Edison	11,196,823	3,737,311
Southern California Edison	8,728,543	4,054,356
Middle South Utilities	8,318,556	2,771,788
Consolidated Edison	7,732,822	4,865,934
Texas Utilities	7,306,658	2,738,377

10 LARGEST DIVERSIFIED FINANCIAL COMPANIES

	Assets	*Revenues*
Federal National Mortgage Assn.	$62,095,903	$5,861,559
Aetna Life & Casualty	39,630,600	13,531,900
American Express	25,103,000	7,211,000
Travelers	23,982,300	9,800,800
Merrill Lynch & Co.	17,682,251	4,038,182
H.F. Ahmanson	15,048,826	1,564,248
INA	11,028,906	5,162,258
Great Western Financial	10,646,435	1,173,973
First Boston	10,314,389	291,536
Loews	9,914,071	4,776,219

Estimated Annual Retail and Wholesale Sales by Kind of Business

(in millions of dollars)

Kind of business	1981	1980
Retail trade, total	$1,038,790	$951,902
Building materials, hardware, garden supply, and mobile home dealers	53,164	49,616
Automotive dealers	180,722	162,309
Furniture, home furnishings, and equipment stores	45,701	43,416
General merchandise group stores	127,494	117,227
Food stores	237,586	217,047
Gasoline service stations	101,665	93,624
Apparel and accessory stores	47,755	44,426
Eating and drinking places	94,070	85,842
Drug stores and proprietary stores	32,999	30,504
Liquor stores	17,461	17,083
Merchant wholesale trade, total	1,174,072	1,055,168
Total, (excluding farm-product raw materials)	1,048,484	932,941
Durable goods, total	499,970	448,040
Motor vehicles and automotive parts and supplies	94,728	84,227
Furniture and home furnishings	16,624	15,321
Lumber and other construction materials	34,061	34,514
Electrical goods	54,181	47,542
Hardware, plumbing, heating and supplies	30,316	27,136
Machinery, equipment, supplies	148,210	130,282
Scrap and waste materials	15,783	17,220
Nondurable goods, total	674,102	607,128
Total (excluding farm-product raw materials)	548,514	484,901
Paper and paper products	24,381	21,296
Drugs, drug proprietaries, and druggists' sundries	15,812	13,626
Apparel, piece goods, and notions	27,091	25,121
Groceries and related products	167,675	152,551
Beer, wine, distilled alcoholic beverages	35,857	32,554
Miscellaneous nondurable goods	70,638	68,382
Tobacco and tobacco products	12,666	11,366

Source: Department of Commerce, Bureau of the Census.

50 Companies With Largest Number of Stockholders

Company	Stockholders	Company	Stockholders
American Telephone & Telegraph	3,055,000	Chrysler Corporation	213,000
General Motors	1,122,000	Niagara Mohawk Power	210,000
Exxon Corporation	776,000	Atlantic Richfield	206,000
International Business Machines	742,000	Northeast Utilities	199,000
General Electric	502,000	Standard Oil (Indiana)	192,000
General Telephone & Electronics	476,000	Virginia Electric & Power	191,000
Texaco, Inc.	384,000	Middle South Utilities	188,000
Sears, Roebuck	354,000	Ohio Edison	183,000
Southern Company	351,000	Occidental Petroleum	176,000
Ford Motor	342,000	Long Island Lighting	175,000
American Electric Power	340,000	Union Electric	175,000
Gulf Oil	302,000	Consumers Power	169,000
Mobil Corporation	292,000	Westinghouse Electric	168,000
Commonwealth Edison	275,000	Pennsylvania Power & Light	165,000
Philadelphia Electric	267,000	BankAmerica	165,000
Pacific Gas & Electric	255,000	International Telephone & Telegraph	153,000
Standard Oil of California	247,000	Southern California Edison	152,000
E. I. du Pont de Nemours	243,000	Union Carbide	150,000
Tenneco, Inc.	238,000	Dow Chemical	144,000
United States Steel	236,000	Columbia Gas System	139,000
Detroit Edison	235,000	Duquesne Light	138,000
Public Service Electric & Gas	233,000	Pan American World Airways	136,000
Eastman Kodak	221,000	General Public Utilities	136,000
Consolidated Edison	219,000	Transamerica Corporation	130,000
RCA Corporation	214,000	Bethlehem Steel	128,000

Note: As of early 1982. *Source:* New York Stock Exchange.

50 Leading Stocks in Market Value

Stock	Market value (millions)	Listed shares (millions)	Stock	Market value (millions)	Listed shares (millions)
American Telephone & Telegraph	$ 47,989	815.1	General Telephone & Electronics	5,396	168.6
International Business Machines	33,549	589.9	Dow Chemical	5,342	203.5
Exxon Corporation	28,211	906.4	Sears, Roebuck	5,247	325.4
Schlumberger, N.V.	16,850	302.2	Marathon Oil	5,124	61.6
Standard Oil (Indiana)	15,825	304.3	Standard Oil (Ohio)	5,018	120.9
Standard Oil of California	14,668	342.1	Union Pacific	5,010	96.4
Shell Oil	13,595	309.0	Reynolds (R.J.) Industries	4,928	104.6
General Electric	13,338	231.5	Caterpillar Tractor	4,917	88.6
General Motors	11,710	303.2	Superior Oil	4,896	132.8
Eastman Kodak	11,569	162.7	Hewlett-Packard	4,865	122.8
Atlantic Richfield	11,225	239.5	Digital Equipment	4,726	54.5
Mobil Corporation	10,317	425.4	SmithKline Corporation	4,512	66.7
Texaco, Inc.	9,052	274.3	Teledyne, Inc.	4,479	32.3
E. I. du Pont de Nemours	8,779	234.1	Pacific Telephone & Telegraph	4,462	224.5
Gulf Oil	7,496	211.9	Tenneco, Inc.	4,343	130.1
Johnson & Johnson	6,953	187.3	Coca-Cola Company	4,310	124.0
Procter & Gamble	6,677	82.9	Eli Lilly	4,258	76.0
Union Oil of California	6,531	173.6	Pfizer, Inc.	4,004	75.2
Merck & Company	6,433	75.9	Cities Service	3,910	85.0
Minnesota Mining & Manufacturing	6,431	118.0	American Express	3,895	88.3
Phillips Petroleum	6,255	154.4	International Telephone & Telegraph	3,879	130.4
Halliburton Company	6,156	118.1	Weyerhaeuser Company	3,730	128.6
American Home Products	6,132	168.6	Aetna Life & Casualty	3,575	81.2
Morris (Philip), Inc.	6,113	125.4	Tandy Corporation	3,566	105.6
Getty Oil	5,721	88.5	**Total**	**$431,602**	**9,895.7**
Sun Company	5,635	123.8			

NOTE: As of Dec. 31, 1981. Of the 1,534 common stocks listed on the New York Stock Exchange at the end of 1981, the 50 issues with the largest market value totaled $432 billion, or 39% of the total value of common stocks listed. The five largest common issues were valued at $142 billion, or 13% of the total. Six corporations joined the list in 1981: Pacific Telephone & Telegraph, Pfizer, Inc., American Express, International Telephone & Telegraph, Aetna Life & Casualty, and Tandy Corporation. *Source:* New York Stock Exchange.

National Labor Organizations With Membership Over 100,000

Members[1]	Union
1,357,000	Automobile, Aerospace and Agricultural Implement Workers of America, International Union, United
160,000	Bakery, Confectionary, and Tobacco Workers International Union
145,000	Boilermakers, Iron Ship Builders, Blacksmiths, Forgers and Helpers, International Brotherhood of
135,000	Bricklayers and Allied Craftsmen, International Union of
184,000	Bridge, Structural, and Ornamental Iron Workers, International Association of
105,000	California State Employees' Association (Ind.)
784,000	Carpenters and Joiners of America, United Brotherhood of
n.a.	Classified School Employees, American Association of (Ind.)
455,000	Clothing and Textile Workers Union, Amalgamated
551,000	Communications Workers of America
1,684,000	Education Association, National (Ind.)
233,000	Electrical, Radio and Machine Workers, International Union of
162,000	Electrical, Radio and Machine Workers of America, United (Ind.)
1,041,000	Electrical Workers, International Brotherhood of
178,000	Fire Fighters, International Association of
1,300,000	Food and Commercial Workers International Union, United
255,000	Government Employees, American Federation of
200,000	Government Employees, National Association of (Ind.)
400,000	Hotel Employees and Restaurant Employees International Union
608,000	Laborers' International Union of North America
323,000	Ladies' Garment Workers' Union, International
230,000	Letter Carriers, National Association of
754,000	Machinists and Aerospace Workers, International Association of
102,000	Maintenance of Way Employes, Brotherhood of
245,000	Mine Workers of America, United (Ind.)
299,000	Musicians, American Federation of
180,000	Nurses' Association; American (Ind.)
107,000	Office and Professional Employees International Union
154,000	Oil, Chemical and Atomic Workers International Union
423,000	Operating Engineers, International Union of
164,000	Painters and Allied Trades of the United States and Canada, International Brotherhood of
275,000	Paperworkers International Union, United
352,000	Plumbing and Pipe Fitting Industry of the United States and Canada, United Association of Journeymen and Apprentices of the
150,000	Police, Fraternal Order of (Ind.)
125,000	Postal and Federal Employees, National Alliance of (Ind.)
251,000	Postal Workers Union, American
122,000	Printing and Graphic Communications Union, International
180,000	Railway, Airline and Steamship Clerks, Freight Handlers, Express and Station Employes, Brotherhood of
215,000	Retail, Wholesale and Department Store Union
151,000	Rubber, Cork, Linoleum and Plastic Workers of America, United
650,000	Service Employees International Union
161,000	Sheet Metal Workers' International Association
1,098,000	State, County and Municipal Employees of America, American Federation of
1,238,000	Steelworkers of America, United
551,000	Teachers, American Federation of
1,891,000	Teamsters, Chauffeurs, Warehousemen and Helpers of America, International Brotherhood of (Ind.)
162,000	Transit Union, Amalgamated
130,000	Transport Workers Union of America
190,000	Transportation Union, United
112,000	Woodworkers of America, International

1. 1980. NOTE: Unless indicated by Ind. (Independent), all unions are affliated with the AFL-CIO. n.a.=not available. *Source:* Department of Labor, Bureau of Labor Statistics.

Job Satisfaction in Decline

According to surveys taken by the National Opinion Research Center, 85% of male and 83% of female workers claimed to be "satisfied" with their jobs in 1980 (the figures include "very satisfied," "somewhat satisfied," and "fairly satisfied" responses).

Survey results show a four and five percent drop, respectively, from the 1978 figures. Job satisfaction in 1980 was at its lowest point since 1962, when 84% of male and 81% of female workers reported that they were satisfied.

The most satisfied workers (male and female) were those 60 years old and over and those who had attended graduate school (both groups reported 90% satisfied). The most dissatisfied workers were those of both sexes between the ages of 18 and 29 (76% satisfied).

Strikes and Lockouts

Year	Strikes and lockouts	Workers involved (thousands)	Man-days idle (thousands)	Year	Strikes and lockouts	Workers involved (thousands)	Man-days idle (thousands)
1895	1,255	407	n.a.	1950	4,843	2,410	38,800
1900	1,839	568	n.a.	1955	4,320	2,650	28,200
1905	2,186	302	n.a.	1960[1]	3,333	1,320	19,100
1915	1,593	n.a.	n.a.	1965	3,963	1,550	23,300
1920	3,411	1,463	n.a.	1970	5,716	3,305	66,414
1925	1,301	428	n.a.	1975	5,031	1,746	31,237
1930	637	183	3,320	1978	4,230	1,623	36,992
1935	2,014	1,120	15,500	1979	4,827	1,727	34,754
1940	2,508	577	6,700	1980	3,885	1,366	33,289
1945	4,750	3,470	38,000	1981[2]	2,577	1,082	24,670

1. First year for which figures include Alaska and Hawaii. 2. Preliminary. NOTE: n.a. = not available. *Source:* Department of Labor, Bureau of Labor Statistics.

Persons in the Labor Force

Year	Labor force[1]		Percent of labor force in		Year	Labor force[1]		Percent of labor force in	
	Number (thousands)	%total population aged 10 and over	Farm occupation	Nonfarm occupation		Number (thousands)	%total population aged 10 and over	Farm occupation	Nonfarm occupation
1830	3,932	45.5	70.5	29.5	1910	37,371	52.2	31.0	69.0
1840	5,420	46.6	68.6	31.4	1920	42,434	51.3	27.0	73.0
1850	7,697	46.8	63.7	36.3	1930	48,830	49.5	21.4	78.6
1860	10,533	47.0	58.9	41.1	1940	52,966	52.4	17.0	83.0
1870	12,925	44.4	53.0	47.0	1950	59,671	53.4	11.5	88.5
1880	17,392	47.3	49.4	50.6	1960	69,877	55.3	5.9	94.1
1890	23,318	49.2	42.6	57.4	1970	82,897	55.5	2.9	97.1
1900	29,073	50.2	37.5	62.5	1980	106,066	62.0	2.7	97.3

1. For 1830 to 1930, the data relate to the population and gainful workers at ages 10 and over. For 1940 to 1970, the data relate to the population and labor force at ages 14 and over; for 1980, the data relate to the population and labor force at age 16 and over. The farm and nonfarm percentages relate only to the experienced civilian labor force. *Source:* Department of Commerce, Bureau of the Census.

Women in the Labor Force

(16 years of age and over; in thousands)

Labor force status	1981	1980	1979	1978	1977	1976
In the labor force:	46,696	44,574	43,391	41,878	39,952	38,414
16 to 19 years of age	4,211	4,331	4,481	4,462	4,267	4,138
20 years and over	42,485	40,243	38,910	37,416	35,685	34,276
Employed	43,000	41,283	40,446	38,882	36,685	35,095
16 to 19 years of age	3,411	3,587	3,748	3,702	3,486	3,365
20 years and over	39,590	37,696	36,698	35,180	33,199	31,730
Unemployed	3,696	3,291	2,945	2,996	3,267	3,320
16 to 19 years of age	800	744	733	760	781	773
20 years and over	2,895	2,547	2,212	2,236	2,486	2,547
Not in the labor force:	42,922	41,871	41,692	41,887	42,510	42,789
Women as percent of labor force	43.0	42.6	42.2	41.7	41.0	40.5
Total civilian population	89,618	86,445	85,083	83,765	82,462	81,203

Source: Department of Labor, Women's Bureau.

Service Employment Tops Production Jobs

For the first time in the history of the American economy, employment in the consumer, financial, and service industries has topped the total employment in the production industry. These industries, the most rapidly growing sectors of the job market, employed 24.3 million workers by April of 1982. This was 300,000 more than were employed in the goods-producing sector, which included manufacturing, construction, and mining.

Employed Persons 16 Years and Over, by Race and Occupational Groups

Race and occupational group	1981 Number	1981 Percent distribution	1980 Number	1980 Percent distribution	Percent change, 1980–81
WHITE					
White-collar workers	48,147,000	54.3	47,267,000	53.9	1.9
Professional and technical workers	14,794,000	16.7	14,444,000	16.5	2.4
Managers and administrators, except farm	10,867,000	12.2	10,512,000	12.0	3.4
Sales workers	6,075,000	6.8	5,963,000	6.8	1.9
Clerical workers	16,410,000	18.5	16,350,000	18.6	0.4
Blue-collar workers	27,191,000	30.7	27,327,000	31.2	−0.5
Craft and kindred workers	11,590,000	13.1	11,683,000	13.3	−0.8
Operatives, except transport	8,836,000	10.0	8,884,000	10.1	−0.5
Transport equipment operatives	2,938,000	3.3	2,984,000	3.4	−1.5
Nonfarm laborers	3,826,000	4.3	3,776,000	4.3	1.3
Private household workers	709,000	.8	706,000	.8	0.4
Service workers, except private household	10,105,000	11.4	9,887,000	11.3	2.2
Farm workers	2,558,000	2.9	2,527,000	2.9	1.2
Total	**88,709,000**	**100.0**	**87,715,000**	**100.0**	**1.1**
BLACK AND OTHER					
White-collar workers	4,802,000	41.1	41,614,000	39.8	4.1
Professional and technical workers	1,625,000	13.9	1,524,000	13.2	6.6
Managers and administrators, except farm	673,000	5.8	627,000	5.4	7.3
Sales workers	350,000	3.0	340,000	2.9	2.9
Clerical workers	2,154,000	18.4	2,124,000	18.3	1.4
Blue-collar workers	4,071,000	34.8	4,124,000	35.6	−1.3
Craft and kindred workers	1,072,000	9.2	1,105,000	9.5	−3.0
Operatives, except transport	1,704,000	14.6	1,680,000	14.5	1.4
Transport equipment operatives	538,000	4.6	548,000	4.7	−1.8
Nonfarm laborers	757,000	6.5	791,000	6.8	−4.3
Private household workers	339,000	2.9	358,000	3.1	−5.3
Service workers, except private household	2,285,000	19.5	2,277,000	19.6	0.4
Farm workers	192,000	1.6	214,000	1.8	−10.3
Total	**11,688,000**	**100.0**	**11,588,000**	**100.0**	**0.9**

Source: Department of Labor, Bureau of Labor Statistics.

Mothers Participating in Labor Force
(figures in percentage)

Year	Mothers with children: Under 18 years	6 to 17 years	Under 6 years[1]
1950	21.6	32.8	13.6
1955	27.0	38.4	18.2
1965	35.0	45.7	25.3
1975	47.4	54.8	38.9
1976	48.8	56.2	39.7
1977	50.7	58.3	40.9
1978	52.9	60.0	43.7
1979	54.5	61.6	45.4
1980	56.6	64.4	46.6
1981	58.1	65.5	48.9

1. May also have older children. NOTE: For 1950 and 1955, data are for April; for 1965 and 1975–81, data are for March. *Source:* Department of Labor, Women's Bureau.

Women in the Working Population

Year[1]	Number (thousands)	Percent of female population aged 10 and over[1]	Percent of total working population aged 10 and over[1]
1890	4,006	17.4	17.2
1900	5,319	18.8	18.3
1910	7,445	21.5	19.9
1920	8,637	21.4	20.4
1930	10,752	22.0	22.0
1940	12,845	25.4	24.3
1950	18,412	33.9	17.3
1960[2]	23,272	37.8	19.4
1970	31,583	43.4	22.5
1979	44,375	51.0	26.6
1980	45,646	51.6	26.9
1981	46,873	52.2	27.7

1. For 1880–1930, data relate to population and gainful workers at ages 10 and over; for 1940, to ages 14 and over; for 1950–78, to population at ages 16 and over. 2. Beginning in 1960, figures include Alaska and Hawaii. *Sources:* Department of Commerce, Bureau of the Census, and Department of Labor, Bureau of Labor Statistics.

Selected Job Prospects in the 1980s

Occupation	Estimated employment 1980[1]	Percent change 1980–90[2]	Employment prospects[3]
Accountants and auditors	900,000	25–34	Employment is expected to increase faster than average as managers rely more on accounting information to make business decisions. College graduates will be in greater demand than applicants who lack this training.
All-round machinists	303,000	16–29	Employment is expected to increase about as fast as average due to growing demand for machined metal parts. Many openings are likely in maintenance shops of manufacturing plants.
Architects	79,500	33–41	Employment is expected to rise faster than average but competition for jobs is likely.
Assemblers	1,670,000	19–31	Employment is expected to increase as fast as average due to growing demand for consumer products and industrial equipment. Since most jobs are in durable goods industries, however, flucuations and national defense spending often affect job opportunities.
Automobile mechanics	845,000	24–33	Employment is expected to increase faster than average due to growing number of automobiles and the present trend toward keeping them longer. Job opportunities will be plentiful.
Carpenters	970,000	15–27	Employment is expected to grow as fast as average due to increasing construction of new structures and alteration and maintenance of old ones. Carpenters with all-round training will have best prospects.
College and university faculty	691,000	–9	Employment is expected to decline due to decreasing enrollments and budgetary constraints. Keen competition is expected in all but a few disciplines and many of the available openings will be part-time or short term. Good job prospects are expected for engineering and computer science faculty.
Computer operating personnel	558,000	22–30	Employment of console and peripheral operators is expected to rise faster than average as use of computers expands. Employment of keypunch operators is expected to decline, however, due to use of more efficient direct data entry techniques.
Computer service technicians	83,000	93–112	Employment is expected to grow much faster than average as more computer equipment is used. Very good opportunities are expected for persons with post-secondary school training in electronics.
Dental assistants	140,000	38–42	Employment is expected to grow faster than average as dentists increasingly use chair-side assistants. Excellent opportunities are expected for full and part-time jobs.
Dentists	126,000	23	Employment is expected to grow as fast as average due to population growth, increased awareness of importance of dental care, and expansion of prepayment arrangements.
Electricians	560,000	20–28	Employment is expect to increase as fast as average as more electricians are needed to install electrical fixtures and wiring in new and renovated buildings, and to maintain electrical systems used by industry.
Electrical engineers	325,000	35–47	Employment is expected to increase faster than average due to growing demand for computers, communications equipment, military electronics, and electrical and electronic consumer goods, as well as increased research and development in power generation.
Engineering and science technicians	885,000	24–33	Employment is expect to grow faster than average as more technicians will be needed to assist growing number of engineers and scientists. Favorable job opportunities are expected particularly for graduates of postsecondary school training programs.
Health services administrators	220,000	43–53	Employment is expected to grow faster than average as demand for health care increases and health services management becomes more complex. Advanced degree required for best positions in hospitals.

Kindergarten and elementary school teachers	1,600,000	18–19	Employment is expected to grow as fast as average. Job prospects may improve in the late 1980's due to rising enrollments in lower grades. Outlook for qualified elementary school teachers is likely to be good unless the number of job seekers increases.
Librarians	135,000	3–5	Little change is expected in employment in school, public, and academic libraries due to declining enrollments and budget constraints. Keen competition for jobs is expected. Best opportunities will be for librarians with scientific or technical qualifications.
Physicians and osteopathic physicians	424,000	32	New physicians should have little difficulty in establishing practices in most areas.
Programmers	228,000	49–60	Employment is expected to grow much faster than average as computer usage expands, particularly in accounting, business management, data processing services, and research and development. Best prospects will be for college graduates with degree in computer science or related fields.
Registered nurses	1,105,000	40–47	Employment is expected to grow faster than average. Favorable job prospects are expected in rural and big city hospitals. Competition may exist in suburban hospitals and in areas with many training facilities.
Retail trade sales workers	3,300,000	19–27	Employment is expected to grow as fast as average. High turnover should create many openings for full-time, part-time, and temporary workers.
Secondary school teachers	1,200,000	–14	Keen competition is expected due to sharply declining enrollments coupled with a continued oversupply of new college graduates qualified to teach. Generally, favorable opportunities will exist for persons qualified to teach special education, vocational subjects, mathematics, and the natural and physical sciences.
Secretaries	2,500,000	28–37	Employment is expected to grow faster than average. Job prospects should be excellent with good opportunities for part-time and temporary work.
Systems analysts	205,000	68–80	Employment is expected to grow much faster than average as computer capabilities are increased and computers are used to solve a greater variety of problems. Excellent prospects are expected for graduates of computer-related curriculums.

1. Reflects estimates from the Bureau's 1980–90 National Industry-Occupation Matrix. In this edition employment represents a count of jobs. In earlier editions, employment referred to a count of people. 2. Rates of change for most occupations are from the 1980–90 National Industry-Occupation Matrix. When a different source was used, only one rate is available. 3. For most occupations, the rate of change in employment is compared to the average for all occupations, which is projected to be 17 to 25 percent. *Source:* Department of Labor, Bureau of Labor Statistics.

Employed Persons by Major Occupations, 1981

(in thousands)

Occupations	Total employed	Percent distribution: Female	Percent distribution: Black and other
White-collar workers	**52,949**	**53.5**	9.1
Professional and technical	16,419	44.6	9.9
Accountants	1,126	38.5	9.9
Architects	93	4.3	10.8
Computer programmers	367	29.4	10.4
Computer systems analysts	213	25.8	8.0
Engineers	1,537	4.4	7.3
Aeronautical and astronautical engineers	84	1.2	6.0
Civil engineers	190	1.6	7.9
Electrical and electronic engineers	380	3.9	7.6
Industrial engineers	237	11.4	7.6
Mechanical engineers	252	2.8	5.6
Lawyers and judges	581	14.1	4.6
Librarians, archivists, and curators	192	82.8	5.7
Life and physical scientists	311	21.9	10.6
Biological scientists	59	40.7	11.9
Chemists	138	21.7	15.2
Operations and systems researchers and analysts	199	26.1	7.0
Personnel and labor relations workers	441	49.9	10.9
Dentists	130	4.6	6.2
Pharmacists	152	25.7	9.2
Physicians, medical and osteopathic	454	13.7	14.5
Registered nurses	1,339	96.8	12.3

Occupations	Total employed	Percent distribution: Female	Percent distribution: Black and other
Therapists	251	70.5	12.0
Health technologists and technicians	643	72.3	14.9
Clergy	282	5.0	7.8
Economists	160	25.0	6.9
Psychologists	117	48.7	9.4
Social workers	390	63.8	21.0
Recreation workers	121	57.9	17.4
Teachers, college and university	585	35.2	9.2
Teachers, except college and university	3,197	70.6	10.1
Adult education teachers	76	42.1	9.2
Elementary school teachers	1,412	83.6	11.4
Prekindergarten and kindergarten teachers	245	98.4	15.5
Secondary school teachers	1,231	51.3	8.0
Engineering and science technicians	1,141	18.8	9.9
Airplane pilots	81	1.2	1.2
Vocational and educational counselors	188	53.7	18.1
Writers, artists, and entertainers	1,388	39.8	6.3
Athletes and kindred workers	135	43.0	7.4
Designers	218	29.4	6.4
Editors and reporters	205	50.2	4.9
Musicians and composers	145	24.8	5.5
Painters and sculptors	211	50.7	5.7
Photographers	101	23.8	7.9
Public relations specialists and publicity writers	123	45.5	4.9
Managers and administrators, except farm	11,540	27.5	5.8
Bank officials and financial managers	696	37.5	5.5
Buyers and purchasing agents	476	35.1	6.1
Buyers, wholesale and retail trade	195	43.6	6.7
Health administrators	219	49.8	6.8
Office managers n.e.c.	504	70.6	4.0
Officials and administrators, public administration n.e.c.	476	29.0	10.3
Restaurant, cafeteria, and bar managers	727	40.3	9.9
Sales managers and department heads, retail trade	346	40.2	6.6
Sales managers, except retail trade	374	13.9	2.7
School administrators, elementary and secondary	291	36.8	10.0
School administrators, college	139	35.3	8.6
Sales workers	6,425	45.4	5.4
Insurance agents, brokers and underwriters	595	23.9	6.2
Real estate agents and brokers	562	49.8	3.0
Stock and bond sales agents	159	17.0	3.1
Sales representatives, manufacturing industries	416	20.0	4.1
Sales representatives, wholesale trade	971	11.9	2.9
Sales clerks, retail trade	2,431	71.2	7.7
Sales workers, except clerks, retail trade	525	19.6	3.6
Clerical workers	18,564	80.5	11.6
Bank tellers	569	93.5	7.6
Billing clerks	153	88.2	10.5
Bookkeepers	1,961	91.1	6.3
Cashiers	1,660	86.2	11.8
Counter clerks, except food	360	76.4	10.3
File clerks	315	83.8	22.9
Insurance adjusters, examiners, and investigators	191	58.1	9.9
Library attendants and assistants	152	82.2	14.5
Mail carriers, post office	242	15.7	13.6
Computer and peripheral equipment operators	564	63.8	15.8
Key punch operators	248	93.5	19.4
Payroll and timekeeping clerks	231	81.0	9.5
Postal clerks	269	37.9	26.4
Receptionists	675	97.3	8.6
Secretaries	3,917	99.1	7.2
Shipping and receiving clerks	525	22.5	14.7
Statistical clerks	370	80.3	15.1
Stock clerks and storekeepers	528	34.8	13.1
Teachers aides, except school monitors	381	92.9	19.2
Telephone operators	308	92.9	17.2
Typists	1,031	96.3	17.8
Blue-collar workers	**31,261**	**18.6**	**13.0**
Craft and kindred workers	12,662	6.3	8.5
Carpenters	1,122	1.9	5.8
Brickmasons and stonemasons	152	—	12.5
Electricians	684	1.6	7.9
Excavating, grading, and road machinery operators	422	0.5	12.3
Painters, construction and maintenance	471	5.7	10.2
Plumbers and pipefitters	472	0.4	7.6
Structural metal craft workers	82	—	3.7
Roofers and slaters	139	—	13.7
Blue-collar worker supervisors n.e.c.	1,816	11.3	7.6
Machinists and job setters	668	4.0	8.5
Metal craft workers, excluding mechanics, machinists, and job setters	626	4.3	7.2
Sheetmetal workers and tinsmiths	157	3.2	6.4
Tool and die makers	175	2.3	2.9
Automobile body repairers	204	1.0	7.8
Automobile mechanics	1,045	0.6	8.9
Mechanics, except automobiles	2,159	2.5	8.1
Heavy equipment mechanics, including diesel	1,007	1.8	7.2
Household appliance and accessory installers and mechanics	132	4.5	9.1
Compositors and typesetters	174	35.1	8.6
Printing press operators	166	11.4	7.8
Bakers	135	41.5	13.3
Crane, derrick, and hoist operators	143	0.7	15.4
Decorators and window dressers	126	72.2	7.9
Stationary engineers	182	1.6	8.2
Telephone installers and repairers	326	9.8	9.2
Operatives, except transport	10,540	19.8	16.2
Assemblers	1,167	52.4	17.1
Checkers, examiners and inspectors, manufacturing	800	53.8	13.8
Garage workers and gas station attendants	349	5.7	10.9
Packers and wrappers, excluding meat and produce	589	63.2	21.1
Precision machine operatives	352	12.8	9.9
Sewers and stitchers	807	96.0	21.6
Textile operatives	300	61.0	26.7
Welders and flame cutters	728	4.7	13.2

Transport equipment operatives	3,476	8.9	15.5
Bus drivers	360	47.2	21.1
Delivery and route workers	563	8.5	9.4
Taxicab drivers and chauffeurs	164	9.8	28.7
Truck drivers	1,878	2.7	13.9
Nonfarm laborers	4,583	11.5	16.5
Service workers	**13,438**	**62.1**	**19.5**
Private households	1,047	96.5	32.4
Service workers, except private households	12,391	59.2	18.4
Cleaning workers	2,489	38.6	28.0
Food service workers	4,682	66.2	14.0
Bartenders	315	47.3	5.1
Cooks	1,393	51.9	19.7
Waiters	1,477	89.3	7.3
Health service workers	1,995	89.2	24.3
Dental assistants	143	97.2	6.3
Health aides, excluding nursing	317	84.2	21.5
Nursing aides, orderlies and attendants	1,131	86.6	29.0
Practical nurses	403	97.8	19.9
Personal service workers	1,766	76.0	14.0
Protective service workers	1,459	10.1	13.8
Fire fighters	214	0.9	8.9
Guards	607	13.7	18.8
Police and detectives	512	5.7	10.7
Farm workers	**2,749**	**17.8**	**6.9**
Farmers and farm managers	1,485	11.3	2.4
Farm laborers, wage workers	969	15.9	15.1
Total employed	**100,397**	**42.8**	**11.6**

NOTE: n.e.c. = "not elsewhere classified" and designates broad categories of occupations that cannot be more specifically identified. *Source:* Department of Labor, Bureau of Labor Statistics.

Manufacturing Industries—Gross Average Weekly Earnings and Hours Worked

	1982[1]		1981		1980		1975		1970		1958	
Industry	Earnings	Hours worked	Earnings	Hours worked	Earnings	Hours worked	Earnings	Hours worked	Earnings	Hours worked	Earnings	Hours worked
All manufacturing[2]	$332.60	38.9	$318.00	39.8	$288.62	39.7	$189.51	39.4	$133.73	39.8	$82.71	39.2
Durable goods	356.72	39.2	342.91	40.2	310.78	40.1	205.09	39.9	143.07	40.3	89.27	39.5
Primary metal industries	439.67	38.5	437.81	40.5	391.78	40.1	246.80	40.0	159.17	40.5	101.11	38.3
Iron and steel foundries	362.84[3]	37.6[3]	355.39	39.4	328.00	40.0	220.99	40.4	151.03	40.6	86.86	37.6
Nonferrous foundries	336.54[3]	39.5[3]	319.20	40.1	291.27	39.9	190.03	39.1	138.16	39.7	90.85	39.5
Fabricated metal products	343.49	38.9	330.46	40.3	300.98	40.4	201.60	40.0	143.67	40.7	89.78	39.9
Hardware, cutlery, hand tools	327.86[3]	38.8[3]	306.14	39.4	275.89	39.3	187.07	39.3	132.33	40.1	82.92	39.3
Other hardware	352.52[3]	39.3[3]	318.67	39.1	286.21	39.1	195.42	39.4	133.46	40.2	84.32	39.4
Structural metal products	338.98[3]	39.6[3]	320.80	40.2	291.85	40.2	202.61	40.2	142.61	40.4	92.63	40.1
Electric and electronic equipment	319.45	39.1	304.04	39.9	276.21	39.8	180.91	39.5	130.54	39.8	83.95	39.6
Machinery, except electrical	367.06	39.3	360.33	40.9	328.00	41.0	219.22	40.9	154.95	41.1	94.33	39.8
Transportation equipment	455.84	40.7	424.95	40.9	379.61	40.6	242.61	40.3	163.22	40.3	100.40	40.0
Motor vehicles and equipment	509.22[3]	42.9[3]	450.31	40.9	394.00	40.0	262.68	40.6	170.07	40.3	101.24	39.7
Lumber and wood products	291.85	38.3	270.90	38.7	252.18	38.5	167.35	39.1	117.51	39.7	69.09	38.6
Furniture and fixtures	235.21	37.1	226.94	38.4	209.17	38.1	142.13	37.9	108.58	39.2	69.95	39.3
Nondurable goods	300.31	38.6	280.74	39.1	255.45	39.0	168.78	38.8	120.43	39.1	74.11	38.8
Textile mill products	218.46	37.6	218.59	39.6	203.31	40.1	133.28	39.2	97.76	39.9	57.51	38.6
Apparel and other textile products	182.50	35.3	177.07	35.7	161.42	35.4	111.97	35.1	84.37	35.3	54.05	35.1
Leather and leather products	188.86	35.5	183.63	36.1	169.09	36.7	120.80	37.4	92.63	37.2	57.25	36.7
Food and kindred products	313.24	39.6	294.97	39.8	271.95	39.7	184.17	40.3	127.98	40.5	79.15	40.8
Tobacco manufactures	387.92	36.7	344.54	38.8	294.89	38.1	171.38	38.0	110.00	37.8	62.17	39.1
Paper and allied products	393.86	41.9	365.50	42.5	330.85	42.2	207.58	41.6	144.14	41.9	87.99	41.9
Printing and publishing	321.63	36.8	305.11	37.3	279.36	37.1	198.32	37.0	147.78	37.7	94.62	38.0
Chemicals and allied products	409.63	40.8	379.39	41.6	344.45	41.5	219.63	40.9	153.50	41.6	93.20	40.7
Petroleum and allied products	549.19	43.9	491.62	43.2	422.18	41.8	267.07	41.6	182.76	42.7	111.66	40.9

1. July preliminary. 2. Average weekly earnings in 1919 = $21.84; 1929 = $24.76; 1932 = $16.89; 1939 = $23.64. Average hours worked per week in 1914 = 49.4; 1919 = 46.3; 1929 = 44.2; 1932 = 38.3; 1939 = 37.7. 3. June preliminary. *Source:* Department of Labor, Bureau of Labor Statistics.

Nonmanufacturing Industries—Gross Average Weekly Earnings and Hours Worked

Industry	1982[1] Earnings	1982[1] Hours worked	1980 Earnings	1980 Hours worked	1975 Earnings	1975 Hours worked	1970 Earnings	1970 Hours worked	1958 Earnings	1958 Hours worked
Bituminous coal and lignite mining	$517.45	40.3	$437.09	40.5	$284.53	39.2[2]	$186.41	40.8	$97.57	33.3
Metal mining	487.91	39.7	415.53	40.5	250.72	42.3	165.68	42.7	94.96	38.6
Nonmetallic minerals	383.21	43.3	327.87	43.6	213.09	43.4	155.11	44.7	88.33	43.3
Telephone communications	415.20	40.0	350.54	40.2	221.18	38.4	131.60	39.4	78.72	38.4
Radio and TV broadcasting	330.37	37.8	283.46	38.1	214.50	39.0	147.45	38.2	100.70	38.0
Electric, gas, and sanitary services	442.21	41.6	371.13	41.7	246.79	41.2	172.64	41.5	98.57	40.9
Local and suburban transportation	300.27	39.2	274.22	39.4	196.89	40.1	142.30	42.1	87.29	43.0
Wholesale trade	308.80	32.2	267.96	38.5	188.75	38.6	137.60	40.0	84.02	40.2
Retail trade	164.65	30.1	147.38	30.2	108.22	32.4	82.47	33.8	54.10	38.1
Hotels, tourist courts, motels	152.11	30.3	135.73	30.5	89.64	31.9	68.16	34.6	40.89	39.7
Laundries and dry cleaning plants	171.52	33.5	151.09	33.8	106.05	35.0	77.47	35.7	45.28	38.7
General building contracting	379.70	36.9	332.84	36.1	254.88	36.0	184.40	36.3	96.92	35.5

1. June preliminary. 2. 11-month average. *Source:* Department of Labor, Bureau of Labor Statistics.

Median Income Comparisons of Year-Round Workers by Educational Attainment 1981

(persons 25 years and over)

Years of school completed	Median income Women	Median income Men	Income gap in dollars	Women's income as a percent of men's	Percent men's income exceeded women's
Elementary school:					
Less than 8 years	$8,419	$12,866	$4,447	65.4	52.8
8 years	9,723	16,084	6,361	60.5	65.4
High School:					
1 to 3 years	10,043	16,938	6,895	59.3	68.7
4 years	12,332	20,598	8,266	59.9	67.0
College:					
1 to 3 years	14,343	22,565	8,222	63.6	57.3
4 years or more	17,795	28,174	10,379	63.2	58.3

Source: Department of Commerce, Bureau of the Census.

Characteristics of Households With Female Householder, 1981

Characteristics	Number of households
All female householders	23,684,000
MARITAL STATUS	
Married, husband present	1,821,000
Married, husband absent	2,590,000
Widowed	9,203,000
Divorced	5,254,000
Single (never married)	4,816,000
RACE AND SPANISH ORIGIN OF HOUSEHOLDER	
White	19,137,000
Black	4,174,000
Spanish origin[1]	1,101,000
SIZE OF HOUSEHOLD	
1 person	11,683,000
2 persons	5,643,000
3 persons	3,274,000
4 persons or more	3,083,000

Income bracket	number of households
RELATED CHILDREN UNDER 18	
No related children	16,573,000
1 or more related children	7,110,000
TOTAL HOUSEHOLD INCOME IN 1980	
Under $2,500	1,449,000
$2,500 to $4,999	4,996,000
$5,000 to $7,499	3,560,000
$7,500 to $9,999	2,579,000
$10,000 to $14,999	4,121,000
$15,000 to $24,999	4,373,000
$25,000 to $49,000	2,327,000
$50,000 and over	277,000
Median income	$9,280
Mean income	$12,446

1. Persons of Spanish origin may be of any race. *Source:* Department of Commerce, Bureau of the Census.

Occupations of Employed Women
(16 years of age and over)

Occupations	1981[1] (percent)	1980[1] (percent)	1979[1] (percent)	1978[1] (percent)	1977[1] (percent)	1976[1] (percent)
Professional and technical workers	17.0	16.8	16.1	15.6	15.9	16.0
Managers and administrators (except farm)	7.4	6.9	6.4	6.1	5.9	5.5
Sales workers	6.8	6.8	6.9	6.9	6.8	6.7
Clerical workers	34.7	35.1	35.0	34.6	34.7	34.9
Craft and kindred workers	1.9	1.8	1.8	1.8	1.6	1.6
Operatives, except transport	9.7	10.0	10.8	11.1	11.2	11.3
Transport equipment operatives	.7	.7	.7	.7	.6	.6
Nonfarm laborers	1.2	1.2	1.3	1.3	1.2	1.1
Private household workers	2.3	2.5	2.6	2.9	3.1	3.1
Service workers	17.1	17.0	17.2	17.7	17.9	17.9
Farmers and farm managers	.4	.4	.3	.3	.3	.3
Farm laborers and supervisors	.7	.8	.9	1.0	1.0	1.0

1. Annual averages. NOTE: Details may not add up to totals because of rounding. *Source:* Department of Labor, Women's Bureau.

Employment by Marital Status and Sex, March 1982
(in thousands)

Marital status and sex (persons 16 years and over)	Population	Civilian labor force				
					Unemployed	
		Number	Labor force participation rate	Employed	Number	Percent of labor force
Men	82,101	61,666	75.9	55,313	6,354	10.3
Never married	23,063	16,160	70.4	13,133	3,028	18.7
Married, wife present	50,293	39,502	79.6	36,986	2,516	6.4
Other ever married	8,745	6,004	69.4	5,195	810	13.5
Married, wife absent	2,279	1,768	79.2	1,491	277	15.7
Widowed	1,861	519	27.9	457	61	11.9
Divorced	4,605	3,718	81.5	3,247	471	12.7
Women	90,436	47,095	52.1	42,895	4,200	8.9
Never married	18,980	11,801	62.2	10,326	1,476	12.5
Married, husband present	50,281	25,756	51.2	23,927	1,828	7.1
Other ever married	21,174	9,538	45.0	8,641	896	9.4
Married, husband absent	3,479	2,087	60.0	1,785	302	14.5
Widowed	10,796	2,287	21.2	2,152	135	5.9
Divorced	6,899	5,164	74.9	4,705	459	8.9
Total: Both sexes	**172,537**	**108,762**	**63.4**	**98,208**	**930**	**9.7**

NOTE: Due to rounding, sums of individual items may not equal totals. *Source:* Department of Labor, Bureau of Labor Statistics.

Earnings Distribution of Full-Time Workers, by Sex, 1980
(persons 15 years old and over as of March 1981)

Earnings group	Number		Distribution (percent)		Likelihood of a woman in each earnings group (percent)[1]
	Women	Men	Women	Men	
Less than $3,000	570,000	924,000	2.5	2.2	1.1
$3,000 to $4,999	706,000	571,000	3.1	1.4	2.2
$5,000 to $6,999	2,106,000	1,288,000	9.2	3.1	3.0
$7,000 to $9,999	5,506,000	3,286,000	24.1	7.8	3.1
$10,000 to $14,999	8,089,000	8,366,000	35.4	20.0	1.8
$15,000 to $19,999	3,691,000	8,571,000	16.1	20.5	0.8
$20,000 to $24,999	1,414,000	7,550,000	6.2	18.0	0.3
$25,000 to $49,999	728,000	9,777,000	3.2	23.3	0.1
$50,000 and over	49,000	1,545,000	0.2	3.7	0.1
Total with earnings	**22,859,000**	**41,881,000**	**100.0**	**100.0**	**1.0**

1. Figures obtained by dividing percentages for women by percentages for men. *Source:* Department of Commerce, Bureau of the Census.

Comparison of Median Earnings of Full-Time Workers by Sex
(persons 15 years and over as of March 1981)

Year	Median earnings: Women	Median earnings: Men	Earnings gap in current dollars	Women's earnings as a percent of men's	Percent men's earnings exceeded women's	Earnings gap in constant 1980 dollars
1960	$3,257	$5,368	$2,111	60.7	64.8	$5,874
1965	3,828	6,388	2,560	60.0	66.9	6,686
1970	5,323	8,966	3,643	59.4	68.4	7,731
1972	5,903	10,202	4,299	57.9	72.8	8,468
1973	6,335	11,186	4,851	56.6	76.6	8,995
1974	6,970	11,889	4,919	58.6	70.6	8,219
1975	7,504	12,758	5,254	58.8	70.0	8,044
1976	8,099	13,455	5,356	60.2	66.1	7,753
1977	8,618	14,626	6,008	58.9	69.7	8,169
1978	9,350	15,730	6,380	59.4	68.2	8,058
1979	10,169	17,045	6,876	59.7	67.6	7,806
1980	11,197	18,612	7,415	60.2	66.2	7,415

Source: Department of Commerce, Bureau of the Census.

Composition of the Civilian Labor Force and Unemployment

Race, sex, and age	July 1982: Civilian labor force: Number (thousands)	July 1982: Civilian labor force: Percent distribution	July 1982: Unemployed: Number (thousands)	July 1982: Unemployed: Percent distribution	July 1982: Unemployed: Rate	July 1981: Civilian labor force: Number (thousands)	July 1981: Civilian labor force: Percent distribution	July 1981: Unemployed: Number (thousands)	July 1981: Unemployed: Percent distribution	July 1981: Unemployed: Rate
White	96,493	87.3	8,356	77.4	8.7	95,126	87.5	5,956	76.1	6.3
Men, 20 years and older	51,292	46.4	4,037	37.4	7.9	50,698	46.7	2,541	32.5	5.0
Women, 20 years and older	37,845	34.2	2,777	25.7	7.3	36,612	33.7	2,131	27.2	5.8
Teenagers, 16 to 19 years	7,356	6.7	1,542	14.3	21.0	7,816	7.2	1,284	16.4	16.4
Black and other	14,027	12.7	2,433	22.6	17.3	13,539	12.5	1,867	23.9	13.8
Men, 20 years and older	6,784	6.1	1,063	10.0	15.7	6,484	6.0	762	9.7	11.8
Women, 20 years and older	6,247	5.7	897	8.3	14.4	6,062	5.6	741	9.5	12.2
Teenagers, 16 to 19 years	997	0.9	473	4.4	47.4	993	0.9	364	4.7	36.7
All races										
Men, 20 years and older	58,076	52.5	5,100	47.3	8.8	57,182	52.6	3,303	42.2	5.8
Women, 20 years and older	44,092	40.0	3,674	34.1	8.3	42,674	39.3	2,872	36.7	6.7
Teenagers, 16 to 19 years	8,353	7.6	2,015	18.7	24.1	8,809	8.1	1,648	21.1	18.7
Total	**110,520**	**100.0**	**10,789**	**100.0**	**9.8**	**108,665**	**100.0**	**7,823**	**100.0**	**7.2**

NOTE: Totals may not add due to rounding. *Source:* Department of Labor, Bureau of Labor Statistics.

Advertising Expenditures by Medium
(in billions)

Medium	1981[1] Amt.	1981[1] % of total	1980 Amt.	1980 % of total	1975 Amt.	1975 % of total	1970 Amt.	1970 % of total	1960 Amt.	1960 % of total	1950 Amt.	1950 % of total
Newspapers	$17.4	28.5	$15.5	28.5	$8.4	29.9	$5.8	29.3	$3.7	31.0	$2.1	36.4
Magazines	3.5	5.8	3.1	5.8	1.5	5.2	1.3	6.8	0.9	7.9	0.5	9.0
Business Papers	1.8	3.0	1.7	3.1	0.9	3.3	0.7	3.8	0.6	5.1	0.3	4.4
Radio	4.2	6.9	3.7	6.8	2.0	7.0	1.3	6.5	0.7	5.8	0.6	10.6
Television	12.7	20.6	11.4	20.9	5.3	18.6	3.7	18.7	1.6	13.3	0.2	3.0
Direct mail	8.8	14.3	7.6	13.9	4.2	14.8	2.7	13.9	1.8	15.3	0.8	14.1
Outdoor	0.7	1.1	0.6	1.1	0.3	1.2	0.2	1.2	0.2	1.7	0.1	2.5
Miscellaneous[2]	12.1	19.7	10.9	19.9	5.6	20.0	3.9	19.8	2.4	19.8	1.1	20.0
Total	**61.3**	**100.0**	**54.5**	**100.0**	**28.2**	**100.0**	**19.6**	**100.0**	**11.9**	**100.0**	**5.7**	**100.0**

1. Preliminary. 2. Includes regional farm papers. *Sources:* McCann-Erickson, Inc., and *Advertising Age.*

Leading Advertising Agencies in World Billings

(in millions of dollars)

Agency	1981	1980
Young & Rubicam	$2,355.0	$2,273.0
J. Walter Thompson Co.	2,212.7	2,120.7
Ogilvy & Mather	1,933.8	1,661.9
McCann-Erickson	1,849.2	1,792.1
Ted Bates & Co.	1,578.1	1,404.1
BBDO International	1,400.0	1,305.0
Leo Burnett Co.	1,336.0	1,154.5
SSC&B	1,168.3	1,203.0
Foote, Cone & Belding	1,153.3	1,118.8
Doyle Dane Bernbach	1,150.0	1,004.0

Source: Reprinted with permission from the March 24, 1982, issue of *Advertising Age.* Copyright © 1982 by Crain Communications, Inc.

Unemployment Rate, 1981

Race and age	Women[1]	Men[1]
All races:	7.9	7.4
16 to 19 years	19.0	20.1
20 years and over	6.8	6.3
White	6.9	6.5
16 to 19 years	16.6	17.9
20 years and over	5.9	5.6
Minority races	14.3	14.1
16 to 19 years	38.3	37.5
20 years and over	12.4	12.1

1. Annual averages. *Source:* Department of Labor, Women's Bureau.

Percent Unemployed in the Civilian Labor Force

Year	Percent Unemployed	Year	Percent Unemployed
1920	5.2	1976	7.7
1922	6.7	1978	6.0
1924	5.0	1979	5.8
1926	1.8	1980	7.1
1928	4.2	1981	7.6
1930	8.7	Jan.	7.4
1932	23.6	Feb.	7.3
1934	21.7	March	7.3
1936	16.9	April	7.3
1938	19.0	May	7.5
1940	14.6	June	7.4
1942	4.7	July	7.2
1944	1.2	Aug.	7.3
1946	3.9	Sept.	7.6
1948	3.8	Oct.	8.0
1950	5.3	Nov.	8.3
1952	3.0	Dec.	8.8
1954	5.5	1982	
1956	4.1	Jan.	8.5
1958	6.8	Feb.	8.8
1960	5.5	March	9.0
1962	5.5	April	9.4
1964	5.2	May	9.5
1966	3.8	June	9.5
1968	3.6	July	9.8
1970	4.9	Aug.	9.8
1972	5.6	Sept.	10.1
1974	5.6		

NOTE: Estimates prior to 1940 are based on sources other than direct enumeration. *Source:* Department of Labor, Bureau of Labor Statistics.

Employment and Unemployment

(in millions of persons)

Category	1981	1980	1979	1975	1970	1959	1950	1945	1941	1932	1929
EMPLOYMENT STATUS[1]											
Total noninstitutional population	172.3	169.8	167.0	155.3	140.3	117.9	106.6	105.5	101.5	—	—
Total labor force	110.8	109.0	107.0	96.0	86.0	70.9	63.9	65.3	57.5	51.3	49.4
Percent of population	64.3	64.2	64.1	61.8	61.3	60.2	59.9	61.9	56.7	—	—
Civilian labor force	108.7	106.9	105.0	93.8	82.8	68.4	62.2	53.9	55.9	51.0	49.2
Employed	100.4	99.3	98.8	85.8	78.7	64.6	58.9	52.8	50.4	38.9	47.6
Agriculture	3.4	3.4	3.3	3.4	3.5	5.6	7.2	8.6	9.1	10.2	10.5
Nonagricultural industries	97.0	95.9	95.5	82.4	75.2	59.1	51.8	44.2	41.3	28.8	37.2
Unemployed	8.3	7.6	6.1	7.9	4.1	3.7	3.3	1.0	5.6	12.1	1.6
Percent of labor force	7.6	7.1	5.8	8.5	4.9	5.5	5.3	1.9	9.9	23.6	3.2
Not in labor force	61.5	60.8	59.9	59.4	54.3	47.0	42.8	40.2	44.0	—	—
INDUSTRY											
Total nonagricultural employment	91.1	90.4	89.8	76.9	70.9	53.3	45.2	40.4	36.5	23.6	31.3
Goods-producing industries	25.5	25.7	26.5	22.6	23.6	20.4	18.5	17.5	16.0	8.6	13.3
Mining	1.1	1.0	1.0	0.8	0.6	0.7	0.9	0.8	1.0	0.7	1.1
Construction	4.2	4.3	4.5	3.5	3.6	3.0	2.4	1.1	1.8	1.0	1.5
Manufacturing: Durable goods	12.1	12.2	12.8	10.7	11.2	9.4	8.1	9.1	7.0	—	—
Nondurable goods	8.1	8.1	8.3	7.6	8.2	7.3	7.1	6.5	6.2	—	—
Services-producing industries	65.6	64.7	63.4	54.3	47.3	32.9	26.7	22.9	20.6	15.0	18.0
Transportation and public utilities	5.2	5.1	5.1	4.5	4.5	4.0	4.0	3.9	3.3	2.8	3.9
Trade: Wholesale	5.4	5.3	5.1	4.4	4.0	3.1	2.6	1.9	2.0	—	—
Retail	15.2	15.0	15.0	12.6	11.0	8.0	6.8	5.4	5.3	—	—
Finance, insurance, and real estate	5.3	5.2	5.0	4.2	3.6	2.5	1.9	1.5	1.5	1.3	1.5
Services	18.6	17.9	17.9	13.9	11.5	7.1	5.4	4.2	3.9	2.9	3.4
Federal government	2.8	2.9	2.8	2.7	2.7	2.2	1.9	2.8	1.3	0.6	0.5
State and local government	13.3	13.4	13.2	11.9	9.8	5.9	4.1	3.1	3.3	2.7	2.5

1. For 1929–45, figures on employment status relate to persons 14 years and over; beginning in 1950, 16 years and over. NOTE: Figures may not add to totals because of rounding. *Source:* Department of Labor, Bureau of Labor Statistics.

Livestock on Farms
(in thousands)

Type	1982	1981	1980	1975	1970	1965	1960	1950	1945
Cattle[1]	115,691	114,321	111,192	132,028	112,369	109,000	96,236	77,963	85,573
Dairy cows[1]	10,998	10,860	10,779	11,220	13,303	16,981	19,527	23,853	27,770
Sheep[1]	11,552	11,287	11,065	14,515	20,423	25,127	33,170	29,826	39,609
Swine[2]	58,601	64,512	67,353	54,693	57,046	56,106	59,026	58,937	59,373
Chickens[2]	383,220	392,110	400,585	384,101	422,000	401,000	369,000	457,000	516,000
Turkeys[3]	3,415	3,749	3,705	3,014	6,715	6,100	5,633	5,124	7,082

1. As of Jan. 1. 2. As of Jan. 1 the previous year for 1945–60 and Dec. 1 for 1965–81. 3. Turkey breeder hens for 1975–81 as of Dec. 1. *Source:* Department of Agriculture, Economics and Statistics Service.

Agricultural Output by States, 1981 Crops

State	Corn (1,000 bu)	Wheat (1,000 bu)	Cotton (1,000 ba[1])	Potatoes (1,000 cwt)	Tobacco (1,000 lb)	Cattle[2] (1,000 head)	Swine[3] (1,000 head)
Alabama	34,100	24,860	418	2,085	—	1,950	540
Alaska	—	—	—	—	—	9	3
Arizona	4,550	21,844	1,613	1,456	—	1,000	170
Arkansas	3,185	67,650	620	—	—	2,100	600
California	35,750	107,085	3,500	20,886	—	5,000	160
Colorado	108,230	87,394	—	13,904	—	3,025	330
Connecticut	—	—	—	486	5,175	102	10
Delaware	15,023	1,720	—	1,248	—	35	40
Florida	17,985	—	18	6,565	22,834	2,350	257
Georgia	69,000	46,010	165	—	120,960	1,950	1,520
Hawaii	—	—	—	—	—	228	55
Idaho	6,820	89,780	—	80,040	—	1,850	150
Illinois	1,452,540	92,500	—	525	—	2,800	6,450
Indiana	654,000	62,100	—	887	16,280	1,750	4,100
Iowa	1,739,900	4,485	—	270	—	6,850	16,300
Kansas	158,760	305,000	—	—	—	6,000	1,770
Kentucky	149,000	28,560	—	—	510,225	2,600	1,040
Louisiana	2,409	11,550	735	128	45	1,450	130
Maine	—	—	—	26,520	—	145	10
Maryland	72,450	5,617	—	312	29,900	405	250
Massachusetts	—	—	—	743	1,818	96	49
Michigan	273,600	41,500	—	8,503	—	1,450	690
Minnesota	744,700	144,025	—	14,947	—	3,880	4,300
Mississippi	6,440	24,000	1,570	—	—	1,950	370
Missouri	213,400	115,500	161	—	6,580	5,400	3,400
Montana	850	172,830	—	1,739	—	2,900	200
Nebraska	802,700	106,200	—	2,472	—	7,250	4,100
Nevada	—	1,850	1	3,480	—	700	13
New Hampshire	—	—	—	—	—	74	9
New Jersey	12,375	2,352	—	2,066	—	100	45
New Mexico	9,000	9,000	127	945	—	1,500	62
New York	74,400	7,040	—	12,240	—	1,959	165
North Carolina	140,910	15,990	94	2,542	793,315	1,160	1,980
North Dakota	41,553	331,700	—	20,125	—	2,000	280
Ohio	360,000	72,600	—	2,073	21,760	1,900	2,050
Oklahoma	3,850	172,800	410	—	—	5,800	245
Oregon	2,750	77,380	—	21,710	—	1,900	78
Pennsylvania	134,400	9,720	—	5,250	25,160	2,100	750
Rhode Island	—	—	—	800	—	8	6
South Carolina	33,060	14,350	165	—	149,580	700	490
South Dakota	180,600	88,970	—	702	—	3,900	1,710
Tennessee	55,040	37,400	315	279	161,119	2,500	900
Texas	127,530	183,400	5,821	2,381	—	13,700	700
Utah	1,650	8,856	—	1,276	—	920	40
Vermont	—	—	—	147	—	355	9
Virginia	56,250	17,160	—	2,320	155,139	1,850	640
Washington	12,875	168,350	—	52,380	—	1,580	60
West Virginia	6,256	360	—	—	2,250	620	52
Wisconsin	378,000	5,518	—	18,190	26,071	4,450	1,380
Wyoming	5,060	8,430	—	1,060	—	1,390	33
Total	**8,200,951**	**2,793,436**	**15,733**	**333,682**	**2,048,211**	**115,691**	**58,691**

1. 480-lb net-weight bales. 2. Number on farms as of Jan. 1, 1982. 3. Number on farms as of Dec. 1, 1981. *Source:* Department of Agriculture, Statistical Reporting Service.

Farm Income
(in millions of dollars)

Year	Cash receipts from marketings: Crops	Cash receipts from marketings: Livestock, livestock products	Government payments	Total cash income
1920	$6,644	$5,956	—	$12,600
1925	5,545	5,476	—	11,021
1930	3,868	5,187	—	9,055
1935	2,977	4,143	$ 573	7,693
1940	3,469	4,913	723	9,105
1945	9,655	12,008	742	22,405
1950	12,356	16,105	283	28,744
1955	13,523	15,967	229	29,719
1960	15,259	18,989	702	34,950
1965	17,479	21,886	2,463	41,828
1970	20,977	29,532	3,717	54,226
1974	51,065	41,326	531	92,922
1975	45,813	43,089	807	89,709
1976	49,032	46,323	734	96,089
1977	48,569	47,635	1,819	98,023
1978	57,676	58,810	3,030	115,516
1979	63,128	68,583	1,375	133,086
1980	71,739	67,796	1,285	140,820
1981	74,984	68,483	1,932	145,399

Source: Department of Agriculture, Economics and Statistics Service. NOTE: Figures are latest available.

Consumption of Principal Foods[1]
(in pounds per capita)

Foods	1981[1]	1957–59 avg	1935–39 avg
Red meats	44.5	131.4	109.8
Poultry	62.4	33.5	15.6
Eggs	33.6	45.2	36.4
Fluid milk and cream[2]	245.7	312.8	300.9
Cheese	18.0	7.9	5.6
Butter	4.3	8.2	17.0
Margarine	11.2	8.9	2.9
Fats and oils	57.3	48.6	49.3
Fresh fruits	90.0	91.8	136.1
Processed fruits	55.0	49.7	25.5
Fresh vegetables	75.2	92.6	95.7
Processed vegetables	60.7	49.9	29.5
Potatoes, sweet potatoes[3]	114.8	115.2	151.5
Sugar	79.4	96.1	97.5
Corn products[4]	120.5	46.1	51.9
Wheat flour	117.0	120.0	160.0
Coffee	7.7	11.7	11.8
Cocoa products	2.9	2.8	3.5

1. As of August 1982. Except where noted, consumption is from commercial sources and is in terms of retail weight. 2. Includes milk and cream produced and consumed on farms. 3. Farm-weight equivalent of fresh and processed use. 4. Farm-weight equivalent of corn for all food use except fresh. *Source:* Department of Agriculture, Economic Research Service.

Government Employment and Payrolls

Year and function	Employees (in thousands): Total	Federal[1]	State	Local	October payrolls (in millions): Total	Federal[1]	State	Local
1940	4,474	1,128	3,346		$566	$177	$389	
1945	6,556	3,375	3,181		1,110	642	468	
1950	6,402	2,117	1,057	3,228	1,528	613	218	96
1955	7,432	2,378	1,199	1,436	2,265	846	326	1,093
1960	8,808	2,421	1,527	4,860	3,333	1,118	524	1,691
1965	10,589	2,588	2,028	5,973	4,884	1,484	849	2,551
1970	13,028	2,881	2,755	7,392	8,334	2,428	1,612	4,294
1972	13,759	2,795	2,957	8,007	9,950	2,710	1,937	5,303
1973	14,139	2,786	3,013	8,339	11,027	3,102	2,158	5,857
1975	14,973	2,890	3,271	8,813	13,224	3,584	2,653	6,987
1976	15,012	2,843	3,343	8,826	13,924	3,565	2,894	7,465
1977	15,614	2,848	3,491	9,274	15,338	3,918	3,195	8,225
1978	15,628	2,885	3,539	9,204	16,483	4,344	3,483	8,656
1979	15,971	2,869	3,699	9,403	18,077	4,728	3,869	9,480
1980	16,213	2,898	3,753	9,562	19,935	5,205	4,285	10,445
1981, total	15,976	2,865	3,726	9,385	$21,199	5,245	4,667	11,287
National defense and international relations	999	999	(2)	(2)	1,794	1,794	(2)	(2)
Postal service	665	665	(2)	(2)	1,192	1,192	(2)	(2)
Education	6,794	18	1,603	5,173	8,041	39	1,768	6,234
Instructional employees	3,767	(2)	470	3,298	5,609	(2)	814	4,795
Highways	535	4	246	284	697	11	354	333
Health and hospitals	1,652	257	684	712	2,078	451	837	789
Police protection	718	56	74	589	1,099	123	125	851
Local fire protection	312	(2)	(2)	312	409	(2)	(2)	409
Sewerage and sanitation	222	(2)	1	221	284	(2)	1	283
Local parks and recreation	220	(2)	(2)	220	184	(2)	(2)	184
Natural resources	498	277	185	36	755	483	234	38
Financial administration	426	106	127	193	564	182	174	208
All other	2,935	483	807	1,645	4,103	970	1,174	1,959

1. Civilians only. 2. Not applicable. *Source:* Department of Commerce, Bureau of the Census.

Receipts and Outlays of the Federal Government

(in millions of dollars)

From 1789 to 1842, the federal fiscal year ended Dec. 31; from 1844 to 1976, on June 30; and beginning 1977, on Sept. 30.

	Receipts						Outlays					
		Internal revenue										
Year	Customs (including tonnage tax)[1]	Income and profits tax	Other	Miscellaneous taxes and receipts	Total receipts	Net receipts[2]	Department of Defense (Army, 1789–1950)	Department of the Navy	Interest on public debt	All other	Net outlays[3]	Surplus (+) or deficit (–)
1789–1791	$ 4	—	—	—	$ 4	$ 4	$ 1	—	$ 2	$ 1	$ 4	—
1800	9	—	$ –1	$ 1	11	11	3	$ 3	3	1	11	—
1810	9	—	—	1	9	9	2	2	3	1	8	$ +1
1820	15	—	—	3	18	18	3	4	5	6	18	—
1830	22	—	—	3	25	25	5	3	2	5	15	+10
1840	14	—	—	6	20	20	7	6	—	11	24	–4
1850	40	—	—	4	44	44	9	8	4	18	40	+4
1860	53	—	—	3	56	56	16	12	3	32	63	–7
1865	85	—	209	39	334	334	1,031	123	77	66	1,298	–964
1870	195	—	185	32	411	411	58	22	129	101	310	+101
1880	187	—	124	23	334	334	38	14	96	120	268	+66
1890	230	—	143	31	403	403	45	22	36	215	318	+85
1900	233	—	295	39	567	567	135	56	40	290	521	+46
1910	334	—	290	52	675	675	190	123	21	359	694	–19
1915	210	$ 80	335	72	698	683	202	142	23	379	746	–63
1918	180	2,314	872	299	3,665	3,645	4,870	1,279	190	6,339	12,677	–9,032
1929	602	2,331	607	493	4,033	3,862	426	365	678	1,658	3,127	+734
1933	251	746	858	225	2,080	1,997	435	349	689	3,125	4,598	–2,602
1939	319	2,189	2,972	188	5,668	4,979	695	673	941	6,533	8,841	–3,862
1943	324	16,094	6,050	934	23,402	21,947	42,526	20,888	1,808	14,146	79,368	–57,420
1944	431	34,655	7,030	3,325	45,441	43,563	49,438	26,538	2,609	16,401	94,986	–51,423
1945	355	35,173	8,729	3,494	47,750	44,362	50,490	30,047	3,617	14,149	98,303	–53,941
1950	423	28,263	11,186	1,439	41,311	36,422	5,789	4,130	5,750	23,875	39,544	–3,122
1956[4]	705	56,639	20,564	389	78,297	74,547	35,693	—	6,787	27,981	70,460	+4,087
1960	1,123	67,151	28,266	1,190	97,730	92,492	43,969	—	9,180	39,075	92,223	+269
1965	1,478	79,792	39,996	1,598	122,863	116,833	47,179	—	11,346	59,904	118,430	–1,596
1970	2,494	138,689	65,276	3,424	209,883	193,743	78,360	—	19,304	98,924	196,588	–2,845
1975	3,782	202,146	108,371	6,711	321,010	280,997	87,471	—	32,665	205,969	326,105	–45,108
1979	7,640	322,995	166,848	9,154	506,721	465,955	117,900	—	59,837	315,870	493,607	–27,652
1980	7,482	359,927	192,436	12,797	572,641	520,050	136,138	—	74,860	368,013	579,011	–58,961
1981	8,523	406,583	235,088	13,796	663,991	602,612	159,183	—	95,589	405,772	660,544	–57,932

1. Beginning 1933, tonnage tax is included in "Other receipts." 2. Net receipts equal total receipts less (a) appropriations to federal old-age and survivors' insurance trust fund beginning fiscal year 1939 and (b) refunds of receipts beginning fiscal year 1933. 3. Includes Air Force 1950–65 (in millions): 1950—$3,521; 1956—$16,750; 1960—$19,065; 1965—$18,471. 4. Beginning 1956, computed on unified budget concepts; not strictly comparable with preceding figures. *Source:* Department of the Treasury, Bureau of Government Financial Operations.

Social Welfare Expenditures Under Public Programs
(in millions of dollars)

Year and source of funds	Social insurance	Public aid	Health and medical programs	Veterans' programs	Education	Housing	Other social welfare	All health and medical care[1]	Total social welfare	Total social welfare as: Percent of gross national product	Total social welfare as: Percent of total gov't outlays
FEDERAL											
1950	$ 2,103	$ 1,103	$ 604	$ 6,386	$ 157	$ 15	$ 174	$ 1,362	$ 10,541	4.0	26.2
1955	6,385	1,504	1,150	4,772	485	75	252	1,948	14,623	3.9	22.3
1960	14,307	2,117	1,737	5,367	868	144	417	2,918	24,957	5.0	28.1
1965	21,807	3,594	2,781	6,011	2,470	238	812	4,625	37,712	5.7	32.6
1970	45,246	9,649	4,775	8,952	5,876	582	2,259	16,600	77,337	8.1	40.1
1975	99,715	27,205	8,513	16,570	8,629	2,541	4,264	34,645	167,436	11.5	53.8
1978	147,252	40,013	11,566	19,570	10,884	4,887	5,949	53,851	240,121	11.8	55.3
1979[2]	163,744	43,612	12,150	20,266	12,097	5,802	6,449	60,420	264,118	11.4	55.0
STATE AND LOCAL											
1950	2,844	1,393	1,460	480	6,518	([3])	274	1,704	12,967	4.9	59.2
1955	3,450	1,499	1,953	62	10,672	15	367	2,473	18,017	4.7	55.3
1960	4,999	1,984	2,727	112	16,758	33	723	3,478	27,337	5.5	60.1
1965	6,316	2,690	3,466	20	25,638	80	1,254	4,911	39,464	6.0	60.4
1970	9,446	6,839	5,132	127	44,970	120	1,886	8,791	68,519	7.1	64.0
1975	23,298	14,122	9,195	449	72,234	631	2,683	17,847	122,612	8.4	63.7
1978	27,683	19,381	11,364	174	90,708	337	4,614	24,441	154,261	7.6	62.7
1979[2]	29,844	21,037	12,346	190	96,182	424	4,192	27,272	164,215	7.1	60.4
TOTAL											
1950	4,947	2,496	2,064	6,866	6,674	15	448	3,065	23,508	8.9	37.4
1955	9,835	3,003	3,103	4,834	11,157	89	619	4,421	32,640	8.6	32.7
1960	19,307	4,101	4,464	5,479	17,626	177	1,139	6,395	52,293	10.5	38.4
1965	28,123	6,283	6,246	6,031	28,108	318	2,066	9,535	77,175	11.7	42.2
1970	54,691	16,488	9,907	9,078	50,846	701	4,145	25,391	145,856	15.2	48.2
1975	123,013	41,326	17,708	17,019	80,863	3,172	6,947	52,492	290,047	20.0	57.4
1978	174,935	59,394	22,930	19,744	101,592	6,133	10,563	78,292	394,383	19.3	57.8
1979[2]	193,588	64,649	24,496	20,455	108,279	6,500	10,640	87,692	428,333	18.5	56.8
PERCENT OF TOTAL, BY TYPE											
1950	21.0	10.6	8.8	29.2	28.4	0.1	1.9	13.0	100.0	([3])	([3])
1955	30.1	9.2	9.5	14.8	34.2	0.3	1.9	13.5	100.0	([3])	([3])
1960	36.9	7.8	8.5	10.5	33.7	0.3	2.2	12.2	100.0	([3])	([3])
1965	36.4	8.1	8.1	7.8	36.4	0.4	2.7	12.4	100.0	([3])	([3])
1970	37.5	11.3	6.7	6.2	34.9	0.5	3.0	17.2	100.0	([3])	([3])
1975	42.4	14.2	6.1	5.9	27.9	1.1	2.4	18.1	100.0	([3])	([3])
1978	44.4	15.1	5.8	5.0	25.8	1.3	2.7	19.8	100.0	([3])	([3])
1979[2]	45.2	15.1	5.7	4.8	25.3	1.5	2.5	20.5	100.0	([3])	([3])
FEDERAL PERCENT OF TOTAL											
1950	42.5	44.2	29.2	93.0	2.3	100.0	38.9	44.4	44.8	([3])	([3])
1955	64.9	50.1	37.1	98.7	4.3	83.7	40.7	44.1	44.8	([3])	([3])
1960	74.1	51.6	38.9	98.0	4.9	81.2	36.6	45.6	47.7	([3])	([3])
1965	77.5	57.2	44.5	99.7	8.8	74.9	39.3	48.5	48.9	([3])	([3])
1970	82.7	58.5	48.2	98.6	11.6	82.9	54.5	65.4	53.0	([3])	([3])
1975	81.1	65.8	48.1	97.4	10.7	80.1	61.4	66.0	57.7	([3])	([3])
1978	84.2	67.4	50.4	99.2	10.7	93.5	56.3	68.8	60.9	([3])	([3])
1979[2]	84.6	67.5	49.6	99.1	11.2	93.2	60.6	68.9	61.7	([3])	([3])

1. Combines health and medical programs with medical services provided in connection with social insurance, public aid, veterans, and other social welfare programs. 2. Preliminary. 3. Not applicable. NOTE: Figures are latest available. *Source:* Department of Health and Human Services. *Social Security Bulletin,* November 1981.

Surplus of Dairy Products Continues to Grow

When President Reagan authorized the distribution of over 280 million pounds of surplus cheese, butter, and nonfat dried milk to the needy in 1982, he tapped a vast reservoir of dairy products. The surplus is the result of two related factors: the federal government continues to pay $2 billion a year for the controversial milk price support program, and the country's dairymen continue to produce 10% more milk than consumers buy.

Every two weeks the overstock grows by about 40 million pounds, costing taxpayers nearly $100 million a year in shipping and storage costs. According to Agriculture Department estimates, if a train were loaded with the surplus, it would stretch from Washington, D.C., to New York City.

Per Capita Social Welfare Expenditures Under Public Programs

Year	Social insurance	Public aid	Health and medical programs	Veterans' programs	Education	Other social welfare	All health and medical care[1]	Total[2]	Total social welfare (in millions)[3]
1950	$ 32.19	$ 16.26	$ 13.44	$ 44.18	$ 43.47	2.92	$ 19.97	$ 152.56	$ 23,421
1955	58.71	17.98	18.58	28.46	66.68	3.71	26.47	194.66	32,512
1960	105.35	22.46	24.45	29.52	96.43	6.24	35.03	285.42	52,106
1965	142.29	31.95	31.76	30.30	142.73	10.50	48.48	391.15	76,929
1970	262.47	79.48	47.75	43.27	244.94	19.98	121.65	701.27	145,484
1975	565.51	190.81	81.76	77.89	373.20	32.07	238.58	1,335.89	289,336
1977	729.63	242.56	92.94	85.86	427.52	41.31	308.30	1,639.66	360,077
1978	786.26	268.06	103.49	88.36	458.31	47.67	347.19	1,775.73	393,456
1979	862.63	289.25	109.60	90.74	484.24	47.61	389.33	1,911.92	427,327
PERCENTAGE INCREASE FOR 1979 FROM—									
1950	2,580	1,679	716	106	1,014	1,530	1,850	1,153	1,725
1955	1,383	1,509	490	220	626	1,183	1,371	882	1,215
1960	719	1,188	348	208	402	663	1,011	570	720
1965	506	805	245	200	239	353	703	389	456
1970	229	264	130	110	98	138	220	173	194
1975	52	52	34	17	30	48	63	43	48
1977	18	19	18	6	13	15	27	17	19
1978	10	8	6	3	6	0	12	8	9

1. Combines health and medical programs with medical services provided in connection with social insurance, public aid, veterans', vocational rehabilitation, and antipoverty programs. 2. Includes housing, now shown. 3. Excludes expenditures abroad for education, veterans' benefits, civil service retirement benefits, and certain other items. Figures are latest available. *Source:* Department of Health and Human Services. *Social Security Bulletin,* November 1981.

Contributions to International Organizations

(for fiscal year 1981 in millions of dollars)

Organization	Amount[1]
United Nations and Specialized Agencies	$262.84
United Nations	109.67
Food and Agricultural Organization	25.45
International Atomic Energy Agency	17.28
International Civil Aviation Organization	3.51
International Labor Union	23.63
International Telecommunications Union	3.28
UNESCO	32.62
World Health Organization	41.15
World Meteorological Organization	3.53
Others	2.72
United Nations Peacekeeping Forces	69.00
United Nations Force in Cyprus	9.00
United Nations Disengagement Observer Force	50.00
Multinational Forces and Observers	10.00
Inter-American Organizations	71.90
Organization of American States	36.73
Pan American Health Organization	23.98
Inter-American Institute for Cooperation on Agriculture	8.72
Inter-American Tropical Tuna Commission	2.03
Others	.44
Regional Organizations	32.10
NATO Civilian Headquarters	12.92
Organization for Economic Cooperation and Development	18.19
Others	.99
Other International Organizations	11.24
Customs Cooperation Council	1.67
General Agreement on Tariffs and Trade	2.16
International Institute for Cotton	2.28
Others	5.13
Special Voluntary Programs	651.43
Consultative Group on International Agricultural Research	35.00
Intergovernmental Committee for Migration—Special Voluntary	5.00
International Atomic Energy Agency—Technical Assistance Fund	12.37[2]
Organization of American States—Special Development Assistance Fund	6.00
Organization of American States—Special Multilateral Fund (education and science)	6.50
United Nations Children's Fund	35.95
United Nations Development Program	125.80
United Nations Environmental Program	9.98[3]
UN/FAO World Food Program	153.49
United Nations Fund for Drug Abuse Control	2.15
United Nations Fund for Population Activities	32.00
United Nations High Commissioner for Refugees (5 programs)	105.50
8 Special programs	33.25
United Nations Relief and Works Agency	62.00
World Health Organization—Special Programs	9.40
Others	17.04
Total	**1,098.51**

1. Estimated. 2. Includes cash, commodities and services and $5.1 million for Safeguard Program. 3. Includes cash, commodities, and services. *Source:* Department of State.

Foreign Assistance
(in millions of dollars)

Calendar years	Economic Assistance (net): Net new grants	Net new credits	Net other assistance	Total	Military grants (net)	Net assistance[1]
July 1945–50[2]	$18,413	$ 8,086	—	$ 26,498	$ 1,981	$ 28,479
1951–55	10,459	556	$ 541	11,556	14,464	26,020
1956–60	8,291	1,503	2,226	12,021	11,327	23,348
1961–65	9,384	5,522	576	15,482	7,831	23,313
1966–70	8,808	9,430	−564	17,674	12,028	29,702
1971–75	12,939	7,524	−725	19,737	16,693	36,430
1976	2,279	3,275	−54	5,501	1,339	6,841
1977	2,280	2,861	−39	5,102	766	5,868
1978	2,676	3,691	−52	6,315	817	7,132
1979	3,050	3,296	−69	6,277	1,070	7,347
1980	3,959	4,637	−69	8,526	1,529	10,055
1981	4,183	4,178	−11	8,350	919	9,269
Total postwar period	**86,721**	**54,559**	**1,759**	**143,040**	**70,764**	**213,804**

1. Excludes investment in international nonmonetary financial institutions of $9,337 million. 2. Includes transactions after V-J Day (Sept. 2, 1945). NOTE: Detail may not add to total due to rounding. *Source:* Department of Commerce, Bureau of Economic Analysis.

The Public Debt

Year	Gross debt: Amount (in millions)	Gross debt: Per capita	Year	Gross debt: Amount (in millions)	Gross debt: Per capita
1800 (Jan. 1)	$ 83	$ 15.87	1950	$256,087[2]	$1,688.30
1860 (June 30)	65	2.06	1955	272,807[2]	1,650.63
1865	2,678	75.01	1960	284,093[2]	1,572.31
1900	1,263	16.60	1965	313,819[2]	1,612.70
1920	24,299	228.23	1970	370,094[2]	1,807.09
1925	20,516	177.12	1975	533,189	2,496.90
1930	16,185	131.51	1978	771,544	3,521.78
1935	28,701	225.55	1979	826,519	3,736.86
1940	42,968	325.23	1980	907,701	3,969.55
1945	258,682	1,848.60	1981[1]	997,855	4,329.52

1. Preliminary, Sept. 30, 1981. 2. Adjusted to exclude issues to the International Monetary Fund and other international lending institutions to conform to the budget presentation. *Source:* Department of the Treasury, Bureau of Government Financial Operations.

Domestic Freight Traffic by Major Carriers
(in millions of ton-miles)[1]

Year	Railroads: Ton-miles	Railroads: % of total	Inland waterways[2]: Ton-miles	Inland waterways[2]: % of total	Motor trucks: Ton-miles	Motor trucks: % of total	Oil pipelines: Ton-miles	Oil pipelines: % of total	Air carriers: Ton-miles	Air carriers: % of total
1940	379,201	61.3	118,057	19.1	62,043	10.0	59,277	9.6	14	—
1945	690,809	67.3	142,737	13.9	66,948	6.5	126,530	12.3	91	—
1950	596,940	56.2	163,344	15.4	172,860	16.3	129,175	12.1	318	—
1955	631,385	49.5	216,508	17.0	223,254	17.5	203,244	16.0	481	—
1960	579,130	44.1	220,253	16.8	285,483	21.7	228,626	17.4	778	—
1965	708,700	43.3	262,421	16.0	359,218	21.9	306,393	18.7	1,910	0.1
1970	771,168	39.8	318,560	16.4	412,000	21.3	431,000	22.3	3,274	0.2
1975	759,000	36.7	342,210	16.5	454,000	22.0	507,300	24.6	3,732	0.2
1976	799,876	36.3	372,865	16.9	510,000	23.2	515,100	23.4	3,900	0.2
1977	833,994	36.1	368,275	15.9	555,000	24.1	546,000	23.7	4,181	0.2
1978	867,982	35.1	409,316	16.6	602,000	24.4	585,800	23.7	4,630	0.2
1979[3]	927,000	35.7	431,000	16.6	628,000	24.2	605,000	23.3	4,439	0.2
1980[3]	932,000	37.2	420,000	16.9	567,000	22.6	588,000	23.1	4,528	0.2
1981[3]	926,000	37.5	423,000	17.1	565,000	22.9	553,000	22.4	4,657	0.2

1. Mail and express included, except railroads for 1970. 2. Rivers, canals, and domestic traffic on Great Lakes. 3. Preliminary. *Sources:* Interstate Commerce Commission; Civil Aeronautics Board; Association of American Railroads, and Transportation Association of America.

Intercity Passenger Traffic
(in millions of passenger-miles)

Year	Railroads		Buses		Air carriers		Inland waterways[1]		Total commercial	Private airplanes
	Miles	% of total	Miles	% of total	Miles	% of total	Miles	% of total		
1940	24,766	67.1	9,800	26.5	1,052	2.8	1,317	3.6	36,935	—
1945	93,535	74.3	27,027	21.4	3,362	2.7	2,056	1.6	125,980	—
1950	32,481	46.3	26,436	37.7	10,072	14.3	1,190	1.7	70,179	—
1955	28,695	36.5	25,519	32.4	22,741	28.9	1,738	2.2	78,693	—
1960	21,574	28.6	19,327	25.7	31,730	42.1	2,688	3.6	75,319	2,228
1965	17,557	17.9	23,775	24.2	53,719	54.7	3,101	3.2	98,152	4,364
1970	10,903	7.3	25,300	16.9	109,499	73.1	4,000	2.7	149,702	9,101
1975	10,075	5.8	25,000	14.2	136,432	77.7	4,000	2.3	175,507	11,500
1976	11,000	5.8	25,000	13.2	150,000	78.9	4,000	2.1	190,000	13,000
1977	10,400	5.1	25,900	12.7	164,200	80.3	4,000	1.9	204,500	12,100
1978	10,500	4.6	25,400	11.1	189,100	82.6	4,000	1.7	229,000	12,700
1979	11,600	4.6	26,600	10.5	210,300	83.3	4,000	1.6	252,500	15,500
1980	11,500	4.7	27,700	11.4	204,368	83.9	4,000	1.6	243,600	15,600
1981[2]	11,800	4.8	27,200	11.1	201,297	82.5	4,000	1.6	240,300	14,700

1. Rivers, canals, and Great Lakes. 2. Preliminary. NOTE: Beginning in 1970, data include Alaska and Hawaii. n.a. = not available. *Sources:* Interstate Commerce Commission; Civil Aeronautics Board; Association of American Railroads, and Transportation Association of America.

Tonnage Handled by Principal U.S. Ports
(over 10 million tons annually; in thousands of tons)

Port	1980	1979	Port	1980	1979
New Orleans	177,316	167,135	St. Louis (Metropolitan)	24,529	21,644
New York	166,991	163,621	Paulsboro, N.J.	22,790	24,061
Houston	108,937	117,551	Toledo Harbor, Ohio	22,263	26,256
Valdez Harbor, Alaska	85,973	65,452	Boston	22,034	26,243
Baton Rouge, La.	79,347	76,703	Seattle	21,289	20,039
Norfolk Harbor, Va.	54,218	48,651	Newport News, Va.	20,821	11,509
Beaumont, Tex.	52,261	58,137	Freeport, Tex.	20,131	19,984
Baltimore Harbor	50,042	51,445	Detroit	19,268	24,996
Tampa Harbor, Fla.	48,625	47,885	Huntington, W. Va.	19,227	16,503
Philadelphia	47,883	54,866	Conneaut Harbor, Ohio	18,655	21,478
Corpus Christi Ship Channel, Tex.	45,001	—	Richmond, Calif.	18,560	18,978
Duluth–Superior, Minn.	41,435	47,725	Tacoma Harbor, Wash.	17,162	15,193
Corpus Christi, Tex.	39,107	46,423	Indiana, Ind.	16,899	18,419
Long Beach, Calif.	38,780	33,347	Jacksonville, Fla.	15,644	15,278
Mobile, Ala.	37,569	35,265	Cleveland	14,045	19,470
Pittsburgh	36,586	40,881	Everglades, Fla.	13,288	13,031
Lake Charles, La.	34,850	35,951	Portland, Me.	12,848	13,26[illegible]
Chicago	32,993	38,693	Savannah, Ga.	12,293	13,52[illegible]
Los Angeles	30,151	31,749	New Castle, Del.	11,457	14,75[illegible]
Port Arthur, Tex.	29,797	32,773	Memphis, Tenn.	11,452	12,34[illegible]
Portland, Ore.	29,314	29,146	Escanaba, Mich.	11,241	13,45[illegible]
Texas City, Tex.	25,949	35,954	Cincinnati	10,833	12,01[illegible]
Marcus Hook, Pa.	25,696	32,700	St. Paul	10,528	11,24[illegible]
Pascagoula, Miss.	25,434	25,289	Ashtabula, Ohio	10,075	14,60[illegible]

Source: Department of the Army, Corps of Engineers.

Annual Railroad Carloadings

Year	Total	Year	Total	Year	Total	Year	Total
1920	33,754,000	1945	41,918,000	1970	27,160,000	1977	23,173,000
1925	34,783,000	1950	38,903,000	1973	27,338,000	1978	23,373,000
1930	30,173,000	1955	37,636,000	1974	26,184,000	1979	23,876,000
1935	22,015,000	1960	30,441,000	1975	23,217,000	1980	22,598,000
1940	36,358,000	1965	29,248,000	1976	23,457,000	1981	21,618,000

Source: Association of American Railroads.

Estimated Motor Vehicle Registration, 1981

(in thousands; excluding publicly owned vehicles)

State	Autos[1]	Trucks and buses	Motor-cycles	Total	State	Autos[1]	Trucks and buses	Motor-cycles	Total
Alabama	2,140	886	78	3,104	Montana	455	268	36	759
Alaska	158	101	8	267	Nebraska	849	431	87	1,367
Arizona	1,458	589	102	2,149	Nevada	492	195	21	708
Arkansas	1,072	558	35	1,665	New Hampshire	604	120	43	767
California	14,019	3,725	761	18,505	New Jersey	4,360	511	109	4,980
Colorado	1,765	605	115	2,485	New Mexico	702	395	55	1,152
Connecticut	2,022	167	75	2,264	New York	6,978	1,010	216	8,204
Delaware	324	78	12	414	North Carolina	3,421	1,196	122	4,739
D.C.	257	22	5	284	North Dakota	370	268	32	670
Florida	6,398	1,484	222	8,104	Ohio	6,536	1,454	283	8,273
Georgia	2,938	912	114	3,964	Oklahoma	1,844	885	133	2,862
Hawaii	525	57	7	589	Oregon	1,579	548	95	2,222
Idaho	531	330	61	922	Pennsylvania	5,897	1,234	215	7,346
Illinois	6,390	1,250	328	7,968	Rhode Island	557	83	27	667
Indiana	2,900	959	190	4,049	South Carolina	1,541	479	43	2,063
Iowa	1,670	661	233	2,664	South Dakota	371	237	38	646
Kansas	1,404	634	110	2,148	Tennessee	2,597	738	85	3,420
Kentucky	1,813	791	66	2,670	Texas	7,606	3,181	331	11,118
Louisiana	2,016	847	81	2,944	Utah	682	318	65	1,065
Maine	525	219	50	794	Vermont	280	80	29	389
Maryland	2,393	464	84	2,941	Virginia	3,137	567	91	3,795
Massachusetts	3,320	489	113	3,922	Washington	2,344	962	153	3,459
Michigan	5,326	1,256	258	6,840	West Virginia	978	406	43	1,427
Minnesota	2,345	797	171	3,313	Wisconsin	2,449	568	176	3,193
Mississippi	1,269	366	30	1,665	Wyoming	282	197	23	502
Missouri	2,447	846	112	3,405	**Total**	**124,336**	**35,424**	**5,972**	**165,732**

1. Includes taxicabs. NOTE: Publicly owned vehicles are as follows: autos, 812,432; trucks and buses, 1,630,976; motorcycles, 29,322; total vehicles, 2,472,730. Figures are latest available. *Source:* Department of Transportation, Federal Highway Administration.

Passenger Car Production by Makes

Companies and models	1981	1980	1979	1975	1970	1965
American Motors Corporation	109,319	164,765	184,636	323,704	276,127	346,367
Chrysler Corporation						
Plymouth	365,502	293,100	372,461	443,550	699,031	679,539
Dodge	325,932	326,506	380,745	354,482	405,699	547,531
Chrysler	57,340	82,440	181,427	102,940	158,614	224,061
Imperial	—	—	—	1,930	10,111	16,422
Total	**748,774**	**638,535**	**934,633**	**902,902**	**1,273,455**	**1,467,553**
Ford Motor Company						
Ford	892,043	929,627	1,375,775	1,301,414	1,647,918	2,164,902
Mercury	360,969	324,528	509,450	405,104	310,463	355,404
Lincoln	67,185	52,793	151,960	101,520	58,771	45,470
Total	**1,320,197**	**1,306,948**	**2,037,185**	**1,808,038**	**2,017,152**	**2,565,776**
General Motors Corporation						
Chevrolet	1,445,353	1,760,030	2,214,955	1,687,091	1,504,614	2,587,509
Pontiac	521,302	575,365	731,570	523,469	422,212	860,652
Oldsmobile	838,333	783,230	1,004,515	654,342	439,632	650,801
Buick	839,960	783,575	787,123	535,820	459,931	653,838
Cadillac	259,135	203,991	345,794	278,404	152,859	196,595
Total	**3,904,083**	**4,106,191**	**5,083,957**	**3,679,126**	**2,979,248**	**4,949,395**
Checker Motors Corporation	3,010	3,340	4,766	3,181	4,146	6,136
Volkswagen of America	167,755	197,106	173,192	—	—	—
Industry total	**6,253,138**	**6,416,885**	**8,418,369**	**6,716,951**	**6,550,128**	**9,335,227**

Source Automotive News, Jan. 11, 1982, and Motor Vehicle Manufacturers Association of the United States.

Passenger Car Data

	1980	1970	1960	1950	1940
U.S. passenger cars and taxis registered (thousands)	121,724	89,280	61,671	40,339	27,466
Total mileage of U.S. passenger cars (millions)	1,111,950	901,000	588,083	363,613	249,600
Total fuel consumption of U.S. passenger cars (millions of gallons)	73,375	65,784	41,169	24,305	16,323
World registration of cars, trucks, and buses (thousands)	411,113	248,900	126,908	70,424	n.a.
U.S. registration of cars, trucks, and buses (thousands)	155,890	108,407	73,858	49,162	32,453
U.S. share of world registration of cars, trucks, and buses	37.9%	44.0%	58.2%	69.8%	n.a.

NOTE: n.a. = not available. *Source:* Motor Vehicle Manufacturers Association of the U.S.

Domestic Passenger Car Sales

Company and model	1981	1980	1979
American Motors	136,682	149,438	162,057
Spirit	33,504	49,723	54,356
Concord	59,846	64,991	85,432
Pacer	111	2,083	8,168
Eagle	43,221	32,641	14,101
Chrysler Corp.	729,873	660,017	942,207
Total Plymouth	325,598	251,312	325,523
Horizon	75,377	78,823	84,668
TC3	51,815	53,791	62,072
Reliant/Volare	196,997	104,836	167,091[1]
Plymouth	1,409	13,682	746
Total Chrysler	93,869	139,748	248,840
LeBaron	36,311	65,519	99,588
LeBaron K	10,680	—	—
Cordoba	23,904	44,908	61,801
New Yorker	5,894	—	—
Chrysler	17,080	29,321	87,451
Total Imperial	4,649	2,497	—
Total Dodge	305,757	266,460	367,844
Omni	56,038	61,240	69,888
024	51,743	46,658	54,490
Aries	149,653	80,876	—
Dodge 400	3,150	—	—
Diplomat	25,598	33,157	45,131
Miranda/Magnum	13,947	27,595	24,784
Dodge	5,628	16,934	28,303
Aspen	—	55,092	117,777
Ford Motor	1,380,600	1,475,232	2,132,644
Ford Division	977,220	1,074,675	1,491,374
Pinto	10,037	142,467	187,708
EXP	54,502	—	—
Escort	284,907	60,196	—
Mustang	154,985	225,290	304,053
Fairmont	182,909	285,272	338,819
Granada	106,996	88,371	141,737
LTD II	—	3,012	26,700
Thunderbird	69,775	127,248	215,698
Ford	113,109	142,819	245,565
L-M Division	403,380	400,557	641,270
Total Mercury	339,550	330,853	509,999
Bobcat	2,169	26,821	44,674
LN7	18,217	—	—
Lynx	92,809	18,196	—
Zephyr	50,603	87,032	99,335
Cougar	46,750	31,710	3,955
XR7	28,706	51,857	121,184
Capri	47,151	62,592	90,850
Mercury	53,145	52,645	94,654
Total Lincoln	63,830	69,704	131,271
Continental/Versailles	4,919	4,219	13,586[2]
Lincoln	29,178	30,114	60,797
Mark VI	29,733	35,371	56,888[3]
General Motors	3,796,696	4,116,482	4,911,875
Buick Division	722,617	720,368	714,508
Skyhawk	—	5,388	18,768
Skylark	200,460	175,741	115,000
Century FWD	2,691	145,894[4]	62,210[4]
Regal Sedan	123,676	145,894	—
Regal Coupe	208,329	199,207	249,379
LeSabre	82,263	89,429	129,554
Electra	57,234	61,792	88,195
Riviera	47,964	42,917	51,402
Cadillac Division	230,665	213,002	314,034
Cimarron	14,604	—	—
Seville	22,724	34,709	45,317
Cadillac	138,948	126,151	206,164
Eldorado	54,389	52,142	62,553
Chevrolet Division	1,442,281	1,747,534	2,152,603
Chevette	346,307	373,988	375,724
Cavalier/Monza	88,072	150,320[5]	141,564[5]
Citation	300,184	374,706[6]	308,437[6]
Camaro	94,606	116,824	204,742
Celebrity	1,361	—	—
Malibu	211,130	267,732	344,233
Monte Carlo	161,158	165,638	265,877
Chevrolet	210,424	261,819	449,001
Corvette	29,039	36,507	38,631
Oldsmobile Division	848,739	820,681	949,488
Starfire	—	5,334	18,611
Omega	109,981	87,262	50,098
Cutlass Ciera	2,882	—	—
Cutlass	187,952	210,784	114,092
Supreme	266,070	258,789	404,068
Olds 88	158,662	147,997	233,699
Olds 98	84,583	73,464	92,075
Toronado	38,609	37,051	46,845
Pontiac Division	552,394	614,897	781,042
T-1000	55,868	—	—
J-2000/Sunbird	75,884	132,630	89,107
Phoenix	82,825	98,952	80,857
Firebird	52,188	81,592	149,211
6000	1,325	—	—
Bonneville/LeMans	73,988	77,911	114,993[7]
Grand Prix	128,236	118,414	175,573
Pontiac	82,620	105,398	171,301
Volkswagen	162,445	177,106	166,839
Industry total	**6,206,296**	**6,578,275**	**8,315,622**

1. Volare only. 2. Versailles only. 3. Includes Mark V. 4. Century. 5. Monza only. 6. Citation/Nova. 7. LeMans only. *Source: Automotive News,* Jan. 11, 1982.

Domestic and Export Factory Sales of Motor Vehicles
(in thousands)

	From plants in United States[1]								
	Passenger cars			Motor trucks and buses			Total motor vehicles		
Year	Total	Domestic	Exports	Total	Domestic	Exports	Total	Domestic	Exports
1965	9,306	9,101	205	1,752	1,616	136	11,058	10,717	341
1970	6,547	6,187	360	1,692	1,566	126	8,239	7,753	486
1975	6,713	6,073	640	2,272	2,003	269	8,985	8,076	909
1977	9,201	8,513	688	3,442	3,179	263	12,643	11,692	951
1978	9,165	8,493	672	3,706	3,416	290	12,871	11,909	962
1979	8,419	7,678	741	3,037	2,741	296	11,456	10,419	1,037
1980	6,400	5,840	560	1,667	1,464	203	8,067	7,304	763
1981	6,255	5,749	506	1,701	1,513	188	7,956	7,262	694

1. Excludes factory sales to all Federal government agencies. *Source:* Motor Vehicle Manufacturers Association of the U.S.

Balance of International Payments
(in billions of dollars)

Item	1981	1980	1979	1975	1970	1965	1960	1955	1949
Exports of goods and services (excluding transfers under military grants)	$376.0	$344.7	$228.9	$155.7	$65.7	$41.1	$28.9	$19.9	$15.8
Merchandise, adjusted, excluding military	236.3	224.0	184.5	107.1	42.5	26.5	19.7	14.4	12.2
Transfers under U.S. military agency sales contracts	9.3	8.2	6.6	3.9	1.5	0.8	0.3	0.2	n.s.s.
Receipts of income on U.S. investments abroad	90.1	75.9	66.7	25.4	11.8	7.4	4.6	2.6	1.5
Other services	40.3	36.5	31.1	19.3	9.9	6.4	4.3	2.7	2.1
Imports of goods and services	–362.7	–333.9	–281.9	–132.6	–60.0	–32.8	–23.7	–17.8	–9.6
Merchandise, adjusted, excluding military	–264.1	–249.3	–211.8	–98.0	–39.9	–21.5	–14.8	–11.5	–6.9
Direct defense expenditures	–11.3	–10.7	–8.6	–4.8	4.9	–3.0	–3.1	–2.9	–0.6
Payments of income on foreign assets in U.S.	–53.3	–43.2	–33.2	–12.6	–5.5	–2.1	–1.2	–0.5	–0.3
Other services	–33.9	–30.7	–28.3	–17.2	–9.8	–6.2	–4.6	–2.8	–1.8
Unilateral transfers, excluding military grants, net	–6.8	–7.0	–5.6	–4.6	–3.3	–2.9	–2.3	–2.5	–5.6
U.S. Government assets abroad, net	–106.6	–84.8	–62.6	–3.5	–1.6	–1.6	–1.1	–0.3	–0.7
U.S. private assets abroad, net	–96.3	–71.5	–57.7	–35.4	–10.2	–5.3	–5.1	–1.3	–0.6
U.S. assets abroad, official reserve, net	–5.2	–8.2	–1.1	–0.6	2.5	1.2	2.1	0.2	–0.3
Foreign assets in U.S., net	74.4	50.3	38.9	15.6	6.4	0.7	2.3	–1.4	0.2
Statistical discrepancy	24.6	29.6	21.1	5.5	–0.2	–0.5	–1.0	0.4	0.7
Balance on goods and services	13.3	10.8	7.1	23.1	5.7	8.3	5.1	2.2	6.2
Balance on goods, services, and remittances	11.0	8.4	5.0	21.3	4.1	7.2	4.5	1.6	5.6
Balance on current account	6.6	3.7	1.4	18.4	2.4	5.4	2.8	–0.3	0.6

NOTE: n.s.s. = not shown separately. – denotes debits. *Source:* Department of Commerce, Bureau of Economic Analysis.

Exports and General Imports by Countries and Areas
($25 million and over; value in millions)

	Exports, including re-exports				General imports			
Area and country	1981	1970	1960	1950	1981	1970	1960	1950
NORTH AND SOUTH AMERICA								
Canada	$39,564	$9,079	$3,810	$2,039	$45,912	$11,092	$2,901	$1,960
20 Latin American Republics	38,950	5,695	3,577	2,720	32,055	4,779	3,528	2,910
Argentina	2,192	441	359	148	1,125	172	98	206
Bolivia	189	46	25	21	177	25	9	35
Brazil	3,798	840	464	365	4,470	670	570	715
Chile	1,465	300	203	73	603	157	193	160

Area and country	Exports, including re-exports 1981	1970	1960	1950	General imports 1981	1970	1960	1950
Colombia	1,771	395	253	237	822	269	299	313
Costa Rica	373	94	45	27	366	117	35	25
Cuba	(1)	(1)	225	464	(1)	(1)	357	406
Dominican Republic	772	143	42	43	926	184	110	38
Ecuador	854	127	57	29	1,021	109	65	34
El Salvador	308	64	43	33	259	48	32	51
Guatemala	559	100	64	44	348	87	59	54
Haiti	301	34	25	25	277	32	18	23
Honduras	349	89	35	24	433	102	34	20
Mexico	17,789	1,704	831	526	13,799	1,218	443	315
Nicaragua	184	77	30	19	140	61	21	19
Panama	844	208	90	112	296	76	24	10
Paraguay	108	18	9	3	48	11	8	6
Peru	1,486	214	147	76	1,223	340	183	49
Uruguay	163	41	63	41	158	19	21	106
Venezuela	5,445	759	567	406	5,566	1,082	948	324
OTHER WESTERN HEMISPHERE								
Bahamas	441	173	49	7	1,261	82	8	1
Barbados	149	22	6	1	81	9	1	(1)
Belize	69	—	—	—	43	—	—	—
Bermuda	150	92	32	10	18	1	2	(1)
French West Indies	69	15	4	3	20	9	(1)	(1)
Guyana	106	25	12	3	104	43	11	1
Jamaica	479	218	48	9	368	187	54	2
Leeward and Windward Islands	282	32	6	1	32	6	2	2
Netherlands Antilles	499	126	65	70	2,625	416	265	158
Suriname	138	35	18	7	179	56	30	13
Trinidad and Tobago	688	84	36	6	2,216	232	55	9
EUROPE								
Western Europe	65,377	14,463	7,204	3,280	51,879	11,169	4,187	1,368
Austria	484	74	80	106	382	120	49	16
Belgium and Luxembourg	5,765	1,195	467	291	2,297	696	364	140
Cyprus	86	—	—	—	4	—	—	—
Denmark	887	227	146	65	850	284	98	12
Finland	613	99	56	21	524	114	52	35
France	7,341	1,483	699	475	5,854	942	396	132
Germany, West	10,277	2,741	1,272	(2)	11,382	3,127	897	—
Gibraltar	53	—	—	—	1	—	—	—
Greece	676	203	103	107	359	52	33	17
Iceland	71	13	12	6	198	47	10	4
Ireland	1,025	112	43	47	498	135	28	2
Italy	5,360	1,353	715	369	5,191	1,316	393	109
Malta	33	—	—	—	11	—	—	—
Netherlands	8,595	1,651	817	251	2,370	528	213	85
Norway	892	196	108	95	2,478	142	66	41
Portugal	1,075	126	45	34	238	92	35	21
Spain	3,397	712	208	46	1,534	353	88	50
Sweden	1,842	543	301	99	1,714	399	170	71
Switzerland	3,022	700	254	130	2,448	459	198	110
Turkey	789	315	178	84	261	70	60	61
United Kingdom	12,439	2,536	1,487	548	12,846	2,194	993	335
Yugoslavia	648	168	88	43	438	96	41	19
Soviet Bloc	4,338	354	194	27	1,555	226	81	81
Bulgaria	258	15	73	857	34	2	1	2
Czechoslovakia	83	22	5	11	67	24	12	27
Germany, East	296	32	4	(2)	48	9	3	(2)
Hungary	78	28	2	3	129	6	2	2
Poland	682	70	143	9	365	98	39	11
Romania	504	66	1	2	560	13	1	(1)
U.S.S.R.	2,432	119	39	1	347	72	23	38
ASIA AND OCEANIA								
Total Asia and Oceania	70,285	11,294	4,700	1,691	95,510	9,103	2,987	1,846
Near East	14,964	1,423	532	228	18,543	10,515	312	131
Bahrain	297	12	8	7	35	8	3	2
Iran	300	326	156	38	64	67	51	24
Iraq	914	22	37	10	164	3	27	12
Israel	2,521	592	130	(2)	1,243	150	27	(2)
Jordan	727	63	20	1	2	(1)	92	8
Kuwait	976	62	41	3	86	25	124	42
Lebanon	296	64	45	28	19	13	3	4

Area and country	Exports, including re-exports 1980	1970	1960	1950	General imports 1980	1970	1960	1950
Oman	180	—	—	—	348	—	—	—
Qatar	157	—	—	—	115	—	—	—
Saudi Arabia	7,327	141	46	34	14,392	20	65	24
Syria	143	11	38	11	83	2	7	12
United Arab Emirates	1,077	—	—	—	1,993	—	—	—
Yemen Arab Republic	44	—	—	—	([1])	—	—	—
Far East	48,885	8,682	1,979	1	73,616	8,682	2,406	1,360
Bangladesh	158	—	—	—	85	—	—	—
Brunei	45	10[3]	—	—	329	([1 3])	—	—
Burma	34	—	—	—	15	—	—	—
China, People's Rep. of	3,603	—	—	37	1,895	([1])	([1])	146
China (Taiwan)	4,305	527	278	40	8,072	549	20	3
Hong Kong	2,635	406	125	104	5,389	944	139	5
India	1,748	574	642	217	1,202	298	228	259
Indonesia	1,302	266	100	85	6,022	182	216	156
Japan	21,823	4,652	1,447	418	37,655	5,875	1,149	182
Korea, South	5,116	643	231	([2])	5,227	370	5	([2])
Macao	1	—	—	—	154	—	—	—
Malaysia[4]	1,537	67	18	([2])	2,185	270	156	([2])
Pakistan	492	328	170	31	174	80	36	31
Philippines	1,787	373	307	247	1,974	472	307	236
Singapore	3,003	240	42	([2])	2,114	81	19	([2])
Sri Lanka	91	12	14	7	154	26	39	66
Thailand	1,170	155	71	29	946	100	56	75
Australia	5,242	986	423	115	2,464	611	142	141
New Zealand and Samoa	940	135	78	29	717	222	119	65
Papua New Guinea	55	18	1	([1])	50	12	([1])	—
AFRICA								
Total Africa	11,097	1,425	793	376	27,068	1,067	534	494
Algeria	717	62	28	16	5,038	10	1	5
Angola	268	38	11	7	904	68	26	13
Botswana	6	—	—	—	132	63	—	—
Burundi	4	—	—	—	28	—	—	—
Cameroon	152	19	—	5	625	25	6	—
Canary Islands	160	22	14	6	3	4	([1])	([1])
Congo	25	—	—	—	286	—	—	—
Egypt	2,159	77	151	34	397	23	32	55
Ethiopia	62	26	12	3	83	67	27	12
Gabon	128	7	—	—	432	9	—	—
Ghana	154	59	17	6	246	91	52	61
Guinea	([1])	7	—	—	96	77	—	—
Ivory Coast	130	36	—	—	345	92	—	—
Kenya	150	34	—	—	52	23	—	—
Liberia	128	46	36	25	113	51	39	21
Libya	813	108	43	([1])	5,301	39	([1])	([1])
Madagascar	16	7[5]	3	4	70	32[5]	13	8
Morocco	429	89	36	—	36	10	10	—
Mozambique	35	22	10	8	83	18	4	3
Nigeria	1,523	129	26	6	9,249	71	40	35
Rwanda	6	—	—	—	41	—	—	—
Senegal	42	8	—	—	1	1	—	—
Sierra Leone	26	8	—	—	45	8	—	—
South Africa[6]	2,912	563	288	129	2,445	290	108	142
Sudan	208	—	—	—	58	—	—	—
Swaziland	7	—	—	—	66	—	—	—
Tanzania	48	12	—	—	19	24	—	—
Uganda	7	4	—	—	101	48	—	—
Zaire	141	62	27	41	423	41	58	46
Zambia	68	—	—	—	114	—	—	—
Zimbabwe	32	—	—	—	109	—	—	—
Summary:								
Developed countries	135,840	29,877	13,250	6,010	141,070	29,259	8,605	3,858
Developing countries	88,972	12,993	7,131	4,193	116,454	10,442	5,965	4,767
Total	**233,739[8]**	**43,224[7]**	**20,575[7]**	**10,275[7]**	**260,982[8]**	**39,952[7]**	**14,654[7]**	**8,852[7]**

1. Less than $500,000. 2. Not applicable. 3. Includes Bhutan, Maldives, and Portuguese Timor. 4. Excludes Sarawak and Sabah, which are included with Singapore through 1960. 5. Includes French Indian Ocean areas. 6. South-West Africa, Bechuanaland, and Swaziland included for 1950 and 1960; South-West Africa (Namibia) included for 1970 and 1981. 7. Includes Communist areas in Europe and Asia. 8. Includes exports to Communist areas in Europe and Asia, $7,950,900,000; imports, $3,454,600,000. *Source:* Department of Commerce, Bureau of the Census, Foreign Trade Division.

Imports of Leading Commodities
(value in millions of dollars)

Commodity	1981	1980
Food and live animals	$15,238	$15,766
Cattle, except for breeding	182	228
Meat and preparations	1,996	2,346
Dairy products and eggs	357	321
Fish	2,962	2,612
Grains and feed for animals	381	331
Vegetables and fruit	2,587	2,048
Sugar, cane or beet	2,142	1,988
Coffee, green	2,622	3,872
Cocoa beans	466	395
Tea	133	131
Beverages and tobacco	3,138	2,785
Alcoholic beverages	2,399	2,232
Tobacco, unmanufactured	427	422
Crude materials, inedible, except fuels	11,193	10,516
Hides and skins, except fur skins	101	88
Fur skins, undressed	168	143
Crude rubber	778	816
Wood—simply worked	2,033	2,134
Wood pulp	1,778	1,725
Textile fibers and wastes	344	242
Industrial diamonds	118	119
Ores and metal scrap	3,838	3,716
Iron ore and concentrates	951	773
Nonferrous metal ores and concentrates	2,038	1,952
Precious metal ores and concentrates, except gold	419	558
Mineral fuels and related materials	81,417	82,924
Petroleum products	75,577	77,637
Natural gas	5,720	5,155
Animal and vegetable oils and fats	479	533
Chemicals	9,446	8,594
Organic chemicals	2,974	2,541
Inorganic chemicals	2,359	2,313
Medicinal and pharmaceutical products	583	509
Fertilizers, manufactured	1,181	1,104
Machinery and transport equipment	69,627	60,558
Machinery	38,212	31,915
Transport equipment	31,415	28,643
Automobiles, buses, trucks	22,111	19,163
Motor vehicle parts	4,106	4,972
Aircraft and parts	2,585	1,885
Other manufactured goods	26,179	23,760
Paper and manufactures	3,875	3,587
Glass, glassware, and pottery	1,349	1,228
Gem diamonds	2,198	2,252
Metals and manufactures	22,333	18,726
Iron and steel-mill products	10,347	6,693
Nonferrous metals	6,952	7,623
Precious metals, except gold	1,581	2,440
Other metal manufactures	4,170	3,732
Textile yarn and fabrics	3,046	2,499
Clothing	7,536	6,431
Footwear	3,019	2,809
Scientific and controlling instruments	1,655	1,418
Clocks and watches	1,276	1,127
Baby carriages, toys, games, and sporting goods	2,167	1,914
Artworks and antiques	2,056	2,672
Other transactions	7,296	7,225
Total	**$261,305**	**$244,871**

Exports of Leading Commodities
(value in millions of dollars)

Commodity	1981	1980
Food and live animals	$30,291	$27,744
Meat and preparations	1,482	1,293
Dairy products and eggs	433	255
Grains and preparations	19,457	18,079
Wheat, including wheat flour	8,073	6,586
Rice	1,527	1,285
Vegetables and fruit	3,314	2,930
Feed for animals	2,739	2,878
Beverages and tobacco	2,915	2,663
Cigarettes	1,229	1,055
Beverages	229	273
Crude materials, inedible, except fuels	20,993	23,791
Hides and skins, except fur skins	700	694
Soybeans, other oilseeds, peanuts	6,200	5,883
Synthetic rubber	625	695
Logs and lumber	2,059	2,675
Pulpwood and wood pulp	2,315	2,454
Raw cotton, excluding wastes	2,260	2,864
Ores and metal scrap	2,718	4,518
Mineral fuels and related materials	10,279	7,982
Coal	6,006	4,772
Petroleum and products	3,696	2,833
Animal and vegetable oils and fats	1,750	1,946
Soybean oil	489	705
Chemicals	21,187	20,740
Chemical elements and compounds	9,202	8,636
Medicines and pharmaceuticals	2,165	1,932
Fertilizers	1,735	2,265
Plastic materials and resins	3,809	3,884
Machinery and transport equipment	95,736	84,629
Machinery	62,946	55,790
Power generating machinery	9,465	8,428
Aircraft engines, parts	2,349	1,915
Automotive engines, parts	1,975	1,688
Agricultural machinery, including tractors, and parts	5,003	4,576
Office machines, computers	9,810	8,709
Metalworking machinery	2,158	1,756
Textile and leather machinery	685	693
Transport equipment	32,791	28,839
Motor vehicles and parts	16,214	14,590
Aircraft, spacecraft, accessories	14,738	12,816
Other manufactured goods	16,748	16,347
Tires and tubes	584	511
Paper and manufactures	2,961	2,831
Nonmetallic mineral manufactures	2,194	2,209
Metals and manufactures	9,616	10,167
Iron and steel-mill products	2,801	2,998
Nonferrous base metals	2,046	2,964
Other manufactures of metals	4,769	4,205
Textile yarns and fabrics	3,619	3,632
Clothing	1,232	1,203
Scientific instruments	5,980	5,256
Photographic supplies	1,501	1,507
Printed matter	1,297	1,097
Other transactions	8,428	8,496
Total	**$233,739**	**$220,783**

Source: Department of Commerce, Bureau of the Census, Foreign Trade Division.

The following material was compiled from information provided by the American Red Cross, the American Heart Association, and Edumed, Inc.

First aid is the rendering of prompt and knowledgeable treatment to a person who has been injured or suddenly taken ill and for whom no immediate medical attention is available. Depending on circumstances, effective first aid can mean the difference between life and death or between temporary and permanent disability. Artificial respiration and treatment for shock that sets in after a serious accident are also important factors in the success of first aid. The best course of action to follow after taking emergency measures is to summon assistance from the local police or fire department or from the nearest available doctor.

Burns

Burns are classified according to first degree (reddened skin), second degree (blisters develop), and third degree (deep tissue damage). Face, feet, and hands are critical areas. For first-degree and small second-degree burns, submerge affected area in cold water until pain subsides. Apply protective bandage. *Do not break blisters.* For third-degree burns, apply thick, sterile dressing, elevate the extremities, and obtain medical help immediately.

Eye burns: For burns of the eye, wash thoroughly with water for 15 minutes—hold the eyelid open and pour the water from the inside corner out. Put a clean pad over both closed eyelids (not only injured eye), bandage, and get medical help.

Poisoning

Speed and a clear head are vital in first aid for poison intake. If the victim loses consciousness, call for an emergency squad and give artificial respiration or cardiopulmonary resuscitation (CPR) if needed. If the victim is conscious and not in convulsions, dilute the swallowed poison with a glass of water or milk, but stop at signs of nausea.

Next, call your physician or local poison-control center. Be ready to supply information on what poison, and how much of it, was taken and the weight and age of the victim, and to take down instructions for treatment and antidotes. (Antidotes suggested on a poison-container label should not be given without approval by your physician or poison-control center.)

If vomiting occurs, save a vomit specimen along with the container label for the attending physician.

Shock

Shock is caused by many types of severe injuries and severe illnesses—poisoning, damage to the respiratory system, and loss of body fluids resulting from vomiting, dysentery, or burns. It is prudent to give shock care to all seriously injured individuals.

The symptoms are: pale or bluish skin that is cold to the touch (in the case of dark-skinned persons, examine the color of the mucous membranes inside the mouth or under the eyelids, or of the nail beds); moist or clammy skin; weakness of the injured person; rapid pulse; increased rate of breathing, which may be shallow, possibly deep, and irregular; severe thirst; vomiting or retching from nausea.

With possible neck or back injury, a victim should not be moved. Otherwise, a person in shock should be kept lying down and covered only enough to keep him from losing body heat. (*Do not* add extra heat, because raising the body's surface temperature is harmful.)

A patient with severe injuries of the lower face and jaw or who is unconscious should be placed on the side, with care taken to prevent suffocation from vomit and blood. When in doubt about the proper position, keep the person lying flat. Fluids may be given by mouth if the victim has no head or abdominal injury, if the victim would probably not need surgery and if medical help will not be available for an hour or more. But fluids *should not* be given to persons who are unconscious, are vomiting, or are having convulsions.

Cardiac Pulmonary Resuscitation (CPR) for Cardiac Arrest[1]

The most common signal of a heart attack is uncomfortable pressure, squeezing, fullness, or pain in the center of the chest behind the breastbone; others may be sweating, nausea, shortness of breath or a feeling of weakness. These signals may subside and return. If these signals persist, activate the emergency medical services system or take the victim to the nearest hospital with 24-hour emergency cardiac care.

Airway: Determine if the collapsed person is conscious by shaking his shoulder and shouting "Are you all right?". If there is no response, you must open his airway. Be sure he is lying flat on his back. If you have to roll him over, move his entire body as a total unit.

To open the airway, lift up his neck (or chin) gently with one hand while pushing down on the forehead with the other to tilt the head back. Place your ear close to the victim's mouth. Look at his chest and stomach for movement. Listen for sounds of breathing. Feel for breath on your cheek.

If none of these signs is present, the victim is not breathing.

Breathing: Use the mouth-to-mouth technique. Turn the hand on the victim's forehead and pinch his nose shut while maintaining the head tilt with the heel of the hand. The other hand should remain under the victim's neck (or chin), lifting up.

Immediately give four quick, full breaths in rapid succession.

Check Pulse: After giving four quick breaths, locate the victim's carotid pulse to see if his heart is beating. Take the hand that is under the victim's neck and locate the voice box. Slide the tips of your index and middle fingers into the groove beside the voice box. Feel for the pulse.

If you cannot find the pulse, you must provide artificial circulation in addition to rescue breathing. Activate the emergency medical services system.

Chest Compression: To perform external chest compression, kneel at the victim's side near his chest. Locate the notch at the lowest portion of the sternum (breastbone). Place the heel of one hand about 1 to 1 ½ inches from that tip and the other on top of the first. Be sure to keep the fingers off the chest wall. You may find it easier to do by interlocking the fingers.

Bring your shoulders directly over the victim's sternum as you compress downward, keeping your arms straight. Depress the sternum about 1 ½ to 2 inches for an adult victim. Relaxation must follow compression immediately and be of equal time. Do *not* remove your hands from the sternum.

If you are the only rescuer, you must provide both rescue breathing and chest compression at the ratio of 15 chest compressions to 2 quick breaths. You must compress at the rate of 80 times per minute, since you will lose compressions when you take time to interpose these breaths.

If there is another rescuer, position yourselves on opposite sides of the victim. One should interpose a breath after every fifth compression; the other should compress the chest at a rate of 60 compressions per minute.

For Infants and Small Children: Do not exaggerate the backward position of the head tilt because it might block breathing passages.

Do not try to pinch off the nose. Cover both the mouth and nose if the victim is not breathing. Use small breaths with less volume to inflate the lungs. Give one small breath every 3 seconds.

Only one hand is used for compression. The other is slipped under the child to provide a firm support for his back.

For infants, use only the *tips* of the index and middle fingers to compress the chest at mid-sternum, depressing between ½ to ¾ inch at a rate of 100 times per minute.

For small children, use only the *heel* of one hand to compress the chest at midsternum, depressing between ¾ and 1 ½ inches, depending on the size of the child. The rate should be 80 times per minute.

For both infants and small children, breaths should be interposed after every fifth chest compression.

Neck Fracture: If the victim is injured in a diving or automobile accident, the possibility of a neck fracture should be considered. The airway should be opened by using a modified jaw thrust, keeping the victim's head in a fixed, neutral position.

The Heimlich Maneuver[2]

Food-Choking

Food-choking is caused by a piece of food lodging in the throat creating a blockage of the airway, making it impossible for the victim to breathe or speak. The victim will die of strangulation in four minutes if you do not act to save him.

Using the Heimlich Maneuver, you exert pressure that forces the diaphragm upward, compresses the air in the lungs, and expels the object blocking the breathing passage.

The victim should see a physician immediately after the rescue. Performing the Maneuver could result in injury to the victim. However, he will survive only if his airway is quickly cleared.

If no help is at hand, victims should attempt to perform the Heimlich Maneuver on themselves by pressing their own fists upward into the abdomen as described.

What to Look for: The victim of food-choking: (1) Cannot speak or breathe, (2) turns blue, (3) collapses.

Performing the Heimlich Maneuver with the rescuer standing and the victim standing or sitting: Stand behind the victim and wrap your arms around his waist.

Place your fist thumb side against the victim's abdomen, slightly above the navel and below the rib cage.

Grasp your fist with your other hand and press into the victim's abdomen with a **quick upward thrust.**

(When the victim is sitting, the rescuer stands behind the victim's chair and performs the Maneuver in the same manner.)

With the rescuer kneeling and the victim lying face up: Facing the victim, kneel astride his hips.

With one of your hands on top of the other, place the heel of your bottom hand on the abdomen slightly above the navel and below the rib cage.

Press into the victim's abdomen with a **quick upward thrust.**

Repeat several times if necessary.

Drowning

The Heimlich Maneuver is the first step used to treat drowning in order to get water out of the victim's lungs.

With the rescuer kneeling and the victim lying face up. Facing the victim, kneel astride his or her hips. Turn the victim's head to the side. This allows water to drain out of the victim's mouth when you perform the Heimlich Maneuver.

With one of your hands on top of the other, place the heel of your bottom hand on the abdomen slightly above the navel and below the rib cage.

Press into the victim's abdomen with a **quick upward thrust.**

Repeat until water no longer flows out. If the victim has not started breathing, proceed with mouth to mouth resuscitation.

Severe Bleeding

Shock and loss of consciousness may occur from the rapid loss of as little as a quart of blood. A preferred technique is to direct pressure by hand over a dressing since it prevents loss of blood from the body without interference with normal blood circulation. In an emergency, in the absence of compresses, the bare hand or fingers may be used, but only until a compress can be applied.

Apply direct pressure by placing the palm of the hand on a dressing directly over the entire area of an open wound on any surface part of the body. In most instances this technique will stop the bleeding.

A thick pad of cloth held between the hand and the wound helps to control the bleeding by absorbing the blood and allowing it to clot.

Do not disturb blood clots after they have formed within the cloth. If blood soaks through the entire pad without clotting, do not remove the pad, but add additional thick layers of cloth and continue to direct pressure even more firmly.

(Continued on page 95)

1. © 1977 American Heart Association. 2. © 1976 Edumed, Inc. Teaching slides, posters, wallet cards, and other instructional materials on the Heimlich Maneuver are now available. To obtain these send a self-addressed, stamped envelope to: Edumed, Inc., Box 52, Cincinnati, Ohio 45201. Heimlich Maneuver instruction for the treatment of choking and drowning can be found in the book, "Dr. Heimlich's Home Guide to Emergency Medical Situations" by Henry J. Heimlich, M.D. and Lawrence Galton (Simon and Schuster).

Sources of Sodium in the Diet

Source: "Technical Paper of Sources of Sodium in the Diet," Water Quality Association

Introduction

Sodium is essential in human nutrition. It plays a vital role in growth, development, and in the maintenance of many bodily functions. Further, though our total sodium intake is usually far larger than the body requires, a person in normal health readily excretes the excess.

In certain physiological conditions, however, normal control functions fail, or are unable to deal with otherwise ordinary amounts of sodium. In such cases, certain drugs may be useful. In addition, the physician may also restrict the amount of sodium ingested.

A typical normal adult takes in 3000 to 6000 milligrams of sodium a day, which is approximately 1/10 to 1/5 ounce. Most of it comes from common salt (sodium chloride). But even unsalted foods, and some everyday medicinals, may contain substantial amounts.

Sodium in Natural Water Supplies

Every natural water supply contains sodium, with the concentration depending upon the exposure of the water to soluble sodium compounds present in the earth or in the atmosphere. Rainwater may contain only a few milligrams per liter (mg/l) of sodium, while water from brackish or saline wells may contain several thousand mg/l. A liter is the equivalent of 1.0567 quarts or just over four 8-ounce glassfuls.

The sodium content of a natural water supply can be determined only by an actual analysis of that supply, but the sodium added by ion exchange water softening can be calculated from the hardness in the supply.

Water Softening and Sodium

It is well known that in ion exchange water softening the chief components of water hardness (calcium and magnesium ions) are removed along with other heavy metal cations and are exchanged for sodium.

Sodium is exchanged not only in household ion exchange softening, but significantly, in ion exchange softening conducted **on a community or municipal basis.** In municipal softening, each milligram of hardness as $CaCO_3$ is replaced by 0.46 milligrams of sodium as Na.

Compared to the sodium added by softening the "average" water **cow's milk** (517 mg/l) and **skim milk** (541 mg/l) contain over ten times this much sodium; **low fat milk,** with 2% dry milk solids added (636 mg/l), contains over 12 times this much sodium, and **human milk** (170 mg/l) contains over three times this much sodium.

Sodium in Common Foods and Beverages

The data in the following table demonstrate the usual range of sodium in common foods. Despite the care with which the table was prepared, it cannot be totally accurate. Variations in sodium content may be even greater than indicated. However, the table does show an important principle: The amount of sodium almost invariably increases with the degree of preparation.

For additional information, the Water Quality Association offers an "Easy-to-Use Guide to Sodium in Food, Medicine, and Water." Individual copies at $1.50 each may be obtained by writing Water Quality Association, 4151 Naperville Road, Lisle, Illinois 60532.

Typical Sodium Contents of Some Common Foods

Food	*Degree of prep.	mg. Sodium per serving	Serving or measure	Weight basis
Apples	R	0.5–3.5	1 medium	3 per lb
Apricots, fresh	R	0.9	2 medium	10 per lb
Asparagus, spears	R	3.5	½ cup	2 cups cooked per lb
Asparagus, spears, canned	O	560	½ cup	1 ½ cup/14.5 oz
Asparagus, frozen	O	1.3–12	½ cup	2 cups/10 oz
Bacon, raw	O	103	1 slice	30 slices per lb
Baking Powder, Phosphate	O	243	1 teaspoon	1 teasp./2.7 g
Bananas	R	0.6–6	1 medium	3 per lb
Beans, baked Navy and Pork	O	950	¾ cup	1 ½ cup/14 oz
Beans, canned, baked	O	1130	¾ cup	2 cups/18 oz
Beans, w/tomato sauce	O	796	¾ cup	1 ½ cup/14 oz
Beans, green	R	0.1–2.3	½ cup	3 cups cooked per lb
Beans, green, canned	O	465	½ cup	2 cups/lb
Beans, green, frozen	O	1.0–1.5	½ cup	3 cups/lb
Beans, lima	R	0.2	½ cup	3 cups/lb

Food	*Degree of prep.	mg. Sodium per serving	Serving or measure	Weight basis
Beans, lima, canned	O	235	½ cup	3 cups/lb
Beans, lima, frozen	O	114–235	½ cup	3 cups/lb
Beef, corned	O	1850	5 oz.	—
Beef, hash, corned, canned	O	610	½ cup	2 cups/lb
Beef, dried	O	1220	1 oz	—
Beef, lean	R	72–92	5 oz	—
Beef, lean, Koshered	R	2270	5 oz	—
Beef, steak	R	98	5 oz	—
Beef, stew, canned	D	22	1 cup	2 cups/lb
Beets	R	32–124	½ cup	2 cups/lb
Beets, canned	O	41	½ cup	2 cups/lb
Beverages, alcoholic				
Beer	O	28	12 fl oz	—
Beer, dark	O	15	12 fl oz	—
Beer, light	O	56	12 fl oz	—
Beer & ale, various	O	3.1–80	12 fl oz	—
Brandy	O	0.9	1 fl oz	—
Gin	O	.24	1 fl oz	—
Rum	O	0.6	1 fl oz	—
Whiskey, blended	O	.09	1 fl oz	—
Whiskey, bonded	O	.03	1 fl oz	—
Wine (average)	O	2.1	1 fl oz	—
Wine Port	O	1.2	1 fl oz	—
Wine, Sauterne	O	3.0	1 fl oz	—
Beverages, carbonated*				
Coca-Cola		3.5–7.0	12 fl oz	—
Creme Soda		3.5	12 fl oz	—
Dr. Pepper		10.5	12 fl oz	—
Ginger Ale		7–28	12 fl oz	—
Canada Dry		63	12 fl oz	—
Grape Soda		42	12 fl oz	—
Lemon-Lime Soda		24.5	12 fl oz	—
Orange Crush		7	12 fl oz	—
Orange Soda		81	12 fl oz	—
Pepsi-Cola		35–49	12 fl oz	—
Root Beer		3.5–28	12 fl oz	—
Royal Crown Cola		17.5	12 fl oz	—
Seven-Up		3.5	12 fl oz	—
Strawberry Soda		17.5	12 fl oz	—
White Rock		3.5	12 fl oz	—
Blueberries	R	1	1 cup	1 cup/5 oz
Bouillon cube, beef	O	908	1 cube	15 cubes/2 oz
Bread, Rye & Wheat	O	112	1 slice	24 slices/lb
Bread, White	O	112	1 thin slice	21 slices/lb
Bread, White	O	129	1 reg. slice	18 slices/lb
Bread, White enriched	O	161	1 reg. slice	18 slices/lb
Bread, Whole Wheat	O	152–211	1 slice	20 slices/lb
Broccoli	R	11–18	¾ cup	8 stalks/lb
Broccoli, frozen	O	15	¾ cup	2 cups/10 oz
Brussels Sprouts	R	6.4–8.5	½ cup	2 cups/10 oz
Brussels Sprouts, frozen	O	6.4–23	½ cup	2 cups/10 oz
Butter, salted	O	42	1 pat	96 pats or teasp./lb
Butter, sweet	O	1	1 pat	96 pats or teasp./lb
Cabbage	R	3.2–14	½ cup shredded R	3½ cups shredded/lb
Cabbage		4.5–19	½ cup cooked	2½ cups cooked/lb
Candy				
Caramel, soft	D	16	1 pc.	50 pcs./14 oz
Milk Chocolate	O	18	1 bar-¾ oz	
Gum Drops	O	36	½ cup	2½ cups/lb
Bar, Baby Ruth	O	60	1 bar-1¼ oz	—
Bar, Milky Way	O	78	1 bar-1¼ oz	—
Carrots	R	68	½ cup	2¼ cups diced or shredded/lb
Carrots		75	½ cup cooked	2 cups cooked/lb
Carrots, canned	O	318	½ cup	2 cups/lb
Cashew nuts, roasted in oil, salted	O	226	4 oz	—
Catsup, tomato	O	204	1 tablespoon	—
Celery	R	172–259	1 cup raw diced	2½ cups/lb
Celery flakes, dehyd.	O	34.5	1 tablespoon	—

Food	*Degree of prep.	mg. Sodium per serving	Serving or measure	Weight basis
Celery Salt	O	672	1 teaspoon	—
Celery Seed	O	3	1 teaspoon	—
Cereals				
Bran, all-bran	O	340–395	1 oz	1 pkg./1 oz
Cornflakes	O	186	1 cup-1 oz	1 cup/oz
Oats, Oatmeal	R	0.2	¼ cup uncooked	5½ cups/lb
Rice, Puffed	O	.13	½ oz.-1 cup	2 cups/oz
Wheat Flakes	O	367	1 cup-1 oz	1 cup/oz
Grape Nuts	O	186	¼ cup-1 oz	¼ cup/oz
Muffets	O	1.5	2 biscuits	24 biscuits/lb
Puffed Wheat	O	.56	½ oz.-1 cup	2 cups/oz
Shredded Wheat	O	0.5	2 biscuits	19 biscuits/lb
Cheese, Am. Swiss	O	201	1 slice	16 slices/lb
Cheese, Cheddar	O	173–198	1 slice	16 slices/lb
Cheese, Cottage	O	330	½ cup	16 fl. oz./lb
Cheese, Cream, Phila.	O	212	3 oz pkg.	—
Cheese, Parmesan powd.	O	14.3	1 teaspoon	—
Cheese, Velveeta Cheese	O	910	1"x1¼"x2"	—
Cherries	R	4.5	1 cup	3 cups/lb
Cherries, sweet, dark canned	D	1.2	½ cup	16 fl oz/1 lb 1 oz
Chicken	R	106	5 oz	—
Chicken, light meat	R	77	5 oz	—
Chicken, light meat breast	R	111	5 oz	—
Chicken, dark meat	R	114	5 oz	—
Chicken, leg meat	R	156	5 oz	—
Chocolate syrup, Hershey	O	10.6	1 tablespoon	13 fl oz/lb
Cloves, whole	O	1.4	10 whole	—
Coffee, instant, Nescafe, dry	O	.84	1 teaspoon	—
Coffee, reg. roasted dry	O	0.2	2 tablespoons	—
Corn, sweet	R	.15–.7	½ cup	—
Corn, sweet, frozen	R	65–80	½ cup	3 cups/lb
Corn, sweet yellow, canned	O	252	½ cup	2 cups/lb
Crackers, Graham	O	100	1 dbl. cracker	32 dbl. crackers/lb
Crackers, Rye, Ry-Krisp	O	95	1 triple cracker	36 triple crackers/8 oz
Crackers, Soda	O	138	1–4 pc. cracker	36x4 crackers/lb
Cucumber, pickle, dill	O	318	1 pickle ½" diam. x 2½"	—
Duck, breast	R	97	5 oz	—
Duck, leg	R	136	5 oz	—
Eggs, whole	R	36–62	1 med.	10 avg. eggs w/out shell/lb
Frankfurters	O	610	1 med.	8/lb
Fruit cocktail, canned in syrup	O	10	½ cup	2 cups/lb
Goose, breast	R	108	5 oz	
Goose, leg	R	136	5 oz	—
Ham, cured	O	1560	5 oz	—
Ice Cream	O	43–68	¼ pt	1 pt/9.5 oz
Lamb (Lean)	R	128	5 oz	—
Lamb chop	R	129–139	5 oz	—
Lamb leg	R	111	5 oz	—
Liver, beef	R	75–492	5 oz	—
Liver, calf	R	156	5 oz	—
Liver, chicken	R	119	5 oz	—
Margarine	O	52	1 pat	96 pats or teasp./lb
Mayonnaise	O	560	½ cup	2½ cups/lb
Milk, Cows				
Milk, Condensed, sweeted	O	444	1 cup	—
Milk, Evaporated	O	246	1 cup	—
Milk, Whole	R	122–127	1 cup	—
Mushrooms, sliced	R	3–7	¼ cup	1¼ cup/lb
Mushrooms, canned	O	283	¼ cup	1¼ cup/lb
Mustard, Prep paste	O	57	1 teaspoon	—
Olives, ripe, pickled	O	33	1 medium	8/oz
Olives, stuffed, pickled	O	70	1 medium	11/oz
Onion, cooked	O	8–11	½ cup	2 cups/lb
Onion Soup, cream of canned	D	72	1 cup	—
Parsley flakes	O	4.4	1 tablespoon	—
Parsnips	R	9–11	½ cup	2 cups/lb
Peanut butter	O	16	1 tablespoon	—

Food	*Degree of prep.	mg. Sodium per serving	Serving or measure	Weight basis
Peanuts, roasted in oil and salted	O	520	1/4 lb	—
Peas	R	1.1–9.1	1/4 cup	1 cup/lb
Peas, frozen	O	27–295	1/2 cup	1 cup/lb
Peas, canned, less liquor	O	306	1/2 cup	2 cups/lb
Pea, Soup, canned	D	28–69	1 cup	—
Pork, lean	R	82	5 oz	—
Pork, med. lean	R	97	5 oz	—
Pork, 10% protein	R	60	5 oz	—
Potatoes	R	7.5–9.8	1 medium	3/lb
Potato chips	O	384	1/4 lb	—
Pretzels	O	1925	1/4 lb	—
Raisins, seedless	O	30	1 cup	3 1/4 cups/lb
Salmon, canned	O	1190	1–7 3/4 oz can	—
Sardines, canned, various	O	424–806	1–3 3/4 oz can	—
Sauerkraut, canned	O	690	1/2 cup	2 cups/lb
Sausage-breakfast	O	1000	1/4 lb	—
Sausage-bolona		370	1 slice	16 slices/lb
Sausage-pork		840–870	1/4 lb or 4 links	—
Shrimp	R	159	1/4 lb	—
Spinach	R	24–165	1/2 cup	1 1/2 to 2 cups/lb.
Spinach, frozen	O	30–43	1/2 cup	3 cups/lb.
Sweet Potatoes	R	13.4	1/2 cup	2 1/2 cups/lb
Sweet Potatoes, canned	O	66	1/2 cup	—
Tomato juice	O	250	1/2 cup	—
Tomato Soup, canned diluted as served	O	900	1 cup	—
Tongue, beef	R	71–142	5 oz	—
Tuna, canned	O	1580	7 oz can	—
Turkey, breast	R	57	5 oz	—
Turkey, leg meat	R	131	5 oz	—
Veal, fillet	R	152	5 oz	—
Veal, lean	R	68	5 oz	—
Veal, muscle	R	163–278	5 oz	—
Worcestershire Sauce	O	84	1 teaspoon	—

NOTE: 1 level teaspoon of table salt weighs approximately 7,000 milligrams. This amount of salt would contain approx. 2800 mg. of sodium. R = Raw or fresh foods, O = Ordinary commercial production processes, D = Dietetic foods. Also note that in beverages, considerable variation may be found between bottling plants, depending on the sodium content of the local water.

Sodium in Drinking Water of the 50 Largest Cities

State and city†	Sodium in city water (mg per 8-oz glass)	Sodium added by ion exchange softening* (mg per 8-oz glass)
Alabama		
Birmingham	2.1	9.4
Arizona		
Phoenix (74%)	25	26.9
Tucson	10.4	20
California		
Long Beach	29.3	9.2
Los Angeles	16	16.5
Oakland	2.8	12.2
San Diego (57%)	23.6	17.9
San Francisco	1	3.3
San Jose (80%)	6.8	21.9
Colorado		
Denver	3.5	8
Washington, D.C.	2.1	14.6
Florida		
Jacksonville	3.3	27.9
Miami	4	8.2
Georgia		
Atlanta	0.5	2.6
Hawaii		
Honolulu (57%)	9.6	6.6
Illinois		
Chicago	0.9	14.4
Indiana		
Indianapolis	2.6	29.5
Kentucky		
Louisville	6.1	10.8
Louisiana		
New Orleans	4.2	8.9
Maryland		
Baltimore	0.8	6.1
Massachusetts		
Boston	0.5	1.4
Michigan		
Detroit	0.9	10.8
Minnesota		
Minneapolis	1.4	7
Missouri		
Kansas City	8.9	7.5

State and city†	Sodium in city water (mg per 8-oz glass)	Sodium added by ion exchange softening* (mg per 8-oz glass)
St. Louis	5.2	8.5
Nebraska		
Omaha	15.3	15.6
New Jersey		
Newark	0.8	4.2
New Mexico		
Albuquerque	10.4	10.6
New York		
Buffalo	2.2	14.4
New York City	1.4	3.5
North Carolina		
Charlotte	0.9	3
Ohio		
Cincinnati	4.2	16.5
Cleveland	2.6	12.5
Columbus	4.2	11.1
Toledo	2.8	7.3
Oklahoma		
Oklahoma City	19.8	15.1
Tulsa	1	9.4
Oregon		
Portland	0.2	.04
Pennsylvania		
Philadelphia	1.4	9.2
Pittsburgh	2.6	7.5
Tennessee		
Memphis	2.6	4.2
Nashville	.09	8.5
Texas		
Austin	7.8	11.8
Dallas	9.2	8.5
El Paso (97%)	28.3	10.8
Fort Worth	4.7	16
Houston (83%)	19.3	7.5
San Antonio (unknown %)	1.8	23.8
Washington		
Seattle	0.3	2.3
Wisconsin		
Milwaukee	0.9	13.9

†100% of supply unless noted. *Based on softening to zero hardness.

Physicians, Dentists, and Nurses
(numbers in thousands)

Profession	1979	1978	1977	1976	1975	1970	1965	1960
Physicians, number	473	454	438	426	409	348	305	275
Rate per 100,000 resident population[1]	210	204	198	194	188	166	153	148
Active (exc. physicians in Federal serv.)	399	381	362	351	338	282	255	n.a.
Rate per 100,000 resident population[1]	177	172	165	161	155	135	129	n.a.
Doctors of medicine[2]	455	437	421	409	394	334	292	260
Doctors of osteopathy	18	17	17[3]	16[3]	15[3]	14	13	14
Physicians admitted to U.S. as immigrants[4]	3.0	4.4	7.1	8.1	7.1	3.2	2.0	1.6
Dentists, number[5]	124	121	118	n.a.	n.a.	116	109	103
Active (excl. dentists in Federal service)	118	115	113	110	108	96	86	85
Rate per 100,000 resident population[1]	54	53	52	52	50	47	45	47
Nurses, number (active registered)	1,075	1,059	1,011	961	906	700	613	504
Rate per 100,000 resident population[1]	490	487	465	449	427	345	319	282

1. Based on Bureau of the Census population estimates. 2. Excludes non-Federal physicians with temporary foreign addresses. 3. Estimated. 4. Immigration and Naturalization Service figures. 5. Beginning 1960, excludes graduates of year stated. Beginning in 1976, excludes inactive dentists. NOTE: n.a. = not available. *Source:* Statistical Abstract of the United States, 1981.

Physicians—Median Earnings
(in thousands of dollars)

Field of practice	Unincorporated				Incorporated			
	1976	1977	1978	1979	1976	1977	1978	1979
All physicians[1]	52.4	52.6	54.7	60.6	75.6	78.3	82.3	86.3
General practitioners	43.7	46.0	45.7	50.5	58.7	63.4	71.0	70.8
Internists	53.6	59.6	53.7	69.3	66.9	73.5	73.6	79.8
General surgeons	61.4	56.7	62.5	65.8	78.4	81.6	88.8	88.6
Obstetricians-gynecologists	63.4	57.3	63.7	75.8	89.2	92.9	88.4	95.3
Pediatricians	45.9	49.2	49.1	53.7	56.6	62.5	67.1	67.0
Family practitioners	50.7	54.8	58.1	67.3	59.4	69.4	66.9	68.0
Orthopedic surgeons	n.a.	71.7	n.a.	96.7	n.a.	98.8	n.a.	119.9

1. Includes specialties not shown separately. Unincorporated: Represents net income from practice after payment of tax-deductible professional expenses but before payment of income taxes. Incorporated: Comprises office-based, patient care doctors of medicine (M.D.'s) of all ages who are shareholders of a medical corporation. Earnings include salary, bonuses (if any), and funds set aside by corporation for individual's retirement. NOTE: n.a. = not available. *Source: Statistical Abstract of the United States, 1981.*

Estimated Safe and Adequate Daily Dietary Intakes of Additional Selected Vitamins and Minerals[1]

	Age (years)	Vitamins			Trace Elements[2]						Electrolytes		
		Vitamin K (µg)	Biotin (µg)	Pantothenic Acid (mg)	Copper (mg)	Manganese (mg)	Fluoride (mg)	Chromium (mg)	Selenium (mg)	Molybdenum (mg)	Sodium (mg)	Potassium (mg)	Chloride (mg)
Infants	0–0.5	12	35	2	0.5–0.7	0.5–0.7	0.1–0.5	0.01–0.04	0.01–0.04	0.03–0.06	115–350	350–925	275–700
	0.5–1	10–20	50	3	0.7–1.0	0.7–1.0	0.2–1.0	0.02–0.06	0.02–0.06	0.04–0.08	250–750	425–1275	400–1200
Children and Adolescents	1–3	15–30	65	3	1.0–1.5	1.0–1.5	0.5–1.5	0.02–0.08	0.02–0.08	0.05–0.1	325–975	550–1650	500–1500
	4–6	20–40	85	3–4	1.5–2.0	1.5–2.0	1.0–2.5	0.03–0.12	0.03–0.12	0.06–0.15	450–1350	775–2325	700–2100
	7–10	30–60	120	4–5	2.0–2.5	2.0–3.0	1.5–2.5	0.05–0.2	0.05–0.2	0.1–0.3	600–1800	1000–3000	925–2775
	11+	50–100	100–200	4–7	2.0–3.0	2.5–5.0	1.5–2.5	0.05–0.2	0.05–0.2	0.15–0.5	900–2700	1525–4575	1400–4200
Adults		70–140	100–200	4–7	2.0–3.0	2.5–5.0	1.5–4.0	0.05–0.2	0.05–0.2	0.15–0.5	1100–3300	1875–5625	1700–1500

1. Because there is less information on which to base allowances, these figures are not given in the main table of the RDA and are provided in the form of ranges of recommended intakes. 2. Since the toxic levels for many trace elements may be only several times usual intakes, the upper levels for the trace elements given in this table should not be habitually exceeded. NOTE: µg—microgram; mg—milligram. *Source: Recommended Dietary Allowances*, Ninth Edition (1980), with the permission of the National Academy of Sciences, Washington, D.C.

Recommended Dietary Allowances

The Recommended Dietary Allowances (RDA) given in the tables are the latest established by the National Academy of Sciences Committee on Dietary Allowances as recommendations for the average daily amounts of nutrients for healthy population groups. They should not be confused with requirements for a specific individual.

Differences in the nutrient requirements of individuals are ordinarily unknown. Therefore, RDA (except for energy) are estimated to exceed the requirements of most individuals. Intake below the recommended allowance for a nutrient is not necessarily inadequate, but the risk of its being inadequate is increased if intake falls below the level recommended as safe.

Special needs for nutrients arising from such problems as premature birth, inherited metabolic disorders, infections, chronic diseases, and the use of medications are not covered by the RDA.

These dietary allowances form the basis for the RDA set by the Food and Drug Administration and are found on food labels as "U.S.R.D.A." The nutritional label lists the percentage of the RDA for protein and any of 17 vitamins and minerals found in the product. This does not represent all the required nutrients.

Because individual foods are not nutritionally complete, RDA should be met by eating a wide variety of selected foods in your diet.

Allowance for Energy

The recommended allowances for energy are estimates of the average needs of population groups, not recommended intakes for individuals. These needs vary from person to person and are not easily predictable without detailed information about physical characteristics and activity of the individual. Hence, the average energy needs for each age and sex are provided only as guidelines and are not repeated in the general table of recommended allowances.

Adjustments in RDA

The RDA does not take into account special needs that may require special attention. Some of these considerations are:

Physical Activity. This increases energy expenditure. Here, the increased need for a nutrient that may be related to carbohydrate utilization is generally met by consuming a larger amount of food. Attention must be given to salt and water losses due to sweating, which if prolonged, may lead to a loss of other nutrients.

Climate. There is little evidence that nutrient requirements, other than those for energy, are altered when individuals are exposed to heat or cold. Therefore, adjustments in dietary allowances to compensate for temperature changes are not considered necessary. However, exposures to temperatures that increase sweating will also increase the need for water and salt.

Aging. It is evident from studies of adult populations that body composition changes throughout life, with fat increasing and metabolically active tissues being slowly reduced. This reduction accounts for the fall in basal energy metabolism, often with an even greater reduction in physical activity.

As a result, less food is needed to meet energy requirements, and, unless food choices are made with great care, the amounts of essential nutrients may fall below desirable levels. It is important for older people to make sure that the smaller quantities of food that they eat are selected to provide the needed amounts of essential nutrients.

It is also important that physical activity be continued in adult life and into old age.

Mean Heights and Weights and Recommended Energy Intake

Category	Age (years)	Weight (lb)	Weight (kg)	Height (in.)	Height (cm)	Energy needs (with range) (kcal)	Energy needs (MJ)
Infants	0.0–0.5	13	6	24	60	kg X 115 (95–145)	kg X .48
	0.5–1.0	20	9	28	71	kg X 105 (80–135)	kg X .44
Children	1–3	29	13	35	90	1300 (900–1800)	5.5
	4–6	44	20	44	112	1700 (1300–2300)	7.1
	7–10	62	28	52	132	2400 (1650–3300)	10.1
Males	11–14	99	45	62	157	2700 (2000–3700)	11.3
	15–18	145	66	69	176	2800 (2100–3900)	11.8
	19–22	154	70	70	177	2900 (2500–3300)	12.2
	23–50	154	70	70	178	2700 (2300–3100)	11.3
	51–75	154	70	70	178	2400 (2000–2800)	10.1
	76 +	154	70	70	178	2050 (1650–2450)	8.6
Females	11–14	101	46	62	157	2200 (1500–3000)	9.2
	15–18	120	55	64	163	2100 (1200–3000)	8.8
	19–22	120	55	64	163	2100 (1700–2500)	8.8
	23–50	120	55	64	163	2000 (1600–2400)	8.4
	51–75	120	55	64	163	1800 (1400–2200)	7.6
	76 +	120	55	64	163	1600 (1200–2000)	6.7
Pregnancy						+ 300	
Lactation						+ 500	

The energy allowances for the young adults are for men and women doing light work. The allowances for the two older age groups represent mean energy needs over these age spans, allowing for a 2% decrease in basal (resting) metabolic rate per decade and a reduction in activity of 200 kcal/day for men and women between 51 and 75 years, 500 kcal for men over 75 years, and 400 kcal for women over 75. The customary range of daily energy output is shown for adults in parentheses, and is based on a variation in energy needs of ± 400 kcal at any one age, emphasizing the wide range of energy intakes appropriate for any group of people. Energy allowances for children through age 18 are based on median energy intakes of children these ages followed in longitudinal growth studies. The values in parentheses are 10th and 90th percentile of energy intake, to indicate the range of energy consumption among children of these ages. NOTE: kg—kilogram; cm—centimeter; kcal—kilocalorie; MJ—megajoule. 1 kcal is equivalent to 4.18 kilojoules. 1 megajoule is equal to 1000 kilojoules. *Source: Recommended Dietary Allowances,* Ninth Edition (1980), with the permission of the National Academy of Sciences, Washington, D.C.

Desirable Weights[1]

Height[2] in	Height[2] cm	Weight[3] Men lb		Weight[3] Men kg		Weight[3] Women lb		Weight[3] Women kg	
58	147	—	—	—	—	102	(92–119)	46	(42–54)
60	152	—	—	—	—	107	(96–125)	49	(44–57)
62	158	123	(112–141)	56	(51–64)	113	(102–131)	51	(46–59)
64	163	130	(118–148)	59	(54–67)	120	(108–138)	55	(49–63)
66	168	136	(124–156)	62	(56–71)	128	(114–146)	58	(52–66)
68	173	145	(132–166)	66	(60–75)	136	(122–154)	62	(55–70)
70	178	154	(140–174)	70	(64–79)	144	(130–163)	65	(59–74)
72	183	162	(148–184)	74	(67–84)	152	(138–173)	69	(63–79)
74	188	171	(156–194)	78	(71–88)	—	—	—	—
76	193	181	(164–204)	82	(74–93)	—	—	—	—

1. Desirable weights for men and women of different heights, based on evidence from insurance statistics of weight in relation to longevity. According to the National Center for Health Statistics, the average American male adult is 70 in. tall (178 cm) and the average female is 64 in. tall (163 cm). Accordingly, the average desirable weights are 154 lb (70 kg) and 120 lb (55 kg) throughout adult life. 2. Without shoes. 3. Without clothes. Average weight ranges in parentheses. *Source: Recommended Dietary Allowances,* 9th Edition (1980), with permission of the National Academy of Sciences, Washington, D.C.

SEVERE BLEEDING

(Continued from page 88)

Tourniquet Warning. The use of a tourniquet is dangerous, and the tourniquet should be used only for a severe life-threatening hemorrhage that cannot be controlled by other means.

The decision to apply a tourniquet is in reality a decision to risk sacrifice of a limb in order to save life. Once a tourniquet is applied, care by a physician is imperative. (NOTE: A tourniquet should be at least two inches wide.)

Recommended Daily Dietary Allowances[1]

Designed for the maintenance of good nutrition of practically all healthy persons in the U.S. (revised 1979)

						Fat-Soluble Vitamins			Water-Soluble Vitamins							Minerals					
Persons	Age (years)	Wgt. (lbs)	Wgt. (kg)	Hgt. (in.)	Hgt. (cm)	Vitamin A μg R.E.[2]	Vitamin D (μg)[3]	Vitamin E (mgα T.E.)[4]	Ascorbic Acid (mg)	Folacin[5] (μg)	Niacin[5] (mg)	Riboflavin (mg)	Thiamin (mg)	Vitamin B_6 (mg)	Vitamin B_{12} (μg)	Calcium (mg)	Phosphorus (mg)	Iodine (μg)	Iron (mg)	Magnesium (mg)	Zinc (mg)
Infants	0.0–0.5	13	6	24	60	420	10	3	35	30	6	0.4	0.3	0.3	0.5[6]	360	240	40	10	50	3
	0.5–1.0	20	9	28	71	400	10	4	35	45	8	0.6	0.5	0.6	1.5	540	360	50	15	70	5
Children	1–3	29	13	35	90	400	10	5	45	100	9	0.8	0.7	0.9	2.0	800	800	70	15	150	10
	4–6	44	20	44	112	500	10	6	45	200	11	1.1	0.9	1.3	2.5	800	800	90	10	200	10
	7–10	62	28	52	132	700	10	7	45	300	16	1.4	1.2	1.6	3.0	800	800	120	10	250	10
Males	11–14	99	45	62	157	1,000	10	8	50	400	18	1.6	1.4	1.8	3.0	1,200	1,200	150	18	350	15
	15–18	145	66	69	176	1,000	10	10	60	400	18	1.7	1.4	2.0	3.0	1,200	1,200	150	18	400	15
	19–22	154	70	70	177	1,000	7.5	10	60	400	19	1.7		2.2	3.0	800	800	150	10	350	15
	23–50	154	70	70	178	1,000	5	10	60	400	18	1.6	1.4	2.2	3.0	800	800	150	10	350	15
	51+	154	70	70	178	1,000	5	10	60	400	16	1.4	1.2	2.2	3.0	800	800	150	10	350	15
Females	11–14	101	46	62	157	800	10	8	50	400	15	1.3	1.1	1.8	3.0	1,200	1,200	150	18	300	15
	15–18	120	55	64	163	800	10	8	60	400	14	1.3	1.1	2.0	3.0	1,200	1,200	150	18	300	15
	19–22	120	55	64	163	800	7.5	8	60	400	14	1.3	1.1	2.0	3.0	800	800	150	18	300	15
	23–50	120	55	64	163	800	5	8	60	400	13	1.2	1.0	2.0	3.0	800	800	150	18	300	15
	51+	120	55	64	163	800	5	8	60	400	13	1.2	1.0	2.0	3.0	800	800	150	10	300	15
Pregnant	—	—	—	—	—	+200	+5	+2	+20	+400	+2	+0.3	+0.4	+0.6	+1.0	+400	+400	+25	[7]	+150	+5
Lactating	—	—	—	—	—	+400	+5	+3	+40	+100	+5	+0.5	+0.5	+0.5	+1.0	+400	+400	+50	[7]	+150	+10

1. Allowances provide for individual variances among most normal persons living in the United States under usual environmental stresses. 2. Retinol equivalents. 1 Retinol equivalent = 1 μg retinol. 3. As cholecalciferol. 10 μg cholecalciferol = 400 I.U. vitamin D. 4. αtocopherol equivalents. 1 mg d-α-tocopherol = 1 α T.E. 5. Although expressed as niacin, the average 1 mg of niacin is derived from each 60 mg of dietary tryptophan. 6. The RDA for vitamin B12 in infants is based on average concentration of the vitamin in human milk. 7. Cannot be met by ordinary diets: use of supplemental iron is recommended. NOTE: mg—milligram; μg—microgram; IU—International Units; lbs—pounds; Wgt.—Weight; Hgt.—Height. *Source: Recommended Dietary Allowances*, Ninth Edition (1980), with the permission of the National Academy of Sciences, Washington, D.C.

Calories, Minerals, and Vitamins of Selected Foods

Food and amount	Energy (calories)	Nutrients: Protein (gm)	Nutrients: Fat (gm)	Minerals: Calcium (mg)	Minerals: Iron (mg)	Vitamins: Vitamin A (IU)	Vitamins: Vitamin B_1 (thiamin) (mg)	Vitamins: Vitamin B_2 (riboflavin) (mg)	Vitamins: Niacin (mg)	Vitamins: Vitamin C (ascorbic acid) (mg)
Apple, 1 medium, raw	80	—	1	10	.4	120	.04	.03	.1	6
Applesauce, 1 cup, canned, unsweetened	100	—	—	10	1.2	100	.05	.02	.1	2
Bacon, 2 slices, crisp	85	4	8	2	.5	—	.08	.05	.8	—
Banana, 1 medium	100	1	—	10	.8	230	.06	.07	.8	12
Beans, snap green, 1 cup cooked	30	2	—	63	.8	680	.09	.11	.6	15
Beans, red kidney, 1 cup canned	230	15	1	74	4.6	10	.13	.10	1.5	—
Beans, baked, pork and molasses, 1 cup	385	16	12	161	5.9	—	.15	.10	1.3	—
Beef cuts, cooked: Chuck, boned, 3 ounces	245	23	16	10	2.9	30	.04	.18	3.6	—
Hamburger, 3 ounces	235	20	17	9	2.6	30	.07	.17	4.4	—
Rib roast, 3 ounces boned	375	17	33	8	2.2	70	.05	.13	3.1	—
Round, 3 ounces boned	220	24	13	10	3.0	20	.07	.19	4.8	—
Sirloin, 3 ounces boned	330	20	27	9	2.5	50	.05	.15	4.0	—
Beef stew with vegetables, 1 cup	220	16	11	29	2.9	2,400	.15	.17	4.7	17
Beets, 1 cup cooked	55	2	—	24	.9	30	.05	.07	.5	10
Breads: Cracked wheat, average slice	65	2	1	22	.5	—	.08	.06	.8	—
Italian, average slice, enriched	85	3	—	5	.7	—	.12	.07	1.0	—
Raisin, average slice enriched	65	2	1	18	.6	—	.09	.06	.6	—
Rye (American), average slice	60	2	—	19	.5	—	.07	.05	.7	—
White, average slice enriched	70	2	1	21	.6	—	.10	.06	.8	—
Whole wheat, average slice	65	3	1	24	.8	—	.09	.03	.8	—
Butter, 1 tbsp	100	—	12	3	—	430	—	—	—	—
Cabbage, 1 cup, raw, coarsely shredded	15	1	—	34	.3	90	.04	.04	.2	33
Cake: Sponge, average slice	195	5	4	20	1.1	300	.09	.14	.6	—
Pound, average slice	160	2	10	6	.5	80	.05	.06	.4	—
Candies: Caramels, 1 ounce	115	1	3	42	.4	—	.01	.05	.1	—
Chocolate, milk, 1 ounce	145	2	9	65	.3	80	.02	.10	.1	—
Cantaloupe, ½ melon	80	2	—	38	1.1	9,240	.11	.08	1.6	90
Carrot, raw, 1 average size	30	1	—	27	.5	7,930	.04	.04	.4	6
Catsup, 1 tbsp	15	—	—	3	.1	210	.01	.01	.2	2
Cheese: Cheddar, 1 ounce	115	7	9	204	.2	300	.01	.11	—	—
Cottage, creamed, 1 cup	235	28	10	135	.3	370	.05	.37	.3	—
Cottage, uncreamed, 1 cup	125	25	1	46	.3	40	.04	.21	.2	—
Cream cheese, 1 ounce	100	2	10	23	.3	400	—	.06	—	—
Swiss, natural, 1 ounce	105	8	8	272	—	240	.01	.10	—	—
Swiss, process, 1 ounce	95	7	7	219	.2	230	—	.08	—	—
Chicken, broiled, 3 ounces	115	20	3	8	1.4	80	.05	.16	7.4	—

Food and amount	Energy (calories)	Nutrients: Protein (gm)	Nutrients: Fat (gm)	Minerals: Calcium (mg)	Minerals: Iron (mg)	Vitamins: Vitamin A (IU)	Vitamins: Vitamin B_1 (thiamin) (mg)	Vitamins: Vitamin B_2 (riboflavin) (mg)	Vitamins: Niacin (mg)	Vitamins: Vitamin C (ascorbic acid) (mg)
Chicken, fried, ½ breast, 3.3 ounces	160	26	5	9	1.3	70	.04	.17	11.6	—
Chicken, canned, boned, 3 ounces	170	18	10	18	1.3	200	.03	.11	3.7	3
Clams, raw, 3 ounces	65	11	1	59	5.2	90	.08	.15	1.1	8
Cocoa, 1 cup, homemade	220	9	9	298	.8	320	.10	.44	.4	2
Coffee; black, 1 cup	—	—	—	—	—	—	—	—	—	—
Cola, carbonated, 12 ounces	145	—	—	—	—	—	—	—	—	—
Corn, average ear	70	2	1	2	.5	310	.09	.08	1.1	7
Corn flakes, 1 cup	95	2	—	3	.6	1,180	.29	.35	2.9	9
Crabmeat, canned, 3 ounces	85	15	2	38	.7	—	.07	.07	1.6	—
Crackers, Graham, 4	110	2	3	11	1.0	—	.04	.16	1.0	—
Saltines, 4	50	1	1	2	.5	—	.05	.05	.4	—
Cream: Light, table, 1 cup	470	6	46	231	.1	1,730	.08	.36	.1	2
Heavy, whipping, 1 cup	820	5	88	154	.1	3,500	.05	.26	.1	1
Sour, 1 cup	495	7	48	268	.1	1,820	.08	.34	.2	2
Whipped topping (pressurized), 1 cup	155	2	13	61	—	550	.02	.04	—	—
Doughnut, 1 plain	100	1	5	10	.4	20	.05	.05	.4	—
Egg: Raw or cooked in shell, 1	80	6	6	28	1.0	260	.04	.14	—	—
Omelet, scrambled, 1	95	6	7	47	.9	310	.04	.16	—	—
Frankfurter, 1	170	7	15	3	.8	—	.08	.11	1.4	—
Fruit cocktail, 1 cup canned	195	1	—	23	1.0	360	.05	.03	1.0	5
Grapefruit: Raw, ½	45	1	—	19	.5	10	.05	.02	.2	44
Canned, syrup, 1 cup	180	2	—	33	.8	30	.08	.05	.5	76
Juice, fresh, 1 cup	95	1	—	22	.5	20	.10	.05	.5	93
Haddock, breaded, fried, 3 ounces	140	17	5	34	1.0	—	.03	.06	2.7	2
Honey, strained, 1 tbsp.	65	—	—	1	.1	—	—	.01	.1	—
Ice cream, 1 cup	270	5	14	176	.1	540	.05	.33	.1	1
Jellies, 1 tbsp	50	—	—	4	.3	—	—	.01	—	1
Lamb: Rib chop, boned, 4 ounces	400	25	33	10	1.5	—	.14	.25	5.6	—
Leg roast, 3 ounces, boned	235	22	16	9	1.4	—	.13	.23	4.7	—
Lemon, 1 medium	20	1	—	19	.4	10	.03	.01	.1	39
Liver: Beef, fried, 2 ounces	130	15	6	6	5.0	30,280	.15	2.37	9.4	15
Luncheon meat: Boiled ham, 2 ounces	135	11	10	6	1.6	—	.25	.09	1.5	—
Canned, spiced or unspiced, 2 ounces	165	8	14	5	1.2	—	.18	.12	1.6	—
Macaroni, enriched, 1 cup	155	5	1	11	1.3	—	.20	.11	1.5	—
Macaroni and cheese, 1 cup	430	17	22	362	1.8	860	.20	.40	1.8	—
Margarine, 1 tbsp	100	—	12	3	—	470	—	—	—	—
Mayonnaise, 1 tbsp	100	—	11	3	.1	40	—	.01	—	—
Milk: Whole, 1 cup	150	8	8	291	.1	310	.09	.40	.2	2
Skim (non-fat), 1 cup	85	8	—	302	.1	500	.09	.34	.2	2

Buttermilk, 1 cup	100	8	2	285	.1	80	.08	.38	.1	2
Mushrooms, canned, 1 cup	40	5	—	15	1.2	—	.04	.60	4.8	4
Nuts: Almonds, 1 cup shelled	850	26	77	332	6.7	—	.34	1.31	5.0	—
Peanuts, roasted, 1 cup	840	37	72	107	3.0	—	.46	.19	24.8	—
Oatmeal, 1 cup cooked	130	5	2	22	1.4	—	.19	.05	.2	—
Oils, salad, cooking, 1 tbsp	120	—	14	—	—	—	—	—	—	—
Orange, 1 medium	65	1	—	54	.5	260	.13	.05	.5	66
Orange juice, fresh, 1 cup	110	2	—	27	.5	500	.22	.07	1.0	124
Frozen, diluted with 3 parts water, 1 cup	120	2	—	25	.2	540	.23	.03	.9	120
Oysters, raw, 1 cup	160	20	4	226	13.2	740	.34	.43	6.0	—
Pancake, wheat, 1 average	60	2	2	27	.4	30	.06	.07	.5	—
Peach, raw, 1 medium	40	1	—	9	.5	1,330	.02	.05	1.0	7
Peanut butter, 1 tbsp	95	4	8	9	.3	—	.02	.02	2.4	—
Peas, green, 1 cup	110	8	—	30	3.0	960	.43	.14	2.7	21
Pie: Apple, 4-inch wedge	345	3	15	11	.9	40	.15	.11	1.3	2
Cherry, 4-inch wedge	350	4	15	19	.9	590	.16	.12	1.4	—
Lemon meringue, 4-inch wedge	305	4	12	17	1.0	200	.09	.12	.7	4
Pineapple, raw, 1 cup diced	80	1	—	26	.8	110	.14	.05	.3	26
Pineapple juice, canned, 1 cup	140	1	—	38	.8	130	.13	.05	.5	23
Pizza (cheese), 4¾-inch wedge	145	6	4	86	1.1	230	.16	.18	1.6	4
Pork: Roast, 3 ounces	310	21	24	9	2.7	—	.78	.22	4.8	—
Chop, with bone, 2.7 ounces	305	19	25	9	2.7	—	.75	.22	4.5	—
Potatoes: Baked, 1 medium	145	4	—	14	1.1	—	.15	.07	2.7	31
French fried, deep fat, 10 pieces	135	2	7	8	.7	—	.07	.04	1.6	11
Mashed with milk, 1 cup	135	4	2	50	.8	40	.17	.11	2.1	21
Potato chips, 10	115	1	8	8	.4	—	.04	.01	1.0	3
Prune juice, 1 cup canned	195	1	—	36	1.8	—	.03	.03	1.0	5
Rice: White, enriched, 1 cup cooked	225	4	—	21	1.8	—	.23	.02	2.1	—
Puffed, 1 cup	60	1	—	3	.3	—	.07	.01	.7	—
Salad dressings: Mayonnaise type, 1 tbsp	65	—	6	2	—	30	—	—	—	—
French, 1 tbsp	65	—	6	2	.1	—	—	—	—	—
French, low calorie, 1 tbsp	15	—	1	2	.1	—	—	—	—	—
Salmon: Canned, 3 ounces	120	17	5	167	.7	60	.03	.16	6.8	—
Sardines, canned, 3 ounces	175	20	9	372	2.5	190	.02	.17	4.6	—
Spaghetti, 1 cup cooked	155	5	1	11	1.3	—	.20	.11	1.5	—
Spinach, 1 cup cooked	40	5	1	167	4.0	14,580	.13	.25	.9	50
Sugar, 1 teaspoon	15	—	—	—	—	—	—	—	—	—
Tomato juice, canned, 1 cup	45	2	—	17	2.2	1,940	.12	.07	1.9	39
Tuna fish, 3 ounces	170	24	7	7	1.6	70	.04	.10	10.1	—
Veal, 3-ounce cutlet	185	23	9	9	2.7	—	.06	.21	4.6	—
Yogurt, from lowfat milk, 8-oz. container, plain	145	12	4	415	.2	150	.10	.49	.3	2

NOTE: Gm—gram; Mg—milligram; IU—International Unit. A dash in a column indicates little or no basis for assigning value. *Source:* Department of Agriculture, Science and Education Administration.

Communicable Diseases

Disease	Incubation period[1]	Period of communicability
Chickenpox (varicella)	2 to 3 weeks	From 5 days before appearance of vesicles to 6 days after
Common Cold	12 to 72 hours; usually 24 hrs	From 1 day before onset to 5 days after
Conjunctivitis	1 to 3 days	During course of active infection
Diphtheria	2 to 5 days	Usually 2 weeks or less; seldom more than 4 weeks
Dysentery, amebic	2 to 4 weeks (varies widely)	During intestinal infection; possibly for years if untreated
Enterobiasis (pinworm)	3 to 6 weeks	Not directly transmitted
Food poisoning: Botulism	12 to 36 hours	Not applicable
Salmonella infection	6 to 72 hours; usually 36	3 days to 3 weeks (extremely variable)
Staphylococcus intoxication	2 to 4 hours	Not applicable
German measles (rubella)	8 to 10 days; usually 14	1 week before and at least 4 days after onset of rash
Gonorrhea	2 to 5 days; sometimes longer	Indefinite unless treated
Hepatitis (serum)	45 to 160 days; usually 80 to 100	Many weeks before onset of symptoms
Herpes Simplex	Up to 2 weeks	As long as 7 weeks after recovery
Impetigo contagiosa	4 to 10 days; sometimes longer	Until lesions are healed
Infectious mononucleosis	Varies 2 to 6 weeks	Unknown
Influenza	Usually 1 to 3 days	Probably limited to 3 days from clinical onset
Measles (rubeola)	10 days (to onset): 14 days (to rash)	From beginning of prodromal period to 4 days after onset of rash
Meningitis, meningococcal	2 to 10 days	Usually 1 day after appropriate medication
Mumps	12 to 26 days; commonly 18	From 6 days before distinctive symptoms up to 9 days after
Pediculosis	Apprx. 2 weeks	While lice remain alive
Pneumonia: Bacterial	Usually 1 to 3 days	Unknown
Viral	Believed to be 1 to 3 days	Unknown
Poliomyelitis	3 to 21 days; commonly 7 to 12	7 to 10 days before and after onset of symptoms
Rabies	2 to 8 weeks or longer	From animals, 3 to 5 days before onset and during course of the disease
Respiratory (acute viral)	Few days to 1 week or more	Duration of active disease
Ringworm (of body)	4 to 10 days	As long as lesions are present
(Athlete's foot)	Unknown	As long as lesions are present
Scarlet fever and streptococcal sore throat	1 to 3 days	Uncomplicated cases apprx. 10 to 21 days; in untreated cases, weeks or months
Smallpox	7 to 17 days; commonly 10 to 12	During first week
Syphilis	10 days to 10 weeks; usually 3 weeks	Variable and indefinite
Tetanus	4 days to 3 weeks	Not applicable
Trichinosis	2 to 28 days after ingestion of infected meat; usually 9 days	Not directly transmitted
Tuberculosis	4 to 12 weeks (to primary phase)	As long as tubercle bacilli are discharged by patient
Typhoid fever	1 to 3 weeks, average 2 weeks	As long as typhoid bacilli appear in excreta; 2 to 5% of patients become permanent carriers
Whooping cough (pertussis)	Commonly 7 days, almost uniformly within 10 days, and not exceeding 21 days	From 7 days after exposure to 3 weeks after onset of typical paroxysms

1. Usual limits. NOTE: This list is incomplete, but includes those diseases that are most common and widespread.

Sunbathing and Skin Cancer

Scientists agree that ultraviolet radiation from the sun is the leading cause of skin cancer, which is responsible for an estimated 6,500 to 7,500 deaths in the United States every year. Sunlamps also can produce ultraviolet radiation, and the Food and Drug Administration is developing performance standards for them to reduce potential hazards.

Most dermatologists consider excessive sunbathing foolhardy. To the argument that the sun stimulates the production of vitamin D on the skin, the experts reply that you can get all the vitamin D you need from proper diet.

To the contention that the use of sunscreen lotions will promote a tan without burning, the experts say that a tanned skin is a damaged skin. Besides, they add, whether you burn or tan, there always is a chance that ultraviolet radiation will damage the DNA and initiate the cancer formation process.

People can reduce the potential hazard from the sun by not exposing themselves to it unnecessarily for extended periods between 10 a.m. and 2 p.m. when most ultraviolet radiation reaches the earth's surface.

HEADLINE HISTORY

In any broad overview of history, arbitrary compartmentalization of facts is self-defeating (and makes locating interrelated people, places, and things that much harder). Therefore, Headline History is designed as a "timeline"—a chronology that highlights both the march of time and interesting, sometimes surprising, juxtapositions.

Also see related sections of *Information Please*, particularly the Statistical History of the United States, Inventions and Discoveries, Countries of the World, etc.

B.C.

Before Christ or Before Common Era (B.C.E.)

4500–3000 B.C. Sumerians in the Tigris and Euphrates valleys develop a city-state civilization; first phonetic writing (**c.3500 B.C.**). Egyptian agriculture develops. Western Europe is neolithic, without metals or written records. Earliest recorded date in Egyptian calendar (**4241 B.C.**). First year of Jewish calendar (**3760 B.C.**). Copper used by Egyptians and Sumerians.

3000–2000 B.C. Pharaonic rule begins in Egypt. Cheops, 4th dynasty (**2700–2675 B.C.**). The Great Sphinx of Giza. Earliest Egyptian mummies. Papyrus. Phoenician settlements on coast of what is now Syria and Lebanon. Semitic tribes settle in Assyria. Sargon, first Akkadian king, builds Mesopotamian empire. The Gilgamesh epic (**c.3000 B.C.**). Abraham leaves Ur (**c.2000 B.C.**). Systematic astronomy in Egypt, Babylon, India, China.

2000–1500 B.C. Hyksos invaders drive Egyptians from Lower Egypt (**17th century B.C.**). Amosis I frees Egypt from Hyksos (**c.1600 B.C.**). Assyrians rise to power—cities of Ashur and Nineveh. Twenty-four-character alphabet in Egypt. Israelites enslaved in Egypt. Cuneiform inscriptions used by Hittites. Peak of Minoan culture on Isle of Crete—earliest form of written Greek. Hammurabi, king of Babylon, develops oldest existing code of laws (**18th century B.C.**). In Britain, Stonehenge erected on some unknown astronomical rationale.

1500–1000 B.C. Ikhnaton develops monotheistic religion in Egypt (**c.1375 B.C.**). His successor, Tutankhamen, returns to earlier gods. Moses leads Israelites out of Egypt into Canaan—Ten Commandments. Greeks destroy Troy (**c.1193 B.C.**). End of Greek civilization in Mycenae with invasion of Dorians. Chinese civilization develops under Shang dynasty. Olmec civilization in Mexico—stone monuments; picture writing.

000–900 B.C. Solomon succeeds King David, builds Jerusalem temple. After Solomon's death, kingdom divided into Israel and Judah. Hebrew elders begin to write Old Testament books of Bible. Phoenicians colonize Spain with settlement at Cadiz.

00–800 B.C. Phoenicians establish Carthage (**c.810 B.C.**). The *Iliad* and the *Odyssey*, perhaps composed by Greek poet Homer.

00–700 B.C. Prophets Amos, Hosea, Isaiah. First recorded Olympic games (**776 B.C.**). Legendary founding of Rome by Romulus (**753 B.C.**). Assyrian king Sargon II conquers Hittites, Chaldeans, Samaria (end of Kingdom of Israel). Earliest written music. Chariots introduced into Italy by Etruscans.

00–600 B.C. End of Assyrian Empire (**616 B.C.**)—Nineveh destroyed by Chaldeans (Neo-Babylonians) and Medes (**612 B.C.**). Founding of Byzantium by Greeks (**c.660 B.C.**). Building of the Acropolis in Athens. Solon, Greek lawgiver (**640–560 B.C.**). Sappho of Lesbos, Greek poetess. Lao-Tse, Chinese philosopher and founder of Taoism (born **c.604 B.C.**).

00–500 B.C. Babylonian king Nebuchadnezzar builds empire, destroys Jerusalem (**586 B.C.**). Babylonian Captivity of the Jews (starting **587 B.C.**). Hanging Gardens of Babylon. Cyrus the Great of Persia creates great empire, conquers Babylon (**539 B.C.**), frees the Jews. Athenian democracy develops. Aeschylus, Greek dramatist (**525–465 B.C.**). Confucius (**551–479 B.C.**) develops philosophy-religion in China. Buddha (**563–483 B.C.**) founds Buddhism in India.

0–400 B.C. Greeks defeat Persians: battles of Marathon (**490 B.C.**), Thermopylae (**480 B.C.**), Salamis (**480 B.C.**). Peloponnesian Wars between Athens and Sparta (**431–404 B.C.**)—Sparta victorious. Pericles comes to power in Athens (**462

Some Ancient Civilizations

Name	Approximate dates	Location	Major cities
Akkadian	2350–2230 B.C.	Mesopotamia, parts of Syria, Asia Minor, Iran	Akkad, Ur, Erich
Assyrian	1800–889 B.C.	Mesopotamia, Syria	Assur, Nineveh, Calah
Babylonian	1728–1686 B.C. (old) 625–539 B.C. (new)	Mesopotamia, Syria, Palestine	Babylon
Cimmerian	750–500 B.C.	Caucasus, northern Asia Minor	—
Egyptian	2850–715 B.C.	Nile valley	Thebes, Memphis, Tanis
Etruscan	900–396 B.C.	Northern Italy	—
Greek	900–200 B.C.	Greece	Athens, Sparta, Thebes, Mycenae, Corinth
Hittite	1640–1200 B.C.	Asia Minor, Syria	Hattusas, Nesa
Lydian	700–547 B.C.	Western Asia Minor	Sardis, Miletus
Mede	835–550 B.C.	Iran	Media
Minoan	3000–1100 B.C.	Crete	Knossos
Persian	559–330 B.C.	Iran, Asia Minor, Syria	Persepolis, Pasargadae
Phoenician	1100–332 B.C.	Palestine (colonies: Gibralter, Carthage Sardinia)	Tyre, Sidon, Byblos
Phrygian	1000–547 B.C.	Central Asia Minor	Gordion
Roman	500 B.C.- A.D. 300	Italy, Mediterranean region, Asia Minor, western Europe	Rome, Byzantium
Scythian	800–300 B.C.	Caucasus	—
Sumerian	3200–2360 B.C.	Mesopotamia	Ur, Nippur

B.C.). Flowering of Greek culture during the Age of Pericles (**450–400 B.C.**). Sophocles, Greek dramatist (**496–c.406 B.C.**). Hippocrates, Greek "Father of Medicine" (born **460 B.C.**). Xerxes I, king of Persia (rules **485–465 B.C.**).

400–300 B.C. Pentateuch—first five books of the Old Testament evolve in final form. Philip of Macedon assassinated (**336 B.C.**) after conquering Greece; succeeded by son, Alexander the Great (**356–323 B.C.**), who destroys Thebes (**335 B.C.**), conquers Tyre and Jerusalem (**332 B.C.**), occupies Babylon (**330 B.C.**), invades India, and dies in Babylon. His empire is divided among his generals; one of them, Seleucis I, establishes Middle East empire with capitals at Antioch (Syria) and Seleucia (in Iraq). Trial and execution of Greek philosopher Socrates (**399 B.C.**). Dialogues recorded by his student, Plato. Euclid's work on geometry (**323 B.C.**). Aristotle, Greek philosopher (**354–322 B.C.**). Demosthenes, Greek orator (**384–322 B.C.**). Praxiteles, Greek sculptor (**400–330 B.C.**).

300–251 B.C. First Punic War (**264–241 B.C.**): Rome defeats the Carthaginians and begins its domination of the Mediterranean. Temple of the Sun at Teotihuacan, Mexico (**c.300 B.C.**). Invention of Mayan calendar in Yucatán —more exact than older calendars. First Roman gladiatorial games (**264 B.C.**). Archimedes, Greek mathematician (**287–212 B.C.**).

250–201 B.C. Second Punic War (**219–201 B.C.**): Hannibal, Carthaginian general (**246–142 B.C.**), crosses the Alps (**218 B.C.**), reaches gates of Rome (**211 B.C.**), retreats, and is defeated by Scipio Africanus at Zama (**202 B.C.**). Great Wall of China built (**c.215 B.C.**).

200–151 B.C. Romans defeat Seleucid King Antiochus III at Thermopylae (**191 B.C.**)—beginning of Roman world domination. Maccabean revolt against Seleucids (**167 B.C.**).

150–101 B.C. Third Punic War (**149–146 B.C.**): Rome destroys Carthage, killing 450,000 and enslaving the remaining 50,000 inhabitants. Roman armies conquer Macedonia, Greece, Anatolia, Balearic Islands, and southern France. Venus de Milo (**c.140 B.C.**). Cicero, Roman orator (**106–43 B.C.**).

100–51 B.C. Julius Caesar (**100–44 B.C.**) invades Britain (**55 B.C.**) and conquers Gaul (France) (**c.50 B.C.**). Spartacus leads slave revolt against Rome (**71 B.C.**). Romans conquer Seleucid empire. Roman general Pompey conquers Jerusalem (**63 B.C.**). Cleopatra on Egyptian throne (**51–31 B.C.**). Chinese develop use of paper (**c.100 B.C.**). Virgil, Roman poet (**70–19 B.C.**). Horace, Roman poet (**65–8 B.C.**).

50–1 B.C. Caesar crosses Rubicon to fight Pompey (50 B.C.). Herod made Roman governor of Judea (47 B.C.). Caesar murdered (44 B.C.). Caesar's nephew, Octavian, defeats Mark Antony and Cleopatra at Battle of Actium (31 B.C.), and establishes Roman empire as Emperor Augustus—rules 27 B.C.-A.D. 14. Birth of Jesus Christ (variously given from 4 B.C. to A.D. 7). Ovid, Roman poet (43 B.C.-A.D. 18).

A.D.

The Christian or Common Era (C.E.)

1–49 After Augustus, Tiberius becomes emperor (dies, 37), succeeded by Caligula (assassinated, 42), who is followed by Claudius. Crucifixion of Jesus (probably 30). Han dynasty in China founded by Emperor Kuang Wu Ti. Buddhism introduced to China.

50–99 Claudius poisoned (54), succeeded by Nero (commits suicide, 68). Missionary journeys of Paul the Apostle (34–60). Jews revolt against Rome; Jerusalem destroyed (70). Roman persecutions of Christians begin (64). Colosseum built in Rome (71–80). Trajan (rules 98–116); Roman empire extends to Mesopotamia, Arabia, Balkans. First Gospels of St. Mark, St. John, St. Matthew.

100–149 Hadrian rules Rome (117–138); codifies Roman law, establishes postal system, builds wall between England and Scotland. Jews revolt under Bar Kokhba (122–135); final *Diaspora* (dispersion) of Jews begins.

150–199 Marcus Aurelius (rules Rome 161–180). Oldest Mayan temples in Central America (c.200). Mayan civilization develops writing, astronomy, mathematics.

200–249 Goths invade Asia Minor (c.220). Roman persecutions of Christians increase. Persian (Sassanid) empire re-established. End of Chinese Han dynasty.

250–299 Increasing invasions of the Roman empire by Franks and Goths. Buddhism spreads in China.

300–349 Constantine the Great (rules 312–337) reunites eastern and western Roman empires, with new capital (Constantinople) on site of Byzantium (330); issues Edict of Milan legalizing Christianity (313); becomes a Christian on his deathbed (337). Council of Nicaea (325) defines orthodox Christian doctrine. First Gupta dynasty in India (c.320).

350–399 Huns (Mongols) invade Europe (c.360). Theodosius the Great (rules 392–395)—last emperor of a united Roman empire. Roman empire permanently divided in 395: western empire ruled from Rome; eastern empire ruled from Constantinople.

400–449 Western Roman empire disintegrates under weak emperors. Alaric, king of the Visigoths, sacks Rome (410). Attila, Hun chieftain, attacks Roman provinces (433). St. Patrick returns to Ireland (432). St. Augustine's *City of God* (411).

450–499 Vandals destroy Rome (455). Western Roman empire ends as Odoacer, German chieftain, overthrows last Roman emperor, Romulus Augustulus, and becomes king of Italy (476). Ostrogothic kingdom of Italy established by Theodoric the Great (493). Clovis, ruler of the Franks, is converted to Christianity (496). First schism between western and eastern churches (484). Peak of Mayan culture in Mexico (c.460).

500–549 Eastern and western churches reconciled (519). Justinian I, the Great (483–565), becomes Byzantine emperor (527), issues his first code of civil laws (529), conquers North Africa, Italy, and part of Spain. Plague spreads through Europe (from 542). Arthur, semi-legendary king of the Britons (killed, c.537). Boëthius, Roman scholar (executed, 524).

550–599 Beginnings of European silk industry after Justinian's missionaries smuggle silkworms out of China (553). Mohammed, founder of Islam (570–632). Buddhism in Japan (c.560). St. Augustine of Canterbury brings Christianity to Britain (597). After killing about half the population, plague in Europe subsides (594).

600–649 Mohammed flees from Mecca to Medina (the *Hegira*); first year of the Muslim calendar (622). Muslim empire grows (634). Arabs conquer Jerusalem (637), destroy Alexandrian library (641), conquer Persians (641). Fatima, Mohammed's daughter (606–632).

650–699 Arabs attack North Africa (670), destroy Carthage (697). Venerable Bede, English monk (672–735).

700–749 Arab empire extends from Lisbon to China (by 716). Charles Martel, Frankish leader, defeats Arabs at Tours/Poitiers, halting Arab advance in Europe (732). Charlemagne (742–814).

750–799 Caliph Harun al-Rashid rules Arab empire (786–809): the "golden age" of Arab culture. Vikings begin attacks on Britain (790), land in

Ireland (**795**). Charlemagne becomes king of the Franks (**771**). City of Machu Picchu flourishes in Peru.

800–849 Charlemagne (Charles the Great) crowned first Holy Roman Emperor in Rome (**800**). Arabs conquer Crete, Sicily, and Sardinia (**826–827**). Charlemagne dies (**814**), succeeded by his son, Louis the Pious, who divides France among his sons (**817**).

850–899 Norsemen attack as far south as the Mediterranean but are repulsed (**859**), discover Iceland (**861**). Alfred the Great becomes king of Britain (**871**), defeats Danish invaders (**878**). Russian nation founded by Vikings under Prince Rurik, establishing capital at Novgorod (**855–879**).

900–949 Vikings discover Greenland (**c.900**). Arab Spain under Abd ar-Rahman III becomes center of learning (**912–961**).

950–999 Eric the Red establishes first Viking colony in Greenland (**982**). Mieczyslaw I becomes first ruler of Poland (**960**). Hugh Capet elected King of France in **987**; Capetian dynasty to rule until **1328**. Musical notation systematized (**c.990**). Vikings and Danes attack Britain (**988–999**). Holy Roman Empire founded by Otto I, King of Germany since **936**, crowned by Pope John XII in **962**.

---

c.1000 Hungary and Scandinavia converted to Christianity. Viking raider Leif Ericson discovers North America, calls it *Vinland*. Chinese invent gunpowder. *Beowulf,* Old English epic.

1009 Moslems destroy Holy Sepulchre in Jerusalem.

1013 Danes control England. Canute takes throne (**1016**), conquers Norway (**1028**), dies (**1035**); kingdom divided among his sons: Harold Harefoot (England), Sweyn (Norway), Hardecanute (Denmark).

1040 Macbeth murders Duncan, king of Scotland.

1053 Robert Guiscard, Norman invader, establishes kingdom in Italy, conquers Sicily (**1072**).

1054 Final separation between Eastern (Orthodox) and Western (Roman) churches.

1055 Seljuk Turks, Asian nomads, move west, capture Baghdad, Armenia (**1064**), Syria, and Palestine (**1075**).

1066 William of Normandy invades England, defeats last Saxon king, Harold II, at Battle of Hastings, crowned William I of England ("the Conqueror").

1073 Emergence of strong papacy when Gregory VII is elected. Conflict with English and French kings and German emperors will continue throughout medieval period.

1095 *(See* special material on "The Crusades.")

Omar Khayyám, *Persian poet* (1027?–1123)
El Cid, *Spanish national hero* (1040–1099)
Peter Abelard, *French theologian* (1079–1142)
Judah Halevi, *Jewish poet* (1085–1140)

1150–67 Universities of Paris and Oxford founded in France and England.

1162 Thomas à Becket named Archbishop of Canterbury, murdered by Henry II's men (**1170**). Troubadours (wandering minstrels) glorify romantic concepts of feudalism.

1189 Richard I ("the Lionhearted") succeeds Henry II in England, killed in France (**1199**), succeeded by King John.

1211 Genghis Khan invades China, captures Peking (**1214**), conquers Persia (**1218**), invades Russia (**1223**), dies (**1227**).

1215 King John forced by barons to sign Magna Carta at Runneymede, limiting royal power.

1233 The Inquisition begins as Pope Gregory IX assigns Dominicans responsibility for combatting heresy. Torture used (**1252**). Ferdinand and Isabella establish Spanish Inquisition (**1478**). Tourquemada, Grand Inquisitor, forces conversion or expulsion of Spanish Jews (**1492**). Forced conversion of Moors (**1499**). Inquisition in Portugal (**1531**). First Protestants burned at the stake in Spain (**1543**). Spanish Inquisition abolished (**1834**).

1241 Mongols defeat Germans in Silesia, invade Poland and Hungary, with-

Thomas à Becket, *English prelate and martyr* (1118–1170)
Moses Maimonides, *Jewish philosopher* (1135–1204)
Genghis Khan, *Mongol emperor* (1162–1227)
St. Francis of Assisi, *founder of Franciscans* (1182–1226)
Roger Bacon, *English scientist* (1214–1294)
Kublai Khan, *Mongol ruler* (1216–1294)
St. Thomas Aquinas, *Catholic theologian* (1225–1274)
Marco Polo, *Venetian explorer* (1254–1323)
Dante Alighieri, *Italian poet* (1265–1321)

THE CRUSADES (1096–1291)

In **1095** Pope Urban II calls for war to rescue Holy Land from Moslem infidels at Council of Clermont. *First Crusade* (**1096**) —about 500,000 peasants led by Peter the Hermit prove so troublesome that Byzantine Emperor Alexius ships them to Asia Minor; only 25,000 survive return after massacre by Seljuk Turks. Followed by organized army, led by nobility, which reaches Constantinople (**1097**), conquers Jerusalem (**1099**), Acre (**1104**), establishes Latin Kingdom protected by Knights of St. John the Hospitaller (**1100**), and Knights Templar (**1123**). Seljuk Turks start series of counterattacks (**1144**). *Second Crusade* (**1146**) led by King Louis VIII of France and Emperor Conrad III. Crusaders perish in Asia Minor (**1147**).

Saladin controls Egypt (**1171**), unites Islam in Holy War *(Jihad)* against Christians, recaptures Jerusalem (**1187**). *Third Crusade* (**1189**) under kings of France, England, and Germany fails to reduce Saladin's power. *Fourth Crusade* (**1200–1204**) —French knights sack Greek Christian Constantinople, establish Latin empire in Byzantium. Greeks re-establish Orthodox faith (**1262**).

Children's Crusade (**1212**)—Only 1 of 30,000 French children and about 200 of 20,000 German children survive to return home. Other Crusades—against Egypt (**1217**), *Sixth* (**1228**), *Seventh* (**1248**), *Eighth* (**1270**). Mamelukes conquer Acre, end of the Crusades (**1291**).

draw from Europe after Ughetai, Mongol leader, dies.
1251 Kublai Khan governs China, becomes ruler of Mongols **(1259)**, establishes Yuan dynasty in China **(1280)**, invades Burma **(1287)**, dies **(1294)**.
1271 Marco Polo of Venice travels to China, in court of Kublai Khan **(1275–1292)**, returns to Genoa **(1295)** and writes *Travels.*
1295 English King Edward I summons the Model Parliament.

Duns Scotus, *Scottish theologian* (1265–1308)
Giotto, *Italian painter* (1276–1337)

1312–37 Mali Empire reaches its height in Africa under King Mansa Musa.
1337–1453 Hundred Years' War—English and French kings fight for control of France.
c.1325 The beginning of the Renaissance in Italy: writers Dante, Petrarch, Boccaccio; painter Giotto. Development of *No* drama in Japan. Aztecs establish capital on site of modern Mexico City. Peak of Moslem culture in Spain. Small cannon in use.
1347–1351 At least 25 million people die in Europe's "Black Death" (bubonic plague).
1368 Ming dynasty begins in China.
1376–82 John Wycliffe, pre-Reformation religious reformer and followers translate Latin bible into English.
1378 The Great Schism **(to 1417)**—rival popes in Rome and Avignon, France, fight for control of Roman Catholic Church.
c.1387 Chaucer's *Canterbury Tales.*

1415 Henry V defeats French at Agincourt. Jan Hus, Bohemian preacher and follower of Wycliffe, burned at stake in Constance as heretic.
1418–60 Portugal's Prince Henry the Navigator sponsors exploration of Africa's coast.
1428 Joan of Arc leads French against English, captured by Burgundians **(1430)** and turned over to the English, burned at the stake as a witch after ecclesiastical trial **(1431)**.
1438 Inca rule in Peru.
1450 Florence becomes center of Renaissance arts and learning under the Medicis.
1453 Turks conquer Constantinople, end of the Byzantine empire. Hundred Years' War between France and England ends.
1455 The Wars of the Roses, civil wars between rival noble factions, begin in England **(to 1485)**. Having invented printing with movable type at Mainz, Germany, Johann Gutenberg completes first bible.
1462 Ivan the Great rules Russia until **1505** as first czar; ends payment of tribute to Mongols.
1492 Moors conquered in Spain by troops of Ferdinand and Isabella. Columbus discovers Caribbean islands, returns to Spain **(1493)**. Second voyage to Dominica, Jamaica, Puerto Rico **(1493–1496)**. Third voyage to Orinoco **(1498)**. Fourth voyage to Honduras and Panama **(1502–1504)**.
1497 Vasco da Gama sails around Africa and discovers sea route to India **(1498)**. Establishes Portuguese colony in India **(1502)**. John Cabot, employed by England, reaches and explores Canadian coast. Michelangelo's *Bacchus* sculpture.

Leonardo da Vinci, *Renaissance artistic and scientific genius* (1452–1519)
Vasco da Gama, *Portuguese explorer* (1460–1524)
Juan Ponce de León, *Spanish explorer* (1460–1521)
Hans Holbein (the Elder), *German painter* (1465?–1524)
Niccolo Machiavelli, *Italian author* (1468–1527)
Albrecht Dürer, *German painter* (1471–1528)
Nicolaus Copernicus, *Polish scientist* (1473–1543)
Michelangelo Buonarroti, *Italian painter, sculptor, architect* (1475–1564)
Cesare Borgia, *Renaissance prince* (1476–1507)
Titian, *Italian painter* (1477–1576)
Sir Thomas More, *English statesman* (1478–1535)
Lucrezia Borgia, *Italian patron of the arts* (1480–1519)
Ferdinand Magellan, *Portuguese explorer* (1480–1521)
Martin Luther, *German Reformation leader* (1483–1546)
Raphael, *Italian painter* (1483–1520)
Ulrich Zwingli, *Swiss humanist* (1484–1531)
Hernando Cortes, *Spanish Conquistador* (1485–1547)
Andrea del Sarto, *Florentine painter* (1486–1531)
Thomas Cranmer, *English churchman* (1489–1556)
François Rabelais, *French writer* (1490–1553)
Jacques Cartier, *French explorer* (1491–1557)
St. Ignatius de Loyola, *founder of Jesuits* (1491–1556)
Paracelsus, *Swiss physician* (1493–1541)
Correggio, *Italian painter* (1494–1534)
Hans Holbein (the Younger) *German painter* (1497–1543)
Hernando De Soto, *Spanish explorer* (1499–1542)

Guillaume de Machaut, *French composer* (1300–1377)
Petrarch (Francesco Petrarca), *Italian poet* (1304–1374)
Giovanni Boccaccio, *Florentine novelist* (1313–1375)
John Wycliffe, *English church reformer* (1320–1384)
Geoffrey Chaucer, *English writer* (c.1340–1400)
Jan Hus, *Bohemian religious reformer* (c.1369–1415)
Thomas à Kempis, *German mystic* (1380–1471)
Donatello, *Italian sculptor* (1386–1466)
Fra Angelico, *Italian painter* (1387–1455)
Johann Gutenberg, *inventor of movable type* (1398–1468)
Luca della Robbia, *Italian sculptor* (1400–1482)
Guillaume Dufay, *French composer* (c.1400–1474)
Fra Filippo Lippi, *Italian painter* (1406–1469)
Joan of Arc, *French saint and national heroine* (1412–1431)
Tomas de Torquemada, *Spanish Inquisitor* (1420–1498)
Giovanni Bellini, *Italian painter* (1430–1516)
François Villon, *French poet* (1431–1465?)
Sandro Botticelli, *Italian painter* (1444–1510)
Lorenzo de'Medici, *Renaissance ruler* (1449–1492)
Hieronymus Bosch, *Dutch painter* (1450–1516)
Josquin des Prés, *Dutch composer* (1450–1521)
Isabella I, *Queen of Spain* (1451–1504)
Christopher Columbus, *Italian explorer* (1451–1506)
Amerigo Vespucci, *Italian navigator* (1451–1512)
Savonarola, *Italian churchman* (1452–1498)

1501 First black slaves in America brought to Spanish colony of Santo Domingo.
c.1503 Leonardo da Vinci paints the *Mona Lisa.*
1506 St. Peter's Church started in Rome; designed and decorated by such artists and architects as Bramante, Michelangelo, da Vinci, Raphael, and Bernini before its completion in **1626**.
1509 Henry VIII ascends English throne. Michelangelo paints the ceiling of the Sistine Chapel.
1517 Turks conquer Egypt, control Arabia. Martin Luther posts his 95 theses denouncing church abuses on church door in Wittenberg—start of the Reformation in Germany.
1519 Ulrich Zwingli begins Reformation in Switzerland. Hernando Cortes conquers Mexico for Spain. Charles I of Spain is chosen Holy Roman Emperor Charles V. Portuguese explorer Fernando Magellan sets out to circumnavigate the globe.
1520 Luther excommunicated by Pope Leo X. Suleiman I ("the Magnificent") becomes Sultan of Turkey, invades Hungary **(1521)**, Rhodes **(1522)**, attacks Austria **(1529)**, annexes Hungary **(1541)**, Tripoli **(1551)**, makes peace with Persia **(1553)**, destroys Spanish fleet **(1560)**, dies **(1566)**. Magellan reaches the Pacific, is killed by Philippine natives **(1521)**. One of his ships under Juan Sebastián del Cano continues around the world, reaches Spain **(1522)**.
1524 Verrazano, sailing under the French flag, explores the New England coast and New York Bay.
1527 Troops of the Holy Roman Empire attack Rome, imprison Pope Clement VII—the end of the Italian Renaissance. Castiglione writes *The Courtier.* The Medici expelled from Florence.
1532 Pizarro marches from Panama to Peru, kills the Inca chieftain, Atahualpa, of Peru **(1533)**. Machiavelli's *Prince* published posthumously.
1535 Reformation begins as Henry VIII makes himself head of English Church after being excommunicated by Pope. Sir Thomas More executed as traitor for refusal to acknowledge king's religious authority. Jacques Cartier sails up the St. Lawrence River, basis of French claims to Canada.
1536 Henry VIII executes second wife, Anne Boleyn. John Calvin establishes Presbyterian form of Protestantism in Switzerland, writes *Institutes of the Christian Religion.* Danish and Norwegian Reformations. Michelangelo's *Last Judgment.*
1541 John Knox leads Reformation in Scotland, establishes Presbyterian church **(1560)**.
1543 Publication of *On the Revolution of Heavenly Bodies* by Polish scholar Nicolaus Copernicus—giving his theory that the earth revolves around the sun.
1545 Council of Trent to meet intermittently until **1563** to define Catholic dogma and doctrine, reiterate papal authority.
1547 Ivan IV ("the Terrible") crowned as Czar of Russia, begins conquest of Astrakhan and Kazan **(1552)**, battles nobles (boyars) for power **(1564)**, kills his son **(1580)**, dies, and is succeeded by a son who gives power to Boris Godunov **(1584)**.
1553 Roman Catholicism restored in England by Queen Mary I, who rules until **1558**. Religious radical Michael Servetus burned as heretic in Geneva by order of John Calvin.
1554 Benvenuto Cellini completes the bronze *Perseus.*
1556 Akbar the Great becomes Mogul emperor of India, conquers Afghanistan **(1581)**, continues wars of conquest (until **1605**).
1558 Queen Elizabeth I ascends the throne (rules to **1603**). Restores Protestantism, establishes state Church of England (Anglicanism). Renaissance will reach height in England—Shakespeare, Marlowe, Spenser.
1561 Persecution of Huguenots in France stopped by Edict of Orleans. French religious wars begin again with massacre of Huguenots at Vassy. St. Bartholomew's Day Massacre—thousands of Huguenots murdered **(1572)**. Amnesty granted **(1573)**. Persecution continues periodically until Edict of Nantes **(1598)** gives Huguenots religious freedom (until **1685**).
1568 Protestant Netherlands revolts against Catholic Spain; independence will be acknowledged by Spain in **1648**. High point of Dutch Renaissance—painters Rubens, Van Dyck, Hals, and Rembrandt.
1570 Japan permits visits of foreign ships. Queen Elizabeth I excommunicated by Pope. Turks attack Cyprus and war on Venice. Turkish fleet defeated at Battle of Lepanto by Spanish and Italian fleets **(1571)**. Peace of Constantinople **(1572)** ends Turkish attacks on Europe.
1580 Francis Drake returns to England after circumnavigating the globe. Knighted by Queen Elizabeth I **(1581)**. Montaigne's *Essays* published.
1583 William of Orange rules The Netherlands; assassinated on orders of Philip II of Spain **(1584)**.

Benvenuto Cellini, *Florentine sculptor* (1500–1571)
Nostradamus, *French astrologer* (1503–1566)
John Knox, *Scottish church reformer* (1505–1572)
St. Francis Xavier, *Jesuit missionary* (1506–1552)
John Calvin, *Swiss theologian* (1509–1564)
Giorgio Vasari, *Italian art historian* (1511–1574)
Andreas Vesalius, *Dutch anatomist* (1515–1564)
Andrea Palladio, *Italian architect* (1518–1580)
Tintoretto (Jacopo Robusti), *Italian painter* (1518–1594)
Pieter Brueghel (the Elder), *Dutch painter* (1520–1569)
Pierre de Ronsard, *French poet* (1524–1585)
Giovanni Palestrina, *Italian composer* (1526–1594)
Paolo Veronese, *Italian painter* (1528–1588)
Queen Elizabeth, *English ruler* (1533?–1603)
Michel de Montaigne, *French author* (1533–1592)
El Greco, *Spanish-Greek painter* (1542–1614)
Tycho Brahe, *Danish astronomer* (1546–1601)
Miguel de Cervantes, *Spanish writer* (1547–1616)
Giordano Bruno, *Italian philosopher* (1548–1600)
Sir Walter Raleigh, *English courtier* (1552–1618)
Edmund Spenser, *English poet* (1552–1599)
Giovanni Gabrieli, *Italian composer* (c.1557–1612)
Francis Bacon, *English philosopher* (1561–1626)
Christopher Marlowe, *English dramatist* (1564–1593)
Galileo Galilei, *Italian scientist* (1564–1642)
William Shakespeare, *English dramatist and poet* (1564–1616)
Michelangelo da Caravaggio, *Italian painter* (c.1565–1609)
Claudio Monteverdi, *Italian composer* (1567–1643)
Johannes Kepler, *German astronomer* (1571–1630)
John Donne, *English poet* (1573–1631)
Inigo Jones, *English architect* (1573–1652)
Ben Jonson, *English dramatist* (1573–1637)
Peter Paul Rubens, *Flemish painter* (1577–1652)
William Harvey, *English physician and anatomist* (1578–1657)

1587 Mary, Queen of Scots, executed for treason by order of Queen Elizabeth I. Monteverdi's *First Book of Madrigals*.
1588 Defeat of the Spanish Armada by English. Henry, King of Navarre and Protestant leader, recognized as Henry IV, first Bourbon king of France. Converts to Roman Catholicism in **1593** in attempt to end religious wars.
1590 Henry IV enters Paris, wars on Spain **(1595)**, marries Maria de Medici **(1600)**, assassinated **(1610)**. Spenser's *The Faerie Queen,* El Greco's *St. Jerome.* Galileo's experiments with falling objects.
1598 Boris Godunov becomes Russian Czar. Tycho Brahe describes his astronomical experiments.

1600 Giordano Bruno burned as a heretic. Ieyasu rules Japan, moves capital to Edo (Tokyo). Shakespeare's *Hamlet* begins his most productive decade. English East India Company established to develop overseas trade.
1607 Jamestown, Virginia, established—first permanent English colony on American mainland.
1609 Samuel de Champlain establishes French colony of Quebec.
1611 Gustavus Adolphus elected King of Sweden. King James Version of the Bible published in England. Rubens paints his *Descent from the Cross.*
1614 John Napier discovers logarithms.
1618 Start of the Thirty Years' War (to **1648**)—Protestant revolt against Catholic oppression; Denmark, Sweden, and France will invade Germany in later phases of war. Kepler proposes his Third Law of planetary motion.
1620 Pilgrims, after three-month voyage in *Mayflower,* land at Plymouth Rock. Francis Bacon's *Novum Organum.*
1633 Inquisition forces Galileo to recant his belief in Copernican theory.
1642 English Civil War. Cavaliers, supporters of Charles I, against Roundheads, parliamentary forces. Oliver Cromwell defeats Royalists **(1646)**. Parliament demands reforms. Charles I offers concessions, brought to trial **(1648)**, beheaded **(1649)**. Cromwell becomes Lord Protector **(1653)**. Rembrandt paints his *Night Watch.*
1644 End of Ming Dynasty in China—Manchus come to power. Descartes' *Principles of Philosophy.* John Milton's *Areopagitica* on the freedom of the press.
1648 End of the Thirty Years' War. German population about half of what it was in **1618** because of war and pestilence.
1658 Cromwell dies; his son, Richard, resigns and Puritan government collapses.
1660 English Parliament calls for the restoration of the monarchy; invites Charles II to return from France.
1661 Charles II is crowned King of England. Louis XIV begins personal rule as absolute monarch; starts to build Versailles.
1664 British take New Amsterdam from the Dutch. English limit "Nonconformity" with re-established Anglican Church. Isaac Newton's experiments with gravity.
1665 Great Plague in London kills 75,000.
1666 Great Fire of London. Molière's *Misanthrope.*
1683 War of European powers against the Turks (to **1699**). Vienna withstands three-month Turkish siege; high point of Turkish advance in Europe.

Frans Hals, *Dutch painter* (1581–1666)
Phineas Fletcher, *English dramatist* (1582–1650)
Francis Beaumont, *English dramatist* (1584–1616)
Cardinal Richelieu, *French prelate* (1585–1642)
Thomas Hobbes, *English philosopher* (1588–1679)
John Winthrop, *first governor of Massachusetts* (1588–1649)
Robert Herrick, *English poet* (1591–1674)
Johann Amos Comenius, *Moravian educational reformer* (1592–1670)
Peter Stuyvesant, *Dutch administrator in America* (1592–1672)
George Herbert, *English poet* (1593–1633)
Izaak Walton, *English biographer* (1593–1683)
Nicola Amati, *Italian violin maker* (1594–1684)
Nicolas Poussin, *French painter* (1594–1665)
Pocahontas, *Indian princess* (1595–1617)
René Descartes, *French philosopher* (1596–1650)
Oliver Cromwell, *English general and statesman* (1599–1658)
Anthony Van Dyck, *Flemish painter* (1599–1641)
Diego Velázquez, *Spanish painter* (1599–1660)
Pedro Calderón de la Barca, *Spanish dramatist* (1600–1681)
Roger Williams, *American religious leader* (1604–1683)
Pierre Corneille, *French dramatist* (1606–1684)
Rembrandt van Rijn, *Dutch painter* (1606–1669)

THE FOUNDING OF THE AMERICAN NATION

Colonization of America begins: Jamestown, Va. **(1607)**; Pilgrims in Plymouth **(1620)**; Massachusetts Bay Colony **(1630)**; New Netherland founded by Dutch West India Company **(1623)**, captured by English **(1664)**. Delaware established by Swedish trading company **(1638)**, absorbed later by Penn family. Proprietorships by royal grants to Lord Baltimore (Maryland, **1632**); Captain John Mason (New Hampshire, **1635**); Sir William Berkeley and Sir George Carteret (New Jersey, **1663**); friends of Charles II (the Carolinas, **1663**); William Penn (Pennsylvania, **1682**); James Oglethorpe and others (Georgia, **1732**).

Increasing conflict between colonists and Britain on western frontier because of royal edict limiting western expansion **(1763)**, and regulation of colonial trade and increased taxation of colonies (Writs of Assistance allow search for illegal shipments, **1761**; Sugar Act, **1764**; Currency Act, **1764**; Stamp Act, **1765**; Quartering Act, **1765**; Duty Act, **1767**.) Boston Massacre **(1770)**. Lord North attempts conciliation **(1770)**. Boston Tea Party **(1773)**, followed by punitive measures passed by Parliament—the "Intolerable Acts."

First Continental Congress **(1774)** sends "Declaration of Rights and Grievances" to King, urges colonies to form Continental Association. Paul Revere's Ride and Lexington and Concord battle between Massachusetts minutemen and British **(1775)**.

Second Continental Congress **(1775)**, while sending "olive branch" to the king, begins to raise army, appoints Washington commander-in-chief, and seeks alliance with France. Some colonial legislatures urge their delegates to vote for independence. Declaration of Independence **(July 4, 1776)**.

Major Battles of the Revolutionary War: *Long Island:* Howe defeats Putnam's division of Washington's Army in Brooklyn Heights, but Americans escape across East River **(1776)**. *Trenton and Princeton:* Washington defeats Hessians at Trenton, British at Princeton, winters at Morristown **(1776–77)**. Howe winters in Philadelphia; Washington at Valley Forge **(1777–78)**. Burgoyne surrenders British army to General Gates at *Saratoga* **(1777)**.

France recognizes American independence **(1778)**. The War moves south: Savannah captured by British **(1778)**; Charleston occupied **(1780)**; Americans fight successful guerrilla actions under Marion, Pickens, and Sumter. In the West, George Rogers Clark attacks Forts Kaskaskia and Vincennes **(1778–1779)**, defeating British in the region. Cornwallis surrenders at *Yorktown,* Virginia **(Oct. 19, 1781)**. By **1782**, Britain is eager for peace because of conflicts with European nations. *Peace of Paris* **(1783)**: Britain recognizes American independence.

1685 James II succeeds Charles II in England, calls for freedom of conscience **(1687)**. Protestants fear restoration of Catholicism and demand "Glorious Revolution." William of Orange invited to England and James II escapes to France **(1688)**. William III and his wife, Mary, crowned. In France, Edict of Nantes of 1598, granting freedom of worship to Huguenots (French Protestants), is revoked by Louis XIV; thousands of Protestants flee.

1689 Peter the Great becomes Czar of Russia—attempts to westernize nation and build Russia as military power. Defeats Charles XII of Sweden at Poltava **(1709)**. Beginning of the French and Indian Wars (to **1763**), campaigns in America linked to a series of wars between France and England for domination of Europe.

1690 William III of England defeats former King James II and Irish rebels at Battle of the Boyne in Ireland. John Locke's *Human Understanding*.

John Milton, *English poet* (1608–1674)
François de La Rouchefoucauld, *French author* (1613–1680)
Henry More, *English philosopher* (1614–1687)
Cyrano de Bergerac, *French poet* (1619–1655)
Andrew Marvell, *English poet* (1621–1678)
Molière (Jean-Baptiste Poquelin), *French dramatist* (1622–1673)
Blaise Pascal, *French philosopher* (1623–1662)
Robert Boyle, *English scientist* (1627–1691)
John Bunyan, *English author* (1628–1688)
John Dryden, *English dramatist* (1631–1700)
John Locke, *English philosopher* (1631–1704)
Luca Giordano, *Italian painter* (1632–1705)
Anton van Leeuwenhoek, *Dutch zoologist* (1632–1723)

Jan Vermeer, *Dutch painter* (1632–1675)
Baruch Spinoza, *Dutch philosopher* (1632–1677)
Christopher Wren, *English architect* (1632–1723)
Samuel Pepys, *English diarist* (1633–1703)
Jean Baptiste Lully, *French composer* (1639–1687)
Jean Racine, *French dramatist* (1639–1699)
Sir Isaac Newton, *English philosopher and mathematician* (1642–1727)
William Penn, *founder of Pennsylvania* (1644–1718)
Antonio Stradivari, *Italian violin maker* (1644–1737)
Gottfried W. von Leibniz, *German scientist* (1646–1716)
Arcangelo Corelli, *Italian composer* (1653–1713)
Jacques Bernoulli, *Swiss scientist* (1654–1705)

Edmund Halley, *English astronomer* (1656–1742)
Henry Purcell, *English composer* (1658–1695)
Daniel Defoe, *English author* (1659–1731)
Alessandro Scarlatti, *Italian composer* (1659–1725)
Cotton Mather, *Massachusetts churchman* (1663–1728)
François Couperin, *French composer* (1668–1733)
Giovanni Battista Vico, *Italian philosopher* (1668–1744)
William Congreve, *English dramatist* (1670–1730)
Peter the Great, *Russian czar* (1672–1725)
Antonio Vivaldi, *Italian composer* (1678–1741)

George Phillip Telemann, *German composer* (1681–1767)
Jean Philippe Rameau, *French composer* (1683–1764)
Jean Antoine Watteau, *French painter* (1684–1721)
J.S. Bach, *German composer* (1685–1750)
George Frederick Handel, *German-English composer* (1685–1759)
Domenico Scarlatti, *Italian composer* (1685–1757)
Gabriel Fahrenheit, *German physicist* (1686–1736)
Alexander Pope, *English poet* (1688–1744)
Emanuel Swedenborg, *Swedish mystic* (1688–1772)
Baron de Montesquieu, *French philosopher* (1689–1755)
François de Voltaire, *French philosopher* (1694–1778)
Canaletto (Antonio Canale), *Italian painter* (1697–1768)
William Hogarth, *English painter* (1697–1764)

1701 War of the Spanish Succession begins—the last of Louis XIV's wars for domination of the continent. The Peace of Utrecht **(1714)** will end the conflict and mark the rise of the British Empire. Called Queen Anne's War in America, it ends with the British taking New Foundland, Acadia, and Hudson's Bay Territory from France, and Gibraltar and Minorca from Spain.

1704 Deerfield (Conn.) Massacre of English colonists by French and Indians. Bach's first cantata. Jonathan Swift's *Tale of a Tub. Boston News Letter* —first newspaper in America.

1707 United Kingdom of Great Britain formed—England, Wales, and Scotland joined by parliamentary Act of Union.

1729 J. S. Bach's *St. Matthew's Passion.* Isaac Newton's *Principia* translated from Latin into English.

1735 John Peter Zenger, New York editor, acquitted of libel in New York, establishing press freedom.

1740 Capt. Vitus Bering, Dane employed by Russia, discovers Alaska.

1746 British defeat Scots under Stuart Pretender Prince Charles at Culloden Moor. Last battle fought on British soil.

1751 Publication of the *Encyclopédie* begins in France, the "bible" of the Enlightenment.

1755 Samuel Johnson's *Dictionary* first published. Great earthquake in Lisbon, Portugal—over 60,000 die.

1756 Seven Years' War (called French and Indian War in America) (to **1763**), in which Britain and Prussia defeat France, Spain, Austria, and Russia.

François Boucher, *French painter* (1703–1770)
Jonathan Edwards, *American theologian* (1703–1758)
John Wesley, *founder of Methodism* (1703–1791)
Benjamin Franklin, *American statesman* (1706–1790)
Henry Fielding, *English novelist* (1707–1754)
Leonhard Euler, *Swiss mathematician* (1707–1783)
Linnaeus (Carl von Linné), *Swedish botanist* (1707–1778)
Samuel Johnson, *English author* (1709–1784)
William Boyce, *English composer* (1710–1779)
Giovanni Pergolesi, *Italian composer* (1710–1736)
David Hume, *Scottish philosopher* (1711–1776)

France loses North American colonies; Spain cedes Florida to Britain in exchange for Cuba. In India, over 100 British prisoners die in "Black Hole of Calcutta."

1757 Beginning of British Empire in India as Robert Clive, British commander, defeats Nawab of Bengal at Plassey.

1759 British capture Quebec from French. Voltaire's *Candide*. Haydn's *Symphony No. 1*.

1762 Catherine II ("the Great") becomes Czarina of Russia. J. J. Rousseau's *Social Contract*. Mozart tours Europe as six-year-old prodigy.

1765 James Watt invents the steam engine.

1769 Sir William Arkwright patents a spinning machine—an early step in the Industrial Revolution.

1772 Joseph Priestley and Daniel Rutherford independently discover nitrogen. Partition of Poland—in 1772, 1793, and 1795, Austria, Prussia, and Russia divide land and people of Poland, end its independence.

1775 The American Revolution (*see* "The Founding of the American Nation"). Priestley discovers hydrochloric and sulfuric acids.

1776 Adam Smith's *Wealth of Nations*. Edward Gibbon's *Decline and Fall of the Roman Empire*. Thomas Paine's *Common Sense*. Fragonard's *Washerwoman*. Mozart's *Haffner Serenade*.

1778 Capt. James Cook discovers Hawaii. Franz Mesmer uses hypnotism.

1781 Immanuel Kant's *Critique of Pure Reason*. Herschel discovers Uranus.

1783 End of Revolutionary War (*see* special material on "The Founding of the American Nation"). William Blake's poems. Beethoven's first printed works.

1784 Crimea annexed by Russia. John Wesley's *Deed of Declaration*, the basic work of Methodism.

1785 Russians settle Aleutian Islands.

1787 The Constitution of the United States signed. Lavoisier's work on chemical nomenclature. Mozart's *Don Giovanni*.

1788 French *Parlement* presents grievances to Louis XVI who agrees to convening of Estates-General in 1789—not called since 1613. Goethe's *Egmont*. Laplace's *Laws of the Planetary System*.

1789 French Revolution (*see* special material on the "French Revolution"). In U.S., George Washington elected President with all 69 votes of the Electoral College, takes oath of office in New York City. Vice President: John Adams. Secretary of State: Thomas Jefferson. Secretary of Treasury: Alexander Hamilton.

George Washington, *first American President* (1732–1799)

.H. Fragonard, *French painter* (1732–1800)

osef Haydn, *Austrian composer* (1732–1809)

ranz Anton Mesmer, *Austrian hypnotist* (1733–1815)

oseph Priestley, *English scientist* (1733–1804)

ohn Adams, *American President* (1735–1826)

aniel Boone, *American frontiersman* (1735–1820)

atrick Henry, *American patriot* (1736–1799)

ames Watt, *Scottish inventor* (1736–1819)

ohn S. Copley, *American painter* (1737–1815)

dward Gibbon, *English historian* (1737–1794)

Thomas Paine, *American author and patriot* (1737–1809)

William Herschel, *English astronomer* (1738–1822)

Prince Potemkin, *Russian statesman* (1739–1791)

James Boswell, *Scottish writer* (1740–1795)

Marquis de Sade, *French libertine and writer* (1741–1814)

Benedict Arnold, *American general and traitor* (1741–1801)

Luigi Boccherini, *Italian composer* (1743–1805)

Antoine Lavoisier, *French chemist* (1743–1794)

Jean-Paul Marat, *French revolutionist* (1743–1793)

Thomas Jefferson, *American President* (1743–1826)

Jean-Baptiste de Lamark, *French scientist* (1744–1829)

Alessandro Volta, *Italian scientist* (1745–1827)

Francisco de Goya, *Spanish painter* (1746–1828)

Johann Pestalozzi, *Swiss educator* (1746–1827)

John Paul Jones, *American naval officer* (1747–1792)

Jeremy Bentham *English economist* (1748–1832)

Jacques David, *French painter* (1748–1825)

Count Casimir Pulaski, *Polish-American patriot* (1748–1779)

Johann Wolfgang von Goethe, *German writer* (1749–1832)

Jean-Jacques Rousseau, *French philosopher* (1712–1778)

Denis Diderot, *French encyclopedist* (1713–1784)

Laurance Sterne, *English novelist* (1713–1768)

K.P.E. Bach, *German composer* (1714–1788)

David Garrick, *English actor* (1717–1779)

Horace Walpole, *English statesman and novelist* (1717–1797)

Thomas Chippendale, *English artisan* (1718?–1779)

Bernardo Canaletto, *Italian painter* (1720–1780)

Giambattista Piranesi, *Italian artist* (1720–1778)

Baron von Münchhausen, *German anecdotist* (1720–1797)

Mme. de Pompadour, *French courtesan* (1721–1764)

Tobias Smollet, *English novelist* (1721–1771)

Samuel Adams, *American patriot* (1722–1803)

Joshua Reynolds, *English painter* (1723–1792)

Adam Smith, *English economist* (1723–1790)

Immanuel Kant, *German philosopher* (1724–1804)

Giovanni Casanova, *Italian adventurer* (1725–1798)

Thomas Gainsborough, *English painter* (1727–1788)

Oliver Goldsmith, *English writer* (1728–1774)

Catherine II (Catherine the Great), *Russian empress* (1729–1796)

Edmund Burke, *English statesman* (1729–1797)

William Cowper, *English poet* (1731–1800)

RENCH REVOLUTION (1789–1799)

Revolution begins when Third Estate (Commons) delegates wear not to disband until France has a constitution. Paris ob storms Bastille, symbol of royal power (July 14, 1789). ational Assembly votes for Constitution, Declaration of the ghts of Man, a limited monarchy, and other reforms (1789–). Legislative Assembly elected, Revolutionary Commune rmed, and French Republic proclaimed (1792). War of the st Coalition—Austria, Prussia, Britain, Netherlands, and Spain fight to restore French nobility (1792–97). Start of series of wars between France and European powers that will last, almost without interruption, for 23 years. Louis XVI and Marie Antoinette executed. Committee of Public Safety begins Reign of Terror as political control measure. Interfactional rivalry leads to mass killings. Danton and Robespierre executed. Third French Constitution sets up Directory government (1795).

1790 H.M.S. *Bounty* mutineers settle on Pitcairn Island. Aloisio Galvani experiments on electrical stimulation of the muscles. Philadelphia temporary capital of U.S. as Congress votes to establish new capital on Potomac. U.S. population about 3,929,000, including 698,000 slaves. Lavoisier formulates *Table of 31 chemical elements.*

1791 U.S. Bill of Rights ratified. Boswell's *Life of Johnson.*

1794 Kosciusko's uprising in Poland quelled by the Russians. In U.S., Whiskey Rebellion in Pennsylvania as farmers object to liquor taxes. U.S. Navy and Post Office Department established.

1796 Napoleon Bonaparte, French general, defeats Austrians. In the U.S., Washington's Farewell Address **(Sept. 17)**; John Adams elected President; Thomas Jefferson, Vice President. Edward Jenner introduces smallpox vaccination.

1798 Napoleon extends French conquests to Rome and Egypt.

1799 Napoleon leads coup that overthrows Directory, becomes First Consul —one of three who rule France.

James Madison, *American President* (1751–1836)
Richard Brinsley Sheridan, *Irish dramatist* (1751–1816)
Fanny Burney, *English writer* (1752–1840)
Betsy Ross, *American flagmaker* (1752–1836)
C. de Talleyrand-Périgord, *French statesman* (1754–1838)
Marie Antoinette, *French queen* (1755–1793)
Alexander Hamilton, *American statesman* (1755–1804)
Gilbert Stuart, *American painter* (1755–1828)
Aaron Burr, *American statesman* (1756–1836)
Wolfgang Amadeus Mozart, *Austrian composer* (1756–1791)
William Blake, *English poet* (1757–1827)
Marquis de Lafayette, *French general in America* (1757–1834)

James Monroe, *American President* (1758–1831)
Horatio Nelson, *English admiral* (1758–1805)
Maximilien de Robespierre, *French revolutionist* (1758–1794)
Noah Webster, *American lexicographer* (1758–1843)
Robert Burns, *Scottish poet* (1759–1796)
Katsuhika Hokusai, *Japanese artist* (1760–1849)
Luigi Cherubini, *Italian composer* (1760–1842)
Robert Fulton, *American inventor* (1765–1815)
Eli Whitney, *American inventor* (1765–1825)
John Dalton, *English chemist* (1766–1844)
T. R. Malthus, *English economist* (1766–1834)
John Quincy Adams, *American President* (1767–1848)
Andrew Jackson, *American President* (1767–1845)

Jacques Lafitte, *French pirate* (1767–1844)
Tecumseh, *American Indian chief* (1768?–1813)
Napoleon Bonaparte, *French emperor* (1769–1821)
Duke of Wellington, *English general* (1769–1852)
Ludwig van Beethoven, *German composer* (1770–1827)
G. W. F. Hegel, *German philosopher* (1770–1831)
William Wordsworth, *English writer* (1770–1850)
Robert Owen, *English social reformer* (1771–1858)
Walter Scott, *Scottish novelist* (1771–1832)
Friedrich von Schlegel, *German philosopher* (1772–1829)

Prince K. von Metternich, *Austrian statesman* (1773–1859)
Jane Austen, *English novelist* (1775–1817)
J. W. Turner, *English painter* (1775–1851)
John Constable, *English painter* (1776–1837)
Henry Clay, *American statesman* (1777–1852)
Heinrich von Kleist, *German poet* (1777–1811)
Karl von Clausewitz, *German military strategist* (1780–1831)
J.A. Ingres, *French painter* (1780–1867)
Nicolo Paganini, *Italian composer* (1782–1840)
Daniel Webster, *American statesman* (1782–1852)
Simón Bolívar, *Latin American patriot* (1783–1830)
Washington Irving, *American writer* (1783–1859)
Stendhal (Marie Henri Beyle), *French novelist* (1783–1842)
J. J. Audubon, *American naturalist* (1785–1851)

1800 Napoleon conquers Italy, firmly establishes himself as First Consul in France. In the U.S., Federal Government moves to Washington. Robert Owen's social reforms in England. William Herschel discovers infrared rays. Alessandro Volta produces electricity.

1801 Austria makes temporary peace with France. United Kingdom of Great Britain and Ireland established with one monarch and one parliament; Catholics excluded from voting.

1803 U.S. negotiates Louisiana Purchase from France: For $15 million, U.S. doubles its domain, increasing its territory by 827,000 sq mi. (2,144,500 sq km), from Mississippi River to Rockies and from Gulf of Mexico to British North America.

1804 Haiti declares independence from France; first black nation to gain freedom from European colonial rule. Napoleon proclaims himself emperor of France, systematizes French law under *Code Napoleon.* In the U.S., Alexander Hamilton is mortally wounded in duel with Aaron Burr. Lewis and Clark expedition begins exploration of what is now northwestern U.S.

1805 Lord Nelson defeats the French-Spanish fleets in the Battle of Trafalgar. Napoleon victorious over Austrian and Russian forces at the Battle of Austerlitz.

1807 Robert Fulton makes first successful steamboat trip on *Clermont* between New York City and Albany.

Davy Crockett, *American frontiersman* (1786–1836)
Carl Maria von Weber, *German composer* (1786–1826)
Louis Daguerre, *French photographic pioneer* (1787–1851)
Lord Byron, *English poet* (1788–1824)
Arthur Schopenhauer, *German philosopher* (1788–1860)
James Fenimore Cooper, *American writer* (1789–1851)
Michael Faraday, *English physicist* (1791–1867)
Samuel F. B. Morse, *American inventor* (1791–1872)

1808 French armies occupy Rome and Spain, extending Napoleon's empire. Britain begins aiding Spanish guerrillas against Napoleon in Peninsular War. In the U.S., Congress bars importation of slaves. Beethoven's *Fifth* and *Sixth Symphonies* performed.

1812 Napoleon's Grand Army invades Russia in June. Forced to retreat in winter, most of Napoleon's 600,000 men are lost. In the U.S., war with Britain declared over freedom of the seas for U.S. vessels. U.S.S. *Constitution* sinks British frigate. (*See* special material on the "War of 1812.")

1814 French defeated by allies (Britain, Austria, Russia, Prussia, Sweden, and Portugal) in War of Liberation. Napoleon exiled to Elba, off Italian coast. Bourbon King Louis XVIII takes French throne. George Stephenson builds first practical steam locomotive.

1815 Napoleon returns: "Hundred Days" begin. Napoleon defeated by Wellington at Waterloo, banished again to St. Helena in South Atlantic. Congress of Vienna: victorious allies change the map of Europe.

1817 Simón Bolívar establishes independent Venezuela, as Spain loses hold on South American countries. Bolívar named President of Colombia (**1819**). Peru, Guatemala, Panama, and Santo Domingo proclaim independence from Spain (**1821**).

1820 Missouri Compromise—Missouri admitted as slave state but slavery barred in rest of Louisiana Purchase north of 36°30′ N.

1822 Greeks proclaim a republic and independence from Turkey. Turks invade Greece. Russia declares war on Turkey (**1828**). Greece also aided by France and Britain. War ends and Turks recognize Greek independence (**1829**). Brazil becomes independent of Portugal. Schubert's *Eighth Symphony* ("The Unfinished").

1823 U.S. Monroe Doctrine warns European nations not to interfere in Western Hemisphere.

1824 Mexico becomes a republic, three years after declaring independence from Spain. Beethoven's *Ninth Symphony*.

1825 First passenger-carrying railroad in England.

1830 French invade Algeria. Louis Philippe becomes "Citizen King" as revolution forces Charles X to abdicate. Mormon church formed in U.S. by Joseph Smith.

1831 Polish revolt against Russia fails. Belgium separates from the Netherlands. In U.S., Nat Turner leads unsuccessful slave rebellion.

1833 Slavery abolished in British Empire.

1834 Charles Babbage invents "analytical engine," precursor of computer. McCormick patents reaper.

1836 Boer farmers start "Great Trek"—Natal, Transvaal, and Orange Free State founded in South Africa. Mexican army besieges Texans in Alamo. Entire garrison, including Davy Crockett and Jim Bowie, wiped out. Texans gain independence from Mexico after winning Battle of San Jacinto. Dickens's *Pickwick Papers*.

1837 Victoria becomes Queen of Great Britain. Mob kills Elijah P. Lovejoy, Illinois abolitionist publisher.

1839 First Opium War (to **1842**) between Britain and China, over importation of drug into China.

1840 Lower and Upper Canada united.

1841 U.S. President Harrison dies (**April 4**) one month after inauguration; John Tyler becomes first Vice President to succeed to Presidency.

1844 Democratic convention calls for annexation of Texas and acquisition of Oregon ("Fifty-four-forty-or-fight"). Five Chinese ports opened to U.S. ships. Samuel F. B. Morse patents telegraph.

1845 Congress adopts joint resolution for annexation of Texas.

1846 Failure of potato crop causes famine in Ireland. U.S. declares war on Mexico. California and New Mexico annexed by U.S. Brigham Young leads Mormons to Great Salt Lake. W. T. Morton uses ether as anesthetic. Sewing machine patented by Elias Howe.

1848 Revolt in Paris: Louis Philippe abdicates; Louis Napoleon elected President of French Republic. Revolutions in Vienna, Venice, Berlin, Milan, Rome, and Warsaw. Put down by royal troops in **1848–49**. U.S.-Mexico War ends; Mexico cedes claims to Texas, California, Arizona, New Mexico, Utah, Nevada. U.S. treaty with Britain sets Oregon Territory boundary at 49th parallel. Karl Marx and Friedrich Engels' *Communist Manifesto*.

1849 California gold rush begins.

Percy Bysshe Shelley, *English poet* (1792–1822)
Gioacchino Rossini, *Italian composer* (1792–1868)
Sam Houston, *Texas political leader* (1793–1863)
John Keats, *English poet* (1795–1821)
Thomas Carlyle, *British historian* (1795–1881)
Heinrich Heine, *German poet* (1797–1856)
Ando Hiroshige, *Japanese painter* (1797–1858)
Franz Schubert, *Austrian composer* (1797–1828)
Adam Mickiewicz, *Polish poet* (1798–1855)
Auguste Comte, *French philosopher* (1798–1857)
Ferdinand Delacroix, *French painter* (1798–1863)
Honoré de Balzac, *French novelist* (1799–1850)
Aleksander Pushkin, *Russian poet* (1799–1837)
John Henry Newman, *English prelate* (1801–1890)
Brigham Young, *Mormon leader* (1801–1877)
Lajos Kossuth, *Hungarian patriot* (1802–1894)
Alexander Dumas, père, *French novelist* (1802–1870)
Victor Hugo, *French novelist* (1802–1885)
Ralph Waldo Emerson, *American philosopher* (1803–1882)
Hector Berlioz, *French composer* (1803–1869)
Benjamin Disraeli, *British statesman* (1804–1881)
Nathaniel Hawthorne, *American novelist* (1804–1864)
George Sand, *French writer* (1804–1876)
Giuseppe Mazzini, *Italian patriot* (1805–1872)
Hans Christian Andersen, *Danish writer* (1805–1875)
Alexis de Tocqueville, *French writer* (1805–1859)
Elizabeth Barrett Browning, *English poet* (1806–1861)
John Stuart Mill, *English philosopher* (1806–1873)
Giuseppe Garibaldi, *Italian patriot* (1807–1882)
Henry Wadsworth Longfellow, *American poet* (1807–1882)
Honoré Daumier, *French artist* (1808–1879)

WAR OF 1812

British interference with American trade, impressment of American seamen, and "War Hawks" drive for western expansion lead to war. American attacks on Canada foiled; U.S. Commodore Perry wins battle of Lake Erie (**1813**). British capture and burn Washington (**1814**) but fail to take Fort McHenry at Baltimore. Andrew Jackson repulses assault on New Orleans after treaty of Ghent ends war (**1815**). War settles little but strengthens U.S. as independent nation.

1850 Henry Clay opens great debate on slavery, warns South against secession.

1851 Herman Melville's *Moby Dick.* Harriet Beecher Stowe's *Uncle Tom's Cabin.*

1852 South African Republic established. Louis Napoleon proclaims himself Napoleon III ("Second Empire").

1853 Crimean War begins as Turkey declares war on Russia. Commodore Perry reaches Tokyo.

1854 Britain and France join Turkey in war on Russia. In U.S., Kansas-Nebraska Act permits local option on slavery; rioting and bloodshed. Japanese allow American trade. Antislavery men in Michigan form Republican Party. Tennyson's *Charge of the Light Brigade.* Thoreau's *Walden.*

1855 Armed clashes in Kansas between pro- and anti-slavery forces. Florence Nightingale nurses wounded in Crimea. Walt Whitman's *Leaves of Grass.*

1856 Flaubert's *Madame Bovary.*

1857 Supreme Court, in Dred Scott decision, rules that a slave is not a citizen. Financial crisis in Europe and U.S. Great Mutiny (Sepoy Rebellion) begins in India. India placed under crown rule as a result.

1858 Pro-slavery constitution rejected in Kansas. Abraham Lincoln makes strong antislavery speech in Springfield, Ill.: ". . . this Government cannot endure permanently half slave and half free." Lincoln-Douglas debates. First trans-Atlantic telegraph cable completed by Cyrus W. Field.

1859 John Brown raids Harpers Ferry; is captured and hanged. Work begins on Suez Canal. Unification of Italy starts under leadership of Count Cavour, Sardinian premier. Joined by France in war against Austria. Edward Fitzgerald's *Rubaiyat of Omar Khayyam.* Charles Darwin's *Origin of Species.* J. S. Mill's *On Liberty*

1861 U.S. Civil War begins as attempts at compromise fail *(see* special material on "The Civil War"). Congress creates Colorado, Dakota, and Nevada territories; adopts income tax; Lincoln inaugurated. Serfs emancipated in Russia. Pasteur's theory of germs. Independent Kingdom of Italy proclaimed under Sardinian King Victor Emmanuel II.

1863 French capture Mexico City; proclaim Archduke Maximilian of Austria emperor.

1865 Lincoln fatally shot at Ford's Theater by John Wilkes Booth. Vice President Johnson sworn as successor. Booth caught and dies of gunshot wounds; four conspirators are hanged. Joseph Lister begins antiseptic surgery. Gregor Mendel's Law of Heredity. Lewis Carroll's *Alice's Adventures in Wonderland.*

1866 Alfred Nobel invents dynamite. Seven Weeks' War: Austria defeated by Prussia and Italy.

1867 Austria-Hungary Dual Monarchy established. French leave Mexico; Maximilian executed. Dominion of Canada established. U.S. buys Alaska from Russia for $7,200,000. South African diamond field discovered. Volume I of Marx's *Das Kapital.* Strauss's *Blue Danube.*

1868 Revolution in Spain; Queen Isabella deposed, flees to France. In U.S., Fourteenth Amendment giving civil rights to blacks is ratified. Georgia under military government after legislature expels blacks.

Abraham Lincoln, *American president* (1809–1865)
Nicolai Gogol, *Russian writer* (1809–1852)
Edgar Allan Poe, *American writer* (1809–1849)
Alfred, Lord Tennyson, *English poet* (1809–1892)
William Ewart Gladstone, *British statesman* (1809–1898)
Charles Darwin, *English scientist* (1809–1882)
Felix Mendelssohn, *German composer* (1809–1847)
Louis Braille, *French inventor of touch alphabet for blind* (1809–1852)
Frédéric Chopin, *Polish composer* (1810–1849)
Robert Schumann, *German composer* (1810–1856)
Phineas T. Barnum, *American showman* (1810–1891)
Harriet Beecher Stowe, *American writer* (1811–1896)
William M. Thackeray, *English novelist* (1811–1863)
Franz Liszt, *Hungarian composer* (1811–1896)
Robert Browning, *English poet* (1812–1889)
Charles Dickens, *English novelist* (1812–1870)
Alfred Krupp, *German munitions magnate* (1812–1887)
Sören Kierkegaard, *Danish philosopher* (1813–1855)
Giuseppe Verdi, *Italian composer* (1813–1901)
Richard Wagner, *German composer* (1813–1883)
Otto von Bismarck, *Prussian statesman* (1815–1898)
Charlotte Brontë, *English writer* (1816–1855)

THE CIVIL WAR (1861–1865)
(The War Between the States or the War of the Rebellion)

Apart from the matter of slavery, the Civil War arose out of both the economic and political rivalry between an agrarian South and an industrial North and the issue of the right of states to secede from the Union.

1861 After South Carolina secedes **(Dec. 20, 1860)**, Mississippi, Florida, Alabama, Georgia, Louisiana, and Texas follow, forming the Confederate States of America, with Jefferson Davis as president **(Jan.-March)**. War begins as Confederates fire on Fort Sumter **(April 12)**. Lincoln calls for 75,000 volunteers. Southern ports blockaded by superior Union naval forces. Virginia, Arkansas, Tennessee, and North Carolina secede to complete 11-state Confederacy. Union army advancing on Richmond repulsed at first Battle of Bull Run **(July)**.

1862 Edwin M. Stanton named Secretary of War **(Jan.)**. Grant wins first important Union victory in West, at Fort Donelson; Nashville falls **(Feb.)**. Ironclads, Union's *Monitor* and Confederate's *Virginia (Merrimac)* duel at Hampton Roads **(March)**. New Orleans falls to Union fleet under Farragut; city occupied **(April)**. Grant's army escapes defeat at Shiloh. Memphis falls as Union gunboats control upper Mississippi **(June)**. Confederate general Robert E. Lee victorious at second Battle of Bull Run **(Aug.)**. Union army under McClellan halts Lee's attack on Washington in the Battle of Antietam **(Sept.)**. Lincoln removes McClellan for lack of aggressiveness. Burnside's drive on Richmond fails at Fredericksburg **(Dec.)**. Union forces under Rosecrans chase Bragg through Tennessee; battle of Murfreesboro **(Oct.-Jan. 1863)**.

1863 Lee defeats Hooker at Chancellorsville; "Stonewall" Jackson, Confederate general, dies **(May)**. Confederate invasion of Pennsylvania stopped at Gettysburg by George Meade—Lee loses 20,000 men—the greatest battle of the War **(July)**. It and the Union victory at Vicksburg mark the war's turning point. Union general George H. Thomas, the "Rock of Chickamauga," holds Bragg's forces on Georgia-Tennessee border **(Sept.)**. Sherman, Hooker, and Thomas drive Bragg back to Georgia. Tennessee restored to the Union **(Nov.)**.

1864 Ulysses S. Grant named commander-in-chief of Union forces **(March)**. In the Wilderness campaign, Grant forces Lee's Army of Northern Virginia back toward Richmond **(May-June)**. Sherman's Atlanta campaign and "march to the sea" **(May-Sept.)**. Farragut's victory at Mobile Bay **(Aug.)**. Hood's Confederate army defeated at Nashville. Sherman takes Savannah **(Dec.)**.

1865 Sheridan defeats Confederates at Five Forks; Confederates evacuate Richmond **(April)**. On **April 9**, Lee surrenders to Grant at Appomattox.

1869 First U.S. transcontinental rail route completed. James Fisk and Jay Gould attempt to control gold market causes Black Friday panic. Suez Canal opened. Mendeleev's periodic table of elements.

1870 Franco-Prussian War (to **1871**): Napoleon III capitulates at Sedan. Revolt in Paris; Third Republic proclaimed.

1871 France surrenders Alsace-Lorraine to Germany; war ends. German Empire proclaimed with Prussian King as Kaiser Wilhelm I. Fighting with Apaches begins in American West. Boss Tweed corruption exposed in New York. The Chicago Fire, with 250 deaths and $196-million damage. Stanley meets Livingston in Africa.

1872 Congress gives amnesty to most Confederates. Jules Verne's *Around the World in 80 Days.*

1873 Economic crisis in Europe. U.S. establishes gold standard.

1875 First Kentucky Derby.

1876 Sioux kill Gen. George A. Custer and 264 troopers at Little Big Horn River. Alexander Graham Bell patents the telephone.

1877 After Presidential election of **1876**, Electoral Commission gives disputed Electoral College votes to Rutherford B. Hayes despite Tilden's popular majority. Russo-Turkish war (ends in **1878** with power of Turkey in Europe broken). Reconstruction ends in the American South. Thomas Edison patents phonograph.

1878 Congress of Berlin revises Treaty of San Stefano ending Russo-Turkish War; makes extensive redivision of southeastern Europe. First commercial telephone exchange opened in New Haven, Conn.

1880 U.S.-China treaty allows U.S. to restrict immigration of Chinese labor.

1881 President Garfield fatally shot by assassin; Vice President Arthur succeeds him. Charles J. Guiteau convicted and executed (in **1882**).

1882 Terrorism in Ireland after land evictions. Britain invades and conquers Egypt. Germany, Austria, and Italy form Triple Alliance. In U.S., Congress adopts Chinese Exclusion Act. Rockefeller's Standard Oil Trust is first industrial monopoly. In Berlin, Robert Koch announces discovery of tuberculosis germ.

1883 Congress creates Civil Service Commission. Brooklyn Bridge and Metropolitan Opera House completed.

1885 British Gen. Charles G. "Chinese" Gordon killed at Khartoum in Egyptian Sudan.

1886 Bombing at Haymarket Square, Chicago, kills seven policemen and injures many others. Eight alleged anarchists accused—three imprisoned, one commits suicide, four hanged. (In **1893**, Illinois Governor Altgeld, critical of trial, pardons three survivors.) Statue of Liberty dedicated. Geronimo, Apache Indian chief, surrenders.

1887 Queen Victoria's Golden Jubilee. Sir Arthur Conan Doyle's first Sherlock Holmes story, "A Study in Scarlet."

1888 Historic March blizzard in Northeast U.S.—many perish, property damage exceeds $25 million. George Eastman's box camera (the Kodak). J.B. Dunlop invents pneumatic tire. Jack the Ripper murders in London.

1889 Second (Socialist) International founded in Paris. Indian Territory in Oklahoma opened to settlement. Thousands die in Johnstown, Pa., flood. Mark Twain's *A Connecticut Yankee in King Arthur's Court.*

1890 Congress votes Sherman Antitrust Act. Sitting Bull killed in Sioux uprising.

1892 Battle between steel strikers and Pinkerton guards at Homestead, Pa.; union defeated after militia intervenes. Silver mine strikers in Idaho fight non-union workers; U.S. troops dispatched. Diesel engine patented.

1894 Sino-Japanese War begins (ends in **1895** with China's defeat). In France, Capt. Alfred Dreyfus convicted on false treason charge (pardoned in **1906**). In U.S., Jacob S. Coxey of Ohio leads "Coxey's Army" of unemployed on Washington. Eugene V. Debs calls general strike of rail workers to support Pullman Company strikers; strike broken, Debs jailed for six months. Thomas A. Edison's kinetoscope given first public showing in New York City.

1895 X-rays discovered by German physicist, Wilhelm Roentgen.

1896 Supreme Court's *Plessy* v. *Ferguson* decision—"separate but equal"

Henry David Thoreau, *American writer* (1817–1862)
Ivan Turgenev, *Russian writer* (1818–1883)
Karl Marx, *German political philosopher* (1818–1883)
Queen Victoria, *British monarch* (1819–1901)
George Eliot, *English novelist* (1819–1880)
Walt Whitman, *American poet* (1819–1892)
Friedrich Engels, *German political philosopher* (1820–1895)
Florence Nightingale, *English nurse* (1820–1910)
Charles Baudelaire, *French poet* (1821–1867)
Feodor Dostoevsky, *Russian writer* (1821–1881)
Gustave Flaubert, *French novelist* (1821–1880)
Mary Baker Eddy, *founder of Christian Science* (1821–1910)
Ulysses S. Grant, *American President* (1822–1885)
Gregor Mendel, *Austrian scientist* (1822–1884)
Louis Pasteur, *French scientist* (1822–1895)
Alexandre Dumas, fils, *French writer* (1824–1895)
Johann Strauss, *Austrian "waltz king"* (1825–1899)
Stephen Foster, *American composer* (1826–1864)
Joseph Lister, *English surgeon* (1827–1912)
Henrik Ibsen, *Norwegian dramatist* (1828–1906)
Leo Tolstoi, *Russian novelist* (1828–1910)
Jules Verne, *French author* (1828–1905)
William Booth, *Salvation Army founder* (1829–1912)
Emily Dickinson, *American poet* (1830–1886)
James Clerk Maxwell, *Scottish astronomer and physicist* (1831–1879)
Louisa May Alcott, *American author* (1832–1888)
Horatio Alger, *American author* (1834–1899)
Lewis Carroll (Charles Lutwidge Dodgson), *English author* (1832–1898)

PANISH-AMERICAN WAR (1898–1899)

War fires stoked by "jingo journalism" as American people ıpport Cuban rebels against Spain. American business sees conomic gain in Cuban trade and resources and American ower zones in Latin America. Outstanding events: Submane mine explodes U.S. battleship *Maine* in Havana Harbor eb. 15); 260 killed; responsibility never fixed. Congress deares independence of Cuba (**April 19**). Spain declares war on .S. (**Apr. 24**); Congress (**Apr. 25**) formally declares nation has been at war with Spain since Apr. 21. Commodore George Dewey wins seven-hour battle of Manila Bay (**May 1**). Spanish fleet destroyed off Santiago, Cuba (**July 3**); city surrenders (**July 17**). Treaty of Paris (ratified by Senate in **1899**) ends war. U.S. given Guam and Puerto Rico and agrees to pay Spain $20 million for Philippines. Cuba independent of Spain; under U.S. military control for three years until **May 20, 1902**. Yellow fever is eradicated and political reforms achieved.

doctrine. Alfred Nobel's will establishes prizes for peace, science, and literature. Marconi receives first wireless patent in Britain. William Jennings Bryan delivers "Cross of Gold" speech at Democratic Convention in Chicago. First modern Olympic games held in Athens, Greece.

1898 Chinese "Boxers," anti-foreign organization, established. They stage uprisings against Europeans in **1900**; U.S. and other Western troops relieve Peking legations. Spanish-American War (*see* special material on the "Spanish-American War"). Pierre and Marie Curie discover radium and polonium.

1899 Boer War (or South African War). Conflict between British and Boers (descendants of Dutch settlers of South Africa). Causes rooted in long-standing territorial disputes and in friction over political rights for English and other "uitlanders" following 1886 discovery of vast gold deposits in Transvaal. (British victorious as war ends in **1902**.) Casualties: 5,774 British dead, about 4,000 Boers. Union of South Africa established in **1908** as confederation of colonies; becomes British dominion in **1910**.

1900 Hurricane ravages Galveston, Tex.; 6,000 drown. Sigmund Freud's *The Interpretation of Dreams.*

1901 Queen Victoria dies; succeeded by son, Edward VII. As President McKinley begins second term, he is shot fatally by anarchist Leon Czolgosz. Theodore Roosevelt sworn in as successor.

1902 Enrico Caruso's first gramophone recording.

1903 Wright brothers, Orville and Wilbur, fly first powered, controlled, heavier-than-air plane at Kitty Hawk, N.C. Henry Ford organizes Ford Motor Company.

1904 Russo-Japanese War—competition for Korea and Manchuria: In **1905**, Port Arthur surrenders to Japanese and Russia suffers other defeats; President Roosevelt mediates Treaty of Portsmouth, N.H., ending war with concessions for Japan. *Entente Cordiale:* Britain and France settle their international differences. General theory of radioactivity by Rutherford and Soddy. New York City subway opened.

1905 General strike in Russia; first workers' soviet set up in St. Petersburg. Sailors on battleship *Potemkin* mutiny; reforms including first Duma (parliament) established by Czar's "October Manifesto." Albert Einstein's special theory of relativity and other key theories in physics. Franz Lehar's *Merry Widow.*

1906 San Francisco earthquake and three-day fire; 500 dead. Roald Amundsen, Norwegian explorer, fixes magnetic North Pole.

1907 Second Hague Peace Conference, of 46 nations, adopts 10 conventions on rules of war. Financial panic of **1907** in U.S.

1908 Earthquake kills 150,000 in southern Italy and Sicily. U.S. Supreme Court, in Danbury Hatters' case, outlaws secondary union boycotts.

1909 North Pole reached by American explorers Robert E. Peary and Matthew Henson.

1910 Boy Scouts of America incorporated.

1911 First use of aircraft as offensive weapon in Turkish-Italian War. Italy defeats Turks and annexes Tripoli and Libya. Chinese Republic proclaimed after revolution overthrows Manchu dynasty. Sun Yat-sen named president. Mexican Revolution: Porfirio Diaz, president since 1877, replaced by Francisco Madero. Triangle Shirtwaist Company fire in New York; 145 killed. Richard Strauss's *Der Rosenkavalier.* Irving Berlin's *Alexander's Ragtime Band.* Amundsen reaches South Pole.

1912 Balkan Wars **(1912–13)** resulting from territorial disputes: Turkey defeated by alliance of Bulgaria, Serbia, Greece, and Montenegro; London peace treaty **(1913)** partitions most of European Turkey among the victors. In second war **(1913)**, Bulgaria attacks Serbia and Greece and is defeated after Romania intervenes and Turks recapture Adrianople. *Titanic* sinks on maiden voyage; over 1,500 drown.

1913 Suffragettes demonstrate in London. Garment workers strike in New York and Boston; win pay raise and shorter hours. Sixteenth Amendment (income tax) and 17th (popular election of U.S. senators) adopted. Bill creating U.S. Federal Reserve System becomes law. Stravinsky's *The Rite of Spring.*

1914 World War I begins (*see* special material on "World War I"). Panama Canal officially opened. Congress sets up Federal Trade Commission, passes Clayton Antitrust Act. U.S. Marines occupy Veracruz, Mexico, intervening in civil war to protect American interests.

1915 U.S. protests German submarine actions and British blockade of Germany. U.S. banks lend $500 million to France and Britain. D. W. Griffith's film *Birth of a Nation.* Albert Einstein's *General Theory of Relativity.*

1916 Congress expands armed forces. Tom Mooney arrested for San Francisco bombing (pardoned in **1939**). Pershing fails in raid into Mexico in

Edouard Manet, *French painter* (1832–1883)
Johannes Brahms, *German composer* (1833–1897)
Alfred Nobel, *Swedish industrialist* (1833–1896)
Edgar Dégas, *French painter* (1834–1917)
James McNeill Whistler, *American painter* (1834–1903)
Dmitri Mendeleev, *Russian chemist* (1834–1907)
Mark Twain (Samuel L. Clemens), *American author* (1835–1910)
Camille Saint-Saëns, *French composer* (1835–1910)
Andrew Carnegie, *American industrialist* (1835–1919)
W. S. Gilbert, *English librettist* (1836–1911)
Bret Harte, *American novelist* (1836–1902)
Winslow Homer, *American painter* (1836–1910)
Sitting Bull, *American Indian chief* (1837–1890)
J. P. Morgan, *American financier* (1837–1913)
Georges Bizet, *French composer* (1838–1875)
Paul Cézanne, *French painter* (1839–1906)
John D. Rockefeller, *American industrialist* (1839–1937)
Thomas Hardy, *English novelist* (1840–1928)
Emile Zola, *French novelist* (1840–1902)
Claude Monet, *French painter* (1840–1926)
Pierre Renoir, *French painter* (1840–1919)
Auguste Rodin, *French sculptor* (1840–1917)
Peter Ilich Tchaikovsky, *Russian composer* (1840–1893)
Ambrose Bierce, *American author* (1842–1914)
William James, *American philosopher* (1842–1910)
Arthur Sullivan, *English composer* (1842–1900)
Henry James, *American novelist* (1843–1916)
Edvard Grieg, *Norwegian composer* (1843–1907)
Sarah Bernhardt, *French actress* (1844–1923)
Anatole France (Jacques Anatole Thibault), *French author* (1844–1924)
Gerard Manley Hopkins, *English poet* (1844–1899)
Friedrich Nietzsche, *German philosopher* (1844–1900)
Nikolai Rimski-Korsakov, *Russian composer* (1844–1908)

quest of rebel Pancho Villa. U.S. buys Virgin Islands from Denmark for $25 million. President Wilson re-elected with "he kept us out of war" slogan. "Black Tom" explosion at munitions dock in Jersey City, N.Y., $40,000,000 damages; traced to German saboteurs. Margaret Sanger opens first birth control clinic. Easter Rebellion in Ireland put down by British troops.

1917 First U.S. combat troops in France as U.S. declares war (**April 6**). Russian Revolution—climax of long unrest under czars. February Revolution—Czar forced to abdicate, liberal government created. Kerensky becomes prime minister and forms provisional government (**July**). In October Revolution, Bolsheviks seize power in armed coup d'état led by Lenin and Trotsky. Kerensky flees. Revolutionaries execute the czar and his family (**1918**). Reds set up Third International in Moscow (**1919**). Balfour Declaration promises Jewish homeland in Palestine. Sigmund Freud's *Introduction to Psychoanalysis.*

1918 Russian Civil War between Reds (Bolsheviks) and Whites (anti-Bolsheviks); Reds win in **1920**. Allied troops (U.S., British, French) intervene (**March**); leave in **1919**. Japanese hold Vladivostok until 1922. World-wide influenza epidemic strikes; by **1920**, nearly 20 million are dead. In U.S. alone, 500,000 perish.

1919 Third International (Comintern) establishes Soviet control over international Communist movements. Paris peace conference. Versailles Treaty, incorporating Wilson's draft Covenant of League of Nations, signed by Allies and Germany; rejected by U.S. Senate. Congress formally ends war in **1921**. Eighteenth (Prohibition) Amendment adopted. Alcock and Brown make first trans-Atlantic non-stop flight.

1920 League of Nations holds first meeting at Geneva, Switzerland. U.S. Dept. of Justice "red hunt" nets thousands of radicals; aliens deported. Woman suffrage (19th) amendment ratified. First Agatha Christie mystery. Sinclair Lewis's *Main Street.*

1921 Reparations Commission fixes German liability at 132 billion gold marks. German inflation begins. Major treaties signed at Washington Disarmament Conference limit naval tonnage and pledge to respect territorial integrity of China. Irish Free State formed in southern Ireland as self-governing dominion of British Empire. In U.S., Nicola Sacco and Bartolomeo Vanzetti, Italian-born anarchists, convicted of armed robbery murder; case stirs world-wide protests; they are executed in **1927**.

1922 Mussolini marches on Rome; forms Fascist government. Irish Free State officially proclaimed.

1923 Adolf Hitler's "Beer Hall Putsch" in Munich fails; in **1924** he is sentenced to five years in prison where he writes *Mein Kampf;* released after eight months. Occupation of Ruhr by French and Belgian troops to enforce reparations payments. Widespread Ku Klux Klan violence in U.S. George Gershwin's *Rhapsody in Blue.*

1924 Death of Lenin; Stalin wins power struggle, rules as Soviet dictator until death in **1953**. Italian Fascists murder Socialist leader Giacomo Matteotti. Interior Secretary Albert B. Fall and oilmen Harry Sinclair and Edward L. Doheny are charged with conspiracy and bribery in the Teapot Dome scandal, involving fraudulent leases of naval oil reserves. In **1931**,

Wilhelm Conrad Roentgen, *German discoverer of X-rays* (1845–1923)
Gabriel Fauré, *French composer* (1845–1924)
Thomas Alva Edison, *American inventor* (1847–1931)
Alexander Graham Bell, *American inventor* (1847–1922)
Paul Gauguin, *French painter* (1848–1903)
August Strindberg, *Swedish dramatist* (1849–1912)
Luther Burbank, *American horticulturist* (1849–1926)
Guy de Maupassant, *French author* (1850–1893)
Robert Louis Stevenson, *English author* (1850–1894)
Vincent van Gogh, *Dutch painter* (1853–1890)
George Eastman, *American photographic pioneer* (1854–1932)
George Bernard Shaw, *Irish dramatist* (1856–1950)
Oscar Wilde, *Anglo-Irish author* (1856–1900)
Sigmund Freud, *Austrian founder of psychoanalysis* (1856–1939)
Robert E. Peary, *American explorer* (1856–1920)
Booker T. Washington, *American educator* (1856–1915)
Joseph Conrad, *Anglo-Polish novelist* (1857–1924)
Giacomo Puccini, *Italian composer* (1858–1924)
Theodore Roosevelt, *American President* (1858–1919)
Max Planck, *German physicist* (1858–1947)

WORLD WAR I (1914–1918)

Imperial, territorial, and economic rivalries lead to the "Great War" between the Central Powers (Austria-Hungary, Germany, Bulgaria, and Turkey) and the Allies (U.S., Britain, France, Russia, Belgium, Serbia, Greece, Romania, Montenegro, Portugal, Italy, Japan). About 10 million combatants killed, 20 million wounded.

1914 Austrian Archduke Francis Ferdinand and wife assassinated in Sarajevo by Serbian nationalist, Gavrilo Princip (**June 28**). Austria declares war on Serbia (**July 28**). Germany declares war on Russia (**Aug. 1**), on France (**Aug. 3**), invades Belgium (**Aug. 4**). Britain declares war on Germany (**Aug. 4**). Germans defeat Russians in Battle of Tannenberg on Eastern Front (**Aug.**). First Battle of the Marne (**Sept.**). German drive stopped 25 miles from Paris. By end of year, war on the Western Front is "positional" in the trenches.

1915 German submarine blockade of Great Britain begins (**Feb.**). Dardanelles Campaign—British land in Turkey (**April**), withdraw from Gallipoli (**Dec. to Jan. 1916**). Germans use gas at second Battle of Ypres (**April-May**). *Lusitania* sunk by German submarine—1,198 lost, including 128 Americans (**May 7**). On Eastern Front, German and Austrian "great offensive" conquers all of Poland and Lithuania; Russians lose 1 million men by **Sept. 6**). "Great Fall Offensive" by Allies results in little change from 1914 (**Sept.-Oct.**). Britain and France declare war on Bulgaria (**Oct. 14**).

1916 Battle of Verdun—Germans and French each lose about 350,000 men (**Feb.**). Extended submarine warfare begins (**March**). British-German sea battle of Jutland (**May**); British lose more ships, but German fleet never ventures forth again. On Eastern front, the Brusilov offensive demoralizes Russians, costs them 1 million men (**June-Sept.**). Battle of the Somme—British lose over 400,000; French, 200,000; Germans, about 450,000; all with no strategic results (**July-Nov.**). Romania declares war on Austria-Hungary (**Aug. 27**). Bucharest captured (**Dec.**).

1917 U.S. declares war on Germany (**April 6**). Submarine warfare at peak (**April**). On Italian Front, Battle of Caporetto—Italians retreat, losing 600,000 prisoners and deserters (**Oct.-Dec.**). On Western Front, Battles of Arras, Champagne, Ypres (third battle), etc. First large British tank attack (**Nov.**). U.S. declares war on Austria-Hungary (**Dec. 7**). Armistice between new Russian Bolshevik government and Germans (**Dec. 15**).

1918 Great offensive by Germans (**March-June**). Americans' first important battle role at Château-Thierry—as they and French stop German advance (**June**). Second Battle of the Marne (**July-Aug.**)—start of Allied offensive at Amiens, St. Mihiel, etc. Battles of the Argonne and Ypres panic German leadership (**Sept.-Oct.**). British offensive in Palestine (**Sept.**). Germans ask for armistice (**Oct. 4**). British armistice with Turkey (**Oct.**). German Kaiser abdicates (**Nov.**). Hostilities cease on Western Front (**Nov. 11**).

Fall is sentenced to year in prison; Doheny and Sinclair acquitted of bribery. Nathan Leopold and Richard Loeb convicted in "thrill killing" of Bobby Franks in Chicago; defended by Clarence Darrow; sentenced to life imprisonment. (Loeb killed by fellow convict in **1936**; Leopold paroled in **1958**, dies in **1971**.)

1925 Nellie Tayloe Ross elected governor of Wyoming; first woman governor elected in U.S. Locarno conferences seek to secure European peace by mutual guarantees. John T. Scopes convicted and fined for teaching evolution in a public school in Tennessee "Monkey Trial"; sentence set aside. John Logie Baird, Scottish inventor, transmits human features by television. Adolf Hitler publishes Volume I of *Mein Kampf*.

1926 General strike in Britain brings nation's activities to standstill. U.S. marines dispatched to Nicaragua during revolt; they remain until **1933**. Gertrude Ederle of U.S. is first woman to swim English Channel.

1927 German economy collapses. Socialists riot in Vienna; general strike follows acquittal of Nazis for political murder. Trotsky expelled from Russian Communist Party. Charles A. Lindbergh flies first successful solo non-stop flight from New York to Paris. Ruth Snyder and Judd Gray convicted of murder of Albert Snyder; they are executed at Sing Sing prison in **1928**. *The Jazz Singer*, with Al Jolson, first part-talking motion picture.

1928 Kellogg-Briand Pact, outlawing war, signed in Paris by 65 nations. Alexander Fleming discovers penicillin. Richard E. Byrd starts expedition to Antarctic; returns in **1930**.

1929 Trotsky expelled from U.S.S.R. Lateran Treaty establishes independent Vatican City. In U.S., stock market prices collapse, with U.S. securities losing $26 billion—first phase of Depression and world economic crisis. St. Valentine's Day gangland massacre in Chicago.

1930 Britain, U.S., Japan, France, and Italy sign naval disarmament treaty. Nazis gain in German elections. Cyclotron developed by Ernest O. Lawrence, U.S. physicist.

1931 Spain becomes a republic with overthrow of King Alfonso XIII. German industrialists finance 800,000-strong Nazi party. British parliament enacts statute of Westminster, legalizing dominion equality with Britain. Mukden Incident begins Japanese occupation of Manchuria. In U.S., Hoover proposes one-year moratorium of war debts. Harold C. Urey discovers heavy hydrogen. Gangster Al Capone sentenced to 11 years in prison for tax evasion (freed in **1939**; dies in **1947**).

1932 Nazis lead in German election with 230 Reichstag seats. Famine in U.S.S.R. In U.S., Congress sets up Reconstruction Finance Corporation to stimulate economy. Veterans march on Washington—most leave after Senate rejects payment of cash bonuses; others removed by troops under Douglas MacArthur. U.S. protests Japanese aggression in Manchuria. Amelia Earhart is first woman to fly Atlantic solo. Charles A. Lindbergh's baby son kidnapped, killed. (Bruno Richard Hauptmann arrested in **1934**, convicted in **1935**, executed in **1936**.)

1933 Hitler appointed German chancellor, gets dictatorial powers. Reichstag fire in Berlin; Nazi terror begins. *(See* special material on "The Holocaust.") Germany and Japan withdraw from League of Nations. Giuseppe Zangara executed for attempted assassination of President-elect Roosevelt in which Chicago Mayor Cermak is fatally shot. Roosevelt inaugurated ("the only thing we have to fear is fear itself"); launches New Deal. Prohibition repealed. U.S.S.R. recognized by U.S.

Arthur Conan Doyle, *English writer* (1859–1930)
Knut Hamsun, *Norwegian novelist* (1859–1952)
Henri Bergson, *French philosopher* (1859–1941)
John Dewey, *American philosopher* (1859–1952)
Georges Seurat, *French painter* (1859–1891)
Pierre Curie, *French physicist* (1859–1906)
Anton Chekhov, *Russian dramatist* (1860–1904)
Gustav Mahler, *German composer* (1860–1911)
Rabindranath Tagore, *Indian poet* (1861–1941)
Alfred North Whitehead, *British philosopher-mathematician* (1861–1947)
Edith Wharton, *American author* (1862–1937)
Claude Debussy, *French composer* (1862–1918)
David Lloyd George, *British statesman* (1863–1945)
Henry Ford, *American automobile pioneer* (1863–1947)
William Randolph Hearst, *American newspaper magnate* (1863–1951)
Henri Toulouse-Lautrec, *French painter* (1864–1901)
George Washington Carver, *American botanist* (1864–1943)
Richard Strauss, *German composer* (1864–1949)
Rudyard Kipling, *English writer* (1865–1936)
William Butler Yeats, *Irish poet* (1865–1939)
Jean Sibelius, *Finnish composer* (1865–1957)
Sun Yat-sen, *Chinese statesman* (1866–1927)
Benedetto Croce, *Italian philosopher* (1866–1952)

THE HOLOCAUST (1933–1945)

"Holocaust" is the term describing the Nazi annihilation of about 6 million Jews (two thirds of the pre-World War II European Jewish population), including 4,500,000 from Russia, Poland, and the Baltic; 750,000 from Hungary and Romania; 290,000 from Germany and Austria; 105,000 from The Netherlands; 90,000 from France; 54,000 from Greece, etc.

The Holocaust was unique in its being *genocide*—the systematic destruction of a people solely because of religion, race, ethnicity, or nationality—on an unmatched scale. Along with the Jews, another 9 to 10 million people—Gypsies, Slavs (Poles, Ukrainians, and Belorussians)—were exterminated.

The only comparable act of genocide in modern times was launched in April 1915, when an estimated 600,000 Armenians were massacred by the Turks.

1933 Hitler named German Chancellor (**Jan.**). Dachau, first concentration camp, established (**March**). Boycotts against Jews begin (**April**).

1935 Anti-Semitic Nuremberg Laws passed by Reichstag (**Sept.**).

1937 Buchenwald concentration camp opens (**July**).

1938 Extension of anti-Semitic laws to Austria after annexation (**March**). *Kristallnacht* (Night of Broken Glass)—anti-Semitic riots in Germany and Austria (**Nov. 9**). 26,000 Jews sent to concentration camps; Jewish children expelled from schools (**Nov.**). Expropriation of Jewish property and businesses (**Dec.**).

1940 As war continues, Nazi acts against Jews extended to German-conquered areas.

1941 Deportation of German Jews begins; massacres of Jews in Odessa and Kiev—68,000 killed (**Nov.**); in Riga and Vilna—almost 60,000 killed (**Dec.**).

1942 Unified Jewish resistance in ghettos begins (**Jan.**). 300,000 Jews from Warsaw Ghetto deported to Treblinka death camp (**July**).

1943 Warsaw Ghetto uprisings (**Jan.** and **April**); Ghetto exterminated (**May**).

1944 476,000 Hungarian Jews sent to Auschwitz (**May-June**). D-day (**June 6**). Soviet Army liberates Maidanek death camp (**July**). Nazis try to hide evidence of death camps (**Nov.**).

1945 Americans liberate Buchenwald, Bergen-Belsen camps (**April**). Nuremberg War Crimes Trial (**Nov. 1945** to **Oct. 1946**).

1934 Chancellor Dollfuss of Austria assassinated by Nazis. Hitler becomes Führer. U.S.S.R. admitted to League of Nations. Dionne sisters, first quintuplets to survive beyond infancy, born in Canada.

1935 Saar incorporated into Germany after plebiscite. Nazis repudiate Versailles Treaty, introduce compulsory military service. Mussolini invades Ethiopia; League of Nations invokes sanctions. Roosevelt opens second phase of New Deal in U.S., calling for social security, better housing, equitable taxation, and farm assistance. Huey Long assassinated in Louisiana.

1936 Germans occupy Rhineland. Italy annexes Ethiopia. Rome-Berlin Axis proclaimed (Japan to join in **1940**). Trotsky exiled to Mexico. King George V dies; succeeded by son, Edward VIII, who soon abdicates to marry American-born divorcée, and is succeeded by brother, George VI. Spanish civil war begins. (Franco's fascist forces defeat Loyalist forces by **1939**, when Madrid falls.) War between China and Japan begins, to continue through World War II. Japan and Germany sign anti-Commintern pact; joined by Italy in **1937**.

1937 Hitler repudiates war guilt clause of Versailles Treaty; continues to build German power. Italy withdraws from League of Nations. U.S. gunboat *Panay* sunk by Japanese in Yangtze River. Japan invades China, conquers most of coastal area. Amelia Earhart lost somewhere in Pacific on round-the-world flight.

1938 Hitler marches into Austria; political and geographical union of Germany and Austria proclaimed. Munich Pact—Britain, France, and Italy agree to let Germany partition Czechoslovakia. Germany occupies Sudetenland, about one third of Czechoslovakia. Douglas "Wrong-Way" Corrigan flies from New York to Dublin.

1939 Germany occupies Bohemia and Moravia; renounces pacts with Poland and England and concludes 10-year non-aggression pact with U.S.S.R. Russo-Finnish War begins; Finns to lose one tenth of territory in **1940** peace treaty. World War II begins (*see* special material on "World War II"). In U.S., Roosevelt submits $1,319-million defense budget, proclaims U.S. neutrality, and declares limited emergency. Einstein writes FDR about feasibility of atomic bomb. New York World's Fair opens.

1940 Trotsky assassinated in Mexico. Estonia, Latvia, and Lithuania annexed by U.S.S.R. U.S. trades 50 destroyers for leases on British bases in Western Hemisphere. Selective Service Act signed.

1941 Japanese surprise attack on U.S. fleet at Pearl Harbor brings U.S. into World War II. Manhattan Project (atomic bomb research) begins. Roosevelt enunciates "four freedoms," signs lend-lease act, declares national emergency, promises aid to U.S.S.R.

Wilbur Wright, *American aviation pioneer* (1867–1912)
Arturo Toscanini, *Italian conductor* (1867–1957)
Marie (Sklodowska) Curie, *Polish-French scientist* (1867–1937)
Maxim Gorki, *Russian writer* (1868–1936)
Robert A. Millikan, *American physicist* (1869–1953)
Mohandas Gandhi, *Indian leader* (1869–1948)
André Gide, *French author* (1869–1951)
Henri Matisse, *French painter* (1869–1954)
Frank Lloyd Wright, *American architect* (1869–1959)
Nikolai Lenin, *Russian revolutionist* (1870–1924)
Orville Wright, *American aviation pioneer* (1871–1948)
Rasputin, *Russian monk* (1871–1916)
Stephen Crane, *American author* (1871–1900)
Theodore Dreiser, *American novelist* (1871–1945)
Marcel Proust, *French author* (1871–1922)
Bertrand Russell, *English philosopher* (1872–1970)
Enrico Caruso, *Italian tenor* (1873–1921)
Chaim Weizmann, *first president of Israel* (1874–1952)

WORLD WAR II (1939–1945)

Axis powers (Germany, Italy, Japan, Hungary, Romania, Bulgaria) *vs.* Allies (U.S., Britain, France, U.S.S.R., Australia, Belgium, Brazil, Canada, China, Denmark, Greece, Netherlands, New Zealand, Norway, Poland, South Africa, Yugoslavia).

1939 Germany invades Poland and annexes Danzig; Britain and France give Hitler ultimatum (**Sept. 1**), declare war (**Sept. 3**). Disabled German pocket battleship Admiral Graf Spee blown up off Montevideo, Uruguay, on Hitler's orders (**Dec. 17**). Limited activity ("Sitzkrieg") on Western Front.

1940 Nazis invade Netherlands, Belgium, and Luxembourg (**May 10**). Chamberlain resigns as Prime Minister; Churchill takes over (**May 10**). Germans cross French frontier (**May 12**) using air/tank/infantry "Blitzkrieg" tactics. Dunkerque evacuation—about 335,000 out of 400,000 Allied soldiers rescued from Belgium by British civilian and naval craft (**May 26-June 3**). Italy declares war on France and Britain; invades France (**June 10**). Germans enter Paris; city undefended (**June 14**). France and Germany sign armistice at Compiègne (**June 22**). Nazis bomb Coventry, England (**Nov. 14**).

1941 Germans launch attacks in Balkans. Yugoslavia surrenders—General Mihajlovic continues guerrilla warfare; Tito leads left-wing guerrillas (**April 17**). Nazi tanks enter Athens; remnants of British Army quit Greece (**April 27**). Hitler attacks Russia (**June 22**). Atlantic Charter—FDR and Churchill agree on war aims (**Aug. 14**). Japanese attacks on Pearl Harbor, Philippines, Guam force U.S. into war; U.S. Pacific fleet crippled (**Dec. 7**). U.S. and Britain declare war on Japan. Germany and Italy declare war on U.S.; Congress declares war on those countries (**Dec. 11**).

1942 British surrender Singapore to Japanese (**Feb. 15**). U.S. forces on Bataan peninsula in Philippines surrender (**April 9**). U.S. and Filipino troops on Corregidor island in Manila Bay surrender to Japanese (**May 6**). Village of Lidice in Czechoslovakia razed by Nazis (**June 10**). U.S. and Britain land in French North Africa (**Nov. 8**).

1943 Casablanca Conference—Churchill and FDR agree on unconditional surrender goal (**Jan. 14–24**). German 6th Army surrenders at Stalingrad—turning point of war in Russia (**Feb. 1–2**). Remnants of Nazis trapped on Cape Bon, ending war in Africa (**May 12**). Mussolini deposed; Badoglio named premier (**July 25**). Allied troops land on Italian mainland after conquest of Sicily (**Sept. 3**). Italy surrenders (**Sept. 8**). Nazis seize Rome (**Sept. 10**). Cairo Conference: FDR, Churchill, Chiang Kai-shek pledge defeat of Japan, free Korea (**Nov. 22–26**). Teheran Conference: FDR, Churchill, Stalin agree on invasion plans (**Nov. 28-Dec. 1**).

1944 U.S. and British troops land at Anzio on west Italian coast and hold beachhead (**Jan. 22**). U.S. and British troops enter Rome (**June 4**). D-Day—Allies launch Normandy invasion (**June 6**). Hitler wounded in bomb plot (**July 20**). Paris liberated (**Aug. 25**). Athens freed by Allies (**Oct. 13**). Americans invade Philippines (**Oct. 20**). Germans launch counteroffensive in Belgium—Battle of Bulge (**Dec. 16**).

1945 Yalta Agreement signed by FDR, Churchill, Stalin—establishes basis for occupation of Germany, returns to Soviet Union lands taken by Germany and Japan; U.S.S.R. agrees to friendship pact with China (**Feb. 11**). Mussolini killed at Lake Como (**April 28**). Admiral Doenitz takes command in Germany; suicide of Hitler announced (**May 1**). Berlin falls (**May 2**). V-E Day—Germany signs unconditional surrender terms at Rheims (**May 7**). Potsdam Conference—Truman, Churchill, Attlee (after **July 28**), Stalin establish council of foreign ministers to prepare peace treaties; plan German postwar government and reparations (**July 17-Aug. 2**). A-bomb blasts Hiroshima (**Aug. 6**). U.S.S.R. declares war on Japan (**Aug. 8**). Nagasaki hit by A-bomb (**Aug. 9**). Japan surrenders (**Aug. 14**). V-J Day—Japanese sign surrender terms aboard battleship *Missouri* (**Sept. 2**).

1942 Declaration of United Nations signed in Washington. Women's military services established. Enrico Fermi achieves nuclear chain reaction. Japanese and persons of Japanese ancestry moved inland from Pacific Coast. Coconut Grove nightclub fire in Boston kills 491.

1943 President freezes prices, salaries, and wages to prevent inflation. Income tax withholding introduced.

1944 G.I. Bill of Rights enacted. Bretton Woods Conference creates International Monetary Fund and World Bank. Dumbarton Oaks Conference—U.S., British Commonwealth, and U.S.S.R. propose establishment of United Nations.

1945 Yalta Conference (Roosevelt, Churchill, Stalin) plans final defeat of Germany (**Feb.**). Germany surrenders (**May 7**). San Francisco Conference establishes U.N. (**April-June**). FDR dies (**April 12**). Potsdam Conference (Truman, Churchill, Stalin) establishes basis of German reconstruction (**July-Aug**). Japan surrenders (**Sept. 2**).

1946 First meeting of U.N. General Assembly opens in London (**Jan. 10**). League of Nations dissolved (**April**). Italy abolishes monarchy (**June**). Verdict in Nuremberg war trial: 12 Nazi leaders (including 1 tried in absentia) sentenced to hang; 7 imprisoned; 3 acquitted (**Oct. 1**). Goering commits suicide a few hours before 10 other Nazis are executed (**Oct. 15**). Winston Churchill's "Iron Curtain" speech warns of Soviet expansion.

1947 Britain nationalizes coal mines (**Jan. 1**). Peace treaties for Italy, Romania, Bulgaria, Hungary, Finland signed in Paris (**Feb. 10**). Soviet Union rejects U.S. plan for U.N. atomic-energy control (**March 4**). Truman Doctrine proposed—the first significant U.S. attempt to "contain" communist expansion (**March 12**). Marshall Plan for European recovery proposed—a coordinated program to help European nations recover from ravages of war (**June**). (By **1951**, this "European Recovery Program" had cost $11 billion.) India and Pakistan gain independence from Britain (**Aug. 15**). Cominform (Communist Information Bureau) founded under Soviet auspices to rebuild contacts among European Communist parties, missing since dissolution of Comintern in **1943** (**Sept.**). (Yugoslav party expelled in **1948** and Cominform disbanded in **1956**.)

1948 Gandhi assassinated in New Delhi by Hindu fanatic (**Jan. 30**). Communists seize power in Czechoslovakia (**Feb. 23–25**). Burma and Ceylon granted independence by Britain. Organization of American States (OAS) Charter signed at Bogotá, Colombia (**April 30**). Nation of Israel proclaimed; British end Mandate at midnight; Arab armies attack (**May 14**). Berlin airlift begins (**June 21**); ends **May 12, 1949**. Stalin and Tito break (**June 28**). Independent Republic of Korea is proclaimed, following election supervised by U.N. (**Aug. 15**). Verdict in Japanese war trial: Tojo and six others sentenced to hang (hanged **Dec. 23**); 18 imprisoned (**Nov. 12**). United States of Indonesia established as Dutch and Indonesians settle conflict (**Dec. 27**). Alger Hiss, former U.S. State Department official, indicted on perjury charges after denying passing secret documents to communist spy ring. Convicted in second trial (**1950**) and sentenced to five-year prison term.

1949 Cease-fire in Palestine (**Jan. 7**). Truman proposes Point Four Program to help world's backward areas (**Jan. 20**). Israel signs armistice with Egypt (**Feb. 24**). Start of North Atlantic Treaty Organization (NATO)—treaty signed by 12 nations (**April 4**). German Federal Republic (West Germany) established (**Sept. 21**). Truman discloses Soviet Union has set off atomic explosion (**Sept. 23**). Communist People's Republic of China formally proclaimed (**Oct. 1**).

1950 Truman orders development of hydrogen bomb (**Jan. 31**). Korean War *(see* special material on the "Korean War"). Assassination attempt on President Truman by Puerto Rican nationalists (**Nov. 1**). Brink's robbery in Boston; almost $3 million stolen (**Jan. 17**).

1951 Six nations agree to Schuman Plan to pool European coal and steel (**March 19**)—in effect **Feb. 10, 1953**. Julius and Ethel Rosenberg sentenced to death for passing atomic secrets to Russians (**March**). Japanese peace treaty signed in San Francisco by 49 nations (**Sept. 8**). Color television introduced in U.S.

1952 George VI dies; his daughter becomes Elizabeth II (**Feb. 6**). NATO

Winston Churchill, *British statesman* (1874–1965)
Gertrude Stein, *American writer* (1874–1946)
Arnold Schönberg, *Austrian composer* (1874–1951)
Guglielmo Marconi, *Italian physicist* (1874–1935)
Thomas Mann, *German novelist* (1875–1955)
Carl G. Jung, *Swiss psychiatrist* (1875–1961)
Carl Sandburg, *American poet* (1878–1967)
Martin Buber, *Jewish philosopher* (1878–1965)
Joseph Stalin, *Russian dictator* (1879–1953)
Leon Trotsky, *Russian revolutionist* (1879–1940)
Paul Klee, *Swiss painter* (1879–1940)
Albert Einstein, *German-American physicist* (1879–1955)
Douglas MacArthur, *American general* (1880–1964)
Pablo Picasso, *Spanish-born French painter* (1881–1973)
Béla Bartók, *Hungarian composer* (1881–1945)
Alexander Fleming, *English scientist* (1881–1955)
Franklin D. Roosevelt, *American President* (1882–1945)
Eamon de Valera, *Irish statesman* (1882–1975)
James Joyce, *Irish author* (1882–1941)
Georges Braque, *French painter* (1882–1963)
Igor Stravinsky, *Russian composer* (1882–1971)
Benito Mussolini, *Italian dictator* (1883–1945)
Franz Kafka, *Czechoslovakian-born Austrian author* (1883–1924)
John Maynard Keynes, *English economist* (1883–1946)
Walter Gropius, *German architect* (1883–1969)
Harry S. Truman, *American President* (1884–1972)
Eduard Benes, *Czechoslovakian statesman* (1884–1948)
D. H. Lawrence, *English writer* (1885–1930)

KOREAN WAR (1950–1953)

1950 North Korean Communist forces invade South Korea (**June 25**). U.N. calls for cease-fire and asks U.N. members to assist South Korea (**June 27**). Truman orders U.S. forces into Korea (**June 27**). North Koreans capture Seoul (**June 28**). Gen. Douglas MacArthur designated commander of unified U.N. forces (**July 8**). Pusan Beachhead—U.N. forces counterattack and capture Seoul (**Aug.-Sept.**), capture Pyongyang, North Korean capital (**Oct.**). Chinese Communists enter war (**Oct. 26**), force U.N. retreat toward 39th parallel (**Dec.**).

1951 Gen. Matthew B. Ridgeway replaces MacArthur after he threatens Chinese with massive retaliation (**April 11**). Armistice negotiations (**July**) continue with interruptions until **June 1953**.

1953 Armistice signed (**June 26**). Chinese troops withdraw from North Korea (**Oct. 26, 1958**), but over 200 violations of armistice noted to **1959**.

conference approves European army **(Feb.)**. AEC announces "satisfactory" experiments in hydrogen-weapons research; eyewitnesses tell of blasts near Enewetak **(Nov.)**.

1953 Gen. Dwight D. Eisenhower inaugurated President of United States **(Jan. 20)**. Stalin dies **(March 5)**. Malenkov becomes Soviet Premier; Beria, Minister of Interior; Molotov, Foreign Minister **(March 6)**. Dag Hammarskjold begins term as U.N. Secretary-General **(April 10)**. Edmund Hillary, of New Zealand, and Tenzing Norkay, of Nepal, reach top of Mt. Everest **(May 29)**. East Berliners rise against Communist rule; quelled by tanks **(June 17)**. Egypt becomes republic ruled by military junta **(June 18)**. Julius and Ethel Rosenberg executed in Sing Sing prison **(June 19)**. Korean armistice signed **(July 27)**. Moscow announces explosion of hydrogen bomb **(Aug. 20)**.

1954 First atomic submarine *Nautilus,* launched **(Jan. 21)**. Five U.S. Congressmen shot on floor of House as Puerto Rican nationalists fire from spectators' gallery; all five recover **(March 1)**. Army *vs.* McCarthy inquiry—Senate subcommittee report blames both sides **(Apr. 22-June 17)**. Dien Bien Phu, French military outpost in Vietnam, falls to Vietminh army **(May 7)**. *(See* special material on the "Vietnam War.") U.S. Supreme Court (in *Brown* v. *Board of Education of Topeka*) unanimously bans racial segregation in public schools **(May 17)**. Eisenhower launches world atomic pool without Soviet Union **(Sept. 6)**. Eight-nation Southeast Asia defense treaty (SEATO) signed at Manila **(Sept. 8)**. West Germany is granted sovereignty, admitted to NATO and Western European Union **(Oct. 23)**. Dr. Jonas Salk starts innoculating children against polio. Algerian War of Independence against France begins **(Nov.)**; France struggles to maintain colonial rule until 1962 when it agrees to Algeria's independence.

1955 Nikolai A. Bulganin becomes Soviet Premier, replacing Malenkov **(Feb. 8)**. Churchill resigns; Anthony Eden succeeds him **(April 6)**. Federal Republic of West Germany becomes a sovereign state **(May 5)**. Warsaw Pact, east European mutual defense agreement, signed **(May 14)**. Argentina ousts Perón **(Sept. 19)**. President Eisenhower suffers coronary thrombosis in Denver **(Sept. 24)**. Martin Luther King, Jr., leads black boycott of Montgomery, Ala., bus system **(Dec. 1)**; desegregated service begun **(Dec. 21)**. AFL and CIO become one organization—AFL-CIO **(Dec. 5)**.

1956 Nikita Khrushchev, First Secretary of U.S.S.R. Communist Party, denounces Stalin's excesses **(Feb. 24)**. First aerial H-bomb tested over Namu islet, Bikini Atoll—10 million tons TNT equivalent **(May 21)**. Worker's uprising against Communist rule in Poznan, Poland, is crushed **(June 28–30)**. Egypt takes control of Suez Canal **(July 26)**. Israel launches attack

Ezra Pound, *American poet* (1885–1972)
Sinclair Lewis, *American novelist* (1885–1951)
Alban Berg, *Austrian composer* (1885–1935)
Niels Bohr, *Danish physicist* (1885–1962)
David Ben-Gurion, *Israeli statesman* (1886–1973)
Chiang Kai-shek, *Chinese statesman* (1887–1975)
Le Corbusier (C.E. Jeanneret), *Swiss-born French architect* (1887–1965)
T. S. Eliot, *Anglo-American poet* (1888–1965)
Eugene O'Neill, *American dramatist* (1888–1953)
Ludwig Wittgenstein, *Austrian philosopher* (1889–1951)
Adolf Hitler, *German dictator* (1889–1945)
Charles Chaplin, *English screen actor-director* (1889–1977)
Dwight D. Eisenhower, *American President* (1890–1969)
Charles de Gaulle, *French soldier and statesman* (1890–1970)
Sergei Prokofiev, *Russian composer* (1891–1953)
Frederick Banting, *Canadian discoverer of insulin* (1891–1941)

'IETNAM WAR (1950–1975)

U.S., South Vietnam, and Allies versus North Vietnam and ational Liberation Front (Viet Cong). Outstanding events:

950 President Truman sends 35-man military advisory group › aid French fighting to maintain colonial power in Vietnam.

354 After defeat of French at Dienbienphu, Geneva Agreeents **(July)** provide for withdrawal of French and Vietminh to ither side of demarcation zone (DMZ) pending reunification lections, which are never held. Presidents Eisenhower and ennedy (from **1954** onward) send civilian advisors and, later, ilitary personnel to train South Vietnamese.

960 Communists form National Liberation Front in South.

963 Ngo Dinh Diem, South Vietnam's premier, slain in coup **lov. 1)**.

961–1963 U.S. military advisors rise from 2,000 to 15,000.

964 North Vietnamese torpedo boats reportedly attack U.S. estroyers in Gulf of Tonkin **(Aug. 2)**. President Johnson orders taliatory air strikes. Congress approves Gulf of Tonkin resotion **(Aug. 7)** authorizing President to take necessary steps › "maintain peace."

965 U.S. planes begin combat missions over South Vietnam. **June,** 23,000 American advisors committed to combat. By d of year over 184,000 U.S. troops in area.

966 B-52s bomb DMZ, reportedly used by North Vietnam for ntry into South **(July 31)**.

967 South Vietnam National Assembly approves election of guyen Van Thieu as President **(Oct. 21)**.

968 U.S. has almost 525,000 men in Vietnam. In Tet offenve **(Jan.-Feb.)**, Viet Cong guerrillas attack Saigon, Hue, and me provincial capitals. President Johnson orders halt to S. bombardment of North Vietnam **(Oct. 31)**. Saigon and L.F. join U.S. and North Vietnam in Paris peace talks.

969 President Nixon announces Vietnam peace offer **(May 14)** —begins troop withdrawals **(June)**. Viet Cong forms Provisional Revolutionary Government. U.S. Senate calls for curb on commitments **(June 25)**. Ho Chi Minh, 79, North Vietnam president, dies **(Sept. 3)**; collective leadership chosen. Some 6,000 U.S. troops pulled back from Thailand and 1,000 marines from Vietnam (announced **Sept. 30**). Massive demonstrations in U.S. protest or support war policies **(Oct. 15)**.

1970 Nixon announces sending of troops to Cambodia **(April 30)**. Last U.S. troops removed from Cambodia **(June 29)**.

1971 Congress bars use of combat troops, but not air power, in Laos and Cambodia **(Jan. 1)**. South Vietnamese troops, with U.S. air cover, fail in Laos thrust. Many American ground forces withdrawn from Vietnam combat. *New York Times* publishes Pentagon papers, classified material on expansion of war **(June)**.

1972 Nixon responds to North Vietnamese drive across DMZ by ordering mining of North Vietnam ports and heavy bombing of Hanoi-Haiphong area **(April 1)**. Nixon orders "Christmas bombing" of north to get North Vietnamese back to conference table **(Dec.)**.

1973 President orders halt to offensive operations in North Vietnam **(Jan. 15)**. Representatives of North and South Vietnam, U.S., and N.L.F. sign peace pacts in Paris, ending longest war in U.S. history **(Jan. 27)**.

1974 Both sides accuse each other of frequent violations of cease-fire agreement.

1975 Full-scale warfare resumes. Communists victorious **(April 30)**. South Vietnam Premier Nguyen Van Thieu resigns **(April 21)**. American troops evacuated **(April 30)**. More than 140,000 Vietnamese refugees leave by air and sea, many to settle in U.S. Provisional Revolutionary Government takes control **(June 6)**.

1976 Election of National Assembly paves way for reunification of North and South.

on Egypt's Sinai peninsula and drives toward Suez Canal (**Oct. 29**). British and French invade Egypt at Port Said (**Nov. 5**). Cease-fire forced by U.S. pressure stops British, French, and Israeli advance (**Nov. 6**). Revolt starts in Hungary—Soviet troops and tanks crush anti-Communist rebellion (**Nov.**).

1957 Eisenhower Doctrine calls for aid to Mideast countries which resist armed aggression from Communist-controlled nations (**Jan. 5**). Eisenhower sends troops to Little Rock, Ark., to quell mob and protect school integration (**Sept. 24**). Russians launch *Sputnik I,* first earth-orbiting satellite—the Space Age begins (**Oct. 4**).

1958 Army's Jupiter-C rocket fires first U.S. earth satellite, *Explorer I,* into orbit (**Jan. 31**). Egypt and Syria merge into United Arab Republic (**Feb. 1**). European Economic Community (Common Market) established by Rome Treaty becomes effective **Jan. 1, 1958**. Khrushchev becomes Premier of Soviet Union as Bulganin resigns (**Mar. 27**). Gen. Charles de Gaulle becomes French premier (**June 1**), remaining in power until **1969**. New French constitution adopted (**Sept. 28**), de Gaulle elected president of 5th Republic (**Dec. 21**). Eisenhower orders U.S. Marines into Lebanon at request of President Chamoun, who fears overthrow (**July 15**).

1959 Cuban President Batista resigns and flees—Castro takes over (**Jan. 1**). Tibet's Dalai Lama escapes to India (**Mar. 31**). St. Lawrence Seaway opens, allowing ocean ships to reach Midwest (**April 25**).

1960 American U-2 spy plane, piloted by Francis Gary Powers, shot down over Russia (**May 5**). Khrushchev kills Paris summit conference because of U-2 (**May 16**). Powers sentenced to prison for 10 years (**Aug. 19**)—freed in **February 1962** in exchange for Soviet spy. Top Nazi murderer of Jews, Adolf Eichmann, captured by Israelis in Argentina (**May 23**)—executed in Israel in **1962**. Communist China and Soviet Union split in conflict over Communist ideology. Belgium starts to break up its African colonial empire, gives independence to Belgian Congo (Zaire) on **June 30**. Cuba begins confiscation of $770 million of U.S. property (**Aug. 7**).

1961 U.S. breaks diplomatic relations with Cuba (**Jan. 3**). John F. Kennedy inaugurated President of U.S. (**Jan. 20**). Kennedy proposes Alliance for Progress—10-year plan to raise Latin American living standards (**Mar. 13**). Moscow announces putting first man in orbit around earth, Maj. Yuri A. Gagarin (**April 12**). Cuba invaded at Bay of Pigs by an estimated 1,200 anti-Castro exiles aided by U.S.; invasion crushed (**April 17**). First U.S. spaceman, Navy Cmdr. Alan B. Shepard, Jr., rockets 116.5 miles up in 302-mile trip (**May 5**). Virgil Grissom becomes second American astronaut, making 118-mile-high, 303-mile-long rocket flight over Atlantic (**July 21**). Gherman Stepanovich Titov is launched in Soviet spaceship *Vostok II;* makes 17½ orbits in 25 hours, covering 434,960 miles before landing safely (**Aug. 6**). East Germans erect Berlin Wall between East and West Berlin to halt flood of refugees (**Aug. 13**). U.S.S.R. fires 50-megaton hydrogen bomb, biggest explosion in history (**Oct. 29**).

1962 Lt. Col. John H. Glenn, Jr., is first American to orbit earth—three times in 4 hr 55 min (**Feb. 20**). Adolf Eichmann hanged in Israel for his part in Nazi extermination of six million Jews (**May 31**). France transfers sovereignty to new republic of Algeria (**July 3**). Cuban missile crisis—U.S.S.R. to build missile bases in Cuba; Kennedy orders Cuban blockade, lifts blockade after Russians back down (**Aug.-Nov.**). James H. Meredith, escorted by Federal marshals, registers in University of Mississippi (**Oct. 1**). Pope John XXIII opens Second Vatican Council (**Oct. 11**)—Council holds four sessions, finally closing Dec. 8, 1965. Cuba releases 1,113 prisoners of 1961 invasion attempt (**Dec. 24**).

1963 France and West Germany sign treaty of cooperation ending four centuries of conflict (**Jan. 22**). Pope John XXIII dies (**June 3**)—succeeded June 21 by Cardinal Montini, who becomes Paul VI. U.S. Supreme Court rules no locality may require recitation of Lord's Prayer or Bible verses in public schools (**June 17**). Civil rights rally held by 200,000 blacks and whites in Washington, D.C. (**Aug. 28**). Washington-to-Moscow "hot line" communications link opens, designed to reduce risk of accidental war (**Aug. 30**). President Kennedy shot and killed by sniper in Dallas, Tex. Lyndon B. Johnson becomes President same day (**Nov. 22**). Lee Harvey Oswald, accused assassin of President Kennedy, is shot and killed by Jack Ruby, Dallas nightclub owner (**Nov. 24**).

1964 U.S. Supreme Court rules that Congressional districts should be roughly equal in population (**Feb. 17**). Jack Ruby convicted of murder in slaying of Lee Harvey Oswald; sentenced to death by Dallas jury (**March 14**) —conviction reversed **Oct. 5, 1966**; Ruby dies **Jan. 3, 1967**, before second trial can be held. Three civil rights workers—Schwerner, Goodman, and Cheney—murdered in Mississippi (**June**). Twenty-one arrests result in trial and conviction of seven by Federal jury. President's Commission on the Assassination of President Kennedy issues Warren Report con-

Tito (Josip Broz), *Yugoslavian President* (1892–1980)
Haile Selassie, *Ethiopian emperor* (1892–1975)
Hermann Goering, *Nazi leader* (1893–1946)
Mao Zedong, *Chinese Communist leader* (1893–1976)
Nikita Khrushchev, *Russian leader* (1894–1971)
Martha Graham, *American dancer* (1894–)
Paul Hindemith, *German-American composer* (1895–1963)
Bertolt Brecht, *German dramatist* (1898–1956)
Ernest Hemingway, *American author* (1898–1961)
Federico García Lorca, *Spanish author* (1899–1936)
Francis Poulenc, *French composer* (1899–1963)
Kurt Weill, *German-American composer* (1900–1950)
Aaron Copland, *American composer* (1900–)
Werner Heisenberg, *German physicist* (1901–)
Walt Disney, *American cartoonist* (1901–1966)
Enrico Fermi, *Italian-American physicist* (1901–1954)
John Steinbeck, *American novelist* (1902–1968)
Dmitri Shostakovich, *Russian composer* (1906–1975)
W. H. Auden, *English poet* (1907–1973)
Albert Camus, *French author* (1913–1960)
John F. Kennedy, *American President* (1917–1963)

cluding that Lee Harvey Oswald acted alone.

1965 Rev. Dr. Martin Luther King, Jr., and more than 2,600 other blacks arrested in Selma, Ala., during three-day demonstrations against voter-registration rules **(Feb. 1)**. Malcolm X, black-nationalist leader, shot to death at Harlem rally in New York City **(Feb. 21)**. U.S. Marines land in Dominican Republic as fighting persists between rebels and Dominican army **(April 28)**. Medicare, senior citizens' government medical assistance program, begins **(July 1)**. Blacks riot for six days in Watts section of Los Angeles: 34 dead, over 1,000 injured, nearly 4,000 arrested, fire damage put at $175 million **(Aug. 11–16)**. Power failure in Ontario plant blacks out parts of eight northeastern states of U.S. and two provinces of southeastern Canada **(Nov. 9)**.

1966 Black teen-agers riot in Watts, Los Angeles; two men killed and at least 25 injured **(March 15)**. Michael E. De Bakey implants artificial heart in human for first time at Houston hospital; plastic device functions and patient lives **(April 21)**.

1967 Three Apollo astronauts—Col. Virgil I. Grissom, Col. Edward White II, and Lt. Cmdr. Roger B. Chaffee—killed in spacecraft fire during simulated launch **(Jan. 27)**. Israeli and Arab forces battle; six-day war ends with Israel occupying Sinai Peninsula, Golan Heights, Gaza Strip, and east bank of Suez Canal **(June 5)**. Red China announces explosion of its first hydrogen bomb **(June 17)**. Racial violence in Detroit; 7,000 National Guardsmen aid police after night of rioting. Similar outbreaks occur in New York City's Spanish Harlem, Rochester, N.Y., Birmingham, Ala., and New Britain, Conn. **(July 23)**. Thurgood Marshall sworn in as first black U.S. Supreme Court justice **(Oct. 2)**. Dr. Christiaan N. Barnard and team of South African surgeons perform world's first successful human heart transplant **(Dec. 3)**—patient dies 18 days later.

1968 North Korea seizes U.S. Navy ship *Pueblo;* holds 83 on board as spies **(Jan. 23)**. President Johnson announces he will not seek or accept presidential renomination **(March 31)**. Martin Luther King, Jr., civil rights leader, is slain in Memphis **(April 4)**—James Earl Ray, indicted in murder, captured in London on **June 8**. In **1969** Ray pleads guilty and is sentenced to 99 years. Sen. Robert F. Kennedy is shot and critically wounded in Los Angeles hotel after winning California primary **(June 5)**—dies **June 6**. Sirhan B. Sirhan convicted **1969**. Czechoslovakia is invaded by Russians and Warsaw Pact forces to crush liberal regime **(Aug. 20)**.

1969 Richard M. Nixon is inaugurated 37th President of the U.S. **(Jan. 20)**. Apollo 11 astronauts—Neil A. Armstrong, Edwin E. Aldrin, Jr., and Michael Collins—take man's first walk on moon **(July 20)**. Sen. Edward M. Kennedy pleads guilty to leaving scene of fatal accident at Chappaquiddick, Mass. **(July 18)** in which Mary Jo Kopechne was drowned—gets two-month suspended sentence **(July 25)**.

1970 Biafra surrenders after 32-month fight for independence from Nigeria **(Jan. 12)**. Rhodesia severs last tie with British Crown and declares itself a racially segregated republic **(March 1)**. Four students at Kent State University in Ohio slain by National Guardsmen at demonstration protesting April 30 incursion into Cambodia **(May 4)**. Senate repeals Gulf of Tonkin resolution **(June 24)**.

1971 Supreme Court rules unanimously that busing of students may be ordered to achieve racial desegregation **(April 20)**. Anti-war militants attempt to disrupt government business in Washington **(May 3)**—police and military units arrest as many as 12,000; most are later released. Twenty-sixth Amendment to U.S. Constitution lowers voting age to 18. U.N. seats Communist China and expels Nationalist China **(Oct. 25)**.

1972 President Nixon makes unprecedented eight-day visit to Communist China **(Feb.)**. Britain takes over direct rule of Northern Ireland in bid for peace **(March 24)**. Okinawa reverts to Japan after 27 years of U.S. rule **(May 14)**. Gov. George C. Wallace of Alabama is shot by Arthur H. Bremer at Laurel, Md., political rally **(May 15)**—Wallace paralyzed for life from the waist down. Bremer is sentenced to 63 years in prison on **Aug. 4**. Five men are apprehended by police in attempt to bug Democratic National Committee headquarters in Washington D.C.'s Watergate complex—start of the Watergate scandal **(June 17)**. Supreme Court rules that death penalty is unconstitutional **(June 29)**. Bobby Fischer becomes first American world chess champion, defeating Boris Spassky of U.S.S.R. **(Sept. 1)**. Eleven Israeli athletes at Olympic Games in Munich are killed after eight members of an Arab terrorist group invade Olympic Village; five guerrillas and one policeman are also killed **(Sept. 5)**.

1973 Great Britain, Ireland, and Denmark enter European Common Market **(Jan. 1)**. Indians hold 10 hostages after seizing settlement of Wounded Knee, S.D., demand Government discuss their grievances **(Feb. 28)**—surrender on **May 9**. Nixon, on national TV, accepts responsibility, but not blame, for Watergate; accepts resignations of advisers H. R. Haldeman and John D. Ehrlichman, fires John W. Dean III as counsel. **(April 30)**. Greek military junta abolishes monarchy and proclaims republic **(June 1)**. U.S. bombing of Cambodia ends, marking official halt to 12 years of combat activity in Southeast Asia **(Aug. 15)**. Violent military coup in Chile deposes President Salvador Allende Gossens, who reportedly commits suicide **(Sept. 11)**. Fourth and biggest Arab-Israeli War begins as Egyptian and Syrian forces attack Israel as Jews mark Yom Kippur, holiest day in their calendar. **(Oct. 6)**. Spiro T. Agnew resigns as Vice President and then, in Federal Court in Baltimore, pleads no contest to charges of evasion of income taxes on $29,500 he received in 1967 while Governor of Maryland. He is fined $10,000 and put on three years' probation **(Oct. 10)**. In the "Saturday Night Massacre," Nixon fires special Watergate prosecutor Archibald Cox and Deputy Attorney General William D. Ruckelshaus; Attorney General Elliot L. Richardson resigns **(Oct. 20)**. Egypt and Israel sign U.S.-sponsored cease-fire accord **(Nov. 11)**.

1974 Patricia Hearst, 19-year-old daughter of publisher Randolph Hearst, kidnapped by Symbionese Liberation Army. **(Feb. 5)**—Bloodless coup restores Portuguese democracy **(April 25)**. House Judiciary Committee adopts three articles of impeachment charging President Nixon with obstruction of justice, failure to uphold laws, and refusal to produce material subpoenaed by the committee **(July 30)**. Richard M. Nixon announces he will resign the next day, the first President to do so **(Aug. 8)**. Vice President Gerald R. Ford of Michigan is sworn in as 38th President of the U.S. **(Aug. 9)**. Ford grants "full, free, and absolute pardon" to ex-President Nixon **(Sept. 8)**.

1975 John N. Mitchell, H. R. Haldeman, John D. Ehrlichman, and Robert C. Mardian found guilty of Watergate cover-up. Mitchell, Haldeman, and Ehrlichman are sentenced on Feb. 21 to 30 months-8 years in jail and Mardian to 10 months-3 years **(Jan. 1)**. American merchant ship *Mayaguez*, seized by Cambodian forces, is rescued in operation by U.S. Navy and Marines, 38 of whom are killed **(May 15)**. *Apollo* and *Soyuz* spacecraft take off for U.S.-Soviet link-up in space **(July 15)**. President Ford escapes assassination attempt in Sacramento, Calif., **(Sept. 5)**. Patricia Hearst apprehended by FBI. **(Sept. 18)**. President Ford escapes second assassination attempt in 17 days. **(Sept. 22)**.

1976 Supreme Court rules that blacks and other minorities are entitled to retroactive job seniority **(March 24)**. Ford signs Federal Election Campaign Act **(May 11)**. Many killed and wounded when South African police fire on students in Soweto, near Johannesburg. **(June 16)**. Francis E. Meloy, Jr., U.S. Ambassador to Lebanon, assassinated in Beirut; all Americans advised to leave country as civil war continues; deaths exceed 30,000 **(June 17)**. Supreme Court rules that death penalty is not inherently cruel or unusual and is a constitutionally acceptable form of punishment **(July 3)**. Nation celebrates Bicentennial **(July 4)**. Israeli airborne commandos attack Uganda's Entebbe Airport and free 103 hostages held by pro-Palestinian hijackers of Air France plane; one Israeli and several Ugandan soldiers killed in raid **(July 4)**. Britain's Ambassador to Ireland and aide are killed when land mine explodes under their car in Dublin **(July 22)**. Mysterious disease that eventually claims 29 lives strikes American Legion convention in Philadelphia **(Aug. 4)**. Jimmy Carter elected U.S. President **(Nov. 2)**.

1977 First woman Episcopal priest ordained **(Jan. 1)**. Scientists identify previously unknown bacterium as cause of mysterious "legionnaire's disease" **(Jan. 18)**. Astronomers discover water outside of Earth's galaxy, indicating possibility of life in outer space **(Jan. 19)**. New Chinese Government allows films, plays, and artists previously banned by Cultural Revolution **(Jan. 21)**. Carter pardons Vietnam draft evaders **(Jan. 21)**. Supreme Court upholds use of racial quotas in state reapportionment plans **(March 1)**. U.S. extends its control of the seas to 200-mile limit **(March 1)**. NASA reports planet Uranus has five rings **(March 30)**. Spain legalizes Communist Party after 38-year ban **(April 9)**. Scientists report using bacteria in lab to make insulin **(May 23)**. Tongsun Park identified as Korean agent who allegedly spent millions to influence U.S. officials **(June 4)**. Soviets charge Anatoly Shcharansky, Jewish human-rights activist, with treason **(June 4)**. Laetrile found useless as cancer cure **(June 15)**. Supreme Court rules that states are not required to spend Medicaid funds on elective abortions **(June 20)**. Deng Xiaoping, purged Chinese leader, restored to power as "Gang of Four" is expelled from Communist Party **(July 22)**. First oil from Alaska's Prudhoe Bay fields pours from 799-mile pipeline at ice-free port of Valdez **(July 28)**. Tongsun Park charged by U.S. Justice Department with influence-buying **(Sept. 8)**. Nuclear-proliferation pact, curbing spread of nuclear weapons, signed by 15 countries, including U.S. and U.S.S.R.

(Sept. 21). Thirty-eight persons killed as earthen dam at Toccoa, Ga., collapses during heavy rains **(Nov. 6)**. Inquiry into prison death of Steven Biko, black leader, absolves South African security police; U.S. State Department expresses shock **(Dec. 2)**. Carter names G. William Miller to replace Arthur F. Burns as Federal Reserve Board Chairman **(Dec. 28)**.

1978 President chooses Federal Appeals Court Judge William H. Webster as FBI director **(Jan. 19)**. Soviet spy satellite with atomic reactor breaks up over northwest Canada **(Jan. 24)**; Rhodesia's Prime Minister Ian D. Smith and three black leaders agree on transfer to black majority rule **(Feb. 15)**. Former Italian Premier Aldo Moro kidnapped by left-wing terrorists, who kill five bodyguards **(March 16)**; he is found slain **(May 9)**. U.S. Senate approves Panama Canal neutrality treaty **(March 16)**; votes treaty to turn canal over to Panama by year 2000 **(April 18)**. Supreme Court upholds corporate spending in elections under constitutional right of free speech **(April 26)**. All 51 construction workers killed in collapse of power plant cooling tower under construction at St. Mary's, W. Va. **(April 27)**. David Berkowitz pleads guilty and gets 25 years to life in each of New York's six "Son of Sam" killings **(May 8)**. Californians in referendum approve Proposition 13 for nearly 60% slash in property tax revenues **(June 6)**. Mormon Church ends ban on blacks **(June 9)**. Supreme Court, in Bakke case, bars quota system in college admissions, but affirms constitutionality of programs giving advantage to minorities **(June 28)**; Justices support affirmative action to remedy past discrimination in employment **(July 3)**. Baby girl born in England from egg fertilized outside womb in what is believed world's first such case **(July 26)**. Pope Paul VI, dead at 80, mourned **(Aug. 6)**; new Pope, John Paul I, 65, dies unexpectedly after 34 days in office **(Sept. 28)**; succeeded by Karol Cardinal Wojtyla of Poland as John Paul II **(Oct. 16)**. "Framework for Peace" in Middle East signed by Egypt's President Anwar el-Sadat and Israeli Premier Menachem Begin after 13-day conference at Camp David led by President Carter **(Sept. 17)**. Senate extends deadline for equal rights amendment ratification until June 30, 1982 **(Oct. 8)**. Republicans score gains in Congressional and state elections; Democrats retain political domination **(Nov. 8)**. 911 in cult die in mass murder-suicide in Guyanan jungle after California Congressman and four others perish in ambush **(Nov. 20)**. U.S. and China agree to begin diplomatic relations; Carter reassures Taiwan **(Dec. 15)**.

1979 Oil spills pollute ocean waters in Atlantic and Gulf of Mexico **(Jan. 1, June 8, July 21)**. Ohio agrees to pay $675,000 to families of dead and injured in Kent State University shootings **(Jan. 4)**. Vietnam and Cambodian insurgents it backs announce fall of Phnom Penh, Cambodian capital, and collapse of Pol Pot regime **(Jan. 7)**. Shah leaves Iran after year of turmoil **(Jan. 16)**; revolutionary forces under Moslem leader, Ayatollah Ruhollah Khomeini, take over **(Feb. 1, et seq.)**. Senior Deputy Prime Minister of China, Deng Xiaoping, acclaimed on visit to U.S.; confers with President Carter **(Jan. 28-Feb. 5)**. Chinese invade Vietnam **(Feb. 18)**; withdraw troops **(March 5)**; report 20,000 casualties, with probably 5,000 deaths **(May 2)**. Conservatives win British election; Margaret Thatcher new Prime Minister **(March 28)**. Nuclear power plant accident at Three Mile Island, Pa., releases radioactivity **(March 28)**. Former Prime Minister Zulfikar Ali Bhutto hanged in Pakistan **(April 4)**. Los Angeles court orders Lee Marvin to pay $104,000 to singer with whom actor lived out of wedlock for six years **(April 18)**. Bishop Abel T. Muzorewa wins interracial Rhodesia election **(April 24)**. Florida executes John Arthur Spenkelink, 30, for murder after pleas fail, first involuntary execution in nation since 1967 **(May 25)**. Millions cheer Pope on triumphal visit to native Poland **(June 2–10)**. Carter and Brezhnev sign SALT II agreement **(June 14)**. Supreme Court upholds Federal ban on controversial cancer drug laetrile **(June 18)**. Supreme Court upholds preference for blacks in jobs **(June 27)**. China signs three-year trade treaty with U.S. **(July 7)**. House committee finds conspiracy in John Kennedy assassination **(July 17)**. Nicaraguan President Gen. Anastasio Somoza Debayle resigns and flees to Miami **(July 17)**; Sandinists form government **(July 19)**. Andrew Young resigns as U.N. delegate from U.S. after reprimand for unauthorized talks with P.L.O. **(Aug 15)**. Carter lifts controls on price of domestic crude oil **(Aug. 17)**. Earl Mountbatten of Burma, 79, British World War II hero, and three others killed by blast on fishing boat off Irish coast **(Aug. 27)**; two I.R.A. members accused **(Aug. 30)**. Spacecraft *Pioneer II* gets first close photos of Saturn **(Sept. 1)**. Carter approves controversial Tellico hydroelectric dam on Little Tennessee River **(Sept. 25)**. Vietnamese start offensive against Pol Pot regime in Cambodia **(Sept. 25)**. Thousands cheer Pope on visit to Ireland and U.S. (**Sept. 29-Oct. 7**). Chilean Supreme Court bars extradition of three indicted in U.S. for planning murder of Chilean exile leader (**Oct. 1**). W. A. Boyle, 78, former UMW president, again sentenced to life after new trial in Yablonski killings (**Oct. 11**). Nevada executes Jesse Walter Bishop, 46, Las Vegas casino murderer, in state's first execution in 18 years (**Oct. 22**). Congress votes stand-by gasoline rationing (**Oct. 23**). U.S. surgeons operate on deposed Shah of Iran (**Oct. 24**); Shah dies at 60 (**July 27, 1980**). Park Chung Hee, 62, South Korean President for 18 years, assassinated by intelligence chief (**Oct. 26**). Iranian militants seize U.S. embassy in Teheran and hold hostages (**Nov. 4**). Lane Kirkland succeeds George Meany as AFL-CIO president (**Nov. 19**). Eleven rock fans killed in crush at Cincinnati's Riverfront Coliseum (**Dec. 3**). Soviet invasion of Afghanistan stirs world protests (**Dec. 27**).

1980 Indira Gandhi wins landslide victory in India (**Jan. 6**). Scientists announce gene splitting produces natural virus-fighting substance (**Jan. 16**). Soviet arrests dissident nuclear physicist Andrei D. Sakharov and wife (**Jan. 22**). Shigato Nakano, Japanese Army chief, resigns in spy inquiry (**Jan. 28**). Six U.S. Embassy aides escape from Iran with Canadian help (**Jan. 29**). FBI's two-year undercover operation "Abscam" (for Arab scam) implicates public officials (**Feb. 2**). U.S. creates 40 million-acre wildlife refuge in Alaska (**Feb. 12**). Supreme Court upholds CIA's right to censor employees' writings (**Feb. 19**). Terrorists hold diplomats hostage for 61 days in Bogota embassy (**Feb. 27-April 27**). Dr. Herman Tarnower, 69, "Scarsdale diet" doctor, slain (**March 10**). John Wayne Gacy, 37, convicted in Chicago in murders of 33 young men and boys (**March 12**). Indiana jury clears Ford Motor Co. in three Pinto deaths (**March 13**). Robert Muncie enthroned as 102nd Archbishop of Canterbury (**March 25**). Congress approves "windfall" tax on oil profits (**March 27**). Thousands of Cubans find refuge in U.S. (**April 6** et seq.). U.S. breaks diplomatic ties with Iran (**April 7**). Two Soviet astronauts rendezvous with space station (**April 9**). John B. Anderson, Republican, declares independent candidacy in Presidential campaign (**April 24**). Eight U.S. servicemen are killed and five are injured as helicopter and cargo plane collide in abortive desert raid to rescue American hostages in Teheran (**April 25**). Cyrus R. Vance resigns as U.S. Secretary of State (**April 28**); Senator Edmund S. Muskie of Maine succeeds him (**April 29**). Georgia Federal court jury acquits Bert Lance, former U.S. Budget Director, on nine bank fraud charges (**April 30**). Death toll 17 in Miami race rioting after acquittal of four white former policemen in fatal beating of black (**May 17**). First women graduate from service academies (**May 21, 28**). Congress votes $3.3 million for draft registration (**June 12, 25**). High court upholds patents for new forms of life (**June 16**). Crack in Milan church wall endangers da Vinci's *Last Supper* (**June 16**). Carter approves shipment of nuclear fuel to India (**June 19**). Congress votes $20-billion synthetic fuels program (**June 26**). Supreme Court upholds limits on Federal aid for abortions (**June 30**). Justices approve affirmative action for minority contractors in Federal works program (**July 2**). Republican National Convention nominates Reagan-Bush slate (**July 16, 17**). Olympic games open in Moscow, boycotted by U.S. and other nations (**July 19**). U.S. strengthens guidelines for bilingual education (**Aug. 5**). Democratic Convention renominates Carter and Mondale (**Aug. 13, 14**). Vatican rules married Anglican priests can join Catholic clergy (**Aug. 20**). Polish workers end 18-day walkout with Government pledges of political and economic concessions (**Sept. 1**). Anastasio Somoza Debayle, ousted Nicaragua ruler, and two aides assassinated in Asunción, Paraguay capital (**Sept. 17**). Iraqi troops hold 90 square miles of Iran after invasion (**Sept. 19**); as scale of warfare grows, U.N. Security Council appeals to both sides to cease fighting (**Sept. 23**); New law gives Gandhi Government in India power to imprison without trial (**Sept. 23**). Aleksei N. Kosygin, 76, ailing Soviet Prime Minister, resigns (**Oct. 23**). Carter and Reagan meet in nationally televised debate (**Oct. 28**).

Ronald Reagan elected President in Republican sweep (**Nov. 4**). *Voyager 1* discovers 15th Saturn moon (**Nov. 8**). Polish Supreme Court backs trade union charter (**Nov. 9**). U.S. rejects higher tariffs for Japanese cars (**Nov. 10**. 300,000 greet Pope on visit to West Germany (**Nov. 15**). U.S. Judge dismisses two Philadelphia Abscam convictions (**Nov. 26**); Federal jury convicts two in Brooklyn trial (**Dec. 3**). President Carter signs bill to protect Alaska lands (**Dec. 2**). Federal Appeals Court upsets "Wilmington 10" convictions (**Dec. 4**). Three U.S. nuns and lay workers found slain in El Salvador (**Dec. 4**). John Lennon of Beatles shot dead in New York (**Dec. 8**). Justice Department drops case against L. Patrick Gray 3rd, former FBI head, accused of authorizing illegal break-ins (**Dec. 11**). Collector pays $5 million for Leonardo de Vinci notebook (**Dec. 12**).

1981 Swiss scientist reports first cloning of a mammal (**Jan. 4**). Scheduled U.S.-China air passenger service restored after 32-year hiatus (**Jan. 7**). Philippine President Ferdinand E. Marcos ends martial law and frees 341 prisoners **(Jan. 17)**. U.S.-Iran agreement frees 52 hostages held in Tehran since Nov. 4, 1979 **(Jan. 18)**; hostages welcomed back in U.S. **(Jan. 25)**. Ronald Reagan takes oath as 40th President **(Jan. 20)**. Edward M. Kennedys announce divorce plans **(Jan. 21)**. Chinese leaders of Cultural Revolution get long sentences after trial **(Jan. 25)**. President Reagan ends remaining controls on oil and gasoline **(Jan. 26)**. Supreme Court, 8–0, approves televising of trials in state courts **(Jan. 26)**. U.S. revokes proposed rules for bilingual teaching in public schools **(Feb. 2)**. Army Gen. Wojciech Jaruzelski named Prime Minister of Poland **(Feb. 9)**. U.S. jury convicts 10 accused Puerto Rico terrorists in Chicago trial **(Feb. 11)**. Missing symphony that Mozart wrote at age 9 discovered **(Feb. 13)**. Pope John Paul II visits Far East **(Feb. 16–27)**. Reagan offers sweeping economic reform program **(Feb. 18)**. Owners and builders of Three Mile Island nuclear reactor agree to $35-million settlement **(Feb. 21)**. Jean W. Harris, 57, convicted in slaying of "Scarsdale Diet" doctor **(Feb. 24)**; she is sentenced to 15 years **(March 20)**. John Lennon of Beatles leaves $5.5-million estate in Britain **(Feb. 28)**. Twelve members of Parliament quit British Labour Party to form Social Democrats **(March 2)**; party organized formally with wide public support **(March 26)**. Berrigan brothers and six other antinuclear activists found guilty in damage to missile nose cones at General Electric Company plant in Pennsylvania **(March 6)**. President Reagan wounded by gunman, with press secretary and two law-enforcement officers **(March 30)**. Test in Norway of new drug, timolol, suggests that it may reduce heart fatalities **(April 1)**. Rioting sweeps London black district for two nights **(April 11–12)**. Space shuttle *Columbia* succeeds in test flight **(April 12)**. Polish farmers win right to form independent union **(April 17)**. Supreme Court widens restrictions on search of homes **(April 21)**. Senator Harrison A. Williams of New Jersey convicted in Abscam case **(May 1)**. Japan agrees to limit automobile exports to U.S. **(May 1)**. Hunger strikers die in Belfast prison protest **(May 5–July 13)**; street battles erupt. François Mitterand, Socialist, elected French President **(May 10)**. Congress approves $695.5-billion Reagan budget **(May 14)**. Pope John Paul II wounded by gunman **(May 14)**. Supreme Court expands protection for criminal defendants against self-incrimination **(May 18)**. Peter Sutcliffe, 35, Yorkshire truck driver, sentenced to life for each of 13 killings of women over five years **(May 22)**. Two anti-Castro Cubans acquitted in retrial in killing of former Chilean Ambassador Orlando Letelier and aide **(May 30)**. Craig S. Crimmins, 22, stagehand, convicted of killing violinst at Metropolitan Opera **(June 4)**. Israeli planes destroy Iraqi atomic reactor **(June 8)**. French Socialists win control of Parliament **(June 14** and **21)**. Supreme Court Justice Potter Stewart announces retirement **(June 16)**. Iran's President Abolhassan Bani-Sadr removed from office **(June 22)**; he flees to France and is granted asylum **(July 29)**. Supreme Court rules, 4–4, that former President Nixon and three top aides may be required to pay monetary damages for unconstitutional wiretap of home telephone of former national security aide **(June 22)**. Court, 6–3, decides that registration for draft can exclude women **(June 23)**. Congress supports Reagan's $35.5-billion budget cuts designed to reverse government's expansion **(June 26–July 31)**. High court, 7–2, backs State Department revocation of former C.I.A. agent's passport **(June 29)**. Administration ends import quotas on shoes from Taiwan and South Korea **(June 30)**. United Auto Workers Union rejoins A.F.L.-C.I.O. 13 years after split **(July 1)**. Reagan nominates Judge Sandra Day O'Connor, 51, of Arizona as first woman on Supreme Court **(July 7)**. Disorders break out in major British cities **(July 12)**; thousands under arrest **(July 14)**. Three hundred dead as Israelis bomb Beirut in attack on Palestinian guerrilla targets **(July 17)**. More than 110 die in collapse of aerial walkways in lobby of Hyatt Regency Hotel in Kansas City; 188 injured **(July 18)**. *Washington Star* ends publication **(July 23)**. Millions around world view wedding of Prince Charles of Britain, 32, and Lady Diana Spencer, 20 **(July 29)**. Congress backs Reagan on tax reductions **(July 29–Aug. 4)**. Major league baseball strike ends after seven weeks **(July 31)**. Panama's leader, Gen. Omar Torrijos Herrera, 52, dies in plane crash **(Aug. 1)**. Air controllers strike, disrupting flights **(Aug. 3 et seq.)**; Government dismisses strikers **(Aug. 11)**. E. I. du Pont de Nemours & Company wins battle to buy Conoco **(Aug. 5)**. President orders production of neutron weapons **(Aug. 6)**. Three former Congressmen are first defendants sentenced in Federal Abscam investigation into political corruption **(Aug. 13)**. California extends aerial spraying of orchards to fight spread of Mediterranean fruit fly **(Aug. 23 et seq.)**. U.S. vetoes U.N. rebuke to South Africans over raid into Angola **(Aug. 31)**.

(For later events, *See* Current Events, 1981–82, in Table of Contents.)

WORLD STATISTICS

Area and Population by Country

Mid-1981 Estimates

Country	Area[1]	Population
Afghanistan	251,000	16,750,000
Albania	11,100	2,875,000
Algeria	919,951	20,000,000
Andorra	175	35,000
Angola	481,350	7,450,000
Antigua and Barbuda	171	80,000
Argentina	1,072,067	28,400,000
Australia	2,967,909	15,100,000
Austria	32,375	7,515,000
Bahamas	4,404	225,000
Bahrain	240	375,000
Bangladesh	55,126	92,600,000
Barbados	166	275,000
Belgium	11,781	9,870,000
Belize	8,867	175,000
Benin	43,483	3,725,000
Bhutan	18,000	1,350,000
Bolivia	424,162	5,900,000
Botswana	222,000	900,000
Brazil	3,286,470	124,500,000
Bulgaria	42,823	8,925,000
Burma	261,789	37,500,000
Burundi	10,747	4,450,000
Cambodia	70,000	7,000,000
Cameroon	183,569	8,800,000
Canada	3,851,809	24,450,000
Cape Verde	1,557	340,000
Central African Republic	241,313	2,500,000
Chad	495,752	4,650,000
Chile	286,396	11,500,000
China, People's Republic of[2]	3,691,521	1,020,000,000
China, Republic of[3]	13,592	18,350,000
Colombia	455,355	28,575,000
Comoros	692	375,000
Congo	132,046	1,625,000
Costa Rica	19,652	2,350,000
Cuba	44,218	9,850,000
Cyprus	3,572	650,000
Czechoslovakia	49,374	15,400,000
Denmark[4]	16,615	5,130,000
Djibouti	8,996	335,000
Dominica	300	85,000
Dominican Republic	18,704	5,575,000
Ecuador	105,685	8,950,000
Egypt	386,872	44,750,000
El Salvador	8,260	5,150,000
Equatorial Guinea	10,830	380,000
Ethiopia	457,142	33,000,000
Fiji	7,055	650,000
Finland	130,119	4,825,000
France	212,973	54,250,000
Gabon	102,317	560,000
Gambia	4,016	640,000
Germany, East[5]	40,646	16,750,000
Germany, West[6]	95,815	61,750,000
Ghana	92,100	12,400,000
Greece	50,547	9,800,000
Grenada	133	110,000
Guatemala	42,042	7,700,000
Guinea	94,925	5,300,000
Guinea-Bissau	13,948	590,000
Guyana	83,000	925,000
Haiti	10,714	5,200,000
Honduras	43,277	3,950,000
Hungary	35,919	10,725,000
Iceland	39,702	235,000
India[7]	1,229,737	700,000,000
Indonesia[8]	735,268	153,000,00
Iran	636,363	41,000,000
Iraq	172,000	14,000,000
Ireland	26,600	3,480,00
Israel	7,992[9]	4,000,00
Italy	116,304	56,500,00
Ivory Coast	124,502	8,500,00
Jamaica	4,411	2,250,00
Japan	143,574	118,500,00
Jordan	37,297	3,475,00
Kenya	224,960	17,600,00
Kiribati	264	60,00
Korea, North	46,768	18,750,00
Korea, South	38,031	39,350,00
Kuwait	7,780	1,550,00
Laos	91,429	3,900,00
Lebanon	4,015	2,700,00
Lesotho	11,720	1,400,00
Liberia	43,000	2,150,00
Libya	679,536	3,250,00
Liechtenstein	61	30,00
Luxembourg	999	365,00
Madagascar	230,035	9,190,00
Malawi	45,747	6,275,00
Malaysia	128,328	14,750,0
Maldives	115	160,0
Mali	464,873	7,350,0
Malta	122	375,0
Mauritania	419,229	1,725,0
Mauritius	787	950,0
Mexico	761,600	72,900,0
Monaco	([10])	30,0
Mongolia	604,250	1,725,0
Morocco	171,953	21,275,0
Mozambique	303,073	11,100,0
Nauru	8.2	8,0
Nepal	54,362	15,325,0
Netherlands	13,967	14,350,0
New Zealand[11]	103,736	3,175,0
Nicaragua	57,143	2,900,0
Niger	489,206	5,650,0
Nigeria	356,700	82,250,0
Norway	125,182	4,125,0
Oman[12]	82,000	950,0
Pakistan[13]	342,750	85,500,0
Panama	29,306	2,000,0
Papua New Guinea	183,540	3,250,0
Paraguay	157,047	3,375,0
Peru	496,222	18,850,0
Philippines	115,707	50,500,0
Poland	120,359	36,300,
Portugal	35,340	10,000,0
Qatar	4,000	260,0
Romania	91,700	22,700,0
Rwanda	10,169	5,200,
St. Lucia	238	125,
St. Vincent and the Grenadines	250	150,
San Marino	23.6	20,
São Tomé and Príncipe	372	90,

Country	Area[1]	Population
Saudi Arabia	873,000	9,700,000
Senegal	76,124	5,950,000
Seychelles	171	70,000
Sierra Leone	27,925	3,675,000
Singapore	238	2,500,000
Solomon Islands	11,500	250,000
Somalia	246,155	5,150,000
South Africa[14]	318,861	23,500,000
Spain[15]	194,885	37,850,000
Sri Lanka	25,332	15,250,000
Sudan	967,491	19,150,000
Suriname	63,251	410,000
Swaziland	6,704	600,000
Sweden	173,665	8,330,000
Switzerland	15,941	6,475,000
Syria	71,498	9,650,000
Tanzania[16]	362,820	19,000,000
Thailand	198,455	49,000,000
Togo	21,853	2,800,000
Tonga	290	100,000
Trinidad and Tobago	1,980	1,200,000
Tunisia	63,379	6,650,000
Turkey	301,380	47,500,000
Tuvalu	10	7,000
Uganda	91,134	14,000,000
U.S.S.R.	8,649,489	269,850,000
United Arab Emirates	32,000	800,000
United Kingdom	94,249	55,850,000
United States	3,540,939	232,000,000
Upper Volta	105,870	7,170,000
Uruguay	68,548	2,950,000
Vanuatu (New Hebrides)	5,700	125,000
Vatican City State	([17])	1,000
Venezuela	352,143	14,700,000
Vietnam	126,436	56,250,000
Western Samoa	1,133	160,000
Yemen, People's Democratic Republic of[18]	111,000	2,100,000
Yemen Arab Republic	75,290	8,575,000
Yugoslavia	98,766	22,412,000
Zaire	905,063	28,150,000
Zambia	290,724	6,100,000
Zimbabwe	150,333	7,850,000

1. Square miles. 2. Including Manchuria and Tibet. 3. Excluding Quemoy and Matsu. 4. Excluding Faeroe Islands and Greenland. 5. Including East Berlin. 6. Excluding West Berlin. 7. Including Jammu and Kashmir and Sikkim. 8. Including Portuguese East Timor, annexed in 1976, and Irian Jaya (former Netherlands New Guinea and later West Irian). 9. Excluding territory occupied in 1967 war. 10. 0.65 square mile. 11. Excluding dependencies. 12. Excluding Kuria Muria Islands. 13. Excluding Jammu and Kashmir. 14. Excluding South-West Africa (Namibia), Bophuthatswana, Transkei, Venda, and Ciskei. 15. Including Balearic and Canary Islands. 16. Including Zanzibar. 17. 0.17 square mile. 18. Excluding Perim and Kamaran Islands.

Largest Cities of the World

Census figures and population estimates in the following table are based on data reflecting different years. Some cities include metropolitan areas or contiguous suburbs, while others report only those residing within precise geographical or physical boundaries. Therefore, the ratings in this listing must be considered approximate.

City	Population	Year
Shanghai	11,000,000	1979E
Mexico City	9,200,000	1979E
Calcutta	9,165,650	1980C
Peking	9,000,000	1979E
Sao Paulo, Brazil	8,584,896	1980C
Tokyo	8,350,000	1980E
Seoul, South Korea	8,400,000	1980E
Bombay	8,202,759	1980C
Moscow	8,011,000	1979C
Manila	7,500,000	1977E
New York	7,071,639	1980C
London	6,696,000	1981E
Jakarta, Indonesia	6,500,000	1981E
Teheran, Iran	6,000,000	1980E
Cairo	5,423,000	1979E
Rio de Janeiro	5,184,292	1980C
Karachi, Pakistan	5,100,000	1981C
Bangkok, Thailand	5,000,000	1980E
Lima, Peru	4,990,000	1979E
Leningrad	4,588,000	1979C

Source: United Nations *Demographic Yearbook, 1979,* and official estimates. NOTE: E = estimate: C = census.

Some Other Large Foreign Cities

City	Population	Year[1]
Addis Ababa, Ethiopia	1,275,000	1980E
Ahmedabad, India	2,515,195	1980C
Alexandria, Egypt	2,317,705	1976C
Algiers	2,500,000	1979E
Alma Ata, U.S.S.R.	910,000	1979C
Amsterdam	957,700	1979E
Ankara, Turkey	2,561,765	1980C
Antwerp, Belgium	197,000	1979E
Athens	3,000,000[2]	1981E
Auckland, New Zealand	818,000[2]	1981E
Baghdad, Iraq	3,205,600	1977E
Baku, U.S.S.R.	1,550,000	1979C
Badung, Indonesia	1,201,730	1971C
Bangalore, India	2,913,537	1980C
Barcelona	1,725,000	1981E
Barranquilla, Colombia	868,000	1979E
Belfast, Northern Ireland	345,800	1980E
Belgrade, Yugoslavia	1,000,000	1980E
Belo Horizonte, Brazil	1,814,990	1980C
Berlin[3]	3,046,000	1980E
Bern, Switzerland	142,800	1979E
Birmingham, England	1,006,000	1981E
Bogotá, Colombia	4,500,000	1982E
Bonn, West Germany	285,000	1977E
Brasilia, Brazil	1,202,683	1980C
Brisbane, Australia	1,000,000[2]	1980E
Brussels	1,000,000	1981E
Bucharest	1,830,000	1979E
Budapest	2,100,000	1980E
Buenos Aires	3,000,000	1980E

City	Population	Year[1]
Calgary, Canada	592,743[2]	1981C
Cali, Colombia	1,189,000	1979E
Canton, China	2,300,000	1970E
Cape Town, South Africa	892,000	1980E
Caracas, Venezuela	3,000,000[2]	1981E
Casablanca, Morocco	2,350,000	1979E
Chongqing (Chungking), China	3,500,000	1970E
Cologne, West Germany	795,000	1980E
Copenhagen	660,000	1980E
Córdoba, Argentina	781,600	1975E
Dacca, Bangladesh	2,500,000	1980E
Damascus, Syria	1,200,000	1980E
Delhi, India	6,196,414	1980C
Dnepropetrovsk, U.S.S.R.	1,066,000	1979C
Donetsk, U.S.S.R.	1,021,000	1979C
Dresden, East Germany	516,000	1980E
Dublin	550,000	1980E
Düsseldorf, West Germany	590,000	1980E
Edinburgh, Scotland	419,200	1981E
Edmonton, Canada	657,057[2]	1981C
Florence, Italy	453,293	1981C
Frankfurt, West Germany	630,000	1980E
Fukuoka, Japan	1,039,300[2]	1977E
Geneva	152,700	1980E
Genoa, Italy	760,300	1981C
Glasgow, Scotland	762,200	1981E
Gorki, U.S.S.R.	1,344,000	1979C
Guadalajara, Mexico	1,813,000	1978E
Guatemala City	1,250,000	1980E
Guayaquil, Ecuador	1,100,000	1980E
The Hague	671,500	1979E
Haifa, Israel	230,000	1979E
Hamburg, West Germany	1,650,000	1980E
Harbin, China	2,750,000	1970E
Havana	2,000,000	1979E
Helsinki, Finland	484,000	1981E
Ho Chi Minh City (Saigon), Vietnam	3,450,000	1979E
Hyderabad, India	1,607,396	1971C
Hyderabad, Pakistan	795,000	1981C
Ibadan, Nigeria	847,000	1975E
Istanbul	2,990,680	1980C
Jerusalem	412,000	1981E
Johannesburg, South Africa	1,500,000	1980E
Kanpur, India	1,685,308	1980C
Kharkov, U.S.S.R.	1,444,000	1979C
Kiev, U.S.S.R.	2,144,000	1979C
Kinshasa, Zaire	2,500,000	1979E
Kobe, Japan	1,375,000	1980E
Kuala Lumpur, Malaysia	1,000,000	1980E
Kuibyshev, U.S.S.R.	1,216,000	1979C
Kunming, China	1,700,000	1970E
Lagos, Nigeria	4,000,000[2]	1980E
Lahore, Pakistan	2,900,000	1981C
La Paz, Bolivia	700,000	1980E
Lausanne, Switzerland	131,000	1980E
Leipzig, East Germany	563,000	1980E
Liège, Belgium	224,000	1979E
Lisbon	861,500	1979E
Liverpool, England	510,300	1981E
Lódz, Poland	830,800	1980E
Luda, China	4,000,000	1970E
Lyons, France	462,841	1975C
Madras, India	4,276,635	1971C
Madrid	3,275,000	1981E
Manchester, England	449,200	1981E
Marseilles, France	914,356	1975C
Mecca, Saudi Arabia	500,000	1980E
Medellín, Colombia	1,748,000	1979E
Melbourne	2,760,000	1980E
Milan, Italy	1,634,638	1981C
Minsk, U.S.S.R.	1,276,000	1979C
Monterrey, Mexico	1,054,000	1978E
Montevideo, Uruguay	1,250,000	1975E
Montreal	2,828,349[2]	1981C
Munich, West Germany	1,300,000	1980E
Nagoya, Japan	2,100,000	1980E
Nanjing (Nanking), China	2,000,000	1970E
Nantes, France	263,689	1975C
Naples, Italy	1,210,503	1981C
Nice, France	346,620	1975C
Novosibirsk, U.S.S.R.	1,312,000	1979C
Odessa, U.S.S.R.	1,046,000	1979C
Osaka, Japan	2,650,000	1980E
Oslo	457,300	1979E
Ottawa	717,978[2]	1981C
Paris	2,150,000	1980E
Port-au-Prince, Haiti	790,000	1980E
Porto Alegre, Brazil	1,158,709	1980C
Prague	1,182,000	1981E
Pusan, South Korea	3,160,000	1980E
Pyongyang, North Korea	1,500,000	1976E
Quebec	576,075[2]	1981C
Quezon City, Philippines	994,700	1975E
Quito, Ecuador	800,000	1980E
Rangoon, Burma	2,200,000	1979E
Recife, Brazil	1,240,897	1980C
Riyadh, Saudi Arabia	1,250,000	1980E
Rome	2,830,569	1981C
Rosario, Argentina	750,500	1975E
Rostov-on-Don, U.S.S.R.	934,000	1979C
Rotterdam	1,014,800	1979E
Salvador, Brazil	1,525,831[2]	1980C
Santiago, Chile	3,850,000	1980E
Santo Domingo, Dominican Republic	1,250,000	1979E
Sapporo, Japan	1,400,000	1980E
Seville, Spain	630,000	1981E
Sheffield, England	536,800	1981E
Shenyang, China	3,750,000[2]	1970E
Singapore, Singapore	2,450,000	1977E
Sofia, Bulgaria	1,000,000	1979E
Stockholm	1,400,000	1980E
Stuttgart, West Germany	582,000	1980E
Surabaja, Indonesia	1,556,255	1971
Sverdlovsk, U.S.S.R.	1,211,000	1979
Sydney, Australia	3,230,000	1980
Taipei, Taiwan	2,250,000	1981
Tashkent, U.S.S.R.	1,779,000	1979
Tbilisi, U.S.S.R.	1,066,000	1979
Tel Aviv-Jaffa, Israel	336,000	1979
Tianjin (Tientsin), China	4,280,000	1970
Toronto	2,998,947[2]	1981
Tunis, Tunisia	960,000[2]	1976
Turin, Italy	1,103,520	1981
Valparaiso, Chile	248,500	1978
Valencia, Spain	770,000	1981
Vancouver, Canada	1,268,183[2]	1981
Venice	358,400	1978
Vienna	1,580,600	1978
Volgograd, U.S.S.R.	929,000	1979
Warsaw	1,576,600	1980
Wellington, New Zealand	342,000[2]	1981
Winnipeg, Canada	584,842[2]	1981
Yokohama, Japan	2,775,000	1980
Zurich	377,300	1980

1. E = estimated; C = census. 2. Figure is for metropolitan area and may include suburbs or some rural population. 3. We Berlin, 1,900,000; East Berlin, 1,046,000. NOTE: The population of many other cities will be found throughout the Wor History section under individual countries. *See* Table of Contents.

Expectation of Life by Age and Sex for Selected Countries

		Average future lifetime in years at stated age											
		Males						Females					
Country	Period	0	1	10	20	40	60	0	1	10	20	40	60
NORTH AMERICA													
United States	1975	68.7	68.9	60.3	50.8	32.6	16.8	76.5	76.6	67.9	58.1	39.0	21.8
Canada	1970–72	69.3	69.8	61.2	51.7	33.2	17.0	76.4	76.6	67.9	58.2	39.0	21.4
Mexico	1975	62.8	68.0	59.2	49.9	32.7	17.9	66.6	69.3	62.6	53.1	35.3	19.1
Trinidad and Tobago	1970	64.1	65.6	57.3	47.8	29.5	13.6	68.1	69.3	60.9	51.3	32.7	16.3
CENTRAL AND SOUTH AMERICA													
Brazil	1960–70	57.6	—	56.2	47.0	30.0	15.0	61.1	—	58.9	49.7	32.5	16.6
Chile	1969–70	60.5	64.9	56.7	47.3	29.9	15.5	66.0	70.0	62.2	52.7	34.5	18.0
Costa Rica	1972–74	66.3	69.1	61.3	51.8	33.8	17.4	70.5	72.7	64.9	55.2	36.5	19.2
Ecuador	1962–74	54.9	60.5	55.5	47.1	31.3	16.2	58.1	62.8	58.0	49.3	33.0	17.3
Guatemala	1963–65	48.3	52.5	51.3	43.2	28.1	14.8	49.7	53.4	52.8	44.6	29.2	14.7
Panama	1970	64.3	66.4	59.9	50.8	33.4	17.0	67.5	69.4	62.7	53.6	36.1	19.9
Peru	1960–65	52.6	—	53.9	45.3	29.3	14.8	55.5	—	55.9	47.3	31.4	16.1
Uruguay	1963–64	65.5	68.0	59.5	50.0	31.7	15.9	71.6	73.7	65.2	55.5	36.7	19.5
Venezuela[1]	1975	65.0	67.3	59.6	50.2	32.6	17.1	69.7	71.5	63.8	54.2	35.6	18.9
EUROPE													
Austria	1977	68.5	—	60.1	50.7	32.3	16.1	75.6	—	67.0	57.2	37.9	20.1
Belgium	1968–72	67.8	68.4	59.9	50.3	31.6	15.2	74.2	74.5	65.9	56.1	36.9	19.2
Cyprus	1973	70.0	70.7	62.1	52.3	33.5	16.5	72.9	74.2	65.7	55.8	36.4	18.5
Czechoslovakia	1970	66.2	67.0	58.4	49.9	30.6	14.6	72.9	72.6	64.9	55.2	35.9	18.3
Denmark[2]	1977–78	71.5	71.3	62.6	52.9	34.0	17.3	77.5	77.1	68.3	58.5	39.1	21.6
Finland	1978	68.5	68.0	59.3	49.7	31.1	15.4	77.1	76.7	67.8	58.0	38.6	20.4
France	1977	69.7	69.7	61.0	51.4	33.0	17.1	77.9	77.6	68.9	59.1	39.9	22.0
Germany, East[3]	1976	68.8	69.0	60.4	50.8	32.2	15.9	74.4	74.3	65.6	55.9	36.6	18.8
Germany, West[3]	1976–78	69.0	69.2	60.6	51.1	32.5	16.0	75.6	75.7	67.0	57.2	38.0	20.2
Greece	1970	70.1	72.2	63.8	54.1	35.1	17.5	73.6	75.3	66.9	57.1	37.8	19.3
Hungary	1978	66.6	67.5	58.8	49.1	30.8	15.3	73.3	73.8	65.1	55.3	36.1	18.7
Ireland	1970–72	68.8	69.2	60.6	51.0	32.1	15.6	73.5	73.8	65.1	55.3	40.8	18.7
Italy	1970–72	69.0	70.1	61.6	52.0	33.2	16.7	74.9	75.8	67.1	57.3	38.1	20.2
Netherlands	1977	72.0	71.8	63.2	53.5	34.4	17.4	78.4	78.1	69.4	59.6	40.2	22.1
Norway	1977–78	72.3	72.0	63.3	53.7	34.7	17.8	78.7	78.3	69.5	59.7	40.2	21.9
Poland	1970–72	66.8	68.0	59.4	49.8	31.6	15.5	73.8	74.6	66.0	56.2	37.0	19.3
Portugal	1974	65.3	67.2	59.0	49.6	31.5	15.4	72.0	73.5	65.3	55.6	36.5	18.7
Spain	1970	69.7	—	62.0	52.4	33.7	17.0	75.0	—	66.9	57.1	38.0	20.1
Sweden	1974–78	72.2	71.9	63.2	53.5	34.7	17.7	78.1	77.7	68.9	59.1	39.7	21.6
Switzerland	1968–73	70.3	70.5	62.0	52.4	33.6	16.7	76.2	76.2	67.6	57.8	38.4	20.4
U.S.S.R.	1971–72	64.0	—	—	—	—	—	74.0	—	—	—	—	—
United Kingdom													
England and Wales	1974–76	69.6	—	—	—	—	—	75.8	—	—	—	—	—
Northern Ireland	1975–77	67.5	67.9	59.3	49.7	31.2	14.9	73.8	74.2	65.5	55.7	36.4	19.0
Scotland	1971–73	67.2	67.8	59.2	49.8	31.3	15.0	73.6	74.1	65.4	55.6	36.3	18.9
Yugoslavia	1970–72	65.4	68.0	59.7	50.1	31.8	15.7	70.2	72.8	64.6	54.9	35.8	18.2
ASIA													
Bangladesh	1974	45.8	53.5	50.5	42.5	28.1	14.4	46.6	53.5	50.3	42.2	27.7	14.1
India	1961–70	46.4	52.3	48.8	41.1	25.9	13.6	44.7	50.2	47.7	39.9	25.4	13.8
Iran	1973–76	57.6	63.5	59.1	49.7	31.4	16.1	57.4	64.0	60.9	51.6	33.7	17.9
Israel	1978	71.5	71.8	63.2	53.6	34.7	17.7	75.0	75.2	66.5	56.8	37.4	19.5
Japan[4]	1974	71.2	71.0	62.5	52.8	33.0	17.0	76.3	76.0	67.4	57.5	38.3	20.3
Korea, South	1970	63.0	66.0	58.0	49.0	31.0	16.0	67.0	69.0	61.0	52.0	34.0	17.0
Pakistan	1962	53.7	60.6	57.0	47.8	30.8	15.6	48.8	53.9	51.7	42.9	27.7	15.5
Sri Lanka	1967	64.8	67.4	60.5	51.2	33.2	17.0	66.9	68.9	62.4	53.0	35.0	17.8
Syria	1970	54.5	60.7	56.4	47.4	30.5	15.2	58.7	64.1	59.5	50.5	33.3	17.3
AFRICA													
Egypt	1960	51.6	56.2	56.6	47.7	30.5	15.1	53.8	59.9	62.0	52.9	35.0	18.0
Kenya	1969	46.9	52.6	51.0	43.0	28.3	14.5	51.2	56.6	54.1	45.7	30.3	15.7
South Africa (white population)	1959–61	64.7	65.9	57.5	48.0	30.2	15.0	71.7	72.5	64.1	54.4	35.5	18.6
OCEANIA													
Australia[5]	1965–67	67.6	68.1	59.5	50.0	31.4	15.8	74.2	74.4	65.8	56.0	36.9	19.5
New Zealand	1970–72	68.5	—	—	—	—	—	74.6	—	—	—	—	—

1. Figures for male and female together. 2. Excluding data for Faeroe Islands and Greenland. 3. Includes relevant data relating to Berlin. No separate data have been supplied. 4. Japanese nationals in Japan only. 5. Excludes full-blooded aborigines. NOTE: Figures are latest available. *Source:* United Nations *Demographic Yearbook, 1979.*

Estimates of World Population by Regions

Year	North America[1]	Latin America[2]	Europe[3]	U.S.S.R.	Asia[4]	Africa	Oceania	World total
	Estimated population in millions							
1650	1	7	103	[5]	257	100	2	470
1750	1	10	144	[5]	437	100	2	694
1850	26	33	274	[5]	656	100	2	1,091
1900	81	63	423	[5]	857	141	6	1,571
1930	134	108	355[6]	179	1,120[7]	164	10	2,070
1950	166	164	392[6]	180	1,380[7]	219	13	2,513
1960	199	215	425[6]	214	1,683[7]	275	16	3,027
1970	226	283	460[6]	244	2,091[7]	354	19	3,678
1975	236	323	474[6]	254	2,319[7]	406	21	4,033
1977	240	340	478[6]	259	2,413[7]	430	22	4,182
1978	242	349	480[6]	262	2,461[7]	442	22	4,258
1979	244	359	482	264	2,509[7]	456	23	4,336
1981	254	370	487[6]	268	2,691[7]	484	23	4,577

1. U.S. (including Alaska and Hawaii), Bermuda, Canada, Greenland, and St. Pierre and Miquelon. 2. Mexico, Central and South America, and Caribbean Islands. 3. Includes Russia 1650–1900. 4. Excludes Russia (U.S.S.R.). 5. Included in Europe. 6. Excludes European Turkey, which is included in Asia. 7. Includes both Asian and European Turkey. NOTE: Figures are latest available. *Sources:* W.F. Willcox, 1650–1900; United Nations, 1930–79. United States Department of Commerce, Bureau of the Census, 1981.

Crude Birth and Death Rates for Selected Countries
(per 1,000 population)

Country	Birth rates 1981	1980	1975	1970	1965	Death rates 1981	1980	1975	1970	1965
Australia	15.8	15.3	16.9	20.6	19.6	7.3	7.4	7.9	9.0	8.8
Austria	12.4	12.0	12.5	15.2	17.9	12.3	12.2	12.8	13.4	13.0
Belgium	12.6	12.7	12.2	14.7	16.4	11.2	11.6	12.2	12.3	12.5
Canada	n.a.	15.4	15.8	17.4	21.4	n.a.	7.2	7.4	7.3	7.5
Czechoslovakia	15.5	16.4	19.6	15.9	16.4	11.7	12.1	11.5	11.6	10.0
Denmark	10.4	11.2	14.2	14.4	18.2	11.0	10.9	10.1	9.8	10.1
El Salvador	n.a.	34.7	38.9	40.0	46.5	n.a.	7.9	7.9	9.9	10.6
Finland	13.2	13.1	13.9	14.0	17.0	9.1	9.3	9.3	9.6	7.9
France	14.9	14.8	14.1	16.8	17.7	10.3	10.2	10.6	10.7	11.1
Germany, East	14.2	14.6	10.8	13.9	16.5	13.9	14.2	14.3	14.1	13.3
Germany, West	10.1	10.0	9.7	11.4	17.9	11.7	11.6	12.1	12.1	11.2
Greece	n.a.	15.4	15.7	16.5	17.7	n.a.	9.1	8.9	8.4	7.9
Hungary	13.3	13.9	18.4	14.7	13.1	13.5	13.6	12.4	11.6	10.7
Ireland	n.a.	21.9	21.5	21.8	22.2	n.a.	9.7	10.6	11.4	11.5
Israel	n.a.	24.1	28.2	26.9	25.4	n.a.	6.7	7.1	7.1	6.2
Italy	10.9	11.2	14.8	16.8	19.2	9.5	9.7	9.9	9.7	10.0
Japan	13.0	13.7	17.2	18.9	18.6	6.2	6.2	6.4	6.9	7.1
Luxembourg	12.0	11.5	11.2	13.2	15.6	11.1	11.5	12.2	12.3	11.8
Malta	15.0	16.0	18.3	16.3	17.6	8.6	8.8	8.8	9.4	9.4
Mauritius	25.1	27.0	25.1	26.0	35.4	6.8	7.2	8.1	7.8	8.6
Mexico	n.a.	n.a.	37.5	42.1	45.3	n.a.	n.a.	7.2	9.6	9.5
Netherlands	12.5	12.8	13.0	18.3	19.9	8.1	8.1	8.3	8.4	8.0
New Zealand	16.3	n.a.	18.4	22.1	22.8	8.0	n.a.	8.1	8.8	8.7
Norway	12.8	12.5	14.1	16.6	17.5	9.9	10.1	9.9	10.0	9.1
Panama	n.a.	26.8	32.3	37.2	39.1	n.a.	n.a.	n.a.	8.8[1]	7.3
Poland	18.9	19.5	18.9	16.8	17.3	9.2	9.8	8.7	8.2	7.4
Portugal	n.a.	16.4	19.1	20.0	22.9	n.a.	9.9	10.4	10.8	10.1
Singapore	17.0	17.3	17.8	23.0	31.1	5.3	5.2	5.1	5.2	5.6
Spain	14.1	16.1	19.1	19.5	21.3	7.6	7.7	8.2	8.3	8.7
Sweden	11.3	11.7	12.6	13.7	15.9	11.1	11.0	10.8	9.9	10.1
Switzerland	n.a.	11.3	12.3	15.8	18.7	n.a.	9.2	8.7	9.1	9.3
Tunisia	n.a.	n.a.	36.6	36.4	44.3	n.a.	n.a.	n.a.	17.6[1]	11.8
United Kingdom	13.1	13.5	12.5	16.3	18.4	n.a.	11.8	11.9	11.8	11.5
United States	15.9	16.2	14.8	18.3	19.4	8.7	8.9	8.9	9.4	9.4
Yugoslavia	16.7	17.0	18.2	17.8	20.9	9.0	9.0	8.7	8.9	8.7

1. 1969–70 figure. NOTE: n.a. = not available. *Source:* United Nations, *Monthly Bulletin of Statistics,* July 1982.

Suicide Rates for Selected Countries
(per 100,000 population)

Country	Year	Rate	Country	Year	Rate	Country	Year	Rate
Angola	1972	1.0	Guatemala	1977	1.9	Singapore	1978	11.4
Australia	1977	11.1	Hong Kong	1978	8.3	South Africa		
Argentina	1977	7.8	Hungary	1978	43.1	Black	1971	5.6
Austria	1978	24.8	Iceland	1978	11.6	White	1971	14.5
Barbados	1977	1.6	Ireland	1976	5.7	Spain	1976	4.1
Belgium	1976	16.6	Israel	1978	5.6	Sweden	1978	19.0
Bulgaria	1978	13.6	Italy	1972	5.8	Switzerland	1978	23.9
Canada	1977	14.2	Jamaica	1971	1.0	Trinidad and		
Chile	1976	5.7	Japan	1978	17.7	Tobago	1977	8.7
Costa Rica	1978	4.1	Mexico	1975	1.7	Turkey	1971	1.9
Cuba	1971	15.0	Netherlands	1978	9.7	United Kingdom		
Czechoslovakia	1977	21.3	New Zealand	1976	9.2	England and		
Denmark	1978	23.3	Norway	1977	11.4	Wales	1977	8.0
Ecuador	1976	2.7	Panama	1977	1.9	Northern		
Egypt	1976	0.1	Paraguay	1977	1.8	Ireland	1977	4.6
El Salvador	1971	8.7	Peru	1972	1.8	Scotland	1977	8.1
Finland	1975	25.0	Philippines	1974	1.1	United States	1976	12.5
France	1977	16.5	Poland	1978	13.3	Uruguay	1978	10.5
Germany, East	1970	30.5	Portugal	1975	8.5	Venezuela	1977	4.6
Germany, West	1978	22.2	Puerto Rico	1977	9.5	Yugoslavia	1977	14.5
Greece	1978	2.9	Romania	1978	66.5			

NOTE: figures are latest available. *Source:* United Nations *Demographic Yearbook, 1979.*

Cost of Living of United Nations Personnel in Selected Cities as Reflected by Index of Retail Prices, 1981
(New York City = 100)

City	Index	City	Index	City	Index
Addis Ababa, Ethiopia	99	Dar es Salaam, Tanzania	113	New Delhi, India	81
Algiers, Algeria	140	Geneva	138	Nicosia, Cyprus	77
Amman, Jordan	116	Guatemala City, Guatemala	99	Paris	117
Ankara, Turkey	72	The Hague, the Netherlands	117	Port-au-Prince, Haiti	97
Athens	106	Havana	87	Quito, Ecuador	80
Baghdad, Iraq	104	Jakarta, Indonesia	109	Rabat, Morocco	101
Bangkok, Thailand	84	Kabul, Afghanistan	77	Rangoon, Burma	75
Beirut, Lebanon	99	Islamabad, Pakistan	88	Rio de Janeiro	81
Belgrade, Yugoslavia	92	Katmandu, Nepal	83	Rome	88
Bogotá, Colombia	107	Kingston, Jamaica	72	San José, Costa Rica	49
Bonn, West Germany	114	Kinshasha, Zaire	134	San Salvador, El Salvador	98
Brazzaville, Congo	111	La Paz, Bolivia	104	Santiago, Chile	132
Brussels, Belgium	116	Lagos, Nigeria	112	Seoul, South Korea	137
Budapest	69	Lima, Peru	104	Sofia, Bulgaria	100
Buenos Aires	110	London	123	Sydney, Australia	101
Cairo	97	Madrid	102	Tokyo	156
Caracas, Venezuela	141	Manila	92	Tripoli, Libya	158
Colombo, Sri Lanka	76	Mexico City	100	Tunis, Tunisia	105
Copenhagen	117	Montevideo, Uruguay	123	Vienna	115
Dacca, Bangladesh	82	Montreal	82	Vientiane, Laos	83
Dakar, Senegal	114	Nairobi, Kenya	88	Warsaw	71
Damascus, Syria	135	Nassau, Bahamas	113	Washington, D.C.	95

Source: United Nations, *Monthly Bulletin of Statistics, March 1982.*

Trade With Developing Countries Increases

Thirty-eight percent of all United States exports now go to the developing world. As important as the OPEC market is, the non-OPEC developing countries (excluding China) absorb 30% of total U.S. exports around the world.

In addition, the United States now imports increasing amounts of its raw materials from the developing countries: more than half its rubber, tin, manganese, and very substantial quantities of its cobalt, tungsten, and petroleum.

Value of Exports and Imports
(in millions of U.S. dollars)

Country	Exports[1]	Imports[1]
Afghanistan	729[2]	924[2]
Algeria	13,656[2]	10,811[2]
Argentina	8,054[2]	10,619[2]
Australia	21,680	23,652
Austria	15,846	21,049
Bahamas	4,834[2]	5,481[2]
Bahrain	3,602[2]	3,484[2]
Bangladesh	791	2,594
Barbados	194	571
Belgium–Luxembourg	55,646	62,133
Benin	26[3]	267[3]
Bolivia	1,033[2]	833[2]
Brazil	22,771	23,543
Bulgaria	10,372[2]	9,650[2]
Burma	465[2]	352[2]
Burundi	71	167
Cameroon	1,384[2]	1,602[2]
Canada	69,922	65,797
Cape Verde	2[3]	44[3]
Central African Republic	79[4]	70[4]
Chile	3,931	6,379
Colombia	3,925[2]	4,739[2]
Congo	510[4]	291[4]
Costa Rica	963[2]	1,528[2]
Cuba	3,967[2]	4,509[2]
Cyprus	562	1,166
Czechoslovakia	14,706	14,958
Denmark	15,735	17,530
Dominican Republic	1,199	1,450
Ecuador	2,013[4]	1,986[4]
Egypt	3,233	8,839
El Salvador	720[2]	976[2]
Ethiopia	418[4]	567[4]
Fiji	311	632
Finland	14,015	14,201
France	101,392	120,689
Gabon	1,477[4]	532[4]
Gambia	27	125
Germany, East	17,312[2]	19,082[2]
Germany, West	176,085	163,907
Ghana	1,096[3]	993[3]
Greece	4,241	8,885
Guatemala	1,520[2]	1,598[2]
Guinea–Bissau	14[4]	61[4]
Guyana	389[2]	417[2]
Haiti	188[4]	266[4]
Honduras	806[2]	1,019[2]
Hungary	8,712	9,128
Iceland	887	1,033
India	7,560	13,194
Indonesia	21,909[2]	10,834[2]
Iran	14,251[2]	12,247[2]
Iraq	11,061[3]	4,213[3]
Ireland	7,786	10,596
Israel	5,416	7,787
Italy	75,214	91,011
Ivory Coast	2,515[4]	2,493[4]
Jamaica	982	1,509
Japan	152,016	143,288
Jordan	736	3,179
Kenya	1,172	2,069
Korea, South	21,254	26,125
Kuwait	19,767[2]	6,560[2]
Liberia	601[2]	535[2]
Libya	16,076[4]	5,311[4]
Madagascar	394[4]	641[4]
Malawi	284	362
Malaysia	14,345[2]	12,139[2]
Mali	149[4]	359[4]
Malta	497[2]	938[2]
Mauritania	194[2]	264[2]
Mauritius	326	553
Mexico	15,301[2]	19,416[2]
Morocco	2,249[2]	4,185[2]
Netherlands	68,756	66,111
New Zealand	5,563	5,684
Nicaragua	448[2]	883[2]
Nigeria	17,331[4]	10,991[4]
Norway	17,992	15,646
Oman	3,202[2]	1,732[2]
Pakistan	2,880	5,348
Panama	315	1,540
Papua New Guinea	1,031[2]	1,023[2]
Paraguay	296	506
Peru	3,364[2]	2,541[2]
Philippines	5,722	7,946
Poland	13,249	15,475
Portugal	4,632[2]	9,299[2]
Qatar	5,698[2]	1,429[2]
Romania	12,230[2]	13,201[2]
Rwanda	115[4]	190[4]
Saudi Arabia	120,240	35,244
Senegal	536[4]	931[4]
Sierra Leone	206[4]	316[4]
Singapore	20,993	27,571
Solomon Islands	73[2]	74[2]
Somalia	141[2]	275[2]
Spain	20,338	32,159
Sri Lanka	1,036	1,803
Sudan	658	1,529
Suriname	514[2]	504[2]
Sweden	28,597	28,857
Switzerland	27,051	30,689
Syria	2,103	5,040
Tanzania	508[2]	1,226[2]
Thailand	6,999	9,911
Togo	218[4]	518[4]
Tonga	7[4]	29[4]
Trinidad and Tobago	4,077[2]	3,178[2]
Tunisia	2,189	3,479
Turkey	4,721	8,944
Uganda	309[4]	167[4]
U.S.S.R.	76,449[2]	68,522[2]
United Arab Emirates	20,742[2]	8,752[2]
United Kingdom	115,149[2]	119,935[2]
United States	228,961	271,269
Upper Volta	90[2]	358[2]
Uruguay	1,019	1,646
Vanuatu	38[3]	56[3]
Venezuela	19,221[2]	10,671[2]
Western Samoa	18[4]	73[4]
Yemen, People's Democratic Republic of	248[4]	393[4]
Yemen Arab Republic	14[4]	1,492[4]
Yugoslavia	10,929	15,757
Zaire	662	672
Zambia	1,402[2]	1,090[2]
Zimbabwe	1,423[2]	1,322[2]

1. 1981 unless otherwise indicated. 2. 1980. 3. 1978. 4. 1979. *Source:* United Nations, *Monthly Bulletin of Statistics,* July 1982.

Consumer Price Indexes for Selected Countries

(1967—100)

Country	Total indexes 1980	1979	1975	1970	Average annual percent change. 1975–1980	Indexes for Selected Items, 1980: Food[1]	Clothing	Housing[2]	Transportation
Australia	295.5	268.3	178.7	109.8	10.6	291.8	301.4	321.8	n.a.
Austria	203.3	191.2	157.2	110.6	5.3	186.5	178.3	233.2	216.6
Canada	243.5	221.0	160.1	112.4	8.7	289.9	195.5	242.9	233.1
France	294.2	259.1	178.9	117.1	10.4	294.8	267.0	309.4	337.4
Germany, West	175.8	169.9	144.1	107.0	4.1	159.0	178.9	181.7	183.9
Italy	403.2	332.7[3]	186.9	109.2	16.6	382.3	437.3	385.6	480.9
Japan	281.8	261.5	204.5	119.3	6.5	288.2	288.7	226.7	297.5
Netherlands	237.4	222.3[3]	175.3	115.5	6.0	197.8	256.5	244.2	223.9
Sweden	270.6	238.0	164.3	112.0	10.5	282.4	197.2	314.9	n.a.
United Kingdom	423.6	359.0	216.5	117.4	14.4	468.0	306.4	421.5	450.3
United States	246.8	217.4	161.2	116.3	8.9	254.6	178.4	263.3	249.7

1. Restaurant meals, alcohol, and tobacco are included for some countries, excluded for others. 2. Includes shelter, utilities, and household furnishings and operations. However, actual coverage and measurement methods vary significantly from country to country. 3. Preliminary. NOTE: n.a. = not available. *Source:* United States Department of Labor, Bureau of Labor Statistics.

Energy, Petroleum, and Coal, by Country

Country	Energy consumed[1] (coal equiv.): Total (mil. metric tons) 1980	Total 1970	Per capita (kilograms) 1980	Per capita 1970	Electric energy production[2] (bil. kwh) 1980	1970	Crude petroleum production[3] (mil. metric tons) 1979	1970	Coal production[4] (mil. metric tons) 1979	1970
Algeria	15.0	3.0	808	212	6.2	2.0	54.5	49.0	z	z
Argentina	49.2	37.9	1,818	1,595	40.6	21.7	24.3	20.0	.7	.6
Australia	88.2	64.1	6,032	5,123	95.9	53.9[6]	21.6	8.5[7]	74.8	45.2
Austria	31.2	24.6	4,160	3,319	42.0	30.0	1.7	2.8	n.a.	—
Bahrain	5.5	.6	15,275	2,698	1.1[8]	.2[8]	2.6	3.8	n.a.	n.a.
Bangladesh	4.1	n.a.	46	n.a.	2.6	n.a.	n.a.	n.a.	n.a.	—
Belgium	59.5	54.2	6,037	5,608	53.6	30.5	n.a.	n.a.	6.1	11.4
Brazil	93.6	41.5	761	449	137.4[5]	45.5[5]	8.0	8.0	4.6	2.4
Bulgaria	50.3	32.1	5,678	3,775	34.8	19.5	.2	.3	.3	.4
Burma	2.2	1.6	63	59	1.4	.6	1.5	.8	z	z
Canada	245.2	187.2	10,241	8,779	366.7[5]	204.7[5]	73.3	60.4	28.0	11.6
Chile	10.9	10.4	985	1,113	11.5	7.6	.8	1.5	.9	1.4
China, People's Republic of	565.5	347.7	602	429	300.6[8]	107.0[8]	106.2	23.9	635.0	360.0[9, 10]
China, Republic of[11]	37.7[12]	15.3	2,202[12]	1,055	40.7[13]	14.0	n.a.	n.a.	2.7	4.5
Colombia	21.2	12.1	769	589	20.6	8.8	6.5	11.3	5.0	2.3
Cuba	13.1	8.5	1,328	1,000	9.8	4.9	.2	.2	n.a.	n.a.
Czechoslovakia	99.3	77.4	6,482	5,402	74.1	45.2	.1	.2	28.8[14]	28.2[14]
Denmark	26.7	26.8	5,224	5,420	25.4	20.0	.4	—	n.a.	n.a.
Ecuador	5.0	1.7	598	282	3.2	.9	10.9	.2	n.a.	n.a.
Egypt	20.8	8.7	496	260	18.5	7.6	24.9	16.4	n.a.	—
Ethiopia	.9	.7	29	27	.7	.5[15]	n.a.	n.a.	n.a.	n.a.
Finland	24.5	18.7	5,135	4,070	38.6[5]	21.2[5]	n.a.	n.a.	n.a.	n.a.
France[16]	233.7	193.6	4,351	3,814	257.8	147.0	1.2	2.3	19.9[14]	37.8[14]
Germany, East	124.0	104.5	7,408	6,128	98.8	67.7	.1	.1	.1	1.0
Germany, West	352.5	311.1	5,727	5,124	368.8	242.6	4.8	7.5	86.3	116.3[17]
Greece	20.5	9.8	2,137	1,109	22.4	9.8	n.a.	—	n.a.	n.a.
Hong Kong	7.3	3.8	1,433	952	12.6[8]	5.1[8]	n.a.	n.a.	n.a.	n.a.
Hungary	41.2	29.0	3,850	2,809	23.9	14.5	2.0	1.9	3.0[14]	4.2[14]
India	126.4	76.4	191	142	116.3	61.2[18]	12.8	6.8	103.4	73.7
Indonesia	33.3	13.8	220	116	7.1	2.3	78.3	42.6	.3	.2
Iran	46.7	27.2	1,246	947	17.2	7.0	153.3	191.3	.9	.5[9, 19]
Iraq	7.9	5.7	606	603	8.0	2.8	168.6	76.5[20]	n.a.	n.a.
Ireland	10.2	7.7	2,955	2,628	10.9	6.1[18]	n.a.	n.a.	.1	.2
Israel	9.2	5.9	2,367	1,986	12.5	6.9	z	5.0[21]	n.a.	n.a.
Italy	189.3[22]	142.0[22]	3,318[22]	2,647[22]	186.3[22]	117.4[22]	1.7	1.4	z	.3
Japan	408.0	317.4	3,494	3,098	612.0	359.5[18]	.5	.8	17.6	39.7[23]
Korea, North	48.5	28.5	2,710	2,050	35.0[8]	16.5[8]	n.a.	n.a.	35.0	21.8[9]

Country	Energy consumed[1] (coal equiv.) Total (mil. metric tons) 1980	1970	Per capita (kilograms) 1980	1970	Electric energy production[2] (bil. kwh) 1980	1970	Crude petroleum production[3] (mil. metric tons) 1979	1970	Coal production[4] (mil. metric tons) 1979	1970
Korea, South	54.3	20.9	1,422	648	40.0	9.6	n.a.	n.a.	18.2	12.4
Kuwait	9.1[24]	4.4[24]	6,720[24]	5,855[24]	9.3[24]	2.7[24]	126.0[24]	150.6[24]	n.a.	n.a.
Libya	6.5	1.3	2,180	672	3.1[8]	.4[8]	99.3	159.8	n.a.	n.a.
Malaysia	11.3	6.1	838	582	9.0	3.5	12.8	.9	n.a.	n.a.
Mexico	127.3	53.5	1,770	1,055	64.2[5]	28.7[5]	74.9	21.5	6.9	3.0
Morocco	6.9	2.9	340	184	4.8	1.9	z	z	.7	.4
Netherlands	87.8	59.9	6,208	4,595	64.8	40.9	1.3	1.9	n.a.	4.3
Nigeria	11.1	2.7	144	49	5.0	1.6	114.5	54.2	.2	.1
Norway	26.3	17.9	6,437	4,616	84.0	57.6	18.3	—	.3	.5
Pakistan	18.0	10.7[25]	218	82[25]	16.1	8.7[6,25]	.5	.5	1.3	1.3[6,10]
Peru	11.0	8.0	619	596	9.8	5.5	10.3	3.6	z	.2
Philippines	15.3	9.7	316	263	18.0	8.7	1.3	—	.3	z
Poland	198.8	137.5	5,586	4,226	121.9	64.5	.4	.4	201.0	140.1
Portugal	10.9	6.4	1,097	712	15.0	7.5	n.a.	n.a.	.2	.3
Romania	102.3	61.4	4,593	3,032	67.5	35.1	12.3	13.4	7.5	6.4
Saudi Arabia	12.4[24]	3.8[24]	1,479[24]	608[24]	9.0[24]	1.1[24]	476.0[24]	188.4[24]	n.a.	n.a.
South Africa[26]	85.7	56.7	2,595	2,241	95.8	50.8	n.a.	n.a.	95.4	54.6
Soviet Union	1,485.7	991.4	5,595	4,084	1,295.0	740.9	590.9	353.0[7]	495.0	432.7
Spain	95.0	49.5	2,539	1,467	110.2	56.5	.9	.2	11.7[14]	10.8[14]
Sudan	1.2	n.a.	65	n.a.	1.0	.4	n.a.	n.a.	n.a.	n.a.
Sweden	43.8	46.4	5,269	5,769	96.3	60.6	n.a.	n.a.	z	z
Switzerland	23.7[27]	20.2[27]	3,708[27]	3,222[27]	48.2[5,27]	33.2[5,27]	n.a.	n.a.	n.a.	n.a.
Syria	9.4	2.4	1,047	386	3.4	.9	8.9	4.2	n.a.	n.a.
Tanzania	1.0	.8	55	57	.7	.5	n.a.	n.a.	z	z
Thailand	17.2	6.7	371	183	15.0	4.5	z	z[9]	n.a.	n.a.
Trinidad and Tobago	5.8	5.0	5,105	4,907	1.8	1.2	11.1	7.2	n.a.	n.a.
Tunisia	3.4	1.5	536	288	2.8	.8	5.5	4.2	n.a.	n.a.
Turkey	33.1	16.5	737	472	23.3	8.6	2.6	3.5	4.5	4.6
United Arab Emirates	4.4	.6	5,449	2,537	4.5[8]	.1[8,28]	89.8	37.7	n.a.	n.a.
United Kingdom	276.2	278.7	4,942	5,029	281.5	249.0	77.6	.1	122.4[14]	147.1[14]
United States	2,369.7	2,227.1	10,410	10,870	2,356[5]	1,640[5]	419.9	475.3	665.7	550.4
Venezuela	47.0	24.3	3,375	2,362	31.0	12.7	123.5	194.3	.1	z
Vietnam	7.8	12.6	148	300	3.9	2.1	n.a.	n.a.	6.0	3.0
Yugoslavia	45.8	28.7	2,049	1,409	58.9	26.0	4.1	2.9	.4	.6
Zaire	1.9	1.5	67	68	4.4	3.2	1.0	—	.1	.1
Zambia	2.8	2.0	475	464	8.9[5]	.9[5]	n.a.	n.a.	.6	.6
World total	n.a.	**6,820.1**	n.a.	**1,892**	n.a.	**4,923**	**3,123**	**2,277**	**2,698**	**2,143**

1. Based on apparent consumption of coal, lignite, petroleum products, natural gas, and hydro and nuclear electricity. 2. Comprises production by utilities generating primarily for public use, and production by industrial establishments generating primarily for own use. Relates to production at generating centers, including station use and transmission losses. 3. Includes shale oil, but excludes natural gasoline. 4. Excludes lignite and brown coal, except as noted. 5. Net production, i.e. excluding station use. 6. Year ending June 30. 7. Includes gas condensates. 8. Excludes production by industrial establishments for own use. 9. Data from United States Bureau of Mines. 10. Includes lignite and brown coal. 11. Source: United States Bureau of the Census. Data from Republic of China publications. 12. For 1978. 13. For 1979. 14. Includes slurries. 15. Year ending Sept. 10. 16. Includes Monaco. 17. Includes low grade coal at its hard-coal equivalent. 18. Year beginning April. 19. Year beginning March 21. 20. Data from Organization of Petroleum Exporting Countries (OPEC). 21. Includes estimated production in the occupied Sinai Peninsula (1970, 4.9 million metric tons). 22. Includes San Marino. 23. Includes brown coal. 24. Includes share of production and consumption in the Neutral Zone. 25. Includes Bangladesh. 26. Includes Botswana, Lesotho, Namibia, and Swaziland. 27. Includes Liechtenstein. 28. Abu Dhabi only. NOTES: metric ton = 1.1023 short tons. n.a. = not available. z = less than 50,000 metric tons. A dash equals zero. *Sources:* Except as noted, Statistical Office of the United Nations, New York, *Statistical Yearbook* (copyright); and *1979 Yearbook of World Energy Statistics.* (Copyright.)

Wheat and Rice—Production by Country

(in thousands of metric tons)[1]

COUNTRY	Wheat 1980	1979	1978	1977	1971–75 average	Rice[1] 1980	1979	1978	1977	1971–75 average
Afghanistan	2,700	2,663	2,813	2,652	2,533	421	439	428	400	405
Argentina	7,830	8,100	8,100	5,390	6,936	266	312	310	320	302
Australia	10,800	15,697	18,086	9,370	10,104	613	692	490	530	331
Austria	1,201	850	1,195	1,072	965	n.a.	n.a.	n.a.	—	—

COUNTRY	Wheat 1980	1979	1978	1977	1971–75 average	Rice[1] 1980	1979	1978	1977	1971–75 average
Bangladesh	1,200	494	348	259	109	20,990	18,403	19,582	19,441	16,793
Belgium	877[2]	1,015[2]	1,022[2]	795[2]	958[2]	n.a.	n.a.	n.a.	(1)	(1)
Brazil	2,614	2,927	2,691	2,066	1,934	9,746	7,589	7,296	8,994	7,012
Bulgaria	3,700	3,355	3,466	3,028	3,123	75[3]	73	61	68	63
Burma	74	41	92	75	39	13,317	10,448	10,500	9,462	8,386
Cambodia	n.a.	n.a.	n.a.	—	—	1,000[3]	850	1,500[3]	1,800[3]	1,569
Canada	19,131	17,185	21,146	19,862	15,092	n.a.	n.a.	n.a.	(1)	(1)
Chile	966	995	893	1,219	1,050	95	181	105	120	64
China, People's Republic of[3]	54,158	62,803	52,002	45,001	36,601	142,301	146,967	138,202	129,470	121,532
Colombia	41	42	38	29	58	1,892	1,933	1,715	1,307	1,231
Cuba	n.a.	n.a.	n.a.	(1)	(1)	500	425	458	459	375
Czechoslovakia	5,100	3,736	5,601	5,214	4,860	n.a.	n.a.	n.a.	(1)	(1)
Denmark	648	589	642	606	566	n.a.	n.a.	n.a.	(1)	(1)
Ecuador	23	31	29	40	57	356	303	233	328	241
Egypt	1,796	1,856	1,943	1,699	1,821	2,348	2,507	2,358	2,275	2,396
Ethiopia	469	449	429	605	648	n.a.	n.a.	n.a.	(1)	(1)
Finland	284	208	241	295	516	n.a.	n.a.	n.a.	(1)	(1)
France	23,668	19,393	20,970	17,350	17,022	27	20	35	23	56
Germany, East	3,600	3,116	3,147	2,914	2,797	n.a.	n.a.	n.a.	(1)	(1)
Germany, West	8,156	8,061	8,118	7,235	7,132	n.a.	n.a.	n.a.	(1)	(1)
Greece	2,931	2,397	2,660	1,766	1,934	78	93	93	94	87
Hungary	5,500[3]	3,709	5,677	5,319	4,299	40[3]	41	23	35	64
India	31,564	35,508	31,749	29,010	24,172	83,000[3]	63,611	80,660	79,006	64,510
Indonesia	n.a.	n.a.	n.a.	(1)	(1)	28,680	26,283	25,781	23,356	21,151
Iran	6,000	5,800	5,700	5,517	4,644	1,150	1,420	1,280	1,400	1,265
Iraq	1,300	880	910	696	1,318	220[3]	284	172	199	172
Ireland	235	260	247	250	264	n.a.	n.a.	n.a.	(1)	(1)
Israel	250	133	169	220	252	n.a.	n.a.	n.a.	(1)	(1)
Italy	9,291	9,140	9,332	6,347	9,528	911	1,014	979	693	950
Japan	583	541	367	236	280	12,189	14,948	16,349	17,000	15,689
North Korea[3]	380	370	350	310	292	4,800	4,800	4,500	4,610	3,195
Korea, South	92	42	36	45	123	6,000	7,881	8,352	8,291	5,915
Laos	n.a.	n.a.	n.a.	(1)	(1)	1,000	925	796	847	865
Madagascar	1[3]	1[3]	—	(1)	(1)	2,327	2,250	1,914	2,154	1,855
Malaysia	n.a.	n.a.	n.a.	(1)	(1)	2,129	2,098	1,498	1,922	1,942
Mexico	2,645	2,339	2,785	2,456	2,264	463	500	402	567	476
Nepal	440	415	411	362	275	2,444	2,060	2,339	2,282	2,365
Netherlands	882	836	792	661	676	n.a.	n.a.	n.a.	(1)	(1)
New Zealand	325	295	329	354	297	n.a.	n.a.	n.a.	(1)	(1)
Pakistan	10,805	9,950	8,367	9,144	7,222	4,800	4,824	4,908	4,424	3,598
Panama	n.a.	n.a.	n.a.	(1)	(1)	199	170	162	186	157
Peru	85	104	113	120	124	423	557	468	587	516
Philippines	n.a.	n.a.	n.a.	(1)	(1)	7,431	7,236	7,198	6,895	5,386
Poland	4,200	4,187	6,029	5,308	5,605	n.a.	n.a.	n.a.	(1)	(1)
Portugal	377	233	255	229	624	155	135	135	112	151
Romania	6,470	4,676	6,243	6,463	5,399	65	60	58	47	57
South Africa	1,470	2,090	1,690	1,860	1,735	3[3]	3[3]	3[3]	3[3]	3
Soviet Union	98,100	90,211	120,824	92,165	88,935	2,800	2,394	2,096	2,217	1,753
Spain	5,901	4,082	4,806	4,064	4,564	433	427	401	379	368
Sri Lanka	n.a.	n.a.	n.a.	(1)	(1)	2,383	1,917	1,890	1,677	1,355
Sweden	1,291	1,030	1,290	1,522	1,352	n.a.	n.a.	n.a.	(1)	(1)
Switzerland	403	425	408	323	386	n.a.	n.a.	n.a.	(1)	(1)
Syria	2,229	1,319	1,651	1,217	1,249	n.a.	n.a.	n.a.	(1)	(1)
Thailand	n.a.	n.a.	n.a.	(1)	(1)	18,000	15,758	17,530	13,921	13,948
Turkey	17,455	17,619	16,764	16,720	12,372	367	363	305	270	248
United Kingdom	8,147	7,170	6,613	5,274	5,045	n.a.	n.a.	n.a.	(1)	(1)
United States	64,492	58,080	48,322	55,420	47,702	6,580	5,985	6,040	4,501	4,579
Uruguay	300	430	174	173	354	289	248	226	228	148
Venezuela	1	1	1	1	1	681	653	502	496	256
Vietnam	n.a.	n.a.	n.a.	(1)	(1)	10,000[3]	10,742	10,040	10,885	10,732
Yugoslavia	5,078	4,512	5,355	5,595	5,177	34[3]	34	34	36	33
World total	444,534	428,065	449,372	390,697	358,794	399,779	376,378	385,885	369,729	329,180

1. Rice data cover rough and paddy, except as noted. Data for each country pertain to the calendar year in which all or most of the crop was harvested. 2. Includes Luxembourg. 3. FAO estimate. NOTES: metric ton = 1.1023 short tons, n.a. = not available. *Source:* Food and Agriculture Organization of the United Nations, Rome, *1980 FAO Production Yearbook*, vol. 34 (copyright).

Corn, Meat, and Sugar—Production by Country

(in thousands of metric tons)

Country	Corn 1980	Corn 1979	Corn 1978	Meat[1] 1978	Meat[1] 1977	Meat[1] 1971–76 average	Sugar[2] 1980	Sugar[2] 1979	Sugar[2] 1978
Argentina	6,410	8,700	9,500	3,540	3,269	2,683	1,710	1,411	1,397
Australia	127	169	130	2,843[3]	2,722[3]	2,268[3]	3,315	2,963	2,902
Austria	1,293	1,347	1,166	504[4]	492	460	435	397	357
Belgium[5]	35	37	37	921	872	855	912	830	728
Brazil	20,377	16,309	13,569	3,148	3,343	2,909	8,300	7,020	7,767
Bulgaria	3,300[4]	3,223	2,236	466[4]	453	387	230	240	180
Canada	5,462	4,983	4,032	1,635	1,687	1,578	115	133	123
Chile	405	489	257	248	253	247	63	104	132
China, People's Republic of[4]	59,705	60,099	53,107	17,017	16,536	13,899	3,673	3,582	3,213
Colombia	813	870	862	547[4]	531[4]	518[4]	1,230	1,105	1,027
Cuba	95[4]	95[4]	95[4]	208[4]	202[4]	200[4]	6,787	8,048	7,457
Czechoslovakia	700	949	619	1,214[4]	1,136	1,053	810	920	885
Denmark	n.a.	n.a.	n.a.	1,031	987	962	464	492	442
Dominican Republic	49	38	49	62	59	55	1,090	1,200	1,199
Egypt	3,230	2,938	3,117	292[4]	284[4]	273	662	668	635
El Salvador	537	523	507	48	47	41[6]	207	277	288
Ethiopia	1,144	1,067	982	343[4]	338[4]	337	164	166	157
France	9,219	10,222	9,531	3,507[4]	3,414	3,382	4,250	4,313	4,065
Germany, East	2[4]	6	2	1,616[4]	1,608	1,395	770	720	780
Germany, West	672	741	617	3,999[4]	3,856	3,651	2,935	3,087	2,997
Ghana	339	365	340	29[4]	27[4]	32[4]	8	6	8
Greece	1,223	731	537	341	343	306	198	311	354
Guatemala	1,058	941	906	93	83	77	398	377	410
Hungary	7,000[4]	7,396	6,655	1,031[4]	1,002	894	482	510	551
India	6,400	5,578	6,199	646[4]	642[4]	620[4]	4,300	6,367	7,018
Indonesia	3,600	3,606	4,029	328[4]	326[4]	301	1,403	1,307	1,105
Iran	60[4]	57	60	366[4]	358[4]	331[4]	600	450	620
Ireland	n.a.	n.a.	n.a.	556	551	469	187	190	204
Italy	6,493	6,260	6,221	2,075[4]	2,000	1,812	1,892	1,707	1,620
Japan	3	5	7	1,590[4]	1,526	1,288	727[4]	710	712
Kenya	1,900[4]	1,800	2,169	181[4]	164[4]	161[4]	420	322	258
Malaysia	13	13	12	62[7]	63[7]	62[7]	90	75	55
Mexico	11,081	8,124	10,930	1,033	1,028	899	2,950	3,078	3,072
Morocco	333	312	390	135	133	159	360[4]	345	398
Netherlands	5	5	5	1,444	1,369	1,221	951	915	1,034
Nigeria	1,550[4]	1,500[4]	1,480[4]	339[4]	330[4]	314[4]	35	35	31
Pakistan	963	875	799	570[4]	559	424	625	660	936
Peru	425	646	623	186	182	190	550	715	856
Philippines	3,117	3,167	2,855	535	518	484	2,450	2,269	2,335
Poland	91	181	119	2,601	2,279	2,261	1,160	1,724	1,763
Portugal	468	456	499	252	249	224	5[4]	10	10
Romania	11,180	12,425	10,208	1,108[4]	1,165	978	570	570	603
South Africa	10,230	8,240	9,930	744[4]	708	683	1,622	2,079	2,082
Soviet Union	9,700	8,373	8,951	13,085[4]	12,732	12,258	7,600	7,500	9,100
Spain	2,297	2,212	1,969	1,358	1,310	1,106	949	719	1,143
Sweden	n.a.	n.a.	n.a.	459	455	417	327	358	327
Switzerland	108	134	105	417[4]	413	374	96	108	99
Thailand	3,150	3,300	2,791	363[4]	352[4]	365[4]	1,086	1,845	1,624
Turkey	1,150	1,350	1,300	624[4]	616	563	1,000	1,052	1,079
Uganda	500[4]	500[4]	660[4]	94[4]	93[4]	84	5	4	10
United Kingdom	1[4]	1	2	2,005	2,133	2,186	1,210	1,254	1,111
United States	168,855	201,655	184,614	17,605	18,013	16,936	5,207	6,096	5,353
Uruguay	119	71	172	405	404	393	86	73	102
Venezuela	584	848	804	384	372	313	371	351	402
Vietnam	520[4]	475	485	550[4]	511[4]	470[4]	130[4]	102	87
Yugoslavia	9,106	10,084	7,585	1,057[4]	1,048	850	805	851	753
Zaire	500[4]	430	500	60[4]	59[4]	55[6]	50[4]	55	52
Zimbabwe	1,600	1,200	1,616	171[4]	189[4]	163[4]	300[4]	299	309
World total	**392,249**	**418,598**	**390,104**	**104,360**	**102,494**	**93,407**	**85,431**	**88,329**	**90,258**

1. Beef and veal (incl. buffalo meat), pork (incl. bacon and ham), and mutton and lamb (incl. goat meat). Refers to meat from animals slaughtered within the national boundaries irrespective of origin of animals, and relates to commercial and farm slaughter. In terms of carcass weight. Excludes lard, tallow, and edible offals, except as noted. 2. Beet and cane. Data generally in terms of raw sugar. 3. Year ending June 30. 4. FAO estimate. 5. Includes Luxembourg for corn and meat. 6. Excludes data for 1971. 7. West Malaysia only. NOTES: Data for each country pertain to the calendar year in which all or most of the crop was harvested. Metric ton = 1.1023 short tons. n.a. = not available. *Sources:* Statistical Office of the United Nations, New

York, *Statistical Yearbook*, (copyright), and Food and Agriculture Organization of the United Nations, Rome, *1980 FAO Production Yearbook*, vol. 34 (copyright).

Communications

(telephones, mail, newspapers, radio, and television)

Country	Telephones, in use[1] 1978 (thousands)	Telephones per 100 population, 1978	Pieces of mail sent domestic,[2] 1978 (millions)	Daily newspapers,[3] 1977			Receiving sets, 1977	
					Circulation			
				Number	Total (thousands)	Copies per 1,000 population	Radios per 1,000 population[4]	TV sets per 1,000 population[5]
Algeria	346	1.9	219	4	236	13	173[9]	31
Argentina	2,404	9.1	620[9]	142[9]	2,682[9, 10]	n.a.	384	177
Australia	6,266	44.0	2,282[11]	60	4,365	310	1,037	357
Austria	2,443[12]	32.5[12]	1,673	31	2,529	336	275[13]	262[9, 13]
Bangladesh	101	.1	261	28[9]	350[9, 14]	n.a.	6	—
Belgium	3,271	33.2	2,941	27	2,369	241	415[13]	286[13]
Bolivia	49[15]	.9[15]	6	13[9]	150[9]	26[9]	74	8
Brazil	5,525	4.5	2.760	299[9]	4,895[9]	45[9]	158[7]	98
Bulgaria	1,032	11.6	n.a.	12	2,083	237	148[13]	180[13]
Burma	34	.1	79	7[9]	329[9]	11[9]	22	—
Cambodia	71[7]	11.2[7]	1[15]	17[9]	n.a.	n.a.	14[7]	4
Canada	15,293	64.8	5,867[16]	122	5,150	221	1,043	430
Chile	467[12]	4.8[12]	86[8]	42	n.a.	n.a.	188	68[9]
China, People's Republic of	n.a.	n.a.	n.a.	n.a.	n.a.	n.a.	16[17]	1[15]
China, Republic of[18]	2,099	12.2	734	31[9]	n.a.	n.a.	90[9]	78
Colombia	1,410	5.4	119[19]	42[9]	1,330[9, 20]	n.a.	117	74
Costa Rica	175	8.2	9[12]	6[9]	210[9]	104[9]	75	77
Cuba	321[12]	3.3[12]	61[8]	16[9]	n.a.	n.a.	197	83
Cyprus	92	15.0	14	13[9]	72[9, 21]	n.a.	331	105[13]
Czechoslovakia	2,981	19.6	2,216[15, 22]	29	4,453	296	248[13]	363
Denmark	2,907[23]	56.9[23]	1,268[12, 16]	49	1,840	362	825	471
Dominican Republic	139[12]	2.8[12]	6[6]	10[9]	208[9, 24]	n.a.	42	33[9]
Ecuador	240	3.0	7[12]	37[25]	350[25]	46[25]	279[17]	45
Egypt	473[12]	1.2[12]	185	10[9]	3,012[9]	79[9]	136	26
El Salvador	78	1.8	11[26]	12[9]	331[9, 27]	n.a.	333	35
Ethiopia	80	.3	12[26]	2	35	1	7	1
Finland	2,127	44.7	643	59	2,235	472	398[13]	400[9]
France	19,870	37.2	11,801[12]	96	10,863	205	330[9, 13]	278[9, 13]
Germany, East	2,956	17.6	938	39	8.317	496	895	325[13]
Germany, West	24,743	40.4	12,368[13]	412	25,968	423	332[9, 13]	300[9, 13]
Ghana	65	.7	58[16]	4[9]	435[9]	42[9]	105	4
Greece	2,487	26.6	294	112	n.a.	n.a.	296	127[9]
Guatemala	71[12]	1.2[12]	27[9]	9[9]	214[9, 28]	n.a.	43	23
Honduras	19[9]	.7[9]	22	8[9]	140[9, 28]	n.a.	57[9]	17[9]
Hong Kong	1,251[12]	27.8[12]	174[16]	83	1,393[14]	n.a.	556	193
Hungary	1,143	10.7	1,647[8]	27	2,585	243	242[13]	236[9, 13]
Iceland	100	44.4	19[8]	6	123	554	293[13]	241[9]
India	2,096[12]	.3[12]	7,707[16]	929	10,672[29]	n.a.	33[13]	1[13]
Indonesia	347[12]	.3[12]	208	178[9]	2,358[9, 30]	n.a.	37	7
Iran	829[12]	2.3[12]	858[31]	23[9]	473[9, 32]	n.a.	62	55
Iraq	320[12]	2.6[12]	46	7[9]	202[9, 28]	n.a.	168	40
Ireland	554	17.2	320[9, 12, 16]	7	702	220	300[9]	207[9, 13]
Israel	993	27.1	316[12, 16]	24[9]	801[9, 32]	231[9]	208	137[9, 13]
Italy	17,088	30.1	5,190	72	5,491	97	236[13]	225[15]
Jamaica	111[12]	5.3[12]	68[12]	3	101	49	270[9]	58
Japan	48,646	42.4	12,417[12, 16]	177	62,221	546	571	242[13]
Kenya	156	1.0	110[26]	3[9]	154[9]	11[9]	37	4
Korea, South	2,387	6.5	780	44	7,169	197	400	96[13]
Kuwait	170	14.3	6[16]	7	180	159	487	478
Lebanon	192[17]	6.8[17]	n.a.	33[9]	281[9, 33]	n.a.	540[9]	147
Luxembourg	192	53.9	49	7[9]	150[9, 34]	n.a.	506	247
Madagascar	29[12]	.4[12]	100	12	n.a.	n.a.	120	1
Malaysia	434	3.3	377[8, 35]	37[9]	1,834[9, 20]	n.a.	119	53
Mexico	4,140	6.2	1,068[9]	352	3,994[9, 36]	n.a.	301[1]	84
Morocco	216	1.1	105	10[9]	190[9, 24]	n.a.	88	33[13]

				Daily newspapers,[3] 1977			Receiving sets, 1977	
					Circulation			
Country	Telephones, in use[1] 1978 (thousands)	Telephones per 100 population, 1978	Pieces of mail sent domestic,[2] 1978 (millions)	Number	Total (thousands)	Copies per 1,000 population[4]	Radios per 1,000 population[5]	TV sets per 1,000 population[5]
Netherlands	6,341	45.3	3,913	67[9]	4,371[9 31]	n.a.	614	325
New Zealand	1.715	54.5	588[8 16]	39[9]	848[9 39]	n.a.	878	263
Nigeria	128	.2[12]	976[8]	19[9]	527[9 39]	n.a.	79	7
Norway	1,636	40.2	1,064[11]	82	1,740	430	326	275[13]
Pakistan	259[9]	.3[9]	552[12]	103[9]	965[9 40]	n.a.	66	8
Panama	155[12]	8.6[12]	7[15]	6[9]	136[9]	79[9]	157	116
Paraguay	48	1.7	n.a.	4[9]	106[9]	39[9]	67	20
Peru	420	2.7	n.a.	30	828	51	134	50
Phillippines	600	1.3	n.a.	17[9]	919[9 41]	n.a.	43	19
Poland	3,095	8.8	1.730[8 9]	44	8,331	240	241[13]	207[13]
Portugal	1.175[12]	12.0[12]	431	28	527	54	164[9]	94[9 13]
Puerto Rico	561[12]	16.9[12]	n.a.	4[9]	430[9]	134[9]	549[9]	162
Romania	1,196[7]	5.6[7]	730[12]	34	3,711	171	143[13]	146[13]
Saudi Arabia	185[12]	2.4[12]	56	12[9]	143[9 34]	n.a.	29	32
Singapore	475	20.4	123	10	497	215	168	285
South Africa	2,320	9.8	1,483	24[9]	1,728[9]	66[9]	96[9]	n.a.
Soviet Union	20,943[42]	8.0[42]	5,925	686	102,462	396	481[7]	217[7]
Spain	10,311	28.0	3,618	143	4,710	128	259[9]	206[9]
Sri Lanka	74	.5	591[16]	22	n.a.	n.a.	72	—
Sudan	62[12]	.3[12]	27[8]	4[9]	26[9 43]	n.a.	83	6
Sweden	6,160	74.4	2,613[8]	112	4,358	528	1,005	370[13]
Switzerland	4,292	67.7	3,020	91	2,622	414	790	348
Syria	212	2.6	23[15]	7[9]	65[9 28]	n.a.	218[17]	32
Thailand	409	.9	213	23	n.a.	n.a.	129	17
Trinidad and Tobago	75[12]	6.7[12]	21[44]	3[9]	144[9 43]	n.a.	246	112
Tunisia	158	2.7	75	5	232[4 45]	n.a.	143	36
Turkey	1,379[12]	3.2[12]	608[12]	493	n.a.	n.a.	101	54[13]
United Kingdom	23,182	41.5	9.337[8 16 26 46]	n.a.	22,900	410	716	390
United States	169,027	77.0	88,970[6 7 8]	1,829	62,159	287	2,048	623
Uruguay	270	9.6	17[12]	26	n.a.	n.a.	571	126
Venezuela	847[12]	6.5[12]	202[19]	54	2,263	178	414	120
Vietnam	47[15 47]	.3[15 47]	59[15 26 47]	5	250	5	24[17 47]	—
Yugoslavia	1,556[12]	7.1[12]	665	26	2,085	96	209[13]	170[12]
Zimbabwe	197[12]	2.9[12]	105	3[1]	116[7]	18[7]	39[9]	11[9]
World Total	**448,201**	**10.5**	n.a.	n.a.	n.a.	n.a.	n.a.	n.a.

1. Comprises public and private telephones installed which can be connected to a central exchange. 2. Items mailed for distribution within national territories. Comprises letters, postcards, printed matter, merchandise samples, small packets, and phonopost packets. Includes mail carried without charge, but excludes ordinary packages, and insured letters and boxes. 3. Publications containing general news and appearing at least 4 times a week; may range in size from a single sheet to 50 or more pages. Circulation data refer to average circulation per issue or number of printed copies per issue and include copies sold outside the country. 4. Data cover estimated number of receivers in use, except as noted, and apply to all types of receivers for radio broadcasts to the public, including receivers connected to a radio "redistribution system" but excluding television sets. 5. Estimated number of sets in use, except as noted. 6. Includes ordinary packages as well as insured letters and boxes. 7. For 1975. 8. Excludes small packets. 9. For 1976. 10. 117 dailies. 11. Year beginning July 1. 12. For 1977. 13. Number of licenses issued. 14. 19 dailies. 15. For 1973. 16. Year beginning April 1. 17. For 1970. 18. Source: U.S. Bureau of the Census. Data from Republic of China publications. 19. For 1974. 20. 35 dailies. 21. 10 or more dailies. 22. Domestic and foreign. 23. Includes Faeroe Islands and Greenland. 24. 7 dailies. 25. For 1978. 26. Excludes postcards. 27. 9 dailies. 28. 5 dailies. 29. 603 dailies. 30. 50 dailies. 31. For 1971. 32. 20 dailies. 33. 15 dailies. 34. 6 dailies. 35. Data refer to West Malaysia only. 36. 146 dailies. 37. 56 dailies. 38. 37 dailies. 39. 8 dailies. 40. 21 dailies. 41. 16 dailies. 42. Excludes telephone systems of the military forces. 43. 2 dailies. 44. For 1972. 45. 4 dailies. 46. Excludes printed matter. 47. Data are for former Rep. of South Vietnam. NOTE: n.a. = not available. *Sources:* Except as noted, Statistical Office of the United Nations, New York, *Statistical Yearbook* (copyright), and United Nations Educational, Scientific, and Cultural Organization, Paris, *Statistical Yearbook* (copyright).

World Population to Level at 10.5 Billion in 2110

The world's population will most likely stabilize at 10.5 billion in the year 2110, according to a 1981 United Nations Fund for Population Activities report. This forecast revises earlier predictions by others that the population would increase to 14 or 16 billion before stabilizing. The lower assessment is a result of improved world population control.

The over-all growth rate of 1.73% between 1975 and 1980 will decline to 1.5% annually by the year 2000. However, there is a sharp difference in the growth for industrialized and nonindustrialized nations. People in industrialized countries, who accounted for 24% of the world's population in 1980, will account for only 13% in the year 2110.

The U.S. population will level off in the year 2060 at 320 million, while the U.S.S.R. will stabilize in 2100 at 380 million. The forecast predicts that by 2110 there will be 6.3 billion people in South Asia and Africa.

International Treaties, Agreements, and Organizations

Association of Southeast Asian Nations

A non-military alliance of Thailand, Malaysia, Singapore, Indonesia, and the Philippines, formed in Bangkok in 1967. Its goal of regional economic integration along the lines of the European Economic Community has not been achieved. However, cooperation on international, political, and economic issues has been evolving. ASEAN took its first major political stand in January 1979 when it condemned Vietnam's invasion of Cambodia.

Papua New Guinea now has observer status in the ASEAN.

Alliance for Progress Agreement

Embodied in the Declaration of Punta del Este, adopted Aug. 17, 1961, by the U.S. and 19 other American republics, Cuba abstaining. The U.S. agreed to provide most of $20 billion needed over the next 10 years for Latin-American economic development. The other nations pledged themselves to increase their own contributions to economic and social development and to make the reforms necessary for all to share fully in the benefits gained under the Alliance for Progress.

Central Treaty Organization (CENTO)

Created in 1955 to provide a defense shield on the northern tier of the Middle East against Soviet penetration. Its original members were Turkey, Iran, U.K., Pakistan, and Iraq (which withdrew in 1959). In 1958, the U.S. signed a declaration of collective security to cooperate with the member states. CENTO was known as the Baghdad Pact until 1958, when its headquarters were moved to Ankara, Turkey. Iran and Pakistan withdrew in 1979.

Commonwealth of Nations

An association of equal and independent nations and subordinate areas formerly part of the old British Empire and united by their symbolic allegiance to the Crown. Member nations gained equal status with the U.K. under the Statute of Westminster of 1931, which formally initiated the Commonwealth. Its members consult and cooperate and share trade and other economic benefits. For a list of members, *see* Countries of the World by Groupings.

Arab League

Formed at Cairo on March 22, 1945, as a loose confederation of Arab states seeking Arab unity. Founding members were Egypt, Iraq, Jordan, Lebanon, Saudi Arabia, Syria, and the Yemen Arab Republic, joined later by Algeria, Bahrain, Djibouti, Kuwait, Libya, Mauritania, Morocco, Oman, Qatar, Somalia, the Sudan, Tunisia, the United Arab Emirates, the Yemen People's Democratic Republic, and the Palestine Liberation Organization. Military cooperation has been hampered by differences among the members, except in the Suez Canal crisis of 1956. The league has proved more effective in economic and cultural affairs. A permanent secretariat was set up at Cairo.

The European Community

In 1950, the then French Foreign Minister, Robert Schumann, proposed a "Community" of the French and German coal and steel industries, with membership open to other European countries. The *European Coal and Steel Community (ECSC)* was established in 1952; it eliminated customs duties and reduced currency and trade restrictions on coal, iron ore, and scrap. Original members were France, Germany, Italy, Belgium, the Netherlands, and Luxembourg.

By 1955, discussions began on other ways of increasing European economic integration. The *European Economic Community* (the *Common Market* or *EEC*) was established by a treaty, signed in Rome in 1957, by the original members of the ECSC. In 1970, the U.K., Ireland, Denmark, and Norway were invited to join. All except Norway did so in 1972; the enlarged "Community of the Nine" formally came into existence on January 1, 1973. Greece became the tenth EEC member in 1979 and joined formally Jan. 1, 1981.

The purposes of the EEC include the removal of trade barriers, coordination of economic policies, and increased mobility of labor and capital among its members—much of which had been achieved by 1978. Its aim is eventual economic union of the member nations and ultimate political confederation.

A second treaty was signed in Rome in 1957 establishing the *European Atomic Energy Community (Euratom)* to integrate activities of member nations concerned with nuclear power and technology.

The three Communities (ECSC, EEC, and Euratom) make up the *European Community,* with a Council of Ministers and a European Parliament. A European Court of Justice and the European Investment Bank also function within the European Community. (*See* R.C. Mowat, *Creating the European Community,* 1973.)

European Free Trade Association (EFTA)

Formed in 1959 (formally begun 1960) to promote economic growth and fair competition, equalize the supply of raw materials among the member states, and to expand world trade. Members now include Austria, Iceland, Norway, Portugal, Sweden, Switzerland, and Finland (associate). Denmark and the U.K., originally members, withdrew before becoming members of the EEC in 1973: at that time a new trade agreement was made between the EFTA and the Common Market. By 1966, custom duties between members had virtually been eliminated. The EFTA is based in Geneva.

Marshall Plan (European Recovery Program)

Proposed in June 1947 by Gen. George C. Marshall, U.S. Secretary of State, to meet the need for integrated recovery efforts against "hunger, poverty, desperation, and chaos" in Europe. A July conference of 16 nations (the U.S.S.R. and its satellites refusing to participate) estimated four-year-aid requirements at $22.4 billion. In April 1948, Congress appropriated $5.4 billion. The U.S. established the Economic Cooperation Administration; European nations set up the Organization for European Economic Cooperation (OEEC). Each participating country set aside, in its own currency, sums matching the aid it received. The ERP ended in December 1951, a year ahead of schedule, with a total cost of $11 billion. Emphasis by then had been shifted to rearmament. (*See* S.E. Harris, ed., *Foreign Economic Policy for the U.S.*, 1948, 1968.)

The Helsinki Agreement

Popular name for declaration adopted Aug. 1, 1975, by 35 nations—including the United States and the Soviet Union—participating in the Conference on Security and Cooperation in Europe held at Helsinki, Finland. The declaration particularly stressed "fundamental rights, economic and social progress and well-being for all peoples," as well as the need for joint action to promote world peace and security. The participating states reaffirmed their full support for the United Nations and pledged to respect each other's "sovereign equality and individuality. . . . " They pledged to broaden and deepen détente, and renounced the "threat or use of force" and subversion in settling international disputes.

Outstanding in the declaration was the section on cooperation in humanitarian and cultural fields. The signers pledged themselves to respect "fundamental freedoms, including the freedom of thought, conscience, religion or belief."

Among the stated objectives were: Freer movement among persons, institutions, and organizations; wider exchange of information; increased cultural exchanges and broader dissemination of books, films, other media, and artistic works. The agreement was reviewed in an eight-month conference at Belgrade, Yugoslavia, ending in March 1978, which was attended by representatives of the U.S. and Canada, 32 European countries, and the Vatican. After bitter debate, the conference adopted a summary document that did not mention human rights or other issues dividing East and West.

Another review conference began in Madrid in the autumn of 1980 and adjourned the following July 24 until Oct. 27 without reaching agreement on the major issues of human rights or military security. The protracted negotiations ranged from terrorism to measures to ease emigration, and a proposal to hold a later conference on military security in Europe. The Madrid conference resumed as scheduled but adjourned March 12, 1982, with East and West at loggerheads over the issue of martial law in Poland. The parting exchange of charges reflected widely varying interpretations of the 1975 Helsinki accords that were under review.

North Atlantic Treaty Organization (NATO)

Set up April 4, 1949, under a regional defense treaty for the North Atlantic area stating that "an armed attack against one . . . shall be considered an attack against . . . all" and that participating nations will take necessary joint counteraction under the United Nations Charter, including the use of armed force. The founding members were the U.S., Canada, Iceland, Norway, Great Britain, the Netherlands, Denmark, Belgium, Luxembourg, Portugal, France, and Italy. Greece, Turkey, and West Germany were added later. Spain formally became the 16th member on May 30, 1982. NATO marked the first time that the United States pledged to go to war to support allies before the outbreak of hostilities. The member nations are represented on the governing NATO Council. Its organization comprises their top foreign, economic, defense, and financial ministers. Its major military commands are SACEUR for Europe and SACLANT for the Atlantic Ocean area. (*See* James Huntley, *The NATO Story*, 1969.)

Organization of American States (OAS)

Created in April 1948 as a regional agency working with the UN to promote peace, justice, hemispheric solidarity, and economic development; and to defend the sovereignty of member nations. Original members were Argentina, Bolivia, Brazil, Chile, Colombia, Costa Rica, Cuba, Dominica, the Dominican Republic, Ecuador, El Salvador, Guatemala, Haiti, Honduras, Mexico, Nicaragua, Panama, Paraguay, Peru, the U.S., Uruguay, and Venezuela. Barbados, Grenada, Jamaica, Santa Lucia, Surinam, and Trinidad and Tobago were admitted later. In 1962 Cuba was suspended. The permanent body of the OAS is the General Secretariat, formerly the Pan-American Union Headquarters, Washington, D.C.

Organization of African Unity (OAU)

Founded in May 1963 by 32 African countries, the OAU has grown to include most independent African countries; South Africa is specifically excluded; as was Rhodesia; Zimbabwe, formerly Rhodesia, was admitted as 50th member upon gaining independence in 1980. On Feb. 22, 1982, the Polisario Front (guerrillas fighting Morocco) was admitted as the 51st member. Its charter reflects historical Pan-African concern for the political sovereignty, economic advancement, and cultural cooperation of all African peoples. The charter affirms allegiance to United Nations principles; its key section emphasizes the eradication of colonialism and promotion of international cooperation. The OAU has assisted in the relaxation or settlement of border disputes and helped resolve internal crises. In economic cooperation, it has stressed transportation and telecommunications. It maintains a close relationship with the U.N. OAU headquarters are at Addis Ababa, Ethiopia.

Organization for Economic Cooperation and Development (OECD)

Founded in 1961 to encourage world trade and economic progress and aid underdeveloped nations. The OECD superseded the Organization for European Economic Cooperation, which had been established under the Marshall Plan in 1948. Members are Australia, Austria, Belgium, Canada, Denmark, Finland, France, West Germany, Greece, Iceland, Ireland, Italy, Japan, Luxembourg, the Netherlands, New Zealand, Norway, Portugal, Spain, Sweden, Switzerland, Turkey, the U.K. and the U.S. (Yugoslavia has a special association). Its structure is consultative; its decisions, not binding.

Organization of Petroleum Exporting Countries (OPEC)

Founded in 1960 at Baghdad, Iraq, to advance its members' interests in trade and development and in relations with other oil-producing nations. Venezuela took the initiative; other founders were Iran, Iraq, Kuwait, and Saudi Arabia. They were joined by Algeria, Ecuador, Gabon, Indonesia, Libya, Nigeria, Qatar, and the United Arab Emirates. Through such practices as the 1973–74 embargo, OPEC has maintained high oil prices and has generally fixed the price of oil in international trade.

Panama Canal Treaties

Approved by the U.S. Senate in March and April of 1978. The basic treaty provides for turning the canal over to Panama by the year 2000. Until noon Dec. 31, 1999, the canal will be operated by a new U.S. agency, the Panama Canal Commission, with five Americans and four Panamanians on the board. Until 2000 the U.S. will have primary responsibility for defending the canal; Panama will assume jurisdiction over the 533-square-mile Canal Zone.

The Neutrality Treaty, also effective Dec. 31, 1999, provides that the U.S. and Panama will each have the right to defend the canal against threats to its neutrality or the peaceful passage of ships. A Senate reservation gave the U.S. the unilateral right to use force if necessary to reopen the canal or restore its operations. The Senate specified that any intervention would be only to keep the canal open, not to interfere in Panama's internal affairs. (See *Panama.*)

The Potsdam Declaration

Issued at Potsdam, Germany, July 26, 1945, after a conference of President Truman, Prime Minister Churchill (later, Clement Attlee), and Prime Minister Stalin. Pending entry of the U.S.S.R. into the war against Japan, it was issued in the names of Truman, Churchill, and Chiang Kai-shek (reached by radio). The declaration, designed to clarify and implement the Yalta Agreement, demanded unconditional surrender of Japan and outlined surrender terms. It called for elimination of "irresponsible militarism" and for Allied occupation until Japan's war-making power was destroyed. Other major points included "stern justice" for war criminals, democratic reforms, and respect for fundamental human rights. Successful U.S. testing of the atom bomb was revealed to Stalin at Potsdam.

The Rio Treaty

Signed at Rio de Janeiro on September 2, 1947, by 19 American states. Formally the Inter-American Treaty of Mutual Assistance, it provides for peaceful settlement of disputes in the Western Hemisphere and common action against aggressors, whether American or an outside nation, within a defense zone encircling North and South America and including Greenland and Antarctica. Canada, Ecuador, and Nicaragua did not sign, but Ecuador, Nicaragua, and Trinidad-Tobago joined later. In 1964 the members suspended Cuba. Countries in alliance now total 21.

Strategic Arms Limitation Talks (SALT I)

Two agreements limiting American and Soviet nuclear weapons were signed in Moscow in 1972 after three years of negotiations. One was a five-year interim pact limiting some offensive strategic weapons and the number of launchers for intercontinental ballistic missiles carrying nuclear warheads. The other, a treaty of indefinite duration, restricted antiballistic or defensive missiles to 200 on each side. (That number was reduced to 100 in a 1974 amendment.) The agreements were signed by President Richard M. Nixon and Leonid I. Brezhnev, the Soviet Communist Party leader. The talks originated with discussions at Glassboro, N.J., in 1967 between President Lyndon B. Johnson and the Soviet Prime Minister, Aleksei N. Kosygin. On Nov. 24, 1974, President Gerald R. Ford reached agreement in principle with Mr. Brezhnev at Vladivostok on limiting the numbers of all offensive strategic weapons and delivery systems until Dec. 31, 1985.

(SALT II)

A treaty resulting from the second round of strategic arms limitation talks was signed in Vienna on June 18, 1979, by President Carter and Soviet leader Brezhnev and went to the U.S. Senate for ratification. The treaty runs to 1985 and limits each side to 2,400 intercontinental ballistic missile launchers and long-range bombers within six months. The U.S. is already under this ceiling, but the Russians will have to destroy 100 of their launchers or bombers. By the end of 1981, a new ceiling of 2,250 is to come into effect. The treaty allows each country to develop one new missile and to modernize its existing weapons within certain restrictions. Each side would verify the other's compliance by its own technical means. The agreement ran into sharp opposition in the Senate. A substantial increase in spending on armaments appeared to be the price many senators would set for their affirmative votes. President Carter delayed ratification efforts indefinitely following the Soviet invasion of Afghanistan in December 1979. Controversy over the treaty continued well into the Reagan Administration and it remained unratified.

Treaty for a Partial Nuclear Test Ban

Agreement, effective Oct. 10, 1963, signed in Moscow Aug. 8, 1963, by the U.S., U.K., and the U.S.S.R. Although over 100 nations have since signed, France and China have not. The treaty banned nuclear testing in the atmosphere, in outer space, or under water. The signatories can withdraw under certain conditions.

Warsaw Pact

Signed May 14, 1955, by Albania, Bulgaria, Czechoslovakia, East Germany, Hungary, Poland, Romania, and the U.S.S.R. Albania, barred from meetings in 1962, withdrew in 1968 after ideological differences. The pact is the Communist equivalent of NATO, providing that an attack on one shall be regarded as an attack on all.

The Yalta Agreement

Signed Feb. 11, 1945, at conference of President Roosevelt and Prime Ministers Churchill and Stalin. The U.S., U.K., and the U.S.S.R. agreed to require Germany's unconditional surrender and on dividing Germany into separate zones for occupation, with France invited to join as the fourth occupying power. The agreement pledged disarmament of Germany, breakup of the arms industry, punishment of war criminals, reparations for destruction by the Germans, and the wiping out of nazism and militarism. The conference also agreed on terms for Russia to enter the war against Japan. (See R.F. Fenno, ed., *The Yalta Conference*, 2nd ed., 1972.)

START

Strategic Arms Reduction Talks between representatives of the United States and the Soviet Union began in Geneva on June 29, 1982. The meeting was the first on strategic weapons between the two powers in more than three years. Washington had wanted to delay negotiations until it could build up a wide range of weapons. Rising antinuclear sentiment in the United States and Europe, however, prompted it to enter the talks earlier. The START discussions deal basically with intercontinental ballistic missiles and long-range bombers, and are a complement to Soviet-American talks on European-based intermediate-range missiles, which began in Geneva in November, 1981. In opening the talks, the U.S. delegation presented a letter from President Reagan appealing for a reversal of the trend toward increasingly unstable strategic relations, blaming a Soviet buildup for the instability but terming the talks an opportunity "to reverse this process and to reduce substantially both the numbers and destructive potential of nuclear forces." The President said the discussions "must immediately focus on the most destabilizing elements of the strategic balance," which the United States has defined as land-based missiles.

America has proposed that each side reduce its missile warheads to no more than 5,000, roughly a one-third reduction. The Soviet Union would have to make greater cuts in its intercontinental ballistic missile force than would the United States. But the Americans say they would have to cut back on sea-launched missiles to a similar degree.

In response to the American proposals, the Soviet offered to make substantial cuts in long-range missile and bomber forces. But in return Moscow demanded that the United States agree to forgo the deployment of new medium-range missiles in Europe and to accept stringent restrictions on all future cruise missile deployment. Administration officials branded the Soviet proposals unacceptable, but neither side formally rejected the other's proposals.

As the negotiations went on toward autumn, it became evident to Administration officials that the pincipal Soviet goal in the Geneva talks was to limit American cruise missiles while preparing to deploy large numbers of its own. The cruise missile is of critical importance because of its versatility and relative safety to its operators. Basically, it is an uncrewed aircraft with more features of an aircraft than of a missile, having wings and a turbine engine. It has a range of from 200 miles to over 1,200. The cruise can be launched from ships, submarines, ground stations and crewed aircraft.

A Moscow spokesman said no arms control agreement could be of "any value" if the United States began a new race in cruise missiles while seeking to reduce the heavy land-based missiles in which the Soviet Union has an advantage. United States programs called for the deployment of 8,000 land-, sea- and air-based cruise missiles, beginning in December, 1982. Several Washington officials said the Soviet Union was still several years from being able to deploy this weapon. Thus, the Soviet is trying to curtail American cruise missiles while stepping up their own program, which has closed the gap with the United States from ten years to five.

In the Moscow START proposals, all 3,800 prospective U.S. air-launched cruise missiles and some sea-launched ones are counted within an unspecified limit on nuclear warheads and bombs. The American proposals for a limit of 5,000 nuclear warheads includes only missile warheads, and not bombs or cruise missiles.

Administration officials believe that the Soviet proposal in the talks on medium-range nuclear forces would ban deployment of the ground-launched cruise missile and the new Pershing missile. In Europe the Russians already have a large number of medium-range ballistic missiles and thus have no interest in developing cruise missiles for that theater. —*A.P.R.*

Countries of the World by Groupings

KEY

1—Member of the Organization of American States (OAS)
2—Member of the Organization of African Unity (OAU)
3—Member of the Organization of Petroleum Exporting Countries (OPEC)
4—Member of the North Atlantic Treaty Organization (NATO)
5—Member of the Association of Southeast Asian Nations
6—Member of the Central Treaty Organization (CENTO)
7—Member of the Arab League
8—Member of the Warsaw Pact
9—Member of the European Economic Community (EEC)
10—Member of the European Free Trade Association (EFTA)
11—Member of British Commonwealth of Nations
12—Member of the Economic Community of West African States (ECOWAS)
13—Member of the Organization for Economic Cooperation and Development (OECD)
14—Member of Inter-American Treaty of Reciprocal Assistance (Rio Pact)

NORTH AMERICA

Canada: 4, 11, 13
Mexico: 1, 14
United States: 1, 4, 13, 14

SOUTH AMERICA

Argentina: 1, 14
Bolivia: 1, 14
Brazil: 1, 14
Chile: 1, 14
Colombia: 1, 14
Ecuador: 1, 3, 14
Guyana: 11
Paraguay: 1, 14
Peru: 1, 14
Suriname: 1
Uruguay: 1, 14
Venezuela: 1, 3, 14

CENTRAL AMERICA

Belize: 11
Costa Rica: 1, 14
El Salvador: 1, 14
Guatemala: 1, 14
Honduras: 1, 14
Nicaragua: 1, 14
Panama: 1, 14

CARIBBEAN REGION

Antigua and Barbuda: 11
Bahamas: 11
Barbados: 1, 11
Cuba
Dominica: 1, 11
Dominican Republic: 1, 14
Grenada: 1, 11
Haiti: 1, 14
Jamaica: 1, 11
St. Lucia: 1, 11
St. Vincent and the Grenadines: 11
Trinidad and Tobago: 1, 11, 14

EUROPE

Albania
Andorra
Austria: 10, 13
Belgium: 4, 9, 13
Bulgaria: 8
Cyprus: 11
Czechoslovakia: 8
Denmark: 4, 9, 13
Finland: 10 (assoc. mem.), 13
France: 4, 9, 13
Germany, East: 8
Germany, West: 4, 9, 13
Greece: 4, 9, 13
Hungary: 8
Iceland: 4, 10, 13
Ireland: 9, 13
Italy: 4, 9, 13
Liechtenstein
Luxembourg: 4, 9, 13
Malta: 11
Monaco
Netherlands: 4, 9, 13
Norway: 4, 10, 13
Poland: 8
Portugal: 4, 10, 13
Romania: 8
San Marino
Spain: 4, 13
Sweden: 10, 13
Switzerland, 10, 13
U.S.S.R.: 8
United Kingdom: 4, 6, 9, 11, 13
Vatican City State
Yugoslavia

MIDDLE EAST

Bahrain: 7
Iran: 3
Iraq: 3, 7
Israel
Jordan: 7
Kuwait: 3, 7
Lebanon: 7
Oman: 7
Qatar: 3, 7
Saudi Arabia: 3, 7
Syria: 7
Turkey: 4, 6, 13
United Arab Emirates: 3, 7
Yemen, People's Democratic Republic of: 7
Yemen Arab Republic: 7

FAR EAST

China, People's Republic of
China, Republic of
Japan: 13
Korea, North
Korea, South
Mongolia
Philippines: 5

SOUTHEAST ASIA

Cambodia
Indonesia: 3, 5
Laos
Malaysia: 5, 11
Singapore: 5, 11
Thailand: 5
Vietnam

SOUTH ASIA

Afghanistan
Bangladesh: 11
Bhutan
Burma
India: 11
Maldives
Nepal
Pakistan
Sri Lanka: 11

OCEANIA

Australia: 11
Fiji: 11
Kiribati: 11
Nauru: 11
New Zealand: 11,13
Papua New Guinea: 11
Solomon Islands: 11
Tonga: 11
Tuvalu: 11
Vanuatu (New Hebrides)
Western Samoa: 11

AFRICA

Algeria: 2, 3, 7
Angola: 2
Benin: 2, 12
Bophuthatswana
Botswana: 2, 11
Burundi: 2
Cameroon: 2, 12
Cape Verde: 2
Central African Republic: 2
Chad: 2, 12
Comoro Islands: 2
Congo: 2
Djibouti: 7
Egypt: 2, 7
Equatorial Guinea: 2
Ethiopia: 2
Gabon: 2, 3
Gambia: 2, 11, 12
Ghana: 2, 11, 12
Guinea: 12
Guinea-Bissau: 2, 12
Ivory Coast: 2, 12
Kenya: 2, 11
Lesotho: 2, 11
Liberia: 2, 12
Libya: 2, 3, 7
Madagascar: 2
Malawi: 2, 11
Mali: 2, 12
Mauritania: 2, 7, 12
Mauritius: 2, 11
Morocco: 2, 7
Mozambique: 2
Niger: 2, 12
Nigeria: 2, 3, 11, 12
Rwanda: 2
Sao Tomé and Príncipe: 2
Senegal: 2, 12
Seychelles: 11
Sierra Leone: 2, 11, 12
Somalia: 2, 7
South Africa, Rep. of
Sudan: 2, 7
Swaziland, 2, 11
Tanzania: 2, 11
Togo: 2, 12
Transkei
Tunisia: 2, 7
Uganda: 2, 11
Upper Volta: 2, 12
Venda
Zaire: 2
Zambia: 2, 11
Zimbabwe: 2,11

Countries, Territories, and Dependencies

For later developments, *see* Current Events

Economic data for each country have been drawn from reports of the United States State Department, the World Bank and the National Foreign Assessment Center. Population figures for countries are mid-1982 estimates.

AFGHANISTAN

Democratic Republic of Afghanistan
President: Babrak Karmal (1979)
Premier: Sultan Ali Kishtmand (1981)
Area: 251,000 sq mi. (650,090 sq km)
Population (est. 1982): 16,750,000 (average annual growth rate: 1.4%)
Density per square mile: 66.7
Capital: Kabul
Largest cities (est. 1979): Kabul, 891,700; Kandahar, 243,000; Herat, 163,000
Monetary unit: Afghani
Languages: Pushtu and Dari Persian (both official)
Religion: Islam (Sunni, 80%; Shiite, 20%)
National name: Jamhouri Democratike Afghanistan
Literacy rate (1981): 10%
Economic summary: Gross national product (1979): $3.4 billion. Average annual growth rate (1976–79): 4.5%. Per capita income (1979): $225. Land used for agriculture: 12%; labor force: 68%; principal products: wheat, grains, cotton, fruits, nuts. Labor force in industry: 10%; major products: carpets and textiles. Natural resources: natural gas, oil, coal, copper, sulfur, lead, zinc, iron, salt, precious and semi-precious stones. Exports: fresh and dried fruits, natural gas, carpets. Imports: petroleum products, and food supplies. Major trading partners: U.S.S.R., and Soviet bloc countries.

Geography. Afghanistan, approximately the size of Texas, lies wedged between the U.S.S.R., China, Pakistan, and Iran. The country is split east to west by the Hindu Kush mountain range, rising in the east to heights of 24,000 feet (7,315 m). With the exception of the southwest, most of the country is covered by high snow-capped mountains and is traversed by deep valleys.

Government. A Marxist "people's republic" was created by the coup of April 27, 1978. Pending adoption of a new Constitution, a 35-member Revolutionary Council is headed by Babrak Karmal, general secretary of the Central Committee of the People's Democratic Party of Afghanistan, the only authorized political party.

History. Darius I and Alexander the Great were the first conquerors to use Afghanistan as the gateway to India. Islamic conquerors arrived in the 7th century and Genghis Khan and Tamerlane followed in the 13th and 14th centuries. Tamerlane's descendant, Baber, used Kabul as the base for the campaign that created the Mogul empire in India. Afghanistan was torn by tribal warfare until Ahmed Shah of Persia established an emirate in 1747 that unified the country.

In the 19th century, Afghanistan became a battleground in the rivalry of imperial Britain and Czarist Russia for the control of Central Asia. The Afghan Wars (1838–42 and 1878–81) fought against the British by Dost Mohammed and his son and grandson ended in victory for the invaders despite the 1840 massacre of the British at Kabul and later fierce battles in the Khyber Pass.

Afghanistan regained autonomy by the Anglo-Russian agreement of 1907 and full independence by the Treaty of Rawalpindi in 1919. Emir Amanullah founded the kingdom in 1926.

The 1973 coup that ousted King Mohammed Zahir Shah also cut off a 10-year experiment in democracy when Mohammed Daud seized all powers. The April 27, 1978, coup that brought Noor Mohammed Taraki to power resulted not only in the death of Daud but also, according to press reports, in the deaths of thousands of officials and supporters of his government.

Taraki's attempts to create a Marxist state with Soviet aid brought armed resistance from conservative Muslim opposition. Rebels kidnapped U.S. Ambassador Adolph Dubs in an attempt to ransom comrades held by the Taraki government. Dubs was killed on Feb. 14, 1979, when Afghan police attacked his captors and Soviet advisers ignored U.S. appeals for restraint.

Taraki resigned on Sept. 16, 1979, reportedly because of poor health, and was succeeded by Prime Minister Hafizullah Amin. As disorder spread, it was announced on Dec. 28 that Amin had been killed and replaced by Babrak Karmal, who had called for Soviet troops under a mutual defense treaty. Pakistan and other Moslem nations called for a U.N. Security Council session and charged that Amin had been executed on Dec. 27 by Soviet troops already present in Kabul. The Council's call for immediate withdrawal of an estimated 40,000 Soviet troops was vetoed by the U.S.S.R. on Jan. 8, 1980.

With 85,000 reported in the invasion force by June, the U.S.S.R. and government forces were still unable to quell the rebels. Despite cuts in U.S. exports of high-technology goods and restrictions on food exports, together with a boycott of the Moscow Olympics by Western and Moslem nations, the Soviet Union refused to withdraw its troops.

Resistance by six Afghan guerrilla organizations continued to be strong late in 1981, with U.S. official sources estimating 10,000 to 12,000 Soviet casualties since the beginning of the Soviet occupation. Soviet-U.S. contacts were reported to have met with failure as Moscow insisted that only Western recognition of the Karmal regime would bring about a Soviet withdrawal.

The United States charged the Soviet Union with the use of chemical weapons in Afghanistan. Deputy Secretary of State Walter J. Stoessel testified in 1982 that at least 3,000 Afghans had been killed by chemical weapons.

ALBANIA

People's Socialist Republic of Albania
President of Presidium: Haxhi Leshi (1953)
Premier: Adil Carcani (1982)
Area: 11,100 sq mi. (28,748 sq km)
Population (est. 1982): 2,875,000 (average annual growth rate: 2.1%)
Density per square mile: 259.0
Capital and largest city (est. 1980): Tirana, 200,000
Monetary unit: Lek
Language: Albanian
Religions: Historically Islam 70%; Greek Orthodox, 20%; Roman Catholic, 10%
National name: Republika Popullore Socialiste e Shqipërisë
Literacy rate (1981): 70%
Economic summary: Gross national product (1972): $1.2 billion. Average annual growth rate (1970–78): 4.2%. Per capita income (1980): n.a. Land used for agriculture: 43%; labor force: 61%; principal products: wheat, corn, potatoes, sugar beets, cotton, tobacco. Labor force in industry: 18%; major products: textiles, timber, construction materials, fuels, semi-processed minerals. Exports: minerals, metals, fuels, foodstuffs, agricultural materials. Imports: machinery, equipment, and spare parts, minerals, metals, fuels, construction materials, foodstuffs. Major trading partners: East European countries.

Geography. Albania is situated on the eastern shore of the Adriatic Sea, with Yugoslavia to the north and east and Greece to the south. Slightly larger than Maryland, it is a mountainous country, mostly over 3,000 feet (914 m) above sea level, with a narrow, marshy coastal plain crossed by several rivers. The centers of population are contained in the interior mountain plateaus and basins.

Government. Under the Constitution that Albania adopted in 1946, supreme power is vested in the popularly elected National Assembly, to which the Cabinet, headed by the Premier, is responsible. The 240 members of the National Assembly all belong to the Labor Party and Democratic Front. The only political party is Labor (Communist), led by First Secretary Enver Hoxha.

History. Albania proclaimed its independence on Nov. 28, 1912, after a history of Roman, Byzantine, and Turkish domination.

A battlefield in World War I, Albania reasserted its independence in 1920. A chief, Ahmet Zogu, proclaimed himself president in 1925 and monarch (King Zog) in 1928. Italy, under Benito Mussolini, drove him into exile in 1939 and annexed the country. The Communists under Enver Hoxha established a government in 1944, issuing a Constitution in 1946 (amended in 1950) declaring the country a people's republic. Close relations with the U.S.S.R. ended in 1961 with the Soviet-Chinese rupture. Thereafter, Albania functioned as a Peking satellite, receiving massive Chinese aid to offset the Soviet boycott.

In 1967, the regime closed all of the nation's 2,169 churches and mosques in a move to make the country "the first atheist state in the world."

Albania's long alliance with China ended with the announcement in 1978, that China was cutting off all aid to its one-time partner. Albanian criticism of Peking following the death of Mao Zedong was cited as the reason, but Tirana called the action "arbitrary." There was no indication from Tirana that Albania was ready to return to the Soviet sphere.

ALGERIA

Democratic and Popular Republic of Algeria
President: Chadli Bendjedid (1979)
Prime Minister: Mohammed Benahmed Abdelghani (1979)
Area: 919,951 sq mi. (2,382,673 sq km)
Population (est. 1982): 20,000,000 (average annual growth rate: 3.1%)
Density per square mile: 21.7
Capital: Algiers
Largest cities (est. 1979): Algiers, 2,500,000; Oran, 600,000; Constantine, 500,000; Annaba, 300,000
Monetary unit: Dinar
Languages: Arabic (official), French
Religion: Islam
National name: République Algérienne Democratiqe et Populaire—El Djemhouria El Djazaïria Demokratia Echaabia
Literacy rate (1981): 25%
Economic summary: Gross national product (1980): $36.4 billion. Average annual growth rate (1970–79): 2.8%. Per capita income (1980): $1,920. Land used for agriculture: 3%; labor force: 19%; principal products: wheat, barley, oats, wine, fruits, olives, vegetables, livestock. Labor force in industry: 20%; major products: petroleum, gas, petrochemicals, fertilizers, iron and steel, textiles, transport equipment. Natural resources: petroleum, natural gas, iron ore, phosphates, lead, zinc, mercury. Exports: petroleum and gas. Imports: food, capital and consumer goods. Major trading partners: U.S., West Germany, France, Italy.

Geography. Nearly four times the size of Texas, Algeria is bordered on the west by Morocco and on the east by Tunisia and Libya. To the south are Mauritania, Mali, and Niger. Low plains cover small areas near the Mediterranean coast, with 68% of the country a plateau between 2,625 and 5,250 feet (800 and 1,600 m) above sea level. The highest point is Mount Tahat in the Sahara, which rises 9,850 feet (3,000 m).

Government. Algeria is governed by the President, whose term runs for 5 years. A new Constitution was approved on Nov. 19, 1976.

A National Popular Assembly of 281 members exercises legislative power, serving for a five-year term. The National Liberation Front, which led the struggle for independence from France, is the only legal party.

History. As ancient Numidia, Algeria became a Roman colony at the close of the Punic Wars (145 B.C.). Conquered by the Vandals about A.D. 440, it fell from a high state of civilization to virtual barbarism, from which it partly recovered after invasion by the Moslems about 650.

In 1492 the Moors and Jews, who had been expelled from Spain, settled in Algeria. Falling under Turkish control in 1518, Algiers served for three centuries as the headquarters of the Barbary pirates. The French took Algeria in 1830 and made it a part of France in 1848.

The fight by Algerian nationalists for independence had widespread political, diplomatic, military, and financial repercussions in France. Politically, it brought Gen. Charles de Gaulle to power when the army and extremist French colonist virtually seceded, set up a "Committee of Public Safety," and demanded that de Gaulle be given power. Ironically, it was de Gaulle who resolved to end the fighting by granting Algeria self-determination and independence, while his former army and French colonial supporters in Algeria joined to create the Secret Army Organization (OAS), a terrorist group that tried to block independence. But metropolitan France, weary of continued warfare, voted by some 15 million to 5 million in January 1961 to approve de Gaulle's proposals.

On July 5, 1962, Algeria was proclaimed independent. In October 1963, Ahmed Ben Bella was elected President. He began to nationalize foreign holdings and aroused opposition. He was overthrown in a military coup on June 19, 1965, by Col. Houari Boumediène, who suspended the Constitution and sought to restore financial stability. While retaining close economic and financial relations with France and the U.S., Algeria entered the Arab bloc and joined the war against Israel in 1967. Thereafter, the U.S.S.R. stepped up development aid.

Friction with Morocco intensified in 1976 as Algeria opposed the annexation of the Spanish Sahara by Morocco and Mauritania following a mass invasion of the former Spanish colony by Moroccan civilians. Algeria formally recognized a Saharan Arab Democratic Republic—composed of Polisario front leaders who fought unsuccessfully for an independent Sahara—on Feb. 27, 1976. The move was accompanied by a break in diplomatic relations with Morocco.

From an agricultural economy closely linked to France even after independence, Algeria became an exporter of energy in the form of petroleum products and then liquefied natural gas. The U.S. replaced France as Algeria's chief trading partner in 1976, buying 40% of Algerian crude oil production. In common with other oil-exporting countries in 1977 and 1978, however, Algeria slowed its general industrial expansion and shifted investment toward increasing oil and gas output and strengthening agriculture. Non-energy industry had proved too costly in relation to income produced and agricultural imports had become a drain on a weakened economy.

Boumediène died in December 1978 after a long illness. Chadli Bendjedid, Secretary-General of the National Liberation Front, took the presidency in a smooth transition of power. On July 4, 1979, he released from house arrest former President Ahmed Ben Bella, who had been confined for 14 years since his overthrow.

Algeria, chosen by Iran to represent it in negotiations in November 1980 with the United States, was able to secure the eventual release of 52 Americans who had been held hostage in the U.S. Embassy in Teheran. The hostages were flown to Algiers on Jan. 20, 1981, and turned over to U.S. custody, ending 444 days in captivity.

ANDORRA

Valleys of Andorra
Episcopal Co-Prince: Msgr. Joan Martí y Alanis, Bishop of Urgel
French Co-Prince: François Mitterrand, President of France (1981)
First Syndic: Julià Reiq-Ribó (1981)
Area: 175 sq mi. (453 sq km)
Population (est. 1982): 35,000 (average annual growth rate: 4.1%)
Density per square mile: 200.0
Capital (est. 1981): Andorra la Vella, 13,500
Monetary units: French franc and Spanish peseta
Languages: Catalán (official); French, Spanish
Religion: Roman Catholic
National names: Les Vallées d'Andorre-Valls d'Andorra
Literacy rate (1981): 10–15%
Economic summary: Land used for agriculture: 4%; labor force: 20%; principal products: oats, barley, cattle, sheep. Labor force in industry: 80%; major products: tobacco products and electric power; tourism. Natural resources: water power, mineral water. Major trading partners: Spain and France.

Geography. Andorra lies high in the Pyrenees Mountains on the French-Spanish border. The country is drained by the Valira River.

Government. A General Council of 28 members, elected for four years, chooses the First Syndic and Second Syndic. In 1976 the Andorran Democratic Party, the principality's first political party, was formed.

History. An autonomous and semi-independent co-principality, Andorra has been under the joint suzerainty of the French state and the Spanish bishops of Urgel since 1278.

ANGOLA

People's Republic of Angola
President: José Eduardo dos Santos (1979)
Area: 481,350 sq mi. (1,246,700 sq km)
Population (est. 1982): 7,450,000 (average annual growth rate: 2.5%)
Density per square mile: 15.5
Capital and largest city (est. 1980): Luanda, 500,000
Monetary unit: Kwanza
Languages: Bantu, Portuguese (official)
Religions: Animist, 45%; Roman Catholic, 43%; Protestant, 12%
Literacy rate (1981): 15%
Economic summary: Gross national product (1980): $3.3 billion. Average annual growth rate (1970–79): −9.6%. Per capita income (1980): $470. Principal agricultural products: coffee, sisal, corn, cotton, sugar, tobacco, bananas. Major industrial products: oil, diamonds, processed fish, tobacco, textiles, cement, processed food and sugar. Natural resources: diamonds, gold, iron, oil. Exports: oil, coffee, diamonds, fish and fish products, iron ore, timber, corn. Imports: machinery and electrical equipment, bulk iron, steel and metals, textiles, clothing. Major trading partners: Cuba, U.S.S.R., Portugal, U.S.

Geography. Angola, more than three times the size of California, extends for more than 1,000 miles (1,609 km) along the South Atlantic in southwestern Africa. Zaire is to the north and east; Zambia to the east, and South-West Africa (Namibia) to the south. A plateau averaging 6,000 feet (1,829 m) above sea level rises abruptly from the coastal lowlands. Nearly all the land is desert or savanna, with hardwood forests in the northeast.

Government. A Marxist "people's republic" is the recognized government, but large areas in the east and south are held by the Union for the Total Independence of Angola (Unita), led by Jonas Savimbi. President José Eduardo dos Santos heads the only official party, the Popular Movement for the Liberation of Angola-Workers Party. The Popular Movement won out over Savimbi's group and a third element in an internal struggle after Portugal granted its former colony independence on Nov

11, 1975. Elections promised at the time of independence have never taken place, and the government relies heavily on Soviet support and Cuban troops, while Savimbi receives aid from South Africa.

History. Discovered by the Portuguese navigator Diego Cao in 1482, Angola became a link in trade with India and the Far East. Later it was a major source of slaves for Portugal's New World colony of Brazil. Development of the interior began after the Treaty of Berlin in 1885 fixed the colony's borders, and British and Portuguese investment pushed mining, railways, and agriculture.

Following World War II, independence movements began but were sternly suppressed by military force. The April revolution of 1974 brought about a reversal of Portugal's policy, and the next year President Francisco da Costa Gomes signed an agreement to grant independence to Angola. The plan called for election of a constituent assembly and a settlement of differences by the MPLA and the National Front for the Liberation of Angola (FNLA) and the National Union for the Total Independence of Angola (UNITA).

Despite covert aid to FNLA by the U.S. and open support by neighboring Zaire for the Front's leader, Holden Roberto, the MPLA had the initial advantage of strength in the capital region. Cuban troops were introduced in October and soon routed the poorly trained and equipped FNLA and UNITA forces.

The Organization of African Unity, split over the issue earlier, recognized the MPLA government led by Agostinho Neto on Feb. 11, 1976, and the People's Republic of Angola became the 47th member of the organization.

The new government nationalized 19 major industries on May 19, mostly Portuguese-owned. This, together with Lisbon's objection to the refueling of Cuban troop transports in the Azores, led to a break between the former mother country and Angola.

Although militarily victorious, Neto's regime had yet to consolidate its power in opposition strongholds in the east and south. Less militantly Marxist than their colleagues in the former East African colony of Mozambique, the new leaders sought help from both the Western and Eastern worlds.

In March 1977, Zairean refugees in Angola invaded Zaire's Shaba Province, bringing charges by Zairean President Mobutu Sese Seko that the unsuccessful invasion was Soviet-backed with the collaboration of Angola. The Neto regime, the U.S.S.R., and Cuba all denied complicity. In May 1978, another invasion took place, and this time the U.S. and France joined Mobutu in accusing Angola, the U.S.S.R., and Cuba, all of which again denied guilt.

Neto died in Moscow of cancer on Sept. 10, 1979. The Planning Minister, José Eduardo dos Santos, was named President.

In March 1981, President Reagan asked Congress to repeal a 1976 ban on military aid to UNITA rebels led by Joseph Savimbi but strong opposition caused the administration to abandon its efforts. U.S. firms doing business with Angola, led by Gulf Oil, which has exploited the Cabinda oil field since its discovery, have supported the central government and urged establishment of diplomatic relations between Washington and Luanda.

Portugal's estrangement ended in April 1982 with the visit of Portuguese President Antonio Ramalho Eanes, the first Western head of state to visit Luanda since independence, who denounced South Africa's "undeclared war" against Angola. Chester A. Crocker, U.S. Assistant Secretary of State, came to Luanda in January to discuss Namibian independence with Angolan officials but Washington made it clear that diplomatic recognition must await withdrawal of Cuban troops.

ANTIGUA AND BARBUDA

Sovereign: Queen Elizabeth II
Governor-General: Sir Wilfred E. Jacobs (1981)
Prime Minister: Vere Bird (1981)
Area: 171 sq mi. (442 sq km)
Population (est. 1982): 80,000 (average annual growth rate: 1.3%)
Density per square mile: 467.8
Capital and largest city (est. 1980): St. John's, 25,000
Monetary unit: East Caribbean dollar
Language: English
Religions: Anglican and Roman Catholic
Literacy rate: 88%
Member of Commonwealth of Nations
Economic summary: Gross national product (1980): $100 million. Average annual growth rate (1970–79): −2.6%. Per capita income (1980): $1,270. Land used for agriculture: 54%; principal product: cotton. Major industry: tourism. Exports: clothing, rum, lobsters. Imports: fuel, food, machinery. Major trading partners: U.K., U.S.

Geography. Antigua, the larger of the two main islands, is low-lying except for a range of hills in the south that rise to their highest point at Boggy Peak (1,319 ft; 402 m). Deforested and without major streams, the island is subject to droughts despite a mean annual rainfall of 44 inches. Barbuda is a coral island, well wooded.

Government. Executive power is held by the Governor-General acting for the sovereign, but actual power is held by the Prime Minister. A 17-member Parliament is elected by universal suffrage. The Antigua Labor Party, led by Prime Minister Bird, holds 14 seats and the remainder are held by the opposition Progressive Labor Movement.

History. Antigua was discovered by Christopher Columbus in 1493 and named for the Church of Santa Maria la Antigua in Seville. Colonized by Britain in 1632, it joined the West Indies Federation in 1958. With the breakup of the Federation, it became one of the West Indies Associated States in 1967, self-governing in internal affairs. Full independence was granted Nov. 1, 1981.

ARGENTINA

Argentine Republic
President: Maj. Gen. Reynaldo Bignone (1982)
Area: 1,072,067 sq mi. (2,776,654 sq km)
Population (est. 1982): 28,400,000 (average annual growth rate: 1.6%)
Density per square mile: 26.5
Capital: Buenos Aires
Largest cities (est. 1980): Buenos Aires, 3,000,000; (est. 1975 by U.N.): Córdoba, 781,600; Rosario, 750,500; La Plata, 391,200; San Miguel de Tucumán, 321,600

Monetary unit: Peso
Language: Spanish
Religion: Predominantly Roman Catholic
National name: República Argentina
Literacy rate (1981): 85%
Economic summary: Gross national product (1980): $66.4 billion. Average annual growth rate (1970–79): 1.0%. Per capita income (1980): $2,390. Land used for agriculture: 57%; labor force: 19%; principal products: grains, oilseeds, livestock products. Labor force in industry: 25%; major products: processed foods, motor vehicles, consumer durables, textiles, chemicals. Natural resources: minerals, lead, zinc, tin, copper, iron, manganese, oil, uranium. Exports: meats, corn, wheat, wool, hides. Imports: machinery, fuel and lubricating oils, iron and steel. Major trading partners: U.S., Brazil, Italy, West Germany, Japan.

Geography. With an area slightly less than one third of the United States and second in South America only to its eastern neighbor, Brazil, in size and population, Argentina is a plain, rising from the Atlantic to the Chilean border and the towering Andes peaks. Aconcagua (23,034 ft.; 7,021 m) is the highest peak in the world outside Asia. It is bordered also by Bolivia and Paraguay on the north, and by Uruguay on the east.

The northern area is the swampy and partly wooded Gran Chaco, bordering on Bolivia and Paraguay. South of that are the rolling, fertile pampas, rich for agriculture and grazing and supporting most of the population. Next southward is Patagonia, a region of cool, arid steppes with some wooded and fertile sections.

Government. Argentina is a federal union of 22 provinces, one national territory, and the Federal District. Under the Constitution of 1853 (restored by a Constituent National Convention in 1957 and amended in 1972), the President and Vice President were elected every four years by direct vote. The President appointed his Cabinet. The Vice President presided over the Senate but had no other powers. The Congress consisted of two houses: a 69-member Senate and a 243-member Chamber of Deputies. All legislators were elected by direct vote for four-year terms.

Political parties, suspended, along with Congress since the military coup of March 24, 1976, were revived by presidential decree in July 1982, and Argentina hoped for a restoration of elected government.

History. Discovered in 1516 by Juan Díaz de Solis, Argentina developed slowly under Spanish colonial rule. Buenos Aires was settled in 1580; the cattle industry was thriving as early as 1600.

Invading British forces were expelled in 1806–07, and when Napoleon conquered Spain, the Argentinians set up their own government in the name of the Spanish King in 1810. On July 9, 1816, independence was formally declared.

As in World War I, Argentina proclaimed neutrality at the outbreak of World War II, but in the closing phase declared war on the Axis on March 27, 1945, and became a founding member of the United Nations. Juan D. Perón, an army colonel, emerged as the strongman of the postwar era, winning the Presidential elections of 1946 and 1951.

Opposition to Perón's increasing authoritarianism, fanned by worsening relations with the Roman Catholic Church, led to a coup by the armed forces that sent Perón into exile in 1955. The Peronist Party and Congress dissolved, and Argentina entered a long period of military dictatorships with brief intervals of constitutional government.

In the first free election since 1951, a Perón-endorsed candidate, Hector Campora, narrowly won the Presidency in 1973. He resigned July 13, seven weeks after his inauguration, in an effort to hand power back to Perón. The former dictator returned from exile and, with his third wife, Maria Estela (Isabel) Martinez de Perón, as Vice-Presidential candidate, swept the election on Sept. 23, 1973, winning 61% of the vote.

Perón died of a heart attack at the age of 78 on July 1, 1974. His widow became the hemisphere's first woman chief of state, but she took over a nation racked by acute economic and political polarization reflected in mounting civil disorders.

Mrs. Perón was re-elected head of the Peronist movement Aug. 24, 1975, at a tumultuous party Congress at which 118 of 238 delegates walked out before the vote. In mid-September she announced she would take a month-long leave of absence to recover from nervous strain and turned the presidential duties over to Italo A. Luder, president of the Senate.

Returning on October 16, Mrs. Perón was greeted with demands for her resignation as both the economic recession and terrorism increased.

The long-anticipated military revolt came March 24, 1976, with a junta composed of Army Lt. Gen. Jorge Rafaél Videla, Adm. Eduardo Massera, and Air Force Brig. Gen. Orlando Agosti taking power. Mrs. Perón and her closest advisers were arrested and subsequently charged with misuse of government funds, while thousands of Peronist government officials and labor leaders were placed under detention.

Videla took office as President on March 29 and suspended the Justicialista (Peronist) Party as well as all others and decreed new security laws and censorship.

Political murders and terrorism under the Videla regime mounted, together with allegations of police torture.

The twin plagues of inflation and terrorism continued in 1980, the former somewhat diminished by stringent economic measures. From a 1978 record 169.5% increase in the cost of living, the 1979 increase was held to below 90%, with unemployment at less than 4%.

Gen. Roberto Eduardo Viola, former Army Chief of Staff, was sworn in as President on March 29, 1981. Earlier, he had visited Washington and assured members of Congress that he would try to improve Argentina's human-rights record. On July 6, Viola released Mrs. Perón from house arrest and she left for Spain.

New fears for the economy arose when the government announced a 30% devaluation of the peso in June, making a total of 64% for the year and triggering new inflation.

The deteriorating economy was believed to have led the junta to depose Viola in December 1981 but his health was cited officially. Lt. Gen. Leopoldo Galtieri, commander of the army, was named president with economic reform as his first priority —Argentine reserves had fallen to $700,000 at year end and foreign debt had risen to $30 billion. But Galtieri's austerity program soon brought protestors into the streets, denouncing military government.

Hostile crowds changed to cheering mobs, however, after Galtieri landed thousands of troops on the Falkland Islands on April 2 and reclaimed the Malvinas, their Spanish name, as national territory. The cheering died when Britain reacted with unexpected force, shooting down Argentine planes and torpedoing the ancient **General Belgrano,** flagship of the fleet. By May 21, when 5,000 British marines and paratroops landed from the British armada, the superior power of an industrialized European nation had made the outcome clear to even the most patriotic Argentines.

Galtieri resigned three days after the surrender of the island garrison on June 14. Maj. Gen. Reynaldo Bignone, a 62-year-old retired division commander, took office as President on July 1. Civilian rule was promised by early 1984 and on July 16 Bignone lifted the six-year ban on political parties.

AUSTRALIA

Commonwealth of Australia
Sovereign: Queen Elizabeth II
Governor-General: Sir Ninian Stephen (1982)
Prime Minister: Malcolm Fraser (1975)
Area: 2,967,909 sq mi. (7,686,843 sq km)
Population (est. 1982): 15,100,000 (average annual growth rate: 1.3%)
Density per square mile: 5.1
Capital (est. 1980): Canberra, 225,000
Largest cities (est. 1980 for metropolitan area): Sydney, 3,230,000; Melbourne, 2,760,000; Brisbane, 1,000,000; Adelaide, 935,000; Perth, 400,000; Hobart (on Tasmania), 170,000
Monetary unit: Australian dollar
Language: English
Religions: Anglican, 36%; Roman Catholic, 33%; Methodist, 7%; Presbyterian, 7%.
Literacy rate (1981): 99%
Member of Commonwealth of Nations
Economic summary: Gross national product (1980): $142.2 billion. Average annual growth rate (1970–79): 1.4%. Per capita income (1980): $9,820. Land used for agriculture: 64%; labor force: 14%; principal products: wool, meat, cereals, sugar, wine grapes, sheep, cattle, dairy products. Labor force in industry: 32%; major products: machinery, motor vehicles, iron and steel, textiles, chemicals. Natural resources: gold, iron ore, bauxite, zinc, lead, tin, coal, oil, uranium, timber. Exports: agricultural products, metal ores, wool, coal. Imports: manufactured raw materials, capital equipment, consumer goods. Major trading partners: Japan, U.S., U.K., New Zealand.

Geography. The continent of Australia, with the island state of Tasmania, is approximately equal in area to the United States (excluding Alaska and Hawaii), and is nearly 50% larger than Europe (excluding the U.S.S.R.).

Mountain ranges run from north to south along the east coast, reaching their highest point in Mount Kosciusko (7,308 ft; 2,228 m). The western half of the continent is occupied by a desert plateau that rises into barren, rolling hills near the west coast. It includes the Great Victoria Desert to the south and the Great Sandy Desert to the north. The Great Barrier Reef, extending about 1,245 miles (2,000 km), lies along the northeast coast.

The island of Tasmania (26,178 sq mi.; 67,800 sq km) is off the southeastern coast.

Government. The Federal Parliament consists of a bicameral legislature. The House of Representatives has 124 members elected for three years by popular vote. The Senate has 64 members elected by popular vote for six years. One half of the Senate is elected every three years. Voting is compulsory at 18. Supreme federal judicial power is vested in the High Court of Australia, which consists of seven justices, appointed by the Governor-General in Council. Each of the states has its own judicial system.

The major political parties are the Liberal Party (54 seats in the House of Representatives), led by Prime Minister Malcolm Fraser; Australian Labor Party (51 seats), led by William G. Hayden; National Country Party (20 seats), led by J. Douglas Anthony.

History. Dutch, Portuguese, and Spanish ships sighted Australia in the 17th century; the Dutch landed at the Gulf of Carpentaria in 1606. In 1642, Abel Tasman (for whom Tasmania was named) proved that Australia was not part of the Antarctic Continent. Australia was called New Holland, Botany Bay, and New South Wales until about 1820.

Captain James Cook, in 1770, claimed possession for Great Britain. A British penal colony was set up at what is now Sydney, then Port Jackson, in 1788, and about 161,000 transported English convicts were settled there until the system was suspended in 1839.

Free settlers established six colonies: New South Wales (1786), Tasmania (then Van Diemen's Land) (1825), Western Australia (1829), South Australia (1834), Victoria (1851), and Queensland (1859).

Sheep raising and wheat growing built the economy, and the white population, which had dwindled to 34,000 in 1820, grew to 400,000 by 1850. Discovery of gold in Victoria in 1851 led immigrants to pour in. The six colonies became states and in 1901 federated into the Commonwealth of Australia with a Constitution that incorporated British parliamentary tradition and U.S. federal experience. Australia became known for liberal legislation: free compulsory education, protected trade unionism with industrial conciliation and arbitration, the "Australian" ballot facilitating selection, the secret ballot, women's suffrage, maternity allowances, and sickness and old age pensions.

The Labor Government of Prime Minister Gough Whitlam, elected in 1972, was itself a victim of the twin economic troubles that hit Australia along with most of the rest of the world—inflation and recession. Opposition parties blocked passage of government budget requests to force Whitlam to resign and, in what was called an unconstitutional action, Governor-General Sir John Kerr dissolved both houses of Parliament in November, 1975. Kerr asked Malcolm Fraser, the Liberal Party chief, to form a caretaker government until a new general election in December. Kerr resigned in 1977.

Following a narrow re-election victory in October 1980, Fraser embarked on a program of spending cuts and incentive to private industry. He announced a 10% cut in federal employment and plans to return government bookshops, home loans, and other activities to private industry.

By mid-1982, however, world recession was slowing the resources boom and for the first time in years Australia reported a drop in employment and a record $3.4-billion trade deficit for the year ending June 30.

Australian External Territories

Norfolk Island (14 sq mi.; 36.3 sq km) was placed under Australian administration in 1914. Population in 1981 was 2,175.

The Ashmore and Cartier Islands (.8 sq mi.), situated in the Indian Ocean off the northwest coast of Australia, came under Australian administration in 1934. In 1938 the islands, which are uninhabited, were annexed to the Northern Territory.

The Australian Antarctic Territory (2,360,000 sq mi.; 6,112,400 sq km), comprises all the islands and territories, other than Adélie Land, situated south of lat. 60° S and lying between long. 160° to 45° E. It came under Australian administration in 1936.

Heard Island and the McDonald Islands (158 sq mi.; 409.2 sq km), lying in the sub-Antarctic, were placed under Australian administration in 1947. The islands are uninhabited.

The Cocos (Keeling) Islands (5.5 sq mi.; 14.2 sq. km) consist of 27 small coral islands lying in the Indian Ocean. They came under Australian administration in 1955. Population in 1981 was 555.

Christmas Island (52 sq mi.; 134.7 sq km) is situated in the Indian Ocean. It came under Australian administration in 1958. Population in 1981 was 2,871.

Coral Sea Islands (400,000 sq mi.; 1,036,000 sq km, but only a few sq mi. of land) became a territory of Australia in 1969. There is no permanent population on the islands.

AUSTRIA

Republic of Austria
President: Rudolf Kirchschläger (1974)
Chancellor: Bruno Kreisky (1970)
Area: 32,375 sq mi. (83,851 sq km)
Population (est. 1982): 7,515,000 (average annual growth rate: 0.0%)
Density per square mile: 232.1
Capital: Vienna
Largest cities (est. 1978): Vienna, 1,580,600; (est. 1976 by U.N.): Graz, 250,900; Linz, 208,000; Salzburg, 139,000; Innsbruck, 120,400
Monetary unit: Schilling
Language: German
Religion: Roman Catholic, 88%
Literacy rate (1981): 98%
National name: Republik Österreich
Economic summary: Gross national product (1980): $76.5 billion. Average annual growth rate (1970–79): 3.5%. Per capita income (1980): $10,230. Land used for agriculture: 20%; labor force: 18%; principal products: livestock, forest products, grains, sugar beets, potatoes. Labor force in industry: 49%; principal products: iron and steel, chemicals, machinery, paper and pulp. Natural resources: iron ore, petroleum, timber, magnesite, aluminum, coal, lignite, cement, copper. Exports: iron and steel products, timber, paper, textiles, electrotechnical machines, chemical products. Imports: machinery, chemicals, iron and steel, textiles and clothing, petroleum. Major trading partners: West Germany, Italy, Switzerland, U.K., U.S.

Geography. Slightly smaller than Maine, Austria includes much of the mountainous territory of the eastern Alps (about 75% of the area). The country contains many snowfields, glaciers, and snow-capped peaks, the highest being the Grossglockner (12,530 ft; 3,819 m). The Danube is the principal river. Forests and woodlands cover about 40% of the land area.

Almost at the heart of Europe, Austria has as its neighbors Italy, Switzerland, West Germany, Czechoslovakia, Hungary, Yugoslavia, and Liechtenstein.

Government. Austria is a federal republic composed of nine provinces (Bundesländer), including Vienna. The President is elected by the people for a term of six years. The bicameral legislature consists of the Bundesrat, with 58 members chosen by the provincial assemblies, and the Nationalrat, with 183 members popularly elected for four years. Presidency of the Bundesrat revolves every six months, going to the provinces in alphabetical order.

The major political parties are the Social Democratic Party (95 of 183 seats in Nationalrat), led by Chancellor Bruno Kreisky; People's Party (77 seats); Freiheitliche Partei (11 seats).

History. Settled in prehistoric times, the Central European land that is now Austria was overrun in pre-Roman times by various tribes, including the Celts. Charlemagne conquered the area in 788 and encouraged colonization and Christianity. In 1252, Ottokar, King of Bohemia, gained possession, only to lose the territories to Rudolf of Hapsburg in 1278. Thereafter, until World War I, Austria's history was largely that of its ruling house, the Hapsburgs.

Austria emerged from the Congress of Vienna in 1815 as the Continent's dominant power. The *Ausgleich* of 1867 provided for a dual sovereignty, the empire of Austria and the kingdom of Hungary, under Francis Joseph I, who ruled until his death on Nov. 21, 1916. He was succeeded by his grandnephew, Charles I.

During World War I, Austria-Hungary was one of the Central Powers with Germany, Bulgaria, and Turkey, and the conflict left the country in political chaos and economic ruin. Austria, shorn of Hungary, was proclaimed a republic in 1918, and the monarchy was dissolved in 1919.

A parliamentary democracy was set up by the Constitution of Nov. 10, 1920. To check the power of Nazis advocating union with Germany, Chancellor Engelbert Dollfuss in 1933 established a dictatorship, but was assassinated by the Nazis on July 25, 1934. Kurt von Schuschnigg, his successor, struggled to keep Austria independent, but on March 12, 1938, German troops occupied the country, and Hitler proclaimed its *Anschluss* (union) with Germany, annexing it to the Third Reich.

After World War II, the U.S. and Britain declared the Austrians a "liberated" people. But the Russians prolonged the occupation. Finally Austria concluded a state treaty with the U.S.S.R. and the other occupying powers and regained its independence on May 15, 1955. The second Austrian republic, established Dec. 19, 1945, on the basis of the 1920 Constitution (amended in 1929), was declared by the federal parliament to be permanently neutral. Austria became a member of the Council of Europe in 1956.

Vienna has become a headquarters for international organizations, such as the International Atomic Energy Agency and the Organization of Petroleum Exporting Countries (OPEC). In June

1979, Presidents Jimmy Carter and Leonid Brezhnev met in Vienna to sign the second U.S.-Soviet Strategic Arms Limitation Treaty—SALT II.

BAHAMAS

Commonwealth of the Bahamas
Sovereign: Queen Elizabeth II
Governor-General: Sir Gerald Cash (1979)
Prime Minister: Lynden O. Pindling (1967)
Area: 4,404 sq mi. (11,406 sq km)
Population (est. 1982): 225,000 (average annual growth rate: 2.8%)
Density per square mile: 56.8
Capital and largest city (est. 1981 for metropolitan area): Nassau, 135,500
Monetary unit: Bahamian dollar
Language: English
Religions: Baptist, 29%; Anglican, 23%; Roman Catholic, 23%; Methodist, 7%
Literacy rate: Not known
Member of Commonwealth of Nations
Economic summary: Gross national product (1980): $800 million. Average annual growth rate (1970–79): −4.7%. Per capita income (1980): $3,300. Principal agricultural products: fruits, vegetables. Major industrial products: fish, petroleum, pharmaceutical products; tourism. Natural resources: salt, aragonite, timber. Exports: pharmaceuticals, cement, rum. Imports: foodstuffs, manufactured goods. Major trading partners: U.S., U.K., Canada.

Geography. The Bahamas are an archipelago of about 700 islands and 2,400 uninhabited islets and cays lying 50 miles off the east coast of Florida. They extend from northwest to southeast for about 760 miles (1,223 km). Only 22 of the islands are inhabited; the most important is New Providence (80 sq mi.; 207 sq km), on which Nassau is situated. Other islands include Grand Bahama, Abaco, Eleuthera, Andros, Cat Island, San Salvador (or Watling's Island), Exuma, Long Island, Crooked Island, Acklins Island, Mayaguana, and Inagua.

The islands are mainly flat, few rising above 200 feet (61 m). There are a few streams and one large lake (on Inagua).

Government. The Bahamas moved toward greater autonomy in 1968 after the overwhelming victory in general elections of the Progressive Liberal Party, led by Prime Minister Lynden O. Pindling. The black leader's party won 29 seats in the House of Assembly to only 7 for the predominantly white United Bahamians, who had controlled the islands for decades before Pindling became Prime Minister in 1967.

With its new mandate from the 85%-black population, Pindling's government negotiated a new constitution with Britain under which the colony became the Commonwealth of the Bahama Islands in 1969. On July 10, 1973, The Bahamas became an independent nation as the Commonwealth of the Bahamas.

In the 1982 election, Pindling's Progressive Liberal Party won 32 of 43 seats in Parliament; the Free National Movement, 11.

History. The islands were reached by Columbus in October 1492, and were a favorite pirate area in the early 18th century. The Bahamas were a crown colony from 1717 until they were granted internal self-government in 1964.

BAHRAIN

State of Bahrain
Amir: Sheik Isa bin-Sulman al-Khalifa (1961)
Prime Minister: Khalifa bin Sulman al-Khalifa (1970)
Area: 240 sq mi. (622 sq km)
Population (est. 1982): 375,000 (average annual growth rate: 4.7%)
Density per square mile: 1,562.5
Capital (est. 1980): Manama, 150,000
Monetary unit: Bahrain dinar
Languages: Arabic (official); English
Religion: Islam
Literacy rate (1981): 40%
Economic summary: Gross national product (1980): $2.4 billion. Average annual growth rate (1970–79): 0.7%. Per capita income (1980): $5,560. Land used for agriculture: 5%; labor force: 5%; principal products: eggs, vegetables, fruits. Labor force in industry: 90%; major products: oil, aluminum, fish. Natural resources: oil, fish. Exports: oil, aluminum, fish. Imports: machinery, oil-industry equipment, motor vehicles, foodstuffs. Major trading partners: Saudi Arabia, U.S., U.K., Japan.

Geography. Bahrain is an archipelago in the Persian Gulf off the coast of Saudi Arabia. The islands for the most part are level expanses of sand and rock.

Government. A new Constitution was approved in 1973. It created the first elected parliament in the country's history. Called the National Council, it consisted of 30 members elected by male citizens for four-year terms, plus up to 14 Cabinet ministers as ex-officio members. In August 1975, the Amir dissolved the National Council.

History. A sheikdom that passed from the Persians to the al-Khalifa family from Arabia in 1782, Bahrain became, by treaty, a British protectorate in 1820. It has become a major Middle Eastern oil center and, through use of oil revenues, is one of the most developed of the Persian Gulf sheikdoms. The Amir, Sheik Isa bin-Sulman al-Khalifa, who succeeded to the post in 1961, is a member of the original ruling family. Bahrain announced its independence on Aug. 14, 1971.

BANGLADESH

People's Republic of Bangladesh
President: A. F. N. Ahsanuddin Chowdhury (1982)
Martial Law Administrator: Lieut. Gen. H.M. Ershad (1982)
Area: 55,126 sq mi. (142,776 sq km)
Population (est. 1982): 92,600,000 (average annual growth rate: 2.6%)
Density per square mile: 1,679.8
Capital and largest city (est. 1980): Dacca, 2,500,000
Monetary unit: Taka
Principal languages: Bengali (official), English
Religions: Islam, 85%; Hindu, 13%
Literacy rate (1980): 23%
Member of Commonwealth of Nations
Economic summary: Gross national product (1980): $11.2 billion. Average annual growth rate (1970–79): 0.8%. Per capita income (1980): $120. Land used for agriculture: 66%; labor force, 75%; principal products: rice, jute, tea, sugar, wheat. Labor force in industry, 11%; major products: jute goods, textiles, leather, sugar, fertilizer, paper, pharmaceuticals. Natural resources: natural gas. Exports: jute goods, jute, tea, leather, seafood. Imports: food grains, fuels, raw cotton, yarn, manufactured goods.

Major trading partners: U.S., U.S.S.R., Japan.

Geography. Bangladesh, on the northern coast of the Bay of Bengal, is surrounded by India, with a small common border with Burma in the southeast. It is approximately the size of Wisconsin. The country is low-lying riverine land traversed by the many branches and tributaries of the Ganges and Brahmaputra rivers. Elevation averages less than 600 feet (183 m) above sea level. Tropical monsoons and frequent floods and cyclones inflict heavy damage in the delta region.

Government. On March 24, 1982, Gen. Hossain Mohammed Ershad ousted President Abdus Sattar, ending three years of civilian rule. He suspended the Constitution and declared himself Martial Law Administrator, appointing former Chief Justice A. F. N. Ahsanuddin Chowdhury as ceremonial President. Gen Ershad later announced that military rule would continue for at least two years.

History. Like West Pakistan and India, the former East Pakistan was part of imperial British India until Britain withdrew in 1947. The two Pakistans were united by religion (Islam), but their peoples were separated by culture, physical features, and 1,000 miles of Indian territory. Bangladesh consists primarily of East Bengal (West Bengal is part of India and its people are primarily Hindu) plus the Sylhet district of the Indian state of Assam. For almost 25 years after independence from Britain, its history was as part of Pakistan (*see* Pakistan).

The East Pakistanis unsuccessfully sought greater autonomy from West Pakistan. The first general elections in Pakistani history, in December 1970, saw virtually all 171 seats of the region (out of 300 for both East and West Pakistan) go to Sheik Mujibur Rahman's Awami League, with the rest to other similarly independence-minded minor parties.

Attempts to write an all-Pakistan Constitution to replace the military regime of Gen. Yahya Khan failed. General strikes in East Pakistan followed at Mujibur's direction; he also told his followers to stop paying taxes. Yahya bloodily put down his revolt in March 1971. An estimated one million Bengalis were killed in the fighting or later slaughtered. Ten million more took refuge in India.

In December 1971, India invaded East Pakistan, routed the West Pakistani occupation forces, and created Bangladesh. The U.S. opposed its violent creation, but recognized Bangladesh in April 1972 and provided several hundred million dollars in relief aid.

In February 1974, Pakistan agreed to recognize the independence of Bangladesh. India, Pakistan, and Bangladesh signed an agreement two months later that provided for release of all Pakistani prisoners, improved conditions for the Bihari minority seeking to emigrate from Bangladesh to Pakistan, and negotiations to restore normal communication among the three states.

The charismatic Mujibur had a following of millions and near-dictatorial powers, but he failed to cope with poverty, starvation, sporadic political violence, and widespread government corruption.

Before dawn on Aug. 15, 1975, Mujibur, his wife, and several relatives were assassinated in a coup led by young Army officers. As president, they installed Khondakar Mushtaque Ahmed, a founder of the Awami League who was then Minister of Foreign Trade and Commerce.

A military coup forced Ahmed from power Nov. 6, 1975, and installed former Supreme Court Chief Justice Abu Sadat Mohammed Sayem as president and "chief martial law administrator." On Nov. 30, 1976, Gen Ziaur Rahman, Army Chief of Staff, took over Sayem's powers and blocked the national elections scheduled for early 1977. On April 21, 1977, Ziaur became president following Sayem's resignation. Two years later, Ziaur ended the martial law originally imposed in 1975 and in 1979 permitted parliamentary elections, in which his Bangladesh Nationalist Party won an absolute majority.

On May 30, 1981, Ziaur was killed by a group of army officers in an attempted coup. Vice President Abdus Sattar assumed power and was elected President Nov. 15. On March 24, 1982, Gen. Hossain Mohammad Ershad, army chief of staff, took control in a bloodless coup, arresting more than 200 officials he said were guilty of corruption.

BARBADOS

Sovereign: Queen Elizabeth II
Governor-General: Sir Deighton L. Ward (1976)
Prime Minister: J. M. G. Adams (1976)
Area: 166 sq mi. (431 sq km)
Population (est. 1982): 275,000 (average annual growth rate: 0.5%)
Density per square mile: 1,656.6
Capital and largest city (est. 1980): Bridgetown, 8,000
Monetary unit: Barbados dollar
Language: English
Religions: Anglican, 53%; Methodist, 9%; Roman Catholic, 4%
Literacy rate (1981): 90%
Member of Commonwealth of Nations
Economic summary: Gross national product (1980): $760 million. Average annual growth rate (1970–79): 2.1%. Per capita income (1980): $3,040. Land used for agriculture: 60%; principal products: sugar cane, subsistence foods. Major industrial products: light manufactures, sugar milling, tourism. Exports: sugar and sugar cane byproducts, clothing. Imports: foodstuffs, machinery, manufactured goods. Major trading partners: U.S., Caribbean nations, U.K., Canada.

Geography. An island in the Atlantic about 30 miles (483 km) north of Venezuela, Barbados is onl 21 miles long (34 km) and 14 miles across (23 km at its widest point. It is circled by fine beaches an narrow coastal plains. The highest point is Moun Hillaby (1,105 ft; 337 m) in the north central area

Government. The Barbados legislature dates fron 1627. It is bicameral, with a Senate of 21 appointe members and an Assembly of 27 elected members

The major political parties are the Barbado Labor Party (17 seats in Assembly), led by Prim Minister J. M. G. Adams; Democratic Labor Part (10 seats), led by Errol Barrow.

History. Barbados, with a population 90% blac was settled by the British in 1627. It became crown colony in 1885. It was a member of the Fec eration of the West Indies from 1958 to 1962. Bri ain granted the colony independence on Nov. 3 1966, and it became a parliamentary democracy

While retaining membership in the Commo wealth of Nations and economic ties with Britai Barbados seeks broader economic and political r lations with Western Hemisphere countries. Dipl matic ties with Cuba were established in 1972.

BELGIUM

Kingdom of Belgium
Sovereign: King Baudouin I (1951)
Premier: Wilfried Martens (1981)
Area: 11,781 sq mi. (30,513 sq km)
Population (est. 1982): 9,870,000 (average annual growth rate: 0.1%)
Density per square mile: 837.8
Capital: Brussels
Largest cities (est. 1981): Brussels, 1,000,000; **(est. 1979):** Ghent, 243,500; Liège, 224,000; Charleroi, 224,000; Antwerp, 197,000
Monetary unit: Belgian franc
Languages: Dutch, 56%; French, 32%; bilingual (Brussels), 11%
Religion: Roman Catholic, 97%
National name: Royaume de Belgique—Koninkrijk van België
Literacy rate (1981): 97%
Economic summary: Gross national product (1980): $119.8 billion. Average annual growth rate (1970–79): 2.9%. Per capita income (1980): $12,180. Land used for agriculture: 28%; labor force: 3.2%; principal products: livestock, poultry, grain, sugar beets, flax, tobacco, potatoes, vegetables, fruits. Labor force in industry: 35%; major products: fabricated metal, iron and steel, coal, textiles, chemicals. Exports: iron and steel products, precious stones, textile products. Imports: nonelectrical machinery, motor vehicles, textiles, chemicals, fuels. Major trading partners: West Germany, France, Netherlands, U.K., U.S., Italy.

Geography. A neighbor of France, West Germany, the Netherlands, and Luxembourg, Belgium has about 40 miles of seacoast on the North Sea at the Strait of Dover. In area, it is approximately the size of Maryland. The northern third of the country is a plain extending eastward from the seacoast. North of the Sambre and Meuse Rivers is a low plateau; to the south lies the heavily wooded Ardennes plateau, attaining an elevation of about 2,300 feet (700 m).

The Schelde River, which rises in France and flows through Belgium, emptying into the Schelde estuaries, enables Antwerp to be an ocean port.

Government. Belgium, a parliamentary democracy under a constitutional monarch, consists of nine provinces. Its bicameral legislature has a Senate, with its 181 members elected for four years—106 by general election, 50 by provincial councillors and 25 by the Senate itself. The 212-member Chamber of Representatives is directly elected for four years by proportional representation. There is universal suffrage, and those who do not vote are fined.

Belgium joined the North Atlantic Alliance in 1949 and is a member of the European Community. NATO and the European Community have their headquarters in Brussels.

The sovereign, Baudouin I, was born Sept. 7, 1930, the son of King Leopold III and Queen Astrid. He became King on July 17, 1951, after the abdication of his father. He married Doña Fabiola de Mora y Aragón on Dec. 15, 1960. Since he has no children, his brother, Prince Albert, is heir to the throne.

The major political parties are the Flemish-Speaking Social Christian Party (22 Senators, 43 Representatives); French-Speaking Social Christian Party (8 Senators, 18 Representatives); Flemish-Speaking Socialist Party (22 Senators, 26 Representatives); French-Speaking Socialist Party (18 Senators, 35 Representatives); Flemish-Speaking Liberal Party (4 Senators, 28 Representatives); Flemish People's Party (10 Senators, 20 Representatives); French-Speaking Liberal Party (11 Senators, 24 Representatives.)

History. Belgium occupies part of the Roman province of Belgica, named after the Belgae, a people of ancient Gaul. The area was conquered by Julius Caesar in 57–50 B.C., then was overrun by the Franks in the 5th century. It was part of Charlemagne's empire in the 8th century, then in the next century was absorbed into Lotharingia and later into the Duchy of Lower Lorraine. In the 12th century it was partitioned into the Duchies of Brabant and Luxembourg, the Bishopric of Liège, and the domain of the Count of Hainaut, which included Flanders.

The rise of the wool industry brought prosperity and power to the country, particularly to the semi-independent cities—Ghent, Bruges, and Ypres. In the 16th century, Belgium, with most of the area of the Low Countries, passed to the Duchy of Burgundy and was the marriage portion of Archduke Maximilian of Hapsburg and the inheritance of his grandson, Charles V, who incorporated it into his empire. Then, in 1555, they were united with Spain.

By the treaty of Utrecht in 1713, the country's sovereignty passed to Austria. During the wars that followed the French Revolution, Belgium was occupied and later annexed to France. But with the downfall of Napoleon, the Congress of Vienna in 1815 gave the country to the Netherlands. The Belgians revolted in 1830 and declared their independence.

Germany's invasion of Belgium in 1914 set off World War I. The Treaty of Versailles (1919) gave the areas of Eupen, Malmédy, and Moresnet to Belgium. Leopold III succeeded Albert, King during World War I, in 1934. In World War II, Belgium was overwhelmed by Nazi Germany, and Leopold III was made prisoner. When he attempted to return in 1950, Socialists and Liberals revolted. He abdicated July 16, 1951, and his son, Baudouin, became King the next day.

The country has long been torn by language disputes between the Dutch-speaking Flemish people and the French-speaking Walloons. In 1972, a major clash occurred over transferring six small hamlets from Flemish to Walloon administrative jurisdiction. When a balancing change was not implemented, the government fell. A new one under Edmond Leburton was formed; this, in turn, was replaced in 1974 by one under Léo Tindemans of the Flemish Social Christian party.

A financial crisis, building for more than a year, brought down the government on March 31, 1981, when Socialists in the majority coalition opposed the suspension of the automatic linkage of wage increases to rising prices. Premier Wilfried Martens proposed that after the suspension, wage increases should be given in fixed amounts, eliminating the indexing system which Belgium pioneered. Mark Eyskens, taking office on April 6, retained Socialist support by instituting a temporary price freeze, thus blocking wage hikes without dismantling the wage-price linkage.

Eyskens' government fell on Sept. 21 in a dispute over the management of the state-controlled Cockerill-Sambre steel company, with French-speaking Socialists in his coalition insisting on maintenance of employment, despite heavy losses. Liberal gains and Socialist losses in the ensuing elections brought a new Christian Democratic-Liberal coalition headed by former Premier Wilfried Martens to office on Dec. 17. Faced with unemployment above 10%, Martens won Parliamentary approval of special powers permitting him to deal with the economic crisis with tax cuts and other special measures.

BELIZE

Sovereign: Queen Elizabeth II
Governor-General: Minita Gordon (1981)
Prime Minister: George C. Price (1981)
Area: 8,867 sq mi. (22,965 sq km)
Population (est. 1982): 175,000 (average annual growth rate: 1.8%)
Density per sq mi.: 19.7
Capital (est. 1980): Belmopan, 4,500
Largest city (est. 1980): Belize City, 40,000
Monetary unit: Belize dollar
Languages: English (official) and Spanish
Religions: 50% Roman Catholic; Anglican, and other Protestant sects
Literacy rate (1981): 80%
Member of Commonwealth of Nations
Economic summary: Gross national product (1980): $160 million. Average annual growth rate (1970–79): 2.1%. Per capita income (1980): $1,080. Land used for agriculture: 35%; labor force: 39%; principal products: sugar cane, citrus fruits, corn, molasses, rice, bananas, livestock. Labor force in industry: 20%; major products: timber, processed foods, furniture, rum, soap. Natural resource: timber. Exports: sugar, molasses, clothing, lumber, citrus fruits, fish. Imports: fuels, transportation equipment, foodstuffs, textiles, machinery. Major trading partners: U.S., U.K., Trinidad and Tobago.

Geography: Belize (formerly British Honduras) is situated on the Caribbean Sea south of Mexico and east and north of Guatemala. In area, it is about the size of New Hampshire. Most of the country is heavily forested with mahogany, cedar, and logwood. Mangrove swamps and cays along the coast give way to hills and mountains in the interior. The highest point is Victoria Peak, 3,681 feet (11,220 m).

Government. Formerly the colony of British Honduras, Belize became a fully independent commonwealth on Sept. 21, 1981, after having been self-governing since 1964. Executive power is nominally wielded by Queen Elizabeth II through an appointed Governor-General but effective power is held by the Prime Minister, who is responsible to an 18-member parliament elected by universal suffrage. The major parties are the People's United Party (13 of 18 seats), led by Prime Minister George Price, and the United Democratic Party (5 seats), led by Dean Russell Lindo.

History. Once a part of the Mayan empire, the area was deserted until British timber cutters began exploiting valuable hardwoods in the 17th century. Efforts by Spain to dislodge British settlers, including a major naval attack in 1798, were defeated. The territory was formally named a British colony in 1862 but administered by the Governor of Jamaica until 1884.

Guatemala has long made claims to the territory and refused to recognize Britain's efforts to grant independence to Belize. Fear of Guatemala caused many inhabitants to oppose independence until a tentative agreement was reached between Britain, Belize, and Guatemala in March 1981 that would offer access to the Caribbean through Belizean territory for Guatemala. The agreement broke down, however, and 1,600 British troops remained to protect the new state after the flag-raising ceremony on Sept. 21, 1981.

BENIN

People's Republic of Benin
President: Col. Mathieu Kerekou (1972)
Area: 43,483 sq mi. (112,622 sq km)
Population (est. 1982): 3,725,000 (average annual growth rate: 2.6%)
Density per square mile: 85.7
Capital: Porto-Novo, 125,000 (est. 1980).
Largest city (est. 1980): Cotonou, 225,000
Monetary unit: Franc CFA
Ethnic groups: Fons and Adjas, Baribas, Yorubas, Mahis
Languages: French, African languages
Religions: Animist, Christian, Islam
National name: République Populaire du Benin
Literacy rate (1981): 20%
Economic summary: Gross national product (1980): $1.1 billion. Average annual growth rate (1970–79): 0.6%. Per capita income (1980): $300. Labor force in agriculture: 70%; principal products: oil palms, peanuts, cotton, coffee, tobacco, corn, rice, livestock, fish. Major industrial products: processed palm oil, palm kernel oil. Natural resources: low-grade iron ore, limestone, some offshore oil. Exports: palm and agricultural products. Imports: clothing, consumer goods, lumber, fuels, foodstuffs, machinery, transportation equipment. Major trading partners: France and other Western European countries.

Geography. This West African nation on the Gulf of Guinea, between Togo on the west and Nigeria on the east, is about the size of Tennessee. It is bounded also by Upper Volta and Niger on the north. The land consists of a narrow coastal strip that rises to a swampy, forested plateau and then to highlands in the north. A hot and humid climate blankets the entire country.

Government. The change in name from Dahomey to Benin was announced by President Mathieu Kerekou in November 1975. Benin commemorates an African kingdom that flourished in the 17th century. At the same time, Kerekou announced the formation of a political organization, the Party of the People's Revolution of Benin, to mark the first anniversary of his declaration of a "new society" guided by Marxist-Leninist principles.

History. One of the smallest and most densely populated states in Africa, Benin was annexed by the French in 1893. The area was incorporated into French West Africa in 1904. It became an autonomous republic within the French Community in 1958, and on Aug. 1, 1960, was granted its independence within the Community.

Gen. Christophe Soglo deposed the first president, Hubert Maga, in an army coup in 1963. He dismissed the civilian government in 1965, proclaiming himself chief of state. A group of young army officers seized power in December 1967, deposing Soglo. They promulgated a new Constitution in 1968.

In December 1969, Benin had its fifth coup of the decade, with the army again taking power. In May 1970, a three-man presidential commission was created to take over the government. The commission had a six-year term; each member serves as president for two years. Maga turned over power as scheduled to Justin Ahomadegbe in May 1972, but six months later yet another army coup ousted the triumvirate and installed Lt. Col. Mathieu Kerekou as President.

BHUTAN

Kingdom of Bhutan
Ruler: King Jigme Singye Wangchuk (1972)
Area: 18,000 sq mi. (46,620 sq km)
Population (est. 1982): 1,350,000 (average annual growth rate: 2.3%)
Density per square mile: 75.0
Capital (est. 1980): Thimphu, 10,000
Monetary unit: Ngultrum
Language: Dzongkha
Religions: Buddhist, 75%; Hindu, 25%
National name: Druk-yul
Literacy rate: Insignificant
Economic summary: Gross national product (1980): $110 million. Average annual growth rate (1970–79): –0.1%. Per capita income (1980): $80. Labor force in agriculture: 99%; principal products: rice, barley, wheat, potatoes, fruit. Major industrial product: handicrafts. Natural resources: timber, hydroelectric power. Exports: fruits and vegetables, timber, coal. Imports: textiles, cereals, vehicles. Major trading partner: India.

Geography. Mountainous Bhutan, half the size of Indiana, is situated on the southeast slope of the Himalayas, bordered on the north and east by Tibet and on the south and west by India. The landscape consists of a succession of lofty and rugged mountains running generally from north to south and separated by deep valleys. In the north, towering peaks reach a height of 24,000 feet (7,315 m).

Government. Bhutan is a constitutional monarchy. The King rules with a Council of Ministers and a nine-member Advisory Council, of whom five are elected by the people; two represent the monastic order and two are named by the King. There is a National Assembly (Parliament), which meets semiannually, but no political parties.

History. After almost a century of conflict, British troops invaded the country in 1865 and negotiated an agreement under which Britain undertook to pay an annual allowance to Bhutan on condition of good behavior. A treaty with India in 1949 increased this subsidy and placed Bhutan's foreign affairs under Indian control.

In the 1960s, Bhutan undertook modernization, abolishing slavery and the caste system, emancipating women, breaking up estates, and limiting farms to 30 acres.

BOLIVIA

Republic of Bolivia
President: Hernán Siles Zuazo (1982)
Area: 424,162 sq mi. (1,098,581 sq km)
Population (est. 1982): 5,900,000 (average annual growth rate, 2.6%) (Indian, 53%; mestizo, 32%; white, 15%)
Density per square mile: 13.9
Judicial capital (est. 1979): Sucre, 90,000
Administrative capital (est. 1980): La Paz, 700,000
Largest cities (est. 1976 by U.N.): Santa Cruz, 237,100; Cochabamba, 194,150; Oruro, 124,100
Monetary unit: Peso boliviano
Languages: Spanish, Quechua, Aymara
Religion: Roman Catholic, 94%
National name: República de Bolivia
Literacy rate (1981): 40%
Economic summary: Gross national product (1980): $3.2 billion. Average annual growth rate (1970–79): 2.3%. Per capita income (1980): $570. Labor force in agriculture: 70%; principal products: potatoes, corn, rice, sugar cane, bananas. Labor force in industry: 10%; major products: refined petroleum, processed foods, tin, textiles, clothing. Natural resources: petroleum, natural gas, tin, lead, zinc, copper, tungsten, bismuth, antimony, gold, sulfur, silver, iron ore. Exports: tin, petroleum, lead, zinc, silver, antimony, gold, coffee, sugar, cotton, natural gas. Imports: foodstuffs, chemicals, capital goods, pharmaceuticals, transport equipment. Major trading partners: Western European and Latin American countries, U.S., Japan.

Geography. Landlocked Bolivia, equal in size to California and Texas combined, lies to the west of Brazil. Its other neighbors are Peru and Chile on the west and Argentina and Paraguay on the south.

The country is a low alluvial plain throughout 60% of its area toward the east, drained by the Amazon and Plata river systems. The western part, enclosed by two chains of the Andes, is a great plateau—the Altiplano, with an average altitude of 12,000 feet (3,658 m). More than 80% of the population lives on the plateau, which also contains La Paz. At an altitude of 11,910 feet (3,630 m), it is the highest capital city in the world.

Lake Titicaca, half the size of Lake Ontario, is one of the highest large lakes in the world, at an altitude of 12,507 feet (3,812 m). Islands in the lake hold ruins of the ancient Incas.

Government. Faltering steps toward the restoration of civilian government were abruptly halted on July 17, 1980, when Gen. Luis García Meza Tejada seized power in the 189th coup in Bolivia's 155 years of independence. He chose a 15-member cabinet—only two civilians among them—to replace the interim administration of Bolivia's first woman President, Lydia Gueiler Tejada.

History. Famous since Spanish colonial days for its mineral wealth, modern Bolivia was once a part of the ancient Incan Empire. After the Spaniards defeated the Incas in the 16th century, Bolivia's predominantly Indian population was reduced to slavery. The country won its independence in 1825 and was named after Simón Bolívar, the famed liberator.

Since 1825 Bolivia has had more than 60 revolutions, 70 Presidents, and 11 Constitutions.

Harassed by internal strife, Bolivia lost great slices of territory to three neighbor nations. Several thousand square miles and its outlet to the Pacific were taken by Chile after the War of the Pacific (1879–84). In 1903 a piece of Bolivia's Acre province, rich in rubber, was ceded to Brazil. And in 1938, after a war with Paraguay, Bolivia gave up claim to nearly 100,000 square miles of the Gran Chaco.

Great prosperity came with World War II and its demand for two important Bolivian products, tin and wolframite. But rising prices provoked strikes that were ruthlessly broken and promoted growth of the leftist National Revolutionary Movement. The movement seized power in 1943 but was ousted by a moderate government in 1947.

In 1965 a guerrilla movement mounted from Cuba and headed by Maj. Ernesto (Ché) Guevara began a revolutionary war. With the aid of U.S. military advisers, the Bolivian army, helped by the peasants, smashed the guerrilla movement, wounding and capturing Guevara on Oct. 8, 1967, and shooting him to death the next day.

Bolivia's first elections in 11 years were authorized in July 1977 by Col. Hugo Banzer Suarez, who had seized the presidency seven years before. Gen. Juan Pereda Asbun, his claimed victory disputed as fraudulent, declared himself the winner with the backing of the armed forces. In August 1978, the U.S. suspended military aid to Bolivia (the combined economic and military-aid program of $56.1 million for fiscal 1979 was the largest in Latin America) as a protest against Pereda's coup. Although he had ruled out elections before 1980, Pereda yielded to external and internal pressure and permitted presidential and congressional elections on July 1, 1979.

Former President Hernan Siles Suazo led in the voting but failed to win a majority, and the Congress chose Walter Guevara Arze as provisional President pending new elections. But in November 1979, Col. Alberto Natusch staged a coup that lasted only 16 days. An interm civilian regime, led by Lydia Gueiler Tejada, was installed.

Gen. Luis Garcia Meza seized power on July 17, 1980, and launched a bloody dictatorship which U.S. Senator Dennis DeConcini, Arizona Democrat, asserted was deeply involved in cocaine traffic. The United States cut off military aid to Bolivia in 1980, conditioning its restoration on a return to civilian rule.

Garcia Meza was forced to resign Aug. 4, 1981, by an army revolt that installed a junta headed by Maj. Gen. Celso Torrelio Villa. Torrelio resigned July 15, 1982, under pressure from the military for his failure to solve Bolivia's economic problems. His successor, Gen. Guido Vildoso Calderón, the 10th president in four years, was forced to resign by the military on Sept. 17 after 58 days in office. His departure cleared the way for a return to civilian government.

BOPHUTHATSWANA

See South Africa

BOTSWANA

Republic of Botswana
President: Quett Masire (1980)
Area: 222,000 sq mi. (576,000 sq km)
Population (est. 1982): 900,000 (average annual growth rate: 4.6%)
Density per square mile: 4.5
Capital and largest city (est. 1981): Gaborone, 60,000
Monetary unit: Pula
Languages: English, Setswana
Religions: Christian, 60%; Animist
Member of Commonwealth of Nations
Literacy rate (1981): 54%
Economic summary: Gross national product (1980): $730 million. Average annual growth rate (1970–79): 12.0%. Per capita income (1980): $910. Land used for agriculture: 1%; principal products: livestock, sorghum, corn, millet, cowpeas, beans. Major industrial products: diamonds, copper, nickel, salt, soda ash, potash, coal, frozen beef; tourism. Natural resources: diamonds, copper, nickel, salt, soda ash, potash, coal. Exports: diamonds, cattle, animal products, copper, nickel. Imports: foodstuffs, vehicles, textiles, petroleum products. Major trading partners: South Africa, U.K.

Geography. Twice the size of Arizona, Botswana is in south central Africa, bounded by South-West Africa, Zambia, Zimbabwe, and South Africa. Most of the country is near-desert, with the Kalahari occupying the western part of the country. The eastern part is hilly, with salt lakes in the north.

Government. The Botswana Constitution provides, in addition to the unicameral National Assembly, for a House of Chiefs, which has a voice on bills affecting tribal affairs. There is universal suffrage.

The major political parties are the Democratic Party (29 of 32 elective seats in 36-man Legislative Assembly), led by President Quett Masire; National Front (2 seats), led by Kenneth Koma; People's Party (1 seat), led by Kenneth Nkhwa.

History. Botswana is the land of the Batawana tribes, which, when threatened by the Boers in Transvaal, asked Britain in 1885 to establish a protectorate over the country, then known as Bechuanaland. In 1961, Britain granted a Constitution to the country. Self-government began in 1965, and on Sept. 30, 1966, the country became independent. Since 1975, it has been an associate member of the European Common Market.

BRAZIL

Federative Republic of Brazil
President: Gen. João Baptista de Oliveira Figueiredo (1979)
Area: 3,286,470 sq mi. (8,511,957 sq km)
Population (est. 1982): 124,500,000 (average annual growth rate, 2.3%) (approx.: white, 60%; mestizo, 26%; black, 11%)
Density per square mile: 37.9
Capital (1980 census): Brasilia, 1,202,683
Largest cities (1980 census): São Paulo, 8,584,896; Rio de Janeiro, 5,184,292; Belo Horizonte, 1,814,990; Recife, 1,240,897; Porto Alegre, 1,158,709; Salvador, 1,525,831
Monetary unit: Cruzeiro
Language: Portuguese
Religion: Roman Catholic, 91%
National name: Brasil
Literacy rate (1981): 45%
Economic summary: Gross national product (1980): $243.2 billion. Average annual growth rate (1970–79): 6.1%. Per capita income (1980): $2,050. Land used for agriculture: 4%; labor force: 36%; principal products: coffee, rice, beef, corn, milk, sugar cane, soybeans, cocoa. Labor force in industry: 23%; major products: steel, chemicals, petrochemicals, machinery, motor vehicles, cement, lumber. Natural resources: iron ore, manganese, bauxite, nickel, other industrial metals. Exports: coffee, iron ore, soybeans, sugar, wood, beef, cocoa beans, footwear. Imports: wheat, copper, aluminum, petroleum, machinery chemicals, pharmaceuticals. Major trading partners: U.S.

West Germany, Argentina, Japan.

Geography. Brazil covers nearly half of South America, extends 2,965 miles (4,772 km) north-south, 2,691 miles (4,331 km), east-west, and borders every nation on the continent except Chile and Ecuador. It is the fifth largest country in the world, ranking after the U.S.S.R., Canada, China, and the U.S.

More than a third of Brazil is drained by the Amazon and its more than 200 tributaries. The Amazon is navigable for ocean steamers to Iquitos, Peru, 2,300 miles (3,700 km) upstream. Southern Brazil is drained by the Plata system—the Paraguay, Uruguay, and Paraná Rivers. The most important stream entirely within Brazil is the Sao Francisco, navigable for 1,000 miles (1,903 km), but broken near its mouth by the 275-foot (84 m) Paulo Afonso Falls.

Government. Under the Constitution, Brazil is a union of 22 states, 4 territories, and 1 federal district. The President is elected for a six-year term by an electoral college made up of members of the National Congress. The National Congress is composed of two houses—the Senate, whose members serve eight-year terms, and the Chamber of Deputies, elected for four-year terms. Members of Congress are elected by equal, direct, compulsory, and secret suffrage under proportional representation.

The military took control in 1964, ousting the last elected civilian President and installing a series of military men (with the Congress ratifying the junta's choice).

The major political parties are the Partido Democrático Social, led by Senator José Sarney (the pro-government party formerly called ARENA, for Aliança Renovadora Nacional); Partido do Movimento Democrático Brasileiro, led by Representative Ulysses Guimarães; Partido Popular, led by Senator Tancredo Neves; Partido Trabalhista Brasileiro, led by Yvette Vargas; Partido Democrático Trabalhista, led by Leonel Brizolla; and Partido dos Trabalhadores, led by Luiz Inacio Silva.

History. Brazil is the only Latin American nation deriving its language and culture from Portugal. Adm. Pedro Alvares Cabral claimed the territory for the Portuguese in 1500. He brought to Portugal a cargo of wood, pau-brasil, from which the land received its name. Portugal began colonization in 1532 and made the area a royal colony in 1549.

During the Napoleonic wars, King João VI, then Prince Regent, fled the country in 1807 in advance of the French armies and in 1808 set up his court in Rio de Janeiro. João was drawn home in 1820 by a revolution, leaving his son as Regent. When Portugal sought to reduce Brazil again to colonial status, the prince declared Brazil's independence on Sept. 7, 1822, and became Pedro I, Emperor of Brazil.

Harassed by his parliament, Pedro I abdicated in 1831 in favor of his five-year-old son, who became Emperor in 1840 as Pedro II. The son was a popular monarch, but discontent built up and, in 1889, following a military revolt, he had to abdicate. Although a republic was proclaimed, Brazil was under two military dictatorships during the next four years. A revolt permitted a gradual return to stability under civilian Presidents.

The President during World War I, Wenceslau Braz, cooperated with the Allies and declared war on Germany. The President from 1926 to 1930, Washington Luiz Pereira da Souza, was overthrown by a revolutionary group under Getulio Vargas, who took over as provisional President.

Vargas' 1934 Constitution curtailed states' rights and established a nationalistic policy. In 1937, Vargas seized absolute power and adopted another Constitution, extending his term indefinitely. In World War II, Brazil cooperated with the Western Allies, welcoming Allied air bases, patrolling the South Atlantic, and joining the invasion of Italy after declaring war on the Axis.

Vargas was overthrown on Oct. 29, 1945. Succeeding presidents were Gen. Eurico Gaspar Dutra (1945–50); Getulio Vargas (1950–54); João Cafe Filho (1954–55); Juscelino Kubitschek de Oliveira (1955–60); Janio Quadros (1960); João Goulart (1960–63); Gen. Humberto de Alencar Castelo Branco (1963–66); Gen. Arthur Costa e Silva (1966–69); Gen. Emilio Garrastazu Médici (1970–74).

In 1974, Gen. Ernesto Geisel was elected President. The election was the freest in a decade and the least violent in many years. Press censorship was relaxed under a policy of "decompression."

Relations with the U.S. remained cool following Geisel's 1977 repudiation of a mutual defense pact after a U.S. State Department report cited the military regime's repression of human rights, and Brazil emphasized that President Carter was coming on his own request when he visited Brazil in March. The U.S. also opposed Brazil's purchase of German nuclear equipment capable of reprocessing spent nuclear fuel into weapons-grade plutonium.

National elections on Nov. 15, 1978, saw the ruling ARENA party lose its majority by a slight margin in popular voting but it retained control of both houses of Congress by a narrow edge. In the 1979 presidential election, Geisel's hand-picked candidate, Gen. João Baptista de Oliveira Figueiredo, was elected.

Figueiredo pledged a return to democracy and granted amnesty to 5,000 political exiles, but he aroused international protest when his government sentenced Luiz da Silva, leader of a strike that shut down automobile production in 1980, to a three-and-a-half-year term in 1981. Da Silva was freed in March 1982, however, and was the leader of one of six parties that were to be permitted to contest national, state, and local elections in November in fulfillment of Figueiredo's pledge.

Economically, Brazil succeeded in slowing its perennial inflation rate from 95% in 1981 to a hoped-for 75% at the beginning of 1982, the result of severe governmental restrictions. But by mid-1982, the annual inflation rate was up to 99.5%, with the prospect of a $3-billion trade surplus cut in half, and more borrowing expected to add to Brazil's $65-billion foreign debt.

BULGARIA

People's Republic of Bulgaria
Chairman of the State Council: Todor Zhivkov (1971)
Prime Minister (Chairman of Council of Ministers): Grisha Filipov (1981)
Area: 42,823 sq mi. (110,912 sq km)
Population (est. 1982): 8,925,000 (average annual growth rate: 0.4%)
Density per square mile: 208.4
Capital: Sofia
Largest cities (est. 1979): Sofia, 1,000,000; **(est. 1978 by U.N.):** Plovdiv, 328,000; Varna, 275,000; Ruse, 168,000; Burgas, 162,000; Stara Zagora, 129,000

Monetary unit: Lev
Language: Bulgarian
Religions: Orthodox, 85%; Islam, 13%
National name: Narodna Republika Bulgariya
Literacy rate (1981): 95%
Economic summary: Gross national product (1980): $37.4 billion. Average annual growth rate (1970–79): 5.6%. Per capita income (1980): $4,150. Labor force in agriculture: 23%; principal products: grains, tobacco, fruits, vegetables. Labor force in industry: 35%; major products: processed agricultural products, machinery, textiles, clothing. Natural resources: metals, minerals, lumber. Exports: machinery and transport equipment, fuels, minerals, raw materials, agricultural products. Imports: machinery and transportation equipment, fuels, raw materials, metals, agricultural raw materials. Major trading partners: U.S.S.R., Soviet bloc countries.

Geography. Two mountain ranges and two great valleys mark the topography of Bulgaria, a country the size of Tennessee. Situated on the Black Sea in the eastern part of the Balkan peninsula, it shares borders with Yugoslavia, Romania, Greece, and Turkey. The Balkan belt crosses the center of the country, almost due east-west, rising to a height of 7,800 feet (2,377 m). The Rhodope range breaks off from the Balkans in the west, curves, and then straightens out to run nearly parallel along the southern border. Between the two ranges, is the valley of the Maritsa, Bulgaria's principal river. Between the Balkan range and the Danube, which forms most of the northern boundary with Romania, is the Danubian tableland.

Southern Dobruja, a fertile region of 2,900 square miles (7,511 sq km), below the Danube delta, is an area of low hills, fens, and sandy steppes.

Government. The present Constitution has been in effect since May 18, 1971. The National Assembly, consisting of 400 members elected for five-year terms, is the governing body. It elects the State Council and the Council of Ministers.

The Communist Party is led by the chairman of the State Council, Todor Zhivkov.

History. The first Bulgarians, a tribe of wild horsemen akin to the Huns, crossed the Danube from the north in A.D. 679 and subjugated the Slavic population of Moesia. They adopted a Slav dialect and Slavic customs and twice conquered most of the Balkan peninsula between 893 and 1280. After the Serbs subjected their kingdom in 1330, the Bulgars gradually fell prey to the Turks, and from 1396 to 1878 Bulgaria was a Turkish province. In 1878, Russia forced Turkey to give the country its independence; but the European powers, fearing that Bulgaria might become a Russian dependency, intervened. By the Treaty of Berlin in 1878, Bulgaria became autonomous under Turkish sovereignty.

In 1887, Prince Ferdinand of Saxe-Coburg-Gotha was elected ruler of Bulgaria; on Oct. 5, 1908, he declared the country independent and took the title of Tsar.

Bulgaria joined Germany in World War I and lost. On Oct. 3, 1918, Tsar Ferdinand abdicated in favor of his son, Tsar Boris III. Boris assumed dictatorial powers in 1934–35. When Hitler awarded Bulgaria southern Dobruja, taken from Romania in 1940, the weak but land-hungry Boris joined the Nazis in war the next year and occupied parts of Yugoslavia and Greece. Later the Germans tried to force Boris to send his troops against the Russians. Boris resisted and died under mysterious circumstances on Aug. 28, 1943.

Simeon II, infant son of Boris, became nominal ruler under a regency. Russia declared war on Bulgaria on Sept. 5, 1944. An armistice was agreed to three days later, after Bulgaria had declared war on Germany. Russian troops streamed in the next day, and under an informal armistice a coalition "Fatherland Front" Cabinet was set up under Kimon Georgiev.

A peace treaty negotiated in 1947 permitted Bulgaria to keep southern Dobruja. A Constitution was adopted in 1947 establishing a Soviet-type people's republic.

BURMA

Socialist Republic of the Union of Burma
President: San Yu (1981)
Prime Minister: U Maung Maung Kha (1977)
Area: 261,789 sq mi. (678,036 sq km)
Population (est. 1982): 37,500,000 (average annual growth rate: 2.5%)
Density per square mile: 143.2
Capital: Rangoon
Largest cities (est. 1980): Rangoon, 2,200,000 (est. 1977 for metropolitan area by U.N.): Mandalay, 458,000; Moulmein, 188,000; Bassein, 138,000; Pegu, 135,000
Monetary unit: Kyat
Language: Burmese
Religions: Buddhist, 80%; Christian, Islam, Hindu
National name: Pyidaungsu Socialist Thammada Myanma Naingngandau
Literacy rate (1981): 70%
Economic summary: Gross national product (1980): $5.9 billion. Average annual growth rate (1970–79): 2.0%. Per capita income (1980): $180. Labor force in agriculture: 67%; principal products: sugar cane, corn, rice, peanuts. Labor force in industry: 9%; major products: textiles, footwear, processed agricultural products, wood and wood products, refined petroleum. Natural resources: timber, nickel, cobalt, copper, gold, rubies, sapphires, jade. Exports: rice, teak. Imports: machinery and transportation equipment, textiles, manufactured goods. Major trading partners: Singapore, Western European countries, China, U.K., Japan.

Geography. Burma occupies the northwest portion of the Indochinese peninsula. India lies to the northwest and China to the northeast. Bangladesh, Laos, and Thailand are also neighbors. The Bay of Bengal touches the southwestern coast.

Slightly smaller than Texas, the country is divided into three natural regions: the Arakan Yoma, a long, narrow mountain range forming the barrier between Burma and India; the Shan Plateau in the east, extending southward into Tenasserim; and the Central Basin, running down to the flat fertile delta of the Irrawaddy in the south. This delta contains a network of intercommunicating canals and nine principal river mouths.

Government. On March 2, 1962, the government of U Nu was overthrown and replaced by a Revolutionary Council, which assumed all power in the state. Gen. U Ne Win, as chairman of the Revolutionary Council, became the chief executive.

A new Constitution was approved in 1973 and took effect Jan. 4, 1974. Under it, Burma is a Socialist Democratic Republic with a 475-seat unicameral legislature called the People's Congress. In 1972, Ne Win and his colleagues resigned their military titles and thereafter ruled as "civilians." In 1974, Ne Win dissolved the Revolutionary Council and became President under the new Constitution. He voluntarily relinquished the presidency on Nov. 9, 1981, but retained leadership of the Burmese Socialist Program Party, the only legal party. San Yu was elected President by the People's Congress.

History. In 1612, the British East India Company sent agents to Burma, but the Burmese long resisted efforts of British traders, and Dutch and Portuguese as well, to establish posts on the Bay of Bengal. By the Anglo-Burmese War in 1824–26 and two following wars, the British East India Company expanded to the whole of Burma by 1886. Burma was annexed to India. It became a separate colony in 1937.

During World War II, Burma was a key battleground; the 800-mile Burma Road was the Allies' vital supply line to China. The Japanese invaded the country in December 1941, and by May 1942 had occupied most of it, cutting the Burma Road. After one of the most difficult campaigns of the war, Allied forces liberated most of Burma prior to the Japanese surrender in August 1945.

Burma became independent on Jan. 4, 1948. The new government was soon faced by armed uprisings of Communists and of Karen tribesmen. In 1949 the Karen rebels won a large degree of autonomy. In 1951 and 1952 the Socialists achieved power, and Burma became the first Asian country to introduce social legislation.

In 1968, after the government had made headway against the Communist rebels, the military regime adopted a policy of strict nonalignment and followed "the Burmese Way" to socialism. But the insurgents, reportedly numbering several thousand and armed by China, continued active.

BURUNDI

Republic of Burundi
Head of Government: Lt. Col. Jean-Baptiste Bagaza (1978)
Area: 10,747 sq mi. (27,834 sq km)
Population (est. 1982): 4,450,000 (average annual growth rate: 2.7%)
Density per square mile: 414.1
Capital and largest city (1979 census): Bujumbura, 151,000
Monetary unit: Burundi franc
Languages: Kirundi (official), French
Religions: Roman Catholic, 60%; Animist, 30%; Protestant, 8%
National name: Republika Y'Uburundi
Literacy rate (1981): 20% (est.)
Economic summary: Gross national product (1980): $830 million. Average annual growth rate (1970–79): 1.5%. Per capita income (1980): $200. Principal agricultural products: coffee, tea, cotton, food crops. Major industrial products: light consumer goods. Natural resources: nickel, uranium, cobalt, unexploited copper and platinum deposits. Exports: coffee, tea, hides. Imports: textiles, food, transport equipment, petroleum products. Major trading partners: U.S., Belgium, West Germany, France

Geography. Wedged among Tanzania, Zaire, and Rwanda in east central Africa, Burundi occupies a high plateau divided by several deep valleys. It is equal in size to Maryland.

Government. Legislative and executive power is vested in the president.

Burundi's first Constitution, approved July 11, 1974, placed UPRONA (Unity and National Progress), the only political party, in control of national policy and automatically made Lt. Gen. Michel Micombero president.

History. Burundi was once part of German East Africa. An integrated society developed among the Watusi, a tall, warlike people and nomad cattle raisers, and the Bahutu, a Bantu people, who were subject farmers. Belgium won a League of Nations mandate in 1923, and subsequently Burundi, with Rwanda, was transferred to the status of a United Nations trust territory.

In 1962, Burundi gained independence and became a kingdom under Mwami Mwambutsa IV, with his son, Louis Rwangasore, as premier. Shortly after, the son was assassinated. The second man to succeed him, Pierre Ngendandumwe, who took office in 1963, was assassinated in 1965 when an unsuccessful coup against the Watusi led to the massacre of many Bahutus.

Crown Prince Charles, returning from Europe, rallied Watusi extremists, ousted the premier, suspended the Constitution, and renewed relations with Communist China. He deposed his father in 1966, reigned as Ntare V, with Micombero as premier. Three months later, Micombero, in a military coup, overthrew the Mwami and established a republic, installing himself as president.

One of Africa's worst tribal wars, which became genocide, occurred in Burundi in April 1972, following the return of Ntare. He was given a safe-conduct promise in writing by Micombero but was "judged and immediately executed" by the Burundi leader. His return was apparently attended by an invasion of exiles of Burundi's Hutu tribe. Although Hutus make up 85% of the population, they have been dominated for centuries by the minority Tutsi tribe of Micombero. Whether Hutus living in Burundi joined the invasion is unclear, but after it failed, the victorious Tutsis proceeded to massacre some 100,000 persons in six weeks, with possibly 100,000 more slain by summer.

On Nov. 1, 1976, a military coup led by Lt. Col. Jean-Baptiste Bagaza ousted Micombero, who was serving his second term. Bagaza assumed the presidency Nov. 3, suspended the Constitution, and announced that a 30-member Supreme Revolutionary Council would be the governing body.

Early in 1977, the Council gave Bagaza a mandate for a renewable five-year term and proposed its own dissolution, once UPRONA is reorganized.

CAMBODIA

People's Republic of Kampuchea
President: Heng Samrin (1979)
Prime Minister: Chan Sy (1982)
Area: 70,000 sq mi. (181,300 sq km)
Population (est. 1982): 7,000,000 (average annual growth rate: 1.9%)
Density per square mile: 100.0
Capital and largest city (est. 1980 for metropolitan area): Phnom Penh, 500,000
Monetary unit: Riel

Ethnic groups: Khmer, 93%; Vietnamese, 4%; Chinese, 3%
Languages: Khmer (official), French, Vietnamese, Chinese
Religion: Theravada Buddhist
Literacy rate: Not known
Economic summary: Gross national product (1971): $500 million. Principal agricultural products: rice, rubber, corn. Major industrial products: fish, wood and wood products, milled rice. Natural resources: timber, gemstones, iron ore, manganese, phosphate. Exports: natural rubber, rice, pepper, wood. Imports: foodstuffs, fuel, machinery. Major trading partners: China, North Korea, Vietnam, U.S.S.R.

Geography. Situated on the Indochinese peninsula, Cambodia is bordered by Thailand and Laos on the north and Vietnam on the east and south. The Gulf of Siam is off the western coast. The country, the size of Missouri, consists chiefly of a large alluvial plain ringed in by mountains and on the east by the Mekong River. The plain is centered on Lake Tonle Sap, which is a natural storage basin of the Mekong.

Government. A bloodless coup toppled Prince Sihanouk in 1970. It was led by Lon Nol and Prince Sisowath Sirik Matak, Sihanouk's cousin. Sihanouk moved to Peking to head a government-in-exile. On Oct. 9, 1970, Lon Nol proclaimed himself President.

The Lon Nol regime was overthrown in April 1975 by Pol Pot, a leader of the Communist Khmer Rouge forces, who instituted a xenophobic reign of terror. Pol Pot was in turn ousted on Jan. 8, 1979, by Heng Samrin, a dissident backed by strong Vietnamese forces.

History. Cambodia came under Khmer rule about A.D. 600. Under the Khmers, magnificent temples were built at Angkor. The Khmer kingdom once ruled over most of Southeast Asia, but attacks by the Thai and the Vietnamese almost annihilated the empire until the French joined Cambodia, Laos, and Vietnam into French Indochina.

Under Norodom Sihanouk, enthroned in 1941, and particularly under Japanese occupation during World War II, nationalism revived. After the ouster of the Japanese, the Cambodians sought independence, but the French returned in 1946, granting the country a Constitution in 1947 and independence within the French Union in 1949. Sihanouk won full military control during the French-Indochinese War in 1953. He abdicated in 1955 in favor of his parents, remaining head of the government, and when his father died in 1960, became chief of state without returning to the throne. In 1963, he sought a guarantee of Cambodia's neutrality from all parties to the Vietnam War.

Sihanouk first favored the Communist-backed Vietcong in Vietnam, but in 1967 he accused the Communists of planning a revolt and veered away from them. In 1968 he announced that under certain conditions he would not oppose "hot pursuit" by American troops of Communist forces across the Cambodian border.

On March 18, 1970, while Sihanouk was abroad trying to get North Vietnamese and the Vietcong out of border sanctuaries near Vietnam, anti-Vietnamese riots occurred, and Sihanouk was overthrown, a move legalized by the legislature. The historically anti-Vietnamese Cambodians largely stayed with the government.

North Vietnamese and Vietcong units in border sanctuaries began moving deeper into Cambodia, threatening rapid overthrow of Lon Nol. President Nixon sent South Vietnamese and U.S. troops across the border on April 30. U.S. ground forces, limited to 30-kilometer penetration, withdrew by June 30.

The Vietnam peace agreement of 1973 stipulated withdrawal of foreign forces from Cambodia, but fighting continued between Hanoi-backed insurgents and U.S.-supplied government troops. U.S. air support for the government forces was ended by Congress on Aug. 15, 1973. Lon Nol made overtures for a negotiated settlement, but neither Sihanouk nor leaders of the Khmer Rouge rebels would deal with him.

Fighting continued through 1974, then reached a quick climax early in 1975. In January, the rebels cut off the Mekong River as a supply route to Phnom Penh and fought their way to the outskirts of the capital and began shelling it. In February, the U.S. Congress ignored a request from President Ford for $222 million to supplement Phnom Penh's dwindling arms stores, but a U.S. food airlift to the besieged capital went forward.

As government troops fell back in bitter fighting, Lon Nol fled by air April 1, leaving the government under the interim control of Premier Long Boret. On April 16, the government's capitulation ended the five-year war, but not the travails of war-ravaged Cambodia.

Khieu Samphan, an early Khmer Rouge leader, appeared to be the strong man of the new regime. Sihanouk, the nominal chief of state, returned from exile in Peking in 1975 for the first time since the 1970 coup. A new Constitution was proclaimed in December 1975, establishing a 250-member People's Assembly, a State Presidium headed by Pol Pot, and a Supreme Judicial Tribunal. Samphan replaced Sihanouk as head of state in April 1976, and the former monarch became a virtual prisoner.

In the next two years, from 2 million to 4 million Cambodians are estimated to have died under the brutality of the regime. Border clashes with Vietnam developed into a Vietnamese invasion and by the end of 1978 the Pol Pot government appeared to be collapsing.

Sihanouk, held under house arrest since 1976, was freed by Pol Pot early in 1979 and sent as a spokesman for the regime to protest the Vietnamese invasion before the U.N. Security Council. Sihanouk eloquently attacked Vietnam while conceding that the Pol Pot regime was inhumane. His call for Vietnam's withdrawal was barred only by a Soviet veto.

Despite the capture of Phnom Penh on Jan. 8 by Heng Samrin, a dissident Khmer Rouge backed by Vietnamese troops, fighting continued in isolated areas. Retreating Pol Pot forces and refugees totaling 40,000 were driven into Thailand by May. Thai authorities forced 15,000 to return, admitting that "several hundred" may have been killed by waiting Vietnamese troops.

Due largely to the support of China and the Association of Southeast Asian Nations (ASEAN), the defeated regime retained the Cambodian seat at the United Nations. A conference on Cambodia met at the United Nations, July 13–17, 1981, and approved unanimously a resolution calling for Vietnamese withdrawal.

The 92-nation conference also asked for U.N.-supervised elections and guarantee of Cambodian independence. Vietnam and the Soviet Union together with all Soviet bloc supporters, boycotted the conference.

On June 22, 1982, meeting in Kuala Lumpur, Malaysia, Sihanouk signed an agreement with Sa

Son, his former prime minister, and Khieu Samphan to form a government of national unity. Sihanouk was to be head of state of Democratic Kampuchea, the rebel regime that still holds Cambodia's United Nations seat; Khieu was to be vice president, and Son prime minister. Sihanouk said of his partnership with his old foes, the Khmer Rouge, "We have to choose between letting the Vietnamese colonize Cambodia or working with the Khmer Rouge."

On July 7, Vietnam announced the withdrawal of a "significant number" of its 200,000 troops from Cambodia after a dry-season campaign that had gained control of some rebel territory, but rebels claimed to have recovered most of their losses immediately.

CAMEROON

United Republic of Cameroon
President: Ahmadou Ahidjo (1960)
Prime Minister: Paul Biya (1975)
Area: 183,569 sq mi. (475,442 sq km)
Population (est. 1982): 8,800,000 (average annual growth rate: 2.9%)
Density per square mile: 47.9
Capital: Yaoundé
Largest cities (est. 1980): Douala, 500,000; Yaoundé, 350,000
Monetary unit: Franc CFA
Languages: French and English (both official); Foulbé, Bamiléke, Ewondo, Donala, Mungaka, Bassa
Religions: Animist, Christian, Islam
National name: République Unie du Cameroun
Literacy rate (1981): 50%
Economic summary: Gross national product (1980): $5.7 billion. Average annual growth rate (1970–79): 3.1%. Per capita income (1980): $675. Land used for agriculture: 35%; labor force: 80%; principal products: coffee, cocoa, tropical agricultural products. Labor force in industry: 10–15%. Major products: small manufacturing, consumer goods, aluminum. Natural resources: timber, some oil, bauxite. Exports: cocoa, coffee, timber, aluminum, cotton. Imports: consumer goods, machinery, food, beverages, tobacco, fuel. Major trading partners: France, U.S., Western European nations.

Geography. Cameroon is a West African nation on the Gulf of Guinea, bordered by Nigeria, Chad, the Central African Republic, the Congo, Equatorial Guinea, and Gabon. It is nearly twice the size of Oregon.

The interior consists of a high plateau, rising to 4,500 feet (1,372 m), with the land descending to a lower, densely wooded plateau and then to swamps and plains along the coast. Mount Cameroon (13,350 ft.; 4,069 m), near the coast, is the highest elevation in the country. The main rivers are the Benue, Nyong, and Sanaga.

Government. After a 1972 plebiscite, a unitary nation was formed out of East and West Cameroon to replace the former Federal Republic. A Constitution was adopted, providing for election of a president every five years and of a 120-seat National Assembly, whose nominal five-year term can be extended or shortened by the president. The Cameroon National Union is the only political party.

History. The United Republic of Cameroon is inhabited by Hamitic and Semitic peoples in the north, where Islam is the principal religion, and by Bantu peoples in the central and southern regions, where native animism prevails. The tribes were conquered by many invaders.

The land escaped colonial rule until 1884, when treaties with tribal chiefs brought the area under German domination. After World War I, the League of Nations gave the French a mandate over 80% of the area, and the British 20% adjacent to Nigeria. After World War II, when the country came under a U.N. trusteeship in 1946, self-government was granted, and the Cameroun People's Union emerged as the dominant party by campaigning for reunification of French and British Cameroon and for independence. Accused of being under Communist control, it waged a campaign of revolutionary terror from 1955 to 1958, when it was crushed. In British Cameroon, unification was pressed also by the leading party, the Kamerun National Democratic Party, led by John Foncha.

France set up Cameroun as an autonomous state in 1957, and the next year its legislative assembly voted for independence by 1960. In 1959 a fully autonomous government of Cameroun was formed under Ahmadou Ahidjo. Cameroun became an independent republic on Jan. 1, 1960, adopted a Constitution in a referendum in February, and chose a National Assembly in April. The Assembly elected Ahidjo president. A federal Constitution was approved in 1961, and the Federal Republic of Cameroon came into being in October, headed by Ahidjo and Foncha.

Ahidjo was re-elected in 1975 for a fourth five-year term. Paul Biya was named prime minister.

CANADA

See separate Canada section

CAPE VERDE

Republic of Cape Verde
President: Aristides Pereira (1975)
Premier: Maj. Pedro Pires (1975)
Area: 1,557 sq mi. (4,033 sq km)
Population: (est. 1982): 340,000 (average annual growth rate: 2.6%)
Density per square mile: 218.4
Capital (est. 1980): Praia, 35,000
Largest city (est. 1980): Mindelo, 50,000
Monetary unit: Cape Verde escudo
Language: Portuguese
Religions: Mainly Roman Catholic; Protestant, and Christian Racionalist
National name: República de Cabo Verde.
Literacy rate (1981): 20% (est.)
Economic summary: Gross national product (1980): $100 million. Average annual growth rate (1970–79): 4.8%. Per capita income (1980): $300. Principal agricultural products: bananas, corn, sugar cane, sweet potatoes. Major industry: fishing, salt mining. Natural resources: salt, siliceous rock, minerals. Exports: fish and shellfish, bananas, salt. Imports: machinery, textiles, petroleum products. Major trading partners: Portugal, U.K., Japan, neighboring African states.

Geography: Cape Verde, only slightly larger than Rhode Island, is an archipelago in the Atlantic 385 miles (620 km) west of Dakar, Senegal.

The islands are divided into two groups: Barlavento in the north, comprising Santo Antão (291 sq mi.; 754 sq km), Boa Vista (240 sq mi.; 622 sq km), São Nicolau (132 sq mi.; 342 sq km), São Vicente (88 sq mi.; 246 sq km), Sal (83 sq mi.; 298 sq km), and Santa Luzia (13 sq mi.; 34 sq km); and Sotavento in the south, consisting of São Tiago (383 sq mi.; 992 sq km), Fogo (184 sq mi.; 477 sq km), Maio (103 sq mi.; 267 sq km), and Brava (25 sq mi.; 65 sq km). The islands are mostly mountainous, with the land deeply scarred by erosion. There is an active volcano on Fogo.

Government. The islands became independent on July 5, 1975, under an agreement negotiated with Portugal in 1974. The 56-member National Assembly chose Aristides Pereira as President and Maj. Pedro Pires as Premier. All members of the Assembly belong to the African Party for the Independence of Portuguese Guinea and Cape Verde, then the only party that entered candidates in the election. It is committed to union with Guinea-Bissau, another former Portuguese colony.

History. Uninhabited upon their discovery in 1456, the Cape Verde islands became part of the Portuguese empire in 1495. A majority of their modern inhabitants are of mixed Portuguese and African ancestry. A coaling station developed during the 19th century on the island of São Vicente has grown in recent years to an oil and gasoline storage depot for ships and aircraft.

CENTRAL AFRICAN REPUBLIC

Head of Government: Gen. André Kolingba (1981)
Area: 241,313 sq mi. (625,000 sq km)
Population (est. 1982): 2,500,000 (average annual growth rate, 2.6%)
Density per square mile: 10.4
Capital and largest city (est. 1981): Bangui, 375,000
Monetary unit: Franc CFA
Ethnic groups: Mandja-Baya, Banda, Mbaka, Azande
Languages: French (official) and Sango
Religions: Animist, 60%; Christian, 35%; Islam, 5%
National name: République Centrafricain
Member of French Community
Literacy rate (1981): 20% (est.)
Economic summary: Gross national product (1980): $680 million. Average annual growth rate (1970–79): 0.9%. Per capita income (1980): $300. Land used for agriculture: 15%; labor force: 80%; principal products: cotton, coffee, peanuts, food crops, livestock. Major industrial products: timber, textiles, soap, cigarettes, processed food. Natural resources: diamonds, uranium, timber. Exports: diamonds, cotton, timber, coffee. Imports: machinery and electrical equipment, petroleum products, textiles. Major trading partners: France, Yugoslavia, Japan, U.S.

Geography. Situated about 500 miles north (805 km) of the equator, the Central African Republic is a landlocked nation bordered by Cameroon, Chad, the Sudan, Zaire, and the Congo. Twice the size of New Mexico, it is covered by tropical forests in the south and semidesert land in the east. The Ubangi and Shari are the largest of many rivers.

Government. On Dec. 4, 1976, the Central African Republic became the Central African Empire. Marshal Jean-Bédel Bokassa, who had ruled the republic since he took power in a military coup Dec. 31, 1965, was declared Emperor Bokassa I. He was overthrown in a coup on Sept. 20, 1979. Former President David Dacko, returned to power and changed the country's name back to the Central African Republic. An army coup on Sept. 1, 1981, deposed Dacko and suspended the Constitution and all political parties. A Military Committee of National Redress was set up to run the country.

History. As the colony of Ubangi-Shari, what is now the Central African Republic was united with Chad in 1905 and joined with Gabon and the Middle Congo in French Equatorial Africa in 1910. After World War II a rebellion in 1946 forced the French to grant self-government. In 1958 the territory voted to become an autonomous republic within the French Community, but on Aug. 13, 1960, President David Dacko proclaimed the republic's independence from France.

Dacko undertook to move the country into Peking's orbit, but was overthrown in a coup on Dec. 31, 1965, by the then Col. Jean-Bédel Bokassa, Army Chief of Staff. In August 1977, the U.S. State Department protested the Emperor's jailing of American and British newsmen.

Bokassa staged an elaborate coronation ceremony on the first anniversary of the Empire, inviting 3,500 guests to see him place a diamond-studded crown on his head and sit on a 2.5-ton gilded bronze throne in the shape of an eagle. The cost of the ceremony was one fourth of the annual foreign-exchange earnings of the country, one of the 25 poorest in the world.

CHAD

Republic of Chad
President: Hissen Habré (1982)
Area: 495,752 sq mi. (1,284,000 sq km)
Population (est. 1982): 4,650,000 (average annual growth rate, 2.3%)
Density per square mile: 9.4
Capital and largest city (est. 1979): N'djamena, 300,000
Monetary unit: Franc CFA
Ethnic groups: Baguirmiens, Kanembous, Saras, Massas, Arabs, Toubous, Goranes
Languages: French (official), Sara, Kanembou, Ouddai, Massa, Arabic, Gorane
Religions: Islam, 45%; Animist, 45%; Christian, 10%
National name: République de Tchad
Literacy rate (1981): 10%
Economic summary: Gross national product (1980): $530 million. Average annual growth rate (1970–79): −2.4%. Per capita income (1980): $120. Land used for agriculture: 17%; labor force: 90%; principal products: cotton, cattle, fish, sugar, subsistence crops. Labor force in industry: 4%; major products: livestock and livestock products, beer, bicycle and radio assembly, textiles, cigarettes. Natural resources: petroleum, unexploited uranium, kaolin. Exports: cotton, livestock and animal products. Imports: food, motor vehicles and parts, petroleum products, machinery, cement, textiles. Major trading partners: France and central African countries.

Geography. A landlocked country in north central Africa, Chad is about 85% the size of Alaska. Its neighbors are Niger, Libya, the Sudan, the Central African Empire, Cameroon, and Nigeria.

Lake Chad, from which the country gets its name, lies on the western border with Niger and

Nigeria. In the north is a desert that runs into the Sahara.

Government. After a coup on April 13, 1975, a nine-member military council took over all governmental functions, including those of the 75-member Legislative Assembly. Political parties were banned.

History. Chad was absorbed into the colony of French Equatorial Africa, as part of Ubangi-Shari, in 1910. France began the country's development after 1920, when it became a separate colony. In 1946, French Equatorial Africa was admitted to the French Union. By referendum in 1958 the Chad territory became an autonomous republic within the French Union.

An independence movement led by the first Premier and President, François (later Ngarta) Tombalbaye, achieved complete independence on Aug. 11, 1960.

A six-year sub-Sahara drought caused mass migrations, thousands of deaths, and famine conditions for some 2 million Chadians in 1974. International relief efforts were disrupted October 25, when President Tombalbaye ordered rejection of U.S. grain shipments.

Tombalbaye was killed in the 1975 coup and was succeeded by Gen. Félix Malloum, who faced a Libyan-financed rebel movement, the Chadian National Liberation Front (Frolinat), throughout his tenure in office. A ceasefire backed by Libya, Niger, and the Sudan early in 1978 failed to end the fighting, and French military aid, both troops and supplies, was increased.

Nine rival groups meeting in Lagos, Nigeria, in March 1979 agreed to form a provisional government headed by Goukouni Oueddi, a former Frolinat leader. Fighting broke out again in Chad in March 1980, when Defense Minister Hissen Habré challenged Goukouni and seized the capital. By the year's end, Libyan troops supporting Goukouni recaptured N'djamena, and Libyan President Muammar el-Qaddafi, in January 1981, proposed a merger of Chad with Libya.

In June, the Organization of African Unity asked that an international peace-keeping force replace Libyan troops and that elections be held, to which Goukouni agreed in November. In April 1982 the O.A.U. warned Goukouni to negotiate with Habré and hold elections by June 30 or face a pullout of the peace-keeping force. Without waiting for the deadline, Habré's troops seized N'djamena on June 7, sending Goukouni into Libyan exile.

CHILE

Republic of Chile
President: Gen. Augusto Pinochet Ugarte (1973)
Area: 286,396 sq mi. (741,766 sq km)
Population (est. 1982): 11,500,000 (average annual growth rate: 1.3%)
Density per square mile: 40.1
Capital: Santiago
Largest cities (est. 1980): Santiago, 3,850,000; Viña del Mar, 262,100; Valparaiso, 248,200; Talcahuano, 204,100; Concepción, 172,800; Antofagasta, 157,000
Monetary unit: Peso
Language: Spanish
Religion: Roman Catholic
National name: República de Chile
Literacy rate (1977): 90%
Economic summary: Gross national product (1980): $24.0 billion. Average annual growth rate (1970–79): 0.8%. Per capita income (1980): $2,160. Land used for agriculture: 21%; labor force 20%; principal products: grains, fruits, potatoes, vegetables, wine, livestock. Labor force in industry: 22%; major products: processed fish, transportation equipment, iron and steel, pulp, paper. Natural resources: copper, timber, iron ore, nitrates. Exports: copper, iron ore, paper and wood products, fruits. Imports: sugar, wheat, vehicles, petroleum, capital goods. Major trading partners: U.S., Japan, West Germany and Brazil.

Geography. Situated south of Peru and west of Bolivia and Argentina, Chile fills a narrow 1,800-mile (2,897 km) strip between the Andes and the Pacific. Its area is nearly twice that of Montana.

One third of Chile is covered by the towering ranges of the Andes. In the north is the mineral-rich Atacama Desert, between the coastal mountains and the Andes. In the center is a 700-mile-long (1,127 km) valley, thickly populated, between the Andes and the coastal plateau. In the south, the Andes border on the ocean.

At the southern tip of Chile's mainland is Punta Arenas, the southernmost city in the world, and beyond that lies the Strait of Magellan and Tierra del Fuego, an island divided between Chile and Argentina. The southernmost point of South America is Cape Horn, a 1,390-foot (424-m) rock on Horn Island in the Wollaston group, which belongs to Chile.

The Juan Fernández Islands, in the South Pacific about 400 miles (644 km) west of the mainland, and Easter Island, about 2,000 miles (3,219 km) west, are Chilean possessions.

Government. Under the pre-coup Constitution, the nation elected a President every six years, a Senate of 50 members every eight years (one-half renewable every four years), and a Chamber of Deputies of 150 members every four years.

Leftist parties were abolished immediately after the 1973 military coup that ousted President Salvador Allende Gossens. Other parties were placed "in recess," and on March 12, 1977, the government officially dissolved them.

History. Chile was originally under the control of the Incas in the north and the fierce Araucanian people in the south. In 1541, a Spaniard, Pedro de Valdivia, founded Santiago. Chile won its independence from Spain in 1818 under Bernardo O'Higgins and an Argentinian, José de San Martin. O'Higgins, dictator until 1823, laid the foundations of the modern state with a two-party system and a centralized government.

The dictator from 1830 to 1837, Diego Portales, fought a war with Peru in 1836–39 that expanded Chilean territory. The Conservatives were in power from 1831 to 1861. Then the Liberals, winning a share of power for the next 30 years, disestablished the church and limited presidential power. Chile fought the War of the Pacific with Peru and Bolivia from 1879 to 1883, winning Antofagasta, Bolivia's only outlet to the sea, and extensive areas from Peru. A revolt in 1890 led by Jorge Montt overthrew, in 1891, José Balmaceda and established a parliamentary dictatorship that existed until a new Constitution was adopted in 1925. Industralization began before World War I and led to the formation of Marxist groups.

Juan Antonio Ríos, President during World War II, was originally pro-Nazi but in 1944 led his country into the war on the side of the U.S. After the war, Gabriel González Videla, elected by a coalition including the Communists, turned on them. The Communist Party was outlawed until 1958.

A small abortive army uprising in 1969 raised fear of military intervention to prevent a Marxist, Salvador Allende Gossens, from taking office after his election to the presidency on Sept. 4, 1970, with 36.3% of the vote in a three-way battle. Dr. Allende was the first President in a non-Communist country freely elected on a Marxist-Leninist program.

Allende quickly established relations with Cuba and the People's Republic of China and nationalized several American companies. He promised compensation but imposed retroactive taxes to cancel out most claims, leading to cool but proper relations with the U.S. By 1972, inflation was running over 100% annually.

A middle-class general strike led to a military coup Sept. 11, 1973, then to Allende's overthrow and mysterious death in an army assault on the presidential palace. More than 2,700 deaths were reported in the coup, and many thousands were arrested. The coup ended a 46-year era of constitutional government in Chile, which had boasted the longest such record in Latin America.

The takeover was led by a four-man junta headed by Army Chief of Staff Augusto Pinochet Ugarte, who assumed the office of President and governed under a state of siege that was kept in force by extensions every six months. In March 1978, Pinochet lifted the state of siege because of "support for government" by the public, reported by a Gallup poll to be 75%.

Committed to "exterminate Marxism," the junta embarked on a right-wing dictatorship. It suspended parliament, banned political activity, and broke relations with Cuba.

The Human Rights Commission of the Organization of American States charged the junta with "most grave violations" of basic liberties, but the O.A.S. voted in May 1975 not to hear the report until further evidence was supplied. In July, Chile denied entry to a U.N. investigatory panel. On June 9, 1978, the government reversed that policy to permit the U.N. Human Rights Commission to send an investigative mission to Cuba.

In 1974, it was disclosed that the U.S. Central Intelligence Agency had secretly aided Allende's opponents before his election and had later worked covertly to "destabilize" his government.

In 1977, Pinochet, in a speech marking his fourth year in power, promised elections by 1985 if conditions warranted. Earlier, he had abolished DINA, the secret police, and decreed an amnesty for political prisoners, an action Amnesty International said might affect only 200–400 of some 1,500 political prisoners. In 1978, Pinochet permitted the deportation of Michael V. Townley to the U.S., where he and three Cuban exiles were charged with the murder of Orlando Letellier, a former Chilean foreign minister who had taken refuge in Washington.

Townley, given a reduced sentence in May 1979 because he gave evidence to convict the Cubans, testified that all four had been ordered to act by the secret police. A Chilean court refused to extradite three Chilean officers the U.S. accused of complicity in the assassination.

Pinochet was inaugurated on March 11, 1981, for an eight-year term as President, at the end of which, according to the Constitution adopted six months earlier, the junta would nominate a civilian as successor.

CHINA

People's Republic of China
Head of State: Ye Jianying (1978)
Premier: Zhao Ziyang (1980)
Area: 3,691,521 sq mi. (9,561,000 sq km)[1]
Population (est. 1982): 1,020,000,000 (average annual growth rate, 1.3%)
Density per square mile: 276.3
Capital: Peking
Largest cities (est. 1979): Shanghai, 11,000,000; Peking, 9,000,000; **(est. 1970):** Tianjin (Tientsin), 4,280,000; Wuhan, 4,250,000; Luda (Port Arthur and Dairen), 4,000,000; Shenyang (Mukden), 3,750,000; Chongqing (Chungking), 3,500,000; Harbin, 2,750,000; Taiyuan, 2,725,000; Canton, 2,300,000; Nanjing (Nanking), 2,000,000
Monetary unit: Yuan
Language: Chinese, (Mandarin, Cantonese, and local dialects)
Religions: Principally Confucianist, Buddhist, and Taoist
National name: Zhonghua Renmin Gongheguo
Literacy rate (1981): 25%
Economic summary: Gross national product (1980): $283.3 billion. Average annual growth rate (1970–79): 2.8%. Per capita income (1980): $290. Land used for agriculture: 11%; labor force: 75%; principal products: rice, wheat, grains, cotton. Major industrial products: iron and steel, textiles, armaments, petroleum. Natural resources: coal, natural gas, limestone, marble. Exports: agricultural products, oil, minerals, metals, manufactured goods. Imports: grains, chemical fertilizer, steel, industrial raw materials, machinery and equipment. Major trading partners: Japan, Hong Kong, U.S., West Germany, Australia, Romania, Canada, U.S.S.R., U.K., France.

1. Including Manchuria and Tibet.

Geography. China, which occupies the eastern part of Asia, is slightly larger in area than the U.S. Its coastline is roughly a semicircle, about 2,150 miles (3,460 km) long. The greater part of the country is mountainous, and only in the lower reaches of the Yellow and Yangtze Rivers are there extensive low plains.

The principal mountain ranges are the Tien Shan, to the northwest; the Kunlun chain, running south of the Taklimakan and Gobi Deserts; and the Trans-Himalaya, connecting the Kunlun with the borders of China and Tibet. Manchuria is largely an undulating plain connected with the north China plain by a narrow lowland corridor. Inner Mongolia contains the relatively fertile southern and eastern portions of the Gobi. The large island of Hainan (13,500 sq mi.; 34,965 sq km) lies off the southern coast.

Hydrographically, China proper consists of three great river systems. The northern part of the country is drained by the Yellow River (Huang Ho), 2,900 miles long (4,667 km) and mostly unnavigable. The central part is drained by the Chang Jiang (Yangtze Kiang), the fourth longest river in the world 3,602 miles (5,797 km). The Xi Jiang (Si Kiang) in the south is 1,236 miles long (1,989 km) and navigable for a considerable distance. In addition, the Amur (2,704 mi.; 4,352 km) forms part of the northeastern boundary.

Provinces and Regions of China

Name	Area (sq mi.)	Area (sq km)	Capital
Provinces			
Anhui (Anhwei)	54,015	139,900	Hefei (Hofei)
Fujian (Fukien)	47,529	123,100	Fuzhou (Fukien)
Gansu (Kansu)	137,104	355,100	Lanzhou (Lanchow)
Guangdong (Kwangtung)	89,344	231,400	Canton
Guizhou (Kweichow)	67,181	174,000	Guiyang (Kweiyang)
Hebei (Hopei)	81,479	211,030	Shijiazhuang (Shitikiachwang)
Heilongjiang (Heilungkiang)[1]	178,996	463,600	Harbin
Henan (Honan)	64,479	167,000	Zhengzhou (Chengchow)
Hubei (Hupeh)	72,394	187,500	Wuhan
Hunan	81,274	210,500	Changsha
Jiangsu (Kiangsu)	40,927	106,000	Nanjing (Nanking)
Jiangxi (Kiangsi)	63,629	164,800	Nanchang
Jilin (Kirin)[1]	72,201	187,000	Changchun
Liaoning[1]	53,301	138,050	Shenyang
Quinghai (Chinghai)	278,378	721,000	Xining (Sining)
Shaanxi (Shensi)	75,598	195,800	Xian (Sian)
Shandong (Shantung)	59,189	153,300	Jinan (Tsinan)
Shanxi (Shansi)	60,656	157,100	Taiyuan
Sichuan (Szechwan)	219,691	569,000	Chengdu (Chengtu)
Yunnan	168,417	436,200	Kunming
Zhejiang (Chekiang)	39,305	101,800	Hangzhou (Hangchow)
Autonomous Region			
Guangxi Zhuang (Kwangsi Chuang)	85,096	220,400	Nanning
Nei Monggol (Inner Mongolia)[1]	454,633	1,177,500	Hohhot (Huhehot)
Ningxia Hui	30,039	77,800	Yinchuan (Yinchwan)
Xinjiang Uygur (Sinkiang Uighur)[1]	635,829	1,646,800	Urumqi (Urumchi)
Xizang (Tibet)	471,660	1,221,600	Lhasa

1. Together constitute (with Taiwan) what has been traditionally known as Outer China, the remaining territory forming the historical China Proper. NOTE: Names are in Pinyin, with conventional spelling in parentheses.

Government. With 3,040 deputies, elected for four-year terms by universal suffrage, the National People's Congress is the chief legislative organ. A State Council has the executive authority. The Congress elects the Premier and Deputy Premiers. All ministries are under the State Council, headed by the Premier.

The Communist Party controls the government.

History. By 2000 B.C., the Chinese were living in the Hwang Ho basin, and they had achieved an advanced stage of civilization by 1200 B.C. The great philosophers Lao-tse, Confucius, Mo Ti, and Mencius lived during the Chou dynasty (1122–249 B.C.). The warring feudal states were first united under Emperor Ch'in Shih Huang Ti, during whose reign (246–210 B.C.) work was begun on the Great Wall. Under the Han dynasty (206 B.C.-A.D. 220) China prospered and traded with the West.

In the T'ang dynasty (618–907), often called the golden age of Chinese history, painting, sculpture, and poetry flourished, and printing made its earliest known appearance.

The Mings, last of the native rulers (1368–1644), overthrew the Mongol, or Yuan, dynasty (1280–1368) established by Kublai Khan. The Mings in turn were overthrown in 1644 by invaders from the north, the Manchus.

China closely restricted foreign activities, and by the end of the 18th century only Canton and the Portuguese port of Macao were open to European merchants. Following the Anglo-Chinese War of 1839–42, however, several treaty ports were opened, and Hong Kong was ceded to Britain. Treaties signed after further hostilities (1856–60) weakened Chinese sovereignty and removed foreigners from Chinese jurisdiction. The disastrous Chinese-Japanese War of 1894–95 was followed by a scramble for Chinese concessions by European powers, leading to the Boxer Rebellion (1900), suppressed by an international force.

The death of the Empress Dowager Tzu Hsi in 1908 and the accession of the infant Emperor Hsüan T'ung (Pu-Yi) were followed by a nationwide rebellion led by Dr. Sun Yat-sen, who became first President of the Provisional Chinese Republic in 1911. The Manchus abdicated on Feb. 12, 1912. Dr. Sun resigned in favor of Yuan Shih-k'ai, who suppressed the republicans but was forced by a serious rising in 1915–16 to abandon his intention of declaring himself Emperor. Yuan's death in June 1916 was followed by years of civil war between rival militarists and Dr. Sun's republicans.

Nationalist forces, led by Gen. Chiang Kai-shek and with the advice of Communist experts, soon occupied most of China, setting up a Kuomintang regime in 1928. Internal strife continued, however, and Chiang broke with the Communists.

An alleged explosion on the South Manchurian Railway on Sept. 18, 1931, brought invasion of Manchuria by Japanese forces, who installed the last Manchu Emperor, Henry Pu-Yi, as nominal ruler of the puppet state of "Manchukuo." Japanese efforts to take China's northern provinces in July 1937 were resisted by Chiang, who meanwhile had succeeded in uniting most of China behind him. Within two years, however, Japan seized most of the ports and railways. The Kuomintang government retreated first to Hankow and then to Chungking, while the Japanese set up a puppet government at Nanking headed by Wang Jingwei.

Japan's surrender in 1945 touched off civil war between Nationalist forces under Chiang and Communist forces led by Mao Zedong, the party chairman. Despite U. S. aid, the Chiang forces were overcome by the Maoists, backed by the Soviet bloc, and were expelled from the mainland. The Mao regime, established in Peking as the new capital, proclaimed the People's Republic of China on Oct. 1, 1949, with Zhou Enlai as Premier.

The soviet-type government, after prolonged negotiations, signed a 30-year treaty of friendship and mutual aid with the U.S.S.R. on Feb. 14, 1950. Its published terms provided for return of the Changchun railroad to China and the eventual return of Port Arthur and Dairen, occupied by Soviet troops. Later in the year, Chinese troops invaded Tibet and began its subjugation, a campaign that brought China into conflict with India. After the Korean War began in June 1950, China led the Communist bloc in supporting North Korea, and on Nov. 26, 1950, the Mao regime intervened openly.

A deterioration of relations between Peking and Moscow was indicated in 1958 when Peking emerged as an independent center of Communist power, challenging the leadership role of the U.S.S.R. in the Soviet bloc.

In 1958, Mao undertook the "Great Leap Forward" campaign, which combined the establishment of rural communes with a crash program of village industrialization. These efforts also failed, causing Mao to lose influence to Liu Shaoqi, who became President in 1959, to Premier Zhou, and to Party Secretary Deng Xiaoping. Meanwhile China's backing of subversive movements in Asia soured relations with India and Burma, although it very nearly achieved the conquest of Indonesia, and culminated in war on the borders of India late in 1962. By the next year, the break with the U.S.S.R. was complete.

Zhou proposed the movement that became known as the Cultural Revolution at the party congress in 1964, the same year China exploded its first atomic (fission) bomb (it produced a fusion bomb in 1967).

Mao moved to Shanghai, and from that base he and his supporters waged their own Cultural Revolution. President Liu and the party secretary, Deng, took over, and their followers denounced hundreds of party and government officials at rallies and in wall posters. Then, in 1966, Chen became director of the Cultural Revolution; the Army Chief of Staff, Lo Ruiqing, was purged; and Lin replaced Liu as second in the hierarchy. In the spring of 1966 the Mao group formed Red Guard units dominated by youths and students, closing the schools to free the students for agitation.

The Red Guards campaigned against "old ideas, old culture, old habits, and old customs." Often they were no more than uncontrolled mobs, and brutality was frequent. Early in 1967 efforts were made to restore control. The Red Guards were urged to return home. Schools started opening. But the height of violence was only reached in September 1967 when in Canton the opposing factions used tanks and artillery against each other.

Persistent overtures by the Nixon Administration (relaxed trade and travel restrictions) abruptly climaxed in an invitation to a U.S. table tennis team to visit Peking in April 1971. This was followed by the dramatic announcement in July that Henry Kissinger, Mr. Nixon's national security adviser, had secretly visited Peking and reached agreement on a visit by the President to China.

The movement toward reconciliation, which signaled the end of the U.S. containment policy toward China, provided irresistible momentum for Chinese admission to the U.N. Despite U.S. opposition to expelling Taiwan (Nationalist China), the world body overwhelmingly ousted Chiang in seating Peking.

Mr. Nixon went to Peking for a week early in 1972, meeting Mao as well as Chou. The summit ended with a historic communiqué on February 28, in which both nations promised to work toward improved relations. They differed over Vietnam as well as Taiwan, although the U.S. noted it was withdrawing from Vietnam and said its ultimate goal was withdrawal from Taiwan as well, with interim reductions of those forces as tension in the area diminished.

In 1973, the U.S. and China agreed to set up "liaison offices" in each other's capitals, which constituted de facto diplomatic relations. Full diplomatic relations were barred by China as long as the U.S. continued to recognize Nationalist China.

The National People's Congress held its first meeting in a decade in Peking, Jan. 13–17, 1975. With Mao absent, it re-elected Zhou as Premier. It approved a government realignment that placed Marshal Ye Jianying in the post of Defense Minister, vacant since Lin's death. It revised the 1954 Constitution to reassert the primacy of the Communist Party and to specify limited rights of citizens to strike and demonstrate, to hold private farm plots, and to work for themselves.

Zhou predicted in a keynote address that "fierce contention" between the U.S. and the U.S.S.R. "is bound to lead to world war some day." He said there is "no détente, let alone lasting peace in the world today."

The same warnings against détente were made during President Ford's visit to China, Dec. 8–12, 1975, by Vice Premier Deng Xiaoping. Deng served as chief host because Zhou was now seriously ill with cancer and Mao, visibly failing, saw the visitor only briefly.

On Jan. 8, 1976, amid a national outpouring of grief, Zhou died. Demonstrations in the capital turned into near riots when mourners suspected the government of trying to suppress the display of emotion. Deng, who had been rehabilitated by Zhou and designated as his successor, was supplanted within a month by Hua Guofeng, former Minister of Public Security. Hua, believed to be a compromise between radicals and the moderates represented by the ousted Deng, became permanent Premier in April. In October he was named successor to Mao as Chairman of the Communist Party.

Mao died September 10, apparently of Parkinson's disease, and China for the second time in a year went into a period of national mourning. Almost immediately afterward, a campaign against his widow, Jiang Qing, and three of her "radical" colleagues began. The "Gang of Four" was denounced for having undermined the party, the government, and the economy.

Jiang was brought to trail in 1980 and sentenced on Jan. 25, 1981, to die within two years unless she showed repentance, in which case she would be imprisoned for life. She showed no remorse at the trial, shouting defiance as she was taken away.

While the despised four were reviled throughout China, there was evidence by late 1976 that Deng was to be rehabilitated. At the Central Committee meeting of 1977, Deng was reinstated as Deputy Premier, Chief of Staff of the Army, and member of the Central Committee of the Politburo. He was ranked behind Ye Jianying, the Defense Minister, in the third-ranking place in the government.

At the same time, Jiang Qing, Wang Hongwen, Zhang Chunqiao, and Yao Wenyuan—the notorious "Gang of Four"—were removed from all official posts and banished from the party. The final resolution of the committee meeting declared national unity restored and "a new leap forward taking shape in the national economy."

In August 1977, the 11th national Communist Party Congress and the election of a new Politburo took place as U.S. Secretary of State Cyrus Vance visited China to call for efforts by both China and the U.S. to normalize relations.

The Fifth National People's Congress adopted a new Constitution on March 5, 1978, strengthening civil rights such as free speech and the right to file complaints against the government. The Congress also approved a 10-year plan to increase farm production and add 120 industrial complexes to the nation's industrial base. Hua Guofeng was affirmed as Premier despite rumors that Deputy Premier Deng might take the post.

In May 1978, expulsion of ethnic Chinese by Vietnam produced an open rupture. China withdrew aid technicians and announced a complete cutoff, disclosing for the first time that it had given $10 billion to Vietnam in the past 20 years. Peking sided with Cambodia in the border fighting that flared between Vietnam and Cambodia, charging Hanoi with aggression.

On Aug. 12, 1978, China and Japan signed a treaty of peace and friendship, a treaty attacked by Moscow as hostile to the Soviet Union. Peking and Washington then announced that they would open full diplomatic relations on Jan. 1, 1979. Over Congressional objections, the Carter administration abrogated the Taiwan defense treaty, the last obstacle to full relations. Deputy Premier Deng sealed the agreement with a visit to the United States that coincided with the opening of embassies in both capitals on March 1.

Peking protested Congressional guarantees of Taiwan's defense that were inserted in legislation governing future U.S. relations with the island. The Chinese nevertheless went ahead with the drafting of a trade pact that gave them most-favored-nation status. China agreed to pay $80 million compensation for American property seized after the 1949 Communist take-over of the mainland.

A near proxy war with the Soviet Union erupted on Deng's return from the U.S. as 200,000 to 300,000 Chinese troops invaded Vietnam to avenge alleged violations of Chinese territory. The action was seen as more a reaction to Vietnam's invasion of Cambodia, where China had been the dominant outside influence since 1975. While the Soviet Union stepped up supply airlifts, the Chinese inflicted damage on the northern border, then withdrew.

At home, a political trend that had seen a "freedom wall" in Peking where individuals could publish their opinions without censorship was dampened. But if individual expression was curbed, the leadership encouraged a radical shift from traditional Marxism toward private enterprise in every phase of the national economy.

The first People's Congress in five years marked the culmination of Deng's post-Mao modernization efforts. On Sept. 10, the Congress confirmed Zhao Ziyang, an economic planner, as Premier replacing Hua Guofeng, who had held the post since 1976. Hua retained his chairmanship of the Communist Party.

At the Central Committee meeting of June 27–29, 1981, another Deng protégé, Hu Yaobang, was elevated to the party chairmanship and Hua retired. The 66-year-old Hu had served as party Secretary-General, a post he retained. Deng became chairman of the military commission of the central committee, giving him control over the army. The committee's 215 members concluded the session with a statement holding Mao Zedong responsible for the "grave blunder" of the Cultural Revolution.

Teng's triumph was somewhat dulled by the recognition that his modernization program had outpaced Chinese resources. The 1981 budget had to be reduced by $9.8 billion to $64.6 billion, cutting capital spending for oil and coal production and even for defense. Inflation was blamed for casualties such as the Baoshan steel plant in Shanghai, which was to have been a showpiece of industrial modernization.

Despite economic problems, foreign investment gained during 1981 and, on Dec. 16 of that year, Japan signed a $1.4-billion aid agreement providing funds to complete the first phase of the Baoshan plant, a refinery at Daqing and four other projects.

In April 1982, a new draft constitution proposed the re-establishment of the office of president, last held by Liu, and the return of the military to parliamentary rather than party control. It also proposed the removal of political power of the communes, leaving them as economic units, with political functions restored to elected town officials.

A clash with the United States over the continuation of U.S. arms to Taiwan required a peace-making visit by Vice President George Bush to Peking, but despite Chinese protests, incoming Secretary of State George Schultz affirmed in July that U.S. F-5E fighter planes would continue to be made in Taiwan under license. On Aug. 17, however, the United States signed a joint communiqué with China pledging that arms sales to Taiwan would not be increased and would instead be gradually decreased pending a "final resolution" of the Taiwan problem.

CHINA (TAIWAN)

Republic of China
President: Chiang Ching-kuo (1978)
Premier: Sun Yun-suan (1978)
Area: 13,592 sq mi. (35,203 sq km)[1]
Population (est. 1982): 18,350,000 (average annual growth rate: 1.8%)
Density per square mile: 1,350.1
Capital: Taipei
Largest cities (est. 1981): Taipei, 2,250,000; **(est. 1980):** Kaohsiung, 1,250,000; Taichung, 579,000; Tainan, 557,000; Chilung (Keelung), 342,300.
Monetary unit: New Taiwan dollar
Language: Chinese (Mandarin) and various dialects
Religions: Confucianist, Buddhist, Christian, Taoist
Literacy rate (1981): 90%
Economic summary: Gross national product (1979): $32 billion. Average annual growth rate (1970–77): 5.5%. Per capita income (1980): $2,160. Land used for agriculture: 24%; labor force: 22%; principal products: rice, sweet potatoes, sugar cane, bananas, pineapples, citrus fruits. Labor force in industry: 42%; major products: textiles, clothing, chemicals, processed foods, electronic equipment, cement, ships, plywood. Natural resources: timber, camphor. Exports: textiles, electrical machinery, plywood. Imports: machinery, basic metals, crude oil,

chemicals. Major trading partners: U.S., Japan.

1. Excluding Quemoy and Matsu.

Geography. The Republic of China today consists of the island of Taiwan, an island 100 miles (161 km) off the Asian mainland in the Pacific; two offshore islands, Quemoy and Matsu; and the nearby islets of the Pescadores chain. It is slightly larger than the combined areas of Massachusetts and Connecticut.

Taiwan is divided by a central mountain range that runs from north to south, rising sharply on the east coast and descending gradually to a broad western plain, where cultivation is concentrated.

Government. The President and the Vice President are elected by the National Assembly for a term of six years. There are five major governing bodies called Yuans: Executive, Legislative, Judicial, Control, and Examination. Taiwan's internal affairs are administered by the Taiwan Provincial Government under the supervision of the Provincial Assembly, which is popularly elected.

The majority and ruling party is the Kuomintang (Nationalist Party) led by President Chiang Ching-kuo. There are also two minority parties: the China Democratic Socialist Party and the Young China Party.

History. Taiwan was inhabited by aborigines of Malayan descent when Chinese from the areas now designated as Fukien and Kwangtung began settling it beginning in the 7th century, becoming the majority.

The Portuguese explored the area in 1590, naming it The Beautiful (Formosa). In 1624 the Dutch set up forts in the south, the Spanish in the North. The Dutch threw out the Spanish in 1641 and controlled the island until 1661, when the Chinese General Koxinga took it over, established an independent kingdom, and expelled the Dutch. The Manchus seized the island in 1683 and held it until 1895, when it passed to Japan after the first Sino-Japanese War. Japan developed and exploited it, and it was heavily bombed by American planes during World War II, after which it was restored to China.

After the defeat of its armies on the mainland, the Nationalist Government of Generalissimo Chiang Kai-shek retreated to Taiwan in December 1949. With only 15% of the population consisting of the 1949 immigrants, Chiang dominated the island, maintaining a 600,000-man army in the hope of eventually recovering the mainland. Japan renounced its claim to the island by the San Francisco Peace Treaty of 1951.

By stationing a fleet in the Strait of Formosa the U.S. prevented a mainland invasion in 1953, and in 1955 the U.S. signed a mutual defense treaty by which it is committed to defend Taiwan and the neighboring islands.

The "China seat" in the U.N., which the Nationalists held with U.S. help for over two decades, was lost in October 1971, when the People's Republic of China was admitted and Taiwan ousted by the world body.

President Nixon's summit meeting with Chinese leaders and the 1972 Sino-American communiqué further eroded Taiwan's position. In it, the U.S. said its eventual goal was complete withdrawal of its forces from Taiwan and progressive cutbacks as tensions in the area eased. With the end of U.S. participation in the war in Vietnam, withdrawal of U.S. air-support forces on the island began in 1973.

Chiang died at 87 of a heart attack on April 5, 1975. His son, Chiang Ching-kuo, continued as Premier and dominant power in the Taipei regime. He assumed the presidency in 1978, and Sun Yun-suan became Premier.

President Carter's announcement that the U.S. would recognize only the People's Republic of China after Jan. 1, 1979, and that the U.S. defense treaty would end aroused protests in Taiwan and in the U.S. Congress. Against Carter's wishes, Congress, in a bill governing future relations with Taiwan, guaranteed U.S. action in the event of an attack on the island. The legislation also provided for the continuation of trade and other relations through an American Institute in Taipei, housed in the former American Embassy.

Although the U.S. had assured Taiwan of continuing arms aid, a communiqué on Aug. 17, 1982, signed by Washington and Peking and promising a gradual reduction of such aid, cast a shadow over Taiwan. The Nationalist government protested that the communiqué contradicted the "letter and the spirit" of the Taiwan Relations Act by which the U.S. Congress sought to assure Taiwan's defense.

COLOMBIA

Republic of Colombia
President: Belisario Betancur Cuartas (1982)
Area: 455,355 sq mi. (1,179,369 sq km)
Population (est. 1982): 28,575,000 (average annual growth rate, 1.6%) (mestizo, 68%; white, 20%; Indian, 7%; black, 5%)
Density per square mile: 62.8
Capital: Bogotá
Largest cities (est. 1982): Bogotá, 4,500,000; **(est. 1980):** Medellín, 1,748,000; Cali, 1,189,000; Baranquilla, 868,000; Bucaramanga, 443,000; Cartagena, 355,000
Monetary unit: Peso
Language: Spanish
Religion: Roman Catholic
National name: República de Colombia
Literacy rate (1981): 75%
Economic summary: Gross national product (1980): $31.6 billion. Average annual growth rate (1970–79): 3.7%. Per capita income (1980): $1,180. Land used for agriculture: 30%; labor force: 30%; principal products: coffee, bananas, rice, corn, sugar cane, cotton, tobacco, flowers. Labor force in industry: 15%; major products: textiles, processed food, clothing and footwear, beverages, chemicals, metal products, cement. Natural resources: petroleum, natural gas, coal, iron ore, nickel, gold, copper, emeralds. Exports: coffee, fuel oil, cotton, tobacco, sugar, textiles. Imports: machinery, electrical equipment, chemical products, metals and metal products, transportation equipment. Major trading partners: U.S., West Germany, Japan, Venezuela, Netherlands.

Geography. Colombia, in the northwestern part of South America, is the only country on that continent that borders on both the Atlantic and Pacific Oceans. It is nearly equal to the combined areas of California and Texas.

Through the western half of the country, three Andean ranges run north and south, merging into one at the Ecuadorean border. The eastern half is a low, jungle-covered plain, drained by spurs of the

Amazon and Orinoco, inhabited mostly by isolated, tropical-forest Indian tribes. The fertile plateau and valley of the eastern range are the most densely populated parts of the country.

Government. Colombia's President, who appoints his own Cabinet, serves for a four-year term. The Senate, the upper house of Congress, has 114 members elected for four years by direct vote. The House of Representatives of 199 members is directly elected for four years.

The major political parties are the Liberal Party (60 of 114 seats in Senate, 114 of 199 seats in House), Conservative Party (51 seats in Senate, 84 seats in House), and a leftist coalition (1 seat in Senate, 1 seat in House).

History. Spaniards in 1510 founded Darien, the first permanent European settlement on the American mainland. In 1538 the Spaniards established the colony of New Granada, the area's name until 1861. After a 14-year struggle, in which Simón Bolívar's Venezuelan troops won the battle of Boyacá in Colombia on Aug. 7, 1819, independence was attained in 1824. Bolívar united Colombia, Venezuela, Panama, and Ecuador in the Republic of Greater Colombia (1819–30), but lost Venezuela and Ecuador to separatists. Bolívar's Vice President, Francisco de Paula Santander, founded the Liberal Party as the Federalists while Bolívar established the Conservatives as the Centralists.

Santander's presidency (1832–36) re-established order, but later periods of Liberal dominance (1849–57 and 1861–80), when the Liberals sought to disestablish the Roman Catholic Church, were marked by insurrection and even civil war. Rafael Nuñez, in a 15-year-presidency, restored the power of the central government and the church, which led in 1899 to a bloody civil war and the loss in 1903 of Panama over ratification of a lease to the U.S. of the Canal Zone. For 21 years, until 1930, the Conservatives held power as revolutionary pressures built up.

The Liberal administrations of Enrique Olaya Herrera and Alfonso López (1930–38) were marked by social reforms that failed to solve the country's problems, and in 1946, insurrection and banditry broke out, claiming hundreds of thousands of lives by 1958. Laureano Gómez (1950–53); the Army Chief of Staff, Gen. Gustavo Rojas Pinilla (1953–56), and a military junta (1956–57) sought to curb disorder by repression.

Subsequent Presidents were Alberto Lleras Camargo (1957–62); Guillermo León Valencia (1962–66); Carlos Lleras Restrepo (1966–70); Misael Pastrana Borrero (1970–74); and Alfonso López Michelson (1974–78).

Julio César Turbay Ayala, Liberal Party candidate in 1978, won a narrow victory—approximately 140,000 of a total of nearly 2.5 million votes—over the Conservative Party candidate. The Liberals also retained control of both the Senate and House.

Government efforts to stamp out the Movement of April 19 (M-19), an urban guerrilla organization, intensified in 1981 with the capture of some of the leaders. A general amnesty failed to bring an end to the movement, but its efforts to impede the 1982 national elections on March 14 had little effect as the voting was called the most peaceful in years. Although the Liberals won a solid majority, a party split enabled Belisario Betancur Cuartas, the Conservative candidate, to win the presidency on May 31. After his inauguration, he ended the state of siege that had existed almost continously for 34 years and renewed Turbay's amnesty offer.

COMOROS

Federal and Islamic Republic of the Comoros
President: Ahmed Abdallah (1978)
Premier: Salim Ben Ali (1978)
Area: 692 sq mi. (1,792 sq km)
Population (est. 1982): 375,000 (average annual growth rate: 3.5%)
Density per square mile: 541.9
Capital and largest city (est. 1980): Moroni (on Grande Comoro), 20,000
Monetary unit: Franc CFA
Language: French
Religions: Islam and Christian
National name: État Comorien
Literacy rate (1981): 20%
Economic summary: Gross national product (1980): $100 million. Average annual growth rate (1970–79): –4.3%. Per capita income (1980): $300. Principal agricultural products: perfume essences, copra, coconuts, cloves, vanilla, cinnamon, yams; major industrial products: perfume distillations. Exports: perfume essences, vanilla, copra, cloves. Imports: foodstuffs, fuels, chemicals, cotton textiles, cement. Major trading partners: France, Madagascar, West Germany, Kenya, Italy.

Geography. The Comoros Islands—Grande Comoro, Anjouan, Mohéli, and Mayotte (which retains ties to France)—are an archipelago of volcanic origin in the Indian Ocean between Mozambique and Madagascar.

Government. A coup by foreign mercenaries on May 13, 1978, deposed President Ali Soilih, who had held power since 1975. A "political and military directorate" headed by Ahmed Abdallah and Mohammed Ahmed governed until the adoption of a constitution on Oct. 1 ushered in a republic. With the resignation of Ahmed two days later, Abdallah became president.

History. Under French rule since 1886, the Comoros declared themselves independent July 6, 1975. However, Mayotte, with a Christian majority, voted against joining the other, mainly Islamic, islands, in the move to independence and remains French.

A month after independence, Justice Minister Ali Soilih staged a coup with the help of mercenaries, overthrowing the new nation's first president, Ahmed Abdallah. Soilih lowered the voting age to 14, destroyed all records and killed many Comorans. He was overthrown on May 13, 1978, when a small boatload of French mercenaries, some of whom had aided him three years earlier, seized government headquarters.

CONGO

People's Republic of the Congo
President: Col. Denis Sassou-Nguessou (1979)
Prime Minister: Col. Louis-Sylvain Ngoma (1975)
Area: 132,046 sq mi. (342,000 sq km)
Population (est. 1982): 1,625,000 (average annual growth rate, 2.8%)
Density per sq mi.: 12.3

Capital and largest city (est. 1977): Brazzaville, 310,000
Monetary unit: Franc CFA
Ethnic groups: Vilis, Bakongo, Batekes, Mbochis
Languages: French, Lingala, Kokongo
Religions: Animist, 47%; Roman Catholic, 41%; Protestant, 10%
National name: République Populaire du Congo
Member of French Community
Literacy rate (1981): 10% (est.)
Economic summary: Gross national product (1980): $1.1 billion. Average annual growth rate (1970–79): −0.2%. Per capita income (1980): $730. Principal agricultural products: sugar cane, wood, coffee, cocoa, peanuts, tobacco. Labor force in industry: 20%; major products: crude oil, cigarettes, soap, beverages, milled sugar. Natural resources: wood, potash, petroleum, natural gas. Exports: oil, lumber, tobacco, veneer and plywood. Imports: machinery, transportation equipment, manufactured consumer goods, iron and steel, foodstuffs. Major trading partners: France and other Western European countries.

Geography. The Congo is situated in west central Africa astride the Equator. It borders on Gabon, Cameroon, the Central African Republic, Zaire, and the Angola exclave of Cabinda, with a short stretch of coast on the South Atlantic. Its area is nearly three times that of Pennsylvania.

Most of the inland is tropical rain forest, drained by tributaries of the Zaire (Congo) River, which flows south along the eastern border with Zaire to Stanley Pool. The narrow coastal plain rises to highlands separated from the inland plateaus by the 200-mile-wide Niari River Valley, which gives passage to the coast.

Government. Since the coup of September 1968 the country has been governed by a National Council of the Revolution. The Congolese Labor Party is the only party.

History. The inhabitants of the former French Congo, mainly Bantu peoples with Pygmies in the north, were subjects of several kingdoms in earlier times.

The Frenchman Pierre Savorgnan de Brazza signed a treaty with Makoko, ruler of the Bateke people, in 1880, which established French control. The area, with Gabon and Ubangi-Shari, was constituted the colony of French Equatorial Africa in 1910. It joined Chad in supporting the Free French cause in World War II. The Congo proclaimed its independence without leaving the French Community in 1960.

Maj. Marien Ngouabi, head of the National Council of the Revolution, took power as president on Jan. 1, 1969. He was sworn in for a second five-year term in 1975. A visit to Moscow by Ngouabi in March ended with the signing of a Soviet-Congolese economic and technical aid pact.

A four-man commando squad assassinated Ngouabi in Brazzaville on March 18, 1977. Five days later the assassination of Émile Cardinal Biayenda, Archbishop of Brazzaville, was announced. Former President Alphonse Massamba-Débat, accused of plotting both deaths, was executed.

Col. Joachim Yhombi-Opango, Army Chief of Staff, assumed the presidency on April 4. In June, the new government agreed to resume diplomatic relations with the U.S., ending a 12-year rift. Yombhi-Opango resigned on Feb. 4, 1979, and was replaced by Col. Denis Sassou-Neguessou.

COSTA RICA

Republic of Costa Rica
President: Luis Alberto Monge Alvarez (1982)
Area: 19,652 sq mi. (50,898 sq km)
Population (est. 1982): 2,350,000 (average annual growth rate, 2.9%)
Density per square mile: 119.6
Capital and largest city (est. 1980 for metropolitan area): San José, 800,000
Monetary unit: Colón
Language: Spanish
Religion: Roman Catholic
National name: República de Costa Rica
Literacy rate (1981): 90%
Economic summary: Gross national product (1980): $3.8 billion. Average annual growth rate (1970–79): 3.2%. Per capita income (1980): $1,730. Land used for agriculture: 8%; labor force: 33%; principal products: bananas, coffee, sugar cane, rice, corn, cocoa, livestock. Labor force in industry: 20%; major products: processed foods, textiles and clothing, construction materials, fertilizer. Natural resource: timber. Exports: coffee, bananas, beef, sugar, cacao. Imports: manufactured products, machinery, transportation equipment, chemicals, foodstuffs, fuels, fertilizer. Major trading partners: U.S., Central American countries, West Germany, Japan.

Geography. This Central American country lies between Nicaragua to the north and Panama to the south. Its area slightly exceeds that of Vermont and New Hampshire combined.

Most of Costa Rica is tableland, from 3,000 to 6,000 feet (914 to 1,829 m) above sea level. Cocos Island (10 sq mi.) (26 sq km), about 300 miles (483 km) off the Pacific Coast, is under Costa Rican sovereignty; although it is mostly tropical jungle, it is of potential strategic importance in defense of the Panama Canal.

Government. Under the 1949 Constitution, the president and the one-house Legislative Assembly of 57 members are elected for terms of four years.

The army was abolished in 1949. There is a civil guard of 3,000 and a rural guard of 2,500.

The major political parties are the National Liberation Party (33 of 57 seats in the Legislative Assembly), led by Armando Arauz; Unity Party (18 seats), led by Rafael A. Grillo; Communist Party (4 seats); Pueblo Unido Party (1 seat); Movimiento Nacional Party (1 seat).

History. Costa Rica was inhabited by 25,000 Indians when Columbus discovered it and probably named it in 1502. Few of the Indians survived the Spanish conquest, which began in 1563. The region was administered as a Spanish province. Costa Rica achieved independence in 1821 but was absorbed for two years by Agustín de Iturbide in his Mexican Empire. It was established as a republic in 1848.

Except for the military dictatorship of Tomás Guardia from 1870 to 1882, Costa Rica has enjoyed one of the most democratic governments in Latin America.

Rodrigo Carazo Odio, leader of a four-party coalition called the Unity Party, won the presidency in February 1978, campaigning on the government's having allowed Robert L. Vesco, a fugitive U.S. financier, to find asylum in Costa Rica. His tenure was marked by a disastrous decline in the economy, which forced postponement of foreign debt payments at the end of 1981. Luis Alberto Monge Alvarez, a former union organizer and cofounder of the National Liberation Party, swept to victory in the Feb. 7, 1982, national elections.

CUBA

Republic of Cuba
President (1976) and Premier (1959): Fidel Castro
Area: 44,218 sq mi. (114,524 sq km)
Population (est. 1982): 9,850,000 (average annual growth rate, 0.8%)
Density per square mile: 222.8
Capital: Havana
Largest cities (est. 1980): Havana, 2,000,000; **(est. 1975 by U.N.):** Santiago de Cuba, 315,800; Camagüey, 221,800; Holguín, 151,900; Guantánamo, 148,800; Santa Clara, 146,650
Monetary unit: Peso
Language: Spanish
Religion: Roman Catholic
National name: República de Cuba
Literacy rate (1981): 96%
Economic summary: Gross national product (1979): $13.9 billion. Average annual growth rate (1970–78): 4.7%. Land used for agriculture: 35%; labor force: 33%; principal products: sugar, tobacco, coffee, rice, meat, vegetables, fruits. Labor force in industry: 17%; major products: refined oil products, textiles, chemicals, processed food, metals, light consumer products. Natural resources: metals, primarily nickel. Exports: sugar, nickel, shellfish, tobacco. Imports: capital goods, industrial raw materials, petroleum, foodstuffs. Major trading partners: U.S.S.R., other Communist bloc countries.

Geography. The largest island of the West Indies group (equal in area to Pennsylvania), Cuba is also the westernmost—just west of Hispaniola (Haiti and the Dominican Republic), and 90 miles (145 km) south of Key West, Fla., at the entrance to the Gulf of Mexico.

The island is mountainous in the southeast and south central area (Sierra Maestra). Elsewhere it is flat or rolling.

Government. There have been no national elections since 1958. Fidel Castro heads the Council of Ministers, the chief governing body.

The only political party is the Cuban Communist Party, with a 100-member Central Committee, a Politbureau of 8, and a Secretariat of 6.

History. Arawak Indians inhabiting Cuba when Columbus discovered the island in 1492 died off from diseases brought by sailors and settlers. By 1511, Spaniards under Diego Velásquez were founding settlements that served as bases for Spanish exploration. Cuba soon after served as an assembly point for treasure looted by the conquistadores, attracting French and English pirates.

Black slaves and free laborers were imported to work sugar and tobacco plantations, and waves of chiefly Spanish immigrants maintained a European character in the island's culture. Early slave rebellions and conflicts between colonials and Spanish rulers laid the foundation for an independence movement that turned into open warfare from 1867 to 1878. The poet, José Marti, in 1895 led the struggle that finally ended Spanish rule, thanks largely to U.S. intervention in 1898 after the sinking of the battleship *Maine* in Havana harbor.

A treaty in 1899 made Cuba an independent republic under U.S. protection. The U.S. occupation, which ended in 1902, suppressed yellow fever and brought large American investment. From 1906 to 1909, Washington invoked the Platt Amendment to the treaty, which gave it the right to intervene in order to suppress any revolt. U.S. troops came back in 1912 and again in 1917 to restore order. The Platt Amendment was abrogated in 1934.

Gerardo Machado, President during the Depression, planned vast social reforms but abandoned them. Fulgencio Batista, an army sergeant, led a revolt in 1934 that overthrew the Machado regime and developed into a Batista dictatorship. A succession of constitutionally elected Presidents—Ramón Grau San Martín, Carlos Mendieta, Miguel Mariano Gómez, Carlos Prío Socarrás—pushed through social reforms, hampered by overwhelming corruption manipulated by Batista, who seized power in 1952.

Fidel Castro staged a hopeless revolt in 1953. Captured and paroled, he went to Oriente Province and, aided by an Argentinian adventurer, Ernesto (Ché) Guevara, rebuilt his forces and waged a guerrilla war. The U.S. withdrew support from Batista in 1958. With funds from Soviet sources, Castro bought off the leaders of Batista's army. This and popular support from the intellectual and laboring classes demoralized the army, and Castro's forces grew as he marched on Havana. Batista fled to the Dominican Republic on Jan. 1, 1959.

Executions and torture by the new Castro regime caused a world outcry. Castro antagonized the U.S. in 1959 by confiscating U.S. investments in banks and industries and by seizing large U.S. landholdings, turning them at first into collective farms, then into Soviet-type state farms.

The U.S. broke off relations on Jan. 3, 1961, and Castro disclosed his alliance with the U.S.S.R. and the Soviet bloc. Thousands of Cubans fled to the U.S. From their ranks an invasion force was recruited by an all-party coalition financed and guided by the U.S. Central Intelligence Agency and trained in Florida and Guatemala. A landing in the Bay of Pigs, Cuba, on April 17, 1961, failed when President Kennedy refused it air support under Soviet and Latin American pressure.

In 1962 the U.S.S.R. built missile sites in Cuba and provided Castro's army with troops, planes, and submarines. Alarmed, Kennedy on Oct. 22, 1962, served notice that the U.S. was willing to risk war to enforce a demand that the Soviet Union remove weapons and troops threatening U.S. security. The U.S. confronted Soviet vessels with U.S. warships. Soviet Premier Nikita Khrushchev agreed to remove the missiles, and the blockade was lifted on November 20. Shortly before Christmas, Castro released 1,113 Bay of Pigs prisoners.

U.S.-Cuban relations began to thaw with negotiation of a 1973 agreement to end air hijacking. Except for political refugees, criminal hijackers will be extradited to their home country or tried for the crime where they land; also, both nations pledged to forbid attacks on the other to be mounted from their territory.

U.S. curbs on travel by Cuba'a United Nations delegation were eased in 1975 and the U.S. joined 15 Latin American republics in voting to scrap economic and diplomatic sanctions the O.A.S. had imposed against Cuba in 1964.

Despite Cuba's intervention in Africa, the Carter administration signed fishing agreements with Havana in 1977, removed restrictions on travel to the island, and eased the 1960 embargo to permit Cuba to buy essential goods.

In September 1977, Cuban diplomats opened an interests section in the old Cuban embassy in Washington and 10 Americans—later 20—opened a similar office in the former U.S. embassy in Havana. Hopes that full diplomatic relations would be restored were shattered early in 1978 when Washington charged that 10,000 to 11,000 Cubans were fighting for the Marxist government of Ethiopia.

Late in 1978, Castro offered to free 3,600 remaining political prisoners if the U.S. would accept them, to which he later added 7,000 former prisoners and up to 50,000 persons having relatives living abroad. Small numbers began to leave, but both Castro and Cuban exiles complained that U.S. immigration processing was too slow.

Emigration increased dramatically after April 1, 1980, when Castro, irritated at the granting of asylum to would-be refugees by the Peruvian embassy, removed the guards and allowed 10,000 Cubans to swarm into the embassy grounds. As an airlift began taking them to Costa Rica for distribution to other countries, Castro insisted that they must go directly to their final destination. He ordered the port of Mariel opened and a "freedom flotilla" of small boats from the U.S. arrived to find that the government had consigned criminals, homosexuals, and others considered undesirable to be taken along with relatives of Cuban-Americans. Departures soared past 125,000 despite efforts by the Carter administration to halt the traffic and they stopped only when Castro, embarrassed by the reported application of 1 million Cubans to join the exodus, closed the port Sept. 26.

At the second Party Congress in December, Castro voiced willingness to improve relations with the new Reagan administration, but was rebuffed by Secretary of State Alexander M. Haig, Jr., who denounced Cuba in January 1981 as a proxy for Soviet subversion in the Caribbean. Haig later named Cuba as the source of arms and training for leftist guerrillas in El Salvador and threatened to "go to the source," a threat that Castro used as justification for mustering a new territorial force of 500,000 as a supplement to regular forces.

Despite a report by the U.S. Congress' Joint Economic Committee in April 1982 that the 20-year embargo against Cuba had served only to drive the island into greater dependence on Moscow, the Reagan administration banned tourist travel to Cuba and tightened the embargo. Secret contacts—a meeting between Haig and Cuban Vice President Carlos Rafael Rodriguez and another between Castro and U.S. Ambassador at Large Vernon Walters—brought no improvement in relations. In August, the U.S. House of Representatives passed a bill authorizing Radio Marti to broadcast internal Cuban news to Cuba. Castro pledged retaliation that could disrupt radio broadcasting throughout the U.S.

CYPRUS

Republic of Cyprus
President: Spyros Kyprianou (1977)
Area: 3,572 sq mi (9,251 sq km)
Population (est. 1982): 650,000 (average annual growth rate: 1.0%) (Turkish, 18%)
Density per square mile: 182.0
Capital and largest city (est. 1980): Nicosia, 160,000
Monetary unit: Cyprus pound
Languages: Greek, Turkish, English
Religions: Greek Orthodox, 77%; Islam, 18%
National name: Kypriaki Dimokratia—Kibris Cumhuriyeti
Member of Commonwealth of Nations
Literacy rate (1981): 89%
Economic summary: Gross national product (1980): $2.2 billion. Average annual growth rate (1970–78): 1.4%. Per capita income (1980): $3,560. Land used for agriculture: 47%; labor force: 36%; principal products: vine products, citrus, potatoes, other vegetables. Labor force in industry: 47%; major products: beverages, footwear, clothing, cement, asbestos mining. Natural resources: copper, asbestos, gypsum, building stone, marble, clay, salt. Exports: asbestos, copper, pyrites, citrus, raisins. Imports: manufactured goods, machinery and transportation equipment, petroleum products, foodstuffs. Major trading partners: U.K., Lebanon, Libya.

Geography. The third largest island in the Mediterranean (one and one half times the size of Delaware), Cyprus lies off the southern coast of Turkey and the western shore of Syria. Most of the country consists of a wide plain lying between two mountain ranges that cross the island. The highest peak is Mount Olympus at 6,406 feet (1,953 m).

Government. Under the republic's Constitution, for the protection of the Turkish minority the vice president as well as three of the 10 Cabinet ministers must be from the Turkish community, while the House of Representatives is elected by each community separately, 70% Greek Cypriote and 30% Turkish Cypriote representatives.

The Greek and Turkish communities are self-governing in questions of religion, education, and culture. Other governmental matters are under the jurisdiction of the central government. Each community is entitled to a Communal Chamber.

The Greek Communal Chamber, which had 23 members, was abolished in 1965 and its function was absorbed by the Ministry of Education. The Turkish Communal Chamber, however, has continued to function.

The following is a breakdown of the 35 seats held by Greeks: Democratic Front of Spyros Kyprianou (8); AKEL Progressive Party of the Working People (12); Democratic Rally (12); Socialist Party of Dr. Vassos Lyssarides (3). The 15 Turkish members have not attended sessions of the House since 1964.

History. Cyprus was the site of early Phoenician and Greek colonies. For centuries its rule passed through many hands. It fell to the Turks in 1571, and a large Turkish colony settled on the island.

In World War I, on the outbreak of hostilities with Turkey, Britain annexed the island. It was declared a crown colony in 1925.

For centuries the Greek population, regarding Greece as its mother country, has sought self-determination and reunion with it *(enosis)*. The resulting quarrel with Turkey threatened NATO. Cyprus became an independent nation on Aug. 16, 1960, with Britain, Greece, and Turkey as guarantor powers.

After troubled years, a crisis was averted in 1968 when an American mediator, Cyrus R. Vance, induced Turkey, Greece, and Cyprus to accept a solution proposed by U.N. Secretary General U Thant for withdrawal of the Greek troops and the dismantling of Turkish invasion forces. The ethnic blocs began long direct negotiations for a new Constitution.

Archbishop Makarios, president since 1959, was overthrown July 15, 1974, by a military coup led by the Cypriot National Guard. The new regime named Nikos Giorgiades Sampson as president and Bishop Gennadios as head of the Cypriot Church to replace Makarios. The rebels were led by rightist Greek officers who supported *enosis*.

Diplomacy failed to resolve the crisis. Turkey invaded Cyprus by sea and air July 20, 1974, asserting its right to protect the Turkish Cypriote minority. Greece rejected a Turkish demand for withdrawal of the 650 Greek officers who had engineered the coup. The crisis forced resignation of the military junta that had ruled Greece for seven years.

Geneva talks involving Greece, Turkey, Britain, and the two Cypriote factions failed in mid-August, and the Turks subsequently gained control of 40% of the island. Greece made no armed response to the superior Turkish force, but bitterly suspended military participation in the NATO alliance.

On Cyprus, U.S. Ambassador Rodger P. Davies was shot to death in August during Greek Cypriote riots. The tension continued after Makarios returned to become President on Dec. 7, 1974. He offered self-government to the Turkish minority, but rejected any solution "involving transfer of populations and amounting to partition of Cyprus."

Turkish Cypriots proclaimed a separate state in the northern part of the island and proposed a "bi-regional federation." Some 200,000 Greek Cypriots demanded return to their homes in the Turkish zone and an estimated three fourths of the 45,000 ethnic Turks in the Greek zone crossed into the Turkish area.

Makarios died on Aug. 3, 1977, and Spyros Kiprianou was elected to serve the remaining five months of his term. Kiprianou, running unopposed, won a full five-year term in 1978.

Despite intense pressure from the U.S. and other NATO allies anxious to end the dispute that kept both Greece and Turkey from functioning as defenders of the strategic eastern Mediterranean, intercommunal negotiations have remained deadlocked.

CZECHOSLOVAKIA

Czechoslovak Socialist Republic
President: Gustav Husak (1975)
Premier: Lubomir Strougal (1970)
Area: 49,374 sq mi. (127,877 sq km)
Population (est. 1982): 15,400,000 (average annual growth rate: 0.4%) (Czech, 64%; Slovak, 30%)
Density per square mile: 311.9
Capital: Prague
Largest cities (est. 1981): Prague, 1,182,000; Bratislava, 381,000; Brno, 371,000; Ostrava, 322,000; Kosice, 203,000; Plzeň, 171,000
Monetary unit: Koruna
Languages: Czech, Slovak, Hungarian
Religions: Roman Catholic, 70%; Czechoslovak Church, 8%; Protestant, 7%; Greek Orthodox, 5%.
National name: Ceskoslovenská Socialistická Republika
Literacy rate (1981): 100%
Economic summary: Gross national product (1980): $89.3 billion. Average annual growth rate (1970–79): 4.1%. Per capita income (1980): $5,820. Labor force in agriculture: 14%; principal products: wheat, rye, oats, corn, barley, potatoes, sugar beets, hogs, cattle, horses. Labor force in industry: 39%; major products: iron and steel, machinery and equipment, cement, textiles, motor vehicles, armaments, chemicals, ceramics. Natural resources: coal/coke, timber, lignite, uranium, magnesite. Exports: machinery, fuels and raw materials, consumer goods. Imports: machinery, equipment, fuels, raw materials, food, consumer goods. Major trading partners: U.S.S.R. and Soviet bloc, West Germany, Austria, U.K.

Geography. Czechoslovakia lies in central Europe, a neighbor of East and West Germany, Poland, the U.S.S.R., Hungary, and Austria. It is equal in size to New York State. The principal rivers—the Elbe, Danube, Oder, and Moldau—are vital commercially to this landlocked country, for both waterborne commerce and agriculture, which flourishes in fertile valleys irrigated by these rivers and their tributaries.

Government. Since 1969 the supreme organ of the state has been the Federal Assembly, which has two equal chambers: the Chamber of People, with 200 deputies, and the Chamber of Nations, with 150 deputies (75 from the Czech Socialist Republic and 75 from the Slovak Socialist Republic). The chief executive is the President, who is elected by the Federal Assembly for a five-year term. The Premier and his Cabinet are appointed by the President but are responsible to the Federal Assembly.

The major political parties are the Communist Party, led by First Secretary Gustav Husak in both republics; Socialist Party; People's Party in the Czech Socialist Republic; Slovak Freedom Party and Slovak Reconstruction Party in the Slovak Socialist Republic. Together with trade unions, youth organizations, and other organizations, they form the National Front.

History. Probably about the 5th century A.D., Slavic tribes from the Vistula basin settled in the region of modern Czechoslovakia. Slovakia came under Magyar domination. The Czechs founded the kingdom of Bohemia, the Premyslide dynasty, which ruled Bohemia and Moravia from the 10th to the 16th century. One of the Bohemian kings, Charles IV, Holy Roman Emperor, made Prague an imperial capital and a center of Latin scholarship. The Hussite movement founded by Jan Hus (1369?–1415) linked the Slavs to the Reformation and revived Czech nationalism, previously under German domination. A Hapsburg, Ferdinand I, ascended the throne in 1526. The Czechs rebelled in 1618. Defeated in 1620, they were ruled for the next 300 years as part of the Austrian Empire.

In World War I, Czech and Slovak patriots, notably Thomas G. Masaryk and Milan Stefanik, promoted Czech-Slovak independence from abroad while their followers fought against the Central Powers. On Oct. 28, 1918, Czechoslovakia proclaimed itself a republic. Shortly thereafter Masaryk was unanimously elected first President.

Hitler provoked the country's German minority in the Sudetenland, led by Konrad Henlein, to agitate for autonomy. At the Munich Conference on Sept. 30, 1938, France and the U.K., seeking to avoid World War II, agreed that the Nazis could take the Sudetenland. Dr. Eduard Beneš, who had succeeded Masaryk, resigned on Oct. 5, 1938, and fled to London. Czechoslovakia became a state within the German orbit and was known as Czecho-Slovakia. In March 1939, the Nazis occupied the country. Beneš organized a government-in-exile in London in 1940.

Soon after Czechoslovakia was liberated in World War II and the government returned in April 1945, it was obliged to cede Ruthenia to the

U.S.S.R. In 1946, a Communist, Klement Gottwald, formed a six-party coalition Cabinet. Pressure from Moscow increased until Feb. 23–25, 1948, when the Communists seized complete control in a coup. Following constituent assembly elections in which the Communists and their allies were unopposed, a new Constitution was adopted.

Beneš refused to sign it and resigned; he died mysteriously on Sept. 3, 1948. The Constitution was promulgated June 9. Thereafter, agriculture was collectivized, industry almost completely socialized, and foreign trade conducted chiefly with the Soviet bloc. Industrialization was intensified and concentrated upon heavy industry. The "people's democracy" was converted into a "socialist" state by a new Constitution adopted June 11, 1960.

After the death of Stalin and the relaxing of Soviet controls, Czechoslovakia witnessed a nationalist awakening. In 1968 conservative Stalinists were driven from power and replaced by more liberal, reform-minded Communists.

In more orthodox circles of the U.S.S.R. and its European satellites, fears arose that the trend was undermining Communist rule. Soviet military maneuvers on Czechoslovak soil in May 1968 were followed in July by a meeting of the U.S.S.R. with Poland, Bulgaria, East Germany, and Hungary in Warsaw that demanded an accounting, which Prague refused. Czechoslovak-Soviet talks on Czechoslovak territory, at Cierna, in late July led to an accord. But the Russians charged that the Czechoslovaks had reneged on pledges to modify their policies, and on Aug. 20–21, troops of the five powers, estimated at 600,000, executed a lightning invasion and occupation.

Soviet secret police seized the top Czechoslovak leadership and detained it for several days in Moscow. But Soviet efforts to establish a puppet regime failed. President Ludvik Svoboda negotiated an accord providing for a gradual troop withdrawal in return for "normalization" of political policy.

The purge of liberals was virtually completed in 1970. Only Svoboda remained from 1968. Husak, who became Secretary General of the Communist Party in 1969, promised no show trials, but most liberals were punished. Czechoslovakia signed a new friendship treaty with the U.S.S.R. that codified the "Brezhnev doctrine," under which Russia can invade any Eastern European socialist nation that threatens to leave the satellite camp.

Continuing ferment surfaced early in 1975 with publication in the West of a long letter of protest against repression written by Alexander Dubcek, First Secretary of the Czechoslovak Communist Party during the 1968 "Prague Spring." The letter, addressed to the Presidium of Czechoslovakia's Federal Assembly, charged that the regime had purged thousands of creative workers. Dubcek was later reported transferred to a menial forester's job.

One of the most vigorous of the Eastern European groups formed to support human rights in the wake of the 1975 Helsinki Conference on Security and Cooperation in Europe was the Czech "Charter 77," an association of 240 intellectuals who signed a New Year manifesto protesting the suppression of freedom. Detentions of the signers began immediately, and a second manifesto appeared on January 8 with 300 signatures condemning the official reaction to the first. On Jan. 28, the government offered to let five of the dissidents leave the country, but they refused.

Charter 77 adherents marked their first anniversary with a manifesto Jan. 1, 1978, calling for open debate on the observance of human rights in Czechoslovakia. Enough of the group remained in May 1981 for the government to jail 36 persons in the biggest roundup of dissidents since 1971, as part of the precautions against any show of sympathy for Polish workers. The Czech Communist Party was among the most severe of the Eastern European states in condemning what Husak called an attempted "counterrevolutionary coup" in Poland.

DENMARK

Kingdom of Denmark
Sovereign: Queen Margrethe II (1972)
Premier: Poul Schlüter (1982)
Area: 16,615 sq mi. (43,033 sq km)[1]
Population (est. 1982): 5,130,000[1] (average annual growth rate: 0.1%)
Density per square mile: 308.8
Capital: Copenhagen
Largest cities (est. 1980): Copenhagen, 660,000; (est. 1976 by U.N.): Arhus, 246,100; Odense, 167,900; Alborg, 154,600
Monetary unit: Krone
Language: Danish
Religion: Lutheran (established)
National name: Kongeriget Danmark
Literacy rate (1981): 99%
Economic summary: Gross national product (1980): $66.4 billion. Average annual growth rate (1970–79): 2.1%. Per capita income (1980): $12,950. Labor force in agriculture: 9%; principal products: meat, dairy products, fish, fur. Labor force in industry: 33%; major products: industrial and construction equipment, electronics, furniture, textiles. Natural resources: oil and gas, zinc, lead, iron ore, coal, molybdenum, cryolite, uranium. Exports: meat and dairy products, industrial machinery, textiles and clothing, chemical products, transportation equipment. Imports: industrial raw materials, fuel, machinery and equipment, transport equipment, petroleum, chemicals, textile fibers. Major trading partners: West Germany, Sweden, U.K., U.S.

1. Excluding Faeroe Islands and Greenland.

Geography. Smallest of the Scandinavian countries (half the size of Maine), Denmark occupies the Jutland peninsula, which extends north from Germany between the tips of Norway and Sweden. To the west is the North Sea and to the east the Baltic.

The country also consists of several Baltic islands; the two largest are Sjaelland, the site of Copenhagen, and Fyn. The narrow waters off the north coast are called the Skagerrak and those off the east, the Kattegat.

Government. Denmark has been a constitutional monarchy since 1849. Legislative power is held jointly by the Sovereign and parliament. The Constitution of 1953 provides for a unicameral parliament called the Folketing, consisting of 179 popularly elected members who serve for four years. The Cabinet is presided over by the Sovereign, who appoints the Prime Minister.

The Sovereign, Queen Margrethe II, was born April 16, 1940, and became Queen—the first in Denmark's history—Jan. 15, 1972, the day after her father, King Frederik IX, died at 72 in the 25th year of his reign. Margrethe was the eldest of his three daughters (by Princess Ingrid of Sweden).

The nation's Constitution was amended in 1953 to permit her to succeed her father in the absence of a male heir to the throne. (Denmark was ruled six centuries ago by Margrethe I, but she was never crowned Queen since there was no female right of succession.) Margrethe's sisters are Benedikte (born 1944) and Anne Marie (born 1946), now the former Queen of Greece.

The major political parties are the Social Democratic Party (59 seats in the Folketing), led by former Premier Anker Jørgensen; Conservative Party (26 seats), led by Premier Poul Schlüter; Socialist People's Party (21 seats), led by Gert Petersen; Liberal Democratic Party (20 seats), led by Henning Christophersen; Progress Party (16 seats), led by Mogens Glistrup; Center Democratic Party (15 seats); Radical Liberal Party (9 seats).

History. Denmark emerged with establishment of the Norwegian dynasty of the Ynglinger in Jutland at the end of the 8th century. Danish mariners played a major role in the raids of the Vikings, or Norsemen, on Western Europe and particularly England. The country was Christianized by St. Ansgar and Harald Blaatand (Bluetooth)—the first Christian king—in the 10th century. Harald's son, Sweyn, conquered England in 1013. His son, Canute the Great, who reigned from 1014 to 1035, united Denmark, England, and Norway under his rule; the southern part of Sweden was part of Denmark until the 17th century. On Canute's death, civil war tore the country until Waldemar I (1157–82) re-established Danish hegemony over the north.

In 1282, the nobles won the Great Charter, and Eric V was forced to share power with parliament and a Council of Nobles. Waldemar IV (1340–75) restored Danish power, checked only by the Hanseatic League of north German cities allied with ports from Holland to Poland. His daughter, Margrethe, in 1397 united under her rule Denmark, Norway, and Sweden. But Sweden later achieved autonomy and in 1523, under Gustavus I, independence.

Denmark supported Napoleon, for which it was punished at the Congress of Vienna in 1815 by the loss of Norway to Sweden. In 1864, Bismarck, together with the Austrians, made war on the little country as an initial step in the unification of Germany. Denmark was neutral in World War I.

In 1939, Denmark signed a 10-year pact with Hitler, but less than a year later it was invaded by the Nazis. King Christian X reluctantly cautioned his countrymen to accept the occupation, but there was widespread resistance against the Nazis. In 1944, Iceland declared its independence from Denmark, ending a union that had existed since 1380.

Liberated by British troops in May 1945, the country staged a fast recovery in both agriculture and manufacturing and was a leader in liberalizing trade. It joined the United Nations in 1945 and NATO in 1949.

The Social Democrats largely ran Denmark after the war but were ousted in 1973 when, in an election dominated by protests against high taxes, all established parties lost heavily. The big winner was the new Progress Party. A minority government was formed by the Liberal Democrats, with their leader, Poul Hartling, as Premier. After losing a vote of confidence in January 1975, Hartling resigned and was succeeded by Anker Jørgensen, a Social Democrat who was Premier in 1972–73.

Outlying Territories of Denmark

FAEROE ISLANDS

Status: Autonomous part of Denmark
Commissioner: L. Groth (1972)
Area: 540 sq mi. (1,399 sq km)
Population (est. 1982): 43,000 (average annual growth rate: 1.8%)
Density per square mile: 79.9
Capital (1977 census): Thorshavn, 11,600
Monetary unit: Faeroese krone
Literacy rate (1981): 80%
Economic summary: Gross national product (1980): $440 million. Average annual growth rate (1970–79): 5.6%. Per capita income (1980): $10,620. Principal agricultural products: sheep and cattle. Major industrial product: fish. Exports: fish and fish products. Imports: machinery and transport equipment, foodstuffs, petroleum and petroleum products. Major trading partners: Denmark, U.S., Norway, U.K.

This group of 21 islands, lying in the North Atlantic about 200 miles (322 km) northwest of the Shetland Islands, joined Denmark in 1386 and has since been part of the Danish kingdom. The islands were occupied by British troops during World War II, after the German occupation of Denmark.

The Faeroes have home rule under a bill enacted in 1948; they also have two representatives in the Danish Folketing.

GREENLAND

Status: Autonomous part of Denmark
Premier: Jonathan Motzfeldt
Area: 840,000 sq mi. (incl. 708,069 sq mi. covered by icecap) (2,175,600 sq km).
Population (est. 1982): 50,000 (average annual growth rate: 0.6%)
Capital (est. 1979): Godthaab, 8,800
Monetary unit: Krone
Literacy rate (1981): 99%
Economic summary: Gross national product (1980): $430 million. Average annual growth rate (1970–79): 4.4%. Per Capita Income (1980): $8,290. Principal agricultural products: hay, sheep, garden produce. Major industries: mining, slaughtering, fishing, sealing. Natural resource: cryolite. Exports: fish and fish products, metalic ores and concentrates. Imports: petroleum and petroleum products, machinery and transport equipment, foodstuffs. Major trading partners: Denmark, U.S., Finland, West Germany, U.K.

Greenland, the world's largest island, was colonized in 985–86 by Eric the Red. Danish sovereignty, which covered only the west coast, was extended over the whole island in 1917. In 1941 the U.S. signed an agreement with the Danish minister in Washington, placing it under U.S. protection during World War II but maintaining Danish sovereignty. A definitive agreement for the joint defense of Greenland within the framework of NATO was signed in 1951. A large U.S. air base at Thule in the far north was completed in 1953.

Under 1953 amendments to the Danish Constitution, Greenland became part of Denmark, with two representatives in the Danish Folketing. On May 1, 1979, Greenland gained home rule, with its own local parliament (Landsting), replacing the Greenland Provincial Council.

In February 1982, Greenlanders voted to withdraw from the European Community, which they had joined as part of Denmark in 1973. Danish

Premier Anker Jørgensen said he would support the request, but with reluctance.

Greenland is the world's only source of natural cryolite, important in making aluminum.

DJIBOUTI

Republic of Djibouti
President: Gouled Aptidon Hassan (1977)
Prime Minister: Gourad Hamadou Barkat (1978)
Area: 8,996 sq mi. (23,300 sq km)
Population (est. 1982): 335,000 (average annual growth rate: 4.1%)
Density per sq mi.: 37.2
Capital (est. 1980): Djibouti, 200,000
Monetary unit: Djibouti franc
Languages: Arabic, French, Afar, Somali
Religion: Islam
Literacy rate (1981): 5%
Economic summary: Gross national product (1980): $170 million. Average annual growth rate (1970–79): –4.9%. Per capita income (1980): $480. Principal agricultural products: goats, sheep, camels. Industries: port and maritime support, construction. Exports: hides, cattle, coffee (in transit from Ethiopia). Imports: machinery, transport equipment, foodstuffs. Major trading partners: France, Ethiopia, Japan, Belgium, U.K.

Geography. Djibouti lies in northeastern Africa on the Gulf of Aden at the southern entrance to the Red Sea. It borders on Ethiopia and Somalia. The country, the size of Massachusetts, is mainly a stony desert, with scattered plateaus and highlands.

Government. On May 8, 1977, the population of the French Territory of the Afars and Issas voted by more than 98% for independence. Voters also approved a 65-member interim Constituent Assembly. France transferred sovereignty to the new nation of Djibouti on June 27. Later in the year it became a member of the Organization of African Unity and the Arab League. The People's Progress Assembly is the only political party.

History. The territory that is now Djibouti was acquired by France between 1843 and 1886 by treaties with the Somali sultans. Small, arid, and sparsely populated, Djibouti is important chiefly because of the capital city's port, the terminal of the Djibouti-Addis Ababa railway that carries 60% of Ethiopia's foreign trade.

Originally known as French Somaliland, the colony voted in 1958 and 1967 to remain under French rule. It was renamed the Territory of the Afars and Issas in 1967 and took the name of its capital city on attaining independence.

Somali rebels in Ethiopia's Ogaden Province cut the railway to Djibouti in June 1977 and there was fear that the new nation might be absorbed by Somalia. In July 1980, Djibouti granted base rights to United States ships and planes in exchange for undisclosed amounts of aid.

DOMINICA

Republic of Dominica
President: Aurelius Marie (1980)
Prime Minister: Mary Eugenia Charles (1980)
Area: 300 sq mi. (777 sq km)
Population: (est. 1982): 85,000 (average annual growth rate: 0.6%)
Density per square mile: 283.3
Capital and largest city (est. 1981): Roseau, 20,000
Monetary unit: East Caribbean dollar
Languages: English and French patois
Religions: Roman Catholic, Anglican, Methodist
National name: Republica Dominicana
Member of Commonwealth of Nations
Literacy rate (1981): 80%
Economic summary: Gross national product (1980): $50 million. Average annual growth rate (1970–79): –3.2%. Per capita income (1980): $620. Labor force in agriculture: 50%; principal products: bananas, citrus fruits, coconuts, cocoa. Major industries: agricultural processing; tourism. Exports: bananas, lime juice, oil, cocoa. Imports: machinery and equipment, foodstuffs, manufactured goods, cement. Major trading partners: U.K. and Caribbean countries.

Geography. Dominica is an island of the Lesser Antilles in the Caribbean south of Guadeloupe and north of Martinique.

Government. Dominica is a republic, with a president elected by the House of Assembly as head of state and a prime minister appointed by the president on the advice of the Assembly. The Freedom Party (17 of 21 seats in the Assembly) is led by Prime Minister Mary Eugenia Charles. The Opposition Democratic Labor Party holds two seats and independents the remaining two.

History. Discovered by Columbus in 1493, Dominica was claimed by Britain and France until 1815, when Britain asserted sovereignty. Dominica, along with other Windward Isles, became a self-governing member of the West Indies Associated States in free association with Britain in 1967.

Full independence was granted on Nov. 3, 1978, in ceremonies at which the first Prime Minister, Patrick R. John, declared a socialist course for the new republic. John aroused strong opposition when he proposed laws curbing the right to strike and freedom of the press. During a demonstration in Roseau in May 1979, police fired at the crowd, killing three. After a general strike, John dissolved the Assembly and set new elections for Dec. 1, but continued disorder forced his resignation and replacement by Oliver Seraphin.

Dissatisfaction over the slow pace of reconstruction after Hurricane David struck the island in September 1979 brought a landslide victory for the opposition Freedom Party in July 1980. The vote gave the prime ministership to Mary Eugenia Charles, a strong advocate of free enterprise.

DOMINICAN REPUBLIC

President: Salvador Jorge Blanco (1982)
Area: 18,704 sq mi. (48,442 sq km)
Population (est. 1982): 5,575,000 (average annual growth rate: 2.7%) (approx.): mestizo, 75%; white, 15%; Negro, 10%
Density per square mile: 298.1
Capital: Santo Domingo
Largest cities (est. 1981): Santo Domingo, 1,250,000; **(1970 census):** Santiago de los Caballeros, 155,151
Monetary unit: Peso
Language: Spanish
Religion: Roman Catholic

National name: República Dominicana
Literacy rate (1981): 68%
Economic summary: Gross national product (1980): $6.2 billion. Average annual growth rate (1970–79): 3.7%. Per capita income (1980): $1,140. Land used for agriculture: 14%; labor force: 73%; principal products: sugar cane, coffee, cocoa, tobacco, rice, corn. Labor force in industry: 8%; major products: processed sugar, textiles, cement, nickel, bauxite, and gold mining. Natural resources: nickel, bauxite, gold, silver. Exports: sugar, nickel, coffee, tobacco, cocoa, bauxite. Imports: foodstuffs, petroleum, industrial raw materials, capital equipment. Major trading partner: U.S.

Geography. The Dominican Republic in the West Indies, occupies the eastern two thirds of the island of Hispaniola, which it shares with Haiti. Its area equals that of Vermont and New Hampshire combined.

Crossed from northwest to southeast by a mountain range with elevations exceeding 10,000 feet (3,048 m), the country has fertile, well-watered land in the north and east, where nearly two thirds of the population lives. The southwest part is arid and has poor soil, except around Santo Domingo.

Government. The president is elected by direct vote every four years. Legislative powers rest with a Senate and a Chamber of Deputies, both elected by direct vote, also for four years. All citizens must vote when they reach 18 years of age, or even earlier if they are married.

The major political parties are the Dominican Revolutionary Party, the party of the Administration, led by Dr. José Francisco Peña Gomez; the Reformist Party, led by former President Joaquín Balaguer; Dominican Liberation Party, led by Juan Bosch; Partido Quisquellano Demócrata, led by Elías Wessin y Wessin; Movimiento de Integración Democrática Anti-Releccionista, led by Augusto Lora.

History. The Dominican Republic was discovered by Columbus in 1492. He named it La Española, and his son, Diego, was its first viceroy. The capital, Santo Domingo, founded in 1496, is the oldest European settlement in the Western Hemisphere. Spain ceded the colony to France in 1795, and Haitian blacks under Toussaint L'Ouverture conquered it in 1801.

In 1808 the people revolted and the next year captured Santo Domingo, setting up the first republic. Spain regained title to the colony in 1814. In 1821 the people overthrew Spanish rule, but in 1822 they were reconquered by the Haitians. They revolted again in 1844, threw out the Haitians, and established the Dominican Republic, headed by Pedro Santana. Uprisings and Haitian attacks led Santana to make the country a province of Spain from 1861 to 1865. The U.S. Senate refused to ratify a treaty of annexation. Disorder continued until the dictatorship of Ulíses Heureaux; in 1916, when disorder broke out again, the U.S. sent in a contingent of marines, who remained until 1934.

A sergeant in the Dominican army trained by the marines, Rafaél Leonides Trujillo Molina, overthrew Horacio Vásquez in 1930 and established a dictatorship that lasted until his assassination 31 years later.

After Trujillo's assassination on May 30, 1961, disorders forced out the President, Joaquín Balaguer, but a governing council, in spite of an abortive military coup, steered the country to a return to constitutional government.

A new Constitution was adopted in 1962, and the first free elections since 1924 put Juan Bosch, a leftist leader, in office. A planned program of reforms with U.S. support was cut off by a right-wing military coup that replaced Bosch with a civilian triumvirate.

Leftists rebelled April 24, 1965, and President Lyndon Johnson sent in 400 marines to help evacuate U.S. citizens. After an OAS ceasefire request May 6, a compromise installed Hector Garcia-Godoy as provisional president. Balaguer won in free elections in 1966 against Bosch, and an OAS force of 9,000 U.S. troops and 2,000 from other countries withdrew. Balaguer restored political and economic stability and launched a 15-year development program.

Balaguer's longtime support for free elections faltered in May 1978, when the army suspended the counting of ballots as he trailed in a fourth-term bid. After a warning from President Jimmy Carter, however, Balaguer accepted the victory of Antonio Guzmán of the opposition Dominican Revolutionary Party.

Guzmán began a rural development and land reform program. In June 1981, Guzmán announced that he would not seek re-election at the end of his term in August 1982.

Salvador Jorge Blanco of the Dominican Revolutionary Party was elected President on May 16, 1982, defeating Balaguer and Bosch. Guzman shot himself on July 4 and Vice President Jacobo Majluta Azar took office until Jorge Blanco's inauguration on Aug. 16.

ECUADOR

Republic of Ecuador
President: Osvaldo Hurtado Larrea (1981)
Area: 105,685 sq mi. (273,724 sq km)
Population (est. 1982): 8,950,000 (average annual growth rate: 3.1%)
Density per square mile: 81.6
Capital: Quito
Largest cities (est. 1980): Guayaquil, 1,100,000; Quito, 800,000; Cuenca, 135,000
Monetary unit: Sucre
Languages: Spanish, Quéchua, Jibaro
Religion: Roman Catholic
National name: República del Ecuador
Literacy rate (1981): 57%
Economic summary: Gross national product (1980): $10.2 billion. Average annual growth rate (1970–79): 5.4%. Per capita income (1980): $1,220. Land used for agriculture: 15%; labor force: 56%; principal products: bananas, coffee, cocoa, sugar cane, fruits, corn, potatoes, rice. Labor force in industry: 18%; major products: processed foods, textiles, chemicals, fish, petroleum. Natural resources: petroleum, fish, timber, minerals. Exports: petroleum, bananas, coffee, cocoa, fish products. Imports: agricultural and industrial machinery, industrial raw materials, building supplies, chemical products, transportation and communication equipment. Major trading partners: U.S., Latin American and Western European countries, Japan.

Geography. Ecuador, equal in area to Nevada, is in the northwest part of South America fronting on the Pacific. To the north is Colombia and to the east and south is Peru. Two high and parallel ranges of the Andes, traversing the country from north to south, are topped by tall volcanic peaks. The highest is Chimborazo at 20,577 feet (6,272 m).

The Galápagos Islands (or Colón Archipelago) (3,029 sq mi.; 7,845 sq km) in the Pacific Ocean about 600 miles (966 km) west of the South American mainland, became part of Ecuador in 1832.

Government. A 1978 Constitution returned Ecuador to civilian government after eight years of military rule. Under its terms, the President is elected by universal suffrage to a term of five years and a House of Representatives of 69 members popularly elected for the same period.

History. The tribes in the northern highlands of Ecuador formed the Kingdom of Quito around A.D. 1000 It was absorbed, by conquest and marriage, into the Inca Empire. Pizarro conquered the land in 1532, and through the 17th century a thriving colony was built by exploitation of the Indians. The first revolt against Spain occurred in 1809. Ecuador then joined Venezuela, Colombia, and Panama in a confederacy founded by Simón Bolívar and known as Greater Colombia.

On the collapse of this union in 1830, Ecuador became independent. Subsequent history was one of revolts and dictatorships; it had 48 presidents during the first 131 years of the republic. Conservatives ruled until the Revolution of 1895 ushered in nearly a half century of Radical Liberal rule, during which the church was disestablished and freedom of worship, speech, and press was introduced.

In 1970, following six months of strife between university students and police, President José María Velasco Ibarra, who was elected in 1968 for the fifth time, took supreme powers to "avoid social and economic chaos." He closed universities, jailed some professors and businessmen, and demanded "reform" of the Supreme Court. Opposition political leaders were arrested and a military shake-up ensued.

Velasco was ousted nine months later by a junta, which sharply increased fees charged to foreign oil companies.

A three-man military junta headed by Vice Adm. Alfredo Poveda, which had taken power in a 1976 coup, agreed to a free presidential election on July 16, 1978. Jaime Roldós Aguilera won the runoff on April 29, 1979, backed by a "center leftist" coalition, the Concentration of Popular Forces.

The 40-year-old President, his wife and Ecudador's minister of defense died in the crash of a small plane May 24, 1981. Vice President Osvaldo Hurtado Larrea became President. In March, Roldos had reached a truce with Peru in a border clash which had broken out January 28 in the Cordillera del Condor mountains. In February, Ecuador released without charge a U.S. tuna boat seized a month earlier and fined $1.2 million for unauthorized entry into the 200-mile "economic zone" claimed by Ecuador.

EGYPT

Arab Republic of Egypt
President: Hosni Mubarak (1981)
Premier: Ahmed Fuad Mohieddin (1982)
Area: 386,872 sq mi. (1,001,998 sq km)
Population (est. 1982): 44,750,000 (average annual growth rate: 3.0%)
Density per square mile: 115.7
Capital: Cairo
Largest cities (est. 1979): Cairo, 5,423,000; **(1976 census):** Alexandria, 2,317,705; Giza, 1,246,713; Shubra el Khema, 393,700; El Mahalla el Kubra, 292,853; Tanta, 284,636; Port Said, 262,620; Mansura, 257,866
Monetary unit: Egyptian pound
Language: Arabic
Religions: Islam, 93%; Christian (mostly Copt), 7%
Literacy rate (1981): 44%
Economic summary: Gross national product (1980): $23.1 billion. Average annual growth rate (1970–79): 5.3%. Per capita income (1980): $580. Land used for agriculture: 3%; labor force: 50%; principal products: cotton, wheat, rice, corn. Labor force in industry: 13%; major products: textiles, processed foods, tobacco manufactures, chemicals, fertilizer, petroleum and petroleum products. Natural resources: manganese ore, phosphates, petroleum, gold, nickel, tungsten. Exports: cotton, rice, petroleum, cement, potatoes. Imports: foodstuffs, machinery, fertilizers, woods. Major trading partners: West Germany, Italy, France, U.K., U.S.

Geography. Egypt, at the northeast corner of Africa on the Mediterranean Sea, is bordered on the west by Libya, on the south by the Sudan, and on the east by the Red Sea and Israel. It is nearly one and one half times the size of Texas.

The historic Nile flows through the eastern third of the country. On either side of the Nile valley are desert plateaus, spotted with oases. In the north, toward the Mediterranean, plateaus are low, while south of Cairo they rise to a maximum of 1,015 feet (309 m) above sea level. At the head of the Red Sea is the Sinai Peninsula, between the Suez Canal and Israel.

Navigable throughout its course in Egypt, the Nile is used largely as a means of cheap transport for heavy goods. The principal port is Alexandria.

The Nile delta starts 100 miles (161 km) south of the Mediterranean and fans out to a sea front of 155 miles between the cities of Alexandria and Port Said. From Cairo north, the Nile branches into many streams, the principal ones being the Damietta and the Rosetta.

Except for a narrow belt along the Mediterranean, Egypt lies in an almost rainless area, in which high daytime temperatures fall quickly at night.

Government. Executive power is held by the President, who can appoint one or more Vice Presidents.

The major political parties are the National Democratic Party, Free Socialist Party, Nationalist Progressive Party, and Independent Front.

History. Egyptian history dates back to about 4000 B.C., when the kingdoms of upper and lower Egypt, already highly civilized, were united. Egypt's "Golden Age" coincided with the 18th and 19th dynasties (16th to 13th centuries B.C.), during which the empire was established. Persia conquered Egypt in 525 B.C.; Alexander the Great subdued it in 332 B.C.; and then the dynasty of the Ptolemies ruled the land until 30 B.C., when Cleopatra, last of the line, committed suicide and Egypt became a Roman province. From 641 to 1517 the Arab caliphs ruled Egypt, and then the Turks took it for their Ottoman Empire.

Napoleon's armies occupied the country from 1798 to 1801. In 1805, Mohammed Ali, leader of a band of Albanian soldiers, became Pasha of Egypt. After completion of the Suez Canal in 1869, the French and British took increasing interest in

Egypt.

British troops occupied Egypt in 1882, and British resident agents became its actual administrators, though it remained under nominal Turkish sovereignty. In 1914, this fiction was ended, and Egypt became a protectorate of Britain.

Egyptian nationalism forced Britain to declare Egypt an independent, sovereign state on Feb. 28, 1922, although the British reserved rights for the protection of the Suez Canal and the defense of Egypt. In 1936, by an Anglo-Egyptian treaty of alliance, all British troops and officials were to be withdrawn, except from the Suez Canal Zone. When World War II started, Egypt remained neutral. British imperial troops finally ended the Nazi threat to Suez in 1942 in the battle of El Alamein, west of Alexandria.

In 1951, Egypt abrogated the 1936 treaty and the 1899 Anglo-Egyptian condominium of the Sudan (*See* Sudan.) Rioting and attacks on British troops in the Suez Canal Zone followed, reaching a climax in January 1952. The army, led by Gen. Mohammed Naguib, seized power on July 23, 1952. Three days later, King Farouk abdicated in favor of his infant son. The monarchy was abolished and a republic proclaimed on June 18, 1953, with Naguib holding the posts of Provisional President and Premier. He relinquished the latter in 1954 to Gamal Abdel Nasser, leader of the ruling military junta. Naguib was deposed seven months later and Nasser confirmed as President in a referendum on June 23, 1956.

Nasser's policies embroiled his country in continual conflict. In 1956, the U.S. and Britain withdrew their pledges of financial aid for the building of the Aswan High Dam. In reply, Nasser nationalized the Suez Canal and expelled British oil and embassy officials. Israel, barred from the Canal and exasperated by terrorist raids, invaded the Gaza Strip and the Sinai Peninsula. Britain and France, after demanding Egyptian evacuation of the Canal Zone, attacked Egypt on Oct. 31, 1956. Worldwide pressure forced Britain, France, and Israel to halt the hostilities. A U.N. emergency force occupied the Canal Zone, and all troops were evacuated in the spring of 1957.

On Feb. 1, 1958, Egypt and Syria formed the United Arab Republic, which was joined by Yemen in an association known as the United Arab States. However, Syria withdrew from the United Arab Republic in 1961 and Egypt dissolved its ties with Yemen in the United Arab States. On Sept. 2, 1971, Egypt finally shed the name United Arab Republic.

On June 5, 1967, Israel invaded the Sinai Peninsula, the East Bank of the Jordan River, and the zone around the Gulf of Aqaba. Only a U.N. cease-fire on June 10 saved the Arabs from complete rout.

Nasser declared the 1967 cease-fire void along the Canal in April 1969 and began a war of attrition. Egyptian artillery fire across the canal sparked Israeli "deep penetration" raids that attempted to topple Nasser. He went to Moscow in January 1970, and by March, Russians were flying planes with Egyptian markings to defend the Nile delta and were manning some antiaircraft missiles. An estimated 10,000 to 12,000 Russians were in Egypt in 1970. Missiles were moved into the Canal Zone, challenging Israeli air superiority. The U.S. peace plan of June 19, 1970, resulted in Egypt's agreement to reinstate the cease-fire for at least three months, (from August) and to accept Israel's existence within "recognized and secure" frontiers that might emerge from U.N.-mediated talks. In return, Israel accepted the principle of withdrawing from occupied territories.

Then, on Sept. 28, 1970, Nasser died, at 52, of a heart attack. The new President was Anwar el-Sadat, an associate of Nasser and a former newspaper editor.

The Aswan High Dam, whose financing by the U.S.S.R. was its first step into Egypt, was completed and dedicated in January 1971.

In July 1972, Sadat ordered the expulsion of Soviet "advisors and experts" from Egypt because the Russians had not provided the sophisticated weapons he felt were needed to retake territory lost to Israel in 1967. Moscow pulled out virtually all of its 18,000 men.

The fourth Arab-Israeli war broke out Oct. 6, 1973, while Israelis were commemorating Yom Kippur, the Jewish high holy day. Egypt swept deep into the Sinai, while Syria strove to throw Israel off the Golan Heights. Arab oil-producing countries cut off shipments to the U.S. and other Western nations, precipitating a worldwide energy crisis.

A U.N.-sponsored truce was accepted on October 22 after an Israeli thrust across the Suez into Egypt itself cut off Egyptian forces in the Sinai. In January 1974, both sides agreed to a settlement negotiated by U.S. Secretary of State Henry A. Kissinger that gave Egypt a narrow strip along the entire Sinai bank of the Suez Canal. In June, President Nixon made the first visit by a U.S. President to Egypt and full diplomatic relations were established together with an Egyptian-American economic commission to channel aid to Egypt, including nuclear power reactors. The Suez Canal was cleared and reopened on June 5, 1975.

Kissinger pursued "shuttle diplomacy" between Cairo and Jerusalem to extend areas of agreement. Israel yielded on three points—the possession of the Mitla and Giddi passes in the Sinai and the Abu Rudeis oil field in the peninsula—and both sides committed themselves to annual renewal of the U.N. peacekeeping force in the Sinai.

Sadat, defying Arab charges of betrayal in dealing with Israel, gained U.S. aid and the security to turn his attention to an economy beset by 30% inflation and serious unemployment. A 1976 referendum gave Sadat, running unopposed for a second six-year term, a 99.9% vote of approval.

In 1977, Saudi Arabia and other Arabian Gulf states agreed to lend Egypt $1.5 billion. A consortium of the International Monetary Fund, the European Economic Community, and others recommended loans and credits of $13.1 billion for 1977–80.

In the most audacious act of his career, Sadat flew to Jerusalem at the invitation of Prime Minister Menachem Begin and pleaded before Israel's Knesset on Nov. 20, 1977, for a permanent peace settlement. The Arab world reacted with fury—only Morocco, Tunisia, Sudan, and Oman approved —and Egyptian Foreign Minister Ismail Fahmy resigned. Hope for progress cooled when political talks in Jerusalem snagged, and Sadat ordered his negotiators home Jan. 17, 1978. The Egyptian was angered by Begin's defense of new settlements on the West Bank and his refusal to discuss the ultimate status of the West Bank and Gaza Strip, which Sadat proposed be placed under Jordanian and Egyptian administration respectively.

Sadat maintained an image of cooperation while Begin reflected intransigence, a perception shared by the U.S. Congress as it voted for Carter's requested package sale of jet fighters to Egypt, Saudi Arabia, and Israel over Israeli protests.

Egyptian and Israeli officials met in the Sinai desert on April 26, 1979, to implement the peace treaty calling for the phased withdrawal of occupation forces from the peninsula. On May 27, ahead of schedule, Israel turned over the gateway town of El Arish to Egyptian administration. By mid-1980, two thirds of the Sinai was transferred, but progress here was not matched in the other area covered by the treaty—the negotiation of Arab autonomy in the Gaza Strip and the West Bank.

Sadat halted further autonomy talks in August 1980 because of continued Israeli settlement of the West Bank. A year later he went to Washington to urge President Reagan to recognize the Palestine Liberation Organization as a means of resuming the talks. There were indications that the Reagan administration might yield, but the process was arrested on Oct. 6, 1981, with the assassination of Sadat by extremist Muslim soldiers at a parade in Cairo. Vice President Hosni Mubarak, a former Air Force chief of staff, was confirmed by the parliament as president the next day.

Although feared unrest in Egypt did not occur in the wake of the assassination, and Israel completed the return of the Sinai to Egyptian control on April 25, 1982, Mubarak was unable to revive the autonomy talks. Israel's invasion of Lebanon in June imposed a new strain on him, but Arab nations showed sympathy to the new leader, which they had withheld from Sadat.

Suez Canal. The Suez Canal, in Egyptian territory between the Arabian Desert and the Sinai Peninsula, is an artificial waterway about 100 miles (161 km) long between Port Said on the Mediterranean and Suez on the Red Sea. Construction work, directed by the French engineer Ferdinand de Lesseps, was begun April 25, 1859, and the Canal was opened Nov. 17, 1869. The cost was 432,807,882 francs. The concession was held by an Egyptian joint stock company, *Compagnie Universelle du Canal Maritime de Suez,* in which the British government held 353,504 out of a total of 800,000 shares. The concession was to expire Nov. 17, 1968, but the company was nationalized July 26, 1956, by unilateral action of the Egyptian government.

The Canal was closed in June 1967 after the Arab-Israeli conflict. With the help of the U.S. Navy, work was begun on clearing the Canal in 1974, after the cease-fire ending the Arab-Israeli war. It was reopened to traffic June 5, 1975.

EL SALVADOR

Republic of El Salvador
President: Alvaro Alfredo Magaña (1982)
Area: 8,260 sq mi. (21,393 sq km)
Population (est. 1982): 5,150,000 (average annual growth rate: −2.4%)
Density per square mile: 623.5
Capital: San Salvador
Largest cities (est. 1980): San Salvador, 430,000; (est. 1969): Santa Ana, 168,000
Monetary unit: Colón
Language: Spanish
Religion: Roman Catholic
National name: República de El Salvador
Literacy rate (1981): 40%
Economic summary: Gross national product (1980): $2.7 billion. Average annual growth rate (1970–79): 1.4%. Per capita income (1980): $590. Land used for agriculture: 32%; labor force: 50%; principal products: coffee, cotton, corn, sugar, rice, beans. Labor force in industry: 14%; major products: processed foods, clothing and textiles, petroleum products. Natural resources: timber, balsam, gold, silver, coal, copper, iron, zinc, mercury, sulfur. Exports: coffee, cotton, sugar. Imports: machinery, automotive vehicles, petroleum, foodstuffs, fertilizer. Major trading partners: U.S., Caribbean countries, Japan.

Geography. Situated on the Pacific coast of Central America, El Salvador has Guatemala to the west and Honduras to the north and east. It is the smallest of the Central American countries, its area equal to that of Massachusetts, and the only one without an Atlantic coastline.

Most of the country is a fertile volcanic plateau about 2,000 feet (607 m) high. There are some active volcanoes and many scenic crater lakes.

Government. The Constitution provides for a President, popularly elected for five years and ineligible to succeed himself, and a unicameral legislature, the National Assembly, consisting of 52 members elected by popular suffrage for two years.

A 60-member Constituent Assembly was elected on March 28, 1982, charged with the drafting of a new Constitution. A coalition of rightist parties won 36 seats and the opposition Christian Democrats won 24. The Assembly elected Dr. Alvaro Alfredo Magaña as provisional president, but the rightist majority retained control of the budget and all executive and judicial appointments.

History. Pedro de Alvarado, a lieutenant of Cortés, conquered El Salvador in 1525. El Salvador, with the other countries of Central America, declared its independence from Spain on Sept. 15, 1821, and was part of a federation of Central American states until that union was dissolved in 1838. Its independent career for several decades thereafter was marked by numerous revolutions and wars against other Central American republics.

In 1931, the first free election in 20 years was held, but Gen. Maximiliano Hernández Martínez took power in December of that year and maintained a dictatorship until he was ousted in 1944. For nearly two decades, politics remained turbulent and unstable, until the 1962 elections.

The new President, Julio Adalberto Rivera, restored free elections. In 1968, a drop in exports of coffee and cotton produced a slump. Widespread unemployment in El Salvador and land hunger in Honduras resulted in a conflict between the two nations in 1969. Deportation from Honduras of several thousand Salvadorans led to an invasion by El Salvador. Under threats of economic sanctions and military intervention, El Salvador withdrew its troops.

Presidential elections in 1972 gave none of four candidates a clear majority; therefore, the National Assembly, in which the National Conciliation Party had an overwhelming majority, proclaimed its candidate, Col. Arturo Armando Molina, as President.

The 1977 presidential elections were marked by at least eight deaths and massive protest demonstrations by the National Opposition Union, which charged extensive voter fraud. Gen. Carlos Humberto Romero, candidate of the governing National Conciliation Party, claimed victory over Lt. Col. Ernesto Claramount, the National Opposition Union candidate, who chose exile rather than prison after the election.

On Oct. 15, 1979, a junta composed of two army officers and three civilians deposed the President, Gen. Carlos Humberto Romero, seeking to halt increasingly violent clashes between leftist and rightist forces. The military officers were Col. Jaime Abdul Gutierrez Avendaño and Col. Adolfo Arnoldo Majano. The civilian members resigned in January and were replaced by two Christian Democrats, José Napoleón Duarte and José Antonio Morales Ehrlich, and a non-party member, José Ramón Avalos Navarrete. The junta strove to halt civil strife but found itself attacked from the left as too conservative and from the right as too liberal, with bloody conflicts continuing.

On Dec. 4, 1980, three American nuns and an American lay worker were killed in an ambush near San Salvador, causing the Carter administration to suspend all aid pending an investigation. The naming of José Napoleón Duarte as president brought a resumption of U.S. aid.

Leftist guerrillas announced a "final offensive" aimed at victory before the Reagan administration took office Jan. 20, but Salvadoran forces beat down rebel attacks. The new U.S. administration sent 56 military advisers and increased military and economic aid to the beleaguered government and launched a campaign to dissuade other countries from supporting the rebels, asserting that the guerrillas were receiving Soviet arms via Cuba and Nicaragua. Violence from both the right and left continued, with the death toll averaging 1,000 a month.

Defying guerrilla threats, voters on March 28, 1982, elected a rightist majority to a constituent assembly that dismissed Duarte and replaced him with a centrist physician, Dr. Alvaro Alfredo Magaña. The rightist majority repealed the laws permitting expropriation of land, and critics charged that the land-reform program begun under Duarte was dead. Even though fighting continued, with reports of government violations of human rights, the Reagan administration asked certification of El Salvador's eligibility for resumed foreign aid, and this was approved by Congress.

EQUATORIAL GUINEA

Republic of Equatorial Guinea
Head of junta: Lieut. Col. Teodoro Obiang Nguema Mbasogo (1979)
Area: 10,830 sq mi. (28,051 sq km)
Population (est. 1982): 380,000 (average annual growth rate: 2.1%)
Density per square mile: 35.1
Capital and largest city (est. 1974): Malabo, 25,000
Monetary unit: Ekuele
Languages: Spanish, Fang, Bubi
Religions: Roman Catholic, Protestant, Animist
National name: Républica de Guinea Ecuatorial
Literacy rate (1981): 38%
Economic summary: Gross national product (1980): $100 million. Per capita income (1980): $417. Land used for agriculture: 85–90%; labor force: 95%; principal products: cocoa, wood, coffee. Natural resource: wood. Exports: cocoa, wood, coffee. Imports: foodstuffs, chemicals, textiles, machinery. Major trading partner: Spain.

Geography. Equatorial Guinea, formerly Spanish Guinea, consists of Rio Muni (10,045 sq mi.; 26,117 sq km), on the western coast of Africa, and several islands in the Gulf of Guinea, the largest of which is Bioko (formerly Fernando Po) (785 sq mi.; 2,033 sq km). The other islands are Pagalu (formerly Annobón), Corisco, Elobey Grande, and Elobey Chico. The total area is twice that of Connecticut.

Government. The Constitution of 1973 was suspended after a coup on Aug. 3, 1979. A Supreme Military Council, headed by the president, exercises all power. Political parties are banned.

History. Fernando Po and Annobón came under Spanish control in 1778. From 1827 to 1844, with Spanish consent, Britain administered Fernando Po, but in the latter year Spain reclaimed the island. Río Muni was given to Spain in 1885 by the Treaty of Berlin.

Negotiations with Spain led to independence on Oct. 12, 1968.

In 1969, anti-Spanish incidents in Río Muni, including the tearing down of a Spanish flag by national troops, caused 5,000 Spanish residents to flee for their safety, and diplomatic relations between the two nations became strained. A month later, President Masie Nguema Biyogo Negue Ndong charged that a coup had been attempted against him. He seized dictatorial powers and arrested 80 opposition politicians and even several of his Cabinet ministers and the secretary of the National Assembly.

A coup on Aug. 3, 1979, deposed Masie, and a junta led by Lieut. Col. Teodoro Obiang Nguema Mbasogo took over the government. Obiang expelled Soviet technicians and reinstated cooperation with Spain.

ETHIOPIA

Head of State: Lt. Col. Mengistu Haile Mariam (1977)
Area: 457,142 sq mi. (1,183,998 sq km)
Population (est. 1982): 33,000,000 (average annual growth rate: 1.9%)
Density per square mile: 72.2
Capital: Addis Ababa
Largest cities (est. 1980): Addis Ababa, 1,275,000; Asmara, 425,000
Monetary unit: Birr
Languages: Amharic (official), Galligna, Tigrigna
Religions: Copt (Christian), Islam
Literacy rate (1981): 5%
Economic summary: Gross national product (1980): $4.3 billion. Average annual growth rate (1970–79): 0.3%. Per capita income (1980): $140. Land used for agriculture: 65%; labor force: 90%; principal products: coffee, barley, wheat, corn, sugar cane, cotton, oilseeds, livestock. Labor force in industry: 10%; Major industrial products: cement, cotton textiles, refined sugar, processed foods, refined oil. Natural resources: potash, salt, gold, copper, platinum. Exports: coffee, hides and skins, oilseeds. Imports: petroleum. Major trading partners: Saudi Arabia, Japan, Italy, West Germany, Iran, U.K., France, U.S.

Geography. Ethiopia is in east central Africa, bordered on the west by the Sudan, the east by Somalia and Djibouti, the south by Kenya, and the north by the Red Sea. It is nearly three times the size of California.

Over its main plateau land, Ethiopia has several high mountains, the highest of which is Ras Dashan at 15,158 feet (4,620 m). The Blue Nile, or Abbai, rises in the northwest and flows in a great semicircle east, south, and northwest before entering the Sudan. Its chief reservoir, Lake Tana, lies in the northwestern part of the plateau.

Government. A provisional military government headed by a 120-member officers' committee (the Dirgue) deposed Ethiopia's traditional monarchy in 1974, suspended parliament, and ruled by decree. It proclaimed Ethiopia a socialist state.

History. Black Africa's oldest state, Ethiopia can trace 2,000 years of recorded history. Its now-deposed royal line claimed descent from King Menelik I, traditionally believed to have been the son of the Queen of Sheba and King Solomon. The present nation is a consolidation of smaller kingdoms that owed feudal allegiance to the Ethiopian Emperor.

Hamitic peoples migrated to Ethiopia from Asia Minor in prehistoric times. Semitic traders from Arabia penetrated the region in the 7th century B.C. Its Red Sea ports were important to the Roman and Byzantine Empires. Coptic Christianity came to the country in A.D. 341, and a variant of that communion became Ethiopia's state religion.

Ancient Ethiopia reached its peak in the 5th century, then was isolated by the rise of Islam and weakened by feudal wars. Modern Ethiopia emerged under Emperor Menelik II, who established its independence by routing an Italian invasion in 1896. He expanded Ethiopia by conquest.

Disorders that followed Menelik's death brought his daughter to the throne in 1917, with his cousin, Tafari Makonnen, as Regent, heir presumptive, and strongman. When the Empress died in 1930, Tafari was crowned Emperor Haile Selassie I.

As Regent, Haile Selassie outlawed slavery. As Emperor, he worked for centralization of his diffuse realm, in which 70 languages are spoken, and for moderate reform. In 1931, he granted a Constitution, revised in 1955, that created a parliament with an appointed Senate and an elected Chamber of Deputies, and a system of courts. But basic power remained with the Emperor.

Bent on colonial empire, fascist Italy invaded Ethiopia on Oct. 3, 1935, forcing Haile Selassie into exile in May 1936. Ethiopia was annexed to Eritrea, then an Italian colony, and Italian Somaliland to form Italian East Africa, losing its independence for the first time in recorded history. In 1941, British troops routed the Italians, and Haile Selassie returned to Addis Ababa.

The Emperor's gradual reforms failed to make headway against key problems. Although 85% of Ethiopians were subsistence farmers, feudal laws vested ownership of 55% of its land in the crown, the church, and the nobility; there was strong pressure for land reform. There was also mounting insurgency in Eritrea, a culturally distinct province where Christians and Moslems have long vied for control, which the United Nations placed under Ethiopian rule in 1952. Violent agitation for Eritrean independence was begun in 1969 by the Moslem-led Eritrean Liberation Front, which used Arab-supplied arms to field a 4,000-man guerrilla force.

Deep discontent erupted in the fall of 1973. A long drought had caused famine that killed 100,000 peasants and drove thousands of others to cities, where food was scarce and inflation was rampant. Charges of mismanagement of drought relief sparked riots in Addis Ababa in 1974, and unpaid troops in Asmara, capital of Eritrea, mutinied to protest conditions. The Cabinet headed by Prime Minister Aklilou Habte-wold resigned.

The Emperor named Endalkachew Makonnen, a moderate, as Prime Minister and agreed to call a constitutional convention. But there was a general strike, students rioted, and mutiny spread to the air force. In mid-April, with disorders growing, army and police units arrested over 200 prominent persons. Late in June the army took virtual control of Addis Ababa and made more arrests.

Endalkachew was ousted on July 24, arrested, and later executed. Under his successor, Michael Imru, a draft Constitution proposing a constitutional monarchy was put forward, but power shifted relentlessly to a new Armed Forces Committee.

In August, the Armed Forces Committee nationalized Haile Selassie's palace and estates and directed him not to leave Addis Ababa. On Sept. 12, 1974, He was peacefully deposed after nearly 58 years as Regent and Emperor. The 82-year-old "Lion of Judah" was placed under guard. Parliament was dissolved and the Constitution suspended.

On December 20, the Armed Forces Committee announced that Ethiopia would become a socialist state directed by one political organization called the Supreme Progressive Council. All financial concerns were nationalized in 1975 and the regime proclaimed nationalization of all rural land, ending 2,000 years of feudal tenure.

On Aug. 27, 1975, Haile Selassie died in a small apartment in his former Addis Ababa palace where he had been treated as a state prisoner. He was 83.

After the coup, revolt in Eritrea escalated from guerrilla conflict to open war. The Eritrean Liberation Front, armed by Libya and other Arab states, demanded full independence. The regime tried and failed to negotiate with the Front and then began vigorous military action. Some 22,000 government troops were in combat in Eritrea by February 1975, and 6,000 deaths, mostly of civilians, were said to have resulted in March.

U.S. military aid, which had been going to Ethiopia since World War II, was suspended after the 1974 coup and only briefly resumed in 1976 as the military government turned increasingly toward the U.S.S.R. In retaliation for the Carter Administration's ruling out further aid to Ethiopia because of human rights violations, the regime in April and May of 1977 shut down the Kagnew communications center in Asmara and other U.S. military and diplomatic offices, ordering some 300 Americans to leave.

Lt. Col. Mengistu Haile Mariam was named head of state Feb. 2, 1977, to replace Brig. Gen. Teferi Benti, who was killed in a factional fight of the Dirgue after having ruled since 1974. The government was losing its fight to hold Eritrea and in the southeastern region of Ogaden, Somali guerrillas backed by Somali regular forces threatened the ancient city of Harar. In October, the U.S.S.R. announced it would end military aid to Somalia and henceforth back its new ally, Ethiopia. This, together with the intervention of Cuban troops in Ogaden, turned the tide for Mengistu. By March 1978, the badly beaten Somalis had retreated to their homeland.

In late July 1978, the Ethiopian government reported that it had gained its first victory over Eritrean rebels in three years in a campaign aimed at cutting them off from their supply lines to the Sudan. In both Eritrea and Ogaden, however, guerrilla resistance was still strong in 1980 and large areas were reported under only sporadic government control.

FIJI

Sovereign: Queen Elizabeth II
Governor General: Sir George Cakobau (1973)
Prime Minister: Sir Kamisese Mara (1970)
Area: 7,055 sq mi. (18,272 sq km)
Population (est. 1982): 650,000 (average annual growth rate: 1.8%)
Density per square mile: 92.1
Capital (1981): Suva (on Viti Levu), 65,000
Monetary unit: Fijian dollar
Languages: Fijian, Hindustani, English
Religions: Christian, Hindu, Islam
Member of Commonwealth of Nations
Literacy rate (1981): 80%
Economic summary: Gross national product (1980): $1.2 billion. Average annual growth rate (1970–79): 3.0%. Per capita income (1980): $1,850. Average rate of inflation (1975–77): 9.3%. Labor force in agriculture: 44%; principal products: sugar, copra, bananas, ginger. Labor force in industry: 16%; major industrial products: refined sugar, gold, lumber. Natural resources: timber, fish, gold, copper. Exports: sugar, copra. Imports: foodstuffs, machinery, manufactured goods, fuels, chemicals. Major trading partners: U.K., New Zealand, U.S.

Geography. Fiji consists of more than 500 islands in the southwestern Pacific Ocean about 1,960 miles (3,152 km) from Sydney, Australia. The two largest islands are Viti Levu (4,109 sq mi.; 10,642 sq km) and Vanua Levu (2,242 sq mi.; 5,807 sq km). The island of Rotuma (18 sq mi.; 47 sq km), about 400 miles (644 km) to the north, is a dependency of Fiji. Overall, Fiji is nearly as large as New Jersey.

The largest islands in the group are mountainous and volcanic, with the tallest peak being Mount Victoria (4,341 ft; 1,323 m) on Viti Levu. The islands in the south have dense forests on the windward side and grasslands on the leeward.

Government. Executive authority is vested in the Cabinet and legislative authority in a bicameral 74-member Parliament. The major political parties are the Alliance Party, led by Prime Minister Sir Kamisese Mara; National Federation Party, led by Jai Ram Reddy, and Fijian Nationalist Party, led by Sakeasi Butadroka.

History. In 1874, an offer of cession by the Fijian chiefs was accepted, and Fiji was proclaimed a possession and dependency of the British Crown.

During World War II, the archipelago was an important air and naval station on the route from the U.S. and Hawaii to Australia and New Zealand.

Fiji became independent on Oct. 10, 1970. The next year it joined the five-island South Pacific Forum, which intends to become a permanent regional group to promote collective diplomacy of the newly independent members. The Forum also includes Western Samoa, Tonga, Nauru, and the self-governing segments of the Cook Islands.

FINLAND

Republic of Finland
President: Mauno H. Koivisto (1982)
Premier: Kalevi Sorsa (1982)
Area: 130,119 sq mi. (337,009 sq km)
Population (est. 1982): 4,825,000 (average annual growth rate: 0.4%) (Finnish, 93%; Swedish, 6%)
Density per square mile: 37.0
Capital: Helsinki
Largest cities (est. 1981): Helsinki, 484,000; Tampere, 166,250; Turku, 163,500
Monetary unit: Markka
Languages: Finnish, Swedish
Religions: Lutheran, 98%; Orthodox, 1.6%
National name: Suomen Tasavalta—Republiken Finland
Literacy rate (1981): 99%
Economic summary: Gross national product (1980): $47.3 billion. Average annual growth rate (1970–79): 2.2%. Per capita income (1980): $9,720. Land used for agriculture: 8%; labor force: 12%; principal products: dairy products, cereals, sugar beets, potatoes. Labor force in industry: 33%; major products: metal manufactures, forestry and wood products, refined copper, ships. Natural resource: timber. Exports: timber, paper and pulp, ships, machinery, iron and steel, clothing, footwear. Imports: foodstuffs, petroleum and petroleum products, chemicals, transportation equipment, iron and steel, machinery, textile yarns. Major trading partners: Western European countries, U.S.S.R., Sweden.

Geography. Finland stretches 700 miles (1,127 km) from the Gulf of Finland on the south to Soviet Petsamo, north of the Arctic Circle. The U.S.S.R. extends along the entire eastern frontier. In area, Finland is three times the size of Ohio.

Off the southwest coast are the Aland Islands, controlling the entrance to the Gulf of Bothnia. Finland has more than 60,000 lakes. Of the few rivers, only the Oulu (Ulea) is navigable to any important extent.

The Swedish-populated Aland Islands (581 sq mi.; 1,505 sq km) have an autonomous status under a law passed in 1951.

Government. The president, chosen for six years by the popularly elected Electoral College of 300 members, appoints the Cabinet. The one-chamber Diet, the Eduskunta, consists of 200 members elected for four-year terms by proportional representation.

The major political parties are the Social Democratic Party (52 seats in the Eduskanta), led by Premier Kalevi Sorsa; Conservative Party (46 seats); Center Party (37 seats); People's Democratic League (Communist) (35 seats); Swedish People's Party (10 seats); Christian League (9 seats); Rural Party (7 seats); Liberal Party (4 seats). Premier Sorsa leads a coalition of Social Democratic, Communist, Center, and Swedish People's Party members totaling 134 seats.

History. At the end of the 7th century, the Finns came to Finland from their Volga settlements, taking the country from the Lapps, who retreated northward. The Finns' repeated raids on the Scandinavian coast impelled Eric IX, the Swedish King, to conquer the country in 1157 and bring it into contact with Western Christendom. By 1809 the whole of Finland was conquered by Alexander I of Russia, who set up Finland as a Grand Duchy.

The first period of Russification (1809–1905) resulted in a lessening of the powers of the Finnish Diet. The Russian language was made official, and the Finnish military system was superseded by the Russian. The pace of Russification was intensified from 1908 to 1914. When Russian control was weakened as a consequence of the March Revolution of 1917, the Diet on July 20, 1917, proclaimed Finland's independence, which became complete on Dec. 6, 1917.

Finland rejected Soviet territorial demands, and the U.S.S.R. attacked on Nov. 30, 1939. The Finns made an amazing stand of three months and finally capitulated, ceding 16,000 square miles (41,440 sq km) to the U.S.S.R. Under German pressure, the Finns joined the Nazis against Russia in 1941, but were defeated again and ceded the Petsamo area to the U.S.S.R. In 1948, a 20-year treaty of friendship and mutual assistance was signed by the two nations and renewed for another 20 years in 1970.

In 1970 Finland entered into a trade agreement with the enlarged European Economic Community (Common Market) and also with Comecom, the Communist East European Economic Group.

Helsinki was the site in 1975 of a summit conference of 35 heads of government convened for the signing of a European security agreement.

After 25 years in office, President Urho K. Kekkonen resigned in October 1981 because of ill health. Premier Mauno Koivisto, leader of the Social Democratic Party, was elected President on Jan. 26, 1982, and was sworn in the next day. Radio Moscow hailed Koivisto's victory as a "clear shift to the left" because he won decisively over a conservative rival with support from Finnish Communists. On Feb. 17, Kalevi Sorsa, a Social Democrat, took office as Premier, heading the same center-left coalition Koivisto had led.

FRANCE

French Republic
President: François Mitterrand (1981)
Premier: Pierre Mauroy (1981)
Area: 212,973 sq mi. (551,600 sq km)
Population (est. 1982): 54,250,000 (average annual growth rate: 0.4%)
Density per square mile: 254.7
Capital: Paris
Largest cities (est. 1980): Paris, 2,150,000; **(1975 census):** Marseilles, 914,356; Lyons, 462,841; Toulouse, 383,176; Nice, 346,620; Nantes, 263,689; Strasbourg, 257,300; Bordeaux, 226,281
Monetary unit: Franc
Religion (est.): Roman Catholic, 90%; Protestant, Jewish, Islam, and others, 10%
National name: République Française
Literacy rate (1981): 97%
Economic summary: Gross national product (1980): $627.7 billion. Average annual growth rate (1970–79): 3.0%. Per capita income (1980): $11,730. Land used for agriculture: 35%; labor force: 9%; principal products: cereals, feed grains, livestock and dairy products, wine, fruits, vegetables. Labor force in industry: 35%; major products: chemicals, automobiles, processed foods, iron and steel, aircraft, textiles, clothing. Natural resources: coal, iron ore, bauxite, fish, forests. Exports: textiles and clothing, iron and steel products, machinery and transport equipment, agricultural products. Imports: machinery, crude petroleum, iron and steel products, chemicals, foodstuffs, agricultural products. Major trading partners: West Germany, Italy, U.S., Belgium-Luxembourg, U.K., Netherlands.

Geography. France (80% the size of Texas) is second in size to the U.S.S.R. among Europe's nations. In the Alps near the Italian and Swiss borders is Europe's highest point—Mont Blanc (15,781 ft; 4,810 m). The forest-covered Vosges Mountains are in the northeast, and the Pyrenees are along the Spanish border.

Except for extreme northern France, which is part of the Flanders plain, the country may be described as four river basins and a plateau. Three of the streams flow west—the Seine into the English Channel, the Loire into the Atlantic, and the Garonne into the Bay of Biscay. The Rhône flows south into the Mediterranean. For about 100 miles (161 km), the Rhine is France's eastern border.

West of the Rhône and northeast of the Garonne lies the central plateau, covering about 15% of France's area and rising to a maximum elevation of 6,188 feet (1,886 m). In the Mediterranean, about 115 miles (185 km) east-southeast of Nice, is Corsica (3,367 sq mi.; 8,721 sq km).

Government. The president is elected for seven years by universal suffrage. He appoints the premier, and the Cabinet is responsible to Parliament. The president has the right to dissolve the National Assembly or to ask Parliament for reconsideration of a law. The Parliament consists of two houses: the National Assembly and the Senate.

The major political parties are the Socialists (267 of 491 seats in the National Assembly), led by Pierre Joxe; Rally for the Republic (79 seats), led by Claude Labbe; Union for French Democracy (52 seats), led by Jean-Claude Gaudin; and Communists (43 seats), led by André Lajoinie. Forty-two other members are affiliated with the various parties, while the remainder do not belong to any group.

History. The history of France, as distinct from ancient Gaul, begins with the Treaty of Verdun (843), dividing the territories corresponding roughly to France, Germany, and Italy among the three grandsons of Charlemagne. Julius Caesar had conquered part of Gaul in 57–52 B.C., and it remained Roman until Franks invaded it in the 5th century.

Charles the Bald, inheritor of *Francia Occidentalis,* founded the Carolingian dynasty, which ruled over a kingdom increasingly feudalized. By 987, the crown passed to Hugh Capet, a princeling who controlled only the Île-de-France, the region surrounding Paris. For 350 years, an unbroken Capetian line added to its domain and consolidated royal authority until the accession in 1328 of Philip VI, first of the Valois line. France was then the most powerful nation in Europe, with a population of 15 million.

The missing pieces in Philip's domain were the French provinces still held by the Plantagenet kings of England, who also claimed the French crown. Beginning in 1338, the Hundred Years' War eventually settled the contest. English longbows defeated French armored knights at Crécy (1346) and the English also won the second landmark battle at Agincourt (1415), but the final victory went to the French peasant girl, Joan of Arc, at Orléans (1429).

Absolute monarchy reached its apogee in the reign of Louis XIV (1643–1715), the Sun King, whose brilliant court was the center of the Western world. Neither Louis XV, nor his grandson, Louis XVI, could sustain the role, however, and the Ancien Régime tottered under the weight of an outmoded society, crushing taxes, and the infiltration of egalitarian philosophy. The monarchy lost French Canada in the Battle of Quebec Sept. 13, 1759, and in its last gasp under Louis XVI aided the American British colonists to gain their freedom.

Revolution plunged France into a blood bath be-

Rulers of France

Name	Born	Ruled[1]
CAROLINGIAN DYNASTY		
Pepin the Short	c. 714	751–768
Charlemagne[2]	742	768–814
Louis I the Debonair[3]	778	814–840
Charles I the Bald[4]	823	840–877
Louis II the Stammerer	846	877–879
Louis III[5]	c. 863	879–882
Carloman[5]	?	879–884
Charles II the Fat[6]	839	884–887[7]
Eudes (Odo), Count of Paris	?	888–898
Charles III the Simple[8]	879	893–923[9]
Robert I[10]	c. 865	922–923
Rudolf (Raoul), Duke of Burgundy	?	923–936
Louis IV d'Outremer	c. 921	936–954
Lothair	941	954–986
Louis V the Sluggard	c. 967	986–987
CAPETIAN DYNASTY		
Hugh Capet	c. 940	987–996
Robert II the Pious[11]	c. 970	996–1031
Henry I	1008	1031–1060
Philip I	1052	1060–1108
Louis VI the Fat	1081	1108–1137
Louis VII the Young	c.1121	1137–1180
Philip II (Philip Augustus)	1165	1180–1223
Louis VIII the Lion	1187	1223–1226
Louis IX (St. Louis)	1214	1226–1270
Philip III the Bold	1245	1270–1285
Philip IV the Fair	1268	1285–1314
Louis X the Quarreler	1289	1314–1316
John I[12]	1316	1316
Philip V the Tall	1294	1316–1322
Charles IV the Fair	1294	1322–1328
HOUSE OF VALOIS		
Philip VI	1293	1328–1350
John II the Good	1319	1350–1364
Charles V the Wise	1337	1364–1380
Charles VI the Well-Beloved	1368	1380–1422
Charles VII	1403	1422–1461
Louis XI	1423	1461–1483
Charles VIII	1470	1483–1498
Louis XII the Father of the People	1462	1498–1515
Francis I	1494	1515–1547
Henry II	1519	1547–1559
Francis II	1544	1559–1560
Charles IX	1550	1560–1574
Henry III	1551	1574–1589
HOUSE OF BOURBON		
Henry IV of Navarre	1553	1589–1610
Louis XIII	1601	1610–1643
Louis XIV the Great	1638	1643–1715
Louis XV the Well-Beloved	1710	1715–1774
Louis XVI	1754	1774–1792[13]
Louis XVII (Louis Charles de France)[14]	1785	1793–1795
FIRST REPUBLIC		
National Convention	—	1792–1795
Directory (Directoire)	—	1795–1799
CONSULATE		
Napoleon Bonaparte[15]	1769	1799–1804
FIRST EMPIRE		
Napoleon I	1769	1804–1815[16]
RESTORATION OF HOUSE OF BOURBON		
Louis XVIII le Désiré	1755	1814–1824
Charles X	1757	1824–1830[17]
BOURBON-ORLEANS LINE		
Louis Philippe ("Citizen King")	1773	1830–1848[18]
SECOND REPUBLIC		
Louis Napoleon[19]	1808	1848–1852
SECOND EMPIRE		
Napoleon III (Louis Napoleon)	1808	1852–1870[20]
THIRD REPUBLIC (PRESIDENTS)		
Louis Adolphe Thiers	1797	1871–1873
Marie E. P. M. de MacMahon	1808	1873–1879
François P. J. Grévy	1807	1879–1887
Sadi Carnot	1837	1887–1894
Jean Casimir-Périer	1847	1894–1895
François Félix Faure	1841	1895–1899
Émile Loubet	1838	1899–1906
Clement Armand Fallières	1841	1906–1913
Raymond Poincaré	1860	1913–1920
Paul E. L. Deschanel	1856	1920–1920
Alexandre Millerand	1859	1920–1924
Gaston Doumergue	1863	1924–1931
Paul Doumer	1857	1931–1932
Albert Lebrun	1871	1932–1940
VICHY GOVERNMENT (CHIEF OF STATE)		
Henri Philippe Pétain	1856	1940–1944
PROVISIONAL GOVERNMENT (PRESIDENTS)		
Charles de Gaulle	1890	1944–1946
Félix Gouin	1884	1946–1946
Georges Bidault	1899	1946–1947
FOURTH REPUBLIC (PRESIDENTS)		
Vincent Auriol	1884	1947–1954
René Coty	1882	1954–1959
FIFTH REPUBLIC (PRESIDENTS)		
Charles de Gaulle	1890	1959–1969
Georges Pompidou	1911	1969–1974
Valéry Giscard d'Estaing	1926	1974–1981
François Mitterrand	1916	1981–

1. For Kings and Emperors through the Second Empire, year of end of rule is also that of death, unless otherwise indicated. 2. Crowned Emperor of the West in 800. His brother, Carloman, ruled as King of the Eastern Franks from 768 until his death in 771. 3. Holy Roman Emperor 814–840. 4. Holy Roman Emperor 875–877 as Charles II. 5. Ruled jointly 879–882. 6. Holy Roman Emperor 881–887 as Charles III. 7. Died 888. 8. King 893–898 in opposition to Eudes. 9. Died 929. 10. Not counted in regular line of Kings of France by some authorities. Elected by nobles but killed in Battle of Soissons. 11. Sometimes called Robert I. 12. Posthumous son of Louis X; lived for only five days. 13. Executed 1793. 14. Titular King only. He died in prison according to official reports, but many pretenders appeared during the Bourbon restoration. 15. As First Consul, Napoleon held the power of government. In 1804, he became Emperor. 16. Abdicated first time June 1814. Re-entered Paris March 1815,

after escape from Elba; Louis XVIII fled to Ghent. Abdicated second time June 1815. He named as his successor his son, Napoleon II, who was not acceptable to the Allies. He died 1821. 17. Died 1836. 18. Died 1850. 19. President; became Emperor in 1852. 20. Died 1873.

ginning in 1789 and ending with a new authoritarianism under Napoleon Bonaparte, who had successfully defended the infant republic from foreign attack and then made himself First Consul in 1799 and Emperor in 1804. Napoleon set patterns in government, education, and law visible today, and his conquests spread them throughout Europe.

The Congress of Vienna (1815) sought to restore the pre-Napoleonic order in the person of Louis XVIII, but industrialization and the middle class, both fostered under Napoleon, built pressure for change, and a revolution in 1848 drove Louis Philipe, last of the Bourbons, into exile.

A second republic elected as its president Prince Louis Napoleon, a nephew of Napoleon I, who declared the Second Empire in 1852 and took the throne as Napoleon III. His opposition to the rising power of Prussia ignited the Franco-Prussian War (1870–71), ending in his defeat and abdication.

A new France emerged from World War I as the continent's dominant power. But four years of hostile occupation had reduced northeast France to ruins. The postwar Third Republic was plagued by political instability and economic chaos.

From 1919, French foreign policy aimed at keeping Germany weak through a system of alliances, but it failed to halt the rise of Adolf Hitler and the Nazi war machine. On May 10, 1940, mechanized Nazi troops attacked, and, as they approached Paris, Italy joined with Germany. The Germans marched into an undefended Paris and Marshal Henri Philippe Pétain signed an armistice June 22. France was split into an occupied north and an unoccupied south, the latter becoming a totalitarian state with Pétain as its chief.

Allied armies liberated France in August 1944. The French Committee of National Liberation, formed in Algiers in 1943, established a provisional government in Paris headed by Gen. Charles de Gaulle. The Fourth Republic was born Dec. 24, 1946.

The Empire became the French Union; the National Assembly was strengthened and the presidency weakened; and France joined the North Atlantic Treaty Organization. A war against communist insurgents in Indochina was abandoned after the defeat at Dien Bien Phu. A new rebellion in Algeria (*see* Algeria) threatened a military coup, and on June 1, 1958, the Assembly invited de Gaulle to return as premier with extraordinary powers. He drafted a new Constitution for a Fifth Republic, adopted Sept. 28, which strengthened the presidency and reduced legislative power. He was elected president Dec. 21.

The new president negotiated the independence of Algeria on July 5, 1962. De Gaulle cultivated the former colonies along with other new nations of what he called the Third World—nations aligned with neither the West nor the Soviet bloc—as a base for French leadership. In 1960, de Gaulle exploded an atomic bomb; in 1963 he negotiated a Franco-German friendship treaty; and the following year he recognized Peking, at the same time improving relations with the U.S.S.R.

De Gaulle took France out of NATO in 1967 and expelled all foreign-controlled troops from the country. He later went on to attempt to achieve a long—cherished plan of regional reform. This, however, aroused wide opposition. He decided to stake his fate on a referendum. At the voting in April 1969, the electorate defeated the plan. His successor, Georges Pompidou, de Gaulle's premier for six years, reversed the de Gaulle policy of opposing the unification of Europe.

Pompidou continued the de Gaulle policies of seeking to expand France's influence in the Mideast and Africa, selling arms to South Africa (despite the U.N. embargo), to Libya, and to Greece, and in 1971 he endorsed British entry into the Common Market.

Pompidou died of cancer in April 1974 and the special election to choose a successor was won by Valéry Giscard d'Estaing, who had served as de Gaulle's Finance Minister but was not a Gaullist party member.

Jacques Chirac, the Gaullist Premier, resigned in 1976 because he said he lacked power to deal with growing economic problems and Giscard refused to delegate presidential authority. Chirac's successor was Raymond Barre, a technician without political background.

A surprise victory in parliamentary elections in 1978, resulting from a split between Socialists and Communists, gave Giscard a solid majority, but the following year a cut in subsidies to industry generated a wave of strikes and the worst rioting in Paris since the student rebellion of 1968. Giscard concentrated on foreign policy, attacking the U.S. at the Tokyo economic summit of 1979 for failing to conserve oil and continuing his criticism at the Venice summit the following year. To the further annoyance of the Carter Administration, he met with Soviet President Leonid I. Brezhnev in Warsaw earlier without prior consultation with Washington.

Giscard's African strongman image began to fade with the collapse of his one-time protégé, Jean-Bedel Bokassa, whose Central African Empire dissolved in a cloud of scandal in 1979. Alleged gifts of diamonds to the French President by the short-lived Emperor Bokassa became the basis of a whispering campaign against Giscard, worsened by Government efforts to suppress it legally. The defeat of President Goukouni Oueddi of Chad by Libyan-aided dissidents in January 1981, despite the presence of French troops, added no luster to Giscard's African record.

Mitterrand's stunning defeat on May 10 of the Gaullist alliance that had held power since 1958 was attributed to the challenger's skill in maintaining the Communists' support while holding them at arm's length and to the failure of Giscard to hold Gaullist support. Chirac only reluctantly supported the President in the final round of voting after having run against him in the first.

Mitterrand's ultimate triumph came in the final round of parliamentary voting when his Socialist Party, which in 1971 had polled only 5% of the votes in a similar election, swept to absolute power in the Assembly with 285 of the 491 seats. The Gaullist Rassemblement pour la République (Rally for the Republic) was cut in half, together with its allied Union pour la Democratie Française (Union for French Democracy), and the Communists fell to their lowest strength since World War II.

Although Communist support was not needed, Mitterrand named four Communist ministers to his 44-member Cabinet, the first since the postwar period and the cause for some alarm among NATO allies. Mitterrand reassured Vice President George Bush in June, pointing to the statement signed by the Communist Party as the price of joining the government, endorsing Western European defense against the Soviet Union and calling for Soviet withdrawal from Afghanistan. Mitterrand also met with German Chancellor Helmut Schmidt to support the stationing of U.S. nuclear weapons in Western Europe.

The victors immediately moved to carry out campaign pledges to nationalize major industries, halt nuclear testing, suspend nuclear power plant construction, and impose new taxes on the rich. Premier Pierre Mauroy called for the nationalization of military production of the Dassault-Breguet aircraft corporation, the Sacinor and Usinor steel companies, some remaining privately owned commercial banks, and the major manufacturing companies in generators, chemicals, glass appliances, and nonferrous metals.

Mauroy said the government would negotiate for subsequent takeover of important foreign-owned businesses such as Honeywell-Bull computers and ITT-France (U.S.) and Roussel-Uclaf (a West German-controlled drug and chemical business).

The Socialist program also called for a job-creation program to ease unemployment, which reached 1.8 million in June. The program was to be partly financed by income surtaxes and taxes on expense-account spending and luxury hotels and restaurants.

On Feb. 11, 1982, the nationalization bills became law. Acquisition of the five major industries targeted by the law was estimated to cost $7 billion and the government announced an immediate program to spend $1.6 billion to aid the weakest of the five—the steel, electronics, and textile-chemical conglomerates. A reaction to the Socialist innovations brought opposition victories in four parliamentary by-elections in January and an opposition sweep in local elections in March, when the Socialist-Communist-alliance won majorities in only 37 of France's 95 departments.

At the Versailles summit of the industrialized nations in June, overshadowed by war in the Falkland Islands and Lebanon, Mitterrand sought U.S. agreement to the extension of French credit and technology for the construction of a Soviet gas pipeline to supply Western Europe. Despite U.S. disapproval, Mitterrand ordered French manufacturers to supply even U.S.-licensed technology to the project.

The first regional assembly was elected in Corsica on Aug. 8, with pro-government Socialists and Communists winning only 23 of 61 seats. Another element of Mitterrand's decentralizing plans, the breakdown of Paris into 20 units, announced June 30, aroused such strong opposition that the government hastily retreated.

Overseas Departments and Territories of France

FRENCH GUIANA (including ININI)

Status: Overseas Department
Prefect: Maxime Gonzalvo (1981)
Area: 35,135 sq mi. (91,000 sq km)
Population (est. 1982): 70,000 (average annual growth rate: 2.5%)
Capital (est. 1980): Cayenne, 35,000
Monetary unit: Franc
Language: Creole
Religion: Roman Catholic
Literacy rate (1981): 73%
Economic summary: Gross national product (1980): $180 million. Average annual growth rate (1970–79): 0.4%. Per capita income (1980): $2,880. Labor force in agriculture: 21%; principal agricultural products: rice, corn, manioc, cocoa, bananas, sugar cane. Labor force in industry: 8%; major industrial products: timber, rum, rosewood essence, gold mining. Natural resources: bauxite, timber, cinnabar, low-grade iron ore. Exports: shrimp, timber, rum, rosewood essence. Imports: food, consumer and producer goods, petroleum. Major trading partners: U.S., France, Martinique.

French Guiana, lying north of Brazil and east of Suriname on the northeast coast of South America, was first settled in 1604. Penal settlements, embracing the area around the mouth of the Maroni River and the Iles du Salut (including Devil's Island), were founded in 1852; they have since been abolished.

During World War II, French Guiana at first adhered to the Vichy government, but the Free French took over in 1943. French Guiana accepted in 1958 the new Constitution of the French Fifth Republic and remained an Overseas Department of the French Republic.

FRENCH POLYNESIA

Status: Overseas Territory
High Commissioner: Paul Cousseran (1977)
Area: 1,544 sq mi. (4,000 sq km)
Population (est. 1982): 160,000 (average annual growth rate: 2.2%)
Monetary unit: Pacific financial community franc
Language: French
Religions: Protestant, 55%; Roman Catholic, 32%.
Capital (est. 1980): Papeete (on Tahiti), 25,000
Economic summary: Gross national product (1980): $1.0 billion. Average annual growth rate (1970–78): 2.8%. Per capita income (1980): $6,780. Principal agricultural product: coconuts. Major industries: tourism, maintenance of French nuclear test base. Exports: coconut products, mother of pearl, vanilla. Imports: fuels, foodstuffs, equipment. Major trading partners: France, U.S.

The term French Polynesia is applied to the scattered French possessions in the South Pacific—Mangareva (Gambier), Makatea, the Marquesas Islands, Rapa, Rurutu, Rimatara, the Society Islands, the Tuamotu Archipelago, Tubuai, Raivavae, and the island of Clipperton—which were organized into a single colony in 1903. There are 120 islands, of which 25 are uninhabited.

The High Commissioner is assisted by a Council of Government and a popularly elected Territorial Assembly. The principal and most populous island —Tahiti, in the Society group—was claimed as French in 1768. In 1958, French Polynesia voted in favor of the new Constitution of the French Fifth Republic and remained an Overseas Territory of the French Republic. The natives are mostly Maoris.

The Pacific Nuclear Test Center on the atoll of Mururoa, 744 miles (1,200 km) from Tahiti, was completed in 1966.

GUADELOUPE

Status: Overseas Department
Prefect: Robert Miguet (1982)
Area: 687 sq mi. (1,779 sq km)
Population (est. 1982): 330,000 (average annual growth

rate: −0.7%)
Capital (est. 1980): Basse-Terre, 15,800
Largest city (est. 1980): Pointe-à-Pitre, 25,000
Monetary unit: Franc
Languages: French, Creole patois
Religions: Roman Catholic
Literacy rate (1981): 70%
Economic summary: Gross national product (1980): $1.3 billion. Average annual growth rate (1970–79): 5.1%. Per capita income (1980): $3,870. Land used for agriculture: 24%; labor force: 25%; principal agricultural products: sugar cane, bananas, rum, pineapples. Major industries: construction, public works. Exports: sugar, fruits and vegetables, bananas. Imports: foodstuffs, clothing, consumer goods, petroleum. Major trading partner: France.

Guadeloupe, in the West Indies about 300 miles (483 km) southeast of Puerto Rico, was discovered by Columbus in 1493. It consists of the twin islands of Basse-Terre and Grande-Terre and five dependencies—Marie-Galante, Les Saintes, La Désirade, St. Barthélemy, and the northern half of St. Martin. The volcano Soufrière (4,813 ft; 1,467 m), also called La Grande Soufrière, is the highest point on Guadeloupe. Violent activity in 1976 and 1977 caused thousands to flee their homes.

French colonization began in 1635. In 1958, Guadeloupe voted in favor of the new Constitution of the French Fifth Republic and remained an Overseas Department of the French Republic.

MAHORÉ

Status: Territorial collectivity
Prefect: Yves Bonnet (1982)
Area: 146 sq mi. (378 sq km)
Population (est. 1980): 48,600
Capital: Dzaoudzi (about 4,100)
Principal products: vanilla, essential oils, copra

The most populous of the Comoro Islands in the Indian Ocean, with a Christian majority, Mahoré (formerly Mayotte) voted in 1974 and 1976 against joining the other, predominantly Moslem islands, in declaring themselves independent. It continues to retain its ties to France.

MARTINIQUE

Status: Overseas Department
Prefect: Jean Chevance (1981)
Area: 431 sq mi. (1,116 sq km)
Population (est. 1982): 315,000 (average annual growth rate: −0.8%)
Capital (1974 census): Fort-de-France 98,800
Monetary unit: Franc
Languages: French, Creole patois
Religion: Roman Catholic
Literacy rate (1981): 70%
Economic summary: Gross national product (1980): $1.5 billion. Average annual growth rate (1970–79): 4.3%. Per capita income (1980): $4,640. Land used for agriculture: 31%; labor force: 23%; principal agricultural products: sugar cane, bananas, rum, pineapples. Labor force in industry: 9%; major industries: sugar, rum, oil, cement, tourism. Natural resource: fish. Exports: bananas, refined petroleum products, rum, sugar, pineapples. Imports: foodstuffs, clothing and other consumer goods, petroleum products. Major trading partners: France, U.S.

Martinique, lying in the Lesser Antilles about 300 miles (483 km) northeast of Venezuela, was probably discovered by Columbus in 1502 and was taken for France in 1635. Following the Franco-German armistice of 1940, it had a semiautonomous status until 1943, when authority was relinquished to the Free French. The area, administered by a Prefect assisted by an elected council, is represented in the French Parliament. In 1958, Martinique voted in favor of the new Constitution of the French Fifth Republic and remained an Overseas Department of the French Republic.

NEW CALEDONIA AND DEPENDENCIES

Status: Overseas Territory
High Commissioner: Christian Nucci (1981)
Area: 8,548 sq mi. (22,139 sq km)[1]
Population (est. 1982): 150,000 (average annual growth rate: 0.5%)
Capital (est. 1980 for metropolitan area): Nouméa, 75,000
Monetary unit: Pacific financial community franc
Language: Melanesian and Polynesian dialects
Religion: Christian
Literacy rate: Not known
Economic summary: Gross national product (1980): $1.1 billion. Average annual growth rate (1970–78): −4.9%. Per capita income (1980): $7,830. Principal agricultural products: coffee, vegetables, beef. Major industrial product: nickel. Natural resources: nickel, chromite, iron ore. Exports: nickel, coffee. Imports: mineral fuels, machinery, transport equipment, foodstuffs. Major trading partners: France, Japan, U.S., Australia.

1. Including dependencies.

New Caledonia (6,466 sq mi.; 16,747 sq km), about 1,070 miles (1,722 km) northeast of Sydney, Austrialia, was discovered by Capt. James Cook in 1774 and annexed by France in 1853. The government also administers the Isle of Pines, the Loyalty Islands (Uvéa, Lifu, and Maré), the Belep Islands, the Huon Island group, and the Chesterfield Islands.

New Caledonia chose in 1958 to remain an Overseas Territory of the French Republic. The natives are Melanesians; about one third of the population is white and one fifth Indochinese and Javanese.

RÉUNION

Status: Overseas Department
Prefect: Michel Levallois (1981)
Area: 970 sq mi. (2,510 sq km)
Population (est. 1982): 500,000 (average annual growth rate, 1975–79: 0.7%)
Capital (est. 1981): Saint-Denis, 105,000
Monetary unit: Franc
Languages: French, Creole
Religion: Roman Catholic
Economic summary: Gross national product (1980): $2.0 billion. Average annual growth rate (1970–79): −0.9%. Principal agricultural products: sugar cane, vanilla, bananas, perfume plants. Major industrial products: rum, cigarettes, processed sugar. Exports: sugar, perfume essences, rum, molasses. Imports: manufactured goods, foodstuffs, beverages, machinery and transportation equipment, petroleum products. Major trading partners: France, Mauritius.

Discovered by Portuguese navigators in the 16th century, the island of Réunion, then uninhabited, was taken as a French possession in 1642. It is located about 450 miles (724 km) east of Madagascar, in the Indian Ocean. In 1958, Réunion approved the Constitution of the Fifth French Republic and remained an Overseas Department of the French Republic.

ST. PIERRE AND MIQUELON

Status: Overseas Department
Prefect: Philippe Parant (1982)
Area: 93 sq mi. (242 sq km)
Population (est. 1982): 6,000
Capital (est. 1981): Saint Pierre, 5,800
Economic summary: Major industries: fishing, canneries. Exports: petroleum products, cattle, fish. Major trading partners: Canada, France, U.S.

The sole remnant of the French colonial empire in North America, these islands were first occupied by the French in 1604. Their only importance arises from proximity to the Grand Banks, located 10 miles south of Newfoundland, making them the center of the French Atlantic cod fisheries. On July 19, 1976, the islands became an Overseas Department of the French Republic.

SOUTHERN AND ANTARCTIC LANDS

Status: Overseas Territory
Administrator: Francis Jacquemont
Area: 169,614 sq mi. (439,300 sq km)
Capital: Port-au-Français

This territory is uninhabited except for the personnel of scientific bases. It consists of Adélie Land (166,752 sq mi.; 431,888 sq km) on the Antarctic mainland and the following islands in the southern Indian Ocean: the Kerguelen and Crozet archipelagos and the islands of Saint-Paul and New Amsterdam.

WALLIS AND FUTUNA ISLANDS

Status: Overseas Territory
Administrator Superior: Robert Thill (1982)
Area: 77 sq mi. (200 sq km)
Population (est. 1982): 9,200
Capital (1980): Wallis (on Uvea), 600

The two islands groups in the South Pacific between Fiji and Samoa were settled by French missionaries at the beginning of the 19th century. A protectorate was established in the 1880s. Following a referendum by the Polynesian inhabitants, the status was changed to that of an Overseas Territory in 1961.

GABON

Gabonese Republic
President: Omar Bongo (1967)
Premier: Léon Mébiame (1975)
Area: 102,317 sq mi. (265,001 sq km)
Population (est. 1982): 560,000 (average annual growth rate: 1.3%)
Density per square mile: 5.5
Capital and largest city (est. 1978): Libreville, 225,200
Monetary unit: Franc CFA
Ethnic groups: Bateke, Obamba, Bakota, Shake, Pongwés, Adumas, Chiras, Punu, and Lumbu
Languages: French (official) and Bantu dialects
Religions: Animist, Christian, Islam
National name: République Gabonaise
Member of French Community
Literacy rate (1981): 20%
Economic summary: Gross national product (1980): $2.4 billion. Average annual growth rate (1970–79): 5.2%. Per capita income (1980): $3,680. Labor force in agriculture:70%; principal products: cocoa, coffee, wood, palm, rice, bananas, peanuts. Labor force in industry: 30%; major products: petroleum, natural gas, processed wood, manganese, uranium. Natural resources: wood, petroleum, iron ore, manganese, uranium. Exports: crude petroleum, wood and wood products, minerals, coffee. Imports: mining and road-building machinery, electrical equipment, foodstuffs, textiles, transport vehicles. Major trading partners: France, U.S., West Germany.

Geography. This West African land with the Atlantic as its western border is also bounded by Equatorial Guinea, Cameroon, and the Congo. Its area is slightly less than Kentucky's.

From mangrove swamps on the coast, the land becomes divided plateaus in the north and east and mountains in the north. Most of the country is covered by a dense tropical forest.

Government. The president is elected for a seven-year term. Legislative powers are exercised by a National Assembly, which is elected for a seven-year term. After his conversion to Islam in 1973, President Bongo changed his given name, Albert Bernard, to Omar. The Parti Démocratique Gabonais (all National Assembly seats) is led by President Bongo. He was re-elected without opposition in 1973 and in 1980.

History. Little is known of Gabon's history, even in oral tradition, but Pygmies are believed to be the original inhabitants. Now there are many tribal groups in the country, the largest being the Fang people who constitute a third of the population.

Gabon was first visited by the Portuguese navigator Diego Cam in the 15th century. In 1839, the French founded their first settlement on the left bank of the Gabon Estuary and gradually occupied the hinterland during the second half of the 19th century. It was organized as a French territory in 1888 and became an autonomous republic within the French Union after World War II and an independent republic on Aug. 17, 1960.

Immense resources in oil, uranium, manganese, and iron help give Gabon's inhabitants a per capita annual income of $225 to $250, the highest in black Africa. To speed exploitation of a billion-ton iron ore reserve in the Belinga-Mekambo region, the government began work in 1969 on a 350-mile railroad leading from the coast into the area. The project was initiated by President León Mba, who died in 1967, and has been continued by his hand-picked successor, Omar Bongo.

In 1974, Bongo negotiated 60% control of an iron-ore venture half-owned by the Bethlehem Steel Corp. In October of that year, he visited Peking and concluded an economic and technical agreement with China.

GAMBIA

Republic of the Gambia
President: Sir Dawda K. Jawara (1970)
Area: 4,016 sq mi. (10,403 sq km)
Population (est. 1982): 640,000 (average annual growth rate: 2.8%)
Density per square mile: 159.4
Capital and largest city (est. 1980) Banjul, 48,000

Monetary unit: Dalasi
Languages: Native tongues, English (official)
Religions: Islam, Christian, Animist
Member of Commonwealth of Nations
Literacy rate (1981): 10%
Economic summary: Gross national product (1980): $150 million. Average annual growth rate (1970–79): 0.4%. Per capita income (1980): $250. Land used for agriculture: 55%; labor force: 85%; principal products: peanuts, rice, palm kernels. Major industrial products: processed peanuts. Natural resources: fish. Exports: peanuts and peanut products, fish. Imports: textiles, foodstuffs, tobacco, machinery, petroleum products. Major trading partners: Western European countries.

Geography. Situated on the Atlantic coast in westernmost Africa and surrounded on three sides by Senegal, Gambia is twice the size of Delaware. The Gambia River flows for 200 miles (322 km) through Gambia on its way to the Atlantic. The country, the smallest on the continent, averages only 20 miles (32 km) in width.

Government. The president's five-year term is linked to the 35-member unicameral House of Representatives, from which he appoints his Cabinet members and the vice president.

The major political party is the People's Progressive Party (29 seats in House of Representatives), led by President Jawara.

History. During the 17th century, Gambia was settled by various companies of English merchants. Slavery was the chief source of revenue until it was abolished in 1807. Gambia became a crown colony in 1843 and an independent nation within the Commonwealth of Nations on Feb. 18, 1965.

Full independence was approved in a 1970 referendum, and on April 24 of that year Gambia proclaimed itself a republic.

President Dawda K. Jawara won overwhelming re-election to his fifth term on May 5, 1982, in a vote that was also seen as an endorsement of his proposal for a confederation with Senegal.

GERMANY, EAST

German Democratic Republic
Chairman of Council of State: Erich Honecker (1976)
Chairman of Council of Ministers: Willi Stoph (1976)
Area: 40,646 sq mi. (195,273 sq km)[1]
Population (est. 1982): 16,750,000 (average annual growth rate: 0.0%)
Density per square mile: 41.2
Capital: Berlin (eastern sector)
Largest cities (est. 1980): East Berlin, 1,146,000; Leipzig, 563,000; Dresden, 516,000; Karl-Marx Stadt, 317,000; Magdeburg, 289,000; Halle, 232,000; Rostock, 230,000; Erfurt, 230,000
Monetary unit: Mark of the Deutsche Demokratische Republik
Language: German
Religions: Protestant, 53%; Roman Catholic, 8%
National name: Deutsche Demokratische Republik
Literacy rate (1981): 99%
Economic summary: Gross national product (1980): $120.9 billion. Average annual growth rate (1970–79): 4.7%. Per capita income (1980): $7,180. Land used for agriculture: 43%; labor force: 9%; principal products: grains, potatoes, sugar beets, meat and dairy products. Labor force in industry: 39%; major products: steel, chemicals, machinery, electrical and precision engineering products, fishing vessels. Natural resources: brown coal, potash, uranium. Exports: machinery and equipment, chemical products, textiles, clothing. Imports: raw materials, fuels, agricultural products, machinery and equipment. Major trading partners: U.S.S.R., Soviet bloc, West Germany.

1. Including East Berlin (156 square miles), which has been incorporated into the German Democratic Republic.

Geography. East Germany lies on the Baltic Sea with Poland to the east and Czechoslovakia to the south. The border with West Germany is roughly a line running south from Lübeck for about 250 miles. The main river is the Elbe, which flows from Dresden in the southeast to the North Sea in the northwest. The Oder and Neisse Rivers form the border with Poland. Most of the country, which is the size of Tennessee, is situated in the north German plain.

Government. The People's Chamber, composed of 500 deputies elected for five-year terms, chooses the chairman and Council of State and the chairman and Council of Ministers, which carries on executive functions.

The major political party is the Socialist Unity (Communist) Party, led by Secretary General Erich Honecker. Others are Christian Democratic Union, Liberal Democratic Party, Democratic Farmers' Party, National Democratic Party.

History. (For history before 1945, *see* Germany, West.) The area now occupied by East Germany, as well as adjacent areas in Eastern Europe, consists of Mecklenburg, Brandenburg, Lusatia, Saxony, and Thuringia. Soviet armies conquered the five territories by 1945. In the division of 1945 they were allotted to the U.S.S.R. Soviet forces created a State controlled by the secret police with a single party, the Socialist Unity (Communist) Party. The Russians appropriated East German plants to restore their war-ravaged industry.

When the Federal Republic of Germany was established in West Germany, the East German states adopted a more centralized constitution for the Democratic Republic of Germany, and it was put into effect on Oct. 7, 1949. The U.S.S.R. thereupon dissolved its occupation zone, but Soviet troops remained. The Western Allies declared that the East German Republic was a Soviet creation undertaken without self-determination and refused to recognize it. It was recognized only within the Soviet bloc.

In 1953, the U.S.S.R. transferred control of East Germany from the military commander to a civilian commissioner and announced a more liberal policy. Continued austerity and political repression led to workers' riots in East Berlin and other cities, allegedly instigated by the Soviet secret police as part of a power struggle within the Kremlin. Soviet troops ruthlessly reestablished order.

In 1955, Walter Ulbricht, hard-line dictator, won Soviet recognition of the East German republic and joined the Warsaw Treaty Organization, organiz- ing troops under the guise of police forces. In the middle and late 1960s, East Germany also came to enjoy economic prosperity.

East German troops took part in the Soviet-bloc occupation of Czechoslovakia in August 1968, but reportedly were withdrawn after the U.S.S.R. questioned whether the 1945 Potsdam agreements permitted German troops on foreign soil.

A constitution adopted in April 1968 reaffirmed one-party rule and narrowed civil rights. Ulbricht continued pressure on West Berlin, opposed liberalization in Czechoslovakia and other parts of the Soviet bloc, impeded Bonn's establishment of ties with East Europe, and pressured Bonn to acknowledge the existence of the two German states.

Talks between the two German states on normalization began in 1970, with the East seeking recognition of its existence and the West wanting easing of pressure on Berlin. West Germany's nonaggression treaty with the U.S.S.R. was cooly received by Ulbricht. In 1971 he resigned and rapprochement between the two Germanys accelerated with agreement on a variety of issues (for details, *see* Germany, West). By 1973, normal relations were established, and the two states entered the United Nations.

A new Constitution unanimously approved by the East German parliament on Sept. 27, 1974, pointedly deleted any reference to eventual reunification of the two Germanys, a principle maintained in the West German constitution.

The 25-year diplomatic hiatus between East Germany and the U.S. ended Sept. 4, 1974, with the establishment of formal relations.

The East German government has repeatedly challenged the Western powers' right of access to Berlin, most recently at the time of President Carter's July 15, 1978, visit to West Berlin. Autobahn traffic between the city and West Germany was deliberately slowed and, as in a similar 1977 case, the U.S., U.K., and France protested to the U.S.S.R. and the East Germans that such action was illegal under the 1971 Four Power Agreement.

Increased Soviet action in Africa in 1978 revealed that East Germany as well as Cuba was actively engaged as a Soviet agent. Defense Minister Heinz Hoffmann visited Angola just before the invasion of Zaire's Shaba Province was launched in May. In Angola, 1,000 East German troops were reported serving with the army, and a small number of pilots were flying combat strikes.

Chairman of the Council of State Erich Honecker gave strong backing to the Soviet Union's stern policy toward Poland as the workers' demand for democratic rights advanced in 1980 and 1981. On Oct. 28, 1980, he closed the border, which had been open between the two states for 10 years, permitting only certified relatives or invited friends to visit. Five million Poles had visited East Germany in the previous year, largely to find cheaper and more abundant consumer goods.

In February 1981, Honecker, in a surprise gesture, declared at his party's 16th Congress that German reunification might eventually be possible, something the Communist regime had ruled out 10 years earlier. He also eased border restrictions on exchanges with West Germany imposed a few months before.

ERMANY, WEST

deral Republic of Germany
esident: Karl Carstens (1979)
ancellor: Helmut Kohl (1982)
ea: 95,815 sq mi. (248,161 sq km)[1]
pulation (est. 1982): 61,750,000 (average annual growth rate: 0.0%)
nsity per square mile: 644.5
pital (est. 1977): Bonn, 285,000
Largest cities (est. 1980): Hamburg, 1,650,000; Munich, 1,300,000; Cologne, 975,000; Essen, 650,000; Frankfurt, 630,000; Dortmund, 610,000; Düsseldorf, 590,000; Stuttgart, 582,000; Bremen, 555,000; Hannover, 535,000
Monetary unit: Deutsche Mark
Language: German
Religions: Protestant, 49%; Roman Catholic, 45%
National name: Bundesrepublik Deutschland
Literacy rate (1980): 99%
Economic summary: Gross national product (1980): $827.8 billion. Average annual growth rate (1970–79): 2.6%. Per capita income (1980): $13,590. Land used for agriculture: 33%; labor force: 5%; principal products: grains, potatoes, sugar beets. Labor force in industry: 43%; major products: iron, steel, coal, cement, chemicals, machinery, ships, vehicles. Natural resources: timber, coal, potash. Exports: machines and machine tools, chemicals, motor vehicles, iron and steel products. Imports: manufactured and agricultural products, raw materials, fuels. Major trading partners: France, Netherlands, Belgium-Luxembourg, Italy, U.S., U.K.

1. Excluding West Berlin (184 square miles with 1980 population of 1,900,000).

Geography. The Federal Republic of Germany occupies the western half of the central European area historically regarded as German. This was the part of Germany occupied by the United States, Britain, and France after World War II, when the eastern half of prewar Germany was split roughly between a Soviet-occupied zone, which became the present German Democratic Republic, and an area annexed by Poland.

West Germany's neighbors are France, Belgium, Luxembourg, and the Netherlands on the west, Switzerland and Austria on the south, Czechoslovakia and East Germany on the east, and Denmark on the north.

The northern plain, the central hill country, and the southern mountain district constitute the main physical divisions of West Germany, which is slightly smaller than Oregon. The Bavarian plateau in the southwest averages 1,600 feet (488 m) above sea level, but it reaches 9,721 feet (2,963 m) in the Zugspitze Mountains, the highest point in the country.

Important navigable rivers are the Danube, rising in the Black Forest and flowing east across Bavaria into Austria, and the Rhine, which rises in Switzerland and flows across the Netherlands in two channels to the North Sea and is navigable by smaller vessels as far as Cologne. The Rhine and the Elbe, which also empties into the North Sea, are navigable within Germany for ships of 400 tons. The Weser, flowing into the North Sea, and the Main and Mosel (Moselle), both tributaries of the Rhine, are also important.

Government. Under the Constitution of May 23, 1949, the Federal Republic was established as a parliamentary democracy. The Parliament consists of the Bundesrat, an upper chamber representing and appointed by the 10 Länder, or states (plus West Berlin), and the Bundestag, a lower house elected for four years by universal suffrage. Each house has non-voting representatives from West Berlin. The entire legislature elects the President of the Republic for a five-year term; the Bundestag alone chooses the Chancellor, or Prime Minister. Each of the Länder and West Berlin have a legislature popularly elected for a four-year or five-year term.

The major political parties are the Christian

Democratic Union-Christian Social Union (226 of 497 seats in the Bundestag), led by Chancellor Helmut Kohl; Social Democratic Party (218 seats) led by former Chancellor Willy Brandt; and the Free Democratic Party (53 seats), led by Foreign Minister Hans-Dietrich Genscher. Kohl's government is a coalition with the Free Democrats.

History. Immediately before the Christian era, when the Roman Empire had pushed its frontier to the Rhine, what is now Germany was inhabited by several tribes believed to have migrated from Central Asia between the 6th and 4th centuries B.C. One of these tribes, the Franks, attained supremacy in western Europe under Charlemagne, who was crowned Holy Roman Emperor A.D. 800. By the Treaty of Verdun (843), Charlemagne's lands east of the Rhine were ceded to the German Prince Louis. Additional territory acquired by the Treaty of Mersen (870) gave Germany approximately the area it maintained throughout the Middle Ages. For several centuries after Otto the Great was crowned King in 936, the German rulers were also usually heads of the Holy Roman Empire.

Relations between state and church were changed by the Reformation, which began with Martin Luther's 95 theses, and came to a head in 1547, when Charles V scattered the forces of the Protestant League at Mühlberg. Freedom of worship was guaranteed by the Peace of Augsburg (1555), but a Counter Reformation took place later, and a dispute over the succession to the Bohemian throne brought on the Thirty Years' War (1618–48), which devastated Germany and left the empire divided into hundreds of small principalities virtually independent of the Emperor.

Meanwhile, Prussia was developing into a state of considerable strength. Frederick the Great (1740–86) reorganized the Prussian army and defeated Maria Theresa of Austria in a struggle over Silesia. After the defeat of Napoleon at Waterloo (1815), the struggle between Austria and Prussia for supremacy in Germany continued, reaching its climax in the defeat of Austria in the Seven Weeks' War (1866) and the formation of the Prussian-dominated North German Confederation (1867).

The architect of German unity was Otto von Bismarck, a conservative, monarchist, and militaristic Prussian Junker who had no use for "empty phrase-making and constitutions." From 1862 until his retirement in 1890 he dominated not only the German but also the entire European scene. He unified all Germany in a series of three wars against Denmark (1864), Austria (1866), and France (1870–71), which many historians believe were instigated and promoted by Bismarck in his zeal to build a nation through "blood and iron."

On Jan. 18, 1871, King Wilhelm I of Prussia was proclaimed German Emperor in the Hall of Mirrors at Versailles. The North German Confederation, created in 1867, was abolished, and the Second German Reich, consisting of the North and South German states, was born. With a powerful army, an efficient bureaucracy, and a loyal bourgeoisie, Chancellor Bismarck consolidated a powerful centralized state.

Wilhelm II dismissed Bismarck in 1890 and embarked upon a "New Course," stressing an intensified colonialism and a powerful navy. His chaotic foreign policy culminated in the diplomatic isolation of Germany and the disastrous defeat in World War I (1914–18).

The Second German Empire collapsed following the defeat of the German armies in 1918, the naval mutiny at Kiel, and the flight of the Kaiser to the Netherlands on November 10. The Social Democrats, led by Friedrich Ebert and Philipp Scheidemann, crushed the Communists and established a moderate republic with Ebert as President.

The Weimar Constitution of 1919 provided for a President to be elected for seven years by universal suffrage and a bicameral legislature, consisting of the Reichsrat, representing the states, and the Reichstag, representing the people. It contained a model Bill of Rights. It was weakened, however, by a provision that enabled the President to rule by decree.

President Ebert died Feb. 28, 1925, and on April 26, Field Marshal Paul von Hindenburg was elected president.

The mass of Germans regarded the Weimar Republic as a child of defeat, imposed upon a Germany whose legitimate aspirations to world leadership had been thwarted by a world conspiracy. Added to this were a crippling currency debacle, a tremendous burden of reparations, and acute economic distress.

Adolf Hitler, an Austrian war veteran and a fanatical nationalist, fanned discontent by promising a Greater Germany, abrogation of the Treaty of Versailles, restoration of Germany's lost colonies, and destruction of the Jews. When the Social Democrats and the Communists refused to combine against the Nazi threat, President Hindenburg made Hitler chancellor on Jan. 30, 1933.

With the death of Hindenburg on Aug. 2, 1934, Hitler repudiated the Treaty of Versailles and began full-scale rearmament. In 1935 he withdrew Germany from the League of Nations, and the next year he reoccupied the Rhineland and signed the anti-Comintern pact with Japan, at the same time strengthening relations with Italy. Austria was annexed in March 1938. By the Munich agreement in September 1938 he gained the Czech Sudetenland, and in violation of this agreement he completed the dismemberment of Czechoslovakia in March 1939. But his invasion of Poland on Sept. 1, 1939, precipitated World War II.

On May 8, 1945, Germany surrendered unconditionally to Allied and Soviet military commanders and on June 5 the four-nation Allied Control Council became the *de facto* government of Germany. (For details of World War II, *see* Headline History.)

At the Berlin (or Potsdam) Conference (July 17–Aug. 2, 1945) President Truman, Premier Stalin and Prime Minister Clement Attlee of Britain set forth the guiding principles of the Allied Control Council. They were Germany's complete disarmament and demilitarization, destruction of its war potential, rigid control of industry, and decentralization of the political and economic structure. Pending final determination of territorial questions at a peace conference, the three victors agreed in principle to the ultimate transfer of the city of Königsberg (now Kaliningrad) and its adjacent area to the U.S.S.R. and to the administration by Poland of former German territories lying generally east of the Oder-Neisse Line.

For purposes of control Germany was divided in 1945 into four national occupation zones, each headed by a Military Governor.

The Western powers were unable to agree with the U.S.S.R. on any fundamental issue. Work of the Allied Control Council was hamstrung by repeated Soviet vetoes; and finally, on March 20, 194[illegible] Russia walked out of the Council. Meanwhile, the U.S. and Britain had taken steps to merge the

Rulers of Germany and Prussia

Name	Born	Ruled[1]
KINGS OF PRUSSIA		
Frederick I[2]	1657	1701–1713
Frederick William I	1688	1713–1740
Frederick II the Great	1712	1740–1786
Frederick William II	1744	1786–1797
Frederick William III	1770	1797–1840
Frederick William IV	1795	1840–1861
William I	1797	1861–1871[3]
EMPERORS OF GERMANY		
William I	1797	1871–1888
Frederick III	1831	1888–1888
William II	1859	1888–1918[4]
HEADS OF THE REICH		
Friedrich Ebert[5]	1871	1919–1925
Paul von Hindenburg[5]	1847	1925–1934
Adolf Hitler[6 7]	1889	1934–1945
Karl Doenitz[6]	1891	1945–1945
GERMAN FEDERAL REPUBLIC (WEST) (PRESIDENTS)		
Theodor Heuss	1884	1949–1959[9]
Heinrich Luebke	1895	1959–1969[8]
Gustav Heinemann[10]	1899	1969–1974
Walter Scheel	1919	1974–1979
Karl Carstens	1914	1979–
GERMAN DEMOCRATIC REPUBLIC (EAST)		
Wilhelm Pieck[5]	1876	1949–1960
Walter Ulbricht[11]	1893	1960–1973
Willi Stoph[12]	1914	1973–1976
Erich Honecker[17]	1912	1976–

1. Year of end of rule is also that of death, unless otherwise indicated. 2. Was Elector of Brandenburg (1688–1701) as Frederick III. 3. Became Emperor of Germany in 1871. 4. Died 1941. 5. President. 6. Führer. 7. Named Chancellor by President Hindenburg in 1933. 8. Died 1972. 9. Died 1963. 10. Died 1976. 11. Chairman of Council of State. Died 1973. 12. Chairman of Council of State.

zones economically (Bizone); and on May 31, 1948, the U.S., Britain, France, and the Benelux countries agreed to set up a German state comprising the three Western Zones.

The U.S.S.R. reacted by clamping a blockade on all ground communications between the Western Zones and Berlin, an enclave in the Soviet Zone. The Western Allies countered by organizing a gigantic airlift to fly supplies into the beleaguered city, assigning 60,000 men to it. The U.S.S.R. was finally forced to lift the blockade on May 12, 1949.

The Federal Republic of Germany was proclaimed on May 23, 1949, with its capital at Bonn. In free elections, West German voters gave a majority in the Constituent Assembly to the Christian Democrats, with the Social Democrats largely making up the opposition. Konrad Adenauer became chancellor, and Theodor Heuss of the Free Democrats was elected first president.

With admission into the European Coal and Steel Community and later into the Common Market, West Germany prospered. In 1950 a West Berlin Constitution provided for autonomous municipal government and representation in the Bundestag.

Agreements in Paris in 1954 giving the Federal Republic full independence and complete sovereignty came into force on May 5, 1955. Under it, West Germany and Italy became members of the Brussels treaty organization created in 1948 and renamed the Western European Union. West Germany also became a member of NATO. In 1955 the U.S.S.R. recognized the Federal Republic. The Saar territory, under an agreement between France and West Germany, held a plebiscite and despite economic links to France voted to rejoin West Germany. It became a state of West Germany on Jan. 1, 1957.

In 1963, Chancellor Adenauer concluded a treaty of mutual cooperation and friendship with France and then retired. He was succeeded by his chief inner-party critic, Ludwig Erhard, who was followed in 1966 by Kurt Georg Kiesinger. He, in turn, was succeeded in 1969 by Willy Brandt, former mayor of West Berlin.

The division between West Germany and East Germany was intensified when the Communists erected the Berlin Wall in 1961. In 1968, the East German Communist leader, Walter Ulbricht, imposed restrictions on West German movements into West Berlin. The Soviet-bloc invasion of Czechoslovakia in August 1968 added to the tension.

A treaty with the U.S.S.R. was signed in Moscow in August 1970 in which force was renounced and respect for the "territorial integrity" of present European states declared.

Three months later, West Germany signed a similar treaty with Poland, renouncing force and setting Poland's western border as the Oder-Neisse Line. It subsequently resumed formal relations with Czechoslovakia in a pact that "voided" the Munich treaty that gave Nazi Germany the Sudetenland.

Both German states were admitted to the United Nations in 1973.

Brandt, winner of a Nobel Peace Prize for his foreign policies, was forced to resign in 1974 when an East German spy was discovered to be one of his top staff members. Succeeding him was a moderate Social Democrat, Helmut Schmidt.

The Christian Social Union of Bavaria broke its 30-year alliance with the Christian Democratic Party in 1979 to run its leader, Franz Josef Strauss, in a three-way race against the Christian Democrats' Ernst Albrecht and Chancellor Schmidt in the 1980 elections. Schmidt, campaigning on a tough policy of stationing U.S. nuclear weapons in West Germany despite Soviet threats, won the Oct. 5 contest easily with a new coalition majority of 271.

Schmidt had made an unsuccessful trip to Moscow four months before the vote to urge President Leonid I. Brezhnev to withdraw from Afghanistan. He canceled a scheduled visit to East Germany in August because of the Soviet and East bloc pressure on the Polish labor movement. Smarting from Reagan Administration criticism of German defense weakness, Schmidt threatened to resign in May 1981 in order to win Bundestag approval of the stationing of U.S. nuclear weapons in West Germany.

At the "big seven" economic summit in Ottawa in July, Schmidt forcefully presented European demands for lower U.S. interest rates, without success. A year later when the eighth economic summit convened at Versailles, he was no more successful despite the serious decline in the German economy. Schmidt staunchly backed U.S. military strategy in Europe nevertheless, staking his political fate on the strategy of placing U.S. nuclear missiles in Germany unless the Soviet Union reduced its arsenal of intermediate missiles.

The chancellor also strongly opposed nuclear freeze proposals and won 2-1 support for his stand at the convention of Social Democrats in April. But the nuclear issue, as well as economic problems, contributed to a Social Democratic defeat in Schmidt's hometown bastion, Hamburg, in which state elections in June put the opposition Christian Democrats in first place. The anti-nuclear "Greens" ran third and the Free Democrats, partners in Schmidt's federal coalition, failed to win a seat. Speculation arose that the Free Democrats may desert the Socialists and join with the Christian Democrats in Bonn to unseat Schmidt, the elder statesman of Western Europe.

BERLIN

Status: West Berlin: State of West Germany; East Berlin: capital of East Germany
Governing Mayor, West Berlin: Richard von Weizsäcker (1981)
Mayor, East Berlin: Erhard Krack
Area: 340 square miles (West Berlin, 184; East Berlin, 156
Population (est. 1980): 3,046,000 (West Berlin, 1,900,000; East Berlin, 1,146,000)

Berlin, the capital of prewar Germany, lies entirely within the borders of East Germany. After the war, the city was occupied by the forces of the U.S., Britain, France, and the U.S.S.R. The three western sectors, now known as West Berlin, contain 55% of the area and two thirds of the population.

West Berlin is a state of the Federal Republic of Germany, but supreme authority remains in the hands of the three Western powers in accordance with postwar agreements. The government is composed of the governing mayor, the 11-member Senate (his Cabinet), and the House of Representatives, a popularly elected legislative body that elects the governing mayor and the Senate.

East Berlin is governed by a City Assembly elected by Communist Party members, and a Magistrat (City Council) chosen by the Assembly and headed by the mayor. In violation of the Four Power Agreements, the Soviet Sector has been incorporated into the German Democratic Republic and is now the capital of that country.

Major anti-Communist riots broke out in East Berlin in June 1953 and, since Aug. 13, 1961, the Soviet Sector has been virtually sealed off by a Communist-built wall, 26½ miles (43 km) long, running through the city. It was built to stem the flood of refugees seeking freedom in the West, 200,000 having fled in 1961 before the wall was erected.

GHANA

Republic of Ghana
Chairman of Provisional National Defense Council: Flight Lt. Jerry Rawlings (1981)
Area: 92,100 sq mi. (238,537 sq km)
Population (est. 1982): 12,400,000 (average annual growth rate: 3.2%)
Density per square mile: 134.6
Capital: Accra
Largest cities (est. 1980): Accra, 1,000,000; **(est. 1972):** Kumasi, 342,982; Sekondi-Takoradi, 161,071
Monetary unit: Cedi
Languages: Native tongues (Twi, Fanti, Ga, Ewe, Dagbani); English
Religions: Christian 43%, Islam 12%, Animist 38%
Literacy rate (1981): 25% (in English)
Member of Commonwealth of Nations
Economic summary: Gross national product (1980): $4.9 billion. Average annual growth rate (1970–79): −3.0%. Per capita income (1980): $420. Land used for agriculture: 19%; labor force: 60%; principal products: cocoa, timber, coconuts, coffee, subsistence crops, rubber. Labor force in industry: 17%; major products: mining products, lumber, light manufactured goods, fish, aluminum. Natural resources: gold, diamonds, bauxite, manganese, fish. Exports: cocoa beans and products, gold, timber, manganese ore. Imports: textiles and manufactured goods, food, fuels, transport equipment. Major trading partners: U.K., Western European countries, U.S.

Geography. A West African country bordering on the Gulf of Guinea, Ghana has the Ivory Coast to the west, Upper Volta to the north, and Togo to the east. It compares in size to Oregon.

The coastal belt, extending about 270 miles (435 km), is sandy, marshy, and generally exposed. Behind it is a gradually widening grass strip. The forested plateau region to the north is broken by ridges and hills. The largest river is the Volta.

Government. Ghana returned to military rule after two years of constitutional government when Flight Lt. Jerry Rawlings, who led a coup in 1979 and stepped down voluntarily, seized power on Dec. 31, 1981. Rawlings heads a Provisional National Defense Council, which exercises all power.

History. Created an independent country on March 6, 1957, Ghana is the former British colony of the Gold Coast. The area was first seen by Portuguese traders in 1470. They were followed by the English (1553), the Dutch (1595), and the Swedes (1640). British rule over the Gold Coast began in 1820, but it was not until after quelling the severe resistance of the Ashanti in 1901 that it was firmly established. British Togoland, formerly a colony of Germany, was incorporated into Ghana by referendum in 1956. As the result of a plebiscite, Ghana became a republic on July 1, 1960.

Premier Kwame Nkrumah attempted to take leadership of the Pan-African Movement, holding the All-African People's Congress in his capital, Accra, in 1958 and organizing the Union of African States with Guinea and Mali in 1961. But he oriented his country toward the Soviet Union and China and built an autocratic rule over all aspects of Ghanaian life.

In February 1966, while Nkrumah was visiting Peking and Hanoi, he was deposed by a military coup led by Gen. Emmanuel K. Kotoka. The U.S. recognized the new regime and gave it financial aid. In April 1967, a military junta was crushed, but Kotoka was killed. The military leaders took steps to restore civilian rule and a new Constitution was approved in May 1969.

Another military group took over in January 1972. Its leader, Col. Ignatius Acheampong, pro claimed himself Head of State and chairman of the National Redemption Council, which replaced Parliament. The new regime proposed a union government of military, police, and civilian elements in a referendum approved by the voters in March 1978. Before the plan could be implemented, however, Lt. Gen. Frederick W. K. Akuffo of the military governing council ousted Acheampong on July 5. The shift was apparently related to food shortages and Ghana's raging inflation, running at an annual rate of more than 100%.

A military coup led by Flight Lieutenant Jerry Rawlings, imprisoned after an earlier attempt, overthrew Akuffo on June 4, 1979. Rawlings promised that the election of a civilian president would go ahead as scheduled, and Hilla Limann, candidate of the People's National Party, became President-elect in July.

Rawlings, who had been retired from the Air Force by Limann, staged a coup on Dec. 31, 1981, charging the civilian government with corruption and repression. As chairman of the Provisional National Defense Council, Rawlings instituted an austerity program aimed at 'total economic independence" by reducing budget deficits and slowing the 116% inflation rate recorded in 1981.

GREECE

Hellenic Republic
President: Constantine Karamanlis (1980)
Premier: Andreas Papandreou (1981)
Area: 50,547 sq mi. (130,917 sq km)
Population (est. 1982): 9,800,000 (average annual growth rate: 0.7%)
Density per square mile: 193.9
Capital: Athens
Largest cities (est. 1981 for metropolitan area): Athens, 3,000,000; **(1971 census):** Salonika, 345,799; Piraeus, 187,362; Péristéri, 118,413; Patrai, 111,607
Monetary unit: Drachma
Language: Greek
Religion: Greek Orthodox
National name: Ellinikí Dimokratía
Literacy rate (1981): 86%
Economic summary: Gross national product (1980): $42.2 billion. Average annual growth rate (1970–79): 4.1%. Per capita income (1980): $4,520. Land used for agriculture: 29%; labor force: 31%; principal products: grains, fruits, vegetables, olives, olive oil, tobacco, cotton, livestock, dairy products. Labor force in industry: 30%; major products: textiles, metals, chemicals, electrical equipment, cement, glass. Natural resources: bauxite, lignite, forests. Exports: fruits, minerals, textiles, tobacco. Imports: machinery and automotive equipment, petroleum, consumer goods, chemicals, meat, live animals. Major trading partners: West Germany, Italy, France, Saudi Arabia.

Geography. Greece, on the Mediterranean Sea, is the southernmost country on the Balkan Peninsula in Eastern Europe. It is bordered on the north by Albania, Yugoslavia, and Bulgaria; on the west by the Ionian Sea; and on the east by the Aegean Sea and Turkey. It is slightly smaller than Alabama.

North central Greece, Epirus, and western Macedonia all are mountainous. The main chain of the Pindus Mountains rises to 9,000 feet (2,743 m) in places, separating Epirus from the plains of Thessaly. Mt. Olympus, rising to 9,570 feet (2,909 m) in the north near the Aegean Sea, is the highest point in the country. Greek Thrace is mostly a lowland region separated from European Turkey by the lower Evros River.

Among the many islands are the Ionian group off the west coast; the Cyclades group to the southeast; other islands in the eastern Aegean, including the Dodecanese Islands, Euboea, Lesbos, Samos, and Chios; and Crete, the fourth largest Mediterranean island.

Government. A referendum in December 1974, five months after the collapse of a military dictatorship, ended the Greek monarchy and established a republic. Ceremonial executive power is held by the president; the Premier heads the government and is responsible to a 300-member unicameral Parliament.

The major political parties are the Panhellenic Socialist Movement (172 of 300 seats in Parliment), led by Premier Andreas Papandreou; New Democracy Party (115 seats), led by Evangelos Averoff-Tossiza; and Communist Party (13 seats), led by Harilaos Florakis.

History. Greece, with a recorded history going back to 766 B.C., reached the peak of its glory in the 5th century B.C., and by the middle of the 2nd century B.C., it had declined to the status of a Roman province. It remained within the Eastern Roman Empire until Constantinople fell to the Crusaders in 1204.

In 1453, the Turks took Constantinople, and by 1460 Greece was a Turkish province. The insurrection made famous by the poet Lord Byron broke out in 1821, and in 1827 Greece won independence with sovereignty guaranteed by Britain, France, and Russia.

The protecting powers chose Prince Otto of Bavaria as the first king of modern Greece in 1832 to reign over an area only slightly larger than the Peloponnese Peninsula. Chiefly under the next king, George I, chosen by the protecting powers in 1863, Greece acquired much of its present territory. During his 57-year reign, a period in which he encouraged parliamentary democracy, Thessaly, Epirus, Macedonia, Crete, and most of the Aegean islands were added from the disintegrating Turkish empire. An unsuccessful war against Turkey after World War I brought down the monarchy, to be replaced by a republic in 1923.

Two military dictatorships and a financial crisis brought George II back from exile, but only until 1941, when Italian and German invaders defeated tough Greek resistance. After British and Greek troops liberated the country in October 1944, Communist guerrillas staged a long campaign in which the government received U.S. aid under the Truman Doctrine, the predecessor of the Marshall Plan.

A military junta seized power in April 1967, sending young King Constantine II into exile December 14. Col. George Papadopoulos, as premier, converted the government to republican form in 1973 and as President ended martial law. He was moving to restore democracy when he was ousted in November of that year by his military colleagues. The regime of the "colonels," which had tortured its opponents and scoffed at human rights, resigned July 23, 1974, after having bungled an attempt to seize Cyprus.

Former Premier Karamanlis returned from exile to become premier of Greece's first civilian government since 1967. The election in November gave him 54% backing, and a new republican Constitution was adopted June 7, 1975.

Greece cut its military ties with the North Atlantic Treaty Organization in 1974 because of U.S. failure to restrain Turkey from invading Cyprus. It was not until Oct. 20, 1980, that Greece returned as a military partner in NATO, even then with some public protest. A lengthy dispute with Turkey over air and sea rights in the Aegean advanced toward settlement with the return to the alliance. An air-rights agreement was announced in March 1981, and the demarcation of the continental shelf in order to resolve oil-exploration problems was expected to follow.

On Jan. 1, 1981, Greece became the 10th member of the European Community. On Oct. 18, the first Socialist government in Greek history won power, and the new Premier, Andreas Papandreou, immediately called for the removal of U.S. bases and threatened to end Greek military participation in NATO because of the alliance's alleged failure to guarantee Greek borders adjoining Turkey. By May 1982, however, Papandreou had retreated from his stand and conferred with U.S. Secretary of State Alexander M. Haig, Jr., about the future of the bases.

GRENADA

State of Grenada
Sovereign: Queen Elizabeth II
Governor General: Paul Scoon (1978)
Prime Minister: Maurice Bishop (1979)
Area: 133 sq mi. (344 sq km)
Population (est. 1982): 110,000 (black, 84%; mixed, 11%) (average annual growth rate, 1.0%)
Density per square mile: 827.1
Capital and largest city (est. 1978): St. George's, 30,000
Monetary unit: East Caribbean dollar
Ethnic groups: Caribs and Indians
Language: English
Religions: Roman Catholic, 64%; Anglican, 22%
Member of Commonwealth of Nations
Literacy rate: Not known
Economic summary: Gross national product (1980): $80 million. Average annual growth rate (1970–79): –1.3%. Per capita income (1980): $690. Land used for agriculture: 44%; labor force: 40%; principal products: spices, cocoa, bananas. Exports: nutmeg, cocoa beans, bananas, mace. Imports: foodstuffs, machinery, building materials. Major trading partners: U.K., West Indies countries, West Germany, Netherlands, U.S.

Geography. Grenada (the first "a" is pronounced as in "gray") is the most southerly of the Windward Islands, about 100 miles (161 km) from the South American coast. It is a volcanic island traversed by a mountain range, the highest peak of which is Mount St. Catherine (2,756 ft.; 840 m).

History. Grenada was discovered by Columbus in 1498. After more than 200 years of British rule, most recently as part of the West Indies Associated States, it became independent Feb. 7, 1974.

The country began its independence in chaos, as opponents of Prime Minister Eric M. Gairy's curbs on civil liberties—notably the professionals and educated class, as well as some union leaders and businessmen—paralyzed Grenada with a general strike that ended after two weeks when Gairy promised to disband his secret police force.

In 1975, Grenada became a member of the Organization of American States. In June 1977, it was host to the OAS General Assembly.

The government of Prime Minister Gairy was ousted March 13, 1979, by the New Jewel Movement of Maurice Bishop. Bishop, a protégé of Cuban President Fidel Castro, invited Cuban military advisers to Grenada and on June 20, 1980, called on Grenadians to join a "people's militia" to fight a "people's war" against imperialism.

GUATEMALA

Republic of Guatemala
President: Gen. José Efraín Ríos Montt (1982)
Area: 42,042 sq mi. (108,889 sq km)
Population (est. 1982): 7,700,000 (average annual growth rate: 3.1%)
Density per square mile: 183.2
Capital and largest city (est. 1982): Guatemala City, 1,250,000
Monetary unit: Quetzal
Languages: Spanish, Indian dialects
Religion: Roman Catholic
National name: República de Guatemala
Literacy rate (1981): 30%
Economic summary: Gross national product (1980): $6.9 billion. Average annual growth rate (1970–79): 3.1%. Per capita income (1980): $1,110. Land used for agriculture: 14%; labor force: 53%; principal products: corn, beans, coffee, cotton, cattle, sugar, bananas, essential oils, timber. Labor force in industry: 12%; principal products: prepared foods, textiles, construction materials, tires, pharmaceuticals. Natural resources: nickel, timber, shrimp. Exports: coffee, cotton, sugar, meat, bananas. Imports: manufactured products, machinery, transportation equipment, chemicals, fuels. Major trading partners: U.S., Central American nations, West Germany, Japan, Venezuela.

Geography. The northernmost of the Central American nations, Guatemala is the size of Tennessee. Its neighbors are Mexico on the north, west, and east and Belize, Honduras, and El Salvador on the east. The country consists of two main regions—the cool highlands with the heaviest population and the tropical area along the Pacific and Caribbean coasts. The principal mountain range rises to the highest elevation in Central America and contains many volcanic peaks. Volcanic eruptions are frequent.

The Petén region in the north contains important resources and archaeological sites of the Mayan civilization.

Government. The Constitution was suspended and political parties banned by a military junta that seized power on March 23, 1982. Gen. José Efraín Ríos Montt announced the retirement of the other two members of the junta and his assumption of sole power June 9.

History. Once the site of the ancient Mayan civilization, Guatemala, conquered by Spain in 1524, set itself up as a republic in 1839. From 1898 to 1920 the dictator Manuel Estrada Cabrera ran the country, and from 1931 to 1944, Gen. Jorge Ubico Castaneda was the strongman. In 1944 the National Assembly elected Gen. Federico Ponce president but he was overthrown in October. In December Dr. Juan José Arévalo was elected as the head of a leftist regime that continued to press its reform program. Jacobo Arbenz Guzmán, administration candidate with pro-Communist leanings, won the 1950 elections.

Arbenz expropriated the large estates, including plantations of the United Fruit Company, and exterminated his political enemies. With covert U.S. backing, a revolt was led by Col. Carlos Castillo Armas, and Arbenz took refuge in Havana. Castillo Armas became president but was assassinated in 1957. Constitutional government was restored in 1958, and Gen. Miguel Ydigoras Fuentes was elected president. He was host to the Cuban force that trained for the disastrous landing at the Bay of Pigs in April 1961.

In 1963 the Ydigoras government was overthrown by Enrique Peralta Azurdia, who ruled until 1966, when elections, under a new Constitution, led to Congress's choice of Dr. Julio César Méndez Montenegro.

A wave of terrorism, by left and right, began in 1967, and in August 1968 U.S. Ambassador John Gordon Mein was killed when he resisted kidnappers. Fear of anarchy led to the election in 1970 of Army Chief of Staff Carlos Araña Osorio, who had put down a rural guerrilla movement at the cost of nearly 3,000 lives. Araña, surprisingly, pledged social reforms when he took office. Another military candidate, Gen. Kjell Laugerud, won the presidency in 1974 amid renewed political violence.

A devastating earthquake on Feb. 4, 1976, killed 22,000 and injured 74,000, doing little damage to the country's growing industrial base, however.

Despite an agreement with Britain signed in 1981, providing for the negotiation of territorial claims and recognition of the independence of Belize, the former British Honduras, Guatemala refused to recognize its new neighbor and continued to assert claims against Belize after its independence was declared on Sept. 21, 1981.

The administration of Gen. Romeo Lucas Garcia, elected president in 1978, ended in a coup by a three-man military junta on March 23, 1982. Lucas Garcia was charged by Amnesty International with responsibility for at least 5,000 political murders in a reign of brutality and corruption that brought a cutoff of U.S. military aid in 1978. Hopes for improvement under the junta faded when Gen. José Efraín Ríos Montt took sole power in June and declared a state of siege on July 1 to pursue a war of extermination against the newly unified leftist guerrillas. Amid reports of massacres, thousands of Guatemalans sought refuge in Mexico.

GUINEA

Revolutionary People's Republic of Guinea
President: Ahmed Sékou Touré (1958)
Premier: Louis Lansana Béavogui (1972)
Area: 94,925 sq mi. (245,857 sq km)
Population (est. 1982): 5,300,000 (average annual growth rate: 1.9%)
Density per square mile: 55.8
Capital and largest city (est. 1980): Conakry, 765,000
Monetary unit: Syli
Languages: French (official), native tongues (Malinké, Susu, Fulani)
Religions: Islam and Animist
National name: République Populaire Revolutionnaire de Guinée
Literacy rate (1981): 10%
Economic summary: Gross national product (1980): $1.6 billion. Average annual growth rate (1970–79): 0.6%. Per capita income (1980): $290. Principal agricultural products: rice, cassava, millet, corn, coffee, bananas, palm products, pineapples. Major industrial products: bauxite, alumina, light manufactured and processed goods. Natural resources: bauxite, iron ore, diamonds, gold, water power. Exports: bauxite, alumina, pineapples, bananas, coffee. Imports: petroleum, machinery, transport equipment, foodstuffs, textiles. Major trading partners: Communist bloc, Western Europe, U.S.

Geography. Guinea, in West Africa on the Atlantic, is also bordered by Guinea-Bissau, Senegal, Mali, the Ivory Coast, Liberia, and Sierra Leone. Slightly smaller than Oregon, the country consists of a coastal plain, a mountainous region, a savanna interior, and a forest area in the Guinea Highlands. The highest peak is Mount Nimba at about 6,000 feet (1,829 m).

Government. The National Assembly has 150 members elected by universal suffrage from a list prepared and presented by the Parti Démocratique de Guinée, the only political party, led by President Ahmed Sékou Touré, Secretary General of the party.

History. Previously part of French West Africa, Guinea achieved independence by rejecting the new French Constitution, and on Oct. 2, 1958, became an independent state with Sékou Touré as president. Touré led the country into being the first avowedly Marxist state in Africa. Diplomatic relations with France were suspended in 1965, with the Soviet Union replacing France as the country's chief source of economic and technical assistance.

In 1966, when a Ghanaian military coup deposed Kwame Nkrumah as President, Touré welcomed him to Guinea and declared him joint president and party leader. The titles proved to be only honorary. Touré accused Ghana of being an American imperialist puppet, and the U.S. Embassy in his capital, Conakry, was sacked. In retaliation the United States ended financial aid. An exchange of letters between the Guinean and U.S. presidents restored relations.

Prosperity came in 1969 after the start of exploitation of bauxite deposits. Touré was re-elected to a seven-year term in 1974 and again in 1981.

GUINEA-BISSAU

Republic of Guinea-Bissau
President of Revolutionary Council: Joao Bernardo Vieira (1980)
Area: 13,948 sq mi. (36,125 sq km)
Population (est. 1982): 590,000 (average annual growth rate: 1.9%)
Density per square mile: 42.3
Capital and largest city (est. 1979 for metropolitan area): Bissau, 109,500
Monetary unit: Guinea-Bissau peso
Language: Portugese
Religions: Animist, 66%; Islam, 30%; Roman Catholic, 4%
National name: Guiné Bissau
Literacy rate (1981): 5%
Economic summary: Gross national product (1980): $130 million. Average annual growth rate (1970–78): 2.9%. Per capita income (1980): $160. Labor force in agriculture: 90%; principal products: palm oil, root crops, rice, coconuts, peanuts. Natural resources: potential bauxite deposits. Exports: peanuts, coconuts, shrimp, fish, wood.

Imports: foodstuffs, manufactured goods, fuels, transportation equipment. Major trading partner: Portugal.

Geography. A neighbor of Senegal and Guinea in West Africa, on the Atlantic coast, Guinea-Bissau is about half the size of South Carolina.

The country is a low-lying coastal region of swamps, rain forests, and mangrove-covered wetlands, with about 25 islands off the coast. The Bijagos archipelago extends 30 miles (48 km) out to sea. Internal communications depend mainly on deep estuaries and meandering rivers, since there are no railroads. Bissau, the capital, is the main port.

Government. The 15-member Council of State was elected in 1977 by a National Assembly of 150 members chosen from regional councils elected from lists provided by the sole political party, the African Party for the Independence of Guinea-Bissau and Cape Verde.

History. Guinea-Bissau was discovered in 1446 by the Portuguese Nuno Tristao, and colonists in the Cape Verde Islands obtained trading rights in the territory. In 1879 the connection with the Cape Verde Islands was broken. Early in the 1900s the Portuguese managed to pacify some tribesmen, although resistance to colonial rule remained.

The African Party for the Independence of Guinea-Bissau and Cape Verde was founded in 1956 and several years later began guerrilla warfare that grew increasingly effective. By 1974 the rebels controlled most of the countryside, where they formed a government that was soon recognized by scores of countries. The military coup in Portugal in April 1974 brightened the prospects for freedom, and in August the Lisbon government signed an agreement granting independence to the province as of Sept. 10. The new republic took the name Guinea-Bissau. Its government was immediately recognized by the United States.

In November 1980, Premier Joao Bernardo Vieira headed a coup that deposed Luis Cabral, President since 1974. A Revolutionary Council assumed the powers of government, with Vieira as its head.

GUYANA

Cooperative Republic of Guyana
President: Forbes Burnham (1980)
Prime Minister: Ptolemy A. Reid (1980)
Area: 83,000 sq mi. (214,969 sq km)
Population (est. 1982): 925,000 (average annual growth rate: 1.5%) (East Indian, 50%; African, 31%; mixed 10%; Amerindian, 5%)
Density per square mile: 11.1
Capital and largest city (est. 1981): Georgetown, 200,000
Monetary unit: Guyana dollar
Languages: English (official), Hindi, Urdu
Religions: Hindu, 37%; Protestant, 32%; Roman Catholic, 13%
Member of Commonwealth of Nations
Literacy rate (1981): 86%
Economic summary: Gross national product (1980): $550 million. Average annual growth rate (1970–79): 0.0%. Per capita income (1980): $690. Labor force in agriculture: 29%; principal products: sugar, rice. Labor force in industry: 31%; major products: bauxite, alumina. Natural resources: bauxite, gold, diamonds, hardwood timber, shrimp. Exports: sugar, bauxite, alumina, rice, shrimp. Imports: consumer and manufactured goods. Major trading partners: U.K., U.S., Caribbean nations.

Geography. Guyana is situated on the northern coast of South America east of Venezuela, west of Suriname, and north of Brazil. The country consists of a low coastal area and the Guiana Highlands in the south. There is an extensive north-south network of rivers. Guyana is the size of Idaho.

Government. Guyana, formerly British Guiana, proclaimed itself a republic on Feb. 23, 1970, ending its tie with Britain while remaining in the Commonwealth.

Guyana has a unicameral legislature, the National Assembly, with 53 members directly elected for four-year terms and 12 elected by local councils. A 24-member Cabinet is headed by the President.

The major political parties are the People's National Congress (41 of 53 seats in National Assembly), led by President Forbes Burnham; People's Progressive Party (10 seats), led by Dr. Cheddi B. Jagan.

History. British Guiana won internal self-government in 1952. The next year the People's Progressive Party, headed by Cheddi B. Jagan, an East Indian dentist, won the elections and Jagan became Prime Minister. British authorities deposed him for alleged Communist connections. A coalition ousted Jagan in 1964, installing a moderate Socialist, Forbes Burnham, a black, as Prime Minister. On May 26, 1966, the country became an independent member of the Commonwealth and resumed its traditional name, Guyana.

The government nationalized mining operations of the U.S.-owned Reynolds Metals Co. in 1975.

In 1978, the International Monetary Fund approved an $18.7-million loan for Guyana, which is trying to overcome a $60-million deficit in balance of payments.

One of the most bizarre incidents in modern history occurred when 911 persons died in a mass murder-suicide on Nov. 19, 1978, at a remote settlement in Guyana founded by a U.S. sect known as the People's Temple. The victims were either shot or forced to drink poisoned Kool-Aid by the Rev. Jim Jones, for whom the site, Jonestown, was named.

Jones ordered his followers to die after his aides had killed U.S. Representative Leo J. Ryan of California and three newsmen who accompanied Ryan on an investigative trip to the colony.

HAITI

Republic of Haiti
Life President: Jean-Claude Duvalier (1971)
Area: 10,714 sq mi. (27,750 sq km)
Population (est. 1982): 5,200,000 (average annual growth rate: 2.2%)
Density per square mile: 485.3
Capital and largest city (est. 1979): Port-au-Prince, 790,000
Monetary unit: Gourde
Languages: French, Creole
Religion: Roman Catholic
National name: République d'Haïti
Literacy rate (1981): 12%
Economic summary: Gross national product (1980): $1.3 billion. Average annual growth rate (1970–79): 1.8%. Per

capita income (1980): $270. Land used for agriculture: 31%; labor force: 79%; principal products: coffee, sugar cane, rice, corn, sorghum. Labor force in industry: 7%; major products: refined sugar, textiles, flour, cement, bauxite, light assembly products. Natural resource: bauxite. Exports: coffee, light industrial products, bauxite, sugar, essential oils, sisal. Imports: consumer goods, foodstuffs, industrial equipment, petroleum products, construction materials. Major trading partner: U.S.

Geography. Haiti, in the West Indies, occupies the western third of the island of Hispaniola, which it shares with the Dominican Republic. About the size of Maryland, Haiti is two thirds mountainous, with the rest of the country marked by great valleys, extensive plateaus, and small plains. The most densely populated region is the Cul-de-Sac plain near Port-au-Prince.

Government. In 1964, the late President, François Duvalier, known as "Papa Doc," made himself president for life. His son, Jean-Claude, then 19, known as "Baby Doc," inherited the title on his father's death on April 21, 1971. Under a Constitution revised in 1964, the president in periods of crisis may dismiss the National Assembly and Cabinet and govern by decree. The Parti d'Unité Nationale (57 of the 58 seats in the National Assembly), led by President Duvalier, is the only legal party in the country.

History. Discovered by Columbus, who landed at Môle Saint Nicolas on Dec. 6, 1492, Haiti in 1697 became a French possession known as Saint Domingue. An insurrection among a slave population of 500,000 in 1791 ended with a declaration of independence by Pierre-Dominique Toussaint 'Ouverture in 1801. Napoleon Bonaparte suppressed the independence movement, but it eventually triumphed in 1804 under Jean-Jacques Dessalines, who gave the new nation the aboriginal name Haiti.

Its prosperity dissipated in internal strife as well s disputes with neighboring Santo Domingo durng a succession of 19th-century dictatorships, a bankrupt Haiti accepted a U.S. customs receivership from 1905 to 1941. Direct U.S. rule from 1915 to 1930 brought a measure of stability and a population growth that made Haiti the most densely populated nation in the hemisphere.

In 1949, after four years of democratic rule by President Dumarsais Estimé, dictatorship returned under Gen. Paul Magloire, who was succeeded by rançois Duvalier in 1957.

Duvalier established a dictatorship based on secret police, known as the "Ton-ton Macoutes," who unned down opponents of the regime. Duvalier's on, Jean-Claude, or "Baby Doc," succeeded his ther in 1971 as ruler of the poorest nation in the Western Hemisphere.

Limited economic improvement followed an increase in foreign investment under the new regime 150 foreign companies established Haitian branches to take advantage of low wages. A steady xodus of refugees continued toward the United ates, reaching a high of 15,000 in 1980. Previous- denied refugee status, Haitian "boat people" ere accorded the same temporary entrance rights Cubans who arrived by boat.

On May 27, 1980, Duvalier married Michelle ennett in a wedding attended by 5,000 guests d estimated to cost from $3 million to $5 million.

HONDURAS

Republic of Honduras
Provisional President: Dr. Roberto Suazo Córdova (1982)
Area: 43,277 sq mi. (112,088 sq km)
Population (est. 1982): 3,950,000 (average annual growth rate: 4.1%) (60% mestizo)
Density per square mile: 91.3
Capital and largest city (est. 1980): Tegucigalpa, 375,000
Monetary unit: Lempira
Languages: Spanish, some Indian dialects, English in Bay Islands Department
Religion: Roman Catholic
National name: República de Honduras
Literacy rate (1970): 47%
Economic summary: Gross national product (1980): $2.1 billion. Average annual growth rate (1970–79): 0.5%. Per capita income (1980): $560. Labor force in agriculture: 59%; principal products: bananas, coffee, corn, beans, cotton, sugar cane, tobacco. Labor force in industry: 14%; major products: processed agricultural products, textiles and clothing, wood products. Natural resources: timber, gold, silver, lead, zinc, antimony. Exports: bananas, coffee, lumber, meat, petroleum products. Imports: manufactured goods, machinery, transportation equipment, chemicals, petroleum. Major trading partners: U.S., Caribbean countries, West Germany, Venezuela, Japan.

Geography. Honduras, in the north central part of Central America, has a 400-mile (644-km) Caribbean coastline and a 40-mile (64-km) Pacific frontage. Its neighbors are Guatemala to the west, El Salvador to the south, and Nicaragua to the east. Honduras is slightly larger than Tennessee.

Generally mountainous, the country is marked by fertile plateaus, river valleys, and narrow coastal plains.

Government. Paz Garcia stepped down in favor of the elected President, Roberto Suazo Córdova, who ended a decade of military rule when he took office on Jan. 29, 1982. Despite the return of parliamentary democracy, Honduras faced severe economic problems and tension on the Nicaraguan border, where Nicaragua alleged that soldiers of the former Somoza regime were using Honduran bases to stage raids against their homeland.

History. Columbus discovered Honduras on his last voyage in 1502. Honduras, with four other countries of Central America, declared its independence from Spain in 1821 and was part of a federation of Central American states until 1838. In that year it seceded from the federation and became a completely independent country.

U.S. Marines intervened in 1903 and 1923. In 1931, 1932, and 1937, major revolutions were crushed by force.

In July 1969, El Salvador invaded Honduras after Honduran landowners had deported several thousand Salvadorans. The fighting left 1,000 dead and tens of thousands homeless. By threatening economic sanctions and military intervention, the OAS induced El Salvador to withdraw.

In 1971, Ramon Ernesto Cruz, a lawyer, diplomat, and teacher, became Honduras's first freely elected president since 1949. But strongman Oswaldo López Arellano, citing "chaos and weakness" under the coalition, again seized control (for the third time in two decades). He served until his ouster in 1975.

On Aug. 7, 1978, the military ousted Juan Alberto Melgar Castro as president, naming Gen. Policarpo Paz Garcia as chief of state. This was the second military-originated change of government in three years resulting from charges of corruption.

HUNGARY

Hungarian People's Republic
President: Pál Losonczi (1967)
Premier: Gyorgy Lazar (1975)
Area: 35,919 sq mi. (93,030 sq km)
Population (est. 1982): 10,725,000 (average annual growth rate: 0.0%)
Density per square mile: 298.6
Capital: Budapest
Largest cities (est. 1980): Budapest, 2,100,000; (est. 1978): Miskolc, 210,000; Debrecen, 198,000; Szeged, 177,000; Pécs, 170,000; Györ, 125,000
Monetary unit: Forint
Language: Magyar
Religions: Roman Catholic, 60%; Protestant, atheist
National name: Magyar Népköztársaság
Literacy rate (1981): 97%
Economic summary: Gross national product (1980): $45.0 billion. Average annual growth rate (1970–79): 4.8%. Per capita income (1980): $4,180. Land used for agriculture: 75%; labor force: 20%; principal products: corn, wheat, potatoes, sugar beets, vegetables, wine grapes, fruits. Labor force in industry: 33%; major products: precision and measuring equipment, pharmaceuticals, textiles, transport equipment. Natural resources: some bauxite and brown coal. Exports: machinery and tools, industrial and consumer goods, raw materials. Imports: machinery, raw materials. Major trading partners: U.S.S.R., Warsaw Pact countries.

Geography. This central European country the size of Indiana is bordered by Austria to the west, Czechoslovakia to the north, the U.S.S.R. and Romania to the east, and Yugoslavia to the south.

Most of Hungary is a fertile, rolling plain lying east of the Danube River and drained by the Danube and Tisza rivers. In the extreme northwest is the Little Hungarian Plain. South of that area is Lake Balaton (250 sq mi.; 648 sq km).

Government. Hungary is a People's Republic with legislative power vested in the unicameral National Assembly, whose 352 members are elected directly for four-year terms. The supreme body of state power is the 21-member Presidential Council elected by the National Assembly. The supreme administrative body is the Council of Ministers, headed by the Premier.

The Hungarian Socialist Workers (Communist) Party, led by János Kádár, is the only political party.

History. About 2,000 years ago, Hungary was part of the Roman provinces of Pannonia and Dacia. In A.D. 896 it was invaded by the Magyars, who founded a kingdom. Christianity was accepted during the reign of Stephen I (St. Stephen) (997–1038).

The peak of Hungary's great period of medieval power came during the reign of Louis I the Great (1342–82), whose dominions touched the Baltic, Black, and Mediterranean seas.

War with the Turks broke out in 1389, and for more than 100 years the Turks advanced through the Balkans. When the Turks smashed a Hungarian army in 1526, western and northern Hungary accepted Hapsburg rule to escape Turkish occupation. Transylvania became independent under Hungarian princes. Intermittent war with the Turks was waged until a peace treaty was signed in 1699.

After the suppression of the 1848 revolt against Hapsburg rule, led by Louis Kossuth, the dual monarchy of Austria-Hungary was set up in 1867.

The dual monarchy was defeated with the other Central Powers in World War I. After a short-lived republic in 1918, the chaotic Communist rule of 1919 under Béla Kun ended with the Romanians occupying Budapest on Aug. 4, 1919. When the Romanians left, Adm. Nicholas Horthy entered the capital with a national army. The Treaty of Trianon of June 4, 1920, cost Hungary 68% of its land and 58% of its population. Meanwhile, the National Assembly had restored the legal continuity of the old monarchy; and, on March 1, 1920, Horthy was elected Regent.

Following the German invasion of Russia on June 22, 1941, Hungary joined the attack against the Soviet Union, but the war was not popular and Hungarian troops were almost entirely withdrawn from the eastern front by May 1943. German occupation troops set up a puppet government after Horthy's appeal for an armistice with advancing Soviet troops on Oct. 15, 1944, had resulted in his overthrow. The German regime soon fled the capital, however, and on December 23 a provisional government was formed in Soviet-occupied eastern Hungary. On Jan. 20, 1945, it signed an armistice in Moscow. Early the next year, the National Assembly approved a constitutional law abolishing the thousand-year-old monarchy and establishing a republic.

By the Treaty of Paris (1947), Hungary had to give up all territory it had acquired since 1937 and to pay $300 million reparations to the U.S.S.R., Czechoslovakia, and Yugoslavia. In 1948 the Communist Party, with the support of Soviet troops seized control. Hungary was proclaimed a People's Republic and one-party state in 1949. Industry was nationalized, the land collectivized into state farms, and the opposition terrorized by the secret police.

The terror, modeled after that of the U.S.S.R., reached its height with the trial of Jozsef Cardinal Mindszenty, Roman Catholic primate. He confessed to fantastic charges under duress of drugs or brainwashing and was sentenced to life imprisonment in 1949. Protests were voiced in all parts of the world.

On Oct. 23, 1956, anti-Communist revolution broke out in Budapest. To cope with it, the Communists set up a coalition government and called former Premier Imre Nagy back to head it. But he and most of his ministers were swept by the logic of events into the anti-Communist opposition, and he declared Hungary a neutral power, withdrawing from the Warsaw Treaty and appealing to the United Nations for help.

One of his ministers, János Kádár, established a counter-regime and asked the U.S.S.R. to send in military power. Soviet troops and tanks suppressed the revolution in bloody fighting after 190,000 people had fled the country and Mindszenty, freed from jail, had taken refuge in the U.S. Embassy. By treachery, Nagy and some of his ministers were abducted by the Soviet occupation troops and executed.

Kádár was succeeded as Premier, but not party secretary, by Gyula Kallai in 1965. Continuing his program of national reconciliation, Kádár emptied prisons, reformed the secret police, and eased travel restrictions.

Hungary developed the reputation of being the freest East European state, with Kádár's new motto —"If you're not against us, you're with us"—replacing previous police state suspicions. Significant Western capitalist investment was welcomed and some capitalistic methods embraced.

After 15 years' asylum in the U.S. Embassy, Mindszenty, under an agreement between the Vatican and the Hungarian regime, was allowed to travel into exile to Rome in 1971. In a move applauded by Kádár, Pope Paul VI removed Mindszenty from his honorary post as Primate of Hungary in 1974. The Cardinal died in Vienna in 1975.

Relations with the U.S. improved in 1972 when World War II debt claims between the two nations were settled. On Jan. 6, 1978, the U.S. returned to Hungary, over anti-Communist protests, the 977-year-old crown of St. Stephen, held at Fort Knox since World War II.

ICELAND

Republic of Iceland
President: Vigdis Finnbogadottir (1980)
Prime Minister: Gunnar Thoroddsen (1980)
Area: 39,702 sq mi. (102,828 sq km)
Population (est. 1982): 235,000 (average annual growth rate: 1.0%)
Density per square mile: 5.9[1]
Capital and largest city (est. 1980): Reykjavik, 83,500
Monetary unit: New króna
Language: Icelandic
Religion: Evangelical Lutheran
National name: Lydveldid Island
Literacy rate (1981): 99%
Economic summary: Gross national product (1980): $2.6 billion. Average annual growth rate (1970–79): 2.8%. Per capita income (1980): $11,330. Labor force in agriculture: 9%; fishing and fish processing: 13%; principal agricultural products: livestock, hay, fodder, cheese. Labor force in industry: 29%; major products: processed aluminum, fish. Natural resources: fish, diatomite, hydroelectric and geothermal power. Exports: fish, animal products, aluminum. Imports: petroleum products, machinery and transportation equipment, petroleum, food, textiles. Major trading partners: U.S., U.S.S.R., Western European countries.

1. Including some offshore islands.

Geography. Iceland, a bleak island about the size of Kentucky, lies in the north Atlantic Ocean east of Greenland and just touches the Arctic Circle. It is one of the most volcanic regions in the world.

Small fresh-water lakes are to be found throughout the island, and there are many natural phenomena, including hot springs, geysers, sulfur beds, canyons, waterfalls, and swift rivers. More than 13% of the area is covered by snowfields and glaciers, and most of the people live in the 7% of the island comprising fertile coastlands.

Government. The president is elected for four years by popular vote. Executive power resides in the prime minister and his Cabinet. The Althing (Parliament) is composed of 60 members in two houses. They elect 20 of themselves to constitute the Upper House, the remaining 40 representing the Lower House.

The major political parties are the Independence Party (22 of 60 seats in the Althing), led by Geir Hallgrimsson; Progressive Party (17 seats), led by Steingrimur Hermannsson; People's Alliance (11 seats), led by Svavar Gestsson; Social Democratic Party (10 seats), led by Kjartan Johannsson. Prime Minister Gunnar Thoroddsen of the Independence Party leads a coalition of the Progressives and the People's Alliance supported by a few of his own party.

History. Iceland was first settled shortly before 900, mainly by Norse. A Constitution drawn up about 930 created a form of democracy and provided for an Althing, or General Assembly.

In 1262–64, Iceland came under Norwegian rule and passed to ultimate Danish control through the formation of the Union of Kalmar in 1483. In 1874, Icelanders obtained their own Constitution. In 1918, Denmark recognized Iceland as a separate state with unlimited sovereignty but still nominally under the Danish king.

On June 17, 1944, after a popular referendum, the Althing proclaimed Iceland an independent republic.

The British occupied Iceland in 1940, immediately after the German invasion of Denmark. In 1942, the U.S. took over the burden of protection. Iceland refused to abandon its neutrality in World War II and thus forfeited charter membership in the United Nations, but it cooperated with the Allies throughout the conflict. Iceland joined the North Atlantic Treaty Organization in 1949.

Iceland unilaterally extended its territorial waters from 12 to 50 nautical miles in 1972, precipitating a running dispute with Britain known as the "cod war." Icelandic warships harassed British trawlers, which then received aid from British gunboats; some trawlers were shelled, and Icelandic and British warships collided in 1973. The World Court ruled in 1974 that the 50-mile limit could not be applied unilaterally, but Iceland rejected the ruling.

An agreement calling for registration of all British trawlers fishing within 200 miles of Iceland and a 24-hour time limit on incursions was finally reached in 1976.

INDIA

Republic of India
President: Zail Singh (1982)
Prime Minister: Indira Gandhi (1980)
Area: 1,229,737 sq mi. (3,185,019 sq km)
Population (1982 census): 700,000,000 (average annual growth rate: 2.1%)
Density per square mile: 569.2
Capital (1980 census): New Delhi, 619,417
Largest cities (1980 census): Calcutta, 9,165,650; Greater Bombay, 8,202,759; Delhi, 6,196,414; Madras, 4,276,635; Bangalore, 2,913,537; Ahmedabad, 2,515,195; Kanpur, 1,685,308
Monetary unit: Rupee
Principal languages; Hindi (official), Bengali, Sindhi, Gujarati, Kannarese, Kashmiri, Malayalam, Marathi, Oriya, Punjabi, Tamil, Telugu, Urdu, Kannada, Assamese (all recognized by the Constitution)
Religions: Hindu, 83%; Islam, 11%; Christian, 3%; Sikh, 2%
National name: Bharat
Literacy rate (1971): 29%
Member of Commonwealth of Nations
Economic summary: Gross national product (1980): $159.4 billion. Average annual growth rate (1970–79): 1.6%. Per capita income (1980): $240. Land used for agriculture:

Political Subdivisions of Republic of India

Subdivisions	Area sq mi.	Population 1981 census
STATES		
Andhra Pradesh	106,052	53,403,619
Assam	30,400	19,902,826
Bihar	67,198	69,823,154
Gujarat	72,154	33,960,905
Haryana	16,670	12,850,902
Himachal Pradesh	10,880	4,237,569
Jammu and Kashmir[1]	85,861	5,981,600
Karnataka	74,122	37,043,451
Kerala	15,003	25,403,217
Madhya Pradesh	171,210	52,131,117
Maharashtra	118,530	62,693,898
Manipur	8,628	1,433,691
Meghalaya	8,700	1,327,874
Nagaland	6,236	773,287
Orissa	60,182	26,272,054
Punjab	21,630	16,609,755
Rajasthan	132,151	34,102,912
Sikkim	2,744	315,682
Tamil Nadu	50,132	48,297,456
Tripura	4,022	2,060,189
Uttar Pradesh	113,452	110,858,019
West Bengal	33,928	54,485,560
UNION TERRITORIES		
Andaman and Nicobar Islands	3,215	188,254
Arunachal Pradesh	31,400	628,050
Chandigarh	44	450,061
Dadra and Nagar-Haveli	189	103,677
Delhi	573	6,196,414
Goa, Daman, and Diu	1,619	1,082,117
Lakshadweep	11	40,237
Mizoram	8,100	487,774
Pondicherry	196	604,136

1. Status in dispute with Pakistan.

50%; labor force: 70%; principal products: rice, wheat, oilseeds, cotton, tea. Major industrial products: jute, processed food, steel, machinery, transport machinery, cement. Natural resources: Iron ore, coal, manganese, mica, bauxite, limestone. Exports: engineering goods, textiles and clothing, tea. Imports: machinery and transport equipment, petroleum, edible oils, fertilizers. Major trading partners: U.S., U.K., U.S.S.R., Japan.

Geography. One third the area of the United States, the Republic of India occupies most of the subcontinent of India in south Asia. It borders on China in the northeast. Other neighbors are Pakistan on the west, Nepal and Bhutan on the north, and Burma and Bangladesh on the east.

The country contains a large part of the great Indo-Gangetic plain, which extends from the Bay of Bengal on the east to the Afghan frontier on the Arabian Sea on the west. This plain is the richest and most densely settled part of the subcontinent. Another distinct natural region is the Deccan, a plateau of 2,000 to 3,000 feet (610 to 914 m) in elevation, occupying the southern portion of the subcontinent.

Forming a part of the republic are several groups of islands—the Laccadives (14 islands) in the Arabian Sea and the Andamans (204 islands) and the Nicobars (19 islands) in the Bay of Bengal.

India's three great river systems, all rising in the Himalayas, have extensive deltas. The Ganges flows south and then east for 1,540 miles (2,478 km) across the northern plain to the Bay of Bengal; part of its delta, which begins 220 miles (354 km) from the sea, is within the republic. The Indus, starting in Tibet, flows northwest for several hundred miles in the Kashmir before turning southwest toward the Arabian Sea; it is important for irrigation in Pakistan. The Brahmaputra, also rising in Tibet, flows eastward, first through India and then south into Bangladesh and the Bay of Bengal.

Government. India is a federal republic. It is also a member of the Commonwealth of Nations, a status defined at the 1949 London Conference of Prime Ministers, by which India recognizes the Queen as head of the Commonwealth. Under the Constitution effective Jan. 26, 1950, India has a parliamentary type of government.

The constitutional head of the state is the President, who is elected every five years. He is advised by the Prime Minister and a Cabinet based on a majority of the bicameral Parliament, which consists of a Council of States (Rajya Sabha), representing the constituent units of the republic and a House of the People (Lok Sabha), elected every five years by universal suffrage.

The major political parties are Congress Party I (351 of 542 seats in the Lok Sabha), led by Prime Minister Indira Gandhi; Lok Dal (secular Janata) Party (41 seats), led by former Prime Minister Charan Singh; Congress II (anti-Gandhi) Party (13 seats); Communist (Marxist independent) Party (3[illegible] seats); Communist (pro-Soviet) Party of India (1[illegible] seats).

History. The Aryans, or Hindus, who invaded India between 2400 and 1500 B.C. from the northwest found a land already well civilized. Buddhism was founded in the 6th century B.C. and spread through northern India. The earliest exact date in Indian history is 327 B.C., when Alexander the Great invaded India.

In 1526, Moslem invaders founded the great Mogul empire, centered on Delhi, which lasted, at least in name, until 1857. Akbar the Great (1542–1605) strengthened this empire and became the ruler of a greater portion of India than had ever before acknowledged the suzerainty of one man. The long reign of his great-grandson, Aurangzeb (1658–1707), represents both the culmination of Mogul power and the beginning of its decay.

Vasco da Gama, the Portuguese explorer, visited India first in 1498, and for the next 100 years the Portuguese had a virtual monopoly on trade with the subcontinent. Meanwhile, the English founded the East India Company, which set up its first factory at Surat in 1612 and began expanding its influence, fighting the Indian rulers and the French

Dutch, and Portuguese traders simultaneously.

Bombay, taken from the Portuguese, became the seat of English rule in 1687. The defeat of French and Islamic armies by Lord Clive in the decade ending in 1760 laid the foundation of the British Empire in India. From then until 1858, when the administration of India was formally transferred to the British Crown following the Sepoy Mutiny of native troops in 1857, the East India Company suppressed native uprisings and extended British rule.

After World War I, in which the Indian states sent more than 6 million troops to fight beside the Allies, Indian nationalist unrest rose to new heights under the leadership of a little Hindu lawyer, Mohandas K. Gandhi, called Mahatma Gandhi. His tactics called for nonviolent revolts against British authority. He soon became the leading spirit of the All-India Congress Party, which was the spearhead of revolt. In 1919 the British gave added responsibility to Indian officials, and in 1935 India was given a federal form of government and a measure of self-rule.

In 1942, with the Japanese pressing hard on the eastern borders of India, the British War Cabinet tried and failed to reach a political settlement with nationalist leaders. The Congress Party took the position that the British must quit India. In 1942, fearing mass civil disobedience, the government of India carried out widespread arrests of Congress leaders, including Gandhi.

Gandhi was released in 1944 and negotiations for a settlement were resumed. Finally, in February 1947, the Labor government announced its determination to transfer power to "responsible Indian hands" by June 1948 even if a Constitution had not been worked out.

Lord Mountbatten as Viceroy, by June 1947, achieved agreement on the partitioning of India along religious lines (a plan previously opposed by the predominant Hindus and by Britain) and on the splitting of the provinces of Bengal and the Punjab, which the Moslems had claimed.

The Indian Independence Act, passed quickly by the British Parliament, received royal assent on July 18, 1947, and on August 15 the Indian Empire passed into history.

Jawaharlal Nehru, leader of the Congress Party, was made Prime Minister. Before an exchange of populations could be arranged, bloody riots occurred among the communal groups, and armed conflict broke out over rival claims to the princely state of Jammu and Kashmir. Peace was restored only with the greatest difficulty. In 1949 a Constitution, along the lines of the U.S. Constitution, was approved making India a sovereign republic. Under a federal structure the states were organized on linguistic lines.

The dominance of the Congress Party contributed to stability. In 1956 the republic absorbed the former French settlements. Five years later, it forcibly annexed the Portuguese enclaves of Goa, Damao, and Diu.

Communist China provoked a border dispute in 1957 that proceeded by local skirmishes until Oct. 20, 1962, when the Chinese mounted a massive offensive against Ladakh in the Kashmir and against the North East Frontier Agency. After gaining much territory claimed by India, the Chinese announced a cease-fire on Nov. 20, 1962.

Nehru died in 1964. His successor, Lal Bahadur Shastri, died on Jan. 10, 1966, a few hours after having concluded talks with President Ayub Khan of Pakistan. Nehru's daughter, Indira Gandhi, became Prime Minister, and she continued his policy of nonalignment.

In 1971 the Pakistani Army moved in to quash the independence movement in East Pakistan that was supported by clandestine aid from India, and some 10 million Bengali refugees poured across the border into India, creating social, economic, and health problems. In August, India signed a friendship treaty with the U.S.S.R. and quantities of Soviet arms began to enter India. After numerous border incidents, India invaded East Pakistan and in two weeks forced the surrender of the Pakistani army and took 93,000 prisoners. East Pakistan was established as an independent state and renamed Bangladesh.

India moved further toward the U.S.S.R. in 1973 with a 15-year economic, technological, and trade cooperation agreement.

India startled the world in 1974 by exploding an atomic device made of plutonium it had surreptitiously removed from a peaceful reactor given by Canada.

In the summer of 1975, the world's largest democracy veered suddenly toward authoritarianism when a judge in Allahabad, Mrs. Gandhi's home constituency, found her landslide victory in the 1971 elections invalid because civil servants had illegally aided her campaign. Amid demands for her resignation, Mrs. Gandhi decreed a state of emergency on June 26 and ordered mass arrests of her critics, including all opposition party leaders except the Communists.

Legislation extending the emergency indefinitely passed Parliament July 23. Opposition members walked out after the vote. Unhampered Congress Party majorities successively enacted: a bill forbidding courts to invalidate the government's emergency decrees; a constitutional amendment retroactively barring lawsuits challenging the elections of high government officers, including the Prime Minister, and a bill retroactively wiping out Mrs. Gandhi's conviction in the 1971 election case.

In 1976, India and Pakistan formally renewed diplomatic relations.

Despite strong opposition to her repressive measures and particularly the resentment against compulsory birth control programs, Mrs. Gandhi in 1977 announced parliamentary elections for March. At the same time, she freed most political prisoners, including her former Deputy Prime Minister, Morarji R. Desai, and L. K. Advani, a right-wing Hindu nationalist.

The landslide victory of Desai and his allies unseated Mrs. Gandhi and also defeated a bid for office by her son, Sanjay, himself a focus of much criticism as the recipient of official favors. Taking office, the 81-year-old Desai promised to "drive fear from the society" and restore morality to government.

In state elections in April, Desai's Janata Party toppled the Congress Party in eight of 10 states where the Congress Party had held power, as in the national government, since independence.

In July, Neelam Sanjiva Reddy was elected President, replacing Fakhruddin Ali Ahmed, who died February 11.

Desai moved away from Mrs. Gandhi's pro-Soviet policy, receiving a visit from President Carter Jan. 1–3, 1978, and himself visiting Carter in June. A dispute over the supply of enriched uranium to India, in which the U.S. Nuclear Regulatory Agency sought greater safeguards over its use, was resolved by Carter in India's favor in the hope that India would eventually sign the Non-Proliferation Treaty. Desai's success abroad was not matched at home, however, as economic problems and party squabbles lowered enthusiasm for the new regime.

One of the unifying factors of the Janata Party was the threat of a comeback attempt by former Prime Minister Gandhi, who regrouped a faction of the Congress Party under her leadership. Her announcement in May 1979 that she would not run for a seat in Parliament released the Janata Party's shaky bonds. The party had already been split over the inclusion of a right-wing Hindu element. Deputy Prime Minister Charan Singh's formation of a new "secular" Janata Party brought down the Desai government in mid-July and he became Prime Minister. However, he resigned the next month, but agreed to stay on and head a caretaker government.

Mrs. Gandhi staged a spectacular comeback in elections in January 1980. She followed her triumph with victories in eight of nine state legislative elections. Returned to power, Mrs. Gandhi showed a less hostile attitude toward the United States, condemning the Soviet invasion of Afghanistan and obtaining from the Carter administration approval for continued uranium shipments for India's nuclear program. She suffered a personal blow in the death of her son, Sanjay, a close personal aide, in a plane crash on June 23.

The visit of Soviet President Leonid I. Brezhnev to India in December 1980 altered Mrs. Gandhi's stand on Afghanistan to an acceptance of the Soviet assertion that its troops were there only because of U.S. and Soviet "interference" in that country. A joint statement called for dismantling all foreign bases in the Indian Ocean but named only one, the U.S. naval base on Diego Garcia Island.

A dispute with Washington over nuclear fuel supplies for a U.S. reactor at Tarapur was resolved in July 1982 when Mrs. Gandhi visited President Reagan. The U.S. Senate had previously barred aid to India and Pakistan if they exploded a nuclear device, and India had balked at inspection of Tarapur. To circumvent the problem, Reagan approved the sale of fuel by France, which would insure international inspection of the reactor, but not of a reprocessing plant, which would have been covered if the fuel were supplied by the United States.

Despite a widening trade deficit and a 1980–81 economic growth rate slowed to 4.5% from the 7.5% achieved the year before, the government raised defense spending by $1 billion from a previous $4.5 billion. In April, the purchase of 40 Mirage 2000 fighters from France was announced, at a cost of $800 million.

Native States. Most of the 560-odd native states and subdivisions of pre-1947 India acceded to the new nation, and the central government pursued a vigorous policy of integration. This took three forms: merger into adjacent provinces, conversion into centrally administered areas, and grouping into unions of states. Finally, under a controversial reorganization plan effective Nov. 1, 1956, the unions of states were abolished and merged into adjacent states, and India became a union of 15 states and 8 centrally administered areas. A 16th state was added in 1962, and in 1966, the Punjab was partitioned into two states.

The status of the large princely state of Jammu and Kashmir on the northwest frontier is in dispute with Pakistan. It is 85% Islamic, but its Hindu ruling prince acceded to India, which took over administration following invasion by Moslem troops in late 1947. The part occupied by India was incorporated into India in 1957.

The controversy over Jammu and Kashmir was waged in the halls of the U.N. until 1965, when India announced that its civil servants would assume administration of the state. Pakistan sent guerrillas into the territory, and India, in response, invaded in August 1965. In September the U.N. sponsored a cease-fire and stationed observers to make sure it was honored, but there were violations.

The U.S.S.R. intervened and arranged a meeting in Tashkent between Prime Minister Shastri of India and President Ayub Khan of Pakistan. With the U.S.S.R. as mediator, they reached an interim settlement, the Declaration of Tashkent, in January 1966. It provided for the withdrawal of troops, observance of the U.N. cease-fire, and continued attempts to resolve their disputes by diplomatic means.

Resolution of the territorial dispute over Kashmir grew out of peace negotiations following the two-week India-Pakistan war of 1971. After sporadic skirmishing, an accord reached July 3, 1972, committed both powers to withdraw troops from a temporary cease-fire line after the border was fixed. Agreement on the border was reached Dec. 7, 1972.

In April 1975, the Indian Parliament voted to make the 300-year-old kingdom of Sikkim a full-fledged Indian state, and the annexation took effect May 16.

Situated in the Himalayas, Sikkim was a virtual dependency of Tibet until the early 19th century. Under an 1890 treaty between China and Great Britain, it became a British protectorate, and was made an Indian protectorate after Britain quit the subcontinent.

INDONESIA

Republic of Indonesia

President and Prime Minister: General Suharto (1969)[1]

Area: 735,268 sq mi. (1,904,344 sq km)[2]

Population (est. 1982): 153,000,000 (average annual growth rate: 2.1%)

Density per square mile: 208.1

Capital: Jakarta

Largest cities (est. 1981): Jakarta, 6,500,000; **(1971 census):** Surabaja, 1,556,255; Bandung, 1,201,730; Semarang, 646,590; Medan, 635,562; Palembang, 582,961

Monetary unit: Rupiah

Languages: Bahasa Indonesia (official), Dutch, and more than 60 regional languages

Religions: Islam, 89%; Christian, 7%; Hindu, Buddhist

National name: Republik Indonesia

Literacy rate (1981): 60% (est.)

Economic summary: Gross national product (1980): $61.8 billion. Average annual growth rate (1970–79): 4.6%. Per capita income (1980): $420. Land used for agriculture: 11%; labor force: 64%; principal products: rice, cassava, soybeans, copra, rubber, coffee, palm oil, tea. Labor force in industry: 7%; major products: textiles, food and beverages, light manufactures, cement, fertilizer. Natural resources: oil, timber, nickel, natural gas, tin, bauxite, copper. Exports: petroleum and liquid natural gas, timber, rubber, coffee, tin. Imports: rice, wheat, textiles, chemicals, iron and steel. Major trading partners: Japan, U.S., Saudi Arabia, West Germany.

1. General Suharto served as Acting President of Indonesia from 1967 to 1969. 2. Includes West Irian (former Netherlands New Guinea), renamed Irian Jaya in March 1973

(159,355 sq mi.; 412,731 sq km), and former Portuguese Timor (5,763 sq mi.; 14,925 sq km), annexed in 1976.

Geography. Indonesia is part of the Malay archipelago in Southeast Asia with an area nearly three times that of Texas. It consists of the islands of Sumatra, Java, Madura, Borneo (except Sarawak in the north), the Celebes, the Moluccas, and about 30 smaller archipelagos, totaling 13,677 islands, of which about 6,000 are inhabited. Its neighbor to the north is Malaysia and to the east Papua New Guinea.

A backbone of mountain ranges extends throughout the main islands of the archipelago. Earthquakes are frequent, and there are many active volcanoes.

Government. The President is elected by the People's Consultative Assembly, whose 920 members include the functioning legislative arm, the 464-member House of Representatives. Meeting at least once every five years, the Assembly has broad policy functions. The House, 100 of whose members are appointed by the President, meets at least once annually. General Suharto was elected unopposed to a third five-year term in 1978.

The major political parties are Sekber Golkar, 246 of 464 contested seats in the House; Islamic United Development Party, 94 seats; Democratic Party, 24 seats.

History. Indonesia is inhabited by Malayan and Papuan peoples ranging from the more advanced Javanese and Balinese to the more primitive Dyaks of Borneo. Invasions from China and India contributed Chinese and Indian admixtures.

During the first few centuries of the Christian era, most of the islands came under the influence of Hindu priests and traders, who spread their culture and religion. Moslem invasions began in the 13th century, and most of the area was Moslem by the 15th. Portuguese traders arrived early in the 16th century but were ousted by the Dutch about 1595. After Napoleon subjugated the Netherlands homeland in 1811, the British seized the islands but returned them to the Dutch in 1816. In 1922 the islands were made an integral part of the Netherlands kingdom.

In World War II, the Japanese military occupation with nominal native self-government continued until August 1945. About the time of the Japanese surrender, a self-styled Indonesian Republic headed by Achmed Sukarno took over effective control of parts of Sumatra and Java. Allied forces, mostly British Indian troops, moved in, and fought the nationalists until November 1946, when Dutch-Indonesian parleys resulted in a draft agreement that contemplated the formation by Jan. 1, 1949, of a Netherlands-Indonesian Union. This would consist on the one hand of the Netherlands, the Netherlands Antilles, and Surinam and on the other of the United States of Indonesia, which was to be a sovereign nation composed of three equal states—the Republic of Indonesia, East Indonesia, and Borneo. Differences of interpretation ensued, and the Dutch resorted to force in July 1947. Both sides issued cease-fire orders the next month in response to a call from the U.N. Security Council.

On Nov. 2, 1949, Dutch and Indonesian leaders agreed upon the terms of union. Sukarno was elected president of the federation and the first all-Indonesian Cabinet was formed with Mohammed Hatta as premier. The transfer of sovereignty took place at Amsterdam on December 27, 1949.

In 1963, Netherlands New Guinea was transferred to Indonesia, and renamed West Irian. In 1973 it became Irian Jaya.

Sukarno, who had himself declared "President for Life," launched a series of guerrilla raids in 1963 to scuttle formation of the new Federation of Malaysia. A treaty between Indonesia and Malaysia in 1966 ended the open conflict.

Early in 1966, Moslem students led an anti-Communist campaign that is believed to have assassinated more than 300,000 Indonesians suspected of Communist ties. Sukarno was forced in March 1966 to yield power to General Suharto, army Chief of Staff. He began a series of trials of Sukarno's associates. The Communist Party was outlawed. Sukarno was forced to give up all power on Feb. 22, 1967, and Suharto became acting President the next month.

He ended hostilities with Malaysia and established close ties with the West. Suharto introduced a "New Order" emphasizing austerity and fiscal responsibility and with Western aid of $200 million —one third provided by the U.S.—began rebuilding the country. In 1968, the Consultative Assembly elected Suharto president for a five-year term.

Suharto also permitted national elections, which moved the nation back toward representative government. The Consultative Assembly elected him unanimously for a second five-year term in 1973.

The economic and political stability achieved by the Suharto regime was tested by external events in 1975. Tightening of world money markets put serious pressures on ambitious industrial development plans underwritten by Pertamina, the state-owned oil company. Communist triumphs in Vietnam and Cambodia encouraged Jakarta toward a policy of non-alignment with any great power and toward closer relationships with other members of the Association of Southeast Asian Nations, a regional grouping of five non-Communist states.

Indonesia annexed the former Portuguese half of the island of Timor in 1976 after the provisional government of the area requested annexation.

Despite a heavy debt burden, Indonesia registered a $2.7-billion surplus in its balance of payments for 1980–81.

IRAN

Islamic Republic of Iran
President: Hojatolislam Mohammed Ali Khamenei (1981)
Prime Minister: Mir Hussein Moussavi Khamenei (1981)
Area: 636,363 sq mi. (1,648,180 sq km)
Population (est. 1982): 41,000,000 (average annual growth rate: 3.1%) (Iranian, Kurdish, Azerbaijani)
Density per square mile: 64.4
Capital: Teheran
Largest cities (est. 1980) (1976 census): Teheran, 6,000,000; Isfahan, 671,825; Mashed, 670,180; Tabriz, 598,576
Monetary unit: Rial
Languages: Farsi (Persian), Kurdish, Azerbaijani
Religions: Shi'ite Moslem, 93%; Sunni Moslem, 5%
Literacy rate (1976): 37% (est.)
Economic summary: Gross national product (1979): $81.7 billion. Per capita income (1980): n.a. Land used for agriculture: 14%; labor force: 33%; principal products: wheat, barley, rice, sugar beets, cotton, dates, raisins, sheep, goats. Labor force in industry: 21%; major products: crude and refined oil, textiles, cement, processed foods, steel and copper fabrication. Natural resources: oil, gas, iron, copper. Exports: petroleum,

carpets, fruits and nuts. Imports: machinery, military supplies, foodstuffs, pharmaceuticals. Major trading partners: Japan, West Germany, U.K., Italy, Netherlands, Spain, France.

Geography. Iran, a Middle Eastern country south of the Caspian Sea and north of the Persian Gulf, is three times the size of Arizona. It shares borders with Iraq, Turkey, the U.S.S.R., Afghanistan, and Pakistan.

In general, the country is a plateau averaging 4,000 feet (1,219 m) in elevation. There are also maritime lowlands along the Persian Gulf and the Caspian Sea. The Elburz Mountains in the north rise to 18,603 feet (5,670 m) at Mt. Damavend. From northwest to southeast, the country is crossed by a desert 800 miles (1,287 km) long.

Government. The Pahlavi dynasty was overthrown on Feb. 11, 1979, by followers of the Ayatollah Ruhollah Khomeini. After a referendum endorsed the establishment of a republic, Khomeini drafted a Constitution calling for a President to be popularly elected every four years, an appointed Prime Minister, and a unicameral National Consultative Assembly, popularly elected every four years.

Khomeini also instituted a Revolutionary Council to insure the adherence to Islamic principles in all phases of Iranian life. The Council formally handed over its powers to the Assembly after the organization of the legislature in July 1980, but continued to exercise power as a sort of shadow government.

History. Oil-rich Iran was called Persia before 1935. Its key location blocks the lower land gate to Asia and also stands in the way of traditional Russian ambitions for access to the Indian Ocean. After periods of Assyrian, Median, and Achaemenidian rule, Persia became a powerful empire under Cyrus the Great, reaching from the Indus to the Nile at its zenith in 525 B.C. It fell to Alexander in 331–30 B.C. and to the Seleucids in 312–02 B.C., and a native Persian regime arose about 130 B.C. Another Persian regime arose about A.D. 224, but it fell to the Arabs in 637. In the 12th century, the Mongols took their turn ruling Persia, and in the early part of the 18th century, the Turks occupied the country.

An Anglo-Russian convention of 1907 divided Persia into two spheres of influence. British attempts to impose a protectorate over the entire country were defeated in 1919. Two years later, Gen. Reza Pahlavi seized the government and was elected hereditary Shah in 1925. Subsequently he did much to modernize the country and abolished all foreign extraterritorial rights.

Increased pro-Axis activity led to Anglo-Russian occupation of Iran in 1941 and deposition of the Shah in favor of his son, Mohammed Reza Pahlavi.

Ali Razmara became premier in 1950 and pledged to restore efficient and honest government, but he was assassinated after less than nine months in office and Mohammed Mossadegh took over. Mossadegh was ousted in August 1953, by Fazollah Zahedi, whom the Shah had named premier.

Iran established closer relations with the U.S. and the West, and the U.S. began a vast program of economic and military aid. In 1955 the country joined the Central Treaty Organization. The government undertook a broad program of reform, especially agrarian land reform, distributing crown lands and estates to the landless peasants.

Iran's oil profits financed an extraordinary modernization program of education, industrialization, and construction.

Iran led nine other members of OPEC in raising oil prices at the end of 1976, and the refusal of Saudi Arabia and the United Arab Emirates to go along resulted in a 38% drop in Iranian oil exports. The loss of revenues forced the government to curtail its aid program.

Opposition to the Shah spread, despite the imposition of martial law in September 1978, and massive demonstrations demanded the return of the exiled Ayatollah Ruhollah Khomeini. Riots and strikes continued despite the appointment of an opposition leader, Shahpur Bakhtiar, as premier on Dec. 29. The Shah and his family left Iran on Jan. 16, 1979, for a "vacation," leaving power in the hands of a regency council.

Khomeini returned on Feb. 1 to a nation in turmoil as military units loyal to the Shah continued to support Bakhtiar and clashed with revolutionaries. Khomeini appointed Mehdi Bazargan as premier of a provisional government and in two days of fighting, revolutionaries forced the military to capitulate on Feb. 11.

The new government began a program of nationalization of insurance companies, banks, and industries both locally and foreign-owned. Oil production fell amid the political confusion.

Khomeini, ignoring opposition, proceeded with his plans for revitalizing Islamic traditions. He urged women to return to the veil, or chador; banned alcohol and mixed bathing, and prohibited music from radio and television broadcasting, declaring it to be "no different from opium."

Revolutionary militants invaded the U.S. Embassy in Teheran on Nov. 4, 1979, seized staff members as hostages, and precipitated an international crisis.

Khomeini refused all appeals, even a unanimous vote by the U.N. Security Council demanding immediate release of the hostages. On a New Year's trip to Teheran, U.N. Secretary-General Kurt Waldheim never saw Khomeini, and a subsequent U.N. commission of inquiry met a similar rebuff.

Election of Abolhassan Bani-Sadr as President on Jan. 25, 1980, raised hopes that his moderate stance might bring a change.

Iranian hostility toward Washington was reinforced by the Carter administration's ineffective economic boycott and deportation order against Iranian students in the U.S., the break in diplomatic relations and ultimately an aborted U.S. raid in April aimed at rescuing the hostages.

Even the death of the deposed Shah Mohammed Reza Pahlavi on July 17 had no effect. As the first anniversary of the embassy seizure neared, Khomeini and his followers insisted on their original conditions: guarantee by the U.S. not to interfere in Iran's affairs, cancellation of U.S. damage claims against Iran, release of $8 billion in frozen Iranian assets, an apology, and the return of the assets held by the former imperial family.

These conditions were largely met in an agreement signed by Deputy Secretary of State Warren Christopher in Teheran on Jan. 19 and the 52 American hostages were released the following day, ending 444 days in captivity. The $8 billion was subject to claims of U.S. creditors, however, and the delivery of the late Shah's assets under U.S. control was made subject to court decisions.

From the release of the hostages onward, Bani-Sadr and the conservative clerics of the dominant Islamic Republican Party clashed with growing frequency. He was stripped of his command of the armed forces by Khomeini on June 6 and ousted as President on June 22. Bani-Sadr went into hiding and emerged in Paris, vowing to fight Khomeini. On June 28, four Cabinet members and 68 other prominent Khomeini backers were killed by a bomb planted in the Islamic Republican Party headquarters. On July 24, Prime Minister Mohammed Ali Rajai was elected overwhelmingly to the Presidency.

Rajai and Prime Minister Mohammed Javad Bahonar were killed on Aug. 30 by a bomb in Bahonar's office.

Hojatolislam Mohammed Ali Khamenei, a clergyman, leader of the Islamic Republican Party and spokesman for Khomeini, was elected President on Oct. 2, 1981. The insurgent Mujahedeen-i-Khalq, accused by the government of killing 300 officials in pre-election violence, announced a government in exile, headquartered in Paris with Bani-Sadr as provisional president.

The sporadic war with Iraq regained momentum in 1982, as Iran launched an offensive in March and regained much of the border area occupied by Iraq in late 1980. On May 24, Iran claimed the recapture of Khurramshahr, the last sizable Iranian town in Iraqi hands, and in July Iranian troops were moving into Iraqi territory. Khomeini rejected Iraqi bids for a truce, insisting that Iraq's President Saddam Hussein must leave office first. The Iranian resurgence was credited in part to Soviet and Syrian arms and, surprisingly, to $27-million worth of arms bought from Israel and acknowledged publicly by Israeli authorities.

War costs weighed heavily on Iran's economy, causing under-the-counter sale of Iranian oil at prices well below OPEC minimums. Oil exports, which had fallen in the wake of the revolution and were reported at only 500,000 barrels a day at the beginning of 1982, were estimated at above 1 million by April, when the United States resumed buying for the first time since 1979.

IRAQ

Republic of Iraq
President: Saddam Hussein (1979)
Area: 172,000 sq mi. (445,480 sq km)
Population (est. 1982): 14,000,000 (average annual growth rate: 3.3%) (Arab, 75%; Kurdish, 15%; Iranian, 3.8%)
Density per square mile: 81.4
Capital: Baghdad
Largest cities (est. 1977): Baghdad, 3,205,600; (1965 census): Basra, 310,950, Mosul, 264,146; Kirkuk, 175,303; An Najaf, 134,027
Monetary unit: Iraqi dinar
Languages: Arabic and Kurdish
Religions: Islam, 96%; Christian, 3%
National name: Al Jumhouriya Al Iraqia
Literacy rate (1981): 30%
Economic summary: Gross national product (1980): $39.5 billion. Average annual growth rate (1970–79): 9.3%. Per capita income (1980): $3,020. Average rate of inflation (1976–78): 10%. Land used for agriculture, 18%; labor force, 30%; principal products: livestock, wheat, barley, cotton, fruits, vegetables. Labor force in industry: 27%; major products: petroleum, cement, textiles. Natural resources: oil, natural gas, phosphates, sulfur. Exports: petroleum, dates. Imports: manufactured goods, food grains, machinery, construction materials, livestock. Major trading partners: France, Italy, U.S.S.R., Japan, West Germany, Turkey, Brazil, U.K.

Geography. Iraq, a triangle of mountains, desert, and fertile river valley, is bounded on the east by Iran, on the north by Turkey, the west by Syria and Jordan, and the south by Saudi Arabia and Kuwait. It is twice the size of Idaho.

The country has arid desertland west of the Euphrates, a broad central valley between the Euphrates and Tigris, and mountains in the northeast. The fertile lower valley is formed by the delta of the two rivers, which join about 120 miles (193 km) from the head of the Persian Gulf. The gulf coastline is 26 miles (42 km) long. The only port for seagoing vessels is Basra, which is on the Shatt-al-Arab River near the head of the Persian Gulf.

Government. Since the coup d'etat of July 1968, Iraq has been governed by the Arab Ba'ath Socialist Party through a Council of Command of the Revolution headed by the President. There is also a Council of Ministers headed by the President.

History. From earliest times Iraq was known as Mesopotamia—the land between the rivers—for it embraces a large part of the alluvial plains of the Tigris and Euphrates.

An advanced civilization existed by 4000 B.C. Sometime after 2000 B.C. the land became the center of the ancient Babylonian and Assyrian empires. It was conquered by Cyrus the Great of Persia in 538 B.C., and by Alexander in 331 B.C. After an Arab conquest in A.D. 637–40, Baghdad became capital of the ruling caliphate. The country was cruelly pillaged by the Mongols in 1258, and during the 16th, 17th, and 18th centuries was the object of repeated Turkish-Persian competition.

Nominal Turkish suzerainty imposed in 1638 was replaced by direct Turkish rule in 1831. In World War I, an Anglo-Indian force occupied most of the country, and Britain was given a mandate over the area in 1920. The British recognized Iraq as a kingdom in 1922 and terminated the mandate in 1932 when Iraq was admitted to the League of Nations. In World War II, Iraq generally adhered to its 1930 treaty of alliance with Britain, but in 1941, British troops were compelled to put down a pro-Axis revolt led by Premier Rashid Ali.

Iraq became a charter member of the Arab League in 1945, and Iraqi troops took part in the Arab invasion of Palestine in 1948. The 1930 treaty of alliance with Britain was terminated in 1955, and replaced by a defense cooperation agreement.

Faisal II, born on May 2, 1935, succeeded his father, Ghazi I, who was killed in an automobile accident on April 4, 1939. Faisal and his uncle, Crown Prince Abdul-Ilah, were assassinated in August 1958 in a swift revolutionary coup that brought to power a military junta headed by Abdul Karem Kassim. The short-lived "Arab Union," formed by the federation of Iraq and Jordan in February 1958, came abruptly to an end with recognition by the United Arab Republic (Egypt) of the rebel government of Iraq. Kassim, in turn, was overthrown and killed in a coup staged March 8, 1963, by the Ba'ath Socialist Party.

President Abdel Salam Arif, a leader in the March coup, staged another coup in November, driving the Ba'ath members of the revolutionary council from power. He adopted a new constitution in 1964. In 1966, he, two Cabinet members, and other supporters died in a helicopter crash. His brother, Gen. Abdel Rahman Arif, assumed the presidency, crushed the opposition, and won an indefinite extension of his term in 1967. His regime was ousted in July 1968 by a junta led by Maj. Gen. Ahmed Hassan al-Bakr.

In 1970, the Baghdad government announced a settlement of the 8½-year sporadic war with the Kurds of northeastern Iraq (who spread over the border into Turkey and Iran). The Kurdish rebellion flared anew in 1974, following collapse of an Iraqi plan for Kurdish self-rule. The rebels, armed and reinforced from Iran, withstood Soviet-supplied Iraqi forces for 11 months until Iran ended its aid under an agreement with Iraq and 200,000 Kurds fled to Iran.

A long-standing dispute over control of the Shatt al-Arab waterway between Iraq and Iran broke into full-scale war on Sept. 20, 1980. Iraqi planes attacked Iranian airfields and the Abadan refinery, and Iraqi ground forces moved into Iranian territory. Within a week, the waterway was blocked and Iraqi bombing of Kharg Island in the Persian Gulf halted Iranian oil exports.

Jordan offered the port of Aqaba and overland transport to enable Iraq to obtain supplies, but Iran, already suffering from trade embargos resulting from its holding U.S. diplomats as hostages, was hit harder. Despite the smaller size of its armed forces, Iraq took and held the initiative by seizing Abadan and Khurramshahr together with substantial Iranian territory by December and beating back Iranian counterattacks in January. Peace efforts by the Islamic nations, the nonaligned, and the United Nations failed as 1981 wore on and the war stagnated.

The Israeli surprise bombing attack on Iraq's Oshirak nuclear reactor outside Baghdad on July 7 rallied the Arab world almost unanimously behind Iraq and the U.N. Security Council's condemnation of the raid on June 19 won a unanimous vote.

Despite equally strong Arab support in the war against Iran—financial contributions from Saudi Arabia and other oil producers were estimated in 1982 to have reached $22 billion—the balance of the war appeared to be tipping against the smaller Iraqi army in midyear. Syria, which had openly sided with Iran in the war, closed its border in April and shut down the pipeline carrying Iraqi oil to the Mediterranean.

IRELAND

President: Patrick J. Hillery (1976)
Taoiseach (Prime Minister): Charles J. Haughey (1982)
Area: 26,600 sq mi. (68,894 sq km)
Population (est. 1982): 3,480,000 (average annual growth rate, 1.5%)
Density per square mile: 130.8
Capital: Dublin
Largest cities (est. 1980): Dublin, 550,000; **(1971 census):** Cork, 128,235
Monetary unit: Irish pound (punt)
Languages: Irish, English
Religions: Roman Catholic, 95%; Protestant, 5%
National name: Eire
Literacy rate (1981): 99%
Economic summary: Gross national product (1980): $16.1 billion. Average annual growth rate (1970–79): 2.3%. Per capita income (1980): $4,880. Land used for agriculture, 67%; labor force in agriculture and fishing: 26%; principal products: cattle and dairy products, potatoes, barley, sugar beets, hay, silage, wheat. Labor force in industry: 26%; major products: processed foods, beverages, textiles, chemicals and pharmaceuticals, machinery and construction equipment. Natural resources: zinc, lead, natural gas, barite, copper, gypsum, limestone, dolomite, peat, silver. Exports: livestock, meat, dairy products, machinery, chemicals, textiles, and clothing. Imports: grains, petroleum products, machinery, chemicals, textile yarn, cereals. Major trading partners: U.K., Western European countries, U.S., Canada.

Geography. Ireland is situated in the Atlantic Ocean and separated from Britain by the Irish Sea. Half the size of Arkansas, it occupies the entire island except for the six northern counties of Ulster.

Ireland resembles a basin—a central plain rimmed with mountains, except in the Dublin region. The mountains are low, with the highest peak, Carrantuohill in County Kerry, rising to 3,415 feet (1,041 m).

The principal river is the Shannon, which begins in the north central area, flows south and southwest for about 240 miles (386 km), and empties into the Atlantic.

Government. Ireland is a parliamentary democracy. The National Parliament (Oireachtas) consists of the president and two Houses, the House of Representatives (Dáil Éireann) and the Senate (Seanad Éireann), whose members serve for a maximum term of five years. The House of Representatives has 166 members elected by proportional representation; the Senate has 60 members of whom 11 are nominated by the prime minister, 6 by the universities and the remaining 43 from five vocational panels. The prime minister (Taoiseach), who is the head of government, is appointed by the president on the nomination of the House of Representatives, to which he is responsible.

The major political parties are Fianna Fáil (81 of 166 seats in the Dáil), led by Prime Minister Charles J. Haughey; Fianna Gael (63 seats), led by former Prime Minister Garret FitzGerald; Labor Party (15 seats), led by Michael O'Leary; Independents (7 seats).

History. In the Stone and Bronze Ages, Ireland was inhabited by Picts in the north and a people called the Erainn in the south, the same stock, apparently, as in all the isles before the Anglo-Saxon invasion of Britain. About the fourth century B.C., tall, red-haired Celts arrived from Gaul or Galicia. They subdued and assimilated the inhabitants and established a Gaelic civilization.

By the beginning of the Christian Era, Ireland was divided into five kingdoms—Ulster, Connacht, Leinster, Meath, and Munster. St. Patrick introduced Christianity in 432 and the country developed into a center of Gaelic and Latin learning. Irish monasteries, the equivalent of universities, attracted intellectuals as well as the pious and sent out missionaries to many parts of Europe and, some believe, to North America.

Norse depredations along the coasts, starting in 795, ended in 1014 with Norse defeat at the Battle of Clontarf by forces under Brian Borv. In the the 12th century, the Pope gave all Ireland to the English Crown as a papal fief. In 1171, Henry II of England was acknowledged "Lord of Ireland," but local sectional rule continued for centuries, and English control over the whole island was not reasonably absolute until the 17th century. By the Act of Union (1800), England and Ireland became the "United Kingdom of Great Britain and Ireland."

A steady decline in the Irish economy followed

in the next decades. The population had reached 8.25 million when the great potato famine of 1846–48 took many lives and drove millions to emigrate to America. By 1921 it was down to 4.3 million.

In the meantime, anti-British agitation continued along with demands for Irish home rule. The advent of World War I delayed the institution of home rule and resulted in the Easter Rebellion in Dublin (April 24–29, 1916), in which Irish nationalists unsuccessfully attempted to throw off British rule. Guerrilla warfare against British forces followed proclamation of a republic by the rebels in 1919.

The Irish Free State was established as a dominion on Dec. 6, 1921, with the six northern counties as part of the United Kingdom. Ireland was neutral in World War II.

In 1948, Éamon de Valera, American-born leader of the Sinn Fein, who had won establishment of the Free State in 1921 in negotiations with Britain's David Lloyd George, was defeated by John A. Costello, who demanded final independence from Britain. The Republic of Ireland was proclaimed on April 18, 1949. It withdrew from the Commonwealth but in 1955 entered the United Nations. Since 1949 the prime concern of successive governments has been economic development.

De Valera, who retired in 1973 after two terms in the largely ceremonial presidency, died Aug. 29, 1975, at the age of 92.

Through the 1960s, two antagonistic currents dominated Irish politics. One sought to bind the wounds of the rebellion and civil war. The other was the effort of the outlawed extremist Irish Republican Army to bring Northern Ireland into the republic. Despite public sympathy for unification of Ireland, the Dublin government dealt rigorously with IRA guerrillas caught inside the republic's borders.

The 1973 election brought to power Liam Cosgrave, at the head of a coalition of the Fine Gael and the Labor Party, unseating the Fianna Fáil, which had governed for 35 of 41 years of the republic. Cosgrave cooperated with the British government in attempts to control IRA terrorism and, after the assassination of the British Ambassador to Ireland in 1976, pushed through an Emergency Powers Act to strengthen police and court powers in combating terrorists.

The 1977 election gave the Fianna Fáil a record 84 seats in the Dáil and put John Lynch into the prime minister's post.

Although Lynch drew protests from Britain and Ulster for publicly advocating unification in 1978, he resigned on Dec. 5, 1979, amid intra-party complaints that he was too conciliatory on the issue. Health Minister Charles J. Haughey, the party's choice to suceed Lynch, was under no such handicap. An ardent nationalist, he had been forced to resign as Finance Minister in 1970 because he was accused of smuggling weapons to IRA rebels in the North.

Elections on June 11, 1981, failed to provide Haughey with a majority and Garret M. D. FitzGerald, leader of the Fine Gael, was elected Prime Minister by 81 to 78 with the support of 15 Labor Party members and one independent Socialist added to his own party's 65 members. Other independents abstained, among them Kieran Doherty, a prisoner in Northern Ireland's Maze Prison, who with another prisoner had won election to the Southern Parliament (the Republic's Constitution extends citizenship to anyone born in Northern Ireland). Doherty died after a hunger strike on Aug. 3, one of nine Maze prisoners to do so.

FitzGerald resigned Jan. 27, 1982, after his presentation of an austerity budget aroused the opposition of independents who had backed him previously. His party lost two seats in the subsequent election and the opposition Fianna Fail won eight but still required support of a splinter party and independents to achieve a majority. Former Prime Minister Charles J. Haughey was sworn in on March 9 and presented a budget with nearly a $1-billion deficit, with additional public spending aimed at stimulating the lagging economy.

ISRAEL

State of Israel
President: Yitzhak Navon (1978)
Prime Minister: Menachem Begin (1977)
Area: 7,992 sq mi. (20,699 sq km)
Population (est. 1982): 4,000,000 (average annual growth rate: 1.9%)
Density per square mile: 500.5
Capital: Jerusalem
Largest cities (est. 1981): Jerusalem, 412,000[1]; (est. 1979): Tel Aviv, 336,000; Haifa, 230,000; Ramat Gan, 120,000
Monetary unit: Shekel
Languages: Hebrew, Arabic, English
Religions: Jewish, 85%; Islam, Christian
National name: Medinat Israel
Literacy rate (1981): 88% (Jews), 48% (Arabs)
Economic summary: Gross national product (1980): $17.4. Average annual growth rate (1970–79): 1.6%. Per capita income (1980): $4,500. Land used for agriculture: 20%; labor force: 6%; principal products: citrus and other fruits, vegetables, beef, dairy and poultry products. Labor force in industry: 25%; major products: processed foods, cut diamonds, clothing and textiles, chemicals, metal products, transport and electrical equipment, plastics. Natural resources: sulfur, limestone, rock salt, phosphates, potash, bromine. Exports: polished diamonds, citrus and other fruits, clothing and textiles, processed foods, fertilizer and chemical products. Imports: military equipment, rough diamonds, chemicals, oil, machinery, iron and steel, cereals, textiles, vehicles, ships, aircraft. Major trading partners: U.S., West Germany, U.K., Switzerland, France, Italy.

1. Includes East Jerusalem.

Geography. Israel, slightly smaller than Massachusetts, lies at the eastern end of the Mediterranean Sea. It is bordered by Egypt on the west, Syria and Jordan on the east, and Lebanon on the north.

Northern Israel is largely a plateau traversed from north to south by mountains and broken by great depressions, also running from north to south.

The maritime plain of Israel is remarkably fertile. The southern Negev region, which comprises almost half the total area, is largely a wide desert steppe area. The National Water Project irrigation scheme is now transforming it into fertile land. The Jordan, the only important river, flows from the north through Lake Hule (Waters of Merom) and Lake Kinneret (Sea of Galilee or Sea of Tiberias), finally entering the Dead Sea, 1,290 feet (393 m) below sea level. This "sea," which is actually a salt lake (394 sq mi.; 1,020 sq km), has no outlet, its water balance being maintained by evaporation.

Government. Israel, which does not have a written constitution, has a republican form of government headed by a president elected for a five-year term by the Knesset. He may serve no more than two terms. The Knesset has 120 members elected by universal suffrage under proportional representation for four years. The government is administered by the Cabinet, which is headed by the prime minister.

The Knesset decided in June 1950 that Israel would acquire a constitution gradually through the years by the enactment of fundamental laws. Israel grants automatic citizenship to every Jew who desires to settle within its borders, subject to control of the Knesset.

The major political parties are Likud (48 of 120 seats in the Knesset), led by Prime Minister Menachem Begin; Labor Alignment (50 seats), led by Shimon Peres; National Religious Party (6 seats), led by Yossef Burg; Agudath Israel (4 seats); Communist Party (4 seats).

History. Palestine, cradle of two great religions and homeland of the modern state of Israel, was known to the ancient Hebrews as the "Land of Canaan." Palestine's name derives from the Philistines, a people who occupied the southern coastal part of the country in the 12th century B.C.

A Hebrew kingdom established in 1000 B.C. was later split into the kingdoms of Judah and Israel; they were subsequently invaded by Assyrians, Babylonians, Egyptians, Persians, Macedonians, Romans, and Byzantines. The Arabs took Palestine from the Byzantine Empire A.D. 634–40. With the exception of a Frankish Crusader kingdom from 1099 to 1187, Palestine remained under Moslem rule until the 20th century (Turkish rule from 1516), when British forces under Gen. Sir Edmund Allenby defeated the Turks and captured Jerusalem Dec. 9, 1917. The League of Nations granted Britain a mandate to govern Palestine, effective in 1923.

Jewish colonies—Jews from Russia established one as early as 1882—multiplied after Theodor Herzl's 1897 call for a Jewish state. The Zionist movement received official approval with the publication of a letter Nov. 2, 1917, from Arthur Balfour, British Foreign Secretary, to Lord Rothschild, a British Jewish leader. Balfour promised support for the establishment of a Jewish homeland in Palestine on the understanding that the civil and religious rights of non-Jewish Palestinians would be safeguarded.

A 1937 British proposal called for an Arab and a Jewish state separated by a mandated area incorporating Jerusalem and Nazareth. Arabs opposed this, demanding a single state with minority rights for Jews, and a 1939 British White Paper retreated, offering instead a single state with further Jewish immigration to be limited to 75,000. Although the White Paper satisfied neither side, further discussion ended on the outbreak of World War II, when the Jewish population stood at nearly 500,000, or 30% of the total. Illegal and legal immigration during the war brought the Jewish population to 678,000 in 1946, compared with 1,269,000 Arabs. Unable to reach a compromise, Britain turned the problem over to the United Nations in 1947, which on November 29 voted for partition—despite strong Arab opposition.

Britain did not help implement the U.N. decision and withdrew on expiration of its mandate May 14, 1948. Zionists had already seized control of areas designated as Jewish, and, on the day of British departure, the Jewish National Council proclaimed the State of Israel.

U.S. recognition came within hours. The next day, Jordanian and Egyptian forces invaded the new nation. At the cease-fire Jan. 7, 1949, Israel increased its original territory by 50%, taking western Galilee, a broad corridor through central Palestine to Jerusalem, and part of modern Jerusalem. (In April 1950, Jordan annexed areas of eastern and central Palestine that had been designated for an Arab state, together with the old city of Jerusalem.)

Chaim Weizmann and David Ben-Gurion, became Israel's first president and prime minister. The new government was admitted to the U.N. May 11, 1949.

The next clash with Arab neighbors came when Egypt nationalized the Suez Canal in 1956 and barred Israeli shipping. Coordinating with an Anglo-French force, Israeli troops seized the Gaza Strip and drove through the Sinai to the east bank of the Suez Canal, but withdrew under U.S. and U.N. pressure. In 1967, Israel threatened retaliation against Syrian border raids, and Syria asked Egyptian aid. Egypt demanded the removal of U.N. peace-keeping forces from Suez, staged a national mobilization, closed the Gulf of Aqaba, and moved troops into the Sinai. On June 5, with a simultaneous air attack against Syrian, Jordanian, and Egyptian bases and in a six-day war totally defeated its Arab enemies. Expanding its territory by 200%, Israel at the cease-fire held the Golan Heights, the West Bank of the Jordan River, the Old City, and all of the Sinai and the east bank of the Suez Canal.

Israel insisted that Jerusalem remain a unified city and that peace negotiations be conducted directly, something the Arab states had refused to do because it would constitute a recognition of their Jewish neighbor.

Egypt's President Gamal Abdel Nasser renounced the 1967 cease-fire in 1969 and began a "war of attrition" against Israel, firing Soviet artillery at Israeli forces on the east bank of the canal. Nasser died of a heart attack on Sept. 28, 1970, and was succeeded by Anwar el-Sadat.

In the face of Israeli reluctance even to discuss the return of occupied territories, the fourth Mideast war erupted Oct. 6, 1973, with a surprise Egyptian and Syrian assault on the Jewish high holy day of Yom Kippur. Initial Arab gains were reversed when a cease-fire took effect two weeks later, but Israel suffered heavy losses in manpower.

U.S. Secretary of State Henry A. Kissinger arranged a disengagement of forces on both the Egyptian and Syrian fronts. Geneva talks, aimed at a lasting peace, foundered, however, when Israel balked at inclusion of the Palestine Liberation Organization, a guerrilla front increasingly active in terrorism directed against Israel.

At home, criticism of the ruling Labor Party's lack of preparedness cost it five seats in 1973 election, and Prime Minister Golda Meir was forced to head a minority government until her retirement on April 10, 1974. Yitzhak Rabin, a former general formed a successor government, which won narrow approval in the Knesset and, in October assembled a majority coalition.

In the same month, the PLO won recognition as the "representative of the Palestine people" in a resolution passed by the U.N. General Assembly and at an Arab summit meeting in Rabat, Morocco.

A second-stage Sinai withdrawal signed by Israel and Egypt in September 1975 required Israel to give up the strategic Mitla and Gidi passes and to return the captured Abu Rudeis oil fields. Egypt guaranteed passage of Israeli cargoes through the reopened Suez Canal, and both sides renounced force in the settlement of disputes. Two hundred U.S. civilian technicians were stationed in a widened U.N. buffer zone to monitor and warn either side of truce violations.

A U.S. commitment to give Israel $400 million in economic aid and $1 billion in weapons was then disclosed, along with the assurance of a coordinated U.S.-Israeli position in any renewed Geneva negotiations. Nevertheless, an estrangement between Washington and Jerusalem, which began with the 1974 Arab oil boycott, persisted and the solidity of the alliance became increasingly an issue in domestic politics.

For the Israelis, the July 4, 1976, rescue of 103 hostages in a hijacked Air France airliner at Entebbe, Uganda, was a stunning victory against Arab terrorism. The hijacking was the first in a year and a half to be carried out by Palestinians, in this case the Popular Front for the Liberation of Palestine. Rabin contravened government policy in opening negotiations with the terrorists but secretly prepared a commando raid on the airport. When he learned that the hostages faced death in any event, Rabin launched the airborne raid, which killed the terrorists and a score of Ugandan soldiers, losing only two hostages and one rescuer.

With no progress toward permanent peace and rampant inflation causing severe economic strain, the malaise in the Labor Party deepened in early 1977 when Rabin confessed to maintaining an illegal bank account in the United States. He resigned April 8 and Defense Minister Shimon Peres was named the party's leader for general elections May 17, in which the Labor Party was defeated for the first time since Israel's founding.

Menachem Begin, 63, took office June 21 as the leader of the Likud, a coalition of conservative parties. Begin founded the Irgun Zvai Leumi (National Military Organization) to fight British rule during the Palestine Mandate. His election victory provoked a wave of negative reaction throughout the Arab world and misgivings on the part of Western proponents of a Mideast peace. Attempting to modify his image, the Likud platform on the inauguration of the new government omitted an election claim of permanent sovereignty over the West Bank and agreed to suspend the application of Israeli law to the occupied territories in general while peace negotiations were under way.

A dramatic breakthrough in the tortuous history of Mideast peace efforts occurred Nov. 9, 1977, when Egypt's President Sadat declared his willingness to go anywhere to talk peace. Begin on November 15 extended an invitation to the Egyptian leader to address the Knesset. Sadat's arrival in Israel four days later raised worldwide hopes. But optimism ebbed even before Begin was invited to Ismailia by Sadat, December 25–26.

An Israeli peace plan unveiled by Begin on his return, and approved by the Knesset, offered to end military administration in the West Bank and the Gaza Strip, with a degree of Arab self-rule but no relinquishment of sovereignty by Israel. Sadat severed talks on January 18 and, despite U.S. condemnation, Begin approved new West Bank settlements by Israelis. Dissidents within the cabinet, notably Defense Minister Ezer Weizman, kept the door open for negotiations, however, and a foreign ministerial meeting of the two antagonists with U.S. Secretary of State Cyrus Vance took place in England on July 18.

A PLO raid on Israel's coast on March 11, 1978, killed 30 civilians and provoked a full-scale invasion of southern Lebanon by Israel three days later to attack PLO bases. Israel withdrew three months later, turning over strongpoints to Lebanese Christian militia wherever possible rather than to a U.N. peacekeeping force installed in the area.

Peace talks resumed their painful progress in October as Israeli Foreign Minister Moshe Dayan and Egyptian Defense Minister Kamel Hassan Ali, with the participation of President Carter, agreed on a U.S. draft treaty.

On March 14, 1979, after a visit by Carter, the Knesset approved a final treaty, and 12 days later Begin and Sadat signed the document, together with Carter, in a White House ceremony. Israel began its withdrawal from the Sinai on May 25 by handing over the coastal town of El Arish and the two countries opened their border on May 29, the same day Israeli navy landing craft transited the Suez Canal for the first time.

On Palestinian automony, there was little progress. On Feb. 10, 1980, Israel inflamed Arab opinion with the Cabinet's approval of Jewish settlements in Hebron, until then an exclusively Arab West Bank city. A right-wing Israeli terrorist campaign that maimed three Arab West Bank mayors and finally, the Knesset's passage of a law annexing East Jerusalem further antagonized the Arabs and stalled the autonomy talks. The Jerusalem action drew a unanimous condemnation—in which the U.S. joined—from the U.N. Security Council and caused the last eight countries still maintaining embassies in Jerusalem to remove them in response to a Council appeal.

One of the most difficult periods in Israel's history began with a confrontation with Syria over the placing by Syria of Soviet surface-to-air missiles in the Bekaa Valley of Lebanon in April 1981. President Reagan dispatched Philip C. Habib to prevent a clash. While Habib was seeking a settlement, Begin ordered a bombing raid against an Iraqi nuclear reactor on June 7, invoking the theory of preemptive self-defense because he said Iraq was planning to make nuclear weapons to attack Israel. Only through strenuous diplomatic efforts was the U.S. able to stave off Arab demands for sanctions against Israel in the Security Council in a vote on June 19 that condemned the action.

Begin's belligerency was credited with his narrow victory over Shimon Peres' Labor Party on June 30. He followed it with a bombing raid against PLO headquarters in Beirut on July 17 that killed 300 persons and injured 700. Begin's assertion that the attack was again in self-defense against PLO raids and bombardment across the border caused questions even among his supporters and drew the strongest criticism of Israel yet from Washington.

Although Israel withdrew its last settlers from the Sinai in April 1982 and agreed to a Sinai "peace patrol" composed of troops from four West European nations, the fragile peace engineered by Habib in Lebanon was shattered on June 9 by a massive Israeli assault on southern Lebanon. The attack was in retaliation for what Israel charged was a PLO attack that critically wounded the Israeli ambassador to London six days earlier.

Israeli armor swept through UNIFIL lines in southern Lebanon, destroyed PLO strongholds in Tyre and Sidon, and reached the suburbs of Beirut on June 10. Air strikes destroyed Syrian missile sites in the Bekaa Valley and resulted in Israeli claims of downing 25 Soviet-made Syrian jets. As

Israeli troops ringed Moslem East Beirut, where 5,000 PLO guerrillas were believed trapped, Habib sought to negotiate a safe exit for them. The Arab world loudly protested the entire action, estimated by Lebanon to have cost the lives of 10,000 civilians by mid-July, but no Arab nation would accept the Palestinian militants Israel insisted must leave Lebanon.

Begin's belligerence for the first time brought large antiwar demonstrations in Israel and a hostile reception by the U.S. Congress when he visited President Reagan in mid-June. The economic consequences of an indefinite military occupation of Lebanon were foreboding in the context of Israel's budget deficit and a 1981 inflation rate of 100%.

ITALY

Italian Republic
President: Sandro Pertini (1978)
Premier: Giovanni Spadolini (1981)
Area: 116,304 sq mi. (301,225 sq km)
Population (est. 1982): 56,500,000 (average annual growth rate: 0.3%)
Density per square mile: 485.8
Capital: Rome
Largest cities (1981 census): Rome, 2,830,569; Milan, 1,634,638; Naples, 1,210,503; Turin, 1,103,520; Genoa, 760,300; Palermo, 699,691; Bologna, 455,853; Florence, 453,293; Catania, 378,521; Bari, 370,781
Monetary unit: Lira
Language: Italian
Religion: Roman Catholic
National name: Repubblica Italiana
Literacy rate: Not known
Economic summary: Gross national product (1980): $369.0 billion. Average annual growth rate (1970–79): 2.2%. Per capita income (1980): $6,480. Land used for agriculture: 50%; labor force: 14%; principal products: wheat, rice, grapes, olives, citrus fruits. Labor force in industry: 38%; major products: automobiles, machinery, chemicals, textiles, shoes. Natural resources: fish, dwindling natural gas reserves. Exports: machinery and transport equipment, textiles, foodstuffs, chemicals, footwear. Imports: machinery and transport equipment, foodstuffs, ferrous and nonferrous metals, wool, cotton, petroleum. Major trading partners: West Germany, France, Netherlands, U.K.

Geography. Italy is a long peninsula shaped like a boot bounded on the west by the Tyrrhenian Sea and on the east by the Adriatic. Slightly larger than Arizona, it has for neighbors France, Switzerland, Austria, and Yugoslavia.

Approximately 600 of Italy's 708 miles (1,139 km) of length are in the long peninsula that projects into the Mediterranean from the fertile basin of the Po River. The Apennine Mountains, branching off from the Alps between Nice and Genoa, form the peninsula's backbone, and rise to a maximum height of 9,560 feet (2,912 m) at the Gran Sasso d'Italia (Corno). The Alps form Italy's northern boundary.

Several islands form part of Italy. Sicily (9,926 sq mi.; 25,708 sq km) lies off the toe of the boot, across the Strait of Messina, with a steep and rockbound northern coast and gentler slopes to the sea in the west and south. Mount Etna, an active volcano, rises to 10,741 feet (3,274 m), and most of Sicily is more than 500 feet (3,274 m) in elevation. Sixty-two miles (100 km) southwest of Sicily lies Pantelleria (45 sq mi.; 117 sq km), and south of that are Lampedusa and Linosa. Sardinia (9,301 sq mi.; 24,090 sq km), which is just south of Corsica and about 125 miles (200 km) west of the mainland, is mountainous, stony, and unproductive.

Italy has many northern lakes, lying below the snow-covered peaks of the Alps. The largest are Garda (143 sq mi.; 370 sq km), Maggiore (83 sq mi.; 215 sq km), and Como (55 sq mi.; 142 sq km).

The Po, the principal river, flows from the Alps on Italy's western border and crosses the Lombard plain to the Adriatic.

Government. The president is elected for a term of seven years by Parliament in joint session with regional representatives. The president nominates the premier and, upon the premier's recommendations, the members of the Cabinet. Parliament is composed of two houses: a Senate with 315 elective members and a Chamber of Deputies of 630 members elected by the people for a five-year term.

The major political parties are: Christian Democratic Party (262 seats of 630 in Chamber of Deputies), led by Ciriaco Demita; Communist Party (201 seats), led by Enrico Berlinguer; Socialist Party (62 seats), led by Bettino Craxi; Social Movement Party (30 seats), led by Giorgio Almirante; Social Democratic Party (20 seats), led by Pietro Longo; Radical Party (18 seats), led by Marco Pannella; Republican Party (16 seats), led by Premier Giovanni Spadolini; Liberal Party (9 seats), led by Valerio Zanone; and Proletarian Unity Party (6 seats), led by Lucio Magri.

History. Until A.D. 476, when the German Odoacer became head of the Roman Empire in the west, the history of Italy was largely the history of Rome. From A.D. 800 on, the Holy Roman Emperors, Popes, Normans, and Saracens all vied for control over various segments of the Italian peninsula. Numerous city states, such as Venice and Genoa, and many small principalities flourished in the late Middle Ages.

In 1713, after the War of the Spanish Succession, Milan, Naples, and Sardinia were handed over to Austria, which lost some of its Italian territories in 1735. After 1800, Italy was unified by Napoleon, who crowned himself King of Italy in 1805; but with the Congress of Vienna in 1815, Austria once again became the dominant power in Italy.

Austrian armies crushed Italian uprisings in 1820, 1821, and 1831. In the 1830s Giuseppe Mazzini, brilliant liberal nationalist, organized the Risorgimento (Resurrection), which laid the foundation for Italian unity.

Disappointed Italian patriots looked to the House of Savoy for leadership. Count Camille di Cavour (1810–61), Premier of Sardinia in 1852 and the architect of a united Italy, joined England and France in the Crimean War (1853–56), and in 1859 helped France in a war against Austria, thereby obtaining Lombardy. By plebiscite in 1860, Modena, Parma, Tuscany, and the Romagna voted to join Sardinia. In 1860, Giuseppe Garibaldi conquered Sicily and Naples and turned them over to Sardinia. Victor Emmanuel II, King of Sardinia, was proclaimed King of Italy in 1861.

Allied with Germany and Austria-Hungary in the Triple Alliance of 1882, Italy declared its neutrality upon the outbreak of World War I on the ground that Germany had embarked upon an offensive war. In 1915, Italy entered the war on the side of the Allies.

Benito (Il Duce) Mussolini, a former Socialist, organized discontented Italians in 1919 into the Fascist Party to "rescue Italy from Bolshevism." He led his Black Shirts in a march on Rome and, on Oct. 28, 1922, became premier. He transformed Italy into a dictatorship, embarking on an expansionist foreign policy with the invasion and annexation of Ethiopia in 1935 and allying himself with Adolf Hitler in the Rome-Berlin Axis in 1936. He was executed by Partisans on April 28, 1945 at Dongo on Lake Como.

Following the overthrow of Mussolini's dictatorship and the armistice with the Allies (Sept. 3, 1943), Italy joined the war against Germany as a co-belligerent. King Victor Emmanuel III abdicated May 9, 1946, and left the country after having installed his son as King Humbert II. A plebiscite rejected monarchy, however, and on June 13, King Humbert followed his father into exile.

The peace treaty of Sept. 15, 1947, required Italian renunciation of all claims in Ethiopia and Greece and the cession of the Dodecanese to Greece and of five small Alpine areas to France. Much of the Istrian Peninsula, including Fiume and Pola, went to Yugoslavia.

The Trieste area west of the new Yugoslav territory was made a free territory (until 1954, when the city and a 90-square-mile zone were transferred to Italy and the rest to Yugoslavia).

The government of Mario Rumor fell in 1974. After a 51-day crisis, a government was formed under Aldo Moro, a left-centrist Christian Democrat who had been Premier three times before.

Withdrawal of the Socialists from Moro's coalition—the 32nd government since World War II—brought his resignation Jan. 7, 1976. In the June elections, the Communists gained but the Christian Democrats still led and, warned by the U.S. and West Germany against a Communist coalition, they chose to govern as a minority under Giulio Andreotti. Petro Ingrao, a Communist, became President of the Chamber of Deputies, however, and Communists won 7 of 26 parliamentary chairmanships.

Andreotti had Communist cooperation in imposing wage limits and taxes to meet International Monetary Fund conditions for a $530-million loan. He also got Communist backing to combat a wave of kidnappings and political terrorism that culminated in the seizure of former Premier Moro in Rome on March 16, 1978, by the ultra-left Red Brigades. The discovery on May 9 of Moro's bullet-ridden body near the site of his kidnapping caused worldwide shock.

A second political shock was the resignation of President Giovanni Leone on June 15, six months before the end of his term, because of his involvement in Lockheed bribery scandals. Eighty-one-year-old Sandro Pertini became Italy's first Socialist president.

Tacit Communist support that had enabled Andreotti to govern ended on March 31, 1979, as the Communists insisted on seats in Andreotti's fifth cabinet and joined with the Socialists to defeat the government. Elections in June produced only one surprise—a drop in Communist strength in national voting for the first time since the beginning of the republic. The 4% loss went to splinter parties rather than to the Christian Democrats.

Disaster and scandal brought the long reign of the Christian Democrats to an end when Italy's 40th premier since World War II, Arnaldo Forlani, was forced to resign in the wake of disclosure that many high-ranking Christian Democrats and civil servants belonged to a secret Masonic lodge known as "P-2." The scandal followed the disastrous earthquake that struck southern Italy on Nov. 23, 1980, killing 3,105, injuring 7,671, and leaving 1,575 missing and presumed dead. Delay in providing relief for survivors, amid reports of theft of supplies, cast a pall over the nation.

When the Socialists deserted the coalition, Forlani was forced to resign on May 26, 1981, leaving to Giovanni Spadolini of the small Republican Party the task of forming a new government. Spadolini declared his intention to outlaw the secret lodge, combat Italy's 20% inflation by cutting social services and government borrowing, fight the terrorism plaguing society, and support NATO's plans for the stationing of nuclear weapons in Western Europe.

A resurgence of terrorism occurred with the kidnapping of Brig. Gen. James L. Dozier, U.S. commander of the NATO land forces headquarters in Verona. He was freed by Italian commandos on Jan. 28, 1982, after 42 days of captivity in a Red Brigade hideout. A total of 385 terrorists were arrested in a nationwide crackdown.

Religion. Although Italy is predominantly Roman Catholic, religious freedom is permitted. Catholic religious teaching is given in all elementary and intermediate schools. Relations with the Church were regulated until 1977, by the treaty with the Holy See of Feb. 11, 1929, which established the temporal power of the Pope over Vatican City. In November 1977, a new accord replaced the 1929 Corcordat; Catholicism is no longer to be considered as the state religion and Vatican influence on education and marriage has been reduced.

IVORY COAST

Republic of Ivory Coast
President: Félix Houphouët-Boigny (1960)
Area: 124,502 sq mi. (322,462 sq km)
Population (est. 1982): 8,500,000 (average annual growth rate: 3.3%)
Density per square mile: 68.3
Capital and largest city (est. 1981): Abidjan, 1,500,000
Monetary unit: Franc CFA
Ethnic groups: Agnis, Baoulés, Senoufos, Kroumen, Mandes, Dan-Gouros
Languages: French and African languages
Religions: Animist, 65%; Christian, 23%; Islam, 12%
National name: République de la Côte d'Ivoire
Literacy rate: Not known
Economic summary: Gross national product (1980): $9.9 billion. Average annual growth rate (1970–79): 1.3%. Per capita income (1980): $1,150. Labor force in agriculture: 85%; principal products: coffee, cocoa, timber, palm oil, sugar, bananas. Major industrial products: food, textiles, shoes, metals. Natural resources: petroleum, iron ore. Exports: coffee, cocoa, tropical woods. Imports: raw materials, consumer goods, fuels. Major trading partners: France, U.S., Western European countries.

Geography. The Ivory Coast, in western Africa on the Gulf of Guinea, is a little larger than New Mexico. Its neighbors are Liberia, Guinea, Mali, Upper Volta, and Ghana.

The country consists of a coastal strip in the south, dense forests in the interior, and savannas in the north. Rainfall is heavy, especially along the coast.

Government. The government is headed by a President who is elected every five years by popular vote, together with a National Assembly of 147 members.

The Parti Démocratique de la Côte d'Ivoire, a member of the Rassemblement Démocratique Africain, is the only political party.

History. The Ivory Coast attracted both French and Portuguese merchants in the 15th century. French traders set up establishments early in the 19th century, and in 1842, the French obtained territorial concessions from local tribes, gradually extending their influence along the coast and inland. The area was organized as a territory in 1893, became an autonomous republic in the French Union after World War II, and achieved independence on Aug. 7, 1960.

The Ivory Coast formed a customs union in 1959 with Dahomey (Benin), Niger, and Upper Volta. The country is one of the most prosperous and stable in West Africa.

JAMAICA

Sovereign: Queen Elizabeth II
Governor-General: Sir Florizel Glasspole (1973)
Prime Minister: Edward P. G. Seaga (1980)
Area: 4,411 sq mi. (11,424 sq km)
Population (est. 1982): 2,250,000 (average annual growth rate: 1.2%)
Density per square mile: 510.1
Capital and largest city (est. 1981): Kingston, 200,000
Monetary unit: Jamaican dollar
Language: English
Religions: Anglican, Baptist, Roman Catholic
Member of Commonwealth of Nations
Literacy rate (1981): 40%
Economic summary: Gross national product (1980): $2.3 billion. Average annual growth rate (1970–79): −3.7%. Per capita income (1980): $1,030. Land used for agriculture: 21%; labor force: 30% (includes fishing and mining); principal products: sugar cane, citrus fruits, bananas, pimentos, coconuts, coffee, cocoa. Labor force in industry: 12%; major products: bauxite, textiles, processed foods, light manufactures. Natural resources: bauxite, gypsum, limestone. Exports: alumina, bauxite, sugar, bananas, citrus fruits, rum, cocoa. Imports: fuels, machinery, transport and electrical equipment, food, fertilizer. Major trading partners: U.S., U.K., Canada.

Geography. Jamaica is an island in the West Indies, 90 miles (145 km) south of Cuba and 100 miles (161 km) west of Haiti. It is a little smaller than Connecticut.

The island is made up of a plateau and the Blue Mountains, a group of volcanic hills, in the east. Blue Mountain (7,402 ft.; 2,256 m) is the tallest peak.

Government. The legislature is a 60-member House of Representatives elected by universal suffrage and an appointed Senate of 21 members. The Prime Minister is appointed by the Governor-General and must, in the Governor-General's opinion, be the person best able to command the confidence of a majority of the members of the House of Representatives.

The major political parties are the Jamaica Labor Party (52 seats in the House of Representatives), led by Prime Minister Edward P. G. Seaga; and the People's National Party (8 seats), led by former Prime Minister Michael Manley.

History. Jamaica was inhabited by Arawak Indians when Columbus discovered it in 1494 and named it St. Iago. It remained under Spanish rule until 1655, then became a British possession. The island prospered from wealth brought by buccaneers to their base, Port Royal, the capital, until the city disappeared in the sea in 1692 after an earthquake. The Arawaks died off from disease and exploitation, and slaves, mostly black, were imported to work sugar plantations. Abolition of the slave trade (1807), emancipation of the slaves (1833), and a gradual drop in sugar prices led to depressed economic conditions that resulted in an uprising in 1865.

The following year Jamaica's status was changed to that of a colony, and conditions improved considerably. Introduction of banana cultivation made the island less dependent on the sugar crop for its well-being. Overpopulation and problems inherited from the colonial era, such as illiteracy, produced chronic substantial unemployment, leading to much emigration to the Caribbean countries and to the U.S.

On May 5, 1953, Jamaica attained internal autonomy, and in 1958 it led in organizing the West Indies Federation. This effort at Caribbean unification failed. A nationalist labor leader, Sir Alexander Bustamente, led a campaign for withdrawal from the Federation. As the result of a popular referendum in 1961, Jamaica became independent on Aug. 6, 1962.

Michael Manley became Prime Minister in 1972 and initiated a socialist program, with higher taxes on land and luxuries and on the production of bauxite. In 1977, the government agreed to buy 51% of the Kaiser and Reynolds bauxite operations in Jamaica, ending a dispute with the U.S. companies over heavy taxes imposed earlier.

Elections on Oct. 30, 1980, offered a sharp contrast between Manley's socialism trending toward the Cuban model of his friend, Fidel Castro, and the aggressive capitalism of Labor Party leader Edward P. G. Seaga. A campaign marked by violence ended with 57% of the popular vote and 51 of 60 House seats for Seaga, who immediately banished the Cuban ambassador. Seaga was the first foreign head of government to visit the newly installed President Reagan, on Jan. 28, 1981, to appeal for aid. The International Monetary Fund granted a loan of $650 million in April and a group of industrialized nations, together with the Interamerican Development Bank, offered credits of $350,000.

JAPAN

Emperor: Hirohito (1926)
Prime Minister: Zenko Suzuki (1980)
Area: 143,574 sq mi. (371,857 sq km)
Population (est. 1982): 118,500,000 (average annual growth rate: 0.7%)
Density per square mile: 825.4
Capital: Tokyo
Largest cities (est. 1980)[1]: Tokyo, 8,350,000; Yokohama, 2,775,000; Osaka, 2,650,000; Nagoya, 2,100,000; Kyoto, 1,475,000; Sapporo, 1,400,000; Kobe, 1,375,000; Sukuoka, 1,100,000

Monetary unit: Yen
Language: Japanese
Religions: Shintoist, Buddhist, Christian
National name: Nippon
Literacy rate (1981): 99%
Economic summary: Gross national product (1980): $1,152.9 billion. Average annual growth rate (1970–79): 3.9%. Per capita income (1980): $9,890. Land used for agriculture, 16%; labor force, including fishing, 11%; principal products: rice, vegetables, fruits, meat, natural silk. Labor force in industry: 34%; major products: machinery and equipment, metals and metal products, textiles, autos, chemicals, electrical and electronic equipment. Natural resource: fish. Exports: machinery and equipment, automobiles, metals and metal products, textiles. Imports: fossil fuels, metal ore, raw materials, foodstuffs, machinery and equipment. Major trading partners: U.S., Southeast Asian, Middle Eastern, and Western European countries.

1. Except for Tokyo, figures refer to *shi*, a minor division that may include some scattered or rural population as well as an urban center.

Geography. An archipelago extending more than 2,360 miles (3,776 km) from north to south in the Pacific, Japan is separated from the east coast of Asia by the Sea of Japan. It is approximately the size of Montana.

Japan's four main islands are Honshu, Hokkaido, Kyushu, and Shikoku. The Ryukyu chain to the southwest was U.S.-occupied and the Kuriles to the northeast are Russian-occupied. The surface of the main islands consists largely of mountains separated by narrow valleys. There are about 50 more or less active volcanoes, of which the best-known is Mount Fuji.

Government. Japan's Constitution, promulgated on Nov. 3, 1946, replaced the Meiji Constitution of 1889. The 1946 Constitution, sponsored by the U.S. during its occupation of Japan, brought fundamental changes to the Japanese political system, including the abandonment of the Emperor's divine rights. The Diet (Parliament) consists of a House of Representatives of 511 members, elected for four years, and a House of Councilors of 252 members, half of whom are elected every three years for six-year terms. Executive power is vested in the Cabinet, which is headed by a Prime Minister, nominated by the Diet from its members.

Emperor Hirohito, who was born April 29, 1901, succeeded his father, Yoshihito, on Dec. 25, 1926. He was married on Jan. 26, 1924, to Princess Nagako, born in 1903. They have two sons—Crown Prince Akihito (born Dec. 23, 1933) and Prince Hitachi (born Nov. 28, 1935)—and four daughters. Succession to the Japanese throne is in the male line only.

The major political parties are the Liberal Democratic Party (287 of 511 seats in the House of Representatives), led by Prime Minister Zenko Suzuki; Socialist Party (104 seats), led by Kazuo Asukada; Clean Government (Komeito) Party (34 seats), led by Yoshikatsu Takeiri; Communist Party (29 seats), led by Sanzo Nosaka; Democratic Socialist Party (32 seats), led by Ikko Kasuga; New Liberal Club (10 seats).

History. A series of legends attributes creation of Japan to the sun goddess, from whom the later emperors were allegedly descended. The first of them was Jimmu Tenno, supposed to have ascended the throne in 660 B.C.

Recorded Japanese history begins with the first contact with China in the 5th century A.D. Japan was then divided into strong feudal states, all nominally under the Emperor, but with real power often held by a court minister or clan. In 1185, Yoritomo, chief of the Minamoto clan, was designated Shogun (Generalissimo) with the administration of the islands under his control. A dual government system —Shogun and Emperor—continued until 1867.

First contact with the West came about 1542, when a Portuguese ship off course arrived in Japanese waters. Portuguese traders, Jesuit missionaries, and Spanish, Dutch, and English traders followed. Suspicious of Christianity and of Portuguese support of a local Japanese revolt, the shoguns prohibited all trade with foreign countries; only a Dutch trading post at Nagasaki was permitted. Western attempts to renew trading relations failed until 1853, when Commodore Matthew Perry sailed an American fleet into Tokyo Bay.

Japan now quickly made the transition from a medieval to a modern power. Feudalism was abolished and industrialization was speeded. An imperial army was established with conscription. The shogun system was abolished in 1868 by Emperor Meiji, and parliamentary government was established in 1889. After a brief war with China in 1894–95, Japan acquired Formosa (Taiwan), the Pescadores Islands, and part of southern Manchuria. China also recognized the independence of Korea (Chosen), which Japan later annexed (1910).

In 1904–05, Japan defeated Russia in the Russo-Japanese War, gaining the territory of southern Sakhalin (Karafuto) and Russia's port and rail rights in Manchuria. In World War I, Japan, which took a negligible part in military operations, seized Germany's Pacific islands and leased areas in China. The Treaty of Versailles then awarded it a mandate over the islands.

At the Washington Conference of 1921–22, Japan agreed to respect Chinese national integrity. The series of Japanese aggressions that was to lead to the nation's downfall began in 1931 with the invasion of Manchuria. The following year, Japan set up this area as a puppet state, "Manchukuo," under Emperor Henry Pu-Yi, last of China's Manchu dynasty. On Nov. 25, 1936, Japan joined the Axis by signing the anti-Comintern pact. The invasion of China came the next year and the Pearl Harbor attack on the U.S. on Dec. 7, 1941.

(For details of World War II (1939–45), *see* Headline History.)

Japan surrendered formally on Sept. 2, 1945, aboard the battleship *Missouri* in Tokyo Bay after atomic bombs had hit Hiroshima and Nagasaki. Southern Sakhalin and the Kurile Islands reverted to the U.S.S.R., and Formosa (Taiwan) and Manchuria to China. The Pacific islands remained under U.S. occupation. General of the Army Douglas MacArthur was appointed Supreme Commander for the Allied Powers on Aug. 14, 1945.

A new Japanese Constitution went into effect in 1947. In 1949, many of the responsibilities of government were returned to the Japanese. Full sovereignty was granted to Japan by the Japanese Peace Treaty in 1951.

The treaty took effect on April 28, 1952, when Japan returned to full status as a nation. It was admitted into the United Nations in 1958.

Following the visit of Prime Minister Eisaku Sato to Washington in 1969, the U.S. agreed to return Okinawa and other Ryukyu Islands to Japan in 1972, and both nations renewed the security treaty in 1970.

When President Nixon opened a dialogue with Peking in 1972. Prime Minister Kakuei Tanaka, who succeeded Sato in 1972, quickly established diplomatic relations with the mainland Chinese and severed ties with Formosa.

President Ford visited Japan Nov. 18–24, 1974, the first U.S. President to do so. Substantive results were minimized by Tanaka's domestic political troubles. Tanaka resigned two days after Ford's departure, and was succeeded by Takeo Miki, a compromise choice from the progressive wing of the Liberal Democrats.

While economic recovery continued in 1976, the Lockheed scandal pursued the ruling Liberal Democrats. With the disclosure by the U.S. Senate that $6.3 million in "promotion" money had been paid by the aircraft company to Yoshio Kodama, a rightwing political "fixer," Miki was placed under strong pressure to investigate the ultimate recipients. The scandal cost the party its control of the House of Representatives in the December election, but nine independents affiliated with the Liberal Democrats to provide a narrow majority. Miki resigned, turning over leadership to Takeo Fukuda.

Fukuda, concentrating on economic recovery, achieved a record year in 1977, with exports exceeding imports by $9 billion, nearly twice the previous record of $5.1 billion in 1972.

Visiting Washington in May 1978, Fukuda promised "massive efforts" to reduce Japan's surplus, by cutting automobile, color television, and steel exports and by buying U.S. aircraft. In return, like other U.S. trade partners, he urged Washington to curb inflation at home and support the dollar in foreign markets.

On Aug. 12, 1978, Japan and China signed a treaty of peace and friendship. This pact followed an 8-year, $20-billion economic pact in which Japanese business leaders agreed to provide China with modern technology in return for Chinese natural resources.

Despite pledges to its economic partners at the Bonn summit of industrial powers in July 1978 that it would reduce its trade surplus, Japan reported an all-time high figure of $18.3 billion for the year.

But, Japan's oil bill of $39.5 billion for the year ended March 31, 1980, produced a record trade deficit of $14.4 billion in contrast to a $13.4 billion surplus the previous year.

A $6-billion favorable balance in trade with the U.S. brought strong pressure from the U.S. auto industry and unions for a reduction in exports of Japanese cars although an earlier voluntary restraint on television exports was dropped.

Masayoshi Ohira, Prime Minister since November 1978, died on June 12, 1980, and in national elections held June 22, the ruling Liberal Democrats reversed an eight-year decline in public support, winning a firm parliamentary majority. The party chose Zenko Suzuki, a little-known 66-year-old follower of Ohira, as the new Prime Minister.

Suzuki's first contact with the Reagan Administration, in May 1981, went badly as reports of a U.S.-Japan "alliance" and weapons build-up emerged from the White House, causing the resignation of Masayoshi Ito as Foreign Minister for "misinterpreting" events. The sinking of a Japanese freighter by a U.S. nuclear submarine in the China Sea on April 9 and the statement by Former U.S. Ambassador Edwin O. Reischauer that U.S. ships carrying nuclear weapons regularly entered Japanese ports in the 1960s despite the Constitutional ban so aroused public opinion that Secretary of State Alexander M. Haig, Jr., canceled plans to visit Tokyo on his Far East tour in June.

Announcement on June 19 that Japan's gross national product grew at a rate of nearly 5% for the fiscal year ending March 31 brought new demands for increased imports of manufactured goods by Japan, which international trade experts charged was still creating barriers against trade despite repeated promises by Tokyo to relax such restrictions. To placate the ailing U.S. automobile industry, Japan announced that it would limit exports of cars to the United States to 1,680,000 units for the year ending March 31, 1982.

The same figure was agreed to by Japan for the following year, and for the first time, Japanese automobile exports declined for the 12-month period ending March 31, 1982. In an effort to remove nontariff trade barriers, which U.S. businessmen held responsible for their inability to increase sales in Japan, the Suzuki government appointed a special ombudsman with authority to cut red tape. Despite this, Japan registered an average monthly trade surplus with the U.S. of $1.77 billion for the first half of 1982.

Under continued U.S. prodding, Tokyo announced a $707-million increase in defense spending for fiscal 1982 and $745 million for fiscal 1983, still below the target figure of 1% of the gross national product, which Suzuki pledged would be reached by 1985. A group of politicians and intellectuals appealed for a greater defense budget, pointing out that when the 1960 defense treaty was signed with the U.S., Japan's G.N.P. was only 8% of that of its partner. Now, they pointed out, the smaller country had advanced to more than half of the U.S. figure.

JORDAN

The Hashemite Kingdom of Jordan
Ruler: King Hussein I (1952)
Prime Minister: Mudar Badran (1980)
Area: 37,297 sq mi. (96,599 sq km)[1]
Population (est. 1982): 3,475,000 (average annual growth rate: 3.2%)
Density per square mile: 93.2
Capital: Amman
Largest cities (est. 1981): Amman, 650,000; **(est. 1977 by U.N.):** Zarka, 263,500; Irbid, 136,800
Monetary unit: Jordanian dinar
Language: Arabic
Religions: Islam, 93%; Christian, 7%
National name: Al Mamlaka al Urduniya al Hashemiyah
Literacy rate (1981): 55%
Economic summary: Gross national product (1980): $3.3 billion (East Bank only). Average annual growth rate (1970–79): 6.0%. Per capita income (1980): $1,420. Land used for agriculture: 11%; labor force: 23%; principal products: wheat, fruits, vegetables, olive oil. Labor force in industry: 67%; major products: phosphate, refined petroleum products, cement. Natural resources: phosphate, potash. Exports: fruits, vegetables, phosphate. Imports: petroleum products, textiles, capital goods, motor vehicles, foodstuffs. Major trading partners: U.S., U.K., West Germany, Japan, Lebanon, Saudi Arabia.

1. Includes territory occupied by Israel in 1967 war.

Geography. The Middle East kingdom of Jordan is bordered on the west by Israel and the Dead Sea, on the north by Syria, on the east by Iraq, and on the south Saudi Arabia. It is comparable in size to Indiana.

Arid hills and mountains make up most of the country. The southern section of the Jordan River flows through the country.

Government. Jordan is a constitutional monarchy with a bicameral parliament. Its Chamber of Deputies of 60 members is elected for four years by the people, and the 30 members of the Senate are appointed by the King.

All political parties were banned in 1957.

History. In biblical times, the country that is now Jordan contained the lands of Edom, Moab, Ammon, and Bashan. In A.D. 106 it became part of the Roman province of Arabia and in 633–36 was conquered by the Arabs.

Taken from the Turks by the British in World War I, Jordan (formerly known as Transjordan) was separated from the Palestine mandate in 1920, and in 1921, placed under the rule of Abdullah ibn Hussein.

In 1923, Britain recognized Jordan's independence, subject to the mandate. In 1946, grateful for Jordan's loyalty in World War II, Britain abolished the mandate. That part of Palestine occupied by Jordanian troops was formally incorporated by action of the Jordanian Parliament in 1950.

King Abdullah was assassinated in 1951. His son Talal was deposed as mentally ill the next year. Talal's son Hussein, born Nov. 14, 1935, succeeded him.

From the beginning of his reign, Hussein had to steer a careful course between his powerful neighbor to the west, Israel, and rising Arab nationalism, frequently a direct threat to his throne. Riots erupted when he joined the Central Treaty Organization (the Baghdad Pact) in 1955, and he incurred further unpopularity when Britain, France, and Israel attacked the Suez Canal in 1956, forcing him to place his army under nominal command of the United Arab Republic of Egypt and Syria.

The 1961 breakup of the UAR eased Arab national pressure on Hussein, who was the first to recognize Syria after it reclaimed its independence. Jordan was swept into the 1967 Arab-Israeli war, however, and lost the old city of Jerusalem and all of its territory west of the Jordan river, the West Bank. Embittered Palestinian guerrilla forces virtually took over sections of Jordan in the aftermath of defeat, and open warfare broke out between the Palestinians and government forces in 1970.

Despite intervention of Syrian tanks, Hussein's Bedouin army defeated the Palestinians, suffering heavy casualties. A U.S. military alert and Israeli armor massed on the Golan Heights contributed psychological weight, but the Jordanians alone drove out the Syrians and invited the departure of 12,000 Iraqui troops who had been in the country since the 1967 war. Ignoring protests from other Arab states, Hussein by mid-1971 crushed Palestinian strength in Jordan and shifted the problem to Lebanon, where many of the guerrillas had fled.

In October 1974, Hussein concurred in an Arab summit resolution calling for an independent Palestinian state and endorsing the Palestine Liberation Organization as the "sole legitimate representative of the Palestinian people." This apparent reversal of policy changed with the growing disillusion of Arab states with the P.L.O., however, and by 1977 Hussein referred again to the unity of people on both banks of the Jordan.

As Egypt and Israel neared final agreement on a peace treaty early in 1979, Hussein met with Yassir Arafat, the PLO leader, on March 17 and issued a joint statement of opposition. Although the U.S. pressed Jordan to break Arab ranks on the issue, Hussein elected to side with the great majority, cutting ties with Cairo and joining the boycott against Egypt.

On June 15, 1978, Hussein, who had celebrated his 25th anniversary on the throne, married Elizabeth Halaby, 26, daughter of Najeeb Halaby, former president of Pan American World Airways. In an unexpected gesture, the monarch's fourth wife —his previous wife was killed and the first two divorced—was proclaimed Queen and given the name Noor al-Hussein.

Hussein visited Washington in July, and despite his refusal to soften his opposition to the Camp David agreements, he won the Carter administration's promise to sell Jordan U.S. tanks.

In September 1980, Jordan declared itself with Iraq in its conflict with Iran and, despite threats from Syria, opened ports to war shipments for Iraq unable to go directly to Baghdad because of the blocking of the Shatt al-Arab waterway.

KAMPUCHEA

See Cambodia

KENYA

Republic of Kenya
President: Daniel arap Moi (1978)
Area: 224,960 sq mi. (582,646 sq km)
Population (est. 1982): 17,600,000 (average annual growth rate: 4.1%)
Density per square mile: 78.2
Capital: Nairobi
Largest cities (est. 1980): Nairobi, 835,000; Mombasa, 400,000
Monetary unit: Kenyan shilling
Languages: Swahili (official), Bantu, Kikuyu, English
Religions: Protestant, 33%; Roman Catholic, 17%; Islam, 24%; Animist
Literacy rate (1981): 27%
Member of Commonwealth of Nations
Economic summary: Gross national product (1980): $6.6 billion. Average annual growth rate (1970–79): 2.6%. Per capita income (1980): $420. Land used for agriculture: 10–15%; labor force in agriculture: 23%; principal products: coffee, sisal, tea, pyrethrum, cotton, livestock. Labor force in industry: 14%; major products: plastic goods, furniture, batteries, textiles, soap, cigarettes, refined oil. Natural resources: wildlife. Exports: coffee, tea, livestock products, pyrethrum, tanning extract. Imports: machinery, transport equipment, crude oil, paper and paper products, iron and steel products, textiles. Major trading partners: Western European countries, Japan, Iran, U.S., Zambia, Uganda.

Geography. Kenya lies on the equator in east central Africa on the coast of the Indian Ocean. It is twice the size of Nevada. Kenya's neighbors are Tanzania, Uganda, the Sudan, Ethiopia, and Somalia.

In the north, the land is arid; the southwestern corner is in the fertile Lake Victoria Basin; and a length of the eastern depression of Great Rift Valley separates western highlands from those that rise from the lowland coastal strip. Large game reserves have been developed.

Government. Under its Constitution of 1963, amended in 1964, Kenya has a one-house National Assembly of 171 members, elected for five years by universal suffrage. Since 1969, the president has been chosen by a general election.

The Kenya African National Union, led by the president, is the only political party.

President Jomo Kenyatta died in his sleep on Aug. 22, 1978. Vice President Daniel Arap Moi was elected to succeed him on Oct. 10.

History. Kenya, formerly a British colony and protectorate, was made a crown colony in 1920. The whites' domination of the rich plateau area, the White Highlands, long regarded by the Kikiyu people as their territory, was a factor leading to native terrorism, called the Mau Mau movement, in 1952. In 1954 the British began preparing the territory for African rule and independence. In 1961 Jomo Kenyatta was freed from banishment to become leader of the Kenya African National Union.

Internal self-government was granted in 1963; Kenya became independent on Dec. 12, 1963, with Kenyatta the first president. Kenya obtained economic and technical assistance from Communist China beginning in 1964 and later a World Bank loan.

In 1967, Kenya, Uganda, and Tanzania agreed to establish an East African trading community and a development bank. Kenya also sought to end dominance of retail trade by the Indian community of 188,000. In 1968 it began a drive against the Asians, and 20,000 left the country. In 1972, Kenyatta ordered all Asians with Kenyan passports to leave, allegedly because of foreign-currency manipulations.

KIRIBATI

Republic of Kiribati
Sovereign: Queen Elizabeth II
Governor General: Reginald J. Wallace (1980)
President: Ieremia Tabai (1979)
Area: 264 sq mi. (683 sq km)
Population (est. 1982): 60,000 (average annual growth rate: 1.1%)
Density per square mile: 227.3
Capital (est. 1974): Bairiki (on Tarawa Atoll), 17,100
Monetary unit: Australian dollar
Language: English
Religions: Roman Catholic, 48%; Protestant, 45%
Member of Commonwealth of Nations
Literacy rate: Not known
Economic summary: Gross national product (1980): $50 million. Per Capita Income (1980): $770. Principal agricultural products: copra, vegetables. Exports: phosphates, copra. Imports: foodstuffs, fuel, transportation equipment. Major trading partners: New Zealand, Australia.

Geography. Kiribati, formerly the Gilbert Islands, consists of three widely separated main groups of Southwest Pacific islands, the Gilberts on the equator, the Phoenix Islands to the east, and the Line Islands further east. Ocean Island, producer of phosphates, which constitute 99% of the new nation's annual income of $18 million, is also included in the two million square miles of ocean, which will give Kiribati an important fishery resource.

Government. The president holds executive power. The legislature consists of a House Assembly with 37 members.

History. A British protectorate since 1892, the Gilbert and Ellice Islands became a colony in 1915–16. The two island groups were separated in 1975 and given internal self-government.

Tarawa and others of the Gilbert group were occupied by Japan during World War II. Tarawa was the site of one of the bloodiest battles in U.S. Marine Corps history when Marines landed in November 1943 to dislodge the Japanese defenders.

Princess Anne, representing Queen Elizabeth II, presented the independence documents to the new government on July 12, 1979.

KOREA, NORTH

Democratic People's Republic of Korea
President: Marshal Kim Il Sung (1972)
Premier: Yi Chong Ok (1977)
Area: 46,768 sq mi. (121,129 sq km)
Population (est. 1982): 18,750,000 (average annual growth rate: 3.2%)
Density per square mile: 400.9
Capital and largest city (est. 1976): Pyongyang, 1,500,000
Monetary unit: Won
Language: Korean
Religions: None
National name: Chosun Minchu-chui Inmin Konghwa-guk
Literacy rate (1981): 90% (est.)
Economic summary: Gross national product (1980): $19.7 billion. Average annual growth rate (1970–79): 3.8%. Per capita income (1979): $750. Land used for agriculture: 17%; labor force, 48%; principal products: corn, rice, vegetables. Major industrial products: machines, electric power, chemicals, textiles, processed foods, metallurgical products. Natural resources: coal, iron ore. Exports: minerals, chemical and metallurgical products. Imports: machinery and equipment, petroleum, foodstuffs, coking coal. Major trading partners: U.S.S.R., China, Japan.

Geography. Korea is a 600-mile (966 km) peninsula jutting from Manchuria and China (and a small portion of the U.S.S.R.) into the Sea of Japan and the Yellow Sea off eastern Asia. North Korea occupies an area slightly smaller than Pennsylvania north of the 38th parallel.

The country is almost completely covered by a series of north-south mountain ranges separated by narrow valleys. The Yalu River forms part of the northern border with Manchuria.

Government. The elected Supreme People's Assembly, as the chief organ of government, chooses a Presidium and a Cabinet. The Cabinet, which exercises executive authority, is subject to approval by the Assembly and the Presidium.

The Korean Workers (Communist) Party, led by President Kim Il Sung, is the only political party.

History. According to myth, Korea was founded in 2333 B.C. by Tangun. In the 17th century, it became a vassal of China and was isolated from all but Chinese influence and contact until 1876, when Japan forced Korea to negotiate a commercial treaty, opening the land to the U. S. and Europe. Japan achieved control as the result of its war with China (1894–95) and with Russia (1904–05) and annexed Korea in 1910. Japan developed the country but never won over the Korean nationalists.

After the Japanese surrender in 1945, the country was divided into two occupation zones, the U.S.S.R. north of and the U.S. south of the 38th parallel. When the cold war developed between the U.S. and U.S.S.R., trade between the zones was cut off. In 1948, the division between the zones was made permanent with the establishment of separate regimes in the north and south. By mid-1949, the U.S. and U.S.S.R. withdrew all troops. The Democratic People's Republic of Korea (North Korea) was established on May 1, 1948. The Communist Party, headed by Kim Il Sung, was established in power.

On June 25, 1950, the North Korean army launched a surprise attack on South Korea. On June 26, the U.N. Security Council condemned the invasion as aggression and ordered withdrawal of the invading forces. On June 27, President Harry S. Truman ordered air and naval units into action to enforce the U.N. order. The British government did the same, and soon a multinational U.N. command was set up to aid the South Koreans. The North Korean invaders took Seoul and pushed the South Koreans into the southeast corner of their country.

Gen. Douglas MacArthur, U.N. commander, made an amphibious landing at Inchon on September 15 behind the North Korean lines, which resulted in the complete rout of the North Korean army. The U.N. forces drove north across the 38th parallel, approaching the Yalu River. Then Communist China entered the war, forcing the U.N. forces into headlong retreat. Seoul was lost again, then regained; ultimately the war stabilized near the 38th parallel but dragged on for two years while the belligerents negotiated. An armistice was agreed to on July 27, 1953.

North Korea became embroiled with the U.S. again on Jan. 23, 1968, when it seized the American intelligence ship *Pueblo* and its crew of 83. After more than a year, the crew was released.

When a U.S. helicopter strayed across the 38th parallel July 13, 1977, and was shot down by North Koreans, with the loss of three crewmen, the reaction was much more restrained. President Carter acknowledged U.S. error and, after seven hours of talks at Panmunjom, the North Koreans sent back the three bodies and the lone survivor.

Although Kim appears to be revered, economic troubles have beset his rigidly collectivist country. World bankers say a record of unpaid accounts due the U.S.S.R., as well as non-Communist states, has demolished North Korea's international credit standing. Its armed forces, numbering 467,000, are about three fourths of the South's military establishment, but the North's 600-plane air force holds a 3-to-1 edge over its potential foe, who has relied on U.S. air support in the event of war.

President Carter, visiting Seoul from June 29 to July 1, 1979, proposed that the U.S., North Korea, and South Korea meet "to promote dialogue and reduce tensions in the area," possibly leading to reunification of the two Koreas. Pyongyang's official party newspaper rejected the proposal, saying the North favors reunification talks but without the "alien interference" of the U.S.

Kim again rejected as a 'foolish burlesque" an invitation on Jan. 12, 1981, by South Korea's military chief, Chun Doo Hwan, to hold reunification talks in Seoul. Kim refused again when Chun repeated the invitation on March 3 during his inauguration as President of the Southern republic.

KOREA, SOUTH

Republic of Korea
President: Chun Doo Hwan (1980)
Premier: Yoo Chang Soon (1982)
Area: 38,031 sq mi. (98,500 sq km)
Population (est. 1982): 39,350,000 (average annual growth rate: 1.6%)
Density per square mile: 1,034.7
Capital: Seoul
Largest cities (est. 1980): Seoul, 8,400,000; Pusan, 3,160,000; Taegu, 1,600,000; Inchon, 1,100,000; Kwangju, 725,000; Taejon, 650,000; Chonju, 370,000; **(1975 census):** Pusan, 2,453,200; Taegu, 1,310,800; Inchon, 800,000; Kwangju, 607,700; Taejon, 506,700; Chonju, 311,400
Monetary unit: Won
Language: Korean
Religions: Buddhist, 39%; Christian, 19%; Confucian, 13%
National name: Dae Han Min Kook
Literacy rate (1981): 90%
Economic summary: Gross national product (1980): $58.6 billion. Average annual growth rate (1970–79): 8.1%. Per capita income (1980): $1,520. Land used for agriculture: 23%; labor force, including fishing, 36%; principal products: rice, barley. Labor force in industry: 24%; major products: clothing and textiles, processed foods, chemical fertilizers, chemicals, plywood, steel, electronics equipment. Natural resources: iron and copper ore, tungsten, graphite, limestone, coal, gold, silver. Exports: clothing and textiles, electric machinery, footwear, steel. Imports: oil, steel, grains, textiles, organic chemicals, machinery. Major trading partners: U.S., Japan.

Geography. Slightly larger than Indiana, South Korea lies below the 38th parallel on the Korean peninsula. It is mountainous in the east; in the west and south are many harbors on the mainland and offshore islands.

Government. A national referendum in October 1980 approved a new Constitution that provides for election of the President by an electoral college chosen by popular vote. The term of office is for seven years, limited to one term. A unicameral National Assembly has 276 members, 184 elected directly by popular vote, the remainder appointed in proportion to party strength in the election.

Major parties are the Democratic Justice Party (151 of 276 National Assembly seats), led by Premier Yoo Chang Soon; the opposition Democratic Korea Party (81 seats), led by Yoo Chi Song, and the Korea National Party (25 seats); Independents hold 11 seats and the remaining eight are held by splinter parties.

History. South Korea came into being in the aftermath of World War II as the result of a 1945 agreement making the 38th parallel the boundary between a northern zone occupied by the U.S.S.R. and a southern zone occupied by U.S. forces. (For details, *see* North Korea.)

Elections were held in the U.S. zone in 1948 for a national assembly, which adopted a republican Constitution and elected Syngman Rhee president. The new republic was proclaimed on August 15 and was recognized as the legal government of Korea by the U.N. on Dec. 12, 1948.

On June 25, 1950, South Korea was attacked by North Korean Communist forces. U.S. armed intervention was ordered on June 27 by President Harry S. Truman, and on the same day the U.N. invoked military sanctions against North Korea. Gen. Douglas MacArthur was named commander of the U.N.

forces. U.S. and South Korean troops fought a heroic holding action but, by the first week of August, they had been forced back to a 4,000-square-mile beachhead in southeast Korea.

There they stood off superior North Korean forces until September 15, when a major U.N. amphibious attack was launched far behind the Communist lines at Inchon, port of Seoul. By September 30, U.N. forces were in complete control of South Korea. They then invaded North Korea and were nearing the Manchurian and Siberian borders when several hundred thousand Chinese Communist troops entered the conflict in late October. U.N. forces were then forced to retreat below the 38th parallel.

On May 24, 1951, U.N. forces recrossed the parallel and had made important new inroads into North Korea when truce negotiations began on July 10. An armistice was finally signed at Panmunjom on July 27, 1953, leaving a devastated Korea in need of large-scale rehabilitation.

The U.S. and South Korea signed a mutual-defense treaty on Oct. 1, 1953.

Rhee, president since 1948, resigned in 1960 in the face of rising disorders. PoSun Yun was elected to succeed him, but political instability continued. In 1961, Gen. Park Chung Hee took power. He built up the country, maintaining an average economic growth rate of 8.5%. The U.S. stepped up military aid, building up South Korea's armed forces to 600,000 men. The South Koreans sent 50,000 troops to Vietnam, at U.S. expense.

In mid-1972, following President Nixon's summit meetings in Moscow and Peking, the two Koreas issued a mutual declaration setting a goal of peaceful reunification. (For details, *see* Korea, North).

In 1977, tension between Seoul and Washington also arose over human rights as South Korean dissidents appealed for U.S. support in their demands that Park rescind both the 1972 Constitution and his 1975 emergency powers. Park responded to pressure by releasing 14 political detainees.

A growing scandal over Korean bribery of U.S. Congressmen accelerated in 1977 with testimony by a defecting ex-Director of the KCIA who named a Washington influence man, Tongsun Park, as a KCIA agent. Two former Democratic Representatives, Richard T. Hanna of California and Otto E. Passman of Louisiana, were indicted in 1978 for accepting bribes, with Hanna sentenced to six months in prison.

A Congressional investigation in 1978 charged four Democratic Representatives, Charles H. Wilson, Edward R. Roybal, and John J. McFall of California, and Edward J. Patten of New Jersey, with having accepted money improperly from Park.

Park's assassination on Oct. 26, 1979, by Kim Jae Kyu, head of the Korean Central Intelligence Agency, brought a liberalizing trend as Choi Kyu Hah, the new President, freed imprisoned dissidents. The release of opposition leader Kim Dae Jung in February 1980 generated anti-government demonstrations that turned into riots by May. Choi resigned on Aug. 16. Chun Doo Wha, head of a military Special Committee for National Security Measures, was the sole candidate as the electoral college confirmed him as President on Aug. 27. On Sept. 17, Kim Dae Jung was sentenced to death by a military court on charges of high treason. Chun commuted the sentence on Jan. 23, 1981, and lifted martial law the next day.

Elected to a full seven-year term on Feb. 11, Chun had visited Washington on Feb. 2 to receive President Reagan's assurance that U.S. troops would remain in South Korea and that the sale of U.S. F-16 jet aircraft would be authorized to modernize the Republic's air force. General elections on March 25 gave the ruling Democratic Justice Party a solid majority of the National Assembly.

Chun marked his first anniversary in March 1982 by freeing 2,863 political prisoners, but renewed political unrest in Pusan two weeks later brought a government crackdown. For the first time since the Korean War, curfew was lifted in Seoul in preparation for the nation's role as host of the 1988 Summer Olympic Games, as a major refurbishing of the capital began.

KUWAIT

State of Kuwait

Emir: Sheik Jaber al-Ahmad al-Sabah (1977)
Prime Minister: Sheik Sa'ad Abdullah al-Sabah (1978)
Area: 7,780 sq mi. (20,150 sq km)
Population (est. 1982): 1,550,000 (average annual growth rate: 6.2%)
Density per square mile: 199.2
Capital (est. 1980): Kuwait, 60,000
Largest city (est. 1980): Hawalli, 152,000
Monetary unit: Kuwaiti dinar
Languages: Arabic and English
Religions: Islam, 95%; Christian, 5%
National name: Dowlat al Kuwait
Literacy rate (1981): 60%
Economic summary: Gross national product (1980): $30.9 billion. Average annual growth rate (1970–79): 1.4%. Per capita income (1980): $22,840. Land used for agriculture: 1%. Labor force in industry: 22%; major products: crude and refined oil, fertilizer, chemicals, building materials, shrimp. Natural resources: petroleum, fish, shrimp. Exports: crude and refined petroleum, shrimp. Imports: foodstuffs, automobiles, building materials, machinery, textiles. Major trading partners: U.S., Japan, U.K., West Germany.

Geography. Kuwait is situated northeast of Saudi Arabia at the northern end of the Persian Gulf, south of Iraq. It is slightly larger than Hawaii. The low-lying land is mainly sandy and barren.

Government. Sheik Jaber al-Ahmad al-Sabah rules as Emir of Kuwait and appoints the Prime Minister, who appoints his Cabinet (Council of Ministers). The National Assembly, consists of 50 members elected by adult males. There are no political parties in Kuwait.

History. Kuwait obtained British protection in 1897 when the Sheik feared that the Turks would take over the area. In 1961, Britain ended the protectorate, giving Kuwait independence, but agreed to give military aid on request. Iraq immediately threatened to occupy the area and Sheik Sabah al-Salem al-Sabah called in British troops in 1961. Soon afterward the Arab League sent in troops, replacing the British. The prize was oil.

Oil was discovered in the 1930s. Kuwait proved to have 20% of the world's known oil resources. It has been a major producer since 1946, the world's second largest oil exporter, with the main concession held by a British-American concern. The Sheik, who gets half the profits, devotes most of them to the education, welfare, and modernization of his kingdom. In 1966, Sheik Sabah designated a relative, Jaber al-Ahmad al-Sabah, as his successor.

By 1968, the sheikdom had established a model welfare state, and it sought to establish dominance among the sheikdoms and emirates of the Persian Gulf.

Kuwait contributed generously to Egypt and Jordan after the 1967 war with Israel and supported the 1973 war against Israel with funds and by joining the Arab oil boycott of Western nations.

In 1975, the government nationalized Kuwaiti operations of Gulf Oil and British Petroleum. The acquisition, which cost about $180 million, gave Kuwait full control of an estimated 60 billion barrels of petroleum reserves.

In 1981, the World Bank classed Kuwait as the world's richest country, with a per capita gross national product of $15,970.

LAOS

Lao People's Democratic Republic
President: Souphanouvong (1975)
Premier: Kaysone Phomvihane (1975)
Area: 91,429 sq mi. (236,800 sq km)
Population (est. 1982): 3,900,000 (average annual growth rate: 1.7%)
Density per square mile: 42.7
Capital and largest city (est. 1978): Vientiane, 200,000
Monetary unit: New kip
Languages: Lao (official); French, English
Religion: Buddhist
Literacy rate (1981): 15%
Economic summary: Gross national product: (1980): $300 million. Per capita income (1977): $70. Land used for agriculture, 8%; labor force, 85%; principal products: rice, corn, vegetables. Major industrial products: tin, timber, tobacco, textiles, electric power. Natural resources: tin, timber, hydroelectric power. Exports: electric power, forest products, tin concentrates, coffee. Imports: rice, foodstuffs, petroleum products, machinery, transport equipment. Major trading partners: Thailand, U.S.S.R., Malaysia, France, China, Vietnam.

Geography. A landlocked nation in Southeast Asia occupying the northwestern portion of the Indochinese peninsula, Laos is surrounded by China, Vietnam, Cambodia, Thailand, and Burma. It is twice the size of Pennsylvania.

Laos is a mountainous country, especially in the north, where peaks rise above 8,000 feet (2,438 m). Dense forests cover the northern and eastern areas. The Mekong River, which forms the boundary with Burma and Thailand, flows through the country for 300 miles (483 km) of its course.

Government. Laos is a people's democratic republic with executive power in the hands of the premier. The monarchy was abolished Dec. 2, 1975, when the Pathet Lao ousted a coalition government and King Sisavang Vatthana abdicated. The King was appointed "Supreme Adviser" to the President, the former Prince Souphanouvong. Former Prince Souvanna Phouma, Premier since 1962, was made an "adviser" to the government. The Lao People's Revolutionary Party (Pathet Lao), led by President Souphanouvong and Premier Kaysone Phomvihane, is the only political party.

History. Laos became a French protectorate in 1893, and the territory was incorporated into the union of Indochina. A strong nationalist movement developed during World War II, but France reestablished control in 1946 and made the King of Luang Prabang constitutional monarch of all Laos. France granted semiautonomy in 1949 and then, spurred by the Viet Minh rebellion in Vietnam, full independence within the French Union in 1950. In 1951, Prince Souphanouvong organized the Pathet Lao, a Communist independence movement, in North Vietnam. The Viet Minh in 1953 established the Pathet Lao in power at Samneua. Viet Minh and Pathet Lao forces invaded central Laos, and civil war resulted.

By the Geneva agreements of 1954 and an armistice of 1955, two northern provinces were given the Pathet Lao, the royal regime the rest. Full sovereignty was given the kingdom by the Paris agreements of Dec. 29, 1954. In 1957, Prince Souvanna Phouma, the royal Premier, and the Pathet Lao leader, Prince Souphanouvong, the Premier's half-brother, agreed to re-establishment of a unified government, with Pathet Lao participation and integration of Pathet Lao forces into the royal army. The agreement broke down in 1959, and armed conflict broke out again.

In 1960, the struggle became three-way as Gen. Phoumi Nosavan, controlling the bulk of the royal army, set up in the south a pro-Western revolutionary government headed by Prince Boun Gum. General Phoumi took Vientiane in December, driving Souvanna Phouma into exile in Cambodia. The Soviet bloc supported Souvanna Phouma. In 1961, a cease-fire was arranged and the three princes agreed to a coalition government headed by Souvanna Phouma.

But North Vietnam, the U.S. (in the form of Central Intelligence Agency personnel), and China remained active in Laos after the settlement. North Vietnam used a supply line (Ho Chi Minh trail) running down the mountain valleys of eastern Laos into Cambodia and South Vietnam, particularly after the U.S.-South Vietnamese incursion into Cambodia in 1970 stopped supplies via Cambodian seaports.

An agreement, reached in 1973 revived coalition government. Royal Laotian rule continued in populous areas, the Pathet Lao controlled the mountainous east, and the two groups exercised joint rule over Vientiane Province. With Souvanna Phouma as premier and Souphanouvong as president of a 42-member National Political Council representing both factions, joint operation of the government began.

Laotian officials confirmed in March 1979 the presence of 30,000 Vietnamese troops in Laos and their use of the country as a staging area for the Vietnamese invasion of Cambodia. They also confirmed that 1,000 Laotian troops were in Cambodia in support of the Heng Samrin regime, which overthrew the Pol Pot government in January.

LEBANON

Republic of Lebanon
President: Amin Gemayel (1982)
Premier: Shafiq al-Wazan (1980)
Area: 4,015 sq mi. (10,400 sq km)
Population (est. 1982): 2,700,000 (average annual growth rate: 2.6%)
Density per square mile: 672.5
Capital: Beirut
Largest cities (est. 1975): Beirut, 1,172,000; (est. 1964): Tripoli, 127,600

Monetary unit: Lebanese pound
Languages: Arabic (official); French, English
Religions: Christian and Islam
National name: Al-Joumhouriya al-Lubnaniya
Literacy rate (1981): 86%
Economic summary: Gross national product: n.a. Per capita income: n.a. Land used for agriculture: 27%; labor force: 49%; principal products: fruits, wheat, corn, barley, potatoes, tobacco, olives, onions. Labor force in industry: 11%; major products: processed foods, textiles, cement, chemicals, refined oil; tourism. Exports: fruits, vegetables, textiles. Imports: metals, machinery, foodstuffs. Major trading partners: U.S., Western European and Arab countries.

Geography. Lebanon lies at the eastern end of the Mediterranean Sea north of Israel and west of Syria. It is four fifths the size of Connecticut.

The Lebanon Mountains, which parallel the coast on the west, cover most of the country, while on the eastern border is the Anti-Lebanon range. Between the two lies the El Bika Valley, the principal agricultural area.

Government. Lebanon is governed by a President, elected by Parliament for a six-year term, and a Cabinet of Ministers appointed by the President but responsible to Parliament.

Parliament has 99 members elected for a four-year term by universal suffrage and chosen by proportional division of religious groups.

Party breakdown of the Chamber of Deputies is difficult because of the religious groupings required by law and because many deputies join in major parliamentary blocs.

History. In ancient times Lebanon was the mountainous hinterland of the Phoenician coast towns. From the 7th to the 11th century there infiltrated into southern Lebanon the heretics of Islam, who finally coalesced into the Druse community.

In the 19th century the Turkish Sultanate encouraged the Druses to wage civil war against the Christian Maronites. After a massacre of 2,500 Christians in 1860, Lebanon was occupied by the French for a year. From 1864 to 1914, a Christian military government ruled the area under nominal Turkish sovereignty. After World War I, France received a League of Nations mandate over Syria and Lebanon. The French drew a Lebanese border in 1920 to offset predominantly Moslem Syria and proclaimed the area a republic under French control on May 23, 1926. Complete independence came on Nov. 26, 1941. Lebanon joined the Arab League and took part in the invasion of Palestine on May 15, 1948.

In 1958, a civil war broke out, with the Moslems Kamal Jumblatt and Saeb Salam leading the opposition to the Maronite Christian government. Threatened with defeat, President Camille Chamoun obtained the intervention of U.S. military forces. In September, a Maronite Christian military man, Gen. Fouad Chehab, took over the presidency. After a U.N. resolution demanded it, the U.S. forces withdrew.

Palestinian guerrillas using Lebanese territory drew Lebanon into conflict with Israel. Terrorist assaults on Israel's northern settlements drew punitive raids against guerrillas in Lebanon by Israeli.

Intensifying civil war through 1976 led to the ousting of President Suleiman Franjieh by Parliament in May. Franjieh refused to step down until the end of his six-year term in October when his successor, Elias Sarkis, took office.

At the time of Sarkis' inauguration, Lebanon was divided into a northern sector, controlled by Syrian troops who had entered the country to restore order, and a coastal region under Christian control, with enclaves where leftist Moslems and the Palestine Liberation Organization dominated. With the economy shattered and an estimated 40,000 dead in 18 months of war, many felt that the country might be dismembered.

A new crisis began for Lebanon on March 14, 1978, with the invasion of Israeli forces across the entire 60-mile northern border. The invasion was in retaliation for a PLO terrorist raid on Israel and the chief targets were PLO bases in southern Lebanon. On March 19, the U.N. Security Council called for immediate withdrawal and authorized a 4,000-man peace-keeping force to occupy the area, a force later enlarged to 6,000.

Israeli troops withdrew by June but turned over more strongpoints to Lebanese Christian militia than to UNIFIL, the U.N. force. Israel asserted that UNIFIL was allowing PLO guerrillas to infiltrate the border region, threatening Israel as well as the Lebanese Christians in the area. Efforts to establish a Lebanese army "presence" in southern Lebanon failed.

Tension escalated in April 1981 when Israeli jets intervened for the first time in fighting between Syrian troops and Christian militia east of Beirut, shooting down two Syrian helicopters. Syria then moved Soviet surface-to-air (SAM-6) missiles into the Bekaa Valley and Israel announced that it would use force if necessary to remove them. While a special U.S. Mideast peace envoy, Philip C. Habib, sought to mediate, Israel on July 17 bombed a densely populated section of Beirut, claiming that it was done in retaliation for PLO rockets and artillery fired from Lebanon into northern Israel.

The bombing left 300 dead and 800 wounded and brought an appeal by the Security Council for a cease-fire. Not until July 24 was Habib able to win Begin's consent to a cease-fire, difficult to arrange because the Israeli Prime Minister refused to negotiate with the PLO.

On June 6, 1982, Lebanon suffered a total invasion by Israel, bent on revenge for a PLO attack on the Israeli ambassador to London. Within four days, the invaders had surrounded Beirut after destroying Tyre and Sidon, two coastal strongholds of the Palestinian guerrillas. The Israelis laid siege to Moslem West Beirut, where some 5,000 or 6,000 PLO guerrillas were trapped, and pounded the city with bombs and artillery.

Habib was finally able to negotiate the dispersal of most of the PLO to other Arab nations and Israel pulled back some of its forces. The violence seemed to have come to an end when, on Sept. 14, Bashir Gemayel, the 34-year-old President-elect, was killed when a bomb destroyed his Phalangist Party headquarters, resulting in the death of 26 others.

The day after Gemayel's assassination, Israel troops moved into west Beirut in force. On Sept. 17 it was revealed that hundreds of Palestinians had been massacred in two refugee camps, reportedly by Christian militiamen. Israel denied responsibility for the killings although its troops had been stationed in the area. Despite worldwide shock, at first Israel refused to authorize an inquiry into the incident, but bowing to public outrage, later ordered a full-scale investigation.

On Sept. 20, Amin Gemayel, older brother of Bashir Gemayel, was elected President by the parliament.

cally abdicated" by siding with the opposition party, exiled him to the Netherlands, and named his Queen and her seven-year-old son as Regent.

The King returned after a compromise with Jonathan in which the new Constitution would name him head of state but forbid his participation in politics.

LESOTHO

Kingdom of Lesotho
Sovereign: King Moshoeshoe II (1966)
Prime Minister: Chief Leabua Jonathan (1966)
Area: 11,720 sq mi. (30,355 sq km)
Population (est. 1982): 1,400,000 (average annual growth rate: 2.2%)
Density per square mile: 119.5
Capital and largest city (est. 1976): Maseru, 14,700
Monetary unit: Loti
Languages: English and Sesotho (official)
Religions: Roman Catholic, 39%; Lesotho Evangelical Church, 24%; Anglican, 10%; non-Christian, 18%
Member of Commonwealth of Nations
Literacy rate (1981): 40%
Economic summary: Gross national product (1980): $520 million. Average annual growth rate (1970–79): 9.5%. Per capita income (1980): $390. Land used for agriculture: 15%; labor force: 87%; principal products: corn, wheat, sorghum, barley, livestock. Labor force in industry: 2%. Natural resources: diamonds. Exports: wool, mohair, wheat, cattle, diamonds, hides and skins. Imports: corn, building materials, clothing, vehicles, machinery. Major trading partner: South Africa.

Geography. Mountainous Lesotho, the size of Maryland, is surrounded by the Republic of South Africa in the east central part of that country except for short borders on the east and south with two discontinuous units of the Republic of Transkei. The Drakensberg Mountains in the east are Lesotho's principal chain. Elsewhere the region consists of rocky tableland.

Government. There is a 93-member interim National Assembly made up of 60 representatives of various political parties, 22 leading chiefs, and 11 appointees.

The major political parties are the Basotho National Party, led by Prime Minister Leabua Jonathan and the Basutoland Congress Party led by G. P. Ramoreboli.

History. Lesotho (formerly Basutoland) was constituted a native state under British protection by a treaty signed with the native chief Moshesh in 1843. It was annexed to Cape Colony in 1871, but in 1884 it was restored to direct control by the Crown.

The colony of Basutoland became the independent nation of Lesotho on Oct. 4, 1966.

In the 1970 elections, Ntsu Mokhehle, head of the Basutoland Congress Party, claimed a victory, but Jonathan declared a state of emergency, suspended the Constitution, and arrested Mokhehle. The major issue in the election was relations with South Africa, with Jonathan for close ties to the surrounding white nation, while Mokhehle was for a more independent policy. Jonathan jailed 45 opposition politicians, declared the King had "techni-

LIBERIA

Republic of Liberia
President: Gen. Samuel K. Doe (1980)
Area: 43,000 sq mi. (111,370 sq km)
Population (est. 1982): 2,150,000 (average annual growth rate: 3.2%)
Density per square mile: 50.0
Capital and largest city (est. 1978): Monrovia, 229,300
Monetary unit: Liberian dollar
Languages: English (official) and tribal dialects
Religions: Protestant Christian, Islam, Catholic, Animist
Literacy rate (1981): 24%
Economic summary: Gross national product (1980): $980 million. Average annual growth rate (1970–79): 0.5%. Per capita income (1980): $520. Land used for agriculture: 20%; labor force: 75%; principal products: rubber, rice, palm oil, cassava, coffee, cocoa. Labor force in industry: 25%; major products: iron ore, diamonds, processed rubber, processed food, construction materials. Natural resources: iron ore, rubber, timber, diamonds. Exports: iron ore, rubber, timber, diamonds. Imports: machinery, petroleum products, transport equipment, foodstuffs. Major trading partners: U.S., West Germany, Netherlands, Italy, Belgium.

Geography. Lying on the Atlantic in the southern part of West Africa, Liberia is bordered by Sierra Leone, Guinea, and the Ivory Coast. It is comparable in size to Tennessee.

Most of the country is a plateau covered by dense tropical forests, which thrive under an annual rainfall of about 160 inches a year.

Government. Since April 25, 1980, Liberia has been under military rule by the 17-member People's Redemptive Council, which suspended the Constitution after overthrowing the civilian government.

History. Liberia was founded in 1822 as a result of the efforts of the American Colonization Society to settle freed American slaves in West Africa. In 1847, it became the Free and Independent Republic of Liberia.

The government of Africa's first republic was modeled after that of the United States, and Joseph J. Roberts of Virginia was elected the first president. He laid the foundations of a modern state and initiated efforts, never too successful but pursued for more than a century, to bring the aboriginal inhabitants of the territory to the level of the emigrants. The English-speaking descendants of U.S. blacks, known as Americo-Liberians, were the intellectual and ruling class. The indigenous inhabitants, divided, constitute 99% of the population.

The country's only big enterprises are the million-acre concession granted in 1925 to the Firestone Plantations Co. for rubber cultivation, and a large iron ore concession developed by the Republic Steel Corp., beginning in 1951. After 1920, considerable progress was made toward opening up the interior, a process that was spurred in 1951 by the establishment of a 43-mile (69-km) railroad to the Bomi Hills from Monrovia.

In July 1971, while serving his sixth term as president, William V. S. Tubman died following surgery and was succeeded by his long-time associate, Vice President William R. Tolbert, Jr.

Tolbert was ousted in a military coup carried out April 12, 1980, by army enlisted men led by Master Sgt. Samuel K. Doe. Tolbert and 27 other high officials were executed and a civilian Cabinet was briefly installed. But on April 25, the 17-member People's Redemptive Council, an exclusively military body, suspended the Constitution and assumed all executive power. Doe and his colleagues based their action on the grievances of "native" Liberians against corruption and misrule by the Americo-Liberians who had ruled the country since its founding.

LIBYA

Socialist People's Libyan Arab Jamahiriya
Head of State: Col. Muammar el-Qaddafi (1969)
Secretary-General of the General People's Congress: Muhammad al-Zarruq Rajah (1981)
Premier: Jadallah Azzuz et Talhi (1979)
Area: 679,536 sq mi. (1,759,998 sq km)
Population (est. 1982): 3,250,000 (average annual growth rate: 5.4%)
Density per square mile: 4.8
Capital: Tripoli
Largest cities (est. 1980): Tripoli, 1,000,000; **(1973 census):** Benghazi, 282,192
Monetary unit: Libyan dinar
Language: Arabic
Religion: Islam
National name: Al-Jumhuria al-Arabia al-Libya
Literacy rate (1981): 35%
Economic summary: Gross national product (1980): $25.7 billion. Average annual growth rate (1970–79): −1.6%. Per capita income (1980): $8,640. Land used for agriculture: 7%; labor force: 20%; principal products: wheat, barley, olives, dates, citrus fruits, peanuts. Labor force in industry: 10%; major products: petroleum, processed foods, textiles, handicrafts. Natural resources: petroleum, natural gas. Export: petroleum. Imports: machinery, foodstuffs, manufactured goods. Major trading partners: Italy, West Germany, U.S., U.K., France.

Geography. Libya stretches along the northeastern coast of Africa between Tunisia and Algeria on the west and Egypt on the east; to the south are the Sudan, Chad, and Niger. It is one sixth larger than Alaska.

A greater part of the country lies within the Sahara. Along the Mediterranean coast and farther inland is arable plateau land.

Government. In a bloodless coup d'etat on Sept. 1, 1969, the military seized power in Libya. King Idris I, who had ruled since 1951, was deposed and the Libyan Arab Republic proclaimed. The official name was changed in 1977 to the Socialist People's Libyan Arab Jamahiriya. The Revolutionary Council that had governed since the coup was renamed the General Secretariat of the General People's Congress. The Arab Socialist Union Organization is the only political party.

History. Libya was a part of the Turkish dominions from the 16th century until 1911. Following the outbreak of hostilities between Italy and Turkey in that year, Italian troops occupied Tripoli; Italian sovereignty was recognized in 1912.

Libya was the scene of much desert fighting during World War II. After the fall of Tripoli on Jan. 23, 1943, it came under Allied administration. In 1949, the U.N. voted that Libya should become independent by 1952.

Discovery of oil in the Libyan Desert promised financial stability and funds for economic development.

On July 21, 1977, a four-day war broke out between Libya and Egypt, with Egypt charging that Libyans had attacked a frontier post. Superior Egyptian air power and armor inflicted losses on their opponents and the clash ended after Algerian President Houari Boumediène intervened as peacemaker.

Another military adventure by President Muammar el-Qaddafi ended ignominiously in April 1979 with the defeat of a Libyan force of 2,000 sent to the aid of Uganda's President Idi Amin against Ugandan rebels and Tanzanian forces. Qaddafi offered asylum to the ousted Amin and his family.

The United States closed its embassy in Tripoli on Feb. 7 amid growing U.S.-Libyan tension. Four members of the Libyan embassy in Washington were expelled on May 11 for threatening Libyan students in the United States.

Libyan troops supporting Chad's President Goukoumi Oueddi entered the capital city of Djamena on Dec. 16, 1980. After a visit to Benghazi in January by Oueddi, Libya announced a merger of the two nations despite protests from France and African nations.

The Reagan Administration, accusing Libya of supporting international terrorism, closed the Libyan embassy in Washington on May 6, 1981. After talks with Libyan officials in July, the U.S. concluded that no improvement in relations was possible, although U.S. oil companies remained active in Libya and 2,000 U.S. citizens continued to work there.

On Aug. 19, 1981, two U.S. Navy F-14's shot down two Soviet-made SU 22's of the Libyan air force that had attacked them in air space above the Gulf of Sidra, claimed by Libya but held to be international by the U.S. In December, Washington asserted that Libyan "hit squads" had been dispatched to the U.S. and security was drastically tightened around President Reagan and other officials. Reagan requested remaining American citizens to leave Libya and nearly all did by Dec. 15. When the Mobil Oil Company abandoned its operations in April 1962, only four U.S. firms were still in Libya, using Libyan or third-country personnel.

In June, Qaddafi's aid to President Goukoumi Oueddi of Chad proved insufficient to fend off the victorious forces of former Chadian Defense Minister Hissene Habré, who routed Oueddi and forced him to seek refuge in Tripoli.

LIECHTENSTEIN

Principality of Liechtenstein
Ruler: Prince Franz Josef II (1938)
Prime Minister: Hans Brunhart (1978)
Area: 61 sq mi. (157 sq km)
Population (est. 1982): 30,000 (average annual growth rate: 1.7%)

Density per square mile: 491.8
Capital and largest city (est. 1980): Vaduz, 4,600
Monetary unit: Swiss franc
Language: German (Alemannish dialect)
Religion: Roman Catholic
Literacy rate (1981): 100%
Economic summary: Per capita income (1978): $14,000. Labor force in agriculture: 4%; principal products: livestock, vegetables, corn, wheat, potatoes, grapes. Labor force in industry: 55%; major products: high-technology products, building equipment, food products, machinery, industrial goods. Natural resources: timber, hydroelectric power, salt. Exports: manufactured metal products, machines and instruments, textiles, chemical products. Imports: raw materials, machinery, processed foods and goods. Major trading partners: Finland, Switzerland and other Western European countries.

Geography. Tiny Liechtenstein, not quite as large as Washington, D.C., lies on the east bank of the Rhine River south of Lake Constance between Austria and Switzerland. It consists of low valley land and Alpine peaks. Falknis (8,401 ft; 2,561 m) and Naatkopf (8,432 ft; 2,570 m) are the tallest.

Government. The Constitution of 1921, amended in 1972, provides for a legislature, the Landtag, of 15 members elected by direct male suffrage.

The ruler, Prince Franz Josef II, was born in 1906 and succeeded his great-uncle, Franz I, in 1938. In 1943 he married Countess Gina Wilczek of Austria.

The major political parties are the Homeland Union (8 of 15 seats in the Landtag) and the Progressive Citizens Party (7 seats).

History. Founded in 1719, Liechtenstein was a member of the German Confederation from 1815 to 1866, when it became an independent principality. It abolished its army in 1868 and has managed to stay neutral and undamaged in all European wars since then. It also remained free of ties until after World War I. Since then, it has been oriented toward Switzerland.

LUXEMBOURG

Grand Duchy of Luxembourg
Ruler: Grand Duke Jean (1964)
Premier: Pierre Werner (1979)
Area: 999 sq mi. (2,586 sq km)
Population (est. 1982): 365,000. (Luxembourgian, French, German) (average annual growth rate: 0.3%)
Density per square mile: 365.4
Capital and largest city (est. 1980): Luxembourg, 80,000
Monetary unit: Luxembourg franc
Languages: Letzeburgesch, French, German
Religion: Mainly Roman Catholic
National name: Grand-Duché de Luxembourg
Literacy rate (1981): 98%
Economic summary: Gross national product (1980): $5.2 billion. Average annual growth rate (1970–79): 3.5%. Per capita income (1980): $14,510. Land used for agriculture: 25%; labor force: 6%; principal products: livestock, dairy products, wine. Labor force in industry: 46%; major products: steel, rubber, synthetic fibers. Natural resource: Iron ore. Export: steel. Imports: machinery, textiles, transport equipment, plastics. Major trading partners: European Common Market countries.

Geography. Luxembourg is a neighbor of Belgium on the west, West Germany on the east, and France on the south. The Ardennes Mountains extend from Belgium into the northern section of Luxembourg.

Government. Luxembourg's unicameral legislature, the Chamber of Deputies, consists of 59 members elected for five years.

The major political parties are the Christian Social Party (24 of 59 seats in Chamber of Deputies), led by Jacques Senter; Socialist-Labor (14 seats), led by Robert Krieps; Democratic Party (15 seats), led by Colette Flesch; Social Democratic Party (5 seats), led by Henry Cravatte; Communist Party (5 seats), led by René Urbany.

History. Sigefroi, Count of Ardennes, an offspring of Charlemagne, was Luxembourg's first sovereign ruler. In 1060, the country came under the rule of the House of Luxembourg. From the 15th to the 18th century, Spain, France, and Austria held it in turn. The Congress of Vienna in 1815 made it a Grand Duchy and gave it to William I, King of the Netherlands. In 1839 the Treaty of London ceded the western part of Luxembourg to Belgium.

The eastern part, continuing in personal union with the Netherlands and a member of the German Confederation, became autonomous in 1848 and a neutral territory by decision of the London Conference of 1867, governed by its Grand Duke. Germany occupied the duchy in World Wars I and II. Allied troops liberated the enclave in 1944.

In 1961, Prince Jean, son and heir of Grand Duchess Charlotte, was made head of state, acting for his mother. She abdicated in 1964, and Prince Jean became Grand Duke.

By a customs union between Belgium and Luxembourg, which came into force on May 1, 1922, to last for 50 years, customs frontiers between the two countries were abolished. On Jan. 1, 1948, a customs union with Belgium and the Netherlands (Benelux) came into existence. On Feb. 3, 1958, it became an economic union.

MADAGASCAR

Democratic Republic of Madagascar
President and Head of State: Comdr. Didier Ratsiraka (1975)
Prime Minister: Lt. Col. Desiré Rakotoarijaona (1977)
Area: 230,035 sq mi. (595,791 sq km)
Population (est. 1982): 9,190,000 (average annual growth rate: 2.5%)
Density per square mile: 40.1
Capital and largest city (est. 1980): Antananarivo, 550,000
Monetary unit: Malagasy franc
Languages: Malagasy, French
Ethnic groups: Merina (or Hova), Betsimisaraka, Betsileo, Tsimihety, Antaisaka, Sakalava, Antandroy
Religions: Animist, 55%; Catholic, 21%; Protestant, 18%; Islam, 7%
National name: Repoblika Demokratika Malagasy
Literacy rate (1981): 45%
Economic summary: Gross national product (1980): $1.4 billion. Average annual growth rate (1970–79): 3.0%. Per capita income (1980): $350. Land used for agriculture: 63%; labor force: 26%; principal products: rice, livestock, coffee, vanilla, sugar, cloves, cotton, sisal, peanuts, tobacco. Labor force in industry: 15%; major products:

processed food, textiles, refined petroleum products, assembled automobiles, soap, mining products. Natural resources: graphite, chromium, coal, bauxite, ilmenite, tar sands, semiprecious stones. Exports: coffee, cloves, vanilla. Imports: consumer goods, foodstuffs, crude petroleum, rice. Major trading partners: France, U.S.

Geography. Madagascar lies in the Indian Ocean off the southeast coast of Africa opposite Mozambique. The world's fourth-largest island, it is twice the size of Arizona. The country's low-lying coastal area gives way to a central plateau. The once densely wooded interior has largely been cut down.

Government. The Constitution of Dec. 30, 1975, approved by referendum following a military coup, provides for direct election by universal suffrage of a president for a seven-year term, a Supreme Council of the Revolution as a policy-making body, a unicameral People's National Assembly of 137 members (elected for five-year terms), and a military Committee for Development. The new constitution followed a period of martial rule that began with the suspension of the republic's original bicameral legislature in 1972.

History. The present population is of black and Malay stock, with perhaps some Polynesian, called Malagasy. The French took over a protectorate in 1885, and then in 1894–95 ended the monarchy, exiling Queen Rànavàlona III to Algiers. A colonial administration was set up, to which the Comoro Islands were attached in 1908, and other territories later. In World War II, the British occupied Madagascar, which retained ties to Vichy France.

An autonomous republic within the French Community since 1958, Madagascar became an independent member of the Community in 1960. In May 1973, an army coup led by Maj. Gen. Gabriel Ramanantsoa ousted Philibert Tsiranana, president since 1959.

With unemployment and inflation both high, Ramanantsoa resigned Feb. 5, 1975. His leftist-leaning successor, Interior Minister Richard Ratsimandrava, an Army lieutenant colonel, was killed six days later by a machine-gun ambush in Antananarivo, the capital.

On June 15, 1975, Comdr. Didier Ratsiraka was named President. He announced that he would follow a socialist course and, after nationalizing banks and insurance companies, declared all mineral resources nationalized.

MALAWI

Republic of Malawi
Life President: Hastings Kamuzu Banda (1966)
Area: 45,747 sq mi. (118,484 sq km)
Population (est. 1982): 6,275,000 (average annual growth rate: 3.0%)
Density per square mile: 137.2
Capital (1977 census): Lilongwe, 102,900
Largest city (1977 census): Blantyre, 222,200
Monetary unit: Kwacha
Languages: English (official), Chichewa
Religion: Animist, 65%; Christian, 33%
Member of Commonwealth of Nations
Literacy rate (1981): 15%
Economic summary: Gross national product (1980): $1.4 billion. Average annual growth rate (1970–79): 3.0%. Per capita income (1980): $230. Average rate of inflation (1974–78): 10%. Land used for agriculture: 30%; labor force: 48%; principal products: tobacco, tea, sugar, corn, peanuts. Labor force in industry: 21%; major products: food, beverages, tobacco, textiles, footwear. Natural resource: limestone. Exports: tobacco, tea, sugar, peanuts. Imports: machinery, transport equipment, building and construction materials, fuel. Major trading partners: U.K., U.S., South Africa, Netherlands, Japan, West Germany.

Geography. Malawi is a landlocked country the size of Pennsylvania in southeastern Africa, surrounded by Mozambique, Zambia, and Tanzania. Lake Malawi, formerly Lake Nyasa, occupies most of the country's eastern border. The north-south Rift Valley is flanked by mountain ranges and high plateau areas.

Government. Under a Constitution that came into effect on July 6, 1966, the president is the sole head of state; there is neither a prime minister nor a vice president. The National Assembly has 87 members.

There is only one national party—the Malawi Congress Party (all 87 seats in the National Assembly), led by President Hastings K. Banda.

History. The first European to make extensive explorations in the area was David Livingstone in the 1850s and 1860s. In 1884, Cecil Rhodes's British South African Company received a charter to develop the country. The company came into conflict with the Arab slavers in 1887–89. After Britain annexed the Nyasaland territory in 1891, making it a protectorate in 1892, Sir Harry Johnstone, the first high commissioner, using Royal Navy gunboats, wiped out the slavers.

Nyasaland became the independent nation of Malawi on July 6, 1964. Two years later, it became a republic within the Commonwealth of Nations.

Dr. Hastings K. Banda, Malawi's first Prime Minister, became its first President. He pledged to follow a policy of "discretionary nonalignment." Banda alienated much of Black Africa by maintaining good relations with such white-ruled nations as South Africa and Rhodesia. He argued that his landlocked country had to rely on white-ruled countries for access to the sea and trade.

MALAYSIA

Paramount Ruler: Sultan Haji Ahmad Shah, Sultan of Pahang (1979)
Prime Minister: Mahathir Bin Mohamed (1981)
Area: 128,328 sq mi. (332,370 sq km)
Population (est. 1982): 14,750,000 (average annual growth rate: 2.3%)
Density per square mile: 114.9
Capital: Kuala Lumpur
Largest cities (est. 1980 by U.N.): Kuala Lumpur, 1,000,000; George Town (Pinang), 300,000; Ipoh, 275,000
Monetary unit: Ringgit
Languages: Malay (official), Chinese, Tamil, English
Religions: Islam, (official), Buddhist, Hindu, Christian, Confucian, Taoist
Member of Commonwealth of Nations
Literacy rate (1981): 46%
Economic summary: Gross national product (1980): $22.4 billion. Average annual growth rate (1970–79): 5.4%. Per capita income (1980): $1,670. Labor force: 12%; principal products: natural rubber, palm oil, tin, petroleum, rice,

timber. Major industrial products: processed rubber, timber, and palm oil, tin, petroleum, light manufactures, electronics equipment. Natural resources: tin, oil, copper, timber. Exports: natural rubber, palm oil, tin, timber, petroleum. Imports: machinery, transport equipment, chemicals. Major trading partners: Japan, Singapore, U.S., Western European countries.

Geography. Malaysia is at the southern end of the Malay Peninsula in southeast Asia. The nation also includes Sabah and Sarawak on the island of Borneo to the southeast. Its area slightly exceeds that of New Mexico.

Most of Malaysia is covered by dense jungle and swamps, with a mountain range running the length of the peninsula. Extensive forests provide ebony, sandalwood, teak, and other woods.

Government. Malaysia is a sovereign constitutional monarchy within the Commonwealth of Nations. The Paramount Ruler is elected for a five-year term by the hereditary rulers of the states from among themselves. He is advised by the prime minister and his cabinet. There is a bicameral legislature. The Senate, whose role is comparable more to that of the British House of Lords than to the U.S. Senate, has 68 members, partly appointed by the Paramount Ruler to represent minority and special interests, and partly elected by the legislative assemblies of the various states.

The House of Representatives, or lower house, is made up of 154 members, who are elected for five-year terms.

The major political parties are the National Front, a coalition of 10 parties (133 of 154 seats in the House of Representatives); Democratic Action Party (86 seats); Islamic Party (5 seats); Independents (8 seats).

History. Malaysia came into existence on Sept. 16, 1963, as a federation of Malaya, Singapore, Sabah (North Borneo), and Sarawak. In 1965, Singapore withdrew from the federation. Since 1966, the 11 states of former Malaya have been known as West Malaysia, and Sabah and Sarawak have been known as East Malaysia.

The Union of Malaya was established April 1, 1946, being formed from the Federated Malay States of Negri Sembilan, Pahang, Perak, and Selangor; the Unfederated Malay States of Johore, Kedah, Kelantan, Perlis, and Trengganu; and two of the Straits Settlements—Malacca and Penang. The Malay states had been brought under British administration during the late 19th and early 20th centuries.

It became the Federation of Malaya on Feb. 1, 1948, and the Federation attained full independence within the Commonwealth of Nations in 1957.

Sabah, constituting the extreme northern portion of the island of Borneo, was a British protectorate administered under charter by the British North Borneo Company from 1881 to 1946, when it assumed the status of a colony. It was occupied by Japanese troops from 1942 to 1945.

Sarawak extends along the northwestern coast of Borneo for about 500 miles (805 km). In 1841, part of the present territory was granted by the Sultan of Brunei to Sir James Brooke. Sarawak continued to be ruled by members of the Brooke family until the Japanese occupation.

From 1963, when Malaysia became independent, it was the target of guerrilla infiltration from Indonesia, but beat off invasion attempts. In 1966, when Sukarno fell and the Communist Party was liquidated in Indonesia, hostilities ended.

In the late 1960s, the country was torn by communal rioting directed against Chinese and Indians, who controlled a disproportionate share of the country's wealth. Beginning in 1968, the government moved to achieve greater economic balance through a rural development program.

Malaysia felt the impact of the "boat people" fleeing Vietnam early in 1978. Because the refugees were mostly ethnic Chinese, the government was apprehensive about any increase of a minority that previously had been the source of internal conflict in the country. In November, authorities banned landings and reversed the order only after several hundred refugees drowned when their fragile boats were towed offshore by Malaysian police. By August 1980, the number of refugees was reported down to 20,000 from a high of 76,500 in July 1979.

MALDIVES

Republic of Maldives
President: Maumoon Abdul Gayoom (1978)
Area: 115 sq mi. (298 sq km)
Population (est. 1982): 160,000 (average annual growth rate: 3.0%)
Density per square mile: 1,391.3
Capital and largest city (est. 1978): Malé, 29,600
Monetary unit: Maldivian rupee
Language: Divehi
Religion: Islam
Literacy rate: Largely illiterate
Economic summary: Gross national product (1980): $40 million. Average annual growth rate (1970–79): −0.7%. Per capita income (1980): $260. Principal agricultural products: coconuts, millet. Labor force in industry: 50%; major products: fish, processed coconuts. Natural resource: fish. Export: fish. Imports: rice, sugar. Major trading partners: Japan, Sri Lanka, Singapore.

Geography. The Republic of Maldives is a group of atolls in the Indian Ocean about 500 miles (805 km) southwest of Sri Lanka. Its 1,087 coral islets stretch over an area of 45,000 square miles (116,550 sq km).

Government. The 9-member Cabinet is headed by the president. The Majlis (Parliament) is a unicameral legislature consisting of 48 members. Eight of these are appointed by the president. The others are elected for three-year terms, 2 from the capital island of Malé and 2 from each of the 19 administrative atolls.

There are no political parties in the Maldives.

History. The Maldives (formerly called the Maldive Islands) are inhabited by an Islamic seafaring people. Originally the islands were under the suzerainty of Ceylon. They came under British protection in 1887 and were a dependency of the then colony of Ceylon until 1948. The independence agreement with Britain was signed July 26, 1965.

For centuries a sultanate, the islands adopted a republican form of government in 1952, but the sultanate was restored in 1954. In 1968, however, as the result of a referendum, a republic was again established in the islands.

Ibrahim Nasir, president since 1968, was removed from office by the Majlis in November 1978 and replaced by Maumoon Abdul Gayoom. A national referendum confirmed the new leader.

MALI

Republic of Mali
Chief of State (1968) and Head of Government (1969): Gen. Moussa Traoré
Area: 464,873 sq mi. (1,204,021 sq km)
Population (est. 1982): 7,350,000 (average annual growth rate, 2.7%)
Density per square mile: 15.8
Capital and largest city (est. 1980): Bamako, 450,000
Monetary unit: Mali franc
Ethnic groups: Bambara, Peul, Soninke, Malinke, Songhai, Dogon, Senoufo, Minianka, Berbers, and Moors
Languages: French (official), African languages
Religions: Islam, 65%; Animist, 30%; Christian
National name: République de Mali
Literacy rate (1981): 5%
Economic summary: Gross national product (1980): $1.3 billion. Average annual growth rate (1970–79): 2.5%. Per capita income (1980): $190. Principal agricultural products: millet, sorghum, corn, rice, sugar, cotton, peanuts, livestock. Major industrial products: processed foods, textiles, cigarettes, fish. Natural resources: bauxite, iron ore, maganese, lithium, phosphate, kaolin, salt, limestone, gold. Exports: livestock, peanuts, dried fish, cotton, skins. Imports: textiles, vehicles, petroleum products, machinery, sugar. Major trading partners: Western European countries, U.S.S.R., China.

Geography. Most of Mali, in West Africa, lies in the Sahara. A landlocked country four fifths the size of Alaska, it is bordered by Guinea, Senegal, Mauritania, Algeria, Niger, Upper Volta, and the Ivory Coast.

The only fertile area is in the south, where the Niger and Senegal Rivers provide irrigation.

Government. The army overthrew the government on Nov. 19, 1968, and formed a provisional government. The Military Committee of National Liberation consists of 14 members and forms the decision-making body.

In late 1969 an attempted coup was foiled, and Lt. Moussa Traoré, president of the Military Committee took over as chief of state and later as head of government, ousting Capt. Yoro Diakité as Premier.

The Malian People's Democratic Union, established in 1976, is the only political party.

History. Subjugated by France by the end of the 19th century, this area became a colony in 1904 (named French Sudan in 1920) and in 1946 became part of the French Union. On June 20, 1960, it became independent and, under the name of Sudanese Republic, was federated with the Republic of Senegal in the Mali Federation. However, Senegal seceded from the Federation on Aug. 20, 1960, and the Sudanese Republic then changed its name to the Republic of Mali on September 22.

In the 1960s, Mali concentrated on economic development, continuing to accept aid from both Soviet bloc and Western nations, as well as international agencies. In the late 1960s, it began retreating from close ties with China. But a purge of conservative opponents brought greater power to President Modibo Keita, and in 1968 the influence of the Chinese and their Malian sympathizers increased. By a treaty signed in Peking in 1968, China agreed to help build a railroad from Mali to Guinea, providing Mali with vital access to the sea.

Mali, with Mauritania, the Ivory Coast, Senegal, Dahomey (Benin), Niger, and Upper Volta signed a treaty establishing the Economic Community for West Africa to promote economic development among the seven nations. It came into force on Jan. 1, 1973.

A six-year sub-Sahara drought devastated Mali before disastrously heavy rains began in 1974. Emergency shipments from a dozen nations and international organizations helped alleviate a famine that affected 1.8 million Malians and killed thousands.

MALTA

Republic of Malta
President: Agatha Barbara (1982)
Prime Minister: Dom Mintoff (1971)
Area: 122 sq mi. (316 sq km)
Population (est. 1982): 375,000 (average annual growth rate: 1.6%)
Density per square mile: 3,073.8
Capital (est. 1979): Valetta, 14,000
Largest city (est. 1979): Sliema, 20,100
Monetary unit: Maltese pound
Languages: Maltese and English
Religion: Roman Catholic
National name: Repubblika Ta Malta
Member of Commonwealth of Nations
Literacy rate (1981): 83%
Economic summary: Gross national product (1980): $1.2 billion. Average annual growth rate (1970–79): 11.0%. Per capita income (1980): $3,470. Land used for agriculture, 45%; labor force: 6%; principal products: fodder crops, potatoes, onions, fruits and vegetables. Labor force in industry: 27%; major products: textiles, yarn, knitted goods, processed foods, plastics, electronic equipment. Natural resources: limestone, salt. Exports: textiles, yarns, manufactured goods, ships. Imports: manufactured goods, machinery, transport equipment. Major trading partners: West Germany, U.K., Italy.

Geography. The five Maltese islands—with a combined land area smaller than Philadelphia—are in the Mediterranean about 60 miles (97 km) south of the southeastern tip of Sicily.

Government. The government is headed by a Prime Minister, responsible to a 65-member House of Representatives elected by universal suffrage.

The major political parties are Malta Labor Party (34 of 65 seats in House of Representatives), led by Prime Minister Dom Mintoff; Nationalist Party (31 seats), led by Edward Fenech Adami.

History. The strategic importance of Malta was recognized by the Phoenicians, who occupied it, as did in their turn the Greeks, Carthaginians, and Romans. The apostle Paul was shipwrecked there in A.D. 58.

The Knights of St. John (Malta), who obtained the three habitable Maltese islands of Malta, Gozo, and Comino from Charles V in 1530, reached their highest fame when they withstood an attack by superior Turkish forces in 1565.

Napoleon seized Malta in 1798, but the French forces were ousted by British troops the next year, and British rule was confirmed by the Treaty of Paris in 1814.

Malta was heavily attacked by German and Italian aircraft during World War II, but was never invaded by the Axis.

Malta became an independent nation on Sept. 21, 1964, and a republic Dec. 13, 1974, but remained in the British Commonwealth. The Governor-General, Sir Anthony Mamo, was sworn in as first president and Dom Mintoff remained prime minister.

The new government proposed a seven-year plan to end economic dependence on foreign military bases by 1980. It called for a $568-million investment program to create 20,000 new jobs. Britain withdrew its last troops from Malta in 1979, thus ending its annual subsidy of $33 million for use of the island's port facilities.

For a time, Libya appeared to be substituting for Britain as a source of outside income, as President Muammar el-Qaddafi extended generous credits and concessionary prices for oil on condition that Malta's Labor government keep the North Atlantic Treaty Organization from using the island's port facilities. But a conflict over oil rights, in which Libyan ships threatened a Maltese-licensed drilling rig in the waters between Malta and Libya in August 1980 forced Mintoff to break with Qaddafi, expel most of the Libyan military advisers, and negotiate a treaty of friendship and aid with Italy.

MAURITANIA

Islamic Republic of Mauritania
Chief of State and Head of Government: Lt. Col. Mohamed Khouna Ould Haydalla (1980)
Premier: Lieut. Col. Maaouya Ould Sidi Ahmed Taya (1981)
Area: 419,229 sq mi. (1,085,803 sq km)
Population (est. 1982): 1,725,000 (average annual growth rate: 1.9%)
Density per square mile: 4.1
Capital and largest city (est. 1977): Nouakchott, 135,000
Monetary unit: Ouguyia
Ethnic groups: Moors; a black minority (Poulars, Soninkes, and Wolofs)
Languages: Arabic and French
Religion: Islam
National name: République Islamique de Mauritanie
Literacy rate (1981): 17%
Economic summary: Gross national product (1980): $530 million. Average annual growth rate (1970–79): −0.7%. Per capita income (1980): $320. Principal agricultural products: livestock, millet, maize, wheat, dates, rice. Major industrial products: iron ore, processed fish. Natural resources: copper, iron ore, gypsum, fish. Exports: iron ore, fish, copper. Imports: foodstuffs, petroleum, capital goods. Major trading partners: France, Spain, U.S., U.K., Italy.

Geography. Mauritania, three times the size of Arizona, is situated in northwest Africa with about 350 miles (592 km) of coastline on the Atlantic Ocean. It is bordered by Morocco on the north, Algeria and Mali on the east, and Senegal on the south.

The country is mostly desert, with the exception of the fertile Senegal River valley in the south and grazing land in the north.

Government. An Army coup on July 10, 1978, deposed Moktar Ould Daddah, who had been President since Mauritania's independence in 1960. Since then, a 13-man Committee for National Recovery has exercised executive and legislative power, having replaced the National Assembly and the single political party that existed before the coup.

History. Mauritania was first explored by the Portuguese. The French organized the area as a territory in 1904.

Mauritania became an independent nation on Nov. 28, 1960, and was admitted to the United Nations in 1961 over the strenuous opposition of Morocco, which claimed the territory. With Moors, Arabs, Berbers, and blacks frequently in conflict, the government in the late 1960s sought to make Arab culture dominant to unify the land.

Mauritania and Morocco planned to divide the territory of the former Spanish Sahara after the departure of the colonial administration. Mauritanian troops moved into the territory but encountered resistance from the Polisario Front, a Saharan independence movement backed by Algeria. Mauritania broke diplomatic relations with Algeria in 1976, after Algerian recognition of the area as an independent state.

The task of pacifying one-third of the former Spanish Sahara (the exact amount of territory acquired by Mauritania in the division with Morocco is unknown) proved a heavy burden. Increased military spending and rising casulaties contributed to the discontent that brought down the civilian government of Ould Daddah in 1978. His military replacement, Lt. Col. Moustapha Saleck, was forced to resign after Premier Ahmed Bouceif and other military leaders were killed in a plane crash on May 27, 1979. Lt. Col. Mohamed Mahmoud Ould Louly held power for only six months and was removed by the junta on Jan. 4, 1980, for unsatisfactory performance. Lt. Col. Mohamed Khouna Ould Haydalla was named new chief of state and government.

MAURITIUS

Sovereign: Queen Elizabeth II
Governor-General: Sir Dayendranath Burrenchobay (1978)
Prime Minister: Aneerood Jugnauth (1982)
Area: 787 sq mi. (2,040 sq km)
Population (est. 1982): 950,000 (average annual growth rate: 1.7%) (Indian, 51%; Creole, 33%)
Density per square mile: 1,207.1
Capital and largest city (est. 1980): Port Louis, 155,000
Monetary unit: Mauritian rupee
Languages: English (official), French, Creole, Hindi, Urdu, Chinese
Religions: Hindu, 51%, Christian (mainly Roman Catholic), 30%; Islam, 16%; Buddhist, 3%
Member of Commonwealth of Nations
Literacy rate (1981): 70%
Economic summary: Gross national product (1980): $1.0 billion. Average annual growth rate (1970–79): 6.4%. Per capita income (1980): $1,060. Land used for agriculture: 50%; labor force: 50%; principal products: sugar cane, rice. Labor force in industry: 6%; major products: processed sugar and tea, tobacco, cut diamonds, textiles, electronic equipment. Natural resources: iron ore, gypsum, fish. Exports: sugar, tea, molasses. Imports: foodstuffs, manufactured goods. Major trading partners: Western European countries, U.S., U.K.

Geography. Mauritius is a mountainous island in the Indian Ocean east of Madagascar.

Government. Mauritius is a member of the British Commonwealth, with Queen Elizabeth II as head of state. She is represented by a governor-general, who chooses the prime minister from the unicameral Legislative Assembly. The Legislative Assembly has 70 members, 62 of whom are elected by direct suffrage. The remaining 8 are chosen from among the unsuccessful candidates.

The major parties are the Mouvement Militant Mauricien (62 of 70 seats in the Legislative Assembly), led by Prime Minister Aneerood Jugnauth, and the opposition Labor Party (8 seats), led by former Prime Minister Sir Seewoosagur Ramgoolam.

History. Mauritius was seized from France by British troops in 1810 and ceded to Britain by the Treaty of Paris in 1814. Until 1903, Mauritius and the Seychelles were administered as a single colony. The colony of Mauritius became an independent nation on March 12, 1968.

The nation has an Indian majority, descendants of laborers imported from India to work the sugar plantations after the abolition of slavery in 1834. The native blacks speak French and are Roman Catholics.

On June 11, 1982, the Labor Party government of Sir Seewoosagur Ramgoolam, who had ruled Mauritius since independence, was routed by the opposition Mouvement Militant Mauricien, which won all 62 elective seats in the Assembly. The victors campaigned for the recovery of Diego Garcia island, separated from Mauritius during the colonial period and leased by Britain to the United States for a naval base.

MEXICO

United Mexican States

President: Miguel de la Madrid Hurtado (1982)
Area: 761,600 sq mi. (1,972,547 sq km)
Population (est. 1982): 72,900,000 (average annual growth rate: 2.4%) (55% mestizo; 29% Indian)
Density per square mile: 95.7
Capital: Mexico City
Largest cities (est 1979): Mexico City, 9,200,000; **(est. 1978 by U.N.):** Guadalajara, 1,813,000; Monterrey, 1,054,000; Puebla de Zaragoza, 678,000
Monetary unit: Peso
Languages: Spanish, Indian languages
Religion: Mainly Roman Catholic
National name: Estados Unidos Mexicanos
Literacy rate (1981): 65% (est.)
Economic summary: Gross national product (1980): $144.0 billion. Average annual growth rate (1970–79): 1.9%. Per capita income (1980): $2,130. Land used for agriculture, 12%; labor force: 33%; principal products: corn, cotton, coffee, sugar cane, vegetables. Labor force in industry: 33%; major products: processed foods, chemicals, basic metals and metal products, petroleum. Natural resources: petroleum, silver, copper, gold, lead, zinc, natural gas, timber. Exports: coffee, cotton, sugar, shrimp, cattle and meat, petroleum, sulfur. Imports: machinery, equipment, industrial vehicles, intermediate goods. Major trading partners: U.S., Japan, Western European countries.

Geography. The United States' neighbor to the south, Mexico is about one fifth its size. Baja California in the west, an 800-mile (1,287-km) peninsula, forms the Gulf of California. In the east are the Gulf of Mexico and the Bay of Campeche, which is formed by Mexico's other peninsula, the Yucatán.

Mexico is a great, high plateau, open to the north, with mountain chains on east and west and with ocean-front lowlands lying outside of them.

Government. The President, who is popularly elected for six years and is ineligible to succeed himself, governs with a Cabinet of ministers. Congress has two houses—a 400-member Chamber of Deputies, elected for three years, and a 64-member Senate, elected for six years.

Each of the 31 states has considerable autonomy, with a popularly elected governor, a legislature, and a local judiciary. The President of Mexico appoints the governor of the Federal District.

The major parties are the Partido Revolucionario Institucional (64 of 64 seats in the Senate and 299 of 400 seats in the Chamber of Deputies); Partido Acción Nacional (56 of 400 seats in Chamber); Partido Socialista Unificado de Mexico (16 seats); Partido Popular Socialista (10 seats); Partido Socialista de los Trabajadores (Socialist Workers Party) (10 seats); and Partido Democrata Mexicano (9 seats). The formerly separate Communist Party merged in 1981 with others to form the Partido Socialista Unificado de Mexico.

History. At least two civilized races—the Mayas and later the Toltecs—preceded the wealthy Aztec empire, conquered in 1519–21 by the Spanish under Hernando Cortés. Spain ruled for the next 300 years until 1810 (the date was Sept. 16 and is now celebrated as Independence Day), when the Mexicans first revolted. They continued the struggle and finally won independence in 1821.

From 1821 to 1877, there were two emperors, several dictators, and enough presidents and provisional executives to make a new government on the average of every nine months. Mexico lost Texas (1836), and after defeat in the war with the U.S. (1846–48) it lost the area comprising the present states of California, Nevada, and Utah, most of Arizona and New Mexico, and parts of Wyoming and Colorado.

In 1855, the Indian patriot Benito Juárez began a series of liberal reforms, including the disestablishment of the Catholic Church, which had acquired vast property. A subsequent civil war was interrupted by the French invasion of Mexico (1861), the crowning of Maximilian of Austria as Emperor (1864), and then his overthrow and execution by forces under Juárez, who again became President in 1867.

The years after the fall of the dictator Porfirio Diaz (1877–80 and 1884–1911) were marked by bloody political-military strife and trouble with the U.S., culminating in the punitive expedition into northern Mexico (1916–17) in unsuccessful pursuit of the revolutionary Pancho Villa. Since a brief period of civil war in 1920, Mexico has enjoyed a period of gradual agricultural, political, and social reforms. Relations with the U.S. were again disturbed in 1938 when all foreign oil wells were expropriated. Agreement on compensation was finally reached in 1941.

Lázaro Cardenas (1934–40), president during the oil seizures, also began a program of distributing land to the peasants and of broad labor reforms. Manuel Avila Camacho, president during World War II, followed Cardenas' policy at home but cooperated closely with the United Nations, and established cordial relations with the U.S. His policy was followed by his immediate successors, Miguel Alemán, Adolfo Ruíz Cortines, and Adolfo López Mateos. López Mateos redefined Mexican foreign policy as "independent" rather than neutral or partial, a course followed by Gustavo Díaz Ordaz, who became president in 1964.

Luis Echeverría Alvarez, who was elected president in 1970, worked vigorously in Latin America and elsewhere in the underdeveloped world to promote more benefits for developing nations from the raw materials they export.

Mexico and Venezuela proposed formation of a Latin American economic system (SELA) to promote regional economic development, and the organization held its first meeting in Caracas in 1976.

The country's oil reserves were estimated to be the world's fifth largest in 1981, following the discovery of a huge offshore field in the Gulf of Mexico. It was here that the world's biggest oil spill was capped in March 1980 after 3.1 million barrels were lost in nine months. The disaster caused a dispute with the United States when Mexico refused to pay the cost of cleaning up Texas beaches. Another conflict arose over the Mexican navy's seizure of U.S. fishing boats off the West Coast in the summer of 1980, causing the Carter Administration to ban importation of Mexican tuna.

With the election of Ronald Reagan as U.S. President, a new era of "personal relationship" was proclaimed by him and López Portillo at a border meeting on Jan. 5, 1981. López Portillo came to Washington in June, and after a long meeting with Reagan at Camp David, a new U.S. immigration policy designed to ease Mexican concerns was disclosed. As elaborated later, the program called for 100,000 "guest workers" to be admitted from Mexico over a two-year test period. Also proposed was an increase to 40,000 a year in visas for legal immigration from Mexico, with the possibility of borrowing additional visas from the Canadian allotment, historically never filled.

López Portillo also pressed for economic, rather than military, aid to combat Communist penetration of the Caribbean area. With Venezuela, he led the way in pledging oil to help poor nations in the region. He urged Reagan to follow his policy and invited him to a 22-nation conference on aid for developing nations sponsored by Mexico at Cancun in October 1981. Reagan accepted after assurances that Cuba, with which López Portillo maintained friendly relations, would not be invited.

The last year of López Portillo's presidency was shadowed by economic problems caused by falling oil prices. Instead of an expected $20 billion in oil export earnings for 1981, the actual figure was only $12 billion. In February 1982, a 41% devaluation of the peso pushed the inflation rate to 75% the following month. Cuts of $5.7 billion in the 1982 budget of $72 billion and the suspension of a $30-billion nuclear energy program were projected to reduce the economic growth rate to zero through mid-1983, in contrast to recent annual growth rates of 8%.

Miguel de la Madrid Hurtado, candidate of the ruling Partido Revolucionario Institucional, won the July 4 election for the presidential term beginning Dec. 1. De la Madrid, 47, was formerly Secretary of Planning and Budget and Deputy Director General of Pemex.

MONACO

Principality of Monaco
Ruler: Prince Rainier III (1949)
Minister of State: Jean Herly (1981)
Area: 0.73 square mile (465 acres)
Population (est. 1982): 30,000, of whom 5,500 are Monégasque citizens (average annual growth rate: 0.8%)
Density per square mile: 41,095.9
Capital: Monaco-Ville
Monetary unit: French franc
Languages: French and Monégasque
Religion: Roman Catholic
National name: Principauté de Monaco
Literacy rate (1981): 99%

Geography. Monaco is a tiny, hilly wedge driven into the French Mediterranean coast nine miles east of Nice.

Government. Prince Albert of Monaco gave the principality a Constitution in 1911, creating a National Council of 18 members popularly elected for five years. The head of government is the Minister of State.

Prince Rainier III, born May 31, 1923, succeeded his grandfather, Louis II, on the latter's death, May 9, 1949. Rainier was married April 18, 1956, to Grace Kelly, U.S. actress. A daughter, Princess Caroline Louise Marguerite, was born on Jan. 23, 1957 (married to Philippe Junot June 28, 1978 and divorced in 1980); a son, Prince Albert Louis Pierre, on March 14, 1958; and Princess Stéphanie Marie Elisabeth, on Feb. 1, 1965. Princess Grace died Sept. 14, 1982, of injuries received the day before when the car she was driving went off the road near Monte Carlo. She was 52. Her daughter Stephanie suffered neck injuries.

The special significance attached to the birth of descendants to Prince Rainier stems from a clause in the Treaty of July 17, 1919, between France and Monaco stipulating that in the event of vacancy of the Crown, the Monégasque territory would become an autonomous state under a French protectorate.

The National and Democratic Union (all 18 seats in National Council), led by Auguste Medecin, is the only political party.

History. The Phoenicians, and after them the Greeks, had a temple on the Monacan headland honoring Hercules. From *Monoikos,* the Greek surname for this mythological strong man, the principality took its name. After being independent for 800 years, Monaco was annexed to France in 1793 and was placed under Sardinia's protection in 1815. In 1861, it went under French guardianship but continued to be independent.

By a treaty in 1918, France stipulated that the French government be given a veto over the succession to the throne.

Monaco is a little land of pleasure with a tourist business that runs as high as 1.5 million visitors a year. It had popular gaming tables as early as 1856. Five years later, a 50-year concession to operate the games was granted to François Blanc, of Bad Homburg. This concession passed into the hand of a private company in 1898.

Monaco's practice of providing a tax shelter for French businessmen resulted in a dispute between the countries. When Rainier refused to end the practice, France retaliated with a customs tax. In 1967, Rainier took control of the Société des Bains de Mer, operator of the famous Monte Carlo gambling casino, in a program to increase hotel and convention space. He paid $8 million to Greek shipping magnate Aristotle Onassis for his shares.

MONGOLIA

Mongolian People's Republic
Chairman of Presidium of the Great People's Khural (President): Yumjaagiin Tsedenbal (1974)
Chairman of Council of Ministers (Premier): Jambyn Batmunkh (1974)
Area: 604,250 sq mi. (1,565,000 sq km)
Population (est. 1982): 1,725,000 (average annual growth rate: 0.8%)
Density per square mile: 2.9
Capital and largest city (est. 1981): Ulan Bator, 435,000
Monetary unit: Tugrik
Language: Mongolian
Religion: Lamaistic Buddhism
National name: Bugd Nairamdakh Mongol Ard Uls
Literacy rate (1981): 80%
Economic summary: Gross national product (1980): $1.5 billion. Average annual growth rate (1970–79): 3.1%. Per capita income: n.a. Principal agricultural products: livestock, wheat, oats, barley. Major industrial products: animal products, building materials, minerals. Natural resources: coal, copper, molybdenum. Exports: livestock, animal products, nonferrous metals. Imports: machinery and equipment, clothing, petroleum, sugar, tea. Major trading partners: U.S.S.R. and Soviet bloc countries.

Geography. Mongolia lies in eastern Asia between Soviet Siberia on the north and China on the south. It is slightly larger than Alaska.

The productive regions of Mongolia—a tableland ranging from 3,000 to 5,000 feet (914 to 1,524 m) in elevation—are in the north, which is well drained by numerous rivers, including the Hovd, Onon, Selenga, and Tula.

Much of the Gobi Desert falls within Mongolia. One of several mountain ranges, the Altai, contains the highest peak in the country—Tabun Bogdo at 14,288 feet (4,355 m).

Government. The Mongolian People's Republic is a socialist state. The highest organ of state power is the Great People's Khural (Parliament), which is elected for a term of four years and is convened once a year. The Great People's Khural elects the Presidium, which consists of a chairman, two vice chairmen, a secretary, and six members. The Council of Ministers is set up by the Great People's Khural and consists of a chairman, vice chairmen, and ministers.

The Mongolian People's Revolutionary Party, led by President Yumjaagiin Tsedenbal, is the only political party.

History. The Mongolian People's Republic, formerly known as Outer Mongolia, is a Soviet satellite. It contains the original homeland of the historic Mongols, whose power reached its zenith during the 13th century under Kublai Khan. The area accepted Manchu rule in 1689, but after the Chinese Revolution of 1911 and the fall of the Manchus in 1912, the northern Mongol princes expelled the Chinese officials and declared independence under the Khutukhtu, or "Living Buddha."

In 1921, Soviet troops entered the country and facilitated the establishment of a republic by Mongolian revolutionaries in 1924 after the death of the last Living Buddha. China, meanwhile, continued to claim Outer Mongolia but was unable to back the claim with any strength. Under the 1945 Chinese-Russian Treaty, China agreed to give up Outer Mongolia, which, after a plebiscite, became a nominally independent country.

Allied with the U.S.S.R. in its dispute with China, Mongolia has mobilized troops along its borders since 1968 when the two powers became involved in border clashes on the Kazakh-Sinkiang frontier to the west and on the Amur and Ussuri Rivers. A 20-year treaty of friendship and cooperation, signed in 1966, entitled Mongolia to call upon the U.S.S.R. for military aid in the event of invasion.

MOROCCO

Kingdom of Morocco
Ruler: King Hassan II (1961)
Premier: Maati Bouabid (1981)
Area: 171,953 sq mi. (445,358 sq km)
Population (est. 1982): 21,275,000 (average annual growth rate: 2.9%)
Density per square mile: 123.7
Capital: Rabat
Largest cities (est. 1980): Casablanca, 2,350,000; Marrakech, 1,225,000; Rabat, 865,000; Meknes, 775,000; Fez, 745,000
Monetary unit: Dirham
Languages: Arabic, French, Spanish
Religions: Chiefly Islam
National name: al-Mamlaka al-Maghrebia
Literacy rate (1981): 38%
Economic summary: Gross national product (1980): $17.4 billion. Average annual growth rate (1970–79): 3.5%. Per capita income (1980): $860. Land used for agriculture; 32%; labor force: 50%; products: barley, wheat, citrus fruits, vegetables, sugar beets, wool. Labor force in industry, 15%; major products: textiles, fish, chemicals. Natural resources: phosphates, iron, manganese, lead, fisheries. Exports: phosphates, citrus fruits, vegetables, canned fruits and vegetables, canned fish, carpets. Imports: capital goods, fuels, foodstuffs, petroleum products. Major trading partners: France, West Germany, Italy.

Geography. Morocco, about one tenth larger than California, is just south of Spain across the Strait of Gibraltar and looks out on the Atlantic from the northwest shoulder of Africa. Algeria is to the east and Mauritania to the south.

On the Atlantic coast there is a fertile plain. The Mediterranean coast is mountainous. The Atlas Mountains, running northeastward from the south to the Algerian frontier, average 11,000 feet (3,353 m) in elevation.

Government. The King, after suspending the 1962 Constitution and dissolving Parliament in 1965, promulgated a new Constitution in 1972. He continued to rule by decree until June 3, 1977, when the first free elections since 1962 took place. The 264-member Chamber of Deputies has 176 elected seats, with the balance chosen by local councils and groups.

A coalition of independents loyal to the King and small right-wing parties has 114 of the 176 elected seats in the Chamber of Deputies; Istiqlal, which participates in the government, 45 seats; Socialist

Union of Popular Forces, 16 seats; and the Communist Party of Progress and Socialism, one seat.

History. Morocco was once the home of the Berbers, who helped the Arabs invade Spain in A.D. 711 and then revolted against them and gradually won control of large areas of Spain for a time after 739.

The country was ruled successively by various native dynasties and maintained regular commercial relations with Europe, even during the 17th and 18th centuries when it was the headquarters of the famous Salé pirates. In the 19th century, there were frequent clashes with the French and Spanish. Finally, in 1904, France and Spain divided Morocco into zones of French and Spanish influence, and these were established as protectorates in 1912.

Meanwhile, Morocco had become the object of big-power rivalry, which almost led to a European war in 1905 when Germany attempted to gain a foothold in the rich mineral country. By terms of the Algeciras Conference (1906), Morocco was internationalized economically, and France's privileges were limited.

The Tangier Statute, concluded by Britain, France, and Spain in 1923, created an international zone at the port of Tangier, permanently neutralized and demilitarized. In World War II, Spain occupied the zone, ostensibly to ensure order, but was forced to withdraw in 1945.

Sultan Mohammed V was deposed by the French in 1953 and replaced by his uncle, but nationalist agitation forced his return in 1955. On his death on Feb. 26, 1961, his son, Hassan, became King.

France and Spain recognized the independence and sovereignty of Morocco in 1956. Later the same year, the Tangier international zone was abolished.

In the Middle East war of 1967, Morocco joined the Arab states in their attack on Israel.

In 1975, tens of thousands of Moroccans crossed the border into Spanish Sahara to back their government's contention that the northern part of the territory was historically part of Morocco. At the same time, Mauritania occupied the southern half of the territory in defiance of Spanish threats to resist such a takeover. Abandoning its commitment to self-determination for the territory, Spain withdrew, and only Algeria protested. Algerian recognition of a Saharan republic in 1976 led to a break in relations among the three North African states, and Algerian-backed Polisario Front guerrillas continued to fight Moroccan and Mauritanian forces, preventing exploitation of the region's rich phosphate deposits.

Although Polisario guerrillas were still active in 1977, Hassan dispatched 1,500 troops to Zaire in April to help President Mobuto Sese Seko defeat an invasion from Angola. Radical African states criticized Morocco, but most hailed the successful operation, in which France supplied the airlift.

In the May 1978 invasion of Zaire's Shaba Province, Morocco once again supplied troops, this time only a small number, who were transported to Zaire by the U.S. Air Force.

Hassan, under pressure from other African leaders at the Organization of African Unity summit in Nairobi, Kenya, in mid-1981, agreed to a cease-fire with a referendum under international supervision to decide the future of the Sahara territory. The referendum was never carried out, but in February 1982, foreign ministers of the O.A.U. voted to admit the Polisario Front as the organization's 51st member, under the name of the Sahara Arab Democratic Republic. Morocco led a walkout of 19 members. Morocco's continued boycott threatened to split the O.A.U. when a summit conference in Tripoli, Libya, was unable to open for lack of a quorum.

MOZAMBIQUE

People's Republic of Mozambique
President: Samora Moises Machel (1975)
Area: 303,073 sq mi. (784,959 sq km)
Population (est. 1982): 11,100,000 (average annual growth rate: 2.7%)
Density per square mile: 36.6
Capital and largest city (est. 1980): Maputo, 750,000
Monetary unit: Metical
Languages: Portuguese (official); Bantu languages
Religions: Animist, 66%; Christian, 22%; Islam, 11%
National name: República Popular de Moçambique
Literacy rate (1974): 15% (est.)
Economic summary: Gross national product (1980): $2.8 billion. Average annual growth rate (1970–79): –5.3%. Per capita income (1980): $270. Principal agricultural products: cotton, cashew nuts, sugar, tea, copra, wheat, peanuts. Labor force in industry: 5%; major products: processed foods, petroleum products, beverages, textiles, tobacco. Natural resources: coal, iron ore, fluorite, tantalite, timber. Exports: cashew nuts, cotton, sugar, mineral and timber products, tea, copra. Imports: machinery and electrical equipment, cotton textiles, vehicles, petroleum products, iron and steel. Major trading partners: Portugal, South Africa, U.S., U.K., West Germany.

Geography. Mozambique stretches for 1,535 miles (2,470 km) along Africa's southeast coast. It is nearly twice the size of California. Tanzania is to the north; Malawi, Zambia, and Zimbabwe to the west; and South Africa and Swaziland to the south.

The country is generally a low-lying plateau broken up by 25 sizable rivers that flow into the Indian Ocean. The largest is the Zambezi, which provides access to central Africa. The principal ports are Maputo and Beira, which is the port for Zimbabwe.

Government. After having been under Portuguese colonial rule for 470 years, Mozambique became independent on June 25, 1975. It is a Marxist state. The first President, Samora Moises Machel, is a militant Maoist and a former nurse who headed the National Front for the Liberation of Mozambique (FRELIMO) in its 10-year guerrilla war for independence.

History. Mozambique was discovered by Vasco da Gama in 1498, although the Arabs had penetrated into the area as early as the 10th century. It was first colonized in 1505, and by 1510, the Portuguese had control of all the former Arab sultanates on the east African coast.

FRELIMO was organized in 1963. Guerrilla activity had become so extensive by 1973 that Portugal was forced to dispatch 40,000 troops to fight the rebels. A cease-fire was signed in September 1974, when Portugal agreed to grant Mozambique independence.

After a brief period of cooperation with neighboring white-ruled Rhodesia, Mozambique closed its border in 1976, cutting off Rhodesia's most direct link to the sea. A series of border clashes between Rhodesian forces and guerrillas based in Mozambique continued until Zimbabwe achieved independence in April 1980, when rail and highway communications between the two countries were reopened.

NAMIBIA

See South Africa

NAURU

Republic of Nauru
President and Premier: Hammer DeRoburt (1978)
Area: 8.2 sq mi. (21 sq km)
Population (est. 1982): 8,000 (average annual growth rate: 1.7%)
Density per square mile: 1,000.0
Capital: Yaren
Monetary unit: Australian dollar
Languages: Nauruan, English
Religions: Protestant, 60%; Catholic, 33%
Special relationship within the Commonwealth of Nations
Literacy rate (1981): 99%
Economic summary: Gross national product (1977): $155 million. Per capita income (1977): $21,400. Major industrial products: phosphates. Natural resources: phosphates. Exports: phosphates. Imports: foodstuffs, fuel. Major trading partners: Australia, New Zealand, U.K., Japan.

Geography. Nauru (pronounced NAH oo roo) is an island in the Pacific just south of the equator, about 2,500 miles (4,023 km) southwest of Honolulu.

Government. Legislative power is invested in a popularly elected 18-member Parliament, which elects the President from among its members. Executive power rests with the President, who is assisted by a five-member Cabinet.

History. Nauru was annexed by Germany in 1888. It was placed under joint Australian, New Zealand, and British mandate after World War I, and in 1947 it became a U.N. trusteeship administered by the same three powers. On Jan. 31, 1968, Nauru became an independent republic.

NEPAL

Kingdom of Nepal
Ruler: King Birendra Bír Bikram Shah Dev. (1972)
Prime Minister: Surya Bahadur Thapa (1979)
Area: 54,362 sq mi. (140,797 sq km)
Population (est. 1982): 15,325,000 (average annual growth rate: 2.4%)
Density per square mile: 281.9
Capital and largest city (est. 1976): Katmandu, 171,400
Monetary unit: Nepalese rupee
Languages: Nepali (official), Newari, Bhutia
Religions: Hindu, 89%; Buddhist, 8%
Literacy rate (1981): 12%
Economic summary: Gross national product (1980): $2.0 billion. Average annual growth rate (1970–79): 0.3%. Per capita income (1980): $140. Labor force in agriculture: 95%; principal products: rice, maize, wheat, millet, jute, sugar cane, oilseed, potatoes. Labor force in industry: 5%; major products: cigarettes, bricks, sugar, lumber, jute, hydroelectric power, cement. Natural resources: water, timber, hydroelectric potential. Exports: rice and food products, and timber. Imports: textiles, manufactured goods, construction materials, fuel. Major trading partner: India.

Geography. A landlocked country the size of Arkansas, lying between India and the Tibetan Autonomous Region of China, Nepal contains Mount Everest (29,028 ft.; 8,848 m), the tallest mountain in the world. Along its southern border, Nepal has a strip of level land that is partly forested, partly cultivated. North of that is the slope of the main section of the Himalayan range, including Everest and many other peaks higher than 20,000 feet (6,096 m).

Government. A new Constitution promulgated by King Mahendra in 1962 provided for a unicameral legislature called the National Panchayat. All political parties were banned in 1960.

History. The Kingdom of Nepal was unified in 1768 by King Prithwi Narayan Shah. A commercial treaty was signed with Britain in 1792, and in 1816, after more than a year's hostilities, the Nepalese agreed to allow British residents to live in Katmandu, the capital. In 1923, Britain recognized the absolute independence of Nepal. Between 1846 and 1951, the country was ruled by the Rana family, which always held the office of prime minister. In 1951, however, the King took over all power and proclaimed a constitutional monarchy.

Mahendra Bir Bikram Shah became King in 1955. Nepal and China settled their differences in 1956, and thereafter Nepal accepted economic aid from the Chinese. The U.S. and the U.S.S.R. also provide aid.

After Mahendra, who had ruled since 1955, died of a heart attack in 1972, Prince Birendra, at 26, succeeded to the throne.

In the first election in 22 years, on May 2, 1980, voters approved the continued autocratic rule by the King with the advice of a partyless Parliament. The King promised, however, that he would eventually permit the election of a new legislature to which the Prime Minister and Cabinet would be responsible.

THE NETHERLANDS

Kingdom of the Netherlands
Sovereign: Queen Beatrix (1980)
Premier: Andries van Agt (1977)
Area: 13,967 sq mi. (36,175 sq km)
Population (est. 1982): 14,350,000 (average annual growth rate: 0.7%)
Density per square mile: 1,027.4
Capital: Amsterdam; seat of government: The Hague
Largest cities (est. 1979): Rotterdam, 1,014,800; Amsterdam, 957,700; The Hague, 671,500; Utrecht, 476,400
Monetary unit: Guilder
Language: Dutch
Religions: Roman Catholic, 40%; Dutch Reformed, 24%; unaffiliated, 24%
National name: Koninkrijk der Nederlanden
Literacy rate (1981): 98%
Economic summary: Gross national product (1980): $161.4 billion. Average annual growth rate (1970–79): 2.2%. Per capita income (1980): $11,470. Land used for agriculture: 70%; labor force, 10%; principal products: wheat, barley,

sugar beets, potatoes, flax, bulbs, meat and dairy products. Labor force in industry: 30%; major products: metal fabrication, textiles, chemicals, electronic equipment. Exports: foodstuffs, machinery, natural gas, chemicals, petroleum products, textiles. Imports: machinery, crude petroleum, chemicals, textiles, mineral ores. Major trading partners: West Germany, Belgium, France, U.K.

Geography. The Netherlands, on the coast of the North Sea, has West Germany to the east and Belgium to the south. It is twice the size of New Jersey.

Part of the great plain of north and west Europe, the Netherlands has maximum dimensions of 190 by 160 miles (360 by 257 km) and is low and flat except in Limburg in the southeast, where some hills rise to 300 feet (92 m). About half the country's area is below sea level, making the famous Dutch dikes a requisite to the use of much land. Reclamation of land from the sea through dikes has continued through recent times.

All drainage reaches the North Sea, and the principal rivers—Rhine, Maas (Meuse), and Schelde—have their sources outside the country. The Rhine is the most heavily used waterway in Europe.

Government. The Netherlands and its former colony of the Netherlands Antilles form the Kingdom of the Netherlands.

The Netherlands is a constitutional monarchy with a bicameral Parliament. The Upper Chamber has 75 members elected for six years by representative bodies of the provinces, half of the members retiring every three years. The Lower Chamber has 150 members elected by universal suffrage for four years. The two Chambers have the right of investigation and interpellation; the Lower Chamber can initiate legislation and amend bills.

The Sovereign, Queen Beatrix Wilhelmina Armgard, born Jan. 31, 1938, was married on March 11, 1966, to Claus von Amsberg, a former West German diplomat. The marriage drew public criticism because of the bridegroom's service in the German army during World War II. In 1967, Beatrix gave birth to a son, Willem-Alexander Claus George Ferdinand, the first male heir to the throne since 1884. She also has two other sons, Johan Friso Bernhard Christian David, born in 1968, and Constantijn Christof Frederik Aschwin, born the next year.

Premier Andries van Agt leads a minority government. The Christian Appeal (48 of 150 seats in the Lower Chamber), led by van Agt, is the largest of 10 parties. Other major parties are the opposition Labor Party (44 seats), led by former Prime Minister Joop den Uyl; the Liberal Party for Freedom and Democracy (26 seats), and Democrats '66 (17 seats).

History. Julius Caesar found the low-lying Netherlands inhabited by Germanic tribes—the Nervii, Frisii, and Batavi. The Batavi on the Roman frontier did not submit to Rome's rule until 13 B.C., and then only as allies.

A part of Charlemagne's empire in the 8th and 9th centuries A.D., the area later passed into the hands of Burgundy and the Austrian Hapsburgs, and finally in the 16th century came under Spanish rule.

When Philip II of Spain suppressed political liberties and the growing Protestant movement in the Netherlands, a revolt led by William of Orange broke out in 1568. Under the Union of Utrecht (1579), the seven northern provinces became the Republic of the United Netherlands.

The Dutch East India Company was established in 1602, and by the end of the 17th century Holland was one of the great sea and colonial powers of Europe.

The nation's independence was not completely established until after the Thirty Years' War (1618–48), after which the country's rise as a commercial and maritime power began. In 1814, all the provinces of Holland and Belgium were merged into one kingdom, but in 1830 the southern provinces broke away to form the Kingdom of Belgium. A liberal Constitution was adopted by the Netherlands in 1848.

In spite of its neutrality in World War II, the Netherlands was invaded by the Nazis in May 1940, and the East Indies were later taken by the Japanese. The nation was liberated in May 1945. In 1948, after a reign of 50 years, Queen Wilhelmina resigned and was succeeded by her daughter Juliana.

In 1949, after a four-year war, the Netherlands granted independence to the East Indies, which became the Republic of Indonesia. In 1963, it turned over the western half of New Guinea to the new nation, ending 300 years of Dutch presence in Asia. Attainment of independence by Suriname on Nov. 25, 1975, left the Dutch Antilles as the Netherlands' only overseas territory.

Prime Minister Andries van Agt ended a seven-month constitutional crisis in December 1977 when he was able to form a center-right majority coalition. Early in 1980, Queen Juliana announced her intention to abdicate on her 71st birthday, April 30, in favor of the 42-year-old Crown Princess Beatrix. Beatrix was invested as Queen on April 30 in a ceremony marred by protests of Amsterdam squatters against eviction.

Van Agt lost his narrow majority in elections on May 26, 1981, in which the major issue was the deployment of U.S. cruise missiles on Dutch soil. Public opposition to the missiles forced the Netherlands, along with Belgium, to reverse its position in 1982 despite the Prime Minister's personal support for the NATO decision to deploy the new weapons in Western Europe. Van Agt lost his centrist coalition in May 1982 in a dispute over economic policy, and new parliamentary elections were scheduled for Sept. 8.

Netherlands Autonomous Country

NETHERLANDS ANTILLES

Status: Part of the Kingdom of the Netherlands
Governor: Bernardito M. Leito (1970)
Premier: Domenico F. Martina
Area: 817 sq mi. (821 sq km)
Population (est. 1982): 260,000 (average annual growth rate: 1.0%)
Capital (est. 1978): Willemstad, 152,000
Literacy rate (1981): 95%
Economic summary: Gross national product (1980): $1.1 billion. Average annual growth rate (1970–79): 0.9%. Per capita income: $4,290. Principal agricultural products: pigs, goats. Major industries: oil refining, tourism. Natural resource: phosphate. Export: petroleum. Import: petroleum. Major trading partners: U.S., Venezuela.

Geography. The Netherlands Antilles comprise two groups of Caribbean islands 500 miles (805 km) apart: one, about 40 miles (64 km) off the Venezuelan coast, consists of Curaçao (173 sq mi.; 448 sq km), Bonaire (95 sq mi.; 246 sq km), and Aruba (69 sq mi.; 179 sq km); the other, lying to the northeast, consists of three small islands with a total area of 34 square miles (88 sq km). The Dutch acquired Curaçao from Spain in 1643.

Government. There is a constitutional government formed by the Governor and Cabinet and an elected Legislative Council. The area has complete autonomy in domestic affairs.

NEW ZEALAND

Dominion of New Zealand
Sovereign: Queen Elizabeth II
Governor-General: Sir David S. Beattie (1980)
Prime Minister: Robert D. Muldoon (1975)
Area: 103,736 sq mi. (268,676 sq km) (excluding dependencies)
Population (est. 1982): 3,175,000 (average annual growth rate: 0.1%) (European, 90%; Maori and other Polynesian, 10%)
Density per square mile: 30.6
Capital: Wellington
Largest cities (est. 1981 for metropolitan area): Auckland, 818,000; Wellington, 342,000; Christchurch, 321,000; Dunedin, 115,000
Monetary unit: New Zealand dollar
Languages: English, Maori
Religions: Church of England, 35%; Presbyterian, 22%; Roman Catholic, 16%
Member of Commonwealth of Nations
Literacy rate (1981): 98%
Economic summary: Gross national product (1980): $23.2 billion. Average annual growth rate (1970–79): 0.5%. Per capita income (1980): $7,090. Labor force in agriculture: 13%; principal products: wool, meat, dairy products, livestock. Labor force in industry: 33%; major products: processed foods, textiles, machinery, transport equipment, wood and paper products. Natural resources: forests, coal, gold, tungsten, iron ore, asbestos. Exports: meat, dairy products, wool. Imports: machinery, minerals, chemicals, consumer goods. Major trading partners: Australia, U.K., Japan, U.S.

Geography. New Zealand, about 1,250 miles (2,012 km) east of Australia, consists of two main islands and a number of smaller, outlying islands so scattered that they range from the tropical to the antarctic. The country is the size of Colorado.

New Zealand's two main components are North Island and South Island, separated by Cook Strait, which varies from 16 to 190 miles (26 to 396 km) in width. North Island (44,281 sq mi.; 114,688 sq km) is 515 miles (829 km) long and volcanic in its south-central part. It contains many hot springs and beautiful geysers. South Island (58,093 sq mi.; 150,461 sq km) has the Southern Alps along its west coast, with Mount Cook (12,349 ft; 3,764 m) the highest point.

The largest of the outlying islands are the Auckland Islands (234 sq mi.; 606 sq km), Campbell Island (44 sq mi.; 114 sq km), the Antipodes Islands (24 sq mi.; 62 sq km), and the Kermadec Islands (13 sq mi.; 34 sq km).

Government. New Zealand was granted self-government in 1852, a full parliamentary system and ministries in 1856, and dominion status in 1907. The Queen is represented by a Governor-General, and the Cabinet is responsible to a unicameral Parliament of 92 members, who are elected by popular vote for three years.

The major political parties are the National Party (47 of 92 seats in the House of Representatives), led by Prime Minister Robert D. Muldoon; Labor Party (43 seats) led by Wallace E. Rowling; and Social Credit Party (2 seats).

History. New Zealand was discovered and named in 1642 by Abel Tasman, a Dutch navigator. Captain James Cook explored the islands in 1769. In 1840, Britain formally annexed them.

From the first, the country has been in the forefront in instituting social welfare legislation. It adopted old age pensions (1898); a national child welfare program (1907); social security for the aged, widows, and orphans, along with family benefit payments; minimum wages; a 40-hour week and unemployment and health insurance (1938); and socialized medicine (1941).

New Zealand supported U.S. policy in Vietnam and supplied military aid to South Vietnam in the orientation of its policy toward the U.S. and Asian neighbors after Britain's entry into the European Common Market. To replace the lost British market —the once prosperous islands had fallen into a local recession since 1972—New Zealand sought to sell more agricultural products to Japan. In 1978, Prime Minister Muldoon announced a pact with Japan enlarging quotas for New Zealand beef, reducing the tariffs on New Zealand fish, and providing for Japanese purchase of butter, skim milk, and other food products.

Cook Islands and Overseas Territories

The Cook Islands (93 sq mi.; 241 sq km) were placed under New Zealand administration in 1901. They achieved self-governing status in association with New Zealand in 1965. Population in 1978 was about 19,600. The seat of government is on Rarotonga Island.

The island's chief exports are citrus juice, clothing, canned fruit, and pineapple juice. Nearly all of the trade is with New Zealand.

Niue (100 sq mi.; 259 sq km) was formerly administered as part of the Cook Islands. It was placed under separate New Zealand administration in 1901 and achieved self-governing status in association with New Zealand in 1974. The capital is Alofi. Population in 1980 was about 3,300.

Niue exports passion fruit, copra, plaited ware, honey, and limes. Its principal trading partner is New Zealand.

The Ross Dependency (160,000 sq mi.; 414,400 sq km), an Antarctic region, was placed under New Zealand administration in 1923.

Tokelau (4 sq mi.; 10 sq km) was formerly administered as part of the Gilbert and Ellice Islands colony. It was placed under New Zealand administration in 1925. Its population is about 1,600.

NICARAGUA

Republic of Nicaragua
Executive power is held by the three-member Directorate of the Sandinista Front (1979)
Area: 57,143 sq mi. (148,000 sq km)

Population (est. 1982): 2,900,000 (average annual growth rate: 3.2%) (mestizo, 70%; white, 17%; black, 9%; Indian, 4%)
Density per square mile: 50.7
Capital and largest city (est. 1978): Managua, 517,500
Monetary unit: Cordoba
Language: Spanish
Religion: Roman Catholic
National name: República de Nicaragua
Literacy rate (1981): 87%
Economic summary: Gross national product (1980): $1.9 billion. Average annual growth rate (1970–79): −1.6%. Per capita income (1980): $720. Land used for agriculture: 7%; labor force: 43%; principal products: cotton, coffee, sugar cane, rice, corn, beans, cattle. Labor force in industry: 13%; major products: processed foods, chemicals, metal products, clothing and textiles. Natural resources: timber, fisheries. Exports: cotton, coffee, chemical products, meat, sugar. Imports: food and non-food agricultural products, chemicals and pharmaceuticals, transport equipment, clothing, petroleum. Major trading partners: U.S., Caribbean and Western European countries.

Geography. Largest but most sparsely populated of the Central American nations, Nicaragua borders on Honduras to the north and Costa Rica to the south. It is slightly larger than New York State.

Nicaragua is mountainous in the west, with fertile valleys. A plateau slopes eastward toward the Caribbean.

Two big lakes—Nicaragua, about 100 miles long (161 km), and Managua, about 38 miles long (61 km)—are connected by the Tipitapa River. The Pacific coast is bald and rocky. The Caribbean coast, swampy and indented, is aptly called the "Mosquito Coast."

Government. A nine-member Directorate for the Sandinista National Liberation Front has replaced the five-member junta that took power July 19, 1979, with the overthrow of President Anastasio Somoza Debayle. Although members of the Directorate share authority in principle, Daniel Ortega Saavedra, a member of the original junta, dominates the Directorate as its "coordinator."

History. Nicaragua, which established independence in 1838, was first visited by the Spaniards in 1522. The chief of the country's leading Indian tribe at that time was called Nicaragua, from whom the nation derived its name. A U.S. naval force intervened in 1909 after two American citizens had been executed, and a few U.S. Marines were kept in the country from 1912 to 1925. The Bryan-Chamorro Treaty of 1916 (terminated in 1970) gave the U.S. an option on a canal route through Nicaragua, and naval bases. Disorder after the 1924 elections brought in the marines again.

A guerrilla leader, Gen. César Augusto Sandino, began fighting the occupation force in 1927. He fought the U.S. troops successfully until their withdrawal in 1933. They trained Gen. Anastasio (Tacho) Somoza García to head a National Guard. In 1934, Somoza assassinated Sandino and overthrew the Liberal President Juan Batista Sacassa, establishing a military dictatorship with himself as president. He spurred the economic development of the country, meanwhile enriching his family through estates in the countryside and investments in air and shipping lines. On his assassination in 1956, he was succeeded by his son Luis, who alternated with trusted family friends in the presidency until his death in 1967. Another son, Maj. Gen. Anastasio Somoza Debayle, became President in 1967.

One of the worst earthquakes in Nicaragua's history struck Managua on Dec. 23, 1972, destroying an estimated 90% of its commercial establishments and 70% of its housing. Over 6,000 were killed, 20,000 injured, and 300,000 made homeless, and 60,000 were jobless as a result. Rebuilding costs were put at $772 million. Somoza obtained loans from the U.S. and international banks totaling $127 million for the reconstruction of Managua. Shortly afterward, he declared martial law after leftist guerrillas had kidnapped 14 prominent officials.

Although the Somoza regime was cited in 1977 by a U.S. State Department report for human-rights violations and Nicaragua's Catholic hierarchy testified to the government's repression and terror, it was not until 1978 that the Carter Administration moved to cut military aid to Somoza.

The situation was aggravated by the murder on January 10 of Pedro Joaquin Chamorro, editor of an opposition newspaper, causing student strikes and wide public protest. In an uncharacteristic response, Somoza made concessions to protesters and announced an inquiry into Chamorro's death. On May 16, the U.S. Congress acted to restore $12 million in military aid to Nicaragua.

Sandinista guerrillas, leftists who took their name from Gen. Sandino, launched a civil war in May 1979, occupying parts of Managua and holding several provincial towns. Somoza ordered bombings to drive the rebels out, an action that embittered Nicaraguans of all classes. He defied appeals by the U.S. and the Organization of American States to step down and permit a peaceful transition to an all-party government.

Although the original five-member junta included two non-Sandinista members who resigned in April 1980, and were replaced by two other non-Sandinistas, exclusive power was moving to the Sandinista Directorate. The prominence of Cuban President Fidel Castro at the celebration of the first anniversary of the revolution and the indefinite delay of elections strengthened debate over the true political color of the Sandinistas. U.S. Congressional doubts delayed release of $75 million in aid until September 1980, when President Jimmy Carter certified that Nicaragua was not "exporting violence."

On Jan. 23, 1981, the Reagan Administration suspended aid after the U.S. Ambassador to El Salvador claimed that Nicaragua was supplying Salvadoran rebels.

In March 1982, the State Department published aerial photographs to back its charges that Nicaragua, with the aid of the Soviet Union and Cuba, was the source of the arms build-up for the Salvadoran rebels. The charges, denied by the Sandinista leadership, lost credibility when a Nicaraguan "defector" presented by the State Department as an informant refused to verify the charges and the issue was rendered moot by the completion of the Salvadoran elections on March 28. Nicaragua was one of a minority of leftist Latin nations that advocated negotiation with the Salvadoran insurgents.

NIGER

Republic of Niger
Chief of State: Col. Seyni Kountché (1974)
Area: 489,206 sq mi. (1,267,044 sq km)

Population (est. 1982): 5,650,000 (average annual growth rate: 2.9%)
Density per square mile: 11.5
Capital and largest city (est. 1977): Niamey, 225,000
Monetary unit: Franc CFA
Ethnic groups: Hausa, 54%; Djerma and Songhai, 24%; Peul, 11%
Languages: French (official); Hausa, Songhai; Arabic
Religions: Islam, 85%; Animist and Christian
National name: République du Niger
Literacy rate (1981): 6%
Economic summary: Gross national product (1980): $1.8 billion. Average annual growth rate (1970–79): −1.2%. Per capita income (1980): $330. Land used for agriculture: 3%; labor force: 90%; principal products: peanuts, cotton, livestock, millet, sorghum, vegetables. Major industrial products: uranium, cement, bricks, light industrial products. Natural resources: uranium, coal, iron. Exports: uranium, peanuts, livestock, hides, skins. Imports: fuels, machinery, transport equipment, foodstuffs, consumer goods. Major trading partners: France, other Western European countries, Nigeria.

Geography. Niger, in West Africa's Sahara region, is four fifths the size of Alaska. It is surrounded by Mali, Algeria, Libya, Chad, Nigeria, Benin, and Upper Volta.

The Niger River in the southwest flows through the country's only fertile area. Elsewhere the land is semiarid.

Government. After a military coup on April 15, 1974, Col. Seyni Kountché suspended the Constitution and instituted rule by decree. Previously, the President was elected by direct universal suffrage for a five-year term and a National House of Assembly of 50 members was elected for the same term.

The Parti Progressiste Nigérien-Rassemblement Démocratique Africain, the only political party, was dissolved in 1974.

History. Niger was incorporated into French West Africa in 1896. There were frequent rebellions, but when order was restored in 1922, the French made the area a colony. In 1958, the voters approved the French Constitution and voted to make the territory an autonomous republic within the French Community. The republic adopted a Constitution in 1959 and the next year withdrew from the Community, proclaiming its independence.

The 1974 army coup ousted President Hamani Diori, who had held office since 1960. He was charged with having mishandled relief for the terrible drought that had devastated Niger and five neighboring sub-Saharan nations for several years. An estimated 2 million people were starving in Niger, but 200,000 tons of imported food, half U.S.-supplied, substantially ended famine conditions by the year's end. The new President, Lt. Col. Seyni Kountché, Chief of Staff of the army, installed a 12-man military government. A predominantly civilian government was formed by Kountché in 1976.

NIGERIA

Federal Republic of Nigeria
President: Alhaji Shehu Shagari (1979)
Area: 356,700 sq mi. (923,853 sq km)
Population (est. 1982): 82,250,000[1] (average annual growth rate: 3.3%)
Density per square mile: 230.6
Capital: Abuja
Largest cities (est. 1980): Lagos (metropolitan area): 4,000,000; (est. 1975 by U.N.): Ibadan, 847,000; Ogbomosho, 432,000; Kano, 399,000
Monetary unit: Naira
Languages: English (official) and native tongues
Religions: Islam, 47%; Christian, 34%; Animist
Member of Commonwealth of Nations
Literacy rate (1981): 25% (est.)
Economic summary: Gross national product (1980): $85.5 billion. Average annual growth rate (1970–79): 5.3%. Per capita income (1980): $1,010. Land used for agriculture: 13%; labor force: 70%; principal products: peanuts, cotton, cocoa, rubber, yams, cassava, livestock. Labor force in industry: 10%; major products: crude oil, natural gas, coal, tin, processed rubber, cotton, petroleum, wood, hides, textiles, cement, footwear, chemicals. Natural resources: petroleum, tin, columbite, iron ore, coal, limestone, lead, zinc, timber. Exports: oil, cocoa, palm products, rubber, timber, tin. Imports: machinery and transport equipment, manufactured goods, chemicals. Major trading partners: U.K., Western European countries, U.S.

1. While U.N. and similar sources continue to report figures in this area, interpretations of election data by demographers suggest that, in reality, the population of Nigeria is close to 100 million.

Geography. Nigeria, one third larger than Texas and black Africa's most populous nation, is situated on the Gulf of Guinea in West Africa. Its neighbors are Benin, Niger, Cameroon, and Chad.

The lower course of the Niger River flows south through the western part of the country into the Gulf of Guinea. Swamps and mangrove forests border the southern coast; inland are hardwood forests.

Government. After 12 years of military rule, a new Constitution re-established democratic government in 1978. The president, directly elected for a four-year term, holds executive power. Legislative power is divided between a 100-seat Senate and a 449-seat House of Representatives, whose members are also elected for four years.

The major parties are the National Party of Nigeria (36 of 100 seats in the Senate and 168 of 149 seats in the House), led by President Alhaji Shehu Shagari; United Party of Nigeria (26 seats in Senate and 111 in House), led by Chief Obafemi Awolowo; Nigerian People's Party (16 seats in Senate, 79 in House) led by Former President Nmandi Azikiwe; Great Nigerian People's Party (8 seats in Senate, 48 in House), led by Alhaji Woziri Ibrahim; and People's Redemption Party (7 seats in Senate, 49 in House), led by Alhaji Aminew Kano.

History. Between 1879 and 1914, private colonial developments by the British, with reorganizations of the Crown's interest in the region, resulted in the formation of Nigeria as it exists today. During World War I, native troops of the West African frontier force joined with French forces to defeat the German garrison in the Cameroons.

Nigeria became independent on Oct. 1, 1960.

Organized as a loose federation of self-governing states, the independent nation faced an overwhelming task of unifying a country with 250 ethnic and linguistic groups.

Rioting broke out again in 1966, the military commander was seized, and Col. Yakubu Gowon took power. Also in that year, the Moslem Hausas in the north massacred the predominantly Christian Ibos in the east, many of whom had been driven from the north. Thousands of Ibos took refuge in the Eastern Region. The military government there asked Ibos to return to the region and, in May 1967, the assembly voted to secede from the federation and set up the Republic of Biafra. Civil war broke out.

In January 1970, after 31 months of civil war, Biafra surrendered to the federal government. An estimated one million persons, mostly Ibos of the defeated state, were homeless and hungry, but a massive international relief operation kept the death toll down. The overall cost of the civil war was estimated at $840 million.

Gowon's nine-year rule was ended in 1975 by a bloodless coup that made Army Brigadier Muritala Rufai Mohammed the new chief of state. Mohammed was assassinated the next year 1976 by a group of seven young officers, who failed to seize control of the government. The 20-member Supreme Military Council chose Lt. Gen. Olusegun Obasanjo, Chief of Staff of the armed forces, as the new head of the Council and President.

The return of civilian leadership was established with the election of Alhaji Shehu Shagari, a former finance minister, as president in 1979.

Shagari was forced to cut the 1982 budget by 10% because of diminishing oil revenues. Foreign currency reserves, which had stood at $3.5 billion at the end of 1980, had fallen by nearly $1 billion by mid-1982 and Nigeria was hoping to raise oil production to offset the lower prices. Output had been increased from 700,000 barrels a day in August 1980 to 1.3 million a day at the end of the year but trade deficits were still running at an annual rate of nearly $1 billion.

NORWAY

Kingdom of Norway
Sovereign: King Olav V (1957)
Prime Minister: Käre Willoch (1981)
Area: 125,182 sq mi. (324,219 sq km)
Population (est. 1982): 4,125,000 (average annual growth rate: 0.3%)
Density per square mile: 33.0
Capital: Oslo
Largest cities (est. 1979): Oslo, 457,300; Bergen, 212,750; Trondheim, 135,550; Stavanger, 88,100
Monetary unit: Krone
Language: Norwegian
Religions: Evangelical Lutheran (state), 94%
National name: Kongeriket Norge
Literacy rate (1981): 100%
Economic summary: Gross national product (1980): $51.6 billion. Average annual growth rate (1970–79): 3.7%. Per capita income (1980): $12,650. Land used for agriculture: 3%; labor force, including fishing: 7%; principal products: dairy products, livestock, grain, vegetables, fruits, furs, wool. Labor force in industry: 29%; major products: oil and gas, fish, pulp and paper, ships, aluminum, iron, steel, nickel, fertilizers, transportation equipment, hydroelectric power, petrochemicals, electronic equipment. Natural resources: fish, timber, hydroelectric power, ores, oil, gas. Exports: oil, natural gas, ships, fish products, chemicals, pulp and paper. Imports: machinery, motor vehicles, foodstuffs, iron and steel, textiles and clothing. Major trading partners: U.K., Sweden, West Germany, U.S., Denmark.

Geography. Norway is situated in the western part of the Scandinavian peninsula. It extends about 1,100 miles (1,770 km) from the North Sea along the Norwegian Sea to more than 300 miles (483 km) above the Arctic Circle, the farthest north of any European country. It is slightly larger than New Mexico. Sweden borders on most of the eastern frontier, with Finland and the U.S.S.R. in the northeast.

Nearly 70% of Norway is uninhabitable and covered by mountains, glaciers, moors, and rivers. The hundreds of deep fiords that cut into the coastline give Norway an overall oceanfront of more than 12,000 miles (19,312 km). Nearly 150,000 islands off the coast form a breakwater and make a safe coastal shipping channel.

Government. Norway is a constitutional hereditary monarchy. Executive power is vested in the King together with a Cabinet, or Council of State, consisting of a Prime Minister and at least seven other members. The Storting, or Parliament, is composed of 155 members elected by the people under proportional representation. The Storting discusses and votes on political and financial questions, but divides itself into two sections (Lagting and Odelsting) to discuss and pass on legislative matters. The King cannot dissolve the Storting before the expiration of its term.

The sovereign is Olav V, born July 2, 1903, only son of Haakon VII and Princess Maud (1869–1938), third daughter of Edward VII of England. He succeeded to the throne on the death of his father Sept. 20, 1957. He married Princess Märtha of Sweden (1901–1954) on March 21, 1929. Their children are Princess Ragnhild Alexandra (born 1930), Princess Astrid (born 1932), and Crown Prince Harald (born 1937). In 1968, the Crown Prince married Sonja Haraldsen, a commoner.

The major political parties are the Labor Party (66 of 155 seats in the Storting), led by former Prime Minister Gro Harlem Brundtland; Conservative Party (53 seats), led by Prime Minister Käre Willoch; Christian Democratic Party (15 seats), led by Lars Korvald; Center Party (11 seats), led by Käre Kristiansen; Socialist Left Party (4 seats), led by Hanna Kranmo; Party of Progress (4 seats), led by Carl I. Hagen; and Liberal Party (2 seats), led by Odd-Einar Dorum.

History. Norwegians, like the Danes and Swedes, are of Teutonic origin. The Norsemen, also known as Vikings, ravaged the coasts of northwestern Europe from the 8th to the 11th century.

In 1815, Norway fell under the control of Sweden. The union of Norway, inhabited by fishermen, sailors, merchants, and peasants, and Sweden, an aristocratic country of large estates and tenant farmers, was not a happy one, but it lasted for nearly a century. In 1905, the Norwegian Parliament arranged a peaceful separation and invited a Danish prince to the Norwegian throne—King Haakon VII. A treaty with Sweden provided that all disputes be settled by arbitration and that no fortifications be erected on the common frontier.

When World War I broke out, Norway joined with Sweden and Denmark in a decision to remain neutral and to cooperate in the joint interest of the three countries. In World War II, Norway was invaded by the Germans on April 9, 1940. It resisted for two months before the Nazis took over complete control. King Haakon and his government fled to London, where they established a government-in-exile. Maj. Vidkun Quisling, whose name is now synonymous with traitor or fifth columnist, was the most notorious Norwegian collaborator with the Nazis. He was executed by the Norwegians on Oct. 24, 1945.

Despite severe losses in the war, Norway recovered quickly. The country led the world in social experimentation. A neighbor of the U.S.S.R., Norway sought to retain good relations with the Soviet Union without losing its identity with the West. It entered the North Atlantic Treaty Organization in 1949.

Verification of U.S. and Soviet oil strikes in separated areas of Norway's sector of the North Sea bottom led the Storting in 1975 to impose stiff tax and royalty rates on concession holders. Following discovery of a North Sea field expected to produce 900,000 barrels a day by 1984, Parliament in 1976 approved establishment of a national refining and distributing company to market petroleum products at home and abroad.

Dependencies of Norway

Svalbard (23,957 sq mi.; 62,049 sq km), in the Arctic Ocean about 360 miles north of Norway, consists of the Spitsbergen group and several smaller islands, including Bear Island, Hope Island, King Charles Land, and White Island (or Gillis Land). It came under Norwegian administration in 1925. The population in 1979 was 3,640.

Bouvet Island (23 sq mi.; 60 sq km), in the South Atlantic about 1,600 miles south-southwest of the Cape of Good Hope, came under Norwegian administration in 1928.

Jan Mayen Island (144 sq mi.; 273 sq km), in the Arctic Ocean between Norway and Greenland, came under Norwegian administration in 1929.

Peter I Island (96 sq mi.; 249 sq km), lying off Antarctica in the Bellinghausen Sea, came under Norwegian administration in 1931.

Queen Maud Land, a section of Antarctica, came under Norwegian administration in 1939.

OMAN

Sultanate of Oman
Sultan: Qabus Bin Said (1970)
Area: 82,000 sq mi. (212,380 sq km)
Population (est. 1982): 950,000[1] (average annual growth rate: 3.1%)
Density per square mile: 11.6
Capital (est. 1973): Muscat, 15,000
Largest city (est. 1973): Matrah, 18,000
Monetary unit: Omani rial
Language: Arabic
Religion: Islam
National name: Saltanat Oman
Literacy rate (1981): 10%
Economic summary: Gross national product (1980): $3.9 billion. Average annual growth rate (1970–79): 3.8%. Per capita income (1980): $4,380. Principal agricultural products: dates, alfalfa, onions, wheat, tobacco, bananas. Major industries: petroleum drilling, fishing, construction. Natural resources: oil, asbestos, marble, copper, limestone, chromium, manganese, iron. Exports: oil. Imports: machinery and transport equipment, food, mineral fuels, tobacco. Major trading partners: U.K., U.S., India, Australia, China, Japan.

1. Excluding the Kuria Muria Islands.

Geography. Oman is a 1,000-mile-long (1,609-km) coastal plain at the southeastern tip of the Arabian peninsula lying on the Arabian Sea and the Gulf of Oman. The interior is a plateau. The country is the size of Kansas.

Government. The Sultan of Oman (formerly called Muscat and Oman), an absolute monarch, is assisted by a council of ministers, six specialized councils, a consultative council and personal advisers.

There are no political parties.

History. Although Oman is an independent state under the rule of the Sultan, it has been under British protection since the early 19th century.

Muscat, the capital of the geographical area known as Oman, was occupied by the Portuguese from 1508 to 1648. Then it fell to Persian princes and later was regained by the Sultan.

The Kuria Muria Islands, formerly part of Aden, were given to Oman by the British in 1967.

In a palace coup on July 23, 1970, the Sultan, Sa'id bin Taimur, who had ruled since 1932, was overthrown by his son, who promised to establish a modern government and use new-found wealth to aid the people of this very isolated state.

PAKISTAN

Islamic Republic of Pakistan
President: Gen. Mohammad Zia ul-Haq (1978)
Area: 342,750 sq mi. (877,723 sq km)[1]
Population (est. 1982): 85,500,000 (average annual growth rate: 2.9%)
Density per square mile: 249.5
Capital (1972 census): Islamabad, 77,000
Largest cities (1981 census for metropolitan area): Karachi, 5,100,000; Lahore, 2,900,000; Faisalabad, (Lyallpur) 1,920,000; Rawalpindi, 920,000; Hyderabad, 795,000
Monetary unit: Pakistan rupee
Principal languages: Urdu (national), English (official), Punjabi, Sindhi, Pashtu, and Baluchi
Religions: Islam, 97%; Hindu, Christian
Literacy rate (1980): 24%
Economic summary: Gross national product (1980): $24.9 billion. Average annual growth rate (1970–79): 1.5%. Per capita income (1980): $300. Land used for agriculture: 24%; labor force: 52%; principal products: wheat, rice, cotton. Labor force in industry: 21%; major products: cotton textiles, processed foods, tobacco, chemicals, natural gas. Natural resources: natural gas, limited petroleum, iron ore. Exports: raw and manufactured cotton, rice, carpets, leather, petroleum products. Imports: food grains, edible oil, crude oil, machinery, chemicals, transport equipment. Major trading partners: U.S., U.K., West Germany, Saudi Arabia, Japan, China.

1. Excluding Kashmir and Jammu.

Geography. Pakistan is situated in the western part of the Indian subcontinent, with Afghanistan and Iran on the west, India on the east, and the Arabian Sea on the south.

Nearly twice the size of California, Pakistan consists of towering mountains, including the Hindu Kush in the west, a desert area in the east, the

Punjab plains in the north, and an expanse of alluvial plains. The 1,000-mile-long (1,609 km) Indus River flows through the country from the Kashmir to the Arabian Sea.

Government. On July 5, 1977, martial law returned to Pakistan when Gen. Mohammad Zia ul-Haq, Army Chief of Staff, ousted the civilian government of Prime Minister Zulfikar Ali Bhutto. Zia declared himself Chief Administrator of Martial Law as head of a four-man council. The national and state assemblies were dissolved and all political parties banned, while the Chief Justices of the four states replaced the governors.

History. Pakistan was one of the two original successor states to British India. For almost 25 years following independence in 1947, it consisted of two separate regions. East and West Pakistan, but now comprises only the western sector. It consists of Sind, Baluchistan, the former North-West Frontier Province, western Punjab, the princely state of Bahawalpur, and several other smaller native states.

The British became the dominant power in the region in 1797 following Lord Clive's military victory, but rebellious tribes kept the northwest in turmoil. In the northeast, the formation of the Moslem League in 1906 estranged the Moslems from the Hindus. In 1930, the league, led by Mohammed Ali Jinnah, demanded creation of a Moslem state wherever Moslems were in the majority. He supported Britain during the war. Afterward, the league received almost a unanimous Moslem vote in 1946 and Britain agreed to the formation of Pakistan as a separate dominion.

Pakistan was proclaimed a republic March 23, 1956. Iskander Mirza, then Governor General, was elected Provisional President and H. S. Suhrawardy became the first non-Moslem League Prime Minister.

In 1958, Mirza surrendered his power to Gen. Ayub Khan, who purged corrupt and inefficient officeholders, broke up the feudal land system, eliminated much of the black market, tax evasion, and hoarding, and revolutionized education. In 1969, Gen. Yahya Khan ousted Ayub and took over as President.

The election of 1970 set the stage for civil war when Sheik Muuibur called general strikes, which turned bloody, and told East Pakistanis to stop paying taxes to the central government. West Pakistan troops moved in and fighting began. The independent state of Bangladesh, or Bengali nation, was proclaimed March 26, 1971.

The intervention of Indian troops protected the new state and brought Yahya down. Bhutto took over and accepted Bangladesh as an independent entity.

Diplomatically, 1976 saw the resumption of formal relations between India and Pakistan. At the same time, civilian air traffic between the two nations was restored after an 11-year interruption.

Pakistan's first elections under civilian rule took place in March 1977 and provoked bitter opposition protest when Bhutto's party was declared to have won 155 of the 200 elected seats in the 216-member National Assembly. A rising tide of violent protest and political deadlock led to a military takeover on July 5. Gen. Mohammed Zia ul-Haq became Chief Martial Law Administrator.

Bhutto was tried and convicted for the 1974 murder of a political opponent, and despite worldwide protests was executed on April 4, 1979, touching off riots by his supporters. Zia, who had declared himself President on Sept. 16, 1978, a month after Fazel Elahi Chaudhry left office upon the completion of his 5-year term.

In April 1981, a five-year U.S. military and economic aid program, with $500 million to be delivered in the first year, was accepted by Pakistan, which had rejected a two-year, $400-million package offered by the Carter administration as inadequate to meet the Soviet threat. While Zia continued to repress political opposition at home, he became increasingly active in world affairs. Pakistan took the leadership in Islamic efforts to settle the war between Iran and Iraq and in opposing the Soviet presence in Afghanistan and the Soviet-backed Vietnamese invasion of Cambodia.

In January 1982, Saudi Arabia was reported to have pledged $500 million to Pakistan to help pay for the first six of a total of 40 U.S. F-16 jet fighters. In February, Zia extended the 28-month ban on all political activity and the next month announced that general elections—once expected to take place before the end of 1982—would be indefinitely postponed.

PANAMA

Republic of Panama
President: Ricardo de la Espriella (1982)
Area: 29,306 sq mi. (75,903 sq km)
Population (est. 1982): 2,000,000 (average annual growth rate: 2.3%) (mestizo, 65%; black, 13%; white, 11%; Indian, 10%)
Density per square mile: 68.2
Capital and largest city (est. 1980): Panama City, 400,000
Monetary unit: Balboa
Language: Spanish (official)
Religion: Roman Catholic, 86%, Protestant
National name: República de Panamá
Literacy rate (1981): 82%
Economic summary: Gross national product (1980): $3.2 billion. Average annual growth rate (1970–79): 1.3%. Per capita income (1980): $1,730. Land used for agriculture: 24%; labor force: 29%; principal products: bananas, corn, sugar, rice, cattle. Labor force in industry: 18%; major industrial products: refined petroleum, sugar. Natural resources: copper (unexploited). Exports: bananas, refined petroleum, sugar, shrimp. Imports: crude oil, crude petroleum, chemicals, food. Major trading partners: U.S., West Germany, Ecuador.

Geography. The southernmost of the Central American nations, Panama is south of Costa Rica and north of Colombia. The Panama Canal bisects the isthmus at its narrowest and lowest point, allowing passage from the Caribbean Sea to the Pacific Ocean.

Panama is slightly smaller than South Carolina. It is marked by a chain of volcanic mountains in the west, moderate hills in the interior, and a low range on the east coast. There are extensive forests in the fertile Caribbean area.

Government. In 1972, a new Constitution was approved by a new 505-seat National Assembly of Community Representatives (corregidores), which was created in the first election in five years. The Charter provides for indirect election of the President by the Assembly for a six-year term.

History. Visited by Columbus in 1502 on his fourth voyage and explored by Balboa in 1513, Panama was the principal transshipment point for Spanish treasure and supplies to and from South and Central America in colonial days. In 1821, when Central America revolted against Spain, Panama joined Colombia, which already had declared its independence. For the next 82 years, Panama attempted unsuccessfully to break away from Colombia. After U. S. proposals for canal rights over the narrow isthmus had been rejected by Colombia, Panama proclaimed its independence with U.S. backing in 1903.

For canal rights in perpetuity, the U.S. paid Panama $10 million and agreed to pay $250,000 each year, increased to $430,000 after devaluation of the U.S. dollar in 1933 and was further increased under a revised treaty signed in 1955. In exchange, the U.S. got the Canal Zone—a 10-mile-wide strip across the isthmus—and a considerable degree of influence in Panama's affairs.

In 1968, Dr. Arnulfo Arias was elected President for the third time in three decades. And for the third time, he was thrown out of office by the military. A two-man junta, Col. José M. Pinilla and Col. Bolivar Urrutia, took control. They were ousted by Gen. Omar Torrijos Herrera, who named a new junta, with Demetrio Lakas Bahas as President.

Panama and the U.S. agreed in 1974 to negotiate the eventual reversion of the canal to Panama, despite strongly expressed opposition in the U.S. Congress. The texts of two treaties—one governing the transfer of the canal and the other guaranteeing its neutrality after transfer—were negotiated by August 1977 and were signed by Torrijos and President Carter in Washington on September 7. A Panamanian referendum approved the treaties by more than two thirds on October 23, but further changes were insisted upon by the U.S. Senate.

The principal change was a reservation sponsored by Senator Dennis De Concini, an Arizona Democrat, specifying that despite the neutrality treaty's specification that only Panama shall maintain forces in its territory after transfer of the canal Dec. 31, 1999, the U.S. should have the right to use military force to keep the canal operating if it should become obstructed. After lengthy debate, the Senate approved the neutrality treaty on March 16, 1978, by 68–32 and by the same vote approved the basic treaty governing the transfer on April 18. On June 16, Carter and Torrijos exchanged instruments of ratification in Panama City.

The basic treaty provides an increase from the present $2.3 million a year in royalties to $10 million a year during the transition period, with an additional annual payment of $10 million if it can be obtained from tolls. It also requires the use of more Panamanians as canal employees in the interim and pledges the U.S. not to pursue the development of another canal without the agreement of Panama.

The death of Torrijos in a plane crash on July 31, 1981, left a power vacuum. President Aristides Royo, named by Torrijos in 1978 to a six-year term, clashed with the leadership of the National Guard and was unable to harmonize factions within the ruling Democratic Revolutionary Party. On July 30, 1982, Royo resigned in favor of Vice President Ricardo de la Espriella amid speculation that the National Guard might resume military rule.

Panama Canal. First conceived by the Spaniards in 1534, when King Charles V of Spain ordered a survey of a waterway across the Isthmus, a construction concession was granted by the Colombian government in 1878 to St. Lucien N. B. Wyse, representing a French company. Two years later, the French Canal Company, inspired by Ferdinand de Lesseps, began construction of what was to have been a sea-level canal. The effort ended in bankruptcy nine years later and the United States ultimately paid the French $40 million for their rights and assets.

The U.S. project, built on territory controlled by the United States, and calling for the creation of an interior lake connected to both oceans by locks, got under way in 1904. Completed in 1914, the Canal is 40.27 miles long and lifts ships 85 feet above sea level through a series of three locks on the Pacific and Atlantic sides. Enlarged in later years, each lock now measures 1,000 feet in length, 110 feet in width, and 40 feet in depth of water.

PAPUA NEW GUINEA

Sovereign: Queen Elizabeth II
Governor General: Sir Tore Lokoloko (1977)
Prime Minister: Michael Somare (1982)
Area: 183,540 sq mi. (475,369 sq km)
Population (est. 1982): 3,250,000 (average annual growth rate: 2.2%)
Density per square mile: 17.7
Capital and largest city (est. 1980): Port Moresby, 120,000
Monetary unit: Kina
Languages: English, Melanesian pidgin, and 717 distinct native languages
Religions: Roman Catholic, 31%; Lutheran, 27%; Anglican, United Church
Member of Commonwealth of Nations
Literacy rate (1982): 15%
Economic summary: Gross national product (1980): $2.4 billion. Average annual growth rate (1970–79): 0.3%. Per Capita Income (1980): $780. Labor force in agriculture, including fishing: 85%; principal products: sweet potatoes, coffee, copra, palm oil, cocoa, tea, rubber, cattle. Major industrial products: soap, concrete products, clothing, light fabricated metal products, paint, furniture. Natural resources: copper, gold, silver, timber, tuna. Exports: copper, coffee and cocoa beans, copra, timber. Imports: food, machinery, transport equipment, fuels, chemicals. Major trading partners: Australia, U.K., Japan.

Geography. Papua New Guinea occupies the eastern half of the island of New Guinea, just north of Australia, and many outlying islands. The Indonesian province of Irian Jaya is to the west. To the north and east are the islands of Manus, New Britain, New Ireland, and Bougainville, all part of Papua New Guinea.

Papua New Guinea is about one tenth larger than California. Its mountainous interior has only recently been explored. The high-plateau climate is temperate, in contrast to the tropical climate of the coastal plains. Two major rivers, the Sepik and the Fly, are navigable for shallow-draft vessels.

Government. Papua New Guinea attained independence Sept. 16, 1975, ending a United Nations trusteeship under the administration of Australia. Parliamentary democracy was established by a

Constitution that invests power in a 109-member national legislature.

The Pangu Party, People's Progress Party, and United Party are the largest of half a dozen political parties.

History. The eastern half of New Guinea was first visited by Spanish and Portuguese explorers in the 16th century, but a permanent European presence was not established until 1884, when Germany declared a protectorate over the northern coast and Britain took similar action in the south. Both nations formally annexed their protectorates and, in 1901, Britain transferred its rights to a newly independent Australia. Australian troops invaded German New Guinea in World War I and retained control under a League of Nations mandate that eventually became a United Nations trusteeship, incorporating a territorial government in the southern region, known as Papua.

Australia granted limited home rule in 1951 and, in 1964, organized elections for the first House of Assembly. Autonomy in internal affairs came nine years later.

Just before independence, dissidents on the island of Bougainville, whose copper resources provide the chief foreign earnings for the central government, declared their intention to secede. The central government responded by taking direct control in October 1975, amid warnings from Australia that it would oppose secession. Prime Minister Michael Somare met with pro-secessionists early in 1976 and, after conceding extra powers for a restored provincial government, resolved the dispute.

Somare lost a vote of confidence on March 11, 1980, and was succeeded by Sir Julius Chan, head of the People's Progress Party and former Finance Minister. After the elections of June 1982, he was chosen prime minister by the new legislature.

PARAGUAY

Republic of Paraguay
President: Gen. Alfredo Stroessner (1954)
Area: 157,047 sq mi. (406,752 sq km)
Population (est. 1982): 3,375,000 (average annual growth rate: 2.4%) (mestizo, 95%; white, 3%; Indian, 2%)
Density per square mile: 21.9
Capital and largest city (est. 1980): Asunción, 530,000
Monetary unit: Guaraní
Languages: Spanish (official), Guaraní
Religion: Roman Catholic (official)
National name: República del Paraguay
Literacy rate (1981): 40%
Economic summary: Gross national product (1980): $4.1 billion. Average annual growth rate (1970–79): 5.3%. Per capita income (1980): $1,340. Labor force in agriculture: 53%; principal products: oilseeds, cotton, wheat, sweet potatoes, tobacco, corn, rice, sugar cane. Labor force in industry: 19%; major products: packed meats, crushed oilseeds, beverages, textiles, light consumer goods, cement. Natural resource: timber. Exports: cotton, oilseeds, meat products, tobacco, timber, coffee, essential oils. Imports: fuels and lubricants, machinery and motors, motor vehicles, beverages, tobacco, foodstuffs. Major trading partners: Argentina, Brazil, West Germany, U.S., Netherlands.

Geography. California-size Paraguay is surrounded by Brazil, Bolivia, and Argentina in south central South America. Eastern Paraguay, between the Paraná and Paraguay Rivers, is upland country with the thickest population settled on the grassy slope that inclines toward the Paraguay River. The greater part of the Chaco region to the west is covered with marshes, lagoons, dense forests, and jungles.

Government. The President is elected by popular vote for five years. The legislature is bicameral, consisting of a Senate of 30 members and a Chamber of Representatives of 60 members. There is also a Council of State, whose members are nominated by the government.

The governing Partido Colorado was further strengthened in 1977 when the Partido Liberal Unido, a merger of the Partido Liberal Radical and Partido Liberal, was declared illegal.

History. In 1526 and again in 1529, Sebastian Cabot explored Paraguay when he sailed up the Paraná and Paraguay Rivers. From 1608 until their expulsion from the Spanish dominions in 1767, the Jesuits maintained an extensive establishment in the south and east of Paraguay. In 1811, Paraguay revolted against Spanish rule and became a nominal republic under two Consuls.

Actually, Paraguay was governed by three dictators during the first 60 years of independence. The third, Francisco López, waged war against Brazil and Argentina in 1864–65, a conflict in which the male population was almost wiped out. A new Constitution in 1870, designed to prevent dictatorships and internal strife, failed to do so, and not until 1912 did a period of comparative economic and political stability begin. The dispute between Paraguay and Bolivia over the Chaco region led to war in 1932 and was finally settled by the 1935 Buenos Aires Peace Conference, which gave most of the Chaco to Paraguay.

After World War II, politics became particularly unstable. Juan Natalicio González was elected President in 1948. Successive revolts on Jan. 30 and Feb. 26, 1949, ousted him and his successor. The leader of the second revolt, Felipe Molas López, was elected President in April but gave way to Federico Chaves. Re-elected in 1953, Chaves was ousted by the army, and Gen. Alfredo Stroessner was elected to complete his term.

Stroessner ruled under a state of siege until 1965, when the dictatorship was relaxed and exiles returned. The Constitution was revised in 1967 to permit Stroessner to be re-elected, and press freedom was briefly restored before the regime again moved to repress opposition.

Although oil exploration begun by U.S. companies in the Chaco boreal in 1974 has been fruitless, Paraguay found prosperity in another form of energy when construction started in 1978 on the Itaipu Dam on the Parana River as a joint Paraguayan-Brazilian project. The largest hydroelectric development in the world when completed in 1988, Itaipu will generate 12.6 megawatts of electricity, surpassing the U.S. Grand Coulee Dam. With 40,000 Paraguayans working around the clock building the $12-billion project, unemployment has virtually disappeared.

The Stroessner regime was criticized by the U.S. State Department during the Carter administration as a violator of human rights, but unlike Argentina and Uruguay, Paraguay did not suffer cuts in U.S. military aid. The criticism is credited with having reduced the number of political prisoners to a "few hundred."

PERU

Republic of Peru
President: Fernando Belaúnde Terry (1980)
Premier: Manuel Ulloa (1980)
Area: 496,222 sq mi. (1,285,216 sq km)
Population (1982): 18,850,000 (average annual growth rate: 2.8%) (white and mestizo, 52%; Indian, 46%)
Density per square mile: 38.0
Capital: Lima
Largest cities (est. 1979 for metropolitan area): Lima, 4,900,000; **(est. 1978):** Arequipa, 410,000; Trujillo, 350,000; Chiclayo, 260,000; Piura, 165,000; Cuzco, 150,000
Monetary unit: Sol
Languages: Spanish, Quéchua
Religion: Roman Catholic
National name: República del Perú
Literacy rate (1981): 45%
Economic summary: Gross national product (1980): $16.5 billion. Average annual growth rate (1970–79): 0.2%. Per capita income (1980): $930. Land used for agriculture: 2%; labor force: 42%; principal products: corn, sugar, cotton, coffee, wool. Labor force in industry: 13%; major products: processed minerals, fish meal, refined petroleum, textiles. Natural resources: minerals and metals, fish, petroleum, timber. Exports: copper, fish products, cotton, sugar, coffee, lead, silver, zinc, wool, iron ore. Imports: machinery, foodstuffs, chemicals, pharmaceuticals. Major trading partners: U.S., Japan, Western European, and Latin American countries.

Geography. Peru, in western South America, extends for nearly 1,500 miles (2,414 km) along the Pacific Ocean. Colombia and Ecuador are to the north, Brazil and Bolivia to the east, and Chile to the south.

Five sixths the size of Alaska, Peru is divided by the Andes Mountains into three sharply differentiated zones. To the west is the coastline, much of it arid, extending 50 to 100 miles (80 to 160 km) inland. The mountain area, with peaks over 20,000 feet (6,096 m), lofty plateaus, and deep valleys, lies centrally. Beyond the mountains to the east is the heavily forested slope leading to the Amazonian plains.

Government. The President, elected by universal suffrage for a five-year term, holds executive power. A Senate of 60 members and a Chamber of Deputies of 180 members, both elected for five-year terms, share legislative power.

The major political parties are: Acción Popular (98 of 180 seats in the Chamber and 26 of 60 seats in the Senate), led by President Fernando Belaúnde Terry; Partido Popular Cristiano (10 Chamber seats and 6 Senate seats), led by Luis Bedoya Reyes; and the opposition Partido Aprista Peruano (58 Chamber seats and 18 Senate seats), led by Luis Alberto Sanchez. The Partido Popular Cristiano is allied with Belaúnde.

History. Peru was once part of the great Incan empire and later the major vice-royalty of Spanish South America. It was conquered in 1531–33 by Francisco Pizarro. On July 28, 1821, Peru proclaimed its independence, but the Spanish were not finally defeated until 1824. For a hundred years thereafter, revolutions were frequent, and a new war was fought with Spain in 1864–66.

Peru emerged from 20 years of dictatorship in 1945 with the inauguration of President José Luis Bustamente y Rivero after the first free election in many decades. But he served for only three years and was succeeded in turn by Gen. Manuel A. Odria, Manuel Prado y Ugarteche, and Fernando Belaúnde Terry. On Oct. 3, 1968, Belaúnde was overthrown by Gen. Juan Velasco Alvarado.

Velasco nationalized the nation's second biggest bank and turned two large newspapers over to Marxists in 1970, but he also allowed a new agreement with a copper-mining consortium of four American firms.

On May 31, 1970, the country suffered the hemisphere's worst natural disaster, an earthquake which, together with a mud slide it caused, took an estimated 50,000 lives.

The World Bank granted Peru $470 million in credits in 1973, which appeared to end a boycott by international financial institutions in which the U.S. has a strong influence. American copper and fishing firms were seized in 1974, but compensation was paid. Peru also became in 1974 the first nation in the Western Hemisphere to receive Soviet military advisers.

On Aug. 29, 1975, Velasco was replaced in a bloodless coup by his Premier, Gen. Francisco Morales Bermúdez. To meet International Monetary Fund requirements for the extension of credit, Morales decreed a severe economic austerity program in 1977, touching off student and leftist demonstrations. Even stiffer measures, ranging from 50% to 100% increases in the prices of essentials, were ordered in 1978.

Fulfilling a pledge to restore civilian government, Morales scheduled elections for May 18, 1980, in which Belaúnde Terry, the last civilian President, won 43% of the vote in a field of 15 candidates. Allied with the small Partido Popular Cristiano, Belaúnde Terry's Acción Popular party was assured of a parliamentary majority. In one of his first moves, the new President returned to private ownership newspapers that had been seized under the Morales regime.

THE PHILIPPINES

Republic of the Philippines
President (1965): Ferdinand E. Marcos
Prime Minister: César Virata (1981)
Area: 115,707 sq mi. (299,681 sq km)
Population (est. 1982): 50,500,000 (average annual growth rate: 2.5%)
Density per square mile: 436.4
Capital: Quezon City
Largest cities (est. 1977 for metropolitan area): Manila, 7,500,000 **(est. 1975 by U.N.):** Quezon City, 994,700; Davao, 515,500; Cebu, 418,500
Monetary unit: Peso
Languages: Pilipino, English, Spanish; dialects: Tagalog, Visayan
Religions: Roman Catholic, 85%; Islam, 4%; Aglipayan (Independent Philippine Christian), 4%; Protestant, 3%
National name: Republika ng Pilipinas
Literacy rate (1981): 83%
Economic summary: Gross national product (1980): $34.4 billion. Average annual growth rate (1970–79): 3.9%. Per capita income (1980): $720. Land used for agriculture: 53%; labor force: 47%; principal products: rice, corn, coconuts, sugar cane, bananas, tobacco. Labor force in industry: 12%; major products: processed agricultural products, textiles, chemicals and chemical products. Natural resources: forests, metallic and non-metallic minerals. Exports: coconut products, sugar, logs and lumber, copper concentrates, bananas, garments, nickel.

Imports: petroleum, industrial equipment, wheat. Major trading partners: U.S., Japan.

Geography. The Philippine Islands are an archipelago of over 7,000 islands lying about 500 miles (805 km) off the southeast coast of Asia. The overall land area is comparable to that of Arizona. The northernmost island, Y'Ami, is 65 miles (105 km) from Taiwan, while the southernmost, Saluag, is 40 miles (64 km) east of Borneo.

Only about 7% of the islands are larger than one square mile, and only one third have names. The largest are Luzon in the north (40,420 sq mi.; 04,687 sq km), Mindanao in the south (36,537 sq mi.; 94,631 sq km), Samar (5,124 sq mi.; 13,271 sq km), Negros (4,903 sq mi.; 12,699 sq km), and Palawan (4,550 sq km).

The islands are of volcanic origin, with the larger ones crossed by mountain ranges. The highest peak is Mount Apo (9,690 ft; 2,954 m) on Mindanao.

Government. President Ferdinand E. Marcos proclaimed a new Constitution in 1973, replacing the previous presidential style of government with a parliamentary system. The president became the symbolic head of state and the prime minister the head of government, with Marcos holding both posts. Marcos has ruled by decree since Sept. 21, 1972, and the new Constitution dissolved the previous legislature. A new National Assembly of 186 elected and 31 appointed members was chosen April 7, 1978. Its powers are limited, within the framework of what Marcos has called "constitutional authoritarianism."

History. Fernando Magellan, the Portuguese navigator in the service of Spain, discovered the Philippines in 1521. Twenty-one years later, a Spanish exploration party named the group of islands in honor of Prince Philip, later Philip II of Spain. Spain retained possession of the islands for the next 350 years.

The Philippines were ceded to the U.S. in 1899 by the Treaty of Paris after the Spanish-American War. Meanwhile, the Filipinos, led by Emilio Aguinaldo, had declared their independence. They continued guerrilla warfare against U.S. troops until the capture of Aguinaldo in 1901. By 1902, peace was established except among the Moros.

The first U.S. civilian Governor-General was William Howard Taft (1901–04). The Jones Law (1916) provided for the establishment of a Philippine Legislature composed of an elective Senate and House of Representatives. The Tydings-McDuffie Act (1934) provided for a transitional period until 1946, at which time the Philippines would become completely independent.

Under a Constitution approved by the people of the Philippines in 1935, the Commonwealth of the Philippines came into being, with Manuel Quezon y Molina as president.

On Dec. 8, 1941, the Philippines were invaded by Japanese troops. Following the fall of Bataan and Corregidor, Quezon established a government-in-exile, which he headed until his death in 1944. He was succeeded by Vice President Sergio Osmeña.

U.S. forces led by Gen. Douglas MacArthur reinvaded the Philippines in October 1944 and, after the liberation of Manila in February 1945, Osmeña re-established the government.

The Philippines achieved full independence on July 4, 1946. Manuel A. Roxas y Acuña was elected first president. Subsequent presidents have been Elpidio Quirino (1948–53), Ramón Magsaysay (1953–57). Carlos P. García (1957–61), Diosdado Macapagal (1961–65), and Ferdinand E. Marcos (since Dec. 30, 1965).

Marcos became the first president in Philippine history to win re-election in 1969, when he overwhelmingly defeated Sergio Osmeña, Jr., with campaign promises to become less dependent on the U.S. and to establish ties with Communist countries. The campaign violence led to 59 deaths. After his inauguration, the worst peacetime riots in Philippine history occurred when a student-led demonstration tried to storm the presidential palace, with 5 dead and 157 injured, to protest government corruption.

Political, civil, and religious unrest was responsible for the deaths of almost 500 persons in 1971, and disastrous month-long rains that caused enormous flooding added to the toll in 1972. In September 1972, Marcos declared martial law and arrested hundreds of political opponents, journalists, and leftists.

Nearly 8,000 persons died Aug. 17, 1976, when an earthquake measuring 8 on the Richter scale hit Mindanao and other southern islands. The disaster temporarily quelled a rebellion by the Moslem majority in Mindanao, but fighting resumed until a truce was reached in December. Rebel representatives and Manila officials signed an agreement in Tripoli in 1977, providing a degree of autonomy for the Moslem region.

The Philippines was one of six nations criticized by the U.S. State Department for human-rights violations in a report made public in 1977, although the department recommended continuing aid because of the importance of U.S. bases in the Philippines. Marcos at first declared he would reject any aid and threatened to close the bases but later softened, saying they could remain if the U.S. pledged that the bases would be used to defend the Philippines in the event of an attack. He also announced that he would phase out the military tribunals he established in 1972 and in two months freed about 1,000 of 4,774 prisoners being held for military trial.

Political restraints were eased for the legislative elections of 1978. The suppressed Liberal Party and other opposition groups formed the People's Force Party and contested the 21 seats assigned to Manila. Amid charges of fraud, Marcos' New Society Movement won all 21. Marcos freed many political prisoners before his inauguration as prime minister on June 12 and pledged to move toward "making democracy real", although he retained his powers under martial law.

Marcos, who had freed the last of the national leaders still in detention, former Senator Benigno S. Aquino, Jr., in 1980 and permitted him to go to the United States, ended eight years of martial law on January 17, 1981. On April 7, a plebiscite approved changes to the 1973 Constitution establishing a ministerial government and authorizing re-election of the President. On June 16, Marcos won a second six-year term with 86% of the vote as most opposition parties boycotted the election.

In January 1982, an anti-Marcos coalition was formed by Aquino and former Senator Salvador Laurel. It was joined by former President Macapagal and his Liberal Party and the Filipino Democratic Party, together with Moslem leaders from Mindanao. On Feb. 28, Marcos added to the liberalizing spirit by declaring that the Communist

Party could again become legal if it renounced violence. He later retracted the offer, saying the Communists would also have to win 10% of the vote in a national election.

POLAND

Polish People's Republic
President of the Council of State: Henryk Jablonski (1972)
Premier: Gen Wojciech Jaruzelski (1981)
Area: 120,359 sq mi. (311,730 sq km)
Population (est. 1982): 36,300,000 (average annual growth rate: 0.9%)
Density per square mile: 301.6
Capital: Warsaw
Largest cities (est. 1980): Warsaw, 1,576,600; Lodz, 830,800; Krakow, 706,100; Wroclaw, 609,100; Poznan, 545,600; Gdansk, 443,200; Szczecin, 388,000; Katowice, 351,300
Monetary unit: Zloty
Language: Polish (more than 90%)
Religions: Roman Catholic, Greek Orthodox, Protestant, Jewish
National name: Polska Rzeczpospolita Ludowa
Literacy rate (1981): 98%
Economic summary: Gross national product (1980): $139.8 billion. Average annual growth rate (1970–79): 5.2%. Per capita income (1980): $3,900. Labor force in agriculture: 27%; principal products: grains, sugar beets, potatoes, hogs and other livestock. Labor force in industry: 32%; major products: iron and steel, chemicals, textiles, processed foods, transport equipment. Natural resources: coal, sulfur, copper, natural gas. Exports: fuels, machinery and equipment, agricultural products, light industrial products. Imports: machinery and equipment, fuels, raw materials, agricultural and food products. Major trading partners: Communist bloc countries, U.K., Italy, U.S., West Germany, France.

Geography. Poland, a country the size of New Mexico in north central Europe, borders on East Germany to the west, Czechoslovakia to the south, and the U.S.S.R. to the east. In the north is the Baltic Sea.

Most of the country is a plain with no natural boundaries except the Carpathian Mountains in the south and the Oder and Neisse Rivers in the east. Other major rivers, which are important to commerce, are the Vistula, Warta, and Bug.

Government. The 1952 Constitution describes Poland as a people's republic. The supreme organ of state authority is the Sejm (Parliament), which is composed of 460 members elected for four years.

The major political parties are the Polish United Workers' (Communist) Party (255 of 460 seats in the Sejm), led by First Secretary Wojciech Jaruzelski; United Peasant Party (117 seats), led by Stefan Malinowski; Democratic Party (39 seats), led by Edward Kowalczyk; non-party members and Catholic organizations (49 seats).

History. Little is known about Polish history before the 11th century, when King Boleslaus I (the Brave) ruled over Bohemia, Saxony, and Moravia. Mongol invasions in 1241 and 1259 were repelled. Meanwhile, the Teutonic knights of Prussia conquered part of Poland and barred the latter's access to the Baltic. The knights were defeated by Wladislaus II at Tannenberg in 1410 and became Polish vassals, and Poland regained a Baltic shoreline. Poland reached the peak of power between the 14th and 16th centuries, scoring military successes against the Russians and Turks. In 1683, John III (John Sobieski) turned back the Turkish tide at Vienna.

An elective monarchy failed to produce strong central authority, and Prussia, Russia, and Austria were able to carry out a first partition of the country in 1772, a second in 1792, and a third in 1795–96. For more than a century thereafter, there was no Polish state, but the Poles never ceased their efforts to regain their independence.

Poland was formally reconstituted in November 1918, with Marshal Josef Pilsudski as Chief of State. In 1919, Ignace Paderewski, the famous pianist and patriot, became the first premier. In 1926, Pilsudski seized complete power in a coup and ruled dictatorially until his death on May 12, 1935, when he was succeeded by Marshal Edward Smigly-Rydz.

Despite a 10-year nonaggression pact signed in 1934, Hitler attacked Poland on Sept. 1, 1939. Russian troops invaded from the east on September 17, and on September 28 a German-Russian agreement divided Poland between Russia and Germany. Wladyslaw Raczkiewicz formed a government-in-exile in France, which moved to London after France's defeat in 1940.

All of Poland was occupied by Germany after the Nazi attack on the U.S.S.R. in June 1941. On July 30, 1941, the government-in-exile signed an agreement with the U.S.S.R. in which the latter voided all German-Soviet agreements effected after Sept. 1, 1939.

The legal Polish government soon fell out with the Russians, however, and, in 1944, a Communist-dominated Polish Committee of National Liberation received Soviet recognition. Moving to Lublin after that city's liberation, it proclaimed itself the Provisional Government of Poland. Some former members of the Polish government in London joined with the Lublin government to form the Polish Government of National Unity, which Britain and the U.S. recognized.

On Aug. 2, 1945, in Berlin, President Harry S. Truman, Joseph Stalin and Prime Minister Clement Attlee of Britain established a new *de facto* western frontier for Poland along the Oder and Neisse Rivers. (The border was finally agreed to by West Germany in a nonaggression pact signed Dec. 7, 1970.) On Aug. 16, 1945, the U.S.S.R. and Poland signed a treaty delimiting the Soviet-Polish frontier. Under these agreements, Poland was shifted westward. In the east it lost 69,860 square miles (180,934 sq km) with 10,772,000 inhabitants; in the west it gained (subject to final peace-conference approval) 38,986 square miles (100,973 sq km) with a prewar population of 8,621,000.

In 1946, a unicameral Parliament was established by referendum. Then, in 1947, the government bloc won a huge majority in government-controlled elections, opposition was suppressed and the Sovietization of Poland begun, with Soviet Marshal Konstantin Rokossovsky as Defense Minister and army commander.

A new Constitution in 1952 made Poland a "people's democracy" of the Soviet type. In 1955, Poland, which had joined the Council for Economic Mutual Assistance in 1949, became a member of the Warsaw Treaty Organization, and its foreign policy became identical with that of the U.S.S.R. The government undertook persecution of the Roman Catholic Church as a remaining source of opposition and in 1953 arrested the primate, Stefan Cardinal Wyszynski. But in June 1956, worker and student riots in Poznan forced reconsideration of the repression.

Wladyslaw Gomulka was elected leader of the United Workers (Communist) Party in 1956. He denounced the Stalinist terror, ousted many Stalinists, relieved Rokossovsky, freed Wyszynski, and improved relations with the church. Most collective farms were dissolved, and the press became freer.

Much as the Poznan bread riots of 1956 brought Gomulka to power, so pre-Christmas rioting in 1970 in Gdansk and other Baltic coastal towns caused Gomulka to fall and elevated Edward Gierek to the key post of party boss. Cause of the worker riots was steep rises in food prices.

Another increase in the summer of 1976 again resulted in widespread riots.

As a result of the riots, the government in 1977 revised its economic goals to put more emphasis on production of consumer goods and reduced foreign borrowing for capital investment, slowing industrial development.

An event of profound importance to Poland's 90% Catholic population was the election in October 1978 of Karol Cardinal Wojtila of Krakow as Pope John Paul II. His visit to his homeland from June 2 to June 11, 1979, was the first papal journey to a Marxist state.

A strike that began in shipyards and spread to other industries in August 1980 produced a stunning victory for workers on Aug. 31 when the economically hard-pressed government accepted for the first time in a Marxist state the right of workers to organize in independent unions. In addition, the strikers won curbs on media censorship and the privileges of Communist Party members over ordinary workers in state enterprises. The strike was supported financially by Western unions and vocally by Pope John Paul II.

The strike also led to major changes in Polish leadership. Edward Babuich, who became Premier early in 1980, was replaced by Jozef Pinkowski, and Edward Gierek, longtime Communist Party head, was ousted in favor of Stanislaw Kania.

Led by Solidarity, a free union founded by Lech Walesa, workers launched a drive for liberty and improved conditions. A national strike for a five-day week in January 1981 led to the dismissal of Premier Pinkowski and the naming of the fourth Premier in less than a year, Gen. Wojciech Jaruzelski. He and Kania defended workers' gains against Soviet and Polish hardline criticism, but warned of the deteriorating economy, which required Western creditors in April to defer repayment of $2.6 billion of $27 billion in foreign debt. In July, for the first time within the Soviet bloc, an emergency party congress voted by secret ballot and confirmed Kania and moderate leaders, rejecting right-wing, pro-Soviet members of the Politburo.

The new freedom was short-lived. Pressed by Moscow, the Communist Party's central committee ousted Kania on Oct. 18 and replaced him with Jaruzelski, who now held the posts of first secretary of the party, premier, defense minister, and commander in chief of the armed forces. The central committee called for an "immediate end" to all strikes, to be enforced by martial law if necessary. When a general strike was called for the first time since March, the government used the army to insure distribution of food and fuel.

Antistrike legislation was approved on Dec. 2 and martial law declared on Dec. 13, when Walesa was arrested. Ten days later, President Reagan ordered sanctions against the Polish government, stopping food shipments and cutting commercial air traffic. In a New Year message, Pope John Paul II criticized military rule and Polish bishops formally protested the government's action. On Jan. 11, 1982, NATO foreign ministers condemned the Soviet role in Poland and hinted at sanctions against Moscow and suspension of negotiations on Poland's foreign debts.

Despite demands for declaring Poland in default, Congress in February authorized payment of $3.5 million in interest charges to U.S. banks that had given loans to Poland for food purchases. Poland's economic situation remained desperate and its internal political climate so tense that the government postponed indefinitely a papal visit set for August.

PORTUGAL

Portuguese Republic
President: Gen. António Ramalho Eanes (1976)
Premier: Francisco Pinto Balsemao (1980)
Area: 35,340 sq mi. (91,531 sq km)
Population (est. 1982): 10,000,000 (average annual growth rate: 0.6%)
Density per square mile: 283.0
Capital: Lisbon
Largest cities (est. 1979): Lisbon, 861,500; **(est. 1975 by U.N.):** Opporto, 335,700
Monetary unit: Escudo
Language: Portuguese
Religion: Roman Catholic
National name: República Portuguesa
Literacy rate (1981): 70%
Economic summary: Gross national product (1980): $23.1 billion. Average annual growth rate (1970–79): 1.1%. Per capita income (1980): $2,350. Land used for agriculture: 48%; labor force: 31%; principal products: grains, potatoes, olives, wine grapes. Labor force in industry: 35%; major products: textiles, footwear, wood pulp, paper, cork, metal products, refined oil, chemicals, canned fish, wine. Natural resources: fish, cork, tungsten ore. Exports: cotton, textiles, cork and cork products, canned fish, wine, timber and timber products, resin. Imports: petroleum, cotton, industrial machinery, iron and steel, chemicals. Major trading partners: Western European countries, U.S.

Geography. Portugal occupies the western part of the Iberian Peninsula, bordering on the Atlantic Ocean to the west and Spain to the north and east. It is slightly smaller than Indiana.

The country is crossed by many small rivers, and also by three large ones that rise in Spain, flow into the Atlantic, and divide the country into three geographic areas. The Minho (Miño in Spain) River, part of the northern boundary, cuts through a mountainous area that extends south to the vicinity of the Douro (Duero) River. South of the Douro, the mountains slope to the plains about the Tagus (Tejo) River. The remaining division is the southern one of Alentejo.

The Azores, stretching over 340 miles (547 km) in the Atlantic, consist of nine islands divided into three groups, with a total area of 924 square miles (2,393 sq km). The nearest continental land is Cape da Roca, Portugal, about 900 miles (1,448 km) to the east. The Azores are an important station on

Atlantic air routes, and Britain and the U.S. established air bases there during World War II.

Madeira, consisting of two inhabited islands, Madeira and Porto Santo, and two groups of uninhabited islands, lies in the Atlantic about 535 miles (861 km) southwest of Lisbon.

Government. A new Constitution, adopted in April 1976, provides for popular election of a President for a five-year term and for a legislature, the Assembly of the Republic, for four years.

The major political parties are the Democratic Alliance (136 of 250 seats in the Assembly), led by Premier Francisco Pinto Balsemao; Socialist Party (73 seats), led by former Premier Mário Soares, and Communist Party (40 seats), led by Alvaro Cunhal.

History. Portugal was a part of Spain until it won its independence in the middle of the 12th century. King John I (1385–1433) unified his country at the expense of the Castilians and the Moors of Morocco. The expansion of Portugal was brilliantly coordinated by John's son, Prince Henry the Navigator. In 1488, Bartolomew Diaz reached the Cape of Good Hope, proving that the Far East was accessible by sea. In 1498, Vasco da Gama reached the west coast of India. By the middle of the 16th century, the Portuguese Empire included West and East Africa, Brazil, Persia, Indochina, and Malaya.

In 1581, Philip II of Spain invaded Portugal and held it for 60 years, precipitating a catastrophic decline of Portuguese commerce. Courageous and shrewd explorers, the Portuguese proved to be inefficient and corrupt colonizers. By the time the Portuguese dynasty was restored in 1640, Dutch, English, and French competitors began to seize the lion's share of the world's colonies and commerce. Portugal retained Angola and Mozambique in Africa, and Brazil (until 1822).

The corrupt King Carlos, who ascended the throne in 1889, made Joao Franco the Premier with dictatorial power in 1906. In 1908, Carlos and his heir were shot dead on the streets of Lisbon. The new King, Manoel II, was driven from the throne in the Revolution of 1910 and Portugal became a French-style republic.

Traditionally friendly to Britain, Portugal fought in World War I on the Allied side in Africa as well as on the Western Front. Weak postwar governments and a revolution in 1926 brought Antonio Oliveira Salazar to power. He kept Portugal neutral in World War II but gave the Allies naval and air bases after 1943.

Portugal lost the tiny remnants of its Indian empire—Goa, Daman, and Diu—to Indian military occupation in 1961, the year an insurrection broke out in Angola. For the next 13 years, Salazar, who died in 1970, and his successor, Marcello Caetano, fought independence movements amid growing world criticism. Leftists in the armed forces, weary of a losing battle, launched the "Happy Revolution" of April 25, 1974. They installed Gen. António de Spínola as Provisional President with promises of peace in Africa and reforms at home.

Spínola's moderate left Cabinet failed to satisfy the military leadership, who named Col. Vasco dos Santos Gonçalves as Premier on July 14. After Spínola's resignation on Sept. 30, Gen, Francisco da Costa Gomez, Chief of Staff of the armed forces, became President of an increasingly leftist regime.

Anti-Communist violence in rural areas and pressure from non-Communists in the government and military forced Gonçalves out on Aug. 29, 1975, and he was replaced by the more moderate Vice Adm. José Pinheiro. Elections under a new Constitution in 1976 gave Gen. António Ramalho Eanes, Army Chief of Staff, a landslide victory even though he campaigned for a program of economic austerity. With Mário Soares as Premier, tough economic policies slowed inflation but proved unpopular with legislators, who forced Soares out on July 27, 1978.

Pursuit of economic austerity measures brought down Soares' centrist successor, Carlos Alberto Mota Pinto, less than a year later, giving Portugal its first woman Premier, Maria Lurdes Pintassilgo, who acted as caretaker until the victory of Francisco Manoel Lumbrales de Sá Carneiro's Democratic Alliance on Dec. 2, 1979. Sá Carneiro's coalition of his own Social Democratic Party, the Christian Democrats and the small Popular Monarchist Party won a majority of three seats, the first absolute majority for a governing party since the 1974 revolution.

On Dec. 4, 1980, Sá Carneiro, who had increased his coalition's majority in parliamentary elections in October, died in an air crash while campaigning against the re-election of President Eanes. Three days later, Eanes won a second four-year term with 57% of the popular vote, a victory for the left-leaning general that countered the rightward trend led by Sá Carneiro.

Francisco Pinto Balsemao, the new Premier, continued the drafting of a permanent Constitution, which was expected to be completed by late 1982. Changes already agreed to by Parliament were the replacement of the Council of the Revolution by a Council of State and the appointment of general officers by the government rather than the individual services, a strengthening of civilian control.

Portuguese Overseas Territory

After the April 1974 revolution, the military junta moved to grant independence to the territories, beginning with Portuguese Guinea in September 1974, which became the Republic of Guinea-Bissau.

Mozambique and Angola followed, leaving only Portuguese Timor and Macao of the former Empire. Despite Lisbon's objections, Indonesia annexed Timor.

MACAO

Status: Territory
Governor: Adm. Vasco Almeida Costa (1981)
Area: 6 sq mi. (15.5 sq km)
Population (est. 1982): 300,000 (average annual growth rate: 1.7%)
Capital (1970 census): Macao, 241,413
Monetary unit: Patacá
Literacy rate (1981): 99% (excluding Chinese)
Economic summary: Gross national product (1980): $550 million. Annual average growth rate (1970–79): 15%. Land used for agriculture: 10%; labor force: 5%; principal products: rice and vegetables; Labor force in industry: 30%; major products: textiles, fireworks, fish products. Exports: textiles and clothing, manufactured goods, foodstuffs. Imports: consumer goods, foodstuffs. Major trading partners: Hong Kong, China, U.S., West Germany, France.

Macao comprises the peninsula of Macao and the two small islands of Taipa and Colôane on the South China coast, about 35 miles (53 km) from

Hong Kong. Established by the Portuguese in 1557, it is the oldest European outpost in the China trade, but Portugal's sovereign rights to the port were not recognized by China until 1887, and its boundaries are still not delimited. The port has been eclipsed in importance by Hong Kong, but it is still a busy distribution center and also has an important fishing industry.

QATAR

State of Qatar
Ruler: Sheik Khalifa bin Hamad al-Thani (1972)
Area: 4,000 sq mi. (19,360 sq km)
Population (est. 1982): 260,000 (average annual growth rate: 4.0%)
Density per square mile: 65.0
Capital (est. 1981): Doha, 190,000
Monetary unit: Qatari riyal
Language: Arabic
Religion: Islam
Literacy rate (1981): 25%
Economic summary: Gross national product (1980): $6.0 billion. Average annual growth rate (1970–79): −1.2%. Per capita income (1980): $26,080. Major industrial product: oil. Natural resource: oil. Export: oil. Major trading partners: U.K., U.S., France, Japan, West Germany.

Geography. Qatar occupies a small peninsula that extends into the Persian Gulf from the east side of the Arabian Peninsula. Saudi Arabia is to the west and the United Arab Emirates to the south. The country is mainly barren.

Government. Qatar, one of the Persian Gulf states, lies between Bahrain and United Arab Emirates. For a long time, it was under Turkish protection, but in 1916, the sultan accepted British protection. After the discovery of oil in the 1940s and its exploitation in the 1950s and 1960s, political unrest spread to the sheikdoms. Qatar declared its independence in 1971. The next year the current Sheik, Khalifa bin Hamad al-Thani, ousted his cousin in a bloodless coup.

ROMANIA

Socialist Republic of Romania
President: Nicolae Ceausescu (1967)
Premier: Constantin Dascalescu (1982)
Area: 91,700 sq mi. (237,500 sq km)
Population (est. 1982): 22,700,000 (Romanian, 88%; Hungarian, 8%) (average annual growth rate: 0.7%)
Density per square mile: 247.5
Capital: Bucharest
Largest cities (est. 1979): Bucharest, 1,830,000; Brasov, 300,000; Timisoara, 281,000; Constanta, 280,000; Cluj-Napoca, 275,000; Iasi, 263,000; Galati, 253,000
Monetary unit: Leu
Languages: Romanian, Hungarian, Serbian, German, Turkish
Religions: Romanian Orthodox, 70%; Greek Orthodox, 10%
National name: Republica Socialista România
Literacy rate (1981): 99%
Economic summary: Gross national product (1980): $52.0 billion. Average annual growth rate (1970–79): 9.2%. Per capita income (1980): $2,340. Land used for agriculture: 63%; labor force: 36%; principal products: corn, wheat, oil, seeds, potatoes. Labor force in industry: 26%; major products: power, mining, forestry, metal production and processing, chemicals, food processing, textiles. Natural resources: oil, timber, natural gas, coal. Exports: machinery, minerals and metals, foodstuffs, lumber, fuel, manufactures. Imports: machinery, rolled steel, iron ore, coke and coking coal, minerals. Major trading partners: U.S.S.R., East Germany, West Germany.

Geography. A country in southeastern Europe slightly smaller than Oregon, Romania is bordered on the west by Hungary and Yugoslavia, on the north and east by the U.S.S.R., on the east by the Black Sea, and on the south by Bulgaria.

The Carpathian Mountains divide Romania's upper half from north to south and connect near the center of the country with the Transylvanian Alps, running east and west.

North and west of these ranges lies the Transylvanian plateau, and to the south and east are the plains of Moldavia and Walachia. In its last 190 miles (306 km), the Danube River flows through Romania only. It enters the Black Sea in northern Dobruja, just south of the border with the Soviet Union.

Government. The supreme body of state power and the sole legislative body is the Grand National Assembly, with 465 members elected for five-year terms. It elects a State Council, which provides for the continuity of state power and settles problems between sessions of the Assembly. The supreme executive and administrative body is the Council of Ministers elected by the Assembly.

The Communist Party, led by Secretary General Nicolae Ceausescu, is the only political party.

History. Most of Romania was the Roman province of Dacia from about A.D. 100 to 275. From the 6th to the 12th century, wave after wave of barbarian conquerors—Vlachs, Bulgars, and others—passed over the area. By the 15th century, the main Romanian principalities of Moldavia and Walachia had become satellites within the Ottoman Empire, although they retained much independence. After the Russo-Turkish War of 1828–29, they became Russian protectorates. In 1848, the Romanians rebelled but were suppressed by the Russians. The nation became a kingdom in 1881 after the Congress of Berlin.

King Ferdinand ascended the throne in 1914. At the start of World War I, Romania proclaimed its neutrality, but later joined the Allied side and in 1916 declared war on the Central Powers. The armistice of Nov. 11, 1918, gave Romania vast territories from Russia and the Austro-Hungarian Empire.

The gains of World War I, making Romania the largest Balkan state, included Bessarabia, Transylvania, and Bukovina. The Banat, a Hungarian area, was divided with Yugoslavia.

In 1925, Crown Prince Carol renounced his rights to the throne, and when King Ferdinand died in 1927, Carol's son, Michael (Mihai) became King under a regency. However, Carol returned from exile in 1930, was crowned King Carol II, and gradually became a powerful political force in the country. In 1938, he abolished the democratic Constitution of 1923.

In 1940, the country was reorganized along Fascist lines, and the Fascist Iron Guard became the nucleus of the new totalitarian party. On June 27, the Soviet Union occupied Bessarabia and northern Bukovina. By the Axis-dictated Vienna Award of

1940, two fifths of Transylvania went to Hungary, after which Carol dissolved Parliament and granted the new premier, Ion Antonescu, full power. He abdicated and again went into exile.

Romania subsequently signed the Axis Pact on Nov. 23, 1940, and the following June joined in Germany's attack on the Soviet Union, reoccupying Bessarabia. Following the invasion of Romania by the Red Army in August 1944, King Michael led a coup that ousted the Antonescu government. An armistice with the Soviet Union was signed in Moscow on Sept. 12, 1944.

A Communist-dominated government bloc won elections in 1946, Michael abdicated on Dec. 30, 1947, and Romania became a "people's republic." In 1955, Romania joined the Warsaw Treaty Organization and the United Nations. A decade later, with the adoption of a new Constitution emphasizing national autonomy, and especially after Nicolae Ceausescu came to power in 1967, Bucharest became an increasingly dissident voice in the Soviet bloc.

Alone of the Warsaw Pact members, Romania maintained ties with China and Albania after the two broke with Moscow. Almost as annoying to the Soviet leadership was Ceausescu's continuing of ties with Israel, a relationship that made possible the secret preparations for the visit to Israel by Egypt's President Anwar el-Sadat in November 1977. Ceausescu also exchanged cultural and scientific accords with Washington in 1974 and visited the United States in 1978. In a New Year's Day speech, 1980, the Romanian leader became the first and only Eastern European voice to protest the Soviet invasion of Afghanistan.

Despite his liberal international record, at home Ceausescu has harshly suppressed dissidents calling for freedom of expression in the wake of the Helsinki agreements.

RWANDA

Republic of Rwanda
President: Maj. Gen. Juvénal Habyarimana (1973)
Area: 10,169 sq mi. (26,338 sq km)
Population (est. 1982): 5,200,000 (average annual growth rate: 3.2%)
Density per square mile: 511.4
Capital and largest city (est. 1981): Kigali, 155,000
Monetary unit: Rwanda franc
Languages: Kinyarwanda and French
Religions: Roman Catholic, 45%; Protestant, 10%; Animist
Literacy rate (1981): 25%
Economic summary: Gross national product (1980): $1.0 billion. Average annual growth rate (1970–79): 1.6%. Per capita income (1980): $200. Land used for agriculture: 33%; labor force: 95%; principal products: coffee, tea, pyrethrum, beans, potatoes. Labor force in industry: less than 5%; major products: processed foods, light consumer goods, minerals. Natural resources: cassiterite, wolfram. Exports: coffee, tea, pyrethrum, wolfram. Imports: textiles, foodstuffs, machinery, and equipment. Major trading partners: U.S., Belgium, West Germany, Kenya.

Geography. Rwanda, in east central Africa, is surrounded by Zaire, Uganda, Tanzania, and Burundi. It is slightly smaller than Maryland.

Steep mountains and deep valleys cover most of the country. Lake Kivu in the northwest, at an altitude of 4,829 feet (1,472 m) is the highest lake in Africa. Extending south of it are the Virunga Mountains, which include Volcan Karisimbi (14,187 ft.; 4,324 m), Rwanda's highest point.

Government. Grégoire Kayibanda was President from 1962 until he was overthrown in a bloodless coup on July 5, 1973, by the military led by Gen. Juvénal Habyarimana.

In a plebiscite in December 1978, Habyarimana was elected to a five-year term as president and a new constitution adopted that provides for an elected Assembly and a single official party, the National Revolutionary Development Movement.

History. Rwanda, which was part of German East Africa, was first visited by European explorers in 1854. During World War I, it was occupied in 1916 by Belgian troops. After the war, it became a Belgian League of Nations mandate, along with Burundi, under the name of Ruanda-Urundi. The mandate was made a U.N. trust territory in 1946. Until the Belgian Congo achieved independence in 1960, Ruanda-Urundi was administered as part of that colony.

Ruanda became the independent nation of Rwanda on July 1, 1962.

ST. LUCIA

Commonwealth of St. Lucia
Sovereign: Queen Elizabeth II
Governor-General: Boswell Williams (1980)
Prime Minister: John Compton (1982)
Area: 238 sq mi. (616 sq km)
Population (est 1982): 125,000 (average annual growth rate: 1.4%)
Density per square mile: 525.2
Capital (est. 1979): Castries, 45,000
Monetary unit: East Caribbean dollar
Languages: English, patois
Religion: Roman Catholic 91%; Anglican, 3%; Seventh-day Adventist, 2%
Member of Commonwealth of Nations
Literacy rate (1981): 80%
Economic summary: Gross national product (1980): $110 million. Average annual growth rate (1970–79): 2.8%. Per capita income (1980): $850. Labor force in agriculture: 50%; principal products: bananas, coconuts, sugar, cocoa, spices. Major industrial products: processed limes. Exports: bananas, cocoa. Imports: foodstuffs, machinery and equipment, fertilizers, petroleum products. Major trading partners: U.K., U.S., Canada.

Geography. One of the Windward Isles of the Eastern Caribbean, St. Lucia lies just south of Martinique. It is of volcanic origin. A chain of wooded mountains runs from north to south, and from them flow many streams into fertile valleys.

Government. A governor-general represents the sovereign, Queen Elizabeth II. A prime minister is head of government, chosen by a 17-member House of Assembly elected by universal suffrage for a maximum term of five years.

History. Discovered by Spain in 1503 and ruled by Spain and then France, St. Lucia became a British territory in 1803. With other Windward Isles, St. Lucia was granted home rule in 1967 as one of the West Indies Associated States. On Feb. 22, 1979,

St. Lucia achieved full independence in ceremonies boycotted by the opposition St. Lucia Labor Party, which had advocated a referendum before cutting ties with Britain.

Unrest and a strike by civil servants forced Prime Minister John Compton to hold elections in July, in which his United Workers Party lost its majority for the first time in 15 years.

A Labor Party government was ousted in turn by Compton and his followers, who won 14 of 17 seats in elections in May 1982. Labor seats fell from 12 to 2, with one seat won by the Progressive Labor Party.

Formerly dependent on a single crop, bananas, St. Lucia has sought to lower its chronic unemployment and payments deficit. The government provided tax incentives to a U.S. corporation, Amerada Hess, to facilitate location of a $150-million oil refinery and transhipment terminal on the island.

ST. VINCENT

Sovereign: Queen Elizabeth II
Governor-General: Sir Sydney Gunn-Munro (1979)
Prime Minister: Milton Cato (1979)
Area: 150 sq mi. (389 sq km)
Population (est. 1982): 150,000 (average annual growth rate: 2.9%)
Density per square mile: 1,000.0
Capital and largest city (est. 1979): Kingstown, 23,650
Monetary unit: East Caribbean dollar
Language: English
Religions: Anglican, 47%; Methodist, 28%; Roman Catholic, 13%
Member of Commonwealth of Nations
Literacy rate (1981): 80%
Economic summary: Gross national product (1980): $60 million. Average annual growth rate (1970–79): −1.7%. Per capita income (1980): $520. Land used for agriculture: 50%; labor force: 40%; principal products: bananas, arrowroot, coconuts. Major industry: food processing. Exports: bananas, arrowroot, copra. Imports: fertilizers, machinery and equipment, chemicals, fuels, clothing. Major trading partners: U.K., U.S., Canada, Caribbean nations.

Geography. St. Vincent, chief island of the Commonwealth, is 18 miles (29 km) long and 11 miles (18 km) wide. One of the Windward Islands in the Lesser Antilles, it is 100 miles (161 km) west of Barbados. The island is mountainous and well forested. The Grenadines, a chain of nearly 600 islets with a total area of only 17 square miles (27 sq km), extend for 60 miles (96 km) from northeast to southwest between St. Vincent and Grenada, southernmost of the Windwards.

St. Vincent is dominated by the volcano La Soufrière, part of a volcanic range running north and south, which rises to 4,048 feet (1,234 m). The volcano erupted over a 10-day period in April 1979, causing the evacuation of the northern two thirds of the island. (There is also a volcano of the same name on Basse-Terre, Guadeloupe, which became violently active in 1976 and 1977.)

Government. A Governor-General represents the sovereign, Queen Elizabeth II. A Prime Minister, elected by a 13-member unicameral legislature, holds executive power. The Labor Party, led by Prime Minister Milton Cato, holds 11 of the 13 seats.

History. Discovered by Columbus in 1498, and alternately claimed by Britain and France, St. Vincent became a British colony by the Treaty of Paris in 1783. The islands won home rule in 1969 as part of the West Indies Associated States and achieved full independence Oct. 26, 1979. Prime Minister Milton Cato's government quelled a brief rebellion Dec. 8, 1979, three days after elections had given the ruling Labor Party 11 of 13 seats in the Assembly. The rebellion was attributed to economic problems following the eruption of La Soufrière in April, 1979. Unlike a 1902 eruption which killed 2,000, there was no loss of life but widespread losses to agriculture.

SAN MARINO

Most Serene Republic of San Marino
Co-Regents: Two selected every six months by Grand and General Council
Area: 23.6 sq mi. (62 sq km)
Population (est. 1982): 20,500 (mostly Italian) (average annual growth rate: 1.6%)
Density per square mile: 868.6
Capital and largest city (est. 1980 for metropolitan area): San Marino, 8,500
Monetary unit: Italian lira
Language: Italian
Religion: Roman Catholic
National name: Repubblica di San Marino
Literacy rate (1981): 97%
Economic summary: Land used for agriculture: 74%; principal products: wheat and other grains, grapes, fruits, vegetables. Major industrial products: textiles, paper, leather, cement and other building materials. Exports: building stone, lime, chestnuts, wheat, hides, baked goods. Imports: manufactured consumer goods. Major trading partner: Italy.

Geography: One tenth the size of New York City, San Marino is surrounded by Italy. It is situated in the Apennines, a little inland from the Adriatic Sea near Rimini.

Government. The country is governed by two coregents. Executive power is exercised by two secretaries of state—one for foreign and political affairs and one for internal affairs. In 1959, the Grand Council granted women the vote.

The major political parties are the Christian Democratic Party (26 of 60 seats in the Grand and General Council); Communist Party (16 seats); Socialist Party (8 seats); United Socialist Party (7 seats); Democratic Socialist Party (2 seats); and Committee for the Defense of the Republic (1 seat).

History. According to tradition, San Marino was founded about A.D. 350 and had good luck for centuries in staying out of the many wars and feuds on the Italian peninsula. It is the oldest republic in the world.

A person born in San Marino remains a citizen and can vote no matter where he lives.

SÃO TOMÉ AND PRÍNCIPE

Democratic Republic of Sao Tomé and Príncipe
President: Manuel Pinto da Costa (1975)
Area: 372 sq mi. (964 sq km)
Population (est. 1982): 90,000 (average annual growth rate: 1.1%)

Density per square mile: 241.9
Capital and largest city (est. 1977): Sao Tomé, 20,000
Monetary unit: Dobra
Language: Portuguese
Religions: Roman Catholic, Evangelical Protestant, Seventh-Day Adventist
Literacy rate (1981): 10%
Economic summary: Gross national product (1980): $60 million. Average annual growth rate (1970–79): –0.2%. Per capita income (1980): $490. Principal agricultural products: cocoa, copra, coconuts, palm oil, coffee, bananas. Major industrial products: timber, copra. Exports: cocoa, coffee, copra, palm oil. Imports: foodstuffs, textiles, machinery, electrical equipment, fuels, lubricants. Major trading partners: Netherlands, Portugal, U.S., West Germany.

Geography. The tiny volcanic islands of Sao Tomé and Príncipe lie in the Gulf of Guinea about 150 miles (241 km) off West Africa. Sao Tomé (about 330 sq mi.; 855 sq km) is covered by a dense mountainous jungle, out of which have been carved large plantations. Príncipe (about 40 sq mi.; 104 sq km) consists of jagged mountains. Other islands in the republic are Pedras Tinhosas and Rolas.

Government. The Constitution grants supreme power to a People's Assembly composed of members elected for four years. The Assembly chooses the President of the republic from candidates named by the Movement for the Liberation of Sao Tomé and Príncipe, the only legal party.

History. Sao Tomé and Príncipe were discovered by Portuguese navigators in 1771 and settled by the end of the century. Intensive cultivation by slave labor made the islands a major producer of sugar during the 17th century but output declined until the introduction of coffee and cacao in the 19th century brought new prosperity. The island of Sao Tomé was the world's largest producer of cacao in 1908 and the crop is still the most important. An exile liberation movement was formed in 1953 after Portuguese landowners quelled labor riots by killing several hundred African workers.

The Portuguese revolution of 1974 brought the end of the overseas empire and the new Lisbon government transferred power to the liberation movement on July 12, 1975. Most of the 4,000 Portuguese inhabitants departed during the transition period.

SAUDI ARABIA

Kingdom of Saudi Arabia

Ruler and Prime Minister: King Fahd Bin Abdul-Aziz (1982)
Area: 873,000 sq mi. (2,261,070 sq km)
Population (est. 1982): 9,700,000 (average annual growth rate: 2.8%)
Density per square mile: 11.1
Capital: Riyadh
Largest cities (est. 1980): Riyadh, 1,250,000; Jeddah, 750,000; Mecca, 500,000
Monetary unit: Riyal
Language: Arabic
Religion: Islam
National name: Al-Mamlaka al-'Arabiya as-Sa'udiya
Literacy rate (1981): 20% (est.)
Economic summary: Gross national product (1980): $100.9 billion. Average annual growth rate (1970–79): 9.6%. Per Capita Income (1980): $11,260. Labor force in agriculture: 28%; principal products: dates, grains, livestock. Labor force in industry: 39%; major products: petroleum, cement, plastic products, furniture. Natural resource: oil. Exports: petroleum and petroleum products. Imports: manufactured goods, transport equipment, construction materials, processed food. Major trading partners: U.S., Western European countries, Japan, West Germany.

Geography. The Middle East oil-producing country of Saudi Arabia occupies most of the Arabian Peninsula, with the Red Sea and the Gulf of Aqaba on the west and the Persian Gulf on the east. Neighbors are Jordan, Iraq, and Kuwait in the north, and, along the perimeter from southwest to east, the two Yemens, Oman, and the United Arab Emirates. The country is more than three times the size of Texas.

Saudi Arabia's oil region lies along the Persian Gulf. The country is mostly desert. The Asir Mountains inland rise to a height of 9,000 feet (2,743 m).

Government. Saudi Arabia is a monarchy whose legitimacy rests on *Shariah* (the Law of Islam) and custom. A Council of Ministers was formed in 1953. It acts as a Cabinet under the leadership of the King and is composed of 21 ministries.

Royal and ministerial decrees account for most of the promulgated legislation, treaties, and conventions.

There are no political parties in Saudi Arabia.

History. Mohammed united the Arabs in the 7th century, and his followers, led by the caliphs, founded a great empire, with its capital at Medina. Later, the caliphate capital was transferred to Damascus and then Baghdad, but Arabia retained its importance because of the holy cities of Mecca and Medina. In the 16th and 17th centuries, the Turks established at least nominal rule over much of Arabia, and in the middle of the 18th century, it was divided into separate principalities.

The Kingdom of Saudi Arabia is almost entirely the creation of King Ibn Saud (1882–1953). A descendant of earlier Wahabi rulers, he seized Riyadh, the capital of Nejd, in 1901 and set himself up as leader of the Arab nationalist movement. By 1906 he had established Wahabi dominance in Nejd. He conquered Hejaz in 1924–25, consolidating it and Nejd into a dual kingdom in 1926. In 1932, Hejaz and Nejd became a single kingdom, which was officially named Saudi Arabia. A year later the region of Asir was incorporated into the kingdom.

Oil was discovered in 1936, and commercial production began during World War II. Saudi Arabia was neutral until nearly the end of the war, but it was permitted to be a charter member of the United Nations. The country joined the Arab League in 1945 and took part in the 1948–49 war against Israel, but followed a moderate policy afterward. In 1951, the U.S. was allowed to build an air base at Dhahran.

On Ibn Saud's death in 1953, his eldest son, Saud, began an 11-year reign marked by an increasing hostility toward the radical Arabism of Egypt's Gamal Abdel Nasser. In 1964, the ailing Saud was deposed and replaced by the Premier, Crown Prince Faisal, who gave vocal support but no military help to Egypt in the 1967 Mideast war.

Faisal's assassination by a deranged kinsman in 1975 shook the Middle East, but failed to alter his kingdom's course. His successor was his brother,

Prince Khalid. Khalid gave influential support to Egypt during negotiations on Israeli withdrawal from the Sinai desert.

Saudi Arabia exercised a moderating influence in the Organization for Petroleum Exporting Countries (OPEC) to restrain prices. In July 1979 President Carter disclosed Crown Prince Fahd's promise to increase Saudi oil production by one million barrels a day for three months to ease the world oil shortage.

Although Carter had hoped that Saudi Arabia would support the Egyptian-Israeli peace treaty—the U.S. sold 60 F-15 fighters to the Saudis in 1978 and sent a fleet to the Arabian Sea when border clashes between the two Yemens alarmed Riyadh—Arab solidarity doomed this hope in 1979. Saudi Arabia joined the majority in condemning Egypt, broke diplomatic relations with Cairo and canceled its commitment to pay for $525 million worth of F-15's for Egypt.

A takeover by an unknown group of the Grand Mosque in Mecca on Nov. 20, 1979, spread fears that the Saudi monarchy might be under internal threat. On Jan. 9, 1980, 63 persons—41 Saudis and the remainder aliens—were beheaded for their participation in the takeover. A tightening of Islamic law and a shakeup in the Army's top command were linked to the incident.

Saudi concern over possible Iranian attack after the outbreak of the war between Iran and Iraq, added to the tension created by the Soviet invasion of Afghanistan, prompted a Saudi request for U.S. arms. Despite Israeli protests, Washington announced on April 21, 1981, that it would sell five Advance Warning and Command Systems (AWAC) planes to the Saudis, together with seven KC-135 tanker planes, which would increase the range of 62 F-15 fighter-interceptors already delivered.

Sheik Ahmed Zaki Yamani, the oil minister, earlier announced that his government would maintain the 10.3-million-barrels-a-day oil production rate it set when the Iran-Iraq war cut the output of those countries. The Saudi action was a key element in the reduction of world oil prices—part of the arms deal—but Congressional approval of the controversial plane sales did not come until Oct. 28. By then, a cut in Saudi production resulted in a total for 1981 of only 9.8 million barrels per day, a decrease from the 9.9 million rate of 1980.

King Khalid died of a heart attack June 13, 1982, and was succeeded by his half-brother, Prince Fahd Bin Abdul-Aziz, 60, who had exercised the real power throughout Khalid's reign. King Fahd, a pro-Western modernist, chose his 58-year-old half-brother, Abdulla, as Crown Prince.

SENEGAL

Republic of Senegal
President: Abdou Diouf (1981)
Premier: Habib Thiam (1981)
Area: 76,124 sq mi. (197,161 sq km)
Population (est. 1982): 5,950,000 (average annual growth rate: 2.7%)
Density per square mile: 78.2
Capital and largest city (est. 1978): Dakar, 915,000
Monetary unit: Franc CFA
Ethnic groups: Wolofs, Sereres, Peuls, Tukulers, and others
Languages: French (official); Wolof, Serer, other tribal dialects
Religion: Islam, 86%; Animist, 9%; Christian, 5%
National name: République du Sénégal
Literacy rate (1981): 60%
Economic summary: Gross national product (1980): $2.6 billion. Average annual growth rate (1970–79): 0.1%. Per capita income (1980): $450. Land used for agriculture: 12%; labor force: 80%; principal products: peanuts, millet, cotton, rice, sorghum. Labor force in industry: 8%; major products: peanut oil, fertilizer, cement, processed food and fish, refined petroleum. Natural resources: fish, phosphate. Exports: peanuts, phosphate rock, canned fish. Imports: foodstuffs, consumer goods, machinery, transport equipment. Major trading partners: France, Western European countries, African neighbors.

Geography. The capital of Senegal, Dakar, is the westernmost point in Africa. The country, slightly smaller than South Dakota, surrounds Gambia on three sides and is bordered on the north by Mauritania, on the east by Mali, and on the south by Guinea and Guinea-Bissau.

Senegal is mainly a low-lying country, with a semidesert area in the north and northeast and forests in the southwest. The largest rivers include the Senegal in the north and the Gambia in the central region.

Government. There is a National Assembly of 100 members, elected every five years. There is universal suffrage and a constitutional guarantee of equality before the law.

The major political party is the Socialist Party, led by President Abdou Diouf. Legal opposition was reconstituted in 1974 with formation of the Senegalese Democratic Party, headed by Abdoulaye Wade, which urged reduction in French and Western influences. Other opposition parties include the African Independence Party and the Republican Party.

History. The Portuguese had some stations on the banks of the Senegal River in the 15th century, and the first French settlement was made at Saint-Louis about 1650. The British took parts of Senegal at various times, but the French gained possession in 1840 and organized the Sudan as a territory in 1904. In 1946, together with other parts of French West Africa, Senegal became part of the French Union. On June 20, 1960, it became an independent republic federated with the Sudanese Republic in the Mali Federation, from which it withdrew two months later.

On Jan. 1, 1973, Senegal joined with six other states to create the West African Economic Community to promote economic development within the region.

SEYCHELLES

Republic of Seychelles
President: Albert René (1977)
Area: 171 sq mi. (443 sq km)
Population (est. 1982): 70,000 (average annual growth rate: 1.9%)
Density per square mile: 409.4
Capital (est. 1977): Victoria, 23,000
Monetary unit: Seychelles rupee
Languages: English, French (both official), Creole patois
Religions: Roman Catholic, 90%; Anglican, 8%
Member of Commonwealth of Nations
Literacy rate (1981): 65%
Economic summary: Gross national product (1980): $120 million. Average annual growth rate (1970–79): 3.8%. Per capita income (1980): $1,770. Land used for agriculture:

54%; labor force: 27%; principal products: vanilla, copra, cinnamon. Labor force in industry: 55%; major products: processed copra and vanilla, coconut oil. Exports: cinnamon, vanilla, copra. Imports: food, tobacco, manufactured goods, machinery, petroleum products, textiles, transport equipment. Major trading partners: U.K., Kenya, India, South Africa, Burma.

Geography. Seychelles consists of an archipelago of about 100 islands in the Indian Ocean northeast of Madagascar. The principal islands are Mahé (55 sq mi.; 142 sq km), Praslin (15 sq mi.; 38 sq km), and La Digue (4 sq mi.; 10 sq km). The Aldabra, Farquhar, and Desroches groups are included in the territory of the republic.

Government. Seized from France by Britain in 1810, the Seychelles Islands remained a colony until June 29, 1976. The state is an independent republic within the Commonwealth.

On June 5, 1977, Prime Minister Albert René ousted the islands' first President, James Mancham, suspending the Constitution and the 25-member National Assembly. Mancham, whose "lavish spending" and flamboyance were cited by René in seizing power, charged that Soviet influence was at work. The new president denied this and, while more left than his predecessor, pledged to keep the Seychelles in the Commonwealth.

A new Cabinet was formed with members only from Seychelles People's United Party, none from Mancham's Seychelles Democratic Party.

A third unsuccessful attempted coup against René attracted international attention when a group of 50 South African mercenaries posing as rugby players attacked the Victoria airport on Nov. 25, 1981. They caused extensive damage before they hijacked an Air India plane and returned to South Africa, where all but five were freed. Only after widespread African protest did the Pretoria government, which denied any responsibility for the attack, reverse the decision and order all the mercenaries tried as hijackers.

SIERRA LEONE

Republic of Sierra Leone
President: Dr. Siaka P. (1971)
Area: 27,925 sq mi. (72,326 sq km)
Population (est. 1982): 3,675,000 (average annual growth rate: 2.2%)
Density per square mile: 131.6
Capital and largest city (est. 1974): Freetown, 314,340
Monetary unit: Leone
Languages: English (official), Mende, Temne, Creole
Religions: Animist, 54%; Islam, 40%; Christian, 6%
Member of Commonwealth of Nations
Literacy rate (1981): 10%
Economic summary: Gross national product (1980): $950 million. Average annual growth rate (1970–79): −1.2%. Per capita income (1980): $270. Land used for agriculture: 6%; labor force: 75%; principal products: coffee, cocoa, ginger, rice. Labor force in industry: 15%; major products: diamonds, bauxite, beverages, cigarettes, construction goods. Natural resources: diamonds, bauxite, chromite, iron ore, rutile. Exports: diamonds, iron ore, palm kernels, cocoa, coffee. Imports: food, petroleum products, chemicals, machinery. Major trading partners: U.K., U.S., Western European and Communist countries, Japan.

Geography. Sierra Leone, on the Atlantic Ocean in West Africa, is half the size of Illinois. Guinea, in the north and east, and Liberia, in the south, are its neighbors.

Mangrove swamps lie along the coast, with wooded hills and a plateau in the interior. The eastern region is mountainous.

Government. Sierra Leone became an independent nation on April 27, 1961, and declared itself a republic, with former Prime Minister Siaka P. Stevens as president for a seven-year term, on April 19, 1971.

Sierra Leone became a one party state under the aegis of the All Peoples Congress Party in April 1978.

History. The coastal area of Sierra Leone was ceded to English settlers in 1788 as a home for blacks discharged from the British armed forces and also for runaway slaves who had found asylum in London. The British protectorate over the hinterland was proclaimed in 1896.

After elections in 1967, the British Governor-General replaced Sir Albert Margai, head of SLPP, which had held power since independence, with Dr. Stevens, head of APC, as prime minister. The Army took over the government; then another coup in April 1968 restored civilian rule and put the military leaders in jail.

A coup attempt early in 1971 by the army commander was apparently foiled by loyal army officers, but the then Prime Minister Stevens called in troops of neighboring Guinea's army, under a 1970 mutual defense pact, to guard his residence. After perfunctorily blaming the U.S. for the coup attempt, Stevens switched Governors-General, changed the Constitution, and ended up with a republic, of which he was first president. He was accused of taking "sweeping dictatorial powers," but was re-elected in 1978.

SINGAPORE

Republic of Singapore
President: C.V. Devan Nair (1981)
Prime Minister: Lee Kuan Yew (1959)
Area: 238 sq mi. (616 sq km)
Population (est. 1982): 2,500,000 (average annual growth rate: 1.2%) (Chinese, 76%; Malay, 15%; Indian, 7%)
Density per square mile: 10,504.2
Capital (est. 1982): Singapore, 2,450,000
Monetary unit: Singapore dollar
Languages: Malay, Chinese (Mandarin), Tamil, English
Religions: Islam, Christian, Buddhist, Hindu, Confucianist, Taoist
Member of Commonwealth of Nations
Literacy rate (1980): 84%
Economic summary: Gross national product (1980): $10.7 billion. Average annual growth rate (1970–79): 6.7%. Per capita income (1980): $4,480. Land used for agriculture: 22%; labor force: 2%; principal products: poultry, hogs, orchids, vegetables, fruits. Labor force in industry: 27%; major industries: petroleum refining, oil exploration, ship repair, rubber processing, electronics and other light industry. Exports: petroleum products, rubber, manufactured goods. Imports: capital equipment, manufactured goods, petroleum. Major trading partners: U.S., Japan, Malaysia, Hong Kong, Thailand.

Geography. The Republic of Singapore consists of the main island of Singapore, off the southern tip of the Malay Peninsula between the South China Sea and the Indian Ocean, and 54 nearby islands.

There are extensive mangrove swamps extending inland from the coast, which is broken by many inlets.

Government. The head of state is the President. There is a Cabinet, headed by the Prime Minister, and a Parliament of 75 members elected by universal suffrage.

The People's Action Party, led by Prime Minister Lee Kuan Yew, is the ruling political party in Parliament, holding all but one seat.

History. Singapore, founded in 1819 by Sir Stamford Raffles, became a separate crown colony of Britain in 1946, when the former colony of the Straits Settlements was dissolved. The other two settlements—Penang and Malacca—were transferred to the Union of Malaya, and the small island of Labuan was transferred to North Borneo. The Cocos (or Keeling) Islands were transferred to Australia in 1955 and Christmas Island in 1958.

Singapore attained full internal self-government in 1959. On Sept. 16, 1963, it joined Malaya, Sabah (North Borneo), and Sarawak in the Federation of Malaysia. It withdrew from the Federation on Aug. 9, 1965, and proclaimed itself a republic the next month.

SOLOMON ISLANDS

Sovereign: Queen Elizabeth II
Governor-General: Baddeley Devesi (1978)
Prime Minister: Solomon Mamaloni (1981)
Area: 11,500 sq mi. (29,785 sq km)
Population (est. 1982): 250,000 (average annual growth rate: 3.4%)
Density per square mile: 21.7
Capital and largest city (est. 1981): Honiara (on Guadalcanal), 19,000
Monetary unit: Solomon Islands dollar
Languages: Pidgin English, English, Melanesian dialects
Religions: Anglican, 34%; Roman Catholic, 19%; South Seas Evangelical, 17%; other Protestant, 25%
Member of British Commonwealth.
Literacy rate (1981): 60%
Economic summary: Gross national product (1980): $110 million. Average annual growth rate (1970–79): 2.3%. Per Capita Income (1980): $460. Principal agricultural products: copra, palm oil, rice, cocoa, cattle, spices. Major industrial products: processed fish, timber, jute, soap, canned meat, handicrafts. Natural resources: fish, timber. Exports: fish, timber, copra, palm oil. Imports: machinery and transport equipment, foodstuffs, fuel, manufactured goods. Major trading partners: Japan, Australia, U.K.

Geography: Lying east of New Guinea, this island nation consists of the southern islands of the Solomon group: Guadalcanal, Malaita, Santa Isabel, San Cristóbal, Choiseul, New Georgia, and numerous smaller islands.

Government. After 85 years of British rule, the Solomons achieved independence July 7, 1978. The Crown is represented by a Governor-General and legislative power is vested in a unicameral legislature of 38 members, led by the Prime Minister.

History. Discovered in 1567 by Alvaro de Mendana, the Solomons were not visited again for about 200 years. In 1886, Great Britain and Germany divided the islands between them. In 1914, Australian forces took over the German islands and the Solomons became an Australian mandate in 1920. In World War II, most of the islands were occupied by the Japanese. American forces landed on Guadalcanal on Aug. 7, 1942. The islands were the scene of several important U.S. naval and military victories. They are still largely undeveloped, with only 60 miles of paved road and fewer than 1,000 motor vehicles.

SOMALIA

Somali Democratic Republic
President: Maj. Gen. Mohamed Siad Barre (1969)
Area: 246,155 sq mi. (637,541 sq km)
Population (est. 1982): 5,150,000 (average annual growth rate: 3.5%)
Density per square mile: 20.9
Capital and largest city (est. 1981): Mogadishu, 500,000
Monetary unit: Somali shilling
Language: Somali
Religion: Islam
National name: Al Jumhouriya As-Somalya Dimocradia
Literacy rate (1981): 10%
Economic summary: Gross national product (1978): $470 million. Average annual growth rate (1970–77): –1.1%. Per capita income (1978): $187. Labor force in agriculture: 30%; principal products: livestock, bananas, sorghum, peanuts, sugar cane, cotton, maize. Labor force in industry: 3%; major products: textiles, meat, fish, canned fruit juices. Natural resources: timber, uranium. Exports: livestock, skins and hides, bananas. Imports: textiles, construction materials and equipment, machinery, manufactured goods, transport equipment. Major trading partners: Arab countries, Italy.

Geography. Somalia, situated in the Horn of Africa, lies along the Gulf of Aden and the Indian Ocean. It is bounded by Djibouti in the northwest, Ethiopia in the east, and Kenya in the southwest. In area it is slightly smaller than Texas.

Generally arid and barren, Somalia has two chief rivers, the Shebeli and the Juba.

Government. Maj. Gen. Mohamed Siad Barre took power on Oct. 21, 1969, in a bloodless coup that established a Supreme Revolutionary Council as the governing body, replacing a parliamentary government. On July 1, 1976, Barre dissolved the Council, naming its members to the Somali Socialist Party, organized that day as the nation's only legal political party. In December 1979, a 171-member People's Assembly was elected under a new Constitution adopted in August. The Assembly confirmed Barre as President for a six-year term.

History. From the 7th to the 10th century, Arab and Persian trading posts were established along the coast of present-day Somalia. Nomadic tribes occupied the interior, occasionally pushing into Ethiopian territory. In the 16th century, Turkish rule extended to the northern coast and the Sultans of Zanzibar gained control in the south.

After British occupation of Aden in 1839, the Somali coast became its source of food. The French established a coaling station in 1862 at the site of Djibouti and the Italians planted a settlement in

Eritrea. Egypt, which for a time claimed Turkish rights in the area, was succeeded by Britain. By 1920, a British protectorate and an Italian protectorate occupied what is now Somalia. The British ruled the entire area after 1941, with Italy returning in 1950 to serve as United Nations trustee for its former territory.

In mid-1960, Britain and Italy granted independence to their respective sectors, enabling the two to join as the Republic of Somalia on July 1. Somalia broke diplomatic relations with Britain in 1963 when the British granted the Somali-populated Northern Frontier District of Kenya to the Republic of Kenya.

On Oct. 15, 1969, President Abdi Rashid Ali Shermarke was assassinated and the army seized power, dissolving the legislature and arresting all government leaders. Maj. Gen. Mohamed Siad Barre, as President of a renamed Somali Democratic Republic, leaned heavily toward the U.S.S.R.

In 1977, Somalia openly backed rebels in the westernmost area of Ethiopia, the Ogaden desert, which had been seized by Ethiopia at the turn of the century. The action was an embarrassment to the U.S.S.R., which was heavily involved in Ethiopia's new Marxist government after the ouster of Emperor Haile Selassie in 1974.

After denying Barre's pleas for aid, the U.S.S.R. announced in 1977 the cutoff of military aid to Somalia and the providing of "defensive weapons" to Ethiopia. Somalia then expelled an estimated 1,500 Soviet military and civilian aides and broke diplomatic relations with Cuba, which had furnished military advisers to the Ethiopian troops fighting in the Ogaden.

Somalia acknowledged defeat in an eight-month war against the Ethiopians, having lost many of what had become a 32,000-man army and most of its tanks and planes. In March 1978, the U.S. agreed to supply $7 million in food over six months, in addition to $6 million in emergency food relief provided in December. The U.S. refused to consider weapons sales, however, unless Somalia gave up all claims to northern Kenya, the Ogaden, and the Republic of Djibouti, all once claimed as "Greater Somalia." Barre refused to do this.

A U.S. announcement on Jan. 9, 1980, that bases for U.S. ships and planes in the Indian Ocean would be sought in Somalia, Oman, and Kenya, brought a request from Somalia for $1 billion worth of modern arms and an equal amount of economic aid. In August, an agreement was signed giving the U.S. use of military bases in Somalia in return for $25 million in military aid in 1981 and more in subsequent years.

SOUTH AFRICA

Republic of South Africa
State President: Marais Viljoen (1979)
Prime Minister: Pieter W. Botha (1978)
Area: 318,861 sq mi. (825,850 sq km)
Population (est. 1982): 23,500,000[1] (average annual growth rate: 2.4%) (black, 68%; white, 18%; colored [mixed], 10%; Asian, 3%)
Density per square mile: 73.7[1]
Administrative capital: Pretoria
Legislative capital: Cape Town
Judicial capital: Bloemfontein
Largest cities (est. 1980): Johannesburg, 1,500,000; Cape Town, 892,000; Pretoria, 600,000; Bloemfontein, 180,000; **(est. 1975):** Durban, 837,000; Port Elizabeth, 468,800
Monetary unit: Rand
Languages: English, Afrikaans, Bantu languages
Religions (1970): Dutch Reformed, 16%; Methodist, 10%; Roman Catholic, 9%; Anglican, 8%; other Christian, 55%
National name: Republiek van Suid-Afrika
Literacy rate (1981): 99% (whites), 50% (Africans)
Economic summary: Gross national product (1980): $67.0 billion. Average annual growth rate (1970–79): 0.6%. Per capita income (1980): $2,290. Labor force in agriculture: 53%; principal products: corn, wool, wheat, sugar cane, tobacco, citrus fruits. Labor force in industry: 15%; major products: assembled automobiles, machinery, textiles, iron and steel, chemicals, fertilizer, fish. Natural resources: gold, diamonds, platinum, uranium, coal, iron ore, asbestos, manganese. Exports: gold, wool, diamonds, corn, uranium, sugar, fruits, hides and skins, asbestos, fish products. Imports: motor vehicles, machinery, metals, petroleum products, chemicals, textiles. Major trading partners: U.S., West Germany, Japan, U.K.

1. Excluding South-West Africa (Namibia), Transkei, Bophuthatswana, Venda, and Ciskei.

Geography. South Africa, on the continent's southern tip, is washed by the Atlantic Ocean on the west and by the Indian Ocean on the south and east. Its neighbors are South-West Africa (Namibia) in the northwest, Zimbabwe and Botswana in the north, and Mozambique and Swaziland in the northeast. Bophuthatswana, Transkei, Ciskei, and Venda are independent enclaves within South Africa, which occupies an area nearly three times that of California.

The country has a high interior plateau, or veld, nearly half of which averages 4,000 feet (1,219 m) in elevation.

There are no important mountain ranges, although the Great Escarpment, separating the veld from the coastal plain, rises to over 11,000 feet (3,350 m) in the Drakensberg Mountains in the east. The principal river is the Orange, rising in Lesotho and flowing westward for 1,300 miles (2,092 km) to the Atlantic.

The southernmost point of Africa is Cape Agulhas, located in Cape Province about 100 miles (161 km) southeast of the Cape of Good Hope.

Government. The Republic is divided into four provinces (Cape, Transvaal, Orange Free State, and Natal), each with a Provincial Council. Parliament consists of a 177-member House of Assembly and a multiracial 54-member President's Council. Members have five-year terms unless Parliament is dissolved earlier. The President is chosen by Parliament for a seven-year term.

Ten "Bantustans," or black homclands, exist within the country. They have unicameral legislatures elected by black voters. (Only whites vote in parliamentary elections.)

The major political parties are the National Party (126 of 177 seats in the House of Assembly), led by Prime Minister Pieter W. Botha; Progressive Federal Party (27 seats), led by Frederick van Zyl Slabbert; Conservative Party (16 seats), led by Dr. Andries Treurnight; and New Republic Party (8 seats), led by Vause Raw.

History. The Dutch East India Company landed the first settlers on the Cape of Good Hope in 1652, launching a colony that by the end of the 18th century numbered only about 15,000. Known as Boers or Afrikaners, speaking a Dutch dialect known as Afrikaans, the settlers as early as 1795 tried to establish an independent republic.

After occupying the Cape Colony in that year, Britain took permanent possession in 1814 at the end of the Napoleonic wars, bringing in 5,000 settlers. Anglicization of government and the freeing of slaves in 1833 drove about 12,000 Afrikaners to make the "great trek" north and east into African tribal territory, where they established the republics of the Transvaal and the Orange Free State.

The discovery of diamonds in 1867 and gold nine years later brought an influx of "outlanders" into the republics and spurred Cecil Rhodes to plot annexation. Rhodes's scheme of sparking an "outlander" rebellion to which an armed party under Leander Starr Jameson would ride to the rescue misfired in 1895, forcing Rhodes to resign as prime minister of the Cape colony. What British expansionists called the "inevitable" war with the Boers eventually broke out on Oct. 11, 1899.

The defeat of the Boers in 1902 led in 1910 to the Union of South Africa, composed of four provinces, the two former republics and the old Cape and Natal colonies. Louis Botha, the first Prime Minister and a Boer, allied the dominion with Britain in World War I. The Unionist Party, led by Jan Christiaan Smuts, advocated a pro-British line and a more liberal racial policy in the period between wars, while the Afrikaner Nationalist Party urged withdrawal from the Commonwealth and racial separation.

Smuts brought the nation into World War II on the Allied side against Nationalist opposition, and South Africa became a charter member of the United Nations in 1945, but refused to sign the Universal Declaration of Human Rights. Apartheid—racial separation—dominated domestic politics as the Nationalists gained power and imposed greater restrictions on Bantus, Coloreds, and Asians.

Afrikaner hostility to Britain triumphed in 1961 with the declaration on May 31 of the Republic of South Africa and the severing of ties with the Commonwealth. Nationalist Prime Minister H. F. Verwoerd's government in 1963 asserted the power to restrict freedom of those who opposed rigid racial laws. Three years later, amid increasing racial tension and criticism from the outside world, Verwoerd was assassinated. His Nationalist successor, Balthazar J. Vorster, launched a campaign of conciliation toward conservative black African states, offering development loans and trade concessions.

A critical issue was South-West Africa, where South African rule was challenged by the United Nations when it asserted responsibility for the territory in 1974 under the name Namibia. African demands for immediate freedom for Namibia led to an attempt to expel South Africa from the U.N. in 1974, a move blocked by a U.S., British, and French veto. The General Assembly barred South Africa from its seat anyway, and the seat has remained empty.

Economic restrictions tightened on South Africa following a vote by the Security Council imposing a mandatory embargo on arms in retaliation for South Africa's crackdown on opponents of apartheid. Although the U.S., Britain, and France vetoed mandatory economic sanctions against South Africa, U.S. and European businesses, unions, and church groups acted to cut trade with it.

Scandal rocked the Nationalist government in 1979 with the disclosure of the diversion of secret propaganda funds by former Information Minister Connie Mulder. Mulder's linking of Vorster with the scandal forced Vorster's resignation on June 4, 1979, from the State Presidency to which he had been elected after leaving the prime ministership in September.

The new Prime Minister, Peter W. Botha, moved toward a more liberal racial policy by easing job restrictions on blacks and extending black union rights. He appointed a multiracial advisory council, to assist in a proposed Constitutional revision and to replace the largely ceremonial Senate. The new group, composed of 39 whites, 15 Asians and mixed bloods, but including no blacks, met for the first time on Feb. 3, 1981.

Botha's policy brought right-wing defection from the ruling party in parliamentary elections on April 29, as the Nationalist popular vote dropped from nearly 65% in 1977 to 55% and the number of seats from 137 to 131. Although winning no seats, the splinter right Herstigte (Reconstituted) Nationalist Party gained nearly 10% in the popular vote. At the same time, the opposition Progressive Federal Party, capitalizing on urban whites' support for faster change, gained nine seats for a total of 26 in the new Parliament.

Negotiations for the independence of Namibia, stalled since 1978, made no progress in the Botha government's first encounter with the Reagan Administration. Foreign Minister Roelof F. Botha conferred with President Reagan and high U.S. officials in May. According to leaked State Department documents, he was offered "strategic cooperation" in return for a commitment to genuine independence in Namibia and movement away from apartheid at home.

In a split over future parliamentary representation, 18 right-wing Nationalists were expelled by Botha when they opposed sharing power with nonwhites. They formed a new party, the Conservatives. On July 30, Botha presented to the Nationalist party convention in Bloemfontein a plan for separate white, colored, and Asian chambers in order to give 2.5 million South Africans of mixed blood and 800,000 Asians a political voice. There was no provision for national representation of the 21 million black South Africans. The government also proposed that a new president with full executive powers be chosen by the three chambers, with the white chamber controlling the election.

BOPHUTHATSWANA

Republic of Bophuthatswana
President: Chief Lucas Mangope (1977)
Area: 15,610 sq mi. (40,430 sq km)
Population (est. 1982): 1,325,000 (average annual growth rate: 2.4%)
Density per square mile: 80.4
Capital: Mmabatho
Largest city (est. 1980): Ga-Rankuwa, 50,000
Monetary unit: South African rand
Languages: Central Tswana, English, Afrikaans
Religions: Methodist, Lutheran, Anglican, and Bantu Christian

Geography. Bophuthatswana consists of half a dozen discontinuous areas within the boundaries of South Africa, most of them in the northern sector near Botswana.

Government. The republic has a 99-member Legislative Assembly, approximately half of whom are elected and the others appointed. President Mangope's Democratic Party is the majority party.

History. Bophuthatswana was given independence

by South Africa on Dec. 6, 1977, following Transkei as the second "homeland" to be established by Pretoria. The new state and Transkei are recognized only by South Africa and each other.

Mangope, as chief minister in the pre-independence period, sought linkage of the six units into a consolidated area, but was unable to achieve his objective. A second issue, the citizenship of Tswanas in South Africa who wished to remain South African nationals, was settled by enabling them to have citizenship in South African homelands not yet independent.

About two thirds of the population of Bophuthatswana live permanently or as migrants in white areas of South Africa.

Economy. Bophuthatswana is richer than many other South African homelands, as it has more than half of the republic's platinum deposits. All foreign trade is included with South Africa's, and it is economically dependent at present on that country.

CISKEI

Republic of Ciskei
President: Chief Lennox Leslie Wongama Sebe (1981)
Area: 3,200 sq mi. (8,300 sq km)
Population (est. 1982): 675,000
Density per square mile: 21.1
Capital (est. 1980): Zwelitsha, 30,750
Largest city (est. 1980): Mdantsane, 159,000
Monetary unit: South African rand
Languages: Xhosa (official) and English
Religions: Methodist, Lutheran, Anglican, and Bantu Christian

Geography. Ciskei is surrounded by South Africa on three sides, with the Indian Ocean on the south. From a subtropical coastal strip, the land rises through grasslands to the mountainous escarpment that edges the South African interior plateau.

Government. Legislative power is vested in a National Assembly with 22 elected seats. Thirty-three hereditary chiefs complete the membership of the Assembly. The President holds executive power. South Africa's State President retains the power to legislate by proclamation and has veto power over the budget. The Ciskei National Independence Party holds all elective seats in the Assembly.

History. Oral tradition ascribes the origin of the Cape Nguni peoples to the central lakes area of Africa. They arrived in what is now Ciskei in the mid-17th century. White settlers from the Cape Colony first entered the territory a century later, but the Dutch East India Colony sought unsuccessfully to discourage white penetration. Nine wars between whites and the inhabitants, by now known as Xhosas, occurred between 1779 and 1878.

A Ciskeian territorial authority was established in 1961, with 84 chiefs and an executive council exercising limited self-government. In 1972, 20 elected members were added to the legislative assembly and a chief minister and six cabinet members elected by the assembly to function as an executive.

A proposed Constitution was approved by referendum on Oct. 30, 1980, and independence ceremonies held on Dec. 4. No government outside South Africa recognized the new state. A new capital was to be built at Bisho, formerly a settlement called Yellow-wood, and the South African government was expected to cede additional territory that will double Ciskei's area.

Economy. A subsistence agricultural economy has been superseded by commuter and migratory labor, which accounted for 64% of national income in 1977. There is some light industry and a potential for exploitation of limestone and other minerals.

SOUTH-WEST AFRICA (NAMIBIA)

Status: Mandate
Area: 318,261 sq mi. (824,296 sq km)
Population (est. 1982): 1,000,000 (average annual growth rate: 3.0%)
Density per square mile: 3.1
Administrator-General: Danie Hough (1980)
Capital (est. 1980): Windhoek, 85,000
Summer capital (est. 1980): Swakopmund 17,500
Monetary unit: South African rand
National name: Suidwes-Afrika/Namibië; South-West Africa/Namibia
Literacy rate: Not known
Economic summary: Gross national product (1980): $1.4 billion. Average annual growth rate (1970–79): 0.3%. Land used for agriculture: 30%; labor force: 68%; principal products: corn, millet, sorghum, livestock. Labor force in industry: 4%; major products: canned meat, dairy products, tanned leather, textiles, clothing. Natural resources: diamonds, copper, lead, zinc, uranium, fish. Exports: diamonds, copper, lead, zinc, beef cattle, karakul pelts. Imports: construction materials, fertilizer, grain, foodstuffs. Major trading partner: South Africa.

Geography. The mandate, bounded on the north by Angola and Zambia and on the east by Botswana and South Africa, was discovered by the Portuguese explorer Diaz in the late 15th century. It is for the most part a portion of the high plateau of southern Africa with a general elevation of from 3,000 to 4,000 feet.

History. The territory became a German colony in 1884 but was taken by South African forces in 1915, becoming a South African mandate by the terms of the Treaty of Versailles.

South Africa's application for incorporation of the territory was rejected by the U.N. General Assembly in 1946 and South Africa was invited to prepare a trusteeship agreement instead. By a law passed in 1949, however, the territory was brought into much closer association with South Africa—including representation in its Parliament.

In 1969, South Africa extended its laws to the mandate over the objection of the U.N., particularly its black African members. When South Africa refused to withdraw them, the Security Council condemned it.

Under a 1974 Security Council resolution, South Africa was required to begin the transfer of power to the Namibians by May 30, 1975, or face U.N. action, but 10 days before the deadline Prime Minister Balthazar J. Vorster rejected U.N. supervision. He said, however, that his government was prepared to negotiate Namibian independence, but not with the South-West African People's Organization, the principal black separatist group. Meanwhile, the all-white legislature of South-West Africa eased several laws on apartheid in public places.

Despite international opposition, the Turnhalle

Conference in Windhoek drafted a constitution to organize an interim government based on racial divisions, a proposal overwhelmingly endorsed by white voters in the territory in 1977. At the urging of ambassadors of the five Western members of the Security Council—the U.S., Britain, France, West Germany, and Canada—South Africa on June 11 announced rejection of the Turnhalle constitution and acceptance of the Western proposal to include the South-West Africa People's Organization (SWAPO) in negotiations.

With the approval of SWAPO, a militant nationalist group, Justice Marthinus T. Steyn was appointed by South Africa to serve as administrator of the territory during the transition to independence. At the same time, Pretoria announced that it would retain control of Walvis Bay, the territory's only deepwater port.

Apartheid laws were repealed by Steyn, and South-West representation in the South African parliament ended.

Although negotiations continued between South Africa, the western powers, neighboring black African states, and internal political groups, there was still no agreement in late 1982 on a final independence plan.

TRANSKEI

Republic of Transkei

President: Paramount Chief Daliwonga Matanzima (1980)
Prime Minister: Paramount Chief George Matanzima (1979)
Area: 15,831 sq mi. (41,002 sq km)
Population (est. 1982): 2,400,000 (growth rate: 2.2%)
Density per square mile: 157.9
Capital (est. 1980): Umtala, 32,500
Monetary unit: South African rand
Languages: English, Xhosa, Southern Sotho
Religions: Christian, 66%; tribal, 24%
Freedom House classifications: Capitalist pre-industrial, dominant party
Economic summary: Gross domestic product: $150 million. Per capita income: $86. Principal agricultural products: tea, corn, sorghum, dry beans. Major industrial products: timber, textiles. Natural resource: timber. Exports: timber, tea, sacks. Imports: foodstuffs, machines, equipment. Major trading partner: South Africa.

Geography. Transkei occupies three discontinuous enclaves within southeast South Africa that add up to twice the size of Massachusetts. It has a 270-mile (435 km) coastline on the Indian Ocean. A port is being developed at Port St. Johns. The capital, Umtata, is connected by rail to the South African port of East London, 100 miles (161 km) to the southwest.

Government. Transkei was granted independence by South Africa as of Oct. 26, 1976. A constitution called for organization of a parliament composed of 75 representative chiefs and 75 elected members, with a ceremonial president and executive power in the hands of a prime minister.

The Organization of African States and the chairman of the United Nations Special Committee Against Apartheid denounced the new state as a sham and urged governments not to recognize it.

History. British rule was established over the Transkei region between 1866 and 1894, and the Transkeian Territories were formed in 1903. Under the Native Land Act of 1913, the Territories were reserved for black occupation. In 1963, Transkei was given internal self-government and a legislature that elected Paramount Chief Kaiser Matanzima as Chief Minister, a post he retained in elections in 1968 and 1973.

Economy. Some 60% of Transkei is cultivated, producing corn, wheat, beans, and sorghum. Grazing is important. Some light industry has been established.

VENDA

Republic of Venda

President: Chief Patrick R. Mphephu (1979).
Area: 2,448 sq mi. (6,340 sq km)
Population (est. 1982): 400,000 (average annual growth rate: 2.4%)
Density per square mile: 214.5
Capital: Thohoyandou
Largest town (est. 1980): Makearela, 2,500
Monetary unit: South African rand
Languages: Venda, English, Afrikaans
Religions: Christian, tribal
Economic summary: Gross domestic product: $156 million. Per capita income: $312. Principal agricultural products: meat, tea, fruit, sisal, corn. Major industrial products: timber, graphite, magnetite.

Geography. Venda is composed of two noncontiguous territories in northeast South Africa with a total area of about half that of Connecticut. It is mountainous but fertile, well-watered land, with a climate ranging from tropical to subtropical.

Government. The third of South Africa's homelands to be granted independence, Venda became a separate republic on Sept. 13, 1979, unrecognized by any government other than South Africa and its sister homelands, Transkei and Bophuthatswana. The President is popularly elected. An 84-seat legislature is half elected, half appointed.

History. The first European reached Venda in 1816, but the isolation of the area prevented its involvement in the wars of the 19th century between blacks and whites and with other tribes. Venda came under South African administration after the Boer War in 1902. Limited home rule was granted in 1962. Chief Patrick R. Mphephu, leader of one of the 27 tribes that historically made up the Venda nation, became Chief Minister of the interim government in 1973 and President upon independence in 1979.

SOVIET UNION

Union of Soviet Socialist Republics

Chairman of Presidium (President): Leonid I. Brezhnev (1977)
Chairman of Council of Ministers (Premier): Nikolai A. Tikhonov (1980)
Area: 8,649,489 sq mi. (22,402,200 sq km)
Population (est. 1982): 269,850,000 (average annual growth rate: 0.8%) (Russian, 52%; Ukrainian, 17%; Uzbek, 5%; Byelorussian, 4%; Kazak, 3%; Tatar, 2%)
Density per square mile: 31.2
Capital: Moscow
Largest cities (1979 census): Moscow, 8,011,000; Leningrad, 4,588,000; Kiev, 2,144,000; Tashkent, 1,779,000; Baku, 1,550,000; Kharkov, 1,444,000; Gorki, 1,344,000; Novosibirsk, 1,312,000; Minsk, 1,276,000; Kuibyshev, 1,216,000; Sverdlovsk, 1,211,000;

Republics of the U.S.S.R.

Republic and capital	Area sq mi.	Population est. 1980 (thousands)
Russian S.F.S.R. (Moscow)	6,593,391	138,400
Ukraine (Kiev)	233,089	49,936
Kazakhstan (Alma-Ata)	1,064,092	14,900
Byelorussia (Minsk)	80,154	9,600
Uzbekistan (Tashkent)	158,069	15,774
Georgia (Tbilisi)	26,872	5,000
Azerbaijan (Baku)	33,475	6,117
Lithuania[1] (Vilnius)	25,174	3,400
Moldavia (Kishinev)	13,012	4,000
Latvia[1] (Riga)	24,595	2,500
Kirghizia (Frunze)	76,641	3,600
Tadzhikistan (Duschambe)	55,019	3,900
Armenia (Erevan)	11,506	3,080
Turkmenistan (Ashkhabad)	188,417	2,840
Estonia[1] (Tallinn)	17,413	1,470

1. Soviet jurisdiction not recognized by the United States.

Dnepropetrovsk, 1,066,000; Tbilisi, 1,066,000; Odessa, 1,046,000; Chelyabinsk, 1,031,000; Donetsk, 1,021,000; Yerevan, 1,019,000; Omsk, 1,014,000

Monetary unit; Ruble

Languages: *See* Population, above

Religions: Russian Orthodox (predominant), Islam, Roman Catholic, Jewish, Lutheran

National name: Soyuz Sovyetskikh Sotsialisticheskikh Respublik

Literacy rate (1981): 95%

Economic summary: Gross national product (1980): $1,212.0 billion. Average annual growth rate (1970–79): 4.1%. Per capita income (1980): $4,550. Land used for agriculture: 10%; labor force: 22%; principal products: wheat, rye, corn, oats, potatoes, sugar beets, cotton and flax, cattle, pigs, sheep. Labor force in industry: 78%; major products: ferrous and nonferrous metals, fuels and power, building materials, chemicals, machinery. Natural resources: fossil fuels, water power, timber, manganese, lead, zinc, nickel, mercury, potash, phosphate. Exports: petroleum and petroleum products, natural gas, machinery and equipment, manufactured goods. Imports: grain, machinery and equipment, foodstuffs, raw materials, consumer manufactures. Major trading partners: Soviet bloc, Western industrialized countries.

Geography. The U.S.S.R. is the largest unbroken political unit in the world, occupying more than one seventh of the land surface of the globe. The greater part of its territory is a vast plain stretching from eastern Europe to the Pacific Ocean. This plain, relieved only occasionally by low mountain ranges (notably the Urals), consists of three zones running east and west: the frozen marshy tundra of the Arctic; the more temperate forest belt; and the steppes or prairies to the south, which in southern Soviet Asia become sandy deserts.

The topography is more varied in the south, particularly in the Caucasus between the Caspian and Black Seas, and in the Tien-Pamir mountain system bordering Afghanistan, Sinkiang, and Mongolia. Mountains (Stanovoi and Kolyma) and great rivers (Amur, Yenisei, Lena) also break up the sweep of the plain in Siberia.

In the west, the major rivers are the Volga, Dnieper, Don, Kama, and Southern Bug.

Government. Legislative authority is vested in the Supreme Soviet of the U.S.S.R., which consists of two chambers—the Soviet of the Union, with 767 members, and the Soviet of Nationalities, with 750 members. All members of the Supreme Soviet are elected for five years by the people.

A Presidium is elected by the Supreme Soviet to deal with state matters when the latter is not in session. It consists of a chairman, first vice chairman, 15 vice chairmen (one for each union republic), 21 members, and a secretary. The chairman of the Presidium is sometimes referred to as the President.

Executive authority rests with the Council of Ministers. It is appointed by the Supreme Soviet and includes a chairman, a first vice chairman, and various vice chairmen, chairmen of state committees, ministers, etc. The chairman of the Council of Ministers is often referred to as the Premier.

Judicial authority is vested in the Supreme Court of the U.S.S.R. It consists of a chairmen, vice chairman, members, and people's assessors, who are elected by the Supreme Soviet for five years.

Each of the 15 union republics and the 20 autonomous republics has a Supreme Soviet (with a Presidium), a Council of Ministers, and a Supreme Court. Each of the eight autonomous regions has a Soviet of People's Deputies.

The Communist Party of the Soviet Union is the only party. It is the basic power in the country and today has a membership of 17,480,000.

The supreme organ of the party is the Party Congress, which meets at least once in five years. It elects a Central Committee, consisting of 320 members and 151 candidate members, to carry on party work between sessions of the Congress.

Within the Central Committee is a Political Bureau (Politburo), which was called the Presidium from 1952 to 1966. It functions between sessions of the Central Committee. Also within the Central Committee is the Secretariat. The present General Secretary of the Central Committee, Leonid I. Brezhnev, has served since Oct. 15, 1964. Named President in June 1977 to succeed Nikolai V. Podgorny, he is the first man in Soviet history to hold both posts simultaneously.

History. Tradition says the Viking Rurik came to Russia in A.D. 862 and founded the first Russian dynasty in Novgorod. The various tribes were united by the spread of Christianity in the 10th and 11th centuries; Vladimir "the Saint" was converted in 988. During the 11th century, the grand dukes of Kiev held such centralizing power as existed. In 1240, Kiev was destroyed by the Mongols, and the Russian territory was split into numerous smaller dukedoms, out of which three large centers emerged—Galicia, Moscow, and Novgorod. The early dukes of Moscow extended their dominions through their office of tribute collector for the Mongols.

In the late 15th century, Duke Ivan III acquired Novgorod and Tver and threw off the Mongol yoke. Ivan IV, the Terrible (1533–84), first Muscovite Tsar, is considered to have founded the Russian state. He crushed the power of rival princes and boyars (great landowners), but Russia remained largely medieval until the reign of Peter the Great (1682–1725), grandson of the first Romanov Tsar, Michael (1613–45). Peter made extensive reforms aimed at westernization and, through his defeat of Charles XII of Sweden at the Battle of Poltava in 1709, he extended Russia's boundaries to the west.

Catherine the Great (1762–96) continued Peter's westernization program and also expanded Russian territory, acquiring the Crimea and part of Poland. During the reign of Alexander I (1801–25), Napoleon's attempt to subdue Russia was defeated (1812–13), and new territory was gained, including Finland (1809) and Bessarabia (1812). Alexander originated the Holy Alliance, which for a time crushed Europe's rising liberal movement.

Alexander II (1855–81) pushed Russia's borders to the Pacific and into central Asia. Serfdom was abolished in 1861, but heavy restrictions were imposed on the emancipated class. Revolutionary strikes following Russia's defeat in the war with Japan forced Nicholas II (1894–1917) to grant a representative national body (Duma), elected by narrowly limited suffrage. It met for the first time in 1906, little influencing Nicholas in his reactionary course.

World War I demonstrated tsarist corruption and inefficiency and only patriotism held the poorly equipped army together for a time. Disorders broke out in Petrograd (now Leningrad) in March 1917, and defection of the Petrograd garrison launched the revolution. Nicholas II was forced to abdicate on March 15, 1917, and he and his family were killed by revolutionists on July 16, 1918.

A provisional government under the successive premierships of Prince Lvov and a moderate, Alexander Kerensky, lost ground to the radical, or Bolshevik, wing of the Socialist Democratic Labor Party. On Nov. 7, 1917, the Bolshevik revolution, engineered by N. Lenin[1] and Leon Trotsky, overthrew the Kerensky government and authority was vested in a Council of People's Commissars, with Lenin as Premier.

1. N. Lenin was the pseudonym taken by Vladimir Ilich Ulyanov. It is sometimes given as Nikolai Lenin or V.

The humiliating Treaty of Brest-Litovsk (March 3, 1918) concluded the war with Germany, but civil war and foreign intervention delayed Communist control of all Russia until 1920. A brief war with Poland in 1920 resulted in Russian defeat.

The Union of Soviet Socialist Republics was established as a federation on Dec. 30, 1922.

The death of Lenin on Jan. 21, 1924, precipitated an intraparty struggle between Joseph Stalin, General Secretary of the party, and Trotsky, who favored swifter socialization at home and fomentation of revolution abroad. Trotsky was dismissed as Commissar of War in 1925 and banished from the Soviet Union in 1929. He was murdered in Mexico City on Aug. 21, 1940, by a political agent.

Stalin further consolidated his power by a series of purges in the late 1930s, liquidating prominent party leaders and military officers. Stalin assumed the premiership May 6, 1941.

Soviet foreign policy, at first friendly toward Germany and antagonistic toward Britain and France and then, after Hitler's rise to power in 1933, becoming anti-Fascist and pro-League of Nations, took an abrupt turn on Aug. 24, 1939, with the signing of a nonaggression pact with Nazi Germany. The next month, Moscow joined in the German attack on Poland, seizing territory later incorporated into the Ukrainian and Byelorussian S.S.R.'s. The war with Finland, 1939-40, added territory to the Karelian S.S.R. set up March 31, 1940; the annexation of Bessarabia and Bukovina from Romania became part of the new Moldavian S.S.R. on Aug. 2, 1940; and the annexation of the Baltic republics of Estonia, Latvia, and Lithuania in June 1940 (still unrecognized by the U.S.) created the 14th, 15th, and 16th Soviet Republics. (The number of so-called "Union" republics was reduced to 15 in 1956 when the Karelian S.S.R. became one of the 20 Autonomous Soviet Socialist Republics based on ethnic groups.)

Rulers of Russia Since 1533

Name	Born	Ruled[1]
Ivan IV the Terrible	1530	1533–1584
Theodore I	1557	1584–1598
Boris Godunov	c.1551	1598–1605
Theodore II	1589	1605–1605
Demetrius I[2]	?	1605–1606
Basil IV Shuiski	?	1606–1610[3]
"Time of Troubles"	—	1610–1613
Michael Romanov	1596	1613–1645
Alexis I	1629	1645–1676
Theodore III	1656	1676–1682
Ivan V[4]	1666	1682–1689[5]
Peter I the Great[4]	1672	1682–1725
Catherine I	c.1684	1725–1727
Peter II	1715	1727–1730
Anna	1693	1730–1740
Ivan VI	1740	1740–1741[6]
Elizabeth	1709	1741–1762
Peter III	1728	1762–1762
Catherine II the Great	1729	1762–1796
Paul I	1754	1796–1801
Alexander I	1777	1801–1825
Nicholas I	1796	1825–1855
Alexander II	1818	1855–1881
Alexander III	1845	1881–1894
Nicholas II	1868	1894–1917[7]
PROVISIONAL GOVERNMENT (PREMIERS)		
Prince Georgi Lvov	1861	1917–1917
Alexander Kerensky	1881	1917–1917
U.S.S.R. (PREMIERS)		
N. Lenin	1870	1917–1924
Aleksei Rykov	1881	1924–1930
Vyacheslav Molotov	1890	1930–1941
Joseph Stalin[8]	1879	1941–1953
Georgi M. Malenkov	1902	1953–1955
Nikolai A. Bulganin	1895	1955–1958
Nikita S. Khrushchev	1894	1958–1964
PRESIDENTS		
Leonid I. Brezhnev	1906	1964–

1. For Tsars through Nicholas II, year of end of rule is also that of death, unless otherwise indicated. 2. Also known as Pseudo-Demetrius. 3. Died 1612. 4. Ruled jointly until 1689, when Ivan was deposed. 5. Died 1696. 6. Died 1764. 7. Killed 1918. 8. General Secretary of Communist Party, 1924–53.

The Soviet-German collaboration ended abruptly with a lightning attack by Hitler on June 22, 1941, which seized 500,000 square miles of Russian territory before Soviet defenses, aided by U.S. and British arms, could halt it. The Soviet resurgence at Stalingrad from November 1942 to February 1943 marked the turning point in a long battle, ending in the final offensive of January 1945.

Then, after denouncing a 1941 nonaggression pact with Japan in April 1945, when Allied forces were nearing victory in the Pacific, the Soviet Union declared war on Japan on Aug. 8, 1945, and quickly occupied Manchuria, Karafuto, and the Kurile islands.

Postwar territorial acquisitions include the Carpatho-Ukraine (12,617 sq mi.; 32,678 sq km) obtained from Czechoslovakia June 29, 1945, incorporated into the Ukrainian S.S.R.; the Republic of Tannu Tuva in central Asia (64,000 sq mi.; 165,760 sq km), incorporated early in 1945 into the Russian Soviet Federal Socialist Republic (R.S.F.S.R.); Karafuto or southern Sakhalin (13,935 sq mi.; 36,092 sq km) and the Kurile Islands (3,944 sq mi.; 10,215 sq km), occupied by Soviet troops in August 1945 and incorporated into the R.S.F.S.R.; the northern part of eastern Prussia (about 7,000 sq mi.; 18,130 sq km), placed under *de facto* Soviet administration at the Potsdam Conference and incorporated into the R.S.F.S.R.; the Petsamo district of Finland, obtained *de jure* under the 1947 treaty and incorporated into the R.S.F.S.R.; and Poland east of the Curzon Line (69,860 sq mi.; 180,937 sq km), under terms of the Soviet-Polish treaty of Aug. 16, 1945, incorporated into the Ukrainian and Byelorussian S.S.R.'s.

The U.S.S.R. built a cordon of Communist states running from Poland in the north to Albania and Bulgaria in the south, including East Germany, Czechoslovakia, Hungary, and Romania, composed of the territories Soviet troops occupied at the war's end. With its Eastern front solidified, the Soviet Union launched a political offensive against the non-Communist West, moving first to block the Western access to Berlin. The Western powers countered with an airlift, completed unification of West Germany, and organized the defense of Western Europe in the North Atlantic Treaty Organization.

Stalin died on March 6, 1953, and was succeeded the next day by G. M. Malenkov as Premier. His chief rivals for power—Lavrenti P. Beria (chief of the secret police), Nikolai A. Bulganin, and Lazar M. Kaganovich—were named first deputies. Beria was purged in July and executed on Dec. 23, 1953.

The new power in the Kremlin was Nikita S. Khrushchev, First Secretary of the party. He replaced Malenkov with Bulganin in the premiership and then removed Malenkov, Kaganovich, and Vyacheslav M. Molotov from the Politburo. At the 20th Party Congress in 1956, Khrushchev denounced the "personality cult" of Stalin and in 1958 unseated Bulganin to become head of the government as well as of the party.

Khrushchev formalized the Eastern European system into a Council for Mutual Economic Assistance (Comecon) and a Warsaw Pact Treaty Organization as a counterweight to NATO. Tiny Albania was allowed to break away to join China in contesting Soviet domination of the Communist world, as Yugoslavia had done earlier. However, no mercy was shown to the Hungarians who rebelled in 1956, nor to the Czechs in their political struggle for liberation 12 years later.

In its technological race with the U.S., the Soviet Union exploded a hydrogen bomb in 1953, developed an intercontinental ballistic missile by 1957, sent the first satellite into space (Sputnik I) in 1957, and put Yuri Gagarin in the first orbital flight around the earth in 1961. On July 24, 1975, the 44-hour linkup of a Soviet Soyuz space vehicle (and two crewmen) with a U.S. Apollo spacecraft and its crew of three) demonstrated—for the first time openly—the level of Soviet space capability.

Khrushchev's downfall stemmed from his decision to place Soviet nuclear missiles in Cuba and then, when challenged by the U.S., backing down and removing the weapons. He was also blamed for the ideological break with China after 1963.

Khrushchev was forced into retirement on Oct. 15, 1964, and was replaced by Leonid I. Brezhnev as First Secretary of the Party and Aleksei N. Kosygin as Premier.

President Nixon visited the U.S.S.R. for summit talks in May 1972, concluding agreements on strategic-arms limitation and a declaration of principles on future U.S.-Soviet relations. The welcome given Nixon at a time when the U.S. was bombing North Vietnam, a Soviet ally, was regarded as proof that 25 years of cold war had ended.

The 1972 Strategic Arms Limitation Treaty (SALT I) set a ceiling of 200 anti-ballistic missiles (ABM's) for each side and the U.S.S.R. was frozen at 1,618 land-based intercontinental missiles (ICBM's), with the U.S. held to 1,054. Submarine-based missiles were restricted by a complicated formula giving the U.S.S.R. a numerical advantage, balanced by permitting the U.S. more warheads for its more reliable and accurate missiles.

Brezhnev visited the U.S. in 1973 to discuss further arms limitations, but a return visit to Moscow by Nixon the following year failed to produce an expected permanent treaty. The two sides agreed to reduce ABM's to 100 each and to restrict underground nuclear testing (air, sea, and space tests were already prohibited), but there was no agreement to stop the proliferation of multi-warhead missiles (MIRV's).

Presidents Gerald R. Ford and Brezhnev met in Vladivostok in November 1974 and reached tentative agreements to be incorporated into a treaty at the Geneva SALT talks in 1975. They proposed a ceiling of 2,400 ICBM's for each side, of which no more than 1,320 could have MIRV's. There was hard bargaining but no decision on verification methods nor on whether the new U.S. subsonic Cruise missile and the Soviet Backfire bomber should be covered.

President Carter, actively pursuing both human rights and disarmament, joined with the Soviet Union in September 1977 to declare that the SALT I accord, which would have expired Oct. 1 without further action, be maintained in effect while the two sides sought a new agreement (SALT II).

Desire for détente appeared to moderate the Kremlin's policies toward the U.S. after the 1972 summit. There was a near-confrontation during the Arab-Israeli war of October 1973, when a Soviet threat to intervene to aid trapped Egyptian forces led Washington to call a world-wide nuclear alert, but the crisis was eased when the United Nations approved a U.S.-U.S.S.R. truce plan. The Kremlin made no overt move to capitalize on the fall of U.S.-backed governments in Indochina in the spring of 1975, but hailed the war's end as an incentive to improvement in relations with the U.S.

Brezhnev's 1977 election to the presidency followed publication of a new Constitution supplanting the one adopted in 1936. It specified the dominance of the Communist Party, previously unstated, and in what was taken to be a weapon against dissidents, declared that "rights and freedoms shall be inseparable from the performance by citizens of their duties." This was thought to restrict dissidents when they cited constitutional guarantees of individual freedom.

Although Brezhnev promised an end to the "illegal repressions" of the Stalin era, the issue of human rights remained a major one in both domestic and foreign policy. Dissidents continued to cite the Helsinki Agreement, and Carter's public support for Anatoly Shcharansky drew the angry charge from Brezhnev that Carter was conducting "ideological warfare" against the U.S.S.R. Amid the verbal fireworks, there was serious concern about the extent to which human rights might become an obstacle to SALT negotiations and to Soviet-U.S. relations in general.

The State Department warned, after Brezhnev had complained of SALT delays, that Soviet military aid to Ethiopia threatened all U.S.-Soviet relations. The Soviet news agency, Tass, said on February 26 that Soviet aid to Ethiopia was to counter Somali aggression and would end with a ceasefire. Similar friction occurred following the invasion of Zaire in May by rebels from Soviet-allied Angola, culminating in a speech by Carter to graduates of the U.S. Naval Academy telling the Russians they must "choose either confrontation or cooperation."

A crisis arose July 10 when, despite warnings from the Carter Administration, the government brought two prominent Jewish dissidents to trial, only two days before the opening of a new round of SALT negotiations in Geneva. Amid worldwide protest, a Moscow judge sentenced Anatoly Scharansky to three years in prison and 10 years in a forced labor camp on charges of treason. Scharansky, a leading spokesman for Jews seeking to emigrate to Israel, was accused of passing classified information to U.S. agents.

Aleksandr Ginzburg, manager of a fund established by exiled writer Aleksandr Solzhenytsin to aid political prisoners, was sentenced to eight years in a labor camp. Ginzburg was found guilty of "anti-Soviet agitation."

Carter condemned the action and temporarily halted the export of high technology goods to the Soviet Union. In April 1979, the issue was partly resolved with the exchange of Ginzburg and four other dissidents for two Soviet spies held by the United States. For 1979, the final count of Soviet Jews allowed to emigrate was 51,320, the highest number since emigration was permitted.

Carter and the ailing Brezhnev signed the SALT II treaty in Vienna on June 18, 1979, setting ceilings on each nation's arsenal of intercontinental ballistic missiles. Doubts about Senate ratification grew, and became a certainty on Dec. 27, when Soviet troops invaded Afghanistan. Despite protests from the Moslem and Western worlds, Moscow insisted that Afghan President Hafizullah Amin had asked for aid in quelling a rebellion.

In the face of evidence that Amin had been liquidated by Soviet advisers before the troops arrived, the Soviet Union vetoed a Security Council resolution on Jan. 7, 1980, that called for a withdrawal. Carter ordered a freeze on grain exports and high-technology equipment and stated that his "opinion of the Russians has changed more drastically in the last week than even in the previous two-and-a-half years."

On Jan. 20, Carter called for a world boycott of the Summer Olympic Games scheduled for Moscow. The boycott, less than complete, nevertheless marred the first Olympics to be held in Moscow as the United States, Canada, Japan, and to a partial extent all the western allies except France and Italy shunned the event.

Through 1981, an estimated 100,000 Soviet troops remained in Afghanistan, with guerrilla resistance continuing, and Moscow's motives still unclear. The invasion was regarded by some U.S. theoreticians as having been prompted by the weak response of the Carter administration to the seizure of the U.S. Embassy in Teheran. Others suggested that Soviet leaders were only routinely backing a Marxist regime threatened with overthrow. With Iran racked by internal struggles, there was also the opportunity for Soviet military power to intervene from a flanking position, possibly gaining for Moscow both Iranian oil and the access to the Indian Ocean, coveted since tsarist days.

While the Soviet Union maintained a stony defense in the face of criticism from Western Europe and the U.S., and a summit meeting of 37 Islamic nations that unanimously condemned the "imperialist invasion" of Afghanistan, the growing crisis in Poland increasingly drew world attention. The Kremlin adopted an equally unyielding policy, sternly warning Warsaw against concessions to Polish workers and threatening military intervention.

The Reagan Administration took an initial hard line, with Secretary of State Alexander M. Haig, Jr., talking of a total trade embargo in the event of a Soviet military move into Poland. But at the Party's 26th Congress on Feb. 23, 1981, Brezhnev appeared to soften his approach with a call for an East-West summit and new arms-control talks.

Making no direct response, Reagan lifted the Carter-imposed embargo on grain sales to the Soviet Union on April 24. Although Soviet officials minimized the effect of a two-thirds cut in U.S. grain deliveries over 15 months, it had forced the slaughter of cattle, resulting in subsequent meat and milk shortages. A third successive bad harvest accentuated the food problem.

In reaction to Soviet repression in Poland in December 1981, Reagan ordered economic sanctions aimed at blocking construction of a gas pipeline between the Soviet Union and Western Europe and Japan. Despite the tension between Moscow and Washington, Strategic Arms Reduction Talks (START) began in Geneva between U.S. and Soviet delegations in mid—1982. Negotiations on intermediate missile reduction also continued in Geneva.

A Brezhnev-Reagan summit was originally expected to launch the new disarmament round, but the Soviet leader's precarious health prevented him from traveling. A long absence from public view early in the year gave rise to rumors that he was near death and that the government was being run by a high-level committee. A noticeable Soviet indecisiveness in the Lebanese crisis, even after Brezhnev's reappearance, gave credence to the "government by committee" theory.

SPAIN

Spanish State

Ruler: King Juan Carlos I (1975)

Premier: Leopoldo Calvo Sotelo (1981)

Area: 194,885 sq mi. (504,750 km)[1]
Population (est. 1982): 37,850,000 (average annual growth rate: 0.7%) (Spanish, Basque, Catalan, Galician)
Density per square mile: 194.2
Capital: Madrid
Largest cities (est. 1981): Madrid, 3,275,000; Barcelona, 1,725,000; Valencia, 770,000; Seville, 630,000; Zaragoza, 600,000; Vizcaya (Bilbao), 450,000
Monetary unit: Peseta
Languages: Spanish, Basque, Catalan, Galician
Religion: Roman Catholic
National name: Estado Español
Literacy rate (1981): 97%
Economic summary: Gross national product (1980): $199.8 billion. Average annual growth rate (1970–79): 3.0%. Per capita income (1980): $5,350. Land used for agriculture: 41%; labor force: 19%; principal products: cereals, vegetables, citrus fruits, wine, olives and olive oil, livestock. Labor force in industry: 37%; major products: processed foods, textiles, footwear, petro-chemicals, steel, automobiles, ships. Natural resources: coal, lignite, water power, uranium, mercury, pyrites, fluorospar, gypsum, iron ore, zinc, lead, tungsten, copper. Exports: fresh fruits, iron and steel products, textiles, footwear, automobiles, fruits and vegetables. Imports: machinery and transportation equipment, chemicals, fuels, automobiles, iron, steel. Major trading partners: Western European nations, U.S.

1. Including the Balearic and Canary Islands.

Geography. Spain occupies 85% of the Iberian Peninsula in southwestern Europe, which it shares with Portugal; France is to the northeast, separated by the Pyrenees. The Bay of Biscay lies to the north, the Atlantic Ocean to the west, and the Mediterranean Sea to the south and east. Africa is less than 10 miles (16 km) south at the Strait of Gibraltar.

A broad central plateau slopes to the south and east, crossed by a series of mountain ranges and river valleys.

Principal rivers are the Ebro in the northeast, the Tejo in the central region, and the Guadalquivir in the south.

Off Spain's east coast in the Mediterranean are the Balearic Islands (1,936 sq mi.; 5,014 sq km), the largest of which is Majorca. Sixty miles (97 km) west of Africa are the Canary Islands (2,808 sq mi.; 7,273 sq km).

Government. King Juan Carlos I (born Jan. 5, 1938) succeeded Generalissimo Francisco Franco Bahamonde as Chief of State Nov. 22, 1975.

The Cortes, or Parliament, consists of a Chamber of Deputies of 350 members and a Senate of 208, all elected by universal suffrage. The new Cortes, replacing one that was largely appointed or elected by special constituencies, was organized under a constitution adopted by referendum Dec. 6, 1978.

The major political parties are the 12-party coalition of the Union of the Democratic Center (167 of 350 seats in the Chamber of Deputies, 120 of 208 elected Senate seats), led by Leopoldo Calvo Sotelo; Spanish Socialist Workers Party (121 seats in Chamber, 65 in Senate); Communist Party (23 seats in Chamber, none in Senate), led by Santiago Carrillo; Democratic Coalition (9 seats in Chamber, 2 in Senate); Convergencia i Unió (Catalonian Party) (9 seats in Chamber, 1 in Senate); Basque Party (7 seats in Chamber, 8 in Senate); Andalusian Socialist Party (5 seats in Chamber).

History. Spain, originally inhabited by Celts, Iberians, and Basques, became a part of the Roman Empire in 201 B.C., when it was conquered by Scipio Africanus. In A.D. 412, the barbarian Visigothic leader Ataulf crossed the Pyrenees and ruled Spain, first in the name of the Roman emperor and then independently. In 711, the Moslems under Tariq entered Spain from Africa and within a few years completed the subjugation of the country. In 732, the Franks, led by Charles Martel, defeated the Moslems near Poitiers, thus preventing the further expansion of Islam in southern Europe. Internal dissension of Spanish Islam invited a steady Christian conquest from the north.

Aragon and Castile were the most important Spanish states from the 13th to the 15th century, consolidated by the marriage of Ferdinand II and Isabella I in 1469. The last Moslem stronghold, Granada, was captured in 1492. Roman Catholicism was established as the official state religion and the Jews (1492) and the Moslems (1502) expelled.

In the era of exploration, discovery, and colonization, Spain amassed tremendous wealth and a vast colonial empire through the conquest of Peru by Pizarro (1532–33) and of Mexico by Cortés (1519–21). The Spanish Hapsburg monarchy became for a time the most powerful in the world.

In 1588, Philip II sent his Invincible Armada to invade England, but its destruction cost Spain its supremacy on the seas and paved the way for England's colonization of America. Spain then sank rapidly to the status of a second-rate power and never again played a major role in European politics. Its colonial empire in the Americas and the Philippines vanished in wars and revolutions during the 18th and 19th centuries.

In World War I, Spain maintained a position of neutrality. In 1923, Gen. Miguel Primo de Rivera became dictator. In 1930, King Alfonso XIII revoked the dictatorship, but a strong antimonarchist and republican movement led to his leaving Spain in 1931.[2] The new Constitution declared Spain a workers' republic, broke up the large estates, separated church and state, and secularized the schools. The elections held in 1936 returned a strong Popular Front majority, with Manuel Azaña as President.

On July 18, 1936, a conservative army officer in Morocco, Francisco Franco Bahamonde, led a mutiny against the government. The civil war that followed lasted three years and cost the lives of nearly a million people. Franco was aided by Fascist Italy and Nazi Germany, while Soviet Russia helped the Loyalist side. Several hundred leftist Americans served in the Abraham Lincoln Brigade on the side of the republic. The war ended when Franco took Madrid on March 28, 1939.

Franco became head of the state, national chief of the Falange Party (the governing party), and Premier and Caudillo (leader). In a referendum in 1947, the Spanish people approved a Franco-drafted succession law declaring Spain a monarchy again. Franco, however, continued as Chief of State.

In 1969, Franco and the Cortes designated Prince Juan Carlos Alfonso Victor María de Borbón (who married Princess Sophia of Greece on May 14, 1962) to become King of Spain when the provisional government headed by Franco came to an end. He is the grandson of Alfonso XIII and the son

2. However, he did not abdicate. In 1941, shortly before his death, he renounced his claim to the throne in favor of his third son, Don Juan.

of Don Juan, pretender to the throne.

In 1967 Spain concluded its first economic-social development plan, which had raised levels of living dramatically within a decade and, combined with Spanish migration to higher-wage countries in Western Europe, had virtually eradicated unemployment. A new Constitution, adopted in 1966, allowed for the direct election of one fourth of the Cortes.

Franco died of a heart attack on Nov. 20, 1975, after more than a year of ill health, and Juan Carlos was proclaimed King two days later.

Over strong rightist opposition, the government legalized the Communist Party in advance of the 1977 elections. Premier Adolfo Suaraz Gonzalez's Union of the Democratic Center, a coalition of a dozen centrist and rightist parties, claimed 34.3% of the popular vote in the election.

The Spanish Socialist Workers Party (PSOE) ran the strongest opposition campaign to win 28.5% of the vote, with the Communists following at 9% and the right-wing Popular Alliance trailing with 8.2%.

Under pressure from Catalonian and Basque nationalists, Suárez granted home rule to these regions in 1979, but centrists backed by him did poorly in the 1980 elections for local assemblies in the two areas. Economic problems persisted, along with new incidents of terrorism, and Suárez resigned on Jan. 29, 1981, recommending Leopoldo Calvo Sotelo as his successor.

While the Cortes was debating Calvo's confirmation, 200 right-wing Civil Guardsmen invaded the chamber on Feb. 23 and held the Cabinet and 350 legislators hostage. King Juan Carlos made a televised appeal for support of the government, the attempt failed and the Prime Minister was subsequently confirmed by a vote of 186–158.

Spain formally entered the North Atlantic Treaty Organization as the 16th member of the Western alliance on Dec. 10 and in 1982 was expected to become a member of the European Economic Community, bringing to an end the international isolation that had marked the Franco era. Old problems persisted at home, however, with Basque violence culminating in permanent suspension of construction of the nation's first nuclear power plant at Lemoniz, near Bilbao, on May 3 after the murder of the plant's director.

Reflecting the end of the economic boom years in which Spain had been catching up with industrialized Europe, unemployment in 1982 was expected to exceed 16%, an increase of 2% over 1981. In April, the government announced a $5-billion public works program to alleviate the situation, with emphasis on Andalusia in the south and Estremadura in the west, both regions particularly hurt by economic recession.

SRI LANKA

Democratic Socialist Republic of Sri Lanka
President: J. R. Jayawardene (1978)
Prime Minister: Ranasinghe Premadasa (1978)
Area: 25,332 sq mi. (65,610 sq km)
Population (est. 1982): 15,250,000 (average annual growth rate: 1.8%)
Density per square mile: 602.0
Capital: Sri Jayewardenapura Kotte (Colombo)
Largest cities (est. 1980): Sri Jayewardenapura Kotte, 640,000; **(est. 1977):** Dehiwela, 169,000; Jaffna, 118,000
Monetary unit: Sri Lanka rupee
Languages: Sinhala, Tamil, English
Religions: Buddhist, 67%; Hindu, 18%; Christian, 8%; Islam, 7%
Member of Commonwealth of Nations
Literacy rate (1970): 82% (est.)
Economic summary: Gross national product (1980): $4.0 billion. Average annual growth rate (1970–79): 2.5%. Per capita income (1980): $270. Land used for agriculture: 25%; labor force: 53%; principal products: tea, coconuts, rubber, rice, spices. Labor force in industry: 15%; major products: consumer goods, textiles, chemicals, paper and paper products. Natural resources: limestone, graphite, gems. Exports: tea, rubber, petroleum products. Imports: petroleum, machinery, transport equipment, sugar. Major trading partners: Saudi Arabia, Iran, Pakistan.

Geography. An island in the Indian Ocean off the southeast tip of India, Sri Lanka is about half the size of Alabama. Most of the land is flat and rolling; mountains in the south central region rise to over 8,000 feet (2,438 m).

Government. After 24 years as a British dominion, Ceylon became an independent republic and reverted to the traditional name Sri Lanka (resplendent island) on May 22, 1972. A new Constitution was adopted, replacing that of 1948.

The new Constitution set up the National State Assembly, a 168-member unicameral legislature that serves for six years unless dissolved earlier.

The major political parties are the United National Party (141 of 168 seats in the National Assembly), led by Prime Minister Ranasinghe Premadasa; Tamil United Liberation Front (17 seats); Sri Lanka Freedom Party (9 seats), led by Maithrapala Senanayake. (Former Prime Minister Mrs. Sirimavo R.D. Bandaranaike has sought to split the Freedom Party, but no official alignment was expected for elections tentatively scheduled for 1983.

History. Following Portuguese and Dutch rule, Ceylon became an English crown colony in 1798. The British developed coffee, tea, and rubber plantations and granted six Constitutions between 1798 and 1924. The Constitution of 1931 gave a large measure of self-government.

Ceylon became a self-governing dominion of the Commonwealth of Nations in 1948. Rioting by the Tamils seeking a separate state within a federal system occurred in 1958 and 1961, resulting in the outlawing of their party. In 1962, the Prime Minister, Mrs. Bandaranaike, a radical, nationalized Western oil and other business facilities and became embroiled with the U.S. and Britain over compensation. She was ousted in the 1965 elections by a multiparty coalition.

Following considerable pre-election violence, Mrs. Bandaranaike was returned to power in a landslide victory in 1970, with her three-party leftist coalition capturing over two thirds of parliament. An important factor was the 800,000 youths 18-to-21 years old given the vote for the first time; they proved largely left-leaning.

Worsening economic conditions and charges of corruption combined to produce a crushing defeat for Mrs. Bandaranaike in general elections of 1977. Junius Richard Jayawardene, 73-year-old leader of the small United National Party, became Prime Minister.

Amid opposition criticism, Jayawardene was sworn in as president on Feb. 3, 1978, in a constitutional change to the presidential system of government. He named his deputy party leader, Ranasinghe Premadasa, as prime minister.

In April 1982, the National Assembly met for the first time in the new capital, Sri Jayewardenapura Kotte. The administrative departments of the government are expected to move in as buildings become available. Sri Jayewardenapura Kotte, a suburb of Colombo, was the capital before the Portuguese colonial period and its name has nothing to do with President Jayawardene.

SUDAN

Democratic Republic of the Sudan
President: (1971) and Prime Minister (1977): Field Marshal Gaafar Mohamed Nimeiri
Area: 967,491 sq mi. (2,505,802 sq km)
Population (est. 1982): 19,150,000 (average annual growth rate: 2.8%)
Density per square mile: 19.8
Capital: Khartoum
Largest cities (est. 1980): Khartoum, 1,600,000; **(est. 1973):** Omdurman, 250,000; Port Sudan, 130,000
Monetary unit: Sudanese pound
Languages: Arabic, English, tribal dialects
Religions: Islam, 66%; Animist, 29%; Christian, 5%
National name: Jamhuryat es-Sudan Al Demogratia
Literacy rate (1981): 20%
Economic summary: Gross national product (1980): $8.6 billion. Average annual growth rate (1970–79): 1.5%. Per capita income (1980): $470. Land used for agriculture: 3%; labor force: 78%; principal products: cotton, peanuts, sesame seeds, gum arabic, sorghum, wheat sugar cane. Labor force in industry: 10%; major products: cement, textiles, pharmaceuticals, shoes, processed foods. Natural resources: some iron ore, copper, chrome, industrial metals. Exports: cotton, peanuts, gum arabic, livestock. Imports: textiles, petroleum products, vehicles, tea, wheat. Major trading partners: U.K., West Germany, Italy, India, China, France, Japan.

Geography. The Sudan, in northeast Africa, is the largest country on the continent, measuring about one fourth the size of the United States. Its neighbors are Chad and the Central African Republic on the west, Egypt and Libya on the north, Ethiopia on the east, and Kenya, Uganda, and Zaire on the south. The Red Sea washes about 500 miles of the eastern coast.

The country extends from north to south about 1,200 miles (1,931 km) and west to east about 1,000 miles (1,609 km). The northern region is a continuation of the Libyan Desert. The southern region is fertile, abundantly watered, and, in places, heavily forested. It is traversed from north to south by the Nile, all of whose great tributaries are partly or entirely within its borders.

Government. Under the 1975 Constitution, executive power is vested in a president elected by universal suffrage for a term of six years. Legislative authority is exercised by a 350-member People's Assembly. The Sudanese Socialist Union is the only authorized political party.

History. The early history of the Sudan (known as the Anglo-Egyptian Sudan between 1898 and 1955) is linked with that of Nubia, where a powerful local kingdom was formed in Roman times with its capital at Dongola. After conversion to Christianity in the 6th century, it joined with Ethiopia and resisted Mohammedanization until the 14th century. Thereafter the area was broken up into many small states until 1820–22, when it was conquered by Mohammed Ali, Pasha of Egypt. Egyptian forces were evacuated during the Mahdist revolt (1881–98), but the Sudan was reconquered by the Anglo-Egyptian expeditions of 1896–98, and in 1899 became an Anglo-Egyptian condominium, which was reaffirmed by the Anglo-Egyptian treaty of 1936.

Egypt and Britain agreed in 1953 to grant self-government to the Sudan under an appointed Governor-General. An all-Sudanese Parliament was elected in November-December 1953, and an all-Sudanese government was formed. In December 1955, the Parliament declared the independence of the Sudan, which, with the approval of Britain and Egypt, was proclaimed on Jan. 1, 1956.

In October 1969, Maj. Gen. Gaafar Mohamed Nimeiri, the president of the Council for the Revolution, took over as prime minister. He was elected the nation's first president in 1971 by a reported 98.6% of the vote in a national referendum. His term was for six years.

On March 2, 1973, eight Palestinian terrorists invaded the Saudi Arabian embassy in Khartoum and killed one Belgian and two American diplomats after their demands for the release of Arab terrorist prisoners in different countries were refused. The terrorists surrendered after three days and were captured, but Nimeiri postponed bringing them to trial in the face of Arab calls for their release.

The terrorists were convicted of murder June 24, 1974, but Nimeiri freed them the next day and turned them over to the Palestine Liberation Army, which flew them to Cairo. The U.S. withdrew its Ambassador in protest, but he returned in October 1974 after the men were imprisoned in Egypt.

In 1976, a third attempted coup against Nimeiri left 1,000 rebels and loyal troops dead after a fierce battle in Khartoum. Nimeiri accused President Muammar el Qaddifi of Libya of having instigated the attempt and broke relations with Libya. Firing squads executed 81 convicted rebels.

Nimeiri also charged Soviet involvement in the attempt and in 1977 expelled 90 Soviet advisers. He moved closer to Egypt—he was one of the few Arab leaders who supported Sadat's dramatic visit to Israel in November 1977—and the U.S. Nimeiri publicly backed the Eritrean rebel movement in 1977 in its fight against the pro-Soviet Ethiopian central government, which accused him of giving material aid as well as moral support to the rebels.

SURINAME

Republic of Suriname
President: L. F. Ramdat Misier (1982)
Prime Minister: Henri N. Neyhorst (1982)
Area: 63,251 sq mi. (163,820 sq km)
Population (est. 1982): 410,000 (average annual growth rate: −1.5%) (Hindi, 37%; Creole, 31%; Indonesian, 15%; Bush Negro, 10%)
Density per square mile: 6.5
Capital and largest city (est. 1980): Paramaribo, 70,000
Monetary unit: Suriname guilder
Language: Dutch, Surinamese (lingua franca)
Religions: Protestant, Roman Catholic, Hindu, Islam
Literacy rate (1981): 80%

Economic summary: Gross national product (1980): $1 billion. Average annual growth rate (1970–79): 6.4%. Per capita income (1980): $2,840. Land used for agriculture: 0.3%; labor force: 29%; principal products: rice, citrus fruits, sugar, coffee. Labor force in industry: 15%; major products: aluminum, alumina, processed foods, lumber, bricks, cigarettes. Natural resources: bauxite, iron ore, timber, fish, shrimp. Exports: bauxite, alumina, aluminum, lumber and wood products. Imports: capital equipment, petroleum, iron and steel, cotton, flour, meat, dairy products. Major trading partners: U.S., Western European countries.

Geography. Suriname lies on the northeast coast of South America, with Guyana to the west, French Guiana to the east, and Brazil to the south. It is about one tenth larger than Michigan. The principal rivers are the Corantijn on the Guyana border, the Marowijne in the east, and the Suriname, on which the capital city of Paramaribo is situated. The Tumuc-Humac Mountains are on the border with Brazil.

Government. Suriname, formerly known as Dutch Guiana, became an independent republic on Nov. 25, 1975. The first prime minister, Henck A. E. Arron, was ousted by a seven-man military junta on Feb. 25, 1980, and replaced by Dr. Henk R. Chin A Sen.

Chin A Sen was elevated to the office of President by the junta on Aug. 14, 1980, and the 39-member National Assembly was abolished. A military cabinet was designated to conduct the government.

History. England established the first European settlement on the Suriname River in 1650 but transferred sovereignty to the Dutch in 1667 in the Treaty of Breda, by which the British acquired New York. Colonization was confined to a narrow coastal strip, and until the abolition of slavery in 1863, African slaves furnished the labor for the plantation economy. After 1870, laborers were imported from British India and the Dutch East Indies.

In 1948, the colony was integrated into the Kingdom of the Netherlands and two years later was granted full home rule in other than foreign affairs and defense. After race rioting over unemployment and inflation, the Netherlands offered complete independence in 1973. Henck A. E. Arron, leader of a coalition of Creole (Surinamese of African descent) parties, advocated independence, while Jaggernath Lachmon, leader of the Surinamese of East Indian descent, urged delay.

Arron retained power in the first post-independence elections in 1977 but held only a one-seat margin over Lachmon's group early in 1980. He had promised early elections when seven Army sergeants and a lieutenant staged a coup on Feb. 25 and installed a civilian, Dr. Henk R. Chin A Sen, as Prime Minister. A subsequent military intervention made Chin A Sen President, abolishing the legislature and instituting a military government.

SWAZILAND

Kingdom of Swaziland
Ruler: Vacant
Prime Minister: Prince Mabandla Dlamini (1979)
Area: 6,704 sq mi. (17,363 sq km)
Population (est. 1982): 600,000 (average annual growth rate: 2.8%)
Density per square mile: 89.5
Capital and largest city (est. 1976): Mbabane, 23,000
Monetary unit: Lilangeni
Languages: English and Siswati (official)
Religions: Christian, 60%; Animist, 40%
Member of Commonwealth of Nations
Literacy rate (1981): 25%
Economic summary: Gross national product (1980): $380 million. Average annual growth rate (1970–79): 4.4%. Per capita income (1980): $680. Land used for agriculture: 8%; labor force: 31%; principal products: corn, livestock, sugar cane, citrus fruits, cotton, rice, pineapples. Labor force in industry: 25%; major products: milled sugar, ginned cotton, processed meat and wood, iron ore. Natural resources: iron ore, asbestos, coal. Exports: sugar, wood products, iron ore, asbestos, citrus fruits, meat products, cotton. Imports: motor vehicles, fuels and lubricants, foodstuffs, clothing. Major trading partners: South Africa, U.K., U.S.

Geography. Swaziland, 85% the size of New Jersey, is surrounded by South Africa and Mozambique. The country consists of a high veld in the west and a series of plateaus descending from 6,000 feet (1,829 m) to a low veld of 1,500 feet (457 m).

Government. In 1967, a new Constitution established King Sobhuza II as head of state and provided for an Assembly of 24 members elected by universal suffrage, together with a Senate of 12 members—half appointed by the Assembly and half by the King. In 1973, the King renounced the Constitution, suspended political parties, and took total power for himself. In 1977, he replaced the Parliament with an assembly of tribal leaders. The Parliament reconvened in 1979.

History. Bantu peoples migrated southwest to the area of Mozambique in the 16th century. A number of clans broke away from the main body in the 18th century and settled in Swaziland. In the 19th century they organized as a tribe, partly because they were in constant conflict with the Zulu. Their ruler, Mswazi, applied to the British in the 1840s for help against the Zulu. The British and the Transvaal governments guaranteed the independence of Swaziland in 1881.

South Africa held Swaziland as a protectorate from 1894 to 1899, but after the Boer War, in 1902, Swaziland was transferred to British administration. The Paramount Chief was recognized as the native authority in 1941.

In 1963, the territory was constituted a protectorate, and on Sept. 6, 1968, it became the independent nation of Swaziland.

King Sobhuza died in August 1982, the world's longest-reigning monarch.

SWEDEN

Kingdom of Sweden
Sovereign: King Carl XVI Gustaf (1973)
Prime Minister: Olof Palme (1982)
Area: 173,665 sq mi. (449,792 sq km)
Population (est. 1982): 8,330,000 (average annual growth rate: 0.1%)
Density per square mile: 48.0
Capital: Stockholm

Largest cities (est. 1980): Stockholm, 1,400,000; Göteborg, 700,000; Malmö, 450,000
Monetary unit: Krona
Language: Swedish
Religion: Swedish Lutheran, 95%
National name: Konungariket Sverige
Literacy rate (1981): 99%
Economic summary: Gross national product (1980): $111.9 billion. Average annual growth rate (1970–79): 1.1%. Per capita income (1980): $13,520. Principal agricultural products: dairy products, grains, sugar beets, potatoes, wood. Labor force in industry: 33%; major products: machinery, instruments, metal products, automobiles. Natural resources: forests, iron ore, hydroelectric power, unmined uranium. Exports: machinery, motor vehicles, wood pulp, paper products, iron and steel products. Imports: machinery, petroleum, yarns, foodstuffs, iron and steel, chemicals. Major trading partners: Norway, West Germany, U.K., Denmark, Finland, U.S.

Geography. Sweden occupies the eastern part of the Scandinavian peninsula, with Norway to the west, Finland and the Gulf of Bothnia to the east, and Denmark and the Baltic Sea in the south. It is one tenth larger than California.

The country slopes eastward and southward from the Kjólen Mountains along the Norwegian border, where the peak elevation is Kebnekaise at 6,965 feet (2,123 m) in Lapland. In the north are mountains and many lakes. To the south and east are central lowlands and south of them are fertile areas of forest, valley, and plain.

Along Sweden's rocky coast, chopped up by bays and inlets, are many islands, the largest of which are Gotland and Öland.

Government. Sweden is a constitutional monarchy. Under the 1975 Constitution, the Riksdag is the sole governing body. The prime minister is the political chief executive.

In 1967, agreement was reached on part of a new Constitution after 13 years of work. It provided for a single-house Riksdag of 350 members (later amended to 349 seats) to replace the 104-year old bicameral Riksdag. The members are popularly elected for three years. Ninety-two present members of the Riksdag are women.

The King, Carl XVI Gustaf, was born April 30, 1946, and succeeded to the throne Sept. 19, 1973, on the death at 90 of his grandfather, Gustaf VI Adolf. Carl Gustaf was married on June 19, 1976, to Silvia Sommerlath, a West German commoner. They have three children: Princess Victoria, born July 14, 1977; Prince Carl Philip, born May 13, 1979; and Princess Madeline, born June 10, 1982. Under the new Act of Succession, effective Jan. 1, 1980, the first child of the reigning monarch, regardless of sex, is heir to the throne.

The major political parties are the Social Democratic Party (166 seats in the Riksdag), led by Prime Minister Olof Palme; Conservative Party (86 seats), led by Ulf Adelsohn; Center Party (21 seats), led by former Prime Minister Thorbjörn Fälldin; Liberal Party (21 seats), led by former Prime Minister Olla Ullsten; Communist Party (20 seats), led by Lars Werner.

History. The earliest historical mention of Sweden is found in Tacitus' *Germania,* where reference is made to the powerful king and strong fleet of the Suiones. Toward the end of the 10th century, Olaf Sköttkonung established a Christian stronghold in Sweden. Around 1400, an attempt was made to unite the northern nations into one kingdom, but this led to bitter strife between the Danes and the Swedes.

In 1520, the Danish King, Christian II, conquered Sweden and in the "Stockholm Bloodbath" put leading Swedish personalities to death. Gustavus Vasa (1523–60) broke away from Denmark and fashioned the modern Swedish state.

Sweden played a leading role in the second phase (1630–35) of the Thirty Years' War (1618–48). By the Treaty of Westphalia (1648), Sweden obtained western Pomerania and some neighboring territory on the Baltic. In 1700, a coalition of Russia, Poland, and Denmark united against Sweden and by the Peace of Nystad (1721) forced it to relinquish Livonia, Ingria, Estonia, and parts of Finland.

Sweden emerged from the Napoleonic Wars with the acquisition of Norway from Denmark and with a new royal dynasty stemming from Marshal Jean Bernadotte of France, who became King Charles XIV (1818–44). The artificial union between Sweden and Norway led to an uneasy relationship, and the union was finally dissolved in 1905.

Sweden maintained a position of neutrality in both World Wars.

An elaborate structure of welfare legislation, imitated by many larger nations, began with the establishment of old-age pensions in 1911. Economic prosperity based on its neutralist policy enabled Sweden, together with Norway, to pioneer in public health, housing, and job security programs.

Forty-four years of Socialist government were ended in 1976 with the election of a conservative coalition headed by Thorbjörn Fälldin, a 50-year-old sheep farmer. The surprise conservative victory was credited to public opposition to a nuclear power program backed by the Socialists and to a program that would have given control of all businesses to labor unions within 20 years.

Nuclear-power policy dominated Swedish policy in the ensuing years. Fälldin resigned on Oct. 5, 1978, when his conservative parties partners demanded less restrictions on nuclear power, and his successor, Ola Ullsten, resigned a year later after failing to achieve a consensus on the issue. Returned to office by his coalition partners, Fälldin said he would follow the course directed by a national referendum. On March 23, 1980, voters backed the development of 12 nuclear plants and use of them for at least 25 years to supply 40% of national energy needs while the search for alternative sources continued.

SWITZERLAND

Swiss Confederation
President: Kurt Furgler (1982)
Vice President: Pierre Aubert (1982)
Area: 15,941 sq mi. (41,288 sq km)
Population (est. 1982): 6,475,000 (average annual growth rate: −0.3%) (Swiss, 85%; Italian, 8%; German, 2%; Spanish, 2%; French, 1%—figures by place of birth)
Density per square mile: 406.2
Capital: Bern
Largest cities (est. 1980): Zurich, 377,300; Basel, 183,200; Geneva, 152,700; Lausanne, 131,000; Winterthur, 86,400
Monetary unit: Swiss franc
Languages: German, 65%; French, 18%; Italian, 12%;

Romansch, 1%
Religions: Roman Catholic, 49%; Protestant, 48%
National name: Schweiz/Suisse/Svizzera
Literacy rate (1981): 98%
Economic summary: Gross national product (1980): $106.3 billion. Average annual growth rate (1970–79): 0.2%. Per capita income (1980): $16,440. Land used for agriculture: 26%; labor force: 7%; principal products: cheese and other dairy products, livestock, fruits, grains, wine. Labor force in industry: 38%; major products: watches and clocks, precision instruments, machinery, chemicals, pharmaceuticals, textiles, generators, turbines. Natural resources: water power, timber, salt. Exports: electrical machinery, chemicals, precision instruments, textiles, foodstuffs, textile yarns, dyestuffs, chemicals. Imports: transport equipment, metals and metal products, foodstuffs, chemicals, textile yarns. Major trading partners: West Germany, France, U.S., Italy, U.K.

Geography. Switzerland, in central Europe, is the land of the Alps. Its tallest peak is the Dufourspitze at 15,203 feet (4,634 m) on the Swiss side of the Italian border, one of 10 summits of the Monte Rose massif in the Pennine Alps. The tallest peak in all of the Alps, Mont Blanc (15,771 ft; 4,807 m), is actually in France.

Most of Switzerland comprises a mountainous plateau bordered by the great bulk of the Alps on the south and by the Jura Mountains on the northwest. About one fourth of the total area is covered by mountains and glaciers.

The country's largest lakes—Geneva, Constance (Bodensee), and Maggiore—straddle the French, German-Austrian, and Italian borders, respectively.

The Rhine, navigable from Basel to the North Sea, is the principal inland waterway. Other rivers are the Aare and the Rhône.

Switzerland, twice the size of New Jersey, is surrounded by France, West Germany, Austria, Liechtenstein, and Italy.

Government. The Swiss Confederation consists of 26 sovereign cantons, of which three are divided into half-cantons. Federal authority is vested in a bicameral legislature. The Ständerat, or State Council, consists of 46 members, two from each canton. The lower house, the Nationalrat, or National Council, has 200 deputies, elected for four-year terms.

Executive authority rests with the Bundesrat, or Federal Council, consisting of seven members chosen by parliament. The parliament elects the President, who serves for one year and is succeeded by the Vice President. The federal government regulates foreign policy, railroads, postal service, and the national mint. Each canton reserves for itself important local powers.

A constitutional amendment adopted in 1971 by referendum gave women the vote in federal elections and the right to hold federal office. An equal rights amendment passed in a national referendum June 14, 1981, barring discrimination against women under canton as well as federal law, ending the legal basis for barring women's votes in the last canton which maintained the restriction.

The major political parties are the Social Democratic Party (51 of 200 seats in National Council), led by Helmut Hubacher; Radical Democratic Party (51 seats), led by Yann Richter; Christian-Democratic Party (44 seats), led by Hans Wyer; People's Party (23 seats), led by Fritz Hofmann. These four parties constitute the ruling coalition.

History. Called Helvetia in ancient times, Switzerland in the Middle Ages was a league of cantons of the Holy Roman Empire. Fashioned around the nucleus of three German forest districts of Schwyz, Uri, and Unterwalden, the Swiss Confederation slowly added new cantons. In 1648 the Treaty of Westphalia gave Switzerland its independence from the Holy Roman Empire.

French revolutionary troops occupied the country in 1798 and named it the Helvetic Republic, but Napoleon in 1803 restored its federal government. By 1815, the French- and Italian-speaking peoples of Switzerland had been granted political equality.

In 1815, the Congress of Vienna guaranteed the neutrality and recognized the independence of Switzerland. In the revolutionary period of 1847, the Catholic cantons seceded and organized a separate union called the *Sonderbund.* In 1848 the new Swiss Constitution established a union modeled upon that of the U.S. The Federal Constitution of 1874 established a strong central government while maintaining large powers of control in each canton.

National unity and political conservatism grew as the country prospered from its neutrality. Its banking system became the world's leading repository for international accounts. Strict neutrality was its policy in World Wars I and II. Geneva was the seat of the League of Nations (later the European headquarters of the United Nations) and of a number of international organizations.

In 1971, the Swiss Supreme Court ruled that Swiss banks must show U.S. tax officials records of U.S. citizens suspected of tax fraud, thus significantly modifying a 1934 law that had seemed to forbid any bank disclosures.

SYRIA

Syrian Arab Republic
President: Hafez al-Assad (1971)
Premier: Abdel Raouf al-Kasm (1980)
Area: 71,498 sq mi. (185,180 sq km)
Population (est. 1982): 9,650,000 (average annual growth rate: 3.4%)
Density per square mile: 135.0
Capital: Damascus
Largest cities (est. 1980): Damascus, 1,200,000; **(est. 1978 by U.N.):** Aleppo, 878,000; Homs, 306,000; Hama, 180,000
Monetary unit: Syrian pound
Language: Arabic
Religions: Islam, 85%; Christian, 14%
National name: Al-Jamhouriya al Arabiya As-Souriya
Literacy rate (1981): 40%
Economic summary: Gross national product (1980): $12.0 billion. Average annual growth rate (1970–79): 4.6%. Per capita income (1980): $1,340. Land used for agriculture: 47%; labor force: 32%; principal products: cotton, wheat, sugar beets, sheep, goats. Labor force in industry: 29%; major products: textiles, cement, glass, petroleum, processed food, soap. Natural resources: chrome, manganese, asphalt, iron ore, rock salt, phosphate, oil, natural gas. Exports: petroleum, textiles, tobacco, fruits and vegetables, cotton. Imports: machinery and metal products, textiles, fuels, foodstuffs. Major trading partners: Italy, Romania, West Germany, U.S.S.R., U.S., Iraq.

Geography. Slightly larger than North Dakota, Syria lies at the eastern end of the Mediterranean

Sea. It is bordered by Lebanon and Israel on the west, Turkey on the north, Iraq on the east, and Jordan on the south.

Coastal Syria is a narrow plain, in back of which is a range of coastal mountains, and still farther inland a steppe area. In the east is the Syrian Desert, and in the south is the Jebel Druze Range. The highest point in Syria is Mount Hermon (9,232 ft; 2,814 m) on the Lebanese border.

Government. Syria's first permanent Constitution was approved in 1973, replacing a provisional charter that had been in force for 10 years. It provided for an elected People's Council as the legislature. No national religion is specified, although Islamic law is the basis of the state law.

In the first election in 10 years, in 1973, the Ba'ath Arab Socialist Party of President Hafez al-Assad, running on a unified National Progressive ticket with the Communist and Socialist parties, won 70% of the vote and a commensurate proportion of the seats for a four-year term in the People's Council. In the 1977 Council elections, the ruling Ba'athists won 125 of the now 195 seats; the National Progressive Front coalition, 34 seats; various rightist candidates, 36 seats.

History. Ancient Syria was conquered by Egypt about 1500 B.C., and after that by Hebrews, Phoenicians, Assyrians, Chaldeans, Persians, and Greeks. From 64 B.C. until the Arab conquest in A.D. 636, it was part of the Roman Empire except during brief periods. The Arabs made it a trade center for their extensive empire, but it suffered severely from the Mongol invasion in 1260 and fell to the Ottoman Turks in 1516. Syria remained a Turkish province until World War I.

A secret Anglo-French pact of 1916 put Syria in the French zone of influence. The League of Nations gave France a mandate over Syria after World War I, but the French were forced to put down several nationalist uprisings. In 1930, France recognized Syria as an independent republic, but still subject to the mandate. After nationalist demonstrations in 1939, the French High Commissioner suspended the Syrian Constitution. In 1941, British and Free French forces invaded Syria to eliminate Vichy control. During the rest of World War II, Syria was an Allied base.

Again in 1945, nationalist demonstrations broke into actual fighting, and British troops had to restore order. Syrian forces met a series of reverses while participating in the Arab invasion of Palestine in 1948. In 1958, Egypt and Syria formed the United Arab Republic, with Gamal Abdel Nasser of Egypt as President. However, Syria became independent again on Sept. 29, 1961, following a revolution.

In the war of 1967, Israel quickly vanquished the Syrian army. Before acceding to the U.N. cease-fire, the Israeli forces took over control of the fortified Golan Heights commanding the Sea of Galilee.

Syria joined Egypt in attacking Israel in October 1973 in the fourth Arab-Israeli war, but was pushed back from initial successes on the Golan Heights to end up losing more land. However, in the settlement worked out by U.S. Secretary of State Henry A. Kissinger in 1974, the Syrians recovered all the territory lost in 1973 and a token amount of territory, including the deserted town of Quneitra, lost in 1967.

Resumption of relations with the U.S. in 1974 moderated Syria's tone, but not the goals of its policy toward Israel. Syria initiated a resolution declaring the Palestine Liberation Organization to be the sole representative of the Palestinian people, a measure that was adopted by the U.N. General Assembly in October 1974 and became the vehicle for legitimizing the insurgent organization. As Israeli-Egyptian peace negotiations continued, Syria's hostility toward Egypt increased.

At the Arab League conference in Baghdad in March 1979, Syria demanded even harsher measures against Egypt than the break in diplomatic relations and economic boycott proposed by the conference. Syria asked that the boycott, including oil supplies, be applied to the U.S. as well.

Syrian troops, in Lebanon since 1976 as part of an Arab peace-keeping force whose other members subsequently departed, intervened increasingly during 1980 and 1981 on the side of Moslem Lebanese in their clashes with Christian militants supported by Israel. When Israeli jets shot down Syrian helicopters operating in Lebanon in April 1981, Syria moved Soviet-built surface-to-air (SAM 6) missiles into Lebanon's Bekaa Valley. Israel demanded that the missiles be removed because they violated a 1976 understanding between the governments. The demand, backed up by bombing raids, prompted the Reagan Administration to send veteran diplomat Philip C. Habib as a special envoy to avert a new conflict between the nations.

Habib's carefully engineered cease-fire was shattered by a new Israeli invasion in June 1982, when Israeli aircraft bombed Bekaa Valley missile sites, claiming to destroy all of them along with 25 Syrian planes that had sought to defend the sites. On the ground, Syrian army units were driven back by Israeli armor along the Lebanese coast. The Syrians, who were equipped with Soviet weapons, were outfought everywhere by U.S.-equipped Israelis.

TANZANIA

United Republic of Tanzania
President: Julius K. Nyerere (1964)
Prime Minister: Cleopa D. Msuya (1981)
Area: 362,820 sq mi. (939,704 sq km)[1]
Population (est. 1982): 19,000,000 (average annual growth rate: 3.2%)
Density per square mile: 52.4
Capital and largest city (est. 1980): Dar es Salaam, 900,000
Monetary unit: Tanzanian shilling
Languages: Swahili, Bantu, Arabic, English
Religions: Animist, 35%; Christian, 31%; Islam, 31%
Member of Commonwealth of Nations
Literacy rate (1981): 61%
Economic summary: Gross national product (1980): $4.8 billion. Average annual growth rate (1970–79): 0.8%. Per capita income (1980): $260. Land used for agriculture: 60%; labor force: 90%; Principal products: sugar, maize, rice, wheat, cotton, coffee, sisal, cashew nuts, tea, tobacco, pyrethrum, cloves. Major industrial products: textiles, light manufactures, refined oil, processed agricultural products, diamonds, cement, fertilizer. Natural resources: hydroelectric potential, unexploited iron and coal, natural gas. Exports: coffee, cotton, sisal, diamonds, cloves, cashew nuts. Imports: manufactured goods, textiles, machinery and transport equipment, crude oil, foodstuffs. Major trading partners: U.K., China, India, Hong Kong, West Germany, U.S., Japan.

1. Including Zanzibar.

Geography. Tanzania is in East Africa on the Indian Ocean. To the north are Uganda and Kenya; to the west, Burundi, Rwanda, and Zaire; and to the south, Mozambique, Zambia, and Malawi. Its area is three times that of New Mexico.

Tanzania contains three of Africa's best-known lakes—Victoria in the north, Tanganyika in the west, and Nyasa in the south. Mount Kilimanjaro in the north, 19,340 feet (5,895 m), is the highest point on the continent.

Government. Under the republican form of government, Tanzania has a President elected by universal suffrage who appoints the Cabinet ministers. The 218-member National Assembly is composed of 96 elected members from the mainland, 10 members appointed by the President (from both Tanganyika and Zanzibar), 35 national members (elected by the National Assembly after nomination by various national institutions), 32 members of the Zanzibar Revolutionary Council, 20 other Zanzibar members appointed by the President in agreement with the President of Zanzibar, and up to 20 other Zanzibar members appointed by the President in agreement with the first Vice President, who represents Zanzibar.

The Tanganyika African National Union, the only authorized party on the mainland, and the Afro-Shirazi Party, the only party in Zanzibar and Pemba, merged in 1977 as the Revolutionary Party (Chama Cha Mapinduzi) and elected Julius K. Nyerere as its head.

History. Arab traders first began to colonize the area in A.D. 700. Portuguese explorers reached the coastal regions in 1500 and held some control until the 17th century, when the Sultan of Oman took power. With what are now Burundi and Rwanda, Tanganyika became the colony of German East Africa in 1885. After World War I, it was administered by Britain under a League of Nations mandate and later as a U.N. trust territory.

Although not mentioned in old histories until the 12th century, Zanzibar was believed always to have had connections with southern Arabia. The Portuguese made it one of their tributaries in 1503 and later established a trading post, but they were driven out by Arabs from Oman in 1698. Zanzibar was declared independent of Oman in 1861 and, in 1890, it became a British protectorate.

Tanganyika became independent on Dec. 9, 1961; Zanzibar, on Dec. 10, 1963. On April 26, 1964, the two nations merged into the United Republic of Tanganyika and Zanzibar. The name was changed to Tanzania six months later.

In 1975, the 1,163-mile (1,872 km) Tanzam railway linking the Tanzanian port of Dar es Salaam with Zambia was officially opened. Built and financed by China, the railway provided a direct route for Zambian copper exports to the sea, replacing a longer route through white-ruled Rhodesia to Mozambique.

In 1977, Tanzania closed its border with Kenya because of a dispute over the operation of East African Airways, an entity of the East African Community. The breakup of the airline left the East African Posts and Telecommunications Corporation as the only community agency still functioning.

An invasion by Ugandan troops in November 1978 was followed by a counterattack in January 1979, in which 5,000 Tanzanian troops were joined by 3,000 Ugandan exiles opposed to President Idi Amin. Within a month, full-scale war developed and the Tanzania/exile force pushed north and captured Kampala on April 11.

Nyerere kept troops in Uganda in open support of former Ugandan President Milton Obote, despite protests from opposition groups, until the national elections in December 1980. Although Obote asked that the Tanzanians remain after his victory in order to control guerrilla resistance, Nyerere ordered their withdrawal in May 1981, citing the $1-million-a-month drain on his precarious finances.

THAILAND

Kingdom of Thailand
Ruler: King Bhumibol Adulyadej (1946)
Premier: Gen. Prem Tinsulanonda (1980)
Area: 198,455 sq mi. (514,000 sq km)
Population (est. 1982): 49,000,000 (average annual growth rate: 2.1%) (incl. 2.5 million of Chinese descent born in Thailand)
Density per square mile: 246.9
Capital and largest city (est. 1980): Bangkok, 5,000,000
Monetary unit: Baht
Languages: Thai (Siamese), Chinese, English
Religions: Buddhist, 95%; Islam, 4%
National name: Muang Thai
Literacy rate (1981): 82%
Economic summary: Gross national product (1980): $31.1 billion. Average annual growth rate (1970–79): 4.4%. Per capita income (1980): $670. Land used for agriculture: 71%; labor force: 78%; principal products: rice, rubber, corn, tapioca, sugar, pineapples. Labor force in industry: 7%; major products: processed food, textiles, wood, cement, tin, tungsten. Natural resources: fish, natural gas, forests, fluorite, tin, tungsten. Exports: rice, tapioca, sugar, rubber, tin, textiles. Imports: machinery and transport equipment, fertilizer, crude oil, fuels and lubricants, base metals, chemicals. Major trading partners: Japan, U.S., Singapore, West Germany, Netherlands, U.K., Hong Kong.

Geography. Thailand occupies the western half of the Indochinese peninsula and the northern two thirds of the Malay peninsula in southeast Asia. Its neighbors are Burma on the north and west, Laos on the east, and Cambodia and Malaysia on the south. Thailand is about three fourths the size of Texas.

Most of the population is supported in the fertile central alluvial plain, which is drained by the Chao Phnaya River and its tributaries.

Government. King Bhumibol Adulyadej, who was born Dec. 5, 1927, second son of Prince Mahidol of Songkhla, succeeded to the throne on June 9, 1946, when his brother, King Ananda Mahidol, died of a gunshot wound. He was married on April 28, 1950, to Queen Sirikit; their son, Vajiralongkorn, born July 28, 1952, is the Crown Prince.

After three years of civilian government ended with a military coup on Oct. 6, 1976, Thailand reverted to military rule. The junta permitted national elections in 1979, however, which confirmed the junta's designated premier, Gen. Kriangsak Chamanan. When Chamanan resigned on March 12, 1980, the National Assembly was allowed to elect his successor. Political parties, banned after the coup, gained limited freedom in 1980.

History. The Thais first began moving down into their present homeland from the Asiatic continent in the 6th century A.D. and by the end of the 13th century ruled most of the western portion. During the next 400 years, the Thais fought sporadically with the Cambodians and the Burmese. The British obtained recognition of paramount interest in Thailand in 1824, and in 1896 an Anglo-French accord guaranteed the independence of Thailand.

A coup in 1932 changed the absolute monarchy into a representative government with universal suffrage. After five hours of token resistance on Dec. 8, 1941, Thailand yielded to Japanese occupation and became one of the springboards in World War II for the Japanese campaign against Malaya.

After the fall of its pro-Japanese puppet government in July 1944, Thailand pursued a policy of passive resistance against the Japanese, and after the Japanese surrender, Thailand repudiated the declaration of war it had been forced to make against Britain and the U.S. in 1942. By a treaty signed with Britain and India in 1946, Thailand renounced all wartime acquisitions of Malayan territory.

Thailand's major problem in the late 1960s was suppressing guerrilla action by Communist invaders in the north.

Although Thailand had received $2 billion in U.S. economic and military aid since 1950 and had sent troops (paid by the U.S.) to Vietnam while permitting U.S. bomber bases on its territory, the collapse of South Vietnam and Cambodia in the spring of 1975 brought rapid changes in the country's diplomatic posture.

At the Thai government's insistence, the U.S. agreed to withdraw all 23,000 U.S. military personnel remaining in Thailand by March 1976. Diplomatic relations with China were established in 1975. Meanwhile, overtures toward an accommodation with the new regime in South Vietnam were initiated.

Thailand protested vigorously when 1,100 U.S. Marines were airlifted to Thai bases May 14, 1975, for use in the rescue of the crew of the cargo ship Mayaguez after its seizure by a Cambodian gunboat. The marines were withdrawn the next day, and Thailand later accepted a U.S. apology for unauthorized use of its territory.

In 1973, when Field Marshal Thanom Kittikachorn resigned under the pressure of massive student demonstrations, Thailand returned to a civilian government and in 1975 had its first general elections. Premier Seni Pramoj, was ousted in 1976 by Admiral Sa-Ngad Chaloryu and the National Administrative Reform Council after rioting by leftist students. The junta appointed Thanin Kraivichien, a supreme court justice, as premier and appointed a 340-member National Assembly, 110 of them military officers.

As insurgent activity increased and skirmishes along the Cambodian border continued despite Thai efforts to make peace with the Communist regime in Phnom Penh, the military, in 1977, ousted Thanin as "weak," replacing him with Gen. Kriangsak Chamanan.

Refugees from Laos, Cambodia, and Vietnam flooded into Thailand in 1978 and 1979, and despite efforts by the United States and other Western countries to resettle them, a total of 130,000 Laotian and Vietnamese refugees were living in camps along the Cambodian border in mid-1980. A drive by Vietnamese occupation forces on western Cambodian areas loyal to the Pol Pot government, culminating in invasions of Thai territory in late June, drove an estimated 100,000 Cambodians across the line as refugees, adding to the 200,000 of their countrymen already in Thailand. The total of 430,000 were being fed by United Nations and church relief organizations but the Thai government complained of the burden of their presence.

The Vietnamese incursions, notwithstanding Hanoi's claim that the troops were only seeking guerrillas hidden in the refugee camps, prompted a Thai appeal to Washington for military aid. In July, 35 reconditioned tanks and other weapons were flown to Thailand, and the Carter administration pledged its help in the event of a larger attack.

By November 1980, U.N. officials said that 150,000 Cambodians had gone back to their homeland, and on Dec. 16 the Red Cross announced that it would end food distribution across the border and henceforth feed only the 90,000 refugees remaining in camps on the Thai side.

On April 3, 1981, a military coup against the Prem government failed. King Bhumibol Adulyadej took refuge outside Bangkok with Prem and his cabinet and the rebels found neither public nor sufficient military support.

TONGA

Kingdom of Tonga

Sovereign: King Taufa'ahau Tupou IV (1965)

Prime Minister: Prince Fatafehi Tu'ipelehake (1965)

Area: 290 sq mi. (751 sq km)

Population (est. 1982): 100,000 (average annual growth rate: 2.1%)

Density per square mile: 370.4

Capital (est. 1976): Nuku'alofa, 18,300

Monetary unit: Pa'anga

Languages: Tongan, English

Religions: Free Wesleyan, 47%; Roman Catholic, 16%; Free Church of Tonga, 14%; Mormon, 9%; Church of Tonga, 9%

Member of Commonwealth of Nations

Literacy rate (1981): 95%

Economic summary: Gross national product (1980): $50 million. Average annual growth rate (1970–78): 1.2%. Per Capita Income (1980): $520. Land used for agriculture: 80%; labor force: 75%; principal products: yams, taro, papaya, pineapples, coconuts, tobacco, peanuts, bananas, copra. Major industrial products: copra, desiccated coconut. Natural resources: fish, timber. Exports: copra, coconut products, bananas. Imports: manufactures, foodstuffs, machinery, petroleum. Major trading partners: New Zealand, Australia, Netherlands, Norway.

Geography. Situated east of the Fiji Islands in the South Pacific, Tonga (also called the Friendly Islands) consists of some 150 islands, of which 36 are inhabited.

Most of the islands contain active volcanic craters; others are coral atolls.

Government. Tonga is a constitutional monarchy. Executive authority is vested in the Sovereign, a Privy Council, and a Cabinet headed by the Prime Minister. Legislative authority is vested in the Legislative Assembly.

History. The present dynasty of Tonga was founded in 1831 by Taufa'ahau Tupou, who took the name George I. He consolidated the kingdom by conquest and in 1875 granted a Constitution.

In 1900, his great-grandson, George II, signed a treaty of friendship with Britain, and the country became a British protected state. The treaty was revised in 1959.

Queen Salote Tupou reigned from 1918 to 1964 and was succeeded by her son, who became King Taufa'ahau Tupou IV.

Tonga became independent on June 4, 1970.

TOGO

Republic of Togo
President: Gen. Gnassingbé Eyadema (1967)
Area: 21,853 sq mi. (56,599 sq km)
Population (est. 1982): 2,800,000 (average annual growth rate: 3.0%)
Density per square mile: 128.1
Capital and largest city (est. 1980): Lomé, 285,000
Monetary unit: Franc CFA
Languages: Ewé, Mina (south), Kabyé, Cotocoli (north), French (official), and many dialects
Religions: Animist, 60%; Christian, 25%; Islam, 8%
National name: République Togolaise
Literacy rate: Not known
Economic summary: Gross national product (1980): $1.0 billion. Average annual growth rate (1970–79): 1.2%. Per capita income (1980): $410. Land used for agriculture: 15%; labor force: 90%; principal products: yams, manioc, millet, sorghum, cocoa, coffee, rice, cotton. Labor force in industry: 22%; major products: phosphate, textiles. Natural resources: marble, iron, manganese, phosphate, limestone. Exports: phosphate, cocoa, coffee. Imports: consumer goods, fuels, machinery, foodstuffs. Major trading partners: France, U.K., West Germany, Netherlands.

Geography. Togo, twice the size of Maryland, is on the south coast of West Africa bordering on Ghana to the west, Upper Volta to the north and Benin to the east.

The Gulf of Guinea coastline, only 32 miles long (51 km), is low and sandy. The only port is at Lomé. The Togo hills traverse the central section.

Government. The government of Nicolas Grunitzky was overthrown in a bloodless coup on Jan. 13, 1967, led by Lt. Col. Etienne Eyadema (now Gen. Gnassingbé Eyadema). A National Reconciliation Committee was set up to rule the country. In April, however, Eyadema dissolved the Committee and took over as President. In December 1979, a 67-member National Assembly was voted in by national referendum. The Assembly of the Togolese People is the only political party.

History. Brazilians were the first traders to settle in Togo. Established as a German colony (Togoland) in 1884, the area was split between the British and the French as League of Nations mandates after World War I and subsequently administered as U. N. trusteeships. The British portion voted for incorporation with Ghana.

Togo became independent on April 27, 1960. Sylvanus Olympio, its first President, was assassinated in 1963 and succeeded by Nicolas Grunitzky.

TRANSKEI

See South Africa

TRINIDAD AND TOBAGO

Republic of Trinidad and Tobago
President: Ellis Clarke (1976)
Prime Minister: George M. Chambers (1981)
Area: 1,980 sq mi. (5,128 sq km)
Population (est. 1982): 1,200,000 (average annual growth rate: 1.5%) (black, 43%; East Indian, 40%; mixed, 14%)
Density per square mile: 606.1
Capital and largest city (est. 1976): Port-of-Spain, 47,300
Monetary unit: Trinidad and Tobago dollar
Languages: English (official); Hindi, French, Spanish
Religions: Roman Catholic, 31%; Protestant, 27%; Islam, 13%; Hindu, 6%
Member of Commonwealth of Nations
Literacy rate (1981): 95%
Economic summary: Gross national product (1980): $5.1 billion. Average annual growth rate (1970–79): 4.5%. Per capita income (1980): $4,370. Land used for agriculture: 26%; labor force: 13%; principal products: sugar cane, cocoa, coffee, rice, bananas. Labor force in industry: 33%; major products: petroleum, processed food, cement; tourism. Natural resources: petroleum. Exports: petroleum, ammonia, fertilizer. Imports: crude oil, foodstuffs, machinery and equipment. Major trading partners: U.S., U.K., Saudi Arabia, Japan.

Geography. Trinidad and Tobago lies in the Caribbean Sea off the northeast coast of Venezuela. The area of the two islands is slightly less than that of Delaware.

Trinidad, the larger, is mainly flat and rolling, with mountains in the north that reach a height of 3,085 feet (940 m) at Mount Aripo. Tobago is heavily forested with hardwood trees.

Government. The legislature consists of a 24-member Senate and a 36-member House of Representatives.

The major political parties are the People's National Movement, led by Prime Minister George M. Chambers (26 seats in the House of Representatives); United Labor Front (8 seats), led by Basdeo Panday; Democratic Action Congress (2 seats).

History. Trinidad was discovered by Columbus in 1498 and remained in Spanish possession, despite raids by other European nations, until it capitulated to the British in 1797 during a war between Britain and Spain.

Trinidad was ceded to Britain in 1802, and in 1899 it was united with Tobago as a colony. From 1958 to 1962, Trinidad and Tobago was a part of the West Indies Federation, and on Aug. 31, 1962, it became independent.

On Aug. 1, 1976, Trinidad and Tobago cut its ties with Britain and became a republic, remaining within the Commonwealth and recognizing Queen Elizabeth II only as head of that organization.

TUNISIA

Republic of Tunisia
President: Habib Bourguiba (1957)
Premier: Mohammed Mzali (1980)
Area: 63,379 sq mi. (164,152 sq km)
Population (est. 1982): 6,650,000 (average annual growth rate: 2.7%)
Density per square mile: 104.9
Capital and largest city (est. 1976 for metropolitan area): Tunis, 960,000

Monetary unit: Tunisian dinar
Languages: Arabic, French
Religions: Predominantly Islam; Roman Catholic, Jewish, Greek Orthodox
National name: Al-Djoumhouria Attunusia
Literacy rate (1981): 50%
Economic summary: Gross national product (1980): $8.3 billion. Average annual growth rate (1970–79): 5.7%. Per capita income (1980): $1,310. Land used for agriculture: 28%; labor force: 40%; principal products: wheat, olives, citrus fruits, grapes, dates. Labor force in industry: 21%; major products: crude oil, olive oil, textiles, and leather, chemical fertilizers, petroleum. Natural resources: oil, phosphates, iron ore, lead, zinc. Exports: petroleum, phosphates, textiles. Imports: machinery and equipment, consumer goods, foodstuffs. Major trading partners: France, West Germany, Italy, Greece.

Geography. Tunisia, at the northernmost bulge of Africa, thrusts out toward Sicily to mark the division between the eastern and western Mediterranean Sea. Twice the size of South Carolina, it is bordered on the west by Algeria and by Libya on the south.

Coastal plains on the east rise to a north-south escarpment which slopes gently to the west. Saharan in the south, Tunisia is more mountainous in the north, where the Atlas range continues from Algeria.

Government. Executive power is vested by the Constitution in the president, elected for five years and eligible for re-election to two additional terms. Legislative power is vested in a National Assembly elected by universal suffrage.

In 1975, the National Assembly amended the Constitution to make Habib Bourguiba President for life. At 71, Bourguiba was re-elected to a fourth five-year term when he ran unopposed in 1974. The only party, the Socialist Destourian, is led by Bourguiba.

History. Tunisia was settled by the Phoenicians and Carthaginians in ancient times. Except for an interval of Vandal conquest in A.D. 439–533, it was part of the Roman Empire until the Arab conquest of 648–69. It was ruled by various Arab and Berber dynasties until the Turks took it in 1570–74. French troops occupied the country in 1881, and the Bey signed a treaty acknowledging a French protectorate.

Nationalist agitation forced France to grant internal autonomy to Tunisia in 1955 and to recognize Tunisian independence and sovereignty in 1956. The Constituent Assembly deposed the Bey on July 25, 1957, declared Tunisia a republic, and elected Habib Bourguiba as President.

Bourguiba maintained a pro-Western foreign policy that earned him enemies. Tunisia refused to break relations with the U.S. during the Israeli-Arab war in June 1967, and it cracked down on anti-U.S. demonstrators.

Tunisia ended its traditionally neutral role in the Arab world when it joined with the majority of Arab League members to condemn Egypt for concluding a peace treaty with Israel. The Tunisian capital was offered as the temporary headquarters of the League, following the expulsion of Egypt and the shutting of the Cairo offices. At the League's first session in Tunis on June 28, 1979, Tunisian Minister of Information Chedli Klibi was elected Secretary-General to replace Mahmoud Riad of Egypt, who resigned.

TURKEY

Republic of Turkey
President and Head of National Security Council: Gen. Kenan Evren (1980)
Prime Minister: Bülent Ulusu (1981)
Area: 301,380 sq mi. (incl. 9,121 in Europe) (780,576 sq km)
Population (est. 1982): 47,500,000 (average annual growth rate: 2.2%)
Density per square mile: 157.6
Capital: Ankara
Largest cities (1980 census): Istanbul, 2,990,680; Ankara, 2,561,765; Izmir, 1,049,000; Adana, 834,050; Bursa, 657,500; Gaziantep, 510,650
Monetary unit: Turkish lira
Language: Turkish
Religion: Islam
National name: Türkiye Cumhuriyeti
Literacy rate (1981): 62%
Economic summary: Gross national product (1980): $66.1 billion. Average annual growth rate (1970–79): 3.5%. Per capita income (1980): $1,460. Land used for agriculture: 35%; labor force: 60%; principal products: cotton, tobacco, cereals, sugar beets, fruits, nuts. Labor force in industry: 16%; major products: textiles, processed foods, steel, petroleum. Natural resources: coal, chromite, copper, boron, oil. Exports: cotton, tobacco, fruits, nuts, livestock products, textiles. Imports: crude oil, machinery, transport equipment, metals, mineral fuels, fertilizer, chemicals, crude oil. Major trading partners: West Germany, Iraq, France, Italy, U.S.S.R., U.S.

Geography. Turkey is at the northeastern end of the Mediterranean Sea in southeast Europe and southwest Asia. To the north is the Black Sea and to the west the Aegean Sea. Its neighbors are Greece and Bulgaria to the west, the U.S.S.R. to the north, Iran to the east, and Syria and Iraq to the south. Overall, it is more than twice the size of Montana.

The Dardanelles, the Sea of Marmara, and the Bosporus divide the country.

Turkey in Europe comprises an area about equal to the state of Massachusetts. It is hilly country drained by the Maritsa River and its tributaries.

Turkey in Asia, or Anatolia, about the size of Texas, is roughly a rectangle in shape with its short sides on the east and west. Its center is a treeless plateau rimmed by mountains.

Government. The President is elected by the Grand National Assembly for a seven-year term and is not eligible for re-election.

In a military coup on Sept. 11, 1980, led by Gen. Kenan Evren, the Army Chief of Staff, Premier Süleyman Demirel was ousted, the Grand National Assembly dissolved and the Constitution suspended. Demirel, former Premier Bülent Ecevit, and some 100 legislators and political figures were detained. Martial law was declared and all political parties were dissolved.

In October 1981, a Constituent Assembly, consisting of the six-member National Security Council and members appointed by them, was organized to draft a new constitution. Evren said the new Constitution would be submitted to a referendum in the fall of 1982 and the election of a representative government would take place by late 1983 or the spring of 1984 at the latest.

History. The Ottoman Turks first appeared in the early 13th century in Anatolia, subjugating Turkish and Mongol bands pressing against the eastern borders of Byzantium. They gradually spread through the Near East and Balkans, capturing Constantinople in 1453 and storming the gates of Vienna two centuries later. At its height, the Ottoman Empire stretched from the Persian Gulf to western Algeria.

Defeat of the Turkish navy at Lepanto by the Holy League in 1571 and failure of the siege of Vienna heralded the decline of Turkish power. By the 18th century, Russia was seeking to establish itself as the protector of Christians in Turkey's Balkan territories. Russian ambitions were checked by Britain and France in the Crimean War (1854–56), but the Russo-Turkish War (1877–78) gave Bulgaria virtual independence and Romania and Serbia liberation from their nominal allegiance to the Sultan.

Turkish weakness stimulated a revolt of young liberals known as the Young Turks in 1909. They forced Sultan Abdul Hamid to grant a constitution and install a liberal government. Reforms were no barrier to further defeats, however, in a war with Italy (1911–12) and the Balkan Wars (1912–13). Under the influence of German military advisors, Turkey signed a secret alliance with Germany on Aug. 2, 1914, that led to a declaration of war by the Allied powers and the ultimate humiliation of the occupation of Turkish territory by Greek and other Allied troops.

In 1919, the new Nationalist movement, headed by Mustafa Kemal, was organized to resist the Allied occupation and, in 1920, a National Assembly elected him President of both the Assembly and the government. Under his leadership, the Greeks were driven out of Smyrna, and other Allied forces were withdrawn.

The present Turkish boundaries (with the exception of Alexandretta, ceded to Turkey by France in 1939) were fixed by the Treaty of Lausanne (1923) and later negotiations. The caliphate and sultanate were separated, and the sultanate was abolished in 1922. On Oct. 29, 1923, Turkey formally became a republic, with Mustafa Kemal, who took the name Kemal Atatürk, as its first President. The caliphate was abolished in 1924, and Atatürk proceeded to carry out an extensive program of reform, modernization, and industrialization.

Gen. Ismet Inönü was elected to succeed Atatürk in 1938 and was re-elected in 1939, 1943, and 1946. Defeated in 1950, he was succeeded by Celâl Bayar. In 1939, a mutual assistance pact was concluded with Britain and France. Neutral during most of World War II Turkey, on Feb. 23, 1945, declared war on Germany and Japan, but took no active part in the conflict.

Turkey became a full member of NATO in 1952.

In 1971, the Turkish military demanded the ouster of Ismet Inönü, Premier since 1961, who was replaced by Nihat Erim. He pushed through a law that forbade growing of opium poppies after 1972.

After Bülent Ecevit, a liberal, became Premier in 1974, the government required bulk-harvesting of all poppies and consignment of dried "poppy hay" to legal refineries abroad, maintaining that the method would prevent farmers from diverting raw opium to illicit channels. The system was continued after conservative Premier Süleyman Demirel took over the government in 1975.

Turkey invaded Cyprus by sea and air July 20, 1974, following the failure of diplomatic efforts to resolve the crisis caused by the ouster of Archbishop Makarios.

Talks in Geneva involving Greece, Turkey, Britain, and Greek Cypriot and Turkish Cypriot leaders broke down in mid-August. Turkey unilaterally announced a cease-fire August 16, after having gained control of 40% of the island. Turkish Cypriots established their own state in the north on Feb. 13, 1975.

U.S.-Turkish relations, excellent for a generation, were seriously damaged when Congress voted to end arms sales to Turkey in 1975 because arms the U.S. had supplied for mutual defense had been used in the invasion of Cyprus. Congress maintained the ban despite warnings from President Ford that it would imperil the future of 20 U.S. air and intelligence bases in Turkey and could affect Turkey's role as NATO's anchor in the Eastern Mediterranean.

In July 1975, after a 30-day warning, Turkey took over control of all the installations except the big joint defense base at Incirlik, which it reserved for "NATO tasks alone." Some 7,000 U.S. military men remained on duty under Turkish orders, but relations between Ankara and Washington hit a 30-year low.

In August 1978, the Carter administration won a reluctant Congressional reversal of the arms embargo, but a year later there was renewed Congressional opposition to granting military aid because Turkey had balked at allowing U.S. U-2 reconnaissance planes to use its air space. The planes were to check on Soviet compliance with SALT II, the strategic arms limitation treaty. Ecevit said the U-2's would be acceptable only if the Soviet Union agreed to their presence.

Economic problems and civil disturbances plagued the government in 1979, and a $1.45-billion aid package organized by the U.S. and Western European nations—conditioned on economic reforms—was advanced to help Turkey finance imports. Meanwhile, the Soviet Union agreed to build an atomic power plant for Turkey and supply fuel for it, the first such agreement with a NATO member. Moscow also increased its oil shipments to Turkey.

After conservative gains in the elections of Oct. 14, 1979, Ecevit resigned and Demirel returned to power at the head of a minority government. Strikes and terrorism, stimulated by continuing inflation and rising unemployment, brought Turkey to the brink of anarchy in 1980. In March, a mission of the Organization for Economic Cooperation and Development abandoned efforts to negotiate Ankara's request for a $3-billion loan to stabilize the economy.

The establishment of a military government in September 1980 brought a measure of internal stability.

An International Monetary Fund report in early 1982 said consumer price increases had slowed to an annual rate of 31% compared with 90% a year earlier, and that the gross national product in 1981 had grown 4.25% after a year of negative growth. The military regime was subjected to criticism for its suppression of human rights, however, particularly for the arrest of former Premier Ecevit in April on charges that he had made political statements in interviews with foreign media.

TUVALU

Sovereign: Queen Elizabeth II
Governor-General: Sir Fiatau Penitala Teo (1978)
Prime Minister: Tomasi Puapua (1981)

Area: 10 sq mi. (26 sq km)
Population (est. 1982): 7,000 (average annual growth rate: 1.4%)
Density per square mile: 700.0
Capital and largest city (est. 1979): Funafuti, 2,200
Monetary unit: Australian dollar
Languages: Samoan and Gilbertese
Member of the Commonwealth of Nations
Literacy rate (1981): 50%
Economic summary: Gross national product (1980): $4 million. Per Capita Income (1980): $570. Principal agricultural products: copra and coconuts. Export: copra. Imports: food and mineral fuels. Major trading partners: Australia, U.K.

Geography. Formerly the Ellice Islands, Tuvalu consists of nine small islands scattered over 500,000 square miles of the western Pacific, just south of the equator.

Government. Official executive power is vested in a Governor-General, representing the Queen, who is appointed by her on the recommendation of the Tuvalu government. Actual executive power lies with a Prime Minister, who is responsible to a House of Assembly composed of eight elected members.

History. The Ellice Islands became a British protectorate in 1892 and were annexed by Britain in 1915–16 as part of the Gilbert and Ellice Islands Colony. The Ellice Islands were separated in 1975, given home rule, and renamed Tuvalu. Full independence was granted on Sept. 30, 1978.

UGANDA

Republic of Uganda
President: Milton Obote (1980)
Prime Minister: Otema Alimadi (1980)
Area: 91,134 sq mi. (236,036 sq km)
Population (est. 1982): 14,000,000 (average annual growth rate: 3.2%)
Density per square mile: 153.6
Capital and largest city (est. 1980): Kampala, 500,000
Monetary unit: Ugandan shilling
Languages: English (official), Swahili, Luganda, Ateso, Luo
Religions: Christian, 63%; Islam, 6%
Member of Commonwealth of Nations
Literacy rate (1981): 30%
Economic summary: Gross national product (1980): $3.8 billion. Average annual growth rate (1970–79): −3.5%. Per capita income (1980): $280. Land used for agriculture: 21%; labor force: 90%; principal products: coffee, tea, cotton, tobacco, sugar, fish. Labor force in industry: 3%; major products: processed agricultural products, copper, cement, shoes, fertilizer, sheet iron, beverages. Natural resources: copper, miscellaneous minerals. Exports: coffee, cotton, tea. Imports: petroleum products, machinery, transport equipment, metals, food. Major trading partners: U.S., U.K., Kenya.

Geography. Uganda, twice the size of Pennsylvania, is in east central Africa. It is bordered on the west by Zaire, on the north by the Sudan, on the east by Kenya, and on the south by Tanzania and Rwanda.

The country, which lies across the Equator, is divided into three main areas—swampy lowlands, a fertile plateau with wooded hills, and a desert region. Lake Victoria forms part of the southern border.

Government. Executive power is held by the President, chosen for a five-year term by the party winning a majority in parliamentary elections. Legislative power is held by the National Assembly. Major parties are the Uganda People's Congress (72 of 126 seats), led by Dr. A. M. Obote; the Democratic Party (53 seats); and the Uganda Patriotic Movement (1 seat).

History. Uganda was first visited by European explorers as well as Arab traders in 1844. An Anglo-German agreement of 1890 declared it to be in the British sphere of influence in Africa, and the Imperial British East Africa Company was chartered to develop the area. The company did not prosper financially, and in 1894 a British protectorate was proclaimed.

Uganda became independent on Oct. 9, 1962. As its first president, the country chose Mutesa II, King of the ancient kingdom of Buganda. Dr. Milton Obote had been Prime Minister. In 1965, he suspended the Constitution and assumed the powers of the government, later abolishing the offices of President and Vice President.

Obote in 1970 passed laws declaring that 40,000 British Asians—Asian-born persons, mostly Indian, who lived in Uganda but chose British citizenship in 1962 rather than Ugandan—needed a variety of passes and permits to remain in the country. In 1971, Idi Amin, an unpredictable army sergeant, ousted Obote and made himself President. The next year, he began expelling the Asians. He also expelled Israeli advisors rather than pay Israel's military aid bill and applauded Hitler's treatment of Jews.

With his country's potentially rich agricultural economy in turmoil, partly because of large purchases of weapons for its 20,000-man army, Amin nationalized all land in 1975, without compensation to former owners.

In 1976, Amin had himself proclaimed President for Life by the Defense Council, which replaced the Council of Ministers as Uganda's ruling body.

An Israeli commando raid against Entebbe airport on July 4, 1976, freed 103 hostages in a hijacked French airliner that had been held at the airport for a week by Palestinian guerrillas. Hostages, and the government of Israel, charged that Amin had collaborated with the hijackers.

The world condemned Amin's atrocities—Amnesty International reported in 1977 that 300,000 may have died under his rule, including Cabinet ministers and church leaders. Few African leaders denounced him, however, until President Julius K. Nyuerere of Tanzania launched an invasion in November 1978, with the tacit acquiescence of most of Africa. Libya's chief, Muammar el-Qaddafi, came to Amin's defense with troops and arms, but the Libyans only temporarily halted the invaders. Kampala was taken on April 11, 1979, and Amin fled to Libya.

A brief interim government in which Yusufe Lule and Godfrey Binaisa served as President in rapid succession ended when a Military Commission, headed by Paulo Muwanga, took power on May 12, 1980. Elections on Dec. 10–11, the first in 18 years, restored constitutional government.

UNION OF SOVIET SOCIALIST REPUBLICS

See Soviet Union

UNITED ARAB EMIRATES

Head of State: Sheik Zayed Bin Sultan Al-Nahayan (1971)
Prime Minister: Sheik Rashid bin Said al-Maktoum (1979)
Area: 32,000 sq mi. (82,880 sq km)
Population (est. 1982): 800,000 (Arab, 42%; South Asian, 50%) (average annual growth rate: 11.3%)
Density per square mile: 25.0
Capital and largest city (est. 1975): Abu Dhabi, 95,000
Monetary unit: Dirham
Language: Arabic
Religion: Islam
Literacy rate (1975): 25% (est.)
Economic summary: Gross national product (1980): $26.9 billion. Average annual growth rate (1970–79): 2.4%. Per capita income (1980): $30,070. Land used for agriculture: 8%; labor force: 10%; principal products: vegetables, meats, dates, tobacco, fruit. Labor force in industry: 65%; major products: fish, light manufactures, petroleum, construction materials. Natural resources: oil. Exports: petroleum, pearls, fish. Imports: consumer goods, food. Major trading partners: U.K., Japan, U.S., India.

Geography. The United Arab Emirates, in the eastern part of the Arabian Peninsula, extends along part of the Gulf of Oman and the southern coast of the Persian Gulf. The nation is the size of Maine. Its neighbors are Saudi Arabia in the west and south, Qatar in the north, and Oman in the east. Most of the land is barren and sandy.

Government. The United Arab Emirates was formed in 1971 by seven emirates known as the Trucial States—Abu Dhabi (the largest), Dubai, Sharjah, Ajman, Fujairah, Ras al Khaimah and Umm al-Qaiwain.

The loose federation allows joint policies in foreign relations, defense, and development, with each member state keeping its internal local system of government headed by its own ruler. A 40-member legislature consists of eight seats each for Abu Dhabi and Dubai, six seats each for Ras al Khaimah and Sharjah, and four each for the others. It is a member of the Arab League.

History. Originally the area was inhabited by a seafaring people who were converted to Islam in the seventh century. Later, a dissident sect, the Carmathians, established a powerful sheikdom, and its army conquered Mecca. After the sheikdom disintegrated, its people became pirates.

Threatening the sultanate of Muscat and Oman early in the 19th century, the pirates provoked the intervention of the British, who in 1820 enforced a partial truce and in 1853 a permanent truce. Thus what had been called the Pirate Coast was renamed the Trucial Coast.

UNITED KINGDOM

United Kingdom of Great Britain and Northern Ireland
Sovereign: Queen Elizabeth II (1952)
Prime Minister: Margaret Thatcher (1979)
Area: 94,250 sq mi. (244,108 sq km)
Population (est. 1982): 55,850,000 (average annual growth rate: 0.1% (English, Scottish, Welsh, Northern Irish)
Density per square mile: 592.6
Capital: London, England
Largest cities (est. 1981): Greater London, 6,696,000; Birmingham, 1,006,000; Glasgow, 762,200; Leeds, 705,000; Sheffield, 536,800; Liverpool, 510,300; Bradford, 457,700; Manchester, 510,300; Edinburgh, 419,200; Bristol, 419,200
Monetary unit: Pound sterling (£)
Languages: English, Welsh, Gaelic
Religions: Church of England (established church); Church of Wales (disestablished); Church of Scotland (established church—Presbyterian); Church of Ireland (disestablished); Roman Catholic; Methodist; Congregational; Baptist; Jewish
Literacy rate (1981): 99%
Economic summary: Gross national product (1980): $442.8 billion. Average annual growth rate (1970–79): 1.9%. Per capita income (1980): $7,920. Land used for agriculture: 30%; principal products: cereals, livestock and livestock products. Major industrial products: steel, heavy engineering and metal manufactures, textiles, motor vehicles and aircraft, electronics, chemicals. Natural resources: coal, oil, gas. Exports: machinery, transport equipment, chemicals, petroleum, foodstuffs. Imports: foodstuffs, petroleum, machinery, chemicals, crude materials. Major trading partners: Western European nations, U.S., West Germany, France.

Geography. The United Kingdom, consisting of England, Wales, Scotland, and Northern Ireland, is twice the size of New York State. England, in the southeast part of the British Isles, is separated from Scotland on the north by the granite Cheviot Hills; from them the Pennine chain of uplands extends south through the center of England, reaching its highest point in the Lake District in the northwest. To the west along the border of Wales—a land of steep hills and valleys—are the Cambrian Mountains, while the Cotswolds, a range of hills in Gloucestershire, extend into the surrounding shires.

The remainder of England is plain land, though not necessarily flat, with the rocky sand-topped moors in the southwest, the rolling downs in the south and southeast, and the reclaimed marshes of the low-lying fens in the east central districts.

Scotland is divided into three physical regions—the Highlands, the Central Lowlands, containing two-thirds of the population, and the Southern Uplands. The western Highland coast is intersected throughout by long, narrow sea-lochs, or fiords. Scotland also includes the Outer and Inner Hebrides and other islands off the west coast and the Orkney and Shetland Islands off the north coast.

Wales is generally hilly; the Snowdon range in the northern part culminates in Mount Snowdon (3,560 ft, 1,085 m), highest in both England and Wales.

Important rivers flowing into the North Sea are the Thames, Humber, Tees, and Tyne. In the west are the Severn and Wye, which empty into the Bristol Channel and are navigable, as are the Mersey and Ribble.

Government. The United Kingdom is a constitutional monarchy, with a Queen and a Parliament that has two houses: the House of Lords with about 830 hereditary peers, 26 spiritual peers, about 270 life peers and peeresses, and 9 law-lords, who are hereditary, or life, peers, and the House of Commons, which since 1974 has had 635 popularly elected members. Supreme legislative power is vested in Parliament, which sits for five years unless sooner dissolved.

The executive power of the Crown is exercised by the Cabinet, headed by the Prime Minister. The latter, normally the head of the party commanding

Area and Population of United Kingdom

Subdivision	Area sq mi.	Area sq km	Population (est. 1980)
England and Wales	58,381	151,207	49,300,000
Scotland	30,416	78,777	5,200,000
Northern Ireland	5,452	14,121	1,500,000
Total	**94,249**	**244,105**	**56,000,000**

a majority in the House of Commons, is appointed by the Sovereign, with whose consent he or she in turn appoints the rest of the Cabinet. All ministers must be members of one or the other house of Parliament; they are individually and collectively responsible to the Crown and Parliament. The Cabinet proposes bills and arranges the business of Parliament, but it depends entirely on the votes in the House of Commons. The Lords cannot hold up "money" bills, but they can delay other bills for a maximum of one year.

By the Act of Union (1707), the Scottish Parliament was assimilated with that of England, and Scotland is now represented in Commons by 71 members. The Secretary of State for Scotland, a member of the Cabinet, is responsible for the administration of Scottish affairs.

The major political parties are the Conservative Party (334 of the 635 seats in the House of Commons), led by Prime Minister Margaret Thatcher; Labor Party (238 seats), led by Michael Foote; Social Democrats (30 seats), led by Roy Jenkins; Liberal Party (12 seats), led by David Steel; Ulster Unionists and other Northern Irish parties (12 seats); Scottish Nationalist Party (2 seats); Welsh Nationalist Party (2 seats). The Speaker and three deputies do not normally vote.

Ruler: Queen Elizabeth II, born April 21, 1926, elder daughter of King George VI and Queen Elizabeth, succeeded to the throne on the death of her father on Feb. 6, 1952; married Nov. 20, 1947, to Prince Philip, Duke of Edinburgh, born June 10, 1921; their children are Prince Charles[1] (heir presumptive), born Nov. 14, 1948; Princess Anne, born Aug. 15, 1950; Prince Andrew, born Feb. 19, 1960; and Prince Edward, born March 10, 1964. The Queen's sister is Princess Margaret, born Aug. 21, 1930. Prince William Arthur Philip Louis, son of the Prince and Princess of Wales and second in line to the throne, was born June 21, 1982.

History. Roman invasions of the 1st century B.C. brought Britain into contact with the Continent. When the Roman legions withdrew in the 5th century A.D., Britain fell easy prey to the invading hordes of Angles, Saxons, and Jutes from Scandinavia and the Low Countries. Seven large kingdoms were established, and the original Britons were forced into Wales and Scotland. It was not until the 11th century that the country finally became united under the Danish King Canute. Following the death of Edward the Confessor (1066), a dispute about the succession arose, and William, Duke of Normandy, invaded England, defeating the Saxon King, Harold II, at the Battle of Hastings (1066). The Norman conquest introduced Norman law and feudalism.

The reign of Henry II (1154–89), first of the Plantagenets, saw an increasing centralization of royal power at the expense of the nobles, but in 1215 John (1199–1216) was forced to sign the Magna Carta, which awarded the people, especially the nobles, certain basic rights. Edward I (1272–1307) continued the conquest of Ireland, reduced Wales to subjection and made some gains in Scotland. In 1314, however, English forces led by Edward II were ousted from Scotland after the Battle of Bannockburn. The late 13th and early 14th centuries saw the development of a separate House of Commons with tax-raising powers.

Edward III's claim to the throne of France led to the Hundred Years' War (1338–1453) and the loss of almost all the large English territory in France. In England, the great poverty and discontent caused by the war were intensified by the Black Death, a plague that reduced the population by about one third. The Wars of the Roses (1455–85), a struggle for the throne between the House of York and the House of Lancaster, ended in the victory of Henry Tudor (Henry VII) at Bosworth Field (1485).

During the reign of Henry VIII (1509–47), the Church in England asserted its independence from the Roman Catholic Church. Under Edward VI and Mary, the two extremes of religious fanaticism were reached, and it remained for Henry's daughter, Elizabeth I (1558–1603), to set up the Church of England on a moderate basis. In 1588, the Spanish Armada, a fleet sent out by Catholic King Philip II of Spain, was defeated by the English and destroyed during a storm. During Elizabeth's reign, England became a world power.

Elizabeth's heir was a Stuart—James VI of Scotland—who joined the two crowns as James I (1603–25). The Stuart kings incurred large debts and were forced either to depend on Parliament for taxes or to raise money by illegal means. In 1642, war broke out between Charles I and a large segment of the Parliament; Charles was defeated and executed in 1649, and the monarchy was then abolished. After the death in 1658 of Oliver Cromwell, the Lord Protector, the Puritan Commonwealth fell to pieces and Charles II was placed on the throne in 1660. The struggle between the King and Parliament continued, but Charles II knew when to compromise. His brother, James II (1685–88), possessed none of his ability and was ousted by the Revolution of 1688, which confirmed the primacy of Parliament. James's daughter, Mary, and her husband, William of Orange, were now the rulers.

Queen Anne's reign (1702–14) was marked by the Duke of Marlborough's victories over France at Blenheim, Oudenarde, and Malplaquet in the War of the Spanish Succession. England and Scotland meanwhile were joined by the Act of Union (1707). Upon the death of Anne, the distant claims of the elector of Hanover were recognized, and he became King of Great Britain and Ireland as George I.

The unwillingness of the Hanoverian kings to rule resulted in the formation by the royal ministers of a Cabinet, headed by a Prime Minister, which directed all public business. Abroad, the constant wars with France expanded the British Empire all over the globe, particularly in North America and India. This imperial growth was checked by the revolt of the American colonies (1775–81).

1. The title Prince of Wales, which is not inherited, was conferred on Prince Charles by his mother on July 26, 1958. The investiture ceremony took place on July 1, 1969. The previous Prince of Wales was Prince Edward Albert, who held the title from 1911 to 1936 before he became Edward VIII.

Rulers of England and Great Britain

Name	Born	Ruled[1]
SAXONS[2]		
Egbert[3]	c. 775	828–839
Ethelwulf	?	839–858
Ethelbald	?	858–860
Ethelbert	?	860–866
Ethelred I	?	866–871
Alfred the Great	849	871–899
Edward the Elder	c. 870	899–924
Athelstan	895	924–939
Edmund I the Deed-doer	921	939–946
Edred	c. 925	946–955
Edwy the Fair	c. 943	955–959
Edgar the Peaceful	943	959–975
Edward the Martyr	c. 962	975–979
Ethelred II the Unready	968	979–1016
Edmund II Ironside	c. 993	1016–1016
DANES		
Canute	995	1016–1035
Harold I Harefoot	c.1016	1035–1040
Hardecanute	c.1018	1040–1042
SAXONS		
Edward the Confessor	c.1004	1042–1066
Harold II	c.1020	1066–1066
HOUSE OF NORMANDY		
William I the Conqueror	1027	1066–1087
William II Rufus	c.1056	1087–1100
Henry I Beauclerc	1068	1100–1135
Stephen of Blois	c.1100	1135–1154
HOUSE OF PLANTAGENET		
Henry II	1133	1154–1189
Richard I Coeur de Lion	1157	1189–1199
John Lackland	1167	1199–1216
Henry III	1207	1216–1272
Edward I Longshanks	1239	1272–1307
Edward II	1284	1307–1327
Edward III	1312	1327–1377
Richard II	1367	1377–1399[4]
HOUSE OF LANCASTER		
Henry IV Bolingbroke	1367	1399–1413
Henry V	1387	1413–1422
Henry VI	1421	1422–1461[5]
HOUSE OF YORK		
Edward IV	1442	1461–1483[5]
Edward V	1470	1483–1483
Richard III	1452	1483–1485
HOUSE OF TUDOR		
Henry VII	1457	1485–1509
Henry VIII	1491	1509–1547
Edward VI	1537	1547–1553
Jane (Lady Jane Grey)[6]	1537	1553–1553
Mary I ("Bloody Mary")	1516	1553–1558
Elizabeth I	1533	1558–1603
HOUSE OF STUART		
James I[7]	1566	1603–1625
Charles I	1600	1625–1649
COMMONWEALTH		
Council of State	—	1649–1653
Oliver Cromwell[8]	1599	1653–1658
Richard Cromwell[8]	1626	1658–1659[9]
RESTORATION OF HOUSE OF STUART		
Charles II	1630	1660–1685
James II	1633	1685–1688[10]
William III[11]	1650	1689–1702
Mary II[11]	1662	1689–1694
Anne	1665	1702–1714
HOUSE OF HANOVER		
George I	1660	1714–1727
George II	1683	1727–1760
George III	1738	1760–1820
George IV	1762	1820–1830
William IV	1765	1830–1837
Victoria	1819	1837–1901
HOUSE OF SAXE-COBURG[12]		
Edward VII	1841	1901–1910
HOUSE OF WINDSOR[12]		
George V	1865	1910–1936
Edward VIII	1894	1936–1936[13]
George VI	1895	1936–1952
Elizabeth II	1926	1952–

1. Year of end of rule is also that of death, unless otherwise indicated. 2. Dates for Saxon kings are still subject of controversy. 3. Became King of West Saxons in 802; considered (from 828) first King of all England. 4. Died 1400. 5. Henry VI reigned again briefly 1470–71. 6. Nominal Queen for 9 days; not counted as Queen by some authorities. She was beheaded in 1554. 7. Ruled in Scotland as James VI (1567–1625). 8. Lord Protector. 9. Died 1712. 10. Died 1701. 11. Joint rulers (1689–1694). 12. Name changed from Saxe-Coburg to Windsor in 1917. 13. Was known after his abdication as the Duke of Windsor; died 1972.

Struggles with France broke out again in 1793 and, during the Napoleonic Wars, which ended at Waterloo (1815), Britain was pitted at one time against almost all of Europe.

The Victorian era, named after Queen Victoria (1837–1901), saw the growth of a democratic system of government that had begun with the Reform Bill of 1832. The two important wars in Victoria's reign were the Crimean War against Russia (1853–56) and the Boer War (1899–1902), the latter enormously extending Britain's influence in Africa.

Increasing uneasiness at home and abroad marked the reign of Edward VII (1901–10). Within four years after the accession of George V in 1910, Britain entered World War I when Germany invaded Belgium. The nation was led by coalition Cabinets, headed first by Herbert Asquith and then, starting in 1916, by the Welsh statesman David Lloyd George. Postwar labor unrest culminated in the general strike of 1926.

King Edward VIII succeeded to the throne on Jan. 20, 1936, at his father's death, but abdicated on Dec. 11, 1936 (in order to marry an American divorcee, Wallis Warfield Simpson) in favor of his brother, who became George VI.

The efforts of Prime Minister Neville Chamberlain to stem the rising threat of Nazism in Germany

British Prime Ministers Since 1770

Name	Term
Lord North (Tory)	1770–1782
Marquis of Rockingham (Whig)	1782–1782
Earl of Shelburne (Whig)	1782–1783
Duke of Portland (Coalition)	1783–1783
William Pitt, the Younger (Tory)	1783–1801
Henry Addington (Tory)	1801–1804
William Pitt, the Younger (Tory)	1804–1806
Baron Grenville (Whig)	1806–1807
Duke of Portland (Tory)	1807–1809
Spencer Perceval (Tory)	1809–1812
Earl of Liverpool (Tory)	1812–1827
George Canning (Tory)	1827–1827
Viscount Goderich (Tory)	1827–1828
Duke of Wellington (Tory)	1828–1830
Earl Grey (Whig)	1830–1834
Viscount Melbourne (Whig)	1834–1834
Sir Robert Peel (Tory)	1834–1835
Viscount Melbourne (Whig)	1835–1841
Sir Robert Peel (Tory)	1841–1846
Earl Russell (Whig)	1846–1852
Earl of Derby (Tory)	1852–1852
Earl of Aberdeen (Coalition)	1852–1855
Viscount Palmerston (Liberal)	1855–1858
Earl of Derby (Conservative)	1858–1859
Viscount Palmerston (Liberal)	1859–1865
Earl Russell (Liberal)	1865–1866
Earl of Derby (Conservative)	1866–1868
Benjamin Disraeli (Conservative)	1868–1868
William E. Gladstone (Liberal)	1868–1874
Benjamin Disraeli (Conservative)	1874–1880
William E. Gladstone (Liberal)	1880–1885
Marquis of Salisbury (Conservative)	1885–1886
William E. Gladstone (Liberal)	1886–1886
Marquis of Salisbury (Conservative)	1886–1892
William E. Gladstone (Liberal)	1892–1894
Earl of Rosebery (Liberal)	1894–1895
Marquis of Salisbury (Conservative)	1895–1902
Earl Balfour (Conservative)	1902–1905
Sir H. Campbell-Bannerman (Liberal)	1905–1908
Herbert H. Asquith (Liberal)	1908–1915
Herbert H. Asquith (Coalition)	1915–1916
David Lloyd George (Coalition)	1916–1922
Andrew Bonar Law (Conservative)	1922–1923
Stanley Baldwin (Conservative)	1923–1924
James Ramsay MacDonald (Labor)	1924–1924
Stanley Baldwin (Conservative)	1924–1929
James Ramsay MacDonald (Labor)	1929–1931
James Ramsay MacDonald (Coalition)	1931–1935
Stanley Baldwin (Coalition)	1935–1937
Neville Chamberlain (Coalition)	1937–1940
Winston Churchill (Coalition)	1940–1945
Clement R. Attlee (Labor)	1945–1951
Sir Winston Churchill (Conservative)	1951–1955
Sir Anthony Eden (Conservative)	1955–1957
Harold Macmillan (Conservative)	1957–1963
Sir Alec Frederick Douglas-Home (Conservative)	1963–1964
Harold Wilson (Labor)	1964–1970
Edward Heath (Conservative)	1970–1974
Harold Wilson (Labor)	1974–1976
James Callaghan (Labor)	1976–1979
Margaret Thatcher (Conservative)	1979–

failed with the German invasion of Poland on Sept. 1, 1939, which was followed by Britain's entry into World War II on September 3. Allied reverses in the spring of 1940 led to Chamberlain's resignation and the formation of another coalition war Cabinet by the Conservative leader, Winston Churchill, who led Britain through most of World War II. Churchill resigned shortly after V-E Day, May 7, 1945, but then formed a "caretaker" government that remained in office until after the parliamentary elections in July, which the Labor Party won overwhelmingly. The government formed by Clement R. Attlee began a moderate socialist program.

For details of World War II (1939–45), *see* Headline History.

In 1951, Churchill again became Prime Minister at the head of a Conservative government. George VI died Feb. 6, 1952, and was succeeded by his daughter Elizabeth II.

Churchill stepped down in 1955 in favor of Sir Anthony Eden, who resigned on grounds of ill health in 1957, and was succeeded by Harold Macmillan and Sir Alec Douglas-Home. In 1964, Harold Wilson led the Labor Party to victory.

Wilson, the first Labor Prime Minister in 13 years, was a skilled strategist from the party's center who instituted no great changes domestically. His ambition for success abroad was thwarted by the French veto of Britain's bid for entry into the European Economic Community and by his own inept handling of the unilateral declaration of independence by Southern Rhodesia, the last sizable British colony.

A lagging economy brought the Conservatives back to power in 1970. Prime Minister Edward Heath won Britain's admission to the European Community, a move affirmed by 67.2% in the nation's first referendum. Heath narrowly lost a February 1974 election overshadowed by a coal strike, returning Wilson to the leadership and the first minority government since 1929.

Party elections after Wilson's announcement of his intention to retire elevated James Callaghan from the Foreign Ministry to the Prime Minister's office in 1976.

Despite economic troubles, unemployment, and continuing conflict in Northern Ireland and Rhodesia, Britons in June 1977 celebrated the Silver Jubilee of Queen Elizabeth II with genuine affection. The Queen's first grandchild, Peter Mark Andrew Phillips, son of Princess Anne, was born November 14. On May 24, 1978, the first divorce in the immediate royal family in more than 150 years took place when Princess Margaret's 18-year marriage to the Earl of Snowdon was legally ended.

Margaret Thatcher became Britain's first woman Prime Minister as the Conservatives won 339 seats for a 43-seat majority in elections on May 3, 1979. The 53-year-old, Oxford-educated daughter of a grocer campaigned for lower taxes, curbs on labor unions, and less government at home coupled with a more decisive foreign policy.

Mrs. Thatcher moved quickly to implement her domestic program but was blocked by African and U.S. resistance from granting early recognition to the Muzorewa government in Zimbabwe (Rhodesia). In September 1979, a bold initiative by her foreign minister, Lord Carrington, brought all parties in the conflict to a conference in London at which she threatened and cajoled the white minority and black factions until all agreed on a new Constitution. The successful conduct of elections in February and the transfer of sovereignty on April 18, 1980, was a political triumph for the Conservatives.

A similar gamble, with Mrs. Thatcher threatening to pull Britain out of the European Economic Community, brought a major reduction in the British contribution to the E.E.C. Although the victory avoided sharp increases in food prices, the dispute strengthened the growing sentiment in Britain for withdrawal from the E.E.C.

Despite rising income from North Sea oil production, the economy sagged in 1980 and continued to slide in 1981 as the government pursued a harsh deflationary policy. With unemployment nearing 2.5 million, rioting broke out in London, Liverpool, Manchester, and other cities. Lack of jobs and discontent among black and Asian minorities were blamed for the upheavals, which resulted in thousands of arrests, but Mrs. Thatcher called only for stronger police measures and public discipline.

An Argentine invasion of the Falkland Islands on April 2, 1982, involved Britain in a war 8,000 miles from the home islands. Although Argentina had long claimed the Falklands, known as the Malvinas in Spanish, negotiations were in progress until a month before the invasion. The Thatcher government responded to the invasion with a 40-ship task force, which sailed from Portsmouth on April 5. U.S. efforts to settle the dispute failed and United Nations efforts collapsed as the Argentine military government ignored Security Council resolutions calling for a withdrawal of its forces.

The war came only 10 days after the Royal Navy had announced plans to cut its strength by 10,000 men—to 62,000 by 1986—and to rely more on submarines than surface ships with the purchase for $13.5 billion of the Trident II nuclear submarine missile system from the United States.

When more than 11,000 Argentine troops on the Falklands surrendered on June 14, Mrs. Thatcher declared her intention to garrison the islands indefinitely at an estimated cost of $37 million per month, together with a naval presence. Although four ships were lost to Argentine air attack during the fighting, they were expected to be replaced.

The military victory bolstered Conservative fortunes at least temporarily, but economic problems continued for the government. Unemployment rose to a record 2.91 million in mid-June and a strike by British Railways workers paralyzed the state-owned system in July, a system already operating at a $300-million annual deficit despite subsidies of $1.5 billion.

NORTHERN IRELAND

Status: Part of United Kingdom
Secretary of State: James Prior (1981)
Area: 5,452 sq mi. (14,121 sq km)
Population (est. 1982): 1,500,000
Density per square mile: 279.7
Capital and largest city (est. 1980): Belfast, 345,800
Monetary Unit: British pound sterling
Languages: English, Gaelic
Religions: Roman Catholic, 35%; Presbyterian, 29%; Church of Ireland, 24%; Methodist, 5%

Geography. Northern Ireland comprises the counties of Antrim, Armagh, Down, Fermanagh, Londonderry, and Tyrone, which make up predominantly Protestant Ulster and form the northern part of the island of Ireland, westernmost of the British Isles. It is slightly larger than Connecticut.

Government. Northern Ireland is an integral part of the United Kingdom (it has 12 representatives in the British House of Commons), but under the terms of the Government of Ireland Act in 1920, it had a semiautonomous government. But in 1972, after three years of internal strife which resulted in over 400 dead and thousands injured, Britain suspended the Ulster parliament. The Ulster counties became governed directly from London after an attempt to return certain powers to an elected Assembly in Belfast.

The Northern Ireland Assembly was dissolved in 1975 and a Constitutional Convention was elected to write a Constitution acceptable to Protestants and Catholics. The convention failed to reach agreement and closed down the next year.

The major political parties are the United Ulster Unionist Coalition (Protestant) (46 of 78 delegates to the Constitutional Convention); Social Democratic Labor Party (Catholic) (17 delegates); Alliance Party (8 delegates); New Unionist Party of Northern Ireland (Protestant) (5 delegates).

History. Ulster was part of Catholic Ireland until the reign of Elizabeth I (1558–1603) when, after crushing three Irish rebellions, the crown confiscated lands in Ireland and settled in Ulster the Scot Presbyterians who became rooted there. Another rebellion in 1641–51, crushed as brutally by Oliver Cromwell, resulted in the settlement of Anglican Englishmen in Ulster. Subsequent political policy favoring Protestants and disadvantaging Catholics encouraged further settlement in Northern Ireland.

But the North did not separate from the South until William Gladstone presented in 1886 his proposal for home rule in Ireland as a means of settling the Irish Question. The Protestants in the North, although they had grievances like the Catholics in the South, feared domination by the Catholic majority. Industry, moreover, was concentrated in the north and dependent on the British market.

When World War I began, civil war threatened between the regions. Northern Ireland, however, did not become a political entity until the six counties accepted the Home Rule Bill of 1920. This set up a semiautonomous Parliament in Belfast and a Crown-appointed Governor advised by a Cabinet of the Prime Minister and eight ministers, as well as a 12-member representation in the House of Commons in London.

As the Republic of Ireland gained its sovereignty, relations improved between North and South, although the Irish Republican Army, outlawed in recent years, continued the struggle to end the partition of Ireland. In 1966–69, communal rioting and street fighting between Protestants and Catholics occurred in Londonderry, fomented by extremist nationalist Protestants, who feared the Catholics might attain a local majority, and by Catholics demonstrating for civil rights.

Rioting, terrorism, and sniping killed more than 2,100 people from 1969 through 1982. and the religious communities, Catholic and Protestant, became hostile armed camps. British troops were brought in to separate them but themselves became a target of Catholics.

In 1973, a new British charter created a 78-member Assembly elected by proportional representation that gave more weight to Catholic strength. It created a Province Executive with committee chairmen of the Assembly heading all government departments except law enforcement, which remained under London's control. Assembly elections in 1973 produced a majority for the new Constitution that included Catholic assemblymen.

Ulster's leaders agreed in 1973 to create an 11-member Executive Body with six seats assigned to Unionists (Protestants) and four to members of Catholic parties. Unionist leader Brian Faulkner headed the Executive. Also agreed to was a Council of Ireland, with 14 seats evenly divided between Dublin and Belfast, which could act only by unanimous vote.

Although the Council lacked real authority, its creation sparked a general strike by Protestant extremists in 1974. The two-week strike caused Faulkner's resignation from the Executive and resumption of direct rule from London.

In April 1974, London instituted a new program that responded to some Catholic grievances, but assigned more British troops to cut off movement of arms and munitions to Ulster's violence-racked cities.

Violence continued unabated, with new heights reached early in 1976 when the British government announced the end of special privileges for political prisoners in Northern Ireland. British Prime Minister James Callaghan visited Belfast in July and pledged that Ulster would remain part of the United Kingdom unless a clear majority wished to separate.

In October 1977, the 1976 Nobel Prize for Peace was awarded to Mairead Corrigan and Betty Williams for their campaign for peace in Northern Ireland. Intermittent violence continued, however, and on Aug. 27, 1979, an I.R.A. bomb killed Earl Mountbatten as he was sailing off southern Ireland. The death of the 79-year-old cousin of the Queen, a World War II hero and the last Viceroy of India, shocked the world. Mrs. Thatcher visited Ulster two days later and denounced terrorism. After Mountbatten's state funeral in Westminster Abbey on Sept. 5, Mrs. Thatcher met with Irish Premier John Lynch to discuss security measures against the I.R.A. Lynch urged an attack on the "root cause," the division of Ireland.

New talks aimed at a restoration of home rule in Northern Ireland began and quickly ended in January 1980. In May, Mrs. Thatcher met with the new Prime Minister of the Irish Republic, Charles Haughey, but she insisted that the future of Ulster must be decided only by its people and the British Parliament. Haughey declared that an internal solution "cannot and will not succeed."

Civil disturbances reached new heights in the summer of 1981 as Irish nationalist prisoners went on hunger strikes in Maze Prison to attain their demands for "political" status.

Ten nationalists died before the strike ended in August as families of fasters asked that they be fed. Although the government rejected any compromise, new prison rules promulgated in November permitted all prisoners to wear their own clothing and all but a handful of the I.R.A. convicts ended their five-year "blanket protest" in which they had worn blankets rather than prison-issue clothing.

In April 1982, Northern Ireland Secretary of State James Prior announced plans for reorganizing an elected assembly with proportional representation and a 70% majority in the Assembly to insure adequate representation of the Catholic minority. It was denounced by Protestant political leaders, who insisted on simple majority rule and by the Republic of Ireland, which called it "unworkable."

Dependencies of the United Kingdom

ANGUILLA

See West Indies Associated States

BERMUDA

Status: Self-governing dependency
Governor: John David Gibbons (1981)
Prime Minister: J. David Gibbons (1977)
Area: 20 sq mi. (52 sq km)
Population (est. 1982): 60,000 (average annual growth rate: 2.6%)
Capital (est. 1978): Hamilton, 2,500
Monetary unit: Bermuda dollar
Literacy rate (1981): 98%
Economic summary: Gross national product (1980): $660 million. Average annual growth rate (1970–79): 1.6%. Per capita income (1980): $11,050. Land used for agriculture: 8%; labor force: 1%; principal products: bananas, vegetables, citrus fruits, dairy products. Labor force in industry: 6.2%; major products: structural concrete, paints, perfumes, furniture. Natural resource: limestone. Exports: semi-tropical produce, light manufactures. Imports: foodstuffs, fuel, machinery. Major trading partners: U.S., U.K., Canada.

Bermuda is an archipelago of about 360 small islands, 580 miles (934 km) east of North Carolina. The largest is (Great) Bermuda, or Long Island. Discovered by Juan de Bermúdez, a shipwrecked Spaniard, early in the 16th century, the islands were settled in 1612 by an offshoot of the Virginia Company and became a crown colony in 1684.

In 1940, sites on the islands were leased for 99 years to the U.S. for air and navy bases. Bermuda is also the headquarters of the West Indies and Atlantic squadron of the Royal Navy.

In 1968, Bermuda was granted a new Constitution, its first Prime Minister, and autonomy, except for foreign relations, defense, and internal security. The predominantly white United Bermuda Party has retained power in three elections against the opposition—the black-led Progressive Laborites—although Bermuda's population is 60% black. Serious rioting occurred in December 1977 after two blacks were hanged for a series of murders, including the 1973 assassination of the Governor, Sir Richard Sharples, and British troops were summoned to restore order.

BRITISH ANTARCTIC TERRITORY

Status: Dependency
High Commissioner: Rex Masterson Hunt (1980)
Area: 500,000 sq mi. (1,395,000 sq km)
Population (1976): 55

The British Antarctic Territory consists of the South Shetland Islands, South Orkney Islands, and Nearby Graham Land on the Antarctic continent, largely uninhabited. They were dependencies of the British crown colony of the Falkland Islands but received a separate administration in 1962, being governed by a British-appointed High Commissioner who is Governor of the Falklands.

BRITISH INDIAN OCEAN TERRITORY

Status: Dependency
Commissioner: W. N. Wenban-Smith
Administrator: P. A. Raftery (1981)
Administrative headquarters: Victoria, Seychelles
Area: 85 sq mi, (220 sq km)

This dependency, consisting of the Chagos Archipelago and other small island groups, was formed in 1965 by agreement with Mauritius and the Seychelles. There is no permanent civilian population in the territory.

BRITISH VIRGIN ISLANDS

Status: Dependency
Governor: D. R. Barwick
Area: 59 sq mi. (153 sq km)
Population (est. 1979): 12,000
Capital (est. 1975): Road Town (on Tortola): 3,500
Monetary unit: U.S. dollar

Some 36 islands in the Caribbean Sea northeast of Puerto Rico and west of the Leeward Islands, the British Virgin Islands are economically interdependent with the U.S. Virgin Islands to the south. They were formerly part of the administration of the Leeward Islands. They received a separate administration in 1956 as a crown colony. In 1967 a new Constitution was promulgated that provided for a ministerial system of government headed by the Governor. The principal islands are Tortola, Virgin Gorda, Anegada and Jost Van Dyke.

BRUNEI

Status: Associated state
Sultan: Hassanel Bolkiah (1968)
High Commissioner: Vacant
Area: 2,226 sq mi. (5,765 sq km)
Population (est. 1982): 250,000 (average annual growth rate: 5.6%)
Capital (est. 1978): Bandar Seri Begawan, 70,000
Monetary unit: Brunei dollar
Literacy rate (1981): 45%
Economic summary: Gross national product (1980): $2.6 billion. Average annual growth rate (1970–79): 4.6%. Per capita income (1980): $11,890. Land used for agriculture: 3%; labor force: 31%; principal agricultural products: rubber, rice, pepper. Labor force in industry: 33%; major industrial products: crude petroleum, liquefied natural gas. Natural resources: petroleum, natural gas. Exports: crude petroleum, liquefied natural gas. Imports: machinery, transport equipment, manufactured goods, foodstuffs. Major trading partners: Japan, U.S., U.K., Singapore.

A sultanate on the northwest coast of the island of Borneo on the South China Sea, Brunei consists of two prongs into the territory of Sarawak, East Malaysia. It was a powerful state from the 16th to the 19th century, ruling over the northern part of Borneo and adjacent island chains. But it fell into decay and lost Sarawak in 1841, becoming a British protectorate in 1888 and a British dependency in 1905.

The Sultan regained control over internal affairs by a Constitution he instituted in 1959, along with an agreement with the Crown delegating responsibility for defense and foreign affairs. Britain, which will be responsible for foreign affairs until the end of 1983, when Brunei will become independent, is represented by a High Commissioner; government is by a Privy Council and Council of Ministers, both presided over by the Sultan, and a Legislative Council.

Sultan Bolkiah was crowned in 1968 at the age of 22. He succeeded his father, Sir Omar Ali Saifuddin, who had abdicated.

Most of the inhabitants are Malays, Borneans, and Chinese. The majority of the population lives in and around the capital, situated on the Brunei River nine miles from its mouth.

CAYMAN ISLANDS

Status: Dependency
Governor: G. P. Lloyd
Area: 118 sq mi. (306 sq km)
Population (est. 1982): 15,000
Capital (est. 1980): Georgetown (on Grand Cayman), 7,600
Monetary unit: Cayman Islands dollar

This dependency consists of three islands—Grand Cayman (76 sq mi; 197 sq km), Cayman Brac (22 sq mi; 57 sq km), and Little Cayman (20 sq mi; 52 sq km)—situated about 180 miles (290 km) northwest of Jamaica. They were dependencies of Jamaica until 1959, when they became a unit territory within the Federation of the West Indies. In 1962, upon the dissolution of the Federation, the Cayman Islands became a British dependency.

The islands' chief export is turtle products.

CHANNEL ISLANDS

Status: Crown dependencies
Lieutenant Governor of Jersey: Gen. Sir Peter Whiteley (1980)
Lieutenant Governor of Guernsey: Air Chief Marshal Sir Peter Le Cheminant
Area: 75 sq mi. (194 sq km)
Population (est. 1982): 130,000
Capital of Jersey: St. Helier
Capital of Guernsey: St. Peter Port
Monetary units: Guernsey pound; Jersey pound

This group of islands, lying in the English Channel off the northwest coast of France, is the only portion of the Duchy of Normandy belonging to the English Crown, to which it has been attached since the conquest of 1066. It was the only British possession occupied by Germany during World War II.

For purposes of government, the islands are divided into the Bailiwick of Jersey (45 sq mi.; 117 sq km) and the Bailiwick of Guernsey (30 sq mi.; 78 sq km), including Alderney (3 sq mi.; 7.8 sq km); Sark (2 sq mi.; 5.2 sq km), Herm, Jethou, etc. The islands are administered according to their own laws and customs by local governments. Acts of Parliament in London are not binding on the islands unless they are specifically mentioned. The Queen is represented in each Bailiwick by a Lieutenant Governor.

English is now the language in daily use, although the French patois is still spoken by some people. New legislation is drafted in English, but French has been retained for ceremonial purposes in the legislative bodies.

FALKLAND ISLANDS AND DEPENDENCIES

Status: Dependency
Governor: Rex Masterson Hunt (1980)
Area: 4,700 sq mi. (12,173 sq km)
Population: est. (1982): 2,000
Capital (est. 1978): Stanley (on East Falkland), 1,100
Monetary unit: Falkland Island pound

This sparsely inhabited dependency consists of a group of islands in the South Atlantic, about 250 miles (402 km) east of the South American mainland. The largest islands are East Falkland and West Falkland. Dependencies are South Georgia Island (1,450 sq mi.; 3,756 sq km), the South Sandwich Islands, and other islets. Three former dependencies—Graham Land, the South Shetland Islands, and the South Orkney Islands—were established as a new British dependency, the British Antarctic Territory, in 1962.

The chief industry is sheep raising and, apart from the production of wool, hides and skins, and tallow, there are no known resources. The whaling industry is carried on from South Georgia Island.

The chief export is wool.

GIBRALTAR

Status: Self-governing dependency
Governor: Sir William Jackson (1978)
Chief Minister: Sir Joshua Hassan
Area: 2.25 sq mi. (5.8 sq km)
Population (est. 1982): 30,000 (average annual growth rate: 0.8%)
Monetary unit: Gibraltar pound
Literacy rate: Negligible
Economic summary: Gross national product (1980): $150 million. Average annual growth rate (1970–79): 4.6%. Exports: re-exports of tobacco, petroleum, wine. Imports: manufactured goods, fuels, foodstuffs. Major trading partners: U.K., Morocco, Portugal, Netherlands.

Gibraltar, at the south end of the Iberian Peninsula, is a rocky promonotory commanding the western entrance to the Mediterranean. Aside from its strategic importance, it is also a free port, naval base, and coaling station. It was captured by the Arabs crossing from Africa into Spain in A.D. 711. In the 15th century, it passed to the Moorish ruler of Granada and later became Spanish. It was captured by an Anglo-Dutch force in 1704 during the War of the Spanish Succession and passed to Great Britain by the Treaty of Utrecht in 1713. Most of the inhabitants of Gibraltar are of Spanish, Italian, and Maltese descent.

Spanish efforts to recover Gibraltar culminated in a referendum in 1967 in which the residents voted overwhelmingly to retain their link with Britain. Spain sealed Gibraltar's land border in 1969 and did not open communications until April 1980, after the two governments had agreed to solve their dispute in keeping with a United Nations resolution calling for restoration of the "Rock" to Spain.

HONG KONG

Status: Dependency
Governor: Sir Edward Youde (1982)
Area: 398 sq mi. (1,031 sq km)
Population (est. 1982): 5,250,000 (average annual growth rate: 2.3%)
Density per sq mi.: 13,191.0
Capital (1976 census): Victoria (Hong Kong Island), 501,700
Monetary unit: Hong Kong dollar
Literacy rate (1981): 75%
Economic summary: Gross national product (1980): $21.5 billion. Average annual growth rate (1970–79): 6.5%. Per capita income (1980): $4,210. Land used for agriculture: 14%: labor force, 3%; principal products: vegetables, rice, dairy products. Labor force in industry: 51%; major industrial products: textiles, clothing, toys, transistor radios, watches, electronic components. Exports: clothing, textiles, toys, watches, transistor radios, electronic components. Imports: raw materials, consumer goods, food. Major trading partners: U.S., U.K., Japan, West Germany, China.

The crown colony of Hong Kong comprises the island of Hong Kong (32 sq mi.; 83 sq km), Stonecutters' Island, Kowloon Peninsula, and the New Territories on the adjoining mainland. The island of Hong Kong, located at the mouth of the Pearl River about 90 miles (145 km) southeast of Canton, was ceded to the Britain in 1841.

Stonecutters' Island and Kowloon were annexed in 1860, and the New Territories, which are mainly agricultural lands, were leased from China in 1898 for 99 years. Hong Kong was attacked by Japanese troops Dec. 7, 1941, and surrendered the following Christmas. It remained under Japanese occupation until August 1945.

Possessing an excellent natural harbor, the only safe deep-sea anchorage between Shanghai and Southeast Asia, Hong Kong is the transshipment center for trade throughout southern China and the western Pacific.

The cities of Victoria and Kowloon contain the greater part of the population, which is overwhelmingly Chinese. Besides those Chinese engaged in agriculture or industry, many live in sampans or junks either in Victoria harbor or neighboring bays, supporting themselves by fishing or by performing labor on the wharves.

In 1974, Hong Kong rescinded a policy of accepting illegal immigrants from China that had, since 1968, made the crowded city a sanctuary for thousands of Chinese refugees.

ISLE OF MAN

Status: Dependency
Lieutenant Governor: Sir John Paul
Area: 227 sq mi. (588 sq km)
Population (est. 1982): 70,000
Capital (est. 1976): Douglas, 20,300
Monetary unit: Isle of Man pound

Situated in the Irish Sea, equidistant from Scotland, Ireland, and England, the Isle of Man is administered according to its own laws by a government composed of the Lieutenant Governor, a Legislative Council, and a House of Keys, one of the most ancient legislative assemblies in the world.

The chief exports are beef and lamb, fish, and livestock.

LEEWARD ISLANDS

See British Virgin Islands; Montserrat; West Indies Associated States

MONTSERRAT

Status: Dependency
Governor: D. K. H. Dale
Area: 40 sq mi. (104 sq km)
Population (est. 1978): 13,500
Capital (est. 1975): Plymouth, 1,260
Monetary unit: East Caribbean dollar

The island of Montserrat is in the Lesser Antilles of the West Indies. Until 1956, it was a division of the Leeward Islands. It did not join the West Indies Associated States established in 1967.

The chief exports are cattle, potatoes, cotton, lint, recapped tires, mangoes, tomatoes.

PITCAIRN ISLAND

Status: Dependency
Governor: R. J. Stratton (1980)
Island Magistrate: Ivan Christian
Area: 1.75 sq mi. (4.5 sq km)
Population (est. 1980): 63
Capital: Adamstown

Pitcairn Island, in the South Pacific about midway between Australia and South America, consists of the island of Pitcairn and the three uninhabited islands of Henderson, Duicie, and Oeno. The island of Pitcairn was settled in 1790 by British mutineers from the ship *Bounty,* commanded by Capt. William Bligh. It was annexed as a British colony in 1838. Overpopulation forced removal of the settlement to Norfolk Island in 1856, but about 40 persons soon returned.

The colony is governed by a 10-member Council presided over by the Island Magistrate, who is elected for a three-year term.

ST. HELENA

Status: Dependency
Governor: G. D. Massingham
Area: 47 sq mi. (122 sq km)
Population (est 1979): 7,300
Capital (est. 1978): Jamestown, 1,500
Monetary unit: Pound sterling

St. Helena is a volcanic island in the South Atlantic about 1,100 miles (1,770 km) from the west coast of Africa. It is famous as the place of exile of Napoleon (1815–21).

It was taken for England in 1659 by the East India Company and was brought under the direct government of the Crown in 1834.

St. Helena has two dependencies: Ascension (34 sq mi.; 88 sq km), an island about 700 miles (1,127 km) northwest of St. Helena; and Tristan da Cunha (40 sq mi.; 104 sq km), a group of six islands about 1,500 miles (2,414 km) south-southwest of St. Helena.

ST. KITTS-NEVIS

See West Indies Associated States

TURKS AND CAICOS ISLANDS

Status: Dependency
Governor: Christopher Turner
Area: 193 sq mi. (500 sq km)
Population (est. 1978): 6,200
Capital (est. 1977): Grand Turk, 2,900
Monetary unit: U.S. dollar

These two groups of islands are situated at the southeast end of the Bahamas. The principal islands in the Turks group are Grand Turk and Salt Cay; the principal ones in the Caicos group are South Caicos, East Caicos, Middle (or Grand) Caicos, North Caicos, Providenciales, and West Caicos.

The Turks and Caicos Islands were dependencies of Jamaica until 1959, when they became a unit territory within the Federation of the West Indies. In 1962, when Jamaica became independent, the Turks and Caicos became a British crown colony. The present Constitution has been in force since 1969.

Chief exports in 1974 were crayfish (73%) and conch (25%).

VIRGIN ISLANDS

See British Virgin Islands

WEST INDIES ASSOCIATED STATES

Status: Self-governing territories in free association with the United Kingdom, which is responsible for defense and external affairs. The British Government conducts its affairs with the West Indies Associated States through an official representative, whose office is in Bridgetown, Barbados.
British Representative: J. S. Arthur (1978)
Area: St. Christopher (Kitts)-Nevis-Anguilla, 153 sq mi. (397 sq km)
Population (est. 1980): St. Christopher (Kitts)-Nevis-Anguilla, 70,000
Capitals: St. Christopher (Kitts)-Nevis-Anguilla: Basseterre (on St. Kitts), 15,900
Monetary unit: East Caribbean dollar
Economic summary: St. Christopher–Nevis–Anguilla: Gross domestic product (1977): $32 million. Per capita income: $580. Principal agricultural products: sugar, cotton. Major industries: sugar processing, salt extraction. Exports: sugar, molasses. Imports: foodstuffs, manufactured goods. Major trading partners: U.S., U.K., Japan.

The West Indies Associated States were established in 1967 and consisted of Antigua and St. Kitts-Nevis-Anguilla of the Leeward Islands, and Dominica, Grenada, St. Lucia, and St. Vincent of the Windward Islands. Statehood for St. Vincent was held up until 1969 because of local political uncertainties. (Grenada became independent in 1974, Dominica in 1978, St. Lucia and St. Vincent in 1979, and Antigua (known as Antigua and Barbuda) in 1981.

Two members of the Leeward group—the British Virgin Islands and Montserrat—did not become Associated States.

Each of the Associated States is fully self-governing in its internal affairs.

The association between Britain and each state is to be free and voluntary. As a guarantee of its voluntary nature, association will be terminable by either party. On termination of association, the state would become independent of Britain.

In 1967, Anguilla declared its independence from the St. Kitts-Nevis-Anguilla federation. Britain however, did not recognize this action. In February 1969, Anguilla voted to cut all ties with Britain and become an independent republic. In March, Britain landed troops on the island and, on March 30, a truce was signed. In July 1971, Anguilla became a dependency of Britain and two months later Britain ordered the withdrawal of all its troops.

A new Constitution for Anguilla, effective in February 1976, provides for separate administration and a government of elected representatives. The Associated State of St. Kitts-Nevis-Anguilla remains in being, but Anguilla has a separate relationship with Britain.

WINDWARD ISLANDS

See West Indies Associated States

UPPER VOLTA

Republic of Upper Volta
President of Military Committee of Reform for National Progress: Col. Sayé Zerbo

Area: 105,870 sq mi. (274,200 sq km)
Population (est 1982): 7,170,000 (average annual growth rate, 0.6%)
Density per square mile: 67.7
Capital and largest city (est. 1980): Ouagadougou, 235,000
Monetary unit: Franc CFA
Ethnic groups: Mossis, Bobos
Languages: French, African languages
Religion: Animist, 50%; Islam, 17%; Roman Catholic, 8%
National name: République de Haute-Volta
Literacy rate (1981): 10%
Economic summary: Gross national product (1980): $1.1 billion. Average annual growth rate (1970–79): −1.2%. Per capita income (1980): $190. Labor force in agriculture: 95%; principal products: millet, sorghum, corn, rice, livestock, peanuts, sugar cane, cotton. Major industrial products: processed agricultural products, light industrial items, brick, brewed products. Natural resources: manganese, limestone, marble, gold, uranium, bauxite, copper. Exports: livestock, peanuts, cotton. Imports: textiles, food and consumer goods, transport equipment, machinery, fuels. Major trading partners: Ivory Coast, France, Ghana, Western European nations.

Geography. Slightly larger than Colorado, Upper Volta is a landlocked country in West Africa. Its neighbors are the Ivory Coast, Mali, Niger, Benin, Togo, and Ghana. The country consists of extensive plains, low hills, high savannas, and a desert area in the north.

Government. Under a Constitution adopted by referendum in 1977, executive power is vested in a President elected by popular vote for a four-year term. Legislative power rests with a 57-member National Assembly elected for four years.

History. Upper Volta consists chiefly of the lands of the Mossi Empire, where France established a protectorate over the Kingdom of Ouagadougou in 1897. Upper Volta became a separate colony in 1919, was partitioned among Niger, the Sudan, and the Ivory Coast in 1933 and was reconstituted in 1947. An autonomous republic within the French Community, it became independent on Aug. 5, 1960.

President Maurice Yameogo was deposed on Jan. 3, 1966, by a military coup led by Col. Sangoulé Lamizana, who dissolved the National Assembly and suspended the Constitution. A new Constitution was adopted later that year and a new Assembly was elected. However, dissension within the Volta Democratic Union, the major party, led to renewed military rule. Constitutional rule returned in 1978 with the election of an Assembly and a presidential vote in June in which Gen. Lamizana won by a narrow margin over three other candidates.

In 1973, Upper Volta formed, with six other nations, the Economic Community for West Africa to promote economic development in the region.

On Nov. 25, 1980, there was a bloodless coup which placed Gen. Lamizana under house arrest. Col. Sayé Zerbo took charge as the President of the Military Committee of Reform for National Progress.

URUGUAY

Oriental Republic of Uruguay
President: Gen. Gregorio Alvarez (1981)
Area: 68,548 sq mi. (177,539 sq km)
Population (est. 1982): 2,950,000 (average annual growth rate: 0.6%)
Density per square mile: 43.0
Capital and largest city (est. 1980): Montevideo, 1,250,000
Monetary unit: New peso
Language: Spanish
Religion: Roman Catholic
National name: República Oriental del Uruguay
Literacy rate (1981): 90%
Economic summary: Gross national product (1980): $8.2 billion. Average annual growth rate (1970–79): 2.9%. Per capita income (1980): $2,820. Land used for agriculture: 85%; labor force: 20%; principal products: livestock, grains. Labor force in industry: 29%; major products: processed meats, wool and hides, textiles, shoes, handbags and leather wearing apparel, cement, refined petroleum. Natural resources: hydroelectric power potential. Exports: meat, hides, wool, textiles. Imports: crude petroleum, transportation equipment, chemicals, machinery, metals. Major trading partners: U.S., Brazil, Argentina.

Geography. Uruguay, on the east coast of South America south of Brazil and east of Argentina, is comparable in size to the State of Washington.

The country consists of a low, rolling plain in the south and a low plateau in the north. It has a 120-mile (193 km) Atlantic shore line, a 235-mile (378 km) frontage on the Rio de la Plata, and 270 miles (435 km) on the Uruguay River, its western boundary.

Government. The President serves for a term of five years. He appoints a Council of 11 ministers to assist him. Before it was dissolved, Congress consisted of the Senate and the House of Deputies. Members remained in office for five years.

In June 1973, President Juan María Bordaberry yielded to military pressure and dissolved Congress, thus ending 40 years of constitutional rule. His decree announced creation of a Council of State to perform Congressional functions, oversee presidential activities, and formulate constitutional reforms for a national plebiscite.

Political activity has been banned since 1973.

History. Juan Díaz de Solis, a Spaniard, discovered Uruguay in 1516, but the Portuguese were first to settle it when they founded Colonia in 1680. After a long struggle, Spain wrested the country from Portugal in 1778. Uruguay revolted against Spain in 1811, only to be conquered in 1816–20 by the Portuguese from Brazil. Independence was reasserted with Argentine help in 1825, and the republic was set up in 1830.

Independence, however, did not restore order, and a revolt in 1836 touched off nearly 50 years of factional strife, with occasional armed intervention from Argentina and Brazil.

Alberto Heber, who became President in 1966, vigorously championed reform, and a referendum authorized revision of the Constitution to vest executive powers in a President and a Cabinet of Ministers. Oscar Diego Gestido, elected President later that year, devoted much effort to improving the ailing economy. But he died the next year and was succeeded by Jorge Pacheco Areco.

Siege-state regulations were instituted after the Tupámaros first urban guerrilla organization launched a series of spectacular kidnappings, bank and casino robberies (one gold haul netted over $250,000), and arms raids on military arsenals to embarrass what was then the most democratic government in South America. In 1970, the Tupámaros kidnapped a U.S. aid adviser, Dan Mitrione, and killed him when their ransom demands were not met.

The continuing economic, political, and guerrilla problems precipitated impeachment proceedings against Pacheco in 1971. A bitterly fought election followed, with Juan María Bordaberry, Pacheco's hand-picked choice, the winner.

Disputes between the government and the military, coupled with worsening economic problems (the peso was devalued 32 times during Bordaberry's first three years in office), led to a military revolt in February 1973 that ended in an agreement with Bordaberry in which the military promised to maintain the constitutional system but virtually took over control of the government.

Despite the military takeover, inflation soared at a 100% yearly rate and the Tupámaros continued to be active. Their assassinations and bombings were matched by government repression; an estimated 3,500 persons were arrested on political charges in the year after Congress was dissolved, and the press was kept tightly in line.

Military leaders, citing Bordaberry's opposition to the return of constitutional government, removed him from office in 1976. The National Council of 25 military officers and 21 civilians designated Aparicio Méndez to take over the Presidency for a five-year term.

Although the government in 1977 reported that sentences for political prisoners would be reduced, Amnesty International estimated that 5,000 such prisoners were being held in Uruguay, more than in any other Latin nation. The Carter Administration cut economic aid from $220,000 to $25,000 and eliminated military sales credits of $3 million for Uruguay because of the human-rights situation. The Uruguayan government then declared that it would refuse any U.S. aid.

In November 1980, voters rejected a draft Constitution that would have given the military permanent power. The Council designated Gen. Gregorio Alvarez, retired commander in chief of the army, as President in September 1981, and shortly afterward a promised discussion of the restoration of a civilian government foundered in a dispute between military leaders and politicians.

VANUATU

Republic of Vanuatu
President: George Sokomanu (1980)
Prime Minster: Rev. Walter Lini (1980)
Area: 5,700 sq mi. (14,763,sq km)
Population (est. 1982): 125,000 (average annual growth rate: 2.7%)
Density per square mile: 21.9
Capital (est. 1979): Vila, 15,000
Monetary unit: Vatu
Religions: Presbyterian, 40%; Roman Catholic, 16%; Anglican, 14%; other Christian, 15%; Animist, 15%
Literacy rate (1981): 15%
Economic Summary: Gross national product (1980): $60 million. Per Capita Income (1980): $530. Average annual growth rate (1970–78): 1.9%. Principal agricultural products: copra, cocoa, coffee, livestock. Exports: copra, cocoa, coffee, frozen fish. Imports: food. Major trading partners: France, U.S., Japan.

Geography. Formerly known as the New Hebrides, Vanuatu is an archipelago of some 80 islands lying between New Caledonia and Fiji in the South Pacific. Largest of the islands is Espiritu Santo (875 sq mi.; 2,266 sq km); others are Efate, Malekula, Malo, Pentecost, and Tanna. The population is largely Melanesian of mixed blood.

Government. The constitution by which Vanuatu achieved independence on July 30, 1980, vests executive authority in a President, elected by an electoral college for a five-year term. A unicameral legislature of 39 members exercises legislative power. The Vanuaaku party, led by Prime Minister Walter Lini, holds 26 seats.

History. The islands were discovered by Pedro Fernandes de Queiros of Portugal in 1606 and were charted and named by the British navigator James Cook in 1774. Conflicting British and French interests were resolved by a joint naval commission that administered the islands from 1887. A condominium government was established in 1906.

The islands' plantation economy, based on imported Vietnamese labor, was prosperous until the 1920s, when markets for its products declined. The New Hebrides escaped Japanese occupation in World War II and the French population was among the first to support the Gaullist Free French movement.

A brief rebellion by French settlers and plantation workers on Espiritu Santo led by Jimmy Stevens in May 1980 threatened the scheduled independence of the islands. Britain sent a company of Royal Marines and France a contingent of 50 policemen to quell the revolt, which the new government said was financed by the Phoenix Foundation, a right-wing U.S. group. With the British and French forces replaced by soldiers from Papua New Guinea, independence ceremonies took place on July 30. The next month it was reported that Stevens had been arrested and the revolt quelled.

VATICAN CITY STATE

Ruler: Pope John Paul II (1978)
Area: 0.17 sq mi. (0.44 sq km)
Population (est. 1982): 1,000 (Italian, 85%; Swiss and others, 15%)
Density per square mile: 5,882.4
Monetary unit: Lira
Languages: Latin, Italian
Religion: Roman Catholic
National name: Stato della Città del Vaticano

Geography. The Vatican City State is situated on the Vatican hill, on the right bank of the Tiber River, within the commune of Rome.

Government. The Pope has full legal, executive, and judicial powers. Executive power over the area is in the hands of a Commission of Cardinals appointed by the Pope. The College of Cardinals is the Pope's chief advisory body, and upon his death the cardinals elect his successor for life. The cardinals themselves are created for life by the Pope.

In the Vatican the central administration of the Roman Catholic Church throughout the world is carried on by 11 congregations, three tribunals, three main secretariats, and numerous councils, committees, and commissions. In its diplomatic relations, the Holy See is represented by the Papal Secretary of State.

History. The Vatican City State, sovereign and independent, is the survivor of the papal states that in 1859 comprised an area of some 17,000 square miles (44,030 sq km). During the struggle for Italian unification, from 1860 to 1870, most of this area became part of Italy.

By an Italian law of May 13, 1871, the temporal power of the Pope was abrogated, and the territory of the Papacy was confined to the Vatican and Lateran palaces and the villa of Castel Gandolfo. The Popes consistently refused to recognize this arrangement and, by the Lateran Treaty of Feb. 11, 1929, between the Vatican and the Kingdom of Italy, the exclusive dominion and sovereign jurisdiction of the Holy See over the city of the Vatican was again recognized, thus restoring the Pope's temporal authority over the area.

The first session of Ecumenical Council Vatican II was opened by John XXIII on Oct. 11, 1962, to plan and set policies for the modernization of the Roman Catholic Church. Pope Paul VI continued the Council, opening the second session on Sept. 29, 1963.

On Aug. 26, 1978, Cardinal Albino Luciani was chosen by the College of Cardinals to succeed Paul VI, who had died of a heart attack on Aug. 6. The new Pope, who took the name John Paul I, was born on Oct. 17, 1912, at Forno di Canale in Italy. (For a listing of all the Popes, *see* the Index.)

Only 34 days after his election, John Paul I died of a heart attack, ending the shortest reign in 373 years. On Oct. 16, Cardinal Karol Wojtyla, 58, was chosen Pope and took the name John Paul II. The first Polish Pope was also the first to have been named from a communist nation.

John Paul II visited his homeland in June 1979, exhorting millions to "never lose your spiritual freedom" and telling workers that Christ would not accept that man be considered "merely as a means of production." The trip was a triumph for the warm, outgoing Pontiff despite the Polish government's undisguised efforts to dampen the public impact of his visit.

A visit to the Irish Republic and to the United States in September and October 1979, followed by a 12-nation African tour in May 1980 and a visit in July to Brazil, the most populous Catholic nation, further established John Paul's image as a "people's" Pope. But he also used his travels to preach a more conservative doctrine, cautioning U.S. nuns against seeking priestly functions and sternly opposing abortion and contraception. During his African journey, he reaffirmed long-ignored canon laws against political roles for the clergy. On May 13, 1981, a Turkish terrorist shot the Pope in St. Peter's Square, the first assassination attempt against the pontiff in modern times. Mehmet Ali Agca was sentenced on July 22 to life imprisonment by an Italian Court.

In October 1981, the Pope named a new temporary head of the powerful Society of Jesus, which normally chooses its own leader. The action was seen both as a reversal of the decentralizing trend of Vatican II and as a curbing of political activism by Jesuits. However, the Pope relented and in February 1982 announced that he would permit an election of a permanent director of the order later in the year.

A controversial trip to Britain, the first by a reigning Pope, was almost canceled in June because of the war with Argentina over the Falkland Islands. To offset criticism in Catholic Argentina, the Pontiff also made a hastily arranged visit to Buenos Aires.

VENEZUELA

Republic of Venezuela
President: Luis Herrera Campíns (1979)
Area: 352,143 sq mi. (912,050 sq km)
Population (est. 1982): 14,700,000 (average annual growth rate: 2.8%) (mestizo, 69%; white, 20%; black, 9%; Indian, 2%)
Density per square mile: 41.7
Capital: Caracas
Largest cities (est. 1981 for metropolitan area): Caracas, 3,000,000; (est. 1977): Maracaibo, 820,000; Valencia, 455,000; Barquiisimeto, 444,000
Monetary unit: Bolívar
Language: Spanish
Religion: Roman Catholic
National name: República de Venezuela
Literacy rate (1970): 70%
Economic summary: Gross national product (1980): $54.2 billion. Average annual growth rate (1970–79): 2.7%. Per capita income (1980): $3,630. Land used for agriculture, 4%; labor force, 24%; principal products: rice, coffee, corn, sugar, bananas, dairy, meat, and poultry products. Labor force in industry, 23%; principal products: refined petroleum products, iron and steel, paper products, aluminum, textiles, transport equipment. Natural resources: petroleum, natural gas, iron ore, gold, hydroelectric power. Exports: petroleum, iron ore, coffee. Imports: industrial machinery and equipment, manufactures, chemicals, foodstuffs. Major trading partners: U.S., Canada, West Germany, Japan.

Geography. Venezuela, a third larger than Texas, occupies most of the northern coast of South America on the Caribbean Sea. It is bordered by Colombia to the west, Guyana to the east, and Brazil to the south.

Mountain systems break Venezuela into four distinct areas: (1) the Maracaibo lowlands; (2) the mountainous region in the north and northwest; (3) the Orinoco basin, with the llanos (vast grass-covered plains) on its northern border and great forest areas in the south and southeast; (4) the Guiana Highlands, south of the Orinoco, accounting for nearly half the national territory. About 80% of Venezuela is drained by the Orinoco and its tributaries.

Government. Venezuela is a federal republic consisting of 20 states, the Federal District, two territories and 72 islands in the Caribbean. There is a bicameral Congress, the 52 members of the Senate and the 213 members of the Chamber of Deputies being elected by popular vote to five-year terms. The President is also elected for five years. He must be a Venezuelan by birth and over 30 years old. He is not eligible for re-election until 10 years after the end of his term.

The major political parties are the Democratic Action Party, with 23 of 52 Senate seats and 83 of 213 seats in the Chamber of Deputies; Social Christian Party, with 22 Senate seats and 83 Chamber seats, People's Electoral Movement, Democratic Republican Union.

History. Columbus discovered Venezuela on his third voyage in 1498. A subsequent Spanish explorer gave the country its name, meaning "Little Venice." There were no important settlements until

Caracas was founded in 1567. Simón Bolívar, who led the liberation of much of the continent from Spain, was born in Caracas in 1783. With Bolívar taking part, Venezuela was one of the first South American colonies to revolt against Spain, in 1810, but it was not until 1821 that independence was won. Federated at first with Colombia and Ecuador, the country set up a republic in 1830 and then sank for many decades into a condition of revolt, dictatorship, and corruption.

From 1908 to 1935, Gen. Juan Vicente Gómez ruled tyrannically, picking satellites to alternate with him in the presidential palace. Thereafter, there was a struggle between democratic forces and those backing a return to strong-man rule. Dr. Rómulo Betancourt and the liberal Acción Democrática Party won a majority of seats in a constituent assembly to draft a new Constitution in 1946. A well-known writer, Rómulo Gallegos, candidate of Betancourt's party, easily won the presidential election of 1947. But, the army ousted Gallegos the next year and instituted a military junta.

The country overthrew the dictatorship in 1958 and thereafter enjoyed democratic government. Rafael Caldera Rodríguez, President from 1969 to 1974, legalized the Communist Party and established diplomatic relations with Moscow.

Venezuela and neighboring Guyana in 1970 called a 12-year moratorium on their border dispute (Venezuela claims 50,000 square miles of Guyana's 83,000).

As a charter member of the Organization of Petroleum Exporting Countries (OPEC), Venezuela shared the benefits of the tripled oil prices engineered by OPEC, but did not join the 1973 Arab oil boycott. President Carlos Andrés Pérez took office in 1974, committed to give all Venezuelans a stake in the oil bonanza that made his country the richest in South America.

In 1976, Venezuela nationalized 21 oil companies, mostly subsidiaries of U.S. firms, offering compensation of $1.28 billion. Oil income in that year was $9.9 billion, and although production decreased 2.2%, revenue remained at the same level in 1977 because of higher prices, largely financing an ambitious social welfare program.

Despite his difficulties at home, Pérez continued to play an active foreign role in extending economic aid to Latin neighbors, in backing the human-rights policy of President Carter, and in supporting Carter's return of the Panama Canal to Panama.

Opposition Christian Democrats capitalized on Pérez's domestic problems to elect Luis Herrera Campíns President in Venezuela's fifth consecutive free election, on Dec. 3, 1978. At his inauguration in March 1979, Herrera called for "fiscal discipline" to reduce a record foreign debt of $7.4 billion despite soaring oil revenues.

Herrera Campins at first supported U.S. policy in Central America, lining up with the majority of Latin nations behind the Christian Democratic government of José Napoleón Duarte in El Salvador, but he later shifted toward a "political solution" that would include the insurgents. In March 1982, he assailed Reagan's policy as "interventionist."

When the Falklands war broke out, Venezuela became one of the most vigorous advocates of the Argentine cause and one of the sharpest critics of the U.S. decision to back Britain. Herrera's position here was thought to be related to the renewal of Venezuela's claims to much of neighboring Guyana, claims that, like Argentina's to the Falkland Islands, rested on inherited Spanish rights.

VIETNAM

Socialist Republic of Vietnam
President: Truong Chinh (1981)
Premier: Pham Van Dong (1976)
Area: 126,436 sq mi. (327,469 sq km)
Population (est. 1982): 56,250,000 (average annual growth rate: 2.5%)
Density per square mile: 444.9
Capital Hanoi
Largest cities (est. 1979): Ho Chi Minh City (Saigon),[1] 3,450,000; Hanoi, 2,600,000; (est. 1973): Da Nang, 492,200; Nha Trang, 216,200; Qui Nho'n, 213,750; Hue, 209,000; **(1960 census):** Haiphong, 182,490
Monetary unit: Dong
Languages: Vietnamese, French, Chinese
Religions: Buddhist, Roman Catholic, Cao-Dai, Hoa-Hao, Confucian, Animist
National name: Công Hòa Xa Hôi Chú Nghia Viêt Nam
Literacy rate: Not known
Economic summary: Gross national product (1978): $8.9 billion. Per capita income (1980): n.a. Land used for agriculture: 14%; labor force: 70%; principal products: rice, rubber, fruits and vegetables, corn, sugar cane, fish. Labor force in industry, 8%; major products: processed foods, textiles, cement, chemical fertilizers, glass, tires. Natural resources: forests, coal. Exports: agricultural products, coal, mineral ores. Imports: petroleum, steel products, railroad equipment, chemicals, medicines, raw cotton, fertilizer, grain. Major trading partners: U.S.S.R., Soviet bloc nations, Japan.

1. Includes suburb of Cholon.

Geography. Vietnam occupies the eastern and southern part of the Indochinese peninsula in Southeast Asia, with the South China Sea along its entire coast. China is to the north and Laos and Cambodia to the west. Long and narrow on a north-south axis, Vietnam is about twice the size of Arizona.

The Mekong River delta lies in the south and the Red River delta in the north. Heavily forested mountain and plateau regions make up most of the country.

Government. Less than a year after the capitulation of the former Republic of Vietnam (South Vietnam) on April 30, 1975, a joint National Assembly convened with 249 deputies representing the North and 243 representing the South. The Assembly set July 2, 1976, as the official reunification date. Hanoi became the capital and Ton Duc Thang, President of the Northern regime since 1969, became President of the new republic.

(By 1981, the National Assembly had increased to 496 members.)

Pham Van Dong, Premier in Hanoi since 1955, took over the new administration, and the Northern flag, anthem, and crest became the symbols of the new Vietnam.

Dang Cong san Vietnam (Communist Party), led by First Secretary Le Duan, is the ruling political party. There are also the Socialist Party and the Democratic Party.

History. The Vietnamese are descendants of Mongoloid nomads from China and migrants from Indonesia. They recognized Chinese suzerainty until the 15th century, an era of nationalistic expansion, when Cambodians were pushed out of the southern area of what is now Vietnam.

A century later, the Portuguese were the first Europeans to enter the area. France established its influence early in the 19th century and within 80 years conquered the three regions into which the country was then divided—Cochin-China in the south, Annam in the center, and Tonkin in the north.

France first unified Vietnam in 1887, when a single governor-generalship was created, followed by the first physical links between north and south—a rail and road system. Even at the beginning of World War II, however, there were internal differences among the three regions.

Japan took over military bases in Vietnam in 1940 and a pro-Vichy French administration remained until 1945. A veteran Communist leader, Ho Chi Minh, organized an independence movement known as the Vietminh to exploit a confused situation. At the end of the war, Ho's followers seized Hanoi and declared a short-lived republic, which ended with the arrival of French forces in 1946.

Paris proposed a unified government within the French Union under the former Annamite emperor, Bao Dai. Cochin-China and Annam accepted the proposal, and Bao Dai was proclaimed emperor of all Vietnam in 1949. Ho and the Vietminh withheld support, and the revolution in China gave them the outside help needed for a war of resistance against French and Vietnamese troops armed largely by the U.S.

A bitter defeat at Dien Bien Phu in northwest Vietnam on May 5, 1954, broke the French military campaign and brought the division of Vietnam at the conference of Geneva that year.

In the new South, Ngo Dinh Diem, Premier under Bao Dai, deposed the monarch in 1955 and established a republic with himself as President. Diem used strong U.S. backing to create an authoritarian regime that suppressed all opposition but could not eradicate the Northern-supplied Communist Viet Cong.

Skirmishing grew into a full-scale war, with escalating U.S. involvement. A military coup, U.S.-inspired in the view of many, ousted Diem Nov. 1, 1963, and a kaleidoscope of military governments followed. The most savage fighting of the war occurred in early 1968, during the Tet holidays.

Although the Viet Cong failed to overthrow the Saigon government, U.S. public reaction to the apparently endless war forced a limitation of U.S. troops to 550,000 and a new emphasis on shifting the burden of further combat to the South Vietnamese. Ho Chi Minh's death on Sept. 3, 1969, brought a quadrumvirate to replace him but no flagging in Northern will to fight.

U.S. bombing and invasion of Cambodia in the summer of 1970—an effort to destroy Viet Cong bases in the neighboring state—marked the end of major U.S. participation in the fighting. Most American ground troops were withdrawn from combat by mid-1971 as heavy bombing of the Ho Chi Minh trail from North Vietnam appeared to cut the supply of men and matériel to the South.

Secret negotiations for peace by Secretary of State Henry A. Kissinger with North Vietnamese officials during 1972 after heavy bombing of Hanoi and Haiphong brought the two sides near agreement in October. When the Northerners demanded the removal of the South's President Nguyen Van Thieu as their price, President Nixon ordered the "Christmas bombing" of the North. The conference resumed and a peace settlement was signed in Paris on Jan. 27, 1973. It called for release of all U.S. prisoners, withdrawal of U.S. forces, limitation of both sides' forces inside South Vietnam, and a commitment to peaceful reunification.

Despite Chinese and Soviet endorsement, the agreement foundered. U.S. bombing of Communist-held areas in Cambodia was halted by Congress in August 1973, and in the following year Communist action in South Vietnam increased.

An armored attack across the 17th parallel in January 1975 panicked the South Vietnamese army and brought the invasion within 40 miles of Saigon by April 9. Thieu resigned on April 21 and fled, to be replaced by Vice President Tran Van Huong, who quit a week later, turning over the office to Gen. Duong Van Minh. "Big Minh" surrendered Saigon on April 30, ending a war that took 1.3 million Vietnamese and 56,000 American lives, at the cost of $141 billion in U.S. aid.

"Re-education" of former South Vietnamese government and army personnel began immediately. By mid-1976, virtually all foreigners were expelled, even those married to Vietnamese.

On May 3, 1977, the U.S. and Vietnam opened negotiations in Paris to normalize relations. One of the first results was the withdrawal of U.S. opposition to Vietnamese membership in the United Nations, formalized in the Security Council on July 20. Two major issues remained to be settled, however: the return of the bodies of some 2,500 U.S. servicemen missing in the war and the claim by Hanoi that former President Nixon had promised reconstruction aid under the 1973 agreement.

Negotiations failed to resolve these issues, and the question of recognition appeared to have been shelved indefinitely when the U.S. expelled the Vietnamese Ambassador to the United Nations, Dinh Ba Thi, early in 1978. Thi was accused of complicity in an espionage case in which a U.S. citizen and a Vietnamese refugee were later convicted of delivering U.S. intelligence to Hanoi.

The new year also brought an intensification of border clashes between Vietnam and Cambodia and accusations by China that Chinese residents of Vietnam were being subjected to persecution. Peking cut off all aid and withdrew 800 technicians.

By June, 133,000 ethnic Chinese were reported to have fled Vietnam, and a year later as many as 500,000 of the 1.8 million Vietnamese of Chinese ancestry were believed to have escaped. Half of these had gone by land or sea to China, where the government made it clear that no more refugees were welcome and tens of thousands more had survived boat passage to Thailand, Malaysia, Indonesia, or Hong Kong. U.S. officials said 100,000 may have died. Survivors said they had paid up to $5,000 in bribes to leave Vietnam, and U.S. and British officials charged Hanoi with a deliberate extortion policy.

Replying to worldwide criticism, Premier Pham Van Dong said only that he would try to limit the outflow. Other Vietnamese officials dismissed the "boat people" as misfits.

Hanoi was undoubtedly preoccupied with a continuing war in Cambodia, where 60,000 Vietnamese troops were aiding the Heng Samrin regime in suppressing the last forces of the pro-Chinese Pol Pot regime. In early 1979, Vietnam was conducting a two-front war, defending its northern border against a Chinese invasion and at the same time supporting its army in Cambodia.

Only a Soviet veto prevented Vietnam from being labeled an aggressor by the U.N. Security Council as Prince Shihanouk of Cambodia, released from house arrest by the Pol Pot regime, presented the case against Hanoi after the fall of Phnom Penh. Vietnam's ambassador, backed by the Soviet Union and the Soviet bloc, sought condemnation of Peking's invasion but could find no sympathizers.

Despite Hanoi's claims of total victory, resistance in Cambodia continued through 1982, prompting Vietnamese troops to raid guerrilla and refugee camps across the Thai border. Vietnam's second conflict, on its border with China, also flared sporadically.

Hanoi permitted four U.S. veterans of the Indochina war to visit Vietnam in December 1981 to discuss the missing U.S. servicemen and the effects of Agent Orange, a defoliant used during the war that veterans have claimed caused permanent damage to their health. Foreign Minister Nguyen Co Thach asked the men to continue to act as a liaison group for further discussion of the missing servicemen and, by implication, to promote recognition by the United States. State department officials concurred in the visit, but warned that diplomatic relations are "out of the question" as long as Vietnamese troops occupy Cambodia.

Economic troubles mounted for Vietnam in 1982, marked by a government shakeup that put Vo Van Kiet in charge of economic planning after a party congress admitted serious errors in economic policy. The government was seeking to reschedule its foreign hard-currency debts of $1.4 billion owed primarily to Japan and the International Monetary Fund.

(For a Vietnam War chronology, see Headline History.)

WESTERN SAMOA

Independent State of Western Samoa
Head of State: Malietoa Tanumafili II (1962)
Prime Minister: Vacant
Area: 1,133 sq mi. (2,934 sq km)
Population (est. 1982): 160,000 (average annual growth rate: 0.7%)
Density per square mile: 141.2
Capital and largest city (1980): Apia, 33,400
Monetary unit: Tala
Languages: Samoan and English
Religions: Congregational, 50%; Roman Catholic, 22%; Methodist, 16%
National name: Samoa i Sísífo
Member of Commonwealth of Nations
Literacy rate (1981): 90%
Economic summary: Gross national product (1978): $70 million. Per capita income (1978): $450. Land used for agriculture: 50%; labor force: 50%; principal products: copra, cocoa, bananas, timber. Labor force in industry: 10%; major products: timber, light industrial products. Natural resource: timber. Exports: copra, cocoa, bananas, timber. Imports: food, manufactured goods, machinery. Major trading partners: West Germany, New Zealand, Australia, Japan.

Geography. Western Samoa, the size of Rhode Island, is in the South Pacific Ocean about 2,200 miles (3,540 km) south of Hawaii midway to Sydney, Australia, and about 800 miles (1,287 km) northeast of Fiji. The larger islands in the Samoan chain are mountainous and of volcanic origin. There is little level land except in the coastal areas, where most cultivation takes place.

Government. Western Samoa has a 47-member Legislature, consisting mainly of the titleholders (chiefs) of family or tribal groups, with two members elected by universal suffrage to represent those not belonging to such groups. When the present Chiefs of State die, successors will be elected by the Legislature.

History. The Samoan islands were discovered in the 18th century and visited by Dutch and French traders. Toward the end of the 19th century, conflicting interests of the U.S., Britain, and Germany resulted in a treaty signed in 1899. It recognized the paramount interests of the U.S. in those islands east of 171° west longitude (American Samoa) and Germany's interests in the other islands (Western Samoa); the British withdrew in return for recognition of their rights in Tonga and the Solomons.

New Zealand occupied Western Samoa in 1914, and was granted a League of Nations mandate. In 1947, the islands became a U.N. trust territory administered by New Zealand.

Western Samoa became independent on Jan. 1, 1962.

YEMEN

People's Democratic Republic of Yemen
President: Ali Nasser Mohamed (1980)
Area: 111,000 sq mi. (287,490 sq km)[1]
Population (est. 1982): 2,100,000 (average annual growth rate: 2.8%)
Density per square mile: 18.9[1]
National capital and largest city (est. 1980): Aden, 343,000
Administrative capital: Madinat ash Sha'b
Monetary unit: Yemen dinar
Language: Arabic
Religion: Islam
National name: Jumhurijah al-Yemen al Dimuqratiyah al Sha'abijah
Literacy rate (1981): 10%
Economic summary: Gross national product (1980): $810 million. Average annual growth rate (1973–78): 12.7%. Per capita income (1980): $420. Land used for agriculture: 0.3%; labor force: 80%; principal products: sorghum, millet, wheat, cotton, coffee. Labor force in industry: 2–3%; major products: refined oil products, salt, fish meal, cloth. Natural resource: fish. Exports: petroleum products, textiles, cotton. Imports: crude oil, foodstuffs, manufactured goods. Major trading partners: U.K., Japan, Yemen Arab Republic.

1. Excluding Perim and Kamaran islands.

Geography. Formerly known as Southern Yemen, the People's Democratic Republic of Yemen extends along the southern part of the Arabian Peninsula on the Gulf of Aden and the Indian Ocean. It is comparable in size to Nevada. The Yemen Arab Republic is to the northwest, Saudi Arabia to the north, and Oman to the east.

A 700-mile (1,130-km) narrow coastal plain gives way to a mountainous region and then a plateau area.

Government. On June 22, 1969, President Qahtan Mohammed al Shaabi resigned and was replaced by a five-man Presidential Council.

A Constitution published in 1970 changed the state's name from Southern Yemen and established a 111-seat legislature, the People's Supreme Council of which Ali Nasser is chairman, and thus head of state. The only legal political party is the Yemeni Socialist Party.

History. The People's Republic of Southern Yemen was established Nov. 30, 1967, when Britain granted independence to the Federation of South Arabia. This Federation consisted of the state (once the colony) of Aden and 16 of the 20 states of the Protectorate of South Arabia (once the Aden Protectorate). The four states of the Protectorate that did not join the Federation later became part of Southern Yemen.

Salim Robea Ali, chairman of the Presidential Council since its establishment in 1969, was ousted and executed June 26, 1978, two days after the assassination of President Ahmed Hussein al-Ghashmi of the Yemen Arab Republic. Premier Ali Nasser Mohammed assumed the added duty of Council head.

Abdul Fattah Ismail, Secretary General of the ruling party who was elected President by the Supreme Council on Dec. 27, 1978, reversed Robea's movement toward reconciliation with the Yemen Arab Republic and an accommodation with Saudi Arabia. Despite Fattah Ismail's acquiescence to the continuing build-up of Soviet military strength in the country in conjunction with the Soviet invasion of Afghanistan, he proved to be an embarrassment to Moscow. His sudden resignation on April 21, 1980, was reported to have stemmed from the new Soviet desire to win friends in the Yemen Arab Republic and Saudi Arabia.

YEMEN ARAB REPUBLIC

President: Col. Ali Abdulla Saleh (1978)
Premier: Abdel Karim al-Iriani (1980)
Area: 75,290 sq mi. (195,000 sq km)
Population (est. 1982): 8,575,000 (average annual growth rate: 2.3%)
Density per square mile: 113.9
Capital and largest city (est. 1980): San'a', 210,000
Monetary unit: Rial
Language: Arabic
Religion: Islam
National name: Al Jamhuriya al Arabiya Yamaniya
Literacy rate (1981): 15% (est.)
Economic summary: Gross national product (1980): $2.7 billion. Per capita income (1980): $460. Land used for agriculture: 20%; labor force: 95%; principal products: wheat, sorghum, cattle, sheep, cotton, fruits. Major industrial products: consumer goods, construction materials. Natural resources: traces of copper, sulfur, coal, quartz. Exports: cotton, coffee, hides and skins. Imports: textiles and other manufactured consumer goods, petroleum and petroleum products, sugar, grain, flour. Major trading partners: China, Yemen (Aden), U.S.S.R., Japan, U.K., Australia.

Geography. The Yemen Arab Republic occupies the southwestern tip of the Arabian Peninsula, with its western coast on the Red Sea opposite Ethiopia. Its neighbors are Saudi Arabia to the north and east and the People's Democratic Republic of Yemen to the south. Its area is slightly less than that of South Dakota.

A north-south coastal plain 20–50 miles wide (32–80 km) lies in the west; eastward, there are the interior highlands, which attain a height of 12,000 feet (3,660 m), and the expanse of the Rub 'al-Khali Desert.

Government. The country's first permanent Constitution was submitted to the National Assembly in 1971. It provided for a 179-member legislature, the Consultative Council, 20 of whose members would be chosen by the President and the rest elected every four years. A five-man executive Presidential Council was to be chosen by the Consultative Council.

A merger agreement between Yemen and the People's Democratic Republic of Yemen (Southern Yemen) was signed by the two states in 1972 after bitter border clashes between them over a five-year period. A new Constitution was to be drafted, but meanwhile the joint government was to be "republican, nationalist, and democratic," ruled by a single, merged Presidential Council and unified legislative, executive, and judicial branches.

In 1974, the army ousted the government in a bloodless coup and suspended the Constitution and its various legislative bodies.

History. The history of Yemen dates back to the Minaean kingdom (1200–650 B.C.). It accepted Islam in A.D. 628, and in the 10th century came under the control of the Rassite dynasty of the Zaidi sect. The Turks occupied the area from 1538 to 1630 and from 1849 to 1918. The sovereign status of Yemen was confirmed by treaties signed with Saudi Arabia and Britain in 1934.

Yemen joined the Arab League in 1945 and established diplomatic relations with the U.S. in 1946.

In 1962, a military revolt of elements favoring President Gamal Abdel Nasser of Egypt broke out. A ruling junta proclaimed a republic, and Yemen became an international battleground, with Egypt and the U.S.S.R. supporting the revolutionaries, and King Saud of Saudi Arabia and King Hussein of Jordan the royalists. The civil war continued until the war between the Arab states and Israel broke out in June 1967. Nasser had to pull out many of his troops and agree to a cease-fire and withdrawal of foreign forces. The war finally ended with the defeat of the royalists in mid-1969.

In 1977, Col. Ibrahim al-Hamidi was assassinated after three years as head of government and was succeeded by Lt. Col. Ahmed Hussein al-Ghashmi as head of the Presidential Council. On June 24, 1978, al-Ghashmi was killed by a bomb as he received the credentials of a new ambassador from the People's Democratic Republic of Yemen. The People's Council elected Col. Ali Abdulla Saleh as President on July 17.

YUGOSLAVIA

Socialist Federal Republic of Yugoslavia
President: Sergej Krajger (1981)
President of Federal Executive Council (Premier): Milka Planinc (1982)
Area: 98,766 sq mi. (255,804 sq km)
Population (1982 census): 22,412,000 (average annual growth rate: 0.8%) (Serbian, 36%; Croatian, 18%; Moslem, 9%; Slovene, 8%; Albanian, 8%; Macedonian, 6%)
Density per square mile: 226.9
Capital: Belgrade
Largest cities (est. 1980): Belgrade, 1,000,000; (1971 census): Zagreb, 566,224; Skopje, 312,980; Sarajevo, 243,980; Ljubljana, 173,853; Split, 152,905
Monetary unit: Dinar

Languages: Serbo-Croatian, Slovene, Macedonian (all official)
Religions: Greek Orthodox, 41%; Roman Catholic, 32%; Islam, 12%
National name: Socijalisticka Federativna Republika Jugoslavija
Literacy rate (1961): 61%
Economic summary: Gross national product (1980): $58.6 billion. Average annual growth rate (1970–79): 5.4%. Per capita income (1980): $2,620. Land used for agriculture: 33%; labor force: 29%; principal products: corn, wheat, tobacco, sugar beets. Labor force in industry: 52%; major products: wood, processed food, nonferrous metals, machinery, textiles. Natural resources: bauxite, timber, antimony, chromium, lead, zinc, asbestos, mercury, cadmium. Exports: raw materials, equipment, consumer goods. Imports: raw materials, equipment, consumer goods. Major trading partners: U.S.S.R., West Germany, Italy, U.S.

Geography. Yugoslavia fronts on the eastern coast of the Adriatic Sea opposite Italy. Its neighbors are Austria, Italy, and Hungary to the north, Romania and Bulgaria to the east, and Greece and Albania to the south. It is slightly larger than Wyoming.

About half of Yugoslavia is mountainous. In the north, the Dinaric Alps rise abruptly from the sea and progress eastward as a barren limestone plateau called the Karst. Montenegro is a jumbled mass of mountains, containing also some grassy slopes and fertile river valleys. Southern Serbia, too, is mountainous. A rich plain in the north and northeast, drained by the Danube, is the most fertile area of the country.

Government. Yugoslavia is a federal republic composed of six socialist republics—Serbia (which includes the provinces of Vojvodina and Kosovo), Croatia, Slovenia, Bosnia-Herzegovina, Macedonia, and Montenegro. Actual administration is carried on by the Federal Executive Council and its secretaries.

The League of Communists and the Socialist Alliance of the Working People are the major political parties.

History. Yugoslavia was formed Dec. 1, 1918, from the patchwork of Balkan states and territories where World War I began with the assassination of Archduke Ferdinand of Austria at Sarajevo on June 28, 1914. The new Kingdom of Serbs, Croats, and Slovenes included the former kingdoms of Serbia and Montenegro; Bosnia-Herzegovina, previously administered jointly by Austria and Hungary; Croatia-Slavonia, a semi-autonomous region of Hungary, and Dalmatia, formerly administered by Austria. King Peter I of Serbia became the first monarch, his son acting as Regent until his accession as Alexander I on Aug. 16, 1921.

Croatian demands for a federal state forced Alexander to assume dictatorial powers in 1929 and to change the country's name to Yugoslavia. Serbian dominance continued despite his efforts, amid the resentment of other regions. A Macedonian associated with Croatian dissidents assassinated Alexander in Marseilles, France, on Oct. 9, 1934, and his cousin, Prince Paul, became Regent for the King's son, Prince Peter.

Paul's pro-Axis policy brought Yugoslavia to sign the Axis Pact on March 25, 1941, and opponents overthrew the government two days later. On April 6 the Nazis occupied the country, and the young King and his government fled. Two guerrilla armies—the Chetniks under Draza Mihajlovic supporting the monarchy and the Partisans under Tito (Josip Broz) leaning toward the U.S.S.R.—fought the Nazis for the duration of the war. In 1943, Tito established an Executive National Committee of Liberation to function as a provisional government.

Tito won the election held in the fall of 1945, as monarchists boycotted the vote. A new Assembly abolished the monarchy and proclaimed the Federal People's Republic of Yugoslavia, with Tito as Prime Minister.

Ruthlessly eliminating opposition, the Tito government executed Mihajlovic in 1946. With Soviet aid, Tito annexed the greater part of Italian Istria under the 1947 peace treaty with Italy but failed in his claim to the key port of Trieste. Zone B of the former free territory of Trieste went to Yugoslavia in 1954.

Tito broke with the Soviet bloc in 1948 and Yugoslavia has since followed a middle road, combining orthodox Communist control of politics and general overall economic policy with a varying degree of freedom in the arts, travel, and individual enterprise. Tito, who became President in 1953 and President for life under a revised Constitution adopted in 1963, has played a major part in the creation of a "non-aligned" group of states, the so-called "third world."

The Marshal supported his one-time Soviet mentors in their quarrel with Communist China, but even though he imprisoned the writer Mihajlo Mihajlov and other dissenters at home, he criticized Soviet repression of Czecholovakia in 1968.

Tito welcomed President Nixon to Yugoslavia in 1970 for the first U.S. Presidential visit, and he went to the U.S. the following year, but the relationship has been touchy.

Tito's death on May 4, 1980, three days before his 88th birthday, removed from the scene the last World War II leader. A rotating presidency designed to avoid internal dissension was put into effect immediately, and the feared clash of Yugoslavia's multiple nationalities and regions appeared to have been averted. On May 15, Cvijetin Mijatovic of the Serbian republic began a one-year term. A collective presidency, rotated annually among the six republics and two autonomous provinces of the federal republic, was to continue to govern according to a constitutional change made in 1974.

In March 1981, the Albanian minority, which forms 80 per cent of the population of the autonomous province of Kosovo, backed Albanian students demonstrating against conditions at the university. By April, the demonstrations had swelled to riots in which 11 were killed as 100,000 people demanded the status of a separate republic, which would enable Kosovo to secede from the Yugoslav federation. Unrest continued in 1982, with 1,700 ethnic Albanians arrested by midyear for "anti-Yugoslav activities."

ZAIRE

Republic of Zaire
President: Mobutu Sese Seko (1965)
Prime Minister: Joseph Nsigna (1981)
Area: 905,063 sq mi. (2,344,113 sq km)
Population (est. 1982): 28,150,000 (average annual growth rate: 2.8%)
Density per square mile: 31.1

Capital: Kinshasa
Largest cities (est. 1979): Kinshasa, 2,500,000; (est. 1974 by U.N.): Kananga, 601,250; Luluabourg, 506,000; Lubumbashi, 403,600
Monetary unit: Zaire
Languages: French; Bantu dialects, mainly Swahili, Lingala, Ishiluba, and Kikongo
Religions: Animist, 50%; Roman Catholic, Protestant, Islam
Ethnic groups: Bantu, Sudanese, Nilotics, Pygmies, Hamites
National name: République du Zaïre
Literacy rate (1981): 40%
Economic summary: Gross national product (1980): $6.3 billion. Average annual growth rate (1970–79): −2.6%. Per capita income (1980): $220. Land used for agriculture: 2%; labor force: 70–80%; principal products: coffee, palm oil, rubber, tea, cotton, cocoa, manioc, bananas, plantains, vegetables, fruits. Major industrial products: processed and unprocessed minerals. Natural resources: copper, cobalt, zinc, industrial diamonds, manganese, tin, gold, rare metals, bauxite, iron, coal, 13% of world hydroelectric potential. Exports: copper, cobalt, diamonds, petroleum, coffee. Imports: consumer goods, foodstuffs, mining and other machinery, transport equipment. Major trading partners: Belgium, West Germany, U.S.

Geography. Zaire is situated in west central Africa and is bordered by the Congo, the Central African Empire, the Sudan, Uganda, Rwanda, Burundi, Tanzania, Zambia, Angola, and the Atlantic Ocean. It is one quarter the size of the U.S.

The principal rivers are the Ubangi and Bomu in the north and the Zaire (Congo) in the west, which flows into the Atlantic. The entire length of Lake Tanganyika lies along the eastern border with Tanzania and Burundi.

Government. Under the Constitution approved by referendum in 1967 and amended in 1974, the third Constitution since 1960, the president and a unicameral Legislature are elected by universal suffrage for five-year terms.

In 1971, the government proclaimed that the Democratic Republic of the Congo would be known as the Republic of Zaire, since the Congo River's name had been changed to the Zaire. In addition, President Joseph D. Mobutu took the name Mobutu Sese Seko and Katanga Province became Shaba.

There is only one political party: the Popular Movement of the Revolution, led by President Mobutu.

History. Formerly the Belgian Congo, this territory was inhabited by ancient Negrito peoples (Pygmies), who were pushed into the mountains by Bantu and Nilotic invaders. The American correspondent Henry M. Stanley navigated the Congo River in 1877 and opened the interior to exploration. Commissioned by King Leopold II of the Belgians, Stanley made treaties with native chiefs that enabled the King to obtain personal title to the territory at the Berlin Conference of 1885.

Criticism of forced labor under royal exploitation prompted Belgium to take over administration of the Congo, which remained a colony until agitation for independence forced Brussels to grant freedom on June 30, 1960. Moise Tshombe, Premier of the then Katanga Province seceded from the new republic on July 11, and another mining province, South Kasai, followed. Belgium sent paratroopers to quell the civil war, and with President Joseph Kasavubu and Premier Patrice Lumumba of the national government in conflict, the United Nations flew in a peacekeeping force.

Kasavubu staged an army coup in 1960 and handed Lumumba over to the Katangan forces. A U.N. investigating commission found that Lumumba had been killed by a Belgian mercenary in the presence of Tshombe. Dag Hammarskjold, U.N. Secretary-General, died in a plane crash en route to a peace conference with Tshombe on Sept. 17, 1961.

U.N. Secretary-General U Thant submitted a national reconciliation plan in 1962 that Tshombe rejected. Tshombe's troops fired on the U.N. force in December, and in the ensuing conflict Tshombe capitulated on Jan. 14, 1963. The peacekeeping force withdrew, and, in a complete about-face, Kasavubu named Tshombe Premier to fight a spreading rebellion. Tshombe used foreign mercenaries and, with the help of Belgian paratroops airlifted by U.S. planes, defeated the most serious opposition, a Communist-backed regime in the northeast.

Kasavubu abruptly dismissed Tshombe in 1965 and was himself ousted by Gen. Joseph-Desiré Mobutu, Army Chief of Staff. The new President nationalized the Union Minière, the Belgian copper mining enterprise that had been a dominant force in the Congo since colonial days. The plane carrying the exiled Tshombe was hijacked in 1967 and he was held prisoner in Algeria until his death from a heart attack was announced June 29, 1969.

Mobutu eliminated opposition to win election in 1970 to a term of seven years, which was renewed in a 1977 election. He invited U.S., South African, and Japanese investment to replace Belgian interests. In 1975, he nationalized much of the economy, barred religious instruction in schools, and decreed the adoption of African names.

In the Angolan civil war of 1975–76, Mobutu backed the National Front for the Liberation of Angola, whose leader, Holden Roberto, is related to him by marriage. The Zairean government opposed the recognition of the Soviet-backed Popular Movement for the Liberation of Angola and reluctantly accepted its victory.

On March 8, 1977, invaders from Angola calling themselves the Congolese National Liberation Front pushed into Shaba and threatened the important mining center of Kolwezi. France and Belgium responded to Mobutu's pleas for help with weapons, but the U.S. gave only nonmilitary supplies.

In April, France flew 1,500 Moroccan troops to Shaba to defeat the invaders, who were, Mobutu charged, Soviet-inspired, and Cuban-led. U.S. intelligence sources, however, confirmed Soviet and Cuban denials of any participation and identified the rebels as former Katanga gendarmes who had fled to Angola after their 1963 defeat.

On May 15, 1978, a new assault from Angola resulted in the capture of Kolwezi and the death of 100 whites and 300 blacks. In this second invasion, France and Belgium intervened directly as 1,000 Foreign Legion paratroopers repelled the Katangese and 1,750 Belgian soldiers helped evacuate 2,000 Europeans. The U.S. supplied 18 air transports for both the troop movement and the evacuation. This time President Carter himself backed Mobutu's renewed assertions of Soviet-Cuban participation.

France led in organizing Western aid for the restoration of the shattered mining operations at Kolwezi, an important part of the Shaba industry that is the mainstay of Zaire's economy.

ZAMBIA

Republic of Zambia
President: Kenneth D. Kaunda (1964)
Prime Minister: Nalumino Mundia (1981)
Area: 290,724 sq mi. (752,975 sq km)
Population (est. 1982): 6,100,000 (average annual growth rate: 3.2%)
Density per square mile: 21.0
Capital: Lusaka
Largest cities (est. 1980 for metropolitan area): Lusaka, 684,000; (est. 1979 by U.N.): Kitwe, 325,000; Ndola, 307,000; Chingola, 183,000; Mufulira, 178,000
Monetary unit: Kwacha
Languages: English and local dialects
Religions: Animist, Roman Catholic, Protestant, Hindu, Islam
Member of Commonwealth of Nations
Literacy rate (1981): 28%
Economic summary: Gross national product (1980): $3.2 billion. Average annual growth rate (1970–79): –1.9%. Per capita income (1980): $560. Land used for agriculture: 5%; labor force: 9%; principal products: corn, tobacco, cotton, sugar cane. Labor force in industry: 15%; major products: copper, cobalt, chemicals, textiles, fertilizers. Natural resources: copper, zinc, lead, cobalt, coal. Exports: copper, zinc, lead, cobalt, tobacco. Imports: manufactured goods, machinery and transport equipment, foodstuffs. Major trading partners: Western European countries, Japan, China, South Africa.

Geography. Zambia, a landlocked country in south central Africa, is about one tenth larger than Texas. It is surrounded by Angola, Zaire, Tanzania, Malawi, Mozambique, Zimbabwe, Botswana, and South-West Africa (Namibia). The country is mostly a plateau that rises to 8,000 feet (2,434 m) in the east.

Government. Zambia (formerly Northern Rhodesia) is governed by a president, elected by universal suffrage, and a Legislative Assembly, consisting of 105 members elected by universal suffrage and up to 10 additional members nominated by the president.

In 1972, the Assembly passed a law making the ruling United National Independence Party, led by President Kenneth D. Kaunda, the only legal political party.

History. Empire builder Cecil Rhodes obtained mining concessions in 1889 from King Lewanika of the Barotse and sent settlers to the area soon thereafter. It was ruled by the British South Africa Company, which he established, until 1924, when the British government took over the administration.

From 1953 to 1964, Northern Rhodesia was federated with Southern Rhodesia and Nyasaland in the Federation of Rhodesia and Nyasaland. On Oct. 24, 1964, Northern Rhodesia became the independent nation of Zambia.

Kenneth Kaunda, the first president, kept Zambia within the Commonwealth of Nations. The country's economy, dependent on copper exports, was threatened when Rhodesia declared its independence from British rule in 1965 and defied U.N. sanctions, which Zambia supported, an action that deprived Zambia of its trade route through Rhodesia. The U.S., Britain, and Canada organized an airlift in 1966 to ship gasoline into Zambia. In 1967, Britain agreed to finance new trade routes for Zambia.

Kaunda visited China in 1967, and China later agreed to finance a 1,000-mile railroad from the copper fields to Dar es Salaam in Tanzania. A pipeline was opened in 1968 from Ndola in Zambia's copper belt to the Indian Ocean at Dar es Salaam, ending the three-year oil drought.

In 1969, Kaunda announced the nationalization of the foreign copper-mining industry, with Zambia to take 51% (over $1 billion, estimated), and an agreement was reached with the companies on payment. He then announced a similar takeover of foreign oil producers.

Zambia suffered heavy damage from bombing raids by the former Rhodesian air force on Zimbabwean guerrilla bases and on its transportation links. These actions, combined with falling prices for copper and cobalt, forced Kaunda to declare a state of economic austerity in January 1981.

A strike by copper-belt workers, directed partly against cuts in consumer subsidies and partly at UNIP, the regime's single party, brought a quick victory for the workers after they shut down production. In February, Kaunda installed a new Prime Minister and a new party chief, both more acceptable to the powerful copper-belt unions, and in April, UNIP readmitted union leaders who had been expelled at the time of the strike.

ZIMBABWE

President: Rev. Canaan Banana (1980)
Prime Minister: Robert Mugabe (1980)
Area: 150,333 sq mi. (389,362 sq km)
Population (est. 1982): 7,850,000 (average annual growth rate: 3.5%) (black, 96%; white, 4%)
Density per square mile: 52.2
Capital: Harare (Salisbury)
Largest cities (est. 1980 for metropolitan area): Harare, 655,000; Bulawayo, 375,000
Monetary unit: Zimbabwean dollar
Languages: English (official), Sindebele, Shona
Religions: Christian, 20%; Animist
Literacy rate (1981): 30% (blacks), 99% (whites)
Economic summary: Gross national product (1980): $4.6 billion. Average annual growth rate (1970–79): –1.7%. Per capita income (1980): $630. Land used for agriculture: 6%; labor force: 35%; principal agricultural products: tobacco, corn, sugar, cotton, livestock. Labor force in industry: 25%; major products: steel, textiles, chemicals, vehicles, gold, copper. Natural resources: gold, copper, cobalt, nickel, tin, asbestos. Exports: gold, tobacco, asbestos, copper, meat, chrome, nickel, clothing, sugar. Imports: machinery, petroleum products, wheat, transport equipment. Major trading partner: South Africa.

Geography. Zimbabwe, a landlocked country in south central Africa, is slightly smaller than California. It is bordered by Botswana on the west, Zambia on the north, Mozambique on the east, and South Africa on the south.

A high veld up to 6,000 feet (1,829 m) crosses the country from northeast to southwest. This is flanked by a somewhat lower veld that contains ranching country. Tropical forests that yield hardwoods lie in the southeast.

In the north, on the border with Zambia, is the 175-mile-long (128-m) Kariba Lake, formed by the Kariba Dam across the Zambezi River. It is the site of one of the world's largest hydroelectric projects.

Government. Executive power rests with the 26-member Cabinet, headed by the Prime Minister. The President, elected by a majority of the House of Assembly, exercises formal executive powers. The legislature is composed of a 100-member House of Assembly, 80 of whom are elected by black voters and 20 by whites, and a 40-member Senate. Black House members elect 14 Senators and whites elect 10. Ten tribal chiefs—five from Mashonaland and five from Matabeleland—are elected by their peers and six appointed by the President complete the Senate membership.

Major political parties are the Zimbabwe African National Union (57 seats in the House of Assembly), led by Prime Minister Robert Mugabe; Zimbabwe African People's Union (20 seats), led by Joshua Nkomo; and the United African National Council (3 seats), led by former Prime Minister Abel Muzorewa. The Republican Front, led by former Prime Minister Ian Smith, holds 17 of the 20 seats reserved for whites.

History. Zimbabwe, formerly called Rhodesia, was colonized by Cecil Rhodes's British South Africa Company at the end of the 19th century. In 1923, European settlers voted in a referendum to become the self-governing British colony of Southern Rhodesia rather than merge with what was then the Union of South Africa. After a brief federation with Northern Rhodesia and Nyasaland in the post-World War II period, Southern Rhodesia chose to remain a colony when its two partners voted for independence in 1963.

On Nov. 11, 1965, the white-minority government of Rhodesia unilaterally declared its independence from Britain.

In 1967, Rhodesia became the first country against which the United Nations ever imposed mandatory sanctions. The U.S. stopped virtually all trade with Rhodesia. The country refused to cave in, but began a slow movement toward meeting the demands of the black Africans. The white-minority regime of Prime Minister Ian Smith withstood British pressure, economic sanctions, guerrilla attacks, and a right-wing assault.

On March 1, 1970, Rhodesia formally proclaimed itself a republic, and within the month nine nations, including the U.S., closed their consulates there.

Heightened guerrilla war and a withdrawal of South African military aid—particularly helicopters—marked the beginning of the collapse of Smith's 11 years of resistance in the spring of 1976. Under pressure from South Africa's Prime Minister, Johannes Vorster, Smith agreed with U.S. Secretary of State Henry A. Kissinger that majority rule should come within two years.

In the fall, Smith met with black nationalist leaders in Geneva. The meeting broke up six weeks later when the Rhodesian Premier insisted that whites must retain control of the police and armed forces during the transition to majority rule. A British proposal called for Britons to take over these powers.

Divisions between Rhodesian blacks—Bishop Abel Muzorewa of the African National Congress and Ndabaningi Sithole as moderates versus Robert Mugabe and Joshua Nkomo of the Patriotic Front as advocates of guerrilla force—sharpened in 1977 and no agreement was reached. In July, with white residents leaving in increasing numbers and the economy showing the strain of war, Smith rejected outside mediation and called for general elections in order to work out an "internal solution" of the transfer of power.

On March 3, 1978, Smith, Muzorewa, Sithole, and Chief Jeremiah Chirau signed an agreement to transfer power to the black majority by Dec. 31, 1978. They constituted themselves an Executive Council, with chairmanship rotating but Smith retaining the title of Prime Minister. Blacks were named to each cabinet ministry, serving as co-ministers with the whites already holding these posts. African nations and the Patriotic Front leaders immediately denounced the action, but Western governments were more reserved, although none granted recognition to the new regime.

Despite continuing fighting, white voters ratified a new constitution on Jan. 30, 1979, enfranchising all blacks, establishing a black majority Senate and Assembly, and changing the country's name to Zimbabwe Rhodesia. A general election on April 24 gave Muzorewa's party 67.3% of the vote, and although the Patriotic Front urged a boycott, more than 60% of the eligible blacks went to the polls.

As black African states refused recognition and the United Nations sanctions remained in force, Muzorewa agreed to negotiate with Mugabe and Nkomo in British-sponsored talks beginning Sept. 9. By December, all parties accepted a new draft constitution, a cease-fire, and a period of British administration pending a general election. Lord Christopher Soames arrived on Dec. 12 to head the government, followed by British and Commonwealth troops who were to serve as peace-keeping forces as Patriotic Front guerrillas were grouped at 40 assembly points throughout the country.

The United Nations Security Council ended sanctions on Dec. 21, the day the formal agreement was signed by all parties.

In voting completed on Feb. 29, 1980, Mugabe's ZANU-Patriotic Front party won 57 of the 80 Assembly seats reserved for blacks. Nkomo's ZAPU-Patriotic Front party won 20 seats and Muzorewa's United African National Council only three. In an earlier vote on Feb. 14, the Rhodesian Front won all 20 seats reserved for whites in the Assembly.

At a ceremony on April 18, Prince Charles of Britain handed to President-elect Rev. Canaan Banana the symbols of independence. Mugabe, a Marxist, had already pledged his support for continuation of the existing free-market economy. Britain announced a two-year $165-million aid program for the new government, and the United States, opening the first embassy in Salisbury, offered $15 million for rural rehabilitation and $2 million to rebuild rural clinics.

In January 1981, Mugabe dismissed Nkomo as Home Minister and his onetime rival left the government in protest. At the same time, the Prime Minister discharged Edgar Z. Tekere, Manpower and Planning Minister, who had been tried and acquitted of the murder of a white farmer.

Mugabe survived both tests and scored an unprecedented triumph when, in response to his appeal for economic aid, Western nations pledged $1.8 billion for the next three years. The United States promised to give $225 million in grants in addition to $50 million in low-interest loans to replace war-damaged housing. Despite the successes of the new government, whites continued to leave the country in 1981, threatening Zimbabwe's farm and industrial production.

(For late reports, see Current Events of 1981–82)

CANADA

Sovereign: Queen Elizabeth II
Governor General: Edward R. Schreyer (1979)
Prime Minister: Pierre Elliott Trudeau (1980)
Area: 3,851,809 sq mi. (9,976,186 sq km)
Population (est. 1982): 24,450,000 (British, 44.6%; French, 28.7%; other European, 23%) (growth rate, 1979–80, 0.9%)
Density per square mile: 6.3
Capital: Ottawa, Ont.
Largest cities (1981 census; metropolitan areas): Toronto, 2,998,947; Montreal, 2,828,349; Vancouver, 1,268,183; Ottawa, 717,978; Edmonton, 657,057; Calgary, 592,743; Winnipeg, 584,842; Quebec, 576,075; Hamilton, 542,095; St. Catherines–Niagara, 304,353; Kitchener, 287,801; London, 283,668; Halifax, 277,727
Monetary Unit: Canadian dollar
Languages: English, French
Religions: Roman Catholic, 46.2%; United Church, 17.5%; Anglican, 11.8%; Presbyterian, 4%; Lutheran, 3.3%, Baptist, 3.1%; others, 14.1%
Gross national product (1979): $228.4 billion
Average annual growth rate (1970–78): 3.0%
Freedom House classifications: Capitalist industrial, multi-party decentralized

Geography. Covering most of the northern part of the North American continent and with an area larger than that of the United States, Canada has an extremely varied topography. The northeastern region, including most of Quebec, northern Ontario and Manitoba, and the Northwest Territories, with Hudson Bay in the center, is an important source of minerals, wood pulp, and water power. In the east the mountainous maritime provinces have an irregular coast line on the Gulf of St. Lawrence and the Atlantic. The St. Lawrence plain, covering most of southern Quebec and Ontario, and the interior continental plain, covering southern Manitoba and Saskatchewan and most of Alberta, are the principal cultivable areas. They are separated by a forested plateau rising from lakes Superior and Huron.

Westward toward the Pacific, most of British Columbia, Yukon, and part of western Alberta are covered by parallel mountain ranges including the Rockies. The Pacific border of the coast range is ragged with fiords and channels. The highest point in Canada is Mount Logan (19,850 ft; 6,050 m), which is in the Yukon.

Canada has an abundance of large and small lakes. In addition to the Great Lakes on the U.S. border, there are 9 others that are more than 100 miles long (161 km) and 35 that are more than 50 miles long (80 km).

The two principal river systems are the Mackenzie and the St. Lawrence. The St. Lawrence, with its tributaries, is navigable for over 1,900 miles (3,058 km).

Government. Canada, a self-governing member of the Commonwealth of Nations, is a federation of 10 provinces and two territories whose powers were spelled out in the British North America Act of 1867. With the passing of the Constitution Act of 1981, the act and the Constitutional amending power were transferred from the British government to Canada so that the Canadian Constitution is now entirely in the hands of the Canadians.

Actually the Governor General acts only with the advice of the Canadian Prime Minister and the Cabinet, who also sit in the federal Parliament. The Parliament has two houses: a Senate of 104 members appointed for life, and a House of Commons of 282 members apportioned according to provincial population. Elections are held at least every five years or whenever the party in power is voted down in the House of Commons or considers it expedient to appeal to the people. The Prime Minister is the leader of the majority party in the House of Commons—or, if no single party holds a majority, the leader of the party able to command the support of a majority of members of the House. Laws must be passed by both houses of Parliament and signed by the Governor General in the Queen's name.

The 10 provincial governments are nominally headed by Lieutenant Governors appointed by the federal government, but the executive power in each actually is vested in a Cabinet headed by a Premier, who is leader of the majority party. The provincial legislatures are composed of one-house assemblies whose members are elected for four-year terms. They are known as Legislative Assemblies, except in Newfoundland, where it is the House of Assembly, and in Quebec, where it is the National Assembly.

The judicial system consists of a Supreme Court in Ottawa (established in 1875), with appellate jurisdiction, and a Supreme Court in each province, as well as county courts with limited jurisdiction in most of the provinces. The Governor General in Council appoints these judges.

The major political parties are the Liberal (146 of 282 seats in House of Commons), led by Prime Minister Pierre Elliott Trudeau; Progressive Conservative Party (100 seats), led by former Prime Minister Charles Joseph Clark; and New Democratic Party (32), led by John Edward Broadbent. One Independent holds a seat and there are three vacancies.

History. The Norse explorer Leif Ericson probably reached the shores of Canada (Labrador or Nova Scotia) in A.D. 1000, but the history of the white man in the country actually began in 1497, when John Cabot, an Italian in the service of Henry VII of England, reached Newfoundland or Nova Scotia. Canada was taken for France in 1534 by Jacques Cartier. The actual settlement of New France, as it was then called, began in 1604 at Port Royal in what is now Nova Scotia; in 1608, Quebec was founded. France's colonization efforts were not very successful, but French explorers by the end of the 17th century had penetrated beyond the Great Lakes to the western prairies and south along the Mississippi to the Gulf of Mexico. Meanwhile, the English Hudson's Bay Company had been established in 1670. Because of the valuable fisheries and fur trade, a conflict developed between the French and English; in 1713, Newfoundland, Hudson Bay, and Nova Scotia (Acadia) were lost to England.

During the Seven Years' War (1756–63), England extended its conquest, and the British Maj. Gen. James Wolfe won his famous victory over Gen. Louis Montcalm outside Quebec on Sept. 13, 1759. The Treaty of Paris in 1763 gave England control.

At that time the population of Canada was almost entirely French, but in the next few decades, thou-

Canadian Governors General and Prime Ministers Since 1867

Term of office	Governor General	Term	Prime Minister	Party
1867–1868	Viscount Monck[1]	1867–1873	Sir John A. Macdonald	Conservative
1869–1872	Baron Lisgar	1873–1878	Alexander Mackenzie	Liberal
1872–1878	Earl of Dufferin	1878–1891	Sir John A. Macdonald	Conservative
1878–1883	Marquess of Lorne	1891–1892	Sir John J. C. Abbott	Conservative
1883–1888	Marquess of Lansdowne	1892–1894	Sir John S. D. Thompson	Conservative
1888–1893	Baron Stanley of Preston	1894–1896	Sir Mackenzie Bowell	Conservative
1893–1898	Earl of Aberdeen	1896	Sir Charles Tupper	Conservative
1898–1904	Earl of Minto	1896–1911	Sir Wilfrid Laurier	Liberal
1904–1911	Earl Grey	1911–1917	Sir Robert L. Borden	Conservative
1911–1916	Duke of Connaught	1917–1920	Sir Robert L. Borden	Unionist
1916–1921	Duke of Devonshire	1920–1921	Arthur Meighen	Unionist
1921–1926	Baron Byng of Vimy	1921–1926	W. L. Mackenzie King	Liberal
1926–1931	Viscount Willingdon	1926	Arthur Meighen	Conservative
1931–1935	Earl of Bessborough	1926–1930	W. L. Mackenzie King	Liberal
1935–1940	Baron Tweedsmuir	1930–1935	Richard B. Bennett	Conservative
1940–1946	Earl of Athlone	1935–1948	W. L. Mackenzie King	Liberal
1946–1952	Viscount Alexander	1948–1957	Louis S. St. Laurent	Liberal
1952–1959	Vincent Massey	1957–1963	John G. Diefenbaker	Progressive-Conservative
1959–1967	George P. Vanier			
1967–1973	Roland Michener	1963–1968	Lester B. Pearson	Liberal
1974–1979	Jules Léger	1968–1979	Pierre Elliott Trudeau	Liberal
1979–	Edward R. Schreyer	1979–1980	Charles Joseph Clark	Conservative
		1980–	Pierre Elliott Trudeau	Liberal

1. Became Governor General of British North America in 1861.

sands of British colonists emigrated to Canada from the British Isles and from the American colonies. In 1849, the right of Canada to self-government was recognized. By the British North America Act of 1867, the Dominion of Canada was created through the confederation of Upper and Lower Canada, Nova Scotia, and New Brunswick. Prince Edward Island joined the Dominion in 1873.

In 1869 Canada purchased from the Hudson's Bay Company the vast middle west (Rupert's Land) from which the provinces of Manitoba (1870), Alberta, and Saskatchewan (1905) were later formed. In 1871, British Columbia joined the Dominion. The country was linked from coast to coast in 1885 by the Canadian Pacific Railway.

During the formative years between 1866 and 1896, the Conservative Party, led by Sir John A. Macdonald, governed the country, except during the years 1873–78. In 1896, the Liberal Party took over and, under Sir Wilfrid Laurier, an eminent French Canadian, ruled until 1911.

In World War I, more than 500,000 Canadian soldiers fought for the Allied cause. After the Treaty of Versailles, Canada, a full-fledged nation, was admitted to the League of Nations and appointed its own representatives in foreign countries. By the Statute of Westminster in 1931 the British Dominions, including Canada, were formally declared to be partner nations with Britian, "equal in status, in no way subordinate to each other," and bound together only by allegiance to a common Crown.

Newfoundland became Canada's 10th province on March 31, 1949, following a plebiscite. Besides the provinces, Canada includes two territories—the Yukon Territory, the area north of British Columbia and east of Alaska, and the Northwest Territories, including all of Canada north of 60° north latitude except Yukon and the northernmost sections of Quebec and Newfoundland. This area includes all of the Arctic north of the mainland, Norway having recognized Canadian sovereignty over the Svendrup Islands in the Arctic in 1931.

The Liberal Party, led by William Lyon Mackenzie King, dominated Canadian politics from 1921 until 1957, when it was succeeded by the Progressive Conservatives. The Liberals, under the leadership of Lester B. Pearson, returned to power in 1963. Pearson remained Prime Minister until 1968, when he retired and was replaced by a former law professor, Pierre Elliott Trudeau. Trudeau maintained Canada's defensive alliance with the United States, but began moving toward a more independent policy in world affairs.

Trudeau set about creating what he termed a "just society," stressing domestic reforms. His election was considered in part a response to the most serious problem confronting the country, the division between French- and English-speaking Canadians, which had led to a separatist movement in the predominantly French province of Quebec. Trudeau, himself a French Canadian, supported programs for bilingualism and an increased measure of provincial autonomy, although he would not tolerate the idea of separatism. In 1974, the provincial government voted to make French the official language of Quebec.

Capturing the Quebec provincial government from the long-entrenched local Liberal Party, René Lévesque and his separatist Parti Québécois pledged that they would seek independence for the province. He shocked English-speaking Canadians with a New York speech two months after his election in which he said the question was not when but *how* Quebec would attain independence.

Conflicts over the law establishing French as the dominant language in Quebec, particularly in schooling, kept separatism as a national issue, but by-elections in 1977 produced easy victories for Trudeau's ruling Liberals in four Quebec seats in the national legislature, and polls showed a decline in separatist support both in the province and elsewhere in Canada. Early in 1978, Trudeau declared that he would use force to prevent any illegal declaration of independence by Lévesque.

Economic problems appeared to take precedence over politics in 1978, as the Sun Life Assurance Company of Canada, the nation's largest insurance firm, announced that it would move its headquarters from Montreal to Toronto. Many businesses had left the province earlier, but Sun Life was the first to cite the language law as the reason for its departure.

Despite Trudeau's removal of price and wage controls in 1978, continuing inflation and a high rate of unemployment caused him to delay elections until May 22, 1979, the first time since 1935 that a Canadian government had retained office for the allowable five-year term. The delay gave Trudeau no advantage—the Progressive Conservatives under Charles Joseph Clark defeated the Liberals everywhere except in Quebec, New Brunswick, and Newfoundland. The Liberals actually won the larger share of the popular vote with 40%, but because their strength was concentrated in Quebec they won only 114 seats to the Conservatives' 136 and 36% of the popular vote.

Clark took office as the head of Canada's fifth minority government in the last 20 years, needing the support of 26 New Democratic Party members and six Social Credit members to obtain an absolute majority in the 282-seat House.

Trudeau's defeat after 11 years in power was attributed to 9.8% inflation, to western opposition to his energy policies, and, in the opinion of some, public distaste over a sensational autobiography written by the Prime Minister's estranged wife. Trudeau's proposed changes in the Canadian constitution aroused the opposition of provincial premiers.

Clark's government collapsed after only six months when a motion to defeat the Tory budget carried by 139–133 on Dec. 13, 1979. On the same day, the Quebec law making French the exclusive official language of the province—an issue which had been expected to provide Clark's first major internal test—was voided by the Canadian Supreme Court.

In national elections Feb. 18, 1980, the resurgent Liberals under Trudeau scored an unexpectedly big victory, winning 146 seats (147 when a vacancy was filled a month later), while the Conservatives fell from 136 to 103 and the New Democrats won 32 seats. The House became a three-party legislature for the first time in half a century when the Social Credit party failed to win a single seat.

Trudeau promised to hold down energy costs—an 18-cents-a-gallon gasoline tax proposal was blamed for the Tory defeat—and to renew his efforts to reform ferderal-provincial relations. The Quebec challenge suffered a setback shortly after Trudeau took power when a referendum for the negotiation of a separate status for the province went down to a crushing defeat.

Resolving a dispute that had occupied Trudeau since the beginning of his tenure, Queen Elizabeth II, in Ottawa on April 17, 1982, signed the Constitution Act, cutting the last legal tie between Canada and Britain. Since 1867, the British North America Act had required approval of the British Parliament for any Canadian constitutional change. Provincial agreement had been achieved by compromise except in the case of Quebec, which sued but lost a Supreme Court decision holding that one province could not block a new Constitution.

The new charter was approved by the federal House of Commons, 246–24, on Dec. 2, 1981, and by a 59–23 vote of the Senate six days later. The Constitution retains Queen Elizabeth as Queen of Canada and keeps Canada's membership in the Commonwealth. A Bill of Rights, subject to overriding provincial legislation, was criticized as deficient in protecting the rights of women and Canada's native peoples, although equality before the law is guaranteed "without discrimination based on race, national or ethnic origin, color, religion, sex, age or mental or physical disability."

Despite assurance of French-language schooling and federal services to French-speaking Canadians anywhere in the nation, Quebec's Premier Lévesque boycotted the signing ceremony and told a crowd of protesters in Montreal, "We are no longer Canadians."

As a concession to Western provinces, the charter granted exclusive jurisdiction over natural resources to provincial governments but forbade the fixing of different prices for energy consumed within a province and energy exported to other provinces.

Canada's oil and gas industry was hard hit in 1982 by the aftereffects of the 1980 National Energy Program, designed to increase home ownership in a predominantly foreign-controlled business, which had slowed investment for new production. Additional blows were the withdrawal of Shell Explorer, Inc. from the multi-billion-dollar Alsands project to extract oil from Alberta tar sands, crippling the project, and the decision by the U.S.-

Population of Canada by Provinces and Territories

Province	1981 (Census)	1980 (Jan. Estimate)	1979 (Jan. Estimate)	1971 (Census)	1961 (Census)
Alberta	2,237,724	2,053,100	1,985,200	1,627,874	1,331,944
British Columbia	2,744,467	2,611,700	2,555,800	2,184,621	1,629,082
Manitoba	1,026,241	1,026,200	1,029,900	988,247	921,686
New Brunswick	696,403	704,800	699,200	634,557	597,936
Newfoundland	567,681	577,400	572,900	522,104	457,853
Nova Scotia	847,442	851,000	845,400	788,960	737,007
Ontario	8,625,107	8,543,300	8,479,900	7,703,106	6,236,092
Prince Edward Island	122,506	123,900	122,300	111,641	104,629
Quebec	6,438,403	6,288,300	6,289,600	6,027,764	5,259,211
Saskatchewan	968,313	965,300	952,500	926,242	925,181
Northwest Territories	45,741	43,100	43,100	34,807	22,998
Yukon Territory	23,153	21,800	21,800	18,388	14,628
Total	**24,343,181**	**23,809,800**	**23,597,600**	**21,568,311**	**18,238,247**
Rural	—	—	—	5,157,525	5,537,857
Urban	—	—	—	16,410,785	12,700,390

Source: Statistics Canada.

owned Northwest Energy Corporation to delay for two years the building of a gas pipeline from Canada's Prudhoe Bay to the United States. Energy Minister Marc Lalonde, on May 31, announced a $2-billion relief measure to lower royalties on oil and gas and to allow higher sales prices for newly-discovered oil.

On June 14, Trudeau rejected any general economic relief measures, however, even though unemployment reached 9.6% in April, the highest in 40 years, and the Liberals' national popularity rating stood at 31%, the lowest since 1976.

Economy. Agriculture, including horticulture, fruit growing, and the raising of stock and poultry, is the largest single industry. Canada is one of the world's greatest wheat-exporting countries; production is concentrated in Manitoba, Saskatchewan, and Alberta.

Stock raising and dairy farming have grown greatly since 1920. Ontario and Quebec are the most important dairying provinces.

Canadian manufactures rely mainly on domestic raw materials; growing industries that depend largely on material imported in a raw or semi-finished state include the manufacture of automobiles, sugar, and rubber goods, as well as the iron and steel industry in Nova Scotia, Quebec, and Ontario. The latter two provinces account for more than 80% of all manufactures. The abundance of cheap water power is one of the chief factors in the growth of Canadian industry.

The most important industries in terms of output are pulp and paper, nonferrous-metals smelting and refining, petroleum products, meatpacking, motor vehicles, and sawmill products.

Canada's mineral resources are both rich and varied. Metals come mainly from two widely separated regions, the mountain ranges of the Pacific coast and the province of Ontario. Copper ore also exists in Quebec, Manitoba, and Newfoundland. Production of petroleum centers in Alberta. There are deposits of uranium in the Northwest Territories.

The total area of land covered by forests is estimated at 1,300,000 square miles (3,367,000 sq km), of which only 435,000 square miles (1,126,650 sq km) are commercially productive and accessible. The manufacture of pulp and paper is one of the leading industries.

Fishing, Canada's oldest industry, is carried on along the Atlantic and Pacific coasts and on the inland lakes.

Chief exports in 1980 were motor vehicles (15%), machinery (10%), cereals (7%), crude oil and products (6%), natural gas (6%), nonferrous metals (6%), metal ores (6%), chemicals (6%), wood pulp (5%), newsprint (5%), timber (5%). Leading customers were U.S. (63%), Japan (6%). Leading suppliers were U.S. (70%), Japan (4%).

In 1981, Canada's inflation rate was 12.5% and unemployment remained at 7.6%.

Government of Canada

Governor General and Commander-in-Chief: His Excellency The Right Honorable Edward R. Schreyer

GOVERNOR GENERAL'S HOUSEHOLD

Secretary to the Governor General and Secretary General of the Order of Canada, and Secretary General of the Order of Military Merit: Esmond U. Butler, Esq., C.V.O.
Comptroller of the Household: D. C. McKinnon, C.V.O.
Director of Honors: Roger de C. Nantel, Esq. C.D.
Administrative Secretary: Edmond A.C. Joly de Lotbiniere
Cultural Advisor to the Governor General: Vacant
Press Secretary: René Chertier

THE CANADIAN MINISTRY

Prime Minister: The Right Hon. Pierre Trudeau
Deputy Prime Minister and Minister of Finance: The Hon. Allan MacEachen
Minister of Transport: The Hon. Jean-Luc Pepin
Minister of Justice and State for Social Development: The Hon. Jean Chrétien
Minister of Indian Affairs and Northern Development: The Hon. John Munro
Minister of State for Economic Development and Senate House Leader: The Hon. H. A. (Bud) Olson
Minister of Industry, Trade and Commerce: The Hon. Herb Gray
Minister of Agriculture: The Hon. Eugene Whelan
Minister of Consumer and Corporate Affairs and Postmaster General: The Hon. André Ouellet
Minister of Energy, Mines and Resources: The Hon. Marc Lalonde
Leader of the Government in the Senate: The Hon. Ray Perrault
Minister of Fisheries and Oceans: The Hon. Roméo Le Blanc
Minister of State for Science and Technology and Minister of the Environment: The Hon. John Roberts
Minister of National Health and Welfare: The Hon. Monique Bégin
Minister of Supply and Services: The Hon. Jean-Jacques Blais
Secretary of State and Minister of Communications: The Hon. Francis Fox
Minister of National Defense: The Hon. Gilles Lamontagne
Minister of Regional Economic Expansion: The Hon. Pierre De Bané
Minister of State for the Wheat Board: The Hon. Hazen Argue
Minister of Labor and Minister of State for Sports: The Hon. Gerald Regan
Secretary of State for External Affairs: The Hon. Mark MacGuigan
Solicitor General: The Hon. Robert Kaplan
Minister of State for Multiculturalism: The Hon. James Fleming
Minister of National Revenue: The Hon. William Rompkey
Minister of State in the Department of Finance: The Hon. Pierre Bussières
Minister of State for Small Business: The Hon. Charles Lapointe
Minister of State for Trade: The Hon. Ed Lumley
President of the Privy Council and Government House Leader: The Hon. Yvon Pinard
President of the Treasury Board: The Hon. Donald Johnston
Minister of Employment and Immigration and Minister of State for the Status of Women: The Hon. Lloyd Axworthy
Minister of Public Works with Responsibility for C.M.H.C.: The Hon. Paul Cosgrove
Minister of State for Mines: The Hon. Judy Erola
Minister of State: The Hon. Jack Austin
Minister of Labor: The Hon. Charles L. Caccia
Minister of State: The Hon. Serge Joyal
Minister of Veterans Affairs: The Hon. W. Bennett Campbell

Provinces and Territories

ALBERTA

Capital: Edmonton
Lieut. Governor: The Hon. Frank Lynch-Staunton
Premier: The Hon. Peter Lougheed
Provincial Treasurer: Hon. Louis D. Hyndman
Atty. General: Hon. Neil Crawford
Entered Confederation: September 1, 1905
Provincial flower: Wild rose (1930)
Population (1981 census): 2,237,724
Area: 255,285 sq mi. (661,188 sq km)
Largest cities (1981): Edmonton (metro 657,057); Calgary (metro 592,743); Lethbridge (53,378); Medicine Hat (39,843); Red Deer (45,693)
Provincial parks: 59 (468.26 sq mi.)
Province revenue (1981–82): $7.961 billion[1]
Province expenditure (1981–82): $8.719 billion

1. Excludes funds allocated to Alberta Heritage Trust Fund and Natural Gas Rebates Fund.

Alberta was inhabited by various Indian groups for at least 10,000 years. European explorers first appeared in the 1750s to extend the fur trade. By the last quarter of the 18th century the Hudson's Bay Company and the North West Company had established trading posts. From 1821, when the companies merged, until 1870 the Hudson's Bay Company governed the area. In 1870 it was transferred to the Dominion of Canada, and officially became a province in 1905.

Alberta today has become the most dynamic and fastest growing of Canada's ten provinces. Economic progress, spurred on in recent years by developments in the energy resources sector is rapidly transforming the province into a leading North American economic region. Out of a Gross Domestic Product of $42.3 billion in 1980, the net value of production of commodity producing industries was $28 billion. The relative shares of this production were: mining (particularly oil and natural gas), 55.2%; construction, 23.7%; manufacturing, 12.8%; agriculture, 6.1%; electric power 1.9%; other including logging, fisheries, and trapping, 0.3%.

Among Alberta's attractions are Elk Island National Park, Banff and Jasper National Parks in the Rocky Mountains, Wood Buffalo National Park which straddles the Alberta-Northwest Territories border, Dinosaur Provincial Park, fur trading post of Rocky Mountain House, Provincial Museum and Archives of Alberta in Edmonton, and Heritage Park in Calgary.

BRITISH COLUMBIA

Capital: Victoria
Lieut. Governor: The Hon. Henry P. Bell-Irving
Premier: The Hon. William R. Bennett
Deputy Premier: The Hon. Grace McCarthy
Minister of Finance: The Hon. Hugh A. Curtis
Atty. General: The Hon. L. Allan Williams
Entered Confederation: July 20, 1871
Provincial flower: Dogwood (1956)
Population (1981 census): 2,744,467
Area: 366,255 sq mi. (948,601 sq km)
Largest cities (1981 census): Vancouver (metro 1,268,183); Victoria (metro 233,481); **(Oct. 1981 est.):** Burnaby (149,610); Surrey (132,945); Richmond (119,600)
Provincial parks: 356 (19,630 sq mi.)
Province revenue (1981–82): $6.7 billion
Province expenditure (1981–82): $6.6 billion

British Columbia was one of the last regions of the North American continent to be explored and settled, with the impetus coming from the fur trade and the gold that lay in its mountains. Spanish ships visited the coast in 1774, followed by Capt. James Cook, whose account of the fur wealth led to the influx of fur traders. The first trading post was established in 1805 at McLeod Lake. The gold strike of 1858 made Fort Victoria into a city, opened up the mainland to settlement, and resulted in its proclamation as the Colony of British Columbia in 1858. With the arrival of the Canadian Pacific Railway at Port Moody in 1885, a new era opened with permanent railroad and lumbering settlements established along the route.

The chief elements of the province's economy are: forest industries, mining, tourism, shipping, and agriculture, with forest industries the leader. The mining sector is also a large contributor to the economy with copper, crude oil, molybdenum, zinc lead, and natural gas the most valuable products.

Among British Columbia's attractions are the re-created gold rush town of Barkerville, Pacific Rim National Park, the fur trading post of Fort St. James, and Fort Langley where the province's salmon export industry began.

MANITOBA

Capital: Winnipeg
Lieut. Governor: Hon. Pearl McGonigal
Premier: Hon. Howard Pawley
Minister of Finance: Hon. Vic Schroeder
Atty. General: Hon. Roland Penner
Entered Confederation: July 15, 1870
Provincial flower: Prairie crocus (1906)
Population (1981 census): 1,026,241
Area: 251,000 sq mi. (650,090 sq km)
Largest cities (1981 census): Winnipeg (metro 584,842); **(1980):** Brandon (34,901); Thompson (17,291); Portage la Prairie (12,555); Selkirk (9,862)
Provincial parks: 56 (3,960 sq mi.)
Province revenue (1982–83): $2,495,000,000
Province expenditure (1982–83): $2,830,000,000

Sir Thomas Button, an English explorer, came through Hudson Bay in 1612. After its foundation in 1670, the Hudson's Bay Company began to build forts in the area. Britain's claim to the Hudson Bay region was recognized by the Treaty of Utrecht in 1713, but meanwhile the French entered Manitoba from the east. La Verendrye explored and built several forts in Manitoba between 1733 and 1738. Later, British and French traders from Montreal reopened trade routes in southern and central Manitoba. In 1783, the North West Company based in Montreal began to compete for furs with the Hudson's Bay Company. A fur war ensued which ended in 1821 when the companies merged. The first European settlement of Manitoba came in 1812 when Thomas Douglas, 5th earl of Selkirk, received a grant of land on the Red River from the Hudson's Bay Company. The Dominion of Canada acquired all of the Hudson's Bay Company territory in 1869–70 and part of it became the province of Manitoba under the Manitoba Act of 1870.

Its southern farmlands are the backbone of the province's economy. Wheat is the main crop. Mineral production and forest products are other leading contributors to the economy. The major minerals are nickel, copper, oil, cement, zinc, and sand/gravel. Pulpwood for paper manufacture accounts for 60% of the timber cut. Manufacturing accounts for more than one third of the value of goods and services produced in the province every year.

Among Manitoba's attractions are Lower Fort Garry near Selkirk, restored to recreate a 19th century Hudson's Bay Company post, and Riding Mountain National Park.

NEW BRUNSWICK

Capital: Fredericton
Lieut. Governor: The Hon. Dr. George F.G. Stanley
Premier: The Hon. Richard B. Hatfield
Minister of Finance: The Hon. Fernand G. Dube
Minister of Justice: The Hon. Rodman E. Logan
Entered Confederation: July 1, 1867
Provincial flower: Purple violet (1936)
Coat of Arms: Assigned by Queen Victoria in 1868
Motto: Spem Reduxit (Hope Restored)
Provincial flag: Adopted 1965
Provincial tartan: Adopted 1959
Geographic center: Boiestown
Number of counties: 15
Language: French is the first language of 36% of the population. New Brunswick is the only officially bilingual province in Canada.
Population (1981 census): 696,403
Area: 28,354 sq mi. (73,437 sq km)
Largest cities (1981): St. John (metro 120,900); Moncton (83,900); Fredericton (47,800); Bathurst (15,700); Edmundston (11,800); Campbellton (8,200)
Provincial parks: 58 (83.68 sq mi.)
Province revenue (1980–81): $1,534.9 million
Province expenditure (1980–81): $1,505.2 million

New Brunswick is one of the four original provinces making up the national Confederation in 1867. It was first known to Europeans as a portion of a region called Acadia, settled by the French. By the mid-18th century, British expansion on the neighboring Nova Scotian peninsula led to confrontation with the French. The Acadians were expelled after the British victory of 1755. A British proclamation of 1763 incorporated the area into Nova Scotia but in 1784 it was separated from it and was established as the province of New Brunswick. The first English settlement was established at Maugerville in 1792. During the American Revolution, 14,000 Loyalists settled on the banks of the St. John and St. Croix rivers. Responsible home government was granted by Britain in 1848 and New Brunswick entered the Confederation in 1867.

Since approximately 90% of the province is forested, it is no surprise that New Brunswick's major industries are forest-related, including the manufacture of pulp and paper. Fishing is another economic mainstay on the Bay of Fundy and northeast coasts with herring, lobster, and cod the top catches. New Brunswick is also an important mining center, ranking first in the nation in the production of antimony and bismuth, with zinc following second, silver third, lead fourth, and copper fifth. New Brunswick agriculture and potatoes are synonymous. The potato industry ranks first, followed by the dairy industry. Food processing is a major employer. Tourism is a growing sector.

Among the province's attractions are King's Landing, a recreated Loyalist village where approximately 70 buildings and a costumed staff portray the 1780–1890 era; Village Historique Acadien which depicts the Acadian way of life between 1780–1880; Fundy and Kouchibouguac National Parks; F.D. Roosevelt's summer home on Campobello Island; the N.B. Museum, one of the oldest in the country; more than 90 covered bridges; beaches; golf courses; numerous crafts festivals.

NEWFOUNDLAND

Capital: St. John's
Lieut. Governor: Hon. W. A. Paddon
Premier: The Hon. A. Brian Pickford
Minister of Finance: The Hon. Dr. John Collins
Minister of Justice: Hon. G. Ottenheimer
Entered Confederation: March 31, 1949
Provincial flower: Pitcher plant (1954)
Population (1981 census): 567,681
Area: 156,185 sq mi. (404,520 sq km)
Largest cities: St. John's (86,576); Corner Brook (35,198); Stephenville (10,284); Mount Pearl (10,193); Conception Bay South (9,743)
Provincial parks: 72 (3,099.0 sq mi.)
Province revenue (1982–83 est.): $1,724,136,000
Province expenditure (1982–83 est.): $1,718,730,000

John Cabot, sailing under the English flag, reached the island of Newfoundland in 1497 and is its official discoverer. His enthusiastic reports led to international rivalries over the region, with English, French, Basque, and Portuguese fishermen contesting for catches. By 1600 England and France were the chief rivals. Attempts at colonization during the 17th century were met with hostility by the English fishermen and after 1634 by the English crown. In 1699 Parliament prohibited settlement except for maintaining fisheries. French-English rivalries were settled by treaties in 1713 and 1783 recognizing British sovereignty. The island's population increased despite repressive legislation, and in 1729 Britain appointed a naval governor and in 1792 established a judicial system. With the appointment of a resident governor and council in 1824, it was acknowledged as a settled colony. A popularly elected assembly was established in 1832 and in 1855 the island was granted full responsible government. Between 1864 and 1869 and again in 1895, the subject of Newfoundland joining the Canadian Confederation was broached but was rejected at the polls. Not until 1948, in the second of two referenda, was there a clear majority for confederation. The administration of Labrador remained unsettled until 1927 when it was awarded to Newfoundland.

Newfoundland's economy is dependent upon mineral production, pulp and paper products, and fish products, with mining playing the major role as a consequence of western Labrador's vast iron reserves. Oil has been discovered at the Hybernia Well, some 200 miles offshore from St. John's on Eastern Grand Banks.

Among Newfoundland's attractions are an ancient Indian burial ground at Port aux Choix and a Norse settlement at L'Anse aux Meadows.

NORTHWEST TERRITORIES

Capital: Yellowknife
Commissioner: John H. Parker
Deputy Commissioner: Robert S. Pilot
Created: July 15, 1870
Reconstituted: Sept. 1, 1905
Flower: Mountain avens (1959)
Population (1981 census): 45,741
Area: 1,304,903 sq mi. (3,379,698 sq km)
Largest cities: Yellowknife (9,483); Inuvik (3,147); Hay River (2,863); Frobisher Bay (2,333); Fort Smith (2,298)
Territories revenue (Fiscal 1981): $335,027,000
Territories expenditure (Fiscal 1981): $327,129,000

The Athabascan Indian people have lived in the forested and barrenland regions of what is now the Northwest Territories during the last 2,500 years. The Inuit (Eskimo) have lived in the Arctic regions for about 1,000 years.

Many believe the first Europeans to visit the Northwest Territories were the Norse. According to their history, they sailed by an icy and mountainous land they called Helluland, which was probably what we now call Baffin Island.

In the late 16th century, British trading companies began searching for a shorter more secure shipping route to the Pacific Ocean and the Orient, and Arctic exploration began. In 1576 Martin Frobisher took possession of Baffin Island. In 1668 the ship *Nonsuch* entered Hudson Bay to establish a trade in furs. This led to the establishment of the Hudson's Bay Company in 1670, a company which continues to this day.

In 1818 the British Admiralty began a serious effort to find the Northwest Passage. Ten expeditions were mounted over the next 30 years. But it wasn't until 1903, when *The Gjoa*, commanded by Norwegian Roald Amundsen, sailed from Europe, that the Passage was finally navigated, after three winters in the Arctic.

Meanwhile land expeditions by Sir John Franklin, Thomas Simpson, and others had resulted in exploration and mapping of the Mackenzie District and northern coastline during the 1820s and 1830s.

Commercial ventures followed in the footsteps of the explorers. Many fur trading posts were established in the Mackenzie Valley. Whaling fleets began in Baffin Bay, Hudson Bay and later the western Arctic.

Not far behind were the missionaries, followed by the Royal Canadian Mounted Police, who were made responsible for maintaining law and order.

In 1920 oil was struck north of Fort Norman. There was a dramatic increase in traffic on the Mackenzie River. The introduction of the airplane increased the demand for fuel and the refinery expanded at Norman Wells in 1939.

The first gold brick was poured in 1938 at Yellowknife and two gold mines are still producing. Mining became the principal industry. Today lead and zinc are the main products. They are mined in Pine Point. Exploration for oil and gas is proceeding at a high pitch with good potential for the future.

There has been an evolution toward more responsible government in the Northwest Territories. In 1967 Yellowknife was named capital of the N.W.T. and the Territorial Government was located there. By 1970 most provincial-type responsibilities had been transferred from the federal government to the Territorial Government. The exception was and still is nonrenewable resources which remain with the federal administration. The Territorial Council has developed from a combination of elected representatives and federal appointees to a fully elected legislative assembly with up to seven of its members responsible for government departments and forming an Executive Committee or cabinet along with the Commissioner and Deputy Commissioner who are public servants.

Among the Northwest Territories' attractions are Wood Buffalo National Park, which straddles the Alberta-Northwest Territories border, home of the largest herd of bison on the continent; Nahanni National Park with its spectacular Virginia Falls; and Auyuittuq, on Baffin Island, Canada's first national park above the Arctic Circle.

NOVA SCOTIA

Capital: Halifax
Lieut. Governor: The Hon. John Elvin Shaffner
Premier: The Hon. John M. Buchanan
Mayor: His Worship Ron Wallace
Minister of Finance: The Hon. Joel Matheson
Atty. General: The Hon. Henry W. How
Entered Confederation: July 1, 1867
Provincial flower: Trailing Arbutus (1901) "Mayflower"
Population (1981 census): 847,442
Area: Land 20,402 sq mi.; water, 1,023 sq mi. Total: 21,425 sq mi. (55,491 sq km)
Highest Point: 1,747 ft
Origin of Name: Latin for New Scotland. Derived from the Latin charter by which New Scotland was granted to Sir Wm. Alexander (afterwards Earl of Stirling) in 1621
Slogan: Canada's Ocean Playground
Flag: Consists of the ancient Arms granted in 1625 by King Charles I, with the cross of Saint Andrew extended in a rectangle three-quarters as wide as its length. Colors: Red, yellow, royal blue, and white
Tartan: The Nova Scotia tartan was the first provincial tartan in Canada. Originally designed in 1953, the popular tartan was registered in 1956 in Her Majesty's Register Office in Edinburgh, Scotland. Colors: red, gold, blue, white, and green
No. of counties: 18
Largest cities (1981 census): Halifax (metro 277,727); (1980): Dartmouth (65,341); Sydney (30,645); Glace Bay (21,836); Truro (12,840)
Provincial parks: 103 (25.1 sq mi.)
Province revenue: $1,564,793,297. Recoveries: $154,195,945
Province expenditure: $1,769,553,365

Nova Scotia is one of the four British colonies federated into the Dominion of Canada in 1867. It was the site of the first permanent North American settlement north of Florida, established by the French in 1605. The 17th and 18th centuries were characterized by struggles for power between the British and French. In 1713 the French began construction of Louisbourg fortress and Halifax was founded in 1749 as a counterbalance. In 1848 Nova Scotia became the first British colony to have a government responsible to the people through elected representatives. There was economic and political opposition to the proposed confederation with Ontario, Quebec, and New Brunswick, but the union was carried out in 1867.

The chief components of the province's economy are fisheries, agriculture (livestock, poultry, dairying), the pulp industry, and mining (coal and industrial minerals).

Among Nova Scotia's attractions are Fort Ann, the first national historic park; the restored fortress of Louisbourg; Champlain's habitation at Port Royal; the Halifax Citadel; Alexander Graham Bell National Historic Park; and Cape Breton Highlands National Park.

ONTARIO

Capital: Toronto
Lieut. Governor: The Hon. John Black Aird
Premier: The Hon. William G. Davis
Provincial Treasurer: The Hon. Frank S. Miller
Atty. General: The Hon. Roy McMurtry
Entered Confederation: July 1, 1867
Provincial flower: White trillium (1937)
Population (1981 census): 8,625,107
Area: 412,582 sq mi. (1,068,587 sq km)
Largest cities (1981 census): Toronto (metro 2,998,947); Ottawa (metro 717,978); Hamilton (metro 542,095); **(1980)** North York (558,389); Scarborough (387,149)
Provincial parks: 127 (20,503.8 sq mi.)
Province revenue (1981–82): $18.9 billion
Province expenditure (1981–82): $20.4 billion

The first known white man in the province was the French explorer Étienne Brûlé on an expedition to the Ottawa River in 1610-11. He was followed by Samuel de Champlain, other French explorers, fur traders, and missionaries. France established Fort Frontenac (present-day Kingston) in 1673 to provide military protection to its fur empire. However, no French colonization had taken place, except for a small farming settlement near Detroit, by the time Canada was ceded to Great Britain in 1763. The Quebec Act of 1774 established Ontario as part of an extended colony ruled from Quebec. The Constitution Act of 1791 divided Quebec colony into Lower Canada (French–Quebec) and Upper Canada (Loyalist–Ontario). John Graves Simcoe, the first lieutenant governor of Upper Canada fixed the capital at York (now Toronto). In 1841 the provinces were united. Responsible cabinet government was achieved in 1848. Canadian federation—in1867—was brought about in large part by John A. Macdonald and George Brown, Ontario politicians.

Leading elements of the province's economy are agriculture, mining (the province mines 51% of the world's nickel), forest products, and manufacturing (steel, automobiles, industrial machinery).

Among Ontario's attractions are Upper Canada Village near Morrisburg, a recreation of a 19th century Ontario community; Fort Henry at Kingston, and Fort George at Niagara Falls; and "Canada's Wonderland," the nation's first theme park located in Maple.

PRINCE EDWARD ISLAND

Capital: Charlottetown
Lieut. Governor: The Hon. J.A. Doiron
Premier: The Hon. James M. Lee
Minister of Finance: The Hon. Lloyd G. MacPhail
Atty. General: The Hon. George R. McMahon
Entered Confederation: July 1, 1873
Provincial flower: Lady's slipper (1947)
Population (1981 census): 122,506
Area: 2,184 sq mi. (5,657 sq km)
Largest cities: Charlottetown (17,063); Summerside (8,592); Sherwood (5,602); St. Elanors (2,495); Parkdale (2,172)
Provincial parks: 40 (12.2 sq mi.)
Province revenue (1982–83 est.): $380,883,900
Province expenditure (1982–83 est.): $386,878,700

John Cabot may have seen the island in 1497 but Jacques Cartier, the French navigator, is credited with its discovery in June 1534. Samuel de Champlain claimed it for France in 1603 but it was not colonized until 1720. The British occupied the island in 1758 and it was formally ceded to Great Britain in 1763. Representative government reached the island in 1851. A conference in 1864 to discuss the possible union of the three Maritime Provinces was the forerunner of the Quebec Conference of 1864 which resulted in the founding of the Dominion of Canada. Thus Prince Edward Island has been known as the "Cradle of Confederation" although it did not join the union until 1873.

Agriculture is the basic element in the island's economy, followed by the tourist industry and fisheries. Manufacturing and processing are becoming more important, especially electronic equipment and frozen french fries.

Among the province's attractions are Province House in Charlottetown, which is a national historic site; 1,100 miles of pink, sandy beaches; and Fort Amherst National Historic Park, with a full-sized reproduction of a Micmac Indian village nearby.

QUEBEC

Capital: Quebec City
Lieut. Governor: The Hon. Jean-Pierre Côté
Premier: Rene Levesque
Vice Premier: Jacques-Yvan Morin
Minister of Finance: Jacques Parizeau
Minister of Justice: Marc-André Bédard
Entered Confederation: July 1, 1867
Provincial flower: White garden (Madonna) lily (1963)
Population (1981 census): 6,438,403
Area: 594,860 sq mi. (1,540,687 sq km)
Largest cities (1981 census): Montreal (metro. 2,802,547); Laval (246,243); Quebec (metro 542,158) **(1980)** Longueuil (122,429); St. Léonard (78,452)
Provincial parks: 100
Province revenue (1982–83): $19,670,000,000
Province expenditure (1982–83): $22,655,000,000

Jacques Cartier landed at present-day Gaspé in 1534 and took possession of the land in the name of the King of France. New France began with the founding of Quebec City by Samuel de Champlain in 1608, Trois-Rivière in 1616, and Montreal in 1642. Following capitulation of the French army to the British in 1760, the land was ceded to Britain in 1763. The Quebec Act of 1774 created what is now Quebec and tried to fuse British and French institutions in the new political entity. In 1791 Canada was divided into Lower Canada (French) and Upper Canada (English). An attempt to unite them in 1822 failed but in 1841 an Act of Union joined the provinces and in 1867 the British North American Act created the Confederation of Canada.

The economy of the province breaks down as follows: 61% service industries, 30% manufacturing-processing industries, 8% agricultural-extractive. Iron ore, electric power, and forest products (pulp and paper plants) are the chief resources.

Among the province's attractions are Cartier-

Brebeuf Park in Quebec City, which marks Jacques Cartier's first wintering spot in the New World; La Mauricie National Park in the Laurentian Mountains; Forillon National Park, on the Gaspé peninsula; and Laurentide Park, established for the conservation of caribou.

SASKATCHEWAN

Capital: Regina
Lieut. Governor: The Hon. Irwin McIntosh
Premier: The Hon. Grant Devine
Minister of Finance: The Hon. Robert Andrew
Atty. General: The Hon. Gary Lane
Entered Confederation: September 1, 1905
Provincial flower: Western red lily (1941)
Provincial bird emblem: Prairie sharp-tailed grouse
Population (1981 census): 968,313
Area: 251,700 sq mi. (651,903 sq km)
Largest cities (1981 census): Regina (metro 164,313); Saskatoon (metro 154,210); Moose Jaw (33,357), Prince Albert (30,906); Yorkton (15,158)
Provincial and Regional parks: 116 (2,191 sq mi.)
National Park: 1 (1,500 sq mi.)
Province revenue (1981–82): $2,287,546,000
Province expenditure (1981–82): $2,285,189,380

The first white man known to see the Saskatchewan River was Henry Kelsey in 1691. The area which became the Province of Saskatchewan was first granted to the Hudson's Bay Company. In 1868 it was surrendered back to the British crown by the Rupert's Land Act to be turned over to the newly formed Dominion of Canada, which was done in 1870. In 1873 Canada created the North West Mounted Police to maintain law and order. The territories were granted an executive council in 1875 and by 1897 had won responsible parliamentary government. Saskatchewan entered the Confederation in 1905 under the Saskatchewan Act.

The chief elements of the province's economy are agriculture, oil, gas, potash, coal and uranium.

Among its attractions are Prince Albert National Park, Cypress Hills Provincial Park, and Fort Walsh, the first headquarters of the North West Mounted police, R.C.M.P. Training Depot, Provincial and Western Development Museums.

YUKON TERRITORY

Capital: Whitehorse
Commissioner: Douglas Bell
Created a separate territory: June 1898
Flower: Fireweed (1957)
Population (1981 census): 23,153
Area: 207,076 sq mi. (536,327 sq km)
Largest cities: Whitehorse (14,814); Faro (1,652); Watson (748)
Government revenue[1] (1981): $98,150,000
Government expenditures[1] (1981): $94,273,000

The Yukon was among the last areas of the North American continent to be explored by white men. Two explorers for the Hudson's Bay Company, John Bell and Robert Campbell, first entered the region around 1840. Fort Yukon was established in 1847 on the Yukon River in what was Russian territory. It was relocated in 1867 after the United States purchased Alaska from Russia, and it was relocated again in 1890. It was a center for a small fur trade. Gold discoveries in the 1870s brought some prospectors into the area, but it was the discovery of rich deposits in Bonanza Creek in 1896 that led to the gold rush of 1898. In the same year the Canadian Parliament separated the rapidly growing area from the Northwest Territories and gave it separate territorial status.

The territory's economy is dependent upon mining, with tourism, a rapidly expanding industry, second. Logging is carried out in some southern areas.

Among the Yukon's attractions are Klune National Park, (a World Heritage Site) which contains Canada's highest peak, Mount Logan; Dawson City, the old gold rush boom town, which has been restored; and the Dempster Highway, the only publicly accessible land link to the Arctic Ocean.

1. Includes Crown corporations

Party Standings—House of Commons

Thirty-second Parliament—Speaker, Jeanne Sauvé; The Clerk of the House of Commons, C.B. Koester

Province	Lib.[1]	P.C.[2]	N.D.P.[3]	S.Cr.[4]	Ind.	Vacancies	Seats by provinces
Alberta	0	20	—	—	1	—	21
British Columbia	—	16	12	—	—	—	28
Manitoba	2	5	7	—	—	—	14
New Brunswick	7	3	—	—	—	—	10
Newfoundland	5	2	—	—	—	—	7
Nova Scotia	5	6	—	—	—	—	11
Ontario	51[5]	36	5	—	—	3	95
Prince Edward Island	2	2	—	—	—	—	4
Quebec	74	1	—	—	—	—	75
Saskatchewan	—	7	7	—	—	—	14
Yukon/NWT	—	2	1	—	—	—	3
National totals	**146[5]**	**100**	**32**		**1**	**3**	**282**

1. Liberal Party—Leader, Rt. Hon. Pierre Elliott Trudeau. 2. Progressive Conservative Party—Leader, Joseph Clark. 3. New Democratic Party—Leader, John Edward Broadbent. 4. Social Credit Party—Leader, Fabien Roy. 5. Includes 1 Liberal-Labor member. NOTE: Last three General Elections were held on July 8, 1974, May 22, 1979 and Feb. 18, 1980. The legal duration is five years.

Principal Trading Partners in 1981
(in millions of Canadian dollars)

Selected countries	Imports	Exports
United States	$54,208.9	$55,462.1
United Kingdom	2,234.7	3,382.7
Belgium/Luxembourg	296.9	853.6
France	848.6	1,001.3
West Germany	1,607.5	1,319.8
Italy	695.6	925.2
Netherlands	295.5	1,168.5
Norway	—	428.2
U.S.S.R.	—	1,866.9
Saudi Arabia	2,272.8	—
Republic of South Africa	—	261.5
India	107.0	348.4
Japan	4,039.0	4,509.5
People's Republic of China	—	1,006.8
Australia	496.3	827.5
Brazil	430.3	—
Venezuela	2,385.1	829.3
Mexico	—	735.2
Total selected countries	**$69,918.2**	**$74,926.5**
Total all countries	**$78,875.9**	**$83,698.4**

National Holidays

	1981	1982	1983
New Year's Day	Jan. 1	Jan. 1	Jan. 1
Good Friday	April 17	April 9	April 1
Easter Monday	April 20	April 12	April 4
Victoria Day	May 18	May 24	May 23
Dominion Day	July 1	July 1	July 1
Labor Day	Sept. 7	Sept. 6	Sept. 5
Thanksgiving	Oct. 12	Oct. 11	Oct. 10
Remembrance Day	Nov. 11	Nov. 11	Nov. 11
Christmas Day	Dec. 25	Dec. 25	Dec. 25

National Flag and Motto

The National Flag of Canada, otherwise known as the Canadian Flag, was approved by Parliament and proclaimed by Her Majesty the Queen on February 15, 1965, and is described as a red flag of the proportions two by length and one by width, containing in its center a white square the width of the flag, bearing a single red maple leaf.

The Flag is flown on land daily from sunrise to sunset at all federal government buildings, airports, and military bases and establishments within and outside Canada, and may appropriately be flown or displayed by individuals and organizations.

The Canada Shipping Act provides that the National Flag is the proper national colors for all Canadian ships and boats; and it is the flag flown on Canadian Naval vessels.

The motto—*A mari usque ad mare* ("From sea to sea")—is from the Latin version of Psalm LXXII: 8: "He shall have dominion also from sea to sea, and from the river unto the ends of the earth."

Canadian Museums and Related Institutions

Region	Art galleries	History museums	Restorations	Science and technology museums	Living science museums[1]	General museums	Community museums	Archives	Other institutions[2]	Total
Atlantic	10	9	65	8	2	3	44	14	5	160
Quebec	11	19	16	4	11	1	27	11	6	106
Ontario	35	22	73	14	12	3	106	19	9	293
Central	19	39	45	10	8	7	113	12	8	261
British Columbia	11	12	14	9	8	2	49	7	6	118
Yukon and Northwest Territories	—	—	2	—	—	1	3	1	—	7
Total	**86**	**101**	**215**	**45**	**41**	**17**	**342**	**64**	**34**	**945**

1. Aquaria, zoos, botanical gardens, arboretums, and conservatories. 2. Including nature park museums or nature centers. *Source:* Statistics Canada, July 1979, based on a 1976 survey. NOTE: Data are latest available.

Percentage Distribution of Canadian Population by Provinces and Territories

Province or territory	1980 (est.)	1979	1971	1961	1951	1941	1931
Alberta	8.69	8.50	7.55	7.30	6.71	6.92	7.05
British Columbia	11.02	10.86	10.13	8.93	8.32	7.11	6.69
Manitoba	4.30	4.36	4.58	5.05	5.54	6.34	6.75
New Brunswick	2.96	2.96	2.94	3.28	3.68	3.97	3.94
Newfoundland	2.42	2.42	2.42	2.51	2.58	—	—
Nova Scotia	3.56	3.58	3.66	4.04	4.59	5.02	4.94
Ontario	35.84	35.92	35.71	34.19	32.82	32.92	33.07
Prince Edward Island	0.52	0.52	0.52	0.58	0.70	0.83	0.85
Quebec	26.36	26.55	27.95	28.84	28.95	28.96	27.70
Saskatchewan	4.05	4.05	4.29	5.07	5.94	7.79	8.88
Northwest Territories	0.18	0.18	0.16	0.13	0.11	0.10	0.09
Yukon Territory	0.09	0.09	0.09	0.08	0.06	0.04	0.04
Totals	**100.00**	**100.00**	**100.00**	**100.00**	**100.00**	**100.00**	**100.00**

Canadian Motor Vehicle Registrations, 1980

Province or territory	Passenger cars[1]	Motor trucks	Motor buses	Motor-cycles	Other motor vehicles[2]	Total motor vehicles
Alberta	1,141,901	457,011	7,304	52,863	(3)	1,659,079
British Columbia	1,181,147	449,210[4]	(5)	42,218[6]	(3)	1,672,575
Manitoba	458,457	180,147	358[7]	16,678[6]	795[8]	656,435
New Brunswick	252,915	89,864	1,557	11,315	8,585	364,236
Newfoundland	146,821	60,521	n.a.	4,856[6]	n.a.	212,198
Nova Scotia	364,416	144,476	1,351	18,649	704	529,596
Ontario	3,708,694	812,890	20,620	98,475	(3)	4,640,679
Prince Edward Island	47,608	18,992	433	1,644	(3)	68,677
Quebec	2,547,500	396,406	16,103	128,670	39,224	3,127,903
Saskatchewan	393,205	273,146	4,731	11,754	778	683,614
N.W.T.	6,069	9,092	112	978[6]	69	16,320
Yukon T.	6,778	10,975	(5)	580[6]	(3)	18,333
Total	**10,255,511**	**2,902,730**	**52,569**	**388,680**	**50,155**	**13,649,645**

1. Includes taxis and for-hire cars. 2. Ambulances, fire trucks, etc. 3. Included with passenger cars or trucks. 4. Includes taxicabs. 5. Included in trucks. 6. Includes mopeds. 7. Excludes school buses which are licensed as passenger cars. 8. Includes only antique vehicles and vehicles for road testing. n.a. = not available. *Source:* Statistics Canada.

Canadian Consumer Price Index
(1971 – 100)

Year	Food	Housing	Clothing	Trans-portation	Health and personal care	Recreation, reading and education	Tobacco and alcohol	All-item index
1963	80.0	74.8	80.3	76.9	73.5	75.4	78.9	77.2
1964	81.3	76.0	82.4	77.8	75.8	76.6	80.4	78.6
1965	83.4	77.3	83.8	80.7	79.4	77.9	81.7	80.5
1966	88.7	79.5	87.0	82.6	81.8	80.1	83.7	83.5
1967	89.9	82.9	91.4	86.1	86.0	84.1	85.8	86.5
1968	92.8	86.7	94.1	88.3	89.5	88.3	93.6	90.0
1969	96.7	91.2	96.7	92.4	93.8	93.5	97.2	94.1
1970	98.9	95.7	98.5	96.1	98.0	96.8	98.4	97.2
1971	100.0	100.0	100.0	100.0	100.0	100.0	100.0	100.0
1972	107.6	104.7	102.6	102.6	104.8	102.8	102.7	104.8
1973	123.3	111.4	107.7	105.3	109.8	107.1	106.0	112.7
1974	143.4	121.1	118.0	115.8	119.4	116.4	111.8	125.0
1975	161.9	133.2	125.1	129.4	133.0	128.5	125.3	138.5
1976	166.2	145.7	132.0	143.3	144.3	136.2	134.3	148.9
1977	180.1	161.9	141.0	153.3	155.1	142.7	143.8	160.8
1978	208.0	170.8	146.4	162.2	166.2	148.2	155.5	175.2
1979	235.4	186.2	159.9	178.0	181.2	158.4	166.7	191.2
1980	260.6	201.4	178.7	200.7	199.3	173.5	185.3	210.6
1981	290.4	226.4	191.4	237.6	221.0	191.0	209.2	236.9

Source: Statistics Canada

Growth Statistics
(in Canadian dollars)

Year	Exports (including re-exports (millions of dollars)	Imports (millions of dollars)	Industry selling price indexes for manufacturing (1971=100)	Railway gross revenues[1] (millions of dollars)	Railway operating expenses[1] (millions of dollars)	Tons of revenue freight carried one mile[1] (millions)	Freight carried on Welland Canal (thousands of tons)	Vessels other than coastal entered & cleared (thousands of reg net tons)
1901	n.a.	n.a.	n.a.	$ 73	$ 50	n.a.	562	26,030
1911	n.a.	n.a.	n.a.	189	131	16,048	2,302	47,430
1921	$ 814	$ 799	n.a.	458	423	26,622	2,792	54,649
1941	1,640	1,449	n.a.	538	404	49,982	12,002	64,766
1951	3,963	4,085	n.a.	1,089	978	64,300	14,696	100,259
1961	5,896	5,771	82.4	1,156	1,053	65,828	28,489	156,987
1965	8,767	8,633	n.a.	1,369	1,288	87,052	53,437	199,454
1966	10,326	9,866	n.a.	1,476	1,367	94,944	59,137	202,170
1967	11,411	11,075	n.a.	1,514	1,438	92,239	52,850	197,422
1968	13,624	12,358	92.3	1,528	1,433	93,147	58,105	204,777
1969	14,890	14,130	95.8	1,579	1,496	94,688	53,532	197,391
1970	16,819	13,952	98.1	1,672	1,570	108,210	57,035	217,621
1971	17,820	15,618	100.0	1,797	1,693	119,412	57,206	228,561
1972	20,140	18,669	104.4	1,843	1,750	119,135	58,236	243,376
1973	25,301	23,303	116.1	2,029	1,935	125,471	60,959	244,466
1974	32,441	31,692	138.1	2,476	2,394	133,554	47,501	227,175
1975	33,245	34,691	153.7	2,619	2,669	131,048	54,295	231,354
1976	38,397	37,444	161.6	3,058	2,927	132,599	58,369	248,502
1977	44,554	42,156	174.3	3,388	3,186	137,745	65,079	264,425
1978	53,183	30,102	190.4	3,723	3,526	141,737	65,671	277,433
1979	65,514	62,724	217.9	4,601	4,259	152,085	66,165	301,562
1980	75,515	68,710	247.2	5,174	4,832	156,247	n.a.	n.a.

1. Six major railways, representing about 95% of the industry in terms of operating revenues and other performance indicators. NOTE: n.a. = not available. *Source:* Statistics Canada.

Growth Statistics
(in Canadian dollars)

Year	Motor vehicle regis-trations (thousands)	Tele-phones in use (thousands)	Post office and money order revenue (thousands)	Index numbers of weekly earnings[1] 1961 = 100	Strikes and lockouts: Em-ployees affected (thousands)	Strikes and lockouts: Time lost working days (thousands)	Federal finance: Total revenue (millions of dollars)	Federal finance: Total expendi-ture (millions of dollars)	Federal finance: Net debt (millions of dollars)
1901	n.a.	n.a.	3,421	n.a.	24	738	53	58	268
1911	22	303	9,147	n.a.	29	1,821	118	123	340
1921	465	902	26,331	n.a.	28	1,049	436	528	2,341
1931	1,201	1,364	30,416	n.a.	11	204	356	442	2,262
1941	1,573	1,562	40,383	34.1	87	434	872	1,250	3,649
1951	2,872	3,114	90,455	64.0	103	902	3,113	2,901	11,645
1961	5,517	6,014	202,004	100.0	98	1,335	5,618	5,958	12,437
1965	6,669	7,445	263,704	116.2	172	2,350	7,180	7,218	15,504
1966	7,035	7,883	275,994	127.8	411	5,178	7,696	7,735	15,543
1967	7,482	8,358	295,529	130.6	252	3,975	8,358	8,780	15,965
1968	7,877	8,818	337,023	140.3	224	5,083	9,029	9,824	16,760
1969	8,254	9,296	374,902	150.8	307	7,752	10,163	11,938	17,336
1970	8,497	9,750	444,069	162.8	262	6,540	12,321	11,928	16,943
1971	9,022	10,269	432,911	176.7	240	2,867	12,803	13,182	17,322
1972	9,481	10,987	504,211	191.4	706	7,754	14,227	14,841	17,937
1973	10,158	11,677	563,159	205.4	348	5,776	16,602	16,121	17,456
1974	11,002	12,454	591,133	227.6	581	9,255	19,383	20,056	18,128
1975	11,443	13,165	617,743	261.7	506	11,480	24,909	26,055	19,275
1976	11,786	13,885	568,190	295.8	1,571[2]	11,685	29,956	33,978	23,296
1977	12,547	14,488	774,860	326.2	218	3,742	32,721	39,011	29,586
1978	12,975	15,172	945,763	350.3	402	7,393	32,866	42,902	39,622
1979	13,338	15,839	1,108,543	381.6	463	7,834	35,216	46,923	55,807
1980	n.a.	n.a.	1,483,211	419.6	441	8,975	40,054	52,364	68,595

1. In manufacturing. 2. This figure includes 830,000 affected by "day of protest." NOTE: n.a. = not available. *Source:* Statistics Canada

Estimates of the Civilian Labor Force and Its Main Components, Annual Averages
(in thousands)

Year	Civilian population[1]	Civilian labor force[1]: Employed	Civilian labor force[1]: Unemployed	Civilian labor force[1]: Total labor force	Persons not in the labor force[1]	Unemployment rate percent	Participation rate percent
1967	13,874	7,379	315	7,694	6,179	4.1	55.5
1968	14,264	7,537	382	7,919	6,344	4.8	55.5
1969	14,638	7,780	382	8,162	6,475	4.7	55.8
1970	15,016	7,879	495	8,374	6,642	5.9	55.8
1971	15,388	8,079	552	8,631	6,757	6.4	56.1
1972	15,747	8,329	562	8,891	6,856	6.3	56.5
1973	16,125	8,759	520	9,279	6,846	5.6	57.5
1974	16,562	9,137	525	9,662	6,900	5.4	58.3
1975	16,470	9,363	697	10,060	6,410	6.9	61.1
1976	16,873	9,572	736	10,308	6,565	7.1	61.1
1977	17,250	9,754	862	10,616	6,634	8.1	61.5
1978[2]	17,381	9,972	911	10,882	6,499	8.4	62.6
1979[2]	17,691	10,369	838	11,207	6,484	7.5	63.3
1980[2]	18,004	10,655	867	11,522	6,483	7.5	64.0
1981[2]	18,295	10,933	898	11,830	6,464	7.6	64.7

1. 14 years of age, or over. 2. 15 years of age, or over. *Source:* Statistics Canada.

Highest Elevations

Province or territory	Height in feet	Height in meters
Alberta—Mount Columbia	12,294	3,747
British Columbia—Mt. Fairweather	15,300	4,663
Manitoba—Baldy Mountain	2,729	832
New Brunswick—Mount Carleton	2,690	820
Newfoundland—Cirque Mt., Labrador Penin.	5,160	1,573
Nova Scotia—North Barren Mt., Cape Breton Island	1,747	532
Ontario—Ogidaki Mt.	2,183	665
Prince Edward Island—highest point Queens County	465	142
Quebec—Mt. Jacques Cartier, Gaspé Penin.	4,160	1,268
Saskatchewan—Cypress Hills	4,546	1,386
Northwest Territories—Mt. Sir James MacBrien	9,062	2,762
Yukon Territory—Mount Logan	19,850	6,050

Air Distances Between Cities
(via Air Canada)

From	To	Miles[1]	From	To	Miles[1]
Gander	Montreal	1,109	Montreal	Toronto	326
Gander	Toronto	1,494	Montreal	Vancouver	2,444
Halifax	Moncton	120	Montreal	Windsor	521
Halifax	Montreal	571	Ottawa	Winnipeg	1,174
Halifax	North Bay	1,034	St. John's, Nfld.	Montreal	1,147
Halifax	Ottawa	665	Sydney	Halifax	200
Halifax	Toronto	897	Toronto	Chicago	435
Halifax	Vancouver	3,015	Toronto	Cleveland	195
Halifax	Winnipeg	1,893	Toronto	Edmonton	1,693
Lethbridge	Calgary	124	Toronto	New York	375
Lethbridge	Edmonton	301	Toronto	Tampa	1,119
Montreal	Boston	778	Toronto	Vancouver	2,118
Montreal	Edmonton	2,019	Toronto	Winnipeg	942
Montreal	Goose Bay	824	Vancouver	Victoria	47
Montreal	Moncton	451	Winnipeg	Calgary	750
Montreal	New York	350	Winnipeg	Edmonton	753
Montreal	Ottawa	94			

1. Statute miles. *Source:* Air Canada.

Mileage Between Principal Points in Canada

(via rail or water)

Approximate distances by rail or water	Nfld. St. John's	N.S. Halifax	P.E.I. Charlottetown	N.B. Saint John	N.B. Fredericton	Que. Quebec	Que. Montreal	Ont. Ottawa	Ont. Toronto	Ont. Thunder Bay	Man. Winnipeg	Sask. Regina	Sask. Saskatoon	Alta. Calgary	Alta. Edmonton	B.C. Vancouver	B.C. Victoria	B.C. Pr. Rupert
St. John's	0	930	1,041	1,081	1,094	1,466	1,563	1,675	1,897	2,521	2,797	3,153	3,268	3,531	3,646	4,262	4,362	4,543
Halifax	930	0	239	279	292	664	761	873	1,095	1,719	1,995	2,351	2,466	2,729	2,844	3,460	3,560	3,741
Charlottetown	1,041	239	0	215	230	600	684	795	1,018	1,653	1,950	2,305	2,421	2,772	2,751	3,413	3,498	3,707
Saint John	1,081	279	215	0	67	425	482	594	816	1,470	1,894	2,250	2,374	2,726	2,699	3,368	3,324	3,655
Fredericton	1,094	292	230	67	0	403	454	565	788	1,423	1,753	2,108	2,224	2,575	2,554	3,216	3,301	3,510
Quebec City	1,466	664	600	425	403	0	164	276	498	1,152	1,521	1,877	1,992	2,353	2,323	2,995	2,898	3,279
Montreal	1,563	761	684	482	454	164	0	112	334	988	1,357	1,713	1,828	2,244	2,151	2,886	2,900	3,115
Ottawa	1,675	873	795	594	565	276	112	0	247	887	1,301	1,658	1,772	2,133	2,098	2,775	2,789	3,054
Toronto	1,897	1,095	1,018	816	788	498	334	247	0	809	1,233	1,590	1,704	2,065	2,030	2,707	2,755	2,986
Thunder Bay	2,521	1,719	1,653	1,470	1,423	1,152	988	877	809	0	424	781	895	1,256	1,221	1,898	1,967	2,177
Winnipeg	2,797	1,995	1,950	1,894	1,753	1,521	1,357	1,301	1,233	424	0	356	471	832	797	1,474	1,548	1,753
Regina	3,153	2,351	2,305	2,250	2,108	1,877	1,713	1,658	1,590	781	356	0	161	476	487	1,118	1,193	1,443
Saskatoon	3,268	2,466	2,421	2,374	2,224	1,992	1,828	1,772	1,704	895	471	161	0	399	326	1,097	1,131	1,282
Calgary	3,531	2,729	2,772	2,726	2,575	2,353	2,244	2,133	2,065	1,256	832	476	399	0	195	642	727	1,151
Edmonton	3,646	2,844	2,751	2,699	2,554	2,323	2,151	2,098	2,030	1,221	797	487	326	195	0	771	846	956
Vancouver	4,262	3,460	3,413	3,368	3,216	2,995	2,886	2,775	2,707	1,898	1,474	1,118	1,097	642	771	0	85	546
Victoria	4,362	3,560	3,498	3,324	3,301	2,898	2,900	2,789	2,755	1,967	1,548	1,193	1,131	727	846	85	0	631
Prince Rupert	4,543	3,741	3,707	3,655	3,510	3,279	3,115	3,054	2,986	2,177	1,753	1,443	1,282	1,151	956	546	641	0

Land and Fresh Water Areas of Canada

Province, territory, or district	Land		Fresh water		Total		Percent of total area
	Sq miles	Sq km	Sq miles	Sq km	Sq miles	Sq km	
Alberta	248,800	644,392	6,485	16,976	255,285	661,188	6.6
British Columbia	359,279	930,533	6,976	18,068	366,255	948,601	9.5
Manitoba	211,775	548,497	39,225	101,593	251,000	650,090	6.5
New Brunswick	27,835	72,093	519	1,344	28,354	73,437	0.7
Newfoundland	143,045	370,487	413,140	34,033	156,185	404,520	4.1
Nova Scotia	20,402	52,841	1,023	2,650	21,425	55,491	0.6
Ontario	344,092	891,198	68,490	177,389	412,582	1,068,587	10.7
Prince Edward Island	2,184	5,657	—	—	2,184	5,657	0.1
Quebec	523,860	1,356,797	71,000	183,890	594,860	1,540,687	15.4
Saskatchewan	220,182	570,271	31,518	81,632	251,700	651,903	6.5
Northwest Territories	1,253,438	3,246,404	51,465	133,294	1,304,903	3,379,698	33.9
Franklin	541,753	1,403,140	7,500	19,425	549,253	1,422,565	14.3
Keewatin	218,460	565,811	9,700	25,123	228,160	590,134	5.9
Mackenzie	493,225	1,277,453	34,265	88,746	527,490	1,366,199	13.7
Yukon Territory	205,346	531,846	1,730	4,481	207,076	536,327	5.4
Totals	**3,560,238**	**9,221,017**	**291,571**	**755,169**	**3,851,809**	**9,976,186**	**100.0**

Canada's 20 Tallest Buildings

City	Building	Stories	Height ft	Height m
Toronto	CN Tower	—	1,821	555
Toronto	First Bank Tower	72	952	290
Toronto	Commerce Court West	57	784	239
Toronto	Toronto–Dominion Tower	56	758	231
Calgary	Calgary Tower	—	626	191
Montreal	Place Victoria	47	624	190
Montreal	Place Ville Marie	42	616	188
Montreal	Canadian Imperial Bank of Commerce	43	604	184
Toronto	Royal Trust Tower	46	600	183
Toronto	Royal Bank Plaza—South Tower	41	589	180
Vancouver	Harbour Center (incl. 100-ft pylon)	32	581	177
Toronto	Manulife Centre	53	545	166
Calgary	Scotia Centre	38	504	154
Calgary	Bank of Montreal	45	500	152
Calgary	Nova Building	37	500	152
Montreal	Le Complexe Desjardins La Tour du Sud	40	498	152
Toronto	Two Bloor West	34	486	148
Toronto	Commerce Court North	34	476	145
Toronto	Simpson Tower	33	473	144
Toronto	Sun Life Centre	35	470	143

Average Temperature and Precipitation Data

Station	Temperature °C Mean Jan.	Mean July	Extreme Max.	Extreme Min.	Average frost date Last in spring	First in fall	Average total annual precip. (mm)	Aver. ann. snow-fall (cm)
St. John's A, Nfld.	−3.8	15.3	30.6	−23.3	June 3	Oct. 12	1511.5	363.7
Charlottetown A, P.E.I.	−6.7	18.4	34.4	−27.8	May 17	Oct. 15	1127.8	305.1
Halifax, N.S.	−3.2	18.3	34.4	−25.0	May 1	Nov. 1	1318.8	210.8
Sydney A, N.S.	−4.4	17.9	35.0	−25.6	May 23	Oct. 16	1340.9	288.0
Yarmouth A, N.S.	−2.7	16.4	30.0	−21.0	May 2	Oct. 24	1283.2	204.5
Chatham A, N.B.	−9.3	19.2	37.8	−35.0	May 22	Sept. 21	1051.2	309.4
Moncton A, N.B.	−7.9	18.6	37.2	−32.2	May 23	Sept. 23	1099.3	313.7
Saint John A, N.B.	−7.1	17.1	34.4	−36.7	May 18	Oct. 2	1400.3	204.7
Fort Chimo A, Que.	−23.4	11.4	32.2	−46.7	June 27	Aug. 30	483.8	236.7
Montreal McGill, Que.	−8.9	21.6	36.1	−33.9	April 22	Oct. 23	999.0	243.1
Quebec A, Que.	−11.6	19.2	35.6	−36.1	May 18	Sept. 28	1088.6	326.6
Schefferville (Knob Lake) A, Que.	−22.7	12.6	31.7	−50.6	June 18	Aug. 31	722.5	335.5
Sherbrooke, Que.	−9.6	20.1	36.7	−41.1	May 12	Sept. 27	972.6	244.6
London A, Ont.	−6.0	20.5	36.7	−31.7	May 9	Oct. 6	924.5	201.2
Ottawa A, Ont.	−10.9	20.7	37.8	−36.1	May 11	Oct. 1	850.9	215.6
Thunder Bay A, Ont.	−14.8	17.5	37.2	−41.1	May 31	Sept. 10	738.5	222.0
Toronto, Ont.	−4.4	21.8	40.6	−32.8	April 20	Oct. 30	789.9	141.0
Churchill A., Man.	−27.6	12.0	33.9	−45.0	June 22	Sept. 12	396.6	183.9
The Pas A, Man.	−22.4	17.9	36.7	−49.4	May 28	Sept. 20	449.7	157.2
Winnipeg A, Man.	−18.3	19.7	40.6	−45.0	May 25	Sept. 21	535.2	131.3
Regina A, Sask.	−17.3	18.9	43.3	−50.0	May 27	Sept. 12	397.9	114.8
Saskatoon A, Sask.	−18.7	18.8	40.0	−47.8	May 27	Sept. 15	352.6	112.5
Beaverlodge CDA, Alta.	−14.9	15.6	36.7	−47.8	May 22	Sept. 7	454.7	183.6
Calgary A, Alta.	−10.9	16.5	36.1	−45.0	May 28	Sept. 12	437.1	153.9
Edmonton Ind. A, Alta.	−14.7	17.5	34.4	−48.3	May 14	Sept. 19	446.5	132.1
Kamloops A, B.C.	−6.0	20.9	40.6	−37.2	May 5	Sept. 28	260.6	77.0
Prince George A, B.C.	−11.8	14.9	34.4	−50.0	June 10	Aug. 28	620.7	233.4
Prince Rupert, B.C.	1.8	13.6	32.2	−21.1	April 19	Nov. 5	2414.5	113.0
Vancouver A, B.C.	2.4	17.4	33.3	−17.8	March 31	Oct. 30	1068.1	52.3
Dawson, Y.T.	−28.6	15.5	35.0	−58.3	May 26	Aug. 27	325.5	136.4
Whitehorse A, Y.T.	−18.9	14.1	34.4	−52.2	June 5	Sept. 1	260.3	127.8
Coppermine, N.W.T.	−29.4	9.3	32.2	−50.0	June 27	Aug. 21	216.3	101.9
Fort Simpson A, N.W.T.	−27.6	16.1	35.0	−53.3	May 31	Aug. 29	343.2	137.9
Frobisher Bay A, N.W.T.	−26.2	7.9	24.4	−45.6	June 30	Aug. 29	415.2	246.9
Resolute A, N.W.T.	−32.6	4.3	18.3	−52.2	July 10	July 20	136.4	78.7

A = Airport, Ind. A = Industrial Airport CDA = Canada Department of Agriculture. *Source: Canada Year Book 1980–81,* Statistics Canada.

Canadian Church Membership

Religious group	Churches	Members	Clergy
Protestant and others[1]	17,385	4,445,902	17,883
Roman Catholics	5,729	10,123,329	12,986
Jewish congregations	112	305,000	n.a.
Eastern churches[2]	238	430,170	170
Polish National Catholic, Armenian churches	18	31,000	15
Buddhist	15	2,543	10
Miscellaneous	19	4,603	13
Total	**23,516**	**15,342,547**	**31,077**

1. Includes such groups as Latter-Day Saints and Jehovah's Witnesses. 2. Includes Coptic church. NOTE: n.a. = not available. *Source: Yearbook of American and Canadian Churches 1982.*

Major Canadian Awards, 1981

Governor General's Literary Awards

Fiction: English: Mavis Gallant, *Home Truth: Selected Canadian Stories;* French: Deny Chabot, *La Province Lunaire*
Poetry: English: F.R. Scott, *The Collected Poems of F.R. Scott;* French: Michel Beaulieu, *Visages*
Drama: English: Sharon Pollock, *Blood Relations;* French: Marie Laberge, *C'Etait Avant La Guerre L'Anse à Gilles*
Nonfiction: English: George Colef, *Caribou and the Barren-Lands;* French: Madeleine Ouellette-Michalska, *L'Echappee des Discours de L'Oeil*

Juno Award Winners

Female Vocalist: Anne Murray
Male Vocalist: Bruce Cockburn
Group: Loverboy
Country Female Vocalist: Anne Murray
Country Male Vocalist: Ronnie Hawkins
Country Group: The Good Brothers
Best New Female Vocalist: Shari Ulrich
Best New Male Vocalist: Eddie Schwartz
Best New Group: Saga
Folksinger: Bruce Cockburn
Instrumental Artist: Liona Boyd
Composer: Mike Reno and Paul Dean for *Turn Me Loose*
Best Jazz Recording: The Brass Connection for *The Brass Connection*
Best Classical Recording: L'Orchestre Symphonique de Montréal for Ravel, *Daphnis et Chloe*

Actra Awards

Earle Grey Award for Best Acting Performance in Television in a Leading Role Lally Cadeau, *You've Come a Long Way, Katie*
Andrew Allan Award for Best Acting Performance in Radio: Mary Pirie, *Party Girl (Sunday Matinee)*
Du Maurier Award for Best New Performer in Canadian Television: Leslie Toth for *Once*
Gordon Sinclair Award for Outspoken Opinions and Integrity in Broadcasting: Stephen Lewis
Foster Hewitt Award for Excellence in Sportscasting: Brian Williams
Best Supporting Actor in Television: Ken James, *You've Come A Long Way, Katie*
Best Variety Performance—Television: Evelyn Hart and David Peregrine for *Belong (Arts Benefit)*
Best Variety Performance—Radio: Roger Abbott, Dave Broadfoot, Don Ferguson, Luba Goy, John Morgan, *Air Farce*
Best Host/Interviewer—Television: Adrienne Clarkson, *Hebron (Fifth Estate)*
Best Host/Interviewer—Radio: Don Harron, *Morningside* and Jay Ingram, *Quirks and Quarks*
Best Writer—Television Drama: Tony Sheer, *Final Edition (For the Record)*
Best Writer—Radio Drama: Erika Ritter, *Automatic Pilot (Festival Theatre)*
Best Writer—Television Variety: Roger Abbott, Dave Broadfoot, Don Ferguson, Gord Holtam, John Morgan, Rick Olsen, *Air Farce*
Best Writer—Radio Variety: Philip Bedard, Glen Davis, Larry Lalonde, *The Continuing Adventures of John Locke, Private Eye*
Best Writer—Television Documentary/Public Affairs: Donald Brittain, *The Most Dangerous Spy (We Stand on Guard for Thee)*
Best Writer—Radio Documentary/Public Affairs: Jurgen Hesse, *Leon Trotsky in Exile (Ideas)*
Best Children's Television Program: *Switchback* , a CBC production, Nijole Kuzmickas, producer
Best Radio Program of the Year: *This Year in Jerusalem,* a CBC production, produced by Charlotte Odele and Dawna Treibicz
Best Television Program of the Year: *Just Another Missing Kid,* a CBC production, produced by John Zaritsky
The John Drainie Award for Distinguished Contribution to Broadcasting: Mavor Moore

The Royal Bank Award

In 1967, as a Canadian centennial project, The Royal Bank of Canada established the Royal Bank Award to honor "a Canadian citizen or person domiciled in Canada whose outstanding achievement is of such importance that it is contributing to human welfare and the common good." The award consists of a gold medal and a cash grant of $100,000.

1967 Dr. Wilder Penfield, neurosurgeon
1968 Dr. C. J. Mackenzie, engineer
1969 His Eminence Paul-Emile Cardinal Léger
1970 Morley Callaghan, novelist
1971 Arthur Erickson, architect
1972 Dr. Gustave Gingras, rehabilitation expert
1973 Dr. J. A. Corry, educationalist
1974 Jean Gascon, actor/director
1975 Dr. R. Keith Downey and Dr. Baldur R. Stefansson, agricultural scientists
1976 Mary Pack, organizer of the Canadian Arthritis and Rheumantism Society
1977 Dr. W. A. Paddon and Dr. Gordon W. Thomas, frontier medical pioneers
1978 Dr. H. Northrop Frye, literary scholar
1979 Dr. Lotta Hitschmanova, founder and executive director, Unitarian Service Committee of Canada
1980 Dr. Jacques Genest, founder and director, Clinical Research Institute of Montreal
1981 Harry E. Foster, founder and president, Canadian Special Olympics Inc.
1982 Rt. Rev. Georges-Henri Levesque, o.p., social scientist

Federal Courts

Federal courts in Canada include the Supreme Court of Canada, the Federal Court of Canada, and various specialized tribunals such as the Tax Review Board, the Court Martial Appeal Court, and the Immigration Appeal Board. These courts and tribunals are created by Parliament.

Canada's Population Is Moving West

Two of Canada's western provinces, Alberta and British Columbia, were the only ones to experience growth rates above the national average, according to census figures. While Canada's population increased by 12.9% between 1971 and 1981, Alberta's rose by 37.5% and British Columbia's by 25.6%. The four western provinces, including Manitoba and Saskatchewan, which only had small population gains, increased their share of the total population during the decade, while all of the other regions' shares dropped.

U.S. Passport and Customs Information

Source: Department of State, Passport Services and Department of the Treasury, Customs Service

Passports

With a few exceptions, a passport is required for all United States citizens to depart from and enter the United States and to enter most foreign countries. A United States citizen is not required by United States laws or regulations to have a valid passport for travel to or in North, South, or Central America, except Cuba. It is, however, recommended that a passport be obtained for travel to Central and South America since many of the countries require that United States citizens be in possession of a valid passport. United States travelers should carry documentary evidence of their United States citizenship and identity to facilitate re-entry into the United States. Travelers should check passport and visa requirements with consular officials of the countries to be visited well in advance of their departure date.

Applications for passport may be made to any Passport Agent; to a clerk of any Federal court or State court of record, or a judge or clerk or any probate court, accepting applications; or at a Post Office selected to accept passport applications. Passport agencies are located in Boston; Chicago; Honolulu; Houston; Los Angeles; Miami; New Orleans; New York; Philadelphia; San Francisco; Seattle; Stamford, Conn.; and Washington, D.C.

A first passport must be applied for in person. Applicants must present evidence of citizenship (e.g., a birth certificate), personal identification (e.g., driver's license), two identical photographs taken within six months (2 x 2 inches, with the image size measured from the bottom of the chin to the top of the head [including hair] not less than 1 inch nor more than 1⅜ inches, signed in the center on the reverse; vending machine photographs not acceptable), plus the application. A fee of $10 plus a $5 execution fee is charged.

You may apply by mail if you have been the bearer of a passport issued within eight years prior to the date of a new application; are able to submit your most recent United States passport with your new application; your previous passport was not issued before your 18th birthday. If you are eligible to apply by mail, include your previous passport, completed and signed Application for Passport by Mail, new signed photographs, and the $10 passport fee. The $5 execution fee is not required when applying by mail.

If you claim citizenship by naturalization, a Certificate of Naturalization is required.

Passports may be amended to show a married name or legal change of name, to correct descriptive data, or to exclude a person previously included.

Any alterations by the bearer other than change of address and notification data appearing in the passport are forbidden.

Your passport is valid for five years from date of issue unless specifically limited by the Secretary of State to a shorter period of validity.

The passport is a traveler's principal means of identification abroad, and its loss is very serious. It

U.S. Travel Industry Statistics

Volume, receipts, employment	1981	1980	1979	1975
Domestic travel volume[1] (in millions of passenger-miles)				
Automobile	1,176.3	975.9	996.0	n.a.
Air	201.2	189.8	200.6	131.8
Bus	27.2	17.5	17.1	n.a.
Rail	4.7	4.7	4.8	3.8
Total (millions)	**1,409.4**	**1,187.9**	**1,218.5**	**n.a.**
Industry receipts[2] (in billions of dollars)				
Transportation	$130.5	$114.5	$ 90.1	$ 57.7
Lodging	26.6	25.1	23.5	13.7
Food service	94.1	82.2	75.1	51.4
Amusements	31.7	28.3	25.8	18.0
Total (billions)	**$282.9**	**$250.1**	**$214.5**	**$140.8**
Employment[3] (in millions of jobs)				
Transportation	1.06	1.06	1.05	1.02
Lodging	1.06	1.01	1.02	.82
Food service	4.83	4.82	4.58	3.33
Total (millions)	**6.95**	**6.89**	**6.65**	**5.17**

1. Includes: Auto: Main rural road passenger-miles; Air: Domestic certified air carrier revenue passenger-miles; Bus: All intercity bus passenger-miles; Rail: Amtrak passenger-miles. 2. Includes: Transportation: Air and rail transportation companies, gasoline service stations; Lodging: Commercial lodging places; Food Service: Eating and drinking places; Amusements: Amusement and recreation services. 3. Includes: Transportation: Air transportation, intercity highway transportation and gasoline service stations; Lodging: Commercial lodging places; Food Service: Eating and drinking places. NOTE: n.a. = not available. *Source:* U.S. Travel Data Center, Washington, D.C.

should be reported immediately to the nearest United States embassy or consular office. Loss of a passport in the United States should be reported in writing to Passport Services, Department of State, Washington, D.C. 20524, or the nearest Passport Agency.

NOTE: The period of validity of passports, passport fees, and criteria for use of the passport-by-mail and amendment procedures may change. This information should be checked with your nearest Passport official.

Customs

United States residents must declare all articles acquired abroad and in their possession at the time of their return. In addition, articles acquired in the U.S. Virgin Islands, American Samoa, or Guam and not accompanying you must be declared at the time of your return. The wearing or use of an article acquired abroad does *not* exempt it from duty. Customs declaration forms are distributed on vessels and planes, and should be prepared in advance of arrival for presentation to the customs inspectors.

If you have not exceeded the duty-free exemption allowed, you may make an oral declaration to the customs inspector. A written declaration is necessary when (1) total fair retail value of articles exceeds $300 (keep your sales slips); (2) over 1 liter of liquor, 200 cigarettes, or 100 cigars are included; (3) items are not intended for your personal or household use, or articles brought home for another person; and (4) when a customs duty or internal revenue tax is collectible on any article in your possession.

An exception to the above are regulations applicable to articles purchased in the Virgin Islands, American Samoa, or Guam where you may receive a customs exemption of $600. Not more than $300 of this exemption may be applied to merchandise obtained elsewhere than in these islands. Four liters of alcoholic beverages and 1000 cigarettes may be included provided not more than one liter and 200 cigarettes were acquired elsewhere than in these islands. Articles acquired in and sent from these islands to the United States may be claimed under your duty-free personal exemption if properly declared at the time of your return.

Articles accompanying you, in excess of your personal exemption, up to $600 will be assessed at a flat rate of duty of 10% based on fair retail value in country of acquisition. (If articles were acquired in the insular possessions, the flat rate of duty is 5% and these goods may accompany you or be shipped home.) These articles must be for your personal use or for use as gifts and not for sale. This provision may be used every 30 days, excluding the day of your last arrival. Any items which have a "free" duty rate will be excluded before duty is calculated.

Other exemptions include in part: automobiles, boats, planes, or other vehicles taken abroad for noncommercial use. Foreign-made personal articles (e.g., watches, cameras, etc.) taken abroad should be registered with Customs before departure. Gifts of not more than $25 can be shipped back to the United States tax and duty free ($40 if mailed from the Virgin Islands, American Samoa, or Guam). Household effects and tools of trade which you take out of the United States are duty free at time of return.

Prohibited and restricted articles include in part: absinthe, narcotics and dangerous drugs, obscene articles and publications, seditious and treasonable materials, hazardous articles (e.g., fireworks, dangerous toys, toxic and poisonous substances, and switchblade knives), biological materials of public health or veterinary importance, fruit, vegetables and plants, meats, poultry and products thereof, birds, monkeys, and turtles.

If you understate the value of an article you declare, or if you otherwise misrepresent an article in your declaration, you may have to pay a penalty in addition to payment of duty. Under certain circumstances, the article could be seized and forfeited if the penalty is not paid.

If you fail to declare an article acquired abroad, not only is the article subject to seizure and forfeiture, but you will be liable for a personal penalty in an amount equal to the value of the article in the United States. In addition, you may also be liable to criminal prosecution.

If you carry more than $5,000 into or out of the United States in currency (either United States or foreign money), negotiable instruments in bearer form, or travelers checks, a report must be filed with United States Customs at the time you arrive or depart with such amounts.

As U.S. restrictions on travel to Cuba, North Korea, Vietnam, and Cambodia have been eased, the Office of Foreign Assets Control (FAC) issued a general license, effective March 21, 1977, which allows visitors to those countries to purchase a max-

Price Index Figures for Domestic Travel and Selected Components, 1976–1981

(1967 = 100)

	1976	1977	1978	1979	1980	1981
Travel price index	169.9	187.8	203.3	234.3	283.2	319.7
Gasoline	177.9	188.2	196.3	265.6	369.1	410.9
Common carrier transportation fares						
Taxicab	176.9	189.9	203.5	221.7	259.5	283.1
Intercity train	165.3	180.6	194.6	212.4	250.1	297.9
Air	172.2	182.0	190.6	205.8	284.8	358.4
Bus	196.9	223.5	240.2	260.0	297.1	339.8
Lodging	172.9	187.0	212.7	245.8	280.7	312.8
Food service	186.1	200.3	218.4	242.9	267.0	291.0
Entertainment services	127.4	166.2	175.4	187.6	201.0	216.3
Incidentals	—	161.5	168.7	178.0	193.3	206.1

Source: U.S. Travel Data Center.

imum of $100 worth of goods. This amount is based on retail value in the country where acquired. These articles must be for personal use—not for resale—and must accompany the traveler on his entry into the U.S. This allowance may be used only once every 6 months.

Expenditures of U.S. Travelers to Foreign Countries

(in millions of dollars)

Type of expense	1980	1979	1978	1977	1975
Transportation fare payments	$6,111	$5,162	$4,680	$4,473	$3,726
Foreign flag carriers	3,607	3,184	2,896	2,748	2,263
U.S. flag carriers	2,504	1,978	1,784	1,725	1,463
Travel payments in foreign countries	10,397	9,413	8,475	7,451	6,417
Canada	1,817	1,599	1,407	1,433	1,306
Mexico	2,564	2,460	2,121	1,918	1,637
Mexican border zone	1,416	1,291	1,128	1,165	1,047
Total overseas areas	6,016	5,354	4,947	4,100	3,474
Europe and Mediterranean[1]	3,412	3,185	2,942	2,398	1,918
Western Europe	3,021	2,842	2,600	2,103	1,709
United Kingdom	903	826	771	585	404
France	383	355	287	233	226
Italy	360	300	260	240	194
Switzerland	150	158	153	145	121
West Germany	322	283	220	203	174
Austria	104	84	75	73	65
Denmark	49	54	70	51	43
Sweden	42	38	52	40	29
Norway	51	47	49	37	44
Netherlands	95	71	65	49	60
Belgium and Luxembourg	44	50	37	34	39
Spain	173	200	213	151	135
Portugal	69	58	53	37	19
Ireland	103	115	110	97	55
Greece	139	163	140	102	73
Other Western Europe	34	40	45	26	28
Other Europe and Mediterranean	391	343	342	295	209
Israel	179	157	144	146	57
Other[2]	212	186	198	149	152
Caribbean Area and Central America	1,134	1,019	888	790	787
Bermuda	191	164	136	123	118
Bahama	262	224	198	158	161
Jamaica	118	122	118	100	118
Other British West Indies	189	190	153	144	103
Netherlands West Indies	157	138	114	106	97
Other West Indies and Central America	217	181	169	159	190
South America	392	288	306	254	242
Other overseas areas	1,078	862	811	658	527
Japan	185	142	155	149	131
Hong Kong	145	137	113	87	75
Australia and New Zealand	234	153	123	92	54
Other	514	430	420	330	267
Total expenses[3]	**16,508**	**14,575**	**13,155**	**11,924**	**10,143**

1. Includes Algeria, Cyprus, Egypt, Israel, Lebanon, Libya, Malta, Morocco, Syria, Tunisia, and Turkey. 2. Includes U.S.S.R. 3. Cruise passenger fare payments included in transportation payments (predominantly foreign flag carriers). Shore expenditures included in regional and country totals. *Source:* Department of Commerce, Bureau of Economic Analysis.

Foreign Currency Exchange

Visitors to foreign countries can usually change their U.S. dollars into the appropriate currency at their point of departure. Most airports have currency exchange facilities, generally open from 9:00 A.M. to 10:00 P.M. The Deak-Perera Group, the largest private organization specializing in foreign money exchange, has offices in some airports. It is generally advisable for an American traveling to a foreign destination to have a small amount of the foreign currency on hand on arrival. Currency can usually be exchanged at foreign entry points.

Visitors to the United States can usually exchange their currency into U.S. dollars at their port of entry. A large number of banks also exchange foreign currency during normal banking hours.

Expenditures of Visitors in U.S.
(in millions of dollars)

Country or region of permanent residence	1980	1979	1978	1977	1975
Transportation—U.S. Flag Carriers	$2,053	$1,677	$1,238	$1,025	$ 767
Expenditures in U.S.	10,090	8,383	7,186	6,150	4,697
Canada	2,428	2,092	2,248	2,150	1,561
Mexico	2,554	1,869	1,459	1,316	1,311
U.S. border area	1,646	1,160	954	967	972
Overseas Visitors	5,108	4,422	3,479	2,684	1,825
Western Europe	1,942	1,715	1,323	1,003	611
United Kingdom	469	375	308	205	144
Germany	500	440	333	263	145
France	216	180	140	121	68
Italy	96	84	70	61	41
Netherlands	108	97	84	57	36
Belgium	n.a.	48	34	29	14
Sweden	n.a.	n.a.	54	40	23
Switzerland	n.a.	n.a.	72	51	32
Other	n.a.	n.a.	228	176	108
Caribbean and Central America	417	375	322	276	206
South America	977	793	660	455	303
Other Areas	1,772	1,539	1,174	950	705
Japan	774	699	539	450	410
Total expenditures	**12,143**	**10,060**	**8,424**	**7,175**	**5,464**

NOTE: n.a. = not available. *Source:* Department of Commerce, Bureau of Economic Analysis.

Travelers from the U.S. to Foreign Countries[1] by Country and Region Visited
(in thousands)

Country or region visited	1980	1979	1978	1977	1975
Canada[2]	10,963[3]	10,909	11,277	11,451	12,499
Mexico[4]	4,144	4,000[4]	3,073	2,735	2,786
Total Overseas	8,163	7,835	7,790	7,390,	6,354
Europe and Mediterranean	3,934	4,068	4,105	3,920	3,185
Western Europe	3,746	3,866	3,914	3,663	2,990
Austria	420	419	426	359	377
Belgium-Luxembourg	243	257	234	240	289
Denmark	181	206	271	238	230
France	888	943	882	786	809
Greece	284	309	284	257	178
Ireland	239	278	296	303	191
Italy	749	718	718	715	650
Netherlands	395	379	363	317	416
Norway	118	137	165	147	135
Portugal	185	195	195	134	95
Spain	368	443	524	334	370
Sweden	135	136	213	180	150
Switzerland	529	535	572	620	567
United Kingdom	1,580	1,617	1,725	1,559	1,199
West Germany	787	864	765	768	733
Other Western Europe	159	167	219	122	142
Israel	289	258	277	316	138
Other Europe and Mediterranean[5]	497	509	606	489	515
Caribbean Area and Central America	2,624	2,533	2,365	2,203	2,065
South America	594	434	515	483	447
Other Overseas Areas	1,011	800	805	784	657
Total	**23,270**	**22,744**	**22,140**	**21,576**	**21,639**

1. Excludes travel by military personnel and other government employees stationed abroad; also excludes cruise travelers. 2. Visitors staying one or more nights. 3. Preliminary figure. 4. Mexican National Tourist Council. Visitors staying one or more nights. 5. Includes the U.S.S.R. *Sources:* Department of Commerce, Bureau of Economic Analysis, and *Statistics Canada.*

International Tourist Arrivals and Receipts, 1980–1981

Area	Arrivals (millions) 1980[1]	Arrivals (millions) 1981[2]	Receipts (billions) 1980[1]	Receipts (billions) 1981[2]
Africa	6.0	6.2	2.0	2.5
Americas	54.9	57.3	20.8	22.9
East Asia and the Pacific	15.5	17.0	7.0	8.0
Europe	195.0	202.0	62.0	68.5
Middle East	5.5	6.0	2.5	3.0
South Asia	1.7	2.0	1.0	1.2
Total	**279.0**	**290.0**	**95.3**	**106.1**

1. Revised estimates. 2. Preliminary estimates. *Source:* World Tourist Organization.

Volume of Domestic Travel by U.S. Residents

(in millions of person-trips)

Domestic Travel	1981
Mode of Transportation:	
Auto, truck, recreational vehicle	966.2
Airplane	146.5
Bus	23.3
Train	11.7
Other	17.9
Purpose of trip:	
Visiting friends and relatives	426.5
Other pleasures	416.9
Business and convention	160.1
Other	162.1
Type of trip:	
Vacation	737.5
Weekend	552.0
Total person–trips	**1,165.6**

Source: U.S. Travel Data Center, Washington, D.C.

Object of Travel by Passport Recipients[1]

Object	1981	1980	1979	1978
Personal reasons	43.5%	41.2%	48.6%	48.5%
Pleasure	26.8	27.5	17.4	25.4
Business	4.5	5.3	6.4	5.1
Education	1.9	2.6	2.9	2.3
Religious	.27	.4	.4	.3
Scientific	.06	.09	.04	.05
Health	.02	.03	.02	.03
Government	4.4	4.5	4.6	4.4
Not Stated	18.6	18.3	19.5	13.9

1. Percentages rounded off. *Source: Summary of Passport Statistics,* Department of State, Passport Services, Bureau of Consular Affairs.

Passport Recipients by Sex and Age Groups, 1981

Age group	Male	Female	Total
Under 5	48,230	64,680	112,910
5–14	90,460	119,980	210,440
15–24	183,040	292,100	475,140
25–44	583,050	537,340	1,120,390
45–59	377,630	341,830	719,460
60–69	183,510	200,260	383,770
70–Over	86,530	113,706	200,236
Total	**1,552,450**	**1,669,896**	**3,222,346**

Source: Summary of Passport Statistics: Department of State, Passport Services, Bureau of Consular Affairs.

Average Daily Temperatures (°F) in Tourist Cities

Location	January High	January Low	April High	April Low	July High	July Low	October High	October Low
U.S. CITIES								
(See Weather and Climate Section)								
CANADA								
(See Canadian Section)								
MEXICO								
Acapulco	85	70	87	71	89	75	88	74
Mexico City	66	42	78	52	74	54	70	50
OVERSEAS								
Australia (Sydney)	78	65	71	58	60	46	71	56
Austria (Vienna)	34	26	57	41	75	59	55	44
Bahamas (Nassau)	77	65	81	69	88	75	85	73
Bermuda (Hamilton)	68	58	71	59	85	73	79	69
Brazil (Rio de Janeiro)	84	73	80	69	75	63	77	66
Denmark (Copenhagen)	36	29	50	37	72	55	53	42
Egypt (Cairo)	65	47	83	57	96	70	86	65
France (Paris)	42	32	60	41	76	55	59	44
Germany (Berlin)	35	26	55	38	74	55	55	41
Greece (Athens)	54	42	67	52	90	72	74	60

Location	January		April		July		October	
	High	Low	High	Low	High	Low	High	Low
Hong Kong	64	56	75	67	87	78	81	73
India (Calcutta)	80	55	97	76	90	79	89	74
Italy (Rome)	54	39	68	46	88	64	73	53
Israel (Jerusalem)	55	41	73	50	87	63	81	59
Japan (Tokyo)	47	29	63	46	83	70	69	55
Nigeria (Lagos)	88	74	89	77	83	74	85	74
Netherlands (Amsterdam)	40	34	52	43	69	59	56	48
Puerto Rico (San Juan)	81	67	84	69	87	74	87	73
South Africa (Cape Town)	78	60	72	53	63	45	70	52
Spain (Madrid)	47	33	64	44	87	62	66	48
United Kingdom (London)	44	35	56	40	73	55	58	44
United Kingdom (Edinburgh)	43	35	50	39	65	52	53	44
U.S.S.R. (Moscow)	21	9	47	31	76	55	46	34
Venezuela (Caracas)	75	56	81	60	78	61	79	61
Yugoslavia (Belgrade)	37	27	64	45	84	61	65	47

State and City Tourism Offices

The following is a selected list of state, tourism offices. Where a toll-free 800 number is available, it is given. However, the numbers are subject to change.

ALABAMA
Bureau of Publicity and Information
532 S. Perry St.
Montgomery, AL 36130-2051
205-832-5510 or 800-633-5761

ALASKA
Alaska Division of Tourism
Pouch E
Juneau, AK 99811
907-465-2010

ARIZONA
Arizona Office of Tourism
Suite 506
3507 N. Central Ave.
Phoenix, AZ 85012
602-255-3618

ARKANSAS
Arkansas Department of Parks and Tourism
1 Capitol Mall
Little Rock, AR 72201
501-371-7777 or 800-643-8383

CALIFORNIA
California Office of Tourism
Department of Economics and Business Development
1030 13th St.
Suite 200
Sacramento, CA 95814
916-322-1396

COLORADO
Office of Tourism
Colorado Division of Commerce and Development
1313 Sherman St., Room 500
Denver, CO 80203
303-866-2205

CONNECTICUT
Tourism Promotion Service
Connecticut Department of Commerce
210 Washington St.
Hartford, CT 06106
203-566-3385 or 800-243-1685

DELAWARE
Delaware State Travel Service
Delaware Development Office
630 State College Rd.
Dover, DE 19901
302-736-4254 or 800-441-8846

DISTRICT OF COLUMBIA
Washington Convention and Visitors Association
Suite 250
1575 Eye Street, NW
Washington, D.C. 20005
202-789-7000

FLORIDA
Department of Commerce Visitors Inquiry
126 Van Buren St.
Tallahassee, FL 32301
904-487-1462

GEORGIA
Tourist Division
P.O. Box 1776
Atlanta, GA 30301
404-656-3590 or 800-241-8444

HAWAII
Hawaii Visitors Bureau
2270 Kalakana Ave., Suite 801
Honolulu, HI 96815
808-823-1811

IDAHO
Economic Community Affairs
State Capitol Bldg., Rm. 108
Boise, ID 83720
208-334-2470
800-635-7820

ILLINOIS
Office of Tourism
222 South College
Springfield, IL 62706
217-782-7139

INDIANA
Tourism Development Division
440 North Meridian
Indianapolis, IN 46204
317-232-8860

IOWA
Tourism and Travel Division
250 Jewett Bldg.
Des Moines, IA 50309
515-281-3100 or 3679

KANSAS
Tourist Division
Department of Economic Development
503 Kansas Ave., 6th Floor
Topeka, KS 66603
913-296-2009

KENTUCKY
Department of Economic Development
Office of Tourism
Capital Plaza Tower
Frankfort, KY 40601
502-564-4930

LOUISIANA
Office of Tourism
P.O. Box 44291, Capitol Station
Baton Rouge, LA 70804
504-925-3860
800-535-8388

MAINE
Maine Publicity Bureau
97 Winthrop St.
Hallowell, ME 04347
207-289-2423

MARYLAND
Office of Tourist Development
1748 Forest Dr.
Annapolis, MD 21401
301-269-3517 or
800-638-5252 (out of state)

MASSACHUSETTS
Division of Marketing
100 Cambridge St.
Boston, MA 02202
617-727-3201

MICHIGAN
Travel Bureau
Department of Commerce
P.O. Box 30226
Law Bldg.
Lansing, MI 48909
517-373-1195 or
800-248-5700
or for latest recorded information on special seasonal activities,
800-248-5708

MINNESOTA
Tourism Division
480 Cedar St., Hanover Bldg.
St. Paul, MN 55101
612-296-5029 or
800-328-1461

MISSISSIPPI
Division of Tourism
Department of Economic Development
P.O. Box 849
Jackson, MS 39205
601-354-6715 or
800-647-2290

MISSOURI
Missouri Division of Tourism
308 E. High St.
P.O. Box 1055
Jefferson City, MO 65102
314-751-4133 or
800-325-0733

MONTANA
Travel Promotion
Department of Commerce
1424 9th Ave.
Helena, MT 59620
406-449-2654 or
800-548-3390

NEBRASKA
Division of Tourism
Department of Economic Development
P.O. Box 94666, State Office Bldg.
Lincoln, NE 68509
402-471-3111 or
800-228-4307

NEVADA
Department of Economic Development
Division of Tourism
1100 E. William St.
Suite 106
Carson City, NV 89710
702-885-4322

NEW HAMPSHIRE
Office of Vacation Travel
P.O. Box 856
Concord, NH 03301
603-271-2665
or for recorded weekly events, ski conditions, foliage reports
800-258-3608

NEW JERSEY
Division of Travel and Tourism
GN 384
Trenton, NJ 08625
609-292-2470

NEW MEXICO
Commerce and Industry Department
Travel Division
Bataan Memorial Bldg.
Santa Fe, NM 87503
505-827-5571 or
800-545-2040

NEW YORK
New York State Department of Commerce
Division of Tourism
99 Washington Ave.
Albany, NY 12245
518-474-4116

NORTH CAROLINA
Travel and Tourism Division
Department of Commerce
430 North Salisbury St.
Raleigh, NC 27611
919-733-4171

NORTH DAKOTA
North Dakota Tourism Promotion
State Highway Department
1050 East Interstate Ave.
Bismarck, ND 58505
701-224-2525 or
800-437-2077 (out of state)

OHIO
Ohio Office of Travel
P.O. Box 1001
Columbus, OH 43216
614-466-8844 or
800-848-1300 (out of state)

OKLAHOMA
Oklahoma Division of Marketing Services
505 Will Rogers Bldg.
Oklahoma City, OK 73105
405-521-2464

OREGON
Travel Information Section
101 Transportation Bldg.
Salem, OR 97310
503-378-6309 or
800-547-7842

PENNSYLVANIA
Bureau of Travel Development
416 Forum Building
Harrisburg, PA 17120
717-787-5453 or
800-323-1717

RHODE ISLAND
Department of Economic Development
Tourist Division
7 Jackson Walkway
Providence, RI 02903
401-277-2601 or
800-556-2484

SOUTH CAROLINA
South Carolina Division of Tourism
Box 71
Columbia, SC 29202
803-758-8735

SOUTH DAKOTA
South Dakota Division of Tourism
221 South Central
Pierre, SD 57501
605-773-3301 or
1-800-843-1930

TENNESSEE
Department of Tourism Development
601 Broadway
Nashville, TN 37203
615-741-2158

TEXAS
Travel Information Services
State Highway Department
Austin, TX 78763
512-465-7401

UTAH
Utah Travel Council
Council Hall, Capitol Hill
Salt Lake City, UT 84114
801-533-5681

VERMONT
Agency of Development and Community Affairs
Travel Division
61 Elm St.
Montpelier, VT 05602
802-828-3236

VIRGINIA
Virginia State Travel Service
6 North Sixth St.
Richmond, VA 23219
804-786-4484

WASHINGTON
Washington State Dept. of Commerce and Economic

Development
General Administration Bldg.
G-3
Olympia, WA 98504
206-753-5630 or
800-541-9274

WASHINGTON, D.C.
See District of Columbia

WEST VIRGINIA
Travel Development—GOECD
1900 Washington St., East
Charleston, WV 25305
304-348-2286 or
800-624-9110

WISCONSIN
Division of Tourism
Box 7606
Madison, WI 53707
608-266-2161

WYOMING
Wyoming Travel Commission
Frank Norris, Jr. Travel Center
Cheyenne, WY 82002
307-777-7777 or
800-443-2784

Information Sources for Travel

Many government and private organizations provide tourist information as a public service. Almost all of the 50 states and the various territories of the U.S. have government-financed tourism offices to provide information about their areas. Many states have welcome centers located on major highways near their borders. Nearly every city has a visitor's bureau, convention center, or chamber of commerce—people very willing to inform visitors about their city or region. Travel agencies—which are business organizations financed by commissions from airlines, cruise lines, hotels, and other elements of the travel industry—make available a variety of travel brochures and general information, almost always without charge. International travel organizations, like American Express, also offer travel information.

Libraries and bookstores have many tour guides to the United States on their shelves. Among the best known are:

Fodor's USA (1 volume and 11 regional guides) (David McKay)
Exxon Travel Club Guides (Exxon Travel Club) 7 guides on U.S., Canada, Mexico, Caribbean and Bahamas/Bermuda.
Mobil Travel Guides (7 volumes) (Mobil Oil Corp. and Rand McNally)
National Park Guide (Rand McNally)

Some publications covering accommodations are:

Hosteling U.S.A. (American Youth Hostels)
Country Inns and Back Roads (Berkshire Traveller Press)
National Directory of Budget Motels (Pilot Industries)
Hotel and Motel Red Book (American Hotel and Motel Association)
Where to Stay USA (Frommer/Pasmantier) For camping—including recreational vehicles and trailers. Accommodations in all 50 states from $3 to $25 per night.
Campground and Trailer Park Guide (Rand McNally)
KOA Kampground Directory and RV Buyers Guide (Kampgrounds of America)
Woodall's Campground Directory (Woodall)

Many foreign governments maintain tourist offices in major American cities. International airlines generally have available detailed information about cities and countries along their routes. Travel agencies and international travel organizations like American Express and Thomas Cook also offer travel information, almost always without charge.

Libraries and bookstores have many guides to specific countries. Among the best known are:

Baedeker's Guides (Prentice-Hall) 9 world guides featuring pull-out maps.
Blue Guides (W.W. Norton) 24 world guides.
$-A-Day Guides (Frommer/Pasmantier) 14 in-depth U.S. and World guides to low-cost tourist accommodations and facilities.
Dollarwise Guides (Frommer/Pasmantier) 11 U.S. and World guides to the best tourist values in every price range, from budget to deluxe, with emphasis on the medium-priced.
The Arthur Frommer Guides (Frommer/Pasmantier) 17 pocket-size guides to U.S. and foreign cities covering tourist accommodations and facilities in all price ranges.
Special Editions (Frommer/Pasmantier): **How to Beat the High Cost of Travel** and **Arthur Frommer's Speakeasy Phrasebook** (Spring 1982) A traveler's guide to French, German, Italian, and Spanish.
Fodor's Europe (David McKay) (plus 35 guides to individual countries)
Fodor's City Guides (5 guides to U.S. and world cities)
Fodor's Budget Europe (10 world guides)
Fielding's Europe (Fielding)
Let's Go: Europe (Harvard Student Agencies) (plus 5 guides to individual countries)
Michelin Guides (Michelin Tyre Co.)
Eurail Guide (Saltzman)
Nagel's Guides (Nagel) (60 guides in English)

Homes of the Presidents and Presidential Libraries–Museums

Source: American Automobile Association *Tour Books* and *Information Please* questionnaires. NOTE: Admission fees and visiting hours are subject to change.

GEORGE WASHINGTON

George Washington Birthplace National Monument: Washingtons Birthplace, Va. 22575. Open: daily 9–5 (closed Jan. 1, Dec. 25). Free.

Mount Vernon: on George Washington Memorial Parkway, Mount Vernon, Va. 22121 (16 mi. south of Washington, D.C.). Open: March 1–Oct. 31 daily 9–5; Nov. 1–Feb. 28–daily 9–4. Adm.: $3; 6–11s, $1.50; senior citizens, $2.50.
Washington's home.

JOHN ADAMS and JOHN QUINCY ADAMS

John Adams and John Quincy Adams Birthplaces: 133 and 141 Franklin St., Quincy, Mass. 02169. Open: April 19–Oct. 15, daily 9–5. Free. Tour of grounds while houses undergo restoration.
Family home of the Adamses.

Adams National Historic Site: 135 Adams St., Quincy, Mass. 02169. Open: April 19–Nov. 10—daily

9–5. Adm.: 50¢; under 16s, free.

Home of Adams family from 1788 to 1927; built in 1731. Contains furnishings used by four Adams generations.

THOMAS JEFFERSON

Monticello: on Route 53, 3 mi. southeast of Charlottesville, Va. 22902. Open: March 1–Oct. 31—daily 8–5; Nov. 1–Feb. 28—daily. 9–4:30 (closed Dec. 25). Adm.: $3; 6–11s, $1.

Home of Jefferson; begun in 1769; finished in 1809. National shrine contains Jefferson mementos.

JAMES MADISON

Montpelier: Montpelier Station, Va., 22957; on Route 20, 5 mi. west of Orange, Va. Estate not open to public, but graveyard may be visited.

Madison's home.

JAMES MONROE

Ash Lawn: off Route 53, 2½ mi. beyond Monticello, near Charlottesville, Va. 22901. Open: daily, March–Oct. 9–6, Nov.-Feb. 10–5. (closed Jan. 1, Thanksgiving, Dec. 25). Adm.: $2.50; 6–11s, 75¢.

Monroe's home from 1799 to 1823; a working farm planned in 1798 by Jefferson; craft demonstrations; owned by College of William and Mary.

ANDREW JACKSON

The Hermitage: off I–40 east on U.S. 70N, 12 mi. east of Nashville, Tenn. 37076. Open: daily 9–5 (closed Dec. 25). Adm.: $3; 6–13s, $1.

Jackson's home.

MARTIN VAN BUREN

Martin Van Buren National Historic Site (Lindenwald): on Route 9H, 2 mi. south of Kinderhook, N.Y. 12106. Open: daily, Memorial Day-Sept. 30.

Van Buren's home from 1839 to 1862. Designated a National Historic Site in 1974, the house is now undergoing restoration by the National Park Service.

WILLIAM HENRY HARRISON

Berkeley Plantation (Harrison's Landing): halfway between Richmond and Williamsburg, Va., on Virginia Route 5. Open daily 8–5 (closed Dec. 25). Adm.: $4.50; 6–12s, $1.75.

Birthplace of William Henry Harrison and ancestral home of Benjamin Harrison. Site of first official Thanksgiving in America, in 1619.

JOHN TYLER

Sherwood Forest: on Virginia Route 5, 20 mi. west of Colonial Williamsburg, Charles City, Va. 23030. Open: by appointment only. Adm.: $4.50; 6–12s, $1.50; students and senior citizens, $3.25.

Tyler's home; built circa 1730, it is the longest frame residence in America—300 feet in length. Original furnishings. Still occupied by Tyler family.

FRANKLIN PIERCE

Franklin Pierce Homestead: near junction of Routes 9 and 31, northwest of Hillsboro, N.H. 03244. Open: Memorial Day-Labor Day, wkds. and hldys., 10–5. Donations.

Pierce's home.

JAMES BUCHANAN FOUNDATION

Wheatland: 1120 Marietta Ave., Route 23, Lancaster, Pa. 17603. Open: April 1–Nov. 30, daily, 10–4:30 (closed Thanksgiving). Adm.: $2.75; under 12s, 65¢; students, $1.40; group rate, $1.40.

Restored 1828 mansion of nation's only bachelor President. Contains American Empire and Victorian decorative-arts collections.

ABRAHAM LINCOLN

Lincoln Home National Historic Site: 526 South 7th St., Springfield, Ill. 62703. Open: daily, 8–5 (closed Jan. 1, Dec. 25). Free.

House is only home owned by Lincoln.

ANDREW JOHNSON

Andrew Johnson National Historic Site: Greeneville, Tenn. 37743. Open: daily 9–5 (closed Dec. 25). Adm. to Homestead (June 1–Sept. 15): 50¢; under 16s and senior citizens, free.

Contains two houses where Johnson lived, tailor shop where he worked, and Andrew Johnson National Cemetery.

ULYSSES S. GRANT

U. S. Grant Home State Historic Site: 510 Bouthillier, Galena, Ill. 61036. Open: daily 9–5 (closed Jan. 1, Thanksgiving, Dec. 25). Free.

RUTHERFORD B. HAYES PRESIDENTIAL CENTER

Rutherford B. Hayes Library, Home, and Museum: 1337 Hayes Ave., Fremont, Ohio 43420. Museum open: Mon.-Sat 9–5, Sun and hldys. 1:30–5. Adm.: $1.50; 7–12s, 75¢. Library open: Mon.-Sat. 9–5 (closed Sun.); free. Home open (tours only): Tues.-Sat. 9–5; Sun., Mon. and hldys. 1:30–5. Adm.; $1.50; 7–12s, 75¢. All three sites closed Jan. 1, Thanksgiving, and Dec. 25. Library also closed on legal holidays.

Estate is known as Spiegel Grove. It contains Hayes' home, his tomb, and White House gates.

JAMES A. GARFIELD

Lawnfield: 8095 Mentor Ave., Mentor, Ohio 44060. Open: May 1-Oct. 31, Tues.-Sat. 9–5, Sun. and hldys. 1–5. Adm.: $2; 12–17s and senior citizens, $1.

Garfield's home and Lake County Historical Society Museum.

BENJAMIN HARRISON

Benjamin Harrison Memorial Home: 1230 North Delaware St., Indianapolis, Ind. 46202. Open: Mon.-Sat. 10–3:30, Sun. 12:30–3:30 (closed Jan. 1, Thanksgiving, Dec. 25). Adm.: $1.50; students, 75¢.

Harrison's home; completed in 1875.

THEODORE ROOSEVELT

Theodore Roosevelt Birthplace National Historic Site: 28 E. 20th St., New York, N.Y. 10003. Open: Wed.-Sun. 9–4:30 (closed natl. hldys.). Adm.: 50¢; under 16s and senior citizens, free.

Sagamore Hill National Historic Site: 3 mi. east of Oyster Bay, L.I., N.Y. 11771, via E. Main St. Open: daily 9:30–4:30 (Nov.-April); 9:30–5 (May-Oct.); (closed Jan. 1, Thanksgiving, Dec. 25). Adm.: 50¢; under 16s and senior citizens, free.

Roosevelt's home and rural estate.

WOODROW WILSON

Birthplace of Woodrow Wilson: Coalter and Frederick Sts., Staunton, Va. 24401. Open: daily 9–5 (closed Sun., Dec.-Feb.; Jan. 1, Thanksgiving, Dec.

25). Adm.: $2; 6–16s and students, $1; senior citizens, $1.50.

Woodrow Wilson House: 2340 S St. N.W., Washington, D.C. 20008. Open: Tues.-Fri. 10–2; Sat., Sun., hldys. 12–4 (closed Jan. 1–March 15, Thanksgiving, Dec. 25). Adm.: $2; students and senior citizens, $1.

Wilson retired to this house after his second term and died here three years later in 1924.

WARREN G. HARDING

Warren G. Harding Home and Museum: 380 Mt. Vernon Ave., Marion, Ohio 43302, Open: Memorial Day to Labor Day, Wed.-Sat. 9:30–5; Sun. 12–5 (closed Mon., Tues.) Sept.-Oct. open Sat. and Sun. only. Adm.: $1; 6–12s, 50¢.

CALVIN COOLIDGE

Calvin Coolidge Birthplace and Historic Plymouth Village: Route 100A, Plymouth, Vt. 05056. Open: mid-May to mid-Oct.—daily 9:30–5:30. Adm.: $1; under 15s, free.

HERBERT HOOVER

Herbert Hoover National Historic Site: ½ mi. north of I-80, exit 254, West Branch, Iowa 52358. Grounds open daily 8–5. (closed Jan. 1, Thanksgiving, Dec. 25). Free.

Restored two-room cottage where Hoover was born; replica of his father's blacksmith shop, school, Quaker Meetinghouse, gravesite.

Herbert Hoover Presidential Library–Museum: Interstate 80, West Branch, Iowa 52358. Open: Sept.–May, Mon.-Sat. 9–5, Sun. 12–5; Memorial Day–Labor Day, Mon.-Sat. 8–6, Sun. 10–6. (closed Jan. 1, Thanksgiving, Dec. 25). Adm.: 75¢; under 16s, free.

Exhibits portray Hoover as engineer, public servant, and humanitarian. Located in surrounding park are birthplace cottage. Quaker Meeting House, replica of Jesse Hoover's blacksmith shop, and graves of President and Mrs. Hoover.

FRANKLIN D. ROOSEVELT

Home of Franklin D. Roosevelt National Historic Site: on U.S. 9, south end of Hyde Park, N.Y. 12538. Open: daily 9–5 (closed Jan. 1, Dec. 25). Adm.: $1.50; under 16s and senior citizens, free.Fee includes admission to Vanderbilt Mansion and the Library–Museum. NOTE: As a result of a fire in January 1982, access to the home may be limited.

Franklin D. Roosevelt Library and Museum: 259 Albany Post Road, Hyde Park, N.Y. 12538. Open: daily 9–5; summer 9–6 (closed Jan. 1, Dec. 25). Adm.: $1.50, includes admission to Roosevelt Home and Vanderbilt Mansion Under 16s and senior citizens, free. Archives open Mon-Fri. 9–5 (closed natl. hldys).

Exhibits feature lives and special interests of Franklin D. and Eleanor Roosevelt. Archives contain historic papers of President and Mrs. Roosevelt and of prominent figures in his Administration. Near the Library are Roosevelt family home, which is open to public, and graves of President and Mrs. Roosevelt.

HARRY S. TRUMAN

Harry S. Truman Birthplace State Historic Site: Truman Ave. & 11th St., Lamar, Mo. 64759. Open: Mon.-Sat. 10–4; Sun. 12–5 (closed Jan. 1, Easter, Thanksgiving, Dec. 25). Free.

Harry S. Truman Library and Museum: U.S. Highway 24 and Delaware St., Independence, Mo. 64050. Open: daily, 9–5; Memorial Day weekend to Labor Day weekend, 9–7 (closed Jan. 1, Thanksgiving, Dec. 25). Adm.: $1; under 16s, free.

Copy of Truman's White House office, United Nations Charter Table, and state gifts. Film programs. Mural by Thomas Hart Benton decorates entrance hall. Truman's gravesite is in the courtyard.

DWIGHT D. EISENHOWER

Eisenhower Birthplace State Historical Site: 208 E. Day St., Denison, Tex. 75020. Open: June 1–Aug. 31, daily, 8–5; Sept. 1–May 31, daily, 10–12, 1–5 (closed Jan. 1, Dec. 25). Adm.: 50¢; 6–12s, 25¢.

Dwight D. Eisenhower Center: Kansas Highway 15, Abilene, Kan. 67410. Open: daily 9–4:45 (closed Jan. 1, Thanksgiving, Dec. 25). Adm.: Library, free; museum, 75¢.

Exhibits of paintings and memorabilia relating to Eisenhower Administration are on display in Library and Museum. Place of Meditation, where Eisenhower is buried, and his boyhood home are nearby and are open to visitors.

JOHN F. KENNEDY

John F. Kennedy National Historic Site: 83 Beals St., Brookline, Mass. 02146. Open: daily 10–4:30 (closed Jan. 1, Thanksgiving, Dec. 25). Adm.: 50¢; under 16s and senior citizens, free.

Kennedy's birthplace.

John Fitzgerald Kennedy Library: Columbia Point on Dorchester Bay, Boston, Mass. 02125. Open: Daily, 9–5 (closed Jan. 1, Thanksgiving, Dec. 25). Adm.: $1.50; under 16s, free.

Research rooms, exhibits and educational activities relating to Kennedy, his times and Administration.

LYNDON B. JOHNSON

Lyndon B. Johnson National Historical Park: P.O. Box 329, Johnson City, Tex. 78636. Open: daily 9–5; LBJ Ranch, 10–4 (closed Jan. 1, Dec. 25). Free.

Site includes LBJ Ranch, birthplace and family cemetery at Stonewall (15 miles west of Johnson City) and his boyhood home and grandfather's ranch headquarters in Johnson City.

Lyndon Baines Johnson Library: 2313 Red River, Austin, Tex. 78705. Open daily 9–5 (closed Dec. 25). Free.

Documents, photographs, art objects, audio tapes, films, and memorabilia concerning the Presidency are exhibited. Audio tapes and film recreate four decades of U.S. history. Archives house 34 million documents. Replica of Oval Office during Johnson's Presidency is on view.

GERALD R. FORD

Gerald R. Ford Library: 1000 Beal Ave., Ann Arbor, Mich. 48109. Open: Mon.-Fri., 9–5 (closed Jan. 1, Washington's Birthday, Memorial Day, July 4, Labor Day, Columbus Day, Veterans Day, Thanksgiving, and Dec. 25). Free.

Documents and audio-visual materials of Ford's Presidency and service in House of Representatives.

Gerald R. Ford Museum: 303 Pearl St., N.W., Grand Rapids, Mich. 49504. Open: Mon.-Sat. 9–4:45, Sun. 12–4:45 (closed Jan.1, Thanksgiving, and Dec. 25) Adm.: 75¢; under 16s and school groups, free.

Exhibits relating to Ford's career, the Presidency and American politics.

Road Mileages Between U.S. Cities[1]

Cities	Birming-ham	Boston	Buffalo	Chicago	Cleveland	Dallas	Denver
Birmingham, Ala.	—	1,194	947	657	734	653	1,318
Boston, Mass.	1,194	—	457	983	639	1,815	1,991
Buffalo, N.Y.	947	457	—	536	192	1,387	1,561
Chicago, Ill.	657	983	536	—	344	931	1,050
Cleveland, Ohio	734	639	192	344	—	1,205	1,369
Dallas, Tex.	653	1,815	1,387	931	1,205	—	801
Denver, Colo	1,318	1,991	1,561	1,050	1,369	801	—
Detroit, Mich.	754	702	252	279	175	1,167	1,301
El Paso, Tex.	1,278	2,358	1,928	1,439	1,746	625	652
Houston, Tex.	692	1,886	1,532	1,092	1,358	242	1,032
Indianapolis, Ind.	492	940	510	189	318	877	1,051
Kansas City, Mo.	703	1,427	997	503	815	508	616
Los Angeles, Calif.	2,078	3,036	2,606	2,112	2,424	1,425	1,174
Louisville, Ky.	378	996	571	305	379	865	1,135
Memphis, Tenn.	249	1,345	965	546	773	470	1,069
Miami, Fla.	777	1,539	1,445	1,390	1,325	1,332	2,094
Minneapolis, Minn.	1,067	1,402	955	411	763	969	867
New Orleans, La.	347	1,541	1,294	947	1,102	504	1,305
New York, N.Y.	983	213	436	840	514	1,604	1,780
Omaha, Neb.	907	1,458	1,011	493	819	661	559
Philadelphia, Pa.	894	304	383	758	432	1,515	1,698
Phoenix, Ariz.	1,680	2,664	2,234	1,729	2,052	1,027	836
Pittsburgh, Pa.	792	597	219	457	131	1,237	1,411
St. Louis, Mo.	508	1,179	749	293	567	638	871
Salt Lake City, Utah	1,805	2,425	1,978	1,458	1,786	1,239	512
San Francisco, Calif.	2,385	3,179	2,732	2,212	2,540	1,765	1,266
Seattle, Wash.	2,612	3,043	2,596	2,052	2,404	2,122	1,373
Washington, D.C.	751	440	386	695	369	1,372	1,635

Cities	Detroit	El Paso	Houston	Indian-apolis	Kansas City	Los Angeles	Louisville
Birmingham, Ala.	754	1,278	692	492	703	2,078	378
Boston, Mass.	702	2,358	1,886	940	1,427	3,036	996
Buffalo, N.Y.	252	1,928	1,532	510	997	2,606	571
Chicago, Ill.	279	1,439	1,092	189	503	2,112	305
Cleveland, Ohio	175	1,746	1,358	318	815	2,424	379
Dallas, Tex.	1,167	625	242	877	508	1,425	865
Denver, Colo.	1,310	652	1,032	1,051	616	1,174	1,135
Detroit, Mich.	—	1,696	1,312	290	760	2,369	378
El Paso, Tex.	1,696	—	756	1,418	936	800	1,443
Houston, Tex.	1,312	756	—	1,022	750	1,556	981
Indianapolis, Ind.	290	1,418	1,022	—	487	2,096	114
Kansas City, Mo.	760	936	750	487	—	1,609	519
Los Angeles, Calif.	2,369	800	1,556	2,096	1,609	—	2,128
Louisville, Ky.	378	1,443	981	114	519	2,128	—
Memphis, Tenn.	756	1,095	586	466	454	1,847	396
Miami, Fla.	1,409	1,957	1,237	1,225	1,479	2,757	1,111
Minneapolis, Minn.	698	1,353	1,211	600	466	2,041	716
New Orleans, La.	1,101	1,121	365	839	839	1,921	725
New York, N.Y.	671	2,147	1,675	729	1,216	2,825	785
Omaha, Neb.	754	1,015	903	590	204	1,733	704
Philadelphia, Pa.	589	2,065	1,586	647	1,134	2,743	703
Phoenix, Ariz.	1,986	402	1,158	1,713	1,226	398	1,749
Pittsburgh, Pa.	288	1,778	1,395	360	847	2,456	416
St. Louis, Mo.	529	1,179	799	239	255	1,864	264
Salt Lake City, Utah	1,721	877	1,465	1,545	1,128	728	1,647
San Francisco, Calif.	2,475	1,202	1,958	2,299	1,882	403	2,401
Seattle, Wash.	2,339	1,760	2,348	2,241	1,909	1,150	2,355
Washington, D.C.	526	1,997	1,443	565	1,071	2,680	601

1. These figures represent estimates and are subject to change.

Road Mileages Between U.S. Cities

Cities	Memphis	Miami	Minne-apolis	New Orleans	New York	Omaha	Phila-delphia
Birmingham, Ala.	249	777	1,067	347	983	907	894
Boston, Mass.	1,345	1,539	1,402	1,541	213	1,458	304
Buffalo, N.Y.	965	1,445	955	1,294	436	1,011	383
Chicago, Ill.	546	1,390	411	947	840	493	758
Cleveland, Ohio	773	1,325	763	1,102	514	819	432
Dallas, Tex.	470	1,332	969	504	1,604	661	1,515
Denver, Colo.	1,069	2,094	867	1,305	1,780	559	1,698
Detroit, Mich.	756	1,409	698	1,101	671	754	589
El Paso, Tex.	1,095	1,957	1,353	1,121	2,147	1,015	2,065
Houston, Tex.	586	1,237	1,211	365	1,675	903	1,586
Indianapolis, Ind.	466	1,225	600	839	729	590	647
Kansas City, Mo.	454	1,479	466	839	1,216	204	1,134
Los Angeles, Calif.	1,847	2,757	2,041	1,921	2,825	1,733	2,743
Louisville, Ky.	396	1,111	716	725	785	704	703
Memphis, Tenn.	—	1,025	854	401	1,134	658	1,045
Miami, Fla.	1,025	—	1,801	892	1,328	1,683	1,239
Minneapolis, Minn.	854	1,801	—	1,255	1,259	373	1,177
New Orleans, La.	401	892	1,255	—	1,330	1,043	1,241
New York, N.Y.	1,134	1,328	1,259	1,330	—	1,315	93
Omaha, Neb.	658	1,683	373	1,043	1,315	—	1,233
Philadelphia, Pa.	1,045	1,239	1,177	1,241	93	1,233	—
Phoenix, Ariz.	1,464	2,359	1,644	1,523	2,442	1,305	2,360
Pittsburgh, Pa.	810	1,250	876	1,118	386	932	304
St. Louis, Mo.	295	1,241	559	696	968	459	886
Salt Lake City, Utah	1,556	2,571	1,243	1,743	2,282	967	2,200
San Francisco, Calif.	2,151	3,097	1,997	2,269	3,036	1,721	2,954
Seattle, Wash.	2,363	3,389	1,641	2,606	2,900	1,705	2,818
Washington, D.C.	902	1,101	1,114	1,098	229	1,170	140

Cities	Phoenix	Pitts-burgh	St. Louis	Salt Lake City	San Francisco	Seattle	Wash-ington
Birmingham, Ala.	1,680	792	508	1,805	2,385	2,612	751
Boston, Mass.	2,664	597	1,179	2,425	3,179	3,043	440
Buffalo, N.Y.	2,234	219	749	1,978	2,732	2,596	386
Chicago, Ill.	1,729	457	293	1,458	2,212	2,052	695
Cleveland, Ohio	2,052	131	567	1,786	2,540	2,404	369
Dallas, Tex.	1,027	1,237	638	1,239	1,765	2,122	1,372
Denver, Colo.	836	1,411	871	512	1,266	1,373	1,635
Detroit, Mich.	1,986	288	529	1,721	2,475	2,339	526
El Paso, Tex.	402	1,778	1,179	877	1,202	1,760	1,997
Houston, Tex.	1,158	1,395	799	1,465	1,958	2,348	1,443
Indianapolis, Ind.	1,713	360	239	1,545	2,299	2,241	565
Kansas City, Mo.	1,226	847	255	1,128	1,882	1,909	1,071
Los Angeles, Calif.	398	2,456	1,864	728	403	1,150	2,680
Louisville, Ky.	1,749	416	264	1,647	2,401	2,355	601
Memphis, Tenn.	1,464	810	295	1,556	2,151	2,363	902
Miami, Fla.	2,359	1,250	1,241	2,571	3,097	3,389	1,101
Minneapolis, Minn.	1,644	876	559	1,243	1,997	1,641	1,114
New Orleans, La.	1,523	1,118	696	1,743	2,269	2,626	1,098
New York, N.Y.	2,442	386	968	2,282	3,036	2,900	229
Omaha, Neb.	1,305	932	459	967	1,721	1,705	1,178
Philadelphia, Pa.	2,360	304	886	2,200	2,954	2,818	140
Phoenix, Ariz.	—	2,073	1,485	651	800	1,482	2,278
Pittsburgh, Pa.	2,073	—	599	1,899	2,653	2,517	241
St. Louis, Mo.	1,485	599	—	1,383	2,137	2,164	836
Salt Lake City, Utah	651	1,899	1,383	—	754	883	2,110
San Francisco, Calif.	800	2,653	2,137	754	—	817	2,864
Seattle, Wash.	1,482	2,517	2,164	883	817	—	2,755
Washington, D.C.	2,278	241	836	2,110	2,864	2,755	—

Air Distances Between U.S. Cities in Statute Miles

Cities	Birmingham	Boston	Buffalo	Chicago	Cleveland	Dallas	Denver
Birmingham, Ala.	—	1,052	776	578	618	581	1,095
Boston, Mass.	1,052	—	400	851	551	1,551	1,769
Buffalo, N. Y.	776	400	—	454	173	1,198	1,370
Chicago, Ill.	578	851	454	—	308	803	920
Cleveland, Ohio	618	551	173	308	—	1,025	1,227
Dallas, Tex.	581	1,551	1,198	803	1,025	—	663
Denver, Colo.	1,095	1,769	1,370	920	1,227	663	—
Detroit, Mich.	641	613	216	238	90	999	1,156
El Paso, Tex.	1,152	2,072	1,692	1,252	1,525	572	557
Houston, Tex.	567	1,605	1,286	940	1,114	225	879
Indianapolis, Ind.	433	807	435	165	263	763	1,000
Kansas City, Mo.	579	1,251	861	414	700	451	558
Los Angeles, Calif.	1,802	2,596	2,198	1,745	2,049	1,240	831
Louisville, Ky.	331	826	483	269	311	726	1,038
Memphis, Tenn.	217	1,137	803	482	630	420	879
Miami, Fla.	665	1,255	1,181	1,188	1,087	1,111	1,726
Minneapolis, Minn.	862	1,123	731	355	630	862	700
New Orleans, La.	312	1,359	1,086	833	924	443	1,082
New York, N. Y.	864	188	292	713	405	1,374	1,631
Omaha, Neb.	732	1,282	883	432	739	586	488
Philadelphia, Pa.	783	271	279	666	360	1,299	1,579
Phoenix, Ariz.	1,456	2,300	1,906	1,453	1,749	887	586
Pittsburgh, Pa.	608	483	178	410	115	1,070	1,320
St. Louis, Mo.	400	1,038	662	262	492	547	796
Salt Lake City, Utah	1,466	2,099	1,699	1,260	1,568	999	371
San Francisco, Calif.	2,013	2,699	2,300	1,858	2,166	1,483	949
Seattle, Wash.	2,082	2,493	2,117	1,737	2,026	1,681	1,021
Washington, D.C.	661	393	292	597	306	1,185	1,494

Cities	Detroit	El Paso	Houston	Indianapolis	Kansas City	Los Angeles	Louisville
Birmingham, Ala.	641	1,152	567	433	579	1,802	331
Boston, Mass.	613	2,072	1,605	807	1,251	2,596	826
Buffalo, N. Y.	216	1,692	1,286	435	861	2,198	483
Chicago, Ill.	238	1,252	940	165	414	1,745	269
Cleveland, Ohio	90	1,525	1,114	263	700	2,049	311
Dallas, Tex.	999	572	225	763	451	1,240	726
Denver, Colo.	1,156	557	879	1,000	558	831	1,038
Detroit, Mich.	—	1,479	1,105	240	645	1,983	316
El Paso, Tex.	1,479	—	676	1,264	839	701	1,254
Houston, Tex.	1,105	676	—	865	644	1,374	803
Indianapolis, Ind.	240	1,264	865	—	453	1,809	107
Kansas City, Mo.	645	839	644	453	—	1,356	480
Los Angeles, Calif.	1,983	701	1,374	1,809	1,356	—	1,829
Louisville, Ky.	316	1,254	803	107	480	1,829	—
Memphis, Tenn.	623	976	484	384	369	1,603	320
Miami, Fla.	1,152	1,643	968	1,024	1,241	2,339	919
Minneapolis, Minn.	543	1,157	1,056	511	413	1,524	605
New Orleans, La.	939	983	318	712	680	1,673	623
New York, N. Y.	482	1,905	1,420	646	1,097	2,451	652
Omaha, Neb.	669	878	794	525	166	1,315	580
Philadelphia, Pa.	443	1,836	1,341	585	1,038	2,394	582
Phoenix, Ariz.	1,690	346	1,017	1,499	1,049	357	1,508
Pittsburgh, Pa.	205	1,590	1,137	330	781	2,136	344
St. Louis, Mo.	455	1,034	679	231	238	1,589	242
Salt Lake City, Utah	1,492	689	1,200	1,356	925	579	1,402
San Francisco, Calif.	2,091	995	1,645	1,949	1,506	347	1,986
Seattle, Wash.	1,938	1,376	1,891	1,872	1,506	959	1,943
Washington, D.C.	396	1,728	1,220	494	945	2,300	476

Source: National Geodetic Survey.

Air Distances Between U.S. Cities in Statute Miles

Cities	Memphis	Miami	Minneapolis	New Orleans	New York	Omaha	Philadelphia
Birmingham, Ala.	217	665	862	312	864	732	783
Boston, Mass.	1,137	1,255	1,123	1,359	188	1,282	271
Buffalo, N. Y.	803	1,181	731	1,086	292	883	279
Chicago, Ill.	482	1,188	355	833	713	432	666
Cleveland, Ohio	630	1,087	630	924	405	739	360
Dallas, Tex.	420	1,111	862	443	1,374	586	1,299
Denver, Colo.	879	1,726	700	1,082	1,631	488	1,579
Detroit, Mich.	623	1,152	543	939	482	669	443
El Paso, Tex.	976	1,643	1,157	983	1,905	878	1,836
Houston, Tex.	484	968	1,056	318	1,420	794	1,341
Indianapolis, Ind.	384	1,024	511	712	646	525	585
Kansas City, Mo.	369	1,241	413	680	1,097	166	1,038
Los Angeles, Calif.	1,603	2,339	1,524	1,673	2,451	1,315	2,394
Louisville, Ky.	320	919	605	623	652	580	582
Memphis, Tenn.	—	872	699	358	957	529	881
Miami, Fla.	872	—	1,511	669	1,092	1,397	1,019
Minneapolis, Minn.	699	1,511	—	1,051	1,018	290	985
New Orleans, La.	358	669	1,051	—	1,171	847	1,089
New York, N. Y.	957	1,092	1,018	1,171	—	1,144	83
Omaha, Neb.	529	1,397	290	847	1,144	—	1,094
Philadelphia, Pa.	881	1,019	985	1,089	83	1,094	—
Phoenix, Ariz.	1,263	1,982	1,280	1,316	2,145	1,036	2,083
Pittsburgh, Pa.	660	1,010	743	919	317	836	259
St. Louis, Mo.	240	1,061	466	598	875	354	811
Salt Lake City, Utah	1,250	2,089	987	1,434	1,972	833	1,925
San Francisco, Calif.	1,802	2,594	1,584	1,926	2,571	1,429	2,523
Seattle, Wash.	1,867	2,734	1,395	2,101	2,408	1,369	2,380
Washington, D.C.	765	923	934	966	205	1,014	123

Cities	Phoenix	Pittsburgh	St. Louis	Salt Lake City	San Francisco	Seattle	Washington
Birmingham, Ala.	1,456	608	400	1,466	2,013	2,082	661
Boston, Mass.	2,300	483	1,038	2,099	2,699	2,493	393
Buffalo, N. Y.	1,906	178	662	1,699	2,300	2,117	292
Chicago, Ill.	1,453	410	262	1,260	1,858	1,737	597
Cleveland, Ohio	1,749	115	492	1,568	2,166	2,026	306
Dallas, Tex.	887	1,070	547	999	1,483	1,681	1,185
Denver, Colo.	586	1,320	796	371	949	1,021	1,494
Detroit, Mich.	1,690	205	455	1,492	2,091	1,938	396
El Paso, Tex.	346	1,590	1,034	689	995	1,376	1,728
Houston, Tex.	1,017	1,137	679	1,200	1,645	1,891	1,220
Indianapolis, Ind.	1,499	330	231	1,356	1,949	1,872	494
Kansas City, Mo.	1,049	781	238	925	1,506	1,506	945
Los Angeles, Calif.	357	2,136	1,589	579	347	959	2,300
Louisville, Ky.	1,508	344	242	1,402	1,986	1,943	476
Memphis, Tenn.	1,263	660	240	1,250	1,802	1,867	765
Miami, Fla.	1,982	1,010	1,061	2,089	2,594	2,734	923
Minneapolis, Minn.	1,280	743	466	987	1,584	1,395	934
New Orleans, La.	1,316	919	598	1,434	1,926	2,101	966
New York, N. Y.	2,145	317	875	1,972	2,571	2,408	205
Omaha, Neb.	1,036	836	354	833	1,429	1,369	1,014
Philadelphia, Pa.	2,083	259	811	1,925	2,523	2,380	123
Phoenix, Ariz.	—	1,828	1,272	504	653	1,114	1,983
Pittsburgh, Pa.	1,828	—	559	1,668	2,264	2,138	192
St. Louis, Mo.	1,272	559	—	1,162	1,744	1,724	712
Salt Lake City, Utah	504	1,668	1,162	—	600	701	1,848
San Francisco, Calif.	653	2,264	1,744	600	—	678	2,442
Seattle, Wash.	1,114	2,138	1,724	701	678	—	2,329
Washington, D.C.	1,983	192	712	1,848	2,442	2,329	—

Source: National Geodetic Survey.

Air Distances Between World Cities in Statute Miles

Cities	Berlin	Buenos Aires	Cairo	Calcutta	Cape Town	Caracas	Chicago
Berlin	—	7,402	1,795	4,368	5,981	5,247	4,405
Buenos Aires	7,402	—	7,345	10,265	4,269	3,168	5,598
Cairo	1,795	7,345	—	3,539	4,500	6,338	6,129
Calcutta	4,368	10,265	3,539	—	6,024	9,605	7,980
Cape Town, South Africa	5,981	4,269	4,500	6,024	—	6,365	8,494
Caracas, Venezuela	5,247	3,168	6,338	9,605	6,365	—	2,501
Chicago	4,405	5,598	6,129	7,980	8,494	2,501	—
Hong Kong	5,440	11,472	5,061	1,648	7,375	10,167	7,793
Honolulu, Hawaii	7,309	7,561	8,838	7,047	11,534	6,013	4,250
Istanbul	1,078	7,611	768	3,638	5,154	6,048	5,477
Lisbon	1,436	5,956	2,363	5,638	5,325	4,041	3,990
London	579	6,916	2,181	4,947	6,012	4,660	3,950
Los Angeles	5,724	6,170	7,520	8,090	9,992	3,632	1,745
Manila	6,132	11,051	5,704	2,203	7,486	10,620	8,143
Mexico City	6,047	4,592	7,688	9,492	8,517	2,232	1,691
Montreal	3,729	5,615	5,414	7,607	7,931	2,449	744
Moscow	1,004	8,376	1,803	3,321	6,300	6,173	4,974
New York	3,965	5,297	5,602	7,918	7,764	2,132	713
Paris	545	6,870	1,995	4,883	5,807	4,736	4,134
Rio de Janeiro	6,220	1,200	6,146	9,377	3,773	2,810	5,296
Rome	734	6,929	1,320	4,482	5,249	5,196	4,808
San Francisco	5,661	6,467	7,364	7,814	10,247	3,904	1,858
Shanghai, China	5,218	12,201	5,183	2,117	8,061	9,501	7,061
Stockholm	504	7,808	2,111	4,195	6,444	5,420	4,278
Sydney, Australia	10,006	7,330	8,952	5,685	6,843	9,513	9,272
Tokyo	5,540	11,408	5,935	3,194	9,156	8,799	6,299
Warsaw	320	7,662	1,630	4,048	5,958	5,517	4,667
Washington, D.C.	4,169	5,218	5,800	8,084	7,901	2,059	597

Cities	Hong Kong	Honolulu	Istanbul	Lisbon	London	Los Angeles	Manila
Berlin	5,440	7,309	1,078	1,436	579	5,724	6,132
Buenos Aires	11,472	7,561	7,611	5,956	6,916	6,170	11,051
Cairo	5,061	8,838	768	2,363	2,181	7,520	5,704
Calcutta	1,648	7,047	3,638	5,638	4,947	8,090	2,203
Cape Town, South Africa	7,375	11,534	5,154	5,325	6,012	9,992	7,486
Caracas, Venezuela	10,167	6,013	6,048	4,041	4,660	3,632	10,620
Chicago	7,793	4,250	5,477	3,990	3,950	1,745	8,143
Hong Kong	—	5,549	4,984	6,853	5,982	7,195	693
Honolulu, Hawaii	5,549	—	8,109	7,820	7,228	2,574	5,299
Istanbul	4,984	8,109	—	2,012	1,552	6,783	5,664
Lisbon	6,853	7,820	2,012	—	985	5,621	7,546
London	5,982	7,228	1,552	985	—	5,382	6,672
Los Angeles, Calif.	7,195	2,574	6,783	5,621	5,382	—	7,261
Manila	693	5,299	5,664	7,546	6,672	7,261	—
Mexico City	8,782	3,779	7,110	5,390	5,550	1,589	8,835
Montreal	7,729	4,910	4,789	3,246	3,282	2,427	8,186
Moscow	4,439	7,037	1,091	2,427	1,555	6,003	5,131
New York	8,054	4,964	4,975	3,364	3,458	2,451	8,498
Paris	5,985	7,438	1,400	904	213	5,588	6,677
Rio de Janeiro	11,021	8,285	6,389	4,796	5,766	6,331	11,259
Rome	5,768	8,022	843	1,161	887	6,732	6,457
San Francisco	6,897	2,393	6,703	5,666	5,357	347	6,967
Shanghai, China	764	4,941	4,962	6,654	5,715	6,438	1,150
Stockholm	5,113	6,862	1,348	1,856	890	5,454	5,797
Sydney, Australia	4,584	4,943	9,294	11,302	10,564	7,530	3,944
Tokyo	1,794	3,853	5,560	6,915	5,940	5,433	1,866
Warsaw	5,144	7,355	863	1,715	899	5,922	5,837
Washington, D.C.	8,147	4,519	5,215	3,562	3,663	2,300	8,562

Source: Encyclopaedia Britannica.

Air Distances Between World Cities in Statute Miles

Cities	Mexico City	Montreal	Moscow	New York	Paris	Rio de Janeiro	Rome
Berlin	6,047	3,729	1,004	3,965	545	6,220	734
Buenos Aires	4,592	5,615	8,376	5,297	6,870	1,200	6,929
Cairo	7,688	5,414	1,803	5,602	1,995	6,146	1,320
Calcutta	9,492	7,607	3,321	7,918	4,883	9,377	4,482
Cape Town, South Africa	8,517	7,931	6,300	7,764	5,807	3,773	5,249
Caracas, Venezuela	2,232	2,449	6,173	2,132	4,736	2,810	5,196
Chicago	1,691	744	4,974	713	4,134	5,296	4,808
Hong Kong	8,782	7,729	4,439	8,054	5,985	11,021	5,768
Honolulu	3,779	4,910	7,037	4,964	7,438	8,285	8,022
Istanbul	7,110	4,789	1,091	4,975	1,400	6,389	843
Lisbon	5,390	3,246	2,427	3,364	904	4,796	1,161
London	5,550	3,282	1,555	3,458	213	5,766	887
Los Angeles	1,589	2,427	6,003	2,451	5,588	6,331	6,732
Manila	8,835	8,186	5,131	8,498	6,677	11,259	6,457
Mexico City	—	2,318	6,663	2,094	5,716	4,771	6,366
Montreal	2,318	—	4,386	320	3,422	5,097	4,080
Moscow	6,663	4,386	—	4,665	1,544	7,175	1,474
New York	2,094	320	4,665	—	3,624	4,817	4,281
Paris	5,716	3,422	1,544	3,624	—	5,699	697
Rio de Janeiro	4,771	5,097	7,175	4,817	5,699	—	5,684
Rome	6,366	4,080	1,474	4,281	697	5,684	—
San Francisco	1,887	2,539	5,871	2,571	5,558	6,621	6,240
Shanghai, China	8,022	7,053	4,235	7,371	5,754	11,336	5,677
Stockholm	5,959	3,667	762	3,924	958	6,651	1,234
Sydney, Australia	8,052	9,954	9,012	9,933	10,544	8,306	10,136
Tokyo	7,021	6,383	4,647	6,740	6,034	11,533	6,135
Warsaw	6,365	4,009	715	4,344	849	6,467	817
Washington, D.C.	1,887	488	4,858	205	3,829	4,796	4,434

Cities	San Francisco	Shanghai	Stockholm	Sydney	Tokyo	Warsaw	Washington
Berlin	5,661	5,218	504	10,006	5,540	320	4,169
Buenos Aires	6,467	12,201	7,808	7,330	11,408	7,662	5,218
Cairo	7,364	5,183	2,111	8,952	5,935	1,630	5,800
Calcutta	7,814	2,117	4,195	5,685	3,194	4,048	8,084
Cape Town, South Africa	10,247	8,061	6,444	6,843	9,156	5,958	7,901
Caracas, Venezuela	3,904	9,501	5,420	9,513	8,799	5,517	2,059
Chicago	1,858	7,061	4,278	9,272	6,299	4,667	597
Hong Kong	6,897	764	5,113	4,584	1,794	5,144	8,147
Honolulu	2,393	4,941	6,862	4,943	3,853	7,355	4,519
Istanbul	6,703	4,962	1,348	9,294	5,560	863	5,215
Lisbon	5,666	6,654	1,856	11,302	6,915	1,715	3,562
London	5,357	5,715	890	10,564	5,940	899	3,663
Los Angeles	347	6,438	5,454	7,530	5,433	5,922	2,300
Manila	6,967	1,150	5,797	3,944	1,866	5,837	8,562
Mexico City	1,887	8,022	5,959	8,052	7,021	6,365	1,887
Montreal	2,539	7,053	3,667	9,954	6,383	4,009	488
Moscow	5,871	4,235	762	9,012	4,647	715	4,858
New York	2,571	7,371	3,924	9,933	6,740	4,344	205
Paris	5,558	5,754	958	10,544	6,034	849	3,829
Rio de Janeiro	6,621	11,336	6,651	8,306	11,533	6,467	4,796
Rome	6,240	5,677	1,234	10,136	6,135	817	4,434
San Francisco	—	6,140	5,361	7,416	5,135	5,841	2,442
Shanghai, China	6,140	—	4,825	4,899	1,097	4,951	7,448
Stockholm	5,361	4,825	—	9,696	5,051	501	4,123
Sydney, Australia	7,416	4,899	9,696	—	4,866	9,696	9,758
Tokyo	5,135	1,097	5,051	4,866	—	5,249	6,772
Warsaw	5,841	4,951	501	9,696	5,249	—	4,457
Washington, D.C.	2,442	7,448	4,123	9,758	6,772	4,457	—

Source: Encyclopedia Britannica.

The Seven Wonders of the World

(Not all classical writers list the same items as the Seven Wonders, but most of them agree on the following.)

The Pyramids of Egypt. A group of three pyramids, *Khufu, Khafra,* and *Menkaura* at Giza, outside modern Cairo, is often called the first wonder of the world. The largest pyramid, built by Khufu (Cheops), a king of the fourth Dynasty, had an original estimated height of 482 ft (now approximately 450 ft). The base has sides 755 ft long. It contains 2,300,000 blocks; the average weight of each is 2.5 tons. Estimated date of construction is 2800 B.C. Of all the Seven Wonders, the pyramids alone survive.

Hanging Gardens of Babylon. Often listed as the second wonder, these gardens were supposedly built by Nebuchadnezzar about 600 B.C. to please his queen, Amuhia. They are also associated with the mythical Assyrian Queen, Semiramis. Archeologists surmise that the gardens were laid out atop a vaulted building, with provisions for raising water. The terraces were said to rise from 75 to 300 ft.

The Walls of Babylon, also built by Nebuchadnezzar, are sometimes referred to as the second (or the seventh) wonder instead of the Hanging Gardens.

Statue of Zeus (Jupiter) at Olympia. The work of Phidias (5th century B.C.), this colossal figure in gold and ivory was reputedly 40 ft high. All trace of it is lost, except for reproductions on coins.

Temple of Artemis (Diana) at Ephesus. A beautiful structure, begun about 350 B.C. in honor of a non-Hellenic goddess who later became identified with the Greek goddess of the same name. The temple, with Ionic columns 60 ft high, was destroyed by invading Goths in A.D. 262.

Mausoleum at Halicarnassus. This famous monument was erected by Queen Artemisia in memory of her husband, King Mausolus of Caria in Asia Minor, who died in 353 B.C. Some remains of the structure are in the British Museum. This shrine is the source of the modern word "mausoleum."

Colossus at Rhodes. This bronze statue of Helios (Apollo), about 105 ft high, was the work of the sculptor Chares, who reputedly labored for 12 years before completing it in 280 B.C. It was destroyed during an earthquake in 224 B.C.

Pharos of Alexandria. The seventh wonder was the Pharos (lighthouse) of Alexandria, built by Sostratus of Cnidus during the 3rd century B.C. on the island of Pharos off the coast of Egypt. It was destroyed by an earthquake in the 13th century.

Famous Structures

Ancient

The *Great Sphinx of Egypt,* one of the wonders of ancient Egyptian architecture, adjoins the pyramids of Giza and has a length of 240 ft. It was built in the 4th dynasty.

Other Egyptian buildings of note include the *Temples of Karnak* and *Edfu* and the *Tombs at Beni Hassan.*

The *Parthenon of Greece,* built on the Acropolis in Athens, was the chief temple to the goddess Athena. It was believed to have been completed by 438 B.C. The present temple remained intact until the 5th century A.D. Today, though the Parthenon is in ruins, its majestic proportions are still discernible.

Other great structures of ancient Greece were the *Temples at Paestum* (about 540 and 420 B.C.); the *Temple of Poseidon* (about 460 B.C.); the *Temple of Apollo* at Corinth (about 540 B.C.); the *Temple of Apollo* at Bassae (about 450–420 B.C.); the famous *Erechtheum* atop the Acropolis (about 421–405 B.C.); the *Temple of Athena Niké* at Athens (about 426 B.C.); the *Olympieum* at Athens (174 B.C.–A.D. 131); the *Athenian Treasury* at Delphi (about 515 B.C.); the *Propylaea* of the Acropolis at Athens (437–432 B.C.); the *Theater of Dionysus* at Athens (about 350–325 B.C.); the *House of Cleopatra* at Delos (138 B.C.) and the *Theater* at Epidaurus (about 325 B.C.).

The *Colosseum (Flavian Amphitheater) of Rome,* the largest and most famous of the Roman amphitheaters, was opened for use A.D. 80. Elliptical in shape, it consisted of three stories and an upper gallery, rebuilt in stone in its present form in the third century A.D. Its seats rise in tiers, which in turn are buttressed by concrete vaults and stone piers. It could seat between 40,000 and 50,000 spectators. It was principally used for gladiatorial combat.

The *Pantheon* at Rome, begun by Agrippa in 27 B.C. as a temple, was rebuilt in its present circular form by Hadrian (A.D. 110–25). Literally the Pantheon was intended as a temple of "all the gods." It is remarkable for its perfect preservation today, and it has served continuously for 20 centuries as a place of worship.

Famous Roman arches include the *Arch of Constantine* (about A.D. 315) and the *Arch of Titus* (about A.D. 80).

Later European

St. Mark's Cathedral in Venice (1063–67), one of the great examples of Byzantine architecture, was begun in the 9th century. Partly destroyed by fire in 976, it was later rebuilt as a Byzantine edifice.

Other famous Byzantine examples of architecture are *St. Sophia* in Istanbul (A.D. 532–37); *San Vitale* in Ravenna (542); *St. Paul's Outside the Walls,* Rome (5th century); the *Kremlin* baptism and marriage church, Moscow (begun in 1397); and *St. Lorenzo Outside the Walls*, Rome, begun in 588.

The *Cathedral Group* at Pisa (1067–1173), one of the most celebrated groups of structures built in Romanesque style, consists of the cathedral, the cathedral's baptistery, and the *Leaning Tower*. This trio forms a group by itself in the northwest corner of the city. The cathedral and baptistery are built in varicolored marble. The campanile *(Leaning Tower)* is 179 ft. high and leans more than 16 ft out of the perpendicular. There is little reason to believe that the architects intended to have the tower lean.

Other examples of Romanesque architecture include the *Vézelay Abbey* in France (1130); the *Church of Notre-Dame-du-Port* at Clermont-Ferrand in France (1100); the *Church of San Zeno* (begun in 1138) at Verona, and *Durham Cathedral* in England.

The *Alhambra* (1248–1354), located in Granada, Spain, is universally esteemed as one of the greatest masterpieces of Moslem architecture. Designed as a palace and fortress for the Moorish monarchs of Granada, it is surrounded by a heavily fortified wall more than a mile in perimeter. The location of the Alhambra in the Sierra Nevada provides a magnificent setting for this jewel of Moorish Spain.

The *Tower of London* is a group of buildings and towers covering 13 acres along the north bank of the Thames. The central *White Tower*, begun in 1078 during the reign of William the Conqueror, was originally a fortress and royal residence, but was later used as a prison. The *Bloody Tower* is associated with Anne Boleyn and other notables.

Westminster Abbey, in London, was begun in 1045 and completed in 1065. It was rebuilt and enlarged in 1245–50.

Notre-Dame de Paris (begun in 1163), one of the great examples of Gothic architecture, is a twin-towered church with a steeple over the crossing and immense flying buttresses supporting the masonry at the rear of the church.

Other famous Gothic structures are *Chartres Cathedral* (12th century); *Sainte Chapelle*, Paris (1246–48); *Laon Cathedral*, France (1160–1205); *Reims Cathedral* (about 1210–50; rebuilt after its almost complete destruction in World War I); *Rouen Cathedral* (13th–16th centuries); *Amiens Cathedral* (1218–69); *Beauvais Cathedral* (begun 1247); *Salisbury Cathedral* (1220–60); *York Minster* or the *Cathedral of St. Peter* (begun in the 7th century); *Milan Cathedral* (begun 1386); and *Cologne Cathedral* (13th–19th centuries; badly damaged in World War II.

The Duomo (cathedral) in Florence was founded in 1298, completed by Brunelleschi and consecrated in 1436. The oval-shaped dome dominates the entire structure.

The *Vatican* is a group of buildings in Rome comprising the official residence of the Pope. The *Basilica of St. Peter*, the largest church in the Christian world, was begun in 1450. The *Sistine Chapel*, begun in 1473, is noted for the art masterpieces of Michelangelo, Botticelli, and others. The *Basilica of the Savior* (known as *St. John Lateran*) is the first-ranking Catholic Church in the world, for it is the cathedral of the Pope.

Other examples of Renaissance architecture are the *Palazzo Riccardi*, the *Palazzo Pitti* and the *Palazzo Strozzi* in Florence; the *Farnese Palace* in Rome; *Palazzo Grimani* (completed about 1550) in Venice; the *Escorial* (1563–93) near Madrid; the *Town Hall* of Seville (1527–32); the *Louvre*, Paris; the *Château* at Blois, France; *St. Paul's Cathedral*, London (1675–1710; badly damaged in World War II); the *École Militaire*, Paris (1752); the *Pazzi Chapel*, Florence, designed by Brunelleschi (1429); the Palace of *Fontainebleau* and the *Château de Chambord* in France.

The *Palace of Versailles*, containing the famous Hall of Mirrors, was built during the reign of Louis XIV and served as the royal palace until 1793.

Outstanding European buildings of the 18th and 19th centuries are the *Superga* at Turin, the *Hôtel-Dieu* in Lyons, the *Belvedere Palace* at Vienna, the *Royal Palace* of Stockholm, the *Opera House* of Paris (1863–75); the *Bank of England*, the *British Museum*, the *University of London*, and the *Houses of Parliament*, all in London; the *Panthéon*, the *Church of the Madeleine*, the *Bourse*, and the *Palais de Justice* in Paris.

The *Eiffel Tower*, in Paris, was built for the Exposition of 1889 by Alexandre Eiffel. It is 984 ft high.[1]

1. 1,056 ft, including the television tower.

Asiatic and African

The *Taj Mahal* (1632–50), at Agra, India, built by Shah Jahan as a tomb for his wife, is considered by some as the most perfect example of the Mogul style and by others as the most beautiful building in the world. Four slim white minarets flank the building, which is topped by a white dome; the entire structure is of marble.

Other examples of Indian architecture are the temples at Benares and Tanjore.

Among famed Moslem edifices are the *Dome of the Rock* or *Mosque of Omar*, Jerusalem (A.D. 691); the *Citadel* (1166), and the *Tombs of the Mamelukes* (15th century), in Cairo; the *Tomb of Humayun* in Delhi; the *Blue Mosque* (1468) at Tabriz, and the *Tamerlane Mausoleum* at Samarkand.

Angkor Wat, outside the city of Angkor Thom, Cambodia, is one of the most beautiful examples of Cambodian or Khmer architecture. The sanctuary was built during the 12th century.

Great Wall of China (228 B.C.?), designed specifically as a defense against nomadic tribes, has numerous large watch towers which could be called buildings. It was erected by Emperor Ch'in Shih Huang Ti and is 1,400 miles long. Built mainly of earth and stone, it varies in height between 18 and 30 ft.

Typical of Chinese architecture are the pagodas or temple towers. Among some of the better-known pagodas are the *Great Pagoda of the Wild Geese* at Sian (founded in 652); *Nan t'a* (11th century) at Fang Shan; the *Pagoda of Sung Yueh Ssu* (A.D. 523) at Sung Shan, Honan.

Other well-known Chinese buildings are the *Drum Tower* (1273), the *Three Great Halls* in the Purple Forbidden City (1627), *Buddha's Perfume Tower* (19th century), the *Porcelain Pagoda*, and the *Summer Palace*, all at Peking.

United States

Rockefeller Center, in New York City, extends from 5th Ave. to the Avenue of the Americas between 48th and 52nd Sts. (and halfway to 7th Ave. between 47th and 51st Sts.). It occupies more than 22 acres and has 19 buildings.

The Cathedral of St. John the Divine, at 112th St. and Amsterdam Ave. in New York City, was begun in 1892 and is now in the final stages of completion. When completed, it will be the largest cathedral in the world: 601 ft long, 146 ft wide at the nave, 320 ft wide at the transept. The east end is designed in

Romanesque-Byzantine style, and the nave and west end are Gothic.

St. Patrick's Cathedral, at Fifth Ave. and 50th St. in New York City, has a seating capacity of 2,500. The nave was opened in 1877, and the cathedral was dedicated in 1879.

Louisiana Superdome, in New Orleans, is the largest arena in the history of mankind. The main area can accommodate up to 95,000 people. It is the world's largest steel-constructed room. Unobstructed by posts, it covers 13 ac. and reaches 27 stories at its peak.

World Trade Center, in New York City, was dedicated in 1973. Its twin towers are 110 stories high (1,350 ft), and the complex contains over 9 million sq ft of office space. A restaurant is on the 107th floor of the No. Tower.

World's Highest Dams

Name	River	Maximum height		Reservoir capacity		Year completed
		feet	meters	Thousands of acre feet	millions of cubic meters	
Rogun	Vakhsh, U.S.S.R.	1066	325	9,404	11,600	UC(1985)
Nurek	Vakhsh, U.S.S.R.	984	300	8,512	10,500	UC(1985)
Grande Dixence	Dixence, Switzerland	935	285	324	400	1962
Inguri	Inguri, U.S.S.R.	892	272	801	1,100	UC(1985)
Chicoasén	Grijalva, Mexico	869	265	1,346	1,660	1981
Vaiont	Vaiont, Italy	869	265	137	169	1961
Tehri	Bhagirathi, India	856	261	2,869	3,540	UC(1990)
Kinshaw	Tons, India	830	253	1,946	2,400	UC(1985)
Mica	Columbia, Canada	794	242	20,000	24,670	1972
Sayano-Shushensk	Yenisei, U.S.S.R.	794	242	25,353	31,300	1980
Mihoesti	Aries, Romania	794	242	5	6	UC(1983)
Chivor	Batá, Colombia	778	237	661	815	1975
Mauvoisin	Drance de Bagnes, Switzerland	777	237	146	180	1957
Oroville	Feather, California	770	235	3,538	4,299	1968
Chirkey	Sulak, U.S.S.R.	764	233	2,252	2,780	1977
Bhakra	Sutlej, India	741	226	8,002	9,870	1963
El Cajón	Humuya, Honduras	741	226	4,580	5,650	UC(1985)
Hoover	Colorado, Arizona–Nevada	726	221	28,537	35,200	1936
Contra	Verzasca, Switzerland	722	220	70	86	1965
Dabaklamm	Dorferbach, Austria	722	220	191	235	UC(1989)
Piva (Mratinje)	Piva, Yugoslavia	722	220	713	880	1975
Dworshak	N. Fk. Clearwater, Idaho	717	219	3,453	4,259	1974
Glen Canyon	Colorado, Arizona	710	216	27,000	33,305	1964
Toktogul	Naryn, U.S.S.R.	705	215	15,800	19,500	1978
Daniel Johnson	Manicouagan, Canada	703	214	115,000	141,851	1968
San Rogue	Agno, Philippines	689	210	803	990	UC(—)
Luzzone	Brenno di Luzzone, Switzerland	682	208	71	87	1963
Keban	Firat, Turkey	679	207	25,110	31,000	1974
Dez	Dez, Abi, Iran	666	203	2,707	3,340	1963
Almendra	Tormes-Douro, Spain	662	202	2,148	2,649	1970
Köelbrein	Malta, Austria	656	200	166	205	1977
Karun	Karun, Iran	656	200	2,351	2,900	1976
Altinkaya	Kizil Irmak, Turkey	640	195	4,672	5,763	UC(1986)
New Bullards Bar	No. Yuba, California	637	194	960	1,184	1968
Lakwar	Yamuna, India	630	192	470	580	UC(1985)
New Melones	Stanislaus, California	625	191	2,400	2,960	1979
Itaipu	Paraná, Brazil/Paraguay	623	190	23,510	29,000	UC(1983)
Kurobe 4	Kurobe, Japan	610	186	162	199	1964
Swift	Lewis, Washington	610	186	756	932	1958
Mossyrock	Cowlitz, Washington	607	185	1,300	1,603	1963
Oymopinar	Manavgat, Turkey	607	185	251	310	UC(1983)
Atatürk	Firat, Turkey	604	184	38,914	48,000	UC(1990)
Shasta	Sacramento, California	602	183	4,552	5,615	1945
Bennett, WAC	Peace, Canada	600	183	57,006	70,309	1967
Karakaya	Firat, Turkey	591	180	7,767	9,580	UC(1986)
Tignes	Isère, France	591	180	186	230	1952
Amir Kabir (Karad)	Karadj, Iran	591	180	166	205	1962
Tachien	Tachia, Taiwan	591	180	207	255	1974
Dartmouth	Mitta-Mitta, Australia	591	180	3,243	4,000	1978
Ököy	Gediz, Turkey	591	180	762	940	UC(1986)
Emosson	Barberine, Switzerland	590	180	184	225	1974
Zillergründl	Ziller, Austria	590	180	73	90	UC(1987)
Los Leones	Los Leones, Chile	587	179	86	106	UC(1982)
New Don Pedro	Tuolumne, California	585	178	2,030	2,504	1971
Alpa-Gera	Cormor, Italy	584	178	53	65	1965

Name	River	Maximum height		Reservoir capacity		Year completed
		feet	meters	Thousands of acre feet	millions of cubic meters	
Kopperston Tailings 3	Jones Branch, West Virginia	580	177	—	—	1963
Takase	Takase, Japan	577	176	62	76	1979
Nader Shah	Marun, Iran	574	175	1,313	1,620	1978
Hasan Ugurlu	Yesil Irmak, Turkey	574	175	874	1,078	1980
Mazar	Mazar, Ecuador	574	175	405	500	UC(1982)
Hungry Horse	S.Fk., Flathead, Montana	564	172	3,468	4,278	1953
Longyangxia	Huanghe, China	564	172	20,025	24,700	UC(1983)
Cabora Bassa	Zambezi, Mozambique	561	171	51,075	63,000	1974
Maqarin	Yarmuk, Jordan	561	171	259	320	UC(1986)
Amaluza	Paute, Equador	558	170	81	100	UC(1982)
Idikki	Periyar, India	554	169	1,618	1,996	1974
Charvak	Chirchik, U.S.S.R.	552	168	1,620	2,000	1970
Gura Apelor Retezat	Riul Mare, Romania	552	168	182	225	1980
Grand Coulee	Columbia, Washington	550	168	9,386	11,578	1942
Boruca	Terraba, Costa Rica	548	167	12,128	14,960	UC(1983)
Vidraru	Arges, Romania	545	166	380	465	1965
Lake LaSalle	Big Thunder, Indiana	541	165	—	—	1962
Kremasta (King Paul)	Achelöus, Greece	541	165	3,850	4,750	1965

NOTE: UC = under construction, ( ) Estimated year of completion. *Source:* Department of the Interior, Bureau of Reclamation.

World's Largest Dams

Dam	Location	Volume (thousands)		Year completed
		Cubic meters	Cubic yards	
New Cornelia Tailings	Arizona	209,500	274,026	1973
Pati (Chapetón)	Argentina	200,000	261,590	UC(1998)
Tarbella	Pakistan	121,720	159,203	1976
Fort Peck	Montana	96,049	125,628	1940
Yacyretá-Apipe	Paraguay/Argentina	81,000	105,944	UC(1988)
Guri (Raul Leoni)	Venezuela	78,000	102,014	UC(1985)
Rogun	U.S.S.R.	75,500	98,750	UC(1985)
Atatürk	Turkey	75,000	98,096	UC(1990)
Oahe	South Dakota	70,339	92,000	1963
Mangla	Pakistan	65,651	85,872	1967
Gardiner	Canada	65,440	85,592	1968
Afsluitdijk	Netherlands	63,400	82,927	1932
Oroville	California	59,639	78,008	1968
San Luis	California	59,383	77,670	1967
Nurek	U.S.S.R.	58,000	75,861	UC(1985)
Garrison	North Dakota	50,843	66,500	1956
Cochita	New Mexico	50,230	65,698	1975
Tabka (Thawra)	Syria	46,000	60,168	1976
Bennett W.A.C.	Canada	43,733	57,201	1967
Tucuruí	Brazil	43,000	56,242	UC(1983)
Boruca	Costa Rica	43,000	56,242	UC(1983)
High Aswan (Sadd–el–Aali)	Egypt	43,000	56,242	1970
San Rogue	Philippines	43,000	56,242	UC(—)
Kiev	U.S.S.R.	42,841	56,034	1964
Dantiwada Left Embankment	India	41,040	53,680	1965
Saratov	U.S.S.R.	40,400	52,843	1967
Mission Tailings 2	Arizona	40,088	52,435	1973
Fort Randall	South Dakota	38,380	50,200	1956
Kanev	U.S.S.R.	37,860	49,520	1976
Mosul	Iraq	36,000	47,086	UC(1982)
Kakhovka	U.S.S.R.	35,640	46,617	1955
Itumbiara	Brazil	35,600	46,563	1980
Lauwerszee	Netherlands	35,575	46,532	1969
Beas	India	35,418	46,325	1974
Oosterschelde	Netherlands	35,000	45,778	UC(1986)

NOTE: UC = under construction, ( ) = estimated year of completion. *Source:* Department of the Interior, Bureau of Reclamation.

World's Largest Hydroelectric Plants

Name of dam	Location	Rated capacity (MW) Present	Rated capacity (MW) Ultimate	Year of initial operation
Itaipu	Brazil/Paraguay	—	12,600	UC(1983)
Grand Coulee	Washington	6,430	10,080	1942
Guri (Raul Leoni)	Venezuela	2,800	10,060	1968
Tucurui	Brazil	—	6,480	UC(1982)
Sayano-Shushensk	U.S.S.R.	—	6,400	1980
Corpus-Christi	Argentina/Paraguay	—	6,000	UC(1990)
Krasnoyarsk	U.S.S.R.	6,096	6,096	1968
LaGrande 2	Canada	—	5,328	UC(1982)
Churchill Falls	Canada	5,225	5,225	1971
Bratsk	U.S.S.R.	4,100	4,600	1964
Ust'—Ilimsk	U.S.S.R.	3,675	4,500	1974
Cabora Bassa	Mozambique	2,075	4,150	1974
Yacyretá-Apipe	Argentina/Paraguay	—	4,050	UC(1986)
Rogun	U.S.S.R.	—	3,600	UC(1985)
Randolph-Hunting	Virginia	—	3,575	UC(1991)
Paulo Afonso	Brazil	1,524	3,409	1955
Pati (Chapetón)	Argentina	—	3,300	UC(1990)
Brumley Gap	Virginia	3,200	3,200	1973
Inga I	Zaire	360	2,820	1974
Gezhouba	China	—	2,715	UC(1986)
John Day	Oregon-Washington	2,160	2,700	1969
Nurek	U.S.S.R.	900	2,700	1976
Revelstoke	Canada	—	2,700	UC(1983)
Sáo Simao	Brazil	2,680	2,680	1979
Ilha Solteira	Brazil	2,650	2,650	1973
LaGrande 4	Canada	—	2,637	UC(1984)
Mica	Canada	1,736	2,610	1976
Volgograd - 22nd Congress	U.S.S.R.	2,560	2,560	1958
Itaparica	Brazil	—	2,500	UC(1985)
Bennett W.A.C.	Canada	2,116	2,416	1969
Chicoasén	Mexico	—	2,400	1980
Atatürk	Turkey	—	2,400	UC(1990)
LaGrande 3	Canada	—	2,304	UC(1982)
Volga—V.I. Lenin	U.S.S.R.	2,300	2,300	1955
Iron Gates I	Romania/Yugoslavia	2,300	2,300	1970
Fos do Areia	Brazil	2,250	2,250	UC(1983)
Itumbiara	Brazil	—	2,124	UC(1982)
Bath County	Virginia	—	2,100	UC(1985)
High Aswan (Saad-el-Aali)	Egypt	2,100	2,100	1967
Tarbella	Pakistan	1,400	2,100	1977
Piedra de Aquila	Argentina	—	2,100	UC(1989)
Chief Joseph	Washington	2,069	2,069	1956
Salto Santiago	Brazil	—	2,031	1980
McNary	Oregon	980	2,030	1954
Green River	North Carolina	—	2,000	1980
Tehri	India	—	2,000	UC(1990)
Cornwall	New York	—	2,000	1978
Ludington	Michigan	1,979	1,979	1973
Robert Moses-Niagara	New York	1,950	1,950	1961
Salto Grande	Argentina/Uruguay	—	1,890	1979

Note: MW = Megawatts, UC = under construction , ( ) = estimated year of initial operation. *Source:* Department of the Interior, Bureau of Reclamation.

How Old Is Man?

Paleoanthropologists (anthropologists who specialize in the study of fossil man) disagree on when humans first were differentiated from their pre-human ancestors. Estimates range from 2 to 3.8 million years ago, based on such criteria as brain size, knee joints indicating an ability to walk on two legs, and tool-making ability.

The oldest footprints of a human-like animal were found by Dr. Mary Leakey in 1979 in the Laetoli area of northern Tanzania, East Africa. The 3.6-million-year age of the footprints was determined by radioactive dating of the rock layer in which they were found.

The old concept of a single line of development from ape to man has been replaced by the generally accepted theory that there were at least three different forms of early man and near man in Africa, where most scientists agree humans first emerged.

United States Tallest Buildings

City	Building	Stories	Height ft	Height m
Chicago	Sears Tower	110	1,454	443
New York	World Trade Center	110	1,377	419
New York	Empire State	102	1,250	381
Chicago	Standard Oil (Indiana)	80	1,136	346
Chicago	John Hancock Center	100	1,127	343
New York	Chrysler	77	1,046	319
New York	American International	66	952	290
New York	Citicorp Center	59	915	279
New York	40 Wall Tower	71	900	274
Chicago	Water Tower Place	74	859	262
Los Angeles	United California Bank	62	858	261
San Francisco	Transamerica Pyramid	61	853	260
Chicago	First National Bank	60	851	259
New York	RCA	70	850	259
Pittsburgh	U.S. Steel Headquarters	64	841	256
New York	Chase Manhattan	60	813	248
New York	Pan Am	59	808	246
New York	Woolworth	55	792	241
Boston	John Hancock Tower	60	790	241
San Francisco	Bank of America	52	779	237
Minneapolis	IDS Tower	57	775	236
New York	One Liberty Plaza	54	775	236
New York	One Penn Plaza	57	774	236
Atlanta	Peachtree Plaza	73	754	230
New York	Exxon	54	750	229
Boston	Prudential Tower	52	750	229
Detroit	Detroit Plaza Hotel	73	747	228
Los Angeles	Security Pacific Plaza	55	743	226
New York	One Astor Plaza	54	730	222
New York	Marine Midland	52	724	221
Houston	One Shell Plaza	50	714	218
Dallas	First International	56	710	216
Cleveland	Terminal Tower	52	708	216
New York	Union Carbide	52	707	215
New York	General Motors	50	705	215
New York	Metropolitan Life	50	700	213

NOTE: Does not include buildings under construction and not completed in 1981. Height does not include TV towers and antennas. *Source: Information Please* questionnaires to building managements.

Notable Tunnels

Railroad, excluding subways

Name	Location	Length mi.	Length km	Year completed
Seikan	Tsugara Strait, Japan	33.1	53.3	UC
Simplon (I and II)	Alps, Switzerland-Italy	12.3	19.8	1906 & 1922
Kammon Straits	Honshu to Kyoshu Islands, Japan	11.6	18.7	UC
Apennine	Genoa, Italy	11.5	18.5	1934
St. Gotthard	Swiss Alps	9.3	14.9	1881
Lötschberg	Swiss Alps	9.1	14.6	1911
Nakayama	Komochi Mountain, Japan	8.8	14.2	UC
Mont Cénis	French Alps	8.5[1]	13.7	1871
New Cascade	Cascade Mountains, Washington	7.8	12.6	1929
Vosges	Vosges, France	7.0	11.3	1940
Arlberg	Austrian Alps	6.3	10.1	1884
Moffat	Rocky Mountains, Colorado	6.2	9.9	1928
Shimuzu	Shimuzu, Japan	6.1	9.8	1931
Rimutaka	Wairarapa, New Zealand	5.5	8.9	1955

Vehicular

Name	Location	Length mi.	Length km	Year completed
St. Gotthard	Alps, Switzerland	10.2	16.4	1980
Mt. Blanc	Alps, France-Italy	7.5	12.1	1965
Mt. Ena	Japan Alps, Japan	5.3	8.5	1976[2]
Great St. Bernard	Alps, Switzerland-Italy	3.4	5.5	1964
Mount Royal	Montreal, Canada	3.2	5.1	1918
Lincoln	Hudson River, New York-New Jersey	2.5	4.0	1937
Queensway Road	Mersey River, Liverpool, England	2.2	3.5	1934
Brooklyn-Battery	East River, New York City	2.1	3.4	1950
Holland	Hudson River, New York-New Jersey	1.7	2.7	1927
Hampton Roads	Norfolk, Virginia	1.4	2.3	1957
Queens-Midtown	East River, New York City	1.3	2.1	1940
Liberty Tubes	Pittsburgh, Pennsylvania	1.2	1.9	1923
Baltimore Harbor	Baltimore, Maryland	1.2	1.9	1957
Allegheny Tunnels	Pennsylvania Turnpike	1.2	1.9	1940[3]

1. Lengthened to its present 8.5 miles in 1881. 2. Parallel tunnel begun in 1976. 3. Parallel tunnel built in 1965, twin tunnel in 1966. NOTE: UC = under construction. *Source:* American Society of Civil Engineers and International Bridge, Tunnel & Turnpike Association.

Notable Modern Bridges

Suspension

Name	Location	Length of main span, ft	m	Year completed
Humber	Hull, Britain	4,626	1,410	1981
Verrazano-Narrows	Lower New York Bay	4,260	1,298	1964
Golden Gate	San Francisco Bay	4,200	1,280	1937
Mackinac Straits	Michigan	3,800	1,158	1957
Bosporus	Istanbul	3,524	1,074	1973
George Washington	Hudson River at New York City	3,500	1,067	1931
Ponte 25 de Abril	Tagus River at Lisbon	3,323	1,013	1966
Forth Road	Queensferry, Scotland	3,300	1,006	1964
Severn	Severn River at Beachley, England	3,240	988	1966
Tacoma Narrows	Puget Sound at Tacoma, Wash.	2,800	853	1950
Kanmon Strait	Kyushu-Honshu, Japan	2,336	712	1973
Angostura	Orinoco River at Ciudad Bolívar, Venezuela	2,336	712	1967
Transbay (twin spans)	San Francisco Bay	2,310	704	1936
Bronx-Whitestone	East River, New York City	2,300	701	1939
Pierre Laporte	St. Lawrence River at Quebec, Canada	2,190	668	1970
Delaware Memorial (twin bridges)	Delaware River near Wilmington, Del.	2,150	655	1951, 1968
Seaway Skyway	St. Lawrence River at Ogdensburg, N.Y.	2,150	655	1960
Gas Pipe Line	Atchafalaya River, Louisiana	2,000	610	1951
Walt Whitman	Delaware River at Philadelphia	2,000	610	1957
Tancarville	Seine River at Tancarville, France	1,995	608	1959
Lillebaelt	Lillebaelt Strait, Denmark	1,969	600	1970
Ambassador International	Detroit River at Detroit	1,850	564	1929
Throgs Neck	East River, New York City	1,800	549	1961
Benjamin Franklin	Delaware River at Philadelphia	1,750	533	1926
Skjomen	Narvik, Norway	1,722	525	1972
Kvalsund	Hammerfest, Norway	1,722	525	1977
Kleve-Emmerich	Rhine River at Emmerich, West Germany	1,640	500	1965
Bear Mountain	Hudson River at Peekskill, N.Y.	1,632	497	1924
Wm. Preston Lane, Jr., Memorial (twin bridges)	Near Annapolis, Md.	1,600	488	1952, 1973
Williamsburg	East River, New York City	1,600	488	1903
Newport	Narragansett Bay at Newport, R.I.	1,600	488	1969
Brooklyn	East River, New York City	1,595	486	1883

Cantilever

Name	Location	ft	m	Year completed
Quebec Railway	St. Lawrence River at Quebec, Canada	1,800	549	1917
Forth Railway (twin spans)	Queensferry, Scotland	1,710	521	1890
Minato Ohashi	Osaka, Japan	1,673	510	1974
Commodore John Barry	Chester, Pa.	1,644	501	1974
Greater New Orleans	Mississippi River, Louisiana	1,576	480	1958
Howrah	Hooghly River at Calcutta	1,500	457	1943
Transbay Bridge	San Francisco Bay	1,400	427	1936
Baton Rouge	Mississippi River, Louisiana	1,235	376	1968
Tappan Zee	Hudson River at Tarrytown, N.Y.	1,212	369	1955
Longview	Columbia River at Longview, Wash.	1,200	366	1930
Patapsco River	Baltimore Outer Harbor Crossing	1,200	366	1976
Queensboro	East River, New York City	1,182	360	1909

Steel Arch

Name	Location	ft	m	Year completed
New River Gorge	Fayetteville, W. Va.	1,700	518	1977
Bayonne	Kill Van Kull at Bayonne, N.J.	1,675	510	1931
Sydney Harbor	Sydney, Australia	1,670	509	1932
Fremont	Portland, Ore.	1,255	383	1973
Zdákov	Vltava River, Czechoslovakia	1,244	380	1967
Port Mann	Fraser River at Vancouver, British Columbia	1,200	366	1964
Thatcher Ferry	Panama Canal, Panama	1,128	344	1962
Laviolette	St. Lawrence River, Trois Rivieres, Quebec	1,100	335	1967
Runcorn-Widnes	Mersey River, England	1,082	330	1961
Birchenough	Sabi River at Fort Victoria, Rhodesia	1,080	329	1935

Name	Location	Length of main span, ft	m	Year completed
Cable-Stayed				
Second Hooghly	Calcutta	1,500	457	UC
St.-Nazaire	Loire River, St.-Nazaire, France	1,325	404	1975
Stretto di Rande	Spain	1,312	400	UC
Luling	Missippi River, Luling, La.	1,235	376	UC
Düsseldorf-Flehe	Rhine River, West Germany	1,205	367	UC
Yamatogawa	Osaka, Japan	1,165	355	UC
Duisburg-Neuenkamp	Duisburg, West Germany	1,148	350	1970
Mesopotamia	Corrientes, Argentina	1,116	340	1972
West Gate	Lower Yarra River at Melbourne, Australia	1,102	336	1970
Zárate	Paraná River, Argentina	1,083	330	1976
Brazo Largo	Paraná River, Argentina	1,083	330	1977
Köhlbrand	Hamburg, West Germany	1,066	325	1974
Kniebrücke	Rhine River at Düsseldorf, West Germany	1,050	320	1969
Brotonne[1]	Seine River, France	1,050	320	1976
Erskine	Clyde River at Glasgow, Scotland	1,000	305	1971
Continuous Truss				
Astoria	Columbia River at Astoria, Oregon	1,232	376	1966
Oshima	Oshima Island, Japan	1,066	325	1976
Croton Reservoir	Croton, N.Y.	1,052	321	1970
Tenmon	Kumamoto, Japan	984	300	1966
Kuronoseto	Nagashima-Kyushu, Japan	984	300	1974
Ravenswood	Ohio River, Ravenswood, W. Va.	902	275	UC
Dubuque	Mississippi River at Dubuque, Iowa	845	258	1943
Braga Memorial	Taunton River at Somerset, Mass.	840	256	1966
Graf Spee	Germany	839	256	1936
Concrete Arch				
KRK	Zagreb, Yugoslavia	1,280	390	1979
Gladesville	Parramatta River at Sydney, Australia	1,000	305	1964
Amizade	Paraná River at Foz do Iguassu, Brazil	951	290	1964
Arrábida	Porto, Portugal	886	270	1963
Sandö	Angerman River at Kramfors, Sweden	866	264	1943
Shibenik	Krka River, Yugoslavia	808	246	1966
Fiumarella	Catanzaro, Italy	758	231	1961
Zaporozhe	Old Dnepr River, U.S.S.R.	748	228	1952
Novi Sad	Danube River, Yugoslavia	692	211	1961

1. Concrete bridge. NOTE: UC = under construction. *Source: Encyclopaedia Britannica*, American Society of Civil Engineers, and International Bridge, Tunnel & Turnpike Association.

Famous Ship Canals

Name	Location	Length (miles)[1]	Width (feet)	Depth (feet)	Locks	Year opened
Albert	Belgium	80.0	53.0	16.5	6	1939
Amsterdam–Rhine	Netherlands	45.0	164.0	41.0	3	1952
Beaumont–Port Arthur	United States	40.0	200.0	34.0	—	1916
Chesapeake and Delaware	United States	19.0	250.0	27.0	—	1927
Houston	United States	43.0	300.0	34.0	—	1914
Kiel (Nord-Ostsee Kanal)	Germany	61.3	144.0	36.0	4	1895
Panama	Canal Zone	50.7	110.0	41.0	12	1914
St. Lawrence Seaway	U.S. and Canada	2,400.0[2]	(3)	—	—	1959
Montreal to Prescott	U.S. and Canada	11.5	80.0	30.0	7	1959
Welland	Canada	27.5	80.0	27.0	8	1931
Sault Ste. Marie	Canada	1.2	60.0	16.8	1	1895
Sault Ste. Marie	United States	1.6	80.0	25.0	4	1915
Suez	Egypt	100.6[4]	197.0	36.0	—	1869

1. Statute miles. 2. From Montreal to Duluth. 3. 442–550 feet; there are 11.5 miles of locks, 80 feet wide and 30 feet deep. 4. From Port Said lighthouse to entrance channel in Suez roads. *Source:* American Society of Civil Engineers.

UNITED NATIONS

The 157 Members of the United Nations

Country	Joined U.N.[1]
Afghanistan	1946
Albania	1955
Algeria	1962
Angola	1976
Antigua and Barbuda	1981
Argentina	1945
Australia	1945
Austria	1955
Bahamas	1973
Bahrain	1971
Bangladesh	1974
Barbados	1966
Belgium	1945
Belize	1981
Benin	1960
Bhutan	1971
Bolivia	1945
Botswana	1966
Brazil	1945
Bulgaria	1955
Burma	1948
Burundi	1962
Byelorussian S.S.R.	1945
Cambodia	1955
Cameroon	1960
Canada	1945
Cape Verde	1975
Central African Republic	1960
Chad	1960
Chile	1945
China[2]	1945
Colombia	1945
Comoros	1975
Congo	1960
Costa Rica	1945
Cuba	1945
Cyprus	1960
Czechoslovakia	1945
Denmark	1945
Djibouti	1977
Dominica	1978
Dominican Republic	1945
Ecuador	1945
Egypt	1945
El Salvador	1945
Equatorial Guinea	1968
Ethiopia	1945
Fiji	1970
Finland	1955
France	1945
Gabon	1960
Gambia	1965
Germany, East	1973
Germany, West	1973
Ghana	1957
Greece	1945
Grenada	1974
Guatemala	1945
Guinea	1958
Guinea-Bissau	1974
Guyana	1966
Haiti	1945
Honduras	1945
Hungary	1955
Iceland	1946
India	1945
Indonesia	1950
Iran	1945
Iraq	1945
Ireland	1955
Israel	1949
Italy	1955
Ivory Coast	1960
Jamaica	1962
Japan	1956
Jordan	1955
Kenya	1963
Kuwait	1963
Laos	1955
Lebanon	1945
Lesotho	1966
Liberia	1945
Libya	1955
Luxembourg	1945
Madagascar	1960
Malawi	1964
Malaysia	1957
Maldives	1965
Mali	1960
Malta	1964
Mauritania	1961
Mauritius	1968
Mexico	1945
Mongolia	1961
Morocco	1956
Mozambique	1975
Nepal	1955
Netherlands	1945
New Zealand	1945
Nicaragua	1945
Niger	1960
Nigeria	1960
Norway	1945
Oman	1971
Pakistan	1947
Panama	1945
Papua New Guinea	1975
Paraguay	1945
Peru	1945
Philippines	1945
Poland	1945
Portugal	1955
Qatar	1971
Romania	1955
Rwanda	1962
St. Lucia	1979
St. Vincent and the Grenadines	1980
Sao Tomé and Principe	1975
Saudi Arabia	1945
Senegal	1960
Seychelles	1976
Sierra Leone	1961
Singapore	1965
Solomon Islands	1978
Somalia	1960
South Africa	1945
Spain	1955
Sri Lanka	1955
Sudan	1956
Suriname	1975
Swaziland	1968
Sweden	1946
Syria	1945
Tanzania	1961
Thailand	1946
Togo	1960
Trinidad and Tobago	1962
Tunisia	1956
Turkey	1945
Uganda	1962
Ukrainian S.S.R.	1945
U.S.S.R.	1945
United Arab Emirates	1971
United Kingdom	1945
United States	1945
Upper Volta	1960
Uruguay	1945
Vanuatu	1981
Venezuela	1945
Vietnam	1977
Western Samoa	1976
Yemen Arab Republic	1947
Yemen, People's Dem. Republic of	1967
Yugoslavia	1945
Zaire	1960
Zambia	1964
Zimbabwe	1980

1. The U.N. officially came into existence on Oct. 24, 1945. 2. On Oct. 25, 1971, the U.N. voted membership to the People's Republic of China, which replaced the Republic of China (Taiwan) in the world body.

11 Countries Are Not Members of U.N.

Eleven countries do not hold membership in the United Nations. They are: Andorra, the Republic of China (Taiwan), Kiribati, North Korea, South Korea, Liechtenstein, Monaco, Nauru, Switzerland, Tonga, and Tuvalu.

Member Countries' Assessments to U.N. Budget, 1982

Country	Total	Country	Total	Country	Total
Afghanistan	$ 72,135	Ghana	$ 216,407	Papua New Guinea	$ 72,135
Albania	72,135	Greece	2,524,741	Paraguay	72,135
Algeria	865,626	Grenada	72,135	Peru	432,813
Angola	72,135	Guatemala	144,270	Philippines	721,355
Argentina	5,626,565	Guinea	72,135	Poland	8,944,795
Australia	13,200,786	Guinea-Bissau	72,135	Portugal	1,370,574
Austria	5,121,617	Guyana	72,135	Qatar	216,407
Bahamas	72,135	Haiti	72,135	Romania	1,514,845
Bahrain	72,135	Honduras	72,135	Rwanda	72,135
Bangladesh	288,542	Hungary	2,380,470	São Tomé and Príncipe	72,135
Barbados	72,135	Iceland	216,407	Saudi Arabia	4,183,856
Belgium	8,800,524	India	4,328,127	Senegal	72,135
Benin	72,135	Indonesia	1,154,168	Seychelles	72,135
Bhutan	72,135	Iran	4,688,804	Sierra Leone	72,135
Bolivia	72,135	Iraq	865,626	Singapore	577,084
Botswana	72,135	Ireland	1,154,168	Solomon Islands	72,135
Brazil	9,161,201	Israel	1,803,387	Somalia	72,135
Bulgaria	1,154,168	Italy	24,886,727	South Africa	3,029,689
Burma	72,135	Ivory Coast	216,407	Spain	12,263,025
Burundi	72,135	Jamaica	144,270	Sri Lanka	144,270
Byelorussian SSR	2,813,283	Japan	69,105,752	St. Lucia	72,135
Cambodia	72,135	Jordan	72,135	St. Vincent and the	
Cameroon	72,135	Kenya	72,135	Grenadines	72,135
Canada	23,660,425	Kuwait	1,442,709	Sudan	72,135
Cape Verde	72,135	Laos	72,135	Suriname	72,135
Central African Republic	72,135	Lebanon	216,407	Swaziland	72,135
Chad	72,135	Lesotho	72,135	Sweden	9,449,743
Chile	504,949	Liberia	72,135	Syria	216,407
China	11,685,942	Libya	1,659,116	Tanzania	72,135
Colombia	793,490	Luxembourg	360,678	Thailand	721,355
Comoros	72,135	Madagascar	72,135	Togo	72,135
Congo	72,135	Malawi	72,135	Trinidad and Tobago	216,407
Costa Rica	144,270	Malaysia	649,220	Tunisia	216,407
Cuba	793,490	Maldives	72,135	Turkey	2,164,064
Cyprus	72,135	Mali	72,135	Uganda	72,135
Czechoslovakia	5,987,242	Malta	72,135	Ukrainian S.S.R.	10,531,775
Denmark	5,338,023	Mauritania	72,135	U.S.S.R.	80,070,338
Djibouti	72,135	Mauritius	72,135	United Arab Emirates	721,355
Dominica	72,135	Mexico	5,482,294	United Kingdom	32,172,407
Dominican Republic	216,407	Mongolia	72,135	United States	180,338,601
Ecuador	144,270	Morocco	360,678	Upper Volta	72,135
Egypt	504,949	Mozambique	72,135	Uruguay	288,542
El Salvador	72,135	Nepal	72,135	Venezuela	3,606,773
Equatorial Guinea	72,135	Netherlands	11,758,077	Vietnam	216,407
Ethiopia	72,135	New Zealand	1,947,657	Western Samoa	72,135
Fiji	72,135	Nicaragua	72,135	Yemen Arab Republic	72,135
Finland	3,462,502	Niger	72,135	Yemen, People's Dem.	
France	45,156,786	Nigeria	1,154,168	Republic of	72,135
Gabon	144,270	Norway	3,606,773	Yugoslavia	3,029,689
Gambia	72,135	Oman	72,135	Zaire	144,270
Germany, East	10,026,827	Pakistan	504,949	Zambia	144,270
Germany, West	59,944,552	Panama	144,270	Zimbabwe	144,270

United Nations Headquarters

The first regular session of the General Assembly held at Central Hall, Westminster, London, voted that interim headquarters of the Organization should be located in New York. From London the U.N. moved to Hunter College in the Bronx. In August 1946, an interim headquarters was set up at Lake Success on Long Island, in a part of the Sperry Gyroscope Co.'s plant. The New York City building at Flushing Meadows, site of the 1939 World's Fair, was converted for the use of the General Assembly. The search for a permanent home ended in December 1946, when the General Assembly accepted an offer from John D. Rockefeller, Jr., of $8,500,000[1] for the purchase of the present Headquarters site—an 18-acre tract in Manhattan, alongside the East River. The U.S. Government lent the U.N. $65,000,000 interest free, which is being repaid in annual installments.

Architectural plans drawn up by an international Board of Design were approved by the Assembly, and construction began in September 1948. By mid-1950, the 39-story Secretariat Building was ready for occupancy, and in the spring of 1951 "United Nations, New York" became the Organization's permanent address. The other main structures are the Conference Building, the General Assembly Hall, and the Dag Hammarskjold Library. All are interconnected.

1. This amount paid for two-thirds of the land; New York City gave one-third.

Preamble of the United Nations Charter

The Charter of the United Nations was adopted at the San Francisco Conference of 1945. The complete text may be obtained by writing to the United Nations Sales Section, United Nations, New York, N.Y. 10017, and enclosing $1.

We the peoples of the United Nations determined to save succeeding generations from the scourge of war, which twice in our lifetime has brought untold sorrow to mankind, and

To reaffirm faith in fundamental human rights, in the dignity and worth of the human person, in the equal rights of men and women and of nations large and small, and

To establish conditions under which justice and respect for the obligations arising from treaties and other sources of international law can be maintained, and

To promote social progress and better standards of life in larger freedom, and for these ends

To practice tolerance and live together in peace with one another as good neighbors, and

To unite our strength to maintain international peace and security, and

To insure, by the acceptance of principles and the institution of methods, that armed force shall not be used, save in the common interest, and

To employ international machinery for the promotion of the economic and social advancement of all peoples, have resolved to combine our efforts to accomplish these aims.

Accordingly, our respective Governments, through representatives assembled in the city of San Francisco, who have exhibited their full powers found to be in good and due form, have agreed to the present Charter of the United Nations and do hereby establish an international organization to be known as the United Nations.

Principal Organs of the United Nations

Secretariat

This is the directorate on U.N. operations, apart from political decisions. All members contribute to its upkeep. Its staff of over 6,000 specialists is recruited from member nations on the basis of as wide a geographical distribution as possible. The staff works under the Secretary-General, whom it assists and advises.

Secretaries-General

Javier Pérez de Cuéllar, Peru, Jan. 1, 1982.
Kurt Waldheim, Austria, Jan. 1, 1972, to Dec. 31, 1981.
U Thant, Burma, Nov. 3, 1961, to Dec. 31, 1971.
Dag Hammarskjöld, Sweden, April 11, 1953, to Sept. 17, 1961.
Trygve Lie, Norway, Feb. 1, 1946, to April 10, 1953.

General Assembly

The General Assembly is the world's forum for discussing matters affecting world peace and security, and for making recommendations concerning them. It has no power of its own to enforce decisions.

The Assembly is composed of the 51 original member nations and those admitted since, a total of 153. Each nation has one vote. On major questions involving international peace and security, a two-thirds majority of those present and voting is required. Decisions on other questions are made by a simple majority.

The Assembly's agenda can be as broad as the Charter. It can make recommendations to member nations, the Security Council, or both. Emphasis is given questions relating to international peace and security brought before it by any member, the Security Council, or nonmembers.

The Assembly also maintains a broad program of international cooperation in economic, social, cultural, educational, and health fields, and for assisting in human rights and freedoms.

Among other duties, the Assembly has functions relating to the trusteeship system, and considers and approves the U.N. Budget. Every member contributes to operating expenses according to its means.

Security Council

The Security Council is the primary instrument for establishing and maintaining international peace. Its main purpose is to prevent war by settling disputes between nations.

Under the Charter, the Council is permitted to dispatch a U.N. force to stop aggression. All member nations undertake to make available armed forces, assistance, and facilities to maintain international peace and security.

Any member may bring a dispute before the Security Council or the General Assembly. Any nonmember may do so if it accepts the charter obligations of pacific settlement.

The Security Council has 15 members. There are five permanent members: the United States, the Soviet Union, Britain, France, and China and 10 temporary members elected by the General Assembly for two-year terms, with different regions of the world rotating.

Voting on procedural matters requires a nine-vote majority to carry. However, on questions of substance, the vote of each of the five permanent members is required. Thus, any one of the five possess a veto.

Current temporary members are (term expires Dec. 31, 1982): Ireland, Japan, Panama, Spain, Uganda; (term expires Dec. 31, 1983): Guyana, Jordan, Poland, Togo, Zaire.

Economic and Social Council

This council is composed of 54 members elected by the General Assembly to 3-year terms. It works closely with the General Assembly as a link with groups formed within the U.N. to help peoples in such fields as education, health, and human rights. It insures that there is no overlapping and sets up commissions to deal with economic conditions and collect facts and figures on conditions over the world. It issues studies and reports and may make recommendations to the Assembly and specialized agencies.

Functional Commissions

Statistical Commission; Population Commission; Commission for Social Development; Commission on Human Rights; Commission on the Status of Women; Commission on Narcotic Drugs.

Regional Commissions

Economic Commission for Europe; Economic

and Social Commission for Asia and the Pacific; Economic Commission for Latin America; Economic Commission for Africa; Economic Commission for Western Asia.

Trusteeship Council

This council supervises territories administered by various nations and placed under an international trusteeship system by the United Nations. Each nation is charged with developing the self-government of the territory and preserving and advancing the cultural, political, economic, and other forms of welfare of the people.

The Trusteeship Council is currently composed of 5 members: 1 member—the United States—that administers a trust territory, and 4 members—China, France, the Soviet Union, and the United Kingdom—that are permanent members of the Security Council but do not administer trust territories.

The following countries ceased to be administering members because of the independence of territories they had administered: Italy and France in 1960, Belgium in 1962, New Zealand and the United Kingdom in 1968 and Australia in 1975. France and the U. K. became nonadministering members.

As of December 1980, there was only one trust territory: the Trust Territory of the Pacific Islands (administered by the United States).

International Court of Justice

The International Court of Justice sits at The Hague, the Netherlands. Its 15-judge bench was established to hear disputes among states, who must agree to accept its verdicts. Its judges, charged with administering justice under international law, deal with cases ranging from disputes over territory to those concerning rights of passage.

Following are the members of the Court and the years in which their terms expire:

President: Taslim Olawale Elias, Nigeria (1985)
Vice President: Jose Sette Camara, Brazil (1988)
Manfred Lachs, Poland (1985)
Herman Mosler, West Germany (1985)
Shigeru Oda, Japan (1985)
Abdallah Fikri El-Khani, Syria (1985)
Platon Dmitrievich Morozov, U.S.S.R. (1988)
Roberto Ago, Italy (1988)
Stephen Schwebel, U.S. (1988)
Mohammed Bedjaoui, Algeria (1988)
Nagendra Singh, India (1991)
Jose Maria Ruda, Argentina (1991)
Robert Y. Jennings, United Kingdom (1991)
Guy Ladreit de Lacharriere, France (1991)
Keba Mbaye, Senegal (1991)

Agencies of the United Nations

INTERNATIONAL ATOMIC ENERGY AGENCY (IAEA)

Established: Statute for IAEA, approved on Oct. 26, 1956, at a conference held at U.N. Headquarters, New York, came into force on July 29, 1957. The Agency is under the aegis of the U.N., but unlike the following, it is not a specialized agency.

Purpose: To promote the peaceful uses of atomic energy; to ensure that assistance provided by it or at its request or under its supervision or control is not used in such a way as to further any military purpose.

Headquarters: P.O. Box 100 A-1400, Vienna, Austria.

FOOD AND AGRICULTURE ORGANIZATION OF THE UNITED NATIONS (FAO)

Established: October 16, 1945, when constitution became effective.

Purpose: To raise nutrition levels and living standards; to secure improvements in production and distribution of food and agricultural products.

Headquarters: Via delle Terme di Caracalla, 00100, Rome, Italy.

GENERAL AGREEMENT ON TARIFFS AND TRADE (GATT)

Established: Jan. 1, 1948.

Purpose: An International Trade Organization (ITO) was planned when the U.N. Agencies were first set up. Although this agency has not materialized, some of its objectives have been embodied in an international commercial treaty, the General Agreement on Tariffs and Trade. Its purpose is to sponsor trade negotiations.

Headquarters: Centre William Rappard, 154 Rue de Lausanne, 1211 Geneva 21, Switzerland.

INTERNATIONAL BANK FOR RECONSTRUCTION AND DEVELOPMENT (IBRD) (WORLD BANK)

Established: December 27, 1945, when Articles of Agreement drawn up at Bretton Woods Conference in July 1944 came into force. Began operations on June 25, 1946.

Purpose: To assist in reconstruction and development of economies of members by facilitating capital investment and by making loans to governments and furnishing technical advice.

Headquarters: 1818 H St., N.W., Washington, D.C. 20433.

INTERNATIONAL CIVIL AVIATION ORGANIZATION (ICAO)

Established: April 4, 1947, after working as a provisional organization since June 1945.

Purpose: To study problems of international civil aviation; to establish international standards and regulations; to promote safety measures, uniform regulations for operation, simpler procedures at international borders, and the use of new technical methods and equipment. It has evolved standards for meteorological services, traffic control, communications, radio beacons and ranges, search and rescue organization, and other facilities. It has brought about much simplification of customs, immigration, and public health regulations as they apply to international air transport. It drafts international air law conventions, and is concerned with economic aspects of air travel.

Headquarters: International Aviation Square, 1000 Sherbrooke St. West, Montreal, Quebec, H3A 2R2, Canada.

INTERNATIONAL DEVELOPMENT ASSOCIATION (IDA)

Established: Sept. 24, 1960. An affiliate of the World Bank, IDA has the same officers and staff as the Bank.

Purpose: To further economic development of its members by providing finance on terms which bear less heavily on balance of payments of members than those of conventional loans.

Headquarters: 1818 H St., N.W., Washington, D.C. 20433.

INTERNATIONAL FINANCE CORPORATION (IFC)

Established: Charter of IFC came into force on July 20, 1956. Although IFC is affiliated with the World Bank, it is a separate legal entity, and its funds are entirely separate from those of the Bank. However, membership in the Corporation is open only to Bank members.

Purpose: To further economic development by encouraging the growth of productive private enterprise in its member countries, particularly in the less developed areas; to invest in productive private enterprises in association with private investors, without government guarantee of repayment where sufficient private capital is not available on reasonable terms; to serve as a clearing house to bring together investment opportunities, private capital (both foreign and domestic), and experienced management.

Headquarters: 1818 H St., N.W., Washington, D.C. 20433.

INTERNATIONAL FUND FOR AGRICULTURAL DEVELOPMENT (IFAD)

Established: June 18,1976. Began operations in December 1977.

Purpose: To mobilize additional funds for agricultural and rural development in developing countries through projects and programs directly benefiting the poorest rural populations.

Headquarters: 107 Via del Serafico, 00142 Rome, Italy.

INTERNATIONAL LABOR ORGANIZATION (ILO)

Established: April 11, 1919, when constitution was adopted as Part XIII of Treaty of Versailles. Became specialized agency of U.N. in 1946.

Purpose: To contribute to establishment of lasting peace by promoting social justice; to improve labor conditions and living standards through international action; to promote economic and social stability. The U.S. withdrew from the ILO in 1977 and resumed membership in 1980.

Headquarters: 4 route des Morillons, CH-1211 Geneva 22, Switzerland.

INTERNATIONAL MARITIME ORGANIZATION (IMO)

Established: March 17, 1958.

Purpose: To give advisory and consultative help to promote international cooperation in maritime navigation and to encourage the highest standards of safety and navigation. Its aim is to bring about a uniform system of measuring ship tonnage; systems now vary widely in different parts of the world. Other activities include cooperation with other U.N. agencies on matters affecting the maritime field.

Headquarters: 101–104 Piccadilly, London, W1V OAE, England.

INTERNATIONAL MONETARY FUND (IMF)

Established: Dec. 27, 1945, when Articles of Agreement drawn up at Bretton Woods Conference in July 1944 came into force. Fund began operations on March 1, 1947.

Purpose: To promote international monetary cooperation and expansion of international trade; to promote exchange stability; to assist in establishment of multilateral system of payments in respect of currency transactions between members.

Headquarters: 700 19th St., N.W., Washington, D.C. 20431.

INTERNATIONAL TELECOMMUNICATION UNION (ITU)

Established: 1865. Became specialized agency of U.N. in 1947.

Purpose: To extend technical assistance to help members keep up with present day telecommunication needs; to standardize communications equipment and procedures; to lower costs. It also works for orderly sharing of radio frequencies and makes studies and recommendations to benefit its members.

Headquarters: Place des Nations, 1211 Geneva 20, Switzerland.

UNITED NATIONS EDUCATIONAL, SCIENTIFIC, AND CULTURAL ORGANIZATION (UNESCO)

Established: Nov. 4, 1946, when twentieth signatory to constitution deposited instrument of acceptance with government of U.K.

Purpose: To promote collaboration among nations through education, science, and culture in order to further justice, rule of law, and human rights and freedoms without distinction of race, sex, language, or religion.

Headquarters: UNESCO House, 7 Place de Fontenoy, 75700, Paris, France.

UNIVERSAL POSTAL UNION (UPU)

Established: Oct. 9, 1874. Became specialized agency of U.N. in 1947.

Purpose: To facilitate reciprocal exchange of correspondence by uniform procedures by all UPU members; to help governments modernize and speed up mailing procedures.

Headquarters: Weltpostrasse 4, 3000 Berne 15, Switzerland.

WORLD HEALTH ORGANIZATION (WHO)

Established: April 7, 1948, when 26 members of the U.N. had accepted its constitution, adopted July 22, 1946, by the International Health Conference in New York City.

Purpose: To aid attainment by all people of highest possible level of health.

Headquarters: 20 Avenue Appia, 1211 Geneva, Switzerland.

WORLD INTELLECTUAL PROPERTY ORGANIZATION (WIPO)

Established: April 26, 1970, when its Convention came into force. Originated as International Bureau of Paris Union (1883) and Berne Union (1886), later succeeded by United International Bureau for the Protection of Intellectual Property (BIRPI). Became a specialized agency of the U.N. in December 1974.

Purpose: To promote legal protection of intellectual property, including artistic and scientific works, artistic performances, sound recordings, broadcasts, inventions, trademarks, industrial designs, and commercial names.

Headquarters: 32 Chemin des Colombettes, 1211 Geneva 20, Switzerland.

WORLD METEOROLOGICAL ORGANIZATION (WMO)

Established: March 23, 1950, succeeding the International Meteorological Organization, a nongovernmental organization founded in 1878.

Purpose: To promote international exchange of weather reports and maximum standardization of observations; to help developing countries establish weather services for their own economic needs; to fill gaps in observation stations; to promote meteorological investigations affecting jet aircraft, satellites, energy resources, etc.

Headquarters: 41 Avenue Giuseppe Motta, Geneva, Switzerland.

The Year in Energy—1982

All good things must come to an end, and the worldwide petroleum glut that had actually driven oil prices downward in the recent past began to show definite signs of abating during 1982. The cost of a gallon of gas at the pump, that most meaningful of price indicators, made a few headlines by dropping just below one dollar early in the year. However, by mid-summer "normal" price trends were once again in effect, although supplies were adequate and no shortages could be detected. In their automobiles and in their industries, Americans had obviously learned the value of energy conservation: the latest statistics available from the US Department of Energy (DOE) showed that drivers had cut back roughly seven percent in their gasoline consumption, mainly through the use of smaller cars and generally more conservative driving habits. Industrial energy consumption also dropped appreciably, but the country was still far from being self-sufficient in fuel production. Oil and natural gas continued to constitute the largest fraction (about 70%) of our fuel consumption, and our imports of petroleum fuels (in terms of crude oil) continued near their 1981 levels of some 5.7 million barrels per day.

The road to energy self-sufficiency clearly lies in the development of viable synthetic fuels (Synfuels) based on our enormous coal and shale oil reserves, as well as on alternate energy sources based on alcohol derived from the biomass, and a number of advances in this direction were reported during 1982. Formation of the Synfuels Corporation was signed into law by President Reagan; the new entity will supervise two shale-oil plants to be located in Colorado, where much of the oil-bearing mineral is found. However, one major oil company announced curtailment of its oil-from-shale project. Research continues, nonetheless: a newly developed catalyst based on oxides of chromium, cobalt and molybdenum can convert shale oil to jet fuel in a single step. This could eventually prove to be an important breakthrough since economics will be the deciding factor as to whether shale oil ever becomes a commercial reality. Incidentally, the US has enough shale oil reserves to satisfy all of our fuel needs for 100 years, based on current consumption rates.

Research leading to the production of liquid or gaseous fuels from coal also continued during 1982, but at a much slower pace than that anticipated during the height of the energy crunch. Still, commercial coal gasification plants gained approval for Federal loan guarantees, a step which was seen as speeding up the exploitation of this synthetic fuel source.

Ethyl alcohol, or ethanol, is another important synfuel, but one which is still too expensive (about $2.00 a gallon) to find all but limited uses in automotive gasohols. It may get cheaper: Canadian scientists have discovered a new yeast, *Pachysolen tannophilus,* which is able to ferment 5-carbon sugars such as xylose into ethanol. Traditional fermentation processes rely on ordinary brewers' yeast, which can only convert 6-carbon sugars such as glucose. Unfortunately, the cheap and abundant biomass feedstocks (wood wastes, agricultural residues) that could be a major source of ethanol fuel contain about one-half of their available sugars in the 6-carbon varieties; 25–30% of the remaining sugars are thought to be of the 5-carbon type. *P. tannophilus* can ferment both the glucose and xylose sugars, leading to increased process yields and, eventually, lower costs.

Let There Be Light

Petroleum producers have long been searching for an inexpensive and nonpolluting way to dispose of the hydrogen sulfide (H_2S) that they must remove from some of their high-sulfur crude oils. A Swiss researcher may have found it for them, even though he wasn't really looking at all. Actually, he was experimenting with ways to split water into hydrogen and oxygen photochemically, using catalysts such as cadmium sulfide (CdS), the stuff of photographic light meters. One of his test solutions inadvertently became contaminated with H_2S, but when he exposed it to sunlight it very efficiently converted the smelly (odor of rotten eggs) pollutant to hydrogen gas, a potentially important fuel in its own right, and elemental sulfur. The process is still under development, but it looks very promising.

Solar energy has also been used, for the first time, to drive a magnetohydrodynamic (MHD) generator, according to scientists at Ben Gurion University in Israel. The new process, called Liquid Metal MHD or LMMHD, relies on solar panels to heat a volatile liquid such as freon, which in turn drives a liquid metal (sodium) through an MHD chamber, generating electricity. The system has no moving parts, and can use the Sun's energy or any other source of waste industrial heat between 200–600°F as its driving force. Efficiency should be between 13 to 15%. A ten kilowatt pilot model is under construction.

Along slightly different lines, Georgia Tech has used a large mirror to concentrate the Sun's rays to 1380°F, utilizing the heat to drive an external combustion Stirling Cycle engine developing 20 kw of electricity. An American company has developed an improved solar collector, which operates under vacuum and has a corrugated surface made up of many semicylindrical glass tubes. The efficiency of the new collector is so high, claims its inventor, that it can even produce useful amounts of heat on a cloudy day in Boston. Before rushing out to install a rooftop collector, however, make sure you are aware of all the necessary safety precautions, including adequate insulation *behind* the collecting panel. At least one house fire has been attributed to charring of underlying roof beams caused by a collector that had been allowed to remain dry too long.

Fission Down, Fusion Coming Up

In 1982, water-cooled nuclear (fission) reactors produced only about three percent of America's total energy requirements, although they did account for a greater fraction of our electric power needs. However, there is serious concern, both pro and con, that nuclear power as we now know it may have reached a dead end. Directly or indirectly, the well-known accident at the Three Mile Island (TMI) generating station near Harrisburg, Pennsylvania has led to the cancellation or deferral of up to 80 nuclear power plants. "Hot" cleanup, or the decontamination of 660,000 gallons of slightly radioactive water resulting from the TMI accident, has begun, with some financial assistance provided by the federal government. However, restarting of the second TMI reactor (not affected by the accident) was delayed pending an evaluation of the "psychological impact" the incident may have had on local residents. The direct effects of any radiation released during the accident may not be known for years, but an analysis of the Windscale reactor accident, which occurred in Britain in 1957, published in 1982, might provide a clue: analysts predicted that 10 to 20 persons will die of cancer over the next few decades as a result of that early disaster. However, radioactive releases at TMI were about 1000 times smaller than they were at Windscale.

As fission-based nuclear power waned in the US, prospects for an early success for fusion power appeared somewhat brighter in 1982. Thermonuclear fusion is the reaction that occurs in hydrogen bombs, and in the Sun. Research has been going on for many years seeking ways to control this reaction in such a way as to permit the extraction of heat for the generation of electric power. Doing this requires that mixtures of deuterium and tritium (isotopes of ordinary hydrogen) be heated to about one hundred million degrees, a temperature at which they can "fuse" to form helium. Currently, the two most promising ways of accomplishing this are to constrict a hot gas plasma by means of a powerful magnetic field, as in the Princeton Large Torus (Tokamak), the Elmo Bumpy Torus at Oak Ridge National Laboratory and the ZT-40 device at Los Alamos, and by so-called "inertial fusion", in which appropriate gas mixtures are blasted by ultrahigh-powered laser beams. Proponents of both schemes claimed to have advanced the state of the art in 1982, but the long-sought goal of breakeven power (net power output equal to power input) had not yet been achieved. Some idea of the magnitude of the problem can be grasped by considering the size of the equipment involved: SHIVA is a 20-arm, 10-kilojoule laser located at the Livermore Laboratory in California. It is the largest laser now in use in the US, producing infrared light with an instantaneous power greater than the entire US electrical grid. It has yet to come within several orders of magnitude of the breakeven point, and researchers now predict that it will take a 3000–4000 kilojoule laser (300–400 times as big as SHIVA) to drive a prototype inertial fusion power plant.

Several nations are now building large magnetic fusion facilities. Besides the Tokamak Fusion Test Reactor at Princeton, tokamaks are being assembled by the Russians (who invented the device), the Japanese and a consortium of European countries. All are scheduled for initial operation in the 1980s. Stay tuned.

Down-To-Earth Power

Less exotic, but equally promising, are prospects for power from the Earth itself. Geothermal power, which taps the heat of volcanically heated strata deep below the surface, has been used in Europe, Iceland and parts of the United States for many years. Now a new potential source of geothermal energy has been discovered in Oregon. About 2500 feet deep inside that state's inactive Newberry Volcano, scientists have found a thermal gradient (the change in temperature with depth) as high as 700°F per mile. This is about 20 times higher than the average for the rest of the world, according to the men and women who dared to poke a hole into the dormant Northwestern volcano. Equally brave (dedicated? deranged?) geologists drilled almost 300 feet into Hawaii's Kilauea Iki Lava Lake to reach magma as hot as 1800°F, recovering a complete core sample and returning it to the surface. When water was injected into magma hotter than 1300°F, energy was extracted at a rate about five and one-half times the power density (amount of power produced divided by thermal contact area) of a commercial electric generating station. Exploitation of this huge geothermal energy source is still 10 to 20 years away, however. Ocean thermal energy conversion (OTEC) may be somewhat nearer at hand, since the US Department of Commerce simplified licensing procedures for the process in 1982. OTEC uses the difference in temperature between surface and deep ocean waters as an infinite source of energy. It is conceivable that a 40 to 80 megawatt plant could be operational in US waters by 1986 to 1988, possibly off Hawaii or Guam. That's understandable—who'd want to plug into a volcano when they could collect their kilowatts at Waikiki?

Konrad J.A. Kundig

Tips on Buying Wood for Home Heating

Wood is usually sold by the cord or fraction thereof. There is a standard cord, face cord, short cord, long cord, a solid cord, and maybe others.

The standard cord should be specified when you order wood. It is a pile of wood measuring four feet high, eight feet wide, and four feet long. A face cord measures four feet high by eight feet wide but the pieces may be any length. So a face cord of stove-length (16 in.) wood would be only one third of a standard cord. The term "short cord" is another way of saying "face cord."

When buying cord, be sure that the pile you measure is tightly stacked with all the wood pieces lying in the same direction. Otherwise, you will pay for the air space instead of wood. Even piled carefully, a cord has only 80 cubic feet of solid wood in it, although its dimensions measure 128 cubic feet.

Pound for pound, most species of wood produce about the same amount of heat if the wood is dry. Some species of wood are lighter than others, so a cord of wood such as aspen will weigh about half as much as a cord of dry white oak and will therefore have about half the heat value.

Ask the seller how long the wood was "air-dried" and whether it was cut to length and split before drying. If the answers are "at least nine months" and "yes," respectively, you can assume that you'll get fair heat value for the weight.

World Production, Trade, and Consumption of Commercial Energy, 1980
(in million metric tons of coal equivalent)

Activity	World	Developed countries[1]	Developing countries[2]	Centrally planned economic[3]	U.S.	U.S.S.R.	Saudi Arabia
Total primary energy production	9,338	3,419	2,821	3,099	2,090	1,939	730
Imports of commercial energy	3,270	2,403	611	256	528	27	3
Exports of commercial energy	3,247	623	2,190	434	100	338	692
Total energy consumption							
Solid fuel	2,654	1,133	130	1,390	619	515	—
Liquid fuels	4,506	1,025	2,423	1,058	695	878	729
Natural gas	1,879	1,054	220	605	711	516	0.9
Hydro/nuclear electricity	300	207	48	45	66	30	—
Total commercial energy in kg per capita	**1,955**	**6,035**	**459**	**1,977**	**10,410**	**5,595**	**1,677**

1. Australia, Canada, Israel, Japan, New Zealand, South Africa, U.S., Western Europe (incl. Yugoslovia). 2. Developing market economies of Africa, Caribbean, Middle East (incl. Turkey), Far East, etc. 3. Albania, Bulgaria, Czechoslovakia, East Germany, Hungary, Poland, Romania, U.S.S.R. *Source:* United Nations, *1980 Yearbook of World Energy Statistics* (Statistical Papers, Series J No. 24).

World's Ten Largest Electric Energy Producers, 1980
(in billion kilowatt hours)

Country	Production			
	Hydro	Nuclear	Thermal	Total
United States	282,794[1]	251,115	1,822,230	2,356,139
U.S.S.R.	180,000	60,000	1,055,000	1,295,000
Japan	93,022[1]	83,220	435,798	612,040
West Germany	18,400	41,500	308,872	368,772
Canada	250,998	35,880	79,799	366,677
China	55,600	—	245,000	300,600
United Kingdom	5,240	37,088	242,807	285,135
France	69,870	60,882	127,000	257,752
Italy	51,600[1]	2,300	132,405	186,305
Poland	2,500	—	119,360	121,860
Sub-total	1,010,024	571,985	4,687,631	6,150,280
All others	735,551	100,972	1,115,030	2,088,913
World total	**1,743,575**	**672,957**	**5,802,661**	**8,239,193**

1. Production from geothermal sources included. *Source:* United Nations, *1980 Yearbook of World Energy Statistics* (Statistical Papers, Series J No. 24).

Per Capita Electric Energy Consumption, 1980
(20 highest per capita consumers)

Country	kwh per capita[1]	Population (thousands)[2]	Production plus net imports[3]
Norway	20,327	4,092	85,726
Canada	14,179	24,033	396,898
Iceland	13,061	229	3,004
Christmas Island	11,667	3	35
Sweden	11,510	8,322	98,950
Luxembourg	10,906	365	4,164
United States	10,469	223,186	2,386,360
Guam	9,583	106	1,150
Turks & Caicos Islands	9,000	6	9
Finland	8,329	4,784	40,961
New Caledonia	8,312	137	1,280
U.S. Virgin Islands	7,684	96	730
New Zealand	7,091	3,152	21,982
Kuwait	6,816	1,418	9,270
Netherlands Antilles	6,759	243	1,825
Qatar	6,591	225	1,450
Australia	6,558	14,676	95,881
Switzerland	6,258	6,328	56,718
West Germany	6,082	61,388	387,883
East Germany	5,960	16,759	102,800
World	**1,884**	**4,415,000**	**8,401,827**

1. Production plus net imports divided by total population. 2. Estimate. 3. In billion kilowatt hours. NOTE: Data on consumption are derived from the formula "production plus imports minus exports." Accordingly, apparent consumption may occasionally be only an indication of the magnitude of actual gross inland availability. Where relatively small populations are involved, large fluctuations in per capita consumption series may derive from small quantitative variations. *Source:* United Nations, *1980 Yearbook of World Energy Statistics* (Statistical Papers, Series J No. 24).

U.S. Energy Supply and Disposition
(in quadrillion Btus)

Activity and fuel	1981[1]	1980	1979	1978	1975	1970	1965	1960
SUPPLY								
Production								
Crude Oil and Lease Condensate	18.13	18.25	18.10	18.43	17.73	20.40	16.52	14.93
Natural Gas Plant Liquids	2.27	2.27	2.29	2.25	2.37	2.51	1.88	1.46
Natural Gas[2]	20.10	19.70	20.08	19.49	19.64	21.67	15.78	12.66
Coal[3]	18.70	18.88	17.65	15.04	15.19	15.05	13.38	11.12
Nuclear Power	2.90	2.70	2.75	2.98	1.90	0.24	0.04	0.01
Hydropower	2.73	2.91	2.95	2.96	3.15	2.63	2.06	1.60
Other[4]	0.13	0.11	0.09	0.07	0.07	0.02	0.01	(Z)
Total Production	**64.95**	**64.82**	**63.91**	**61.21**	**60.06**	**62.51**	**49.67**	**41.78**
Imports								
Crude Oil[5]	9.35	11.06	13.83	13.46	8.72	2.81	2.65	2.20
Refined Petroleum Products[6]	3.31	3.38	4.11	4.36	4.23	4.66	2.75	1.80
Natural Gas	0.90	1.03	1.30	0.99	0.98	0.85	0.47	0.16
Other[7]	0.32	0.28	0.39	0.44	0.19	0.07	0.04	0.07
Total Imports	13.87	15.75	19.62	19.26	14.11	8.39	5.92	4.23
Adjustments[8]	−0.57	−0.54	−1.66	−0.36	−1.08	−1.41	−0.74	−0.44
Total Supply	**78.25**	**80.03**	**81.87**	**80.11**	**73.09**	**69.49**	**54.85**	**45.57**
DISPOSITION								
Consumption								
Refined Petroleum Products[9]	32.00	34.25	37.12	37.97	32.73	29.52	23.25	19.92
Natural Gas[2]	19.93	20.44	20.67	20.00	19.95	21.79	15.77	12.39
Coal[5]	16.01	15.67	15.11	13.85	12.82	12.66	11.89	10.12
Nuclear Power	2.90	2.70	2.75	2.98	1.90	0.24	0.04	0.01
Hydropower[10]	2.97	3.13	3.17	3.17	3.22	2.65	2.06	1.65
Other	0.13	0.11	0.09	0.07	0.07	0.02	0.01	(Z)
Net Imports of Coal Coke	−0.02	−0.04	0.07	0.13	0.01	−0.06	−0.02	−0.01
Total Consumption	**73.91**	**76.27**	**78.97**	**78.15**	**70.71**	**66.83**	**52.99**	**44.08**
Exports								
Coal[3]	2.94	2.47	1.78	1.10	1.79	1.94	1.38	1.02
Other[11]	1.39	1.29	1.12	0.85	0.60	0.73	0.48	0.46
Total Exports	**4.34**	**3.76**	**2.90**	**1.95**	**2.39**	**2.66**	**1.86**	**1.48**
Total Disposition	**78.25**	**80.03**	**81.87**	**80.11**	**73.09**	**69.49**	**54.85**	**45.57**

1. Preliminary. 2. Dry marketed gas. 3. Includes bituminous, lignite, and anthracite coal. 4. Geothermal, wood, refuse, and other vegetal fuels used for electricity generation at utilities. 5. Includes imports of crude oil for the Strategic Petroleum Reserve. 6. Also includes imports of unfinished oils and natural gas plant liquids. 7. Includes bituminous, lignite, and anthracite coal, as well as coke made from coal, and hydropower. 8. A balancing item. Includes stock changes, losses, gains, miscellaneous blending compounds, unaccounted for supply, and shipments of anthracite coal to U.S. Armed Forces in Europe. 9. Refined petroleum products supplied includes natural gas plant liquids and crude oil burned as fuel. 10. Includes industrial generation of hydropower and net electricity imports. 11. Includes crude oil, refined petroleum products, natural gas, coke made from coal, and hydropower. (Z) = Less than 0.005 quadrillion Btu. NOTE: The sum of the components may not equal the total due to independent rounding. *Source:* Energy Information Administration, Annual Report to Congress 1981, Volume 2.

Comparing Energy Sources[1]
(converting energy sources into BTU equivalents)

One British Thermal Unit (BTU) = the amount of heat needed to increase the temperature of one pound of water by 1° F. (252 calories).

	BTU (in thousands)
Bituminous Coal and Lignite	
Production, average/short ton	23,500.0
Consumption, average/short ton	22,800.0
Electricity generation/short ton	21,630.0
Anthracite, short ton	25,400.0
Crude petroleum, barrel (42 gallons)	5,800.0
Natural gas, dry, cubic foot	1.021
Nuclear power, kilowatt-hour	10.66
Hydropower[2] kilowatt-hour	10.38

1. For helpful conversion factors, *see* the "Science" section of this *Almanac.* 2. Calculated from national average heat rates for fossil-fueled steam-electric plants.

Production of Crude Petroleum by Countries

(in thousands of 42-gallon barrels)

Area and country	Est. 1982[1]	1981	Est. percent change
Western Hemisphere	5,712,980	5,794,375	−1.4
Argentina	175,200	182,500	−4.0
Bolivia	9,490	8,760	+8.3
Brazil	86,870	71,905	+20.8
Canada	419,385	507,715	−17.4
Chile	16,790	14,600	+15.0
Colombia	45,625	45,625	—
Ecuador	74,825	80,300	−6.8
Guatemala	1,825	1,825	—
Mexico	885,855	792,780	+11.7
Peru	73,000	68,985	+5.8
Trinidad and Tobago	87,600	87,600	—
United States	3,156,885	3,125,860	+1.0
Venezuela	680,360	805,920	−15.6
Western Europe	980,390	930,385	+5.4
Austria	9,855	9,855	—
Denmark	6,570	2,190	+200.0
France	12,775	12,045	+6.1
West Germany	31,755	31,390	+1.2
Greece	5,475	—	—
Italy	12,775	14,600	−12.5
Netherlands	9,855	9,125	+8.0
Norway	186,516	195,640	−4.7
Spain	6,205	8,395	−26.1
United Kingdom	699,340	647,875	+7.9
Middle East	5,150,880	6,030,530	−14.6
Abu Dhabi[2]	365,000	455,520	−24.8
Bahrain	16,790	16,425	+2.2
Dubai	135,780	130,305	+4.2
Iran	384,345	489,830	−21.5
Iraq	491,655	197,830	+148.5
Israel	365	365	—
Kuwait	255,500	517,935	−50.7
Neutral Zone[3]	106,580	193,085	−44.8
Oman	118,990	118,990	—
Qatar	142,350	180,675	−21.2
Saudi Arabia	3,050,670	3,650,000	−16.4
Sharjah[2]	2,555	2,920	−12.5
Syria	62,050	60,225	+3.0
Turkey	18,250	16,425	+11.1
Asia–Pacific	996,450	1,027,475	−3.0
Australia	150,380	146,730	+2.5
Brunei	60,225	60,225	—
Burma	10,950	10,950	—
India	124,100	105,850	+17.4
Indonesia	537,280	593,490	−9.5
Japan	2,920	3,285	−11.1
Malaysia	100,740	98,915	+1.8
New Zealand	3,285	2,190	+50.0
Pakistan	3,650	3,650	—
Philippines	1,825	1,095	+66.7
Taiwan	1,095	1,095	—
Africa	1,536,285	2,082,325	−26.2
Algeria	255,500	328,500	−22.2
Angola	10,950	10,950	—
Cabinda[4]	36,500	36,500	—
Cameroon	35,040	30,295	+15.7
Congo	29,200	28,105	+3.9
Egypt	231,775	211,700	+9.5
Gabon	51,100	54,020	−5.4
Ghana	730	730	—
Ivory Coast	2,190	1,460	+50.0
Libya	257,325	592,760	−56.6
Morocco	365	365	—
Nigeria	574,510	737,665	−22.1
Tunisia	43,800	42,340	+3.4
Zaire	7,300	6,935	+5.3
Communist bloc	5,290,675	5,321,700	−1.3
China	730,000	737,300	−1.0
Romania	83,950	83,950	—
U.S.S.R.	4,425,625	4,434,750	−0.2
Other	51,100	65,700	−22.2
World total	**19,667,660**	**21,186,790**	**−7.2**

1. Based on Jan.–Feb. average. 2. A state within the United Arab Emirates. 3. Shared by Kuwait and Saudi Arabia. 4. An enclave in West Africa on Atlantic coast between the Congo and Angola. *Source: Oil & Gas Journal,* May 10, 1982.

U.S. Motor Vehicle Fuel Consumption

(1980 estimate)

Type of vehicle	Total travel (million vehicle miles)	Number of registered vehicles	Average miles traveled per vehicle	Fuel consumed (thousand gallons)	Average fuel consumption per vehicle (gallons)	Average miles per gallon
All passenger vehicles	1,136,287	127,977,053	8,879	74,810,354	585	15.19
Total personal passenger vehicles	1,129,887	127,448,252	8,865	73,734,754	579	15.32
Cars	1,111,887	121,723,650	9,135	73,374,754	603	15.15
Motorcycles	18,000	5,724,602	3,144	360,000	63	50.00
All buses	6,400	528,801	12,103	1,075,600	2,034	5.95
Commercial	3,500	106,821	32,765	696,000	6,516	5.03
School and other nonrevenue	2,900	421,980	6,872	379,600	900	7.64
All cargo vehicles	384,570	33,637,241	11,433	40,149,500	1,194	9.58
Single unit trucks	324,570	32,232,241	10,070	29,240,500	907	11.10
Combinations	60,000	1,405,000	42,705	10,909,000	7,764	5.50
All motor vehicles	**1,520,857**	**161,614,294**	**9,410**	**114,959,854**	**711**	**13.23**

Source: Department of Transportation, Federal Highway Administration.

Petroleum Imported Directly[1] from OPEC[2] Countries, 1971–1981

(thousand barrels per day)

Year	Saudi Arabia	Iran	Venezuela	Libya	Indonesia	United Arab Emirates	Algeria	Nigeria	Other OPEC[3]	Total OPEC
1971	128	112	1,020	58	112	79	15	102	47	1,673
1972	190	142	960	123	164	73	92	251	68	2,063
1973	486	223	1,135	164	213	71	136	459	106	2,993
1974	461	469	979	4	300	74	190	713	88	3,280
1975	715	280	703	232	390	117	282	762	121	3,601
1976	1,230	299	700	453	539	254	432	1,025	134	5,066
1977	1,380	535	690	723	541	335	559	1,143	287	6,193
1978	1,144	555	645	654	573	385	649	919	226	5,751
1979	1,356	304	690	658	420	281	636	1,080	212	5,637
1980	1,252	8	460	550	337	179	481	846	121	4,233
1981[4]	1,128	0	404	320	364	83	310	622	88	3,318

1. Excludes indirect imports from OPEC countries which refers to U.S. imports of refined petroleum products, primarily from Caribbean and West European areas, which were refined from crude oil produced in OPEC countries. 2. Organization of Petroleum Exporting Countries. 3. Includes Ecuador, Gabon, Iraq, Kuwait, and Qatar. 4. Preliminary. NOTE: Includes data for individual countries prior to their entrance into OPEC. Data include imports for Strategic Petroleum Reserve, which began in 1977. Sum of components may not equal total due to independent rounding. *Source:* 1960 through 1975—U.S. Dept. of the Interior, Bureau of Mines, *Mineral Industry Surveys,* "Petroleum Statement Annual"; 1976 through 1979—U.S. Dept. of Energy, Energy Information Administration, *Energy Data Reports,* "Petroleum Statement, Annual"; 1980—U.S. Dept. of Energy, Energy Information Administration, *Energy Data Reports,* "Monthly Petroleum Statement."

Largest Nuclear Power Plants in the United States

(over a million kilowatts)

Location	Operating utility	Capacity (kilowatts)	Year operative
Daisy, Tenn. (Unit 1)	Tennessee Valley Authority	1,148,000	1980
Prescott, Ore. (Unit 1)	Portland General Electric Co.	1,130,000	1976
Bridgman, Mich. (Unit 2)	Indiana & Michigan Electric Co.	1,100,000	1978
Salem, N.J. (Unit 2)	Public Service Electric & Gas, N.J.	1,100,000	1981
Salem, N.J. (Unit 1)	Public Service Electric and Gas, N.J.	1,090,000	1977
Decatur, Ala. (Unit 1)	Tennessee Valley Authority	1,065,000	1974
Decatur, Ala. (Unit 2)	Tennessee Valley Authority	1,065,000	1975
Decatur, Ala. (Unit 3)	Tennessee Valley Authority	1,065,000	1977
Peach Bottom, Pa. (Unit 2)	Philadelphia Electric Co.	1,065,000	1974
Peach Bottom, Pa. (Unit 3)	Philadelphia Electric Co.	1,065,000	1974
Bridgman, Mich. (Unit 1)	Indiana & Michigan Electric Co.	1,054,000	1975
Zion, Ill. (Unit 1)	Commonwealth Edison Co.	1,040,000	1973
Zion, Ill. (Unit 2)	Commonwealth Edison Co.	1,040,000	1974

Source: Nuclear Regulatory Commission.

Radiation Doses

Radiation doses were originally measured in *roentgens,* (r), a unit of exposure to X-ray or gamma-ray radiation in the air. The roentgen drew its name from Wilhelm Conrad Roentgen (1845–1923), who discovered X-rays in 1895 and who received the first Nobel Prize in physics in 1901.

Today, the *rad* (ra) is the unit commonly used for measuring the amount of radiation to which the whole body, as contrasted with a single organ, is exposed.

The *millirad* is one-thousandth of a rad. Most scientists believe that a dose of a few millirads is safe, but there is significant controversy over the threshold at which a dose becomes hazardous.

The *rem* (for "roentgen equivalent, man") is a measure of ionizing radiation of the type that produces the same damage to human beings as one roentgen of approximately 200 kilowatts of X-radiation.

Millirem is the term used to describe the amount of absorption of radiation by humans. The average American is exposed to 100–200 millirems of radiation per year from man-made and natural sources. A normal chest X-ray exposes one to 20–30 millirems.

Warning on Taking Catalytic Equipped Vehicles Abroad

Catalytic equipped vehicles (1976 or later model) driven outside the United States, Canada, or Mexico will not, in most cases, meet EPA standards when brought back to the U.S. As unleaded fuel generally is not available in other countries, the catalytic converter will become inoperative and will have to be replaced. Contact Environmental Protection Agency, Public Information Center (PM-215), Washington, D.C. 20460, for details and exceptions.

Annual Cost of Fuel
(Based on driving 10,000 miles per year)

	Price Per Gallon						
MPG	$1.60	$1.70	$1.80	$1.90	$2.00	$2.10	$2.20
50	320	340	360	380	400	420	440
45	355	377	400	422	444	466	488
40	400	425	450	475	500	525	550
35	458	486	515	543	572	601	629
30	533	566	599	633	666	699	733
25	640	680	720	760	800	840	880
20	800	850	900	950	1,000	1,050	1,100
15	1,067	1,134	1,201	1,267	1,334	1,401	1,467
10	1,600	1,700	1,800	1,900	2,000	2,100	2,200

Be Wary of Gas Gadgets

With most motorists concerned about getting more miles per gallon of gasoline, the promoters of "miracle" devices and additives are having a field day. But be wary of the claims, warns the Automotive Information Council (AIC), because most of them will do nothing for the car's mileage.

The auto manufacturers have used their best engineering know-how to gain maximum miles per gallon, not only for competitive but for regulatory reasons. If there was a product on the market which would increase the mileage, the car companies would be using it.

Buying Gasoline—Converting Liters to Gallons[1]
(Rounded-off Figures)

Liters	Gallons	Liters	Gallons	Liters	Gallons	Liters	Gallons
1	.3	26	6.9	51	13.5	76	20.1
2	.5	27	7.1	52	13.7	77	20.3
3	.8	28	7.4	53	14.0	78	20.6
4	1.1	29	7.7	54	14.3	79	20.9
5	1.3	30	7.9	55	14.5	80	21.1
6	1.6	31	8.2	56	14.8	81	21.4
7	1.8	32	8.5	57	15.0	82	21.7
8	2.1	33	8.7	58	15.3	83	21.9
9	2.4	34	9.0	59	15.6	84	22.2
10	2.6	35	9.2	60	15.9	85	22.5
11	2.9	36	9.5	61	16.1	86	22.7
12	3.2	37	9.8	62	16.4	87	23.0
13	3.4	38	10.0	63	16.6	88	23.2
14	3.7	39	10.3	64	16.9	89	23.5
15	4.0	40	10.6	65	17.2	90	23.8
16	4.2	41	10.8	66	17.4	91	24.0
17	4.5	42	11.1	67	17.7	92	24.3
18	4.8	43	11.4	68	18.0	93	24.6
19	5.0	44	11.6	69	18.2	94	24.8
20	5.3	45	11.9	70	18.5	95	25.1
21	5.5	46	12.2	71	18.8	96	25.4
22	5.8	47	12.4	72	19.0	97	25.6
23	6.1	48	12.7	73	19.3	98	25.9
24	6.3	49	12.9	74	19.6	99	26.1
25	6.6	50	13.2	75	19.8	100	26.4

1. For precise conversion: 1 liter=.2642 gallons. 1 gallon=3.785 liters. Multiplying prices per liter by 3.785 gives price per gallon.

Beware of Underinflated Tires

Survey after survey by tire companies and other sources show that up to 90% of the tires on the road are underinflated, many to the point of being not only wasteful of gas, but of being dangerous.

Improper air pressure not only cuts into gas mileage by about 5% but it also reduces the life of a tire because of heat build-up caused by too much sidewall flexing.

Some motorists try to guess the tire pressure by looking at the tires. That system won't work with radials, which have a natural appearance of being too low, so the car owner becomes accustomed to that look. But put one tire inflated to 24 pounds next to one with 16 pounds, a difference of one third, and the tires will look virtually the same. Therefore, it is important to check the air pressure with a gauge.

The Year in Science—1982

New discoveries and revised interpretations of information gathered in previous years provided ample subject matter for lively scientific discussions during 1982. How old are the first true primates? Did they live in trees or walk upright on the ground, and what effect might this have had on their intellectual development? What was early man's diet like; did our ancestors in fact operate primitive slaughterhouses? Were the dinosaurs wiped out by the impact of a giant meteor, or did their extinction take place gradually? Will there be a new volcano in California? Do free quarks exist? Does God? Or at least, did his script for creation follow Genesis or Darwin? These are just a few of the controversies that arose over the past year. None were resolved. But then, for scientists, questions have always been far more important than answers.

Once Upon a Time . . .

In what sounded like a replay of the 1920s Scopes "monkey trial", the question of evolution *vs.* creation was brought before a court of law. The State of Arkansas enacted a law that mandated equal treatment, by public school teachers, of Darwinian theory and Biblical creation. Scientists from around the world were called to testify. The term "creation science" became a part of our vocabulary. Some of the more interesting arguments in favor of the State came, ironically, from a respected scientist born in India, a practicing Hindu. In the end, the Court ruled in favor of evolution, but the entire exercise created a lot more heat than light.

Undaunted by all the courtroom drama, paleontologists continued to dig up new information about early life forms. The oldest known true plant seeds, dating from 360 million years B.C., were discovered in West Virginia. Before the advent of seed-bearing plants, all flora reproduced by means of spores, as do ferns and mushrooms today. Other early seed fossils have been discovered before, but none that are quite this old.

The second specimen of some of the earliest mammals to be found in North America were unearthed in Arizona. Not much can be determined about the species since only a part of a jawbone was found, but the animals are thought to be a type of Morganucodontid, perhaps a distant relative of the platypus. The tooth structure of the mouse-sized creature indicates that it probably ate plants and lived on land, about 180 million years ago. Three more early mammalian fossils were also found in 1982. These are about 120 million years old, and may represent critical steps in the transition from primitive to more advanced animal forms, bridging the gap between the Jurassic and Cretaceous Periods. The specimens had not been named yet, but it appeared that they represented land-dwelling, plant-eating small mammals.

The first true primates may have evolved much later than originally thought. Fifty million year old fossils of *Cantius Trigonodus,* which resembled the modern-day bush baby, were discovered in Wyoming. Most early fossils are characterized by their teeth, but the interesting features of this creature are its forward-looking eyes and its grasping big toe. If the animal could live in trees and raise its young there, so the thinking goes, the greater amount of parent-child contact would have provided more opportunities for adolescent learning, hence faster brain development.

The role of *Ramapithecus* in early man's evolution was cast into doubt in 1982. Fossils found in Pakistan and thought to be 8–13 million years old suggest that Ramapithecus was not a hominid, but rather an ancient indirect ancestor of the orangutan. If this is so, then the man-ape split must have taken place several million years later than previously thought, i.e., it occurred seven to nine million years ago. Also, the common ancestor for Asian and African homon*oids* (which include both man and ape) must therefore be at least 13 million years old. Other workers still maintain that *Ramapithecus* was on the direct line of human evolution, that he was a ground dweller, possibly a bipedal hunter or scavenger, and that he came down out of the trees about six million years ago.

To confuse the issue some more, 1982 brought the first fossil evidence that ape-men walked upright long before the evolution of a large human brain. A four-million year old fossil may be another specimen of *Australopithicus afarensis,* the same species as the famous Lucy, found in 1979. If it is, it pushes the advent of upright-walking, small-brained creatures back another 300,000 years. *A. afarensis'* brain, incidentally, was about the size of a modern chimpanzee's. In any event, the latest fossil find included both a skull segment and a portion of a femur, or thigh bone. The former pinned down the brain size, the latter definitely indicated bipedal walking.

Fossils from the Olduvai and Koobi Fora sites in Eastern Africa provided more evidence that early man was using tools to butcher animals. Two human species, *Homo habilis* and *Australopithicus boisei,* coexisted in the area about 1.5–2.0 million years ago. They are thought to be responsible for some animal bone fossils that bear distinct markings of primitive stone cutting tools. The finding is considered important because of its implications regarding early human diets, i.e., they ate meat as well as plants, and that the hominids seem to have worked in groups and might therefore have been able to develop a language.

In a related set of findings, the remains of 90 giant gelada baboons have been found, dating back to between 400,000 and 700,000 years ago. All the skeletons were found together, and all had apparently had their skulls crushed. This may therefore be the first evidence of ritual (?) butchering of non-human primates by early hominids. Also, researchers at the University of California at Berkeley have used an electron microscope to prove that humans used cutting tools on animal tissues at least 1.79 million years ago. It is possible that the tool marks resulted from an attempt to skin the animals for their hides, but if they do represent actual butchering, then man's carnivorous diet goes back at least that far. Pass the steak, please.

Early man (or woman) was cutting other things besides baboons, or so it seems. A specimen of *Homo erectus* about 300,000 years old was also examined under an electron microscope and found to have been scalped. It is not known whether the scalping was punitive or whether it was part of a burial ritual. One thing is certain, it did not follow some sort of prehistoric cowboys-and-Indians confrontation; the specimen was found in Africa.

But early American residents did account for some archeological news in 1982—it was established that Del Mar Man, one of the earliest Californians, actually lived about 11,000 years ago, not 48,000 years ago as had previously been thought. That means he probably was a descendant of the first Americans who migrated across the then-dry Bering Straits from Asia around 13,000 B.C.

At about the same time, early Europeans built what may be the first sanctuary or shrine. A stone-age culture known as Magdalenian III flourished in Spain 14,000 years ago and was probably responsible for the structure. The most curious feature of the site, discovered in 1982, is an apparent monument, carved on opposite sides with a human and an animal face. Earlier grave sites, from Neanderthal Man, ca. 50,000 B.C., are known to exist, but the discovery in Spain is the first evidence of what may have been organized worship.

Here Today, Gone Tomorrow?

Why did the dinosaurs, and most other living creatures, suddenly disappear at the end of the Cretaceous Period, 65 million years ago? Evidence presented a few years ago seems to indicate that a giant meteor struck the Earth at about that time. Its great dust cloud could have been dense enough to block out sunlight, disrupting the food chain. The evidence continues to mount: to date, more than two dozen samples of clay from scattered parts of the world have been analyzed. All have been found to be rich in iridium, a metal that is rare on Earth, but relatively common in meteorites. Cretaceous/Tertiary boundary clays have also yielded a type of feldspar crystal known as sanadine, which is known to form at high temperatures and could have resulted from volcanism or an impact event. Tiny meteoritic grains known as microtektites have also been linked with iridium and other rare metal anomalies: are they also linked to the Cretaceous/Tertiary extinction? Many scientists favor the impact theory, but there are several pieces of contradictory evidence. If a meteor struck the Earth 65,000,000 years ago, where is its crater? In order to cause the massive dust cloud needed for the observed extinctions, the object must have been at least a mile in diameter. Even if it struck the sea, some trace of the impact should still be discernible. Also, careful studies of fossils found in Wyoming and Montana, dating to the Cretaceous/Tertiary boundary, show that at least in that case, extinction took place much more gradually than the impact theory would predict. There is still a lot of controversy on the subject but the best current consensus seems to be that yes, some sort of impact was probably responsible for the iridium data, but its connection with the observed extinctions remains tenuous, at best. Incidentally, there have been six major extinctions over the span of geological time, the most recent one occurring only 6,000 to 10,000 years ago: even if a meteor wiped out the dinosaurs, what caused the other extinctions?

Other ancient meteorites, or their remains, made scientific news in 1982. First, what appear to be traces of a very old impact feature were found in Canada. It may have been responsible for the formation of the continental shields about 3.9–4.0 billion years ago. Second, satellite photos have revealed a partially sand-covered meteor crater in the western Sahara desert. The scientific significance of the discovery lies in its ability to provide clues about the restructuring of the sandy, crater-pocked surface of Mars. Finally, micropaleontologists have confirmed the presence of levo- or l-type amino acids in certain types of meteorites called carbonaceous chondrites. Since amino acids are the basis for proteins and since only l-type amino acids are found in animal tissues on Earth, does the chondrite evidence imply that our earliest amino acids were imported from outer space? And if so, from where?

Genetic Juggling

Speaking of amino acids, British scientists in 1982 fabricated the longest piece of genetic material to date: 514 paired nucleotides in length. The synthesized gene is similar but not identical to the chain responsible for producing human leucocyte interferon. All three types of human interferon have now been produced in genetically engineered bacteria. Leucocyte and fibroblast interferons had been produced earlier; now immune, or gamma interferon completes the list. Gamma is the smallest interferon, and so far has been the most difficult to produce. It may be more active in fighting cancer than its other two chemical cousins.

The sequence of all of the 7,433 nucleotides that make up the poliomyelytis virus have been "read". This may lead to the development of better polio vaccines.

More Volcanoes?

Mt. St. Helens has retreated to the relative obscurity of rebuilding its peak: periodic minor eruptions continued to replace the material lost as a result of the mountain's spectacular earlier explosion. But there may be more to come. In a large caldera (volcanic crater) in the Mammoth Lakes region of California, near Yosemite National Park, geologists have noted a few signs of possible volcanic activity. The evidence comes in the form of seismic rumbles from magma bodies moving up from 7–8 kilometers beneath the surface to about 3 kilometers down. When the slowly rising magma hits the water table, boom.

California also recorded its deepest earthquake yet, some 58 kilometers (36 miles) down. It didn't pose any danger to the surface, but it did confirm a well-defined dipping zone deep below the state. Elsewhere, the first volcanic submarine hot springs have been found off the Oregon coast. Surrounding rocks appear glassy and may be less than 100 years old.

Volcanoes have been postulated as one potential cause for a future "greenhouse effect", in which the atmosphere will get continuously hotter because surface heat cannot escape through thick clouds. A more commonly postulated cause would be the buildup of carbon dioxide in the atmosphere from the burning of fossil fuels. Use of these fuels (coal, oil, gas) since 1880 is thought to be responsible for a global warming of 0.4°C over the past century.

(Continued on page 354)

Table of Geological Periods

It is now generally assumed that planets are formed by the accretion of gas and dust in a cosmic cloud, but there is no way of estimating the length of this process. Our earth acquired its present size, more or less, between 4,000 and 5,000 million years ago. Life on earth originated about 2,000 million years ago, but there are no good fossil remains from periods earlier than the Cambrian, which began about 550 million years ago. The largely unknown past before the Cambrian Period is referred to as the Pre-Cambrian and is subdivided into the Lower (or older) and Upper (or younger) Pre-Cambrian—also called the Archaeozoic and Proterozoic Eras.

The known geological history of the earth since the beginning of the Cambrian Period is subdivided into three "eras," each of which comprises a number of "periods." They, in turn, are subdivided into "subperiods." In a subperiod, a certain section may be especially well known because of rich fossil finds. Such a section is called a "formation," and it is usually identified by a place name.

Paleozoic Era

This era began 550 million years ago and lasted for 355 million years. The name was compounded from Greek *palaios* (old) and *zoön* (animal).

Period	Duration[1]	Subperiods	Events
Cambrian (from *Cambria,* Latin name for Wales)	70	Lower Cambrian Middle Cambrian Upper Cambrian	Invertebrate sea life of many types, proliferating during this and the following period
Ordovician (from Latin *Ordovices,* people of early Britain)	85	Lower Ordovician Upper Ordovician	
Silurian (from Latin *Silures,* people of early Wales)	40	Lower Silurian Upper Silurian	First known fishes; gigantic sea scorpions
Devonian (from Devonshire in England)	50	Lower Devonian Upper Devonian	Proliferation of fishes and other forms of sea life; land still largely lifeless
Carboniferous (from Latin *carbo* = coal + *fero* = to bear)	85	Lower or Mississippian Upper or Pennsylvanian	Period of maximum coal formation in swampy forests; early insects and first known amphibians
Permian (from district of Perm in Russia)	25	Lower Permian Upper Permian	Early reptiles and mammals; earliest form of turtles

Mesozoic Era

This era began 195 million years ago and lasted for 135 million years. The name was compounded from Greek *mesos* (middle) and *zoön* (animal). Popular name: Age of Reptiles.

Period	Duration[1]	Subperiods	Events
Triassic (from *trias* = triad)	35	Lower or Buntsandstein (from German *bunt* = colorful + *Sandstein* = sandstone) Middle or Muschelkalk (from German *Muschel* = clam + *Kalk* = limestone) Upper or Keuper (old miners' term)	Early saurians
Jurassic (from Jura Mountains)	35	Lower or Black Jurassic, or Lias (from French *liais* = hard stone) Middle or Brown Jurassic, or Dogger (old provincial English for ironstone) Upper or White Jurassic, or Malm (Middle English for sand)	Many sea-going reptiles; early large dinosaurs; somewhat later, flying reptiles (pterosaurs), earliest known birds
Cretaceous (from Latin *creta* = chalk)	65	Lower Cretaceous Upper Cretaceous	Maximum development of dinosaurs; birds proliferating; oppossum-like mammals

Cenozoic Era

This era began 60 million years ago and includes the geological present. The name was compounded from Greek *kainos* (new) and *zoön* (animal). Popular name: Age of Mammals.

Period	Duration[1]	Subperiods	Events
Tertiary (originally thought to be the third of only three periods)	c. 60	Paleocene (from Greek *palaios* = old + *kainos* = new)	First mammals other than marsupials
		Eocene (from Greek *eos* = dawn + *kainos* = new)	Formation of amber; rich insect fauna; early bats
		Oligocene (from Greek *oligos* = few + *kainos* = new)	Steady increase of large mammals
		Miocene (from Greek *meios* = less + *kainos* = new)	
		Pliocene (from Greek *pleios* = more + *kainos* = new)	Mammals closely resembling present types; protohumans
Pleistocene (from Greek *pleistos* = most + *kainos* = new) (popular name: Ice Age)	1	Four major glaciations, named Günz, Mindel, Riss, and Würm, originally the names of rivers. Last glaciation ended 10,000 to 15,000 years ago	Various forms of early man
Holocene (from Greek *holos* = entire + *kainos* = new)		The present	The last 3,000 years are called "history"

1. In millions of years.

Chemical Elements

Element	Symbol	Atomic no.	Atomic weight	Specific gravity	Melting point °C	Boiling point °C	Number of isotopes[1]	Discoverer	Year
Actinium	Ac	89	227[2]	10.07[2]	1050	3200±300	11	Debierne	1899
Aluminum	Al	13	26.9815	2.6989	660.37	2467	8	Wöhler	1827
Americium	Am	95	243[6]	13.67	994±4	2607	13[3]	Seaborg et al.	1944
Antimony	Sb	51	121.75	6.691	630.74	1750	29	Early historic times	—
Argon	Ar	18	39.948	1.7837[4]	−189.2	−185.7	8	Rayleigh and Ramsay	1894
Arsenic (gray)	As	33	74.9216	5.73	817 (28 atm.)	613[5]	14	Albertus Magnus	1250?
Astatine	At	85	~210	—	302	337	21	Corson et al.	1940
Barium	Ba	56	137.34	3.5	725	1640	25	Davy	1808
Berkelium	Bk	97	247[6]	14.00[7]	—	—	8[3]	Seaborg et al.	1949
Beryllium	Be	4	9.01218	1.848	1278±5	2970 (5 mm.)	6	Vauquelin	1798
Bismuth	Bi	83	208.9806	9.747	271.3	1560±5	19	Geoffroy	1753
Boron	B	5	10.81	2.37[8]	2300	2550[5]	6	Gay-Lussac and Thénard; Davy	1808
Bromine	Br	35	79.904	3.12[4]	−7.2	58.78	19	Balard	1826
Cadmium	Cd	48	112.40	8.65	320.9	765	22	Stromeyer	1817
Calcium	Ca	20	40.08	1.55	839±2	1484	14	Davy	1808
Californium	Cf	98	251[6]	—	—	—	12[3]	Seaborg et al.	1950
Carbon	C	6	12.011	1.8–3.5[9]	~3550	4827	7	Prehistoric	—
Cerium	Ce	58	140.12	6.771	798±3	3257	19	Berzelius and Hisinger; Klaproth	1803
Cesium	Cs	55	132.9055	1.873	28.40	678.4	22	Bunsen and Kirchhoff	1860
Chlorine	Cl	17	35.453	1.56[4]	−100.98	−34.6	11	Scheele	1774
Chromium	Cr	24	51.996	7.18–7.20	1857±20	2672	9	Vauquelin	1797
Cobalt	Co	27	58.9332	8.9	1495	2870	14	Brandt	c.1735
Copper	Cu	29	63.546	8.96	1083.4±0.2	2567	11	Prehistoric	—
Curium	Cm	96	247[6]	13.51[2]	1340±40	—	13[3]	Seaborg et al.	1944
Dysprosium	Dy	66	162.50	8.540	1409	2335	21	Boisbaudran	1886
Einsteinium	Es	99	254[6]	—	—	—	12[3]	Ghiorso et al	1952
Erbium	Er	68	167.26	9.045	1522	2510	16	Mosander	1843
Europium	Eu	63	151.96	5.283	822±5	1597	21	Demarcay	1896
Fermium	Fm	100	257[6]	—	—	—	10[3]	Ghiorso et al	1953
Fluorine	F	9	18.9984	1.108[4]	−219.62	−188.14	6	Moissan	1886
Francium	Fr	87	223[6]	—	27[2]	677[2]	21	Perey	1939
Gadolinium	Gd	64	157.25	7.898	1311±1	3233	17	Marignac	1880
Gallium	Ga	31	69.72	5.904	29.78	2403	14	Boisbaudran	1875
Germanium	Ge	32	72.59	5.323	937.4	2830	17	Winkler	1886
Gold	Au	79	196.9665	19.32	1064.43	2807	21	Prehistoric	—
Hafnium	Hf	72	178.49	13.31	2227±20	4602	17	Coster and von Hevesy	1923
Helium	He	2	4.00260	0.1785[4]	−272.2 (26 atm.)	−268.934	5	Janssen	1868
Holmium	Ho	67	164.9303	8.781	1470	2720	29	Delafontaine and Soret	1878
Hydrogen	H	1	1.0080	0.070[4]	−259.14	−252.87	3	Cavendish	1766

Element	Symbol	Atomic no.	Atomic weight	Specific gravity	Melting point °C	Boiling point °C	Number of isotopes[1]	Discoverer	Year
Indium	In	49	114.82	7.31	156.61	2080	34	Reich and Richter	1863
Iodine	I	53	126.9045	4.93	113.5	184.35	24	Courtois	1811
Iridium	Ir	77	192.22	22.42	2410	4130	25	Tennant	1803
Iron	Fe	26	55.847	7.894	1535	2750	10	Prehistoric	—
Krypton	Kr	36	83.80	3.733[4]	−156.6	−152.30±0.10	23	Ramsay and Travers	1898
Lanthanum	La	57	138.9055	6.166	920±5	3454	19	Mosander	1839
Lawrencium	Lr	103	257[6]	—	—	—	20[3]	Ghiorso et al.	1961
Lead	Pb	82	207.2	11.35	327.502	1740	29	Prehistoric	—
Lithium	Li	3	6.941	0.534	180.54	1347	5	Arfvedson	1817
Lutetium	Lu	71	174.97	9.835	1656±5	3315	22	Urbain	1907
Magnesium	Mg	12	24.305	1.738	648.8±0.5	1090	8	Black	1755
Manganese	Mn	25	54.9380	7.21–7.44[10]	1244±3	1962	11	Gahn, Scheele, and Bergman	1774
Mendelevium	Md	101	256[6]	—	—	—	3[3]	Ghiorso et al.	1955
Mercury	Hg	80	200.59	13.546	−38.87	356.58	26	Prehistoric	—
Molybdenum	Mo	42	95.94	10.22	2617	4612	20	Scheele	1778
Neodymium	Nd	60	144.24	6.80 & 7.004[10]	1010	3127	16	von Welsbach	1885
Neon	Ne	10	20.179	0.89990 (g/1 0°C/1 atm)	−248.67	−246.048	8	Ramsay and Travers	1898
Neptunium	Np	93	237.0482	20.25	640±1	3902	15[3]	McMillan and Abelson	1940
Nickel	Ni	28	58.71	8.902	1453	2732	11	Cronstedt	1751
Niobium (Columbium)	Nb	41	92.9064	8.57	2468±10	4742	24	Hatchett	1801
Nitrogen	N	7	14.0067	0.808[4]	−209.86	−195.8	8	Rutherford	1772
Nobelium	No	102	254[6]	—	—	—	7[3]	Ghiorso et al.	1957
Osmium	Os	76	190.2	22.57	3045±30	5027±100	19	Tennant	1803
Oxygen	O	8	15.9994	1.14[4]	−218.4	−182.962	8	Priestley	1774
Palladium	Pd	46	106.4	12.02	1552	3140	21	Wollaston	1803
Phosphorus	P	15	30.9738	1.82 (white)	44.1	280	7	Brand	1669
Platinum	Pt	78	195.09	21.45	1772	3827±100	32	Ulloa	1735
Plutonium	Pu	94	244[6]	19.84	641	3232	16[3]	Seaborg et al.	1940
Polonium	Po	84	210[6]	9.32	254	962	34	Curie	1898
Potassium	K	19	39.102	0.862	63.65	774	10	Davy	1807
Praseodymium	Pr	59	140.9077	6.772	931±4	3212	15	von Welsbach	1885
Promethium	Pm	61	145[6]	—	~1080	2460?	14	Marinsky et al.	1945
Protactinium	Pa	91	231.0359	15.37[2]	<1600	—	14	Hahn and Meitner	1917
Radium	Ra	88	226.0254	5.0?	700	1140	15	P. and M. Curie	1898
Radon	Rn	86	222[6]	4.4[4]	−71	−61.8	20	Dorn	1900
Rhenium	Re	75	186.2	21.02	3180	5627[7]	21	Noddack, Berg, and Tacke	1925
Rhodium	Rh	45	102.9055	12.41	1966±3	3727±100	20	Wollaston	1803
Rubidium	Rb	37	85.4678	1.532	38.89	688	20	Bunsen and Kirchoff	1861
Ruthenium	Ru	44	101.07	12.44	2310	3900	16	Klaus	1844
Samarium	Sm	62	150.4	7.536	1072±5	1778	17	Boisbaudran	1879
Scandium	Sc	21	44.9559	2.989	1539	2832	15	Nilson	1879
Selenium	Se	34	78.96	4.79 (gray)	217	684.9±1	20	Berzelius	1817
Silicon	Si	14	28.086	2.33	1410	2355	8	Berzelius	1824
Silver	Ag	47	107.868	10.50	961.93	2212	27	Prehistoric	—
Sodium	Na	11	22.9898	0.971	97.81±0.03	882.9	7	Davy	1807
Strontium	Sr	38	87.62	2.54	769	1384	18	Davy	1808
Sulfur	S	16	32.06	2.07[11]	112.8	444.674	10	Prehistoric	—
Tantalum	Ta	73	180.9479	16.654	2996	5425± 100	19	Ekeberg	1801
Technetium	Tc	43	98.9062	11.50[2]	2172	4877	23	Perrier and Segrè	1937
Tellurium	Te	52	127.60	6.24	449.5±0.3	989.8±3.8	29	von Reichenstein	1782
Terbium	Tb	65	158.9254	8.234	1360±4	3041	24	Mosander	1843
Thallium	Tl	81	204.37	11.85	303.5	1457±10	28	Crookes	1861
Thorium	Th	90	232.0381	11.72	1750	4790	12	Berzelius	1828
Thulium	Tm	69	168.9342	9.314	1545±15	1727	18	Cleve	1879
Tin	Sn	50	118.69	7.31 (white)	231.9681	2270	28	Prehistoric	—
Titanium	Ti	22	47.90	4.55	1660±10	3287	9	Gregor	1791
Tungsten (Wolfram)	W	74	183.85	19.3	3410±20	5660	22	J. and F. d'Elhuyar	1783
Uranium	U	92	238.029	~18.95	1132.3±0.8	3818	15	Peligot	1841
Vanadium	V	23	50.9414	6.11	1890±10	3380	9	del Rio	1801
Xenon	Xe	54	131.30	3.52[4]	−111.9	−107.1±3	31	Ramsay and Travers	1898
Ytterbium	Yb	70	173.04	6.972	824±5	1193	16	Marignac	1878
Yttrium	Y	39	88.9059	4.457	1523±8	3337	21	Gadolin	1794
Zinc	Zn	30	65.38	7.133	419.58	907	15	Prehistoric	—
Zirconium	Zr	40	91.22	6.506[2]	1852±2	4377	20	Klaproth	1789

1. Isotopes are different forms of the same element having the same atomic number but different atomic weights. 2. Calculated figure. 3. Artificially produced. 4. Liquid. 5. Sublimation point. 6. Mass number of the isotope of longest known life. 7. Estimated. 8. Amorphous. 9. Depending on whether amorphous, graphite or diamond. 10. Depending on allotropic form. 11. Rhombic. ~ Is approximately. < Is less than. NOTE: There is a dispute between groups at the Lawrence Berkeley Laboratory of the University of California and at the Dubna Laboratory in the Soviet Union concerning the discovery of elements 104, 105, and 106. The Lawrence Berkeley Laboratory claims that 104 and 105 were discovered in 1969 and 1970, respectively, by Ghiorso et al. and has suggested the names Rutherfordium and Hahnium. The U.S. laboratory claims also that Ghiorso et al. discovered element 106 in 1974. No name has yet been suggested for this element. Names will not be official until the controversy is resolved and they have been approved by the International Union for Pure and Applied Chemistry.

THE YEAR IN SCIENCE

(Continued from page 350)

One-half of the observed rise in temperature has occurred during the past 15 years. There is no cause for concern yet, but when the over-all temperature rise reaches 2°C it could trigger changes in the Antarctic ice sheet that would flood low-lying coastal areas. NASA launched the Solar Mesosphere Explorer (MSE) satellite. Its sole function will be to study the Earth's ozone layer, which exists between 15 and 34 miles in altitude. Changes in the ozone layer have been attributed to the use of chlorofluorocarbon aerosol propellants, but since these have been restricted in recent years, the danger may be decreasing. MSE will seek to find out.

Konrad J.A. Kundig

Atomic Energy

Just as the Space Age is said to have started with the orbiting of Sputnik I, the Atomic Age is said to have started with the explosion of a test bomb on July 16, 1945, near Alamogordo, N.M., at 5:30 A.M. local time. The bomb was placed on top of a steel tower, and observers were stationed in bunkers 10,000 yards away. The explosion vaporized the steel tower, produced a mushroom cloud rising to 40,000 feet, and melted the desert sand into glass for distances up to 800 yards from the tower.

The first operational use of an atom bomb took place only three weeks later, when a uranium bomb was exploded over Hiroshima, Japan, on Aug. 6, 1945. The bomb, cylindrical in shape, 10 feet long with a diameter of 2 feet 4 inches, weighed about 9,000 pounds. Its explosive force was equal to 20,000 tons of TNT, hence the term "20-kiloton bomb." Three days later another atomic bomb, this time of plutonium, was exploded over Nagasaki.

Of course, the Atomic Age did not begin with the explosion of the test bomb at Alamogordo, just as the Space Age did not begin with the orbiting of the first artificial satellite. In both cases these visible feats were just experiments which proved the theory that had been built up patiently over decades.

At the turn of the century, scientists began to wonder whether the atoms of the chemical elements might not be composed of smaller particles. This was actually a contradiction in terms, because the Greek word *atomos,* from which the word *atom* was derived, meant "indivisible." But there were some indications of particles smaller than an atom —the electrons. In 1905, Albert Einstein suggested that matter might just be "condensed energy" and gave the conversion formula $E = mc^2$, in which E represents the energy, m the mass, and c the velocity of light. If this formula was correct, a small piece of matter should represent enormous amounts of energy.

Fission and Fusion

As is now generally known, atomic energy can be released in two ways. One is the *fission* of elements with very heavy atoms, such as uranium and plutonium, which will split when struck by a neutron, a sub-atomic particle. The splitting of the heavy atom releases more neutrons, which are then available to split other atoms—the so-called chain reaction. The other way of obtaining atomic energy is *fusion;* four light atoms (hydrogen) are fused together into the next heavier element (helium). The fusion reaction requires enormous heat and very high pressures. These pressures, coupled with very high temperatures, can most easily be produced by exploding a fission bomb, which is the reason why it is often said that a fission bomb is the trigger for a fusion (hydrogen) bomb.

Interestingly enough, the fusion reaction was discovered first, though only on paper. For the period from, say, 1910 to 1930, most physicists believed that the release of atomic energy, if it could be done, would be of no practical value. They asserted that causing the release would require more energy than could be obtained. Most astronomers, on the other hand, were convinced that atomic energy was released in the sun and the other stars because there was no other way to account for the energy the stars radiated into space. Trying to account for the energy radiated by the stars led to theoretical papers predicting what we now call the fusion reaction. At the time (1930), atomic fission was still unknown; it was discovered first by Enrico Fermi in 1934. But nobody yet knew that the sudden bursts of energy observed in the experiments were due to the fission of the uranium-235 atom. This was established (by way of calculation) by Dr. Lise Meitner. Once it was known what happened, the way to a premeditated release of atomic energy was clear.

But nobody could be quite certain whether the release would take the form of an explosion or whether it would be slow enough to be used to generate power. American scientists proceeded under the assumption that the release would be sudden and violent (and the Alamogordo test proved them right), while Professor Heisenberg in Germany thought the slow release to be more likely, which is the reason why the Germans did not start a large-scale atomic energy project.

Atoms for Peace

The *peaceful* Atomic Age can be said to have been born in 1954, when the original U.S. Atomic Energy Act was amended to release many so-called "secrets" of nuclear energy so that nuclear power plants could be built and radioactive isotopes be used in medicine. The next year, the first International Conference on the Peaceful Uses of the Atom was convened at Geneva, bringing together scientists from all over the world to discuss what hitherto had been considered to be secret.

Actually there was little that was really secret about nuclear energy. When the results of the 1938 experiments were brought to the United States, scientists from different parts of the world openly stated that the possibility of atomic bombs was inherent in the scientific findings.

Once the veil of "secrecy" had been dispelled by revision of the Atomic Energy Act and the Geneva meeting, construction of plants to produce electricity by controlled fission of uranium atoms got under way in the United States and several other industrialized nations. Electric power was first produced as a result of nuclear fission in December 1951 at the National Reactor Testing Station in Idaho. When a reactor was connected to a generator, the nuclear power plant produced enough electricity for about 50 homes.

Scientific Inventions, Discoveries, and Theories

Most inventions are the results of the discoveries, theories, experiments, and improvements of many people. This list tries to suggest the development of certain particularly important ideas. In some instances, it tries to connect the fundamental theory with the ultimate practical invention.

Abacus: *See* Calculating machine
Adding machine: *See* Calculating machine; Computer
Adrenaline: (isolation of) Jokichi Takamine, U.S., 1901
Air brake: George Westinghouse, U.S., 1868
Air conditioning: Willis Carrier, U.S., 1911
Airplane: (first powered, sustained, controlled flight) Orville and Wilbur Wright, U.S., 1903. *See also* Jet propulsion, aircraft
Airship: (non-rigid) Henri Giffard, France, 1852; (rigid) Ferdinand von Zeppelin, Germany, 1900
Aluminum manufacture: (by electrolytic action) Charles M. Hall, U.S., 1866
Anesthetic: (first use of anesthetic—ether—on man) Crawford W. Long, U.S., 1842
Antibiotics: (first demonstration of antibiotic effect) Louis Pasteur, Jules-François Joubert, France, 1887; (penicillin, first modern antibiotic) Alexander Fleming, England, 1928
Antiseptic: (surgery) Joseph Lister, England, 1867
Antitoxin, diphtheria: Emil von Behring, Germany, 1890
Atomic theory: (ancient) Leucippus, Democritus, Greece, c.500 B.C.; Lucretius, Rome, c.100 B.C.; (modern) John Dalton, England, 1808
Automobile: (first with internal combustion engine, 250 rpm) Karl Benz, Germany, 1885; (first with practical high-speed internal combustion engine, 900 rpm) Gottlieb Daimler, Germany, 1885; (first true automobile, not carriage with motor) René Panhard, Emile Lavassor, France, 1891; (carburetor, spray) Charles E. Duryea, U.S., 1892
Bacteria: Anton van Leeuwenhoek, The Netherlands, 1683
Bakelite: *See* Plastics
Balloon, hot-air: Joseph and Jacques Montgolfier, France, 1783
Ball-point pen: *See* Pen
Barometer: Evangelista Torricelli, Italy, 1643
Bicycle: Karl D. von Sauerbronn, Germany, 1816; (first modern model) James Starley, England, 1884
Bifocal lens: *See* Lens, bifocal
Blood, circulation of: William Harvey, England, 1628
Braille: Louis Braille, France, 1829
Bullet: (conical) Claude Minié, France, 1849
Calculating machine: (Abacus) China, c.190; (logarithms: made multiplying easier and thus calculators practical) John Napier, Scotland, 1614; (slide rule) William Oughtred, England, 1632; (digital calculator) Blaise Pascal, 1642; (multiplication machine) Gottfried Leibnitz, Germany, 1671; (important 19th-century contributors to modern machine) Frank S. Baldwin, Jay R. Monroe, Dorr E. Felt, W. T. Ohdner, William Burroughs, all U.S.; ("analytical engine" design, included concepts of programming, taping) Charles Babbage, England, 1835. *See also* Computer
Camera: (hand-held) George Eastman, U.S., 1888; (Polaroid Land) Edwin Land, U.S., 1948. *See also* Photography
Carburetor: *See* Automobile
Celanese: *See* Fibers, man-made
Celluloid: *See* Plastics
Classification of plants and animals: (by genera and species) Carolus Linnaeus, Sweden, 1737–53
Clock, pendulum: Christian Huygens, The Netherlands, 1656
Combustion: (nature of) Antoine Lavoisier, France, 1777
Computer: (differential analyzer, mechanically operated) Vannevar Bush, U.S., 1928; (Mark I, first information-processing digital computer) Howard Aiken, U.S., 1944; (ENIAC, Electronic Numerical Integrator and Calculator, first all-electronic) J. Presper Eckert, John W. Mauchly, U.S., 1946; (stored-program concept) John von Neumann, U.S., 1947
Conditioned reflex: Ivan Pavlov, Russia, c.1910
Converter, Bessemer: William Kelly, U.S., 1851
Cosmetics: Egypt, c.4000 B.C.
Cotton gin: Eli Whitney, U.S., 1793
Crossbow: China, c.300 B.C.
Cyclotron: Ernest O. Lawrence, U.S., 1931
Deuterium: (heavy hydrogen) Harold Urey, U.S., 1931
DNA: (deoxyribonucleic acid) Friedrich Meischer, Germany, 1869; (determination of double-helical structure) F. H. Crick, England, James D. Watson, U.S., 1953
Dynamite: Alfred Nobel, Sweden, 1867
Electric generator (dynamo): (laboratory model) Michael Faraday, England, 1832; Joseph Henry, U.S., c.1832; (hand-driven model) Hippolyte Pixii, France, 1833; (alternating-current generator) Nikola Tesla, U.S., 1892
Electric lamp: (arc lamp) Sir Humphrey Davy, England, 1801; (fluorescent lamp) A. E. Becquerel, France, 1867; (incandescent lamp) Sir Joseph Swann, England, Thomas A. Edison, U.S., contemporaneously, 1870s; (carbon arc street lamp) Charles F. Brush, U.S., 1879; (first widely marketed incandescent lamp) Thomas A. Edison, U.S., 1879; (mercury vapor lamp) Peter Cooper Hewitt, U.S., 1903; (neon lamp) Georges Claude, France, 1911; (tungsten filament) Irving Langmuir, U.S., 1915
Electric motor: *See* Motor
Electromagnet: William Sturgeon, England, 1823
Electron: Sir Joseph J. Thompson, England, 1897
Elevator, passenger: (safety device permitting use by passengers) Elisha G. Otis, U.S., 1852; (elevator utilizing safety device) 1857
$E = mc^2$: (equivalence of mass and energy) Albert Einstein, Switzerland, 1905
Engine, internal combustion: No single inventor. Fundamental theory established by Sadi Carnot, France, 1824; (two-stroke) Étienne Lenoir, France, 1860; (ideal operating cycle for four-stroke) Alphonse Beau de Rochet, France, 1862; (operating four-stroke) Nikolaus Otto, Germany, 1876; (diesel) Rudolf Diesel, Germany, 1892; (rotary) Felix Wankel, Germany, 1956. *See also* Automobile
Engine, steam: *See* Steam engine
Evolution: (by natural selection) Charles Darwin, England, 1859
Falling bodies, law of: Galileo Galilei, Italy, 1590
Fermentation: (micro-organisms as cause of) Louis Pasteur, France, c,1860
Fibers, man-made: (nitrocellulose fibers treated to change flammable nitrocellulose to harmless cel-

lulose, precursor of rayon) Sir Joseph Swann, England, 1883; (rayon) Count Hilaire de Chardonnet, France, 1889; (Celanese) Henry and Camille Dreyfuss, U.S., England, 1921; (research on polyesters and polyamides, basis for modern man-made fibers) U.S., England, Germany, 1930s; (nylon) Wallace H. Carothers, U.S., 1935

Fountain pen: *See* Pen

Geometry, elements of: Euclid, Alexandria, Egypt, c.300 B.C.

Gravitation, law of: Sir Isaac Newton, England, c.1665 (published 1687)

Gunpowder: China, c.700

Gyrocompass: Elmer A. Sperry, U.S., 1905

Gyroscope: Léon Foucault, France, 1852

Helicopter: Igor Sikorsky, U.S., 1939

Helium first observed on sun: Sir Joseph Lockyer, England, 1868

Heredity, laws of: Gregor Mendel, Austria, 1865

Induction, electric: Joseph Henry, U.S., 1828

Insulin: Sir Frederick G. Banting, J. J. R. MacLeod, Canada, 1922

Intelligence testing: Alfred Binet, Theodore Simon, France, 1905

Isotopes: (concept of) Frederick Soddy, England, 1912; (stable isotopes) J. J. Thompson, England, 1913; (existence demonstrated by mass spectrography) Francis W. Ashton, 1919

Jet propulsion, aircraft: Sir Frank Whittle, England, 1930

Laser: (theoretical work on) Charles H. Townes, Arthur L. Schawlow, U.S., N. Basov, A. Prokhorov, U.S.S.R., 1958; (first working model) T. H. Maiman, U.S., 1960

Lens, bifocal: Benjamin Franklin, U.S., c.1760

Light, nature of: (wave theory) Christian Huygens, Denmark, 1678; (electromagnetic theory) James Clerk Maxwell, England, 1873

Light, speed of: (theory that light has finite velocity) Olaus Roemer, Denmark, 1675

Lightning rod: Benjamin Franklin, U.S., 1752

Linotype: *See* Printing

Lithography: *See* Printing

Locomotive: (steam-powered) Richard Trevithick, England, 1804; (first practical, due to multiple-fire-tube boiler) George Stephenson, England, 1829; (largest steam-powered) Union Pacific's "Big Boy," U.S., 1941

Logarithms: *See* Calculating machine

Loom: (horizontal, two-beamed) Egypt, c.4400 B.C.; (Jacquard drawloom, pattern controlled by punch cards) Jacques de Vaucanson, France, 1745, Joseph-Marie Jacquard, 1801; (flying shuttle) John Kay, England, 1733; (power-driven loom) Edmund Cartwright, England, 1785

Machine gun: James Puckle, England, 1718; Richard J. Gatling, U.S., 1861

Match: (phosphorus) François Derosne, France, 1816; (friction) Charles Sauria, France, 1831; (safety) J. E. Lundstrom, Sweden, 1855

Mendelian law: *See* Heredity

Microscope: (compound) Zacharias Janssen, The Netherlands, 1590; (electron) Vladimir Zworykin et al., U.S., Canada, Germany, 1932–1939

Motion pictures: Thomas A. Edison, U.S., 1893

Motion pictures, sound: Product of various inventions. First picture with synchronized musical score: *Don Juan,* 1926; with spoken dialogue: *The Jazz Singer,* 1927; both Warner Bros.

Motor, electric: Michael Faraday, England, 1822; (alternating-current) Nikola Tesla, U.S., 1892

Motor, gasoline: *See* Engine, internal combustion

Motorcycle: (motor tricycle) Edward Butler, England, 1884; (gasoline-engine motorcycle) Gottieb Daimier, Germany, 1885

Neptunium: (first transuranic element, synthesis of) Edward M. McMillan, Philip H. Abelson, U.S., 1940

Neutron: James Chadwick, England, 1932

Neutron-induced radiation: Enrico Fermi et al., Italy, 1934

Nitroglycerin: Ascanio Sobrero, Italy, 1846

Nuclear fission: Otto Hahn, Fritz Strassmann, Germany, 1938

Nuclear reactor: Enrico Fermi et al., U.S., 1942

Nylon: *See* Fibers, man-made

Ohm's law: (relationship between strength of electric current, electromotive force, and circuit resistance) Georg S. Ohm, Germany, 1827

Ozone: Christian Schönbein, Germany, 1839

Paper: China, c.100 B.C.

Parachute: Louis S. Lenormand, France, 1783

Pen: (fountain) Lewis E. Waterman, U.S., 1884; (ball-point, for marking on rough surfaces) John H. Loud, U.S., 1888; (ball-point, for handwriting) Lazlo Biro, Argentina, 1944

Penicillin: *See* Antibiotics

Periodic law: (that properties of elements are functions of their atomic weights) Dmitri Mendeleev, Russia, 1869

Periodic table: (arrangement of chemical elements based on periodic law) Dmitri Mendeleev, Russia, 1869

Phonograph: Thomas A. Edison, U.S., 1877

Photography: (first paper negative, first photograph, on metal) Joseph Nicéphore Niepce, France, 1816–1827; (discovery of fixative powers of hyposulfite of soda) Sir John Herschel, England, 1819; (first direct positive image on silver plate, the daguerreotype) Louis Daguerre, based on work with Niepce, France, 1839; (first paper negative from which a number of positive prints could be made) William Talbot, England, 1841. Work of these four men, taken together, forms basis for all modern photography. (First color images) Alexandre Becquerel, Claude Niepce de Saint-Victor, France, 1848–60; (commercial color film with three emulsion layers, Kodachrome) U.S., 1935. *See also* Camera

Plastics: (first material, nitrocellulose softened by vegetable oil, camphor, precursor to Celluloid) Alexander Parkes, England, 1855; (Celluloid, involving recognition of vital effect of camphor) John W. Hyatt, U.S., 1869; (Bakelite, first completely synthetic plastic) Leo H. Baekeland, U.S., 1910; (theoretical background of macromolecules and process of polymerization on which modern plastics industry rests) Hermann Staudinger, Germany, 1922. *See also* Fibers, man-made

Plow, forked: Mesopotamia, before 3000 B.C.

Plutonium, synthesis of: Glenn T. Seaborg, Edwin M. McMillan, Arthur C. Wahl, Joseph W. Kennedy, U.S., 1941

Polaroid Land camera: *See* Camera

Polio, vaccine against: (vaccine made from dead virus strains) Jonas E. Salk, U.S., 1954; (vaccine made from live virus strains) Albert Sabin, U.S., 1960

Positron: Carl D. Anderson, U.S., 1932

Pressure cooker: (early version) Denis Papin, France, 1679

Printing: (block) Japan, c.700; (movable type) Korea, c.1400; Johann Gutenberg, Germany, c.1450 (lithography, offset) Aloys Senefelder, Germany, 1796; (rotary press) Richard Hoe, U.S., 1844; (linotype) Ottman Mergenthaler, U.S. 1884

Programming, information: *See* Calculating machine
Propeller, screw: Sir Francis P. Smith, England, 1836; John Ericsson, England, worked independently of and simultaneously with Smith, 1837
Proton: Ernest Rutherford, England, 1919
Psychoanalysis: Sigmund Freud, Austria, c.1904
Quantum theory: Max Planck, Germany, 1901
Rabies immunization: Louis Pasteur, France, 1885
Radar: (limited to one-mile range) Christian Hulsmeyer, Germany, 1904; (pulse modulation, used for measuring height of ionosphere) Gregory Breit, Merle Tuve, U.S., 1925; (first practical radar—radio detection and ranging) Sir Robert Watson-Watt, England, 1934–35
Radio: (electromagnetism, theory of) James Clerk Maxwell, England, 1873; (spark coil, generator of electromagnetic waves) Heinrich Hertz, Germany, 1886; (first practical system of wireless telegraphy) Guglielmo Marconi, Italy, 1895; (vacuum electron tube, basis for radio telephony) Sir John Fleming, England, 1904; (triode amplifying tube) Lee de Forest, U.S., 1906; (regenerative circuit, allowing long-distance sound reception) Edwin H. Armstrong, U.S., 1912; (frequency modulation—FM) Edwin H. Armstrong, U.S., 1933
Radioactivity: (X-rays) William K. Roentgen, Germany, 1895; (radioactivity of uranium) Henri Becquerel, France, 1896; (radioactive elements, radium and polonium in uranium ore) Marie Sklodowska-Curie, Pierre Curie, France, 1898; (classification of alpha and beta particle radiation) Pierre Curie, France, 1900; (gamma radiation) Paul-Ulrich Villard, France, 1900; (carbon dating) Willard F. Libby et al., U.S., 1955
Rayon: *See* Fibers, man-made
Reaper: Cyrus McCormick, U.S., 1834
Relativity: (special and general theories of) Albert Einstein, Switzerland, Germany, U.S., 1905–53
Revolver: Samuel Colt, U.S., 1835
Rifle: (muzzle-loaded) Italy, Germany, c.1475; (breech-loaded) England, France, Germany, U.S., c.1866; (bolt-action) Paul von Mauser, Germany, 1889; (automatic) John Browning, U.S., 1918
Roller bearing: (wooden for cartwheel) Germany or France, c.100 B.C.
Rubber: (vulcanization process) Charles Goodyear, U.S., 1839
Safety match: *See* Match
Solar system, universe: (sun-centered universe) Nicolaus Copernicus, Warsaw, 1543; (establishment of planetary orbits as elliptical) Johannes Kepler, Germany, 1609; (infinity of universe) Giordano Bruno, Italian monk, 1584
Spectrum: (heterogeneity of light) Sir Isaac Newton, England, 1665–66
Spermatozoa: Anton van Leeuwenhoek, The Netherlands, 1683
Spinning: (spinning wheel) India, introduced to Europe in Middle Ages; (Saxony wheel, continuous spinning of wool or cotton yarn) England, c.1500–1600; (spinning jenny) James Hargreaves, England, 1764; (spinning frame) Sir Richard Arkwright, England, 1769; (spinning mule, completed mechanization of spinning, permitting production of yarn to keep up with demands of modern looms) Samuel Crompton, England, 1779
Steam engine: (first commercial version based on principles of French physicist Denis Papin) Thomas Savery, England, 1639; (atmospheric steam engine) Thomas Newcomen, England, 1705; (steam engine for pumping water from collieries) Savery, Newcomen, 1725; (modern condensing, double-acting) James Watt, England, 1782
Steam engine, railroad: *See* Locomotive
Steamship: Claude de Jouffroy d'Abbans, France, 1783; James Rumsey, U.S., 1787; John Fitch, U.S., 1790. All preceded Robert Fulton, U.S., 1807, credited with launching first commercially successful steamship
Sulfa drugs: (parent compound, para-aminobenzenesulfanomide) Paul Gelmo, Austria, 1908; (antibacterial activity) Gerhard Domagk, Germany, 1935
Syphilis, test for: *See* Wassermann test
Tank, military: Sir Ernest Swinton, England, 1914
Telegraph: Samuel F. B. Morse, U.S., 1837
Telephone: Alexander Graham Bell, U.S., 1876
Telescope: Hans Lippershey, The Netherlands, 1608
Television: (mechanical disk-scanning method) successfully demonstrated by J. L. Baird, England, C. F. Jenkins, U.S., 1926; (electronic scanning method) Vladimir K. Zworykin, U.S., 1928; (color, all-electronic) Zworykin, 1925; (color, mechanical disk) Baird, 1928; (color, compatible with black and white) George Valensi, France, 1938; (color, sequential rotating filter) Peter Goldmark, U.S., first introduced, 1951; (color, compatible with black and white) commercially introduced in U.S., National Television Systems Committee, 1953
Thermometer: (open-column) Galileo Galilei, c.1593; (clinical) Santorio Santorio, Padua, c.1615; (mercury, also Fahrenheit scale) Gabriel D. Fahrenheit, Germany, 1714; (centigrade scale) Anders Celsius, Sweden, 1742; (absolute-temperature, or Kelvin, scale) William Thompson, Lord Kelvin, England, 1848
Tire, pneumatic: Robert W. Thompson, England, 1845; (bicycle tire) John B. Dunlop, Northern Ireland, 1888
Toilet, flush: Product of Minoan civilization, Crete, c.2000 B.C. Alleged invention by "Thomas Crapper" is untrue.
Tractor: Benjamin Holt, U.S., 1900
Transformer, electric: William Stanley, U.S., 1885
Transistor: John Bardeen, William Shockley, Walter Brattain, U.S., 1948
Uncertainty principle: (that position and velocity of an object cannot both be measured exactly, at the same time) Werner Heisenberg, Germany, 1927
Vaccination: Edward Jenner, England, 1796
Vacuum tube: *See* Radio
Van Allen (radiation) Belt: (around the earth) James Van Allen, U.S., 1958
Vitamins: (hypothesis of disease deficiency) Sir F. G. Hopkins, Casimir Funk, England, 1912; (vitamin A) Elmer V. McCollum, M. Davis, U.S., 1912–14; (vitamin B) Elmer V. McCollum, U.S., 1915–16; (thiamin, B_1) Casimir Funk, England, 1912; (riboflavin, B_2) D. T. Smith, E. G. Hendrick, U.S., 1926; (niacin) Conrad Elvehjem, U.S., 1937; (B_6) Paul Gyorgy, U.S., 1934; (vitamin C) C. A. Holst, T. Froelich, Norway, 1912; (vitamin D) Elmer V. McCollum, U.S., 1922; (folic acid) Lucy Wills, England, 1933
Wassermann test: (for syphilis) August von Wassermann, Germany, 1906
Weaving, cloth: *See* Loom
Wheel: (cart, solid wood) Mesopotamia, c.3800–3600 B.C.
Windmill: Persia, c.600
X-ray: *See* Radioactivity
Xerography: Chester Carlson, U.S., 1938
Zero: India, c.600; (absolute zero, cessation of all molecular energy) William Thompson, Lord Kelvin, England, 1848

WEIGHTS & MEASURES

Measures and Weights

Source: Department of Commerce, National Bureau of Standards.

The International System (Metric)

The International System of Units is a modernized version of the metric system, established by international agreement, i.e. provides a logical and interconnected framework for all measurements in science, industry, and commerce. The system is built on a foundation of seven basic units, and all other units are derived from them. (Use of metric weights and measures was legalized in the United States in 1866, and our customary units of weights and measures are defined in terms of the meter and kilogram.)

Length. Meter. The meter is defined as 1,650,763.73 wavelengths in vacuum of the orange-red line of the spectrum of krypton-86.

Time. Second. The second is defined as the duration of 9,192,631,770 cycles of the radiation associated with a specified transition of the cesium 133 atom.

Mass. Kilogram. The standard for the kilogram is a cylinder of platinum-iridium alloy kept by the International Bureau of Weights and Measures at Paris. A duplicate at the National Bureau of Standards serves as the mass standard for the United States. The kilogram is the only base unit still defined by a physical object.

Temperature. Kelvin. The kelvin is defined as the fraction 1/273.16 of the thermodynamic temperature of the triple point of water; that is, the point at which water forms an interface of solid, liquid and vapor. This is defined as 0.01°C on the Centigrade or Celsius scale and 32.02°F on the Fahrenheit scale. The temperature 0°K is called "absolute zero."

Electric Current. Ampere. The ampere is defined as that current that, if maintained in each of two long parallel wires separated by one meter in free space, would produce a force between the two wires (due to their magnetic fields) of 2×10^{-7} newton for each meter of length. (A newton is the unit of force which when applied to one kilogram mass would experience an acceleration of one meter per second per second.)

Luminous Intensity. Candela. The candela is defined as the luminous intensity of 1/600,000 of a square meter of a cavity at the temperature of freezing platinum (2,042K).

Amount of Substance. Mole. The mole is the amount of substance of a system that contains as many elementary entities as there are atoms in 0.012 kilograms of carbon-12.

Tables of Metric Weights and Measures

LINEAR MEASURE

10 millimeters (mm) = 1 centimeter (cm)
10 centimeters = 1 decimeter (dm) = 100 millimeters
10 decimeters = 1 meter (m) = 1,000 millimeters
10 meters = 1 dekameter (dam)
10 dekameters = 1 hectometer (hm) = 100 meters
10 hectometers = 1 kilometer (km) = 1,000 meters

AREA MEASURE

100 square millimeters (mm^2) = 1 sq centimeter (cm^2)
10,000 square centimeters = 1 sq meter (m^2) = 1,000,000 sq millimeters
100 square meters = 1 are (a)
100 ares = 1 hectare (ha) = 10,000 sq meters
100 hectares = 1 sq kilometer (km^2) = 1,000,000 sq meters

VOLUME MEASURE

10 milliliters (ml) = 1 centiliter (cl)
10 centiliters = 1 deciliter (dl) = 100 milliliters
10 deciliters = 1 liter (l) = 1,000 milliliters
10 liters = 1 dekaliter (dal)
10 dekaliters = 1 hectoliter (hl) = 100 liters
10 hectoliters = 1 kiloliter (kl) = 1,000 liters

CUBIC MEASURE

1,000 cubic millimeters (mm^3) = 1 cu centimeter (cm^3)
1,000 cubic centimeters = 1 cu decimeter (dm^3) = 1,000,000 cu millimeters
1,000 cubic decimeters = 1 cu meter (m^3) = 1 stere = 1,000,000 cu centimeters = 1,000,000,000 cu millimeters

WEIGHT

10 milligrams (mg) = 1 centigram (cg)
10 centigrams = 1 decigram (dg) = 100 milligrams
10 decigrams = 1 gram (g) = 1,000 milligrams
10 grams = 1 dekagram (dag)
10 dekagrams = 1 hectogram (hg) = 100 grams
10 hectograms = 1 kilogram (kg) = 1,000 grams
1,000 kilograms = 1 metric ton (t)

Tables of Customary U.S. Weights and Measures

LINEAR MEASURE

12 inches (in.) = 1 foot (ft)
3 feet = 1 yard (yd)
5 1/2 yards = 1 rod (rd), pole, or perch (16 1/2 ft)
40 rods = 1 furlong (fur) = 220 yds = 660 ft
8 furlongs = 1 statute mile (mi.) = 1,760 yds = 5,280 ft
3 land miles = 1 league
5,280 feet = 1 statute or land mile
6,076.11549 feet = 1 international nautical mile

AREA MEASURE

144 square inches = 1 sq ft
9 square feet = 1 sq yd = 1,296 sq in.
30 1/4 square yards = 1 sq rd = 272 1/4 sq ft
160 square rods = 1 acre = 4,840 sq yds = 43,560 sq ft
640 acres = 1 sq mi.
1 mile square = 1 section (of land)
6 miles square = 1 township = 36 sections = 36 sq mi.

CUBIC MEASURE

1,728 cubic inches = 1 cu ft
27 cubic feet = 1 cu yd

LIQUID MEASURE

When necessary to distinguish the liquid pint or quart from the dry pint or quart, the word "liquid" or the abbreviation "liq" should be used in combination with the name or abbreviation of the liquid unit.

4 gills (gi) = 1 pint (pt) (= 28.875 cu in.)
2 pints = 1 quart (qt) (= 57.75 cu in.)
4 quarts = 1 gallon (gal) (= 231 cu in.) = 8 pts = 32 gills

APOTHECARIES FLUID MEASURE

60 minims (min.) = 1 fluid dram (fl dr) (= 0.2256 cu in.)
8 fluid drams = 1 fluid ounce (fl oz) (= 1.8047 cu in.)
16 fluid ounces = 1 pt (= 28.875 cu in.) = 128 fl drs
2 pints = 1 qt (= 57.75 cu in.) = 32 fl oz = 256 fl drs
4 quarts = 1 gal (= 231 cu in.) = 128 fl oz = 1,024 fl drs

DRY MEASURE

When necessary to distinguish the dry pint or quart from the liquid pint or quart; the word "dry" should be used in combination with the name or abbreviation of the dry unit.

2 pints = 1 qt (=67.2006 cu in.)
8 quarts = 1 peck (pk) (=537.605 cu in.) = 16 pts
4 pecks = 1 bushel (bu) (= 2,150.42 cu in.) = 32 qts

AVOIRDUPOIS WEIGHT

When necessary to distinguish the avoirdupois dram from the apothecaries dram, or to distinguish the avoirdupois dram or ounce from the fluid dram or ounce, or to distinguish the avoirdupois ounce or pound from the troy or apothecaries ounce or pound, the word "avoirdupois" or the abbreviation "avdp" should be used in combination with the name or abbreviation of the avoirdupois unit.
(The "grain" is the same in avoirdupois, troy, and apothecaries weights.)

27 11/32 grains = 1 dram (dr)
16 drams = 1 oz = 437 1/2 grains
16 ounces = 1 lb = 256 drams = 7,000 grains
100 pounds = 1 hundredweight (cwt)[1]
20 hundredweights = 1 ton (tn) = 2,000 lbs[1]

In "gross" or "long" measure, the following values are recognized:

112 pounds = 1 gross or long cwt[1]
20 gross or long hundredweights = 1 gross or long ton = 2,240 lbs[1]

1. When the terms "hundredweight" and "ton" are used unmodified, they are commonly understood to mean the 100-pound hundredweight and the 2,000-pound ton, respectively; these units may be designated "net" or "short" when necessary to distinguish them from the corresponding units in gross or long measure.

UNITS OF CIRCULAR MEASURE

Second (") = —
Minute (') = 60 seconds
Degree (°) = 60 minutes
Right angle = 90 degrees
Straight angle = 180 degrees
Circle = 360 degrees

TROY WEIGHT

24 grains = 1 pennyweight (dwt)
20 pennyweights = 1 ounce troy (oz t) = 480 grains
12 ounces troy = 1 pound troy (lb t) = 240 pennyweights = 5,760 grains

APOTHECARIES WEIGHT

20 grains = 1 scruple (s ap)
3 scruples = 1 dram apothecaries (dr ap) = 60 grains
8 drams apothecaries = 1 ounce apothecaries (oz ap) = 24 scruples = 480 grains
12 ounces apothecaries = 1 pound apothecaries (lb ap) = 96 drams apothecaries = 288 scruples = 5,760 grains

GUNTER'S OR SURVEYOR'S CHAIN MEASURE

7.92 inches = 1 link (li)
100 links = 1 chain (ch) = 4 rods = 66 ft
80 chains = 1 statute mile = 320 rods = 5,280 ft

Metric and U.S. Equivalents

1 angstrom[1] (light wave measurement)	0.1 millimicron 0.000 1 micron 0.000 000 1 millimeter 0.000 000 004 inch
1 cable's length	120 fathoms 720 feet 219.456 meters
1 centimeter	0.3937 inch
1 chain (Gunter's or surveyor's)	66 feet 20.1168 meters
1 decimeter	3.937 inches
1 dekameter	32.808 feet
1 fathom	6 feet 1.8288 meters
1 foot	0.3048 meter
1 furlong	10 chains (surveyor's) 660 feet 220 yards 1/8 statute mile 201.168 meters

1 inch	2.54 centimeters
1 kilometer	0.621 mile
1 league (land)	3 statute miles 4.828 kilometers
1 link (Gunter's or surveyor's)	7.92 inches 0.201 168 meter
1 meter	39.37 inches 1.094 yards
1 micron	0.001 millimeter 0.000 039 37 inch
1 mil	0.001 inch 0.025 4 millimeter
1 mile (statute or land)	5,280 feet 1.609 kilometers
1 mile (nautical international)	1.852 kilometers 1.151 statute miles 0.999 U.S. nautical miles
1 millimeter	0.03937 inch
1 millimicron (mμ)	0.001 micron 0.000 000 039 37 inch
1 nanometer	0.001 micrometer or 0.000 000 039 37 inch
1 point (typography)	0.013 837 inch 1/72 inch (approximately) 0.351 millimeter
1 rod, pole, or perch	16 1/2 feet 5.0292 meters
1 yard	0.9144 meter

AREAS OR SURFACES

1 acre	43,560 square feet 4,840 square yards 0.405 hectare
1 are	119.599 square yards 0.025 acre
1 hectare	2.471 acres
1 square centimeter	0.155 square inch
1 square decimeter	15.5 square inches
1 square foot	929.030 square centimeters
1 square inch	6.4516 square centimeters
1 square kilometer	0.386 square mile 247.105 acres
1 square meter	1.196 square yards 10.764 square feet
1 square mile	258.999 hectares
1 square millimeter	0.002 square inch
1 square rod, square pole or square perch	25.293 square meters
1 square yard	0.836 square meters

CAPACITIES OR VOLUMES

1 barrel, liquid	31 to 42 gallons[2]
1 barrel, standard for fruits, vegetables, and other dry commodities except cranberries	7,056 cubic inches 105 dry quarts 3.281 bushels, struck measure
1 barrel, standard, cranberry	5.286 cubic inches 86 45/64 dry quarts 2.709 bushels, struck measure
1 bushel (U.S.) struck measure	2,150.42 cubic inches 35.238 liters
1 bushel, heaped (U.S.)	2,747.715 cubic inches 1.278 bushels, struck measure[3]
1 cord (firewood)	128 cubic feet
1 cubic centimeter	0.061 cubic inches
1 cubic decimeter	61.024 cubic inches
1 cubic foot	7.481 gallons 28.316 cubic decimeters
1 cubic inch	0.554 fluid ounce 4.433 fluid drams 16.387 cubic centimeters
1 cubic meter	1.308 cubic yards
1 cubic yard	0.765 cubic meter
1 cup, measuring	8 fluid ounces 1/2 liquid pint
1 dram, fluid or liquid (U.S.)	1/8 fluid ounces 0.226 cubic inch 3.697 milliliters 1.041 British fluid drachms
1 dekaliter	2.642 gallons 1.135 pecks
1 gallon (U.S.)	231 cubic inches 3.785 liters 0.833 British gallon 128 U.S. fluid ounces
1 gallon (British Imperial)	277.42 cubic inches 1.201 U.S. gallons 4.546 liters 160 British fluid ounces
1 gill	7.219 cubic inches 4 fluid ounces 0.118 liter
1 hectoliter	26.418 gallons 2.838 bushels
1 liter	1.057 liquid quarts 0.908 dry quart 61.024 cubic inches
1 milliliter	0.271 fluid drams 16.231 minims 0.061 cubic inch
1 ounce, fluid or liquid (U.S.)	1.805 cubic inch 29.574 milliliters 1.041 British fluid ounces

1 peck	8.810 liters
1 pint, dry	33.600 cubic inches 0.551 liter
1 pint, liquid	28.875 cubic inches 0.473 liter
1 quart, dry (U.S.)	67.201 cubic inches 1.101 liters 0.969 British quart
1 quart, liquid (U.S.)	57.75 cubic inches 0.946 liter 0.833 British quart
1 quart (British)	69.354 cubic inches 1.032 U.S. dry quarts 1.201 U.S. liquid quarts
1 tablespoon, measuring	3 teaspoons 4 fluid drams 1/2 fluid ounce
1 teaspoon, measuring	1/3 tablespoon 1 1/3 fluid drams
1 assay ton[4]	29.167 grams
1 carat	200 milligrams 3.086 grains
1 dram, apothecaries	60 grains 3.888 grams
1 dram, avoirdupois	27 11/32 (=27.344) grains 1.772 grams
1 grain	64.798 91 milligrams
1 gram	15.432 grains 0.035 ounce, avoirdupois
1 hundredweight, gross or long[5]	112 pounds 50.802 kilograms
1 hundredweight, net or short	100 pounds 45.359 kilograms
1 kilogram	2.205 pounds
1 microgram [μg (the Greek letter mu in combination with the letter g)]	0.000 001 gram
1 milligram	0.015 grain
1 ounce, avoirdupois	437.5 grains 0.911 troy or apothecaries ounce 28.350 grams
1 ounce, troy or apothecaries	480 grains 1.097 avoirdupois ounces 31.103 grams
1 pennyweight	1.555 grams
1 point	0.01 carat 2 milligrams
1 pound, avoirdupois	7,000 grains 1.215 troy or apothecaries pounds 453.592 37 grams
1 pound, troy or apothecaries	5,760 grains 0.823 avoirdupois pound 373.242 grams
1 ton, gross or long[5]	2,240 pounds 1.12 net tons 1.016 metric tons
1 ton, metric	2,204.623 pounds 0.984 gross ton 1.102 net tons
1 ton, net or short	2,000 pounds 0.893 gross ton 0.907 metric ton

1. The angstrom is basically defined as 10^{-10} meter. 2. There is a variety of "barrels" established by law or usage. For example, federal taxes on fermented liquors are based on a barrel of 31 gallons; many state laws fix the "barrel for liquids" at 31 1/2 gallons; one state fixes a 36-gallon barrel for cistern measurement; federal law recognizes a 40-gallon barrel for "proof spirits"; by custom, 42 gallons comprise a barrel of crude oil or petroleum products for statistical purposes, and this equivalent is recognized "for liquids" by four states. 3. Frequently recognized as 1 1/4 bushels, struck measure. 4. Used in assaying. The assay ton bears the same relation to the milligram that a ton of 2,000 pounds avoirdupois bears to the ounce troy; hence the weight in milligrams of precious metal obtained from one assay ton of ore gives directly the number of troy ounces to the net ton. 5. The gross or long ton and hundredweight are used commercially in the United States to only a limited extent, usually in restricted industrial fields. These units are the same as the British "ton" and "hundredweight."

Miscellaneous Units of Measure

Acre: An area of 43,560 square feet. Originally, the area a yoke of oxen could plow in one day.

Agate: Originally a measurement of type size (5 1/2 points). Now equal to 1/14 inch. Used in printing for measuring column length.

Ampere: Unit of electric current. A potential difference of one volt across a resistance of one ohm produces a current of one ampere.

Astronomical Unit (A.U.): 93,000,000 miles, the average distance of the earth from the sun. Used in astronomy.

Bale: A large bundle of goods. In the U.S., the approximate weight of a bale of cotton is 500 pounds. The weight varies in other countries.

Board Foot (fbm): 144 cubic inches (12 in. x 12 in. x 1 in.). Used for lumber.

Bolt: 40 yards. Used for measuring cloth.

Btu: British thermal unit. Amount of heat needed to increase the temperature of one pound of water by one degree Fahrenheit (252 calories).

Carat (c): 200 milligrams or 3.086 grains troy.

Originally the weight of a seed of the carob tree in the Mediterranean region. Used for weighing precious stones. *See also* Karat.

Chain (ch): a chain 66 feet or one-tenth of a furlong in length, divided into 100 parts called links. One mile is equal to 80 chains. Used in surveying and sometimes called Gunter's or surveyor's chain.

Cubit: 18 inches or 45.72 cm. Derived from distance between elbow and tip of middle finger.

Decibel: Unit of relative loudness. One decibel is the smallest amount of change detectable by the human ear.

Ell, English: 1 1/4 yards or 1/32 bolt. Used for measuring cloth.

Freight Ton (also called Measurement Ton): 40 cubic feet of merchandise. Used for cargo freight.

Great Gross: 12 gross or 1728.

Gross: 12 dozen or 144.

Hand: 4 inches or 10.16 cm. Derived from the width of the hand. Used for measuring the height of horses at withers.

Hertz: Modern unit for measurement of electromagnetic wave frequencies (equivalent to "cycles per second").

Hogshead: (hhd): 2 liquid barrels or 14,653 cubic inches.

Horsepower: The power needed to lift 33,000 pounds a distance of one foot in one minute (about 1 1/2 times the power an average horse can exert). Used for measuring power of steam engines, etc.

Karat (kt): A measure of the purity of gold, indicating how many parts out of 24 are pure. For example, 18 karat gold is 3/4 pure. Sometimes spelled *carat*.

Knot: Not a distance, but the rate of speed of one nautical mile per hour. Used for measuring speed of ships.

League: Rather indefinite and varying measure, but usually estimated at 3 miles in English-speaking countries.

Light-Year: 5,880,000,000,000 miles, the distance light travels in a year at the rate of 186,281.7 miles per second. (If an astronomical unit were represented by one inch, a light-year would be represented by about one mile.) Used for measurements in interstellar space.

Magnum: Two-quart bottle. Used for measuring wine, etc.

Ohm: Unit of electrical resistance. A circuit in which a potential difference of one volt produces a current of one ampere has a resistance of one ohm.

Parsec: Approximately 3.26 light-years of 19.2 trillion miles. Term is combination of first syllables of *par*allax and *sec*ond, and distance is that of imaginary star when lines drawn from it to both earth and sun form a maximum angle or parallax of one second (1/3600 degree). Used for measuring interstellar distances.

Pi (π): 3.14159265+. The ratio of the circumference of a circle to its diameter. For practical purposes, the value is used to four decimal places: 3.1416.

Pica: 1/6 inch or 12 points. Used in printing for measuring column width, etc.

Pipe: 2 hogsheads. Used for measuring wine and other liquids.

Point: .013837 (approximately 1/72) inch or 1/12 pica. Used in printing for measuring type size.

Quintal: 100,000 grams or 220.46 pounds avoirdupois.

Quire: Used for measuring paper. Sometimes 24 sheets but more often 25. There are 20 quires in a ream.

Ream: Used for measuring paper. Sometimes 480 sheets, but more often 500 sheets.

Roentgen: Dosage unit of radiation exposure produced by X-rays.

Score: 20 units.

Sound, Speed of: Usually placed at 1,088 ft per second at 32°F at sea level. It varies at other temperatures and in different media.

Span: 9 inches or 22.86 cm. Derived from the distance between the end of the thumb and the end of the little finger when both are outstretched.

Square: 100 square feet. Used in building.

Stone: Legally 14 pounds avoirdupois in Great Britain.

Therm: 100,000 BTU's.

Township: U. S. land measurement of almost 36 square miles. The south border is 6 miles long. The east and west borders, also 6 miles long, follow the meridians, making the north border slightly less than 6 miles long. Used in surveying.

Tun: 252 gallons, but often larger. Used for measuring wine and other liquids.

Watt: Unit of power. The power used by a current of one ampere across a potential difference of one volt equals one watt.

Kelvin Scale

Absolute zero, −273.16° on the Celsius (Centigrade) scale, is 0° Kelvin. Thus, degrees Kelvin are equivalent to degrees Celsius plus 273.16. The freezing point of water, 0°C. and 32°F., is 273.16°K. The conversion formula is K° = C° + 273.16.

Conversion of Miles to Kilometers and Kilometers to Miles

Miles	Kilometers	Miles	Kilometers	Miles	Kilometers	Kilometers	Miles	Kilometers	Miles	Kilometers	Miles
1	1.6	8	12.8	60	96.5	1	0.6	8	4.9	60	37.2
2	3.2	9	14.4	70	112.6	2	1.2	9	5.5	70	43.4
3	4.8	10	16.0	80	128.7	3	1.8	10	6.2	80	49.7
4	6.4	20	32.1	90	144.8	4	2.4	20	12.4	90	55.9
5	8.0	30	48.2	100	160.9	5	3.1	30	18.6	100	62.1
6	9.6	40	64.3	1,000	1609	6	3.7	40	24.8	1,000	621
7	11.2	50	80.4			7	4.3	50	31.0		

Bolts and Screws: Conversion from Fractions of an Inch to Millimeters

Inch	mm	Inch	mm	Inch	mm	Inch	mm
1/64	0.40	17/64	6.75	33/64	13.10	49/64	19.45
1/32	0/79	9/32	7.14	17/32	13.50	25/32	19.84
3/64	1.19	19/64	7.54	35/64	13.90	51/64	20.24
1/16	1.59	5/16	7.94	9/16	14.29	13/16	20.64
5/64	1.98	21/64	8.33	37/64	14.69	53/64	21.03
3/32	2.38	11/32	8.73	19/32	15.08	27/32	21.43
7/64	2.78	23/64	9.13	39/64	15.48	55/64	21.83
1/8	3.18	3/8	9.53	5/8	15.88	7/8	22.23
9/64	3.57	25/64	9.92	41/64	16.27	57/64	22.62
5/32	3.97	13/32	10.32	21/32	16.67	29/32	23.02
11/64	4.37	27/64	10.72	43/64	17.06	59/64	23.42
3/16	4.76	7/16	11.11	11/64	17.46	15/16	23.81
13/64	5.16	29/64	11.51	45/64	17.86	61/64	24.21
7/32	5.56	15/32	11.91	23/32	18.26	31/32	24.61
15/64	5.95	31/64	12.30	47/64	18.65	63/64	25.00
1/4	6.35	1/2	12.70	3/4	19.05	1	25.40

U.S.—Metric Cooking Conversions

U.S. customary system				Metric			
Capacity		Weight		Capacity		Weight	
1/5 teaspoon	1 milliliter	1 fluid oz	30 milliliters	1 milliliter	1/5 teaspoon	1 gram	.035 ounce
1 teaspoon	5 ml		28 grams	5 ml	1 teaspoon	100 grams	3.5 ounces
1 tablespoon	15 ml	1 pound	454 grams	15 ml	1 tablespoon	500 grams	1.10 pounds
1/5 cup	50 ml			34 ml	1 fluid oz	1 kilogram	2.205 pounds
1 cup	240 ml			100 ml	3.4 fluid oz		35 oz
2 cups (1 pint)	470 ml			240 ml	1 cup		
4 cups (1 quart)	.95 liter			1 liter	34 fluid oz		
4 quarts (1 gal.)	3.8 liters				4.2 cups		
					2.1 pints		
					1.06 quarts		
					0.26 gallon		

Cooking Measurement Equivalents

16 tablespoons = 1 cup
12 tablespoons = 3/4 cup
10 tablespoons + 2 teaspoons = 2/3 cup
8 tablespoons = 1/2 cup
6 tablespoons = 3/8 cup
5 tablespoons + 1 teaspoon = 1/3 cup
4 tablespoons = 1/4 cup

2 tablespoons = 1/8 cup
2 tablespoons + 2 teaspoons = 1/6 cup
1 tablespoon = 1/16 cup
2 cups = 1 pint
2 pints = 1 quart
3 teaspoons = 1 tablespoon
48 teaspoons = 1 cup

Prefixes and Multiples

Prefix	Symbol	Equivalent	Multiple/ submultiple	Prefix	Symbol	Equivalent	Multiple/ submultiple
atto	a	quintillionth part	10^{-18}	deci	d	tenth part	10^{-1}
femto	f	quadrillionth part	10^{-15}	deka	da	tenfold	10
pico	p	trillionth part	10^{-12}	hecto	h	hundredfold	10^{2}
nano	n	billionth part	10^{-9}	kilo	k	thousandfold	10^{3}
micro	μ	millionth part	10^{-6}	mega	M	millionfold	10^{6}
milli	m	thousandth part	10^{-3}	giga	G	billionfold	10^{9}
centi	c	hundredth part	10^{-2}	tera	T	trillionfold	10^{12}

Common Formulas

Circumference

Circle: $C=\pi d$, in which π is 3.1416 and *d* the diameter.

Area

Triangle: $A=\frac{ab}{2}$, in which *a* is the base and *b* the height.

Square: $A=a^2$, in which *a* is one of the sides.

Rectangle: $A=ab$, in which *a* is the base and *b* the height.

Trapezoid: $A=\frac{h(a+b)}{2}$, in which *h* is the height, *a* the longer parallel side, and *b* the shorter.

Regular pentagon: $A=1.720a^2$, in which *a* is one of the sides.

Regular hexagon: $A=2.598a^2$, in which *a* is one of the sides.

Regular octagon: $A=4.828a^2$, in which *a* is one of the sides.

Circle: $A=\pi r^2$, in which π is 3.1416 and *r* the radius.

Volume

Cube: $V=a^3$, in which *a* is one of the edges.

Rectangular prism: $V=abc$, in which *a* is the length, *b* the width, and *c* the depth.

Pyramid: $V=\frac{Ah}{3}$, in which *A* is the area of the base and *h* the height.

Cylinder: $V=\pi r^2 h$, in which π is 3.1416, *r* the radius of the base, and *h* the height.

Cone: $V=\frac{\pi r^2 h}{3}$, in which π is 3.1416, *r* the radius of the base, and *h* the height.

Sphere: $V=\frac{4\pi r^3}{3}$, in which π is 3.1416 and *r* the radius.

Miscellaneous

Speed per second acquired by falling body: $v=32t$, in which *t* is the time in seconds.

Distance in feet traveled by falling body: $d=16t^2$, in which *t* is the time in seconds.

Speed of sound in feet per second through any given temperature of air: $V=\frac{1087\sqrt{273+t}}{16.52}$, in which *t* is the temperature Centigrade.

Cost in cents of operation of electrical device: $C=\frac{Wtc}{1000}$, in which *W* is the number of watts, *t* the time in hours, and *c* the cost in cents per kilowatt-hour.

Conversion of matter into energy (Einstein's Theorem): $E=mc^2$, in which *E* is the energy in ergs, *m* the mass of the matter in grams, and *c* the speed of light in centimeters per second. ($c^2=9\cdot10^{20}$).

Decimal Equivalents of Common Fractions

1/2	.5000	1/10	.1000	2/7	.2857	3/11	.2727	5/9	.5556	7/11	.6364
1/3	.3333	1/11	.0909	2/9	.2222	4/5	.8000	5/11	.4545	7/12	.5833
1/4	.2500	1/12	.0833	2/11	.1818	4/7	.5714	5/12	.4167	8/9	.8889
1/5	.2000	1/16	.0625	3/4	.7500	4/9	.4444	6/7	.8571	8/11	.7273
1/6	.1667	1/32	.0313	3/5	.6000	4/11	.3636	6/11	.5455	9/10	.9000
1/7	.1429	1/64	.0156	3/7	.4286	5/6	.8333	7/8	.8750	9/11	.8182
1/8	.1250	2/3	.6667	3/8	.3750	5/7	.7143	7/9	.7778	10/11	.9091
1/9	.1111	2/5	.4000	3/10	.3000	5/8	.6250	7/10	.7000	11/12	.9167

Conversion Factors

To change	To	Multiply by	To change	To	Multiply by
acres	hectares	.4047	liters	pints (dry)	1.8162
acres	square feet	43,560	liters	pints (liquid)	2.1134
acres	square miles	.001562	liters	quarts (dry)	.9081
atmospheres	cms. of mercury	76	liters	quarts (liquid)	1.0567
BTU	horsepower-hour	.0003931	meters	feet	3.2808
BTU	kilowatt-hour	.0002928	meters	miles	.0006214
BTU/hour	watts	.2931	meters	yards	1.0936
bushels	cubic inches	2150.4	metric tons	tons (long)	.9842
bushels (U.S.)	hectoliters	.3524	metric tons	tons (short)	1.1023
centimeters	inches	.3937	miles	kilometers	1.6093
centimeters	feet	.03281	miles	feet	5280
circumference	radians	6.283	miles (nautical)	miles (statute)	1.1516
cubic feet	cubic meters	.0283	miles (statute)	miles (nautical)	.8684
cubic meters	cubic feet	35.3145	miles/hour	feet/minute	88
cubic meters	cubic yards	1.3079	millimeters	inches	.0394
cubic yards	cubic meters	.7646	ounces avdp.	grams	28.3495
degrees	radians	.01745	ounces	pounds	.0625
dynes	grams	.00102	ounces (troy)	ounces (avdp)	1.09714
fathoms	feet	6.0	pecks	liters	8.8096
feet	meters	.3048	pints (dry)	liters	.5506
feet	miles (nautical)	.0001645	pints (liquid)	liters	.4732
feet	miles (statute)	.0001894	pounds ap or t	kilograms	.3782
feet/second	miles/hour	.6818	pounds avdp	kilograms	.4536
furlongs	feet	660.0	pounds	ounces	16
furlongs	miles	.125	quarts (dry)	liters	1.1012
gallons (U.S.)	liters	3.7853	quarts (liquid)	liters	.9463
grains	grams	.0648	radians	degrees	57.30
grams	grains	15.4324	rods	meters	5.029
grams	ounces avdp	.0353	rods	feet	16.5
grams	pounds	.002205	square feet	square meters	.0929
hectares	acres	2.4710	square kilometers	square miles	.3861
hectoliters	bushels (U.S.)	2.8378	square meters	square feet	10.7639
horsepower	watts	745.7	square meters	square yards	1.1960
hours	days	.04167	square miles	square kilometers	2.5900
inches	millimeters	25.4000	square yards	square meters	.8361
inches	centimeters	2.5400	tons (long)	metric tons	1.1060
kilograms	pounds avdp or t	2.2046	tons (short)	metric tons	.9072
kilometers	miles	.6214	tons (long)	pounds	2240
kilowatts	horsepower	1.341	tons (short)	pounds	2000
knots	nautical miles/hour	1.0	watts	BTU/hour	3.4129
knots	statute miles/hour	1.151	watts	horsepower	.001341
liters	gallons (U.S.)	.2642	yards	meters	.9144
liters	pecks	.1135	yards	miles	.0005682

Fahrenheit and Celsius (Centigrade) Scales

Zero on the Fahrenheit scale represents the temperature produced by the mixing of equal weights of snow and common salt.

	F	C
Boiling point of water	212°	100°
Freezing point of water	32°	0°
Absolute zero	−459.6°	−273.1°

Absolute zero is theoretically the lowest possible temperature, the point at which all molecular motion would cease.

To convert Fahrenheit to Celsius (Centigrade), subtract 32 and multiply by 5/9.

To convert Celsius (Centigrade) to Fahrenheit, multiply by 9/5 and add 32.

° Centigrade	° Fahrenheit	° Centigrade	° Fahrenheit
−273.1	−459.6	30	86
−250	−418	35	95
−200	−328	40	104
−150	−238	45	113
−100	−148	50	122
− 50	− 58	55	131
− 40	− 40	60	140
− 30	− 22	65	149
− 20	− 4	70	158
− 10	14	75	167
0	**32**	80	176
5	41	85	185
10	50	90	194
15	59	95	203
20	68	**100**	**212**
25	77		

Roman Numerals

Roman numerals are expressed by letters of the alphabet and are rarely used today except for formality or variety.

There are three basic principles for reading Roman numerals:

1. A letter repeated once or twice repeats its value that many times. (XXX=30, CC=200, etc.).

2. One or more letters placed after another letter of greater value increases the greater value by the amount of the smaller. (VI=6, LXX=70, MCC=1200, etc.).

3. A letter placed before another letter of greater value decreases the greater value by the amount of the smaller. (IV=4, XC=90, CM=900, etc.).

Letter	Value	Letter	Value	Letter	Value	Letter	Value	Letter	Value
I	1	VII	7	XXX	30	LXXX	80	$\overline{V}$	5,000
II	2	VIII	8	XL	40	XC	90	$\overline{X}$	10,000
III	3	IX	9	L	50	C	100	$\overline{L}$	50,000
IV	4	X	10	LX	60	D	500	$\overline{C}$	100,000
V	5	XX	20	LXX	70	M	1,000	$\overline{D}$	500,000
VI	6							$\overline{M}$	1,000,000

Mean and Median

The mean, also called the average, of a series of quantities is obtained by finding the sum of the quantities and dividing it by the number of quantities. In the series 1,3,5,18,19,20,25, the mean or average is 13—i.e., 91 divided by 7.

The median of a series is that point which so divides it that half the quantities are on one side, half on the other. In the above series, the median is 18.

The median often better expresses the common-run, since it is not, as is the mean, affected by an excessively high or low figure. In the series 1,3,4,7,-55, the median of 4 is a truer expression of the common-run than is the mean of 14.

Prime Numbers Between 1 and 1,000

1	2	3	5	7	11	13	17	19	23
29	31	37	41	43	47	53	59	61	67
71	73	79	83	89	97	101	103	107	109
113	127	131	137	139	149	151	157	163	167
173	179	181	191	193	197	199	211	223	227
229	233	239	241	251	257	263	269	271	277
281	283	293	307	311	313	317	331	337	347
349	353	359	367	373	379	383	389	397	401
409	419	421	431	433	439	443	449	457	461
463	467	479	487	491	499	503	509	521	523
541	547	557	563	569	571	577	587	593	599
601	607	613	617	619	631	641	643	647	653
659	661	673	677	683	691	701	709	719	727
733	739	743	751	757	761	769	773	787	797
809	811	821	823	827	829	839	853	857	859
863	877	881	883	887	907	911	919	929	937
941	947	953	967	971	977	983	991	997	(1009)

Definitions of Gold Terminology

The term "fineness" defines a gold content in parts per thousand. For example, a gold nugget containing 885 parts of pure gold, 100 parts of silver, and 15 parts of copper would be considered 885-fine.

The word "karat" indicates the proportion of solid gold in an alloy based on a total of 24 parts. Thus, 14-karat (14K) gold indicates a composition of 14 parts of gold and 10 parts of other metals.

The term "gold-filled" is used to describe articles of jewelry made of base metal which are covered on one or more surfaces with a layer of gold alloy. No article having a gold alloy portion of less than one twentieth by weight may be marked "gold-filled." Articles may be marked "rolled gold plate" provided the proportional fraction and fineness designations are also shown.

Electroplated jewelry items carrying at least 7 millionths of an inch of gold on significant surfaces may be labeled "electroplate." Plate thicknesses less than this may be marked "gold flashed" or "gold washed."

Portraits and Designs of U.S. Paper Currency[1]

Currency	Portrait	Design on back	Currency	Portrait	Design on back
$1	Washington	ONE between obverse and reverse of Great Seal of U.S.	$50	Grant	U.S. Capitol
$2[2]	Jefferson	Monticello	$100	Franklin	Independence Hall
$2[3]	Jefferson	"The Signing of the Declaration of Independence"	$500	McKinley	Ornate FIVE HUNDRED
$5	Lincoln	Lincoln Memorial	$1,000	Cleveland	Ornate ONE THOUSAND
$10	Hamilton	U.S. Treasury Building	$5,000	Madison	Ornate FIVE THOUSAND
$20	Jackson	White House	$10,000	Chase	Ornate TEN THOUSAND
			$100,000[4]	Wilson	Ornate ONE HUNDRED THOUSAND

1. Denominations of $500 and higher were discontinued in 1969. 2. Discontinued in 1966. 3. New issue, April 13, 1976. 4. For use only in transactions between Federal Reserve System and Treasury Department.

Astronomical Terms

Planet is the term used for a body in orbit around the Sun. Its origin is Greek; even in antiquity it was known that a number of "stars" did not stay in the same relative positions to the others. There were five such restless "stars" known—Mercury, Venus, Mars, Jupiter, and Saturn—and the Greeks referred to them as *planetes,* a word which means "wanderers." That the earth is one of the planets was realized later. The additional planets were discovered after the invention of the telescope.

Satellite (or *moon*) is the term for a body in orbit around a planet. As long as our own Moon was the only moon known, there was no need for a general term for the moons of planets. But when Galileo Galilei discovered the four main moons of the planet Jupiter, Johannes Kepler (in a letter to Galileo) suggested "satellite" (from the Latin *satelles,* which means attendant) as a general term for such bodies. The word is used interchangeably with "moons": astronomers speak and write about the moons of Neptune, Saturn, etc. A satellite may be any size.

Orbit is the term for the path traveled by a body in space. It comes from the Latin *orbis,* which means circle, circuit, etc., and *orbita,* which means a rut or a wheel track. Theoretically, four mathematical figures are possible orbits: two are open (hyperbola and parabola) and two are closed (ellipse and circle), but in reality all closed orbits are ellipses. These ellipses can be nearly circular, as are the orbits of most planets, or very elongated, as are the orbits of most comets. In these orbits, the Sun is in one focal point of the ellipse, and the other focal point is empty. In the orbits of satellites, the planet stands in one focal point of the orbit. The *primary* of an orbit is the body in the focal point. For planets, the point of the orbit closest to the Sun is the *perihelion,* and the point farthest from the Sun is the *aphelion.* For orbits around the Earth, the corresponding terms are *perigee* and *apogee;* for orbits around other planets, corresponding terms are coined when necessary.

Two heavenly bodies are in *inferior* or *superior conjunction* when they have the same Right Ascension, or are in the same meridian; that is, when one is due north or south of the other. If the bodies appear near each other as seen from the Earth, they will rise and set at the same time. They are in *opposition* when they are opposite each other in the heavens: when one rises as the other is setting. *Greatest elongation* is the greatest apparent angular distance from the Sun, when a planet is most favorably suited for observation. Mercury can be seen with the naked eye only at about this time. An *occultation* of a planet or star is an eclipse of it by some other body, usually the Moon.

Stars are the basic units of population in the universe. Our Sun is the nearest star. Stars are very large (our Sun has a diameter of 865,400 miles—a comparatively small star). Stars are composed of intensely hot gasses, deriving their energy from nuclear reactions going on in their interiors.

Galaxies are immense systems containing billions of stars. All that you can see in the sky (with a very few exceptions) belongs to our galaxy—a system of roughly 100 billion stars. The few exceptions are other galaxies. Our own galaxy, the rim of which we see as the "Milky Way," is about 100,000 light-years in diameter and about 10,000 light-years in thickness. Its shape is roughly that of a thick lens; more precisely it is a "spiral nebula," a term first used for other galaxies when they were discovered and before it was realized that these were separate and distant galaxies. The spiral galaxy nearest to ours is in the constellation An-

Astronomical Constants

Light-year (distance traveled by light in one year)	5,880,000,000,000 mi.
Parsec (parallax of one second, for stellar distances)	3.259 light-yrs.
Velocity of light	186,281.7 mi./sec.
Astronomical unit (A.U.), or mean distance earth-to-sun	ca. 93,000,000 mi.[1]
Mean distance, earth to moon	238,860 mi.
General precession	50″.26
Obliquity of the ecliptic	23° 27′ 8″.26–0″.4684(t – 1900)[2]
Equatorial radius of the earth	3963.34 statute mi.
Polar radius of the earth	3949.99 statute mi.
Earth's mean radius	3958.89 statute mi.
Oblateness of the earth	1/297
Equatorial horizontal parallax of the moon	57′ 2″.70
Earth's mean velocity in orbit	18.5 mi./sec.
Sidereal year	365d.2564
Tropical year	365d.2422
Sidereal month	27d.3217
Synodic month	29d.5306
Mean sidereal day	23h56m4s.091 of mean solar time
Mean solar day	24h3m56s.555 of sidereal time

1. Actual mean distance derived from radar bounces: 92,935,700 mi. The value of 92,897,400 mi. (based on parallax of 8″.80) is used in calculations. 2. *t* refers to the year in question, for example, 1983.

dromeda. It is somewhat larger than our own galaxy and is visible to the naked eye.

Recent developments in radio astronomy have revealed additional celestial objects that are still incompletely understood.

Quasars ("quasi-stellar" objects), originally thought to be peculiar stars in our own galaxy, are now believed to be the most remote objects in the Universe. Spectral studies of quasars indicate that some are 9 billion light years away and moving away from us at the incredible rate of 150,000 miles per second. Quasars emit tremendous amounts of light and microwave radiation. Although they appear to be far smaller than ordinary galaxies, some quasars emit as much as 100 times more energy. Some astronomers believe that quasars are the cores of violently exploding galaxies.

Pulsars are believed to be rapidly spinning neutron stars, so crushed by their own gravity that a million tons of their matter would hardly fill a thimble. Pulsars are so named because they emit bursts of radio energy at regular intervals. Some have pulse rates as rapid as 10 per second.

A *black hole* is the theoretical end-product of the total gravitational collapse of a massive star or group of stars. Crushed even smaller than an incredibly dense neutron star, such a body may become so dense that not even light can escape its gravitational field. It has been suggested that black holes may be detectable in proximity to normal stars when they draw matter away from their visible neighbors. Strong sources of X-rays in our galaxy and beyond may also indicate the presence of black holes. One possible black hole now being studied is the invisible companion to a supergiant star in the constellation Cygnus.

Origin of the Universe

Evidence uncovered in recent years tends to confirm that the universe began its existence about 15 billion years ago as a dense, hot globule of gas expanding rapidly outward. At that time, the universe contained nothing but hydrogen and a small amount of helium. There were no stars and no planets. The first stars probably began to condense out of the primordial hydrogen when the universe was about 100 million years old and continued to form as the universe aged. The Sun arose in this way 4.6 billion years ago. Many stars came into being before the Sun was formed; many others formed after the Sun appeared. This process continues, and through telescopes we can now see stars forming out of compressed pockets of hydrogen in outer space.

Birth and Death of a Star

When a star begins to form as a dense cloud of gas, the individual hydrogen atoms fall toward the center of the cloud under the force of the star's gravity. As they fall, they pick up speed, and their

The Brightest Stars

Star	Constellation	Mag.	Dist. (l.-y.)	Star	Constellation	Mag.	Dist. (l.-y.)
Sirius	Canis Major	−1.6	8	Antares	Scorpius	1.2	170
Canopus	Carina	−0.9	650	Fomalhaut	Piscis Austrinus	1.3	27
Alpha Centauri	Centaurus	+0.1	4	Deneb	Cygnus	1.3	465
Vega	Lyra	0.1	23	Regulus	Leo	1.3	70
Capella	Auriga	0.2	42	Beta Crucis	Crux	1.5	465
Arcturus	Boötes	0.2	32	Eta Carinae	Carina	1–7	—
Rigel	Orion	0.3	545	Alpha-one Crucis	Crux	1.6	150
Procyon	Canis Minor	0.5	10	Castor	Gemini	1.6	44
Achernar	Eridanus	0.6	70	Gamma Crucis	Crux	1.6	—
Beta Centari	Centaurus	0.9	130	Epsilon Canis Majoris	Canis Major	1.6	325
Altair	Aquila	0.9	18	Epsilon Ursae Majoris	Ursa Major	1.7	50
Betelgeuse	Orion	0.9	300	Bellatrix	Orion	1.7	215
Aldebaran	Taurus	1.1	54	Lambda Scorpii	Scorpius	1.7	205
Spica	Virgo	1.2	190	Epsilon Carinae	Carina	1.7	325
Pollux	Gemini	1.2	31	Mira	Cetus	2–10	250

Conversion of Universal Time (U. T.) to Civil Time

U.T.	E.D.T.[1]	E.S.T.[2]	C.S.T.[3]	M.S.T.[4]	P.S.T.[5]	U.T.	E.D.T.[1]	E.S.T.[2]	C.S.T.[3]	M.S.T.[4]	P.S.T.[5]
00	*8P	*7P	*6P	*5P	*4P	12	8A	7A	6A	5A	4A
01	*9P	*8P	*7P	*6P	*5P	13	9A	8A	7A	6A	5A
02	*10P	*9P	*8P	*7P	*6P	14	10A	9A	8A	7A	6A
03	*11P	*10P	*9P	*8P	*7P	15	11A	10A	9A	8A	7A
04	M	*11P	*10P	*9P	*8P	16	N	11A	10A	9A	8A
05	1A	M	*11P	*10P	*9P	17	1P	N	11A	10A	9A
06	2A	1A	M	*11P	*10P	18	2P	1P	N	11A	10A
07	3A	2A	1A	M	*11P	19	3P	2P	1P	N	11A
08	4A	3A	2A	1A	M	20	4P	3P	2P	1P	N
09	5A	4A	3A	2A	1A	21	5P	4P	3P	2P	1P
10	6A	5A	4A	3A	2A	22	6P	5P	4P	3P	2P
11	7A	6A	5A	4A	3A	23	7P	6P	5P	4P	3P

1. Eastern Daylight Time. 2. Eastern Standard Time, same as Central Daylight Time. 3. Central Standard Time, same as Mountain Daylight Time. 4. Mountain Standard Time, same as Pacific Daylight Time. 5. Pacific Standard Time. NOTES: *denotes previous day. N = noon. M = midnight.

Data for Sun, Moon, and Planets

	Mean distance from Sun in millions of miles	Period of revolution around the Sun	Eccentricity of orbit	Inclination to ecliptic ° ′	Diameter (miles)	Period of rotation on axis	Inclination of equator to orbit plane °	Surface gravity (earth = 1)	Density H_2O = 1	Number of satellites	Mean velocity in orbit (mi./sec.)	Max. stellar mag.
Sun	—	—	—	—	865,400	24d.64[2]	7.2	28	1.4	0	—	−26.7
Moon	—	(27d.322)[1]	0.05	5 8	2,160	27d.322	6.7	0.16	3.3	0	0.63	−12.6
Mercury	36.00	87d.969	0.21	7 0	3,100	58.66d	7	0.28	3.8	0	30	−1.2
Venus	67.27	224d.701	0.01	3 24	7,700	243.2d	—	0.85	5.1	0	22	−4.4
Earth	93.00	365d.256	0.02	0 0	7,927[3]	23h56m	23.4	1.00	5.5	1	18.5	—
Mars	141.71	1y.881	0.09	1 51	4,200	24h37m	25.2	0.38	4.0	2	15	−2.8
Jupiter	483.88	11y.862	0.05	1 18	88,700[3]	9h50m [2]	3.1	2.6	1.3	16	8	−2.5
Saturn	887.14	29y.458	0.06	2 29	75,100[3]	16h39m [2]	26.8	1.2	0.7	21+	6	−0.4
Uranus	1783.98	84y.013	0.05	0 46	32,000	12.8h	98	1.1	1.3	5	4	+5.7
Neptune	2795.46	164y.794	0.01	1 46	27,700	18h.2	29	1.4	2.2	2	3	+7.8
Pluto	3675.27	248y.430	0.25	17 9	1,500(?)	6d8h(?)	—	—	>1.0	1	<3	+14

1. Period of revolution around the earth. 2. Voyager 1 and 2 data. 3. The equatorial diameters of the earth, Jupiter, and Saturn are given; polar diameters are: earth, 7,900.0 mi., Jupiter 82,789 mi., Saturn 67,170 mi. OTHER DATA ON THE EARTH: Equatorial circumference, 24,902.4 mi.; total area, 196,949,970 sq mi.; mass, 6.6 sextillion tons; mean diameter, 7,917.8 mi.

energy increases. The increase in energy heats the gas. When this process has continued for some millions of years, the temperature reaches about 20 million degrees Fahrenheit. At this temperature, the hydrogen within the star ignites and burns in a continuing series of nuclear reactions in which all the elements in the universe are manufactured from hydrogen and helium. The onset of these reactions marks the birth of a star. When a star begins to exhaust its hydrogen supply, its life nears an end. The first sign of old age is a swelling and reddening of its outer regions. Such an aging, swollen star is called a red giant. The Sun, a middle-aged star, will probably swell to a red giant in 5 billion years, vaporizing the earth and any creatures that may be left on its surface. When all its fuel has been exhausted, a star cannot generate sufficient pressure at its center to balance the crushing force of gravity. The star collapses under the force of its own weight; if it is a small star, it collapses gently and remains collapsed. Such a collapsed star, at its life's end, is called a white dwarf. The Sun will probably end its life in this way. A different fate awaits a large star. Its final collapse generates a violent explosion, blowing the innards of the star out into space. There, the materials of the exploded star mix with the primeval hydrogen of the universe. Later in the history of the galaxy, other stars are formed out of this mixture. The Sun is one of these stars. It contains the debris of countless other stars that exploded before the Sun was born.

Formation of the Solar System

The Sun, like other stars, seems to have been formed 4.6 billion years ago from a cloud of hydrogen mixed with small amounts of other substances that had been manufactured in the bodies of other stars before the Sun was born. This was the parent cloud of the solar system. The dense hot gas at the center of the cloud gave rise to the Sun; the outer regions of the cloud—cooler and less dense—gave birth to the planets.

Our solar system consists of one star (the Sun), nine planets and all their moons, several thousand minor planets called asteroids or planetoids, and an equally large number of comets.

The Sun

All the stars, including our Sun, are gigantic balls of superheated gas, kept hot by atomic reactions in their centers. In our Sun, this atomic reaction is hydrogen fusion: four hydrogen atoms are combined to form one helium atom. The temperature at the core of our Sun must be 20 million degrees centigrade, the surface temperature is around 6,000 degrees centigrade, or about 11,000 degrees Fahrenheit. The diameter of the sun is 865,400 miles, and its surface area is approximately 12,000 times that of the Earth. Compared with other stars, our Sun is just a bit below average in size and temperature. Its fuel supply (hydrogen) is estimated to last for another 5 billion years.

Our Sun is not motionless in space; in fact it has two proper motions. One is a seemingly straight-line motion in the direction of the constellation Hercules at the rate of about 12 miles per second. But since the Sun is a part of the Milky Way system and since the whole system rotates slowly around its own center, the Sun also moves at the rate of 175 miles per second as part of the rotating Milky Way system.

In addition to this motion, the Sun rotates on its axis. Observing the motion of sun spots (darkish areas which look like enormous whirling storms) and solar flares, which are usually associated with sun spots, has shown that the rotational period of our Sun is just short of 25 days. But this figure is valid for the Sun's equator only; the sections near the Sun's poles seem to have a rotational period of 34 days. Naturally, since the Sun generates its own heat and light, there is no temperature difference between poles and equator.

What we call the Sun's "surface" is technically known as the photosphere. Since the whole Sun is a ball of very hot gas, there is really no such thing as a surface; it is a question of visual impression. The next layer outside the photosphere is known as the chromosphere, which extends several thousand miles beyond the photosphere. It is in steady motion, and often enormous prominences can be seen to burst from it, extending as much as 100,000 miles into space. Outside the chromosphere is the corona. The corona consists of very tenuous gases (essentially hydrogen) and makes a magnificent sight when the Sun is eclipsed.

The Moon

Mercury and Venus do not have any moons. Therefore, the Earth is the planet nearest the Sun to be orbited by a moon.

The next planet farther out, Mars, has two very small moons. Jupiter has four major moons and twelve minor ones. Saturn, the ringed planet, has fifteen known moons, of which one (Titan) is larger than the planet Mercury. Uranus has five known moons (four of them large) as well as rings, while Neptune has one large and one small moon. Pluto has one moon, discovered in 1978. Some astronomers still consider Pluto to be a "runaway moon" of Neptune.

Our own Moon, with a diameter of 2,160 miles, is one of the larger moons in our solar system and is especially large when compared with the planet that it orbits. In fact, the common center of gravity of the Earth-Moon system is only about 1,000 miles below the Earth's surface. The closest our Moon can come to us (its perigee) is 221,463 miles; the farthest it can go away (its apogee) is 252,710 miles. The period of rotation of our Moon is equal to its period of revolution around the Earth. Hence from Earth we can see only one hemisphere of the Moon. Both periods are 27 days, 7 hours, 43 minutes and 11.47 seconds. But while the rotation of the Moon is constant, its velocity in its orbit is not, since it moves more slowly in apogee than in perigee. Consequently, some portions near the rim which are not normally visible will appear briefly. This phenomenon is called "libration," and by taking advantage of the librations, astronomers have succeeded in mapping approximately 59% of the lunar surface. The other 41% can never be seen from the earth but has been mapped by American and Russian Moon-orbiting spacecraft.

Though the Moon goes around the Earth in the time mentioned, the interval from new Moon to new Moon is 29 days, 12 hours, 44 minutes and 2.78 seconds. This delay of nearly two days is due to the fact that the Earth is moving around the Sun, so that the Moon needs two extra days to reach a spot in its orbit where no part is illuminated by the Sun, as seen from Earth.

If the plane of the Earth's orbit around the Sun (the ecliptic) and the plane of the Moon's orbit around the Earth were the same, the Moon would be eclipsed by the Earth every time it is full, and the Sun would be eclipsed by the Moon every time the Moon is "new" (it would be better to call it the "black Moon" when it is in this position). But because the two orbits do not coincide, the Moon's shadow normally misses the Earth and the Earth's shadow misses the Moon. The inclination of the two orbital planes to each other is 5 degrees. The tides are, of course, caused by the Moon with the help of the Sun, but in the open ocean they are surprisingly low, amounting to about one yard. The very high tides which can be observed near the shore in some places are due to funnelling effects of the shorelines. At new Moon and at full Moon the tides raised by the Moon are reinforced by the Sun; these are the "spring tides." If the Sun's tidal power acts at right angles to that of the Moon (quarter moons) we get the low "neap tides."

Our Planet Earth

The Earth, circling the Sun at an average distance of 93 million miles, is the fifth largest planet and the third from the Sun. It orbits the Sun at a speed of 67,000 miles per hour, making one revolution in 365 days, 5 hours, 48 minutes, and 45.51 seconds. The Earth completes one rotation on its axis every 23 hours, 56 minutes, and 4.09 seconds. Actually a bit pear-shaped rather than a true sphere, the Earth has a diameter of 7,927 miles at the Equator and a few miles less at the poles. It has an estimated mass of about 6.6 sextillion tons, with an average density of 5.52 grams per cubic centimeter. The Earth's surface area encompasses 196,949,970 square miles, of which about three-fourths is water.

Origin of the Earth. The Earth, along with the other planets, is believed to have been born 4.5 billion years ago as a solidified cloud of dust and gases left over from the creation of the Sun. For perhaps 500 million years, the interior of the Earth stayed solid and relatively cool, perhaps 2000° F. The main ingredients, according to the best available evidence, were iron and silicates, with small amounts of other elements, some of them radioactive. As millions of years passed, energy released by radioactive decay—mostly of uranium, thorium, and potassium—gradually heated the Earth, melting some of its constituents. The iron melted before the silicates, and, being heavier, sank toward the center. This forced upward the silicates that it found there. After many years, the iron reached the center, almost 4,000 miles deep, and began to accumulate. No eyes were around at that time to view the turmoil which must have taken place on the face of the Earth—gigantic heaves and bubbling of the surface, exploding volcanoes, and flowing lava covering everything in sight. Finally, the iron in the center accumulated as the core. Around it, a thin but fairly stable crust of solid rock formed as the Earth cooled. Depressions in the crust were natural basins in which water, rising from the interior of the planet through volcanoes and fissures, collected to form the oceans. Slowly the Earth acquired its present appearance.

The Earth Today. As a result of radioactive heating over millions of years, the Earth's molten *core* is probably fairly hot today, around 11,000° F. By comparison, lead melts at around 800° F. Most of the Earth's 2,100-mile-thick core is liquid, but there is evidence that the center of the core is solid. The liquid outer portion, about 95% of the core, is constantly in motion, causing the Earth to have a magnetic field that makes compass needles point north and south. The details are not known, but the latest evidence suggests that planets which have a magnetic field probably have a solid core or a partially liquid one.

Outside the core is the Earth's *mantle,* 1,800 miles thick, and extending nearly to the surface. The mantle is composed of heavy silicate rock, similar to that brought up by volcanic eruptions. It is somewhere between liquid and solid, slightly yielding, and therefore contributing to an active, moving Earth. Most of the Earth's radioactive material is in the thin *crust* which covers the mantle, but some is in the mantle and continues to give off heat. The crust's thickness ranges from 5 to 25 miles.

Continental Drift. A great deal of recent evidence confirms the long-disputed theory that the continents of the Earth, made mostly of relatively light granite, float in the slightly yielding mantle, like logs in a pond. For many years it had been noticed that if North and South America could be pushed toward western and southern Europe and western Africa, they would fit like pieces in a jigsaw puzzle. Today, there is little question—the continents have drifted widely and continue to do so.

In 10 million years, the world as we know it may be unrecognizable, with California drifting out to sea, Florida joining South America, and Africa moving farther away from Europe and Asia.

The Earth's Atmosphere. The thin blanket of atmosphere that envelops the Earth extends several hundred miles into space. From sea level—the very bottom of the ocean of air—to a height of about 60 miles, the air in the atmosphere is made up of the same gases in the same ratio: about 78% nitrogen, 21% oxygen, and the remaining 1% being a mixture of argon, carbon dioxide, and tiny amounts of neon, helium, krypton, xenon, and other gases. The atmosphere becomes less dense with increasing altitude: more than three-fourths of the Earth's huge envelope is concentrated in the first 5 to 10 miles above the surface. At sea level, a cubic foot of the atmosphere weighs about an ounce and a quarter. The entire atmosphere weighs 5,700,000,000,000,000 tons, and the force with which gravity holds it in place causes it to exert a pressure of nearly 15 pounds per square inch. Going out from the Earth's surface, the atmosphere is divided into five regions. The regions, and the heights to which they extend, are: *Troposphere,* 0 to 7 miles (at middle latitudes); *stratosphere,* 7 to 30 miles; *mesosphere,* 30 to 50 miles; *thermosphere,* 50 to 400 miles; and *exosphere,* above 400 miles. The boundaries between each of the regions are known respectively as the *tropopause, stratopause, mesopause,* and *thermopause.* Alternate terms often used for the layers above the troposhere are *ozonosphere* (for stratosphere) and *ionosphere* for the remaining upper layers.

The Seasons. Seasons are caused by the 23.4 degree tilt of the Earth's axis, which alternately turns the North and South Poles toward the Sun. Times when the Sun's apparent path crosses the Equator are known as *equinoxes.* Times when the Sun's apparent path is at the greatest distance from the Equator are known as *solstices.* The lengths of the days are most extreme at each solstice. If the Earth's axis were perpendicular to the plane of the Earth's orbit around the Sun, there would be no seasons, and the days always would be equal in length. Since the Earth's axis is at an angle, the Sun strikes the Earth directly at the Equator only twice a year: in March (vernal equinox) and September (autumnal equinox). In the Northern Hemisphere, spring begins at the vernal equinox, summer at the summer solstice, fall at the autumnal equinox, and winter at the winter solstice. The situation is reversed in the Southern Hemisphere.

Mercury

Mercury is the planet nearest the Sun. Appropriately named for the wing-footed Roman messenger of the gods, Mercury whizzes around the Sun at a speed of 30 miles per second, completing one circuit in 88 days. The planet rotates on its axis over a period of nearly 59 days. Daytime on cratered Mercury is hot, about 800 degrees F., although at night the temperature may fall to room temperature. Mercury has no moons, but it does have a trace of atmosphere and a weak magnetic field, according to findings of Mariner 10. Until this spacecraft flew by Mercury in 1974 and 1975, very little was known about the planet, primarily because of its short angular distance from the Sun as seen from Earth, which puts it too close to the Sun to be easily observed.

• Mercury is a naked eye object at morning or evening twilight when it is at greatest elongation.

Venus

Although Venus is Earth's nearest neighbor, little is known about this planet because it is permanently covered by thick clouds. In 1962, Soviet and American space probes, coupled with Earth-based radar and infrared spectroscopy, began slowly unraveling some of the mystery surrounding Venus. According to the latest results, Venus' atmosphere is about 96% carbon dioxide, exerting a pressure at the surface 90.5 times greater than Earth's. Walking on Venus would be as difficult as walking a half-mile beneath the ocean. Because of the thick blanket of carbon dioxide, a "greenhouse effect" exists on Venus: Venus intercepts twice as much of the Sun's light as does the Earth. The light enters freely through carbon dioxide gas and is changed to heat radiation in molecular collisions. But carbon dioxide prevents the heat from escaping. Consequently, the temperature of the surface of Venus is over 800 degrees F., hot enough to melt lead. The atmosphere appears to have five distinct layers and to flash almost continuously with lightning. Radar bounced off the planet recently revealed what appear to be large craters and an immense, 900-mile-long canyon. Venus rotates in retrograde motion for a reason not yet known.

In March 1982, the Soviet *Venera 13* and *14* landing craft made the first actual test samples of the Venusian surface by x-ray fluorescence spectroscopy which gave an element-by-element analysis. The terrestrial samples revealed a terrain of basaltic uplands and lowlands.

The Soviets have announced plans to place two more Venera landers on Venus in 1986.

• Venus is the brightest of all the planets and is often visible in the morning or evening, when it is frequently referred to as the Morning Star or Evening Star. At its brightest, it can sometimes be seen with the naked eye in full daylight, if one knows where to look.

Mars

Mars, on the other side of the Earth from Venus, is Venus' direct opposite in terms of physical properties. Its atmosphere is cold, thin, and transparent, and readily permits observation of the planet's features. We know more about Mars than any other planet except Earth. Mars is a forbidding, rugged planet with huge volcanoes and deep chasms. The largest volcano, Olympus Mons rises 78,000 feet above the surface, higher than Mount Everest. The plains of Mars are pockmarked by the hits of thousands of meteors over the years. Most of our information about Mars comes from the Mariner 9 spacecraft, which orbited the planet in 1971. Mariner 9, photographing 100% of the planet, uncovered spectacular geological formations, including a Martian Grand Canyon that dwarfs the one on Earth. The spacecraft's cameras also recorded what appeared to be dried riverbeds, suggesting the onetime presence of water on the planet. The latter idea gives encouragement to scientists looking for life on Mars, for where there is water, there may be life. However, by 1979, no evidence of life has been found. Temperatures near the equator range from −17 degrees F. in the daytime to −130 degrees F. at night. Mars rotates upon its axis in nearly the same period as Earth—24 hours, 37 minutes—so that a Mars day is almost identical to an Earth day. Mars takes 687 days to make one trip around the Sun. Because of its eccentric orbit Mars' distance from the Sun can vary by about 36 million miles. Its distance from Earth can vary by as much as 200 million miles. The atmosphere of Mars is much thinner than Earth's; atmospheric pressure is about 1% that of our planet. Its gravity is one-third of Earth's. Major constituents are carbon dioxide and nitrogen. Water vapor and oxygen are minor constituents. Mars' polar caps, composed mostly of carbon dioxide, recede and advance according to the Martian seasons. Mars was named for the Roman god of war, because when seen from Earth its distinct red color reminded the ancient people of blood. We know now that the reddish hue reflects the oxidized (rusted) iron in the surface material. The landing of two robot Viking spacecraft on the surface of Mars in 1976 provided more information about Mars in a few months than in all the time that has gone before.

Jupiter

Jupiter, with an equatorial diameter of 88,000 miles, is the largest of a group of planets which differ markedly from the terrestrial planets. The others in the group are Saturn, Uranus, and Neptune. All are large, with very dense atmospheres, and indeed may be giant balls of gas without any perceptible surfaces. They all whirl rapidly around their axes, but more slowly around the Sun, resulting in short days and long years. They have many moons. Majestic Jupiter, named for the king of the Roman gods, rotates so fast that it is greatly flattened at the poles. According to Pioneers 10 and 11, which flew past Jupiter in 1974 and 1975, this planet is a whirling ball of liquid hydrogen with perhaps an Earth-sized iron core. Other atmospheric constituents are helium, methane, and ammonia. Its clouds are probably ammonia ice crystals, becoming ammonia droplets deeper towards the "surface." Temperatures range from perhaps minus 300 degrees F. at the tops of the cloud decks to 100,000 degrees F. or more deep down at the center. The pressure at the center of the planet is estimated to be a crushing 10 million pounds per square inch. The Great Red Spot, a 13,000-mile-wide storm that may have been raging for thousands of years, was found by Voyagers 1 and 2 in 1979 to be cooler at the top than the surrounding clouds, indicating that the Red Spot may tower high above them. Jupiter has 16 satellites. The four largest moons, called Galilean moons, are Europa, Ganymede, Io, and Callisto. *Voyagers 1 and 2* found them to be very different from each other in terms of surface relief, volcanic activity, and other characteristics.

• Even when nearest the Earth, Jupiter is still almost 400 million miles away. But because of its size, it may rival Venus in brilliance when near. Jupiter's four large moons may be seen through field glasses, moving rapidly around Jupiter and changing their position from night to night.

Saturn

Saturn, the second largest planet in the solar system, is the least dense. It would float in an ocean if there were one big enough to hold it. Aside from its rings, Saturn is very similar to Jupiter except that it is probably colder, being twice as far from the Sun. Recent radar observations of Saturn's rings indicate that they are no more than 10 miles thick, and probably composed of chunks of rock and ice averaging a meter in size. Saturn's ring system begins about 7000 miles from the planet's disk, and extends out to about 35,000 miles. Recent observations have shown Saturn to have between 21 and 23 moons, more than any other planet. The two *Voyager* probes that examined Jupiter in 1979 flew by Saturn in 1980 and 1981. *Voyager 2* will encounter Uranus in 1986.

• Saturn is the last of the planets visible to the naked eye. Saturn is never an object of overwhelming brilliance, but it looks like a bright star. The rings can be seen with a small telescope.

Uranus and Neptune

Little is known about the distant giant planets Uranus and Neptune, but they are believed to be similar to Saturn and Jupiter. Being twice as far from the Sun as Saturn, Uranus must be a grim frozen world, and Neptune, 11 A.U. beyond Uranus, must be even colder and darker. The axis of Uranus is tilted at 98 degrees, so it goes around the Sun nearly lying on its side. In 1977, American astronomers made the startling discovery that Uranus has rings, like Saturn. The first Voyager to Uranus may take pictures of the rings in 1986. Uranus has five known moons; Neptune, two. Neptune's Triton, Jupiter's Ganymede and Callisto, and Saturn's Titan are the four largest moons in the solar system.

• Uranus and Neptune can—on rare occasion—become bright enough to be seen with the naked eye, if one knows exactly where to look; normally, they are objects for good field glasses or small portable telescopes.

Pluto

Pluto, the outermost and smallest planet in the solar system, looks more like a terrestrial planet than a gaseous planet. But so little is known about it, that it is difficult to classify. Appropriately named for the Roman god of the underworld, it must be frozen, dark, and dead.

In 1978, light curve studies gave evidence of a moon revolving around Pluto with the same period as Pluto's rotation. Therefore, it stays over the same point on Pluto's surface. In addition, it keeps the same face toward the planet. The discovery of this moon of 500–600 miles in diameter reduces the previously estimated diameter of Pluto to little more than 1,500 miles, making the pair more like a double planet than any other in the solar system. Previously, the Earth-Moon system held this distinction. The density of Pluto is slightly greater than that of water.

Pluto was predicted by calculation when Percival Lowell noticed irregularities in the orbits of Uranus and Neptune. Clyde Tombaugh discovered the planet in 1930, precisely where Lowell predicted it would be. The name Pluto was chosen because the first two letters represent the initials of Percival Lowell.

• Pluto has the most eccentric orbit in the solar system, bringing it at times closer to the Sun

The First Ten Minor Planets (Asteroids)

Name	Year of discovery	Mean distance from sun (millions of miles)	Orbital period (years)	Diameter (miles)	Magnitude
1. Ceres	1801	257.0	4.60	485	7.4
2. Pallas	1802	257.4	4.61	304	8.0
3. Juno	1804	247.8	4.36	118	8.7
4. Vesta	1807	219.3	3.63	243	6.5
5. Astraea	1845	239.3	4.14	50	9.9
6. Hebe	1847	225.2	3.78	121	8.5
7. Iris	1847	221.4	3.68	121	8.4
8. Flora	1847	204.4	3.27	56	8.9
9. Metis	1848	221.7	3.69	78	8.9
10. Hygeia	1849	292.6	5.59	40(?)	9.5

than Neptune. Pluto is now approaching the perihelion of its orbit, and for the rest of this century will be closer to the Sun than Neptune. Even then, it can be seen only with a large telescope.

The Asteroids

Between the orbits of Mars and Jupiter are an estimated 30,000 pieces of rocky debris, known collectively as the asteroids, or planetoids. The first and, incidentally, the largest was discovered during the New Year's night of 1801 by the Italian astronomer Father Piazzi, and its orbit was calculated by the German mathematician Karl Friedrich Gauss. (Gauss invented a new method of calculating orbits on that occasion.) A German amateur astronomer, the physician Olbers, discovered the second asteroid. The number now known, catalogued, and named is around 1,600; the estimated total is about 20 times that figure. A few asteroids do not move in orbits beyond the orbit of Mars, but in orbits which cross the orbit of Mars. The first of them was named Eros because of this peculiar orbit. It had become the rule to bestow female names on the asteroids, but when it was found that Eros crossed the orbit of a major planet, it received a male name. Since then around two dozen orbit-crossers have been discovered, and they are often referred to as the "male asteroids." A few of them—Albert, Adonis, Apollo, Amor, and Icarus—cross the orbit of the Earth, and two of them may come closer than our Moon; but the crossing is like a bridge crossing a highway, not like two highways intersecting. Hence there is very little danger of collision from these bodies. They are all small, three to five miles in diameter, and therefore very difficult objects to identify, even when quite close. Some scientists believe the asteroids represent the remains of an exploded planet.

Comets

Comets, according to the noted astronomer, Fred L. Whipple, are enormous "snowballs" of frozen gases (mostly carbon dioxide, methane, and water vapor) and contain very little solid material. The whole behavior of comets can then be explained as the behavior of frozen gas being heated by the Sun. When the comet Kohoutek made its first appearance to man in 1973, its behavior seemed to confirm this Whipple theory of the make-up of comets.

Kohoutek will probably not appear in view for another 75,000 years. The next comet large and brilliant enough to be very easily seen is predicted for 1986, when Halley's comet will approach perihelion (the point of its orbit closest to the Sun) again.

Since comets appear in the sky without any warning, people in classical times and especially during the Middle Ages believed that they had a special meaning, which, of course, was bad. Since a natural catastrophe of some sort or a military conflict occurs every year, it was quite simple to blame the comet that happened to be visible. But even in the past, there were some people who used logical reasoning. When, in Roman times, a comet was blamed for the loss of a battle and hence was called a "bad omen," a Roman writer observed that the victors in the battle probably did not think so.

Up until the middle of the sixteenth century, comets were believed to be phenomena of the upper atmosphere; they were usually "explained" as "burning vapors" which had risen from "distant swamps." That nobody had ever actually seen burning vapors rise from a swamp did not matter.

But a large comet which appeared in 1577 was carefully observed by Tycho Brahe, a Danish astronomer who is often, and with the best of reasons, called "eccentric" but who insisted on precise measurements for everything. It was Tycho Brahe's accumulation of literally thousands of precise measurements which later enable his younger collaborator, Johannes Kepler, to discover the laws of

21 Famous Comets

Year and no.	Name of comet	Period (years)
1744	De Chéseaux's Comet	—
1806	Biela's Comet	6.7
1811 I	Great Comet of 1811	3000
1812	Di Vico's Comet	70.7
1815	Olbers' Comet	74.0
1819 I	Encke's Comet	3.3
1819	Pons-Winnecke Comet	6.0
1835 III	Halley's Comet	76.3
1843 I	Great Comet of 1843	512.4
1844 II	Great Comet of 1844	102,050
1858 VI	Donati's Comet	2,040(?)
1864 II	Great Comet of 1864	2,800,000
1871 III	Tuttle's Comet	13.8
1874 III	Coggia's Comet	6,000(?)
1879	Brorsen's Comet	5.6
1881 II	Tebbutt's Comet	—
1889 VI	Swift's 2nd Comet	7.0
1892 III	Holmes' Comet	6.9
1923	d'Arrest's Comet	6.6
1925 II	Comet Schwassmann-Wachmann	16.2
1973 I	Comet Kohoutek	75,000(?)

planetary motion. Measuring the motion of the comet of 1577, Tycho Brahe could show that it had been far beyond the atmosphere, even though he could not give figures for the distance. Tycho Brahe's work proved that comets were astronomical and not meteorological phenomena.

In 1682, the second Astronomer Royal of Great Britain, Dr. Edmond Halley, checked the orbit of a bright comet that was in the sky then and compared it with earlier comet orbits which were known in part. Halley found that the comet of 1682 was the third to move through what appeared to be the same orbit. And the three appearances were roughly 76 years apart. Halley concluded that this was the same comet, moving around the Sun in a closed orbit, like the planets. He predicted that it would reappear in 1758 or 1759. Halley himself died in 1742, but a large comet appeared sixteen years after his death as predicted and was immediately referred to as "Halley's comet."

In the Spring of 1973, the discovery of comet Kohoutek, apparently headed for a close-Christmastime rendezvous with the Sun, created worldwide excitement. The comet was a visual disappointment, but turned out to be a treasure trove of information on these little-understood celestial objects. Given an unprecedented advance notice of nine months on the advent of the fiery object, scientists were able to study the comet in visible, ultraviolet and infrared light; with optical telescopes, radio telescopes, and radar. They observed it from the ground, from high-flying aircraft, with instruments aboard unmanned satellites, with sounding rockets, and telescopes and cameras on the Earth-orbiting Skylab space station.

Astronomers refer to comets as "periodic" or as "non-periodic" comets, but the latter term does not mean that these comets have no period; it merely means that their period is not known. The actual periods of comets run from 3.3 years (the shortest known) to many thousands of years. Their orbits are elliptical, like those of the planets, but they are very eccentric, long and narrow ellipses. Only comet Schwassmann-Wachmann has an orbit which has such a low eccentricity (for a cometary orbit) that it could be the orbit of a minor planet.

When a comet, coming from deep space, approaches the Sun, it is at first indistinguishable from a minor planet. Somewhere between the orbits of Mars and Jupiter its outline becomes fuzzy; it is said to develop a "coma" (the word used here is the Latin word *coma,* which means "hair," not the phonetically identical Greek word which means "deep sleep"). Then, near the orbit of Mars, the comet develops its tail, which at first trails behind. This grows steadily as the comet comes closer and closer to the Sun. As it rounds the Sun (as first noticed by Girolamo Fracastoro) the tail always points away from the Sun so that the comet, when moving away from the Sun, points its tail ahead like the landing lights of an airplane.

The reason for this behavior is that the tail is pushed in these directions by the radiation pressure of the Sun. It sometimes happens that a comet loses its tail at perihelion; it then grows another one. Although the tail is clearly visible against the black of the sky, it is very tenuous. It has been said that if the tail of Halley's comet could be compressed to the density of iron, it would fit into a small suitcase.

Although very low in mass, comets are among the largest members of the solar system. The nucleus of a comet may be up to 10,000 miles in diameter; its coma between 10,000 and 50,000 miles in diameter; and its tail as long as 28 million miles.

Meteors and Meteorites

The term "meteor" for what is usually called a "shooting star" bears an unfortunate resemblance to the term "meteorology," the science of weather and weather forecasting. This resemblance is due to an ancient misunderstanding which wrongly considered meteors an atmospheric phenomenon. Actually, the streak of light in the sky that scientists call a meteor is essentially an astronomical phenomenon: the entry of a small piece of cosmic matter into our atmosphere.

The distinction between "meteors" and "fireballs" (formerly also called "bolides") is merely one of convenience; a fireball is an unusually bright meteor. Incidentally, it also means that a fireball is larger than a faint meteor.

Bodies which enter our atmosphere become visible when they are about 60 miles above the ground. The fact that they grow hot enough to emit light is not due to the "friction" of the atmosphere, as one can often read. The phenomenon responsible for the heating is one of compression. Unconfined air cannot move faster than the speed of sound. Since the entering meteorite moves with 30 to 60 times the speed of sound, the air simply cannot get out of the way. Therefore, it is compressed like the air in the cylinder of a Diesel engine and is heated by compression. This heat—or part of it—is transferred to the moving body. The details of this process are now fairly well understood as a result of re-entry tests with ballistic-missile nose cones.

The average weight of a body producing a faint "shooting star" is only a small fraction of an ounce. Even a bright fireball may not weigh more than 2 or 3 pounds. Naturally, the smaller bodies are worn to dust by the passage through the atmosphere; only rather large ones reach the ground. Those that are found are called meteorites. (The "meteor," to repeat, is the term for the light streak in the sky.)

The largest meteorite known is still imbedded in the ground near Grootfontein in SW Africa and is estimated to weight 70 tons. The second largest known is the 34-ton Anighito (on exhibit in the Hayden Planetarium, New York), which was found by Admiral Peary at Cape York in Greenland. The

Important Meteor Showers

Approx. date	Name of meteor stream	Radiant in constellation
Jan. 1–4	Quadrantids	Boötes
Feb. 5–10	Alpha Aurigids	Auriga
March 10–12	Zeta Boötids	Boötes
April 19–23	Lyrids	Hercules
May 1–6	May Aquarids	Aquarius
May 30	Eta Pegasids	Pegasus
June 27–30	Pons-Winnecke meteors	Draco
July 14	Alpha Cygnids	Cygnus
July 26–31	Delta Aquarids	Aquarius
Aug. 10–14	Perseids	Cassiopeia
Aug. 10–20	Kappa Cygnids	Cygnus
Aug. 21–31	Zeta Draconids	Draco
Sept. 22	Alpha Aurigids	Auriga
Oct. 2	Quadrantids	Boötes
Oct. 9	Giacobinids	Draco
Oct. 18–23	Orionids	Orion
Nov. 14–18	Leonids	Leo
Dec. 10–13	Geminids	Gemini

The 88 Recognized Constellations

In astronomical works, the Latin names of the constellations are used. The letter N or S following the Latin name indicates whether the constellation is located to the north or south of the Zodiac. The letter Z indicates that the constellation is within the Zodiac.

Latin name	Letter	English version
Andromeda	N	Andromeda
Antlia	S	Airpump
Apus	S	Bird of Paradise
Aquarius	Z	Water Bearer
Aquila	N	Eagle
Ara	S	Altar
Aries	Z	Ram
Auriga	N	Charioteer
Boötes	N	Herdsmen
Caelum	S	Sculptor's Tool
Camelopardalis	N	Giraffe
Cancer	Z	Crab
Canes Venatici	N	Hunting Dogs
Canis Major	S	Great Dog
Canis Minor	S	Little Dog
Capricornus	Z	Goat (or Sea-Goat)
Carina	S	Keel (of Argo)[1]
Cassiopeia	N	Cassiopeia
Centaurus	S	Centaur
Cepheus	N	Cepheus
Cetus	S	Whale
Chamaeleon	S	Chameleon
Circinus	S	Compasses
Columba	S	Dove
Coma Berenices	N	Berenice's Hair
Corona Australis	S	Southern Crown
Corona Borealis	N	Northern Crown
Corvus	S	Crow (Raven)
Crater	S	Cup
Crux	S	Southern Cross
Cygnus	N	Swan

Latin name	Letter	English version
Delphinus	N	Dolphin
Dorado	S	Swordfish (Goldfish)
Draco	N	Dragon
Equuleus	N	Filly
Eridanus	S	Eridanus (river)
Fornax	S	Furnace
Gemini	Z	Twins
Grus	S	Crane
Hercules	N	Hercules
Horologium	S	Clock
Hydra	N	Sea Serpent
Hydrus	S	Water Snake
Indus	S	Indian
Lacerta	N	Lizard
Leo	Z	Lion
Leo Minor	N	Little Lion
Lepus	S	Hare
Libra	Z	Scales
Lupus	S	Wolf
Lynx	N	Lynx
Lyra	N	Lyre (Harp)
Mensa	S	Table (mountain)
Microscopium	S	Microscope
Monoceros	S	Unicorn
Musca	S	Southern Fly
Norma	S	Rule (straightedge)
Octans	S	Octant
Ophiuchus	N	Serpent-Bearer
Orion	S	Orion

Latin name	Letter	English version
Pavo	S	Peacock
Pegasus	N	Pegasus
Perseus	N	Perseus
Phoenix	S	Phoenix
Pictor	S	Painter (or his Easel)
Pisces	Z	Fishes
Piscis Austrinus	S	Southern Fish
Puppis	S	Poop (of Argo)[1]
Pyxis	S	Mariner's Compass
Reticulum	S	Net
Sagitta	N	Arrow
Sagittarius	Z	Archer
Scorpius	Z	Scorpion
Sculptor	S	Sculptor
Scutum	N	Shield
Serpens	N	Serpent
Sextans	S	Sextant
Taurus	Z	Bull
Telescopium	S	Telescope
Triangulum	N	Triangle
Triangulum Australe	S	Southern Triangle
Tucana	S	Toucan
Ursa Major	N	Big Dipper
Ursa Minor	N	Little Dipper
Vela	S	Sail (of Argo)[1]
Virgo	Z	Virgin
Volans	S	Flying Fish
Vulpecula	N	Fox

1. The original constellation Argo Navis (the Ship Argo) has been divided into Carina, Puppis, and Vela. Normally the brightest star in each constellation is designated by alpha, the first letter of the Greek alphabet, the second brightest by beta, the second letter of the Greek alphabet, and so forth. But the Greek letters run through Carina, Puppis, and Vela as if it were still one constellation.

largest meteorite found in the United States is the Willamette meteorite (found in Oregon, weight ca. 15 tons), but large portions of this meteorite weathered away before it was found. Its weight as it struck the ground may have been 20 tons.

All these are iron meteorites (an iron meteorite normally contains about 7% nickel), which form one class of meteorites. The other class consists of the stony meteorites, and between them there are the so-called "stony irons." The so-called "tektites" consist of glass similar to our volcanic glass obsidian, and because of the similarity, there is doubt in a number of cases whether the glass is of terrestrial or of extra-terrestrial origin.

Though no meteorite larger than the Grootfontein is actually known, we do know that the Earth has, on occasion, been struck by much larger bodies. Evidence for such hits are the meteorite craters, of which an especially good example is located near the Cañon Diablo in Arizona. Another meteor crater in the United States is a rather old crater near Odessa, Texas. A large number of others are known, especially in eastern Canada; and for many "probables," meteoric origin has now been proved.

The meteor showers are caused by multitudes of very small bodies travelling in swarms. The Earth travels in its orbit through these swarms like a car driving through falling snow. The point from which the meteors seem to emanate is called the *radiant* and is named for the constellation in that area. The Perseid meteor shower in August is the most spectacular of the year, boasting at peak roughly 60 meteors per hour under good atmospheric conditions. The presence of a bright moon diminishes the number of visible meteors.

The Constellations

Constellations are groupings of stars which form patterns that can be easily recognized and remembered, for example, Orion and the Big Dipper. Actually, the stars of the majority of all constellations do not "belong together." Usually they are at greatly varying distances from the Earth and just happen to lie more or less in the same line of sight as seen from our solar system. But in a few cases the stars of a constellation are actually associated; most of the bright stars of the Big Dipper travel together and form what astronomers call an open cluster.

If you observe a planet, say Mars, for one complete revolution, you will see that it passes successively through twelve constellations. All planets (except Pluto at certain times) can be observed only in these twelve constellations, which form the so-called Zodiac, and the Sun also moves through the signs of the Zodiac, though the Sun's apparent

Symbols

☉ the sun	♀ Venus	♃ Jupiter	♆ Neptune	occultation	☽ first quarter
☾ the moon	⊕ the earth	♄ Saturn	♇ Pluto	☍ opposition	○ full moon
☿ Mercury	♂ Mars	♅ Uranus	☌ conjunction	● new moon	☾ last quarter

movement is actually caused by the movement of the Earth.

Although the constellations are due mainly to the optical accident of line of sight and have no real significance, astronomers have retained them as reference areas. It is much easier to speak of a star in Orion than to give its geometrical position in the sky. During the Astronomical Congress of 1928, it was decided to recognize 88 constellations. A description of their agreed-upon boundaries was published at Cambridge, England, in 1930, under the title *Atlas Céleste.*

The Auroras

The "northern lights" *(Aurora borealis)* as well as the "southern lights" *(Aurora australis)* are upper-atmosphere phenomena of astronomical origin. The auroras center around the magnetic (not the geographical) poles of the Earth, which explains why, in the Western Hemisphere, they have been seen as far to the south as New Orleans and Florida while the equivalent latitude in the Eastern Hemisphere never sees an aurora. The northern magnetic pole happens to be in the Western Hemisphere.

The lower limit of an aurora is at about 50 miles. Upper limits have been estimated to be as high as 400 miles. Since about 1880, a connection between the auroras on Earth and the sun spots has been suspected and has gradually come to be accepted. It was said that the sun spots probably eject "particles" (later the word *electrons* was substituted) which on striking the Earth's atmosphere, cause the auroras. But this explanation suffered from certain difficulties. Sometimes a very large sun spot group on the Sun, with individual spots bigger than the Earth itself, would not cause an aurora. Moreover, even if a sun spot caused an aurora, the time that passed between the appearance of the one and the occurrence of the other was highly unpredictable.

This problem of the time lag is, in all probability, solved by the discovery of the Van Allen layer by artificial satellite *Explorer I.* The Van Allen layer is a double layer of charged sub-atomic particles around the Earth. The inner layer, with its center some 1,500 miles from the ground, reaches from about 40°N. to about 40°S. and does not touch the atmosphere. The outer layer, much larger and with its center several thousand miles from the ground, does touch the atmosphere in the vicinity of the magnetic poles.

It seems probable that the "leakage" of electrons from the outer Van Allen layer causes the auroras. A new burst of electrons from the Sun seems to be caught in the outer layer first. Under the assumption that all electrons are first caught in the outer layer, the time lag can be understood. There has to be an "overflow" from the outer layer to produce an aurora.

The Atmosphere

Astronomically speaking, the presence of our atmosphere is deplorable. Though reasonably transparent to visible light, the atmosphere may absorb as much as 60% of the visible and near-visible light. It is opaque to most other wave-lengths, except certain fairly short radio waves. In addition to absorbing much light, our atmosphere bends light rays entering at a slant (for a given observer) so that the true position of a star close to the horizon is not what it seems to be. One effect is that we see the Sun above the horizon before it actually is. And the unsteady movement of the atmosphere causes the "twinkling" of the stars, which may be romantic but is a nuisance when it comes to observing.

The composition of our atmosphere near the ground is 78% nitrogen and 21% oxygen, the remaining 1% consisting of other gases, most of it argon. The composition stays the same to an altitude of at least 70 miles (except that higher up two impurities, carbon dioxide and water vapor, are missing), but the pressure drops very fast. At 18,000 feet, half of the total mass of the atmosphere is below, and at 100,000 feet, 99% of the mass of the atmosphere is below. The upper limit of the atmosphere is usually given as 120 miles; no definitive figure is possible, since there is no boundary line between the incredibly attenuated gases 120 miles up and space.

Astronomical Telescopes

Optical telescopes used in astronomy are of two basic kinds: refracting and reflecting. In the *refractor telescope,* a lens is used to collect light from a distant object and bring it to a focus. A second lens, the eyepiece, then magnifies the image which may be examined visually or photographed directly. The *reflector telescope* uses a concave mirror instead of a lens, which reflects the light rays back toward the upper end of the telescope where they are magnified and observed or photographed. Most large optical telescopes now being built are reflectors.

Radio telescopes are used to study radio waves coming from outside the Earth's atmosphere. The waves are gathered by an antenna or "dish," which is a parabolic reflecting surface made of metal or finely meshed wire. Radio signals have been received from the Sun, Moon, and planets, and from the center of our galaxy and other galaxies. Radio signals are the means by which the distant and mysterious quasars and pulsars were recently discovered.

Space Telescope Eagerly Awaited

There is a heavy anticipated demand for use of the Space Telescope, when the U.S. Space Shuttle brings the 10-ton satellite into a 500-kilometer (310.5-mile) high orbit in late 1983. The 2.4-meter (7-ft-10½-in.) Space Telescope is designed to last past the end of this century and is to be serviced about every two and a half years by Space Shuttle astronauts. It will be taken back to earth occasionally for overhaul and relaunching during its 20-year lifetime.

Chinese Calendar

The Chinese lunar year is divided into 12 months of 29 or 30 days. The calendar is adjusted to the length of the solar year by the addition of extra months at regular intervals.

The years are arranged in major cycles of 60 years. Each successive year is named after one of 12 animals. These 12-year cycles are continuously repeated. The Chinese New Year is celebrated at the first new moon after the sun enters Aquarius—sometime between Jan. 21 and Feb. 19.

Rat	Ox	Tiger	Cat (Rabbit)	Dragon	Snake	Horse	Sheep (Goat)	Monkey	Rooster	Dog	Pig
1864	1865	1866	1867	1868	1869	1870	1871	1872	1873	1874	1875
1876	1877	1878	1879	1880	1881	1882	1883	1884	1885	1886	1887
1888	1889	1890	1891	1892	1893	1894	1895	1896	1897	1898	1899
1900	1901	1902	1903	1904	1905	1906	1907	1908	1909	1910	1911
1912	1913	1914	1915	1916	1917	1918	1919	1920	1921	1922	1923
1924	1925	1926	1927	1928	1929	1930	1931	1932	1933	1934	1935
1936	1937	1938	1939	1940	1941	1942	1943	1944	1945	1946	1947
1948	1949	1950	1951	1952	1953	1954	1955	1956	1957	1958	1959
1960	1961	1962	1963	1964	1965	1966	1967	1968	1969	1970	1971
1972	1973	1974	1975	1976	1977	1978	1979	1980	1981	1982	1983
1984	1985	1986	1987	1988	1989	1990	1991	1992	1993	1994	1995

Eclipses of the Sun and the Moon, 1983

June 11: Total eclipse of the Sun. Visible in Madagascar, extreme southeast Asia, Indonesia, Australia, and the western part of New Zealand.

June 25: Partial Eclipse of the Moon. The beginning of the umbral phase visible in extreme eastern Australia, New Zealand, Antarctica, the Pacific Ocean, South America, North America except the northern part, and the western Atlantic Ocean, the end visible in South America except the northeastern part, North America except the northeastern part, Antarctica, the Pacific Ocean, New Zealand, and Australia except the extreme northwestern part.

December 4: Annular eclipse of the Sun. Visible in the extreme northeastern part of North America, northeastern part of South America, British Isles, Iceland, Southern Europe, Africa, and southwestern Asia.

December 19–20. Penumbral eclipse of the Moon. The beginning of the penumbral phase will be visible in South America except the southern tip, North America, the Arctic regions, Greenland, the Atlantic Ocean, Africa, Europe, Asia except the far eastern part, and the western part of the Indian Ocean; the end will be visible in Africa except the eastern part, Europe, South America, the Atlantic Ocean, North America, the Arctic regions, the eastern part of the Pacific Ocean, and extreme western and northern Asia.

Phenomena, 1983

Configurations of Sun, Moon, and Planets

NOTE: The hour listings are in Universal Time. For conversion to United States time zones, see conversion table in this section.

JANUARY

d	h	
2	16	Earth at perihelion
6	04	LAST QUARTER
6	18	Mercury stationary
7	10	Mercury 2° N of Venus
7	12	Saturn 2° S of Moon
9	22	Jupiter 2° S of Moon
10	07	Uranus 2° S of Moon
12	01	Neptune 0° 6 N of Moon
14	05	NEW MOON
14	05	Moon at apogee
15	19	Venus 1° 8 N of Moon
16	03	Mercury in inferior conjunction
17	04	Mars 3° N of Moon
18	13	Vesta 0° 8 S of Moon
22	06	FIRST QUARTER
27	10	Mercury stationary
28	11	Moon at perigee
28	22	FULL MOON

FEBRUARY

d	h	
3	00	June in conjunction with Sun
3	21	Saturn 2° S of Moon
4	19	LAST QUARTER
6	13	Jupiter 1° 5 S of Moon
6	16	Uranus 2° S of Moon
7	07	Pluto stationary
8	09	Neptune 0° 8 N of Moon
8	20	Mercury greatest elong. W
10	08	Moon at apogee
10	15	Mercury 2° N of Moon
13	01	NEW MOON
13	08	Saturn stationary
15	02	Venus 4° N of Moon
15	06	Mars 5° N of Moon
15	15	Uranus 5° N of Antares
15	19	Vesta 0° 3 S of Moon
17	05	Jupiter 5° N of Antares
17	14	Jupiter 0° 8 N of Uranus
18	22	Venus 0° 5 S of Mars
20	18	FIRST QUARTER
25	22	Moon at perigee
27	09	FULL MOON

MARCH

d	h	
3	06	Saturn 1° 7 S of Moon
6	00	Uranus 1° 8 S of Moon
6	03	Jupiter 1° 0 S of Moon
6	13	LAST QUARTER
7	17	Neptune 1° 0 N of Moon
9	23	Moon at apogee
14	13	Uranus stationary
14	18	NEW MOON
16	02	Vesta 0° 3 S of Moon
16	06	Mars 5° N of Moon
17	06	Venus 5° N of Moon
21	05	Equinox
22	02	FIRST QUARTER
25	22	Moon at perigee
26	11	Mercury in superior conjunction
28	01	Jupiter stationary
28	19	FULL MOON
30	14	Saturn 1° 5 S of Moon

APRIL

d	h	
1	05	Neptune stationary
2	09	Uranus 1° 6 S of Moon
2	13	Jupiter 0° 6 S of Moon
4	01	Neptune 1° 3 N of Moon
5	09	LAST QUARTER
6	18	Moon at apogee
9	12	Mercury 1° 4 N of Mars
10	19	Uranus 5° N of Antares
13	08	NEW MOON

14 15 Mercury 6° N of Moon
14 18 Vesta in conjunction with Sun
16 07 Venus 4° N of Moon
18 18 Pluto at opposition
20 09 FIRST QUARTER
21 08 Moon at perigee
21 08 Mercury greatest elong. E (20°)
21 19 Saturn at opposition
22 13 Venus 7° N of Aldebaran
26 19 Saturn 1° 6 S of Moon
27 07 FULL MOON
29 17 Uranus 1° 5 S of Moon
29 19 Jupiter 0° 6 S of Moon

MAY

1 09 Neptune 1° 5 N of Moon
2 04 Mercury stationary
4 13 Moon at apogee
5 04 LAST QUARTER
6 06 Jupiter 6° N of Antares
7 21 Pallas stationary
12 17 Mercury in inferior conjunction
12 19 NEW MOON
16 01 Venus 1° 5 N of Moon
16 13 Jupiter 0° 8 N of Uranus
16 16 Moon at perigee
19 14 FIRST QUARTER
23 23 Saturn 1° 8 S of Moon
24 23 Mercury stationary
26 19 FULL MOON
26 21 Jupiter 0° 8 S of Moon
26 23 Uranus 1° 6 S of Moon
27 22 Jupiter at opposition
28 16 Neptune 1° 6 N of Moon
29 01 Uranus at opposition
31 05 Venus 4° S of Pollux

JUNE

1 08 Moon at apogee
3 11 Mars in conjunction with Sun
3 21 LAST QUARTER
8 06 Mercury greatest elong. W. (24°)
9 10 Mercury 0° 8 S of Moon
11 05 NEW MOON (Eclipse)
13 06 Moon at perigee
14 11 Venus 1° 5 S of Moon
16 07 Venus greatest elong. E (45°)
17 20 FIRST QUARTER
19 17 Neptune at opposition
20 03 Saturn 2° S of Moon
21 06 Mercury 4° N of Aldebaran
21 23 Solstice
22 21 Jupiter 1° 2 S of Moon
23 03 Uranus 1° 7 S of Moon
24 22 Neptune 1° 5 N of Moon
25 09 FULL MOON (Eclipse)
28 06 Ceres stationary
28 23 Moon at apogee

JULY

2 13 Saturn stationary
3 12 LAST QUARTER
6 10 Earth at aphelion
8 06 Pallas at opposition
9 16 Mercury in superior conjunction
9 23 Venus 0° 7 S of Regulus
10 12 NEW MOON
11 10 Moon at perigee
13 08 Venus 6° S of Moon
14 08 Pluto stationary
17 03 FIRST QUARTER
17 09 Saturn 2° S of Moon
19 15 Venus greatest brilliancy
19 23 Jupiter 1° 4 S of Moon
20 07 Uranus 1° 7 S of Moon
22 02 Neptune 1° 5 N of Moon
24 23 FULL MOON
26 07 Moon at apogee
29 13 Jupiter stationary

AUGUST

1 02 Mercury 0° 4 N. of Regulus
1 12 Venus stationary
2 01 LAST QUARTER
4 12 Mars 6° S of Pollux
6 06 Mercury 6° N of Venus
7 12 Mars 1° 8 S of Moon
8 19 NEW MOON
8 19 Moon at perigee
10 01 Venus 12° S of Moon
10 11 Mercury 6° S of Moon
13 18 Saturn 1° 9 S of Moon
14 05 Ceres at opposition
14 08 Uranus stationary
15 13 FIRST QUARTER
16 06 Jupiter 1° 3 S of Moon
16 13 Uranus 1° 6 S of Moon
18 07 Neptune 1° 5 N of Moon
19 16 Mercury greatest elong. E (27°)
22 09 Moon at apogee
23 15 FULL MOON
25 05 Venus in inferior conjunction
29 20 Pallas stationary
31 11 LAST QUARTER

SEPTEMBER

1 19 Mercury stationary
5 02 Mars 3° S of Moon
5 14 Venus 13° S of Moon
6 05 Moon at perigee
7 03 NEW MOON
7 20 Mercury 10° S of Moon
8 12 Neptune stationary
10 07 Saturn 1° 7 S of Moon
12 18 Jupiter 0° 9 S of Moon
12 21 Uranus 1° 3 S of Moon
14 02 FIRST QUARTER
14 08 Venus stationary
14 14 Neptune 1° 7 N of Moon
14 19 Venus 9° S of Mars
15 16 Mercury in inferior conjunction
18 17 Moon at apogee
22 07 FULL MOON
23 15 Equinox
24 01 Mercury stationary
24 03 Juno stationary
24 22 Jupiter 0° 4 N of Uranus
28 21 Mars 0° 9N of Regulus
29 20 LAST QUARTER

OCTOBER

1 07 Venus greatest brilliancy
1 10 Mercury greatest elong. W (18°)
3 07 Venus 9° S of Moon
3 16 Mars 4° S of Moon
4 11 Moon at perigee
5 03 Mercury 4° S of Moon
6 11 NEW MOON
7 07 Venus 4° S of Regulus
7 13 Ceres stationary
7 23 Saturn 1° 4 S of Moon
10 08 Uranus 1° 0 S of Moon
10 11 Jupiter 0° 4 S of Moon
11 22 Neptune 2° N of Moon
13 01 Jupiter 5° N of Antares
13 20 FIRST QUARTER
16 08 Moon at apogee
21 22 FULL MOON
23 11 Pluto in conjunction with Sun
24 05 Juno at opposition
25 12 Vesta stationary
23 13 Venus 1° 7 S of Mars
29 04 LAST QUARTER
30 17 Mercury in superior conjunction
31 06 Saturn in conjunction with Sun

NOVEMBER

1 03 Moon at perigee
1 04 Mars 4° S of Moon
1 06 Venus 5° S of Moon
4 20 Venus greatest elong. W (47°)
4 22 NEW MOON
6 20 Uranus 0° 7 S of Moon
7 07 Jupiter 0° 2 N of Moon
8 09 Neptune 2° N of Moon
12 16 FIRST QUARTER
13 03 Moon at apogee
20 04 Mercury 1° 8 S of Uranus
20 07 Mercury 3° N of Antares
20 12 FULL MOON
26 02 Moon at perigee
26 06 Mercury 3° S of Jupiter
27 11 LAST QUARTER
29 15 Venus 4° N of Spica
29 15 Mars 4° S of Moon
30 21 Venus 2° S of Moon

DECEMBER

2 03 Uranus in conjunction with Sun
2 04 Saturn 0° 9 S of Moon
2 23 Juno stationary
3 07 Mercury 4° S of Neptune
4 12 NEW MOON (Eclipse)
5 19 Neptune 2° N of Moon
6 03 Mercury 0° 9 S of Moon
11 01 Moon at apogee
12 13 FIRST QUARTER
13 10 Vesta at opposition
13 21 Mercury greatest elong. E (21°)
14 13 Jupiter in conjunction with Sun
17 11 Venus 0° 2 N of Saturn
20 02 FULL MOON (Penumbral Eclipse)
21 10 Neptune in conjunction with Sun
21 20 Mercury stationary
22 11 Solstice
22 18 Moon at perigee
26 19 LAST QUARTER
27 08 Mars 4° N of Spica
28 00 Mars 3° S of Moon
29 16 Saturn 0° 6 S of Moon
30 19 Venus 0° 7 N of Moon
31 08 Mercury in inferior conjunction
31 18 Uranus 0° 4 S of Moon

The Year in Space—1982

While there were no spectacular headlines to match last year's twin blockbusters of the first Space Shuttle launching and the close-up looks at Jupiter and Saturn provided by the Voyager series, 1982 still provided sufficient new data, some of it gathered from earlier satellites and only recently analyzed, to keep astronomers, astrophysicists and aerospace engineers busy. The Space Shuttle *Columbia* completed its initial series of test flights, changing as it did so from an experimental research vehicle to an operational, if exotic, space transport bus. Elsewhere, new knowledge was gained about our solar system, and about the universe beyond. A number of questions appeared to have found satisfactory answers but, not surprisingly, several new ones have popped up. A few well-established "facts", some of which having profound implications regarding the structure and origin of matter, and of the universe itself, have been shaken thoroughly. For space scientists, 1982 was an exciting year.

Shuttle 3, 4 . . . and Counting

The basic aims of the initial series of Space Shuttle flights were quite simple: aside from delivering a limited number of scientific and military instrument packages, the main objective of *Columbia's* first four missions was to prove that a reusable manned spaceship would work. And work it does: after a thorough examination and a little body and fender repair to replace some missing heat shielding tiles, Astronauts Joe Engle and Richard Truly took the ship back into space for *Columbia's* second mission on November 12, 1981. A balky fuel cell cut their planned 124-hour flight short by more than one half, but over 90% of the mission's goals were satisfactorily accomplished. The spaceship's third flight began on March 22, 1982 with Astronauts Jack R. Lousma and C. Gordon Fullerton at the controls. Shuttle-3 carried a cargo weighing 21,000 pounds, four times that of its predecessor. As usual, there were a few glitches: recall that Shuttle-1 had computers that wouldn't talk to each other; Shuttle-2 had its fuel cell problems; in Shuttle-3's case, it was the weather. While the second flight had to be cut short, the third was extended by more than a day waiting for skies to clear over Edwards Air Force Base, the prime landing site. When the weatherman refused to cooperate, Lousma and Fullerton brought their "bird" home to roost at White Sands Missile Range, New Mexico. Shuttle-4, piloted by Astronauts Ken Mattingly and Henry Hartsfield, completed the initial series of test flights after its launching on June 27. That accomplished, the Space Shuttle was declared operational and ready for the relatively mundane business of trucking people and things from Down Here to Up There, and *vice versa.*

One interesting future Shuttle mission may be to rescue Solar Max, a Sun-studying satellite crippled by faulty electrical circuits. Fortunately, Max was designed with a series of plug-in modules much like the circuit boards in a modern TV set. The malfunctioning modules have been identified and new ones can be completed in time for the March, 1984 rescue. Plans now call for an astronaut to "walk" out to Max, stop it from tumbling by means of his (or her) back-pack transporter jets, then bring it back to the Shuttle's cargo bay, where it can be repaired. More over, Buck Rogers, the Yanks are coming.

A Long, Hard Look

Another mission for some future Shuttle flight will be to carry the Space Telescope, now being readied, into orbit. Since its vision won't be obscured by the atmosphere, the telescope will be able to see a lot farther, and detect much fainter objects, than its earthbound counterparts. If all goes as planned, the telescope will observe light that has travelled 14 billion light-years to reach us. Does such light exist, that is, is the universe as we know it even that old? The question was brought up through new estimates of the Hubble constant, which is a measure of the size, and therefore the age, of the universe. Strange behavior of the X-ray spectra of quasar 1525+227 indicate that the Hubble constant should be closer to 85 or 100, rather than the commonly accepted value of about 50. If the larger value is correct, it would mean that the universe is only about one-half as old as we think it is.

Most astronomers subscribe to the Original Big Bang Theory of the creation of the universe, which states, in elaborate mathematical terms, that the origin consisted of a "singularity" containing only energy at an infinite temperature. Now, a modification of the theory proposes that there wasn't a singularity after all, but something called a de Sitter space. This would have had a very high but finite density, 3×10^{93} grams per cubic centimeter, and a finite temperature, 5×10^{31}°Kelvin. Our universe, and presumably others as well, would have existed in the de Sitter space as primordial bubbles, the surfaces of which would have had properties (called Hawking radiation) similar to the "event horizons" postulated to exist at the boundaries of black holes. Weird. A number of interesting and puzzling oddities were found during the year: The first X-ray burster was detected in a binary system. The burster is thought to be a neutron star whose periodic emissions are caused by matter drawn in from its celestial dancing partner. Two more quasars whose components are apparently moving apart faster than the speed of light have been detected. That brings the total of such "superluminous" objects to six, but it's still not clear whether or not the observed velocities are just an optical illusion. The year also saw the discovery of a "quasi-quasar" object simply called Markarian 335. It looks something like a galaxy, but is more like a number of nebulosities bunched together. The strange thing is that one of the blobs in the bunch seems to be moving around. The hottest known white dwarf star to date has been located in the constellation Ursa Major; it may be a binary with a temperature estimated at 100,000°C. But the strangest discovery of the year was not a star or a quasar, but nothing. Or at least very nearly nothing. One region in the direction of the constellation Boötes is practically devoid of galaxies. It is one million cubic parsecs in extent. (One parsec equals 3.258 light-years.) Space is supposed to contain a fairly uniform dispersion of galaxies and other cosmic flotsam, but there it is: a great big hole in the sky. Strange.

The question of whether our universe is open or closed also came up again. Combined studies of the universe and particle physics point to an open universe, or one that is continually expanding. However, if massive neutrinos (one kind of elementary particle, postulated, but not yet found) exist, the density of the universe may be altered enough to close it.

In Our Neighborhood

Our own solar system provided its share of exciting space news during 1982. Recent analyses of photographs taken by the research satellite P78–1 back in 1979 revealed what appeared to be a comet striking the Sun. The photos clearly show an object approaching the corona, disappearing into it and producing a large halo. No effects were felt on Earth, and the event was not related to the strange spiral sunspot observed early in the year. The sunspot was quite large, about 50,000 miles across, but within a few days it changed to a roughly circular shape and faded away.

Venus was the object of a lot of astronomical attention, principally by the Russian landers Venera 13 and 14. Both unmanned probes transmitted photographs of the Venusian surface: it appeared to be flat and rocky, with a few scattered boulders. In one striking picture, the surface looks as though it had been formed by successive volcanic events, with several of the uppermost rock layers clearly discernible. This, and other evidence from previous US and Soviet Venus probes may mean that the planet has undergone recent volcanism, or perhaps that it is still active. Further indications of volcanic activity came in the form of X-ray fluorescence data sent back by the most recent Venera lander, in which the surface rocks were found to be quite similar to ordinary basalt. The Venusian atmosphere consists mostly of carbon dioxide, but Venera data also indicate measurable concentrations of hydrogen, water, hydrogen sulfide, carbonyl sulfide and sulfur hexafluoride. Nasty. Neither of the Venera probes lasted more than a few hours on the planet's surface, not surprising in that temperatures on Venus are around 890°F and the atmospheric pressure is about 90 times that on the surface of the Earth. Very Nasty.

Something Old, Something New

The Viking 1 Mars orbiter is still working five years after its launching. That's about 20 times its original design life. The satellite is being allowed to loaf along in semi-retirement, sending back only about one picture per week, plus some Martian meteorological data. That information, incidentally, is being logged automatically by computer, since all of the original Viking staff members have long since gone into separate orbits of their own. Meanwhile, something may be orbiting around the ninth asteroid, Metis. Earth telescope observations may have detected a tiny (36-mile diameter) moonlet orbiting around its 95-mile "planet" at a distance of some 687 miles. It hasn't been confirmed yet, but its period appears to be about 4.61 days.

The closer we look, the more we see, at least so it seems at the Saturn ring system. First, the system was thought to consist of a few fairly well-defined rings separated by visible divisions. Voyager 1 showed that there were many more, perhaps a few hundred. Now, Voyager 2 data seems to indicate that the real number is up in the thousands, maybe even tens of thousands. Voyager 2 data is still being scrutinized, and more baffling information continues to pour out of the computers. Saturn's moon count is now at 17, officially, but there are almost certainly up to six more floating around. Strangely, no tiny moons have been found in positions that would explain the oddly braided appearance of the planet's outer F ring. In fact, Voyager 2 photos failed to see any more evidence of braiding at all. The latest pictures did confirm the existence of "spokes" in the larger rings, but final explanations are far from established. The rings themselves are not flat and smooth, but seem to vary in thickness. Passing moons are probably responsible for the recently discovered "density waves", which look almost exactly like the spiral grooves on a phonograph record. Those same gravitational effects may also cause the eccentricity found in the divisions between major rings.

Saturn's moons are being mapped, one by one. As of the date of this publication, at least partial maps of Iapetus, Tethys, Enceladus, Dione and Rhea have been prepared by NASA.

Having given us such dramatic pictures of Jupiter and Saturn, Voyager 2 is now well on its way to Uranus, a journey that will cover some one billion miles and take about four years. It has about a 60% chance of making the trip intact. Not bad, considering it will then have been in service for nine and one-half years and covered two billion miles in all. Not even Volkswagens last that long.

Konrad J.A. Kundig

Lightning Caused by Cosmic Rays

Cosmic rays from space probably provide the extra electric potential that triggers a lightning stroke, according to a report made by Johns Hopkins scientists in the late seventies. Such rays, very high-energy particles moving at almost the speed of light, hit the upper atmosphere as an "air shower." When such a shower passes through a thunderhead, it releases electrons from oxygen and nitrogen atoms through ionization of the air. The free electrons are accelerated by the electric field already existing within the cloud, concentrating enough negative electric charge at the bottom of the cloud to generate a lightning stroke. The first stroke generated is a preliminary "leader stroke" of low luminosity. It travels the zigzag path of least electrical resistance to the ground. When the leader stroke is about 50 yards above the ground, an electric charge leaps up to meet it. These strokes complete the circuit between the cloud and the ground, clearing the way for the powerful return stroke, usually the first lightning seen. Often other strokes follow so quickly that they may seem to be one single stroke.

Manned Space Flight Projects

Mercury. *Project Mercury,* America's first manned space program, was designed to further knowledge about man's capabilities in space. *Mercury 9,* with astronaut Gordon L. Cooper, was the longest flight. It proved conclusively that man can live and work in space for at least 34 hours, despite the high-gravity forces of launch and re-entry, and weightlessness.

Gemini. *Gemini* was an extension of *Project Mercury,* to determine the effects of prolonged space flight on man—two weeks or longer. "Walks in space" provided invaluable information for astronauts' later walks on the Moon. The *Gemini* spacecraft, twice as large as the *Mercury* capsule, accommodated two astronauts.

Apollo. *Apollo* was the designation for the United States' effort to land a man on the Moon and return him safely to Earth. The goal was successfully accomplished with *Apollo 11* on July 20, 1969, culminating eight years of rehearsal and centuries of dreaming. Astronauts Neil A. Armstrong and Col. Edwin E. Aldrin, Jr., scooped up and brought back the first lunar rocks ever seen on Earth—about 47 pounds. Six *Apollo* flights followed, ending with Apollo 17 in December, 1972. The last three *Apollos* carried mechanized vehicles called lunar rovers for wide-ranging surface exploration of the Moon by astronauts. The rendezvous and docking of an *Apollo* spacecraft with a Russian *Soyuz* craft in Earth orbit on July 18, 1975, closed out the *Apollo* program.

Skylab. America's first Earth-orbiting space station. *Project Skylab* was designed to demonstrate that men can work and live in space for prolonged periods without ill effects. Originally the spent third stage of a Saturn 5 moon rocket, *Skylab* measured 118 feet from stem to stern, and carried the most varied assortment of experimental equipment ever assembled in a single spacecraft. Three three-man crews visited the space stations, spending more than 740 hours observing the Sun and bringing home more than 175,000 solar pictures. These were the first recordings of solar activity above Earth's obscuring atmosphere. *Skylab* also evaluated systems designed to gather information on Earth's resources and environmental conditions. *Skylab* biomedical findings indicated that man adapts well to space for at least a period of three months, provided he has a proper diet and adequately programmed exercise, sleep, work, and recreation periods. *Skylab* orbited Earth at a distance of about 300 miles. Five years after the last *Skylab* mission, the 77-ton space station's orbit began to deteriorate faster than expected, owing to unexpectedly high sunspot activity. On July 11, 1979, the parts of *Skylab* that did not burn up in the atmosphere came crashing down on parts of Australia and the Indian Ocean. No one was hurt.

Space Shuttle. The *Space Shuttle* is a new manned space transportation system developed by NASA to reduce the cost of using space for commercial, scientific, and defense needs. In effect, the *Shuttle* is a manned rocket which, after depositing its payload in space, can be flown back to Earth like a conventional airplane and be available for re-use. Because of its versatility and large cargo-carrying capacity, the *Space Shuttle* can combine missions. For example, on one trip to space the *Shuttle* might place a weather satellite and a scientific satellite into different orbits, and then retrieve a communications satellite and return it to Earth for servicing. Or, if the repairs required by the communications satellite were relatively simple, the *Shuttle* might carry technicians who would repair it in orbit. Although most of its cargoes will be unmanned, the *Shuttle* can serve as an inhabited Earth-orbiting laboratory for up to 30 days. The *Space Shuttle Columbia* was successfully launched on April 12, 1981. *See* The Year in Space, p. 379, for details.

Unmanned Planetary and Lunar Programs

Lunar Orbiter. Series of spacecraft designed to orbit the Moon, taking pictures and obtaining data in support of the subsequent manned Apollo landings. The U.S. launched five *Lunar Orbiters* between Aug. 10, 1966 and Aug. 2, 1967.

Mariner. Designation for a series of spacecraft designed to fly past or orbit the planets, particularly Mercury, Venus, and Mars. *Mariners* provided the early information on Venus and Mars. *Mariner 9,* orbiting Mars in 1971, returned the most startling photographs of that planet to date, and helped pave the way for a *Viking* landing in 1976. *Mariner 10* explored Venus and Mercury in 1973 and was the first probe to use a planet's gravity to whip it toward another.

Pioneer. Designation for the United States' first series of sophisticated interplanetary spacecraft. *Pioneers 10* and *11* reached Jupiter in 1973 and 1974 and continued on to explore Saturn and the other outer planets. *Pioneer 11,* renamed *Pioneer Saturn,* examined the Saturn system in September 1979. Significant discoveries were the finding of a small new moon and a narrow new ring. In 1986, *Pioneer 10* will be the first man-made object to escape the solar system. *Pioneer Venus 1* and *2* reached Venus in 1978 and provided detailed information about that planet's surface and atmosphere.

Ranger. NASA's earliest moon exploration program. Spacecraft were designed for a crash landing on the Moon, taking pictures and returning scientific data up to the moment of impact. Provided the first closeup views of the lunar surface. The *Rangers* provided more than 17,000 closeup pictures, giving us more information about the Moon in a few years than in all the time that had gone before.

Surveyor. Series of unmanned spacecraft designed to land gently on the Moon and provide information on the surface in preparation for the manned lunar landings. Their legs were instrumented to return data on the surface hardness of the Moon. *Surveyor* dispelled the fear that Apollo spacecraft might sink several feet or more into the lunar dust.

Viking. Designation for two spacecraft designed to conduct detailed scientific examination of the planet Mars, including a search for life. *Viking 1* landed on July 20, 1976; *Viking 2,* Sept. 3, 1976. More was learned about the Red Planet in a few short months than in all the time that had gone before. But the question of life on Mars remains unresolved.

Voyager. Designation for two spacecraft designed to explore Jupiter and the other outer planets. *Voyager 1* and *Voyager 2* passed Jupiter in 1979 and sent back startling color TV images of that planet and its moons. They took a total of about 33,000 pictures. *Voyager 2* will continue on a trajectory that will take it to Uranus in 1986. *Voyager 1* passed Saturn November 1980 and *Voyager 2* passed Saturn August 1981.

Notable Unmanned Lunar and Interplanetary Probes

Spacecraft	Launch date	Destination	Remarks
Pioneer 1 (U.S.)	Oct. 11, 1958	Moon	Max. alt.: 71,300 mi. Flight duration: 43 h 17.5 min
Pioneer 3 (U.S.)	Dec. 6, 1958	Moon	Max. alt.: 66,654 mi. Discovered outer Van Allen layer.
Lunik 1 (U.S.S.R.)	Sept. 12, 1959	Moon	Landed in area of Mare Serenitatis.
Pioneer 5 (U.S.)	March 11, 1960	Interplanetary	Orbited sun between Earth & Venus. Radio transmission over record distance of 20 million miles.
Ranger 4 (U.S.)	April 23, 1962	Moon	730-lb probe. Impacted on Moon's far side April 26. No transmission.
Mariner 2 (U.S.)	Aug. 27, 1962	Venus	Venus probe. Successful mid-course correction. Passed 21,648 mi. from Venus Dec. 14, 1962. Reported 800°F. surface temp. Contact lost Jan. 3, 1963 at 54 million mi.
Ranger 7 (U.S.)	July 28, 1964	Moon	Impacted near Crater Guericke 68.5 h after launch. Sent 4,316 pictures during last 15 min of flight as close as 1,000 ft above lunar surface.
Mariner 4 (U.S.)	Nov. 28, 1964	Mars	After mid-course correction, passed behind Mars July 14, 1965, taking 22 pictures from about 6,000 mi.
Ranger 8 (U.S.)	Feb. 17, 1965	Moon	809 lb. After 64.9 h, crashed into Mare Tranquilitatis, 2.59° N of lunar equator. Sent 7,137 pictures.
Ranger 9 (U.S.)	March 21, 1965	Moon	After 64.5 h, hit Crater Alphonsus. Sent 5,814 pictures.
Zond 3 (U.S.S.R.)	July 18, 1965	Moon	Sent close-ups of 3 million sq mi. of Moon. Now in solar orbit.
Venera 3 (U.S.S.R.)	Nov. 16, 1965	Venus	2,112 lb. Entered Venus atmosphere (March 1, 1966). No data sent.
Pioneer 6 (U.S.)	Dec. 16, 1965	Interplanetary	Successfully orbiting Sun (every 311 days) to check space conditions between Earth & Venus. Perihelion: 75.6 million mi. Aphelion: 90.7 million mi.
Luna 9 (U.S.S.R.)	Jan. 31, 1966	Moon	3,428 lb. Instrument capsule of 220 lb soft-landed Feb. 3, 1966. Sent back about 30 pictures.
Luna 10 (U.S.S.R.)	March 31, 1966	Moon	540 lb. Orbit achieved April 2, 1966.
Surveyor 1 (U.S.)	May 30, 1966	Moon	Landed June 2, 1966. Sent almost 10,400 pictures, a number after surviving the 14-day lunar night.
Lunar Orbiter 1 (U.S.)	Aug. 10, 1966	Moon	Orbited Moon Aug. 14. 21 pictures sent.
Pioneer 7 (U.S.)	Aug. 17, 1966	Sun Orbit	Orbiting sun (400 days). Perihelion: 92 million mi. Aphelion: 102 million mi.
Luna 11 (U.S.S.R.)	Aug. 24, 1966	Moon	Moon orbit achieved Aug. 27.
Luna 12 (U.S.S.R.)	Oct. 22, 1966	Moon	Moon orbit achieved Oct. 25 for 3.5 h. Transmission difficulties.
Lunar Orbiter 2 (U.S.)	Nov. 7, 1966	Moon	Orbit achieved Nov. 10. Sent hundreds of excellent pictures.
Luna 13 (U.S.S.R.)	Dec. 21, 1966	Moon	Soft-landed 80 h after launch. Good pictures. Drove spike into Moon's surface.
Lunar Orbiter 3 (U.S.)	Feb. 4, 1967	Moon	Orbited Moon Feb. 8. Terminated Oct. 9, 1967. Excellent pictures.
Surveyor 3 (U.S.)	April 17, 1967	Moon	Soft-landed 65 h after launch on Oceanus Procellarum. Scooped and tested lunar soil.
Lunar Orbiter 4 (U.S.)	May 4, 1967	Moon	Achieved orbit May 7. Changed orbit on command.
Venera 4 (U.S.S.R.)	June 12, 1967	Venus	Arrived Oct. 17. Instrument capsule sent temperature and chemical data.
Mariner 5 (U.S.)	June 14, 1967	Venus	Fly-by Oct. 19, confirming Mariner 2 and Venera 4 findings
Surveyor 4 (U.S.)	July 14, 1967	Moon	Contact lost 2.5 min before landing
Explorer 35 (U.S.)	July 19, 1967	Moon	Orbit July 22. Perilune: 500 mi.; apolune: 4000 mi.
Lunar Orbiter 5 (U.S.)	Aug. 2, 1967	Moon	Orbited Aug. 5, Perilune: 125 mi.; apolune: 3,760 mi. Time 3 h 50 min. After filming, was crashed on Moon.
Surveyor 5 (U.S.)	Sept. 8, 1967	Moon	Landed near lunar equator Sept. 10. Radiological analysis of lunar soil. Mechanical claw for digging soil.
Surveyor 6 (U.S.)	Nov. 7, 1967	Moon	Landed in Sinus Medii Nov. 10. Jumped 8 ft to photograph original position. Sent back 11,524 pictures.
Pioneer 8 (U.S.)	Dec. 12, 1967	Sun Orbit	Achieved Solar orbit. Stopped functioning April 28, 1968.
Surveyor 7 (U.S.)	Jan. 6, 1968	Moon	Landed near Crater Tycho Jan. 10. Soil analysis. Sent 3,343 pictures.
Zond 4 (U.S.S.R.)	March 2, 1968	Unknown	Achieved parking orbit but was unable to leave. Re-entered March 3.
Zond 5 (U.S.S.R.)	Sept. 14, 1968	Moon	Circumlunar flight
Pioneer 9 (U.S.)	Nov. 8, 1968	Sun Orbit	Achieved orbit. Six experiments returned solar radiation data.
Zond 6 (U.S.S.R.)	Nov. 10, 1968	Moon	Circumlunar flight

Spacecraft	Launch date	Destination	Remarks
Venera 5 (U.S.S.R.)	Jan. 5, 1969	Venus	Landed May 16, 1969. Returned atmospheric data.
Venera 6 (U.S.S.R.)	Jan. 10, 1969	Venus	Landed May 17, 1969. Sent data as Venera 5.
Mariner 6 (U.S.)	Feb. 24, 1969	Mars	Came within 2000 mi. of Mars July 31, 1969. Sent back data & TV pictures.
Mariner 7 (U.S.)	March 27, 1969	Mars	Came within 2000 mi. of Mars Aug. 5, 1969. Sent back data & TV pictures.
Luna 15 (U.S.S.R.)	July 13, 1969	Moon	Lunar orbiter landed on Moon July 21, 1969 after completing varying orbits.
Zond 7 (U.S.S.R.)	Aug. 8, 1969	Moon	Circumlunar. Recovered Aug. 14, 1969.
Pioneer E (U.S.)	Aug. 27, 1969	Inter-planetary	To obtain data on particles and magnetic fields, but failed to achieve orbit.
Venera 7 (U.S.S.R.)	Aug. 17, 1970	Venus	Reached Venus Dec. 15, 1970. Sent data, apparently from surface, for 58 min.
Luna 16 (U.S.S.R.)	Sept. 12, 1970	Moon	Soft-landed Sept. 20, scooped up rock, returned to earth Sept. 24.
Zond 8 (U.S.S.R.)	Oct. 20, 1970	Moon	Circumlunar. Photographed Moon and Earth. Returned Oct. 27, 1970.
Luna 17 (U.S.S.R.)	Nov. 10, 1970	Moon	Soft-landed on Sea of Rains Nov. 17. Lunokhod 1, self-propelled vehicle, used for first time. Sent TV photos, made soil analysis, etc.
Mars 2 (U.S.S.R.)	May 19, 1971	Mars	Reached Mars Nov. 27. Dropped landing capsule on surface.
Mars 3 (U.S.S.R.)	May 28, 1971	Mars	Like Mars 2. Capsule landed Dec. 2. TV transmission cut short.
Mariner 9 (U.S.)	May 30, 1971	Mars	First craft to orbit Mars, Nov. 13. 7,300 pictures, 1st close-ups of Mars' moon. Transmission ended Oct. 27, 1972.
Luna 19 (U.S.S.R.)	Sept. 28, 1971	Moon	Orbited Moon, making measurements & taking photos. Soft-landed Feb. 21 in Sea of Fertility. Returned Feb. 25 with rock samples.
Pioneer 10 (U.S.)	March 3, 1972	Jupiter	620-million-mile flight path through asteroid belt passed Jupiter Dec. 3, 1973, to give man first close-up of planet. In 1986, will become first man-made object to escape solar system.
Venera 8 (U.S.S.R.)	March 27, 1972	Venus	Landed July 22. Sent signals for 50 min. Capsule burned or crushed because of surface heat and pressure. Sent data on atmosphere and surface.
Luna 21 (U.S.S.R.)	Jan. 8, 1973	Moon	Soft-landed Jan. 16. Lunokhod 2 (moon-car) scooped up soil samples, returned them to Earth Jan. 27.
Pioneer 11 (U.S.)	April 6, 1973	Jupiter	Flew by 25,000 mi. from Jupiter Dec. 3, 1974—3 times closer than Pioneer 10.
Mars 4 (U.S.S.R.)	July 21, 1973	Mars	Arrived Feb. 1974, briefly sending back photos
Mars 5 (U.S.S.R.)	July 25, 1973	Mars	Sister craft of Mars 4
Mariner 10 (U.S.)	Nov. 3, 1973	Venus, Mercury	Passed Venus Feb. 5, 1974. Arrived Mercury March 29, 1974, for man's first close-up look at planet. First time gravity of one planet (Venus) used to whip spacecraft toward another (Mercury).
Luna 22 (U.S.S.R.)	May 29, 1974	Moon	Orbited Moon June 2, 1974
Venera 9 (U.S.S.R.)	June 8, 1975	Venus	Soft-landed Oct. 25, 1976. Photographed surface of planet.
Venera 10 (U.S.S.R.)	June 14, 1975	Venus	(See Venera 9)
Viking 1 (U.S.)	Aug. 20, 1975	Mars	Carrying life-detection labs. Landed July 20, 1976, for detailed scientific research, including pictures.
Viking 2 (U.S.)	Sept. 9, 1975	Mars	Like Viking 1. Landed Sept. 3, 1976.
Luna 24 (U.S.S.R.)	Aug. 9, 1976	Moon	Soft-landed Aug. 18, 1976. Returned soil samples Aug. 22, 1976.
Voyager 1 (U.S.)	Sept. 5, 1977	Jupiter, Saturn, Uranus	Fly-by mission. Reached Jupiter in March 1979; passed Saturn Nov. 1980; to reach Uranus 1986.
Voyager 2 (U.S.)	Sept. 20, 1977	Jupiter, Saturn, Uranus	Like Voyager 1. Encountered Jupiter in July 1979; flew by Saturn Aug. 1981; to pass Uranus 1986; then perhaps Neptune.
Pioneer Venus 1 (U.S.)	May 20, 1978	Venus	Arrived Dec. 4 and orbited Venus, photographing surface and atmosphere.
Pioneer Venus 2 (U.S.)	Aug. 8, 1978	Venus	Four-part multi-probe, landed Dec. 9.
Venera 11 (U.S.S.R.)	Sept. 9, 1978	Venus	Soft-landed Dec. 25, 1978. Transmitted data for 95 minutes.
Venera 12 (U.S.S.R.)	Sept. 14, 1978	Venus	Like Venera 11. Landed Dec. 21 and transmitted data for 1 hour 50 minutes.
Venera 13 (U.S.S.R.)	Oct. 30, 1981	Venus	Landed March 1, 1982. Took first X-ray fluorescence analysis of the planet's surface. Transmitted data 2 hours 7 minutes.
Venera 14 (U.S.S.R.)	Nov. 4, 1981	Venus	Landed March 5, 1982. Like Venera 13, took X-ray fluorescence analysis of Venusian soil.

Notable Manned Space Flights

Designation and country	Date	Astronauts	Orbit: perigee/apogee (km)	Orbital period (min)	Number of orbits	Flight time (h/min)	Remarks
Vostok 1(U.S.S.R.)	April 12, 1961	Yuri A. Gagarin	181/327	89.1	1	1/48	First manned orbital flight
MR III(U.S.)	May 5, 1961	Alan B. Shepard, Jr.	—	—	([1])	0/15	Range 486 km (302 mi.), peak 187 km (116.5 mi.); capsule recovered
MR IV (U.S.)	July 21, 1961	Virgil I. Grissom	—	—	([1])	0/16	Range 487 km, peak 190 km; capsule lost
Vostok 2 (U.S.S.R.)	Aug. 6–7, 1961	Gherman S. Titov	178/257	88.6	17.5	25/18	First long-duration flight
MA VI (U.S.)	Feb. 20, 1962	John H. Glenn, Jr.	161/261	88.5	3	4/55	First American in orbit
MA VII (U.S.)	May 24, 1962	M. Scott Carpenter	161/268	88.3	3	4/56	Overshot landing area; otherwise fine
Vostok 3 (U.S.S.R.)	Aug. 11–15, 1962	Andrian G. Nikolavev	173/221	88.1	64	94/22	Vostoks 3 and 4 approached within 5 km
MA VIII (U.S.)	Oct. 3, 1962	Walter M. Schirra, Jr.	161/283	88.5	6	9/13	First splashdown close to aiming point
MA IX (U.S.)	May 15–16, 1963	L. Gordon Cooper, Jr.	161/267	88.4	22	34/20	Longest Mercury flight
Vostok 5 (U.S.S.R.)	June 14–19, 1963	Valery F. Bykovsky	180/235	88.4	81	119/6	Longest Russian orbital flight to date
Vostok 6 (U.S.S.R.)	June 16–19, 1963	Valentina V. Tereshkova	183/233	88.3	48	70/50	First orbital flight by female cosmonaut
Voskhod 1 (U.S.S.R.)	Oct. 12, 1964	Vladimir M. Komarov; Konstantin P. Feoktistov; Boris G. Yegorov	177/409	90.1	16	24/17	First 3-man orbital flight; also first flight without space suits
Voskhod 2 (U.S.S.R.)	March 18, 1965	Alexei A. Leonov; Pavel I. Belyayev	174/495	90.9	17	26/2	First "space walk" (by Leonov), 10 min
GT III (U.S.)	March 23, 1965	Virgil I. Grissom; John W. Young	161/224	88.3	3	4/53	First manned test of Gemini spacecraft
GT IV (U.S.)	June 3–7, 1965	James A. McDivitt; Edward H. White 2d	161/282	89.0	62	97/48	First American "space walk" (by White), lasting slightly over 20 min
GT VI (U.S.)	Dec. 15–16, 1965	Walter M. Schirra, Jr.; Thomas P. Stafford	151/258	88.7	16	25/52	Orbit was extended to 298 km to make rendezvous with orbiting GT VII
GT VIII (U.S.)	March 16–17, 1966	Neil A. Armstrong; David R. Scott	160/270	88.8	6.5	10/42	Only Gemini flight cut short by malfunction: one thruster kept firing after rendezvous and docking with an orbiting Agena rocket had been accomplished
GT IX (U.S.)	June 3–6, 1966	Thomas P. Stafford; Eugene A. Cernan	167/169	90.0	44	72/21	Rendezvous (but no docking)
GT X (U.S.)	July 18–21, 1966	John W. Young; Michael Collins	165/274	88.8	43	70/47	Docking with orbiting Agena rocket
GT XI (U.S.)	Sept. 12–15, 1966	Charles Conrad, Jr.; Richard F. Gordon, Jr.	161/281	89.0	44	71/17	Docking with orbiting Agena on first orbit; apogee of orbit then extended to 1,368 km (850 mi.)
GT XII (U.S.)	Nov. 11–15, 1966	James A. Lovell, Jr.; Edwin E. Aldrin, Jr.	161/282	89.0	59	94/33	Docking with Agena visually, without computer; co-pilot outside spacecraft for total of 5½ hours
Soyuz 1 (U.S.S.R.)	April 23, 1967	Vladimir M. Komarov	201/224	88.6	17	26/40	First test of Soyuz spacecraft; crashed after re-entry, killing Komarov
Apollo 7 (U.S.)	Oct. 11–22, 1968	Walter M. Schirra, Jr.; Donn F. Eisele; R. Walter Cunningham	233/285	89.9	163	260/9	First manned test of Apollo command module; first live TV transmissions from orbit

Soyuz 3 (U.S.S.R.)	Oct. 26–30, 1968	Georgi T. Beregovoi	204/224	88.6	64	94/51	First manned rendezvous and possible docking by Soviet cosmonaut
Apollo 8 (U.S.)	Dec. 21–27, 1968	Frank Borman; James A. Lovell, Jr.; William A. Anders	—	—	10³	147/00	First spacecraft in circumlunar orbit; TV transmissions from this orbit
Soyuz 5 (U.S.S.R.)	Jan. 15–18, 1969	Boris V. Volynov; Alexei S. Yeliseyev; Yevgeny V. Khrunov	208/232	88.8	49	72/46	Rendezvoused and docked with Soyuz 4; Khrunov and Yeliseyev perform EVA and transfer to Soyuz 4
Apollo 9 (U.S.)	Mar. 3–13, 1969	James A. McDivitt; David R. Scott; Russell L. Schweikart	197/508	91.5	151	241/1	First manned flight of Lunar Module
Apollo 10 (U.S.)	May 18–26, 1969	Thomas P. Stafford; Eugene A. Cernan; John W. Young	—	—	—	192/3	First descent to within 9 miles of Moon's surface by manned craft
Apollo 11 (U.S.)	July 16–24, 1969	Neil A. Armstrong; Edwin E. Aldrin, Jr.; Michael Collins	—	—	—	195/18	First manned landing and EVA on Moon; soil and rock samples collected; experiments left on lunar surface
Soyuz 6 (U.S.S.R.)	Oct. 11–16, 1969	Gorgiy Shonin; Valriy Kabasov	186/221	88.4	80	118/42	Three spacecraft and seven men put into earth orbit simultaneously for first time
Apollo 12 (U.S.)	Nov. 14–24, 1969	Charles Conrad, Jr.; Richard F. Gordon, Jr.; Alan Bean	—	—	—	244/36	Manned lunar landing mission; investigated Surveyor 3 spacecraft; collected lunar samples. EVA time: 15 h 30 min
Apollo 13 (U.S.)	April 11–17, 1970	James A. Lovell, Jr.; Fred W. Haise, Jr.; John L. Swigert, Jr.	—	—	—	142/54	Third manned lunar landing attempt; aborted due to pressure loss in liquid oxygen in service module and failure of fuel cells
Soyuz 9 (U.S.S.R.)	June 1–17, 1970	Andreiyan Nikolayez; Vitaly Sevastianov	236/249	89.3	287	424/59	Mission to test man's ability to withstand long periods of weightlessness
Apollo 14 (U.S.)	Jan. 31–Feb. 9, 1971	Alan B. Shepard; Stuart A. Roosa; Edgar D. Mitchell	—	—	—	216/42	Third manned lunar landing: returned largest amount of lunar material
Soyuz 10 (U.S.S.R.)	April 22–24, 1971	Vladimir A. Shatalov; Alexei S. Yeliseyev; Nikolai Rukavishnikov	208/246	88.9	—	47/46	Linked up for 5½ hours with orbiting space station, Salyut 1
Soyuz 11 (U.S.S.R.)	June 6–30, 1971	Georgiy Tomofeyevich Dobrovolskiy; Vladislav Nikolayevich Volkov; Viktor Ivanovich Patsyev	185/217	88.3	—	569/40	Linked up with first space station, Salyut 1. Astronauts died just before re-entry due to loss of pressurization in spacecraft
Apollo 15 (U.S.)	July 26–Aug. 7, 1971	David R. Scott; James B. Irwin; Alfred M. Worden	—	—	—	295/12	Fourth manned lunar landing; first use of Lunar Rover propelled by Scott and Irwin; first live pictures of LM lift-off from Moon; exploration time: 18 hours
Apollo 16 (U.S.)	April 16–27, 1972	John W. Young; Thomas K. Mattingly; Charles M. Duke, Jr.	—	—	—	265/51	Fifth manned lunar landing; second use of Lunar Rover Vehicle, propelled by Young and Duke. Total exploration time on the Moon was 20 h 14 min, setting new record. Mattingly's in-flight "walk in space" was 1 h 23 min. Approximately 213 lb of lunar rock returned

Designation and country	Date	Astronauts	Orbit: perigee/apogee (km)	Orbital period (min)	Number of orbits	Flight time (h/min)	Remarks
Apollo 17 (U.S.)	Dec. 7–19, 1972	Eugene A. Cernan; Ronald E. Evans; Harrison H. Schmitt	—	—	—	301/51	Sixth and last manned lunar landing; third to carry lunar rover. Cernan and Schmitt, during three EVA's, completed total of 22 h 05 min 3 sec. USS Ticonderoga recovered crew and about 250 lbs of lunar samples.
Skylab SL-1 (U.S.)	May 14, 1973	—	423/440	93.4	—	—	Unmanned portion of Skylab comprised of Orbital Workshop (OWS), Airlock Module (AM), Multiple Docking Adapter (MDA), Apollo Telescope Mount (ATM), Instrument Unit (IU), and Payload Shroud (PS)
Skylab SL-2 (U.S.)	May 25-June 22, 1973	Charles Conrad, Jr.; Joseph P. Kerwin; Paul J. Weitz	401/424	93.2	—	672/50	First manned Skylab launch. Established Skylab Orbital Assembly and conducted scientific and medical experiments
Skylab SL-3 (U.S.)	July 28-Sept. 25, 1973	Alan L. Bean, Jr.; Jack R. Lousma; Owen K. Garriott	401/424	93.2	—	1427/9	Second manned Skylab launch. New crew remained in space for 59 days, continuing scientific and medical experiments and earth observations from orbit.
Skylab SL-4 (U.S.)	Nov. 16, 1973-Feb. 8, 1974	Gerald Carr; Edward Gibson; William Pogue	401/424	93.2	—	2017/16	Third manned Skylab launch; obtained medical data on crew for use in extending the duration of manned space flight; crews "walked in space" 4 times, totaling 44 h 40 min. Longest space mission yet—84 d 1 h 16 min. Splashdown in Pacific, Feb. 9, 1974.
Soyuz 12 (U.S.S.R.)	Sept. 27–29, 1973	Vasily G. Lazarev; Oleg K. Makarov	202/231	88.7	—	50/12	Two-day test flight. First Soviet manned flight since ill-fated Soyuz 11.
Soyuz 13 (U.S.S.R.)	Dec. 18–26, 1973	Pyotr Klimuk; Valentin Lebedev	188/246	88.9	—	188/55	Modified spacecraft to be used for rendezvous with U.S. spacemen in 1975
Soyuz 14 (U.S.S.R.)	July 3–19, 1974	Pavel Popovich; Yuri Artyukhin	201/338	89.9	—	377/29	Crewmen spent two weeks on board Soviet space station Salyut 3
Soyuz 17 (U.S.S.R.)	Jan. 11–Feb. 9, 1975	Col. Aleksey Gubarev; Georgi Grechko				709/20	Crew spent 30 days in Salyut 4 space station, which was launched Dec. 26, 1974 and placed in Earth orbit
Apollo/Soyuz Test Project (U.S. and U.S.S.R.)	July 15–24, 1975 (U.S.)	U.S.: Brig. Gen. Thomas P. Stafford, Vance D. Brand, Donald K. Slayton	152/166	87.7 89.0 (docked)	138 (docked)	216/05	World's first international manned rendezvous and docking in space; aimed at developing a space rescue capability.
	July 15–21, 1975 (U.S.S.R.)	U.S.S.R.: Col. A. A. Leonov, V. N. Kubasov	191/218	91.0 89.0 (docked)	138 (docked)	223/35	Apollo and Soyuz docked and crewmen exchanged visits on July 17, 1975. Mission duration for Soyuz: 142 h 31

							min. For Apollo: 217 h, 28 min.
Soyuz 21 (U.S.S.R.)	July 6–Aug. 24, 1976	Col. Boris Volynov; Lt. Col. Vitali Zholobov	114/409	89.7	—	1218/24	Crew spent 50 days aboard Salyut 5 space station, which was launched June 22
Soyuz 24 (U.S.S.R.)	Feb. 7–25, 1977	Col. V. Gorbatko; Lt. Col. Yuri Glaszkov	173/323	89.5	—	425/23	Docked and transferred to Salyut 5 on Feb. 8. Returned Feb. 25
Soyuz 31 (U.S.S.R.)	Aug. 26–Nov. 2, 1978	Valery Bykovsky; Sigmund Jaehn	337/353	91.4	—	1632/0[2]	Docked with Salyut 6 and Soyuz 29; crew returned in Soyuz 29 on Sept. 3, 1978
Soyuz 33 (U.S.S.R.)	April 11–12, 1979	N. Rukavishnikov; G. Ivanov	—	—	—	—	Commander veteran of Soyuz 16
Soyuz 35 (U.S.S.R.)	April 9–Oct. 11, 1981	Valery Ryumin; Leonid Popov	—	—	—	—	Docked with Salyut 6; Crew set record of 185 days duration in space.
Soyuz T2 (U.S.S.R.)	June 5–9, 1980	Lt. Col. Yuri V. Mayyshev; Vladimir V. Aksenov	—	—	—	—	Docked with Salyut 6; tested new model spacecraft, T2
Columbia (U.S.)	April 12–14, 1981	Capt. Robert L. Crippen; John W. Young	—	—	—	54/20	Maiden voyage of *Space Shuttle,* the first spacecraft designed specifically for re-use up to 100 times.

1. Suborbital flight. 2. Approximate time. 3. Number of orbits around moon. NOTE: The letters MR stand for Mercury (capsule) and Redstone (rocket); MA, for Mercury and Atlas (rocket); GT, for Gemini (capsule) and Titan-II (rocket). The first astronaut listed in the Gemini and Apollo flights is the command pilot. The Mercury capsules had names: MR-III was *Freedom 7,* MR-IV was *Liberty Bell 7,* MA-VI was *Friendship 7,* MA-VII was *Aurora 7,* MA-VIII was *Sigma 7,* and MA-IX was *Faith 7.* The figure 7 referred to the fact that the first group of U.S. astronauts numbered seven men. Only one Gemini capsule had a name: GT-III was called *Molly Brown* (after the Broadway musical *The Unsinkable Molly Brown*); thereafter the practice of naming the capsules was discontinued.

Some Major U.S. Space Projects
Scientific Satellites

Biosatellite. Earth-orbiting biological laboratory, carrying a variety of plants and animals into space to determine effects of weightlessness (zero gravity). *Biosatellite 1,* launched Dec. 14, 1966, was unrecovered. *Biosatellite 2,* launched Sept. 7, 1967, was highly successful. The last in the series, *Biosatellite 3,* launched June 29, 1969, was returned to Earth because of the deteriorating condition of its primate passenger.

Explorer. Largest group of satellites in U.S. space program, used for a variety of scientific purposes in atmosphere, ionosphere and interplanetary space. *Explorer 1,* launched July 1, 1958, was America's first successful satellite. It confirmed the existence of the Van Allen radiation belts which girdle the Earth. First Explorer weighed about 18 lb; current spacecraft average about 100 lb, but some weigh as much as 500 lb. Orbits and design vary.

High Energy Astronomy Observatory (HEAO). Series of space platforms designed for research in high-energy astrophysics—the domain of peculiar astronomical objects such as quasars, pulsars, and black holes in space. Weighing 2,200 lb, *HEAO-1* was launched into a 225-mile Earth orbit Aug. 12, 1977, to perform a detailed X-ray survey of the celestial sphere. After *HEAO-3,* 1979, HEAO scientific instruments will be carried into space by NASA's Space Shuttle.

Nimbus. Advanced meteorological satellites for detailed global weather and atmosphere soundings. Equipped with advanced television cameras and a high resolution infrared camera system, Nimbus can provide both day and night pictures of Earth's cloud cover. The first *Nimbus 1* was launched Aug. 28, 1964.

Relay. Communications satellite system designed to demonstrate feasibility of intercontinental and transoceanic transmission of television and radio signals with a medium-altitude (up to 12,000 miles) radio-equipped satellite. *Relay I* was launched Dec. 13, 1962.

Solar Maximum Mission (S.M.M.). Designed to study solar flares. The 5,100-lb spacecraft is the first to be built so that it could be repaired or retrieved by astronauts flying the space shuttle. The spacecraft, nicknamed Solar Max, was launched into a 356-mile high orbit on Feb. 14, 1980. In January 1981, mechanical failure resulted in the inability to point the craft's instruments precisely for observing solar events. However, much important information was already returned.

Syncom. First communications satellite to be placed in a synchronous Earth orbit for global communication. Three Syncom satellites were launched between Feb. 14, 1963, and Aug. 19, 1964.

Vanguard. Earth-orbiting geodetic survey satellites. *Vanguard 1,* launched March 17, 1958, determined that Earth is slightly pear-shaped.

CALENDAR & HOLIDAYS

1983

JANUARY

S	M	T	W	T	F	S
–	–	–	–	–	–	1
2	3	4	5	6	7	8
9	10	11	12	13	14	15
16	17	18	19	20	21	22
23	24	25	26	27	28	29
30	31					

1—New Year's Day
6—Epiphany

FEBRUARY

S	M	T	W	T	F	S
–	–	1	2	3	4	5
6	7	8	9	10	11	12
13	14	15	16	17	18	19
20	21	22	23	24	25	26
27	28					

2—Groundhog Day
12—Lincoln's Birthday
14—St. Valentine's Day
16—Ash Wednesday
21—Washington's Birthday
27—Purim

MARCH

S	M	T	W	T	F	S
–	–	1	2	3	4	5
6	7	8	9	10	11	12
13	14	15	16	17	18	19
20	21	22	23	24	25	26
27	28	29	30	31		

17– St. Patrick's Day
27—Palm Sunday
29—1st Day of Passover

APRIL

S	M	T	W	T	F	S
–	–	–	–	–	1	2
3	4	5	6	7	8	9
10	11	12	13	14	15	16
17	18	19	20	21	22	23
24	25	26	27	28	29	30

1—Good Friday
3—Easter
24—Daylight Savings Time begins

MAY

S	M	T	W	T	F	S
1	2	3	4	5	6	7
8	9	10	11	12	13	14
15	16	17	18	19	20	21
22	23	24	25	26	27	28
29	30	31				

8—Mother's Day
12—Ascension Day
18—1st Day of Shabuoth
22—Pentecost
29—Trinity Sunday
30—Memorial Day

JUNE

S	M	T	W	T	F	S
–	–	–	1	2	3	4
5	6	7	8	9	10	11
12	13	14	15	16	17	18
19	20	21	22	23	24	25
26	27	28	29	30		

14—Flag Day
19—Father's Day

JULY

S	M	T	W	T	F	S
–	–	–	–	–	1	2
3	4	5	6	7	8	9
10	11	12	13	14	15	16
17	18	19	20	21	22	23
24	25	26	27	28	29	30
31						

4—Independence Day

AUGUST

S	M	T	W	T	F	S
–	1	2	3	4	5	6
7	8	9	10	11	12	13
14	15	16	17	18	19	20
21	22	23	24	25	26	27
28	29	30	31			

SEPTEMBER

S	M	T	W	T	F	S
–	–	–	–	1	2	3
4	5	6	7	8	9	10
11	12	13	14	15	16	17
18	19	20	21	22	23	24
25	26	27	28	29	30	

5—Labor Day
8—1st Day of Rosh Hashana
11– Grand Parent's Day
17—Yom Kippur
22—1st Day of Sukkoth

OCTOBER

S	M	T	W	T	F	S
–	–	–	–	–	–	1
2	3	4	5	6	7	8
9	10	11	12	13	14	15
16	17	18	19	20	21	22
23	24	25	26	27	28	29
30	31					

10—Columbus Day
30—Daylight Savings Time ends
31—Halloween

NOVEMBER

S	M	T	W	T	F	S
–	–	1	2	3	4	5
6	7	8	9	10	11	12
13	14	15	16	17	18	19
20	21	22	23	24	25	26
27	28	29	30			

1—All Saints' Day
1—Election Day
11—Veterans Day
24—Thanksgiving Day
27—1st Sunday of Advent

DECEMBER

S	M	T	W	T	F	S
–	–	–	–	1	2	3
4	5	6	7	8	9	10
11	12	13	14	15	16	17
18	19	20	21	22	23	24
25	26	27	28	29	30	31

1—1st Day of Hanukkah
25—Christmas

Seasons for the Northern Hemisphere, 1983

Eastern Standard Time

March 20, 11:30 p.m., sun enters sign of Aries; spring begins

June 21, 6:09 p.m., sun enters sign of Cancer; summer begins

Sept. 23, 9:42 a.m., sun enters sign of Libra; fall begins

Dec. 22, 5:30 a.m., sun enters sign of Capricorn; winter begins

1982

JANUARY

S	M	T	W	T	F	S
–	–	–	–	–	1	2
3	4	5	6	7	8	9
10	11	12	13	14	15	16
17	18	19	20	21	22	23
24	25	26	27	28	29	30
31						

FEBRUARY

S	M	T	W	T	F	S
–	1	2	3	4	5	6
7	8	9	10	11	12	13
14	15	16	17	18	19	20
21	22	23	24	25	26	27
28						

MARCH

S	M	T	W	T	F	S
–	1	2	3	4	5	6
7	8	9	10	11	12	13
14	15	16	17	18	19	20
21	22	23	24	25	26	27
28	29	30	31			

APRIL

S	M	T	W	T	F	S
–	–	–	–	1	2	3
4	5	6	7	8	9	10
11	12	13	14	15	16	17
18	19	20	21	22	23	24
25	26	27	28	29	30	

MAY

S	M	T	W	T	F	S
–	–	–	–	–	–	1
2	3	4	5	6	7	8
9	10	11	12	13	14	15
16	17	18	19	20	21	22
23	24	25	26	27	28	29
30	31					

JUNE

S	M	T	W	T	F	S
–	–	1	2	3	4	5
6	7	8	9	10	11	12
13	14	15	16	17	18	19
20	21	22	23	24	25	26
27	28	29	30			

JULY

S	M	T	W	T	F	S
–	–	–	–	1	2	3
4	5	6	7	8	9	10
11	12	13	14	15	16	17
18	19	20	21	22	23	24
25	26	27	28	29	30	31

AUGUST

S	M	T	W	T	F	S
1	2	3	4	5	6	7
8	9	10	11	12	13	14
15	16	17	18	19	20	21
22	23	24	25	26	27	28
29	30	31				

SEPTEMBER

S	M	T	W	T	F	S
–	–	–	1	2	3	4
5	6	7	8	9	10	11
12	13	14	15	16	17	18
19	20	21	22	23	24	25
26	27	28	29	30		

OCTOBER

S	M	T	W	T	F	S
–	–	–	–	–	1	2
3	4	5	6	7	8	9
10	11	12	13	14	15	16
17	18	19	20	21	22	23
24	25	26	27	28	29	30
31						

NOVEMBER

S	M	T	W	T	F	S
–	1	2	3	4	5	6
7	8	9	10	11	12	13
14	15	16	17	18	19	20
21	22	23	24	25	26	27
28	29	30				

DECEMBER

S	M	T	W	T	F	S
–	–	–	1	2	3	4
5	6	7	8	9	10	11
12	13	14	15	16	17	18
19	20	21	22	23	24	25
26	27	28	29	30	31	

1984

JANUARY

S	M	T	W	T	F	S
1	2	3	4	5	6	7
8	9	10	11	12	13	14
15	16	17	18	19	20	21
22	23	24	25	26	27	28
29	30	31				

FEBRUARY

S	M	T	W	T	F	S
–	–	–	1	2	3	4
5	6	7	8	9	10	11
12	13	14	15	16	17	18
19	20	21	22	23	24	25
26	27	28	29			

MARCH

S	M	T	W	T	F	S
–	–	–	–	1	2	3
4	5	6	7	8	9	10
11	12	13	14	15	16	17
18	19	20	21	22	23	24
25	26	27	28	29	30	31

APRIL

S	M	T	W	T	F	S
1	2	3	4	5	6	7
8	9	10	11	12	13	14
15	16	17	18	19	20	21
22	23	24	25	26	27	28
29	30					

MAY

S	M	T	W	T	F	S
–	–	–	–	1	2	3
4	5	6	7	8	9	10
11	12	13	14	15	16	17
18	19	20	21	22	23	24
25	26	27	28	29	30	31

JUNE

S	M	T	W	T	F	S
–	–	–	–	–	1	2
3	4	5	6	7	8	9
10	11	12	13	14	15	16
17	18	19	20	21	22	23
24	25	26	27	28	29	30

JULY

S	M	T	W	T	F	S
1	2	3	4	5	6	7
8	9	10	11	12	13	14
15	16	17	18	19	20	21
22	23	24	25	26	27	28
29	30	31				

AUGUST

S	M	T	W	T	F	S
–	–	–	1	2	3	4
5	6	7	8	9	10	11
12	13	14	15	16	17	18
19	20	21	22	23	24	25
26	27	28	29	30	31	

SEPTEMBER

S	M	T	W	T	F	S
–	–	–	–	–	–	1
2	3	4	5	6	7	8
9	10	11	12	13	14	15
16	17	18	19	20	21	22
23	24	25	26	27	28	29
30						

OCTOBER

S	M	T	W	T	F	S
–	1	2	3	4	5	6
7	8	9	10	11	12	13
14	15	16	17	18	19	20
21	22	23	24	25	26	27
28	29	30				

NOVEMBER

S	M	T	W	T	F	S
–	–	–	–	1	2	3
4	5	6	7	8	9	10
11	12	13	14	15	16	17
18	19	20	21	22	23	24
25	26	27	28	29	30	31

DECEMBER

S	M	T	W	T	F	S
–	–	–	–	–	–	1
2	3	4	5	6	7	8
9	10	11	12	13	14	15
16	17	18	19	20	21	22
23	24	25	26	27	28	29
30	31					

PERPETUAL CALENDAR

1800 ... 4	1844 ... 9	1888 ... 8	1932 ... 13	1976 ... 12	2020 ... 11
1801 ... 5	1845 ... 4	1889 ... 3	1933 ... 1	1977 ... 7	2021 ... 6
1802 ... 6	1846 ... 5	1890 ... 4	1934 ... 2	1978 ... 1	2022 ... 7
1803 ... 7	1847 ... 6	1891 ... 5	1935 ... 3	1979 ... 2	2023 ... 1
1804 ... 8	1848 ... 14	1892 ... 13	1936 ... 11	1980 ... 10	2024 ... 9
1805 ... 3	1849 ... 2	1893 ... 1	1937 ... 6	1981 ... 5	2025 ... 4
1806 ... 4	1850 ... 3	1894 ... 2	1938 ... 7	1982 ... 6	2026 ... 5
1807 ... 5	1851 ... 4	1895 ... 3	1939 ... 1	1983 ... 7	2027 ... 6
1808 ... 13	1852 ... 12	1896 ... 11	1940 ... 9	1984 ... 8	2028 ... 14
1809 ... 1	1853 ... 7	1897 ... 6	1941 ... 4	1985 ... 3	2029 ... 2
1810 ... 2	1854 ... 1	1898 ... 7	1942 ... 5	1986 ... 4	2030 ... 3
1811 ... 3	1855 ... 2	1899 ... 1	1943 ... 6	1987 ... 5	2031 ... 4
1812 ... 11	1856 ... 10	1900 ... 2	1944 ... 14	1988 ... 13	2032 ... 12
1813 ... 6	1857 ... 5	1901 ... 3	1945 ... 2	1989 ... 1	2033 ... 7
1814 ... 7	1858 ... 6	1902 ... 4	1946 ... 3	1990 ... 2	2034 ... 1
1815 ... 1	1859 ... 7	1903 ... 5	1947 ... 4	1991 ... 3	2035 ... 2
1816 ... 9	1860 ... 8	1904 ... 13	1948 ... 12	1992 ... 11	2036 ... 10
1817 ... 4	1861 ... 3	1905 ... 1	1949 ... 7	1993 ... 6	2037 ... 5
1818 ... 5	1862 ... 4	1906 ... 2	1950 ... 1	1994 ... 7	2038 ... 6
1819 ... 6	1863 ... 5	1907 ... 3	1951 ... 2	1995 ... 1	2039 ... 7
1820 ... 14	1864 ... 13	1908 ... 11	1952 ... 10	1996 ... 9	2040 ... 8
1821 ... 2	1865 ... 1	1909 ... 6	1953 ... 5	1997 ... 4	2041 ... 3
1822 ... 3	1866 ... 2	1910 ... 7	1954 ... 6	1998 ... 5	2042 ... 4
1823 ... 4	1867 ... 3	1911 ... 1	1955 ... 7	1999 ... 6	2043 ... 5
1824 ... 12	1868 ... 11	1912 ... 9	1956 ... 8	2000 ... 14	2044 ... 13
1825 ... 7	1869 ... 6	1913 ... 4	1957 ... 3	2001 ... 2	2045 ... 1
1826 ... 1	1870 ... 7	1914 ... 5	1958 ... 4	2002 ... 3	2046 ... 2
1827 ... 2	1871 ... 1	1915 ... 6	1959 ... 5	2003 ... 4	2047 ... 3
1828 ... 10	1872 ... 9	1916 ... 14	1960 ... 13	2004 ... 12	2048 ... 11
1829 ... 5	1873 ... 4	1917 ... 2	1961 ... 1	2005 ... 7	2049 ... 6
1830 ... 6	1874 ... 5	1918 ... 3	1962 ... 2	2006 ... 1	2050 ... 7
1831 ... 7	1875 ... 6	1919 ... 4	1963 ... 3	2007 ... 2	2051 ... 1
1832 ... 8	1876 ... 14	1920 ... 12	1964 ... 11	2008 ... 10	2052 ... 9
1833 ... 3	1877 ... 2	1921 ... 7	1965 ... 6	2009 ... 5	2053 ... 4
1834 ... 4	1878 ... 3	1922 ... 1	1966 ... 7	2010 ... 6	2054 ... 5
1835 ... 5	1879 ... 4	1923 ... 2	1967 ... 1	2011 ... 7	2055 ... 6
1836 ... 13	1880 ... 12	1924 ... 10	1968 ... 9	2012 ... 8	2056 ... 14
1837 ... 1	1881 ... 7	1925 ... 5	1969 ... 4	2013 ... 3	2057 ... 2
1838 ... 2	1882 ... 1	1926 ... 6	1970 ... 5	2014 ... 4	2058 ... 3
1839 ... 3	1883 ... 2	1927 ... 7	1971 ... 6	2015 ... 5	2059 ... 4
1840 ... 11	1884 ... 10	1928 ... 8	1972 ... 14	2016 ... 13	2060 ... 12
1841 ... 6	1885 ... 5	1929 ... 3	1973 ... 2	2017 ... 1	2061 ... 7
1842 ... 7	1886 ... 6	1930 ... 4	1974 ... 3	2018 ... 2	2062 ... 1
1843 ... 1	1887 ... 7	1931 ... 5	1975 ... 4	2019 ... 3	2063 ... 2

DIRECTIONS: The number given with each year in the key above is number of calendar to use for that year

1

JANUARY

S	M	T	W	T	F	S
1	2	3	4	5	6	7
8	9	10	11	12	13	14
15	16	17	18	19	20	21
22	23	24	25	26	27	28
29	30	31				

FEBRUARY

S	M	T	W	T	F	S
			1	2	3	4
5	6	7	8	9	10	11
12	13	14	15	16	17	18
19	20	21	22	23	24	25
26	27	28				

MARCH

S	M	T	W	T	F	S
			1	2	3	4
5	6	7	8	9	10	11
12	13	14	15	16	17	18
19	20	21	22	23	24	25
26	27	28	29	30	31	

APRIL

S	M	T	W	T	F	S
						1
2	3	4	5	6	7	8
9	10	11	12	13	14	15
16	17	18	19	20	21	22
23	24	25	26	27	28	29
30						

MAY

S	M	T	W	T	F	S
	1	2	3	4	5	6
7	8	9	10	11	12	13
14	15	16	17	18	19	20
21	22	23	24	25	26	27
28	29	30	31			

JUNE

S	M	T	W	T	F	S
				1	2	3
4	5	6	7	8	9	10
11	12	13	14	15	16	17
18	19	20	21	22	23	24
25	26	27	28	29	30	

JULY

S	M	T	W	T	F	S
						1
2	3	4	5	6	7	8
9	10	11	12	13	14	15
16	17	18	19	20	21	22
23	24	25	26	27	28	29
30	31					

AUGUST

S	M	T	W	T	F	S
		1	2	3	4	5
6	7	8	9	10	11	12
13	14	15	16	17	18	19
20	21	22	23	24	25	26
27	28	29	30	31		

SEPTEMBER

S	M	T	W	T	F	S
					1	2
3	4	5	6	7	8	9
10	11	12	13	14	15	16
17	18	19	20	21	22	23
24	25	26	27	28	29	30

OCTOBER

S	M	T	W	T	F	S
1	2	3	4	5	6	7
8	9	10	11	12	13	14
15	16	17	18	19	20	21
22	23	24	25	26	27	28
29	30	31				

NOVEMBER

S	M	T	W	T	F	S
			1	2	3	4
5	6	7	8	9	10	11
12	13	14	15	16	17	18
19	20	21	22	23	24	25
26	27	28	29	30		

DECEMBER

S	M	T	W	T	F	S
					1	2
3	4	5	6	7	8	9
10	11	12	13	14	15	16
17	18	19	20	21	22	23
24	25	26	27	28	29	30
31						

2

JANUARY

S	M	T	W	T	F	S
	1	2	3	4	5	6
7	8	9	10	11	12	13
14	15	16	17	18	19	20
21	22	23	24	25	26	27
28	29	30	31			

FEBRUARY

S	M	T	W	T	F	S
				1	2	3
4	5	6	7	8	9	10
11	12	13	14	15	16	17
18	19	20	21	22	23	24
25	26	27	28			

MARCH

S	M	T	W	T	F	S
				1	2	3
4	5	6	7	8	9	10
11	12	13	14	15	16	17
18	19	20	21	22	23	24
25	26	27	28	29	30	31

APRIL

S	M	T	W	T	F	S
1	2	3	4	5	6	7
8	9	10	11	12	13	14
15	16	17	18	19	20	21
22	23	24	25	26	27	28
29	30					

MAY

S	M	T	W	T	F	S
		1	2	3	4	5
6	7	8	9	10	11	12
13	14	15	16	17	18	19
20	21	22	23	24	25	26
27	28	29	30	31		

JUNE

S	M	T	W	T	F	S
					1	2
3	4	5	6	7	8	9
10	11	12	13	14	15	16
17	18	19	20	21	22	23
24	25	26	27	28	29	30

JULY

S	M	T	W	T	F	S
1	2	3	4	5	6	7
8	9	10	11	12	13	14
15	16	17	18	19	20	21
22	23	24	25	26	27	28
29	30	31				

AUGUST

S	M	T	W	T	F	S
			1	2	3	4
5	6	7	8	9	10	11
12	13	14	15	16	17	18
19	20	21	22	23	24	25
26	27	28	29	30	31	

SEPTEMBER

S	M	T	W	T	F	S
						1
2	3	4	5	6	7	8
9	10	11	12	13	14	15
16	17	18	19	20	21	22
23	24	25	26	27	28	29
30						

OCTOBER

S	M	T	W	T	F	S
	1	2	3	4	5	6
7	8	9	10	11	12	13
14	15	16	17	18	19	20
21	22	23	24	25	26	27
28	29	30	31			

NOVEMBER

S	M	T	W	T	F	S
				1	2	3
4	5	6	7	8	9	10
11	12	13	14	15	16	17
18	19	20	21	22	23	24
25	26	27	28	29	30	

DECEMBER

S	M	T	W	T	F	S
						1
2	3	4	5	6	7	8
9	10	11	12	13	14	15
16	17	18	19	20	21	22
23	24	25	26	27	28	29
30	31					

3

JANUARY

S	M	T	W	T	F	S
		1	2	3	4	5
6	7	8	9	10	11	12
13	14	15	16	17	18	19
20	21	22	23	24	25	26
27	28	29	30	31		

FEBRUARY

S	M	T	W	T	F	S
					1	2
3	4	5	6	7	8	9
10	11	12	13	14	15	16
17	18	19	20	21	22	23
24	25	26	27	28		

MARCH

S	M	T	W	T	F	S
					1	2
3	4	5	6	7	8	9
10	11	12	13	14	15	16
17	18	19	20	21	22	23
24	25	26	27	28	29	30
31						

APRIL

S	M	T	W	T	F	S
	1	2	3	4	5	6
7	8	9	10	11	12	13
14	15	16	17	18	19	20
21	22	23	24	25	26	27
28	29	30				

MAY

S	M	T	W	T	F	S
			1	2	3	4
5	6	7	8	9	10	11
12	13	14	15	16	17	18
19	20	21	22	23	24	25
26	27	28	29	30	31	

JUNE

S	M	T	W	T	F	S
						1
2	3	4	5	6	7	8
9	10	11	12	13	14	15
16	17	18	19	20	21	22
23	24	25	26	27	28	29
30						

JULY

S	M	T	W	T	F	S
	1	2	3	4	5	6
7	8	9	10	11	12	13
14	15	16	17	18	19	20
21	22	23	24	25	26	27
28	29	30	31			

AUGUST

S	M	T	W	T	F	S
				1	2	3
4	5	6	7	8	9	10
11	12	13	14	15	16	17
18	19	20	21	22	23	24
25	26	27	28	29	30	31

SEPTEMBER

S	M	T	W	T	F	S
1	2	3	4	5	6	7
8	9	10	11	12	13	14
15	16	17	18	19	20	21
22	23	24	25	26	27	28
29	30					

OCTOBER

S	M	T	W	T	F	S
		1	2	3	4	5
6	7	8	9	10	11	12
13	14	15	16	17	18	19
20	21	22	23	24	25	26
27	28	29	30	31		

NOVEMBER

S	M	T	W	T	F	S
					1	2
3	4	5	6	7	8	9
10	11	12	13	14	15	16
17	18	19	20	21	22	23
24	25	26	27	28	29	30

DECEMBER

S	M	T	W	T	F	S
1	2	3	4	5	6	7
8	9	10	11	12	13	14
15	16	17	18	19	20	21
22	23	24	25	26	27	28
29	30	31				

4

JANUARY

S	M	T	W	T	F	S
			1	2	3	4
5	6	7	8	9	10	11
12	13	14	15	16	17	18
19	20	21	22	23	24	25
26	27	28	29	30	31	

FEBRUARY

S	M	T	W	T	F	S
						1
2	3	4	5	6	7	8
9	10	11	12	13	14	15
16	17	18	19	20	21	22
23	24	25	26	27	28	

MARCH

S	M	T	W	T	F	S
						1
2	3	4	5	6	7	8
9	10	11	12	13	14	15
16	17	18	19	20	21	22
23	24	25	26	27	28	29
30	31					

APRIL

S	M	T	W	T	F	S
		1	2	3	4	5
6	7	8	9	10	11	12
13	14	15	16	17	18	19
20	21	22	23	24	25	26
27	28	29	30			

MAY

S	M	T	W	T	F	S
				1	2	3
4	5	6	7	8	9	10
11	12	13	14	15	16	17
18	19	20	21	22	23	24
25	26	27	28	29	30	31

JUNE

S	M	T	W	T	F	S
1	2	3	4	5	6	7
8	9	10	11	12	13	14
15	16	17	18	19	20	21
22	23	24	25	26	27	28
29	30					

JULY

S	M	T	W	T	F	S
		1	2	3	4	5
6	7	8	9	10	11	12
13	14	15	16	17	18	19
20	21	22	23	24	25	26
27	28	29	30	31		

AUGUST

S	M	T	W	T	F	S
					1	2
3	4	5	6	7	8	9
10	11	12	13	14	15	16
17	18	19	20	21	22	23
24	25	26	27	28	29	30
31						

SEPTEMBER

S	M	T	W	T	F	S
	1	2	3	4	5	6
7	8	9	10	11	12	13
14	15	16	17	18	19	20
21	22	23	24	25	26	27
28	29	30				

OCTOBER

S	M	T	W	T	F	S
			1	2	3	4
5	6	7	8	9	10	11
12	13	14	15	16	17	18
19	20	21	22	23	24	25
26	27	28	29	30	31	

NOVEMBER

S	M	T	W	T	F	S
						1
2	3	4	5	6	7	8
9	10	11	12	13	14	15
16	17	18	19	20	21	22
23	24	25	26	27	28	29
30						

DECEMBER

S	M	T	W	T	F	S
	1	2	3	4	5	6
7	8	9	10	11	12	13
14	15	16	17	18	19	20
21	22	23	24	25	26	27
28	29	30	31			

5

JANUARY

S	M	T	W	T	F	S
				1	2	3
4	5	6	7	8	9	10
11	12	13	14	15	16	17
18	19	20	21	22	23	24
25	26	27	28	29	30	31

FEBRUARY

S	M	T	W	T	F	S
1	2	3	4	5	6	7
8	9	10	11	12	13	14
15	16	17	18	19	20	21
22	23	24	25	26	27	28

MARCH

S	M	T	W	T	F	S
1	2	3	4	5	6	7
8	9	10	11	12	13	14
15	16	17	18	19	20	21
22	23	24	25	26	27	28
29	30	31				

APRIL

S	M	T	W	T	F	S
			1	2	3	4
5	6	7	8	9	10	11
12	13	14	15	16	17	18
19	20	21	22	23	24	25
26	27	28	29	30		

MAY

S	M	T	W	T	F	S
					1	2
3	4	5	6	7	8	9
10	11	12	13	14	15	16
17	18	19	20	21	22	23
24	25	26	27	28	29	30
31						

JUNE

S	M	T	W	T	F	S
	1	2	3	4	5	6
7	8	9	10	11	12	13
14	15	16	17	18	19	20
21	22	23	24	25	26	27
28	29	30				

JULY

S	M	T	W	T	F	S
			1	2	3	4
5	6	7	8	9	10	11
12	13	14	15	16	17	18
19	20	21	22	23	24	25
26	27	28	29	30	31	

AUGUST

S	M	T	W	T	F	S
						1
2	3	4	5	6	7	8
9	10	11	12	13	14	15
16	17	18	19	20	21	22
23	24	25	26	27	28	29
30	31					

SEPTEMBER

S	M	T	W	T	F	S
		1	2	3	4	5
6	7	8	9	10	11	12
13	14	15	16	17	18	19
20	21	22	23	24	25	26
27	28	29	30			

OCTOBER

S	M	T	W	T	F	S
				1	2	3
4	5	6	7	8	9	10
11	12	13	14	15	16	17
18	19	20	21	22	23	24
25	26	27	28	29	30	31

NOVEMBER

S	M	T	W	T	F	S
1	2	3	4	5	6	7
8	9	10	11	12	13	14
15	16	17	18	19	20	21
22	23	24	25	26	27	28
29	30					

DECEMBER

S	M	T	W	T	F	S
		1	2	3	4	5
6	7	8	9	10	11	12
13	14	15	16	17	18	19
20	21	22	23	24	25	26
27	28	29	30	31		

6

JANUARY

S	M	T	W	T	F	S
					1	2
3	4	5	6	7	8	9
10	11	12	13	14	15	16
17	18	19	20	21	22	23
24	25	26	27	28	29	30
31						

FEBRUARY

S	M	T	W	T	F	S
	1	2	3	4	5	6
7	8	9	10	11	12	13
14	15	16	17	18	19	20
21	22	23	24	25	26	27
28						

MARCH

S	M	T	W	T	F	S
	1	2	3	4	5	6
7	8	9	10	11	12	13
14	15	16	17	18	19	20
21	22	23	24	25	26	27
28	29	30	31			

APRIL

S	M	T	W	T	F	S
				1	2	3
4	5	6	7	8	9	10
11	12	13	14	15	16	17
18	19	20	21	22	23	24
25	26	27	28	29	30	

MAY

S	M	T	W	T	F	S
						1
2	3	4	5	6	7	8
9	10	11	12	13	14	15
16	17	18	19	20	21	22
23	24	25	26	27	28	29
30	31					

JUNE

S	M	T	W	T	F	S
		1	2	3	4	5
6	7	8	9	10	11	12
13	14	15	16	17	18	19
20	21	22	23	24	25	26
27	28	29	30			

JULY

S	M	T	W	T	F	S
				1	2	3
4	5	6	7	8	9	10
11	12	13	14	15	16	17
18	19	20	21	22	23	24
25	26	27	28	29	30	31

AUGUST

S	M	T	W	T	F	S
1	2	3	4	5	6	7
8	9	10	11	12	13	14
15	16	17	18	19	20	21
22	23	24	25	26	27	28
29	30	31				

SEPTEMBER

S	M	T	W	T	F	S
			1	2	3	4
5	6	7	8	9	10	11
12	13	14	15	16	17	18
19	20	21	22	23	24	25
26	27	28	29	30		

OCTOBER

S	M	T	W	T	F	S
					1	2
3	4	5	6	7	8	9
10	11	12	13	14	15	16
17	18	19	20	21	22	23
24	25	26	27	28	29	30
31						

NOVEMBER

S	M	T	W	T	F	S
	1	2	3	4	5	6
7	8	9	10	11	12	13
14	15	16	17	18	19	20
21	22	23	24	25	26	27
28	29	30				

DECEMBER

S	M	T	W	T	F	S
			1	2	3	4
5	6	7	8	9	10	11
12	13	14	15	16	17	18
19	20	21	22	23	24	25
26	27	28	29	30	31	

7

JANUARY

S	M	T	W	T	F	S
						1
2	3	4	5	6	7	8
9	10	11	12	13	14	15
16	17	18	19	20	21	22
23	24	25	26	27	28	29
30	31					

FEBRUARY

S	M	T	W	T	F	S
		1	2	3	4	5
6	7	8	9	10	11	12
13	14	15	16	17	18	19
20	21	22	23	24	25	26
27	28					

MARCH

S	M	T	W	T	F	S
		1	2	3	4	5
6	7	8	9	10	11	12
13	14	15	16	17	18	19
20	21	22	23	24	25	26
27	28	29	30	31		

APRIL

S	M	T	W	T	F	S
					1	2
3	4	5	6	7	8	9
10	11	12	13	14	15	16
17	18	19	20	21	22	23
24	25	26	27	28	29	30

MAY

S	M	T	W	T	F	S
1	2	3	4	5	6	7
8	9	10	11	12	13	14
15	16	17	18	19	20	21
22	23	24	25	26	27	28
29	30	31				

JUNE

S	M	T	W	T	F	S
			1	2	3	4
5	6	7	8	9	10	11
12	13	14	15	16	17	18
19	20	21	22	23	24	25
26	27	28	29	30		

JULY

S	M	T	W	T	F	S
					1	2
3	4	5	6	7	8	9
10	11	12	13	14	15	16
17	18	19	20	21	22	23
24	25	26	27	28	29	30
31						

AUGUST

S	M	T	W	T	F	S
	1	2	3	4	5	6
7	8	9	10	11	12	13
14	15	16	17	18	19	20
21	22	23	24	25	26	27
28	29	30	31			

SEPTEMBER

S	M	T	W	T	F	S
				1	2	3
4	5	6	7	8	9	10
11	12	13	14	15	16	17
18	19	20	21	22	23	24
25	26	27	28	29	30	

OCTOBER

S	M	T	W	T	F	S
						1
2	3	4	5	6	7	8
9	10	11	12	13	14	15
16	17	18	19	20	21	22
23	24	25	26	27	28	29
30	31					

NOVEMBER

S	M	T	W	T	F	S
		1	2	3	4	5
6	7	8	9	10	11	12
13	14	15	16	17	18	19
20	21	22	23	24	25	26
27	28	29	30			

DECEMBER

S	M	T	W	T	F	S
				1	2	3
4	5	6	7	8	9	10
11	12	13	14	15	16	17
18	19	20	21	22	23	24
25	26	27	28	29	30	31

8

JANUARY

S	M	T	W	T	F	S
1	2	3	4	5	6	7
8	9	10	11	12	13	14
15	16	17	18	19	20	21
22	23	24	25	26	27	28
29	30	31				

FEBRUARY

S	M	T	W	T	F	S
			1	2	3	4
5	6	7	8	9	10	11
12	13	14	15	16	17	18
19	20	21	22	23	24	25
26	27	28	29			

MARCH

S	M	T	W	T	F	S
				1	2	3
4	5	6	7	8	9	10
11	12	13	14	15	16	17
18	19	20	21	22	23	24
25	26	27	28	29	30	31

APRIL

S	M	T	W	T	F	S
1	2	3	4	5	6	7
8	9	10	11	12	13	14
15	16	17	18	19	20	21
22	23	24	25	26	27	28
29	30					

MAY

S	M	T	W	T	F	S
		1	2	3	4	5
6	7	8	9	10	11	12
13	14	15	16	17	18	19
20	21	22	23	24	25	26
27	28	29	30	31		

JUNE

S	M	T	W	T	F	S
					1	2
3	4	5	6	7	8	9
10	11	12	13	14	15	16
17	18	19	20	21	22	23
24	25	26	27	28	29	30

JULY

S	M	T	W	T	F	S
1	2	3	4	5	6	7
8	9	10	11	12	13	14
15	16	17	18	19	20	21
22	23	24	25	26	27	28
29	30	31				

AUGUST

S	M	T	W	T	F	S
			1	2	3	4
5	6	7	8	9	10	11
12	13	14	15	16	17	18
19	20	21	22	23	24	25
26	27	28	29	30	31	

SEPTEMBER

S	M	T	W	T	F	S
						1
2	3	4	5	6	7	8
9	10	11	12	13	14	15
16	17	18	19	20	21	22
23	24	25	26	27	28	29
30						

OCTOBER

S	M	T	W	T	F	S
	1	2	3	4	5	6
7	8	9	10	11	12	13
14	15	16	17	18	19	20
21	22	23	24	25	26	27
28	29	30	31			

NOVEMBER

S	M	T	W	T	F	S
				1	2	3
4	5	6	7	8	9	10
11	12	13	14	15	16	17
18	19	20	21	22	23	24
25	26	27	28	29	30	

DECEMBER

S	M	T	W	T	F	S
						1
2	3	4	5	6	7	8
9	10	11	12	13	14	15
16	17	18	19	20	21	22
23	24	25	26	27	28	29
30	31					

9

JANUARY

S	M	T	W	T	F	S
	1	2	3	4	5	6
7	8	9	10	11	12	13
14	15	16	17	18	19	20
21	22	23	24	25	26	27
28	29	30	31			

FEBRUARY

S	M	T	W	T	F	S
				1	2	3
4	5	6	7	8	9	10
11	12	13	14	15	16	17
18	19	20	21	22	23	24
25	26	27	28	29		

MARCH

S	M	T	W	T	F	S
					1	2
3	4	5	6	7	8	9
10	11	12	13	14	15	16
17	18	19	20	21	22	23
24	25	26	27	28	29	30
31						

APRIL

S	M	T	W	T	F	S
	1	2	3	4	5	6
7	8	9	10	11	12	13
14	15	16	17	18	19	20
21	22	23	24	25	26	27
28	29	30				

MAY

S	M	T	W	T	F	S
			1	2	3	4
5	6	7	8	9	10	11
12	13	14	15	16	17	18
19	20	21	22	23	24	25
26	27	28	29	30	31	

JUNE

S	M	T	W	T	F	S
						1
2	3	4	5	6	7	8
9	10	11	12	13	14	15
16	17	18	19	20	21	22
23	24	25	26	27	28	29
30						

JULY

S	M	T	W	T	F	S
	1	2	3	4	5	6
7	8	9	10	11	12	13
14	15	16	17	18	19	20
21	22	23	24	25	26	27
28	29	30	31			

AUGUST

S	M	T	W	T	F	S
				1	2	3
4	5	6	7	8	9	10
11	12	13	14	15	16	17
18	19	20	21	22	23	24
25	26	27	28	29	30	31

SEPTEMBER

S	M	T	W	T	F	S
1	2	3	4	5	6	7
8	9	10	11	12	13	14
15	16	17	18	19	20	21
22	23	24	25	26	27	28
29	30					

OCTOBER

S	M	T	W	T	F	S
		1	2	3	4	5
6	7	8	9	10	11	12
13	14	15	16	17	18	19
20	21	22	23	24	25	26
27	28	29	30	31		

NOVEMBER

S	M	T	W	T	F	S
					1	2
3	4	5	6	7	8	9
10	11	12	13	14	15	16
17	18	19	20	21	22	23
24	25	26	27	28	29	30

DECEMBER

S	M	T	W	T	F	S
1	2	3	4	5	6	7
8	9	10	11	12	13	14
15	16	17	18	19	20	21
22	23	24	25	26	27	28
29	30	31				

10

JANUARY

S	M	T	W	T	F	S
		1	2	3	4	5
6	7	8	9	10	11	12
13	14	15	16	17	18	19
20	21	22	23	24	25	26
27	28	29	30	31		

FEBRUARY

S	M	T	W	T	F	S
					1	2
3	4	5	6	7	8	9
10	11	12	13	14	15	16
17	18	19	20	21	22	23
24	25	26	27	28	29	

MARCH

S	M	T	W	T	F	S
						1
2	3	4	5	6	7	8
9	10	11	12	13	14	15
16	17	18	19	20	21	22
23	24	25	26	27	28	29
30	31					

APRIL

S	M	T	W	T	F	S
		1	2	3	4	5
6	7	8	9	10	11	12
13	14	15	16	17	18	19
20	21	22	23	24	25	26
27	28	29	30			

MAY

S	M	T	W	T	F	S
				1	2	3
4	5	6	7	8	9	10
11	12	13	14	15	16	17
18	19	20	21	22	23	24
25	26	27	28	29	30	31

JUNE

S	M	T	W	T	F	S
1	2	3	4	5	6	7
8	9	10	11	12	13	14
15	16	17	18	19	20	21
22	23	24	25	26	27	28
29	30					

JULY

S	M	T	W	T	F	S
		1	2	3	4	5
6	7	8	9	10	11	12
13	14	15	16	17	18	19
20	21	22	23	24	25	26
27	28	29	30	31		

AUGUST

S	M	T	W	T	F	S
					1	2
3	4	5	6	7	8	9
10	11	12	13	14	15	16
17	18	19	20	21	22	23
24	25	26	27	28	29	30
31						

SEPTEMBER

S	M	T	W	T	F	S
	1	2	3	4	5	6
7	8	9	10	11	12	13
14	15	16	17	18	19	20
21	22	23	24	25	26	27
28	29	30				

OCTOBER

S	M	T	W	T	F	S
			1	2	3	4
5	6	7	8	9	10	11
12	13	14	15	16	17	18
19	20	21	22	23	24	25
26	27	28	29	30	31	

NOVEMBER

S	M	T	W	T	F	S
						1
2	3	4	5	6	7	8
9	10	11	12	13	14	15
16	17	18	19	20	21	22
23	24	25	26	27	28	29
30						

DECEMBER

S	M	T	W	T	F	S
	1	2	3	4	5	6
7	8	9	10	11	12	13
14	15	16	17	18	19	20
21	22	23	24	25	26	27
28	29	30	31			

11

JANUARY

S	M	T	W	T	F	S
			1	2	3	4
5	6	7	8	9	10	11
12	13	14	15	16	17	18
19	20	21	22	23	24	25
26	27	28	29	30	31	

FEBRUARY

S	M	T	W	T	F	S
						1
2	3	4	5	6	7	8
9	10	11	12	13	14	15
16	17	18	19	20	21	22
23	24	25	26	27	28	29

MARCH

S	M	T	W	T	F	S
1	2	3	4	5	6	7
8	9	10	11	12	13	14
15	16	17	18	19	20	21
22	23	24	25	26	27	28
29	30	31				

APRIL

S	M	T	W	T	F	S
			1	2	3	4
5	6	7	8	9	10	11
12	13	14	15	16	17	18
19	20	21	22	23	24	25
26	27	28	29	30		

MAY

S	M	T	W	T	F	S
					1	2
3	4	5	6	7	8	9
10	11	12	13	14	15	16
17	18	19	20	21	22	23
24	25	26	27	28	29	30
31						

JUNE

S	M	T	W	T	F	S
	1	2	3	4	5	6
7	8	9	10	11	12	13
14	15	16	17	18	19	20
21	22	23	24	25	26	27
28	29	30				

JULY

S	M	T	W	T	F	S
			1	2	3	4
5	6	7	8	9	10	11
12	13	14	15	16	17	18
19	20	21	22	23	24	25
26	27	28	29	30	31	

AUGUST

S	M	T	W	T	F	S
						1
2	3	4	5	6	7	8
9	10	11	12	13	14	15
16	17	18	19	20	21	22
23	24	25	26	27	28	29
30	31					

SEPTEMBER

S	M	T	W	T	F	S
		1	2	3	4	5
6	7	8	9	10	11	12
13	14	15	16	17	18	19
20	21	22	23	24	25	26
27	28	29	30			

OCTOBER

S	M	T	W	T	F	S
				1	2	3
4	5	6	7	8	9	10
11	12	13	14	15	16	17
18	19	20	21	22	23	24
25	26	27	28	29	30	31

NOVEMBER

S	M	T	W	T	F	S
1	2	3	4	5	6	7
8	9	10	11	12	13	14
15	16	17	18	19	20	21
22	23	24	25	26	27	28
29	30					

DECEMBER

S	M	T	W	T	F	S
		1	2	3	4	5
6	7	8	9	10	11	12
13	14	15	16	17	18	19
20	21	22	23	24	25	26
27	28	29	30	31		

12

JANUARY

S	M	T	W	T	F	S
				1	2	3
4	5	6	7	8	9	10
11	12	13	14	15	16	17
18	19	20	21	22	23	24
25	26	27	28	29	30	31

FEBRUARY

S	M	T	W	T	F	S
1	2	3	4	5	6	7
8	9	10	11	12	13	14
15	16	17	18	19	20	21
22	23	24	25	26	27	28
29						

MARCH

S	M	T	W	T	F	S
	1	2	3	4	5	6
7	8	9	10	11	12	13
14	15	16	17	18	19	20
21	22	23	24	25	26	27
28	29	30	31			

APRIL

S	M	T	W	T	F	S
				1	2	3
4	5	6	7	8	9	10
11	12	13	14	15	16	17
18	19	20	21	22	23	24
25	26	27	28	29	30	

MAY

S	M	T	W	T	F	S
						1
2	3	4	5	6	7	8
9	10	11	12	13	14	15
16	17	18	19	20	21	22
23	24	25	26	27	28	29
30	31					

JUNE

S	M	T	W	T	F	S
		1	2	3	4	5
6	7	8	9	10	11	12
13	14	15	16	17	18	19
20	21	22	23	24	25	26
27	28	29	30			

JULY

S	M	T	W	T	F	S
				1	2	3
4	5	6	7	8	9	10
11	12	13	14	15	16	17
18	19	20	21	22	23	24
25	26	27	28	29	30	31

AUGUST

S	M	T	W	T	F	S
1	2	3	4	5	6	7
8	9	10	11	12	13	14
15	16	17	18	19	20	21
22	23	24	25	26	27	28
29	30	31				

SEPTEMBER

S	M	T	W	T	F	S
			1	2	3	4
5	6	7	8	9	10	11
12	13	14	15	16	17	18
19	20	21	22	23	24	25
26	27	28	29	30		

OCTOBER

S	M	T	W	T	F	S
					1	2
3	4	5	6	7	8	9
10	11	12	13	14	15	16
17	18	19	20	21	22	23
24	25	26	27	28	29	30
31						

NOVEMBER

S	M	T	W	T	F	S
	1	2	3	4	5	6
7	8	9	10	11	12	13
14	15	16	17	18	19	20
21	22	23	24	25	26	27
28	29	30				

DECEMBER

S	M	T	W	T	F	S
			1	2	3	4
5	6	7	8	9	10	11
12	13	14	15	16	17	18
19	20	21	22	23	24	25
26	27	28	29	30	31	

13

JANUARY

S	M	T	W	T	F	S
					1	2
3	4	5	6	7	8	9
10	11	12	13	14	15	16
17	18	19	20	21	22	23
24	25	26	27	28	29	30
31						

FEBRUARY

S	M	T	W	T	F	S
	1	2	3	4	5	6
7	8	9	10	11	12	13
14	15	16	17	18	19	20
21	22	23	24	25	26	27
28	29					

MARCH

S	M	T	W	T	F	S
		1	2	3	4	5
6	7	8	9	10	11	12
13	14	15	16	17	18	19
20	21	22	23	24	25	26
27	28	29	30	31		

APRIL

S	M	T	W	T	F	S
					1	2
3	4	5	6	7	8	9
10	11	12	13	14	15	16
17	18	19	20	21	22	23
24	25	26	27	28	29	30

MAY

S	M	T	W	T	F	S
1	2	3	4	5	6	7
8	9	10	11	12	13	14
15	16	17	18	19	20	21
22	23	24	25	26	27	28
29	30	31				

JUNE

S	M	T	W	T	F	S
			1	2	3	4
5	6	7	8	9	10	11
12	13	14	15	16	17	18
19	20	21	22	23	24	25
26	27	28	29	30		

JULY

S	M	T	W	T	F	S
					1	2
3	4	5	6	7	8	9
10	11	12	13	14	15	16
17	18	19	20	21	22	23
24	25	26	27	28	29	30
31						

AUGUST

S	M	T	W	T	F	S
	1	2	3	4	5	6
7	8	9	10	11	12	13
14	15	16	17	18	19	20
21	22	23	24	25	26	27
28	29	30	31			

SEPTEMBER

S	M	T	W	T	F	S
				1	2	3
4	5	6	7	8	9	10
11	12	13	14	15	16	17
18	19	20	21	22	23	24
25	26	27	28	29	30	

OCTOBER

S	M	T	W	T	F	S
						1
2	3	4	5	6	7	8
9	10	11	12	13	14	15
16	17	18	19	20	21	22
23	24	25	26	27	28	29
30	31					

NOVEMBER

S	M	T	W	T	F	S
		1	2	3	4	5
6	7	8	9	10	11	12
13	14	15	16	17	18	19
20	21	22	23	24	25	26
27	28	29	30			

DECEMBER

S	M	T	W	T	F	S
				1	2	3
4	5	6	7	8	9	10
11	12	13	14	15	16	17
18	19	20	21	22	23	24
25	26	27	28	29	30	31

14

JANUARY

S	M	T	W	T	F	S
						1
2	3	4	5	6	7	8
9	10	11	12	13	14	15
16	17	18	19	20	21	22
23	24	25	26	27	28	29
30	31					

FEBRUARY

S	M	T	W	T	F	S
		1	2	3	4	5
6	7	8	9	10	11	12
13	14	15	16	17	18	19
20	21	22	23	24	25	26
27	28	29				

MARCH

S	M	T	W	T	F	S
			1	2	3	4
5	6	7	8	9	10	11
12	13	14	15	16	17	18
19	20	21	22	23	24	25
26	27	28	29	30	31	

APRIL

S	M	T	W	T	F	S
						1
2	3	4	5	6	7	8
9	10	11	12	13	14	15
16	17	18	19	20	21	22
23	24	25	26	27	28	29
30						

MAY

S	M	T	W	T	F	S
	1	2	3	4	5	6
7	8	9	10	11	12	13
14	15	16	17	18	19	20
21	22	23	24	25	26	27
28	29	30	31			

JUNE

S	M	T	W	T	F	S
				1	2	3
4	5	6	7	8	9	10
11	12	13	14	15	16	17
18	19	20	21	22	23	24
25	26	27	28	29	30	

JULY

S	M	T	W	T	F	S
						1
2	3	4	5	6	7	8
9	10	11	12	13	14	15
16	17	18	19	20	21	22
23	24	25	26	27	28	29
30	31					

AUGUST

S	M	T	W	T	F	S
		1	2	3	4	5
6	7	8	9	10	11	12
13	14	15	16	17	18	19
20	21	22	23	24	25	26
27	28	29	30	31		

SEPTEMBER

S	M	T	W	T	F	S
					1	2
3	4	5	6	7	8	9
10	11	12	13	14	15	16
17	18	19	20	21	22	23
24	25	26	27	28	29	30

OCTOBER

S	M	T	W	T	F	S
1	2	3	4	5	6	7
8	9	10	11	12	13	14
15	16	17	18	19	20	21
22	23	24	25	26	27	28
29	30	31				

NOVEMBER

S	M	T	W	T	F	S
			1	2	3	4
5	6	7	8	9	10	11
12	13	14	15	16	17	18
19	20	21	22	23	24	25
26	27	28	29	30		

DECEMBER

S	M	T	W	T	F	S
					1	2
3	4	5	6	7	8	9
10	11	12	13	14	15	16
17	18	19	20	21	22	23
24	25	26	27	28	29	30
31						

The Calendar

History of the Calendar

The purpose of a calendar is to reckon time in advance, to show how many days have to elapse until a certain event takes place—the harvest, a religious festival, or whatever. The earliest calendars, naturally, were crude, and they must have been strongly influenced by the geographical location of the people who made them. In the Scandinavian countries, for example, where the seasons are pronounced, the concept of the year was determined by the seasons, specifically by the end of winter. The Norsemen, before becoming Christians, are said to have had a calendar consisting of ten months of 30 days each.

But in warmer countries, where the seasons are less pronounced, the Moon became the basic unit for time reckoning; an old Jewish book actually makes the statement that "the Moon was created for the counting of the days." All the oldest calendars of which we have reliable information were lunar calendars, based on the time interval from one new moon to the next—a so-called "lunation." But even in a warm climate there are annual events that pay no attention to the phases of the Moon. In some areas it was a rainy season; in Egypt it was the annual flooding of the Nile. It was, therefore, necessary to regulate daily life and religious festivals by lunations, but to take care of the annual event in some other manner.

The calendar of the Assyrians was based on the phases of the Moon. The month began with the first appearance of the lunar crescent, and since this can best be observed in the evening, the day began with sunset. They knew that a lunation was 29½ days long, so their lunar year had a duration of 354 days, falling eleven days short of the solar year.[1] After three years such a lunar calendar would be off by 33 days, or more than one lunation. We know that the Assyrians added an extra month from time to time, but we do not know whether they had developed a special rule for doing so or whether the priests proclaimed the necessity for an extra month from observation. If they made every third year a year of 13 lunations, their three-year period would cover 1,091½ days (using their value of 29½ days for one lunation), or just about four days too short. In one century this mistake would add up to 133 days by their reckoning (in reality closer to 134 days), requiring four extra lunations per century.

We now know that an eight-year period, consisting of five years with 12 months and three years with 13 months would lead to a difference of only 20 days per century, but we do not know whether such a calendar was actually used.

The best approximation that was possible in antiquity was a 19-year period, with seven of these 19 years having 13 months. This means that the period contained 235 months. This, still using the old value for a lunation, made a total of 6,932½ days, while 19 solar years added up to 6,939.7 days, a difference of just one week per period and about five weeks per century. Even the 19-year period required constant adjustment, but it was the period that became the basis of the religious calendar of the Jews. The Arabs used the same calendar at first, but Mohammed forbade shifting from 12 months to 13 months, so that the Islamic religious calendar, even today, has a lunar year of 354 days. As a result the Islamic religious festivals run through all the seasons of the year three times per century.

The Egyptians had a traditional calendar with 12 months of 30 days each. At one time they added five extra days at the end of every year. These turned into a five-day festival because it was thought to be unlucky to work during that time.

When Rome emerged as a world power, the difficulties of making a calendar were well known, but the Romans complicated their lives because of their superstition that even numbers were unlucky. Hence their months were 29 or 31 days long, with the exception of February, which had 28 days. However, four months of 31 days, seven months of 29 days, and one month of 28 days added up to only 355 days. Therefore, the Romans invented an extra month called Mercedonius of 22 or 23 days. It was added every second year.

Even with Mercedonius, the Roman calendar was so far off that Caesar, advised by the astronomer Sosigenes, ordered a sweeping reform in 45 B.C. One year, made 445 days long by imperial decree, brought the calendar back in step with the seasons. Then the solar year (with the value of 365 days and 6 hours) was made the basis of the calendar. The months were 30 or 31 days in length, and to take care of the six hours, every fourth year was made a 366-day year. Moreover, Caesar decreed, the year began with the first of January, not with the vernal equinox in late March.

This was the Julian calendar, named after Julius Caesar. It is still the calendar of the Eastern Orthodox churches.

However, the year is 11½ minutes shorter than the figure written into Caesar's calendar by Sosigenes, and after a number of centuries, even 11½ minutes add up. *See* table.

While Caesar could decree that the vernal equinox should not be used as the first day of the new year, the vernal equinox is still a fact of Nature that could not be disregarded. One of the first (as far as we know) to become alarmed about this was Roger Bacon. He sent a memorandum to Pope Clement IV, who apparently was not impressed. But Pope Sixtus IV (reigned 1471 to 1484) decided that another reform was needed and called the German astronomer Regiomontanus to Rome to advise him. Regiomontanus arrived in 1475, but one year later he died in an epidemic, one of the recurrent outbreaks of the plague. The Pope himself survived, but his reform plans died with Regiomontanus.

Less than a hundred years later, in 1545, the Council of Trent authorized the then Pope, Gregory XIII, to reform the calendar once more. Most of the mathematical and astronomical work was done by Father Christopher Clavius, S.J. The immediate correction, advised by Father Clavius and ordered by Pope Gregory XIII, was that Thursday, Oct. 4, 1582, was to be the last day of the Julian calendar. The next day was Friday, with the date of October 15. For long-range accuracy, a formula suggested by the Vatican librarian Aloysius Giglio (latinized into Lilius) was adopted: every fourth year is a leap year *unless* it is a century year like 1700 or 1800. Century years can be leap years *only* when they are divisible by 400 (e.g., 1600).

1. The correct figures are: lunation: 29 d, 12 h, 44 min, 2.8 sec (29.530585 d); solar year: 365 d, 5 h, 48 min, 46 sec (365.242216 d); 12 lunations: 354 d, 8 h, 48 min, 34 sec (354.3671 d).

Drift of the Vernal Equinox in the Julian Calendar

Date	Julian year	Date	Julian year	Date	Julian year
March 21	325 A.D.	March 17	837 A.D.	March 13	1349 A.D.
March 20	453 A.D.	March 16	965 A.D.	March 12	1477 A.D.
March 19	581 A.D.	March 15	1093 A.D.	March 11	1605 A.D.
March 18	709 A.D.	March 14	1221 A.D.		

This rule eliminates three leap years in four centuries, making the calendar sufficiently correct for all ordinary purposes.

Unfortunately, all the Protestant princes in 1582 chose to ignore the papal bull; they continued with the Julian calendar. It was not until 1698 that the German professor Erhard Weigel persuaded the Protestant rulers of Germany and of the Netherlands to change to the new calendar. In England the shift took place in 1752, and in Russia it needed the revolution to introduce the Gregorian calendar in 1918.

The average year of the Gregorian calendar, in spite of the leap year rule, is about 26 seconds longer than the earth's orbital period. But this discrepancy will need 3,323 years to build up to a single day.

Modern proposals for calendar reform do not aim at a "better" calendar, but at one that is more convenient to use, especially for commercial purposes. A 365-day year cannot be divided into equal halves or quarters; the number of days per month is haphazard; the months begin or end in the middle of a week; a holiday fixed by date (e.g., the Fourth of July) will wander through a week; a holiday fixed in another manner (e.g., Easter) can fall on thirty-five possible dates. The Gregorian calendar, admittedly, keeps the calendar dates in reasonable unison with astronomical events, but it still is full of minor annoyances. Moreover, you need a calendar every year to look up dates; an ideal calendar should be one that you can memorize for one year and that is valid for all other years, too.

In 1834 an Italian priest, Marco Mastrofini, suggested taking one day out of every year. It would be made a holiday and *not* be given the name of a weekday. That would make every year begin with January 1 as a Sunday. The leap-year day would be treated the same way, so that in leap years there would be two unnamed holidays at the end of the year.

About a decade later the philosopher Auguste Comte also suggested a 364-day calendar with an extra day, which he called Year Day.

Since then there have been other unsuccessful attempts at calendar reform.

Time and Calendar

The two natural cycles on which time measurements are based are the year and the day. The year is defined as the time required for the Earth to complete one revolution around the Sun, while the day is the time required for the Earth to complete one turn upon its axis. Unfortunately the Earth needs 365 days plus about six hours to go around the Sun once, so that the year does not consist of so and so many days; the fractional day has to be taken care of by an extra day every fourth year.

But because the Earth, while turning upon its axis, also moves around the Sun there are two kinds of days. A day may be defined as the interval between the highest point of the Sun in the sky on two successive days. This, averaged out over the year, produces the customary 24-hour day. But one might also define a day as the time interval between the moments when a certain point in the sky, say a conveniently located star, is directly overhead. This is called:

Sidereal time. Astronomers use a point which they call the "vernal equinox" for the actual determination. Such a sidereal day is somewhat shorter than the "solar day," namely by about 3 minutes and 56 seconds of so-called "mean solar time."

Apparent solar time is the time based directly on the Sun's position in the sky. In ordinary life the day runs from midnight to midnight. It begins when the Sun is invisible by being 12 hours from its zenith. Astronomers use the so-called "Julian Day," which runs from noon to noon; the concept was invented by the astronomer Joseph Scaliger, who named it after his father Julius. To avoid the problems caused by leap-year days and so forth, Scaliger picked a conveniently remote date in the past and suggested just counting days without regard to weeks, months, and years. The Julian Day 2,440,225.5 is Jan. 1, 1969. The reason for having the Julian Day run from noon to noon is the practical one that astronomical observations usually extend across the midnight hour, which would require a change in date (or in the Julian Day number) if the astronomical day, like the civil day, ran from midnight to midnight.

Mean solar time, rather than apparent solar time, is what is actually used most of the time. The mean solar time is based on the position of a fictitious "mean sun." The reason why this fictitious sun has to be introduced is the following: the Earth turns on its axis regularly; it needs the same number of seconds regardless of the season. But the movement of the Earth around the Sun is not regular because the Earth's orbit is an ellipse. This has the result (as explained in the section The Seasons) that the Earth moves faster in January and slower in July. Though it is the Earth that changes velocity, it looks to us as if the Sun did. In January, when the Earth moves faster, the *apparent* movement of the Sun looks faster. The "mean sun" of time measurements, then, is a sun that moves regularly all year round; the real Sun will be either ahead of or behind the "mean sun." The difference between the real Sun and the fictitious mean sun is called the *equation of time.*

When the real Sun is west of the mean sun we have the "sun fast" condition, with the real Sun crossing the meridian ahead of the mean sun. The opposite is the "sun slow" situation when the real Sun crosses the meridian after the mean sun. Of course, what is observed is the real Sun. The equation of time is needed to establish mean solar time, kept by the reference clocks.

But if all clocks were actually set by mean solar time we would be plagued by a welter of time differences that would be "correct" but a major nuisance. A clock on Long Island, correctly showing mean solar time for its location (this would be *local*

The Names of the Days

Latin	Saxon	English	French	Italian	Spanish	German
Dies Solis	Sun's Day	Sunday	Dimanche	domenica	domingo	Sonntag
Dies Lunae	Moon's Day	Monday	Lundi	lunedì	lunes	Montag
Dies Martis	Tiw's Day	Tuesday	Mardi	martedì	martes	Dienstag
Dies Mercurii	Woden's Day	Wednesday	Mercredi	mercoledì	miércoles	Mittwoch
Dies Jovis	Thor's Day	Thursday	Jeudi	giovedì	jueves	Donnerstag
Dies Veneris	Frigg's Day	Friday	Vendredi	venedrì	viernes	Freitag
Dies Saturni	Seterne's Day	Saturday	Samedi	sabato	sábado	Sonnabend

NOTE: The Romans gave one day of the week to each planet known, the Sun and Moon being considered planets in this connection. The Saxon names are a kind of translation of the Roman names: Tiw was substituted for Mars, Woden (Wotan) for Mercury, Thor for Jupiter (Jove), Frigg for Venus, and Seterne for Saturn. The English names are adapted Saxon. The Spanish and Italian names, which are normally not capitalized, and the French are derived from the Latin. The German names follow the Saxon pattern with two exceptions: Wednesday is Mittwoch (Middle of the Week), and Saturday is Sonnabend (Sunday's Eve).

civil time), would be slightly ahead of a clock in Newark, N.J. The Newark clock would be slightly ahead of a clock in Trenton, N.J., which, in turn, would be ahead of a clock in Philadelphia. This condition actually prevailed in the past until 1883, when *standard time* was introduced. Standard time is the correct mean solar time for a designated meridian, and this time is used for a certain area to the east and west of this meridian. In the U.S. four meridians have been designated to supply standard times; they are 75°, 90°, 105°, and 120° west of Greenwich. The 75° meridian determines Eastern Standard Time. It happens to run through Camden, N.J., where standard time, therefore, is also mean solar time and local civil time. The 90° meridian (which happens to pass through the western part of Memphis, Tenn.) determines Central Standard Time, the 105° meridian (passing through Denver) determines Mountain Standard Time, and the 120° meridian (which runs through Lake Tahoe) determines Pacific Standard Time.

Canada, extending over more territory from west to east, adds one time zone on either side: Atlantic Standard Time (based on 60° west of Greenwich) for New Brunswick, Nova Scotia, and Quebec, and Yukon Standard Time (determined by the 135° meridian) for its extreme West. Alaska, extending still farther to the west, adds two more time zones, Alaska Standard Time (determined by the 150° meridian that passes through Anchorage) and Nome Standard Time, based on the 165° meridian just east of Nome.

In general the Earth is divided into 24 such time zones, which run one hour apart. For practical purposes the time zones sometimes show indentations, and there are a few "subzones" that differ from the neighboring zone by only half an hour, e.g., Newfoundland.

The date line. While the time zones are based on the natural event of the Sun crossing the meridian, the date must be an arbitrary decision. The meridians are traditionally counted from the meridian of the observatory of Greenwich in England, which is called the zero meridian. The logical place for changing the date is 12 hours, or 180° from Greenwich. Fortunately, the 180th meridian runs mostly through the open Pacific. The date line makes a zigzag in the north to incorporate the eastern tip of Siberia into the Siberian time system and then another one to incorporate a number of islands into the Alaska time system. In the south there is a similar zigzag for the purpose of tying a number of British-owned islands to the New Zealand time system. Otherwise the date line is the same as 180° from Greenwich. At points to the east of the date line the calendar is one day earlier than at points to the west of it. A traveller going eastward across the date line from one island to another would not have to re-set his watch because he would stay inside the time zone (provided he does so where the date line does *not* coincide with the 180° meridian), but it would be the same time of the previous day.

The Seasons

The seasons are caused by the tilt of the Earth's axis (23.4°) and not by the fact that the Earth's orbit around the Sun is an ellipse. The average distance of the Earth from the Sun is 93 million miles; the difference between aphelion (farthest away) and perihelion (closest to the Sun) is 3 million miles, so that perihelion is about 91.4 million miles from the Sun. The Earth goes through the perihelion point a few days after New Year, just when the northern hemisphere has winter. Aphelion is

The Names of the Months

January: named after Janus, protector of the gateway to heaven
February: named after Februalia, a time period when sacrifices were made to atone for sins
March: named after Mars, the god of war, presumably signifying that the campaigns interrupted by the winter could be resumed
April: from *aperire,* Latin for "to open" (buds)
May: named after Maia, the goddess of growth of plants
June: from *juvenis,* Latin for "youth"
July: named after Julius Caesar
August: named after Augustus, the first Roman Emperor
September: from *septem,* Latin for "seven"
October: from *octo,* Latin for "eight"
November: from *novem,* Latin for "nine"
December: from *decem,* Latin for "ten"

NOTE: The earliest Latin calendar was a 10-month one; thus September was the seventh month, October, the eighth, etc. July was originally called Quintilis, as the fifth month; August was originally called Sextilis, as the sixth month.

passed during the first days in July. This by itself shows that the distance from the Sun is not important within these limits. What is important is that when the Earth passes through perihelion, the northern end of the Earth's axis happens to tilt away from the Sun, so that the areas beyond the Tropic of Cancer receive only slanting rays from a Sun low in the sky.

The tilt of the Earth's axis is responsible for four lines you find on every globe. When, say, the North Pole is tilted away from the Sun as much as possible, the farthest points in the North which can still be reached by the Sun's rays are 23½° from the pole. This is the Arctic Circle. The Antarctic Circle is the corresponding limit 23.4° from the South Pole; the Sun's rays cannot reach beyond this point when we have mid-summer in the North.

When the Sun is vertically above the equator, the day is of equal length all over the Earth. This happens twice a year, and these are the "equinoxes" in March and in September. After having been over the equator in March, the Sun will seem to move northward. The northernmost point where the Sun can be straight overhead is 23.4° north of the equator. This is the Tropic of Cancer; the Sun can never be vertically overhead to the north of this line. Similarly the Sun cannot be vertically overhead to the south of a line 23.4° south of the equator—the Tropic of Capricorn.

This explains the climatic zones. In the belt (the Greek word *zone* means "belt") between the Tropic of Cancer and the Tropic of Capricorn, the Sun can be straight overhead; this is the tropical zone. The two zones where the Sun cannot be overhead but will be above the horizon every day of the year are the two temperate zones; the two areas where the Sun will not rise at all for varying lengths of time are the two polar areas, Arctic and Antarctic.

Holidays

Religious and Secular, 1983

Since 1971, by federal law, Washington's Birthday, Memorial Day, Columbus Day, and Veterans' Day have been celebrated on Mondays to create three-day weekends for federal employees. Many states now observe these holidays on the same Mondays. (*See* page 398.) The dates given for the holidays listed below are the traditional ones.

New Year's Day, Saturday, Jan. 1. A legal holiday in all states and the District of Columbia, New Year's Day has its origin in Roman times, when sacrifices were offered to Janus, the two-faced Roman deity who looked back on the past and forward to the future.

Epiphany, Thursday, Jan. 6. Falls the twelfth day after Christmas and commemorates the manifestation of Jesus as the Son of God, as represented by the adoration of the Magi, the baptism of Jesus, and the miracle of the wine at the marriage feast at Cana. Epiphany originally marked the beginning of the carnival season preceding Lent, and the evening (sometimes the eve) is known as Twelfth Night.

Lincoln's Birthday, Saturday, Feb. 12. A legal holiday in many states, this day was first formally observed in Washington, D.C., in 1866, when both houses of Congress gathered for a memorial address in tribute to the assassinated President.

St. Valentine's Day, Monday, Feb. 14. This day is the festival of two third-century martyrs, both named St. Valentine. It is not known why this day is associated with lovers. It may derive from an old pagan festival about this time of year, or it may have been inspired by the belief that birds mate on this day.

Shrove Tuesday, Feb. 15. Falls the day before Ash Wednesday and marks the end of the carnival season, which once began on Epiphany but is now usually celebrated the last three days before Lent. In France, the day is known as Mardi Gras (Fat Tuesday), and Mardi Gras celebrations are also held in several American cities, particularly in New Orleans. The day is sometimes called Pancake Tuesday by the English because fats, which were prohibited during Lent, had to be used up.

Ash Wednesday, Feb. 16. The first day of the Lenten season, which lasts 40 days. Having its origin sometime before A.D. 1000, it is a day of public penance and is marked in the Roman Catholic Church by the burning of the palms blessed on the previous year's Palm Sunday. With his thumb, the priest then marks a cross upon the forehead of each worshipper. The Anglican Church and a few Protestant groups in the United States also observe the day, but generally without the use of ashes.

Washington's Birthday, Tuesday, Feb. 22. The birthday of George Washington is celebrated as a legal holiday in every state of the Union, the Distict of Columbia, and all territories. The observance began in 1796.

Purim (Feast of Lots), Sunday, Feb. 27. (14 Adar). A day of joy and feasting celebrating deliverance of the Jews from a massacre planned by the Persian Minister Haman. The Jewish Queen Esther interceded with her husband, King Ahasuerus, to spare the life of her uncle, Mordecai, and Haman was hanged on the same gallows he had built for Mordecai. The holiday is marked by the reading of the Book of Esther (megillah), and by the exchange of gifts, donations to the poor, and the presentation of Purim plays.

St. Patrick's Day, Thursday, March 17. St. Patrick, patron saint of Ireland, has been honored in America since the first days of the nation. There are many dinners and meetings but perhaps the most notable part of the observance is the annual St. Patrick's Day parade on Fifth Avenue in New York City.

Palm Sunday, March 27. Is observed the Sunday before Easter to commemorate the entry of Jesus into Jerusalem. The procession and the ceremonies introducing the benediction of palms probably had their origin in Jerusalem.

First Day of Passover (Pesach), Tuesday, March 29. (15 Nisan). The Feast of the Passover, also called the Feast of Unleavened Bread, commemorates the escape of the Jews from Egypt. As the

Jews fled they ate unleavened bread, and from that time the Jews have allowed no leavening in the houses during Passover, bread being replaced by matzoth.

Good Friday, April 1. This day commemorates the Crucifixion, which is retold during services from the Gospel according to St. John. A feature in Roman Catholic churches is the Liturgy of the Passion; there is no Consecration, the Host having been consecrated the previous day. The eating of hot cross buns on this day is said to have started in England.

Easter Sunday, April 3. Observed in all Christian churches, Easter commemorates the Resurrection of Jesus. It is celebrated on the first Sunday after the full moon which occurs on or next after March 21 and is therefore celebrated between March 22 and April 25 inclusive. This date was fixed by the Council of Nicaea in A.D. 325. The Orthodox Church celebrates Easter on May 8, 1983.

Ascension Day, Thursday, May 12. Took place in the presence of His apostles 40 days after the Resurrection of Jesus. It is traditionally held to have occurred on Mount Olivet in Bethany.

First Day of Shavuot (Hebrew Pentecost), Wednesday, May 18. (6 Sivan). This festival, sometimes called the Feast of Weeks, or of Harvest, or of the First Fruits, falls 50 days after Passover and originally celebrated the end of the seven-week grain harvesting season. In later tradition, it also celebrated the giving of the Law to Moses on Mount Sinai.

Pentecost (Whitsunday), May 22. This day commemorates the descent of the Holy Ghost upon the apostles 50 days after the Resurrection. The sermon by the Apostle Peter, which led to the baptism of 3,000 who professed belief, originated the ceremonies that have since been followed. "Whitsunday" is believed to have come from "white Sunday" when, among the English, white robes were worn by those baptized on the day.

Memorial Day, Monday, May 30. Also known as Decoration Day, Memorial Day is a legal holiday in most of the states and in the territories, and is also observed by the armed forces. In 1868, Gen. John A. Logan, Commander in Chief of the Grand Army of the Republic, issued an order designating the day as one in which the graves of soldiers would be decorated. The holiday was originally devoted to honoring the memory of those who fell in the Civil War, but is now also dedicated to the memory of all war dead.

Flag Day, Tuesday, June 14. This day commemorates the adoption by the Continental Congress on June 14, 1777, of the Stars and Stripes as the U.S. flag. Although it is a legal holiday only in Pennsylvania, President Truman, on Aug. 3, 1949, signed a bill requesting the President to call for its observance each year by proclamation.

Independence Day, Monday, July 4. The day of the adoption of the Declaration of Independence in 1776, celebrated in all states and territories. The observance began the next year in Philadelphia.

Labor Day, Monday, Sept. 5. Observed the first Monday in September in all states and territories, Labor Day was first celebrated in New York in 1882 under the sponsorship of the Central Labor Union, following the suggestion of Peter J. McGuire, of the Knights of Labor, that the day be set aside in honor of labor.

First Day of Rosh Hashana (Jewish New Year), Thursday, Sept. 8. (1 Tishri). This day marks the beginning of the Jewish year 5744 and opens the Ten Days of Penitence closing with Yom Kippur.

Yom Kippur (Day of Atonement), Saturday, Sept. 17. (10 Tishri). This day marks the end of the Ten Days of Penitence that began with Rosh Hashana. It is described in *Leviticus* as a "Sabbath of rest," and synagogue services begin the preceding sundown, resume the following morning, and continue to sundown.

First Day of Sukkot (Feast of Tabernacles), Thursday, Sept. 22. (15 Tishri). This festival, also known as the Feast of the Ingathering, originally celebrated the fruit harvest, and the name comes from the booths or tabernacles in which the Jews lived during the harvest, although one tradition traces it to the shelters used by the Jews in their wandering through the wilderness. During the festival many Jews build small huts in their back yards or on the roofs of their houses.

Simhat Torah (Rejoicing of the Law), Friday, Sept. 30. (23 Tishri). This joyous holiday falls on the eighth day of Sukkot. It marks the end of the year's reading of the Torah (Five Books of Moses) in the synagogue every Saturday and the beginning of the new cycle of reading.

Columbus Day, Wednesday, Oct. 12. A legal holiday in many states, commemorating the discovery of America by Columbus in 1492. Quite likely the first celebration of Columbus Day was that organized in 1792 by the Society of St. Tammany, or Columbian Order, more widely known as Tammany Hall.

Halloween, Monday, Oct. 31. Eve of All Saints' Day, formerly called All Hallows and Hallowmass. Halloween is traditionally associated in some countries with old customs such as bonfires, masquerading, and the telling of ghost stories. These are old Celtic practices that marked the beginning of winter.

All Saints' Day, Tuesday, Nov. 1. A Roman Catholic and Anglican holiday celebrating all saints, known and unknown.

Election Day, (legal holiday in certain states), Tuesday, Nov. 8. Since 1845, by Act of Congress, the first Tuesday after the first Monday in November is the date for choosing Presidential electors. State elections are also generally held on this day.

Veterans Day, Friday, Nov. 11. Armistice Day was established in 1926 to commemorate the signing in 1918 of the Armistice ending World War I. On June 1, 1954, the name was changed to Veterans Day to honor all men and women who have served America in its armed forces.

Thanksgiving, Thursday, Nov. 24. Observed nationally on the fourth Thursday in November by Act of Congress (1941), the first such national proclamation having been issued by President Lincoln in

1863, on the urging of Mrs. Sarah J. Hale, editor of *Godey's Lady's Book.* Most Americans believe that the holiday dates back to the day of thanks ordered by Governor Bradford of Plymouth Colony in New England in 1621, but scholars point out that days of thanks stem from ancient times.

First Sunday of Advent, Nov. 27. Advent is the season in which the faithful must prepare themselves for the advent of the Saviour on Christmas. The four Sundays before Christmas are marked by special church services.

First Day of Hanukkah (Festival of Lights), Thursday, Dec. 1. (25 Kislev). This festival was instituted by Judas Maccabaeus in 165 B.C. to celebrate the purification of the Temple of Jerusalem, which had been desecrated three years earlier by Antiochus Epiphanes, who set up a pagan altar and offered sacrifices to Zeus Olympius. In Jewish homes, a light is lighted on each night of the eight-day festival.

Christmas (Feast of the Nativity), Sunday, Dec. 25. The most widely celebrated holiday of the Christian year, Christmas is observed as the anniversary of the birth of Jesus. Christmas customs are centuries old. The mistletoe, for example, comes from the Druids, who, in hanging the mistletoe, hoped for peace and good fortune. Use of such plants as holly comes from the ancient belief that such plants

National Holidays Around the World, 1983

Afghanistan	Aug. 19	Greece	March 25	Papua New Guinea	Sept. 16
Albania	Nov. 29	Grenada	Feb. 7	Paraguay	May 14
Algeria	Nov. 1	Guatemala	Sept. 15	Peru	July 28
Angola	Nov. 11	Guinea	Oct. 2	Philippines	June 12
Antigua and Barbuda	Nov. 1	Guinea-Bissau	Sept. 12	Poland	July 22
Argentina	May 25	Guyana	Feb. 23	Portugal	June 10
Australia	Jan. 26	Haiti	Jan. 1	Qatar	Sept. 3
Austria	Oct. 26	Honduras	Sept. 15	Romania	Aug. 23
Bahamas	July 10	Hungary	April 4	Rwanda	July 1
Bahrain	Dec. 16	Iceland	June 17	St. Lucia	Dec. 13
Bangladesh	March 26	India	Jan. 26	St. Vincent and the Grenadines	Oct. 27
Barbados	Nov. 30	Indonesia	Aug. 17		
Belgium	July 21	Iran	April 1	Sao Tomé and Príncipe	July 12
Belize	Sept. 20	Iraq	July 14	Saudi Arabia	Sept. 23
Benin	Nov. 30	Ireland	March 17	Senegal	April 4
Bhutan	Dec. 17	Israel	April 18[1]	Seychelles	June 5
Bolivia	Aug. 6	Italy	June 2	Sierra Leone	April 19
Botswana	Sept. 30	Ivory Coast	Dec. 7	Singapore	Aug. 9
Brazil	Sept. 7	Jamaica	Aug. 1[2]	Somalia	Oct. 21
Bulgaria	Sept. 9	Japan	April 29	South Africa	May 31
Burma	Jan. 4	Jordan	May 25	Spain	Oct. 12
Burundi	July 1	Kenya	Dec. 12	Sri Lanka	Feb. 4
Cambodia	April 17	Kuwait	Feb. 25	Sudan	Jan. 1
Cameroon	May 20	Laos	Dec. 2	Suriname	Nov. 25
Canada	July 1	Lebanon	Nov. 22	Swaziland	Sept. 6
Cape Verde	Sept. 12	Lesotho	Oct. 4	Sweden	April 30
Central African Republic	Dec. 1	Liberia	July 26	Syria	April 17
Chad	April 13	Libya	Sept. 1	Tanzania	April 26
Chile	Sept. 18	Luxembourg	June 23	Thailand	Dec. 5
China	Oct. 1	Madagascar	June 26	Togo	April 27
Colombia	July 20	Malawi	July 6	Trinidad and Tobago	Aug. 31
Congo	Aug. 15	Malaysia	Aug. 31	Tunisia	June 1
Costa Rica	Sept. 15	Maldives	July 26	Turkey	Oct. 29
Cuba	Jan. 1	Mali	Sept. 22	Uganda	Oct. 9
Cyprus	Oct. 1	Malta	March 31	U.S.S.R.	Nov. 7
Czechoslovakia	May 9	Mauritania	Nov. 28	United Arab Emirates	Dec. 2
Denmark	April 16	Mauritius	March 12	United States	July 4
Djibouti	June 27	Mexico	Sept. 16	Upper Volta	Dec. 11
Dominican Republic	Feb. 27	Mongolia	July 11	Uruguay	Aug. 25
Ecuador	Aug. 10	Morocco	March 3	Venezuela	July 5
Egypt	July 23	Mozambique	June 25	Vietnam	Sept. 2
El Salvador	Sept. 15	Nepal	Dec. 28	Western Samoa	June 1
Equatorial Guinea	March 5	Netherlands	April 30	Yemen, People's Dem. Republic of	Oct. 14
Ethiopia	Sept. 12	New Zealand	Feb. 6		
Fiji	Oct. 10	Nicaragua	Sept. 15	Yemen Arab Republic	Sept. 26
Finland	Dec. 6	Niger	Dec. 18	Yugoslavia	Nov. 29
France	July 14	Nigeria	Oct. 1	Zaire	June 30
Gabon	Aug. 17	Norway	May 17	Zambia	Oct. 24
Gambia	Feb. 18	Oman	Nov. 18	Zimbabwe	April 18
Germany, East	Oct. 7	Pakistan	March 23		
Ghana	March 6	Panama	Nov. 3		

1. Changes yearly according to Hebrew calendar. 2. Celebrated on first Monday in August. *Source:* United Nations.

blossomed at Christmas. Comparatively recent is the Christmas tree, first set up in Germany in the 17th century, and the use of candles on trees developed from the belief that candles appeared by miracle on the trees at Christmas. Colonial Manhattan Islanders introduced the name Santa Claus, a corruption of the Dutch name for the 4th-century Asia Minor St. Nicholas.

Legal Holidays in the 50 States, D.C., and Puerto Rico

HOLIDAYS WIDELY OBSERVED

January 1, New Year's Day: All states, D.C., Puerto Rico.

February 12, Lincoln's Birthday: Alaska, California, Colorado, Connecticut, Florida, Illinois, Indiana, Iowa, Kansas, Kentucky, Maryland, Missouri, Montana, New Jersey, New Mexico, New York, Utah, Vermont, Washington, West Virginia.

February (first Monday), Lincoln's Birthday: Delaware, Oregon.

February (second Monday), Lincoln Day: Arizona.

February (third Monday), Washington's Birthday: All states,[3] D.C., Puerto Rico. Called **Washington Day** in Arizona. Called **Presidents' Day** in Hawaii, Nebraska, Pennsylvania, South Dakota. Called **Washington-Lincoln Day** in Ohio, Wisconsin, Wyoming.

May 25, Memorial Day: New Mexico.

May 28, Memorial Day: Puerto Rico.

May 30, Memorial Day: Delaware,[2] Illinois, Maryland, New Hampshire, South Dakota, Vermont.

May (last Monday), Memorial Day: All states,[3] D.C., except those listed above, and Alabama, Mississippi, South Carolina.

July 4, Independence Day: All states, D.C., Puerto Rico.

September (1st Monday), Labor Day: All states, D.C., Puerto Rico.

October 12, Columbus Day: Maryland, Puerto Rico.

October (2nd Monday), Columbus Day: All states,[2] D.C., except Alaska, Iowa, Maryland, Michigan, Mississippi, Nevada, North Carolina, North Dakota, Oregon, South Carolina, Washington, Puerto Rico. Also called **Fraternal Day** in Alabama. Called **Discoverers' Day** in Hawaii, **Farmers' Day** in Florida, **Pioneers' Day** in South Dakota.

November (4th Thursday), Thanksgiving Day: All states, D.C., Puerto Rico.

November, Day after Thanksgiving: Nebraska, Illinois, New Hampshire.

November (first Tuesday after the first Monday), Election Day: Arkansas, California, Colorado, D.C., Delaware, Florida, Hawaii, Idaho, Illinois, Indiana, Kentucky, Louisiana, Maryland, Missouri, Montana, New Hampshire, New Jersey, New York, Oklahoma, Pennsylvania, Rhode Island, South Carolina, Tennessee, Texas, Virginia, West Virginia, Wisconsin, Wyoming, Puerto Rico.

November 11, Veterans' Day: All states, D.C., Puerto Rico. Called **Armistice Day** and **Veterans' Day** in New Mexico.

December 25, Christmas: All states, D.C., Puerto Rico.

OTHER HOLIDAYS

January 6, Three Kings' Day: Puerto Rico.

January 8, Battle of New Orleans Day: Louisiana.

January 11, De Hostos' Birthday: Puerto Rico.

January 15, Martin Luther King Day: Connecticut, D.C., Florida, Illinois, Kentucky, Louisiana,[3] Maryland, Massachusetts, New Jersey, Pennsylvania, South Carolina,[1] Michigan.[2]

January 19, Robert E. Lee's Birthday: Arkansas, Florida, Georgia, Kentucky, Louisiana,[3] South Carolina.[1] Called **Confederate Heroes Day** in Texas, also in honor of Jefferson Davis and other Confederate heroes.

January (third Sunday), Martin Luther King Day: New York.

January (third Monday), Martin Luther King Day: Ohio.

January (third Monday), Robert E. Lee's Birthday: Alabama, Mississippi. **Lee-Jackson Day** in Virginia.

January 30, F. D. Roosevelt's Birthday: Kentucky.

February or March (1 day before Ash Wednesday), Mardi Gras (Shrove Tuesday): Alabama, Louisiana (in some parishes).

February 15, Susan B. Anthony's Birthday: Florida.

February 19, Robert E. Lee Day: Kentucky.

March (first Tuesday), Town Meeting Day: Vermont.

March 2, Texas Independence Day: Texas.

March 17, Evacuation Day: Massachusetts (in Suffolk Co. only).

March or April (2 days before Easter), Good Friday: Connecticut, Delaware, Florida, Hawaii, Indiana, Louisiana, Maryland, New Jersey, North Dakota, Pennsylvania, Tennessee, Wisconsin (11 a.m.-3 p.m.).

March or April (1 day after Easter), Easter Monday: North Carolina.

March 20, (First Day of Spring), Youth Day: Oklahoma.

March 22, Abolition Day: Puerto Rico.

March 25, Maryland Day: Maryland.

March 26, Prince Jonah Kuhio Kalanianaole Day: Hawaii.

March (last Monday), Seward's Day: Alaska.

April 2, Pascua Florida Day: Florida.

April 13, Thomas Jefferson's Birthday: Alabama, Oklahoma.

April 16, De Diego's Birthday: Puerto Rico.

April (third Monday), Patriots' Day: Maine, Mass.

April 21, San Jacinto Day: Texas.

April 22, Arbor Day: Nebraska, Delaware.

April 22, Oklahoma Day: Oklahoma.

April 26, Confederate Memorial Day: Florida, Georgia.

April (4th Monday), Fast Day: New Hampshire.

April (last Monday), Arbor Day: Wyoming.

April (last Monday), Confederate Memorial Day: Alabama, Mississippi.

April (last Friday), Arbor Day: Utah.

May (1st Tuesday after the first Monday), Primary Election Day: Indiana.

May (2nd Sunday), Mother's Day: Arizona, Okla.

May 1, Bird Day: Oklahoma.

May 4, Rhode Island Independence Day: Rhode Island.

May 8, Truman Day: Missouri.

May 10, Confederate Memorial Day: South Carolina.[1]

May 11, Minnesota Day: Minnesota.

May 20, Mecklenburg Independence Day: North Carolina.

June (first Monday), Jefferson Davis's Birthday: Alabama, Mississippi.

June (second Sunday), Flag Day: New York.

June (third Sunday), Father's Day: Arizona.

June 3, Jefferson Davis's Birthday: Florida, Georgia, South Carolina, also called **Confederate Memorial Day** in Kentucky and Louisiana.[3]

June 9, Senior Citizens Day: Oklahoma.

June 11, King Kamehameha I Day: Hawaii.
June 14, Flag Day: Pennsylvania.
June 15, Separation Day: Delaware.
June 17, Bunker Hill Day: Massachusetts (in Suffolk Co. only).
June 19, Emancipation Day: Texas.
June 20, West Virginia Day: West Virginia.
July 17, Muñoz Rivera's Birthday: Puerto Rico.
July 24, Pioneer Day: Utah.
July 25, Constitution Day: Puerto Rico.
July 27, Barbosa's Birthday: Puerto Rico.
August (first Sunday), American Family Day: Arizona, Minnesota.
August (first Monday), Colorado Day: Colo.
August (second Monday), Victory Day: Rhode Island.
August 16, Bennington Battle Day: Vermont.
August (third Friday), Admission Day: Hawaii.
August 27, Lyndon B. Johnson's Birthday: Texas.
August 30, Huey P. Long Day: Louisiana.[3]
September (first Tuesday), Primary Election Day: Wisconsin.
September, (second Tuesday), Primary Election Day: Wyoming.
September 9, Admission Day: California.
September 12, Defenders' Day: Maryland.
September 16, Cherokee Strip Day: Oklahoma.
September 23, Grito de Lares: Puerto Rico.
September (1st Saturday after full moon), Indian Day: Oklahoma.
October 10, Oklahoma Historical Day: Oklahoma.
October 18, Alaska Day: Alaska.
October 31, Nevada Day: Nevada.
November 1, All Saints' Day: Louisiana.[3]
November (first Tuesday), Election Day: Montana.
November 4, Will Rogers Day: Oklahoma.
November (week of the 16th), Oklahoma Heritage Week: Oklahoma.
November 19, Discovery Day: Puerto Rico.
November 29, Nellie Tayloe Ross's Birthday: Wyoming.
December 7, Delaware Day: Delaware.
December 10, Wyoming Day: Wyoming.

1. Optional, two of three allowed. 2. Third Monday in Michigan. 3. In Louisiana, observed only if proclaimed by governor.

Movable Holidays, 1983–1991

CHRISTIAN AND SECULAR

Year	Ash Wednesday	Easter	Pentecost	Labor Day	Election Day	Thanksgiving	1st Sun. Advent
1983	Feb. 16	April 3	May 22	Sept. 5	Nov. 8	Nov. 24	Nov. 27
1984	March 7	April 22	June 10	Sept. 3	Nov. 6	Nov. 22	Dec. 2
1985	Feb. 20	April 7	May 26	Sept. 2	Nov. 5	Nov. 28	Dec. 1
1986	Feb. 12	March 30	May 18	Sept. 1	Nov. 4	Nov. 27	Nov. 30
1987	March 4	April 19	June 7	Sept. 7	Nov. 3	Nov. 26	Nov. 29
1988	Feb. 17	April 3	May 22	Sept. 5	Nov. 8	Nov. 24	Nov. 27
1989	Feb. 8	March 26	May 14	Sept. 4	Nov. 7	Nov. 23	Dec. 3
1990	Feb. 28	April 15	June 3	Sept. 3	Nov. 6	Nov. 22	Dec. 2
1991	Feb. 13	March 31	May 19	Sept. 2	Nov. 5	Nov. 28	Dec. 1

Shrove Tuesday: 1 day before Ash Wednesday
Palm Sunday: 7 days before Easter
Maundy Thursday: 3 days before Easter
Good Friday: 2 days before Easter
Holy Saturday: 1 day before Easter
Ascension Day: 10 days before Pentecost
Trinity Sunday: 7 days after Pentecost
Corpus Christi: 11 days after Pentecost

NOTE: Easter is celebrated on May 8, 1983, by the Orthodox Church.

JEWISH

Year	Purim[1]	1st day Passover[2]	1st day Shavuot[3]	1st day Rosh Hashana[4]	Yom Kippur[5]	1st day Sukkot[6]	Simhat Torah[7]	1st day Hanukkah[8]
1983	Feb. 27	March 29	May 18	Sept. 8	Sept. 17	Sept. 22	Sept. 30	Dec. 1
1984	March 18	April 17	June 6	Sept. 27	Oct. 6	Oct. 11	Oct. 19	Dec. 19
1985	March 7	April 6	May 26	Sept. 16	Sept. 25	Sept. 30	Oct. 8	Dec. 8
1986	March 25	April 24	June 13	Oct. 4	Oct. 13	Oct. 18	Oct. 26	Dec. 27
1987	March 15	April 14	June 3	Sept. 24	Oct. 3	Oct. 8	Oct. 16	Dec. 16
1988	March 3	April 2	May 22	Sept. 12	Sept. 21	Sept. 26	Oct. 4	Dec. 4
1989	March 21	April 20	June 9	Sept. 30	Oct. 9	Oct. 14	Oct. 22	Dec. 23
1990	March 11	April 10	May 30	Sept. 20	Sept. 29	Oct. 4	Oct. 12	Dec. 12
1991	Feb. 28	March 30	May 19	Sept. 9	Sept. 18	Sept. 23	Oct. 1	Dec. 2

1. Feast of Lots. 2. Feast of Unleavened Bread. 3. Hebrew Pentecost; or Feast of Weeks, or of Harvest, or of First Fruits. 4. Jewish New Year. 5. Day of Atonement. 6. Feast of Tabernacles, or of the Ingathering. 7. Rejoicing of the Law. 8. Festival of Lights.

Length of Jewish holidays (O=Orthodox, C=Conservative, R=Reform):

Passover: O & C, 8 days (holy days: first 2 and last 2); R, 7 days (holy days: first and last)
Shavuot: O & C, 2 days; R, 1 day
Rosh Hashana: O & C, 2 days; R, 1 day.
Yom Kippur: All groups, 1 day
Sukkot: All groups, 7 days (holy days: O & C, first 2; R, first only) O & C observe two additional days: Shemini Atseret (Eighth Day of the Feast) and Simhat Torah R observes Shemini Atseret but not Simhat Torah
Hanukkah: All groups, 8 days

NOTE: All holidays begin at sundown on the evening before the date given.

MILITARY

Average Military Strength—Man Years[1]

(in thousands)

Year	Army	Air Force	Navy	Marine Corps	Total
1941	755	[2]	218	44	1,017
1942	1,992	[2]	416	89	2,498
1943	5,224	[2]	1,206	232	6,662
1944	7,507	[2]	2,386	398	10,290
1945	8,131	[2]	3,205	473	11,809
1950	632	415	412	80	1,539
1951	1,090	584	566	153	2,394
1952	1,597	899	789	219	3,504
1953	1,536	971	809	237	3,554
1954	1,477	939	767	242	3,425
1955	1,311	958	692	217	3,178
1960	871	828	617	173	2,489
1962	1,018	864	656	187	2,725
1965	966	844	669	190	2,668
1966	1,073	844	716	221	2,854
1969	1,510	886	759	311	3,465
1970	1,432	834	732	295	3,293
1971	1,238	763	656	234	2,891
1972	955	749	604	202	2,510
1973	839	706	580	198	2,323
1974	788	672	556	191	2,207
1975	779	628	545	193	2,145
1976	775	600	529	194	2,098
1977	779	577	527	190	2,073
1978	777	570	530	191	2,068
1979	765	565	527	188	2,045
1980	762	561	525	185	2,033
1981	769	561	531	186	2,050

1. Data represent averages of month-end strengths including both current and preceding fiscal years' figures, each weighted one half. 2. Air Force data prior to June 30, 1948, included with Army data. NOTE: Detail may not add to totals due to rounding. *Source:* Department of Defense, Selected Manpower Statistics, Fiscal Year 1980.

History of the Armed Services

Source: Department of Defense.

U.S. Army

On June 14, 1775, the Continental Congress "adopted" the New England Army—a mixed force of militia and volunteers besieging the British in Boston—by appointing a committee to draft "Rules and regulations for the government of the Army" and voting to raise 10 rifle companies as a reinforcement. The next day, it appointed Washington commander-in-chief of the "Continental forces to be raised for the defense of liberty," and he took command at Boston on July 3, 1775. The Continental Army that fought the Revolution was our first national military organization, and hence the Army is the senior service. After the war, the Continental Army was radically reduced but enough survived to form a small Regular Army of about 700 men under the Constitution in 1789, a nucleus for expansion in the 1790s to successfully meet threats from the Indians and from France. From these humble beginnings, the U.S. Army has developed, normally expanding rapidly by absorbing citizen soldiers in wartime and contracting just as rapidly after each war.

U.S. Navy

The antecedents of the U.S. Navy go back to September 1775, when Gen. Washington commissioned 7 schooners and brigantines to prey on British supply vessels bound for the Colonies or Canada. On Oct. 13, 1775, a resolve of the Continental Congress called for the purchase of 2 vessels for the purpose of intercepting enemy transports. With its passage a Naval Committee of 7 men was formed, and they rapidly obtained passage of legislation calling for procurement of additional vessels. The Continental Navy was supplemented by privateers and ships operated as state navies, but soon after the British surrender it was disestablished.

In 1794, because of dissatisfaction with the payment of tribute to the Barbary pirates, Congress authorized construction of 6 frigates. The first,

United States, was launched May 10, 1797, but the Navy still remained under the control of the Secretary of War until April 1798, when the Navy Department was created under the Secretary of the Navy with Cabinet rank.

U.S. Air Force

Until creation of the National Military Establishment in September 1947, which united the services under one department, military aviation was a part of the U.S. Army. In the Army, aeronautical operations came under the Signal Corps from 1907 to 1918, when the Army Air Service was established. In 1926, the Army Air Corps came into being and remained until 1941, when the Army Air Forces succeeded it as the Army's air arm. On Sept. 18, 1947, the U.S. Air Force was established as an independent military service under the National Military Establishment. At that time, the name "Army Air Forces" was abolished.

U.S. Coast Guard

Our country's oldest continuous seagoing service, the U.S. Coast Guard, traces its history back to 1790, when the first Congress authorized the construction of ten vessels for the collection of revenue. Known first as the Revenue Marine, and later as the Revenue Cutter Service, the Coast Guard received its present name in 1915 under an act of Congress combining the Revenue Cutter Service with the Life-Saving Service. In 1939, the Lighthouse Service was also consolidated with this unit. The Bureau of Marine Inspection and Navigation was transferred temporarily to the Coast Guard in 1942, permanently in 1946. Through its antecedents, the Coast Guard is one of the oldest organizations under the federal government and, until the Navy Department was established in 1798, served as the only U.S. armed force afloat. In times of peace, it operates under the Department of Transportation, serving as the nation's primary agency for promoting marine safety and enforcing federal maritime laws. In times of war, or on direction of the President, it is attached to the Navy Department.

U.S. Marine Corps

Founded in 1775 and observing its official birthday on Nov. 10, the U.S. Marine Corps was developed to serve on land, on sea, and in the air.

Marines have fought in every U.S. war. From an initial two battalions in the Revolution, the Corps reached a peak strength of six divisions and five aircraft wings in World War II. Its present strength is three active divisions and aircraft wings and a Reserve division/aircraft wing team. In 1947, the National Security Act set Marine Corps strength at not less than three divisions and three aircraft wings.

Service Academies

U.S. Military Academy

Source: U.S. Military Academy.

Established in 1802 by an act of Congress, the U.S. Military Academy is located on the west bank of the Hudson River some 50 miles north of New York City. To gain admission a candidate must first secure a nomination from an authorized source. These sources, and the number of cadetships allocated to each, are:

Congressional

Representatives	5 each
Senators	5 each
Other: Vice Presidential	5
District of Columbia	5
Puerto Rico	6
Am. Samoa, Guam, Virgin Is.	1 each

Military-Service-Connected Nominations (Each Class)

Presidential	100
Enlisted members of Army	85
Enlisted members of Army Reserve/ National Guard	85
Sons and daughters of deceased and disabled veterans (approximately)	10
Honor military, naval schools and ROTC	20
Sons and daughters of persons awarded the Medal of Honor	(unlimited)

Any number of applicants can meet the requirements for a *nomination* in these categories. *Appointments* (offers of admission), however, can only be made to the number of applicants shown above.

Candidates may be nominated for vacancies during the year preceding the day of admission, which occurs in early July. The best time to apply is during the junior year in high school.

Candidates must be citizens of the U.S., be unmarried, be at least 17 but not yet 22 years old on July 1 of the year admitted, have a secondary-school education or its equivalent, and be able to meet the academic, medical, and physical aptitude requirements. Academic qualification is determined by an analysis of entire scholastic record, and performance on either the American College Testing (ACT) Assessment Program Test or the College Entrance Examination Board Scholastic Aptitude Test (SAT). Entrance requirements and procedures for appointment are described in the Admissions Bulletin, available without charge from Admissions, U.S. Military Academy, West Point, N.Y. 10996.

Cadets are members of the Regular Army. As such they receive full scholarships and annual salaries from which they pay for their uniforms, textbooks, and incidental expenses. Upon successful completion of the four-year course, the graduate receives the degree of Bachelor of Science and is commissioned a second lieutenant in the Regular Army with a requirement to serve as an officer for a minimum of five years.

U.S. Naval Academy

Source: U.S. Naval Academy.

The Naval School, established in 1845 at Fort Severn, Annapolis, Md., was renamed the U.S. Naval Academy in 1850. A four-year course was adopted a year later.

The Superintendent is a rear admiral. A civilian academic dean heads the academic program. A captain heads the 4,500-man Brigade of Midshipmen and military, professional, and physical training. The faculty is half military and half civilian.

Graduates are awarded the Bachelor of Science or Bachelor of Science in Engineering and are commissioned as officers in the U.S. Navy or Marine Corps.

Applicants *must* obtain a nomination from an official source in order to be considered by the Naval Academy for an appointment. The principle sources are: U.S. Senators, Representatives, the Vice President, the Mayor of Washington, D. C., and the Resident Commissioner of Puerto Rico may each have 5 midshipmen at the Academy at any one time. Ten candidates may be nominated for each vacancy. Well over half of the more than 1,300 appointments as midshipmen made annually originate from these sources.

The President appoints the 65 best-qualified sons and daughters of deceased or disabled veterans, or sons and daughters of prisoners of war or servicemen missing in action, and the 100 best-qualified sons and daughters of officers and enlisted men in the regular Armed Services. He also appoints sons and daughters of Medal of Honor holders.

The Secretary of the Navy awards 170 (85 + 85) appointments to regular and reserve personnel of the Navy or Marine Corps; 150 to congressional alternate nominees, all on a competitive, best-qualified basis; and 20 outstanding graduates of NROTC or Honor Naval and Military Schools. He may also make additional appointments each year, to bring the Brigade up to authorized strength, from among qualified congressional and competitive nominees, again on a best-qualified basis. Three fourths of these additional appointments must, by law, be congressional nominees.

There are also limited numbers of appointments available from the Philippines, Canal Zone, Virgin Islands, Guam, American Samoa, and the American republics.

To have basic eligibility for admission, candidates must be citizens of the U.S., of good moral character, at least 17 and not more than 22 years of age on July 1 of their entering year, in the top 40% of their high school class, and unmarried.

In order to be considered for admission, a candidate must obtain a nomination from one of the sources of appointments listed above. The Admissions Board at the Naval Academy examines the candidate's school record, College Board or ACT scores, recommendations from school officials, extracurricular activities, and evidence from other sources concerning his or her character, leadership potential, academic preparation, and physical fitness. Qualification for admission is based on all of the above factors.

Tuition, board, lodging, and medical and dental care are provided. Midshipmen receive over $460 a month for books, uniforms, and personal needs.

For a catalogue or answers to specific questions, write: Superintendent, U.S. Naval Academy, (Attention: Candidate Guidance), Annapolis, Md. 21402.

U.S. Air Force Academy

Source: U.S. Air Force Academy.

The bill establishing the Air Force Academy was signed by President Eisenhower on April 1, 1954. The first class of 306 cadets was sworn in on July 11, 1955, at Lowry Air Force Base, Denver, the Academy's temporary location. The Cadet Wing moved into the Academy's permanent home north of Colorado Springs in 1958.

Cadets receive four years of academic, military, and physical education to prepare them for leadership as officers in the Air Force. The Academy is authorized a total of 4,544 cadets. Each new class averages 1,500. This includes approximately 1,325 men and 175 women. The candidates for the Academy must be at least 17 but less than 22 on July 1 of the year for which they seek admission, must be a United States citizen, be single, and be able to meet the mental and physical requirements. A candidate is required to take the following examinations and tests: (1) the Service Academies' Qualifying Medical Examination; (2) either the American College Testing (ACT) Assessment Program test or the College Entrance Examination Board Scholastic Aptitude Test (SAT), and (3) a Physical Aptitude Examination.

Cadets receive their entire education at government expense and, in addition, are paid $460 per month base pay. From this sum, they pay for their uniforms, textbooks, tailoring, laundry, entertainment tickets, etc. Upon completion of the four-year course, leading to a Bachelor of Science degree, a cadet who meets the qualifications is commissioned a second lieutenant in the regular U.S. Air Force. Many go on to pilot or navigator training. For details on admissions, write: Director of Cadet Admissions, USAF Academy, Colo. 80840.

U.S. Coast Guard Academy

Source: U.S. Coast Guard Academy.

The U.S. Coast Guard Academy, New London, Conn., was founded on July 31, 1876, to serve as the "School of Instruction" for the Revenue Cutter Service, predecessor to the Coast Guard.

The J.C. Dobbin, a converted schooner, housed the first Coast Guard Academy, and was succeeded in 1878 by the barque Chase, a ship built for cadet training. First winter quarters were in a sail loft at New Bedford, Mass. The school was moved in 1900 to Curtis Bay, Md., to provide a more technical education, and in 1910 was moved back to New England to Fort Trumbull, New London, Conn. In 1932 the Academy moved to its present location in New London.

The Academy today offers a four-year curriculum for the professional and academic training of cadets, which leads to a Bachelor of Science degree and a commission as ensign in the Coast Guard.

Cadets receive appointment through nationwide competition, which includes either the December administration of the College Entrance Examination Board tests, or the American College Testing (ACT) Program tests. Applications must be submitted to the Coast Guard not later than December 15 and to the College Entrance Examination Board, 30 days prior to the tests.

Women were admitted to the Coast Guard Academy for the first time during 1976 as members of the Class of 1980. Candidates must be between 17 and 22 years of age, physically sound, and unmarried. They must agree to remain unmarried until graduation and to serve at least five years on active duty. Cadets receive $4,140 per year to cover their uniform and incidental expenses and are furnished their rations and quarters. Applications may be made to Director of Admissions, U.S. Coast Guard Academy, New London, Conn. 06320.

U.S. Merchant Marine Academy

Source: U.S. Merchant Marine Academy.

The U.S. Merchant Marine Academy, situated at Kings Point, N.Y., on the north shore of Long Island, was dedicated Sept. 30, 1943. It is maintained by the Department of Transportation under direction of the Maritime Administration.

The Academy has a complement of approximately 1,100 men and women representing every state, D.C., the Canal Zone, Puerto Rico, Guam, American Samoa, and the Virgin Islands. It is also authorized to admit up to 12 candidates from the Western Hemisphere and 30 other foreign students at any one time.

Candidates are nominated by Senators and members of the House of Representatives. Nominations to the Academy are governed by a state and territory quota system based on population and the results of the College Entrance Examination Board tests.

A candidate must be a citizen not less than 17 and not yet 22 years of age by July 1 of the year in which admission is sought. Fifteen high school credits, including 3 units in mathematics (from algebra, geometry and/or trigonometry), 1 unit in science (physics or chemistry) and 3 in English are required.

The course is four years and includes one year of practical training aboard a merchant ship. Study includes marine engineering including nuclear studies, navigation, satellite navigation and communications, electricity, ship construction, naval science and tactics, economics, business, languages, history, etc.

Upon completion of the course of study, a graduate receives a Bachelor of Science degree, a license as a merchant marine deck or engineering officer, and a commission as an ensign in the Naval Reserve.

The National Guard

Source: Departments of the Army and the Air Force, National Guard Bureau.

The National Guard of the U.S. originated with the Old North and East Regiments of the Colonial Militia in Massachusetts in 1636. It is the oldest military force in the country. Guardsmembers have served overseas in every major conflict in which the U.S. has participated.

As of March 31, 1982, the Army and Air National Guard totaled about 500,000 men and women serving in 3,684 Army and Air Guard units in all 50 states, Puerto Rico, the Virgin Islands, and the District of Columbia. ANG units 334 (current Mar. 31, 1982), ARNG units, 3,350.

In peacetime, the National Guard is commanded by the governors of the respective states/territories and may be called to state active duty by the governor to assist in state emergencies, disasters, and civil disturbances. During a war or national emergency, the National Guard may be called to active duty by the President or Congress. The National Guard serves as the primary source of augmentation for the Army and the Air Force.

Budget requests for fiscal 1983 are $2.9 billion for the Army National Guard and $2.4 billion for the Air National Guard. Additional money is appropriated directly for the National Guard by the states. Substantial support is also provided by state, county, and municipal governments in land, police and fire protection, maintenance of roads, and the provision of direct county and municipal fiscal support to local units.

The Army National Guard provides 28% of the Army's entire organized structure and about 46% of its combat elements. That support consists of 8 combat divisions, 22 separate combat brigades, 4 armored cavalry units, 2 special forces groups, 1 infantry group arctic recon, 16 major command headquarters, and 1,195 other separate battalions, companies, headquarters, and detachments.

Army National Guard forces are an integral part of the nation's first-line defenses. For example, the 29th Infantry Brigade in the Hawaii National Guard is a round-out brigade for the active Army's 25th Infantry Division. Under the round-out concept, National Guard units work and train with the active Army unit to which they would be assigned upon mobilization. Under the total force policy, the program for increasing readiness is continually being improved. In 1981, 98 Army National Guard units deployed overseas to participate in realistic contingency mission-oriented training. An additional four units participated in an exchange with units from England and Norway, and selected individuals from other units with a NATO contingency mission participated in orientation training in Germany. In order to improve readiness of the individual soldier, the Skill Qualification Training (Test) Program has been implemented. National Guard units take part in Joint Chiefs of Staff and Army exercises with the active forces to develop further the readiness of both units and individuals.

A totally new program implemented in the Army National Guard now provides opportunities for military personnel to seek full-time active duty careers in various duty positions with the Army National Guard. The new Full-Time Manning (FTM) program offers both officer and enlisted (male and female) personnel recurring tours of active duty in an Active Duty Guard/Reserve (AGR) status which could eventually lead to a 20-year active duty retirement identical to that authorized active Army personnel. Positions are located in all States at both State and local unit level. Duties encompass the areas of training, supply, administration, and maintenance. Applicants must be members of the Army National Guard to be considered for FTM positions, and generally qualified to perform the duties required of the position for which applying.

The Air National Guard has 91 flying units and 243 specialized ground support units which, upon mobilization, would be gained by one of six major commands of the USAF. The gaining major commands are Tactical Air Command (TAC), Strategic Air Command (SAC), Military Airlift Command (MAC), Air Force Communications Command (AFCC), Pacific Air Forces (PACAF), and Alaskan Air Command (AAC).

Air National Guard flying units support four mission areas: strategic with aerial refuelers in the offensive role and in the defensive role with interceptors; general purpose with tactical fighters, reconnaissance, electronic warfare and close air support; mobility with tactical airlift; and defense wide with rescue and recovery. These are supported by combat communications, flight facilities, tactical air control, electronics installation, civil engineering, medical, and weather units.

The National Guard is administered by the National Guard Bureau, a joint Army and Air Force office in the Pentagon. Chief of the Bureau is Lt. Gen. LaVern E. Weber of Oklahoma.

The Army National Guard offers its young men and women a broad spectrum of educational opportunities. These not only include skill training associated with their military assignment, but in many instances embrace civilian occupations as well. The list of skills is not limited to those that are equipment oriented but includes management, medical, and other career fields. Some of these educational opportunities may even be pursued in civilian institutions, specifically that of the Clinical Specialist, which is compatible with a Licensed Practical Nurse or Licensed Vocational Nurse.

Participation in the military education system by Army National Guard personnel is not limited to initial entry-skill-level training. There are opportunities available to become a qualified aviator, improve managerial and leadership abilities through attending courses designed for middle managers, and, finally, there are the courses offered at the prestigious Senior Service Colleges that address the needs of personnel at the executive level and positions of greater responsibilities.

If openings exist, young men and women between the ages of 17 and 35 may enlist for a period of six years. In certain circumstances the period of active participation may be less than six years. Upon enlistment, they serve a minimum of 12 weeks on active duty, training with the U.S. Army or the U.S. Air Force, depending upon which branch of the National Guard they choose. The remainder of their term of enlistment is spent in part-time training with their Guard unit.

A woman between the ages of 17 and 35 who has no previous military experience may also enlist in the National Guard for a period of six years. Women in the Army National Guard will receive basic training at either Fort McClellan, Ala., Fort Dix, N.J., or Fort Jackson, S.C.; women in the Air National Guard train at Lackland Air Force Base, Tex. Advanced training takes place at appropriate training centers.

Guard members receive a full day's pay of their military rank for each unit training assembly attended. Additionally, they receive a day's pay of their military rank for each day of their 15 days of annual training, plus any other days on active duty for training at military schools or special assignments. All such training counts toward retirement eligibility at age 60 with 20 or more years of qualifying service.

Pay Grades of Enlisted Personnel

Army ranks[1]	Air Force ranks	Marine ranks	Navy and Coast Guard ranks	Pay grades
Command Sergeant Major and Staff Sergeant Major	Chief Master Sergeant	Sergeant Major and Master Gunnery Sergeant	Master Chief Petty Officer	E-9
1st Sergeant and Master Sergeant	Senior Master Sergeant	1st Sergeant and Master Sergeant	Senior Chief Petty Officer	E-8
Sergeant 1st Class	Master Sergeant	Gunnery Sergeant	Chief Petty Officer	E-7
Staff Sergeant	Technical Sergeant	Staff Sergeant	Petty Officer 1st Class	E-6
Sergeant	Staff Sergeant	Sergeant	Petty Officer 2nd Class	E-5
Corporal	Sergeant and Senior Airman	Corporal	Petty Officer 3rd Class	E-4
Private 1st Class	Airman 1st Class	Lance Corporal	Seaman	E-3
Private	Airman	Private 1st Class	Seaman Apprentice	E-2
Private	Airman/Basic	Private	Seaman Recruit	E-1

1. Army specialist pay grades correspond to numbers: Specialist 4 (E-4), etc. *Source:* Department of Defense

NATO and Warsaw Pact Military Balance, 1981–1982

Category	NATO	(of which) U.S.	Warsaw Pact	(of which) U.S.S.R.
Total manpower in uniform (in thousands)	4,933	2,049	4,788	3,673
Ground forces available in peacetime (division equivalents).	89	5	78	41
Main battle tanks available in peacetime	17,053	3,000	26,300	13,000
Tactical aircraft in operational service:				
Fighter/ground attack	2,293	492	1,755	1,170
Interceptors	572	0	1,490	0
Reconnaisance	397	60	524	360
Fighters	204	90	665	665
Bombers	81	0	365	365

Missile strength (all theaters)	Intercontinental ballistic missiles	Submarine launched ballistic missiles	Long-range bombers
United States[1]	1,052	576	316
Soviet Union[1]	1,398	989	150

1. 1981. *Source:* International Institute for Strategic Studies, London.

Monthly Basic Pay and Allowance for Quarters Rates by Pay Grades, Effective Oct. 1981

	Pay rates														Allowance for quarters		
	Years of service														Without dependents		
Pay Grade	Under 2	2	3	4	6	8	10	12	14	16	18	20	22	26	Full rate[1]	Partial rate[2]	With dependents
COMMISSIONED OFFICERS																	
0–10	4506.60	4665.30	4665.30	4665.30	4665.30	4844.10	4844.10	5215.20	5215.20	5588.10	5588.10	5961.90	5961.90	6333.90	489.00	50.70	611.70
0–9	3994.20	4098.90	4186.20	4186.20	4186.20	4292.70	4292.70	4471.20	4471.20	4844.10	4844.10	5215.20	5215.20	5588.10	489.00	50.70	611.70
0–8	3617.70	3726.00	3814.50	3814.50	3814.50	4098.90	4098.90	4292.70	4292.70	4471.20	4665.30	4844.10	5038.20	5038.20	489.00	50.70	611.70
0–7	3006.00	3210.60	3210.60	3210.60	3354.30	3354.30	3549.00	3549.00	3726.00	4098.90	4380.60	4380.60	4380.60	4380.60	489.00	50.70	611.70
0–6	2228.10	2448.30	2608.20	2608.20	2608.20	2608.20	2608.20	2608.20	2696.70	3123.60	3283.20	3354.30	3549.00	3849.00	438.90	39.60	535.50
0–5	1782.00	2092.80	2237.10	2237.10	2237.10	2237.10	2305.20	2428.80	2591.40	2785.50	2945.40	3034.20	3140.40	3140.40	404.70	33.00	487.20
0–4	1502.10	1828.80	1951.20	1951.20	1986.90	2075.10	2216.40	2341.20	2448.30	2555.40	2626.20	2626.20	2626.20	2626.20	360.30	26.70	434.70
0–3	1395.90	1560.60	1668.30	1845.90	1934.10	2004.00	2111.70	2216.40	2271.00	2271.00	2271.00	2271.00	2271.00	2271.00	316.80	22.20	390.90
0–2	1217.10	1329.30	1596.90	1650.60	1685.10	1685.10	1685.10	1685.10	1685.10	1685.10	1685.10	1635.10	1685.10	1685.10	275.10	17.70	348.00
0–1	1056.60	1099.80	1329.30	1329.30	1329.30	1329.30	1329.30	1329.30	1329.30	1329.30	1329.30	1329.30	1329.30	1329.30	214.80	13.20	279.60
COMMISSIONED OFFICERS WITH OVER 4 YEARS ACTIVE SERVICE AS ENLISTED MEMBERS																	
0–3E	0.00	0.00	0.00	1845.90	1934.10	2004.00	2111.70	2216.40	2305.20	2305.20	2305.20	2305.20	2305.20	2305.20	—	—	—
0–2E	0.00	0.00	0.00	1650.60	1685.10	1738.50	1828.80	1899.00	1951.20	1951.20	1951.20	1951.20	1951.20	1951.20	—	—	—
0–1E	0.00	0.00	0.00	1329.30	1419.90	1472.40	1525.50	1578.60	1650.60	1650.60	1650.60	1650.60	1650.60	1650.60	—	—	—
WARRANT OFFICERS																	
W-4	1422.00	1525.50	1525.50	1560.60	1631.40	1703.40	1774.80	1899.00	1986.90	2057.10	2111.70	2180.40	2253.60	2428.80	347.10	25.20	419.10
W-3	1292.70	1402.20	1402.20	1419.90	1436.70	1541.70	1631.40	1685.10	1738.50	1790.70	1845.90	1917.30	1986.90	2057.10	309.60	20.70	381.60
W-2	1132.20	1224.60	1224.60	1260.30	1329.30	1402.20	1455.00	1508.40	1560.60	1615.20	1668.30	1721.10	1790.70	1790.70	269.10	15.90	342.60
W-1	943.20	1081.50	1081.50	1171.80	1224.60	1277.40	1329.30	1384.20	1436.70	1489.50	1541.70	1596.90	1596.90	1596.90	243.00	13.80	314.70
ENLISTED MEMBERS																	
E–9	0.00	0.00	0.00	0.00	0.00	0.00	1653.90	1691.40	1729.80	1769.70	1809.00	1844.10	1941.30	2130.00	261.90	18.60	368.70
E–8	0.00	0.00	0.00	0.00	0.00	1387.50	1426.60	1464.30	1502.70	1542.00	1577.70	1616.40	1711.50	1902.30	241.50	15.30	340.50
E–7	968.70	1045.50	1084.50	1122.00	1160.70	1197.30	1236.00	1274.10	1331.70	1369.50	1408.20	1426.50	1522.20	1711.50	205.50	12.00	316.80
E–6	833.10	908.40	946.50	986.40	1023.00	1060.50	1099.20	1155.90	1192.20	1230.60	1249.20	1249.20	1249.20	1249.20	186.60	9.90	291.60
E–5	731.40	796.20	834.60	870.90	927.90	965.70	1004.40	1041.30	1060.50	1060.50	1060.50	1060.50	1060.50	1060.50	179.40	8.70	267.90
E–4	682.20	720.30	762.30	821.70	854.40	854.40	854.40	854.40	854.40	854.40	854.40	854.40	854.40	854.40	158.10	8.10	235.50
E–3	642.60	677.70	705.00	732.90	732.90	732.90	732.90	732.90	732.90	732.90	732.90	732.90	732.90	732.90	141.30	7.80	205.50
E–2	618.30	618.30	618.30	618.30	618.30	618.30	618.30	618.30	618.30	618.30	618.30	618.30	618.30	618.30	124.80	7.20	205.50
E–1	551.40	551.40	551.40	551.40	551.40	551.40	551.40	551.40	551.40	551.40	551.40	551.40	551.40	551.40	117.90	6.90	205.50

1. Payment of the full rate of basic allowance for quarters at these rates for members of the uniformed services to personnel without dependents is authorized by 37 U.S. Code 403 and Part IV of Executive Order 11157, as amended. 2. Payment of the partial rate of basic allowance for quarters at these rates to members of the uniformed services without dependents who, under 37 U.S. Code 403(b) or 403(c), are not entitled to the full rate of basic allowance for quarters, is authorized by 37 U.S. Code 1009(d) and Part IV of Executive Order 11157, as amended. The Chairman of the Joint Chiefs and the military heads of each service receive $4,176.04 a month. The senior enlisted persons of the Air Force, Army, Coast Guard, Marine Corps and Navy each get $2,589.00 regardless of length of service. Note: Basic pay is limited to $4,176 by Level V of the executive schedule. *Source:* Department of Defense.

Extra Pay for Service During Hostilities

Act of March 3, 1847, during the Mexican War, provided for $2 a month extra pay for "distinguished service." This continued beyond the war and applied in the Civil War.

In the Spanish-American War, there was a 20% increase in enlisted men's pay for war service.

In World War I, additional incentive pay was offered for all types of services. Among these items was pay for certificate of merit of $2 a month. By the law passed in 1920, the reasons for additional pay had expanded. Recipients of the Medal of Honor, Distinguished Service Cross, and Distinguished Service Medal received $2 a month extra, while each bar in lieu of these medals also added another $2 a month. Added to this was a foreign service bonus of 20%.

Act of June 30, 1944, authorized $5 a month to enlisted men qualified as expert infantrymen and $10 to those qualified as combat infantrymen. Amounts were payable for the duration of war and 6 months thereafter.

By the Act of July 6, 1945, for the duration of war and for 6 months thereafter, enlisted men entitled to wear Medical Badges received additional pay of $10 a month.

Act of July 10, 1952, authorized $45 a month for each month beginning after May 31, 1950, for which the member was entitled to receive basic pay and during which he was a member of a combat unit in Korea.

The Combat Duty Pay Act of 1952 was repealed by the Uniformed Services Pay Act of 1963, which authorized special pay for duty subject to hostile fire under certain conditions at the rate of $55 (now $65) a month.

Family Separation Allowance

Military members with dependents in grades E-4 (over 4 years of service) and above are entitled to an allowance of $30 a month in addition to allowances or per diem when on a permanent change of station, with movement of dependents not authorized and dependents not residing near his station; or be on board ship or temporary duty for more than 30 days, with dependents not residing near the temporary duty station.

A second type of family separation allowance at the rate equal to the quarters allowance for a member in the same grade without dependents is payable to a member with dependents when assigned to permanent duty outside the United States or in Alaska when government quarters, or quarters under the jurisdiction of a uniformed service, are not available to the member. Further, the member's dependents must not be residing at or near his permanent duty station and are not authorized to movement to or near the permanent duty station at Government expense.

Allowances for Subsistence

Officers receive $94.39 per month. Enlisted personnel receive allowances for subsistence under the following provisions: (1) when rations in kind are not available, $5.09 per day; (2) when on leave or authorized to mess separately, $4.50 per day; (3) when assigned to duty under emergency conditions where no messing facilities of the U.S. are available, $6.73 per day.

Veterans' Benefits

Although benefits of various kinds date back to Colonial days, veterans of World War I were the first to receive disability compensation, allotments for dependents, life insurance, medical care, and vocational rehabilitation. In 1940, these benefits were slowly broadened.

The following benefits available to veterans require certain minimum periods of active duty during qualifying periods of service and, except for service personnel, are applicable only to those whose discharges are not dishonorable.

Unemployment allowances. Every effort is being made to secure employment for Vietnam veterans. Unemployment benefits are administered by the U.S. Department of Labor.

Loans. GI loans are made for a variety of purposes, such as: to buy or build a home; to purchase a mobile home with or without a lot; and to refinance a home presently owned and occupied by the veteran. The VA will guarantee the lender against loss up to 60% of a home loan with a maximum of $25,000. On mobile home loans, the amount of the guaranty is 50% of the loan with a maximum of $17,500. The interest rate may not exceed the maximum rate set by the VA and in effect when the loan is made.

Compensation and rehabilitation benefits. These are available to those having some service-connected illness or disability.

Disability compensation. The VA pays from $58 to $1,130 per month, and for specific conditions up to $3,223 per month, plus allowances for dependents, where the disability is rated 30% or more.

Vocational rehabilitation. Necessary training expenses, special equipment, etc., toward a definite job objective are paid for, plus a monthly allowance of up to $282, with increased amounts for dependents, in addition to compensation.

Medical and dental care. This includes care in VA and, in certain instances, in non-VA, or other federal hospitals. It also covers outpatient treatment at a VA field facility or, in some cases, by an approved private physician or dentist. Full domiciliary care is also provided where necessary. Nursing home care may be provided at certain VA medical facilities or in approved community nursing homes. Hospital and other medical care may also be provided for the spouse and child dependents of a veteran who is permanently and totally disabled due to a service-connected disability; or for survivors of a veteran who dies from a service-connected disability; or for survivors of a veteran who at the time of death had a total disability, permanent in nature, resulting from a service-connected disability. These latter benefits are usually provided in non-federal facilities. Eligibility criteria for these benefits vary, and veterans and/or their dependents or survivors should always apply in advance. Contact the nearest VA medical facility.

Dependents' Educational Assistance. The VA pays $311 a month for up to 45 months of schooling to sons and daughters of veterans who died of service-connected causes or who were permanently and totally disabled from service-connected causes or while permanently and totally disabled or who are missing in action, captured in the line of duty, or forcibly detained or interned in line of duty by a foreign power for more than 90 days. Students must usually be between 18 and 26.

Spouses of veterans whose deaths are adjudged to be service-connected, and spouses of veterans who are permanently and totally disabled due to service-connected causes or who are prisoners of war or are missing in action are also eligible for this educational benefit.

Veterans readjustment education. Veterans who served on active duty for at least 181 days after Jan. 31, 1955, but before Jan. 1, 1977, may receive monthly educational assistance under the new GI Bill for post-Korean conflict veterans, varying from $311 for single full-time students to $422 for veterans with two dependents, plus $26 for each additional dependent. Veterans and servicepersons who initially entered the military on or after Jan. 1, 1977, may receive educational assistance under a contributory plan. Individuals contribute $50 to $75 from military pay, up to a maximum of $2,700. Participants receive monthly payments for the number of months they contributed, or for 36 months, whichever is less.

Pensions. The Veterans Pension Act of 1959, effective July 1, 1960, provides a sliding-scale formula for pension benefits for wartime veterans totally disabled from non-service-connected causes. These benefits are based on need. Surviving spouses and orphans of Mexican Border service, World War II, Korea, and Vietnam veterans have the same eligibility status.

Insurance. The VA life insurance programs have approximately 8.3 million policyholders with total coverage of about $102.4 billion. Detailed information on NSLI (National Service Life Insurance), USGLI (United States Government Life Insurance), and VMLI (Veterans Mortgage Life Insurance) may be obtained at any VA Office. Information regarding SGLI (Servicemen's Group Life Insurance) and VGLI (Veterans Group Life Insurance) may be obtained from the VA Center, P.O. Box 8079, Philadelphia, Pa. 19101, or the Office of Servicemen's Group Life Insurance, 212 Washington St., Newark, N.J. 07102

Highest Ranking Officers in the Armed Forces

ARMY[1]
Generals: John W. Vessey, Jr., Chairman of the Joint Chiefs of Staff; Edward C. Meyer, Chief of Staff; Bernard W. Rogers, Supreme Allied Commander, Europe; Frederick J. Kroesen, Donn A. Starry, John A. Wickham, Jr., Glenn K. Otis, Donald R. Keith, Richard E. Cavazos.

AIR FORCE
Generals: James R. Allen; Wilbur L. Creech; Bennie L. Davis; William Y. Smith; Robert T. Marsh; Charles A. Gabriel; Richard L. Lawson; James V. Hartinger; Billy M. Minter; James P. Mullins; Thomas M. Ryan, Jr.

NAVY
Admirals: James D. Watkins, Chief of Naval Operations; Bobby R. Inman; Robert L.J. Long; Harry D. Train II; William J. Crowe, Jr.; William N. Small; John G. Williams, Jr.; George E.R. Kinnear, II; Sylvester R. Foley, Jr.

MARINE CORPS
Generals: Robert H. Barrow, Commandant of the Marine Corps; Paul X. Kelly, Assistant Commandant of the Marine Corps and Chief of Staff.
Lieutenant Generals: Richard E. Carey; Adolph G. Schwenk; John H. Miller; William J. White; Edward J. Bronars; Harold A. Hatch; John K. Davis.

COAST GUARD
Admiral: James S. Gracey, Commandant.
Vice Admirals: Benedict L. Stabile, Vice Commandant; Wayne E. Caldwell, Commander, Atlantic Area; Charles E. Larkin, Commander, Pacific Area.

1. On March 15, 1978, George Washington, the commander of the Continental Army in the American Revolution and our first President, was promoted to the newly-created rank of General of the Armies of the United States. Congress authorized this title two years ago to make it clear that Washington is the Army's senior general. *Source:* Department of Defense.

Blacks in the Armed Forces

(As of Dec. 31, except 1977, June 30, and 1978 and 1979, Sept. 30[1])

Item	1980	1979	1978	1977	1976	1975	1970	1965
Total Armed Forces (1,000)	2,037	2,013	2,048	2,063	2,059	2,071	2,861	2,816
Officers (1,000)	279	274	274	281	279	283	389	337
Enlisted (1,000)	1,759	1,739	1,774	1,782	1,780	1,788	2,472	2,478
Black personnel (1,000)	359	382	353	322	314	299	279	267
Officers (1,000)	12	13	12	11	10	9	8	6
Enlisted (1,000)	347	369	342	311	303	290	271	261
Percent Black								
Officers	4.3	4.7	4.3	3.9	3.6	3.2	2.2	1.9
Enlisted	21.2	21.2	19.3	17.4	17.1	16.2	11.0	10.5

1. Includes women. Officers include warrant officers. *Source:* U.S. Dept. of Defense, Office of Equal Opportunity. Through 1972, *The Black in the Armed Forces, Statistical Fact Book,* 1972; thereafter, unpublished data.

Defense Budget by Major Programs

(Current millions of dollars)

Military programs	Change 1982–83[2]	1983	1982[2]	1981	1980
Strategic forces	+ 6.9	23.1	16.2	12.7	11.1
General purpose forces	+18.5	106.5	88.0	68.3	52.4
Intelligence and communications	+ 4.0	18.0	14.0	11.2	9.1
Airlift and sealift	+ 0.3	4.4	4.0	2.9	2.1
Guard and reserve forces	+ 2.8	14.3	11.6	9.9	7.9
Research and development	+ 3.2	20.1	16.9	14.2	11.8
Central supply and maintenance	+ 3.0	22.2	19.2	17.6	15.3
Training, medical, other general personnel activities	+ 4.5	44.2	39.8	35.0	29.3
Administrative and associated activities	+ 0.7	4.3	3.6	3.4	2.5
Support of other nations[1]	− 0.1	0.9	1.0	0.9	0.6
Total	**+43.7**	**258.0**	**214.2**	**176.1**	**142.2**

1. Excluding Military Assistance Program. 2. Figures are latest available and are subject to change. NOTE: Figures represent Total Obligational Authority (TOA), that is, the value of the direct Defense program for each fiscal year regardless of the method of financing (which could include balances available from prior years or resources available from sale of items from inventory). *Source:* Department of Defense.

Budget Outlays for National Defense Functions

(in billions of dollars, except as indicated[6])

item	1981	1980	1979	1978	1977	1976	1975	1974	1970
Defense Dept., military	158.6	132.8	115.0	103.0	95.7	88.0	85.0	77.6	77.2
Military personnel	37.0	30.8	28.4	27.1	25.7	25.1	25.0	23.7	23.0
Percent of military	23.3	23.2	24.7	26.3	26.9	28.5	29.4	30.6	29.9
Active forces	33.8	28.5	26.3	25.1	23.9	23.3	23.2	22.1	22.0
Reserve forces	3.2	2.3	2.1	2.0	1.9	1.8	1.7	1.6	1.1
Military retirees	13.8	11.9	10.3	9.2	8.2	7.3	6.2	5.1	2.8
Operation, maintenance	53.8	44.8	36.4	33.6	30.6	27.9	26.3	22.5	21.6
Procurement[2]	34.1	29.0	25.4	20.0	18.2	16.0	16.0	15.2	21.6
Army	6.8	5.4	4.5	3.2	2.6	1.4	2.5	2.6	5.2
Navy[3]	14.3	12.4	11.8	9.2	8.5	8.0	8.1	7.3	7.9
Air Force	12.7	10.9	8.9	7.3	6.9	6.5	5.3	5.4	8.4
Research and develop	15.2	13.1	11.2	10.5	9.8	8.9	8.9	8.6	7.2
Military construction	2.5	2.5	2.1	1.9	1.9	2.0	1.5	1.4	1.2
Family housing	1.9	1.7	1.5	1.4	1.4	1.2	1.1	.9	.6
Civil defense	(7)	(7)	(7)	(7)	.1	.1	.1	.1	.1
Other[4]	.3	−1.0	−.2	−.8	−.2	−.4	−.1	−.2	−1.0
Atomic energy activities[5]	3.6	2.9	2.5	2.1	1.9	1.6	1.5	1.5	1.4
Defense-related activities[7]	—	.1	.1	.2	−.1	−.1	−.9	−1.3	—
Total	**162.1**	**135.9**	**117.7**	**105.2**	**97.5**	**89.4**	**85.5**	**77.8**	**78.6**

1. Less than $50 million. 2. Includes other defense agencies not shown separately. 3. Includes Marine Corps. 4. Revolving and management funds, trust funds, special foreign currency program, allowances, and offsetting receipts. 5. Defense activities only. 6. For years ending June 30 except, beginning 1977, ending Sept. 30. 1981 data are estimates. 7. After 1977, Civil Defense figures are included in Defense-related activities. *Source:* Office of Management and Budget.

Department of Defense Outlays by Branch of Service

	Outlays (in millions of dollars)					Percent distribution			
Year	Total	Army	Navy	Air Force	Other	Army	Navy	Air Force	Other
1965	47,098	11,552	13,339	18,146	4,061	24.5	28.3	38.5	8.6
1970	78,349	25,147	22,656	25,233	5,313	32.1	28.9	32.2	6.8
1975	84,988	23,678	28,299	26,709	6,303	27.9	33.3	31.4	7.4
1976	87,950	25,025	30,404	28,248	4,272	28.5	34.6	32.1	4.9
1977	94,810	24,231	31,287	28,356	10,936	25.6	33.0	29.9	11.5
1978	102,682	26,250	33,573	29,344	13,515	25.6	32.7	28.6	13.2
1979	113,464	29,068	37,951	32,506	13,939	25.6	33.4	28.6	12.3
1980	134,210	33,034	42,886	39,639	18,651	24.6	32.0	29.5	13.9

Source: Department of the Treasury.

U.S. Military Actions Other Than Declared Wars

Hawaii (1893): U.S. Marines, ordered to land by U.S. Minister John L. Stevens, aided the revolutionary Committee of Safety in overthrowing the native government. Stevens then proclaimed Hawaii a U.S. protectorate. Annexation, resisted by the Democratic administration in Washington, was not formally accomplished until 1898.

China (1900): Boxers (a group of Chinese revolutionists) occupied Peking and laid siege to foreign legations. U.S. troops joined an international expedition which relieved the city.

Panama (1903): After Colombia had rejected a proposed agreement for relinquishing sovereignty over the Panama Canal Zone, revolution broke out, aided by promoters of the Panama Canal Co. Two U.S. warships were standing by to protect American privileges. The U.S. recognized the Republic of Panama on November 6.

Dominican Republic (1904): When the Dominican Republic failed to meet debts owed to the U.S. and foreign creditors, President Theodore Roosevelt declared the U.S. intention of exercising "international police power" in the Western Hemisphere whenever necessary. The U.S. accordingly administered customs and managed debt payments of the Dominican Republic from 1905 to 1907.

Nicaragua (1911): The possibility of foreign control over Nicaragua's canal route led to U.S. intervention and agreement. The U.S. landed Marines in Nicaragua (Aug. 14, 1912) to protect American interests there. A small detachment remained until 1933.

Mexico (1914): Mexican dictator Victoriano Huerta, opposed by President Woodrow Wilson, had the support of European governments. An incident involving unarmed U.S. sailors in Tampico led to the landing of U.S. forces on Mexican soil. Veracruz was bombarded by the Navy to prevent the landing of munitions from a German vessel. At the point of war, both powers agreed to mediation by Argentina, Brazil, and Chile. Huerta abdicated, and Venustiano Carranza succeeded to the presidency.

Haiti (1915): U.S. Marines imposed a military occupation. Haiti signed a treaty making it a virtual protectorate of the U.S. until troops were withdrawn in 1934.

Mexico (1916): Raids by Pancho Villa cost American lives on both sides of the border. President Carranza consented to a punitive expedition led by Gen. John J. Pershing, but antagonism grew in Mexico. Wilson withdrew the U.S. force when war with Germany became imminent.

Dominican Republic (1916): Renewed intervention in the Dominican Republic with internal administration by U.S. naval officers lasted until 1924.

Korea (1950): In this undeclared war, which terminated with the July 27, 1953, truce at Panmunjom and the establishment of a neutral nations' supervisory commission, the U.S. and 15 member-nations of the U.N. came to the aid of the Republic of South Korea, whose 38th-parallel border was crossed by the invading Russian Communist-controlled North Koreans, who were later joined by the Chinese Communists.

Lebanon (1958): Fearful of the newly formed U.A.R. abetting the rebels of his politically and economically torn country, President Camille Chamoun appealed to the U.S. for military assistance. U.S. troops landed in Beirut in mid-July and left before the end of the year, after internal and external quiet were restored.

Dominican Republic (1965): On April 28, when a political coup-turned-civil war endangered the lives of American nationals, President Lyndon B. Johnson rushed 400 marines into Santo Domingo, the beginning of an eventual U.S. peak-commitment of 30,000 troops, constituting the preponderant military strength of the OAS-created Inter-American Peace Force, and 6,500 troops, including 5,000 Americans, remained until after the peaceful inauguration of President Joaquín Balaguer on July 1, 1966, and the entire force left the country on September 20.

Vietnam: This longest war in U.S. history began with economic and technical assistance after 1954 Geneva accords ending the Indochinese War. By 1964 it had escalated into a major conflict.

This involvement spanning the administrations of five Presidents led to domestic discontent in the late 1960s. By April 1969, U.S. troop strength reached a peak of 543,400. Peace negotiations began in Paris in 1968 but proved fruitless. Finally, on Jan. 27, 1973, a peace accord was signed in Paris by the U.S., North and South Vietnam, and the Vietcong. Within 60 days, U.S. POWs were returned, and the U.S. withdrew all military forces from South Vietnam.

U.S. Casualties in Major Wars

War	Branch of service	Numbers engaged	Battle deaths	Other deaths	Total deaths	Wounds not mortal	Total casualties
Revoluntionary War 1775 to 1783	Army	n.a.	4,044	n.a.	n.a.	6,004	n.a.
	Navy	n.a.	342	n.a.	n.a.	114	n.a.
	Marines	n.a.	49	n.a.	n.a.	70	n.a.
	Total	**n.a.**	**4,435**	**n.a.**	**n.a.**	**6,188**	**n.a.**
War of 1812 1812 to 1815	Army	n.a.	1,950	n.a.	n.a.	4,000	n.a.
	Navy	n.a.	265	n.a.	n.a.	439	n.a.
	Marines	n.a.	45	n.a.	n.a.	66	n.a.
	Total	**286,730**	**2,260**	**n.a.**	**n.a.**	**4,505**	**n.a.**

War	Branch of service	Numbers engaged	Battle deaths	Other deaths	Total deaths	Wounds not mortal	Total casualties
Mexican War 1846 to 1848	Army	n.a.	1,721	11,550	13,271	4,102	17,373
	Navy	n.a.	1	n.a.	n.a.	3	n.a.
	Marines	n.a.	11	n.a.	n.a.	47	n.a.
	Total	78,718	1,733	n.a.	n.a.	4,152	n.a.
Civil War[2] 1861 to 1865	Army	2,128,948	138,154	221,374	359,528	280,040	639,568
	Navy	84,415	2,112	2,411	4,523	1,710	6,233
	Marines		148	312	460	131	591
	Total	2,213,363	140,414	224,097	364,511	281,881	646,392
Spanish-American War 1898	Army	280,564	369	2,061	2,430	1,594	4,024
	Navy	22,875	10	0	10	47	57
	Marines	3,321	6	0	6	21	27
	Total	306,760	385	2,061	2,446	1,662	4,108
World War I 1917 to 1918	Army	4,057,101	50,510	55,868	106,378	193,663	300,041
	Navy	599,051	431	6,856	7,287	819	8,106
	Marines	78,839	2,461	390	2,851	9,520	12,371
	Total	4,734,991	53,402	63,114	116,516	204,002	320,518
World War II 1941 to 1946	Army[3]	11,260,000	234,874	83,400	318,274	565,861	884,135
	Navy	4,183,466	36,950	25,664	62,614	37,778	100,392
	Marines	669,100	19,733	4,778	24,511	67,207	91,718
	Total	16,112,566	291,557	113,842	405,399	670,846	1,076,245
Korean War 1950 to 1953	Army	2,834,000	27,704	9,429	37,133	77,596	114,729
	Navy	1,177,000	458	4,043	4,501	1,576	6,077
	Marines	424,000	4,267	1,261	5,528	23,744	29,272
	Air Force	1,285,000	1,200	5,884	7,084	368	7,452
	Total	5,720,000	33,629	20,617	54,246	103,284	157,530
War in Southeast Asia[4]	Army	4,386,000	30,867	7,252	38,119	96,802	134,921
	Navy[5]	1,842,000	1,605	911	2,516	4,178	6,694
	Marines	794,000	13,066	1,685	14,749	51,392	66,141
	Air Force	1,740,000	1,715	603	2,318	931	3,249
	Total	8,744,000	47,253	10,449	57,702	153,303	211,005

1. Excludes captured or interned and missing in action who were subsequently returned to military control. 2. Union forces only. Totals should probably be somewhat larger as data or disposition of prisoners are far from complete. Final Confederate deaths, based on incomplete returns, were 133,821, to which should be added 26,000–31,000 personnel who died in Union prisons. 3. Army data include Air Force. 4. As of Sept. 30, 1977. 5. Includes a small number of Coast Guard. NOTE: All data are subject to revision. For wars before World War I, information represents best data from available records. However, due to incomplete records and possible difference in usage of terminology, reporting systems, etc., figures should be considered estimates. n.a. = not available. *Source:* Department of Defense.

Casualties in World War I

Country	Total mobilized forces	Killed or died[1]	Wounded	Prisoners or missing	Total casualties
Austria-Hungary	7,800,000	1,200,000	3,620,000	2,200,000	7,020,000
Belgium	267,000	13,716	44,686	34,659	93,061
British Empire[2]	8,904,467	908,371	2,090,212	191,652	3,190,235
Bulgaria	1,200,000	87,500	152,390	27,029	266,919
France[2]	8,410,000	1,357,800	4,266,000	537,000	6,160,800
Germany	11,000,000	1,773,700	4,216,058	1,152,800	7,142,558
Greece	230,000	5,000	21,000	1,000	27,000
Italy	5,615,000	650,000	947,000	600,000	2,197,000
Japan	800,000	300	907	3	1,210
Montenegro	50,000	3,000	10,000	7,000	20,000
Portugal	100,000	7,222	13,751	12,318	33,291
Romania	750,000	335,706	120,000	80,000	535,706
Russia	12,000,000	1,700,000	4,950,000	2,500,000	9,150,000
Serbia	707,343	45,000	133,148	152,958	331,106
Turkey	2,850,000	325,000	400,000	250,000	975,000
United States	4,734,991	116,516	204,002	—	320,518

1. Includes deaths from all causes. 2. Official figures. NOTE: For additional U.S. figures, *see* the table on U.S. Casualties in Major Wars in this section.

Casualties in World War II

Country	Men in war	Battle deaths	Wounded
Australia	1,000,000	26,976	180,864
Austria	800,000	280,000	350,117
Belgium	625,000	8,460	55,513[1]
Brazil[2]	40,334	943	4,222
Bulgaria	339,760	6,671	21,878
Canada	1,041,080	32,412	53,145
China[3]	17,250,521	1,324,516	1,762,006
Czechoslovakia	—	6,683[4]	8,017
Denmark	—	4,339	—
Finland	500,000	79,047	50,000
France	—	201,568	400,000
Germany	20,000,000	3,250,000[4]	7,250,000
Greece	—	17,024	47,290
Hungary	—	147,435	89,313
India	2,393,891	32,121	64,354
Italy	3,100,000	149,496[4]	66,716
Japan	9,700,000	1,270,000	140,000
Netherlands	280,000	6,500	2,860
New Zealand	194,000	11,625[4]	17,000
Norway	75,000	2,000	—
Poland	—	664,000	530,000
Romania	650,000[5]	350,000[6]	—
South Africa	410,056	2,473	—
U.S.S.R.	—	6,115,000[4]	14,012,000
United Kingdom	5,896,000	357,116[4]	369,267
United States	16,112,566	291,557	670,846
Yugoslavia	3,741,000	305,000	425,000

1. Civilians only. 2. Army and navy figures. 3. Figures cover period July 7, 1937–Sept. 2, 1945, and concern only Chinese regular troops. They do not include casualties suffered by guerrillas and local military corps. 4. Deaths from all causes. 5. Against Soviet Russia; 385,847 against Nazi Germany. 6. Against Soviet Russia; 169,822 against Nazi Germany. NOTE: The figures in this table are unofficial estimates obtained from various sources. For additional U.S. Figures, *see* the tables on U.S. Casualties in Major Wars in this section.

Women in the Armed Services

(In thousands except percent. As of June 30 except, beginning 1977, as of Sept. 30)

Item	1980	1979	1978	1977	1976	1975	1974	1970	1965
TOTAL MILITARY	**2,037**	**2,027**	**2,062**	**2,074**	**2,082**	**2,128**	**2,162**	**3,066**	**2,655**
Women	170	151	134	119	109	97	75	42	31
Percent	8.3	7.4	6.5	5.7	5.2	4.6	3.5	1.4	1.2
Officers, total	257	274	274	276	281	292	303	402	339
Women	21.5	19	17	15	14	14	13	13	11
Percent	8.1	6.9	6.2	5.4	5.0	4.6	4.3	3.3	3.1
Enlisted personnel	1,610	1,753	1,788	1,798	1,801	1,836	1,860	2,664	2,317
Women	149	132	117	104	95	83	62	28	20
Percent	9.2	7.5	6.5	5.8	5.3	4.5	3.3	1.1	.9

Source: U.S. Department of Defense.

U.S. Navy Combatant Vessels, 1982

Type	Number	Type	Number
Carriers	13	Mine warfare	3
Destroyers	84	Patrol ships	6
Cruisers	27	Amphibious warfare	60
Frigates	84	Auxiliaries	80
Submarines	130	Total	487

NOTE: As of May 1981, exact figures are classified information. *Source:* Department of Navy.

Military Spending and Strengths of World Nations, 1981

	Expenditures				Manpower					
Country	Total (millions)	Per person	% of govt spending	% of GNP[1] (1980)	Total in armed forces	Army	Navy	Air Forces	Estimated reservists[2]	Para-military forces
United States	$171,023	$759	23.7	5.5	2,049,100	775,000	716,100[3]	558,000	879,400	56,600
Canada	4,990	205	9.1	1.7	79,500[4]	13,000	5,500	15,300	23,300	—
U.S.S.R.	133,000[5]	508[5]	n.a.	12–14	3,673,000	1,825,000	443,000	475,000	5,200,000	560,000
China	56,941[6]	56[6]	n.a.	9.0	4,750,000	3,900,000	360,000	490,000	n.a.	12,000
NATO (not including U.S. and Canada)										
Belgium	3,560	359	9.0	3.3	89,500	65,000	4,400	20,100	155,500	16,000
Britain	28,660	512	12.3	5.1	343,646	176,248	74,687	92,701	276,400	6,900
Denmark	1,520	295	7.1	2.4	32,600	19,300	5,700	7,600	57,500	73,300
France	26,008	483	20.5	3.9	504,600	321,320	69,600	103,460	450,000	88,900
Germany, West[7]	25,000	405	22.6	3.2	495,000	335,200	36,500	106,000	750,000	—
Greece	1,770[6]	236[6]	19.8[6]	5.1	193,500	150,000	19,000	24,500	390,000	34,000
Italy	8,887	155	5.1	2.4	366,000	255,000	42,000	69,000	738,000	193,900
Luxembourg	51	140	3.3	1.0	690	690	—	—	—	500
Netherlands	4,930	348	9.5	3.4	102,800	67,000	16,800	19,000	171,000	12,700
Norway	1,570[6]	383[6]	10.8[6]	2.9	37,000	18,000	9,000	10,000	162,000	85,000
Portugal	944	94	10.9	3.8	70,926	47,000	13,426	10,500	n.a.	37,300
Turkey	3,106	67	19.0	4.2	569,000	470,000	46,000	53,000	470,000	120,000
WARSAW PACT[8] (not including U.S.S.R.)										
Bulgaria	1,340	151	6.0	3.4	149,000	105,000	10,000	34,000	240,000	175,000
Czechoslovakia	3,520[6]	229[6]	7.6[6]	4.0	194,000	140,000	—	54,000	325,000	157,500
Germany, East	6,960	415	8.5	6.1	167,000	113,000	16,000	38,000	305,000	70,200
Hungary	1,240	115	3.9	2.3	101,000	80,000	—	21,000	143,000	75,000
Poland	4,670[6]	131[6]	6.0[6]	3.2	319,500	210,000	22,500	87,000	605,000	72,000
Romania	1,350	61	2.3	1.3	184,500	140,000	10,500	34,000	300,000	37,000
OTHER EUROPEAN COUNTRIES										
Austria	870	116	3.8	1.2	50,300	46,000	—	4,300	910,000	—
Finland	713	149	5.1	1.5	39,900	34,400	2,500	3,000	700,000	—
Ireland	285[6]	86[6]	3.3[6]	1.6[9]	14,012	12,428	890	694	22,500	—
Spain	3,980	105	12.0	2.9[9]	342,000	255,000	49,000	38,000	1,085,000	104,000
Sweden	3,790	455	7.7	3.2	64,300	44,500	10,000	9,800	500,000	5,000
Switzerland	1,840	154	20.2	1.9[9]	20,500	—	—	—	621,500	—
Yugoslavia	3,470	154	56.9[6]	n.a.	252,500	190,000	17,500	45,000	500,000	2,020,000

MIDDLE EAST										
Algeria	914	47	5.3[6]	1.9[9]	101,000	90,000	4,000	7,000	100,000	10,000
Egypt	2,168[9]	54[9]	n.a.	13.2[9]	367,000	235,000	20,000	27,000	335,000	139,000
Iran	4,200[6]	110[6]	12.3[6]	n.a.	195,000	150,000	10,000	35,000	400,000	75,000
Iraq	2,700[6]	202[6]	24.0[6]	10.9[9]	252,250	210,000	4,250	38,000	250,000	79,800
Israel	7,340	1,835	30.6	23.2	172,000	135,000	9,000	28,000	504,000	4,500
Jordan	420	127	25.0	12.2[9]	67,500	60,000	300	7,200	35,000	11,000
Libya	448[10]	162[10]	19.5[10]	1.8[10]	55,000	45,000	5,000	5,000	n.a.	5,000
Saudi Arabia	27,695	2,664	31.0	15.0[6]	51,700	35,000	2,200	14,500	n.a.	36,500
Syria	2,389	261	30.8	13.1	222,500	170,000	2,500	50,000	102,500	9,800
AFRICA										
Ethiopia	385[6]	17[6]	n.a.	n.a.	230,000	225,000[11]	1,500	3,500	20,000	169,000
Morocco	1,210	56	16.7	6.7	120,000	107,000	5,000	8,000	n.a.	30,000
Nigeria	1,702[6]	22[6]	8.7[6]	n.a.	156,000	140,000	6,000	10,000	2,000	—
South Africa	2,556[6]	89[6]	18.1[6]	3.9[9]	92,700	76,000	6,400	10,300	157,000	145,000
Sudan	245[6]	13[6]	12.7[6]	n.a.	71,000	68,000	1,500	1,500	n.a.	3,500
Zimbabwe	444[6]	6[6]	22.0[6]	n.a.	34,000	33,000	—	1,000	16,000	40,000
ASIA–OCEANIA (not including People's Republic of China)										
Australia	3,900[6]	272[6]	9.7[6]	2.8[9]	72,591	32,850	17,300	22,441	63,800	—
China (Taiwan)	1,672[5]	95[5]	48.3[5]	8.3[5]	451,000	310,000	35,000	67,000	1,170,000	100,000
India	5,119	7	16.9	3.8	1,104,000	944,000	47,000	113,000	240,000	300,000
Indonesia	2,387	5	12.3[6]	3.4[9]	273,000	195,000	52,000	26,000	n.a.	82,000
Japan	11,497	98	5.0	0.9	243,000	155,000	44,000	44,000	41,600	—
Korea, North	1,470	74	14.7	11.2[9]	782,000	700,000	31,000	51,000	300,000	38,000
Korea, South	4,400	113	36.0[6]	5.7	601,600	520,000	49,000	32,600	1,240,000	2,800,000
Malaysia	2,250	157	23.0	3.4[9]	102,000	90,000	30,000	6,000	51,000	90,000
New Zealand	426[6]	135[6]	3.9[6]	1.8[6]	12,913	5,675	2,843	4,395	9,800	—
Pakistan	1,540[6]	17	n.a.	7.2[9]	450,600	420,000	13,000	17,600	513,000	109,100
Philippines	863	17	13.0[6]	2.0	112,800	70,000	26,000	16,800	124,000	110,500
Singapore	574[6]	239[6]	16.5[6]	6.1	42,000	35,000	3,000	4,000	50,000	37,500
Thailand	1,279	26	18.7	4.3[9]	238,100	160,000	35,000	43,100	500,000	44,500
LATIN AMERICA										
Argentina	3,380[6]	12.3[6]	15.1[6]	0.9[9]	185,500	130,000	36,000	19,500	250,000	43,000
Brazil	1,540[6]	13[6]	6.8[6]	0.7	272,550	182,750	47,000	42,800	560,000	185,000
Colombia	31[6]	12[6]	9.3[6]	0.8[9]	70,000	57,000	9,200	3,800	70,000	50,000
Cuba	1,100[6]	114[6]	n.a.	8.5	227,000	200,000	11,000	16,000	130,000	18,000
Mexico	1,166	17	1.1[6]	0.7[9]	119,500	95,000	20,000	4,500	250,000	—
Peru	430[9]	25[9]	n.a.	3.1[9]	130,000	75,000	15,000	40,000	n.a.	25,000
Venezuela	1,399	85	n.a.	2.3	40,800	27,000	9,000	4,800	n.a.	20,000

1. Based on local currency, GNP estimated where official figures are unavailable. 2. Reservists with recent training. 3. Includes Marine Corps. 4. Includes 46,000 not identified by service. 5. 1977 figure. 6. 1980 figure. 7. Includes aid to West Berlin. 8. This section is not directly comparable to others. Difficulty of calculating suitable exchange rates makes conversion to dollars impractical. 9. 1979 figure. 10. 1978 figure. 11. Includes 150,000 People's Militia. NOTE: n.a. = not available. *Source:* International Institute for Strategic Studies, London.

U.S. Military Sales Deliveries to Foreign Governments
(in millions of dollars)

Country	1980	1979	1978	1977	1960-1969
Argentina	18.2	6.9	10.7	6.8	57.7
Australia	185.1	133.0	150.6	28.7	457.4
Austria	6.6	4.3	1.9	28.2	42.1
Belgium	289.7	146.5	27.6	5.8	76.4
Bolivia	2.1	(3)	.1	(3)	.5
Brazil	8.0	7.7	7.8	8.5	61.9
Cambodia	—	—	—	—	—
Canada	88.2	72.0	71.3	65.7	308.2
Chile	4.3	7.8	11.1	56.0	18.5
China (Taiwan)	222.0	183.2	135.9	139.4	29.1
Colombia	4.1	5.0	1.9	.9	2.6
Denmark	208.6	17.6	12.0	19.9	52.0
Dominican Republic	.1	(3)	.1	(3)	.9
Ecuador	10.9	8.1	7.8	9.1	2.7
Egypt	203.8	192.0	50.8	10.5	.1
Ethiopia	—	—	—	61.7	.2
France	11.3	2.8	4.4	5.2	258.9
Germany	419.7	240.2	211.0	274.8	2,471.1
Greece	155.1	127.4	125.0	259.6	22.7
Guatemala	2.3	3.6	2.4	2.2	2.0
Honduras	.6	.9	.5	.4	.2
India	6.6	1.3	1.2	1.4	19.3
Indonesia	89.5	6.2	6.3	25.4	.6
Iran[1]	—	1,413.8	1,669.1	2,416.6	237.8
Israel	622.3	377.2	828.6	869.5	158.9
Italy	35.9	30.2	29.9	38.1	322.8
Japan	91.2	29.7	37.2	25.9	179.6
Jordan	176.7	80.2	105.8	101.0	74.7
Korea[3]	300.0	404.2	413.6	176.9	2.2
Kuwait	87.1	71.7	188.8	157.7	—
Laos[3]	—	—	—	—	—
Lebanon	16.0	7.9	8.7	.4	1.7
Liberia	.6	.5	(3)	.4	.4
Libya	—	—	(3)	—	17.3
Malaysia	4.7	3.3	3.4	2.3	3.9
Mexico	2.5	.4	.5	3.6	8.2
Morocco	65.2	134.5	87.5	33.7	9.8
Netherlands	354.6	87.6	52.3	19.9	74.3
New Zealand	18.7	5.7	4.2	3.2	52.8
Nicaragua	(3)	(3)	.8	.4	.6
Nigeria	6.2	5.9	5.9	2.0	.4
Norway	228.3	22.9	26.2	31.2	101.9
Pakistan	53.1	59.1	44.9	39.5	40.3
Panama	.2	.3	.2	.2	(3)
Paraguay	.1	(3)	(3)	.2	.1
Peru	14.9	13.9	13.6	26.0	16.4
Philippines[3]	15.3	25.5	34.5	31.5	3.5
Portugal	1.3	.7	1.2	.3	5.9
Saudi Arabia	2,724.7	2,471.5	2,368.9	1,502.1	126.6
Singapore	18.4	81.6	9.3	15.2	.8
South Vietnam	—	—	—	—	(3)
Spain	57.4	80.1	57.6	164.5	60.0
Sweden	5.6	1.5	4.5	15.7	29.7
Switzerland	21.2	301.5	48.3	45.0	50.5
Thailand[3]	202.6	85.9	93.4	17.7	.5
Tunisia	9.7	42.0	1.5	3.2	1.6
Turkey	137.1	129.9	158.7	35.0	1.5
U.K.	295.0	234.8	100.8	103.8	948.4
Uruguay	.8	.9	1.2	5.3	1.5
Venezuela	7.5	5.1	4.3	43.7	71.9
Yemen	77.0	72.8	27.3	22.0	—
Yugoslavia	.6	.4	.2	1.4	8.9
Zaire	9.8	6.8	10.9	7.4	1.4
Other countries	38.0	19.2	84.2	2.0	19.9
International Organizations	61.2	30.6	39.3	47.7	166.5
Total	**7,698.3**	**7,506.3**	**7,407.7**	**7,022.4**	**6,688.3**

1. Change between 1978 and 1979 reflects values adjusted for cancellation and program reductions agreed to by the governments of the United States and Iran. 2. Includes MAP and MASF programs for military assistance deliveries. 3. Less than $50,000.—Represents zero. *Source:* U.S. Defense Security Assistance Agency.

Strengths of Military Formations, 1981–1982

Type of unit	U.S.	U.S.S.R.	China	West Germany	India	Egypt	Israel
Division: Armored							
Men	18,300	11,000	9,200	17,000	15,000	11,000	—
Tanks	324	335[1]	270	300	200	300	—
Mechanized							
Men	18,500	14,000	12,700[2]	17,500	17,500	12,000	—
Tanks	216	266[1]	30[2]	250	—	190	—
Airborne							
Men	16,800	7,000	9,000	8,000–9,000	—	—	—
Brigade: Armored							
Men	4,500	1,300[3]	1,200[3]	4,500	6,000	3,500	3,500
Tanks	108	95[3]	90[3]	110	150	96	80–100
Mechanized							
Men	4,800	2,300[3]	2,000	5,000	4,500	3,500	3,500
Tanks	54	40[3]	—	54	—	36	36–40
Squadron:							
Fighter Aircraft	18–24	12–15	9–10	15–21	12–20	10–12	15–20

1. Tank strengths are for Soviet division in Eastern Europe: other divisions have fewer. 2. Infantry division. 3. Strength of a regiment, which is equivalent formation in Soviet and Chinese command structures. Particularly in West European countries, "regiment" often describes a battalion-size unit. It is so used here. *Source:* International Institute for Strategic Studies, London.

Insignia and Ranks of the Armed Forces

Army, Air Force, and Marines: Insignia	Army, Air Force, and Marines: Rank	Navy and Coast Guard: Insignia	Navy and Coast Guard: Rank	Stripes[1]
Five silver stars	General of the Army, AF	Five silver stars	Fleet Admiral	1—4—0
Four silver stars	General	Four silver stars	Admiral	1—3—0
Three silver stars	Lieutenant General	Three silver stars	Vice Admiral	1—2—0
Two silver stars	Major General	Two silver stars	Rear Admiral	1—1—0
One silver star	Brigadier General	One silver star	Commodore[2]	1—0—0
Silver eagle	Colonel	Silver eagle	Captain	0—4—0
Silver oak leaf	Lieutenant Colonel	Silver oak leaf	Commander	0—3—0
Gold oak leaf	Major	Gold oak leaf	Lt. Commander	0—2—1
Two silver bars	Captain	Two silver bars	Lieutenant	0—2—0
One silver bar	First Lieutenant	One silver bar	Lieutenant (jg)	0—1—1
One gold bar	Second Lieutenant	One gold bar	Ensign	0—1—0
Silver bar with 4 enamel bands[3]	Chief Warrant Officer (W-4)	Silver bar with 3 enamel bands[3]	Chief Warrant Officer (W-4)	0—1—0[4]
Silver bar with 3 enamel bands[3]	Chief Warrant Officer (W-3)	Silver bar with 2 enamel bands[3]	Chief Warrant Officer (W-3)	0—1—0[5]
Silver bar with 2 enamel bands[3]	Chief Warrant Officer (W-2)	Gold bar with 3 enamel bands[3]	Chief Warrant Officer (W-2)	0—1—0[6]
Silver bar with 1 enamel band[3]	Warrant Officer (W-1)	Gold bar with 2 enamel bands[3]	Warrant Officer (W-1)	0—0—1[6]

1. Of gold embroidery; first figure is number of 2-in. stripes, second is number of 1/2-inch strips, third is number of 1/4-in. stripes. 2. The Navy rank of Commodore became effective Sept. 15, 1981, although the first Navy officer will not be promoted to the rank until Fiscal Year 1983. Until Fiscal Year 1983, the Navy will retain its system of upper-half (0–8) and lower-half (0–7) Rear Admirals. The Coast Guard will continue to have Rear Admirals at both 0–7 and 0–8 grades. 3. Navy and Marine Corps use same size insignia as Army when worn on shoulder straps, but miniature size on shirt collars. Enamel bands are black for Army, scarlet for Marines, medium blue for Air Force, and blue for Navy and Coast Guard. 4. One break. 5. Two breaks. 6. Three breaks.

Pay Grades of Commissioned Officers and Warrant Officers

Rank: Army, Air Force, and Marine Corps	Rank: Navy, Coast Guard, and National Oceanic and Atmospheric Adm. (NOAA)	Rank: Public Health Service	Pay grade
General	Admiral[1]	—	0–10
Lieutenant General	Vice Admiral	Surgeon General	0–9
Major General	Rear Admiral (Navy) and Rear Admiral (upper half) (Coast Guard and National Oceanic and Atmospheric Administration	Deputy Surgeon General, Assistant Surgeon General having rank of Major General	0–8
Brigadier General	Commodore (NOAA)[2] (Navy) and Rear Admiral (lower half) (Coast Guard)	Assistant Surgeon General having rank of Brigadier General	0–7
Colonel	Captain	Director Grade	0–6
Lieutenant Colonel	Commander	Senior Grade	0–5
Major	Lieutenant Commander	Full Grade	0–4
Captain	Lieutenant	Senior Assistant Grade	0–3
First Lieutenant	Lieutenant (Junior Grade)	Assistant Grade	0–2
Second Lieutenant	Ensign	Junior Assistant Grade	0–1
Chief Warrant Officer	Chief Warrant Officer[1]	—	W–4
Chief Warrant Officer	Chief Warrant Officer[1]	—	W–3
Chief Warrant Officer	Chief Warrant Officer[1]	—	W–2
Warrant Officer	Warrant Officer[1]	—	W–1

1. Not applicable to National Oceanic and Atmospheric Administration (NOAA). *Source:* Department of Defense. 2. The Defense Officer Personnel Management Act (Public Law 96–513;94 Stat. 2835) effective Sept. 15, 1981, established a new officer grade of Commodore in the Navy and assigns officers in that grade to pay grade 0–7. Following a period of transition, attainment of the grade of Rear Admiral will be by selection from officers in the grade of Commodore and officers so selected will be assigned to pay grade 0–8.

Soviet Sub Is World's Fastest

A new type of Soviet submarine can travel almost an unprecedented 50 miles per hour under water. Dubbed the *"Alpha"* by the U.S. Navy, the submarine can dive to more than 3,000 feet or three times deeper than an American submarine.

The Soviet sub's hull is made of titanium metal which is nonmagnetic and therefore helps it to avoid detection from the air. Titanium is lightweight and has a very high tensile strength which contributes to the *Alpha's* deep-diving ability.

Arms Exports and Imports, Supplier and Recipient Countries
(in millions of constant 1977 dollars)

Country	1978	1977	1976	1972-75	1969-71
SUPPLIERS					
Canada	$ 74	$ 70	$ 127	$ 704	$ 881
China, Mainland	130	110	148	1,876	902
Czechoslovakia	744	600	465	1,550	523
France	1,256	1,300	1,058	3,789	885
Germany, West	814	850	687	1,374	646
Poland	325	240	243	924	723
U.S.S.R.	6,609	6,500	5,607	20,623	6,454
United Kingdom	1,024	950	820	2,719	711
United States	6,237	6,900	6,242	23,051	15,470
RECIPIENTS—Developed countries					
Australia	232	140	84	537	391
Canada	214	170	190	668	153
Czechoslovakia	102	250	317	1,471	370
Germany, East	270	500	581	2,231	602
Germany, West	269	470	555	3,155	1,179
Hungary	242	170	222	782	184
Italy	121	150	179	612	311
Japan	158	130	190	370	322
Poland	149	370	412	1,742	555
Romania	223	170	148	668	184
Soviet Union	768	525	402	1,221	925
United Kingdom	139	150	253	470	747
United States	111	120	116	752	870
RECIPIENTS—Developing countries					
Algeria	581	460	338	191	120
Brazil	148	140	190	428	184
Cambodia	37	10	5	1,019	173
China: Taiwan	176	180	169	509	1,074
Cuba	288	100	137	341	106
Egypt	214	220	158	2,579	1,696
Greece	279	480	555	618	870
India	260	725	518	969	733
Indonesia	83	60	84	102	75
Iran	1,955	2,400	2,221	3,996	1,074
Iraq	1,396	1,500	1,058	2,544	248
Israel	884	1,100	1,058	2,712	996
Jordan	158	120	148	257	263
Korea, North	18	110	84	833	357
Korea, South	512	290	359	1,013	1,252
Laos	n.a.	40	n.a.	529	366
Libya	1,768	1,200	1,058	1,437	270
Nigeria	37	10	52	178	62
Pakistan	158	220	201	560	294
Peru	139	420	243	434	151
Saudi Arabia	930	925	497	953	204
Spain	102	290	190	557	287
Syria	768	775	555	3,559	334
Turkey	195	140	328	703	1,157
Vietnam, Socialist Rep.	—	5	42	2,325	1,282
Vietnam, South	(2)	(2)	(2)	7,559	4,105
World, total[1]	**19,177**	**19,300**	**17,352**	**60,669**	**27,917**

1. Includes countries, not shown separately. 2. Absorbed by Vietnam Socialist Republic in 1976. n.a. = Not available. — Represents zero. Note: Figures shown are latest available. *Source:* U.S. Arms Control and disarmament Agency, World Military Expenditures and Arms Transfers, annual.

The XM-1 Battle Tank

The XM-1 is the Army's new main battle tank. It has been named the Abrams tank in honor of the late Gen. Creighton W. Abrams, Army Chief of Staff.

The Abrams tank has a crew of four, a turbine engine, weighs 60 tons, and can travel at 45 miles per hour on a road and can go 30 miles per hour cross country. The top speed of the former main battle tank, the M-60, is 30 miles per hour.

At present, the XM-1 has a 105-millimeter gun. There are plans to replace this in 1984 with a new West German 120-millimeter gun now being developed. 7,058 of the new tanks are scheduled to be built.

Major Religions of the World

Judaism

The determining factors of Judaism are: descendance from Israel, the *Torah,* and Tradition.

The name Israel (Jacob, a patriarch) also signifies his descendants as a people. During the 15th–13th centuries B.C., Israelite tribes, coming from South and East, gradually settled in Palestine, then inhabited by Canaanites. They were held together by Moses, who gave them religious unity in the worship of *Jahweh,* the God who had chosen Israel to be his people.

Under Judges, the 12 tribes at first formed an amphictyonic covenant. Saul established kingship (circa 1050 B.C.), and under David, his successor (1000–960 B.C.), the State of Israel comprised all of Palestine with Jerusalem as religio-political center. A golden era followed under Solomon (965–926 B.C.), who built *Jahweh* a temple.

After Solomon's death, the kingdom separated into Israel in the North and Judah in the South. A period of conflicts ensued, which ended with the conquest of Israel by Assyria in 722 B.C. The Babylonians defeated Judah in 586 B.C., destroying Jerusalem and its temple, and deporting many to Babylon.

The era of the kings is significant also in that the great prophets worked in that time, emphasizing faith in *Jahweh* as both God of Israel and God of the universe, and stressing social justice.

When the Persians permitted the Jews to return from exile (539 B.C.), temple and cult were restored in Jerusalem. The Persian rulers were succeeded by the Seleucides. The Maccabaean revolt against these Hellenistic kings gave independence to the Jews in 128 B.C., which lasted till the Romans occupied the country.

Important groups that exerted influence during these times were the Sadducees, priests in the temple in Jerusalem; the Pharisees, teachers of the Law in the synagogues; Essenes, a religious order (from whom Dead Sea Scrolls, discovered in 1947, came); Apocalyptists, who were expecting the heavenly Messiah; and Zealots, who were prepared to fight for national independence.

When the latter turned against Rome in A.D. 66, Roman armies under Titus suppressed the revolt, destroying Jerusalem and its temple in A.D. 70. The Jews were scattered in the *diaspora* (Dispersion), subject to oppressions until the Age of the Enlightenment (18th century) brought their emancipation, although persecutions did not end entirely.

The fall of the Jerusalem temple was an important event in the religious life of the Jews, which now developed around *Torah* (Law) and synagogue. Around A.D. 100 the Sacred Scriptures were codified. Synagogue worship became central, with readings from *Torah* and prophets. Most important prayers are the *Shema* (Hear) and the Prayer of the 18 Benedictions.

Religious life is guided by the commandments contained in the *Torah:* circumcision and *Sabbath,* as well as other ethical and ceremonial commandments.

The *Talmud,* based on the *Mishnah* and its interpretations, took shape over many centuries in the Babylonian and Palestinian Schools. It was a strong binding force of Judaism in the Dispersion.

In the 12th century, Maimonides formulated his "13 Articles of Faith," which carried great authority. Fundamental in this creed are: belief in God and his oneness *(Shema),* belief in the changeless

Estimated Membership of the Principal Religions of the World

Statistics of the world's religions are only very rough approximations. Aside from Christianity, few religions, if any, attempt to keep statistical records; and even Protestants and Catholics employ different methods of counting members. All persons of whatever age who have received baptism in the Catholic Church are counted as members, while in most Protestant Churches only those who "join" the church are numbered. The compiling of statistics is further complicated by the fact that in China one may be at the same time a Confucian, a Taoist, and a Buddhist. In Japan, one may be both a Buddhist and a Shintoist.

Religion	North America[1]	South America	Europe	Asia	Africa	Oceania[2]	World
Total Christian	238,028,500	174,112,000	340,780,400	95,787,240	130,917,000	18,158,000	997,783,140
Roman Catholic	133,889,000	161,489,000	177,187,300	55,027,000	48,024,500	4,445,000	580,061,800
Eastern Orthodox	4,782,000	514,000	53,035,600	2,328,000	13,106,000	409,000	74,174,600
Protestant	99,357,500	12,109,000	110,557,500	38,432,240	69,786,500	13,304,000	343,546,740
Jewish[3]	6,295,340	585,800	4,057,120	3,492,860	176,900	76,500	14,684,520
Muslim	386,200	254,000	15,945,000	429,766,000	145,714,700	92,000	592,157,900
Zoroastrian	2,750	2,600	12,000	257,000	700	1,000	276,050
Shinto	60,000	90,000	—	58,003,000	1,200	—	58,154,200
Taoist	16,000	10,000	—	30,260,000	—	—	30,286,000
Confucian	97,100	70,000	—	153,887,500	1,500	24,000	154,080,100
Buddhist	197,250	194,450	194,500	255,741,000	25,000	35,000	256,387,200
Hindu	96,500	852,000	425,000	478,073,000	1,379,800	415,000	481,241,300
Totals	**245,179,640**	**176,170,850**	**361,414,020**	**1,505,267,600**	**278,216,800**	**18,801,500**	**2,585,050,410**

1. Includes Central America and West Indies. 2. Includes Australia and New Zealand, as well as islands of the South Pacific. 3. Includes total Jewish population, whether or not related to the synagogue. *Source: Britannica Book of the Year, 1982.*

Torah, in the words of Moses and the prophets, belief in reward and punishment, the coming of the Messiah, and the resurrection of the dead.

Judaism is divided into theological schools, the main divisions of which are Orthodox, Conservative, and Reform.

Christianity

Christianity is founded upon Jesus Christ, to whose life the New Testament writings testify. Jesus, a Jew, was born in about 7 B.C. and assumed his public life, after his 30th year, in Galilee. The Gospels tell of many extraordinary deeds that accompanied his ministry. He proclaimed the Kingdom of God, a future reality that is at the same time already present. Nationalistic-Jewish expectations of the Messiah he rejected. Rather, he referred to himself as the "Son of Man," the Christ, who has power to forgive sins now and who shall also come as Judge at the end of time. Jesus set forth the religio-ethical demands for participation in the Kingdom of God as change of heart and love of God and neighbor.

At the Last Supper he signified his death as a sacrifice, which would inaugurate the New Covenant, by which many would be saved. Circa A.D. 30 he died on a cross in Jerusalem. The early Church carried on Jesus' proclamation, the apostle Paul emphasizing his death and resurrection.

The person of Jesus is fundamental to the Christian faith since it is believed that in his life, death, and resurrection, God's revelation became historically tangible. He is seen as the turning point in history, and man's relationship to God as determined by his attitude to Jesus.

Historically Christianity thus arose out of Judaism, claiming fulfillment of the promises of the Old Testament in Jesus. The early Church designated itself as "the true Israel," which expected the speedy return of Jesus. The mother church was at Jerusalem, but churches were soon founded in many other places. The apostle Paul was instrumental in founding and extending a Gentile Christianity that was free from Jewish legalism.

The new religion spread rapidly throughout the eastern and western parts of the Roman Empire. In coming to terms with other religious movements within the Empire, Christianity began to take definite shape as an organization in its doctrine, liturgy, and ministry circa A.D. 200. In the 4th century the Catholic Church had taken root in countries stretching from Spain in the West to Persia and India in the East. Christians had been repeatedly subject to persecution by the Roman state, but finally gained tolerance under Constantine the Great (A.D. 313). Since that time, the Church became favored under his successors and in 380 the Emperor Theodosius proclaimed Christianity the State religion. Paganism was suppressed and public life was gradually molded in accordance with Christian ethical demands.

It was in these years also that the Church was able to achieve a certain unity of doctrine. Due to differences of interpretation of basic doctrines concerning Christ, which threatened to divide the Catholic Church, a standard Christian Creed was formulated by bishops at successive Ecumenical Councils, the first of which was held in A.D. 325 (Nicaea). The chief doctrines formulated concerned the doctrine of the Trinity, i.e., that there is one God in three persons: Father, Son, and Holy Spirit (Constantinople, A.D. 381); and the nature of Christ as both divine and human (Chalcedon, A.D. 541).

Through differences and rivalry between East and West the unity of the Church was broken by schism in 1054. In 1517 a separation occurred in the Western Church with the Reformation. From the major Protestant denominations [Lutheran, Presbyterian, Anglican (Episcopalian)], many Free Churches separated themselves in an age of individualism.

In the 20th century, however, the direction is toward unity. The Ecumenical Movement led to the formation of the World Council of Churches in 1948 (Amsterdam), which has since been joined by many Protestant and Orthodox Churches.

Through its missionary activity Christianity has spread to most parts of the globe.

Eastern Orthodoxy

Eastern Orthodoxy comprises the faith and practice of Churches stemming from ancient Churches in the Eastern part of the Roman Empire. The term covers Orthodox Churches in communion with the See of Constantinople, Uniate Churches in communion with Rome, and Nestorian and Monophysite Churches.

The Orthodox, Catholic, Apostolic Church is the direct descendant of the Byzantine State Church and consists of a series of independent national churches that are united by Doctrine, Liturgy, and Hierarchical organization (deacons and priests, who may either be married or be monks before ordination, and bishops, who must be celibates). The heads of these Churches are patriarchs or metropolitans; the Patriarch of Constantinople is only "first among equals." Rivalry between the Pope of Rome and the Patriarch of Constantinople, aided by differences and misunderstandings that existed for centuries between the Eastern and Western parts of the Empire, led to a schism in 1054. Repeated attempts at reunion have failed in past centuries. The mutual excommunication pronounced in that year was lifted in 1965, however, and because of greater interaction in theology between Orthodox Churches and those in the West, a climate of better understanding has been created in the 20th century. First contacts were with Anglicans and Old Catholics. Orthodox Churches belong to the World Council of Churches.

The Eastern Orthodox Churches recognize only the canons of the seven Ecumenical Councils (325–787) as binding for faith and they reject doctrines that have been added in the West.

The central worship service is called the Liturgy, which is understood as representation of God's acts of salvation. Its center is the celebration of the Eucharist, or Lord's Supper.

In their worship *icons* (sacred pictures) are used that have a sacramental meaning as representation. The Mother of Christ, angels, and saints are highly venerated.

The number of sacraments in the Orthodox Church is the same as in the Western Catholic Church.

Orthodox Churches are found in the Balkans and the Soviet Union also, since the 20th century, in Western Europe and other parts of the world, particularly in America.

Eastern Orthodoxy also includes the Uniate Churches that recognize the authority of the Pope but keep their own traditional liturgies and those Churches dating back to the 5th century that emancipated themselves from the Byzantine State

Church: the Nestorian Church in the Near East and India with approximately half a million members and the Monophysite Churches with some 17 million members (Coptic, Ethiopian, Syrian, Armenian, and the Mar Thoma Church in India).

Roman Catholicism

Roman Catholicism comprises the belief and practice of the Roman Catholic Church. The Church stands under the authority of the Bishop of Rome, the Pope, and is ruled by him and bishops who are held to be, through ordination, successors of Peter and the Apostles, respectively. Fundamental to the structure of the Church is the juridical aspect: doctrine and sacraments are bound to the power of jurisdiction and consecration of the hierarchy. The Pope, as the head of the hierarchy of archbishops, bishops, priests, and deacons, has full ecclesiastical power, granted him by Christ, through Peter. As successor to Peter, he is the Vicar of Christ. The powers that others in the hierarchy possess are delegated.

Roman Catholics believe their Church to be the one, holy, catholic, and apostolic Church, possessing all the properties of the one, true Church of Christ.

The faith of the Church is understood to be identical with that taught by Christ and his Apostles and contained in Bible and Tradition, i.e. the original deposit of faith, to which nothing new may be added. New definitions of doctrines, such as the Immaculate Conception of Mary (1854) and the bodily Assumption of Mary (1950), have been declared by Popes, however, in accordance with the principle of development (implicit-explicit doctrine).

At Vatican Council I (1870) the Pope was proclaimed "endowed with infallibility, *ex cathedra,* i.e., when exercising the office of Pastor and Teacher of all Christians."

The center of Roman Catholic worship is the celebration of the Mass, the Eucharist, which is the commemoration of Christ's sacrificial death and of his resurrection. Other sacraments are Baptism, Confirmation, Confession, Matrimony, Ordination, and Extreme Unction, seven in all. The Virgin Mary and saints, and their relics, are highly venerated and prayers are made to them to intercede with God, in whose presence they are believed to dwell.

The Roman Catholic Church is the largest Christian organization in the world, found in most countries. Some 8 million belong to the Uniate rites, the vast majority to the Latin rite.

Since Vatican Council II (1962–65), and the effort to "update" the Church, many interesting changes and developments have been taking place.

Protestantism

Protestantism comprises the Christian churches that separated from Rome during the Reformation in the 16th century, initiated by an Augustinian monk, Martin Luther. "Protestant" was originally applied to followers of Luther, who protested at the Diet of Spires (1529) against the decree which prohibited all further ecclesiastical reforms. Subsequently, Protestantism came to mean rejection of attempts to tie God's revelation to earthly institutions, and a return to the Gospel and the Word of God as sole authority in matters of faith and practice. Central in the biblical message is the justification of the sinner by faith alone. The Church is understood as a fellowship and the priesthood of all believers stressed.

The Augsburg Confession (1530) was the principal statement of Lutheran faith and practice. It became a model for other Confessions of Faith, which in their turn had decisive influence on Church polity. Major Protestant denominations are the Lutheran, Reformed (Calvinist), Presbyterian, and Anglican (Episcopal). Smaller ones are the Mennonite. Schwenkfeldians, and Unitarians. In Great Britain and America there are the Congregationalists, Baptists, Quakers, Methodists, and other free church types of communities. (In regarding themselves as being faithful to original biblical Christianity, these Churches differ from such religious bodies as Unitarians, Mormons, Jehovah's Witnesses, and Christian Scientists, who either teach new doctrines or reject old ones.)

Since the latter part of the 19th century, national councils of churches have been established in many countries, e.g. the Federal Council of Churches of Christ in America in 1908. Denominations across countries joined in federations and world alliances, beginning with the Anglican Lambeth Conference in 1867.

Protestant missionary activity, particularly strong in the last century, resulted in the founding of many younger churches in Asia and Africa. The Ecumenical Movement, which originated with Protestant missions, aims at unity among Christians and churches.

Islam

Islam is the religion founded in Arabia by Mohammed between 610 and 632. Its more than 600 million adherents are found in countries stretching from Morocco in the West to Indonesia in the East.

Mohammed was born in A.D. 570 at Mecca and belonged to the Quraysh tribe, which was active in caravan trade. At the age of 25 he joined the caravan trade from Mecca to Syria in the employment of a rich widow, Khadiji, whom he married. Critical of the idolatry of the inhabitants of Mecca, he began to lead a contemplative life in the deserts. There he received a series of revelations. Encouraged by Khadiji, he gradually became convinced that he was given a God-appointed task to devote himself to the reform of religion and society. Idolatry was to be abandoned.

The *Hegira (Hijra)* (migration) of Mohammed from Mecca, where he was not honored, to Medina, where he was well received, occurred in 622 and marks the beginning of the Muslim era. In 630 he marched on Mecca and conquered it. He died at Medina in 632. His grave there has since been a place of pilgrimage.

Mohammed's followers, called Moslems, revered him as the prophet of *Allah* (God), beside whom there is no other God. Although he had no close knowledge of Judaism and Christianity, he considered himself succeeding and completing them as the seal of the Prophets. Sources of the Islamic faith are the *Qur'an,* regarded as the uncreated, eternal Word of God, and Tradition *(hadith)* regarding sayings and deeds of the prophet.

Islam means surrender to the will of *Allah.* He is the all-powerful, whose will is supreme and determines man's fate. Good deeds will be rewarded at the Last Judgment in paradise and evil deeds will be punished in hell.

The Five Pillars, primary duties, of Islam are: witness; confessing the oneness of God and of Mohammed, his prophet; prayer, to be performed five times a day; almsgiving to the poor and the mosque (house of worship); fasting during daylight hours in the month of Ramadan; and pilgrimage to Mecca at least once in the Moslem's lifetime.

The practice of Holy War *(jihad)*, at first responsible for the rapid growth of the new religion, could not be maintained. Mohammed curtailed the practice of polygamy by limiting it to four wives. In modern times the position of women has improved, due to Western influence. The eating of pork and drinking of intoxicants is forbidden.

Islam, upholding the law of brotherhood, succeeded in uniting an Arab world that had disintegrated into tribes and castes. Disagreements concerning the succession of the prophet caused a great division in Islam between *Sunnis* and *Shias.* Among these, other sects arose *(Wahhabi).* Doctrinal issues also led to the rise of different schools of thought in theology. Nevertheless, since Arab armies turned against Syria and Palestine in 635, Islam has expanded successfully under Mohammed's successors. Its rapid conquests in Asia and Africa are unsurpassed in history. Turning against Europe, Moslems conquered Spain in 713. In 1453 Constantinople fell into their hands and in 1529 Moslem armies besieged Vienna. Since then, Islam has lost its foothold in Europe.

In modern times it has made great gains in Africa.

Hinduism

In India alone there are more than 300 million adherents of Hinduism. In contrast to other religions, it has no founder. Considered the oldest religion in the world, it dates back, perhaps, to prehistoric times.

Hinduism is hard to define, there being no common creed, no one doctrine to bind Hindus together. Intellectually there is complete freedom of belief, and one can be monotheist, polytheist, or atheist. What matters is the social system: a Hindu is one born into a caste.

As a religion, Hinduism is founded on the sacred scriptures, written in Sanskrit and called the *Vedas* (*Veda*-knowledge). There are four Vedic books, among which the *Rig Veda* is the most important. It speaks of many gods and also deals with questions concerning the universe and creation. The dates of these works are unknown (1000 B.C.?).

The *Upanishads* (dated 1000–300 B.C.), commentaries on the Vedic texts, have philosophical speculations on the origin of the universe, the nature of deity, of *atman* (the human soul), and its relationship to *Brahman* (the universal soul).

Brahman is the principle and source of the universe who can be indicated only by negatives. As the divine intelligence, he is the ground of the visible world, a presence that pervades all beings. Thus the many Hindu deities came to be understood as manifestations of the one *Brahman* from whom everything proceeds and to whom everything ultimately returns. The religio-social system of Hinduism is based on the concept of reincarnation and transmigration in which all living beings, from plants below to gods above, are caught in a cosmic system that is an everlasting cycle of becoming and perishing.

Life is determined by the law of *karma,* according to which rebirth is dependent on moral behavior in a previous phase of existence. The doctrine of transmigration thus provides a rationale for the caste system. In this view, life on earth is regarded as transient *(maya)* and a burden. The goal of existence is liberation from the cycle of rebirth and redeath and entrance into the indescribable state of what in Buddhism is called *nirvana* (extinction of passion).

Further important sacred writings are the Epics *(puranas),* which contain legendary stories about gods and men. They are the *Mahabharata* (composed between 200 B.C. and A.D. 200) and the *Ramayana.* The former includes the *Bhagavad-Gita* (Song of the Lord), its most famous part, that tells of devotion to *Krishna* (Lord), who appears as an *avatar* (incarnation) of the god *Vishnu,* and of the duty of obeying caste rules. The work begins with a praise of the *yoga* (discipline) system.

The practice of Hinduism consists of rites and ceremonies, performed within the framework of the caste system and centering on the main socio-religious occasions of birth, marriage, and death. There are many Hindu temples, which are dwelling places of the deities and to which people bring offerings. There are also places of pilgrimages, the chief one being Benares on the Ganges, most sacred among the rivers in India.

In modern times work has been done to reform and revive Hinduism. One of the outstanding reformers was Ramakrishna (1836-86), who inspired many followers, one of whom founded the Ramakrishna mission, which seeks to convert others to its religion. The mission is active both in India and in other countries.

Buddhism

Founded in the 6th century B.C. in northern India by Gautama Buddha, who was born in southern Nepal as son to a king. His birth is surrounded by many legends, but Western scholars agree that he lived from 563 to 483 B.C. Warned by a sage that his son would become an ascetic or a universal monarch, the king confined him to his home. He was able to escape and began the life of a homeless wanderer in search of peace, passing through many disappointments until he finally came to the Tree of Enlightenment, under which he lived in meditation till enlightenment came to him and he became a Buddha (enlightened one).

Now he understood the origin of suffering, summarized in the *Four Noble Truths,* which constitutes the foundation of Buddhism. The Four are the truth of suffering, which all living beings must endure; of the origin of suffering, which is craving and which leads to rebirth; that it can be destroyed; and of the way that leads to cessation of pain, i.e., the *Noble Eightfold Way,* which is the rule of practical Buddhism: right views, right intention, right speech, right action, right livelihood, right effort, right concentration, and right ecstasy.

Nirvana is the goal of all existence, the state of complete redemption, into which the redeemed enters. Buddha's insight can free every man from the law of reincarnation through complete emptying of the self.

The nucleus of Buddha's church or association was originally formed by monks and lay-brothers, whose houses gradually became monasteries used as places for religious instruction. The worship service consisted of a sermon, expounding of Scripture, meditation, and confession. At a later stage pilgrimages to the holy places associated with the Buddha came into being, as well as veneration of relics.

In the 3rd century B.C., King Ashoka made Buddhism the State religion of India but, as centuries passed, it gradually fell into decay through splits, persecutions, and the hostile Brahmans. Buddhism spread to countries outside India, however.

At the beginning of the Christian era, there occurred a split that gave rise to two main types: *Hinayana* (Little Vehicle), or southern Buddhism, and *Mahayana* (Great Vehicle), or northern Buddhism. The former type, more individualistic, survived in Ceylon and southern Asia. *Hinayana* retained more closely the original teachings of the Buddha, which did not know of a personal god or soul. *Mahayana,* more social, polytheistic, and developing a pluralistic pompous cult, was strong in the Himalayas, Tibet, Mongolia, China, Korea, and Japan.

In the present century, Buddhism has found believers also in the West and Buddhist associations have been established in Europe and the U. S.

Confucianism

Confucius (K'ung Fu-tzu), born in the state of Lu (northern China), lived from 551 to 479 B.C. Tradition, exaggerating the importance of Confucius in life, has depicted him as a great statesman but, in fact, he seems to have been a private teacher. Anthologies of ancient Chinese classics, along with his own Analects *(Lun Yu),* became the basis of Confucianism. These Analects were transmitted as a collection of his sayings as recorded by his students, with whom he discussed ethical and social problems. They developed into men of high moral standing, who served the State as administrators.

In his teachings, Confucius emphasized the importance of an old Chinese concept *(li)* , which has the connotation of proper conduct. There is some disagreement as to the religious ideas of Confucius, but he held high the concepts handed down from centuries before him. Thus he believed in Heaven *(T'ien)* and sacrificed to his ancestors. Ancestor worship he indeed encouraged as an expression of filial piety, which he considered the loftiest of virtues.

Piety to Confucius was the foundation of the family as well as the State. The family is the nucleus of the State, and the "five relations," between king and subject, father and son, man and wife, older and younger brother, and friend and friend, are determined by the virtues of love of fellow men, righteousness, and respect.

An extension of ancestor worship may be seen in the worship of Confucius, which became official in the 2nd century B.C. when the emperor, in recognition of Confucius' teachings as supporting the imperial rule, offered sacrifices at his tomb.

Mencius (Meng Tse), who lived around 400 B.C., did much to propagate and elaborate Confucianism in its concern with ordering society. Thus, for two millennia, Confucius' doctrine of State, with its emphasis on ethics and social morality, rooted in ancient Chinese tradition and developed and continued by his disciples, has been standard in China and the Far East.

With the revolution of 1911 in China, however, students, burning Confucius in effigy, called for the removel of "the old curiosity shop."

Shintoism

Shinto, the Chinese term for the Japanese *Kami no Michi,* i.e., the Way of the Gods, comprises the religious ideas and cult indigenous to Japan. *Kami,* or gods, considered divine forces of nature that are worshipped, may reside in rivers, trees, rocks, mountains, certain animals, or, particularly, in the sun and moon. The worship of ancestors, heroes, and deceased emperors was incorporated later.

After Buddhism had come from Korea, Japan's native religion at first resisted it. Then there followed a period of compromise and amalgamation with Buddhist beliefs and ceremonies, resulting, since the 9th century A.D., in a syncretistic religion, a Twofold Shinto. Buddhist deities came to be regarded as manifestations of Japanese deities and Buddhist priests took over most of the Shinto shrines.

In modern times Shinto regained independence from Buddhism. Under the reign of the Emperor Meiji (1868–1912) it became the official State religion, in which loyalty to the emperor was emphasized. The line of succession of emperors is traced back to the first Emperor Jimmu (660 B.C.) and beyond him to the Sun-goddess *Amaterasuomikami.*

The centers of worship are the shrines and temples in which the deities are believed to dwell and believers approach them through *torii* (gateways). Most important among the shrines is the imperial shrine of the Sun-goddess at Ise, where state ceremonies were once held in June and December. The *Yasukuni* shrine of the war dead in Tokyo is also well known.

Acts of worship consist of prayers, clapping of hands, acts of purification, and offerings. On feast days processions and performances of music and dancing take place and priests read prayers before the gods in the shrines, asking for good harvest, the well-being of people and emperor, etc. In Japanese homes there is a god-shelf, a small wooden shrine that contains the tablets bearing the names of ancestors. Offerings are made and candles lit before it.

After World War II the Allied Command ordered the disestablishment of State Shinto. To be distinguished from State Shinto is Sect Shinto, consisting of 13 recognized sects. These have arisen in modern times, gaining large followings. Most important among them is *Tenrikyo* in Tenri City (Nara), in which healing by faith plays a central role.

Taoism

Taoism, a religion of China, was, according to tradition, founded by Lao Tse, a Chinese philosopher, long considered one of the prominent religious leaders from the 6th century B.C.

Data about him are for the most part legendary, however, and the *Tao Te Ching* (the classic of the Way and of its Power), traditionally ascribed to him, is now believed by many scholars to have originated in the 3rd century B.C. The book is composed in short chapters, written in aphoristic rhymes. Central are the word *Tao,* which means way or path and, in a deeper sense, signifies the principle that underlies the reality of this world and manifests itself in nature and in the lives of men, and the word *Te* (power).

The virtuous man draws power from being absorbed in *Tao,* the ultimate reality within an ever-changing world. By non-action and keeping away from human striving it is possible for man to live in harmony with the principles that underlie and govern the universe. *Tao* cannot be comprehended by reason and knowledge, but only by inward quiet.

Besides the *Tao Te Ching,* dating from approximately the same period, there are two Taoist works, written by Chuang Tse and Lieh Tse.

Theoretical Taoism of this classical philosophical movement of the 4th and 3rd centuries B.C. in China differed from popular Taoism, into which it gradually degenerated. The standard of theoretical Taoism was maintained in the classics, of course, and among the upper classes it continued to be alive until modern times.

Religious Taoism is a form of religion dealing with deities and spirits, magic and soothsaying. In the 2nd century A.D. it was organized with temples, cult, priests, and monasteries and was able to hold its own in the competition with Buddhism that came up at the same time.

After the 7th century A.D., however, Taoist religion further declined. Split into numerous sects, which often operate like secret societies, it has become a syncretistic folk religion in which some of the old deities and saints live on.

History of Leading Religious Groups in the United States

(50,000 members or over)

Source: Yearbook of American and Canadian Churches, 1982.

BAPTIST

American Baptist Association: A group of independent Missionary Baptist Churches, mainly in the South, Southeast, and Southwest, organized in 1905. Members (1981): 1,500,000. Headquarters: 4605 N. State Line Ave., Texarkana, Tex. 75501.

American Baptist Churches in the U.S.A.: Formerly known as the Northern Baptist Convention and the American Baptist Convention, this body changed its name in 1973. Although national missionary organizational developments began in 1814 with the establishment of the American Baptist Foreign Mission Society, the Convention was not formed until 1907. Members (1979): 1,600,521. Headquarters: Valley Forge, Pa. 19481.

Baptist General Conference: Formerly known as the Swedish Baptist General Conference of America. It has operated as a general conference since 1879. Members (1980): 133,385. Headquarters: 2002 S. Arlington Heights Rd., Arlington Heights, Ill. 60005.

Baptist Missionary Association of America: Formerly called the North American Baptist Association. It was organized in 1950 in Little Rock, Ark. Members (1980): 224,533. Office of president: Rt. 2, Box 272, Corinth, Miss. 38834.

Conservative Baptist Association of America: Organized in 1947. Adherents regard the Bible as infallible. Local churches are independent, autonomous, and free from ecclesiastical or political authority. Members (1979): 225,000. Headquarters: Geneva Rd., Box 66, Wheaton, Ill. 60187.

Free Will Baptists: A body of evangelical Baptists, organized in 1727 in the South and 1780 in the North. Members (1980): 227,888. Headquarters: 1134 Murfreesboro Rd., Nashville, Tenn. 37217.

General Association of Regular Baptist Churches: Founded in 1932 in Chicago by a group of churches which had withdrawn from the Northern Baptist Convention (now the American Baptist Convention) because of doctrinal differences. Members (1981): 243,000. Headquarters: 1300 N. Meacham Rd., Schaumburg, Ill. 60195.

General Baptists (General Association of): An Arminian group of Baptists, organized in England in 1607 and transplanted to the colonies in 1714. It died out along the Seaboard, but revived in the Midwest in 1823. Members (1980): 74,159. Headquarters: 100 Stinson Dr., Poplar Bluff, Mo. 63901.

National Baptist Convention, U.S.A.: The older and parent convention of Black Baptists. This body is to be distinguished from the National Baptist Convention of America, usually referred to as the "unincorporated" body. Members (1958): 5,500,000. Office of president: 405 E. 31st St., Chicago, Ill. 60616.

National Baptist Convention of America: This is a body usually referred to as the "unincorporated" convention, not to be confused with the "incorporated" National Baptist Convention, U.S.A., Inc., from which this body withdrew. Organized in 1880. Members (1956): 2,668,799. Office of president: 954 Kings Rd., Jacksonville, Fla. 32204.

National Primitive Baptist Convention: A group of Baptists having local associations and a National Convention. Organized in 1907. Members (1975): 250,000. Headquarters: Box 2355, Tallahassee, Fla.

North American Baptist Association: *See* Baptist Missionary Association of America.

Primitive Baptists: A large group of Baptists, largely through the South, who are opposed to all centralization and to modern missionary societies. Members (1960): 72,000. Headquarters: Cayce Publishing Co., S. Second St., Thornton, Ariz., 71766.

Progressive National Baptist Convention: A body that held its organizational meeting in Cincinnati in 1961 and its first annual session in Philadelphia in 1962. Members (1967): 521,692. Office of president: Savannah Grove Baptist Church, 312 S. Main St., Sumter, S.C. 29150.

U. S. Church Membership

Religious group	Members
Protestant bodies and others	73,479,341
Roman Catholics	51,207,579
Jewish congregations[1]	5,920,000
Eastern churches	3,822,590
Old Catholic, Polish National Catholic, Armenian churches	923,985
Buddhist Churches of America	60,000
Miscellaneous	161,185
Total[2]	135,574,680

1. Includes Orthodox, Conservative, and Reform. 2. As reported in the *1982 Yearbook* from statistics furnished by 218 religious bodies in the United States.

Southern Baptist Convention: In 1845, Southern Baptists withdrew from the General Missionary Convention over the question of slavery and other matters and formed the Southern Baptist Convention. Members (1980): 13,600,126. Office of recording secretary: 127 9th Ave. N., Nashville, Tenn. 37234.

United Free Will Baptist Church: A body which set up its organization in 1870. Members (1952): 100,000. Headquarters: Kinston College, 1000 University St., Kinston, N.C. 28501.

CATHOLIC AND ORTHODOX

American Carpatho-Russian Orthodox Greek Catholic Church: This church is a self-governing diocese in communion with the Ecumenical Patriarchate of Constantinople. On Sept. 19, 1938, the late Patriarch Benjamin I canonized the diocese in the name of the Orthodox Church of Christ. Members (1976): 100,000. Headquarters: Johnstown, Pa. 15906.

Antiochian Orthodox Christian Archdiocese of North America: Formed in 1975 by merger of the Antiochian Orthodox Christian Archdiocese of New York and All North America (formerly the Syrian Antiochian Orthodox Archdiocese of New York and North America) and the Antiochian Orthodox Archdiocese of Toledo, Ohio, and Dependencies in North America. The new Archdiocese is under the jurisdiction of the Patriarch of Antioch. Members (1977): 152,000. Headquarters: 358 Mountain Rd., Englewood, N.J. 07631.

Armenian Apostolic Church of America: The Armenian Church divided into two separate dioceses in 1933 because of a dispute regarding the political activities of the prelate at that time, and because of the status of the church in Soviet Armenia. Since 1956, this diocese has been under the jurisdiction of the Holy See of Cilicia, Beirut, Lebanon. Members (1972): 125,000. Headquarters: 138 E. 39th St., New York, N.Y. 10016.

Armenian Church of America, Diocese of the (including Diocese of California): The American branch of the Ancient Church of Armenia. Established in the U. S. in 1889. Diocesan organization is under the jurisdiction of the Holy See of Etchmiadzin, Armenia, U.S.S.R. Members (1979): 450,000. Headquarters: St. Vartan Cathedral, 630 Second Ave., New York, N.Y. 10016.

Bulgarian Eastern Orthodox Church (Diocese of North and South America and Australia): A Synod of the Bulgarian Eastern Orthodox Church, established as the Bulgarian Orthodox Mission in 1909. Became a canonical metropolitan archdiocese in 1947. Members (1971): 86,000. Headquarters: 550A W. 50th St., New York, N.Y. 10019; 1953 Stockbridge Rd., Akron, Ohio, 44313.

Coptic Orthodox Church: Part of the ancient Coptic Orthodox Church of Egypt. Egyptian immigrants have formed many parishes in the United States. Members (1980): 100,000. Office of correspondent: 427 West Side Ave., Jersey City, N.J. 07304.

Greek Orthodox Archdiocese of North and South America: Greek-speaking Orthodox Christians have parishes in the U. S., Canada, and South America. These are under the Ecumenical Patriarchate of Constantinople. Members (1977): 1,950,000. Headquarters: 8–10 E. 79th St., New York, N.Y. 10021.

North American Old Roman Catholic Church: A body with the doctrine of the Old Catholics; identical with the Roman Catholic Church in most worship and discipline. It is not under Papal jurisdiction. Members (1980): 61,263. Office of presiding archbishop: 4200 N. Kedvale Ave., Chicago, Ill. 60641.

Orthodox Church in America (The Russian Orthodox Greek Catholic Church of America): This body entered Alaska in 1792. In 1872, its headquarters were moved from Sitka to San Francisco and, in 1905, to New York. Members (1978): 1,000,000. Office of primate: Box 675, Syosset, N.Y. 11791.

Polish National Catholic Church of America: After long dissatisfaction with Roman Catholic administration and ideology, this group was organized in 1897. Members (1960): 282,411. Headquarters: 529 E. Locust St., Scranton, Pa. 18505.

Roman Catholic Church: The largest single group of Christians in the U. S., the Roman Catholic Church is under the spiritual leadership of the Pope. This group dates back to the priests who accompanied Columbus on his second voyage to the New World. A settlement, later discontinued, was made at St. Augustine, Fla. The continuous history of this Church in the colonies began at St. Mary's in 1634, in Maryland. Members (1981): 51,207,579. National Conference of Catholic Bishops, 1312 Massachusetts Ave., N.W., Washington, D.C. 20005.

Russian Orthodox Church in the U.S.A., Patriarchial Parishes of the: This autonomous body is the direct canonical successor of the Orthodox Catholic mission established in Alaska by the Russian Orthodox Church in 1793. It is under the spiritual jurisdiction of the Patriarch of Moscow and all Russia, His Holiness Pimen. In 1962 an administration was established for the Orthodox Mission in Puerto Rico and the Spanish-speaking people in the United States. Members (1975): 51,500. Headquarters: St. Nicholas Patriarchal Cathedral, 15 E. 97th St., New York, N.Y. 10029.

Russian Orthodox Church Outside Russia: The governing body was set up in Constantinople. In 1950, it came to the U. S. Members (1955): 55,000. Headquarters: 75 E. 93rd St., New York, N.Y. 10028.

Serbian Eastern Orthodox Church for the U.S.A. and Canada: This body of the Eastern Orthodox Church is autonomous. Members (1967): 65,000. Chancery: St. Sava Monastery, Box 519, Libertyville, Ill. 60048.

Syrian Antiochian Orthodox Archdiocese of New York and North America: *See* Antiochian Orthodox Christian Archdiocese of New York and All North America.

Ukrainian Orthodox Church in the U.S.A.: This church was organized in the U.S. in 1919. Members (1966): 87,745. Headquarters: South Bound Brook, N.J. 08880.

JEWISH

Jews arrived in the colonies before 1650. The first congregation is recorded in 1654, in New York

City, the Shearith Israel (Remnant of Israel). Members (1980): 5,920,000.

Following are the major Jewish organizations:

Central Conference of American Rabbis (Reform): 790 Madison Ave., New York, N.Y. 10021
Rabbinical Alliance of America (Orthodox): 156 Fifth Ave., New York, N.Y. 10011
Rabbinical Assembly (Conservative): 3080 Broadway, New York, N.Y. 10027
Rabbinical Council of America (Orthodox): 1250 Broadway, New York, N.Y. 10001
Synagogue Council of America: 432 Park Ave. South, New York, N.Y. 10016
Union of American Hebrew Congregations (Reform): 838 Fifth Ave., New York, N.Y. 10021
Union of Orthodox Jewish Congregations of America: 45 W. 36th St., New York, N.Y. 10018
Union of Orthodox Rabbis of the United States and Canada: 235 E. Broadway, New York, N.Y. 10002
United Synagogue of America (Conservative): 155 Fifth Ave., New York, N.Y. 10010

LUTHERAN

American Lutheran Church: This church is the result of the merger in 1960 of the American Lutheran Church, the Evangelical Lutheran Church, and the United Evangelical Lutheran Church. In 1963, the Lutheran Free Church merged with The American Lutheran Church. Members (1980): 2,353,229. Headquarters: 422 S. Fifth St., Minneapolis, Minn. 55415.

Evangelical Lutheran Churches, Association of: Formed in 1976, this group is made up mainly of former affiliates of the Lutheran Church-Missouri Synod, plus some new and some formerly independent congregations. Its members have joined together to be in mission and ministry. Members (1980): 107,782. Headquarters: 12015 Manchester Rd., St. Louis, Mo. 63131.

Lutheran Church—Missouri Synod: This body, the largest constituent part of the Evangelical Lutheran Synodical Conference of North America, was organized in 1847. It is the leader in the conservative group among the Lutherans. Members (1980): 2,625,650. Headquarters: 500 N. Broadway, St. Louis, Mo. 63102.

Lutheran Church in America: This body was organized in 1962 by the consolidation of the American Evangelical Lutheran Church (1874), the Augustana Evangelical Lutheran Church (1860), the Finnish Evangelical Lutheran Church (1890), and the United Lutheran Church in America (1918). Members (1980): 2,923,260. Headquarters: 231 Madison Ave., New York, N.Y. 10016.

Wisconsin Evangelical Lutheran Synod: This body was organized in Wisconsin in 1850. Members (1980): 407,043. Office of president: 3512 W. North Ave., Milwaukee, Wis. 53208.

METHODIST

African Methodist Episcopal Church: This church began in 1787 in Philadelphia when persons in a Methodist Episcopal Church withdrew. In 1816, the denomination was started. Members (1980): 2,050,000. Office of senior bishop: 1002 Kirkwood Ave., Nashville, Tenn. 37203.

African Methodist Episcopal Zion Church: This group was organized in 1796, having withdrawn from the John Street Methodist Church, New York. (1980): 1,134,176. Office of senior bishop: 3752 Springhill Ave., Mobile, Ala. 36608.

Christian Methodist Episcopal Church: In 1870, the General Conference of the M.E. Church, South, approved the request of its black membership for the formation of their conferences into a separate body. Members (1981): 786,707. Office of secretary: Box 74, Memphis, Tenn. 38101.

Free Methodist Church of North America: This body, organized in 1860, grew out of a movement in the Genesee Conference of the Methodist Episcopal Church about 1850 towards a more original Methodism. Members (1979): 67,394. Headquarters: 901 College Ave., Winona Lake, Ind. 46590.

United Methodist Church: The United Methodist Church was formed in April, 1968, by the union of the Methodist Church and the Evangelical United Brethren Church. The two churches shared a common historical and spiritual heritage. The Methodist Church resulted in 1939 from the unification of three branches of Methodism—the Methodist Episcopal Church; the Methodist Episcopal Church South; and the Methodist Protestant Church. The Methodist movement began in 18th-century England under the preaching of John Wesley, but the so-called Christmas Conference of 1784 in Baltimore is regarded as the date on which the organized Methodist Church was founded as an ecclesiastical organization. The Evangelical United Brethren Church was formed in 1946 with the merger of the Evangelical Church and the Church of the United Brethren in Christ, both of which had their beginnings in Pennsylvania in the evangelistic movement of the 18th and early 19th centuries. Members (1980): 9,584,711. Office of Secretary of General Conference, Perkins School of Theology, Southern Methodist University, Dallas, Tex. 75222.

PRESBYTERIAN

Cumberland Presbyterian Church: An outgrowth of the Great Revival of 1800, the Cumberland Presbytery was organized in 1810 in Tennessee. A union with the Presbyterian Church, U.S.A., in 1906, was only partially successful, and the Cumberland Presbyterian Church continued as a separate denomination. Members (1980): 96,553. Office of moderator: 7225 Old Clinton Pike, Knoxville, Tenn. 37921.

Presbyterian Church in America: Formed in Birmingham, Ala., in 1973 after separating from the Presbyterian Church in the United States, this body believes the Bible is the only infallible rule of faith and practice. It is committed to the Reformed Faith as set forth in the Westminster Confession and Catechisms. Members (1980): 90,991. Office of stated clerk: Box 312, Brevard, N.C. 28712.

Presbyterian Church in the United States: This body is a branch of the Presbyterian Church established in separate existence in 1861. Members (1980): 838,485. Headquarters: 341 Ponce de Leon Ave., NE, Atlanta, Ga. 30365.

United Presbyterian Church in the United States of America: This group was formed in 1958 by a merger of the Presbyterian Church in the U.S.A. (dating from 1706) and the United Presbyterian Church of North America (established in 1858). Members (1980): 2,423,601. Headquarters: 475 Riverside

Dr., New York, N.Y. 10115.

OTHER RELIGIOUS BODIES

Apostolic Overcoming Holy Church of God: A black body incorporated in Alabama in 1919. It is evangelistic in purpose and emphasizes sanctification, holiness, and divine healing. Members (1956): 75,000. Office of secretary, 909 Jasper Rd. W., Birmingham, Ala. 35204.

Assemblies of God: A pentecostal, evangelical, missionary denomination which grew out of the spiritual revivals of the early 1900's. The organization is composed of self-governing churches. Founded in Arkansas in 1914. Members (1980): 1,732,371. Headquarters: 1445 Boonville Ave., Springfield, Mo. 65802.

Bahá'í Faith: Baháís are followers of Bahá'u'lláh (1817–1892), whose religion upholds the basic principle of progressive revelation, religious unity and a new world order. There is a spiritual and administrative world center in Haifa, Israel. Headquarters, 536 Sheridan Rd., Wilmette, Ill. 60091.

Buddhist Churches of America: Organized in 1914 as the Buddhist Mission of North America, this body was incorporated in 1942 under the present name and represents the Jodo Shinshu Sect of Buddhism in this country. Members (1975): 60,000. Headquarters: 1710 Octavia St., San Francisco, Calif. 94109.

Christian and Missionary Alliance: An evangelical, evangelistic, and missionary movement organized in 1887. It stresses "the deeper Christian life and consecration to the Lord's service." Members (1980): 189,710. Headquarters: 350 N. Highland Ave., Nyack, N.Y. 10960.

Christian Church (Disciples of Christ): In the revival period of the early nineteenth century, a movement resulted in the establishment of a fellowship called "Christians" or "Disciples." This movement calls for the reunion of the church on the basis of a return to New Testament faith and order. It is congregational in government. Members (1980): 1,177,984. Headquarters: 222 S. Downey Ave., Box 1986, Indianapolis, Ind. 46206.

Christian Churches and Churches of Christ: This fellowship, congregational in polity, has its origin in the movement to "restore the New Testament church in doctrine, ordinances and life." Members (1981): 1,063,254. North American Christian Convention, Box 39456, Cincinnati, Ohio 45231.

Christian Congregation: Incorporated in 1887, denomination provides ministerial affiliation for independent clergymen. Members (1980): 89,379. Office of general superintendent: 804 W. Hemlock St., LaFollette, Tenn. 37766.

Christian Reformed Church in North America: A group of Dutch Calvinists which dissented from the Reformed Church in America in 1857 and which was strengthened by later accessions from the same source and by immigration. Members (1980): 213,995. Office of stated clerk: William P. Brink, 2850 Kalamazoo Ave., S.E., Grand Rapids, Mich. 49560.

Church of Christ, Scientist: Founded by Mary Baker Eddy in 1879 to reinstate the healing power of original Christianity. As defined by Mrs. Eddy, her religion is the scientific system of divine healing.[1] Headquarters: Christian Science Church Center, Boston, Mass. 02115.

Church of God: Inaugurated by Bishop A. J. Tomlinson, who served as General Overseer 1903–43. Episcopal in administration. Members (1978): 75,890. Headquarters: 2504 Arrow Wood Dr., S.E., Huntsville, Ala. 35803.

Church of God (Anderson, Ind.): This group is one of the largest of the groups which have taken the name "Church of God." It originated about 1880 and emphasizes Christian unity. Members (1980): 176,429. Headquarters: Box 2420, Anderson, Ind. 46018.

Church of God (Cleveland, Tenn.): This church is one of the large groups which use the name "Church of God." Organized in 1886 in Tennessee as the Christian Union, it was reorganized in 1902 as the Holiness Church, and in 1907 under its present name. Members (1980): 435,012. Headquarters: Keith St. at 25th., N.W., Cleveland, Tenn. 37311.

Church of God in Christ: Organized in Arkansas in 1895, by C. P. Jones and C. H. Mason, who believed there was no salvation without holiness; incorporated 1897. Members (1965): 425,000. Headquarters: 938 Mason St., Memphis, Tenn. 38126.

Church of God in Christ, International: Organized in 1969 in Kansas City, Mo., by 14 bishops of the Church of God in Christ of Memphis, Tenn., after disagreement over polity and governmental authority. Church is Wesleyan in theology. Members (1971): 501,000. Headquarters: 170 Adelphi St., Brooklyn, N.Y. 11025.

Church of God of Prophecy: Organized in 1903 at Murphy, N. C. Doctrine stresses justification by faith and the second coming of Christ. Members (1981): 72,977. Headquarters: Bible Place, Cleveland, Tenn. 37311.

Church of the Brethren: German pietists from Krefeld, Germany, under the leadership of Peter Becker, entered the colonies in 1719, and settled at Germantown, Philadelphia, Pa. They hold to the principles of nonviolence, temperance, and the expression of religion through the good life. Members (1980): 170,839. Headquarters: 1451 Dundee Ave., Elgin, Ill. 60120.

Church of the Nazarene: One of the larger holiness bodies, organized in Pilot Point, Tex., in 1908. It is in general accord with the early doctrines of Methodism and emphasizes entire sanctification. Members (1980): 484,276. Headquarters: 6401 The Paseo, Kansas City, Mo. 64131.

Churches of Christ: This body is made up of a large group of churches, formerly reported with the Disciples of Christ but, since the religious census of 1906, reported separately. They are strictly congregational and have no organization larger than the local congregation. Members (1979): 1,600,000.

1. Membership figure not available. The manual of the church forbids "the numbering of people and the reporting of such statistics for publication."

Community Churches, National Council of: This body was formed in 1946 by the merger of the Biennial Council of Community Churches, a black group, with white churches which had the name of the present Council. Its members are ecumenically minded, congregationally governed, non-creedal Protestant churches. Members (1979): 190,000. Headquarters: 89 E. Wilson Bridge Rd., Worthington, Ohio, 43085.

Congregational Christian Churches: *See* United Church of Christ.

Congregational Christian Churches, National Association of: Organized in Detroit, Mich., in 1955 to continue the Congregational way of faith and order in church life. It has no doctrinal requirements, and participation by member churches is voluntary. Members (1981): 104,000. Headquarters: Box 1620, Oak Creek, Wis. 53154.

Disciples of Christ: *See* Christian Church.

Episcopal Church, The: This group entered the colonies with the earliest settlers as the Church of England. It became autonomous, adopted its present name in 1789. It is an integral part of the Anglican Communion. In 1967, the General Convention adopted "The Episocal Church" as an alternate name. Members (1980): 2,786,004. Headquarters: 815 Second Ave., New York, N.Y. 10017.

Evangelical and Reformed Church: *See* United Church of Christ.

Evangelical Covenant Church of America: This church has its roots in historical Christianity as it emerged in the Protestant Reformation in the biblical instruction of the Lutheran State Church of Sweden. Organized in 1885 in Chicago. Prior to 1957, it was known as the Evangelical Mission Covenant Church of America. Members (1980): 77,737. Headquarters: 5101 N. Francisco Ave., Chicago, Ill. 60625.

Evangelical Free Church of America: Organized in the 1880's in Boone, Iowa, as the Swedish Evangelical Free Mission. Later the name was changed to the Evangelical Free Church of America. In 1950, the Evangelical Free Church Association merged with this group. Members (1979): 77,592. Headquarters: 1515 E. 66th St., Minneapolis, Minn. 55423.

Evangelical United Brethren Church: *See* United Methodist Church under Methodist Churches.

Friends United Meeting: The Five Years Meeting of Friends was formed in 1902 by 11 Yearly Meetings entering into a loose confederation. Since then, two of the original Yearly Meetings have withdrawn (Kansas and Oregon) and two American and three Yearly Meetings outside the U. S. have joined. In 1965, the name was changed to Friends United Meeting. Members (1980): 60,745. Office of presiding clerk: 101 Quaker Hill Dr., Richmond, Ind. 47374.

Independent Fundamental Churches of America: Organized in 1930 by representatives of various independent churches. Members (1980): 120,446. Headquarters: 1860 Mannheim Rd., Westchester, Ill. 60153.

International Church of the Foursquare Gospel: An evangelistic missionary body organized by Aimee Semple McPherson in 1927. The parent church is Angelus Temple, 1100 Glendale Blvd., Los Angeles, Calif. 90026. Members (1963): 89,215.

Jehovah's Witnesses: A group calling themselves primitive Christians. They believe that the Kingdom under Christ will replace all earthly governments. Members (1980): 565,309. Headquarters: 25 Columbia Heights, Brooklyn, N.Y. 11201.

Latter-day Saints, Church of Jesus Christ of: Organized in 1830. A group in which the Bible, the Book of Mormon, the Doctrine and Covenants, and the Pearl of Great Price are regarded as the word of God. Their belief is summed up in 13 Articles of Faith written by Joseph Smith. Members (1980): 2,811,000. Headquarters: 50 E. North Temple St., Salt Lake City, Utah, 84150.

Latter-day Saints, Reorganized Church of Jesus Christ of: A division among the Latter-day Saints (non-Mormon) occurred on the death of Joseph Smith in 1844. His son, Joseph Smith, became presiding officer of this group, which has headquarters at Independence, Mo. Members (1980): 190,087. Headquarters: the Auditorium, Box 1059, Auditorium, Independence, Mo. 64051.

Mennonite Church: The largest group of the Mennonites who began arriving in the U. S. in 1683, settling in Germantown, Pa. They derive their name from Menno Simons, born 1496. Members (1980): 99,511. Headquarters: 528 E. Madison St., Lombard, Ill. 60148.

Moravian Church in America (Unitas Fratrum): In 1735, Moravian missionaries of the pre-Reformation faith of John Hus came to Georgia, in 1740 to Pennsylvania, and in 1753 to North Carolina. Members: Northern Province (1980): 32,724. Headquarters: 69 W. Church St., P.O. Box 1245, Bethlehem, Pa. 18018; Southern Province (1980): 21,057. Headquarters: 459 S. Church St., Winston-Salem, N.C. 27108.

Old Order Amish Church: Members of this group worship in private homes and adhere to the older forms of worship and attire. Members (1980): 80,250.

Pentecostal Church of God: Organized in 1919 at Chicago, Ill. The first convention was held in October, 1933. Members (1980): 113,000. Headquarters: Messenger Plaza, 221 Main St., Joplin, Mo. 64801.

Pentecostal Holiness Church: This body grew out of the holiness movement in the South and Middle West from 1895 to 1900. Members (1977): 86,103. Headquarters: Box 12609, Oklahoma City, Okla. 73157.

Plymouth Brethren (also known as Christian Brethren): This orthodox and evangelical movement began in Britain in the 1820s and has since become worldwide. It is made of up two groups—the smaller "exclusive" branch, which stresses the interdependency of congregations, and the "open" branch, in which each assembly is guided by local elders. Members (1980): 98,000.

Reformed Church in America: This group was established by the earliest Dutch settlers of New York as the Reformed Protestant Dutch Church in 1628. Members (1980): 345,532. Headquarters: 475 Riverside Dr., New York, N.Y. 10115.

Salvation Army: An evangelistic organization, with a military government, first set up by General William Booth in England in 1865 and introduced into the U.S. in 1880. Members (1980): 417,359. Headquarters: 120–30 W. 14th St., New York, N.Y. 10011.

Seventh-day Adventists: This body developed out of an interdenominational movement in the early decades of the 19th century, but was not formally organized until 1863. Their two cardinal points of faith are belief in the personal, imminent, premillennial return of Christ and observance of the seventh day as the Sabbath. Members (1980): 571,141. Headquarters: 6840 Eastern Ave., N.W., Washington, D.C. 20012.

Triumph the Church and Kingdom of God in Christ (International): Organized by Elder E. D. Smith in Georgia in 1902. This group emphasizes the sanctification and the Second Coming of Christ. Members (1972): 54,307. Headquarters: Rt. 4, Box 386, Birmingham, Ala. 35210.

Unitarian Universalist Association: This association is the result of a merger in 1961 of the American Unitarian Association, formed in 1825, and the Universalist Church in America, organized in the 1770's. Members (1979): 139,052. Headquarters, 25 Beacon St., Boston, Mass. 02108.

United Church of Christ: A merger in 1961 of the Evangelical and Reformed Church and the Congregational Christian Churches. Members (1980): 1,736,244. Headquarters: 105 Madison Ave., New York, N.Y. 10016.

United Pentecostal Church, International: Pentecostal Church, Inc., and Pentecostal Assemblies of Jesus Christ merged in 1945 at St. Louis. Members (1980): 465,000. Headquarters: 8855 Dunn Rd., Hazelwood, Mo. 63042.

Wesleyan Church: Originated through the uniting of the Pilgrim Holiness Church (1897) and the Wesleyan Methodist Church of America (1843) in 1968. Members (1980): 103,160. Headquarters: Box 2000, Marion, Ind. 46952.

Other Religious Groups

(1,000–50,000 members)

Advent Christian Church (1980: 29,838)
Albanian Orthodox Archdiocese in America (1978: 40,000)
Albanian Orthodox Diocese of America (1981: 5,285)
American Rescue Workers (1978: 2,140)
Anglican Orthodox Church (1972: 2,630)
Apostolic Christian Church (Nazarean) (1979: 2,497)
Apostolic Christian Churches of America (1981: 11,556)
Apostolic Faith (1980: 4,100)
Apostolic Lutheran Church of America (1974: 9,384)
Associate Reformed Presbyterian Church (General Synod) (1980: 31,518)
Beachy Amish Mennonite Church (1980: 5,338)
Berean Fundamental Church (1976: 4,269)
Bethel Ministerial Association (1971: 5,000)
Bible Church of Christ, (1980: 3,095)
Bible Protestant Church (1978: 2,077)
Bible Way Church of Our Lord Jesus Christ World Wide (1970: 30,000)
Brethren Church (Ashland, Ohio) (1978: 15,802)
Brethren in Christ Church (1979: 15,283)
Christ Catholic Church (1980: 1,453)
Christadelphians (1964: 15,800)
Christian Catholic Church (Evangelical-Protestant) (1980: 2,500)
Christian Church of North America, General Council (1981: 12,500)
Christian Nation Church U.S.A. (1976: 2,000)
Christian Union (1979: 5,463)
Church of Christ (1972: 2,400)
Church of God General Conference (Oregon, Ill.) (1980: 5,890)
Church of God (7th Day) (1960: 2,000)
Church of God (Seventh Day), Denver (1980: 3,940)
Church of God by Faith (1973: 4,500)
Church of God in Christ (Mennonite) (1980: 7,259)
Church of God of the Mountain Assembly (1977: 3,125)
Church of Illumination (1963: 9,000)
Church of Jesus Christ (Bickertonites) (1979: 2,567)
Church of Our Lord Jesus Christ of the Apostolic Faith (1954: 45,000)
Church of the Lutheran Brethren of America (1980: 10,523)
Church of the Lutheran Confession (1980: 9,426)
Churches of Christ in Christian Union (1980: 11,943)
Churches of God, General Conference (1980: 34,638)
Congregational Holiness Church (1966: 4,859)
Conservative Congregational Christian Conference (1980: 24,410)
Duck River (and Kindred) Association of Baptists (1975: 8,632)
Estonian Evangelical Lutheran Church (1980: 8,316)
Ethical Culture Movement (1980: 4,000)
Evangelical Church of North America (1980: 13,088)
Evangelical Congregational Church (1981: 27,567)
Evangelical Friends Alliance (1975: 25,531)
Evangelical Lutheran Church in America (Eielsen Synod) (1957: 2,500)
Evangelical Lutheran Synod (1980: 19,885)
Evangelical Mennonite Brethren Conference (1980: 4,329)
Evangelical Mennonite Church (1980: 3,762)
Evangelical Methodist Church (1974: 10,502)
Free Christian Zion Church of Christ (1956: 22,260)
Free Lutheran Congregations, Association of (1980: 14,738)
Friends General Conference (1974: 26,184)
Full Gospel Assemblies, International (1981: 3,500)
General Church of the New Jerusalem (1971: 2,143)
General Conference of Mennonite Brethren Churches (1980: 17,813)
General Convention, The Swedenborgian Church (1980: 2,842)
General Conference of the Evangelical Baptist Church (1952: 2,200)
Grace Brethren Churches, Fellowship of (1979: 40,680)
Grace Gospel Fellowship (1980: 4,000)
Holy Apostolic and Catholic Church of the East (Assyrian) (1981: 30,000)
Holy Ukrainian Autocephalic Orthodox Church in Exile (1965: 4,800)
House of God, Which Is the Church of the Living God, the Pillar and Ground of the Truth (1956: 2,350)
Hungarian Reformed Church in America (1978: 10,500)
Hutterian Brethren (1980: 3,684)
International Pentecostal Church of Christ (1980: 2,619)
Latvian Evangelical Lutheran Church in America (1980: 14,274)
Liberal Catholic Church—Province of the United States of America (1973: 2,393)
Mennonite Church, The General Conference (1980: 36,736)
Metropolitan Community Churches, Universal Fellowship of (1980: 28,700)

Missionary Church, The (1980: 23,505)
National Spiritual Alliance of the U.S.A., The (1971: 3,230)
National Spiritualist Association of Churches (1976: 5,168)
Netherlands Reformed Congregations (1980: 5,000)
New Apostolic Church of North America (1980: 27,986)
North American Baptist Conference (1980: 43,041)
Old German Baptist Brethren (1980: 5,092)
Old Order (Wisler) Mennonite (1980: 9,731)
Open Bible Standard Churches (1981: 44,549)
(Original) Church of God, The (1971: 20,000)
Orthodox Presbyterian Church, The (1980: 16,590)
Pentecostal Assemblies of the World (1960: 4,500)
Pentecostal Free-Will Baptist Church, The (1980: 9,280)
Pillar of Fire (1949: 5,100)
Primitive Methodist Church, U.S.A. (1980: 10,138)
Protestant Conference (Lutheran), The (1980: 1,325)
Protestant Reformed Churches in America (1980: 4,544)
Reformed Baptists (1980: 2,500)
Reformed Church in the United States (1980: 3,660)
Reformed Episcopal Church (1977: 6,211)
Reformed Methodist Union Episcopal Church (1976: 3,800)
Reformed Presbyterian Church, Evangelical Synod (1977: 25,448)
Reformed Presbyterian Church of North America (1977: 4,878)
Reformed Zion Union Apostolic Church (1965: 16,000)
Religious Society of Friends (Conservative) (1979: 1,832)
Religious Society of Friends (Unaffiliated Meetings) (1980: 6,386)
Romanian Orthodox Episcopate of America, The (1980: 40,000)
Schwenkfelder Church, The (1981: 2,763)
Second Cumberland Presbyterian Church in U.S. (1959: 30,000)
Separate Baptists in Christ (1972: 7,496)
Seventh-Day Baptist General Conference (1979: 5,125)
Social Brethren (1975: 1,784)
Southern Methodist Church (1977: 11,000)
Syrian Orthodox Church of Antioch (Archdiocese of the U.S.A. and Canada) (1980: 30,000)
Ukrainian Orthodox Church in America (Ecumenical Patriarchate) (1977: 25,000)
United Brethren in Christ (1976: 28,035)
United Holy Church of America (1960: 28,980)
Unity of the Brethren (1964: 6,142)
Vedanta Society of New York (1980: 1,000)
Volunteers of America (1978: 36,634)

Roman Catholic Pontiffs

St. Peter, of Bethsaida in Galilee, Prince of the Apostles, was the first Pope. He lived first in Antioch and then in Rome for 25 years. In AD 64 or 67, he was martyred. St. Linus became the second Pope.

Name	Birthplace	Reigned From	To
St. Linus	Tuscia	67	76
St. Anacletus (Cletus)	Rome	76	88
St. Clement	Rome	88	97
St. Evaristus	Greece	97	105
St. Alexander I	Rome	105	115
St. Sixtus I	Rome	115	125
St. Telesphorus	Greece	125	136
St. Hyginus	Greece	136	140
St. Pius I	Aquileia	140	155
St. Anicetus	Syria	155	166
St. Soter	Campania	166	175
St. Eleutherius	Epirus	175	189
St. Victor I	Africa	189	199
St. Zephyrinus	Rome	199	217
St. Callistus I	Rome	217	222
St. Urban I	Rome	222	230
St. Pontian	Rome	230	235
St. Anterus	Greece	235	236
St. Fabian	Rome	236	250
St. Cornelius	Rome	251	253
St. Lucius I	Rome	253	254
St. Stephen I	Rome	254	257
St. Sixtus II	Greece	257	258
St. Dionysius	Unknown	259	268
St. Felix I	Rome	269	274
St. Eutychian	Luni	275	283
St. Caius	Dalmatia	283	296
St. Marcellinus	Rome	296	304
St. Marcellus I	Rome	308	309
St. Eusebius	Greece	309[1]	309[1]
St. Meltiades	Africa	311	314
St. Sylvester I	Rome	314	335
St. Marcus	Rome	336	336
St. Julius I	Rome	337	352
Liberius	Rome	352	366
St. Damasus I	Spain	366	384
St. Siricius	Rome	384	399
St. Anastasius I	Rome	399	401
St. Innocent I	Albano	401	417
St. Zozimus	Greece	417	418
St. Boniface I	Rome	418	422
St. Celestine I	Campania	422	432
St. Sixtus III	Rome	432	440
St. Leo I (the Great)	Tuscany	440	461
St. Hilary	Sardinia	461	468
St. Simplicius	Tivoli	468	483
St. Felix III (II)[2]	Rome	483	492
St. Gelasius I	Africa	492	496
Anastasius II	Rome	496	498
St. Symmachus	Sardinia	498	514
St. Hormisdas	Frosinone	514	523
St. John I	Tuscany	523	526
St. Felix IV (III)	Samnium	526	530
Boniface II	Rome	530	532
John II	Rome	533	535
St. Agapitus I	Rome	535	536
St. Silverius	Campania	536	537
Vigilius	Rome	537	555
Pelagius I	Rome	556	561
John III	Rome	561	574
Benedict I	Rome	575	579
Pelagius II	Rome	579	590
St. Gregory I (the Great)	Rome	590	604
Sabinianus	Tuscany	604	606
Boniface III	Rome	607	607
St. Boniface IV	Marsi	608	615
St. Deusdedit (Adeodatus I)	Rome	615	618
Boniface V	Naples	619	625
Honorius I	Campania	625	638
Severinus	Rome	640	640
John IV	Dalmatia	640	642
Theodore I	Greece	642	649
St. Martin I	Todi	649	655
St. Eugene I[3]	Rome	654	657
St. Vitalian	Segni	657	672
Adeodatus II	Rome	672	676
Donus	Rome	676	678
St. Agatho	Sicily	678	681
St. Leo II	Sicily	682	683
St. Benedict II	Rome	684	685

Name	Birthplace	Reigned From	Reigned To
John V	Syria	685	686
Conon	Unknown	686	687
St. Sergius I	Syria	687	701
John VI	Greece	701	705
John VII	Greece	705	707
Sisinnius	Syria	708	708
Constantine	Syria	708	715
St. Gregory II	Rome	715	731
St. Gregory III	Syria	731	741
St. Zachary	Greece	741	752
Stephen II (III)[4]	Rome	752	757
St. Paul I	Rome	757	767
Stephen III (IV)	Sicily	768	772
Adrian I	Rome	772	795
St. Leo III	Rome	795	816
Stephen IV (V)	Rome	816	817
St. Paschal I	Rome	817	824
Eugene II	Rome	824	827
Valentine	Rome	827	827
Gregory IV	Rome	827	844
Sergius II	Rome	844	847
St. Leo IV	Rome	847	855
Benedict III	Rome	855	858
St. Nicholas I (the Great)	Rome	858	867
Adrian II	Rome	867	872
John VIII	Rome	872	882
Marinus I	Gallese	882	884
St. Adrian III	Rome	884	885
Stephen V (VI)	Rome	885	891
Formosus	Portus	891	896
Boniface VI	Rome	896	896
Stephen VI (VII)	Rome	896	897
Romanus	Gallese	897	897
Theodore II	Rome	897	897
John IX	Tivoli	898	900
Benedict IV	Rome	900	903
Leo V	Ardea	903	903
Sergius III	Rome	904	911
Anastasius III	Rome	911	913
Landus	Sabina	913	914
John X	Tossignano	914	928
Leo VI	Rome	928	928
Stephen VII (VIII)	Rome	928	931
John XI	Rome	931	935
Leo VII	Rome	936	939
Stephen VIII (IX)	Rome	939	942
Marinus II	Rome	942	946
Agapitus II	Rome	946	955
John XII	Tusculum	955	964
Leo VIII[5]	Rome	963	965
Benedict V[5]	Rome	964	966
John XIII	Rome	965	972
Benedict VI	Rome	973	974
Benedict VII	Rome	974	983
John XIV	Pavia	983	984
John XV	Rome	985	996
Gregory V	Saxony	996	999
Sylvester II	Auvergne	999	1003
John XVII	Rome	1003	1003
John XVIII	Rome	1004	1009
Sergius IV	Rome	1009	1012
Benedict VIII	Tusculum	1012	1024
John XIX	Tusculum	1024	1032
Benedict IX[6]	Tusculum	1032	1044
Sylvester III	Rome	1045	1045
Benedict IX (2nd time)	—	1045	1045
Gregory VI	Rome	1045	1046
Clement II	Saxony	1046	1047

Name	Birthplace	Reigned From	Reigned To
Benedict IX (3rd time)	—	1047	1048
Damasus II	Bavaria	1048	1048
St. Leo IX	Alsace	1049	1054
Victor II	Germany	1055	1057
Stephen IX (X)	Lorraine	1057	1058
Nicholas II	Burgundy	1059	1061
Alexander II	Milan	1061	1073
St. Gregory VII	Tuscany	1073	1085
Bl. Victor III	Benevento	1086	1087
Bl. Urban II	France	1088	1099
Paschal II	Ravenna	1099	1118
Gelasius II	Gaeta	1118	1119
Callistus II	Burgundy	1119	1124
Honorius II	Fiagnano	1124	1130
Innocent II	Rome	1130	1143
Celestine II	Città di Castello	1143	1144
Lucius II	Bologna	1144	1145
Bl. Eugene III	Pisa	1145	1153
Anastasius IV	Rome	1153	1154
Adrian IV	England	1154	1159
Alexander III	Siena	1159	1181
Lucius III	Lucca	1181	1185
Urban III	Milan	1185	1187
Gregory VIII	Benevento	1187	1187
Clement III	Rome	1187	1191
Celestine III	Rome	1191	1198
Innocent III	Anagni	1198	1216
Honorius III	Rome	1216	1227
Gregory IX	Anagni	1227	1241
Celestine IV	Milan	1241	1241
Innocent IV	Genoa	1243	1254
Alexander IV	Anagni	1254	1261
Urban IV	Troyes	1261	1264
Clement IV	France	1265	1268
Bl. Gregory X	Piacenza	1271	1276
Bl. Innocent V	Savoy	1276	1276
Adrian V	Genoa	1276	1276
John XXI[7]	Portugal	1276	1277
Nicholas III	Rome	1277	1280
Martin IV[8]	France	1281	1285
Honorius IV	Rome	1285	1287
Nicholas IV	Ascoli	1288	1292
St. Celestine V	Isernia	1294	1294
Boniface VIII	Anagni	1294	1303
Bl. Benedict XI	Treviso	1303	1304
Clement V	France	1305	1314
John XXII	Cahors	1316	1334
Benedict XII	France	1334	1342
Clement VI	France	1342	1352
Innocent VI	France	1352	1362
Bl. Urban V	France	1362	1370
Gregory XI	France	1370	1378
Urban VI	Naples	1378	1389
Boniface IX	Naples	1389	1404
Innocent VII	Sulmona	1404	1406
Gregory XII	Venice	1406	1415
Martin V	Rome	1417	1431
Eugene IV	Venice	1431	1447
Nicholas V	Sarzana	1447	1455
Callistus III	Jativa	1455	1458
Pius II	Siena	1458	1464
Paul II	Venice	1464	1471
Sixtus IV	Savona	1471	1484
Innocent VIII	Genoa	1484	1492
Alexander VI	Jativa	1492	1503
Pius III	Siena	1503	1503
Julius II	Savona	1503	1513
Leo X	Florence	1513	1521

Name	Birthplace	Reigned From	To	Name	Birthplace	Reigned From	To
Adrian VI	Utrecht	1522	1523	Innocent XII	Spinazzola	1691	1700
Clement VII	Florence	1523	1534	Clement XI	Urbino	1700	1721
Paul III	Rome	1534	1549	Innocent XIII	Rome	1721	1724
Julius III	Rome	1550	1555	Benedict XIII	Gravina	1724	1730
Marcellus II	Montepulciano	1555	1555	Clement XII	Florence	1730	1740
Paul IV	Naples	1555	1559	Benedict XIV	Bologna	1740	1758
Pius IV	Milan	1559	1565	Clement XIII	Venice	1758	1769
St. Pius V	Bosco	1566	1572	Clement XIV	Rimini	1769	1774
Gregory XIII	Bologna	1572	1585	Pius VI	Cesena	1775	1799
Sixtus V	Grottammare	1585	1590	Pius VII	Cesena	1800	1823
Urban VII	Rome	1590	1590	Leo XII	Genga	1823	1829
Gregory XIV	Cremona	1590	1591	Pius VIII	Cingoli	1829	1830
Innocent IX	Bologna	1591	1591	Gregory XVI	Belluno	1831	1846
Clement VIII	Florence	1592	1605	Pius IX	Senegallia	1846	1878
Leo XI	Florence	1605	1605	Leo XIII	Carpineto	1878	1903
Paul V	Rome	1605	1621	St. Pius X	Riese	1903	1914
Gregory XV	Bologna	1621	1623	Benedict XV	Genoa	1914	1922
Urban VIII	Florence	1623	1644	Pius XI	Desio	1922	1939
Innocent X	Rome	1644	1655	Pius XII	Rome	1939	1958
Alexander VII	Siena	1655	1667	John XXIII	Sotto il Monte	1958	1963
Clement IX	Pistoia	1667	1669	Paul VI	Concesio	1963	1978
Clement X	Rome	1670	1676	John Paul I	Forno di Canale	1978	1978
Bl. Innocent XI	Como	1676	1689	John Paul II	Wadowice, Poland	1978	
Alexander VIII	Venice	1689	1691				

1. Or 310. 2. He should be called Felix II, and his successors of the same name should be numbered accordingly. The discrepancy was caused by the erroneous insertion in some lists of the name of St. Felix of Rome, Martyr. 3. He was elected during the exile of St. Martin I, who endorsed him as Pope. 4. After St. Zachary died, a Roman priest named Stephen was elected but died before his consecration as Bishop of Rome. His name is not included in all lists for this reason. In view of this historical confusion, the *National Catholic Almanac* lists the true Stephen II as Stephen II (III), the true Stephen III as Stephen III (IV), etc. 5. Confusion exists concerning the legitimacy of claims. If the deposition of John was invalid, Leo was an antipope until after the end of Benedict's reign. If the deposition of John was valid, Leo was the legitimate Pope and Benedict an antipope. 6. If the triple removal of Benedict IX was not valid, Sylvester III, Gregory VI, and Clement II were antipopes. 7. Elimination was made of the name of John XX in an effort to rectify the numerical designation of Popes named John. The error dates back to the time of John XV. 8. The names of Marinus I and Marinus II were construed as Martin. In view of these two pontificates and the earlier reign of St. Martin I, this pontiff was called Martin IV. *Source: National Catholic Almanac,* from *Annuarto Pontificio.*

Books of the Bible

OLD TESTAMENT — STANDARD VERSIONS

Genesis
Exodus
Leviticus
Numbers
Deuteronomy
Joshua
Judges
Ruth
I Samuel
II Samuel
I Kings
II Kings
I Chronicles
II Chronicles
Ezra
Nehemiah
Esther
Job
Psalms
Proverbs
Ecclesiastes
Song of Solomon
Isaiah
Jeremiah
Lamentations
Ezekiel
Daniel
Hosea
Joel
Amos
Obadiah
Jonah
Micah
Nahum
Habakkuk
Zephaniah
Haggai
Zechariah
Malachi

NEW TESTAMENT — STANDARD VERSIONS

Matthew
Mark
Luke
John
Acts
Romans
Corinthians
Galatians
Ephesians
Philippians
Colossians
Thessalonians
Timothy
Titus
Philemon
Hebrews
James
Peter
John
Jude
Revelation

OLD TESTAMENT — DOUAY VERSION[1]

Genesis
Exodus
Leviticus
Numbers
Deuteronomy
Josue
Judges
Ruth
I Kings
II Kings
III Kings
IV Kings
I Paralipomenon
II Paralipomenon
I Esdras
II Esdras
Tobias
Judith
Esther
Job
Psalms
Proverbs
Ecclesiastes
Canticle of Canticles
Wisdom
Ecclesiasticus
Isaias
Jeremias
Lamentations
Baruch
Ezechiel
Daniel
Osee
Joel
Amos
Abdias
Jonas
Micheas
Nahum
Habacuc
Sophonias
Aggeus
Zacharias
Malachias
I Machabees
II Machabees

1. In the Douay Version of the Bible, the books of the New Testament are the same as those of the Authorized (King James) Version, except that the Revelation of St. John is called the Apocalypse of St. John in the Douay Version.

World and U.S. Extremes of Climate

Highest recorded temperature

	Place	Date	Degree Fahrenheit	Degree Centigrade
World (Africa)	El Azizia, Libya	Sept. 13, 1922	136	58
North America (U.S.)	Death Valley, Calif.	July 10, 1913	134	57
Asia	Tirat Tsvi, Israel	June 21, 1942	129	54
Australia	Cloncurry, Queensland	Jan. 16, 1889	128	53
Europe	Seville, Spain	Aug. 4, 1881	122	50
South America	Rivadavia, Argentina	Dec. 11, 1905	120	49
Antarctica	Esperanza, Palmer Peninsula	Oct. 20, 1956	58	14

Lowest recorded temperature

	Place	Date	Degree Fahrenheit	Degree Centigrade
World (Antarctica)	Vostok	Aug. 24, 1960	−127	−88
Asia	Verkhoyansk/Oimekon	Feb. 6, 1933	−90	−68
Greenland	Northice	Jan. 9, 1954	−87	−66
North America (excl. Greenland)	Snag, Yukon, Canada	Feb. 3, 1947	−81	−63
Europe	Ust 'Shchugor, U.S.S.R.	n.a.	−67	−55
South America	Sarmiento, Argentina	Jan. 1, 1907	−27	−33
Africa	Ifrane, Morocco	Feb. 11, 1935	−11	−24
Australia	Charlotte Pass, N.S.W.	July 22, 1947	−8	−22
United States	Prospect Creek, Alaska	Jan. 23, 1971	−80	−62

Greatest rainfalls

	Place	Date	Inches	Centimeters
1 minute (U.S.)	Unionville, Md.	—	1.23	3.1
20 minutes (Romania)	Curtea-de-Arges	—	8.1	20.6
42 minutes (U.S.)	Holt, Mo.	—	12	30
12 hours (Indian Ocean)	Belouve, La Réunion	—	53	135
24 hours (Indian Ocean)	Cilaos, La Réunion	—	74	188
5 days (Indian Ocean)	Cilaos, La Réunion	—	152	386
1 month (India)	Cherrapunji	—	366	930
1 month (U.S.)	Kukui, Maui, Hawaii	—	460	1,168
12 months (India)	Cherrapunji	—	1,042	2,647

Greatest snowfalls

	Place	Date	Inches	Centimeters
1 month (U.S.)	Tamarack, Calif.	Jan. 1911	390	991
24 hours (U.S.)	Silver Lake, Colo.	April 14–15, 1921	76	193
19 hours (France)	Bessans	—	68	173
1 storm (U.S.)	Mt. Shasta Ski Bowl, Calif.	—	189	480
1 season (U.S.)	Paradise Ranger Sta., Wash.	—	1,122	2,850

NOTE: n.a. = not available. *Source:* National Oceanic and Atmospheric Administration, Environmental Data Service.

Tropical Storms and Hurricanes, 1886–1981

	Jan.–April	May	June	July	Aug.	Sept.	Oct.	Nov.	Dec.	Total
Number of tropical storms (incl. hurricanes)	3	14	51	61	186	268	173	34	5	795
Number of tropical storms that reached hurricane intensity	1	3	21	32	135	176	85	18	2	473

Climate of Selected U.S. Cities, 1981

(T = trace)

Month	Temperature, °F				Precipitation			Percentage possible sunshine	Percentage relative humidity, afternoon
	Average daily maximum	Average daily minimum	Record high	Record low	Rainfall, inches	Snowfall, inches	Days with precipitation		
Bakersfield, California (Kern County Air Terminal): lat. 35° 25′ N, long. 119° 03′ W; elevation: 475 ft									
January	61.0	42.5	79	31	0.93	0.0	4	n.a.	56
April	77.3	53.1	101	42	0.56	0.0	4	n.a.	32
July	101.5	71.7	107	64	0.00	0.0	0	n.a.	15
October	76.6	53.3	89	44	0.83	0.0	4	n.a.	34
Annual	79.3	56.2	112	31	6.07	0.0	38	n.a.	37
Caribou, Maine (Municipal Airport): lat. 46° 52′ N, long. 68° 01′ W; elevation: 624 ft									
January	15.0	−3.8	40	−27	1.68	35.2	13	n.a.	64
April	48.9	30.1	71	11	2.17	1.4	10	n.a.	53
July	77.3	55.2	87	43	2.62	0.0	9	n.a.	54
October	48.5	32.2	64	23	6.28	2.6	15	n.a.	64
Annual	50.4	32.1	89	−27	46.69	123.5	163	n.a.	61
Charleston, South Carolina (Municipal Airport): lat. 32° 54′ N, long. 80° 02′ W; elevation: 40 ft									
January	54.6	28.5	70	13	0.93	0.0	4	84	39
April	79.8	55.1	93	41	1.87	0.0	6	68	48
July	91.6	75.4	99	67	12.66	0.0	14	66	64
October	75.9	52.2	91	34	1.95	0.0	8	66	49
Annual	75.4	53.2	101	13	49.44	0.0	92	72	51
Chicago, Illinois (O'Hare International Airport): lat. 41° 59′ N, long. 87° 54′ W; elevation: 658 ft									
January	31.0	14.1	53	−9	0.10	2.0	4	49	62
April	63.2	40.4	84	22	6.14	0.0	15	49	61
July	82.3	62.6	94	51	4.50	0.0	10	59	62
October	60.1	38.0	76	17	1.80	T	9	52	58
Annual	58.7	38.9	96	−11	39.19	28.7	121	54	61
Dallas-Fort Worth, Texas (Regional Airport): lat. 32° 54′ N, long. 97° 02′ W; elevation: 551 ft									
January	55.5	33.6	77	21	0.58	T	7	54	55
April	79.5	58.8	91	37	2.69	0.0	6	62	60
July	97.0	74.7	103	71	1.81	0.0	3	79	50
October	75.3	56.8	93	38	14.18	0.0	13	45	66
Annual	76.2	54.6	104	10	44.60	T	82	65	57
Denver, Colorado (Stapleton International Airport): lat. 39° 45′ long. 104° 52′ W; elevation: 5,283 ft									
January	52.0	22.6	69	13	0.29	4.1	2	80	35
April	70.2	42.5	84	28	1.01	2.9	4	82	29
July	90.0	61.7	100	53	0.90	0.0	7	68	32
October	65.2	40.0	81	20	0.79	2.8	7	61	40
Annual	67.4	40.7	100	−12	12.59	51.3	82	67	36
Duluth, Minnesota (International Airport): lat. 46° 50′ N, long. 92° 11′ W; elevation: 1,428 ft									
January	21.4	2.3	43	−23	0.32	4.7	7	68	62
April	48.3	30.0	67	11	4.48	4.3	15	48	63
July	75.7	55.3	88	42	3.26	0.0	12	62	65
October	47.7	33.2	64	12	3.59	1.4	14	42	73
Annual	48.5	31.0	88	−26	28.37	55.9	136	52	66

Month	Temperature, °F				Precipitation			Percentage possible sunshine	Percentage relative humidity, afternoon
	Average daily maximum	Average daily minimum	Record high	Record low	Rainfall, inches	Snowfall, inches	Days with precipitation		
Great Falls, Montana (International Airport): lat. 47° 29′ N, long. 111° 22′ W; elevation: 3,663 ft									
January	44.2	23.4	62	5	0.34	4.1	4	58	52
April	58.3	34.7	75	23	0.05	0.1	3	57	30
July	81.5	51.4	101	42	1.04	0.0	11	79	29
October	56.0	34.6	75	14	1.06	7.9	10	49	46
Annual	59.2	35.1	101	−24	13.86	37.6	98	60	42
Kansas City, Missouri (International Airport): lat. 39° 19′ N, long. 94° 43′ W; elevation: 973 ft									
January	40.8	19.8	68	6	0.49	4.0	1	74	49
April	72.3	49.9	85	33	1.94	0.0	9	63	57
July	86.1	70.4	96	60	8.43	0.0	12	52	73
October	64.2	46.4	87	26	4.14	0.0	7	51	56
Annual	64.3	44.7	96	−13	42.07	12.4	98	59	60
Los Angeles, California (International Airport): lat. 33° 56′ N, long. 118° 24′ W; elevation: 97 ft									
January	67.5	51.5	81	44	1.51	0.0	4	n.a.	66
April	67.8	54.5	92	49	0.46	0.0	3	n.a.	64
July	78.3	65.0	96	62	0.00	0.0	0	n.a.	62
October	72.7	57.8	93	51	0.40	0.0	2	n.a.	60
Annual	71.7	57.4	104	43	11.39	0.0	26	n.a.	64
Miami, Florida (International Airport): lat. 25° 49′ N, long. 80° 17′ W; elevation: 7 ft									
January	71.2	48.2	80	32	0.61	0.0	4	78	48
April	83.9	71.6	90	68	0.05	0.0	1	85	51
July	92.6	77.3	98	74	2.78	0.0	16	87	58
October	86.4	73.0	92	66	1.62	0.0	10	93	60
Annual	83.5	67.9	98	32	50.79	0.0	114	85	57
New Orleans, Louisiana (International Airport): lat. 29° 59′ N, long. 90° 15′ W; elevation: 4 ft									
January	59.3	37.7	76	17	0.94	0.0	6	66	56
April	81.5	61.2	88	44	2.28	0.0	7	50	61
July	93.9	76.0	101	71	1.92	0.0	11	76	65
October	80.7	61.4	91	44	2.03	0.0	7	55	64
Annual	79.1	59.6	101	17	54.51	0.0	103	61	61
New York, New York (Central Park): lat. 40° 47′ N, long. 73° 58′ W; elevation: 132 ft									
January	32.2	20.8	50	5	0.49	7.7	6	n.a.	54
April	61.1	46.2	81	36	2.77	0.0	13	n.a.	54
July	84.1	70.5	97	63	5.32	0.0	10	n.a.	58
October	61.6	47.6	70	39	3.74	0.0	8	n.a.	58
Annual	60.9	47.9	97	5	34.57	17.7	117	n.a.	56
Phoenix, Arizona (Sky Harbor International Airport): lat. 33° 26′ N, long. 112° 01′ W; elevation: 1,110 ft									
January	70.4	47.9	81	38	0.71	0.0	3	84	32
April	88.8	63.1	100	49	0.20	0.0	1	87	15
July	105.6	84.8	111	78	1.14	0.0	4	89	22
October	85.7	61.5	96	48	1.34	0.0	3	87	20
Annual	88.0	64.0	114	34	6.72	0.0	28	88	21
Salt Lake City, Utah (International Airport): lat. 40° 47′ N, long. 111° 57′ W; elevation: 4,221 ft									
January	35.8	28.3	50	24	0.64	8.9	5	12	77
April	64.7	42.0	82	31	0.45	0.3	9	73	35

Month	Temperature, °F: Average daily maximum	Average daily minimum	Record high	Record low	Precipitation: Rainfall, inches	Snowfall, inches	Days with precipitation	Percentage possible sunshine	Percentage relative humidity, afternoon
July	92.7	63.6	100	53	0.33	0.0	6	79	19
October	60.4	40.5	78	31	3.91	4.4	13	55	50
Annual	65.1	43.4	101	7	16.59	41.3	99	59	44
San Francisco, California (International Airport): lat. 37° 37′ N, long. 122° 23′ W; elevation: 8 ft									
January	57.4	44.7	67	36	5.92	0.0	13	n.a.	67
April	65.4	46.9	92	42	0.24	0.0	4	n.a.	55
July	71.9	51.4	89	49	T	0.0	0	n.a.	52
October	66.8	50.3	82	43	2.35	0.0	6	n.a.	60
Annual	65.8	49.6	92	36	23.47	T	74	n.a.	60
Seattle, Washington (Seattle-Tacoma Airport): lat. 47° 27′ N, long. 122° 18′ W; elevation: 400 ft									
January	50.5	38.2	64	29	2.42	0.0	14	31	76
April	57.1	42.1	73	34	1.58	0.0	15	45	60
July	72.3	54.3	87	47	1.38	0.0	5	48	51
October	57.0	44.8	64	38	6.40	0.0	13	48	68
Annual	60.0	45.3	99	26	35.40	1.1	155	48	61
Washington, D.C. (National Airport): lat. 38° 51′ N, long. 77° 02′ W; elevation: 10 ft									
January	40.5	25.5	63	11	0.38	4.2	4	47	52
April	72.2	51.9	86	39	2.63	0.0	13	59	51
July	87.8	72.6	98	61	5.69	0.0	12	69	59
October	67.3	49.3	87	37	3.64	0.0	8	54	58
Annual	67.5	50.4	98	11	30.67	5.9	108	58	55

NOTE: n.a. = not available. *Source:* Department of Commerce, National Oceanic and Atmospheric Administration, Environmental Data Service.

Other Recorded Extremes

Highest average annual temperature (World): Dallol, Ethiopia (1960–66), 94°F (34.4°C). **(U.S.):** Key West, Fla. (30-year normal), 78.2°F (25.7°C).

Lowest average annual temperature (Antarctica): Plateau Station −70°F (−56.7°C). **(U.S.):** Barrow, Alaska (30-year normal), 9.3°F (−12.6°C).

Greatest average yearly rainfall (U.S.): Mt. Waialeale, Kauai, Hawaii (1912–58), 460 in. (1,168 cm). **(India):** Cherrapunji (74-year avg), 450 in. (1,143 cm).

Minimum average yearly rainfall (Chile): Arica (59-year avg), 0.03 in. (0.08 cm) (no rainfall for 14 consecutive years). **(U.S.):** Death Valley, Calif. (49-year avg), 1.63 in. (4.14 cm). (Bagdad, Calif., holds the U.S. record for the longest period with no measurable rain, 767 days, from Oct. 3, 1912 to Nov. 8, 1914).

Hottest summer avg in Western Hemisphere (U.S.): Death Valley, Calif., 98°F (36.7°C).

Longest hot spell (W. Australia): Marble Bar, 100°F (37.8°C) (or above) for 162 consecutive days.

Largest hailstone (U.S.): Potter, Neb., 1½ lb (.68 kg).

Wind Chill Factors

Wind speed (mph)	Thermometer reading (degrees Fahrenheit): 35	30	25	20	15	10	5	0	−5	−10	−15	−20	−25	−30	−35	−40	−45
5	33	27	21	19	12	7	0	−5	−10	−15	−21	−26	−31	−36	−42	−47	−52
10	22	16	10	3	−3	−9	−15	−22	−27	−34	−40	−46	−52	−58	−64	−71	−77
15	16	9	2	−5	−11	−18	−25	−31	−38	−45	−51	−58	−65	−72	−78	−85	−92
20	12	4	−3	−10	−17	−24	−31	−39	−46	−53	−60	−67	−74	−81	−88	−95	−103
25	8	1	−7	−15	−22	−29	−36	−44	−51	−59	−66	−74	−81	−88	−96	−103	−110
30	6	−2	−10	−18	−25	−33	−41	−49	−56	−64	−71	−79	−86	−93	−101	−109	−116
35	4	−4	−12	−20	−27	−35	−43	−52	−58	−67	−74	−82	−89	−97	−105	−113	−120
40	3	−5	−13	−21	−29	−37	−45	−53	−60	−69	−76	−84	−92	−100	−107	−115	−123
45	2	−6	−14	−22	−30	−38	−46	−54	−62	−70	−78	−85	−93	−102	−109	−117	−125

NOTES: This chart gives equivalent temperatures for combinations of wind speed and temperatures. For example, the combination of a temperature of 10° Fahrenheit and a wind blowing at 10 mph has a cooling power equal to −9° F. Wind speeds of higher than 45 mph have little additional cooling effect.

Weather Glossary

blizzard: storm characterized by strong winds, low temperatures, and large amounts of snow.

cyclone: circulation of winds rotating counterclockwise in the northern hemisphere and clockwise in the southern hemisphere. Hurricanes and tornadoes are both examples of cyclones.

drizzle: uniform close precipitation of tiny drops with diameter of less than .02 inch.

flash flood: dangerous rapid rise of water levels in streams, rivers, or over land area.

gale warning: winds in the 33–48 knot (38–55 mph) range forecast.

heavy snow warnings: issued when 4 inches or more of snow are expected to fall in a 12-hour period or when 6 inches or more are anticipated in a 24-hour period.

hurricane: devastating cyclonic storm; winds over 74 mph near storm center; usually tropical in origin; called cyclone in Indian Ocean, typhoon in the Pacific.

hurricane warning: winds in excess of 64 knots (74 mph) in connection with hurricane.

snow flurries: snow falling for a short time at intermittent periods; accumulations are usually small.

snow squall: brief, intense falls of snow, usually accompanied by gusty winds.

storm warnings: winds greater than 48 knots (55 mph) are forecast.

temperature-humidity index (THI): measure of personal discomfort based on the combined effects of temperature and humidity. Most people are uncomfortable when the THI is 75. A THI of 80 produces acute discomfort for almost everyone.

tidal waves: series of ocean waves caused by earthquakes; can reach speeds of 600 mph; they grow in height as they reach shore and can crest as high as 100 feet.

thunder: the sound produced by the rapid expansion of air heated by lightning.

tornado: dangerous whirlwind associated with the cumulonimbus clouds of severe thunderstorms; winds up to 300 mph.

tornado warning: tornado has actually been detected by radar or sighted in designated area.

tornado watch: potential exists in the watch area for storms that could contain tornadoes.

tsunami: *see* tidal waves.

warning: the designated condition is imminent.

wind-chill factor: combined effect of temperature and wind speed as compared to equivalent temperature in calm air.

Tornadoes That Caused Outstanding Damage

Date	Number of tornadoes	Deaths	Property losses	States in which storms occurred
1884, Feb. 19	60	800	(1)	Mississippi, Alabama, North and South Carolina, Tennessee, Kentucky, Indiana
1917, May 26–27	(1)	249	$ 5,555,000	Illinois, Indiana, Arkansas, Kentucky, Tennessee, Alabama, Mississippi
1920, April 20	6	220	3,525,000	Mississippi, Alabama, Tennessee
1924, April 29–30	22	115	4,372,300	Oklahoma, Arkansas, Alabama, Georgia, Louisiana, North and South Carolina, Virginia
1924, June 28	4	96	13,050,000	Ohio and Pennsylvania
1925, March 18	8	792	17,872,000	Missouri, Illinois, Indiana, Kentucky, Tennessee, Alabama
1927, May 8–9	36	227	7,877,000	Texas, Louisiana, Missouri, Nebraska, Indiana, Michigan
1932, March 21	27	321	5,514,000	Alabama, Mississippi, Georgia, Tennessee
1936, April 5–6	22	498	21,800,000	Arkansas, Alabama, Tennessee, Georgia, South Carolina
1944, June 23	4	153	5,160,000	Pennsylvania, West Virginia, Maryland
1947, April 9–10	8	167	10,030,750	Texas, Oklahoma, Kansas
1952, March 21–22	31	343	15,327,100	Arkansas, Tennessee, Missouri, Mississippi, Alabama, Kentucky
1953, June 7–9	12	234	93,230,840	Michigan, Ohio, and New England states
1953, May 11	1	114	39,500,000	Texas
1955, May 25	13	102	11,747,500	Oklahoma and Kansas
1965, April 11–12	47	257	200,000,000	Iowa, Illinois, Wisconsin, Michigan, Indiana, Ohio
1968, May 15	7	63	65,000,000	Arkansas, Iowa, Illinois
1970, May 11	1	26	135,000,000	Texas
1971, Feb. 21	(1)	117	17,000,000	Louisiana, Mississippi
1973, March 31	2	9	115,000,000	Georgia, South Carolina
1973, May 26–28	96	22	(1)	Hawaii and 18 states in South, Southwest, Midwest, and East
1974, April 3–4	144	307	500,000,000+	13 states in East, South, and Midwest
1975, May 6	3	3	400,000,000+	Nebraska
1977, April 4	7	22	15,000,000	Alabama
1978, Dec. 3	13	4	100,000,000+	Louisiana and Arkansas
1979, April 10	10	54	(1)	Texas and Oklahoma
1979, Oct. 3	1	3	200,000,000	Connecticut
1980, May 13	1	5	40,000,000	Michigan
1980, Aug. 9–11	29	0	50,000,000+	Texas
1981, April 4	1	3	12,900,000	Wisconsin

1. Not definitely known; believed to be large. NOTE: Additional storms may be listed in the *Current Events* section. *Source:* Data for 1884–1953, reprinted from *Tornadoes of the United States,* by S. D. Flora, copyright 1954, by University of Oklahoma Press. Used by permission. Also, Department of Commerce, National Oceanic and Atmospheric Administration.

Devastating North Atlantic Hurricanes of the 20th Century

The following is a selected list of North Atlantic hurricanes based on casualties, damage, and general public interest. Facts about each storm are taken from Weather records, although in some cases only estimates of wind speed are available. Data given in this list pertain only to U.S. land areas except where indicated otherwise.

Date	Areas hardest hit	Land stations with highest wind speed	Deaths (U.S. only)	Est. damage (millions)	Remarks
1900, Aug. 27-Sept. 15	Galveston, Tex.	Galveston, Tex. (120[1] mph)	6,000	$30	Damage due to both winds and storm wave. Galveston Is. inundated.
1909, Sept. 10–21	Louisiana and Mississippi	New Orleans, La. (53 mph)	350	5	Winds 50–75 mi. W of New Orleans, where deaths occurred, were stronger than 68 mph.
1915, Aug. 5–23	East Texas and Louisiana	Galveston, Tex. (120 mph)	275	50	Water 5–6 ft deep in Galveston business district. 90% of homes demolished. Warnings issued well ahead of time.
1915, Sept. 22-Oct. 1	Mid-Gulf Coast	Burrwood, La. (140 mph)	275	13	Many casualties due to persons insisting on staying in low-lying areas despite warnings.
1919, Sept. 2–15	Florida, Louisiana, and Texas	Sand Key, Fla. (84[1] mph)	287	22	488 persons drowned at sea.
1926, Sept. 11–22	Florida and Alabama	Miami, Fla. (138 mph)	243	112	Most deaths were in Miami area. Said to have been one of most destructive storms of century.
1928, Sept. 6–20	Southern Florida	Lake Okeechobee, Fla. (75[1] mph)	1,836	25	1,870 injured. Nearly all deaths were in Lake Okeechobee area. Winds estimated as high as 160 mph caused Lake to overflow into populated areas.
1935, Aug. 29-Sept. 10	Southern Florida	Tampa, Fla. (86 mph)	408	6	Sustained winds over Florida Keys est. 150–200 mph. Remembered as "Labor Day Storm."
1938, Sept. 10–22	Long Island and Southern New England	Blue Hills Obs., Mass. (183 mph)	600	306	Unusually destructive. Storm center moved as fast as 56 mph at times. 1,754 injured.
1944, Sept. 9–16	North Carolina to New England	Cape Henry, Va. (150[1] mph)	46	100	344 deaths at sea. Shipping lanes were crowded with war-time activity.
1944, Oct. 12–23	Florida	Dry Tortugas Is. (120 mph)	18	100	About 300 were killed in Cuba area before storm reached U.S. Evacuation of thousands from threatened areas in Fla. prevented higher toll.
1947, Sept. 4–21	Florida and Mid-Gulf Coast	Hillsboro Light, Fla. (155 mph)	51	110	Wind damage especially heavy Along Gulf Coast and Florida east coast.
1954, Aug. 25–31	North Carolina to New England	Block Island, R.I. (135 mph)	60	461	"CAROL"—more damage than any other single storm to this date. Water and high waves flooded low-lying areas; 1,000 injuries in Long Island–New England area.
1954, Sept. 2–14	New Jersey to New England	Block Island, R.I. (87 mph)	21	40	"EDNA"—New England again heavily hit. Gusts of 120 mph at Martha's Vineyard, Mass.
1954, Oct. 5–18	South Carolina to New York	New York, N.Y. (113 mph) (See Remarks)	95	252	"HAZEL"—several N.C. localities had winds of 130–150 mph with unusually heavy wave damage resulting. Est. 400–1,000 casualties in Haiti. In Canada there were 78 deaths, mostly due to flooding.
1955, Aug. 7–21	North Carolina to New England	Wilmington, N.C. (83 mph)	184	832	"DIANE"—worst floods in history in Southern New England. 16 in. of rain in Hartford area.
1957, June 25–28	Texas to Alabama	Sabine Pass, Tex. (100 mph)	390	150	"AUDREY"—gave an early start to the hurricane season and wiped out Cameron, La. Two

Date	Areas hardest hit	Land stations with highest wind speed	Deaths (U.S. only)	Est. damage (millions)	Remarks
					weeks later "BERTHA" struck same area.
1960, Aug. 29-Sept. 13	Florida to New England	Ft. Myers, Fla. (92 mph) Block Island, R.I. (130 mph) (See Remarks)	50	500	"DONNA"—hurricane winds from a single storm swept the entire Atlantic seaboard from Florida to New England for the first time in a 75-year record. Winds estimated near 140 mph with gusts 175–180 mph on Central Keys and lower southwest Florida coast. 115 deaths in Antilles, most from flash floods in Puerto Rico.
1961, Sept. 3–15	Texas coast	Port Lavaca, Tex. (145 mph)	46	408	"CARLA"—devastated Texas Gulf Coast Cities with 15-foot tides and 15-inch rains. Gusts to 175 mph at Port Lavaca.
1964, Aug. 20-Sept. 5	Southern Florida, Eastern Virginia	Miami, Fla. (110 mph)	3	129	"CLEO"—first hurricane in Miami area since 1950. Killed 214 in Caribbean Islands.
1964, Aug. 28-Sept. 16	Northeastern Florida, Southern Georgia	St. Augustine, Fla. (125 mph)	5	250	"DORA"—first storm of full hurricane force on record to move inland from east over northeastern Florida.
1965, Aug. 27-Sept. 12	Southern Florida and Louisiana	Port Sulphur, La. (136 mph)	75	1,420	"BETSY"—Damage in Louisiana, $1.2 billion. 27,000 homes destroyed; 17,500 injured or ill, 300,000 evacuated. Gusts of 165 mph at Pine Key, Fla.
1967, Sept. 5–22	Southern Texas	Brownsville, Texas (109 mph gust)	15	200	"BEULAH"—main damage was caused by torrential rains.
1969, Aug. 14–22	Mississippi, Louisiana, Alabama, Virginia, W. Virginia	Oil drilling rig east of Boothville, La. (172 mph)	256	1,420	"CAMILLE"—68 additional persons missing. One of most destructive killer storms ever to hit U.S.
1970, July 23-Aug. 5	Texas coast	Corpus Christi, Tex. (130 mph)	11	453.8	"CELIA"—Costliest storm in history to hit Texas coast. Gusts of 161 mph recorded.
1972, June 14–23	Florida to New York	Key West, Fla. (43 mph)	117	3,097	"AGNES"—Devastating floods with many record-breaking river crests. Pa. hardest hit, with 50 deaths.
1975, Sept. 13–24	Florida and Southern Alabama	Ozark, Ala. (104 mph)	21	490	"ELOISE"—Structures destroyed from Panama City Beach, Fla., to Ft. Walton Beach, Fla. Major flooding from rainfall.
1976, Aug. 6–10	New York, New Jersey, and Southern New England	Bridgeport, Conn. (77 mph gust)	5	100	"BELLE"—Crop damage in the Northeast. Considerable Inland stream and road flooding.
1979, Aug. 25-Sept. 7	Florida to New England	Fort Pierce, Fla. (95 mph gust)	5	320	"DAVID"—1200 deaths in the Dominican Republic. Homes 80 percent destroyed in Dominica.
1979, Aug. 29-Sept. 14	Alabama and Mississippi	Dauphin Island, Alabama (145 mph gust)	5	2300	"FREDERIC"— highest dollar dammage ever in the United States.
1980, Aug. 3–10	Caribbean Islands to Texas Gulf Coast	Port Mansfield, Texas (120 mph gust.)	28	300	"ALLEN"—Highest tides in 61 years. Over 200 killed in Caribbean Islands. Extensive crop damage in Caribbean.

1. Wind-measuring equipment disabled at speed indicated. NOTE: Additional hurricanes may be listed in *News Chronology*. *Source:* Department of Commerce, National Oceanic and Atmospheric Administration.

Tornado Deaths Down

The outstanding feature of the 1981 tornado season was that only 24 fatalities were recorded, the lowest total since 1916.

History of the Income Tax in the United States

Source: Touche Ross & Co.

The nation had few taxes in its early history. From 1791 to 1802, the United States Government was supported by internal taxes on distilled spirits, carriages, refined sugar, tobacco and snuff, property sold at auction, corporate bonds, and slaves. The high cost of the War of 1812 brought about the nation's first sales taxes on gold, silverware, jewelry, and watches. In 1817, however, Congress did away with all internal taxes, relying on tariffs on imported goods to provide sufficient funds for running the Government.

In 1862, in order to support the Civil War effort, Congress enacted the nation's first income tax law. It was a forerunner of our modern income tax in that it was based on the principles of graduated, or progressive, taxation and of withholding income at the source. During the Civil War, a person earning from $600 to $10,000 per year paid tax at the rate of 3%. Those with incomes of more than $10,000 paid taxes at a higher rate. Additional sales and excise taxes were added, and an "inheritance" tax also made its debut. In 1866, internal revenue collections reached their highest point in the nation's 90-year history—more than $310 million, an amount not reached again until 1911.

The Act of 1862 established the office of Commissioner of Internal Revenue. The Commissioner was given the power to assess, levy, and collect taxes, and the right to enforce the tax laws through seizure of property and income and through prosecution. His powers and authority remain very much the same today.

In 1868, Congress again focused its taxation efforts on tobacco and distilled spirits and eliminated the income tax in 1872. It had a short-lived revival in 1894 and 1895. In the latter year, the U.S. Supreme Court decided that the income tax was unconstitutional because it was not apportioned among the states in conformity with the Constitution.

By 1913, with the 16th Amendment to the Constitution, the income tax had become a permanent fixture of the U.S. tax system. The amendment gave Congress legal authority to tax income and resulted in a revenue law that taxed incomes of both individuals and corporations. In fiscal year 1918, annual internal revenue collections for the first time passed the billion-dollar mark, rising to $5.4 billion by 1920. With the advent of World War II, employment increased, as did tax collections—to $7.3 billion. The withholding tax on wages was introduced in 1943 and was instrumental in increasing the number of taxpayers to 60 million and tax collections to $43 billion by 1945.

In 1981, Congress enacted the largest tax cut in U.S. history, including a 25% reduction in individual tax rates over a three-year period. The Economic Recovery Tax Act of 1981 has resulted in numerous changes in the tax law, including the reduction of total taxes for individuals and businesses by approximately $750 billion over a six-year period.

Internal Revenue Service

The Internal Revenue Service (IRS), a bureau of the U.S. Treasury Department, is the federal agency charged with the administration of the tax laws passed by Congress. The IRS functions through a national office in Washington, 7 regional offices, 59 district offices, and 10 service centers.

Operations involving most taxpayers are carried out in the district offices and service centers. District offices are organized into Resources Management, Examination, Collection, Taxpayer Service, and Criminal Investigation. All tax returns are filed with the service centers, where the IRS computer operations are located.

Auditing Tax Returns

Most taxpayers' contacts with IRS arise through the auditing of their tax returns. The Service has been empowered by Congress to inquire about all persons who may be liable for any tax and to obtain for review the books and/or records pertinent to those taxpayers' returns. A wide-ranging audit operation is carried out in the 59 district offices by some 13,000 field agents and 4,000 office auditors.

Selecting Returns for Audit

The primary method used by the IRS in selecting returns for audits is a computer program that measures the probability of tax error in each return. The data base (established by an in-depth audit of randomly selected returns in various income categories) consists of approximately 200–250 individual items of information taken from each return. These 200–250 variables individually or in combination are weighted as relative indicators of potential tax change. Returns are then scored according to the weights given the combinations of variables as they appear on each return. The higher the score, the greater the tax change potential. Other returns are selected for examination on the basis of claims for refund, multi-year audits, related

Internal Revenue Service

	1981	1980	1979	1970	1960	1950
U.S. population (in thousands)	225,865	223,383	220,999	204,878	180,671	152,271
Number of IRS employees	86,156	87,464	86,630	68,098	50,199	55,551
Cost to govt. of collecting $100 in taxes	$0.41	$0.44	$0.46	$0.45	$0.40	$0.59
Tax per capita	$2,686.55	$2,325.04	$2,083.32	$955.31	$507.96	$255.84
Collections by principal sources (in thousands of dollars)						
Total IRS collections	$606,799,120	$519,375,273	$460,412,185	$195,722,096	$91,744,803	$38,957,132
Income and profits taxes						
Individual	332,850,146	287,547,782	251,545,857	103,651,585	44,945,711	17,153,308
Corporation	73,733,156	72,379,610	71,447,876	35,036,983	22,179,414	10,854,351
Employment taxes	152,885,816	128,330,480	112,849,874	37,449,188	11,158,589	2,644,575
Estate and gift taxes	6,910,386	6,498,381	5,519,074	3,680,076	1,626,348	706,227
Alcohol taxes	5,688,413	5,704,768	5,647,924	4,746,382	3,193,714	2,219,202
Tobacco taxes	2,583,857	2,446,416	2,495,517	2,094,212	1,931,504	1,328,464
Manufacturers' excise taxes	6,089,000	6,487,421	7,057,612	6,683,061	4,735,129	1,836,053
All other taxes	26,058,329	9,980,417	3,848,450	2,380,609	2,004,394	2,214,951

NOTE: For fiscal year ending September 30th.

return audits, and other audits initiated by the IRS as a result of informants' information, special compliance programs, and the information document matching program.

During 1980, the IRS initiated a new method to group individual returns for examination selection purposes. Total positive income, the sum of all positive income amounts appearing on a return, with losses treated as zero is the newly utilized factor. This new method replaces the adjusted gross income method of classifying returns. In a similar manner, total gross receipts is used for business returns.

The Appeals Process

The IRS attempts to resolve tax disputes through an administrative appeals system. Taxpayers who, after audit of their tax returns, disagree with a proposed change in their tax liabilities are entitled to an independent review of their cases. Taxpayers are able to seek an immediate, informal appeal with the Appeals Office. If, however, the dispute arises from a field audit and the amount in question exceeds $2,500, a taxpayer must submit a written protest. Alternatively, the taxpayer can wait for the examiner's report and then request consideration by the Appeals Office and file a protest if necessary. Taxpayers may represent themselves or be represented by an attorney, accountant, or any other advisor authorized to practice before the IRS. Taxpayers can forego their right to the above process and await receipt of a deficiency notice. At this juncture, taxpayers can either (1) not pay the deficiency and petition the Tax Court by a required deadline or (2) pay the deficiency and file a claim for refund with the District Director's office. If the claim is denied, a suit for refund may be brought either in the District Court or the Court of Claims within a specified period. A third option is to let the IRS assess the tax and then submit a compromise offer on Form 656. In 1981, 53,260 cases were disposed of by agreement through the administrative process. The Tax Court tried 1,818 cases, and the U.S. District Courts and the Court of Claims tried 289 cases.

Federal Individual Income Tax

The Federal individual income tax is levied on the world-wide income of U.S. citizens and resident aliens and on certain types of U.S. source income of non-residents. A new term, "tax table income," was introduced by the Tax Reduction and Simplification Act of 1977. For a non-itemizer, "tax table income" is adjusted gross income (*see below*) less $1,000 for each personal exemptions. If a taxpayer itemizes, tax table income is adjusted gross income minus excess itemized deductions and personal exemptions. Excess itemized deductions are the excess of a taxpayer's itemized deductions on Schedule A, Form 1040, over the zero bracket amount. The zero bracket amount is $2,300 for unmarried individuals and heads of household; $3,400 for married individuals filing jointly and for surviving spouses; $1,700 for married individuals filing separately. The tax tables apply to individuals with taxable income of less than $50,000. Taxpayers with taxable income of $50,000 or more must use Tax Rate Schedule X, Y, or Z to compute their tax. For this purpose tax rates are graduated, for joint returns, from a minimum of 12% on the first $2,100 of taxable income above $3,400 to a maximum of 50% of taxable income above $85,600 (1982 rates).

Who Must File a Return[1]

You must file a return if you are:	and your gross income is at least:
Single (legally separated, divorced, or married living apart from spouse with dependent child) and are under 65	$3,300
Single (legally separated, divorced, or married living apart from spouse with	

dependent child) and are 65 or older	$4,300
A person who can be claimed as a dependent on your parent's return, and who has taxable dividends, interest, or other unearned income	$1,000
A qualifying widow(er) with a dependent child and under 65	$4,400
A qualifying widow(er) with a dependent child and are 65 or older	$5,400
Married, filing jointly, living together at end of year (or at date of death of spouse), and both are under 65	$5,400
Married, filing jointly, living together at end of year (or at date of death of spouse), and one is 65 or older	$6,400
Married, filing jointly, living together at end of year (or at date of death of spouse), and both are 65 or older	$7,400
Married, filing separate return, or married but not living together at end of year	$1,000
A person with income from sources within U.S. possessions	$1,000
Self-employed and your net earnings from self-employment were at least $400	
A person who received any advance earned income credit payments from their employer during 1981	
A person who owes minimum tax, individual retirement arrangement tax, investment credit recapture tax or social security tax on unreported tips	

1. In 1982.

Adjusted Gross Income

Gross income consists of wages and salaries, tips and gratuities, interest, dividends, annuities, rents and royalties, and certain other types of income. Among the items excluded from gross income, and thus not subject to tax, are social security payments, federal and state unemployment compensation (phased out above a base amount), public assistance benefits, interest on exempt securities (mostly state and local bonds), and 60 percent of net capital gains. Net capital gain is the excess of net long-term capital gain over the net short-term capital loss for the year. In addition, the first $100 (up to $200 on a joint return) of eligible dividends received is excluded from gross income. *Adjusted gross income* is determined by subtracting from gross income certain business-type expenses considered necessary in earning income, job-related moving expenses, alimony, and a limited amount of charitable contributions.

Deductions

Taxpayers may itemize deductions or, as previously discussed, take the benefit of the zero bracket amount incorporated in the tax tables and tax rate schedules. In itemizing deductions, the following are the major items that may be deducted (with limits, in some instances): interest payments; state and local general sales, income, and property taxes; medical expenses; charitable contributions; and casualty losses.

Personal Exemptions

Personal exemptions are available to the taxpayer, his spouse, and his dependents. The amount is $1,000 for each individual. Additional exemptions of $1,000 each are granted for persons 65 and over and for the blind.

Credits

The Revenue Act of 1978 grants a credit (a reduction of tax owed) for certain lower-income households with dependent children, with a maximum credit of $500 on $5,000 of earned income. This maximum credit will be reduced if earned income or adjusted gross income exceeds $6,000 and the credit will be zero for families with incomes over $10,000.

The Tax Reform Act of 1976 provided for a credit for child or dependent care expense. Beginning in 1982, the credit is between 20% and 30% (depending on adjusted gross income) of up to $2,400 of employment-related expenses for one qualifying child or dependent and up to $4,800 of expenses for two or more qualifying individuals.

The Revenue Act of 1978 extended the child care credit to include payments to grandparents for care of their grandchildren, provided that the parents are not also entitled to a dependency deduction for the grandparents.

The Tax Reform Act of 1976 also provided for a new expanded and simplified credit for the elderly. A credit of as much as $375 (if single) or $562.50 (if married and filing jointly) may be claimed by persons 65 or older (or persons under age 65 and retired under a public retirement system) who have retirement income. This credit, however, phases out for married couples with adjusted gross income over $10,000 and single persons with adjusted gross income over $7,500.

Expenditures for insulation and other energy-conserving components and for renewable energy

Results of Criminal Action in Tax Fraud Cases

Internal Revenue Service

Action	Number of Defendants					
	1981	1980	1979	1978	1977	1976
Plea of guilty nolo contendere	1,212	1,337	1,270	1,189	1,229	977
Convicted after trial	282	264	342	225	247	216
Acquitted	81	80	86	70	55	77
Nol-prossed or dismissed	142	193	183	119	110	71
Total disposals	1,717	1,874	1,881	1,603	1,641	1,341
Indictments and Informations	1,785	1,832	1,820	1,724	1,636	1,331

Federal Individual Income Tax Rates
Effective January 1, 1982

MARRIED INDIVIDUALS FILING JOINT RETURNS AND SURVIVING SPOUSES:

If taxable income is:	*The tax is:*
Not over $3,400	No tax
Over $3,400 but not over $5,500	12% of the excess over $3,400
Over $5,500 but not over $7,600	$252, plus 14% of the excess over $5,500
Over $7,600 but not over $11,900	$546, plus 16% of the excess over $7,600
Over $11,900 but not over $16,000	$1,234, plus 19% of the excess over $11,900
Over $16,000 but not over $20,200	$2,013, plus 22% of the excess over $16,000
Over $20,200 but not over $24,600	$2,937, plus 25% of the excess over $20,200
Over $24,600 but not over $29,900	$4,037, plus 29% of the excess over $24,600
Over $29,900 but not over $35,200	$5,574, plus 33% of the excess over $29,900
Over $35,200 but not over $45,800	$7,323, plus 39% of the excess over $35,200
Over $45,800 but not over $60,000	$11,457, plus 44% of the excess over $45,800
Over $60,000 but not over $85,600	$17,705, plus 49% of the excess over $60,000
Over $85,600	$30,249, plus 50% of the excess over $85,600

HEADS OF HOUSEHOLDS:

If taxable income is:	*The tax is:*
Not over $2,300	No tax
Over $2,300 but not over $4,400	12% of the excess over $2,300
Over $4,400 but not over $6,500	$252, plus 14% of the excess over $4,400
Over $6,500 but not over $8,700	$546, plus 16% of the excess over $6,500
Over $8,700 but not over $11,800	$898, plus 20% of the excess over $8,700
Over $11,800 but not over $15,000	$1,518, plus 22% of the excess over $11,800
Over $15,000 but not over $18,200	$2,222, plus 23% of the excess over $15,000
Over $18,200 but not over $23,500	$2,958, plus 28% of the excess over $18,200
Over $23,500 but not over $28,800	$4,442, plus 32% of the excess over $23,500
Over $28,800 but not over $34,100	$6,138, plus 38% of the excess over $28,800
Over $34,100 but not over $44,700	$8,152, plus 41% of the excess over $34,100
Over $44,700 but not over $60,600	$12,498, plus 49% of the excess over $44,700
Over $60,600	$20,289, plus 50% of the excess over $60,600

source equipment are eligible for residential energy credits. The residential insulation and energy conservation credit is 15% of the first $2,000 of qualifying expenditures, with a maximum $300 credit. The residential renewable energy source equipment credit is 40% of the first $10,000 of expenditures, with a maximum credit of $4,000.

Other tax credits available to taxpayers include the targeted jobs credit and contributions to candidates for public office credit.

Recent Legislation

1980 Tax Legislation. 1980 saw a rush of tax legislation during the recent "Lame Duck" session of Congress.

A major reform of installment sales reporting (the Installment Sales Revision Act of 1980) was enacted. Under the new law, for dispositions after October 19, 1980, virtually any sale where payment is deferred will automatically qualify for installment treatment. If installment reporting is not desired, an election of normal reporting is required.

Additional legislation passed included the Bankruptcy Tax Act of 1980 which provides new tax rules applicable to debt discharge both for bankrupt and insolvent debtors and for solvent debtors not in bankruptcy.

New legislation affecting estimated tax payments by large corporations is effective for taxable years beginning after December 31, 1980. The new law provides that a corporation which has incurred taxable income of $1,000,000 or more in any one of the three years preceding the taxable year involved cannot rely on certain exceptions, based on the preceding year's tax or taxable income using current year's tax rates unless the estimated tax payments equal at least 60% of the tax shown on the current corporate income tax return. As a result of 1981 tax legislation this minimum percentage payment is gradually increased to 80% over a three-year period.

Sales of U.S. real property after June 18, 1980 by non-resident aliens and foreign corporations are governed by the Foreign Investment in Real Property Tax Act of 1980. With few exceptions, this act attempts to prevent most foreign investors from obtaining tax–free capital gain treatment upon the disposal of U.S. real property interests.

Other significant legislation affects the use of allowable tax credits against the alternative minimum tax; amortization of business start-up costs; and prevention of abuse of certain employee benefit requirements through a device utilizing two or more professional corporations in a partnership structure.

Federal Individual Income Tax Rates Effective January 1, 1982

UNMARRIED INDIVIDUALS:

If taxable income is:	*The tax is:*
Not over $2,300	No tax
Over $2,300 but not over $3,400	12% of the excess over $2,300
Over $3,400 but not over $4,400	$132, plus 14% of the excess over $3,400
Over $4,400 but not over $6,500	$272, plus 16% of the excess over $4,400
Over $6,500 but not over $8,500	$608, plus 17% of the excess over $6,500
Over $8,500 but not over $10,800	$948, plus 19% of the excess over $8,500
Over $10,800 but not over $12,900	$1,385, plus 22% of the excess over $10,800
Over $12,900 but not over $15,000	$1,847, plus 23% of the excess over $12,900
Over $15,000 but not over $18,200	$2,330, plus 27% of the excess over $15,000
Over $18,200 but not over $23,500	$3,194, plus 31% of the excess over $18,200
Over $23,500 but not over $28,800	$4,837, plus 35% of the excess over $23,500
Over $28,800 but not over $34,100	$6,692, plus 40% of the excess over $28,800
Over $34,100 but not over $41,500	$8,812, plus 44% of the excess over $34,100
Over $41,500	$12,068, plus 50% of the excess over $41,500

MARRIED INDIVIDUALS FILING SEPARATE RETURNS:

If taxable income is:	*The tax is:*
Not over $1,700	No tax
Over $1,700 but not over $2,750	12% of the excess over $1,700
Over $2,750 but not over $3,800	$126, plus 14% of the excess over $2,750
Over $3,800 but not over $5,950	$273, plus 16% of the excess over $3,800
Over $5,950 but not over $8,000	$617, plus 19% of the excess over $5,950
Over $8,000 but not over $10,100	$1,006, plus 22% of the excess over $8,000
Over $10,100 but not over $12,300	$1,468, plus 25% of the excess over $10,100
Over $12,300 but not over $14,950	$2,018, plus 29% of the excess over $12,300
Over $14,950 but not over $17,600	$2,787, plus 33% of the excess over $14,950
Over $17,600 but not over $22,900	$3,661, plus 39% of the excess over $17,600
Over $22,900 but not over $30,000	$5,728, plus 44% of the excess over $22,900
Over $30,000 but not over $42,800	$8,852, plus 49% of the excess over $30,000
Over $42,800	$15,124, plus 50% of the excess over $42,800

Crude Oil Windfall Profit Tax Act of 1980. The Crude Oil Windfall Profit Tax of 1980 covers primarily the excise tax provisions affecting domestic oil producers. It is based on windfall profits, which equals the selling price of the oil less base price which is adjusted for inflation and less a limited deduction for state severance taxes on removal of crude oil from the ground. The tax is deductible in arriving at federal taxable income for the taxable year in which the tax is paid or accrued.

Also included in the Act are certain residential energy tax credits, business energy investment credits, and certain other business income tax provisions. Of special significance is the repeal of carryover basis for inherited property so that property acquired from a decedent gets a "stepped up" basis to date of death (or alternate valuation date—6 months after death).

Economic Recovery Tax Act of 1981. The Economic Recovery Tax Act of 1981 enacted on August 13, 1981, has as its chief objective the stimulation of economic growth through the reduction of individual income taxes. The act seeks to encourage savings and provides investment incentives to both individuals and business.

In addition to reducing both the minimum and maximum marginal rates of tax for individuals, the act reduces the maximum tax on capital gains from 28% to 20% for sales or exchanges as of June 10, 1981. Starting in 1982, the act provides for a marriage tax offset deduction of 5% of the lower-paid spouse's salary up to $1,500 and permits an adjustment to gross income for contributions to Individual Retirement Accounts of up to $2,000 per working spouse regardless of pension coverage by an employer. It also exempts cumulative interest income of up to $1,000 ($2,000 joint return) on special one-year "All-Saver" certificates issued between October 1, 1981, and December 31, 1982. The act revived the stock option as a compensation technique by providing that qualified incentive stock options exercised after 1980 will not be taxed to the employee until sold. Starting in 1982, individual income earned abroad is allowed a flat $75,000 exclusion from gross income. In addition, reasonable housing expenses in excess of a base amount can be excluded from gross income.

The act also increases the amount of depreciation deduction for real property acquired after 1980 by allowing an accelerated 15-year recovery period. The Accelerated Cost Recovery System section of the act provides for a faster writeoff of capital expenditures for property acquired or placed in service retroactive to January 1, 1981. For tangible personal property, assets are grouped into four classes with recovery periods of 3, 5, 10, and 15 years. As an incentive for research and ex-

Federal Income Tax Comparisons

Taxes at Selected Rate Brackets After Standard Deductions/Zero Bracket Amounts[2]

Adjusted gross income	Single return listing no dependents				Joint return listing two dependents			
	1982	1980	1972[1]	1967	1982	1980	1972[1]	1967
$ 3,000	$ 0	$ 0	$ 141	$ 333	$−300[3]	$−300[3]	$ 0	$ 4
5,000	216	250	495	667	$−500[3]	−500[3]	102	286
10,000	1,043	1,177	1,545	1,742	322	374	901	1,114
15,000	2,100	2,345	2,703	3,334	1,090	1,242	1,820	2,172
20,000	3,442	3,837	4,255	5,350	2,013	2,265	3,010	3,428
25,000	5,012	5,562	6,090	7,730	3,137	3,497	4,380	4,892

1. A 2.5% surcharge was in effect. 2. For comparison purposes, tax rate schedules were used. 3. Refund based on Earned Income credit for families with dependent children.

Returns Filed and Examined

Internal Revenue Service

Category	Returns filed for calendar year 1980	Returns examined 1981	Percent coverage
Individual, total	93,052,000	1,644,104	1.7
1040A, TPI[1] under $10,000	28,222,000	149,419	.53
Non 1040A, TPI under $10,000	8,553,000	150,829	1.76
TPI $10,000 under $25,000, simple	21,071,000	128,953	.61
TPI $10,000 under $25,000, complex	11,694,000	365,450	3.13
TPI $25,000 under $50,000	14,901,000	471,802	3.17
TPI $50,000 and over	2,249,000	176,033	7.83
Schedule C-TGR[2] under $25,000 (business)	2,324,000	33,085	1.42
Schedule C-TGR $25,000 under $100,000 (business)	1,758,000	69,984	3.98
Schedule C-TGR $100,000 and over (business)	886,000	63,114	7.12
Schedule F-TGR under $25,000 (farm)	640,000	9,472	1.48
Schedule F-TGR $25,000 under $100,000 (farm)	559,000	14,655	2.62
Schedule F-TGR $100,000 and over (farm)	195,000	11,308	5.80
Fiduciary	1,876,000	9,197	.49
Partnerships	1,362,000	22,113	1.62
Corporation, total[3]	2,124,000	107,363	5.05
Assets not reported	126,000	4,017	3.19
Under $100,000[4]	1,014,000	26,393	2.60
$100,000 under $1 million	779,000	42,245	5.42
$1 million under $10 million	165,000	23,681	14.35
$10 million under $100 million	27,000	7,001	25.93
$100 million and over	5,000	4,026	80.52
Small business corporation	528,000	9,356	1.77
Form 1120 DISC	9,000	1,460	16.22
Estate, total	147,000	27,097	18.43
Gross estate under $300,000	93,000	8,115	8.73
Gross estate $300,000 and over	55,000	18,982	34.51
Gift	215,000	5,897	2.74
Income, estate and gift, total	99,313,000	1,826,587	1.84
Excise	875,000	72,191	8.25
Employment	26,387,000	31,332	.12
Miscellaneous	—	182	—
Service Center corrections	—	—	—

NOTE: Total may not add because of rounding. Individual income classes for 1981 are not comparable to those for 1980 due to a change from adjusted gross income (AGI) to total positive income (TPI) for grouping returns by income levels. 1. Total positive income. 2. Total gross receipts. 3. Includes 8,000 Forms 1120F not allocated to corporation classes. 4. Balance sheet assets.

perimentation, the act provides for a 25% tax credit for certain such expenditures made after June 30, 1981.

In the Estate and Gift Tax area, the unified credit for post–1976 lifetime and death transfers is gradually increased from $47,000 in 1981 to 192,800 in 1987, the equivalent of a 600,000 exemption. The maximum rate of 70% on taxable transfers will be reduced 5% a year starting in 1982 to 50% in 1985 and thereafter.

Tax Errors

In 1981, 57.1 million taxpayers filed a Form 1040, a 3.3% increase over 1980. In 1981, 36.9 million taxpayers filed a Form 1040A, 1.9% fewer than in 1980. 39% of all individual taxpayers used the short form 1040A.

Error rates rose from 1980 to 1981:

1980	Form 1040	7.5%
1980	Form 1040A	6.3%
1981	Form 1040	8.0%
1981	Form 1040A	6.7%

Federal Corporation Taxes

For tax years beginning after 1978, the old corporate system of normal tax, surtax, and surtax exemption is replaced by a graduated tax rate structure that provides for tax reductions to stimulate the economy. The new rates are graduated over the first four $25,000 amounts of taxable income as follows:

1982

Taxable income	Tax	Percent over excess
$0 to $25,000[1]	$ 0	16% over $0
$25,000 to $50,000	$ 4,000	19% over $25,000
$50,000 to $75,000	$ 8,750	30% over $50,000
$75,000 to $100,000	$16,250	40% over $75,000
$100,000 and over	$26,250	46% over $100,000

1. Rates will decrease after 1982.

The Tax Reform Act of 1976 made certain changes affecting the taxation of corporations. Foreign tax advantages are denied to companies that participate in international boycotts. The foreign tax credit, deferral of earnings of foreign subsidiaries, and benefits derived through Domestic International Sales Corporations (DISC) are denied in proportion to income attributable to boycott activity. The amount of any illegal payments to a foreign official may not be deducted.

DISC is exempt from all federal taxes, but DISC shareholders are deemed to have received as a dividend 50% of the corporation's net income every taxable year. Thus, use of a DISC permitted deferral of tax on one-half of DISC income. The 1976 Tax Reform Act reduced this deferral and permits DISC benefits only to the extent that gross export receipts exceed 67% of the average for a four-year base. Full DISC benefits are retained for those having taxable income of $100,000 or less for a taxable year, but phase out at $150,000.

The tax law provides for a credit for investments in depreciable personal property. The 10% credit as well as the $100,000 limitation on used property eligible for the credit has been made permanent by the Revenue Act of 1978. There is an additional 1% credit if the employer established an Employee Stock Ownership Plan (ESOP) meeting specified criteria. An additional half percent credit is available if employee contributions to an ESOP match the half percent. The tax liability credit limitation is increased over a transitional period. The 1978 Energy Tax Act provides for certain additional investment credits.

In 1978, the targeted jobs credit replaced the new jobs credit. The credit may be elected by employers who hire individuals from certain target groups. The credit is equal to 50% of the first $6,000 of qualified first-year wages and 25% of the first $6,000 of qualified second-year wages paid to each such individual. However, the targeted credit may not exceed 90% of the employer's tax liability net of certain credits.

State Corporation Income and Franchise Taxes

All states but Nevada, South Dakota, Texas, Washington, and Wyoming impose a tax on corporation net income. The majority of states impose the tax at flat rates ranging from 3% to 12%. Several states have adopted a graduated basis of rates for corporations.

Nearly all states follow the federal law in defining net income. However, many states provide for varying exclusions and adjustments.

A state is empowered to tax all of the net income of its domestic corporations. With regard to nonresident corporations, however, it may only tax the net income on business carried on within its boundaries. Corporations are, therefore, required to apportion their incomes among the states where they do business and pay a tax to each of these states. Nearly all states provide an apportionment to their domestic corporations, too, in order that they not be unduly burdened.

Several states tax unincorporated businesses separately.

Federal Estate and Gift Taxes

A Federal Estate Tax Return must be filed for the estate of every U.S. citizen or resident whose gross estate, if the decedent died in 1982, exceeds $225,000. The gross estate filing requirement is increased and phased in from 1983 to 1987 from the present $225,000 to $600,000. An estate tax return must also be filed for the estate of a non-resident, not a citizen, if the value of his gross estate in the U.S. is more than $30,000 at the date of death. The estate tax return is due nine months after the date of death of the decedent, but a reasonable extension of time to file may be obtained for good reason. Tax due is to be paid when the return is filed. The executor of an estate with an interest in closely held business that comprises at least 35% of the adjusted gross estate may pay estate tax attributable to the business in from two to ten equal annual installments. In such a case, a 5-year extension for the payment of estate taxes may be exercised for that portion of the tax attributable to a closely held business.

Under the unified federal estate and gift tax structure, individuals who made taxable gifts during the calendar year are required to file a gift tax return by April 15 of the following year.

The Tax Reform Act of 1976 replaced the old $30,000 gift tax exemption and $60,000 estate tax exemption with a unified credit. This credit is used for both estate and gift taxes. Any part of the credit used to offset gift taxes is not available to offset estate taxes. As a result, although they are still taxable as gifts, lifetime transfers no longer cushion the impact of progressive estate tax rates. Lifetime transfers and transfers made at death are cumulated for estate tax rate purposes. Gift taxes are computed by applying the uniform rate schedule to lifetime taxable transfers (after deducting the unified credit) and subtracting the taxes payable for prior taxable periods. In general, estate taxes are computed by applying the uniform rate schedule to cumulated transfers and subtracting the gift taxes paid. An appropriate adjustment is made for taxes on lifetime transfers—such as gifts within three years of death—in a decedent's estate.

Among the deductions allowed in computing the amount of the estate subject to tax are funeral expenditures, administrative costs, claims and bequests to religious, charitable, and fraternal organizations or government welfare agencies, and state inheritance taxes. A marital deduction is also allowable for both estates and gifts. In 1981 the maximum estate marital deduction was the greater of $250,000 or one-half of the decedent's adjusted gross estate. Also, in 1981, there was a gift marital deduction of $100,000 for the first $100,000 of lifetime gifts made to a spouse, no deduction for the next $100,000 of such gifts, and thereafter a deduction for one half of the aggregate lifetime gifts made to a spouse in excess of $200,000. For transfers made after 1981 during life or death, there is an unlimited marital deduction. An annual gift tax exclusion is provided that permits tax-free gifts to each donee of $10,000 for each year. A husband and wife that agree to treat gifts to third persons as joint gifts can exclude up to $20,000 a year to each donee. An unlimited exclusion for medical expenses and school tuition paid for the benefit of any donee is also available.

Unified Credit— Estate & Gift Taxes

Year	Credit
1981	$ 47,000
1982	62,800
1983	79,300
1984	96,300
1985	121,800
1986	155,800
1987 and after	192,800

Federal Estate and Gift Taxes

Unified Rate Schedule, 1982[1]

If the net amount is:		Tentative tax is:		
From	To	Tax +	%	On excess over
$ 0	$ 10,000	$ 0	18	$ 0
10,000	20,000	1,800	20	10,000
20,000	40,000	3,800	22	20,000
40,000	60,000	8,200	24	40,000
60,000	80,000	13,000	26	60,000
80,000	100,000	18,200	28	80,000
100,000	150,000	23,800	30	100,000
150,000	250,000	38,800	32	150,000
250,000	500,000	70,800	34	250,000
500,000	750,000	155,800	37	500,000
750,000	1,000,000	248,300	39	750,000
1,000,000	1,250,000	345,800	41	1,000,000
1,250,000	1,500,000	448,300	43	1,250,000
1,500,000	2,000,000	555,800	45	1,500,000
2,000,000	2,500,000	780,800	49	2,000,000
2,500,000	3,000,000	1,025,800	53	2,500,000
3,000,000	3,500,000	1,290,800	57	3,000,000
3,500,000	4,000,000	1,575,800	61	3,500,000
4,000,000 and up	—	1,880,800	65	4,000,000

1. The estate and gift tax rates are combined in the single rate schedule effective for the estates of decedents dying, and for gifts made, after Dec. 31, 1976.

State General Sales and Use Taxes[1]

(as of May 1, 1982)

State	Percent rate	State	Percent rate	State	Percent rate
Alabama	4	Kentucky	5	Ohio	5
Arizona	4	Louisiana	3	Oklahoma	2
Arkansas	3	Maine	5	Pennsylvania	6
California	4.75	Maryland	5	Rhode Island	6
Colorado	3	Massachusetts	5	South Carolina	4
Connecticut	7.5	Michigan	4	South Dakota	4
D.C.	6	Minnesota[2]	5	Tennessee[4]	4.5
Florida	5	Mississippi	5	Texas	4
Georgia	3	Missouri	3.125	Utah	4
Hawaii	4	Nebraska	3.5	Vermont[5]	4
Idaho	3	Nevada	5.75	Virginia	3
Illinois[2]	4	New Jersey[3]	5	Washington	5.5
Indiana	4	New Mexico	3.5	West Virginia[4]	5
Iowa	3	New York	4	Wisconsin	5
Kansas	3	North Carolina	3	Wyoming	3
		North Dakota	3		

1. Local and county taxes, if any, are additional. 2. 2% on food and drugs. 3. Footnote 1 does not apply. 4. Continues temporary State Retail Sales Tax for one year at 4.5%. 5. 1% on fuels for residential use. NOTE: Alaska, Delaware, Montana, New Hampshire and Oregon have no statewide sales and use taxes. *Source: Information Please Almanac* questionnaires to the states.

Income Tax Rates in Selected Cities

(Population exceeding 50,000)

City	Percent rate	Year begun	City	Percent rate	Year begun
Akron, Ohio	2	1962	Lakewood, Ohio	1.75	1968
Allentown, Pa.	1	1958	Lancaster, Pa.	0.5	1959
Altoona, Pa.	1	1948	Lansing, Mich.	1	1968
Baltimore	(1)	1966	Lexington, Ky.	2	1952
Bethlehem, Pa.	1	1957	Lima, Ohio	1	1959
Birmingham, Ala.	1	1970	Lorain, Ohio	1	1967
Canton, Ohio	2	1954	Louisville, Ky.	2.2	1948
Cincinnati	2	1954	Mansfield, Ohio	1	1966
Cleveland	2	1967	New York	0.9–4.3	1966
Cleveland Heights, Ohio	2	1968	Owensboro, Ky.	1	1960
Columbus, Ohio	1.5	1947	Parma, Ohio	2	1967
Covington, Ky.	2.5	1956	Philadelphia	4.3125	1939
Dayton, Ohio	1.75	1949	Pontiac, Mich.	1	1968
Detroit	2	1965	Reading, Pa.	1	1969
District of Columbia	2–11	1947	Saginaw, Mich.	1	1965
Elyria, Ohio	1.5	1969	St. Louis	1	1948
Erie, Pa.	1	1948	Scranton, Pa.	2.6	1948
Euclid, Ohio	1.5	1967	Springfield, Ohio	2	1948
Flint, Mich.	1	1965	Toledo, Ohio	1.5	1946
Gadsden, Ala.	2	1956	Warren, Ohio	1	1952
Grand Rapids, Mich.	1	1967	Wilkes-Barre, Pa.	1	1966
Hamilton, Ohio	1.5	1960	Wilmington, Del.	1	1970
Harrisburg, Pa.	1	1966	York, Pa.	1	1965
Kansas City, Mo.	1	1964	Youngstown, Ohio	2	1948
Kettering, Ohio	1.75	1968			

1. Tax is 50% of state income tax. NOTE: Rates are for residents only, except in Kentucky, Ohio, and Pennsylvania cities, where non-resident rate is the same. *Source:* Tax Foundation, Inc.

National Clearinghouse for Health Information

The Department of Health and Human Services has opened a National Health Information Clearinghouse to help consumers locate specific information about health. The project has a number of referral specialists to work with questions, get in touch with resource organizations, and refer those sources to the caller or writer. The center will not give medical advice or provide referrals to individual physicians.

For information, write: National Health Information Clearinghouse, P.O. Box 1133, Washington, D.C. 20013, or call 800–336–4797 (in Virginia, 703–522–2590).

Sales Tax Rates in Selected Cities[1]

City	Percent rate	City	Percent rate	City	Percent rate
Amarillo, Tex.	1	Ithaca, N.Y.[2]	3	Richmond, Va.	1
Anaheim, Calif.[2]	1.25	Jefferson City, Mo.	1	Roanoke, Va.	1
Austin, Tex.	1	Lincoln, Neb.	1	Sacramento, Calif.[2]	1.25
Baton Rouge, La.[3]	3	Los Angeles[2]	1.25	St. Louis	1
Berkeley, Calif.[2 4]	1.75	Lynchburg, Va.	1	San Antonio, Tex.	1
Birmingham, Ala.	1	Mobile, Ala.	2	San Diego, Calif.[2]	1.25
Boulder, Colo.	2.15	Montgomery, Ala.	2	San Francisco[2 4]	1.75
Chicago[2]	3	New Orleans[3]	3	Seattle[2]	0.925
Dallas	1	New York	4.25	Shreveport, La.[3]	3
Denver	3	Nome, Alaska	3	Spokane, Wash.[2]	0.925
Duluth, Minn.	1	Norfolk, Va.	1	Springfield, Ill.[2]	2
El Paso	1	Oakland, Calif.[2 4]	1.75	Topeka, Kan.	0.5
Fort Worth	1	Oklahoma City	2	Troy, N.Y.[2]	3
Fresno, Calif.[2]	1.25	Omaha, Neb.	1.5	Tucson, Ariz.	2
Glendale, Calif.[2]	1.25	Pasadena, Calif.[2]	1.25	Tulsa, Okla.	3
Houston	1	Phoenix, Ariz.	1	Washington, D.C.	6
Huntsville, Ala.	2	Rapid City, S.D.	1.5	Yonkers, N.Y.[2]	4

1. Excludes state and county sales taxes unless otherwise indicated. 2. Combined city and county rate. 3. Includes Parish School Board tax. 4. Includes 0.5% imposed by San Francisco Bay Area Rapid Transit District. *Source:* Tax Foundation, Inc.

"Go West, Young Man"

It was not Horace Greeley but John Babsone Lane Soule, editor of the Terre Haute (Indiana) *Express* who gave this advice in 1851. As 100,000 pioneers moved west to Oregon and California in the 1840s, Greeley called their trek "an aspect of insanity."

From 1840 to 1870, about 254,000 emigrants traveled from the Missouri River to the Pacific; 43,000 more stopped in Utah.

In this 30-year period, only 342 emigrants were killed by Indians, while 426 Indians were killed by whites, reports Charles D. Unruh in *The Plains Across* (1979). Nine out of 10 deaths on the trail came from disease; almost as many died from drowning as from Indian action.

The Stages of Invention

Alexander von Humbolt (1769–1859), the German naturalist, said that an invention goes through three stages: doubt of its existence, denial of its importance, and, finally, credit for its discovery going to someone else.

One example of the truth in this perception is the invention of the "Pullman," the railroad sleeping car. The first sleeper was built by Richard Imlay of Philadelphia. It ran between Chambersburg and Harrisburg, Pa., in 1838. At least eight railroads advertised some kind of sleeping car before 1850. Pullman's first car was not built until 1859. George M. Pullman and his friend Ben Field patented the folding upper berth in 1864. Pullman seems to have been a better businessman and a better promoter.

Cold Weather Tire Tip

When the outside temperature drops, so will the air pressure in the tires, which also brings down fuel economy because of increased rolling resistance. According to the Automotive Information Council, tire pressure can drop from 32 pounds at 70 degrees to 26 pounds at freezing.

Selected CB 10-Codes

10–1	Receiving poorly	10–21	Call by phone	10–51	Wrecker needed at . . .
10–2	Receiving well	10–23	Stand by	10–52	Ambulance needed at . . .
10–3	Stop transmitting	10–25	Can you contact?	10–53	Road blocked
10–4	OK, message received	10–26	Disregard last information	10–59	Convoy or escort
10–5	Relay message	10–27	I am moving to channel . . .	10–62	Unable to copy, use phone
10–6	Stand by	10–28	Identify your station	10–66	Message cancellation
10–7	Out of service	10–29	I am leaving this location	10–70	Fire at . . .
10–8	In service	10–30	Does not conform to FCC rules	10–73	Speed Trap at . . .
10–9	Repeat message	10–32	Radio check	10–75	You are causing interference
10–10	Transmission completed, standing by	10–33	Emergency traffic at this station	10–77	ETA (estimated time of arrival
10–11	Speak more slowly	10–34	Trouble here, help needed	10–82	Reserve lodging
10–12	Visitors present	10–36	Correct time is . . .	10–91	Talk closer to mike
10–13	Report road conditions, weather	10–39	Your message delivered	10–92	Have your transmitter checked
10–17	Urgent business	10–44	I have a message for . . .	10–93	Check my frequency
10–20	Location . . .	10–45	All units please report	10–94	Give me a long count
		10–46	Assist motorist	10–200	Police needed at . . .
		10–50	Accident at . . .		

AVIATION

Famous Firsts in Aviation

1782 **First balloon flight.** Jacques and Joseph Montgolfier of Annonay, France, sent up a small smoke-filled balloon about mid-November.

1783 **First hydrogen-filled balloon flight.** Jacques A. C. Charles, Paris physicist, supervised construction by A. J. and M. N. Robert of a 13-ft diameter balloon that was filled with hydrogen. It got up to about 3,000 ft and traveled about 16 mi. in a 45-min flight (Aug. 27).

First human balloon flights. A Frenchman, Jean Pilâtre de Rozier, made the first captive-balloon ascension (Oct. 15). With the Marquis d'Arlandes, Pilâtre de Rozier made the first free flight, reaching a peak altitude of about 500 ft, and traveling about 5½ mi. in 20 min (Nov. 21).

1784 **First powered balloon.** Gen. Jean Baptiste Marie Meusnier developed the first propeller-driven and elliptically-shaped balloon—the crew cranking three propellers on a common shaft to give the craft a speed of about 3 mph.

First woman to fly. Mme. Thible, a French opera singer (June 4).

1793 **First balloon flight in America.** Jean Pierre Blanchard, a French pilot, made it from Philadelphia to near Woodbury, Gloucester County, N.J., in a little over 45 min (Jan. 9).

1794 **First military use of the balloon.** Jean Marie Coutelle, using a balloon built for the French Army, made two 4-hr observation ascents. The military purpose of the ascents seems to have been to damage the enemy's morale.

1797 **First parachute jump.** André-Jacques Garnerin dropped from about 6,500 ft over Monceau Park in Paris in a 23-ft diameter parachute made of white canvas with a basket attached (Oct. 22).

1843 **First air transport company.** In London, William S. Henson and John Stringfellow filed articles of incorporation for the Aerial Transit Company (March 24). It failed

1852 **First dirigible.** Henri Giffard, a French engineer, flew in a controllable (more or less) steam-engine powered balloon, 144 ft long and 39 ft in diameter, inflated with 88,000 cu ft of coal gas. It reached 6.7 mph on a flight from Paris to Trappe (Sept. 24).

1860 **First aerial photographers.** Samuel Archer King and William Black made two photos of Boston, still in existence.

1872 **First gas-engine powered dirigible.** Paul Haenlein, a German engineer, flew in a semi-rigid-frame dirigible, powered by a 4-cylinder internal-combustion engine running on coal gas drawn from the supporting bag.

1873 **First transatlantic attempt.** *The New York Daily Graphic* sponsored the attempt with a 400,000 cu ft balloon carrying a lifeboat. A rip in the bag during inflation brought collapse of the balloon and the project.

1897 **First successful metal dirigible.** An all-metal dirigible, designed by David Schwarz, a Hungarian, took off from Berlin's Tempelhof Field and, powered by a 16-hp Daimler engine, got several miles before leaking gas caused it to crash (Nov. 13).

1900 **First Zeppelin flight.** Germany's Count Ferdinand von Zeppelin flew the first of his long series of rigid-frame airships. It attained a speed of 18 mi. per h and got 3½ mi. before its steering gear failed (July 2).

1903 **First successful heavier-than-air machine flight.** Aviation was really born on the sand dunes at Kitty Hawk, N.C., when Orville Wright crawled to his prone position between the wings of the biplane he and his brother Wilbur had built, opened the throttle of their homemade 12-hp engine and took to the air. He covered 120 ft in 12 sec. Later that day, in one of four flights, Wilbur stayed up 59 sec and covered 852 ft (Dec. 17).

1904 **First airplane maneuvers.** Orville Wright made the first turn with an airplane (Sept. 15); 5 days later his brother Wilbur made the first complete circle.

1905 **First airplane flight over half an hour.** Orville Wright kept his craft up 33 min 17 sec (Oct. 4).

1906 **First European airplane flight.** Alberto Santos-Dumont, a Brazilian, flew a heavier-than-air machine at Bagatelle Field, Paris (Sept. 13).

1908 **First airplane fatality.** Lt. Thomas E. Selfridge, U.S. Army Signal Corps, was in a group of officers evaluating the Wright plane at Fort Myer, Va. He was up about 75 ft with Orville Wright when the propeller hit a bracing wire and was broken, throwing the plane out of control, killing Selfridge and seriously injuring Wright (Sept. 17).

1910 **First licensed woman pilot.** Baroness Raymonde de la Roche of France, who learned to fly in 1909, received ticket No. 36 on March 8.

First flight from shipboard. Lt. Eugene Ely, USN, took a Curtiss plane off from the deck of cruiser *Birmingham* at Hampton Roads, Va., and flew to Norfolk (Nov. 14). The following January, he reversed the process, flying from Camp Selfridge to the deck of the armored cruiser *Pennsylvania* in San Francisco Bay (Jan. 18).

1911 **First U.S. woman pilot.** Harriet Quimby, a magazine writer, who got ticket No. 37.

1913 **First multi-engined aircraft.** Built and flown by Igor Ivan Sikorsky while still in his native Russia.

1914 **First aerial combat.** In August, Allied and German pilots and observers started shooting at each other with pistols and rifles—with negligible results.

1915 **First air raids on England.** German Zeppelins started dropping bombs on four English communities (Jan. 19).

1918 **First U.S. air squadron.** The U.S. Army Air Corps made its first independent raids over enemy lines, in DH-4 planes (British-designed) powered with 400-hp American-designed Liberty engines (April 8).

First regular airmail service. Operated for the Post Office Department by the Army, the first regular service was inaugurated with one round trip a day (except Sunday) between Washington, D.C., and New York City (May 15).

1919 **First transatlantic flight.** The NC-4, one of four Curtiss flying boats commanded by Lt. Comdr. Albert C. Read, reached Lisbon, Portugal, (May 27) after hops from Trepassy Bay, Newfoundland, to Horta, Azores (May 16–17), to Ponta Delgada (May 20). The Liberty-powered craft was piloted by Walter Hinton.

First nonstop transatlantic flight. Capt. John Alcock and Lt. Arthur Whitten Brown, British World War I flyers, made the 1,900 mi. from St. John's, Newfoundland, to Clifden, Ireland, in 16 h 12 min in a Vickers-Vimy bomber with two 350-hp Rolls-Royce engines (June 15–16).

First lighter-than-air transatlantic flight. The British dirigible R-34, commanded by Maj. George H. Scott, left Firth of Forth, Scotland, (July 2) and touched down at Mineola, L.I., 108 h later. The eastbound trip was made in 75 h (completed July 13).

First scheduled passenger service (using airplanes). Aircraft Travel and Transport inaugurated London-Paris service (Aug. 25). Later the company started the first trans-channel mail service on the same route (Nov. 10).

1921 **First naval vessel sunk by aircraft.** Two battleships being scrapped by treaty were sunk by bombs dropped from Army planes in demonstration put on by Brig. Gen. William S. Mitchell (July 21).

First helium balloon. The C-7, non-rigid Navy dirigible was first to use non-inflammable helium as lifting gas, making a flight from Hampton Roads, Va., to Washington, D.C. (Dec. 1).

1922 **First member of Caterpillar Club.** Lt. (later Maj. Gen.) Harold Harris bailed out of a crippled plane he was testing at McCook Field, Dayton, Ohio (Oct. 20), and became the first man to join the Caterpillar Club—those whose lives have been saved by parachute.

1923 **First nonstop transcontinental flight.** Lts. John A. Macready and Oakley Kelly flew a single-engine Fokker T-2 nonstop from New York to San Diego, a distance of just over 2,500 mi. in 26 h 50 min (May 2–3).

First autogyro flight. Juan de la Cierva, a brilliant Spanish mathematician, made the first successful flight in a rotary wing aircraft in Madrid (June 9).

1924 **First round-the-world flight.** Four Douglas Cruiser biplanes of the U.S. Army Air Corps took off from Seattle under command of Maj. Frederick Martin (April 6). 175 days later, two of the planes (Lt. Lowell Smith's and Lt. Erik Nelson's) landed in Seattle after a circuitous route—one source saying 26,345 mi., another saying 27,553 mi.

1926 **First polar flight.** Then-Lt. Cmdr. Richard E. Byrd, acting as navigator, and Floyd Bennett as pilot, flew a trimotor Fokker from Kings Bay, Spitsbergen, over the North Pole and back in 15½ h (May 8–9).

1927 **First solo transatlantic flight.** Charles Augustus Lindbergh lifted his Wright-powered Ryan monoplane, *Spirit of St. Louis,* from Roosevelt Field, L.I., to stay aloft 33 h 39 min and travel 3,600 mi. to Le Bourget Field outside Paris (May 20–21).

First transatlantic passenger. Charles A. Levine was piloted by Clarence D. Chamberlin from Roosevelt Field, L.I., to Eisleben, Germany, in a Wright-powered Bellanca (June 4–5).

1928 **First east-west transatlantic crossing.** Baron Guenther von Huenefeld, piloted by German Capt. Hermann Koehl and Irish Capt. James Fitzmaurice, left Dublin for New York City (April 12) in a single-engine all-metal Junkers monoplane. Some 37 h later, they crashed on Greely Island, Labrador. Rescued.

First U.S.-Australia flight. Sir Charles Kingsford-Smith and Capt. Charles T. P. Ulm, Australians, and two American navigators, Harry W. Lyon and James Warner, crossed the Pacific from Oakland to Brisbane. They went via Hawaii and the Fiji Islands in a trimotor Fokker (May 31–June 8).

First transarctic flight. Sir Hubert Wilkins, an Australian explorer and Carl Ben Eielson, who served as pilot, flew from Point Barrow, Alaska, to Spitsbergen (mid-April).

1929 **First of the endurance records.** With Air Corps Maj. Carl Spaatz in command and Capt. Ira Eaker as chief pilot, an Army Fokker, aided by refueling in the air, remained aloft 150 h 40 min at Los Angeles (Jan. 1–7).

First blind flight. James H. Doolittle proved the feasibility of instrument-guided flying when he took off and landed entirely on instruments (Sept. 24).

First rocket-engine flight. Fritz von Opel, a German auto maker, stayed aloft in his small rocket-powered craft for 75 sec, covering nearly 2 mi. (Sept. 30).

First South Pole flight. Comdr. Richard E. Byrd, with Bernt Balchen as pilot, Harold I. June, radio operator, and Capt. A. C. McKinley, photographer, flew a trimotor Fokker from the Bay of Whales, Little America, over the South Pole and back (Nov. 28–29).

1930 **First Paris–New York nonstop flight.** Dieudonné Coste and Maurice Bellonte, French pilots, flew a Hispano-powered Breguet biplane from Le Bourget Field to Valley Stream, L.I., in 37 h 18 min. (Sept. 2–3).

1931 **First flight into the stratosphere.** Auguste Piccard, a Swiss physicist, and Charles Knipfer, ascended in a balloon from Augsburg, Germany, and reached a height of 51,793 ft in a 17-h flight that terminated on a glacier near Innsbruck, Austria (May 27).

First nonstop transpacific flight. Hugh Herndon and Clyde Pangborn took off from Sabishiro Beach, Japan, dropped their landing gear, and flew 4,860 mi. to near Wenatchee, Wash., in 41 h 13 min. (Oct. 4–5).

1932 **First woman's transatlantic solo.** Amelia Earhart, flying a Pratt & Whitney Wasp-powered Lockheed Vega, flew alone from Harbor Grace, Newfoundland, to Ireland in approximately 15 h (May 20–21).

First westbound transatlantic solo. James A. Mollison, a British pilot, took a de Havilland Puss Moth from Portmarnock, Ireland, to Pennfield, N.B. (Aug. 18).

First woman airline pilot. Ruth Rowland Nichols, first woman to hold three international records at the same time—speed, distance, altitude—was employed by N.Y.-New England Airways.

1933 **First round-the-world solo.** Wiley Post took a Lockheed Vega, *Winnie Mae,* 15,596 mi. around the world in 7 d 18 h 49$^{1}/_{2}$ min (July 15–22).

1937 **First successful helicopter.** Hanna Reitsch, a German pilot, flew Dr. Heinrich Focke's FW-61 in free, fully controlled flight at Bremen (July 4).

1939 **First turbojet flight.** Just before their invasion of Poland, the Germans flew a Heinkel He-178 plane powered by a Heinkel S3B turbojet (Aug. 27).

1942 **First American jet plane flight.** Robert Stanley, chief pilot for Bell Aircraft Corp., flew the Bell XP-59 *Airacomet* at Muroc Army Base, Calif. (Oct. 1).

1947 **First piloted supersonic flight in an airplane.** Capt. Charles E. Yeager, U.S. Air Force, flew the X-1 rocket-powered research plane built by Bell Aircraft Corp., faster than the speed of sound at Muroc Air Force Base, California (Oct. 14).

1949 **First round-the-world nonstop flight.** Capt. James Gallagher and USAF crew of 13 flew a Boeing B-50A Superfortress around the world nonstop from Ft. Worth, returning to same point: 23,452 mi. in 94 h 1 min, with 4 aerial refuelings enroute (Feb. 27–March 2).

1950 **First nonstop transatlantic jet flight.** Col. David C. Schilling (USAF) flew 3,300 mi. from England to Limestone, Maine, in 10 h 1 min (Sept. 22).

1951 **First solo across North Pole.** Charles F. Blair, Jr., flew a converted P-51 (May 29).

1952 **First jetliner service.** De Havilland Comet flight inaugurated by BOAC between London and Johannesburg, South Africa (May 2). Flight, including stops, took 23 h 38 min.

First transatlantic helicopter flight. Capt. Vincent H. McGovern and 1st Lt. Harold W. Moore piloted 2 Sikorsky H-19s from Westover, Mass., to Prestwick, Scotland (3,410 mi.). Trip was made in 5 steps, with flying time of 42 h 25 min (July 15–31).

First transatlantic round trip in same day. British Canberra twin-jet bomber flew from Aldergrove, Northern Ireland, to Gander, Newfoundland, and back in 7 h 59 min flying time (Aug. 26).

1955 **First transcontinental round trip in same day.** Lt. John M. Conroy piloted F-86 Sabrejet across U.S. (Los Angeles–New York) and back—5,085 mi.—in 11 h 33 min 27 sec (May 21).

1957 **First round-the-world, nonstop jet plane flight.** Maj. Gen. Archie J. Old, Jr., USAF, led a flight of 3 Boeing B-52 bombers, powered with 8 10,000-lb. thrust Pratt & Whitney Aircraft J57 engines around the world in 45 h 19 min; distance 24,325 mi.; average speed 525 mph. (Completed Jan. 18.)

1958 **First transatlantic jet passenger service.** BOAC, New York to London (Oct. 4). Pan American started daily service, N.Y. to Paris (Oct. 26).

First domestic jet passenger service. National Airlines inaugurated service between New York and Miami (Dec. 10).

1976 **First regularly-scheduled commercial supersonic transport (SST) flights begin.** Air France and British Airways inaugurate service (January 21). Air France flies the Paris-Rio de Janeiro route; B.A., the London-Bahrain. Both airlines begin SST service to Washington, D.C. (May 24).

1977 **First successful man-powered aircraft.** Paul MacCready, an aeronautical engineer from Pasadena, Calif., was awarded the Kremer Prize for creating the world's first successful man-powered aircraft. The *Gossamer Condor* was flown by Bryan Allen over the required 3-mile course on Aug. 23.

1978 **First successful transatlantic balloon flight.** Three Albuquerque, N.M., men, Ben Abruzzo, Larry Newman, and Maxie Anderson, completed the crossing (Aug. 16. Landed, Aug. 17) in their hot air balloon, *Double Eagle II.*

1979 **First man-powered aircraft to fly across the English Channel.** The Kremer Prize for the Channel crossing was won by Bryan Allen who flew the *Gossamer Albatross* from Folkestone, England to Cap Gris-Nez, France, in 2 h 55 min (June 12).

1980 **First successful balloon flight over the North Pole.** Sidney Conn and his wife Eleanor, in hot-air balloon *Joy of Sound* (April 11).

First nonstop transcontinental balloon flight, and also record for longest overland voyage in a balloon. Maxie Anderson and his son, Kris, completed four-day flight from Fort Baker, Calif., to successful landing outside Matane, Quebec, on May 12 in their helium-filled balloon, *Kitty Hawk.*

First long-distance solar-powered flight. Janice Brown, 98-lb former teacher, flew tiny experimental solar-powered aircraft, *Solar Challenger* six miles in 22-min near Marana, Ariz. (Dec. 3). The craft was powered by a 2.75-hp engine.

First solar-powered aircraft to fly across the English Channel. Stephen R. Ptacek flew the 210-lb *Solar Challenger* at the average speed of 30 mph from Cormeilles-en-Vexin near Paris to the Royal Manston Air Force Base on England's southeastern coast in 5h 30 min (July 7).

Official World Airplane Records

Source: National Aeronautic Association.

Speed Over Measured Straightaway Course

Speed (mph)	Date	Type plane	Pilot	Place
314.32	Dec. 25, 1934	Caudron	Raymond Delmotte (France)	Istres, France
352.39	Sept. 13, 1935	Hughes Special	Howard Hughes (U.S.)	Santa Ana, Calif.
379.63	Nov. 11, 1937	BF-113R	Herman Wurster (Germany)	Augsburg, Germany
469.22	April 26, 1939	ME-109R	Fritz Wendel (Germany)	Augsburg, Germany
606.25	Nov. 7, 1945	Gloster Meteor IV	Group Capt. H. Wilson (U.K.)	Herne Bay, England
615.78	Sept. 7, 1946	Gloster Meteor	Group Capt. E. M. Donalson (U.K.)	Littlehampton, England
650.80	Aug. 25, 1947	Douglas D-558	Maj. Marion Carl, USMC	Muroc AFB, Calif.
670.98	Sept. 15, 1948	North American F-86A	Maj. R. L. Johnson (USAF)	Muroc AFB, Calif.
698.51	Nov. 19, 1952	North American F-86D	Capt. James S. Nash (USAF)	Salton Sea, Calif.
755.14	Oct. 29, 1953	North American YF	Lt. Col. F. K. Everest, Jr. (USAF)	Salton Sea, Calif.
822.27	Aug. 20, 1955	North American F-100C	Col. Horace A. Hanes (U.S.)	Palmdale, Calif.
1,132.14	March 10, 1956	Fairey Delta 2	L. Peter Twiss, D.S.C. (U.K.)	Ford-Chichester, England
1,207.60	Dec. 12, 1957	McDonnell F-101A	Maj. Adrian E. Drew (USAF)	Edwards AFB, Calif.
1,404.09	May 16, 1958	Lockheed F104	Capt. Walter W. Irwin (USAF)	Edwards AFB, Calif.
1,483.85	Oct. 31, 1959	Sukhoi S-66	G. Mossolov (U.S.S.R.)	U.S.S.R.
1,525.96	Dec. 15, 1959	F-106A Delta Wing Monoplane	Maj. Joseph W. Rogers (USAF)	Edwards AFB, Calif.
1,606.32	Nov. 22, 1961	McDonnell F4H	Lt. Col. R. B. Robinson (USMC)	Edwards AFB, Calif.
1,665.89	July 7, 1962	E-166 Jet	G. Mossolov (U.S.S.R.)	U.S.S.R.
2,070.101	May 1, 1965	Lockheed YF-12A Jet	Col. R. L. Stephens (USAF)	Edwards AFB, Calif.
2,196.17	July 28, 1976	Lockheed SR-71	Capt. Eldon W. Joersz (USAF)	Beale AFB, Calif.

Fastest U.S. continental: Capt. Robert G. Sowers (USAF)—Convair B-58 "Hustler"—from Long Beach, Calif., to Kennedy International Airport, N.Y.—2,458.58 statute miles—2 h 0 min 58.71 sec—average speed, 1,214.65 mph—March 5, 1962.

Distance, Straight Line

Distance (mi.)	Date	Crew	From	To
4,911.93	Sept. 27–29, 1929	Costes & Bellonte (France)	Le Bourget, France	Manchuria
5,011.35	July 28–30, 1931	Russel N. Boardman, John Polando (U.S.)	New York	Istanbul
5,656.93	Aug. 5–7, 1933	Maurice Rossi, Paul Codos (France)	New York	Ryack, Syria
6,305.66	July 12–14, 1937	Gromov, Youmachev, Daniline (U.S.S.R.)	Moscow	San Jacinto, Calif.
7,158.44	Nov. 5–7, 1938	Sqd. Ldr. R. Kellett (U.K.)	Ismailia, Egypt	Darwin, Australia
7,916.00	Nov. 19–20, 1945	Col. C. S. Irvine & Lt. Col. G. R. Stanley (U.S.)	Guam	Washington, D. C.
11,235.60	Sept. 29–Oct. 1, 1946	Comdr. Thomas D. Davies, Comdrs. Eugene P. Rankin, Walter S. Reid, Lt. Comdr. Ray A. Tabeling (USN)	Perth, Australia	Columbus, Ohio
12,532.28	Jan. 10–11, 1962	Maj. Clyde P. Evely (USAF)	Kadena, Okinawa	Madrid

Longest light airplane (3,858–6,614 lb) distance: Maximillian A. Conrad—U. S. Piper Comanche 250, Lycoming 0-540-AIAS (250 hp), from Casablanca, Morocco, to Los Angeles, 7,668.48 mi.—June 2–4, 1959.

Distance, Closed Circuit

Distance (mi.)	Date	Crew	Place
6,587.441	March 23–26, 1932	Bossoutrot & Rossi (France)	Oran
7,239.588	May 13–15, 1938	Comdr. Fujita & Sgt. Maj. Takahashi (Japan)	Kisarasu, Japan
8,037.899	July 30–Aug. 1, 1939	Angelo Tondi, Roberto Dagasso, Ferrucio Vignoli (Italy)	Rome
8,854.308	Aug. 1–2, 1947	Lt. Col. O. F. Lassiter (U.S.) Capt. W. J. Valentine (U.S.)	Tampa, Fla.
10,078.84	Dec. 13–14, 1960	Lt. Col. J. R. Grissom (USAF)	Edwards AFB, Calif.
11,336.92	June 6–7, 1962	Capt. William Stevenson (USAF)	Seymour-Johnson, N.C.

Altitude

Height (ft)	Date	Crew	Place
44,819	Sept. 28, 1933	G. Lemoine (France)	Villacoublay, France
47,352	April 11, 1934	Comdr. Renato Donati (Italy)	Rome
49,944	Sept. 28, 1936	Sqd. Ldr. F. R. D. Swain (U.K.)	South Farnborough, England
53,937	June 30, 1937	Fl. Lt. M. J. Adam (U.K.)	Farnborough, England
56,046	Oct. 22, 1938	Col. Mario Pezzi (Italy)	Montecelio

Altitude

Height (ft)	Date	Crew	Place
59,445[1]	March 23, 1948	John Cunningham (U.K.)	Hatfield, England
63,668[1]	May 4, 1953	Walter F. Gibb (U.K.)	Bristol, England
65,889[1]	Aug. 29, 1955	Walter F. Gibb (U.K.)	Bristol, England
70,308[1]	Aug. 28, 1957	Michael Randrup (U.K.)	Luton, England
91,243[1]	May 7, 1958	Maj. H. C. Johnson (USAF)	Palmdale, Calif.
103,389[1]	Nov. 14, 1959	Capt. Joe B. Jordan (USAF)	Edwards AFB, Calif.
314,750[2]	July 17, 1962	Maj. Robert M. White (USAF)	Edwards AFB, Calif.
118,898	July 25, 1973	Alexander Fedotov (U.S.S.R.)	U.S.S.R.
123,524	Aug. 31, 1977	Alexander Fedotov (U.S.S.R.)	U.S.S.R.

1. Jet-propelled aircraft. 2. X-15-1 rocket plane.

World's 50 Busiest Airports in 1981

Airport	Passengers[1]	Airport	Passengers[1]
1 O'Hare International: Chicago	37,992,151	26 Gatwick Airport: London	9,885,847
2 Hartsfield International: Atlanta	37,594,073	27 Schiphol Airport: Amsterdam	9,668,970
3 International: Los Angeles	32,722,534	28 Sea–Tac International: Seattle	9,194,957
4 Heathrow Airport: London	27,512,945	29 McCarran International: Las Vegas	9,138,268
5 Kennedy International: New York	25,752,719	30 Metropolitan: Detroit	9,106,614
6 Dallas/Ft. Worth Airport	25,533,929	31 International: Philadelphia	9,008,529
7 Stapleton International: Denver	22,601,877	32 Kingsford-Smith Airport: Sydney	8,480,851
8 Haneda: Tokyo	21,235,185	33 International: Hong Kong	8,224,509
9 International: Miami	19,848,593	34 Copenhagen Airport Kastrup	8,221,757
10 International: San Francisco	19,848,491	35 Narita: Tokyo	8,210,029
11 La Guardia: New York	18,146,191	36 Zurich Airport	7,973,264
12 International: Osaka	17,087,548	37 Minneapolis-St. Paul International	7,824,031
13 Orly Airport: Paris	17,012,241	38 Dusseldorf Airport	7,218,189
14 Frankfurt/Main: West Germany	16,953,045	39 International: Tampa	7,083,621
15 Boston–Logan International	14,827,684	40 International: Vancouver, B.C.	7,072,400
16 International: Toronto	14,512,400	41 Changi Airport: Rep. of Singapore	6,879,924
17 International: Honolulu	14,344,225	42 Sky Harbor International: Phoenix	6,642,350
18 National Airport: Washington, D.C.	13,870,905	43 International: Montreal	6,226,000
19 International: Mexico City	12,961,727	44 International: New Orleans	6,132,292
20 Intercontinental: Houston	11,601,315	45 International: Orlando	6,072,143
21 Charles de Gaulle: Paris	10,935,700	46 Tullamarine Airport: Melbourne	6,055,135
22 Fiumicino Airport: Rome	10,923,564	47 Munich–Riem Airport	5,915,167
23 Lambert-St. Louis International	10,632,429	48 Ft. Lauderdale–Hollywood International	5,742,070
24 International: Newark	10,181,865	49 Linate International: Milan	5,700,933
25 International: Pittsburgh	10,112,266	50 Sao Paulo International	5,554,176

1. Enplaned, deplaned, and transfer, in millions. *Source:* Airport Operators Council International.

World Airplane Hijackings and Attempts

	Place of flight origin		
Years	U.S.	Foreign	Total
1930–67	12	67	79
1968	22	13	35
1969	40	47	87
1970	27	56	83
1971	27	31	58
1972	31	31	62
1973	2	20	22
1974	7	19	26
1975	12	13	25
1976	4	14	18
1977	6	26	32
1978	13	18	31
1979	13	14	27
1980	22	19	41
1981	8	24	32
Total	**246**	**412**	**658**

Source: Department of Transportation, Federal Aviation Administration.

Disposition of Hijackers of Aircraft in U.S. Commerce, 1930–81[1]

Disposition of case	Number
Convictions	151
United States	140
Foreign	11
Acquittals	5
Committed to mental institution	27
Cases dismissed	11
Prosecution declined	8
Killed or Suicide	23
Cases pending	4
Fugitives[2]	109
Total	**338**

1. Through December 31, 1981. 2. Includes a number of passive companions indicted along with active hijackers. *Source:* Department of Transportation, Federal Aviation Administration.

U. S. Airlines Transport Planes

Manufacturer	Type	Number of passengers	Maximum speed, mph	Typical gross weight, lbs	Wingspan, ft	Maximum length, ft
4-ENGINE						
Boeing	707–120B	100–181	600	258,000	142.4	145.1
Boeing	707–320, –402/Intercontinental	108–189	600	316,000	142.4	152.9
Boeing	707–320B, C/Intercontinental	145	600	336,000	145.8	152.9
Boeing	747–100B/Superjet	442	640	733,000	195.7	231.9
Boeing	747–200B, C/Superjet	442	640	785,000	195.7	231.9
Boeing	747SR/Superjet	512	640	600,000	195.7	231.9
Boeing	747SP/Superjet	321	640	696,000	195.7	184.7
DeHavilland	DHC7	50	270	43,500	93.0	80.6
Douglas	DC–6B	90–100	300	100,000	117.5	106.8
McDonnell Douglas	DC–8/Series 30,40	116–176	600+	315,000	142.3	150.5
McDonnell Douglas	DC–8/Series 50	116–189	600	325,000	142.3	150.5
McDonnell Douglas	DC–8/Super 61	259	600	325,000	142.3	187.4
McDonnell Douglas	DC–8/Super 62	189	600	325,000	148.4	157.4
McDonnell Douglas	DC–8/Super 63	259	600	350,000	148.4	187.4
DeHavilland	DHC–7	50	270	26,700	93.0	80.6
Lockheed	L–188	94	373	113,000	99.0	104.5
Lockheed	L382	Freighter	380	155,000	132.6	97.8
3-ENGINE						
Airbus Industries	A–300	269–345	600	347,100	147.1	175.1
Boeing	727–100	70–131	600+	170,000	108.0	133.1
Boeing	727–200/Advanced	145	600+	191,500	108.0	153.1
McDonnell Douglas	DC–10/Series 10	250–380	600+	455,000	155.3	182.3
McDonnell Douglas	DC–10/Series 30	250–380	600+	572,000	165.3	181.6
McDonnell Douglas	DC–10/Series 40	250–350	600+	572,000	165.3	182.3
Lockheed	L–1011–1/TriStar	240–400	620+	430,000	155.3	177.7
Lockheed	L–1011–100, –200/TriStar	250–400	620+	466,000	155.3	177.7
Lockheed	L–1011–500/TriStar	230–330	620+	496,000	155.3	164.2
2-ENGINE						
Beech	BE18	7–9	236	9,900	49.6	35.2
Beech	B–99	15	285	10,900	45.8	44.6
Boeing	737–100	112	586	111,000	93.0	94.0
Boeing	737–200/Advanced	115	586	116,000	93.0	100.2
Boeing	737–200/Advanced	115	586	125,000	93.0	100.2
British Aircraft Corp.	BAC 111	120	470	98,500	93.5	93.5
Britten Norman	BN2	10	180	6,600	49.0	35.3
Cessna	402	6–10	242	6,885	44.1	36.4
Convair	CV440	44–48	270	52,000	105.0	81.5
Convair	580	50	270	52,000	105.4	81.5
DeHavilland	DHC–6	20	210	12,500	65.0	51.7
Douglas	DC–3	21–30	200	24,800	95.0	64.5
Embraer	EMB 110	15	286	12,500	50.0	49.5
Handley Page	Jetstream	12–18	285	12,500	52.0	47.0
McDonnell Douglas	DC–9/Series 10	90	576	90,700	89.4	104.4
McDonnell Douglas	DC–9/Series 20	90	576	98,000	93.4	104.4
McDonnell Douglas	DC–9 Series 30	115	576	121,000	93.4	119.3
McDonnell Douglas	DC–9/Series 40	125	576	121,000	93.4	125.6
McDonnell Douglas	DC–9/Series 50	139	576	122,000	93.4	133.6
McDonnell Douglas	DC–9/Series 80	167	576	140,000	107.8	149.9
Marcel Dassault	Falcon–10	4–7	600+	10,760	42.9	45.5
Marcel Dassault	Falcon–20	12–14	400	28,660	53.5	56.3
Nihon	YS–11	60	290	54,000	104.9	86.3
Piper	PA–23	6	247	5,200	37.3	31.2
Piper	PA–31	6	247	6,500	40.7	32.6
Short Brothers Harland	SH–330	30	228	22,600	74.7	58.0
Swearingen	SA–226TC	20	300	12,500	46.4	59.4

NOTE: Data show the most-used manufacturers' type and model aircraft used by air carriers and commercial operators as of April 1980. *Source:* Federal Aviation Administration.

Important American Aircraft Types (U.S. Air Force)

Abbreviations: GA—Garrett AiResearch; All—Detroit Diesel Allison Div. of General Motors; Con—Continental; GD—General Dynamics; GE—General Electric; Lyc—Lycoming; RI—Rockwell International; P&W—Pratt & Whitney; PWC—Pratt & Whitney Aircraft of Canada, Ltd; Wr—Curtiss Wright; kt—knots.

Type	Manufacturer	Popular name	Power plant	Crew	Wing-span, ft/in.	Length, ft/in.	Height, ft/in.	Gross weight, lb	Speed, mph
ATTACK									
A-7D	LTV Aerospace	Corsair II	1 All TF41-A-1	1	38/9	46/1	16/0	42,000	698
A-10A	Fairchild Hiller	Thunderbolt II	2 GE TF34-GE-100	1	57/5	53/3	14/6	40,038	449
A-37B	Cessna	Dragonfly	2 GE J85-GE-17A	1	35/8	29/3	8/9	14,000	507
BOMBERS									
B-52D	Boeing	Stratofortress	8 P&W J57-P-29W	6	185/0	156/6	48/4	450,000	650
B-52G	Boeing	Stratofortress	8 P&W J57-P-43W	6	185/0	161/11	40/8	488,000	650
B-52H	Boeing	Stratofortress	8 P&W TF33-P-3	6	185/0	159/3	40/8	488,000	650
FB-111A	GD/Ft. Worth	—	2 P&W TF30-P-7	2	70/0[3]	73/6	17/0	114,000	Mach 2+
FIGHTERS									
F-4D/E	McDonnell Douglas	Phantom II	2 GEJ79-GE-17	2	38/7	63/0	16/5	61,975	Mach 2.2
F-15A/B/C	McDonnell Douglas	Eagle	2 P&W F100-PW-100	1/2	42/8	63/8	18/6	56,000	Mach 2.5
F-5E/F	Northrop	Tiger II	2 J85-GE-21A	1/2	25/3	47/2	13/2	24,676	Mach 1.6
F-16A	GD/Ft. Worth	—	1 P&W F100-PW-200	1	31/0	47/6	16/4	22,000	Mach 2
F-106A	GD/Convair	Delta Dart	1 P&W J75-P-17	1/2	38/3	70/8	20/3	36,000	Mach 2.3
F-111	GD/Ft. Worth	—	2 P&W TF30-P-3/100(F)	2	63/0[4]	73/6	17/0	100,000	Mach 2.5
F-101B	McDonnell Douglas	Voodoo	2 P&W J57-P-55	2	39/8	67/4	18/0	46,500	Mach 1.85
RECONNAISSANCE									
RF-4C	McDonnell Douglas	Phantom II	2 GE J79-GE-17	2	38/7	63/0	16/5	61,795	Mach 2.2
SR-71	Lockheed/Calif.	—	2 P&W J58	2	55/6	107/4	18/5	170,000	Mach 3
U/WU-2	Lockheed/Calif.	—	1 P &W J75	1	80/0	49/6	13/0	19,850	400 kt
OBSERVATION									
0-2A	Cessna		2 Con 10-360-D	2	38/0	29/2	9/5	5,400	199
OV-10A[1]	RI/Columbus	Bronco	2 T76-G-416/417	2	40/0	39/7	15/1	14,466	281
EARLY WARNING COMMAND, CONTROL AND COMMUNICATIONS									
E-3A	Boeing		4 P&W TF33-P-100/A	17	145/9	152/1	42/0	325,000	530
E-4A/B	Boeing	—	4 GE CF6-50E	5	195/7	231/3	63/5	803,000	—
CARGO/TRANSPORT									
C-5A	Lockhead/Georgia	Galaxy	4 GE TF39-GE-1C	7	222/8	245/9	65/1	764,500	550
C-9A	McDonnell Douglas	Nightingale	2 P&W JT8D-9	2–7	93/3	119/3	27/5	108,000	570
C-12A[2]	Beech		2 PWC PT6A-38	2	54/5	43/6	14/6	12,500	260 kt
C-130E/H	Lockheed/Georgia	Hercules	4 All T56-A-7/-15(H)	5	132/6	99/5	38/4	155,000	360
C-140A	Lockheed/Georgia	Jetstar	4 P&W J60-P-5	5	54/4	60/4	20/4	40,921	525
C-141A	Lockheed/Georgia	Starlifter	4 P&W TF33-P-7	4–9	160/7	145/0	39/3	325,000	505
KC-135A	Boeing	Stratotanker	4 P&W J57-P-59W	4	130/9	136/3	38/4	297,000	530
C-137C	Boeing	Stratoliner	4 P&W JT3D-3B	4	145/9	152/9	42/5	328,000	627
CT-39	RI/General Aviation	Sabreliner	2 P&W J60-P-3	2	44/5	43/8	15/9	18,650	595
TRAINERS									
T-33A	Lockheed/Calif.	Shooting Star	1 All J33-A-35	2	38/9	37/7	11/7	15,100	505
T-37B	Cessna	Tweet	2 CAE J69-T-25	2	33/8	29/3	9/2	6,575	425
T-38A	Northrop	Talon	2 GE J85-5	2	25/3	46/4	12/1	12,500	Mach 1.2
T-41C	Cessna	Mescalero	1 CON 10-360-D	2	36/2	26/5	8/9	2,550	142
T-43A	Boeing	—	2 P&W JT8D-9	2	93/0	100/0	37/0	115,500	Mach .7

1. Air Force/Marines. 2. Air Force/Army. 3. Wing extended; 34 ft fully swept. 4. Wing extended; 31.11 ft fully swept. *Source:* Department of the Air Force.

Lower Ozone Levels for Air Passengers

Ozone in airplanes has been linked with respiratory and skin problems. Air passengers usually encounter high ozone levels in aircraft cabins during transoceanic or high-altitude flights. According to new regulations, the ozone levels within an airplane cannot exceed 0.3 parts per million.

Ozone is a gaseous allotrope of oxygen and is a powerful bleaching, poisonous, oxidizing agent with a pungent, irritating odor. It is used commercially to purify and deodorize air, to sterilize water, and as a bleach.

Helicopter Records

Source: National Aeronautic Association.

Distance in Straight Line
International: 2,213.04 mi., 3,561.55 km.
Robert G. Ferry (U.S.) in Hughes YOH-6A helicopter powered by Allison T-63-A-5 engine; from Culver City, Calif., to Daytona Beach, Fla., April 6–7, 1966.

Distance, Closed Circuit
International: 1,739.96 mi; 2,800.20 km.
Jack Schweibold (U.S.) in Hughes YOH-6A helicopter powered by Allison T-62-A-5 engine; Edwards Air Force Base, Calif., March 26, 1966.

Altitude
International: 40,820 ft; 12,442 m.
Jean Boulet (France) in Alouette SA 315-001 "Lama" powered by Artouste IIIB 735 KW engine; Istres, France, June 21, 1972.

Maximum Speed
International: 228.91 mph; 368.4 kph.
Gourguen Karapetyan (U.S.S.R.) in A-10 helicopter powered by 2 TB-3-117 engines; Podmoskovnoye, U.S.S.R., Sept. 21, 1978.

Speed for 100 Km (Closed Circuit)
International: 211.35 mph; 340.15 kph.
Boris Galitsky (U.S.S.R.) in MI-6 helicopter powered by 2 TB-2BM turbine engines; Podmoskovnoye, U.S.S.R., Aug. 26, 1964.

Speed for 500 Km (Closed Circuit)
International: 214.84 mph; 345.74 kph.
Thomas Doyle (U.S.) in Sikorsky S-76 helicopter powered by 2 Allison 250-C-30 engines; West Palm Beach, Fla., Feb. 8, 1982.

Speed for 500 Km (Closed Circuit)
International: 205.688 mph; 331.023 kph.
Galina Rastorgoueva (U.S.S.R.) in A-10 helicopter powered by 2 TV2 117A engines; Ramenskoye, U.S.S.R., Aug. 1, 1975.

Speed for 1,000 Km (Closed Circuit)
International: 200.48 mph; 322.646 kph.
Galina Rastorgoueva (U.S.S.R.) in A-10 helicopter powered by 2 TV2 117A engines; Aug. 13, 1975.

Speed for 2,000 Km (Closed Circuit)
International: 146.09 mph; 235.119 kph.
Inna Kopets (U.S.S.R.) in MI-8 helicopter; Sept. 14, 1967.

Active Pilot Certificates Held
(as of January 1)

Year	Total[1]	Airline transport	Commercial	Private
1970	720,028	31,442	176,585	299,491
1975	733,728	41,002	192,425	305,848
1980	814,667	63,652	182,097	343,276
1981	827,071	69,569	183,442	357,479
1982	764,182	70,311	168,580	328,562

1. Includes other pilot categories—helicopter, glider and lighter-than-air (1982: 16,817): and students (1982: 179,912). *Source:* Department of Transportation, Federal Aviation Administration.

Average Hours and Earnings in Aircraft Industries

Hours and earnings	1981	1980	1979	1978	1975	1970	1965	1960	1955
Average weekly hours									
Aircraft industries	42.5	41.8	42.8	42.1	40.4	41.0	41.2	40.6	41.4
Engines and parts industries	41.7	41.8	42.3	41.7	41.4	40.5	42.1	41.1	40.6
Average weekly earnings									
Aircraft industries	$464.95	$404.21	$357.86	$324.17	$250	$171	$130	$110	$90
Engines and parts industries	$460.37	$393.76	$360.82	$325.26	$249	$166	$133	$112	$86
Average hourly earnings									
Aircraft industries	$10.94	$9.67	$8.46	$7.70	$6.20	$4.17	$3.16	$2.71	$2.17
Engines and parts industries	$11.04	$9.42	$8.53	$7.80	$6.03	$4.10	$3.17	$2.73	$2.13

NOTE: Figures are latest available. *Source:* Department of Transportation, Federal Aviation Administration.

Old Magic and New Science

Over 1,000 years ago, certain "magic" stones protected people against many illnesses including arsenic poisoning—or so Persian pharmacists believed. These "bezoar" stones *(bezoar* meant "to protect against poison") were used by royalty, always afraid of poisoned wine. It is said that Queen Elizabeth I set these stones in her rings; other monarchs wore them on necklaces.

Bezoar stones are really bits of non-digestible hair and other substances, in the stomachs of cud-chewing animals, around which a mineral (sodium hydrogen phosphate) collects. The curative properties of these stones was considered yet another ancient myth—but recent research concerned with arsenic metabolism in the ocean at the Scripps Institution of Oceanography discovered that the partly digested animal hair really *did* absorb arsenite, one form of the poison, like a "chemical sponge." Earlier research at Scripps had discovered that the mineral accumulated in these stones switched phosphate for arsenate, another form of the poison, by means of ion exchange.

U.S. SOCIETIES & ASSOCIATIONS

Source: Information Please questionnaires to organizations.
Names are listed alphabetically according to key word in title; figure in parentheses is year of founding; other figure is membership.

Abortion Federation, National (1976): 110 E. 59th St., New York, N.Y. 10022. Uta Landy, Executive Director.

Abortion Rights Action League, National (1969): 1424 K St., N.W., Washington, D.C. 20005. 145,000; Nanette Falkenberg, Executive Director.

Accountants, American Institute of Certified Public (1887): 1211 Avenue of the Americas, New York, N.Y. 10036. 174,000; Philip B. Chenok, President.

Accountants, National Association of (1919): 919 Third Ave., New York, N.Y. 10022. 96,000; Robert L. Shultis, Executive Director.

Actors' Equity Association (1913): 165 W. 46th St., New York, N.Y. 10036. 30,000; Alan Eisenberg, Executive Secretary.

Aeronautic Association, National (1905): 821 15th St., N.W., Washington, D.C. 20005. 160,000; Ev Langworthy, Executive Director.

Aeronautics and Astronautics, American Institute of (1932): 1290 Avenue of the Americas, New York, N.Y. 10104. 31,000; James J. Harford, Executive Secretary.

African-American Institute, The (1953): 833 United Nations Plaza, New York, N.Y. 10017. Donald B. Easum, President.

AFS International/Intercultural Programs (1947): 313 E. 43rd St., New York, N.Y. 10017. 100,000; William M. Dyal, Jr., President.

Air Force Association (1946): 1750 Pennsylvania Ave., N.W., Washington, D.C. 20006. 170,000; Russell E. Dougherty, Executive Director.

Air Line Pilots Association (1931): 1625 Massachusetts Ave., N.W., Washington, D.C. 20036. 33,000; John J. O'Donnell, President.

Air Pollution Control Association (1907): P.O. Box 2861, Pittsburgh, Pa. 15230. 8,000; William G. Hamlin, Executive Vice President.

Alcohol Problems, American Council on (1900): 6955 University Ave., Des Moines, Iowa 50311. 2,000; William N. Plymat, Executive Director.

Alcoholics Anonymous (1935): P.O. Box 459, Grand Central Station, New York, N.Y. 10163. 1,000,000. Address communications to General Service Office.

America-Mideast Educational and Training Services (1951): 1717 Massachusetts Ave., N.W., Washington, D.C. 20036. 350; Orin D. Parker, President.

American Federation of Labor and Congress of Industrial Organizations (AFL-CIO) (1955): 815 16th St., N.W., Washington, D.C. 20006. 15,000,000; Murray Seeger, Director of Information.

American Friends Service Committee (1917): 1501 Cherry St., Philadelphia, Pa. 19102. Paul E. Brink, Director of Information.

American Indian Affairs, Association on (1923): 432 Park Ave. S., New York, N.Y. 10016. 50,000; Steven Unger, Executive Director.

American Legion (1919): P.O. Box 1055, Indianapolis, Ind. 46206. 2,650,000; Robert W. Spanogle, National Adjutant.

American Legion Auxiliary (1919): 777 N. Meridian St., Indianapolis, Ind. 46204. 940,000; Miriam Junge, National Secretary.

Americans for Democratic Action (1947): 1411 K St., N.W., Washington, D.C. 20005. 75,000; Leon Shull, National Director.

Amnesty International/USA (1961): 304 W. 58th St., New York, N.Y. 10019. 12,000; John G. Healey, Executive Director.

AMVETS (American Veterans of World War II, Korea, and Vietnam) (1944): 4647 Forbes Blvd., Lanham, Md. 20706. 200,000; Morgan S. Ruph, National Executive Director.

AMVETS National Auxiliary (1946): Saco Rd., Old Orchard Beach, Me. 04064. 60,000. Rita J. Potvin, Executive Secretary.

Animal Protection Institute of America (1968): 5894 S. Land Park Dr., P.O. Box 22505, Sacramento Calif. 95822. Belton P. Mouras, President.

Animals, The American Society for the Prevention of Cruelty to (1866): 441 E. 92nd St., New York, N.Y. 10028. 23,000; John F. Kullberg, Executive Director.

Animals, Fund For (1967): 140 W. 57th St., New York, N.Y. 10019. 175,000; Cleveland Amory, President.

Anti-Defamation League of B'nai B'rith (1913): 823 United Nations Plaza, New York, N.Y. 10017. Nathan Perlmutter, National Director.

Anti-Vivisection Society, The American (1883): Suite 204, Noble Plaza, 801 Old York Rd., Jenkintown, Pa. 19046. 15,000; William A. Cave, President.

Arbitration Association, American (1926): 140 W. 51st St., New York, N.Y. 10020. 4,502; E. W. Dippold, Corporate Secretary.

Architects, American Institute of (1857): 1735 New York Ave., N.W., Washington, D.C. 20006. 38,000; David O. Meeker, Jr., Executive Vice President.

Army, Association of the United States (1950): 2425 Wilson Blvd., Arlington, Va. 22201. 142,400; Robert F. Cocklin, Executive Vice President.

Arthritis Foundation (1948): 3400 Peachtree Rd., N.E., Atlanta, Ga. 30326. 71 local chapters; Clifford M. Clarke, President.

Arts and Letters, American Academy and Institute of (1898): 633 W. 155th St., New York, N.Y. 10032. 250; Margaret M. Mills, Executive Director.

Astronomical Society, American (1899): Louisiana State University, Box BK, LSU Observatory, Baton Rouge, La. 70803. 3,700; Arlo U. Landolt, Secretary.

Audubon Society, National (1905): 950 Third Ave., New York, N.Y. 10022. 440,000; Andrew Bihun, Information Services.

Authors League of America (1912): 234 W. 44th St., New York, N.Y. 10036. 10,000; Helen A. Stephenson, Administrator.

Automobile Association, American (1902): 8111 Gatehouse Rd., Falls Church, Va. 22047. 22,300,000; J. B. Creal, President.

Automobile Club, National (1924): One Market Plaza, San Francisco, Calif. 94105. 427,780; Gene Halliburton, President.

Bar Association, American (1898): 1155 E. 60th St., Chicago, Ill. 60637. 280,000; Thomas H. Gonser, Executive Director.

Barber Shop Quartet Singing in America, Society for the Preservation and Encouragement of (1938): Box 575, Kenosha, Wis. 53141. 36,000; Hugh Ingraham, Executive Director.

Bible Society, American (1816): 1865 Broadway, New York, N.Y. 10023. 376,600; Charles W. Baas, Alice E. Ball, John D. Erickson, General Officers.

Big Brothers/Big Sisters of America (1977): 117 S. 17th St., Suite 1200, Philadelphia, Pa. 19103. Betty Larkin, Director of Communications.

Blind, National Federation of the (1940): 1800 Johnson St., Baltimore, Md. 21230. 50,000; Kenneth Jernigan, President.

Blindness, National Society to Prevent (1908): 79 Madison Ave., New York, N.Y. 10016. 26 affiliates; Virginia Boyce, Executive Director.

Blue Cross and Blue Shield Associations (1946 and 1948): 676 St. Clair, Chicago, Ill. 60611. 109 affiliates. Duane R. Carlson, Vice President, Communications.

B'nai B'rith (1843): 1640 Rhode Island Ave., N.W., Washington, D.C. 20036. 500,000; Hank Siegel, Press Officer.

Boy Scouts of America (1910): 1325 Walnut Hill Lane, Irving, Tex. 75062. 4,493,491.

Boys Clubs of America (1906): 771 First Ave., New York, N.Y. 10017. 1,000,000.

Brookings Institution, The (1927): 1775 Massachusetts Ave., N.W., Washington, D.C. 20036. James D. Farrell, Information Editor.

Camp Fire, Inc. (1910): 4601 Madison Ave., Kansas City, Mo. 64112. 500,000; Roberta van der Voort, National Executive Director.

Campers & Hikers Association, National (1949): 7172 Transit Rd., Buffalo, N.Y. 14221. 45,000 families. Fran Opela, National Office Manager.

Camping Association, The American (1910): Bradford Woods, Martinsville, Ind. 46151. 6,000; Armand Ball, Executive Vice President.

Cancer Society, American (1913): 777 Third Ave., New York, N.Y. 10017. 2,300,000 volunteers; Lane W. Adams, Executive Vice President.

CARE (Cooperative for American Relief Everywhere) (1945): 660 First Ave., New York, N.Y. 10016. 26 agencies; Philip Johnston, Executive Director.

Catholic Bishops, National Conference of (1966): 1312 Massachusetts Ave., N.W., Washington, D.C. 20005. 340; Most Rev. John R. Roach, President.

Catholic Charities, National Conference of (1910): 1346 Connecticut Ave., N.W., Washington, D.C. 20036. 2,750 individuals, 850 agencies and institutions; Rev. Msgr. Lawrence Corcoran, Executive Director.

Catholic Conference, United States (1966): 1312 Massachusetts Ave., N.W., Washington, D.C. 20005. Rev. Daniel F. Hoye, General Secretary.

Catholic Daughters of the Americas (1903): 10 W. 71st St., New York, N.Y. 10023. 175,000; Lorraine McMahon, Executive Secretary.

Catholic War Veterans of the U.S.A. (1935): 2 Massachusetts Ave., N.W., Washington, D.C. 20001. 75,000; George G. Baran, National Commander.

Cerebral Palsy Associations, United (1949): 66 E. 34th St., New York, N.Y. 10016. 250 affiliates; Earl H. Cunerd, Executive Director.

Chamber of Commerce of the U.S. (1912): 1615 H St., N.W., Washington, D.C. 20062. 225,000; Richard L. Lesher, President.

Chartered Life Underwriters, American Society of (1929): 270 Bryn Mawr Ave., Bryn Mawr, Pa. 19010. 27,000; John R. Driskill, Executive Vice President.

Chemical Engineers, American Institute of (1908): 345 E. 47th St., New York, N.Y. 10017. 57,000; J. Charles Forman, Executive Director and Secretary.

Chemical Society, American (1876): 1155 16th St., N.W., Washington, D.C. 20036. 120,000; Raymond P. Mariella, Executive Director.

Chess Federation, United States (1939): 186 Rt. 9W, New Windsor, N.Y. 12550. 50,000; Gerard J. Dullea, Executive Director.

Child Welfare League of America (1920): 67 Irving Pl., New York, N.Y. 10003. Edwin F. Watson, Executive Director.

Chiropractic Association, American (1963): 1916 Wilson Blvd., Arlington, Va. 22201. 18,103; G.M. Brassard, Executive Vice President.

Christians and Jews, National Conference of (1928): 43 W. 57th St., New York, N.Y. 10019. 200,000; David Hyatt, President.

Churches, National Council of (1950): 475 Riverside Drive, New York, N.Y. 10115. 32 Protestant and Orthodox communions; Claire Randall, General Secretary.

Civil Engineers, American Society of (1852): 345 E. 47th St., New York, N.Y. 10017. 78,000; Eugene Zwoyer, Executive Director.

Civil Liberties Union, American (1920): 132 W. 43rd St., New York, N.Y. 10036. 200,000; Alan Reitman, Associate Director.

Colleges, Association of American (1915): 1818 R St., N.W., Washington, D.C. 20009. 600 institutions; Mark H. Curtis, President.

Colored Women's Clubs, National Association of (1896): 5808 16th St., N.W., Washington, D.C. 20011. 40,000; Mrs. Otelia E. Champion, National President.

Common Cause (1970): 2030 M St., N.W., Washington, D.C. 20036. 225,000; Archibald Cox, Chairman.

Composers, Authors, and Publishers, American Society of (ASCAP) (1914): One Lincoln Plaza, New York, N.Y. 10023. 30,000; Hal David, President.

Congress of Racial Equality (CORE) (1942): 1916–38 Park Ave., New York, N.Y. 10037. Nationwide network of chapters; Roy Innis, National Director.

Conscientious Objectors, Central Committee for (1948): 2208 South St., Philadelphia, Pa. 19146.

Consumer Federation of America (1968): 1314 14th St., N.W., Washington, D.C. 20005. 220 member organizations; Stephen Brobeck, Executive Director.

Consumers Union (1936): 256 Washington St., Mt. Vernon, N.Y. 10550. 2,800,000 subscribers to *Consumer Reports;* Rhoda H. Karpatkin, Executive Director.

Contract Bridge League, American (1927): P.O. Box 161192, Memphis, Tenn. 38116. 200,000; Richard L. Goldberg, Executive Secretary.

Cooperative League of the U.S.A. (1916): 1828 L St., N.W., Washington, D.C. 20036. 30,000,000 families; E. Morgan Williams, President.

Country Music Association (1958): Box 22299,

Nashville, Tenn. 37202. 6,300; Jo Walker-Meador, Executive Director.

Crime and Delinquency, National Council on (1907): Continental Plaza, 411 Hackensack Ave., Hackensack, N.J. 07601. Nationwide membership; Diana R. Gordon, President.

Daughters of the American Revolution, National Society (1890): 1776 D St., N.W., Washington, D.C. 20006. 208,000; Mrs. Richard Denny Shelby, President General.

Daughters of the Confederacy, United (1894): 328 N. Boulevard, Richmond, Va. 23220. 26,000.

Deaf, National Association of the (1880): 814 Thayer Ave., Silver Spring, Md. 20910 Albert T. Pimentel, Executive Director.

Defenders of Wildlife (1925): 1244 19th St. N.W., Washington, D.C. 20036. 60,000; Anne Marie Ellis, Director of Public Information.

Defense Preparedness Association, American (1919): 1700 N. Moore St., Arlington, Va. 22209. 34,000; H.A. Miley, Jr., President.

Democratic Club, National (1834): Chemists Club, 52 E. 41st St., New York, N.Y. 10017. 500; John G. Treacy, Secretary.

Dental Association, American (1859): 211 E. Chicago Ave., Chicago, Ill. 60611. 138,000; John M. Coady, Executive Director.

Diabetes Association, American (1940): 2 Park Ave., New York, N.Y. 10016. Robert S. Bolan, Executive Vice President.

Dignity (1969): 1500 Massachusetts Ave., N.W., Washington, D.C. 20005. 5,000; Frank Scheuren, President.

Disabled American Veterans (1922): P.O. Box 14301, Cincinnati, Ohio 45214. 700,000; Richard M. Wilson, Assistant National Adjutant for Public Relations.

Ducks Unlimited (1937): Box 66300, Chicago, Ill. 60666. 410,000; Dale E. Whitesell, Executive Vice President.

Eagles, Fraternal Order of (1898): 2401 W. Wisconsin Ave., Milwaukee, Wis. 53233. 850,000; Art Ehrmann, Publications Editor.

Easter Seal Society, The National (1921): 2023 W. Ogden Ave., Chicago, Ill. 60612. 50 affiliated state societies; John R. Garrison, Executive Director.

Eastern Star, Order of, (1876): 1618 New Hampshire Ave., N.W., Washington, D.C. 20009. 3,000,000; Thelma R. Bailey, Most Worthy Grand Matron.

Education Association, National (1857): 1201 16th St., N.W., Washington, D.C. 20036. 1,600,000; Terry Herndon, Executive Director.

Electrochemical Society, The (1902): 10 S. Main St., Pennington, N.J. 08534. 4,476; Donna N. Kimberlin, Administrative Assistant.

Elks of the U.S.A., Benevolent and Protective Order of the (1868): 2750 Lake View Ave., Chicago, Ill. 60614. 1,650,000; Stanley F. Kocur, Grand Secretary.

English-Speaking Union of the United States (1920): 16 E. 69th St., New York, N.Y. 10021. 32,000; John D. Walker, Executive Director.

Euthanasia Foundation, American (1972): 95 N. Birch Rd., Fort Lauderdale, Fla. 33304. Vincent F. Sullivan, Executive Director.

Exploration Geophysicists, Society of (1930): P.O. Box 3098, Tulsa, Okla. 74101. 16,500; John Hyden, Executive Director.

Family Service Association of America (1911): 44 E. 23rd St., New York, N.Y. 10010. 260 member agencies; Robert Rice, Interim General Director.

Farm Bureau Federation, American (1919): 225 Touhy Ave., Park Ridge, Ill. 60068. 3,297,224 member families; J. Patrick Batts, Director of Information.

Fellowship of Reconciliation (1915): Box 271, Nyack, N.Y. 10960. 30,000; Richard Baggett Deats, Executive Secretary.

Fleet Reserve Association (1924): 1303 New Hampshire Ave., N.W., Washington, D.C. 20036. 152,000; Robert W. Nolan, National Executive Secretary.

Foreign Policy Association (1918): 205 Lexington Ave., New York, N.Y. 10016. Thetis Reavis, Vice President for Public Affairs.

Foreign Relations, Council on (1921): 58 E. 68th St., New York, N.Y. 10021. 2,099; Winston Lord, President.

Foreign Study, American Institute for (1965): 102 Greenwich Ave., Greenwich, Conn. 06830. 250,000; Henry C. Kahn, President.

Foreign Trade Council, Inc., National (1914): 10 Rockefeller Plaza, New York, N.Y. 10020. Over 650 companies; Richard W. Roberts, President.

Foster Parents Plan International (1937): Box 400, Warwick, R.I. 02887. George W. Ross, International Executive Director.

4-H Program (early 1900s): Room 5035S, U.S. Department of Agriculture, Washington, D.C. 20250. 5,200,00; Eugene Williams, Deputy Administrator.

Friends of the Earth (1969): 1045 Sansome St., San Francisco, Calif. 94111. 27,000; Rafe Pomerance, President.

Future Farmers of America (1928): 5632 Mt. Vernon Hgwy, Alexandria, Va. 22309. 482,000; Byron F. Rawls, National Advisor.

Future Homemakers of America (1945): 2010 Massachusetts Ave., N.W., Washington, D.C. 20036. 400,000; Mildred Reel, Executive Director.

Gamblers Anonymous Fellowship: Box 17173, Los Angeles, Calif. 90017. 7,000; Jim Z., National Executive Secretary.

Geographic Society, National (1888): 17th and M Sts., N.W., Washington, D.C. 20036. 10,700,000; Gilbert M. Grosvenor, President.

Geriatrics Society, American (1942): 10 Columbus Circle, New York, N.Y. 10019. 8,000; Kathryn S. Henderson, Executive Director.

Gideons International, The (1889): 2900 Lebanon Rd., Nashville, Tenn. 37214. 70,000; M.A. Henderson, Executive Director.

Girl Scouts of the U.S.A. (1912): 830 Third Ave., New York, N.Y. 10022. 2,829,000; Rhoda Pauley, Communications Services.

Girls Clubs of America (1945): 205 Lexington Ave., New York, N.Y. 10016. 220,000; Edith B. Phelps, National Executive Director.

Hadassah, The Women's Zionist Organization of America (1912): 50 W. 58th St., New York, N.Y. 10019. 370,000; Aline Kaplan, Executive Director.

Health, Physical Education, Recreation, and Dance, American Alliance for (1885): 1900 Association Dr., Reston, Va. 22091. 50,000; Ray Ciszek, Executive Vice President.

Hearing and Speech Action, National Association for (1919): 10801 Rockville Pike, Rockville, Md. 20852. 1,000.

Heart Association, American (1924): 7320 Greenville Ave., Dallas, Tex. 75231. 115,000; Dudley Hafner, Executive Vice President.

Hemispheric Affairs, Council on (1975): 1900 L

St., N.W., Washington, D.C. 20036. Laurence R. Birns, Director.

Historical Association, American (1884): 400 A St., S.E., Washington, D.C. 20003. 15,000; Samuel R. Gammon, Executive Director.

Home Economics Association, American (1909): 2010 Massachusetts Ave., N.W., Washington, D.C. 20036. 32,000; Kinsey Green, Executive Director.

Horticultural Society, American (1922): Mt. Vernon, Va. 22121. 35,000; Thomas W. Richards, Executive Vice President.

Hospital Association, American (1898): 840 N. Lake Shore Dr., Chicago, Ill. 60611. 6,271 institutions; J. Alexander McMahon, President.

Humane Association, American (1877): 9725 E. Hampden, Denver, Colo. 80231.

Humane Society of the United States (1954): 2100 L St., N.W., Washington, D.C. 20037. 135,000; Patrick B. Parkes, Vice President for Field Services.

Indian Rights Association (1882): 1505 Race St., Philadelphia, Pa. 19102. 1,400; Sandra L. Cadwalader, Executive Director.

Interfraternity Conference, National (1909): 3901 W. 86th St., Indianapolis, Ind. 46268. 56; Jack L. Anson, Executive Director.

Jaycees, The United States (1920): P.O. Box 7, Tulsa, Okla. 74121. 280,000; Sam Willits, Executive Vice President.

Jewish Appeal, United (1939): 1290 Avenue of the Americas, New York, N.Y. 10104. Irving Bernstein, Executive Vice Chairman.

Jewish Committee, American (1906): 165 E. 56th St., New York, N.Y. 10022. 40,000; Morton Yarmon, Director of Public Relations.

Jewish Community Centers, World Confederation of (1946): 15 E. 26th St., New York, N.Y. 10010. Haim Zipori, Executive Director.

Jewish War Veterans of the U.S.A. (1896): 1712 New Hampshire Ave., N.W., Washington, D.C. 20009.

Jewish Women, National Council of (1893): 15 E. 26th St., New York, N.Y. 10010. Dadie Perlov, Executive Director.

John Birch Society (1958): 395 Concord Ave., Belmont, Mass. 02178. Under 100,000; Ellen Sproul, Clerk of Corporation.

Journalists, Society of Professional, Sigma Delta Chi (1909): 840 N. Lake Shore Dr., Chicago, Ill. 60611. 30,000; Russell C. Tornabene, Executive Officer.

Judaism, American Council for (1943): 307 Fifth Ave., New York, N.Y. 10016. 10,000; Clarence L. Coleman, Jr., President.

Junior Achievement (1919): 550 Summer St., Stamford, Conn. 06901. 5,500,000; Glenn V. Gardinier, National Public Relations Director.

Junior Leagues, Association of (1921): 825 Third Ave., New York, N.Y. 10022. 140,000.

JWB (1917): 15 E. 26th St., New York, N.Y. 10010. 275 affiliated community centers, YM–YWHAs, and camps; Arthur Rotman, Executive Vice President.

Kennel Club, American (1884): 51 Madison Ave., New York, N.Y. 10010. 424 member clubs; Mark T. Mooty, Secretary.

Kiwanis International (1915): 101 E. Erie, Chicago, Ill. 60611. 300,000; J. William Kleindorfer, International Secretary.

Knights of Columbus (1882): One Columbus Plaza, New Haven, Conn. 06507. 1,357,697; Virgil Dechant, Supreme Knight.

Knights of Pythias, Supreme Lodge (1864): 47 N. Grant St., Stockton, Calif. 95202. 124,365; Jule O. Pritchard, Supreme Secretary.

Knights Templar, Grand Encampment of (1816): 14 E. Jackson Blvd., Suite 1700, Chicago, Ill. 60604. 360,000; Paul C. Rodenhauser, Grand Recorder.

La Leche League International (1956): 9616 Minneapolis Ave., Franklin Park, Ill. 60131. 53,543; Betty Wagner, Executive Director.

League of Women Voters of the U.S. (1920): 1730 M St., N.W., Washington, D.C. 20036. 114,000; Harriet Hentges, Executive Director.

Library Association, American (1876): 50 E. Huron St., Chicago, Ill. 60611. 35,257; Robert Wedgeworth, Executive Director.

Life Underwriters, National Association of (1890): 1922 F St., N.W., Washington, D.C. 20006. Jack E. Bobo, Executive Vice President.

Lions Clubs, The International Association of (1917): 300 22nd St., Oak Brook, Ill. 60570. 1,332,490; Roy Schaetzel, Executive Administrator.

Lupus Foundation of America (1976): 11673 Holly Spring Drive., St. Louis, Mo. 63141. 172 chapters and groups; Virginia Masters, Executive Secretary.

Management Associations, American (1923): 135 W. 50th St., New York, N.Y. 10020. 92,000; Joseph P. Keyes, Vice President Public Relations.

Manufacturers, National Association of (1895): 1776 F St., N.W., Washington, D.C. 20006. 13,000; Edmund W. Haskins, Secretary.

March of Dimes Birth Defects Foundation (1938): 1275 Mamaroneck Ave., White Plains, N.Y. 10605. 730 chapters; Charles L. Massey, President.

Marine Corps League (1923): 933 N. Kenmore St., Arlington, Va. 22201. 26,000; C. L. Kammeier, Executive Director.

Masons, Ancient and Accepted Scottish Rite, Northern Masonic Jurisdiction, Supreme Council 33° (1867): 33 Marrett Rd., Lexington, Mass. 02173. 496,824; Lynn J. Sanderson, Grand Secretary General.

Masons, Ancient and Accepted Scottish Rite, Southern Jurisdiction, Supreme Council (1801): 1733 16th St., N.W., Washington, D.C. 20009. 659,500; C. Fred Kleinknecht, Grand Secretary General.

Masons, Royal Arch, International General Grand Chapter (1797): Box 5320, Lexington, Ky. 40505. 450,000; Charles K.A. McGaughey, General Grand Secretary.

Mathematical Society, American (1888): P.O. Box 6248, Providence, R.I. 02940. 19,994; William J. LeVeque, Executive Director.

Mayflower Descendants, General Society of (1897): 4 Winslow St., P.O. Box 297, Plymouth, Mass. 02361. 20,000; Eugene A. Stratton, Historian General.

Mechanical Engineers, American Society of (1880): 345 E. 47th St., New York, N.Y. 10017. 101,162; Burke E. Nelson, Executive Director.

Medical Association, American (1847): 535 N. Dearborn St., Chicago, Ill. 60610.

Mental Health Association, National (1909): 1800 N. Kent St., Arlington, Va. 22209. 1,000,000;

Mining, Metallurgical and Petroleum Engineers, American Institute of (1871): 345 E. 47th St., New York, N.Y. 10017. 86,380; Edward A. Buckley, Executive Director.

Modern Language Association of America (1883): 62 Fifth Avenue., New York, N.Y. 10011. 30,000.

Modern Woodmen of America (1883): Mississippi River at 17th St., Rock Island, Ill. 61201. 500,000; W.B. Foster, President.

Moose, Loyal Order of (1888): Mooseheart, Ill. 60539. 1,767,914; Carl A. Weis, Supreme Secretary.

Motion Picture Arts & Sciences, Academy of (1927): 8949 Wilshire Blvd., Beverly Hills, Calif. 90211. James M. Roberts, Executive Director.

Multiple Sclerosis Society, National (1946): 205 E. 42nd St., New York, N.Y. 10017. Sylvia Lawry, Executive Director.

Muscular Dystrophy Association (1950): 810 Seventh Ave., New York, N.Y. 10019. 1,945,800 volunteers. Jerry Lewis, National Chairman.

Museums, American Association of (1906): 1055 Thomas Jefferson St., N.W., Washington, D.C. 20007. 7,500; Lawrence Reger, Director.

Musicians, American Federation of (1896): 1500 Broadway, New York, N.Y. 10036. 280,000; Victor W. Fuentealba, President.

National Association for the Advancement of Colored People (1909): 1790 Broadway, New York, N.Y. 10019. 450,000; Benjamin L. Hooks, Executive Director.

National Grange, The (1867): 1616 H St., N.W., Washington, D.C. 20006. 400,000; Edward Andersen, Master.

National PTA (National Congress of Parents and Teachers) (1897): 700 N. Rush St., Chicago, Ill. 60611. 5,893,047; Ronald L. Smith, Executive Director.

Newspaper Publishers Association, American (1887): The Newspaper Center, P.O. Box 17407, Dulles International Airport, Washington, D.C. 20041. 1,405; Jerry W. Friedheim, Executive Vice President and General Manager.

Nurses' Association, American (1896): 1101 14th St., N.W. Washington, D.C. 20005. 170,000.

Odd Fellows, Sovereign Grand Lodge, Independent Order of (1819): 422 Trade St., Winston-Salem, N.C. 27101. 1,200,000; Edward T. Rogers, Sovereign Grand Secretary.

Olympic Committee, United States (1921): 1750 Boulder St., Colorado Springs, Colo. 80909. Bob Paul, Director of Communications.

Organization of American States, General Secretariat (1890): 1889 F St., N.W., Washington, D.C. 20006. 28 member nations.

ORT Federation, American (1922): 817 Broadway, New York, N.Y. 10003. 160,000; Donald H. Klein, Executive Vice President.

Overeaters Anonymous (1960): 2190 190th St., Torrance, Calif. 90504. 100,000.

Parents Without Partners (1957): 7910 Woodmont Ave., Bethesda, Md. 20814. 204,000; Louise Spaulding, Interim Office Supervisor.

Parks and Conservation Association, National (1919): 1701 18th St., N.W., Washington, D.C. 20009. 35,000; Paul C. Pritchard, President.

Philatelic Society, American (1886): P.O. Box 800, State College, Pa. 16801. 53,000; Keith A. Wagner, Executive Director.

Philosophical Society, American (1743): 104 S. 5th St., Philadelphia, Pa. 19106. 600; W. J. Bell, Jr., Executive Officer.

Photographic Society of America (1933): 2005 Walnut St., Philadelphia, Pa. 19103. 17,500; Harold J. Vermes, Executive Director.

Physical Society, American (1899): 335 E. 45th St., New York, N.Y. 10017. 32,000; W. W. Havens, Jr., Executive Secretary.

Physics, American Institute of (1931): 335 E. 45th St., New York, N.Y. 10017. 58,300; H. William Koch, Director.

Planned Parenthood Federation of America (1916): 810 Seventh Ave., New York, N.Y. 10019. 189 affiliates.

Political Science, Academy of (1880): 2852 Broadway, New York, N.Y. 10025. 10,500; C. Lowell Harriss, Executive Director.

Professional Engineers, National Society of (1934): 2029 K St., N.W., Washington, D.C. 20006. 80,000; Donald G. Weinert, Executive Director.

Psychiatric Association, American (1844): 1400 K St., N.W., Washington, D.C. 20005. 26,634; H. Keith H. Brodie, President.

Psychological Association, American (1892): 1200 17th St., N.W., Washington, D.C. 20036. 50,000; Michael S. Pallak, Executive Officer.

Public Health Association, American (1872): 1015 15th St., N.W., Washington, D.C. 20005. 30,201; William H. McBeath, M.D., Executive Director.

Puppeteers of America (1937): 5 Cricklewood Path, Pasadena, Calif. 91107. Gayle Schluter, Membership Chairman.

Red Cross, American (1881): 17th and D Sts., N.W., Washington, D.C. 20006. Over 3,000 chapters; George M. Elsey, President.

Rehabilitation Association, National (1925): 633 S. Washington St., Alexandria, Va. 22314. 20,000; David L. Mills, Executive Director.

Reserve Officers Association of the United States (1922): 1 Constitution Ave., N.E., Washington, D.C. 20002. 130,000; J. Milnor Roberts, Executive Director.

Retarded Citizens, Association for (1950): 2501 Avenue J, Arlington, Tex. 76011. 1,900 units; Philip Roos, National Executive Director.

Retired Federal Employees, National Association of (1921): 1533 New Hampshire Ave., N.W., Washington, D.C. 20036. 313,000; L. J. Andolsek, President.

Retired Persons, American Association of (1958): 1909 K St., N.W., Washington, D.C. 20049. 13,500,000; Cyril F. Brickfield, Executive Director.

Rifle Association of America, National (1871): 1600 Rhode Island Ave., N.W., Washington, D.C. 20036. 2,100,000; Harlon B. Carter, Executive Vice President.

Right to Life, National Committee (1973): 419 7th St., N.W., Washington, D.C. 20004. Warren Sweeney, Executive Director.

Rotary International (1905): 1600 Ridge Ave., Evanston, Ill. 60201. 905,000; Herbert A. Pigman, General Secretary.

Safety Council, National (1913): 444 N. Michigan Ave., Chicago, Ill. 60611. Charles C. Vance, Director of Public Relations.

Salvation Army, The (1865): 799 Bloomfield Ave., Verona, N.J. 07044. 417,359; Col. G.E. Murray, National Chief Secretary.

SANE, Citizens for a SANE Nuclear Policy (1957): 711 G St., S.E., Washington, D.C. 20003. 28,000; David Cortright, Executive Director.

Save-the-Redwoods League (1918): 114 Sansome St., San Francisco, Calif. 94104. 50,000; John B. Dewitt, Executive Director.

Science, American Association for the Advancement of (1848): 1515 Massachusetts Ave., N.W., Washington, D.C. 20005. 140,000; Carol L. Rogers, Communications.

Screen Actors Guild (1933): 7750 Sunset Blvd., Hollywood, Calif. 90046. 52,000; Kim Fellner, Information Director.

Seeing Eye (1929): Morristown, N.J. 07960. Stuart Grout, Executive Vice President.

Shrine of North America (Shriners Hospitals) (1872): Box 25356, Tampa, Fla. 33622. 932,744; Charles G. Cumpstone, Jr., Executive Secretary of Fraternal Affairs.

Sierra Club (1892): 530 Bush St., San Francisco, Calif. 94108. 285,000; Michael McCloskey, Executive Director.

Small Business Association, National (1937): 1604 K St., N.W., Washington, D.C. 20006. 40,000; Herbert Liebenson, President.

Social Welfare, National Conference on (1873): 1730 M St., N.W., Washington, D.C. 20036. 4,000; John E. Hansan, Executive Director.

Social Workers, National Association of (1955): 1425 H St., N.W., Washington, D.C. 20005. 90,000; C. Annette Maxey, Executive Director.

Sons of Italy in America, Order (1905): 219 E St., N.E., Washington, D.C. 20002. 90,000; Peter M. Borromeo, National Executive Director.

Sons of the American Revolution, National Society of the (1889): 1000 S. 4th St., Louisville, Ky. 40203. 22,000; John C. Davis, Executive Secretary.

Soroptimist International of the Americas (1921): 1616 Walnut St., Philadelphia, Pa. 19103. 36,000; Mary Helen Madden, Executive Director.

Southern Christian Leadership Conference (1957): 334 Auburn Ave., N.E., Atlanta, Ga. 30303. 1,000,000; 350 chapters, 260 affiliated organizations; Dr. Joseph E. Lowery, President.

Speech-Language-Hearing Association, American (1925): 10801 Rockville Pike, Rockville, Md. 20852. 35,000; Frederick T. Spahr, Executive Director.

Sports Car Club of America (1944): 6750 S. Emporia, Englewood, Colo. 80112. 23,000; Mac DeMere, News Department Manager.

Student Association, United States (1947): 1220 G St., S.E., Washington, D.C. 20003. Frank X. Viggiano, Executive Director.

Surgeons, American College of (1913): 55 E. Erie, St., Chicago, Ill. 60611. 45,000; C. Rollins Hanlon, Director.

Teachers, American Federation of (1916): 11 Dupont Circle, N.W., Washington, D.C. 20036. 550,000; Albert Shanker, President.

Travel Agents, American Society of (ASTA) (1931): 711 Fifth Ave., New York, N.Y. 10022. 18,000; Joseph R. Stone, Chairman.

Travelers Aid Society of New York (1905): 204 E. 39th St., New York, N.Y. 10016. Elizabeth P. Anderson, General Director.

United Negro College Fund (1944): 500 E. 62nd St., New York, N.Y. 10021. Christopher F. Edley, Executive Director.

University Women, American Association of (1881): 2401 Virginia Ave., N.W., Washington, D.C. 20037. 190,000; Quincalee Brown, Executive Director.

Urban League, National (1910): 500 E. 62nd St., New York, N.Y. 10021. 116; James D. Williams, Director of Communications.

Veterans Committee, American (AVC) (1944): 1346 Connecticut Ave., N.W., Suite 930, Washington, D.C. 20036. 25,000; June A. Willenz, Executive Director.

Veterans of Foreign Wars of the U.S. (1899): V.F.W. Bldg., 34th and Broadway, Kansas City, Mo. 64111. V.F.W. and Auxiliary, 2,600,000; Howard E. Vander Clute, Jr., Adjutant General.

Veterinary Medical Association, American (1863): 930 N. Meacham Rd., Schaumburg, Ill. 60196. 35,000; Dr. D. A. Price, Executive Vice President.

War Resisters League (1923): 339 Lafayette St., New York, N.Y. 10012. 10,000; Norma Becker, Chairwoman.

Wildlife Federation, National (1936): 1412 16th St., N.W., Washington, D.C. 20036. 4,600,000; Jay D. Hair, Executive Vice President.

Woman's Christian Temperance Union, National (1874): 1730 Chicago Ave., Evanston, Ill. 60201. 250,000; Martha G. Edgar, President.

Women's American ORT (1927): 1250 Broadway, New York, N.Y. 10001. 145,000; Nathan Gould, National Executive Director.

Women's Clubs, General Federation of (1890): 1734 N St., N.W., Washington, D.C. 20036. 600,000; Mildred Baptista, Executive Director.

Women's International League for Peace and Freedom (1915): 1213 Race St., Philadelphia, Pa. 19107. 10,000; Libby Frank, Executive Director.

Women's Strike for Peace (1961): 145 S. 13th St., Philadelphia, Pa. 19107. 25,000; Ethel Taylor, National Coordinator.

YMCA of the USA (1844): 101 N. Wacker Dr., Chicago, Ill. 60606. 11,000,000; Solon B. Cousins, Executive Director.

Young Women's Christian Association of the U.S.A. (1858 in U.S.A., 1855 in England): 600 Lexington Ave., New York, N.Y. 10022. 2,471,000; Jane Pinkerton, Director of Communications.

Youth Hostels, American (1934): 1332 I St., N.W., Washington, D.C. 20005. 100,000.

Zionist Organization of America (1897): ZOA House, 4 E. 34th St., New York, N.Y. 10016. 135,000; Paul I. Flacks, National Executive Director.

In Search of Legendary Creatures

A new society, the International Society of Cryptozoology, has been formed "to promote scientific inquiry, education and communication among people interested in animals of unexpected form or size, or unexpected occurrence in time or space." "Unexpected" animals include the so-called monsters of many northern lakes, the dinosaurlike mokelembembe of Africa, "Big Foot" of the American Northwest, and the abominable snowman of the Himalayas. The Society's symbol is the okapi, a giraffelike animal that had long been considered extinct until discovered in 1900 in the forests of Zaire (then the Belgian Congo).

Membership is open to laymen as well as scientists. The society's address is 1220 East Copper Street, Tucson, Ariz. 85712.

A Star Hotter Than the Sun

A white dwarf, a tiny, very dense star, has been found to be 20 times hotter than the sun. Its temperature of about 180,000 degrees Fahrenheit makes it the hottest white dwarf known. White dwarfs are the final stage in the evolution of small and medium-size stars. This one is located in the constellation Ursa Major.

GEOGRAPHY

World Geography

Explorations and Discoveries

(All years are A.D. unless B.C. is specified.)

Country or place	Event	Explorer or discoverer	Date
AFRICA			
Sierra Leone	Visited	Hanno, Carthaginian seaman	c. 520 B.C.
Congo River	Mouth discovered	Diogo Cão, Portuguese	c. 1484
Cape of Good Hope	Rounded	Bartolomeu Diaz, Portuguese	1488
Gambia River	Explored	Mungo Park, Scottish explorer	1795
Sahara	Crossed	Dixon Denham and Hugh Clapperton, English explorers	1822–23
Zambezi River	Discovered	David Livingstone, Scottish explorer	1851
Sudan	Explored	Heinrich Barth, German explorer	1852–55
Victoria Falls	Discovered	Livingstone	1855
Lake Tanganyika	Discovered	Richard Burton and John Speke, British explorers	1858
Congo River	Traced	Sir Henry M. Stanley, British explorer	1877
ASIA			
Punjab (India)	Visited	Alexander the Great	327 B.C.
China	Visited	Marco Polo, Italian traveler	c. 1272
Tibet	Visited	Odoric of Pordenone, Italian monk	c. 1325
Southern China	Explored	Niccolò dei Conti, Venetian traveler	c. 1440
India	Visited (Cape route)	Vasco da Gama, Portuguese navigator	1498
Japan	Visited	St. Francis Xavier of Spain	1549
Arabia	Explored	Carsten Niebuhr, German explorer	1762
China	Explored	Ferdinand Richthofen, German scientist	1868
Mongolia	Explored	Nikolai M. Przhevalsky, Russian explorer	1870–73
Central Asia	Explored	Sven Hedin, Swedish scientist	1890–1908
EUROPE			
Shetland Islands	Visited	Pytheas of Massilia (Marseille)	c. 325 B.C.
North Cape	Rounded	Ottar, Norwegian explorer	c. 870
Iceland	Colonized	Norwegian noblemen	c. 890–900
NORTH AMERICA			
Greenland	Colonized	Eric the Red, Norwegian	c. 985
Labrador; Nova Scotia (?)	Discovered	Leif Ericson, Norse explorer	1000
West Indies	Discovered	Christopher Columbus, Italian	1492
North America	Coast discovered	Giovanni Caboto (John Cabot), for British	1497
Pacific Ocean	Discovered	Vasco Núñez de Balboa, Spanish explorer	1513
Florida	Explored	Ponce de León, Spanish explorer	1513
Mexico	Conquered	Hernando Cortés, Spanish adventurer	1519–21
St. Lawrence River	Discovered	Jacques Cartier, French navigator	1534
Southwest U. S.	Explored	Francisco Coronado, Spanish explorer	1540–4
Colorado River	Discovered	Hernando de Alarcón, Spanish explorer	154
Mississippi River	Discovered	Hernando de Soto, Spanish explorer	154
Frobisher Bay	Discovered	Martin Frobisher, English seaman	157

Country or place	Event	Explorer or discover	Date
Maine Coast	Explored	Samuel de Champlain, French explorer	1604
Jamestown, Va.	Settled	John Smith, English colonist	1607
Hudson River	Explored	Henry Hudson, English navigator	1609
Hudson Bay (Canada)	Discovered	Henry Hudson	1610
Baffin Bay	Discovered	William Baffin, English navigator	1616
Lake Michigan	Navigated	Jean Nicolet, French explorer	1634
Arkansas River	Discovered	Jacques Marquette and Louis Jolliet, French explorers	1673
Mississippi River	Explored	Sieur de La Salle, French explorer	1682
Bering Strait	Discovered	Vitus Bering, Danish explorer	1728
Alaska	Discovered	Vitus Bering	1741
Mackenzie River (Canada)	Discovered	Sir Alexander Mackenzie, Scottish-Canadian explorer	1789
Northwest U. S.	Explored	Meriwether Lewis and William Clark	1804–06
Northeast Passage (Arctic Ocean)	Navigated	Nils Nordenskjöld, Swedish explorer	1879
Greenland	Explored	Robert Peary, American explorer	1892
Northwest Passage	Navigated	Roald Amundsen, Norwegian explorer	1906
SOUTH AMERICA			
Continent	Visited	Columbus, Italian	1498
Brazil	Discovered	Pedro Alvarez Cabral, Portuguese	1500
Peru	Conquered	Francisco Pizarro, Spanish explorer	1532–33
Amazon River	Explored	Francisco Orellana, Spanish explorer	1541
Cape Horn	Discovered	Willem C. Schouten, Dutch navigator	1615
OCEANIA			
Papua New Guinea	Visited	Jorge de Menezes, Portuguese explorer	1526
Australia	Visited }	Abel Janszoon Tasman, Dutch navigator	1642
Tasmania	Discovered }		
Australia	Explored	John McDouall Stuart, English explorer	1828
Australia	Explored	Robert Burke and William Wills, Australian explorers	1861
New Zealand	Sighted (and named)	Abel Janszoon Tasman	1642
New Zealand	Visited	James Cook, English navigator	1769
ARCTIC, ANTARCTIC, AND MISCELLANEOUS			
Ocean exploration	Expedition	Magellan's ships circled globe	1519–22
Galápagos Islands	Visited	Diego de Rivadeneira, Spanish captain	1535
Spitsbergen	Visited	Willem Barents, Dutch navigator	1596
Antarctic Circle	Crossed	James Cook, English navigator	1773
Antarctica	Discovered	Nathaniel Palmer, U. S. whaler (archipelago) and Fabian Gottlieb von Bellingshausen, Russian admiral (mainland)	1820–21
Antarctica	Explored	Charles Wilkes, American explorer	1840
North Pole	Reached	Robert E. Peary, American explorer	1909
South Pole	Reached	Roald Amundsen, Norwegian explorer	1911

The Continents

A continent is defined as a large unbroken land mass completely surrounded by water, although in some cases continents are (or were in part) connected by land bridges.

The hypothesis first suggested late in the 19th century was that the continents consist of lighter rocks that rest on heavier crustal material in about the same manner that icebergs float on water. That the rocks forming the continents are lighter than the material below them and under the ocean bottoms is now established. As a consequence of this fact, Alfred Wegener (for the first time in 1912) suggested that the continents are slowly moving, at a rate of about one yard per century, so that their relative positions are not rigidly fixed. Many geologists that were originally skeptical have come to accept this theory of Continental Drift.

When describing a continent, it is important to remember that there is a fundamental difference between a deep ocean, like the Atlantic, and shallow seas, like the Baltic and most of the North Sea, which are merely flooded portions of a continent. Another and entirely different point to remember is that political considerations have often overridden geographical facts when it came to naming continents.

Geographically speaking, Europe, including the British Isles, is a large western peninsula of the continent of Asia; and many geographers, when referring to Europe and Asia, speak of the Eurasian Continent. But traditionally, Europe is counted as a separate continent, with the Ural and the Caucasus mountains forming the line of demarcation between Europe and Asia.

To the south of Europe, Asia has an odd-shaped peninsula jutting westward, which has a large number of political subdivisions. The northern section is taken up by Turkey; to the south of Turkey there are Syria, Iraq, Israel, Jordan, Saudi Arabia, and a number of smaller Arab countries. All this is part of Asia. Traditionally, the island of Cyprus in the Mediterranean is also considered to be part of Asia, while the island of Crete is counted as European.

The large islands of Java, Borneo, and Sumatra and the smaller islands near them are counted as part of "tropical Asia," while New Guinea is counted as related to Australia. In the case of the Americas, the problem arises as to whether they should be considered one or two continents. There are good arguments on both sides, but since there is now a land bridge between North and South America (in the past it was often flooded) and since no part of the sea east of the land bridge is deep ocean, it is more logical to consider the Americas as one continent.

Politically, based mainly on history, the Americas are divided into North America (from the Arctic to the Mexican border), Central America (from Mexico to Panama, with the Caribbean islands), and South America. Greenland is considered a section of North America, while Iceland is traditionally counted as a European island because of its political ties with the Scandinavian countries.

The island groups in the Pacific are often called "Oceania," but this name does *not* imply that scientists consider them the remains of a continent.

Volcanoes of the World

About 500 volcanoes have had recorded eruptions within historical times. Almost two thirds of these are in the Northern Hemisphere. Most volcanoes occur at the boundaries of the earth's crustal plates, such as the famous "Ring of Fire" that surrounds the Pacific Ocean plate. Of the world's active volcanoes, about 60% are along the perimeter of the Pacific, about 17% on mid-oceanic islands, about 14% in an arc along the south of the Indonesian islands, and about 9% in the Mediterranean area, Africa, and Asia Minor. Many of the world's volcanoes are submarine and have unrecorded eruptions.

Pacific "Ring of Fire"

NORTHWEST

Japan: At least 33 active vents.

Aso (5,223 ft; 1,592 m), on Kyushu, has one of the largest craters in the world.

Asama (over 8,300 ft; 2,530 m), on Honshu, is continuously active; violent eruption in 1783.

Azuma (nearly 7,700 ft; 2,347 m), on Honshu, erupted in 1900.

Chokai (7,300 ft; 2,225 m), on Honshu, erupted in 1974 after having been quiescent since 1861.

Fujiyama (Fujisan) (12,385 ft; 3,775 m), on Honshu, southwest of Tokyo. Symmetrical in outline, snow-covered. Regarded as a sacred mountain.

On-take (3,668 ft; 1,118 m), on peninsula of Kyushu. Strong smoke emissions and explosions began November 1973 and continued through 1974.

U.S.S.R.: Kamchatka peninsula, 14–18 active volcanoes. Klyuchevskaya (Kluchev) (15,500 ft; 4,724 m) reported active in 1974.

Kuril Islands: At least 13 active volcanoes and several submarine outbreaks.

SOUTHWEST

New Zealand: Mount Tarawera (3,645 ft; 1,112 m), on North Island, had a severe eruption in 1886 that destroyed the famous Pink and White sinter terraces of Rotomahana, a hot lake.

Ngauruhoe (7,515 ft; 2,291 m), on North Island, emits steam and vapor constantly. Erupted 1974.

Papua New Guinea: Karkar Island (4,920 ft; 1,500 m). Mild eruptions 1974.

Philippine Islands: About 100 eruptive centers; Hibok Hibok, on Camiguin, erupted September 1950 and again in December 1951, when about 750 were reported killed or missing; eruptions continued during 1952–53.

Taal (4,752 ft; 1,448 m), on Luzon. Major eruption in 1965 killed 190; erupted again, 1968.

Volcano Islands: Mount Suribachi (546 ft; 166 m), on Iwo Jima. A sulfurous steaming volcano. Raising of U.S. flag over Mount Suribachi was one of the dramatic episodes of World War II.

NORTHEAST

Alaska: Mount Wrangell (14,163 ft; 4,317 m) and Mount Katmai (about 6,700 ft; 2,042 m). On June 6, 1912, a violent eruption (Nova Rupta) of Mount Katmai occurred, during which the "Valley of Ten Thousand Smokes" was formed.

Aleutian Islands: There are 32 active vents known and numerous inactive cones. Akutan Island (over 4,000 ft; 1,220 m) erupted in 1974, with ash and debris rising over 300 ft.

Great Sitkin (5,741 ft; 1,750 m). Explosive activity February-September 1974, accompanied by earthquake originating at volcano that registered 2.3 on Richter scale.

California, Oregon, Washington: Lassen Peak (10,453 ft; 3,186 m) in California is one of two observed active volcanoes in the U.S. outside Alaska and Hawaii. The last period of activity was 1914–17. Mt. St. Helens (9,677 ft; 2,950 m) in the Cascade Range of southwest Washington became active on March 27, 1980, and erupted on May 18. It last erupted in 1857. Other mountains of volcanic origin include Mount Shasta (California), Mount Hood (Oregon), Mount Mazama (Oregon)—the mountain containing Crater Lake, Mount Rainier (Washington), and Mount Baker (Washington), which has been steaming since October 1975, but gives no sign of an impending eruption.

SOUTHEAST

Chile and Argentina: About 25 active or potentially active.

Colombia: Huila (nearly 18,900 ft; 5,760 m), a vapor-emitting volcano, and Tolima (nearly 18,500 ft; 5,640 m). Eruption of Puracé (15,600 ft; 4,755 m) in 1949 killed 17 people.

Ecuador: Cayambe (nearly 19,000 ft; 5,791 m). Almost on the equator.

Cotopaxi (19,344 ft; 5,896 m). Perhaps highest active volcano in the world. Possesses a beautifully formed cone.

Reventador (11,434 ft; 3,485 m). Observed in active state in late 1973.

El Salvador: Izalco ("beacon of Central America") (7,830 ft; 2,387 m) first appeared in 1770 and is still growing (erupted in 1950, 1956; last erupted in October-November 1966). San Salvador (6,187 ft; 1,886 m) had a violent eruption in 1923. Conchagua (about 4100 ft; 1250 m) erupted with considerable damage early in 1947.

Guatemala: Santa Maria Quezaltenango (12,361 ft; 3,768 m). Frequent activity between 1902–08 and 1922–28 after centuries of quiescence. Most dangerously active vent of Central America. Other volcanoes include Tajumulco (13,814 ft; 4,211 m) and Atitlán (11,633 ft; 3,546 m).

Mexico: Boquerón ("Big Mouth"), on San Benedicto, about 250 mi. south of Lower California. Newest volcano in Western Hemisphere, discovered September 1952.

Colima (about 14,000 ft; 4,270 m), in group that has had frequent eruptions.

Orizaba (Citlaltépetl) (18,701 ft; 5,700 m).

Parícutin (7,450 ft; 2,270 m). First appeared in February 1943. In less than a week, a cone over 140 ft high developed with a crater one quarter mile in circumference. Cone grew more than 1,500 ft (457 m) in 1943. Erupted 1952.

Popocatépetl (17,887 ft; 5,452 m). Large, deep, bell-shaped crater. Not entirely extinct; steam still escapes.

El Chinchonal (7,300 ft 1,005.6 m) about 15 miles from Pichucalco. Long inactive, it erupted in March 1982.

Nicaragua: Volcanoes include Telica, Coseguina, and Momotombo. Between Momotombo on the west shore of Lake Managua and Coseguina overlooking the Gulf of Fonseca, there is a string of more than 20 cones, many still active. One of these, Cerro Negro, erupted in July 1947, with considerable damage and loss of life, and again in 1971.

Concepción (5,100 ft; 1,555 m). Ash eruptions 1973–74.

Mid-oceanic Islands

Canary Islands: Pico de Teide (12,192 ft; 3,716 m), on Tenerife.

Cape Verde Islands: Fogo (nearly 9,300 ft; 2,835 m). Severe eruption in 1857; quiescent until 1951.

Caribbean: La Soufrière (4,813 ft; 1,467 m), on Basse-Terre, Guadeloupe. Also called La Grande Soufrière. Violent activity in July-August 1976 caused evacuation of 73,000 people; renewed activity in April 1977 again caused thousands to flee their homes.

La Soufrière (4,048 ft; 1,234 m), on St. Vincent. Major eruption in 1902 killed over 1,000 people. Eruptions over 10-day period in April 1979 caused evacuation of northern two thirds of island.

Comoros: One volcano, Karthala (nearly 8,000 ft; 2,440 m), is visible for over 100 miles. Last erupted in 1904.

Hawaii: Mauna Loa ("Long Mountain") (13,680 ft; 4,170 m), on Hawaii, discharges from its high side vents more lava than any other volcano. Largest volcanic mountain in the world in cubic content. Area of crater is 3.7 sq mi. Violent eruption in June 1950, with lava pouring 25 miles into the ocean. Last major eruption in July 1975.

Mauna Kea (13,796 ft; 4,205 m), on Hawaii. Highest mountain in state.

Kilauea (4,090 ft; 1,247 m) is a vent in the side of Mauna Loa, but its eruptions are apparently independent. One of the most spectacular and active craters. Crater has an area of 4.14 sq mi. Earthquake in July 1975 caused major eruption. Eruptions began in September 1977 and reached a height of 980 ft (300 m). Activity ended Oct. 1.

Iceland: At least 25 volcanoes active in historical times. Very similar to Hawaiian volcanoes. Askja (over 4,700 ft; 1,433 m) is the largest.

Lesser Antilles (West Indian Islands): Mount Pelée (over 4,500 ft; 1,370 m), northwestern Martinique. Eruption in 1902 destroyed town of St. Pierre and killed approximately 40,000 people.

Réunion Island (east of Madagascar): Piton de la Fournaise (Le Volcan) (8,610 ft; 2,624 m). Large lava flows. Last erupted in 1972.

Samoan archipelago: Savai'i Island had an eruption in 1905 that caused considerable damage. Niuafoo (Tin Can), in the Tonga Islands, has a crater that extends 6,000 feet below and 600 feet above water.

Indonesia

Sumatra: Ninety volcanoes have been discovered; 12 are now active. The most famous, Krakatau, is a small volcanic island in the Sunda Strait. Numerous volcanic discharges occurred in 1883. One extremely violent explosion caused the disappearance of the highest peak and the northern part of the island. Fine dust was carried around the world in the upper atmosphere. Over 36,000 persons lost their lives in resultant tidal waves that were felt as far away as Cape Horn. Active in 1972.

Mediterranean Area

Italy: Mount Etna (10,902 ft; 3,323 m), eastern Sicily. Two new craters formed in eruptions of February-March 1947. Worst eruption in 50 years occurred November 1950-Jaunary 1951. Erupted again in 1974, 1975, 1977, 1978, and 1979.

Stromboli (about 3,000 ft; 914 m), Lipari Islands (north of Sicily). Called "Lighthouse of the Mediterranean." Reported active in 1971.

Mount Vesuvius (4,200 ft; 1,280 m), southeast of Naples. Only active volcano on European mainland. Pompeii buried by an eruption, A.D. 79.

Antarctica

The discovery of two small active volcanoes in 1982 brings to five the total number known on Antarctica. The new ones, 30 miles apart, are on the Weddell Sea side of the Antarctic Peninsula. The largest, Mount Erebus (13,000 ft; 3,962 m), rises from McMurdo Sound. Mount Melbourne (9,000 ft; 2,743 m) is in Victoria Land. The fifth, off the northern tip of the Antartic Peninsula, is a crater known as Deception Island.

World Population, Land Areas, and Elevations

Area	Estimated population, 1979	Approximate Land area sq mi.	Percent of total land area	Population density per sq mi.	Elevation, feet: Highest	Elevation, feet: Lowest	Dimensions, miles: East-West	Dimensions, miles: North-South
WORLD	4,336,000,000	58,451,000	100.0	82.7[1]	Mt. Everest, Asia, 29,028	Dead Sea, Asia, 1,290 below sea level	24,902	24,860
ASIA, incl. Philippines, Indonesia, and European and Asiatic Turkey; excl. Asiatic U.S.S.R.	2,509,000,000	10,678,000	18.2	235.0	Mt. Everest, Tibet-Nepal, 29,028	Dead Sea, Israel-Jordan, 1,290 below sea level	5,400[2]	5,300[2]
AFRICA	456,000,000	11,714,000	20.0	38.9	Mt. Kilimanjaro, Tanzania, 19,340	Lake Assal, Djibouti, 571 below sea level	4,600	5,000
NORTH AMERICA, including Hawaii, Central America, and Caribbean region	364,000,000	9,363,000	16.0	38.9	Mt. McKinley; Alaska, 20,320	Death Valley, Calif., 282 below sea level	3,200[5]	4,000[5]
SOUTH AMERICA	239,000,000	6,885,000	11.8	34.7	Mt. Aconcagua, Arg.-Chile, 23,034	Valdes Peninsula, 131 below sea level	3,200	4,600
ANTARCTICA	—	6,000,000	10.3	—	Vinson Massif, Sentinel Range, 16,863	Sea level	—	—
EUROPE, incl. Iceland; excl. European U.S.S.R. and European Turkey	482,000,000	1,906,000	3.3	252.9	Mont Blanc, France, 15,781	Sea level	3,300[3]	2,400[3]
OCEANIA, incl. Australia, New Zealand, Melanesia, Micronesia, and Polynesia[4]	22,500,000	3,286,000	5.6	6.8	Mauna Kea, Hawaii, 13,796	Lake Eyre, Australia, 38 below sea level	—	—
U.S.S.R., both European and Asiatic	264,000,000	8,649,000	14.8	30.5	Communism Peak, Pamir, 24,547	Caspian Sea, 96 below sea level	5,000	2,500

1. In computing density per square mile, the area of Antarctica is omitted. 2. Including Asiatic U.S.S.R. 3. Including European U.S.S.R. 4. Although Hawaii is geographically part of Oceania, its population is included in the population figure for North America. 5. Excludes Hawaii. *Source:* United Nations *Demographic Yearbook, 1979.*

Some Countries With High Population Densities (per square mile)

Monaco	41,095.9	South Korea	1,034.7	Lebanon	672.5	India	569.2
Singapore	10,504.2	Netherlands	1,027.4	West Germany	644.5	Jamaica	510.1
Bangladesh	1,679.8	Belgium	837.8	Sri Lanka	602.0	Israel	500.5
China, Rep. of	1,350.1	Japan	825.4	United Kingdom	592.6	Italy	485.8

Longitude and Latitude of Foreign Cities

(and time corresponding to 12:00 noon, eastern standard time)

City	Long. ° ′	Lat. ° ′	Time
Aberdeen, Scotland	2 9 w	57 9 n	5:00 p.m.
Adelaide, Australia	138 36 e	34 55 s	2:30 a.m.[1]
Algiers	3 0 e	36 50 n	6:00 p.m.
Amsterdam	4 53 e	52 22 n	6:00 p.m.
Ankara, Turkey	32 55 e	39 55 n	7:00 p.m.
Asunción, Paraguay	57 40 w	25 15 s	1:00 p.m.
Athens	23 43 e	37 58 n	7:00 p.m.
Auckland, New Zeland	174 45 e	36 52 s	5:00 a.m.[1]
Bangkok, Thailand	100 30 e	13 45 n	midnight[1]
Barcelona	2 9 e	41 23 n	6:00 p.m.
Belém, Brazil	48 29 w	1 28 s	2:00 p.m.
Belfast, Northern Ireland	5 56 w	54 37 n	5:00 p.m.
Belgrade, Yugoslavia	20 32 e	44 52 n	6:00 p.m.
Berlin	13 25 e	52 30 n	6:00 p.m.
Birmingham, England	1 55 w	52 25 n	5:00 p.m.
Bogotá, Colombia	74 15 w	4 32 n	12:00 noon
Bombay	72 48 e	19 0 n	10:30 p.m.
Bordeaux, France	0 31 w	44 50 n	6:00 p.m.
Bremen, Germany	8 49 e	53 5 n	6:00 p.m.
Brisbane, Australia	153 8 e	27 29 s	3:00 a.m.[1]
Bristol, England	2 35 w	51 28 n	5:00 p.m.
Brussels	4 22 e	50 52 n	6:00 p.m.
Bucharest	26 7 e	44 25 n	7:00 p.m.
Budapest	19 5 e	47 30 n	6:00 p.m.
Buenos Aires	58 22 w	34 35 s	2:00 p.m.
Cairo	31 21 e	30 2 n	7:00 p.m.
Calcutta	88 24 e	22 34 n	10:30 p.m.
Canton, China	113 15 e	23 7 n	1:00 a.m.[1]
Cape Town, South Africa	18 22 e	33 55 s	7:00 p.m.
Caracas, Venezuela	67 2 w	10 28 n	1:00 p.m.
Cayenne, French Guiana	52 18 w	4 49 n	1:00 p.m.
Chihuahua, Mexico	106 5 w	28 37 n	11:00 a.m.
Chongqing, China	106 34 e	29 46 n	1:00 a.m.[1]
Copenhagen	12 34 e	55 40 n	6:00 p.m.
Córdoba, Argentina	64 10 w	31 28 s	2:00 p.m.
Dakar, Senegal	17 28 w	14 40 n	5:00 p.m.
Darwin, Australia	130 51 e	12 28 s	2:30 a.m.[1]
Djibouti	43 3 e	11 30 n	8:00 p.m.
Dublin	6 15 w	53 20 n	5:00 p.m.
Durban, South Africa	30 53 e	29 53 s	7:00 p.m.
Edinburgh, Scotland	3 10 w	55 55 n	5:00 p.m.
Frankfurt	8 41 e	50 7 n	6:00 p.m.
Georgetown, Guyana	58 15 w	6 45 n	1:15 p.m.
Glasgow, Scotland	4 15 w	55 50 n	5:00 p.m.
Guatemala City, Guatemala	90 31 w	14 37 n	11:00 a.m.
Guayaquil, Ecuador	79 56 w	2 10 s	12:00 noon
Hamburg	10 2 e	53 33 n	6:00 p.m.
Hammerfest, Norway	23 38 e	70 38 n	6:00 p.m.
Havana	82 23 w	23 8 n	12:00 noon
Helsinki, Finland	25 0 e	60 10 n	7:00 p.m.
Hobart, Tasmania	147 19 e	42 52 s	3:00 a.m.[1]
Iquique, Chile	70 7 w	20 10 s	1:00 p.m.
Irkutsk, U.S.S.R.	104 20 e	52 30 n	1:00 a.m.[1]
Jakarta, Indonesia	106 48 e	6 16 s	0:30 a.m.[1]
Johannesburg, South Africa	28 4 e	26 12 s	7:00 p.m.
Kingston, Jamaica	76 49 w	17 59 n	12:00 noon
Kinshasa, Zaire	15 17 e	4 18 s	6:00 p.m.
La Paz, Bolivia	68 22 w	16 27 s	1:00 p.m.
Leeds, England	1 30 w	53 45 n	5:00 p.m.
Leningrad	30 18 e	59 56 n	8:00 p.m.
Lima, Peru	77 2 w	12 0 s	12:00 noon
Lisbon	9 9 w	38 44 n	5:00 p.m.
Liverpool, England	3 0 w	53 25 n	5:00 p.m.
London	0 5 w	51 32 n	5:00 p.m.
Lyons, France	4 50 e	45 45 n	6:00 p.m.
Madrid	3 42 w	40 26 n	6:00 p.m.
Manchester, England	2 15 w	53 30 n	5:00 p.m.
Manila	120 57 e	14 35 n	1:00 a.m.[1]
Marseilles, France	5 20 e	43 20 n	6:00 p.m.
Mazatlán, Mexico	106 25 w	23 12 n	10:00 a.m.
Mecca, Saudi Arabia	39 45 e	21 29 n	8:00 p.m.
Melbourne	144 58 e	37 47 s	3:00 a.m.[1]
Mexico City	99 7 w	19 26 n	11:00 a.m.
Milan, Italy	9 10 e	45 27 n	6:00 p.m.
Montevideo, Uruguay	56 10 w	34 53 s	2:00 p.m.
Moscow	37 36 e	55 45 n	8:00 p.m.
Munich, Germany	11 35 e	48 8 n	6:00 p.m.
Nagasaki, Japan	129 57 e	32 48 n	2:00 a.m.[1]
Nagoya, Japan	136 56 e	35 7 n	2:00 a.m.[1]
Nairobi, Kenya	36 55 e	1 25 s	8:00 p.m.
Nanjing (Nanking), China	118 53 e	32 3 n	1:00 a.m.[1]
Naples, Italy	14 15 e	40 50 n	6:00 p.m.
Newcastle-on-Tyne, Eng.	1 37 w	54 58 n	5:00 p.m.
Odessa, U.S.S.R.	30 48 e	46 27 n	8:00 p.m.
Osaka, Japan	135 30 e	34 32 n	2:00 a.m.[1]
Oslo	10 42 e	59 57 n	6:00 p.m.
Panama City, Panama	79 32 w	8 58 n	12:00 noon
Paramaribo, Surinam	55 15 w	5 45 n	1:30 p.m.
Paris	2 20 e	48 48 n	6:00 p.m.
Peking	116 25 e	39 55 n	1:00 a.m.[1]
Perth, Australia	115 52 e	31 57 s	1:00 a.m.[1]
Plymouth, England	4 5 w	50 25 n	5:00 p.m.
Port Moresby, Papua New Guinea	147 8 e	9 25 s	3:00 a.m.[1]
Prague	14 26 e	50 5 n	6:00 p.m.
Rangoon, Burma	96 0 e	16 50 n	11:30 p.m.
Reykjavik, Iceland	21 58 w	64 4 n	4:00 p.m.
Rio de Janeiro	43 12 w	22 57 s	2:00 p.m.
Rome	12 27 e	41 54 n	6:00 p.m.
Salvador, Brazil	38 27 w	12 56 s	2:00 p.m.
Santiago, Chile	70 45 w	33 28 s	1:00 p.m.
Sao Paulo, Brazil	46 31 w	23 31 s	2:00 p.m.
Shanghai, China	121 28 e	31 10 n	1:00 a.m.[1]
Singapore	103 55 e	1 14 n	0:30 a.m.[1]
Sofia, Bulgaria	23 20 e	42 40 n	7:00 p.m.
Stockholm	18 3 e	59 17 n	6:00 p.m.
Sydney, Australia	151 0 e	34 0 s	3:00 a.m.[1]
Tananarive, Madagascar	47 33 e	18 50 s	8:00 p.m.
Teheran, Iran	51 45 e	35 45 n	8:30 p.m.
Tokyo	139 45 e	35 40 n	2:00 a.m.[1]
Tripoli, Libya	13 12 e	32 57 n	7:00 p.m.
Venice	12 20 e	45 26 n	6:00 p.m.
Veracruz, Mexico	96 10 w	19 10 n	11:00 a.m.
Vienna	16 20 e	48 14 n	6:00 p.m.
Vladivostok, U.S.S.R.	132 0 e	43 10 n	3:00 a.m.[1]
Warsaw	21 0 e	52 14 n	6:00 p.m.
Wellington, New Zealand	174 47 e	41 17 s	5:00 a.m.[1]
Zürich	8 31 e	47 21 n	6:00 p.m.

1. On the following day.

Highest Mountain Peaks of the World

(For U.S. peaks, see Index)

Mountain peak	Range	Location	Height	
			feet	meters
Everest[1]	Himalayas	Nepal-Tibet	29,028	8,848
Godwin Austen (K-2)	Karakoram	India	28,741	8,750
Kanchenjunga	Himalayas	Nepal-Sikkim	28,208	8,598
Lhotse	Himalayas	Nepal-Tibet	27,890	8,501
Makalu	Himalayas	Tibet-Nepal	27,790	8,470
Dhaulagiri I	Himalayas	Nepal	26,810	8,172
Manaslu	Himalayas	Nepal	26,760	8,156
Cho Oyu	Himalayas	Nepal	26,750	8,153
Nanga Parbat	Himalayas	India	26,660	8,126
Annapurna I	Himalayas	Nepal	26,504	8,078
Gasherbrum I	Karakoram	India	26,470	8,068
Broad Peak	Karakoram	India	26,400	8,047
Gasherbrum II	Karakoram	India	26,360	8,033
Gosainthan	Himalayas	Tibet	26,291	8,013
Gasherbrum III	Karakoram	India	26,090	7,952
Annapurna II	Himalayas	Nepal	26,041	7,937
Gasherbrum IV	Karakoram	India	26,000	7,925
Kangbachen	Himalayas	Nepal	25,925	7,902
Gyachung Kang	Himalayas	Nepal	25,910	7,897
Himal Chuli	Himalayas	Nepal	25,895	7,893
Disteghil Sar	Karakoram	India	25,868	7,885
Nuptse	Himalayas	Nepal	25,850	7,829
Kunyang Kish	Karakoram	India	25,760	7,852
Dakum (Peak 29)	Himalayas	Nepal	25,760	7,852
Masherbrum	Karakoram	India	25,660	7,821
Nanda Devi	Himalayas	India	25,645	7,817
Chomolonzo	Himalayas	Nepal-Tibet	25,640	7,815
Rakaposhi	Karakoram	India	25,550	7,788
Batura	Karakoram	India	25,540	7,785
Kanjut Sar	Karakoram	India	25,460	7,760
Kamet	Himalayas	India-Tibet	25,447	7,756
Namche Barwa	Himalayas	Tibet	25,445	7,756
Dhaulagiri II	Himalayas	Nepal	25,427	7,750
Saltoro Kangri	Karakoram	India	25,400	7,742
Gurla Mandhata	Himalayas	Tibet	25,355	7,728
Ulugh Muztagh	Kunlun	Tibet	25,341	7,724
Trivor	Karakoram	India	25,330	7,721
Jannu	Himalayas	Nepal	25,294	7,710
Saser Kangri	Karakoram	India	25,170	7,672
Makalu II	Himalayas	Nepal	25,130	7,660
Chogolisa	Karakoram	India	25,110	7,654
Dhaulagiri IV	Himalayas	Nepal	25,064	7,639
Fang	Himalayas	Nepal	25,013	7,624
Kula Gangri	Himalayas	Tibet	24,783	7,554
Changtse	Himalayas	Tibet	24,780	7,553
Muztagh Ata	Muztagh Ata	China	24,757	7,546
Skyang Kangri	Himalayas	Kashmir	24,750	7,544
Communism Peak	Pamir	U.S.S.R.	24,547	7,482
Victory Peak	Pamir	U.S.S.R.	24,406	7,439
Sia Kangri	Himalayas	Kashmir	24,340	7,419
Chamlang	Himalayas	Nepal	24,012	7,319
Alung Gangri	Himalayas	Tibet	23,999	7,315
Chomo Lhari	Himalayas	Tibet-Bhutan	23,996	7,314
Muztagh (K-5)	Kunlun	China	23,891	7,282
Amne Machin	Kunlun	China	23,490	7,160
Gaurisankar	Himalayas	Nepal-Tibet	23,440	7,145
Lenin Peak	Pamir	U.S.S.R.	23,405	7,134
Korzhenevski Peak	Pamir	U.S.S.R.	23,310	7,105
Kangto	Himalayas	Tibet	23,260	7,090
Dunagiri	Himalayas	India	23,184	7,066
Pauhunri	Himalayas	India-Tibet	23,180	7,065
Aconcagua	Andes	Argentina-Chile	23,034	7,021
Revolution Peak	Pamir	U.S.S.R.	22,880	6,974
Kangchenjhan	Himalayas	India	22,700	6,919
Siniolchu	Himalayas	India	22,620	6,895
Ojos des Salado	Andes	Argentina-Chile	22,588	6,885

Mountain peak	Range	Location	Height feet	meters
Bonete	Andes	Argentina-Chile	22,546	6,872
Simvuo	Himalayas	India	22,346	6,811
Tup	Andes	Argentina	22,309	6,800
Kungpu	Himalayas	Bhutan	22,300	6,797
Falso-Azufre	Andes	Argentina-Chile	22,277	6,790
Moscow Peak	Pamir	U.S.S.R.	22,260	6,785
Veladero	Andes	Argentina	22,244	6,780
Pissis	Andes	Argentina	22,241	6,779
Mercedario	Andes	Argentina-Chile	22,211	6,770
Huascarán	Andes	Peru	22,198	6,766
Tocorpuri	Andes	Bolivia-Chile	22,162	6,755
Karl Marx Peak	Pamir	U.S.S.R.	22,067	6,726
Llullaillaco	Andes	Argentina-Chile	22,057	6,723
Libertador	Andes	Argentina	22,047	6,720
Kailas	Himalayas	Tibet	22,027	6,714
Lingtren	Himalayas	Nepal-Tibet	21,972	6,697
Incahuasi	Andes	Argentina-Chile	21,719	6,620
Carnicero	Andes	Peru	21,689	6,611
Kurumda	Pamir	U.S.S.R.	21,686	6,610
Garmo Peak	Pamir	U.S.S.R.	21,637	6,595
Sajama	Andes	Bolivia	21,555	6,570
Ancohuma	Andes	Bolivia	21,490	6,550
El Muerto	Andes	Argentina-Chile	21,456	6,540
Nacimiento	Andes	Argentina	21,302	6,493
Illimani	Andes	Bolivia	21,184	6,457
Antofalla	Andes	Argentina-Chile	21,129	6,440
Coropuña	Andes	Peru	21,079	6,425
Cuzco (Ausangate)	Andes	Peru	20,995	6,399
Toro	Andes	Argentina-Chile	20,932	6,380
Parinacota	Andes	Bolivia-Chile	20,768	6,330
Chimboraso	Andes	Ecuador	20,702	6,310
Salcantay	Andes	Peru	20,575	6,271
General Manuel Belgrano	Andes	Argentina	20,505	6,250
Chañi	Andes	Argentina	20,341	6,200
Caca Aca	Andes	Bolivia	20,328	6,196
McKinley	Alaska	Alaska	20,320	6,194
Vudor Peak	Pamir	U.S.S.R.	20,118	6,132
Condoriri	Andes	Bolivia	20,095	6,125
Solimana	Andes	Peru	20,069	6,117
Nevada	Andes	Argentina	20,023	6,103

1. The U. S. Air Force Planning Charts list the height of Mt. Everest as 29,141 ft.

Oceans and Seas

Name	Area sq mi.	Area sq km	Average depth feet	Average depth meters	Greatest known depth feet	Greatest known depth meters	Place greatest known depth
Pacific Ocean	64,000,000	165,760,000	13,215	4,028	37,782	11,516	Mindanao Deep
Atlantic Ocean	31,815,000	82,400,000	12,880	3,926	30,246	9,219	Puerto Rico Trough
Indian Ocean	25,300,000	65,526,700	13,002	3,963	24,460	7,455	Sunda Trench
Arctic Ocean	5,440,200	14,090,000	3,953	1,205	18,456	5,625	77° 45′ N; 175° W
Mediterranean Sea[1]	1,145,100	2,965,800	4,688	1,429	15,197	4,632	Off Cape Matapan, Greece
Caribbean Sea	1,049,500	2,718,200	8,685	2,647	22,788	6,946	Off Cayman Islands
South China Sea	895,400	2,319,000	5,419	1,652	16,456	5,016	West of Luzon
Bering Sea	884,900	2,291,900	5,075	1,547	15,659	4,773	Off Buldir Island
Gulf of Mexico	615,000	1,592,800	4,874	1,486	12,425	3,787	Sigsbee Deep
Okhotsk Sea	613,800	1,589,700	2,749	838	12,001	3,658	146° 10′ E; 46° 50′ N
East China Sea	482,300	1,249,200	617	188	9,126	2,782	25° 16′ N; 125° E
Hudson Bay	475,800	1,232,300	420	128	600	183	Near entrance
Japan Sea	389,100	1,007,800	4,429	1,350	12,276	3,742	Central Basin
Andaman Sea	308,100	797,700	2,854	870	12,392	3,777	Off Car Nicobar Island
North Sea	222,100	575,200	308	94	2,165	660	Skagerrak
Red Sea	169,100	438,000	1,611	491	7,254	2,211	Off Port Sudan
Baltic Sea	163,000	422,200	180	55	1,380	421	Off Gotland

1. Includes Black Sea and Sea of Azov. NOTE: For Caspian Sea, *see* Large Lakes of World elsewhere in this section.

World's Greatest Man-Made Lakes[1]

Name of dam	Location	Millions of cubic meters	Thousands of acre-feet	Year completed
Owen Falls	Uganda	204,800	166,000	1954
Kariba	Zimbabwe	181,592	147,218	1959
Bratsk	U.S.S.R.	169,270	137,220	1964
High Aswan (Sadd-el-Aali)	Egypt	168,000	136,200	1970
Akosombo	Ghana	148,000	120,000	1965
Daniel Johnson	Canada	141,851	115,000	1968
Guri (Raul Leoni)	Venezuela	136,000	110,256	UC(1985)
Krasnoyarsk	U.S.S.R.	73,300	59,425	1967
Bennett W.A.C.	Canada	70,309	57,006	1967
Zeya	U.S.S.R.	68,400	55,452	UC(—)
Cabora Bassa	Mozambique	63,000	51,075	1974
LaGrande 2	Canada	61,720	50,037	UC(1982)
LaGrande 3	Canada	60,020	48,659	UC(1982)
Ust'—Ilimsk	U.S.S.R.	59,300	48,075	1980
Volga—V.I. Lenin	U.S.S.R.	58,000	47,020	1955
Caniapiscau	Canada	53,790	43,608	UC(—)
Pati (Chapetón)	Argentina	53,700	43,535	UC(1998)
Upper Wainganga	India	50,700	41,103	UC(1987)
Sáo Felix	Brazil	50,600	41,022	UC(1985)
Bukhtarma	U.S.S.R.	49,740	40,325	1960
Atatürk (Karababa)	Turkey	48,000	38,914	UC(1990)
Cerros Colorados	Argentina	48,000	38,914	1973
Irkutsk	U.S.S.R.	46,000	37,290	1956
Tucuruí	Brazil	36,375	29,489	UC(1983)
Vilyuy	U.S.S.R.	35,900	29,104	1967
Sanmenxia	China	35,400	28,700	1960
Hoover	Nevada–Arizona	35,200	28,537	1936
Sobridinho	Brazil	34,200	27,726	1981
Glen Canyon	Arizona	33,305	27,000	1964
Jenpeg	Canada	31,790	25,772	1975

1. Formed by construction of dams. NOTE: UC = under construction, ( ) = estimated year of completion. *Source:* Department of the Interior, Bureau of Reclamation.

Large Lakes of the World

Name and location	Area		Length		Maximum depth	
	sq mi.	sq km	mi.	km	feet	meters
Caspian Sea, U.S.S.R.-Iran[1]	152,239	394,299	745	1,199	3,104	946
Superior, U.S.-Canada	31,820	82,414	383	616	1,333	406
Victoria, Tanzania–Uganda	26,828	69,485	200	322	270	82
Aral, U.S.S.R.	25,659	66,457	266	428	223	68
Huron, U.S.-Canada	23,010	59,596	247	397	750	229
Michigan, U.S.	22,400	58,016	321	517	923	281
Tanganyika, Tanzania-Zaire	12,700	32,893	420	676	4,708	1,435
Baikal, U.S.S.R.	12,162	31,500	395	636	5,712	1,741
Great Bear, Canada	12,000	31,080	232	373	270	82
Nyasa, Malawi-Mozambique-Tanzania	11,600	30,044	360	579	2,316	706
Great Slave, Canada	11,170	28,930	298	480	2,015	614
Chad,[2] Chad-Niger-Nigeria	9,946	25,760	—	—	23	7
Erie, U.S.-Canada	9,930	25,719	241	388	210	64
Winnipeg, Canada	9,094	23,553	264	425	204	62
Ontario, U.S.-Canada	7,520	19,477	193	311	778	237
Balkash, U.S.S.R.	7,115	18,428	376	605	87	27
Ladoga, U.S.S.R.	7,000	18,130	124	200	738	225
Onega, U.S.S.R.	3,819	9,891	154	248	361	110
Titicaca, Bolivia-Peru	3,141	8,135	110	177	1,214	370
Nicaragua, Nicaragua	3,089	8,001	110	177	230	70
Athabaska, Canada	3,058	7,920	208	335	407	124
Rudolf, Kenya	2,473	6,405	154	248	—	—
Reindeer, Canada	2,444	6,330	152	245	—	—
Eyre, South Australia	2,400[3]	6,216	130	209	varies	varies
Issyk-Kul, U.S.S.R.	2,394	6,200	113	182	2,297	700
Urmia,[2] Iran	2,317	6,001	81	130	49	15
Torrens, South Australia	2,200	5,698	130	209	—	—
Vänern, Sweden	2,141	5,545	87	140	322	98

Name and location	Area		Length		Maximum depth	
	sq mi.	sq km	mi.	km	feet	meters
Winnipegosis, Canada	2,086	5,403	152	245	59	18
Mobutu Sese Seko, Uganda	2,046	5,299	100	161	180	55
Nettilling, Baffin Island, Canada	1,950	5,051	70	113	—	—
Nipigon, Canada	1,870	4,843	72	116	—	—
Manitoba, Canada	1,817	4,706	140	225	22	7
Great Salt, U.S.	1,800	4,662	75	121	15/25	5/8
Kioga, Uganda	1,700	4,403	50	80	about 30	9
Koko-Nor, China	1,630	4,222	66	106	—	—

1. The Caspian Sea is called "sea" because the Romans, finding it salty, named it *Mare Caspium.* Many geographers, however, consider it a lake because it is land-locked. 2. Figures represent high-water data. 3. Varies with the rainfall of the wet season. It has been reported to dry up almost completely on occasion.

Principal Rivers of the World

(For other U.S. rivers, see Index)

River	Source	Outflow	Approx. length	
			miles	km
Nile	Tributaries of Lake Victoria, Africa	Mediterranean Sea	4,180	6,690
Amazon	Glacier-fed lakes, Peru	Atlantic Ocean	3,912	6,296
Mississippi-Missouri-Red Rock	Source of Red Rock, Montana	Gulf of Mexico	3,741	6,020
Yangtze Kiang	Tibetan plateau, China	China Sea	3,602	5,797
Ob	Altai Mts., U.S.S.R.	Gulf of Ob	3,459	5,567
Yellow (Hwang Ho)	Eastern part of Kunlan Mts., west China	Gulf of Chihli	2,900	4,667
Yenisei	Tannu-Ola Mts., western Tuva, U.S.S.R.	Arctic Ocean	2,800	4,506
Paraná	Confluence of Paranaiba and Grande rivers	Río de la Plata	2,795	4,498
Irtish	Altai Mts., U.S.S.R.	Ob River	2,758	4,438
Congo	Confluence of Lualaba and Luapula rivers, Zaire	Atlantic Ocean	2,716	4,371
Amur	Confluence of Shilka (U.S.S.R.) and Argun (Manchuria) rivers	Tatar Strait	2,704	4,352
Lena	Baikal Mts., U.S.S.R.	Arctic Ocean	2,652	4,268
Mackenzie	Head of Finlay River, British Columbia, Canada	Beaufort Sea (Arctic Ocean)	2,635	4,241
Niger	Guinea	Gulf of Guinea	2,600	4,184
Mekong	Tibetan highlands	South China Sea	2,500	4,023
Mississippi	Lake Itasca, Minnesota	Gulf of Mexico	2,348	3,779
Missouri	Confluence of Jefferson, Gallatin, and Madison rivers, Montana	Mississippi River	2,315	3,726
Volga	Valdai plateau, U.S.S.R.	Caspian Sea	2,291	3,687
Madeira	Confluence of Beni and Maumoré rivers, Bolivia-Brazil boundary	Amazon River	2,012	3,238
Purus	Peruvian Andes	Amazon River	1,993	3,207
São Francisco	Southwest Minas Gerais, Brazil	Atlantic Ocean	1,987	3,198
St. Lawrence	Lake Ontario	Gulf of St. Lawrence	1,900	3,058
Yukon	Junction of Lewes and Pelly rivers, Yukon Territory, Canada	Bering Sea	1,900	3,058
Rio Grande	San Juan Mts., Colorado	Gulf of Mexico	1,885	3,034
Brahmaputra	Himalayas	Ganges River	1,800	2,897
Indus	Himalayas	Arabian Sea	1,800	2,897
Danube	Black Forest, W. Germany	Black Sea	1,766	2,842

River	Source	Outflow	Approx. length miles	Approx. length km
Euphrates	Confluence of Murat Nehri and Kara Su rivers, Turkey	Shatt-al-Arab	1,739	2,799
Darling	Central part of Eastern Highlands, Australia	Murray River	1,702	2,739
Zambezi	11°21′S, 24°22′E, Zambia	Mozambique Channel	1,700	2,736
Tocantins	Goiás, Brazil	Pará River	1,677	2,699
Murray	Australian Alps, New South Wales	Indian Ocean	1,609	2,589
Nelson	Head of Bow River, western Alberta, Canada	Hudson Bay	1,600	2,575
Paraguay	Mato Grosso, Brazil	Paraná River	1,584	2,549
Ural	Southern Ural Mts., U.S.S.R.	Caspian Sea	1,574	2,533
Ganges	Himalayas	Bay of Bengal	1,557	2,506
Amu Darya (Oxus)	Nicholas Range, Pamir Mts., U.S.S.R.	Aral Sea	1,500	2,414
Japurá	Andes, Colombia	Amazon River	1,500	2,414
Salween	Tibet, south of Kunlun Mts.	Gulf of Martaban	1,500	2,414
Arkansas	Central Colorado	Mississippi River	1,450	2,333
Colorado	Grand County, Colorado	Gulf of California	1,450	2,333
Dnieper	Valdai Hills, U.S.S.R.	Black Sea	1,419	2,284
Ohio-Allegheny	Potter County, Pennsylvania	Mississippi River	1,306	2,102
Irrawaddy	Confluence of Nmai and Mali rivers, northeast Burma	Bay of Bengal	1,300	2,092
Orange	Lesotho	Atlantic Ocean	1,300	2,092
Orinoco	Serra Parima Mts., Venezuela	Atlantic Ocean	1,281	2,062
Pilcomayo	Andes Mts., Bolivia	Paraguay River	1,242	1,999
Xi Jiang (Si Kiang)	Eastern Yunnan Province, China	China Sea	1,236	1,989
Columbia	Columbia Lake, British Columbia, Canada	Pacific Ocean	1,232	1,983
Don	Tula, R.S.F.S.R., U.S.S.R.	Sea of Azov	1,223	1,968
Sungari	China-North Korea boundary	Amur River	1,215	1,955
Saskatchewan	Canadian Rocky Mts.	Lake Winnipeg	1,205	1,939
Peace	Stikine Mts., British Columbia, Canada	Great Slave River	1,195	1,923
Tigris	Taurus Mts., Turkey	Shatt-al-Arab	1,180	1,899

Highest Waterfalls of the World

Waterfall	Location	River	Height feet	Height meters
Angel	Venezuela	Tributary of Caroní	3,281	1,000
Tugela	Natal, South Africa	Tugela	3,000	914
Cuquenán	Venezuela	Cuquenán	2,000	610
Sutnerland	South Island, N.Z.	Arthur	1,904	580
Takkakaw	British Columbia	Tributary of Yoho	1,650	503
Ribbon (Yosemite)	California	Creek flowing into Yosemite	1,612	491
Upper Yosemite	California	Yosemite Creek, tributary of Merced	1,430	436
Gavarnie	Southwest France	Gave de Pau	1,384	422
Vettisfoss	Norway	Mörkedola	1,200	366
Widows' Tears (Yosemite)	California	Tributary of Merced	1,170	357
Staubbach	Switzerland	Staubbach (Lauterbrunnen Valley)	984	300

Waterfall	Location	River	Height feet	meters
Middle Cascade (Yosemite)	California	Yosemite Creek, tributary of Merced	909	277
King Edward VIII	Guyana	Courantyne	850	259
Gersoppa	India	Sharavati	829	253
Kaieteur	Guyana	Potaro	822	251
Skykje	Norway	In Skykjedal (valley of Inner Hardinger Fjord)	820	250
Kalambo	Tanzania-Zambia	—	720	219
Fairy (Mount Rainier Park)	Washington	Stevens Creek	700	213
Trummelbach	Switzerland	Trummelbach (Lauterbrunnen Valley)	700	213
Aniene (Teverone)	Italy	Tiber	680	207
Cascata delle Marmore	Italy	Velino, tributary of Nera	650	198
Maradalsfos	Norway	Stream flowing into Ejkisdalsvand (lake)	643	196
Feather	California	Fall River	640	195
Maletsunyane	Lesotho	Maletsunyane	630	192
Bridalveil (Yosemite)	California	Yosemite Creek	620	189
Multnomah	Oregon	Multnomah Creek, tributary of Columbia	620	189
Vøringsfos	Norway	Bjoreia	597	182
Nevada (Yosemite)	California	Merced	594	181
Skjeggedal	Norway	Tysso	525	160
Marina	Guyana	Tributary of Kuribrong, tributary of Potaro	500	152
Tequendama	Colombia	Funza, tributary of Magdalena	425	130
King George's	Cape of Good Hope, South Africa	Orange	400	122
Illilouette (Yosemite)	California	Illilouette Creek, tributary of Merced	370	113
Victoria	Rhodesia-Zambia boundary	Zambezi	355	108
Handöl	Sweden	Handöl Creek	345	105
Lower Yosemite	California	Yosemite	320	98
Comet (Mount Rainier Park)	Washington	Van Trump Creek	320	98
Vernal (Yosemite)	California	Merced	317	97
Virginia	Northwest Territories, Canada	South Nahanni, tributary of Mackenzie	315	96
Lower Yellowstone	Wyoming	Yellowstone	310	94

NOTE: Niagara Falls (New York-Ontario), though of great volume, has parallel drops of only 158 and 167 feet.

Large Islands of the World

Island	Location and status	Area sq mi.	sq km
Greenland	North Atlantic (Danish)	839,999	2,175,597
New Guinea	Southwest Pacific (Irian Jaya, Indonesian, west part; Papua New Guinea, east part)	316,615	820,033
Borneo	West mid-Pacific (Indonesian, south part; British protectorate, and Malaysian, north part)	286,914	743,107
Madagascar	Indian Ocean (Malagasy Republic)	226,657	587,042
Baffin	North Atlantic (Canadian)	183,810	476,068
Sumatra	Northeast Indian Ocean (Indonesian)	182,859	473,605
Honshu	Sea of Japan-Pacific (Japanese)	88,925	230,316
Great Britain	Off coast of NW Europe (England, Scotland, and Wales)	88,758	229,883
Ellesmere	Arctic Ocean (Canadian)	82,119	212,688
Victoria	Arctic Ocean (Canadian)	81,930	212,199
Celebes	West mid-Pacific (Indonesian)	72,986	189,034
South Island	South Pacific (New Zealand)	58,093	150,461
Java	Indian Ocean (Indonesian)	48,990	126,884
North Island	South Pacific (New Zealand)	44,281	114,688

Island	Location and status	Area sq mi.	Area sq km
Cuba	Caribbean Sea (republic)	44,218	114,525
Newfoundland	North Atlantic (Canadian)	42,734	110,681
Luzon	West mid-Pacific (Philippines)	40,420	104,688
Iceland	North Atlantic (republic)	39,768	102,999
Mindanao	West mid-Pacific (Philippines)	36,537	94,631
Ireland	West of Great Britain (republic, south part; United Kingdom, north part)	32,597	84,426
Hokkaido	Sea of Japan—Pacific (Japanese)	30,372	78,663
Hispaniola	Caribbean Sea (Dominican Republic, east part; Haiti, west part)	29,355	76,029
Tasmania	South of Australia (Australian)	26,215	67,897
Sri Lanka (Ceylon)	Indian Ocean (republic)	25,332	65,610
Sakhalin (Karafuto)	North of Japan (U.S.S.R.)	24,560	63,610
Banks	Arctic Ocean (Canadian)	23,230	60,166
Devon	Arctic Ocean (Canadian)	20,861	54,030
Tierra del Fuego	Southern tip of South America (Argentinian, east part; Chilean, west part)	18,605	48,187
Kyushu	Sea of Japan—Pacific (Japanese)	16,223	42,018
Melville	Arctic Ocean (Canadian)	16,141	41,805
Axel Heiberg	Arctic Ocean (Canadian)	15,779	40,868
Southampton	Hudson Bay (Canadian)	15,700	40,663

Principal Deserts of the World

Desert	Location	Approximate size	Approx. elevation, ft
Atacama	North Chile	400 mi. long	7,000–13,500
Black Rock	Northwest Nevada	About 1,000 sq mi.	2,000–8,500
Colorado	Southeast California from San Gorgonio Pass to Gulf of California	200 mi. long and a maximum width of 50 mi.	Few feet above to 250 below sea level
Dasht-e-Kavír	Southeast of Caspian Sea, Iran	—	2,000
Dasht-e-Lūt	Northeast of Kerman, Iran	—	1,000
Gobi (Shamo)	Covers most of Mongolia	500,000 sq mi.	3,000–5,000
Great Arabian	Most of Arabia	1,500 mi. long	—
An Nafud (Red Desert)	South of Jauf	400 mi. by avg of 140 mi.	3,000
Dahna	Northeast of Nejd	400 mi. by 30 mi.	—
Rub' al-Khali	South portion of Nejd	Over 200,000 sq mi.	—
Syrian (Al-Hamad)	North of lat. 30°N	—	1,850
Great Australian	Western portion of Australia	About one half the continent	600–1,000
Great Salt Lake	West of Great Salt Lake to Nevada–Utah boundary	About 110 mi. by 50 mi.	4,500
Kalahari	South Africa—South-West Africa	About 120,000 sq mi.	Over 3,000
Kara Kum (Desert of Kiva)	Southwest Turkmen, U.S.S.R.	115,000 sq mi.	—
Kyzyl Kum	Uzbek and Kazakh, U.S.S.R.	Over 100,000 sq mi.	160 near Lake Aral to 2,000 in southeast
Libyan	Libya, Egypt, Sudan	Over 500,000 sq mi.	—
Mojave	North of Colorado Desert and south of Death Valley, southeast California	15,000 sq mi.	2,000
Nubian	From Red Sea to great west bend of the Nile, Sudan	—	2,500
Painted Desert	Northeast Arizona	Over 7,000 sq mi.	High plateau, 5,000
Sahara	North Africa to about lat. 15°N and from Red Sea to Atlantic Ocean	3,200 mi. greatest length along lat. 20°N; area over 3,500,000 sq mi.	440 below sea level to 11,000 above; avg elevation, 1,400–1,600
Takla Makan	South central Sinkiang, China	Over 100,000 sq mi.	—
Thar (Indian)	Pakistan-India	Nearly 100,000 sq mi.	Over 1,000

Interesting Caves and Caverns of the World

Aggtelek. In village of same name, northern Hungary. Large stalactitic cavern about 5 miles long.

Altamira Cave. Near Santander, Spain. Contains animal paintings (Old Stone Age art) on roof and walls.

Antiparos. On island of same name in the Grecian Archipelago. Some stalactites are 20 ft long. Brilliant colors and fantastic shapes.

Blue Grotto. On island of Capri, Italy. Cavern hollowed out in limestone by constant wave action. Now half filled with water because of sinking coast. Name derived from unusual blue light permeating the cave. Source of light is a submerged opening, light passing through the water.

Carlsbad Caverns. Southeast New Mexico. Largest underground labyrinth yet discovered. Three levels: 754, 900, and 1,320 ft below the surface.

Fingal's Cave. On island of Staffa off coast of western Scotland. Penetrates about 200 ft inland. Contains basaltic columns almost 40 ft high.

Ice Cave. Near Dobsina, Czechoslovakia. Noted for its beautiful crystal effects.

Jenolan Caves. In Blue Mountain plateau, New South Wales, Australia. Beautiful stalactitic formations.

Kent's Cavern. Near Torquay, England. Source of much information on Paleolithic man.

Luray Cavern. Near Luray, Va. Has large stalactitic and stalagmitic columns of many colors.

Mammoth Cave. Limestone cavern in central Kentucky. Cave area is about 10 miles in diameter but has at least 150 miles of irregular subterranean passageways at various levels. Temperature remains fairly constant at 54°F.

Peak Cavern or **Devil's Hole.** Derbyshire, England. About 2,250 ft into a mountain. Lowest part is about 600 ft below the surface.

Postojna (Postumia) Grotto. Near Postumia in Julian Alps, about 25 miles northeast of Trieste. Stalactitic cavern, largest in Europe. Piuca (Pivka) River flows through part of it. Caves have numerous beautiful stalactites.

Singing Cave. Iceland. A lava cave; name derived from echoes of people singing in it.

Wind Cave. In Black Hills of South Dakota. Limestone caverns with stalactites and stalagmites almost entirely missing. Variety of crystal formations called "boxwork."

Wyandotte Cave. In Crawford County, southern Indiana. A limestone cavern with five levels of passages; one of the largest in North America. "Monumental Mountain," approximately 135 ft high, is believed to be one of the world's largest underground "mountains."

U.S. Geography

Miscellaneous Data for the United States

Source: Department of the Interior, U.S. Geological Survey.

Highest point: Mount McKinley, Alaska		20,320 ft (6,193 m)
Lowest point: Death Valley, Calif.		282 ft (86 m) below sea level
Approximate mean altitude		2,500 ft (762 m)
Points farthest apart (50 states):		
Log Point, Elliot Key, Fla., and Kure Island, Hawaii		5,852 mi. (9,418 km)
Geographic center (50 states):		
In Butte County, S.D. (west of Castle Rock)	44° 58′ N. lat.	103° 46′ W. long.
Geographic center (48 conterminous states):		
In Smith County, Kan. (near Lebanon)	39° 50′ N. lat.	98° 35′ W. long.
Boundaries:		
Between Alaska and Canada		1,538 mi. (2,475 km)
Between the 48 conterminous states and Canada (incl. Great Lakes)		3,987 mi. (6,416 km)
Between the United States and Mexico		1,933 mi. (3,111 km)

Extreme Points of the United States (50 States)

Extreme point	Latitude	Longitude	Distance[1] mi.	Distance[1] km
Northernmost point: Point Barrow, Alaska	71°23′ N	156°29′ W	2,502	4,027
Easternmost point: West Quoddy Head, Me.	44°49′ N	66°57′ W	1,785	2,873
Southernmost point: Ka Lae (South Cape), Hawaii	18°56′ N	155°41′ W	3,456	5,562
Westernmost point: Cape Wrangell, Alaska (Attu Island)	52°55′ N	172°27′ E	3,620	5,826

1. From geographic center of United States (incl. Alaska and Hawaii), west of Castle Rock, S.D., 44°58′ N. lat., 103°46′ W long.

Highest, Lowest, and Mean Altitudes in the United States

State	Altitude, ft[1]	Highest point	Altitude, ft	Lowest point	Altitude, ft
Alabama	500	Cheaha Mountain	2,407	Gulf of Mexico	Sea level
Alaska	1,900	Mount McKinley	20,320	Pacific Ocean	Sea level
Arizona	4,100	Humphreys Peak	12,633	Colorado River	70
Arkansas	650	Magazine Mountain	2,753	Ouachita River	55
California	2,900	Mount Whitney	14,494	Death Valley	282[2]
Colorado	6,800	Mount Elbert	14,433	Arkansas River	3,350
Connecticut	500	Mount Frissell, on south slope	2,380	Long Island Sound	Sea level
Delaware	60	On Ebright Road	442	Atlantic Ocean	Sea level
D. C.	150	Tenleytown, northwest part	410	Potomac River	1
Florida	100	Sec. 30, T6N, R20W[3]	345	Atlantic Ocean	Sea level
Georgia	600	Brasstown Bald	4,784	Atlantic Ocean	Sea level
Hawaii	3,030	Mauna Kea	13,796	Pacific Ocean	Sea level
Idaho	5,000	Borah Peak	12,662	Snake River	710
Illinois	600	Charles Mound	1,235	Mississippi River	279
Indiana	700	Franklin Township, Wayne County	1,257	Ohio River	320
Iowa	1,100	Sec. 29, T100N, R41W[4]	1,670	Mississippi River	480
Kansas	2,000	Mount Sunflower	4,039	Verdigris River	680
Kentucky	750	Black Mountain	4,145	Mississippi River	257
Louisiana	100	Driskill Mountain	535	New Orleans	5[2]
Maine	600	Mount Katahdin	5,268	Atlantic Ocean	Sea level
Maryland	350	Backbone Mountain	3,360	Atlantic Ocean	Sea level
Massachusetts	500	Mount Greylock	3,491	Atlantic Ocean	Sea level
Michigan	900	Mount Curwood	1,980	Lake Erie	572
Minnesota	1,200	Eagle Mountain	2,301	Lake Superior	602
Mississippi	300	Woodall Mountain	806	Gulf of Mexico	Sea level
Missouri	800	Taum Sauk Mountain	1,772	St. Francis River	230
Montana	3,400	Granite Peak	12,799	Kootenai River	1,800
Nebraska	2,600	Johnson Township, Kimball County	5,426	Southeast corner of state	840
Nevada	5,500	Boundary Peak	13,143	Colorado River	470
New Hampshire	1,000	Mount Washington	6,288	Atlantic Ocean	Sea level
New Jersey	250	High Point	1,803	Atlantic Ocean	Sea level
New Mexico	5,700	Wheeler Peak	13,161	Red Bluff Reservoir	2,817
New York	1,000	Mount Marcy	5,344	Atlantic Ocean	Sea level
North Carolina	700	Mount Mitchell	6,684	Atlantic Ocean	Sea level
North Dakota	1,900	White Butte	3,506	Red River	750
Ohio	850	Campbell Hill	1,550	Ohio River	433
Oklahoma	1,300	Black Mesa	4,973	Little River	287
Oregon	3,300	Mount Hood	11,239	Pacific Ocean	Sea level
Pennsylvania	1,100	Mount Davis	3,213	Delaware River	Sea level
Rhode Island	200	Jerimoth Hill	812	Atlantic Ocean	Sea level
South Carolina	350	Sassafras Mountain	3,560	Atlantic Ocean	Sea level
South Dakota	2,200	Harney Peak	7,242	Big Stone Lake	962
Tennessee	900	Clingmans Dome	6,643	Mississippi River	182
Texas	1,700	Guadalupe Peak	8,749	Gulf of Mexico	Sea level
Utah	6,100	Kings Peak	13,528	Beaverdam Creek	2,000
Vermont	1,000	Mount Mansfield	4,393	Lake Champlain	95
Virginia	950	Mount Rogers	5,729	Atlantic Ocean	Sea level
Washington	1,700	Mount Rainier	14,410	Pacific Ocean	Sea level
West Virginia	1,500	Spruce Knob	4,863	Potomac River	240
Wisconsin	1,050	Timms Hill	1,951	Lake Michigan	581
Wyoming	6,700	Gannett Peak	13,804	Belle Fourche River	3,100
United States	2,500	Mount McKinley (Alaska)	20,320	Death Valley (California)	282[2]

1. Approximate mean altitude. 2. Below sea level. 3. Walton County. 4. Osceola County. *Source:* Department of the Interior U.S. Geological Survey.

Mason and Dixon's Line

Mason and Dixon's Line (often called the Mason-Dixon Line) is the boundary between Pennsylvani[a] and Maryland, running at a north latitude of 39°43′19.11″. The greater part of it was surveyed fro[m] 1763–67 by Charles Mason and Jeremiah Dixon, English astronomers who had been appointed to sett[le] a dispute between the colonies. As the line was partly the boundary between the free and the slave state[s] it has come to signify the division between the North and the South.

Named Summits in the U. S. Over 14,000 Feet Above Sea Level

Name	State	Height	Name	State	Height	Name	State	Height
Mt. McKinley	Alaska	20,320	Mt. Antero	Colo.	14,269	Windom Peak	Colo.	14,087
Mt. St. Elias	Alaska	18,008	Torreys Peak	Colo.	14,267	Mt. Russell	Calif.	14,086
Mt. Foraker	Alaska	17,400	Castle Peak	Colo.	14,265	Mt. Eolus	Colo.	14,084
Mt. Bona	Alaska	16,421	Quandary Peak	Colo.	14,265	Mt. Columbia	Colo.	14,073
Mt. Blackburn	Alaska	16,390	Mt. Evans	Colo.	14,264	Mt. Augusta	Alaska	14,070
Mt. Sanford	Alaska	16,237	Longs Peak	Colo.	14,255	Missouri Mtn.	Colo.	14,067
South Buttress	Alaska	15,885	Mt. Wilson	Colo.	14,246	Humboldt Peak	Colo.	14,064
Mt. Vancouver	Alaska	15,700	White Mtn.	Calif.	14,246	Mt. Bierstadt	Colo.	14,060
Mt. Churchill	Alaska	15,638	North Palisade	Calif.	14,242	Sunlight Peak	Colo.	14,059
Mt. Fairweather	Alaska	15,300	Shavano Peak	Colo.	14,229	Split Mtn.	Calif.	14,058
Mt. Hubbard	Alaska	15,015	Crestone Needle	Colo.	14,197	Handies Peak	Colo.	14,048
Mt. Bear	Alaska	14,831	Mt. Belford	Colo.	14,197	Culebra Peak	Colo.	14,047
East Buttress	Alaska	14,730	Mt. Princeton	Colo.	14,197	Mt. Lindsey	Colo.	14,042
Mt. Hunter	Alaska	14,573	Mt. Yale	Colo.	14,196	Middle Palisade	Calif.	14,040
Mt. Alverstone	Alaska	14,565	Mt. Bross	Colo.	14,172	Little Bear Peak	Colo.	14,037
Browne Tower	Alaska	14,530	Kit Carson Mtn.	Colo.	14,165	Mt. Sherman	Colo.	14,036
Mt. Whitney	Calif.	14,494	Mt. Wrangell	Alaska	14,163	Redcloud Peak	Colo.	14,034
Mt. Elbert	Colo.	14,433	Mt. Shasta	Calif.	14,162	Mt. Langley	Calif.	14,028
Mt. Massive	Colo.	14,421	Mt. Sill	Calif.	14,162	Mt. Tyndall	Calif.	14,018
Mt. Harvard	Colo.	14,420	El Diente Peak	Colo.	14,159	Pyramid Peak	Colo.	14,018
Mt. Rainier	Wash.	14,410	Maroon Peak	Colo.	14,156	Wilson Peak	Colo.	14,017
Mt. Williamson	Calif.	14,375	Tabeguache Mtn.	Colo.	14,155	Mt. Muir	Calif.	14,015
Blanca Peak	Colo.	14,345	Mt. Oxford	Colo.	14,153	Wetterhorn Peak	Colo.	14,015
La Plata Peak	Colo.	14,336	Mt. Sneffels	Colo.	14,150	No. Maroon Pk.	Colo.	14,014
Uncompahgre Pk.	Colo.	14,309	Mt. Democrat	Colo.	14,148	San Luis Peak	Colo.	14,014
Crestone Peak	Colo.	14,294	Capitol Peak	Colo.	14,130	Huron Peak	Colo.	14,005
Mt. Lincoln	Colo.	14,286	Pikes Peak	Colo.	14,110	Mt. of the Holy Cross	Colo.	14,005
Grays Peak	Colo.	14,270	Snowmass Mtn.	Colo.	14,092	Sunshine Peak	Colo.	14,001

Source: Department of the Interior, U.S. Geological Survey.

Post-Eruption Map of Mount St. Helens for Sale

A post-eruption map of Mount St. Helens and vicinity that includes color photographs of the major eruption and aftereffects has been published by the U.S. Geological Survey.

The 30- x 40-inch topographical map shows how the area appears in the wake of the violent eruption of May 18, 1980. Presented at a scale of 1:100,000 (one inch equals about 1.68 miles), the map denotes land managed by federal and state agencies and includes numerical designations for roads within the Gifford Pinchot National Forest, viewpoints, campgrounds, picnic areas, visitor centers and points of interest.

On the reverse side of the map, the Forest Service has prepared a text and color photographs providing a narrative of recent Mount St. Helens volcanic activities.

The map, "Mount St. Helens and Vicinity, March 1981," may be purchased by mail for $1.00 each, from the Branch of Distribution, U.S. Geological Survey, Box 25286, Federal Center, Denver, Colo. 80225. Map orders *must* specify the correct title given here, and a check or money order made payable to the U.S. Geological Survey must be included with your order.

Rivers of the United States

(350 or more miles long)

Alabama (735 mi.; 1,183 km): From junction of Tallapoosa R. and Coosa R. in Alabama to Mobile R.

Altamaha-Ocmulgee (392 mi.; 631 km): From junction of Yellow R. and South R., Newton Co. in Georgia to Atlantic Ocean.

Apalachicola-Chattahoochee (524 mi.; 843 km): From Towns Co. in Georgia to Gulf of Mexico in Florida.

Arkansas (1,459 mi.; 2,348 km): From Lake Co. in Colorado to Mississippi R. in Arkansas.

Brazos (870 mi.; 1,400 km): From junction of Salt Fork and Double Mountain Fork in Texas to Gulf of Mexico.

Canadian (906 mi.; 1,458 km): From Las Animas Co. in Colorado to Arkansas R. in Oklahoma.

Cimarron (600 mi.; 966 km): From Colfax Co. in New Mexico to Arkansas R. in Oklahoma.

Clark Fork-Pend Oreille (505 mi.; 813 km): From Silver Bow Co. in Montana to Columbia R. in British Columbia.

Colorado (1,450 mi.; 2,333 km): From Rocky Mountain National Park in Colorado to Gulf of California in Mexico.

Colorado (840 mi.; 1,352 km): From Borden Co. in Texas to Matagorda Bay.

Columbia (1,243 mi.; 2,000 km): From Columbia Lake in British Columbia to Pacific Ocean (entering between Oregon and Washington).

Colville (350 mi.; 563 km): From Brooks Range in Alaska to Beaufort Sea.

Connecticut (407 mi.; 655 km): From Third Connecticut Lake in New Hampshire to Long Island Sound in Connecticut.

Cumberland (720 mi.; 1,159 km): From junction of Poor and Clover Forks in Harlan Co. in Kentucky to Ohio R.

Delaware (390 mi.; 628 km): From Schoharie County in New York to Liston Point, Delaware Bay.
Gila (630 mi.; 1,014 km): From Catron Co. in New Mexico to Colorado R. in Arizona.
Green (360 mi.; 579 km): From Lincoln Co. in Kentucky to Ohio R. in Kentucky.
Green (730 mi.; 1,175 km): From Sublette Co. in Wyoming to Colorado R. in Utah.
Illinois (420 mi.; 676 km): From St. Joseph Co. in Indiana to Mississippi R. at Grafton in Illinois.
James (sometimes called *Dakota*) (710 mi.; 1,143 km): From Wells Co. in North Dakota to Missouri R. in South Dakota.
Kanawha-New (352 mi.; 566 km): From junction of North and South Forks of New R. in North Carolina, through Virginia and West Virginia (New River becoming Kanawha River), to Ohio River.
Koyukuk (470 mi.; 756 km): From Brooks Range in Alaska to Yukon R.
Kuskokwim (680 mi.; 1,094 km): From Alaska Range in Alaska to Kuskokwim Bay.
Licking (350 mi.; 563 km): From Magoffin Co. in Kentucky to Ohio R. at Cincinnati in Ohio.
Little Missouri (560 mi.; 901 km): From Crook Co. in Wyoming to Missouri R. in North Dakota.
Milk (625 mi.; 1,006 km): From junction of forks in Alberta Province to Missouri R.
Mississippi (2,348 mi.; 3,779 km): From Lake Itasca in Minnesota to mouth of Southwest Pass in Louisiana.
Mississippi-Missouri-Red Rock (3,710 mi.; 5,971 km): From source of Red Rock R. in Montana to mouth of Southwest Pass in Louisiana.
Missouri (2,315 mi.; 3,726 km): From junction of Jefferson R., Gallatin R., and Madison R. in Montana to Mississippi R. near St. Louis.
Missouri-Red Rock (2,533 mi.; 4,076 km): From source of Red Rock R. in Montana to Mississippi R. near St. Louis.
Mobile-Alabama-Coosa (780 mi.; 1,255 km): From junction of Etowah R. and Oostanaula R. in Georgia to Mobile Bay.
Neosho (460 mi.; 740 km): From Morris Co. in Kansas to Arkansas R. in Oklahoma.
Niobrara (431 mi.; 694 km): From Niobrara Co. in Wyoming to Missouri R. in Nebraska.
Noatak (350 mi.; 563 km): From Brooks Range in Alaska to Kotzebue Sound.
North Canadian (760 mi.; 1,223 km): From Union Co. in New Mexico to Canadian R. in Oklahoma.
North Platte (618 mi.; 995 km): From Jackson Co. in Colorado to junction with So. Platte R. in Nebraska to form Platte R.
Ohio (981 mi.; 1,579 km): From junction of Allegheny R. and Monongahela R. at Pittsburgh to Mississippi R. between Illinois and Kentucky.
Ohio-Allegheny (1,306 mi.; 2,102 km): From Potter Co. in Pennsylvania to Mississippi R. at Cairo in Illinois.
Osage (500 mi.; 805 km): From east-central Kansas to Missouri R. near Jefferson City in Missouri.
Ouachita (605 mi.; 974 km): From Polk Co. in Arkansas to Red R. in Louisiana.
Pearl (411 mi.; 661 km): From Neshoba County in Mississippi to Gulf of Mexico (Mississippi-Louisiana).
Pecos (735 mi.; 1,183 km): From Mora Co. in New Mexico to Rio Grande in Texas.
Pee Dee-Yadkin (435 mi.; 700 km): From Watauga Co. in North Carolina to Winyah Bay in South Carolina.
Pend Oreille (490 mi.; 789 km): Near Butte in Montana to Columbia R. on Washington-Canada border.
Porcupine (460 mi.; 740 km): From Yukon Territory, Canada, to Yukon R. in Alaska.
Potomac (383 mi.; 616 km): From Garrett Co. in Maryland to Chesapeake Bay at Point Lookout in Maryland.
Powder (375 mi.; 603 km): From junction of forks in Johnson Co. in Wyoming to Yellowstone R. in Montana.
Red (1,270 mi.; 2,044 km): From junction of forks in Harmon Co. in Oklahoma to Mississippi R. in Louisiana.
Red (officially called *Red River of the North*) (545 mi.; 877 km): From junction of Otter Tail R. and Bois de Sioux R. in Minnesota to Lake Winnipeg in Manitoba.
Republican (445 mi.; 716 km): From junction of North Fork and Arikaree R. in Nebraska to junction with Smoky Hill R. in Kansas to form Kansas R.
Rio Grande (1,885 mi.; 3,034 km): From San Juan Co. in Colorado to Gulf of Mexico.
Roanoke (380 mi.; 612 km): From junction of forks in Montgomery Co. in Virginia to Albemarle Sound in North Carolina.
Sabine (380 mi.; 612 km): From junction of forks in Hunt Co. in Texas to Sabine Lake between Texas and Louisiana.
Sacramento (377 mi.; 607 km): From Siskiyou Co. in California to Suisun Bay.
Saint Francis (425 mi.; 684 km): From Iron Co. in Missouri to Mississippi R. in Arkansas.
Salmon (420 mi.; 676 km): From Custer Co. in Idaho to Snake R.
San Joaquin (350 mi.; 563 km): From junction of forks in Madera Co. in California to Suisun Bay.
San Juan (360 mi.; 579 km): From Archuleta Co. in Colorado to Colorado R. in Utah.
Santee-Wateree-Catawba (538 mi.; 866 km): From McDowell Co. in North Carolina to Atlantic Ocean in South Carolina.
Smoky Hill (540 mi.; 869 km): From Cheyenne Co. in Colorado to junction with Republican R. in Kansas to form Kansas R.
Snake (1,038 mi.; 1,670 km): From Ocean Plateau in Wyoming to Columbia R. in Washington.
South Platte (424 mi ; 682 km): From Park Co. in Colorado to junction with North Platte R. in Nebraska to form Platte R.
Susquehanna (444 mi.; 715 km): From Otsego Lake in New York to Chesapeake Bay in Maryland.
Tanana (620 mi.; 998 km): From Wrangell Mts. in Yukon Territory, Canada, to Yukon R. in Alaska.
Tennessee (652 mi.; 1,049 km): From junction of Holston R. and French Broad R. in Tennessee to Ohio R. in Kentucky.
Tennessee-French Broad (900 mi.; 1,448 km): From Bland Co. in Virginia to Ohio R. at Paducah in Kentucky.
Tombigbee (525 mi.; 845 km): From junction of forks in Itawamba Co. in Mississippi to Mobile R. in Alabama.
Trinity (360 mi.; 579 km): From junction of forks in Dallas Co. in Texas to Galveston Bay.
Wabash (529 mi.; 851 km): From Darke Co. in Ohio to Ohio R. between Illinois and Indiana.
Washita (500 mi.; 805 km): From Hemphill Co. in Texas to Red R. in Oklahoma.
White (720 mi.; 1,159 km): From Madison Co. in Arkansas to Mississippi R.
Wisconsin (430 mi.; 692 km): From Vilas Co. in Wisconsin to Mississippi R.
Yellowstone (671 mi.; 1,080 km): From Park Co. in Wyoming to Missouri R. in North Dakota.
Yukon (1,770 mi.; 2,848 km): From junction of Lewes R. and Pelly R. in Yukon Territory, Canada, to Bering Sea in Alaska.

Longitude and Latitude of U.S. and Canadian Cities

(and time corresponding to 12:00 noon, eastern standard time)

City	Long. w °	'	Lat. n °	'	Time
Albany, N.Y.	73	45	42	40	12:00 noon
Amarillo, Tex.	101	50	35	11	11:00 a.m.
Anchorage, Alaska	149	54	61	13	7:00 a.m.
Atlanta	84	23	33	45	12:00 noon
Atlantic City, N.J.	74	25	39	22	12:00 noon
Austin, Nev.	117	4	39	29	9:00 a.m.
Baker, Ore.	117	50	44	47	9:00 a.m.
Baltimore	76	38	39	18	12:00 noon
Bangor, Me.	68	47	44	48	12:00 noon
Birmingham, Ala.	86	50	33	30	11:00 a.m.
Bismarck, N.D.	100	47	46	48	11:00 a.m.
Boise, Idaho	116	13	43	36	10:00 a.m.
Boston	71	5	42	21	12:00 noon
Buffalo, N.Y.	78	50	42	55	12:00 noon
Calgary, Alberta	114	1	51	1	10:00 a.m.
Carlsbad, N.M.	104	15	32	26	10:00 a.m.
Charleston, S.C.	79	56	32	47	12:00 noon
Charleston, W.Va.	81	38	38	21	12:00 noon
Charlotte, N.C.	80	50	35	14	12:00 noon
Cheyenne, Wyo.	104	52	41	9	10:00 a.m.
Chicago	87	37	41	50	11:00 a.m.
Cincinnati	84	30	39	8	12:00 noon
Cleveland	81	37	41	28	12:00 noon
Columbia, S.C.	81	2	34	0	12:00 noon
Columbus, Ohio	83	1	40	0	12:00 noon
Dallas	96	46	32	46	11:00 a.m.
Denver	105	0	39	45	10:00 a.m.
Des Moines, Iowa	93	37	41	35	11:00 a.m.
Detroit	83	3	42	20	12:00 noon
Dubuque, Iowa	90	40	42	31	11:00 a.m.
Duluth, Minn.	92	5	46	49	11:00 a.m.
Eastport, Me.	67	0	44	54	12:00 noon
El Centro, Calif.	115	33	32	38	9:00 a.m.
El Paso	106	29	31	46	10:00 a.m.
Eugene, Ore.	123	5	44	3	9:00 a.m.
Fargo, N.D.	96	48	46	52	11:00 a.m.
Flagstaff, Ariz.	111	41	35	13	10:00 a.m.
Fresno, Calif.	119	48	36	44	9:00 a.m.
Garden City, Kan.	100	53	37	58	10:00 a.m.
Grand Junction, Colo.	108	33	39	5	10:00 a.m.
Grand Rapids, Mich.	85	40	42	58	12:00 noon
Havre, Mont.	109	43	48	33	10:00 a.m.
Helena, Mont.	112	2	46	35	10:00 a.m.
Honolulu	157	50	21	18	7:00 a.m.
Hoquiam, Wash.	123	54	46	59	9:00 a.m.
Hot Springs, Ark.	93	3	34	31	11:00 a.m.
Idaho Falls, Idaho	112	1	43	30	10:00 a.m.
Indianapolis	86	10	39	46	12:00 noon
Jackson, Miss.	90	12	32	20	11:00 a.m.
Jacksonville, Fla.	81	40	30	22	12:00 noon
Juneau, Alaska	134	24	58	18	9:00 a.m.
Kansas City, Mo.	94	35	39	6	11:00 a.m.
Key West, Fla.	81	48	24	33	12:00 noon
Kingston, Ont.	76	30	44	15	12:00 noon
Klamath Falls, Ore.	121	44	42	10	9:00 a.m.
Knoxville, Tenn.	83	56	35	57	12:00 noon
Lander, Wyo.	108	40	42	50	10:00 a.m.
Las Vegas, Nev.	115	12	36	10	9:00 a.m.
Lewiston, Idaho	117	2	46	24	9:00 a.m.
Lincoln, Neb.	96	40	40	50	11:00 a.m.
London, Ont.	81	34	43	2	12:00 noon
Los Angeles	118	15	34	3	9:00 a.m.
Louisville, Ky.	85	46	38	15	12:00 noon
Manchester, N.H.	71	30	43	0	12:00 noon
Memphis, Tenn	90	3	35	9	11:00 a.m.
Miami, Fla.	80	12	25	46	12:00 noon
Milwaukee	87	55	43	2	11:00 a.m.
Minneapolis	93	14	44	59	11:00 a.m.
Mobile, Ala.	88	3	30	42	11:00 a.m.
Montgomery, Ala.	86	18	32	21	11:00 a.m.
Montpelier, Vt.	72	32	44	15	12:00 noon
Montreal, Que.	73	35	45	30	12:00 noon
Moose Jaw, Sask.	105	31	50	37	10:00 a.m.
Nashville, Tenn.	86	47	36	10	11:00 a.m.
Needles, Calif.	114	36	34	50	9:00 a.m.
Nelson, B.C.	117	17	49	30	9:00 a.m.
New Haven, Conn.	72	55	41	19	12:00 noon
New Orleans	90	4	29	57	11:00 a.m.
New York	73	58	40	47	12:00 noon
Nogales, Ariz.	110	56	31	21	10:00 a.m.
Nome, Alaska	165	30	64	25	6:00 a.m.
North Platte, Neb.	100	46	41	8	11:00 a.m.
Oklahoma City	97	28	35	26	11:00 a.m.
Ottawa, Ont.	75	43	45	24	12:00 noon
Philadelphia	75	10	39	57	12:00 noon
Phoenix, Ariz.	112	4	33	29	10:00 a.m.
Pierre, S.D.	100	21	44	22	11:00 a.m.
Pittsburgh	79	57	40	27	12:00 noon
Port Arthur, Ont.	89	17	48	30	12:00 noon
Portland, Me.	70	15	43	40	12:00 noon
Portland, Ore.	122	41	45	31	9:00 a.m.
Providence, R.I.	71	24	41	50	12:00 noon
Quebec, Que.	71	11	46	49	12:00 noon
Raleigh, N.C.	78	39	35	46	12:00 noon
Reno, Nev.	119	49	39	30	9:00 a.m.
Richfield, Utah	112	5	38	46	10:00 a.m.
Richmond, Va.	77	29	37	33	12:00 noon
Roanoke, Va.	79	57	37	17	12:00 noon
Sacramento, Calif.	121	30	38	35	9:00 a.m.
St. John, N.B.	66	10	45	18	1:00 p.m.
St. Louis	90	12	38	35	11:00 a.m.
Salmon, Idaho	113	54	45	11	10:00 a.m.
Salt Lake City, Utah	111	54	40	46	10:00 a.m.
San Antonio	98	33	29	23	11:00 a.m.
San Diego, Calif.	117	10	32	42	9:00 a.m.
San Francisco	122	26	37	47	9:00 a.m.
San Juan, P.R.	66	10	18	30	1:00 p.m.
Santa Fe, N.M.	105	57	35	41	10:00 a.m.
Sault Ste. Marie, Mich.	84	21	46	30	11:00 a.m.
Savannah, Ga.	81	5	32	5	12:00 noon
Scranton, Pa.	75	39	41	24	12:00 noon
Seattle	122	20	47	37	9:00 a.m.
Shreveport, La.	93	42	32	28	11:00 a.m.
Sioux Falls, S.D.	96	44	43	33	11:00 a.m.
Sitka, Alaska	135	15	57	10	9:00 a.m.
Spokane, Wash.	117	26	47	40	9:00 a.m.
Springfield, Ill.	89	38	39	48	11:00 a.m.
Springfield, Mass.	72	34	42	6	12:00 noon
Springfield, Mo.	93	17	37	13	11:00 a.m.
Syracuse, N.Y.	76	8	43	2	12:00 noon
Tampa, Fla.	82	27	27	57	12:00 noon
Toronto, Ont.	79	24	43	40	12:00 noon
Trinidad, Colo.	104	30	37	10	10:00 a.m.
Victoria, B.C.	123	21	48	25	9:00 a.m.
Watertown, N.Y.	75	55	43	58	12:00 noon
Wichita, Kan.	97	17	37	43	11:00 a.m.
Wilmington, N.C.	77	57	34	14	12:00 noon
Winnipeg, Man.	97	7	49	54	11:00 a.m.

Coastline of the United States

State	Lengths, statute miles General coastline[1]	Tidal shoreline[2]	State	Lengths, statute miles General coastline[1]	Tidal shoreline[2]
Atlantic Coast:			Gulf Coast:		
Maine	228	3,478	Florida (Gulf)	770	5,095
New Hampshire	13	131	Alabama	53	607
Massachusetts	192	1,519	Mississippi	44	359
Rhode Island	40	384	Louisiana	397	7,721
Connecticut	—	618	Texas	367	3,359
New York	127	1,850	Total Gulf coast	1,631	17,141
New Jersey	130	1,792	Pacific Coast:		
Pennsylvania	—	89	California	840	3,427
Delaware	28	381	Oregon	296	1,410
Maryland	31	3,190	Washington	157	3,026
Virginia	112	3,315	Hawaii	750	1,052
North Carolina	301	3,375	Alaska (Pacific)	5,580	31,383
South Carolina	187	2,876	Total Pacific coast	7,623	40,298
Georgia	100	2,344	Arctic Coast:		
Florida (Atlantic)	580	3,331	Alaska (Arctic)	1,060	2,521
Total Atlantic coast	2,069	28,673	Total Arctic coast	1,060	2,521
			States Total	**12,383**	**88,633**

1. Figures are lengths of general outline of seacoast. Measurements made with unit measure of 30 minutes of latitude on charts as near scale of 1:1,200,000 as possible. Coastline of bays and sounds is included to point where they narrow to width of unit measure, and distance across at such point is included. 2. Figures obtained in 1939–40 with recording instrument on largest-scale maps and charts then available. Shoreline of outer coast, offshore islands, sounds, bays, rivers, and creeks is included to head of tidewater, or to point where tidal waters narrow to width of 100 feet. *Source:* Department of Commerce, National Oceanic and Atmospheric Administration, National Ocean Survey.

The Continental Divide

The Continental Divide is a ridge of high ground which runs irregularly north and south through the Rocky Mountains and separates eastward-flowing from westward-flowing streams. The waters which flow eastward empty into the Atlantic Ocean, chiefly by way of the Gulf of Mexico; those which flow westward empty into the Pacific.

Volcanic Eruptions Decrease

During 1981, only 47 of the world's volcanoes erupted, which is the lowest number reported since 1970. According to the Smithsonian Institution's Scientific Event Alert Network, 14 volcanoes erupted explosively as compared to 23 in 1980. The yearly average for active volcanoes is about 60 eruptions per year for the last decade.

MAPS

Maps prepared for Information Please Almanac by Hammond Incorporated

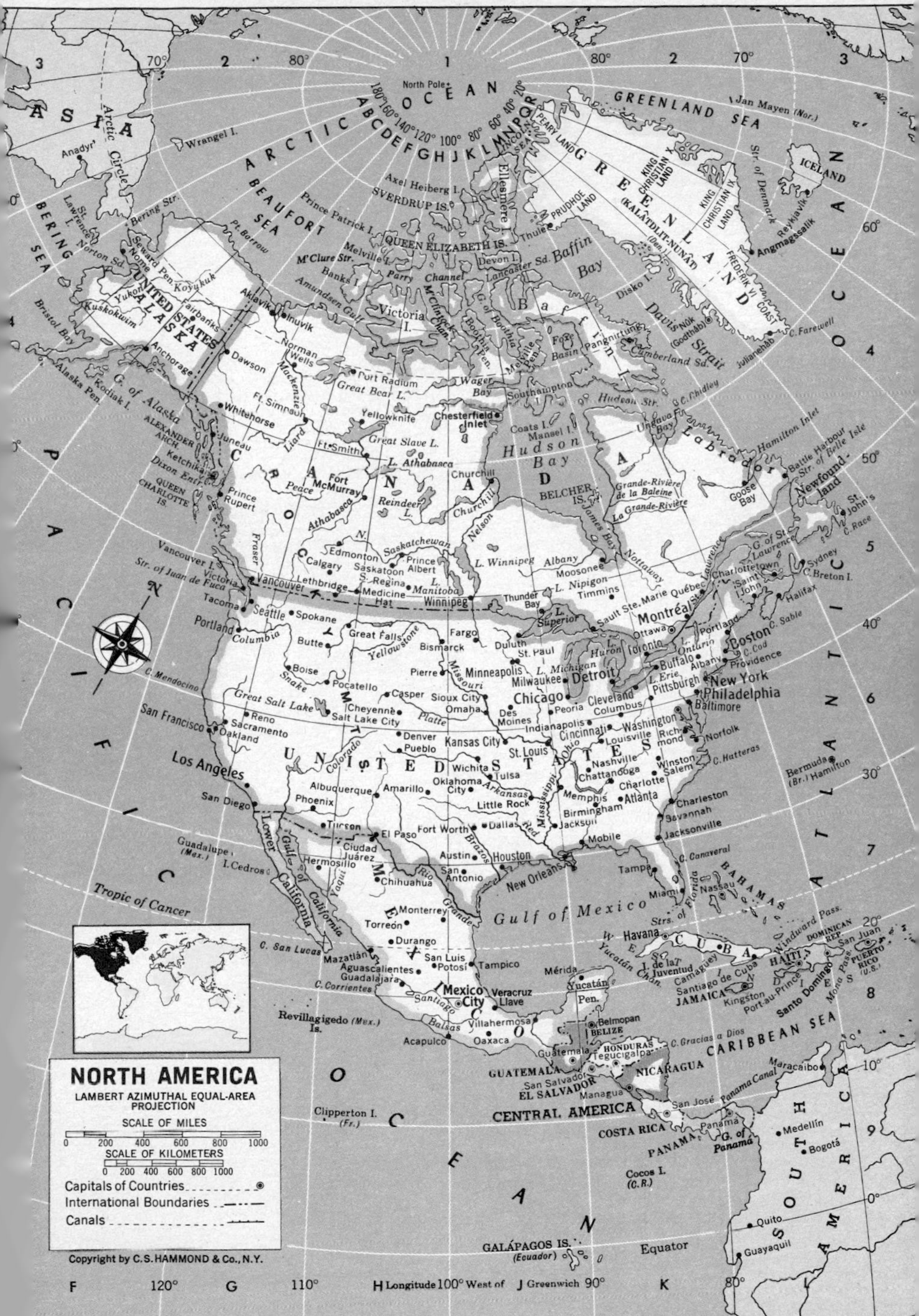

NORTH AMERICA
LAMBERT AZIMUTHAL EQUAL-AREA PROJECTION
SCALE OF MILES
0 200 400 600 800 1000
SCALE OF KILOMETERS
0 200 400 600 800 1000
Capitals of Countries
International Boundaries
Canals
ARCTIC OCEAN
North Pole
GREENLAND SEA
GREENLAND (KALÂTDLIT-NUNÂT) (Den.)
ICELAND
Reykjavík
BEAUFORT SEA
BERING SEA
ASIA
Arctic Circle
Baffin Bay
Davis Strait
Baffin I.
Hudson Bay
Hudson Str.
Labrador
Newfoundland
ATLANTIC OCEAN
PACIFIC OCEAN
CANADA
UNITED STATES
ALASKA
MEXICO
CENTRAL AMERICA
CARIBBEAN SEA
Gulf of Mexico
G. of Alaska
Tropic of Cancer
Equator
SOUTH AMERICA
BAHAMAS
CUBA
JAMAICA
HAITI
DOMINICAN REP.
PUERTO RICO (U.S.)
BELIZE
GUATEMALA
HONDURAS
EL SALVADOR
NICARAGUA
COSTA RICA
PANAMA
GALÁPAGOS IS. (Ecuador)
Anchorage
Fairbanks
Juneau
Whitehorse
Dawson
Yellowknife
Edmonton
Calgary
Vancouver
Victoria
Winnipeg
Regina
Saskatoon
Toronto
Ottawa
Montréal
Québec
Halifax
St. John's
Seattle
Portland
San Francisco
Los Angeles
San Diego
Denver
Chicago
Detroit
Minneapolis
St. Louis
Kansas City
Dallas
Houston
New Orleans
Atlanta
Miami
Washington
Philadelphia
New York
Boston
Havana
Mexico City
Monterrey
Guadalajara
Acapulco
Guatemala
Tegucigalpa
San Salvador
Managua
San José
Panamá
Kingston
Santo Domingo
Port-au-Prince
San Juan
Bogotá
Quito
Guayaquil
Copyright by C.S.HAMMOND & Co., N.Y.
F 120° G 110° H Longitude 100° West of J Greenwich 90° K 80°

WASHINGTON
OREGON
CALIFORNIA
NEVADA
IDAHO
MONTANA
WYOMING
UTAH
COLORADO
ARIZONA
NEW MEXICO
NORTH DAKOTA
SOUTH DAKOTA
NEBRASKA
CANADA
MEXICO
PACIFIC OCEAN
ROCKY MOUNTAINS
Sierra Nevada
Cascade Ra.
Bitterroot Ra.
Seattle
Tacoma
Spokane
Portland
Salem
Eugene
Boise
Sacramento
San Francisco
Oakland
San Jose
Fresno
Los Angeles
Long Beach
San Diego
Reno
Las Vegas
Salt Lake City
Denver
Phoenix
Tucson
Albuquerque
Santa Fe
El Paso
Great Falls
Helena
Billings
Butte
Cheyenne
Casper
Vancouver
Calgary
Saskatoon
Regina
Great Salt Lake
L. Mead
Lake Powell
Gulf of California
Lower California
YELLOWSTONE NAT'L. PARK
GLACIER NAT'L. PARK
YOSEMITE NAT'L. PARK
GRAND CANYON NAT'L. PARK
Mt. Rainier 14,410 ft. (4392 m.)
Mt. Shasta 14,162 ft. (4317 m.)
Mt. Whitney 14,494 ft. (4418 m.)
Borah Pk. 12,662 ft. (3859 m.)
Gannett Pk. 13,804 ft. (4207 m.)
Mt. Elbert 14,433 ft. (4399 m.)
Pikes Peak 14,110 ft. (4301 m.)
Mt. Wilson 14,246 ft. (4342 m.)
Blanca Pk. 14,317 ft. (4364 m.)
Wheeler Peak 13,161 ft. (4011 m.)
ARCTIC OCEAN
U.S.S.R.
BERING SEA
ALASKA
Alaska Range
Brooks Range
Fairbanks
Anchorage
Nome
Juneau
Gulf of Alaska
Mt. McKinley 20,320 ft. (6194 m.)
Mt. St. Elias 18,008 ft. (5489 m.)
Same scale as Alaska map
Attu I.
Kiska I.
Amchitka I.
Aleutian Is.
Atka
Longitude West of Greenwich 156°
HAWAII
PACIFIC OCEAN
Kauai
Oahu
Honolulu
Molokai
Lanai
Maui
Hawaii
Hilo
Mauna Kea 13,796 ft. (4205 m.)
Mauna Loa 13,677 ft. (4169 m.)
Midway Is. (U. S.)
Tropic of Cancer

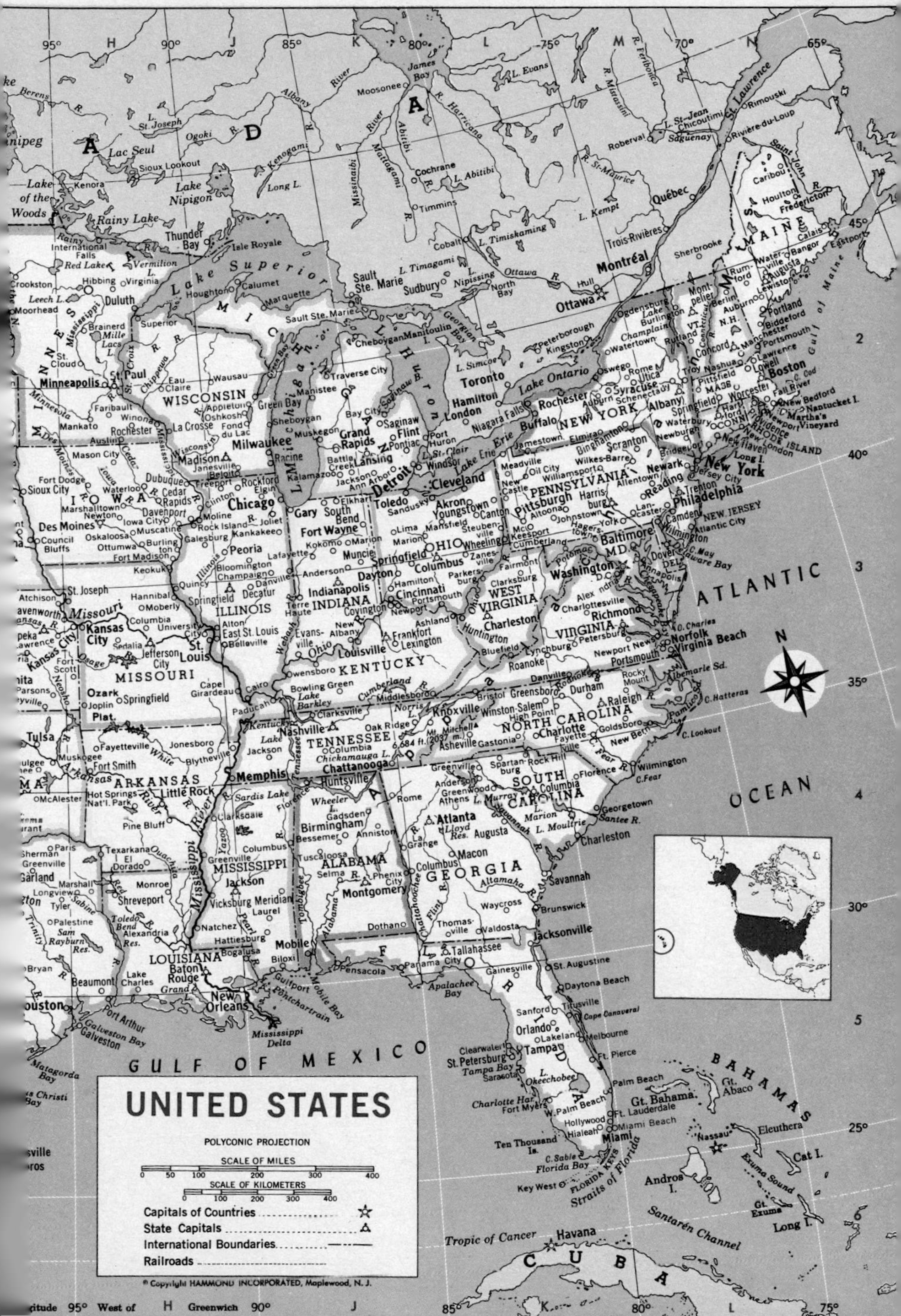
UNITED STATES
POLYCONIC PROJECTION
SCALE OF MILES
0 50 100 200 300 400
SCALE OF KILOMETERS
0 100 200 300 400
Capitals of Countries
State Capitals
International Boundaries
Railroads
© Copyright HAMMOND INCORPORATED, Maplewood, N. J.
ATLANTIC
OCEAN
GULF OF MEXICO
BAHAMAS
CUBA
Longitude 95° West of H Greenwich 90°

CANADA
CONIC PROJECTION
SCALE OF MILES
0 100 200 300 400 500
SCALE OF KILOMETRES
0 100 200 300 400 500
Capitals of Countries
Provincial & Territorial Capitals
Canals
Copyright by C.S. Hammond & Co., N.Y.
GREENLAND
BAFFIN BAY
DAVIS STRAIT
ATLANTIC OCEAN
BEAUFORT SEA
HUDSON BAY
BAFFIN ISLAND
DISTRICT OF FRANKLIN
DISTRICT OF KEEWATIN
DISTRICT OF MACKENZIE
NORTHWEST TERRITORIES
YUKON
BRITISH COLUMBIA
ALBERTA
SASKATCHEWAN
MANITOBA
ONTARIO
QUEBEC
NEWFOUNDLAND
NOVA SCOTIA
NEW BRUNSWICK
ALASKA
UNITED STATES
ROCKY MOUNTAINS
COAST MTS.
Victoria I.
Banks Island
Ottawa
Toronto
Montréal
Québec
Winnipeg
Regina
Edmonton
Victoria
Vancouver
Halifax
Fredericton
Whitehorse
Yellowknife
Churchill
Lake Winnipeg
Lake Superior
Lake Michigan
Lake Huron
Lake Erie
James Bay
Hudson Str.
Great Bear Lake
Great Slave Lake
L. Athabasca
Mt. Logan 19,524
Mt. St. Elias 18,008
Mt. Waddington 13,260
Minneapolis
Detroit
Chicago
Buffalo
New York
Boston
Seattle
Portland
Fairbanks
Juneau
Windsor
London
Hamilton
Kitchener
Niagara Falls
St. Catharines
Sarnia
Chatham
Oshawa
Sherbrooke
Granby
Drummondville
St.-Hyacinthe
Valleyfield
St.-Jean
Laval
Verdun
Lachine
Joliette
Sorel

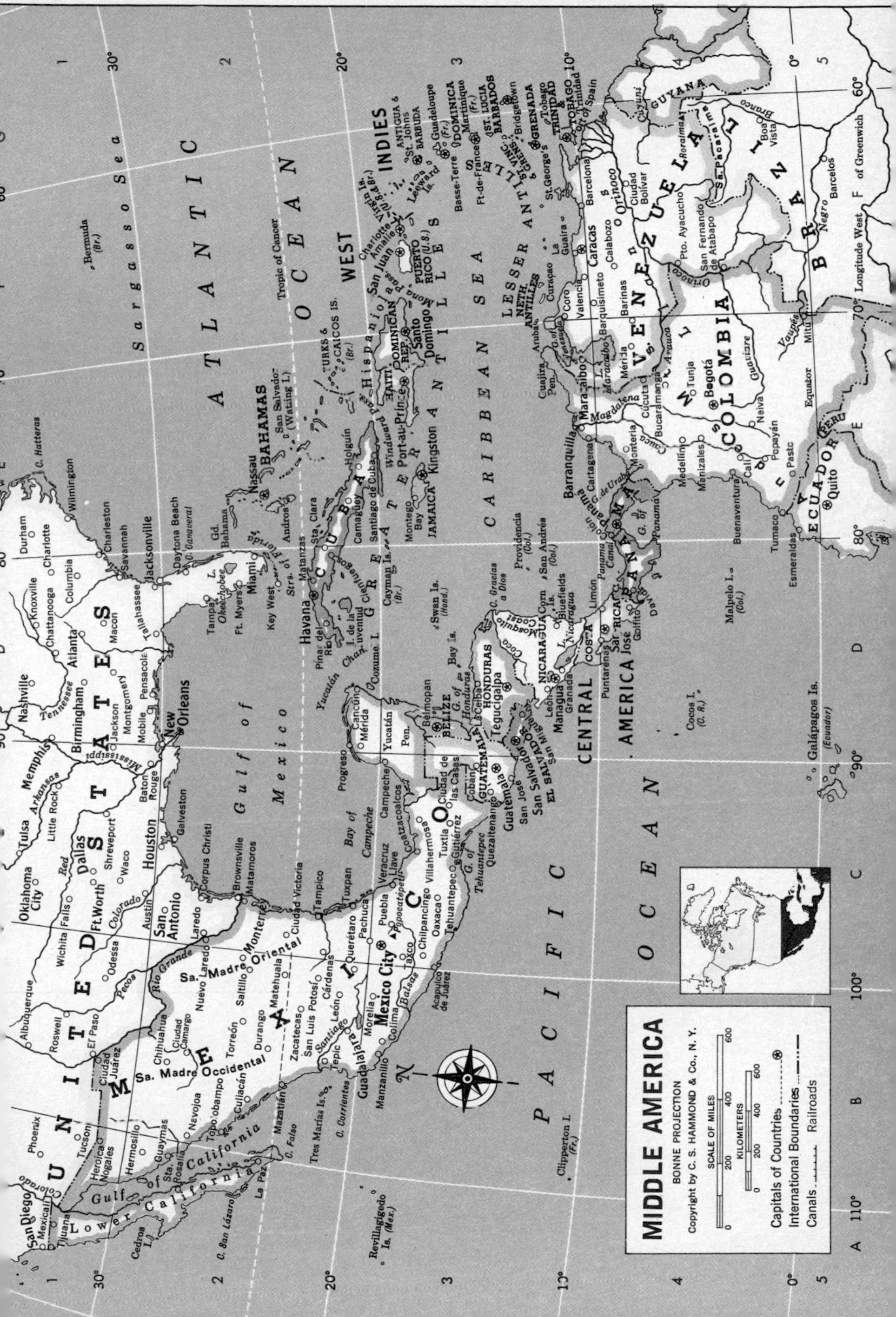

MIDDLE AMERICA
BONNE PROJECTION
Copyright by C. S. HAMMOND & Co., N. Y.
SCALE OF MILES
0 200 400 600
KILOMETERS
0 200 400 600
Capitals of Countries
International Boundaries
Canals
Railroads
Longitude West of Greenwich
UNITED STATES
MEXICO
ATLANTIC OCEAN
PACIFIC OCEAN
Gulf of Mexico
Sargasso Sea
CARIBBEAN SEA
WEST INDIES
GREATER ANTILLES
LESSER ANTILLES
CENTRAL AMERICA
BAHAMAS
CUBA
HAITI
DOMINICAN REP.
PUERTO RICO (U.S.)
JAMAICA
GUATEMALA
BELIZE
HONDURAS
EL SALVADOR
NICARAGUA
COSTA RICA
PANAMA
COLOMBIA
VENEZUELA
ECUADOR
PERU
BRAZIL
GUYANA
NETH. ANTILLES
TURKS & CAICOS IS. (Br.)
Bermuda (Br.)
Tropic of Cancer
Gulf of California
Lower California
Sa. Madre Occidental
Sa. Madre Oriental
Bay of Campeche
Yucatán Pen.
Yucatán Chan.
Mexico City
Guadalajara
Monterrey
Havana
Nassau
Port-au-Prince
Santo Domingo
San Juan
Kingston
Guatemala
Belmopan
Tegucigalpa
San Salvador
Managua
San José
Panamá
Bogotá
Caracas
Quito
Houston
Dallas
Ft. Worth
San Antonio
New Orleans
Miami
Jacksonville
Atlanta
Birmingham
Memphis
Nashville
Oklahoma City
Tulsa
El Paso
Phoenix
Tucson
San Diego
Tijuana
Revillagigedo Is. (Mex.)
Clipperton I. (Fr.)
Cocos I. (C. R.)
Galápagos Is. (Ecuador)
Malpelo I. (Col.)

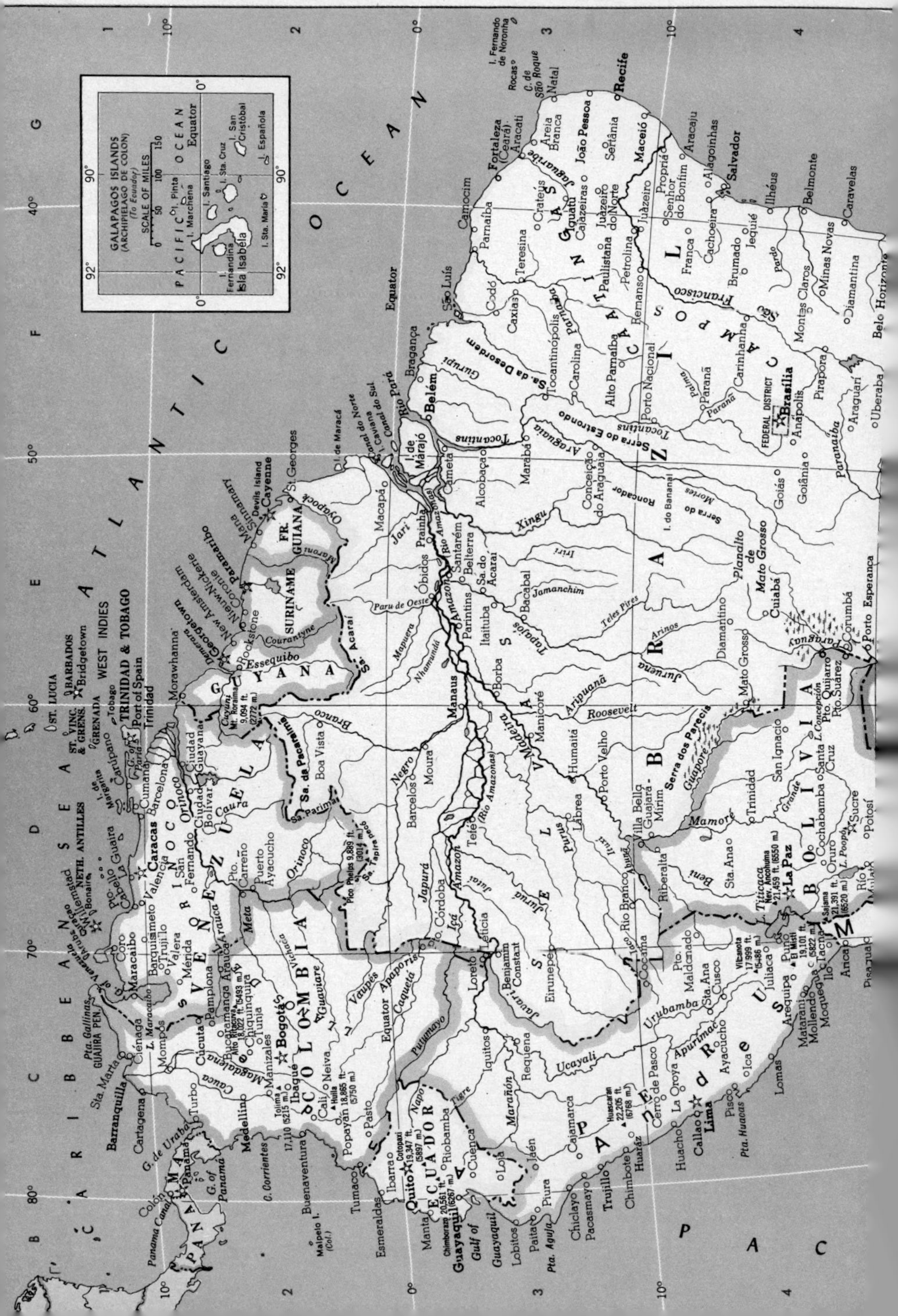
CARIBBEAN SEA
ATLANTIC OCEAN
PACIFIC OCEAN
GALAPAGOS ISLANDS (ARCHIPIELAGO DE COLON) (To Ecuador)
SCALE OF MILES
Equator
WEST INDIES
TRINIDAD & TOBAGO
Port of Spain
BARBADOS
Bridgetown
ST. LUCIA
ST. VINC. & GRENS.
GRENADA
NETH. ANTILLES
VENEZUELA
Caracas
Maracaibo
COLOMBIA
Bogotá
Medellín
Barranquilla
Cartagena
PANAMA
Panamá
Panama Canal
ECUADOR
Quito
Guayaquil
PERU
Lima
Callao
BOLIVIA
La Paz
Sucre
GUYANA
Georgetown
SURINAME
Paramaribo
FR. GUIANA
Cayenne
BRAZIL
Brasília
FEDERAL DISTRICT
Belém
Manaus
Recife
Salvador
Fortaleza (Ceará)
São Luís
Natal
João Pessoa
Maceió
Amazon
Orinoco
Madeira
Xingu
Tocantins
Araguaia
Negro
Purus
Juruá
Ucayali
Marañón
Putumayo
Japurá
Tapajós
Paraná
São Francisco
Mato Grosso
Planalto de Mato Grosso
Serra dos Parecis
Cuiabá
Mt. Roraima 9,094 ft. (2772 m.)
Pico Phelps 9,888 ft. (3014 m.)
Chimborazo 20,561 ft. (6267 m.)
Cotopaxi 19,347 ft. (5897 m.)
Huascarán 22,205 ft. (6768 m.)
Titicaca
Gulf of Guayaquil
I. de Marajó
I. Fernando de Noronha

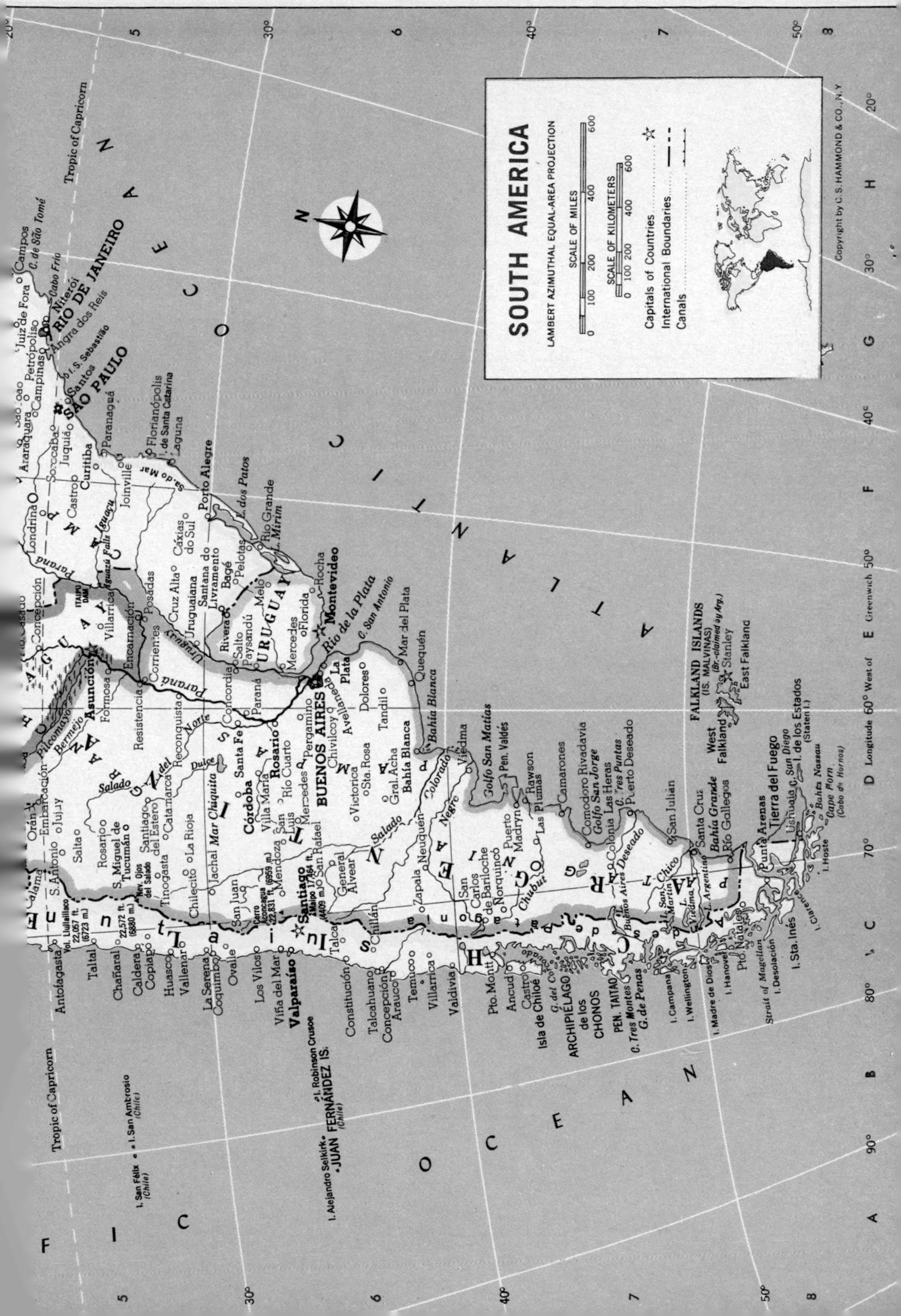
SOUTH AMERICA
LAMBERT AZIMUTHAL EQUAL-AREA PROJECTION
SCALE OF MILES
0 100 200 400 600
SCALE OF KILOMETERS
0 100 200 400 600
Capitals of Countries
International Boundaries
Canals
Copyright by C. S. HAMMOND & CO., N.Y.
PACIFIC OCEAN
ATLANTIC OCEAN
Tropic of Capricorn
ARGENTINA
CHILE
URUGUAY
PARAGUAY
FALKLAND ISLANDS
(IS. MALVINAS)
(Br.-claimed by Arg.)
Stanley
East Falkland
West Falkland
JUAN FERNÁNDEZ IS.
(Chile)
I. Robinson Crusoe
I. Alejandro Selkirk
I. San Félix
I. San Ambrosio
(Chile)
BUENOS AIRES
Montevideo
Asunción
Santiago
Valparaíso
Córdoba
Rosario
Mendoza
Tucumán
La Plata
Mar del Plata
Bahía Blanca
Concepción
Valdivia
Pto. Montt
Isla de Chiloé
ARCHIPIÉLAGO de los CHONOS
PEN. TAITAO
G. de Penas
Strait of Magellan
Punta Arenas
Tierra del Fuego
Ushuaia
I. de los Estados
(Staten I.)
Cape Horn
(Cabo de Hornos)
Río de la Plata
Golfo San Matías
Golfo San Jorge
Bahía Grande
Comodoro Rivadavia
Río Gallegos
Santa Cruz
San Julián
Puerto Deseado
Trelew
Rawson
Puerto Madryn
Viedma
Neuquén
Santa Rosa
Tandil
Santa Fe
Paraná
Corrientes
Resistencia
Posadas
Encarnación
Salta
Jujuy
Antofagasta
Taltal
Chañaral
Copiapó
La Serena
Coquimbo
Talca
Chillán
Temuco
SÃO PAULO
RIO DE JANEIRO
Santos
Curitiba
Porto Alegre
Florianópolis
Pelotas
Rio Grande
L. dos Patos
L. Mirim
Iguaçu Falls
ITAIPU DAM
Cerro Aconcagua 22,831 ft. (6959 m.)
Vol. Llullaillaco 22,057 ft. (6723 m.)
Paraná
Uruguay
Pilcomayo
Bermejo
Salado
Colorado
Negro
Chubut
Deseado
Longitude 60° West of Greenwich
20° 30° 40° 50°
A B C D E F G H
5 6 7 8

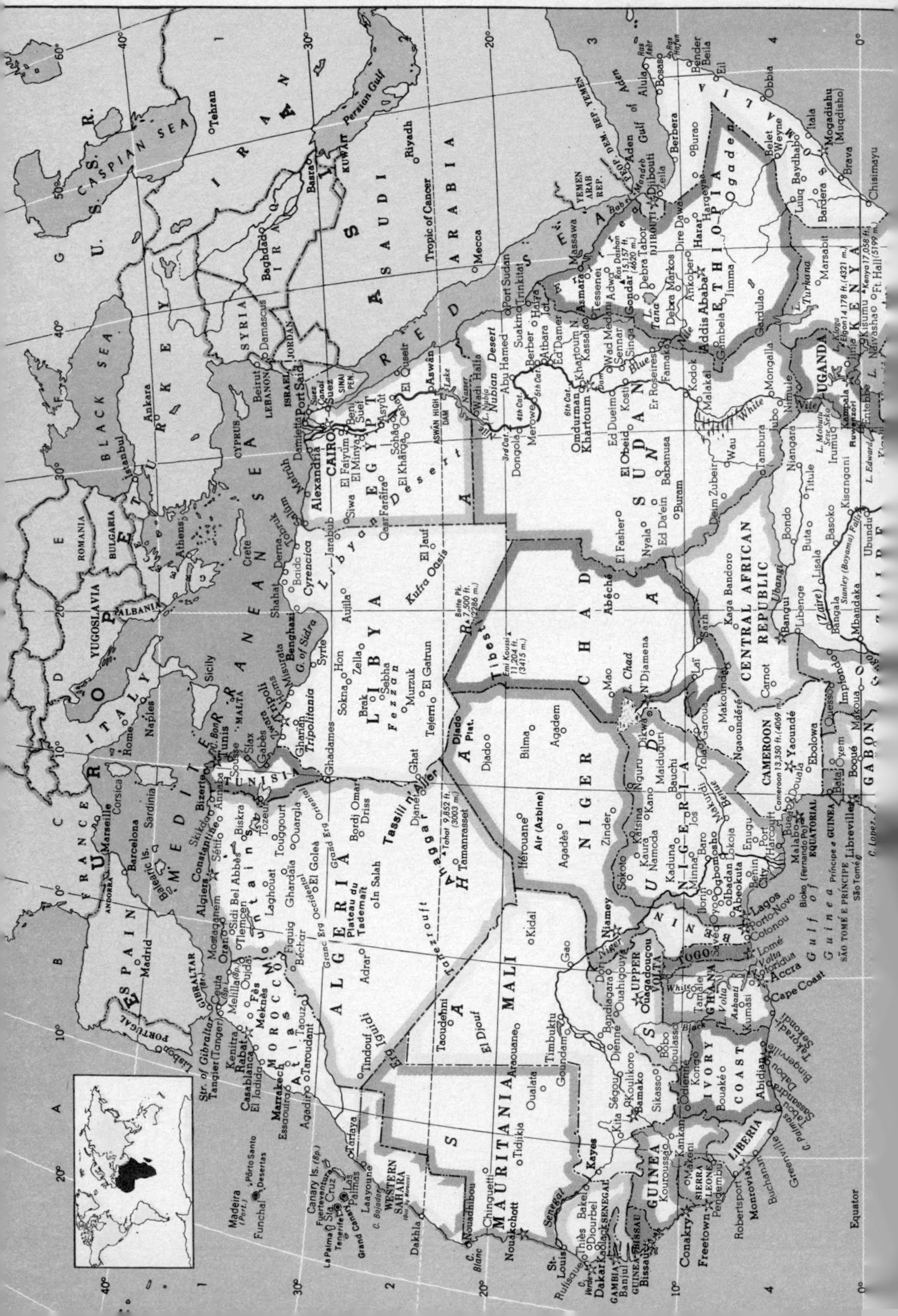

SPAIN
PORTUGAL
FRANCE
ITALY
YUGOSLAVIA
ALBANIA
ROMANIA
BULGARIA
GREECE
TURKEY
U. S. S. R.
BLACK SEA
CASPIAN SEA
IRAN
IRAQ
SYRIA
LEBANON
ISRAEL
JORDAN
KUWAIT
SAUDI ARABIA
Persian Gulf
RED SEA
Gulf of Aden
YEMEN ARAB REP.
PEOP. DEM. REP. YEMEN
MEDITERRANEAN SEA
MOROCCO
ALGERIA
TUNISIA
LIBYA
EGYPT
SUDAN
ETHIOPIA
SOMALIA
KENYA
UGANDA
CHAD
NIGER
MALI
MAURITANIA
WESTERN SAHARA
SENEGAL
GAMBIA
GUINEA-BISSAU
GUINEA
SIERRA LEONE
LIBERIA
IVORY COAST
GHANA
TOGO
BENIN
UPPER VOLTA
NIGERIA
CAMEROON
CENTRAL AFRICAN REPUBLIC
EQUATORIAL GUINEA
GABON
CONGO
ZAIRE
SÃO TOMÉ E PRÍNCIPE
Gulf of Guinea
Tropic of Cancer
Equator
Sahara
Libyan Desert
Nubian Desert
Atlas Mts.
Ahaggar Mts.
Tibesti Mts.
Ogaden
Fezzan
Cyrenaica
Tripolitania
Madrid
Rome
Athens
Ankara
Istanbul
Tehran
Baghdad
Damascus
Beirut
Riyadh
Mecca
Cairo
Alexandria
Port Said
Suez
Aswân
Khartoum
Omdurman
Addis Ababa
Asmara
Djibouti
Aden
Mogadishu
Nairobi
Kampala
Tripoli
Benghazi
Tunis
Algiers
Rabat
Casablanca
Dakar
Nouakchott
Bamako
Ouagadougou
Niamey
N'Djamena
Lagos
Accra
Abidjan
Monrovia
Freetown
Conakry
Bissau
Banjul
Lomé
Porto-Novo
Yaoundé
Bangui
Libreville
Canary Is.
Madeira

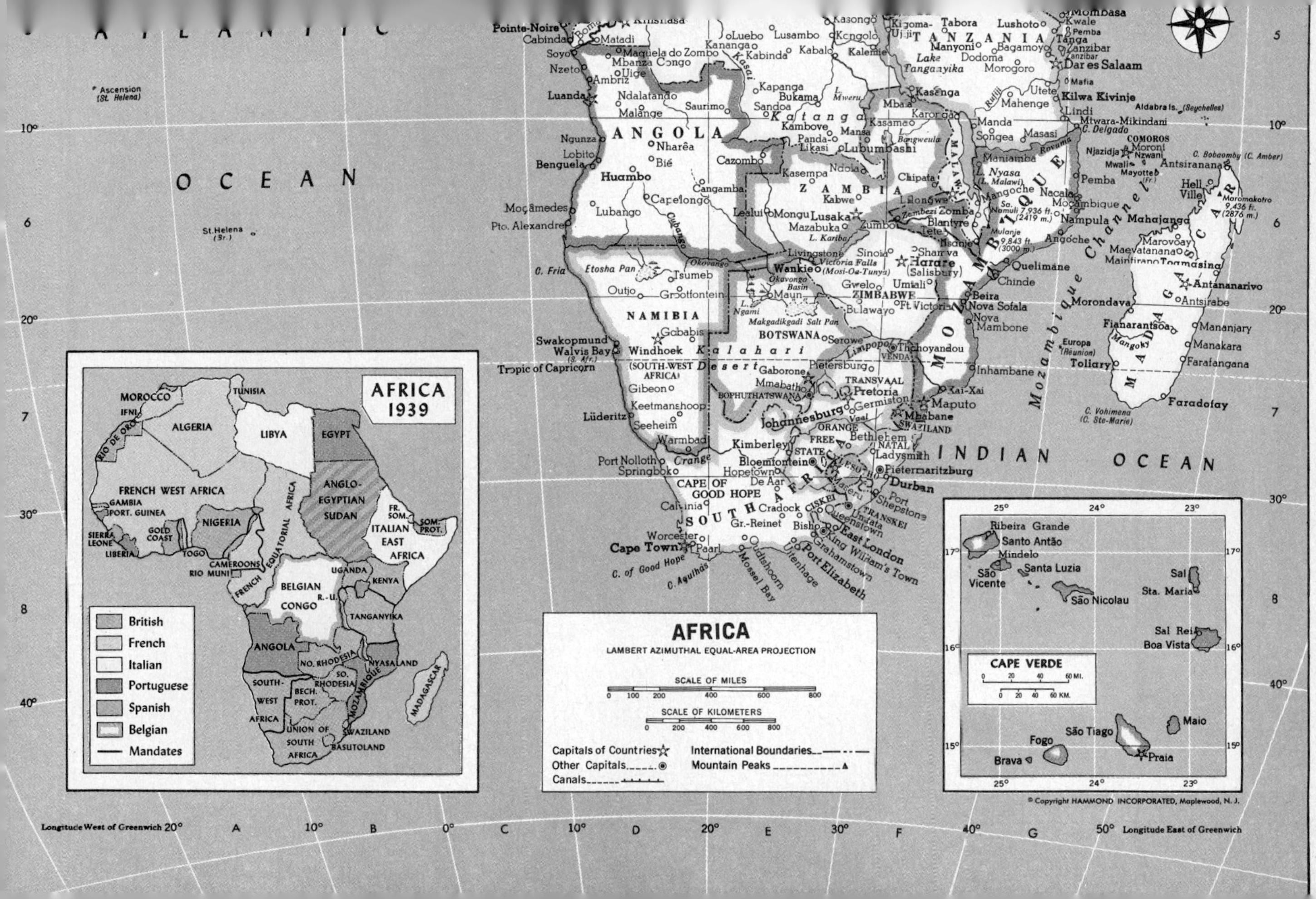
AFRICA
LAMBERT AZIMUTHAL EQUAL-AREA PROJECTION
SCALE OF MILES
0 100 200 400 600 800
SCALE OF KILOMETERS
0 200 400 600 800
Capitals of Countries
Other Capitals
Canals
International Boundaries
Mountain Peaks
ATLANTIC OCEAN
INDIAN OCEAN
Mozambique Channel
Ascension (St. Helena)
St. Helena (Br.)
ANGOLA
ZAMBIA
NAMIBIA (SOUTH-WEST AFRICA)
BOTSWANA
ZIMBABWE
MOZAMBIQUE
TANZANIA
MALAWI
MADAGASCAR
SOUTH AFRICA
SWAZILAND
COMOROS
Kalahari Desert
Katanga
Tropic of Capricorn
Pointe-Noire
Cabinda
Luanda
Benguela
Huambo
Lubango
Moçâmedes
Windhoek
Walvis Bay (S. Afr.)
Swakopmund
Lüderitz
Gaborone
Johannesburg
Pretoria
Bloemfontein
Kimberley
Cape Town
Port Elizabeth
East London
Durban
Pietermaritzburg
Maseru
Mbabane
Maputo
Beira
Quelimane
Nampula
Lusaka
Lubumbashi
Harare (Salisbury)
Bulawayo
Lilongwe
Zomba
Blantyre
Dar es Salaam
Zanzibar
Dodoma
Mombasa
Antananarivo
Mahajanga
Toamasina
Fianarantsoa
Toliary
Moroni
Antsiranana
C. of Good Hope
C. Agulhas
Europa (Réunion)
Aldabra Is. (Seychelles)
AFRICA 1939
British
French
Italian
Portuguese
Spanish
Belgian
Mandates
MOROCCO
IFNI
RIO DE ORO
ALGERIA
TUNISIA
LIBYA
EGYPT
ANGLO-EGYPTIAN SUDAN
FRENCH WEST AFRICA
FRENCH EQUATORIAL AFRICA
ITALIAN EAST AFRICA
FR. SOM.
SOM. PROT.
GAMBIA
PORT. GUINEA
SIERRA LEONE
LIBERIA
GOLD COAST
TOGO
NIGERIA
CAMEROONS
RIO MUNI
BELGIAN CONGO
R.-U.
UGANDA
KENYA
TANGANYIKA
ANGOLA
NO. RHODESIA
SO. RHODESIA
NYASALAND
MOZAMBIQUE
MADAGASCAR
SOUTH-WEST AFRICA
BECH. PROT.
UNION OF SOUTH AFRICA
SWAZILAND
BASUTOLAND
CAPE VERDE
Santo Antão
São Vicente
Mindelo
Santa Luzia
São Nicolau
Sal
Sta. Maria
Sal Rei
Boa Vista
Maio
São Tiago
Praia
Fogo
Brava
Longitude West of Greenwich
Longitude East of Greenwich
© Copyright HAMMOND INCORPORATED, Maplewood, N. J.

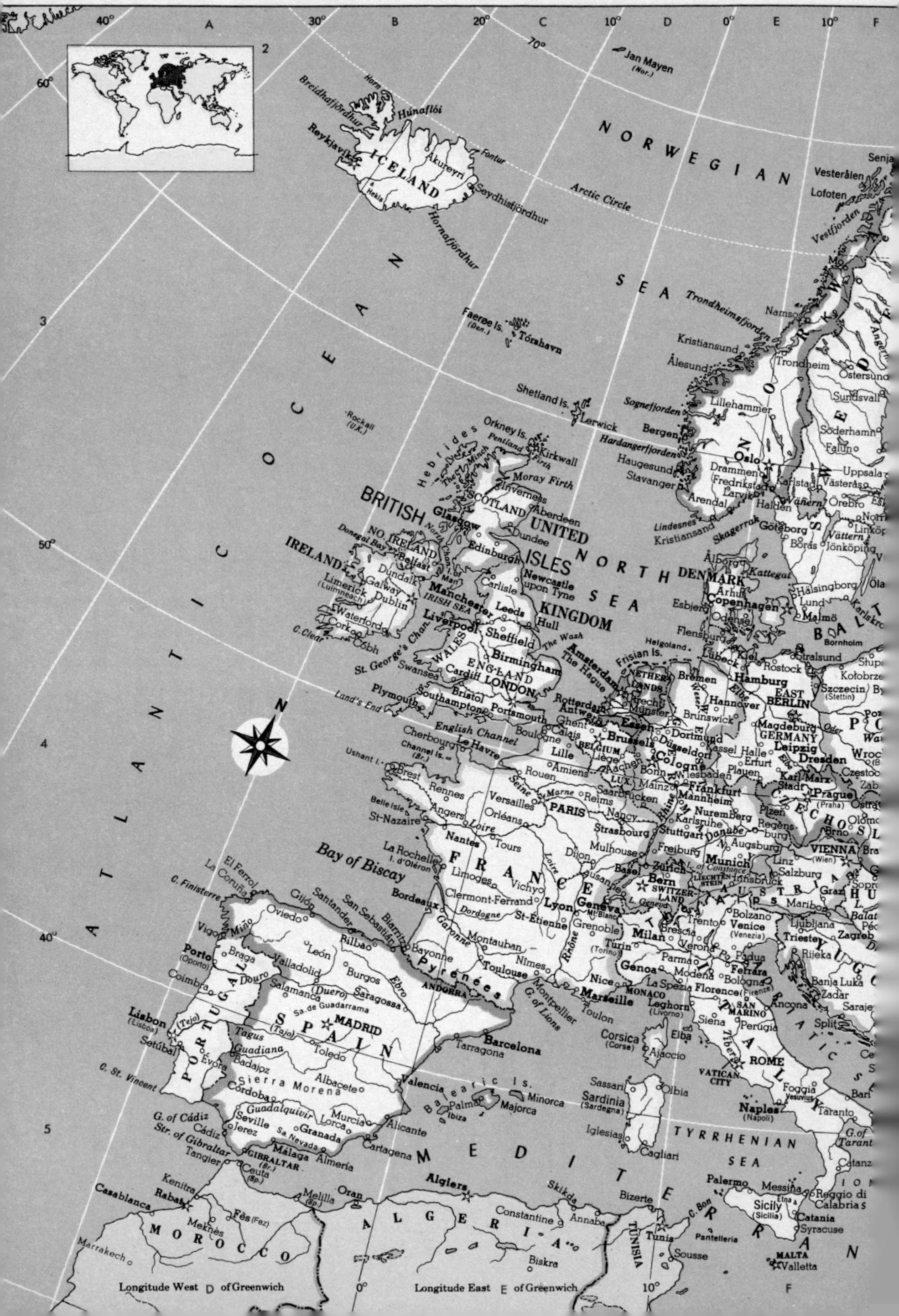

A
B
C
D
E
F
40°
30°
20°
10°
0°
70°
60°
50°
40°
2
3
4
5
Jan Mayen
(Nor.)
Horn
Breidhafjördhur
Húnaflói
Reykjavík
ICELAND
Akureyri
Fontur
Hekla
Seydhisfjördhur
Hornafjördhur
NORWEGIAN
SEA
Arctic Circle
Senja
Vesterålen
Lofoten
Vestfjorden
Mo
Trondheimsfjorden
Namsos
Kristiansund
Ålesund
Trondheim
Östersund
Sundsvall
Lillehammer
Söderhamn
Falun
Faerøe Is.
(Den.)
Tórshavn
Shetland Is.
Lerwick
Sognefjorden
Bergen
Hardangerfjorden
Haugesund
Stavanger
Oslo
Drammen
Fredrikstad
Larvik
Karlstad
Västerås
Uppsala
Arendal
Halden
Vänern
Örebro
Lindesnes
Kristiansand
Skagerrak
Göteborg
Vättern
Linköping
Borås
Jönköping
Ålborg
Kattegat
DENMARK
Århus
Esbjerg
Copenhagen
Odense
Hälsingborg
Lund
Malmö
Bornholm
Rockall
(U.K.)
Orkney Is.
Pentland Firth
Kirkwall
Hebrides
The Minch
Moray Firth
Inverness
BRITISH
SCOTLAND
Aberdeen
Glasgow
UNITED
Dundee
Edinburgh
ISLES
NORTH
SEA
NO. IRELAND
Donegal Bay
Belfast
IRELAND
Dundalk
Newcastle upon Tyne
Limerick
(Luimneach)
Galway
Dublin
Carlisle
Manchester
IRISH SEA
Leeds
KINGDOM
Waterford
Cork
Cobh
C. Clear
Liverpool
Sheffield
Hull
The Wash
WALES
St. George's Chan.
Birmingham
ENGLAND
Swansea
Cardiff
LONDON
Bristol
Plymouth
Southampton
Portsmouth
Land's End
Amsterdam
The Hague
Frisian Is.
Helgoland
Flensburg
Kiel
Lübeck
Rostock
Stralsund
Bremen
Hamburg
NETHERLANDS
Rotterdam
Münster
Hannover
EAST
BERLIN
Szczecin
(Stettin)
Brunswick
Magdeburg
GERMANY
Leipzig
Dresden
Antwerp
Ghent
Essen
Dortmund
Düsseldorf
Kassel
Halle
Erfurt
Brussels
BELGIUM
Liège
Aachen
Cologne
Bonn
Plauen
Karl-Marx-Stadt
Prague
(Praha)
Wiesbaden
Frankfurt
Mainz
Mannheim
LUX.
Saarbrücken
Nuremberg
Regensburg
Karlsruhe
Stuttgart
Danube
Augsburg
Munich
Linz
VIENNA
(Wien)
Salzburg
English Channel
Cherbourg
Le Havre
Channel Is.
(Br.)
Ushant I.
Brest
Boulogne
Calais
Lille
Amiens
Rouen
Seine
Rennes
Versailles
Marne
Reims
PARIS
Belle Isle
Angers
Orléans
St-Nazaire
Loire
Nancy
Strasbourg
Nantes
Tours
Mulhouse
Freiburg
Bay of Biscay
La Rochelle
I. d'Oléron
FRANCE
Dijon
Basel
Zürich
Bern
SWITZERLAND
Lausanne
Limoges
Vichy
Clermont-Ferrand
Lyon
Geneva
Mt. Blanc
Bordeaux
Dordogne
St-Étienne
Grenoble
Garonne
Rhône
Turin
(Torino)
Milan
Brescia
Verona
Venice
(Venezia)
Trento
Bolzano
Innsbruck
AUSTRIA
Graz
Ljubljana
Trieste
Zagreb
Rijeka
Montauban
Bayonne
Biarritz
Nîmes
Toulouse
Montpellier
G. of Lions
Marseille
Toulon
Nice
MONACO
Genoa
Parma
Modena
Padua
Ferrara
Bologna
La Spezia
Florence
(Firenze)
Leghorn
(Livorno)
Siena
SAN MARINO
Perugia
Ancona
Banja Luka
Zadar
Split
Corsica
(Corse)
Ajaccio
Elba
Tiber
ROME
VATICAN CITY
ITALY
El Ferrol
La Coruña
C. Finisterre
Gijón
Santander
San Sebastián
Oviedo
Bilbao
Vigo
Miño
Porto
(Oporto)
Braga
León
Valladolid
Burgos
Ebro
Douro
(Duero)
Coimbra
Salamanca
Saragossa
Pyrénées
ANDORRA
Sa. de Guadarrama
PORTUGAL
Lisbon
(Lisboa)
Tejo
(Tajo)
MADRID
SPAIN
Setúbal
Tagus
Toledo
Guadiana
Évora
Badajoz
Barcelona
Tarragona
C. St. Vincent
Sierra Morena
Albacete
Valencia
Córdoba
Balearic Is.
Minorca
Majorca
Palma
Ibiza
Sassari
Olbia
Sardinia
(Sardegna)
Foggia
Vesuvius
Bari
Naples
(Napoli)
Taranto
G. of Cádiz
Cádiz
Guadalquivir
Seville
Jerez
Lorca
Murcia
Alicante
Granada
Sa. Nevada
Str. of Gibraltar
Tangier
GIBRALTAR
(Br.)
Málaga
Almería
Cartagena
Ceuta
(Sp.)
Iglesias
Cagliari
TYRRHENIAN
SEA
MEDITERRANEAN
Kenitra
Rabat
Casablanca
Melilla
(Sp.)
Oran
Algiers
Skikda
Bizerte
C. Bon
Palermo
Messina
Etna
Reggio di Calabria
Sicily
(Sicilia)
Catania
Syracuse
Meknès
Fès (Fez)
MOROCCO
ALGERIA
Constantine
Annaba
Tunis
TUNISIA
Pantelleria
Sousse
MALTA
Valletta
Marrakech
Biskra
ATLANTIC OCEAN
N
Longitude West
of Greenwich
Longitude East
of Greenwich

EUROPE
LAMBERT AZIMUTHAL EQUAL AREA PROJECTION
SCALE OF MILES
0 100 200 300 400 500
SCALE OF KILOMETERS
0 100 200 300 400 500
Capitals of Countries
International Boundaries
Canals
Copyright by C. S. HAMMOND & CO., N.Y.
BARENTS SEA
White Sea
BLACK SEA
Sea of Azov
CASPIAN SEA
UNION OF SOVIET SOCIALIST REPUBLICS
RUSSIAN SOVIET FEDERATED SOCIALIST REPUBLIC
UKRAINIAN S.S.R.
WHITE RUSSIAN S.S.R.
ESTONIAN S.S.R.
LATVIAN S.S.R.
LITHUANIAN S.S.R.
MOLDAVIAN S.S.R.
GEORGIAN S.S.R.
ARMENIAN S.S.R.
AZERBAIDZHAN S.S.R.
FINLAND
ROMANIA
BULGARIA
GREECE
TURKEY
SYRIA
CYPRUS
IRAN
CRIMEA
KOLA PEN.
KANIN PEN.
Caucasus
Ural
Kolguyev I.
Cheshskaya Bay
Bay of Mezen'
Gulf of Finland
L. Ladoga
L. Onega
L. Peipus
L. Il'men
Rybinsk Res.
Gor'kiy Res.
Kuybyshev Res.
Volgograd Res.
Tsimlyansk Res.
Kremenchug Res.
Kakhovka Res.
Kiev Res.
L. Manych-Gudilo
G. of Kara Bogaz
Murmansk
Archangel
Kandalaksha
Kirovsk
Pechenga
Vadsø
Kem
Onega
Mezen'
Naryan Mar
Vorkuta
Salekhard
Ust Tsilma
Syktyvkar
Kotlas
Nyandoma
Velikiy Ustyug
Petrozavodsk
Sortavala
Joensuu
Kuopio
Vaasa
Oulu
Tornio
Tampere
Turku
Helsinki
Kotka
Vyborg
LENINGRAD
Cherepovets
Vologda
Rybinsk
Yaroslavl
Kostroma
Ivanovo
Kalinin
MOSCOW (Moskva)
Orekhovo Zuyevo
Serpukhov
Tula
Kaluga
Smolensk
Vitebsk
Minsk
Gomel
Pinsk
Brest
Grodno
Białystok
Vilna
Kaunas
Riga
Cēsis
Rēzekne
Jelgava
Daugavpils
Šiauliai
Panevėžys
Tallinn
Narva
Kingisepp
Tartu
Pärnu
Pskov
Velikiye Luki
Bryansk
Orel
Kursk
Voronezh
Tambov
Michurinsk
Penza
Saratov
Engel's
Volgograd (Stalingrad)
Astrakhan
Gur'yev
Ural'sk
Aktyubinsk
Orenburg
Temir
Chelkar
Kuybyshev
Ul'yanovsk
Kazan
Gor'kiy
Dzerzhinsk
Balakhna
Kirov (Vyatka)
Kotel'nich
Izhevsk
Sarapul
Votkinsk Res.
Perm'
Berezniki
Kama Res.
Ufa
Zlatoust
Chelyabinsk
Magnitogorsk
Troitsk
Kustanay
Kurgan
Sverdlovsk
Nizhniy Tagil
Krasnoural'sk
Kirovgrad
Tyumen'
Tobol'sk
Khanty-Mansiysk
Surgut
Berezovo
Kiev
Khar'kov
Poltava
Kremenchug
Dneprodzerzhinsk
Dnepropetrovsk
Zaporozh'ye
Kramatorsk
Donetsk
Makeyevka
Voroshilovgrad
Shakhty
Millerovo
Rostov
Taganrog
Zhdanov
Kirovograd
Krivoy Rog
Nikolayev
Kherson
Odessa
Kishinev
Tiraspol
Bendery
Belgorod Dnestrovskiy
Zhitomir
Rovno
Shepetovka
Vinnitsa
L'vov
Ivano-Frankovsk
Chernovtsy
Przemyśl
Lublin
Mukachevo
Krasnodar
Novorossiysk
Maykop
Armavir
Pyatigorsk
Kislovodsk
Karachayevsk
Elbrus 18,510 ft. (5642 m.)
Ordzhonikidze
Groznyy
Makhachkala
Elista
Kerch
Simferopol'
Sevastopol'
Yalta
Tuapse
Sochi
Sukhumi
Kutaisi
Batumi
Tbilisi
Leninakan
Erivan
Nakhichevan'
Dzhul'fa
Baku
Krasnovodsk
Fort Shevchenko
Satu Mare
Debrecen
Oradea
Cluj-Napoca
Arad
Timişoara
Sibiu
Braşov
Iaşi
Roman
Galaţi
Brăila
Sulina
Constanţa
Ploieşti
Bucharest
Craiova
Iron Gate
Ruse
Pleven
Varna
Sliven
Burgas
Sofia
Plovdiv
Stara Zagora
Niš
Skopje
Edirne
Tekirdağ
ISTANBUL
Bosporus
Sea of Marmara
Dardanelles
Thessaloníki
Lárisa
Vólos
Lésvos
Khíos
Sámos
Athens
Piraeus
Corinth
Kalámai
Rhodes
Iráklion
Khania
Crete
Bursa
Eskişehir
Manisa
İzmir
Afyonkarahisar
Konya
Ankara
Kayseri
Sivas
Maraş
Adana
Tarsus
Mersin
Antalya
Antakya
Aleppo
Latakia
Nicosia
Larnaca
Sinop
Samsun
Trabzon
Erzurum
Ereğli
Kizilirmak
Danube
Dnieper
Dniester
Prut
Siret
Olt
Bug
Vistula
Don
Volga
Oka
Kama
Belaya
Northern Dvina
Pechora
Usa
Ob'
Irtysh
Tobol
Ural
Emba
Araks
Torne
Muonio
Tana
L. Inari
L. Oulu
Gulf of Bothnia
Nordkapp (North Cape)

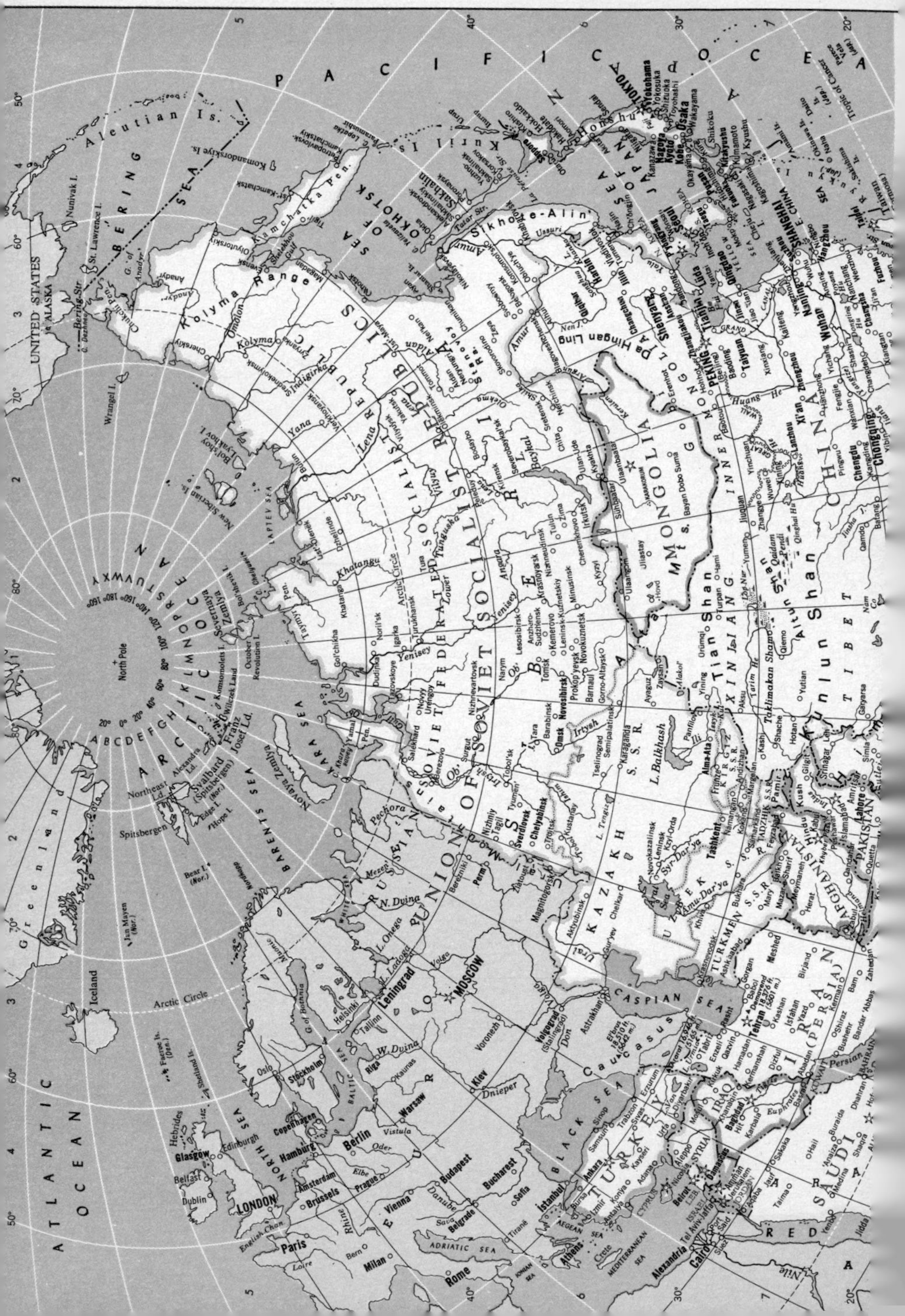

UNION OF SOVIET SOCIALIST REPUBLICS
RUSSIAN SOVIET FEDERATED SOCIALIST REPUBLIC
SIBERIA
ARCTIC OCEAN
ATLANTIC OCEAN
PACIFIC OCEAN
BERING SEA
SEA OF OKHOTSK
SEA OF JAPAN
BARENTS SEA
KARA SEA
LAPTEV SEA
NORTH SEA
BALTIC SEA
BLACK SEA
CASPIAN SEA
ADRIATIC SEA
AEGEAN SEA
MEDITERRANEAN SEA
RED SEA
YELLOW SEA
EAST CHINA SEA
North Pole
Arctic Circle
Tropic of Cancer
Greenland
Iceland
UNITED STATES
ALASKA
Aleutian Is.
Komandorskiye Is.
Kamchatka Pen.
Kuril Is.
Sakhalin
Hokkaido
Honshu
JAPAN
TOKYO
Yokohama
Osaka
Kyoto
Nagoya
Kobe
Kyushu
Shikoku
Sapporo
KOREA
Seoul
Pyongyang
CHINA
PEKING
SHANGHAI
Tianjin
Shenyang
Wuhan
Nanjing
Chongqing
Chengdu
Xi'an
Lanzhou
MONGOLIA
Ulaanbaatar
INNER MONGOLIA
XINJIANG
TIBET
Tian Shan
Altay
Kunlun Shan
Taklimakan Shamo
Altun Shan
Qaidam Pendi
Da Hinggan Ling
Stanovoy Range
Sikhote-Alin'
Kolyma Range
Amur
Lena
Yenisey
Ob'
Irtysh
Angara
Aldan
Kolyma
Indigirka
Yana
Vilyuy
Lower Tunguska
L. Baykal
Vladivostok
Khabarovsk
Magadan
Yakutsk
Irkutsk
Krasnoyarsk
Novosibirsk
Omsk
Norilsk
Tomsk
Barnaul
Novokuznetsk
Chita
New Siberian Is.
Severnaya Zemlya
Franz Josef Ld.
Novaya Zemlya
Svalbard (Spitsbergen) (Nor.)
Wrangel I.
Yamal Pen.
Taymyr Pen.
KAZAKH S.S.R.
UZBEK S.S.R.
TURKMEN S.S.R.
KIRGIZ S.S.R.
TADZHIK S.S.R.
L. Balkhash
Aral Sea
Alma-Ata
Tashkent
Frunze
Karaganda
Semipalatinsk
Sverdlovsk
Chelyabinsk
Perm
Magnitogorsk
Ural Mts.
MOSCOW
Leningrad
Helsinki
Stockholm
Oslo
Copenhagen
Riga
Tallinn
Warsaw
Berlin
Hamburg
Amsterdam
Brussels
Prague
Vienna
Budapest
Bucharest
Belgrade
Sofia
Istanbul
Ankara
Athens
Rome
Milan
Paris
Bern
LONDON
Dublin
Belfast
Glasgow
Edinburgh
Kiev
Volgograd (Stalingrad)
Voronezh
Astrakhan
Dnieper
Volga
Don
Caucasus
TURKEY
SYRIA
IRAQ
IRAN (PERSIA)
AFGHANISTAN
PAKISTAN
SAUDI ARABIA
KUWAIT
Persian Gulf
Baghdad
Tehran
Damascus
Beirut
Cairo
Alexandria
Jerusalem
Amman
ISRAEL
JORDAN
LEB.
CYPRUS
Kabul
Lahore
Meshed
Hindu Kush
Pamir
Hebrides
Shetland Is.
Faeroe Is. (Den.)
Jan Mayen (Nor.)
Bear I. (Nor.)

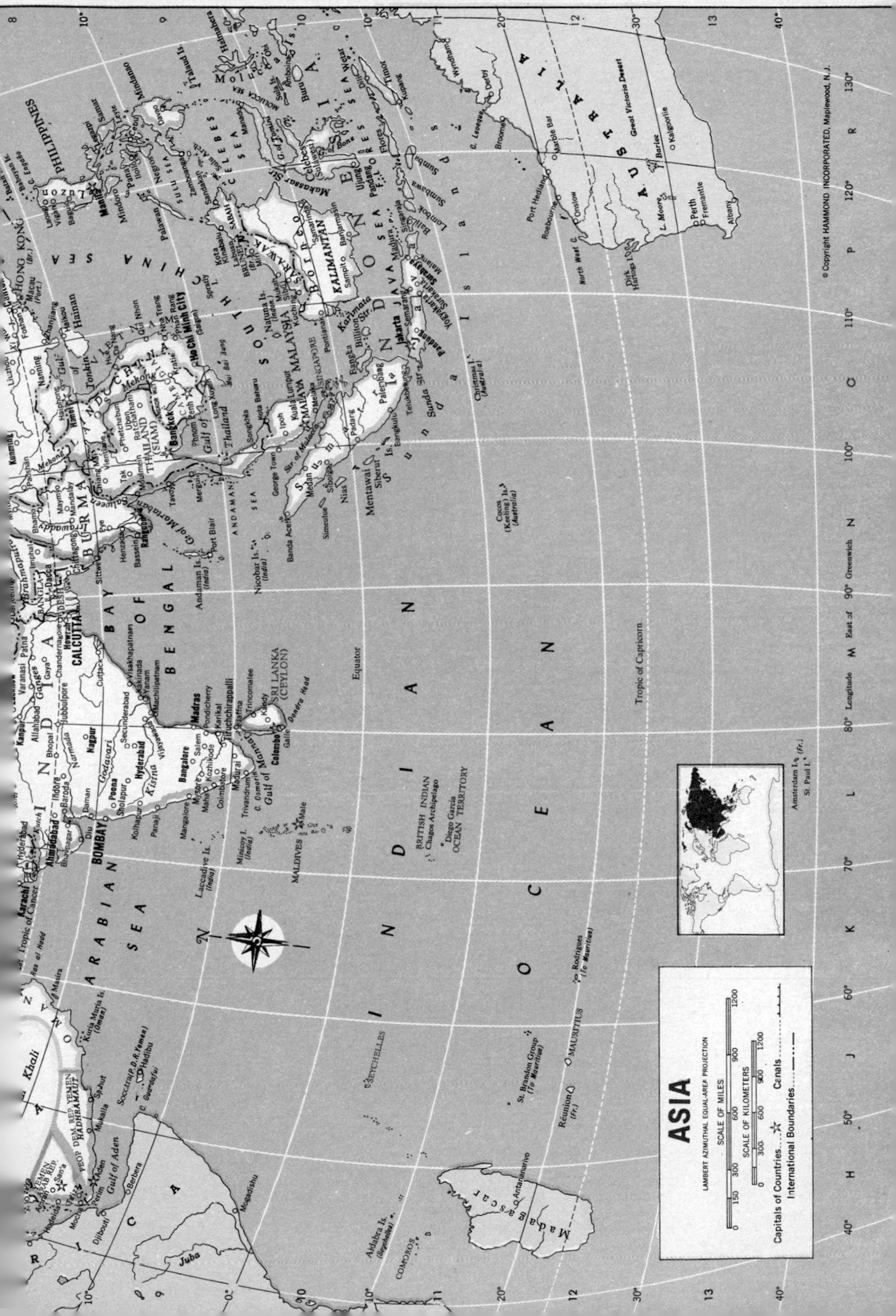
ASIA
LAMBERT AZIMUTHAL EQUAL-AREA PROJECTION
SCALE OF MILES
0 150 300 600 900 1200
SCALE OF KILOMETERS
0 300 600 900 1200
Capitals of Countries
Canals
International Boundaries
© Copyright HAMMOND INCORPORATED, Maplewood, N.J.
INDIAN OCEAN
ARABIAN SEA
BAY OF BENGAL
SOUTH CHINA SEA
INDIA
BURMA
THAILAND (SIAM)
PHILIPPINES
INDONESIA
MALAYSIA
AUSTRALIA
SRI LANKA (CEYLON)
MALDIVES
SEYCHELLES
MAURITIUS
BRITISH INDIAN OCEAN TERRITORY
Madagascar
Equator
Tropic of Capricorn
Tropic of Cancer
Longitude East of Greenwich

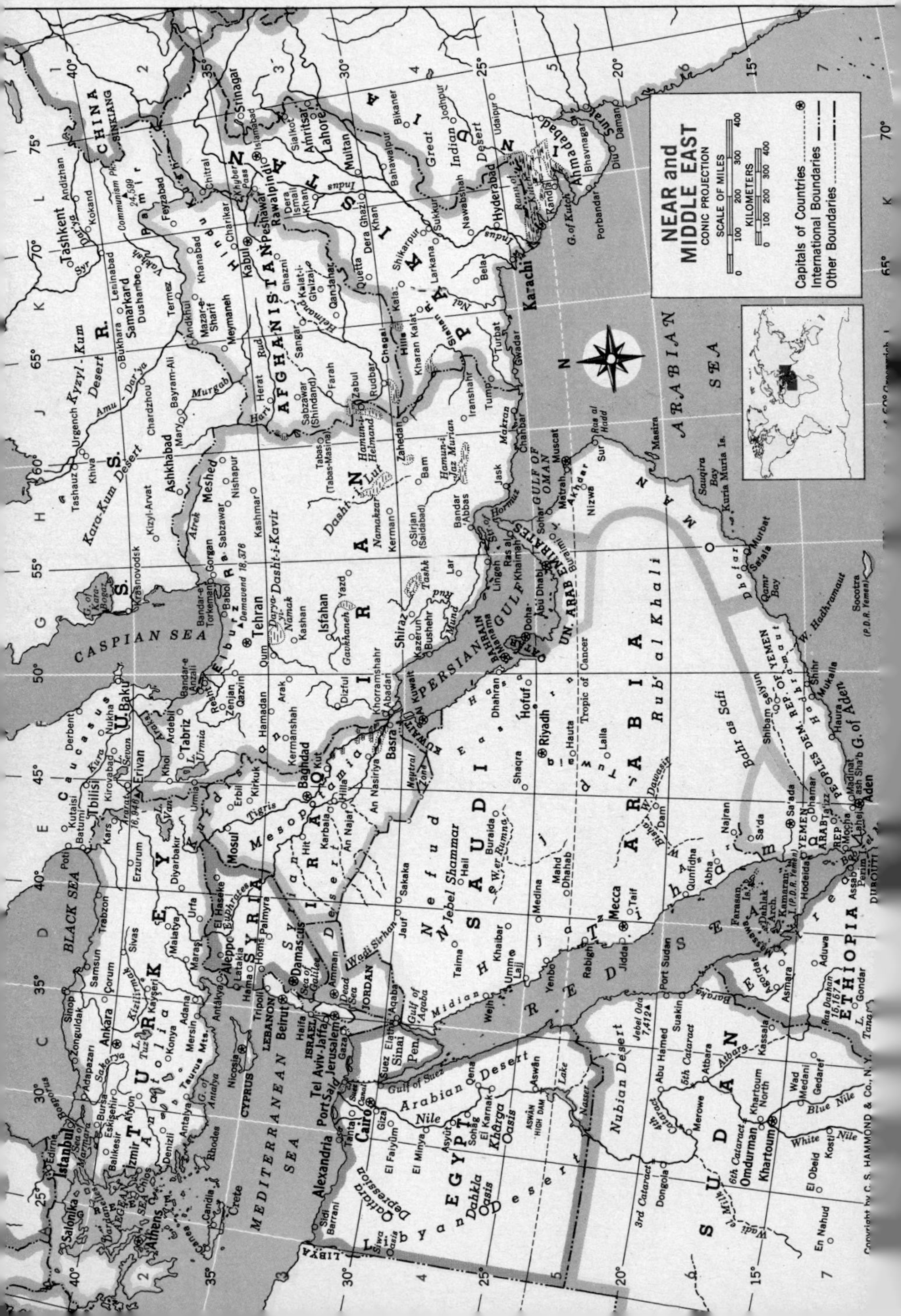
NEAR and MIDDLE EAST
CONIC PROJECTION
SCALE OF MILES
0 100 200 300 400
KILOMETERS
0 100 200 300 400
Capitals of Countries
International Boundaries
Other Boundaries
Copyright by C. S. HAMMOND & Co., N. Y.

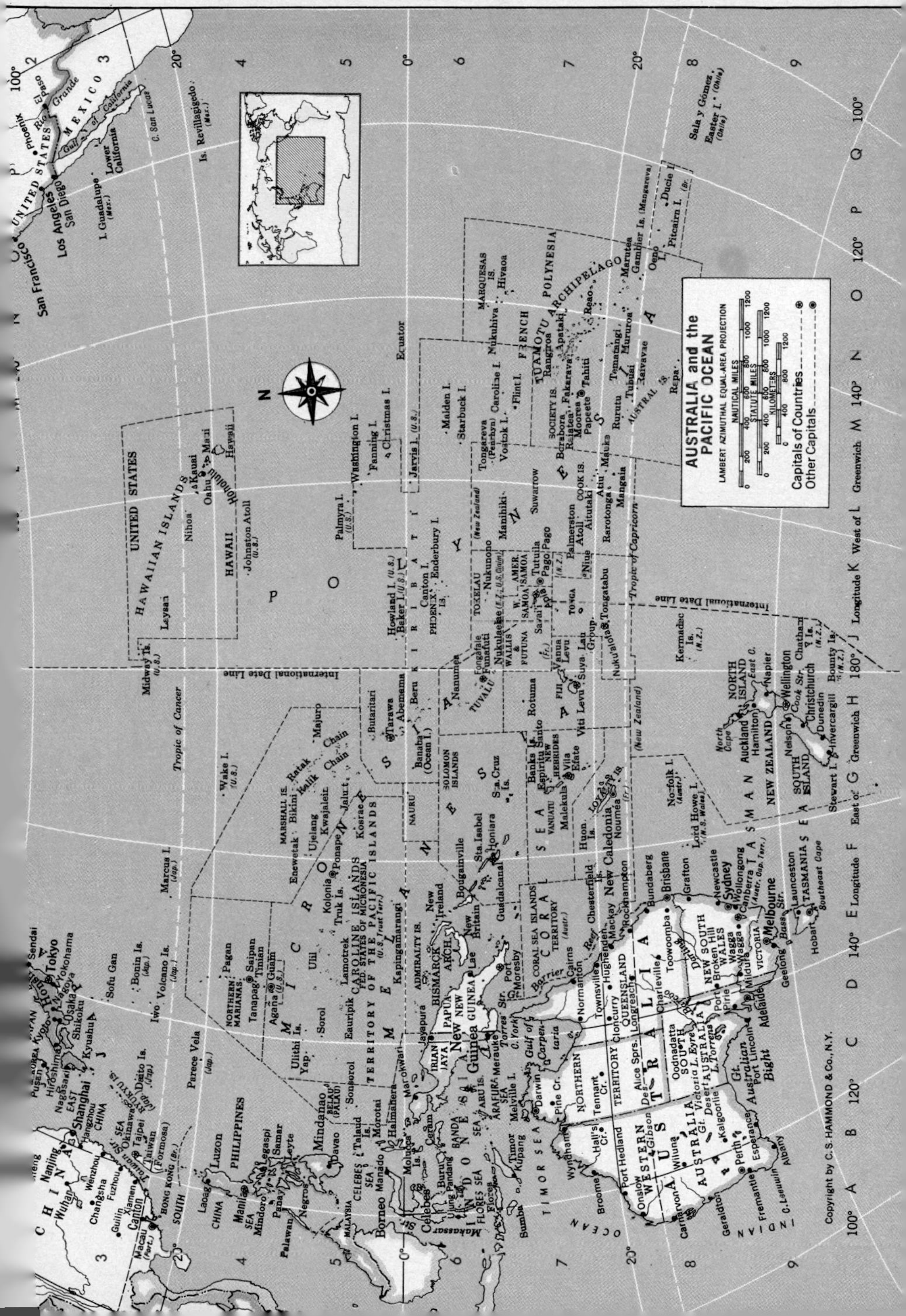
AUSTRALIA and the
PACIFIC OCEAN
LAMBERT AZIMUTHAL EQUAL-AREA PROJECTION
NAUTICAL MILES
STATUTE MILES
KILOMETERS
Capitals of Countries
Other Capitals
Copyright by C.S. HAMMOND & Co., N.Y.
AUSTRALIA
NEW ZEALAND
NEW GUINEA
PHILIPPINES
UNITED STATES
MEXICO
CHINA
HAWAIIAN ISLANDS
MICRONESIA
MELANESIA
POLYNESIA
INDONESIA
TASMAN SEA
CORAL SEA
TIMOR SEA
ARAFURA SEA
Tropic of Cancer
Tropic of Capricorn
Equator
International Date Line
Longitude East of Greenwich
Longitude West of Greenwich

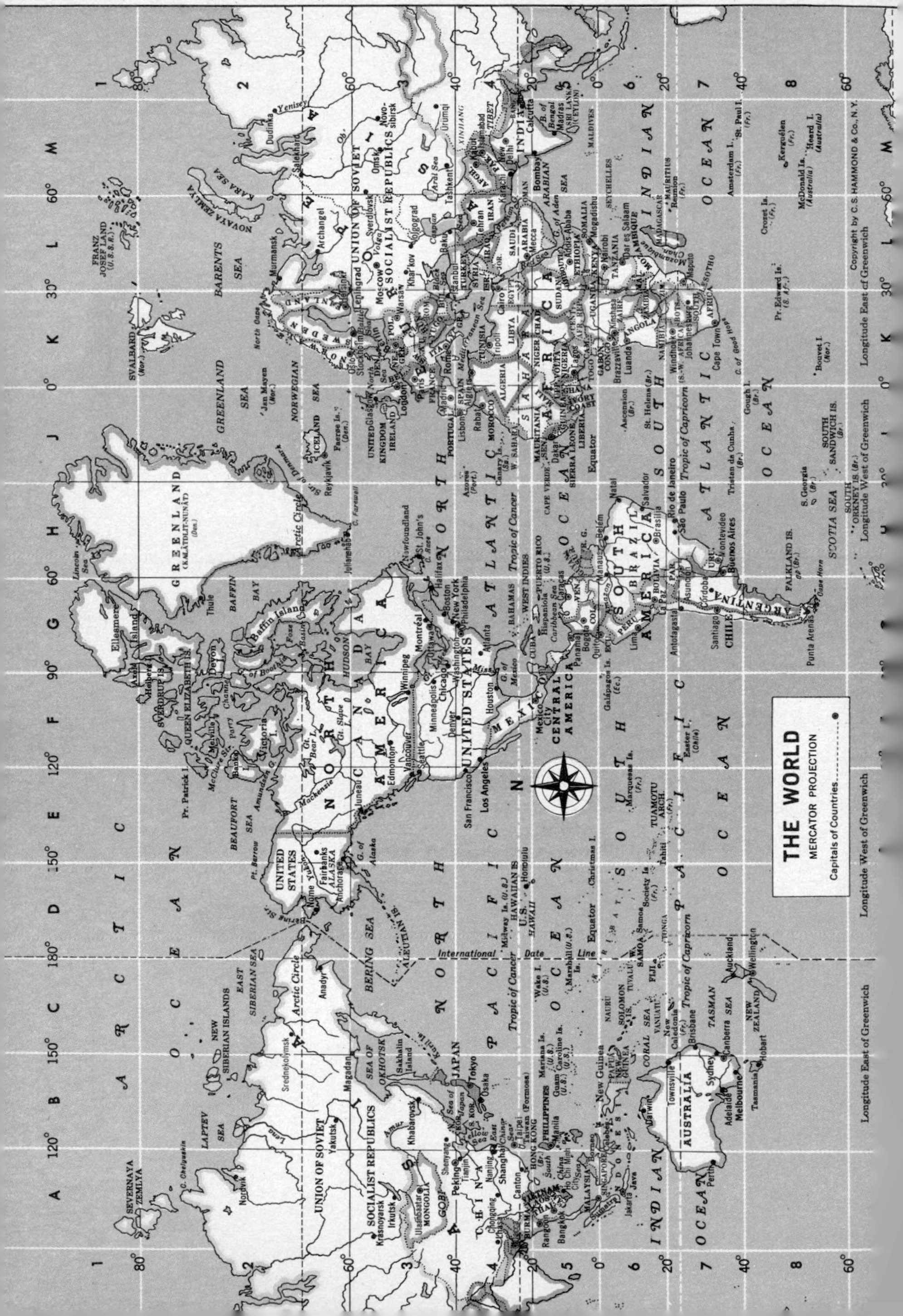
THE WORLD
MERCATOR PROJECTION
Capitals of Countries
Copyright by C. S. HAMMOND & Co., N. Y.
Longitude West of Greenwich
Longitude East of Greenwich
ARCTIC OCEAN
NORTH PACIFIC OCEAN
SOUTH PACIFIC OCEAN
NORTH ATLANTIC OCEAN
SOUTH ATLANTIC OCEAN
INDIAN OCEAN
NORTH AMERICA
SOUTH AMERICA
AFRICA
AUSTRALIA
UNION OF SOVIET SOCIALIST REPUBLICS
International Date Line
Tropic of Cancer
Equator
Tropic of Capricorn
Arctic Circle

Major U.S. Daily Newspapers[1]

City and newspaper	Net paid circulation: Morning[2]	Evening[2]	Sunday
Akron, Ohio: *Beacon Journal*	—	163,409	225,667
Albany, N.Y.: *Times–Union* (M & S); *Knickerbocker News* (E)	83,609	43,400[3]	154,834
Albuquerque, N.M.: *Journal* (M & S); *Tribune* (E)	90,204[4]	44,735[4]	131,745[4]
Allentown, Pa.: *Morning Call; Call–Chronicle* (S)	122,142[3]	—	160,496
Asbury Park, N.J.: *Press*	—	112,912	158,638
Atlanta: *Constitution* (M); *Journal* (E); *Journal and Constitution* (S)	208,289[3]	184,237[3]	499,084
Atlantic City, N.J.: *Press*	73,551	—	77,909
Augusta, Ga.: *Chronicle* (M); *Herald* (E) *Chronicle–Herald* (S)	59,065	18,301	83,899
Austin, Tex.: *American–Statesman*	136,685[3,5]		162,238
Bakersfield, Calif.: *Californian*	73,821[4]	—	82,002[4]
Baltimore: *Sun*	176,954[3]	167,878[3]	382,953
News American	—	141,449[3]	196,438
Bangor, Me.: *News*	79,602	—	—
Baton Rouge, La.: *Advocate* (M & S); *State–Times* (E)	78,904	38,602	122,058
Bergen County (Hackensack), N.J.: *Record* (E); *Sunday Record*	—	148,387[3,4]	214,713[4]
Beaumont, Tex.: *Journal* (M & E); *Enterprise–Journal* (S)	64,595[3]	10,708[3]	78,820
Binghamton, N.Y.: *Sun–Bulletin* (M); *Press* (E &S)	27,616[3]	64,878[3]	83,933
Birmingham, Ala.: *Post–Herald* (M); *News* (E &S)	66,800[3]	168,565[3]	216,012
Boston: *Globe*	502,868[3,5]		751,289
Herald–American	211,930[3]	—	231,106
Christian Science Monitor	153,676[3]	—	—
Bridgeport, Conn: *Telegram* (M); *Post* (E); *Sunday Post*	17,929[3,4]	71,918[3,4]	91,846[4]
Buffalo, N.Y.: *Courier–Express*[13]	127,124	—	265,449
Evening News	—	264,222[3]	186,535
Camden, N.J.: *Courier–Post*	—	128,503[3,4]	118,362[4]
Canton, Ohio: *Repository*	—	62,099[4]	76,860[4]
Cedar Rapids, Iowa: *Gazette*	68,680	—	77,540
Charleston, S.C.: *News & Courier* (M); *Evening Post; News & Courier Post* (S)	68,785[3]	38,600[3]	104,232
Charleston, W. Va.: *Gazette* (M); *Daily Mail* (E); *Gazette–Mail* (S)	54,162	54,455	107,271
Charlotte, N.C.: *Observer* (M & S); *News* (E)	169,291	44,810	241,903
Chattanooga, Tenn: *Times* (M); *News–Free Press* (E & S)	45,929[3]	58,923[3]	107,767
Chicago: *Tribune*	770,798[3,5]		1,107,574
Sun–Times	663,410[3]	—	700,769
Daily Herald (M); *Sunday Herald*	57,326	—	55,495
Cincinnati: *Enquirer* (M & S); *Post* (E)	193,090	147,560	298,257
Cleveland: *Plain Dealer*	405,842	—	448,219
Press[10]	316,147[5]		275,701
Cocoa, Fla.: *Today*	72,577	—	88,759
Colorado Springs, Colo.: *Gazette Telegraph*	34,897	47,416	87,129
Sun	33,137[3]	—	34,664
Columbia, S.C.: *State* (M & S); *Record* (E)	108,620	31,750	136,195
Columbus, Ohio: *Citizen–Journal* (M); *Dispatch* (E & S)	117,178	202,220	340,484
Corpus Christi, Tex.: *Caller* (M & S); *Times* (E)	63,831[3,4]	24,075[3,4]	89,985[4]
Dallas: *News*	308,649	—	380,981
Times Herald	267,579		352,372
Wall Street Journal (Southwest edition)	229,232[3]	—	—
Davenport, Iowa: *Quad City Times*	64,160		83,341
Dayton, Ohio: *Journal Herald* (M); *Daily News* (E & S)	103,452	131,511	221,799
Daytona Beach, Fla.: *Journal* (M); *News* (E); *News–Journal* (S)	58,257	30,467[3]	79,198
Denver: *Post*	258,376	—	356,372
Rocky Mountain News	312,873	—	335,665
Des Moines, Iowa: *Register* (M & S); *Tribune* (E)	205,640	67,596	379,124
Detroit: *News*	629,392[3,5]		825,384
Free Press	627,640[3]	—	758,706
Duluth, Minn.: *News–Tribune* (M & S); *Herald* (E)	47,777	18,281	80,743
Erie, Pa.: *News* (M); *Times* (E); *Times–News* (S)	24,927[3]	50,525[3]	96,220
El Paso, Tex.: *Times* (M & S); *Herald–Post* (E)	57,070[4]	32,435[4]	88,662[4]
Evansville, Ind.: *Courier* (M); *Press* (E); *Courier & Press* (S)	63,453	43,328	116,689
Flint, Mich.: *Journal*	—	108,533[3,4]	111,438[4]

City and newspaper	Net paid circulation Morning[2]	Evening[2]	Sunday
Fort Lauderdale, Fla.: *Sun–Sentinel* (M); *News* (E); *News & Sun–Sentinel* (S)	85,484[3]	96,179[3]	233,560
Fort Myers, Fla.: *News–Press*	78,173	—	91,791
Fort Wayne, Ind.: *Journal–Gazette* (M & S); *News–Sentinel* (E)	56,953[4]	66,477[4]	106,401[4]
Fort Worth: *Star–Telegram*	103,897[3]	126,757[3]	260,710
Fresno, Calif.: *Bee*	137,699[4]	—	156,376[4]
Gary, Ind.: *Post–Tribune*	—	81,663	92,798
Grand Rapids, Mich.: *Press*	—	128,099[4]	155,930[4]
Greensboro, N.C.: *News* (M & S); *Record* (E)	82,981	29,709	115,105
Greensburg, Pa.: *Tribune–Review*	46,974	—	81,066
Greenville, S.C.: *News* (M); *Piedmont* (E & S)	84,298	23,746	112,842
Hammond–East Chicago, Ind.: *Times*	—	69,982[3]	78,351
Harrisburg, Pa.: *Patriot* (M); *Evening News*; *Sunday Patriot News*	46,832[3]	59,687[3]	154,578
Hartford, Conn.: *Courant*	208,845	—	290,254
Honolulu: *Advertiser* (M); *Star–Bulletin* (E); *Star–Bulletin & Advertiser* (S)	85,848	112,716	199,245
Houston: *Chronicle*	393,730[3 5]		481,319
Post	376,879[3]	—	440,135
Indianapolis: *Star* (M & S); *News* (E)	220,947[4]	136,043[4]	361,571[4]
Jackson, Miss.: *Clarion–Ledger* (M); *Daily News* (E); *Clarion Ledger–Daily News* (S)	66,354	40,248	116,724
Jacksonville, Fla.: *Florida Times–Union* (M & S); *Journal* (E)	160,905[3]	43,649[3]	207,724
Kansas City, Mo.: *Times* (M); *Star* (E & S)	287,441	240,529[3]	391,626
Knoxville, Tenn.: *Journal* (M); *News–Sentinel* (E & S)	57,096	100,910	160,163
Lancaster, Pa.: *Intelligencer–Journal* (M); *New Era* (E) *News* (S)	40,770[4]	58,247[4]	136,526[4]
Lansing, Mich.: *State–Journal*	—	73,290	79,994
Las Vegas, Nev.: *Review–Journal*	92,993[3 5]		104,120
Sun	61,670[3]	—	68,918
Lexington, Ky.: *Herald* (M); *Leader* (E); *Herald–Leader* (S)	74,035[3]	32,215[3]	118,177
Little Rock, Ark.: *Arkansas Gazette*	131,929	—	158,202
Arkansas Democrat	69,533	—	126,142
Long Beach, Calif.: *Press–Telegram*	68,282[3]	63,438[3]	137,484
Long Island (Melville), N.Y.: *Newsday*	513,728[3 5]		582,261
Los Angeles: *Times*	1,062,707[3]	—	1,317,817
Herald–Examiner	—	285,656[3]	303,805
Daily News	127,571[3]	—	139,075
Louisville, Ky.: *Courier–Journal* (M & S); *Times* (E)	182,843	143,121	324,624
Lubbock, Tex.: *Avalanche–Journal*	58,628[3]	14,201[3]	81,226
Macon, Ga.: *Telegraph* (M); *News* (E); *Telegraph and News* (S)	52,878[3]	19,064[3]	85,266
Madison, Wis.: *State Journal* (M & S); *Capital Times* (E)	75,423	31,472	126,251
Memphis, Tenn.: *Commercial Appeal* (M & S); *Press Scimitar* (E)	202,272	90,581	284,377
Miami, Fla.: *Herald* (M & S); *News* (E)	435,071	60,905	521,091
Milwaukee: *Sentinel* (M); *Journal* (E & S)	176,680	308,764	516,858
Minneapolis: *Tribune* (M & S); *Star* (E)[6]	239,332[3]	169,184[3]	576,994
Mobile, Ala.: *Register* (M); *Press* (E); *Press–Register* (S)	51,124[4]	50,730[4]	97,132[4]
Modesto, Calif.: *Bee*	69,743[4]	—	76,145[4]
Naperville, Ill.: *Wall Street Journal* (Midwest edition)	578,493[3]	—	—
Nashville, Tenn.: *Tennessean* (M & S); *Banner* (E)	127,296	74,235	246,081
New Haven, Conn.: *Journal–Courier* (M); *Register* (E & S)	36,417[3]	92,423	137,044
New Orleans: *Times–Picayune/States–Item*	280,655[3 4 5]		332,410[4]
New York: *News*	1,540,218[3]	—	2,042,830
Times	947,682[3]	—	1,524,833
Post	904,476[3 5]		601,120[7]
Wall Street Journal (Eastern edition)	772,160[3]	—	—
National edition	2,002,727[3]	—	—
Staten Island Advance	—	73,148[3]	80,999
Women's Wear Daily	61,665[3]	—	—
Newark, N.J.: *Star–Ledger*	415,406[3 4]	—	606,044[4]
Newport News–Hampton, Va.: *Daily Press* (M & S); *Times Herald* (E)	58,706[4]	40,839[4]	104,927[4]
Norfolk–Portsmouth–Virginia Beach–Chesapeake, Va.: *Virginian–Pilot* (M); *Ledger–Star* (E); *Virginian–Pilot/Ledger–Star* (S)	133,237[4]	93,922[4]	211,857[4]
Oakland, Calif.: *Tribune* (E & S); *Eastbay Today* (M)	94,310[3]	120,011[3]	172,549
Oklahoma City: *Daily Oklahoman* (M); *Times* (E); *Sunday Oklahoman*	195,180[3]	85,004[3]	300,358
Omaha, Neb.: *World–Herald*	120,169[3]	104,211[3]	276,431
Orange County (Santa Ana), Calif.: *Register*	251,647[3 5]		286,096

City and newspaper	Net paid circulation: Morning[2]	Evening[2]	Sunday
Orlando, Fla.: *Sentinel Star*	215,015[3,5]		249,974
Palo Alto, Calif.: *Wall Street Journal* (Western edition)	422,842[3]	—	—
Peoria, Ill.: *Journal Star*	101,717[5]		118,798
Philadelphia: *Inquirer*	425,865[3,8]	—	852,611[8]
Daily News	—	230,398[3,8]	—
Phoenix, Ariz.: *Republic* (M & S); *Gazette* (E)	286,984[4]	119,116[4]	432,397[4]
Pittsburgh: *Post–Gazette* (M); *Press* (E & S)	181,397[3]	266,307[3]	616,373
Pontiac, Mich.: *Press*	—	72,258[3]	76,642
Portland, Me.: *Press–Herald* (M); *Express* (E); *Maine Sunday Telegram*	57,329	30,046	124,257
Portland, Ore.: *Oregonian* (M & S);[11] *Oregon Journal* (E)	237,141	100,039[3]	409,641
Providence, R. I.: *Journal* (M & S); *Bulletin* (E)	82,182[3]	137,258[3]	238,908
Quincy, Mass.: *Patriot–Ledger*	—	88,594[3,4]	87,510[4]
Raleigh, N.C.: *News & Observer* (M & S); *Times* (E)	129,240[4]	33,338[4]	170,317[4]
Reading, Pa.: *Times* (M); *Eagle* (E & S)	43,807	42,218	103,288
Richmond, Va.: *Times–Dispatch* (M & S); *News–Leader* (E)	135,240	113,404	218,929
Riverside, Calif.: *Press–Enterprise*	74,666[3]	34,594[3]	115,170
Roanoke, Va.: *Times & World–News*	71,243[3]	47,834[3]	121,572
Rochester, N.Y.: *Democrat & Chronicle* (M & S); *Times–Union* (E)	127,283[3]	113,104[3]	241,545
Rockford, Ill.: *Register Star*	76,532	—	85,735
Sacramento, Calif.: *Bee*	219,216	—	244,841
Union	112,022	—	113,941
St. Louis: *Post–Dispatch*	—	238,099[3]	443,442
Globe–Democrat	261,329[3]	—	250,815[9]
St. Paul: *Pioneer Press* (M & S); *Dispatch* (E)	105,301[3]	112,783[3]	245,622
St. Petersburg, Fla.: *Times* (M & S); *Independent* (E)	259,715	37,985	321,935
Salt Lake City, Utah: *Tribune* (M & S); *Deseret News* (E)	114,800	72,048	183,580
San Antonio: *Express* (M); *News* (E); *Express News* (S)	84,879[3]	75,512[3]	193,635
Light	—	122,319[3]	187,976
San Bernardino, Calif.: *Sun*	80,862	—	84,417
San Diego, Calif.: *Union* (M & S); *Tribune* (E)	216,252[4]	126,308[4]	339,922[4]
San Francisco: *Chronicle* (M); *Examiner* (E); *Examiner & Chronicle* (S)	530,672[3]	155,298[3]	673,029
San Jose, Calif.: *Mercury* (M); *News* (E); *Mercury–News* (S)	163,285[3]	63,544[3]	276,293
Santa Rosa, Calif.: *Press Democrat*	—	67,661[3]	75,120
Sarasota, Fla.: *Herald–Tribune* (M & S); *Journal* (E)	104,177[4]	5,230[3,4]	115,123[4]
Seattle: *Times*	256,888[3,5]		339,921
Post–Intelligencer	191,158[3]	—	209,061
Shreveport, La.: *Times* (M & S); *Journal* (E)	84,305	30,009	120,864
South Bend–Mishawake, Ind.: *Tribune*	—	104,858	124,484
Spokane, Wash.: *Spokesman–Review* (M & S); *Daily Chronicle* (E)	77,627	58,028	129,149
Springfield, Mass.: *Union* (M); *News* (E); *Republican* (S)	70,840	73,645	146,723
Springfield, Mo.: *News* (M); *Leader & Press* (E); *News & Leader* (S)	35,477[3,4]	34,328[3,4]	83,614[4]
Syracuse, N.Y.: *Post–Standard* (M); *Herald–Journal* (E); *Herald–American* (S)	78,760	107,668	234,258
Tacoma, Wash.: *News–Tribune* (E); *News–Tribune & Ledger* (S)	—	107,383	113,123
Tampa, Fla.: *Tribune* (M & S); *Times* (E)[12]	202,363	22,046	256,463
Toledo, Ohio: *Blade*	—	165,034	208,527
Topeka, Kan.: *Capital–Journal*	69,596	—	75,220
Torrance–Redondo Beach–Hermosa Beach–Manhattan Beach, Calif.: *Daily Breeze*	—	85,417	101,568
Trenton, N.J.: *Times*	—	n.a.	n.a.
Trentonian	n.a.	—	n.a.
Tucson, Ariz.: *Daily Star* (M & S); *Citizen* (E)	78,039	68,970	142,265
Tulsa, Okla: *World* (M & S); *Tribune* (E)	130,268[4]	75,769[4]	219,100[4]
Washington, D.C.: *Post*	760,950[3]	—	986,024
West Palm Beach, Fla.: *Post* (M); *Times* (E); *Post–Times* (S)	100,952[3]	27,651[3]	155,614
Wichita, Kan.: *Eagle–Beacon*	124,171	—	183,080
Wilmington, Del.: *News* (M); *Journal* (E); *Sunday News Journal*	54,707[3,4]	74,385[3,4]	121,759[4]
Winston–Salem, N.C.: *Journal* (M & S); *Sentinel* (E)	71,681	34,478	97,511
Worcester, Mass.: *Telegram* (M & S); *Gazette* (E)	55,568[4]	87,329[4]	115,327[4]
Youngstown, Ohio: *Vindicator*	100,222	—	150,222

1. Listing is of cities in which any one edition of a newspaper exceeds an average net paid circulation of 75,000; newspapers of smaller circulation in those cities are also included. 2. Unless otherwise indicated, figures are average Monday-through-Saturday circulation for six-month period ending March 31, 1982. 3. Average Monday-through-Friday circulation. 4. Three-month average for period ending March 31, 1982. 5. All-day newspaper. 6. Merged with Minneapolis Tribune April 5, 1982. 7. Published on Saturday. 8. Three-month average for period ending Jan. 31, 1982. 9. Weekend edition. 10. Ceased publication June 17, 1982. 11. Became all-day newspaper on Sept. 6, 1982, when Oregon Journal ceased publication. 12. Ceased publication August 14, 1982. 13. Ceased publication Sept. 19, 1982. NOTE: n.a. = not available. *Source:* Audit Bureau of Circulations.

Leading Magazines: United States and Canada

Magazine	Circulation[1]
AARP News Bulletin	7,107,362
American Legion Magazine, The	2,587,751
American Rifleman, The	1,185,236
Better Homes and Gardens	8,059,717
Bon Apetit	1,340,653
Boys' Life	1,450,841
Changing Times, The Kiplinger Magazine	1,421,176
Chatelaine	1,065,972
Cosmopolitan	2,848,399
Discovery	1,055,675
Ebony	1,306,549
Elks Magazine, The	1,645,905
Family Circle	7,427,979
Family Handyman, The	1,078,569
Field and Stream	2,023,785
Glamour	2,052,115
Globe	1,912,684
Golf Digest	1,025,088
Good Housekeeping	5,425,790
House & Garden	1,111,539
Hustler	1,238,955
Ladies' Home Journal	5,527,071
Life	1,461,964
McCall's	6,266,090
Mademoiselle	1,186,416
Marvel Comics Group	5,472,724
Mechanix Illustrated	1,602,777
Modern Maturity	7,309,035
Mother Earth News, The	1,072,797
Motorland	1,314,538
National Enquirer	4,602,524
National Geographic Magazine, The	10,861,186
Nation's Business	1,113,573
Newsweek	2,960,073
New Woman	1,306,387
1,001 Home Ideas	1,105,003
Organic Gardening	1,314,536
Outdoor Life	1,535,929
Parents	1,568,221
Penthouse	4,051,969
People Weekly	2,551,642
Playboy	5,013,941
Popular Mechanics	1,611,239
Popular Science	1,803,309
Prevention	2,462,023
Psychology Today	1,188,083
Reader's Digest	17,926,542
Reader's Digest (Canadian English Edition)	1,288,404
Redbook Magazine	4,368,523
Scholastic Magazines	3,126,125
Self	1,029,315
Senior Scholastic Unit	2,299,709
Seventeen	1,480,236
Smithsonian	1,936,726
Southern Living	1,973,219
Sports Illustrated	2,284,800
Star, The	3,515,530
Sunset, The Magazine of Western Living	1,417,333
'Teen	1,122,562
Time, The Weekly Newsmagazine	4,337,988
Today's Education	1,649,494
True Story	1,525,089
TV Guide (U.S.)	17,670,543
U.S. News & World Report	2,063,366
Us	1,107,819
V.F.W. Magazine	1,867,201
Vogue (incl. Vanity Fair)	1,217,453
Woman's Day	7,004,367
Workbasket, The	1,565,992

1. Average total paid circulation for the six-month period ending December 31, 1981. The table lists magazines of over 1,000,000 circulation. *Source:* Audit Bureau of Circulations. Publishers' Statements for six-month period ending December 31, 1981.

English Language Daily and Sunday U.S. Newspapers

(number of newspapers as of Feb. 1, 1982; circulation as reported for Sept. 30, 1981)

State	Morning papers and circulation		Evening papers and circulation		Total M and E and circulation		Sunday papers and circulation	
Alabama	8	204,330	20	535,497	28	739,827	21	692,233
Alaska	2	39,579	6	76,731	8	116,310	2	90,267
Arizona	4	355,585	14	264,331	18	619,916	10	606,793
Arkansas[1]	6	260,197	27	227,437	32	487,634	17	486,602
California[1]	32	3,333,530	95	2,634,370	124	5,967,900	51	5,523,532
Colorado	6	432,966	21	488,031	27	920,997	10	950,059
Connecticut	6	366,012	19	530,197	25	896,209	10	755,306
Delaware	1	54,418	2	97,843	3	152,261	2	145,280
District of Columbia	1	662,978	0	0	1	662,978	1	890,079
Florida[1]	22	1,931,119	31	713,957	52	2,645,076	33	2,781,201
Georgia	10	451,643	27	562,616	37	1,014,259	15	991,305
Hawaii	1	81,802	5	165,547	6	247,349	3	410,215
Idaho	5	114,158	9	98,607	14	212,765	7	191,804
Illinois[1]	12	1,411,183	67	1,343,840	76	2,755,023	24	2,698,946
Indiana	8	447,562	68	1,181,527	76	1,629,089	18	1,201,95[illegible]
Iowa[1]	7	377,060	35	491,404	41	868,464	9	733,445
Kansas[1]	6	241,924	42	338,201	47	580,125	18	493,91[illegible]
Kentucky	5	305,400	21	440,176	26	745,576	11	602,17[illegible]
Louisiana[1]	7	423,515	19	370,562	25	794,077	16	825,03[illegible]

State	Morning papers and circulation		Evening papers and circulation		Total M and E and circulation		Sunday papers and circulation	
Maine	5	220,065	4	71,728	9	291,793	1	122,852
Maryland	8	335,033	8	431,829	16	766,862	4	639,410
Massachusetts[1]	6	812,565	41	1,212,367	46	2,024,932	10	1,595,868
Michigan	8	966,310	45	1,496,225	52	2,462,535	15	2,400,209
Minnesota	8	449,288	22	558,049	30	1,007,337	11	1,000,712
Mississippi	6	130,458	19	269,397	25	399,855	13	325,573
Missouri	9	690,752	40	820,392	49	1,511,144	18	1,391,897
Montana	5	153,782	6	46,938	11	200,720	8	201,946
Nebraska	4	187,431	15	297,460	19	484,891	6	413,074
Nevada	3	104,531	5	125,796	8	230,327	5	234,610
New Hampshire	1	66,091	8	133,095	9	199,186	2	81,092
New Jersey	8	735,049	18	952,035	26	1,687,084	17	1,679,718
New Mexico	1	87,717	19	193,318	20	281,035	14	259,298
New York[1]	24	5,686,141	57	2,350,325	78	8,036,466	35	5,912,101
North Carolina	10	609,571	45	756,091	55	1,365,662	25	1,150,900
North Dakota[1]	3	71,825	8	121,860	10	193,685	4	116,408
Ohio[1]	12	929,466	85	2,350,624	95	3,280,090	29	2,841,254
Oklahoma	7	382,149	46	460,389	53	842,538	43	872,500
Oregon	3	305,555	18	379,990	21	685,545	7	628,829
Pennsylvania[1]	35	1,451,105	67	1,847,006	98	3,298,111	19	2,610,707
Rhode Island	1	77,527	6	236,839	7	314,366	2	239,231
South Carolina[1]	8	390,546	12	216,475	19	607,021	8	505,665
South Dakota	2	46,102	10	123,641	12	169,743	4	122,901
Tennessee[1]	8	469,901	23	593,431	30	1,063,332	16	1,010,782
Texas[1]	28	1,857,018	92	1,593,819	116	3,450,837	97	3,974,982
Utah	1	110,708	5	172,676	6	283,384	5	282,053
Vermont	2	72,507	6	45,885	8	118,392	3	78,792
Virginia	14	580,297	24	575,042	38	1,155,339	15	873,097
Washington[1]	9	495,392	19	677,093	27	1,172,485	17	1,145,949
West Virginia	10	241,437	15	224,822	25	466,259	10	400,219
Wisconsin	4	271,498	32	950,711	36	1,222,209	10	922,480
Wyoming	6	69,538	4	32,207	10	101,745	4	74,755
Total	**408**	**30,552,316**	**1,352**	**30,878,429**	**1,730**	**61,430,745**	**755**	**55,180,004**
Total U.S., Sept. 30, 1980	387	29,414,036	1,388	32,787,804	1,745	62,201,840	736	54,676,173
Total U.S., Sept. 30, 1979	382	28,574,879	1,405	33,648,161	1,763	62,223,040	720	54,379,923
Total U.S., Sept. 30, 1978	355	27,656,739	1,419	34,333,258	1,756	61,989,997	696	53,990,033
Total U.S., Sept. 30, 1977	352	26,742,318	1,435	34,752,822	1,753	61,495,140	668	52,429,234
Total U.S., Sept. 30, 1976	346	25,858,386	1,435	35,118,625	1,762	60,977,011	650	51,565,334
Total U.S., Sept. 30, 1975	339	25,490,186	1,436	35,165,245	1,756	60,655,431	639	51,096,323
Total U.S., Sept. 30, 1974	340	26,144,966	1,449	35,732,231	1,768	61,877,197	641	51,678,726
Total U.S., Sept. 30, 1973	343	26,524,140	1,451	36,623,140	1,774	63,147,280	634	51,717,465
Total U.S., Sept. 30, 1972	337	26,078,386	1,441	36,431,856	1,761	62,510,242	605	50,000,669
Total U.S., Sept. 30, 1970	334	25,933,783	1,429	36,173,744	1,748	62,107,527	586	49,216,602

1. "All-day" newspapers are listed in morning and evening columns but only once in the total, and their circulations are divided between morning and evening figures. Adjustments have been made in state and U.S. total figures. *Source: Editor and Publisher Yearbook, 1982.*

See **the Entertainment and Culture section for additional Media information.**

Electric Cars Have a Long History

Electric cars are expected to be taking a share of the vehicle market after 1985. One new unit can power a car at 55 miles per hour for 150 miles before it has to be recharged. Also in the works are hybrids, which combine electric and gasoline power.

According to the Automotive Information Council (AIC), the first electric vehicle was built in 1839 by Robert Anderson of Aberdeen, Scotland, but the first practical use did not occur until 1886 when one was introduced as a taxicab in England. The battery had 28 bulky cells and the taxi had a top speed of eight miles per hour.

By 1904 electrics were somewhat common on U.S. city streets for short runs. The Electric Vehicle Co. in that year made 2,000 taxis, accounting for one third of the cabs used in New York, Chicago, and Boston.

By 1910 the use of electric vehicles had peaked. They quickly lost ground to the internal-combustion engine with its great improvements such as the self-starter, and the availability of inexpensive gasoline, plus the low price of gasoline-powered mass-assembled cars.

WHERE TO FIND OUT MORE

Reference Books And Other Sources

This cannot be a complete record of all the thousands of available sources of information. Nevertheless, these selected references will enable the reader to locate additional facts about many subjects covered in the *Information Please Almanac.* The editors have chosen sources that they believe will be most helpful to the general reader.

General References

Encyclopedias are a unique category, since they attempt to cover most subjects quite thoroughly. Two most valuable multivolume encyclopedias are the **Encyclopaedia Britannica** and the **Encyclopedia Americana.** Useful one-volume encyclopedias are the **New Columbia Encyclopedia** and the **Random House Encyclopedia.**

Dictionaries and similar "word books" are also unique: **Webster's New International Dictionary** (third edition, unabridged). **Random House Dictionary. Merriam Webster's Collegiate Dictionary** (eighth edition, abridged). **Oxford English Dictionary. Bartlett's Familiar Quotations. Roget's Thesaurus. Modern American Usage.**

There are a number of useful **atlases: New York Times Atlas of the World,** a number of historical atlases (Penguin Books), **Oxford Economic Atlas of the World, Atlas of the Universe** (Rand McNally), **Atlas of the Historical Geography of the U.S.** (Carnegie Institution of Washington and the American Geographical Society), and contemporary road atlases of the U.S. (Rand McNally).

A source of information on virtually all subjects is the United States Government Printing Office. For information write: Superintendent of Documents, Washington, D.C. 20402.

For help on any subject, consult: **Subject Guide to Books in Print, The New York Times Index,** and the **Reader's Guide to Periodical Literature** in your library.

Specific References

America Votes (Congressional Quarterly, Inc.)
American Indian, Reference Encyclopedia of the (Todd Publications)
Antiques, Collectors Encyclopedia of (Crown)
Architecture, Encyclopedia of World (Facts on File)
Art, Encyclopedia of World (McGraw-Hill)
Art, History of (Prentice-Hall)
Art, Oxford Companion to (Oxford University Press)
Art, Who's Who in American (R.R. Bowker)
Art Directory, American (R.R. Bowker)
Associations, Encyclopedia of (Gale Research Co.)
Authors, 1000–1900, European (H.W. Wilson)
Authors, 1600–1900, American (H.W. Wilson)
Authors, Twentieth Century (H.W. Wilson)
Authors Before 1800 (H.W. Wilson)
Authors of the Nineteenth Century, British (H.W. Wilson)
Auto Racing (Morrow)
Banking and Finance, Encyclopedia of (Bankers Publishing Co.)
Baseball Encyclopedia (Information Concepts/Macmillan)
(Baseball) **World Series Records** (The Sporting News)
Basketball, Modern Encyclopedia of (Four Winds Press)
Biographical Dictionary, Chambers (St. Martin's Press)
Biographical Dictionary, Webster's (G. & C. Merriam)
Biography Yearbook, Current (H.W. Wilson)
Birds of America (Audubon)
Book Review Digest, 1905— (H.W. Wilson)
Business Almanac, Dow Jones-Irwin (Dow Jones-Irwin)
Catholic Encyclopedia, New (Publishers Guild/McGraw-Hill)
CB: Citizens Band Radio Service Rules (Government Printing Office)
Chemistry, Encyclopedia of (Van Nostrand Reinhold)
Chemistry and Physics, Handbook of (Chemical Rubber Co.)
Christian Church, Oxford Dictionary of the (Oxford University Press)
Church Annual, Episcopal (Morehouse-Barlow)
Churches, Yearbook of American and Canadian (Abingdon Press)
Climate and Man (U.S. Department of Agriculture)
Communist Affairs, Yearbook on International (Hoover Institution Press)
Composers, Great, 1300–1900; A Biographical and Critical Guide (H.W. Wilson)
Composers Since 1900; A Biographical and Critical Guide (H.W. Wilson)
Congressional Quarterly Directory (Congressional Quarterly, Inc.)
(Consumer) **Agriculture, Yearbook of: Gardening for Food and Fun** (Government Printing Office)
(Consumer) **HELP: The Indispensable Almanac of Consumer Information 1980** (Everest House)
Consumer Sourcebook (Gale Research Co.)
Consumer Reports (Consumers Union)
Dance Encyclopedia (Simon & Schuster)
Drama, Crowell's Handbook of Classical (Crowell)
Ecology Information and Organizations, Guide to (H.W. Wilson)
Energy Factbook 1980–81 (McGraw)
Environment, Living With Our (Government Printing Office)
Environmental Quality Report (Council on Environmental Quality)
Environmental Science (Holt, Rinehart & Winston)
Europa Year Book (Europa Publications)
Facts, Famous First (H.W. Wilson)
Facts on File (Facts on File, Inc.)
Film, Oxford Companion to (Oxford University Press)
Filmgoer's Companion (Hill & Wang)
Fishing: An Encyclopedic Guide to Tackle and Tactics for Fresh and Salt Water (Dutton)
Football, Encyclopedia of (A.S. Barnes & Co.)
Foreign Terms, Dictionary of (Crowell)
Game, Rules of the (Bantam Books)
Geographical Dictionary, Webster's New (G. & C. Merriam)

Geography, Dictionary of (Penguin Books)
Government Manual, U.S. (U.S. Office of the Federal Register)
History, Album of American (Charles Scribner's)
History, Atlas of American (Oxford University Press)
History, Dictionary of American (Charles Scribner's)
History, Documents of American (Appleton-Century-Crofts)
History, Encyclopedia of Latin American (Bobbs-Merrill)
History, Encyclopedia of World (Houghton-Mifflin)
History, Timetables of (Simon & Schuster)
History and Literature, Oxford Companion to Canadian (Oxford University Press)
Ice Hockey A to Z (Lothrop)
Investments, American and Foreign, Manual of (Moody's Investors Service)
Jazz in the Seventies, Encyclopedia of (Horizon)
Jewish Concepts, Encyclopedia of (Hebrew Publishers)
Job Outlook in Brief, The (Government Printing Office)
Libraries, World Guide to (K.G. Saur)
Library Directory, American (R.R. Bowker)
Literary History of the United States (Macmillan)
Literature, Oxford Companion to American (Oxford University Press)
Literature, Oxford Companion to Classical (Oxford University Press)
Literature, Oxford Companion to English (Oxford University Press)
Literature, Reader's Adviser to the Best in (R.R. Bowker)
Literature, Reader's Encyclopedia of American (Crowell)
Medical Adviser, Modern Home (Doubleday)
Museums, Directory of World (Columbia University Press)
Music and Musicians, Handbook of American (Free Press, Div. of Macmillan)
(Music) ASCAP. Biographical Dictionary (American Society of Authors, Composers, and Publishers)
Music, Concise Oxford Dictionary of (Oxford University Press)
Music, Harvard Dictionary of (Harvard University Press)
Musical Terms, Dictionary of (Gordon Press)
Mythology, (Larousse) Greek and Roman (McGraw)
Nations, Handbook of New (Crowell)
Nations, Worldmark Encyclopedia of the (Harper & Row)
Newspapers and Periodicals, Ayer Directory of (Ayer Press)
Pain, Coping With Chronic (Crown Publishers)
Pocket Data Book, U.S.A. (Bureau of Census)
Poetry, Granger's Index to (Columbia University Press)
Politics, Almanac of American (Gambit, Inc.)
Politics, Who's Who in American (R.R. Bowker)
Private Schools, Handbook of (Porter Sargent)
Robert's Rules of Order (Morrow & Co.)
Science, American Men and Women of (R.R. Bowker)
Science and Technology, Asimov's Biographical Encyclopedia of (Doubleday)
Scientific Encyclopedia, Van Nostrand's (Van Nostrand Reinhold)
Sports Dictionary, Webster's (G. & C. Merriam Co.)
Sports, Encyclopedia of (A.S. Barnes & Co.)
States, Book of (Council of State Governments)
Statesman's Yearbook (Burke's Peerage, Ltd.)
Tennis, Encyclopedia of (Viking Press)
Theater, Oxford Companion to the (Oxford University Press)
Theater, Who's Who in the (Gale Research Co.)
United Nations, Demographic Yearbook (U.N. Publishing Service)
United States, Historical Statistics of the (U.S. Department of Commerce)
United States, Statistical Abstract of the (Government Printing Office)
United Nations, Statistical Yearbook of the (U.N. Publishing Service)
Washington Information Directory (Congressional Quarterly, Inc.)
Way Things Work (Simon & Schuster)
Weather Almanac (Gale Research Co.)
Wildlife, Atlas of World (Rand McNally)
Women, Notable American, 1607–1950 (Belknap Press)
Who's Who (British), (St. Martin's Press)
Who's Who in America (Marquis)
World, Harper Encyclopedia of the Modern (Harper & Row)
ZIP Code and Post Office Directory, National (Government Printing Office)

See the full range of publications of Dun & Bradstreet and Standard & Poor's for corporate financial and stockholder information.

For detailed information on American colleges and universities, see the many publications of the **American Council on Education.**

Also see the many specialized **Who's Who** volumes issued by Marquis for biographies of famous contemporaries in many fields.

Most Years Are Actually Longer—By One Leap Second

June 1982 lasted one second longer than usual due to the discrepancy between the average spin rate of the earth and the internationally agreed length of the second. Those concerned about accuracy should have set their clocks back one second at 8 p.m. EDT on June 30, 1982.

According to the international agreement of 1967 establishing Coordinated Universal Time, the second is defined as equal to 9,192,631,770 oscillations of the cesium atom. This number was agreed upon because it equalled the length of the second as derived from the measured length of a full year in 1900.

However, since then, sun time has been getting out of phase with atomic time due to a number of factors that slow the earth and therefore lengthen the day. The most significant of these are lunar gravity, the slight wobble in the earth's spin, solar eruptions, and severe changes in wind patterns and surface features.

T.V. broadcasters, seismologists, and power companies all rely on time precise to within billionths of a second in order to function accurately and efficiently.

There have been other leap seconds—except for 1980, there has been one leap second added to the end of every year since 1972. In addition, another leap second was added in June 1972.

WRITER'S GUIDE

Rules for Correct Punctuation, Capitalization, Abbreviation

Blanche Ormont

Punctuation

Period (.) Use a period: (1) After a statement or command: *Panama is roughly the size of South Carolina. Go to the head of the line.*

(2) After most abbreviations: C.O.D., Ms., U.S. (In familiar abbreviations, where the letters themselves are usually spoken, the period is often omitted: *CIO, NBC, SPCA.*)

(3) With decimals and in dollars and cents: *.05, 22.5, $12.95.* Do not use a period after *percent,* as in *twenty percent;* if cents is written out or the cents sign is used, as in *27 cents, 27¢;* or after Roman numerals, *XXIII, Act III,* except when numbering or listing.

Question Mark (?) Use the question mark after a direct question: *Do you know why the world's climate is changing?* Do not use the question mark after an indirect question or request: *The teacher asked him if he knew the capital of South Dakota. Will you please return this book as soon as possible.*

Exclamation Point (!) Use an exclamation point after an emphatic statement or after a sentence, phrase, or word expressing strong feeling: *You're absolutely wrong! Ouch! That hurts!*

Comma (,) The comma is the most commonly used (and misused) punctuation mark. It indicates a slight separation between words or groups of words and should serve primarily to make the writer's meaning clear. Too many commas may cause the reader to separate words that should be grouped together, or they may unnecessarily slow the movement of a sentence. Too few commas, or misplaced commas, may seriously distort the writer's meaning. Although one should always use good judgment in deciding when and where to use commas, the following rules are generally applicable. Use a comma:

(1) To separate words, phrases, or clauses (a clause is a group of words that has a subject and a predicate) in a series of three or more items: *Tuition, board, lodging, and medical and dental care are provided.* (Note that the comma before the second *and* has been omitted because *medical and dental care* is considered a single unit. However, in some cases it is necessary to insert the comma before *and* to avoid misreading: *The course includes navigation, electricity, ship construction, marine biology, and engineering.*)

Commas are used between two or more adjectives preceding a noun if each separately could modify the noun and if switching the order of the adjectives does not alter the sense: *It was a cold, bleak, rainy day.* Do not use commas if the first adjective qualifies the entire expression following it: *Their constitution established a strong central government.*

Use a comma after *etc.* (abbreviation of *et cetera*) when it is the last of a series within a sentence: *Books, papers, cartons, etc., lay scattered about the room.*

(2) Between independent clauses (clauses that could stand alone as complete sentences) joined by *and, but, for, or, nor: Pluto has the most eccentric orbit in the solar system, and at times it comes closer to the sun than Neptune. A huge fireball appeared in the sky, but the natives were not afraid.* In a short compound sentence—a sentence made up of two or more independent clauses—the comma is often omitted: *The canoe turned over and everyone fell into the water*

(3) To set off introductory words, phrases, or clauses: *Outraged, he slammed the door behind him. During the wars that followed the French Revolution, Belgium was occupied and later annexed to France. Because Bolivia has no access to the sea, foreign trade must pass through free ports in Chile and river ports on the Amazon.*

If the introductory phrase or clause is very short, or if it is the subject of the sentence, do not use a comma: *Because of its beaches the state is a popular resort area. To cross the sea in ancient times was an extraordinary feat.*

Such introductory transitional words as *yes, no, still, nevertheless, moreover, however, therefore, besides, furthermore,* and weak exclamations like *well, oh,* and *why* should be followed by a comma: *No, I cannot go with you. Well, that's a long story. Why, how nice!*

(4) To set off nonessential elements—words, phrases, or clauses that are not closely related to the rest of the sentence and could be left out without drastically changing its meaning: *Hinduism dates back, perhaps, to prehistoric times. The emperor, in recognition of Confucius' teachings, offered sacrifices at his tomb. Gold, which was responsible for California's settlement boom, is still found in that state.*

To determine whether a modifying expression is restrictive or nonrestrictive (essential or nonessential), see if it can be omitted without significantly changing the meaning. If it is essential to the meaning of the sentence, commas are not used: *Delhi residents who would not limit their families were denied government assistance.* The clause "who would not limit their families" is clearly restrictive; if it were removed, the sentence would indicate that *all* Delhi residents were denied government assistance.

Use the comma before *for, although, though, as, since,* and *because* when these words introduce nonrestrictive clauses or phrases: *The Age of Enlightenment brought about the Jews' emancipation, although persecutions did not end entirely.* But: *The famous Dutch dikes are requisite to the use of much land because half of the country's area is below sea level.* (No comma before *because*, which introduces a restrictive clause.)

Appositives are words or phrases that directly follow a noun or pronoun and identify or explain it. If an appositive is nonrestrictive, it is set off by commas: *The fur-bearing chinchilla, a native of the colder plateau regions, is also raised.* If it is restrictive, no commas are used: *The phrase "hot line" refers to the emergency communications link between Washington and Moscow.*

Contrasting expressions introduced by such words and phrases as *not, but not,* and *though not* are usually nonrestrictive and are therefore set off by commas: *Venus, not Mars, is Earth's nearest neighbor.*

When nonrestrictive words, phrases, or clauses occur within a sentence, they must be set off by *two* commas—one before the expression and one after.

(5) In certain conventional places: (a) To separate items in addresses and dates: *He wrote to his aunt at 94 Birch Road, Omaha, Nebraska, on June 12, 1924.* (b) With numbers greater than three figures: *1,422, 12,498,620.* (c) In letters, after salutations (in informal letters) and after the complimentary close: *Dear Aunt Mary, Sincerely yours,.* (d) To set off the name of a person addressed: *John, please close the door. Listen carefully, Sarah, because this is important.* (e) To separate degrees and titles from names: *Margaret Harrison, M.D., Ph.D. Frank Simmons, Treasurer.* (f) To set off direct quotations: *"Happiness," someone said, "is a warm puppy."* With exclamations or very short quotations, no comma is necessary: *"Hi there!" she called. He constantly said "like" and "you know."*

(6) Whenever necessary to avoid misunderstanding: *Several months after, he saw his father.* (Without the comma the sentence changes meaning, turning into the clause *Several months after he saw his father.)*

Semicolon (;) The semicolon is a mark of separation that functions like a weak period or a strong comma. Use a semicolon:

(1) Between two independent clauses which are not joined by a conjunction: *The soil is generally poor; high crop yields are dependent upon large-scale use of fertilizers.*

(2) Between two independent clauses containing one or more commas even if a conjunction is used: *After members of the committee have debated the bill, a vote is taken; and if the vote is favorable, the bill is sent back to the floor of the house.*

(3) Between two main clauses linked by such connecting words as *therefore, however, finally, thus, otherwise, nevertheless,* and by such phrases as *for example, in fact, on the contrary: The first game of lawn tennis in the United States was played in 1874; however, it was not until 1880 that standard measurements for the court were established.*

(4) Between items in a series if one or more are subdivided by commas: *Among the great libraries of the world are the British Museum, with more than 6,000,000 printed volumes; the National Diet Library in Tokyo, containing more than 4,100,000 volumes; and, of course, the United States Library of Congress, whose extensive collections total over 72,466,000 volumes.*

Colon (:) The colon is a mark of anticipation introducing material that follows it. Use a colon:

(1) To introduce a long quotation, explanatory statement, or question: *The Declaration of Independence states: "We hold these truths to be self-evident, that all men are created equal, that they are endowed by their Creator with certain unalienable Rights, that among these are Life, Liberty, and the Pursuit of Happiness." In 1976, the World Health Organization accomplished a major goal: It virtually eliminated one of mankind's most ancient enemies—smallpox. The question we discussed was: What are the real differences between Socialism and Communism?*

(2) To introduce a list of items. The colon here is frequently, though not always, preceded by such phrases as *the following* or *as follows: Among the great Gothic structures of Europe are the following: Chartres Cathedral, Notre Dame de Paris, Milan Cathedral, and Cologne Cathedral.*

(3) In these customary places: (Note preceding use of colon.) After a formal salutation in a letter: *Dear Sir:;* between hours and minutes: *10:15 a.m.;* between volume and page in formal footnotes and bibliography: *The Dictionary of Dates 2:120–142;* between chapter and verse in the Bible: *Genesis 1:10;* between numerical elements in ratios: *4:2;* after the name of a speaker in a play: *Lady Macbeth: Out, damned spot!*

Quotation Marks (" ") Use quotation marks:

(1) To enclose a direct quotation: *"Life," said Julia Ward Howe, who lived to be ninety-one, "is like a cup of tea; the sugar is all at the bottom."*

Quotation marks are always used in *pairs,* before the quoted material and after it. However, if you quote two or more paragraphs, place quotation marks at the beginning of each paragraph and at the end of the entire quotation.

Single marks are used to enclose a quotation within a quotation. *"His constant use of such words as 'cool' and 'far out' has become very tiresome," the teacher remarked.*

(2) To enclose the title of a short literary work—a chapter, article, essay, poem, or short story—and titles of paintings, short musical compositions, and radio and television programs. The titles of longer works should be italicized. (Joyce's collection of short stories *Dubliners* includes the famous story "The Dead.")

(3) To enclose all words or phrases that are borrowed, that the writer does not wish to claim as his own, or that he uses ironically: *The term "the chain of being" was for centuries a descriptive name for the universe. For many of the world's poor, "home" is a tarpaper shack or a large oil pipe.*

(4) To enclose words or phrases which themselves are being discussed: *Many women now prefer the term "feminism" to the earlier phrase "women's lib."*

(5) When quotation marks are used with other punctuation, they appear as follows:

Outside a comma or period. *"I'm tired," she said. "It's been a long day."*

Inside the semicolon or colon: *A foreign phrase commonly misused to describe aristocracy is "hoi polloi"; actually, it means "the common people."*

Outside a question mark or exclamation point if either is part of the quotation—otherwise, inside. *"Get out of here!" she shrieked. Who wrote "The Unfinished Symphony"?*

Apostrophe (') Use an apostrophe:

(1) In contractions to indicate the omission of a letter: *haven't.*

(2) Before an *s* to form the plural of figures and

letters: *Two size 12's. Cross your t's and dot your i's.*

(3) To form possessives: *Mary's house, men's clothing.* If a plural ends in *s,* add only the apostrophe: *girls' sports, hostesses' duties.* If a singular ends in *s,* add the apostrophe and *s: James's car.* However, the second *s* may be omitted, especially if the word would become more difficult to pronounce: *Socrates' teachings.* Be sure never to use the apostrophe with the possessive pronouns *his, hers, its, yours, ours, theirs.*

Hyphen (-) Use a hyphen:

(1) To link many compound words—two or more words considered as a single unit: *secretary-treasurer, bull's-eye, heavy-hearted, cease-fire.* Do not use a hyphen if a compound modifier follows the noun: *This scientist is well known.* (But note use of hyphen in *a well-known scientist.*) Do not use a hyphen in a compound modifier that includes an adverb ending in *-ly* even if it precedes the noun: *richly deserved praise.*

(2) With certain prefixes and suffixes: *self-support, ex-wife, anti-American, co-worker, president-elect, husband-to-be.* When the parts have become merged in general use, the hyphen may be unnecessary: *midsummer, prehistoric, nonaligned.* (Since usage here is often inconsistent, it is wise, when in doubt, to consult a dictionary.)

(3) In compound numbers from twenty-one to ninety-nine and in fractions: *twenty-five, one-third.*

(4) To divide a word *between syllables* at the end of a line.

(5) Wherever misreading might occur, as in *a navy-blue uniform,* or if a prefix ends with a vowel and the root word begins with the same vowel: *re-elected, anti-inflationary, semi-independent.*

Dash (—) The dash indicates greater separation than a comma but lesser separation than parentheses. Use the dash:

(1) To indicate a sudden change in thought or sentence structure: *We rescheduled the picnic for the following Sunday—we hoped it would be a nice day—but it rained again.*

(2) To emphasize parenthetic, appositive, or explanatory matter. *Imagine a device that is only a cubic foot in size—the size of a hat box—containing 40,000 electronic parts!*

(3) To set off a parenthetic or appositive expression that is itself broken by commas: *She was beset by fears—of heights, open spaces, animals, traffic, strangers—and, as a result, she never left her home.*

Parentheses (()) Generally speaking, dashes add emphasis to the material they enclose, while parentheses tend to subordinate it. Use parentheses:

(1) To enclose incidental or explanatory material that may be relevant but is not strictly necessary: *The rivers, lakes, and surrounding seas (except the Black Sea) are rich in fish. During the reign of Henry VIII (1509–47), the Church of England asserted its independence from the Roman Catholic Church.*

(2) Around figures or letters to enumerate items in a series: *Three qualities of good writing are (1) clarity, (2) consistency, and (3) coherence.*

Parenthetical statements within a sentence begin with a small letter and have no end punctuation, except a question mark or exclamation point if needed. If a comma, semicolon, or colon are necessary after the parenthetical material within a sentence, they are placed outside the closing curve. A complete parenthetic sentence within a paragraph but not within another sentence has an initial capital and end punctuation placed within the closing curve: *Although Nigeria was the world's sixth largest oil producer (its 1974 oil revenues totaled $8 billion), the country's per capita income was only $120 per year. (Even so, it remained black Africa's wealthiest nation.) This problem contributed to continuing government instability.*

Brackets ([]) Use brackets to enclose parenthetic comments inserted in a quotation by the person using the quotation: *In his Nobel Lecture, Martin Luther King said, "In a dark, confused world [where war, poverty, and racism exist] the kingdom of God may yet reign in the hearts of men."*

Capitalization

The use of capital letters is quite standardized in general English. Avoid unnecessary capitals, and when in doubt consult a dictionary. As a rule, capitalize the following:

(1) The first word of a complete sentence: *The modern museum originated during the Renaissance.;* of a quoted sentence: *Freud said, "What does a woman want?";* of each line of poetry:

Had we but world enough, and time,
This coyness, lady, were no crime.—Andrew Marvell

(2) Proper names. A proper name is the name of a *particular* person, place, or thing. Capitalize all proper names including adjectives and abbreviations derived from proper names. Among the proper names to be capitalized are the names of specific persons or places: *John F. Kennedy, Vermont, China, Central Park;* organizations, institutions, buildings, and monuments: *the Republican Party, the Bank of America, Harvard University, the Museum of Modern Art, the Lincoln Memorial;* peoples, languages, religions, and political groups: *Africans, Indians, French, Caucasian, Methodist, Communist;* days of the week, months, holidays: *Tuesday, August, New Year's Day, Easter;* historical periods, events, or documents: *the Dark Ages, the Renaissance, the Holocaust, the Civil War, the Magna Carta, the Social Security Act;* geographical names and regions: *Yellowstone National Park, Lake Huron, the South Pole, the Northeast* (when words like *south* and *north* refer to directions rather than regions, they are not capitalized); names of departments of government and of institutions: *Department of Commerce, Police Department, the City Council, the English Department, the Graduate School;* stars, planets, constellations, satellites, except the sun, earth, and moon: *Sirius, Venus, Orion, Viking I, Halley's Comet;* words referring to the Deity, the Bible, and other sacred writings: *Jehovah, the Messiah, the Virgin, Genesis, Lamentations, the Koran.*

(3) Titles preceding proper names and titles of high rank used without the name: *Professor Cohen, Mayor Daley, Sergeant Jones, Aunt Ellen, the Pope, the President, the Secretary of State, the Queen Mother.*

(4) First and last words and all other words, except the articles *a, an, the,* conjunctions, and prepositions in titles of books, plays, poems, articles, movies, etc.: *Wild Animals of the World, Ode to the West Wind, All in the Family, Porgy and Bess.*

(5) The pronoun *I* and the exclamation *O: If I forget thee, O Jerusalem, let my right hand forget her cunning.*—Psalms

Abbreviations

Abbreviations are useful and appropriate in notetaking, in reference works, in statistical tables, and in certain other situations where speed and space-saving are important. In general writing, however, abbreviations should be avoided. A few standard abbreviations that are correct in all writing are the following:

(1) Titles and names: *Mr., Messrs., Mrs., Dr., Esq., Sr., Jr., Ph.D., M.D., LL.D.* Do not use a title both before and after a name: *Mr. James T. Smith* or *James T. Smith, Ph.D.,* not *Mr. James T. Smith, Ph.D.*

Do not abbreviate civil, professional (except *Dr.*), military, or political titles, except when the person's first name or initials are used: *Professor Downey* or *Prof. Charles Downey, General Marshall* or *Gen. G. C. Marshall,* never *Prof. Downey* or *Gen. Marshall.*

First names should, as a rule, be spelled out: *William Shakespeare,* not *Wm. Shakespeare.*

(2) Certain units of measurements: *a.m., p.m., A.D., B.C., mph,* when used with figures, as in *50 mph; No.* with numbers expressed in figures, as in *No. 8.* Write out other expressions for time, weight, and size, as in *three ounces, two miles, four hours,* unless such expressions appear in directions, recipes, or technical writing: *½ tsp salt, 10 ft 2 in.*

(3) Names of organizations, governmental agencies, scientific words, trade names, and other expressions that are familiar to most people and are frequently referred to by their initials: *YMCA, AFL-CIO, FCC, CIA, FBI, NASA, DDT, DNA, CBS, MGM.* Generally no period is used. (Exceptions: *C.O.D., F.O.B.*) Abbreviations like *Co., Inc., Ltd.,* or *Corp.* are correct when they are part of the company name: *Jones Publishing, Inc.*

(4) Certain literary abbreviations: *i.e.* (that is); *e.g.* (for example); *ibid.* (in the same place); *etc.* (and so forth).

In ordinary usage, write out: names of states, countries, months, days of the week; words like *street, road, square* when they are used as part of a proper name: *Maple Street;* and numbers that can be expressed in not more than one or two words: *twenty books, four hundred miles* (but *$3,560.23, 60,211 miles*).

> These are "general" rules of punctuation, capitalization, and abbreviation designed to make writing as clear and "correct" as possible. There are no absolutes. Many publications have modifications of these basic rules that reflect their own special needs.

Forms of Address[1]

By permission, From Webster's New Collegiate Dictionary, © 1981 by G. & C. Merriam Co., Publishers of the Merriam-Webster Dictionaries.

Abbot. *Address:* The Right Reverend _____, O.S.B. (or other initials of the order), Abbot of _____. *Begin:* Right Reverend and Dear Father.

Ambassador (U.S.). *Address:* The Honorable _____ _____, American Ambassador; **(to the U.S.):** His Excellency _____ _____, Ambassador of _____. *Begin:* Sir; *or* Dear Mr. Ambassador.

Archbishop. *Address:* The Most Reverend Archbishop of _____; *or* The Most Reverend _____ _____, Archbishop of _____. *Begin:* Your Excellency; *or* Dear Archbishop _____.

Archdeacon. *Address:* The Venerable the Archdeacon of _____. *Begin:* Venerable Sir.

Armed Forces (U.S.). See *Military and Naval Officers.*

Assemblyman. *Address:* The Honorable _____ _____, The Assembly, State Capitol. *Begin:* Dear Mr. _____.

Associate Justice (Supreme Court). *Address:* Mr. Justice _____, The Supreme Court of the United States. *Begin:* Dear Mr. Justice.

Attorney. *Address:* Mr. _____ _____, Attorney-at-Law; *or* _____ _____, Esq. *Begin:* Dear Mr. _____.

Bishop (Episcopal). *Address:* The Right Reverend _____ _____, Bishop of _____. *Begin:* Right Reverend Sir; *or* Dear Bishop _____.

Bishop (Roman Catholic). *Address:* The Most Reverend _____ _____, Bishop of _____. *Begin:* Your Excellency; *or* Dear Bishop _____.

Bishop (other denominations). *Address:* The Reverend _____ _____. *Begin:* Reverend Sir; *or* Dear Bishop _____.

Brother (Roman Catholic). *Address:* Brother _____ (first name followed by initials of the order). *Begin:* Dear Brother _____.

Cabinet Officer (U.S.). *Address:* The Honorable _____ _____, Secretary of State (or other department); *or* The Honorable _____ _____, Attorney General of the United States. *Begin:* Dear Sir.

Cardinal. *Address:* His Eminence John Cardinal Smith. *Begin:* Your Eminence; *or* Dear Cardinal _____.

Chargé d'Affaires (U.S.). *Address:* _____ _____, Esq., American Chargé d'Affaires. *Begin:* Dear Sir.

Chief Justice (Supreme Court). *Address:* The Chief Justice of the United States. *Begin:* Dear Mr. Chief Justice.

Clergyman (Protestant). *Address:* The Reverend _____ _____; *or* (if a Doctor of Divinity) The Reverend Dr. _____ _____; *Begin:* Dear Sir; *or* Dear Mr. _____; *or* Dear Dr. _____.

Commissioner (of a Department or Bureau). *Address:* The Honorable _____ _____. *Begin:* Dear Mr. _____.

Consul. *Address:* _____ _____, Esq., American Consul. *Begin:* Dear Sir.

Dean (of a Cathedral). *Address:* The Very Reverend _____ _____; *or* Dean _____ _____. *Begin:*

1. Since the relationship between correspondents affects the form of address used in letters, no rigid guidelines can be set down for all occasions. When two salutations are shown, it is to be understood that the formal styling precedes the informal. In salutations where the addressee is a woman, it is to be understood that in formal address Madam may be substituted for Sir, and in informal address Mrs. or Miss or Ms. may be substituted for Mr. 2. From Webster's Eighth New Collegiate Dictionary. NOTE: Forms of Address for foreign dignitaries may be obtained from their United Nations missions in New York City.

Very Reverend Sir; *or* Dear Dean ______.

Dean (of a College or University). *Address:* Dean ______ ______. *Begin:* Dear Dean ______.

Dentist. *Address:* ______ ______, D.D.S. (office address); *or* Dr. ______ ______ (home address). *Begin:* Dear Dr. ______.

Divorced Woman. *Address:* Ordinarily use *Mrs.* with her maiden name as a prename. Some divorced women prefer to resume the *Miss.*[2]

Doctor of Divinity. See *Clergyman.*

Doctor of Philosophy, Laws, etc. *Address:* ______ ______, Ph.D. (LL.D.) (or other degree). *Begin:* Dear Sir; *or* Dear Dr. ______.

Governor. *Address:* The Honorable ______ ______, Governor of ______. *Begin:* Dear Governor ______.

Governor-General of Canada. *Address:* His Excellency The Right Honourable ______ ______ (plus personal rank or title, if any). *Begin:* My Lord; *or* Sir (according to rank).[2]

Governor-General's Wife. *Address:* Her Excellency ______ ______ (plus personal rank or title, if any). *Begin:* Madam.[2]

Judge (Federal). *Address:* The Honorable ______ ______, United States District Judge. *Begin:* Dear Judge ______.

Judge (State or Local). *Address:* The Honorable ______ ______, Judge of the Court of Appeals (or other court). *Begin:* Dear Judge ______.

King. *Address:* The King's Most Excellent Majesty; *or* His Most Gracious Majesty, King ______. *Begin:* Sir; *or* May It Please Your Majesty.[2]

Lieutenant Governor. *Address:* The Honorable ______ ______, Lieutenant Governor of ______. *Begin:* Dear Mr. ______.

Mayor (in Canadian Cities and Towns, and English Boroughs and Cities). *Address:* The Right Worshipful the Mayor of ______ (English cities only); His Worship, The Mayor of ______ (other). *Begin:* Sir.[2]

Mayor (U.S.). *Address:* The Honorable ______ ______, Mayor of ______. *Begin:* Dear Mayor ______.

Member of Parliament (or of a Legislative Council). The ordinary form of address followed by M.P. (or M.L.C.).[2]

Military and Naval Officers (U.S.): *Address:* (full rank) ______ ______, U.S.N. (or U.S.A., U.S.A.F., U.S.M.C., U.S.C.G.). *Begin:* Sir (admirals and generals only); *or* Dear (full rank) ______ (other officers, including admirals and generals); *or* Dear Mr. ______ (lieutenant commander, lieutenant, ensign only).

Minister (to U.S.). *Address:* The Honorable ______ ______, Minister of ______. *Begin:* Sir; *or* Dear Mr. Minister.

Minister of Religion. See *Clergyman, Priest, Rabbi.*

Monsignor. *Address:* The Right Reverend Monsignor ______. *Begin:* Dear Monsignor ______.

Mother Superior of a Sisterhood. *Address:* The Reverend Mother Superior, O.S.F. (or other initials of the order); *Begin:* Reverend Mother; or Dear Reverend Mother.

Nun. See *Sister of a Religious Order.*

Papal Nuncio or Internuncio or Apostolic Delegate. *Address:* His Excellency, The Papal Nuncio (*or* Internuncio *or* Apostolic Delegate) to ______. *Begin:* Your Excellency.[2]

Patriarch (Eastern Church). *Address:* His Beatitude the Patriarch of ______. *Begin:* Most Reverend Lord.

Physician. *Address:* ______ ______, M.D. (office address); *or* Dr. ______ ______ (home address). *Begin:* Dear Dr. ______.

Pope. *Address:* His Holiness Pope ______; *or* His Holiness the Pope. *Begin:* Your Holiness; *or* Most Holy Father.

President of a College or University. *Address:* President ______ ______. *Begin:* Dear President ______.

President of a State Senate. *Address:* The Honorable ______ ______, President of the Senate of ______. *Begin:* Dear Senator ______.[2]

President of the U.S. *Address:* The President. *Begin:* Dear Mr. President.

President of the U.S. (Former). *Address:* The Honorable ______ ______. *Begin:* Dear Mr. ______.

Priest (Roman Catholic). *Address:* The Reverend Father ______; *or* The Reverend ______ ______. *Begin:* Dear Father ______; *or* Dear Father.

Prime Minister of Canada. *Address:* The Right Honourable ______ ______, P.C., Prime Minister of Canada. *Begin:* Sir.[2]

Privy Councillor (of Canada). *Address:* The Honourable ______ ______. *Begin:* Sir.[2]

Professor at a College or University. *Address:* Professor ______ ______. *Begin:* Dear Professor ______.

Queen. *Address:* The Queen's Most Excellent Majesty; *or* Her Gracious Majesty, The Queen. *Begin:* Madam; *or* May It Please Your Majesty.[2]

Rabbi. *Address:* Rabbi ______ ______; *or* Rabbi ______ ______, D.D. (if a Doctor of Divinity). *Begin:* Dear Rabbi ______; *or* Dear Dr. ______.

Representative (State). *Address:* The Honorable ______ ______, House of Representatives, State Capitol. *Begin:* Dear Mr. ______.

Representative (U.S.). *Address:* The Honorable ______ ______, The United States House of Representatives. *Begin:* Dear Mr. ______.

Secretary-General of the U.N. *Address:* His Excellency ______ ______, Secretary-General of the United Nations. *Begin:* Excellency; *or* Dear Mr. Secretary-General; *or* Dear Mr. ______.

Senator (State). *Address:* The Honorable ______ ______, The State Senate, State Capitol. *Begin:* Dear Senator ______.

Senator (U.S.). *Address:* The Honorable ______ ______, United States Senate. *Begin:* Dear Senator ______.

Sister of a Religious Order. *Address:* Sister ______ ______, S.C. (or other initials of the order). *Begin:* Dear Sister ______ ______; *or* Dear Sister.

Speaker of the House of Commons (Canada). *Address:* The Honourable ______ ______, The Speaker of the House of Commons. *Begin:* Dear Mr. Speaker.[2]

Speaker of the House of Representatives (U.S.). *Address:* The Honorable ______ ______, Speaker of the House of Representatives. *Begin:* Dear Mr. Speaker.

Superior of a Brotherhood. *Address:* Brother ______ (first name followed by initials of the order), Superior. *Begin:* Dear Brother ______.

United Nations Representative (Foreign). *Address:* His Excellency ______ ______, Representative of ______ to the United Nations. *Begin:* Excellency; *or* Dear Mr. Ambassador.[2]

United Nations Representative (U.S.). *Address:* The Honorable ______ ______, United States Representative to the United Nations. *Begin:* Sir; *or* Dear Mr. Ambassador.[2]

Veterinarian. *Address:* ______ ______, D.V.M. (office address); or Dr. ______ ______ (home address). *Begin:* Dear Dr. ______.

Vice President of the U.S. *Address:* The Vice President, United States Senate. *Begin:* Dear Mr. Vice President.

Widow. Ordinarily addressed by her former title: as, Mrs. John Doe, not Mrs. Jane Doe, unless the latter form is preferred by the person herself.[2]

Foreign Words and Phrases

(The English meanings given are not necessarily literal translations.)

ab ovo: from the beginning
à bon marché: good bargain; cheap
à deux: for two; between two
a priori: from something previous
à votre santé: to your health
ad infinitum: to infinity; with no end
ad valorem: according to its value
al fresco: outdoors
alma mater: one's college or school
alter ego: other self
amicus curiae: friend of the court
ancien regime: the old order
anno Domini: year of our Lord
ante bellum: before the war
au contraire: on the contrary
au courant: current; up-to-date
auf Wiedersehen: goodbye
bête noire: particular nemesis
bienvenue: welcome
bon mot: a funny or witty saying
bon vivant: a gourmet, an epicure
bona fide: in good faith; genuine; honest
carpe diem: enjoy today; seize the day
carte blanche: unlimited authority
cause célèbre: a cause that generates wide interest
caveat emptor: buy at your own risk; let the buyer beware
circa: about; approximately
chacun à son goût: each to his own taste
combien: how much?
corpus delicti: fundamental fact or facts about the commission of a crime
coup de grâce: finishing blow
cum grano salis: with a grain of salt
d'accord: in accord; agreement
de facto: as a matter of fact; actual
de profundis: out of the depths
Deo gratias: thanks be to God
Deo volente: God willing
dernier cri: the last word
deus ex machina: artificially produced to bring a solution to some extreme difficulty
dramatis personae: characters in a play
ecce homo: this is the man
en masse: all together
en passant: in passing
fait accompli: an accomplished fact
faux pas: a false step; a mistake
flagrante delicto: caught in the act
Gesundheit: good health (God bless you)
habeas corpus: common-law writ to bring a person before a court or judge
hoi polloi: the common people
honi soit qui mal y pense: evil to him who thinks evil of it
hors d'oeuvre: appetizer
idée fixe: fixed idea; obsession
in loco parentis: in place of a parent
ipso facto: by the very fact
je ne sais quoi: I don't know what; an elusive quality
jeunesse dorée: gilded youth
laissez faire: noninterference
l'chaim: to life
maven: an expert; connoisseur
mea culpa: I am to blame
mirabile dictu: wonderful to relate
modus operandi: method of operation; way of working
nom de plume: pen name
non compos mentis: not of sound mind
non sequitur: it does not follow
O tempora! O mores!: What sad times and customs
omnia vincit amor: love conquers all
per annum: by the year
per capita: by the head; individually
per diem: by the day; daily
persona non grata: an unwelcome or unacceptable person
plus ça change, plus c'est le même chose: the more things change, the more they remain the same
post mortem: after death
pro bono publico: for the public good
pro tempore (pro tem): for the time being; temporary
quid pro quo: something done or given in exchange for something else
repondez s'il vous plait: please reply; please answer (abbr. R.S.V.P.)
requiescat in pace: rest in peace
sans souci: without worry or care
savoir faire: know-how; manners for all occasions
semper fidelis: always faithful
shalom: peace
sic transit gloria mundi: so passes the glory of the world
s'il vous plait: if you please; please
sine die: with no day set for the next meeting
sine qua non: indispensable
status (in) quo: state in which anything is
sui generis: in a class by itself
tempus fugit: time flies
tout de suite: immediately
veni, vidi, vici: I came, I saw, I conquered
vis-à-vis: face-to-face

Carbon 14 Dating Technique

The old method for determining the age of a fossil by carbon 14 dating usually required samples so large that the fossil being analyzed was often destroyed. The latest technique developed by the University of Rochester uses a special high-voltage generator to directly measure the carbon 14 remaining in the sample. The advantage of this technique is that it requires only a one-milligram sample for testing.

Copyrights

Source: Library of Congress, Copyright Office.

The copyright law (Title 17 of the United States Code) has been amended by the enactment of a statute for its general revision, Public Law 94-553 (90 Stat. 2541), which was signed by the President on October 19, 1976. The new law superseded the copyright act of 1909, as amended, which remained effective until the new enactment took effect on January 1, 1978.

Under the new law, all copyrightable works, whether published or unpublished, are subject to a single system of statutory protection which gives a copyright owner the exclusive right to reproduce the copyrighted work in copies or phonorecords and distribute them to the public by sale, rental, lease, or lending. Among the other rights given to the owner of a copyright are the exclusive rights to prepare derivative works based upon the copyrighted work, to perform the work publicly if it be literary, musical, dramatic, choreographic, a pantomime, motion picture, or other audiovisual work, and in the case of literary, musical, dramatic, and choreographic works, pantomimes, and pictorial, graphic, or sculptural works, including the individual images of a motion picture or other audiovisual work, to display the copyrighted work publicly. All of these rights are subject to certain exceptions, including the principle of "fair use" which the new statute specifically recognizes.

Special provisions are included which permit compulsory licensing for the recording of musical compositions, noncommercial transmissions by public broadcasters of published musical and graphic works, performances of copyrighted music by jukeboxes, and the secondary transmission of copyrighted works on cable television systems.

Copyright protection under the new law extends to original works of authorship fixed in any tangible medium of expression, now known or later developed, from which they can be perceived, reproduced, or otherwise communicated, either directly or with the aid of a machine or device. Works of authorship include books, periodicals and other literary works, musical compositions with accompanying lyrics, dramas and dramatico-musical compositions, pantomimes and choreographic works, motion pictures and other audiovisual works, and sound recordings.

As a mandatory condition of copyright protection under the law in effect before 1978, all published copies of a work were required to bear a copyright notice. The 1976 Act provides for a notice on published copies, but omission or errors will not immediately result in forfeiture of the copyright, and can be corrected within certain time limits. Innocent infringers misled by the omission or error will be shielded from liability.

Registration in the Copyright Office is not a condition of copyright protection but will be a prerequisite to bringing an action in a court of law for infringement. With certain exceptions, the remedies of statutory damages and attorney's fees will not be available for infringements occurring before registration. Copies or phonorecords published in the United States with notice of copyright are required to be deposited for the collections of the Library of Congress, not as a condition of copyright protection, but under provisions of the law subjecting the copyright owner to certain penalties for failure to deposit after a demand by the Register of Copyrights. Registration is permissive, but may be made either at the time the depository requirements are satisfied or at any other time during the subsistence of the copyright.

For works already under statutory protection, the new law retains the present term of copyright of 28 years from first publication (or from registration in some cases), renewable by certain persons for a second period of protection, but it increases the length of the second period to 47 years. Copyrights in their first term on January 1, 1978, must still be renewed during the last (28th) year of the original copyright term to receive the maximum statutory term of 75 years (a first term of 28 years plus a renewal term of 47 years).

Copyrights in their second term on January 1, 1978, are automatically extended up to a maximum of 75 years, without the need for further renewal. Unpublished works that are already in existence on January 1, 1978, but are not protected by statutory copyright and have not yet gone into the public domain, will generally obtain automatic Federal copyright protection for the author's life, plus an additional 50 years after the author's death, but in any event, for a minimal term of 25 years (that is, until December 31, 2002), and if the work is published before that date, then for an additional term of 25 years, through the end of 2027.

For works created on or after January 1, 1978, the new law provides a term lasting for the author's life, plus an additional 50 years after the author's death. For works made for hire, and for anonymous and pseudonymous works (unless the author's identity is revealed in Copyright Office records), the new term will be 75 years from publication or 100 years from creation, whichever is shorter. The new law provides that all terms of copyright will run through the end of the calendar year in which they would otherwise expire. This will not only affect the duration of copyrights, but also the time-limits for renewal registrations.

Works already in the public domain cannot be protected under the new law. The 1976 Act provides no procedure for restoring protection to works in which copyright has been lost for any reason. In general, works published before September 19, 1906, are not under copyright protection in the United States, at least insofar as any version published before that date is concerned.

The new law requires that all visually perceptible copies published in the United States or elsewhere bear a notice of copyright affixed in such manner and location as to give reasonable notice of the claim of copyright. The notice consists of the symbol © (the letter C in a circle), the word "Copyright," or the abbreviation "Copr.," and the year of first publication of the work, and the name of the owner of copyright in the work. EXAMPLE: © *1983 John Doe.*

The notice of copyright prescribed for sound recordings consists of the symbol ℗ (the letter P in a circle), the year of first publication of the sound recording, and the name of the owner of copyright in the sound recording, placed on the surface of the phonorecord, or on the phonorecord label or container, in such manner and location as to give reasonable notice of the claim of copyright. EXAMPLE: ℗ *1983 Doe Records, Inc.*

A work by a U.S. citizen may obtain copyright protection in all countries that are members of the Universal Copyright Convention (UCC), provided the copyright notice appearing on all copies from the date of first publication includes the symbol ©, together with the name of the copyright owner and the year date of publication. EXAMPLE: © *John Doe 1983.*

Further information and application forms may be obtained free of charge upon request from the Copyright Office, Library of Congress, Washington, D.C. 20559.

Patents

Source: Department of Commerce, Patent and Trademark Office.

A patent, in the most general sense, is a document issued by a government, conferring some special right or privilege. The term is now restricted mainly to patents for inventions; occasionally, land patents.

The grant of a patent for an invention gives the inventor the privilege, for a limited period of time, of excluding others from making, using, or selling a certain article. However, it does not give him the right to make, use, or sell his own invention if it is an improvement on some unexpired patent whose claims are infringed thereby.

In the U.S., the law provides that a patent may be granted, for a term of 17 years, to any person who has invented or discovered any new and useful art, machine, manufacture, or composition of matter, as well as any new and useful improvements thereof. A patent may also be granted to a person who has invented or discovered and asexually reproduced a new and distinct variety of plant (other than a tuber-propagated one) or has invented a new, original and ornamental design for an article of manufacture.

A patent is granted only upon a regularly filed application, complete in all respects; upon payment of the fees; and upon determination that the disclosure is complete and that the invention is new, useful, and, in view of the prior art, unobvious to one skilled in the art. The disclosure must be of such nature as to enable others to reproduce the invention.

A complete application, which must be addressed to the Commissioner of Patents and Trademarks, Washington, D.C. 20231, consists of a specification with one or more claims; oath or declaration; drawing (whenever the nature of the case admits of it); and a basic filing fee of $65, plus certain additional charges for claims. The filing fee is not returned to the applicant if the patent is refused. If the patent is allowed, another fee of $100, plus additional printing charges, is required before the patent is issued. The fees for design patents vary.

Applications are ordinarily considered in the order in which they are received. Patents are not granted for printed matter, for methods of doing business, or for devices for which claims contrary to natural laws are made. Applications for a perpetual-motion machine have been made from time to time, but until a working model is presented that actually fulfills the claim, no patent will be issued.

Trademarks

Source: Department of Commerce, Patent and Trademark Office.

A trademark may be defined as a word, letter, device, or symbol, as well as some combination of these, which is used in connection with merchandise and which points distinctly to the origin of the goods.

Certificates of registration of trademarks are issued under the seal of the Patent and Trademark Office and may be registered by the owner if he is engaged in interstate or foreign commerce, since any Federal jurisdiction over trademarks arises under the commerce clause of the Constitution. Trademarks may be registered by foreign owners who comply with our law, as well as by citizens of foreign countries with which the U.S. has treaties relating to trademarks. American citizens may register trademarks in foreign countries by complying with the laws of those countries. The right to registration and protection of trademarks in many foreign countries is guaranteed by treaties.

General jurisdiction in trademark cases involving Federal Registrations is given to Federal courts. Adverse decisions of examiners on applications for registration are appealable to the Trademark Trial and Appeal Board, whose affirmances, and decisions in *inter partes* proceedings, are subject to court review. Before adopting a trademark, a person should make a search of prior marks to avoid infringing unwittingly upon them.

The duration of a trademark registration is 20 years, but it may be renewed indefinitely for 20-year periods, provided the trademark is still in use at the time of expiration.

Birthstones

Month	Stone	Month	Stone
January	Garnet	July	Ruby or Star Ruby
February	Amethyst	August	Peridot or Sardonyx
March	Aquamarine or Bloodstone	September	Sapphire or Star Sapphire
April	Diamond	October	Opal or Tourmaline
May	Emerald	November	Topaz
June	Pearl, Alexandrite, or Moonstone	December	Turquoise or Zircon

Source: Jewelry Industry Council.

CROSSWORD PUZZLE GUIDE

First Aid to Crossword Puzzlers

We cannot begin to list all the odd words you will meet with in your daily and Sunday crossword puzzles, for such words run into many thousands. But we have tried to include those which turn up most frequently, as well as many others which should be of help to you when you are unable to go any further.

Also, we do not guarantee that the definitions in your puzzle will be exactly the same as ours, although we have checked every word with a standard dictionary and have followed its definition.

In nearly every case, we have used as the key word the principal noun of the definition, rather than any adjective, adjective phrase, or noun used as an adjective. And, to simplify your searching, we have grouped the words according to the number of spaces you have to fill.

For a list of Foreign Phrases, *see* Index. For Rulers of England and Great Britain, France, Germany and Prussia, and Russia, *see* Countries of the World.

Words of Two Letters

Ambary, DA
And (French, Latin), ET
Article (Arabic), AL
  (French), LA, LE, UN
  (Spanish), EL, LA, UN
At the (French), AU
  (Spanish), AL
Behold, LO
Bird: Hawaiian, OO
Birthplace: Abraham's, UR
Bone, OS
Buddha, FO
Butterfly: Peacock, IO
Champagne, AY
Chaos, NU
Chief: Burmese, BO
Coin: Roman, AS
  Siamese, AT
Concerning, RE
Dialect: Chinese, WU
Double (Egy. relig.), KA
Drama: Japanese, NO
Egg (comb. form), OO
Esker, OS
Eye (Scotch), EE
Factor: Amplification, MU
Fifty (Greek), NU
Fish: Carplike, ID
Force, OD
Forty (Greek), MU
From (French, Latin, Spanish), DE
  (Latin prefix), AB
From the (French), DU
God: Babylonian, EA, ZU
  Egyptian sun, RA
  Hindu unknown, KA
  Semitic, EL
Goddess: Babylonian, AI
  Greek earth, GE
Gold (heraldry), OR
Gulf: Arctic, OB
Heart (Egy. relig.), AB
Indian: South American, GE
King: Of Bashan, OG
Language: Artificial, RO
  Assamese, AO
Lava: Hawaiian, AA
Letter: Greek, MU, NU, PI, XI
  Hebrew, HE, PE
Lily: Palm, TI
Measure: Annamese, LY
  Chinese, HO, HU, KO, LI, MU, PU, TO, TU
  Japanese, GO, JO, MO, RI, SE, TO
  Metric land, AR
  Netherlands, EL
  Portuguese, PE
  Siamese, WA
  Swedish, AM
  Type, EM, EN
Monk: Buddhist, BO
Month: Jewish, AB
Mouth, OS
Mulberry: Indian, AL
Native: Burmese, WA
Note: Of Scale, DO, FA, MI, LA, RE, TI
Of (French, Latin, Spanish), DE
Of the (French), DU
One (Scotch), AE
Pagoda: Chinese, TA
Plant: East Indian fiber, DA
Ridge: Sandy, AS, OS
River: Russian, OB
Sloth: Three-toed, AI
Soul (Egy. relig.), BA
Sound: Hindu mystic, OM
Suffix: Comparative, ER
The. *See* Article
To the: French, AU
  Spanish, AL
Tree: Buddhist sacred, BO
Tribe: Assamese, AO
Type: Jumbled, PI
Weight: Annamese, TA
  Chinese, LI
  Danish, ES
  Japanese, MO
  Roman, AS
Whirlwind: Faeroe Is., OE
Yes (German), JA
  (Italian, Spanish), SI
  (Russian), DA

Words of Three Letters

Adherent, IST
Again, BIS
Age, ERA
Antelope: African, GNU, KOB
Apricot: Japanese, UME
Article (German), DAS, DEM, DEN, DER, DES, DIE, EIN
  (French), LES, UNE
  (Spanish), LAS, LOS, UNA
Banana: Polynesian, FEI
Barge, HOY
Bass: African, IYO
Beak, NEB, NIB
Beard: Grain, AWN
Beetle: June, DOR
Being, ENS
Berry: Hawthorn, HAW
Beverage: Hawaiian, AVA
Bird: Australian, EMU
  Crowlike, JAY
  Extinct, MOA
  Fabulous, ROC
  Frigate, IWA
  Parson, POE, TUE, TUI
  Sea, AUK
Blackbird, ANI, ANO
Born, NEE
Bronze: Roman, AES
Bugle: Yellow, IVA
By way of, VIA
Canton: Swiss, URI
Cap: Turkish, FEZ
Catnip, NEP
Character: In "Faerie Queene," UNA
Coin: Afghan, PUL
  Albanian, LEK
  British Guiana, BIT
  Bulgarian, LEV, LEW
  French, ECU, SOU
  Indian, PIE
  Japanese, SEN, YEN
  Korean, WON
  Lithuanian, LIT
  Macao, Timor, AVO
  Palestinian, MIL
  Persian, PUL
  Peruvian, SOL
  Rumanian, BAN, LEU, LEY
  Scandinavian, ORE
  Siamese, ATT
  See also Money of account
Collection: Facts, ANA
Commune: Belgian, ANS, ATH
  Netherlands, EDE, EPE
Community: Russian, MIR
Constellation: Southern, ARA
Contraction: Poetic, EEN, EER, OER
Covering: Apex of roof, EPI
Crab: Fiddler, UCA
Crag: Rocky, TOR
Cry: Crow, rook, raven, CAW
Cup: Wine, AMA
Cymbal, Oriental, TAL, ZEL

Disease: Silkworm, UJI
Division: Danish territorial, AMT
  Geologic, EON
Doctrine, ISM
Dowry, DOT
Dry (French), SEC
Dynasty: Chinese, CHI, HAN, SUI, WEI, YIN
Eagle: Sea, ERN
Earth (comb. form), GEO
Egg: Louse, NIT
Eggs: Fish, ROE
Emmet, ANT
Enzyme, ASE
Equal (comb. form), ISO
Extension: building, ELL
Far (comb. form), TEL
Farewell, AVE
Fiber: Palm, TAL
Finial, EPI
Fish: Carplike, IDE
  Pikelike, GAR
Flatfish, DAB
Fleur-de-lis, LIS, LYS
Food: Hawaiian, POI
Formerly, NEE
Friend (French), AMI
Game: Card, LOO
Garment: Camel-hair, ABA
Gateway, DAR
Gazelle: Tibetan, GOA
Genus: Ducks, AIX
  Grasses, POA
  Grasses (maize), ZEA
  Herbs or shrubs, IVA
  Lizards, UTA
  Rodents (incl. house mice), MUS
  Ruminants (incl. cattle), BOS
  Swine, SUS
Gibbon: Malay, LAR
God: Assyrian, SIN
  Babylonian, ABU, ANU, BEL, HEA, SIN, UTU
  Irish sea, LER
  Phrygian, MEN
  Polynesian, ORO
Goddess: Babylonian, AYA
  Etruscan, UNI
  Hindu, SRI, UMA, VAC
  Teutonic, RAN
Governor: Algerian, DEY
  Turkish, BEY
Grampus, ORC
Grape, UVA
Grass: Meadow, POA
Gypsy, ROM
Hail, AVE
Hare: Female, DOE
Hawthorn, HAW
Hay: Spread for drying, TED
Herb: Japanese, UDO
  Perennial, PIA
  Used for blue dye, WAD
Herd: Whales, GAM, POD
Hero: Spanish, CID
High (music), ALT
Honey (pharm.), MEL
Humorist: American, ADE
I (Latin), EGO
I love (Latin), AMO
Indian: Algonquian, FOX, SAC, WEA
  Chimakuan, HOH
  Keresan, SIA
  Mayan, MAM
  Shoshonean, UTE
  Siouan, KAW, OTO
  South American, ITE, ONA, URO, URU, YAO
  Tierra del Fuego, ONA
  Wakashan, AHT
Ingot, PIG
Inlet: Narrow, RIA
Island: Cyclades, IOS
  Dodecanese, COS, KOS
  (French), ILE
  River, AIT
Jackdaw, DAW
John (Gaelic), IAN
Keelbill, ANI, ANO
Kiln, OST
King: British legendary LUD
Kobold, NIS
Lace: To make, TAT
Lamprey, EEL
Language: Artificial, IDO
  Bantu, ILA
  Siamese, LAO, TAI
Leaf: Palm, OLA, OLE
Leaving, ORT
Left: Cause to turn, HAW
Letter: Greek, CHI, ETA, PHI, PSI, RHO, TAU
  Hebrew, MEM, NUN, SIN, TAV, VAU
Lettuce, COS
Life (comb. form), BIO
Lily: Palm, TOI
Lizard, EFT
Louse: Young NIT
Love (Anglo-Irish), GRA
Lute: Oriental, TAR
Macaw: Bralizian, ARA
Marble, TAW
Match: Shooting (French), TIR
Meadow, LEA
Measure: Abyssinian, TAT
  Algerian, PIK
  Annamese, GON, MAU, NGU, VUO, SAO, TAO, TAT
  Arabian, DEN, SAA
  Belgian, VAT
  Bulgarian, OKA, OKE
  Chinese, FEN, TOU, YIN
  Cloth, ELL
  Cyprus, OKA, OKE, PIK
  Czech, LAN, SAH
  Danish, FOD, MIL, POT
  Dominican Republic, ONA
  Dutch, old, AAM
  East Indian, KIT
  Egyptian, APT, HEN, PIK, ROB
  Electric, MHO, OHM
  Energy, ERG
  English, PIN
  Estonian, TUN
  French, POT
  German, AAM
  Greek, PIK
  Hebrew, CAB, HIN, KOR, LOG
  Hungarian, AKO
  Icelandic, FET
  Indian, GAZ, GUZ, JOW, KOS
  Japanese, BOO, CHO, KEN, RIN, SHO, SUN, TAN
  Malabar, ADY
  Metric land, ARE
  Netherlands, KAN, KOP, MUD, VAT, ZAK
  Norwegian, FOT, POT
  Persian, GAZ, GUZ, MOU, ZAR, ZER
  Polish, CAL
  Rangoon, DHA, LAN
  Roman, PES, URN
  Russian, FUT, LOF
  Scotch, COP
  Siamese, KEN, NIU, RAI, SAT, SEN, SOK, WAH, YOT
  Somaliland, TOP
  Spanish, PIE
  Straits Settlements, PAU, TUN
  Swedish, ALN, FOT, MIL, REF, TUM
  Swiss, POT
  Tunisian, SAA
  Turkish, OKA, OKE, PIK
  Wire, MIL
  Württemberg, IMI
  Yarn, LEA
  Yugoslavian, OKA, RIF
Milk, LAC
Milkfish, AWA
Moccasin, PAC
Money: Yap stone, FEI
Money of Account: Anglo-Saxon, ORA, ORE
  French, SOU
  Indian, LAC
  Japanese, RIN
  Oman, GAJ
  Virgin Islands, BIT
  See also Coin
Monkey: Capuchin, SAI
Morsel, ORT
Mother: Peer Gynt's, ASE
Mountain: Asia Minor, IDA
Mulberry: Indian, AAL, ACH, AWL
Muttonbird: New Zealand, OII
Nahoor, SNA
Native: Mindanao, ATA
Neckpiece, BOA
Newt, EFT
No (Scotch), NAE
Note: Guido's highest, ELA
  Of scale, SOL
Nursemaid: Oriental, AMA, IYA
Ocher: Yellow, SIL
One (Scotch), YIN
Ornament: Pagoda, TEE
Oven: Polynesian, UMU
Ox: Tibetan, YAK
Pagoda: Chinese, TAA
Parrot: Hawk, HIA
  New Zealand, KEA
Part: Footlike, PES
Particle: Electrified, ION
Pasha, DEY
Pass: Mountain, COL
Paste: Rice, AME
Pea: Indian split, DAL
Peasant: Philippine, TAO
Penpoint, NEB, NIB
Piece out, EKE
Pigeon, NUN
Pine: Textile screw, ARA
Pistol (slang), GAT
Pit: Baking, IMU
Plant: Pepper, AVA
Play: By Capek, RUR
Poem: Old French, DIT
Porgy: Japanese, TAI
Priest: Biblical high, ELI
Prince Ethiopian, RAS
Pseudonym: Dickens', BOZ
Queen: Fairy, MAB
Quince: Bengal, BEL
Record: Ship's, LOG
Refuse: Flax (Scotch), PAB, POB
Resin, LAC
Resort, SPA
Revolver (slang), GAT
Right: Cause to turn, GEE
River: Scotch or English, DEE
  (Spanish), RIO
  Swiss, AAR
Room: Harem, ODA
Rootstock: Fern, ROI
Rose (Persian), GUL
Ruff: Female, REE
Rule: Indian, RAJ
Sailor, GOB, TAR
Saint: Female (abbr.), STE
  Mohammedan, PIR
Salt, SAL
Sash: Japanese, OBI
Scrap, ORT
Seed: Poppy, MAW
  Small, PIP
Self, EGO
Serpent: Vedic sky, AHI
Sesame, TIL
Sheep: Female, EWE
  Indian, SHA
  Male, RAM
Sheepfold (Scotch), REE
Shelter, LEE
Shield, ECU
Shooting match (French), TIR
Shrew: European, ERD
Shrub: Evergreen, YEW
Silkworm, ERI

Snake, ASP, BOA
Soak, RET
Son-in-law: Mohammed's, ALI
Sorrel: Wood, OCA
Spade: Long, narrow, LOY
Spirit: Malignant, KER
Spot: Playing-card, PIP
Spread for drying, TED
Spring: Mineral, SPA
Sprite: Water, NIX
Statesman: Japanese, ITO
Stern: Toward, AFT
Stomach: Bird's, MAW
Street (French), RUE
Summer (French), ETE
Sun, SOL
Swamp, BOG, FEN
Swan: Male, COB
Tea: Chinese, CHA
Temple: Shinto, SHA
The. *See* Article
Thing (law), RES
Title: Etruscan, LAR
  Monk's, FRA
  Portuguese, DOM
  Spanish, DON
  Turkish, AGA, BEY
Tool: Cutting, ADZ, AXE
  Mining, GAD
  Piercing, AWL
Tree: Candlenut, AMA
  Central American, EBO
  East Indian, SAJ, SAL
  Evergreen, YEW
  Hawaiian, KOA, KOU
  Indian, BEL, DAR
  Linden, LIN
  New Zealand, AKE
  Philippine, DAO, TUA, TUI
  Rubber, ULE
  South American, APA
Tribe: New Zealand, ATI
Turmeric, REA
Twice, BIS
Twin: Siamese, ENG
Uncle (dialect), EAM, EME
Veil: Chalice, AER, AIR
Vessel: Wine, AMA
Vestment: Ecclesiastical, ALB
Vetch: Bitter, ERS
Victorfish, AKU
Vine: New Zealand, AKA
  Philippine, IYO
Wallaba, APA
Wapiti, ELK
Water (French), EAU
Waterfall, LIN
Watering place: Prussian, EMS
Weave: Designating plain, UNI
Weight: Annamese, CAN
  Bulgarian, OKA, OKE
  Burmese, MOO, VIS
  Chinese, FEN, HAO, KIN, SSU, TAN, YIN
  Cyprus, OKA, OKE
  Danish, LOD, ORT, VOG
  East Indian, TJI
  Egyptian, KAT, OKA, OKE
  English, for wool, TOD
  German, LOT
  Greek, MNA, OKA, OKE
  Indian, SER
  Japanese, FUN, KIN, RIN, SHI
  Korean, KON
  Malacca, KIP
  Mongolian, LAN
  Netherlands, ONS
  Norwegian, LOD
  Polish, LUT
  Rangoon, PAI
  Roman, BES
  Russian, LOT
  Siamese, BAT, HAP, PAI
  Swedish, ASS, ORT
  Turkish, OKA, OKE
  Yugoslavian, OKA, OKE
Whales: Herd, GAM, POD
Wildebeest, GNU
Wing, ALA
Witticism, MOT
Wolframite, CAL
Worm: African, LOA
Wreath: Hawaiian, LEI
Yale, ELI
Yam: Hawaiian, HOI
Yes (French), OUI
Young: Bring forth, EAN
Z (letter), ZED

Words of Four Letters

Aborigine: Borneo, DYAK
Agave, ALOE
Animal: Footless, APOD
Ant: White, ANAI, ANAY
Antelope: African, ASSE, BISA, GUIB, KOBA, KUDU, ORYX, POKU, PUKU, TOPI, TORA
Apoplexy: Plant, ESCA
Apple, POME
Apricot, ANSU
Ardor, ELAN
Armadillo, APAR, PEBA, PEVA, TATU
Ascetic: Mohammedan, SUFI
Association: Chinese, TONG
Astronomer: Persian, OMAR
Avatar: Of Vishnu, RAMA
Axillary, ALAR
Band: Horizontal (heraldry), FESS
Barracuda, SPET
Bark: Mulberry, TAPA
Base: Column, DADO
Bearing (heraldry), ORLE
Beer: Russian, KVAS
Beige, ECRU
Being, ESSE
Beverage: Japanese rice, SAKE
Bird: Asian, MINA, MYNA
  Egyptian sacred, IBIS
  Extinct, DODO, MAMO
  Flightless, KIWI
  Gull-like, TERN
  Hawaiian, IIWI, MAMO
  Parson, KOKO
  Unfledged, EYAS
Birds: As class, AVES
Black, EBON
  (French), NOIR
Blackbird: European, MERL
Boat: Flat-bottomed, DORY
Bone: Forearm, ULNA
Bones, OSSA
Box, Japanese, INRO
Bravo (rare), EUGE
Buffalo: Indian wild, ARNA
Bull (Spanish), TORO
Burden, ONUS
Cabbage: Sliced, SLAW
Caliph: Mohammedan, OMAR
Canoe: Malay, PRAU, PROA
Cap: Military, KEPI
Cape, NESS
Capital: Ancient Irish, TARA
Case: Article, ETUI
Cat: Wild, BALU, EYRA
Chalcedony, SARD
Chamber: Indian ceremonial, KIVA
Channel: Brain, ITER
Cheese: Dutch, EDAM
Chest: Sepulchral stone, CIST
Chieftain: Arab, EMIR
Church: Part of, APSE, NAVE
  (Scotch), KIRK
Claim (law), LIEN
Cluster: Flower, CYME
Coin: Chinese, TAEL, YUAN
  German, MARK
  Indian, ANNA
  Iranian, RIAL
  Italian, LIRA
  Moroccan, OKIA
  Siamese, BAHT
  South American, PESO
  Spanish, DURO, PESO
  Turkish, PARA
Commune: Belgian, AATH
Composition: Musical, OPUS
Compound: Chemical, DIOL
Constellation: Southern, PAVO
Council; Russian, DUMA
Counsel, REDE
Covering: Seed, ARIL
Cross: Egyptian, ANKH
Cry: Bacchanalian, EVOE
Cup (Scotch), TASS
Cupbearer, SAKI
Dagger, DIRK
  Malay, KRIS
Dam: River, WEIR
Dash, ELAN
Date: Roman, IDES
Dawn: Pertaining to, EOAN
Dean: English, INGE
Decay: In fruit, BLET
Deer: Sambar, MAHA
Disease: Skin, ACNE
Disk: Solar, ATEN
Dog: Hunting, ALAN
Drink: Hindu intoxicating, SOMA
Duck, SMEE, SMEW, TEAL
Dynasty: Chinese, CHEN, CHIN, CHOU, CHOW, HSIA, MING, SUNG, TANG, TSIN
  Mongol, YUAN
Eagle: Biblical, GIER
  Sea, ERNE
Egyptian: Christian, COPT
Ear: Pertaining to, OTIC
Entrance: Mine, ADIT
Esau, EDOM
Escutcheon: Voided, ORLE
Eskers, OSAR
Evergreen: New Zealand, TAWA
Fairy: Persian, PERI
Family: Italian, ESTE
Far (comb. form), TELE
Farewell, VALE
Father (French), PERE
Fennel: Philippine, ANIS
Fever: Malarial, AGUE
Fiber: East Indian, JUTE
Firn, NEVE
Fish: Carpike, DACE
  Hawaiian, ULUA
  Herringlike, SHAD
  Mackerellike, CERO
  Marine, HAKE
  Sea, LING, MERO, OPAH
  Spiny-finned, GOBY
Food: Tropical, TARO
Foot: Metric, IAMB
Formerly, ERST
Founder: Of Carthage, DIDO
France: Southern, MIDI
Furze, ULEX
Gaelic, ERSE
Gaiter, SPAT
Game: Card, FARO, SKAT
Garlic: European wild, MOLY
Garment: Hindu, SARI
  Roman, TOGA
Gazelle, CORA

Gem, JADE, ONYX, OPAL, RUBY
Genus: Amphibians (incl. frogs), RANA
  Amphibians (incl. tree toads), HYLA
  Antelopes, ORYX
  Auks, ALCA, URIA
  Bees, APIS
  Birds (American ostriches), RHEA
  Birds (cranes), CRUS
  Birds (magpies), PICA
  Birds (peacocks), PAVO
  Cetaceans, INIA
  Ducks (incl. mallards), ANAS
  Fishes (burbots), LOTA
  Fishes (incl. bowfins), AMIA
  Geese (snow geese), CHEN
  Gulls, XEMA
  Herbs, ARUM, GEUM
  Insects (water scorpions), NEPA
  Lilies, ALOE
  Mammals (mankind), HOMO
  Orchids, DISA
  Owls, ASIO, BUBO, OTUS
  Palms, NIPA
  Sea birds, SULA
  Sheep, OVIS
  Shrubs, Eurasian, ULEX
  Shrubs (hollies), ILEX
  Shrubs (incl. Virginia Willow), ITEA
  Shrubs, tropical, EVEA
  Snakes (sand snakes), ERYX
  Swans, OLOR
  Trees, chocolate, COLA
  Trees (ebony family), MABA
  Trees (incl. maples), ACER
  Trees (olives), OLEA
  Trees, tropical, EVEA
  Turtles, EMYS
Goat: Wild, IBEX, KRAS, TAHR, TAIR, THAR
God: Assyrian, ASUR
  Babylonian, ADAD, ADDU, ENKI, ENZU, IRRA, NABU, NEBO, UTUG
  Celtic, LLEU, LLEW
  Hindu, AGNI, CIVA, DEVA, DEWA, KAMA, RAMA, SIVA, VAYU
  Phrygian, ATYS
  Semitic, BAAL
  Teutonic, HLER
Goddess: Babylonian, ERUA, GULA
  Hawaiian, PELE
  Hindu, DEVI, KALI, SHRI, VACH
Gooseberry: Hawaiian, POHA
Gourd, PEPO
Grafted (heraldry), ENTE
Grandfather (obsolete), AIEL
Grandparents: Pertaining to, AVAL
Grass: Hawaiian, HILO
Gray (French), GRIS
Green (heraldry), VERT
Groom: Indian, SYCE
Half (prefix), DEMI, HEMI, SEMI
Hamlet, DORP
Hammer-head: Part of, PEEN
Handle, ANSA
Harp: Japanese, KOTO
Hartebeest, ASSE, TORA
Hautboy, OBOE
Hawk: Taken from nest (falconry), EYAS
Hearing (law), OYER
Heater: For liquids, ETNA
Herb: Aromatic, ANET, DILL
  Fabulous, MOLY
  Perennial, GEUM, SEGO
  Pot, WORT
  Used for blue dye, WADE, WOAD
Hill: Flat-topped, MESA
  Sand, DENE, DUNE
Hoarfrost, RIME
Hog: Immature female, GILT
Holly, ILEX
House: Cow, BYRE
  (Spanish), CASA
Ice: Floating, FLOE
Image, ICON, IKON
Incarnation: Of Vishnu, RAMA

Indian: Algonquian, CREE, SAUK
  Central American, MAYA
  Iroquoian, ERIE
  Mexican, CORA
  Peruvian, CANA, INCA, MORO
  Shoshonean, HOPI
  Siouan, OTOE
  Southwestern, HOPI, PIMA, YUMA, ZUNI
Insect: Immature, PUPA
Instrument: Stringed, LUTE, LYRE
Ireland, EIRE, ERIN
Jacket: English, ETON
Jail (British), GAOL
Jar, OLLA
Judge: Mohammedan, CADI
Juniper: European, CADE
Kiln, OAST, OVEN
King: British legendary, LUDD, NUDD
Kiss, BUSS
Knife: Philippine, BOLO
Koran: Section of, SURA
Laborer: Spanish American, PEON
Lake: Mountain, TARN
  (Scotch), LOCH
Lamp: Miner's, DAVY
Landing place: Indian, GHAT
Language: Buddhist, PALI
  Japanese, AINU
Latvian, LETT
Layer: Of iris, UVEA
Leaf: Palm, OLAY, OLLA
Legislature: Ukrainian, RADA
Lemur, LORI
Leopard, PARD
Let it stand, STET
Letter: Greek, BETA, IOTA, ZETA
  Hebrew, AYIN, BETH, CAPH, KOPH, RESH, SHIN, TETH, YODH
  Papal, BULL
Lily, ALOE
Literature: Hindu sacred, VEDA
Lizard, GILA
  Monitor, URAN
Loquat, BIWA
Magistrate: Genose or Venetian, DOGE
Man (Latin), HOMO
Mark: Omission, DELE
Marmoset: South American, MICO
Meadow: Fertile, VEGA
Measure: Electric, VOLT, WATT
  Force, DYNE
  Hebrew, OMER
  Printing, PICA
  Spanish or Portuguese, VARA
  Swiss land, IMMI
Medley, OLIO
Merganser, SMEW
Milk (French), LAIT
Molding, GULA
  Curved, OGEE
Mongoose: Crab-eating, URVA
Monk: Tibetan, LAMA
Monkey: African, MONA, WAAG
  Ceylonese, MAHA
  Cochin-China, DOUC
  South American, SAKI, TITI
Monkshood, ATIS
Month: Jewish, ADAR, ELUL, IYAR
Mother (French), MERE
Mountain: Thessaly, OSSA
Mouse: Meadow, VOLE
Mythology: Norse, EDDA
Nail (French), CLOU
Native: Philippine, MORO
Nest: Of pheasants, NIDE
Network, RETE
No (German), NEIN
Noble: Mohammedan, AMIR
Notice: Death, OBIT
Novel: By Zola, NANA
Nursemaid: Oriental AMAH, AYAH, EYAH
Nut: Philippine, PILI
Oak: Holm, ILEX
Oil (comb. form), OLEO

Ostrich: American, RHEA
Oven, KILN, OAST
Owl: Barn, LULU
Ox: Celebes wild, ANOE
  Extinct wild, URUS
Palm, ATAP, NIPA, SAGO
Parliament, DIET
Parrot: New Zealand, KAKA
Pass: Indian mountain, GHAT
Passage: Closing (music), CODA
Peach: Clingstone, PAVY
Peasant: Indian, RYOT
  Old English, CARL
Pepper: Australasian, KAVA
Perfume, ATAR
Persia, IRAN
Person: Extraordinary, ONER
Pickerel or pike, ESOX
Pitcher, EWER
Plant: Aromatic, NARD
  Century, ALOE
  Indigo, ANIL
  Pepper, KAVA
Platform: Raised, DAIS
Plum: Wild, SLOE
Pods: Vegetable, OKRA, OKRO
Poem: Epic, EPOS
Poet: Persian, OMAR
  Roman, OVID
Poison, BANE
  Arrow, INEE
Porkfish, SISI
Portico: Greek, STOA
Premium, AGIO
Priest: Mohammedan, IMAM
Prima donna, DIVA
Prong: Fork, TINE
Pseudonym: Lamb's, ELIA
Queen: Carthaginian, DIDO
  Hindu, RANI
Rabbit, CONY
Race: Of Japan, AINU
Rail: Ducklike, COOT
  North American, SORA
Redshank, CLEE
Refuse: After pressing, MARC
Regiment: Turkish, ALAI
Reliquary, ARCA
Resort: Italian, LIDO
Ridges: Sandy, ASAR, OSAR
River: German, ELBE, ODER
  Italian, ADDA
  Siberian, LENA
Road: Roman, ITER
Rockfish: California, RENA
Rodent: Mouselike, VOLE
  South American, PACA
Rootstock, TARO
Salamander, NEWT
Salmon: Silver, COHO
  Young, PARR
Same (Greek), HOMO
  (Latin), IDEM
Sauce: Fish, ALEC
School: English, ETON
Seaweed, AGAR, ALGA, KELP
Secular, LAIC
Sediment, SILT
Seed: Dill, ANET
  Of vetch, TARE
Serf, ILOT
Sesame, TEEL
Settlement: Eskimo, ETAH
Shark: Atlantic, GATA
  European, TOPE
Sheep: Wild, UDAD
Sheltered, ALEE
Shield, EGIS
Ship: Jason's, ARGO
  Left side of, PORT
  Two-masted, BRIG
Shrine: Buddhist, TOPE
Shrub: New Zealand, TUTU
Sign: Magic, RUNE
Silkworm, ERIA
Skin: Beaver, PLEW

Skink: Egyptian, ADDA
Slave, ESNE
Sloth: Two-toed, UNAU
Smooth, LENE
Snow: Glacial, NEVE
Soapstone, TALC
Society: African secret, EGBO, PORO
Son: Of Seth, ENOS
Song (German), LIED
 Unaccompanied, GLEE
Sound: Lung, RALE
Sour, ACID
Sow: Young, GILT
Spike: Brad-shaped, BROB
Spirit: Buddhist evil, MARA
Stake: Poker, ANTE
Star: Temporary, NOVA
Starch: East Indian, SAGO
Stone: Precious, OPAL
Strap: Bridle, REIN
Strewn (heraldry), SEME
Sweetsop, ATES, ATTA
Sword: Fencing, EPEE, FOIL
Tambourine: African, TAAR
Tapir: Brazilian, ANTA
Tax, CESS
Tea: South American, MATE
Therefore (Latin), ERGO
Thing: Extraordinary, ONER
Three (dice, cards, etc.), TREY
Thrush: Hawaiian, OMAO
Tide, NEAP
Tipster: Racing, TOUT
Tissue, TELA
Title: Etruscan, LARS
 Hindu, BABU
 Indian, RAJA
 Mohammedan, EMIR, IMAM
 Persian, BABA
 Spanish, DONA
 Turkish, AGHA, BABA
Toad: Largest known, AGUA
 Tree, HYLA
Tool: Cutting, ADZE
Track: Deer, SLOT
Tract: Sandy, DENE
Tree: Apple, SORB
 Central American, EBOE
 East Indian, TEAK
 Eucalyptus, YATE
 Guiana and Trinidad, MORA
 Javanese, UPAS
 Linden, LIME, LINN, TEIL, TILL
 Sandarac, ARAR
 Sassafras, AGUE
 Tamarisk salt, ATLE
Tribe: Moro, SULU
Trout, CHAR
Urchin: Street, ARAB
Vessel: Arab, DHOW
Vestment: Ecclesiastical, COPE
Vetch, TARE
Vine: East Indian, SOMA
Violinist: Famous, AUER
Vortex, EDDY
Wampum, PEAG
Wapiti, STAG
Waste: Allowance for, TRET
Watchman: Indian, MINA
Water (Spanish), AGUA
Waterfall, LINN
Wavy (heraldry), ONDE, UNDE
Wax, CERE
 Chinese, PELA
Weed: Biblical, TARE
Weight: Ancient, MINA
 Danish (pl.), ESER
 East Asian, TAEL
 Greek, MINA
 Siamese, BAHT
Well done (rare), EUGE
Whale, CETE
 Killer, ORCA
 White, HUSE, HUSO
Whirlpool, EDDY
Wife: Of Geraint, ENID
Willow: Virginia, ITEA
Wine, PORT
Winged, ALAR
 (Heraldry), AILE
Wings, ALAE
Withered, SERE
Without (French), SANS
Wool: To comb, CARD
Work, OPUS
Wrong: Civil, TORT
Young: Bring forth, YEAN

Words of Five Letters

Abode of dead: Babylonian, ARALU
Aborigine: Borneo DAYAK
Aftersong, EPODE
Aloe, AGAVE
Animal: Footless, APODE
Ant, EMMET
Antelope: African, ADDAX, BEISA, CAAMA, ELAND, GUIBA, ORIBI, TIANG
 Goat, GORAL, SEROW
 Indian, SASIN
 Siberian, SAIGA
Arch: Pointed, OGIVE
Armadillo, APARA, POYOU, TATOU
Arrowroot, ARARU
Artery: Trunk, AORTA
Association: Russian, ARTEL
 Secret, CABAL
Author: English, READE
Automaton, GOLEM, ROBOT
Award: Motion-picture, OSCAR
Basket: Fishing, CREEL
Beer: Russian, KVASS
Bible: Mohammedan, KORAN
Bird: Asian, MINAH, MYNAH
 Indian, SHAMA
 Larklike, PIPIT
 Loonlike, GREBE
 Oscine, VIREO
 South American, AGAMI
 Swimming, GREBE
Black: (French), NOIRE
 (Heraldry), SABLE
Blackbird: European, MERLE, OUSEL, OUZEL
Block: Glacial, SERAC
Blue (heraldry), AZURE
Boat: Eskimo, BIDAR, UMIAK
Bobwhite, COLIN, QUAIL
Bone (comb. form), OSTEO
 Leg, TIBIA
 Thigh, FEMUR
Broom: Twig, BESOM
Brother (French), FRERE
 Moses', AARON
Canoe: Eskimo, BIDAR, KAYAK
Cape: Papal, FANON, ORALE
Caravansary, SERAI
Card: Old playing, TAROT
Caterpillar: New Zealand, AWETO
Catkin, AMENT
Cavity: Stone, GEODE
Cephalopod, SQUID
Cetacean, WHALE
Chariot, ESSED
Cheek: Pertaining to, MALAR
Chieftain: Arab, EMEER
Child (Scotch), BAIRN
Cigar, CLARO
Coating: Seed, TESTA
Cockatoo: Palm, ARARA
Coin: Costa Rican, COLON
 Danish, KRONE
 Ecuadorian, SUCRE
 English, GROAT, PENCE
 French, FRANC
 German, KRONE, TALER
 Hungarian, PENGO
 Icelandic, KRONA
 Indian, RUPEE
 Iraqi, DINAR
 Norwegian, KRONE
 Polish, ZLOTY
 Russian, COPEC, KOPEK, RUBLE
 Swedish, KRONA
 Turkish, ASPER
 Yugoslav, DINAR
Collar: Papal, FANON, ORALE
 Roman, RABAT
Commune: Italian, TREIA
Composition: Choral, MOTET
Compound: Chemical, ESTER
Conceal (law), ELOIN
Council: Ecclesiastical, SYNOD
Court: Anglo-Saxon, GEMOT
 Inner, PATIO
Crest: Mountain, ARETE
Crown: Papal, TIARA
Cuttlefish, SEPIA
Date: Roman, NONES
Decree: Mohammedan, IRADE
 Russian, UKASE
Deposit: Loam, LOESS
Desert: Gobi, SHAMO

Devilfish, MANTA
Disease: Cereals, ERGOT
Disk, PATEN
Dog: Wild, DHOLE, DINGO
Dormouse, LEROT
Drum, TABOR
Duck: Sea, EIDER
Dynasty: Chinese, CHING, LIANG, SHANG
Earthquake, SEISM
Eel, ELVER, MORAY
Ermine: European, STOAT
Ether: Crystalline, APIOL
Fabric: Velvetlike, PANNE
Fabulist, AESOP
Family: Italian, CENCI
Fiber: West Indian, SISAL
Fig: Smyrna, ELEME, ELEMI
Figure: Of speech, TROPE
Finch: European, SERIN
Fish: American small, KILLY
Flower: Garden, ASTER
Friend (Spanish), AMIGO
Fruit: Tropical, MANGO
Fungus: Rye, ERGOT
Furze, GORSE
Gateway, TORAN, TORII
Gem, AGATE, BERYL, PEARL, TOPAZ
Genus: Barnacles, LEPAS
  Bears, URSUS
  Birds (loons), GAVIA
  Birds (nuthatches), SITTA
  Cats, FELIS
  Dogs, CANIS
  Fishes (chiros), ELOPS
  Fishes (perch), PERCA
  Geese, ANSER
  Grasses, STIPA
  Grasses (incl. oats), AVENA
  Gulls, LARUS
  Hares, rabbits, LEPUS
  Hawks, BUTEO
  Herbs, old world, INULA
  Herbs, trailing or climbing, APIOS
  Herbs, tropical, TACCA, URENA
  Horses, EQUUS
  Insects (olive flies), DACUS
  Lice, plant, APHIS
  Lichens, USNEA
  Lizards, AGAMA
  Moles, TALPA
  Mollusks, OLIVA
  Monkeys, CEBUS
  Palms, ARECA
  Pigeons, GOURA
  Plants (amaryllis family), AGAVE
  Ruminants (goats), CAPRA
  Shrubs, Asiatic, SABIA
  Shrubs (heath), ERICA
  Shrubs (incl. raspberry), RUBUS
  Shrubs, tropical, IXORA, TREMA, URENA
  Ticks, ARGAS
  Trees (of elm family), TREMA, ULMUS
  Trees, tropical, IXORA, TREMA
Goat: Bezoar, PASAN
God: Assyrian, ASHIR, ASHUR, ASSUR
  Babylonian, DAGAN, SIRIS
  Gaelic, DAGDA
  Hindu, BHAGA, INDRA, SHIVA
  Japanese, EBISU
  Phillistine, DAGON
  Phrygian, ATTIS
  Teutonic, AEGIR, GYMIR
  Welsh, DYLAN
Goddess: Babylonian, ISTAR, NANAI
  Hindu, DURGA, GAURI, SHREE
Group: Of six, HEXAD
Grove: Sacred to Diana, NEMUS
Growing out, ENATE
Guitar: Hindu, SITAR
Gull: PEWEE, PEWIT
Hartebeest, CAAMA
Headdress: Jewish or Persian, TIARA
  Liturgical, MITER, MITRE
Heath, ERICA
Herb: Grasslike marsh, SEDGE
Heron, EGRET
Hog: Young, SHOAT, SHOTE
Image, EIKON
Indian: Cariban, ARARA
  Iroquoian, HURON
  Mexican, AZTEC, OPATA, OTOMI
  Muskhogean, CREEK
  Siouan, OSAGE, TETON
  Spanish American, ARARA, CARIB
Inflorescence: Racemose, AMENT
Insect: Immature, LARVA
Intrigue, CABAL
Iris: Yellow, SEDGE
Juniper, GORSE, RETEM
Kidneys: Pertaining to, RENAL
King: British legendary, LLUDD
Kite: European, GLEDE
Kobold, NISSE
Land: Cultivated, ARADA, ARADO
Landholder (Scotch), LAIRD, THANE
Language: Dravidian, TAMIL
Lariat, LASSO, REATA
Laughing, RIANT
Lawgiver: Athenian, DRACO, SOLON
Leaf: Calyx, SEPAL
  Fern, FROND
Lemur, LORIS
Letter: English, AITCH
  Greek, ALPHA, DELTA, GAMMA, KAPPA, OMEGA, SIGMA, THETA
  Hebrew, ALEPH, CHETH, GIMEL, SADHE, ZAYIN
Lichen, USNEA
Lighthouse, PHARE
Lizard: Old World, AGAMA
Loincloth, DHOTI
Louse: Plant, APHID
Macaw: Brazilian, ARARA
Mahogany: Philippine, ALMON
Mammal: Badgerlike, RATEL
  Civetlike, GENET
  Giraffelike, OKAPI
  Raccoonlike, COATI
Man (French), HOMME
Marble, AGATE
Mark: Insertion, CARET
Market place: Greek, AGORA
Marsupial: Australian, KOALA
Measure: Electric, FARAD, HENRY
  Energy, JOULE
  Metric, LITER, STERE
  Printing, AGATE
  Russian, VERST
Mixture: Smelting, MATTE
Mohicans: Last of, UNCAS
Molding: Convex, OVOLO, TORUS
Mole, TALPA
Monkey: African, PATAS
  Capuchin, SAJOU
  Howling, ARABA
Monkshood, ATEES
Month: Jewish, NISAN, SIVAN, TEBET
Museum (French), MUSEE
Musketeer, ATHOS
Native: Aleutian, ALEUT
  New Zealand, MAORI
Neckpiece: Ecclesiastical, AMICE
Nerve (comb. form), NEURO
Nest: Eagle's or hawk's, AERIE
  Insect's, NIDUS
Net: Fishing, SEINE
Newsstand, KIOSK
Nitrogen, AZOTE
Noble: Mohammedan, AMEER
Nodule: Stone, GEODE
Nostrils, NARES
Notched irregularly, EROSE
Nymph: Mohammedan, HOURI
Official: Roman, EDILE
Oleoresin, ELEMI
Opening: Mouthlike, STOMA
Oration: Funeral, ELOGE
Ostiole, STOMA
Page: Left-hand, VERSO
  Right-hand, RECTO
Palm, ARECA, BETEL
Park: Colorado, ESTES
Perfume, ATTAR

Philosopher: Greek, PLATO
Pillar: Stone, STELA, STELE
Pinnacle: Glacial, SERAC
Plain, LLANO
Plant: Century, AGAVE
  Climbing, LIANA
  Dwarf, CUMIN
  East Asian perennial, RAMIE
  Medicinal, SENNA
  Mustard family, CRESS
Plate: Communion, PATEN
Poem: Lyric, EPODE
Point: Lowest, NADIR
Poplar, ABELE, ALAMO, ASPEN
Porridge: Spanish American, ATOLE
Post: Stair, NEWEL
Priest: Mohammedan, IMAUM
Protozoan, AMEBA
Queen: (French), REINE
  Hindu, RANEE
Rabbit, CONEY
Rail, CRAKE
Red (heraldry), GULES
Religion: Moslem, ISLAM
Resin, ELEMI
Revoke (law), ADEEM
Rich man, MIDAS, NABOB
Ridge: Sandy, ESKAR, ESKER
River: French, LOIRE, SEINE
Rockfish: California, REINA
Rootstock: Fragrant, ORRIS
Ruff: Female, REEVE
Sack: Pack, KYACK
Salt: Ethereal, ESTER
Saltpeter, NITER, NITRE
Salutation: Eastern, SALAM
Sandpiper: Old World, TEREK
Scented, OLENT
School: Fish, SHOAL
  French public, LYCEE
Scriptures: Mohammedan, KORAN
Seaweeds, ALGAE
Seed: Aromatic, ANISE
Seraglio, HAREM, SERAI
Serf, HELOT
Sheep: Wild, AUDAD
Sheeplike, OVINE
Shield, AEGIS
Shoe: Wooden, SABOT
Shoots: Pickled bamboo, ACHAR
Shot: Billiard, CAROM, MASSE
Shrine: Buddhist, STUPA
Shrub: Burning bush, WAHOO
  Ornamental evergreen, TOYON
  Used in tanning, SUMAC
Silk: Watered, MOIRE
Sister (French), SOEUR
  (Latin), SOROR
Six: Group of, HEXAD
Skeleton: Marine, CORAL
Slave, HELOT
Snake, ABOMA, ADDER, COBRA, RACER
Soldier: French, POILU
  Indian, SEPOY
Sour, ACERB
Spirit: Air, ARIEL
Staff: Shepherd's, CROOK
Starwort, ASTER
Steel (German), STAHL
Stockade: Russian, ETAPE
Stop (nautical), AVAST
Storehouse, ETAPE
Subway: Parisian, METRO
Tapestry, ARRAS
Tea: Paraguayan, YERBA
Temple: Hawaiian, HEIAU
Terminal: Positive, ANODE
Theater: Greek, ODEON, ODEUM
Then (French), ALORS
Thread: Surgical, SETON
Thrush: Wilson's, VEERY
Title: Hindu, BABOO
  Indian, RAJAH, SAHEB, SAHIB
  Mohammedan, EMEER, IMAUM
Tree: Buddhist sacred, PIPAL
  East Indian cotton, SIMAL
  Hickory, PECAN
  Light-wooded, BALSA
  Malayan, TERAP
  Mediterranean, CAROB
  Mexican, ABETO
  Mexican pine, OCOTE
  New Zealand, MAIRE
  Philippine, ALMON
  Rain, SAMAN
  South American, UMBRA
  Tamarack, LARCH
  Tamarisk salt, ATLEE
  West Indian, ACANA
Trout, CHARR
Troy, ILION, ILIUM
Twin: Siamese, CHANG
Vestment: Ecclesiastical, STOLE
Violin: Famous, AMATI, STRAD
Volcano: Mud, SALSE
Wampum, PEAGE
War cry: Greek, ALALA
Wavy (heraldry), UNDEE
Weight: Jewish, GERAH
Wen, TALPA
Wheat, SPELT
Wheel: Persian water, NORIA
Whitefish, CISCO
Willow, OSIER
Window: Bay, ORIEL
Wine, MEDOC, RHINE, TINTA, TOKAY
Winged, ALATE
Woman (French), FEMME
Year: Excess of solar over lunar, EPACT
Zoroastrian, PARSI

Words of Six or More Letters

Agave, MAGUEY
Alkaloid: Crystalline, ESERIN, ESERINE
Alligator, CAYMAN
Amphibole, EDENITE, URALITE
Ant: White, TERMITE
Antelope: African, DIKDIK, DUIKER, GEMSBOK, IMPALA, KOODOO
  European, CHAMOIS
  Indian, NILGAI, NILGAU, NILGHAI, NILGHAU
Ape: Asian or East Indian, GIBBON
Appendage: Leaf, STIPEL, STIPULE
Armadillo, PELUDO, TATOUAY
Arrowroot, ARARAO
Ascetic: Jewish, ESSENE
Ass: Asian wild, ONAGER
Avatar: Of Vishnu, KRISHNA
Babylonian, ELAMITE
Badge: Shoulder, EPAULET
Baldness, ALOPECIA
Barracuda, SENNET
Bark: Aromatic, SINTOC
Bearlike, URSINE
Beetle, ELATER
Bible: Zoroastrian, AVESTA
Bird: Sea, PETREL
  South American, SERIEMA
  Wading, AVOCET, AVOSET
Bone: Leg, FIBULA
Branched, RAMATE
Brother (Latin), FRATER
Bunting: European, ORTOLAN
Call: Trumpet, SENNET
Canoe: Eskimo, BAIDAR, OOMIAK
Caravansary, IMARET
Cat: Asian or African, CHEETAH
  Leopardlike, OCELOT
Cenobite: Jewish, ESSENE
Centerpiece: Table, EPERGNE

Cetacean, DOLPHIN, PORPOISE
Chariot, ESSEDA, ESSEDE
Chief: Seminole, OSCEOLA
Claim: Release as (law), REMISE
Clock: Water, CLEPSYDRA
Cloud, CUMULUS, NIMBUS
Coach: French hackney, FIACRE
Coin: Czech, KORUNA
  Ethiopian, TALARI
  Finnish, MARKKA
  German, THALER
  Greek, DRACHMA
  Haitian, GOURDE
  Honduran, LEMPIRA
  Hungarian, FORINT
  Indo-Chinese, PIASTER
  Netherlands, GUILDER
  Panamanian, BALBOA
  Paraguayan, GUARANI
  Portuguese, ESCUDO
  Russian, COPECK, KOPECK, ROUBLE
  Spanish, PESETA
  Venezuelan, BOLIVAR
Communion: Last holy, VIATICUM
Conceal (law), ELOIGN
Confection, PRALINE
Construction: Sentence, SYNTAX
Convexity: Shaft of column, ENTASIS
Court: Anglo-Saxon, GEMOTE
Cow: Sea, DUGONG, MANATEE
Cylindrical, TERETE
Dagger, STILETTO
  Malay, CREESE, KREESE
Date: Roman, CALENDS, KALENDS
Deer, CARIBOU, WAPITI
Disease: Plant, ERINOSE
Doorkeeper, OSTIARY
Dragonflies: Order of, ODANATA
Drink: Of gods, NECTAR
Drum: TABOUR
  Moorish, ATABAL, ATTABAL
Duck: Fish-eating, MERGANSER
  Sea, SCOTER
Dynasty: Chinese, MANCHU
Eel, CONGER
Edit, REDACT
Envelope: Flower, PERIANTH
Eskimo, AMERIND
Ether: Crystalline, APIOLE
Excuse (law), ESSOIN
Eyespots, OCELLI
Fabric, ESTAMENE, ESTAMIN, ETAMINE
Falcon: European, KESTREL
Figure: Used as column, CARYATID, TELAMON
Fine: For punishment, AMERCE
Fish: Asian fresh-water, GOURAMI
  Pikelike, BARRACUDA
Five: Group of, PENTAD
Fly: African, TSETSE
Foot: Metric, ANAPEST, IAMBUS
Foxlike, VULPINE
Frying pan, SPIDER
Fur, KARAKUL
Galley: Greek or Roman, BIREME, TRIREME
Game: Card, ECARTE
Garment: Greek, CHLAMYS
Gateway, GOPURA, TORANA
Genus: Birds (ravens, crows), CORVUS
  Eels, CONGER
  Fishes, ANABAS
  Foxes, VULPES
  Herbs, ANEMONE
  Insects, CICADA
  Lemurs, GALAGO
  Mints (incl. catnip), NEPETA
  Mollusks, ANOMIA, ASTARTE, TEREDO
  Mollusks (incl. oysters), OSTREA
  Monkeys (spider monkeys), ATELES
  Thrushes (incl. robins), TURDUS
  Trees (of elm family), CELTIS
  Trees (inc. dogwood), CORNUS
  Trees, tropical American, SAPOTA
  Wrens, NANNUS
Gibbon, SIAMANG, WOUWOU
Gland: Salivary, RACEMOSE
Goat: Bezoar, PASANG
Goatlike, CAPRINE
God: Assyrian, ASHSHUR, ASSHUR
  Babylonian, BABBAR, MARDUK, MERODACH, NANNAR, NERGAL, SHAMASH
  Hindu, BRAHMA, KRISHNA, VISHNU
  Tahitian, TAAROA
Goddess: Babylonian, ISHTAR
  Hindu, CHANDI, HAIMAVATI, LAKSHMI, PARVATI, SARASVATI, SARASWATI
Government, POLITY
Governor: Persian, SATRAP
Grandson (Scotch), NEPOTE
Group: Of five, PENTAD
  Of nine, ENNEAD
  Of seven, HEPTAD
Hare: in first year, LEVERET
Harpsichord, SPINET
Herb: Alpine, EDELWEISS
  Chinese, GINSENG
  South African, FREESIA
Hermit, EREMITE
Hero: Legendary, PALADIN
Heron, BITTERN
Horselike, EQUINE
Hound: Short-legged, BEAGLE
House (French), MAISON
Idiot, CRETIN
Implement: Stone, NEOLITH
Incarnation: Hindu, AVATAR
Indian, APACHE, COMANCHE, PAIUTE, SENECA
Inn: Turkish, IMARET
Insects: Order of, DIPTERA
Instrument: Japanese banjolike, SAMISEN
  Musical, CLAVIER, SPINET
Interstice, AREOLA
Ironwood, COLIMA
Juniper: Old Testament, RAETAM
Kettledrum, ATABAL
King: Fairy, OBERON
Kneecap, PATELLA
Knife, MACHETE
Langur: Sumatran, SIMPAI
Legislature: Spanish, CORTES
Lemur: African, GALAGO
  Madagascar, AYEAYE
Letter: Greek, EPSILON, LAMBDA, OMICRON, UPSILON
  Hebrew, DALETH, LAMEDH, SAMEKH
Lighthouse, PHAROS
Lizard, IGUANA
Llama, ALPACA
Lockjaw, TETANUS
Locust, CICADA, CICALA
Macaw: Brazilian, MARACAN
Maid: Of Astolat, ELAINE
Mammal: Madagascar, TENDRAC, TENREC
Man (Spanish), HOMBRE
Marmoset: South American, TAMARIN
Marsupial, BANDICOOT, WOMBAT
Massacre, POGROM
Mayor: Spanish, ALCALDE
Measure: Electric, AMPERE, COULOMB, KILOWATT
Medicine: Quack, NOSTRUM
Member: Religious order, CENOBITE
Molasses, TREACLE
Monkey: African, GRIVET, NISNAS
  Asian, LANGUR
  Philippine, MACHIN
  South American, PINCHE, SAIMIRI, SAMIRI, SAPAJOU
Monster, CHIMERA, GORGON
  (Comb. form), TERATO
  Cretan, MINOTAUR
Month: Jewish, HESHVAN, KISLEV, SHEBAT, TAMMUZ, TISHRI, VEADAR
Mountain: Asia Minor, ARARAT
Mulct, AMERCE
Musketeer, ARAMIS, PORTHOS
Nearsighted, MYOPIC
Net, TRAMMEL
New York City, GOTHAM
Nine: Group of, ENNEAD
Nobleman: Spanish, GRANDEE
Official: Roman, AEDILE
Onyx: Mexican, TECALI
Order: Dragonflies, ODANATA
  Insects, DIPTERA
Organ: Plant, PISTIL

Ornament: Shoulder, EPAULET
Overcoat: Military, CAPOTE
Ox: Wild, BANTENG
Oxidation: Bronze or copper, PATINA
Paralysis: Incomplete, PARESIS
Pear: Alligator, AVOCADO
Persimmon: Mexican, CHAPOTE
Pipe: Peace, CALUMET
Plaid (Scotch), TARTAN
Plain, PAMPAS, STEPPE, TUNDRA
Plant: Buttercup family, ANEMONE
Century, MAGUEY
On rocks, LICHEN
Plowing: Fit for, ARABLE
Poem: Heroic, EPOPEE
Six-lined, SESTET
Point: Highest, ZENITH
Potion: Love, PHILTER, PHILTRE
Protozoan, AMOEBA
Punish, AMERCE
Purple (heraldry), PURPURE
Queen: Fairy, TITANIA
Race: Skiing, SLALOM
Rat, BANDICOOT, LEMMING
Retort, RIPOST, RIPOSTE
Ring: Harness, TERRET
Little, ANNULET
Rodent: Jumping, JERBOA
Spanish American, AGOUTI, AGOUTY
Sailor: East Indian, LASCAR
Salmon: Young, GRILSE
Salutation: Eastern, SALAAM
Sandpiper, PLOVER
Sandy, ARENOSE
Sapodilla, SAPOTA, SAPOTE
Saw: Surgical, TREPAN
Seven: Group of, HEPTAD
Sexes: Common to both, EPICENE
Shawl: Mexican, SERAPE
Sheathing: Flower, SPATHE
Sheep: Wild, AOUDAD, ARGALI
Shipworm, TEREDO
Shoes: Mercury's winged, TALARIA
Shortening: Syllable, SYSTOLE
Shrub, SPIRAEA
Sickle-shaped, FALCATE
Silver (heraldry), ARGENT
Snake, ANACONDA
Speech: Loss of, APHASIA
Spiral, HELICAL
Staff: Bishop's, CROSIER, CROZIER
Stalk: Plant, PETIOLE
State: Swiss, CANTON
Studio, ATELIER
Swan: Young, CYGNET
Swimming, NATANT
Sword-shaped, ENSATE
Terminal: Negative, CATHODE
Third (music), TIERCE
Thrust: Fencing, RIPOST, RIPOSTE
Tile: Pertaining to, TEGULAR
Tomb: Empty, CENOTAPH
Tooth (comb. form), ODONTO
Tower: Mohammedan, MINARET
Tree: African timber, BAOBAB
Black gum, TUPELO
East Indian, MARGOSA
Locust, ACACIA
Malayan, SINTOC
Marmalade, SAPOTE
Urn: Tea, SAMOVAR
Vehicle, LANDAU, TROIKA
Verbose, PROLIX
Viceroy: Egyptian, KHEDIVE
Vulture: American, CONDOR
Warehouse (French), ENTREPOT
Whale: White, BELUGA
Whirlpool, VORTEX
Will: Addition to, CODICIL
Having left, TESTATE
Wind, CHINOOK, MONSOON, SIMOOM, SIMOON, SIROCCO
Window: In roof, DORMER
Wine, BARBERA, BURGUNDY, CABERNET, CHABLIS, CHIANTI, CLARET, MUSCATEL, RIESLING, SAUTERNE, SHERRY, ZINFANDEL
Wolfish, LUPINE
Woman: Boisterous, TERMAGANT
Woolly, LANATE
Workshop, ATELIER
Zoroastrian, PARSEE

Old-Testament Names

(We do not pretend that this list is all-inclusive. We include only those names which in our opinion one meets most often in crossword puzzles.)

Aaron: First high priest of Jews; son of Amram; brother of Miriam and Moses; father of Abihu, Eleazer, Ithamar, and Nadab.

Abel: Son of Adam; slain by Cain.

Abigail: Wife of Nabal; later, wife of David.

Abihu: Son of Aaron.

Abimelech: King of Gerar.

Abner: Commander of army of Saul and Ishbosheth; slain by Joab.

Abraham (or Abram): Patriarch; forefather of the Jews; son of Terah; husband of Sarah; father of Isaac and Ishmael.

Absalom: Son of David and Maacah; revolted against David; slain by Joab.

Achish: King of Gath; gave refuge to David.

Achsa (or Achsah): Daughter of Caleb; wife of Othniel.

Adah: Wife of Lamech.

Adam: First man; husband of Eve; father of Cain, Abel, and Seth.

Adonijah: Son of David and Haggith.

Agag: King of Amalek; spared by Saul; slain by Samuel.

Ahasuerus: King of Persia; husband of Vashti and, later, Esther; sometimes identified with Xerxes the Great.

Ahijah: Prophet; foretold accession of Jeroboam.

Ahinoam: Wife of David.

Amasa: Commander of army of David; slain by Joab.

Amnon: Son of David and Ahinoam; ravished Tamar; slain by Absalom.

Amram: Husband of Jochebed; father of Aaron, Miriam and Moses.

Asenath: Wife of Joseph.

Asher: Son of Jacob and Zilpah.

Balaam: Prophet; rebuked by his donkey for cursing God.

Barak: Jewish captain; associated with Deborah.

Baruch: Secretary to Jeremiah.

Bathsheba: Wife of Uriah; later, wife of David.

Belshazzar: Crown prince of Babylon.

Benaiah: Warrior of David; proclaimed Solomon King.

Ben-Hadad: Name of several kings of Damascus.

Benjamin: Son of Jacob and Rachel.

Bezaleel: Chief architect of tabernacle.

Bilbah: Servant of Rachel; mistress of Jacob.

Bildad: Comforter of Job.

Boaz: Husband of Ruth; father of Obed.

Cain: Son of Adam and Eve; slayer of Abel; father of Enoch.

Cainan: Son of Enos.

Caleb: Spy sent out by Moses to visit Canaan; father of Achsa.

Canaan: Son of Ham.

Chilion: Son of Elimelech; husband of Orpah.

Cush: Son of Ham; father of Nimrod.

Dan: Son of Jacob and Bilhah.

Daniel: Prophet; saved from lions by God.

Deborah: Hebrew prophetess; helped Israelites conquer Canaanites.

Delilah: Mistress and betrayer of Samson.

Elam: Son of Shem.

Eleazar: Son of Aaron; succeeded him as high priest.

Eli: High priest and judge; teacher of Samuel; father of Hophni and Phinehas.
Eliakim: Chief minister of Hezekiah.
Eliezer: Servant of Abraham.
Elihu: Comforter of Job.
Elijah (or Elias): Prophet; went to heaven in chariot of fire.
Elimelech: Husband of Naomi; father of Chilion and Mahlon.
Eliphaz: Comforter of Job.
Elisha (or Eliseus): Prophet; successor of Elijah.
Elkanah: Husband of Hannah; father of Samuel.
Enoch: Son of Cain.
Enoch: Father of Methuselah.
Enos: Son of Seth; father of Cainan.
Ephraim: Son of Joseph.
Esau: Son of Isaac and Rebecca; sold his birthright to his brother Jacob.
Esther: Jewish wife of Ahasuerus; saved Jews from Haman's plotting.
Eve: First woman; created from rib of Adam.
Ezra (or Esdras): Hebrew scribe and priest.
Gad: Son of Jacob and Zilpah.
Gehazi: Servant of Elisha.
Gideon: Israelite hero; defeated Midianites.
Goliath: Philistine giant; slain by David.
Hagar: Handmaid of Sarah; concubine of Abraham; mother of Ishmael.
Haggith: Mother of Adonijah.
Ham: Son of Noah; father of Cush, Mizraim, Phut, and Canaan.
Haman: Chief minister of Ahasuerus; hanged on gallows prepared for Mordecai.
Hannah: Wife of Elkanah; mother of Samuel.
Hanun: King of Ammonites.
Haran: Brother of Abraham; father of Lot.
Hazael: King of Damascus.
Hephzi-Bah: Wife of Hezekiah; mother of Mannaseh.
Hiram: King of Tyre.
Holofernes: General of Nebuchadnezzar; slain by Judith.
Hophni: Son of Eli.
Isaac: Hebrew patriarch; son of Abraham and Sarah; half brother of Ishmael; husband of Rebecca; father of Esau and Jacob.
Ishmael: Son of Abraham and Hagar; half brother of Isaac.
Issachar: Son of Jacob and Leah.
Ithamar: Son of Aaron.
Jabal: Son of Lamech and Adah.
Jabin: King of Hazor.
Jacob: Hebrew patriarch, founder of Israel; son of Isaac and Rebecca; husband of Leah and Rachel; father of Asher, Benjamin, Dan, Gad, Issachar, Joseph, Judah, Levi, Naphtali, Reuben, Simeon, and Zebulun.
Jael: Slayer of Sisera.
Japheth: Son of Noah.
Jehoiada: High priest; husband of Jehoshabeath; revolted against Athaliah and made Joash King of Judah.
Jehoshabeath (or Jehosheba): Daughter of Jehoram of Judah; wife of Jehoiada.
Jephthah: Judge in Israel; sacrificed his only daughter because of vow.
Jesse: Son of Obed; father of David.
Jethro: Midianite priest; father of Zipporah.
Jezebel: Phoenician princess; wife of Ahab; mother of Ahaziah, Athaliah, and Jehoram.
Joab: Commander in chief under David; slayer of Abner, Absalom, and Amasa.
Job: Patriarch; underwent many afflictions; comforted by Bildad, Elihu, Eliphaz and Zophar.
Jochebed: Wife of Amram.
Jonah: Prophet; cast into sea and swallowed by great fish.
Jonathan: Son of Saul; friend of David.
Joseph: Son of Jacob and Rachel; sold into slavery by his brothers; husband of Asenath; father of Ephraim and Manassah.
Joshua: Successor of Moses; son of Nun.
Jubal: Son of Lamech and Adah.
Judah: Son of Jacob and Leah.
Judith: Slayer of Holofernes.
Kish: Father of Saul.
Laban: Father of Leah and Rachel.
Lamech: Son of Methuselah; father of Noah.
Lamech: Husband of Adah and Zillah; father of Jabal, Jubal, and Tubal-Cain.
Leah: Daughter of Laban; wife of Jacob.
Levi: Son of Jacob and Leah.
Lot: Son of Haran; escaped destruction of Sodom.
Maacah: Mother of Absalom and Tamar.
Mahlon: Son of Elimelech; first husband of Ruth.
Manasseh: Son of Joseph.
Melchizedek: King of Salem.
Methuselah: Patriarch; son of Enoch; father of Lamech.
Michal: Daughter of Saul; wife of David.
Miriam: Prophetess; daughter of Amram; sister of Aaron and Moses.
Mizraim: Son of Ham.
Mordecai: Uncle of Esther; with her aid, saved Jews from Haman's plotting.
Moses: Prophet and lawgiver; son of Amram; brother of Aaron and Miriam; husband of Zipporah.
Naaman: Syrian captain; cured of leprosy by Elisha.
Nabal: Husband of Abigail.
Naboth: Owner of vineyard; stoned to death because he would not sell it to Ahab.
Nadab: Son of Aaron.
Nahor: Father of Terah.
Naomi: Wife of Elimelech; mother-in-law of Ruth.
Naphtali: Son of Jacob and Bilhah.
Nathan: Prophet; reproved David for causing Uriah's death.
Nebuchadnezzar (or Nebuchadrezzar): King of Babylon; destroyer of Jerusalem.
Nehemiah: Jewish leader; empowered by Artaxerxes to rebuild Jerusalem.
Nimrod: Mighty hunter; son of Cush.
Noah: Patriarch; Son of Lamech; escaped Deluge by building Ark; father of Ham, Japheth and Shem.
Nun (or Non): Father of Joshua.
Obed: Son of Boaz; father of Jesse.
Og: King of Bashan.
Orpah: Wife of Chilion.
Othniel: Kenezite; judge of Israel; husband of Achsa.
Phinehas: Son of Eleazer.
Phinehas: Son of Eli.
Phut (or Put): Son of Ham.
Potiphar: Egyptian official; bought Joseph.
Rachel: Wife of Jacob.
Rebecca (or Rebekah): Wife of Isaac.
Reuben: Son of Jacob and Leah.
Ruth: Wife of Mahlon, later of Boaz; daughter-in-law of Naomi.
Samson: Judge of Israel; famed for strength; betrayed by Delilah.
Samuel: Hebrew judge and prophet; son of Elkanah.
Sarah (or Sara, Sarai): Wife of Abraham.
Sennacherib: King of Assyria.
Seth: Son of Adam; father of Enos.
Shem: Son of Noah; father of Elam.
Simeon: Son of Jacob and Leah.
Sisera: Canaanite captain; slain by Jael.
Tamar: Daughter of David and Maachah; ravished by Amnon.
Terah: Son of Nahor; father of Abraham.
Tubal-Cain: Son of Lamech and Zillah.
Uriah: Husband of Bathsheba; sent to death in battle by David.
Vashti: Wife of Ahasuerus; set aside by him.
Zadok: High priest during David's reign.
Zebulun (or Zabulon): Son of Jacob and Leah.
Zillah: Wife of Lamech.
Zilpah: Servant of Leah; mistress of Jacob.
Zipporah: Daughter of Jethro; wife of Moses.
Zophar: Comforter of Job.

Kings of Judah and Israel

Kings Before Division of Kingdom

Saul: First King of Israel; son of Kish; father of Ish-Bosheth, Jonathan and Michal.

Ish-Bosheth (or Eshbaal): King of Israel; son of Saul.

David: King of Judah; later of Israel; son of Jesse; husband of Abigail, Ahinoam, Bathsheba, Michal, etc.; father of Absalom, Adonijah, Amnon, Solomon, Tamar, etc.

Solomon: King of Israel and Judah; son of David; father of Rehoboam.

Rheoboam: Son of Solomon; during his reign the kingdom was divided into Judah and Israel.

Kings of Judah (Southern Kingdom)

Rehoboam: First King.

Abijah (or Abijam or Abia): Son of Rehoboam.

Asa: Probably son of Abijah.

Jehoshaphat: Son of Asa.

Jehoram (or Joram): Son of Jehoshaphat; husband of Athaliah.

AHAZIAH: Son of Jehoram and Athaliah.

ATHALIAH: Daughter of King Ahab of Israel and Jezebel; wife of Jehoram.

JOASH (or JEHOASH): Son of Ahaziah.

Amaziah: Son of Joash.

Uzziah (or Azariah): Son of Amaziah.

Jotham: Regent, later King; son of Uzziah.

Ahaz: Son of Jotham.

Hezekiah: Son of Ahaz; husband of Hephzi-Bah.

Manasseh: Son of Hezekiah and Hephzi-Bah.

Amon: Son of Manasseh.

Josiah (or Josias): Son of Amon.

Jehoahaz (or Joahaz): Son of Josiah.

Jehoiachin: Son of Jehoiakim.

Jehoiakim: Son of Josiah.

Zedekiah: Son of Josiah; kingdom overthrown by Babylonians under Nebuchadnezzar.

Kings of Israel (Northern Kingdom)

Jeroboam I: Led secession of Israel.

Nadab: Son of Jeroboam I.

Baasha: Overthrew Nadab.

Elah: Son of Baasha.

Zimri: Overthrew Elah.

Omri: Overthrew Zimri.

Ahab: Son of Omri; husband of Jezebel.

Ahaziah: Son of Ahab.

Jehoram (or Joram): Son of Ahab.

Jehu: Overthrew Jehoram.

Jehoahaz (or Joahaz): Son of Jehu.

Jehoash (or Joash): Son of Jehoahaz.

Jeroboam II: Son of Jehoash.

Zechariah: Son of Jeroboam II.

Shallum: Overthrew Zechariah.

Menahem: Overthrew Shallum.

Pekahiah: Son of Menahem.

Pekah: Overthrew Pekahiah.

Hoshea: Overthrew Pekah; kingdom overthrown by Assyrians under Sargon II.

Prophets

Major.—Isaiah, Jeremiah, Ezekiel, Daniel.

Minor.—Hosea, Obadiah, Nahum, Haggai, Joel, Jonah, Habakkuk, Zechariah, Amos, Micah, Zephaniah, Malachi.

Greek and Roman Mythology

(Most of the Greek deities were adopted by the Romans, although in many cases there was a change of name. In the list below, information is given under the Greek name; the name in parentheses is the Latin equivalent. However, all Latin names are listed with cross references to the Greek ones. In addition, there are several deities which were exclusively Roman.)

Acheron: *See* Rivers.

Achilles: Greek warrior; slew Hector at Troy; slain by Paris, who wounded him in his vulnerable heel.

Actaeon: Hunter; surprised Artemis bathing; changed by her to stag and killed by his dogs.

Admetus: King of Thessaly; his wife, Alcestis, offered to die in his place.

Adonis: Beautiful youth loved by Aphrodite.

Aeacus: One of three judges of dead in Hades; son of Zeus.

Aeëtes: King of Colchis; father of Medea; keeper of Golden Fleece.

Aegeus: Father of Theseus; believing Theseus killed in Crete, he drowned himself, Aegean Sea named for him.

Aegisthus: Son of Thyestes; slew Atreus; with Clytemnestra, his paramour, slew Agamemnon; slain by Orestes.

Aegyptus: Brother of Danaus; his sons, except Lynceus, slain by Danaides.

Aeneas: Trojan; son of Anchises and Aphrodite; after fall of Troy, led his followers eventually to Italy; loved and deserted Dido.

Aeolus: *See* Winds.

Aesculapius: *See* Asclepius.

Aeson: King of Ioclus; father of Jason; overthrown by his brother Pelias; restored to youth by Medea.

Aether: Personification of sky.

Aethra: Mother of Theseus.

Agamemnon: King of Mycenae; son of Atreus; brother of Menelaus; leader of Greeks against Troy; slain on his return home by Clytemnestra and Aegisthus.

Aglaia: *See* Graces.

Ajax: Greek warrior; killed himself at Troy because Achilles' armor was awarded to Odysseus.

Alcestis: Wife of Admetus; offered to die in his place but saved from death by Hercules.

Alcmene: Wife of Amphitryon; mother by Zeus of Hercules.

Alcyone: *See* Pleiades.

Alecto: *See* Furies.

Alectryon: Youth changed by Ares into cock.

Althaea: Wife of Oeneus; mother of Meleager.

Amazons: Female warriors in Asia Minor; supported Troy against Greeks.

Amor: *See* Eros.

Amphion: Musician; husband of Niobe; charmed stones to build fortifications for Thebes.

Amphitrite: Sea goddess; wife of Poseidon.

Amphitryon: Husband of Alcmene.

Anchises: Father of Aeneas.

Ancile: Sacred shield that fell from heavens; palladium of Rome.

Andraemon: Husband of Dryope.

Andromache: Wife of Hector.

Andromeda: Daughter of Cepheus; chained to cliff for monster to devour; rescued by Perseus.

Anteia: Wife of Proetus; tried to induce Bellerophon to elope with her.

Anteros: God who avenged unrequited love.

Antigone: Daughter of Oedipus; accompanied him to Colonus; performed burial rite for Polynices and was buried alive.

Antinoüs: Leader of suitors of Penelope; slain by Odysseus.

Aphrodite (Venus): Goddess of love and beauty; daughter

of Zeus; mother of Eros.

Apollo: God of beauty, poetry, music; later identified with Helios as Phoebus Apollo; son of Zeus and Leto.

Aquilo: *See* Winds.

Arachne: Maiden who challenged Athena to weaving contest; changed to spider.

Ares (Mars): God of war; son of Zeus and Hera.

Argo: Ship in which Jason and followers sailed to Colchis for Golden Fleece.

Argus: Monster with hundred eyes; slain by Hermes; his eyes placed by Hera into peacock's tail.

Ariadne: Daughter of Minos; aided Theseus in slaying Minotaur; deserted by him on island of Naxos and married to Dionysus.

Arion: Musician; thrown overboard by pirates but saved by dolphin.

Artemis (Diana): Goddess of moon; huntress; twin sister of Apollo.

Asclepius (Aesculapius): Mortal son of Apollo; slain by Zeus for raising dead; later deified as god of medicine. Also known as Asklepios.

Astarte: Phoenician goddess of love; variously identified with Aphrodite, Selene, and Artemis.

Astraea: Goddess of Justice; daughter of Zeus and Themis.

Atalanta: Princess who challenged her suitors to a foot race; Hippomenes won race and married her.

Athena (Minerva): Goddess of wisdom; known poetically as Pallas Athene; sprang fully armed from head of Zeus.

Atlas: Titan; held world on his shoulders as punishment for warring against Zeus; son of Iapetus.

Atreus: King of Mycenae; father of Menelaus and Agamemnon; brother of Thyestes, three of whose sons he slew and served to him at banquet; slain by Aegisthus.

Atropos: *See* Fates.

Aurora: *See* Eos.

Auster: *See* Winds.

Avernus: Infernal regions; name derived from small vaporous lake near Vesuvius which was fabled to kill birds and vegetation.

Bacchus: *See* Dionysus.

Bellerophon: Corinthian hero; killed Chimera with aid of Pegasus; tried to reach Olympus on Pegasus and was thrown to his death.

Bellona: Roman goddess of war.

Boreas: *See* Winds.

Briareus: Monster of hundred hands; son of Uranus and Gaea.

Briseis: Captive maiden given to Achilles; taken by Agamemnon in exchange for loss of Chryseis, which caused Achilles to cease fighting, until death of Patroclus.

Cadmus: Brother of Europa; planter of dragon seeds from which first Thebans sprang.

Calliope: *See* Muses.

Calypso: Sea nymph; kept Odysseus on her island Ogygia for seven years.

Cassandra: Daughter of Priam; prophetess who was never believed; slain with Agamemnon.

Castor: *See* Dioscuri.

Celaeno: *See* Pleiades.

Centaurs: Beings half man and half horse; lived in mountains of Thessaly.

Cephalus: Hunter; accidentally killed his wife Procris with his spear.

Cepheus: King of Ethiopia; father of Andromeda.

Cerberus: Three-headed dog guarding entrance to Hades.

Ceres: *See* Demeter.

Chaos: Formless void; personified as first of gods.

Charon: Boatman on Styx who carried souls of dead to Hades; son of Erebus.

Charybdis: Female monster; personification of whirlpool.

Chimera: Female monster with head of lion, body of goat, tail of serpent; killed by Bellerophon.

Chiron: Most famous of centaurs.

Chronos: Personification of time.

Chryseis: Captive maiden given to Agamemnon; his refusal to accept ransom from her father Chryses caused Apollo to send plague on Greeks besieging Troy.

Circe: Sorceress; daughter of Helios; changed Odysseus' men into swine.

Clio: *See* Muses.

Clotho: *See* Fates.

Clytemnestra: Wife of Agamemnon, whom she slew with aid of her paramour, Aegisthus; slain by her son Orestes.

Cocytus: *See* Rivers.

Creon: Father of Jocasta; forbade burial of Polynices; ordered burial alive of Antigone.

Creüsa: Princess of Corinth, for whom Jason deserted Medea; slain by Medea, who sent her poisoned robe; also known as Glaüke.

Creusa: Wife of Aeneas; died fleeing Troy.

Cronus (Saturn): Titan; god of harvests; son of Uranus and Gaea; dethroned by his son Zeus.

Cupid: *See* Eros.

Cybele: Anatolian nature goddess; adopted by Greeks and identified with Rhea.

Cyclopes: Race of one-eyed giants (singular: Cyclops).

Daedalus: Athenian artificer; father of Icarus; builder of Labyrinth in Crete; devised wings attached with wax for him and Icarus to escape Crete.

Danae: Princess of Argos; mother of Perseus by Zeus, who appeared to her in form of golden shower.

Danaïdes: Daughters of Danaüs; at his command, all except Hypermnestra slew their husbands, the sons of Aegyptus.

Danaüs: Brother of Aegyptus; father of Danaïdes; slain by Lynceus.

Daphne: Nymph; pursued by Apollo; changed to laurel tree.

Decuma: *See* Fates.

Deino: *See* Graeae.

Demeter (Ceres): Goddess of agriculture; mother of Persephone.

Diana: *See* Artemis.

Dido: Founder and queen of Carthage; stabbed herself when deserted by Aeneas.

Diomedes: Greek hero; with Odysseus, entered Troy and carried off Palladium, sacred statue of Athena.

Diomedes: Owner of man-eating horses, which Hercules, as ninth labor, carried off.

Dione: Titan goddess; mother by Zeus of Aphrodite.

Dionysus (Bacchus): God of wine; son of Zeus and Semele.

Dioscuri: Twins Castor and Pollux; sons of Leda by Zeus.

Dis: *See* Hades.

Dryads: Wood nymphs.

Dryope: Maiden changed to Hamadryad.

Echo: Nymph who fell hopelessly in love with Narcissus; faded away except for her voice.

Electra: Daughter of Agamemnon and Clytemnestra; sister of Orestes; urged Orestes to slay Clytemnestra and Aegisthus.

Electra: *See* Pleiades.

Elysium: Abode of blessed dead.

Endymion: Mortal loved by Selene.

Enyo: *See* Graeae.

Eos (Aurora): Goddess of dawn.

Epimetheus: Brother of Prometheus; husband of Pandora.

Erato: *See* Muses.

Erebus: Spirit of darkness; son of Chaos.

Erinyes: *See* Furies.

Eris: Goddess of discord.

Eros (Amor or Cupid): God of love; son of Aphrodite.

Eteocles: Son of Oedipus, whom he succeeded to rule alternately with Polynices; refused to give up throne at end of year; he and Polynices slew each other.

Eumenides: *See* Furies.

Euphrosyne: *See* Graces.

Europa: Mortal loved by Zeus, who, in form of white bull, carried her off to Crete.

Eurus: *See* Winds.

Euryale: *See* Gorgons.

Eurydice: Nymph; wife of Orpheus.

Eurystheus: King of Argos; imposed twelve labors on Hercules.

Euterpe: *See* Muses.

Fates: Goddesses of destiny; Clotho (Spinner of thread of life), Lachesis (Determiner of length), and Atropos (Cutter of thread); also called Moirae. Identified by Romans with their goddesses of fate; Nona, Decuma, and Morta; called Parcae.

Fauns: Roman deities of woods and groves.

Faunus: *See* Pan.

Favonius: *See* Winds.

Flora: Roman goddess of flowers.

Fortuna: Roman goddess of fortune.

Furies: Avenging spirits; Alecto, Megaera, and Tisiphone; known also as Erinyes or Eumenides.

Gaea: Goddess of earth; daughter of Chaos; mother of Titans; known also as Ge, Gea, Gaia, etc.

Galatea: Statue of maiden carved from ivory by Pygmalion; given life by Aphrodite.

Galatea: Sea nymph; loved by Polyphemus.

Ganymede: Beautiful boy; successor to Hebe as cupbearer of gods.

Glaucus: Mortal who became sea divinity by eating magic grass.

Glauke: *See* Creüsa.

Golden Fleece: Fleece from ram that flew Phrixos to Colchis; Aeëtes placed it under guard of dragon; carried off by Jason.

Gorgons: Female monsters: Euryale, Medusa, and Stheno; had snakes for hair; their glances turned mortals to stone. *See* Medusa.

Graces: Beautiful goddesses: Aglaia (Brilliance), Euphrosyne (Joy), and Thalia (Bloom); daughters of Zeus.

Graeae: Sentinels for Gorgons; Deino, Enyo, and Pephredo; had one eye among them, which passed from one to another.

Hades (Dis): Name sometimes given Pluto; also, abode of dead, ruled by Pluto.

Haemon: Son of Creon; promised husband of Antigone; killed himself in her tomb.

Hamadryads: Tree nymphs; lived and died with trees they inhabited.

Harpies: Monsters with heads of women and bodies of birds.

Hebe (Juventas): Goddess of youth; cupbearer of gods before Ganymede; daughter of Zeus and Hera.

Hecate: Goddess of sorcery and witchcraft.

Hector: Son of Priam; slayer of Patroclus; slain by Achilles.

Hecuba: Wife of Priam.

Helen: Fairest woman in world; daughter of Zeus and Leda; wife of Menelaus; carried to Troy by Paris, causing Trojan War.

Heliades: Daughters of Helios; mourned for Phaëthon and were changed to poplar trees.

Helios (Sol): God of sun; later identified with Phoebus Apollo.

Helle: Sister of Phrixos; fell from ram of Golden Fleece; water where she fell named Hellespont.

Hephaestus (Vulcan): God of fire; celestial blacksmith; son of Zeus and Hera; husband of Aphrodite.

Hera (Juno): Queen of heaven; wife of Zeus.

Hercules: Hero and strong man; son of Zeus and Alcmene; performed twelve labors or deeds to be free from bondage under Eurystheus; after death, his mortal share was destroyed, and he became immortal. Also known as Herakles or Heracles. Labors: (1) killing Nemean lion; (2) killing Lernaean Hydra; (3) capturing Erymanthian boar; (4) capturing Cerynean hind; (5) killing man-eating Stymphalian birds; (6) procuring girdle of Hippolyte; (7) cleaning Augean stables; (8) capturing Cretan bull; (9) capturing man-eating horses of Diomedes; (10) capturing cattle of Geryon; (11) procuring golden apples of Hesperides; (12) bringing Cerberus up from Hades.

Hermes (Mercury): God of physicians and thieves; messenger of gods; son of Zeus and Maia.

Hero: Priestess of Aphrodite; Leander swam Hellespont nightly to see her; drowned herself at his death.

Hesperus: Evening star.

Hestia (Vesta): Goddess of hearth; sister of Zeus.

Hippolyte: Queen of Amazons; wife of Theseus.

Hippolytus: Son of Theseus and Hippolyte; falsely accused by Phaedra of trying to kidnap her; slain by Poseidon at request of Theseus.

Hippomenes: Husband of Atalanta, whom he beat in foot race by dropping golden apples, which she stopped to pick up.

Hyacinthus: Beautiful youth accidentally killed by Apollo, who caused flower to spring up from his blood.

Hydra: Nine-headed monster in marsh of Lerna; slain by Hercules.

Hygeia: Personification of health.

Hyman: God of marriage.

Hyperion: Titan; early sun god; father of Helios.

Hypermnestra: Daughter of Danaüs; refused to kill her husband Lynceus.

Hypnos (Somnus): God of sleep.

Iapetus: Titan; father of Atlas, Epimetheus, and Prometheus.

Icarus: Son of Daedalus; flew too near sun with wax-attached wings and fell into sea and was drowned.

Io: Mortal maiden loved by Zeus; changed by Hera into heifer.

Iobates: King of Lycia; sent Bellerophon to slay Chimera.

Iphigenia: Daughter of Agamemnon; offered as sacrifice to Artemis at Aulis; carried by Artemis to Tauris where she became priestess; escaped from there with Orestes.

Iris: Goddess of rainbow; messenger of Zeus and Hera.

Ismene: Daughter of Oedipus; sister of Antigone.

Iulus: Son of Aeneas.

Ixion: King of Lapithae; for making love to Hera he was bound to endlessly revolving wheel in Tartarus.

Janus: Roman god of gates and doors; represented with two opposite faces.

Jason: Son of Aeson; to gain throne of Ioclus from Pelias, went to Colchis and brought back Golden Fleece; married Medea; deserted her for Creüsa.

Jocasta: Wife of Laius; mother of Oedipus; unwittingly became wife of Oedipus; hanged herself when relationship was discovered.

Juno: *See* Hera.

Jupiter: *See* Zeus.

Juventas: *See* Hebe.

Lachesis: *See* Fates.

Laius: Father of Oedipus, by whom he was slain.

Laocoön: Priest of Apollo at Troy; warned against bringing wooden horse into Troy; destroyed with his two sons by serpents sent by Athena.

Lares: Roman ancestral spirits protecting descendants and homes.

Lavinia: wife of Aeneas after defeat of Turnus.

Leander: Swam Hellespont nightly to see Hero; drowned in storm.

Leda: Mortal loved by Zeus in form of Swan; mother of Helen, Clytemnestra, Dioscuri.

Lethe: *See* Rivers.

Leto (Latona): Mother by Zeus of Artemis and Apollo.

Lucina: Roman goddess of childbirth; identified with Juno.

Lynceus: Son of Aegyptus; husband of Hypermnestra; slew Danaüs.

Maia: Daughter of Atlas; mother of Hermes.

Maia: *See* Pleiades.

Manes: Souls of dead Romans, particularly of ancestors.

Mars: *See* Ares.

Marsyas: Shepherd; challenged Apollo to music contest and lost; flayed alive by Apollo.

Medea: Sorceress; daughter of Aeëtes; helped Jason obtain Golden Fleece; when deserted by him for Creüsa, killed her children and Creüsa.

Medusa: Gorgon; slain by Perseus, who cut off her head.

Megaera: *See* Furies.

Meleager: Son of Althaea; his life would last as long as brand burning at his birth; Althaea quenched and saved it but destroyed it when Meleager slew his uncles.

Melpomene: *See* Muses.

Memnon: Ethiopian king; made immortal by Zeus; son of Tithonus and Eos.

Menelaus: King of Sparta; son of Atreus; brother of Agamemnon; husband of Helen.

Mercury: *See* Hermes.

Merope: *See* Pleiades.

Mezentius: Cruel Etruscan king; ally of Turnus against Aeneas; slain by Aeneas.

Midas: King of Phrygia; given gift of turning to gold all he touched.

Minerva: *See* Athena.

Minos: King of Crete; after death, one of three judges of dead in Hades; son of Zeus and Europa.

Minotaur: Monster, half man and half beast, kept in Labyrinth in Crete; slain by Theseus.

Mnemosyne: Goddess of memory; mother by Zeus of Muses.

Moirae: *See* Fates.

Momus: God of ridicule.

Morpheus: God of dreams.

Mors: *See* Thanatos.

Morta: *See* Fates.

Muses: Goddesses presiding over arts and sciences: Calliope (epic poetry), Clio (history), Erato (lyric and love poetry), Euterpe (music), Melpomene (tragedy), Polymnia or Polyhymnia (sacred poetry), Terpsichore (choral dance and song), Thalia (comedy and bucolic poetry), Urania (astronomy); daughters of Zeus and Mnemosyne.

Naiads: Nymphs of waters, streams, and fountains.

Napaeae: Wood nymphs.

Narcissus: Beautiful youth loved by Echo; in punishment for not returning her love, he was made to fall in love with his image reflected in pool; pined away and became flower.

Nemesis: Goddess of retribution.

Neoptolemus: Son of Achilles; slew Priam; also known as Pyrrhus.

Neptune: *See* Poseidon.

Nereids: Sea nymphs; attendants on Poseidon.

Nestor: King of Pylos; noted for wise counsel in expedition against Troy.

Nike: Goddess of victory.

Niobe: Daughter of Tantalus; wife of Amphion; her children slain by Apollo and Artemis; changed to stone but continued to weep her loss.

Nona: *See* Fates.

Notus: *See* Winds.

Nox: *See* Nyx.

Nymphs: Beautiful maidens; inferior deities of nature.

Nyx (Nox): Goddess of night.

Oceanids: Ocean nymphs; daughters of Oceanus.

Oceanus: Eldest of Titans; god of waters.

Odysseus (Ulysses): King of Ithaca; husband of Penelope; wandered ten years after fall of Troy before arriving home.

Oedipus: King of Thebes; son of Laius and Jocasta; unwittingly murdered Laius and married Jocasta; tore his eyes out when relationship was discovered.

Oenone: Nymph of Mount Ida; wife of Paris, who abandoned her; refused to cure him when he was poisoned by arrow of Philoctetes at Troy.

Ops: *See* Rhea.

Oreads: Mountain nymphs.

Orestes: Son of Agamemnon and Clytemnestra; brother of Electra; slew Clytemnestra and Aegisthus; pursued by Furies until his purification by Apollo.

Orion: Hunter; slain by Artemis and made heavenly constellation.

Orpheus: Famed musician; son of Apollo and Muse Calliope; husband of Eurydice.

Pales: Roman goddess of shepherds and herdsmen.

Palinurus: Aeneas' pilot; fell overboard in his sleep and was drowned.

Pan (Faunus): God of woods and fields; part goat; son of Hermes.

Pandora: Opener of box containing human ills; mortal wife of Epimetheus.

Parcae: *See* Fates.

Paris: Son of Priam; gave apple of discord to Aphrodite, for which she enabled him to carry off Helen; slew Achilles at Troy; slain by Philoctetes.

Patroclus: Great friend of Achilles; wore Achilles' armor and was slain by Hector.

Pegasus: Winged horse that sprang from Medusa's body at her death; ridden by Bellerophon when he slew Chimera.

Pelias: King of Iolcus; seized throne from his brother Aeson; sent Jason for Golden Fleece; slain unwittingly by his daughters at instigation of Medea.

Pelops: Son of Tantalus; his father cooked and served him to gods; restored to life; Peloponnesus named for him.

Penates: Roman household gods.

Penelope: Wife of Odysseus; waited faithfully for him for ten years while putting off numerous suitors.

Pephredo: *See* Graeae.

Periphetes: Giant; son of Hephaestus; slain by Theseus.

Persephone (Proserpine): Queen of infernal regions; daughter of Zeus and Demeter; wife of Pluto.

Perseus: Son of Zeus and Danaë; slew Medusa; rescued Andromeda from monster and married her.

Phaedra: Daughter of Minos; wife of Theseus; caused the death of her stepson, Hippolytus.

Phaethon: Son of Helios; drove his father's sun chariot and was struck down by Zeus before he set world on fire.

Philoctetes: Greek warrior who possessed Hercules' bow and arrows; slew Paris at Troy with poisoned arrow.

Phineus: Betrothed of Andromeda; tried to slay Perseus but turned to stone by Medusa's head.

Phlegethon: *See* Rivers.

Phosphor: Morning star.

Phrixos: Brother of Helle; carried by ram of Golden Fleece to Colchis.

Pirithous: Son of Ixion; friend of Theseus; tried to carry off Persephone from Hades; bound to enchanted rock by Pluto.

Pleiades: Alcyone, Celaeno, Electra, Maia, Merope, Sterope or Asterope, Taygeta; seven daughters of Atlas; transformed into heavenly constellation, of which six stars are visible (Merope is said to have hidden in shame for loving a mortal).

Pluto (Dis): God of Hades; brother of Zeus.

Plutus: God of wealth.

Pollux: *See* Dioscuri.

Polymnia: *See* Muses.

Polynices: Son of Oedipus; he and his brother Eteocles killed each other; burial rite, forbidden by Creon, performed by his sister Antigone.

Polyphemus: Cyclops; devoured six of Odysseus' men; blinded by Odysseus.

Polyxena: Daughter of Priam; betrothed to Achilles, whom Paris slew at their betrothal; sacrificed to shade of Achilles.

Pomona: Roman goddess of fruits.

Pontus: Sea god; son of Gaea.

Poseidon (Neptune): God of sea; brother of Zeus.

Priam: King of Troy; husband of Hecuba; ransomed Hector's body from Achilles; slain by Neoptolemus.

Priapus: God of regeneration.

Procris: Wife of Cephalus, who accidentally slew her.

Procrustes: Giant; stretched or cut off legs of victims to make them fit iron bed; slain by Theseus.

Proetus: Husband of Anteia; sent Bellerophon to Iobates to be put to death.

Prometheus: Titan; stole fire from heaven for man. Zeus punished him by chaining him to rock in Caucasus where vultures devoured his liver daily.

Proteus: Sea god; assumed various shapes when called on to prophesy.

Psyche: Beloved of Eros; punished by jealous Aphrodite; made immortal and united with Eros.

Pygmalion: King of Cyprus; carved ivory statue of maiden which Aphrodite gave life as Galatea.

Pyramus: Babylonian youth; made love to Thisbe through hole in wall; thinking Thisbe slain by lion, killed himself.

Pyrrhus: *See* Neoptolemus.

Python: Serpent born from slime left by Deluge; slain by Apollo.

Quirinus: Roman war god.

Remus: Brother of Romulus; slain by him.

Rhadamanthus: One of three judges of dead in Hades; son of Zeus and Europa.

Rhea (Ops): Daughter of Uranus and Gaea; wife of Cronus; mother of Zeus; identified with Cybele.

Rivers of Underworld: Acheron (woe), Cocytus (wailing), Lethe (forgetfulness), Phlegethon (fire), Styx (across which souls of dead were ferried by Charon).

Romulus: Founder of Rome; he and Remus suckled in infancy by she-wolf; slew Remus; deified by Romans.

Sarpedon: King of Lycia; son of Zeus and Europa; slain by Patroclus at Troy.

Saturn: *See* Cronus.

Satyrs: Hoofed demigods of woods and fields; companions of Dionysus.

Sciron: Robber; forced strangers to wash his feet, then hurled them into sea where tortoise devoured them; slain by Theseus.

Scylla: Female monster inhabiting rock opposite Charybdis; menaced passing sailors.

Selene: Goddess of moon.

Semele: Daughter of Cadmus; mother by Zeus of Dionysus; demanded Zeus appear before her in all his splendor and was destroyed by his lightnings.

Sibyls: Various prophetesses; most famous, Cumaean sibyl, accompanied Aeneas into Hades.

Sileni: Minor woodland deities similar to satyrs (singular: silenus). Sometimes Silenus refers to eldest of satyrs, son of Hermes or of Pan.

Silvanus: Roman god of woods and fields.

Sinis: Giant; bent pines, by which he hurled victims against side of mountain; slain by Theseus.

Sirens: Minor deities who lured sailors to destruction with their singing.

Sisyphus: King of Corinth; condemned in Tartarus to roll huge stone to top of hill; it always rolled back down again.

Sol: *See* Helios.

Somnus: *See* Hypnos.

Sphinx: Monster of Thebes; killed those who could not answer her riddle; slain by Oedipus. Name also refers to other monsters having body of lion, wings, and head and bust of woman.

Sterope: *See* Pleiades.

Stheno: *See* Gorgons.

Styx: *See* Rivers.

Symplegades: Clashing rocks at entrance to Black Sea; Argo passed through, causing them to become forever fixed.

Syrinx: Nymph pursued by Pan; changed to reeds, from which he made his pipes.

Tantalus: Cruel king; father of Pelops and Niobe; condemned in Tartarus to stand chin-deep in lake surrounded by fruit branches; as he tried to eat or drink, water or fruit always receded.

Tartarus: Underworld below Hades; often refers to Hades.

Taygeta: *See* Pleiades.

Telemachus: Son of Odysseus; made unsuccessful journey to find his father.

Tellus: Roman goddess of earth.

Terminus: Roman god of boundaries and landmarks.

Terpsichore: *See* Muses.

Terra: Roman earth goddess.

Thalia: *See* Graces; Muses.

Thanatos (Mors): God of death.

Themis: Titan goddess of laws of physical phenomena; daughter of Uranus; mother of Prometheus.

Theseus: Son of Aegeus; slew Minotaur; married and deserted Ariadne; later married Phaedra.

Thisbe: Beloved of Pyramus; killed herself at his death.

Thyestes: Brother of Atreus; Atreus killed three of his sons and served them to him at banquet.

Tiresias: Blind soothsayer of Thebes.

Tisiphone: *See* Furies.

Titans: Early gods from which Olympian gods were derived; children of Uranus and Gaea.

Tithonus: Mortal loved by Eos; changed into grasshopper.

Triton: Demigod of sea; son of Poseidon.

Turnus: King of Rutuli in Italy; betrothed to Lavinia; slain by Aeneas.

Ulysses: *See* Odysseus.

Urania: *See* Muses.

Uranus: Personification of Heaven; husband of Gaea; father of Titans; dethroned by his son Cronus.

Venus: *See* Aphrodite.

Vertumnus: Roman god of fruits and vegetables; husband of Pomona.

Vesta: *See* Hestia.

Vulcan: *See* Hephaestus.

Winds: Aeolus (keeper of winds), Boreas (Aquilo) (north wind), Eurus (east wind), Notus (Auster) (south wind), Zephyrus (Favonius) (west wind).

Zephyrus: *See* Winds.

Zeus (Jupiter): Chief of Olympian gods; son of Cronus and Rhea; husband of Hera.

Norse Mythology

Aesir: Chief gods of Asgard.

Andvari: Dwarf; robbed of gold and magic ring by Loki.

Angerbotha (Angrbotha): Giantess; mother by Loki of Fenrir, Hel, and Midgard serpent.

Asgard (Asgarth): Abode of gods.

Ask (Aske, Askr): First man; created by Odin, Hoenir, and Lothur.

Asynjur: Goddesses of Asgard.

Atli: Second husband of Gudrun; invited Gunnar and Hogni to his court, where they were slain; slain by Gudrun.

Audhumla (Audhumbla): Cow that nourished Ymir; created Buri by licking ice cliff.

Balder (Baldr, Baldur): God of light, spring, peace, joy; son of Odin; slain by Hoth at instigation of Loki.

Bifrost: Rainbow bridge connecting Midgard and Asgard.

Bragi (Brage): God of poetry; husband of Ithunn.

Branstock: Great oak in hall of Volsungs; into it, Odin thrust Gram, which only Sigmund could draw forth.

Brynhild: Valkyrie; wakened from magic sleep by Sigurd; married Gunnar; instigated death of Sigurd; killed herself and was burned on pyre beside Sigurd.

Bur (Bor): Son of Buri; father of Odin, Hoenir, and Lothur.

Buri (Bori): Progenitor of gods; father of Bur; created by Audhumla.

Embla: First woman; created by Odin, Hoenir, and Lothur.

Fafnir: Son of Rodmar, whom he slew for gold in Otter's skin; in form of dragon, guarded gold; slain by Sigurd.

Fenrir: Wolf; offspring of Loki; swallows Odin at Ragnarok and is slain by Vitharr.

Forseti: Son of Balder.

Frey (Freyr): God of fertility and crops; son of Njorth; originally one of Vanir.

Freya (Freyja): Goddess of love and beauty; sister of Frey; originally one of Vanir.

Frigg (Frigga): Goddess of sky; wife of Odin.

Garm: Watchdog of Hel; slays, and is slain by, Tyr at Ragnarok.

Gimle: Home of blessed after Ragnarok.

Giuki: King of Nibelungs; father of Gunnar, Hogni, Guttorm, and Gudrun.

Glathsehim (Gladsheim): Hall of gods in Asgard.

Gram (meaning "Angry"): Sigmund's sword; rewelded by Regin; used by Sigurd to slay Fafnir.

Greyfell: Sigmund's horse; descended from Sleipnir.

Grimhild: Mother of Gudrun; administered magic potion to Sigurd which made him forget Brynhild.

Gudrun: Daughter of Giuki; wife of Sigurd; later wife of Atli and Jonakr.

Gunnar: Son of Giuki; in his semblance Sigurd won Brynhild for him; slain at hall of Atli.

Guttorm: Son of Giuki; slew Sigurd at Brynhild's request.

Heimdall (Heimdallr): Guardian of Asgard.

Hel: Goddess of dead and queen of underworld; daughter of Loki.

Hiordis: Wife of Sigmund; mother of Sigurd.

Hoenir: One of creators of Ask and Embla; son of Bur.

Hogni: Son of Giuki; slain at hall of Atli.

Hoth (Hoder, Hodur): Blind god of night and darkness; slayer of Balder at instigation of Loki.

Ithunn (Ithun, Iduna): Keeper of golden apples of youth; wife of Bragi.

Jonakr: Third husband of Gudrun.

Jormunrek: Slayer of Swanhild; slain by sons of Gudrun.

Jotunnheim (Jotunheim): Abode of giants.

Lif and Lifthrasir: First man and woman after Ragnarok.

Loki: God of evil and mischief; instigator of Balder's death.

Lothur (Lodur): One of creators of Ask and Embla.

Midgard (Midgarth): Abode of mankind; the earth.

Midgard Serpent: Sea monster; offspring of Loki; slays, and is slain by, Thor at Ragnarok.

Mimir: Giant; guardian of well in Jotunnheim at root of Yggdrasill; knower of past and future.

Mjollnir: Magic hammer of Thor.

Naglfar: Ship to be used by giants in attacking Asgard at

Ragnarok; built from nails of dead men.

Nanna: Wife of Balder.

Nibelungs: Dwellers in northern kingdom ruled by Giuki.

Niflheim (Nifelheim): Outer region of cold and darkness; abode of Hel.

Njorth: Father of Frey and Freya; originally one of Vanir.

Norns: Demigoddesses of fate: Urth (Urdur) (Past), Verthandi (Verdandi) (Present), Skuld (Future).

Odin (Othin): Head of Aesir; creator of world with Vili and Ve; equivalent to Woden (Wodan, Wotan) in Teutonic mythology.

Otter: Son of Rodmar; slain by Loki; his skin filled with gold hoard of Andvari to appease Rodmar.

Ragnarok: Final destruction of present world in battle between gods and giants; some minor gods will survive, and Lif and Lifthrasir will repeople world.

Regin: Blacksmith; son of Rodmar; foster-father of Sigurd.

Rerir: King of Huns; son of Sigi.

Rodmar: Father of Regin, Otter, and Fafnir; demanded Otter's skin be filled with gold; slain by Fafnir, who stole gold.

Sif: Wife of Thor.

Siggeir: King of Goths; husband of Signy; he and his sons slew Volsung and his sons, except Sigmund; slain by Sigmund and Sinflotli.

Sigi: King of Huns; son of Odin.

Sigmund: Son of Volsung; brother of Signy, who bore him Sinflotli; husband of Hiordis, who bore him Sigurd.

Signy: Daughter of Volsung; sister of Sigmund; wife of Siggeir; mother by Sigmund of Sinflotli.

Sigurd: Son of Sigmund and Hiordis; wakened Brynhild from magic sleep; married Gudrun; slain by Guttorm at instigation of Brynhild.

Sigyn: Wife of Loki.

Sinflotli: Son of Sigmund and Signy.

Skuld: *See* Norns.

Sleipnir (Sleipner): Eight-legged horse of Odin.

Surt (Surtr): Fire demon; slays Frey at Ragnarok.

Svartalfaheim: Abode of dwarfs.

Swanhild: Daughter of Sigurd and Gudrun; slain by Jormunrek.

Thor: God of thunder; oldest son of Odin; equivalent to Germanic deity Donar.

Tyr: God of war; son of Odin; equivalent to Tiu in Teutonic mythology.

Ull (Ullr): Son of Sif; stepson of Thor.

Urth: *See* Norns.

Valhalla (Valhall): Great hall in Asgard where Odin received souls of heroes killed in battle.

Vali: Odin's son: Ragnarok survivor.

Valkyries: Virgins, messengers of Odin, who selected heroes to die in battle and took them to Valhalla; generally considered as nine in number.

Vanir: Early race of gods; three survivors, Njorth, Frey, and Freya, are associated with Aesir.

Ve: Brother of Odin; one of creators of world.

Verthandi: *See* Norns.

Vili: Brother of Odin; one of creators of world.

Vingolf: Abode of goddesses in Asgard.

Vitharr (Vithar): Son of Odin; survivor of Ragnarok.

Volsung: Descendant of Odin, and father of Signy, Sigmund; his descendants were called Volsungs.

Yggdrasill: Giant ash tree springing from body of Ymir and supporting universe; its roots extended to Asgard, Jotunnheim, and Niffheim.

Ymir (Ymer): Primeval frost giant killed by Odin, Vili, and Ve; world created from his body; also, from his body sprang Yggdrasill.

Egyptian Mythology

Aaru: Abode of the blessed dead.

Amen (Amon, Ammdn): One of chief Theban deities; united with sun god under form of Amen-Ra.

Amenti: Region of dead where souls were judged by Osiris.

Anubis: Guide of souls to Amenti; son of Osiris; jackal-headed.

Apis: Sacred bull, an embodiment of Ptah; identified with Osiris as Osiris-Apis or Serapis.

Geb (Keb, Seb): Earth god; father of Osiris; represented with goose on head.

Hathor (Athor): Goddess of love and mirth; cow-headed.

Horus: God of day; son of Osiris and Isis; hawk-headed.

Isis: Goddess of motherhood and fertility; sister and wife of Osiris.

Khepera: God of morning sun.

Khnemu (Khnum, Chnuphis, Chnemu, Chnum): Ram-headed god.

Khonsu (Khensu, Khuns): Son of Amen and Mut.

Mentu (Ment): Solar deity, sometimes considered god of war; falcon-headed.

Min (Khem, Chem): Principle of physical life.

Mut (Maut): Wife of Amen.

Nephthys: Goddess of the dead; sister and wife of Set.

Nu: Chaos from which world was created, personified as a god.

Nut: Goddess of heavens; consort of Geb.

Osiris: God of underworld and judge of dead; son of Geb and Nut.

Ptah (Phtha): Chief deity of Memphis.

Ra: God of the Sun, the supreme god; son of Nut; Pharaohs claimed descent from him; represented as lion, cat, or falcon.

Serapis: God uniting attributes of Osiris and Apis.

Set (Seth): God of darkness or evil; brother and enemy of Osiris.

Shu: Solar deity; son of Ra and Hathor.

Tem (Atmu, Atum, Tum): Solar deity.

Thoth (Dhouti): God of wisdom and magic; scribe of gods; ibis-headed.

Modern Wedding Anniversary Gift List

Anniversary	Gift	Anniversary	Gift	Anniversary	Gift
1st	Clock	10th	Diamond jewelry	19th	Bronze
2nd	China	11th	Fashion jewelry and accessories	20th	Platinum
3rd	Crystal, glass			25th	Sterling Silver Jubilee
4th	Electrical Appliances	12th	Pearls or colored gems	30th	Diamond
5th	Silverware	13th	Textiles, furs	35th	Jade
6th	Wood	14th	Gold jewelry	40th	Ruby
7th	Desk sets, pen and pencil sets	15th	Watches	45th	Sapphire
		16th	Silver hollow ware	50th	Golden Jubilee
8th	Linens, laces	17th	Furniture	55th	Emerald
9th	Leather	18th	Porcelain	60th	Diamond Jubilee

Source: Jewelry Industry Council

AWARDS

Nobel Prizes

The Nobel prizes are awarded under the will of Alfred Bernhard Nobel, Swedish chemist and engineer, who died in 1896. The interest of the fund is divided annually among the persons who have made the most outstanding contributions in the fields of physics, chemistry, and physiology or medicine, who have produced the most distinguished literary work of an idealist tendency, and who have contributed most toward world peace.

In 1968, a Nobel Prize of economic sciences was established by Riksbank, the Swedish bank, in celebration of its 300th anniversary. The prize was awarded for the first time in 1969.

The prizes for physics and chemistry are awarded by the Swedish Academy of Science in Stockholm, the one for physiology or medicine by the Caroline Medical Institute in Stockholm, that for literature by the academy in Stockholm, and that for peace by a committee of five elected by the Norwegian Storting. The distribution of prizes was begun on December 10, 1901, the anniversary of Nobel's death. The amount of each prize varies with the income from the fund and currently is about $180,000. No Nobel prizes were awarded for 1940, 1941, and 1942; prizes for Literature were not awarded for 1914, 1918, and 1943.

PEACE

1901 Henri Dunant (Switzerland); Frederick Passy (France)
1902 Elie Ducommun and Albert Gobat (Switzerland)
1903 Sir William R. Cremer (England)
1904 Institut de Droit International (Belgium)
1905 Bertha von Suttner (Austria)
1906 Theodore Roosevelt (U.S.)
1907 Ernesto T. Moneta (Italy) and Louis Renault (France)
1908 Klas P. Arnoldson (Sweden) and Frederik Bajer (Denmark)
1909 Auguste M. F. Beernaert (Belgium) and Baron Paul H. B. B. d'Estournelles de Constant de Rebecque (France)
1910 Bureau International Permanent de la Paix (Switzerland)
1911 Tobias M. C. Asser (Holland) and Alfred H. Fried (Austria)
1912 Elihu Root (U.S.)
1913 Henri La Fontaine (Belgium)
1915 No award
1916 No award
1917 International Red Cross
1919 Woodrow Wilson (U.S.)
1920 Léon Bourgeois (France)
1921 Karl H. Branting (Sweden) and Christian L. Lange (Norway)
1922 Fridtjof Nansen (Norway)
1923 No award
1924 No award
1925 Sir Austen Chamberlain (England) and Charles G. Dawes (U.S.)
1926 Aristide Briand (France) and Gustav Stresemann (Germany)
1927 Ferdinand Buisson (France) and Ludwig Quidde (Germany)
1928 No award
1929 Frank B. Kellogg (U.S.)
1930 Lars O. J. Söderblom (Sweden)
1931 Jane Addams and Nicholas M. Butler (U.S.)
1932 No award
1933 Sir Norman Angell (England)
1934 Arthur Henderson (England)
1935 Karl von Ossietzky (Germany)
1936 Carlos de S. Lamas (Argentina)
1937 Lord Cecil of Chelwood (England)
1938 Office International Nansen pour les Réfugiés (Switzerland)
1939 No award
1944 International Red Cross
1945 Cordell Hull (U.S.)
1946 Emily G. Balch and John R. Mott (U.S.)
1947 American Friends Service Committee (U.S.) and British Society of Friends' Service Council (England)
1948 No award
1949 Lord John Boyd Orr (Scotland)
1950 Ralph J. Bunche (U.S.)
1951 Léon Jouhaux (France)
1952 Albert Schweitzer (French Equatorial Africa)
1953 George C. Marshall (U.S.)
1954 Office of U.N. High Commissioner for Refugees
1955 No award
1956 No award
1957 Lester B. Pearson (Canada)
1958 Rev. Dominique Georges Henri Pire (Belgium)
1959 Philip John Noel-Baker (England)
1960 Albert John Luthuli (South Africa)
1961 Dag Hammarskjöld (Sweden)
1962 Linus Pauling (U.S.)
1963 Intl. Comm. of Red Cross; League of Red Cross Societies (both Geneva)
1964 Rev. Dr. Martin Luther King, Jr. (U.S.)
1965 UNICEF (United Nations Children's Fund)
1966 No award
1967 No award
1968 René Cassin (France)
1969 International Labour Organization
1970 Norman E. Borlaug (U.S.)
1971 Willy Brandt (West Germany)
1972 No award
1973 Henry A. Kissinger (U.S.); Le Duc Tho (North Vietnam)[1]
1974 Eisaku Sato (Japan); Sean MacBride (Ireland)
1975 Andrei D. Sakharov (U.S.S.R.)
1976 Mairead Corrigan and Betty Williams (both Northern Ireland)
1977 Amnesty International
1978 Menachem Begin (Israel) and Anwar el-Sadat (Egypt)
1979 Mother Teresa of Calcutta (Albania)
1980 Adolfo Pérez Esquivel (Argentina)
1981 Office of the United Nations High Commissioner for Refugees

1. Le Duc Tho refused prize, charging that peace had not yet been really established in South Vietnam.

LITERATURE

1901 René F. A. Sully Prudhomme (France)
1902 Theodor Mommsen (Germany)
1903 Björnstjerne Björnson (Norway)
1904 Frédéric Mistral (France) and José Echegaray (Spain)
1905 Henryk Sienkiewicz (Poland)

1906 Giosuè Carducci (Italy)
1907 Rudyard Kipling (England)
1908 Rudolf Eucken (Germany)
1909 Selma Lagerlöf (Sweden)
1910 Paul von Heyse (Germany)
1911 Maurice Maeterlinck (Belgium)
1912 Gerhart Hauptmann (Germany)
1913 Rabindranath Tagore (India)
1915 Romain Rolland (France)
1916 Verner von Heidenstam (Sweden)
1917 Karl Gjellerup (Denmark) and Henrik Pontoppidan (Denmark)
1919 Carl Spitteler (Switzerland)
1920 Knut Hamsun (Norway)
1921 Anatole France (France)
1922 Jacinto Benavente (Spain)
1923 William B. Yeats (Ireland)
1924 Wladyslaw Reymont (Poland)
1925 George Bernard Shaw (England)
1926 Grazia Deledda (Italy)
1927 Henri Bergson (France)
1928 Sigrid Undset (Norway)
1929 Thomas Mann (Germany)
1930 Sinclair Lewis (U.S.)
1931 Erik A. Karlfeldt (Sweden)
1932 John Galsworthy (England)
1933 Ivan G. Bunin (Russia)
1934 Luigi Pirandello (Italy)
1935 No award
1936 Eugene O'Neill (U.S.)
1937 Roger Martin du Gard (France)
1938 Pearl S. Buck (U.S.)
1939 Frans Eemil Sillanpää (Finland)
1944 Johannes V. Jensen (Denmark)
1945 Gabriela Mistral (Chile)
1946 Hermann Hesse (Switzerland)
1947 André Gide (France)
1948 Thomas Stearns Eliot (England)
1949 William Faulkner (U.S.)
1950 Bertrand Russell (England)
1951 Pär Lagerkvist (Sweden)
1952 François Mauriac (France)
1953 Sir Winston Churchill (England)
1954 Ernest Hemingway (U.S.)
1955 Halldór Kiljan Laxness (Iceland)
1956 Juan Ramón Jiménez (Spain)
1957 Albert Camus (France)
1958 Boris Pasternak (U.S.S.R.) (declined)
1959 Salvatore Quasimodo (Italy)
1960 St.-John Perse (Alexis St.-Léger Léger) (France)
1961 Ivo Andric (Yugoslavia)
1962 John Steinbeck (U.S.)
1963 Giorgios Seferis (Seferiades) (Greece)
1964 Jean-Paul Sartre (France) (declined)
1965 Mikhail Sholokhov (U.S.S.R.)
1966 Shmuel Yosef Agnon (Israel) and Nelly Sachs (Sweden)
1967 Miguel Angel Asturias (Guatemala)
1968 Yasunari Kawabata (Japan)
1969 Samuel Beckett (France)
1970 Aleksandr Solzhenitsyn (U.S.S.R.)
1971 Pablo Neruda (Chile)
1972 Heinrich Böll (Germany)
1973 Patrick White (Australia)
1974 Eyvind Johnson and Harry Martinson (both Sweden)
1975 Eugenio Montale (Italy)
1976 Saul Bellow (U.S.)
1977 Vicente Aleixandre (Spain)
1978 Isaac Bashevis Singer (U.S.)
1979 Odysseus Elytis (Greece)
1980 Czeslaw Milosz (U.S.)
1981 Elias Canetti (Bulgaria)

PHYSICS

1901 Wilhelm K. Roentgen (Germany), for discovery of Roentgen rays
1902 Hendrik A. Lorentz and Pieter Zeeman (Netherlands), for work on influence of magnetism upon radiation
1903 A. Henri Becquerel (France), for work on spontaneous radioactivity; and Pierre and Marie Curie (France), for study of radiation
1904 John Strutt (Lord Rayleigh) (England), for discovery of argon in investigating gas density
1905 Philipp Lenard (Germany), for work with cathode rays
1906 Sir Joseph Thomson (England), for investigations on passage of electricity through gases
1907 Albert A. Michelson (U.S.), for spectroscopic and metrologic investigations
1908 Gabriel Lippmann (France), for method of reproducing colors by photography
1909 Guglielmo Marconi (Italy) and Ferdinand Braun (Germany), for development of wireless
1910 Johannes D. van der Waals (Netherlands), for work with the equation of state for gases and liquids
1911 Wilhelm Wien (Germany), for his laws governing the radiation of heat
1912 Gustaf Dalén (Sweden), for discovery of automatic regulators used in lighting lighthouses and light buoys
1913 Heike Kamerlingh-Onnes (Netherlands), for work leading to production of liquid helium
1914 Max von Laue (Germany), for discovery of diffraction of Roentgen rays passing through crystals
1915 Sir William Bragg and William L. Bragg (England), for analysis of crystal structure by X rays
1916 No award
1917 Charles G. Barkla (England), for discovery of Roentgen radiation of the elements
1918 Max Planck (Germany), discoveries in connection with quantum theory
1919 Johannes Stark (Germany), discovery of Doppler effect in Canal rays and decomposition of spectrum lines by electric fields
1920 Charles E. Guillaume (Switzerland), for discoveries of anomalies in nickel steel alloys
1921 Albert Einstein (Germany), for discovery of the law of the photoelectric effect
1922 Niels Bohr (Denmark), for investigation of structure of atoms and radiations emanating from them
1923 Robert A. Millikan (U.S.), for work on elementary charge of electricity and photoelectric phenomena
1924 Karl M. G. Siegbahn (Sweden), for investigations in X-ray spectroscopy
1925 James Franck and Gustav Hertz (Germany), for discovery of laws governing impact of electrons upon atoms
1926 Jean B. Perrin (France), for work on discontinous structure of matter and discovery of the equilibrium of sedimentation
1927 Arthur H. Compton (U.S.), for discovery of Compton phenomenon; and Charles T. R. Wilson (England), for method of perceiving paths taken by electrically charged particles
1928 In 1929, the 1928 prize was awarded to Sir Owen Richardson (England), for work on the phenomenon of thermionics and discovery of the Richardson Law
1929 Prince Louis Victor de Broglie (France), for discovery of the wave character of electrons
1930 Sir Chandrasekhara Raman (India), for work on

diffusion of light and discovery of the Raman effect

1931 No award

1932 In 1933, the prize for 1932 was awarded to Werner Heisenberg (Germany), for creation of the quantum mechanics

1933 Erwin Schrödinger (Austria) and Paul A. M. Dirac (England), for discovery of new fertile forms of the atomic theory

1934 No award

1935 James Chadwick (England), for discovery of the neutron

1936 Victor F. Hess (Austria), for discovery of cosmic radiation; and Carl D. Anderson (U.S.), for discovery of the positron

1937 Clinton J. Davisson (U.S.) and George P. Thomson (England), for discovery of diffraction of electrons by crystals

1938 Enrico Fermi (Italy), for identification of new radioactivity elements and discovery of nuclear reactions effected by slow neutrons

1939 Ernest Orlando Lawrence (U.S.), for development of the cyclotron

1943 Otto Stern (U.S.), for detection of magnetic momentum of protons

1944 Isidor Isaac Rabi (U.S.), for work on magnetic movements of atomic particles

1945 Wolfgang Pauli (Austria), for work on atomic fissions

1946 Percy Williams Bridgman (U.S.), for studies and inventions in high-pressure physics

1947 Sir Edward Appleton (England), for discovery of layer which reflects radio short waves in the ionosphere

1948 Patrick M. S. Blackett (England), for improvement on Wilson chamber and discoveries in cosmic radiation

1949 Hideki Yukawa (Japan), for mathematical prediction, in 1935, of the meson

1950 Cecil Frank Powell (England), for method of photographic study of atom nucleus, and for discoveries about mesons

1951 Sir John Douglas Cockcroft (England) and Ernest T. S. Walton (Ireland), for work in 1932 on transmutation of atomic nuclei

1952 Edward Mills Purcell and Felix Bloch (U.S.), for work in measurement of magnetic fields in atomic nuclei

1953 Fritz Zernike (Netherlands), for development of "phase contrast" microscope

1954 Max Born (England), for work in quantum mechanics; and Walther Bothe (Germany), for work in cosmic radiation

1955 Polykarp Kusch and Willis E. Lamb, Jr. (U.S.), for atomic measurements

1956 William Shockley, Walter H. Brattain, and John Bardeen (U.S.), for developing electronic transistor

1957 Tsung Dao Lee and Chen Ning Yang (China), for disproving principle of conservation of parity

1958 Pavel A. Cherenkov, Ilya M. Frank, and Igor E. Tamm (U.S.S.R.), for work resulting in development of cosmic-ray counter

1959 Emilio Segre and Owen Chamberlain (U.S.), for demonstrating the existence of the anti-proton

1960 Donald A. Glaser (U.S.), for invention of "bubble chamber" to study subatomic particles

1961 Robert Hofstadter (U.S.), for determination of shape and size of atomic nucleus; Rudolf Mössbauer (Germany), for method of producing and measuring recoil-free gamma rays

1962 Lev D. Landau (U.S.S.R.), for his theories about condensed matter

1963 Eugene Paul Wigner, Maria Goeppert Mayer (both U.S.), and J. Hans D. Jensen (Germany), for research on structure of atom and its nucleus

1964 Charles Hard Townes (U.S.), Nikolai G. Basov, and Aleksandr M. Prochorov (both U.S.S.R.), for developing maser and laser principle of producing high-intensity radiation

1965 Richard P. Feynman, Julian S. Schwinger (both U.S.), and Shinichero Tomonaga (Japan), for research in quantum electrodynamics

1966 Alfred Kastler (France), for work on energy levels inside atom

1967 Hans A. Bethe (U.S.), for work on energy production of stars

1968 Luis Walter Alvarez (U.S.), for study of subatomic particles

1969 Murray Gell-Mann (U.S.), for study of subatomic particles

1970 Hannes Alfvén (Sweden), for theories in plasma physics; and Louis Néel (France), for discoveries in antiferromagnetism and ferrimagnetism

1971 Dennis Gabor (England), for invention of holographic method of three-dimensional imagery

1972 John Bardeen, Leon N. Cooper, and John Robert Schrieffer (all U.S.), for theory of superconductivity, where electrical resistance in certain metals vanishes above absolute zero temperature

1973 Ivar Giaever (U.S.), Leo Esaki (Japan), and Brian D. Josephson (U.K.), for theories that have advanced and expanded the field of miniature electronics

1974 Antony Hewish (England), for discovery of pulsars; Martin Ryle (England), for using radiotelescopes to probe outer space with high degree of precision

1975 James Rainwater (U.S.) and Ben Mottelson and Aage N. Bohr (both Denmark), for showing that the atomic nucleus is asymmetrical

1976 Burton Richter and Samuel C. C. Ting (both U.S.), for discovery of subatomic particles known as J and psi

1977 Philip W. Anderson and John H. Van Vleck (both U.S.), and Nevill F. Mott (U.K.), for work underlying computer memories and electronic devices

1978 Arno A. Penzias and Robert W. Wilson (both (U.S.), for work in cosmic microwave radiation; Piotr L. Kapitsa (U.S.S.R.), for basic inventions and discoveries in low-temperature physics

1979 Steven Weinberg and Sheldon L. Glashow (both U.S.) and Abdus Salam (Pakistan), for developing theory that electromagnetism and the "weak" force, which causes radioactive decay in some atomic nuclei, are facets of the same phenomenon

1980 James W. Cronin and Val L. Fitch (both U.S.), for work concerning the assymetry of subatomic particles

1981 Nicolaas Bloembergen and Arthur L. Schawlow (both U.S.) and Kai M. Siegbahn (Sweden), for developing technologies with lasers and other devices to probe the secrets of complex forms of matter

CHEMISTRY

1901 Jacobus H. van't Hoff (Netherlands), for laws of chemical dynamics and osmotic pressure in solutions

1902 Emil Fischer (Germany), for experiments in sugar and purin groups of substances

1903 Svante A. Arrhenius (Sweden), for his electrolytic theory of dissociation
1904 Sir William Ramsay (England), for discovery and determination of place of inert gaseous elements in air
1905 Adolf von Baeyer (Germany), for work on organic dyes and hydroaromatic combinations
1906 Henri Moissan (France), for isolation of fluorine, and introduction of electric furnace
1907 Eduard Buchner (Germany), discovery of cell-less fermentation and investigations in biological chemistry
1908 Sir Ernest Rutherford (England), for investigations into disintegration of elements
1909 Wilhelm Ostwald (Germany), for work on catalysis and investigations into chemical equilibrium and reaction rates
1910 Otto Wallach (Germany), for work in the field of alicyclic compounds
1911 Marie Curie (France), for discovery of elements radium and polonium
1912 Victor Grignard (France), for reagent discovered by him; and Paul Sabatier (France), for methods of hydrogenating organic compounds
1913 Alfred Werner (Switzerland), for linking up atoms within the molecule
1914 Theodore W. Richards (U.S.), for determining atomic weight of many chemical elements
1915 Richard Willstätter (Germany), for research into coloring matter of plants, especially chlorophyll
1916 No award
1917 No award
1918 Fritz Haber (Germany), for synthetic production of ammonia
1919 No award
1920 Walther Nernst (Germany), for work in thermochemistry
1921 Frederick Soddy (England), for investigations into origin and nature of isotopes
1922 Francis W. Aston (England), for discovery of isotopes in nonradioactive elements and for discovery of the whole number rule
1923 Fritz Pregl (Austria), for method of microanalysis of organic substances discovered by him
1924 No award
1925 In 1926, the 1925 prize was awarded to Richard Zsigmondy (Germany), for work on the heterogeneous nature of colloid solutions
1926 Theodor Svedberg (Sweden), for work on disperse systems
1927 In 1928 the 1927 prize was awarded to Heinrich Wieland (Germany), for investigations of bile acids and kindred substances
1928 Adolf Windaus (Germany), for investigations on constitution of the sterols and their connection with vitamins
1929 Sir Arthur Harden (England) and Hans K. A. S. von Euler-Chelpin (Sweden), for research of fermentation of sugars
1930 Hans Fischer (Germany), for work on coloring matter of blood and leaves and for his synthesis of hemin
1931 Karl Bosch and Friedrich Bergius (Germany), for invention and development of chemical high-pressure methods
1932 Irving Langmuir (U.S.), for work in realm of surface chemistry
1933 No award
1934 Harold C. Urey (U.S.), for discovery of heavy hydrogen
1935 Frédéric and Irène Joliot-Curie (France), for synthesis of new radioactive elements
1936 Peter J. W. Debye (Netherlands), for investigations on dipole moments and diffraction of X rays and electrons in gases
1937 Walter N. Haworth (England), for research on carbohydrates and Vitamin C; and Paul Karrer (Switzerland), for work on carotenoids, flavins, and Vitamins A and B
1938 Richard Kuhn (Germany), for carotinoid study and vitamin research (declined the prize)
1939 Adolf Butenandt (Germany), for work on sexual hormones (declined the prize); and Leopold Ruzicka (Switzerland), for work with polymethylenes
1943 Georg Hevesy De Heves (Hungary), for work on use of isotopes as indicators
1944 Otto Hahn (Germany), for work on atomic fission
1945 Artturi Ilmari Virtanen (Finland), for research in the field of conservation of fodder
1946 James B. Sumner (U.S.), for crystallizing enzymes; John H. Northrop and Wendell M. Stanley (U.S.), for preparing enzymes and virus proteins in pure form
1947 Sir Robert Robinson (England), for research in plant substances
1948 Arne Tiselius (Sweden), for biochemical discoveries and isolation of mouse paralysis virus
1949 William Francis Giauque (U.S.), for research in thermodynamics, especially effects of low temperature
1950 Otto Diels and Kurt Alder (Germany), for discovery of diene synthesis enabling scientists to study structure of organic matter
1951 Glenn T. Seaborg and Edwin H. McMillan (U.S.), for discovery of plutonium
1952 Archer John Porter Martin and Richard Laurence Millington Synge (England), for development of partition chromatography
1953 Hermann Staudinger (Germany), for research in giant molecules
1954 Linus C. Pauling (U.S.), for study of forces holding together protein and other molecules
1955 Vincent du Vigneaud (U.S.), for work on pituitary hormones
1956 Sir Cyril Hinshelwood (England) and Nikolai N. Semenov (U.S.S.R.), for parallel research on chemical reaction kinetics
1957 Sir Alexander Todd (England), for research with chemical compounds that are factors in heredity
1958 Frederick Sanger (England), for determining molecular structure of insulin
1959 Jaroslav Heyrovsky (Czechoslovakia), for development of polarography, an electrochemical method of analysis
1960 Willard F. Libby (U.S.), for "atomic time clock" to measure age of objects by measuring their radioactivity
1961 Melvin Calvin (U.S.), for establishing chemical steps during photosynthesis
1962 Max F. Perutz and John C. Kendrew (England), for mapping protein molecules with X rays
1963 Carl Ziegler (Germany) and Giulio Natta (Italy), for work in uniting simple hydrocarbons into large molecule substances
1964 Dorothy Mary Crowfoot Hodgkin (England), for determining structure of compounds needed in combating pernicious anemia
1965 Robert B. Woodward (U.S.), for work in synthesizing complicated organic compounds
1966 Robert Sanderson Mulliken (U.S.), for research on bond holding atoms together in molecule
1967 Manfred Eigen (Germany), Ronald G. W. Nor-

rish, and George Porter (both England), for work in high-speed chemical reactions

1968 Lars Onsager (U.S.), for development of system of equations in thermodynamics

1969 Derek H. R. Barton (England) and Odd Hassel (Norway), for study of organic molecules

1970 Luis F. Leloir (Argentina), for discovery of sugar nucleotides and their role in biosynthesis of carbohydrates

1971 Gerhard Herzberg (Canada), for contributions to knowledge of electronic structure and geometry of molecules, particularly free radicals

1972 Christian Boehmer Anfinsen, Stanford Moore, and William Howard Stein (all U.S.), for pioneering studies in enzymes

1973 Ernst Otto Fischer (W. Germany) and Geoffrey Wilkinson (U.K.), for work that could solve problem of automobile exhaust pollution

1974 Paul J. Flory (U.S.), for developing analytic methods to study properties and molecular structure of long-chain molecules

1975 John W. Cornforth (Australia) and Vladimir Prelog (Switzerland), for research on structure of biological molecules such as antibiotics and cholesterol

1976 William N. Lipscomb, Jr. (U.S.), for work on the structure and bonding mechanisms of boranes

1977 Ilya Prigogine (Belgium), for contributions to nonequilibrium thermodynamics, particularly the theory of dissipative structures

1978 Peter Mitchell (U.K.), for contributions to the understanding of biological energy transfer

1979 Herbert C. Brown (U.S.) and Georg Wittig (West Germany), for developing a group of substances that facilitate very difficult chemical reactions

1980 Paul Berg and Walter Gilbert (both U.S.) and Frederick Sanger (England), for developing methods to map the structure and function of DNA, the substance that controls the activity of the cell

1981 Roald Hoffmann (U.S.) and Kenichi Fukui (Japan), for applying quantum-mechanics theories to predict the course of chemical reactions

PHYSIOLOGY OR MEDICINE

1901 Emil A. von Behring (Germany), for work on serum therapy against diphtheria

1902 Sir Ronald Ross (England), for work on malaria

1903 Niels R. Finsen (Denmark), for his treatment of lupus vulgaris with concentrated light rays

1904 Ivan P. Pavlov (U.S.S.R.), for work on the physiology of digestion

1905 Robert Koch (Germany), for work on tuberculosis

1906 Camillo Golgi (Italy) and Santiago Ramón y Cajal (Spain), for work on structure of the nervous system

1907 Charles L. A. Laveran (France), for work with protozoa in the generation of disease

1908 Paul Ehrlich (Germany), and Elie Metchnikoff (U.S.S.R.), for work on immunity

1909 Theodor Kocher (Switzerland), for work on the thyroid gland

1910 Albrecht Kossel (Germany), for achievements in the chemistry of the cell

1911 Allvar Gullstrand (Sweden), for work on the dioptrics of the eye

1912 Alexis Carrel (France), for work on vascular ligature and grafting of blood vessels and organs

1913 Charles Richet (France), for work on anaphylaxy

1914 Robert Bárány (Austria), for work on physiology and pathology of the vestibular system

1915 No award

1916 No award

1917 No award

1918 No award

1919 Jules Bordet (Belgium), for discoveries in connection with immunity

1920 August Krogh (Denmark), for discovery of regulation of capillaries' motor mechanism

1921 No award

1922 In 1923, the 1922 prize was shared by Archibald V. Hill (England), for discovery relating to heat-production in muscles; and Otto Meyerhof (Germany), for correlation between consumption of oxygen and production of lactic acid in muscles

1923 Sir Frederick Banting (Canada) and John J. R. Macleod (Scotland), for discovery of insulin

1924 Willem Einthoven (Netherlands), for discovery of the mechanism of the electrocardiogram

1925 No award

1926 Johannes Fibiger (Denmark), for discovery of the Spiroptera carcinoma

1927 Julius Wagner-Jauregg (Austria), for use of malaria inoculation in treatment of dementia paralytica

1928 Charles Nicolle (France), for work on typhus exanthematicus

1929 Christiaan Eijkman (Netherlands), for discovery of the antineuritic vitamins; and Sir Frederick Hopkins (England), for discovery of growth-promoting vitamins

1930 Karl Landsteiner (U.S.), for discovery of human blood groups

1931 Otto H. Warburg (Germany), for discovery of the character and mode of action of the respiratory ferment

1932 Sir Charles Sherrington (England) and Edgar D. Adrian (U.S.), for discoveries of the function of the neuron

1933 Thomas H. Morgan (U.S.), for discoveries on hereditary function of the chromosomes

1934 George H. Whipple, George R. Minot, and William P. Murphy (U.S.), for discovery of liver therapy against anemias

1935 Hans Spemann (Germany), for discovery of the organizer-effect in embryonic development

1936 Sir Henry Dale (England) and Otto Loewi (Germany), for discoveries on chemical transmission of nerve impulses

1937 Albert Szent-Györgyi von Nagyrapolt (Hungary), for discoveries on biological combustion

1938 Corneille Heymans (Belgium), for determining importance of sinus and aorta mechanisms in the regulation of respiration

1939 Gerhard Domagk (Germany), for antibacterial effect of prontocilate

1943 Henrik Dam (Denmark) and Edward A. Doisy (U.S.), for analysis of Vitamin K

1944 Joseph Erlanger and Herbert Spencer Gasser (U.S.), for work on functions of the nerve threads

1945 Sir Alexander Fleming, Ernst Boris Chain, and Sir Howard Florey (England), for discovery of penicillin

1946 Herman J. Muller (U.S.), for hereditary effects of X rays on genes

1947 Carl F. and Gerty T. Cori (U.S.), for work on animal starch metabolism; Bernardo A. Houssay (Argentina), for study of pituitary

1948 Paul Mueller (Switzerland), for discovery of insect-killing properties of DDT
1949 Walter Rudolf Hess (Switzerland), for research on brain control of body; and Antonio Caetano de Abreu Freire Egas Moniz (Portugal), for development of brain operation
1950 Philip S. Hench, Edward C. Kendall (both U.S.), and Tadeus Reichstein (Switzerland), for discoveries about hormones of adrenal cortex
1951 Max Theiler (South Africa), for development of anti-yellow-fever vaccine
1952 Selman A. Waksman (U.S.), for co-discovery of streptomycin
1953 Fritz A. Lipmann (Germany-U.S.) and Hans Adolph Krebs (Germany-England), for studies of living cells
1954 John F. Enders, Thomas H. Weller, and Frederick C. Robbins (U.S.), for work with cultivation of polio virus
1955 Hugo Theorell (Sweden), for work on oxidation enzymes
1956 Dickinson W. Richards, Jr., André F. Cournand (both U.S.), and Werner Forssmann (Germany), for new techniques in treating heart disease
1957 Daniel Bovet (Italy), for development of drugs to relieve allergies and relax muscles during surgery
1958 Joshua Lederberg (U.S.), for work with genetic mechanisms; George W. Beadle and Edward L. Tatum (U.S.), for discovering how genes transmit hereditary characteristics
1959 Severo Ochoa and Arthur Kornberg (U.S.), for discoveries related to compounds within chromosomes, which play a vital role in heredity
1960 Sir Macfarlane Burnet (Australia) and Peter Brian Medawar (England), for discovery of acquired immunological tolerance
1961 Georg von Bekesy (U.S.), for discoveries about physical mechanisms of stimulation within cochlea
1962 James D. Watson (U.S.), Maurice H. F. Wilkins, and Francis H. C. Crick (England), for determining structure of deoxyribonucleic acid (DNA)
1963 Alan Lloyd Hodgkin, Andrew Fielding Huxley (both England), and Sir John Carew Eccles (Australia), for research on nerve cells
1964 Konrad E. Bloch (U.S.) and Feodor Lynen (Germany), for research on mechanism and regulation of cholesterol and fatty acid metabolism
1965 François Jacob, André Lwolff, and Jacques Monod (France), for study of regulatory activities in body cells
1966 Charles Brenton Huggins (U.S.), for studies in hormone treatment of cancer of prostate; Francis Peyton Rous (U.S.), for discovery of tumor-producing viruses
1967 Haldan K. Hartline, George Wald, and Ragnar Granit (U.S.), for work on human eye
1968 Robert W. Holley, Har Gobind Khorana, and Marshall W. Nirenberg (U.S.), for studies of genetic code
1969 Max Delbruck, Alfred D. Hershey, and Salvador E. Luria (U.S.), for study of mechanism of virus infection in living cells
1970 Julius Axelrod (U.S.), Ulf S. von Euler (Sweden), and Sir Bernard Katz (England), for studies of how nerve impulses are transmitted within the body
1971 Earl W. Sutherland, Jr., (U.S.), for research on how hormones work
1972 Gerald M. Edelman (U.S.), and Rodney R. Porter (U.K.), for research on the chemical structure and nature of antibodies
1973 Karl von Frisch and Konrad Lorenz (Austria), and Nikolaas Tinbergen (Netherlands), for their studies of individual and social behavior patterns
1974 George E. Palade and Christian de Duve (both U.S.) and Albert Claude (Belgium), for contributions to understanding inner workings of living cells
1975 David Baltimore, Howard M. Temin and Renato Dulbecco (all U.S.), for work in interaction between tumor viruses and genetic material of the cell
1976 Baruch S. Blumberg and D. Carleton Gajdusek (U.S.), for discoveries concerning new mechanisms for the origin and dissemination of infectious diseases
1977 Rosalyn S. Yalow, Roger C. L. Guillemin, and Andrew V. Schally (all U.S.), for research in role of hormones in chemistry of the body
1978 Daniel Nathans and Hamilton Smith (both U.S.) and Werner Arber (Switzerland), for discovery of restriction enzymes and their application to problems of molecular genetics
1979 Allan McLeod Cormack (U.S.) and Godfrey Newbold Hounsfield (England), for developing computed axial tomography (CAT scan) X-ray technique
1980 Baruj Benacerraf and George D. Snell (both U.S.) and Jean Dausset (France), for discoveries that explain how the structure of cells relates to organ transplants and diseases
1981 Roger W. Sperry and David H. Hubel (both U.S.) and Torsten N. Wiesel (Sweden), for studies vital to understanding the organization and functioning of the brain

ECONOMIC SCIENCE

1969 Ragnar Frisch (Norway) and Jan Tinbergen (Netherlands), for work in econometrics (application of mathematics and statistical methods to economic theories and problems)
1970 Paul A. Samuelson (U.S.), for efforts to raise the level of scientific analysis in economic theory
1971 Simon Kuznets (U.S.), for developing concept of using a country's gross national product to determine its economic growth
1972 Kenneth J. Arrow (U.S.) and Sir John R. Hicks (U.K.), for theories that help to assess business risk and government economic and welfare policies
1973 Wassily Leontief (U.S.), for devising the input-output technique to determine how different sectors of an economy interact
1974 Gunnar Myrdal (Sweden) and Friedrich A. von Hayek (Austria), for pioneering analysis of the interdependence of economic, social and institutional phenomena
1975 Leonid V. Kantorovich (U.S.S.R.) and Tjalling C. Koopmans (U.S.), for work on the theory of optimum allocation of resources
1976 Milton Friedman (U.S.), for work in consumption analysis and monetary history and theory, and for demonstration of complexity of stabilization policy
1977 Bertil Ohlin (Sweden) and James E. Meade (U.K.), for contributions to theory of international trade and international capital movements
1978 Herbert A. Simon (U.S.), for research into the

decision-making process within economic organizations

1979 Sir Arthur Lewis (England) and Theodore Schultz (U.S.), for work on economic problems of developing nations

1980 Lawrence R. Klein (U.S.), for developing models for forecasting economic trends and shaping policies to deal with them

1981 James Tobin (U.S.), for analyses of financial markets and their influence on spending and saving by families and businesses

Major Grammy Awards for Recording in 1981

Source: National Academy of Recording Arts and Sciences.

Record: "Bette Davis Eyes," Kim Carnes (EMI-America)

Album: "Double Fantasy," John Lennon and Yoko Ono (Geffen/Warner Bros.)

Song: "Bette Davis Eyes," Donna Weiss and Jackie DeShannon

New Artist: Sheena Easton (EMI-America)

Pop Vocalists: Lena Horne, "Lena Horne: The Lady and Her Music Live on Broadway" (QWest/Warner Bros.); Al Jarreau, "Breakin' Away" (Warner Bros.)

Pop Group: The Manhattan Transfer, "Boy From New York City" (Atlantic)

Pop Instrumentalists: Mike Post featuring Larry Carlton, "The Theme From Hill Street Blues" (E/A)

Rock Vocalists: Pat Benatar, "Fire and Ice" (Chrysalis); Rick Springfield, "Jessie's Girl" (RCA)

Rock Group: The Police, "Don't Stand So Close to Me" (A&M)

Rock Instrumentalists: The Police, "Behind My Camel" (A&M)

Rhythm and Blues Vocalists: Aretha Franklin, "Hold On I'm Comin' " (Arista); James Ingram, "One Hundred Ways" (A&M)

Rhythm and Blues Group: Quincy Jones, "The Dude" (A&M)

Rhythm and Blues Instrumentalist: David Sanborn, "All I Need Is You" (Warner Bros.)

Rhythm and Blues Song: "Just the Two of Us," Bill Withers, William Salter, and Ralph MacDonald

Country Vocalists: Dolly Parton, "9 to 5" (RCA); Ronnie Milsap, "(There's) No Gettin' Over Me" (RCA)

Country Group: Oak Ridge Boys, "Elvira" (MCA)

Country Instrumentalist: Chet Atkins, "Country—After All These Years" (RCA)

Country Song: Dolly Parton, "9 to 5"

Jazz Vocalists: Ella Fitzgerald, "Digital III at Montreux" (Pablo); Al Jarreau, "Blue Rondo à la Turk" (Warner Bros.)

Jazz Group: The Manhattan Transfer, "Until I Met You (Corner Pocket)" (Atlantic)

Jazz Instrumentalists: Soloist, John Coltrane, "Bye Bye Blackbird" (Pablo); group, Chick Corea and Gary Burton, "Chick Corea and Gary Burton in Concert, Zurich, Oct. 28, 1979" (ECM)

Jazz, Big Band: Gerry Mulligan and His Orchestra, "Walk on the Water" (DRG)

Jazz Fusion: Grover Washington, Jr., "Winelight" (E/A)

Gospel, Contemporary: Imperials, "Priority" (Dayspring/Word)

Gospel, Traditional: J.D. Sumner, James Blackwood, Hovie Lister, Rosie Rozell, and Jake Hess, "The Masters V" (Skylite)

Soul Gospel, Contemporary: Andrae Crouch, "Don't Give Up" (Warner Bros.)

Soul Gospel, Traditional: Al Green, "The Lord Will Make a Way" (Hi-Myrrh/Word)

Inspirational: B.J. Thomas, "Amazing Grace" (Myrrh/Word)

Ethnic or Traditional: B. B. King, "There Must Be a Better World Somewhere" (MCA)

Latin: Clare Fischer, "Guajira Pa' La Jeva" (Pausa)

For Children: "Sesame Country," The Muppets, Glen Campbell, Crystal Gayle, Loretta Lynn, and Tanya Tucker (Sesame St.)

Comedy: Richard Pryor, "Rev. Du Rite" (Laff)

Spoken Word: Orson Welles, "Donovan's Brain" (Radiola)

Instrumental Composition: "The Theme From Hill Street Blues," Mike Post

Instrumental Arrangement: Quincy Jones and Johnny Mandel, "Velas" (A&M)

Motion Picture Score: "Raiders of the Lost Ark," John Williams (Columbia/CBS)

Cast Show Album: "Lena Horne: The Lady and Her Music Live on Broadway" (QWest/Warner Bros.)

Historical Album: "Hoagy Carmichael: From 'Star Dust' to 'Ole Buttermilk Sky' " (Book-of-the-Month Records)

Classical Album: "Mahler: Symphony No. 2 in C Minor," Sir Georg Solti conducting Chicago Symphony Orchestra (London)

Classical, Orchestral Recording: "Mahler: Symphony No. 2 in C Minor," Sir Georg Solti conducting Chicago Symphony Orchestra (London)

Classical, Soloist Without Orchestra: Vladimir Horowitz, "The Horowitz Concerts 1979/80" (RCA)

Classical, Soloists With Orchestra: Isaac Stern, Itzhak Perlman, and Pinchas Zuckerman, "Isaac Stern 60th Anniversary Celebration" (CBS)

Chamber Music: Itzhak Perlman, Lynn Harrell, and Vladimir Ashkenazy, "Tchaikovsky: Piano Trio in A Minor" (Angel)

Classical, Vocal Soloists: Joan Sutherland, Marilyn Horne, and Luciano Pavarotti, "Live From Lincoln Center—Sutherland—Horne—Pavarotti (London)

Classical, Choral: "Haydn: The Creation," Neville Marriner conducting Chorus of the Academy of St. Martin-in-the-Fields and Academy of St. Martin-in-the-Fields (Philips)

Opera: "Janacek: From the House of the Dead," Sir Charles Mackerras conducting Vienna Philharmonic (London)

Producers: Non-classical, Quincy Jones; classical, James Mallinson

National Book Critics Circle Awards, 1982

Fiction: *Rabbit Is Rich,* by John Updike (Alfred A. Knopf)

General nonfiction: *The Mismeasure of Man,* by Stephen Jay Gould (W. W. Norton)

Poetry: *A Coast of Trees,* by A.R. Ammons (W.W. Norton)

Criticism: *A Virgil Thomson Reader* (Houghton Mifflin)

Pulitzer Prize Awards

(For years not listed, no award was made.)

Source: Columbia University.

Pulitzer Prizes in Journalism

MERITORIOUS PUBLIC SERVICE

1918 *New York Times;* also special award to Minna Lewinson and Henry Beetle Hough
1919 *Milwaukee Journal*
1921 *Boston Post*
1922 *New York World*
1923 *Memphis Commercial Appeal*
1924 *New York World*
1926 *Columbus* (Ga.) *Enquirer Sun*
1927 *Canton* (Ohio) *Daily News*
1928 *Indianapolis Times*
1929 *New York Evening World*
1931 *Atlanta Constitution*
1932 *Indianapolis News*
1933 *New York World-Telegram*
1934 *Medford* (Ore.) *Mail Tribune*
1935 *Sacramento Bee*
1936 *Cedar Rapids* (Iowa) *Gazette*
1937 *St. Louis Post-Dispatch*
1938 *Bismarck* (N.D.) *Tribune*
1939 *Miami Daily News*
1940 *Waterbury* (Conn.) *Republican* and *American*
1941 *St. Louis Post-Dispatch*
1942 *Los Angeles Times*
1943 *Omaha World-Herald*
1944 *New York Times*
1945 *Detroit Free Press*
1946 *Scranton* (Pa.) *Times*
1947 *Baltimore Sun*
1948 *St. Louis Post-Dispatch*
1949 (Lincoln) *Nebraska State Journal*
1950 *Chicago Daily News;* and *St. Louis Post-Dispatch*
1951 *Miami Herald;* and *Brooklyn Eagle*
1952 *St. Louis Post-Dispatch*
1953 *Whiteville* (N.C.) *News Reporter;* and *Tabor City* (N.C.) *Tribune*
1954 *Newsday* (Garden City, L.I.)
1955 *Columbus* (Ga.) *Ledger* and *Sunday Ledger-Enquirer*
1956 *Watsonville* (Calif.) *Register-Pajaronian*
1957 *Chicago Daily News*
1958 (Little Rock) *Arkansas Gazette*
1959 *Utica* (N.Y.) *Observer Dispatch* and *Utica Daily Press*
1960 *Los Angeles Times*
1961 *Amarillo* (Tex.) *Globe-Times*
1962 *Panama City* (Fla.) *News-Herald*
1963 *Chicago Daily News*
1964 *St. Petersburg* (Fla.) *Times*
1965 *Hutchinson* (Kan.) *News*
1966 *Boston Globe*
1967 *Louisville Courier-Journal* and *Milwaukee Journal*
1968 *Riverside* (Calif.) *Press-Enterprise*
1969 *Los Angeles Times*
1970 *Newsday* (Garden City, L.I.)
1971 *Winston-Salem* (N.C.) *Journal and Sentinel*
1972 *New York Times*
1973 *Washington Post*
1974 *Newsday* (Garden City, L.I.)
1975 *Boston Globe*
1976 *Anchorage* (Alaska) *Daily News*
1977 *Lufkin* (Tex.) *News*
1978 *Philadelphia Inquirer*
1979 *Point Reyes* (Calif.) *Light*
1980 *Boston Globe*
1981 *Charlotte* (N.C.) *Observer*
1982 *Detroit News*

EDITORIAL

1917 *New York Tribune*
1918 *Louisville Courier-Journal*
1920 Harvey E. Newbranch *(Omaha Evening World-Herald)*
1922 Frank M. O'Brien *(New York Herald)*
1923 William Allen White *(Emporia* [Kan.] *Gazette)*
1924 *Boston Herald* (Frank Buxton); special prize: Frank I. Cobb *(New York World)*
1925 *Charleston* (S.C.) *News and Courier*
1926 *New York Times* (Edward M. Kingsbury)
1927 *Boston Herald* (F. Lauriston Bullard)
1928 Grover Cleveland Hall *(Montgomery* [Ala.] *Advertiser)*
1929 Louis Isaac Jaffe *(Norfolk Virginian-Pilot)*
1931 Charles S. Ryckman *(Fremont* [Neb.] *Tribune)*
1933 *Kansas City* (Mo.) *Star*
1934 E. P. Chase *(Atlantic* [Iowa] *News Telegraph)*
1936 Felix Morley *(Washington Post);* George B. Parker (Scripps-Howard Newspapers)
1937 John W. Owens *(Baltimore Sun)*
1938 W. W. Waymack *(Des Moines Register and Tribune)*
1939 Ronald G. Callvert *(Portland Oregonian)*
1940 Bart Howard *(St. Louis Post-Dispatch)*
1941 Reuben Maury *(New York Daily News)*
1942 Geoffrey Parsons *(New York Herald Tribune)*
1943 Forrest W. Seymour *(Des Moines Register and Tribune)*
1944 *Kansas City* (Mo.) *Star* (Henry J. Haskell)
1945 George W. Potter *(Providence* [R.I.] *Journal-Bulletin)*
1946 Hodding Carter ([Greenville, Miss.] *Delta Democrat-Times*)
1947 William H. Grimes *(Wall Street Journal)*
1948 Virginius Dabney *(Richmond Times-Dispatch)*
1949 John H. Crider *(Boston Herald);* Herbert Elliston *(Washington Post)*
1950 Carl M. Saunders *(Jackson* [Mich.] *Citizen Patriot)*
1951 William H. Fitzpatrick *(New Orleans States)*
1952 Louis LaCoss *(St. Louis Globe-Democrat)*
1953 Vermont C. Royster *(Wall Street Journal)*
1954 *Boston Herald* (Don Murray)
1955 *Detroit Free Press* (Royce Howes)
1956 Lauren K. Soth *(Des Moines Register and Tribune)*
1957 Buford Boone *Tuscaloosa* ([Ala.] *News)*
1958 Harry S. Ashmore *(Arkansas Gazette)*
1959 Ralph McGill *(Atlanta Constitution)*
1960 Lenoir Chambers *(Virginian-Pilot)*
1961 William J. Dorvillier *(San Juan* [P.R.] *Star)*
1962 Thomas M. Storke *(Santa Barbara* [Calif.] *News-Press)*
1963 Ira B. Harkey, Jr. *(Pascagoula* [Miss.] *Chronicle)*
1964 Hazel Brannon Smith *(Lexington* [Miss.] *Advertiser)*
1965 John R. Harrison *(Gainesville* [Fla.] *Daily Sun)*
1966 Robert Lasch *(St. Louis Post-Dispatch)*

1967 Eugene Patterson *(Atlanta Constitution)*
1968 John S. Knight (Knight Newspapers)
1969 Paul Greenberg *(Pine Bluff* [Ark.] *Commercial)*
1970 Philip L. Geyelin *(Washington Post)*
1971 Horance G. Davis, Jr. *(Gainesville* [Fla.] *Sun)*
1972 John Strohmeyer *(Bethlehem* [Pa.] *Globe Times)*
1973 Roger Bourne Linscott *(Berkshire Eagle* [Pittsfield, Mass.])
1974 F. Gilman Spencer *(Trenton* [N.J.] *Trentonian)*
1975 John Daniell Maurice *(Charleston* [W. Va] *Daily Mail)*
1976 Philip P. Kerby *(Los Angeles Times)*
1977 Warren L. Lerude, Foster Church and Norman F. Cardoza *(Reno* [Nev.] *Gazette* and *Nevada State Journal)*
1978 Meg Greenfield *(Washington Post)*
1979 Edwin M. Yoder, Jr. *(Washington Star)*
1980 Robert L. Bartley *(Wall Street Journal)*
1981 Not awarded
1982 Jack Rosenthal *(New York Times)*

CORRESPONDENCE

1929 Paul Scott Mowrer *(Chicago Daily News)*
1930 Leland Stowe *(New York Herald Tribune)*
1931 H. R. Knickerbocker *(Philadelphia Public Ledger* and *New York Evening Post)*
1932 Walter Duranty *(New York Times)*; Charles G. Ross *(St. Louis Post-Dispatch)*
1933 Edgar Ansel Mowrer *(Chicago Daily News)*
1934 Frederick T. Birchall *(New York Times)*
1935 Arthur Krock *(New York Times)*
1936 Wilfred C. Barber *(Chicago Tribune)*
1937 Anne O'Hare McCormick *(New York Times)*
1938 Arthur Krock *(New York Times)*
1939 Louis P. Lochner (Associated Press)
1940 Otto D. Tolischus *(New York Times)*
1941 Group award[1]
1942 Carlos P. Romulo *(Philippines Herald)*
1943 Hanson W. Baldwin *(New York Times)*
1944 Ernie Pyle (Scripps-Howard Newspaper Alliance)
1945 Harold V. (Hal) Boyle (Associated Press)
1946 Arnaldo Cortesi *(New York Times)*
1947 Brooks Atkinson *(New York Times)*
1948 Discontinued

CARTOON

1922 Rollin Kirby *(New York World)*
1924 Jay Norwood Darling *(New York Tribune)*
1925 Rollin Kirby *(New York World)*
1926 D. R. Fitzpatrick *(St. Louis Post-Dispatch)*
1927 Nelson Harding *(Brooklyn Eagle)*
1928 Nelson Harding *(Brooklyn Eagle)*
1929 Rollin Kirby *(New York World)*
1930 Charles R. Macauley *(Brooklyn Eagle)*
1931 Edmund Duffy *(Baltimore Sun)*
1932 John T. McCutcheon *(Chicago Tribune)*
1933 H. M. Talburt *(Washington Daily News)*
1934 Edmund Duffy *(Baltimore Sun)*
1935 Ross A. Lewis *(Milwaukee Journal)*
1937 C. D. Batchelor *(New York Daily News)*
1938 Vaughn Shoemaker *(Chicago Daily News)*
1939 Charles G. Werner *(Daily Oklahoman* [Oklahoma City])
1940 Edmund Duffy *(Baltimore Sun)*
1941 Jacob Burck *(Chicago Times)*
1942 Herbert L. Block (NEA Service)
1943 Jay Norwood Darling *(New York Herald Tribune)*
1944 Clifford K. Berryman *(Washington Evening Star)*
1945 Bill Mauldin (United Features Syndicate)
1946 Bruce Alexander Russell *(Los Angeles Times)*
1947 Vaughn Shoemaker *(Chicago Daily News)*
1948 Reuben L. Goldberg *(New York Sun)*
1949 Lute Pease *(Newark Evening News)*
1950 James T. Berryman *(Washington Evening Star)*
1951 Reg (Reginald W.) Manning *(Arizona Republic* [Phoenix])
1952 Fred L. Packer *(New York Mirror)*
1953 Edward D. Kuekes *(Cleveland Plain Dealer)*
1954 Herbert L. Block *(Washington Post* and *Times-Herald)*
1955 Daniel R. Fitzpatrick *(St. Louis Post-Dispatch)*
1956 Robert York *(Louisville Times)*
1957 Tom Little *(Nashville Tennessean)*
1958 Bruce M. Shanks *(Buffalo Evening News)*
1959 Bill Mauldin *(St. Louis Post-Dispatch)*
1961 Carey Orr *(Chicago Tribune)*
1962 Edmund S. Valtman *(Hartford Times)*
1963 Frank Miller *(Des Moines Register)*
1964 Paul Conrad (formerly of *Denver Post*, later on *Los Angeles Times*)
1966 Don Wright *(Miami News)*
1967 Patrick B. Oliphant *(Denver Post)*
1968 Eugene Gray Payne *(Charlotte* [N.C.] *Observer)*
1969 John Fischetti *(Chicago Daily News)*
1970 Thomas F. Darcy (*Newsday* [Garden City, L.I.])
1971 Paul Conrad *(Los Angeles Times)*
1972 Jeffrey K. MacNelly *(Richmond* [Va.] *News Leader)*
1974 Paul Szep *(Boston Globe)*
1975 Garry Trudeau (Universal Press Syndicate)
1976 Tony Auth *(Philadelphia Inquirer)*
1977 Paul Szep *(Boston Globe)*
1978 Jeffrey K. MacNelly *(Richmond [Va.] News Leader)*
1979 Herbert L. Block *(Washington Post)*
1980 Don Wright *(Miami News)*
1981 Mike Peters *(Dayton* [Ohio] *Daily News)*
1982 Ben Sargent *(Austin* [Tex.] *American-Statesman)*

NEWS PHOTOGRAPHY

1942 Milton Brooks *(Detroit News)*
1943 Frank Noel (Associated Press)
1944 Frank Filan (Associated Press); Earle L. Bunker *(Omaha World-Herald)*
1945 Joe Rosenthal (Associated Press)
1947 Arnold Hardy
1948 Frank Cushing *(Boston Traveler)*
1949 Nat Fein *(New York Herald Tribune)*
1950 Bill Crouch *(Oakland Tribune)*
1951 Max Desfor (Associated Press)
1952 John Robinson and Don Ultang *(Des Moines Register & Tribune)*
1953 William M. Gallagher *(Flint* [Mich.] *Journal)*
1954 Mrs. Walter M. Schau
1955 John L. Gaunt, Jr. *(Los Angeles Times)*
1956 *New York Daily News*
1957 Harry A. Trask *(Boston Traveler)*
1958 William C. Beall *(Washington Daily News)*
1959 William Seaman *(Minneapolis Star)*
1960 Andrew Lopez (United Press International)
1961 Yasushi Nagao (Mainichi Newspapers, Tokyo)
1962 Paul Vathis (Harrisburg [Pa.] bureau of Associated Press)
1963 Hector Rondon (*La Republica*, Caracas, Venezuela)

1. For the public services and the individual achievements of American news reporters in the war zones.

1964 Robert H. Jackson *(Dallas Times Herald)*
1965 Horst Faas (Associated Press)
1966 Kyoichi Sawada (United Press International)
1967 Jack R. Thornell (Associated Press)
1968 News: Rocco Morabito *(Jacksonville* [Fla.] *Journal)*; features: Toshio Sakai (United Press International)
1969 Spot news: Edward T. Adams (Associated Press); features: Moneta Sleet, Jr.
1970 Spot news: Steve Starr (Associated Press); features: Dallas Kinney *(Palm Beach Post)*
1971 Spot news: John Paul Filo (*Valley Daily News and Daily Dispatch* [Tarentum and New Kensington, Pa.]); features: Jack Dykinga *(Chicago Sun-Times)*
1972 Spot news: Horst Faas and Michel Laurent (Associated Press); features: Dave Kennerly (United Press International)
1973 Spot News: Huynh Cong Ut *(Associated Press)*; features: Brian Lanker *(Topeka Capital-Journal)*
1974 Spot news: Anthony K. Roberts (Associated Press); features: Slava Veder (Associated Press)
1975 Spot news: Gerald H. Gay *(Seattle Times)*; features: Matthew Lewis *(Washington Post)*
1976 Spot news: Stanley J. Forman *(Boston Herald-American)*; features: photographic staff of *Louisville Courier-Journal* and *Times)*
1977 Spot news: Neal Ulevich (Associated Press) and Stanley J. Forman *(Boston Herald-American)*; features: Robin Hood *(Chattanooga News-Free Press)*
1978 Spot news: John Blair, freelance, Evansville, Ind.; features: J. Ross Baughman (Associated Press)
1979 Spot news: Thomas J. Kelly, 3rd *(Pottstown* [Pa.] *Mercury)*; features: photographic staff of *Boston Herald American*
1980 Features: Erwin H. Hagler *(Dallas Times Herald)*
1981 Spot news: Larry C. Price *(Fort Worth Star-Telegram)*; features: Taro M. Yamasaki *(Detroit Free Press)*
1982 Spot news: Ron Edmonds (Associated Press); features: John H. White *(Chicago Sun-Times)*

NATIONAL TELEGRAPHIC REPORTING

1942 Louis Stark *(New York Times)*
1944 Dewey L. Fleming *(Baltimore Sun)*
1945 James Reston *(New York Times)*
1946 Edward A. Harris *(St. Louis Post-Dispatch)*
1947 Edward T. Folliard *(Washington Post)*

NATIONAL REPORTING

1948 Bert Andrews *(New York Herald Tribune)*; Nat S. Finney *(Minneapolis Tribune)*
1949 C. P. Trussel *(New York Times)*
1950 Edwin O. Guthman *(Seattle Times)*
1952 Anthony Leviero *(New York Times)*
1953 Don Whitehead (Associated Press)
1954 Richard Wilson (Cowles Newspapers)
1955 Anthony Lewis *(Washington Daily News)*
1956 Charles L. Bartlett *(Chattanooga Times)*
1957 James Reston *(New York Times)*
1958 Relman Morin (Associated Press) and Clark Mollenhoff *(Des Moines Register & Tribune)*
1959 Howard Van Smith *(Miami News)*
1960 Vance Trimble (Scripps-Howard Newspaper Alliance)
1961 Edward R. Cony *(Wall Street Journal)*
1962 Nathan G. Caldwell and Gene S. Graham *(Nashville Tennessean)*
1963 Anthony Lewis *(New York Times)*
1964 Merriman Smith (United Press International)
1965 Louis M. Kohlmeier *(Wall Street Journal)*
1966 Haynes Johnson *(Washington Evening Star)*
1967 Stanley Penn and Monroe Karmin *(Wall Street Journal)*
1968 Howard James *(Christian Science Monitor)*; Nathan K. (Nick) Kotz *(Des Moines Register* and *Minneapolis Tribune)*
1969 Robert Cahn *(Christian Science Monitor)*
1970 William J. Eaton *(Chicago Daily News)*
1971 Lucinda Franks and Thomas Powers (United Press International)
1972 Jack Anderson *(United Feature Syndicate)*
1973 Robert Boyd and Clark Hoyt *(Knight Newspapers)*
1974 Jack White *(Providence* [R.I.] *Journal-Bulletin)*; and James R. Polk *(Washington Star-News)*
1975 Donald L. Barlett and James B. Steele *(Philadelphia Inquirer)*
1976 James Risser *(Des Moines Register)*
1977 Walter Mears (Associated Press)
1978 Gaylord D. Shaw *(Los Angeles Times)*
1979 James Risser *(Des Moines Register)*
1980 Bette Swenson Orsini and Charles Stafford *(St. Petersburg Times)*
1981 John M. Crewdson *(New York Times)*
1982 Rick Atkinson, *(Kansas City* [Mo.] *Times)*

INTERNATIONAL TELEGRAPHIC REPORTING

1942 Laurence Edmund Allen (Associated Press)
1943 Ira Wolfert (North American Newspaper Alliance, Inc.)
1944 Daniel De Luce (Associated Press)
1945 Mark S. Watson *(Baltimore Sun)*
1946 Homer W. Bigart *(New York Herald Tribune)*
1947 Eddy Gilmore (Associated Press)

INTERNATIONAL REPORTING

1948 Paul W. Ward *(Baltimore Sun)*
1949 Price Day *(Baltimore Sun)*
1950 Edmund Stevens *(Christian Science Monitor)*
1951 Keyes Beech and Fred Sparks *(Chicago Daily News)*; Homer Bigart and Marguerite Higgins *(New York Herald Tribune)*, Relman Morin and Don Whitehead (Associated Press)
1952 John M. Hightower (Associated Press)
1953 Austin C. Wehrwein *(Milwaukee Journal)*
1954 Jim G. Lucas (Scripps-Howard Newspapers)
1955 Harrison E. Salisbury *(New York Times)*
1956 William Randolph Hearst, Jr., and Frank Conniff (Hearst newspapers) and Kingsbury Smith (INS)
1957 Russell Jones (United Press)
1958 *New York Times*
1959 Joseph Martin and Philip Santora *(New York Daily News)*
1960 A. M. Rosenthal *(New York Times)*
1961 Lynn Heinzerling (Associated Press)
1962 Walter Lippmann (New York Herald Tribune Syndicate)
1963 Hal Hendrix *(Miami News)*
1964 Malcolm W. Browne (Associated Press) and David Halberstam *(New York Times)*
1965 J. A. Livingston *(Philadelphia Bulletin)*
1966 Peter Arnett (Associated Press)
1967 R. John Hughes *(Christian Science Monitor)*
1968 Alfred Friendly *(Washington Post)*
1969 William Tuohy *(Los Angeles Times)*
1970 Seymour M. Hersh (Dispatch News Service)
1971 Jimmie Lee Hoagland *(Washington Post)*

1972 Peter R. Kann *(Wall Street Journal)*
1973 Max Frankel *(New York Times)*
1974 Hedrick Smith *(New York Times)*
1975 William Mullen and Ovie Carter *(Chicago Tribune)*
1976 Sydney H. Schanberg *(New York Times)*
1978 Henry Kamm *(New York Times)*
1979 Richard Ben Cramer *(Philadelphia Inquirer)*
1980 Joel Brinkley and Jay Mather *(Louisville Courier-Journal)*
1981 Shirley Christian *(Miami Herald)*
1982 John Darnton *(New York Times)*

REPORTING

1917 Herbert B. Swope *(New York World)*
1918 Harold A. Littledale *(New York Evening Post)*
1920 John J. Leary, Jr. *(New York World)*
1921 Louis Seibold *(New York World)*
1922 Kirke L. Simpson (Associated Press)
1923 Alva Johnston *(New York Times)*
1924 Magner White *(San Diego Sun)*
1925 James W. Mulroy and Alvin H. Goldstein *(Chicago Daily News)*
1926 William Burke Miller *(Louisville Courier-Journal)*
1927 John T. Rogers *(St. Louis Post-Dispatch)*
1929 Paul Y. Anderson *(St. Louis Post-Dispatch)*
1930 Russell D. Owen *(New York Times)*; special award: W. O. Dapping *(Auburn* [N.Y.] *Citizen)*
1931 A. B. MacDonald *(Kansas City* [Mo.] *Star)*
1932 W. C. Richards, D. D. Martin, J. S. Pooler, F. D. Webb, J. N. W. Sloan (all of *Detroit Free Press)*
1933 Francis A. Jamieson (Associated Press)
1934 Royce Brier *(San Francisco Chronicle)*
1935 William H. Taylor *(New York Herald Tribune)*
1936 Lauren D. Lyman *(New York Times)*
1937 John J. O'Neill *(New York Herald Tribune)*, William Leonard Laurence *(New York Times)*, Howard W. Blakeslee (Associated Press), Gobind Behari Lal (Universal Service), David Dietz (Scripps-Howard Newspapers)
1938 Raymond Sprigle *(Pittsburg Post-Gazette)*
1939 Thomas L. Stokes *(New York World-Telegram)*
1940 S. Burton Heath *(New York World-Telegram)*
1941 Westbrook Pegler *(New York World-Telegram)*
1942 Stanton Delaplane *(San Francisco Chronicle)*
1943 George Weller *(Chicago Daily News)*
1944 Paul Schoenstein and associates *(New York Journal-American)*
1945 Jack S. McDowell *(San Francisco Call-Bulletin)*
1946 William Leonard Laurence *(New York Times)*
1947 Frederick Woltman *(New York World-Telegram)*
1948 George E. Goodwin *(Atlanta Journal)*
1949 Malcolm Johnson *(New York Sun)*
1950 Meyer Berger *(New York Times)*
1951 Edward S. Montgomery *(San Francisco Examiner)*
1952 George de Carvalho *(San Francisco Chronicle)*
1953 Editorial staff *(Providence Journal and Evening Bulletin)*;[1] Edward J. Mowery *(New York World-Telegram and Sun)*[2]
1954 *Vicksburg* (Miss.) *Sunday Post-Herald*;[1] Alvin Scott McCoy *(Kansas City* [Mo.] *Star)*[2]
1955 Mrs. Caro Brown *(Alice* [Tex.] *Daily Echo)*;[1] Roland Kenneth Towery *(Cuero* [Tex.] *Record)*[2]

1. Reporting under pressure of edition deadlines. 2. Reporting not under pressure of edition deadlines.

1956 Lee Hills *(Detroit Free Press)*;[1] Arthur Daley *(New York Times)*[2]
1957 *Salt Lake Tribune*;[1] Wallace Turner and William Lambert *(Portland Oregonian)*[2]
1958 *Fargo* [N.D.] *Forum*;[1] George Beveridge *(Washington* [D.C.] *Evening Star)*[2]
1959 Mary Lou Werner *(Washington* [D.C.] *Evening Star)*;[1] John Harold Brislin *(Scranton* [Pa.] *Tribune & Scrantonian)*[2]
1960 Jack Nelson *(Atlanta Constitution)*;[1] Miriam Ottenberg *(Washington Evening Star)*[2]
1961 Sançhe de Gramont *(New York Herald Tribune)*;[1] Edgar May *(Buffalo Evening News)*[2]
1962 Robert D. Mullins (*Deseret News*, Salt Lake City); [1] George Bliss *(Chicago Tribune)*[2]
1963 Sylvan Fox, Anthony Shannon, and William Longgood *(New York World-Telegram and Sun)*;[1] Oscar Griffin, Jr. (former editor of *Pecos* [Tex.] *Independent and Enterprise*, now on staff of *Houston Chronicle)*[2]

GENERAL LOCAL REPORTING

1964 Norman C. Miller *(Wall Street Journal)*
1965 Melvin H. Ruder (*Hungry Horse News*, Columbia Falls, Mont.)
1966 Staff of *Los Angeles Times*
1967 Robert V. Cox *(Chambersburg* [Pa.] *Public Opinion)*
1968 Staff of *Detroit Free Press*
1969 John Fetterman *(Louisville Times* and *Courier-Journal)*
1970 Thomas Fitzpatrick *(Chicago Sun-Times)*
1971 Staff of *Akron* (Ohio) *Beacon*
1972 Richard Cooper and John Machacek *(Rochester* [N.Y.] *Times-Union)*
1973 *Chicago Tribune*
1974 Arthur M. Petacque and Hugh F. Hough *(Chicago Sun-Times)*
1975 *Xenia* (Ohio) *Daily Gazette*
1976 Gene Miller *(Miami Herald)*
1977 Margo Huston *(Milwaukee Journal)*
1978 Richard Whitt *(Louisville Courier-Journal)*
1979 Staff of *San Diego* (Calif.) *Evening Tribune*
1980 Staff of *Philadelphia Inquirer*
1981 *Longview* (Wash.) *Daily News*
1982 *Kansas City* (Mo.) *Star* and *Kansas City* (Mo.) *Times*

SPECIAL LOCAL REPORTING

1964 James V. Magee, Albert V. Gaudiosi, and Frederick A. Meyer *(Philadelphia Bulletin)*
1965 Gene Goltz *(Houston Post)*
1966 John A. Frasca *(Tampa Tribune)*
1967 Gene Miller *(Miami Herald)*
1968 J. Anthony Lukas *(New York Times)*
1969 Albert L. Delugach and Denny Walsh *(St. Louis Globe-Democrat)*
1970 Harold Eugene Martin *(Montgomery Advertiser)*
1971 William Hugh Jones *(Chicago Tribune)*
1972 Timothy Leland, Gerard N. O'Neill, Stephen A. Kurkjian, and Ann DeSantis *(Boston Globe)*
1973 Sun Newspapers of Omaha, Neb.
1974 William Sherman *(New York Daily News)*
1975 *Indianapolis Star*
1976 *Chicago Tribune*
1977 Acel Moore and Wendell Rawls, Jr. *(Philadelphia Inquirer)*
1978 Anthony R. Dolan *(Stamford* [Conn.] *Advocate)*
1979 Gilbert M. Gaul and Elliot G. Jaspin *(Pottsville* Pa. *Republican)*

1980 Nils J. Bruzelius, Alexander B. Hawes, Jr., Stephen A. Kurkjian, and Joan Vennochi *(Boston Globe)*
1981 Clark Hallas and Robert B. Lowe (*Arizona Daily Star*, Tucson)
1982 Paul Henderson *(Seattle Times)*

FEATURE WRITING

1979 Jon D. Franklin *(Baltimore Evening Sun)*
1980 Madeleine Blais *(Miami Herald)*
1981 Teresa Carpenter (*Village Voice*, New York)
1982 Saul Pett (Associated Press)

COMMENTARY

1970 Marquis W. Childs *(St. Louis Post-Dispatch)*
1971 William A. Caldwell (*Record* [Hackensack, N.J.])
1972 Mike Royko *(Chicago Daily News)*
1973 David S. Broder *(Washington Post)*
1974 Edwin A. Roberts, Jr. *(National Observer)*
1975 Mary McGrory *(Washington Star)*
1976 Walter W. (Red) Smith *(New York Times)*
1977 George F. Will (*Washington Post* Writers Group)
1978 William Safire *(New York Times)*
1979 Russell Baker *(New York Times)*
1980 Ellen H. Goodman *(Boston Globe)*
1981 Dave Anderson *(New York Times)*
1982 Art Buchwald (*Los Angeles Times* Syndicate)

CRITICISM

1970 Ada Louise Huxtable *(New York Times)*
1971 Harold C. Schonberg *(New York Times)*
1972 Frank Peters, Jr. *(St. Louis Post-Dispatch)*
1973 Ronald Powers *(Chicago Sun-Times)*
1974 Emily Genauer (Newsday Syndicate)
1975 Roger Ebert *(Chicago Sun-Times)*
1976 Alan M. Kriegsman *(Washington Post)*
1977 William McPherson *(Washington Post)*
1978 Walter Kerr *(New York Times)*
1979 Paul Gapp *(Chicago Tribune)*
1980 William A. Henry 3rd *(Boston Globe)*
1981 Jonathan Yardley *(Washington Star)*
1982 Martin Bernheimer *(Los Angeles Times)*

SPECIAL CITATIONS

1938 *Edmonton* (Alberta) *Journal*, special bronze plaque for editorial leadership in defense of freedom of press in Province of Alberta.
1941 *New York Times* for the public educational value of its foreign news report.
1944 Byron Price, Director of the Office of Censorship, for the creation and administration of the newspaper and radio codes. Mrs. William Allen White, for her husband's interest and services during the past seven years as a member of the Advisory Board of the Graduate School of Journalism, Columbia University. Richard Rodgers and Oscar Hammerstein II for their musical *Oklahoma!*
1945 The cartographers of the American press for their war maps.
1947 (Pulitzer centennial year.) Columbia University and the Graduate School of Journalism, for their efforts to maintain and advance the high standards governing the Pulitzer Prize awards. The *St. Louis Post-Dispatch,* for its unswerving adherence to the public and professional ideals of its founder and its leadership in American journalism.
1948 Dr. Frank D. Fackenthal, for his interest and service.
1951 Cyrus L. Sulzberger *(New York Times)* for his exclusive interview with Archbishop Stepinac in a Yugoslav prison.
1952 *Kansas City Star* for coverage of 1951 floods; Max Kase *(New York Journal-American)* for exposures of bribery in college basketball.
1953 *New York Times* for its 17-year publication of "News of the Week in Review"; and Lester Markel, its founder.
1957 Kenneth Roberts for his historical novels.
1958 Walter Lippmann *(New York Herald Tribune)* for his "wisdom, perception and high sense of responsibility" in his commentary on national and international affairs.
1960 Garrett Mattingly, for *The Armada.*
1961 *American Heritage Picture History of the Civil War,* as distinguished example of American book publishing.
1964 Gannett Newspapers, Rochester, N.Y.
1973 James Thomas Flexner for his biography *George Washington.*
1974 Roger Sessions, for his "life's work in music."
1976 John Hohenberg for "services for 22 years as administrator of the Pulitzer Prizes." Scott Joplin for his contributions to American music.
1977 Alex Haley for his novel, *Roots*
1978 E.B.White of *New Yorker* magazine and Richard L. Strout of *Christian Science Monitor*
1982 Milton Babbitt, "for his life's work as a distinguished and seminal American composer"

Pulitzer Prizes in Letters

FICTION[1]

1918 *His Family.* Ernest Poole
1919 *The Magnificent Ambersons.* Booth Tarkington
1921 *The Age of Innocence.* Edith Wharton
1922 *Alice Adams.* Booth Tarkington
1923 *One of Ours.* Willa Cather
1924 *The Able McLaughlins.* Margaret Wilson
1925 *So Big.* Edna Ferber
1926 *Arrowsmith.* Sinclair Lewis
1927 *Early Autumn.* Louis Bromfield
1928 *The Bridge of San Luis Rey.* Thornton Wilder
1929 *Scarlet Sister Mary.* Julia Peterkin

1. Before 1948, award was for novels only.

1930 *Laughing Boy.* Oliver La Farge
1931 *Years of Grace.* Margaret Ayer Barnes
1932 *The Good Earth.* Pearl S. Buck
1933 *The Store.* T. S. Stribling
1934 *Lamb in His Bosom.* Caroline Miller
1935 *Now in November.* Josephine Winslow Johnson
1936 *Honey in the Horn.* Harold L. Davis
1937 *Gone with the Wind.* Margaret Mitchell
1938 *The Late George Apley.* John Phillips Marquand
1939 *The Yearling.* Marjorie Kinnan Rawlings
1940 *The Grapes of Wrath.* John Steinbeck
1942 *In This Our Life.* Ellen Glasgow

1943 *Dragon's Teeth.* Upton Sinclair
1944 *Journey in the Dark.* Martin Flavin
1945 *A Bell for Adano.* John Hersey
1947 *All the King's Men.* Robert Penn Warren
1948 *Tales of the South Pacific.* James A. Michener
1949 *Guard of Honor.* James Gould Cozzens
1950 *The Way West.* A. B. Guthrie, Jr.
1951 *The Town.* Conrad Richter
1952 *The Caine Mutiny.* Herman Wouk
1953 *The Old Man and the Sea.* Ernest Hemingway
1955 *A Fable.* William Faulkner
1956 *Andersonville.* MacKinlay Kantor
1958 *A Death in the Family.* James Agee
1959 *The Travels of Jaimie McPheeters.* Robert Lewis Taylor
1960 *Advise and Consent.* Allen Drury
1961 *To Kill a Mockingbird.* Harper Lee
1962 *The Edge of Sadness.* Edwin O'Connor
1963 *The Reivers.* William Faulkner
1965 *The Keepers of the House.* Shirley Ann Grau
1966 *Collected Stories of Katherine Anne Porter.* Katherine Anne Porter
1967 *The Fixer.* Bernard Malamud
1968 *The Confessions of Nat Turner.* William Styron
1969 *House Made of Dawn.* N. Scott Momaday
1970 *Collected Stories.* Jean Stafford
1972 *Angle of Repose.* Wallace Stegner
1973 *The Optimist's Daughter.* Eudora Welty
1975 *The Killer Angels.* Michael Shaara
1976 *Humboldt's Gift.* Saul Bellow
1978 *Elbow Room.* James Alan McPherson
1979 *The Stories of John Cheever.* John Cheever
1980 *The Executioner's Song.* Norman Mailer
1981 *A Confederacy of Dunces.* John Kennedy Toole
1982 *Rabbit Is Rich.* John Updike

DRAMA

1918 *Why Marry?* Jesse Lynch Williams
1920 *Beyond the Horizon.* Eugene O'Neill
1921 *Miss Lulu Bett.* Zona Gale
1922 *Anna Christie.* Eugene O'Neill
1923 *Icebound.* Owen Davis
1924 *Hell-Bent Fer Heaven.* Hatcher Hughes
1925 *They Knew What They Wanted.* Sidney Howard
1926 *Craig's Wife.* George Kelly
1927 *In Abraham's Bosom.* Paul Green
1928 *Strange Interlude.* Eugene O'Neill
1929 *Street Scene.* Elmer L. Rice
1930 *The Green Pastures.* Marc Connelly
1931 *Alison's House.* Susan Glaspell
1932 *Of Thee I Sing.* George S. Kaufman, Morrie Ryskind, and Ira Gershwin
1933 *Both Your Houses.* Maxwell Anderson
1934 *Men in White.* Sidney Kingsley
1935 *The Old Maid.* Zöe Akins
1936 *Idiot's Delight.* Robert E. Sherwood
1937 *You Can't Take It with You.* Moss Hart and George S. Kaufman
1938 *Our Town.* Thornton Wilder
1939 *Abe Lincoln in Illinois.* Robert E. Sherwood
1940 *The Time of Your Life.* William Saroyan
1941 *There Shall Be No Night.* Robert E. Sherwood
1943 *The Skin of Our Teeth.* Thornton Wilder
1945 *Harvey.* Mary Chase
1946 *State of the Union.* Russel Crouse and Howard Lindsay
1948 *A Streetcar Named Desire.* Tennessee Williams
1949 *Death of a Salesman.* Arthur Miller
1950 *South Pacific.* Richard Rodgers, Oscar Hammerstein II, and Joshua Logan
1952 *The Shrike.* Joseph Kramm
1953 *Picnic.* By William Inge
1954 *The Teahouse of the August Moon.* John Patrick
1955 *Cat on a Hot Tin Roof.* Tennessee Williams
1956 *The Diary of Anne Frank.* Frances Goodrich and Albert Hackett
1957 *Long Day's Journey Into Night.* Eugene O'Neill
1958 *Look Homeward, Angel.* Ketti Frings
1959 *J.B.* Archibald MacLeish
1960 *Fiorello!* George Abbott, Jerome Weidman, Jerry Bock, and Sheldon Harnick
1961 *All the Way Home.* Tad Mosel
1962 *How to Succeed in Business Without Really Trying.* Frank Loesser and Abe Burrows
1965 *The Subject Was Roses.* Frank D. Gilroy
1967 *A Delicate Balance.* Edward Albee
1969 *The Great White Hope.* Howard Sackler
1970 *No Place to Be Somebody.* Charles Gordone
1971 *The Effect of Gamma Rays on Man-in-the-Moon Marigolds.* Paul Zindel
1973 *That Championship Season.* Jason Miller
1975 *Seascape.* Edward Albee
1976 *A Chorus Line.* Conceived by Michael Bennett
1977 *The Shadow Box.* Michael Cristofer
1978 *The Gin Game.* Donald L. Coburn
1979 *Buried Child.* Sam Shepard
1980 *Talley's Folly.* Lanford Wilson
1981 *Crimes of the Heart.* Beth Henley
1982 *A Soldier's Play.* Charles Fuller

HISTORY OF UNITED STATES

1917 *With Americans of Past and Present Days.* J. J. Jusserand, Ambassador of France to United States
1918 *A History of the Civil War, 1861–1865.* James Ford Rhodes
1920 *The War with Mexico.* Justin H. Smith
1921 *The Victory at Sea.* William Sowden Sims in collaboration with Burton J. Hendrick
1922 *The Founding of New England.* James Truslow Adams
1923 *The Supreme Court in United States History.* Charles Warren
1924 *The American Revolution—A Constitutional Interpretation.* Charles Howard McIlwain
1925 *A History of the American Frontier.* Frederic L. Paxson
1926 *The History of the United States.* Edward Channing
1927 *Pinckney's Treaty.* Samuel Flagg Bemis
1928 *Main Currents in American Thought.* Vernon Louis Parrington
1929 *The Organization and Administration of the Union Army, 1861–1865.* Fred Albert Shannon
1930 *The War of Independence.* Claude H. Van Tyne
1931 *The Coming of the War: 1914.* Bernadotte E. Schmitt
1932 *My Experiences in the World War.* John J. Pershing
1933 *The Significance of Sections in American History.* Frederick J. Turner
1934 *The People's Choice.* Herbert Agar
1935 *The Colonial Period of American History.* Charles McLean Andrews
1936 *The Constitutional History of the United*

States. Andrew C. McLaughlin
1937 *The Flowering of New England.* Van Wyck Brooks
1938 *The Road to Reunion, 1865–1900.* Paul Herman Buck
1939 *A History of American Magazines.* Frank Luther Mott
1940 *Abraham Lincoln: The War Years.* Carl Sandburg
1941 *The Atlantic Migration, 1607–1860.* Marcus Lee Hansen
1942 *Reveille in Washington.* Margaret Leech
1943 *Paul Revere and the World He Lived In.* Esther Forbes
1944 *The Growth of American Thought.* Merle Curti
1945 *Unfinished Business.* Stephen Bonsal
1946 *The Age of Jackson.* Arthur M. Schlesinger, Jr.
1947 *Scientists Against Time.* James Phinney Baxter, 3rd
1948 *Across the Wide Missouri.* Bernard DeVoto
1949 *The Disruption of American Democracy.* Roy Franklin Nichols
1950 *Art and Life in America.* Oliver W. Larkin
1951 *The Old Northwest, Pioneer Period 1815–1840.* R. Carlyle Buley
1952 *The Uprooted.* Oscar Handlin
1953 *The Era of Good Feelings.* George Dangerfield
1954 *A Stillness at Appomattox.* Bruce Catton
1955 *Great River: The Rio Grande in North American History.* Paul Horgan
1956 *The Age of Reform.* Richard Hofstadter
1957 *Russia Leaves the War: Soviet-American Relations, 1917–1920.* George F. Kennan
1958 *Banks and Politics in America: From the Revolution to the Civil War.* Bray Hammond
1959 *The Republican Era: 1869–1901.* Leonard D. White, assisted by Jean Schneider
1960 *In the Days of McKinley.* Margaret Leech
1961 *Between War and Peace: The Potsdam Conference.* Herbert Feis
1962 *The Triumphant Empire, Thunder-Clouds Gather in the West.* Lawrence H. Gipson
1963 *Washington, Village and Capital, 1800–1878.* Constance McLaughlin Green
1964 *Puritan Village: The Formation of a New England Town.* Sumner Chilton Powell
1965 *The Greenback Era.* Irwin Unger
1966 *Life of the Mind in America.* Perry Miller
1967 *Exploration and Empire: The Explorer and Scientist in the Winning of the American West.* William H. Goetzmann
1968 *The Ideological Origins of the American Revolution.* Bernard Bailyn
1969 *Origins of the Fifth Amendment.* Leonard W. Levy
1970 *Present at the Creation: My Years in the State Department.* Dean Acheson
1971 *Roosevelt: The Soldier of Freedom.* James McGregor Burns
1972 *Neither Black Nor White. Slavery and Race Relations in Brazil and the United States.* Carl N. Degler
1973 *People of Paradox: An Inquiry Concerning the Origin of American Civilization.* Michael Kammen
1974 *The Americans: The Democratic Experience, Vol. 3.* Daniel J. Boorstin
1975 *Jefferson and His Time.* Dumas Malone
1976 *Lamy of Santa Fe.* Paul Horgan
1977 *The Impending Crisis: 1841–1861.* David M. Potter (posth)
1978 *The Invisible Hand: The Managerial Revolution in American Business.* Alfred D. Chandler Jr.
1979 *The Dred Scott Case: Its Significance in Law and Politics.* Don E. Fehrenbacher
1980 *Been in the Storm So Long.* Leon F. Litwack
1981 *American Education: The National Experience 1783–1876.* Lawrence A. Cremin
1982 *Mary Chestnut's Civil War.* C. Vann Woodward, editor

BIOGRAPHY OR AUTOBIOGRAPHY

1917 *Julia Ward Howe.* Laura E. Richards and Maude Howe Elliott, assisted by Florence Howe Hall
1918 *Benjamin Franklin, Self-Revealed.* William Cabell Bruce
1919 *The Education of Henry Adams.* Henry Adams
1920 *The Life of John Marshall.* Albert J. Beveridge
1921 *The Americanization of Edward Bok.* Edward Bok
1922 *A Daughter of the Middle Border.* Hamlin Garland
1923 *The Life and Letters of Walter H. Page.* Burton J. Hendrick
1924 *From Immigrant to Inventor.* Michael Idvorsky Pupin
1925 *Barrett Wendell and His Letters.* M. A. DeWolfe Howe
1926 *The Life of Sir William Osler.* Harvey Cushing
1927 *Whitman.* Emory Holloway
1928 *The American Orchestra and Theodore Thomas. Charles Edward Russell*
1929 *The Training of an American. The Earlier Life and Letters of Walter H. Page.* Burton J. Hendrick
1930 *The Raven.* Marquis James
1931 *Charles W. Eliot.* Henry James
1932 *Theodore Roosevelt.* Henry F. Pringle
1933 *Grover Cleveland.* Allan Nevins
1934 *John Hay.* Tyler Dennett
1935 *R. E. Lee.* Douglas S. Freeman
1936 *The Thought and Character of William James.* Ralph Barton Perry
1937 *Hamilton Fish.* Allan Nevins
1938 *Pedlar's Progress.* Odell Shepard. *Andrew Jackson.* Marquis James
1939 *Benjamin Franklin.* Carl Van Doren
1940 *Woodrow Wilson. Life and Letters,* Vols. VII and VIII. Ray Stannard Baker
1941 *Jonathan Edwards.* Ola E. Winslow
1942 *Crusader in Crinoline.* Forrest Wilson
1943 *Admiral of the Ocean Sea.* Samuel Eliot Morison
1944 *The American Leonardo: The Life of Samuel F. B. Morse.* Carleton Mabee
1945 *George Bancroft: Brahmin Rebel.* Russel Blaine Nye
1946 *Son of the Wilderness.* Linnie Marsh Wolfe
1947 *The Autobiography of William Allen White*
1948 *Forgotten First Citizen: John Bigelow.* Margaret Clapp
1949 *Roosevelt and Hopkins.* Robert E. Sherwood
1950 *John Quincy Adams and the Foundations of American Foreign Policy.* Samuel Flagg Bemis
1951 *John C. Calhoun: American Portrait.* Margaret Louise Coit
1952 *Charles Evans Hughes.* Merlo J. Pusey
1953 *Edmund Pendleton 1721–1803.* David J. Mays

1954 *The Spirit of St. Louis.* Charles A. Lindbergh
1955 *The Taft Story.* William S. White
1956 *Benjamin Henry Latrobe.* Talbot F. Hamlin
1957 *Profiles in Courage.* John F. Kennedy
1958 *George Washington.* Douglas Southall Freeman (Vols. 1–6) and John Alexander Carroll and Mary Wells Ashworth (Vol. 7)
1959 *Woodrow Wilson, American Prophet.* Arthur Walworth
1960 *John Paul Jones.* Samuel Eliot Morison
1961 *Charles Sumner and the Coming of the Civil War.* David Donald
1963 *Henry James: Vol. II, The Conquest of London, 1870–1881; Vol. III, The Middle Years, 1881–1895.* Leon Edel
1964 *John Keats.* Walter Jackson Bate
1965 *Henry Adams* (3 vols.). Ernest Samuels
1966 *A Thousand Days.* Arthur M. Schlesinger, Jr.
1967 *Mr. Clemens and Mark Twain.* Justin Kaplan
1968 *Memoirs, 1925–1950.* George F. Kennan
1969 *The Man from New York.* B. L. Reid
1970 *Huey Long.* T. Harry Williams
1971 *Robert Frost: The Years of Triumph, 1915–1938.* Lawrance Thompson
1972 *Eleanor and Franklin: The Story of Their Relationship Based on Eleanor Roosevelt's Private Papers.* Joseph P. Lash
1973 *Luce and His Empire.* W. A. Swanberg
1974 *O'Neill, Son and Artist.* Louis Sheaffer
1975 *The Power Broker: Robert Moses and the Fall of New York.* Robert A. Caro
1976 *Edith Wharton: A Biography.* Richard W. B. Lewis
1977 *A Prince of Our Disorder.* John E. Mack
1978 *Samuel Johnson.* Walter Jackson Bate
1979 *Days of Sorrow and Pain: Leo Baeck and the Berlin Jews.* Leonard Baker
1980 *The Rise of Theodore Roosevelt.* Edmund Morris
1981 *Peter the Great.* Robert K. Massie
1982 *Grant: A Biography.* William S. McFeely

POETRY[1]

1918 *Love Songs.* Sara Teasdale
1919 *Old Road to Paradise.* Margaret Widdemer; *Corn Huskers.* Carl Sandburg
1922 *Collected Poems.* Edwin Arlington Robinson
1923 *The Ballad of the Harp-Weaver; A Few Figs from Thistles;* eight sonnets in *American Poetry, 1922, A Miscellany.* Edna St. Vincent Millay
1924 *New Hampshire: A Poem with Notes and Grace Notes.* Robert Frost
1925 *The Man Who Died Twice.* Edwin Arlington Robinson
1926 *What's O'Clock.* Amy Lowell
1927 *Fiddler's Farewell.* Leonora Speyer
1928 *Tristram.* Edwin Arlington Robinson
1929 *John Brown's Body.* Stephen Vincent Benét
1930 *Selected Poems.* Conrad Aiken
1931 *Collected Poems.* Robert Frost
1932 *The Flowering Stone.* George Dillon
1933 *Conquistador.* Archibald MacLeish
1934 *Collected Verse.* Robert Hillyer
1935 *Bright Ambush.* Audrey Wurdemann
1936 *Strange Holiness.* Robert P. T. Coffin
1937 *A Further Range.* Robert Frost
1938 *Cold Morning Sky.* Marya Zaturenska
1939 *Selected Poems.* John Gould Fletcher
1940 *Collected Poems.* Mark Van Doren
1941 *Sunderland Capture.* Leonard Bacon

1. This prize was established in 1922. The 1918 and 1919 awards were made from gifts provided by the Poetry Society.

1942 *The Dust Which Is God.* William Rose Benét
1943 *A Witness Tree.* Robert Frost
1944 *Western Star.* Stephen Vincent Benét
1945 *V-Letter and Other Poems.* Karl Shapiro
1947 *Lord Weary's Castle.* Robert Lowell
1948 *The Age of Anxiety.* W. H. Auden
1949 *Terror and Decorum.* Peter Viereck
1950 *Annie Allen.* Gwendolyn Brooks
1951 *Complete Poems.* Carl Sandburg
1952 *Collected Poems.* Marianne Moore
1953 *Collected Poems 1917–1952.* Archibald MacLeish
1954 *The Waking.* Theodore Roethke
1955 *Collected Poems.* Wallace Stevens
1956 *Poems—North & South.* Elizabeth Bishop
1957 *Things of This World.* Richard Wilbur
1958 *Promises: Poems 1954–1956.* Robert Penn Warren
1959 *Selected Poems, 1928–1958.* Stanley Kunitz
1960 *Heart's Needle.* William Snodgrass
1961 *Times Three: Selected Verse from Three Decades.* Phyllis McGinley
1962 *Poems.* Alan Dugan
1963 *Pictures from Breughel.* William Carlos Williams
1964 *At the End of the Open Road.* Louis Simpson
1965 *77 Dream Songs.* John Berryman
1966 *Selected Poems.* Richard Eberhart
1967 *Live or Die.* Anne Sexton
1968 *The Hard Hours.* Anthony Hecht
1969 *Of Being Numerous.* George Oppen
1970 *Untitled Subjects.* Richard Howard
1971 *The Carrier of Ladders.* William S. Merwin
1972 *Collected Poems.* James Wright
1973 *Up Country.* Maxine Winokur Kumin
1974 *The Dolphin.* Robert Lowell
1975 *Turtle Island.* Gary Snyder
1976 *Self-Portrait in a Convex Mirror.* John Ashbery
1977 *Divine Comedies.* James Merrill
1978 *Collected Poems.* Howard Nemerov: *Poems 1976–1978.*
1979 *Now and Then* Robert Penn Warren.
1980 *Selected Poems.* Donald Rodney Justice
1981 *The Morning of the Poem.* James Schuyler
1982 *The Collected Poems.* Sylvia Plath

GENERAL NONFICTION

1962 *The Making of the President 1960.* Theodore H. White
1963 *The Guns of August.* Barbara W. Tuchman
1964 *Anti-intellectualism in American Life.* Richard Hofstadter
1965 *O Strange New World.* Howard Mumford Jones
1966 *Wandering Through Winter.* Edwin Way Teale
1967 *The Problem of Slavery in Western Culture.* David Brion Davis
1968 *Rousseau and Revolution.* Will and Ariel Durant
1969 *So Human an Animal.* Rene Jules Dubos
The Armies of the Night. Norman Mailer
1970 *Gandhi's Truth.* Erik H. Erikson
1971 *The Rising Sun.* John Toland
1972 *Stilwell and the American Experience in China, 1911–1945.* Barbara W. Tuchman
1973 *Fire in the Lake: The Vietnamese and the Americans in Vietnam.* Frances FitzGerald; and *Children of Crisis* (Vols. 1 and 2). Robert M. Coles
1974 *The Denial of Death.* Ernest Becker
1975 *Pilgrim at Tinker Creek.* Annie Dillard

1976 *Why Survive? Being Old in America.* Robert N. Butler
1977 *Beautiful Swimmers: Watermen, Crabs and the Chesapeake Bay.* William W. Warner
1978 *The Dragons of Eden.* Carl Sagan
1979 *On Human Nature.* Edward O. Wilson
1980 *Gödel, Escher, Bach: An Eternal Golden Braid.* Douglas R. Hofstadter
1981 *Fin-de-Siecle Vienna: Politics and Culture.* Carl E. Schorske
1982 *The Soul of a New Machine.* Tracy Kidder

Pulitzer Prizes in Music

1943 *Secular Cantata No. 2, A Free Song.* William Schuman
1944 *Symphony No. 4* (Op. 34). Howard Hanson
1945 *Appalachian Spring.* Aaron Copland
1946 *The Canticle of the Sun.* Leo Sowerby
1947 *Symphony No. 3.* Charles Ives
1948 *Symphony No. 3.* Walter Piston
1949 *Louisiana Story* music. Virgil Thomson
1950 *The Consul.* Gian Carlo Menotti
1951 Music for opera *Giants in the Earth.* Douglas Stuart Moore
1952 *Symphony Concertante.* Gail Kubik
1954 *Concerto for Two Pianos and Orchestra.* Quincy Porter
1955 *The Saint of Bleecker Street.* Gian Carlo Menotti
1956 *Symphony No. 3.* Ernst Toch
1957 *Meditations on Ecclesiastes.* Norman Dello Joio
1958 *Vanessa.* Samuel Barber
1959 *Concerto for Piano and Orchestra.* John La Montaine
1960 *Second String Quartet.* Elliott Carter
1961 *Symphony No. 7.* Walter Piston
1962 *The Crucible.* Robert Ward
1963 *Piano Concerto No. 1.* Samuel Barber
1966 *Variations for Orchestra.* Leslie Bassett
1967 *Quartet No. 3.* Leon Kirchner
1968 *Echoes of Time and the River.* George Crumb
1969 *String Quartet No. 3.* Karel Husa
1970 *Time's Encomium.* Charles Wuorinen
1971 *Synchronisms No. 6 for Piano and Electronic Sound.* Mario Davidowsky
1972 *Windows.* Jacob Druckman
1973 *String Quartet No. 3.* Elliott Carter
1974 *Notturno.* Donald Martino
1975 *From the Diary of Virginia Woolf.* Dominick Argento
1976 *Air Music.* Ned Rorem
1977 *Visions of Terror and Wonder.* Richard Wernick
1978 *Déjà Vu for Percussion Quartet and Orchestra.* Michael Colgrass
1979 *Aftertones of Infinity.* Joseph Schwantner
1980 *In Memory of a Summer Day.* David Del Tredici
1981 Not awarded
1982 *Concerto for Orchestra.* Roger Sessions

Antoinette Perry (Tony) Awards, 1982

Dramatic play: *The Life and Adventures of Nicholas Nickleby,* adapted by David Edgar
Musical: *Dreamgirls*
Actor (play): Roger Rees, *Nicholas Nickleby*
Actress (play): Zoe Caldwell, *Medea*
Actor (musical): Ben Harney, *Dreamgirls*
Actress (musical): Jennifer Holliday, *Dreamgirls*
Actor, featured (play): Zakes Mokae, *Master Harold . . . and the Boys*
Actress, featured (play): Amanda Plummer, *Agnes of God*
Actor, featured (musical): Cleavant Derricks, *Dreamgirls*
Actress, featured (musical): Liliane Montevecchi, *Nine*
Director (play): Trevor Nunn and John Caird, *Nicholas Nickleby*
Director (musical): Tommy Tune, *Nine*
Score: Maury Yeston, *Nine*
Musical book: Tom Eyen, *Dreamgirls*
Choreography: Michael Bennett and Michael Peters, *Dreamgirls*
Scenic design: John Napier and Dermot Hayes, *Nicholas Nickleby*
Costumes: William Ivey Long, *Nine*
Lighting: Tharon Musser, *Dreamgirls*
Reproduction of a play or musical: *Othello*
Special Awards: Tyrone Guthrie Theater of Minneapolis and Actors Fund of America

Sigma Delta Chi Journalism Awards, 1981

General reporting: David L. Ashenfelter and Sydney P. Freedberg, *Detroit News*
Editorial writing: John T. Senderling, *Dallas Times Herald*
Washington correspondence: Jerome Watson, *Chicago Sun-Times*
Foreign correspondence: Richard Ben Cramer, *Philadelphia Inquirer*
News photography: Ron Edmonds, Associated Press
Editorial cartoon: Paul Conrad, *Los Angeles Times*
Public service in newspaper journalism: *Los Angeles Times*
Magazine reporting: Seymour Hersh, *New York Times Magazine*
Public service in magazine journalism: *National Geographic*
Radio reporting: KVET-AM, Austin, Tex.
Public service in radio reporting: WJR-AM, Detroit
Editorializing on radio: Michal Regunberg, WEEI, Boston
Television reporting: WHAS, Louisville, Ky.
Public service in television reporting: WNBC, New York
Editorializing on television: Jack Hurley, WHIO, Toledo, Ohio
Research about journalism: Robert W. Desmond, for five-volume series on international news gathering

Motion Picture Academy Awards (Oscars)

	Picture	Director	Actress
1928	*Wings,* Paramount	Frank Borzage, *Seventh Heaven;* Lewis Milestone, *Two Arabian Nights*	Janet Gaynor, *Seventh Heaven, Street Angel, Sunrise*
1929	*The Broadway Melody,* M-G-M	Frank Lloyd, *The Divine Lady*	Mary Pickford, *Coquette*
1930	*All Quiet on the Western Front,* Universal	Lewis Milestone, *All Quiet on the Western Front*	Norma Shearer, *The Divorcee*
1931	*Cimarron,* RKO Radio	Norman Taurog, *Skippy*	Marie Dressler, *Min and Bill*
1932	*Grand Hotel,* M-G-M	Frank Borzage, *Bad Girl*	Helen Hayes, *The Sin of Madelon Claudet*
1933	*Cavalcade,* Fox	Frank Lloyd, *Cavalcade*	Katharine Hepburn, *Morning Glory*
1934	*It Happened One Night,* Columbia	Frank Capra, *It Happened One Night*	Claudette Colbert *It Happened One Night*
1935	*Mutiny on the Bounty,* M-G-M	John Ford, *The Informer*	Bette Davis, *Dangerous*
1936	*The Great Ziegfeld,* M-G-M	Frank Capra, *Mr. Deeds Goes to Town*	Luise Rainer, *The Great Ziegfeld*
1937	*The Life of Emile Zola,* Warner Bros.	Leo McCarey, *The Awful Truth*	Luise Rainer, *The Good Earth*
1938	*You Can't Take It with You,* Columbia	Frank Capra, *You Can't Take It with You*	Bette Davis, *Jezebel*
1939	*Gone with the Wind,* Selznick-M-G-M	Victor Fleming, *Gone with the Wind*	Vivien Leigh, *Gone with the Wind*
1940	*Rebecca,* Selznick-UA	John Ford, *The Grapes of Wrath*	Ginger Rogers, *Kitty Foyle*
1941	*How Green Was My Valley,* 20th Century-Fox	John Ford, *How Green Was My Valley*	Joan Fontaine, *Suspicion*
1942	*Mrs. Miniver,* M-G-M	William Wyler, *Mrs. Miniver*	Greer Garson, *Mrs. Miniver*
1943	*Casablanca,* Warner Bros.	Michael Curtiz, *Casablanca*	Jennifer Jones, *The Song of Bernadette*
1944	*Going My Way,* Paramount	Leo McCarey, *Going My Way*	Ingrid Bergman, *Gaslight*
1945	*The Lost Weekend,* Paramount	Billy Wilder, *The Lost Weekend*	Joan Crawford, *Mildred Pierce*
1946	*The Best Years of Our Lives,* Goldwyn-RKO Radio	William Wyler, *The Best Years of Our Lives*	Olivia de Havilland, *To Each His Own*
1947	*Gentleman's Agreement,* 20th Century-Fox	Elia Kazan, *Gentleman's Agreement*	Loretta Young, *The Farmer's Daughter*
1948	*Hamlet,* Rank-Two Cities-U-I	John Huston, *Treasure of Sierra Madre*	Jane Wyman, *Johnny Belinda*
1949	*All the King's Men,* Rossen-Columbia	Joseph L. Mankiewicz, *A Letter to Three Wives*	Olivia de Havilland, *The Heiress*
1950	*All About Eve,* 20th Century-Fox	Joseph L. Mankiewicz, *All About Eve*	Judy Holliday, *Born Yesterday*
1951	*An American in Paris,* M-G-M	George Stevens, *A Place in the Sun*	Vivien Leigh, *A Streetcar Named Desire*
1952	*The Greatest Show on Earth,* DeMille-Paramount	John Ford, *The Quiet Man*	Shirley Booth, *Come Back, Little Sheba*
1953	*From Here to Eternity,* Columbia	Fred Zinnemann, *From Here to Eternity*	Audrey Hepburn, *Roman Holiday*
1954	*On the Waterfront,* Horizon-American Corp., Columbia	Elia Kazan, *On the Waterfront*	Grace Kelly, *The Country Girl*
1955	*Marty,* Hecht and Lancaster, United Artists	Delbert Mann, *Marty*	Anna Magnani, *The Rose Tattoo*
1956	*Around the World in 80 Days,* Michael Todd Co., Inc.-UA	George Stevens, *Giant*	Ingrid Bergman, *Anastasia*
1957	*The Bridge on the River Kwai,* Horizon Picture, Columbia	David Lean, *The Bridge on the River Kwai*	Joanne Woodward, *The Three Faces of Eve*
1958	*Gigi,* Arthur Freed Productions, Inc., M-G-M	Vincente Minnelli, *Gigi*	Susan Hayward, *I Want to Live!*
1959	*Ben-Hur,* M-G-M	William Wyler, *Ben-Hur*	Simone Signoret, *Room at the Top*
1960	*The Apartment,* Mirisch Co., Inc., United Artists	Billy Wilder, *The Apartment*	Elizabeth Taylor, *Butterfield 8*
1961	*West Side Story,* Mirisch Pictures, Inc., and B and P Enterprises, Inc., United Artists	Robert Wise and Jerome Robbins, *West Side Story*	Sophia Loren, *Two Women*

Actor	Supporting Actress	Supporting Actor	
Emil Jannings, *The Way of All Flesh, The Last Command*	—	—	1928
Warner Baxter, *In Old Arizona*	—	—	1929
George Arliss, *Disraeli*	—	—	1930
Lionel Barrymore, *A Free Soul*	—	—	1931
Fredric March, *Dr. Jekyll and Mr. Hyde,* and Wallace Beery, *The Champ*	—	—	1932
Charles Laughton, *The Private Life of Henry VIII*	—	—	1933
Clark Gable, *It Happened One Night*	—	—	1934
Victor McLaglen, *The Informer*	—	—	1935
Paul Muni, *The Story of Louis Pasteur*	Gale Sondergaard, *Anthony Adverse*	Walter Brennan, *Come and Get It*	1936
Spencer Tracy, *Captains Courageous*	Alice Brady, *In Old Chicago*	Joseph Schildkraut, *The Life of Emile Zola*	1937
Spencer Tracy, *Boys Town*	Fay Bainter, *Jezebel*	Walter Brennan, *Kentucky*	1938
Robert Donat, *Goodbye, Mr. Chips*	Hattie McDaniel, *Gone with the Wind*	Thomas Mitchell, *Stagecoach*	1939
James Stewart, *The Philadelphia Story*	Jane Darwell, *The Grapes of Wrath*	Walter Brennan, *The Westerner*	1940
Gary Cooper, *Sergeant York*	Mary Astor, *The Great Lie*	Donald Crisp, *How Green Was My Valley*	1941
James Cagney, *Yankee Doodle Dandy*	Teresa Wright, *Mrs. Miniver*	Van Heflin, *Johnny Eager*	1942
Paul Lukas, *Watch on the Rhine*	Katina Paxinou, *For Whom the Bell Tolls*	Charles Coburn, *The More the Merrier*	1943
Bing Crosby, *Going My Way*	Ethel Barrymore, *None But the Lonely Heart*	Barry Fitzgerald, *Going My Way*	1944
Ray Milland, *The Lost Weekend*	Anne Revere, *National Velvet*	James Dunn, *A Tree Grows in Brooklyn*	1945
Fredric March, *The Best Years of Our Lives*	Anne Baxter, *The Razor's Edge*	Harold Russell, *The Best Years of Our Lives*	1946
Ronald Colman, *A Double Life*	Celeste Holm, *Gentleman's Agreement*	Edmund Gwenn, *Miracle on 34th Street*	1947
Laurence Olivier, *Hamlet*	Claire Trevor, *Key Largo*	Walter Huston, *Treasure of Sierra Madre*	1948
Broderick Crawford, *All the King's Men*	Mercedes McCambridge, *All the King's Men*	Dean Jagger, *Twelve O'Clock High*	1949
José Ferrer, *Cyrano de Bergerac*	Josephine Hull, *Harvey*	George Sanders, *All About Eve*	1950
Humphrey Bogart, *The African Queen*	Kim Hunter, *A Streetcar Named Desire*	Karl Malden, *A Streetcar Named Desire*	1951
Gary Cooper, *High Noon*	Gloria Grahame, *The Bad and the Beautiful*	Anthony Quinn, *Viva Zapata!*	1952
William Holden, *Stalag 17*	Donna Reed, *From Here to Eternity*	Frank Sinatra, *From Here to Eternity*	1953
Marlon Brando, *On the Waterfront*	Eva Marie Saint, *On the Waterfront*	Edmond O'Brien, *The Barefoot Contessa*	1954
Ernest Borgnine, *Marty*	Jo Van Fleet, *East of Eden*	Jack Lemmon, *Mister Roberts*	1955
Yul Brynner, *The King and I*	Dorothy Malone, *Written on the Wind*	Anthony Quinn, *Lust for Life*	1956
Alec Guinness, *The Bridge on the River Kwai*	Miyoshi Umeki, *Sayonara*	Red Buttons, *Sayonara*	1957
David Niven, *Separate Tables*	Wendy Hiller, *Separate Tables*	Burl Ives, *The Big Country*	1958
Charlton Heston, *Ben-Hur*	Shelley Winters, *The Diary of Anne Frank*	Hugh Griffith, *Ben-Hur*	1959
Burt Lancaster, *Elmer Gantry*	Shirley Jones, *Elmer Gantry*	Peter Ustinov, *Spartacus*	1960
Maximilian Schell, *Judgment at Nuremberg*	Rita Moreno, *West Side Story*	George Chakiris, *West Side Story*	1961

	Picture	Director	Actress
1962	*Lawrence of Arabia,* Horizon Pictures, Ltd.-Columbia	David Lean, *Lawrence of Arabia*	Anne Bancroft, *The Miracle Worker*
1963	*Tom Jones,* A Woodfall Production, UA-Lopert Pictures	Tony Richardson, *Tom Jones*	Patricia Neal, *Hud*
1964	*My Fair Lady,* Warner Bros.	George Cukor, *My Fair Lady*	Julie Andrews, *Mary Poppins*
1965	*The Sound of Music,* Argyle Enterprises Production, 20th Century-Fox	Robert Wise, *The Sound of Music*	Julie Christie, *Darling*
1966	*A Man for All Seasons,* Highland Films, Ltd., Production, Columbia	Fred Zinnemann, *A Man for All Seasons*	Elizabeth Taylor, *Who's Afraid of Virginia Woolf?*
1967	*In the Heat of the Night,* Mirisch Corp. Production, United Artists	Mike Nichols, *The Graduate*	Katharine Hepburn, *Guess Who's Coming to Dinner*
1968	*Oliver!,* Columbia Pictures	Sir Carol Reed, *Oliver!*	Katharine Hepburn, *The Lion in Winter, and Barbara Streisand, Funny Girl*
1969	*Midnight Cowboy,* Jerome Hellman-John Schlesinger Production, United Artists	John Schlesinger, *Midnight Cowboy*	Maggie Smith, *The Prime of Miss Jean Brodie*
1970	*Patton,* Frank McCarthy-Franklin J. Schaffner Production, 20th Century-Fox	Franklin J. Schaffner, *Patton*	Glenda Jackson, *Women in Love*
1971	*The French Connection,* D'Antoni Productions, 20th Century-Fox	William Friedkin, *The French Connection*	Jane Fonda, *Klute*
1972	*The Godfather,* Albert S. Ruddy Production, Paramount	Bob Fosse, *Cabaret*	Liza Minnelli, *Cabaret*
1973	*The Sting,* Universal-Bill-Phillips-George Roy Hill Production, Universal	George Roy Hill, *The Sting*	Glenda Jackson, *A Touch of Class*
1974	*The Godfather, Part II,* Coppola Co. Production, Paramount	Francis Ford Coppola, *The Godfather, Part II*	Ellen Burstyn, *Alice Doesn't Live Here Anymore*
1975	*One Flew Over the Cuckoo's Nest,* Fantasy Films Production, United Artists	Milos Forman, *One Flew Over the Cuckoo's Nest*	Louise Fletcher, *One Flew Over the Cuckoo's Nest*
1976	*Rocky,* Robert Chartoff-Irwin Winkler Production, United Artists	John G. Avildsen, *Rocky*	Faye Dunaway *Network*
1977	*Annie Hall,* Jack Rollins-Charles H. Joffe Production, United Artists	Woody Allen, *Annie Hall*	Diane Keaton, *Annie Hall*
1978	*The Deer Hunter,* Michael Cimino Film Production, Universal	Michael Cimino, *The Deer Hunter*	Jane Fonda, *Coming Home*
1979	*Kramer vs. Kramer,* Stanley Jaffe Production, Columbia Pictures	Robert Benton, *Kramer vs. Kramer*	Sally Field, *Norma Rae*
1980	*Ordinary People,* Wildwood Enterprises Production, Paramount	Robert Redford, *Ordinary People*	Sissy Spacek, *Coal Miner's Daughter*
1981	*Chariots of Fire,* Enigma Productions, Ladd Company/Warner Bros.	Warren Beatty, *Reds*	Katharine Hepburn, *On Golden Pond*

Other Academy Awards for 1981

Art direction: *Raiders of the Lost Ark,* Norman Reynolds and Leslie Dilley, art direction; Michael Ford, set decoration
Cinematography: Vittorio Storaro, *Reds*
Costume design: Milena Canonero, *Chariots of Fire*
Documentary (feature): *Genocide;* **short subject:** *Close Harmony*
Editing: Michael Kahn, *Raiders of the Lost Ark*
Foreign-language film: *Mephisto,* Hungary
Music (original score): Vengelis, *Chariots of Fire*
Song: "Arthur's Theme, (Best That You Can Do)", Burt Bacharach, Carole Bayer Sager, Christopher Cross, and Peter Allen, from *Arthur*
Screenplay (original): Colin Welland, *Chariots of Fire.;* **(adapted);** Ernest Thompson, *On Golden Pond*
Short subject (animated): *CRAC;* **(live-action):** *Violet*
Sound: Bill Varney, Steve Maslow, Gregg Landaker, and Roy Charman, *Raiders of the Lost Ark*
Visual effects: Richard Edlund, Kit West, Bruce Nicholson, and Joe Johnston, *Raiders of the Lost Ark*
Makeup: Rick Baker, *An American Werewolf in London*
Irving G. Thalberg Award: Albert R. (Cubby) Broccoli
Jean Hersholt Humanitarian Award: Danny Kaye
Honorary Award: Barbara Stanwyck
Special Achievement—Sound Effects: *Raiders of the Lost Ark*
Gordon E. Sawyer Award: Joseph B. Walker
Special Award: Fuji Photo Film Company, for its extremely high-speed film

Actor	Supporting Actress	Supporting Actor	
Gregory Peck, *To Kill a Mockingbird*	Patty Duke, *The Miracle Worker*	Ed Begley, *Sweet Bird of Youth*	1962
Sidney Poitier, *Lilies of the Field*	Margaret Rutherford, *The V.I.P.s*	Melvyn Douglas, *Hud*	1963
Rex Harrison, *My Fair Lady*	Lila Kedrova, *Zorba the Greek*	Peter Ustinov, *Topkapi*	1964
Lee Marvin, *Cat Ballou*	Shelley Winters, *A Patch of Blue*	Martin Balsam, *A Thousand Clowns*	1965
Paul Scofield, *A Man for All Seasons*	Sandy Dennis, *Who's Afraid of Virginia Woolf?*	Walter Matthau, *The Fortune Cookie*	1966
Rod Steiger, *In the Heat of the Night*	Estelle Parsons, *Bonnie and Clyde*	George Kennedy, *Cool Hand Luke*	1967
Cliff Robertson, *Charly*	Ruth Gordon, *Rosemary's Baby*	Jack Albertson, *The Subject Was Roses*	1968
John Wayne, *True Grit*	Goldie Hawn, *Cactus Flower*	Gig Young, *They Shoot Horses, Don't They?*	1969
George C. Scott, *Patton*	Helen Hayes, *Airport*	John Mills, *Ryan's Daughter*	1970
Gene Hackman, *The French Connection*	Cloris Leachman, *The Last Picture Show*	Ben Johnson, *The Last Picture Show*	1971
Marlon Brando, *The Godfather*	Eileen Heckart, *Butterflies Are Free*	Joel Grey, *Cabaret*	1972
Jack Lemmon, *Save the Tiger*	Tatum O'Neal, *Paper Moon*	John Houseman, *The Paper Chase*	1973
Art Carney, *Harry and Tonto*	Ingrid Bergman, *Murder on the Orient Express*	Robert De Niro, *The Godfather, Part II*	1974
Jack Nicholson, *One Flew Over the Cuckoo's Nest*	Lee Grant, *Shampoo*	George Burns, *The Sunshine Boys*	1975
Peter Finch, *Network*	Beatrice Straight, *Network*	Jason Robards, *All the President's Men*	1976
Richard Dreyfuss, *The Goodbye Girl*	Vanessa Redgrave, *Julia*	Jason Robards, *Julia*	1977
Jon Voight, *Coming Home*	Maggie Smith, *California Suite*	Christopher Walken, *The Deer Hunter*	1978
Dustin Hoffman, *Kramer vs. Kramer*	Meryl Streep, *Kramer vs. Kramer*	Melvyn Douglas, *Being There*	1979
Robert De Niro, *Raging Bull*	Mary Steenburgen, *Melvin and Howard*	Timothy Hutton, *Ordinary People*	1980
Henry Fonda, *On Golden Pond*	Maureen Stapleton, *Reds*	John Gielgud, *Arthur*	1981

"Oscar"

In 1928, the Academy of Motion Picture Arts and Sciences began the annual presentation of its awards for motion picture excellence. The "Oscar" was originally sketched by Cedric Gibbons. The statue is 10 inches tall, weighs 7 pounds, and is made of gold plate over bronze. When Margaret Harrick, the Academy's first executive director, saw the statue, she remarked that it looked like her Uncle Oscar. The nickname stuck, and today the "Oscar" is the most important and sought after of film awards.

American Library Association Awards for Children's Books, 1982

John Newbery Medal for best book: *A Visit to William Blake's Inn: Poems for Innocent and Experienced Travelers,* by Nancy Willard (Harcourt Brace Jovanovich)

Newbery Honor Books: *Ramona Quimby, Age 8,* by Beverly Cleary (William Morrow); *Upon the Head of the Goat: A Childhood in Hungary 1939–1944,* by Aranka Siegal (Farrar, Straus & Giroux)

Randolph Caldecott Medal for best picture book: *Jumanji,* written and illustrated by Chris Van Allsburg (Houghton Mifflin)

Caldecott Honor Books: *A Visit to William Blake's Inn: Poems for Innocent and Experienced Travelers,* Alice and Martin Provensen, illustrators; *On Market Street,* by Arnold Lobel, illustrated by Anita Lobel (Greenwillow Books); *Outside Over There,* written and illustrated by Maurice Sendak (Harper & Row/Ursula Nordstrom); *Where the Buffaloes Begin,* by Olaf Baker, illustrated by Stephen Gammell (Frederick Warne)

New York Drama Critics' Circle Awards

1935–36
Winterset, Maxwell Anderson
1936–37
High Tor, Maxwell Anderson
1937–38
Of Mice and Men, John Steinbeck
Shadow and Substance, Paul Vincent Carroll[1]
1938–39
(No award) *The White Steed,* Paul Vincent Carroll[1]
1939–40
The Time of Your Life, William Saroyan
1940–41
Watch on the Rhine, Lillian Hellman
The Corn Is Green, Emlyn Williams[1]
1941–42
(No award) *Blithe Spirit,* Noel Coward[1]
1942–43
The Patriots, Sidney Kingsley
1943–44
(No award) *Jacobowsky and the Colonel.* Franz Werfel and S. N. Behrman[1]
1944–45
The Glass Menagerie, Tennessee Williams
1945–46
(No award) *Carousel,* Richard Rodgers and Oscar Hammerstein II[2]
1946–47
All My Sons, Arthur Miller
No Exit, Jean-Paul Sartre[1]
Brigadoon, Alan Jay Lerner and Frederick Loewe[2]
1947–48
A Streetcar Named Desire, Tennessee Williams
The Winslow Boy, Terence Rattigan[1]
1948–49
Death of a Salesman, Arthur Miller
The Madwoman of Chaillot, Jean Giraudoux and Maurice Valency[1]
South Pacific, Richard Rodgers, Oscar Hammerstein II, and Joshua Logan[2]
1949–50
The Member of the Wedding, Carson McCullers
The Cocktail Party, T. S. Eliot[1]
The Consul, Gian Carlo Menotti[2]
1950–51
Darkness at Noon, Sidney Kingsley[3]
The Lady's Not for Burning, Christopher Fry[1]
Guys and Dolls, Abe Burrows, Jo Swerling and Frank Loesser[2]
1951–52
I Am a Camera, John Van Druten[4]
Venus Observed, Christopher Fry[1]
Pal Joey, Richard Rodgers, Lorenz Hart, and John O'Hara[2]
Don Juan in Hell, George B. Shaw[5]
1952–53
Picnic, William Inge
The Love of Four Colonels, by Peter Ustinov[1]
Wonderful Town, Joseph Fields, Jerome Chodorov, Betty Comden, Adolph Green, and Leonard Bernstein[2]
1953–54
The Teahouse of the August Moon, John Patrick
Ondine, Jean Giraudoux[1]
The Golden Apple, John Latouche and Jerome Moross[2]
1954–55
Cat on a Hot Tin Roof, Tennessee Williams
Witness for the Prosecution, Agatha Christie[1]
The Saint of Bleecker Street, Gian Carlo Menotti[2]
1955-56
The Diary of Anne Frank, Frances Goodrich and Albert Hackett
Tiger at the Gates, Jean Giraudoux and Christopher Fry[1]
My Fair Lady, Frederick Loewe and Alan Jay Lerner[2]
1956–57
Long Day's Journey Into Night, Eugene O'Neill
Waltz of the Toreadors, Jean Anouilh[1]
The Most Happy Fella, Frank Loesser[2, 6]
1957–58
Look Homeward, Angel, Ketti Frings[7]
Look Back in Anger, John Osborne[1]
The Music Man, Meredith Willson[2]
1958–59
A Raisin in the Sun, Lorraine Hansberry
The Visit, Friedrich Duerrenmatt–Maurice Valency[1]
La Plume de ma Tante, Robert Dhery and Gerard Calvi[2]
1959–60
Toys in the Attic, Lillian Hellman
Five Finger Exercise, Peter Shaffer[1]
Fiorello!, Jerome Weidman, George Abbott, Jerry Bock, and Sheldon Harnick[2]
1960–61
All the Way Home, Tad Mosel[8]
A Taste of Honey, Shelagh Delaney[1]
Carnival, Michael Stewart[2]
1961–62
The Night of the Iguana, Tennessee Williams
A Man for All Seasons, Robert Bolt[1]
How to Succeed in Business Without Really Trying, Abe Burrows, Jack Weinstock, Willie Gilbert, and Frank Loesser[2, 9]
1962–63
Who's Afraid of Virginia Woolf?, Edward Albee
Beyond the Fringe, Alan Bennett, Peter Cook, Jonathan Miller, and Dudley Moore[10]
1963–64
Luther, John Osborne
Hello, Dolly!, Michael Stewart and Jerry Herman[2, 11]
The Trojan Women, Euripides[10, 12]
1964–65
The Subject Was Roses, Frank D. Gilroy
Fiddler on the Roof, Joseph Stein, Jerry Bock, and Sheldon Harnick[2, 13]
1965–66
The Persecution and Assassination of Marat as Performed by the Inmates of the Asylum of Charenton under the Direction of the Marquis de Sade, Peter Weiss
The Man of La Mancha, Dale Wasserman, Mitch Leigh, and Joe Darion
1966–67
The Homecoming, Harold Pinter
Cabaret, Joe Masteroff, John Kander, and Fred Ebb[2, 14]
1967–68
Rosencrantz and Guilderstern Are Dead, Tom Stoppard
Your Own Thing, Donald Driver, Hal Hester, and Danny Apolinar[2]
1968–69
The Great White Hope, Howard Sackler
1776, Sherman Edwards and Peter Stone[2]
1969–70
Borstal Boy, Frank McMahon[15]
The Effect of Gamma Rays on Man-in-the-Moon Marigolds, Paul Zindel[16]
Company, George Furth and Stephen Sondheim[2]
1970–71
Home, David Storey
The House of Blue Leaves, John Guare[16]

Follies, James Goldman and Stephen Sondheim[2]

1971–72

That Championship Season, Jason Miller

Two Gentlemen of Verona, adapted by John Guare and Mel Shapiro[2]

The Screens, Jean Genet[1]

1972–73

The Changing Room, David Storey

The Hot l Baltimore, by Lanford Wilson[16]

A Little Night Music, Hugh Wheeler and Stephen Sondheim[2]

1973–74

The Contractors, David Storey

Short Eyes, Miguel Piñero[16]

Candide, Leonard Bernstein, Hugh Wheeler, and Richard Wilbur[2]

1974–75

Equus, Peter Shaffer

The Taking of Miss Janie, Ed Bullins[16]

A Chorus Line, James Kirkwood and Nicholas Dante[2]

1975–76

Travesties, Tom Stoppard

Streamers, David Rabe[16]

Pacific Overtures, Stephen Sondheim, John Weidman, and Hugh Wheeler[2]

1976–77

Otherwise Engaged, Simon Gray

American Buffalo, David Mamet[16]

Annie, Thomas Meehan, Charles Strouse, and Martin Charnin[2]

1977–78

Da, Hugh Leonard

Ain't Misbehavin', conceived by Richard Maltby, Jr.[2]

1978–79

The Elephant Man, Bernard Pomerance

Sweeney Todd, Hugh Wheeler and Stephen Sondheim[2]

1979–80

Talley's Folly, Lanford Wilson

Evita,[2] Andrew Lloyd Webber and Tim Rice

Betrayal, Harold Pinter[1]

1980–81

A Lesson From Aloes, Athol Fugard

Crimes of the Heart, Beth Henley[16]

1981–82

The Life and Adventures of Nicholas Nickleby, adapted by David Edgar

A Soldier's Play, Charles Fuller[16]

1. Citation for best foreign play. 2. Citation for best musical. 3. Based on a novel by Arthur Koestler. 4. Based on Christopher Isherwood's *Berlin Stories*. 5. For "distinguished and original contribution to the theater." 6. Based on Sidney Howard's *They Knew What They Wanted*. 7. Based on a novel by Thomas Wolfe. 8. Based on James Agee's *A Death in the Family*. 9. Based on a book by Shepherd Mead. 10. Special citation. 11. Based on Thornton Wilder's *The Matchmaker*. 12. Translated by Edith Hamilton. 13. Based on Sholem Aleichem's Tevye stories, translated by Arnold Perl. 14. Based on John Van Druten's *I Am a Camera*, which won the award for the best play in 1951–52. 15. Based on Brendan Behan's autobiography. 16. Citation for best American play.

Major American Book Awards, 1982

Established by Association of American Publishers

Fiction: *Rabbit Is Rich*, by John Updike (Alfred A. Knopf)

First novel: *Dale Loves Sophie to Death*, by Robb Forman Dew (Farrar, Straus & Giroux)

General nonfiction: *The Soul of a New Machine*, by Tracy Kidder (Atlantic/Little, Brown)

Biography/Autobiography: *Mornings on Horseback*, by David McCullough (Simon & Schuster)

History: *People of the Sacred Mountain*, by the Rev. Peter John Powell (Harper & Row)

Science: *Lucy*, by Donald Johanson and Maitland Edey (Simon & Schuster)

Poetry: *Life Supports*, by William Bronk (North Point Press)

Translation: Robert Lyons Danly for *In the Shade of Spring Leaves* (Yale University Press) and Ian Hideo Levy for *The Ten Thousand Leaves* (Princeton University Press)

Children's fiction: *Westmark*, by Lloyd Alexander (E. P. Dutton)

Children's nonfiction: *A Penguin Year*, by Susan Bonners (Delacorte)

Picture book: *Outside Over There*, by Maurice Sendak (Harper & Row)

Book design, pictorial: Susan Mitchell for *Nicaragua*, by Susan Meiselas (Pantheon)

Book design, typographical: Betty Anderson for *Edith Sitwell*, by Victoria Glendinning (Alfred A. Knopf)

Book illustration, collected art: Bill Katz for *The World of Donald Evans*, by Willy Eisenhart (Harlin Quist)

Book illustration, original art: Chris Van Allsburg for *Jumanji* (Houghton Mifflin)

Book illustration, photographs: Deborah Turbeville for *Unseen Versailles* (Doubleday)

Cover design, mass market: Milton Charles for *The Best of John Sladek* (Pocket Books)

Cover design, trade: Fred Marcellino for *African Stories*, by Doris Lessing (Simon & Schuster)

Jacket design: Janet Odgis for *Remembrance of Things Past*, by Marcel Proust (Random House)

National Medal for Literature: John Cheever

Enrico Fermi Award

Named in honor of Enrico Fermi, the atomic pioneer, the $25,000 award is given in recognition of "exceptional and altogether outstanding" scientific and technical achievement in atomic energy.

1954	Enrico Fermi
1956	John von Neumann
1957	Ernest O. Lawrence
1958	Eugene P. Wigner
1959	Glenn T. Seaborg
1961	Hans A. Bethe
1962	Edward Teller
1963	J. Robert Oppenheimer
1964	Hyman G. Rickover
1966	Otto Hahn, Lise Meitner, and Fritz Strassman
1968	John A. Wheeler
1969	Walter H. Zinn
1970	Norris E. Bradbury
1971	Shields Warren and Stafford L. Warren
1972	Manson Benedict
1976	William L. Russell
1978	Harold M. Agnew and Wolfgang K.H. Panofsky
1980	Alvin M. Weinberg and Rudolf E. Peirls
1982	W. Bennett Lewis

Presidential Medal of Freedom

The nation's highest civilian award, the Presidential Medal of Freedom, was established in 1963 by President John F. Kennedy to continue and expand Presidential recognition of meritorious service which, since 1945, had been granted as the Medal of Freedom. Kennedy selected the first recipients, but was assassinated before he could make the presentations. They were made by President Johnson. NOTE: An asterisk following a year denotes a posthumous award.

SELECTED BY PRESIDENT KENNEDY

Marian Anderson (contralto)	1963
Ralph J. Bunche (statesman)	1963
Ellsworth Bunker (diplomat)	1963
Pablo Casals (cellist)	1963
Genevieve Caulfield (educator)	1963
James B. Conant (educator)	1963
John F. Enders (bacteriologist)	1963
Felix Frankfurter (jurist)	1963
Karl Horton (youth authority)	1963
Robert J. Kiphuth (athletic director)	1963
Edwin H. Land (inventor)	1963
Herbert H. Lehman (statesman)	1963*
Robert A. Lovett (statesman)	1963
J. Clifford MacDonald (educator)	1963*
John J. McCloy (banker and statesman)	1963
George Meany (labor leader)	1963
Alexander Meiklejohn (philosopher)	1963
Ludwig Mies van der Rohe (architect)	1963
Jean Monnet (European statesman)	1963
Luis Muñoz-Marín (Governor of Puerto Rico)	1963
Clarence B. Randall (industrialist)	1963
Rudolf Serkin (pianist)	1963
Edward Steichen (photographer)	1963
George W. Taylor (educator)	1963
Alan T. Waterman (scientist)	1963
Mark S. Watson (journalist)	1963
Annie D. Wauneka (public health worker)	1963
E. B. White (author)	1963
Thornton N. Wilder (author)	1963
Edmund Wilson (author and critic)	1963
Andrew Wyeth (artist)	1963

AWARDED BY PRESIDENT JOHNSON

Dean G. Acheson (statesman)	1964
Eugene R. Black (banker)	1969
Detlev W. Bronk (neurophysiologist)	1964
McGeorge Bundy (government service)	1969
Ellsworth Bunker (diplomat)	1968
Clark Clifford (statesman)	1969
Aaron Copland (composer)	1964
Michael E. DeBakey (surgeon)	1969
Willem de Kooning (artist)	1964
Walt Disney (cartoon film producer)	1964
J. Frank Dobie (author)	1964
David Dubinsky (labor leader)	1969
Lena F. Edwards (physician and humanitarian)	1964
Thomas Stearns Eliot (poet)	1964
Ralph Ellison (author)	1969
Lynn Fontanne (actress)	1964
Henry Ford II (industrialist)	1969
John W. Gardner (educator)	1964
W. Averell Harriman (statesman)	1969
Rev. Theodore M. Hesburgh (educator)	1964
Bob Hope (comedian)	1969
John XXIII (Pope)	1963*
Clarence L. Johnson (aircraft engineer)	1964
Edgar F. Kaiser (industrialist)	1969
Frederick R. Kappel (telecommunications executive)	1964
Helen A. Keller (educator)	1964
John Fitzgerald Kennedy (U.S. President)	1963*
Robert W. Komer (government service)	1968
Mary Lasker (philanthropist)	1969
John L. Lewis (labor leader)	1964
Walter Lippmann (journalist)	1964
Eugene M. Locke (diplomat)	1968
Alfred Lunt (actor)	1964
John W. Macy, Jr. (government service)	1969
Ralph McGill (journalist)	1964
Robert S. McNamara (government service)	1968
Samuel Eliot Morison (historian)	1964
Lewis Mumford (urban planner and critic)	1964
Edward R. Murrow (radio-TV commentator)	1964
Reinhold Niebuhr (theologian)	1964
Gregory Peck (actor)	1969
Leontyne Price (soprano)	1964
A. Philip Randolph (labor leader)	1964
Laurance S. Rockefeller (conservationist)	1969
Walt Whitman Rostow (government service)	1969
Deak Rusk (statesman)	1969
Carl Sandburg (poet and biographer)	1964
Merriman Smith (journalist)	1969
John Steinbeck (author)	1964
Helen B. Taussig (pediatrician)	1964
Cyrus R. Vance (government service)	1969
Carl Vinson (legislator)	1964
Thomas J. Watson, Jr. (industrialist)	1964
James E. Webb (NASA administrator)	1968
Paul Dudley White (physician)	1964
William S. White (journalist)	1969
Roy Wilkins (social welfare executive)	1969
Whitney M. Young, Jr. (social welfare executive)	1969

AWARDED BY PRESIDENT NIXON

Edwin E. Aldrin (astronaut)	1969
Apollo 13 Mission Operations Team	1970
Neil A. Armstrong (astronaut)	1969
Earl Charles Behrens (journalist)	1970
Manlio Brosio (NATO secretary general)	1971
Michael Collins (astronaut)	1969
Edward K. "Duke" Ellington (musician)	1969
Edward T. Folliard (journalist)	1970
John Ford (film director)	1973
Samuel Goldwyn (film producer)	1971
Fred Wallace Haise, Jr. (astronaut)	1970
William M. Henry (journalist)	1970*
Paul G. Hoffman (statesman)	1974
William J. Hopkins (White House service)	1971
Arthur Krock (journalist)	1970
Melvin R. Laird (government service)	1974
David Lawrence (journalist)	1970
George Gould Lincoln (journalist)	1970
James A. Lovell, Jr. (astronaut)	1970
Dr. Charles L. Lowman (orthopedist)	1974
Raymond Moley (journalist)	1970
Eugene Ormandy (conductor)	1970
William P. Rogers (diplomat)	1973
Adela Rogers St. Johns (journalist)	1970
John Leonard Swigert, Jr. (astronaut)	1970
John Paul Vann (adviser, Vietnam war)	1972*
DeWitt and Lila Wallace (founders, *Reader's Digest*)	1972

AWARDED BY PRESIDENT FORD

I. W. Abel (labor leader)	1977
John Bardeen (physicist)	1977
Irving Berlin (composer)	1977
Norman Borlaug (agricultural scientist)	1977
Omar N. Bradley (national security)	1977
David K. E. Bruce (diplomat)	1976
Arleigh Burke (national security)	1977
Alexander Calder (sculptor)	1977*
Bruce Catton (historian)	1977
Joseph P. DiMaggio (baseball star)	1977
Ariel Durant (author)	1977

Will Durant (author)	1977
Arthur Fiedler (conductor)	1977
Henry J. Friendly (jurist)	1977
Martha Graham (dancer-choreographer)	1976
Claudia "Lady Bird" Johnson (service to U.S. scenic beauty)	1977
Henry A. Kissinger (statesman)	1977
Archibald MacLeish (poet)	1977
James A. Michener (author)	1977
Georgia O'Keeffe (artist)	1977
Jesse Owens (track champion)	1976
Nelson A. Rockefeller (government service)	1977
Norman Rockwell (illustrator)	1977
Arthur Rubinstein (pianist)	1976
Donald H. Rumsfeld (government service)	1977
Katherine Filene Shouse (service to the performing arts)	1977
Lowell Thomas (radio-TV commentator)	1977
James D. Watson (biochemist)	1977

AWARDED BY PRESIDENT CARTER

Ansel Adams (photographer)	1980
Horace M. Albright (government service)	1980
Roger Baldwin (civil libertarian)	1981
Harold Brown (government service)	1981
Zbigniew Brzezinski (government service)	1981
Rachel Carson (author)	1980*
Lucia Chase (ballet director)	1980
Warren M. Christopher (government service)	1981
Walter Cronkite (TV newscaster)	1981
Kirk Douglas (actor)	1981
Arthur J. Goldberg (government service)	1978
Hubert H. Humphrey (government service)	1980*
Archbishop Iakovos (churchman)	1980
Lyndon B. Johnson (U.S. President)	1980*
Rev. Dr. Martin Luther King, Jr. (civil rights leader)	1977*
Margaret Craig McNamara (educator)	1981
Margaret Mead (anthropologist)	1979*
Karl Menninger (psychiatrist)	1981
Clarence Mitchell, Jr. (civil rights leader)	1980
Edmund S. Muskie (government service)	1981
Esther Peterson (government service)	1981
Roger Tory Peterson (ornithologist)	1980
Adm. Hyman Rickover (national security)	1980
Jonas Salk (medical research)	1977
Beverly Sills (opera singer)	1980
Gerard C. Smith (government service)	1981
Robert S. Strauss (government service)	1981
Elbert Parr Tuttle (government service)	1981
Earl Warren (government service)	1981*
Robert Penn Warren (author and poet)	1980
John Wayne (actor)	1980*
Eudora Welty (author)	1980
Tennessee Williams (playwright)	1980
Andrew M. Young (government service)	1981

AWARDED BY PRESIDENT REAGAN

James H. (Eubie) Blake (composer-pianist)	1981
Ella T. Grasso (Connecticut Governor)	1981*
Philip C. Habib (diplomat)	1982
Bryce N. Harlow (government service)	1981
Walter H. Judd (government service)	1981
Morris I. Leibman (lawyer)	1981
Charles B. Thornton (industrialist)	1981

George Foster Peabody Awards for Broadcasting, 1981

Radio

WJR, Detroit: *Newsfile: A Bankrupt Court*
National Radio Theater, Chicago: *The Odyssey of Homer*
Canadian Broadcasting Corporation: *Carl Sandburg at Connemara*
Timothy and Susan Todd, Middlebury, Vt.: *The Todds' Teddy Bears Picnic*
WQDR-FM, Raleigh, N.C.: *Our Forgotten Warriors: Vietnam Veterans Face the Challenges of the 80's*

Television

Bill Leonard: CBS News
John Goldsmith: WDVM, Washington
NBC and MTM Enterprises: *Hill Street Blues*
Nebraska Educational Television Network and Great Amwell Company: *The Private History of a Campaign That Failed*
CBS and Alan Landsburg Productions: *Bill,* on *General Electric Theater*
Danny Kaye: *An Evening With Danny Kaye and the New York Philharmonic; Zubin Mehta, Music Director,* on PBS; and *Skokie,* on CBS
WNET, New York, and PBS: *Dance in America: Nureyev and the Joffrey Ballet/In Tribute to Nijinsky*
KJRH, Tulsa, Okla.: *Project: China*
Home Box Office and Ms. Magazine: *She's Nobody's Baby: The History of American Women in the 20th Century*
Société Radio-Canada, Montreal: *Klimbo: Le lion et la souris (The Lion and the Mouse)*
ABC and T.A.T. Communications: *The Wave,* on *ABC Theater for Young Americans*
WSMV, Nashville, Tenn.: Series of documentaries including *Crime's Children, Hot Cars, Cold Cash, Split Second Justice,* and *Crime's Carousel*
KATU, Portland, Ore.: Series of documentaries including *Ready on the Firing Line, Out of the Ashes,* and *To Begin Again . . .*
WGBH, Boston, and Granada TV, London: *The Red Army*
Eighth Decade Consortium, Seattle: *Fed Up With Fear*
ABC News: *Viewpoint, Nightline,* and *America Held Hostage: The Secret Negotiations,* with special mention of Ted Koppel
KTEH, San Jose, Calif.: *The Day After Trinity: J. Robert Oppenheimer and the Atomic Bomb*
WLS, Chicago: *Eyewitness News*

Poets Laureate of England

Edmund Spenser	1591–1599
Samuel Daniel	1599–1619
Ben Jonson	1619–1637
William Davenant	1638–1668
John Dryden[1]	1670–1689
Thomas Shadwell	1689–1692
Nahum Tate	1692–1715
Nicholas Rowe	1715–1718
Laurence Eusden	1718–1730
Colley Cibber	1730–1757
William Whitehead	1757–1785
Thomas Warton	1785–1790
Henry James Pye	1790–1813
Robert Southey	1813–1843
William Wordsworth	1843–1850
Alfred Lord Tennyson	1850–1892
Alfred Austin	1896–1913
Robert Bridges	1913–1930
John Masefield	1930–1967
C. Day Lewis	1967–1972
Sir John Betjeman	1972–

1. First to bear the title officially. *Source: Encyclopaedia Britannica.*

Winners of Bollingen Prize in Poetry

($5,000 award is given biennially. It is administered by Yale University and the Bollingen Foundation.)

1949	Ezra Pound
1950	Wallace Stevens
1951	John Crowe Ransom
1952	Marianne Moore
1953	Archibald MacLeish and William Carlos Williams
1954	W. H. Auden
1955	Léonie Adams and Louise Bogan
1956	Conrad Aiken
1957	Allen Tate
1958	E.E. Cummings
1959	Theodore Roethke
1960	Delmore Schwartz
1961	Yvor Winters
1962	John Hall Wheelock and Richard Eberhart
1963	Robert Frost
1965	Horace Gregory
1967	Robert Penn Warren
1969	John Berryman and Karl Shapiro
1971	Richard Wilbur and Mona Van Duyn
1973	James Merrill
1975	Archie Randolph Ammons
1977	David Ignatow
1979	W. S. Merwin
1981	Howard Nemerov and May Swenson

Templeton Foundation Prize for Progress in Religion

Billy Graham, the elder statesman of modern-day evangelists, is the second American to be awarded the Templeton Prize. The $200,000 prize, the largest in the world, was presented May 11, 1982, in London. Mr. Graham indicated that the money would be used for world relief, the education of Third World seminary students, and the evangelical movement in Britain.

The prize, which was inaugurated in 1972 and first presented in 1973, was founded by John M. Templeton, a financial analyst and Presbyterian layman, to honor a person whose work is of pioneering nature and is likely to result in a new and better understanding of God. The first American recipient of the prize was Dr. Ralph Wendell Burhoe, a Chicago scientist and theologian, in 1980.

Prior recipients:

1973 Mother Teresa of Calcutta, founder of the Missionaries of Charity

1974 Brother Roger, Founder and Prior of the Taize Community in France

1975 Dr. Sarvepalli Radhakrishnan, former President of India and Oxford Professor of Eastern Religions and Ethics

1976 H.E. Leon Joseph Cardinal Suenes, Archbishop of Malines-Brussels

1977 Chiara Lubich, Founder of the Focolare Movement, Italy

1978 Prof. Thomas F. Torrence, Edinburgh University

1979 Nikkyo Niwano, The Rissho Kosei-Kai Movement, Japan

For 1982 Emmy Awards see Current Events page 47

Longest Broadway Runs[1]

1. Grease (M) (1972–80)	3,388
2. Fiddler on the Roof (M) (1964–72)	3,242
3. Life With Father (1939–47)	3,224
4. Tobacco Road (1933–41)	3,182
5. A Chorus Line (M) (1974–)	2,976
6. Hello, Dolly! (M) (1964–71)	2,844
7. My Fair Lady (M) (1956–62)	2,717
8. Oh! Calcutta! (M) (1976–) (revival)	2,539
9. Man of La Mancha (M) (1965–71)	2,329
10. Abie's Irish Rose (1922–27)	2,327
11. Annie (M) (1977–)	2,272
12. Oklahoma! (M) (1943–48)	2,212
13. South Pacific (M) (1949–54)	1,925
14. The Magic Show (M) (1974–78)	1,920
15. Pippin (M) (1971–77)	1,908
16. Gemini (1977–81)	1,819
17. Deathtrap (1978–1982)	1,793
18. Harvey (1944–49)	1,775
19. Dancin' (M) (1978–82)	1,774
20. Hair (M) (1968–72)	1,742
21. The Wiz (M) (1975–79)	1,672
22. Born Yesterday (1946–49)	1,642
23. Ain't Misbehavin' (M) (1978–82)	1,604
24. The Best Little Whorehouse in Texas (M) (1978–82)	1,584
25. Mary, Mary (1961–64)	1,572

1. As of Oct. 3, 1982. M = musical. Years are those of opening and closing. *Source: Variety.*

Labors of Hercules

Hercules, hero and strong man, was the son of Zeus and Alcmene. He performed twelve labors or deeds to be free from bondage under Eurystheus. After his death, he became immortal. His twelve mythological labors were: (1) killing the Nemean Lion; (2) killing the Lernaean Hydra; (3) capturing the Cerynean Stag; (4) capturing the Erymanthian Boar; (5) cleaning the Augean Stables; (6) killing the Stymphalian Birds; (7) capturing the Cretan Bull; (8) capturing the Mares of Diomedes; (9) procuring the Girdle of Hippolyta; (10) capturing the Cattle of Geryon; (11) procuring the golden Apples of Hesperides; (12) bringing Cerberus up from Hades.

NOTE: List varies but the 12 given here represent widely accepted tradition.

PEOPLE

Many public figures not listed here may be found elsewhere in the *Information Please Almanac.*

A name in parentheses is the original name or form of name. Localities are places of birth. Dates of birth appear as month/day/year. **Boldface** years in parentheses are dates of **(birth-death).**
Information has been gathered from many sources, including the individuals themselves. However, the *Information Please Almanac* cannot guarantee the accuracy of every individual item.

A

Aalto, Alvar (architect); Kuortane, Finland **(1898–1976)**
Abbott, Bud (William) (comedian); Asbury Park, N.J. **(1898–1974)**
Abbott, George (stage producer); Forestville, N.Y., 6/25/1887
Abel, Walter (actor); St. Paul, 6/6/1898
Abernathy, Ralph (civil rights leader); Linden, Ala., 3/11/1926
Acheson, Dean (statesman); Middletown, Conn. **(1893–1971)**
Acuff, Roy Claxton (musician); nr. Maynardsville, Tenn. 9/15/1903
Adams, Charles Francis (diplomat); Boston **(1807–1886)**
Adams, Don (actor); New York City, 4/19/1927
Adams, Edie (actress); Kingston, Pa., 4/16/1929
Adams, Franklin Pierce (columnist and author); Chicago **(1881–1960)**
Adams, Henry Brooks (historian); Boston **(1838–1918)**
Adams, Joey (comedian); New York City, 1/6/1911
Adams, Maude (Maude Kiskadden) (actress); Salt Lake City, **(1872–1953)**
Adams, Samuel (American Revolutionary patriot); Boston **(1722–1803)**
Adamson, Joy (naturalist); Troppau, Silesia **(1910–1980)**
Addams, Charles (cartoonist); Westfield, N.J., 1/7/1912
Addams, Jane (social worker); Cedarville, Ill. **(1860–1935)**
Adderley, Julian "Cannonball" (jazz saxophonist); Tampa, Fla. **(1928–1975)**
Ade, George (humorist); Kentland, Ind. **(1866–1944)**
Adenauer, Konrad (statesman); Cologne, Germany **(1876–1967)**
Adler, Alfred (psychoanalyst); Vienna **(1870–1937)**
Adler, Larry (musician); Baltimore, 2/10/1914
Adler, Richard (songwriter); New York City, 8/3/1921
Adoree, Renée (Renée La Fonte) (actress); Lille, France **(1898–1933)**
Aeschylus (dramatist); Eleusis (Greece) **(525–456 B.C.)**
Aesop (fabulist); birthplace unknown **(lived c. 600 B.C.)**
Aherne, Brian (actor); King's Norton, England, 5/2/1902
Aiken, Conrad (poet); Savannah, Ga. **(1889–1973)**
Ailey, Alvin (choreographer); Rogers, Tex., 1/5/1931
Albanese, Licia (operatic soprano); Bari, Italy, 7/22/1913
Albee, Edward (playwright); Washington, D.C., 3/12/1928
Albers, Josef (painter); Bottrop, Germany **(1888–1976)**
Albert, Eddie (Edward Albert Heimberger) (actor); Rock Island, Ill., 4/22/1908
Albertson, Jack (actor); Malden, Mass., 6/16/1910(?)
Albright, Lola (actress); Akron, Ohio, 7/20/1925
Alcott, Louisa May (novelist); Germantown, Pa. **(1832–1888)**
Alda, Alan (actor); New York City, 1/28/1936
Alda, Robert (Alphonso d'Abruzzo) (actor); New York City, 2/26/1914
Alden, John (American Pilgrim); England **(1599?–1687)**
Alexander the Great (monarch and conqueror); Pella, Macedonia (now Greece) **(356–323 B.C.)**
Alger, Horatio (author); Revere, Mass. **(1834–1899)**
Algren, Nelson (novelist); Detroit **(1909–1981)**
Allen, Ethan (American Revolutionary soldier); Litchfield, Conn. **(1738–1789)**
Allen, Fred (John Florence Sullivan) (comedian); Cambridge, Mass. **(1894–1956)**
Allen, Gracie (Grace Ethel Cecile Rosalie Allen) (comedienne); San Francisco **(1906–1964)**
Allen, Mel (Melvin Israel) (sportscaster); Birmingham, Ala., 2/14/1913
Allen, Steve (TV entertainer); New York City, 12/26/1921
Allen, Woody (Allen Stewart Konigsberg) (actor, writer, and director); Brooklyn, N.Y., 12/1/1935
Allison, Fran (actress); LaPorte City, Iowa, 1924(?)
Allman, Gregg (singer); Nashville, Tenn., 12/8/1947
Allyson, June (Jan Allyson) (actress); New York City, 10/7/1923
Alonso, Alicia (ballerina); Havana, 12/21/1921(?)
Alpert, Herb (band leader); Los Angeles, 3/31/1935(?)
Alsop, Joseph W., Jr. (journalist); Avon, Conn., 10/11/1910
Alsop, Stewart (journalist); Avon, Conn. **(1914–1974)**
Altman, Robert (film director); Kansas City, Mo., 2/20/1925
Ambler, Eric (suspense writer); London, 6/28/1909
Ameche, Don (Dominic Amici) (actor); Kenosha, Wis., 5/31/1908
Amis, Kingsley (novelist); London, 4/16/1922
Amory, Cleveland (writer and conservationist); Nahant, Mass., 9/2/1917
Amos (Freeman F. Gosden) (radio comedian); Richmond, Va., 5/5/1899
Amsterdam, Morey (actor); Chicago, 12/14/1914
Andersen, Hans Christian (author of fairy-tales); Odense, Denmark **(1805–1875)**
Anderson, Eddie. *See* Rochester
Anderson, Jack (journalist); Long Beach, Calif., 10/19/1922
Anderson, Dame Judith (actress); Adelaide, Australia, 2/10/1898
Anderson, Lindsay (Gordon) (director); Bangalore, India, 4/17/1923
Anderson, Lynn (singer); Grand Forks, N.D., 9/26/1947
Anderson, Marian (contralto); Philadelphia, 2/17/1902
Anderson, Maxwell (dramatist); Atlantic, Pa. **(1888–1959)**
Anderson, Robert (playwright); New York City, 4/28/1917
Andersson, Bibi (actress); Stockholm, 11/11/1935
Andress, Ursula (actress); Switzerland, 3/19/1938
Andrews, Dana (actor); Collins, Miss., 1/1/1909
Andrews, Julie (Julia Wells) (actress and singer); Walton-on-Thames, England, 10/1/1935
Andrews, La Verne (singer); Minneapolis **(1916–1967)**
Andrews, Maxene (singer); Minneapolis, 1/3/1918
Andrews, Patti (singer); Minneapolis, 2/16/1920
Andy (Charles J. Correll) (radio comedian); Peoria, Ill. **(1890–1972)**
Angeles, Victoria de los (Victoria Gamez Cima) (operatic soprano); Barcelona, 11/1/1924
Anka, Paul (singer and composer); Ottawa, 7/30/1941
Ann-Margret (Ann-Margret Olsson) (actress); Valsjobyn, Sweden, 4/28/1941
Annabella (actress); Paris, 1912
Anouilh, Jean (playwright); Bordeaux, France, 6/23/1910
Anthony, Susan Brownell (woman suffragist); Adams, Mass. **(1820–1906)**
Antonioni, Michelangelo (director); Ferrara, Italy, 9/29/1912
Antony, Mark (Marcus Antonius) (statesman); Rome **(83?–30 B.C.)**
Anuszkiewicz, Richard (painter); Erie, Pa., 5/23/1930
Aquinas, St. Thomas (philosopher); nr. Aquino (Italy) **(1225? –1274)**
Arbuckle, Roscoe "Fatty" (actor and director); San Jose, Calif. **(1887–1933)**
Archimedes (physicist and mathematician); Syracuse, Sicily **(287?–212 B.C.)**
Archipenko, Alexandre (sculptor); Kiev, Russia **(1887–1964)**
Arden, Elizabeth (Florence Nightingale Graham) (cosmetics executive); Woodbridge, Canada **(1891–1966)**
Arden, Eve (Eunice Quedens) (actress); Mill Valley, Calif., 4/30/1912
Arendt, Hannah (historian); Hannover, Germany **(1906–1975)**
Aristophanes (dramatist); Athens **448?–380 B.C.)**
Aristotle (philosopher); Stagirus, Macedonia **(384–322 B.C.)**
Arkin, Alan (actor and director); New York City, 3/26/1934
Arledge, Roone (TV executive); Forest Hills, N.Y., 7/8/1931
Arlen, Harold (Hyman Arluck) (composer); Buffalo, N.Y., 2/15/1905
Arlen, Richard (actor); Charlottesville, Va. **(1900–1976)**
Arliss, George (actor); London **(1868–1946)**
Armstrong, Louis ("Satchmo") (musician); New Orleans **(1900–1971)**
Armstrong-Jones, Anthony. *See* Snowden, Earl of
Arnaz, Desi (Desiderio) (actor and producer); Santiago, Cuba, 3/2/1917
Arness, James (James Aurness) (TV actor); Minneapolis, 5/26/1923
Arno, Peter (cartoonist); New York City **(1904–1968)**
Arnold, Benedict (American Revolutionary War General, convicted of treason); Norwich, Conn. **(1741–1801)**
Arnold, Eddy (singer); Henderson, Tenn., 5/15/1918

Arnold, Edward (actor); New York City **(1890–1956)**
Arnold, Matthew (poet and critic); Laleham, England **(1822–1888)**
Arp, Jean (sculptor and painter); Strasbourg (France) **(1887–1966)**
Arquette, Cliff ("Charley Weaver") (actor); Toledo, Ohio **(1905–1974)**
Arrau, Claudio (pianist); Chillán, Chile, 2/6/1903
Arthur, Bea (Bernice Frankel) (actress); New York City, 5/13/1926(?)
Arthur, Jean (Gladys Greene) (actress); New York City, 10/17/1905
Asch, Sholem (novelist); Kutno, Poland **(1880–1957)**
Ashkenazy, Vladimir (concert pianist); Gorki, U.S.S.R., 7/6/1937
Ashley, Elizabeth (actress); Ocala, Fla., 8/30/1939
Ashton, Sir Frederick William Mallandaine (choreographer); Guayaquil, Ecuador, 9/17/1904
Asimov, Isaac (author); Petrovichi, Russia, 1/2/1920
Asner, Edward (actor); Kansas City, Mo., 11/15/1929
Astaire, Fred (Frederick Austerlitz) (dancer and actor); Omaha, Neb., 5/10/1899
Astor, John Jacob (financier); Waldorf (Germany) **(1763–1848)**
Astor, Mary (Lucile Langhanke) (actress); Quincy, Ill., 5/3/1906
Atkins, Chet (guitarist); nr. Luttrell, Tenn., 6/20/1924
Atkinson, Brooks (drama critic); Melrose, Mass., 11/28/1894
Attenborough, Richard (actor); Cambridge, England, 8/29/1923
Attila (King of Huns, called "Scourge of God") **(406?–453)**
Attlee, Clement Richard (statesman); London **(1883–1967)**
Auchincloss, Louis (author); Lawrence, N.Y., 9/27/1917
Auden, W(ystan) H(ugh) (poet); York, England **(1907–1973)**
Audubon, John James (naturalist and painter); Haiti **(1785–1851)**
Auer, Leopold (violinist and teacher); Veszprém, Hungary **(1845–1930)**
Auer, Mischa (actor); St. Petersburg, Russia **(1905–1967)**
Augustine, Saint (Aurelius Augustinus) (philosopher); Numidia (Algeria) **(354–430)**
Augustus (Gaius Octavius) (Roman emperor); Rome **(63 B.C.–A.D. 14)**
Aumont, Jean-Pierre (actor); Paris, 1/5/1913
Austen, Jane (novelist); Steventon, England **(1775–1817)**
Autry, Gene (singer and actor); Tioga, Tex., 9/29/1907
Avalon, Frankie (singer); Philadelphia, 9/18/1940
Avedon, Richard (photographer); New York City, 5/15/1923
Avery, Milton (painter); Altmar, N.Y. **(1893–1965)**
Axelrod, George (playwright); New York City, 6/9/1922
Ayckbourn Alan (playwright); London, 4/12/1939
Ayres, Lew (actor); Minneapolis, 12/28/1908

B

Bacall, Lauren (Betty Joan Perske) (actress); New York City, 9/16/1924
Bach, Johann Sebastian (composer); Eisenach (Germany) **(1685–1750)**
Bacharach, Burt (songwriter); Kansas City, Mo., 5/12/1929
Backus, Jim (actor); Cleveland, 2/25/1913
Bacon, Francis (painter); Dublin, 1910
Bacon, Francis (philosopher and essayist); London **(1561–1626)**
Bacon, Roger (philosopher and scientist); Ilchester, England **(1214?–1294)**
Baedeker, Karl (travel-guidebook publisher); Essen (Germany) **(1801–1859)**
Baez, Joan (folk singer); Staten Island, N.Y., 1/9/1941
Bagnold, Enid (novelist); Rochester, England **(1889–1981)**
Bailey, F. Lee (lawyer); Waltham, Mass., 6/10/1933
Bailey, Pearl (singer); Newport News, Va., 3/29/1918
Bainter, Fay (actress); Los Angeles **(1891–1968)**
Baird, Bil (William B.) (puppeteer); Grand Island, Neb., 8/15/1904
Baker, Carroll (actress); Johnstown, Pa., 5/28/1931
Baker, Josephine (singer and dancer); St. Louis **(1906–1975)**
Baker, Kenny (singer and actor); Monrovia, Calif., 9/30/1912
Baker, Russell (columnist); Loudoun County, Va., 8/14/1925
Balanchine, George (choreographer); St. Petersburg, Russia, 1/9/1904
Balboa, Vasco Nuñez de (explorer); Jerez de los Caballeros (Spain) **(1475–1517)**
Baldwin, Faith (novelist); New Rochelle, N.Y. **(1893–1978)**
Baldwin, James (novelist); New York City, 8/2/1924
Balenciaga, Cristóbal (fashion designer); Guetaria, Spain **(1895–1972)**
Ball, Lucille (Dianne Belmont) (actress and producer); Celoron (nr. Jamestown), N.Y., 8/6/1911
Ballard, Kaye (Catherine Gloria Balotta) (actress); Cleveland, 11/20/1926
Balmain, Pierre (fashion designer); St.-Jean-de-Maurienne, France **(1914–1982)**
Balsam, Martin (actor); New York City, 11/4/1919
Balzac, Honoré de (novelist); Tours, France **(1799–1850)**
Bancroft, Anne (Annemarie Italiano) (actress); New York City, 9/17/1931
Bancroft, George (actor); Philadelphia **(1882–1956)**
Bankhead, Tallulah (actress); Huntsville, Ala. **(1903–1968)**
Banneker, Benjamin (almanacker and mathematician-astronomer on District of Columbia site survey); Ellicott, Md. **(1731–1806)**
Bara, Theda (Theodosia Goodman) (actress); Cincinnati **(1890–1955)**
Barber, Red (Walter Lanier) (sportscaster); Columbus, Miss., 2/17/1908
Barber, Samuel (composer); West Chester, Pa. **(1910–1981)**
Bardot, Brigitte (actress); Paris, 1935
Barenboim, Daniel (concert pianist and conductor); Buenos Aires, 11/15/1942
Barnard, Christiaan N. (heart surgeon); Beauford West, South Africa, 1923
Barnum, Phineas Taylor (showman); Bethel, Conn. **(1810–1891)**
Barrie, Sir James Matthew (author); Kirriemuir, Scotland **(1860–1937)**
Barrie, Wendy (actress); Hong Kong **(1913–1978)**
Barry, Gene (Eugene Klass) (actor); New York City, 6/4/1922
Barry, John (naval officer); County Wexford, Ireland **(1745–1803)**
Barrymore, Diana (actress); New York City **(1921–1960)**
Barrymore, Ethel (Ethel Blythe) (actress); Philadelphia **(1879–1959)**
Barrymore, Georgiana Drew (actress); Philadelphia **(1856–1893)**
Barrymore, John (John Blythe) (actor); Philadelphia **(1882–1942)**
Barrymore, John, Jr. (John Drew Barrymore) (actor); Beverly Hills, Calif., 1932
Barrymore, Lionel (Lionel Blythe) (actor); Philadelphia **(1878–1954)**
Barrymore, Maurice (Herbert Blythe) (actor and playwright); Agra, India **(1847–1905)**
Barthelme, Donald (novelist); Philadelphia, 4/7/1931
Barthelmess, Richard (actor); New York City **(1897–1963)**
Bartholomew, Freddie (actor); London, 3/28/1924
Bartók, Béla (composer); Nagyszentmiklos (Romania) **(1881–1945)**
Barton, Clara (founder of American Red Cross); Oxford, Mass. **(1821–1912)**
Baruch, Bernard Mannes (statesman); Camden, S.C. **(1870–1965)**
Baryshnikov, Mikhail Nikolayevich (ballet dancer); Riga, Latvia, 1/27/1948
Basehart, Richard (actor); Zanesville, Ohio, 8/31/1919
Basie, Count (William) (band leader); Red Bank, N.J., 8/21/1904
Bassey, Shirley (singer); Cardiff, Wales, 1/8/1937
Batchelor, Clarence Daniel (political cartoonist); Osage City, Kan. **(1888–1977)**
Bates, Alan (actor); Allestree, England, 2/17/1934
Baudelaire, Charles Pierre (poet); Paris **(1821–1867)**
Baudouin (King); Palace of Laeken, Belgium, 9/7/1930
Baxter, Anne (actress); Michigan City, Ind., 5/7/1923
Baxter, Warner (actor); Columbus, Ohio **(1891–1951)**
Bean, Orson (Dallas Frederick Burrows) (actor); Burlington, Vt., 7/22/1928
Beardsley, Aubrey Vincent (illustrator); Brighton, England **(1872–1898)**
Beaton, Cecil (photographer and designer); London **(1904–1980)**
Beatty, Warren (actor and producer); Richmond, Va., 3/30/1937
Becket, Thomas à (Archbishop of Canterbury); London **(1118?–1170)**
Beckett, Samuel (playwright); Dublin, 4/13/1906
Beckmann, Max (painter); Leipzig, Germany **(1884–1950)**
Bede, Saint ("The Venerable Bede") (scholar); Monkwearmouth, England **(673–735)**
Beecham, Sir Thomas (conductor); St. Helens, England **(1879–1961)**
Beecher, Henry Ward (clergyman); Litchfield, Conn. **(1813–1887)**
Beerbohm, Sir Max (author); London **(1872–1956)**
Beery, Noah, Jr. (actor); New York City, 8/10/1916
Beery, Wallace (actor); Kansas City, Mo. **(1886–1949)**
Beethoven, Ludwig van (composer); Bonn (Germany) **(1770–1827)**
Begley, Ed (actor); Hartford, Conn. **(1901–1970)**
Belafonte, Harry (singer and actor); New York City, 3/1/1927
Belasco, David (dramatist and producer); San Francisco **(1854–1931)**
Bell, Alexander Graham (inventor); Edinburgh, Scotland **(1847–1922)**
Bellamy, Edward (author); Chicopee Falls, Mass. **(1850–1898)**
Bellamy, Ralph (actor); Chicago, 6/17/1904
Bellini, Giovanni (painter); Venice **(c.1430–1516)**
Bellow, Saul (novelist); Lachine, Quebec, Canada, 7/10/1915
Bellows, George Wesley (painter and lithographer); Columbus, Ohio **(1882–1925)**
Belmondo, Jean-Paul (actor); Neuilly-sur-Seine, France, 4/9/1933
Belushi, John (comedian, actor); Chicago **(1949–1982)**
Benchley, Peter Bradford (novelist); New York City, 5/8/1940
Benchley, Robert Charles (humorist); Worcester, Mass. **(1889–1945)**
Bendix, William (actor); New York City **(1906–1964)**
Benes, Eduard (statesman); Kozlany (Czechoslovakia) **(1884–1948)**
Benét, Stephen Vincent (poet and story writer); Bethlehem, Pa. **(1898–1943)**
Benét, William Rose (poet and novelist); Ft. Hamilton, Brooklyn, N.Y. **(1886–1950)**
Ben-Gurion, David (David Green) (statesman); Plónsk (Poland) **(1886–1973)**
Benjamin, Richard (actor); New York City, 5/22/1938
Bennett, Constance (actress); New York City **(1905–1965)**
Bennett, Enoch Arnold (novelist and dramatist); Hanley, England **(1867–1931)**
Bennett, James Gordon (editor); Keith, Scotland **(1795–1872)**
Bennett, Joan (actress); Palisades, N.J., 2/27/1910
Bennett, Robert Russell (composer); Kansas City, Mo., **(1894–1981)**
Bennett, Tony (Anthony Benedetto) (singer); Astoria, Queens, N.Y., 8/3/1926

Benny, Jack (Benjamin Kubelsky) (comedian); Chicago **(1894–1974)**
Benton, Thomas Hart (painter); Neosho, Mo. **(1889–1975)**
Berg, Gertrude (writer and actress); New York City **(1899–1966)**
Bergen, Candice (actress); Beverly Hills, Calif., 5/9/1946
Bergen, Edgar (ventriloquist); Chicago, **(1903–1978)**
Bergen, Polly (actress and singer); Knoxville, Tenn., 7/14/1930
Bergman, Ingmar (film director); Uppsala, Sweden, 7/14/1918
Bergman, Ingrid (actress); Stockholm **(1918–1982)**
Berle, Milton (Milton Berlinger) (comedian); New York City, 7/12/1908
Berlin, Irving (Israel Baline) (songwriter); Temum, Russia, 5/11/1888
Berlioz, Louis Hector (composer); La Côte-Saint-André, France **(1803–1869)**
Berman, Lazar (concert pianist); Leningrad, 1930.
Berman, Shelley (Sheldon) (comedian); Chicago, 2/3/1926
Bernardi, Herschel (actor); New York City, 1923
Bernhardt, Sarah (Rosine Bernard) (actress); Paris **(1844–1923)**
Bernini, Gian Lorenzo (sculptor and painter); Naples (Italy) **(1598–1680)**
Bernstein, Leonard (conductor); Lawrence, Mass., 8/25/1918
Berry, Chuck (Charles Edward Berry) (singer); San Jose, Calif., 1/15/1926
Betjeman, Sir John (Poet Laureate); London, 8/28/1906
Bickford, Charles (actor); Cambridge, Mass. **(1889–1967)**
Bierce, Ambrose Gwinnett (journalist); Meigs County, Ohio **(1842–1914?)**
Bikel, Theodore (actor and folk singer); Vienna, 5/2/1924
Bing, Sir Rudolf (opera manager); Vienna, 1/9/1902
Bingham, George Caleb (painter); Augusta Co., Va. **(1811–1879)**
Bishop, Joey (Joseph Gottlieb) (comedian); New York City, 2/3/1919
Bismarck-Schönhausen, Prince Otto Eduard Leopold von (statesman); Schönhausen (Germany) **(1815–1898)**
Bisset, Jacqueline (actress); Weybridge, England, 9/13/1944
Bixby, Bill (actor); San Francisco, 1/22/1934
Bizet, Georges (Alexandre César Léopold Bizet) (composer); Paris **(1838–1875)**
Black, Cilla (singer and actress); Liverpool, England, 5/27/1943
Black, Karen (actress); Park Ridge, Ill., 7/1/1942
Black, Shirley Temple (former actress); Santa Monica, Calif., 4/23/1928
Blackman, Honor (actress); London, 8/22/1929
Blackmer, Sidney (actor); Salisbury, N.C. **(1898–1973)**
Blackstone, Sir William (jurist); London **(1723–1780)**
Blaine, Vivian (actress and singer); Newark, N.J., 11/21/1924
Blair, Janet (actress); Altoona, Pa., 4/23/1921
Blake, Amanda (Beverly Louise Neill) (actress); Buffalo, N.Y., 1931
Blake, Eubie (James Hubert) (pianist); Baltimore, 2/7/1883
Blake, Robert (Michael Gubitosi) (actor); Nutley, N.J., 9/18/1933
Blake, William (poet and artist); London **(1757–1827)**
Blanc, Mel(vin Jerome) (actor and voice specialist); San Francisco, 5/30/1908
Blass, Bill (fashion designer); Fort Wayne, Ind., 6/22/1922
Bloch, Ernest (composer); Geneva **(1880–1959)**
Blondell, Joan (actress); New York City **(1909–1979)**
Bloom, Claire (actress); London, 2/15/1931
Bloomgarden, Kermit (producer); Brooklyn, N.Y. **(1904–1976)**
Blue, Monte (actor); Indianapolis **(1890–1963)**
Blyth, Ann (actress); New York City, 8/16/1928
Boccaccio, Giovanni (author); Paris **(1313–1375)**
Boccioni, Umberto (painter and sculptor); Reggio di Calabria, Italy **(1882–1916)**
Bock, Jerry (composer); New Haven, Conn., 11/23/1928
Bogarde, Dirk (Derek Van den Bogaerde) (film actor and director); London, 3/28/1921
Bogart, Humphrey DeForest (actor); New York City **(1899–1957)**
Bogdanovich, Peter (producer and director); Kingston, N.Y., 7/30/1939
Bohlen, Charles E. (diplomat); Clayton, N.Y. **(1904–1974)**
Bohr, Niels (atomic physicist); Copenhagen **(1885–1962)**
Bolger, Ray (dancer and actor); Dorchester, Mass., 1/10/1904
Bolivar, Simón (South American liberator); Caracas, Venezuela **(1783–1830)**
Bologna, Giovanni da (sculptor); Douai (France) **(1529–1608)**
Bombeck, Erma (author, columnist); Dayton, Ohio 2/21/1927
Bonaparte, Napoleon (Emperor of the French); Ajaccio, Corsica (France) **(1769–1821)**
Bond, Julian (Georgia legislator); Nashville, Tenn., 1/14/1940
Bondi, Beulah (actress); Chicago **(1888–1981)**
Bonnard, Pierre (painter); Fontenayaux-Roses, France **(1867–1947)**
Bono, Sonny (Salvatore) (singer); Detroit, 2/16/1935
Boone, Daniel (frontiersman); nr. Reading, Pa. **(1734–1820)**
Boone, Pat (Charles) (singer); Jacksonville, Fla., 6/1/1934
Boone, Richard (actor); Los Angeles **(1917–1981)**
Booth, Edwin Thomas (actor); Bel Air, Md. **(1833–1893)**
Booth, Evangeline Cory (religious leader); London **(1865–1950)**
Booth, John Wilkes (actor; assassin of Lincoln); Harford County, Md. **(1838–1865)**
Booth, Shirley (Thelma Booth Ford) (actress); New York City, 8/30/1907
Bordoni, Irene (actress); Ajaccio (France) **(1895–1953)**
Borge, Victor (pianist and comedian); Copenhagen, 1/3/1909
Borgia, Cesare (nobleman and soldier); Rome **(1475?–1507)**
Borgia, Lucrezia (Duchess of Ferrara); Rome **(1480–1519)**
Borgnine, Ernest (actor); Hamden, Conn., 1/24/1917
Borromini, Francesco (architect); Bissone (Italy) **(1599–1667)**
Bosch, Hieronymus (Hieronymus van Aeken) (painter); Hertogenbosch (Netherlands) **(c.1450–1516)**
Bosley, Tom (actor); Chicago, 10/1/1927
Boswell, Connee (singer); New Orleans **(1907–1976)**
Boswell, James (diarist and biographer); Edinburgh, Scotland **(1740–1795)**
Botticelli, Sandro (Alessandro di Mariano dei Filipepi) (painter); Florence (Italy) **(1444?–1510)**
Boulez, Pierre (conductor); Montbrison, France, 3/26/1925
Bow, Clara (actress); Brooklyn, N.Y. **(1905–1965)**
Bowen, Catherine Drinker (biographer); Haverford, Pa. **(1897–1973)**
Bowie, David (David Robert Jones) (actor and musician), London, 1/8/1947(?)
Bowie, James (soldier); Burke County, Ga. **(1799–1836)**
Bowles, Chester (diplomat); Springfield, Mass., 4/5/1901
Boyd, Bill (William) ("Hopalong Cassidy") (actor); Cambridge, Ohio **(1898–1972)**
Boyd, Stephen (Stephen Millar) (actor); Belfast, Northern Ireland **(1928–1977)**
Boyer, Charles (actor); Figeac, France **(1899–1978)**
Bracken, Eddie (actor); Astoria, Queens, N.Y., 2/7/1920
Bradbury, Ray Douglas (science-fiction writer); Waukegan, Ill., 8/22/1920
Bradlee, Benjamin C. (editor), Boston, 8/26/1921
Bradley, Omar N. (5-star general); Clark, Mo. **(1893–1981)**
Bradley, Thomas (Mayor of Los Angeles); Calvert, Tex., 12/29/1917
Brady, Scott (actor); Brooklyn, N.Y., 9/13/1924
Brahms, Johannes (composer), Hamburg **(1833–1897)**
Braille, Louis (teacher of blind); Coupvray, France **(1809–1862)**
Brailowsky, Alexander (pianist); Kiev, Russia **(1896–1976)**
Bramante, Donato D'Agnolo (architect); Monte Asdrualdo (now Fermignano, Italy) **(1444–1514)**
Brancusi, Constantin (sculptor); Pestisansi, Romania **(1876–1957)**
Brando, Marlon (actor); Omaha, Neb., 4/3/1924
Brandt, Willy (Herbert Frahm) (ex-Chancellor); Lübeck, Germany, 12/18/1913
Braque, Georges (painter); Argenteuil, France **(1882–1963)**
Brazzi, Rossano (actor); Bologna, Italy, 9/18/1916
Brecht, Bertolt (dramatist and poet); Augsburg, Bavaria **(1898–1956)**
Brel, Jacques (singer and composer); Brussels, **(1929–1978)**
Brennan, Walter (actor); Lynn, Mass. **(1894–1974)**
Brent, George (actor); Dublin **(1904–1979)**
Breslin, Jimmy (journalist); Jamaica, Queens, N.Y., 10/17/1930
Breuer, Marcel (architect and designer); Pécs, Hungary **(1902–1981)**
Brewer, Teresa (singer); Toledo, Ohio, 5/7/1931
Brewster, Kingman, Jr. (ex-president of Yale); Longmeadow, Mass., 6/17/1919
Brezhnev, Leonid I. (Communist Party Secretary); Dneprodzerzhinsk, Ukraine, 12/19/1906
Brice, Fanny (Fannie Borach) (comedienne); New York City **(1892–1951)**
Bridges, Beau (actor); Los Angeles, 12/9/1941
Bridges, Lloyd (actor); San Leandro, Calif. 1/15/1913
Brinkley, David (TV newscaster); Wilmington, N.C., 7/10/1920
Britt, May (Maybritt Wilkins) (actress); Sweden, 3/22/1936
Britten, Benjamin (composer); Lowestoft, England **(1913–1976)**
Britton, Barbara (actress); Long Beach, Calif. **(1920–1980)**
Bromfield, Louis (novelist); Mansfield, Ohio **(1896–1956)**
Bronson, Charles (Charles Buchinsky) (actor); Ehrenfield, Pa., 11/3/1922(?)
Brontë, Charlotte (novelist); Thornton, England **(1816–1855)**
Brontë, Emily Jane (novelist); Thornton, England **(1818–1848)**
Bronzino, Agnolo (painter); Monticelli (Italy) **(1503–1572)**
Brook, Peter (director); London, 3/21/1925
Brooke, Rupert (poet); Rugby, England **(1887–1915)**
Brooks, Geraldine (Geraldine Stroock) (actress); New York City **(1925–1977)**
Brooks, Gwendolyn (poet); Topeka, Kan., 6/7/1917
Brooks, Mel (Melvin Kaminsky) (writer and film director); Brooklyn, N.Y., 1926(?)
Broun, Matthew Heywood Campbell (journalist); Brooklyn, N.Y. **(1888–1939)**
Brown, Helen Gurley (author); Green Forest, Ark., 2/18/1922
Brown, James (singer); Augusta, Ga., 5/3/1934
Brown, Joe E. (comedian); Holgate, Ohio **(1892–1973)**
Brown, John (abolitionist); Torrington, Conn. **(1800–1859)**
Brown, John Mason (critic); Louisville, Ky. **(1900–1969)**
Brown, Les (band leader); Reinerton, Pa., 1912
Brown, Pamela (actress); London **(1918–1975)**
Brown, Vanessa (Smylla Brind) (actress); Vienna, 3/24/1928
Browne, Jackson (singer and guitarist); Heidelberg, Germany, 10/9/late 1940s
Browning, Elizabeth Barrett (poet); Durham, England **(1806–1861)**
Browning, Robert (poet); London **(1812–1889)**

Brubeck, Dave (musician); Concord, Calif., 12/6/1920
Bruce, Lenny (comedian); Long Island, N.Y. **(1926–1966)**
Brueghel, Pieter (painter); nr. Breda, Flanders (Netherlands) **(1520?–1569)**
Bruhn, Erik (Belton Evers) (ballet dancer); Copenhagen, 10/3/1928
Brunelleschi, Filippo (architect); Florence (Italy) **(1377–1446)**
Brutus, Marcus Junius (Roman politician); **(85?–42 B.C.)**
Bryan, William Jennings (orator and politician); Salem, Ill. **(1860–1925)**
Bryant, Anita (singer); Barnsdall, Okla., 3/25/1940
Bryant, William Cullen (poet and editor); Cummington, Mass. **(1794–1878)**
Brynner, Yul (Taidje Khan) (actor); Sakhalin Island, Russia, 7/11/1920
Brzezinski, Zbigniew (ex-presidential adviser); Warsaw, 3/28/1928
Buber, Martin (philosopher and theologian); Vienna **(1878–1965)**
Buchanan, Edgar (actor); Humansville, Mo., **(1903–1979)**
Buchholz, Horst (actor); Berlin, 12/4/1933
Buchwald, Art (Arthur) (columnist); Mount Vernon, N.Y., 10/20/1925
Buck, Pearl S(ydenstricker) (author); Hillsboro, W. Va. **(1892–1973)**
Buckley, William F., Jr. (journalist); New York City, 11/24/1925
Buddha. *See* Gautama Buddha
Buffalo Bill (William Frederick Cody) (scout); Scott County, Iowa **(1846–1917)**
Bujold, Genevieve (actress); Montreal, 7/1/1942
Bujones, Fernando (ballet dancer); Miami, Fla., 3/9/1955
Bullins, Ed (playwright); Philadelphia, 7/2/1935
Bumbry, Grace (mezzo-soprano); St. Louis, 1/4/1937
Bunche, Ralph J. (statesman); Detroit **(1904–1971)**
Bundy, McGeorge (educator); Boston, 3/30/1919
Bundy, William Putnam (editor); Washington, D.C., 9/24/1917
Buñuel, Luis (film director); Calanda, Spain, 2/22/1900
Bunyan, John (preacher and author); Elstow, England **(1628–1688)**
Burbank, Luther (horticulturist); Lancaster, Mass. **(1849–1926)**
Burke, Adm. Arleigh A. (ex-Chief of Naval Operations); Boulder, Colo., 10/19/1901
Burke, Billie (comedienne); Washington, D.C. **(1885–1970)**
Burke, Edmund (statesman); Dublin **(1729–1797)**
Burne-Jones, Edward Coley (painter); Birmingham, England **(1833–1898)**
Burnett, Carol (comedienne); San Antonio, 4/26/1936
Burns, George (Nathan Birnbaum) (comedian); New York City, 1/20/1896
Burns, Robert (poet); Alloway, Scotland **(1759–1796)**
Burr, Aaron (political leader); Newark, N.J. **(1756–1836)**
Burr, Raymond (William Stacey Burr) (actor); New Westminster, British Columbia, Canada, 5/21/1917
Burroughs, Edgar Rice (novelist); Chicago **(1875–1950)**
Burrows, Abe (playwright and director); New York City, 12/18/1910
Burstyn, Ellen (Edna Rae Gillooly) (actress); Detroit, 12/7/1932
Burton, Richard (Richard Jenkins) (actor); Pontrhydfen, Wales, 11/10/1925
Bush, Vannevar (scientist); Everett, Mass. **(1890–1974)**
Bushman, Francis X. (actor); Baltimore **(1883–1966)**
Butler, Samuel (author); Langar, England **(1835–1902)**
Buttons, Red (Aaron Chwatt) (actor); New York City, 2/5/1919
Buzzi, Ruth (comedienne); Wequetequock, Conn., 7/24/1936
Byrd, Richard Evelyn (polar explorer); Winchester, Va. **(1888–1957)**
Byrne, Jane (Mayor of Chicago); Chicago, 5/24/1934
Byron, George Gordon (6th Baron Byron) (poet); London **(1788–1824)**

C

Caan, James (actor); The Bronx, N.Y., 3/26/1939
Cabot, John (Giovanni Caboto) (navigator); Genoa (?) **(1450–1498)**
Cabot, Sebastian (navigator); Venice **(1476?–1557)**
Cadmus, Paul (painter and etcher); New York City, 12/17/1904
Caesar, Gaius Julius (statesman); Rome **(100?–44 B.C.)**
Caesar, Sid (comedian); Yonkers, N.Y., 9/8/1922
Cagney, James (actor); New York City, 7/17/1899
Cahn, Sammy (songwriter); New York City, 6/18/1913
Caine, Michael (Maurice J. Micklewhite) (actor); London, 3/14/1933
Calder, Alexander (sculptor); Lawnton, Pa. **(1898–1976)**
Caldwell, Erskine (novelist); White Oak, Ga., 12/17/1903
Caldwell, Sarah (opera director and conductor); Maryville, Mo., 1928
Caldwell, Taylor (novelist); Manchester, England, 9/7/1900
Caldwell, Zoe (actress); Hawthorn, Australia, 9/14/1933
Calhern, Louis (Carl Henry Vogt) (actor); Brooklyn, N.Y. **(1895–1956)**
Calhoun, John Caldwell (statesman); nr. Calhoun Mills, S.C. **(1782–1850)**
Calisher, Hortense (novelist); New York City, 12/20/1911
Callas, Maria (Maria Calogeropoulos) (dramatic soprano); New York City **(1923–1977)**
Calloway, Cab (Cabell) (band leader); Rochester, N.Y., 12/25/1907
Calvet, Corinne (actress); Paris, 4/30/1926
Calvin, John (Jean Chauvin) (religious reformer); Noyon, Picardy **(1509–1564)**
Cambridge, Godfrey (comedian); New York City **(1933–1976)**
Cameron, Rod (Rod Cox) (actor); Calgary, Alberta, Canada, 12/7/1912
Campbell, Glen (singer); nr. Delight, Ark., 4/22/1938
Camus, Albert (author); Mondovi, Algeria **(1913–1960)**
Caniff, Milton (cartoonist); Hillsboro, Ohio, 2/28/1907
Cannon, Dyan (actress); Tacoma, Wash., 1/4/1937
Canova, Judy (comedienne); Jacksonville, Fla., 11/20/1916
Cantinflas (Mario Moreno) (comedian); Mexico City, 8/12/1911
Cantor, Eddie (Edward Iskowitz) (actor); New York City **(1892–1964)**
Cantrell, Lana (singer); Sydney, Australia, 1944
Capote, Truman (novelist); New Orleans, 9/30/1924
Capp, Al (Alfred Gerald Caplin) (cartoonist); New Haven, Conn. **(1909–1979)**
Capra, Frank (film producer, director); Palermo, Italy, 5/18/1897
Caravaggio, Michelangelo Merisi da (painter); Caravaggio (Italy) **(1573–1610)**
Cardin, Pierre (fashion designer); nr. Venice, 7/7/1922
Cardinale, Claudia (actress); Tunis, Tunisia, 1939
Carey, Harry (actor); New York City **(1878–1947)**
Carey, Macdonald (actor); Sioux City, Iowa, 3/15/1913
Carlisle, Kitty (singer and actress); New Orleans, 9/3/1915
Carlson, Richard (actor); Albert Lea, Minn., **(1912–1977)**
Carlyle, Thomas (essayist and historian); Ecclefechan, Scotland **(1795–1881)**
Carmichael, Hoagy (Hoagland Howard) (songwriter); Bloomington, Ind. **(1899–1981)**
Carne, Judy (Joyce Botterill) (singer): Northampton, England, 1939
Carnegie, Andrew (industrialist); Dunfermline, Scotland **(1835–1919)**
Carney, Art (actor); Mt. Vernon, N.Y., 11/4/1918
Carnovsky, Morris (actor); St. Louis, 9/5/1897
Caron, Leslie (actress); Paris, 7/1/1931
Carr, Vikki (singer); El Paso, 7/19/1942
Carracci, Annibale (painter); Bologna (Italy) **(1560–1609)**
Carracci, Lodovico (painter); Bologna (Italy) **(1555–1619)**
Carradine, David (actor); Hollywood, Calif., 12/8/1936
Carradine, John (actor); New York City, 2/5/1906
Carrillo, Leo (actor); Los Angeles **(1881–1961)**
Carroll, Diahann (Carol Diahann Johnson) (singer and actress); Bronx, N.Y., 7/17/1935
Carroll, Leo G. (actor); Weedon, England **(1892–1972)**
Carroll, Lewis (Charles Lutwidge Dodgson) (author and mathematician); Daresbury, England **(1832–1898)**
Carroll, Madeleine (actress); West Bromwich, England, 2/26/1909
Carroll, Pat (comedienne); Shreveport, La., 5/5/1927
Carson, Johnny (TV entertainer); Corning, Iowa, 10/23/1925
Carson, Kit (Christopher) (scout); Madison County, Ky. **(1809–1868)**
Carson, Rachel (biologist and author); Springdale, Pa. **(1907–1964)**
Carter, (Bessie) Lillian (President's mother); Richland, Ga., 8/15/1898
Carter, Jack (comedian); New York City, 1923
Cartier-Brisson, Henri (photographer); Chanteloup, France, 8/22/1908
Cartland, Barbara (author); England, 7/9/1901
Caruso, Enrico (Errico) (tenor); Naples, Italy **(1873–1921)**
Carver, George Washington (botanist); Missouri **(1864–1943)**
Cary, Arthur Joyce Lunel (novelist); Londonderry, Ireland **(1888–1957)**
Casals, Pablo (cellist); Vendrell, Spain **(1876–1973)**
Casanova de Seingalt, Giovanni Jacopo (adventurer); Venice **(1725–1798)**
Cash, Johnny (singer); nr. Kingsland, Ark., 2/26/1932
Cass, Peggy (comedienne); Boston, 5/21/1924
Cassatt, Mary (painter); Allegheny, Pa. **(1844–1926)**
Cassavetes, John (actor and director); New York City, 12/9/1929
Cassidy, David (singer); New York City, 4/12/1950
Cassidy, Jack (actor); Richmond Hill, Queens, N.Y. **(1927–1976)**
Cassini, Oleg (Oleg Lolewski-Cassini) (fashion designer); Paris, 4/11/1913
Castagno, Andrea del (painter); San Martino a Corella (Italy) **(c.1421–1457)**
Castellano, Richard (actor); New York City, 9/2/1934
Castle, Irene (Irene Foote) (actress and dancer); New Rochelle, N.Y. **(1893–1969)**
Castle, Vernon Blythe (dancer and aviator); Norwich, England **(1887–1918)**
Castro Ruz, Fidel (Premier); Mayari, Oriente, Cuba, 8/13/1926
Cather, Willa Sibert (novelist); Winchester, Va. **(1876–1947)**
Cato, Marcus Porcius (called Cato the Elder) (statesman); Tusculum (Italy) **(234–149 B.C.)**
Catt, Carrie Chapman Lane (woman suffragist); Ripon, Wis. **(1859–1947)**
Catton, Bruce (historian); Petoskey, Mich. **(1899–1978)**
Cavallaro, Carmen (band leader); New York City, 1913
Cavett, Dick (Richard) (TV entertainer); Gibbon, Neb., 11/19/1936
Cellini, Benvenuto (goldsmith and sculptor); Florence (Italy) **(1500–1571)**
Cervantes Saavedra, Miguel de (novelist); Alcalá de Henares, Spain **(1547–1616)**
Cézanne, Paul (painter); Aix-en-Provence, France **(1839–1906)**
Chagall, Marc (painter); Vitebsk, Russia, 7/7/1887
Chaliapin, Feodor Ivanovitch (operatic basso); Kazan, Russia **(1873–1938)**
Chamberlain, Arthur Neville (statesman); Edgbaston, England **(1869–1940)**

Chamberlain, Richard (actor); Los Angeles, 3/31/1935(?)
Champion, Gower (choreographer); Geneva, Ill. **(1921–1980)**
Champion, Marge (actress and dancer); Los Angeles, 9/2/1923
Champlain, Samuel de (explorer); nr. Rochefort, France **(1567?–1635)**
Chancellor, John (TV commentator); Chicago, 7/14/1927
Chandler, Raymond (writer); Chicago **(1888–1959)**
Chanel, "Coco" (Gabriel Bonheur) (fashion designer); Issoire, France **(1883–1971)**
Chaney, Lon (actor); Colorado Springs, Colo. **(1883–1930)**
Channing, Carol (actress); Seattle, 1/31/1923
Chaplin, Geraldine (actress); Santa Monica, Calif., 7/31/1944
Chaplin, Sir Charles (actor); London **(1889–1977)**
Charisse, Cyd (Tula Finklea) (dancer and actress); Amarillo, Tex., 3/8/1923
Charlemagne (Holy Roman Emperor); birthplace unknown **(742–814)**
Charles, Ray (Ray Charles Robinson) (pianist, singer, and songwriter); Albany Ga., 9/23/1930
Chase, Chevy (Cornelius Crane Chase) (comedian); New York City, 10/8/1943
Chase, Ilka (author and actress); New York City **(1905–1978)**
Chase, Lucia (founder Ballet Theatre [now American Ballet Theatre]); Waterbury, Conn., 3/24/1907
Chatterton, Ruth (actress); New York City **(1893–1961)**
Chaucer, Geoffrey (poet); London **(1340?–1400)**
Chávez, Carlos (composer); nr. Mexico City **(1899–1978)**
Chavez, Cesar (labor leader); nr. Yuma, Ariz., 3/31/1927
Chayefsky, Paddy (Sidney) (playwright); New York City, **(1923–1981)**
Checker, Chubby (Ernest Evans) (performer); Philadelphia, 10/3/1941
Cheever, John (novelist); Quincy, Mass. **(1912–1982)**
Chekhov, Anton Pavlovich (dramatist and short-story writer); Taganrog, Russia **(1860–1904)**
Cher (Cherilyn LaPiere) (singer); El Centro, Calif., 5/20/1946
Chesterton, Gilbert Keith (author); Kensington, England **(1874–1936)**
Chevalier, Maurice (entertainer); Paris **(1888–1972)**
Chiang Ch'ing (political leader); Chucheng, China, 1913(?)
Chiang Kai-shek (Chief of State); Feng-hwa, China **(1887–1975)**
Child, Julia (food expert); Pasadena, Calif., 8/15/1912
Chippendale, Thomas (cabinet-maker); Otley, England **(1718?–1779)**
Chirico, Giorgio de (painter); Vólos, Greece, **(1888–1978)**
Chisholm, Shirley (ex-Representative); Brooklyn, N.Y., 11/30/1924
Chopin, Frédéric François (composer); nr. Warsaw **(1810–1849)**
Chou En-lai. *See* Zhou Enlai
Christian, Linda (Blanca Rosa Welter) (actress); Tampico, Mexico, 11/13/1924
Christie, Agatha (mystery writer); Torquay, England, **(1890–1976)**
Christie, Julie (actress); Chukua, India, 4/14/1941
Christopher, Jordon (actor and musician); Youngstown, Ohio, 1941
Christy, June (singer); Springfield, Ill., 1925
Churchill, Sarah (actress); London **(1914–1982)**
Churchill, Sir Winston Leonard Spencer (statesman); Blenheim Palace, Oxfordshire, England **(1874–1965)**
Cicero, Marcus Tullius (orator and statesman); Arpinum (Italy) **(106–43 B.C.)**
Cilento, Diane (actress); Queensland, Australia, 10/5/1933
Cimabue, Giovanni (painter); Florence (Italy) **(c.1240–c.1302)**
Cimino, Michael (film director); New York City, 1943(?)
Clair, René (René Chomette (film director); Paris **(1898–1981)**
Claire, Ina (Ina Fagan) (actress); Washington, D.C., 10/15/1895
Clapton, Eric (singer and guitarist); Ripley, England, 3/30/1945
Clark, Dane (Barney Zanville) (actor); New York City, 2/18/1915
Clark, Dick (TV personality); Mt. Vernon, N.Y., 11/30/1929
Clark, Mark W. (general); Madison Barracks, N.Y., 5/1/1896
Clark, Petula (singer); Epsom, England, 11/15/1934
Clark, Roy (country music artist); Meherrin, Va., 4/15/1933
Clark, William (explorer); Caroline County, Va. **(1770–1838)**
Claude Lorrain (Claude Gellée) (painter); Champagne, France **(1600–1682)**
Clay, Henry (statesman); Hanover County, Va. **(1777–1852)**
Clay, Lucius D. (banker, ex-general); Marietta, Ga. **(1897–1978)**
Clayburgh, Jill (actress); New York City, 4/30/1944
Clemenceau, Georges (statesman); Mouilleron-en-Pareds, Vendée, France **(1841–1929)**
Clemens, Samuel L. *See* Mark Twain
Cleopatra (Queen of Egypt); Alexandria, Egypt **(69–30 B.C.)**
Cliburn, Van (Harvey Lavan Cliburn, Jr.) (concert pianist); Shreveport, La., 7/12/1934
Clifford, Clark M. (ex-Secretary of Defense); Ft. Scott, Kan., 12/25/1906
Clift, Montgomery (actor); Omaha, Neb. **(1920–1966)**
Clooney, Rosemary (singer); Maysville, Ky., 5/23/1928
Clurman, Harold (stage producer); New York City **(1901–1980)**
Cobb, Irvin Shrewsbury (humorist); Paducah, Ky. **(1876–1944)**
Cobb, Lee J. (Leo Jacob) (actor); New York City **(1911–1976)**
Coburn, Charles Douville (actor); Savannah, Ga. **(1877–1961)**
Coburn, James (actor); Laurel, Neb., 8/31/1928
Coca, Imogene (comedienne); Philadelphia, 11/18/1908
Cocker, Joe (John Robert Cocker) (singer); Sheffield, England, 5/20/1944
Coco, James (actor); New York City, 3/21/1929
Cocteau, Jean (author); Maison-Lafitte, France **(1891–1963)**
Cody, W. F. *See* Buffalo Bill
Cohan, George Michael (actor and dramatist); Providence, R.I. **(1878–1942)**
Cohen, Leonard (singer and songwriter); Montreal, 1935
Colbert, Claudette (Lily Chauchoin) (actress); Paris, 9/13/1903
Colby, William E. (ex-Director of CIA); St. Paul, 1/4/1920
Cole, Nat "King" (singer); Montgomery, Ala. **(1919–1965)**
Cole, Natalie (singer); Los Angeles, 2/6/1950
Cole, Thomas (painter); Lancashire, England **(1801–1848)**
Coleridge, Samuel Taylor (poet); Ottery St. Mary, England **(1772–1834)**
Colette (Sidonie-Gabrielle Colette) (novelist); St.-Sauveur, France **c.1873–1954)**
Collingwood, Charles (TV commentator); Three Rivers, Mich., 6/4/1917
Collins, Dorothy (Marjorie Chandler) (singer); Windsor, Ontario, Canada, 11/18/1926
Collins, Joan (actress); London, 1933
Collins, Judy (singer); Seattle, 5/1/1939
Colman, Ronald (actor); Richmond, England **(1891–1958)**
Colonna, Jerry (comedian); Boston, 1905
Columbus, Christopher (Cristoforo Colombo) (discoverer of America); Genoa (Italy) **(1451–1506)**
Comden, Betty (writer); New York City, 5/3/1919
Commager, Henry Steele (historian); Pittsburgh, 10/25/1902
Como, Perry (Pierino) (singer); Canonsburg, Pa., 5/18/1913
Compton, Karl Taylor (physicist); Wooster, Ohio **(1887 1954)**
Conant, James B. (educator and statesman); Dorchester, Mass. **(1893–1978)**
Condon, Eddie (jazz musician); Goodland, Ind. **(1905–1973)**
Confucius (K'ung Fu-tzu) (philosopher); Shantung province, China **(c.551–479 B.C.)**
Congreve, William (dramatist); nr. Leeds, England **(1670–1729)**
Connelly, Marc (playwright); McKeesport, Pa. **(1890–1980)**
Connery, Sean (actor); Edinburgh, Scotland, 8/25/1930
Conniff, Ray (band leader); Attleboro, Mass., 11/6/1916
Connors, Chuck (actor); Brooklyn, N.Y., 4/10/1921
Connors, Mike (Krekor Ohanian) (actor); Fresno, Calif., 8/15/1925
Conrad, Joseph (Teodor Jozef Konrad Korzeniowski) (novelist); Berdichev, Ukraine **(1857–1924)**
Conrad, Robert (actor); Chicago, 1935
Conrad, William (actor); Louisville, Ky., 9/27/1920
Conried, Hans (Frank Foster) (actor); Baltimore **(1915–1982)**
Constable, John (painter); East Bergholt, Suffolk, England **(1776–1837)**
Constantine II (ex-king); Athens, 6/2/1940
Conte, Richard (actor); New York City **(1916–1975)**
Converse, Frank (actor); St. Louis, 1938
Conway, Tim (actor); Chagrin Falls, Ohio, 12/15/1933
Coogan, Jackie (actor); Los Angeles, 10/26/1914
Cooke, Alistair (Alfred Alistair); (TV narrator and journalist); Manchester, England, 11/20/1908
Cooley, Denton A(rthur) (heart surgeon); Houston, Tex., 8/22/1920
Coolidge, Rita (singer); Nashville, Tenn., 1944
Cooper, Alice (Vincent Furnier) (rock musician); Detroit, 2/4/1948
Cooper, Gary (Frank James Cooper) (actor); Helena, Mont. **(1901–1961)**
Cooper, Jackie (actor and director); Los Angeles, 9/15/1922
Cooper, James Fenimore (novelist); Burlington, N.J. **(1789–1851)**
Cooper, Peter (industrialist and philanthropist); New York City **(1791–1883)**
Copernicus, Nicolaus (Mikolaj Kopernik) (astronomer); Thorn, Poland **(1473–1543)**
Copland, Aaron (composer); Brooklyn, N.Y., 11/14/1900
Copley, John Singleton (painter); Boston, Mass. **(1738–1815)**
Coppolla, Francis Ford (film director); Detroit, 4/7/1939
Corelli, Franco (operatic tenor); Ancona, Italy, 4/8/1923
Corneille, Pierre (dramatist); Rouen, France **(1606–1684)**
Cornell, Katharine (actress); Berlin **(1893–1974)**
Corot, Jean Baptiste Camille (painter); Paris **(1796–1875)**
Correggio, Antonio Allegri da (painter); Correggio (Italy) **(1494–1534)**
Corsaro, Frank (opera director); New York harbor, 12/22/1924
Cortés (or Cortez), Hernando (explorer); Medellín, Spain **(1485–1547)**
Cosby, Bill (actor); Philadelphia, 7/12/1937
Cosell, Howard (Howard Cohen) (sportscaster); Winston-Salem, N.C., 3/25/1920
Costa-Gavras, Henri (Kostantinos Gavras) (film director); Athens, 1933
Costello, Lou (comedian); Paterson, N.J. **(1908–1959)**
Cotten, Joseph (actor); Petersburg, Va., 5/15/1905
Courbet, Gustave (painter); Ornans, France **(1819–1877)**
Courrèges, André (fashion designer); Pau, France, 3/9/1923
Courtenay, Tom (actor); Hull, England, 2/25/1937
Cousins, Norman (publisher); Union Hill, N.J., 6/24/1915
Cousteau, Jacques-Yves (marine explorer); St. André-de-Cubzac, France, 6/11/1910
Coward, Sir Noel (playwright and actor); Teddington, England **(1899–1973)**
Cowles, Gardner (newspaper publisher); Algona, Iowa, 1/31/1903

Cowper, William (poet); Great Berkhamstead, England **(1731–1800)**
Cozzens, James Gould (novelist); Chicago **(1903–1978)**
Crabbe, Buster (Clarence) (actor); Oakland, Calif., 2/7/1908
Crain, Jeanne (actress); Barstow, Calif., 5/25/1925
Cranach, Lucas, the elder (painter); Kronach (Germany) **(1472–1553)**
Crane, Hart (poet); Garrettsville, Ohio **(1899–1932)**
Crane, Stephen (novelist and poet); Newark, N.J. **(1871–1900)**
Crawford, Broderick (actor); Philadelphia, 12/9/1911
Crawford, Cheryl (stage producer); Akron, Ohio, 9/24/1902
Crawford, Joan (Lucille LeSueur) (actress and business executive); San Antonio **(1908–1977)**
Crenna, Richard (actor); Los Angeles, 11/30/1927
Crespin, Régine (operatic soprano); Marseilles, France, 2/23/1929
Crichton, (John) Michael (novelist); Chicago, 10/23/1942
Crisp, Donald (actor); London **(1880–1974)**
Croce, Benedetto (philosopher); Pescasseroli, Aquila, Italy **(1866–1952)**
Croce, Jim (singer); Philadelphia **(1942–1973)**
Crockett, Davy (David) (frontiersman); Greene County, Tenn. **(1786–1836)**
Cromwell, Oliver (statesman); Huntingdon, England **(1599–1658)**
Cronin, A. J. (Archibald J. Cronin) (novelist); Cardross, Scotland **(1896–1981)**
Cronkite, Walter (TV newscaster); St. Joseph, Mo., 11/4/1916
Cronyn, Hume (actor); London, Ontario, Canada, 7/18/1911
Crosby, Bing (Harry Lillis) (singer, actor); Tacoma, Wash. **(1904–1977)**
Crosby, Bob (musician); Spokane, Wash., 8/23/1913
Crosby, David (singer); Los Angeles, 8/14/1941
Cross, Milton (opera commentator); New York City **(1897–1975)**
Crouse, Russel (playwright); Findlay, Ohio **(1893–1966)**
Cugat, Xavier (band leader); Barcelona, Spain, 1/1/1900
Cukor, George (film director); New York City, 7/7/1899
Cullen, Bill (William Lawrence Cullen) (radio and TV entertainer); Pittsburgh, 2/18/1920
Culp, Robert (actor); Berkeley, Calif., 8/16/1930
Cummings, E. E. (Edward Estlin Cummings) (poet); Cambridge, Mass. **(1894–1962)**
Cummings, Robert (actor); Joplin, Mo., 6/9/1910
Curie, Marie (Marja Sklodowska) (physical chemist); Warsaw **(1867–1934)**
Curtin, Phyllis (soprano); Clarksburg, W.Va., 12/3/1927
Curtis, Tony (Bernard Schwartz) (actor); Bronx, N.Y., 6/3/1925
Curzon, Clifford (concert pianist); London **(1907–1982)**
Custer, George Armstrong (army officer); New Rumley, Ohio **(1839–1876)**

D

Dahl, Arlene (actress); Minneapolis, 8/11/1928
Dailey, Dan (actor and dancer); New York City, **(1917–1978)**
Daley, Richard J. (ex-Mayor of Chicago); Chicago **(1902–1976)**
Dali, Salvador (painter); Figueras, Spain, 5/11/1904
Daly, James (actor); Wisconsin Rapids, Wis. **(1918–1978)**
Daly, John (radio and TV news analyst); Johannesburg, South Africa, 2/20/1914
d'Amboise, Jacques (ballet dancer); Dedham, Mass., 7/28/1934
Damone, Vic (Vito Farinola) (singer); Brooklyn, N.Y., 6/12/1928
Damrosch, Walter Johannes (orchestra conductor); Breslau (Poland) **(1862–1950)**
Dana, Charles Anderson (editor); Hinsdale, N.H. **(1819–1897)**
Dandridge, Dorothy (actress); Cleveland **(1923–1965)**
Dangerfield, Rodney (comedian); Babylon, L.I., N.Y., 1921
Daniels, Bebe (Virginia Daniels) (actress); Dallas **(1901–1971)**
Danilova, Alexandra (ballerina); Peterhof, Russia, 1/20/1904
Dannay, Frederic (novelist, pseudonym Ellery Queen); Brooklyn, N.Y. **(1905–1982)**
Danner, Blythe (actress); Philadelphia, 1944(?)
D'Annunzio, Gabriele (soldier and author); Francaville al Mare, Pescara, Italy **(1863–1938)**
Dante (or **Durante**) **Alighieri** (poet); Florence (Italy) **(1265–1321)**
Danton, Georges Jacques (French Revolutionary leader); Arcis-sur-Aube, France **(1759–1794)**
Darnell, Linda (actress); Dallas **(1921–1965)**
Darren, James (actor); Philadelphia, 6/8/1936
Darrieux, Danielle (actress); Bordeaux, France, 5/1/1917
Darrow, Clarence Seward (lawyer); Kinsman, Ohio **(1857–1938)**
Darwin, Charles Robert (naturalist); Shrewsbury, England **(1809–1882)**
daSilva, Howard (actor); Cleveland, 5/4/1909
Dassin, Jules (film director); Middletown, Conn., 12/18/1911
Daumier, Honoré (caricaturist); Marseilles, France **(1808–1879)**
Dauphin, Claude (actor); Corbeil, France **(1903–1978)**
David, Jacques-Louis (painter); Paris **(1748–1825)**
David (King of Israel and Judah) **(died c. 973 B.C.)**
Davidson, John (singer and actor); Pittsburgh, 12/13/1941
Davies, Marion (Marion Douras) (actress); New York City **(1898?–1961)**
da Vinci, Leonardo (painter and scientist); Vinci, Tuscany (Italy) **(1452–1519)**
Davis, Bette (actress); Lowell, Mass., 4/5/1908
Davis, Elmer Holmes (radio commentator); Aurora, Ind. **(1890–1958)**
Davis, Jefferson (President of the Confederacy); Christian (now Todd) County, Ky. **(1808–1889)**
Davis, Mac (singer); Lubbock, Tex.
Davis, Miles (jazz trumpeter); Alton, Ill., 5/25/1926
Davis, Ossie (actor and writer); Cogdell, Ga., 12/18/1917
Davis, Sammy, Jr. (actor and singer); New York City, 12/8/1925
Davis, Skeeter (Mary Francis Penick) (singer); Dry Ridge, Ky., 12/30/1931
Davis, Stuart (painter); Philadelphia **(1894–1964)**
Day, Dennis (singer); New York City, 5/21/1917
Day, Doris (Doris von Kappelhoff) (singer and actress); Cincinnati, 4/3/1924
Day, Laraine (La Raine Johnson) (actress); Roosevelt, Utah, 10/13/1920
Dayan, Moshe (ex-Defense Minister of Israel); Dagania, Palestine (Jordan) **(1915–1981)**
Dean, James (actor); Marion, Ind. **(1931–1955)**
Dean, Jimmy (singer); Seth Ward, nr. Plainview, Tex., 8/10/1928
De Bakey, Michael E. (heart surgeon); Lake Charles, La., 9/7/1908
de Beauvoir, Simone (novelist and philosopher); Paris, 1/9/1908
Debs, Eugene Victor (Socialist leader); Terre Haute, Ind. **(1855–1926)**
Debussy, Claude Achille (composer); St. Germain-en-Laye, France **(1862–1918)**
De Carlo, Yvonne (Peggy Yvonne Middleton) (actress); Vancouver, B.C., Canada, 9/1/1924
de Chirico, Giorgio (painter); Volos, Greece, **(1888–1978)**
Dee, Ruby (Ruby Ann Wallace) (actress); Cleveland, 10/27/1924(?)
Dee, Sandra (Alexandra Zuck) (actress); Bayonne, N.J., 4/23/1942
Defoe, Daniel (novelist); London **(1659?–1731)**
Degas, Hilaire Germain Edgar (painter); Paris **(1834–1917)**
de Gaulle, Charles André Joseph Marie (soldier and statesman); Lille, France **(1890–1970)**
DeHaven, Gloria (actress); Los Angeles, 7/23/1925
de Havilland, Olivia (actress); Tokyo, 7/1/1916
Dekker, Albert (actor); Brooklyn, N.Y. **(1904–1968)**
De Kooning, Willem (painter); Rotterdam, 4/24/1904
Delacroix, Eugène (painter); Charenton-St. Maurice, France **(1798–1863)**
de la Renta, Oscar (fashion designer); Santo Domingo, Dominican Republic, 7/22/1932
Delaunay, Robert (painter); Paris **(1885–1941)**
De Laurentiis, Dino (film producer); Torre Annunziata, Bay of Naples, Italy, 8/8/1919
Delon, Alain (actor); Sceaux, France, 11/8/1935
Del Rio, Dolores (actress); Durango, Mexico, 8/3/1905
DeLuise, Dom (comedian); Brooklyn, N.Y., 8/1/1933
Demarest, William (actor); St. Paul, 2/27/1892
de Mille, Agnes (choreographer); New York City
De Mille, Cecil Blount (film director); Ashfield, Mass. **(1881–1959)**
Demosthenes (orator); Athens **(385?–322 B.C.)**
Deneuve, Catherine (actress); Paris, 10/22/1943
De Niro, Robert (actor); New York City, 8/17/1943
Dennis, Sandy (actress); Hastings, Neb., 4/27/1937
Denver, John (Henry John Deutschendorf, Jr.) (singer); Roswell, N.M., 12/31/1943
Derain, André (painter); Chatou, Seine-et-Oise, France **(1880–1954)**
Dern, Bruce (actor); Chicago, 6/4/1936
Descartes, René (philosopher and mathematician); La Haye, France **(1596–1650)**
De Seversky, Alexander P. (aviator); Tiflis, Russia **(1894–1974)**
De Sica, Vittorio (film director); Sora, Italy **(1901–1974)**
Desmond, Johnny (composer); Detroit, 11/14/1921
Desmond, William (actor); Dublin **(1878–1949)**
De Soto, Hernando (explorer); Barcarrota, Spain **(1500?–1542)**
De Valera, Eamon (ex-President of Ireland); New York City **(1882–1975)**
Devine, Andy (actor); Flagstaff, Ariz. **(1905–1977)**
De Vries, Peter (novelist); Chicago, 2/27/1910
Dewey, George (admiral); Montpelier, Vt. **(1837–1917)**
Dewey, John (philosopher and educator); Burlington, Vt. **(1859–1952)**
Dewey, Thomas E. (politician); Owosso, Mich. **(1902–1971)**
Dewhurst, Colleen (actress); Montreal, 1926(?)
Diamond, Neil (singer); Brooklyn, N.Y., 1/24/1941
Dickens, Charles John Huffam (novelist); Portsea, England **(1812–1870)**
Dickey, James (poet); Atlanta, 2/2/1923
Dickinson, Angie (Angeline Brown) (actress); Kulm, N.D., 9/30/1932
Dickinson, Emily Elizabeth (poet); Amherst, Mass. **(1830–1886)**
Diddley, Bo (Elias McDaniel) (guitarist); McComb, Miss., 12/30/1928
Diefenbaker, John G. (ex-Prime Minister); Grey County, Ontario, Canada **(1895–1979)**
Dietrich, Marlene (Maria Magdalena von Losch) (actress); Berlin, 12/27/1901
Diggs, Dudley (actor); Dublin **(1879–1947)**
Diller, Phyllis (Phyllis Driver) (comedienne); Lima, Ohio, 7/17/1917
Dillinger, John (American bank robber); prob. Indianapolis **(1902–1934)**
Dillman, Bradford (actor); San Francisco, 4/14/1930
Dine, Jim (painter); Cincinnati, 6/16/1935

Diogenes (philosopher); Sinope (Turkey) **(412?–323 B.C.)**
Dion (Dion DiMucci) (singer); Bronx, N.Y., 7/18/1939
Dior, Christian (fashion designer); Granville, France **(1905–1957)**
Disney, Walt(er) Elias (film animator and producer); Chicago **(1901–1966)**
Disraeli, Benjamin (Earl of Beaconsfield) (statesman); London **(1804–1881)**
Dix, Dorothea (civil rights reformer); Hampden, Me. **(1802–1887)**
Dix, Richard (Ernest Carlton Brimmer) (actor); St. Paul **(1894–1949)**
Dixon, Jeane (Jeane Pinckert) (seer); Medford, Wis., 1918
Doctorow, E.L. (Edgar Laurence) (novelist); New York City, 1/6/1931
Dodgson, C. L. *See* Carroll, Lewis.
Dolin, Anton (dancer); Slinfold, England, 7/27/1904
Domingo, Placido (tenor); Madrid, 1/21/1941
Domino, Fats (Antoine) (musician); New Orleans, 2/26/1928
Donahue, Phil (television personality); Cleveland, 12/21/1935
Donahue, Troy (Merle Johnson) (actor); New York City, 1/27/1938
Donat, Robert (actor); Withington, England **(1905–1958)**
Donatello (Donato Niccolò di Betto Bardi) (sculptor); Florence (Italy) **(c.1386–1466)**
Donne, John (poet); London **(1573–1631)**
Donovan (Donovan Leitch) (singer and songwriter); Glasgow, Scotland, 2/10/1946
Doolittle, James H. (ex-Air Force general); Alameda, Calif., 12/14/1896
Dorati, Antal (orchestra conductor); Budapest, 4/9/1906
Dors, Diana (Diana Fluck) (actress); Swindon, England, 10/23/1931
Dorsey, Jimmy (band leader); Shenandoah, Pa. **(1904–1957)**
Dorsey, Tommy (band leader); Mahonoy Plains, Pa. **(1905–1956)**
Dos Passos, John (author); Chicago **(1896–1970)**
Dostoevski, Fyodor Mikhailovich (novelist); Moscow **(1821–1881)**
Douglas, Helen Gahagan (ex-Representative); Boonton, N.J. **(1900–1980)**
Douglas, Kirk (Issur Danielovitch) (actor); Amsterdam, N.Y., 12/9/1916
Douglas, Melvyn (Melvyn Hesselberg) (actor); Macon, Ga., **(1901–1981)**
Douglas, Mike (Michael D. Dowd, Jr.) (TV personality); Chicago, 8/11/1925
Douglas, Paul (actor); Philadelphia **(1907–1959)**
Douglas, Stephen Arnold (politician); Brandon, Vt. **(1813–1861)**
Dowling, Eddie (Edward Goucher) (actor and stage producer); Woonsocket, R.I., **(1894–1976)**
Downs, Hugh (TV entertainer); Akron, Ohio, 2/14/1921
Doyle, Sir Arthur Conan (novelist and spiritualist); Edinburgh, Scotland **(1859–1930)**
Drake, Alfred (singer and actor); New York City, 10/7/1914
Drake, Sir Francis (navigator); Tavistock, England **(1545–1596)**
Dreiser, Theodore (writer); Terre Haute, Ind. **(1871–1945)**
Dressler, Marie (Leila Koeber) (actress); Cobourg, Ontario, Canada **(1869–1934)**
Dreyfus, Alfred (French army officer); Mulhouse (France) **(1859–1935)**
Dreyfuss, Richard (actor); Brooklyn, N.Y., 10/29/1947
Drury, Allen (novelist); Houston, 9/2/1918
Dryden, John (poet); Northamptonshire, England **(1631–1700)**
Dubček, Alexander (ex-President of Czechoslovakia); Uhroved (Czechoslovakia), 11/27/1921
Dubinsky, David (David Dobnievski) (labor leader); Brest-Litovsk (U.S.S.R.) **(1892–1982)**
Duchamp, Marcel (painter); Blainville, France **(1887–1968)**
Duchin, Peter (pianist and band leader); New York City, 7/28/1937
Duff, Howard (actor); Bremerton, Wash., 11/24/1917
Dufy, Raoul (painter); Le Havre, France **(1877–1953)**
Duke, James B. (industrialist); nr. Durham, N.C. **(1856–1925)**
Duke, Patty (Anna Marie Duke) (actress); New York City, 12/14/1946
Dullea, Keir (actor); Cleveland, 5/30/1936(?)
Dulles, Allen Welsh (ex-Director of CIA); Watertown, N.Y. **(1893–1969)**
Dulles, John Foster (statesman); Washington, D.C. **(1888–1959)**
Dumas, Alexandre (called Dumas fils) (novelist); Paris **(1824–1895)**
Dumas, Alexandre (called Dumas père) (novelist); Villers-Cotterets, France **(1802–1870)**
Du Maurier, Daphne (novelist); London, 5/13/1907
Du Maurier, George Louis Palmella Busson (novelist); Paris **(1834–1896)**
Dumont, Margaret (actress); **(1889–1965)**
Dunaway, Faye (actress); Bascom, Fla., 1/14/1941
Duncan, Isadora (dancer); San Francisco **(1878–1927)**
Duncan, Sandy (actress); Henderson, Tex., 2/20/1946
Dunn, James (actor); Santa Monica, Calif. **(1905–1967)**
Dunne, Irene (actress); Louisville, Ky., 12/20/1904
Dunnock, Mildred (actress); Baltimore, 1/25/(?)
Du Pont, Pierre S. (economist); Paris **(1739–1817)**
Durante, Jimmy (comedian); New York City **(1893–1980)**
Durbin, Deanna (Edna Mae) (actress); Winnipeg, Canada, 12/4/1922
Dürer, Albrecht (painter and engraver); Nürnberg (Germany) **(1471–1528)**
Durrell, Lawrence George (novelist); Julundur, India, 2/27/1912
Duse, Eleonora (actress); Chioggia, Italy **(1859–1924)**
Duvalier, Jean-Claude (President; son of "Papa Doc"); Port-au-Prince, Haiti, 7/3/1951
Duvall, Robert (actor); San Diego, Calif., 1931
Dvořák, Antonín (composer); Nelahozeves (Czechoslovakia) **(1841–1904)**
Dylan, Bob (Robert Zimmerman) (folk singer and composer); Duluth, Minn., 5/24/1941

E

Eagels, Jeanne (actress); Kansas City, Mo. **(1894–1929)**
Eakins, Thomas (painter and sculptor); Philadelphia, **(1844–1916)**
Earhart, Amelia (aviator); Atchison, Kan. **(1898–1937)**
Eastman, George (inventor); Waterville, N.Y. **(1854–1932)**
Eastwood, Clint (actor); San Francisco, 5/31/1931(?)
Ebsen, Buddy (Christian Ebsen, Jr.) (actor); Belleville, Ill., 4/2/1908
Eckstine, Billy (singer); Pittsburgh, 7/8/1914
Eddy, Mary Baker (founder of Christian Science Church); Bow, N.H. **(1821–1910)**
Eddy, Nelson (baritone and actor); Providence, R.I. **(1901–1967)**
Eden, Sir Anthony (Earl of Avon) (ex-Prime Minister); Durham, England **(1897–1977)**
Eden, Barbara (Barbara Huffman) (actress); Tucson, Ariz., 1934
Edison, Thomas Alva (inventor); Milan, Ohio **(1847–1931)**
Edwards, Ralph (TV and radio producer); Merino, Colo., 1913
Edwards, Vincent (actor); Brooklyn, N.Y., 7/7/1928
Egan, Richard (actor); San Francisco, 7/29/1923
Eggar, Samantha (actress); London, 5/3/1939
Eglevsky, André (ballet dancer); Moscow **(1917–1977)**
Ehrlich, Paul (bacteriologist); Strzelin (Poland) **(1854–1915)**
Einstein, Albert (physicist); Ulm, Germany **(1879–1955)**
Eisenhower, Milton S. (educator); Abilene, Kan., 9/15/1899
Eisenstaedt, Alfred (photographer and photojournalist); Dirschau (Poland), 12/6/1898
Ekberg, Anita (actress); Malmö, Sweden, 9/29/1931
Eldridge, Florence (Florence McKechnie) (actress); Brooklyn, N.Y., 9/5/1901
Elgar, Sir Edward (composer); Worcester, England **(1857–1934)**
Elgart, Larry (band leader); New London, Conn., 3/20/1922
El Greco (Domenicos Theotocopoulos) (painter); Candia, Crete (Greece) **(c.1541–1614)**
Eliot, George (Mary Ann Evans) (novelist); Chilvers Coton, England **(1819–1880)**
Eliot, Thomas Stearns (poet); St. Louis **(1888–1965)**
Ellington, Duke (Edward Kennedy) (jazz musician); Washington, D.C. **(1899–1974)**
Elliot, "Mama" Cass (Ellen Naomi Cohen) (singer); Baltimore **(1941–1974)**
Elman, Mischa (violinist); Stalnoye, Ukraine **(1891–1967)**
Emerson, Ralph Waldo (philosopher and poet); Boston **(1803–1882)**
Enesco, Georges (composer); Dorohoi, Romania **(1881–1955)**
Engels, Friedrich (Socialist writer); Barmen (Germany) **(1820–1895)**
Entremont, Philippe (concert pianist); Rheims, France, 6/7/1934
Epicurus (philosopher); Samos (Greece) **(341–270 B.C.)**
Epstein, Sir Jacob (sculptor); New York City **(1880–1959)**
Erasmus, Desiderius (Gerhard Gerhards) (scholar); Rotterdam **(1466?–1536)**
Erhard, Ludwig (ex-Chancellor); Furth, Germany **(1897–1977)**
Erickson, Leif (actor); Alameda, Calif., 10/27/1911
Ericson, Leif (navigator); **(c. 10th century A.D.)**
Erikson, Erik H. (psychoanalyst); Frankfurt, Germany, 6/15/1902
Ernst, Max (painter); Bruhl, Germany **(1891–1976)**
Euclid (mathematician); Megara (Greece) **(c. 300 B.C.)**
Euripides (dramatist); Salamis (Greece) **(c.484–407 B.C.)**
Evans, Dale (Frances Butts) (actress and singer); Uvalde, Tex., 10/31/1912
Evans, Dame Edith (actress); London **(1888–1976)**
Evans, Maurice (actor); Dorchester, England, 6/3/1901
Everett, Chad (actor); South Bend, Ind., 1937
Evers, Charles (civil rights leader); Decatur, Miss., 9/14/1923(?)
Evers, Medgar (civil rights leader); Decatur, Miss. **(1925–1963)**
Ewell, Tom (Yewell Tompkins) (actor); Owensboro, Ky., 4/29/1909

F

Fabian (Fabian Anthony Forte) (singer); Philadelphia, 2/6/1943
Fabray, Nanette (Nanette Fabares) (actress); San Diego, Calif., 10/27/1922
Fadiman, Clifton (literary critic); Brooklyn, N.Y., 5/15/1904
Fairbanks, Douglas (Julius Ullman) (actor); Denver **(1883–1939)**
Fairbanks, Douglas, Jr. (actor); New York City, 12/9/1909
Faith, Percy (conductor); Toronto **(1908–1976)**
Falk, Peter (actor); New York City, 9/16/1927
Falla, Manuel de (composer); Cadiz, Spain **(1876–1946)**
Faraday, Michael (physicist); Newington, England **(1791–1867)**
Farber, Barry (radio broadcaster); Baltimore, Md., 1930
Farentino, James (actor); Brooklyn, N.Y., 2/24/1938
Farmer, James (civil rights leader); Marshall, Tex., 1/12/1920

Farnum, William (actor); Boston **(1876–1953)**
Farrell, Charles (actor); Onset Bay, Mass., 1901
Farrell, Eileen (operatic soprano); Willimantic, Conn., 2/13/1920
Farrell, Glenda (actress); Enid, Okla. **(1904–1971)**
Farrell, James T. (novelist); Chicago **(1904–1979)**
Farrell, Suzanne (Roberta Sue Ficker) (ballerina); Cincinnati, 8/16/1945
Farrow, Mia (actress); Los Angeles, 2/9/1946
Fasanella, Ralph (painter); New York City, 9/2/1914
Fassbinder, Rainer Werner (film and stage director); Bad Wörishofen, West Germany **(1946–1982)**
Fast, Howard (novelist); New York City, 11/11/1914
Faulkner, William (novelist); New Albany, Miss. **(1897–1962)**
Fawcett, Farrah (actress); Corpus Christi, Tex., 2/2/1947(?)
Faye, Alice (Ann Leppert) (actress); New York City, 5/5/1915
Feiffer, Jules (cartoonist); New York City, 1/26/1929
Feininger, Lyonel (painter); New York City **(1871–1956)**
Feldon, Barbara (actress); Pittsburgh, 3/12/1941
Feliciano, José (singer); Larez, Puerto Rico, 9/10/1945
Felker, Clay S. (editor and publisher); St. Louis, 10/2/1925(?)
Fellini, Federico (film director); Rimini, Italy, 1/20/1920
Fender, Freddie (Baldemar Huerta) (singer); San Benito, Tex., 1937
Ferber, Edna (novelist); Kalamazoo, Mich. **(1885–1968)**
Ferguson, Maynard (jazz trumpeter); Verdun, Quebec, Canada, 5/4/1928
Fermi, Enrico (atomic physicist); Rome **(1901–1954)**
Fernandel (Fernand Joseph Desire Contandin) (actor); Marseilles, France **(1903–1971)**
Ferrer, José (actor and director); Santurce, Puerto Rico, 1/8/1912
Ferrer, Mel (actor); Elberon, N.J., 8/25/1917
Fetchit, Stepin (comedian); Key West, Fla., 1902
Fiedler, Arthur (conductor); Boston **(1894–1979)**
Field, Eugene (poet); St. Louis **(1850–1895)**
Field, Marshall (merchant); nr. Conway, Mass. **(1834–1906)**
Field, Sally (actress); Pasadena, Calif., 11/6/1946
Fielding, Henry (novelist); nr. Glastonbury, England **(1707–1754)**
Fields, Gracie (comedienne); Rochdale, England **(1898–1979)**
Fields, Totie (comedienne); Hartford, Conn. **(1931–1978)**
Fields, W. C. (William Claude Dukenfield) (comedian); Philadelphia **(1880–1946)**
Filene, Edward A. (merchant); **(1860–1937)**
Finch, Peter (actor); Kensington, England **(1916–1977)**
Finney, Albert (actor); Salford, England, 5/9/1936
Firkusny, Rudolf (pianist); Napajedla (Czechoslovakia), 2/11/1912
Fischer-Dieskau, Dietrich (baritone); Berlin, 5/28/1925
Fisher, Eddie (Edwin) (singer); Philadelphia, 8/10/1928
Fitzgerald, Barry (William Joseph Shields) (actor); Dublin **(1888–1961)**
Fitzgerald, Edward (radio broadcaster); Troy, N.Y. **(1898(?)–1982)**
Fitzgerald, Ella (singer); Newport News, Va., 4/25/1918
Fitzgerald, F. Scott (Francis Scott Key) (novelist); St. Paul, Minn. **(1896–1940)**
Fitzgerald, Geraldine (actress); Dublin, 11/24/1914
Fitzgerald, Pegeen (radio broadcaster); Norcatur, Kan., 1910
Flack, Roberta (singer); Black Mountain, N.C., 2/10/1940
Flagstad, Kirsten (Wagnerian soprano); Hamar, Norway **(1895–1962)**
Flatt, Lester Raymond (bluegrass musician); Overton County, Tenn. **(1914–1979)**
Flaubert, Gustave (novelist); Rouen, France **(1821–1880)**
Fleming, Sir Alexander (bacteriologist); Lochfield, Scotland **(1881–1955)**
Fleming, Rhonda (Marilyn Louis) (actress); Los Angeles, 8/10/1923
Flynn, Errol (actor); Hobart, Tasmania **(1909–1959)**
Foch, Nina (actress); Leyden, Netherlands, 4/20/1924
Fodor, Eugene (violinist); Turkey Creek, Colo., 3/5/1950
Fonda, Henry (actor); Grand Island, Neb. **(1905–1982)**
Fonda, Jane (actress); New York City, 12/21/1937
Fonda, Peter (actor); New York City, 2/23/1939
Fontaine, Frank (singer and comedian); Cambridge, Mass. **(1920–1979)**
Fontaine, Joan (Joan de Havilland) (actress); Tokyo, 10/22/1917
Fontanne, Lynn (actress); London, 12/6/1887(?)
Fonteyn, Dame Margot (Margaret Hookham) (ballerina); Reigate, England, 5/18/1919
Forbes, Malcolm S(tevenson) (publisher and sportsman); Brooklyn, N.Y., 8/19/1919
Ford, Glenn (Gwyllyn Ford) (actor); Quebec, 5/1/1916
Ford, Henry (industrialist); Greenfield, Mich. **(1863–1947)**
Ford, Henry, II (auto maker); Detroit, 9/4/1917
Ford, John (film director); Cape Elizabeth, Me. **(1895–1973)**
Ford, Paul (actor); Baltimore **(1901–1976)**
Ford, Tennessee Ernie (Ernie Jennings Ford) (singer); Bristol, Tenn., 2/13/1919
Forsythe, John (actor); Carney's Point, N.J., 1/29/1918
Fosdick, Harry Emerson (clergyman); Buffalo, N.Y. **(1878–1968)**
Fosse, Bob (Robert Louis) (choreographer and director); Chicago, 6/23/1927
Foster, Jodie (actress); Los Angeles, 1962
Foster, Stephen Collins (composer); nr. Pittsburgh **(1826–1864)**
Foxx, Redd (John Elroy Sanford) (actor and comedian); St. Louis, 12/9/1922
Foy, Eddie, Jr. (dancer and actor); New Rochelle, N.Y., 2/4/1905
Fra Angelico (Giovanni da Fiesole) (painter); Vicchio in the Mugello, Tuscany (Italy) **(c.1387–1455)**
Fracci, Carla (ballerina); Milan, Italy, 8/20/1936
Fragonard, Jean Honoré (painter); Grasse, France **(1732–1806)**
Frampton, Peter (rock musician); Beckenham, England, 4/20/1950
France, Anatole (Jacques Anatole François Thibault) (author); Paris **(1844–1924)**
Francescatti, Zino (violinist); Marseilles, France, 8/9/1905
Franciosa, Anthony (Anthony Papaleo) (actor); New York City, 10/25/1928
Francis, Arlene (Arlene Francis Kazanjian) (actress); Boston, 10/20/1908
Francis, Connie (Concetta Franconero) (singer); Newark, N.J., 12/12/1938
Francis, Kay (Katherine Edwina Gibbs) (actress); Oklahoma City **(1903–1968)**
Franciscus, James (actor); Clayton, Mo., 1/31/1934
Franck, César Auguste (composer); Liège (Belgium) **(1822–1890)**
Franco Bahamonde, Francisco (Chief of State); El Ferrol, Spain **(1892–1975)**
Franklin, Aretha (singer); Memphis, Tenn., 3/25/1942
Franklin, Benjamin (statesman and scientist); Boston **(1706–1790)**
Frazer, Sir James George (anthropologist); Glasgow, Scotland **(1854–1941)**
Freud, Sigmund (psychoanalyst); Moravia (Czechoslovakia) **(1856–1939)**
Friedan, Betty (Betty Noami Goldstein) (feminist); Peoria, Ill., 2/4/1921
Fromm, Erich (psychoanalyst); Frankfurt-am-Main, Germany **(1900–1980)**
Frost, David (TV entertainer); Tenterden, England, 4/7/1939
Frost, Robert Lee (poet); San Francisco **(1874–1963)**
Fry, Christopher (playwright); Bristol, England, 12/18/1907
Frye, David (impressionist); Brooklyn, N.Y., 1934
Fuller, R(ichard) Buckminster (Jr.) (architect and educator); Milton, Mass., 7/12/1895
Fulton, Robert (inventor); Lancaster County, Pa. **(1765–1815)**
Funt, Allen (TV producer); Brooklyn, N.Y., 9/16/1914
Furness, Betty (Elizabeth) (ex-actress and consumer advocate); New York City, 1/3/1916

G

Gabel, Martin (actor and producer); Philadelphia, 1912
Gabin, Jean (actor); Paris **(1904–1976)**
Gable, (William) Clark (actor); Cadiz, Ohio **(1901–1960)**
Gabo, Naum (sculptor); Briansk, Russia **(1890–1977)**
Gabor, Eva (actress); Budapest, 2/11/1926(?)
Gabor, Zsa Zsa (Sari) (actress); Budapest, 2/6/1923
Gainsborough, Thomas (painter); Sudbury, Suffolk, England **(1727–1788)**
Galbraith, John Kenneth (economist); Iona Station, Ontario, Canada, 10/15/1908
Galilei, Galileo (astronomer and physicist); Pisa (Italy) **(1564–1642)**
Gallico, Paul (novelist); New York City **(1897–1976)**
Gallup, George H. (poll taker); Jefferson, Iowa, 11/18/1901
Galsworthy, John (novelist and dramatist); Coombe, England **(1867–1933)**
Galway, James (flutist); Belfast, Northern Ireland, 12/8/1939
Gambling, John A. (radio broadcaster); New York City, 1930
Gandhi, Indira (Indira Nehru) (Prime Minister); Allahabad, India, 11/19/1917
Gandhi, Mohandas Karamchand (called Mahatma Gandhi) (Hindu leader); Porbandar, India **(1869–1948)**
Gannett, Frank E. (editor and publisher); **(1876–1957)**
Garagiola, Joe (Joseph Henry) (sportscaster); St. Louis, 2/12/1926
Garbo, Greta (Greta Gustafsson) (actress), Stockholm, 9/18/1905
Gardner, Ava (Lucy Johnson) (actress); Smithfield, N.C., 12/24/1922
Gardner, Erle Stanley (novelist); Malden, Mass. **(1889–1970)**
Garfield, John (Jules Garfinkle) (actor); New York City **(1913–1952)**
Garfunkel, Art (Arthur) (singer); Newark, N.J., 11/5/1941
Gargan, William (actor); Brooklyn, N.Y., **(1905–1979)**
Garibaldi, Giuseppe (Italian nationalist leader); Nice, France **(1807–1882)**
Garland, Judy (Frances Gumm) (actress and singer); Grand Rapids, Minn. **(1922–1969)**
Garner, Erroll (jazz pianist); Pittsburgh **(1921–1977)**
Garner, James (James Bumgarner) (actor); Norman, Okla., 4/7/1928
Garner, Peggy Ann (actress); Canton, Ohio, 2/3/1932
Garrett, Betty (actress); St. Joseph, Mo., 5/23/1919
Garrick, David (actor); Hereford, England **(1717–1779)**
Garrison, William Lloyd (abolitionist); Newburyport, Mass. **(1805–1879)**
Garroway, Dave (TV host); Schenectady, N.Y., 7/13/1913
Garson, Greer (actress); County Down, Northern Ireland, 9/29/1912(?)
Gary, John (singer); Watertown, N.Y., 11/29/1932
Gassman, Vittorio (film actor and director); Genoa, Italy, 9/1/1922
Gaudí, Antonio (architect); Reus, Spain **(1852–1926)**
Gauguin, Eugène Henri Paul (painter); Paris **(1848–1903)**
Gautama Buddha (Prince Siddhartha) (philosopher); Kapilavastu (India) **(563?–?483 B.C.)**

Gavin, John (actor, diplomat); Los Angeles, 4/8/1935

Gayle, Crystal (Brenda Gayle Webb) (singer); Paintsville, Ky., 1951

Gaynor, Janet (actress); Philadelphia, 10/6/1906

Gaynor, Mitzi (Francesca Mitzi Marlene de Czanyi von Gerber) (actress); Chicago, 9/4/1931

Gazzara, Ben (Biago Anthony Gazzara) (actor); New York City, 8/28/1930

Gebel-Williams, Gunther (animal trainer); Schweidnitz (Poland), 1934

Geddes, Barbara Bel (actress); New York City, 10/31/1922

Genet, Jean (playwright); Paris, 12/19/1910

Genghis Khan (Temujin) (conqueror); nr. Lake Baikal (U.S.S.R.) **(1162–1227)**

Genn, Leo (actor); London **(1905–1978)**

Gentry, Bobbie (Roberta Streeter) (singer); Chickasaw Co., Miss., 7/27/1944

Gericault, Jean Louis (painter); Rouen, France **(1791–1824)**

Gernreich, Rudi (fashion designer); Vienna, 8/8/1922

Geronimo (Goyathlay) (Apache chieftain); Arizona **(1829–1909)**

Gershwin, George (composer); Brooklyn, N.Y. **(1898–1937)**

Gershwin, Ira (lyricist); New York City, 12/6/1896

Getty, J. Paul (oil executive); Minneapolis **(1892–1976)**

Getz, Stan (saxophonist); Philadelphia, 2/2/1927

Ghiberti, Lorenzo (goldsmith and sculptor); Florence **(1378–1455)**

Giacometti, Alberto (sculptor); Switzerland **(1901–1966)**

Giannini, Giancarlo (actor); La Spezia, Italy, 8/1/1942

Gibbon, Edward (historian); Putney, England **(1737–1794)**

Gibson, Charles Dana (illustrator); Roxbury, Mass. **(1867–1944)**

Gibson, Hoot (Edward) (actor); Tememah, Neb. **(1892–1962)**

Gide, André (author); Paris **(1869–1951)**

Gielgud, Sir John (actor); London, 4/14/1904

Gilbert, John (movie actor); Logan, Utah **(1897–1936)**

Gilbert, Sir William Schwenck (librettist); London **(1836–1911)**

Gilels, Emil (concert pianist); Odessa, Ukraine, 1916

Gillespie, Dizzy (John Birks Gillespie) (jazz trumpeter); Cheraw, S.C., 10/21/1917

Gimbel, Bernard F. (merchant); Vincennes, Ind. **(1885–1966)**

Gingold, Hermione (actress and comedienne); London, 12/9/1897

Ginsberg, Allen (poet); Newark, N.J., 6/3/1926

Giorgione (painter); Castelfranco, (Italy) **(c.1477–1510)**

Giotto di Bondone (painter); Vespignamo (Italy) **(c.1266–1337)**

Giovanni, Nikki (poet); Knoxville, Tenn., 6/7/1943

Giroud, Françoise (French government official); Geneva, 9/21/1916

Gish, Dorothy (actress); Massillon, Ohio **(1898–1968)**

Gish, Lillian (Lillian de Guiche) (actress); Springfield, Ohio, 10/14/1896(?)

Givenchy, Hubert (fashion designer); Beauvais, France, 2/21/1927

Gladstone, William Ewart (statesman); Liverpool, England **(1809–1898)**

Gleason, Jackie (comedian); Brooklyn, N.Y., 2/26/1916

Gleason, James (actor); New York City **(1886–1959)**

Gluck, Christoph Willibald (composer); Erasbach (Germany) **(1714–1787)**

Gobel, George (comedian); Chicago, 5/20/1920

Godard, Jean Luc (film director); Paris, 12/3/1930

Goddard, Paulette (Marion Levy) (actress); Great Neck, N.Y., 6/3/1911

Godfrey, Arthur (entertainer); New York City, 8/31/1903

Goebbels, Joseph Paul (Nazi leader); Rheydt, Germany **(1897–1945)**

Goering, Hermann (Nazi leader); Rosenheim, Germany **(1893–1946)**

Goethals, George Washington (engineer); Brooklyn, N.Y. **(1858–1928)**

Goethe, Johann Wolfgang von (poet); Frankfurt am Main, Germany **(1749–1832)**

Gogol, Nikolai Vasilievich (novelist); nr. Mirgorod, Ukraine **(1809–1852)**

Goldberg, Rube (cartoonist); San Francisco **(1883–1970)**

Golden, Harry (Harry Goldhurst) (author); New York City **(1902–1981)**

Goldsmith, Oliver (dramatist and poet); County Longford, Ireland **(1728–1774)**

Goldwyn, Samuel (Samuel Goldfish) (film producer); Warsaw **(1882–1974)**

Golenpaul, Dan (creator of Information Please radio show and editor of almanac of same name); New York City **(1900–1974)**

Gompers, Samuel (labor leader); London **(1850–1924)**

Goodall, Jane (Baroness van Lawick-Goodall) (ethologist); London, 4/3/1934

Goodman, Benny (clarinetist); Chicago, 5/30/1909

Goodyear, Charles (inventor); New Haven, Conn. **(1800–1860)**

Gordimer, Nadine (novelist and short-story writer); Springs, South Africa, 12/20/1923

Gordon, Max (stage producer); New York City; **(1892–1978)**

Gordon, Ruth (actress); Wollaston, Mass., 10/30/1896

Gordy, Berry, Jr. (record company executive); Detroit, 11/28/1929

Gore, Lesley (singer); Tenafly, N.J., 1946

Goren, Charles H. (bridge expert); Philadelphia, 3/4/1901

Gorki, Maxim (Alexei Maximovich Peshkov) (author); Nizhni Novgorod, Russia **(1868–1936)**

Gorky, Arshile (painter); Armenia **(1904–1948)**

Gormé, Eydie (singer); Bronx, N.Y., 8/16/1932

Gorshin, Frank (actor); Pittsburgh, 4/5/1934

Gosden, Freeman F. *See* Amos

Gould, Chester (cartoonist); Pawnee, Okla., 11/20/1900

Gould, Elliott (Elliott Goldstein) (actor); Brooklyn, N.Y., 8/29/1938

Gould, Glenn (concert pianist); Toronto, **(1932–1982)**

Gould, Morton (composer); Richmond Hill, Queens, N.Y., 12/10/1913

Goulet, Robert (singer); Lawrence, Mass., 11/26/1933

Gounod, Charles François (composer); Paris **(1818–1893)**

Goya y Lucientes, Francisco José de (painter); Fuendetodos, Spain **(1746–1828)**

Grable, Betty (actress); St. Louis **(1916–1973)**

Graham, Bill (Wolfgang Grajonca) (rock impresario); Berlin, 1931

Graham, Billy (William F.) (evangelist); Charlotte, N.C., 11/7/1918

Graham, Katharine Meyer (newspaper publisher); New York City, 6/16/1917

Graham, Martha (choreographer); Pittsburgh, 5/11/1894(?)

Grahame, Gloria (Gloria Hallwood) (actress); Los Angeles **(1929–1981)**

Gramm, Donald (bass-baritone); Milwaukee, 2/26/1927

Granger, Farley (actor); San Jose, Calif., 7/1/1925

Granger, Stewart (James Stewart) (actor); London, 5/6/1913

Grant, Cary (Alexander Archibald Leach) (actor); Bristol, England, 1/18/1904

Grant, Kathryn (actress); Houston, Tex., 1933

Grant, Lee (Lyova Haskell Rosenthal) (actress); New York City, 10/31/1930

Granville, Bonita (actress and producer); New York City, 1923

Grass, Günter (novelist); Danzig (Poland), 10/16/1927

Grauer, Ben (radio and TV announcer); New York City **(1908–1977)**

Graves, Peter (Peter Arness) (actor); Minneapolis, 3/18/1926

Graves, Robert (writer); London, 7/24/1895

Gray, Barry (Bernard Yaroslaw) (radio interviewer); Atlantic City, N.J., 7/2/1916

Gray, Dolores (singer and actress); Chicago, 6/7/1930

Gray, Thomas (poet); London **(1716–1771)**

Grayson, Kathryn (Zelma Hednick) (singer and actress); Winston-Salem, N.C., 2/9/1923

Greco, Buddy (singer); Philadelphia, 8/14/1926

Greco, José (dancer); Montorio nei Frentani, Italy, 12/23/1918

Greeley, Horace (journalist and politician); Amherst, N.H. **(1811–1872)**

Green, Adolph (actor and lyricist); New York City, 12/2/1915

Green, Al (singer); Forrest City, Ark., 4/13/1946

Greene, Graham (novelist); Berkhamsted, England, 10/2/1904

Greene, Lorne (actor); Ottowa, 2/12/1915

Greene, Martyn (actor); London **(1899–1975)**

Greenstreet, Sydney (actor); Sandwich, England **(1879–1954)**

Greenwood, Joan (actress and director); London, 3/4/1921

Greer, Germaine (feminist); Melbourne, 1/29/1939

Gregory, Cynthia (ballerina); Los Angeles, 7/8/1946

Gregory, Dick (comedian); St. Louis, 1932

Greuze, Jean Baptiste (painter); Tournus, France **(1725–1805)**

Grey, Joel (Joel Katz) (actor); Cleveland, 4/11/1932

Grey, Zane (author); Zanesville, Ohio **(1875–1939)**

Grieg, Edvard Hagerup (composer); Bergen, Norway **(1843–1907)**

Grier, Roosevelt (entertainer and former athlete); Cuthbert, Ga., 7/14/1932

Griffin, Merv (TV entertainer); San Mateo, Calif., 7/6/1925

Griffith, Andy (actor); Mount Airy, N.C., 6/1/1926

Griffith, David Lewelyn Wark (film producer); La Grange, Ky. **(1875–1948)**

Grigorovich, Yuri (choreographer); Leningrad, 1/1/1927

Grimes, Tammy (actress); Lynn, Mass., 1/30/1934

Grimm, Jacob (author of fairy tales); Hanau (Germany) **(1785–1863)**

Grimm, Wilhelm (author of fairy tales); Hanau (Germany) **(1786–1859)**

Gris, Juan (José Victoriano González) (painter); Madrid **(1887–1927)**

Grizzard, George (actor); Roanoke Rapids, N.C., 4/1/1928

Gromyko, Andrei A. (diplomat); Starye Gromyki, Russia, 7/5/1909

Gropius, Walter (architect); Berlin **(1883–1969)**

Gropper, William (painter, illustrator); New York City **(1897–1977)**

Grosz, George (painter); Germany **(1893–1959)**

Guardino, Harry (actor); New York City, 12/23/1925

Guggenheim, Meyer (capitalist); Langnau, Switzerland **(1828–1905)**

Guinness, Sir Alec (actor); London, 4/2/1914

Guitry, Sacha (Alexandre) (actor and film director); St. Petersburg, Russia **(1885–1957)**

Gunther, John (author); Chicago **(1901–1970)**

Gutenberg, Johann (printer); Mainz (Germany) **(1400?–?1468)**

Guthrie, Arlo (singer); New York City, 7/10/1947

Guthrie, Woody (folk singer and composer); Okemah, Okla. **(1912–1967)**

Gwenn, Edmund (actor); London **(1875–1959)**

H

Hackett, Bobby (trumpeter); Providence, R.I. **(1915–1976)**

Hackett, Buddy (Leonard Hacker) (comedian and actor); Brooklyn, N.Y., 8/31/1924

Hackman, Gene (actor); San Bernardino, Calif., 1/30/1931

Hagen, Uta (actress); Göttingen, Germany, 6/12/1919

Haggard, Merle (songwriter); Bakersfield, Calif., 4/6/1937
Hagman, Larry (actor); Weatherford, Tex., 1931
Haig, Alexander Meigs, Jr. (ex-Secretary of State and ex-general); Bala-Cynwyd, Pa., 12/2/1924
Haile Selassie (Ras Tafari Makonnen) (ex-Emperor); Ethiopia **(1892–1975)**
Hailey, Arthur (novelist); Luton, England, 4/5/1920
Halberstam, David (journalist); New York City, 4/10/1934
Hale, Edward Everett (clergyman and author); Boston **(1822–1909)**
Hale, Nathan (American Revolutionary officer); Coventry, Conn. **(1755–1776)**
Haley, Alex (writer); Ithaca, N.Y., 8/11/1921
Hall, Monty (TV personality); Winnipeg, Canada, 1923
Hals, Frans (painter); Antwerp (Netherlands) **(1580?–1666)**
Halsey, William Frederick, Jr. (naval officer); Elizabeth, N.J. **(1882–1959)**
Hamill, Pete (journalist); Brooklyn, N.Y., 6/24/1935
Hamilton, Alexander (statesman); Nevis, British West Indies **(1757?–1804)**
Hamilton, George (actor); Memphis, Tenn., 8/12/1939
Hamilton, Margaret (actress); Cleveland, 9/12/1902
Hamlisch, Marvin (composer and pianist); New York City, 6/2/1944
Hammarskjold, Dag (U.N. Secretary-General); Jönköping, Sweden **(1905–1961)**
Hammerstein, Oscar, II (librettist and stage producer); New York City **(1895–1960)**
Hampden, Walter (Walter Hampden Dougherty) (actor); Brooklyn, N.Y. **(1879–1955)**
Hampton, Lionel (vibraharpist and band leader); Birmingham, Ala., 4/20/1914
Hancock, John (statesman); Braintree, Mass. **(1737–1793)**
Hand, Learned (jurist); Albany, N.Y. **(1872–1961)**
Handel, George Frederick (Georg Friedrich Händel) (composer); Halle (Germany) **(1685–1759)**
Handy, William Christopher (blues composer); Florence, Ala. **(1873–1958)**
Hannibal (Carthaginian general); North Africa **(247–182 B.C.)**
Hanson, Howard (conductor); Wahoo, Neb., **(1896–1981)**
Harburg, E. Y. "Yip" (songwriter); New York City, 4/8/1896
Harding, Ann (actress); San Antonio, Tex. **(1902–1981)**
Hardwicke, Sir Cedric (actor); Stourbridge, England **(1893–1964)**
Hardy, Oliver (comedian); Atlanta **(1892–1957)**
Hardy, Thomas (novelist); Dorsetshire, England **(1840–1928)**
Harkness, Edward S. (capitalist); Cleveland **(1874–1940)**
Harlow, Jean (Harlean Carpentier) (actress); Kansas City, Mo. **(1911–1937)**
Harnick, Sheldon (lyricist); Chicago, 4/30/1924
Harper, Valerie (actress); Suffern, N.Y., 8/22/1940(?)
Harriman, W. (William) Averell (ex-Governor of New York); New York City, 11/15/1891
Harris, Barbara (actress); Evanston, Ill., 1935
Harris, Emmylou (singer); Birmingham, Ala., 1949
Harris, Julie (actress); Grosse Pointe Park, Mich., 12/2/1925
Harris, Phil (actor and band leader); Linton, Ind., 6/24/1906
Harris, Richard (actor); Limerick, Ireland, 10/1/1933
Harris, Rosemary (actress); Ashby, England, 9/19/1930
Harris, Roy (composer); Lincoln County, Olka. **(1898–1979)**
Harrison, George (singer and songwriter); Liverpool, England, 2/25/1943
Harrison, Noel (singer and actor); London, 1/29/1936
Harrison, Rex (Reginald Carey) (actor); Huyton, England, 3/5/1908
Hart, Lorenz (lyricist); New York **(1895–1943)**
Hart, Moss (playwright); New York City **(1904–1961)**
Hart, William S. (actor); Newburgh, N.Y. **(1862–1946)**
Harte, Bret (Francis Brett Harte) (author); Albany, N.Y. **(1836–1902)**
Hartford, Huntington (George Huntington Hartford II) (A.&P. heir); New York City, 4/18/1911
Hartford, John (singer and banjoist); New York City, 12/30/1937
Hartman, Elizabeth (actress); Youngstown, Ohio, 12/23/1941
Harvey, Laurence (Larushka Skikne) (actor); Joniskis, Lithuania **(1928–1973)**
Harvey, William (physician); Folkestone, England **(1578–1657)**
Hasso, Signe (actress); Stockholm, 8/15/1915
Haver, June (actress); Rock Island, Ill., 6/10/1926
Havoc, June (June Hovick) (actress); Seattle, 1916
Hawkins, Jack (actor); London **(1910–1973)**
Hawn, Goldie (actress); Washington, D.C., 11/21/1945
Haworth, Jill (actress); Sussex, England, 1945
Hawthorne, Nathaniel (novelist); Salem, Mass. **(1804–1864)**
Hay, John Milton (statesman); Salem, Ind. **(1838–1905)**
Hayakawa, Sessue (actor); Honshu, Japan **(1890–1973)**
Hayden, Melissa (ballerina); Toronto, 4/25/1923
Hayden, Sterling (Sterling Relyea Walter) (actor and writer); Montclair, N.J., 3/26/1916
Haydn, Franz Joseph (composer); Rohrau (Austria) **(1732–1809)**
Hayes, Helen (Helen Hayes Brown) (actress); Washington, D.C., 10/10/1900
Hayes, Isaac (composer); Covington, Tenn., 8/20/1942
Hayward, Louis (actor); Johannesburg, South Africa, 1909
Hayward, Susan (Edythe Marrener) (actress); Brooklyn, N.Y. **(1919?–1975)**
Hayworth, Rita (Margarita Cansino) (actress); New York City, 10/17/1918
Head, Edith (costume designer); Los Angeles, 10/28/1907
Hearst, William Randolph (publisher); San Francisco **(1863–1951)**
Hearst, William Randolph, Jr. (publisher); New York City, 1/27/1908
Heath, Edward (ex-Prime Minister); Broadstairs, England, 7/9/1916
Heatherton, Joey (actress); Rockville Centre, N.Y., 9/14/1944
Hecht, Ben (author); New York City **(1894–1964)**
Heckart, Eileen (actress); Columbus, Ohio, 3/29/1919
Heflin, Van (Emmet Evan Heflin) (actor); Walters, Okla. **(1910–1971)**
Hefner, Hugh (publisher); Chicago, 4/9/1926
Hegel, Georg Wilhelm Friedrich (philosopher); Stuttgart (Germany) **(1770–1831)**
Heifetz, Jascha (concert violinist); Vilna, Russia, 2/2/1901
Heine, Heinrich (Harry) (poet); Düsseldorf (Germany) **(1797–1856)**
Heinemann, Gustav (ex-President of Germany); Schweim, Germany **(1899–1976)**
Heller, Joseph (novelist); Brooklyn, N.Y., 5/1/1923
Hellman, Lillian (playwright); New Orleans, 6/20/1905
Hemingway, Ernest Miller (novelist); Oak Park, Ill. **(1899–1961)**
Hemmings, David (actor); Guilford, England, 11/2/1941
Henderson, Florence (actress); Dale, Ind., 2/14/1934
Henderson, Skitch (Lyle Russell Cedric) (conductor and pianist); Birmingham, England(?), 1/27/1918
Hendrix, Jimi (James Marshall Hendrix) (guitarist); Seattle **(1942–1970)**
Henning, Doug (magician and actor); Winnipeg, Canada, 1947(?)
Henreid, Paul (actor); Trieste, 1/10/1908
Henri, Robert (painter); Cincinnati **(1865–1926)**
Henry, O. (William Sydney Porter) (story writer); Greensboro, N.C. **(1862–1910)**
Henry, Patrick (statesman); Hanover County, Va. **(1736–1799)**
Henson, Jim (puppeteer); Greenville, Miss., 9/24/1936
Hepburn, Audrey (actress); Brussels, Belgium, 5/4/1929
Hepburn, Katharine (actress); Hartford, Conn., 11/8/1909
Hepplewhite, George (furniture designer); England **(?–1786)**
Hepworth, Barbara (sculptor); Wakefield, England **(1903–1975)**
Herbert, Victor (composer); Dublin **(1859–1924)**
Herblock (Herbert L. Block) (political cartoonist); Chicago, 10/13/1909
Herman, Woody (Woodrow Charles) (band leader); Milwaukee, 5/16/1913
Herod (Herodes) (called Herod the Great) (King of Judea) **(73?–4 B.C.)**
Herodotus (historian); Halicarnassus (Turkey) **(c. 484–425 B.C.)**
Hershfield, Harry (humorist and raconteur); Cedar Rapids, Iowa **(1885–1974)**
Hersholt, Jean (actor); Copenhagen **(1886–1956)**
Heston, Charlton (actor); Evanston, Ill., 10/4/1924
Heyerdahl, Thor (ethnologist and explorer); Larvik, Norway, 10/6/1914
Hildegarde (Hildegarde Loretta Sell) (singer); Adell, Wis., 2/1/1906
Hill, Arthur (actor); Melfort, Canada, 8/1/1922
Hillary, Sir Edmund (mountain climber); New Zealand, 7/20/1919
Hiller, Wendy (actress); Bramhall, England, 8/15/1912
Hilliard, Harriet. *See* Nelson, Harriet
Hindemith, Paul (composer); Hanau, Germany **(1895–1963)**
Hines, Earl "Fatha" (jazz pianist); Duquesne, Pa., 12/28/1905
Hines, Jerome (Jerome Heinz) (basso); Los Angeles, 11/8/1921
Hingle, Pat (actor); Denver, 7/19/1924
Hippocrates (physician); Cos, Greece **(c. 460–c. 377 B.C.)**
Hirohito (Emperor); Tokyo, 4/29/1901
Hirschfeld, Al (Albert) (cartoonist); St. Louis, 6/21/1903
Hirschhorn, Joseph Herman (financier, speculator, and art collector); Mitau, Latvia **(1899–1981)**
Hirt, Al (trumpeter); New Orleans, 11/7/1922
Hitchcock, Alfred J. (film director); London **(1899–1980)**
Hitler, Adolf (Adolf Schicklgruber) (German dictator); Braunau, Austria **(1889–1945)**
Hitzig, William Maxwell (physician); Austria, 12/15/1904
Hobson, Laura Z. (Laura K. Zametkin) (novelist); New York City, 1900(?)
Hodges, Eddie (actor); Hattiesburg, Miss., 3/5/1947
Hoffa James R(iddle) (labor leader); Brazil, Ind., 2/14/1913 (presumed dead, 1977)
Hoffman, Dustin (film actor and director); Los Angeles, 8/8/1937
Hofmann, Hans (painter); Germany **(1880–1966)**
Hogarth, William (painter and engraver); London **(1697–1764)**
Holbein, Hans (the Elder) (painter); Augsburg (Germany) **(1465?–1524)**
Holbein, Hans (the Younger) (painter); Augsburg (Germany) **(1497?–1543)**
Holbrook, Hal (actor); Cleveland, 2/17/1925
Holden, William (William Franklin Beedle, Jr.) (actor); O'Fallon, Ill. **(1918–1981)**
Holder, Geoffrey (dancer); Port-of-Spain, Trinidad, 8/1/1930
Holiday, Billie (Eleanora Fagan) (jazz–blues singer); Baltimore **(1915–1959)**

Holliday, Judy (Judith Tuvim) (comedienne); New York City **(1922–1965)**
Holloway, Stanley (actor); London **(1890–1982)**
Holloway, Sterling (actor); Cedartown, Ga., 1905
Holm, Celeste (actress); New York City, 4/29/1919
Holmes, Oliver Wendell (jurist); Boston **(1841–1935)**
Holt, Jack (actor); Winchester, Va. **(1888–1951)**
Holtz, Lou (comedian); San Francisco **(1898–1980)**
Home, Lord (Alexander Frederick Douglas-Home) (diplomat); London, 7/2/1903
Homeier, Skip (actor); Chicago, 1930
Homer, Winslow (painter); Boston, Mass. **(1836–1910)**
Homer (Greek poet) **(c.850 B.C.?)**
Homolka, Oscar (actor); Vienna **(1898–1978)**
Honegger, Arthur (composer); Le Havre, France **(1892–1955)**
Hook, Sidney (philosopher); New York City, 12/20/1902
Hoover, J. Edgar (FBI director); Washington, D.C. **(1895–1972)**
Hope, Bob (Leslie Townes Hope) (comedian); London, 5/29/1903
Hopkins, Anthony (actor); Port Talbot, Wales, 12/31/1937
Hopkins, Johns (financier); Anne Arundel County, Md. **(1795–1873)**
Hopkins, Miriam (actress); Bainbridge, Ga. **(1902–1972)**
Hopper, Dennis (actor); Dodge City, Kan., 5/17/1936
Hopper, Edward (painter); Nyack, N.Y. **(1882–1967)**
Horace (Quintus Horatius Flaccus) (poet); Venosa (Italy) **(65–8 B.C.)**
Horne, Lena (singer); Brooklyn, N.Y., 6/30/1917
Horne, Marilyn (mezzo-soprano); Bradford, Pa., 1/16/1934
Horowitz, Vladimir (pianist); Kiev, Russia, 10/1/1904
Horton, Edward Everett (comedian); Brooklyn, N.Y. **(1887–1970)**
Houdini, Harry (Ehrich Weiss) (magician); Appleton, Wis. **(1874–1926)**
Houseman, John (John Haussmann) (producer, director, and actor); Bucharest, 9/22/1902
Housman, Alfred Edward (poet); Fockburg, England **(1859–1936)**
Houston, Samuel (political leader); Rockbridge County, Va. **(1793–1863)**
Howard, Leslie (Leslie Stainer) (actor); London **(1893–1943)**
Howard, Trevor (actor); Kent, England, 9/29/1916
Howe, Elias (inventor); Spencer, Mass. **(1819–1867)**
Howe, Irving (literary critic); New York City, 6/11/1920
Howe, Julia Ward (poet and reformer); New York City **(1819–1910)**
Howes, Sally Ann (actress); London, 7/20/1934
Hudson, Henry (English navigator) **(?–1611)**
Hudson, Rock (born Roy Scherer, Jr.; took Roy Fitzgerald as legal name) (actor); Winnetka, Ill., 11/17/1925
Hughes, Charles Evans (jurist); Glens Falls, N.Y. **(1862–1948)**
Hughes, Howard (industrialist and film producer); Houston **(1905–1976)**
Hughes, Langston (poet); Joplin, Mo. **(1902–1967)**
Hugo, Victor Marie (author); Besançon, France **(1802–1885)**
Hume, David (philosopher); Edinburgh, Scotland **(1711–1776)**
Humperdinck, Engelbert (Arnold Dorsey) (singer); Madras, India, 5/2/1936
Humperdinck, Engelbert (composer); Siegburg (Germany) **(1854–1921)**
Hunt, H. L. (industrialist); nr. Vandalia, Ill. **(1889–1974)**
Hunt, Marsha (actress); Chicago, 10/17/1917
Hunter, Kim (Janet Cole) (actress); Detroit, 11/12/1922
Hunter, Tab (Arthur Andrew Gelien) (actor); New York City, 7/11/1931
Huntley, Chet (TV newscaster); Cardwell, Mont. **(1911–1974)**
Hurok, Sol (Solomon) (impresario); Pogar, Russia **(1884–1974)**
Hurst, Fannie (novelist); Hamilton, Ohio **(1889–1968)**
Hussein I (King); Jordan, 11/14/1935
Huston, John (film director and writer); Nevada, Mo., 8/5/1906
Huston, Walter (Walter Houghston) (actor); Toronto **(1884–1950)**
Hutchins, Robert M. (educator); Brooklyn, N.Y. **(1899–1977)**
Hutton, Barbara (Woolworth heiress); New York City **(1912–1979)**
Hutton, Betty (Betty Thornburg) (actress); Battle Creek, Mich., 2/26/1921
Hutton, Lauren (model and actress); Charleston, S.C., 1944
Huxley, Aldous (author); Godalming, England **(1894–1963)**
Huxley, Sir Julian S. (biologist and author); London **(1887–1975)**
Huxley, Thomas Henry (biologist); Ealing, England **(1825–1895)**

I

Ian, Janis (singer); New York City, 5/7/1951
Ibsen, Henrik (dramatist); Skien, Norway **(1828–1906)**
Inge, William (playwright); Independence, Kan. **(1913–1973)**
Ingres, Jean Auguste Dominique (painter); Montauban, France **(1780–1867)**
Inness, George (painter); nr. Newburgh, N.Y. **(1825–1894)**
Ionesco, Eugène (playwright); Slatina, Romania, 11/26/1912
Ireland, John (actor); Vancouver, B.C., Canada, 1/30/1915
Irving, Washington (author); New York City **(1783–1859)**
Isherwood, Christopher (novelist and playwright); nr. Disley and High Lane, England, 8/26/1904
Iturbi, José (concert pianist); Valencia, Spain **(1895–1980)**
Ives, Burl (Icle Ivanhoe) (singer); Hunt, Ill., 6/14/1909
Ives, Charles E(dward) (composer); Danbury, Conn. **(1874–1954)**

J

Jackson, Anne (actress); Millvale, Pa., 9/3/1926
Jackson, Glenda (actress); Hoylake, England, 1937(?)
Jackson, Rev. Jesse (civil rights leader); Greenville, S.C., 10/8/1941
Jackson, Kate (actress); Alabama, 1949
Jackson, Mahalia (gospel singer); New Orleans **(1912–1972)**
Jackson, Thomas Jonathan ("Stonewall") (general); Clarksburg, Va. (now W. Va.) **(1824–1863)**
Jacobi, Lou (actor); Toronto, 12/28/1913
Jacobs, Jane (urbanologist); Scranton, Pa., 5/1/1916
Jaffe, Sam (actor); New York City, 3/8/1893
Jagger, Dean (actor); Lima, Ohio, 11/7/1903
Jagger, Mick (Michael Philip) (singer); Dartford, England, 7/26/1944
James, Harry (trumpeter); Albany, Ga., 3/15/1916
James, Henry (novelist); New York City **(1843–1916)**
James, Jesse Woodson (outlaw); Clay County, Mo. **(1847–1882)**
James, William (psychologist); New York City **(1842–1910)**
Jameson, (Margaret) Storm (novelist); Whitby, England, 1897
Janis, Byron (pianist); McKeesport, Pa., 3/24/1928
Jannings, Emil (actor); Brooklyn, N.Y. **(1886–1950)**
Janssen, David (David Meyer) (actor); Naponee, Neb. **(1930–1980)**
Jay, John (statesman and jurist); New York City **(1745–1829)**
Jeanmaire, Renée (dancer); Paris, 4/29/1924
Jenner, Edward (physician); Berkeley, England **(1749–1823)**
Jennings, Waylon (singer); Littlefield, Tex., 1937
Jessel, George (entertainer); New York City **(1898–1981)**
Jessup, Philip C. (jurist); New York City, 1/5/1897
Joan of Arc (Jeanne d'Arc) (saint and patriot); Domremy-la-Pucelle, France **(1412–1431)**
Joffrey, Robert (Abdullah Jaffa Bey Khan) (choreographer); Seattle, 12/24/1930
John, Elton (Reginald Kenneth Dwight) (singer and pianist); Pinner, England, 3/25/1947
Johns, Glynis (actress); Pretoria, South Africa, 10/5/1923
Johns, Jasper (painter and sculptor); Augusta, Ga., 5/15/1930
Johnson, James Weldon (author and educator); Jacksonville, Fla. **(1871–1938)**
Johnson, Philip Cortelyou (architect); Cleveland, Ohio, 7/8/1906
Johnson, Samuel (lexicographer and author); Lichfield, England **(1709–1784)**
Johnson, Van (actor); Newport, R.I., 8/20/1916
Joliot-Curie, Frédéric (physicist); Paris **(1900–1958)**
Joliot-Curie, Irène (Irène Curie) (physicist); France **(1897–1956)**
Jolliet (or **Joliet**), Louis (explorer); Beaupré, Canada **(1645–1700)**
Jolson, Al (Asa Yoelson) (actor and singer); St. Petersburg, Russia **(1886–1950)**
Jones, Carolyn (singer and actress); Amarillo, Tex., 4/28/1933
Jones, Dean (actor); Morgan County, Ala., 1/25/1935
Jones, George (singer); Saratoga, Tex., 9/12/1931
Jones, Inigo (architect); London **(1573–1652)**
Jones, James (novelist); Robinson, Ill. **(1921–1977)**
Jones, James Earl (actor); Arkabutla, Miss., 1/17/1931
Jones, Jennifer (Phyllis Isley) (actress); Tulsa, Okla., 3/2/1919
Jones, John Paul (John Paul) (naval officer); Scotland **(1747–1792)**
Jones, Quincy (composer); Chicago, 3/14/1933
Jones, Shirley (singer and actress); Smithtown, Pa., 3/31/1934
Jones, Tom (Thomas Jones Woodward) (singer); Pontypridd, Wales, 6/7/1940
Jong, Erica (writer); New York City, 3/26/1942
Jonson, Ben (Benjamin) (poet and dramatist); Westminster, England **(1572–1637)**
Joplin, Janis (singer); Port Arthur, Tex. **(1943–1970)**
Jory, Victor (actor); Dawson City, Yukon, Canada **(1902–1982)**
Jourdan, Louis (Louis Gendre) (actor); Marseilles, France, 6/19/1920
Joyce, James (novelist); Dublin **(1882–1941)**
Juárez, Benito Pablo (statesman); Guelatao, Mexico **(1806–1872)**
Juliana (Queen); The Hague, Netherlands, 4/30/1909
Jung, Carl Gustav (psychoanalyst); Basel, Switzerland **(1875–1961)**
Jurado, Katy (actress); Guadalajara, Mexico, 1927

K

Kabalevsky, Dmitri (composer); St. Petersburg, Russia, 12/30/1904
Kádár, János (Communist Party leader); Hungary, 1912
Kahn, Gus (songwriter); Coblenz, Germany **(1886–1941)**
Kahn, Louis I. (architect); Oesel Island, Estonia **(1901–1974)**
Kahn, Madeline (actress); Boston, 9/29/1942
Kaminska, Ida (actress); Odessa, Russia **(1899–1980)**
Kandinsky, Wassily (painter); Moscow **(1866–1944)**
Kanin, Garson (playwright); Rochester, N.Y., 11/24/1912
Kant, Immanuel (philosopher); Königsberg (Germany) **(1724–1804)**
Kantor, MacKinlay (novelist); Webster City, Iowa **(1904–1977)**
Kaplan, Gabe (actor); Brooklyn, N.Y., 1945
Karloff, Boris (William Henry Pratt) (actor); London **(1887–1969)**

Kaufman, George S. (playwright); Pittsburgh **(1889–1961)**
Kaye, Danny (David Daniel Kominski) (comedian); Brooklyn, N.Y., 1/18/1913
Kaye, Sammy (band leader); Cleveland, 3/13/1910
Kazan, Elia (director); Constantinople, Turkey, 9/7/1909
Kazan, Lainie (singer); New York City, 1940
Keach, Stacy (actor); Savannah, Ga., 6/2/1941
Keaton, Buster (Joseph Frank Keaton) (comedian); Piqua, Kan. **(1896–1966)**
Keaton, Diane (actress); Los Angeles, 1/5/1946
Keats, John (poet); London **(1795–1821)**
Keel, Howard (singer and actor); Gillespie, Ill., 4/13/1919
Keeler, Ruby (Lehy Keeler) (actress and dancer); Halifax, Nova Scotia, Canada, 8/25/1910
Kefauver, Estes (legislator); Madisonville, Tenn. **(1903–1963)**
Keith, Brian (actor); Bayonne, N.J., 11/14/1921
Keller, Helen Adams (author and educator); Tuscumbia, Ala. **(1880–1968)**
Kellerman, Sally (actress); Long Beach, Calif., 6/2/1938
Kelly, Emmett (clown); Sedan, Kan., **(1898–1979)**
Kelly, Gene (dancer and actor); Pittsburgh, 8/23/1912
Kelly, Grace (Princess Grace of Monaco) (former actress); Philadelphia **(1929–1982)**
Kelly, Patsy (actress and comedienne); Brooklyn, N.Y., 1/12/1910
Kelly, Walt (cartoonist); Philadelphia **(1913–1973)**
Kemal Ataturk (Mustafa Kemal) (Turkish soldier and statesman); Salonika (Greece) **(1881–1938)**
Kennan, George F. (diplomat); Milwaukee, 2/16/1904
Kennedy, Arthur (actor); Worcester, Mass., 2/17/1914
Kennedy, George (actor); New York City, 2/18/1925
Kennedy, Jacqueline. *See* Onassis, Jacqueline
Kennedy, Joseph P. (financier); Boston **(1888–1969)**
Kennedy, Robert Francis (legislator); Brookline, Mass. **(1925–1968)**
Kennedy, Rose Fitzgerald (President's mother); Boston, 7/22/1890
Kent, Rockwell (painter); Tarrytown Heights, N.Y. **(1882–1971)**
Kenton, Stan (Stanley Newcomb) (jazz musician); Wichita, Kan. **(1912–1979)**
Kepler, Johannes (astronomer); Weil (Germany) **(1571–1630)**
Kerensky, Alexander Fedorovich (statesman); Simbirks, Russia **(1881–1970)**
Kern, Jerome David (composer); New York City **(1885–1945)**
Kerr, Deborah (actress); Helensburgh, Scotland, 9/30/1921
Kesey, Ken (novelist); La Junta, Colo., 9/17/1935
Kettering, Charles F. (engineer and inventor); nr. Loudonville, Ohio **(1876–1958)**
Key, Francis Scott (lawyer and author of national anthem); Frederick (now Carroll) County, Md. **(1779–1843)**
Keyes, Frances Parkinson (novelist); Charlottesville, Va. **(1885–1970)**
Keynes (1st Baron of Tilton) (John Maynard Keynes) (economist); Cambridge, England **(1883–1946)**
Khachaturian, Aram (composer); Tiflis, Russia **(1903–1978)**
Khrushchev, Nikita S. (Soviet leader); Kalinovka, nr. Kursk, Ukraine **(1894–1971)**
Kibbee, Guy (actor); El Paso **(1886–1956)**
Kidd, Michael (choreographer); Brooklyn, N.Y., 1917
Kidd, William (called Captain Kidd) (pirate); Greenock, Scotland **(1645?–1701)**
Kieran, John (writer); New York City **(1892–1981)**
Kiesinger, Kurt Georg (diplomat); Ebingen, Germany, 4/6/1904
Kiley, Richard (actor and singer); Chicago, 3/31/1922
Kilmer, Alfred Joyce (poet); New Brunswick, N.J. **(1886–1918)**
King, Alan (Irwin Alan Kniberg) (entertainer); Brooklyn, N.Y., 12/26/1927
King, B.B. (Riley King) (guitarist); Itta Bena, Miss., 9/16/1925
King, Carole (singer and songwriter); Brooklyn, N.Y., 2/9/1941
King, Coretta Scott (civil rights leader); Marion, Ala., 4/27/1927
King, Martin Luther, Jr. (civil rights leader); Atlanta **(1929–1968)**
King, Pee Wee (Frank) (singer); Abrams, Wis., 2/18/1914
Kingsley, Sidney (Sidney Kirschner) (playwright); New York City, 10/18/1906
Kipling, Rudyard (author); Bombay **(1865–1936)**
Kipnis, Alexander (basso); Ukraine, **(1891–1978)**
Kirby, George (comedian); Chicago, 1923(?)
Kirk, Grayson (educator); Jeffersonville, Ohio, 10/12/1903
Kirk, Lisa (actress and singer); Charleroi, Pa., 1925
Kirk, Phyllis (actress); Plainfield, N.J., 9/18/1930
Kirkland, Gelsey (ballerina); Bethelhem, Pa., 12/29/1952
Kirkpatrick, Ralph (harpsichordist); Leominster, Mass., 6/10/1911
Kirkwood, James (actor); Grand Rapids, Mich. **(1883–1963)**
Kirsten, Dorothy (soprano); Montclair, N.J., 7/6/1919
Kissinger, Henry (Heinz Alfred Kissinger) (ex-Secretary of State); Furth, Germany, 5/27/1923
Kitt, Eartha (singer); North, S.C., 1/26/1928
Klee, Paul (painter); Münchenbuchsee, nr. Bern, Switzerland **(1879–1940)**
Klein, Calvin (fashion designer); Bronx, N.Y., 11/19/1942
Klein, Robert (comedian); Bronx, N.Y., 2/8/1942
Klemperer, Otto (conductor); Breslau (Poland) **(1885–1973)**
Klemperer, Werner (actor); Cologne, Germany, 3/22/1920
Klugman, Jack (actor); Philadelphia, 4/27/1922
Knievel, Evel (Robert Craig) (daredevil motorcyclist); Butte, Mont., 10/17/1938
Knight, Gladys (singer); Atlanta, 5/28/1944
Knight, John S. (publisher); Bluefield, W. Va. **(1894–1981)**
Knopf, Alfred A. (publisher); New York City, 9/12/1892
Knotts, Don (actor); Morgantown, W.Va., 7/21/1924
Knox, John (religious reformer); Haddington, East Lothian, Scotland **(1505–1572)**
Koch, Robert (physician); Klausthal (Germany) **(1843–1910)**
Koestler, Arthur (novelist); Budapest, 9/5/1905
Kokoschka, Oskar (painter); Póchlarn Austria **(1886–1980)**
Kooper, Al (singer and pianist); Brooklyn, N.Y., 2/5/1944
Korman, Harvey (actor); Chicago, 2/15/1927
Kosciusko, Thaddeus (Tadeusz Andrzej Bonawentura Kosciuszko) (military officer); Grand Duchy of Lithuania **(1746–1817)**
Kostelanetz, André (orchestra conductor); St. Petersburg, Russia **(1901–1980)**
Kosygin, Aleksei N. (Premier); St. Petersburg, Russia **(1904–1980)**
Koussevitzky, Serge (Sergei) Alexandrovitch (orchestra conductor); Vishni Volochek, Tver, Russia **(1874–1951)**
Kovacs, Ernie (comedian); Trenton, N.J. **(1919–1962)**
Kramer, Stanley E. (film producer and director); New York City, 9/29/1913
Kraus, Lili (pianist); Budapest, 3/4/1905(?)
Kreisler, Fritz (violinist and composer); Vienna **(1875–1962)**
Kresge, S. S. (merchant); Bald Mount, Pa. **(1867–1966)**
Krips, Josef (orchestra conductor); Vienna **(1902–1974)**
Kristofferson, Kris (singer); Brownsville, Tex., 6/22/1936
Kruger, Otto (actor); Toledo, Ohio **(1885–1974)**
Krupa, Gene (drummer); Chicago **(1909–1973)**
Kubelik, Rafael (conductor); Bychory (Czechoslovakia), 6/29/1914
Kublai Khan (Mongol conqueror) **(1216–1294)**
Kubrick, Stanley (producer and director); New York City, 7/26/1928
Kuralt, Charles (TV journalist); North Carolina, 1934
Kurosawa, Akira (film director); Tokyo, 3/23/1910
Kurtz, Efrem (conductor); St. Petersburg, Russia, 11/7/1900
Ky, Nguyen Cao (ex-Vice President of South Vietnam); Son Tay (Vietnam), 9/8/1930

L

Ladd, Alan (actor); Hot Springs, Ark. **(1913–1964)**
Ladd, Cheryl (actress); Huron, S.D., 4/2/(?)
Lafayette, Marquis de (Marie Joseph Paul Yves Roch Gilbert du Motier) (military officer); Auvergne, France **(1757–1834)**
La Follette, Robert Marin (politician); Primrose, Wis. **(1855–1925)**
La Guardia, Fiorello Henry (Mayor of New York); New York City **(1882–1947)**
Lahr, Bert (Irving Lahrheim) (comedian); New York City **(1895–1967)**
Laine, Frankie (Frank Paul LoVecchio) (singer); Chicago, 3/30/1913
Laird, Melvin (ex-Secretary of Defense); Omaha, Neb., 9/1/1922
Lamarck, Chevalier de (Jean Baptiste Pierre Antoine de Monet) (naturalist); Bazantin, France **(1744–1829)**
Lamarr, Hedy (Hedwig Kiesler) (actress); Vienna, 1915
Lamas, Fernando (actor); Buenos Aires, **(1915–1982)**
Lamb, Charles (Elia) (essayist); London **(1775–1834)**
Lamour, Dorothy (Dorothy Kaumeyer) (actress); New Orleans, 10/10/1914
Lancaster, Burt (actor); New York City, 11/2/1913
Lanchester, Elsa (Elsa Sullivan) (actress); London, 10/28/1902
Landau, Martin (actor); Brooklyn, N.Y. 1925(?)
Landers, Ann (columnist); Sioux City, Iowa, 7/4/1918
Landon, Michael (Michael Orowitz) (actor); Forest Hills, Queens, N.Y., 10/31/1936(?)
Lane, Abbe (singer); New York City, 1933
Lang, Fritz (film director); Vienna **(1890–1976)**
Lang, Paul Henry (music critic); Budapest, 8/28/1901
Lange, Hope (actress); Redding Ridge, Conn., 11/28/1933
Langella, Frank (actor); Bayonne, N.J., 1/1/1940
Langford, Frances (singer); Lakeland, Fla., 4/4/1913
Langmuir, Irving (chemist); Brooklyn, N.Y. **(1881–1957)**
Langtry, Lily (Emily Le Breton) (actress); Island of Jersey **(1852–1929)**
Lansbury, Angela (actress); London, 10/16/1925
Lansing, Robert (actor); San Diego, Calif., 6/5/1929
Lanza, Mario (Alfred Arnold Cocozza) (singer and actor); Philadelphia **(1925–1959)**
Lao-Tzu (or **Lao-Tse**) (Li Erh) (philosopher); Honan Province, China **(c. 604–531** B.C.)
Lardner, Ring (Ringgold Wilmer Lardner) (story writer); Niles, Mich. **(1885–1933)**
La Salle, Sieur de (Robert Cavelier) (explorer); Rouen, France **(1643–1687)**
Lasser, Louise (actress); New York City, 1940(?)

Lauder, Sir Harry (Harry MacLennan) (singer); Portobello, Scotland **(1870–1950)**
Laughton, Charles (actor); Scarborough, England **(1899–1962)**
Laurel, Stan (Arthur Jefferson) (comedian); Ulverston, England **(1890–1965)**
Laurents, Arthur (playwright); New York City, 7/14/1918
Laurie, Piper (Rosetta Jacobs) (actress); Detroit, 1/22/1932
Lavoisier, Antoine-Laurent (chemist); Paris **(1743–1794)**
Lawford, Peter (actor); London, 9/7/1923
Lawrence, Carol (Carol Maria Laraia) (dancer and actress); Melrose Park, Ill., 9/5/1932
Lawrence, David Herbert (novelist); Nottingham, England **(1885–1930)**
Lawrence, Gertrude (Gertrud Klasen) (actress); London **(1900–1952)**
Lawrence, Marjorie (singer); Deans Marsh, Australia **(1908–1979)**
Lawrence, Steve (Sidney Leibowitz) (singer); Brooklyn, N.Y., 7/8/1935
Lawrence, Vicki (actress); Inglewood, Calif., 1949
Lawrence of Arabia (Thomas Edward Lawrence, later changed to Shaw) (author and soldier); Tremadoc, Wales **(1888–1935)**
Leachman, Cloris (actress); Des Moines, Iowa, 4/30/1926(?)
Lean, David (film director); Croydon, England, 3/25/1908
Lear, Edward (nonsense poet); London **(1812–1888)**
le Carré, John (David John Moore Cornwell) (novelist); Poole, England, 10/19/1931
Le Corbusier (Charles Edouard Jeanneret) (architect); La Chaux-de-Fonds, Switzerland **(1887–1965)**
Lederer, Francis (actor); Prague, 11/6/1906
Lee, Christopher (actor); London, 5/27/1922
Lee, Gypsy Rose (Rose Louise Hovick) (entertainer); Seattle **(1919–1970)**
Lee, Manfred B. (novelist, pseudonym Ellery Queen); Brooklyn, N.Y. **(1905–1971)**
Lee, Peggy (Norma Engstrom) (singer); Jamestown, N.D., 5/26/1920
Lee, Robert Edward (Confederate general); Stratford Estate, Va. **(1807–1870)**
Le Gallienne, Eva (actress); London, 1/11/1899
Lehár, Franz (composer); Komárom (Czechoslovakia) **(1870–1948)**
Lehman, Herbert H. (Governor and Senator); New York City **(1878–1963)**
Lehmann, Lotte (soprano); Perleberg (Germany) **(1888–1976)**
Leigh, Janet (Jeanette Morrison) (actress); Merced, Calif., 7/6/1927
Leigh, Vivien (Vivien Mary Hartley) (actress); Darjeeling, India **(1913–1967)**
Leighton, Margaret (actress); nr. Birmingham, England **(1922–1976)**
Leinsdorf, Erich (conductor); Vienna, 2/4/1912
Lemmon, Jack (actor); Boston, 2/8/1925
Lenin, Nicolai (Vladimir Ilich Ulyanov) (Soviet leader); Simbirsk, Russia **(1870–1924)**
Lennon, John (singer and songwriter); Liverpool, England (1940–1980)
Lenya, Lotte (Karoline Blamauer) (singer and actress); Vienna, Austria **(1898–1981)**
Leonard, Sheldon (actor and director); New York City, 2/22/1907
Lerner, Alan Jay (lyricist); New York City, 8/31/1918
Lerner, Max (columnist); Minsk, Russia, 12/20/1902
Le Roy, Mervyn (film producer); San Francisco, 10/15/1900
Leslie, Joan (actress); Detroit, 1/26/1925
Lessing, Doris (novelist); Kermanshah, Iran, 10/22/1919
Lester, Mark (actor); Richmond, England, 1958
Letterman, David (TV personality); Indianapolis, 1944
Levant, Oscar (pianist); Pittsburgh **(1906–1972)**
Levene, Sam (actor); New York City **(1905–1980)**
Levenson, Sam (humorist); New York City **(1911–1980)**
Levi, Carlo (novelist); Turin, Italy **(1902–1975)**
Levine, James (music director, Metropolitan Opera); Cincinnati, 6/23/1943
Levine, Joseph E. (film producer); Boston, 9/9/1905
Lewis, Jerry (Joseph Levitch) (comedian and film director); Newark, N.J., 3/16/1926
Lewis, Jerry Lee (singer); Ferriday, La., 9/29/1935
Lewis, John Llewellyn (labor leader); Lucas, Iowa **(1880–1969)**
Lewis, Meriwether (explorer); Albemarle Co., Va. **(1774–1809)**
Lewis, Shari (Shari Hurwitz) (puppeteer); New York City, 1/17/1934
Lewis, Sinclair (novelist); Sauk Centre, Minn. **(1885–1951)**
Lewis, Ted (entertainer); Circleville, Ohio **(1891–1971)**
Ley, Willy (science writer); Berlin **(1906–1969)**
Liberace (Wladziu Liberace) (pianist); West Allis, Wis., 5/16/1919
Lichtenstein, Roy (painter); New York City, 10/27/1923
Lie, Trygve Halvdan (first U.N. Secretary-General); Oslo **(1896–1968)**
Lightfoot, Gordon (singer and songwriter); Orillia, Ontario, Canada, 11/17/1938
Lillie, Beatrice (Lady Peel) (actress and comedienne); Toronto, 5/29/1898
Lin Yutang (author); Changchow, China **(1895–1976)**
Lind, Jenny (Johanna Maria Lind) (soprano); Stockholm **(1820–1887)**
Lindbergh, Anne Morrow (author); Englewood, N.J., 6/22/1906
Lindbergh, Charles A. (aviator); Detroit **(1902–1974)**
Linden, Hal (actor); New York City, 3/20/1931
Lindfors, Viveca (actress); Uppsala, Sweden, 12/29/1920
Lindsay, Howard (dramatist); Waterford, N.Y. **(1889–1968)**
Lindsay, John Vliet (ex-Mayor of New York City); New York City, 11/24/1921
Lindstrom, Pia (TV newscaster); Stockholm, 11/?/1938
Linkletter, Art (radio-TV personality); Moose Jaw, Saskatchewan, Canada, 7/17/1912
Lipchitz, Jacques (sculptor); Druskieniki, Latvia **(1891–1973)**
Lippmann, Walter (columnist, author, and political analyst); New York City **(1889–1974)**
Lister, (1st Baron of Lyme Regis) (Joseph Lister) (surgeon); Upton, England **(1827–1912)**
Liszt, Franz (composer and pianist); Raiding (Hungary) **(1811–1886)**
Little, Cleavon (actor and comedian); Chickasha, Okla., 6/1/1939
Little, Rich (impressionist); Ottawa, 11/26/1938
Livesey, Roger (actor); Barry, Wales **(1906–1976)**
Livingstone, David (missionary and explorer); Lanarkshire, Scotland **(1813–1873)**
Livingstone, Mary (Sadye Marks) (comedienne); Seattle, 1909
Llewellyn, Richard (novelist); St. David's, Wales
Lloyd, Harold (comedian); Burchard, Neb. **(1894–1971)**
Lloyd George, David (Earl of Dwyfor) (statesman); Manchester, England **(1863–1945)**
Locke, John (philosopher); Somersetshire, England **(1632–1704)**
Lockhart, Gene (actor); London, Ontario, Canada **(1891–1957)**
Lockhart, June (actress); New York City, 6/25/1925
Lockwood, Margaret (actress); Karachi (Pakistan), 9/15/1916
Lodge, Henry Cabot (legislator); Boston **(1850–1924)**
Lodge, Henry Cabot, Jr. (diplomat); Nahant, Mass., 7/5/1902
Loesser, Frank (composer); New York City **(1910–1969)**
Loewe, Frederick (composer); Vienna, 6/10/1904
Logan, Joshua (director and producer); Texarkana, Tex., 10/5/1908
Lollobrigida, Gina (actress); Subiaco, Italy, 1928
Lombard, Carole (Carol Jane Peters) (actress); Ft. Wayne, Ind. **(1908–1942)**
Lombardo, Guy (band leader); London, Ontario, Canada **(1902–1977)**
London, George (baritone); Montreal, 5/30/1920
London, Jack (John Griffith London) (novelist); San Francisco **(1876–1916)**
London, Julie (Julie Peck) (singer and actress); Santa Rosa, Calif., 9/26/1926
Long, Huey Pierce (politician); Winnfield, La. **(1893–1935)**
Longfellow, Henry Wadsworth (poet); Portland, Me. **(1807–1882)**
Longworth, Alice Roosevelt (social figure); New York City **(1884–1980)**
Loos, Anita (novelist); Sissons, Calif., **(1888–1981)**
Lopez, Trini (Trinidad Lopez III) (singer); Dallas, 5/15/1937
Lopez, Vincent (band leader); Brooklyn, N.Y. **(1895–1975)**
Lord, Jack (actor); New York City, 12/30/1930
Loren, Sophia (Sofia Scicolone) (actress); Rome, 9/20/1934
Lorre, Peter (Laszlo Löewenstein) (actor); Rosenberg (Czechoslovakia) **(1904–1964)**
Louise, Tina (actress); New York City, 2/11/1937
Lowell, Amy (poet); Brookline, Mass. **(1874–1925)**
Lowell, James Russell (poet); Cambridge, Mass. **(1819–1891)**
Lowell, Robert (poet); Boston **(1917–1977)**
Loy, Myrna (Myrna Williams) (actress); nr. Helena, Mont., 8/2/1905
Loyola, St. Ignatius of (Iñigo de Oñez y Loyola) (founder of Jesuits); Gúipuzcoa Province, Spain **(1491–1556)**
Lubitsch, Ernst (film director); Berlin **(1892–1947)**
Luce, Clare Boothe (playwright and former Ambassador); New York City, 4/10/1903
Luce, Henry Robinson (editor and publisher); Tengchow, China **(1898–1967)**
Lugosi, Bela (Bela Lugosi Blasko) (actor); Logos, Hungary **(1888–1956)**
Lukas, Paul (actor); Budapest **(1895–1971)**
Lumet, Sidney (film and TV director); Philadelphia, 6/25/1924
Lunt, Alfred (actor); Milwaukee **(1892–1977)**
Lupino, Ida (actress and director); London, 2/4/1918
Luther, Martin (religious reformer); Eisleben (Germany) **(1483–1546)**
Lynde, Paul (comedian); Mt. Vernon, Ohio **(1926–1982)**
Lynley, Carol (actress); New York City, 2/13/1942
Lynn, Jeffrey (actor); Auburn, Mass., 1909
Lynn, Loretta (singer); Butcher's Hollow, Ky., 4/14/1935

M

Maazel, Lorin (conductor); Neuilly, France, 3/5/1930
MacArthur, Charles (playwright); Scranton, Pa. **(1895–1956)**
MacArthur, Douglas (five-star general); Little Rock Barracks, Ark. **(1880–1964)**
MacArthur, James (actor); Los Angeles, 12/8/1937
Macaulay, Thomas Babington (author); Rothley Temple, England **(1800–1859)**
MacDermot, Galt (composer); Montreal, 12/19/1928
MacDonald, James Ramsay (statesman); Lossiemouth, Scotland **(1866–1937)**

MacDonald, Jeanette (actress and soprano); Philadelphia **(1907–1965)**
Macdonald, Ross (Kenneth Millar) (mystery writer); Los Gatos, Calif., 12/13/1915
MacDowell, Edward Alexander (composer); New York City **(1861–1908)**
Macfadden, Bernarr (physical culturist); nr. Mill Spring, Mo. **(1868–1955)**
MacGraw, Ali (actress); New York City, 4/1/1939
Machiavelli, Niccolò (political philosopher); Florence (Italy) **(1469–1527)**
Mack, Ted (TV personality); Greeley, Colo. **(1904–1976)**
MacKenzie, Gisele (Marie Marguerite Louise Gisele LaFleche) (singer and actress); Winnipeg, Manitoba, Canada, 1/10/1927
MacLaine, Shirley (Shirley MacLean Beaty) (actress); Richmond, Va., 4/24/1934
MacLeish, Archibald (poet); Glencoe, Ill. **(1892–1982)**
Macmillan, Harold (ex-Prime Minister); London, 2/10/1894
MacMurray, Fred (actor); Kankakee, Ill., 8/30/1908
MacNeil, Cornell (baritone); Minneapolis, 1925
MacRae, Gordon (singer); East Orange, N.J., 3/12/1921
MacRae, Sheila (comedienne); London, 9/24/1924
Madison, Guy (Robert Moseley) (actor); Bakersfield, Calif., 1/19/1922
Maeterlinck, Count Maurice (author); Ghent, Belgium **(1862–1949)**
Magellan, Ferdinand (Fernando de Magalhaes) (navigator); Sabrosa, Portugal **(1480?–1521)**
Magnani, Anna (actress); Rome **(1908–1973)**
Magritte, René (painter); Belgium **(1898–1967)**
Magsaysay, Ramón (statesman); Iba, Luzon, Philippines **(1907–1957)**
Mahan, Alfred Thayer (naval historian); West Point, N.Y. **(1840–1914)**
Mahler, Gustav (composer and conductor); Kalischt (Czechoslovakia) **(1860–1911)**
Mailer, Norman (novelist); Long Branch, N.J., 1/31/1923
Maillol, Aristide (sculptor); Banyuls-sur-Mer, Rousillon, France **(1861–1944)**
Main, Marjorie (Mary Tomlinson Krebs) (actress); Acton, Ind. **(1890–1975)**
Mainbocher (Main Rousseau Bocher) (fashion designer); Chicago **(1891–1976)**
Majors, Lee (actor); Wyandotte, Mich., 1942
Makarova, Natalia (ballerina); Leningrad, 11/21/1940
Makeba, Miriam (singer); Johannesburg, South Africa, 3/4/1932
Malamud, Bernard (novelist); Brooklyn, N.Y., 4/26/1914
Malden, Karl (Mladen Sekulovich) (actor); Chicago, 3/22/1913
Malone, Dorothy (actress); Chicago, 1/30/1925
Malraux, André (author); Paris **(1901–1976)**
Manchester, Melissa (singer); Bronx, N.Y., 2/15/1951
Manchester, William (writer); Attleboro, Mass., 4/1/1922
Mancini, Henry (composer and conductor); Cleveland, 4/16/1924
Manet, Edouard (painter); Paris **(1832–1883)**
Mangano, Silvana (actress); Rome, 4/21/1930
Mangione, Chuck (hornist, pianist, and composer); Rochester, N.Y., 11/29/1940
Manilow, Barry (singer); Brooklyn, N.Y., 6/17/1946
Mankiewicz, Frank F. (columnist); New York City, 5/16/1924
Mankiewicz, Joseph L. (film writer and director); Wilkes-Barre, Pa., 2/11/1909
Mann, Horace (educator); Franklin, Mass. **(1796–1859)**
Mann, Thomas (novelist); Lübeck, Germany **(1875–1955)**
Mannes, Marya (writer); New York City, 11/14/1904
Mansfield, Jayne (Jayne Palmer) (actress); Bryn Mawr, Pa. **(1932–1967)**
Mansfield, Katherine (story writer); Wellington, New Zealand **(1888–1923)**
Mantovani, Annunzio (conductor); Venice **(1905–1980)**
Mao Zedong (Tse-tung) (Chinese leader); Shao Shan, China **(1893–1976)**
Marat, Jean Paul (French revolutionist); Boudry, Neuchâtel, Switzerland **(1743–1793)**
Marceau, Marcel (mime); Strasbourg, France, 3/22/1923
March, Fredric (Frederick Bickel) (actor); Racine, Wis. **(1897–1975)**
Marconi, Guglielmo (inventor); Bologna, Italy **(1874–1937)**
Marcus Aurelius (Marcus Annius Verus) (Roman emperor); Rome **(121–180)**
Marcuse, Herbert (philosopher); Berlin, **(1898–1979)**
Margaret Rose (Princess); Glamis Castle, Angus, Scotland, 8/21/1930
Margrethe II (Queen); Copenhagen, 4/16/1940
Marie Antoinette (Josèphe Jeanne Marie Antoinette) (Queen of France); Vienna **(1755–1793)**
Marisol (sculptor); Venezuela, 1930
Markham, Edwin (poet); Oregon City, Ore. **(1852–1940)**
Markova, Dame Alicia (Lilian Alice Marks) (ballerina); London, 12/1/1910
Marley, Bob (reggae singer and songwriter); Kingston, Jamaica **(1945–1981)**
Marlowe, Christopher (dramatist); Canterbury, England **(1564–1593)**
Marlowe, Julia (Sarah Frances Frost) (actress); Cumberlandshire, England **(1866–1950)**
Marquand, John Phillips (novelist); Wilmington, Del. **(1893–1960)**
Marquette, Jacques (missionary and explorer); Laon, France **(1637–1675)**
Marriner, Neville (conductor); Lincoln, England, 4/15/1924
Marsh, Jean (actress); Stoke Newington, England, 7/1/1934
Marshall, E.G. (actor); Owatonna, Minn., 6/18/1910
Marshall, George Catlett (general); Uniontown, Pa. **(1880–1959)**
Marshall, Herbert (actor); London **(1890–1968)**
Marshall, John (jurist); nr. Germantown, Va. **(1755–1835)**
Marshall, Penny (actress); New York City, 10/15/1942
Martin, Dean (Dino Crocetti) (singer and actor); Steubenville, Ohio, 6/17/1917
Martin, Dick (actor and comedian); Battle Creek, Mich., 1/30/1922
Martin, Mary (singer and actress); Weatherford, Tex., 12/1/1913
Martin, Steve (comedian); prob. Waco, Tex., 1945(?)
Martin, Tony (Alvin Morris) (singer); San Francisco, 12/25/1913
Martin, William McChesney, Jr. (ex-chairman of Federal Reserve Board); St. Louis, 12/17/1906
Martinelli, Giovanni (tenor); Montagnana, Italy **(1885–1969)**
Marvin, Lee (actor); New York City, 2/19/1924
Marx, Chico (Leonard) (comedian); New York City **(1891–1961)**
Marx, Groucho (Julius) (comedian); New York City **(1890–1977)**
Marx, Harpo (Arthur) (comedian); New York City **(1893–1964)**
Marx, Karl (Socialist writer); Treves (Germany) **(1818–1883)**
Marx, Zeppo (Herbert) (comedian); New York City **(1901–1979)**
Mary Stuart (Queen of Scotland); Linlithgow, Scotland **(1542–1587)**
Masaryk, Jan Garrigue (statesman); Prague (Czechoslovakia) **(1886–1948)**
Masaryk, Thomas Garrigue (statesman); Hodonin (Czechoslovakia) **(1850–1937)**
Masefield, John (poet); Ledbury, England **(1878–1967)**
Masekela, Hugh (trumpeter); Wilbank, South Africa, 4/4/1939
Mason, James (actor); Huddersfield, England, 5/15/1909
Massenet, Jules Emile Frédéric (composer); Montaud, France **(1842–1912)**
Massey, Raymond (actor); Toronto, 8/30/1896
Massine, Léonide (choreographer); Moscow, **(1895–1979)**
Masters, Edgar Lee (poet); Garnett, Kan. **(1869–1950)**
Mastroianni, Marcello (actor); Fontana Liri, Italy, 9/28/1924
Mathis, Johnny (singer); San Francisco, 9/30/1935
Matisse, Henri (painter); Le Cateau, France **(1869–1954)**
Matthau, Walter (Walter Matuschanskayasky) (actor); New York City, 10/1/1920
Mature, Victor (actor); Louisville, Ky., 1/19/1916
Maugham, (William) Somerset (author); Paris **(1874–1965)**
Mauldin, Bill (political cartoonist); Mountain Park, N.M., 10/29/1921
Maupassant, Henri René Albert Guy de (story writer); Normandy, France **(1850–1893)**
Maurois, André (Emile Herzog) (author); Elbeuf, France **(1885–1967)**
Maximilian (Ferdinand Maximilian Joseph) (Emperor of Mexico); Vienna **(1832–1867)**
Maxwell, James Clerk (physicist); Edinburgh, Scotland **(1831–1879)**
May, Elaine (entertainer); Philadelphia, 4/21/1932
May, Rollo (psychologist); Ada, Ohio, 4/21/1909
Mayall, John (singer and songwriter); Manchester, England, 11/29/1933
Mayo, Charles H. (surgeon); Rochester, Minn. **(1865–1939)**
Mayo, Charles W. (surgeon); Rochester, Minn. **(1898–1968)**
Mayo, Virginia (actress); St. Louis, 1920
Mayo, William J. (surgeon); Le Sueur, Minn. **(1861–1939)**
McBride, Mary Margaret (radio personality); Paris, Mo. **(1899–1976)**
McBride, Patricia (ballerina); Teaneck, N.J., 8/23/1942
McCallum, David (actor); Glasgow, Scotland, 9/19/1933
McCambridge, Mercedes (actress); Joliet, Ill., 3/17/1918
McCarthy, Eugene J. (ex-Senator); Watkins, Minn., 3/29/1916
McCarthy, Joseph Raymond (Senator); Grand Chute, Wis. **(1908–1957)**
McCarthy, Kevin (actor); Seattle, 1915
McCarthy, Mary (novelist); Seattle, 6/21/1912
McCartney, Paul (singer and songwriter); Liverpool, England, 6/18/1942
McClellan, George Brinton (general); Philadelphia **(1826–1885)**
McCloy, John J. (lawyer and banker); Philadelphia, 3/31/1895
McClure, Doug (actor); Glendale, Calif., 5/11/1938
McCormack, John (tenor); Athlone, Ireland **(1884–1945)**
McCormack, John W. (ex-Speaker of House); Boston **(1891–1980)**
McCormack, Patty (actress); New York City, 8/21/1945
McCormick, Cyrus Hall (inventor); Rockbridge County, Va. **(1809–1884)**
McCoy, Col. Tim (actor); Saginaw, Mich. **(1891–1978)**
McCracken, James (dramatic tenor); Gary, Ind., 12/16/1926
McCrea, Joel (actor); Los Angeles, 11/5/1905
McCullers, Carson (novelist); Columbus, Ga. **(1917–1967)**
McDowall, Roddy (actor); London, 9/17/1928
McDowell, Malcolm (actor); Leeds, England, 6/19/1943
McGavin, Darren (actor); San Joaquin, Calif., 5/7/1922
McGinley, Phyllis (poet and writer); Ontario, Ore. **(1905–1978)**
McGoohan, Patrick (actor); Astoria, Queens, N.Y., 1928
McGuire, Dorothy (actress); Omaha, Neb., 6/14/1919
McKenna, Siobhan (actress); Belfast, Northern Ireland, 5/24/1923
McKuen, Rod (singer and composer); Oakland, Calif., 4/29/1933
McLaglen, Victor (actor); Tunbridge Wells, Kent, England **(1886–1959)**
McLaughlin, John (guitarist); Yorkshire, England, 1942
McLean, Don (singer and songwriter); New Rochelle, N.Y., 10/2/1945
McLuhan, Marshall (Herbert Marshall) (communications writer); Edmonton, Canada **(1911–1980)**

McMahon, Ed (TV personality); Detroit, 3/6/1923
McNamara, Robert S. (former president of World Bank); San Francisco, 6/9/1916
McQueen, Steve (Terence Stephen McQueen) (actor); Indianapolis **(1930–1980)**
Mead, Margaret (anthropologist); Philadelphia, **(1901–1978)**
Meadows, Audrey (actress); Wu Chang, China, 1922(?)
Meadows, Jayne (actress); Wu Chang, China 9/27/1926
Meany, George (labor leader); New York City **(1894–1980)**
Meara, Anne (actress); New York City, 1929
Medici, Lorenzo de' (called Lorenzo the Magnificent) (Florentine ruler); Florence (Italy) **(1449–1492)**
Meeker, Ralph (Ralph Rathgeber) (actor); Minneapolis, 11/21/1920
Mehta, Zubin (conductor); Bombay, 4/29/1936
Meir, Golda (Golda Myerson, nee Mabovitz) (ex-Premier of Israel); Kiev, Russia **(1898–1978)**
Melanie (Melanie Safka) (singer and songwriter); New York City, 2/3/1947
Melba, Dame Nellie (Helen Porter Mitchell) (soprano); nr. Melbourne **(1861–1931)**
Melchior, Lauritz (Lebrecht Hommel) (heroic tenor); Copenhagen **(1890–1973)**
Mellon, Andrew William (financier); Pittsburgh **(1855–1937)**
Melville, Herman (novelist); New York City **(1819–1891)**
Mencken, Henry Louis (writer); Baltimore **(1880–1956)**
Mendel, Gregor Johann (geneticist); Heinzendorf, Austrian Silesia **(1822–1884)**
Mendeleyev, Dmitri Ivanovich (chemist); Tobolsk, Russia **(1834–1907)**
Mendelssohn-Bartholdy, Jakob Ludwig Felix (composer); Hamburg **(1809–1847)**
Mendès-France, Pierre (ex-Premier); Paris, 1/11/1905
Menjou, Adolphe (actor); Pittsburgh **(1890–1963)**
Mennin, Peter (Peter Mennini) (composer); Erie, Pa., 5/17/1923
Menninger, William C. (psychiatrist); Topeka, Kan. **(1899–1966)**
Menotti, Gian Carlo (composer); Cadegliano, Italy, 7/7/1911
Menuhin, Yehudi (violinist and conductor); New York City, 4/22/1916
Menzies, Robert Gordon (ex-Prime Minister); Jeparit, Australia **(1894–1978)**
Mercer, Johnny (songwriter); Savannah, Ga. **(1909–1976)**
Mercer, Mabel (singer); Burton-on-Trent, England, 1/?/1900
Mercouri, Melina (actress); Athens, 10/18/1925
Meredith, Burgess (actor); Cleveland, 11/16/1908
Merkel, Una (actress); Covington, Ky., 12/10/1903
Merman, Ethel (Ethel Zimmerman) (singer and actress); Astoria, Queens, N.Y., 1/16/1909
Merrick, David (David Margulois) (stage producer); St. Louis, 11/27/1912
Merrill, Dina (actress); New York City, 12/9/1925
Merrill, Gary (actor); Hartford, Conn., 8/2/1914
Merrill, Robert (baritone); Brooklyn, N.Y., 6/4/1919
Merton, Thomas (clergyman and writer); France **(1915–1968)**
Mesmer, Franz Anton (physician); Itzmang, nr. Constance (Germany) **(1733–1815)**
Mesta, Perle (social figure); Sturgis, Mich. **(1889–1975)**
Metternich, Prince Klemens Wenzel Nepomuk Lothar von (statesman); Coblenz (Germany) **(1773–1859)**
Michelangelo Buonarroti (painter, sculptor, and architect); Caprese (Italy) **(1475–1564)**
Michener, James A. (novelist); New York City, 2/3/1907
Midler, Bette (singer); Honolulu, 1945
Mielziner, Jo (stage designer); Paris **(1901–1976)**
Mies van der Rohe, Ludwig (architect and designer); Aachen, Germany **(1886–1969)**
Mikoyan, Anastas I. (diplomat); Sanain, Armenia, **(1895–1978)**
Miles, Sarah (actress); Essex, England, 12/31/1943
Miles, Sylvia (actress); New York City, 9/9/1932
Miles, Vera (Vera Ralston) (actress); nr. Boise City, Okla., 8/23/1930
Milhaud, Darius (composer); Aix-en-Provence, France **(1892–1974)**
Mill, John Stuart (philosopher); London, **(1806–1873)**
Milland, Ray (Reginald Truscott-Jones) (actor); Neath, Wales, 1/3/1907
Millay, Edna St. Vincent (poet); Rockland, Me. **(1892–1950)**
Miller, Ann (Lucille Ann Collier) (dancer and actress); Cherino, Tex., 4/12/1923
Miller, Arthur (playwright); New York City, 10/17/1915
Miller, Glenn (band leader); Clarinda, Iowa **(1909?–1944)**
Miller, Henry (novelist); New York City **(1891–1980)**
Miller, Jason (John Miller) (playwright); New York City, 1939(?)
Miller, Mitch (Mitchell) (musician); Rochester, N.Y., 7/4/1911
Miller, Roger (singer); Fort Worth, 1/2/1936
Millet, Jean François (painter); Gruchy, France **(1814–1875)**
Millett, Kate (feminist); St. Paul, 9/14/1934
Mills, Hayley (actress); London, 4/18/1946
Mills, John (actor); Felixstowe, England, 2/22/1908
Milne, A(lan) A(lexander) (author); London **(1882–1956)**
Milstein, Nathan (concert violinist); Odessa, Russia, 12/31/1904
Milton, John (poet); London **(1608–1674)**
Mimieux, Yvette (actress); Hollywood, Calif., 1/8/1941
Mineo, Sal (actor); New York City **(1939–1976)**
Minnelli, Liza (singer and actress); Hollywood, Calif., 3/12/1946
Minnelli, Vincente (film director); Chicago, 2/28/1913
Minuit, Peter (Governor of New Amsterdam); Wesel (Germany) **(1580–1638)**
Miranda, Carmen (Maria do Carmo da Cunha) (singer and dancer); Lisbon **(1913–1955)**
Miró, Joan (painter); Barcelona, 4/20/1893
Mitchell, Cameron (actor); Dallastown, Pa., 4/11/1918
Mitchell, Guy (actor); Detroit, 2/27/1927
Mitchell, John N. (former Attorney General); Detroit, 9/15/1913
Mitchell, Joni (Roberta Joan Anderson) (singer and songwriter); Ft. MacCleod, Canada, 11/7/1943
Mitchell, Margaret (novelist); Atlanta **(1900–1949)**
Mitchum, Robert (actor); Bridgeport, Conn., 8/6/1917
Mitropoulos, Dimitri (orchestra conductor); Athens **(1896–1960)**
Mix, Tom (actor); Mix Run, Pa. **(1880–1940)**
Modigliani, Amedeo (painter); Leghorn, Italy **(1884–1920)**
Moffo, Anna (soprano); Wayne, Pa., 6/27/1934
Mohammed (prophet); Mecca (Saudi Arabia) **(570–632)**
Molière (Jean Baptiste Poquelin) (dramatist); Paris **(1622–1673)**
Molnar, Ferenc (dramatist); Budapest **(1878–1952)**
Molotov, Vyacheslav M. (V. M. Skryabin) (diplomat); Kukarka, Russia, 3/9/1890
Mondrian, Piet (painter); Amersfoort, Netherlands **(1872–1944)**
Monet, Claude (painter); Paris **(1840–1926)**
Monk, Thelonious (pianist); Rocky Mount, N.C. **(1918–1982)**
Monroe, Marilyn (Norma Jean Mortenson or Baker) (actress); Los Angeles **(1926–1962)**
Monroe, Vaughn (Wilton) (band leader); Akron, Ohio **(1912–1973)**
Monsarrat, Nicholas (novelist); Liverpool, England, **(1910–1979)**
Montaigne, Michel Eyquem de (essayist); nr. Bordeaux, France **(1533–1592)**
Montalban, Ricardo (actor); Mexico City, 11/25/1920
Montand, Yves (Yves Montand Livi) (actor and singer); Mansummano, Italy, 10/13/1921
Montez, Maria (actress); Dominican Republic **(1918–1951)**
Montezuma II (Aztec emperor); Mexico **(1480?–1520)**
Montgomery, Elizabeth (actress); Hollywood, Calif., 4/15/1933
Montgomery, George (George Letz) (actor); Brady, Mont., 1929
Montgomery, Robert (Henry, Jr.) (actor); Beacon, N.Y. **(1904–1981)**
Montgomery of Alamein, 1st Viscount of Hindhead (Sir Bernard Law Montgomery) (military leader); London **(1887–1976)**
Montoya, Carlos (guitarist); Madrid, 12/13/1903
Moore, Clement Clarke (author); New York City **(1779–1863)**
Moore, Garry (Thomas Garrison Morfit) (TV personality); Baltimore, 1/31/1915
Moore, Grace (soprano); Jellico, Tenn. **(1901–1947)**
Moore, Henry (sculptor); Castleford, England, 7/30/1898
Moore, Marianne (poet); Kirkwood, Mo. **(1887–1972)**
Moore, Mary Tyler (actress); Brooklyn, N.Y., 12/29/1937
Moore, Melba (Beatrice) (singer and actress); New York City, 10/27/1945
Moore, Roger (actor); London, 10/14/1927(?)
Moore, Thomas (poet); Dublin **(1779–1852)**
Moore, Victor (actor); Hammonton, N.J. **(1876–1962)**
Moorehead, Agnes (actress); Clinton, Mass. **(1906–1974)**
More, Sir Thomas (statesman and author); London **(1478–1535)**
Moreau, Jeanne (actress); Paris, 1/23/1928
Moreno, Rita (Rosita Dolores Alverio) (actress); Humacao, Puerto Rico, 12/11/1931
Morgan, Dennis (actor); Prentice, Wis., 12/10/1920
Morgan, Helen (singer); Danville, Ohio **(1900?–1941)**
Morgan, Henry (comedian); New York City, 3/31/1915
Morgan, Jane (Florence Currier) (singer); Boston, 1920
Morgan, John Pierpont (financier); Hartford, Conn. **(1837–1913)**
Moriarty, Michael (actor); Detroit, 4/5/1941
Morini, Erica (concert violinist); Vienna, 1/5/1910
Morison, Samuel Eliot (historian); Boston **(1887–1976)**
Morley, Christopher Darlington (novelist); Haverford, Pa. **(1890–1957)**
Morley, Robert (actor); Semley, England, 5/26/1908
Morrison, Jim (James Douglas Morrison) (singer and songwriter); Melbourne, Fla. **(1943–1971)**
Morse, Marston (mathematician); Waterville, Me. **(1892–1977)**
Morse, Robert (actor); Newton, Mass., 5/18/1931
Morse, Samuel Finley Breese (painter and inventor); Charlestown, Mass. **(1791–1872)**
Moses, Grandma (Mrs. Anna Mary Robertson Moses) (painter); Greenwich, N.Y. **(1860–1961)**
Moses, Robert (urban planner); New Haven, Conn., **(1888–1981)**
Mostel, Zero (Samuel Joel Mostel) (actor); Brooklyn, N.Y. **(1915–1977)**
Moussorgsky, Modest Petrovich (composer); Karev, Russia **(1839–1881)**
Moyers, Bill D. (Billy Don) (journalist); Hugo, Okla., 6/5/1934

Moynihan, Daniel Patrick (New York Senator); Tulsa, Okla., 3/16/1927
Mozart, Wolfgang Amadeus (Johannes Chrysostomus Wolfgangus Theophilus Mozart) (composer); Salzburg (Austria) **(1756–1791)**
Mudd, Roger (TV newscaster); Washington, D.C., 2/9/1928
Muggeridge, Malcolm (Thomas) (writer); Croydon, England, 3/24/1903
Muhammad, Elijah (Elijah Poole) (religious leader); Sandersville, Ga. **(1897–1975)**
Mulhare, Edward (actor); Ireland, 1923
Mumford, Lewis (cultural historian and city planner); Flushing, Queens, N.Y., 10/19/1895
Munch, Edvard (painter); Löten, Norway **(1863–1944)**
Muni, Paul (Muni Weisenfreund) (actor); Lemburg (Ukraine) **(1895–1967)**
Munsel, Patrice (soprano); Spokane, Wash., 5/14/1925
Murdoch, Iris (novelist); Dublin, 7/15/1919
Murdoch, Rupert (publisher); Melbourne, 3/11/1931
Murillo, Bartolomé Esteban (painter); Seville, Spain **(1617–1682)**
Murphy, Audie (actor and war hero); Kingston, Tex. **(1924–1971)**
Murphy, George (actor, dancer, and ex-Senator); New Haven, Conn., 7/4/1902
Murray, Arthur (dance teacher); New York City, 4/4/1895
Murray, Kathryn (dance teacher); Jersey City, N.J., 1906
Murray, Ken (Don Court) (producer); New York City, 7/14/1903
Murray, Mae (Marie Adrienne Koenig) (actress); Portsmouth, Va. **(1890–1965)**
Murrow, Edward R. (commentator and government official); Greensboro, N.C. **(1908–1965)**
Mussolini, Benito (Italian dictator); Dovia, Forli, Italy **(1883–1945)**
Myerson, Bess (consumer advocate); Bronx, N.Y., 1924
Myrdal, Gunnar (sociologist and economist); Gustaf Parish, Sweden, 12/6/1898

N

Nabokov, Vladimir (novelist); St. Petersburg, Russia **(1899–1977)**
Nabors, Jim (actor and singer); Sylacauga, Ala., 6/12/1932
Nader, Ralph (consumer advocate); Winsted, Conn., 2/27/1934
Nagel, Conrad (actor); Keokuk, Iowa **(1897–1970)**
Naish, J. Carrol (actor); New York City **(1900–1973)**
Naldi, Nita (Anita Donna Dooley) (actress); New York City **(1899–1961)**
Napoleon Bonaparte. *See* Bonaparte, Napoleon
Nash, Graham (singer); Blackpool, England, 1942
Nash, Ogden (poet); Rye, N.Y. **(1902–1971)**
Nasser, Gamal Abdel (statesman); Beni Mor, Egypt **(1918–1970)**
Nast, Thomas (cartoonist); Landau (Germany) **(1840–1902)**
Nation, Carry Amelia (temperance leader); Garrard County, Ky. **(1846–1911)**
Natwick, Mildred (actress); Baltimore, 6/19/1908
Nazimova, Alla (actress); Yalta, Crimea, Russia **(1879–1945)**
Neagle, Anna (Marjorie Robertson) (actress); London, 10/20/1908
Neal, Patricia (actress); Packard, Ky., 1/20/1926
Neff, Hildegarde (actress); Ulm, Germany, 12/28/1925
Negri, Pola (Appolina Chapulez) (actress); Bromberg (Poland), c. 1897
Nehru, Jawaharlal (first Prime Minister of India); Allahabad, India **(1889–1964)**
Nelson, Barry (actor); San Francisco, 1920
Nelson, David (actor); New York City, 10/24/1936
Nelson, Harriet Hilliard (Peggy Lou Snyder) (actress); Des Moines, Iowa, 1914
Nelson, Ozzie (Oswald) (actor); Jersey City, N.J. **(1907–1975)**
Nelson, Ricky (Eric) (singer and actor); Teaneck, N.J., 5/8/1940
Nelson, Viscount Horatio (naval officer); Burnham Thorpe, England **(1758–1805)**
Nenni, Pietro (Socialist leader); Faenza, Italy **(1891–1980)**
Nero (Nero Claudius Caesar Drusus Germanicus) (Roman emperor); Antium (Italy) **(37–68)**
Nero, Peter (pianist); New York City, 5/22/1934
Nesbitt, Cathleen (actress); Cheshire, England **(1889–1982)**
Nevelson, Louise (sculptor); Kiev, Russia, 9/23/1900
Newhart, Bob (entertainer); Chicago, 9/5/1929
Newhouse, Samuel I. (publisher); New York City **(1895–1979)**
Newley, Anthony (actor and song writer); London, 9/24/1931
Newman, Edwin (news commentator); New York City, 1/25/1919
Newman, Paul (actor and director); Cleveland, 1/26/1925
Newman, Randy (singer); Los Angeles, 11/28/1943
Newton, Huey (black activist); New Orleans, 2/17/1942
Newton, Sir Isaac (mathematician and scientist); nr. Grantham, England **(1642–1727)**
Newton, Wayne (singer); Norfolk, Va., 4/3/1942
Newton-John, Olivia (singer); Cambridge, England, 9/26/1948
Nichols, Mike (Michael Peschkowsky) (stage and film director); Berlin, 11/6/1931
Nicholson, Jack (actor); Neptune, N.J., 4/22/1937
Nietzsche, Friedrich Wilhelm (philosopher); nr. Lützen (Germany) **(1844–1900)**
Nightingale, Florence (nurse); Florence (Italy) **(1820–1910)**
Nijinsky, Waslaw (ballet dancer); Warsaw **(1890–1950)**
Nilsson, Birgit (soprano); West Karup, Sweden, 5/17/1923
Nilsson, Harry (singer and songwriter); Brooklyn, N.Y., 6/15/1941
Nimitz, Chester W. (naval officer); Fredericksburg, Tex. **(1885–1966)**
Nimoy, Leonard (actor); Boston, 3/26/1931
Nin, Anais (author and diarist); Neuilly, France **(1903–1977)**
Niven, David (actor); Kirriemuir, Scotland, 3/1/1910
Nizer, Louis (lawyer and author); London, 2/6/1902
Nobel, Alfred Bernhard (industrialist); Stockholm **(1833–1896)**
Noguchi, Isamu (sculptor); Los Angeles, 11/7/1904
Nolan, Lloyd (actor); San Francisco, 8/11/1902
Nolte, Nick (actor); Omaha, Neb., 1942
Norell, Norman (Norman Levinson) (fashion designer); Noblesville, Ind. **(1900–1972)**
Norstad, Gen. Lauris (ex-commander of NATO forces); Minneapolis, 3/24/1907
North, John Ringling (circus director); Baraboo, Wis., 8/14/1903
North, Sheree (actress); Los Angeles, 1/17/1933
Norton, Eleanor Holmes (New York City government official, lawyer); Washington, D.C., 6/13/1937
Nostradamus (Michel de Notredame) (astrologer); St. Rémy, France **(1503–1566)**
Novaes, Guiomar (pianist); Sao Joao de Boa Vista, Brazil **(1895–1979)**
Novak, Kim (Marilyn Novak) (actress); Chicago, 2/13/1933
Novarro, Ramon (Ramon Samaniegoes) (actor); Durango, Mexico **(1899–1968)**
Nugent, Elliott (actor and director); Dover, Ohio, **(1899–1980)**
Nureyev, Rudolf (ballet dancer); U.S.S.R., 3/17/1938
Nuyen, France (actress); Marseilles, France, 7/31/1939
Nyro, Laura (singer and songwriter); Bronx, N.Y., 1947

O

Oakie, Jack (actor); Sedalia, Mo. **(1903–1978)**
Oates, Joyce Carol (novelist); Lockport, N.Y., 6/16/1938
Oberon, Merle (Estelle Merle O'Brien Thompson) (actress); Tasmania **(1911–1979)**
O'Brian, Hugh (Hugh J. Krampe) (actor); Rochester, N.Y., 4/19/1930
O'Brien, Edmond (actor); New York City, 9/10/1915
O'Brien, Margaret (Angela Maxine O'Brien) (actress); San Diego, Calif., 1/15/1937
O'Brien, Pat (William Joseph O'Brien, Jr.) (actor); Milwaukee, 11/11/1899
O'Casey, Sean (playwright); Dublin **(1881–1964)**
Ochs, Adolph Simon (publisher); Cincinnati **(1858–1935)**
O'Connor, Carroll (actor); New York City, 8/2/1924
O'Connor, Donald (actor); Chicago, 8/28/1925
Odets, Clifford (playwright); Philadelphia **(1906–1963)**
Odetta (Odetta Holmes) (folk singer and actress); Brimingham, Ala., 12/31/1930
Offenbach, Jacques (composer); Cologne, Germany **(1819–1880)**
O'Hara, John (novelist); Pottsville, Pa. **(1905–1970)**
O'Hara, Maureen (Maureen FitzSimons) (actress); Dublin, 8/17/1921
Oistrakh, David (concert violinist); Odessa, Russia **(1908–1974)**
O'Keeffe, Georgia (painter); Sun Prairie, Wis., 11/15/1887
Oland, Warner (actor); Umea, Sweden **(1880–1938)**
Olav V (King of Norway); Sandringham, England, 7/2/1903
Oldenburg, Claes (painter); Stockholm, Sweden, 1/28/1929
Olivier, Lord (Laurence) (actor); Dorking, England, 5/22/1907
Olmsted, Frederick Law (landscape architect); Hartford, Conn. **(1822–1903)**
Olsen, Ole (John Sigvard Olsen) (comedian); Peru, Ind. **(1892–1963)**
Omar Khayyam (poet and astronomer); Nishapur (Iran) **(died c. 1123)**
Onassis, Aristotle (shipping executive); Smyrna, Turkey **(1906–1975)**
Onassis, Christina (shipping executive); New York City, 12/11/1950
Onassis, Jacqueline Kennedy (Jacqueline Bouvier) (President's widow); Southampton, N.Y., 7/28/1929
O'Neal, Ryan (Patrick) (actor); Los Angeles, 4/20/1941
O'Neal, Tatum (actress); Los Angeles, Calif., 1963
O'Neill, Eugene Gladstone (playwright); New York City **(1888–1953)**
O'Neill, Jennifer (actress); Rio de Janeiro, 2/20/1949
Oppenheimer, J. Robert (nuclear physicist); New York City **(1904–1967)**
Orff, Carl (composer); Munich, Germany **(1895–1982)**
Orlando, Tony (singer); New York City, 1944
Ormandy, Eugene (conductor); Budapest, 11/18/1899
Orozco, José Clemente (painter); Zapotlán, Jalisco, Mexico **(1883–1949)**
Orwell, George (Eric Arthur Blair) (British author); Motihari, India **(1903–1950)**
Osborn, Paul (playwright); Evansville, Ind., 9/4/1901
Osborne, John (playwright); London, 12/12/1929
Osler, Sir William (physician); Bondhead, Ontario, Canada **(1849–1919)**
Osmond, Donny (singer); Ogden, Utah, 12/9/1957
Osmond, Marie (singer); Ogden, Utah, 1959

O'Sullivan, Maureen (actress); County Roscommon, Ireland, 5/17/1911
Otis, Elisha (inventor); Halifax, Vt. (1811–1861)
O'Toole, Peter (actor); Connemara, Ireland, 8/2/1933
Ovid (Publius Ovidius Naso) (poet); Sulmona (Italy) (43 B.C.–? A.D. 17)
Owens, Buck (Alvis Edgar Owens) (singer); Sherman, Tex., 8/12/1929

P

Paar, Jack (TV personality); Canton, Ohio, 5/1/1918
Pacino, Al (Alfred) (actor); New York City, 4/25/1940
Packard, Vance (author); Granville Summit, Pa., 5/22/1914
Paderewski, Ignace Jan (pianist and statesman); Kurylowka, Russian Podolia (1860–1941)
Paganini, Nicolò (violinist); Genoa (Italy) (1782–1840)
Page, Geraldine (actress); Kirksville, Mo., 11/22/1924
Page, Patti (Clara Ann Fowler) (singer and entertainer); Claremore, Okla., 11/8/1927
Paige, Janis (actress); Tacoma, Wash., 9/16/1922
Paine, Thomas (political philosopher); Thetford, England (1737–1809)
Palance, Jack (Walter Palanuik) (actor); Lattimer, Pa., 2/18/1920
Paley, William S. (broadcasting executive); Chicago, 9/28/1901
Palladio, Andrea (architect); Padua or Vicenza (Italy) (1508–1580)
Palmer, Betsy (actress); East Chicago, Ind., 1929
Palmer, Lilli (actress); Posen (Poland), 5/24/1914
Palmerston, Henry John Templeton (3rd Viscount) (statesman); Broadlands, England (1784–1865)
Papanicolaou, George N. (physician); Coumi, Greece (1883–1962)
Papas, Irene (actress); Chiliomodion, Greece, 1929
Papp, Joseph (Joseph Papirofsky) (stage producer and director); Brooklyn, N.Y., 6/22/1921
Park, Chung Hee (President of South Korea); Sangmo-ri, Korea (1917–1979)
Parker, Dorothy (Dorothy Rothschild) (author); West End, N.J. (1893–1967)
Parker, Eleanor (actress); Cedarville, Ohio, 6/26/1922
Parker, Fess (actor); Fort Worth, Tex., 1925
Parker, Suzy (model and actress); San Antonio, 10/28/1933
Parkinson, C. (Cyril) Northcote (historian); Durham, England, 7/30/1909
Parks, Bert (Bert Jacobson) (entertainer); Atlanta, 12/30/1914
Parks, Gordon (film director); Ft. Scott, Kan., 11/30/1912
Parnell, Charles Stewart (statesman); Avondale, Ireland (1846–1891)
Parnis, Mollie (Mollie Parnis Livingston) (fashion designer); New York City, 3/18/1905
Parsons, Estelle (actress); Marblehead, Mass., 11/20/1927
Parton, Dolly (singer); Locust Ridge, Tenn. 1/19/1946
Pascal, Blaise (philosopher); Clermont, France (1623–1662)
Pasternak, Boris Leonidovich (author); Moscow (1890–1960)
Pasternak, Joseph (film producer); Silagy-Somlyo, Romania, 9/19/1901
Pasteur, Louis (chemist); Dôle, France (1822–1895)
Patton, George Smith, Jr. (general); San Gabriel, Calif., (1885–1945)
Paul, Les (Lester William Polfus) (guitarist); Waukesha, Wis., 6/9/1915
Paul VI (Giovanni Battista Montini) (Pope); Concesio, nr. Brescia, Italy (1897–1978)
Pauling, Linus Carl (chemist); Portland, Ore., 2/28/1901
Pavarotti, Luciano (tenor); Modena, Italy, 10/12/1935
Pavlov, Ivan Petrovich (physiologist); Ryazan district, Russia (1849–1936)
Pavlova, Anna (ballerina); St. Petersburg, Russia (1885–1931)
Payne, John (actor); Roanoke, Va., 1912
Peale, Norman Vincent (clergyman); Bowersville, Ohio, 5/31/1898
Pearl, Minnie (Sarah Ophelia Colley Cannon) (comedienne and singer); Centerville, Tenn., 10/25/1912
Pears, Peter (tenor); Farnham, England, 6/22/1910
Pearson, Drew (Andrew Russel Pearson) (columnist); Evanston, Ill. (1897–1969)
Pearson, Lester B. (statesman); Toronto (1897–1972)
Peary, Robert Edwin (explorer); Cresson, Pa. (1856–1920)
Peck, Gregory (actor); La Jolla, Calif., 4/5/1916
Peckinpah, Sam (film director); Fresno, Calif., 2/21/1925
Peerce, Jan (tenor); New York City, 1904
Pegler, (James) Westbrook (columnist); Minneapolis, (1894–1969)
Pei, I. M. (architect); Canton, China, 4/26/1917
Penn, Arthur (stage and film director); Philadelphia, 9/27/1922
Penn, William (American colonist); London (1644–1718)
Penney, James C. (merchant); Hamilton, Mo. (1875–1971)
Peppard, George (actor); Detroit, 10/1/1928
Pepys, Samuel (diarist); Bampton, England (1633–1703)
Perelman, S. J. (Sidney J.) (humorist); Brooklyn, N.Y. (1904–1979)
Pericles (statesman); Athens (died 429 B.C.)
Perkins, Osgood (actor); West Newton, Mass. (1892–1937)
Perkins, Tony (Anthony) (actor); New York City, 4/14/1932
Perlman, Itzhak (violinist); Tel Aviv, Israel, 8/31/1945
Perón, Isabel (María Estela Martínez Cartas) (former chief of state); La Rioja, Argentina, 2/4/1931
Perón, Juan D. (statesman); nr. Lobos, Argentina (1895–1974)
Perón, Maria Eva Duarte de (political leader); Los Toldos, Argentina (1919–1952)
Perrine, Valerie (actress and dancer); Galveston, Tex., 9/3/1943
Pershing, John Joseph (general); Linn County, Mo. (1860–1948)
Peters, Bernadette (actress); New York City, 1944
Peters, Jean (actress); Canton, Ohio, 10/15/1926
Peters, Roberta (Roberta Peterman) (soprano); New York City, 5/4/1930
Petrarch (Francesco Petrarca) (poet); Arezzo (Italy) (1304–1374)
Philip (Philip Mountbatten) (Duke of Edinburgh); Corfu, Greece, 6/10/1921
Piaf, Edith (Edith Gassion) (chanteuse); Paris (1916–1963)
Piatigorsky, Gregor (cellist); Ekaterinoslav, Russia (1903–1976)
Piazza, Ben (actor); Little Rock, Ark., 7/30/1934
Piazza, Marguerite (soprano); New Orleans, 5/6/1926
Picasso, Pablo (painter and sculptor); Málaga, Spain (1881–1973)
Pickford, Jack (Jack Smith) (actor); Toronto (1896–1933)
Pickford, Mary (Gladys Mary Smith) (actress); Toronto (1893–1979)
Picon, Molly (actress); New York City, 6/1/1898
Pidgeon, Walter (actor); East St. John, New Brunswick, Canada, 9/23/1898
Pinter, Harold (playwright); London, 10/10/1930
Pinza, Ezio (basso); Rome (1892–1957)
Pirandello, Luigi (dramatist and novelist); nr. Girgenti, Italy (1867–1936)
Pissaro, Camille Jacob (painter); St. Thomas (U.S. Virgin Islands) (1830–1903)
Piston, Walter (composer); Rockland, Me. (1894–1976)
Pitman, Sir (Isaac) James (educator and publisher); Bath, England, 8/14/1901
Pitt, William ("Younger Pitt") (statesman); nr. Bromley, England (1759–1806)
Pitts, ZaSu (actress); Parsons, Kan. (1898–1963)
Pius XII (Eugenio Pacelli) (Pope); Rome (1876–1958)
Pizarro, Francisco (explorer); Trujillo, Spain (1470?–1541)
Plato (Aristocles) (philosopher); Athens (?) (427?–347 B.C.)
Pleasence, Donald (actor); Worksop, England, 10/5/1919
Pleshette, Suzanne (actress); New York City, 1/31/1937
Plimpton, George (author); New York City, 3/18/1927
Plisetskaya, Maya (ballerina); Moscow, 11/20/1925
Plowright, Joan (actress); Brigg, England, 10/28/1929
Plummer, Christopher (actor); Toronto, 12/13/1929
Plutarch (biographer); Chaeronea (Greece) (46?–?120)
Pocahontas (Matoaka) (American Indian princess); Virginia (?) (1595?–1617)
Podhoretz, Norman (author); Brooklyn, N.Y., 1/16/1930
Poe, Edgar Allan (poet and story writer); Boston, Mass. (1809–1849)
Poitier, Sidney (film actor and director); Miami, Fla., 2/20/1927
Polanski, Roman (film director); Paris, 8/18/1933
Pollard, Michael J. (actor); Passaic, N.J., 5/30/1939
Pollock, Jackson (painter); Cody, Wyo. (1912–1956)
Polo, Marco (traveler); Venice (1254?–?1324)
Pompey (Gnaeus Pompeius Magnus) (general); Rome (?) (106–48 B.C.)
Ponce de León, Juan (explorer); Servas, Spain (1460?–1521)
Pons, Lily (coloratura soprano); Cannes, France (1904–1976)
Ponti, Carlo (director); Milan, Italy, 12/11/1913
Pope, Alexander (poet); London (1688–1744)
Porter, Cole (songwriter); Peru, Ind. (1891–1964)
Porter, Katherine Anne (novelist); Indian Creek, Tex. (1891–1980)
Post, Wiley (aviator); Grand Plain, Tex. (1900–1935)
Poston, Tom (actor); Columbus, Ohio, 10/17/1927
Potok, Chaim (author); New York City, 2/17/1929
Pound, Ezra (poet); Hailey, Idaho (1885–1972)
Powell, Adam Clayton, Jr. (Congressman); New Haven, Conn. (1908–1972)
Powell, Dick (actor); Mt. View, Ark. (1904–1963)
Powell, Eleanor (actress and tap dancer); Springfield, Mass. (1912–1982)
Powell, Jane (Suzanne Burce) (actress and singer); Portland, Ore., 4/1/1929
Powell, William (actor); Pittsburgh, 7/29/1892
Power, Tyrone (actor); Cincinnati, Ohio (1914–1958)
Powers, Stephanie (Taffy Paul) (actress); Hollywood, Calif., 11/12/1942
Praxiteles (sculptor); Athens (c.370–c.330 B.C.)
Preminger, Otto (film director and producer); Vienna, 12/5/1906
Prentiss, Paula (Paula Ragusa) (actress); San Antonio, 1939
Presley, Elvis (singer and actor); Tupelo, Miss. (1935–1977)
Preston, Robert (Robert Preston Meservey) (actor); Newton Highlands, Mass., 6/8/1918
Previn, André (conductor); Berlin, 4/6/1929
Previn, Dory (singer); Rahway, N.J., 10/22/1929(?)
Price, Leontyne (Mary) (soprano); Laurel, Miss., 2/10/1927
Price, Ray (country music artist); Perryville, Tex., 1/12/1926
Price, Vincent (actor); St. Louis, 5/27/1911
Pride, Charley (singer); Sledge, Miss., 3/18/1938(?)
Priestley, J. B. (John B.) (author); Bradford, England, 9/13/1894
Priestley, Joseph (chemist); nr. Leeds, England (1733–1804)
Primrose, William (violist); Glasgow, Scotland (1904–1982)

Prince, Harold (stage producer); New York City, 1/30/1928
Prinze, Freddie (actor); New York City (1954–1977)
Pritchett, V(ictor) S(awdon) (literary critic); Ipswich, England, 12/16/1900
Procter, William (scientist); Cincinnati (1872–1951)
Prokofieff, Sergei Sergeevich (composer); St. Petersburg, Russia (1891–1953)
Proust, Marcel (novelist); Paris (1871–1922)
Provine, Dorothy (actress); Deadwood, S. Dak., 1/20/1937
Prowse, Juliet (actress); Bombay, 9/25/1936
Pryor, Richard (comedian); Peoria, Ill., 12/1/1940
Ptolemy (Claudius Ptolemaeus) (astronomer and geographer); Ptolemais Hermii (Egypt) (2nd century A.D.)
Pucci, Emilio (Marchese di Barsento) (fashion designer); Naples, Italy, 11/20/1914
Puccini, Giacomo (composer); Lucca, Italy (1858–1924)
Puente, Tito (band leader); New York City, 4/20/1923
Pulaski, Casimir (military officer); Podolia, Poland (1748–1779)
Pulitzer, Joseph (publisher); Makó (Hungary) (1847–1911)
Pullman, George (inventor); Brockton, N.Y. (1831–1897)
Pusey, Nathan M. (educator); Council Bluffs, Iowa, 4/4/1907
Pushkin, Alexander Sergeevich (poet and dramatist); Moscow (1799–1837)
Puzo, Mario (novelist); New York City, 10/15/1921
Pyle, Ernest Taylor (journalist); Dana, Ind. (1900–1945)
Pythagoras (mathematician and philosopher); Samos (Greece) (6th century B.C.)

Q

Quayle, Anthony (actor); Ainsdale, England, 9/7/1913
Queen, Ellery: pen name of Frederic Dannay and the late Manfred B. Lee.
Quinn, Anthony (actor); Chihuahua, Mexico, 4/21/1916

R

Rabe, David (playwright); Dubuque, Iowa, 3/10/1940
Rabelais, François (satirist); nr. Chinon, France (1494?–1553)
Rabi, I. I. (Isidor Isaac) (physicist); Rymanow (Poland), 7/29/1898
Rachmaninoff, Sergei Wassilievitch (pianist and composer); Oneg Estate, Novgorod, Russia (1873–1943)
Racine, Jean Baptiste (dramatist); La Ferté-Milon, France (1639–1699)
Radner, Gilda (comedienne); Detroit, 6/28/1946
Raft, George (actor); New York City (1895–1980)
Rainer, Luise (actress); Vienna, 1912
Raines, Ella (actress); Snoqualmie Falls, Wash., 8/6/1921
Rainier III (Prince); Monaco, 5/31/1923
Rains, Claude (actor); London (1889–1967)
Raitt, Bonnie (singer); Los Angeles, 1950
Raleigh, Sir Walter (courtier and navigator); London (1552?–1618)
Randall, Tony (Leonard Rosenberg) (actor); Tulsa, Okla., 2/26/1920
Randolph, Asa Philip (labor leader); Crescent City, Fla. (1889–1979)
Raphael (Raffaello Santi) (painter and architect); Urbino (Italy) (1483–1520)
Rasputin, Grigori Efimovich (monk); Tobolsk Province, Russia (1871?–1916)
Rathbone, Basil (actor); Johannesburg, South Africa (1892–1967)
Rather, Dan (TV newscaster); Wharton, Tex., 10/31/1931
Ratoff, Gregory (film director); St. Petersburg, Russia (1897–1960)
Rattigan, Terence (playwright); London (1911–1977)
Rauschenberg, Robert (painter); Port Arthur, Tex., 1925
Ravel, Maurice Joseph (composer); Ciboure, France (1875–1937)
Rawls, Lou (singer); Chicago, 12/1/1935
Ray, Man (painter); Philadelphia (1890–1976)
Ray, Satyajat (film director); Calcutta, 5/2/1922
Rayburn, Gene (TV personality); Christopher, Ill., 12/22/1917
Raye, Martha (Margie Yvonne Reed) (comedienne and actress); Butte, Mont., 8/27/1916
Raymond, Gene (actor); New York City, 8/13/1908
Reasoner, Harry (TV commentator); Dakota City, Iowa, 4/17/1923
Redding, Otis (singer); Dawson, Ga. (1941–1967)
Reddy, Helen (singer); Melbourne, 10/25/1941
Redford, Robert (Charles Robert Redford, Jr.) (actor); Santa Monica, Calif., 8/18/1937
Redgrave, Lynn (actress); London, 3/8/1943
Redgrave, Sir Michael (actor); Bristol, England, 3/20/1908
Redgrave, Vanessa (actress); London, 1/30/1937
Reed, Donna (actress); Denison, Iowa, 1/27/1921
Reed, Rex (critic); Ft. Worth, 10/2/1940
Reed, Walter (army surgeon); Belroi, Va. (1851–1902)
Reese, Della (Deloreese Patricia Early) (singer); Detroit, 7/6/1932
Reeves, Jim (singer); Panola County, Tex. (1923–1964)
Reid, Wallace (actor); St. Louis (1891–1923)
Reiner, Carl (actor); New York City, 3/20/1922
Reiner, Fritz (conductor); Budapest (1888–1963)
Reiner, Robert (actor); Bronx, N.Y., 1945
Reinhardt, Max (Max Goldmann) (theater producer); nr. Vienna (1873–1943)
Remarque, Erich Maria (novelist); Osnabruk, Germany (1898–1970)
Rembrandt (Rembrandt Harmensz van Rijn) (painter); Leyden (Netherlands) (1606–1669)
Remick, Lee (Ann) (actress); Boston, 12/14/1935
Rennert, Günther (opera director and producer); Essen, Germany, 4/1/1911
Rennie, Michael (actor); Bradford, England (1909–1971)
Renoir, Jean (film director and writer); Paris, (1894–1979)
Renoir, Pierre Auguste (painter); Limoges, France (1841–1919)
Resnais, Alain (film director); Vannes, France, 6/3/1922
Resnik, Regina (mezzo-soprano); New York City, 8/30/1922
Respighi, Ottorino (composer); Bologna, Italy (1879–1936)
Reston, James (journalist); Clydebank, Scotland, 11/3/1909
Reuther, Walter (labor leader); Wheeling, W. Va. (1907–1970)
Revere, Paul (silversmith and hero of famous ride); Boston (1735–1818)
Revson, Charles (business executive); Boston (1906–1975)
Reynolds, Burt (actor); Waycross, Ga., 2/11/1936
Renolds, Debbie (Marie Frances Reynolds) (actress); El Paso, 4/1/1932
Reynolds, Sir Joshua (painter); nr. Plymouth, England (1723–1792)
Rhodes, Cecil John (South African statesman); Bishop Stortford, England (1853–1902)
Rice, Elmer (playwright); New York City (1892–1967)
Rice, Grantland (sports writer); Murfreesboro, Tenn. (1880–1954)
Rich, Buddy (Bernard) (drummer); Brooklyn, N.Y., 6/30/1917
Rich, Charlie (singer); Colt, Ark., 12/14/1932
Richardson, Elliot L. (ex-Cabinet member); Boston, 7/20/1920
Richardson, Sir Ralph (actor); Cheltenham, England, 12/19/1902
Richardson, Tony (director); Shipley, England, 6/5/1928
Richelieu, Duc de (Armand Jean du Plessis) (cardinal); Paris (1585–1642)
Richter, Charles Francis (seismologist); Hamilton, Canada, 4/26/1900
Richter, Sviatoslav (pianist); Zhitomir, Ukraine, 3/20/1914
Rickenbacker, Edward V. (aviator); Columbus, Ohio (1890–1973)
Rickles, Don (comedian); New York City, 5/8/1926
Rickover, Vice Admiral Hyman G. (atomic energy expert); Russia, 1/27/1900
Riddle, Nelson (composer); Hackensack, N.J., 6/1/1921
Ridgway, General Matthew B. (ex-Army Chief of Staff); Ft. Monroe, Va., 3/3/1895
Rigg, Diana (actress); Doncaster, England, 7/20/1938
Riley, James Whitcomb (poet); Greenfield, Ind. (1849–1916)
Rimsky-Korsakov, Nikolai Andreevich (composer); Tikhvin, Russia (1844–1908)
Rinehart, Mary (née Roberts) (novelist); Pittsburgh (1876–1958)
Ritchard, Cyril (actor and director); Sydney, Australia (1898–1977)
Ritter, John (Jonathan) (actor); Burbank, Calif., 9/17/1948
Ritter, Tex (Woodward Maurice Ritter) (singer); Panola County, Tex., (1905–1973)
Ritz, Al (Al Joachim) (comedian); Newark, N.J. (1901–1965)
Rivera, Diego (painter); Guanajuato, Mexico (1886–1957)
Rivera, Geraldo (Miguel) (TV newscaster); New York City, 7/3/1943
Rivers, Joan (comedienne); Brooklyn, N.Y., 1935(?)
Rivers, Larry (Yitzroch Loiza Grossberg) (painter); New York City, 8/17/1923
Robards, Jason, Jr. (actor); Chicago, 7/26/1922
Robards, Jason, Sr. (actor); Hillsdale, Mich. (1892–1963)
Robbins, Harold (Harold Rubin) (novelist); New York City, 5/21/1916
Robbins, Jerome (Jerome Rabinowitz) (choreographer); New York City, 10/11/1918
Robbins, Marty (singer); Glendale, Ariz., 12/26/1925
Roberts, (Granville) Oral (evangelist and publisher); nr. Ada, Okla., 1/24/1918
Robertson, Cliff (actor); La Jolla, Calif., 9/9/1925
Robertson, Dale (actor); Oklahoma City, 1923
Robeson, Paul (singer and actor); Princeton, N.J., (1898–1976)
Robespierre, Maximilien François Marie Isidore de (French Revolutionist); Arras, France (1758–1794)
Robinson, Bill "Bojangles" (Luther) (dancer); Richmond, Va. (1878–1949)
Robinson, Edward G. (Emanuel Goldenberg) (actor); Bucharest (1893–1973)
Robinson, Edwin Arlington (poet); Head Tide, Me. (1869–1935)
Robson, Dame Flora (actress); South Shields, England, 3/28/1902
Rochester (Eddie Anderson) (actor); Oakland, Calif. (1905–1977)
Rockefeller, David (banker); New York City, 6/12/1915
Rockefeller, John Davison (capitalist); Richford, N.Y. (1839–1937)
Rockefeller, John Davison, Jr. (industrialist); Cleveland (1874–1960)
Rockefeller, John D., 3rd (philanthropist); New York City (1906–1978)
Rockefeller, Laurance S. (conservationist); New York City, 5/26/1910
Rockwell, Norman (painter and illustrator); New York City, (1894–1978)
Rodgers, Jimmie (singer); Meridian, Miss. (1897–1933)

Rodgers, Richard (composer); New York City **(1902–1979)**
Rodin, François Auguste René (sculptor); Paris **(1840–1917)**
Roentgen, Wilhelm Konrad (physicist); Lennep, Prussia **(1845–1923)**
Rogers, Buddy (Charles) (actor); Olathe, Kan., 8/13/1904
Rogers, Ginger (Virginia McMath) (dancer and actress); Independence, Mo., 7/16/1911
Rogers, Kenny (singer); Houston, 1939(?)
Rogers, Roy (Leonard Slye) (actor); Cincinnati, 11/5/1912
Rogers, Will (William Penn Adair Rogers) (humorist); Oologah, Okla. **(1879–1935)**
Rogers, Will, Jr. (actor); New York City, 10/20/1911
Rogers, William P. (ex-Secretary of State); Norfolk, N.Y., 6/23/1913
Roland, Gilbert (actor); Juarez, Mexico, 12/11/1905
Rolland, Romain (author); Clamecy, France **(1866–1944)**
Rollins, Sonny (saxophonist); New York City, 9/7/1930
Romberg, Sigmund (composer); Szeged (Hungary) **(1887–1951)**
Rome, Harold (composer); Hartford, Conn., 5/27/1908
Romero, Cesar (actor); New York City, 2/15/1907
Romney, George W. (ex-Secretary of HUD); Chihuahua, Mexico, 7/8/1907
Romulo, Carlos P. (diplomat and educator); Manila, 1/14/1899
Ronstadt, Linda (singer); Tucson, Ariz., 7/30/1946
Rooney, Mickey (Joe Yule, Jr.) (actor); Brooklyn, N.Y., 9/23/1920
Roosevelt, Anna Eleanor (reformer and humanitarian); New York City **(1884–1962)**
Rose, Billy (showman); New York City **(1899–1966)**
Rose, Leonard (concert cellist); Washington, D.C., 7/27/1918
Ross, Diana (singer); Detroit, 3/26/1944
Ross, Katharine (actress); Hollywood, Calif., 1/29/1943
Rossellini, Roberto (film director); Rome **(1906–1977)**
Rossetti, Dante Gabriel (painter and poet); London **(1828–1882)**
Rossini, Gioacchino Antonio (composer); Pesaro (Italy) **(1792–1868)**
Rostand, Edmond (dramatist); Marseilles, France **(1868–1918)**
Rostow, Walt Whitman (economist); New York City, 10/7/1916
Rostropovich, Mstislav (cellist and conductor); Baku, U.S.S.R., 8/12/1927
Roth, Lillian (singer); Boston **(1910–1980)**
Roth, Philip (novelist); Newark, N.J., 3/19/1933
Rothko, Mark (Marcus Rothkovich) (painter); Russia **(1903–1970)**
Rouault, Georges (painter); Paris, France **(1871–1958)**
Roundtree, Richard (actor); New Rochelle, N.Y., 9/7/1942
Rousseau, Henri (painter); Laval, France **(1844–1910)**
Rousseau, Jean Jacques (philosopher); Geneva **(1712–1778)**
Rovere, Richard H. (journalist); Jersey City, N.J., 5/5/1915
Rowan, Dan (comedian); Beggs, Okla., 7/2/1922
Rowlands, Gena (actress); Cambria, Wis., 6/19/1936(?)
Rubens, Sir Peter Paul (painter); Siegen (Germany) **(1577–1640)**
Rubenstein, Arthur (concert pianist); Lódz (Poland), 1/28/1887
Rubinstein, Helena (cosmetics executive); Kraków (Poland) **(1882?–1965)**
Rudel, Julius (conductor); Vienna, 3/6/1921
Ruggles, Charles (actor); Los Angeles **(1892–1970)**
Rule, Janice (actress); Norwood, Ohio, 8/15/1931
Runcie, Robert (Alexander Kennedy) (Archbishop of Canterbury); Liverpool, England, 10/2/1921
Runyon, (Alfred) Damon (journalist); Manhattan, Kan. **(1884–1946)**
Rusk, Dean (ex-Sec. of State); Cherokee County, Ga., 2/9/1909
Ruskin, John (art critic); London **(1819–1900)**
Russell, Lord Bertrand (Arthur William) (mathematician and philosopher); Trelleck, Wales **(1872–1970)**
Russell, Jane (actress); Bemidji, Minn., 6/21/1921
Russell, Leon (pianist and singer); Lawton, Okla., 4/2/1941
Russell, Lillian (Helen Louise Leonard) (soprano); Clinton, Iowa **(1861–1922)**
Russell, Nipsy (comedian); Atlanta, 1924(?)
Russell, Rosalind (actress); Waterbury, Conn. **(1912–1976)**
Rustin, Bayard (civil rights leader); West Chester, Pa., 1910
Rutherford, Dame Margaret (actress); London, England **(1892–1972)**
Ryan, Robert (actor); Chicago **(1909–1973)**
Rydell, Bobby (singer); Philadelphia, 1942
Rysanek, Leonie (dramatic soprano); Vienna, 11/14/1928

S

Saarinen, Eero (architect); Finland **(1910–1961)**
Sabin, Albert B. (polio researcher); Bialystok (Poland), 8/26/1906
Sadat, Anwar el- (President); Egypt **(1918–1981)**
Sagan, Françoise (novelist); Cajarc, France, 6/21/1935
Sahl, Mort (Morton Lyon Sahl) (comedian); Montreal, 5/11/1927
Saint, Eva Marie (actress); Newark, N.J., 7/4/1924
Saint-Gaudens, Augustus (sculptor); Dublin **(1848–1907)**
St. James, Susan (actress); Los Angeles, 1946
St. John, Jill (actress); Los Angeles, 8/19/1940
St. Johns, Adela Rogers (journalist and author); Los Angeles, 5/20/1894
Saint-Laurent, Yves (Henri Donat Mathieu) (fashion designer); Oran, Algeria, 8/1/1936
Saint-Saëns, Charles Camille (composer); Paris **(1835–1921)**
Sainte-Marie, Buffy (Beverly) (folk singer); Craven, Saskatchewan, Canada, 2/20/1942(?)
Salinger, J. D. (Jerome David) (novelist); New York City, 1/1/1919
Salisbury, Harrison E. (journalist); Minneapolis, 11/14/1908
Salk, Jonas (polio researcher); New York City, 10/28/1914
Salk, Lee (psychologist); New York City, 1926
Salomon, Haym (American Revolution financier); Leszno, Poland **(1740–1785)**
Sand, George (Amandine Lucille Aurore Dudevant, née Dupin) (novelist); Paris **(1804–1876)**
Sandburg, Carl (poet and biographer); Galesburg, Ill. **(1878–1967)**
Sanders, George (actor); St. Petersburg, Russia **(1906–1972)**
Sands, Tommy (singer); Chicago, 8/27/1937
Sanger, Margaret (birth control leader); Corning, N.Y. **(1883–1966)**
Santayana, George (philosopher); Madrid **(1863–1952)**
Sappho (poet); Lesbos (Greece) **(lived c. 600** B.C.**)**
Sargent, John Singer (painter); Florence, Italy **(1856–1925)**
Sarnoff, David (radio executive); Minsk, Russia **(1891–1971)**
Saroyan, William (novelist); Fresno, Calif. **(1908–1981)**
Sarrazin, Michael (actor); Quebec, 5/22/1940
Sarto, Andrea del (Andrea Domenico d'Agnolo di Francesco) (painter); Florence (Italy) **(1486–1531)**
Sartre, Jean-Paul (existentialist writer); Paris **(1905–1980)**
Sassoon, Vidal (hair stylist); London, 1/(?)/1928
Saul (King of Israel) **(11th century** B.C.**)**
Savalas, Telly (Aristoteles) (actor); Garden City, N.Y., 1/21/1924(?)
Sayao, Bidú (soprano); Rio de Janeiro, 5/11/1902
Scaasi, Arnold (Arnold Isaacs) (fashion designer); Montreal
Schary, Dore (producer and writer); Newark, N.J. **(1905–1980)**
Schell, Maria (actress); Vienna, 1/15/1926
Schell, Maximilian (actor); Vienna, 12/8/1930
Schiaparelli, Elsa (fashion designer); Rome **(1890?–1973)**
Schiff, Dorothy (newspaper publisher); New York City, 3/11/1903
Schildkraut, Joseph (actor); Vienna **(1896–1964)**
Schiller, Johann Christoph Friedrich von (dramatist and poet); Marbach (Germany) **(1759–1805)**
Schippers, Thomas (conductor); Kalamazoo, Mich. **(1930–1977)**
Schlesinger, Arthur M., Jr. (historian); Columbus, Ohio, 10/15/1917
Schneider, Romy (Rose-Marie Albach) (actress); Vienna **(1938–1982)**
Schoenberg, Arnold (composer); Vienna **(1874–1951)**
Schopenhauer, Arthur (philosopher); Danzig (Poland) **(1788–1860)**
Schubert, Franz Peter (composer); Vienna **(1797–1828)**
Schulberg, Budd (novelist); New York City, 3/27/1914
Schulz, Charles M. (cartoonist); Minneapolis, 11/26/1922
Schuman, Robert (statesman); Luxembourg **(1886–1963)**
Schuman, William (composer); New York City, 8/4/1910
Schumann, Robert Alexander (composer); Zwickau (Germany) **(1810–1856)**
Schwartz, Arthur (song writer); Brooklyn, N.Y., 11/25/1900
Schwartz, Maurice (actor); Russia **(1891–1960)**
Schwarzkopf, Elisabeth (soprano); Jarotschin, Poznán (Poland), 12/9/1915
Schweitzer, Albert (humanitarian); Kaysersburg, Upper Alsace **(1875–1965)**
Scofield, Paul (actor); Hurstpierpoint, England, 1/21/1922
Scorsese, Martin (film director); Flushing, N.Y., 11/17/1942
Scott, George C. (actor); Wise, Va., 10/18/1927
Scott, Lizabeth (Emma Matso) (actress); Scranton, Pa., 1923
Scott, Martha (actress); Jamesport, Mo., 9/22/1914
Scott, Randolph (Randolph Crane) (actor); Orange County, Va., 1/23/1903
Scott, Robert Falcon (explorer); Devonport, England **(1868–1912)**
Scott, Sir Walter (novelist); Edinburgh, Scotland **(1771–1832)**
Scott, Zachary (actor); Austin, Tex. **(1914–1965)**
Scotto, Renata (operatic soprano); Savona, Italy, 2/?/1936?
Scruggs, Earl Eugene (bluegrass musician); Cleveland County, N.C., 1/6/1924
Sebastian, John (composer); New York City, 3/17/1944
Seberg, Jean (actress); Marshalltown, Iowa **(1938–1979)**
Sedaka, Neil (singer); Brooklyn, N.Y., 3/13/1939
Seeger, Pete (folk singer); New York City, 5/3/1919
Segal, Erich (novelist); Brooklyn, N.Y., 6/16/1937
Segal, George (actor); New York City, 2/13/1936
Segovia, Andrés (guitarist); Linares, Spain, 2/21/1893
Sellers, Peter (actor); Southsea, England **(1925–1980)**
Selye, Hans (physician); Vienna, 1/26/1907
Selznick, David O. (film producer); Pittsburgh **(1902–1965)**
Sendak, Maurice (Bernard) (children's book author and illustrator); Brooklyn, N.Y., 6/10/1928
Sennett, Mack (Michael Sinnott) (film producer); Richmond, Quebec, Canada **(1880–1960)**
Serkin, Rudolf (pianist); Eger (Hungary), 3/28/1903
Serling, Rod (story writer); Syracuse, N.Y. **(1924–1975)**
Sessions, Roger (composer); Brooklyn, N.Y., 12/28/1896
Seurat, Georges (painter); Paris **(1859–1891)**

Seuss, Dr. (Theodor Seuss Geisel) (author and illustrator); Springfield, Mass., 3/2/1904
Sevareid, Eric (TV commentator); Velva, N.D., 11/26/1912
Severinsen, Doc (band leader); Arlington, Ore., 1927
Sexton, Anne (poet); Newton, Mass. **(1928–1974)**
Shahn, Ben(jamin) (painter); Kaunas, Lithuania **(1898–1969)**
Shakespeare, William (dramatist); Stratford on Avon, England **(1564–1616)**
Shankar, Ravi (sitar player); Benares, India, 4/7/1920
Shanker, Albert (labor leader); New York City, 9/14/1928
Sharif, Omar (Michael Shalhoub) (actor); Alexandria, Egypt, 4/10/1932
Shatner, William (actor); Montreal, 3/22/1931
Shaw, Artie (Arthur Arshawsky) (band leader); New York City, 5/23/1910
Shaw, George Bernard (dramatist); Dublin, **(1856–1950)**
Shaw, Irwin (novelist); Brooklyn, N.Y., 2/27/1913
Shaw, Robert (actor); Lancashire, England **(1927–1978)**
Shaw, Robert (chorale conductor); Red Bluff, Calif., 4/30/1916
Shearer, Moira (ballerina); Dunfermline, Scotland, 1/17/1926
Shearer, Norma (actress); Montreal, 1904
Shearing, George (pianist); London, 8/13/1920
Sheen, Fulton J. (Peter Sheen) (Roman Catholic bishop); El Paso, Ill. **(1895–1979)**
Sheen, Martin (Ramon Estevez) (actor); Dayton, Ohio, 8/3/1940
Shelley, Percy Bysshe (poet); nr. Horsham, England **(1792–1822)**
Shepard, Sam (playwright); Ft. Sheridan, Ill. 11/5/1943
Sheraton, Thomas (furniture designer); Stockton-on-Tees, England **(1751–1806)**
Sheridan, Ann (actress); Denton, Tex. **(1915–1967)**
Sheridan, Philip (army officer); Albany, N.Y. **(1831–1888)**
Sheridan, Richard Brinsley (dramatist); Dublin, **(1751–1816)**
Sherman, William Tecumseh (army officer); Lancaster, Ohio **(1820–1891)**
Sherwood, Robert Emmet (playwright); New Rochelle, N.Y. **(1896–1955)**
Shirer, William L. (journalist and historian); Chicago, 2/23/1904
Sholokhov, Mikhail (novelist); Veshenskaya, Russia, 5/24/1905
Shore, Dinah (Frances Rose Shore) (singer); Winchester, Tenn., 3/1/1917(?)
Short, Bobby (Robert Waltrip Short) (singer and pianist); Danville, Ill., 9/15/1924
Shostakovich, Dmitri (composer); St. Petersburg, Russia **(1906–1975)**
Shriver, Sargent (Robert Sargent Shriver, Jr.) (business executive); Westminster, Md., 11/9/1915
Shulman, Max (novelist); St. Paul, 3/14/1919
Sibelius, Jean (Johann Julius Christian Sibelius) (composer); Tavastehus (Finland) **(1865–1957)**
Sidney, Sylvia (actress); New York City, 8/8/1910
Siepi, Cesare (basso); Milan, Italy, 2/10/1923
Signoret, Simone (Simone Kaminker) (actress); Wiesbaden, Germany, 3/25/1921
Sikorsky, Igor I. (inventor); Kiev, Russia **(1889–1972)**
Sills, Beverly (Belle Silverman) (soprano); Brooklyn, N.Y., 5/25/1929
Silone, Ignazio (Secondo Tranquilli) (novelist); Pescina dei Marsi, Italy **(1900–1978)**
Silverman, Fred (broadcasting executive); New York City, 9/13/1937
Silvers, Phil (Philip Silversmith) (comedian); Brooklyn, N.Y., 5/11/1912
Sim, Alastair (actor); Edinburgh, Scotland **(1900–1976)**
Simenon, Georges (Georges Sim) (mystery writer); Liège, Belgium, 2/13/1903
Simmons, Jean (actress); Crouch Hill, London, 1/31/1929
Simon, Carly (singer and songwriter); New York City, 6/25/1945
Simon, Neil (playwright); Bronx, N.Y., 7/4/1927
Simon, Norton (business executive); Portland, Ore., 2/5/1907
Simon, Paul (singer and songwriter); Newark, N.J., 11/5/1942
Simon, Simone (actress); Marseilles, France, 4/23/1914
Simone, Nina (Eunice Kathleen Waymon) (singer and pianist); Tryon, N.C., 2/21/1933
Simpson, Adele (Adele Smithline) (fashion designer); New York City, 12/8/1903
Sinatra, Frank (singer and actor); Hoboken, N.J., 12/12/1915
Sinclair, Upton Beall (novelist); Baltimore **(1878–1968)**
Singer, Isaac Bashevis (novelist); Radzymin (Poland), 7/14/1904
Siqueiros, David (painter); Chihuahua, Mexico **(1896–1974)**
Sisley, Alfred (painter); Paris **(1839–1899)**
Sitting Bull (Prairie Sioux Indian Chief); on Grand River, S.D. **(c. 1835–1890)**
Skelton, Red (Richard) (comedian); Vincennes, Ind., 7/18/1913
Skinner, B. F. (Burrhus Frederic) (psychologist); Susquehanna, Pa., 3/20/1904
Skinner, Cornelia Otis (writer and actress); Chicago, **(1901–1979)**
Skinner, Otis (actor); Cambridge, Mass. **(1858–1942)**
Slezak, Walter (actor); Vienna, 5/3/1902
Sloan, Alfred P., Jr. (industrialist); New Haven, Conn. **(1875–1966)**
Sloan, John (painter); Lock Haven, Pa. **(1871–1951)**
Smetana, Bedrich (composer); Litomysl (Czechoslovakia) **(1824–1884)**
Smith, Adam (economist); Kirkaldy, Scotland **(1723–1790)**
Smith, Alexis (actress); Penticon, Canada, 6/8/1921
Smith, Alfred Emanuel (politician); New York City **(1873–1944)**
Smith, David (sculptor); Decatur, Ind. **(1906–1965)**
Smith, H. Allen (humorist); McLeansboro, Ill. **(1907–1976)**
Smith, Howard K. (TV commentator); Ferriday, La., 5/12/1914
Smith, Jaclyn (actress); Houston, 10/26/(?)
Smith, John (American colonist); Willoughby, Lincolnshire, England **(1580–1631)**
Smith, Joseph (religious leader); Sharon, Vt. **(1805–1844)**
Smith, Kate (Kathryn) (singer); Greenville, Va., 5/1/1909
Smith, Maggie (actress); Ilford, England, 12/28/1934
Smith, Red (Walter) (sports columnist); Green Bay, Wis. **(1905–1982)**
Smothers, Dick (Richard) (comedian); Governors Island, New York City, 11/20/1939
Smothers, Tom (Thomas) (comedian); Governors Island, New York City, 2/2/1937
Snow, Lord (Charles Percy) (author); Leicester, England **(1905–1980)**
Snowden, Earl of (Anthony Armstrong-Jones) (photographer); London, 3/7/1930
Snyder, Tom (TV personality); Milwaukee, 5/12/1936
Socrates (philosopher); Athens **(469–399 B.C.)**
Solomon (King of Israel); Jerusalem (?) **(died c. 933 B.C.)**
Solon (lawgiver); Salamis (Greece) **(638?–?559 B.C.)**
Solti, Sir Georg (conductor); Budapest, 10/21/1912
Solzhenitsyn, Aleksandr (novelist); Kislovodsk, Russia, 12/11/1918
Sommer, Elke (Elke Schletz) (actress); Berlin, 11/5/1942
Sondheim, Stephen (composer); New York City, 3/22/1930
Sontag, Susan (author and film director); New York City, 1/28/1933
Sophocles (dramatist); nr. Athens **(496?–406 B.C.)**
Sothern, Ann (Harriette Lake) (actress); Valley City, N.D., 1/22/1912
Soul, David (David Solberg) (actor); Chicago, 8/28/(?)
Sousa, John Philip (composer); Washington, D.C. **(1854–1932)**
Soyer, Raphael (painter); Borisoglebsk, Russia, 12/25/1899
Spaak, Paul-Henri (statesman); Brussels **(1899–1972)**
Spacek, Sissy (Mary Elizabeth) (actress); Quitman, Tex., 12/25/1949
Spark, Muriel (novelist); Edinburgh, Scotland, 2/1/1918
Spector, Phil (rock producer); Bronx, N.Y., 12/25/1940
Spencer, Herbert (philosopher); Derby, England **(1820–1903)**
Spender, Stephen (poet); nr. London, 2/28/1909
Spengler, Oswald (philosopher); Blankenburg, Germany **(1880–1936)**
Spenser, Edmund (poet); London **(1552?–1599)**
Spewack, Bella (playwright); Hungary, 1899
Spiegel, Sam (producer); Jaroslaw (Poland), 11/11/1901
Spielberg, Steven (film director); Cincinnati, 12/18/1947
Spillane, Mickey (Frank Spillane) (mystery writer); Brooklyn, N.Y., 3/9/1918
Spinoza, Baruch (philosopher); Amsterdam (Netherlands) **(1632–1677)**
Spivak, Lawrence (TV producer); Brooklyn, N.Y., 1900
Spock, Benjamin (pediatrician); New Haven, Conn., 5/2/1903
Springsteen, Bruce (singer and songwriter); Freehold, N.J., 9/23/1949
Sproul, Robert G. (educator); San Francisco **(1891–1975)**
Stack, Robert (actor); Los Angeles, 1/13/1919
Stafford, Jo (singer); Coalinga, Calif., 1918
Stalin, Joseph Vissarionovich (Iosif V. Dzhugashvili) (Soviet leader); nr. Tiflis, Russia **(1879–1953)**
Stalina, Svetlana Alliluyeva (Stalin's daughter); Moscow, 2/28/1926
Stallone, Sylvester (actor and writer); New York City, 7/6/1946
Stamp, Terrence (actor); London, 1940
Stang, Arnold (comedian); Chelsea, Mass., 1925
Stanislavski (Konstantin Sergeevich Alekseev) (stage producer); Moscow **(1863–1938)**
Stanley, Sir Henry Morton (John Rowlands) (explorer); Denbigh, Wales **(1841–1904)**
Stanley, Kim (Patricia Reid) (actress); Tularosa, N.M., 2/11/1925
Stans, Maurice H. (ex-Secretary of Commerce); Shakope, Minn., 3/22/1908
Stanton, Frank (broadcasting executive); Muskegon, Mich., 3/20/1908
Stanwyck, Barbara (Ruby Stevens) (actress); Brooklyn, N.Y., 7/16/1907
Stapleton, Jean (Jeanne Murray) (actress); New York City, 1/19/1923
Stapleton, Maureen (actress); Troy, N.Y., 6/21/1925
Starker, Janós (cellist); Budapest 7/5/1926
Starr, Kay (Starks) (singer); Dougherty, Okla., 7/21/1922
Starr, Ringo (Richard Starkey) (singer and songwriter); Liverpool, England, 7/7/1940
Stassen, Harold E. (ex-government official); West St. Paul, Minn., 4/13/1907
Steegmuller, Francis (biographer); New Haven, Conn., 7/3/1906
Steele, Tommy (singer); London, 12/17/1936
Stegner, Wallace (Earle) (novelist and critic); Lake Mills, Iowa, 2/18/1909
Steiger, Rod (Rodney) (actor); Westhampton, N.Y., 4/14/1925
Stein, Gertrude (author); Allegheny, Pa. **(1874–1946)**
Steinbeck, John Ernst (novelist); Salinas, Calif. **(1902–1968)**
Steinberg, William (conductor); Cologne, Germany **(1899–1978)**
Steinem, Gloria (feminist); Toledo, Ohio, 3/25/1935(?)
Steinmetz, Charles (electrical engineer); Breslau (Poland) **(1865–1923)**
Stendhal (Marie Henri Beyle) (novelist); Grenoble, France **(1783–1842)**

Sterling, Jan (actress); New York City, 4/3/1923
Stern, Isaac (concert violinist); Kreminiecz, Russia, 7/21/1920
Sterne, Laurence (novelist); Clonmel, Ireland **(1713–1768)**
Stevens, Cat (Steven Georgiou) (singer and songwriter); London, 7/?/1947
Stevens, Connie (Concetta Ingolia) (singer); Brooklyn, N.Y., 8/8/1938
Stevens, George (film director); Oakland, Calif. **(1905–1975)**
Stevens, Risë (mezzo-soprano); New York City, 6/11/1913
Stevens, Stella (actress); Yazoo City, Miss., 10/1/1936
Stevenson, Adlai Ewing (statesman); Los Angeles **(1900–1965)**
Stevenson, McLean (actor); Bloomington, Ind., 11/14/1929(?)
Stevenson, Robert Louis Balfour (novelist and poet); Edinburgh, Scotland **(1850–1894)**
Stewart, James (actor); Indiana, Pa., 5/20/1908
Stewart, Rod (Roderick David) (singer); London, 1/10/1945
Stickney, Dorothy (actress); Dickinson, N.D. 6/21/1903
Stills, Stephen (singer and songwriter); Dallas, 1/3/1945
Stokes, Carl (TV newscaster); Cleveland, 6/21/1927
Stokowski, Leopold (conductor); London **(1882–1977)**
Stone, Edward Durell (architect); Fayetteville, Ark. **(1902–1978)**
Stone, Ezra (actor and producer); New Bedford, Mass., 12/2/1917
Stone, I. F. (Isidor Feinstein Stone) (journalist); Philadelphia, 12/24/1907
Stone, Irving (Irving Tennenbaum) (novelist); San Francisco, 7/14/1903
Stone, Lewis (actor); Worcester, Mass. **(1879–1953)**
Stone, Lucy (woman suffragist); nr. West Brookfield, Mass. **(1818–1893)**
Stone, Sly (Sylvester) (rock musician); 1944
Storm, Gale (actress); Bloomington, Tex., 1922
Stout, Rex (mystery writer); Noblesville, Ind. **(1886–1975)**
Stowe, Harriet Elizabeth Beecher (novelist); Litchfield, Conn. **(1811–1896)**
Stradivari, Antonio (violinmaker); Cremona (Italy) **(1644–1737)**
Strasberg, Lee (stage director); Budanov, Austria **(1901–1982)**
Strasberg, Susan (actress); New York City, 5/22/1938
Straus, Oskar (composer); Vienna **(1870–1954)**
Strauss, Johann (composer); Vienna **(1825–1899)**
Strauss, Lewis L. (naval officer and scientist); Charleston, W. Va. **(1896–1974)**
Strauss, Richard (composer); Munich, Germany **(1864–1949)**
Stravinsky, Igor (composer); Orienbaum, Russia **(1882–1971)**
Streep, Meryl (Mary Louise) (actress); Summit, N.J., 6/22/1949
Streisand, Barbra (singer and actress); Brooklyn, N.Y., 4/24/1942
Stritch, Elaine (actress); Detroit, 2/2/1928
Struthers, Sally Ann (actress); Portland, Ore., 7/28/1948
Stuart, Gilbert Charles (painter); Rhode Island **(1755–1828)**
Stuart, James Ewell Brown (known as Jeb) (Confederate army officer); Patrick County, Va. **(1833–1864)**
Stuyvesant, Peter (Governor of New Amsterdam); West Friesland (Netherlands) **(1592–1672)**
Styron, William (William Clark Styron, Jr.) (novelist); Newport News, Va., 6/11/1925
Sullavan, Margaret Brooke (actress); Norfolk, Va. **(1911–1960)**
Sullivan, Sir Arthur Seymour (composer); London **(1842–1900)**
Sullivan, Barry (Patrick Barry) (actor); New York City, 8/29/1912
Sullivan, Ed (columnist and TV personality); New York City **(1901–1974)**
Sullivan, Francis Loftus (actor); London **(1903–1956)**
Sullivan, Frank (Francis John) (humorist); Saratoga Springs, N.Y. **(1892–1976)**
Sullivan, Louis Henry (architect); Boston, Mass. **(1856–1924)**
Sulzberger, Arthur Ochs (newspaper publisher); New York City, 2/5/1926
Sumac, Yma (singer); Ichocan, Peru, 9/10/1927
Summer, Donna (singer); Boston, 12/31/1948
Sun Yat-sen (statesman); nr. Macao **(1866–1925)**
Susann, Jacqueline (novelist); Philadelphia **(1926?–1974)**
Susskind, David (TV producer); New York City, 12/19/1920
Sutherland, Joan (soprano); Sydney, Australia, 11/7/1926
Suzuki, Pat (actress); Cressey, Calif., 1931
Swados, Elizabeth (composer, playwright); Buffalo, N.Y., 2/5/1951
Swanson, Gloria (Josephine Swenson) (actress); Chicago, 3/27/1899
Swarthout, Gladys (soprano); Deepwater, Mo. **(1904–1969)**
Swayze, John Cameron (news commentator); Wichita, Kan., 4/4/1906
Swift, Jonathan (satirist); Dublin **(1667–1745)**
Swinburne, Algernon Charles (poet); London **(1837–1909)**
Swope, Herbert Bayard (journalist); St. Louis **(1882–1958)**
Sydow, von, Max (Carl Adolf von Sydow) (actor); Lund, Sweden, 4/10/1929
Synge, John Millington (dramatist); nr. Dublin **(1871–1909)**
Szilard, Leo (physicist); Budapest **(1898–1964)**

T

Taft, Robert Alphonso (legislator); Cincinnati **(1889–1953)**
Tagore, Sir Rabindranath (poet); Calcutta **(1861–1941)**
Tallchief, Maria (ballerina); Fairfax, Okla., 1/24/1925
Talleyrand-Périgord, Charles Maurice de (statesman); Paris **(1754–1838)**
Talmadge, Norma (actress); Niagara Falls, N.Y. **(1897–1957)**
Tamerlane (Timur) (Mongol conqueror); nr. Samarkand (U.S.S.R.) **(1336?–1405)**
Tandy, Jessica (actress); London, 6/7/1909
Tarkington, (Newton) Booth (novelist); Indianapolis **(1869–1946)**
Tate, Allen (John Orley) (poet and critic); Winchester, Ky., **(1899–1979)**
Tate, Sharon (actress); Dallas **(1943–1969)**
Tati, Jacques (Jacques Tatischeff) (actor); Pecq, France, 10/9/1908
Taylor, Elizabeth (actress); London, 2/27/1932
Taylor, Estelle (actress); Wilmington, Del. **(1899–1958)**
Taylor, Harold (educator); Toronto, 9/28/1914
Taylor, James (singer and songwriter); Boston, 3/12/1948
Taylor, (Joseph) Deems (composer); New York City **(1885–1966)**
Taylor, Laurette (Laurette Cooney) (actress); New York City **(1884–1946)**
Taylor, Gen. Maxwell D. (former Army Chief of Staff); Keytesville, Mo., 8/26/1901
Taylor, Robert (Spangler Arlington Brugh) (actor); Filley, Neb. **(1911–1969)**
Taylor, Rod (actor); Sydney, Australia, 1/11/1930
Tchaikovsky, Peter (Pëtr) Ilich (composer); Votkinsk, Russia **(1840–1893)**
Teasdale, Sara (poet); St. Louis **(1884–1933)**
Tebaldi, Renata (lyric soprano); Pesaro, Italy, 1/2/1922
Tecumseh (Shawnee Indian chief); nr. Springfield, Ohio **(1768?–1813)**
Teller, Edward (atomic physicist); Budapest, 1/15/1908
Temple, Shirley. *See* Black, Shirley Temple
Tennyson, Alfred (1st Baron Tennyson) (poet); Somersby, England **(1809–1892)**
Terhune, Albert Payson (novelist and journalist); Newark, N.J. **(1872–1942)**
Terry, Ellen Alicia (actress); Coventry, England **(1848–1928)**
Terry-Thomas (Thomas Terry Hoar Stevens) (actor); London, 7/14/1911
Tesla, Nikola (electrician and inventor); Smiljan (Yugoslavia) **(1856–1943)**
Thackeray, William Makepeace (novelist); Calcutta **(1811–1863)**
Thant, U (U.N. statesman); Pantanaw (Burma) **(1909–1974)**
Tharp, Twyla (dancer and choreographer); Portland, Ind., 7/1/1941(?)
Thatcher, Margaret (Prime Minister); Grantham, England, 10/13/1925
Thaxter, Phyllis (actress); Portland, Me., 1921
Thebom, Blanche (mezzo-soprano); Monessen, Pa., 9/19/1919
Theodorakis, Mikis (composer); Chios, Greece, 7/29/1925
Thieu, Nguyen Van (ex-President of South Vietnam); Trithuy (Vietnam) 4/5/1923
Thomas, Danny (Amos Jacobs) (entertainer and TV producer); Deerfield, Mich., 1/6/1914
Thomas, Dylan Marlais (poet); Carmarthenshire, Wales **(1914–1953)**
Thomas, Lowell (explorer, commentator); Woodington, Ohio **(1892–1981)**
Thomas, Marlo (actress); Detroit, 11/21/1943
Thomas, Michael Tilson (conductor); Hollywood, Calif., 12/21/1944
Thomas, Norman Mattoon (Socialist leader); Marion, Ohio **(1884–1968)**
Thomas, Richard (actor); New York City, 6/13/1951
Thompson, Dorothy (writer); Lancaster, N.Y. **(1894–1961)**
Thompson, Sada (actress); Des Moines, Iowa, 9/27/1929
Thoreau, Henry David (naturalist and author); Concord, Mass. **(1817–1862)**
Thorndike, Dame Sybil (actress); Gainsborough, England **(1882–1976)**
Thurber, James Grover (author and cartoonist); Columbus, Ohio **(1894–1961)**
Tibbett, Lawrence (baritone); Bakersfield, Calif. **(1896–1960)**
Tierney, Gene (actress); Brooklyn, N.Y., 11/20/1920
Tiffin, Pamela (actress); Oklahoma City, 10/13/1942
Tillstrom, Burr (puppeteer); Chicago, 10/13/1917
Tintoretto, Il (Jacopo Robusti) (painter); Venice **(1518–1594)**
Tiny Tim (Herbert Khaury) (entertainer); New York City, 1923(?)
Tiomkin, Dmitri (composer); St. Petersburg, Russia **(1894–1979)**
Titian (Tiziano Vecelli) (painter); Pieve di Cadore (Italy) **(1477–1576)**
Tito (Josip Broz or Brozovich) (President of Yugoslavia); Croatia (Yugoslavia) **(1892–1980)**
Tocqueville, Alexis de (writer); Verneuil, France **(1805–1859)**
Todd, Thelma (actress); Lawrence, Mass. **(1905–1935)**
Tolstoi, Count Leo (Lev) Nikolaevich (novelist); Tula Province, Russia **(1828–1910)**
Tomlin, Lily (comedienne); Detroit, 1939(?)
Tone, Franchot (actor); Niagara Falls, N.Y. **(1905–1968)**
Torme, Mel (Melvin) (singer); Chicago, 9/13/1925
Torn, Rip (Elmore Torn, Jr.) (actor and director); Temple, Tex., 2/6/1931
Toscanini, Arturo (orchestra conductor); Parma, Italy **(1867–1957)**
Toulouse-Lautrec (Henri Marie Raymond de Toulouse-Lautrec Monfa) (painter); Albi, France **(1864–1901)**
Toynbee, Arnold J. (historian); London **(1889–1975)**
Tracy, Spencer (actor); Milwaukee **(1900–1967)**
Traubel, Helen (Wagnerian soprano); St. Louis **(1903–1972)**
Travolta, John (actor); Englewood, N.J., 2/18/1954
Treacher, Arthur (actor); Brighton, England **(1894–1975)**
Trevor, Claire (actress); New York City, 1911
Trigère, Pauline (fashion designer); Paris, 11/4/1912

Trilling, Lionel (author and educator); New York City **(1905–1975)**
Trotsky, Leon (Lev Davidovich Bronstein) (statesman); Elisavetgrad, Russia **(1879–1940)**
Trudeau, Pierre Elliott (Prime Minister); Montreal, 10/18/1919
Truffaut, François (film director); Paris, 2/6/1932
Trujillo y Molina, Rafael Leonidas (Dominican Republic dictator); San Cristóbal, Dominican Republic **(1891–1961)**
Truman, Margaret (author); Independence, Mo., 2/17/1924
Tryon, Thomas (actor and novelist); Hartford, Conn., 1/14/1926
Tucker, Forrest (actor); Plainfield, Ind., 2/12/1919
Tucker, Richard (tenor); New York City **(1914–1975)**
Tucker, Sophie (Sophie Abuza) (singer); Boston **(1884?–1966)**
Tudor, Antony (choreographer); London, 4/4/1909
Turgenev, Ivan Sergeevich (novelist); Orel, Russia **(1818–1883)**
Turner, Ike (singer); Clarksdale, Miss., 11/?/1931
Turner, Joseph M.W. (painter); London **(1775–1851)**
Turner, Lana (Julia Jean Mildred Frances Turner) (actress); Wallace, Idaho, 2/8/1920
Turner, Nat (civil rights leader); Southampton County, Va. **(1800–1831)**
Turner, Tina (Annie Mae Bullock) (singer); Brownsville, Tex., 1939
Turpin, Ben (comedian); New Orleans **(1874–1940)**
Tushingham, Rita (actress); Liverpool, England, 3/14/1942
Twain, Mark (Samuel Langhorne Clemens) (author); Florida, Mo. **(1835–1910)**
Tweed, William Marcy (politician); New York City **(1823–1878)**
Twiggy (Leslie Hornby) (model); London, 9/19/1949
Twining, Gen. Nathan F. (former Air Force Chief of Staff); Monroe, Wis., 10/11/1897
Twitty, Conway (Harold Lloyd Jenkins) (singer and guitarist); Friars Point, Miss., 9/1/1933
Tyson, Cicely (actress); New York City, 12/19/1939(?)

U

Udall, Stewart L. (ex-Secretary of the Interior); St. Johns, Ariz., 1/31/1920
Uggams, Leslie (singer and actress); New York City, 5/25/1943
Ulanova, Galina (ballerina); St. Petersburg, Russia, 1/10/1910
Ullmann, Liv (actress); Tokyo, 12/16/1939
Ulric, Lenore (actress); New Ulm, Minn. **(1894–1970)**
Untermeyer, Louis (anthologist and poet); New York City **(1885–1977)**
Updike, John (novelist); Shillington, Pa., 3/18/1932
Urey, Harold C. (physicist); Walkerton, Ind. **(1893–1981)**
Uris, Leon (novelist); Baltimore, 8/3/1924
Ustinov, Peter (actor and producer); London, 4/16/1921
Utrillo, Maurice (painter); Paris **(1883–1955)**

V

Vaccaro, Brenda (actress); Brooklyn, N.Y., 11/18/1939
Valentine, Karen (actress); Santa Rosa, Calif., 1947
Valentino, Rudolph (Rodolpho d'Antonguolla) (actor); Castellaneta, Italy **(1895–1926)**
Valentino (Valentino Garavani) (fashion designer); nr. Milan, Italy, 5/11/1932
Vallee, Rudy (Hubert Vallée) (band leader and singer); Island Pond, Vt., 7/28/1901
Van Allen, James Alfred (space physicist); Mt. Pleasant, Iowa, 9/7/1914
Van Buren, Abigail (Mrs. Morton Phillips) (columnist); Sioux City, Iowa, 7/4/1918
Vance, Vivian (actress); Cherryvale, Kan. **(1912–1979)**
Vanderbilt, Alfred G. (sportsman); London, 9/22/1912
Vanderbilt, Cornelius (financier); Port Richmond, N.Y. **(1794–1877)**
Vanderbilt, Gloria (artist and heiress); New York City, 2/20/1924
Van Doren, Carl (writer and educator); Hope, Ill. **(1885–1950)**
Van Doren, Mamie (actress); Rowena, S.D., 2/6/1933
Van Dyke, Dick (actor); West Plains, Mo., 12/13/1925
Vandyke (or Van Dyck), Sir Anthony (painter); Antwerp (Belgium) **(1599–1641)**
Van Eyck, Jan (painter); Maeseyck (Belgium) **(c.1390–1441)**
van Gogh, Vincent (painter); Groot Zundert, Brabant **(1853–1890)**
van Hamel, Martine (ballerina); Brussels, 11/16/1945
Van Heusen, Jimmy (Edward Chester Babcock) (songwriter); Syracuse, N.Y., 1/26/1913
Van Peebles, Melvin (playwright); Chicago, 9/21/1932
Vaughan, Sarah (singer); Newark, N.J., 3/27/1924
Vaughan Williams, Ralph (composer); Down Ampney, England **(1872–1958)**
Vaughn, Robert (actor); New York City, 11/22/1932
Velázquez, Diego Rodriguez de Silva y (painter); Seville, Spain **(1599–1660)**
Velez, Lupe (Guadelupe Velez de Villalobos) (actress); San Luis Potosi, Mexico **(1908–1944)**
Venturi, Robert (Charles) (architect); Philadelphia, 6/25/1925
Verdi, Giuseppe (composer); Roncole (Italy) **(1813–1901)**
Verdon, Gwen (actress); Culver City, Calif., 1/13/1925
Vereen, Ben (actor and singer); Miami, Fla., 10/10/1946
Vermeer, Jan (or Jan van der Meer van Delft) (painter); Delft (Netherlands) **(1632–1675)**
Verne, Jules (author); Nantes, France **(1828–1905)**
Verrazano, Giovanni da (navigator); Florence (Italy) **(1485?–1528)**
Verrett, Shirley (mezzo-soprano); New Orleans, 5/31/1933
Vespucci, Amerigo (navigator); Florence (Italy) **(1454–1512)**
Vickers, Jon (tenor); Prince Albert, Sask., Canada, 10/29/1926
Vidal, Gore (novelist); West Point, N.Y., 10/3/1925
Vidor, King (film director and producer); Galveston, Tex., 2/8/1895
Villa, Pancho (Doroteo Arango) (bandit); Rio Grande, Mexico **(1877–1923)**
Villella, Edward (ballet dancer); Bayside, Queens, N.Y., 10/1/1936
Villon, François (François de Montcorbier) (poet); Paris **(1431–1463)**
Vinton, Bobby (singer); Canonsburg, Pa., 4/16/1935(?)
Virgil (or Vergil) (Publius Vergilius Maro) (poet); nr. Mantua (Italy) **(70–19 B.C.)**
Vishnevskaya, Galina (soprano); Leningrad, 10/25/1926
Vlaminck, Maurice de (painter); Paris **(1876–1958)**
Voight, Jon (actor); Yonkers, N.Y., 12/29/1938
Voltaire (François Marie Arouet) (author); Paris **(1694–1778)**
von Braun, Wernher (rocket scientist); Wirsitz, Germany **(1912–1977)**
von Furstenberg, Betsy (actress); Neiheim-Heusen, Germany, 8/16/1935
von Fürstenberg, Diane (Diane Simone Michelle Halfin) (fashion designer); Brussels, 12/31/1946
von Hindenburg, Paul (statesman): Posen (Poland) **(1847–1934)**
von Karajan, Herbert (conductor); Salzburg (Austria), 4/5/1908
Vonnegut, Kurt, Jr. (novelist); Indianapolis, 11/11/1922
Von Stroheim, Erich Oswald Hans Carl Maria von Nordenwall (film actor and director); Vienna **(1885–1957)**
Vorster, Balthazar Johannes (Prime Minister); Jamestown, Cape Province, South Africa, 12/13/1915
Vreeland, Diana (Diana Dalziel) (fashion journalist and museum consultant); Paris, 1903(?)

W

Wagner, Lindsay (actress); Los Angeles, 1949
Wagner, Robert (actor); Detroit, 2/10/1930
Wagner, Robert F. (ex-Mayor of New York City); New York City, 4/20/1910
Wagner, Wilhelm Richard (composer); Leipzig (Germany) **(1813–1883)**
Waldheim, Kurt (U.N. Secretary-General); St. Andrae-Wörden, Austria, 12/21/1918
Walker, Clint (actor); Hartford, Ill., 5/30/1927
Walker, Nancy (Ann Myrtle Swoyer); (actress and comedienne); Philadelphia, 5/10/1922
Wallace, DeWitt (publisher); St. Paul **(1889–1981)**
Wallace, George C. (ex-Governor); Clio, Ala., 8/25/1919
Wallace, Irving (novelist); Chicago, 3/19/1916
Wallace, Mike (Myron Wallace) (TV interviewer and commentator); Brookline, Mass., 5/9/1918
Wallach, Eli (actor); Brooklyn, N.Y., 12/7/1915
Waller, Thomas "Fats" (pianist); New York City **(1904–1943)**
Wallis, Hal (film producer); Chicago, 9/14/1899
Waltari, Mika (novelist); Helsinki, Finland, **(1908–1979)**
Walter, Bruno (Bruno Walter Schlesinger) (orchestra conductor); Berlin **(1876–1962)**
Walters, Barbara (TV commentator); Boston, 9/25/1931
Walton, Izaak (author); Stafford, England **(1593–1683)**
Wambaugh, Joseph (author and screenwriter); East Pittsburgh, Pa., 1/22/1937
Wanamaker, John (merchant); Philadelphia **(1838–1922)**
Ward, Barbara (economist); York, England **(1914–1981)**
Warhol, Andy (artist and producer); Cleveland, 8/8/1930(?)
Waring, Fred (band leader); Tyrone, Pa., 6/9/1900
Warner, H. B. (Henry Bryan Warner Lickford) (actor); London **(1876–1958)**
Warren, Earl (Chief Justice of the U.S.); Los Angeles **(1891–1974)**
Warren, Robert Penn (novelist); Guthrie, Ky., 4/24/1905
Warwicke, Dionne (singer); East Orange, N.J., 1941
Washington, Booker Taliaferro (educator); Franklin County, Va. **(1856–1915)**
Waters, Ethel (actress and singer); Chester, Pa. **(1896–1977)**
Waters, Muddy (McKinley Morganfield) (singer and guitarist); Rolling Fork, Miss., 4/4/1915
Watson, Thomas John (industrialist); Campbell, N.Y. **(1874–1956)**
Watt, James (inventor); Greenock, Scotland **(1736–1819)**
Watteau, Jean-Antoine (painter); Valenciennes, France **(1684–1721)**
Watts, André (concert pianist); Nuremberg, Germany, 6/20/1946
Waugh, Alec (Alexander Raban Waugh) (novelist); London **(1898–1981)**
Waugh, Evelyn (satirist); London **(1903–1966)**

Wayne, Anthony (military officer); Waynesboro (family farm), nr. Paoli, Pa. **(1745–1796)**
Wayne, David (David McMeakan) (actor); Traverse City, Mich., 1/30/1914
Wayne, John (Marion Michael Morrison) (actor); Winterset, Iowa, **(1907–1979)**
Weaver, Dennis (actor); Joplin, Mo., 6/4/1925
Weaver, Fritz (actor); Pittsburgh, 1/19/1926
Webb, Clifton (Webb Parmelee Hollenbeck) (actor); Indianapolis **(1893–1966)**
Webb, Jack (film actor and producer); Santa Monica, Calif., 4/2/1920
Weber, Karl Maria Friedrich Ernst von (composer); nr. Lübeck (Germany) **(1786–1826)**
Webster, Daniel (statesman); Salisbury, N.H. **(1782–1852)**
Webster, Noah (lexicographer); West Hartford, Conn. **(1758–1843)**
Weill, Kurt (composer); Dessau, Germany **(1900–1950)**
Weizmann, Chaim (statesman); Grodno Province, Russia **(1874–1952)**
Welch, Raquel (Raquel Tejada) (actress); Chicago, 9/5/1942
Weld, Tuesday (Susan) (actress); New York City, 8/27/1943
Welk, Lawrence (band leader); Strasburg, N.D., 3/11/1903
Welles, Orson (actor and producer); Kenosha, Wis., 5/6/1915
Wellington, Duke of (Arthur Wellesley) (statesman); Ireland **(1769–1852)**
Wells, H(erbert) G(eorge) (author); Bromley, England **(1866–1946)**
Welty, Eudora (novelist); Jackson, Miss., 4/13/1909
Werfel, Franz (novelist); Prague **(1890–1945)**
Werner, Oskar (Josef Schliessmayer) (film actor and director); Vienna, 11/13/1922
Wertmuller, Lina (film director); Rome, 1926(?)
Wesley, John (religious leader); Epworth Rectory, Lincolnshire, England **(1703–1791)**
West, Dame Rebecca (Cicily Fairchild) (novelist); County Kerry, Ireland, 12/25/1892
West, Jessamyn (novelist); nr. North Vernon, Ind., 7/18/1902
West, Mae (actress); Brooklyn, N.Y. **(1893–1980)**
West, Nathanael (Nathan Weinstein) (novelist); New York City **(1902–1940)**
Westinghouse, George (inventor); Central Bridge, N.Y. **(1846–1914)**
Westmoreland, William Childs (ex-Army Chief of Staff); Saxon, S.C., 3/26/1914
Wharton, Edith Newbold (née Jones) (novelist); New York City **(1862–1937)**
Wheeler, Bert (Albert Jerome Wheeler) (comedian); Paterson, N.J. **(1895–1968)**
Whistler, James Abbott McNeill (painter and etcher); Lowell, Mass. **(1834–1903)**
White, E. B. (Elwyn Brooks White) (author); Mt. Vernon, N.Y., 7/11/1899
White, Stanford (architect); New York City **(1853–1906)**
White, Theodore H. (historian); Boston, 5/6/1915
White, William Allen (journalist); Emporia, Kan. **(1868–1944)**
Whitehead, Alfred North (mathematician and philosopher); Isle of Thanet, England **(1861–1947)**
Whiteman, Paul (band leader); Denver **(1891–1967)**
Whitman, Walt (Walter) (poet); West Hills, N.Y. **(1819–1892)**
Whitmore, James (actor); White Plains, N.Y., 10/1/1921
Whitney, Cornelius Vanderbilt (sportsman); New York City, 2/20/1899
Whitney, Eli (inventor); Westboro, Mass. **(1765–1825)**
Whitney, John Hay (publisher); Ellsworth, Me. **(1904–1982)**
Whittier, John Greenleaf (poet); Haverhill, Mass. **(1807–1892)**
Widmark, Richard (actor); Sunrise, Minn., 12/26/1914
Wiesel, Elie (Eliezer) (author); Sighet, Romania, 9/30/1928
Wilbur, Richard (poet); New York City, 3/1/1921
Wilde, Cornel (film actor and producer); New York City, 10/13/1918
Wilde, Oscar Fingal O'Flahertie Wills (author); Dublin **(1854–1900)**
Wilder, Billy (film producer and director); Vienna, 6/22/1906
Wilder, Gene (Jerome Silberman) (actor); Milwaukee, 6/11/1935(?)
Wilder, Thornton (author); Madison, Wis. **(1897–1975)**
Wilding, Michael (actor); Westcliff, England **(1912–1979)**
Wilkins, Roy (civil rights leader); St. Louis **(1901–1981)**
Williams, Andy (singer); Wall Lake, Iowa, 12/3/1930
Williams, Cindy (actress); Van Nuys, Calif., 8/22/(?)
Williams, Edward Bennett (lawyer); Hartford, Conn., 5/31/1920
Williams, Emlyn (actor and playwright); Mostyn, Wales, 11/26/1905
Williams, Esther (actress); Los Angeles, 8/8/1923
Williams, Gluyas (cartoonist); San Francisco **(1888–1982)**
Williams, Hank, Sr. (Hiram King Williams) (singer); Georgiana, Ala. **(1923–1953)**
Williams, Robin (comedian); Chicago, 7/?/1952
Williams, Roger (clergyman); London **(1603?–1683)**
Williams, Tennessee (Thomas L. Williams) (playwright); Columbus, Miss., 3/26/1911
Willkie, Wendell Lewis (lawyer); Elwood, Ind. **(1892–1944)**
Willson, Meredith (composer); Mason City, Iowa, 5/18/1902
Wilson, Don (radio and TV announcer); Lincoln, Neb. **(1900–1982)**
Wilson, Flip (Clerow) (comedian); Jersey City, N.J., 12/8/1933
Wilson, Harold (ex-Prime Minister); Huddersfield, England, 3/11/1916
Wilson, Nancy (singer); Chillicothe, Ohio, 2/20/1937
Wilson, Sloan (novelist); Norwalk, Conn., 5/8/1920
Winchell, Walter (columnist); New York City **(1897–1972)**
Windsor, Duchess of (Bessie Wallis Warfield); Blue Ridge Summit, Pa., 6/19/1896
Windsor, Duke of (formerly King Edward VIII of England); Richmond Park, England **(1894–1972)**
Winkler, Henry (actor); New York City, 10/30/1945
Winter, Johnny (guitarist); Leland, Miss., 2/23/1944
Winters, Jonathan (comedian); Dayton, Ohio, 11/11/1925
Winters, Shelley (Shirley Schrift) (actress); East St. Louis, Ill., 8/18/1922
Winthrop, John (first Governor, Massachusetts Bay Colony); Suffolk, England **(1588–1649)**
Wise, Stephen Samuel (rabbi); Budapest **(1874–1949)**
Withers, Jane (actress); Atlanta, 1927
Wittgenstein, Ludwig (Josef Johann) (philosopher); Vienna **(1889–1951)**
Wodehouse, P(elham) G(renville) (novelist); Guildford, England **(1881–1975)**
Wolfe, Thomas Clayton (novelist); Asheville, N.C. **(1900–1938)**
Wolfe, Tom (journalist); Richmond, Va., 3/2/1931
Wolsey, Thomas (prelate and statesman); Ipswich, England **(1475?–1530)**
Wonder, Stevie (Steveland Judkins, later Steveland Morris) (singer and songwriter); Saginaw, Mich., 5/13/1950
Wong, Anna May (Lu Tsong Wong) (actress); Los Angeles **(1907–1961)**
Wood, Grant (painter); Anamosa, Iowa **(1892–1942)**
Wood, Natalie (Natasha Gurdin) (film actress); San Francisco **(1938–1981)**
Woodward, Joanne (film actress); Thomasville, Ga., 2/27/1930
Woolf, Adeline Virginia (née Stephens) (novelist); London **(1882–1941)**
Woollcott, Alexander (author); Phalanx, N.J. **(1887–1943)**
Woolley, Monty (Edgar Montillion Woolley) (actor); New York City **(1888–1963)**
Woolworth, Frank (merchant); Rodman, N.Y. **(1852–1919)**
Wordsworth, William (poet); Cockermouth, England **(1770–1850)**
Worley, Jo Anne (actress and singer); Lowell, Ind., 9/6/1937
Wouk, Herman (novelist); New York City, 5/27/1915
Wray, Fay (actress); Alberta, Canada, 1907
Wren, Sir Christopher (architect); East Knoyle, England **(1632–1723)**
Wright, Frank Lloyd (architect); Richland Center, Wis. **(1869–1959)**
Wright, Orville (inventor); Dayton, Ohio **(1871–1948)**
Wright, Richard (novelist); nr. Natchez, Miss. **(1908–1960)**
Wright, Teresa (actress); New York City, 10/27/1918
Wright, Wilbur (inventor); Millville, Ind. **(1867–1912)**
Wyatt, Jane (film actress); Campgaw, N.J., 8/12/1912
Wyeth, Andrew (painter); Chadds Ford, Pa., 7/12/1917
Wyler, William (film director); Mulhouse (France), **(1902–1981)**
Wyman, Jane (Sarah Jane Fulks) (actress); St. Joseph, Mo., 1/4/1914
Wynette, Tammy (Wynette Pugh) (singer); Tupelo, Miss. 5/5/1942
Wynn, Ed (Isaiah Edwin Leopold) (comedian); Philadelphia **(1886–1966)**
Wynn, Keenan (actor); New York City, 7/27/1916
Wynter, Dana (actress); London, 6/8/1930

Y

Yeats, William Butler (poet); nr. Dublin **(1865–1939)**
Yevtushenko, Yevgeny (poet); Zima, U.S.S.R., 7/18/1933
York, Michael (actor); Fulmer, England, 3/27/1942
York, Susannah (Fletcher) (actress); London, 1/9/1942
Yorty, Samuel W. (ex-Mayor of Los Angeles); Lincoln, Neb., 10/1/1909
Young, Alan (actor); North Shield, England, 11/19/1919
Young, Brigham (religious leader); Whitingham, Vt. **(1801–1877)**
Young, Gig (Byron Barr) (actor); St. Cloud, Minn. **(1917–1978)**
Young, Loretta (Gretchen Young) (actress); Salt Lake City, Utah, 1/6/1913
Young, Neil (singer and songwriter); Toronto, 11/12/1945
Young, Robert (actor); Chicago, 2/22/1907
Youngman, Henny (comedian); England, 1906

Z

Zanuck, Darryl F. (film producer); Wahoo, Neb. **(1902–1979)**
Zappa, Frank (Francis Vincent Zappa, Jr.) (singer and songwriter); Baltimore, 12/21/1940
Zeffirelli, Franco (director); Florence, Italy, 2/12/1923
Zhou Enlai (Premier); Hualyin, China **(1898–1976)**
Ziegfeld, Florenz (theatrical producer); Chicago **(1869–1932)**
Zimbalist, Efrem (concert violinist); Rostov-on-Don, Russia, 4/9/1889
Zimbalist, Efrem, Jr. (actor); New York City, 11/30/1923
Zola, Emile (novelist); Paris **(1840–1902)**
Zoroaster (religious leader); Persian Empire **(c. 6th century B.C.)**
Zukerman, Pinchas (violinist); Tel Aviv, Israel 7/16/1948
Zweig, Stefan (author); Vienna **(1881–1942)**

Firsts in America

This selection is based on our editorial judgment. Other sources may list different firsts.

Admiral in U.S. Navy: David Glasgow Farragut, 1866.

Air-mail route, first transcontinental: Between New York City and San Francisco, 1920.

Assembly, representative: House of Burgesses, founded in Virginia, 1619.

Bank established: Bank of North America, Philadelphia, 1781.

Birth in America to English parents: Virginia Dare, born Roanoke Island, N.C., 1587.

Botanic garden: Established by John Bartram in Philadelphia, 1728. (Oldest still existing was established in Cambridge, Mass., in 1807.)

Cartoon, colored: "The Yellow Kid," by Richard Outcault, in *New York World,* 1895.

College: Harvard, founded 1636.

College to confer degrees on women: Oberlin (Ohio) College, 1841.

College to establish coeducation: Oberlin (Ohio) College, 1833.

Electrocution of a criminal: William Kemmler in Auburn Prison, Auburn, N.Y., Aug. 6, 1890.

Five and Ten Cents Store: Founded by Frank Woolworth, Utica, N.Y., 1879 (moved to Lancaster, Pa., same year).

Fraternity: Phi Beta Kappa; founded Dec. 5, 1776, at College of William and Mary.

Law to be declared unconstitutional by U.S. Supreme Court: Judiciary Act of 1789. Case: *Marbury* v. *Madison,* 1803.

Library, circulating: Philadelphia, 1731.

Newspaper, illustrated daily: *New York Daily Graphic,* 1873.

Newspaper published daily: *Pennsylvania Packet and General Advertiser,* Philadelphia, Sept., 1784.

Newspaper published over a continuous period: *The Boston News-Letter,* April, 1704.

Newsreel: Pathé Frères of Paris, in 1910, circulated a weekly issue of their *Pathé Journal.*

Oil well, commercial: Titusville, Pa., 1859.

Panel quiz show on radio: *Information Please,* May 17, 1938.

Postage stamps issued: 1847.

Railroad, transcontinental: Central Pacific and Union Pacific railroads, joined at Promontory, Utah, May 10, 1869.

Savings bank: The Provident Institute for Savings, Boston, 1816.

Science museum: Founded by Charleston (S.C.) Library Society, 1773.

Skyscraper: Home Insurance Co., Chicago, 1885 (10 floors, 2 added later).

Slaves brought into America: At Jamestown, Va., 1619, from a Dutch ship.

Sorority: Kappa Alpha Theta, at De Pauw University, 1870.

State to abolish capital punishment: Michigan, 1847.

State to enter Union after original 13: Vermont, 1791.

Steam-heated building: Eastern Hotel, Boston, 1845.

Steam railroad (carried passengers and freight): Baltimore & Ohio, 1830.

Strike on record by union: Journeymen Printers, New York City, 1776.

Subway: Opened in Boston, 1897.

"Tabloid" picture newspaper: *The Illustrated Daily News* (now *The Daily News*), New York City, 1919.

Vaudeville theater: Gaiety Museum, Boston, 1883.

Woman cabinet member: Frances Perkins, Secretary of Labor, 1933.

Woman candidate for President: Victoria Claflin Woodhull, nominated by National Woman's Suffrage Assn. on ticket of Nation Radical Reformers, 1872.

Woman doctor of medicine: Elizabeth Blackwell; M.D. from Geneva Medical College of Western New York, 1849.

Woman elected governor of a state: Mrs. Nellie Tayloe Ross, Wyoming, 1925.

Woman elected to U.S. Senate: Mrs. Hattie Caraway, Arkansas; elected Nov., 1932.

Woman graduate of law school: Mrs. Ada H. Kepley, Union College of Law, Chicago, 1870.

Woman member of U.S. House of Representatives: Jeannette Rankin; elected Nov., 1916.

Woman member of U.S. Senate: Mrs. Rebecca Latimer Felton of Georgia; appointed Oct. 3, 1922.

Woman member of U.S. Supreme Court: Mrs. Sandra Day O'Connor; appointed July 1981.

Woman suffrage granted: Wyoming Territory, 1869.

Written constitution: *Fundamental Orders of Connecticut,* 1639.

Figures and Legends in American Folklore

Appleseed, Johnny (John Chapman, 1774–1847): Massachusetts-born nurseryman; reputed to have spread seeds and seedlings from which rose orchards of the Midwest.

Billy the Kid (William H. Bonney, 1859–1881): New York-born desperado; killed his first man before he reached his teens; after short life of crime in Wild West, was gunned down by Sheriff Pat Garrett; symbol of lawless West.

Boone, Daniel (1734–1820): Frontiersman and Indian fighter, about whom legends of early America have been built; figured in Byron's *Don Juan*.

Brodie, Steve (1863–1901): Reputed to have dived off Brooklyn Bridge on July 23, 1886. (Whether he actually did so has never been proved.)

Buffalo Bill (William F. Cody, 1846–1917): Buffalo hunter and Indian scout; much of legend about him and Wild West stems from his own Wild West show, which he operated in late 19th century.

Bunyan, Paul: Mythical lumberjack; subject of tall tales throughout timber country (that he dug Grand Canyon, for example).

Crockett, David (1786–1836): Frontiersman and member of U.S. Congress, about whom legends have been built of heroic feats; died in defense of Alamo.

Fritchie (or Frietchie), Barbara: Symbol of patriotism; in ballad by John Greenleaf Whittier, 90-year-old Barbara Fritchie defiantly waves Stars and Stripes as "Stonewall" Jackson's Confederate troops march through Frederick, Md.

James, Jesse (1847–1882): Bank and train robber; folklore has given him quality of American Robin Hood.

Jones, Casey (John Luther Jones, 1863–1900): Example of heroic locomotive engineer given to feats of prowess; died in wreck with his hand on brake lever when his Illinois Central "Cannonball" express hit freight train at Vaughan, Miss.

Ross, Betsy (1752–1836): Member of Philadelphia flag-making family; reported to have designed and sewn first American flag. (Report is without confirmation.)

Uncle Sam: Personification of United States and its people; origin uncertain; may be based on inspector of government supplies in Revolutionary War and War of 1812.

Assassinations and Attempts in U. S. Since 1865

Cermak, Anton J. (Mayor of Chicago): Shot Feb. 15, 1933, in Miami by Giuseppe Zangara, who attempted to assassinate Franklin D. Roosevelt; Cermak died March 6.

Ford, Gerald R. (President of U.S.): Escaped assassination attempt Sept. 5, 1975, in Sacramento, Calif., by Lynette Alice (Squeaky) Fromm, who pointed but did not fire .45-caliber pistol.

Ford, Gerald R. (President of U.S.): Escaped assassination attempt in San Francisco, Calif., Sept. 22, 1975, by Sara Jane Moore, who fired one shot from a .38-caliber pistol that was deflected.

Garfield, James A. (President of U.S.): Shot July 2, 1881, in Washington, D.C., by Charles J. Guiteau; died Sept. 19.

Jordan, Vernon E., Jr. (civil rights leader): Shot and critically wounded in assassination attempt May 29, 1980, in Fort Wayne, Ind.

Kennedy, John F. (President of U.S.): Shot Nov. 22, 1963, in Dallas, Tex., allegedly by Lee Harvey Oswald; died same day. Injured was Gov. John B. Connally of Texas. Oswald was shot and killed two days later by Jack Ruby.

Kennedy, Robert F. (U.S. Senator from New York): Shot June 5, 1968, in Los Angeles by Sirhan Bishara Sirhan; died June 6.

King, Martin Luther, Jr. (civil rights leader): Shot April 4, 1968, in Memphis by James Earl Ray; died same day.

Lincoln, Abraham (President of U.S.): Shot April 14, 1865, in Washington, D.C., by John Wilkes Booth; died April 15.

Long, Huey P. (U.S. Senator from Louisiana): Shot Sept. 8, 1935, in Baton Rouge by Dr. Carl A. Weiss; died Sept. 10.

McKinley, William (President of U.S.): Shot Sept. 6, 1901, in Buffalo by Leon Czolgosz; died Sept. 14.

Reagan, Ronald (President of U.S.): Shot in left lung in Washington by John W. Hinckley, Jr., on March 30, 1981; three others also wounded.

Roosevelt, Franklin D. (President-elect of U.S.): Escaped assassination unhurt Feb. 15, 1933, in Miami. *See* Cermak.

Roosevelt, Theodore (ex-President of U.S.): Escaped assassination (though shot) Oct. 14, 1912, in Milwaukee while campaigning for President.

Seward, William H. (Secretary of State): Escaped assassination (though injured) April 14, 1865, in Washington, D.C., by Lewis Powell (or Paine), accomplice of John Wilkes Booth.

Truman, Harry S. (President of U.S.): Escaped assassination unhurt Nov. 1, 1950, in Washington, D.C., as 2 Puerto Rican nationalists attempted to shoot their way into Blair House.

Wallace, George C. (Governor of Alabama): Shot and critically wounded in assassination attempt May 15, 1972, at Laurel, Md., by Arthur Herman Bremer. Wallace paralyzed from waist down.

THE DECLARATION OF INDEPENDENCE

In Congress, July 4, 1776

The unanimous Declaration of the thirteen united States of America.

When in the Course of human events it becomes necessary for one people to dissolve the political bands which have connected them with another, and to assume among the powers of the earth, the separate and equal station to which the Laws of Nature and of Nature's God entitle them, a decent respect to the opinions of mankind requires that they should declare the causes which impel them to the separation.

We hold these truths to be self-evident, that all men are created equal, that they are endowed by their Creator with certain unalienable Rights, that among these are Life, Liberty and the pursuit of Happiness.—That to secure these rights, Governments are instituted among Men, deriving their just powers from the consent of the governed,—That whenever any Form of Government becomes destructive of these ends, it is the Right of the People to alter or to abolish it, and to institute new Government, laying its foundation on such principles and organizing its powers in such form, as to them shall seem most likely to effect their Safety and Happiness. Prudence, indeed, will dictate that Governments long established should not be changed for light and transient causes; and accordingly all experience hath shewn that mankind are more disposed to suffer, while evils are sufferable, than to right themselves by abolishing the forms to which they are accustomed. But when a long train of abuses and usurpations, pursuing invariably the same Object evinces a design to reduce them under absolute Despotism, it is their right, it is their duty, to throw off such Government, and to provide new Guards for their future security.—Such has been the patient sufferance of these Colonies; and such is now the necessity which constrains them to alter their former Systems of Government. The history of the present King of Great Britain is a history of repeated injuries and usurpations, all having in direct object the establishment of an absolute Tyranny over these States. To prove this, let Facts be submitted to a candid world.

He has refused his Assent to Laws, the most wholesome and necessary for the public good.

He has forbidden his Governors to pass Laws of immediate and pressing importance, unless suspended in their operation till his Assent should be obtained; and when so suspended, he has utterly neglected to attend to them.

He has refused to pass other Laws for the accommodation of large districts of people, unless those people would relinquish the right of Representation in the Legislature, a right inestimable to them and formidable to tyrants only.

He has called together legislative bodies at places unusual, uncomfortable, and distant from the depository of their Public Records, for the sole purpose of fatiguing them into compliance with his measures.

He has dissolved Representative Houses repeatedly, for opposing with manly firmness his invasions on the rights of the people.

He has refused for a long time, after such dissolutions, to cause others to be elected; whereby the Legislative Powers, incapable of Annihilation, have returned to the People at large for their exercise; the State remaining in the mean time exposed to all the dangers of invasion from without, and convulsions within.

He has endeavoured to prevent the population of these States; for that purpose obstructing the Laws for Naturalization of Foreigners; refusing to pass others to encourage their migrations hither, and raising the conditions of new Appropriations of Lands.

He has obstructed the Administration of Justice, by refusing his Assent to Laws for establishing Judiciary Powers.

He has made Judges dependent on his Will alone, for the tenure of their offices, and the amount and payment of their salaries.

He has erected a multitude of New Offices, and sent hither swarms of Officers to harass our people, and eat out their substance.

He has kept among us, in times of peace, Standing Armies without the Consent of our legislatures.

He has affected to render the Military independent of and superior to the Civil Power.

He has combined with others to subject us to a jurisdiction foreign to our constitution, and unacknowledged by our laws; giving his Assent to their Acts of pretended Legislation:

For quartering large bodies of armed troops among us:

For protecting them, by a mock Trial, from punishment for any Murders which they should commit on the Inhabitants of these States:

For cutting off our Trade with all parts of the

NOTE: On April 12, 1776, the legislature of North Carolina authorized its delegates to the Continental Congress to join with others in a declaration of separation from Great Britain; the first colony to instruct its delegates to take the actual initiative was Virginia on May 15. On June 7, 1776, Richard Henry Lee of Virginia offered a resolution to the Congress to the effect "that these United Colonies are, and of right ought to be, free and independent States. . . ." A committee, consisting of Thomas Jefferson, John Adams, Benjamin Franklin, Robert R. Livingston, and Roger Sherman was organized to "prepare a declaration to the effect of the said first resolution." The Declaration of Independence was adopted on July 4, 1776.

Most delegates signed the Declaration August 2, but George Wythe (Va.) signed August 27; Richard Henry Lee (Va.), Elbridge Gerry (Mass.), and Oliver Wolcott (Conn.) in September; Matthew Thornton (N. H.), not a delegate until September, in November; and Thomas McKean (Del.), although present on July 4, not until 1781 by special permission, having served in the army in the interim.

world:

For imposing Taxes on us without our Consent:

For depriving us in many cases, of the benefits of Trial by Jury:

For transporting us beyond Seas to be tried for pretended offences:

For abolishing the free System of English Laws in a neighbouring Province, establishing therein an Arbitrary government, and enlarging its Boundaries so as to render it at once an example and fit instrument for introducing the same absolute rule into these Colonies:

For taking away our Charters, abolishing our most valuable Laws and altering fundamentally the Forms of our Governments:

For suspending our own Legislatures, and declaring themselves invested with power to legislate for us in all cases whatsoever.

He has abdicated Government here, by declaring us out of his Protection and waging War against us.

He has plundered our seas, ravaged our Coasts, burnt our towns, and destroyed the lives of our people.

He is at this time transporting large Armies of foreign Mercenaries to compleat the works of death, desolation, and tyranny, already begun with circumstances of Cruelty & Perfidy scarcely paralleled in the most barbarous ages, and totally unworthy the Head of a civilized nation.

He has constrained our fellow Citizens taken Captive on the high Seas to bear Arms against their Country, to become the executioners of their friends and Brethren, or to fall themselves by their Hands.

He has excited domestic insurrections amongst us, and has endeavoured to bring on the inhabitants of our frontiers, the merciless Indian Savages, whose known rule of warfare, is an undistinguished destruction of all ages, sexes and conditions.

In every stage of these Oppressions We have Petitioned for Redress in the most humble terms: Our repeated Petitions have been answered only by repeated injury. A Prince, whose character is thus marked by every act which may define a Tyrant, is unfit to be the ruler of a free people.

Nor have We been wanting in attentions to our Brittish brethren. We have warned them from time to time of attempts by their legislature to extend an unwarrantable jurisdiction over us. We have reminded them of the circumstances of our emigration and settlement here. We have appealed to their native justice and magnanimity, and we have conjured them by the ties of our common kindred to disavow these usurpations, which would inevitably interrupt our connections and correspondence. They too have been deaf to the voice of justice and of consanguinity. We must, therefore, acquiesce in the necessity, which denounces our Separation, and hold them, as we hold the rest of mankind, Enemies in War, in Peace Friends.

We, therefore, the Representatives of the United States of America, in General Congress, Assembled, appealing to the Supreme Judge of the world for the rectitude of our intentions, do, in the Name, and by Authority of the good People of these Colonies, solemnly publish and declare, That these United Colonies are, and of Right ought to be Free and Independent States; that they are Absolved from all Allegiance to the British Crown, and that all political connection between them and the State of Great Britain, is and ought to be totally dissolved; and that as Free and Independent States, they have full Power to levy War, conclude Peace, contract Alliances, establish Commerce, and to do all other Acts and Things which Independent States may of right do.—And for the support of this Declaration, with a firm reliance on the protection of Divine Providence, we mutually pledge to each other our Lives, our Fortunes and our sacred Honor.

John Hancock

New Hampshire
Josiah Bartlett
Wm. Whipple
Matthew Thornton

Rhode Island
Step. Hopkins
William Ellery

Connecticut
Roger Sherman
Sam'el Huntington
Wm. Williams
Oliver Wolcott

New York
Wm. Floyd
Phil. Livingston
Frans. Lewis
Lewis Morris

New Jersey
Richd. Stockton
Jno. Witherspoon
Fras. Hopkinson
John Hart
Abra. Clark

Pennsylvania
Robt. Morris
Benjamin Rush
Benj. Franklin
John Morton
Geo. Clymer
Jas. Smith
Geo. Taylor
James Wilson
Geo. Ross

Massachusetts-Bay
Saml. Adams
John Adams
Robt. Treat Paine
Elbridge Gerry

Delaware
Caesar Rodney
Geo. Read
Tho. M'Kean

Maryland
Samuel Chase
Wm. Paca
Thos. Stone
Charles Carroll of Carrollton

Virginia
George Wythe
Richard Henry Lee
Th. Jefferson
Benj. Harrison
Ths. Nelson, Jr.
Francis Lightfoot Lee
Carter Braxton

North Carolina
Wm. Hooper
Joseph Hewes
John Penn

South Carolina
Edward Rutledge
Thos. Heyward, Junr.
Thomas Lynch, Junr.
Arthur Middleton

Georgia
Button Gwinnett
Lyman Hall
Geo. Walton

Constitution of the United States of America

(Historical text has been edited to conform to contemporary American usage.
The bracketed words are designations for your convenience; they are not part of the Constitution.)

The oldest federal constitution in existence was framed by a convention of delegates from twelve of the thirteen original states in Philadelphia in May, 1787, Rhode Island failing to send a delegate. George Washington presided over the session, which lasted until September 17, 1787. The draft (originally a preamble and seven Articles) was submitted to all thirteen states and was to become effective when ratified by nine states. It went into effect on the first Wednesday in March, 1789, having been ratified by New Hampshire, the ninth state to approve, on June 21, 1788. The states ratified the Constitution in the following order:

Delaware	December 7, 1787	South Carolina	May 23, 1788
Pennsylvania	December 12, 1787	New Hampshire	June 21, 1788
New Jersey	December 18, 1787	Virginia	June 25, 1788
Georgia	January 2, 1788	New York	July 26, 1788
Connecticut	January 9, 1788	North Carolina	November 21, 1789
Massachusetts	February 6, 1788	Rhode Island	May 29, 1790
Maryland	April 28, 1788		

[Preamble]

We the people of the United States, in order to form a more perfect Union, establish justice, insure domestic tranquility, provide for the common defence, promote the general welfare, and secure the blessings of liberty to ourselves and our posterity, do ordain and establish this Constitution for the United States of America.

Article I

Section 1

[Legislative powers vested in Congress.] All legislative powers herein granted shall be vested in a Congress of the United States, which shall consist of a Senate and House of Representatives.

Section 2

[Composition of the House of Representatives.—1.] The House of Representatives shall be composed of members chosen every second year by the people of the several States, and the electors in each State shall have the qualifications requisite for electors of the most numerous branch of the State Legislature.

[Qualifications of Representatives.—2.] No Person shall be a Representative who shall not have attained to the age of twenty-five years, and been seven years a citizen of the United States, and who shall not, when elected, be an inhabitant of that State in which he shall be chosen.

[Apportionment of Representatives and direct taxes—census.[1]—3.] (Representatives and direct taxes shall be apportioned among the several States which may be included within this Union, according to their respective numbers, which shall be determined by adding to the whole number of free persons, including those bound to service for a term of years, and excluding Indians not taxed, three fifths of all other persons.) The actual enumeration shall be made within three years after the first meeting of the Congress of the United States, and within every subsequent term of ten years, in such manner as they shall by law direct. The number of Representatives shall not exceed one for every thirty thousand, but each State shall have at least one Representative; and until such enumeration shall be made, the State of New Hampshire shall be entitled to choose three, Massachusetts eight, Rhode-Island and Providence Plantations one, Connecticut five, New York six, New Jersey four, Pennsylvania eight, Delaware one, Maryland six, Virginia ten, North Carolina five, South Carolina five, and Georgia three.

[Filling of vacancies in representation.—4.] When vacancies happen in the representation from any State, the Executive Authority thereof shall issue writs of election to fill such vacancies.

[Selection of officers; power of impeachment.—5.] The House of Representatives shall choose their Speaker and other officers; and shall have the sole power of impeachment.

Section 3[2]

[The Senate.—1.] The Senate of the United States shall be composed of two Senators from each State, chosen by the Legislature thereof, for six years; and each Senator shall have one vote.

[Classification of Senators; filling of vacancies.—2.] Immediately after they shall be assembled in consequence of the first election, they shall be divided as equally as may be into three classes. The seats of the Senators of the first class shall be vacated at the expiration of the second year, of the second class at the expiration of the fourth year, and of the third class at the expiration of the sixth year, so that one-third may be chosen every second year; and if vacancies happen by resignation, or otherwise, during the recess of the Legislature of any State, the Executive thereof may make temporary appointments (until the next meeting of the Legislature, which shall then fill such vacancies).

[Qualification of Senators.—3.] No person shall be a Senator who shall not have attained to the age of thirty years, and been nine years a citizen of the United States, and who shall not, when elected, be an inhabitant of that State for which he shall be chosen.

[Vice President to be President of Senate.—4.] The Vice President of the United States shall be President of the Senate, but shall have no vote, unless they be equally divided.

[Selection of Senate officers; President pro tempore.—5.] The Senate shall choose their other officers, and also a President pro tempore, in the absence of the Vice President, or when he shall exercise the office of President of the United States.

[Senate to try impeachments.—6.] The Senate

shall have the sole power to try all impeachments. When sitting for that purpose, they shall be on oath or affirmation. When the President of the United States is tried, the Chief Justice shall preside: and no person shall be convicted without the concurrence of two thirds of the members present.

[Judgment in cases of Impeachment.—7.] Judgment in cases of impeachment shall not extend further than to removal from office, and disqualification to hold and enjoy any office of honor, trust, or profit under the United States: but the party convicted shall nevertheless be liable and subject to indictment, trial, judgment and punishment, according to Law.

Section 4

[Control of congressional elections.—1.] The times, places, and manner of holding elections for Senators and Representatives, shall be prescribed in each State by the Legislature thereof; but the Congress may at any time by law make or alter such regulations, except as to the places of choosing Senators.

[Time for assembling of Congress.[3]—2.] The Congress shall assemble at least once in every year, and such meeting shall be on the first Monday in December, unless they shall by law appoint a different day.

Section 5

[Each house to be the judge of the election and qualifications of its members; regulations as to quorum.—1.] Each House shall be the judge of the elections, returns, and qualifications of its own members, and a majority of each shall constitute a quorum to do business; but a smaller number may adjourn from day to day, and may be authorized to compel the attendance of absent members, in such manner, and under such penalties as each House may provide.

[Each house to determine its own rules.—2.] Each House may determine the rules of its proceedings, punish its members for disorderly behavior, and, with the concurrence of two thirds, expel a member.

[Journals and yeas and nays.—3.] Each House shall keep a journal of its proceedings, and from time to time publish the same, excepting such parts as may in their judgment require secrecy; and the yeas and nays of the members of either House on any question shall, at the desire of one fifth of those present, be entered on the journal.

[Adjournment.—4.] Neither House, during the session of Congress, shall, without the consent of the other, adjourn for more than three days, nor to any other place than that in which the two Houses shall be sitting.

Section 6

[Compensation and privileges of members of Congress.—1.] The Senators and Representatives shall receive a compensation for their services, to be ascertained by law, and paid out of the Treasury of the United States. They shall in all cases, except treason, felony, and breach of the peace, be privileged from arrest during their attendance at the session of their respective Houses, and in going to and returning from the same; and for any speech or debate in either House, they shall not be questioned in any other place.

[Incompatible offices; exclusions.—2.] No Senator or Representative shall, during the time for which he was elected, be appointed to any civil office under the authority of the United States, which shall have been created, or the emoluments whereof shall have been increased during such time; and no person holding any office under the United States shall be a member of either House during his continuance in office.

Section 7

[Revenue bills to originate in House.—1.] All bills for raising revenue shall originate in the House of Representatives; but the Senate may propose or concur with amendments as on other bills.

[Manner of passing bills; veto power of President.—2.] Every bill which shall have passed the House of Representatives and the Senate, shall, before it becomes a law, be presented to the President of the United States; if he approve he shall sign it, but if not he shall return it, with his objections to that House in which it shall have originated, who shall enter the objections at large on their journal, and proceed to reconsider it. If after such reconsideration two thirds of that House shall agree to pass the bill, it shall be sent, together with the objections, to the other House, by which it shall likewise be reconsidered, and if approved by two thirds of that House, it shall become a law. But in all such cases the votes of both Houses shall be determined by yeas and nays, and the names of the persons voting for and against the bill shall be entered on the journal of each house, respectively. If any bill shall not be returned by the President within ten days (Sundays excepted) after it shall have been presented to him, the same shall be a law, in like manner as if he had signed it, unless the Congress by their adjournment prevent its return, in which case it shall not be a law.

[Concurrent orders or resolutions, to be passed by President.—3.] Every order, resolution, or vote to which the concurrence of the Senate and House of Representatives may be necessary (except on a question of adjournment) shall be presented to the President of the United States; and before the same shall take effect, shall be approved by him, or being disapproved by him, shall be repassed by two thirds of the Senate and House of Representatives, according to the rules and limitations prescribed in the case of a bill.

Section 8

[General powers of Congress.[4]]

[Taxes, duties, imposts, and excises.—1.] The Congress shall have power to lay and collect taxes, duties, imposts and excises, to pay the debts and provide for the common defense and general welfare of the United States; but all duties, imposts and excises shall be uniform throughout the United States;

[Borrowing of money.—2.] To borrow money on the credit of the United States;

[Regulation of commerce.—3.] To regulate commerce with foreign nations, and among the several States, and with the Indian tribes;

[Naturalization and bankruptcy.—4.] To establish a uniform rule of naturalization, and uniform laws on the subject of bankruptcies throughout the United States;

[Money, weights and measures.—5.] To coin money, regulate the value thereof, and of foreign coin, and fix the standard of weights and measures;

[Counterfeiting.—6.] To provide for the punishment of counterfeiting the securities and current coin of the United States;

[Post offices.—7.] To establish post offices and post roads;

[Patents and copyrights.—8.] To promote the

progress of science and useful arts, by securing for limited times to authors and inventors the exclusive right to their respective writings and discoveries;

[**Inferior courts.—9.**] To constitute tribunals inferior to the Supreme Court;

[**Piracies and felonies.—10.**] To define and punish piracies and felonies commited on the high seas, and offences against the law of nations;

[**War; marque and reprisal.—11.**] To declare war, grant letters of marque and reprisal, and make rules concerning captures on land and water;

[**Armies.—12.**] To raise and support armies, but no appropriation of money to that use shall be for a longer term than two years;

[**Navy.—13.**] To provide and maintain a navy;

[**Land and naval forces.—14.**] To make rules for the government and regulation of the land and naval forces;

[**Calling out militia.—15.**] To provide for calling forth the militia to execute the laws of the Union, suppress insurrections, and repel invasions.

[**Organizing, arming, and disciplining militia.—16.**] To provide for organizing, arming, and disciplining, the militia, and for governing such part of them as may be employed in the service of the United States, reserving to the States, respectively, the appointment of the officers, and the authority of training the militia according to the discipline prescribed by Congress;

[**Exclusive legislation over District of Columbia.—17.**] To exercise exclusive legislation in all cases whatsoever, over such district (not exceeding ten miles square) as may, by cession of particular States, and the acceptance of Congress,become the seat of the Government of the United States, and to exercise like authority over all places purchased by the consent of the Legislature of the State in which the same shall be, for the erection of forts, magazines, arsenals, dock-yards, and other needful buildings; —And

[**To enact laws necessary to enforce Constitution.—18.**] To make all laws which shall be necessary and proper for carrying into execution the foregoing powers, and all other powers vested by this Constitution in the Government of the United States, or in any department or officer thereof.

Section 9

[**Migration or importation of certain persons not to be prohibited before 1808.—1.**] The migration or importation of such persons as any of the States now existing shall think proper to admit, shall not be prohibited by the Congress prior to the year one thousand eight hundred and eight, but a tax or duty may be imposed on such importation, not exceeding ten dollars for each person.

[**Writ of habeas corpus not to be suspended; exception.—2.**] The privilege of the writ of habeas corpus shall not be suspended, unless when in cases of rebellion or invasion the public safety may require it.

[**Bills of attainder and ex post facto laws prohibited.—3.**] No bill of attainder or ex post facto law shall be passed.

[**Capitation and other direct taxes.—4.**] No capitation, or other direct, tax shall be laid, unless in proportion to the census or enumeration herein before directed to be taken.[5]

[**Exports not to be taxed.—5.**] No tax or duty shall be laid on articles exported from any State.

[**No preference to be given to ports of any State; interstate shipping.—6.**] No preference shall be given by any regulation of commerce or revenue to the ports of one State over those of another: nor shall vessels bound to, or from, one State, be obliged to enter, clear, or pay duties in another.

[**Money, how drawn from treasury; financial statements to be published.—7.**] No money shall be drawn from the Treasury, but in consequence of appropriations made by law; and a regular statement and account of the receipts and expenditures of all public money shall be published from time to time.

[**Titles of nobility not to be granted; acceptance by government officers of favors from foreign powers.—8.**] No title of nobility shall be granted by the United States: and no person holding any office of profit or trust under them, shall, without the consent of the Congress, accept of any present, emolument, office, or title, of any kind whatever, from any king, prince, or foreign state.

Section 10

[**Limitations of the powers of the several States.—1.**] No State shall enter into any treaty, alliance, or confederation; grant letters of marque and reprisal; coin money; emit bills of credit; make any thing but gold and silver coin a tender in payment of debts; pass any bill of attainder, ex post facto law, or law impairing the obligation of contracts, or grant any title of nobility.

[**State imposts and duties.—2.**] No State shall, without the consent of the Congress, lay any imposts or duties on imports or exports, except what may be absolutely necessary for executing its inspection laws: and the net produce of all duties and imposts, laid by any State on imports or exports, shall be for the use of the Treasury of the United States; and all such laws shall be subject to the revision and control of the Congress.

[**Further restrictions on powers of States.—3.**] No State shall, without the consent of Congress, lay any duty of tonnage, keep troops, or ships of war in time of peace, enter into any agreement or compact with another state, or with a foreign power, or engage in war, unless actually invaded, or in such imminent danger as will not admit of delay.

Article II

Section 1

[**The President; the executive power.—1.**] The executive power shall be vested in a President of the United States of America. He shall hold his office during the term of four years, and, together with the Vice President, chosen for the same term, be elected, as follows

[**Appointment and qualifications of presidential electors.—2.**] Each State shall appoint, in such manner as the Legislature thereof may direct, a number of electors, equal to the whole number of Senators and Representatives to which the State may be entitled in the Congress: but no Senator or Representative, or person holding an office of trust or profit under the United States, shall be appointed an elector.

[**Original method of electing the President and Vice President.**[6]] (The electors shall meet in their respective States, and vote by ballot for two persons, of whom one at least shall not be an inhabitant of the same State with themselves. And they shall make a list of all the persons voted for, and of the number of votes for each; which list they shall sign and certify, and transmit sealed to the seat of the Government of the United States, directed to the President of the Senate. The President of the Senate shall, in the presence of the Senate and House of Representatives, open all the certificates, and the votes shall then be counted. The person having the greatest number of votes shall be the President, if such number be a majority of the whole number of electors appointed; and if there be more than one who have such majority, and have an equal number of votes, then the House of Representatives shall immediately choose by ballot one of them for President; and if no person have a majority, then from the five highest on the list the said House shall in like manner choose the President. But in choosing the President, the votes shall be taken by States, the representation from each State having one vote; A quorum for this purpose shall consist of a member or members from two thirds of the States, and a majority of all the states shall be necessary to a choice. In every case, after the choice of the President, the person having the greatest number of votes of the electors shall be the Vice President. But if there should remain two or more who have equal votes, the Senate should choose from them by ballot the Vice President.)

[Congress may determine time of choosing electors and day for casting their votes.—3.] The Congress may determine the time of choosing the electors, and the day on which they shall give their votes; which day shall be the same throughout the United States.

[Qualifications for the office of President.[7]—4.] No person except a natural born citizen, or a citizen of the United States, at the time of the adoption of this Constitution, shall be eligible to the office of President; neither shall any person be eligible to that office who shall not have attained to the age of thirty-five years, and been fourteen years a resident within the United States.

[Filling vacancy in the office of President.[8]—5.] In case of the removal of the President from office, or of his death, resignation, or inability to discharge the powers and duties of the said office, the same shall devolve on the Vice President, and the Congress may by law provide for the case of removal, death, resignation or inability, both of the President and Vice President, declaring what officer shall then act as President, and such officer shall act accordingly, until the disability be removed, or a President shall be elected.

[Compensation of the President.—6.] The President shall, at stated times, receive for his services, a compensation, which shall neither be increased nor diminished during the period for which he shall have been elected, and he shall not receive within that period any other emolument from the United States, or any of them.

[Oath to be taken by the President.—7.] Before he enter on the execution of his office, he shall take the following oath or affirmation:—"I do solemnly swear (or affirm) that I will faithfully excute the office of President of the United States, and will to the best of my ability, preserve, protect, and defend the Constitution of the United States."

Section 2

[The President to be commander in chief of army and navy and head of executive departments; may grant reprieves and pardons.—1.] The President shall be Commander in Chief of the Army and Navy of the United States, and of the militia of the several States, when called into the actual service of the United States; he may require the opinion, in writing, of the principal officer in each of the executive departments, upon any subject relating to the duties of their respective offices, and he shall have power to grant reprieves and pardons for offences against the United States, except in cases of impeachment.

[President may, with concurrence of Senate, make treaties, appoint ambassadors, etc.; appointment of inferior officers, authority of Congress over.—2.] He shall have power, by and with the advice and consent of the Senate, to make treaties, provided two thirds of the Senators present concur; and he shall nominate, and by and with the advice and consent of the Senate, shall appoint ambassadors, other public ministers and consuls, judges of the Supreme Court, and all other officers of the United States, whose appointments are not herein otherwise provided for, and which shall be established by law: but the Congress may by law vest the appointment of such inferior officers, as they think proper, in the President alone, in the courts of law, or in the heads of departments.

[President may fill vacancies in office during recess of Senate.—3.] The President shall have power to fill up all vacancies that may happen during the recess of the Senate, by granting commissions which shall expire at the end of their session.

Section 3

[President to give advice to Congress; may convene or adjourn it on certain occasions; to receive ambassadors, etc.; have laws executed and commission all officers.] He shall from time to time give to the Congress information of the state of the Union, and recommend to their consideration such measures as he shall judge necessary and expedient; he may, on extraordinary occasions, convene both Houses, or either of them, and in case of disagreement between them, with respect to the time of adjournment, he may adjourn them to such time as he shall think proper; he shall receive ambassadors and other public ministers: he shall take care that the laws be faithfully executed, and shall commission all the officers of the United States.

Section 4

[All civil officers removable by impeachment.] The President, Vice President, and all civil officers of the United States shall be removed from office on impeachment for, and conviction of, treason, bribery, or other high crimes and misdemeanors.

Article III

Section 1

[Judicial powers; how vested; term of office and compensation of judges.] The judicial Power of the United States, shall be vested in one Supreme Court, and in such inferior courts as the Congress may from time to time ordain and establish. The judges, both of the supreme and inferior courts, shall hold their offices during good behavior, and shall, at stated times, receive for their services, a compensation, which shall not be diminished during their continuance in office.

Section 2

[Jurisdiction of Federal courts.[9]—1.] The judicial power shall extend to all cases, in law and equity, arising under this Constitution, the laws of the United States, and treaties made, or which shall be made, under their authority; to all cases affecting ambassadors, other public ministers and consuls; to all cases of admiralty and maritime jurisdiction; to controversies to which the United States, shall be a party; to controversies between two or more States; between a State and citizens of another State; between citizens of different States, between citizens of the same State claiming lands under grants of different states, and between a State, or the citizens thereof, and foreign states, citizens, or subjects.

[Original and appellate jurisdiction of Supreme Court.—2.] In all cases affecting ambassadors, other public ministers and consuls, and those in which a State shall be party, the Supreme Court shall have original jurisdiction. In all the other cases before mentioned, the Supreme Court shall have appellate jurisdiction, both as to law and fact, with such exceptions, and under such regulations, as the Congress shall make.

[Trial of all crimes, except impeachment, to be by jury.—3.] The trial of all crimes, except in cases of impeachment, shall be by jury; and such trial shall be held in the State where the said crimes shall have been committed; but when not committed within any State, the trial shall be at such place or places as the Congress may by law have directed.

Section 3

[Treason defined; conviction of.—1.] Treason against the United States, shall consist only in levying war against them, or, in adhering to their enemies, giving them aid and comfort. No person shall be convicted of treason unless on the testimony of two witnesses to the same overt act, or on confession in open court.

[Congress to declare punishment for treason; proviso.—2.] The Congress shall have power to declare the punishment of treason, but no attainder of treason shall work corruption of blood, or forfeiture except during the life of the person attainted.

Article IV

Section 1

[Each State to give full faith and credit to the public acts and records of other States.] Full faith and credit shall be given in each State to the public acts, records, and judicial proceedings of every other State. And the Congress may by general laws prescribe the manner in which such acts, records, and proceedings shall be proved, and the effect thereof.

Section 2

[Privileges of citizens.—1.] The citizens of each State shall be entitled to all privileges and immunities of citizens in the several States.

[Extradition between the several States.—2.] A person charged in any State with treason, felony, or other crime, who shall flee from justice, and be found in another State, shall on demand of the Executive authority of the State from which he fled, be delivered up, to be removed to the State having jurisdiction of the crime.

[Persons held to labor or service in one State, fleeing to another, to be returned.—3.] No person held to service or labor in one State, under the laws thereof, escaping into another, shall, in consequence of any law or regulation therein, be discharged from such service or labor, but shall be delivered up on claim of the party to whom such service or labor may be due.

Section 3

[New States.—1.] New States may be admitted by the Congress into this Union; but no new State shall be formed or erected within the jurisdiction of any other State; nor any State be formed by the junction of two or more States, or parts of States, without the consent of the Legislatures of the States concerned as well as of the Congress.

[Regulations concerning territory.—2.] The Congress shall have power to dispose of and make all needful rules and regulations respecting the territory or other property belonging to the United States; and nothing in this Constitution shall be so construed as to prejudice any claims of the United States, or of any particular State.

Section 4

[Republican form of government and protection guaranteed the several States.] The United States shall guarantee to every State in this Union a Republican form of government, and shall protect each of them against invasion; and on application of the Legislature, or of the Executive (when the Legislature cannot be convened) against domestic violence.

Article V

[Ways in which the Constitution can be amended.] The Congress, whenever two thirds of both Houses shall deem it necessary, shall propose amendments to this Constitution, or, on the application of the Legislatures of two thirds of the several States shall call a convention for proposing amendments, which, in either case, shall be valid to all intents and purposes, as part of this Constitution, when ratified by the Legislatures of three fourths of the several States, or by conventions in three fourths thereof, as the one or the other mode of ratification may be proposed by the Congress; provided that no amendment which may be made prior to the year one thousand eight hundred and eight shall in any manner affect the first and fourth clauses in the ninth Section of the first Article; and that no State, without its consent, shall be deprived of its equal suffrage in the Senate.

Article VI

[Debts contracted under the confederation secured.—1.] All debts contracted and engagements entered into, before the adoption of this Constitution, shall be as valid against the United States under this Constitution, as under the Confederation.

[Constitution, laws, and treaties of the United States to be supreme.—2.] This Constituion, and the laws of the United States which shall be made in pursuance thereof; and all treaties made, or which shall be made, under the authority of the United States, shall be the supreme law of the land; and the judges in every State shall be bound thereby, any thing in the Constitution or laws of any State to the contrary notwithstanding.

[Who shall take constitutional oath; no religious test as to official qualification.—3.] The Senators and Representatives before mentioned, and the

1. The clause included in parentheses is amended by the 14th Amendment, Section 2. 2. The first paragraph of this section and the part of the second paragraph included in parentheses are amended by the 17th Amendment. 3. Amended by the 20th Amendment, Section 2. 4. By the 16th Amendment, Congress is given the power to lay and collect taxes on income. 5. See the 16th Amendment. 6. This clause has been superseded by the 12th Amendment. 7. For qualifications of the Vice President, see 12th Amendment. 8. Amended by the 20th Amendment, Sections 3 and 4. 9. This section is abridged by the 11th Amendment. 10. See the 13th Amendment.

members of the several State Legislatures, and all executive and judicial officers, both of the United States and of the several States, shall be bound by oath or affirmation, to support this Constitution; but no religious test shall ever be required as a qualification to any office or public trust under the United States.

Article VII

[Constitution to be considered adopted when ratified by nine States.] The ratification of the conventions of nine States shall be sufficient for the establishment of this Constitution between the States so ratifying the same.

Done in convention by the unanimous consent of the States present the seventeenth day of September in the year of our Lord one thousand seven hundred and eighty seven and of the independence of the United States of America the Twelfth. In witness whereof we have hereunto subscribed our names.

GEORGE WASHINGTON
President and Deputy from Virginia

NEW HAMPSHIRE

John Langdon — Nicholas Gilman

MASSACHUSETTS

Nathaniel Gorham — Rufus King

CONNECTICUT

Wm. Saml. Johnson — Roger Sherman

NEW YORK

Alexander Hamilton

NEW JERSEY

Wil. Livingston — Wm. Paterson
David Brearley — Jona. Dayton

PENNSYLVANIA

B. Franklin — Thomas Mifflin
Robt. Morris — Geo. Clymer
Thos. FitzSimons — Jared Ingersoll
James Wilson — Gouv. Morris

DELAWARE

Geo. Read — Gunning Bedford Jun.
John Dickinson — Richard Bassett
Jaco. Broom

MARYLAND

James McHenry — Dan. of St. Thos. Jenifer
Danl. Carroll

VIRGINIA

John Blair — James Madison, Jr.

NORTH CAROLINA

Wm. Blount — Richd Dobbs Spaight
Hu. Williamson

SOUTH CAROLINA

J. Rutledge — Charles Cotesworth Pinckney
Charles Pinckney — Pierce Butler

GEORGIA

William Few — Abr. Baldwin

Attest: William Jackson, Secretary

Amendments to the Constitution of the United States

(Amendments I to X inclusive, popularly known as the Bill of Rights, were proposed and sent to the states by the first session of the First Congress. They were ratified Dec. 15, 1791.)

Article I

[Freedom of religion, speech, of the press, and right of petition.] Congress shall make no law respecting an establishment of religion, or prohibiting the free exercise thereof; or abridging the freedom of speech, or of the press; or the right of the people peaceably to assemble, and to petition the Government for a redress of grievances.

Article II

[Right of people to bear arms not to be infringed.] A well regulated militia, being necessary to the security of a free State, the right of the people to keep and bear arms, shall not be infringed.

Article III

[Quartering of troops.] No soldier shall, in time of peace be quartered in any house, without the consent of the owner, nor in time of war, but in a manner to be prescribed by law.

Article IV

[Persons and houses to be secure from unreasonable searches and seizures.] The right of the people to be secure in their persons, houses, papers, and effects, against unreasonable searches and seizures, shall not be violated, and no warrants shall issue, but upon probable cause, supported by oath or affirmation, and particularly describing the place to be searched, and the persons or things to be seized.

Article V

[Trials for crimes; just compensation for private property taken for public use.] No person shall be held to answer for a capital, or otherwise infamous crime, unless on a presentment or indictment of a Grand Jury, except in cases arising in the land or naval forces, or in the militia, when in actual service in time of war or public danger; nor shall any person be subject for the same offence to be twice put in jeopardy of life or limb; nor shall be compelled in any criminal case to be a witness, against himself, nor be deprived of life, liberty, or property, without due process of law; nor shall private property be taken for public use, without just compensation.

Article VI

[Civil rights in trials for crimes enumerated.] In all criminal prosecutions, the accused shall enjoy the right to a speedy and public trial, by an impartial jury of the State and district wherein the crime shall have been committed, which district shall have been previously ascertained by law, and to be informed of the nature and cause of the accusation;

to be confronted with the witnesses against him; to have compulsory process for obtaining witnesses in his favor, and to have the assistance of counsel for his defense.

Article VII

[Civil rights in civil suits.] In suits at common law, where the value in controversy shall exceed twenty dollars, the right of trial by jury shall be preserved, and no fact tried by a jury, shall be otherwise re-examined in any court of the United States, than according to the rules of the common law.

Article VIII

[Excessive bail, fines, and punishments prohibited.] Excessive bail shall not be required, nor excessive fines imposed, nor cruel and unusual punishments inflicted.

Article IX

[Reserved rights of people.] The enumeration in the Constitution, of certain rights, shall not be construed to deny or disparage others retained by the people.

Article X

[Powers not delegated, reserved to states and people respectively.] The powers not delegated to the United States by the Constitution, nor prohibited by it to the States, are reserved to the States, respectively, or to the people.

Article XI

(The proposed amendment was sent to the states Mar. 5, 1794, by the Third Congress. It was ratified Feb. 7, 1795.)

[Judicial power of United States not to extend to suits against a State.] The judicial power of the United States shall not be construed to extend to any suit in law or equity, commenced or prosecuted against one of the United States by citizens of another State, or by citizens or subjects of any foreign state.

Article XII

(The proposed amendment was sent to the states Dec. 12, 1803, by the Eighth Congress. It was ratified July 27, 1804.)

[Present mode of electing President and Vice-President by electors.[1]] The electors shall meet in their respective states, and vote by ballot for President and Vice President, one of whom, at least, shall not be an inhabitant of the same state with themselves; they shall name in their ballots the person voted for as President, and in distinct ballots the person voted for as Vice President, and they shall make distinct lists of all persons voted for as President, and of all persons voted for as Vice President, and of the number of votes for each, which lists they shall sign and certify, and transmit sealed to the seat of the government of the United States, directed to the President of the Senate; the President of the Senate shall, in the presence of the Senate and House of Representatives, open all the certificates and the votes shall then be counted; the person having the greatest number of votes for President, shall be the President, if such number be a majority of the whole number of electors appointed; and if no person have such majority, then from the persons having the highest numbers not exceeding three on the list of those voted for as President, the House of Representatives shall choose immediately, by ballot, the President. But in choosing the President, the votes shall be taken by states, the representation from each State having one vote; a quorum for this purpose shall consist of a member or members from two thirds of the states, and a majority of all the states shall be necessary to a choice. And if the House of Representatives shall not choose a President whenever the right of choice shall devolve upon them, before the fourth day of March next following, then the Vice President shall act as President, as in the case of the death or other constitutional disability of the President. The person having the greatest number of votes as Vice President, shall be the Vice President, if such number be a majority of the whole number of electors appointed, and if no person have a majority, then from the two highest numbers on the list, the Senate shall choose the Vice President; a quorum for the purpose shall consist of two thirds of the whole number of Senators, and a majority of the whole number shall be necessary to a choice. But no person constitutionally ineligible to the office of President shall be eligible to that of Vice President of the United States.

Article XIII

(The proposed amendment was sent to the states Feb. 1, 1865, by the Thirty-eighth Congress. It was ratified Dec. 6, 1865.)

Section 1

[Slavery prohibited.] Neither slavery nor involuntary servitude, except as a punishment for crime whereof the party shall have been duly convicted, shall exist within the United States, or any place subject to their jurisdiction.

Section 2

[Congress given power to enforce this article.] Congress shall have power to enforce this article by appropriate legislation.

Article XIV

(The proposed amendment was sent to the states June 16, 1866, by the Thirty-ninth Congress. It was ratified July 9, 1868.)

Section 1

[Citizenship defined; privileges of citizens.] All persons born or naturalized in the United States, and subject to the jurisdiction thereof, are citizens of the United States and of the State wherein they reside. No State shall make or enforce any law which shall abridge the privileges or immunities of citizens of the United States; nor shall any State deprive any person of life, liberty, or property, without due process of law; nor deny to any person within its jurisdiction the equal protection of the laws.

Section 2

[Apportionment of Representatives.] Representatives shall be apportioned among the several States according to their respective numbers, counting the whole number of persons in each State, excluding Indians not taxed. But when the right to vote at any election for the choice of electors for President and Vice President of the United

States, Representatives in Congress, the executive and judicial officers of a State, or the members of the Legislature thereof, is denied to any of the male inhabitants of such State, being twenty-one years of age, and citizens of the United States, or in any way abridged, except for participation in rebellion, or other crime, the basis of representation therein shall be reduced in the proportion which the number of such male citizens shall bear to the whole number of male citizens twenty-one years of age in such State.

Section 3

[Disqualification for office; removal of disability.] No person shall be a Senator or Representative in Congress, or elector of President and Vice President, or hold any office, civil or military, under the United States, or under any State, who, having previously taken an oath, as a member of Congress, or as an officer of the United States, or as a member of any State Legislature, or as an executive or judicial officer of any State, to support the Constitution of the United States, shall have engaged in insurrection or rebellion against the same, or given aid or comfort to the enemies thereof. But Congress may by a vote of two thirds of each House, remove such disability.

Section 4

[Public debt not to be questioned; payment of debts and claims incurred in aid of rebellion forbidden.] The validity of the public debt of the United States, authorized by law, including debts incurred for payment of pensions and bounties for services in suppressing insurrection or rebellion, shall not be questioned. But neither the United States nor any State shall assume or pay any debt or obligation incurred in aid of insurrection or rebellion against the United States, or any claim for the loss or emancipation of any slave; but all such debts, obligations, and claims shall be held illegal and void.

Section 5

[Congress given power to enforce this article.] The Congress shall have power to enforce, by appropriate legislation, the provisions of this article.

Article XV

(The proposed amendment was sent to the states Feb. 27, 1869, by the Fortieth Congress. It was ratified Feb. 3, 1870.)

Section 1

[Right of certain citizens to vote established.] The right of citizens of the United States to vote shall not be denied or abridged by the United States or by any State on account of race, color, or previous condition of servitude.

Section 2

[Congress given power to enforce this article.] The Congress shall have power to enforce this article by appropriate legislation.

Article XVI

(The proposed amendment was sent to the states July 12, 1909, by the Sixty-first Congress. It was ratified Feb. 3, 1913.)

[Taxes on income; Congress given power to lay and collect.] The Congress shall have power to lay and collect taxes on incomes, from whatever source derived, without apportionment among the several States, and without regard to any census or enumeration.

Article XVII

(The proposed amendment was sent to the states May 16, 1912, by the Sixty-second Congress. It was ratified April 8, 1913.)

[Election of United States Senators; filling of vacancies; qualifications of electors.]

The Senate of the United States shall be composed of two Senators from each State, elected by the people thereof, for six years; and each Senator shall have one vote. The electors in each State shall have the qualifications requisite for electors of the most numerous branch of the State Legislatures.

When vacancies happen in the representation of any State in the Senate, the executive authority of such State shall issue writs of election to fill such vacancies: Provided, that the legislature of any State may empower the executive thereof to make temporary appointment until the people fill the vacancies by election as the legislature may direct.

This amendment shall not be so construed as to affect the election or term of any Senator chosen before it becomes valid as part of the Constitution.

Article XVIII[2]

(The proposed amendment was sent to the states Dec. 18, 1917, by the Sixty-fifth Congress. It was ratified by three quarters of the states by Jan. 16, 1919, and became effective Jan. 16, 1920.)

Section 1

[Manufacture, sale, or transportation of intoxicating liquors, for beverage purposes, prohibited.] After one year from the ratification of this article the manufacture, sale, or transportation of intoxicating liquors within, the importation thereof into, or the exportation thereof from the United States and all territory subject to the jurisdiction thereof for beverage purposes is hereby prohibited.

Section 2

[Congress and the several States given concurrent power to pass appropriate legislation to enforce this article.] The Congress and the several States shall have concurrent power to enforce this article by appropriate legislation.

Section 3

[Provisions of article to become operative, when adopted by three fourths of the States.] This article shall be inoperative unless it shall have been ratified as an amendment to the Constitution by the legislatures of the several States, as provided in the Constitution, within seven years from the date of the submission hereof to the States by Congress.

Article XIX

(The proposed amendment was sent to the states June 4, 1919, by the Sixty-sixth Congress. It was ratified Aug. 18, 1920.)

[The right of citizens to vote shall not be denied because of sex.] The right of citizens of the United States to vote shall not be denied or abridged by the United States or by any State on account of sex.

[Congress given power to enforce this article.] Congress shall have power to enforce this article by appropriate legislation.

Article XX

(The proposed amendment, sometimes called the "Lame Duck Amendment," was sent to the states Mar. 3, 1932, by the Seventy-second Congress. It was ratified Jan. 23, 1933; but, in accordance with Section 5, Sections 1 and 2 did not go into effect until Oct. 15, 1933.)

Section 1

[Terms of President, Vice President, Senators, and Representatives.] The terms of the President and Vice President shall end at noon on the twentieth day of January, and the terms of Senators and Representatives at noon on the third day of January, of the years in which such terms would have ended if this article had not been ratified; and the terms of their successors shall then begin.

Section 2

[Time of assembling Congress.] The Congress shall assemble at least once in every year, and such meeting shall begin at noon on the third day of January, unless they shall by law appoint a different day.

Section 3

[Filling vacancy in office of President.] If, at the time fixed for the beginning of the term of the President, the President-elect shall have died, the Vice President-elect shall become President. If a President shall not have been chosen before the time fixed for the beginning of his term, or if the President-elect shall have failed to qualify, then the Vice President shall have qualified; and the Congress may by law provide for the case wherein neither a President-elect nor a Vice President-elect shall have qualified, declaring who shall then act as President, or the manner in which one who is to act shall be selected, and such person shall act accordingly until a President or Vice President shall have qualified.

Section 4

[Power of Congress in Presidential succession.] The Congress may by law provide for the case of the death of any of the persons from whom the House of Representatives may choose a President whenever the right of choice shall have devolved upon them, and for the case of the death of any of the persons from whom the Senate may choose a Vice President whenever the right of choice shall have devolved upon them.

Section 5

[Time of taking effect.] Sections 1 and 2 shall take effect on the 15th day of October following the ratification of this article.

Section 6

[Ratification.] This article shall be inoperative unless it shall have been ratified as an amendment to the Constitution by the legislatures of three fourths of the several States within seven years from the date of its submission.

Article XXI

(The proposed amendment was sent to the states Feb. 20, 1933, by the Seventy-second Congress. It was ratified Dec. 5, 1933.)

Section 1

[Repeal of Prohibition Amendment.] The eighteenth article of amendment to the Constitution of the United States is hereby repealed.

Section 2

[Transportation of intoxicating liquors.] The transportation or importation into any State, territory, or possession of the United States for delivery or use therein of intoxicating liquors, in violation of the laws thereof, is hereby prohibited.

Section 3

[Ratification.] This article shall be inoperative unless it shall have been ratified as an amendment to the Constitution by convention in the several States, as provided in the Constitution, within seven years from the date of the submission thereof to the States by the Congress.

Article XXII

(The proposed amendment was sent to the states Mar. 21, 1947, by the Eightieth Congress. It was ratified Feb. 27, 1951.)

Section 1

[Limit to number of terms a President may serve.] No person shall be elected to the office of the President more than twice, and no person who has held the office of President, or acted as President, for more than two years of a term to which some other person was elected President shall be elected to the office of the President more than once. But this article shall not apply to any person holding the office of President when this article was proposed by the Congress, and shall not prevent any person who may be holding the office of President, or acting as President, during the term within which this article becomes operative from holding the office of President or acting as President during the remainder of such term.

Section 2

[Ratification.] This article shall be inoperative unless it shall have been ratified as an amendment to the Constitution by the legislatures of three fourths of the several States within seven years from the date of its submission to the States by the Congress.

Article XXIII

(The proposed amendment was sent to the states June 16, 1960, by the Eighty-sixth Congress. It was ratified March 29, 1961.)

Section 1

[Electors for the District of Columbia.] The District constituting the seat of Government of the United States shall appoint in such manner as the Congress may direct:

A number of electors of President and Vice President equal to the whole number of Senators and Representatives in Congress to which the District would be entitled if it were a State, but in no event more than the least populous State; they shall be in addition to those appointed by the States, but they shall be considered, for the purposes of the election of President and Vice President, to be electors appointed by a State; and they shall meet in the District and perform such duties as provided by the twelfth article of amendment.

Section 2

[Congress given power to enforce this article.] The Congress shall have the power to enforce this article by appropriate legislation.

Article XXIV

(The proposed amendment was sent to the states Aug. 27, 1962, by the Eighty-seventh Congress. It was ratified Jan. 23, 1964.)

Section 1

[Payment of poll tax or other taxes not to be prerequisite for voting in federal elections.] The right of citizens of the United States to vote in any primary or other election for President or Vice President, for electors for President or Vice President, or for Senator or Representative in Congress, shall not be denied or abridged by the United States or any State by reasons of failure to pay any poll tax or other tax.

Section 2

[Congress given power to enforce this article.] The Congress shall have the power to enforce this article by appropriate legislation.

Article XXV

(The proposed amendment was sent to the states July 6, 1965, by the Eighty-ninth Congress. It was ratified Feb. 10, 1967.)

Section 1

[Succession of Vice President to Presidency.] In case of the removal of the President from office or of his death or resignation, the Vice President shall become President.

Section 2

[Vacancy in office of Vice President.] Whenever there is a vacancy in the office of the Vice President, the President shall nominate a Vice President who shall take office upon confirmation by a majority vote of both Houses of Congress.

Section 3

[Vice President as Acting President.] Whenever the President transmits to the President pro tempore of the Senate and the Speaker of the House of Representatives his written declaration that he is unable to discharge the powers and duties of his office, and until he transmits to them a written declaration to the contrary, such powers and duties shall be discharged by the Vice President as Acting President.

Section 4

[Vice President as Acting President.] Whenever the Vice President and a majority of either the principal officers of the executive departments or of such other body as Congress may by law provide, transmit to the President pro tempore of the Senate and the Speaker of the House of Representatives their written declaration that the President is unable to discharge the powers and duties of his office, the Vice President shall immediately assume the powers and duties of the office as Acting President.

Thereafter, when the President transmits to the President pro tempore of the Senate and the Speaker of the House of Representatives his written declaration that no inability exists, he shall resume the powers and duties of his office unless the Vice President and a majority of either the principal officers of the executive department or of such other body as Congress may by law provide, transmit within four days to the President pro tempore of the Senate and the Speaker of the House of Representatives their written declaration that the President is unable to discharge the powers and duties of his office. Thereupon Congress shall decide the issue, asssembling within forty-eight hours for that purpose if not in session. If the Congress, within twenty-one days after receipt of the latter written declaration, or, if Congress is not in session, within twenty-one days after Congress is required to assemble, determines by two thirds vote of both Houses that the President is unable to discharge the powers and duties of his office, the Vice President shall continue to discharge the same as Acting President; otherwise, the President shall resume the powers and duties of his office.

Article XXVI

(The proposed amendment was sent to the states Mar. 23, 1971, by the Ninety-second Congress. It was ratified July 1, 1971.)

Section 1

[Voting for 18-year-olds.] The right of citizens of the United States, who are 18 years of age or older, to vote shall not be denied or abridged by the Unit ed States or by any state on account of age.

Section 2

[Congress given power to enforce this article.] The Congress shall have power to enforce this article by appropriate legislation.

1. Amended by the 20th Amendment, Sections 3 and 4. 2. Repealed by the 21st Amendment.

The White House

Source: Department of the Interior, U.S. National Park Service.

The White House, the official residence of the President, is at 1600 Pennsylvania Avenue in Washington, D.C. The site, covering about 18 acres, was selected by President Washington and Pierre Charles L'Enfant, and the architect was James Hoban. The design of the residence is said to have been suggested by the Duke of Leinster's house in Ireland. The cornerstone was laid Oct. 13, 1792, and the first residents were President and Mrs. John Adams in November 1800. During the War of 1812, on August 24, 1814, the British set fire to the building. The sandstone exterior was painted white during the course of the reconstruction.

From December 1948 to March 1952, the interior of the White House was rebuilt, and the outer walls were strengthened.

The rooms for public functions are on the first floor; on the second and third are the President's apartments. The most celebrated public room is the East Room, where formal receptions take place. Other public rooms are the Red Room, the Green Room, and the Blue Room. The State Dining Room is used for formal dinners. There are 132 rooms.

The Mayflower Compact

On Sept. 6, 1620, the *Mayflower,* a sailing vessel of about 180 tons, started her memorable voyage from Plymouth, England, with about 100[1] pilgrims aboard, bound for Virginia to establish a private permanent colony in North America. Arriving at what is now Provincetown, Mass., on Nov. 11 (Nov. 21, new style calendar), 41 of the passengers signed the famous "Mayflower Compact" as the boat lay at anchor in that Cape Cod harbor. A small detail of the pilgrims, led by William Bradford, assigned to select a place for permanent settlement landed at what is now Plymouth, Mass., on Dec. 21 (n.s.).

The text of the compact follows:

> In the name of God, Amen. We, whose names are underwritten, the Loyal Subjects of our dread Sovereign Lord, King *James,* by the Grace of God, of *Great Britain, France* and *Ireland,* King, *Defender of the Faith,* &,
>
> Having undertaken for the Glory of God, and Advancement of the Christian Faith, and the Honour of our King and Country, a voyage to plant the first colony in the northern Parts of Virginia; do by these Presents, solemnly and mutually in the Presence of God and one of another, covenant and combine ourselves together into a civil Body Politick, for our better Ordering and Preservation, and Furtherance of the Ends aforesaid; And by Virtue hereof to enact, constitute, and frame, such just and equal Laws, Ordinances, Acts, Constitutions and Offices, from time to time, as shall be thought most meet and convenient for the General good of the Colony; unto which we promise all due Submission and Obedience.
>
> In Witness whereof we have hereunto subscribed our names at *Cape Cod* the eleventh of *November,* in the Reign of our Sovereign Lord, King *James* of *England, France* and *Ireland,* the eighteenth, and of *Scotland* the fifty-fourth. *Anno Domini,* 1620

John Carver	William Mullins	John Billington	Peter Brown
Digery Priest	Thomas English	Thomas Tinker	John Turner
William Brewster	John Howland	Samuel Fuller	Edward Tilly
Edmund Margesson	Stephen Hopkins	Richard Clark	John Craxton
John Alden	Edward Winslow	John Allerton	Thomas Rogers
George Soule	Gilbert Winslow	Richard Warren	John Goodman
James Chilton	Miles Standish	Edward Liester	Edward Fuller
Francis Cooke	Richard Bitteridge	William Bradford	Richard Gardiner
Moses Fletcher	Francis Eaton	Thomas Williams	William White
John Ridgate	John Tilly	Isaac Allerton	Edward Doten
Christopher Martin			

1. Historians differ as to whether 100, 101, or 102 passengers were aboard.

The Monroe Doctrine

The Monroe Doctrine was announced in President James Monroe's message to Congress, during his second term on Dec. 2, 1823, in part as follows:

"In the discussions to which this interest has given rise, and in the arrangements by which they may terminate, the occasion has been deemed proper for asserting as a principle in which rights and interests of the United States are involved, that the American continents, by the free and independent condition which they have assumed and maintain, are henceforth not to be considered as subjects for future colonization by any European power. . . . We owe it, therefore, to candor and to the amicable relations existing between the United States and those powers to declare that we should consider any attempt on their part to extend their system to any portion of this hemisphere as dangerous to our peace and safety. With the existing colonies or dependencies of any European power we have not interfered and shall not interfere. But with the governments who have declared their independence and maintain it, and whose independence we have, on great consideration and on just principles, acknowledged, we could not view any interposition for the purpose of oppressing them or controlling in any other manner their destiny by any European power in any other light than as the manifestation of an unfriendly disposition toward the United States."

Order of Presidential Succession

1. The Vice President
2. Speaker of the House
3. President pro tempore of the Senate
4. Secretary of State
5. Secretary of the Treasury
6. Secretary of Defense
7. Attorney General
8. Secretary of the Interior
9. Secretary of Agriculture
10. Secretary of Commerce
11. Secretary of Labor
12. Secretary of Health and Human Services
13. Secretary of Housing and Urban Development
14. Secretary of Transportation
15. Secretary of Energy
16. Secretary of Education

NOTE: An official cannot succeed to the Presidency unless that person meets the Constitutional requirements.

The Star-Spangled Banner

Francis Scott Key, 1814

O say, can you see, by the dawn's early light,
What so proudly we hail'd at the twilight's last gleaming?
Whose broad stripes and bright stars, thro' the perilous fight,
O'er the ramparts we watch'd, were so gallantly streaming?
And the rockets' red glare, the bombs bursting in air,
Gave proof thro' the night that our flag was still there.
O say, does that star-spangled banner yet wave
O'er the land of the free and the home of the brave?

On the shore dimly seen thro' the mists of the deep,
Where the foe's haughty host in dread silence reposes,
What is that which the breeze, o'er the towering steep,
As it fitfully blows, half conceals, half discloses?
Now it catches the gleam of the morning's first beam,
In full glory reflected, now shines on the stream:
'T is the star-spangled banner: O, long may it wave
O'er the land of the free and the home of the brave!

And where is that band who so vauntingly swore
That the havoc of war and the battle's confusion,
A home and a country should leave us no more?
Their blood has wash'd out their foul footsteps' pollution.
No refuge could save the hireling and slave
From the terror of flight or the gloom of the grave:
And the star-spangled banner in triumph doth wave
O'er the land of the free and the home of the brave.

O thus be it ever when free-men shall stand
Between their lov'd home and the war's desolation;
Blest with vict'ry and peace, may the heav'n-rescued land
Praise the Pow'r that hath made and preserv'd us a nation!
Then conquer we must, when our cause it is just,
And this be our motto: "In God is our trust!"
And the star-spangled banner in triumph shall wave
O'er the land of the free and the home of the brave!

On Sept. 13, 1814, Francis Scott Key visited the British fleet in Chesapeake Bay to secure the release of Dr. William Beanes, who had been captured after the burning of Washington, D.C. The release was secured, but Key was detained on ship overnight during the shelling of Fort McHenry, one of the forts defending Baltimore. In the morning, he was so delighted to see the American flag still flying over the fort that he began a poem to commemorate the occasion. First published under the title "Defense of Fort M'Henry," and later as "The Star-Spangled Banner," the poem soon attained wide popularity as sung to the tune "To Anacreon in Heaven." The origin of this tune is obscure, but it may have been written by John Stafford Smith, a British composer born in 1750. "The Star-Spangled Banner" was officially made the National Anthem by Congress in 1931, although it had been already adopted as such by the Army and the Navy.

The Emancipation Proclamation

January 1, 1863

By the President of the United States of America:

A Proclamation.

Whereas on the 22d day of September, A.D. 1862, a proclamation was issued by the President of the United States, containing, among other things, the following, to wit:

"That on the 1st day of January, A.D. 1863, all persons held as slaves within any State or designated part of a State the people whereof shall then be in rebellion against the United States shall be then, thenceforward, and forever free; and the executive government of the United States, including the military and naval authority thereof, will recognize and maintain the freedom of such persons and will do no act or acts to repress such persons, or any of them, in any efforts they may make for their actual freedom.

"That the executive will on the 1st day of January aforesaid, by proclamation, designate the States and parts of States, if any, in which the people thereof, respectively, shall then be in rebellion against the United States; and the fact that any State or the people thereof shall on that day be in good faith represented in the Congress of the United States by members chosen thereto at elections wherein a majority of the qualified voters of such States shall have participated shall, in the absence of strong countervailing testimony, be deemed conclusive evidence that such State and the people thereof are not then in rebellion against the United States."

Now, therefore, I, Abraham Lincoln, President

of the United States, by virtue of the power in me vested as Commander-in-Chief of the Army and Navy of the United States in time of actual armed rebellion against the authority and government of the United States, and as a fit and necessary war measure for suppressing said rebellion, do, on this 1st day of January, A.D. 1863, and in accordance with my purpose so to do, publicly proclaimed for the full period of one hundred days from the first day above mentioned, order and designate as the States and parts of States wherein the people thereof, respectively, are this day in rebellion against the United States the following, to wit:

Arkansas, Texas, Louisiana (except the parishes of St. Bernard, Plaquemines, Jefferson, St. John, St. Charles, St. James, Ascension, Assumption, Terrebonne, Lafourche, St. Mary, St. Martin, and Orleans, including the city of New Orleans), Mississippi, Alabama, Florida, Georgia, South Carolina, North Carolina, and Virginia (except the forty-eight counties designated as West Virginia, and also the counties of Berkeley, Accomac, Northhampton, Elizabeth City, York, Princess Anne, and Norfolk, including the cities of Norfolk and Portsmouth), and which excepted parts are for the present left precisely as if this proclamation were not issued.

And by virtue of the power and for the purpose aforesaid, I do order and declare that all persons held as slaves within said designated States and parts of States are, and henceforward shall be, free; and that the Executive Government of the United States, including the military and naval authorities thereof, will recognize and maintain the freedom of said persons.

And I hereby enjoin upon the people so declared to be free to abstain from all violence, unless in necessary self-defense; and I recommend to them that, in all cases when allowed, they labor faithfully for reasonable wages.

And I further declare and make known that such persons of suitable condition will be received into the armed service of the United States to garrison forts, positions, stations, and other places, and to man vessels of all sorts in said service.

And upon this act, sincerely believed to be an act of justice, warranted by the Constitution upon military necessity, I invoke the considerate judgment of mankind and the gracious favor of Almighty God.

The Confederate States of America

State	Seceded from Union	Readmitted to Union[1]
1. South Carolina	Dec. 20, 1860	July 9, 1868
2. Mississippi	Jan. 9, 1861	Feb. 23, 1870
3. Florida	Jan. 10, 1861	June 25, 1868
4. Alabama	Jan. 11, 1861	July 13, 1868
5. Georgia	Jan. 19, 1861	July 15, 1870[2]
6. Louisiana	Jan. 26, 1861	July 9, 1868
7. Texas	March 2, 1861	March 30, 1870
8. Virginia	April 17, 1861	Jan. 26, 1870
9. Arkansas	May 6, 1861	June 22, 1868
10. North Carolina	May 20, 1861	July 4, 1868
11. Tennessee	June 8, 1861	July 24, 1866

1. Date of readmission to representation in U.S. House of Representatives. 2. Second readmission date. First date was July 21, 1868, but the representatives were unseated March 5, 1869. NOTE: Four other slave states—Delaware, Kentucky, Maryland, and Missouri—remained in the Union.

Lincoln's Gettysburg Address

The Battle of Gettysburg, one of the most noted battles of the Civil War, was fought on July 1, 2, and 3, 1863. On Nov. 19, 1863, the field was dedicated as a national cemetery by President Lincoln in a two-minute speech that was to become immortal. At the time of its delivery the speech was relegated to the inside pages of the papers, while a two-hour address by Edward Everett, the leading orator of the time, caught the headlines.

The following is the text of the address revised by President Lincoln from his own notes:

Fourscore and seven years ago our fathers brought forth on this continent a new nation conceived in liberty and dedicated to the proposition that all men are created equal. Now we are engaged in a great civil war testing whether that nation, or any nation so conceived and so dedicated, can long endure. We are met on a great battlefield of that war. We have come to dedicate a portion of that field as a final resting-place for those who here gave their lives that that nation might live. It is altogether fitting and proper that we should do this. But, in a larger sense, we cannot dedicate, we cannot consecrate, we cannot hallow this ground. The brave men, living and dead, who struggled here have consecrated it far above our poor power to add or detract. The world will little note nor long remember what we say here, but it can never forget what they did here. It is for us the living rather to be dedicated here to the unfinished work which they who fought here have thus far so nobly advanced. It is rather for us to be here dedicated to the great task remaining before us—that from these honored dead we take increased devotion to that cause for which they gave the last full measure of devotion—that we here highly resolve that these dead shall not have died in vain, that this nation under God shall have a new birth of freedom, and that government of the people, by the people, for the people shall not perish from the earth.

The Early Congresses

At the urging of Massachusetts and Virginia, the First Continental Congress met in Philadelphia on Sept. 5, 1774, and was attended by representatives of all the colonies except Georgia. Patrick Henry of Virginia declared: "The distinctions between Pennsylvanians, New Yorkers and New Englanders are no more. I am not a Virginian but an American." This Congress, which adjourned Oct. 26, 1774, passed intercolonial resolutions calling for extensive boycott by the colonies against British trade.

The following year, most of the delegates from the colonies were chosen by popular election to attend the Second Continental Congress, which assembled in Philadelphia on May 10. As war had already begun between the colonies and England, the chief problems before the Congress were the procuring of military supplies, the establishment of an army and proper defenses, the issuing of continental bills of credit, etc. On June 15, 1775, George Washington was elected to command the Continental army. Congress adjourned Dec. 12, 1776.

Other Continental Congresses were held in Baltimore (1776–77), Philadelphia (1777), Lancaster, Pa. (1777), York, Pa. (1777–78), and Philadelphia (1778–81).

In 1781, the Articles of Confederation, although establishing a league of the thirteen states rather than a strong central government, provided for the continuance of Congress. Known thereafter as the Congress of the Confederation, it held sessions in Philadelphia (1781–83), Princeton, N.J. (1783), Annapolis, Md. (1783–84), and Trenton, N.J. (1784). Five sessions were held in New York City between the years 1785 and 1789.

The Congress of the United States, established by the ratification of the Constitution, held its first meeting on March 4, 1789, in New York City. Several sessions of Congress were held in Philadelphia, and the first meeting in Washington, D.C., was on Nov. 17, 1800.

Presidents of the Continental Congresses

Name	Elected	Born	Died
Peyton Randolph, Va.	Sept. 5, 1774	c.1721	1775
Henry Middleton, S.C.	Oct. 22, 1774	1717	1784
Peyton Randolph, Va.	May 10, 1775	c.1721	1775
John Hancock, Mass.	May 24, 1775	1737	1793
Henry Laurens, S.C.	Nov. 1, 1777	1724	1792
John Jay, N.Y.	Dec. 10, 1778	1745	1829
Samuel Huntington, Conn.	Sept. 28, 1779	1731	1796
Thomas McKean, Del.	July 10, 1781	1734	1817
John Hanson, Md.	Nov. 5, 1781	1715	1783
Elias Boudinot, N.J.	Nov. 4, 1782	1740	1821
Thomas Mifflin, Pa.	Nov. 3, 1783	1744	1800
Richard Henry Lee, Va.	Nov. 30, 1784	1732	1794
John Hancock, Mass.[1]	Nov. 23, 1785	1737	1793
Nathaniel Gorham, Mass.	June 6, 1786	1738	1796
Arthur St. Clair, Pa.	Feb. 2, 1787	1734	1818
Cyrus Griffin, Va.	Jan. 22, 1788	1748	1810

1. Resigned May 29, 1786, never having served, because of continued illness.

The Great Seal of the U.S.

On July 4, 1776, the Continental Congress appointed a committee consisting of Benjamin Franklin, John Adams, and Thomas Jefferson "to bring in a device for a seal of the United States of America." After many delays, a verbal description of a design by William Barton was finally approved by Congress on June 20, 1782. The seal shows an American bald eagle with a ribbon in its mouth bearing the device *E pluribus unum* (One out of many). In its talons are the arrows of war and an olive branch of peace. On the reverse side it shows an unfinished pyramid with an eye (the eye of Providence) above it.

The American's Creed

William Tyler Page

"I believe in the United States of America as a government of the people, by the people, for the people; whose just powers are derived from the consent of the governed; a democracy in a republic; a sovereign Nation of many sovereign States; a perfect union, one and inseparable; established upon those principles of freedom, equality, justice, and humanity for which American patriots sacrificed their lives and fortunes.

"I therefore believe it is my duty to my country to love it, to support its Constitution, to obey its laws, to respect its flag, and to defend it against all enemies."

NOTE: William Tyler Page, Clerk of the U.S. House of Representatives, wrote "The American's Creed" in 1917. It was accepted by the House on behalf of the American people on April 3, 1918.

Item	Unit	1980	1975	1970	1960[2]	1950
1. Population estimates[1]	thousands	226,505	213,540	204,879	180,671	151,684
2. Population abroad		995,546	—	1,737,836	1,374,421	481,545[17]
3. Population per sq mile		64.0	60.2	57.5	50.6	50.7
4. Median age of population	years	30.0	28.8	28.1	29.5	30.2
5. Number of households	thousands	79,108	71,120	63,401	52,799	43,554
6. Average household size		2.75	2.94	3.14	3.33	3.37
7. Homicides		23,044	21,310	16,848	8,464	7,942
8. Rate per 100,000 population		10.2	10.0	8.3	4.7	5.3
9. Suicides		28,290	27,063	23,480	19,041	17,145
10. Rate per 100,000 population		12.2	12.7	11.6	10.6	11.4
11. Number of immigrants		460,300[15]	386,200	373,326	265,398	249,187
Immigrants by selected occupations						
12. Professional[4]		39,500[15]	38,500	46,151	21,940	20,502
13. Farmers[4 5]		800[15]	900	3,839	3,050	17,642
14. Skilled[4 6]		39,500[15]	38,500	46,622	34,135	41,450
15. Laborers[4 7]		13,800[15]	13,000	14,148	12,838	5,693
16. Total Gross National Product—Current prices	billion dollars	2,226.1	1,516.3	977.1	503.7	284.8
17. Per capita Gross National Product—Current prices	dollars	11,536	7,016	4,808	2,788	1,877
Retail prices of selected foods in U.S. cities						
18. Flour—5 lb	¢/unit shown	105	99.5	58.9	55.4	49.1
19. Bread—1 lb	¢/unit shown	50.9	36.0	24.3	20.3	14.3
20. Beef, choice—1 lb	¢/unit shown	237.6	188.5	130.2	105.5	93.6
21. Butter—1 lb	¢/unit shown	187.8	102.5	86.6	74.9	72.9
22. Potatoes—10 lb	¢/unit shown	197.5	134.0	89.7	71.8	46.1
23. Sugar—5 lb	¢/unit shown	213.5	186.0	64.8	58.2	48.7
24. Total labor force[10]	thousands 16 years and over	106,800	94,793	82,049	69,877[11]	59,643[11]
25. Percent of population		64.3	61.8	59.0	56.1[11]	54.1[11]
26. Percent of civilian labor force unemployed[13]	10 years and over	7.1	8.5	4.9	5.5	5.3
Physical output of selected manufactured commodities						
27. Bitominous coal	mil. short tons	776[15]	648	603	416	516
28. Beer	thou. bbl	192,000	158,000	134,654	94,548	88,807
29. Cigarettes	millions	702,000	627,000	562,154	506,127	391,956
30. Total raw steel	thou. short tons	111,800	116,642	131,514	99,282	96,836
31. Total value of new construction put in place	mil. dollars	230,781	132,043	94,855	54,738	33,575
32. Total concerns in business	thousands	2,781	2,679	2,442	2,708	2,687
33. Business failure rate	per 10,000 listed enterprises	42	43	44	57	34
34. Average annual earnings of employees	dollars	14,376[15]	10,836	7,564	4,743	2,992
Average annual earnings per full time employee in selected industries[23]						
35. Services[19]	current $	12,178[15]	9,066	5,946	3,513	2,183
36. Agriculture, Forestry, and Fisheries	current $	9,332[15]	6,232	3,063	1,658	1,282
37. Manufacturing	current $	16,259[15]	11,903	8,150	5,352	3,302
38. Mining[21]	current $	21,077[15]	14,765	9,262	5,676	3,460
39. Construction	current $	16,755[15]	13,448	9,293	5,443	3,333
40. Transportation	current $	22,522[15]	16,060	9,928	6,185	3,714
41. Communications and public utilities	current $	19,785[15]	14,020	8,897	5,681	3,346
42. Wholesale and retail trade	current $	13,601[15]	10,425	7,554	4,597	3,045
43. Finance, insurance, and real estate	current $	14,365[15]	10,618	8,026	5,030	3,223
44. Government	current $	14,607[15]	11,451	7,965	4,676	3,014
45. Total farm population	thousands	7,241	8,864	9,712	15,635	23,048
46. Number of farms	thousands	2,428	2,808	2,954	3,962	5,388
47. Total land in farms	mil. acres	1,042	1,086.0	1,102.8	1,176.9	1,161.4
48. Total value of all farm property	mil. dollars	753,608	358,640	215,042	167,564	101,117[22]
49. Average value per farm of land and buildings	dollars	311,000	142,500	70,485	32,854	14,005
50. Farm wages, per day, with room and board	dollars	20.99[15]	14.80	9.30	6.50	4.45

1940	1930	1920	1910	1900
132,122	123,188	106,461	92,407	76,094
118,933	2,977,128	2,969,451	2,969,565	2,969,834
44.2	41.2	35.6	31.0	25.6
29.0	26.5	25.3	24.1	22.9
34,949	29,905	24,352	20,256	15,964
3.67	4.11	4.34	4.54	4.76
8,329	10,331	5,815	2,161	230
6.3	8.8	6.8	4.6	1.2
18,907	18,323	8,790	7,283	2,036
14.4	15.6	10.2	15.3	10.2
70,756	241,700	430,001	1,041,570	448,572
6,802	8,585	10,540	9,689	2,392
847	8,375	12,192	11,793	5,433
5,710	32,474	55,991	121,847	54,793
2,120	18,080	83,496	216,909	164,261
99.7	90.4	91.5	35.3	18.7
754	734	860	382	246
21.5	23.0	40.5	18.0	12.5
8.0	8.6	11.5	—	—
36.4	42.6	39.5	17.4	13.2
36.0	46.4	70.1	35.9	26.1
23.9	36.0	63.0	17.0	14.0
26.0	30.5	97.0	30.0	30.5
53,011[11]	48,830[12]	41,614[12]	38,167[12]	29,073[12]
52.9[11]	49.5[12]	50.3[12]	53.3[12]	50.2[12]
14.6	8.7	5.2	5.9	5.0
461	468	569	417	212
54,892	3,681	9,200	59,500	39,500
189,373	124,193	48,091	9,782	3,870
66,983	44,591	46,183	28,330	11,227
8,682	8,741	6,749	3,262	—
2,156	2,183	1,821	1,515	1,174
63	122[16]	48	84	92
1,299	1,368	1,236[18]	517[18]	375[18]
953	1,066	912	447	340
407	388	528	223	178
1,432	1,488	1,532	651	487
1,388	1,424	1,684	668	479
1,330	1,526	1,710	804	593
1,756	1,610	1,645	607	505
1,717	1,499	1,238	516	470
1,382	1,569	1,270	630	508
1,725	1,973	1,758	1,301	1,040
1,344	1,553	1,245	725	584
30,547	30,529	31,974	32,077	29,875
6,102	6,295	6,454	6,366	5,740
1,065.1	990.1	958.7	881.4	841.2
41,829	57,689	78,386	40,959	20,365
5,532	7,624	10,295	5,480	2,895
1.30	1.80	2.80	1.05	.75[23]

Statistical Profile of The United States

1900–1980

There are many ways of looking at American history—at the growth of the United States, its people, and its economy. One of the most interesting is to examine certain aspects of American life "by the numbers." This "Statistical Profile" makes such an examination possible. The data at left and following—stripped of the men and women, events, and technological changes that have shaped American society—reveal much that is often hidden in the complex folds of the fabric of history.

Statistical Profile Table—Footnotes

1. Total, including Armed Forces overseas, as of July 1. 2. Beginning with 1960, figures include Alaska and Hawaii. 3. Based on resident population figures, excluding Armed Forces overseas. 4. Like occupations have been grouped as closely as possible to allow for changing definitions over the years. For example, figures for Professional and Skilled workers are combined for 1975 and following. See sources for definitions and further explanation. 5. Includes "Farmers and Farm Managers." 6. Includes craftsmen, foremen, operatives, and kindred workers. 7. Excludes farm and mine laborers. 8. Earnings are calculated for all types of jobs performed in these industries. 9. Because the Air Deregulation Act of 1978 lifted some restrictions on entering new markets, domestic and international operators are no longer considered separately after 1975. Cargo included. 10. 1940–75, includes Armed Forces. 11. Data for persons 14 years old and over. 12. Data for persons 10 years old and over reporting a gainful occupation. 13. Prior to 1950, figures are for persons 14 years old and over. Annual averages. Unemployment percentages for the Depression years are as follows: 1931, 15.9%; 1932, 23.6%; 1933, 24.9%; 1934, 21.7%; 1935, 20.1%; 1936, 16.9%; 1937, 14.3%; 1938, 19.0%; 1939, 17.2%. 14. In 1918, 2,897,167 people were on active military duty. 15. Figure is for 1979. 16. In 1932, the rate reached a high of 154. 17. Estimate. 18. After deduction for unemployment. 19. Includes workers in personal, medical, and other health services, domestic, nonprofit, educational service industries. 20. Figure is for 1974. 21. Includes workers in anthracite coal, bituminous coal, and metal mining. 22. Figure is for 1949. 23. Figure is for 1899. 24. Liveweight production. 25. Figures are annual averages for 1960–64. 26. Figures are annual averages for 1950–54. 27. Figures are annual averages for 1940–44. 28. Figures are annual averages for 1930–34. 29. Figures are annual averages for 1920–24. 30. Figures are annual averages for 1910–14. 31. Figure is for 1907. 32. Figure is for 1902. 33. Figure is for 1921. 34. Duplication has been eliminated where the same passengers were carried on more than one route of an air carrier, but still exists where the same passengers were carried by more than one air carrier. 35. Includes nonrevenue passengers. 36. Figure is for 1957, the first year for large-scale generation of electricity by nuclear power. 37. Figure is for 1922. 38. Preliminary figures. 39. Figure is for 1913. 40. Includes hospital care, professional services, drugs and sundries, eyeglasses and appliances, nursing home care, expenses for prepayment and administration, government public health activities, other health services, and research and medical facilities construction. 41. Figure is for 1969. 42. Figure is for 1959. 43. Figure is for 1978. 44. Figure is for 1901. 45. Figures for 1970 and following are for both color and monochrome sets. 46. Figures are annual averages for 1975–79. 47. Figures are annual averages for 1970–74. 48. Figures are annual averages for 1965–69. 49. Figures are annual averages for 1955–59. 50. Figures are annual averages for 1945–49. 51. Figures are annual averages for 1935–39. 52. Figures are annual averages for 1925–29. 53. Figures are annual averages for 1915–19. 54. Figures are annual averages for 1910–14. 55. In 1945, 12,123,455 people were on active military duty. *Sources: Historical Statistics of the U.S.* and *Statistical Abstract of the United States,* Department of Commerce, Bureau of the Census; *Crime in the United States,* Department of Justice, Federal Bureau of Investigation; Edison Electric Institute; Bureau of Labor Statistics.

	Item	Unit	1980	1975	1970	1960[2]	1950
	Farm Productivity						
51.	Wheat—yield per acre	bushels	33.4	31.0	31.0	25.2[25]	17.3[26]
52.	Wheat—man-hours	100 bushels	9	9	9	12[25]	27[26]
53.	Cotton—yield per acre	pounds	404	473	438	475[25]	296[26]
54.	Cotton—man-hours	bale	8	23	26	47[25]	107[26]
55.	Potatoes—yield per acre	cwt	261	239.0	229.0	194.9[25]	151.2[26]
56.	Potatoes—man-hours	ton	—	4	4	5[25]	8[26]
57.	Cattle—value	head	502	159	179	137	124
58.	Cattle—man-hours	cwt	1.3[46]	1.7[47]	2.1[48]	3.2[49]	4.0[50]
59.	Milk cows—milk per cow	pounds	11,000	10,200.0	9,385.0	7,507.0[25]	5,440.0[26]
60.	Milk cows—man-hours	cwt of milk	0.4	0.6	0.7	1.2[25]	2.2[26]
61.	Total use of electrical energy	mil. kwh	2,286,000	1,918,000	1,641,731	848,723	396,346
62.	Residential	mil. kwh	721,000	—	453,015	196,296	72,200
63.	Commercial	mil. kwh	510,000	—	295,057	121,437	52,091
64.	Industrial	mil. kwh	791,000	—	685,693	415,699	194,835
65.	Value of exports	mil. dollars	220,705	107,591	43,265	20,603	10,816
66.	Value of imports	mil. dollars	239,944	96,940	40,189	15,046	9,125
67.	Passenger car factory sales	thousands	6,400.0	6,713.0	6,546.8	6,674.7	6,665.8
68.	Total motor vehicle registrations	millions	159.1	133.7	108.4	73.9	49.2
69.	Miles of travel by motor vehicles	mil. miles	1,529,000[15]	1,300,100	1,120,705	718,845	458,246
70.	Number of operating railroads		63[15]	341[20]	351	407	471
71.	Railroad passengers	thousands	274,200[15]	270,000	289,469	327,172	488,019
	Air transportation						
72.	Number of operators		63[9]	30	33	42	52
73.	Aircraft in service		2,505	2,267	2,437	1,594	960
74.	Revenue passengers carried[34]	thousands	273,000	189,000	153,408	56,352	17,345
75.	Total school enrollments—elementary and secondary	thousands	48,000[17]	64,872	51,319	41,762	28,492
76.	High school graduates	thousands	3,127	3,133	2,906	1,864	1,200
77.	Illiteracy[11]	percent	.5[15]	—	1.0[41]	2.2[42]	3.2
78.	Total institutions of higher education		2,871[43]	2,747	2,525	1,959	1,863
79.	Bachelor's or first professional degrees conferred		1,010,000	988,000	827,234	389,183	432,058
	Radio and television						
80.	Nuclear plants		75[38]	51	13	4	—
81.	Electricity generated by nuclear power	mil. kwh	—	265,200	181,800	21,808	519
82.	Television sets produced	thousands	17,508	10,637	9,483[45]	5,708	7,464
83.	Households with television sets	thousands	80,000	72,600	63,200	45,750	3,875
84.	Books published		42,377	39,372	36,071	15,012	11,022
85.	Daily newspapers—number		1,745	1,756	1,748	1,763	1,772
86.	Daily newspapers—circulation	thousands	62,202	60,655	62,108	58,882	53,829
87.	Telephones per 1,000 population		791.0	695.0	583.4	407.8	280.9
88.	Average number of daily telephone conversations	thousands	787,000	633,000	485,200	285,386	170,623
89.	Patents issued for inventions		61,800	71,994	64,427	47,170	43,040
90.	Currency in circulation	mil. dollars	137,244	92,095.0	54,351.0	32,064.6	27,156.3
91.	Total social welfare expenditures under public programs	mil. dollars	428,400[15, 38]	290,000	145,893	52,293	23,508
92.	Percent of GNP	percent	18.5[15, 38]	20	15.3	10.6	8.9
93.	Percent of all government expenditures	percent	56.8[15, 38]	57.4	47.8	38.0	37.6
94.	Per capita (actual prices)	dollars	1,912[15, 38]	1336	701	286	153
95.	Per capita health expenditure	dollars	1,017	565.00	343.44	146.30	81.86
96.	Number of physicians		473,000	409,000	348,328	274,833	191,947
97.	Rate per 100,000 population		210	186	166	148	149
	Summary of federal government finances						
98.	Receipts	mil. dollars	520,100.0	281,000.0	193,700.0	92,500.0	40,900.0
99.	Outlays	mil. dollars	579,600.0	324,600.0	196,600.0	92,200.0	43,100.0
100.	Total public debt	mil. dollars	907,000.0	533,200.0	370,918.7	286,300.8	257,357.4
101.	Per capita public debt	dollars	4,063	2,496	1,811	1,585	1,697
102.	Paid civilian employees of the federal government		2,875,866	2,896,944	2,981,574	2,398,704	1,960,708
103.	Military personnel on active duty[54]		2,050,000	2,127,000	3,066,294	2,476,435	1,460,261

Item	Unit	1940	1930	1920	1910	1900
Farm Productivity						
51. Wheat—yield per acre	bushels	17.1[27]	13.5[28]	13.8[29]	14.4[30]	13.9
52. Wheat—man-hours	100 bushels	44[27]	70[28]	90[29]	106[30]	108
53. Cotton—yield per acre	pounds	260[27]	184[28]	155[29]	201[30]	189
54. Cotton—man-hours	bale	182[27]	252[28]	296[29]	276[30]	284
55. Potatoes—yield per acre	cwt	82.1[27]	64.6[28]	64.6[29]	59.8[30]	—
56. Potatoes—man-hours	ton	17[27]	21[28]	23[29]	25[30]	—
57. Cattle—value	head	41	56.36	52.64	24.54	26.50
58. Cattle—man-hours	cwt	3.4[51]	3.3[52]	3.7[53]	3.8[58]	—
59. Milk cows—milk per cow	pounds	4,653.0[27]	4,289.0[28]	4,000.0[29]	3,842.0[30]	—
60. Milk cows—man-hours	cwt of milk	3.1[27]	3.4[28]	3.6[29]	3.8[30]	—
61. Total use of electrical energy	mil. kwh	181,706	115,783	57,125	14,262[31]	6,029[32]
62. Residential	mil. kwh	24,068	11,018	3,190	—	—
63. Commercial	mil. kwh	22,373	13,944	6,150	—	—
64. Industrial	mil. kwh	92,390	61,023	31,500	—	—
65. Value of exports	mil. dollars	4,030	4,013	8,664	1,919	1,499
66. Value of imports	mil. dollars	7,433	3,500	5,784	1,646	930
67. Passenger car factory sales	thousands	3,717.3	2,787.4	1,905.5	181.0	4.1
68. Total motor vehicle registrations	millions	32.4	26.7	9.2	.5	.008
69. Miles of travel by motor vehicles	mil. miles	302,188	206,320	55,027[33]	—	—
70. Number of operating railroads		574	775	1,085	1,306	1,224
71. Railroad passengers	thousands	456,088	707,987	1,269,913	971,683	576,831
Air transportation						
72. Number of operators		19	43	—	—	—
73. Aircraft in service		369	497	—	—	—
74. Revenue passengers carried[34]	thousands	2,523	385[35]	—	—	—
75. Total school enrollments—elementary and secondary	thousands	28,045	28,329	23,278	19,372	16,885
76. High school graduates	thousands	1,221	667	311	156	95
77. Illiteracy[11]	percent	2.9	4.3	6.0	7.7	10.7
78. Total institutions of higher education		1,708	1,409	1,041	951	977
79. Bachelor's or first professional degrees conferred		186,500	122,484	48,622	37,199	27,410
Radio and television						
80. Nuclear plants		—	—	—	—	—
81. Electricity generated by nuclear power	mil. kwh	10[36]	—	—	—	—
82. Television sets produced	thousands	—	—	—	—	—
83. Households with television sets	thousands	—	—	—	—	—
84. Books published		11,328	10,027	8,422	13,470	6,356
85. Daily newspapers—number		1,878	1,942	2,042	—	—
86. Daily newspapers—circulation	thousands	41,132	39,589	27,791	—	—
87. Telephones per 1,000 population		165.1.	162.6	123.4	82.0	17.6
88. Average number of daily telephone conversations	thousands	98,783	83,520	51,814	36,161	7,882
89. Patents issued for inventions		42,238	45,226	37,060	35,141	24,644
90. Currency in circulation	mil. dollars	7,847.5	4,521.0	5,467.6	3,148.7	2,081.2
91. Total social welfare expenditures under public programs	mil. dollars	8,795	4,085	—	1,000[39]	—
92. Percent of GNP	percent	9.2	4.2	—	2.5[39]	—
93. Percent of all government expenditures	percent	49.0	—	—	34.0[39]	—
94. Per capita (actual prices)	dollars	66	33	—	—	—
95. Per capita health expenditure	dollars	29.62	29.49[14]	—	—	—
96. Number of physicians		165,989	153,803	144,977	151,132	132,002
97. Rate per 100,000 population		126	125	137	164	173
Summary of federal government finances						
98. Receipts	mil. dollars	6,900.0	4,057.9	6,648.9	675.5	567.2
99. Outlays	mil. dollars	9,600.0	3,320.2	6,357.7	693.6	520.9
100. Total public debt	mil. dollars	42,967.5	16,185.3	24,299.3	1,146.9	1,263.4
101. Per capita public debt	dollars	325	132	228	12	17
102. Paid civilian employees of the federal government		1,042,420	601,319	655,265	388,708	239,476[44]
103. Military personnel on active duty[54]		458,365[14]	255,648	343,302	139,344[57]	125,923

U.S. Capitol

When the French architect and engineer Maj. Pierre L'Enfant first began to lay out the plans for a new Federal city (now Washington, D.C.), he noted that Jenkins' Hill, overlooking the area, seemed to be "a pedestal waiting for a monument." It was here that the U.S. Capitol would be built. The basic structure as we know it today evolved over a period of more than 150 years. In 1792 a competition was held for the design of a capitol building. Dr. William Thornton, a physician and amateur architect, submitted the winning plan, a simple, low-lying structure of classical proportions with a shallow dome. Later, internal modifications were made by Benjamin Henry Latrobe. After the building was burned by the British in 1814, Latrobe and architect Charles Bulfinch were responsible for its reconstruction. Finally, under Thomas Walter, who was Architect of the Capitol from 1851 to 1865, the House and Senate wings and the imposing cast iron dome topped with the Statue of Freedom were added, and the Capitol assumed the form we see today. It was in the old Senate chamber that Daniel Webster cried out, "Liberty and Union, now and forever, one and inseparable!" In Statuary Hall, which used to be the old House chamber, a small disk on the floor marks the spot where John Quincy Adams was fatally stricken after more than 50 years of service to his country. A whisper from one side of this room can be heard across the vast space of the hall. Visitors can see the original Supreme Court chamber a floor below the Rotunda.

In addition to its historical association, the Capitol Building is also a vast artistic treasure house. The works of such famous artists as Gilbert Stuart, Rembrandt Peale, and John Trumbull are displayed on the walls. The Great Rotunda, with its 180-foot- (54.9-m-) high dome, is decorated with a massive fresco by Constantino Brumidi, which extends some 300 feet (90 m) in circumference. Throughout the building are many paintings of events in U.S. history and sculptures of outstanding Americans. The Capitol itself is situated on a 68-acre (27.5-ha) park designed by the 19th-century landscape architect Frederick Law Olmsted. There are free guided tours of the Capitol, which include admission to the House and Senate galleries. Those who wish to visit the visitors' gallery in either wing without taking the tour may obtain passes from their Senators or Congressmen. Visitors may ride on the monorail subway that joins the House and Senate wings of the Capitol with the Congressional office buildings.

Washington Monument

Construction of this magnificent Washington, D.C., monument, which draws some two million visitors a year, took nearly a century of planning, building, and controversy. Provision for a large equestrian statue of George Washington was made in the original city plan, but the project was soon dropped. After Washington's death it was taken up again, and a number of false starts and changes of design were made. Finally, in 1848, work was begun on the monument that stands today. The design, by architect Robert Mills, then featured an ornate base. In 1854, however, political squabbling and a lack of money brought construction to a halt. Work was resumed in 1880, and the monument was completed in 1884 and opened to the public in 1888. The tapered shaft, faced with white marble and rising from walls 15 feet thick (4.6 m) at the base was modeled after the obelisks of ancient Egypt. The monument, one of the tallest masonry constructions in the world, stands just over 555 feet (169 m). Memorial stones from the 50 States, foreign countries, and organizations line the interior walls. The top, reached only by elevator, commands a panoramic view of the city.

The Liberty Bell

The Liberty Bell was cast in England in 1752 for the Pennsylvania Statehouse (now named Independence Hall) in Philadelphia. It was recast in Philadelphia in 1753. It is inscribed with the words, "Proclaim liberty throughout all the land unto all the inhabitants thereof" (Lev. 25:10). The bell was rung on July 8, 1776, for the first public reading of the Declaration of Independence. Hidden in Allentown during the British occupation of Philadelphia, it was replaced in Independence Hall in 1778. The bell cracked on July 8, 1835, while tolling the death of Chief Justice John Marshall. In 1976 the Liberty Bell was moved to a special exhibition building near Independence Hall.

Arlington National Cemetery

Arlington National Cemetery occupies 612 acres in Virginia on the Potomac River, directly opposite Washington. This land was part of the estate of John Parke Custis, Martha Washington's son, who built the mansion which later became the home of Robert E. Lee. In 1864, Arlington became a military cemetery. Over 184,000 persons, including many thousands of soldiers as well as hundreds of distinguished Americans, are buried there. Expansion of the cemetery began in 1966, using a 180-acre tract of land directly east of the present site.

In 1921, an Unknown American Soldier of World War I was buried in a temporary crypt in the cemetery; the completed Tomb was opened to the public without ceremony in 1932. Two additional Unknowns, one from World War II and one from the Korean War, were buried May 30, 1958. The inscription carved on the side of the Tomb of the Unknown Soldier reads:

HERE RESTS IN
HONORED GLORY
AN AMERICAN
SOLDIER
KNOWN BUT TO GOD

History of the Flag

Source: Encyclopaedia Britannica.

The first official American flag, the Continental or Grand Union flag, was displayed on Prospect Hill, Jan. 1, 1776, in the American lines besieging Boston. It had 13 alternate red and white stripes, with the British Union Jack in the upper left corner.

On June 14, 1777, the Continental Congress adopted the design for a new flag, which actually was the Continental flag with the red cross of St. George and the white cross of St. Andrew replaced on the blue field by 13 stars, one for each state. No rule was made as to the arrangement of the stars, and while they were usually shown in a circle, there were various other designs. It is uncertain when the new flag was first flown, but its first official announcement is believed to have been on Sept. 3, 1777.

The first public assertion that Betsy Ross made the first Stars and Stripes appeared in a paper read before the Historical Society of Pennsylvania on March 14, 1870, by William J. Canby, a grandson. However, Mr. Canby on later investigation found no official documents of any action by Congress on the flag before June 14, 1777. Betsy Ross's own story, according to her daughter, was that Washington, Robert Morris, and George Ross, as representatives of Congress, visited her in Philadelphia in June 1776, showing her a rough draft of the flag and asking her if she could make one. However, the only actual record of the manufacture of flags by Betsy Ross is a voucher in Harrisburg, Pa., for 14 pounds and some shillings for flags for the Pennsylvania navy.

On Jan. 13, 1794, Congress voted to add two stars and two stripes to the flag in recognition of the admission of Vermont and Kentucky to the Union. By 1818, there were 20 states in the Union, and as it was obvious that the flag would soon become unwieldly, Congress voted April 18 to return to the original 13 stripes and to indicate the admission of a new state simply by the addition of a star the following July 4. The 49th star, for Alaska, was added July 4, 1959; and the 50th star, for Hawaii, was added July 4, 1960.

The first Confederate flag, adopted in 1861 by the Confederate convention in Montgomery, Ala., was called the Stars and Bars; but because of its similarity in colors to the American flag, there was much confusion in the Battle of Bull Run. To remedy this situation, Gen. G. T. Beauregard suggested a battle flag, which was used by the Southern armies throughout the war. The flag consisted of a red field on which was placed a blue cross of St. Andrew separated from the field by a white fillet and adorned with 13[1] white stars for the Confederate states. In May 1863, at Richmond, an official flag was adopted by the Confederate Congress. This flag was white and twice as long as wide; the union, two-thirds the width of the flag, contained the battle flag designed for Gen. Beauregard. A broad transverse stripe of red was added Feb. 4, 1865, so that the flag might not be mistaken for a signal of truce.

1. 11 states formally seceded, and unofficial groups in Kentucky and Missouri adopted ordinances of secession. On this basis, these two states were admitted to the Confederacy, although the official state governments remained in the Union.

The Pledge of Allegiance[1] to the Flag

"I pledge allegiance to the Flag of the United States of America, and to the Republic for which it stands, one Nation under God,[2] indivisible, with liberty and justice for all."

1. The original pledge was published in the Sept. 8, 1892, issue of *The Youth's Companion* in Boston. For years, the authorship was in dispute between James B. Upham and Francis Bellamy of the magazine's staff. In 1939, after a study of the controversy, the United States Flag Association decided that authorship be credited to Bellamy. 2. The phrase "under God" was added to the pledge on June 14, 1954.

The Statue of Liberty

The Statue of Liberty ("Liberty Enlightening the World") is a 225-ton, steel-reinforced copper female figure, 152 ft in height, facing the ocean from Liberty[1] Island in New York Harbor. The right hand holds aloft a torch, and the left hand carries a tablet upon which is inscribed: "July IV MDCCLXXVI."

The statue was designed by Fredéric Auguste Bartholdi of Alsace as a gift to the United States from the people of France to memorialize the alliance of the two countries in the American Revolution and their abiding friendship. The French people contributed the $250,000 cost.

The 150-foot pedestal was designed by Richard M. Hunt and built by Gen. Charles P. Stone, both Americans. It contains steel underpinnings designed by Alexander Eiffel of France to support the statue. The $270,000 cost was borne by popular subscription in this country. President Grover Cleveland accepted the statue for the United States on Oct. 28, 1886.

On Sept. 26, 1972, President Richard M. Nixon dedicated the American Museum of Immigration, housed in structural additions to the base of the statue. Some 200 exhibits memorialize the flow of immigrants into the United States, including as many as 5,000 a day on nearby Ellis Island.

On a tablet inside the pedestal is engraved the following sonnet, written by Emma Lazarus (1849–1887):

1. Called Bedloe's Island prior to 1956.

The New Colossus

Not like the brazen giant of Greek fame,
With conquering limbs astride from land to land;
Here at our sea-washed, sunset gates shall stand
A mighty woman with a torch, whose flame
Is the imprisoned lightning, and her name
Mother of Exiles. From her beacon-hand
Glows world-wide welcome; her mild eyes command
The air-bridged harbor that twin cities frame.
"Keep, ancient lands, your storied pomp!" cries she
With silent lips. "Give me your tired, your poor,
Your huddled masses yearning to breathe free,
The wretched refuse of your teeming shore.
Send these, the homeless, tempest-tost to me,
I lift my lamp beside the golden door!"

Biographies of the Presidents

GEORGE WASHINGTON was born on Feb. 22, 1732 (Feb. 11, 1731/2, old style) in Westmoreland County, Va. While in his teens, he trained as a surveyor, and at the age of 20 he was appointed adjutant in the Virginia militia. For the next three years, he fought in the wars against the French and Indians, serving as Gen. Edward Braddock's aide in the disastrous campaign against Fort Duquesne. In 1759, he resigned from the militia, married Martha Dandridge Custis, a widow, and settled down as a gentleman farmer at Mount Vernon, Va.

As a militiaman, Washington had been exposed to the arrogance of the British officers, and his experience as a planter with British commercial restrictions increased his anti-British sentiment. He opposed the Stamp Act of 1765 and after 1770 became increasingly prominent in organizing resistance. A delegate to the Continental Congress, Washington was selected as commander in chief of the Continental Army and took command at Cambridge, Mass., on July 3, 1775.

Inadequately supported and sometimes covertly sabotaged by the Congress, in charge of troops who were inexperienced, badly equipped, and impatient of discipline, Washington conducted the war on the policy of avoiding major engagements with the British and wearing them down by harassing tactics. His able generalship, along with the French alliance and the growing weariness within Britain, brought the war to a conclusion with the surrender of Cornwallis at Yorktown, Va., on Oct. 19, 1781.

The chaotic years under the Articles of Confederation led Washington to return to public life in the hope of promoting the formation of a strong central government. He presided over the Constitutional Convention and yielded to the universal demand that he serve as first President. He was inaugurated on April 30, 1789, in New York, the first national capital. In office, he sought to unite the nation and establish the authority of the new government at home and abroad. Greatly distressed by the emergence of the Hamilton-Jefferson rivalry, Washington worked to maintain neutrality but actually sympathized more with Hamilton. Following his unanimous re-election in 1792, his second term was dominated by the Federalists. His Farewell Address on Sept. 17, 1796 (published but never delivered) rebuked party spirit and warned against "permanent alliances" with foreign powers.

He died at Mount Vernon on Dec. 14, 1799.

JOHN ADAMS was born on Oct. 30 (Oct. 19, old style), 1735, at Braintree (now Quincy), Mass. A Harvard graduate, he considered teaching and the ministry but finally turned to law and was admitted to the bar in 1758. Six years later, he married Abigail Smith. He opposed the Stamp Act, served as lawyer for patriots indicted by the British, and by the time of the Continental Congresses, was in the vanguard of the movement for independence. In 1778, he went to France as commissioner. Subsequently he helped negotiate the peace treaty with Britain, and in 1785 became envoy to London. Resigning in 1788, he was elected Vice President under Washington and was re-elected in 1792.

Though a Federalist, Adams did not get along with Hamilton, who sought to prevent his election to the presidency in 1796 and thereafter intrigued against his administration. In 1798, Adams's independent policy averted a war with France but completed the break with Hamilton and the right-wing Federalists; at the same time, the enactment of the Alien and Sedition Acts, directed against foreigners and against critics of the government, exasperated the Jeffersonian opposition. The split between Adams and Hamilton resulted in Jefferson's becoming the next President. Adams retired to his home in Quincy. He and Jefferson died on the same day, July 4, 1826, the 50th anniversary of the signing of the Declaration of Independence.

His *Defence of the Constitutions of Government of the United States* (1787) contains original and striking, if conservative, political ideas.

THOMAS JEFFERSON was born on April 13 (April 2, old style), 1743, at Shadwell in Goochland (now Albemarle) County, Va. A William and Mary graduate, he studied law, but from the start showed an interest in science and philosophy. His literary skill and political clarity brought him to the forefront of the revolutionary movement in Virginia. As delegate to the Continental Congress, he drafted the Declaration of Independence. In 1776, he entered the Virginia House of Delegates and initiated a comprehensive reform program for the abolition of feudal survivals in land tenure and the separation of church and state.

In 1779, he became governor, but constitutional limitations on his power, combined with his own lack of executive energy, caused an unsatisfactory administration, culminating in Jefferson's virtual abdication when the British invaded Virginia in 1781. He retired to his beautiful home at Monticello, Va., to his family. His wife, Martha Wayles Skelton, whom he married in 1772, died in 1782.

Jefferson's *Notes on Virginia* (1784–85) illustrate his many-faceted interests, his limitless intellectual curiosity, his deep faith in agrarian democracy. Sent to Congress in 1783, he helped lay down the decimal system and drafted basic reports on the organization of the western lands. In 1785 he was appointed minister to France, where the Anglo-Saxon liberalism he had drawn from John Locke, the British philosopher, was stimulated by contact with the thought that would soon ferment in the French Revolution. In 1789, Washington appointed him Secretary of State. While favoring the Constitution and a strengthened central government, Jefferson came to believe that Hamilton contemplated the establishment of a monarchy. Growing differences resulted in Jefferson's resignation on Dec. 31, 1793.

Elected vice president in 1796, Jefferson continued to serve as spiritual leader of the opposition to Federalism, particularly to the repressive Alien and Sedition Acts. He was elected President in 1801 by the House of Representatives as a result of Hamilton's decision to throw the Federalist votes to him rather than to Aaron Burr, who had tied him in electoral votes. He was the first President to be inaugurated in Washington, which he had helped to design.

The purchase of Louisiana from France in 1803, though in violation of Jefferson's earlier constitutional scruples, was the most notable act of his administration. Re-elected in 1804, with the Federalist Charles C. Pinckney opposing him, Jefferson tried desperately to keep the United States out of the Napoleonic Wars in Europe, employing to this end the unpopular embargo policy.

After his retirement to Monticello in 1809, he developed his interest in education, founding the University of Virginia and watching its development with never-flagging interest. He died at Monticello on July 4, 1826. Jefferson had an enormous variety of interests and skills, ranging from education and science to architecture and music.

JAMES MADISON was born in Port Conway, Va., on March 16, 1751 (March 5, 1750/1, old style). A Princeton graduate, he joined the struggle for independence on his return to Virginia in 1771. In the 1770s and 1780s he was active in state politics, where he championed the Jefferson reform program, and in the Continental Congress. Madison was influential in the Constitutional Convention as leader of the group favoring a strong central government and as recorder of the debates; and he subsequently wrote, in collaboration with Alexander Hamilton and John Jay, the *Federalist* papers to aid the campaign for the adoption of the Constitution.

Serving in the new Congress, Madison soon emerged as the leader in the House of the men who opposed Hamilton's financial program and his pro-British leanings in foreign policy. Retiring from Congress in 1797, he continued to be active in Virginia and drafted the Virginia Resolution protesting the Alien and Sedition Acts. His intimacy with Jefferson made him the natural choice for Secretary of State in 1801.

In 1809, Madison succeeded Jefferson as President, defeating Charles C. Pinckney. His attractive wife, Dolley Payne Todd, whom he married in 1794, brought a new social sparkle to the executive mansion. In the meantime, increasing tension with Britain culminated in the War of 1812—a war for which the United States was unprepared and for which Madison lacked the executive talent to clear out incompetence and mobilize the nation's energies. Madison was re-elected in 1812, running against the Federalist De Witt Clinton. In 1814, the British actually captured Washington and forced Madison to flee to Virginia.

Madison's domestic program capitulated to the Hamiltonian policies that he had resisted 20 years before and he now signed bills to establish a United States Bank and a higher tariff.

After his presidency, he remained in retirement in Virginia until his death on June 28, 1836.

JAMES MONROE was born on April 28, 1758, in Westmoreland County, Va. A William and Mary graduate, he served in the army during the first years of the Revolution and was wounded at Trenton. He then entered Virginia politics and later national politics under the sponsorship of Jefferson. In 1786, he married Elizabeth (Eliza) Kortright.

Fearing centralization, Monroe opposed the adoption of the Constitution and, as senator from Virginia, was highly critical of the Hamiltonian program. In 1794, he was appointed minister to France, where his ardent sympathies with the Revolution exceeded the wishes of the State Department. His troubled diplomatic career ended with his recall in 1796. From 1799 to 1802, he was governor of Virginia. In 1803, Jefferson sent him to France to help negotiate the Louisiana Purchase and for the next few years he was active in various negotiations on the Continent.

In 1808, Monroe flirted with the radical wing of the Republican Party, which opposed Madison's candidacy; but the presidential boom came to naught and, after a brief term as governor of Virginia in 1811, Monroe accepted Madison's offer to become Secretary of State. During the War of 1812, he vainly sought a field command and instead served as Secretary of War from September 1814 to March 1815.

Elected President in 1816 over the Federalist Rufus King, and re-elected without opposition in 1820, Monroe, the last of the Virginia dynasty, pursued the course of systematic tranquilization that won for his administrations the name "the era of good feeling." He continued Madison's surrender to the Hamiltonian domestic program, signed the Missouri Compromise, acquired Florida, and with the able assistance of his Secretary of State, John Quincy Adams, promulgated the Monroe Doctrine in 1823, declaring against foreign colonization or intervention in the Americas. He died in New York City on July 4, 1831, the third president to die on the anniversary of Independence.

JOHN QUINCY ADAMS was born on July 11, 1767, at Braintree (now Quincy), Mass., the son of John Adams, the second President. He spent his early years in Europe with his father, graduated from Harvard, and entered law practice. His anti-Jeffersonian newspaper articles won him political attention. In 1794, he became minister to the Netherlands, the first of several diplomatic posts that occupied him until his return to Boston in 1801. In 1797, he married Louisa Catherine Johnson.

In 1803, Adams was elected to the Senate, nominally as a Federalist, but his repeated displays of independence on such issues as the Louisiana Purchase and the embargo caused his party to demand his resignation and ostracize him socially. In 1809, Madison rewarded him for his support of Jefferson by appointing him minister to St. Petersburg. He helped negotiate the Treaty of Ghent in 1814, and in 1815 became minister to London. In 1817 Monroe appointed him Secretary of State where he served with great distinction, gaining Florida from Spain without hostilities and playing an equal part with Monroe in formulating the Monroe Doctrine.

When no presidential candidate received a majority of electoral votes in 1824, Adams, with the support of Henry Clay, was elected by the House in 1825 over Andrew Jackson, who had the original plurality. Adams had ambitious plans of government activity to foster internal improvements and promote the arts and sciences, but congressional obstructionism, combined with his own unwillingness or inability to play the role of a politician, resulted in little being accomplished. After being defeated for re-elected by Jackson in 1828, he successfully ran for the House of Representatives in 1830. There though nominally a Whig, he pursued as ever an independent course. He led the fight to force Congress to receive antislavery petitions and fathered the Smithsonian Institution.

Stricken on the floor of the House, he died on Feb. 23, 1848. His long and detailed *Diary* gives a unique picture of the personalities and politics of the times.

ANDREW JACKSON was born on March 15, 1767, in what is now generally agreed to be Waxhaw, S.C. After a turbulent boyhood as an orphan and a British prisoner, he moved west to Tennessee, where he soon qualified for law practice but found time for such frontier pleasures as horse racing, cockfighting, and dueling. His marriage to Rachel Donelson Robards in 1791 was complicated by subsequent legal uncertainties about the status of her divorce. During the 1790s, Jackson served in the Tennessee Constitutional Convention, the United States House of Representatives and Senate, and on the Tennessee Supreme Court.

After some years as a country gentleman, living at the Hermitage near Nashville, Jackson in 1812 was given command of Tennessee troops sent against the Creeks. He defeated the Indians at Horseshoe Bend in 1814; subsequently he became a major general and won the Battle of New Orleans over veteran British troops, though after the treaty of peace had been signed at Ghent. In 1818, Jackson invaded Florida, captured Pensacola, and hanged two Englishmen named Arbuthnot and Ambrister, creating an international incident. A presidential boom began for him in 1821, and to foster it, he returned to the Senate (1823–25). Though he won a plurality of electoral votes in 1824, he lost in the House when Clay threw his strength to Adams. Four years later, he easily defeated Adams.

As President, Jackson greatly expanded the power and prestige of the presidential office and carried through an unprecedented program of domestic reform, vetoing the bill to extend the United States Bank, moving toward a hard-money currency policy, and checking the program of federal internal improvements. He also vindicated federal authority against South Carolina with its doctrine of nullification and against France on the question of debts. The support given his policies by the workingmen of the East as well as by the farmers of the East, West, and South resulted in his triumphant re-election in 1832 over Clay.

After watching the inauguration of his handpicked successor, Martin Van Buren, Jackson retired to the Hermitage, where he maintained a lively interest in national affairs until his death on June 8, 1845.

MARTIN VAN BUREN was born on Dec. 5, 1782, at Kinderhook, N.Y. After graduating from the village school, he became a law clerk, entered practice in 1803, and soon became active in state politics as state senator and attorney general. In 1820, he was elected to the United States Senate. He threw the support of his efficient political organization, known as the Albany Regency, to William H. Crawford in 1824 and to Jackson in 1828. After leading the opposition to Adams's administration in the Senate, he served briefly as governor of New York (1828–29) and resigned to become Jackson's Secretary of State. He was soon on close personal terms with Jackson and played an important part in the Jacksonian program.

In 1832, Van Buren became vice president; in 1836, President. The Panic of 1837 overshadowed his term. He attributed it to the overexpansion of the credit and favored the establishment of an independent treasury as repository for the federal funds. In 1840, he established a 10-hour day on public works. Defeated by Harrison in 1840, he was the leading contender for the Democratic nomination in 1844 until he publicly opposed immediate annexation of Texas, and was subsequently beaten by the Southern delegations at the Baltimore convention. This incident increased his growing misgivings about the slave power.

After working behind the scenes among the antislavery Democrats, Van Buren joined in the movement that led to the Free-Soil Party and became its candidate for President in 1848. He subsequently returned to the Democratic Party while continuing to object to its pro-Southern policy. He died in Kinderhook on July 24, 1862. His *Autobiography* throws valuable sidelights on the political history of the times.

His wife, Hannah Hoes, whom he married in 1807, died in 1819.

WILLIAM HENRY HARRISON was born in Charles City County, Va., on Feb. 9, 1773. Joining the army in 1791, he was active in Indian fighting in the Northwest, became secretary of the Northwest Territory in 1798 and governor of Indiana in 1800. He married Anna Symmes in 1795. Growing discontent over white encroachments on Indian lands led to the formation of an Indian alliance under Tecumseh to resist further aggressions. In 1811, Harrison won a nominal victory over the Indians at Tippecanoe and in 1813 a more decisive one at the Battle of the Thames, where Tecumseh was killed.

After resigning from the army in 1814, Harrison had an obscure career in politics and diplomacy, ending up 20 years later as a county recorder in Ohio. Nominated for President in 1835 as a military hero whom the conservative politicians hoped to be able to control, he ran surprisingly well against Van Buren in 1836. Four years later, he defeated Van Buren but caught pneumonia and died in Washington on April 4, 1841, a month after his inauguration. Harrison was the first president to die in office.

JOHN TYLER was born in Charles City County, Va., on March 29, 1790. A William and Mary graduate, he entered law practice and politics, serving in the House of Representatives (1817–21), as governor of Virginia (1825–27), and as senator (1827–36). A strict constructionist, he supported Crawford in 1824 and Jackson in 1828, but broke with Jackson over his United States Bank policy and became a member of the Southern state-rights group that cooperated with the Whigs. In 1836, he resigned from the Senate rather than follow instructions from the Virginia legislature to vote for a resolution expunging censure of Jackson from the Senate record.

Elected vice president on the Whig ticket in 1840, Tyler succeeded to the presidency on Harrison's death. His strict-constructionist views soon caused a split with the Henry Clay wing of the Whig party and a stalemate on domestic questions. Tyler's more considerable achievements were his support of the Webster-Ashburton Treaty with Britain and his success in bringing about the annexation of Texas.

After his presidency he lived in retirement in Virginia until the outbreak of the Civil War, when he emerged briefly as chairman of a peace convention and then as delegate to the provisional Congress of the Confederacy. He died on Jan. 18, 1862. He married Letitia Christian in 1813 and, two years after her death in 1842, Julia Gardiner.

JAMES KNOX POLK was born in Mecklenburg County, N.C., on Nov. 2, 1795. A graduate of the University of North Carolina, he moved west to Tennessee, was admitted to the bar, and soon became prominent in state politics. In 1825, he was elected to the House of Representatives, where he opposed Adams and, after 1829, became Jackson's floor leader in the fight against the Bank. In 1835, he became Speaker of the House. Four years later, he was elected governor of Tennessee, but was beaten in tries for re-election in 1841 and 1843.

The supporters of Van Buren for the Democratic

nomination in 1844 counted on Polk as his running mate; but, when Van Buren's stand on Texas alienated Southern support, the convention swung to Polk on the ninth ballot. He was elected over Henry Clay, the Whig candidate. Rapidly disillusioning those who thought that he would not run his own administration, Polk proceeded steadily and precisely to achieve four major objectives—the acquisition of California, the settlement of the Oregon question, the reduction of the tariff, and the establishment of the independent treasury. He also enlarged the Monroe Doctrine to exclude all non-American intervention in American affairs, whether forcible or not, and he forced Mexico into a war that he waged to a successful conclusion.

His wife, Sarah Childress, whom he married in 1824, was a woman of charm and ability. Polk died in Nashville, Tenn., on June 15, 1849.

ZACHARY TAYLOR was born at Montebello, Orange County, Va., on Nov. 24, 1784. Embarking on a military career in 1808, Taylor fought in the War of 1812, the Black Hawk War, and the Seminole War, meanwhile holding garrison jobs on the frontier or desk jobs in Washington. A brigadier general as a result of his victory over the Seminoles at Lake Okeechobee (1837), Taylor held a succession of Southwestern commands and in 1846 established a base on the Rio Grande, where his forces engaged in hostilities that precipitated the war with Mexico. He captured Monterrey in September 1846 and, disregarding Polk's orders to stay on the defensive, defeated Santa Anna at Buena Vista in February 1847, ending the war in the northern provinces.

Though Taylor had never cast a vote for president, his party affiliations were Whiggish and his availability was increased by his difficulties with Polk. He was elected president over the Democrat Lewis Cass. During the revival of the slavery controversy, which was to result in the Compromise of 1850, Taylor began to take an increasingly firm stand against appeasing the South; but he died in Washington on July 9, 1850, during the fight over the Compromise. He married Margaret Mackall Smith in 1810. His bluff and simple soldierly qualities won him the name Old Rough and Ready.

MILLARD FILLMORE was born at Locke, Cayuga County, N.Y., on Jan. 7, 1800. A lawyer, he entered politics with the Anti-Masonic Party under the sponsorship of Thurlow Weed, editor and party boss, and subsequently followed Weed into the Whig Party. He served in the House of Representatives (1833–35 and 1837–43) and played a leading role in writing the tariff of 1842. Defeated for governor of New York in 1844, he became State comptroller in 1848, was put on the Whig ticket with Taylor as a concession to the Clay wing of the party, and became president upon Taylor's death in 1850.

As president, Fillmore broke with Weed and William H. Seward and associated himself with the pro-Southern Whigs, supporting the Compromise of 1850. Defeated for the Whig nomination in 1852, he ran for president in 1856 as candidate of the American, or Know-Nothing Party, which sought to unite the country against foreigners in the alleged hope of diverting it from the explosive slavery issue. Fillmore opposed Lincoln during the Civil War. He died in Buffalo on March 8, 1874.

He was married in 1826 to Abigail Powers, who died in 1853, and in 1858 to Caroline Carmichael McIntosh.

FRANKLIN PIERCE was born at Hillsboro, N.H., on Nov. 23, 1804. A Bowdoin graduate, lawyer, and Jacksonian Democrat, he won rapid political advancement in the party, in part because of the prestige of his father, Gov. Benjamin Pierce. By 1831 he was Speaker of the New Hampshire House of Representatives; from 1833 to 1837, he served in the federal House and from 1837 to 1842 in the Senate. His wife, Jane Means Appleton, whom he married in 1834, disliked Washington and the somewhat dissipated life led by Pierce; in 1842 Pierce resigned from the Senate and began a successful law practice in Concord, N.H. During the Mexican War, he was a brigadier general.

Thereafter Pierce continued to oppose antislavery tendencies within the Democratic Party. As a result, he was the Southern choice to break the deadlock at the Democratic convention of 1852 and was nominated on the 49th ballot. In the election, Pierce overwhelmed Gen. Winfield Scott, the Whig candidate.

As president, Pierce followed a course of appeasing the South at home and of playing with schemes of territorial expansion abroad. The failure of his foreign and domestic policies prevented his renomination; and he died in Concord on Oct. 8, 1869, in relative obscurity.

JAMES BUCHANAN was born near Mercersburg, Pa., on April 23, 1791. A Dickinson graduate and a lawyer, he entered Pennsylvania politics as a Federalist. With the disappearance of the Federalist Party, he became a Jacksonian Democrat. He served with ability in the House (1821–31), as minister to St. Petersburg (1832–33), and in the Senate (1834–45), and in 1845 became Polk's Secretary of State. In 1853, Pierce appointed Buchanan minister to Britain, where he participated with other American diplomats in Europe in drafting the expansionist Ostend Manifesto.

He was elected president in 1856, defeating John C. Frémont, the Republican candidate, and former President Millard Fillmore of the American Party. The growing crisis over slavery presented Buchanan with problems he lacked the will to tackle. His appeasement of the South alienated the Stephen Douglas wing of the Democratic Party without reducing Southern militancy on slavery issues. While denying the right of secession, Buchanan also denied that the federal government could do anything about it. He supported the administration during the Civil War and died in Lancaster, Pa., on June 1, 1868.

The only president to remain a bachelor throughout his term, Buchanan used his charming niece, Harriet Lane, as White House hostess.

ABRAHAM LINCOLN was born in Hardin (now Larue) County, Ky., on Feb. 12, 1809. His family moved to Indiana and then to Illinois, and Lincoln gained what education he could along the way. While reading law, he worked in a store, managed a mill, surveyed, and split rails. In 1834, he went to the Illinois legislature as a Whig and became the party's floor leader. For the next 20 years he practiced law in Springfield, except for a single term (1847–49) in Congress, where he denounced the Mexican War. In 1855, he was a candidate for senator and the next year he joined the new Republican Party.

A leading but unsuccessful candidate for the vice-presidential nomination with Frémont, Lincoln gained national attention in 1858 when, as

Republican candidate for senator from Illinois, he engaged in a series of debates with Stephen A. Douglas, the Democratic candidate. He lost the election, but continued to prepare the way for the 1860 Republican convention and was rewarded with the presidential nomination on the third ballot. He won the election over three opponents.

From the start, Lincoln made clear that, unlike Buchanan, he believed the national government had the power to crush the rebellion. Not an abolitionist, he held the slavery issue subordinate to that of preserving the Union, but soon perceived that the war could not be brought to a successful conclusion without freeing the slaves. His administration was hampered by the incompetence of many Union generals, the inexperience of the troops, and the harassing political tactics both of the Republican Radicals, who favored a hard policy toward the South, and the Democratic Copperheads, who desired a negotiated peace. The Gettysburg Address of Nov. 19, 1863, marks the high point in the record of American eloquence. Lincoln's long search for a winning combination finally brought Generals Ulysses S. Grant and William T. Sherman to the top; and their series of victories in 1864 dispelled the mutterings from both Radicals and Peace Democrats that at one time seemed to threaten Lincoln's re-election. He was re-elected in 1864, defeating Gen. George B. McClellan, the Democratic candidate. His inaugural address urged leniency toward the South: "With malice toward none, with charity for all . . . let us strive on to finish the work we are in; to bind up the nation's wounds . . . " This policy aroused growing opposition on the part of the Republican Radicals, but before the matter could be put to the test, Lincoln was shot by the actor John Wilkes Booth at Ford's Theater, Washington, on April 14, 1865. He died the next morning.

Lincoln's marriage to Mary Todd in 1842 was often unhappy and turbulent, in part because of his wife's pronounced instability.

ANDREW JOHNSON was born at Raleigh, N.C., on Dec. 29, 1808. Self-educated, he became a tailor in Greeneville, Tenn., but soon went into politics, where he rose steadily. He served in the House of Representatives (1843–54), as governor of Tennessee (1853–57), and as a senator (1857–62). Politically he was a Jacksonian Democrat and his specialty was the fight for a more equitable land policy. Alone among the Southern Senators, he stood by the Union during the Civil War. In 1862, he became war governor of Tennessee and carried out a thankless and difficult job with great courage. Johnson became Lincoln's running mate in 1864 as a result of an attempt to give the ticket a nonpartisan and nonsectional character. Succeeding to the presidency on Lincoln's death, Johnson sought to carry out Lincoln's policy, but without his political skill. The result was a hopeless conflict with the Radical Republicans who dominated Congress, passed measures over Johnson's vetoes, and attempted to limit the power of the executive concerning appointments and removals. The conflict culminated with Johnson's impeachment for attempting to remove his disloyal Secretary of War in defiance of the Tenure of Office Act which required senatorial concurrence for such dismissals. The opposition failed by one vote to get the two thirds necessary for conviction.

After his presidency, Johnson maintained an interest in politics and in 1875 was again elected to the Senate. He died near Carter Station, Tenn., on July 31, 1875. He married Eliza McCardle in 1827.

ULYSSES SIMPSON GRANT was born (as Hiram Ulysses Grant) at Point Pleasant, Ohio, on April 27, 1822. He graduated from West Point in 1843 and served without particular distinction in the Mexican War. In 1848 he married Julia Dent. He resigned from the army in 1854, after warnings from his commanding officer about his drinking habits, and for the next six years held a wide variety of jobs in the Middle West. With the outbreak of the Civil War, he sought a command and soon, to his surprise, was made a brigadier general. His continuing successes in the western theaters, culminating in the capture of Vicksburg, Miss., in 1863, brought him national fame and soon the command of all the Union armies. Grant's dogged, implacable policy of concentrating on dividing and destroying the Confederate armies brought the war to an end in 1865. The next year, he was made full general.

In 1868, as Republican candidate for president, Grant was elected over the Democrat, Horatio Seymour. From the start, Grant showed his unfitness for the office. His Cabinet was weak, his domestic policy was confused, many of his intimate associates were corrupt. The notable achievement in foreign affairs was the settlement of controversies with Great Britain in the Treaty of London (1871), negotiated by his able Secretary of State, Hamilton Fish.

Running for re-election in 1872, he defeated Horace Greeley, the Democratic and Liberal Republican candidate. The Panic of 1873 graft scandals close to the presidency created difficulties for his second term.

After retiring from office, Grant toured Europe for two years and returned in time to accede to a third-term boom, but was beaten in the convention of 1880. Illness and bad business judgment darkened his last years, but he worked steadily at the *Personal Memoirs,* which were to be so successful when published after his death at Mount McGregor, near Saratoga, N.Y., on July 23, 1885.

RUTHERFORD BIRCHARD HAYES was born in Delaware, Ohio, on Oct. 4, 1822. A graduate of Kenyon College and the Harvard Law School, he practiced law in Lower Sandusky (now Fremont) and then in Cincinnati. In 1852 he married Lucy Webb. A Whig, he joined the Republican party in 1855. During the Civil War he rose to major general. He served in the House of Representatives from 1865 to 1867 and then confirmed a reputation for honesty and efficiency in two terms as Governor of Ohio (1868–72). His election to a third term in 1875 made him the logical candidate for those Republicans who wished to stop James G. Blaine in 1876, and he was nominated.

The result of the election was in doubt for some time and hinged upon disputed returns from South Carolina, Louisiana, Florida, and Oregon. Samuel J. Tilden, the Democrat, had the larger popular vote but was adjudged by the strictly partisan decisions of the Electoral Commission to have one fewer electoral vote, 185 to 184. The national acceptance of this result was due in part to the general understanding that Hayes would pursue a conciliatory policy toward the South. He withdrew the troops from the South, took a conservative position on financial and labor issues, and urged civil service reform.

Hayes served only one term by his own wish and

spent the rest of his life in various humanitarian endeavors. He died in Fremont on Jan. 17, 1893.

JAMES ABRAM GARFIELD, the last president to be born in a log cabin, was born in Cuyahoga County, Ohio, on Nov. 19, 1831. A Williams graduate, he taught school for a time and entered Republican politics in Ohio. In 1858, he married Lucretia Rudolph. During the Civil War, he had a promising career, rising to major general of volunteers; but he resigned in 1863, having been elected to the House of Representatives, where he served until 1880. His oratorical and parliamentary abilities soon made him the leading Republican in the House, though his record was marred by his unorthodox acceptance of a fee in the DeGolyer paving contract case and by suspicions of his complicity in the Crédit Mobilier scandal.

In 1880, Garfield was elected to the Senate, but instead became the presidential candidate on the 36th ballot as a result of a deadlock in the Republican convention. In the election, he defeated Gen. Winfield Scott Hancock, the Democratic candidate. Garfield's administration was barely under way when he was shot by Charles J. Guiteau, a disappointed office seeker, in Washington on July 2, 1881. He died in Elberon, N.J., on Sept. 19.

CHESTER ALAN ARTHUR was born at Fairfield, Vt., on Oct. 5, 1830. A graduate of Union College, he became a successful New York lawyer. In 1859, he married Ellen Herndon. During the Civil War, he held administrative jobs in the Republican state administration and in 1871 was appointed collector of the Port of New York by Grant. This post gave him control over considerable patronage. Though not personally corrupt, Arthur managed his power in the interests of the New York machine so openly that President Hayes in 1877 called for an investigation and the next year Arthur was suspended.

In 1880 Arthur was nominated for vice president in the hope of conciliating the followers of Grant and the powerful New York machine. As president upon Garfield's death, Arthur, stepping out of his familiar role as spoilsman, backed civil service reform, reorganized the Cabinet, and prosecuted political associates accused of post office graft. Losing machine support and failing to gain the reformers, he was not nominated for a full term in 1884. He died in New York City on Nov. 18, 1886.

STEPHEN GROVER CLEVELAND was born at Caldwell, N.J., on March 18, 1837. He was admitted to the bar in Buffalo, N.Y., in 1859 and lived there as a lawyer, with occasional incursions into Democratic politics, for more than 20 years. He did not participate in the Civil War. As mayor of Buffalo in 1881, he carried through a reform program so ably that the Democrats ran him successfully for governor in 1882. In 1884 he won the Democratic nomination for President. The campaign contrasted Cleveland's spotless public career with the uncertain record of James G. Blaine, the Republican candidate, and Cleveland received enough Mugwump (independent Republican) support to win.

As president, Cleveland pushed civil service reform, opposed the pension grab and attacked the high tariff rates. While in the White House, he married Frances Folsom in 1886. Renominated in 1888, Cleveland was defeated by Benjamin Harrison, polling more popular but fewer electoral votes. In 1892, he was elected over Harrison. When the Panic of 1893 burst upon the country, Cleveland's attempts to solve it by sound-money measures alienated the free-silver wing of the party, while his tariff policy alienated the protectionists. In 1894, he sent troops to break the Pullman strike. In foreign affairs, his firmness caused Great Britain to back down in the Venezuela border dispute.

In his last years Cleveland was an active and much-respected public figure. He died in Princeton, N.J., on June 24, 1908.

BENJAMIN HARRISON was born in North Bend, Ohio, on Aug. 20, 1833, the grandson of William Henry Harrison, the ninth president. A graduate of Miami University in Ohio, he took up the law in Indiana and became active in Republican politics. In 1853, he married Caroline Lavinia Scott. During the Civil War, he rose to brigadier general. A sound-money Republican, he was elected senator from Indiana in 1880. In 1888, he received the Republican nomination for President on the eighth ballot. Though behind on the popular vote, he won over Grover Cleveland in the electoral college by 233 to 168.

As President, Harrison failed to please either the bosses or the reform element in the party. In foreign affairs he backed Secretary of State Blaine, whose policy foreshadowed later American imperialism. Harrison was renominated in 1892 but lost to Cleveland. His wife died in the White House in 1892 and Harrison married her niece, Mary Scott (Lord) Dimmick, in 1896. After his presidency, he resumed law practice. He died in Indianapolis on March 13, 1901.

WILLIAM McKINLEY was born in Niles, Ohio, on Jan. 29, 1843. He taught school, then served in the Civil War, rising from the ranks to become a major. Subsequently he opened a law office in Canton, Ohio, and in 1871 married Ida Saxton. Elected to Congress in 1876, he served there until 1891, except for 1883–85. His faithful advocacy of business interests culminated in the passage of the highly protective McKinley Tariff of 1890. With the support of Mark Hanna, a shrewd Cleveland businessman interested in safeguarding tariff protection, McKinley became governor of Ohio in 1892 and Republican presidential candidate in 1896. The business community, alarmed by the progressivism of William Jennings Bryan, the Democratic candidate, spent considerable money to assure McKinley's victory.

The chief event of McKinley's administration was the war with Spain, which resulted in our acquisition of the Philippines and other islands. With imperialism an issue, McKinley defeated Bryan again in 1900. On Sept. 6, 1901, he was shot at Buffalo, N.Y., by Leon F. Czolgosz, an anarchist, and he died there eight days later.

THEODORE ROOSEVELT was born in New York City on Oct. 27, 1858. A Harvard graduate, he was early interested in ranching, in politics, and in writing picturesque historical narratives. He was a Republican member of the New York Assembly in 1882–84, an unsuccessful candidate for mayor of New York in 1886, a U.S. Civil Service Commissioner under Benjamin Harrison, Police Commissioner of New York City in 1895, and Assistant Secretary of the Navy under McKinley in 1897. He resigned in 1898 to help organize a volunteer regiment, the Rough Riders, and take a more direct part in the war with Spain. He was elected governor of New York in 1898 and vice president in 1900, in spite of lack of enthusiasm on the part of the bosses.

Assuming the presidency of the assassinated McKinley in 1901, Roosevelt embarked on a wide-ranging program of government reform and conservation of natural resources. He ordered antitrust suits against several large corporations, threatened to intervene in the anthracite coal strike of 1902, which prompted the operators to accept arbitration, and, in general, championed the rights of the "little man" and fought the "malefactors of great wealth." He was also responsible for such progressive legislation as the Elkins Act of 1901, which outlawed freight rebates by railroads; the bill establishing the Department of Commerce and Labor; the Hepburn Act, which gave the I.C.C. greater control over the railroads; the Meat Inspection Act; and the Pure Food and Drug Act.

In foreign affairs, Roosevelt pursued a strong policy, permitting the instigation of a revolt in Panama to dispose of Colombian objections to the Panama Canal and helping to maintain the balance of power in the East by bringing the Russo-Japanese War to an end, for which he won the Nobel Peace Prize, the first American to achieve a Nobel prize in any category. In 1904, he decisively defeated Alton B. Parker, his conservative Democratic opponent.

Roosevelt's increasing coldness toward his successor, William Howard Taft, led him to overlook his earlier disclaimer of third-term ambitions and to re-enter politics. Defeated by the machine in the Republican convention of 1912, he organized the Progressive Party (Bull Moose) and polled more votes than Taft, though the split brought about the election of Woodrow Wilson. From 1915 on, Roosevelt strongly favored intervention in the European war. He became deeply embittered at Wilson's refusal to allow him to raise a volunteer division. He died in Oyster Bay, N.Y., on Jan. 6, 1919. He was married twice: in 1880 to Alice Hathaway Lee, who died in 1884, and in 1886 to Edith Kermit Carow.

WILLIAM HOWARD TAFT was born in Cincinnati on Sept. 15, 1857. A Yale graduate, he entered Ohio Republican politics in the 1880s. In 1886 he married Helen Herron. From 1887 to 1890, he served on the Ohio Superior Court; 1890–92, as solicitor general of the United States; 1892–1900, on the federal circuit court. In 1900 McKinley appointed him president of the Philippine Commission and in 1901 governor general. Taft had great success in pacifying the Filipinos, solving the problem of the church lands, improving economic conditions, and establishing limited self-government. His period as Secretary of War (1904–08) further demonstrated his capacity as administrator and conciliator, and he was Roosevelt's hand-picked successor in 1908. In the election, he polled 321 electoral votes to 162 for William Jennings Bryan, who was running for the presidency for the third time.

Though he carried on many of Roosevelt's policies, Taft got into increasing trouble with the progressive wing of the party and displayed mounting irritability and indecision. After his defeat in 1912, he became professor of constitutional law at Yale. In 1921 he was appointed Chief Justice of the United States. He died in Washington on March 8, 1930.

THOMAS WOODROW WILSON was born in Staunton, Va., on Dec. 28, 1856. A Princeton graduate, he turned from law practice to post-graduate work in political science at Johns Hopkins University, receiving his Ph.D. in 1886. He taught at Bryn Mawr, Wesleyan, and Princeton, and in 1902 was made president of Princeton. After an unsuccessful attempt to democratize the social life of the university, he welcomed an invitation in 1910 to be the Democratic gubernatorial candidate in New Jersey, and was elected. His success in fighting the machine and putting through a reform program attracted national attention.

In 1912, at the Democratic convention in Baltimore, Wilson won the nomination on the 46th ballot and went on to defeat Roosevelt and Taft in the election. Wilson proceeded under the standard of the New Freedom to enact a program of domestic reform, including the Federal Reserve Act, the Clayton Antitrust Act, the establishment of the Federal Trade Commission, and other measures designed to restore competition in the face of the great monopolies. In foreign affairs, while privately sympathetic with the Allies, he strove to maintain neutrality in the European war and warned both sides against encroachments on American interests.

Re-elected in 1916 as a peace candidate, he tried to mediate between the warring nations; but when the Germans resumed unrestricted submarine warfare in 1917, Wilson brought the United States into what he now believed was a war to make the world safe for democracy. He supplied the classic formulations of Allied war aims and the armistice of Nov. 11, 1918 was negotiated on the basis of Wilson's Fourteen Points. In 1919 he strove at Versailles to lay the foundations for enduring peace. He accepted the imperfections of the Versailles Treaty in the expectation that they could be remedied by action within the League of Nations. He probably could have secured ratification of the treaty by the Senate if he had adopted a more conciliatory attitude toward the mild reservationists; but his insistence on all or nothing eventually caused the diehard isolationists and diehard Wilsonites to unite in rejecting a compromise.

In September 1919 Wilson suffered a paralytic stroke that limited his activity. After leaving the presidency he lived on in retirement in Washington, dying on Feb. 3, 1924. He was married twice—in 1885 to Ellen Louise Axson, who died in 1914, and in 1915 to Edith Bolling Galt.

WARREN GAMALIEL HARDING was born in Morrow County, Ohio, on Nov. 2, 1865. After attending Ohio Central College, Harding became interested in journalism and in 1884 bought the *Marion* (Ohio) *Star*. In 1891 he married a wealthy widow, Florence Kling De Wolfe. As his paper prospered, he entered Republican politics, serving as state senator (1899–1903) and as lieutenant governor (1904–06). In 1910, he was defeated for governor, but in 1914 was elected to the Senate. His reputation as an orator made him the keynoter at the 1916 Republican convention.

When the 1920 convention was deadlocked between Leonard Wood and Frank O. Lowden, Harding became the dark-horse nominee on his solemn affirmation that there was no reason in his past that he should not be. Straddling the League question, Harding was easily elected over James M. Cox, his Democratic opponent. His Cabinet contained some able men, but also some manifestly unfit for public office. Harding's own intimates were mediocre when they were not corrupt. The impending disclosure of the Teapot Dome scandal in the Interior Department and illegal practices in the Justice Department and Veterans' Bureau, as well as political setbacks, profoundly worried him. On his return from Alaska in 1923, he died unexpectedly in San Francisco on Aug. 2.

JOHN CALVIN COOLIDGE was born in Plymouth, Vt., on July 4, 1872. An Amherst graduate, he went into law practice at Northampton, Mass., in 1897. He married Grace Anna Goodhue in 1905. He entered Republican state politics, becoming successively mayor of Northampton, state senator, lieutenant governor and, in 1919, governor. His use of the state militia to end the Boston police strike in 1919 won him a somewhat undeserved reputation for decisive action and brought him the Republican vice-presidential nomination in 1920. After Harding's death Coolidge handled the Washington scandals with care and finally managed to save the Republican Party from public blame for the widespread corruption.

In 1924, Coolidge was elected without difficulty, defeating the Democrat, John W. Davis, and Robert M. La Follette running on the Progressive ticket. His second term, like his first, was characterized by a general satisfaction with the existing economic order. He stated that he did not choose to run in 1928.

After his presidency, Coolidge lived quietly in Northampton, writing an unilluminating *Autobiography* and conducting a syndicated column. He died there on Jan. 5, 1933.

HERBERT CLARK HOOVER was born at West Branch, Iowa, on Aug. 10, 1874, the first president to be born west of the Mississippi. A Stanford graduate, he worked from 1895 to 1913 as a mining engineer and consultant throughout the world. In 1899, he married Lou Henry. During World War I, he served with distinction as chairman of the American Relief Committee in London, as chairman of the Commission for Relief in Belgium, and as U.S. Food Administrator. His political affiliations were still too indeterminate for him to be mentioned as a possibility for either the Republican or Democratic nomination in 1920, but after the election he served Harding and Coolidge as Secretary of Commerce.

In the election of 1928, Hoover overwhelmed Gov. Alfred E. Smith of New York, the Democratic candidate and the first Roman Catholic to run for the presidency. He soon faced the worst depression in the nation's history, but his attacks upon it were hampered by his devotion to the theory that the forces that brought the crisis would soon bring the revival and then by his belief that there were too many areas in which the federal government had no power to act. In a succession of vetoes, he struck down measures proposing a national employment system or national relief, he reduced income tax rates, and only at the end of his term did he yield to popular pressure and set up agencies such as the Reconstruction Finance Corporation to make emergency loans to assist business.

After his 1932 defeat, Hoover returned to private business. In 1946, President Truman charged him with various world food missions; and from 1947 to 1949 and 1953 to 1955, he was head of the Commission on Organization of the Executive Branch of the Government. He died in New York City on Oct. 20, 1964.

FRANKLIN DELANO ROOSEVELT was born in Hyde Park, N.Y., on Jan. 30, 1882. A Harvard graduate, he attended Columbia Law School and was admitted to the New York bar. In 1910, he was elected to the New York State Senate as a Democrat. Reelected in 1912, he was appointed Assistant Secretary of the Navy by Woodrow Wilson the next year. In 1920, his radiant personality and his war service resulted in his nomination for vice president as James M. Cox's running mate. After his defeat, he returned to law practice in New York. In August 1921, Roosevelt was stricken with infantile paralysis while on vacation at Campobello, New Brunswick. After a long and gallant fight, he recovered partial use of his legs. In 1924 and 1928, he led the fight at the Democratic national conventions for the nomination of Gov. Alfred E. Smith of New York, and in 1928 Roosevelt was himself induced to run for governor of New York. He was elected, and was re-elected in 1930.

In 1932, Roosevelt received the Democratic nomination for president and immediately launched a campaign that brought new spirit to a weary and discouraged nation. He defeated Hoover by a wide margin. His first term was characterized by an unfolding of the New Deal program, with greater benefits for labor, the farmers, and the unemployed, and the progressive estrangement of most of the business community.

At an early stage, Roosevelt became aware of the menace to world peace posed by totalitarian fascism, and from 1937 on he tried to focus public attention on the trend of events in Europe and Asia. As a result, he was widely denounced as a warmonger. He was re-elected in 1936 over Gov. Alfred M. Landon of Kansas by the overwhelming electoral margin of 523 to 8, and the gathering international crisis prompted him to run for an unprecedented third term in 1940. He defeated Wendell L. Willkie.

Roosevelt's program to bring maximum aid to Britain and, after June 1941, to Russia was opposed, until the Japanese attack on Pearl Harbor restored national unity. During the war, Roosevelt shelved the New Deal in the interests of conciliating the business community, both in order to get full production during the war and to prepare the way for a united acceptance of the peace settlements after the war. A series of conferences with Winston Churchill and Joseph Stalin laid down the bases for the postwar world. In 1944 he was elected to a fourth term, running against Gov. Thomas E. Dewey of New York.

On April 12, 1945, Roosevelt died of a cerebral hemorrhage at Warm Springs, Ga., shortly after his return from the Yalta Conference. His wife, Anna Eleanor Roosevelt, whom he married in 1905, was a woman of great ability who made significant contributions to her husband's policies.

HARRY S. TRUMAN was born on a farm near Lamar, Mo., on May 8, 1884. During World War I, he served in France as a captain with the 129th Field Artillery. He married Bess Wallace in 1919. After engaging briefly and unsuccessfully in the haberdashery business in Kansas City, Mo., Truman entered local politics. Under the sponsorship of Thomas Pendergast, Democratic boss of Missouri, he held a number of local offices, preserving his personal honesty in the midst of a notoriously corrupt political machine. In 1934, he was elected to the Senate and was re-elected in 1940. During his first term he was a loyal but quiet supporter of the New Deal, but in his second term, an appointment as head of a Senate committee to investigate war production brought out his special qualities of honesty, common sense, and hard work, and he won widespread respect.

Elected vice president in 1944, Truman became president upon Roosevelt's sudden death in April 1945 and was immediately faced with the problems of winding down the war against the Axis and preparing the nation for postwar adjustment.

The years 1947–48 were distinguished by civil-rights proposals, the Truman Doctrine to contain the spread of Communism, and the Marshall Plan to aid in the economic reconstruction of war-ravaged nations. Truman's general record, highlighted by a vigorous Fair Deal campaign, brought about his unexpected election in 1948 over the heavily favored Thomas E. Dewey.

Truman's second term was primarily concerned with the Cold War with the Soviet Union, the implementing of the North Atlantic Pact, the United Nations police action in Korea, and the vast rearmament program with its accompanying problems of economic stabilization.

On March 29, 1952, Truman announced that he would not run again for the presidency. After leaving the White House, he returned to his home in Independence, Mo., to write his memoirs. He further busied himself with the Harry S. Truman Library there. He died in Kansas City, Mo., on Dec. 26, 1972.

DWIGHT DAVID EISENHOWER was born in Denison, Tex., on Oct. 14, 1890. His ancestors lived in Germany and emigrated to America, settling in Pennsylvania, early in the 18th century. His father, David, had a general store in Hope, Kan., which failed. After a brief time in Texas, the family moved to Abilene, Kan.

After graduating from Abilene High School in 1909, Eisenhower did odd jobs for almost two years. He won an appointment to the Naval Academy at Annapolis, but was too old for admittance. Then he received an appointment in 1910 to West Point, from which he graduated as a second lieutenant in 1915.

He did not see service in World War I, having been stationed at Fort Sam Houston, Tex. There he met Mamie Geneva Doud, whom he married in Denver on July 1, 1916, and by whom he had two sons: Doud Dwight (died in infancy) and John Sheldon Doud.

Eisenhower served in the Philippines from 1935 to 1939 with Gen. Douglas MacArthur. Afterward, Gen. George C. Marshall, the Army Chief of Staff, brought him into the War Department's General Staff and in 1942 placed him in command of the invasion of North Africa. In 1944, he was made Supreme Allied Commander for the invasion of Europe.

After the war, Eisenhower served as Army Chief of Staff from November 1945 until February 1948, when he was appointed president of Columbia University.

In December 1950, President Truman recalled Eisenhower to active duty to command the North Atlantic Treaty Organization forces in Europe. He held this post until the end of May 1952.

At the Republican convention of 1952 in Chicago, Eisenhower won the presidential nomination on the first ballot in a close race with Senator Robert A. Taft of Ohio. In the election, he defeated Gov. Adlai E. Stevenson of Illinois.

Through two terms, Eisenhower hewed to moderate domestic policies. He sought peace through Free World strength in an era of new nationalisms, nuclear missiles, and space exploration. He fostered alliances pledging the United States to resist Red aggression in Europe, Asia, and Latin America. The Eisenhower Doctrine of 1957 extended commitments to the Middle East.

At home, the popular president lacked Republican Congressional majorities after 1954, but he was re-elected in 1956 by 457 electoral votes to 73 for Stevenson.

While retaining most Fair Deal programs, he stressed "fiscal responsibility" in domestic affairs. A moderate in civil rights, he sent troops to Little Rock, Ark., to enforce court-ordered school integration.

With his wartime rank restored by Congress, Eisenhower returned to private life and the role of elder statesman, with his vigor hardly impaired by a heart attack, an ileitis operation, and a mild stroke suffered while in office. He died in Washington on March 28, 1969.

JOHN FITZGERALD KENNEDY was born in Brookline, Mass., on May 29, 1917. His father, Joseph P. Kennedy, was Ambassador to Great Britain from 1937 to 1940.

Kennedy was graduated from Harvard University in 1940 and joined the Navy the next year. He became skipper of a PT boat that was sunk in the Pacific by a Japanese destroyer. Although given up for lost, he swam to a safe island, towing an injured enlisted man.

After recovering from a war-aggravated spinal injury, Kennedy entered politics in 1946 and was elected to Congress. In 1952, he ran against Senator Henry Cabot Lodge, Jr., of Massachusetts, and won.

Kennedy was married on Sept. 12, 1953, to Jacqueline Lee Bouvier, by whom he had three children: Caroline, John Fitzgerald, Jr., and Patrick Bouvier (died in infancy).

In 1957 Kennedy won the Pulitzer Prize for a book he had written earlier, *Profiles in Courage*.

After strenuous primary battles, Kennedy won the Democratic presidential nomination on the first ballot at the 1960 Los Angeles convention. With a plurality of only 118,574 votes, he carried the election over Vice President Richard M. Nixon and became the first Roman Catholic president.

Kennedy brought to the White House the dynamic idea of a "New Frontier" approach in dealing with problems at home, abroad, and in the dimensions of space. Out of his leadership in his first few months in office came the 10-year Alliance for Progress to aid Latin America, the Peace Corps, and accelerated programs that brought the first Americans into orbit in the race in space.

Failure of the U.S.-supported Cuban invasion in April 1961 led to the entrenchment of the Communist-backed Castro regime, only 90 miles from United States soil. When it became known that Soviet offensive missiles were being installed in Cuba in 1962, Kennedy ordered a naval "quarantine" of the island and moved troops into position to eliminate this threat to U.S. security. The world seemed on the brink of a nuclear war until Soviet Premier Khrushchev ordered the removal of the missiles.

A sudden "thaw," or the appearance of one, in the cold war came with the agreement with the Soviet Union on a limited test-ban treaty signed in Moscow on Aug. 6, 1963.

In his domestic policies, Kennedy's proposals for medical care for the aged, expanded area redevelopment, and aid to education were defeated, but on minimum wage, trade legislation, and other measures he won important victories.

Widespread racial disorders and demonstrations led to Kennedy's proposing sweeping civil rights legislation. As his third year in office drew to a close, he also recommended an $11-billion tax cut to bolster the economy. Both measures were pending in Congress when Kennedy, looking forward to a second term, journeyed to Texas for a series of speeches.

While riding in a procession in Dallas on Nov. 22, 1963, he was shot to death by an assassin firing from an upper floor of a building. The alleged assassin, Lee Harvey Oswald, was killed two days later in the Dallas city jail by Jack Ruby, owner of a strip-tease place.

At 46 years of age, Kennedy became the fourth president to be assassinated and the eighth to die in office.

LYNDON BAINES JOHNSON was born in Stonewall, Tex., on Aug. 27, 1908. On both sides of his family he had a political heritage mingled with a Baptist background of preachers and teachers. Both his father and his paternal grandfather served in the Texas House of Representatives.

After his graduation from Southwest Texas State Teachers College, Johnson taught school for two years. He went to Washington in 1932 as secretary to Rep. Richard M. Kleberg. During this time, he married Claudia Alta Taylor, known as "Lady Bird." They had two children: Lynda Bird (Robb) and Luci Baines (Nugent).

In 1935, Johnson became Texas administrator for the National Youth Administration. Two years later, he was elected to Congress as an all-out supporter of Franklin D. Roosevelt, and served until 1949. He was the first member of Congress to enlist in the armed forces after the attack on Pearl Harbor. He served in the Navy in the Pacific and won a Silver Star.

Johnson was elected to the Senate in 1948 after he had captured the Democratic nomination by only 87 votes. He was 40 years old. He became the Senate Democratic leader in 1953. A heart attack in 1955 threatened to end his political career, but he recovered fully and resumed his duties.

At the height of his power as Senate leader, Johnson sought the Democratic nomination for president in 1960. When he lost to John F. Kennedy, he surprised even some of his closest associates by accepting second place on the ticket.

Johnson was riding in another car in the motorcade when Kennedy was assassinated in Dallas on Nov. 22, 1963. He took the oath of office in the presidential jet on the Dallas airfield.

With Johnson's insistent backing, Congress finally adopted a far-reaching civil-rights bill, a voting-rights bill, a Medicare program for the aged, and measures to improve education and conservation. Congress also began what Johnson described as "an all-out war" on poverty.

Amassing a record-breaking majority of nearly 16 million votes, Johnson was elected president in his own right in 1964, defeating Senator Barry Goldwater of Arizona.

The double tragedy of a war in Southeast Asia and urban riots at home marked Johnson's last two years in office. Faced with disunity in the nation and challenges within his own party, Johnson surprised the country on March 31, 1968, with the announcement that he would not be a candidate for re-election. He died of a heart attack suffered at his LBJ Ranch on Jan. 22, 1973.

RICHARD MILHOUS NIXON was born in Yorba Linda, Calif., on Jan. 9, 1913, to Midwestern-bred parents, Francis A. and Hannah Milhous Nixon, who raised their five sons as Quakers.

Nixon was a high school debater and was undergraduate president at Whittier College in California, where he was graduated in 1934. As a scholarship student at Duke University Law School in North Carolina, he graduated third in his class in 1937.

After five years as a lawyer, Nixon joined the Navy in August 1942. He was an air transport officer in the South Pacific and a legal officer stateside before his discharge in 1946 as a lieutenant commander.

Running for Congress in California as a Republican in 1946, Nixon defeated Rep. Jerry Voorhis. As a member of the House Un-American Activities Committee, he made a name as an investigator of Alger Hiss, a former high State Department official, who was later jailed for perjury. In 1950, Nixon defeated Rep. Helen Gahagan Douglas, a Democrat, for the Senate. He was criticized for portraying her as a Communist dupe.

Nixon's anti-Communism, his Western base, and his youth figured in his selection in 1952 to run for vice president on the ticket headed by Dwight D. Eisenhower. Demands for Nixon's withdrawal followed disclosure that California businessmen had paid some of his Senate office expenses. He televised rebuttal, known as "the Checkers speech" (named for a cocker spaniel given to the Nixons), brought him support from the public and from Eisenhower. The ticket won easily in 1952 and again in 1956.

Eisenhower gave Nixon substantive assignments, including missions to 56 countries. In Moscow in 1959, Nixon won acclaim for his defense of U.S. interests in an impromptu "kitchen debate" with Soviet Premier Nikita S. Khrushchev.

Nixon lost the 1960 race for the presidency to John F. Kennedy.

In 1962, Nixon failed in a bid for California's governorship and seemed to be finished as a national candidate. He became a Wall Street lawyer, but kept his old party ties and developed new ones through constant travels to speak for Republicans.

Nixon won the 1968 Republican presidential nomination after a shrewd primary campaign, then made Gov. Spiro T. Agnew of Maryland his surprise choice for vice president. In the election, they edged out the Democratic ticket headed by Vice President Hubert H. Humphrey by 510,314 votes out of 73,212,065 cast.

Committed to wind down the U.S. role in the Vietnamese War, Nixon pursued "Vietnamization"—training and equipping South Vietnamese to do their own fighting. American ground combat forces in Vietnam fell steadily from 540,000 when Nixon took office to none in 1973 when the military draft was ended. But there was heavy continuing use of U.S. air power.

Nixon improved relations with Moscow and reopened the long-closed door to mainland China with a good-will trip there in February 1972. In May of that year, he visited Moscow and signed agreements on arms limitation and trade expansion and approved plans for a joint U.S.-Soviet space mission in 1975.

Inflation was a campaign issue for Nixon, but he failed to master it as president. On Aug. 15, 1971, with unemployment edging up, Nixon abruptly announced a new economic policy: a 90-day wage-price freeze, stimulative tax cuts, a temporary 10% tariff, and spending cuts. A second phase, imposing guidelines on wage, price and rent boosts, was announced October 7.

The economy responded in time for the 1972 campaign, in which Nixon played up his foreign-policy achievements. Played down was the burglary on June 17, 1972, of Democratic national headquarters in the Watergate apartment complex in Washington. The Nixon-Agnew re-election campaign cost a record $60 million and swamped the Democratic ticket headed by Senator George McGovern of South Dakota with a plurality of 17,999,528 out of 77,718,554 votes. Only Massachusetts, with 14 electoral votes, and the District of Columbia, with 3, went for McGovern.

In January 1973, hints of a cover-up emerged at the trial of six men found guilty of the Watergate burglary. With a Senate investigation under way, Nixon announced on April 30 the resignations of his top aides, H. R. Haldeman and John D. Ehrlichman, and the dismissal of White House counsel John Dean III. Dean was the star witness at televised Senate hearings that exposed both a White House cover-up of Watergate and massive illegalities in Republican fund-raising in 1972.

The hearings also disclosed that Nixon had routinely tape-recorded his office meetings and telephone conversations.

On Oct. 10, 1973, Agnew resigned as vice president, then pleaded no-contest to a negotiated federal charge of evading income taxes on alleged bribes. Two days later, Nixon nominated the House minority leader, Rep. Gerald R. Ford of Michigan, as the new vice president. Congress confirmed Ford on Dec. 6, 1973.

In June 1974, Nixon visited Israel and four Arab nations. Then he met in Moscow with Soviet leader Leonid I. Brezhnev and reached preliminary nuclear arms limitation agreements.

But, in the month after his return, Watergate ended the Nixon regime. On July 24 the Supreme Court ordered Nixon to surrender subpoenaed tapes. On July 30, the Judiciary Committee referred three impeachment articles to the full membership. On August 5, Nixon bowed to the Supreme Court and released tapes showing he halted an FBI probe of the Watergate burglary six days after it occurred. It was in effect an admission of obstruction of justice, and impeachment appeared inevitable.

Nixon resigned on Aug. 9, 1974, the first president ever to do so. A month later, President Ford issued an unconditional pardon for any offenses Nixon might have committed as president, thus forestalling possible prosecution.

In 1940, Nixon married Thelma Catherine (Pat) Ryan. They had two daughters, Patricia (Tricia) Cox and Julie, who married Dwight David Eisenhower II, grandson of the former president.

GERALD RUDOLPH FORD was born in Omaha, Neb., on July 14, 1913, the only child of Leslie and Dorothy Gardner King. His parents were divorced in 1915. His mother moved to Grand Rapids, Mich., and married Gerald R. Ford. The boy was renamed for his stepfather.

Ford captained his high school football team in Grand Rapids, and a football scholarship took him to the University of Michigan, where he starred as varsity center before his graduation in 1935. A job as assistant football coach at Yale gave him an opportunity to attend Yale Law School, from which he graduated in the top third of his class in 1941.

He returned to Grand Rapids to practice law, but entered the Navy in April 1942. He saw wartime service in the Pacific on the light aircraft carrier *Monterey* and was a lieutenant commander when he returned to Grand Rapids early in 1946 to resume law practice and dabble in politics.

Ford was elected to Congress in 1948 for the first of his 13 terms in the House. He was soon assigned to the influential Appropriations Committee and rose to become the ranking Republican on the subcommittee on Defense Department appropriations and an expert in the field.

As a legislator, Ford described himself as "a moderate on domestic issues, a conservative in fiscal affairs, and a dyed-in-the-wool internationalist." He carried the ball for Pentagon appropriations, was a hawk on the war in Vietnam, and kept a low profile on civil-rights issues.

He was also dependable and hard-working and popular with his colleagues. In 1963, he was elected chairman of the House Republican Conference. He served in 1963–64 as a member of the Warren Commission that investigated the assassination of John F. Kennedy. A revolt by dissatisfied younger Republicans in 1965 made him minority leader.

Ford shelved his hopes for the Speakership on Oct. 12, 1973, when Nixon nominated him to fill the vice presidency left vacant by Agnew's resignation under fire. It was the first use of the procedures for filling vacancies in the vice presidency laid down in the 25th Amendment to the Constitution, which Ford had helped enact.

Congress confirmed Ford as vice president on Dec. 6, 1973. Once in office, he said he did not believe Nixon had been involved in the Watergate scandals, but criticized his stubborn court battle against releasing tape recordings of Watergate-related conversations for use as evidence.

The scandals led to Nixon's unprecedented resignation on Aug. 9, 1974, and Ford was sworn in immediately as the 38th president, the first to enter the White House without winning a national election.

Ford assured the nation when he took office that "our long national nightmare is over" and pledged "openness and candor" in all his actions. He won a warm response from the Democratic 93rd Congress when he said he wanted "a good marriage" rather than a honeymoon with his former colleagues. In December 1974 Congressional majorities backed his choice of former New York Gov. Nelson A. Rockefeller as his successor in the again-vacant vice presidency.

The cordiality was chilled by Ford's announcement on Sept. 8, 1974, that he had granted an unconditional pardon to Nixon for any crimes he might have committed as president. Although no formal charges were pending, Ford said he feared "ugly passions" would be aroused if Nixon were brought to trial. The pardon was widely criticized.

To fight inflation, the new president first proposed fiscal restraints and spending curbs and a 5% tax surcharge that got nowhere in the Senate and House. Congress again rebuffed Ford in the spring of 1975 when he appealed for emergency military aid to help the governments of South Vietnam and Cambodia resist massive Communist offensives.

In November 1974, Ford visited Japan, South Korea, and the Soviet Union, where he and Soviet leader Leonid I. Brezhnev conferred in Vladivostok and reached a tentative agreement to limit the number of strategic offensive nuclear weapons. It was Ford's first meeting as president with Brezhnev, who planned a return visit to Washington in the fall of 1975.

Politically, Ford's fortunes improved steadily in the first half of 1975. Badly divided Democrats in Congress were unable to muster votes to override his vetoes of spending bills that exceeded his budget. He faced some right-wing opposition in his own party, but moved to pre-empt it with an early announcement—on July 8, 1975—of his intention to be a candidate in 1976.

Early state primaries in 1976 suggested an easy victory for Ford despite Ronald Reagan's bitter attacks on administration foreign policy and defense programs. But later Reagan primary successes threatened the President's lead. At the Kansas City convention, Ford was nominated by the narrow margin of 1,187 to 1,070. But Reagan had moved the party to the right, and Ford himself was regarded as a caretaker president lacking in strength and vision. He was defeated in November by Jimmy Carter.

In 1948, Ford married Elizabeth Anne (Betty) Bloomer. They had four children, Michael Gerald, John Gardner, Steven Meigs, and Susan Elizabeth.

JAMES EARL CARTER, JR., was born in the tiny village of Plains, Ga., Oct. 1, 1924, and grew up on the family farm at nearby Archery. Both parents were fifth-generation Georgians. His father, James Earl Carter, was known as a segregationist, but treated his black and white workers equally. Carter's mother, Lillian Gordy, was a matriarchal presence in home and community and opposed the then-prevailing code of racial inequality. The future President was baptized in 1935 in the conservative Southern Baptist Church and spoke often of being a "born again" Christian, although committed to the separation of church and state.

Carter married Rosalynn Smith, a neighbor, in 1946. Their first child, John William, was born a year later in Portsmouth, Va. Their other children are James Earl III, born in Honolulu in 1950; Donnel Jeffrey, born in New London, Conn., in 1952, and Amy Lynn, born in Plains in 1967.

In 1946 Carter was graduated from the U.S. Naval Academy at Annapolis and served in the nuclear-submarine program under Adm. Hyman G. Rickover. In 1954, after his father's death, he resigned from the Navy to take over the family's flourishing warehouse and cotton gin, with several thousand acres for growing seed peanuts.

Carter was elected to the Georgia Senate in 1962. In 1966 he lost the race for Governor, but was elected in 1970. His term brought a state government reorganization, sharply reduced agencies, increased economy and efficiency, and new social programs, all with no general tax increase. In 1972 the peanut farmer-politician set his sights on the Presidency and in 1974 built a base for himself as he criss-crossed the country as chairman of the Democratic Campaign Committee, appealing for revival and reform. In 1975 his image as a typical Southern white was erased when he won support of most of the old Southern civil-rights coalition after endorsement by Rep. Andrew Young, black Democrat from Atlanta, who had been the closest aide to the Rev. Martin Luther King, Jr. At Carter's 1971 inauguration as Governor he had called for an end to all forms of racial discrimination.

In the 1976 spring primaries, he won 19 out of 31 with a broad appeal to conservatives and liberals, black and white, poor and well-to-do. Throughout his campaigning Carter set forth his policies in his soft Southern voice, and with his electric-blue stare faced down skeptics who joked about "Jimmy Who?" His toothy smile became his trademark. He was nominated on the first roll-call vote of the 1976 Bicentennial Democratic National Convention in New York, and defeated Gerald R. Ford in November. Likewise, in 1980 he was renominated on the first ballot after vanquishing Senator Edward M. Kennedy of Massachusetts in the primaries. At the convention he defeated the Kennedy forces in their attempt to block a party rule that bound a large majority of pledged delegates to vote for Carter. In the election campaign, Carter attacked his rivals, Ronald Reagan and John B. Anderson, independent, with the warning that a Reagan Republican victory would heighten the risk of war and impede civil rights and economic opportunity. In November Carter lost to Reagan, who won 489 Electoral College votes and 51% of the popular tally, to 49 electoral votes and 41% for Carter.

In his one term, Carter fought hard for his programs against resistance from an independent-minded Democratic Congress that frustrated many pet projects although it overrode only two vetoes. Many of his difficulties were traced to his aides' brusqueness in dealing with Capitol Hill and insensitivity to Congressional feelings and tradition. Observers generally viewed public dissatisfaction with the "stagflation" economy as a principal factor in his defeat. Others included his jittery performance in the debate Oct. 28 with Reagan and the final uncertainties in the negotiations for freeing the Iranians' hostages, along with earlier staff problems, friction with Congress, long gasoline lines, and the months-long Iranian crisis, including the abortive sally in April 1980 to free the hostages. The President, however, did deflect criticism resulting from the activities of his brother, Billy. Yet, assessments of his record noted many positive elements. There was, for one thing, peace throughout his term, with no American combat deaths and with a brake on the advocates of force. Regarded as perhaps his greatest personal achievements were the Camp David accords between Israel and Egypt and the resulting treaty—the first between Israel and an Arab neighbor. The treaty with China and the Panama Canal treaties were also major achievements. Carter worked for nuclear-arms control. His concern for international human rights was credited with saving lives and reducing torture, and he supported the British policy that ended internecine warfare in Rhodesia, now Zimbabwe. Domestically, his environmental record was a major accomplishment. His judicial appointments won acclaim; the Southerner who had forsworn racism made 265 choices for the Federal bench that included minority members and women. On energy, he ended by price decontrols the practice of holding U.S. petroleum prices far below world levels. He broke with outmoded liberal ideas to begin the deregulation of airlines, trucks, and banking.

In his final days, the agreement that resulted in freeing the Iranians' hostages was a crowning achievement, although Carter was no longer the President to welcome them on their return. Instead, he traveled to Germany to meet the freed captives as the special envoy of his successor.

RONALD REAGAN, actor turned politician, New Dealer turned conservative, came to the films and politics from a thoroughly middle-American background middle class, Middle West, and small town. He was born in Tampico, Ill., Feb. 6, 1911, the second son of John Edward Reagan and Nelle Wilson Reagan, and the family later moved to Dixon, Ill. The father, of Irish descent, was a shop clerk and merchant with Democratic sympathies. It was an impoverished family; Ronald sold homemade popcorn at highschool games and worked as a lifeguard to earn money for his college tuition. When the father got a New Deal WPA job, the future President became an ardent Roosevelt Democrat.

Reagan won his B.A. degree in 1932 from Eureka (Ill.) College, where a photographic memory aided in his studies and in debating and college theatricals. In a Depression year, he was making $100 a week as a sports announcer for radio station WHO in Des Moines, Iowa, from 1932 to 1937. His career as a film and TV actor stretched from 1937 to 1966, and his salary climbed to $3,500 a week. As a World War II captain in an Army film studio, Reagan recoiled from what he saw as the laziness of Civil Service workers and soon moved to the Right. As president of the Screen Actors Guild, he resisted what he considered a Communist plot to subvert the film industry. With advancing age, Reagan was eased out of leading-man roles and became a television spokesman for the General Electric Company at $150,000.

With oratorical skill his trademark, Reagan became an active Republican, and in 1964 made a dramatic speech supporting Senator Barry Goldwater, who became the party's Presidential nominee. At the behest of a small group of conservative Southern California businessmen, he ran for Governor with a pledge to cut spending, and was elected by almost a million votes over the political veteran, Democratic Gov. Edmund G. Brown, father of the later Governor. But, bowing to the reality of a depleted state treasury, Reagan sponsored a billion-dollar tax increase, then the largest state tax rise in U.S. history. He later rebated $6 billion in property taxes, although there was a net increase of $15 billion in additional taxes from individuals and businesses in his eight years in office. At the end of his second term in 1974, the state budget had grown by $6 billion.

In 1968 Reagan was nosed out by Richard M. Nixon for the G.O.P. presidential nomination and in 1976 by Gerald Ford. In 1980 Reagan won the nomination after a more aggressively conservative campaign.

In the election battle against Jimmy Carter, Reagan rode a tide of resurgent right-wing sentiment among an electorate battered by the winds of unwanted change, longing for a distant, simpler era. Broadening his appeal by espousing moderate policies, Reagan gained much of his success from crossover votes from disaffected Democrats and blue-collar workers. This was reflected by his winning of Hispanic and blue-collar votes in the California campaigns. In a conciliatory convention speech, he expressed a concern for the poor and urged an end to discrimination against women. His selection of George Bush for Vice President and his overtures to Gerald Ford were viewed as tokens of his outreach to a wider audience, as was his campaign appeal to blacks. In general, the Reagan camp made Carter's record the issue.

The incoming Administration immediately set out to "turn the Government around" with a new economic program. In a few months that program had become reality. Despite strenuous opposition in Congress, Reagan triumphed on the major elements of his "supply side" theory to stimulate production and control inflation through tax cuts and sharp reductions in Government spending. Through adroit and daring maneuvering and the exercise of personal charm in television appeals to the public and direct contacts with Congressmen, he won over the converts needed for massive victories. Thus, he achieved the largest budget and tax cuts in recent United States history; many compared the "Reagan revolution" to the early New Deal of Franklin D. Roosevelt.

The President won high acclaim for his nomination of Sandra Day O'Connor of the Arizona Court of Appeals to be the first woman on the Supreme Court. But the choice encountered some opposition from extreme conservatives over her reported stands on abortion and the equal rights amendment. Critics on the Left questioned her judicial fitness.

Barely three months in office, Reagan was the target of an assassin's bullet. On Monday, March 30, he was shot in the chest by a gunman as he walked to his limousine after addressing a meeting at the Washington Hilton Hotel. James S. Brady, the White House press secretary, and two law officers were also wounded. Surgeons removed a .22-caliber bullet that had penetrated Reagan's left lung three inches. The President made a good recovery, and by April he was meeting key aides and working on a limited schedule. On April 11 he walked out of the hospital.

Reagan's second year in office saw the economy sluggish, with persistent high unemployment and interest rates. The initial solid support for his "supply side" economic policies began to erode. Nevertheless, the President won a crucial battle in the early summer of 1982 when Congress voted a Republican-sponsored compromise budget after Democrats and liberals had fought a losing struggle against cuts in social programs. Later in the session, a bipartisan coalition in the House and Senate gave him a major victory by voting his 98.3 billion dollar tax package despite the opposition of Republican conservatives. In foreign policy, Reagan encountered new problems in Israel's invasion of Lebanon; the Argentine aggression in the Falkland Islands, repulsed by the British, and the precipitate resignation of Alexander M. Haig, Jr., as Secretary of State. The President consulted extensively with European leaders and took part in international conferences.

Reagan is devoted to his wife, Nancy, whom he married after his divorce from the screen actress Jane Wyman. The Reagans spend much time together at the White House and Camp David and at their California home and ranch when Presidential duties permit. Reagan enjoys horseback riding and is a connoisseur of fine wines. The children of the first marriage are Maureen, his daughter by Miss Wyman, and Michael, an adopted son. In the present marriage, the children are Patricia and Ronald. *—A.P.R.*

Presidents

Name and (party)[1]	Term	State of birth	Born	Died	Religion	Age at inaug.	Age at death
1. Washington (F)[2]	1789–1797	Va.	2/22/1732	12/14/1799	Episcopalian	57	67
2. J. Adams (F)	1797–1801	Mass.	10/30/1735	7/4/1826	Unitarian	61	90
3. Jefferson (DR)	1801–1809	Va.	4/13/1743	7/4/1826	Deist	57	83
4. Madison (DR)	1809–1817	Va.	3/16/1751	6/28/1836	Episcopalian	57	85
5. Monroe (DR)	1817–1825	Va.	4/28/1758	7/4/1831	Episcopalian	58	73
6. J. Q. Adams (DR)	1825–1829	Mass.	7/11/1767	2/23/1848	Unitarian	57	80
7. Jackson (D)	1829–1837	S.C.	3/15/1767	6/8/1845	Presbyterian	61	78
8. Van Buren (D)	1837–1841	N.Y.	12/5/1782	7/24/1862	Reformed Dutch	54	79
9. W. H. Harrison (W)[3]	1841	Va.	2/9/1773	4/4/1841	Episcopalian	68	68
10. Tyler (W)	1841–1845	Va.	3/29/1790	1/18/1862	Episcopalian	51	71
11. Polk (D)	1845–1849	N.C.	11/2/1795	6/15/1849	Methodist	49	53
12. Taylor (W)[3]	1849–1850	Va.	11/24/1784	7/9/1850	Episcopalian	64	65
13. Fillmore (W)	1850–1853	N.Y.	1/7/1800	3/8/1874	Unitarian	50	74
14. Pierce (D)	1853–1857	N.H.	11/23/1804	10/8/1869	Episcopalian	48	64
15. Buchanan (D)	1857–1861	Pa.	4/23/1791	6/1/1868	Presbyterian	65	77
16. Lincoln (R)[4]	1861–1865	Ky.	2/12/1809	4/15/1865	Liberal	52	56
17. A. Johnson (U)[5]	1865–1869	N.C.	12/29/1808	7/31/1875	([6])	56	66
18. Grant (R)	1869–1877	Ohio	4/27/1822	7/23/1885	Methodist	46	63
19. Hayes (R)	1877–1881	Ohio	10/4/1822	1/17/1893	Methodist	54	70
20. Garfield (R)[4]	1881	Ohio	11/19/1831	9/19/1881	Disciples of Christ	49	49
21. Arthur (R)	1881–1885	Vt.	10/5/1830	11/18/1886	Episcopalian	50	56
22. Cleveland (D)	1885–1889	N.J.	3/18/1837	6/24/1908	Presbyterian	47	71
23. B. Harrison (R)	1889–1893	Ohio	8/20/1833	3/13/1901	Presbyterian	55	67
24. Cleveland (D)[7]	1893–1897	—	—	—	—	55	—
25. McKinley (R)[4]	1897–1901	Ohio	1/29/1843	9/14/1901	Methodist	54	58
26. T. Roosevelt (R)	1901–1909	N.Y.	10/27/1858	1/6/1919	Reformed Dutch	42	60
27. Taft (R)	1909–1913	Ohio	9/15/1857	3/8/1930	Unitarian	51	72
28. Wilson (D)	1913–1921	Va.	12/28/1856	2/3/1924	Presbyterian	56	67
29. Harding (R)[3]	1921–1923	Ohio	11/2/1865	8/2/1923	Baptist	55	57
30. Coolidge (R)	1923–1929	Vt.	7/4/1872	1/5/1933	Congregationalist	51	60
31. Hoover (R)	1929–1933	Iowa	8/10/1874	10/20/1964	Quaker	54	90
32. F. D. Roosevelt (D)[3]	1933–1945	N.Y.	1/30/1882	4/12/1945	Episcopalian	51	63
33. Truman (D)	1945–1953	Mo.	5/8/1884	12/26/1972	Baptist	60	88
34. Eisenhower (R)	1953–1961	Tex.	10/14/1890	3/28/1969	Presbyterian	62	78
35. Kennedy (D)[4]	1961–1963	Mass.	5/29/1917	11/22/1963	Roman Catholic	43	46
36. L. B. Johnson (D)	1963–1969	Tex.	8/27/1908	1/22/1973	Disciples of Christ	55	64
37. Nixon (R)[8]	1969–1974	Calif.	1/9/1913	—	Quaker	56	—
38. Ford (R)	1974–1977	Neb.	7/14/1913	—	Episcopalian	61	—
39. Carter (D)	1977–1981	Ga.	10/1/1924	—	Southern Baptist	52	—
40. Reagan (R)	1981–	Ill.	2/6/1911	—	Disciples of Christ	69	—

1. F—Federalist; DR—Democratic-Republican; D—Democratic; W—Whig; R—Republican; U—Union. 2. No party for first election. The party system in the U.S. made its appearance during Washington's first term. 3. Died in office. 4. Assassinated in office. 5. The Republican National Convention of 1864 adopted the name Union Party. It renominated Lincoln for President; for Vice President it nominated Johnson, a War Democrat. Although frequently listed as a Republican Vice President and President, Johnson undoubtedly considered himself strictly a member of the Union Party. When that party broke apart after 1868, he returned to the Democratic Party. 6. Johnson was not a professed church member; however, he admired the Baptist principles of church government. 7. Second nonconsecutive term. 8. Resigned Aug. 9, 1974.

Vice Presidents

Name and (party)[1]	Term	State of birth	Birth and death dates	President served under
1. John Adams (F)[2]	1789–1797	Massachusetts	1735–1826	Washington
2. Thomas Jefferson (DR)	1797–1801	Virginia	1743–1826	J. Adams
3. Aaron Burr (DR)	1801–1805	New Jersey	1756–1836	Jefferson
4. George Clinton (DR)[3]	1805–1812	New York	1739–1812	Jefferson and Madison
5. Elbridge Gerry (DR)[3]	1813–1814	Massachusetts	1744–1814	Madison
6. Daniel D. Tompkins (DR)	1817–1825	New York	1774–1825	Monroe
7. John C. Calhoun[4]	1825–1832	South Carolina	1782–1850	J. Q. Adams and Jackson
8. Martin Van Buren (D)	1833–1837	New York	1782–1862	Jackson
9. Richard M. Johnson (D)	1837–1841	Kentucky	1780–1850	Van Buren
10. John Tyler (W)[5]	1841	Virginia	1790–1862	W. H. Harrison
11. George M. Dallas (D)	1845–1849	Pennsylvania	1792–1864	Polk
12. Millard Fillmore (W)[5]	1849–1850	New York	1800–1874	Taylor
13. William R. King (D)[3]	1853	North Carolina	1786–1853	Pierce
14. John C. Breckinridge (D)	1857–1861	Kentucky	1821–1875	Buchanan

Name and (party)[1]	Term	State of birth	Birth and death dates	President served under
15. Hannibal Hamlin (R)	1861–1865	Maine	1809–1891	Lincoln
16. Andrew Johnson (U)[5]	1865	North Carolina	1808–1875	Lincoln
17. Schuyler Colfax (R)	1869–1873	New York	1823–1885	Grant
18. Henry Wilson (R)[3]	1873–1875	New Hampshire	1812–1875	Grant
19. William A. Wheeler (R)	1877–1881	New York	1819–1887	Hayes
20. Chester A. Arthur(R)[5]	1881	Vermont	1830–1886	Garfield
21. Thomas A. Hendricks (D)[3]	1885	Ohio	1819–1885	Cleveland
22. Levi P. Morton (R)	1889–1893	Vermont	1824–1920	B. Harrison
23. Adlai E. Stevenson (D)	1893–1897	Kentucky	1835–1914	Cleveland
24. Garrett A. Hobart (R)[3]	1897–1899	New Jersey	1844–1899	McKinley
25. Theodore Roosevelt (R)[5]	1901	New York	1858–1919	McKinley
26. Charles W. Fairbanks (R)	1905–1909	Ohio	1852–1918	T. Roosevelt
27. James S. Sherman (R)[3]	1909–1912	New York	1855–1912	Taft
28. Thomas R. Marshall (D)	1913–1921	Indiana	1854–1925	Wilson
29. Calvin Coolidge (R)[5]	1921–1923	Vermont	1872–1933	Harding
30. Charles G. Dawes (R)	1925–1929	Ohio	1865–1951	Coolidge
31. Charles Curtis (R)	1929–1933	Kansas	1860–1936	Hoover
32. John N. Garner (D)	1933–1941	Texas	1868–1967	F. D. Roosevelt
33. Henry A. Wallace (D)	1941–1945	Iowa	1888–1965	F. D. Roosevelt
34. Harry S. Truman (D)[5]	1945	Missouri	1884–1972	F. D. Roosevelt
35. Alben W. Barkley (D)	1949–1953	Kentucky	1877–1956	Truman
36. Richard M. Nixon (R)	1953–1961	California	1913–	Eisenhower
37. Lyndon B. Johnson (D)[5]	1961–1963	Texas	1908–1973	Kennedy
38. Hubert H. Humphrey (D)	1965–1969	South Dakota	1911–1978	Johnson
39. Spiro T. Agnew (R)[6]	1969–1973	Maryland	1918–	Nixon
40. Gerald R. Ford (R)[7]	1973–1974	Nebraska	1913–	Nixon
41. Nelson A. Rockefeller (R)[8]	1974–1977	Maine	1908–1979	Ford
42. Walter F. Mondale (D)	1977–1981	Minnesota	1928–	Carter
43. George Bush (R)	1981–	Massachusetts	1924–	Reagan

1. F—Federalist; DR—Democratic-Republican; D—Democratic; W—Whig; R—Republican; U—Union. 2. No party for first election. The party system in the U.S. made its appearance during Washington's first term as President. 3. Died in office. 4. Democratic-Republican with J. Q. Adams; Democratic with Jackson. Calhoun resigned in 1832 to become a U.S. Senator. 5. Succeeded to presidency on death of President. 6. Resigned Oct. 10, 1973, after pleading no contest to Federal income tax evasion charges. 7. Nominated by Nixon on Oct. 12, 1973, under provisions of 25th Amendment. Confirmed by Congress on Dec. 6, 1973, and was sworn in same day. He became President Aug. 9, 1974, upon Nixon's resignation. 8. Nominated by Ford Aug. 20, 1974; confirmed by Congress on Dec. 19, 1974, and was sworn in same day.

Burial Places of the Presidents

President	Burial place	President	Burial place
Washington	Mt. Vernon, Va.	Grant	New York City
J. Adams	Quincy, Mass.	Hayes	Fremont, Ohio
Jefferson	Charlottesville, Va.	Garfield	Cleveland, Ohio
Madison	Montpelier Station, Va.	Arthur	Albany, N.Y.
Monroe	Richmond, Va.	Cleveland	Princeton, N.J.
J. Q. Adams	Quincy, Mass.	B. Harrison	Indianapolis
Jackson	The Hermitage, nr. Nashville, Tenn.	McKinley	Canton, Ohio
		T. Roosevelt	Oyster Bay, N.Y.
Van Buren	Kinderhook, N.Y.	Taft	Arlington National Cemetery
W. H. Harrison	North Bend, Ohio	Wilson	Washington National Cathedral
Tyler	Richmond, Va.	Harding	Marion, Ohio
Polk	Nashville, Tenn.	Coolidge	Plymouth, Vt.
Taylor	Louisville, Ky.	Hoover	West Branch, Iowa
Fillmore	Buffalo, N.Y.	F. D. Roosevelt	Hyde Park, N.Y.
Pierce	Concord, N.H.	Truman	Independence, Mo.
Buchanan	Lancaster, Pa.	Eisenhower	Abilene, Kan.
Lincoln	Springfield, Ill.	Kennedy	Arlington National Cemetery
A. Johnson	Greeneville, Tenn.	L. B. Johnson	Stonewall, Tex.

"In God We Trust"

"In God We Trust" first appeared on U.S. coins after April 22, 1864, when Congress passed an act authorizing the coinage of a 2-cent piece bearing this motto. Thereafter, Congress extended its use to other coins. On July 30, 1956, it became the national motto.

Wives and Children of the Presidents

President	Wife's name	Year and place of wife's birth	Married	Wife died	Children of President[1] Sons	Daughters
Washington	Mrs. Martha Dandridge Custis	1732, Va.	1759	1802	—	—
John Adams	Abigail Smith	1744, Mass.	1764	1818	3	2
Jefferson	Mrs. Martha Wayles Skelton	1748, Va.	1772	1782	1	5
Madison	Mrs. Dorothy "Dolley" Payne Todd	1768, N.C.	1794	1849	—	—
Monroe	Elizabeth "Eliza" Kortright	1768, N.Y.	1786	1830	—	2
J. Q. Adams	Louisa Catherine Johnson	1775, England	1797	1852	3	1
Jackson	Mrs. Rachel Donelson Robards	1767, Va.	1791	1828	—	—
Van Buren	Hannah Hoes	1788, N.Y.	1807	1819	4	—
W. H. Harrison	Anna Symmes	1775, N.J.	1795	1864	6	4
Tyler	Letitia Christian	1790, Va.	1813	1842	3	4
	Julia Gardiner	1820, N.Y.	1844	1889	5	2
Polk	Sarah Childress	1803, Tenn.	1824	1891	—	—
Taylor	Margaret Smith	1788, Md.	1810	1852	1	5
Fillmore	Abigail Powers	1798, N.Y.	1826	1853	1	1
	Mrs. Caroline Carmichael McIntosh	1813, N.J.	1858	1881	—	—
Pierce	Jane Means Appleton	1806, N.H.	1834	1863	3	—
Buchanan	(Unmarried)	—	—	—	—	—
Lincoln	Mary Todd	1818, Ky.	1842	1882	4	—
A. Johnson	Eliza McCardle	1810, Tenn.	1827	1876	3	2
Grant	Julia Dent	1826, Mo.	1848	1902	3	1
Hayes	Lucy Ware Webb	1831, Ohio	1852	1889	7	1
Garfield	Lucretia Rudolph	1832, Ohio	1858	1918	5	2
Arthur	Ellen Lewis Herndon	1837, Va.	1859	1880	2	1
Cleveland	Frances Folsom	1864, N.Y.	1886	1947	2	3
B. Harrison	Caroline Lavinia Scott	1832, Ohio	1853	1892	1	1
	Mrs. Mary Scott Lord Dimmick	1858, Pa.	1896	1948	—	1
McKinley	Ida Saxton	1847, Ohio	1871	1907	—	2
T. Roosevelt	Alice Hathaway Lee	1861, Mass.	1880	1884	—	1
	Edith Kermit Carow	1861, Conn.	1886	1948	4	1
Taft	Helen Herron	1861, Ohio	1886	1943	2	1
Wilson	Ellen Louise Axson	1860, Ga.	1885	1914	—	3
	Mrs. Edith Bolling Galt	1872, Va.	1915	1961	—	—
Harding	Mrs. Florence Kling DeWolfe	1860, Ohio	1891	1924	—	—
Coolidge	Grace Anna Goodhue	1879, Vt.	1905	1957	2	—
Hoover	Lou Henry	1875, Iowa	1899	1944	2	—
F. D. Roosevelt	Anna Eleanor Roosevelt	1884, N.Y.	1905	1962	5	1
Truman	Bess Wallace	1885, Mo.	1919	—	—	1
Eisenhower	Mamie Geneva Doud	1896, Iowa	1916	1979	2	—
Kennedy	Jacqueline Lee Bouvier	1929, N.Y.	1953	—	2	1
L. B. Johnson	Claudia Alta "Lady Bird" Taylor	1912, Tex.	1934	—	—	2
Nixon	Thelma Catherine "Pat" Ryan	1912, Nev.	1940	—	—	2
Ford	Mrs. Elizabeth "Betty" Bloomer Warren	1918, Ill.	1948	—	3	1
Carter	Rosalynn Smith	1928, Ga.	1946	—	3	1
Reagan	Jane Wyman	1914, Mo.	1940[2]	—	1[3]	1
	Nancy Davis	1923, N.Y.	1952	—	1	1

1. Includes children who died in infancy. 2. Divorced in 1948. 3. Adopted.

Elections

How a President is Nominated and Elected

The National Conventions of both major parties are held during the summer of a presidential-election year. Earlier, each party selects delegates by primaries, conventions, committees, etc.

For their 1980 National Convention, the Republicans allowed each state a base of 6 delegates at large; the District of Columbia, 14; Puerto Rico, 14; Guam and the Virgin Islands, 4 each. In addition, each state received 3 district delegates for each of its Representatives in the House. This did not apply to the District of Columbia, Puerto Rico, Guam and the Virgin Islands.

Each state was awarded additional delegates at large on the basis of having supported the Republican candidate for President in 1976 and electing Republican candidates for Senator, Governor, and U.S. Representative in the 1976 and 1978 elections.

The number of delegates at the 1980 convention, held in Detroit starting July 14, was 1,997.

Following was the apportionment of delegates:

Ala.	27	Fla.	51	Ky.	27	Mont.	20	Ohio	77	Tex.	80
Alaska	19	Ga.	36	La.	31	Neb.	25	Okla	34	Utah	21
Ariz.	28	Guam	4	Me.	21	Nev.	17	Ore.	29	Vt.	19
Ark.	19	Hawaii	14	Md.	30	N.H.	22	Pa.	83	Va.	51
Calif.	168	Idaho	21	Mass.	42	N.J.	66	P.R.	14	V.I.	4
Colo.	31	Ill.	102	Mich.	82	N.M.	22	R.I.	13	Wash.	37
Conn.	35	Ind.	54	Minn.	34	N.Y.	123	S.C.	25	W. Va.	18
Del.	12	Iowa	37	Miss.	22	N.C.	40	S.D.	22	Wis.	34
D.C.	14	Kan.	32	Mo.	37	N.D.	17	Tenn.	32	Wyo.	19

The Democrats also based the number of delegates on a state's showing in the 1976 and 1978 elections. At the 1980 convention, held in New York City starting Aug. 11, there were 3,331[1] delegates casting votes. Following was the apportionment:

Ala.	45	Fla.	100	Ky.	50	Mont.	19	Ohio	161	Tex.	152
Alaska	11	Ga.	63	La.	51	Neb.	24	Okla.	42	Utah	20
Ariz.	29	Guam	4	Me.	22	Nev.	12	Ore.	39	Vt.	12
Ark.	33	Hawaii	19	Md.	59	N.H.	19	Pa.	185	V.I.	4
Calif.	306	Idaho	17	Mass.	111	N.J.	113	P.R.	41	Va.	64
Canal Zone	4	Ill.	179	Mich.	141	N.M.	20	R.I.	23	Wash.	58
Colo.	40	Ind.	80	Minn.	75	N.Y.	282	S.C.	37	W.Va.	35
Conn.	54	Iowa	50	Miss.	32	N.C.	69	S.D.	19	Wis.	75
Del.	14	Kan.	37	Mo.	77	N.D.	14	Tenn.	55	Wyo.	11
D.C.	19										

1. Includes three votes for Democrats abroad.

The Conventions

At each convention, a temporary chairman is chosen. After a credentials committee seats the delegates, a permanent chairman is elected. The convention then votes on a platform, drawn up by the platform committee.

By the third or fourth day, presidential nominations begin. The chairman calls the roll of states alphabetically. A state may place a candidate in nomination or yield to another state.

Voting, again alphabetically by roll call of states, begins after all nominations have been made and seconded. A simple majority is required in each party, although this may require many ballots.

Finally, the vice-presidential candidate is selected. Although there is no law saying that the candidates *must* come from different states, it is, practically, necessary for this to be the case. Otherwise, according to the Constitution (*see* Amendment XII), electors from that state could vote for only one of the candidates and would have to cast their other vote for some person of another state. This could result in a presidential candidate's receiving a majority electoral vote and his running mate's failing to.

The Electoral College

The next step in the process is the nomination of electors in each state. according to its laws. These electors must not be Federal office holders. In the November election, the voters cast their votes for electors, not for President. In some states, the ballots include only the names of the presidential and vice-presidential candidates; in others, they include only names of the electors. Nowadays, it is rare for electors to be split between parties. The last such occurrence was in North Carolina in 1968[1]; the last before that, in Tennessee in 1948. On three occasions (1824, 1876, and 1888), the presidential candidate with the largest popular vote failed to obtain an electoral-vote majority.

Each state has as many electors as it has Senators and Representatives. For the 1976 election, the total electors were 538, based on 100 Senators, 435 Representatives, plus 3 electoral votes from the District of Columbia as a result of the 23rd Amendment to the Constitution.

On the first Monday after the second Wednesday in December, the electors cast their votes in their respective state capitols. Constitutionally they may vote for someone other than the party candidate but usually they do not since they are pledged to one party and its candidate on the ballot. Should the presidential or vice-presidential candidate die between the November election and the December meetings, the electors pledged to vote for him could vote for whomever they pleased. However, it seems certain that the national committee would attempt to get an agreement among the state party leaders for a replacement candidate.

The votes of the electors, certified by the states, are sent to Congress, where the president of the Senate opens the certificates and has them counted in the presence of both Houses on January 6. The new President is inaugurated at noon on January 20.

Should no candidate receive a majority of the electoral vote for President, the House of Representatives chooses a President from among the three highest candidates, voting, not as individuals, but as states, with a majority (now 26) needed to elect. Should no vice-presidential candidate obtain the majority, the Senate, voting as individuals, chooses from the highest two.

1. In 1956, 1 of Alabama's 11 electoral votes was cast for Walter B. Jones. In 1960, 6 of Alabama's 11 electoral votes and 1 of Oklahoma's 8 electoral votes were cast for Harry Flood Byrd. (Byrd also received all 8 of Mississippi's electoral votes.)

National Political Conventions Since 1856

Opening date	Party	Where held
June 17, 1856	Republican	Philadelphia
June 2, 1856	Democratic	Cincinnati
May 16, 1860	Republican	Chicago
April 23, 1860	Democratic	Charleston and Baltimore
June 7, 1864	Republican[1]	Baltimore
Aug. 29, 1864	Democratic	Chicago
May 20, 1868	Republican	Chicago
July 4, 1868	Democratic	New York City
June 5, 1872	Republican	Philadelphia
June 9, 1872	Democratic	Baltimore
June 14, 1876	Republican	Cincinnati
June 28, 1876	Democratic	St. Louis
June 2, 1880	Republican	Chicago
June 23, 1880	Democratic	Cincinnati
June 3, 1884	Republican	Chicago
July 11, 1884	Democratic	Chicago
June 19, 1888	Republican	Chicago
June 6, 1888	Democratic	St. Louis
June 7, 1892	Republican	Minneapolis
June 21, 1892	Democratic	Chicago
June 16, 1896	Republican	St. Louis
July 7, 1896	Democratic	Chicago
June 19, 1900	Republican	Philadelphia
July 4, 1900	Democratic	Kansas City
June 21, 1904	Republican	Chicago
July 6, 1904	Democratic	St. Louis
June 16, 1908	Republican	Chicago
July 7, 1908	Democratic	Denver
June 18, 1912	Republican	Chicago
June 25, 1912	Democratic	Baltimore
June 7, 1916	Republican	Chicago
June 14, 1916	Democratic	St. Louis
June 8, 1920	Republican	Chicago
June 28, 1920	Democratic	San Francisco
June 10, 1924	Republican	Cleveland
June 24, 1924[2]	Democratic	New York City
June 12, 1928	Republican	Kansas City
June 26, 1928	Democratic	Houston
June 14, 1932	Republican	Chicago
June 27, 1932	Democratic	Chicago
June 9, 1936	Republican	Cleveland
June 23, 1936	Democratic	Philadelphia
June 24, 1940	Republican	Philadelphia
July 15, 1940	Democratic	Chicago
June 26, 1944	Republican	Chicago
July 19, 1944	Democratic	Chicago
June 21, 1948	Republican	Philadelphia
July 12, 1948	Democratic	Philadelphia
July 17, 1948	([3])	Birmingham
July 22, 1948	Progressive	Philadelphia
July 7, 1952	Republican	Chicago
July 21, 1952	Democratic	Chicago
Aug. 20, 1956	Republican	San Francisco
Aug. 13, 1956	Democratic	Chicago
July 25, 1960	Republican	Chicago
July 11, 1960	Democratic	Los Angeles
July 13, 1964	Republican	San Francisco
Aug. 24, 1964	Democratic	Atlantic City
Aug. 5, 1968	Republican	Miami Beach
Aug. 26, 1968	Democratic	Chicago
July 10, 1972	Democratic	Miami Beach
Aug. 21, 1972	Republican	Miami Beach
July 12, 1976	Democratic	New York City
Aug. 16, 1976	Republican	Kansas City, Mo.
Aug. 11, 1980	Democratic	New York City
July 14, 1980	Republican	Detroit

1. The Convention adopted name Union party to attract War Democrats and others favoring prosecution of war. 2. In session until July 10, 1924. 3. States' Rights delegates from 13 Southern states.

National Committee Chairmen Since 1932

Chairman and (state)	Term
REPUBLICAN	
Everett Sanders (Ind.)	1932–34
Henry P. Fletcher (Pa.)	1934–36
John Hamilton (Kan.)	1936–40
Joseph W. Martin, Jr. (Mass.)	1940–42
Harrison E. Spangler (Iowa)	1942–44
Herbert Brownell, Jr. (N.Y.)	1944–46
Carroll Reece (Tenn.)	1946–48
Hugh D. Scott, Jr. (Pa.)	1948–49
Guy G. Gabrielson (N.J.)	1949–52
Arthur E. Summerfield (Mich.)	1952–53
Wesley Roberts (Kan.)	1953–
Leonard W. Hall (N.Y.)	1953–57
Meade Alcorn (Conn.)	1957–59
Thruston B. Morton (Ky.)	1959–61
William E. Miller (N.Y.)	1961–64
Dean Burch (Ariz.)	1964–65
Ray C. Bliss (Ohio)	1965–69
Rogers C. B. Morton (Md.)	1969–71
Robert Dole (Kan.)	1971–73
George H. Bush (Tex.)	1973–74
Mary Louise Smith (Iowa)	1974–77
William E. Brock III (Tenn.)	1977–81
Richard Richards (Utah)	1981–
DEMOCRATIC	
James A. Farley (N.Y.)	1932–40
Edward J. Flynn (N.Y.)	1940–43
Frank C. Walker (Mont.)	1943–44
Robert E. Hannegan (Mo.)	1944–47
J. Howard McGrath (R.I.)	1947–49
William M. Boyle, Jr. (Mo.)	1949–51
Frank E. McKinney (Ind.)	1951–52
Stephen A. Mitchell (Ill.)	1952–54
Paul M. Butler (Ind.)	1955–60
Henry M. Jackson (Wash.)	1960–61
John M. Bailey (Conn.)	1961–68
Lawrence F. O'Brien (Mass.)	1968–69
Fred R. Harris (Okla.)	1969–70
Lawrence F. O'Brien (Mass.)	1970–72
Jean Westwood (Utah)	1972–
Robert S. Strauss (Tex.)	1972–77
Kenneth M. Curtis (Me.)	1977–
John C. White (Tex.)	1977–81
Charles T. Manatt (Calif.)	1981–

Republican National Committee: 310 First St., S.E., Washington, D. C. 20003.
Democratic National Committee: 1625 Massachusetts Ave., N.W., Washington, D.C. 20036.

Presidential Elections, 1789 to 1980

For the original method of electing the President and the Vice President (elections of 1789, 1792, 1796, and 1800), see Article II, Section 1, of the Constitution. The election of 1804 was the first one in which the electors voted for President and Vice President on separate ballots. (See Amendment XII to the Constitution.)

Year	Presidential candidates	Party	Electoral vote
1789[1]	George Washington	(no party)	69
	John Adams	(no party)	34
	Scattering	(no party)	35
	Votes not cast		8
1792	George Washington	Federalist	132
	John Adams	Federalist	77
	George Clinton	Anti-Federalist	50
	Thomas Jefferson	Anti-Federalist	4
	Aaron Burr	Anti-Federalist	1
	Votes not cast		6
1796	John Adams	Federalist	71
	Thomas Jefferson	Dem.-Rep.	68
	Thomas Pinckney	Federalist	59
	Aaron Burr	Dem.-Rep.	30
	Scattering		48
1800[2]	Thomas Jefferson	Dem.-Rep.	73
	Aaron Burr	Dem.-Rep.	73
	John Adams	Federalist	65
	Charles C. Pinckney	Federalist	64
	John Jay	Federalist	1

Year	Presidential candidates	Party	Electoral vote	Vice-presidential candidates	Party	Electoral vote
1804	Thomas Jefferson	Dem.-Rep.	162	George Clinton	Dem.-Rep.	162
	Charles C. Pinckney	Federalist	14	Rufus King	Federalist	14
1808	James Madison	Dem.-Rep.	122	George Clinton	Dem.-Rep.	113
	Charles C. Pinckney	Federalist	47	Rufus King	Federalist	47
	George Clinton	Dem.-Rep.	6	John Langdon	Ind. (no party)	9
	Votes not cast		1	James Madison	Dem.-Rep.	3
				James Monroe	Dem.-Rep.	3
				Votes not cast		1
1812	James Madison	Dem.-Rep.	128	Elbridge Gerry	Dem.-Rep.	131
	De Witt Clinton	Federalist	89	Jared Ingersoll	Federalist	86
	Votes not cast		1	Votes not cast		1
1816	James Monroe	Dem.-Rep.	183	Daniel D. Tompkins	Dem.-Rep.	183
	Rufus King	Federalist	34	John E. Howard	Federalist	22
	Votes not cast		4	James Ross	Ind. (no party)	5
				John Marshall	Federalist	4
				Robert G. Harper	Ind. (no party)	3
				Votes not cast		4
1820	James Monroe	Dem-Rep	231	Daniel D. Tompkins	Dem.-Rep.	218
	John Quincy Adams	Ind. (no party)	1	Richard Stockton	Ind. (no party)	8
	Votes not cast		3	Daniel Rodney	Ind. (no party)	4
				Richard Rush	Ind. (no party)	1
				Robert G. Harper	Ind. (no party)	1
				Votes not cast		3
1824[3]	John Quincy Adams	(no party)	84	John C. Calhoun	(no party)	182
	Andrew Jackson	(no party)	99	Nathan Sanford	(no party)	30
	William H. Crawford	(no party)	41	Nathaniel Macon	(no party)	24
	Henry Clay	(no party)	37	Andrew Jackson	(no party)	13
				Martin Van Buren	(no party)	9
				Henry Clay	(no party)	2
				Votes not cast		1
1828	Andrew Jackson	Democratic	178	John C. Calhoun	Democratic	171
	John Quincy Adams	Natl. Rep.	83	Richard Rush	Natl. Rep.	83
				William Smith	Democratic	7
1832	Andrew Jackson	Democratic	219	Martin Van Buren	Democratic	189
	Henry Clay	Natl. Rep.	49	John Sergeant	Natl. Rep.	49
	John Floyd	Ind. (no party)	11	Henry Lee	Ind. (no party)	11
	William Wirt	Antimasonic[4]	7	Amos Ellmaker	Antimasonic	7
	Votes not cast		2	William Wilkins	Ind. (no party)	30
				Votes not cast		2

Year	Presidential candidates	Party	Electoral vote	Vice-presidential candidates	Party	Electoral vote
1836	Martin Van Buren	Democratic	170	Richard M. Johnson[5]	Democratic	147
	William H. Harrison	Whig	73	Francis Granger	Whig	77
	Hugh L. White	Whig	26	John Tyler	Whig	47
	Daniel Webster	Whig	14	William Smith	Ind. (no party)	23
	W. P. Mangum	Ind. (no party)	11			
1840	William H. Harrison[6]	Whig	234	John Tyler	Whig	234
	Martin Van Buren	Democratic	60	Richard M. Johnson	Democratic	48
				L. W. Tazewell	Ind. (no party)	11
				James K. Polk	Democratic	1
1844	James K. Polk	Democratic	170	George M. Dallas	Democratic	170
	Henry Clay	Whig	105	Theo. Frelinghuysen	Whig	105
1848	Zachary Taylor[7]	Whig	163	Millard Fillmore	Whig	163
	Lewis Cass	Democratic	127	William O. Butler	Democratic	127
1852	Franklin Pierce	Democratic	254	William R. King	Democratic	254
	Winfield Scott	Whig	42	William A. Graham	Whig	42
1856	James Buchanan	Democratic	174	John C. Breckinridge	Democratic	174
	John C. Frémont	Republican	114	William L. Dayton	Republican	114
	Millard Fillmore	American[8]	8	A. J. Donelson	American[8]	8
1860	Abraham Lincoln	Republican	180	Hannibal Hamlin	Republican	180
	John C. Breckinridge	Democratic	72	Joseph Lane	Democratic	72
	John Bell	Const. Union	39	Edward Everett	Const. Union	39
	Stephen A. Douglas	Democratic	12	H. V. Johnson	Democratic	12
1864	Abraham Lincoln[9]	Union[10]	212	Andrew Johnson	Union[15]	212
	George B. McClellan	Democratic	21	G. H. Pendleton	Democratic	21
1868	Ulysses S. Grant	Republican	214	Schuyler Colfax	Republican	214
	Horatio Seymour	Democratic	80	Francis P. Blair, Jr.	Democratic	80
	Votes not counted[11]		23	Votes not counted[11]		23

Year	Presidential candidates	Party	Electoral vote	Popular vote	Vice-presidential candidates and party
1872	Ulysses S. Grant	Republican	286	3,597,132	Henry Wilson—R
	Horace Greeley	Dem., Liberal Rep.	([12])	2,834,125	B. Gratz Brown—D, LR—(47)
	Thomas A. Hendricks	Democratic	42		Scattering—(19)
	B. Gratz Brown	Dem., Liberal Rep.	18		Votes not counted—(14)
	Charles J. Jenkins	Democratic	2		
	David Davis	Democratic	1		
	Votes not counted		17		
1876[13]	Rutherford B. Hayes	Republican	185	4,033,768	William A. Wheeler—R
	Samuel J. Tilden	Democratic	184	4,285,992	Thomas A. Hendricks—D
	Peter Cooper	Greenback	0	81,737	Samuel F. Cary—G
1880	James A. Garfield[14]	Republican	214	4,449,053	Chester A. Arthur—R
	Winfield S. Hancock	Democratic	155	4,442,035	William H. English—D
	James B. Weaver	Greenback	0	308,578	B. J. Chambers—G
1884	Grover Cleveland	Democratic	219	4,911,017	Thomas A. Hendricks—D
	James G. Blaine	Republican	182	4,848,334	John A. Logan—R
	Benjamin F. Butler	Greenback	0	175,370	A. M. West—G
	John P. St. John	Prohibition	0	150,369	William Daniel—P
1888	Benjamin Harrison	Republican	233	5,440,216	Levi P. Morton—R
	Grover Cleveland	Democratic	168	5,538,233	A. G. Thurman—D
	Clinton B. Fisk	Prohibition	0	249,506	John A. Brooks—P
	Alson J. Streeter	Union Labor	0	146,935	Charles E. Cunningham—UL
1892	Grover Cleveland	Democratic	277	5,556,918	Adlai E. Stevenson—D
	Benjamin Harrison	Republican	145	5,176,108	Whitelaw Reid—R
	James B. Weaver	People's[15]	22	1,041,028	James G. Field—Peo
	John Bidwell	Prohibition	0	264,133	James B. Cranfill—P

Year	Presidential candidates	Party	Electoral vote	Popular vote	Vice-presidential candidates and party
1896	William McKinley	Republican	271	7,035,638	Garret A. Hobart—R
	William J. Bryan	Dem., People's[15]	176	6,467,946	Arthur Sewall—D—(149)
					Thomas E. Watson—Peo—(27)
	John M. Palmer	Natl. Dem.	0	133,148	Simon B. Buckner—ND
	Joshua Levering	Prohibition	0	132,007	Hale Johnson—P
1900	William McKinley[16]	Republican	292	7,219,530	Theodore Roosevelt—R
	William J. Bryan	Dem., People's[15]	155	6,358,071	Adlai E. Stevenson—D, Peo
	Eugene V. Debs	Social Democratic	0	94,768	Job Harriman—SD
1904	Theodore Roosevelt	Republican	336	7,628,834	Charles W. Fairbanks—R
	Alton B. Parker	Democratic	140	5,084,491	Henry G. Davis—D
	Eugene V. Debs	Socialist	0	402,400	Benjamin Hanford—S
1908	William H. Taft	Republican	321	7,679,006	James S. Sherman—R
	William J. Bryan	Democratic	162	6,409,106	John W. Kern—D
	Eugene V. Debs	Socialist	0	402,820	Benjamin Hanford—S
1912	Woodrow Wilson	Democratic	435	6,286,214	Thomas R. Marshall—D
	Theodore Roosevelt	Progressive	88	4,126,020	Hiram Johnson—Prog
	William H. Taft	Republican	8	3,483,922	Nicholas M. Butler—R[17]
	Eugene V. Debs	Socialist	0	897,011	Emil Seidel—S
1916	Woodrow Wilson	Democratic	277	9,129,606	Thomas R. Marshall—D
	Charles E. Hughes	Republican	254	8,538,221	Charles W. Fairbanks—R
	A. L. Benson	Socialist	0	585,113	G. R. Kirkpatrick—S
1920	Warren G. Harding[18]	Republican	404	16,152,200	Calvin Coolidge—R
	James M. Cox	Democratic	127	9,147,353	Franklin D. Roosevelt—D
	Eugene V. Debs	Socialist	0	917,799	Seymour Stedman—S
1924	Calvin Coolidge	Republican	382	15,725,016	Charles G. Dawes—R
	John W. Davis	Democratic	136	8,385,586	Charles W. Bryan—D
	Robert M. LaFollette	Progressive, Socialist	13	4,822,856	Burton K. Wheeler—Prog S
1928	Herbert Hoover	Republican	444	21,392,190	Charles Curtis—R
	Alfred E. Smith	Democratic	87	15,016,443	Joseph T. Robinson—D
	Norman Thomas	Socialist	0	267,420	James H. Maurer—S
1932	Franklin D. Roosevelt	Democratic	472	22,821,857	John N. Garner—D
	Herbert Hoover	Republican	59	15,761,841	Charles Curtis—R
	Norman Thomas	Socialist	0	884,781	James H. Maurer—S
1936	Franklin D. Roosevelt	Democratic	523	27,751,597	John N. Garner—D
	Alfred M. Landon	Republican	8	16,679,583	Frank Knox—R
	Norman Thomas	Socialist	0	187,720	George Nelson—S
1940	Franklin D. Roosevelt	Democratic	449	27,244,160	Henry A. Wallace—D
	Wendell L. Willkie	Republican	82	22,305,198	Charles L. McNary—R
	Norman Thomas	Socialist	0	99,557	Maynard C. Krueger—S
1944	Franklin D. Roosevelt[19]	Democratic	432	25,602,504	Harry S. Truman—D
	Thomas E. Dewey	Republican	99	22,006,285	John W. Bricker—R
	Norman Thomas	Socialist	0	80,518	Darlington Hoopes—S
1948	Harry S. Truman	Democratic	303	24,179,345	Alben W. Barkley—D
	Thomas E. Dewey	Republican	189	21,991,291	Earl Warren—R
	J. Strom Thurmond	States' Rights Dem.	39	1,176,125	Fielding L. Wright—SR
	Henry A. Wallace	Progressive	0	1,157,326	Glen Taylor—Prog
	Norman Thomas	Socialist	0	139,572	Tucker P. Smith—S
1952	Dwight D. Eisenhower	Republican	442	33,936,234	Richard M. Nixon—R
	Adlai E. Stevenson	Democratic	89	27,314,992	John J. Sparkman—D
1956[20]	Dwight D. Eisenhower	Republican	457	35,590,472	Richard M. Nixon—R
	Adlai E. Stevenson	Democratic	73	26,022,752	Estes Kefauver—D
1960	John F. Kennedy[22]	Democratic	303	34,226,731	Lyndon B. Johnson—D
	Richard M. Nixon	Republican	219	34,108,157	Henry Cabot Lodge—R

Year	Presidential candidates	Party	Electoral vote	Popular vote	Vice-presidential candidates and party
1964	Lyndon B. Johnson	Democratic	486	43,129,484	Hubert H. Humphrey—D
	Barry M. Goldwater	Republican	52	27,178,188	William E. Miller—R
1968	Richard M. Nixon	Republican	301	31,785,480	Spiro T. Agnew—R
	Hubert H. Humphrey	Democratic	191	31,275,166	Edmund S. Muskie—D
	George C. Wallace	American Independent	46	9,906,473	Curtis F. LeMay—AI
1972	Richard M. Nixon[23]	Republican	520[24]	47,169,911	Spiro T. Agnew—R
	George McGovern	Democratic	17	29,170,383	Sargent Shriver—D
	John G. Schmitz	American	0	1,099,482	Thomas J. Anderson—A
1976	Jimmy Carter	Democratic	297	40,830,763	Walter F. Mondale—D
	Gerald R. Ford	Republican	240[25]	39,147,973	Robert J. Dole—R
	Eugene J. McCarthy	Independent	0	756,631	None
1980	Ronald Reagan	Republican	489	43,899,248	George Bush—R
	Jimmy Carter	Democratic	49	36,481,435	Walter F. Mondale—D
	John B. Anderson	Independent	0	5,719,437	Patrick J. Lucey—I

1. Only 10 states participated in the election. The New York legislature chose no electors, and North Carolina and Rhode Island had not yet ratified the Constitution. 2. As Jefferson and Burr were tied, the House of Representatives chose the President. In a vote by states, 10 votes were cast for Jefferson, 4 for Burr; 2 votes were not cast. 3. As no candidate had an electoral-vote majority, the House of Representatives chose the President from the first three. In a vote by states, 13 votes were cast for Adams, 7 for Jackson, and 4 for Crawford. 4. The Antimasonic Party on Sept. 26, 1831, was the first party to hold a nominating convention to choose candidates for President and Vice-President. 5. As Johnson did not have an electoral-vote majority, the Senate chose him 33–14 over Granger, the others being legally out of the race. 6. Harrison died April 4, 1841, and Tyler succeeded him April 6. 7. Taylor died July 9, 1850, and Fillmore succeeded him July 10. 8. Also known as the Know-Nothing Party. 9. Lincoln died April 15, 1865, and Johnson succeeded him the same day. 10. Name adopted by the Republican National Convention of 1864. Johnson was a War Democrat. 11. 23 Southern electoral votes were excluded. 12. See Election of 1872 in *Unusual Voting Results* under Elections, Presidential, in Index. 13. See Election of 1876 in *Unusual Voting Results* under Elections, Presidential, in Index. 14. Garfield died Sept. 19, 1881, and Arthur succeeded him Sept. 20. 15. Members of People's Party were called Populists. 16. McKinley died Sept. 14, 1901, and Roosevelt succeeded him the same day. 17. James S. Sherman, Republican candidate for Vice President, died Oct. 30, 1912, and the Republican electoral votes were cast for Butler. 18. Harding died Aug. 2, 1923, and Coolidge succeeded him Aug. 3. 19. Roosevelt died April 12, 1945, and Truman succeeded him the same day. 20. One electoral vote from Alabama was cast for Walter B. Jones. 21. Sen. Harry F. Byrd received 15 electoral votes. 22. Kennedy died Nov. 22, 1963, and Johnson succeeded him the same day. 23. Nixon resigned Aug. 9, 1974, and Gerald R. Ford succeeded him the same day. 24. One electoral vote from Virginia was cast for John Hospers, Libertarian Party. 25. One electoral vote from Washington was cast for Ronald Reagan.

Characteristics of Voters in 1980 Presidential Election

(in millions)

Characteristic	Persons of voting age	Persons reporting they voted: Total	Persons reporting they voted: Percent	Persons reporting they did not vote
Male	74,082	43,753	59.1	30,329
Female	83,003	49,312	59.4	33,691
White	137,676	83,855	60.9	53,821
Black	16,423	8,287	50.5	8,136
Spanish origin[1]	8,210	2,453	29.9	5,757
Age: 18–20	12,274	4,387	35.7	7,887
21–24	15,864	6,838	43.1	9,026
25–34	35,733	19,498	54.6	16,235
35–44	25,552	16,460	64.4	9,092
45–54	22,495	15,174	67.5	7,321
55–64	21,074	15,031	71.3	6,043
65–74	15,324	10,622	69.3	4,702
75 and over	8,770	5,055	57.6	3,715
Residence:				
Metropolitan	106,627	62,703	58.8	43,924
Nonmetropolitan	50,459	30,363	60.2	20,096
North and West	106,525	64,963	61.0	41,560
South	50,561	28,103	55.6	22,458
Education:				
8 years or less	22,656	9,643	42.6	13,012
9–11 years	22,477	10,246	45.6	12,232
12 years	61,165	35,998	58.9	25,167
More than 12	50,787	37,179	73.2	13,608
Employed	95,041	58,778	61.8	36,262
Unemployed	6,893	2,838	41.2	4,055
Not in labor force	55,151	31,449	57.0	23,702
Total	**157,085**	**93,066**	**59.2**	**64,020**

Persons of Spanish origin may be of any race. *Source:* Department of Commerce, Bureau of the Census.

Facts About Elections

Candidate with highest popular vote: Nixon (1972), 47,169,911.

Candidate with highest electoral vote: F. D. Roosevelt (1936), 523.

Candidate carrying most states: Nixon (1972), 49.

Candidate running most times: Norman Thomas, 6 (1928, 1932, 1936, 1940, 1944, 1948).

Candidate elected, defeated, then reelected: Cleveland (1884, 1888, 1892).

Presidential Election of 1968

Principal Candidates for President and Vice President
Republican: Richard M. Nixon; Spiro T. Agnew
Democratic: Hubert H. Humphrey; Edmund S. Muskie
American Independent Party: George C. Wallace; Curtis E. LeMay

		Nixon	Humphrey	Wallace		Electoral Vote			Votes at Natl. Convs.	
State	Total	Rep.	Dem.	Am. Ind.	Plurality	R	D	A	Dem.	Rep.
Alabama	1,049,922	146,923	196,579[1]	691,425[2]	494,846 A	—	—	10	32	26
Alaska	83,035	37,600	35,411	10,024	2,189 R	3	—	—	22	12
Arizona	486,936	266,721	170,514	46,573	96,207 R	5	—	—	19	16
Arkansas	619,969	190,759	188,228	240,982	50,223 A	—	—	6	33	18
California	7,251,587	3,467,664	3,244,318	487,270	223,346 R	40	—	—	174	86
Colorado	811,199	409,345	335,174	60,813	74,171 R	6	—	—	35	18
Connecticut	1,256,232	556,721	621,561	76,650	64,840 D	—	8	—	44	16
Delaware	214,367	96,714	89,194	28,459	7,520 R	3	—	—	22	12
D.C.	170,578	31,012	139,566	—	108,554 D	—	3	—	23	9
Florida	2,187,805	886,804	676,794	624,207	210,010 R	14	—	—	63	34
Georgia	1,250,266	380,111	334,440	535,550	155,439 A	—	—	12	43	30
Hawaii	236,218	91,425	141,324	3,469	49,899 D	—	4	—	26	14
Idaho	291,183	165,369	89,273	36,541	76,096 R	4	—	—	25	14
Illinois	4,619,749	2,174,774	2,039,814	390,958	134,960 R	26	—	—	118	58
Indiana	2,123,597	1,067,885	806,659	243,108	261,226 R	13	—	—	63	26
Iowa	1,167,931	619,106	476,699	66,422	142,407 R	9	—	—	46	24
Kansas	872,783	478,674	302,996	88,921	175,678 R	7	—	—	38	20
Kentucky	1,055,893	462,411	397,541	193,098	64,870 R	9	—	—	46	24
Louisiana	1,097,450	257,535	309,615	530,300	220,685 A	—	—	10	36	26
Maine	392,936	169,254	217,312	6,370	48,058 D	—	4	—	27	14
Maryland	1,235,039	517,995	538,310	178,734	20,315 D	—	10	—	49	26
Massachusetts	2,331,752	766,844	1,469,218	87,088	702,374 D	—	14	—	72	34
Michigan	3,306,250	1,370,665	1,593,082	331,968	222,417 D	—	21	—	96	48
Minnesota	1,588,506	658,643	857,738	68,931	199,095 D	—	10	—	52	26
Mississippi	654,509	88,516	150,644	415,349	264,705 A	—	—	7	24	20
Missouri	1,809,502	811,932	791,444	206,126	20,488 R	12	—	—	60	24
Montana	274,404	138,835	114,117	20,015	24,718 R	4	—	—	26	14
Nebraska	536,851	321,163	170,784	44,904	150,379 R	5	—	—	30	16
Nevada	154,218	73,188	60,598	20,432	12,590 R	3	—	—	22	12
New Hampshire	297,298	154,903	130,589	11,173	24,314 R	4	—	—	26	8
New Jersey	2,875,395	1,325,467	1,264,206	262,187	61,261 R	17	—	—	82	40
New Mexico	327,350	169,692	130,081	25,737	39,611 R	4	—	—	26	14
New York	6,791,688	3,007,932	3,378,470[3]	358,864	370,538 D	—	43	—	190	92
North Carolina	1,587,493	627,192	464,113	496,188	131,004 R	12	—	1	59	26
North Dakota	247,882	138,669	94,769	14,244	43,900 R	4	—	—	25	8
Ohio	3,959,698	1,791,014	1,700,586	467,495	90,428 R	26	—	—	115	58
Oklahoma	943,086	449,697	301,658	191,731	148,039 R	8	—	—	41	22
Oregon	819,622	408,433	358,866	49,683	49,567 R	6	—	—	35	18
Pennsylvania	4,747,928	2,090,017	2,259,405	378,582	169,388 D	—	29	—	130	64
Rhode Island	385,000	122,359	246,518	15,678	124,159 D	—	4	—	27	14
South Carolina	666,978	254,062	197,486	215,430	38,632 R	8	—	—	28	22
South Dakota	281,264	149,841	118,023	13,400	31,818 R	4	—	—	26	14
Tennessee	1,248,617	472,592	351,233	424,792	47,800 R	11	—	—	51	28
Texas	3,079,406	1,227,844	1,266,804	584,269	38,960 D	—	25	—	104	56
Utah	422,568	238,728	156,665	26,906	82,063 R	4	—	—	26	8
Vermont	161,404	85,142	70,255	5,104	14,887 R	3	—	—	22	12
Virginia	1,361,491	590,319	442,387	321,833	147,932 R	12	—	—	54	24
Washington	1,304,281	588,510	616,037	96,990	27,527 D	—	9	—	47	24
West Virginia	754,206	307,555	374,091	72,560	66,536 D	—	7	—	38	14
Wisconsin	1,691,538	809,997	748,804	127,835	61,193 R	12	—	—	59	30
Wyoming	127,205	70,927	45,173	11,105	25,754 R	3	—	—	22	12
Total	**73,212,065**	**31,785,480**	**31,275,166**	**9,906,473**	**510,314 R**	**301**	**191**	**46**	**2,622[4]**	**1,333[5]**

1. This vote, cast for Humphrey, is a combination of National Democratic (54,144) and Independent Democratic (142,435). 2. This vote for Wallace was cast as Democratic in Alabama. 3. Contains 3,066,848 Democratic and 311,622 Liberal votes. 4. Includes 23 votes allocated to U.S. territories. 5. Includes 8 votes allocated to U.S. territories.
OTHER CANDIDATES FOR PRESIDENT: New Party, Dick Gregory; Peace and Freedom Party, Eldridge Cleaver; Prohibition Party, E. Harold Munn; Socialist Labor Party, Hennings Blomen; Socialist Workers Party, Fred Halstead.
NATIONAL TOTAL OF OTHER VOTES: 244,946, from 30 states.
Source: America Votes, compiled and edited by Richard M. Scammon.

Presidential Election of 1972

Principal Candidates for President and Vice President
Republican: Richard M. Nixon; Spiro T. Agnew
Democratic: George McGovern; Sargent Shriver
American Party[1]: John G. Schmitz; Thomas J. Anderson

		Nixon	McGovern	Schmitz		Electoral vote			Votes at Natl. Convs.	
State	Total	Republican	Democratic	American	Plurality	R	D	A	Dem.	Rep.
Alabama	1,006,111	728,701	256,923	11,928	471,778 R	9	—	—	37	17
Alaska	95,219	55,349	32,967	6,903	22,382 R	3	—	—	10	12
Arizona	622,926	402,812	198,540	21,208	204,272 R	6	—	—	25	18
Arkansas	651,320	448,541	199,892	2,887	248,649 R	6	—	—	27	18
California	8,367,862	4,602,096	3,475,847	232,554	1,126,249 R	45	—	—	271	96
Colorado	953,884	597,189	329,980	17,269	267,209 R	7	—	—	36	20
Connecticut	1,384,277	810,763	555,498	17,239	255,265 R	8	—	—	51	22
Delaware	235,516	140,357	92,283	2,638	48,074 R	3	—	—	13	12
D.C.	163,421	35,226	127,627	—	92,401 D	—	3	—	15	9
Florida	2,583,283	1,857,759	718,117	—	1,139,642 R	17	—	—	81	40
Georgia	1,174,772	881,496	289,529	812	591,967 R	12	—	—	53	24
Hawaii	270,274	168,865	101,409	—	67,456 R	4	—	—	17	14
Idaho	310,379	199,384	80,826	28,869	118,558 R	4	—	—	17	14
Illinois	4,723,236	2,788,179	1,913,472	2,471	874,707 R	26	—	—	170	58
Indiana	2,125,529	1,405,154	708,568	—	696,586 R	13	—	—	76	32
Iowa	1,225,944	706,207	496,206	22,056	210,001 R	8	—	—	46	20
Kansas	916,095	619,812	270,287	21,808	349,525 R	7	—	—	35	24
Kentucky	1,067,499	676,446	371,159	17,627	305,287 R	9	—	—	47	20
Louisiana	1,051,491	686,852	298,142	52,099	388,710 R	10	—	—	44	8
Maine	417,042	256,458	160,584	—	95,874 R	4	—	—	20	26
Maryland	1,353,812	829,305	505,781	18,726	323,524 R	10	—	—	53	34
Massachusetts	2,458,756	1,112,078	1,332,540	2,877	220,462 D	—	14	—	102	48
Michigan	3,489,727	1,961,721	1,459,435	63,321	502,286 R	21	—	—	132	26
Minnesota	1,741,652	898,269	802,346	31,407	95,923 R	10	—	—	64	26
Mississippi	645,963	505,125	126,782	11,598	378,343 R	7	—	—	25	13
Missouri	1,855,803	1,153,852	697,147	—	456,705 R	12	—	—	73	30
Montana	317,603	183,976	120,197	13,430	63,779 R	4	—	—	17	14
Nebraska	576,289	406,298	169,991	—	236,307 R	5	—	—	24	16
Nevada	181,766	115,750	66,016	—	49,734 R	3	—	—	11	12
New Hampshire	334,055	213,724	116,435	3,386	97,289 R	4	—	—	18	14
New Jersey	2,997,229	1,845,502	1,102,211	34,378	743,291 R	17	—	—	109	40
New Mexico	386,241	235,606	141,084	8,767	94,522 R	4	—	—	18	14
New York	7,165,919	4,192,778	2,951,084	—	1,241,694 R	41	—	—	278	88
North Carolina	1,518,612	1,054,889	438,705	25,018	616,184 R	13	—	—	64	32
North Dakota	280,514	174,109	100,384	5,646	73,725 R	3	—	—	14	12
Ohio	4,094,787	2,441,827	1,558,889	80,067	882,938 R	25	—	—	153	56
Oklahoma	1,029,900	759,025	247,147	23,728	511,878 R	8	—	—	39	22
Oregon	927,946	486,686	392,760	46,211	93,926 R	6	—	—	34	18
Pennsylvania	4,592,106	2,714,521	1,796,951	70,593	917,570 R	27	—	—	182	60
Rhode Island	415,808	220,383	194,645	25	25,738 R	4	—	—	22	8
South Carolina	673,960	477,044	186,824	10,075	290,220 R	8	—	—	32	22
South Dakota	307,415	166,476	139,945	—	26,531 R	4	—	—	17	14
Tennessee	1,201,182	813,147	357,293	30,373	455,854 R	10	—	—	49	26
Texas	3,471,281	2,298,896	1,154,289	6,039	1,144,607 R	26	—	—	130	52
Utah	478,476	323,643	126,284	28,549	197,359 R	4	—	—	19	14
Vermont	186,947	117,149	68,174	—	48,975 R	3	—	—	12	12
Virginia	1,457,019	988,493	438,887	19,721	549,606 R	11[2]	—	—	53	30
Washington	1,470,847	837,135	568,334	58,906	268,801 R	9	—	—	52	24
West Virginia	762,399	484,964	277,435	—	207,529 R	6	—	—	35	18
Wisconsin	1,852,890	989,430	810,174	47,525	179,256 R	11	—	—	67	18
Wyoming	145,570	100,464	44,358	748	56,106 R	3	—	—	11	12
Total	**77,718,554**	**47,169,911**	**29,170,383**	**1,099,482**	**17,999,528 R**	**520**	**17**	**0**	**3,016[3]**	**1,346[4]**

1. Known as American Independent Party and by other names in some states. 2. One Virginia elector cast vote for Libertarian Party. 3. Includes 16 votes allocated to U.S. territories. 4. Includes 11 votes allocated to U.S. territories.

OTHER CANDIDATES FOR PRESIDENT: Communist, Gus Hall, Libertarian Party, John Hospers; People's Party, Benjamin Spock; Prohibition Party, Earle H. Munn; Socialist Labor Party, Louis Fisher; Socialist Workers Party, Linda Jenness.

NATIONAL TOTALS OF OTHER VOTES: People's, 78,756; Social Workers, 66,677; Socialist Labor, 53,814; Communist, 25,595; Prohibition, 13,505; others and scattered, 40,431.

Source: America Votes 10, compiled and edited by Richard M. Scammon.

Presidential Election of 1976

Principal Candidates for President and Vice President
Democratic: Jimmy Carter; Walter F. Mondale
Republican: Gerald R. Ford; Robert J. Dole
Independent: Eugene J. McCarthy

State	Total	Carter	Ford	McCarthy	Plurality	Electoral vote		Votes at Natl. Convs.	
		Dem.	Rep.	Ind.		D	R	Dem.	Rep.
Alabama	1,182,850	659,170	504,070	99	155,100 D	9	—	35	37
Alaska	123,574	44,058	71,555	—	27,497 R	—	3	10	19
Arizona	742,719	295,602	418,642	19,229	123,040 R	—	6	25	29
Arkansas	767,535	498,604	267,903	639	230,701 D	6	—	26	27
California	7,867,117	3,742,284	3,882,244	58,412	139,960 R	—	45	280	167
Colorado	1,081,554	460,801	584,278	26,047	123,477 R	—	7	35	31
Connecticut	1,381,526	647,895	719,261	3,759	71,366 R	—	8	51	35
Delaware	235,834	122,596	109,831	2,437	12,765 D	3	—	12	17
D.C.	168,830	137,818	27,873	—	109,945 D	3	—	17	14
Florida	3,150,631	1,636,000	1,469,531	23,643	166,469 D	17	—	81	66
Georgia	1,467,458	979,409	483,743	991	495,666 D	12	—	50	48
Hawaii	291,301	147,375	140,003	—	7,372 D	4	—	17	19
Idaho	344,071	126,549	204,151	1,194	77,602 R	—	4	16	21
Illinois	4,718,914	2,271,295	2,364,269	55,939	92,974 R	—	26	169	101
Indiana	2,220,362	1,014,714	1,183,958	—	169,244 R	—	13	75	54
Iowa	1,279,306	619,931	632,863	20,051	12,932 R	—	8	47	36
Kansas	957,845	430,421	502,752	13,185	72,331 R	—	7	34	34
Kentucky	1,167,142	615,717	531,852	6,837	83,865 D	9	—	46	37
Louisiana	1,278,439	661,365	587,446	6,588	73,919 D	10	—	41	41
Maine	483,216	232,279	236,320	10,874	4,041 R	—	4	20	20
Maryland	1,439,897	759,612	672,661	4,541	86,951 D	10	—	53	43
Massachusetts	2,547,558	1,429,475	1,030,276	65,637	399,199 D	14	—	104	43
Michigan	3,653,749	1,696,714	1,893,742	47,905	197,028 R	—	21	133	84
Minnesota	1,949,931	1,070,440	819,395	35,490	251,045 D	10	—	65	42
Mississippi	769,361	381,309	366,846	4,074	14,463 D	7	—	24	30
Missouri	1,953,600	998,387	927,443	24,029	70,944 D	12	—	71	49
Montana	328,734	149,259	173,703	—	24,444 R	—	4	17	20
Nebraska	607,668	233,293	359,219	9,409	125,926 R	—	5	23	25
Nevada	201,876	92,479	101,273	—	8,794 R	—	3	11	18
New Hampshire	339,618	147,645	185,935	4,095	38,290 R	—	4	17	21
New Jersey	3,014,472	1,444,653	1,509,688	32,717	65,035 R	—	17	108	67
New Mexico	418,409	201,148	211,419	1,161	10,271 R	—	4	18	21
New York	6,534,170	3,389,558	3,100,791	4,303	288,767 D	41	—	274	154
North Carolina	1,678,914	927,365	741,960	780	185,405 D	13	—	61	54
North Dakota	297,188	136,078	153,470	2,952	17,392 R	—	3	13	18
Ohio	4,111,873	2,011,621	2,000,505	58,258	11,116 D	25	—	152	97
Oklahoma	1,092,251	532,442	545,708	14,101	13,266 R	—	8	37	36
Oregon	1,029,876	490,407	492,120	40,207	1,713 R	—	6	34	30
Pennsylvania	4,620,787	2,328,677	2,205,604	50,584	123,073 D	27	—	178	103
Rhode Island	411,170	227,636	181,249	479	46,387 D	4	—	22	19
South Carolina	802,583	450,807	346,149	289	104,658 D	8	—	31	36
South Dakota	300,678	147,068	151,505	—	4,437 R	—	4	17	20
Tennessee	1,476,345	825,879	633,969	5,004	191,910 D	10	—	46	43
Texas	4,071,884	2,082,319	1,953,300	20,118	129,019 D	26	—	130	100
Utah	541,198	182,110	337,908	3,907	155,798 R	—	4	18	20
Vermont	187,765	78,789	100,387	4,001	21,598 R	—	3	12	18
Virginia	1,697,094	813,896	836,554	—	22,658 R	—	12	54	51
Washington	1,555,534	717,323	777,732	36,986	60,409 R	—	8[1]	53	38
West Virginia	750,964	435,914	314,760	113	121,154 D	6	—	33	28
Wisconsin	2,104,175	1,040,232	1,004,987	34,943	35,245 D	11	—	68	45
Wyoming	156,343	62,239	92,717	624	30,478 R	—	3	10	17
Total	**81,555,889**	**40,830,763**	**39,147,793**	**756,631**	**1,682,970D**	**297**	**240**	**3,008[2]**	**2,259[3]**

1. Ninth Washington elector cast vote for Ronald Reagan. 2. Includes 34 votes allocated to U.S. territories and Democrats abroad. 3. Includes 16 votes allocated to U.S. territories.

OTHER CANDIDATES FOR PRESIDENT: Roger L. MacBride, Libertarian; Lester G. Maddox, American Independent; Thomas J. Anderson, American; Peter Camejo, Socialist Workers; Gus Hall, Communist; Margaret Wright, People's; Lyndon LaRouche, United States Labor; Benjamin C. Bubar, Prohibition; Julius Levin, Socialist Labor; Frank P. Zeidler, Socialist.

NATIONAL TOTALS OF OTHER VOTES: Libertarian, 173,011; American Independent, 170,531; American, 160,773; Socialist Workers, 91,314; Communist, 58,992; People's, 49,024; United States Labor, 40,043; Prohibition, 15,934; Socialist Labor, 9,616; Socialist, 6,038; others and scattered, 45,366.

Source: America Votes 12, compiled and edited by Richard M. Scammon and Alice V. McGillivray.

Presidential Election of 1980

Principal Candidates for President and Vice President
Democratic: Jimmy Carter; Walter F. Mondale
Republican: Ronald Reagan; George Bush
Independent: John B. Anderson; Patrick J. Lucey

		Carter		Reagan		Anderson			Electoral vote		
State	Total	Dem.	Per-cent	Rep.	Per-cent	Independent	Per-cent	Plurality	D	R	I
Alabama	1,341,929	636,730	47	654,192	49	16,481	1	17,462 R	—	9	—
Alaska	157,589	41,842	27	86,112	55	11,156	7	44,270 R	—	3	—
Arizona	873,945	246,843	28	529,688	61	76,952	9	282,845 R	—	6	—
Arkansas	837,582	398,041	48	403,164	48	22,468	3	5,123 R	—	6	—
California	8,585,789	3,083,652	36	4,524,835	53	739,832	9	1,441,183 R	—	45	—
Colorado	1,184,450	368,009	31	652,264	55	130,633	11	284,255 R	—	7	—
Connecticut	1,406,285	541,732	39	677,210	48	171,807	12	135,478 R	—	8	—
Delaware	235,723	105,754	45	111,252	47	16,288	7	5,498 R	—	3	—
D.C.	173,889	130,231	75	23,313	13	16,131	9	106,918 D	3	—	—
Florida	3,686,926	1,419,475	39	2,046,951	56	189,692	5	734,394 R	—	17	—
Georgia	1,596,582	890,733	56	654,168	41	36,055	2	236,565 D	12	—	—
Hawaii	303,287	135,879	45	130,112	43	32,021	11	5,767 D	4	—	—
Idaho	437,431	110,192	25	290,699	67	27,058	6	180,507 R	—	4	—
Illinois	4,749,766	1,981,413	42	2,358,094	50	346,754	7	376,681 R	—	26	—
Indiana	2,242,033	844,197	38	1,255,656	56	111,639	5	411,459 R	—	13	—
Iowa	1,317,661	508,672	39	676,026	51	115,633	9	167,354 R	—	8	—
Kansas	979,786	326,150	33	566,812	58	68,231	7	240,662 R	—	7	—
Kentucky	1,295,627	617,417	48	635,274	49	31,127	2	17,857 R	—	9	—
Louisiana	1,548,591	708,453	46	792,853	51	26,345	2	84,400 R	—	10	—
Maine	523,134	220,974	42	238,522	46	53,450	10	17,548 R	—	4	—
Maryland	1,540,496	726,161	47	680,606	44	119,537	8	45,555 R	10	—	—
Massachusetts	2,524,630	1,053,802	42	1,056,233	42	382,539	15	2,421 R	—	14	—
Michigan	3,909,725	1,661,532	43	1,915,225	49	275,223	7	253,393 R	—	21	—
Minnesota	2,045,780	954,173	47	873,268	43	174,997	9	80,905 D	10	—	—
Mississippi	892,620	429,281	48	441,089	49	12,036	1	11,808 R	—	7	—
Missouri	2,099,824	931,182	44	1,074,181	51	77,920	4	142,999 R	—	12	—
Montana	363,952	118,032	32	206,814	57	29,281	8	88,782 R	—	4	—
Nebraska	639,533	166,424	26	419,214	66	44,854	7	252,790 R	—	5	—
Nevada	243,692	66,666	27	155,017	64	17,651	7	177,026 R	—	3	—
New Hampshire	383,999	108,864	28	221,705	58	49,693	13	112,841 R	—	4	—
New Jersey	2,975,684	1,147,364	39	1,546,557	52	234,632	8	399,193 R	—	17	—
New Mexico	456,237	167,832	37	250,770	55	29,459	6	82,938 R	—	4	—
New York	6,201,959	2,728,372	44	2,893,831	47	467,801	8	165,459 R	—	41	—
North Carolina	1,855,833	875,635	47	915,018	49	52,800	3	39,383 R	—	13	—
North Dakota	301,545	79,189	26	193,695	64	23,640	8	114,506 R	—	3	—
Ohio	4,283,603	1,752,414	41	2,206,545	52	254,472	6	454,131 R	—	25	—
Oklahoma	1,149,708	402,026	35	695,570	60	38,284	3	293,544 R	—	8	—
Oregon	1,181,516	456,890	39	571,044	48	112,389	10	114,154 R	—	6	—
Pennsylvania	4,561,501	1,937,540	42	2,261,872	50	292,921	6	324,332 R	—	27	—
Rhode Island	415,967	198,342	48	154,793	37	59,819	14	43,549 D	4	—	—
South Carolina	893,190	28,220	48	39,277	49	13,868	2	11,456 R	—	8	—
South Dakota	327,703	103,855	32	198,343	61	21,431	7	94,488 R	—	4	—
Tennessee	1,617,616	783,051	48	787,761	49	35,991	2	4,710 R	—	10	—
Texas	4,541,636	1,881,147	41	2,510,705	55	111,613	2	629,558 R	—	26	—
Utah	604,152	124,266	21	439,687	73	30,284	5	315,421 R	—	4	—
Vermont	213,299	81,952	38	94,628	44	31,761	15	12,676 R	—	3	—
Virginia	1,866,032	752,174	40	989,609	53	95,418	5	237,435 R	—	12	—
Washington	1,742,394	650,193	37	865,244	50	185,073	11	215,051 R	—	9	—
West Virginia	737,715	367,462	50	334,206	45	31,691	4	33,256 D	6	—	—
Wisconsin	2,273,221	981,584	43	1,088,845	48	160,657	7	107,261 R	—	11	—
Wyoming	176,713	49,427	28	110,700	63	12,072	7	61,273 R	—	8	—
Total	**86,495,678**	**35,481,435**	**41**	**43,899,248**	**51**	**5,719,437**	**6**	**8,417,813 R**	**49**	**489**	—

NATIONAL TOTALS OF OTHER CANDIDATES FOR PRESIDENT: Ed Clark, Libertarian, 920,859; Barry Commoner, Citizens, 230,377: Gus Hall, Communist, 43,871; John Rarick, American Independent, 41,172; Clifton DeBerry, Socialist Workers, 40,105; Ellen McCormack, Respect for Life, 32,319; Margaret Smith, Peace and Freedom, 18,117; Deirdre Griswold, Workers' World, 13,211; others and write-ins, 55,527. *Source:* Federal Election Commission.

1980 Election Had Lowest Voter Turnout in 32 Years

According to the Federal Election Commission, only 53.95% of the eligible voters in the country cast their ballots in the 1980 presidential election. This was the lowest since the Truman-Dewey election of 1948 when only 51.1% of the voters went to the polls.

The highest voter turnout in the last 50 years was in the Kennedy-Nixon contest of 1960 with 62.8% of the electorate participating.

Qualifications for Voting

The Supreme Court decision of March 21, 1972, declared lengthy requirements for voting in state and local elections unconstitutional and suggested that 30 days was an ample period. Most of the states have changed or eliminated their durational residency requirements to comply with the ruling, as shown.

NO DURATIONAL RESIDENCY REQUIREMENT

Alabama, Arkansas, California, Connecticut,[14] Delaware,[13] District of Columbia,[2] Florida,[17] Georgia,[2] Hawaii,[2] Idaho, Iowa,[6] Louisiana,[2] Maine, Maryland, Massachusetts,[8] Nebraska,[9] New Hampshire,[18] New Mexico,[7] North Carolina, Oklahoma, South Carolina,[2] South Dakota,[10] Tennessee,[12] Texas, Virginia, West Virginia,[2] Wyoming[2]

30-DAY RESIDENCY REQUIREMENT

Alaska, Arizona,[11] Illinois, Indiana, Kentucky,[2] Michigan, Mississippi, Montana, Nevada, New Jersey, New York, North Dakota,[3] Ohio, Pennsylvania, Rhode Island, Utah, Washington

OTHER

Colorado,[1] Kansas, Minnesota[16] and Oregon, 20 days; Missouri,[4] 6 months; Vermont, 17 days;[15] Wisconsin, 10 days

1. 29-day for Presidential elections, 32 for all other. 2. 30-day registration requirement. 3. 10-day for Presidential elections. 4. 28 days in St. Louis County, 4th Wednesday prior to elections in rest of state. 5. 30-day registration requirement for national elections; 45-day for state elections. 6. 10-day registration requirement. 7. 42-day registration requirement. 8. Registration deadline 28 days prior to primary or state elections. 9. Registration requirement, 2nd Friday prior to elections. 10. 15-day registration requirement. 11. 50-day for state. 12. 20-day registration requirement. 13. Must reside in Delaware and register by the last day that the books are open for registration. 14. 21-day registration requirement for elections; 14-day for primaries. 15. Administrative cut-off date for processing applications. 16. Permits registration and voting on election day with approved ID. 17. Must declare residency and D.C. must process within 15 days. Registration stops 30 days before any election and until 15 days after. 18. Registration requirement, 2nd Saturday prior to elections. *Source: Information Please* questionnaires to the states, and League of Women Voters.

Unusual Voting Results

Election of 1872

The presidential and vice-presidential candidates of the Liberal Republicans and the northern Democrats in 1872 were Horace Greeley and B. Gratz Brown. Greeley died Nov. 29, 1872, before his 66 electors voted. In the electoral balloting for President, 63 of Greeley's votes were scattered among four other men, including Brown.

Election of 1876

In the election of 1876 Samuel J. Tilden, the Democratic candidate, received a popular majority but lacked one undisputed electoral vote to carry a clear majority of the electoral college. The crux of the problem was in the 22 electoral votes which were in dispute because Florida, Louisiana, South Carolina, and Oregon each sent in two sets of election returns. In the three southern states, Republican election boards threw out enough Democratic votes to certify the Republican candidate, Hayes. In Oregon, the Democratic governor disqualified a Republican elector, replacing him with a Democrat. Since the Senate was Republican and the House of Representatives Democratic, it seemed useless to refer the disputed returns to the two houses for solution. Instead Congress appointed an Electoral Commission with five representatives each from the Senate, the House, and the Supreme Court. All but one Justice was named, giving the Commission seven Republican and seven Democratic members. The naming of the fifth Justice was left to the other four. He was a Republican who first favored Tilden but, under pressure from his party, switched to Hayes, ensuring his election by the Commission voting 8 to 7 on party lines.

Minority Presidents

Fifteen candidates have become President of the United States with a popular vote less than 50% of the total cast. It should be noted, however, that in elections before 1872, presidential electors were not chosen by popular vote in all states. Adams' election in 1824 was by the House of Representatives, which chose him over Jackson, who had a plurality of both electoral and popular votes, but not a majority in the electoral college.

Besides Jackson in 1824, only two other candidates receiving the largest popular vote have failed to gain a majority in the electoral college—Samuel J. Tilden (D) in 1876 and Grover Cleveland (D) in 1888.

The "minority" Presidents follow:

Vote Received by Minority Presidents

		Electoral	Popular vote
Year	President	Percent	Percent
1824	John Q. Adams	31.8	29.8
1844	James K. Polk (D)	61.8	49.3
1848	Zachary Taylor (W)	56.2	47.3
1856	James Buchanan (D)	58.7	45.3
1860	Abraham Lincoln (R)	59.4	39.9
1876	Rutherford B. Hayes (R)	50.1	47.9
1880	James A. Garfield (R)	57.9	48.3
1884	Grover Cleveland (D)	54.6	48.8
1888	Benjamin Harrison (R)	58.1	47.8
1892	Grover Cleveland (D)	62.4	46.0
1912	Woodrow Wilson (D)	81.9	41.8
1916	Woodrow Wilson (D)	52.1	49.3
1948	Harry S. Truman (D)	57.1	49.5
1960	John F. Kennedy (D)	56.4	49.7
1968	Richard M. Nixon (R)	56.1	43.4

Government Officials

Cabinet Members With Dates of Appointment

Although the Constitution made no provision for a President's advisory group, the heads of the three executive departments (State, Treasury, and War) and the Attorney General were organized by Washington into such a group; and by about 1793, the name "Cabinet" was applied to it. With the exception of the Attorney General up to 1870 and the Postmaster General from 1829 to 1872, Cabinet members have been heads of executive departments.

A Cabinet member is appointed by the President, subject to the confirmation of the Senate; and as his term is not fixed, he may be replaced at any time by the President. At a change in Administration, it is customary for him to tender his resignation, but he remains in office until a successor is appointed.

The table of Cabinet members lists only those members who actually served after being duly commissioned.

The dates shown are those of appointment. "Cont." indicates that the term continued from the previous Administration for a substantial amount of time.

With the creation of the Department of Transportation in 1966, the Cabinet consisted of 12 members. This figure was reduced to 11 when the Post Office Department became an independent agency in 1970 but, with the establishment in 1977 of a Department of Energy, became 12 again. Creation of the Department of Education in 1980 raised the number to 13.

WASHINGTON

Secretary of State	Thomas Jefferson 1789
	Edmund Randolph 1794
	Timothy Pickering 1795
Secretary of the Treasury	Alexander Hamilton 1789
	Oliver Wolcott, Jr. 1795
Secretary of War	Henry Knox 1789
	Timothy Pickering 1795
	James McHenry 1796
Attorney General	Edmund Randolph 1789
	William Bradford 1794
	Charles Lee 1795

J. ADAMS

Secretary of State	Timothy Pickering (Cont.)
	John Marshall 1800
Secretary of the Treasury	Oliver Wolcott, Jr. (Cont.)
	Samuel Dexter 1801
Secretary of War	James McHenry (Cont.)
	Samuel Dexter 1800
Attorney General	Charles Lee (Cont.)
Secretary of the Navy	Benjamin Stoddert 1798

JEFFERSON

Secretary of State	James Madison 1801
Secretary of the Treasury	Samuel Dexter (Cont.)
	Albert Gallatin 1801
Secretary of War	Henry Dearborn 1801
Attorney General	Levi Lincoln 1801
	Robert Smith 1805
	John Breckinridge 1805
	Caesar A. Rodney 1807
Secretary of the Navy	Benjamin Stoddert (Cont.)
	Robert Smith 1801

MADISON

Secretary of State	Robert Smith 1809
	James Monroe 1811
Secretary of the Treasury	Albert Gallatin (Cont.)
	George W. Campbell 1814
	Alexander J. Dallas 1814
	William H. Crawford 1816
Secretary of War	William Eustis 1809
	John Armstrong 1813
	James Monroe 1814
	William H. Crawford 1815
Attorney General	Caesar A. Rodney (Cont.)
	William Pinckney 1811
	Richard Rush 1814
Secretary of the Navy	Paul Hamilton 1809
	William Jones 1813
	B. W. Crowninshield 1814

MONROE

Secretary of State	John Quincy Adams 1817
Secretary of the Treasury	William H. Crawford (Cont.)
Secretary of War	John C. Calhoun 1817
Attorney General	Richard Rush (Cont.)
	William Wirt 1817
Secretary of the Navy	B. W. Crowninshield (Cont.)
	Smith Thompson 1818
	Samuel L. Southard 1823

J. Q. ADAMS

Secretary of State	Henry Clay 1825
Secretary of the Treasury	Richard Rush 1825
Secretary of War	James Barbour 1825
	Peter B. Porter 1828
Attorney General	William Wirt (Cont.)
Secretary of the Navy	Samuel L. Southard (Cont.)

JACKSON

Secretary of State	Martin Van Buren 1829
	Edward Livingston 1831
	Louis McLane 1833
	John Forsyth 1834
Secretary of the Treasury	Samuel D. Ingham 1829
	Louis McLane 1831
	William J. Duane 1833
	Roger B. Taney[3] 1833
	Levi Woodbury 1834
Secretary of War	John H. Eaton 1829
	Lewis Cass 1831
Attorney General	John M. Berrien 1829
	Roger B. Taney 1831
	Benjamin F. Butler 1833
Postmaster General[1]	William T. Barry 1829
	Amos Kendall 1835
Secretary of the Navy	John Branch 1829
	Levi Woodbury 1831
	Mahlon Dickerson 1834

VAN BUREN

Secretary of State	John Forsyth (Cont.)
Secretary of the Treasury	Levi Woodbury (Cont.)
Secretary of War	Joel R. Poinsett 1837
Attorney General	Benjamin F. Butler (Cont.)
	Felix Grundy 1838
	Henry D. Gilpin 1840
Postmaster General	Amos Kendall (Cont.)
	John M. Niles 1840
Secretary of the Navy	Mahlon Dickerson (Cont.)
	James K. Paulding 1838

W. H. HARRISON

Secretary of State	Daniel Webster 1841
Secretary of the Treasury	Thomas Ewing 1841
Secretary of War	John Bell 1841
Attorney General	John J. Crittenden 1841
Postmaster General	Francis Granger 1841
Secretary of the Navy	George E. Badger 1841

TYLER

Secretary of State	Daniel Webster (Cont.)
	Abel P. Upshur 1843
	John C. Calhoun 1844
Secretary of the Treasury	Thomas Ewing (Cont.)

	Walter Forward 1841
	John C. Spencer[3] 1843
	George M. Bibb 1844
Secretary of War	John Bell (Cont.)
	John C. Spencer 1841
	James M. Porter[3] 1843
	William Wilkins 1844
Attorney General	John J. Crittenden (Cont.)
	Hugh S. Legaré 1841
	John Nelson 1843
Postmaster General	Francis Granger (Cont.)
	Charles A. Wickliffe 1841
Secretary of the Navy	George E. Badger (Cont.)
	Abel P. Upshur 1841
	David Henshaw[3] 1843
	Thomas W. Gilmer 1844
	John Y. Mason 1844

POLK

Secretary of State	James Buchanan 1845
Secretary of the Treasury	Robert J. Walker 1845
Secretary of War	William L. Marcy 1845
Attorney General	John Y. Mason 1845
	Nathan Clifford 1846
	Isaac Toucey 1848
Postmaster General	Cave Johnson 1845
Secretary of the Navy	George Bancroft 1845
	John Y. Mason 1846

TAYLOR

Secretary of State	John M. Clayton 1849
Secretary of the Treasury	William M. Meredith 1849
Secretary of War	George W. Crawford 1849
Attorney General	Reverdy Johnson 1849
Postmaster General	Jacob Collamer 1849
Secretary of the Navy	William B. Preston 1849
Secretary of the Interior	Thomas Ewing 1849

FILLMORE

Secretary of State	Daniel Webster 1850
	Edward Everett 1852
Secretary of the Treasury	Thomas Corwin 1850
Secretary of War	Charles M. Conrad 1850
Attorney General	John J. Crittenden 1850
Postmaster General	Nathan K. Hall 1850
	Samuel D. Hubbard 1852
Secretary of the Navy	William A. Graham 1850
	John P. Kennedy 1852
Secretary of the Interior	Thos. M. T. McKennan 1850
	Alex. H. H. Stuart 1850

PIERCE

Secretary of State	William L. Marcy 1853
Secretary of the Treasury	James Guthrie 1853
Secretary of War	Jefferson Davis 1853
Attorney General	Caleb Cushing 1853
Postmaster General	James Campbell 1853
Secretary of the Navy	James C. Dobbin 1853
Secretary of the Interior	Robert McClelland 1853

BUCHANAN

Secretary of State	Lewis Cass 1857
	Jeremiah S. Black 1860
Secretary of the Treasury	Howell Cobb 1857
	Philip F. Thomas 1860
	John A. Dix 1861
Secretary of War	John B. Floyd 1857
	Joseph Holt 1861
Attorney General	Jeremiah S. Black 1857
	Edwin M. Stanton 1860
Postmaster General	Aaron V. Brown 1857
	Joseph Holt 1859
	Horatio King 1861
Secretary of the Navy	Isaac Toucey 1857
Secretary of the Interior	Jacob Thompson 1857

LINCOLN

Secretary of State	William H. Seward 1861
Secretary of the Treasury	Salmon P. Chase 1861
	William P. Fessenden 1864
	Hugh McCulloch 1865
Secretary of War	Simon Cameron 1861
	Edwin M. Stanton 1862
Attorney General	Edward Bates 1861
	James Speed 1864
Postmaster General	Montgomery Blair 1861
	William Dennison 1864
Secretary of the Navy	Gideon Welles 1861
Secretary of the Interior	Caleb B. Smith 1861
	John P. Usher 1863

A. JOHNSON

Secretary of State	William H. Seward (Cont.)
Secretary of the Treasury	Hugh McCulloch (Cont.)
Secretary of War	Edwin M. Stanton (Cont.)
	John M. Schofield 1868
Attorney General	James Speed (Cont.)
	Henry Stanbery 1866
	William M. Evarts 1868
Postmaster General	William Dennison (Cont.)
	Alexander W. Randall 1866
Secretary of the Navy	Gideon Welles (Cont.)
Secretary of the Interior	John P. Usher (Cont.)
	James Harlan 1865
	Orville H. Browning 1866

GRANT

Secretary of State	Elihu B. Washburne 1869
	Hamilton Fish 1869
Secretary of the Treasury	George S. Boutwell 1869
	William A. Richardson 1873
	Benjamin H. Bristow 1874
	Lot M. Morrill 1876
Secretary of War	John A. Rawlins 1869
	William W. Belknap 1869
	Alphonso Taft 1876
	James D. Cameron 1876
Attorney General	Ebenezer R. Hoar 1869
	Amos T. Akerman 1870
	George H. Williams 1871
	Edwards Pierrepont 1875
	Alphonso Taft 1876
Postmaster General	John A. J. Creswell 1869
	Marshall Jewell 1874
	James N. Tyner 1876
Secretary of the Navy	Adolph E. Borie 1869
	George M. Robeson 1869
Secretary of the Interior	Jacob D. Cox 1869
	Columbus Delano 1870
	Zachariah Chandler 1875

HAYES

Secretary of State	William M. Evarts 1877
Secretary of the Treasury	John Sherman 1877
Secretary of War	George W. McCrary 1877
	Alexander Ramsey 1879
Attorney General	Charles Devens 1877
Postmaster General	David M. Key 1877
	Horace Maynard 1880
Secretary of the Navy	Richard W. Thompson 1877
	Nathan Goff, Jr. 1881
Secretary of the Interior	Carl Schurz 1877

GARFIELD

Secretary of State	James G. Blaine 1881
Secretary of the Treasury	William Windom 1881
Secretary of War	Robert T. Lincoln 1881
Attorney General	Wayne MacVeagh 1881
Postmaster General	Thomas L. James 1881
Secretary of the Navy	William H. Hunt 1881
Secretary of the Interior	Samuel J. Kirkwood 1881

ARTHUR

Secretary of State	James G. Blaine (Cont.)
	F. T. Frelinghuysen 1881
Secretary of the Treasury	William Windom (Cont.)
	Charles J. Folger 1881
	Walter Q. Gresham 1884
	Hugh McCulloch 1884
Secretary of War	Robert T. Lincoln (Cont.)
Attorney General	Wayne MacVeagh (Cont.)
	Benjamin H. Brewster 1881
Postmaster General	Thomas L. James (Cont.)
	Timothy O. Howe 1881
	Walter Q. Gresham 1883
	Frank Hatton 1884
Secretary of the Navy	William H. Hunt (Cont.)

	William E. Chandler 1882
Secretary of the Interior	Samuel J. Kirkwood (Cont.)
	Henry M. Teller 1882

CLEVELAND

Secretary of State	Thomas F. Bayard 1885
Secretary of the Treasury	Daniel Manning 1885
	Charles S. Fairchild 1887
Secretary of War	William C. Endicott 1885
Attorney General	Augustus H. Garland 1885
Postmaster General	William F. Vilas 1885
	Don M. Dickinson 1888
Secretary of the Navy	William C. Whitney 1885
Secretary of the Interior	Lucius Q. C. Lamar 1885
	William F. Vilas 1888
Secretary of Agriculture	Norman J. Colman 1889

B. HARRISON

Secretary of State	James G. Blaine 1889
	John W. Foster 1892
Secretary of the Treasury	William Windom 1889
	Charles Foster 1891
Secretary of War	Redfield Proctor 1889
	Stephen B. Elkins 1891
Attorney General	William H. H. Miller 1889
Postmaster General	John Wanamaker 1889
Secretary of the Navy	Benjamin F. Tracy 1889
Secretary of the Interior	John W. Noble 1889
Secretary of Agriculture	Jeremiah M. Rusk 1889

CLEVELAND

Secretary of State	Walter Q. Gresham 1893
	Richard Olney 1895
Secretary of the Treasury	John G. Carlisle 1893
Secretary of War	Daniel S. Lamont 1893
Attorney General	Richard Olney 1893
	Judson Harmon 1895
Postmaster General	Wilson S. Bissell 1893
	William L. Wilson 1895
Secretary of the Navy	Hilary A. Herbert 1893
Secretary of the Interior	Hoke Smith 1893
	David R. Francis 1896
Secretary of Agriculture	Julius Sterling Morton 1893

McKINLEY

Secretary of State	John Sherman 1897
	William R. Day 1898
	John Hay 1898
Secretary of the Treasury	Lyman J. Gage 1897
Secretary of War	Russell A. Alger 1897
	Elihu Root 1899
Attorney General	Joseph McKenna 1897
	John W. Griggs 1898
	Philander C. Knox 1901
Postmaster General	James A. Gary 1897
	Charles E. Smith 1898
Secretary of the Navy	John D. Long 1897
Secretary of the Interior	Cornelius N. Bliss 1897
	Ethan A. Hitchcock 1898
Secretary of Agriculture	James Wilson 1897

T. ROOSEVELT

Secretary of State	John Hay (Cont.)
	Elihu Root 1905
	Robert Bacon 1909
Secretary of the Treasury	Lyman J. Gage (Cont.)
	Leslie M. Shaw 1902
	George B. Cortelyou 1907
Secretary of War	Elihu Root (Cont.)
	William H. Taft 1904
	Luke E. Wright 1908
Attorney General	Philander C. Knox (Cont.)
	William H. Moody 1904
	Charles J. Bonaparte 1906
Postmaster General	Charles E. Smith (Cont.)
	Henry C. Payne 1902
	Robert J. Wynne 1904
	George B. Cortelyou 1905
	George von L. Meyer 1907
Secretary of the Navy	John D. Long (Cont.)
	William H. Moody 1902
	Paul Morton 1904
	Charles J. Bonaparte 1905
	Victor H. Metcalf 1906
	Truman H. Newberry 1908
Secretary of the Interior	Ethan A. Hitchcock (Cont.)
	James R. Garfield 1907
Secretary of Agriculture	James Wilson (Cont.)
Secretary of Commerce and Labor	George B. Cortelyou 1903
	Victor H. Metcalf 1904
	Oscar S. Straus 1906

TAFT

Secretary of State	Philander C. Knox 1909
Secretary of the Treasury	Franklin MacVeagh 1909
Secretary of War	Jacob M. Dickinson 1909
	Henry L. Stimson 1911
Attorney General	George W. Wickersham 1909
Postmaster General	Frank H. Hitchcock 1909
Secretary of the Navy	George von L. Meyer 1909
Secretary of the Interior	Richard A. Ballinger 1909
	Walter L. Fisher 1911
Secretary of Agriculture	James Wilson (Cont.)
Secretary of Commerce and Labor	Charles Nagel 1909

WILSON

Secretary of State	William J. Bryan 1913
	Robert Lansing 1915
	Bainbridge Colby 1920
Secretary of the Treasury	William G. McAdoo 1913
	Carter Glass 1918
	David F. Houston 1920
Secretary of War	Lindley M. Garrison 1913
	Newton D. Baker 1916
Attorney General	James C. McReynolds 1913
	Thomas W. Gregory 1914
	A. Mitchell Palmer 1919
Postmaster General	Albert S. Burleson 1913
Secretary of the Navy	Josephus Daniels 1913
Secretary of the Interior	Franklin K. Lane 1913
	John B. Payne 1920
Secretary of Agriculture	David F. Houston 1913
	Edwin T. Meredith 1920
Secretary of Commerce	William C. Redfield 1913
	Joshua W. Alexander 1919
Secretary of Labor	William B. Wilson 1913

HARDING

Secretary of State	Charles E. Hughes 1921
Secretary of the Treasury	Andrew W. Mellon 1921
Secretary of War	John W. Weeks 1921
Attorney General	Harry M. Daugherty 1921
Postmaster General	Will H. Hays 1921
	Hubert Work 1922
	Harry S. New 1923
Secretary of the Navy	Edwin Denby 1921
Secretary of the Interior	Albert B. Fall 1921
	Hubert Work 1923
Secretary of Agriculture	Henry C. Wallace 1921
Secretary of Commerce	Herbert Hoover 1921
Secretary of Labor	James J. Davis 1921

COOLIDGE

Secretary of State	Charles E. Hughes (Cont.)
	Frank B. Kellogg 1925
Secretary of the Treasury	Andrew W. Mellon (Cont.)
Secretary of War	John W. Weeks (Cont.)
	Dwight F. Davis 1925
Attorney General	Harry M. Daugherty (Cont.)
	Harlan F. Stone 1924
	John G. Sargent 1925
Postmaster General	Harry S. New (Cont.)
Secretary of the Navy	Edwin Denby (Cont.)
	Curtis D. Wilbur 1924
Secretary of the Interior	Hubert Work (Cont.)
	Roy O. West 1928
Secretary of Agriculture	Henry C. Wallace (Cont.)
	Howard M. Gore 1924
	William M. Jardine 1925
Secretary of Commerce	Herbert Hoover (Cont.)
	William F. Whiting 1928
Secretary of Labor	James J. Davis (Cont.)

HOOVER

Secretary of State	Frank B. Kellogg (Cont.)

	Henry L. Stimson 1929
Secretary of the Treasury	Andrew W. Mellon (Cont.)
	Ogden L. Mills 1932
Secretary of War	James W. Good 1929
	Patrick J. Hurley 1929
Attorney General	William D. Mitchell 1929
Postmaster General	Walter F. Brown 1929
Secretary of the Navy	Charles F. Adams 1929
Secretary of the Interior	Ray Lyman Wilbur 1929
Secretary of Agriculture	Arthur M. Hyde 1929
Secretary of Commerce	Robert P. Lamont 1929
	Roy D. Chapin 1932
Secretary of Labor	James J. Davis (Cont.)
	William N. Doak 1930

F. D. ROOSEVELT

Secretary of State	Cordell Hull 1933
	E. R. Stettinius, Jr. 1944
Secretary of the Treasury	William H. Woodin 1933
	Henry Morgenthau, Jr. 1934
Secretary of War	George H. Dern 1933
	Harry H. Woodring 1936
	Henry L. Stimson 1940
Attorney General	Homer S. Cummings 1933
	Frank Murphy 1939
	Robert H. Jackson 1940
	Francis Biddle 1941
Postmaster General	James A. Farley 1933
	Frank C. Walker 1940
Secretary of the Navy	Claude A. Swanson 1933
	Charles Edison 1940
	Frank Knox 1940
	James Forrestal 1944
Secretary of the Interior	Harold L. Ickes 1933
Secretary of Agriculture	Henry A. Wallace 1933
	Claude R. Wickard 1940
Secretary of Commerce	Daniel C. Roper 1933
	Harry L. Hopkins 1938
	Jesse H. Jones 1940
	Henry A. Wallace 1945
Secretary of Labor	Frances Perkins 1933

TRUMAN

Secretary of State	E. R. Stettinius, Jr. (Cont.)
	James F. Byrnes 1945
	George C. Marshall 1947
	Dean Acheson 1949
Secretary of the Treasury	Henry Morgenthau, Jr. (Cont.)
	Frederick M. Vinson 1945
	John W. Snyder 1946
Secretary of Defense	James Forrestal 1947
	Louis A. Johnson 1949
	George C. Marshall 1950
	Robert A. Lovett 1951
Attorney General	Francis Biddle (Cont.)
	Tom C. Clark 1945
	J. Howard McGrath 1949
	James P. McGranery 1952
Postmaster General	Frank C. Walker (Cont.)
	Robert E. Hannegan 1945
	Jesse M. Donaldson 1947
Secretary of the Interior	Harold L. Ickes (Cont.)
	Julius A. Krug 1946
	Oscar L. Chapman 1949
Secretary of Agriculture	Claude R. Wickard (Cont.)
	Clinton P. Anderson 1945
	Charles F. Brannan 1948
Secretary of Commerce	Henry A. Wallace (Cont.)
	W. Averell Harriman 1946
	Charles Sawyer 1948
Secretary of Labor	Frances Perkins (Cont.)
	Lewis B. Schwellenbach 1945
	Maurice J. Tobin 1948
Secretary of War[2]	Henry L. Stimson (Cont.)
	Robert P. Patterson 1945
	Kenneth C. Royall 1947
Secretary of the Navy[2]	James Forrestal (Cont.)

EISENHOWER

Secretary of State	John Foster Dulles 1953
	Christian A. Herter 1959
Secretary of the Treasury	George M. Humphrey 1953
	Robert B. Anderson 1957
Secretary of Defense	Charles E. Wilson 1953
	Neil H. McElroy 1957
	Thomas S. Gates, Jr. 1959
Attorney General	Herbert Brownell, Jr. 1953
	William P. Rogers 1958
Postmaster General	Arthur E. Summerfield 1953
Secretary of the Interior	Douglas McKay 1953
	Frederick A. Seaton 1956
Secretary of Agriculture	Ezra Taft Benson 1953
Secretary of Commerce	Sinclair Weeks 1953
	Lewis L. Strauss[3] 1958
	Frederick H. Mueller 1959
Secretary of Labor	Martin P. Durkin 1953
	James P. Mitchell 1953
Secretary of Health, Education, and Welfare	Oveta Culp Hobby 1953
	Marion B. Folsom 1955
	Arthur S. Flemming 1958

KENNEDY

Secretary of State	Dean Rusk 1961
Secretary of the Treasury	C. Douglas Dillon 1961
Secretary of Defense	Robert S. McNamara 1961
Attorney General	Robert F. Kennedy 1961
Postmaster General	J. Edward Day 1961
	John A. Gronouski 1963
Secretary of the Interior	Stewart L. Udall 1961
Secretary of Agriculture	Orville L. Freeman 1961
Secretary of Commerce	Luther H. Hodges 1961
Secretary of Labor	Arthur J. Goldberg 1961
	W. Willard Wirtz 1962
Secretary of Health, Education, and Welfare	Abraham A. Ribicoff 1961
	Anthony J. Celebrezze 1962

L. B. JOHNSON

Secretary of State	Dean Rusk (Cont.)
Secretary of the Treasury	C. Douglas Dillon (Cont.)
	Henry H. Fowler 1965
	Joseph W. Barr[4] 1968
Secretary of Defense	Robert S. McNamara (Cont.)
	Clark M. Clifford 1968
Attorney General	Robert F. Kennedy (Cont.)
	N. de B. Katzenbach 1965
	Ramsey Clark 1967
Postmaster General	John A. Gronouski (Cont.)
	Lawrence F. O'Brien 1965
	W. Marvin Watson 1968
Secretary of the Interior	Stewart L. Udall (Cont.)
Secretary of Agriculture	Orville L. Freeman (Cont.)
Secretary of Commerce	Luther H. Hodges (Cont.)
	John T. Connor 1964
	A. B. Trowbridge 1967
	C. R. Smith 1968
Secretary of Labor	W. Willard Wirtz (Cont.)
Secretary of Health, Education, and Welfare	Anthony J. Celebrezze (Cont.)
	John W. Gardner 1965
	Wilbur J. Cohen 1968
Secretary of Housing and Urban Development	Robert C. Weaver 1966
	Robert C. Wood[4] 1969
Secretary of Transportation	Alan S. Boyd 1966

NIXON

Secretary of State	William P. Rogers 1969
	Henry A. Kissinger 1973
Secretary of the Treasury	David M. Kennedy 1969
	John B. Connally 1971
	George P. Shultz 1972
	William E. Simon 1974
Secretary of Defense	Melvin R. Laird 1969
	Elliot L. Richardson 1973
	James R. Schlesinger 1973
Attorney General	John N. Mitchell 1969
	Richard G. Kleindienst 1972
	Elliot L. Richardson 1973
	William B. Saxbe 1974
Postmaster General[5]	William M. Blount 1969
Secretary of the Interior	Walter J. Hickel 1969
	Rogers C. B. Morton 1971
Secretary of Agriculture	Clifford M. Hardin 1969
	Earl L. Butz 1971
Secretary of Commerce	Maurice H. Stans 1969
	Peter G. Peterson 1972

	Frederick B. Dent 1973
Secretary of Labor	George P. Shultz 1969
	James D. Hodgson 1970
	Peter J. Brennan 1973
Secretary of Health, Education, and Welfare	Robert H. Finch 1969
	Elliot L. Richardson 1970
	Caspar W. Weinberger 1973
Secretary of Housing and Urban Development	George Romney 1969
	James T. Lynn 1973
Secretary of Transportation	John A. Volpe 1969
	Claude S. Brinegar 1973

FORD

Secretary of State	Henry A. Kissinger (Cont.)
Secretary of the Treasury	William E. Simon (Cont.)
Secretary of Defense	James R. Schlesinger (Cont.)
	Donald H. Rumsfeld 1975
Attorney General	William B. Saxbe (Cont.)
	Edward H. Levi 1975
Secretary of the Interior	Rogers C. B. Morton (Cont.)
	Stanley K. Hathaway 1975
	Thomas S. Kleppe 1975
Secretary of Agriculture	Earl L. Butz (Cont.)
	John Knebel 1976
Secretary of Commerce	Frederick B. Dent (Cont.)
	Rogers C. B. Morton 1975
	Elliot L. Richardson 1976
Secretary of Labor	Peter J. Brennan (Cont.)
	John T. Dunlop 1975
	William J. Usery, Jr. 1976
Secretary of Health, Education and Welfare	Caspar W. Weinberger (Cont.)
	F. David Mathews 1975
Secretary of Housing and Urban Development	James T. Lynn (Cont.)
	Carla A. Hills 1975
Secretary of Transportation	Claude S. Brinegar (Cont.)
	William T. Coleman, Jr. 1975

CARTER

Secretary of State	Cyrus R. Vance 1977
	Edmund S. Muskie 1980
Secretary of the Treasury	W. Michael Blumenthal 1977
	G. William Miller 1979
Secretary of Defense	Harold Brown 1977
Attorney General	Griffin B. Bell 1977
	Benjamin R. Civiletti 1979
Secretary of the Interior	Cecil D. Andrus 1977
Secretary of Agriculture	Bob S. Bergland 1977
Secretary of Commerce	Juanita M. Kreps 1977
	Philip M. Klutznick 1979
Secretary of Labor	F. Ray Marshall 1977
Secretary of Health and Human Services[6]	Joseph A. Califano, Jr. 1977
	Patricia Roberts Harris 1979
Secretary of Housing and Urban Development	Patricia Roberts Harris 1977
	Moon Landrieu 1979
Secretary of Transportation	Brock Adams 1977
	Neil E. Goldschmidt 1979
Secretary of Energy	James R. Schlesinger 1977
	Charles W. Duncan, Jr. 1979
Secretary of Education	Shirley Mount Hufstedler 1979

REAGAN

Secretary of State	Alexander M. Haig, Jr. 1981
	George P. Shultz 1982
Secretary of the Treasury	Donald T. Regan 1981
Secretary of Defense	Caspar W. Weinberger 1981
Attorney General	William French Smith 1981
Secretary of the Interior	James G. Watt 1981
Secretary of Agriculture	John R. Block 1981
Secretary of Commerce	Malcolm Baldrige 1981
Secretary of Labor	Raymond J. Donovan 1981
Secretary of Health and Human Services	Richard S. Schweiker 1981
Secretary of Housing and Urban Development	Samuel R. Pierce, Jr. 1981
Secretary of Transportation	Andrew L. Lewis, Jr. 1981
Secretary of Energy	James B. Edwards 1981
Secretary of Education	T. H. Bell 1981

1. The Postmaster General did not become a Cabinet member until 1829. Earlier Postmasters General were: Samuel Osgood (1789), Timothy Pickering (1791), Joseph Habersham (1795), Gideon Granger (1801), Return J. Meigs, Jr. (1814), and John McLean (1823). 2. On July 26, 1947, the Departments of War and of the Navy were incorporated into the Department of Defense. 3. Not confirmed by the Senate. 4. Recess appointment. 5. The Postmaster General is no longer a Cabinet member. 6. Known as Department of Health, Education, and Welfare until May 1980.

How a Bill Becomes a Law

When a Senator or a Representative introduces a bill, he sends it to the clerk of his house, who gives it a number and title. This is the *first reading,* and the bill is referred to the proper committee.

The committee may decide the bill is unwise or unnecessary and *table* it, thus killing it at once. Or it may decide the bill is worthwhile and hold hearings to listen to facts and opinions presented by experts and other interested persons. After members of the committee have debated the bill and perhaps offered amendments, a vote is taken; and if the vote is favorable, the bill is sent back to the floor of the house.

The clerk reads the bill sentence by sentence to the house, and this is known as the *second reading.* Members may then debate the bill and offer amendments. In the House of Representatives, the time for debate is limited by a *cloture rule,* but there is no such restriction in the Senate for cloture, where 60 votes are required. This makes possible a *filibuster,* in which one or more opponents hold the floor to defeat the bill.

The *third reading* is by title only, and the bill is put to a vote, which may be by voice or roll call, depending on the circumstances and parliamentary rules. Members who must be absent at the time but who wish to record their vote may be paired if each negative vote has a balancing affirmative one.

The bill then goes to the other house of Congress, where it may be defeated, or passed with or without amendments. If the bill is defeated, it dies. If it is passed with amendments, a joint Congressional committee must be appointed by both houses to iron out the differences.

After its final passage by both houses, the bill is sent to the President. If he approves, he signs it, and the bill becomes a law. However, if he disapproves, he *vetoes* the bill by refusing to sign it and sending it back to the house of origin with his reasons for the veto. The objections are read and debated, and a roll-call vote is taken. If the bill receives less than a two-thirds vote, it is defeated and goes no farther. But if it receives a two-thirds vote or greater, it is sent to the other house for a vote. If that house also passes it by a two-thirds vote, the President's veto is *overridden,* and the bill becomes a law.

Should the President desire neither to sign nor to veto the bill, he may retain it for ten days, Sundays excepted, after which time it automatically becomes a law without signature. However, if Congress has adjourned within those ten days, the bill is automatically killed, that process of indirect rejection being known as a *pocket veto.*

Federal Judiciary

Source: Administrative Office of the United States Courts.

SUPREME COURT OF THE U.S.

(Washington, D.C. 20543)
Chief Justice: Warren E. Burger

Associate Justices:
William J. Brennan, Jr.
Byron R. White
Thurgood Marshall
Harry A. Blackmun
Lewis F. Powell, Jr.
William H. Rehnquist
John Paul Stevens
Sandra Day O'Connor

U.S. COURTS OF APPEALS

(CJ indicates Chief Judge)
District of Columbia: Spottswood W. Robinson III, CJ, J.Skelly Wright, Edward Allen Tamm, Robert H. Bork, Patricia M. Wald, Abner J. Mikva, George E. MacKinnon, Malcolm R. Wilkey, Harry T. Edwards, Ruth Bader Ginsburg, all Washington.

First Circuit (Me., Mass., N.H., R.I., Puerto Rico): Frank M. Coffin, CJ, Portland, Me.; Levin H. Campbell, Stephen G. Breyer, both Boston; Hugh H. Bownes, Concord, N.H.

Second Circuit (Conn., N.Y., Vt.): Wilfred Feinbert, CJ, Irving R. Kaufman, Lawerence W. Pierce, Amalya Lyle Kearse, all New York City; Ellsworth A. Van Graafeiland, Rochester, N.Y.; Richard J. Cardamone, Utica, N.Y.; James L. Oakes, Brattleboro, Vt.; Thomas J. Meskill, New Britain, Conn; Jon O. Newman, Hartford, Conn.; Ralph K. Winter, Jr., New Haven, Conn.

Third Circuit (Del., N.J., Pa., Virgin Is.): Collins J. Seitz, CJ, Wilmington, Del.; Arlin M. Adams, Dolores K. Sloviter, Philadelphia; Ruggero J. Aldisert, Joseph F. Weis, Jr., both Pittsburgh; John J. Gibbons, Leonard I. Garth, both Newark, N.J.; James Hunter, III, Camden, N.J.; A. Leon Higginbotham, Jr., Edward R. Becker, Philadelphia.

Fourth Circuit (Md., N.C., S.C., Va., W. Va.): Harrison L. Winter, CJ, Francis D. Murnaghan, Jr., both Baltimore, Md.; John D. Butzner, Jr., Richmond, Va.; Donald Stuart Russell, Spartanburg, S.C.; Robert F. Chapman, Columbia, S.C.; H. Emory Widener, Jr., Abingdon, Va.; Kenneth K. Hall, James M. Sprouse, both Charleston, W. Va.; James Dickson Phillips, Jr., Durham, N.C.; Sam J. Ervin III, Morganton, N.C.

Fifth Circuit (La., Miss., Tex., Canal Zone): Charles Clark, CJ, Jackson, Miss.; John R. Brown, Carolyn D. Randall, both Houston; Albert Tate, Jr., New Orleans; Alvin B. Rubin, Baton Rouge, La.; Thomas G. Gee, Thomas M. Reavley, Samuel D. Johnson, Jerre S. Williams, William L. Garwood, all Austin, Tex.; Irving L. Goldberg, Dallas; Reynaldo G. Garza, Brownsville, Tex.; Henry A. Politz, Shreveport, La.

Sixth Circuit (Ky., Mich., Ohio, Tenn.): George Clifton Edwards, Jr., CJ, Cincinnati, Ohio; Nathaniel R. Jones, Cleveland, Ohio; Gilbert S. Merritt, Nashville, Tenn.; Albert J. Engel, Grand Rapids, Mich.; Pierce Lively, Danville, Ky.; Damon J. Keith, Cornelia G. Kennedy, both Detroit, Mich.; Boyce F. Martin, Jr., Louisville, Ky.

Seventh Circuit (Ill., Ind., Wis.): Walter J. Cummings, CJ, Wilbur F. Pell, Jr., Robert A. Sprecher, William J. Bauer, Harlington Wood, Jr., Richard A. Posner, Richard D. Cudahy, all Chicago; Jesse E. Eschbach, Fort Wayne, Ind.

Eighth Circuit (Ark., Iowa, Minn., Mo., Neb., N.D., S.D.): Donald P. Lay, CJ, Donald R. Ross, both Omaha, Neb.; Gerald W. Heaney, Duluth, Minn.; Myron H. Bright, Fargo, N.D.; Theodore McMillian, St. Louis; Richard Sheppard Arnold, Little Rock, Ark.

Ninth Circuit (Ariz., Calif., Idaho, Mont., Nev., Ore., Wash., Alaska, Hawaii, Guam): James R. Browning, CJ, Joseph T. Sneed, Cecil F. Poole, all San Francisco; Harry Pregerson, Arthur L. Alarcon, Warren J. Ferguson, Dorothy W. Nelson, William A. Norris, Stephen Reinhardt, all Los Angeles; J. Clifford Wallace, San Diego, Calif.; Eugene A. Wright, Jerome Farris, Betty B. Fletcher, all Seattle; Thomas Tang, Mary M. Schroeder, William C. Canby, all Phoenix, Ariz.; Herbert Y. C. Choy, Honolulu; Alfred T. Goodwin, Otto R. Skopil, Jr., both Portland, Ore.; Anthony M. Kennedy, Sacramento, Calif.; J. Blaine Anderson, Boise, Idaho; Procter Hug, Jr., Reno, Nev.; Robert Boochever, Juneau, Alaska.

Tenth Circuit (Colo., Kan., N.M., Okla., Utah, Wyo.): Oliver Seth, CJ, Santa Fe, N.M.; William J. Holloway, Jr., Oklahoma City; Robert H. McWilliams, William E. Doyle, both Denver; James E. Barrett, Cheyenne, Wyo.; James K. Logan, Olathe, Kan.; Monroe G. McKay, Salt Lake City, Utah; Stephanie K. Seymour.

Eleventh Circuit (Ala., Fla., Ga.): John C. Godbold, CJ, Frank M. Johnson, Jr., Montgomery, Ala.; James C. Hill, Albert J. Henderson, Thomas A. Clark, all Atlanta; Paul H. Roney, St. Petersburg, Fla.; Gerald B. Tjoflat, Jacksonville, Fla.; Peter T. Fay, Miami, Fla.; Robert S. Vance, Birmingham, Ala.; Phyllis A. Kravitch, Savannah, Ga.; Joseph W. Hatchett, Tallahassee, Fla.; R. Lanier Anderson, III, Macon, Ga.

U.S. COURT OF CLAIMS

(Washington, D.C. 20005)
Chief Judge: Daniel M. Friedman.
Associate Judges: Oscar H. Davis, Philip Nichols, Jr., Shiro Kashiwa, Marion T. Bennett, Edward S. Smith.

U.S. COURT OF CUSTOMS AND PATENT APPEALS

(Washington, D.C. 20439)
Chief Judge: Howard T. Markey.
Associate Judges: Giles S. Rich, Phillip B. Baldwin, Jack R. Miller, Helen W. Nies.

U.S. COURT OF INTERNATIONAL TRADE

(One Federal Plaza, New York, N.Y. 10007)
Chief Judge: Edward D. Re.
Judges: Paul P. Rao, Morgan Ford, Frederick Landis, James L. Watson, Herbert N. Maletz, Bernard Newman, Nils A. Boe.

U.S. TAX COURT

(Washington, D.C. 20217)
Chief Judge: Theodore Tannenwald, Jr.
Judges: William M. Drennen, Irene F. Scott, William M. Fay, Howard A. Dawson, Jr., Charles R. Simpson, C. Moxley Featherston, Leo H. Irwin, Samuel B. Sterrett, William A. Goffe, Darrell D. Wiles, Richard C. Wilbur, Herbert L. Chabot, Arthur L. Nims, III, Edna G. Parker, Norman O. Tietjens, Bruce M. Forrester, Arnold Raum, Meade Whitaker, Jules G. Korner, III, Perry Shields.

NOTE: To keep abreast of changes see *United States Court Directory 1983.*

Plurality and Majority

In order to win a plurality, a candidate must receive a greater number of votes than anyone running against him. If he receives 50 votes, for example, and two other candidates receive 49 and 2, he will have a plurality of one vote over his closest opponent.

However, a candidate does not have a majority unless he receives more than 50% of the total votes cast. In the example above, the candidate does not have a majority, because his 50 votes are less than 50% of the 101 votes cast.

Members of the Supreme Court of the United States

	Birth		Religious affiliation	Appointment		Oath taken		Service terminated				Death	
Name	Place	Date	(Source: Library of Congress)	From	President	Date	Age	Date	Cause	Years served	Age	Date	Age
CHIEF JUSTICES													
John Jay	N.Y.	1745	Episcopal	N.Y.	Washington	1789	44	1795	resigned	5	49	1829	83
John Rutledge	S.C.	1739	Church of England	S.C.	Washington	1795	55	1795	rejected	0	56	1800	60
Oliver Ellsworth	Conn.	1745	Congregational	Conn.	Washington	1796	50	1800	resigned	4	55	1807	62
John Marshall	Va.	1755	Episcopal	Va.	J. Adams	1801	45	1835	death	34	79	1835	79
Roger B. Taney	Md.	1777	Roman Catholic	Md.	Jackson	1836	59	1864	death	28	87	1864	87
Salmon P. Chase	N.H.	1808	Episcopal	Ohio	Lincoln	1864	56	1873	death	8	65	1873	65
Morrison R. Waite	Conn	1816	Episcopal	Ohio	Grant	1874	57	1888	death	14	71	1888	71
Melville W. Fuller	Me.	1833	Episcopal	Ill.	Cleveland	1888	55	1910	death	21	77	1910	77
Edward D. White	La.	1845	Roman Catholic	La.	Taft	1910	65	1921	death	10	75	1921	75
William H. Taft	Ohio	1857	Unitarian	Conn.	Harding	1921	63	1930	retired	8	72	1930	72
Charles E. Hughes	N.Y.	1862	Baptist	N.Y.	Hoover	1930	67	1941	retired	11	79	1948	86
Harlan F. Stone	N.H.	1872	Episcopal	N.Y.	F. Roosevelt	1941	68	1946	death	4	73	1946	73
Frederick M. Vinson	Ky.	1890	Methodist	Ky.	Truman	1946	56	1953	death	7	63	1953	63
Earl Warren	Calif.	1891	Protestant	Calif.	Eisenhower	1953	62	1969	retired	15	78	1974	83
Warren E. Burger	Minn.	1907	Presbyterian	Va.	Nixon	1969	61	—	—	—	—	—	—
ASSOCIATE JUSTICES													
James Wilson	Scotland	1742	Episcopal	Pa.	Washington	1789	47	1798	death	8	55	1798	55
John Rutledge	S.C.	1739	Church of England	S.C.	Washington	1790	50	1791	resigned	1	51	1800	60
William Cushing	Mass.	1732	Unitarian	Mass.	Washington	1790	57	1810	death	20	78	1810	78
John Blair	Va.	1732	Presbyterian	Va.	Washington	1790	58	1796	resigned	5	64	1800	68
James Iredell	England	1751	Episcopal	N.C.	Washington	1790	38	1799	death	9	48	1799	48
Thomas Johnson	Md.	1732	Episcopal	Md.	Washington	1792	59	1793	resigned	0	60	1819	86
William Paterson	Ireland	1745	Protestant	N.J.	Washington	1793	47	1806	death	13	60	1806	60
Samuel Chase	Md.	1741	Episcopal	Md.	Washington	1796	54	1811	death	15	70	1811	70
Bushrod Washington	Va.	1762	Episcopal	Va.	J. Adams	1799	36	1829	death	30	67	1829	67
Alfred Moore	N.C.	1755	Episcopal	N.C.	J. Adams	1800	45	1804	resigned	3	48	1810	55
William Johnson	S.C.	1771	Presbyterian	S.C.	Jefferson	1804	32	1834	death	30	62	1834	62
Brockholst Livingston	N.Y.	1757	Presbyterian	N.Y.	Jefferson	1807	49	1823	death	16	65	1823	65
Thomas Todd	Va.	1765	Presbyterian	Ky.	Jefferson	1807	42	1826	death	18	61	1826	61
Gabriel Duval	Md.	1752	French Protestant	Md.	Madison	1811	58	1835	resigned	23	82	1844	91
Joseph Story	Mass.	1779	Unitarian	Mass.	Madison	1812	32	1845	death	33	65	1845	65
Smith Thompson	N.Y.	1768	Presbyterian	N.Y.	Monroe	1823	55	1843	death	20	75	1843	75
Robert Trimble	Va.	1777	Protestant	Ky.	J. Q. Adams	1826	49	1828	death	2	51	1828	51
John McLean	N.J.	1785	Methodist-Epis.	Ohio	Jackson	1830	44	1861	death	31	76	1861	76
Henry Baldwin	Conn.	1780	Trinity Church	Pa.	Jackson	1830	50	1844	death	14	64	1844	64
James M. Wayne	Ga.	1790	Protestant	Ga.	Jackson	1835	45	1867	death	32	77	1867	77
Philip P. Barbour	Va.	1783	Episcopal	Va.	Jackson	1836	52	1841	death	4	57	1841	57
John Catron	Pa.	1786	Presbyterian	Tenn.	Jackson	1837	51	1865	death	28	79	1865	79

Name	Birth		Religious affiliation (*Source:* Library of Congress)	Appointment		Oath taken		Service terminated				Death	
	Place	Date		From	President	Date	Age	Date	Cause	Years served	Age	Date	Age
John McKinley	Va	1780	Protestant	Ala.	Van Buren	1837	57	1852	death	14	72	1852	72
Peter V. Daniel	Va.	1784	Episcopal	Va.	Van Buren	1841	57	1860	death	18	76	1860	76
Samuel Nelson	N.Y.	1792	Protestant	N.Y.	Tyler	1845	52	1872	retired	27	80	1873	81
Levi Woodbury	N.H.	1789	Protestant	N.H.	Polk	1845	55	1851	death	5	61	1851	61
Robert C. Grier	Pa.	1794	Presbyterian	Pa.	Polk	1846	52	1870	retired	23	75	1870	76
Benjamin R. Curtis	Mass.	1809	(2)	Mass.	Fillmore	1851	41	1857	resigned	5	47	1874	64
John A. Campbell	Ga.	1811	Episcopal	Ala.	Pierce	1853	41	1861	resigned	8	49	1889	77
Nathan Clifford	N.H.	1803	(1)	Maine	Buchanan	1858	54	1881	death	23	77	1881	77
Noah H. Swayne	Va.	1804	Quaker	Ohio	Lincoln	1862	57	1881	retired	18	76	1884	79
Samuel F. Miller	Ky.	1816	Unitarian	Iowa	Lincoln	1862	46	1890	death	28	74	1890	74
David Davis	Md.	1815	(4)	Ill.	Lincoln	1862	47	1877	resigned	14	61	1886	71
Stephen J. Field	Conn.	1816	Episcopal	Calif.	Lincoln	1863	46	1897	retired	34	81	1899	82
William Strong	Conn.	1808	Presbyterian	Pa.	Grant	1870	61	1880	retired	10	72	1895	87
Joseph P. Bradley	N.Y.	1813	Presbyterian	N.J.	Grant	1870	57	1892	death	21	78	1892	78
Ward Hunt	N.Y.	1810	Episcopal	N.Y.	Grant	1872	62	1882	disabled	9	71	1886	75
John M. Harlan	Ky.	1833	Presbyterian	Ky.	Hayes	1877	44	1911	death	33	78	1911	78
William B. Woods	Ohio	1824	Protestant	Ga.	Hayes	1880	56	1887	death	6	62	1887	62
Stanley Matthews	Ohio	1824	Presbyterian	Ohio	Garfield	1881	56	1889	death	7	64	1889	64
Horace Gray	Mass.	1828	(3)	Mass.	Arthur	1882	53	1902	death	20	74	1902	74
Samuel Blatchford	N.Y.	1820	Presbyterian	N.Y.	Arthur	1882	62	1893	death	11	73	1893	73
Lucius Q. C. Lamar	Ga.	1825	Methodist	Miss.	Cleveland	1888	62	1893	death	5	67	1893	67
David J. Brewer	Asia Minor	1837	Protestant	Kan.	Harrison	1889	52	1910	death	20	72	1910	72
Henry B. Brown	Mass.	1836	Protestant	Mich.	Harrison	1890	54	1906	retired	15	70	1913	77
George Shiras, Jr.	Pa.	1832	Presbyterian	Pa.	Harrison	1892	60	1903	retired	10	71	1924	92
Howell E. Jackson	Tenn.	1832	Baptist	Tenn.	Harrison	1893	60	1895	death	2	63	1895	63
Edward D. White	La.	1845	Roman Catholic	La.	Cleveland	1894	48	1910	promoted	16	65	1921	75
Rufus W. Peckham	N.Y.	1838	Episcopal	N.Y.	Cleveland	1895	57	1909	death	13	70	1909	70
Joseph McKenna	Pa.	1843	Roman Catholic	Calif.	McKinley	1898	54	1925	retired	26	81	1926	83
Oliver W. Holmes	Mass.	1841	Unitarian	Mass.	T. Roosevelt	1902	61	1932	retired	29	90	1935	93
William R. Day	Ohio	1849	Protestant	Ohio	T. Roosevelt	1903	53	1922	retired	19	73	1923	74
William H. Moody	Mass.	1853	Episcopal	Mass.	T. Roosevelt	1906	52	1910	disabled	3	56	1917	63
Horace H. Lurton	Ky.	1844	Episcopal	Tenn.	Taft	1909	65	1914	death	4	70	1914	70
Charles E. Hughes	N.Y.	1862	Baptist	N.Y.	Taft	1910	48	1916	resigned	5	54	1948	86
Willis Van Devanter	Ind.	1859	Episcopal	Wyo.	Taft	1910	51	1937	retired	26	78	1941	81
Joseph R. Lamar	Ga.	1857	Ch. of Disciples	Ga.	Taft	1910	53	1916	death	4	58	1916	58
Mahlon Pitney	N.J.	1858	Presbyterian	N.J.	Taft	1912	54	1922	disabled	10	64	1924	66
James C. McReynolds	Ky.	1862	Disciples of Christ	Tenn.	Wilson	1914	52	1941	retired	26	78	1946	84
Louis D. Brandeis	Ky.	1856	Jewish	Mass.	Wilson	1916	59	1939	retired	22	82	1941	84
John H. Clarke	Ohio	1857	Protestant	Ohio	Wilson	1916	59	1922	resigned	5	65	1945	87
George Sutherland	England	1862	Episcopal	Utah	Harding	1922	60	1938	retired	15	75	1942	80
Pierce Butler	Minn.	1866	Roman Catholic	Minn.	Harding	1923	56	1939	death	16	73	1939	73
Edward T. Sanford	Tenn.	1865	Episcopal	Tenn.	Harding	1923	57	1930	death	7	64	1930	64

Harlan F. Stone	N.H.	1872	Episcopal	N.Y.	Coolidge	1925	52	1941	promoted	16	68	1946	73
Owen J. Roberts	Pa.	1875	Episcopal	Pa.	Hoover	1930	55	1945	resigned	15	70	1955	80
Benjamin N. Cardozo	N.Y.	1870	Jewish	N.Y.	Hoover	1932	61	1938	death	6	68	1938	68
Hugo L. Black	Ala.	1886	Baptist	Ala.	F. Roosevelt	1937	51	1971	retired	34	85	1971	85
Stanley F. Reed	Ky.	1884	Protestant	Ky.	F. Roosevelt	1938	53	1957	retired	19	72	1980	95
Felix Frankfurter	Austria	1882	Jewish	Mass.	F. Roosevelt	1939	56	1962	retired	23	79	1965	82
William O. Douglas	Minn.	1898	Presbyterian	Conn.	F. Roosevelt	1939	40	1975	retired	36	77	1980	81
Frank Murphy	Mich.	1890	Roman Catholic	Mich.	F. Roosevelt	1940	49	1949	death	9	59	1949	59
James F. Byrnes	S.C.	1879	Episcopal	S.C.	F. Roosevelt	1941	62	1942	resigned	1	63	1972	92
Robert H. Jackson	N.Y.	1892	Episcopal	Pa.	F. Roosevelt	1941	49	1954	death	13	62	1954	62
Wiley B. Rutledge	Ky.	1894	Unitarian	Iowa	F. Roosevelt	1943	48	1949	death	6	55	1949	55
Harold H. Burton	Mass.	1888	Unitarian	Ohio	Truman	1945	57	1958	retired	13	70	1964	76
Tom C. Clark	Tex.	1899	Presbyterian	Tex.	Truman	1949	49	1967	retired	17	67	1977	78
Sherman Minton	Ind.	1890	Roman Catholic	Ind.	Truman	1949	58	1956	retired	7	65	1965	74
John M. Harlan	Ill.	1899	Presbyterian	N.Y.	Eisenhower	1955	55	1971	retired	16	72	1971	72
William J. Brennan, Jr.	N.J.	1906	Roman Catholic	N.J.	Eisenhower	1956	50	—	—	—	—	—	—
Charles E. Whittaker	Kan.	1901	Methodist	Mo.	Eisenhower	1957	56	1962	disabled	5	61	1973	73
Potter Stewart	Mich.	1915	Episcopal	Ohio	Eisenhower	1958	43	1981	resigned	23	66	—	—
Byron R. White	Colo.	1917	Episcopal	Colo.	Kennedy	1962	44	—	—	—	—	—	—
Arthur J. Goldberg	Ill.	1908	Jewish	Ill.	Kennedy	1962	54	1965	resigned	2	56	—	—
Abe Fortas	Tenn.	1910	Jewish	Tenn.	Johnson	1965	55	1969	resigned	3	58	1982	71
Thurgood Marshall	Md.	1908	Episcopalian	N.Y.	Johnson	1967	59	—	—	—	—	—	—
Harry A. Blackmun	Ill.	1908	Methodist	Minn.	Nixon	1970	61	—	—	—	—	—	—
Lewis F. Powell, Jr.	Va.	1907	Presbyterian	Va.	Nixon	1972	64	—	—	—	—	—	—
William H. Rehnquist	Wis.	1924	Lutheran	Ariz.	Nixon	1972	47	—	—	—	—	—	—
John Paul Stevens	Ill.	1920	Protestant	Ill.	Ford	1975	55	—	—	—	—	—	—
Sandra Day O'Connor	Tex.	1930	Episcopal	Ariz.	Reagan	1981	51	—	—	—	—	—	—

1. Congregationalist; later Unitarian. 2. Unitarian; then Episcopal. 3. Unitarian or Congregational. 4. Not a member of any church.

Impeachments of Federal Officials

Source: Congressional Directory

The procedure for the impeachment of Federal officials is detailed in Article I, Section 3, of the Constitution. See Index.

The Senate has sat as a court of impeachment in the following cases:

William Blount, Senator from Tennessee; charges dismissed for want of jurisdiction, January 14, 1799.

John Pickering, Judge of the U.S. District Court for New Hampshire; removed from office March 12, 1804.

Samuel Chase, Associate Justice of the Supreme Court; acquitted March 1, 1805.

James H. Peck, Judge of the U.S. District Court for Missouri; acquitted Jan. 31, 1831.

West H. Humphreys, Judge of the U.S. District Court for the middle, eastern, and western districts of Tennessee; removed from office June 26, 1862.

Andrew Johnson, President of the United States; acquitted May 26, 1868.

William W. Belknap, Secretary of War; acquitted Aug. 1, 1876.

Charles Swayne, Judge of the U.S. District Court for the northern district of Florida; acquitted Feb. 27, 1905.

Robert W. Archbald, Associate Judge, U.S. Commerce Court; removed Jan. 13, 1913.

George W. English, Judge of the U.S. District Court for eastern district of Illinois; resigned Nov. 4, 1926; proceedings dismissed.

Harold Louderback, Judge of the U.S. District Court for the northern district of California; acquitted May 24, 1933.

Halsted L. Ritter, Judge of the U.S. District Court for the southern district of Florida; removed from office April 17, 1936.

Senate and House Standing Committees, 97th Congress

Committees of the Senate

Agriculture, Nutrition, and Forestry (17 members)
Chairman: Jesse Helms (N.C.)
Ranking Dem.: Walter D. Huddleston (Ky.)
Appropriations (29 members)
Chairman: Mark O. Hatfield (Ore.)
Ranking Dem.: William Proxmire (Wis.)
Armed Services (17 members)
Chairman: John Tower (Tex.)
Ranking Dem.: John C. Stennis (Miss.)
Banking, Housing, and Urban Affairs (15 members)
Chairman: E.J. (Jake) Garn (Utah)
Ranking Dem.: Donald W. Riegle, Jr. (Mich.)
Budget (22 members)
Chairman: Pete V. Domenici (N.M.)
Ranking Dem.: Ernest F. Hollings (S.C.)
Commerce, Science, and Transportation (17 members)
Chairman: Bob Packwood (Ore.)
Ranking Dem.: Howard W. Cannon (Nev.)
Energy and Natural Resources (20 members)
Chairman: James A. McClure (Idaho)
Ranking Dem.: Henry M. Jackson (Wash.)
Environment and Public Works (16 members)
Chairman: Robert T. Stafford (Vt.)
Ranking Dem.: Jennings Randolph (W.Va.)
Finance (20 members)
Chairman: Robert J. Dole (Kan.)
Ranking Dem.: Russell B. Long (La.)
Foreign Relations (17 members)
Chairman: Charles H. Percy (Ill.)
Ranking Dem.: Claiborne Pell (R.I.)
Governmental Affairs (17 members)
Chairman: William V. Roth, Jr. (Del.)
Ranking Dem.: Thomas F. Eagleton (Mo.)
Judiciary (18 members)
Chairman: Strom Thurmond (S.C.)
Ranking Dem.: Joseph R. Biden, Jr. (Del.)
Labor and Human Resources (16 members)
Chairman: Orrin G. Hatch (Utah)
Ranking Dem.: Edward M. Kennedy (Mass.)
Rules and Administration (12 members)
Chairman: Charles McC. Mathias, Jr. (Md.)
Ranking Dem.: Wendell H. Ford (Ky.)
Small Business (17 members)
Chairman: Lowell P. Weicker, Jr. (Conn.)
Ranking Dem.: Sam Nunn (Ga.)
Veterans' Affairs (12 members)
Chairman: Alan K. Simpson (Wyo.)
Ranking Dem.: Alan Cranston (Calif.)

Select and Special Committees

Aging (15 members)
Chairman: John Heinz (Pa.)
Ranking Dem.: Lawton Chiles (Fla.)
Ethics (6 members)
Chairman: Malcolm Wallop (Wyo.)
Vice Chairman: Howell T. Heflin (Ala.)
Indian Affairs (7 members)
Chairman: William S. Cohen (Me.)
Ranking Dem.: John Melcher (Mont.)
Intelligence (15 members)
Chairman: Barry Goldwater (Ariz.)
Ranking Dem.: Daniel Patrick Moynihan (N.Y.)

Committees of the House

Agriculture (43 members)
Chairman: E. (Kika) de la Garza (Tex.)
Ranking Repub.: William C. Wampler (Va.)
Appropriations (55 members)
Chairman: Jamie L. Whitten (Miss.)
Ranking Repub.: Silvio O. Conte (Mass.)
Armed Services (44 members)
Chairman: Melvin Price (Ill.)
Ranking Repub.: William L. Dickinson (Ala.)
Banking, Finance, and Urban Affairs (44 members)
Chairman: Fernand J. St. Germain (R.I.)
Ranking Repub.: J. William Stanton (Ohio)
Budget (30 members)
Chairman: James R. Jones (Okla.)
Ranking Repub.: Delbert L. Latta (Ohio)
District of Columbia (11 members)
Chairman: Ronald V. Dellums (Calif.)
Ranking Repub.: Stewart B. McKinney (Conn.)
Education and Labor (33 members)
Chairman: Carl D. Perkins (Ky.)
Ranking Repub.: John N. Erlenborn (Ill)
Energy and Commerce (42 members)
Chairman: John D. Dingell (Mich.)
Ranking Repub.: James T. Broyhill (N.C.)
Foreign Affairs (37 members)
Chairman: Clement J. Zablocki (Wis.)
Ranking Repub.: William S. Broomfield (Mich.)
Government Operations (41 members)
Chairman: Jack Brooks (Tex.)
Ranking Repub.: Frank Horton (N.Y.)
House Administration (19 members)
Chairman: Augustus F. Hawkins (Calif.)
Ranking Repub.: Bill Frenzel (Minn.)
Interior and Insular Affairs (40 members)
Chairman: Morris K. Udall (Ariz.)
Ranking Repub.: Manuel Lujan, Jr. (N.M.)
Judiciary (28 members)
Chairman; Peter W. Rodino, Jr. (N.J.)
Ranking Repub.: Robert McClory (Ill.)
Merchant Marine and Fisheries (35 members)
Chairman: Walter B. Jones (N.C.)
Ranking Repub.: Gene Snyder (Ky.)
Post Office and Civil Service (26 members)
Chairman: William D. Ford (Mich.)
Ranking Repub.: Edward J. Derwinski (Ill.)
Public Works and Transportation (46 members)
Chairman: James J. Howard (N.J.)
Ranking Repub.: Don H. Clausen (Calif.)
Rules (16 members)
Chairman: Richard Bolling (Mo.)
Ranking Repub.: James H. Quillen (Tenn.)
Science and Technology (40 members)
Chairman: Don Fuqua (Fla.)
Ranking Repub.: Larry Winn, Jr. (Kan.)
Small Business (40 members)
Chairman: Parren J. Mitchell (Md.)
Ranking Repub.: Joseph M. McDade (Pa.)
Standards of Official Conduct (12 members)
Chairman: Louis Stokes (Ohio)
Ranking Repub.: Floyd D. Spence (S.C.)
Veterans' Affairs (32 members)
Chairman: G.V. (Sonny) Montgomery (Miss.)
Ranking Repub.: John P. Hammerschmidt (Ark.)
Ways and Means (35 members)
Chairman: Dan Rostenkowski (Ill.)
Ranking Repub.: Barber B. Conable, Jr. (N.Y.)

Select Committees

Aging (55 members)
Chairman: Claude Pepper (Fla.)
Ranking Repub.: Matthew J. Rinaldo (N.J.)
Intelligence (14 members)
Chairman: Edward P. Boland (Mass.)
Ranking Repub.: J. Kenneth Robinson (Va.)
Narcotics Abuse and Control (19 members)
Chairman: Leo C. Zeferetti (N.Y.)
Ranking Repub.: Tom Railsback (Ill.)

Speakers of the House of Representatives

Dates served	Congress	Name and state	Dates served	Congress	Name and state
1789–1791	1	Frederick A. C. Muhlenberg (Pa.)	1863–1869	38–40	Schuyler Colfax (Ind.)
1791–1793	2	Jonathan Trumbull (Conn.)	1869–1869	40	Theodore M. Pomeroy (N.Y.)[5]
1793–1795	3	Frederick A. C. Muhlenberg (Pa.)	1869–1875	41–43	James G. Blaine (Me.)
1795–1799	4–5	Jonathan Dayton (N.J.)[1]	1875–1876	44	Michael C. Kerr (Ind.)[6]
1799–1801	6	Theodore Sedgwick (Mass.)	1876–1881	44–46	Samuel J. Randall (Pa.)
1801–1807	7–9	Nathaniel Macon (N.C.)	1881–1883	47	J. Warren Keifer (Ohio)
1807–1811	10–11	Joseph B. Varnum (Mass.)	1883–1889	48–50	John G. Carlisle (Ky.)
1811–1814	12–13	Henry Clay (Ky.)[2]	1889–1891	51	Thomas B. Reed (Me.)
1814–1815	13	Langdon Cheves (S.C.)	1891–1895	52–53	Charles F. Crisp (Ga.)
1815–1820	14–16	Henry Clay (Ky.)[3]	1895–1899	54–55	Thomas B. Reed (Me.)
1820–1821	16	John W. Taylor (N.Y.)	1899–1903	56–57	David B. Henderson (Iowa)
1821–1823	17	Philip P. Barbour (Va.)	1903–1911	58–61	Joseph G. Cannon (Ill.)
1823–1825	18	Henry Clay (Ky.)	1911–1919	62–65	Champ Clark (Mo.)
1825–1827	19	John W. Taylor (N.Y.)	1919–1925	66–68	Frederick H. Gillett (Mass.)
1827–1834	20–23	Andrew Stevenson (Va.)[4]	1925–1931	69–71	Nicholas Longworth (Ohio)
1834–1835	23	John Bell (Tenn.)	1931–1933	72	John N. Garner (Tex.)
1835–1839	24–25	James K. Polk (Tenn.)	1933–1934	73	Henry T. Rainey (Ill.)[7]
1839–1841	26	Robert M. T. Hunter (Va.)	1935–1936	74	Joseph W. Byrns (Tenn.)[8]
1841–1843	27	John White (Ky.)	1936–1940	74–76	William B. Bankhead (Ala.)[9]
1843–1845	28	John W. Jones (Va.)	1940–1947	76–79	Sam Rayburn (Tex.)
1845–1847	29	John W. Davis (Ind.)	1947–1949	80	Joseph W. Martin, Jr. (Mass.)
1847–1849	30	Robert C. Winthrop (Mass.)	1949–1953	81–82	Sam Rayburn (Tex.)
1849–1851	31	Howell Cobb (Ga.)	1953–1955	83	Joseph W. Martin, Jr. (Mass.)
1851–1855	32–33	Linn Boyd (Ky.)	1955–1961	84–87	Sam Rayburn (Tex.)[10]
1855–1857	34	Nathaniel P. Banks (Mass.)	1962–1971	87–91	John W. McCormack (Mass.)[11]
1857–1859	35	James L. Orr (S.C.)	1971–1977	92–94	Carl Albert (Okla.)[12]
1859–1861	36	Wm. Pennington (N.J.)	1977–	95–	Thomas P. O'Neill, Jr. (Mass.)
1861–1863	37	Galusha A. Grow (Pa.)			

1. George Dent (Md.) was elected Speaker pro tempore for April 20 and May 28, 1798. 2. Resigned during second session of 13th Congress. 3. Resigned between first and second sessions of 16th Congress. 4. Resigned during first session of 23rd Congress. 5. Elected Speaker and served the day of adjournment. 6. Died between first and second sessions of 44th Congress. During first session, there were two Speakers pro tempore: Samuel S. Cox (N.Y.), appointed for Feb. 17, May 12, and June 19, 1876, and Milton Sayler (Ohio), appointed for June 4, 1876. 7. Died in 1934 after adjournment of second session of 73rd Congress. 8. Died during second session of 74th Congress. 9. Died during third session of 76th Congress. 10. Died between first and second sessions of 87th Congress. 11. Not a candidate in 1970 election. 12. Not a candidate in 1976 election. *Source:* Congressional Directory.

Floor Leaders of the Senate

Democratic	Republican
Gilbert M. Hitchcock, Neb. (Min. 1919–20)	Charles Curtis, Kan. (Maj. 1925–29)
Oscar W. Underwood, Ala. (Min. 1920–23)	James E. Watson, Ind. (Maj. 1929–33)
Joseph T. Robinson, Ark. (Min. 1923–33, Maj. 1933–37)	Charles L. McNary, Ore. (Min. 1933–44)
Alben W. Barkley, Ky. (Maj. 1937–46, Min. 1947–48)	Wallace H. White, Jr., Me. (Min. 1944–47, Maj. 1947–48)
Scott W. Lucas, Ill. (Maj. 1949–50)	Kenneth S. Wherry, Neb. (Min. 1949–51)
Ernest W. McFarland, Ariz. (Maj. 1951–52)	Styles Bridges, N. H. (Min. 1951–52)
Lyndon B. Johnson, Tex. (Min. 1953–54, Maj. 1955–60)	Robert A. Taft, Ohio (Maj. 1953)
Mike Mansfield, Mont. (Maj. 1961–77)	William F. Knowland, Calif. (Maj. 1953–54, Min. 1955–58)
Robert C. Byrd, W. Va. (Maj. 1977–81, Min. 1981–)	Everett M. Dirksen, Ill. (Min. 1959–69)
	Hugh Scott, Pa. (Min. 1969–1977)
	Howard H. Baker, Jr., Tenn. (Min. 1977–81, Maj. 1981–)

NOTE: Min. = Minority Leader; Maj. = Majority Leader. *Source:* United States Senate, Secretary for the Majority.

Annual Salaries of Federal Officials

President of the U.S.	$200,000[1]	Secretaries of the Army, Navy, Air Force	$60,662
Vice President of the U.S.	79,125[2]	Senators and Representatives	60,662
Cabinet members	69,630	President Pro Tempore of Senate	68,575
Under secretaries of executive departments	55,387	Speaker of the House	79,125
Deputy Secretaries of State, Defense, Treasury	60,662	Majority and Minority Leader of the Senate	68,575
Deputy Attorney General	60,662	Majority and Minority Leader of the House	68,575
Under Secretary of Transportation	60,662	Chief Justice of the United States	96,800
		Associate Justices of the Supreme Court	93,000

1. Plus taxable $50,000 for expenses and a nontaxable sum (not to exceed $100,000 a year) for travel expenses. 2. Plus taxable $10,000 for expenses. NOTE: All salaries shown above are taxable.

Executive Departments and Agencies

Source: U.S. Government Organization Manual.

Unless otherwise indicated, addresses shown are in Washington, D.C.

CENTRAL INTELLIGENCE AGENCY (CIA)
Washington, D.C. (20505)
Established: 1947.
Director: William J. Casey.
Activities: Coordinates intelligence activities of certain government departments and agencies by making recommendations to the National Security Council; correlates and evaluates intelligence and disseminates the results; performs certain additional services for existing intelligence agencies when the National Security Council determines that these can be more efficiently accomplished centrally.

COUNCIL OF ECONOMIC ADVISERS (CEA)
Executive Office Bldg. (20506).
Members: 3.
Established: Feb. 20, 1946.
Chairman: Martin S. Feldstein.
Activities: Assists President in preparation of economic reports to Congress; studies economic trends; appraises government activities on nation's economy; recommends economic policies.

COUNCIL ON ENVIRONMENTAL QUALITY
722 Jackson Pl., N.W. (20006).
Members: 3.
Established: 1969.
Chairman: A. Alan Hill.
Activities: Develops and recommends to President national policies that promote environmental quality.

NATIONAL SECURITY COUNCIL (NSC)
Old Executive Office Bldg. (20506).
Members: 4.
Established: July 26, 1947.
Chairman: The President.
Other members: Vice President; Secretary of State; Secretary of Defense.
Activities: Assesses and appraises objectives, commitments and risks of United States in relation to our actual and potential military power.

OFFICE OF ADMINISTRATION
Executive Office of the President (20500).
Established: Dec. 12, 1977.
Director: John F. W. Rogers.
Activities: Provides the common services for the Executive Office of the President such as mail, payroll, dataprocessing and messengers.

OFFICE OF MANAGEMENT AND BUDGET
Executive Office Bldg. (20503).
Established: July 1, 1970.
Director: David A. Stockman.
Activities: Assists President in preparing budget and formulating fiscal program; supervises administration of budget; coordinates advice on proposed legislation; plans improvements in statistical services; keeps President informed of progress of activities by government agencies so that Congressional appropriations are spent most economically.

OFFICE OF SCIENCE AND TECHNOLOGY POLICY
Executive Office Building (20500).
Established: June 8, 1962.
Director: Benjamin Huberman (acting).
Activities: Advises the President on scientific, engineering, and technological aspects of issues requiring his attention.

OFFICE OF THE UNITED STATES TRADE REPRESENTATIVE
1800 G St., N.W. (20506).
Established: Jan. 15, 1963.
Special Representative: Bill Brock.
Activities: Advises the President on the administration and carrying out of the trade agreements program and on non-tariff barriers to international trade and international commodity agreements; chairs the Trade Expansion Act Advisory Committee.

WHITE HOUSE OFFICE OF POLICY DEVELOPMENT
The White House (20500)
Established: Jan. 21, 1981.
Director: Edwin J. Gray.
Activities: Formulates and coordinates domestic policy recommendations for the President.

Executive Departments

DEPARTMENT OF STATE
2201 C St., N.W. (20520).
Established: 1781 as Department of Foreign Affairs; reconstituted, 1789, following adoption of Constitution; name changed to Department of State Sept. 15, 1789.
Secretary: George P. Schultz.
Deputy Secretary: Kenneth W. Dam.
Chief delegate to U.N.: Jeane J. Kirkpatrick.
Activities: Determines government policy in relation to international problems; formulates measures for promoting friendship with other countries; develops policies and programs for U.S. participation in U.N. and other international organizations; conducts correspondence with our representatives abroad and accredited foreign representatives here; administers Foreign Service, Agency for International Development.

DEPARTMENT OF THE TREASURY
15th St. & Pennsylvania Ave., N.W. (20220).
Established: Sept. 2, 1789.
Secretary: Donald T. Regan.
Deputy Secretary: Richard McNamar.
Treasurer of the U.S.: Angela M. Buchanan.
Comptroller of the Currency: John G. Heimann.
Activities: Manages national finances; grants warrants for money drawn from Treasury pursuant to legal appropriations; handles collection of revenue; keeps and renders public accounts; prepares plans for improvement of revenue and for support of public credit; controls coinage and printing of money; administers Secret Service, Customs Service, Internal Revenue Service, Bureau of Engraving and Printing, Bureau of the Mint, Federal Law Enforcement Training Center, Bureau of the Public Debt.

DEPARTMENT OF DEFENSE

The Pentagon (20301).

Established: July 26, 1947, as National Department Establishment; name changed to Department of Defense on Aug. 10, 1949. Subordinate to Secretary of Defense are Secretaries of Army, Navy, Air Force.

Secretary: Caspar W. Weinberger.

Deputy Secretary: Frank C. Carlucci.

Secretary of Army: John O. Marsh, Jr.

Secretary of Navy: John F. Lehman, Jr.

Secretary of Air Force: Verne Orr.

Commandant of Marine Corps: Gen. Robert H. Barrow.

Joint Chiefs of Staff:[1] Gen. John W. Vessey, Jr., Chairman; Adm. James D. Watkins, Navy; Gen. Charles A. Gabriel, Air Force: Gen. Edward C. Meyer, Army; Gen. Robert H. Barrow, Marine Corps.

Activities: Provides for security of U.S. by establishing integrated policies and procedures; co-ordinates and directs the activities of three separately administered military departments (Army, Navy, and Air Force).

1. Consisting of chairman and chiefs of each service.

DEPARTMENT OF JUSTICE

Constitution Ave. between 9th & 10th Sts., N.W. (20530).

Established: Office of Attorney General was created Sept. 24, 1789. Although he was one of original Cabinet members, he was not executive department head until June 22, 1870, when Department of Justice was established.

Attorney General: William French Smith.

Deputy Attorney General: Edward C. Schmults.

Solicitor General: Rex E. Lee.

Director of FBI: William H. Webster.

Activities: Provides means for enforcing federal laws; investigates and detects violations; represents U.S. in legal matters generally and gives advice and opinions when requested by President or heads of executive departments; directs FBI, Bureau of Prisons, Immigration and Naturalization Service, Drug Enforcement Administration, Marshals Service.

DEPARTMENT OF THE INTERIOR

C St. between 18th & 19th Sts., N.W. (20240).

Established: March 3, 1849.

Secretary: James G. Watt.

Under Secretary: Donald P. Hodel.

Activities: Develops and conserves natural resources of U.S. and territories; supervises public business relating to such offices as Bureau of Land Management, Geological Survey, Bureau of Indian Affairs, National Park Service, Bureau of Mines, Fish and Wildlife Service, Bureau of Land Management, Heritage Conservation and Recreation Service, Water and Power Resources Service.

DEPARTMENT OF AGRICULTURE

Independence Ave. between 12th & 14th Sts., S.W. (20250).

Established: May 15, 1862. Administered by Commissioner of Agriculture until 1889, when it was made executive department.

Secretary: John R. Block.

Deputy Secretary: Richard E. Lyng.

Activities: Conducts comprehensive research and educational program relating to agriculture; provides crop reports, commodity standards, meat inspection and other marketing services; administers national forests; aids in flood control; administers price-support and production-adjustment programs; makes loans to farmers; supervises Farmers Home Administration, Agricultural Marketing Service, Rural Electrification Administration, Federal Grain Inspection Service, Animal and Plant Inspection Service, Food and Nutrition Service, Food Safety and Quality Service, Commodity Credit Corporation, Federal Crop Insurance Corporation, Science and Education Administration, Soil Conservation Service, Office of Environmental Quality, Forest Service, Foreign Agricultural Service, Agricultural Stabilization and Conservation Service, Office of International Cooperation and Development, Rural Telephone Bank.

DEPARTMENT OF COMMERCE

14th St. between Constitution Ave. & E St., N.W. (20230).

Established: Department of Commerce and Labor was created Feb. 14, 1903. On March 4, 1913, all labor activities were transferred out of Department of Commerce and Labor and it was renamed Department of Commerce.

Secretary: Malcolm Baldrige.

Under Secretary: Joseph R. Wright, Jr.

Activities: Fosters and develops foreign and domestic commerce of U.S.; maintains Bureau of the Census, International Trade Administration, Economic Development Administration, Bureau of Economic Analysis, Office of Minority Business Enterprise, Patent and Trademark Office, National Oceanic and Atmospheric Administration (including National Weather Service), National Technical Information Service, National Telecommunications and Information Service, Travel Service, Maritime Administration, National Bureau of Standards, Minority Business Development Agency, Office of Product Technology and Innovation, Office of Industrial Economics.

DEPARTMENT OF LABOR

Frances Perkins Building, 200 Constitution Ave., N.W. (20210).

Established: Bureau of Labor was created in 1884 under Department of the Interior; later became independent department without executive rank. Returned to bureau status in Department of Commerce and Labor, but on March 4, 1913, became independent executive department under its present name.

Secretary: Raymond J. Donovan.

Under Secretary: Malcolm R. Lovell, Jr.

Activities: Promotes welfare of wage earners of U.S., improving working conditions and advancing opportunities for profitable employment; directs collection and collation of statistics concerning labor conditions; promulgates and enforces certain maximum-hour, minimum-wage, child-labor, safety and health standards. Maintains Employment and Training Administration, Labor-Management Services Administration, Employment Standards Administration, Occupational Safety and Health Administration, Bureau of Labor Statistics, Women's Bureau, Mine Safety and Health Administration.

DEPARTMENT OF HEALTH AND HUMAN SERVICES[1]
200 Independence Ave., S.W. (20201).
Established: April 11, 1953, replacing Federal Security Agency created in 1939.[1]
Secretary: Richard S. Schweiker.
Under Secretary: David B. Swoap.
Surgeon General: Dr. C. Everett Koop.
Activities: Supervises and coordinates various organizations within the department. Organizations are: Food and Drug Administration, Office of Human Development Services, Public Health Service, Social Security Administration, Alcohol, Drug Abuse and Mental Health Administration, National Institutes of Health, Center for Disease Control, Health Care Financing Administration, Office of Child Support Enforcement, Health Resources Administration, Office of Community Services.

1. Originally Department of Health, Education and welfare. Name changed in May 1980 when Department of Education was activated.

DEPARTMENT OF HOUSING AND URBAN DEVELOPMENT
451 7th St., S.W. (20410).
Established: 1965, replacing Housing and Home Finance Agency created in 1947.
Secretary: Samuel R. Pierce, Jr.
Under Secretary: Donald I. Hovde.
Activities: Supervises and coordinates New Community Development Corporation, Government National Mortgage Association.

DEPARTMENT OF TRANSPORTATION
400 7th St., S.W. (20590).
Established: Oct. 15, 1966, as result of Department of Transportation Act, which became effective April 1, 1967.
Secretary: Drew Lewis.
Deputy Secretary: Darrell M. Trent.
Activities: Supervises and coordinates activities of Coast Guard, Federal Aviation Administration, Federal Highway Administration, Federal Railroad Administration, St. Lawrence Seaway Development Corporation, National Highway Traffic Safety Administration, Urban Mass Transportation Administration.

DEPARTMENT OF ENERGY
1000 Independence Ave., S.W. (20585).
Established: August 1977.
Secretary: James B. Edwards.
Deputy Secretary: Kenneth Davis.
Activities: Takes over the Federal Energy Administration, the Federal Power Commission, the Energy Research and Development Administration, and functions of other government agencies concerned with energy. Has management responsibility for such projects as Bonneville Dam, the Energy Information Administration, the Energy Regulatory Commission, Economic Regulatory Administration.

DEPARTMENT OF EDUCATION
400 Maryland Avenue, S.W. (20202)
Established: May 4, 1980
Secretary: T. H. Bell.
Under Secretary: William C. Clohan, Jr.
Activities: Administers federally mandated education programs that pertain to elementary and secondary education, post-secondary, vocational and adult education, and special education and rehabilitative services. Supervises National Institute of Education, Fund for the Improvement of Postsecondary Education, Institute of Museum Services, and National Center for Educational Statistics.

Independent Agencies

(Titles and addresses of independent agencies not described below follow on page 643)

ACTION
806 Connecticut Ave., N.W. (20525).
Established: July 1, 1971.
Director: Thomas Weir Pauken.
Activities: Coordinates a system of volunteer services to people in need at home and abroad; administers Peace Corps and VISTA (Volunteers in Service to America).

CIVIL AERONAUTICS BOARD (CAB)
1825 Connecticut Ave., N.W. (20428)
Members: 5.
Established: June 30, 1940.
Chairman: C. Dan McKinnon.
Activities: Regulates economic aspects of U.S. air carrier operation; assists in development of international air transportation; promotes safety in civil aviation.

CONSUMER PRODUCT SAFETY COMMISSION
1111 18th St., N.W. (20207).
Members: 5.
Established: May 14, 1973.
Chairman: Nancy Harvey Steorts.
Activities. Protects the public against unreasonable risks of injury associated with consumer products; assists consumers to evaluate the comparative safety of products; develops uniform safety standards for products; promotes research into causes and prevention of product-related deaths, illnesses, and injuries.

ENVIRONMENTAL PROTECTION AGENCY (EPA)
401 M St., S.W. (20460).
Established: Dec. 2, 1970.
Administrator: Anne M. Gorsuch.
Activities: Coordinates governmental action to assure protection of the environment by abating and controlling pollution.

EQUAL EMPLOYMENT OPPORTUNITY COMMISSION (EEOC)
2401 E St., N.W. (20506).
Members: 5.
Established: July 2, 1965.
Chairman: Clarence Thomas.
Activities: Prohibits employment discrimination based on race, color, religion, sex, or national origin.

FARM CREDIT ADMINISTRATION (FCA)
490 L'Enfant Plaza East, S.W. (20578).
Members: 13.
Established: July 17, 1916.
Chairman of Federal Farm Credit Board: Owen Cooper.
Activities: Supervises and coordinates coopera-

tive credit system for agriculture; provides long- and short-term credit to farmers and their cooperative marketing, purchasing, and business service organizations.

FEDERAL COMMUNICATIONS COMMISSION (FCC)
1919 M St., N.W. (20554).
Members: 7.
Established: 1934.
Chairman: Mark S. Fowler.
Activities: Regulates interstate and foreign communications by wire and radio, including amateur radio and TV; regulates operator's licenses; classifies radio stations and prescribes their services.

FEDERAL DEPOSIT INSURANCE CORPORATION (FDIC)
550 17th St., N.W. (20429)
Members: 3.
Established: June 16, 1933.
Chairman: William M. Isaac.
Activities: Insures (up to $100,000) deposits in national banks, state banks that are members of the Federal Reserve System, and other state banks that qualify for Federal Deposit Insurance.

FEDERAL ELECTION COMMISSION (FEC)
1325 K St., N.W. (20463).
Members: 6.
Established: 1974.
Chairman: Frank Reiche.
Activities: Certifies distribution of public funding of federal elections; regulates compliance with Federal Election Campaign Act; makes available to the public copies of reports filed with the commission.

FEDERAL MARITIME COMMISSION
1100 L St., N.W. (20573).
Members: 5.
Established: Aug. 12, 1961.
Chairman: Alan Green, Jr.
Activities: Regulates waterborne shipping in foreign and domestic offshore commerce of U.S.

FEDERAL MEDIATION AND CONCILIATION SERVICE (FMCS)
2100 K St., N.W. (20427).
Established: 1947.
Director: Kenneth Moffett.
Activities: Assists in labor-management disputes in industries affecting interstate commerce to reach settlements by mediation or conciliation.

FEDERAL RESERVE SYSTEM (FRS), BOARD OF GOVERNORS OF
20th St. & Constitution Ave., N.W. (20551).
Members: 7.
Established: Dec. 23, 1913.
Chairman: Paul A. Volcker.
Activities: Supervises the 12 Federal Reserve banks, 24 branches and member commercial banks; determines country's monetary policy, including setting maximum interest paid by member banks, amount of credit extended for purchase of securities and discount rates charged by members; handles Government deposits and debt issue; regulates open-market operations; issues Federal Reserve notes.

FEDERAL TRADE COMMISSION (FTC)
Pennsylvania Ave. at 6th St., N.W. (20580).
Members: 5.
Established: Sept. 26, 1914.
Chairman: James C. Miller, 3rd.
Activities: Prevents unfair competition, deceptive practices, false advertising, price discrimination, monopolies.

GENERAL SERVICES ADMINISTRATION (GSA)
18th and F Sts., N.W. (20405).
Established: July 1, 1949.
Administrator: Gerald P. Carmen.
Activities: Establishes policy and provides efficient system for management of the government's property and records, including construction and operation of buildings, procurement and distribution of supplies, stockpiling of strategic materials and utilization and disposal of property. Directs National Archives and Records Service, Federal Supply Service, Public Buildings Service, Federal Preparedness Agency, Automated Data and Telecommunications Service.

INTERSTATE COMMERCE COMMISSION (ICC)
12th St. & Constitution Ave., N.W. (20423).
Members: 11.
Established: Feb. 4, 1887.
Chairman: Reese H. Taylor, Jr.
Activities: Regulates railroads, motor carriers, water carriers, and freight forwarders as to rates, through-routes, services, and bills of lading; authorizes mergers or consolidations; authorizes issue of securities by carriers.

NATIONAL AERONAUTICS AND SPACE ADMINISTRATION (NASA)
400 Maryland Ave., S.W. (20546).
Established: 1958.
Administrator: James M. Beggs.
Activities: Conducts research into problems of flight within and outside earth's atmosphere.

NATIONAL FOUNDATION ON THE ARTS AND THE HUMANITIES
2401 E St., N.W. (20506).
Established: 1965.
Chairman: National Endowment for the Arts, Francis S. M. Hodsoll; National Endowment for the Humanities, William J. Bennett.
Activities: Encourages and supports national progress in the humanities and the arts. Also includes National Councils on the Arts and the Humanities, which coordinates activities of the two endowments and related programs of other agencies.

NATIONAL LABOR RELATIONS BOARD (NLRB)
1717 Pennsylvania Ave., N.W. (20570).
Members: 5.
Established: July 5, 1935.
Chairman: John Van Dewater.
Activities: Prevents unfair labor practices by employers or labor organizations; conducts secret ballots among employees to determine bargaining representatives.

NATIONAL SCIENCE FOUNDATION (NSF)
1800 G St., N.W. (20550).
Established: 1950.
Director: Lewis N. Branscomb.
Activities: Awards grants and contracts to sup-

port research in the sciences. Encourages research in areas that can lead to improvements in economic growth, productivity, and environmental quality. Administered by 25-member National Science Board.

NATIONAL TRANSPORTATION SAFETY BOARD
800 Independence Ave., S.W. (20594).
Members: 5.
Established: April 1, 1975.
Chairman: Jim Burnett.
Activities: Conducts investigations into accidents, assesses techniques of accident investigation and recommends safety-improvement measures.

NUCLEAR REGULATORY COMMISSION (NRC)
1717 H St., N.W. (20555) and Bethesda, Md. (20014).
Members: 5.
Established: Jan. 19, 1975.
Chairman: Nunzio J. Palladino.
Activities: Regulates civilian nuclear facilities to assure protection of public health and safety and the environment, and safeguarding of nuclear materials and facilities.

OFFICE OF PERSONNEL MANAGEMENT (OPM)
1900 E St., N.W. (20415).
Member: 3.
Established: Jan. 16, 1883.
Director: Donald J. Devine.
Activities: Provides examinations to test fitness of applicants for positions in competitive service; provides personnel in response to requests from appointing officers; investigates applicants for national security purposes; classifies positions; provides leadership to Federal agencies in personnel matters.

SECURITIES AND EXCHANGE COMMISSION (SEC)
500 N. Capitol St., N.W. (20549).
Members: 5.
Established: June 6, 1934.
Chairman: John S. R. Shad.
Activities: Registers and issues regulations for securities and exchanges; registers securities offered for public sale; penalizes violators of regulations subject to appeal to U.S. Court of Appeals.

SELECTIVE SERVICE SYSTEM (SSS)
600 E. St., N.W. (20435)
Established: Sept. 16, 1940
Director: Maj. Gen. Thomas K. Turnage.
Activities: Authorizes registration of male citizens and all other male persons, except aliens in certain categories, for military service. (Authority to induct registrants expired July 1, 1973.)

SMALL BUSINESS ADMINISTRATION (SBA)
1441 L St., N.W. (20416).
Established: July 30, 1953.
Administrator: James C. Sanders.
Activities: Aids and assists the interests of small business firms to insure a fair share of total government contracts; makes loans to small firms and victims of flood and disaster.

TENNESSEE VALLEY AUTHORITY (TVA)
400 Commerce Ave., Knoxville, Tenn. (37902). Washington office: Woodward Bldg., 15th & H Sts., N.W. (20444).
Members of Board of Directors: 3.
Established: May 18, 1933.
Chairman: Charles H. Dean, Jr.
Activities: Provides navigable channel and flood control of Tennessee River and some of its larger tributaries; disposes of surplus electric power, improves, increases, and cheapens fertilizer production.

U.S. ARMS CONTROL AND DISARMAMENT AGENCY
Department of State Building (20451).
Established: Sept. 26, 1961.
Director: Eugene V. Rostow.
Special Representative for Negotiations: Edward L. Rowny.
Activities: Conducts studies and provides advice relating to arms control and disarmament policy fomulation; prepares for and manages U.S. participation in international negotiations in arms control and disarmament; prepares for, operates, or as needed, directs U.S. participation in international control systems.

U.S. COMMISSION ON CIVIL RIGHTS
1121 Vermont Avenue, N.W. (20425).
Members: 6.
Established: 1957.
Chairman: Clarence M. Pendleton.
Activities: Collects and studies information concerning discrimination or denial of equal protection of the nation's laws because of race, color, religion, sex, age, handicap, or national origin. Complaints about denials of rights are usually referred to the appropriate Federal agencies for action.

U.S. INFORMATION AGENCY
1750 Pennsylvania Ave., N.W. (20547).
Established: April 1, 1978.
Director: Charles Wick.
Activities: Conducts international communication, educational, cultural, and exchange programs with other peoples of the world.

U.S. INTERNATIONAL DEVELOPMENT COOPERATION AGENCY
320 21st. St., N.W. (20523)
Established: Oct. 1, 1979.
Director: M. Peter McPherson.
Activities: Plans and coordinates policy for economic matters affecting relations with developing countries. Administers Agency for International Development, Institute for Scientific & Technological Cooperation, and Overseas Private Investment Corporation.

U.S. INTERNATIONAL TRADE COMMISSION
701 E St., N.W. (20436).
Members: 6.
Established: Sept. 8, 1916.
Chairman: Alfred Eckes.
Activities: Investigates customs laws, unfair competition, and foreign and domestic manufacturing costs; advises the President on duty rates.

U.S. POSTAL SERVICE
475 L'Enfant Plaza West, S.W. (20260).
Postmaster General: William F. Bolger.
Deputy Postmaster General: C. Neil Benson.

Activities: Maintains postal system of U.S.

Established: Office of Postmaster General and temporary post office system created in 1789. Act of Feb. 20, 1792, made detailed provisions for Post Office Department. Postmaster General became Cabinet member in 1829, and Department received executive status in 1872. In 1970 became independent agency headed by 11-member board of governors. Postmaster General, no longer Cabinet member, is chosen by nine governors, who, with Postmaster General, choose Deputy Postmaster General.

VETERANS ADMINISTRATION (VA)
810 Vermont Ave., N.W. (20420).
Established: July 21, 1930.
Administrator: Vacant.
Activities: Administers laws authorizing benefits for veterans and dependents or beneficiaries. Included are hospitals, pensions, insurance, loans, education, etc.

Other Independent Agencies

Administrative Conference of the United States—2120 L St., N.W. (20037).
American Battle Monuments Commission—20 Massachusetts Ave., S.W. (20314).
Appalachian Regional Commission—1666 Connecticut Ave., N.W. (20235).
Board for International Broadcasting—1030 15th St., N.W. (20005).
Commission of Fine Arts—708 Jackson Place, N.W. (20006).
Commodity Futures Trading Commission—2033 K St., N.W. (20581).
Export-Import Bank of the United States—811 Vermont Ave., N.W. (20571).
Federal Council on the Aging—330 Independence Ave. S.W. (20201)
Federal Emergency Management Agency—1725 I St., N.W. (20472).
Federal Home Loan Bank Board—1700 G St., N.W. (20552).
Federal Labor Relations Authority—1900 E St., N.W. (20424).
Inter-American Foundation—1515 Wilson Blvd., Rosslyn, Va. (22209).
Merit Systems Protection Board—1717 H St., N.W. (20419).
National Center for the Prevention and Control of Rape—5600 Fishers Lane, Rockville, Md. (20857).
National Commission on Libraries and Information Science—1717 K St. (20036).
National Credit Union Administration—1776 G St., N.W. (20456).
National Mediation Board—1425 K St., N.W. (20572).
Occupational Safety and Health Review Commission—1825 K St., N.W. (20006).
Panama Canal Commission—425 13th St., N.W. (20004).
Pension Benefit Guaranty Corporation—2020 K St., N.W. (20006).
Postal Rate Commission—2000 L St., N.W. (20268).
President's Committee on Employment of the Handicapped—1111 20th St., N.W. (20210).
President's Council on Physical Fitness and Sports—400 6th St., S.W. (20201).
Railroad Retirement Board (RRB)—844 Rush St., Chicago, Ill. (60611). Washington Liaison Office: Room 444, 425 13th St., N.W. (20004).
U.S. Metric Board—1600 Wilson Blvd., Arlington, Va. (22209).

Legislative Department

ARCHITECT OF THE CAPITOL
U.S. Capitol Building (20515).
Established: First Architect of the Capitol was appointed in 1793; office has been continuous since 1851.
Architect of Capitol: George M. White.
Activities: Architect of the Capitol has charge of structural and mechanical care of Capitol Building and various other government buildings in Washington.

GENERAL ACCOUNTING OFFICE (GAO)
441 G Street, N.W. (20548).
Established: 1921.
Comptroller General: Charles A. Bowsher.
Deputy Comptroller General: Vacant.
Activities: Assists Congress in providing legislative control over receipt, disbursement, and application of public funds.

GOVERNMENT PRINTING OFFICE (GPO)
North Capitol & H Sts., N.W. (20401).
Established: June 23, 1860.
Public Printer: Danford L. Sawyer.
Superintendent of Documents: Raymond Mason Taylor.
Activities: Executes printing and binding orders for Congress and federal agencies; distributes government publications.

LIBRARY OF CONGRESS
10 First St., S.E. (20540).
Established: April 24, 1800.
Librarian of Congress: Daniel J. Boorstin.
Activities: Extends services to members of government and offers facilities for persons engaged in scholarly research.

OFFICE OF TECHNOLOGY ASSESSMENT
600 Pennsylvania Ave., S.E. (20510).
Established: 1972.
Director: John H. Gibbons.
Activities: Helps Congress anticipate and plan for the consequences of the uses of technology.

UNITED STATES BOTANIC GARDEN
Office of Director, 245 First St., S.W. (20024).
Established: 1820.
Director: George M. White (acting).
Activities: Collects, cultivates, and grows various vegetable products for exhibition and study.

Quasi-Official Agencies

American National Red Cross—17th & D Sts., N.W. (20006).
Legal Services Corporation—733 15th St., N.W. (20005).
National Academy of Sciences, National Academy of Engineering, National Research Council, Institute of Medicine—2101 Constitution Ave., N.W. (20418).
National Railroad Passenger Corporation (Amtrak)—400 N. Capitol St., N.W. (20001).
Smithsonian Institution—1000 Jefferson Dr., S.W. (20560).
U.S. Railway Association—955 L'Enfant Plaza North, S.W. (20595).

POSTAL REGULATIONS

Domestic Mail Service

First Class

First-class consists of letters and written and sealed matter. The rate is 20¢ for the first oz; 17¢ for each additional oz, or fraction of an oz, up to 12 oz. Pieces over 12 oz are subject to priority-mail (heavy pieces) rates. Single postcards, 13¢; double postcards, 26¢ (13¢ for each half). The post office sells prestamped single and double postal cards. Consult your postmaster for information on business-reply mail and presort rates.

The weight limit for first-class mail is 70 lb, and the maximum size is 100 in. in combined length and girth.

Weight	Rates
First oz	$ .20
Over 1 oz, but not over 2	.37
Over 2 oz, but not over 3	.54
Over 3 oz, but not over 4	.71
Over 4 oz, but not over 5	.88
Over 5 oz, but not over 6	1.05
Over 6 oz, but not over 7	1.22
Over 7 oz, but not over 8	1.39
Over 8 oz, but not over 9	1.56
Over 9 oz, but not over 10	1.76
Over 10 oz, but not over 11	1.90
Over 11 oz, but not over 12	2.07
Over 12 oz, *see* Priority Mail	

Priority Mail (over 12 oz to 70 lb)

The zone rate applies to mailable matter over 12 oz of any class carried by air. Such matter shall not exceed 100 in. in length and girth combined. Your local post office will supply free official zone tables appropriate to your location.

Airmail

First-class and priority mail receive airmail service.

Express Mail

Express Mail Service is available for any mailable article up to 70 lb, and guarantees next day delivery between major U.S. cities or your money back.

Articles received by 5 p.m. at a postal facility offering Express Mail Service will be delivered by 3 p.m. the next day or, if you prefer, your shipment can be picked up as early as 10 a.m. the next business day. Rates include Insurance, Shipment Receipt, and Record of Delivery at the destination post office.

Consult Postmaster for other Express Mail Services and rates.

The Postal Service will refund, upon application to originating office, the postage for any Express Mail shipments not meeting the service standard except for those delayed by strike or work stoppage.

Second Class

Second-class mail is used primarily by newspapers, magazines, and other periodicals with second-class mailing privileges. For copies mailed by the public, the rate is:

Weight	Rates	Weight	Rates
0 to 1 oz	$ .19	Over 4 to 5 oz	$ .65
Over 1 to 2 oz	.35	Over 5 to 6 oz	.75
Over 2 to 3 oz	.45	Over 6 to 7 oz	.85
Over 3 to 4 oz	.55	Over 7 to 8 oz	.95
Each additional two ounces over 8 oz, add $ .10			

Third Class (under 16 oz)

Third-class mail is used for circulars, books, printed matter, merchandise, seeds, cuttings, bulbs, roots, scions, and plants, and all other mailable matter not in first or second class. There are two rate structures for this class, a single-piece and a bulk rate.

Many community organizations, as well as businesses, find it economical to use this service. Because of the number of categories of third-class mail, you should consult your postmaster for the one best suited to your needs.

Third-Class, Single-Piece Rates

Weight	Rates	Weight	Rates
0 to 1 oz	$ .20	Over 8 to 10 oz	$1.05
Over 1 to 2 oz	.37	Over 10 to 12 oz	1.15
Over 2 to 3 oz	.54	Over 12 to 14 oz	1.25
Over 3 to 4 oz	.71	Over 14 but less than 16 oz	1.35
Over 4 to 6 oz	.85		
Over 6 to 8 oz	.95		

Fourth Class (Parcel Post—16 oz and over)

Fourth-class mail is used for merchandise, books, printed matter, and all other mailable matter not in first, second, or third class. Special fourth-class rates apply to books, library books, publications or records for the blind, and certain controlled-circulation publications.

Packages should be taken to your local post office, where the postage will be determined according to the weight of the package and the distance it is being sent. Information on weight and size limits for fourth-class mail may be obtained there.

Special Fourth-Class Rate

The special fourth-class rate is restricted specifically to books; 16-mm or narrower width films and catalogs of such films (which must be positive prints); printed music, printed objective-test materials, sound recordings, and playscripts and manuscripts for books, periodicals, and music; printed educational reference charts, looseleaf pages, and binders therefor, consisting of medical information for distribution to doctors, hospitals, medical schools, and medical students. The rate is 63¢ for the first lb or fraction, plus 23¢ for each additional lb or fraction through 7 lb, 14¢ for each additional lb or fraction over 7 lb.

Special Services

Registered Mail. When you use registered mail service, you are buying security—the safest way to send valuables. The full value of your mailing must be declared when mailed. You receive a receipt and the movement of your mail is controlled throughout the postal system. For an additional fee, a return receipt showing to whom, when, and where delivered may be obtained.

Fees for articles (in addition to postage)

Value			with Insurance	without Insurance
0.00	to	$ 100	$3.30	$3.25
100.01	to	500	3.60	3.55
500.01	to	1,000	3.90	3.85

For higher values, consult your postmaster.

Certified Mail. Certified mail service provides for a receipt to the sender and a record of delivery at the post office of address. No record is kept at the post office where mailed. It is handled in the ordinary mails and no insurance coverage is provided.

Fee in addition to postage, 75¢.

Return Receipts. Requested at time of mailing:

Showing to whom and date delivered	$ .60
Showing to whom, date, and address where delivered	.70
Requested after mailing:	
Showing to whom and date delivered	3.75

C.O.D. Mail. Consult your postmaster for fees and conditions of mailing.

Insured Mail. Fees, in addition to postage, for coverage against loss or damage:

Liability			Fees
$ .01	to	$20	$ .45
$ 20.01	to	$50	.85
$ 50.01	to	$100	1.25
$100.01	to	$150	1.70
$150.01	to	$200	2.05
$200.01	to	$300	3.45
$300.01	to	$400[1]	4.70

1. Liability for insured mail is limited to $400.

Special Delivery. The payment of the special-delivery fee entitles mail to the most expeditious transportation and delivery. The fee is in addition to the regular postage.

Class of mail	Weight/Fees: Not more than 2 lb	More than 2 lb but not more than 10 lb	More than 10 lb
First-class	$2.10	$2.35	$3.00
All other classes	2.35	3.00	3.40

Special Handling. Payment of the special-handling fee entitles third- and fourth-class matter to the most expeditious handling and transportation, but not special delivery. The fee is in addition to the regular postage.

Weight	Fees
Not more than 10 lb	$ .75
More than 10 lb	1.30

Money Orders. Money orders are used for the safe transmission of money.

Amount of money order			Fees
$ .01	to	$25	$ .75
$25.01	to	$50	1.10
$50.01	to	$500	1.55

Minimum Mail Sizes

All mail must be at least 0.007 in. thick and mail that is 1/4 in. or less in thickness must be at least 3 1/2 in. in height, at least 5 in. long, and rectangular in shape.

Adhesive Stamps Available

Purpose	Form	Denomination and prices
Ordinary postage	Single or sheet	1, 2, 3, 4, 5, 6, 10, 11, 12, 13, 14, 15, 16, 17, 18, 20, 25, 28, 30, 35, 37, 40, and 50¢, $1, 2, and $5.
	Book	6 at 20=$1.20 20 at 20=$4.00
	Coil of 100[1]	20¢
	Coil of 500	1, 2, 3, 5, 6, 10, 12, 13, 15, 16, 17, 18, 20, and $1.00.
	Coil of 3,000	1, 2, 3, 5, 6, 9, 10, 15, 16, and 25¢
International airmail postage	Single or sheet	28, 35, and 40¢

1. Dispenser to hold coil of 100 stamps may be purchased for 10¢

"Junk" Mail

If you want to unclutter your mailbox of unwanted advertising mail or if you want more mail, the Direct Mail Marketing Association Inc. offers a free service allowing consumers to have their names added or deleted from national advertising lists. Copies of a booklet, "How Did They Get My Name?" which explains consumer mailing lists, are available without charge from DMMA, Dept. M, 6 E. 43rd St., New York, N.Y. 10017.

Non-Standard Mail

All first-class mail weighing one ounce or less and all single-piece rate third-class mail weighing one ounce or less is nonstandard (and subject to a 9¢ surcharge in addition to the applicable postage and fees)if any of the following dimensions are exceeded: length—11½ inches; height—6-⅛ inches; thickness—¼ inch, or the piece has a height to length (aspect) ratio which does not fall between 1 to 1.3 and 1 to 2.5 inclusive. (The aspect ratio is found by dividing the length by the height. If the answer is between 1.3 and 2.5 inclusive, the piece has a standard aspect ratio).

International Mail Service

Canada and Mexico—Surface Rates

Weight	Letter mail	Printed matter and small packets
1 oz	$ .20	$ .20
2 oz	.37	.37
3 oz	.54	.54
4 oz	.71	.71
6 oz	1.05	.85
8 oz	1.39	.95
10 oz	1.73	1.14
12 oz	2.07	1.36
14 oz	—	1.58
16 oz	2.58	1.81
Postcards	.13	—

Consult your postmaster for rates for heavier items.

International Airmail

Destination	Letters and letter packages[1]	Post-cards	Aero-gramme[2]
Central America Colombia, Venezuela, Caribbean Islands, Bahamas, Bermuda, St. Pierre and Miquelon	35¢ per half oz through 2 oz 30¢ each additional half oz or fraction	28¢	30¢
All other countries	40¢ per half oz through 2 oz 35¢ each additional half oz or fraction	28¢	30¢

1. Weight limit, 4 lb. 2. No enclosures permitted.

For Canada and Mexico, *see* Surface Rates.

International Money Order Fees

This service available only to certain countries. Consult post office.

Countries Other Than Canada and Mexico—Surface Rates

Ounces	Letter mail	Printed matter	Small packets
1	$ .30	$ .23	$ .23
2	.47	.37	.37
4	.81	.71	.71
8	1.49	.95	.95
16	2.76	1.81	1.81
32	4.80	2.76	2.76
64	7.80	3.86	—
Each additional 32 oz	—	.96	—

International Surface Parcel Post

Weight through lb	Canada, Mexico, Central America, Caribbean Islands, Bahamas, Bermuda, St. Pierre and Miquelon	All other countries
2	$ 3.10	$ 3.25
3	4.10	4.30
	$1.00 each additional lb or fraction	$1.05 each additional lb or fraction

Consult your postmaster for weight and size limits.

For other international services and rates consult your local postmaster.

United Nations Stamps

United Nations stamps are issued in three different currencies, namely, U.S. dollars, Swiss francs, and Austrian schillings. Stamps in all three currencies are available at face value at each of the U.N. Postal Administration offices in New York, Geneva, and Vienna. They may be purchased over the counter, by mail, or by opening a Customer Deposit Account.

Mail orders for mint (unused) stamps and postal stationery may be sent to the U.N. Postal Administration in New York, Geneva, and Vienna. A special order form, listing all available mint issues, is available on request. Write to: United Nations Postal Administration, P.O. Box 5900, Grand Central Station, New York, N.Y. 10017. All mint stamps and postal stationery are sold by the U.N. Postal Administration at face value.

Authorized 2-Letter State Abbreviations

When the Post Office instituted the ZIP Code for mail in 1963, it also drew up a list of two-letter abbreviations for the states which would gradually replace the traditional ones in use. Following is the official list, including the District of Columbia, Guam, Puerto Rico, and the Virgin Islands (note that only capital letters are used):

Alabama	AL	Kentucky	KY	Ohio	OH
Alaska	AK	Louisiana	LA	Oklahoma	OK
Arizona	AZ	Maine	ME	Oregon	OR
Arkansas	AR	Maryland	MD	Pennsylvania	PA
California	CA	Massachusetts	MA	Puerto Rico	PR
Colorado	CO	Michigan	MI	Rhode Island	RI
Connecticut	CT	Minnesota	MN	South Carolina	SC
Delaware	DE	Mississippi	MS	South Dakota	SD
Dist. of Columbia	DC	Missouri	MO	Tennessee	TN
Florida	FL	Montana	MT	Texas	TX
Georgia	GA	Nebraska	NE	Utah	UT
Guam	GU	Nevada	NV	Vermont	VT
Hawaii	HI	New Hampshire	NH	Virginia	VA
Idaho	ID	New Jersey	NJ	Virgin Islands	VI
Illinois	IL	New Mexico	NM	Washington	WA
Indiana	IN	New York	NY	West Virginia	WV
Iowa	IA	North Carolina	NC	Wisconsin	WI
Kansas	KS	North Dakota	ND	Wyoming	WY

The Mail Order Merchandise Rule

The mail order rule adopted by the Federal Trade Commission in October 1975 provides that when you order by mail:

You must receive the merchandise when the seller says you will.

If you are not promised delivery within a certain time period, the seller must ship the merchandise to you no later than 30 days after your order comes in.

If you don't receive it shortly after that 30-day period, you can cancel your order and get your money back.

How the Rule Works

The seller must notify you if the promised delivery date (or the 30-day limit) cannot be met. The seller must also tell you what the new shipping date will be and give you the option to cancel the order and receive a full refund or agree to the new shipping date. The seller must also give you a free way to send back your answer, such as a stamped envelope or a postage-paid postcard. *If you don't answer, it means that you agree to the shipping delay.*

The seller must tell you if the shipping delay is going to be more than 30 days. You then can agree to the delay or, if you do not agree, the seller must return your money by the end of the first 30 days of the delay.

If you cancel a prepaid order, the seller must mail you the refund within seven business days. Where there is a credit sale, the seller must adjust your account within one billing cycle.

It would be impossible, however, for one rule to apply uniformly to such a varied field as mail order merchandising. For example, the rule does not apply to mail order photo finishing, magazine subscriptions, and other serial deliveries (except for the initial shipment); to mail order seeds and growing plants; to COD orders; or to credit orders where the buyer's account is not charged prior to shipment of the merchandise.

The Pony Express

Established in April 1860, the Pony Express provided fast mail service between St. Joseph, Mo., the westernmost extent of the U.S. telegraph line, and Sacramento, Calif. The freighting and stagecoach firm of Russell, Majors & Waddell hired expert riders to ride fleet horses in relays over the 1,838-mile distance. Along the route, there were 157 stations, spaced about 12 miles apart, at which the riders changed horses. Each man changed horses about six times before being replaced by another. The route, which was covered in about ten days, passed through hostile Indian territory, and, during the Paiute War in the summer of 1860, Indians burned a number of stations and killed the occupants. October 24, 1861, the day the first telegram to San Francisco was transmitted, marked the downfall of the Pony Express. No longer the crucial link to the West, the Pony Express was discontinued. Though a financial failure, it remains one of the most colorful episodes of American history.

And Now for the Good News, After the Bomb . . .

The U.S. Postal Service has presented to a Congressional subcommittee a 300-page report on plans for continued delivery of the nation's mail after a nuclear attack. It has even supplied most post offices with 2,000 emergency change-of-address forms for citizens forced to evacuate. If Washington, D.C., is obliterated, the Service's command will shift to one of the five regional postmasters, whose headquarters have already been stocked with $18,000–$20,000 worth of food and medical supplies. Members of the House subcommittee, not surprisingly, wondered how useful these plans would be after the elimination of roads, addresses, and addressees.

1982 Environmental Quality Index

Source: Copyright 1982 by the National Wildlife Federation.
Reprinted from the February-March issue of *National Wildlife* Magazine.

National Wildlife's annual Environmental Quality Index is a subjective analysis of the state of the nation's natural resources. The information included in each section is based on personal interviews, news reports, and the most current scientific studies. The judgments on resource trends represent the collective thinking of the editors and the National Wildlife Federation staff, based on consultation with government experts, private specialists, and academic researchers.

Wildlife: Worse. Suddenly, "multiple use" becomes the opening gun in a new war over wildlife habitat. During the past 15 years new federal laws and programs were established to provide for the orderly development of natural resources while safeguarding wildlife. Last year most of these hard-won laws came under the harsh scrutiny of a new administration. Among the hardest hit were programs dealing with wetlands acquisition and protection. One positive note, Interior Secretary James Watt surprised—and pleased—many of his conservationist-critics when he strongly supported a congressional move to end federal expenditures for developing thousands of miles of fragile barrier islands along the Atlantic and Gulf coasts. Another wildlife problem flared up anew last year: chemical poisoning. NWF Wildlife Director Alan Wentz warned that, unless controls on pesticides are tightened, "we may be returning to an era of indiscriminate chemical use—with resultant damage to wildlife."

Air: Same. The Clean Air Act has worked wonders since 1970 but the heat is on to water it down. Up for congressional renewal, the 11-year-old program was roundly attacked by business, and the administration concurred. Under the administration's plan, it would postpone the deadline from 1985 to 1987 for improved pollution control in the nation's most unhealthful areas; weaken the requirements for coal plant scrubbing devices; and stated its intention to modify standards that would keep national parks pollution-free. It also proposed doubling the amount of permissible levels of certain automobile pollutants which could contribute further to one of the nation's two most uncontrolled forms of air pollution—ozone, or photochemical smog, and acid rain. The administration is openly opposed to any acid rain controls.

Minerals: Same. More lands are open for mineral exploration, and fuel conservation takes a back seat to supply. Despite signs that seemed to indicate that Uncle Sam's emphasis on conservation and renewable energy sources was beginning to pay off, the administration didn't see it that way. Last year, the Reagan budget proposals included slashing the federal government energy conservation program by 86% and reducing funds for the nation's solar energy development efforts by some 70% while increasing federal funds for nuclear power by 30%. To help the nation achieve more energy independence the administration proposed opening up more federal lands and offshore areas to coal, oil, and other mineral development. One of the first areas to succumb was Georges Bank off New England.

Water: Worse: Pollution runoff into surface waters and toxic contamination of underground supplies are still monumental problems. Thirty-seven states have reported that some of their waters will be unable to meet the law's "fishable and swimmable" mandates by 1983 because of such "nonpoint" pollution problems. In addition, according to the General Accounting Office, more than a third of the new municipal treatment facilities do not meet legal standards. The EPA's 1982 water quality budget included no funding for municipal treatment plant construction; cleanup and research funds for the Great Lakes, which provide drinking water for some 22 million people, were cut in half. Budget cuts also took their toll on the nation's hazardous waste cleanup effort. The nation has made some progress; in many areas, waterways are better off than they were a decade ago. And though toxic substances remain a serious problem, about 90% of the country's industrial water polluters are now meeting the mandates of the law.

Forests: Same. Though demand for wood is down, minerals and energy become important forestland products. For several years now, the country's economic problems have decreased pressure on forests by keeping a tight lid on timber demand, and last year was no different. Looking beyond the current slowdown, however, the pressure for increased cuts on national forestlands, along with more minerals and energy production, is as strong as ever. One solution, advanced by the new Assistant Secretary of Agriculture for Environment and Natural Resources, John Crowell, Jr., is more intensive management and more cutting of slower growing, older trees in national forests. "I believe in intensive multiple use," he says and believes that such an objective can be achieved without unduly sacrificing wildlife and recreational values. Environmentalists aren't so sure.

Soil: Worse: Farmland is going, going, going . . . and that includes millions of acres of wildlife habitat, too. Once again last year, the nation's most serious soil problem was erosion and the most alarming agricultural issue was the continued loss of farmland to development. Last year, the Soil Conservation Service reported that erosion was 35% worse than in the Dust Bowl days of the 1930s. The underlying problem is not the weather. It is the failure of the nation's farmers to follow effective antierosion measures. Until the federal government stops subsidizing farmers who ignore good conservation practices, erosion may continue unabated.

Living Space: Worse. When the administration moved to cut off all new acquisitions, Congress and conservationists rebelled. Pressure increased for development on federally owned lands, particularly in the West, and Secretary of the Interior James Watt committed himself to a "good neighbor" policy with the states, including removing administrative obstacles to the development on millions of acres of mostly roadless land being considered for inclusion in the nation's wilderness system. On the positive side President Reagan came out against plans for building an MX missile system that would have inflicted irreparable damage on thousands of acres of desert land in Nevada and Utah. Also decades of feverish highway building ended last year.

Some Endangered Species of the World[1]

Common name	Scientific name	Range
MAMMALS		
Anteater, scaly	*Manis temmincki*	Africa
Bear, brown	*Ursus arctos pruinosus*	China (Tibet)
Bear, brown or grizzly[2]	*Ursus arctos horribilis*	Canada, Western U.S.
Cat, leopard	*Felis bengalensis bengalensis*	Eastern Asia
Cat, tiger	*Felis tigrina*	Costa Rica to northern South America
Cheetah	*Acinonyx jubatus*	Africa to India
Chimpanzee[2]	*Pan troglodytes*	Western and Central Africa
Chinchilla	*Chinchilla brevicaudata boliviana*	Bolivia
Deer, Columbian white-tailed	*Odocoileus virginianus leucurus*	U.S. (Ore., Wash.)
Deer, marsh	*Blastocerus dichotomus*	Argentina, Uruguay, Paraguay, Brazil
Deer, musk	*Moschus moschiferus moschiferus*	Southcentral Asia
Elephant, Asian	*Elephas maximus*	Southcentral and Southeast Asia
Gazelle, Clark's (Dibatag)	*Ammodorcas clarkei*	Somalia, Ethiopia
Gazelle, slender-horned (Rhim)	*Gazella leptoceros*	Sudan, Algeria, Egypt, Libya
Gorilla	*Gorilla gorilla*	Central and western Africa
Ibex, Walia	*Capra walie*	Ethiopia
Jaguar	*Panthera onca*	Central and South America
Kangaroo, red[2]	*Macropus (=Megaleia) rufus*	Australia
Leopard	*Panthera pardus*	Africa, Southern and Eastern Asia
Leopard, snow	*Panthera uncia*	Central Asia
Lion, Asiatic	*Panthera leo persica*	India
Mandrill	*Papio sphinx*	Equatorial West Africa
Monkey, black howler[2]	*Alouatta pigra*	Mexico, Guatemala, Belize
Ocelot	*Felis pardalis*	Central and South America
Orangutan	*Pongo pygmaeus*	Borneo, Sumatra
Otter, southern sea[2]	*Enhydra lutris nereis*	West coast U.S. (Wash.), south to Mexico (Baja Calif.)
Panther, Florida	*Felis concolor coryi*	U.S. (La. and Ark., east to S.C. and Fla.)
Prairie Dog, Utah	*Cynomys parvidens*	U.S. (Utah)
Pronghorn, Sonoran	*Antilocapra americana sonoriensis*	U.S. (Ariz.), Mexico
Rat, Morro Bay kangaroo	*Dipodomys heermanni morroensis*	U.S. (Calif.)
Rhinoceros, great Indian	*Rhinoceros unicornis*	India, Nepal
Sloth, Brazilian three-toed	*Bradypus torquatus*	Brazil
Tiger	*Panthera tigris*	Temperate and tropical Asia
Whale, humpback	*Megaptera novaeangliae*	Oceanic
Wolf, gray	*Canis lupus*	U.S., Mexico
Zebra, mountain	*Equus zebra zebra*	Southern Africa
BIRDS		
Albatross, short-tailed	*Diomedea albatrus*	North Pacific Ocean: Japan, USSR, U.S. (Alas., Calif., Hawaii, Ore., Wash.)
Condor, Andean	*Vultur gryphus*	Colombia to Chile and Argentina
Eagle, bald	*Haliaeetus leucocephalus*	U.S. (except Wash., Ore., Minn., Wis., Mich.[2])
Falcon, Eurasian peregrine	*Falco peregrinus peregrinus*	Europe, Eurasia south to Africa and Mideast
Parakeet, paradise (=beautiful)	*Psephotus pulcherrimus*	Australia
Pelican, brown	*Pelecanus occidentalis*	U.S., (Carolinas to Texas, Calif., West Indies, Central and South America, coastal.)

Common name	Scientific name	Range
Penguin, Galápagos	*Spheniscus mendiculus*	Ecuador (Galápagos Islands)
Stork, white oriental	*Ciconia ciconia boyciana*	China, Japan, Korea, U.S.S.R.
REPTILES		
Alligator, American	*Alligator mississippiensis*	Southeastern U.S. (except Fla., La., certain areas of Ga., S.C., Texas[2])
Crocodile, American	*Crocodylus acutus*	U.S. (Fla.), Mexico, South America, Central America, Caribbean
Iguana, Anegada ground	*Cyclura pinguis*	West Indies, British Virgin Is. (Anegada Is.)
Python, Indian	*Python molurus molurus*	Sri Lanka, India
Snake, Atlantic salt marsh[2]	*Nerodia fasciata taeniata*	U.S. (Fla.)
Tortoise, Indian flap-shell	*Lissemys punctata punctata*	India, Pakistan, Bangladesh
AMPHIBIANS		
Frog, Israel painted	*Discoglossus nigriventer*	Israel
Toad, African viviparous	*Nectophrynoides* spp.	Tanzania, Guinea
Treefrog, Pine Barrens	*Hyla andersonii*	U.S. (Fla.)
FISH		
Catfish, giant	*Pangasianodon gigas*	Thailand
Pike, blue[3]	*Stizostedion vitreum glaucum*	U.S. and Canada (Lakes Erie and Ontario)
Trout, greenback cutthroat[2]	*Salmo clarki stomias*	U.S. (Colo.)

1. Due to space limitations, does not include clams, crustaceans, snails, insects, and plants. 2. Threatened. 3. Extinct. *Source:* Department of the Interior, Fish and Wildlife Service.

Sources of Information

Source: Brooklyn Botanic Garden, *Handbook on The Environment and The Home Gardener.*

Advice on various aspects of conservation programs and problems is available from national, state, and local organizations. Dr. Richard H. Pough, President of the Natural Area Council, has compiled a list of membership organizations that are happy to help smaller groups get started on worthwhile projects in conservation.

America the Beautiful Fund, Inc. 219 Shoreham Building, Washington, D.C. 20005

American Forestry Association, 1319 18th St., N.W., Washington, D.C. 20036

Defenders of Wildlife, 1244 19th St., N.W., Washington, D.C. 20036

Environmental Defense Fund, Inc., 444 Park Ave. South, New York, N.Y. 10016

Friends of the Earth, 208 W. 13th St., New York, N.Y. 10011

Izaak Walton League of America, 1800 N. Kent St., Suite 806, Arlington, VA. 22209

National Audubon Society, 950 Third Ave., New York, N.Y. 10022

National Park and Conservation Association, 1701 18th St., N.W., Washington, D.C. 20009

National Trust for Historic Preservation, 748 Jackson Place, N.W., Washington, D.C. 20006

National Wildlife Federation, 1412 16th St., N.W., Washington, D.C. 20036

Natural Science for Youth Foundation, 763 Silvermine Rd., New Canaan, Conn. 06840

The Nature Conservancy, 1800 N. Kent St., Suite 800, Arlington, Va. 22209

Open Space Institute, Inc., Room 4500, 122 East 42nd St., New York, N.Y. 10168

Sierra Club, 530 Bush St., San Francisco, Calif. 94108

The Wilderness Society, 1901 Pennsylvania Ave., N.W., Washington, D.C. 20006

World Wildlife Fund, 1601 Connecticut Ave., N.W., Washington, D.C. 20009

Don't Eat the Flowers

There are more than 700 species of plants that grow in the United States that have been identified as dangerous if eaten. Among them are some that are commonly favored by gardeners—buttercups, daffodils, lily of the valley, sweet peas, oleander, azalea, bleeding heart, delphinium, and rhododendron. According to a survey of the nation's poison control centers, next to medicines, plants are the leading cause of poisoning in children under five years of age. A threefold increase in plant poisoning, from 1971 levels, is attributed to the house plant explosion and back-to-nature dining.

Another Dust Bowl in the Making?

From Montana to Texas the plowing of more than a million acres of grassland and prairie, much of it within the last three years, is causing concern that a new Dust Bowl is in the making. This trend of plowing up grassland represents a dangerous reversal of several decades of soil conservation practices. Some of the land being plowed was reseeded with Federal funds to restore land damaged by soil erosion during the Dust Bowl years of the mid-30s. According to Neil Sampson, executive vice president of the National Association of Conservation Districts, the nation could lose 25 to 62 million acres of cropland and rangeland to soil erosion in the next 50 years.

Air Pollutant Emissions, by Source
(estimates)

Year and pollutant	Total emissions[1]	Controllable emissions[1]: Transportation: Total	Transportation: Road vehicles	Fuel combustion[2]: Total	Fuel combustion[2]: Electric utilities	Industrial processes	Solid waste disposal	Misc. uncontrollable[1]
1970								
Carbon monoxide	112.7	88.7	78.2	1.4	.2	8.8	6.8	6.8
Sulfur oxides	32.8	.8	.3	24.9	17.5	6.9	.1	.1
Hydrocarbons	32.5	13.4	11.7	1.7	.1	9.5	1.9	6.1
Particulates[3]	24.5	1.3	.8	7.8	4.5	13.1	1.2	1.0
Nitrogen oxides	21.6	8.2	5.8	12.2	5.7	.7	.3	.2
1975								
Carbon monoxide	106.8	90.4	81.3	1.2	.3	8.0	3.2	4.0
Sulfur oxides	28.8	.8	.3	22.9	18.5	5.1	—	—
Hydrocarbons	29.7	12.5	10.8	1.5	.1	10.1	.9	4.6
Particulates[3]	15.1	1.2	.9	5.5	4.1	7.2	.6	.7
Nitrogen oxides	23.1	9.5	7.1	12.7	6.8	.8	.1	.1
1979								
Carbon monoxide	100.7	82.1	72.6	2.1	.3	6.9	2.8	6.8
Sulfur oxides	27.0	1.1	.4	21.6	17.6	4.5	—	—
Hydrocarbons	27.1	9.7	7.9	.2	.1	13.7	.9	2.6
Particulates[3]	10.5	1.5	1.2	2.8	1.7	4.7	.4	1.0
Nitrogen oxides	24.9	10.1	7.4	13.6	8.3	.9	.1	.2

1. In millions of tons. 2. Stationary. 3. Suspended particulate matter (particles of smoke or dust, fumes, and droplets of viscous liquid remaining in the air for varying periods of time and ranging from less than 1 micron [1/25,000 in.] to 100 microns). NOTE: — represents zero. *Source:* Environmental Protection Agency.

Federal Outlays for the Environment by Activity, 1977–1981
(In millions of dollars, except percent, for years ending Sept. 30)

Activity	1981[1]	1980	1979	1978	1977
Pollution abatement and control	$7,723	$7,632	$6,945	$5,934	$5,829
Percent Environmental Protection Agency	71.8	73.4	69.1	68.6	74.9
Aid to State and local governments	5,028	5,177	4,769	3,972	3,967
Research and development	869	782	795	836	786
Standard setting and enforcement	917[2]	791	537	524	426
Reduction of pollution from Federal facilities	510	471	550	431	457
Other	399	411	294	171	192
Protection and enhancement	2,651	2,749	2,614	2,688	1,498
Aid to State and local governments[3]	877	891	856	847	426
City recreation	345	335	338	425	205
Noncity general recreation	130	128	196	158	145
Historic preservation and rehabilitation	92	84	45	39	47
Direct Federal activities[3]	1,774	1,858	1,758	1,841	1,073
Noncity general recreation	488	468	449	372	325
Preservation and protection[4]	397	434	387	647	303
City recreation	204	212	196	132	113
Historic preservation and rehabilitation	111	112	133	63	73
Understanding, describing, and predicting[3]	2,481	2,376	2,423	2,155	1,885
Observation and prediction[5]	913	854	757	744	709
Locate and describe natural resources	655	650	861	688	490
Research on environmental impact on people	351	337	303	266	261
Ecological and other basic environmental research	237	228	266	242	206
Physical environmental surveys	292	281	214	197	199
Total	**12,855**	**12,757**	**11,982**	**10,777**	**9,212**

1. Estimated. Based on January budget estimates. 2. Includes funds for planning, monitoring and surveillance, and technical assistance. 3. Includes activities not shown separately. 4. Unique natural areas and endangered species. 5. Includes weather, ocean, and earthquakes and other disturbances. *Source: Statistical Abstract of the United States, 1981.*

Water Supply of the World[1]

The Antarctic Icecap is the largest supply of fresh water, nearly 2 percent of the world's total of fresh and salt water. As can be seen from the table below, the amount of water in our atmosphere is over ten times as large as the water in all the rivers taken together. The fresh water actually available for human use in lakes and rivers and the accessible ground water amounts to only about one third of one percent of the world's total water supply.

	Surface area (square miles)	Volume (cubic miles)	Percentage of total
Salt Water			
The oceans	139,500,000	317,000,000	97.2
Inland seas and saline lakes	270,000	25,000	0.008
Fresh Water			
Freshwater lakes	330,000	30,000	0.009
All rivers (average level)	—	300	0.0001
Antarctic Icecap	6,000,000	6,300,000	1.9
Arctic Icecap and glaciers	900,000	680,000	0.21
Water in the atmosphere	197,000,000	3,100	0.001
Ground water within half a mile from surface	—	1,000,000	0.31
Deep-lying ground water	—	1,000,000	0.31
Total (rounded)	—	**326,000,000**	**100.00**

1. All figures are estimated. *Source:* Department of the Interior, Geological Survey.

Speed of Animals

Most of the following measurements are for maximum speeds over approximate quarter-mile distances. Exceptions—which are included to give a wide range of animals—are the lion and elephant, whose speeds were clocked in the act of charging; the whippet, which was timed over a 200-yard course; the cheetah over a 100-yard distance; man for a 15-yard segment of a 100-yard run; and the black mamba, six-lined race runner, spider, giant tortoise, three-toed sloth, and garden snail, which were measured over various small distances.

Animal	Speed mph	Animal	Speed mph	Animal	Speed mph
Cheetah	70	Mongolian wild ass	40	Man	27.89
Pronghorn antelope	61	Greyhound	39.35	Elephant	25
Wildebeest	50	Whippet	35.5	Black mamba snake	20
Lion	50	Rabbit (domestic)	35	Six-line race runner	18
Thomson's gazelle	50	Mule deer	35	Squirrel	12
Quarter horse	47.5	Jackal	35	Pig (domestic)	11
Elk	45	Reindeer	32	Chicken	9
Cape hunting dog	45	Giraffe	32	Spider (Tegenearia atrica)	1.17
Coyote	43	White-tailed deer	30	Giant Tortoise	0.17
Gray fox	42	Wart hog	30	Three-toed sloth	0.15
Hyena	40	Grizzly bear	30	Garden snail	0.03
Zebra	40	Cat (domestic)	30		

Source: Natural History Magazine, March 1974, copyright 1974, The American Museum of Natural History; and James Doherty, Curator of Mammals, N.Y. Zoological Society.

Animal Names: Male, Female, and Young

Animal	Male	Female	Young	Animal	Male	Female	Young	Animal	Male	Female	Young
Ass	Jack	Jenny	Foal	Duck	Drake	Duck	Duckling	Sheep	Ram	Ewe	Lamb
Bear	Boar	Sow	Cub	Elephant	Bull	Cow	Calf	Swan	Cob	Pen	Cygnet
Cat	Tom	Queen	Kitten	Fox	Dog	Vixen	Cub	Swine	Boar	Sow	Piglet
Cattle	Bull	Cow	Calf	Goose	Gander	Goose	Gosling	Tiger	Tiger	Tigress	Cub
Chicken	Rooster	Hen	Chick	Horse	Stallion	Mare	Foal	Whale	Bull	Cow	Calf
Deer	Buck	Doe	Fawn	Lion	Lion	Lioness	Cub	Wolf	Dog	Bitch	Pup
Dog	Dog	Bitch	Pup	Rabbit	Buck	Doe	Bunny				

Source: James Doherty, Curator of Mammals, N.Y. Zoological Society.

Winter Sports Gain in National Forests

Department of Agriculture Forest Service officials predict a 23% increase in winter sports in the 154 national forests over the next ten years. This gain is twice the expected increase in sports for other times of the year. Part of the reason is attributed to the growing popularity of the back country in the winter time.

Animal Group Terminology

Source: James Doherty, Curator of Mammals, N.Y. Zoological Society, and *Information Please* data.

ants: colony
bears: sleuth, sloth
bees: grist, hive, swarm
birds: flight, volery
cattle: drove
cats: clutter, clowder
chicks: brood, clutch
clams: bed
cranes: sedge, seige
crows: murder
doves: dule
ducks: brace, team
elephants: herd
elks: gang
finches: charm
fish: school, shoal, draught
foxes: leash, skulk
geese: flock, gaggle, skein
gnats: cloud, horde
goats: trip
gorillas: band
hares: down, husk
hawks: cast
hens: brood
hogs: drift
horses: pair, team
hounds: cry, mute, pack
kangaroos: troop
kittens: kindle, litter
larks: exaltation
lions: pride
locusts: plague
magpies: tidings
mules: span
nightingales: watch
oxen: yoke
oysters: bed
parrots: company
partridges: covey
peacocks: muster, ostentation
pheasants: nest, bouquet
pigs: litter
ponies: string
quail: bevy, covey
rabbits: nest
seals: pod
sheep: drove, flock
sparrows: host
storks: mustering
swans: bevy, wedge
swine: sounder
toads: knot
turkeys: rafter
turtles: bale
vipers: nest
whales: gam, pod
wolves: pack, route
woodcocks: fall

Gestation, Incubation, and Longevity of Certain Animals

Animal	Gestation or incubation, in days & (average)	Longevity, in years & (record exceptions)	Animal	Gestation or incubation, in days & (average)	Longevity, in years & (record exceptions)
Ass	365	18–20 (63)	Horse	329–345 (336)	20–25 (50+)
Bear	180–240[1]	15–30 (47)	Kangaroo	32–39[1]	4–6 (23)
Cat	52–69 (63)	10–12 (26+)	Lion	105–113 (108)	10 (29)
Chicken	22	7–8 (14)	Man	253–303	([2])
Cow	c. 280	9–12 (39)	Monkey	139–270[1]	12–15[1](29)
Deer	197–300[1]	10–15 (26)	Mouse	19–31[1]	1–3 (4)
Dog	53–71 (63)	10–12 (24)	Parakeet (Budgerigar)	17–20 (18)	8 (12+)
Duck	21–35[1](28)	10 (15)	Pig	101–130 (115)	10 (22)
Elephant	510–730 (624)[1]	30–40 (71)	Pigeon	11–19	10–12 (39)
Fox	51–63[1]	8–10 (14)	Rabbit	30–35 (31)	6–8 (15)
Goat	136–160 (151)	12 (17)	Rat	21	3 (5)
Groundhog	31–32	4–9	Sheep	144–152 (151)[1]	12 (16)
Guinea pig	58–75 (68)	3 (6)	Squirrel	44	8–9 (15)
Hamster, golden	15–17	2 (8)	Whale	365–547[1]	—
Hippopotamus	220–255 (240)	30 (49+)	Wolf	60–63	10–12 (16)

1. Depending on kind. 2. For life expectancy charts, *see* Index. *Source:* James Doherty, Curator of Mammals, N.Y. Zoological Society.

Zoological Gardens

North America has more than 30 major zoos, in the United States, Canada, and Mexico. The *Quebec Zoological Society's* collection is made up of Canadian species; Toronto has many exotic species.

The first zoological garden in the United States was established in Philadelphia in 1874. Since that time nearly every large city in the country has acquired a zoo. Among the largest are San Diego's on the West Coast; Chicago's Brookfield Zoo and those of St. Louis and Kansas City in the Middle West; and, in the East, the New York Zoological Society's park in the Bronx. The *National Zoological Park* in Washington, D.C., in a beautiful setting of hills, woods, and streams, was established in 1890 by an act of Congress. The major U.S. zoos now have created large natural-habitat areas for their collections.

In Europe, zoological gardens have long been popular public institutions. The *Jardin d'Acclimatation,* in the Bois de Boulogne, Paris, is the oldest and largest. Others are located at Clères, Ermenonville, Lyons, Marseilles, Maubeuge, Mulhouse, and Nancy.

Germany had about 20 zoological gardens, many of which were developed in the peacetime years between World Wars I and II. Large zoos were located in Berlin and Frankfurt am Main. In Munich, the animals were grouped according to the continent of their origin. At Stellingen near Hamburg, the *Hagenback Garden* became an outstanding show place and distributing center for animals.

The *Schönbrunn* at Vienna is one of the oldest zoos in Europe. The Budapest zoological gardens house a fine collection of European birds. At Antwerp, the *Royal Zoological Society* founded a large menagerie in 1843. It was seriously damaged by German bombs during World War II.

In the British Isles, a popular zoo is in the garden of the *London Zoological Society* in Regent's Park. Although this zoo received a number of direct bomb hits in 1940–41 and again in 1944, it remained open throughout World War II; visitors during this period numbered 6,500,000. Manchester and Clifton have smaller gardens, and the one at Edinburgh is famous for its collection of penguins. The *Dublin Zoo* is noted for its lions, many of which were born there.

The Amsterdam zoo, with its East Indian collection and its aquarium, and the Rotterdam gardens are the two best known in the Netherlands. Built on a high elevation, the *Skansen Zoo* in Stockholm exhibits north European specimens. The most important gardens in the U.S.S.R. are found in Moscow, where northern as well as exotic species are collected. The zoo at Rome has part of its collection confined in barless pits. At Lisbon there is a small zoological garden, and in Madrid a part of the original royal menagerie.

Notable American Zoos

Source: Information Please questionnaires to the zoos.

Atlanta Zoological Park: 800 Cherokee Ave., S.E., Atlanta, Ga. 30315
Audubon Park and Zoological Garden: St. Charles Ave. between Magazine St. and Mississippi River, New Orleans, La. 70178
Baltimore Zoo: Druid Hill Park, Baltimore, Md. 21217
Belle Isle Aquarium and Zoo: Detroit, Mich. Mailing address: Box 39, Royal Oak, Mich. 48068-0039
Bronx Zoo. *See* New York Zoological Park
Buffalo Zoological Gardens: Delaware Park, Buffalo, N.Y. 14214
Burnet Park Zoo: Coleridge and Wilbur Ave., Syracuse, N.Y. 13204
Central Park Zoo: 830 Fifth Ave. at 64th St., New York, N.Y. 10021
Cheyenne Mountain Zoological Park: Cheyenne Mountain Hwy., P.O. Box 158, Colorado Springs, Colo. 80901
Chicago Zoological Park (Brookfield Zoo): First Ave. and 31st St., Brookfield, Ill. 60513
Cincinnati, Zoological Society of: 3400 Vine St., Cincinnati, Ohio 45220
Cleveland Metroparks Zoo: Brookside Park, Cleveland, Ohio 44109
Columbus Zoo: 9990 Riverside Drive, Powell, Ohio 43065
Dallas Zoo: 621 East Clarendon Drive, Dallas, Tex. 75203
Denver Zoological Gardens: City Park, Denver, Colo. 80205
Detroit Zoological Park: Woodward and Ten Mile Road, Royal Oak, Mich. 48068-0039
El Paso Zoological Park: Evergreen and Paisano, El Paso, Tex. 79905
Fort Worth Zoological Park: 2727 Zoological Park Drive, Fort Worth, Tex. 76110
Franklin Park Zoological Gardens: Boston, Mass. 02121
Hogle Zoological Gardens: 2600 East Sunnyside Ave., Salt Lake City, Utah 84108
Houston Zoological Gardens: Hermann Park, P.O. Box 1562, Houston, Tex. 77001
Jacksonville Zoological Park: 8605 Zoo Road, Jacksonville, Fla. 32218
Kansas City Zoo: Swope Park, Kansas City, Mo. 64132
Lincoln Municipal Zoo: 1300 South 27th St., Lincoln, Neb. 68502
Lincoln Park Zoological Gardens: 2200 N. Cannon Drive, Chicago, Ill. 60614
Los Angeles Zoo: 5333 Zoo Drive, Los Angeles, Calif. 90027
Louisville Zoological Garden: 1100 Trevilian Way, Louisville, Ky. 40213
Memphis Zoo and Aquarium: Overton Park, Memphis, Tenn. 38112
Mesker Park Zoo: Bement Ave., Evansville, Ind. 47712
Milwaukee County Zoo: 10001 West Bluemound Road, Milwaukee, Wis. 53226
National Zoological Park: 3000 block of Connecticut Ave. N.W., Washington, D.C. 20008
New York Zoological Park (Bronx Zoo): Bronx River Parkway at Fordham Rd., Bronx, N.Y. 10460
Oakland Zoo: Golf Links Road, off Freeway 580, Oakland, Calif. 94605
Oklahoma City Zoo: 2101 N.E. 50th St., Oklahoma City, Okla. 73111
Philadelphia Zoo: 34th St. and Girard Ave., Philadelphia, Pa. 19104
Pittsburgh Zoo: Highland Park, P.O. Box 5250, Pittsburgh, Pa. 15206
Rio Grande Zoological Park: 903 Tenth St., S.W., Albuquerque, N.M. 87102
St. Louis Zoological Park: Forest Park, St. Louis, Mo. 63110
St. Paul's Como Zoo: Midway Pkwy. and Kaufman Drive, St. Paul, Minn. 55103
San Diego Zoo: Park Blvd. and Zoo Place, P.O. Box 551, San Diego, Calif. 92112
San Francisco Zoo: Sloat Blvd. at Pacific Ocean, San Francisco, Calif., 94132
Seneca Park Zoo: 2222 St. Paul St., Rochester, N.Y. 14621-1097
Staten Island Zoo: 614 Broadway, W. Brighton, Staten Island, New York 10310
Toledo Zoological Gardens: 2700 Broadway, Toledo, Ohio 43609
Washington Park Zoo: 4001 S.W. Canyon Road, Portland, Ore. 97221
Woodland Park Zoological Gardens: 5500 Phinney Ave. N., Seattle, Wash. 98103

The National Park System

Source: Department of the Interior, National Park Service.

The National Park System of the United States is administered by the National Park Service, a bureau of the Department of the Interior. Started with the establishment of Yellowstone National Park in 1872, the system includes not only the most extraordinary and spectacular scenic exhibits in the United States but also a large number of sites distinguished either for their historic or prehistoric importance or scientific interest, or for their superior recreational assets. The number and extent of the various types of areas that make up the system follow.

Type of area	Number	Total acreage[1]
National Parks	48	46,862,644.49
National Monuments	78	4,693,988.34
National Preserves	12	21,993,219.01
National Lakeshores	4	232,130.52
National Rivers[4]	11	525,748.65
National Seashores	10	598,617.72
National Historic Sites	62	17,376.80
National Memorials	23	8,228.10
National Military Parks	10	34,668.22
National Battlefield Parks	3	8,166.80
National Battlefields	10	11,037.97
National Battlefield Site	1	1.00
National Historical Parks	26	150,184.72
National Recreation Areas	17	3,659,040.12
National Parkways	4	160,854.45
National Scenic Trail	1	52,034.25
Other Parks[2]	10	32,026.39
National Capital Parks[3]	1	6,468.88
White House	1	18.07
National Mall	1	146.35
Affiliated Areas	28	45,815.53
Total	**333**	**79,049,188.69**

1. Acreage as of January 1, 1982. Ten national cemeteries administered by the National Park Service are administered in conjunction with associated historical units and are not listed separately. 2. Parks without national designation. 3. Comprises 346 units within the District of Columbia, Maryland, and Virginia. 4. Includes Wild and Scenic Rivers and Riverways.

National Parks

Name, location, and year authorized	Acreage	Outstanding characteristics
Acadia (Maine), 1919	38,631.86	Rugged seashore on Mt. Desert Island and adjacent mainland
Arches (Utah), 1971	39,055.75	Unusual stone arches, windows, pedestals caused by erosion
Badlands (S.D.), 1978	243,302.33	Arid land of fossils, prairie, bison, deer, bighorn, antelope
Big Bend (Tex.), 1935	741,118.40	Mountains and desert bordering the Rio Grande
Biscayne (Fla.), 1980	180,128	Aquatic, coral reef park south of Miami was a national monument, 1968–80
Bryce Canyon (Utah), 1924	35,835.08	Area of grotesque eroded rocks brilliantly colored
Canyonlands (Utah), 1964	377,570.43	Colorful wilderness with impressive red-rock canyons, spires, arches
Capitol Reef (Utah), 1971	241,904.26	Highly colored sedimentary rock formations in high, narrow gorges
Carlsbad Caverns (N.M.), 1930	46,755.33	The world's largest known caves
Channel Islands (Calif.) 1980	249,353.77	Area is rich in marine mammals, sea birds, endangered species and archeology
Crater Lake (Ore.), 1902	160,290.33	Deep blue lake in heart of inactive volcano
Denali (Alaska), 1917	4,698,583.00	Mt. McKinley National Park was renamed and enlarged by Act of Dec. 2, 1980. Contains Mt. McKinley, N. America's highest mountain (20,320 ft)
Everglades (Fla.), 1934	1,398,800.00	Subtropical area with abundant bird and animal life
Gates of the Arctic (Alaska), 1980	7,498,066.00	Diverse north central wilderness contains part of Brooks Range
Glacier (Mont.), 1910	1,013,594.67	Rocky Mountain scenery with many glaciers and lakes
Glacier Bay (Alaska), 1980	3,020,396.00	Park was a national monument (1925–1980) popular for wildlife, whale-watching, glacier-calving, and scenery
Grand Canyon (Ariz.), 1919	1,218,375.24	Mile-deep gorge, 4 to 18 miles wide, 217 miles long
Grand Teton (Wyo.), 1929	310,516.23	Picturesque range of high mountain peaks
Great Smoky Mts. (N.C.-Tenn), 1926	520,269.44	Highest mountain range east of Black Hills; luxuriant plant life
Guadalupe Mountains (Tex.), 1966	76,293.06	Contains highest point in Texas: Guadalupe Peak (8,751 ft)
Haleakala (Hawaii), 1960	28,655.25	World-famous 10,023-ft Haleakala volcano (dormant)
Hawaii Volcanoes (Hawaii), 1916	229,177.03	Spectacular volcanic area; luxuriant vegetation at lower levels
Hot Springs (Ark.), 1921	5,825.79	47 mineral hot springs said to have therapeutic value
Isle Royale (Mich.), 1931	571,796.18	Largest wilderness island in Lake Superior; moose, wolves, lakes
Katmai (Alaska), 1980	3,678,929.00	Expansion may assure brown bear's preservation. Park was national monument 1918–80; is known for fishing, 1912 eruption, bears
Kenai Fjords (Alaska), 1980	567,000	Mountain goats, marine mammals, birdlife are features at this seacoast park near Seward
Kings Canyon (Calif.), 1940	460,136.20	Huge canyons; high mountains; giant sequoias
Kobuk Valley (Alaska), 1980	1,749,037.00	Native culture and anthropology center around the broad Kobuk River in northwest Alaska
Lake Clark (Alaska), 1980	2,633,933.00	Park provides scenic and wilderness recreation across Cook Inlet from Anchorage
Lassen Volcanic (Calif.), 1916	106,372.36	Exhibits of impressive volcanic phenomena
Mammoth Cave (Ky.), 1926	52,369.60	Vast limestone labyrinth with underground river
Mesa Verde (Colo.), 1906	52,085.14	Best-preserved prehistoric cliff dwellings in United States

Name, location, and year authorized	Acreage	Outstanding characteristics
Mount Rainier (Wash.), 1899	235,404.00	Single-peak glacial system; dense forests, flowered meadows
North Cascades (Wash.), 1968	504,780.94	Roadless Alpine landscape; jagged peaks; mountain lakes; glaciers
Olympic (Wash.), 1938	915,425.86	Finest Pacific Northwest rain forest; scenic mountain park
Petrified Forest (Ariz.), 1962	93,492.57	Extensive natural exhibit of petrified wood
Redwood (Calif.), 1968	109,027.04	Coastal redwood forests; contains world's tallest known tree (369.2 ft)
Rocky Mountain (Colo.), 1915	266,942.71	Section of the Rocky Mountains; 107 named peaks over 10,000 ft
Sequoia (Calif.), 1890	402,487.83	Giant sequoias; magnificent High Sierra scenery, including Mt. Whitney
Shenandoah (Va.), 1926	195,057.36	Tree-covered mountains; scenic Skyline Drive
Theodore Roosevelt (N.D.), 1978	70,416.39	Scenic valley of Little Missouri River; T.R. Ranch; Wildlife
Virgin Islands (U.S. V.I.), 1956	14,695.37	Beaches; lush hills; prehistoric Carib Indian relics
Voyageurs (Minn.), 1971	219,128.00	Wildlife, canoeing, fishing, and hiking
Wind Cave (S.D.), 1903	28,292.08	Limestone caverns in Black Hills; buffalo herd
Wrangell-St. Elias (Alaska), 1980	8,331,406.00	Largest Park System area has abundant wildlife, second highest peak in U.S. (Mt. St. Elias); adjoins Canadian park
Yellowstone (Wyo.-Mont.-Idaho), 1872	2,219,822.70	World's greatest geyser area; abundant falls, wildlife, and canyons
Yosemite (Calif.), 1890	760,917.18	Mountains; inspiring gorges and waterfalls; giant sequoias
Zion (Utah), 1919	146,551.10	Multicolored gorge in heart of southern Utah desert

NATIONAL HISTORICAL PARKS

Name and location	*Total acreage*
Appomattox Court House (Va.)	1,318.70
Boston (Mass.)	41.03
Chaco Culture (N.M.)	33,969.40
Chesapeake and Ohio Canal (Md.-W.Va.-D.C.)	20,781.00
Colonial (Va.)	9,315.53
Cumberland Gap (Ky.-Tenn.-Va.)	20,350.90
George Rogers Clark (Ind.)	24.30
Harpers Ferry (W.Va.-Md.)	2,238.64
Independence (Pa.)	44.85
Jean Lafitte (La.)	20,000
Kalaupapa (Hawaii)	10,902.10
Klondike Goldrush (Alaska)	13,270.49
Koloko-Honokohau (Hawaii)	1,250.24
Lowell (Mass.)	137.08
Lyndon B. Johnson (Tex.)	1,477.78
Minute Man (Mass.)	752.35
Morristown (N.J.)	1,677.65
Nez Perce (Idaho)	2,108.89
Puuhonua o Honaunau (Hawaii)	181,80
San Antonio Missions (Tex.)	482.64
San Juan Island (Wash.)	1,751.99
Saratoga (N.Y.)	2,604.93
Sitka (Alaska)	107.71
Valley Forge (Pa.)	3,469.58
War in the Pacific (Guam)	1,919.68
Women's Rights (N.Y.)	2.45

NATIONAL MONUMENTS

Name and location	*Total acreage*
Agate Fossil Beds (Neb.)	3,055.22
Alibates Flint Quarries (Tex.)	1,370.97
Aniakchak (Alaska)	136,955.00
Aztec Ruins (N.M.)	27.14
Bandelier (N.M.)	36,971.20
Black Canyon (Colo.)	13,672.13
Booker T. Washington (Va.)	223.92
Buck Island Reef (U.S. V.I.)	880.00
Cabrillo (Calif.)	143.94
Canyon de Chelly (Ariz.)	83,840.00
Cape Krusenstern (Alaska)	656,685.00
Capulin Mountain (N.M.)	775.38
Casa Grande (Ariz.)	472.50
Castillo de San Marcos (Fla.)	20.48
Castle Clinton (N.Y.)	1.00
Cedar Breaks (Utah)	6,154.60
Chiricahua (Ariz.)	11,088.25
Colorado (Colo.)	20,453.95
Congaree Swamp (S.C.)	15,138.25
Craters of the Moon (Idaho)	53,545.05
Custer Battlefield (Mont.)	765.34
Death Valley (Calif.-Nev.)	2,067,627.68
Devils Postpile (Calif.)	798.46
Devils Tower (Wyo.)	1,346.91
Dinosaur (Utah-Colo.)	211,058.37
Effigy Mounds (Iowa)	1,474.63
El Morro (N.M.)	1,278.72
Florissant Fossil Beds (Colo.)	5,998.09
Fort Frederica (Ga.)	213.72
Fort Jefferson (Fla.)	47,125.00
Fort Matanzas (Fla.)	298.51
Fort McHenry (Md.)	43.26
Fort Pulaski (Ga.)	5,615.50
Fort Stanwix (N.Y.)	15.52
Fort Sumter (S.C.)	66.77
Fort Union (N.M.)	720.60
Fossil Butte (Wyo.)	8,198.00
George Washington Birthplace (Va.)	538.23
George Washington Carver (Mo.)	210.00
Gila Cliff Dwellings (N.M.)	533.13
Grand Portage (Minn.)	709.97
Great Sand Dunes (Colo.)	38,951.50
Hohokam Pima (Ariz.)	1,690.00
Homestead (Neb.)	194.57
Hovenweep (Utah-Colo.)	785.43
Jewel Cave (S.D.)	1,274.56
John Day Fossil Beds (Ore.)	14,011.90
Joshua Tree (Calif.)	559,959.50
Lava Beds (Calif.)	46,559.87
Lehman Caves (Nev.)	640.00
Montezuma Castle (Ariz.)	857.69
Mound City Group (Ohio)	67.50
Muir Woods (Calif.)	553.55
Natural Bridges (Utah)	7,779.14
Navajo (Ariz.)	360.00
Ocmulgee (Ga.)	683.48
Oregon Caves (Ore.)	487.98
Organ Pipe Cactus (Ariz.)	330,688.86
Pecos (N.M.)	364.80
Pinnacles (Calif.)	16,221.77
Pipe Spring (Ariz.)	40.00
Pipestone (Minn.)	281.78
Rainbow Bridge (Utah)	160.00
Russell Cave (Ala.)	310.45

Name and location	Total acreage
Saguaro (Ariz.)	83,576.07
St. Croix Island (Me.)	35.39
Salinas (N.M.)	1,079.94
Scotts Bluff (Neb.)	2,997.08
Statue of Liberty (N.Y.-N.J.)	58.38
Sunset Crater (Ariz.)	3,040.00
Timpanogos Cave (Utah)	250.00
Tonto (Ariz.)	1,120.00
Tumacacori (Ariz.)	16.52
Tuzigoot (Ariz.)	848.78
Walnut Canyon (Ariz.)	2,249.46
White Sands (N.M.)	144,458.24
Wupatki (Ariz.)	35,253.24
Yucca House (Colo.)	10.00

NATIONAL PRESERVES

Aniakchak (Alaska)	466,238.00
Bering Land Bridge (Alaska)	2,774,182.00
Big Cypress (Fla.)	570,000.00
Big Thicket (Tex.)	85,846.01
Denali (Alaska)	1,335,380.00
Gates of the Arctic (Alaska)	943,327.00
Glacier Bay (Alaska)	54,948.00
Katmai (Alaska)	410,473.00
Lake Clark (Alaska)	1,405,847.00
Noatak (Alaska)	6,557,204.00
Wrangell-St. Elias (Alaska)	4,872,953.00
Yukon-Charley Rivers (Alaska)	2,516,821.00

NATIONAL MILITARY PARKS

Chickamauga and Chattanooga (Ga.-Tenn.)	8,102.54
Fort Donelson (Tenn.)	536.09
Fredericksburg and Spotsylvania (Va.)	5,908.64
Gettysburg (Pa.)	3,862.06
Guilford Courthouse (N.C.)	220.25
Horseshoe Bend (Ala.)	2,040.00
Kings Mountain (S.C.)	3,945.29
Pea Ridge (Ark.)	4,300.35
Shiloh (Tenn.)	3,837.50
Vicksburg (Miss.)	1,740.78

NATIONAL BATTLEFIELDS

Antietam (Md.)	3,246.44
Big Hole (Mont.)	655.61
Cowpens (S.C.)	841.04
Fort Necessity (Pa.)	902.80
Monocacy (Md.)	1,647.10
Moores Creek (N.C.)	86.78
Petersburg (Va.)	1,536.26
Stones River (Tenn.)	330.86
Tupelo (Miss.)	1.00
Wilson's Creek (Mo.)	1,749.91

NATIONAL BATTLEFIELD PARKS

Kennesaw Mountain (Ga.)	2,884.38
Manassas (Va.)	4,513.29
Richmond (Va.)	769.13

NATIONAL BATTLEFIELD SITE

Brices Crossroads (Miss.)	1.00

NATIONAL HISTORIC SITES

Abraham Lincoln Birthplace (Ky.)	116.50
Adams (Mass.)	9.17
Allegheny Portage Railroad (Pa.)	1,134.91
Andersonville (Ga.)	475.72
Andrew Johnson (Tenn.)	16.68
Bent's Old Fort (Colo.)	800.00
Carl Sandburg Home (N.C.)	263.52
Christiansted (V.I.)	27.15
Clara Barton (Md.)	8.59
Edgar Allan Poe (Pa.)	0.52
Edison (N.J.)	21.25
Eisenhower (Pa.)	690.46
Eleanor Roosevelt (N.Y.)	180.50
Eugene O'Neill (Calif.)	14.00
Ford's Theatre (Lincoln Museum) (D.C.)	0.29
Fort Bowie (Ariz.)	1,000.00
Fort Davis (Tex.)	460.00
Fort Laramie (Wyo.)	832.49
Fort Larned (Kan.)	718.39
Fort Point (Calif.)	29.00
Fort Raleigh (N.C.)	157.40
Fort Scott (Kan.)	16.86
Fort Smith (Ark.-Okla.)	63.04
Fort Union Trading Post (N.D.-Mont.)	436.45
Fort Vancouver (Wash.)	208.89
Frederick Law Olmsted (Mass.)	1.75
Friendship Hill (Pa.)	675.00
Georgia O'Keeffe (N.M.)	4.00
Golden Spike (Utah)	2,203.20
Grant-Kohrs Ranch (Mont.)	1,502.03
Hampton (Md.)	59.44
Herbert Hoover (Iowa)	186.80
Home of F. D. Roosevelt (N.Y.)	264.01
Hopewell Village (Pa.)	848.06
Hubbell Trading Post (Ariz.)	160.09
James A. Garfield (Ohio)	7.56
Jefferson National Expansion Memorial (Mo.)	90.96
John F. Kennedy (Mass.)	0.09
John Muir (Calif.)	8.90
Knife River Indian Villages (N.D.)	1,293.35
Lincoln Home (Ill.)	12.28
Longfellow (Mass.)	1.98
Maggie L. Walker (Va.)	1.29
Martin Luther King, Jr. (Ga.)	23.16
Martin Van Buren (N.Y.)	39.59
Ninety Six (S.C.)	1,115.08
Palo Alto Battlefield (Tex.)	50.00
Puukohola Heiau (Hawaii)	76.57
Sagamore Hill (N.Y.)	78.00
Saint-Gaudens (N.H.)	148.33
Salem Maritime (Mass.)	9.10
San Juan (P.R.)	53.20
Saugus Iron Works (Mass.)	8.51
Sewall-Belmont House (D.C.)	0.35
Springfield Armory (Mass.)	54.93
Theodore Roosevelt Birthplace (N.Y.)	0.11
Theodore Roosevelt Inaugural (N.Y.)	1.03
Thomas Stone (Md.)	328.25
Tuskegee Institute (Ala.)	74.39
Vanderbilt Mansion (N.Y.)	211.65
Whitman Mission (Wash.)	98.15
William Howard Taft (Ohio)	3.83

NATIONAL MEMORIALS

Arkansas Post (Ark.)	389.18
Arlington House, the Robert E. Lee Memorial (Va.)	27.91
Chamizal (Tex.)	54.90
Coronado (Ariz.)	4,976.77
Desoto (Fla.)	26.84
Federal Hall (N.Y.)	0.45
Fort Caroline (Fla.)	138.88
Fort Clatsop (Ore.)	125.20
General Grant (N.Y.)	0.76
Hamilton Grange (N.Y.)	0.71
John F. Kennedy Center for Performing Arts (D.C.)	17.50
Johnstown Flood (Pa.)	163.47
Lincoln Boyhood (Ind.)	197.60
Lincoln Memorial (D.C.)	163.63
Lyndon Baines Johnson Memorial Grove on the Potomac (D.C.)	17.00

Name and location	*Total acreage*
Mount Rushmore (S.D.)	1,278.45
Roger Williams (R.I.)	4.56
Thaddeus Kosciuszko (Pa.)	0.02
Theodore Roosevelt Island (D.C.)	88.50
Thomas Jefferson Memorial (D.C.)	18.36
USS Arizona Memorial (Hawaii)	0.00
Washington Monument (D.C.)	106.01
Wright Brothers (N.C.)	431.40

NATIONAL CEMETERIES[1]

Antietam (Md.)	11.36
Battleground (D.C.)	1.03
Fort Donelson (Tenn.)	15.34
Fredericksburg (Va.)	12.00
Gettysburg (Pa.)	20.58
Poplar Grove (Va.)	8.72
Shiloh (Tenn.)	10.05
Stones River (Tenn.)	20.09
Vicksburg (Miss.)	116.28
Yorktown (Va.)	2.91

NATIONAL SEASHORES

Assateague Island (Md.-Va.)	39,630.93
Canaveral (Fla.)	57,627.07
Cape Cod (Mass.)	44,596.43
Cape Hatteras (N.C.)	30,319.43
Cape Lookout (N.C.)	28,414.74
Cumberland Island (Ga.)	36,978.28
Fire Island (N.Y.)	19,578.55
Gulf Islands (Fla.-Miss.)	139,775.46
Padre Island (Tex.)	130,696.83
Point Reyes (Calif.)	71,000.00

NATIONAL PARKWAYS

Blue Ridge (Va.-N.C.)	82,328.50
George Washington Memorial (Va.-Md.)	7,141.63
John D. Rockefeller, Jr., Memorial (Wyo.)	23,777.22
Natchez Trace (Miss.-Tenn.-Ala.)	50,194.94

NATIONAL LAKESHORES

Apostle Islands (Wis.)	67,884.84
Indiana Dunes (Ind.)	12,534.82
Pictured Rocks (Mich.)	72,258.86
Sleeping Bear Dunes (Mich.)	79,452.00

NATIONAL SCENIC RIVERS AND RIVERWAYS

Alagnak Wild River (Alaska)	0.00
Big South Fork National River & Recreation Area (Ky.-Tenn.)	122,960.00
Buffalo (Ark.)	94,146.00
Delaware (N.Y.-N.J.-Pa.)	1,973.33
Lower St. Croix (Minn.-Wis.)	9,411.38
New River Gorge (W. Va.)	62,024.00
Obed Wild & Scenic River (Tenn.)	5,250.00
Ozark (Mo.)	81,217.53
Rio Grande Wild & Scenic (Tex.)	9,600.00
St. Croix (Minn.-Wis.)	64,166.41
Upper Delaware (N.Y., N.J.-Pa.)	75,000.00

NATIONAL CAPITAL PARKS

National Capital Parks (D.C.-Va.-Md.)	6,467.85

WHITE HOUSE

White House (D.C.)	18.07

OTHER PARKS

Catoctin Mountain (Md.)	5,768.90
Fort Benton (Mont.)	0.0
Fort Washington Park (Md.)	341.00

1. The National Cemeteries are not independent areas of the National Park System; each is part of a millitary park, battlefield, etc., except Battleground. Their acreage is kept separately. Arlington National Cemetery is under the Department of the Army. *See* Index.

Name and location	*Total acreage*
Frederick Douglass Home (D.C.)	8.08
Greenbelt Park (Md.)	1,175.99
Perry's Victory and International Peace Memorial (Ohio)	25.38
Piscataway (Md.)	4,250.84
Prince William Forest (Va.)	18,571.55
Rock Creek Park (D.C.)	1,754.37
Wolf Trap Farm Park for the Performing Arts (Va.)	130.28

NATIONAL RECREATION AREAS

Amistad (Tex.)	62,451.74
Bighorn Canyon (Wyo.-Mont.)	120,277.86
Chattahoochee River (Ga.)	7,273.73
Chickasaw (Okla.)	9,500.06
Coulee Dam (Wash.)	100,059.00
Curecanti (Colo.)	42,114.47
Cuyahoga Valley (Ohio)	32,460.19
Delaware Water Gap (Pa.-N.J.)	69,628.74
Gateway (N.Y.-N.J.)	26,172.00
Glen Canyon (Ariz.-Utah)	1,236,880.00
Golden Gate (Calif.)	38,676.59
Lake Chelan (Wash.)	61,889.84
Lake Mead (Ariz.-Nev.)	1,496,600.52
Lake Meredith (Tex.)	44,977.63
Ross Lake (Wash.)	117,574.09
Santa Monica Mountains (Calif.)	150,000.00
Whiskeytown-Shasta-Trinity (Calif.)	42,503.43

NATIONAL SCENIC TRAIL

Appalachian (Maine, N.H. Vt., Mass., Conn., N.Y., N.J., Pa., Md., W.Va., Va., N.C., Tenn., Ga.)	52,034.25

NATIONAL MALL

National Mall (D.C.)	146.35

AFFILIATED AREAS

(National Historic Sites unless otherwise noted.)

Afro-American History and Culture (Ohio)	0.00
American Memorial Park (N. Mariana Is.)	0.00
Benjamin Franklin (Pa.)[1]	0.00
Boston African American (Mass.)	0.00
Cherokee Strip Living Museum (Kan.)	6.00
Chicago Portage (Ill.)	91.20
Chimney Rock (Neb.)	83.36
David Berger (Ohio)[1]	0.00
Ebey's Landing (Wash.)	8,000.00
Father Marquette (Mich.)	52.00
Green Springs Historic District (Va.)	0.00
Gloria Dei Church (Pa.)	3.71
Ice Age Scenic Trail (Wisc.)	0.00
Ice Age (Wis.)[2]	32,500.00
Iditarod National Historic Trail (Alaska)	0.00
International Peace Garden (N.D.)	2,330.30
Jamestown (Va.)	20.63
Lewis & Clark Natl. Historic Trail (Ill., Mo., Kan., Neb., Iowa, Idaho, S.D., N.D., Mont., Ore., Wash.)	0.00
McLoughlin House (Ore.)	0.63
Mormon Pioneer Natl. Historic Trail (Ill., Iowa, Neb., Wyo., Utah)	0.00
North Country Nat'l Scenic Trail (N.Y., Pa., Ohio, Mich., Wis., Minn., N.D.)	0.00
Oregon Natl. Historic Trail (Mo., Kan., Neb., Wyo., Idaho, Ore., Wash.)	0.00
Overmountain Victory Trail (Mo. to Ore.)	0.00
Pennsylvania Avenue (D.C.)	0.00
Pinelands Natl. Reserve (N.J.)	0.00
Roosevelt-Campobello International Park (Canada)	2,721.50
St. Paul's Church (N.Y.)	6.09
Touro Synagogue (R.I.)	0.23

1. National Memorial. 2. National Scientific Reserve.

Environmental Glossary

Source: Environmental Protection Agency

abatement: the reduction in degree or intensity of pollution.

acclimation: the physiological and behavioral adjustments of an organism to changes in the environment.

adaptation: a change in structure or habit of an organism that produces better adjustment to its surroundings.

adulterants: chemical impurities or substances that by law do not belong in a food, plant, animal, or pesticide formulation.

aeration: to circulate oxygen through a substance, as in waste water treatment where it aids in purification.

agricultural pollution: the liquid and solid wastes from farming, including: runoff from pesticides, fertilizers, and feedlots; erosion and dust from plowing; animal manure and carcasses, crop residues, and debris.

air pollution: the presence of contaminant substances in the air that do not disperse properly and interfere with human health.

air quality standards: the level of pollutants prescribed by law that cannot be exceeded during a specified time in a defined area.

ambient air: any unconfined portion of the atmosphere; open air.

asbestos: a mineral fiber that can pollute air or water and cause cancer if inhaled or ingested.

A-scale sound level: a measurement of sound approximating the sensitivity of the human ear, used to note the intensity or annoyance of sounds.

attractant: a chemical or agent that lures insects or other pests by stimulating their sense of smell.

biodegradable: any substance that decomposes quickly through the action of microorganisms.

breeder: a nuclear reactor that produces more fuel than it consumes.

carcinogenic: cancer-producing.

catalytic converter: an air pollution abatement device that removes organic contaminants by oxidizing them into carbon dioxide and water.

chilling effect: the lowering of the earth's temperature because of increased particles in the air blocking the sun's rays.

chlorination: the application of chlorine to drinking water, sewage, or industrial waste to disinfect or oxidize undesirable compounds.

combined sewers: a system that carries both sewage and storm water runoff. In dry weather all flow goes to the waste treatment plant. During a storm, only part of the flow is intercepted due to overloading. The remaining mixture of sewage and storm water overflows untreated into the receiving stream.

desalinization: removing salt from ocean or brackish water.

ecological impact: the total effect of an environmental change, natural or man-made, on the community of living things.

ecology: the relationships of living things to one another and to their environment, or the study of such relationships.

effluent: treated or untreated waste material discharged into the environment. Generally refers to water pollution.

emission standard: the maximum amount of discharge legally allowed from a single source, mobile or stationary.

environment: the sum of all external conditions affecting the life, development, and survival of an organism.

fluorocarbons: a gas used as a propellant in aerosols, thought to be modifying the ozone layer in the stratosphere, thereby allowing more harmful solar radiation to reach the earth's surface.

fossil fuels: combustibles—like coal, oil, and natural gas—derived from the remains of ancient plants and animals.

greenhouse effect: the warming of our atmosphere caused by build-up of carbon dioxide, which allows light from the sun's rays to heat the earth, but prevents loss of the heat.

groundwater: the supply of fresh water under the earth's surface that forms a natural reservoir.

habitat: the sum of environmental conditions in a specific place that is occupied by an organism, population, or community.

herbicide: a chemical that controls or destroys undesirable plants.

inversion: an atmospheric condition caused by a layer of warm air preventing the rise of cool air trapped beneath it. This holds down pollutants that might otherwise be dispersed, and can cause an air pollution episode.

nuclear power plant: a device that converts atomic energy into usable power; heat produced by a reactor makes steam to drive electricity-generating turbines.

oil spill: accidental discharge into bodies of water, can be controlled by chemical dispersion, combustion, mechanical containment, and absorption.

organic: referring to or derived from living organisms. In chemistry, any compound containing carbon.

pesticide: any substance used to control pests ranging from rats, weeds, and insects to algae and fungi. Pesticides can accumulate in the food chain and can contaminate the environment if misused.

pollutant: any introduced substance that adversely affects the usefulness of a resource.

pollution: the presence of matter or energy whose nature, location, or quantity produces undesired environmental effects.

radiation: the emission of particles or rays by the nucleus of an atom.

radiation standards: regulations that govern exposure to permissible concentrations of and transportation of radioactive materials.

radioactive: substances that emit rays either naturally or as a result of scientific manipulation.

recycling: converting solid waste into new products by using the resources contained in discarded materials.

refuge, wildlife: an area designated for the protection of wild animals, within which hunting and fishing are either prohibited or strictly controlled.

runoff: water from rain, snow melt, or irrigation that flows over the ground surface and returns to streams. It can collect pollutants from air or land and carry them to the receiving waters.

sanitary landfill, landfilling: protecting the environment when disposing of solid waste. Waste is spread in thin layers, compacted by heavy machinery, and covered with soil daily.

thermal pollution: discharge of heated water from industrial processes that can affect the life processes of aquatic plants and animals.

water pollution: the addition of enough harmful or objectionable material to damage water quality.

GREAT DISASTERS

(For later disasters, see Current Events of 1982)

Earthquakes and Volcanic Eruptions

A.D. 79 **Aug. 24, Italy:** eruption of Mt. Vesuvius buried cities of Pompeii and Herculaneum, killing thousands.

1556 **Jan. 24, Shaanxi (Shensi) Province, China:** most deadly earthquake in history; 830,000 killed.

1755 **Nov. 1, Portugal:** one of the most severe of recorded earthquakes leveled Lisbon and was felt as far away as southern France and North Africa; 10,000–20,000 killed in Lisbon.

1883 **Aug. 26–28, Netherlands Indies:** eruption of Krakatau; violent explosions destroyed two thirds of island. Sea waves occurred as far away as Cape Horn, and possibly England. Estimated 36,000 dead.

1902 **May 8, Martinique, West Indies:** Mt. Pelée erupted and wiped out city of St. Pierre; 40,000 dead.

1906 **April 18, San Francisco:** earthquake accompanied by fire razed more than 4 sq mi.; more than 500 dead or missing; property damage about $250–300 million.

1908 **Dec. 28, Messina, Sicily:** about 85,000 killed and city totally destroyed.

1915 **Jan. 13, Avezzano, Italy:** earthquake left 29,980 dead.

1920 **Dec. 16, Gansu (Kansu) Province, China:** earthquake killed 200,000.

1923 **Sept. 1, Japan:** earthquake destroyed third of Tokyo and most of Yokohama; more than 140,000 killed.

1933 **March 10, Long Beach, Calif.:** 117 left dead by earthquake.

1935 **May 31, India:** earthquake at Quetta killed an estimated 50,000.

1939 **Jan. 24, Chile:** earthquake razed 50,000 sq mi.; about 30,000 killed.

Dec. 27, Northern Turkey: severe quakes destroyed city of Erzingan; about 100,000 casualties.

1946 **April 1, Alaska, Hawaii, West Coast:** earthquake and tsunami (tidal wave) left 173 dead in Hawaii.

1950 **Aug. 15, India:** earthquake affected 30,000 sq mi. in Assam; 20,000–30,000 believed killed.

1963 **July 26, Skoplje, Yugoslavia:** four fifths of city destroyed; 1,011 dead, 3,350 injured.

1964 **March 27, Alaska:** strongest earthquake ever to strike North America hit 80 miles east of Anchorage; followed by seismic wave 50 feet high that traveled 8,445 miles at 450 miles per hour; 117 killed and damage in Alaska and West Coast $500–750 million.

1970 **May 31, Peru:** earthquake left 50,000 dead, 17,000 missing.

1971 **Feb. 9, Los Angeles:** earthquake rocked San Fernando Valley. Death toll 64; damage $1 billion.

1972 **April 10, Iran:** 5,000 killed in earthquake 600 miles south of Teheran.

Dec. 22, Managua, Nicaragua: earthquake devastated city, leaving up to 6,000 dead.

1976 **Feb. 4, Guatemala:** earthquake left over 23,000 dead.

July 28, Tangshan, China: earthquake devastated 20-sq-mi. area of city leaving estimated 242,000 dead.

Aug. 17, Mindanao, Philippines: earthquake and tidal wave left up to 8,000 dead or missing.

1977 **March 4, Bucharest:** earthquake razed most of downtown Bucharest; 1,541 reported dead, over 11,000 injured.

1978 **Sept. 16, Tabas, Iran:** earthquake destroyed city in eastern Iran, leaving 25,000 dead.

1980 **Nov. 23, Naples, Italy:** 2,735 killed when earthquake struck southern Italy.

Floods, Avalanches, and Tidal Waves

1228 **Holland:** 100,000 persons reputedly drowned by sea flood in Friesland.

1642 **China:** rebels destroyed Kaifeng seawall; 300,000 drowned.

1889 **May 31, Johnstown, Pa.:** more than 2,200 died in flood.

1896 **June 15, Sanriku, Japan:** earthquake and tidal wave killed 27,000.

1928 **March 12, Santa Paula, Calif.:** collapse of St. Francis Dam left 450 dead.

1953 **Northwest Europe:** storm followed by floods devastated North Sea coastal areas. Netherlands was hardest hit with 1,794 dead.

1959 **Dec. 2, Frejus, France:** flood caused by collapse of Malpasset Dam left 412 dead.

1960 **Agadir, Morocco:** 10,000–12,000 dead as earthquake set off tidal wave and fire, destroying most of city.

1962 **Jan. 10, Peru:** avalanche down Huascaran, extinct Andean volcano, killed more than 3,000 persons.

1963 **Oct. 9, Italy:** landslide into the Vaiont Dam; flood killed about 2,000.

1966 **Oct. 21, Aberfan, Wales:** avalanche of coal, waste, mud, and rocks killed 144 persons, including 116 children in school.

1969 **Jan. 18–26, Southern California:** floods and mudslides from heavy rains caused widespread property damage; at least 100 dead. Another downpour (Feb. 23–26) caused further floods and mudslides; at least 18 dead.

1970 **Nov. 13, East Pakistan:** 200,000 killed by cyclone-driven tidal wave from Bay of Bengal. Over 100,000 missing.

1971 **Sept. 29, Orissa State, India:** cyclone and tidal wave off Bay of Bengal killed as many as 10,000.

1972 **Feb. 26, Man, W. Va.:** more than 118 died when slag-pile dam collapsed under pressure of torrential rains and flooded 17-mile valley.

June 9–10, Rapid City, S.D.: flash flood caused 237 deaths and $160 million in damage.

June 20, Eastern Seaboard: tropical storm Agnes, in 10-day rampage, caused widespread flash floods. Death toll was 129, 115,000 were left homeless, and damage estimated at $3.5 billion.

1976 **Aug. 1, Loveland, Colo.:** Flash flood along Route 34 in Big Thompson Canyon left 139 dead.

1977 **Nov. 6, Toccoa, Ga.:** rupture of Kelly Barnes Dam left 39 dead.

Nov. 19, Andhra Pradesh State, India: cyclone and flood from Bay of Bengal left 7,000–10,000 dead.

Storms and Weather

(For U.S. tornadoes and hurricanes, see Index)

1864 **Oct. 5, India:** most of Calcutta denuded by cyclone; 70,000 killed.

1930 **Sept. 3. Santo Domingo:** hurricane killed about 2,000 and injured 6,000.

1934 **Sept. 21, Japan:** hurricane killed more than 4,000 on Honshu.

1942 **Oct. 16, India:** cyclone devastated Bengal; about 40,000 lives lost.

1963 **May 28–29, East Pakistan:** cyclone killed about 22,000 along coast.

Oct. 2–7, Caribbean: Hurricane Flora killed up to 7,000 in Haiti and Cuba.

1965 **May 11–12 and June 1–2, East Pakistan:** cyclones killed about 47,000.

Dec. 15, Karachi, Pakistan: cyclone killed about 10,000.

1974 **Sept. 20, Honduras:** Hurricane Fifi struck northern section of country, leaving 8,000 dead, 100,000 homeless.

Dec. 25, Darwin, Australia: cyclone destroyed nearly the entire city, causing mass evacuation.

1977 **Nov. 19, India:** cyclone struck state of Andhra Pradesh, killing 10,000.

Fires and Explosions

1666 **Sept. 2, England:** "Great Fire of London" destroyed St. Paul's Church, etc. Damage £10 million.

1835 **Dec. 16, New York City:** 530 buildings destroyed by fire.

1871 **Oct. 8, Chicago:** the "Chicago Fire" burned 17,450 buildings, killed 250 persons; $196 million damage.

Oct. 8, Peshtigo, Wis.: 1,152 lives lost; 2 billion trees burned.

1872 **Nov. 9, Boston:** fire destroyed 800 buildings; $75-million damage.

1876 **Dec. 5, New York City:** fire in Brooklyn Theater killed more than 300.

1881 **Dec. 8, Vienna:** at least 620 died in fire at Ring Theatre.

1894 **Sept. 1, Minnesota:** forest fire over 480-square-mile area destroyed six towns and killed 480 people.

1900 **May 1, Scofield, Utah:** explosion of blasting powder in coal mine killed 200.

June 30, Hoboken, N.J.: piers of North German Lloyd Steamship line burned; 326 dead.

1903 **Dec. 30, Chicago:** Iroquois Theatre fire killed 602.

1904 **Feb. 7, Baltimore:** business section burned; estimated $125-million damage.

1906 **March 10, France:** explosion in coal mine in Courrières killed 1,060.

1907 **Dec. 6, Monongha, W. Va.:** coal mine explosion killed 361.

Dec. 19, Jacobs Creek, Pa.: explosion in coal mine left 239 dead.

1909 **Nov. 13, Cherry, Ill.:** explosion in coal mine killed 259.

1911 **March 25, New York City:** fire in Triangle Shirtwaist Factory fatal to 145.

1913 **Oct. 22, Dawson, N.M.:** coal mine explosion left 263 dead.

1917 **April 10, Eddystone, Pa.:** explosion in munitions plant killed 133.

Dec. 6, Canada: explosion and fire at Halifax when ammunition ship collided with a vessel; 1,500 dead.

1930 **April 21, Columbus, Ohio:** fire in Ohio State Penitentiary killed 320 convicts.

1937 **March 18, New London, Tex.:** explosion destroyed schoolhouse; 294 killed.

1942 **April 26, Manchuria:** explosion in Honkeiko Colliery killed 1,549.

Nov. 28, Boston: Cocoanut Grove nightclub fire killed 491.

1943 **Sept. 7, Houston:** fire in Gulf Hotel left 55 dead.

1944 **July 6, Hartford, Conn.:** fire and ensuing stampede in main tent of Ringling Brothers Circus killed 168, injured 487.

July 17, Port Chicago, Calif.: 322 killed as ammunition ships explode.

Oct. 20, Cleveland: liquid-gas tanks exploded, killing 130.

1946 **June 5, Chicago:** fire in La Salle hotel fatal to 61.

Dec. 7, Atlanta: fire in Winecoff Hotel killed 119.

1947 **April 16–18, Texas City, Tex.:** most of city destroyed, 561 dead following explosion on ship.

1949 **Sept. 2, China:** fire on Chongqing (Chungking) waterfront killed 1,700.

1953 **Oct. 16, Boston:** explosion and fire aboard U.S.S. *Leyte* killed 37.

1954 **May 26, off Quonset Point, R.I.:** explosion and fire aboard aircraft *Bennington* killed 103 crewmen.

1956 **Aug. 7, Colombia:** about 1,100 reported killed when seven army ammunition trucks exploded at Cali.

Aug. 8, Belgium: 262 died in coal mine fire at Marcinelle.

1958 **Dec. 1, Chicago:** fire at Our Lady of the Angels school killed 95.

1960 **Jan. 21, Coalbrook, South Africa:** coal mine explosion killed 437.

Nov. 13, Syria: 152 children killed in moviehouse fire.

Dec. 19. Brooklyn, N.Y.: blaze on aircraft carrier *Constellation* killed 49 workmen.

1961 **Dec. 17, Niteroi, Brazil:** circus fire fatal to 323.

1962 **Feb. 7, Saarland, West Germany:** coal mine gas explosion killed 298.

1963 **Nov. 9, Japan:** explosion in coal mine at Omuta killed 447.

1965 **May 28, India:** coal mine fire in state of Bihar killed 375.

June 1, near Fukuoka, Japan: coal mine explosion killed 236.

1966 **Oct. 26, off South Vietnam:** fire on U.S. carrier *Oriskany* killed 43.

1967 **May 22, Brussels:** fire in L'Innovation, major department store, left 322 dead.

July 29, off North Vietnam: fire on U.S. carrier *Forrestal* killed 134.

1969 **Jan. 14, Pearl Harbor, Hawaii:** nuclear aircraft carrier *Enterprise* ripped by explosions; 27 dead, 82 injured.

April 6, New Orleans: Taiwanese freighter and string of oil-loaded barges collided in fiery explosion on Mississippi River; 25 dead.

1970 **Nov. 1, Saint-Laurent-du-Pont, France:** fire in dance hall killed 146 young people.

Dec. 30, Wooten, Ky.: coal-dust explosion in coal mine killed 38.

1972 **May 2, Kellogg, Idaho:** fire in Sunshine silver mine killed 91 miners; two men survived.

May 13, Osaka, Japan: 118 people died in fire in

nightclub on top floor of Sennichi department store.
June 6, Wankie, Rhodesia: explosion in coal mine killed 427.
1973 **Nov. 29, Kumamoto, Japan:** fire in Taiyo department store killed 101.
1974 **Feb. 1, Sao Paulo, Brazil:** fire in upper stories of bank building killed 189 persons, many of whom leaped to death.
1975 **Dec. 27, Dhanbad, India:** explosion in coal mine followed by flooding from nearby reservoir left 372 dead.
1977 **Feb. 25, Moscow:** fire in 6,000-bed Hotel Rossiya fatal to at least 45 guests.
May 28, Southgate, Ky.: fire in Beverly Hills Supper Club; 167 dead.
June 26, Columbia, Tenn.: fire believed set by inmate was fatal to 42 prisoners and visitors at Maury County Jail.
Dec. 22, Westwego, La.: explosion destroyed Continental Grain Company plant, killing 36.
1978 **July 11, Tarragona, Spain:** 140 killed at coastal campsite when tank truck carrying liquid gas overturned and exploded.
Aug. 20, Abadan, Iran: nearly 400 killed when arsonists set fire to crowded theater.
1979 **July 12, Saragossa, Spain:** fire in 10-story Hotel Corona de Aragon killed more than 72 guests when a pastry machine exploded.
Dec. 31, Chapais, Quebec, Canada: fire at Opemiska Club fatal to 45 New Year's Eve partygoers.
1980 **Oct. 23, Ortuella, Spain:** explosion leveled elementary school, killing 48, nearly all of them children.
Nov. 21, Las Vegas, Nev.: fire in MGM Grand Hotel left 84 dead.
Dec. 4, Harrison, N.Y.: fire in a Stouffer's Inn conference center fatal to 26, most of them corporation executives.
1981 **Feb. 14, Dublin, Ireland:** fire in Stardust discothèque killed 44.

Shipwrecks

1833 **May 11, *Lady of the Lake:*** bound from England to Quebec, struck iceberg; 215 perished.
1853 **Sept. 29 *Annie Jane:*** emigrant vessel off coast of Scotland; 348 died.
1865 **April 27, *Sultana:*** boiler explosion on Mississippi River steamboat near Memphis, 1,547 killed.
1898 **Nov. 26, *City of Portland:*** Loss of 157 off Cape Cod.
1904 **June 15, *General Slocum:*** excursion steamer burned in East River, New York; 1,021 perished.
1912 **March 5, *Principe de Asturias:*** Spanish steamer struck rock off Sebastien Point; 500 drowned.
April 15, *Titanic:* sank after colliding with iceberg; 1,513 died.
1914 **May 29, *Empress of Ireland:*** sank after collision in St. Lawrence River; 1,024 perished.
1915 **July 24, *Eastland:*** Great Lakes excursion steamer overturned in Chicago River; 812 died.
1928 **Nov. 12, *Vestris:*** British steamer sank in gale off Virginia; 110 died.
1931 **June 14:** French excursion steamer overturned in gale off St. Nazaire; approximately 450 died.
1934 **Sept. 8, *Morro Castle:*** 134 killed in fire off Asbury Park, N.J.
1939 **May 23, *Squalus:*** submarine with 59 men sank off Hampton Beach, N.H.; 33 saved.
June 1, Submarine *Thetis:* sank in Liverpool Bay, England; 99 perished.
1942 **Oct. 2, *Queen Mary:*** rammed and sank a British cruiser; 338 aboard the cruiser died.
1945 **April 9:** U.S. ship, loaded with aerial bombs, exploded at Bari, Italy; at least 360 killed.
1948 **Dec. 3, *Kiangya:*** Chinese refugee ship wrecked in explosion; about 1,000 believed dead.
1949 **Sept. 17, *Noronic:*** Canadian Great Lakes cruise ship burned at Toronto dock; about 130 died.
1951 **April 16, *Affray:*** British submarine sank in English Channel; 75 dead.
1952 **April 26, *Hobson:*** minesweeper collided with aircraft carrier *Wasp* and sank during night maneuvers in mid-Atlantic; 176 persons lost.
1953 **Jan. 9, *Chang Tyong-Ho:*** South Korean ferry foundered off Pusan; 249 reported dead.
Jan. 31, *Princess Victoria:* British ferry sank in Irish Sea; 133 lost.
1956 **July 25, *Andrea Doria:*** Italian liner collided with Swedish liner *Stockholm* off Nantucket Island, Mass., sinking next day; 52, mostly passengers on Italian ship, dead or unaccounted for; over 1,600 rescued.
1962 **April 8, *Dara,*** British liner, exploded and sank in Persian Gulf; 236 persons dead. Caused by time bomb.
1963 **April 10, *Thresher:*** atomic-powered submarine sank in North Atlantic; 129 dead.
May 4: U.A.R. ferry capsized and sank in upper Nile; over 200 died.
1965 **Nov. 13, *Yarmouth Castle:*** cruise ship burned and sank 60 miles northeast of Nassau en route from Miami to Bahamas; 90 dead.
1968 **Late May, *Scorpion:*** nuclear submarine sank in Atlantic 400 miles S.W. of Azores; 99 dead. (Located Oct. 31.)
1970 **Dec. 15:** ferry in Korean Strait capsized; 261 lost.
1976 **Oct. 20, Luling, La.: *George Prince,*** Mississippi River ferry, rammed by Norwegian tanker *Frosta;* 77 dead.
1980 **Jan. 28, *Blackthorn:*** *Coast Guard cutter and Tanker Capricorn* collided under Sunshine Skyway near Tampa, Fla. 23 members of cutter's crew lost.

Aircraft Accidents

1921 **Aug. 24, England:** *ZR-2* British dirigible, broke in two on trial trip near Hull; 62 died.
1925 **Sept. 3, Caldwell, Ohio:** U.S. dirigible *Shenandoah* broke apart; 14 dead.
1930 **Oct. 5, Beauvais, France:** British dirigible R 101 crashed, killing 47.
1933 **April 4, New Jersey Coast:** U.S. dirigible *Akron* crashed; 73 died.
1937 **May 6, Lakehurst, N.J.:** German zeppelin *Hindenburg* destroyed by fire at tower mooring; 36 killed.
1945 **July 28, New York City:** U.S. Army bomber crashed into Empire State Building; 13 dead.
1946 **May 20, New York City:** U.S. Army plane crashed into Manhattan Company building; five dead.
1949 **Nov. 1, Washington, D.C.:** fighter plane rammed airliner, killing 55.
1951 **Dec. 16, Elizabeth, N.J.:** nonscheduled airliner crash killed 56.
1952 **Jan. 22, Elizabeth, N.J.:** 29 killed, including former Secretary of War Robert P. Patterson, when airliner hit apartments; seven of dead were on ground.
Feb. 11, Elizabeth, N.J.: third major air disaster in Elizabeth within two months fatally injured 33.

1953 **June 18, near Tokyo:** crash of U.S. Air Force "Globemaster" killed 129 servicemen.

1955 **Nov. 1, near Longmont, Colo.:** time bomb hidden in luggage destroyed airliner in flight, killing 44.

1956 **June 30, Grand Canyon, Ariz.:** 128 died in collision of TWA Super Constellation and United Airlines DC-7.

1957 **March 17, near Cebu City, Philippines:** President Ramón Magsaysay and 24 others killed in crash.

1959 **Feb. 3, New York City:** American Airlines Lockheed Electra turboprop plane crashed in East River; 65 dead.

1960 **Feb. 25, Rio de Janeiro:** U.S. Navy plane, flying Navy musicians to perform at dinner given by visiting President Eisenhower, collided with Brazilian airliner, killing 61.

Dec. 16, New York City: United and Trans World planes collided in fog, crashed in two boroughs, killing 134 in air and on ground.

1961 **Feb. 15, near Brussels:** 72 on board and farmer on ground killed in crash of Sabena plane; U.S. figure skating team wiped out.

1962 **March 1, New York City:** American Airlines jetliner crashed into Jamaica Bay, near Idlewild Airport, killing all 95 on board.

June 3, Paris: chartered Air France Boeing Jet 707 crashed at Orly Airport; 130 dead.

1965 **Feb. 8, New York City:** Eastern Airlines DC-7B went down in Atlantic shortly after take-off from Kennedy International Airport; 84 dead.

1966 **March 5, Japan:** British airliner caught fire and crashed into Mt. Fuji; 124 dead.

Dec. 24, Binh Thai, South Vietnam: crash of military-chartered plane into village killed 129.

1967 **April 20, Nicosia, Cyprus:** crash of chartered Swiss Turboprop killed 126.

July 19, near Hendersonville, N.C.: Piedmont Airlines Boeing 727 collided with private plane; 82 dead.

1968 **May 3, near Dawson, Tex.:** Braniff airliner crashed; 85 dead.

1969 **March 16, Maracaibo, Venezuela:** Venezuelan jetliner crashed and exploded; 84 crew members and passengers died and 71 were killed on ground.

Sept. 9, Shelbyville, Ind.: Allegheny Airlines jetliner and single-engine plane flown by student pilot collided in air and crashed; 83 dead.

1970 **Feb. 15, Santo Domingo, Dominican Republic:** Dominican Republic jetliner plunged into Caribbean on takeoff; 102 dead.

July 4, Arbucias, Spain: British Comet crashed into mountains while coming in for landing at Barcelona; 112 dead.

July 5, Toronto: Canadian jetliner crashed on landing approach; 109 dead.

Aug. 9, Cuzco, Peru: Peruvian turboprop, with 51 teen-age U.S. students among passengers, crashed shortly after takeoff; 99 dead.

Nov. 14, Huntington, W. Va.: chartered plane carrying 43 players and coaches of Marshall University football team crashed; 75 dead.

1971 **June 6, near Los Angeles:** Air West DC-9 and Navy F-4 fighter collided over San Gabriel Canyon; 49 killed; one Navy crewman parachuted to safety.

July 30, Morioka, Japan: Japanese Boeing 727 and F-86 fighter collided in mid-air; toll was 162.

Sept. 4, near Juneau, Alaska: Alaska Airlines Boeing 727 crashed into Chilkoot Mountains; 111 killed.

1972 **June 18, London:** B.E.A. Trident jetliner plunged into field minutes after take-off from Heathrow Airport; all 118 aboard dead.

Aug. 14, East Berlin, East Germany: Soviet-built East German Ilyushin plane crashed, killing 156.

Dec. 3, Santa Cruz de Tenerife, Canary Islands: Spanish charter jet carrying West German tourists crashed on take-off; all 155 aboard killed.

Dec. 30, Miami, Fla.: Eastern Airlines Lockheed 1011 TriStar Jumbo jet crashed into Everglades; 101 killed, 75 survived.

1973 **Jan. 22, Kano, Nigeria:** 171 Nigerian Moslems returning from Mecca and five crewmen died in crash.

April 10, Hochwald, Switzerland: British airliner carrying tourists to Swiss fair crashed in blizzard; 106 dead.

July 11, Paris: Boeing 707 of Varig Airlines, en route to Rio de Janeiro, crashed near airport, killing 122 of 134 passengers.

July 31, Boston: Delta Airlines jet crashed in heavy fog in landing at Logan International Airport killing 88 of 89 aboard.

1974 **Jan. 31, Pago Pago, Samoa:** Pan American 707 crashed while landing; 97 of 101 persons aboard killed.

March 3, Paris: Turkish DC-10 jumbo jet crashed in forest shortly after take-off; all 346 passengers and crew killed in worst single-plane disaster to date.

Dec. 1, Berryville, Va.: all 92 aboard killed in crash of TWA 727 into wooded area.

Dec. 4, Colombo, Sri Lanka: Dutch DC-8 carrying Moslems to Mecca crashed on landing approach, killing all 191 persons aboard.

1975 **April 4, near Saigon, Vietnam:** Air Force Galaxy C-5A crashed after take-off, killing 172, mostly Vietnamese children.

June 24, New York City: Eastern Airlines Boeing 727, arriving from New Orleans, crashed at Kennedy International Airport, killing 113.

Aug. 3, Agadir, Morocco: Chartered Boeing 707, returning Moroccan workers home after vacation in France, plunged into mountainside; all 188 aboard killed.

Aug. 20, Damascus, Syria: Czech airliner crashed while landing, killing 126 of 128 persons aboard.

1976 **Sept. 10, Zagreb, Yugoslavia:** midair collision between British Airways Trident and Yugoslav charter DC-9 fatal to all 176 persons aboard; worst mid-air collision on record.

1977 **March 27, Santa Cruz de Tenerife, Canary Islands:** Pan American and KLM Boeing 747s collided on runway. All 249 on KLM plane and 333 of 394 aboard Pan Am jet killed. Total of 582 is highest for any type of aviation disaster.

1978 **Jan. 1, Bombay:** Air India 747 with 213 aboard exploded and plunged into sea minutes after takeoff.

Sept. 25, San Diego, Calif.: Pacific Southwest plane collided in midair with Cessna. All 135 on airliner, 2 in Cessna, and 7 on ground killed for total of 144.

Nov. 15, Colombo, Sri Lanka: Chartered Icelandic Airlines DC-8, carrying 249 Moslem pilgrims from Mecca, crashed in thunderstorm during landing approach; 183 killed.

1979 **May 25, Chicago:** American Airlines DC-10 lost left engine upon take-off and crashed seconds later, killing all 272 persons aboard and

three on the ground, in worst U.S. air disaster.
Aug. 15, Ukraine, U.S.S.R.: Two planes collided in mid-air; 150 killed.
Oct. 15, Mexico City: Western Airlines DC-10 crashed on landing, killing 73.
Nov. 26, Jidda, Saudi Arabia: Pakistan International Airlines 707 carrying pilgrims returning from Mecca crashed on take-off; all 156 aboard killed.
Nov. 28, Mt. Erebus, Antarctica: Air New Zealand DC-10 crashed on sightseeing flight; 257 killed.

1980 **Jan. 21, near Laskgarak, Iran:** Iran Air Boeing 727 crashed into mountains, killing all 128 aboard.
March 14, Warsaw: LOT Polish Airlines Ilyushin 62 crashed while attempting landing; 22 boxers and officials of a U.S. amateur boxing team killed along with 65 others.
April 25, Santa Cruz de Tenerife, Canary Islands: Chartered Boeing 727 carrying 138 British vacationers and crew of 8 crashed into mountain while approaching for landing; all killed.
Aug. 19, Riyadh, Saudi Arabia: all 301 aboard Saudi Arabian jet killed when burning plane made safe landing but passengers were unable to escape.

1981 **Dec. 1, Ajaccio, Corsica:** Yugoslav DC-9 Super 80 carrying tourists crashed into mountain on landing approach, killing all 178 aboard.

1982 **July 9, Kenner, La.:** Pan Am 727 crashed minutes after take-off from New Orleans, killing all 145 on board and 9 on ground.

Railroad Accidents

1904 **Aug. 7, Eden, Colo.:** Two-train collision killed 96.

1910 **March 1, Wellington, Wash.:** two trains swept into canyon by avalanche; 96 dead.

1915 **May 22, Gretna, Scotland:** two passenger trains and troop train collided; 227 killed.

1917 **Dec. 12, Modane, France:** nearly 550 killed in derailment of troop train near mouth of Mt. Cenis tunnel.

1918 **Nov. 1, New York City:** derailment of subway train in Malbone St. tunnel in Brooklyn left 92 dead.

1939 **Dec. 22, near Magdeburg, Germany:** more than 125 killed in collision; 99 killed in another wreck near Friedrichshafen.

1943 **Dec. 16, near Rennert, N.C.:** 72 killed in derailment and collision of two Atlantic Coast Line trains.

1944 **March 2, near Salerno, Italy:** 521 suffocated when Italian train stalled in tunnel.
Dec. 31, near Ogden, Utah: 48 killed in collision of two sections of Southern Pacific's Pacific Limited.

1946 **April 25, Naperville, Ill.:** at least 47 killed in collision of two trains of Burlington Railroad.

1949 **Oct. 22, near Nowy Dwor, Poland:** more than 200 reported killed in derailment of Danzig-Warsaw express.

1950 **Feb. 17, Rockville Centre, N.Y.:** head-on crash of two Long Island Rail Road commuter trains killed 30.
Nov. 22, Richmond Hill, N.Y.: 79 died when one Long Island Rail Road commuter train crashed into rear of another.

1951 **Feb. 6, Woodbridge, N.J.:** 85 died when Pennsylvania Railroad commuter train plunged through temporary overpass.

1952 **Oct. 8, Harrow-Wealdstone, England:** two express trains crashed into commuter train; 112 dead.

1953 **Dec. 24, near Sakvice, Czechoslovakia:** two trains crashed; over 100 dead.

1957 **Sept. 1, near Kendal, Jamaica:** about 175 killed when train plunged into ravine.
Sept. 29, near Montgomery, West Pakistan: express train crashed into standing oil train; nearly 300 killed.
Dec. 4, St. John's, England: 92 killed, 187 injured as one commuter train crashed into another in fog.

1958 **Sept. 15, near Bayonne, N.J.:** over 40 killed when Central Railroad of New Jersey train went through open drawbridge.

1960 **Nov. 14, Pardubice, Czechoslovakia:** two trains collided; 110 dead, 106 injured.

1962 **May 3, near Tokyo:** 163 killed and 400 injured when train crashed into wreckage of collision between inbound freight train and outbound commuter train.

1963 **Nov. 9, near Yokohama, Japan:** two passenger trains crashed into derailed freight, killing 162.

1964 **July 26, Custoias, Portugal:** passenger train derailed; 94 dead.

1970 **Feb. 4, near Buenos Aires:** 236 killed when express train crashed into standing commuter train.

1972 **July 21, Seville, Spain:** head-on crash of two passenger trains killed 76.
Oct. 6, near Saltillo, Mexico: train carrying religious pilgrims derailed and caught fire, killing 204 and injuring over 1,000.
Oct. 30, Chicago: two Illinois Central commuter trains collided during morning rush hour; 45 dead and over 200 injured.

1974 **Aug. 30, Zagreb, Yugoslavia:** train entering station derailed, killing 153 and injuring over 60.

1977 **Feb. 4, Chicago:** 11 killed and over 180 injured when elevated train hit rear of another, sending two cars to street.

1982 **Jan. 26, Algeria:** Derailment on Algiers–Oran line leaves up to 120 dead.

Miscellaneous

1955 **June 11, Le Mans, France:** Racing car in Grand Prix hurtled into grandstand, killing 82 spectators.

1967 **Aug. 27, Huron, Ohio:** Sky divers jumping through overcast from off-course plane landed in Lake Erie; 16 killed.

1978 **April 27, St. Mary's, W. Va.:** Scaffolding in powerplant cooling tower under construction collapsed; killing 57 workmen.
Aug. 4, Lac d'Argent, Quebec: Bus carrying handicapped theatergoers plunged into lake, killing 40.

1980 **Jan. 20, Sincelejo, Colombia:** Bleachers at a bullring collapsed, leaving 222 dead.
March 30, Stavanger, Norway: Floating hotel in North Sea collapsed, killing 123 oil workers.
May 9, St. Petersburg, Fla.: *Summit Venture*, 606-foot phosphate carrier, struck Sunshine Skyway Bridge in blinding rain squall; 1,300-foot section of roadway fell into Tampa Bay, taking with it several passenger cars and a Greyhound bus; 35 killed.

1981 **July 18, Kansas City, Mo:** suspended walkway in Hyatt Regency Hotel collapses; 113 dead, 186 injured.

1982 **Feb. 15, off St. John's, Newfoundland:** Ocean Ranger, oil-drilling rig, capsizes and sinks in storm 200 miles at sea; 84 lost.

States and Territories

State flower, bird, etc., are official unless otherwise indicated; dates in parentheses are those of adoption. Largest cities include incorporated places only. Land areas for 1980 are revised figures. For secession and readmission dates of the former Confederate states, *see* Index. For lists of Governors, Senators, and Representatives, *see* Index. For additional state information, *see* the sections on "Business and the Economy," "Taxes," and "U.S. Statistics."

ALABAMA

Capital: Montgomery
Governor: Forrest H. (Fob) James, Jr., D (to Jan. 1983)
Lieut. Governor: George McMillan, D (to Jan. 1983)
Secy. of State: Don Seigleman, D (to Jan. 1983)
Comptroller: J.T. Brassell
Atty. General: Charles A. Graddick, D (to Jan. 1983)
Organized as territory: March 3, 1817
Entered Union & (rank): Dec. 14, 1819 (22)
Present constitution adopted: 1901
Motto: *Audemus jura nostra defendere* (We dare defend our rights)
State flower: Camellia (1959)
State bird: Yellowhammer (1927)
State song: "Alabama" (1931)
State tree: Southern pine (longleaf) (1949)
Nickname: Yellowhammer State
Origin of name: May come from Choctaw meaning "thicket-clearers" or "vegetation-gatherers"
1980 population (1980 census) & (rank): 3,893,888 (22)
1981 population (prov.) & (rank): 3,917,000 (22)
1980 land area & (rank): 50,767 sq mi. (131,487 sq km) (28)
Geographic center: In Chilton Co., 12 mi. SW of Clanton
Number of counties: 67
Largest cities (1980 census): Birmingham, 284,413; Mobile, 200,452; Montgomery, 178,157; Huntsville, 142,513; Tuscaloosa, 75,143; Gadsden, 47,565
State forests: 8 (14,248.58 ac.)
State parks: 22 (45,614 ac.)
Gross receipts (1980–81): $9,162,325,987
Net receipts (1980–81): $7,431,919,841
Net disbursements (1980–81): $6,896,349,280

Spanish explorers are believed to have arrived at Mobile Bay in 1519, and the territory was visited in 1540 by the explorer Hernando de Soto. The first permanent European settlement in Alabama was founded by the French at Fort Louis in 1702. The British gained control of the area in 1763 by the Treaty of Paris, but had to cede almost all the Alabama region to the U.S. after the American Revolution. The Confederacy was founded at Montgomery in February 1861 and, for a time, the city was the Confederate capital.

During the last part of the 19th century, the economy of the state slowly improved. At Tuskegee Institute, founded in 1881 by Booker T. Washington, Dr. George Washington Carver carried out his famous agricultural research.

In the 1950s and '60s, Alabama was the site of such landmark civil-rights actions as the bus boycott in Montgomery (1955–56) and the "Freedom March" from Selma to Birmingham (1965).

Today, Alabama is the leading heavy-industry state in the South. Textiles, iron, and steel lead its manufacturing, which centers around Birmingham, the "Pittsburgh of the South." Industry is growing rapidly in other areas, including the Tennessee River Valley, with its great Muscle Shoals power plant. Manufacturing also includes cement, feed, fertilizer, chemical, rubber, and aluminum products. The state ranks high in the output of poultry, cotton, cattle, hogs, corn, potatoes, peanuts, and fruit.

Points of interest include the George C. Marshall Space Flight Center at Huntsville, Russell Cave National Monument near Bridgeport, and the White House of the Confederacy in Montgomery.

ALASKA

Capital: Juneau
Governor: Jay S. Hammond, R (to Dec. 1982)
Lieut. Governor: Terry Miller, R (to Dec. 1982)
Commissioner of Administration: W. R. Hudson, R (to Dec. 1982)
Atty. General: Wilson L. Condon, D (apptd. by Governor)
Organized as territory: 1912
Entered Union & (rank): Jan. 3, 1959 (49)
Constitution ratified: April 24, 1956
Motto: North to the Future
State flower: Forget-me-not
State tree: Sitka spruce
State bird: Willow ptarmigan
State fish: King salmon
State song: "Alaska's Flag"
Nickname: The state is commonly called "The Last Frontier" or "Land of the Midnight Sun"
Origin of name: Corruption of Aleut word meaning "great land" or "that which the sea breaks against"
1980 population (1980 census) & (rank): 401,851 (50)
1981 population (prov.) & (rank): 412,000 (50)
1980 land area & (rank): 570,833 sq mi. (1,478,458 sq km) (1)
Geographic center: 60 mi. NW of Mt. McKinley
Number of boroughs: 10
Largest cities (1980 census): Anchorage, 174,431; Fairbanks, 22,645; Juneau, 19,528; Sitka, 7,803; Ketchikan, 7,198; Kodiak, 4,756; Bethel, 3,576
State forests: None
State parks: 5; 59 waysides and areas (3.3 million ac.)
General revenue (1980–81): $4,074,327,000
General expenditures (1980–81): $4,699,405,000

Vitus Bering, a Dane working for the Russians, and Alexei Chirikov discovered the Alaskan mainland and the Aleutian Islands in 1741. The tremendous land mass of Alaska—equal to one fifth of the continental U.S.—was unexplored in 1867 when Secretary of State William Seward arranged for its purchase from the Russians for $7,200,000. The transfer of the territory took place on Oct. 18,

1867. Despite a price of about two cents an acre, the purchase was widely ridiculed as "Seward's Folly." The first official census (1880) reported a total of 33,426 Alaskans, all but 430 being of aboriginal stock. The Gold Rush of 1898 resulted in a mass influx of more than 30,000 people. Since then, Alaska has returned billions of dollars' worth of products to the U.S.

In 1968, a large oil and gas reservoir near Prudhoe Bay on the Arctic Coast was found. The Prudhoe Bay reservoir, with an estimated recoverable 10 billion barrels of oil and 27 trillion cubic feet of gas, is twice as large as any other oil field in North America. The Trans-Alaska pipeline was completed in 1977 at a cost of $7.7 billion. On June 20, oil started flowing through the 800-mile-long pipeline from Prudhoe Bay to the port of Valdez.

Other industries important to Alaska's economy are fisheries, wood and wood products, and furs.

Denali National Park and Mendenhall Glacier in North Tongass National Forest are of interest, as is the large totem pole collection at Sitka National Historical Park. The Katmai National Park includes the "Valley of Ten Thousand Smokes," an area of active volcanoes.

ARIZONA

Capital: Phoenix
Governor: Bruce Babbitt, D (to Jan. 1983)
Secy. of State: Rose Mofford, D (to Jan. 1983)
Atty. General: Bob Corbin, R (to Jan. 1983)
State Treasurer: Clark Dierks, R (to Jan. 1983)
Organized as territory: Feb. 24, 1863
Entered Union & (rank): Feb. 14, 1912 (48)
Present constitution adopted: 1911
Motto: *Ditat Deus* (God enriches)
State flower: Flower of saguaro cactus (1931)
State bird: Cactus wren (1931)
State colors: Blue and old gold (1915)
State song: "Arizona," a march song (1919)
State tree: Paloverde (1957)
Nickname: Grand Canyon State
Origin of name: From the Indian "Arizonac," meaning "little spring"
1980 population (1980 census) & (rank): 2,718,425 (29)
1981 population (prov.) & (rank): 2,794,000 (29)
1980 land area & (rank): 113,508 sq mi. (293,986 sq km) (6)
Geographic center: In Yavapai Co., 55 mi. ESE of Prescott
Number of counties: 14
Largest cities (1980 census): Phoenix, 789,704; Tucson, 330,537; Mesa, 152,453; Tempe, 106,743; Glendale, 97,172; Scottsdale, 86,622; Yuma, 42,481
State forests: None
State parks: 16
State revenue (1980): $3,187,000,000
State expenditure (1980): $2,637,000,000

Marcos de Niza, a Spanish Franciscan friar, was the first European to explore Arizona. He entered the area in 1539 in search of the mythical Seven Cities of Gold. Although he was followed a year later by another gold seeker, Francisco Vásquez de Coronado, most of the early settlement was for missionary purposes. In 1776 the Spanish established Fort Tucson. In 1848, after the Mexican War, most of the Arizona territory became part of the U.S., and the southern portion of the territory was added by the Gadsden Purchase in 1853.

In 1973 the world's biggest dam, the New Cornelia Tailings, was completed near Ajo.

Arizona history is rich in legends of America's Old West. It was here that the great Indian chiefs Geronimo and Cochise led their people against the frontiersmen. Tombstone, Ariz., was the site of the West's most famous shoot-out—the gunfight at the O.K. Corral. Today, Arizona has the largest U.S. Indian population; more than 14 tribes are represented on 19 reservations.

Manufacturing has become Arizona's most important industry. Principal products include electrical, communications, and aeronautical items. The state produces over half the country's copper. Agriculture is also important to the state's economy.

State attractions include such famous scenery as the Grand Canyon, the Petrified Forest, and the Painted Desert. Hoover Dam, Lake Mead, Fort Apache, and the reconstructed London Bridge at Lake Havasu City are of particular interest.

ARKANSAS

Capital: Little Rock
Governor: Frank White, R (to Jan. 1983)
Lieut. Governor: Winston Bryant, D (to Jan. 1983)
Secy. of State: Paul Reviere, D (to Jan. 1983)
Atty. General: Steve Clark (to Jan. 1983)
Auditor of State: Julia Highes Jones, D (to Jan. 1983)
Treasurer of State: Jimmie Lou Fisher, D (to Jan. 1983)
Land Commissioner: Bill McCuen, D (to Jan. 1983)
Organized as territory: March 2, 1819
Entered Union & (rank): June 15, 1836 (25)
Present constitution adopted: 1874
Motto: *Regnat populus* (The people rule)
State flower: Apple Blossom (1901)
State tree: Pine (1939)
State bird: Mockingbird (1929)
State insect: Honeybee
State song: "Arkansas" (1963)
Nickname: Land of Opportunity
Origin of name: From the Quapaw Indians
1980 population (1980 census) & (rank): 2,286,435 (33)
1981 population (prov.) & (rank): 2,296,000 (32)
1980 land area & (rank): 52,078 sq mi. (134,883 sq km) (27)
Geographic center: In Pulaski Co., 12 mi. NW of Little Rock
Number of counties: 75
Largest cities (1980 census): Little Rock, 158,461; Fort Smith, 71,626; North Little Rock, 64,288; Pine Bluff, 56,636; Fayetteville, 36,608; Hot Springs, 35,781
State forests: None
State parks: 44
State tax receipts (1981): $1,258,696,977
Taxes from all sources (1981): $2,206,477,650
State general expenditure (1981): $2,146,791,855

Hernando de Soto, in 1541, was among the early European explorers to visit the territory. It was a Frenchman, Henri de Tonty, who in 1686 founded the first permanent white settlement—the Arkansas Post. In 1803 the area was acquired by the U.S. as part of the Louisiana Purchase.

Food products are the state's largest employing sector, with lumber and wood products a close second. Arkansas is also a leader in the production of cotton, rice, and soybeans. The state produces 97% of the nation's high-grade domestic bauxite ore—the source of aluminum. It also has the country's only active diamond mine; located near Murfreesboro, it is operated as a tourist attraction.

Hot Springs National Park is a major state attraction. Its 47 curative springs flow at an average temperature of 147°F year round. Blanchard Springs Caverns, the Arkansas Territorial Capitol Restoration at Little Rock, and Dogpatch U.S.A. near Harrison are of interest. There are two large national forests in Arkansas—the Ouachita and the Ozark—and one of the nation's smallest—the St. Francis.

CALIFORNIA

Capital: Sacramento
Governor: Edmund G. Brown, Jr., D (to Jan. 1983)
Lieut. Governor: Mike Curb, R (to Jan. 1983)
Secy. of State: March Fong Eu, D (to Jan. 1983)
Controller: Ken Cory, D (to Jan. 1983)
Atty. General: George Deukmejian, R (to Jan. 1983)
Treasurer: Jesse M. Unruh, D (to Jan. 1983)
Entered Union & (rank): Sept. 9, 1850 (31)
Present constitution adopted: 1879
Motto: *Eureka* (I have found it)
State flower: Golden poppy (1903)
State tree: California redwoods *(Sequoia sempervirens & Sequoia gigantea)* (1937 & 1953)
State bird: California valley quail (1931)
State animal: California grizzly bear (1953)
State fish: California golden trout (1947)
State insect: California dog-face butterfly (1972)
State colors: Blue and gold (1951)
State song: "I Love You, California" (1951)
Nickname: Golden State
Origin of name: From a book, *Las Sergas de Esplandián,* by Garcia Ordóñez de Montalvo, c. 1500
1980 population (1980 census) & (rank): 23,667,565 (1)
1981 population (prov.) & (rank): 24,196,000 (1)
1980 land area & (rank): 156,299 sq mi. (404,815 sq km) (3)
Geographic center: In Madera Co., 35 mi. NE of Madera
Number of counties: 58
Largest cities (1980 census): Los Angeles, 2,966,850; San Diego, 875,538; San Francisco, 678,974; San Jose, 629,442; Long Beach, 361,334; Oakland, 339,337
State forests: 8 (70,283 ac.)
State parks and beaches: 180 (723,000 ac.)
State general revenue (1980–81): $19,060,712,065
State general expenditure (1980–81): $21,065,545,894

Although California was sighted by Spanish navigator Juan Rodríguez Cabrillo in 1542, its first Spanish mission (at San Diego) was not established until 1769. California became a U.S. Territory in 1847 when Mexico surrendered it to John C. Frémont. On Jan. 24, 1848, James W. Marshall discovered gold at Sutter's Mill, starting the California Gold Rush and bringing settlers to the state in large numbers.

In 1964, the U.S. Census Bureau estimated that California had become the most populous state, surpassing New York. California also leads the country in personal income and consumer expenditures.

Leading industries include manufacturing (transportation equipment, machinery, and electronic equipment), agriculture, and tourism. Principal natural resources include petroleum, cement, and natural gas.

The Bank of America National Trust and Savings Association, founded by the Giannini family, ranks first or second in the world.

Death Valley, in the southeast, is 282 feet below sea level, the lowest point in the nation; and Mt. Whitney (14,495 ft) is the highest point in the contiguous 48 states. Lassen Peak is one of two active U.S. volcanos outside of Alaska and Hawaii; its last eruptions were recorded in 1917. The General Sherman Tree in Sequoia National Park is estimated to be about 3,500 years old and a stand of bristlecone pine trees in the White Mountains may be over 4,000 years old.

Other points of interest include Yosemite National Park, Disneyland, Hollywood, the Golden Gate bridge, San Simeon State Park, and Point Reyes National Seashore.

COLORADO

Capital: Denver
Governor: Richard D. Lamm, D (to Jan. 1983)
Lieut. Governor: Nancy E. Dick, D (to Jan. 1983)
Secy. of State: Mary Estill Buchanan, R (to Jan. 1983)
Treasurer: Roy Romer, D (to Jan. 1983)
Controller: Dan S. Whittemore
Atty. General: J. D. MacFarlane, D (to Jan. 1983)
Organized as territory: Feb. 28, 1861
Entered Union & (rank): Aug. 1, 1876 (38)
Present constitution adopted: 1876
Motto: *Nil sine Numine* (Nothing without Providence)
State flower: Rocky Mountain columbine (1899)
State tree: Colorado blue spruce (1939)
State bird: Lark bunting (1931)
State animal: Rocky Mountain bighorn sheep
State colors: Blue and white (1911)
State gemstone: Aquamarine (1971)
State song: "Where the Columbines Grow" (1915)
Nickname: Centennial State
Origin of name: From the Spanish, meaning "ruddy" or "red"
1970 population & (rank): 2,209,596 (30)
1980 population (1980 census) & (rank): 2,889,735 (28)
1980 land area & (rank): 103,595 sq mi. (268,311 sq km) (8)
Geographic center: In Park Co., 30 mi. NW of Pikes Peak
Number of counties: 63
Largest cities (1980 census): Denver, 492,365; Colorado Springs, 214,821; Aurora, 158,588; Lakewood, 113,808; Pueblo, 101,686; Arvada, 84,576; Boulder, 76,685
State forests: 1 (71,000 ac.)
Total state revenue (1980–81): $3,127,700,000
Total state expenditure (1980–81): $3,303,800,000

First visited by Spanish explorers in the 1500s, the territory was claimed for Spain by Juan de Ulibarri in 1706. The U.S. obtained eastern Colorado as part of the Louisiana Purchase in 1803, the central portion in 1845 with the admission of Texas as a state, and the western part in 1848 as a result of the Mexican War.

Colorado has the highest mean elevation of any state, with more than 1,000 Rocky Mountain peaks over 10,000 feet high and 54 towering above 14,000 feet. Pikes Peak, the most famous of these mountains, was discovered by U.S. Army Lieut. Zebulon M. Pike in 1806.

Gold was first discovered near present-day Denver in 1858 and at Cripple Creek in 1891. Rich silver deposits were also found in 1875.

Once primarily a mining and agricultural state, today Colorado draws the largest segment of its income from manufacturing. Denver is a leader in electronics and space-age industry. Pueblo, the "Pittsburgh of the West," makes iron, steel, brick, tile, and foundry products.

Rich in natural resources, Colorado now produces most of the world's molybdenum. Uranium, vanadium, gold, silver, lead, tin, zinc, and other minerals are also mined. Colorado's highly developed irrigation system promotes farming of wheat, hay, beans, sugar beets, corn, potatoes, barley, and truck vegetables. Cattle and sheep raising is also important.

Tourism has developed into a major industry largely because of Colorado's magnificent scenery. Among the major attractions are Rocky Mountain National Park, Garden of the Gods, Great Sand Dunes and Dinosaur National Monuments, Pikes Peak and Mt. Evans Highways, and Mesa Verde National Park (prehistoric cliff dwellings).

Colorado Springs, with the nearby U.S. Air Force Academy, is probably the most popular tourist center in the Rocky Mountains, while Aspen and Vail have become leading ski resorts.

CONNECTICUT

Capital: Hartford
Governor: William A. O'Neill, D (to Jan. 1983)
Lieut. Governor: Joseph J. Fauliso, D (to Jan. 1983)
Secy. of State: Maura L. Melley, D (to Jan. 1983)
Comptroller: J. Edward Caldwell, D (to Jan. 1983)
Treasurer: Henry E. Parker, D (to Jan. 1983)
Atty. General: Carl R. Ajello, D (to Jan. 1983)
Entered Union & (rank): Jan. 9, 1788 (5)
Present constitution adopted: Dec. 30, 1965
Motto: *Qui transtulit sustinet* (He who transplanted still sustains)
State flower: Mountain laurel (1907)
State tree: White Oak (1947)
State animal: Sperm whale (1975)
State bird: American robin (1943)
State insect: Praying mantis (1977)
State mineral: Garnet (1977)
State song: "Yankee Doodle" (1978)
Official designation: *Constitution State* (1959)
Nickname: Nutmeg State
Origin of name: From an Indian word (Quinnehtukqut) meaning "beside the long tidal river"
1980 population (1980 census) & (rank): 3,107,576 (25)
1981 population (prov.) & (rank): 3,134,000 (25)
1980 land area & (rank): 4,872 sq mi. (12,618 km) (48)
Geographic center: In Hartford Co., at East Berlin
Number of counties: 8
Largest cities (1980 census): Bridgeport, 142,546; Hartford, 136,392; New Haven, 126,109; Waterbury, 103,266; Stamford, 102,453; Norwalk, 77,767
State forests: 30 (137,782 ac.)
State parks: 88 (29,922 ac.)
State and local general revenue (1980–81): $4,789,000,000
State and local general expenditure (1980–81): $4,899,000,000

The Dutch navigator, Adriaen Block, was the first European of record to explore the area, sailing up the Connecticut River in 1614. In 1633, Dutch colonists built a fort and trading post near present-day Hartford, but soon lost control to English Puritans migrating south from the Massachusetts Bay Colony.

English settlements, established in the 1630s at Windsor, Wethersfield, and Hartford, united in 1639 to form the Connecticut Colony and adopted the *Fundamental Orders*, considered the world's first written constitution.

The colony's royal charter of 1682 was exceptionally liberal. When Gov. Edmund Andros tried to seize it in 1687, it was hidden in the Hartford Oak, commemorated in Charter Oak Place.

Connecticut played a prominent role in the Revolutionary War, serving as the Continental Army's major supplier. Sometimes called the "Arsenal of the Nation," the state became one of the most industrialized in the nation. Its early business and industrial pioneers included Eli Whitney, Samuel Colt, and Charles Goodyear.

Today, Connecticut factories produce weapons, sewing machines, jet engines, helicopters, motors, hardware and tools, cutlery, clocks, locks, ball bearings, silverware, and submarines. Hartford, which has the oldest U.S. newspaper still being published —the *Courant*, established 1764— is the insurance capital of the nation.

Poultry, fruit, and dairy products account for the largest portion of farm income, and Connecticut shade-grown tobacco is acknowledged to be the nation's most valuable crop, per acre.

Connecticut is a popular resort area with its 250-mile Long Island Sound shoreline and many inland lakes. Among the major points of interest are the American Shakespeare Theatre in Stratford, Yale University's Gallery of Fine Arts and Peabody Museum. Other famous museums include the P.T. Barnum, Winchester Gun, and American Clock and Watch. The town of Mystic features a recreated 19th-century New England seaport and the Mystic Marinelife Aquarium.

DELAWARE

Capital: Dover
Governor: Pierre S. du Pont IV, R (to Jan. 1985)
Lieut. Governor: Michael N. Castle (to Jan. 1985)
Secy. of State: Glenn C. Kenton, R (Pleasure of Governor)
State Treasurer: Thomas R. Carper, D (to Jan. 1983)
Atty. General: Richard S. Gebelein (to Jan. 1983)
Entered Union & (rank): Dec. 7, 1787 (1)
Present constitution adopted: 1897
Motto: Liberty and independence
State colors: Colonial blue and buff
State flower: Peach blossom
State tree: American holly
State bird: Blue Hen chicken
State insect: Ladybug
State song: "Our Delaware"
Nicknames: Diamond State; First State
Origin of name: From Delaware River and Bay; named in turn for Sir Thomas West, Lord De La Warr
1980 population (1980 census) & (rank): 594,317 (47)
1981 population (prov.) & (rank): 598,000 (47)
1980 land area & (rank): 1,932 sq mi. (5,005 sq km) (49)
Geographic center: In Kent Co., 11 mi. S of Dover
Number of counties: 3
Largest cities (1980 census): Wilmington, 70,195; Newark, 25,247; Dover, 23,512; Elsmere, 6,493; Milford, 5,356; Seaford, 5,256; New Castle, 4,709; Lewes, 2,197
State forests: 3 (6,149 ac.)
State parks: 10
State receipts (1981): $642,311,820[1]
State disbursements (1981): $660,545,397[1]

1. General Funds, do not include Federal funds.

Henry Hudson, sailing under the Dutch flag, is credited with Delaware's discovery in 1609. The following year, Capt. Samuel Argall of Virginia named Delaware for his colony's governor, Thomas West, Baron De La Warr. An attempted Dutch settlement failed in 1631. Swedish colonization began at Fort Christina (now Wilmington) in 1638, but New Sweden fell to Dutch forces led by New Netherlands' Gov. Peter Stuyvesant in 1655.

England took over the area in 1664 and it was transferred to William Penn as the southern Three Counties in 1682. Semiautonomous after 1704, Delaware fought as a separate state in the American Revolution and became the first state to ratify the constitution in 1787.

During the Civil War, although a slave state, Delaware did not secede from the Union.

In 1802, Éleuthère Irénée du Pont established a gunpowder mill near Wilmington that laid the foundation for Delaware's huge chemical industry. Delaware's manufactured products now also include vulcanized fiber, glazed kid and morocco leathers, textiles, paper, dental supplies, metal products, machinery, machine tools, and automobiles.

Delaware also grows a great variety of fruits and vegetables and is a U.S. pioneer in the food-canning industry. Corn, soybeans, potatoes, and hay are important crops. Delaware's broiler chicken farms supply the big Eastern markets, and fishing is another major industry.

Points of interest include the Fort Christina Monument, Hagley Museum, Holy Trinity Church (erected in 1698, the oldest Protestant church in the United States still in use), and Winterthur Museum, in and near Wilmington; central New Castle, an almost unchanged late 18th-century capital; and the Delaware Museum of Natural History.

Popular recreation areas include Cape Henlopen, Delaware Seashore, Trapp Pond State Park, and Rehoboth Beach.

DISTRICT OF COLUMBIA

See listing at end of *50 Largest Cities of the United States.*

FLORIDA

Capital: Tallahassee
Governor: Bob Graham, D (to Jan. 1983)
Lieut. Governor: Wayne Mixson, D (to Jan. 1983)
Secy. of State: George Firestone, D (to Jan. 1983)
Comptroller: Gerald Lewis, D (to Jan. 1983)
Commissioner of Agriculture: Doyle Connor, D (to Jan. 1983)
Atty. General: Jim Smith, D (to Jan. 1983)
Organized as territory: March 30, 1822
Entered Union & (rank): March 3, 1845 (27)
Present constitution adopted: 1969
Motto: In God we trust (1868)
State flower: Orange blossom (1909)
State bird: Mockingbird (1927)
State song: "Suwannee River" (1935)
Nickname: Sunshine State (1970)
Origin of name: From the Spanish, meaning "feast of flowers" (Easter)
1980 population (1980 census) & (rank): 9,746,342 (7)
1981 population (prov.) & (rank): 10,183,000 (7)
1980 land area & (rank): 54,153 sq mi. (140,256 sq km) (26)
Geographic center: In Hernando Co., 12 mi. NNW of Brooksville
Number of counties: 67
Largest cities (1980 census): Jacksonville, 540,920; Miami, 346,865; Tampa, 271,523; St. Petersburg, 238,647; Fort Lauderdale, 153,279; Hialeah, 159,887
State forests: 4 (306,881 ac.)
State parks: 88 (215,820 ac.)
State tax receipts (1980–81): $5,164,196,808
Other state revenue (1980–81): $3,062,711,971
State expenditures (1980–81): $14,994,540,715

In 1513, Ponce de Leon, seeking the mythical "Fountain of Youth," named Florida and claimed it for Spain. Later, Florida would be held at different times by Spain, France, and England until Spain finally sold it to the United States in 1819.

Florida's early 19th-century history as a U.S. territory was scarred by savage wars with the Seminole Indians that did not end until 1842.

One of the nation's fastest-growing states, Florida's population has gone from 2.8 million in 1950 to more than 9.5 million today.

Florida's economy rests on a solid base of tourism, manufacturing, and agriculture. The state entertained more than 35.9 million visitors, who spent about $16.5 billion, in 1979.

Oranges and grapefruit lead Florida's crop list, followed by sugarcane, tomatoes, beans, celery, potatoes, field corn, honey, watermelons, limes, and mangoes. Forestry, truck gardening, commercial fishing, and cattle raising are leading industries. Deep-sea fishing for sport is a leading tourist industry.

Florida is expanding in all industrial areas with the greatest development taking place in the research-oriented Space Age manufacturing. The state produces 80% of the nation's phosphate.

Major tourist attractions are Miami Beach, Palm Beach, St. Augustine (founded in 1565 and the oldest permanent city in the U.S.), Daytona Beach, and Fort Lauderdale, on the East Coast. West Coast resorts include Sarasota, Tampa, Key West, and St. Petersburg. Disney World, located on a 27,000-acre site near Orlando, is a popular attraction.

The John F. Kennedy Space Center at Cape Canaveral, and Everglades National Park, a 5,000-square-mile preserve, also draw many visitors.

GEORGIA

Capital: Atlanta
Governor: George Busbee, D (to Jan. 1983)
Lieut. Governor: Zell Miller, D (to Jan. 1983)
Secy. of State: David Poythress, D (to Jan. 1983)
Comptroller General: Johnnie Caldwell, D (to Jan. 1983)
Atty. General: Michael J. Bowers, D (to Jan. 1983)
Entered Union & (rank): Jan. 2, 1788 (4)
Present constitution adopted: 1977
Motto: Wisdom, justice, and moderation
State flower: Cherokee rose (1916)
State tree: Live oak (1937)
State bird: Brown thrasher (1935)
State song: "Georgia on my Mind" (1922)
Nicknames: Peach State, Empire State of the South
Origin of name: In honor of George II of England
1980 population (1980 census) & (rank): 5,463,105 (13)
1981 population (prov.) & (rank): 5,574,000 (12)
1980 land area & (rank): 58,056 sq mi. (150,365 sq km) (21)
Geographic center: In Twiggs Co., 18 mi. SE of Macon
Number of counties: 159
Largest cities (1980 census): Atlanta, 425,022; Columbus, 169,441; Savannah, 141,634; Macon, 116,860; Albany, 74,550; Augusta, 47,532; Athens, 42,549; Warner Robins, 39,893
State forests: 25,258,000 ac. (67% of total state area)
State parks: 53 (42,600 ac.)
State revenue receipts (1981): $2,944,157,270
State revenue distribution (1981): $2,944,157,270

Hernando de Soto, the Spanish explorer, first traveled parts of Georgia in 1540. British claims later conflicted with those of Spain. After obtaining a royal charter, Gen. James Oglethorpe established the first permanent settlement in Georgia in 1733 as a refuge for English debtors. In 1742, Oglethorpe defeated Spanish invaders in the Battle of

Bloody Marsh.

A Confederate stronghold, Georgia was the scene of extensive military action during the Civil War. Union General William T. Sherman burned Atlanta and destroyed a 60-mile wide path to the coast where he captured Savannah in 1864.

The largest state east of the Mississippi, Georgia is typical of the changing South with an ever-increasing industrial development. Atlanta, largest city in the state, is the communications and transportation center for the Southeast and the area's chief distributor of goods.

Georgia leads the nation in the production of paper and board, tufted textile products, and processed chicken. Other major manufactured products are transportation equipment, food products, apparel, and chemicals.

Important agricultural products are corn, cotton, tobacco, soybeans, eggs, and peaches. Georgia produces twice as many peanuts as the next leading state. From its vast stands of pine come more than half the world's resins and turpentine and 74.4% of the U.S. supply. Georgia is also a leader in the production of marble, kaolin, barite, and bauxite.

Principal tourist attractions in Georgia include the Okefenokee National Wildlife Refuge, Andersonville Prison Park and National Cemetery, Chickamauga and Chattanooga National Military Park, the Little White House at Warm Springs where Pres. Franklin D. Roosevelt died in 1945, Sea Island, the enormous Confederate Memorial at Stone Mountain, Kennesaw Mountain National Battlefield Park, and Cumberland Island National Seashore.

HAWAII

Capital: Honolulu (on Oahu)
Governor: George R. Ariyoshi, D (to Dec. 1982)
Lieut. Governor: Jean King, D (to Dec. 1982)
Comptroller: Hideo Murakami, (to Dec. 1982)
Atty. General: Tany S. Hong, (to Dec. 1982)
Organized as territory: 1900
Entered Union & (rank): Aug. 21, 1959 (50)
Motto: *Ua Mau Ke Ea O Ka Aina I Ka Pono* (The life of the land is perpetuated in righteousness)
State flower: Hibiscus
State song: "Hawaii Ponoi"
State bird: Nene (Hawaiian goose)
Nickname: Aloha State
Origin of name: Uncertain. The islands may have been named by Hawaii Loa, their traditional discoverer. Or they may have been named after Hawaii or Hawaiki, the traditional home of the Polynesians.
1980 population (1980 census) & (rank): 964,691 (39)
1981 population (prov.) & (rank): 981,000 (39)
1980 land area & (rank): 6,425 sq mi. (16,641 sq km) (47)
Geographic center: In Hawaii Co., off Maui Island
Number of counties: 4
Largest cities (1980 census): Honolulu, 365,048; Hilo, 37,017[1]
State parks and historic sites: 65
Total state government revenues (1980–81): $2,102,600,000
Total state government expenditures (1980–81): $2,162,100,000

1. There are no political boundaries to Honolulu or any other place, but statistical boundaries are assigned under state law.

First settled by Polynesians sailing from other Pacific islands in the 6th century, Hawaii was visited in 1778 by British Captain James Cook who called the group the Sandwich Islands.

Hawaii was a native kingdom throughout most of the 19th century when the expansion of the vital sugar industry (pineapple came after 1898) meant increasing U.S. business and political involvement. In 1893, Queen Liliuokalani was deposed and a year later the Republic of Hawaii was established with Sanford B. Dole as president. Then, following its annexation in 1898, Hawaii became a U.S. Territory in 1900.

The Japanese attack on the naval base at Pearl Harbor on Dec. 7, 1941, was directly responsible for U.S. entry into World War II.

Hawaii, 2,100 miles west-southwest of San Francisco, is a 1,600-mile chain of islets and eight main islands—Hawaii, Kahoolawe, Maui, Lanai, Molokai, Oahu, Kauai, and Niihau. Kure (Ocean) Atoll, an islet in the Northwestern Hawaiian Islands, is administratively part of Hawaii.

The temperature is mild and Hawaii's soil is fertile for tropical fruits and vegetables. Cane sugar and pineapple are the chief products. Hawaii also grows coffee, bananas and nuts. The tourist business is Hawaii's largest source of outside income.

Hawaii's highest peak is Mauna Kea (13,796 ft.). Mauna Loa (13,677 ft.) is the largest volcanic mountain in the world in cubic content.

Among the major points of interest are Hawaii Volcanoes National Park (Hawaii), Haleakala National Park (Maui), Puuhonua o Honaunau National Historical Park (Hawaii), Polynesian Cultural Center (Oahu), the U.S.S. *Arizona* Memorial at Pearl Harbor, and Iolani Palace (the only royal palace in the U.S.), Bishop Museum, and Waikiki Beach (all in Honolulu).

IDAHO

Capital: Boise
Governor: John V. Evans, D (to Jan. 1983)
Lieut. Governor: Phil Batt, R (to Jan. 1983)
Secy. of State: Pete T. Cenarrusa, R (to Jan. 1983)
State Auditor: Joe R. Williams, D (to Jan. 1983)
Atty. General: David Leroy, R (to Jan. 1983)
Organized as territory: March 3, 1863
Entered Union & (rank): July 3, 1890 (43)
Present constitution adopted: 1890
Motto: *Esto perpetua* (May you last forever)
State flower: Syringa (1931)
State tree: White pine (1935)
State bird: Mountain bluebird (1931)
State horse: Appaloosa (1975)
State gem: Star garnet (1967)
State song: "Here We Have Idaho"
Nicknames: Gem State; Spud State; Panhandle State
Origin of name: Means "Gem of the Mountains"
1980 population (1980 census) & (rank): 944,038 (41)
1981 population (prov.) & (rank): 959,000 (40)
1980 land area & (rank): 82,413 sq mi. (213,449 sq km) (11)
Geographic center: In Custer Co., at Custer, SW of Challis
Number of counties: 44, plus small part of Yellowstone National Park
Largest cities (1980 census): Boise, 102,160; Pocatello, 46,340; Idaho Falls, 39,590; Lewiston, 27,986; Twin Falls, 26,209; Nampa, 25,112; Coeur d'Alene, 20,054
State forests: 881,000 ac.
State parks: 21 (38,487) ac.
State revenue (1980–81): $2,497,950,517
State expenditure (1980–81): $2,497,077,389

After its acquisition by the U.S. as part of the Louisiana Purchase in 1803, the region was explored by Meriwether Lewis and William Clark in 1805–06. Northwest boundary disputes with Great Britain were settled by the Oregon Treaty in 1846 and the first permanent U.S. settlement in Idaho was established by the Mormons at Franklin in 1860.

After gold was discovered on Orofino Creek in 1860, prospectors swarmed into the territory, but left little more than a number of ghost towns.

In the 1870s, growing white occupation of Indian lands led to a series of battles between U.S. forces and the Nez Percé, Bannock, and Sheepeater tribes.

Mining, lumbering, and irrigation farming have been important for years. Idaho produces more than one third of all the silver mined in the U.S. It also ranks high among the states in antimony, lead, cobalt, garnet, phosphate rock, vanadium, zinc, and mercury.

Idaho's most impressive growth began when World War II military needs made processing agricultural products a big industry, particularly the dehydrating and freezing of potatoes. The state produces about one fourth of the nation's potato crop, as well as wheat, apples, corn, barley, sugar beets, and hops. More money is made from livestock in the state than from all agricultural products.

With the growth of winter sports, tourism now outranks mining in dollar revenue. Idaho's many streams and lakes provide fishing, camping, and boating sites. The nation's largest elk herds draw hunters from all over the world and the famed Sun Valley resort attracts thousands of visitors to its swimming and skiing facilities.

Other points of interest are the Craters of the Moon National Monument; Nez Percé National Historic Park, which includes many sites visited by Lewis and Clark; and the State Historical Museum in Boise.

ILLINOIS

Capital: Springfield
Governor: James R. Thompson, R (to Jan. 1983)
Lieut. Governor: Dave O'Neal, R (to Jan. 1983)
Secy. of State: Jim Edgar, R (to Jan. 1983)
Comptroller: Roland J. Burris, D (to Jan. 1983)
Atty. General: Tyrone C. Fahner, R (to Jan. 1983)
Treasurer: Jerry Cosentino, D (to Jan. 1983)
Organized as territory: Feb. 3, 1809
Entered Union & (rank): Dec. 3, 1818 (21)
Present constitution adopted: 1970
Motto: State sovereignty, national union
State flower: Violet (1908)
State tree: White oak (1973)
State bird: Cardinal (1929)
State insect: Monarch butterfly
State song: "Illinois" (1925)
State slogan: Land of Lincoln
State mineral: Fluorite (1965)
Nickname: Prairie State
Origin of name: From an Indian word and French suffix meaning "tribe of superior men"
1980 population (1980 census) & (rank): 11,426,518 (5)
1981 population (prov.) & (rank): 11,462,000 (5)
1980 land area & (rank): 55,645 sq mi. (144,120 sq km) (24)
Geographic center: In Logan County 28 mi. NE of Springfield
Number of counties: 102
Largest cities (1980 census): Chicago, 3,005,072; Rockford, 139,712; Peoria, 124,160; Springfield, 100,054; Decatur, 94,081; Aurora, 81,293; Joliet, 77,956
Public use areas: 187 (275,000 ac.), incl. state parks, memorials, forests and conservation areas
Total state revenue, all appropriated funds, all sources (fiscal 1980): $14,270,035,651
Total state expenditure, all appropriated funds (fiscal 1981): $13,777,449,742

French explorers Marquette and Joliet, in 1673, were the first Europeans of record to visit the region. In 1699 French settlers established the first permanent settlement at Cahokia, near present-day East St. Louis.

Great Britain obtained the region at the end of the French and Indian War in 1763. The area figured prominently in frontier struggles during the Revolutionary War and in Indian wars during the early 19th century.

Significant episodes in the state's early history include the growing migration of Eastern settlers following the opening of the Erie Canal in 1825; the Black Hawk War, which virtually ended the Indian troubles in the area; and the rise of Abraham Lincoln from farm laborer to President-elect.

Today, Illinois stands high in manufacturing, coal mining, agriculture, and oil production. The sprawling Chicago district (including a slice of Indiana) is a great iron and steel producer, meat packer, grain exchange, and railroad center. Chicago is also famous as a busy long-flight airport city and Great Lakes port.

Illinois ranks first in the nation in export of agricultural products and second in hog production. An important dairying state, Illinois is also a leader in corn, oats, wheat, barley, rye, truck vegetables, and nursery products.

The state manufactures a great variety of industrial and consumer products: railroad cars, clothing, furniture, tractors, liquor, watches, and farm implements are just some of the items made in its factories and plants.

Central Illinois is noted for shrines and memorials associated with the life of Abraham Lincoln. In Springfield are the Lincoln Home, the Lincoln Tomb, and the restored Old State Capitol. Other points of interest are the home of Mormon leader Joseph Smith in Nauvoo and, in Chicago: the Art Institute, Field Museum, Museum of Science and Industry, Shedd Aquarium, Adler Planetarium, Merchandise Mart, and Chicago Portage National Historic Site.

INDIANA

Capital: Indianapolis
Governor: Robert D. Orr, R (to Jan. 1985)
Lieut. Governor: John M. Muntz, R (to Jan. 1985)
Secy. of State: Edwin J. Simcox, R (to Dec. 1982)
Treasurer: Julian L. Ridlen, R (to Feb. 1983)
Atty. General: Linley E. Pearson, R (to Jan. 1985)
Auditor: Charles D. Loos, R (to Dec. 1982)
Organized as territory: May 7, 1800
Entered Union & (rank): Dec. 11, 1816 (19)
Present constitution adopted: 1851
Motto: The Crossroads of America
State flower: Peony (1957)
State tree: Tulip tree (1931)
State bird: Cardinal (1933)
State song: "On the Banks of the Wabash, Far Away" (1913)
Nickname: Hoosier State
Origin of name: Meaning "land of Indians"

1980 population (1980 census) & (rank): 5,490,260 (12)
1981 population (prov.) & (rank): 5,468,000 (13)
1980 land area & (rank): 35,932 sq mi. (93,064 sq km) (38)
Geographic center: In Boone Co., 14 mi. NNW of Indianapolis
Number of Counties: 92
Largest cities (1980 census): Indianapolis, 700,807; Fort Wayne, 172,028; Gary, 151,953; Evansville, 130,496; South Bend, 109,727; Hammond, 93,714; Muncie, 77,216
State parks: 19 (54,126 ac.)
State memorials: 16 (941.977 ac.)
State general revenue (1979–80): $5,335,003,766
State general expenditure (1979–80): $5,524,340,647

First explored for France by La Salle in 1679–80, the region figured importantly in the Franco-British struggle for North America that culminated with British victory in 1763.

George Rogers Clark led American forces against the British in the area during the Revolutionary War and, prior to becoming a state, Indiana was the scene of frequent Indian uprisings until the victory of Gen. William Henry Harrison at Tippecanoe in 1811.

Indiana's 41-mile Lake Michigan waterfront—one of the world's great industrial centers—turns out iron, steel, and oil products. Products include automobile parts and accessories, mobile homes and recreational vehicles, truck and bus bodies, aircraft engines, farm machinery, and fabricated structural steel. Phonograph records, wood office furniture, and pharmaceuticals are also manufactured.

The state is a leader in agriculture with corn the principal crop. Hogs, soybeans, wheat, oats, rye, tomatoes, onions, and poultry also contribute heavily to Indiana's agricultural output. Much of the building limestone used in the U.S. is quarried in Indiana which is also a large producer of coal.

Wyandotte Cave, one of the largest in the U.S., is located in Crawford County in southern Indiana and West Baden and French Lick are well known for their mineral springs. Other attractions include Indiana Dunes National Lakeshore, Indianapolis Motor Speedway, Lincoln Boyhood National Memorial, and the George Rogers Clark National Historical Park.

IOWA

Capital: Des Moines
Governor: Robert D. Ray, R (to Jan. 1983)
Lieut. Governor: Terry Branstad, R (to Jan. 1983)
Secy. of State: Mary Jane Odell, R (to Jan. 1983)
Treasurer: Maurice E. Baringer, R (to Jan. 1983)
Atty. General: Tom Miller, D (to Jan. 1983)
Organized as territory: June 12, 1838
Entered Union & (rank): Dec. 28, 1846 (29)
Present constitution adopted: 1857
Motto: Our liberties we prize and our rights we will maintain
State flower: Wild rose (1897)
State bird: Eastern goldfinch (1933)
State colors: Red, white, and blue (in state flag)
State song: "Song of Iowa"
Nickname: Hawkeye State
Origin of name: Probably from an Indian word meaning "I-o-w-a, this is the place," or "The Beautiful Land"
1980 population (1980 census) & (rank): 2,913,808 (27)
1981 population (prov.) & (rank): 2,899,000 (28)
1980 land area & (rank): 55,965 sq mi. (144,950 sq km) (23)
Geographic center: In Story Co., 5 mi. NE of Ames
Number of counties: 99
Largest cities (1980 census): Des Moines, 191,003; Cedar Rapids, 110,243; Davenport, 103,264; Sioux City 82,003; Waterloo, 75,985; Dubuque, 62,321; Council Bluffs, 56,449; Iowa City, 50,508; Ames, 45,775
State forests: 5 (28,000 ac.)
State parks: 95 (49,237)
Total revenue (1981): $1,930,800,000
Total expenditures (1981): $1,793,100,000

The first Europeans to visit the area were the French explorers, Father Jacques Marquette and Louis Jolliet in 1673. The U.S. obtained control of the area in 1803 as part of the Louisiana Purchase.

During the first half of the 19th century, there was heavy fighting between white settlers and Indians. Lands were taken from the Indians after the Black Hawk War in 1832 and again in 1836 and 1837.

When Iowa became a state in 1846, its capital was Iowa City; the more centrally located Des Moines became the new capital in 1857. At that time, the state's present boundaries were also drawn.

Although Iowa produces a tenth of the nation's food supply, the value of Iowa's manufactured products is almost 2½ times that of its agriculture. Major industries are food and associated products, non-electrical machinery, electrical equipment, printing and publishing, and fabricated products.

Iowa stands in a class by itself as an agricultural state. Its farms sell over $9 billion worth of crops and livestock annually. Iowa leads the nation in all livestock and hog marketings, with about 25% of the pork supply and 12% of the grain-fed cattle. Iowa's forests produce hardwood lumber, particularly walnut, and its mineral products include cement, limestone, sand, gravel, gypsum, and coal.

Tourist attractions include the Herbert Hoover birthplace and library near West Branch; the Amana Colonies; Fort Dodge Historical Museum, Fort, and Stockade; the Iowa State Fair at Des Moines in August; and the Effigy Mounds National Monument at Marquette, a prehistoric Indian burial site.

KANSAS

Capital: Topeka
Governor: John W. Carlin, D (to Jan. 1983)
Lieut. Governor: Paul V. Dugan, D (to Jan. 1983)
Secy. of State: Jack H. Brier, R (to Jan. 1983)
Treasurer: Joan Finney, D (to Jan. 1983)
Atty. General: Robert T. Stephan, R (to Jan. 1983)
Organized as territory: May 30, 1854
Entered Union & (rank): Jan. 29, 1861 (34)
Present constitution adopted: 1859
Motto: *Ad astra per aspera* (To the stars through difficulties)
State flower: Sunflower (1903)
State tree: Cottonwood (1937)
State bird: Western meadow lark (1937)
State animal: Buffalo (1955)
State song: "Home on the Range" (1947)
State march: "The Kansas March" (1935)
Nicknames: Sunflower State; Jayhawk State
Origin of name: From a Siouan word meaning "people of the south wind"
1980 population (1980 census) & (rank): 2,364,236 (32)
1981 population (prov.) & (rank): 2,383,000 (32)
1980 land area & (rank): 81,781 sq mi. (211,814 sq km) (13)

Geographic center: In Barton Co., 15 mi. NE of Great Bend
Number of counties: 105
Largest cities (1980 census): Wichita, 279,835; Kansas City, 161,148; Topeka, 115,266; Overland Park, 81,784; Lawrence, 52,738; Salina, 41,843; Hutchinson, 40,284
State parks: 22 (14,394 ac.)
State operating revenue (1980–81): $2,677,166,000
State operating expenditure (1980–81): $2,687,001,000

Spanish explorer Francisco de Coronado, in 1541, is considered the first European to have traveled this region. La Salle's extensive land claims for France (1682) included present-day Kansas. Ceded to Spain by France in 1763, the territory reverted back to France in 1800 and was sold to the U.S. as part of the Louisiana Purchase in 1803.

Lewis and Clark, Zebulon Pike, and Stephen H. Long explored the region between 1803 and 1819. The first permanent settlements in Kansas were outposts—Fort Leavenworth (1827), Fort Scott (1842), and Fort Riley (1853)—established to protect travelers along the Santa Fe and Oregon Trails.

Just before the Civil War, the conflict between the pro- and anti-slavery forces earned the region the grim title "Bleeding Kansas."

Today, wheat fields, oil well derricks, herds of cattle, and grain storage elevators are chief features of the Kansas landscape. A leading wheat-growing state, Kansas also raises corn, sorghums, oats, barley, soy beans, and potatoes. Kansas stands high in petroleum production and mines zinc, coal, salt, and lead. It is also the nation's leading producer of helium.

Wichita is one of the nation's leading aircraft manufacturing centers, ranking first in production of private aircraft. Kansas City is an important transportation, milling, and meat-packing center.

Points of interest include the Kansas State Historical Society Museum at Topeka, the Eisenhower boyhood home and the new Eisenhower Memorial Museum and Presidential Library at Abilene, John Brown's cabin at Osawatomie, recreated Front Street in Dodge City, Fort Larned (once the most important military post on the Santa Fe Trail), and Fort Leavenworth and Fort Riley, still active military posts.

KENTUCKY

Capital: Frankfort
Governor: John Y. Brown, Jr., D (to Dec. 1983)
Lieut. Governor: Martha Layne Collins, D (to Dec. 1983)
Secy. of the Commonwealth: Francis Jones Mills, D (to Jan. 1984)
State Treasurer: Drexell Davis, D (to Jan. 1984)
State Auditor: James B. Graham, D (to Jan. 1984)
Atty. General: Steven L. Beshear, D (to Jan. 1984)
Entered Union & (rank): June 1, 1792 (15)
Present constitution adopted: 1891
Motto: United we stand, divided we fall
State tree: Coffeetree
State flower: Goldenrod
State bird: Kentucky cardinal
State song: "My Old Kentucky Home"
Nickname: Bluegrass State
Origin of name: From an Iroquoian word "Ken-tah-ten" meaning "land of tomorrow"
1980 population (1980 census) & (rank): 3,660,257 (23)
1981 population (prov.) & (rank): 3,662,000 (23)
1980 land area & (rank): 39,669 sq mi. (102,743 sq km) (37)
Geographic center: In Marion Co., 3 mi. NNW of Lebanon
Number of counties: 120
Largest cities (1980 census): Louisville, 298,840; Lexington, 204,165; Owensboro, 54,450; Covington, 49,563; Bowling Green, 40,450; Paducah, 29,315; Hopkinsville, 27,318
State forests: 9 (44,173 ac.)
State parks: 43 (40,574 ac.)
Total state revenue (1980–81): $3,960,230,000[2]
Total state expenditure (1980–81): $4,055,862,000[1]

1. Figures taken from Kentucky's Financial Report for fiscal year ending June 30, 1980. 2. Five operating funds only.

Kentucky was the first region west of the Allegheny Mountains settled by American pioneers. James Harrod established the first permanent settlement at Harrodsburg in 1774; the following year Daniel Boone, who had explored the area in 1767, blazed the Wilderness Trail and founded Boonesboro.

Politically, the Kentucky region was originally part of Virginia, but early statehood was gained in 1792.

During the Civil War, as a slaveholding state with a considerable abolitionist population, Kentucky was caught in the middle of the conflict, supplying both Union and Confederate forces with thousands of troops.

In recent years, manufacturing has shown important gains, but agriculture and mining are still vital to Kentucky's economy. Kentucky prides itself on producing some of the nation's best tobacco, horses, and whiskey. Corn, soybeans, wheat, fruit, hogs, cattle, and dairy farming are also important.

Among the manufactured items produced in the state are furniture, aluminum ware, brooms, shoes, lumber products, machinery, textiles, and iron and steel products. Kentucky also produces significant amounts of petroleum, natural gas, fluorspar, clay, and stone. However, coal accounts for 90% of the total mineral income.

Louisville, the largest city, famed for the Kentucky Derby at Churchill Downs, is also the location of a large state university, whiskey distilleries, and cigarette factories. The Bluegrass country around Lexington is the home of some of the world's finest race horses. Other attractions are Mammoth Cave, the George S. Patton, Jr., Military Museum at Fort Knox, and Old Fort Harrod State Park.

LOUISIANA

Capital: Baton Rouge
Governor: David C. Treen, R (to March 1984)
Lieut. Governor: Robert L. Freeman, D (to March 1984)
Secy. of State: James H. Brown, Jr., D (to March 1984)
Treasurer: Mary Evelyn Parker, D (to March 1984)
Atty. General: William J. Guste, Jr., D (to March 1984)
Organized as territory: March 26, 1804
Entered Union & (rank): April 30, 1812 (18)
Present constitution adopted: 1974
Motto: Union, justice, and confidence
State flower: Magnolia (1900)
State tree: Bald cypress
State bird: Pelican
State song: "Give Me Louisiana," and "You Are My Sunshine"
Nicknames: Pelican State; Sportsman's Paradise; Creole State; Sugar State
Origin of name: In honor of Louis XIV of France
1980 population (1980 census) & (rank): 4,206,312 (19)
1981 population (prov.) & (rank): 4,308,000 (18)

1980 land area & (rank): 44,521 sq mi. (115,310 sq km) (33)
Geographic center: In Avoyelles Parish, 3 mi. SE of Marksville
Number of parishes (counties): 64
Largest cities (1980 census): New Orleans, 557,927; Baton Rouge, 219,419; Shreveport, 205,820; Lafayette, 81,961; Lake Charles, 75,226; Monroe, 57,597; Alexandria, 51,565
State forests: 1 (8,000 ac.)
State parks: 30 (13,932 ac.)
State general revenue (1982–83 est.): $5,300,000,000
Capital outlay: $1,100,000,000 (1982–83 est.)
State general expenditure (1982–83 est.): $5,300,000,000

Louisiana has a rich, colorful historical background. Early Spanish explorers were Piñeda, 1519; Cabeza de Vaca, 1528; and de Soto in 1541. La Salle reached the mouth of the Mississippi and claimed all the land drained by it and its tributaries for Louis XIV of France in 1682.

Louisiana became a French crown colony in 1731, was ceded to Spain in 1763, returned to France in 1800, and sold by Napoleon to the U.S. as part of the Louisiana Purchase (with large territories to the north and northwest) in 1803.

In 1815, Gen. Andrew Jackson's troops defeated a larger British army in the Battle of New Orleans, neither side aware that the treaty ending the War of 1812 had been signed.

As to total value of its mineral output, Louisiana is a leader in natural gas, salt, petroleum, and sulfur production. Much of the oil and sulfur comes from offshore deposits. The state also produces large crops of sweet potatoes, rice, sugarcane, pecans, soybeans, corn, and cotton.

Leading manufactures include chemicals, processed food, petroleum and coal products, paper, lumber and wood products, transportation equipment, and apparel.

Louisiana marshes supply most of the nation's muskrat fur as well as that of opossum, raccoon, mink, and otter, and large numbers of game birds.

Major points of interest include New Orleans with its French Quarter and Superdome, plantation homes near Natchitoches and New Iberia, Cajun country in the Mississippi delta region, Chalmette National Historical Park, and the state capital at Baton Rouge.

MAINE

Capital: Augusta
Governor: Joseph E. Brennan, D (to Jan. 1983)
Secy. of State: Rodney F. Quinn, D (to Jan. 1983)
Controller: Donald A. Brown (term indefinite)
Atty. General: James Tierney, D (to Jan. 1983)
Entered Union & (rank): March 15, 1820 (23)
Present constitution adopted: 1820
Motto: *Dirigo* (I direct)
State flower: White pine cone and tassel (1895)
State tree: White pine tree (1945)
State bird: Chickadee (1927)
State fish: Landlocked salmon (1969)
State mineral: Tourmaline (1971)
State song: "State of Maine Song" (1937)
Nickname: Pine Tree State
Origin of name: First used to distinguish the mainland from the offshore islands. It has been considered a compliment to Henrietta Maria, Queen of Charles I of England. She was said to have owned the province of Mayne in France.
1980 population (1980 census) & (rank): 1,125,027 (38)
1981 population (prov.) & (rank): 1,133,000 (38)
1980 land area & (rank): 30,995 sq mi. (80,277 sq km) (39)
Geographic center: In Piscataquis Co., 18 mi. N of Dover-Foxcroft
Number of counties: 16
Largest cities (1980 census): Portland, 61,572; Lewiston, 40,481; Bangor, 31,643; Auburn, 23,128; South Portland, 22,712; Augusta, 21,819; Biddeford, 19,638
State forests: 1 (21,000 ac.)
State parks: 26 (247,627 ac.)
State historic sites: 18 (403 ac.)
State total revenue (1981): $1,246,329,521
State total expenditure (1981): $1,234,482,878

John Cabot and his son, Sebastian, are believed to have visited the Maine coast in 1498. However, the first permanent English settlements were not established until more than a century later, in 1623.

The first naval action of the Revolutionary War occurred in 1775 when colonials captured the British sloop *Margaretta* off Machias on the Maine coast. In that same year, the British burned Falmouth (now Portland).

Long governed by Massachusetts, Maine became the 23rd state as part of the Missouri Compromise in 1820.

Maine produced 26.5 million hundred weight of potatoes or 9.4% of the national production in 1981 and 95% of the nation's low-bush blueberries. Farm income is also derived from apples, sweet corn, peas, and beans, with poultry and eggs the largest items.

The state is one of the world's largest pulp-paper producers. It ranks fifth in boot-and-shoe manufacturing. With more than 90% of its area forested, Maine turns out wood products from boats to toothpicks.

Maine leads the world in the production of the familiar flat tins of sardines, producing more than 100 million of them annually. Lobstermen normally catch 80–90% of the nation's true total of lobsters.

A scenic seacoast, beaches, lakes, mountains, and resorts make Maine a popular vacationland. There are more than 2,500 lakes and 5,000 streams, plus 26 state parks, to attract hunters, fishermen, skiers, and campers.

Major points of interest are: Bar Harbor, Allagash National Wilderness Waterway, the Wadsworth-Longfellow House in Portland, Roosevelt Campobello International Park, and the St. Croix Island National Monument.

MARYLAND

Capital: Annapolis
Governor: Harry Hughes, D (to Jan. 1983)
Lieut. Gov.: Samuel W. Bogley, D (to Jan. 1983)
Secy. of State: Fred L. Wineland, D (appointed by governor)
Comptroller of the Treasury: Louis L. Goldstein, D (to Jan. 1983)
Treasurer: William S. James, D (to Jan. 1983)
Atty. General: Stephen H. Sachs, D (to Jan. 1983)
Entered Union & (rank): April 28, 1788 (7)
Present constitution adopted: 1867
Motto: *Fatti maschii, parole femine* (Manly deeds, womanly words)
State flower: Black-eyed susan (1918)
State tree: White oak (1941)
State bird: Baltimore oriole (1947)

State dog: Chesapeake Bay retriever (1964)
State fish: Rockfish (1965)
State insect: Baltimore checkerspot butterfly (1973)
State sport: Jousting (1962)
State song: "Maryland! My Maryland!" (1939)
Nicknames: Free State; Old Line State
Origin of name: In honor of Henrietta Maria (Queen of Charles I of England)
1980 population (1980 census) & (rank): 4,216,975 (18)
1981 population (prov.) & (rank): 4,263,000 (19)
1980 land area & (rank): 9,837 sq mi. (25,477 sq km) (42)
Geographic center: In Prince Georges Co., 4½ mi. NW of Davidsonville
Number of counties: 23, and 1 independent city
Largest cities (1980 census): Baltimore, 786,775; Rockville, 43,811; Hagerstown, 34,132; Bowie, 33,695; Annapolis, 31,740; Frederick, 28,086; Gaithersburg, 26,424
State forests: 10 (120,921 ac.)
State parks: 42 (70,302 ac.)
State general revenue (1982 est.): $2,915,196,000
State general expenditure (1982 est.): $2,925,379,870

In 1608, Chesapeake Bay was explored by Capt. John Smith. Charles I granted a royal charter to Cecil Calvert, Lord Baltimore, in 1632 and English Roman Catholics landed on St. Clement's (now Blakistone Island) in 1634. Religious freedom, granted all Christians in the Toleration act passed by the Maryland assembly in 1649, was ended by a Puritan revolt, 1654–58.

In 1814, when the British unsuccessfully tried to capture Baltimore, the bombardment of Fort McHenry inspired Francis Scott Key to write *The Star Spangled Banner.*

Maryland is almost cut in two by the Chesapeake Bay, and the many estuaries and rivers create one of the longest waterfronts of any state. The Bay produces more seafood—oysters, crabs, clams, fin fish—than any comparable body of water. Important agricultural products, in order of cash value, are chickens, dairy products, corn, cattle, tobacco, and vegetables. Maryland is a leader in vegetable canning. Sand, gravel, lime and cement, stone, coal, and clay are the chief mineral products.

Manufacturing industries produce missiles, airplanes, steel, clothing, and chemicals. Baltimore, home of The Johns Hopkins University and Hospital, ranks as the nation's second port in foreign tonnage. Annapolis, site of the U.S. Naval Academy, has one of the earliest state houses (1772–79) still in regular use by a State government.

Among the popular attractions in Maryland are the Fort McHenry National Monument, Harpers Ferry and Chesapeake and Ohio Canal National Historical Parks, St. Marys City restoration near Leonardtown, USS *Constellation* at Baltimore, U.S. Naval Academy in Annapolis, Assateague Island National Seashore, and Catoctin Mountain and Piscataway parks.

MASSACHUSETTS

Capital: Boston
Governor: Edward King, D (to Jan. 1983)
Lieut. Governor: Thomas P. O'Neill III, D (to Jan. 1983)
Secy. of the Commonwealth: Michael Joseph Connolly, D (to Jan. 1983)
Treasurer & Receiver-General: Robert Q. Crane, D (to Jan. 1983)
Auditor of the Commonwealth: John J. Finnegan, D (to Jan. 1983)
Atty. General: Francis X. Bellotti (to Jan. 1983)
Entered Union & (rank): Feb. 6, 1788 (6)
Motto: *Ense petit placidam sub libertate quietem* (By the sword we seek peace, but peace only under liberty)
State flower: Mayflower (1918)
State tree: American elm (1941)
State bird: Chickadee (1941)
State colors: Blue and gold
State song: "All Hail to Massachusetts" (1966)
State beverage: Cranberry juice (1970)
State horse: Morgan horse (1970)
State insect: Ladybug (1974)
Nicknames: Bay State; Old Colony State
Origin of name: From two Indian words meaning "Great mountain place"
1981 population (prov.) & (rank): 5,773,000 (11)
1980 land area & (rank): 7,824 sq mi. (20,265 sq km) (45)
Geographic center: In Worcester Co., in S part of city of Worcester
Number of counties: 14
Largest cities (1980 census): Boston, 562,994; Worcester, 161,799; Springfield, 152,319; New Bedford, 98,478; Cambridge, 95,322; Brockton, 95,172; Fall River, 94,574
State forests and parks: 129 (242,000 ac.)[1]
State general revenue (1980–81): $6,704,700,000
State general expenditure (1980–81): $6,769,100,000

1. The Metropolitan District Commission, an agency of the Commonwealth serving municipalities in the Boston area, has about 14,000 acres of parkways and reservations under its jurisdiction.

Massachusetts has played a significant role in American history since the Pilgrims, seeking religious freedom, founded Plymouth Colony in 1620.

As one of the most important of the 13 colonies, Massachusetts became a leader in resisting British oppression. In 1773, the Boston Tea Party protested unjust taxation. The Minutemen started the American Revolution by battling British troops at Lexington and Concord on April 19, 1775.

During the 19th century, Massachusetts was famous for the vigorous intellectual activity of famous writers and educators and for its expanding commercial fishing, shipping, and manufacturing interests.

Massachusetts pioneered in the manufacture of textiles and shoes. Today, these industries have been replaced in importance by activity in the electronics and communications equipment fields.

The state's cranberry crop is the nation's largest. Also important are dairy and poultry products, nursery and greenhouse produce, vegetables, and fruit.

Tourism has become an important factor in the economy of the state because of its numerous recreational areas and historical landmarks.

Cape Cod has summer theaters, water sports, and an artists' colony at Provincetown. Tanglewood, in the Berkshires, features the summer concerts of the Boston Symphony.

Among the many other points of interest are Old Sturbridge Village, Minute Man National Historical Park between Lexington and Concord, and, in Boston: Old North Church, Old State House, Faneuil Hall, the USS *Constitution* and the John F. Kennedy Library.

MICHIGAN

Capital: Lansing
Governor: William C. Milliken, R (to Jan. 1983)
Lieut. Governor: James H. Brickley, R (to Jan. 1983)

Secy. of State: Richard H. Austin, D (to Jan. 1983)
Atty. General: Frank J. Kelley, D (to Jan. 1983)
Organized as territory: Jan. 11, 1805
Entered Union & (rank): Jan. 26, 1837 (26)
Present constitution adopted: April 1, 1963, (effective Jan. 1, 1964)
Motto: *Si quaeris peninsulam amoenam circumspice* (If you seek a pleasant peninsula, look around you)
State flower: Apple blossom (1897)
State bird: Robin
State fish: Brook trout (1965)
State gem: Isle Royal Greenstone (Chlorastrolite) (1972)
State stone: Petoskey stone (1965)
Nickname: Wolverine State
Origin of name: From two Indian words meaning "great lake"
1980 population (1980 census) & (rank): 9,262,078 (8)
1981 population (prov.) & (rank): 9,204,000 (8)
1980 land area & (rank): 56,954 sq mi. (147,511 sq km) (22)
Geographic center: In Wexford Co., 5 mi. NNW of Cadillac
Number of counties: 83
Largest cities (1980 census): Detroit, 1,203,339; Grand Rapids, 181,843; Warren, 161,134; Flint, 159,611; Lansing, 130,414; Sterling Heights, 108,999; Ann Arbor, 107,966
State forests: 33 (3,762,184 ac.)
State parks and recreation areas: 92 (216,857 ac.)
State general revenue (1980): $9,518,130,000
State general expenditure (1980): $9,933,024,000

Indian tribes were living in the Michigan region when the first European, Étienne Brulé of France, arrived in 1618. Other French explorers, including Marquette, Jolliet, and La Salle, followed, and the first permanent settlement was established in 1668 at Sault Ste. Marie. France was ousted from the territory by Great Britain in 1763, following the French and Indian War.

After the Revolutionary War, the U.S. acquired most of the region, which remained the scene of constant conflict between the British and U.S. forces and their respective Indian allies through the War of 1812.

Bordering on four of the five Great Lakes, Michigan is divided into Upper and Lower Peninsulas by the Straits of Mackinac, which link Lakes Michigan and Huron. The two parts of the state are connected by the Mackinac Bridge, one of the world's longest suspension bridges. To the north, connecting Lakes Superior and Huron are the busy Sault Ste. Marie Canals.

While Michigan ranks first among the states in production of motor vehicles and parts, it is also a leader in many other manufacturing and processing lines including prepared cereals, machine tools, airplane parts, refrigerators, hardware, steel springs, and furniture.

The state produces important amounts of iron, copper, iodine, gypsum, bromine, salt, lime, gravel, and cement. Michigan's farms grow apples, cherries, pears, grapes, potatoes, and sugar beets and the annual value of its forest products is estimated at $2 billion. With over 36,000 miles of streams, some 11,000 lakes, and a 2,000 mile shoreline, Michigan is a prime area for both commercial and sport fishing.

Points of interest are the automobile plants in Dearborn, Detroit, Flint, Lansing, and Pontiac; Mackinac Island; Pictured Rocks and Sleeping Bear Dunes National Lakeshores, Greenfield Village near Dearborn; and the many summer resorts along both the inland and Great Lakes.

MINNESOTA

Capital: St. Paul
Governor: Albert H. Quie, R (to Jan. 1983)
Lieut. Governor: Lou Wangberg, R (to Jan. 1983)
Secy. of State: Joan Grow (to Jan. 1983)
State Auditor: Arne Carlson, R (to Jan. 1983)
Atty. General: Warren Spannus, D (to Jan. 1983)
State Treasurer: Jim Lord (to Jan. 1983)
Organized as territory: March 3, 1849
Entered Union & (rank): May 11, 1858 (32)
Present constitution adopted: 1858
Motto: L'Etoile du Nord (The North Star)
State flower: Showy lady slipper (1902)
State tree: Red (or Norway) pine
State bird: Common loon (also called Great Northern Diver)
State song: "Hail Minnesota"
Nicknames: North Star State; Gopher State; Land of 10,000 Lakes
Origin of name: From a Dakota Indian word meaning "sky-tinted water"
1980 population (1980 census) & (rank): 4,075,970 (21)
1981 population (prov.) & (rank): 4,094,000 (21)
1980 land area & (rank): 79,548 sq mi. (206,030 sq km) (14)
Geographic center: In Crow Wing Co., 10 mi. SW of Brainerd
Number of counties: 87
Largest cities (1980 census): Minneapolis, 370,951; St. Paul, 270,230; Duluth, 92,811; Bloomington, 81,831; Rochester, 57,890; Edina, 46,073
State forests: 55 (2,984,000 ac.)
State parks: 92 (202,205 ac.)
Total revenue (Fiscal 1981): $5,301,932,000
Total expenditures (Fiscal 1981): $5,663,877,000

Following the visits of several French explorers, fur traders, and missionaries, including Marquette and Jolliet and La Salle, the region was claimed for Louis XIV by Daniel Greysolon, Sieur Duluth, in 1679.

The U.S. acquired eastern Minnesota from Great Britain after the Revolutionary War and 20 years later bought the western part from France in the Louisiana Purchase of 1803. Much of the region was explored by U.S. Army Lt. Zebulon M. Pike before cession of the northern strip of Minnesota bordering Canada by Britain in 1818.

The state is rich in natural resources. A few square miles of land in the north in the Mesabi, Cuyuna, and Vermillion ranges, produce more than 60% of the nation's iron ore. The state's farms rank high in yields of corn, wheat, rye, alfalfa, and sugar beets. Other leading farm products include butter, eggs, milk, potatoes, green peas, barley, and livestock.

Minnesota's factory production includes nonelectrical machinery, fabricated metals, flour-mill products, plastics, electronic computers, scientific instruments, and processed foods.

Minneapolis is the trade center of the Northwest; St. Paul is the nation's biggest publisher of calendars and law books. These "twin cities" are the nation's third largest trucking center. Duluth has the nation's largest inland harbor and now handles a significant amount of foreign trade. Rochester is the home of the Mayo Clinic, an internationally famous medical center.

Today, tourism is a major revenue producer in Minnesota, with fishing, hunting, water sports, and winter sports bringing in millions of visitors each year.

Among the most popular attractions are the St.

Paul Winter Carnival; the Tyrone Guthrie Theatre, the Institute of Arts, Walker Art Center, and Minnehaha Park, in Minneapolis; Voyageurs National Park; North Shore Drive; and the Minnesota Zoological Gardens.

MISSISSIPPI

Capital: Jackson
Governor: William F. Winter, D (to Jan. 1984)
Lieut. Governor: Brad Dye, D (to Jan. 1984)
Secy. of State: Edwin Lloyd Pittman, D (to Jan. 1984)
Treasurer: Bill Cole, D (to Jan. 1984)
Atty. General: William A. (Bill) Allain (to Jan. 1984)
Organized as Territory: April 7, 1798
Entered Union & (rank): Dec. 10, 1817 (20)
Present constitution adopted: 1890
Motto: *Virtute et armis* (By valor and arms)
State flower: Flower or bloom of the magnolia or evergreen magnolia (1952)
State tree: Magnolia (1938)
State bird: Mockingbird (1944)
State song: "Go, Mississippi" (1962)
Nickname: Magnolia State
Origin of name: From an Indian word meaning "Father of Waters"
1980 population (1980 census) & (rank): 2,520,638 (31)
1981 population (prov.) & (rank): 2,531,000 (31)
1980 land area & (rank): 47,233 sq mi. (122,333 sq km) (31)
Geographic center: In Leake Co., 9 mi. WNW of Carthage
Number of counties: 82
Largest cities (1980 census): Jackson, 202,895; Biloxi, 49,311; Hattiesburg, 40,829; Greenville, 40,613; Gulfport, 39,676; Pascagoula, 29,318
State forests: 1 (1,760 ac.)
State parks: 27 (16,763 ac.)
State general and special revenue (1981): $3,534,454,391
State general and special expenditure (1981): $3,540,451,335

First explored for Spain by Hernando de Soto who discovered the Mississippi River in 1540, the region was later claimed by France. In 1699, a French group under Sieur d'Iberville established the first permanent settlement near present-day Biloxi.

Great Britain took over the area in 1763 after the French and Indian War, ceding it to the U.S. in 1783 after the Revolution. Spain did not relinquish its claims until 1798, and in 1810 the U.S. annexed West Florida from Spain, including what is now southern Mississippi.

Mississippi, the stronghold of the Old South, has until the past decade been one of the least industrialized states, with more than half its population making a living from the soil. However, a recent industrialization program has attracted manufacturing industries such as lumber, furniture, paper, food processing, apparel, chemicals, transportation equipment, and machinery.

Cotton, nevertheless, is still king with the state ranking second to Texas in cotton production, though soybeans have become Mississippi's largest crop. Other important farm products are corn, peanuts, pecans, rice, sugarcane, sweet potatoes, and hay. Poultry and eggs are also important.

The state abounds in historical landmarks and is the home of the Vicksburg National Military Park where visitors may see the remains of forts, trenches, and other military relics used in the 1863 Union-army siege of the city. Other National Park Service areas are Brices Cross Roads National Battlefield Site, Tupelo National Battlefield, and part of Natchez Trace National Parkway. Pre-Civil War mansions are the special pride of Natchez, Oxford, Hattiesburg, and Jackson.

MISSOURI

Capital: Jefferson City
Governor: Christopher S. Bond, R (to Jan. 1985)
Lieut. Governor: Kenneth J. Rothman, D (to Jan. 1985)
Secy. of State: James C. Kirkpatrick, D (to Jan. 1985)
Auditor: James F. Antonio, R (to Jan. 1983)
Treasurer: Mel Carnahan, D (to Jan. 1985)
Atty. General: John D. Ashcroft, R (to Jan. 1985)
Organized as territory: June 4, 1812
Entered Union & (rank): Aug. 10, 1821 (24)
Present constitution adopted: 1945
Motto: *Salus populi suprema lex esto* (The welfare of the people shall be the supreme law)
State flower: Hawthorn (1923)
State bird: Bluebird (1927)
State colors: Red, white, and blue (1913)
State song: "Missouri Waltz" (1949)
State rock: Mozarkite (1967)
State mineral: Galena (1967)
Nickname: Show-me State
Origin of name: Named after a tribe called Missouri Indians. "Missouri" means "town of the large canoes."
1980 population (1980 census) & (rank): 4,916,759 (15)
1981 population (prov.) & (rank): 4,941,000 (15)
1980 land area & (rank): 68,945 sq mi. (178,568 sq km) (18)
Geographic center: In Miller Co., 20 mi. SW of Jefferson City
Number of counties: 114, plus 1 independent city
Largest cities (1980 census): St. Louis, 453,085; Kansas City, 448,159; Springfield, 133,116; Independence, 111,806; Columbia, 62,061; Florissant, 55,372
State forests and Tower sites: 93 (265,000 ac.)
State parks: 71 (97,314 ac.)[1]
State cash receipts (1981): $3,641,104,829
State general expenditure (1981): $3,868,163,594

1. Includes 24 historic sites and 1 archaeological site.

De Soto visited the Missouri area in 1541. France's claim to the entire region was based on La Salle's travels in 1682. French fur traders established Ste. Genevieve in 1735 and St. Louis was first settled in 1764.

The U.S. gained Missouri from France as part of the Louisiana Purchase in 1803, and the territory was admitted as a state following the Missouri Compromise of 1820. Throughout the pre-Civil War period and during the war, Missourians were sharply divided in their opinions about slavery and in their allegiances, supplying both Union and Confederate forces with troops. However, the state itself remained in the Union.

Historically, Missouri played a leading role as a gateway to the West, St. Joseph being the eastern starting point of the Pony Express, while the much-traveled Santa Fe and Oregon Trails began in Independence. Now a popular vacationland, Missouri has 11 major lakes and numerous fishing streams, springs, and caves. Bagnell Dam, across the Osage River in the Ozarks, completed in 1931, created one of the largest man-made lakes in the world, covering 65,000 acres of surface area.

Manufacturing, paced by the aerospace industry, provides more income and jobs than any other segment of the economy. Missouri is also a leading producer of transportation equipment, shoes, lead, and beer. Among the major crops are corn, soybeans, wheat, oats, barley, potatoes, tobacco, and cotton.

Points of interest include Mark Twain's boyhood home and Mark Twain Cave (Hannibal), the Harry S. Truman Library and Museum (Independence), the house where Jesse James was killed in St. Joseph, Jefferson National Expansion Memorial (St. Louis), and the Ozark National Scenic Riverway.

MONTANA

Capital: Helena
Governor: Ted Schwinden, D (to Jan. 1985)
Lieut. Governor: George Turman, D (to Jan. 1985)
Secy. of State: Jim Waltermire, R (to Jan. 1985)
Auditor: E. V. "Sonny" Omholt, R (to Jan. 1983)
Atty. General: Michael Greely, D (to Jan. 1985)
Organized as territory: May 26, 1864
Entered Union & (rank): Nov. 8, 1889 (41)
Present constitution adopted: 1972
Motto: *Oro y plata* (Gold and silver)
State flower: Bitterroot (1895)
State tree: Ponderosa pine (1949)
State stones: Sapphire and agate (1969)
State bird: Western meadow lark (1931)
State song: "Montana" (1945)
Nickname: Treasure State
Origin of name: Chosen from Latin dictionary by J. M. Ashley. It is a Latinized Spanish word.
1981 population (prov.) & (rank): 793,000 (44)
1980 land area & (rank): 145,392 sq mi. (376,564 sq km) (4)
Geographic center: In Fergus Co., 12 mi. W of Lewistown
Number of counties: 56, plus small part of Yellowstone National Park
Largest cities (1980 census): Billings, 66,824; Great Falls, 56,725; Butte-Silver Bow, 37,205; Missoula, 33,388; Helena, 23,938; Bozeman, 21,645; Havre, 10,891
State forests: 7 (214,000 ac.)
State parks and recreation areas: 77 (18,273 ac.)
State general revenue (1982–83): $342,800,000
State general expenditure (1982–83): $337,800,000

First explored for France by François and Louis-Joseph Verendrye in the early 1740s, much of the region was acquired by the U.S. from France as part of the Louisiana Purchase in 1803. Before western Montana was obtained from Great Britain in the Oregon Treaty of 1846, American trading posts and forts had been established in the territory.

The major Indian wars (1867–1877) included the famous 1876 Battle of the Little Big Horn, better known as "Custer's Last Stand," in which Cheyennes and Sioux killed George A. Custer and more than 200 of his men in southeastern Montana.

Much of Montana's early history was concerned with mining with copper, lead, zinc, silver, coal, and oil as principal products.

Butte, sitting on the "richest hill in the world," is the center of the area that once supplied half of the U.S. copper.

Fields of grain cover much of Montana's plains; it ranks high among the states in wheat and barley, with rye, oats, flaxseed, sugar beets, and potatoes other important crops. Sheep and cattle raising make significant contributions to the state's economy.

Tourist attractions include hunting, fishing, skiing, and dude ranching. Glacier National Park, on the Continental Divide, is a scenic and vacation wonderland with 60 glaciers, 200 lakes, and many streams with good trout fishing.

Other major points of interest include the Custer Battlefield National Monument, Virginia City, Yellowstone National Park, Museum of the Plains Indians at Browning, and the Fort Union Trading Post and Grant-Kohr's Ranch National Historic Sites.

NEBRASKA

Capital: Lincoln
Governor: Charles Thone, R (to Jan. 1983)
Lieut. Governor: Roland Luedtke, R (to Jan. 1983)
Secy. of State: Allen J. Beermann, R (to Jan. 1983)
Atty. General: Paul L. Douglas, R (to Jan. 1983)
Auditor: Ray A. C. Johnson, R (to Jan. 1983)
Treasurer: Frank Marsh, R (to Jan. 1983)
Organized as territory: May 30, 1854
Entered Union & (rank): March 1, 1867 (37)
Present constitution adopted: Nov. 1, 1875 (extensively amended 1919–20)
Motto: Equality before the law
State flower: Goldenrod (1895)
State tree: Cottonwood (1972)
State bird: Western meadow lark (1929)
State insect: Honey Bee (1975)
State gem stone: Blue agate (1967)
State rock: Prairie agate (1967)
State fossil: Mammoth (1967)
State song: "Beautiful Nebraska" (1967)
Nicknames: Cornhusker State; Beef State; Tree Planters State
Origin of name: From an Oto Indian word meaning "flat water"
1980 population (1980 census) & (rank): 1,570,006 (35)
1981 population (prov.) & (rank): 1,577,000 (35)
1980 land area & (rank): 76,644 sq mi. (198,508 sq km) (15)
Geographic center: In Custer Co., 10 mi. NW of Broken Bow
Number of counties: 93
Largest cities (1980 census): Omaha, 313,911; Lincoln, 171,932; Grand Island, 33,180; North Platte, 24,479; Fremont, 23,979; Hastings, 23,045; Bellevue, 21,813
State forests: None
State parks: 93 areas, 4 categories, 5 major areas
State general revenue (1980–81): $1,828,782,198
State general expenditure (1980–81): $1,495,152,499

French fur traders first visited Nebraska in the early 1700s. Part of the Louisiana Purchase in 1803, Nebraska was explored by Lewis and Clark in 1804–06.

Robert Stuart pioneered the Oregon Trail across Nebraska in 1812–13 and the first permanent settlement was established at Bellevue in 1823. Western Nebraska was acquired by treaty following the Mexican War in 1848. The Union Pacific began its transcontinental railroad at Omaha in 1865. In 1937, Nebraska became the only state in the Union to have a unicameral (one-house) legislature. Members are elected to it without party designation.

Nebraska is a leading grain-producer with bumper crops of rye, corn, and wheat. More varieties of grass, valuable for forage, grow in this state than in any other in the nation.

The state's sizable cattle and hog industries make

Omaha with its surrounding area the nation's largest meat-packing center and the second-largest cattle market in the world.

Manufacturing has become diversified in Nebraska, strengthening the state's economic base. Firms making electronic components, auto accessories, pharmaceuticals, and mobile homes have joined such older industries as clothing, farm machinery, chemicals, and transportation equipment. Oil was discovered in 1939 and natural gas in 1949.

Among the principal attractions are Agate Fossil Beds, Homestead, and Scotts Bluff National Monuments; Chimney Rock National Historic Site; a recreated pioneer village at Minden; the Union stockyards in Omaha; the Stuhr Museum of the Prairie Pioneer with 57 original 19th-century buildings near Grand Island; and the Sheldon Memorial Art Gallery at the University of Nebraska in Lincoln.

NEVADA

Capital: Carson City
Governor: Robert F. List, R (to Jan. 1983)
Lieut. Governor: Myron E. Leavitt, D (to Jan. 1983)
Secy. of State: Wm. D. Swackhamer, D (to Jan. 1983)
State Treasurer: Stan Colton, D (to Jan. 1983)
Controller: Wilson McGowan, R (to Jan. 1983)
Atty. General: Richard H. Bryan, D (to Jan. 1983)
Organized as territory: March 2, 1861
Entered Union & (rank): Oct. 31, 1864 (36)
Present constitution adopted: 1864
Motto: All for Our Country
State flower: Sagebrush (1967)
State tree: Single-leaf pinon (1953)
State bird: Mountain bluebird (1967)
State animal: Desert bighorn sheep (1973)
State colors: Silver and blue (unofficial)
State song: "Home Means Nevada" (1933)
Nicknames: Sagebrush State; Silver State; Battle-born State
Origin of name: Spanish: "snowcapped"
1980 population (1980 census) & (rank): 800,493 (43)
1981 population (prov.) & (rank): 845,000 (43)
1980 land area & (rank): 109,893 sq mi. (284,624 sq km) (7)
Geographic center: In Lander Co., 26 mi. SE of Austin
Number of counties: 16, plus 1 independent city
Largest cities (1980 census): Las Vegas, 164,674; Reno, 100,756; North Las Vegas, 42,739; Sparks, 40,780; Carson City, 32,022; Henderson, 24,363; Boulder City, 9,590
State forests: None
State parks: 20 (150,000 ac., including leased lands)
General fund revenue (1980–81): $342,440,681
General fund expenditure (1980–81): $347,505,475, made possible by surpluses from previous years.

Trappers and traders, including Jedediah Smith and Peter Skene Ogden, entered the Nevada area in the 1820s. In 1843–45, John C. Fremont and Kit Carson explored the Great Basin and Sierra Nevada.

In 1848 following the Mexican War, the U.S. obtained the region and the first permanent settlement was a Mormon trading post near present-day Genoa.

The driest state in the nation with an average annual rainfall of only 3.73 inches, much of Nevada is uninhabited, sagebrush-covered desert.

Nevada was made famous by the discovery of the fabulous Comstock Lode in 1859 and its mines have produced large quantities of gold, silver, copper, lead, zinc, mercury, barite, and tungsten. Oil was discovered in 1954. Copper now far exceeds all other minerals in value of production.

In 1931, the state created two industries, divorce and gambling. For many years, Reno and Las Vegas were the "divorce capitals of the nation." More liberal divorce laws in many states have ended this distinction, but Nevada is the gambling and entertainment capital of the U.S. State gambling taxes account for 45% of tax revenues. Although Nevada leads the nation in per capita gambling revenue, it ranks only fourth in total gambling revenue.

Near Las Vegas, on the Colorado River, stands Hoover Dam, which impounds the waters of Lake Mead, one of the world's largest artificial lakes.

The state's agricultural crop consists mainly of hay, alfalfa seed, barley, and wheat.

Nevada manufactures gaming devices, chemicals, forest products, suntan lotion, and stone-clay-glass products.

Major resort areas flourish in Lake Tahoe, Reno, and Las Vegas. Recreation areas include those at Pyramid Lake, Lake Tahoe, and Lake Mead and Lake Mohave, both in Lake Mead National Recreation Area. Among the other attractions are Hoover Dam, Virginia City, and Lehman Caves National Monument.

NEW HAMPSHIRE

Capital: Concord
Governor: Hugh Gallen, D (to Jan. 1983)
Secy. of State: William M. Gardner, D (to Jan. 1983)
Comptroller: Michael R. Cornelius
Atty. General: Gregory Smith
Entered Union & (rank): June 21, 1788 (9)
Present constitution adopted: 1784
Motto: Live free or die
State flower: Purple lilac (1919)
State tree: White birch (1947)
State bird: Purple finch (1957)
State songs: "Old New Hampshire" (1949) and "New Hampshire, My New Hampshire" (1963)
Nickname: Granite State
Origin of name: From the English county of Hampshire
1980 population (1980 census) & (rank): 920,610 (42)
1981 population (prov.) & (rank): 936,000 (42)
1980 land area & (rank): 8,993 sq mi. (23,292 sq km) (44)
Geographic center: In Belknap Co., 3 mi. E of Ashland
Number of counties: 10
Largest cities (1980 census): Manchester, 90,936; Nashua, 67,865; Concord, 30,400; Portsmouth, 26,254; Dover, 22,377; Rochester, 21,560; Keene, 21,449
State forests & parks: 175 (96,975 ac.)
State revenue (1981): $652,939,551
State expenditure (1981): $922,570,399

Under an English land grant, Capt. John Smith sent settlers to establish a fishing colony at the mouth of the Piscataqua River, near present-day Rye and Dover, in 1623. Capt. John Mason, who participated in the founding of Portsmouth in 1630, gave New Hampshire its name.

After a 38-year period of union with Massachusetts, New Hampshire was made a separate royal colony in 1679. As leaders in the revolutionary cause, New Hampshire delegates received the honor of being the first to vote for the Declaration of Independence on July 4, 1776. New Hampshire is the only state that ever played host at the formal conclusion of a foreign war when, in 1905,

Portsmouth was the scene of the treaty ending the Russo-Japanese War.

Abundant water power early turned New Hampshire into an industrial state and manufacturing is the principal source of income in the state. The most important industrial products are leather goods, electrical and other machinery, textiles, and pulp and paper products.

Dairy and poultry farming and growing fruit, truck vegetables, corn, potatoes, and hay are the major agricultural pursuits.

Tourism, because of New Hampshire's scenic and recreational resources, now brings over $400 million into the state annually.

Vacation attractions include Lake Winnipesaukee, largest of 1,300 lakes and ponds; the 724,000-acre White Mountain National Forest; Daniel Webster's birthplace near Franklin; Strawberry Banke, restored building of the original settlement at Portsmouth; and the famous "Old Man of the Mountain" granite head profile, the state's official emblem, at Franconia.

NEW JERSEY

Capital: Trenton
Governor: Thomas H. Kean (to Jan. 1986)
Secy. of State: Jane Burgio (to Jan. 1986)
Treasurer: Kenneth Biederman (to Jan. 1986)
Atty. General: Irwin I. Kimmelman (to Jan. 1986)
Entered Union & (rank): Dec. 18, 1787 (3)
Present constitution adopted: 1947
Motto: Liberty and prosperity
State flower: Purple violet (1913)
State bird: Eastern goldfinch (1935)
State insect: Honeybee
State tree: Red oak (1950)
State animal: Horse (1977)
State colors: Buff and blue (1965)
State song: None
Nickname: Garden State
Origin of name: From the Channel Isle of Jersey
1980 population (1980 census) & (rank): 7,364,823 (9)
1982 population (prov.) & (rank): 7,404,000 (9)
1980 land area & (rank): 7,468 sq mi. (19,342 sq km) (46)
Geographic center: In Mercer Co., 5 mi. SE of Trenton
Number of counties: 21
Largest cities (1980 census): Newark, 329,248; Jersey City, 223,532; Paterson, 137,970; Elizabeth, 106,201; Trenton, 92,124; Camden, 84,910; Clifton, 77,690
State forests: 11
State parks: 40 (73,483 ac.)
State general revenue (Fiscal 1983): $4,513,911,273
State appropriations (Fiscal 1983): $6,181,906,985

New Jersey's early colonial history was involved with that of New York (New Netherlands), of which it was a part. One year after the Dutch surrender to England in 1664, New Jersey was organized as an English colony under Gov. Philip Carteret.

In the late 1600s the colony was divided between Carteret and William Penn; later it would be administered by the royal governor of New York. Finally, in 1738, New Jersey was separated from New York under its own royal governor, Lewis Morris.

Because of its key location between New York City and Philadelphia, New Jersey saw much fighting during the American Revolution.

Today, New Jersey, an area of wide industrial diversification, is known as the Crossroads of the East. Products from over 15,000 factories can be delivered overnight to almost 60 million people, representing 12 states and the District of Columbia. The greatest single industry is chemicals and New Jersey is one of the foremost research centers in the world. Many large oil refineries are located in northern New Jersey and other important manufactures are pharmaceuticals, instruments, machinery, electrical goods, and apparel.

Of the total land area, 43% is forested and about 24% is devoted to agriculture. The state ranks high in production of almost all garden vegetables. Tomatoes, asparagus, corn, and blueberries are important crops, and poultry farming and dairying make significant contributions to the state's economy.

Tourism is the second largest industry in New Jersey. The state has numerous resort areas on 127 miles of Atlantic coastline. In 1977, New Jersey voters approved legislation allowing legalized casino gambling in Atlantic City. Points of interest include the Walt Whitman House in Camden, the Delaware Water Gap, the Edison National Historic Site in West Orange, and Princeton University.

NEW MEXICO

Capital: Santa Fe
Governor: Bruce King, D (to Jan. 1983)
Lieut. Governor: Roberto A. Mondragon, D (to Jan. 1983)
Secy. of State: Shirley Hooper, D (to Jan. 1983)
Atty. General: Jeff Bingaman, D (to Jan. 1983)
State Auditor: Alvino E. Castillo, D (to Jan. 1983)
State Treasurer: Jan Alan Hartke, D (to Jan. 1983)
Commissioner of Public Lands: Alex J. Armijo, D (to Jan. 1983)
Organized as territory: Sept. 9, 1850
Entered Union & (rank): Jan. 6, 1912 (47)
Present constitution adopted: 1911
Motto: *Crescit eundo* (It grows as it goes)
State flower: Yucca (1927)
State tree: Pinon (1949)
State animal: Black bear (1963)
State bird: Roadrunner (1949)
State fish: Cutthroat trout (1955)
State vegetables: Chile and frijol (1965)
State gem: Turquoise (1967)
State colors: Red and yellow of old Spain (1925)
State song: "O Fair New Mexico" (1917)
Spanish language state song: "Asi Es Nuevo Mejico" (1971)
Nicknames: Land of Enchantment; Sunshine State
Origin of name: From the country of Mexico
1980 population (1980 census) & (rank): 1,302,981 (37)
1981 population (prov.) & (rank): 1,328,000 (37)
1980 land area & (rank): 121,335 sq mi. (314,258 sq km) (5)
Geographic center: In Torrance Co., 12 mi. SSW of Willard
Number of counties: 33
Largest cities (1980 census): Albuquerque, 331,767; Santa Fe, 48,953; Las Cruces, 45,086; Roswell, 39,676; Farmington, 31,222; Clovis, 31,194; Hobbs, 29,153
State-owned forested land: 933,000 ac.
State parks: 29 (105,012 ac.)
State general revenue (1982): $1,114,800,000
State general expenditure (1982): $1,130,200,000

Francisco Vásquez de Coronado, Spanish explorer searching for gold, traveled the region that became New Mexico in 1540–42. In 1598 the first Spanish settlement was established on the Rio

Grande River by Juan de Onate and in 1610 Santa Fe was founded and made the capital of New Mexico.

The U.S. acquired most of New Mexico in 1848, as a result of the Mexican War, and the remainder in the 1853 Gadsden Purchase. Union troops captured the territory from the Confederates during the Civil War. With the surrender of Geronimo in 1886, the Apache Wars and most of the Indian troubles in the area were ended.

Since 1945, New Mexico has been a leader in energy research and development with extensive experiments conducted at Los Alamos Scientific Laboratory and Sandia Laboratories in the nuclear, solar, and geothermal areas.

Minerals are the state's richest natural resource and New Mexico leads the U.S. in output of uranium and potassium salts. Petroleum, natural gas, copper, gold, silver, zinc, lead, and molybdenum also contribute heavily to the state's income.

The principal manufacturing industries include food products, chemicals, transportation equipment, lumber, electrical machinery, and stone-clay-glass products. More than two thirds of New Mexico's farm income comes from livestock products, especially sheep. Cotton, pecans, and sorghum are the most important field crops. Corn, peanuts, beans, onions, and lettuce are also grown.

Tourist attractions in New Mexico include the Carlsbad Caverns National Park, Inscription Rock at El Morro National Monument, the ruins at Fort Union, Billy the Kid mementos at Lincoln, and the White Sands and Gila Cliff Dwellings National Monuments.

NEW YORK

Capital: Albany
Governor: Hugh L. Carey, D (to Jan. 1983)
Lieut. Governor: Mario M. Cuomo, D (to Jan. 1983)
Secy. of State: Basil A. Paterson, D (to Jan. 1983)
Comptroller: Edward V. Regan, R (to Jan. 1983)
Atty. General: Robert Abrams, D (to Jan. 1983)
Entered Union & (rank): July 26, 1788 (11)
Present constitution adopted: 1777 (last revised 1938)
Motto: *Excelsior* (Ever upward)
State animal: Beaver (1975)
State fish: Brook trout (1975)
State gem: Garnet (1969)
State flower: Rose (1955)
State tree: Sugar maple (1956)
State bird: Bluebird
State song: "I Love New York" (1980)
Nickname: Empire State
Origin of name: In honor of the English Duke of York
1980 population (1980 census) & (rank): 17,558,072 (2)
1981 population (prov.) & (rank): 17,602,000 (2)
1980 land area & (rank): 47,377 sq mi. (122,707 sq km) (30)
Geographic center: In Madison Co., 12 mi. S of Oneida and 26 mi. SW of Utica
Number of counties: 62
Largest cities (1980 census): New York, 7,071,639; Buffalo, 357,870; Rochester, 241,741; Yonkers, 195,351; Syracuse, 170,105; Albany, 101,727; Utica, 75,632
State forest preserves: Adirondacks, 2,500,000 ac., Catskills, 250,000 ac.
State parks: 145 (more than 220,000 ac.)
State general fund income (1982–83): $17,369,000
State general fund outgo (1982–83): $17,369,000

Giovanni da Verrazano, Italian-born navigator sailing for France, discovered New York Bay in 1524. Henry Hudson, an Englishman employed by the Dutch, reached the bay and sailed up the river now bearing his name in 1609, the same year that northern New York was explored and claimed for France by Samuel de Champlain.

In 1624 the first permanent Dutch settlement was established at Fort Orange (now Albany); one year later Peter Minuit is said to have purchased Manhattan Island from the Indians for trinkets worth about $24 and founded the Dutch colony of New Amsterdam (now New York City), which was surrendered to the English in 1664.

For a short time, New York City was the U.S. capital and George Washington was inaugurated there as first President on April 30, 1789.

New York's extremely rapid commercial growth may be partly attributed to Governor De Witt Clinton, who pushed through the construction of the Erie Canal (Buffalo to Albany), which was opened in 1825. Today, the 559-mile Governor Thomas E. Dewey Thruway connects New York City with Buffalo and with Connecticut, Massachusetts, and Pennsylvania express highways. Two toll-free superhighways, the Adirondack Northway (linking Albany with the Canadian border) and the North-South-Expressway (crossing central New York from the Pennsylvania border to the Thousand Islands) have been opened.

New York, with the great metropolis of New York City, is the spectacular nerve center of the nation. It is a leader in manufacturing, foreign trade, commercial and financial transactions, book and magazine publishing, and theatrical production.

New York City is not only a national but an international leader. A leading seaport, its John F. Kennedy International Airport is one of the busiest airports in the world. The largest manufacturing center in the country, it had, in 1977, over 21,000 manufacturing establishments employing 610,000 persons and reported $14.6 billion of value added by manufacture. The apparel industry is the city's largest manufacturing employer, with printing and publishing second.

Nearly all the rest of the state's manufacturing is done on Long Island, along the Hudson River north to Albany and through the Mohawk Valley, Central New York, and Southern Tier regions to Buffalo. The St. Lawrence seaway and power projects have opened the North Country to industrial expansion and have given the state a second seacoast. In 1962, the Niagara power development was completed, giving the state the largest hydroelectric installation in the free world.

The state ranks second in the nation in manufacturing with 1,509,900 employees and $44.3 billion in value added by manufacture in 1977. The principal industries are machinery, printing and publishing, instruments, apparel, and food.

The convention and tourist business is one of the state's most important sources of income.

New York farms are famous for dairying, truck gardening, and the raising of potatoes, onions, cabbage, fruits, and poultry. The state is a leading wine producer.

Among the major points of interest are Castle Clinton, Fort Stanwix, and Statue of Liberty National Monuments; Niagara Falls; U.S. Military Academy at West Point; National Historic Sites that include homes of Franklin D. Roosevelt at Hyde Park and Theodore Roosevelt in Oyster Bay and New York City; National Memorials, including Grant's Tomb and Federal Hall in New York City;

Fort Ticonderoga; the Baseball Hall of Fame in Cooperstown; and the United Nations, skyscrapers, museums, theaters, and parks in New York City.

NORTH CAROLINA

Capital: Raleigh
Governor: James B. Hunt, Jr., D (to Jan. 1985)
Lieut. Governor: James C. Greene (to Jan. 1985)
Secy. of State: Thad Eure, D (to Jan. 1985)
Treasurer: Harlan E. Boyles (to Jan. 1985)
Auditor: Edward Renfrow, D (to Jan. 1985)
Atty. General: Rufus Edmisten, D (to Jan. 1985)
Entered Union & (rank): Nov. 21, 1789 (12)
Present constitution adopted: 1971
Motto: *Esse quam videri* (To be rather than to seem)
State flower: Dogwood (1941)
State tree: Pine (1963)
State bird: Cardinal (1943)
State mammal: Gray Squirrel (1969)
State insect: Honeybee (1973)
State Reptile: Turtle (1979)
State gem stone: Emerald (1973)
State shell: Scotch bonnet (1965)
State song: "The Old North State" (1927)
State colors: Red and blue (1945)
Nickname: Tar Heel State
Origin of name: In honor of Charles I of England
1980 population (1980 census) & (rank): 5,881,813 (10)
1981 population (prov.) & (rank): 5,953,000 (10)
1980 land area & (rank): 48,843 sq mi. (126,504 sq km) (29)
Geographic center: In Chatham Co., 10 mi. NW of Sanford
Number of counties: 100
Largest cities (1980 census): Charlotte, 314,447; Greensboro, 155,642; Raleigh, 150,255; Winston-Salem, 131,885; Durham, 100,538; High Point, 63,808
State forests: 1
State parks: 26 (115,051 ac.)
State revenues (1980–81): $3,431,000,000[1]
State expenditure (1980–81): $3,154,000,000[2]

1. Excludes all Federal revenues and expenditures. 2. All expenditures: operating, and capital improvements.

English colonists, sent by Sir Walter Raleigh, unsuccessfully attempted to settle Roanoke Island in 1585 and 1587. Virginia Dare, born there in 1587, was the first child of English parentage born in America.

In 1653 the first permanent settlements were established by English colonists from Virginia near the Roanoke and Chowan Rivers.

The region was established as an English proprietary colony in 1663–65 and its early history was the scene of Culpepper's Rebellion (1677), the Quaker-led Cary Rebellion of 1708, the Tuscarora Indian War in 1711–13, and many pirate raids.

During the American Revolution, there was relatively little fighting within the state, but many North Carolinians saw action elsewhere. Despite considerable pro-Union, anti-slavery sentiment, North Carolina joined the Confederacy.

North Carolina is the nation's largest furniture, tobacco, brick, and textile producer. It holds second place in the Southeast in population and first place in the value of its industrial and agricultural production. This production is highly diversified, with metalworking, chemicals, and paper constituting enormous industries. Tobacco, corn, cotton, hay, peanuts, and truck and vegetable crops are of major importance. It is the country's leading producer of mica and lithium.

Tourism is also important, with travelers and vacationers spending more than $1 billion annually in North Carolina. Sports include year-round golfing, skiing at mountain resorts, both fresh and salt water fishing, and hunting.

Among the major attractions are the Great Smoky Mountains, the Blue Ridge National Parkway, the Cape Hatteras and Cape Lookout National Seashores, the Wright Brothers National Memorial at Kitty Hawk, Guilford Courthouse and Moores Creek National Military Parks, Carl Sandburg's home near Hendersonville, and the Old Salem Restoration in Winston-Salem.

NORTH DAKOTA

Capital: Bismarck
Governor: Allen I. Olson, R (to Jan. 1985)
Lieut. Governor: Ernest M. Sands, R (to Jan. 1985)
Secy. of State: Ben Meier, R (to Jan. 1985)
Auditor: Robert W. Peterson, R (to Jan. 1985)
State Treasurer: John Lesmeister, R (to Jan. 1985)
Atty. General: Bob Wefald, R (to Jan. 1985)
Organized as territory: March 2, 1861
Entered Union & (rank): Nov. 2, 1889 (39)
Present constitution adopted: 1889
Motto: Liberty and union, now and forever: one and inseparable
State tree: American Elm (1947)
State bird: Western meadow lark (1947)
State song: "North Dakota Hymn" (1947)
Nickname: Sioux State; Flickertail State
Origin of name: From the Dakotah tribe, meaning "allies"
1980 population (1980 census) & (rank): 652,717 (46)
1981 population (prov.) & (rank): 658,000 (46)
1980 land area & (rank): 69,300 sq mi (179,486 sq km) (17)
Geographic center: In Sheridan Co., 5 mi. SW of McClusky
Number of counties: 53
Largest cities (1980 census): Fargo, 61,383; Bismarck, 44,485; Grand Forks, 43,765; Minot, 32,843; Jamestown, 16,280; Dickinson, 15,924; Mandan, 15,513
State forests: None
State parks: 14 (14,922.6 ac.)
Total state collections (1981): $540,498,551
Total state disbursements (1981): $436,960,041

North Dakota was explored in 1738–40 by French Canadians led by Vérendrye. In 1803, the U.S. acquired most of North Dakota from France in the Louisiana Purchase. Lewis and Clark explored the region in 1804–06 and the first settlements were made at Pembina in 1812 by Scottish and Irish families while this area was still in dispute between the U.S. and Great Britian.

In 1818, the U.S. obtained the northeastern part of North Dakota by treaty with Great Britain and took possession of Pembina in 1823.

North Dakota is the most rural of all the states, with farms covering more than 90% of the land. Only Kansas produces more wheat and the state's coal and oil reserves are plentiful.

Other agricultural products include barley, rye, oats and flaxseed, sugar beets, and hay; beef cattle, sheep, and hogs are also important to the state's economy.

Recently, manufacturing industries have grown, especially food processing and farm equipment. The state also produces natural gas, lignite, salt, clay, sand, and gravel.

The Garrison Dam on the Missouri River provides extensive irrigation and produces 400,000 kilowatts of electricity for the Missouri Basin areas.

Known for its waterfowl, grouse, and deer hunting and bass, trout, and northern pike fishing, North Dakota has 20 state parks and recreation areas. Points of interest include the International Peace Garden near Dunseith, Fort Union Trading Post National Historic Site, the State Capitol at Bismarck, the Badlands, and Fort Lincoln, now a state park, from which Gen. George Custer set out on his last campaign in 1876.

OHIO

Capital: Columbus
Governor: James A. Rhodes, R (to Jan. 1983)
Lieut. Governor: (Vacant)
Secy. of State: Anthony J. Celebrezze, Jr., D (to Jan. 1983)
Auditor: Thomas E. Ferguson (to Jan. 1983)
Treasurer: Gertrude W. Donahey, D (to Jan. 1983)
Atty. General: William J. Brown, D (to Jan. 1983)
Entered Union & (rank): March 1, 1803 (17)
Present constitution adopted: 1851
Motto: With God, all things are possible
State flower: Scarlet carnation (1904)
State tree: Buckeye (1953)
State bird: Cardinal (1933)
State insect: Ladybug (1975)
State gem stone: Flint (1965)
State song: "Beautiful Ohio"
State drink: Tomato juice (1965)
Nickname: Buckeye State
Origin of name: From an Iroquoian word meaning "great river"
1980 population (1980 census) & (rank): 10,797,624 (6)
1981 population (prov.) & (rank): 10,781,000 (6)
1980 land area & (rank): 41,004 sq mi. (106,201 sq km) (35)
Geographic center: In Delaware Co., 25 mi. NNE of Columbus
Number of counties: 88
Largest cities (1980 census): Cleveland, 573,822; Columbus, 565,032; Cincinnati, 385,457; Toledo, 354,635; Akron, 237,177; Dayton, 203,371; Youngstown, 115,436
State forests: 19 (172,744 ac.)
State parks: 71 (198,027 ac.)
State actual revenue (1980–81): $9,270,217,623
State actual expenditure (1980–81): $9,334,355,300

First explored for France by La Salle in 1669, the Ohio region became British property after the French and Indian War. Ohio was acquired by the U.S. after the Revolutionary War in 1783 and, in 1788, the first permanent settlement was established at Marietta, capital of the Northwest Territory.

The 1790s saw severe fighting with the Indians in Ohio; a major battle was won by Maj. Gen. Anthony Wayne at Fallen Timbers in 1794. In the War of 1812, Commodore Oliver H. Perry defeated the British in the Battle of Lake Erie on Sept. 10, 1813.

Ohio is one of the nation's industrial leaders, ranking third in the value of manufactured products. Important manufacturing centers are located in or near Ohio's major cities. Akron is known for rubber; Canton for roller bearings; Cincinnati for jet engines and machine tools; Cleveland for auto assembly and parts, refining, and steel; Dayton for office machines, refrigeration, and heating and auto equipment; Youngstown and Steubenville for steel; and Toledo for glass and auto parts.

The state's thousands of factories almost overshadow its importance in agriculture and mining. Its fertile soil produces soybeans, corn, oats, grapes, and clover. More than half of Ohio's farm receipts come from dairying and sheep and hog raising. Ohio is the top state in lime production and among the leaders in coal, clay, salt, sand, and gravel. Petroleum, gypsum, cement, and natural gas are also important.

Tourism is a valuable revenue producer, bringing in over $3 billion annually. Attractions include the Indian burial grounds at Mound City Group National Monument, Perry's Victory International Peace Memorial, the Pro Football Hall of Fame at Canton, and the homes of Presidents Grant, Taft, Hayes, Harding, and Garfield.

OKLAHOMA

Capital: Oklahoma City
Governor: George P. Nigh, D (to Jan. 1983)
Lieut. Governor: Spencer Bernard, D (to Jan. 1983)
Secy. of State: Jeannette Edmondson, D (to Jan. 1983)
Treasurer: Leo Winters, D (to Jan. 1983)
Atty. General: Jan Eric Cartwright, D (to Jan. 1983)
Organized as territory: May 2, 1890
Entered Union & (rank): Nov. 16, 1907 (46)
Present constitution adopted: 1907
Motto: *Labor omnia vincit* (Labor conquers all things)
State flower: Mistletoe (1893)
State tree: Redbud (1937)
State bird: Scissor-tailed flycatcher (1951)
State animal: Bison (1972)
State reptile: Mountain boomer lizard (1969)
State stone: Rose Rock (barite rose) (1968)
State colors: Green and white (1915)
State song: "Oklahoma" (1953)
Nickname: Sooner State
Origin of name: From two Choctaw Indian words meaning "red people"
1980 population (1980 census) & (rank): 3,025,290 (26)
1981 population (prov.) & (rank): 3,100,000 (26)
1980 land area & (rank): 68,655 sq mi. (177,817 sq km) (19)
Geographic center: In Oklahoma Co., 8 mi. N of Oklahoma City
Number of counties: 77
Largest cities (1980 census): Oklahoma City, 403,213; Tulsa, 360,919; Lawton, 80,054; Norman, 68,020; Enid, 50,363; Midwest City, 49,559; Muskogee, 40,011
State forests: None
State parks: 28 (88,959 ac.)
Total state revenue (1981): $3,981,892,064
Total state expenditure (1981): $3,849,696,879

Francisco Vásquez de Coronado first explored the region for Spain in 1541. The U.S. acquired most of Oklahoma in 1803 in the Louisiana Purchase from France; the Western Panhandle region became U.S. territory with the annexation of Texas in 1845.

In 1834, Oklahoma was set aside as Indian Territory. It remained so until April 22, 1889, when it was opened to homestead settlement. On that one day 50,000 people swarmed in and the term "Sooners" was applied to those who tried to beat the noon starting gun. Other Oklahoma "Land Rushes" took place through 1901.

Oil has made Oklahoma a rich state and Tulsa one of the world's wealthiest cities per capita. Oil refining, meat packing, food processing, and machinery manufacturing (especially construction and oil equipment) are important industries.

Other minerals produced in Oklahoma include natural gas, helium, gypsum, zinc, cement, coal, copper, and silver.

Oklahoma's rich plains produce bumper yields of wheat, as well as large crops of sorghum, corn, cotton, and peanuts. Its beef cattle herd is among the largest in the nation; more than half of Oklahoma's annual farm receipts are contributed by livestock products.

Tourist attractions include the National Cowboy Hall of Fame in Oklahoma City, the Will Rogers Memorial in Claremore, the Cherokee Cultural Center with a restored Cherokee village, the restored Fort Gibson Stockade near Muskogee, and the Lake Texoma recreation area.

OREGON

Capital: Salem
Governor: Victor G. Atiyeh, R (to Jan. 1983)
Secy. of State: Norma Paulus, R (to Jan. 1985)
Treasurer: Clay Myers, R (to Jan. 1985)
Atty. General: David B. Frohnmayer, R (to Jan. 1985)
Organized as territory: Aug. 14, 1848
Entered Union & (rank): Feb. 14, 1859 (33)
Present constitution adopted: 1859
Motto: The Union (1957)
State flower: Oregon grape (1899)
State tree: Douglas fir (1939)
State animal: Beaver (1969)
State bird: Western meadow lark (1927)
State fish: Chinook salmon (1961)
State rock: Thunderegg (1965)
State colors: Navy blue and gold (1959)
State song: "Oregon, My Oregon" (1927)
Nickname: Beaver State
Origin of name: Unknown. However, it is generally accepted that the name, first used by Jonathan Carver in 1778, was taken from the writings of Maj. Robert Rogers, an English army officer.
1980 population (1980 census) & (rank): 2,633,105 (30)
1981 population (prov.) & (rank): 2,651,000 (30)
1980 land area & (rank): 96,184 sq mi. (249,117 sq km) (10)
Geographic center: In Crook Co., 25 mi. SSE of Prineville
Number of counties: 36
Largest cities (1980 census): Portland, 366,383; Eugene, 105,624; Salem, 89,233; Springfield, 41,621; Corvallis, 40,960; Medford, 39,603; Gresham, 33,005
State forests: 820,000 ac.
State parks: 240 (93,330 ac.)
State general revenue (1981–83 est.): $2,999,169,055
State general expenditure (1981–83 est.): $2,992,136,113

Spanish and English sailors are believed to have sighted the Oregon coast in the 1500s and 1600s. Capt. James Cook, seeking the Northwest Passage, charted some of the coastline in 1778. In 1792, Capt. Robert Gray, in the *Columbia,* discovered the river named after his ship and claimed the area for the U.S.

In 1805 the Lewis and Clark expedition explored the area and John Jacob Astor's fur depot, Astoria, was founded in 1811. Disputes for control of Oregon between American settlers and the Hudson Bay Company were finally resolved in the 1846 Oregon Treaty in which Great Britain gave up claims to the region.

Oregon, with the greatest U.S. reserve of standing timber, has a five-billion-dollar wood processing industry. Its salmon-fishing industry, centered at Astoria at the mouth of the Columbia, is one of the world's largest.

In agriculture, the state leads in growing peppermint, winter pears, fresh plums, prunes, blackberries, boysenberries, filberts, Blue Lake beans, and cover seed crops, and also raises strawberries, hops, wheat and other grains, sugar beets, potatoes, green peas, fiber flax, dairy products, livestock and poultry, apples, pears, and cherries. Oregon is the source of all the nickel produced in the U.S.

With the low-cost electric power provided by Bonneville Dam, McNary Dam, and other dams in the Pacific Northwest, Oregon has developed steadily as a manufacturing state. Leading manufactures are lumber and plywood, metalwork, machinery, aluminum, chemicals, paper, food packing, and electronic equipment.

Crater Lake National Park, Mount Hood, and Bonneville Dam on the Columbia are major tourist attractions. Oregon Dunes National Recreation Area has been established near Florence. Other points of interest include the Oregon Caves National Monument, Cape Perpetua in Siuslaw National Forest, Columbia River Gorge between The Dalles and Troutdale, and Hells Canyon.

PENNSYLVANIA

Capital: Harrisburg
Governor: Richard L. Thornburgh, R (to Jan. 1983)
Lieut. Governor: William W. Scranton III, R (to Jan. 1983)
Secy. of the Commonwealth: William R. Davis (to Jan. 1983)
Auditor General: Al Benedict, D (to Jan. 1985)
Atty. General: Leroy S. Zimmerman, R (to Jan. 1985)
Entered Union & (rank): Dec. 12, 1787 (2)
Present constitution adopted: 1874
Motto: Virtue, liberty, and independence
State flower: Mountain laurel (1933)
State tree: Hemlock (1931)
State bird: Ruffed grouse (1931)
State insect: Firefly (1974)
State dog: Great Dane (1965)
State colors: Blue and gold
State song: None
Nickname: Keystone State
Origin of name: In honor of Adm. Sir. William Penn, father of William Penn. It means "Penn's Woodland."
1980 population (1980 census) & (rank): 11,863,895 (4)
1981 population (prov.) & (rank): 11,871,000 (4)
1980 land area & (rank): 44,888 sq mi. (116,260 sq km) (32)
Geographic center: In Centre Co., 2½ mi. SW of Bellefonte
Number of counties: 67
Largest cities (1980 census): Philadelphia, 1,688,210; Pittsburgh, 423,959; Erie, 119,123; Scranton, 88,117; Reading, 78,686; Bethlehem, 70,419
State forests: 1,930,108 ac.
State parks: 120 (297,438 ac.)
Total estimated revenue subject to general appropriations (1982–83): $7,569,015,000
Total est. appropriations (1982–83): $7,565,875,000

Rich in historic lore, Pennsylvania territory was disputed in the early 1600s among the Dutch, the Swedes, and the English. England acquired the region in 1664 with the capture of New York and in 1681 Pennsylvania was granted to William Penn, a Quaker, by King Charles II.

Philadelphia was the seat of the federal government almost continuously from 1776 to 1800; there the Declaration of Independence was signed in 1776 and the U.S. Constitution drawn up in 1787. Valley Forge, of Revolutionary War fame, and Gettysburg, the turning-point of the Civil War, are both in Pennsylvania. The Liberty Bell is located in Independence Hall in Philadelphia.

Approximately 23% of all American pig iron steel is made in Pennsylvania, which ranks first among the states in steel wire and structural metal production. Other manufactures include machinery, chemicals, storage batteries, motor vehicles and trailers, computers, textiles and apparel, shoes, plastics, and explosives. Pennsylvania produces almost all the nation's anthracite coal. Also important are bituminous coal, cement, stone, petroleum, natural gas, lime, clays, zinc, and iron.

Prosperous farms brought in total receipts of more than $1.3 billion in 1973. The state ranked high in milk cows, chickens, and turkeys. Agricultural products include apples, peaches, potatoes, corn, wheat, barley, buckwheat, and mushrooms.

Tourists now spend approximately $6 billion in Pennsylvania annually. Among the chief attractions: the Gettysburg National Military Park, Valley Forge National Historical Park, Independence National Historical Park in Philadelphia, the Pennsylvania Dutch region, the Eisenhower farm near Gettysburg, and the Delaware Water Gap National Recreation Area.

RHODE ISLAND

Capital: Providence
Governor: J. Joseph Garrahy, D (to Jan. 1983)
Lieut. Governor: Thomas R. Di Luglio, D (to Jan. 1983)
Secy. of State: Robert F. Burns, D (to Jan. 1983)
Controller: James A. Carter (civil service)
Atty. General: Dennis J. Roberts II, D (to Jan. 1983)
Entered Union & (rank): May 29, 1790 (13)
Present constitution adopted: 1843
Motto: Hope
State flower: Violet (unofficial)
State tree: Red maple (official)
State bird: Rhode Island Red (official)
State colors: Blue, white, and gold (in state flag)
State song: "Rhode Island" (1946)
Nickname: The Ocean State
Origin of name: From the Greek island of Rhodes
1980 population (1980 census) & (rank): 947,154 (40)
1981 population (prov.) & (rank): 953,000 (41)
1980 land area & (rank): 1,055 sq mi. (2,732 sq km) (50)
Geographic center: In Kent Co., 1 mi. SSW of Crompton
Number of counties: 5
Largest cities (1980 census): Providence, 156,804; Warwick, 87,123; Cranston, 71,992; Pawtucket, 71,204; East Providence, 50,980; Woonsocket, 45,914
State forests: 11 (20,900 ac.)
State parks: 17 (8,200 ac.)
State general revenue (1980–81): $1,036,019,003
State general expenditure (1980–81): $1,067,094,750

From its beginnings, Rhode Island has been distinguished by its support for freedom of conscience and action, started by Roger Williams, exiled by the Massachusetts Bay Colony Puritans in 1636, and the founder of the present state capital, Providence. Williams was followed by other religious exiles who founded Pocasset, now Portsmouth, in 1638 and Newport in 1639.

The first Baptist church in the U.S. was established in Providence in 1638 and Rhode Island provided a haven for Quakers in 1657 and for Jews from Holland in 1659.

Rhode Island's rebellious, authority-defying nature was further demonstrated by the burnings of the British revenue cutters *Liberty* and *Gaspee* prior to the Revolution, by its early declaration of independence from Great Britain in May 1776, its refusal to participate actively in the War of 1812, and by Dorr's Rebellion of 1842, which protested property requirements for voting.

Rhode Island, smallest of the 50 states, is densely populated and highly industrialized. The state pioneered in the manufacture of jewelry and silverware and still retains first place in the U.S. Other leading industries are primary metal processing, metal products, machinery, rubber and plastics, food processing, chemicals, transportation equipment and electronic equipment.

With more than eight tenths of the population living in urban areas, adjacent areas of the state are involved in dairying and poultry and truck farming. Nursery and greenhouse products, potatoes, corn, apples, oats, and hay lead the crop list.

Newport became famous as the summer capital of society in the mid-19th century. Touro Synagogue (1763) is the oldest in the U.S. Other points of interest include the Roger Williams National Memorial in Providence, Samuel Slater's Mill in Pawtucket, the General Nathaniel Greene Homestead in Coventry, Block Island, and Narragansett Pier.

SOUTH CAROLINA

Capital: Columbia
Governor: Richard W. Riley, D (to Jan. 1983)
Lieut. Governor: Nancy Stevenson, D (to Jan. 1983)
Secy. of State: John T. Campbell, D (to Jan. 1983)
Comptroller General: Earl E. Morris, Jr. (to Jan. 1983)
Atty. General: Daniel R. McLeod, D (to Jan. 1983)
Entered Union & (rank): May 23, 1788 (8)
Present constitution adopted: 1895
Mottoes: *Animis opibusque parati* (Prepared in mind and resources) and *Dum spiro spero* (While I breathe, I hope)
State flower: Carolina yellow jessamine (1924)
State tree: Palmetto tree (1939)
State bird: Carolina wren (1948)
State song: "Carolina" (1911)
Nickname: Palmetto State
Origin of name: In honor of Charles I of England
1980 population (1980 census) & (rank): 3,121,833 (24)
1981 population (prov.) & (rank): 3,167,000 (24)
1980 land area & (rank): 30,203 sq mi. (78,227 sq km) (40)
Geographic center: In Richland Co., 13 mi. SE of Columbia
Number of counties: 46
Largest cities (1980 census): Columbia, 100,385; Charleston, 69,510; North Charleston, 62,534; Greenville, 58,242; Spartanburg, 43,826; Rock Hill, 35,344
State forests: 4 (124,052 ac.)
State parks: 50 (61,726 ac.)
State general fund revenue (1981–82 est.): $1,918,174,826[1]
State general expenditures (1981–82 est.): $1,918,174,826[1]

1. Highway Department has separate funding and expenditures.

Following exploration of the coast in 1521 by De Cordillo, the Spanish tried unsuccessfully to establish a colony near present-day Georgetown in 1526 and the French also failed to colonize Parris Island near Fort Royal in 1562.

The first English settlement was made in 1670 at Albemarle Point on the Ashley River, but poor conditions drove the settlers to the site of Charleston (originally called Charles Town). South Carolina, officially separated from North Carolina in 1729, was the scene of extensive military action during the Revolution and again during the Civil War. The Civil War began in 1861 as South Carolina troops fired on federal Fort Sumter in Charleston Harbor and the state was the first to secede from the Union.

Once primarily agricultural, South Carolina has built so many large textile and other mills that today its factories produce eight times the output of its farms in cash value. Charleston makes asbestos, wood, pulp, and steel products; chemicals, machinery, and apparel are also important.

Farms have become fewer but larger in recent years. South Carolina grows more peaches than any other state except California; it ranks fourth in tobacco. Other farm products include cotton, peanuts, sweet potatoes, soybeans, corn, and oats. Poultry and dairy products are also important revenue producers.

Points of interest include Fort Sumter National Monument, Fort Moultrie, Fort Johnson, and aircraft carrier USS *Yorktown* in Charleston Harbor; the Middleton, Magnolia, and Cypress Gardens in Charleston; Cowpens National Battlefield; and the Hilton Head resorts.

SOUTH DAKOTA

Capital: Pierre
Governor: William J. Janklow, R (to Jan. 1983)
Lieut. Governor: Lowell C. Hansen II, R (to Jan. 1983)
Atty. General: Mark Meierhenry, R (to Jan. 1983)
Secy. of State: Alice Kundert, R (to Jan. 1983)
State Auditor: Vern Larson, R (to Jan. 1983)
State Treasurer: David L. Volk, R (to Jan. 1983)
Organized as territory: March 2, 1861
Entered Union & (rank): Nov. 2, 1889 (40)
Present constitution adopted: 1889
Motto: Under God the people rule
State flower: American pasqueflower (1903)
State grass: Western wheat grass (1970)
State tree: Black Hills spruce (1947)
State bird: Ring-necked pheasant (1943)
State insect: Honeybee (1978)
State animal: Coyote (1949)
State mineral stone: Rose quartz (1966)
State gem stone: Fairburn agate (1966)
State colors: Blue and gold (in state flag)
State song: "Hail! South Dakota" (1943)
State fish: Walleye (1982)
Nicknames: Sunshine State; Coyote State
Origin of name: Same as for North Dakota
1980 population (1980 census) & (rank): 690,768 (45)
1981 population (prov.) & (rank): 686,000 (45)
1980 land area & (rank): 75,952 sq mi. (196,715 sq km) (16)
Geographic center: In Hughes Co., 8 mi. NE of Pierre
Number of counties: 67 (64 county governments)
Largest cities (1980 census): Sioux Falls, 81,343; Rapid City, 46,492; Aberdeen, 25,851; Watertown, 15,649; Brookings, 14,951; Mitchell, 13,916; Huron, 13,000
State forests: None[1]
State parks: 13 plus 39 recreational areas (87,269 ac.)[2]
State general revenue (1981): $233,105,986
State general expenditure (1981): $229,115,896

1. No designated state forests; about 13,000 ac. of state land is forestland. 2. Acreage includes 39 recreation areas and 80 roadside parks, in addition to 12 state parks.

Exploration of this area began in 1743 when Louis-Joseph and François Verendrye came from France in search of a route to the Pacific.

The U.S. acquired the region as part of the Louisiana Purchase in 1803 and it was explored by Lewis and Clark in 1804–06. Fort Pierre, the first permanent settlement, was established in 1817 and, in 1831, the first Missouri River steamboat reached the fort.

Settlement of South Dakota did not begin in earnest until the arrival of the railroad in 1873 and the discovery of gold in the Black Hills the following year.

Agriculture is South Dakota's basic industry today. It normally ranks first in the U.S. in the size of its rye crop and high in spring wheat, flaxseed, oats, and barley. In 1974 South Dakota had 5 million cattle, almost a million sheep, and 2 million hogs.

South Dakota is the nation's second leading producer of gold (Nevada ranks first) and the Homestake Mine is the richest in the U.S. Other minerals produced include berylium, bentonite, granite, silver, petroleum, and uranium.

Processing of foods produced by farms and ranches is the largest South Dakota manufacturing industry, followed by lumber, wood products, and machinery, including farm equipment.

The Black Hills, a great tourist attraction, are the highest mountains east of the Rockies. Mt. Rushmore, in this group, is famous for the likenesses of Washington, Jefferson, Lincoln, and Theodore Roosevelt, which were carved in granite by Gutzon Borglum. The Badlands offer scenic masses of bare rock and clay unrelieved by any vegetation. Other points of interest are Deadwood, where Wild Bill Hickok was killed in 1876; the Crazy Horse Memorial near Custer; and the Corn Palace in Mitchell.

TENNESSEE

Capital: Nashville
Governor: Lamar Alexander, R (to Jan. 1983)
Lieut. Governor: John S. Wilder, D (to Jan. 1985)
Secy. of State: Gentry Crowell, D (to Jan. 1985)
Atty. General: Brooks McLemore, D (to Sept. 1982)
State Treasurer: Harlan Matthews, D (to Jan. 1983)
Entered Union & (rank): June 1, 1796 (16)
Present constitution adopted: 1870; amended 1953, 1960, 1965 and 1973
Motto: "Tennessee—America at its best" (1965)
State flower: Iris (1933)
State tree: Tulip poplar (1947)
State bird: Mockingbird (1933)
State horse: Tennessee walking horse
State animal: Raccoon
State wild flower: Passion flower
State song: "Tennessee Waltz" (1965)
Nickname: Volunteer State
Origin of name: Of Cherokee origin; the exact meaning is unknown
1980 population (1980 census) & (rank): 4,591,120 (17)
1981 population (prov.) & (rank): 4,612,000 (17)
1980 land area & (rank): 41,155 sq mi. (106,591 sq km) (34)
Geographic center: In Rutherford Co., 5 mi. NE of Murfreesboro
Number of counties: 95
Largest cities (1980 census): Memphis, 646,174; Nashville, 455,651; Knoxville, 175,045; Chattanooga, 169,558; Clarksville, 54,777; Jackson, 49,131
State forests: 14 (155,752 ac.)
State parks: 21 (130,000 ac.)
State general revenue (1980): $4,028,000,000
State general expenditure (1980): $3,874,000,000

First visited by the Spanish explorer de Soto in 1541, the Tennessee area would later be claimed by both France and England as a result of the 1670s and 1680s explorations of Marquette and Jolliet, La Salle, and the Englishmen James Needham and Gabriel Arthur.

Great Britain obtained the region following the French and Indian War in 1763 and it was rapidly occupied by settlers moving in from Virginia and the Carolinas.

During 1784–87, the settlers formed the "state" of Franklin, which was disbanded when the region was allowed to send representatives to the North Carolina legislature. In 1790 Congress organized the territory south of the Ohio River and Tennessee joined the Union in 1796.

Although Tennessee joined the Confederacy during the Civil War, there was much pro-Union sentiment in the state, which was the scene of extensive military action.

The state is now predominantly industrial; in 1970, 58.8% of its population lived in urban areas. Among the most important products are chemicals, textiles, apparel, electrical machinery, furniture, and leather goods. Other lines include food processing, lumber, primary metals, and metal products. The state is known as the U.S. hardwood-flooring center and ranks first in the production of marble, zinc, pyrite, and ball clay.

Tennessee is one of the leading tobacco-producing states in the nation and its farming income is also derived from livestock and dairy products as well as corn, cotton, and soybeans.

With six other states, Tennessee shares the extensive federal reservoir developments on the Tennessee and Cumberland River systems. The Tennessee Valley Authority operates a number of dams and reservoirs in the state.

Among the major points of interest: the Andrew Johnson National Historic Site at Greenville, American Museum of Atomic Energy at Oak Ridge, Great Smoky Mountains National Park, The Hermitage (home of Andrew Jackson near Nashville), Rock City Gardens near Chattanooga, and three National Military Parks.

TEXAS

Capital: Austin
Governor: Bill Clements, R (to Jan. 1983)
Lieut. Governor: William P. Hobby, D (to Jan. 1981)
Secy. of State: George Strake, Jr., R (to Jan. 1983)
Comptroller: Bob Bullock (to Jan. 1983)
Atty. General: Mark White, D (to Jan. 1983)
Entered Union & (rank): Dec. 29, 1845 (28)
Present constitution adopted: 1876
Motto: Friendship
State flower: Bluebonnet (1901)
State tree: Pecan (1919)
State bird: Mockingbird (1927)
State song: "Texas, Our Texas" (1930)
Nickname: Lone Star State
Origin of name: From an Indian word meaning "friends"
1980 population (1980 census) & (rank): 14,229,288 (3)
1981 population (prov.) & (rank): 14,766,000 (3)
1980 land area & (rank): 262,017 sq mi. (678,623 sq km) (2)
Geographic center: In McCulloch Co., 15 mi. NE of Brady
Number of counties: 254
Largest cities (1980 census): Houston, 1,595,138; Dallas, 904,078; San Antonio, 785,023; El Paso, 425,259; Fort Worth, 385,164; Austin, 345,496
State forests: 4 (6,306 ac.)
State parks: 83 (64 developed)
State revenue receipts (1980–81): $12,735,320,296
State government cost (1980–81): $11,367,553,831
Total net revenue: (1980–81): $13,421,260,063
Total net expenditures (1980–81): $11,367,553,831

Spanish explorers, including Cabeza de Vaca and Coronado, were the first to visit the region in the 16th and 17th centuries, settling at Ysleta near present-day El Paso in 1682. In 1685, La Salle established a short-lived French colony at Matagorda Bay.

Americans, led by Stephen F. Austin, began to settle along the Brazos River in 1821 when Texas was controlled by Mexico, recently independent from Spain. In 1836, following a brief war between the American settlers in Texas and the Mexican government, and famous for the battles of the Alamo and San Jacinto, the Independent Republic of Texas was proclaimed with Sam Houston as president.

After Texas became the 28th U.S. state in 1845, border disputes led to the Mexican War of 1846–48.

Today, Texas, second only to Alaska in land area, leads all other states in such categories as oil, cattle, sheep, and cotton. Possessing enormous natural resources, Texas is a major agricultural state and an industrial giant.

Sulfur, salt, helium asphalt, graphite, bromine, natural gas, cement, and clays give Texas first place in mineral production—nearly $8 billion in 1973. Chemicals, oil refining, food processing, machinery, and transportation equipment are among the major Texas manfacturing industries.

Texas ranches and farms produce beef cattle, poultry, rice, pecans, peanuts, sorghum, and an extensive variety of fruits and vegetables.

Millions of tourists spend well over $2 billion annually visiting more than 70 state parks, recreations areas, and points of interest such as the Gulf Coast resort area, the Lyndon B. Johnson Space Center in Houston, the Alamo in San Antonio, the state capital in Austin, and the Big Bend and Guadalupe Mountains National Parks.

UTAH

Capital: Salt Lake City
Governor: Scott M. Matheson, D (to Jan. 1984)
Lieut. Governor/Secretary of State: David S. Monson, R (to Jan. 1984)
Atty. General: David Wilkison, R (to Jan. 1984)
Organized as territory: Sept. 9, 1850
Entered Union & (rank): Jan. 4, 1896 (45)
Present constitution adopted: 1896
Motto: Industry
State flower: Sego lily (1911)
State tree: Blue spruce (1933)
State bird: Seagull (1955)
State emblem: Beehive
State song: "Utah, We Love Thee"
Nickname: Beehive State
Origin of name: From the Ute tribe, meaning "people of the mountains"
1970 population & (rank): 1,059,273 (36)
1980 population (1980 census) & (rank): 1,461,037 (36)
1981 population (prov.) & (rank): 1,518,000 (36)
1980 land area & (rank): 82,073 sq mi. (212,569 sq km) (12)

Geographic center: In Sanpete Co., 3 mi. N. of Manti
Number of counties: 29
Largest cities (1980 census): Salt Lake City, 163,697; Provo, 52,210; Ogden, 64,407; Orem, 52,399; Sandy City, 52,210; Bountiful, 32,877; West Jordan, 27,192; Logan, 26,844; Murray, 25,750
State forests: None
State parks: 44 (64,097 ac.)
Total state revenues (Fiscal 1981): $1,563,058,000
Total state expenditures (Fiscal 1981): $1,596,226,000
Cash balance—Unappropriated general fund balance (1981): $24,300,000

The region was first explored for Spain by Franciscan friars, Escalante and Dominguez in 1776. In 1824 the famous American frontiersman Jim Bridger discovered the Great Salt Lake.

Fleeing the religious persecution encountered in eastern and middle-western states, the Mormons reached the Great Salt Lake in 1847 and began to build Salt Lake City. The U.S. acquired the Utah region in the treaty ending the Mexican War in 1848 and the first transcontinental railroad was completed with the driving of a golden spike at Promontory Point in 1869.

Mormon difficulties with the federal government about polygamy did not end until the Mormon Church renounced the practice in 1890, six years before Utah became a state.

In recent years, manufacturing has become Utah's most important industry, ahead of mining, agriculture, and tourism. The state's factories produce transportation equipment, food products, machinery, metal products, and electrical equipment. Utah has also become an important aerospace research and production center and is a leading warehousing and distribution point for much of the western U.S.

Rich in natural resources, Utah has long been a leading producer of copper, gold, silver, lead, zinc, and molybdenum. Oil has also become a major product; with Colorado and Wyoming, Utah shares what have been called the world's richest oil shale deposits.

Ranked eighth among the states in number of sheep in 1973, Utah also produces large crops of apricots and cherries as well as sugar beets, potatoes, onions, alfalfa, winter wheat, and beans. Utah's farmlands and crops require extensive irrigation.

Utah is a great vacationland with 11,000 miles of fishing streams and 147,000 acres of lakes and reservoirs. Among the many tourist attractions are Arches, Bryce Canyon, Canyonlands, Capitol Reef, and Zion National Parks; Dinosaur, Natural Bridges, and Rainbow Bridge National Monuments; the Mormon Tabernacle in Salt Lake City; and Monument Valley.

VERMONT

Capital: Montpelier
Governor: Richard A. Snelling, R (to Jan. 1983)
Lieut. Governor: Madeleine M. Kunin (to Jan. 1983)
Secy. of State: James H. Douglas (to Jan. 1983)
Treasurer: Emory A. Hebard, R (to Jan. 1983)
Auditor of Accounts: Alexander V. Acebo (to Jan. 1983)
Atty. General: John J. Easton, Jr. (to Jan. 1983)
Entered Union & (rank): March 4, 1791 (14)
Present constitution adopted: 1793
Motto: Vermont, Freedom, and Unity
State flower: Red clover (1894)
State tree: Sugar maple (1949)
State bird: Hermit thrush (1941)
State animal: Morgan horse (1961)
State insect: Honeybee (1978)
State song: "Hail, Vermont!" (1938)
Nickname: Green Mountain State
Origin of name: From the French "vert mont," meaning "green mountain"
1980 population (1980 census) & (rank): 511,456 (48)
1981 population (prov.) & (rank): 516,000 (48)
1980 land area & (rank): 9,273 sq mi. (24,017 sq km) (43)
Geographic center: In Washington Co., 3 mi. E of Roxbury
Number of counties: 14
Largest cities (1980 census): Burlington, 37,712; Rutland, 18,436; South Burlington, 10,679; Barre, 9,824; Montpelier, 8,241; St. Albans, 7,308; Winooski, 6,318
State forests: 34 (113,953 ac.)
State parks: 45 (31,325 ac.)
State receipts (1981): $595,310,594
State disbursements (1981): $638,651,364

The Vermont region was explored and claimed for France by Samuel de Champlain in 1609 and the first French settlement was established at Fort Ste. Anne in 1666. The first English settlers moved into the area in 1724 and built Fort Drummer on the site of present-day Brattleboro. England gained control of the area in 1763 after the French and Indian War.

First organized to drive settlers from New York out of Vermont, the Green Mountain Boys, led by Ethan Allen, won fame by capturing Fort Ticonderoga from the British on May 10, 1775, in the early days of the Revolution.

In 1777 Vermont adopted its first constitution abolishing slavery and providing for universal male suffrage without property qualifications. In 1791 Vermont became the first state after the original 13 to join the Union.

Vermont leads the nation in the production of monument granite, marble, and maple syrup. It is also a leader in the production of asbestos and talc.

In ratio to population, Vermont keeps more dairy cows than any other state. Vermont's soil is devoted to dairying, truck farming, and fruit growing because the rugged, rocky terrain discourages extensive farming.

Principal manufactured goods are machine tools, computer components, stone and clay products, lumber, furniture, and paper.

Tourism is a major industry in Vermont. Vermont's many famous ski areas include Stowe, Killington, Mt. Snow, Bromley, Jay Peak, and Sugarbush. Hunting and fishing also attract many visitors to Vermont each year. Among the many points of interest are the Green Mountain National Forest, Bennington Battle Monument, the Calvin Coolidge Homestead at Plymouth, and the Marble Exhibit in Proctor.

VIRGINIA

Capital: Richmond
Governor: Charles S. Robb, D (to Jan. 1986)
Lieut. Governor: Richard J. Davis, D (to Jan. 1986)
Secy. of the Commonwealth: Frederick T. Gray, D (apptd. by Governor)
Acting Comptroller: Vincent Pross, Jr. (apptd. by Governor)
Atty. General: Gerald L. Baliles, D (to Jan. 1986)

Entered Union & (rank): June 25, 1788 (10)
Present constitution adopted: 1970
Motto: *Sic semper tyrannis* (Thus always to tyrants)
State flower: American dogwood (1918)
State bird: Cardinal (1950)
State dog: American foxhound (1966)
State shell: Oyster shell
State song: "Carry Me Back to Old Virginia" (1940)
Nicknames: The Old Dominion; Mother of Presidents
Origin of name: In honor of Elizabeth "Virgin Queen" of England
1980 population (1980 census) & (rank): 5,346,818 (14)
1981 population (prov.) & (rank): 5,430,000 (14)
1980 land area & (rank): 39,703 sq mi. (102,832 sq km) (36)
Geographic center: In Buckingham Co., 5 mi. SW of Buckingham
Number of counties: 95, plus 41 independent cities
Largest cities (1980 census): Norfolk, 266,979; Virginia Beach, 262,199; Richmond, 219,214; Newport News, 144,903; Hampton, 122,617; Chesapeake, 114,486
State forests: 8 (49,566 ac.)
State parks and recreational parks: 22, plus 3 in process of acquisition and/or development (42,722 ac.)[1]
State revenue (1980–81): $5,801,800,000
State expenditure (1980–81): $5,898,400,000

1. Does not include portion of Breaks Interstate Park (Va.-Ky., 1,200 ac.) which lies in Virginia.

The history of America is closely tied to that of Virginia, particularly in the Colonial period. Jamestown, founded in 1607, was the first permanent English settlement in North America and slavery was introduced there in 1619. The surrenders ending both the American Revolution (Yorktown) and the Civil War (Appomattox) occurred in Virginia. The state is called the "Mother of Presidents" because eight chief executives of the United States were born there.

Today, Virginia has a large number of diversified manufacturing industries including chemicals, textiles, food products, and clothing. Other important lines are lumber, paper, furniture, cigarettes, electrical machinery, transportation equipment, and stone-glass-clay products.

Agriculture remains an important sector in the Virginia economy and the state ranks among the leaders in the U.S. in tobacco, peanuts, apples, and sweet potatoes. Other crops include corn, vegetables, barley, and peaches. Famous for its turkeys and Smithfield hams, Virginia also has a large dairy industry.

Coal mining accounts for roughly 70% of Virginia's mineral output, and lime, zinc, and stone are also mined.

Points of interest include Mt. Vernon and other places associated with George Washington; Monticello, home of Thomas Jefferson; Stratford, home of the Lees; Richmond, capital of the Confederacy and of Virginia; and Williamsburg, the restored Colonial capital.

The Chesapeake Bay Bridge-Tunnel spans the mouth of Chesapeake Bay, connecting Cape Charles with Norfolk. Consisting of a series of low trestles, two bridges and two mile-long tunnels, the complex is 18 miles (29 km) long. It was opened in 1964.

Other attractions are the Shenandoah National Park, Fredericksburg and Spotsylvania National Military Park, the Booker T. Washington birthplace near Roanoke, Arlington House (the Robert E. Lee Memorial), the Skyline Drive, and the Blue Ridge National Parkway.

WASHINGTON

Capital: Olympia
Governor: John Spellman (to Jan. 1985)
Lieut. Governor: John A. Cherberg, (to Jan. 1985)
Secy. of State: Ralph Munro (to Jan. 1985)
State Treasurer: Robert S. O'Brien (to Jan. 1985)
Atty. General: Kenneth O. Eikenberry (to Jan. 1985)
Organized as territory: March 2, 1853
Entered Union & (rank): Nov. 11, 1889 (42)
Present constitution adopted: 1889
Motto: *Al-Ki* (Indian word meaning "by and by")
State flower: Rhododendron (1949)
State tree: Western hemlock (1947)
State bird: Willow goldfinch (1951)
State fish: Steelhead trout (1969)
State gem: Petrified wood (1975)
State colors: Green and gold (1925)
State song: "Washington, My Home" (1959)
State dance: Square dance (1979)
Nicknames: Evergreen State; Chinook State
Origin of name: In honor of George Washington
1980 population (1980 census) & (rank): 4,132,180 (20)
1981 population (prov.) & (rank): 4,217,000 (20)
1980 land area & (rank): 66,511 sq mi (172,264 sq km) (20)
Geographic center: In Chelan Co., 10 mi. WSW of Wenatchee
Number of counties: 39
Largest cities (1980 census): Seattle, 493,846; Spokane, 171,300; Tacoma, 158,501; Bellevue, 73,903; Everett, 54,413; Yakima, 49,826; Bellingham, 45,794
State forest lands: 1,922,880 ac.
State parks: 202 (171,700 ac.)[1]
State revenue (1981–83 projected): $13,386,100,000
State expenditure (1981–83 projected): $14,244,800,000

1. Parks and undeveloped areas administered by Parks and Recreation Dept. Game Dept. administers wildlife and recreation areas totaling 762,895 acres.

As part of the vast Oregon Country, Washington territory was visited by Spanish, American, and British explorers—Bruno Heceta for Spain in 1775, the American Capt. Robert Gray in 1792, and Capt. George Vancouver for Britain in 1792–94. Lewis and Clark explored the Columbia River region and coastal areas for the U.S. in 1805–06.

Rival American and British settlers and conflicting territorial claims threatened war in the early 1840s. However, in 1846 the Oregon Treaty set the boundary at the 49th parallel and war was averted.

Washington is a leading lumber producer. Its rugged surface is rich in stands of Douglas fir, hemlock, ponderosa and white pine, spruce, larch, and cedar. The state holds first place in apples, blueberries, hops, and red raspberries and it ranks high in potatoes, winter wheat, pears, grapes, apricots, and strawberries. Livestock and livestock products make important contributions to total farm revenue and the commercial fishing catch of salmon, halibut, and bottomfish makes a significant contribution to the state's economy.

Manufacturing industries in Washington include aircraft and missiles, shipbuilding and other transportation equipment, lumber, food processing, metals and metal products, chemicals, and machinery.

The Columbia River contains one third of the potential water power in the U.S., harnessed by such dams as the Grand Coulee, one of the greatest power producers in the world. Washington has 90 dams throughout the state built for irrigation, power, flood control, and water storage. Its abundance of electrical power makes Washington the nation's largest producer of refined aluminum.

Among the major points of interest: Mt. Rainier, Olympic, and North Cascades. In 1980, Mount St. Helens, a peak in the Cascade Range in Southwestern Washington erupted on May 18th. Also of interest are National Parks; Whitman Mission and Fort Vancouver National Historic Sites; and the Pacific Science Center and Space Needle in Seattle.

WEST VIRGINIA

Capital: Charleston
Governor: John D. Rockefeller IV, D (to Jan. 1985)
Secy. of State: James A. Manchin, D (to Jan. 1985)
State Auditor: Glen Gainer (to Jan. 1985)
Atty. General: Chauncey H. Browning, Jr., D (to Jan. 1985)
Entered Union & (rank): June 20, 1863 (35)
Present constitution adopted: 1872
Motto: *Montani semper liberi* (Mountaineers are always free)
State flower: Rhododendron (1903)
State tree: Sugar maple (1949)
State bird: Cardinal (1949)
State animal: Black bear
State colors: Blue and gold (unofficial)
State songs: "West Virginia, My Home Sweet Home," "The West Virginia Hills," and "This Is My West Virginia" (adopted by Legislature in 1947, 1961 and 1963 as official state songs)
Nickname: Mountain State
Origin of name: Same as for Virginia
1980 population (1980 census) & (rank): 1,950,279 (34)
1981 population (prov.) & (rank): 1,952,000 (34)
1980 land area & (rank): 24,119 sq mi. (62,468 sq km) (41)
Geographic center: In Braxton Co., 4 mi. E of Sutton
Number of counties: 55
Largest cities (1980 census): Charleston, 63,968; Huntington, 63,684; Wheeling, 43,070; Parkersburg, 39,967; Morgantown, 27,605; Weirton, 25,371
State forests: 9 (77,000 ac.)
State parks: 34 (65,861 ac.)
Total state revenue (1980–81): $3,946,331,489
Total state expenditure (1980–81): $3,947,818,633

West Virginia's early history from 1609 until 1863 is largely shared with Virginia, of which it was a part until Virginia seceded from the Union in 1861. Then the delegates of 40 western counties formed their own government, which was granted statehood in 1863.

First permanent settlement dates from 1731 when Morgan Morgan founded Mill Creek. In 1742 coal was discovered on the Coal River, an event that would be of great significance in determining West Virginia's future.

The state usually ranks first in bituminous coal production with about 20% of the U.S. total. It also is a leader in steel, glass, aluminum, and chemical manufactures; natural gas, oil, quarry products, and hardwood lumber.

Poultry, dairy products, cattle, and sheep account for the major portion of farm receipts. Apples, peaches, wheat, corn, and hay are profitable crops. More than 75% of West Virginia is covered with forests.

Tourism is increasingly popular in mountainous West Virginia and visitors spend over $750 million annually. More than a million acres have been set aside in 34 state parks and recreation areas and in 9 state forests.

Major points of interest include Harpers Ferry and Chesapeake and Ohio Canal National Historical Parks, White Sulphur Springs and Berkeley Springs resorts, the scenic railroad at Cass, and the historic homes at Charles Town.

WISCONSIN

Capital: Madison
Governor: Lee Sherman Dreyfus, R (to Jan. 1983)
Lieut. Governor: Russell A. Olson, R (to Jan. 1983)
Secy. of State: Vel R. Phillips, D (to Jan. 1983)
State Treasurer: Charles P. Smith, D (to Jan. 1983)
Atty. General: Bronson C. La Follette, D (to Jan. 1983)
Superintendent of Public Instruction: Herbert J. Grover, Nonpartisan (to July 1985)
Organized as territory: July 4, 1836
Entered Union & (rank): May 29, 1848 (30)
Present constitution adopted: 1848
Motto: Forward
State flower: Wood violet
State tree: Sugar maple
State bird: Robin
State animal: Badger; "wild life" animal: white-tailed deer; "domestic" animal: dairy cow
State insect: Honeybee (1977)
State fish: Musky (Muskellunge)
State song: "On Wisconsin"
State mineral: Galena (1971)
State rock: Red Granite (1971)
Nickname: Badger State
Origin of name: French corruption of an Indian word whose meaning is disputed
1980 population (1980 census) & (rank): 4,705,521 (16)
1981 population (prov.) & (rank): 4,742,000 (16)
1980 land area & (rank): 54,426 sq mi. (140,964 sq km) (25)
Geographic center: In Wood Co., 9 mi. SE of Marshfield
Number of counties: 72
Largest cities (1980 census): Milwaukee, 636,236; Madison, 170,616; Green Bay, 87,899; Racine, 85,725; Kenosha, 77,685; West Allis, 63,982; Appleton, 58,913
State forests: 9 (465,926 ac.)
State parks & scenic trails: 63 parks, 9 trails (61,573 ac.)
State revenue (1980–81): $8,073,918,072
State expenditure (1980–81): $7,374,895,466

The Wisconsin region was first explored for France by Jean Nicolet, who landed at Green Bay in 1634. In 1660 a French trading post and Roman Catholic mission were established near present-day Ashland.

Great Britain obtained the region in settlement of the French and Indian War in 1763; the U.S. acquired it in 1783 after the Revolutionary War. However, Great Britain retained actual control until after the War of 1812. The region was successively governed as part of the territories of Indiana, Illinois, and Michigan between 1800 and 1836, when it became a separate territory.

Wisconsin leads the nation in milk and cheese production. In 1981 the state ranked first in the number of milk cows (1,820,000) and produced nearly 17% of the nation's total output of milk. Other important farm products are peas, beets, corn, potatoes, cabbage, maple sugar, and cranberries.

The chief industrial products of the state are automobiles, machinery, furniture, paper, beer, and processed foods. Wisconsin ranks second among the 47 paper-producing states. Tourism also ranks among the major industries.

Wisconsin pioneered in social legislation, providing pensions for the blind (1907), aid to dependent children (1913), and old-age assistance (1925). In 1932 it was the first state to enact an unemployment compensation law. In labor legislation, the state has also pioneered in important laws, among them the first workmen's compensation law actually to take effect. Wisconsin had the first state-wide primary-election law and the first successful income-tax law.

The state has over 8,500 lakes, of which Winnebago is the largest. Water sports, ice-boating, and fishing are popular, as are skiing and hunting. Public parks and forests take up one seventh of the land, with 63 state parks, 9 state forests, and 2 national forests.

Among the many points of interest are the Apostle Islands National Lakeshore; Ice Age National Scientific Reserve; the Circus World Museum at Baraboo; the Wolf, St. Croix, and Lower St. Croix national scenic riverways; and the Wisconsin Dells.

WYOMING

Capital: Cheyenne
Governor: Ed Herschler, D (to Jan. 1983)
Secy. of State: Thyra G. Thomson, R (to Jan. 1983)
Auditor: James B. Griffith, Jr., R (to Jan. 1983)
Treasurer: Shirley Wittler, D (to Jan. 1983)
Atty. General: Steven F. Freudenthal, D (apptd. by Governor)
Organized as territory: May 19, 1869
Entered Union & (rank): July 10, 1890 (44)
Present constitution adopted: 1890
Motto: Equal rights (1955)
State flower: Indian paintbrush (1917)
State tree: Cottonwood (1947)
State bird: Meadow lark (1927)
State gemstone: Jade (1967)
State insignia: Bucking horse (unofficial)
State song: "Wyoming" (1955)
Nickname: Equality State
Origin of name: From the Delaware Indian word, meaning "mountains and valleys alternating"; the same as the Wyoming Valley in Pennsylvania
1980 population (1980 census) & (rank): 469,557 (49)
1981 population (prov.) & (rank): 492,000 (49)
1980 land area & (rank): 96,989 sq mi. (251,201 sq km) (9)
Geographic center: In Fremont Co., 58 mi. ENE of Lander
Number of counties: 23, plus Yellowstone National Park
Largest cities (1980 census): Casper, 51,016; Cheyenne, 47,283; Laramie, 24,410; Rock Springs, 19,458; Sheridan, 15,146; Green River, 12,807; Gillette, 12,134
State forests: None
State parks: 9 (44,732 ac.)
Estimated income (1981–83): $890,737,287
Estimated expenditure (1981–83): $869,054,972

The U.S. acquired the territory from France as part of the Louisiana Purchase in 1803. John Colter, a fur-trapper, is the first white man known to have entered present Wyoming. In 1807 he explored the Yellowstone area and brought back news of its geysers and hot springs.

Robert Stuart pioneered the Oregon Trail across Wyoming in 1812–13 and, in 1834, Fort Laramie, the first permanent trading post in Wyoming, was built. Western Wyoming was obtained by the U.S. in the 1846 Oregon Treaty with Great Britain and as a result of the treaty ending the Mexican War in 1848.

When the Wyoming Territory was organized in 1869 Wyoming women became the first in the nation to obtain the right to vote. In 1925 Mrs. Nellie Tayloe Ross was elected first woman governor in the United States.

Wyoming's towering mountains and vast plains provide spectacular scenery, grazing lands for sheep and cattle, and rich mineral deposits.

Mining, particularly oil and natural gas, is the most important industry. In January 1981, Wyoming led the nation in sodium carbonate (natrona) and bentonite production, and was second in uranium.

Wyoming ranks second among the states in wool production. In January 1981, its sheep numbered 1,110,000, exceeded only by Texas and California; it also had 1,350,000 cattle. Principal crops include wheat, oats, sugar beets, corn, potatoes, barley, and alfalfa.

Second in mean elevation to Colorado, Wyoming has many attractions for the tourist trade, notably Yellowstone National Park. Cheyenne is famous for its annual "Frontier Days" celebration. Flaming Gorge, the Fort Laramie National Historic Site, and Devils Tower and Fossil Butte National Monuments are other National points of interest.

Self-Governing Areas

PUERTO RICO

Capital: San Juan
Governor: Carlos Romero Barceló, New Progressive Party (to Jan. 1985)
Song: "La Borinqueña"
1970 population: 2,712,033
1980 population (1980 census): 3,196,520
1980 land area: 3,421 sq mi. (8,860 sq km)
Largest cities (1976): San Juan (516,500); Ponce (198,600); Caguas (117,600); Mayagüez (102,500)

Puerto Rico is an island about 100 miles long and 35 miles wide at the northeastern end of the Caribbean Sea. It is a self-governing Commonwealth freely and voluntarily associated with the U.S. Under its Constitution, a Governor and a Legislative Assembly are elected by direct vote for a four-year period. The judiciary is vested in a Supreme Court and lower courts established by law. The people elect a Resident Commissioner to the U.S. House of Representatives, where he has a voice but no vote. The island was formerly an unincorporated territory of the U.S. after being ceded by Spain as a result of the Spanish-American War.

The Commonwealth, established in 1952, has one of the highest standards of living in Latin America. Featuring Puerto Rican economic development is Operation Bootstrap. This program has established over 2,300 new factories and has greatly increased agricultural production, transportation and communications facilities, electric power, housing, and other industries.

The island's chief exports are chemicals, textiles, fish products and petroleum products.

Columbus discovered the island on his second voyage to America in 1493.

GUAM

Capital: Agaña
Governor: Paul M. Calvo
1950 population: 59,498
1960 population: 67,044
1970 population: 84,996
1980 population: 105,917
1980 land area: 212 sq mi. (549 sq km)

Guam, the largest of the Mariana Islands, is independent of the trusteeship assigned to the U.S. in 1947. It was acquired by the U.S. from Spain in 1898 (occupied 1899) and was placed under the Navy Department.

In World War II, Guam was seized by the Japanese on Dec. 11, 1941; but on July 21, 1944, it was once more in U. S. hands.

On Aug. 1, 1950, President Truman signed a bill which granted U.S. citizenship to the people of Guam and established self-government. However, the people do not vote in national elections. In 1972 Guam elected its first delegate to the U.S. Congress. The Executive Branch of the Guam government is under the general supervision of the U.S. Secretary of the Interior. In November 1970, Guam elected its first Governor.

Military installations and tourism are important factors in Guam's economy.

Non-Self-Governing Territories

AMERICAN SAMOA

Capital: Fagatogo (on Tutuila Island)
Governor: Peter Tali Coleman
Lieut. Governor: Tufele Liá
1950 population: 18,937
1960 population: 20,051
1980 est. population: 33,506
1980 land area: 76 sq mi. (197 sq km)

American Samoa, a group of five volcanic islands and two coral atolls located some 2,600 miles south of Hawaii in the South Pacific Ocean, is an unincorporated, unorganized territory of the U.S., administered by the Department of the Interior.

By the Treaty of Berlin, signed Dec. 2, 1899, and ratified Feb. 16, 1900, the U.S. was internationally acknowledged to have rights extending over all the islands of the Samoa group east of longitude 171° west of Greenwich. On April 17, 1900, the chiefs of Tutuila and Aunu'u ceded those islands to the U.S. In 1904, the King and chiefs of Manu'a ceded the islands of Ofu, Olosega and Tau (composing the Manu'a group) to the U.S. Swains Island, some 214 miles north of Samoa, was included as part of the territory by Act of Congress March 4, 1925; and on Feb. 20, 1929, Congress formally accepted sovereignty over the entire group and placed the responsibility for administration in the hands of the President. From 1900 to 1951, by Presidential direction, the Department of the Navy governed the territory. On July 1, 1951, administration was transferred to the Department of the Interior. The first Constitution for the territory was signed on April 27, 1960, and became effective on Oct. 17, 1960. It was revised in 1967.

Congress has provided for a non-voting delegate to sit in the House of Representatives in 1981.

The principal products are canned tuna, pet food, fish meal, mats, and handicrafts.

BAKER, HOWLAND, AND JARVIS ISLANDS

These Pacific islands were not to play a role in the extraterritorial plans of the U.S. until May 13, 1936. President F. D. Roosevelt, at that time, placed them under the control and jurisdiction of the Secretary of the Interior for administration purposes.

Baker Island is a saucer-shaped atoll with an area of approximately one square mile. It is about 1,650 miles from Hawaii.

Howland Island, 36 miles to the northeast, is approximately one and a half miles long and half a mile wide.

Jarvis Island is several hundred miles to the east and is approximately two miles long by one and an eighth miles wide.

Baker, Howland, and Jarvis have been uninhabited since 1942. In 1974, these islands became part of the National Wildlife Refuge System, administered by the U.S. Fish & Wildlife Service, Department of The Interior.

CANTON AND ENDERBURY ISLANDS

Canton and Enderbury islands, the largest of the Phoenix group, are jointly administered by the U.S. and Great Britain after an agreement signed April 6, 1939. The status of Canton and Enderbury was the subject of negotiations between the U.S., U.K., and Gilbert Islands Governments in 1979. The negotiations resulted in the signing on September 20, 1979, of a Treaty of Friendship between the U.S. and the Republic of Kiribati, which, once ratified by the U.S. Senate, will formally renounce the U.S. claim to Canton and Enderbury. The Republic of Kiribati declared its independence on July 12, 1979.

Canton is triangular in shape and the largest of the eight islands of this group. It lies about 1,600 miles southwest of Hawaii and was discovered at the turn of the 18th century by U.S. whalers. After World War II it served as an aviation support facility, and later as a missile tracking station. Since 1967, the island has been utilized by the U.S. Air Force Space and Missile Test Center.

Enderbury is rectangular in shape and is 3.5 miles long by 1.5 miles wide. It is unpopulated and lies about 32 miles southeast of Canton.

JOHNSTON ATOLL

Johnston is a coral atoll about 700 miles southwest of Hawaii. It consists of four small islands—Johnston Island, Sand Island, Hikina Island, and Akau Island—which lie on a reef about 9 miles long in a northeast-southwest direction.

The atoll was discovered by Capt. Charles James Johnston of *H.M.S. Cornwallis* in 1807. In 1858 it was claimed by Hawaii, and later became a U.S. possession.

Johnston Atoll is a Naval Defense Sea Area and Airspace Reservation and is closed to the public.

The administration of Johnston Atoll is under the jurisdiction of the Defense Nuclear Agency, Commander, Johnston Atoll (FCDNA), APO San Francisco, CA 96305.

KINGMAN REEF

Kingman Reef, located about 1,000 miles south of Hawaii, was discovered by Capt. E. Fanning in 1798, but named for Capt. W. E. Kingman, who rediscovered it in 1853. The reef, drying only on its northeast, east and southeast edges, is of atoll character. A small islet, 3 feet high, lies on its east side. The reef is triangular in shape, with its apex northward; it is about 9.5 miles long, east and west, and 5 miles wide, north and south, within the 100-fathom curve.

A United States possession, Kingman Reef is a Defense Sea Area and Airspace Reservation, and is closed to the public. The Airspace Entry Control has been suspended, but is subject to immediate reinstatement without notice. No vessel or aircraft, except those authorized by the Secretary of the Navy, shall be navigated in or above the area within the 3-mile limit.

MIDWAY ISLANDS

Midway Islands, lying about 1,200 miles west-northwest of Hawaii, were discovered by Captain N. C. Brooks of the Hawaiian bark *Gambia* on July 5, 1859, in the name of the United States. The atoll was formally declared a U.S. possession in 1867, and in 1903 Theodore Roosevelt made it a naval reservation.

Midway Islands consist of a circular atoll, 6 miles in diameter, and enclosing two islands. Eastern Island, on its southeast side, is triangular in shape, and about 1.2 miles long. Sand Island on its south side, is about 2 miles long in a northeast-southwest direction.

The Midway Islands are within a naval defensive sea area. The Navy Department maintains an installation and has jurisdiction over the atoll. Permission to enter the Naval Defense Sea Area must be obtained in advance from the Commanding Officer, Naval Air Facility, Midway Islands, FPO San Francisco, CA 96614.

U.S. VIRGIN ISLANDS

Capital: Charlotte Amalie (on St. Thomas)
Governor: Juan Luis
1950 population: 26,665
1960 population: 32,099
1970 population: 62,468 (St. Thomas, 28,960; St. Croix, 31,779; St. John, 1,729)
1980 est. population: 95,214 (St. Croix, 48,916; St. Thomas, 43,828; St. John, 2,470)
1980 land area: 136 sq mi. (352 sq km) (St. Croix, 84 [218 sq km]; St. Thomas, 32 [83 sq km]; St. John, 20 [52 sq km])

The Virgin Islands, consisting of nine main islands and some 75 islets, were discovered by Columbus in 1493. Since 1666, England has held six of the main islands; the other three (St. Croix, St. Thomas, and St. John), as well as about 50 of the islets, were eventually acquired by Denmark, which named them the Danish West Indies. In 1917, these islands were purchased by the U.S. from Denmark for $25 million.

Congress granted U.S. citizenship to Virgin Islanders in 1927; and, in 1931, administration was transferred from the Navy to the Department of the Interior. Universal suffrage was given in 1936 to all persons who could read and write the English language. The Governor was elected by popular vote for the first time in 1970; previously he had been appointed by the President of the U.S. A unicameral 15-man legislature serves the Virgin Islands, and recent Congressional legislation gave the islands a non-voting Representative in Congress.

The "Constitution" of the Virgin Islands is the Revised Organic Act. of 1954 in which the U.S. Congress defines the three branches of the territorial government, i.e., the Executive Branch, the Legislative Branch, and the Judicial Branch. Residents of the islands substantially enjoy the same rights as those enjoyed by mainlanders with one important exception: citizens of the U.S. who are residents may not vote in presidential elections.

About 80% of the population is black, and there is limited farming, fishing, and cattle raising. Industrial products include rum, watches, costume jewelry, clothing, alumina, pharmaceuticals, and petroleum products. Tourism is the principal industry.

WAKE ISLAND

Wake Island, about halfway between Midway and Guam, is an atoll comprising the three islets of Wilkes, Peale, and Wake. They were discovered by the British in 1796 and annexed by the U.S. in 1898. The entire area comprises 3 square miles and has no native population. In 1938, Pan American Airways established a seaplane base and Wake Island has been used as a commercial base since then. On Dec. 8, 1941, it was attacked by the Japanese, who finally took possession on Dec. 23. It was surrendered by the Japanese on Sept. 4, 1945.

The Federal Aviation Administration maintained a station on Wake Island until June 1972, when civil administration of the island was taken over by the U.S. Air Force. In 1962, the area was placed under the jurisdiction of the Department of the Interior.

Trust Territory of the Pacific Islands (Micronesia)

In 1885, Germany assumed a protectorate over the Marshall Islands; and, in 1899, she purchased the Northern Mariana and Caroline Islands from Spain. These islands were occupied by the Japanese in 1914 and were mandated to Japan by the League of Nations in 1919. On April 2, 1947, the U. N. Security Council approved a trusteeship agreement proposed by the U.S. under which the Northern Mariana, Caroline, and Marshall Islands became a Strategic Trust Territory under the administration of the U.S. The measure was approved by the President, with the agreement of Congress, on July 18, 1947. Administration was transferred from the Navy to the Department of the Interior on July 1, 1951. However, during 1953, administration of the islands of the Northern Marianas, except

Rota, was transferred back to the Navy. The Department of the Interior again took over administration of these islands in July, 1962.

In February 1975 a covenant was signed by the U.S. and the Marianas Political Status Commission that would make the 14 islands in the Northern Marianas a commonwealth under American sovereignty. The covenant was overwhelmingly ratified by the people of the islands and was approved by President Ford on March 24, 1976.

On April 9, 1978, in Hilo, Hawaii, the heads of the three Micronesian political status commissions and the U.S. negotiator signed a statement of agreed principles which is intended to form the basis of a free association relationship between the U.S. and Micronesia. A draft Compact of Free Association was initialled by the U.S. and the respective Micronesian commissions in late 1980, and negotiations to terminate the Trusteeship are continuing.

The entire group comprises more than 2,000 islands, but the total land area is only 531 square miles, many of the islands being only tiny coral reefs. The Micronesians are the main ethnic group; however, the inhabitants of two outlying islands, Kapingamarangi and Nukuoro, are Polynesian. The population of the Trust Territory in 1980 was estimated to be 116,974.

MARIANA ISLANDS

The Mariana Islands, east of the Philippines and south of Japan, include the islands of Guam, Rota, Saipan, Tinian, Pagan, Guguan, Agrihan, and Aguijan. Guam, the largest, is independent of the trusteeship, having been acquired by the U.S. from Spain in 1898. (For more information, *see* the entry on Guam in this section.)

Chief crops are copra and fresh fruits and vegetables.

CAROLINE ISLANDS

The Caroline Islands, east of the Philippines and south of the Marianas, include the Yap, Truk, and the Palau groups and the islands of Ponape and Kosrae, as well as many coral atolls.

The islands are composed chiefly of volcanic rock, and their peaks rise 2,000 to 3,000 feet above sea level. Chief exports of the islands are copra, fish products, and handicrafts.

MARSHALL ISLANDS

The Marshall Islands, east of the Carolines, are divided into two chains: the western or Ralik group, including the atolls Jaluit, Kwajalein, Wotho, Bikini, and Enewetak; and the eastern or Ratak group, including the atolls Mili, Majuro, Maloelap, Wotje, and Likiep.

The islands are of the coral-reef type and rise only a few feet above sea level. The chief crop is coconuts; exports include copra, tortoise shell, mother-of-pearl, etc.

Bikini and Enewetak were the scene of several atom-bomb tests after World War II. Enewetak was returned to Trust Territory administration in August 1976. In April 1977, some 55 original inhabitants, the forerunner of 450 returnees, were resettled after an absence of 30 years.

People Living in State of Birth—By State

Total population of each state is shown below, with the percentage still living in the state where they were born. Figures are estimates based on a sample.

State	Total pop.	Percent born in state	State	Total pop.	Percent born in state
Ala.	3,893.9	79.0%	Mont.	786.7	56.9
Alaska	401.9	31.6	Neb.	1,569.8	70.5
Ariz.	2,718.2	32.5	Nev.	800.5	21.3
Ark.	2,286.4	69.1	N.H.	920.6	49.7
Calif.	23,667.9	45.3	N.J.	7,364.8	56.1
Colo.	2,890.0	42.7	N.M.	1,302.9	51.2
Conn.	3,107.6	57.2	N.Y.	17,558.1	69.0
Del.	594.3	52.0	N.C.	5,881.8	75.8
D.C.	638.3	33.7	N.D.	652.7	72.6
Fla.	9,746.3	31.3	Ohio	10,797.6	72.1
Ga.	5,463.1	70.8	Okla.	3,025.3	63.0
Hawaii	964.7	57.8	Ore.	2,633.1	43.7
Idaho	943.9	49.3	Pa.	11,863.9	81.0
Ill.	11,426.5	68.9	R.I.	947.2	67.0
Ind.	5,490.2	71.3	S.C.	3,121.8	72.7
Iowa	2,913.8	76.8	S.D.	690.8	70.5
Kan.	2,363.7	62.3	Tenn.	4,591.1	72.3
Ky.	3,660.8	79.4	Tex.	14,229.2	68.6
La.	4,205.9	78.1	Utah	1,461.0	65.8
Me.	1,124.7	72.9	Vt.	511.4	61.2
Md.	4,217.0	53.4	Va.	5,346.8	60.0
Mass.	5,737.0	71.6	Wash.	4,132.2	47.8
Mich.	9,262.1	71.3	W. Va.	1,949.6	78.6
Minn.	4,076.0	74.7	Wis.	4,705.8	77.2
Miss.	2,520.6	78.5	Wyo.	469.6	38.4
Mo.	4,916.7	69.8	**U.S.**	**226,545.8**	**63.8%**

Source: Bureau of the Census.

Tabulated Data on State Governments

State	Governor: Term, years	Governor: Annual salary	Legislature[1]: Membership U[3]	Membership L[4]	Term, yrs. U[3]	Term, yrs. L[4]	Salaries of members[5]		Highest Court[2]: Members	Term, years	Annual salary[6]
Alabama	4[10]	$66,000[16]	35	105	4	4	$9,000	per annum[16]	9	6	$52,600
Alaska	4	77,760	20	40	4	2	20,076	per annum	5	([8])	77,760
Arizona	4	50,000	30	60	2	2	15,000	per annum	5	6	47,500
Arkansas	2	35,000	35	100	4	2	7,500	per annum[25]	7	8	46,214
California	4	49,100	40	80	4	2	28,110	per annum	7	12	62,935[25]
Colorado	4	60,000	35	65	4	2	14,000	per annum[26]	7	10	50,000
Connecticut	4	42,000	36	151	2	2	17,000	per biennium	6	8	50,800
Delaware	4[9]	35,000	21	41	4	2	11,400	per annum	5	12	52,920
Florida	4[10]	60,498	40	120	4	2	12,000	per annum	7	6	60,453
Georgia	4[9]	68,571	56	180	2	2	7,200	per annum	7	6	55,462
Hawaii	4	59,400	25	51	4	2	13,650	per session	5	10	56,430
Idaho	4	33,000	35	70	2	2	4,200	per annum	5	6	38,000
Illinois	4	58,000	59	118	4–2	2	28,000	per annum	7	10	58,000
Indiana	4[10]	48,000	50	100	4	2	9,600	per annum	5	([24])	42,000
Iowa	4	60,000	50	100	4	2	12,000	per annum	9	8	49,000
Kansas	4	49,500	40	125	4	2	42	per diem[22]	7	6	47,500
Kentucky	4[7]	50,000	38	100	4	2	50	per diem[22]	7	8	49,000
Louisiana	4	73,400	39	105	4	4	16,800	per annum	7	10	66,566
Maine	4	35,000	33	151	2	2	7,000	per biennium[16]	7	7	40,392
Maryland	4[10]	75,000	47	141	4	4	21,000	per annum	7	10	62,500
Massachusetts	4	60,000	40	160	2	2	20,335	per annum	7	Life	50,000
Michigan	4	70,000	38	110	4	2	31,000	per annum[16]	7	8	69,000
Minnesota	4	66,500	67	134	4	2	18,500	per annum[16]	9	6	56,000
Mississippi	4[7]	53,000	52	122	4	4	8,100	per session	9	8	46,000
Missouri	4[10]	55,000	34	163	4	2	15,000	per annum[5]	7	12	50,000
Montana	4	47,023	50	100	4	2	48	per diem[16]	6	8	47,023
Nebraska	4[10]	40,000	49[11]	—	4[11]	—	4,800	per annum	7	6	48,315
Nevada	4	65,000	1	42	4	2	6,240	per biennium	5	6	61,500
New Hampshire	2	51,830	24	([12])	2	2	200	per biennium	5	([13])	49,355
New Jersey	4[10]	85,000	40	80	4[14]	2	18,000	per annum	7	7[15]	78,000
New Mexico	4[7]	50,000	42	70	4	2	40	per diem	5	8	55,000
New York	4	100,000	60	150	2	2	28,788	per annum	7	14	75,600
North Carolina	4[9]	57,864	50	120	2	2	6,936	per annum[16]	7	8	57,012
North Dakota	4	47,000[16]	50	100	4	2	5	per diem[16 23]	5	10	53,900
Ohio	4	50,000	33	99	4	2	22,500	per annum	7	6	58,000
Oklahoma	4	70,000	48	101	4	2	18,000[27]	per annum	([19])	6	53,760
Oregon	4[10]	55,423	30	60	4	2	8,400[27]	per annum	7	6	54,637
Pennsylvania	4[10]	75,000	50	203	4	2	25,000	per annum	7	10	64,500
Rhode Island	2	49,500	50	100	2	2	5	per diem[17]	5	([18])	48,788
South Carolina	4[7]	60,000	46	124	4	2	10,000	per annum	5	10	47,000
South Dakota	4[10]	55,000	35	70	2	2	6,000	per biennium	5	8	52,750
Tennessee	4	68,226	33	99	4	2	8,308	per annum	5	8	58,000
Texas	4	85,500	31	150	4	2	7,200	per annum	([20])	6	71,400
Utah	4	52,000	29	75	4	2	25	per diem[16]	5	10	50,000
Vermont	2	48,800	30	150	2	2	80	per week[21]	5	6	41,000
Virginia	4[7]	75,000	40	100	4	2	8,000	per annum	7	12	63,000
Washington	4	63,000	49	98	4	2	11,200	per annum	9	6	51,500
West Virginia	4	60,000	34	100	4	2	5,136	per annum	5	12	49,000
Wisconsin	4	65,801	33	99	4	2	22,638	per annum	7	10	56,009
Wyoming	4	70,000	30	62	4	2	60	per diem[16]	5	8	63,500

1. General Assembly in Ark., Colo., Conn., Del., Ga., Ind., Ky., Md., Mo., N.C., Ohio, Pa., R.I., S.C., Tenn., Vt., Va., Legislative Assembly in N.D., Ore.; General Court in Mass., N.H.; Legislature in other states. Meets biennially in Calif., Ky., Me., Mont., Nev., N.H., N.J., N.C., N.D., Ore., Pa., Texas, Wash. and Wyo.; meets annually in other states. 2. Court of Appeals in Md., N.Y., Supreme Court of Virginia in Va., Supreme Judicial Court in Me., Mass.; Supreme Court in other states. 3. Upper house: Senate in all states. 4. Lower house: Assembly in Calif., Nev., N.Y., Wis.; House of Delegates in Md., Va., W.Va.; General Assembly in N.J.; House of Representatives in other states. 5. Does not include additional payments for expenses, mileage, special sessions, etc., or additional per diem payments beyond salary shown. 6. In some states, Chief Justice receives a higher salary. 7. Cannot succeed himself. 8. Appointed for 3 years; thereafter subject to approval or rejection on a nonpartisan ballot for 10-year term. 9. May serve only 2 terms, consecutive or otherwise. 10. May not serve 3rd consecutive term. 11. Unicameral legislature. 12. Constitutional number: 375–400. 13. Until 70 years old. 14. When term begins in Jan. of 2nd year following U.S. census, term shall be 2 years. 15. 2nd term receive tenure, mandatory retirement at 70. 16. Plus additional expenses. 17. For 60 days only. 18. Term of good behavior. 19. 9 members in Supreme Court, highest in civil cases; 3 in Court of Criminal Appeals. 20. 9 members in Supreme Court, highest in civil cases; 9 in Court of Criminal Appeals. 21. To limit of $7,500 per biennium; $2,000 for special session. 22. When in session. 23. Plus $180 per month. 24. Appointed for 2 years; thereafter elected popularly for 10-year term. 25. To receive cost of living increase not to exceed 10% in the two year period. 26. Those elected before 1980 receive $12,000 until re-elected. 27. Plus $300 per month when performing official duties. *Source: Information Please* questionnaires to the states.

50 Largest Cities of the United States

Source of population and land area: Bureau of the Census. Telephones; source: American Telephone & Telegraph Co. Other data were supplied by the cities in response to *Information Please* questionnaires.

ALBUQUERQUE, N.M.

Incorporated as city: 1891
Mayor: Harry Kinney (to Dec. 1985)
1970 population & (rank): 244,501 (58)
1980 population (1980 census) & (rank): 331,767 (44)
1970–80 population change: +35.7%
1981 land area: 95.3 sq mi. (247 sq km)
Altitude: 4,958 ft.
Location: Central part of state on Rio Grande River
County: Bernalillo
Churches: 211
City-owned parks: 135
Telephones (Jan. 1, 1979): 308,271
Radio stations: 14
Television stations: 5
Assessed valuation (1980): $1,318,049,290
City tax rate (1981): $22.02 per $1,000
Bonded debt (1981): $113,930,000
Revenue (1981): $86,080,200
Expenditures (1981): $91,778,547
Chamber of Commerce: Albuquerque Chamber of Commerce, 401 2nd St., N.W., Albuquerque, N.M. 87102. Hispanic Chamber of Commerce 407 Rio Grande Blvd., N.W. Albuquerque, N.M. 87104

ATLANTA, GA.

Incorporated as city: 1847
Mayor: Andrew Young (to Jan. 1986)
1970 population & (rank): 495,039 (27)
1980 population (1980 census) & (rank): 425,022 (29)
1970–80 population change: −14.1%
1981 city land area: 131.0 sq mi. (339 sq km)
Altitude: Highest, 1,050 ft; lowest, 940
Location: In northwest central part of state, near Chattahoochee River
Counties: Fulton and De Kalb
Churches (5-county area): 1,500
City-owned parks: 297 (3,178 ac.)
Telephones (Jan. 1, 1979): 907,830
Radio stations (15-county area): AM, 23; FM, 15
Television stations (15-county area): 6 commercial; 2 PBS
Gross assessed valuation (city, 1981): $4,027,553,312
City tax rate (1982): $46.60 per $1,000
Total bonded debt (1981): $174,388,203
Revenue (incl. General Fund, Airport Revenues, Water/Sewer Fund) (1981): $299,313,314
Expenditures (1981): $273,954,844
Chamber of Commerce: Atlanta Chamber of Commerce, 1300 N Omni International, Atlanta, Ga. 30303

Information is gathered on 3 geographic areas: City of Atlanta, 5-county metro area, 15-county SMSA

AUSTIN, TEX.

Incorporated as city: 1839
Mayor: Carole Keeton McClellan (to May, 1983)
1970 population & (rank): 253,539 (56)
1980 population (1980 census) & (rank): 345,496 (42)
1970–80 population change: +36.3%
1981 land area: 116.0 sq mi. (300 sq km)
Altitude: Highest, 425 ft
Location: In south central part of state, on the Colorado River
County: Seat of Travis Co.
Churches: Protestant, 290; Roman Catholic, 19; Jewish, 3
City-owned parks and playgrounds: 137
Telephones (Jan. 1, 1979): 324,658
Radio stations: AM, 6; FM, 12
Television stations: 3 commercial; 1 PBS
Assessed valuation (1981–82): $7,310,868,750
Tax rate (1981–82): $17.00 per $1,000 at 100% assessed valuation
Bonded debt (1981–82): $1,992,545,731
Revenue (1981–82): $117,852,060
Expenditures (1981–82): $115,310,000
Chamber of Commerce: Austin Chamber of Commerce, 901 W Riverside Dr., Austin, Tex. 78701

BALTIMORE, MD.

Incorporated as city: 1797
Mayor: William D. Schaefer (to Dec. 1983)
1970 population & (rank): 905,787 (7)
1980 population (1980 census) & (rank): 786,775 (10)
1970–80 population change: −13.1%
1981 land area: 80.3 sq mi. (208 sq km)
Altitude: Highest, 490 ft; lowest, sea level
Location: On Patapsco River, about 12 mi. from Chesapeake Bay
County: Independent city
Churches: Roman Catholic, 72; Jewish, 50; Protestant and others, 344
City-owned parks: 347 park areas and tracts (6,314 ac.)
Telephones (Jan. 1, 1979): 1,400,808
Radio stations: AM, 11; FM, 9
Television stations: 5
Assessed valuation (1982–83): $3,979,387,638
City tax rate (1982): $59.70 per $1,000
Net bonded debt (March 1982): $474,316,000
Revenue (1982): $1,764,862,177
Expenditures (1980): $1,731,154,967
Chamber of Commerce: Greater Baltimore Committee, 2 Hopkins Plaza, Baltimore, Md. 21201

BIRMINGHAM, ALA.

Incorporated as city: 1871
Mayor: Richard Arrington, Jr. (to Nov. 1983)
1970 population & (rank): 300,910 (48)
1980 population (1980 census) & (rank): 284,413 (50)
1970–80 population change: −5.5%
1981 land area: 98.5 sq mi. (255 sq km)
Altitude: Highest, 1,200 ft.; lowest, 583
Location: In north central part of state in Jones Valley.
County: Seat of Jefferson Co.
Churches: 1,100
City-owned parks and playgrounds: 100 (1,684 ac.)
Telephones (Jan. 1, 1979): 466,176
Radio stations: AM, 16; FM, 4
Television stations: 5

Assessed valuation (1982): $668,446,442
City tax rate (1982): $28.50 per $1,000 assessed value
Bonded debt (June 1981): $135,683,116
Revenue (1981): $84,645,270
Expenditures (1981): $84,585,696
Chamber of Commerce: Chamber of Commerce, 1st Ave. and 21st St., Birmingham, Ala.

BOSTON, MASS.

Incorporated as city: 1822
Mayor: Kevin H. White (to Jan. 1984)
1970 population & (rank): 641,071 (16)
1980 population (1980 census) & (rank): 562,994 (20)
1970–80 population change: −12.2%
1981 land area: 47.2 sq mi. (122 sq km)
Altitude: Highest, 330 ft; lowest, sea level
Location: On Massachusetts Bay, at mouths of Charles and Mystic Rivers
County: Seat of Suffolk Co.
Churches: Protestant, 187; Roman Catholic, 73; Jewish, 28; others, 100
City-owned parks, playgrounds, etc.: 2,276.36 ac.
Telephones (Jan. 1, 1979): 534,287
Radio stations: AM, 9; FM, 8
Television stations: 7
Assessed valuation (1982): $1,908,700,000
City tax rate (1982): $230.90 per $1,000
Gross direct bonded debt (July 1, 1982): $455,533,500
Revenue (1982): $828,480,000
Expenditures (1982): $828,480,000
Chamber of Commerce: Boston Chamber of Commerce, 125 High St., Boston, Mass. 02110

BUFFALO, N.Y.

Incorporated as city: 1832
Mayor: James Griffin (to Dec. 1985)
1970 population & (rank): 462,768 (28)
1980 population (1980 census) & (rank): 357,870 (39)
1970–80 population change: −22.7%
1981 land area: 41.8 sq mi. (198 sq km)
Altitude: Highest, 698 ft; lowest, 571
Location: At east end of Lake Erie, on Niagara River
County: Seat of Erie Co.
Churches: 60 denominations, with over 1,100 churches
County-owned parks: 9 public parks (3,000 ac.)
Telephones (Jan. 1, 1979): 409,914
Radio stations: AM, 13; FM, 14
Television stations: 5 (plus reception from 4 Canadian stations)
Assessed valuation (1980–81): $1,000,496,000
City tax rate (1980–81): $85.16 per $1,000
Total funded debt (long-term, June 30, 1981): $134,547,000
Revenue (general fund, 1980–81): $207,296,996
Expenditures (1980–81): $122,156,475
Chamber of Commerce: Buffalo Area Chamber of Commerce, 107 Delaware Ave., Buffalo, N.Y. 14202

CHARLOTTE, N.C.

Incorporated as city: 1768
Mayor: H. Edward Knox (to Nov. 1983)
1970 population & (rank): 241,420 (60)
1980 population (1980 census) & (rank): 314,447 (47)
1970–80 population change: +30.2%
1981 land area: 139.7 sq mi. (362 sq km)
Altitude: 765 ft
Location: In the southern part of state near the border of South Carolina
County: Seat of Mecklenburg Co.
Churches: Protestant, over 400; Roman Catholic, 8; Jewish, 3; Greek Orthodox, 1
City-owned parks and parkways: 87
Telephones (Jan. 1, 1979): 366,246
Radio stations: AM, 8; FM, 4
Television stations: 4 commercial; 2 PBS
Assessed valuation (1980–81): $6,791,162,390
City tax rate (includes county, 1980–81): $18.02 per $1,000
Bonded debt (June 30, 1981): $199,925,000
Revenue (1981): $86,892,402
Expenditures (1981): $82,330,785
Chamber of Commerce: Greater Charlotte Chamber of Commerce, P.O. Box 32785, Charlotte, N.C., 28232

CHICAGO, ILL.

Incorporated as city: 1837
Mayor: Jane M. Byrne (to April 1983)
1970 population & (rank): 3,369,357 (2)
1980 population (1980 census) & (rank): 3,005,072 (2)
1970–80 population change: −10.8%
1981 land area: 228.1 sq mi. (591 sq km)
Altitude: Highest, 672 ft; lowest, 578.5
Location: On lower west shore of Lake Michigan
County: Seat of Cook Co.
Churches: Protestant, 850; Roman Catholic, 266; Jewish, 61
City-owned parks: 572
Telephones (Jan. 1, 1979): 2,639,826
Radio stations: AM, 17; FM, 19
Television stations: 9
Assessed valuation (1980): $12,098,730,347
Total Chicago tax rate (1980): $97.93 per $1,000
Total gross bonded debt (1980): $368,410,000
Revenue (est. 1982): $1,773,078,818
Expenditures (est. 1982): $1,760,122,933
Chamber of Commerce: Chicago Association of Commerce & Industry, 130 S Michigan Ave., Chicago, Ill. 60603

CINCINNATI, OHIO

Incorporated as city: 1819
Mayor: David S. Mann (to Dec. 1982)
City Manager: Sylvester Murray
1970 population & (rank): 453,514 (30)
1980 population (1980 census) & (rank): 385,457 (32)
1970–80 population change: −15.0%
1981 land area: 78.1 sq mi. (202 sq km)
Altitude: Highest, 960 ft; lowest, 441
Location: In southwestern corner of state on Ohio River
County: Seat of Hamilton Co.
Churches: 850
City-owned parks: 96 (4,345 ac.)
Telephones (Jan. 1, 1979): 961,410
Radio stations: AM, 9; FM, 12 (Greater Cincinnati)
Television stations: 6
Assessed valuation (1981): $2,416,996,340
City tax rate (1981): $11.12 per $1,000
Bonded debt (1981): $177,514,180
Revenue (general fund, 1981): $130,120,000
Expenditures (general fund, 1981): $134,947,579
Chamber of Commerce: Cincinnati Chamber of Commerce, 120 W Fifth St., Cincinnati, Ohio 45202

CLEVELAND, OHIO

Incorporated as city: 1836
Mayor: George V. Voinovich (to Dec. 1985)
1970 population & (rank): 750,879 (10)

1980 population (1980 census) & (rank): 573,822 (18)
1970–80 population change: −23.6%
1981 land area: 79.0 sq mi. (205 sq km)
Altitude: Highest, 865 ft.; lowest, 573
Location: On Lake Erie at mouth of Cuyahoga River
County: Seat of Cuyahoga Co.
Churches: [1] Protestant, 717; Roman Catholic, 162; Jewish, 23; Eastern Orthodox, 18
City-owned parks: 41 (1,930 ac.)
Telephones (Jan. 1, 1979): 924,277
Radio stations: AM, 13; FM, 14
Television stations: 7
Assessed valuation (1982): $3,499,864,285
City tax rate (1981): $70.30 per $1,000
Bonded debt (March 31, 1981): $369,790,000
Revenue (est. 1982): $231,924,000
Expenditures (est. 1982): $231,923,000
Chamber of Commerce: Greater Cleveland Growth Association, 690 Union Commerce Building, Cleveland, Ohio 44115

1. 100-mile area.

COLUMBUS, OHIO

Incorporated as city: 1834
Mayor: Tom Moody (to Jan. 1984)
1970 population & (rank): 540,025 (21)
1980 population (1980 census) & (rank): 565,032 (19)
1970–80 population change: +4.6%
1981 land area: 180.9 sq mi. (469 sq km)
Altitude: Highest, 902 ft; lowest, 702
Location: In central part of state, on Scioto River
County: Seat of Franklin Co.
Churches: Protestant, 412; Roman Catholic, 43; Jewish, 5
City-owned parks: 135 (10,931 ac.)
Telephones (Jan. 1, 1979): 484,446
Radio stations: AM, 8; FM, 6
Television stations: 3 commercial, 2 PBS
Assessed valuation (1981): $4,542,836,000
City tax rate (1981): $48.78 per $1,000
Bonded debt (Dec. 31, 1981): $479,236,000
Revenue (1981): $376,244,974
Expenditures (1981): $415,330,440
Chamber of Commerce: Columbus Area Chamber of Commerce, P.O. Box 1527, Columbus, Ohio 43216

DALLAS, TEX.

Incorporated as city: 1856
Mayor: Jack Evans (to April 1983)
City Manager: Charles Anderson (apptd. Oct. 1981)
1970 population & (rank): 844,401 (8)
1980 population (1980 census) & (rank): 904,078 (7)
1970–80 population change: +7.1%
1981 land area: 333.0 sq mi. (862 sq km)
Altitude: Highest, 750 ft; lowest, 375
Location: In northeastern part of state, on Trinity River
County: Seat of Dallas Co.
Churches: 1,200 (in Dallas Co.)
City-owned parks: 283 (21,012 ac.)
Telephones (Jan. 1, 1979): 838,735
Radio stations: AM, 14; FM, 15
Television stations: 7
Assessed valuation (1980–81): $26,051,000,000
City tax rate (1980–81): $6.38 per $1,000 (at 100% valuation)
Bonded debt (Sept. 30, 1981): $658,634,000
Revenue (1981): $354,388,000
Expenditures (1981): $422,336,000
Chamber of Commerce: Dallas Chamber of Commerce. 1507 Pacific, Dallas, Tex. 75201

DENVER, COLO.

Incorporated as city: 1861
Mayor: William H. McNichols, Jr. (to July 1, 1983)
1970 population & (rank): 514,678 (24)
1980 population (1980 census) & (rank): 492,365 (24)
1970–80 population change: −4.3%
1981 land area: 110.6 sq mi. (287 sq km)
Altitude: Highest, 5,470 ft; lowest, 5,130
Location: In northeast central part of state, on South Platte River
County: Coextensive with Denver Co.
Churches: Protestant, 815; Roman Catholic, 63; Jewish, 13[1]
City-owned parks: 155 (3,600 ac.)
City-owned mountain parks: 40 (13,448 ac.)
Telephones (Jan. 1, 1979): 1,354,374
Radio stations: AM, 18; FM, 13[1]
Television stations: 5
Assessed valuation (1981): $2,337,419,740
City tax rate (1981): $29.34 per $1,000[2]
Bonded debt (1981): $363,940,000[2]
Revenue (1981): $542,767,100[2]
Expenditures (1981): $499,836,800[2]
Chamber of Commerce: Denver Chamber of Commerce, 1301 Welton, Denver, Colo. 80204

1. Metropolitan area. 2. Excluding school district.

DETROIT, MICH.

Incorporated as city: 1815
Mayor: Coleman A. Young (to Jan. 1986)
1970 population & (rank): 1,514,063 (5)
1980 population (1980 census) & (rank): 1,203,339 (6)
1970–80 population change: −20.5%
1981 land area: 135.6 sq mi. (351 sq km)
Altitude: Highest, 685 ft; lowest, 574
Location: In southeastern part of state, on Detroit River
County: Seat of Wayne Co.
Churches: [1] Protestant, 2,204; Roman Catholic, 333; Jewish, 40
City-owned parks: 52 parks (3,843 ac.); 350 sites (5,838 ac.)
Telephones (Jan. 1, 1979): 1,509,894
Radio stations: AM, 17; FM, 37 (7-county area)
Television stations: 11 (incl. Windsor, Ontario, Canada)[1]
Assessed valuation (1981): $5,321,090,420
City tax rate (1981–82): $33.01 per $1,000[2]
Net bonded debt (June 1981): General obligations, (net): $316,640,000
Revenue (1981–82): $1,604,400,000[3]
Expenditures (1981–82): $1,604,400,000[3]
Chamber of Commerce: Greater Detroit Chamber of Commerce, 150 Michigan Ave., Detroit, Mich. 48226

1. Six-county metropolitan area. 2. Excludes school system and county tax. 3. Excludes utilities.

EL PASO, TEX.

Incorporated as city: 1873
Mayor: Jonathan Rogers (to April 1983)
1970 population & (rank): 322,261 (45)
1980 population (1980 census) & (rank): 425,259 (28)
1970–80 population change: +32.0%
1981 land area: 239.2 sq mi. (620 sq km)
Altitude: 4,000 ft
Location: In far western part of state, on Rio Grande
County: Seat of El Paso Co.
Churches: Protestant, 212; Roman Catholic, 36; Jewish, 2; others, 13
City-owned parks: 83 (4,694 ac.)
Telephones (Jan. 1, 1979): 259,609

Radio stations: AM, 9; FM, 5
Television stations: 5
Assessed valuation (1982): $6,764,485,271
City tax rate (1982): $5.31 per $1,000, city; $7.26, El Paso Independent School District: $7.36, Ysleta Independent School District.
Bonded debt (1982): $38,510,000
Revenue (1981–82): $91,851,605
Expenditures (1981–82): $91,851,605
Chamber of Commerce: El Paso Chamber of Commerce, 10 Civic Center Plaza, El Paso, Tex. 79944

FORT WORTH, TEX.

Incorporated as city: 1873
Mayor: Bob Bolen (to April 1983)
City Manager: Robert L. Herchert
1970 population & (rank): 393,455 (33)
1980 population (1980 census) & (rank): 385,164 (33)
1970–80 population change: −21.1%
1981 land area: 240.1 sq mi. (622 sq km)
Altitude: Highest, 780 ft; lowest, 520
Location: In north central part of state, on Trinity River
County: Seat of Tarrant Co.
Churches: Protestant, 392; Roman Catholic, 16; Jewish, 2
City-owned parks: 136 (8,189 ac.; 3,500 ac. in Nature Center)
Telephones (Jan. 1, 1979): 365,150
Radio stations: AM, 6; FM, 8
Television stations: 6 (2 local)
Assessed valuation (1981–82): $5,868,782,068
City tax rate (1981–82): $9.05 per $1,000
Bonded debt (1981–82): $189,848,000
Revenue (1981–82): $127,789,438
Expenditures (1981–82): $127,789,438
Chamber of Commerce: Fort Worth Chamber of Commerce, 700 Throckmorton, Fort Worth, Tex. 76102

HONOLULU, HAWAII

Incorporated as city and county: 1907
Mayor: Eileen R. Anderson (to Jan. 1985)
1970 population & (rank): 324,871 (44)
1980 population (1980 census) & (rank): 365,048[1] (36)
1970–1980 population change: +12.4%
1981 land area: 87.0 sq mi. (225 sq km)
Altitude: Highest, 4,025 ft; lowest, sea level
Location: The city and county government's jurisdiction includes the entire island of Oahu
Churches: Roman Catholic, 33; Buddhist, 32; Jewish, 2; Protestant and others, 328
City-owned parks: 5,279 ac.
Telephones (Jan. 1, 1979): 375,858
Radio stations: AM, 18; FM, 7
Television stations: 5
Assessed valuation (1981): $10,592,000,000 (60% of market value.)
City and county tax rate (1981): $15.23 per $1,000
Bonded debt (June 1981): $193,533,000
Net revenue (1980–81): $375,765,739
Net expenditures (1980–81): $316,887,581; capital improvement budget, $33,895,899
Chamber of Commerce: Chamber of Commerce of Hawaii, 735 Bishop St., Honolulu, Hawaii 96813

1. City and county area.

HOUSTON, TEX.

Incorporated as city: 1837
Mayor: Kathryn J. Whitmire (to Dec. 1983)
1970 population & (rank): 1,233,535 (6)
1980 population (1980 census) & (rank): 1,595,138 (5)
1970–80 population change: +29.2%
1981 land area: 556.4 sq mi. (1,441 sq km)
Altitude: Highest, 120 ft; lowest, sea level
Location: In southeastern part of state, near Gulf of Mexico
County: Seat of Harris Co.
Churches: 1,750[2]
City-owned parks: 259 (5,742 ac., not including parkways)
Telephones (Jan. 1, 1979): 1,436,358
Radio stations: AM, 14; FM, 16[1]
Television stations: 6
Assessed valuation (1981): $29,542,633,000
City tax rate (1981): $.84 per $100
Bonded debt (1981): $588,910,000
Revenue (1981): $520,348,000
Expenditures (1981): $485,784,000
Chamber of Commerce: Houston Chamber of Commerce, 1100 Milam Building, Houston, Tex. 77002

1. Includes annexations since 1970. 2. Metropolitan area (Harris County).

INDIANAPOLIS, IND.

Incorporated as city: 1832 (reincorporated 1838)
Mayor: William H. Hudnut III (to Jan. 1984)
1970 population & (rank): 736,856 (11)
1980 population (1980 census) & (rank): 700,807 (12)
1970–80 population change: −4.9%
1981 land area: 352.0 sq mi. (912 sq km)
Altitude: Highest, 840 ft; lowest, 700
Location: In central part of the state, on West Fork of White River
County: Seat of Marion Co.
Churches: 1,200[1]
City-owned parks: 188 (8,992 ac.)
Telephones (Jan. 1, 1979): 680,183
Radio stations: AM, 9; FM, 13[1]
Television stations: 6[1]
Assessed valuation (1981): (consolidated city), $3,406,194,289; (Marion County) $3,695,225,852
City tax rate (Center Township, 1981): $101.40 per $1,000
Gross debt (consolidated city, Dec. 31, 1981): $190,543,000
Revenue (1981): $237,595,046
Expenditures (1981): $235,551,594
Chamber of Commerce: Indianapolis Chamber of Commerce, 320 N Meridian St., Indianapolis, Ind. 46202

1. Marion County.

JACKSONVILLE, FLA.

Incorporated as city: 1822
Mayor: Jake M. Godbold (to July 1, 1983)
1970 population & (rank): 504,265 (26)
1980 population (1980 census) & (rank): 540,920 (22)
1970–80 population change: +7.3%
1981 land area: 759.6 sq mi. (1,967 sq km)
Altitude: Highest, 71 ft; lowest, sea level
Location: On St. Johns River, 20 miles from Atlantic Ocean
County: Duval
Churches: Protestant, 525; Roman Catholic, 20; Jewish, 4; others, 11
City-owned parks and playgrounds: 138 (1,522 ac.)
Telephones (Jan. 1, 1979): 431,204
Radio stations: AM, 15; FM, 10
Television stations: 6 commercial, 1 PBS
Assessed valuation (1981): $7,413,924,871
City tax rate (1981–82): $19.62 per $1,000 (old county area); $20.07 per $1,000 (old city area)
Bonded debt (1981): $50,075,783
Revenue (1981–82): $1,120,170,750

Expenditures (1981–82): $1,120,170,750
Chamber of Commerce: Jacksonville Area Chamber of Commerce, Jacksonville, Fla. 32202

KANSAS CITY, MO.

Incorporated as city: 1850
Mayor: Richard L. Berkley (to April 1983)
City Manager: Robert A. Kipp (apptd. Jan. 1974)
1970 population & (rank): 507,330 (25)
1980 population (1980 census) & (rank): 448,159 (27)
1970–80 population change: −11.7%
1981 land area: 316.3 sq mi. (819 sq km)
Altitude: Highest, 1,014 ft; lowest, 722
Location: In western part of state, at juncture of Missouri and Kansas Rivers
County: Located in Jackson, Clay, and Platte Co.
Churches: 1,100 churches of all denominations
City-owned parks and playgrounds: 168 (7,500 ac.)
Telephones (Jan. 1, 1979): 351,494
Radio stations: AM, 14; FM, 13[1]
Television stations: 6[1]
Assessed valuation (1980–81): $1,811,988,223
City tax rate (1980–81): $15.20 per $1,000
Bonded debt (1980–81): $68,035,000
Revenue (1980–81): $277,185,650
Expenditures (1980–81): $267,222,186
Budget (gross total, 1981–82): $343,989,006
Chamber of Commerce: Chamber of Commerce of Greater Kansas City, 920 Main St., Kansas City, Mo. 64105

1. Metropolitan area.

LONG BEACH, CALIF.

Founded: 1881
Mayor: Eunice N. Sato (to July 1977)
City Manager: John E. Dever (Jan. 1, 1977)
1970 population & (rank): 358,879 (40)
1980 population (1980 census) & (rank): 361,334 (37)
1970–80 population change: +0.7%
1981 land area: 49.8 sq mi. (129 sq km)
Altitude: Highest, 170 ft; lowest, sea level
Location: On San Pedro Bay, south of Los Angeles
County: In Los Angeles Co.
Churches: 236
City-owned parks: 43 (1,620 ac.)
Telephones: (included in Los Angeles area)
Radio stations: AM, 2; FM, 6
Television stations: 1 (cable)
Assessed valuation (1982): $9,913,928,996
City tax rate (1981–82): none; county, $10 per $1,000
Bonded debt (June 1981): $2,700,000
Revenue (1981–82): $977,310,935
Expenditures (1981–82): $992,304,842
Chamber of Commerce: Long Beach Chamber of Commerce, 50 Oceangate Plaza, Long Beach, Calif. 90802

LOS ANGELES, CALIF.

Incorporated as city: 1850
Mayor: Tom Bradley (to June 1985)
1970 population & (rank): 2,811,801 (3)
1980 population (1980 census) & (rank): 2,966,850 (3)
1970–80 population change: +5.5%
1981 land area: 464.7 sq mi. (1,204 sq km)
Altitude: Highest, 5,081 ft; lowest, sea level
Location: In southwestern part of state, on Pacific Ocean
County: Seat of Los Angeles Co.
Churches: 1,963 of all denominations
City-owned parks: 296 (14,489 ac.)
Telephones (extended area, Jan. 1, 1979): 6,096,663[1]
Radio stations: AM, 32; FM, 40
Television stations: 18
Assessed valuation (1981–82): $72,877,439,927
City tax rate (1981–82): $1.33 per $1,000 (100% valuation)
Gross debt (June 30, 1981): general obligation bonds, $84,255,000; revenue bonds, $2,463,095,000
Revenue (1981–82): $1,414,588,000
Expenditures (1981–82): $1,392,488,000
Chamber of Commerce: Los Angeles Chamber of Commerce, 404 S Bixel St., Los Angeles, Calif. 90017

1. Includes Long Beach, Calif.

LOUISVILLE, KY.

Incorporated as city: 1828
Mayor: Harvey I. Sloane (to Dec. 1985)
1970 population & (rank): 361,706 (38)
1980 population (1980 census) & (rank): 298,840 (49)
1970–80 population change: −17.5%
1981 land area: 60.0 sq mi. (155 sq km)
Altitude: Highest, 565 ft; lowest, 477
Location: In north central part of state, on Ohio River
County: Seat of Jefferson Co.
Churches: 678[1]
City-owned parks and playgrounds: 166 (over 7,000 ac.)
Telephones (Jan. 1, 1979): 576,756
Radio stations: 16
Television stations: 5
Assessed valuation (1981): $3,591,678,150
City tax rate (1981–82): $4.95 per $1,000, real property; $5.66 per $1,000, personal property (exclusive of schools) (city purposes only; exclusive of schools)
Net bonded debt (Jan. 1, 1982): $35,724,000
Revenue (1980–81): $123,450,360
Expenditures (1980–81): $122,978,912
Chamber of Commerce: Louisville Area Chamber of Commerce, 300 W Liberty St., Louisville, Ky. 40202

1. Metropolitan area.

MEMPHIS, TENN.

Incorporated as city: 1826
Mayor: Wyeth Chandler (to Dec. 1983)
1970 population & (rank): 623,988 (17)
1980 population (1980 census) & (rank): 646,174 (14)
1970–80 population change: +3.6%
1981 land area: 264.1 sq mi. (684 sq km)
Altitude: Highest, 331 ft
Location: In southwestern corner of state, on Mississippi River
County: Seat of Shelby Co.
Churches: 1,000
Parks and playgrounds: 169 (5,400 ac.)
Telephones (Jan. 1979): 621,276
Radio stations: AM, 13; FM, 8
Television stations: 5
Assessed valuation (1981): $2,905,373,048
City tax rate (1981): $35.50 per $1,000
Bonded debt (June 30, 1981): $464,887,550
Revenue (1981): $365,682,394
Expenditures (1981): $377,161,743
Chamber of Commerce: Memphis Area Chamber of Commerce, P.O. Box 224, Memphis, Tenn. 38103

MIAMI, FLA.

Incorporated as city: 1896
Mayor: Maurice A. Ferre (to Nov. 1983)
City manager: Howard V. Gary (apptd. April 1981)

1970 population & (rank): 334,859 (42)
1980 population (1980 census) & (rank): 346,865 (41)
1970–80 population change: +3.6%
1981 land area: 34.3 sq mi. (89 sq km)
Altitude: Average, 12 ft
Location: In southeastern part of state, on Biscayne Bay
County: Seat of Dade Co.
Churches: Protestant, 592; Roman Catholic, 53; Jewish, 48
City-owned parks: 94
Telephones (Jan. 1, 1979): 1,066,918
Radio stations: AM, 18; FM, 20
Television stations: 5 commercial, 2 PBS
Assessed valuation (1981–82): $7,302,234,465
City tax rate (1981–82): $10.66 per $1,000
Bonded debt (1981–82): $116,010,000
Revenue (1981–82): $161,627,095
Expenditures (1981–82): $161,627,095
Chamber of Commerce: Greater Miami Chamber of Commerce, 391 N.E. 15th St., Miami, Fla. 33132

MILWAUKEE, WIS.

Incorporated as city: 1846
Mayor: Henry W. Maier (to April 1984)
1970 population & (rank): 717,372 (12)
1980 population (1980 census) & (rank): 636,236 (16)
1970–80 population change: −11.3%
1981 land area: 95.8 sq mi. (248 sq km)
Altitude: 580.60 ft
Location: In southeastern part of state, on Lake Michigan
County: Seat of Milwaukee Co.
Churches: 411
County-owned parks: 14,061 ac.
Telephones (Jan. 1, 1979): 862,735
Radio stations: AM, 9; FM, 12
Television stations: 7
Assessed valuation (1981): $7,459,893,460
City tax rate (1981): $32.72 per $1,000
Gross debt (1981): $198,090,800
Revenue (1981): $459,582,858
Expenditures (1981): $478,449,282
Chamber of Commerce: Metropolitan Milwaukee Association of Commerce, 828 N. Broadway, Milwaukee, Wis. 53202

MINNEAPOLIS, MINN.

Incorporated as city: 1867
Mayor: Donald M. Fraser (to Jan. 1984)
1970 population & (rank): 434,400 (31)
1980 population (1980 census) & (rank): 370,951 (34)
1970–80 population change: −14.6%
1981 land area: 55.1 sq mi. (143 sq km)
Altitude: Highest, 945 ft; lowest, 695
Location: In southeast central part of state, on Mississippi River
County: Seat of Hennepin Co.
Churches: 419
City-owned parks: 153
Telephones (incl. St. Paul, Jan. 1, 1979): 1,610,700
Radio stations: AM, 17; FM, 15 (metro area)
Television stations: 6 (metro area)
Assessed valuation (1982): $2,341,764,115[1]
City tax rate (1982): $105.93 per $1,000
Net debt (Dec. 31, 1981): $315,155,000
Revenue (1981): $315,319,523
Expenditures (1981): $304,546,192
Chamber of Commerce: Greater Minneapolis Chamber of Commerce, 15 S Fifth Street, Minneapolis, Minn. 55402

1. Assessed valuations on majority of properties now range from 16% (homesteads) to 43% (commercial, industrial) of actual market value.

NASHVILLE, TENN.

Incorporated as city: 1806
Mayor: Richard H. Fulton (to Sept. 1983)
1970 population & (rank): 426,029 (32)
1980 population (1980 census) & (rank): 455,651 (25)
1970–80 population change: +7.0%
1981 land area: 479.4 sq mi. (1,242 sq km)
Altitude: Highest, 1,100 ft; lowest, approx. 400 ft
Location: In north central part of state, on Cumberland River
County: Davidson
Churches: Protestant, 739; Roman Catholic, 16; Jewish, 3
City-owned parks: 68 (6,650 ac.)
Telephones (Jan. 1, 1979): 420,995
Radio stations: AM, 11; FM, 8
Television stations: 5
Assessed valuation (1981): $1,955,103,362
City tax rate (1981): $68.30 per $1,000
Bonded debt (June 1981): $195,756,000
Revenue (1981): $322,152,884
Expenditures (1981): $320,265,041
Chamber of Commerce: Nashville Area Chamber of Commerce, 161 Fourth Ave. North, Nashville, Tenn. 37219

NEWARK, N.J.

Incorporated as city: 1836
Mayor: Kenneth A. Gibson (to July 1984)
1970 population & (rank): 381,930 (35)
1980 population (1980 census) & (rank): 329,248 (46)
1970–80 population change: −13.8%
1981 land area: 24.1 sq mi. (62 sq km)
Altitude: Highest, 273.4 ft; lowest, sea level
Location: In northeastern part of state, on Passaic River and Newark Bay
County: Seat of Essex Co.
Churches: Roman Catholic, 32; Jewish, 4; Protestant and others, 250
City-owned parks: 40 (and 20 mini parks); (39.3 ac.)
County-governed parks in city: 7 (743.97 ac.)
Telephones (Jan. 1, 1979): 329,254
Radio stations: AM, 2; FM, 4
Television stations: 2
Assessed valuation (1982): $1,024,987,400
City tax rate (1982): $100.90 per $1,000
Net bonded debt (1982): $52,296,486
Revenue (est. 1982): $293,579,659
Expenditures (est. 1982): $293,579,659
Chamber of Commerce: Greater Newark Chamber of Commerce, 50 Park Place, Newark, N.J. 07102

NEW ORLEANS, LA.

Incorporated as city: 1805
Mayor: Ernest N. Morial (to May 1986)
1970 population & (rank): 593,471 (19)
1980 population (1980 census) & (rank): 557,927 (21)
1970–80 population change: −6.1%
1981 land area: 199.4 sq mi. (516 sq km)
Altitude: Highest, 15 ft; lowest, −4
Location: In southeastern part of state, between Mississippi River and Lake Ponchartrain
Parish: Seat of Orleans Parish
Churches: 644
City-owned parks: 69 (21,000 ac.)
Telephones (Jan. 1, 1979): 754,517
Radio stations: AM, 12; FM, 10
Television stations: 5
Assessed valuation (1981): $698,915,044
City tax rate (1980): $93.57 per $1,000
Bonded debt (Jan. 1981): $150,783,000
Revenue (est. 1981): $280,014,718

Expenditures (est. 1981): $280,014,718
Chamber of Commerce: New Orleans and the River Region Chamber of Commerce, 301 Camp Street, New Orleans, La. 70130.

NEW YORK, N.Y.

Chartered as "Greater New York": 1898
Mayor: Edward Koch (to Dec. 31, 1985)
Borough Presidents: Bronx, Stanley Simon; Brooklyn, Howard Golden; Manhattan, Andrew Stein; Queens, Donald R. Manes; Staten Island, Anthony Gaeta
1970 population & (rank): 7,895,563 (1)[1]
1980 population (1980 census) & (rank): 7,071,639 (1)[1]
1970–80 population change: −10.4%
1981 land area: 301.5 sq mi. (781 sq km) (Queens, 109; Brooklyn, 72; Staten Island, 55; Bronx, 42.5; Manhattan, 23.0)
Altitude: Highest, 410 ft; lowest, sea level
Location: In south of state, at mouth of Hudson River (also known as the North River as it passes Manhattan)
Counties: Consists of 5 counties: Bronx, Kings (Brooklyn), New York (Manhattan), Queens, Richmond (Staten Island)
Churches: Protestant, 1,766; Jewish, 1,256; Roman Catholic 437; Orthodox, 66
City-owned parks: 1,588 (37,372 ac.)
Telephones (Jan. 1, 1979): 5,847,731
Radio stations: AM and FM, 7; AM only, 10; FM only, 12
Television stations: 6 commercial
Assessed valuation (1981–82): $42,545,394,486[2]
City tax rate (1981–82): $89.50 per $1,000
Expenditures (1981–82): $15,042,648,776
Chamber of Commerce: New York Chamber of Commerce and Industry, 65 Liberty St., New York, N.Y. 10005

1. For population of boroughs, *see* Index. 2. Taxable property only.

OAKLAND, CALIF.

Incorporated as city: 1854
Mayor: Lionel J. Wilson (to June 30, 1985)
City Manager: Henry L. Gardner (apptd. June 1981)
1970 population & (rank): 361,561 (39)
1980 population (1980 census) & (rank): 339,337 (43)
1970–80 population change: −6.2%
1981 land area: 53.9 sq mi.
Altitude: Highest, 1,700 ft; lowest, sea level
Location: In west central part of state, on east side of San Francisco Bay
County: Seat of Alameda Co.
Churches: 374, representing over 78 denominations in the City; over 500 churches in Alameda County
City-owned parks: 2,196 ac.
Telephones (Jan. 1, 1979): 589,155[1]
Radio stations: AM, 3; FM, 2
Television stations: 9 commercial; 3 PBS
Assessed valuation (1980–81): $1,609,678,000 (25% of appraised value)
City tax rate (1981–82): $13.14 per $1,000
Bonded debt (est. June 1981): $3,677,000
Revenue (1980–81): $157,866,000
Expenditures (1980–81): $165,022,000
Chamber of Commerce: Oakland Chamber of Commerce, 1939 Harrison St., Suite 400, Oakland, Calif. 94612

1. In East Bay Exchange, which includes Oakland.

OKLAHOMA CITY, OKLA.

Incorporated as city: 1890
Mayor: Mrs. Patience Latting (to April 1983)
City Manager: Scott Johnson
1970 population & (rank): 368,164 (37)
1980 population (1980 census) & (rank): 403,213 (31)
1970–80 population change: +9.5%
1981 land area: 603.6 sq mi. (1,563 sq km)
Altitude: Highest, 1,320 ft; lowest, 1,140
Location: In central part of state, on North Canadian River
County: Seat of Oklahoma Co.
Churches: Roman Catholic, 15; Jewish, 2; Protestant and others, 741
City-owned parks: 132 (3,934 ac.)
Telephones (Jan. 1, 1979): 641,434
Television stations: 7
Radio stations: AM, 10; FM, 14
Assessed valuation (1981–82): $1,106,546,951
City tax rate (1981–82): $21.38 per $1,000
Bonded debt (1981–82): $224,703,670
Revenue (general fund, 1981–82): $142,166,164
Expenditures (general fund, 1981–82): $142,166,164
Chamber of Commerce: Oklahoma City Chamber of Commerce, 1 Santa Fe Plaza, Oklahoma City, Okla. 73102

OMAHA, NEB.

Incorporated as city: 1857
Mayor: Mike Boyle (to June 1985)
1970 population & (rank): 346,929 (41)
1980 population (1980 census) & (rank): 313,911 (48)
1970–80 population change: −9.5%
1981 land area: 90.9 sq mi. (235 sq km)
Altitude: Highest, 1,270 ft
Location: In eastern part of state, on Missouri River
County: Seat of Douglas Co.
Churches: Protestant, 246; Roman Catholic, 44; Jewish, 4
City-owned parks: 99 (3,671.6 ac.)
Telephones (Jan. 1, 1979): 469,200
Radio stations: AM, 7; FM, 6
Television stations: 4
Assessed valuation (1981): $5,486,920,795
City tax rate (1981): $71.41 per $1,000
Bonded debt (1981): $77,487,583
Revenue (1981): $138,761,959
Expenditures (1981): $122,571,665
Chamber of Commerce: Omaha Chamber of Commerce, 1620 Dodge St., Omaha, Neb. 68102

PHILADELPHIA, PA.

First charter as city: 1701
Mayor: William J. Green (to Jan. 1984)
1970 population & (rank): 1,949,996 (4)
1980 population (1980 census) & (rank): 1,688,210 (4)
1970–80 population change: −13.4%
1982 land area: 136.0 sq mi. (352 sq km)
Altitude: Highest, 440 ft; lowest, sea level
Location: In southeastern part of state, at junction of Schuylkill and Delaware Rivers
County: Seat of Philadelphia Co. (coterminous)
Churches: Roman Catholic, 139; Jewish, 70; Protestant and others, 830
City-owned parks: 630 (10,252 ac.)
Telephones (Jan. 1, 1979): 1,706,199
Radio stations: AM, 20; FM, 22
Television stations: 8
Assessed valuation (1982): $5,868,000,000
City and school district tax rate (1981): $67.50 per $1,000
Net bonded debt (June 30, 1981): $1,744,440 (incl. revenue bonds of $437,346,000 for water and sewer; $282,388,000 for gas works; $69,956,000 for airport)
Revenue (1981): $1,123,674,407
Expenditures (1981): $1,089,210,034

Chamber of Commerce: Greater Philadelphia Chamber of Commerce, 1617 John F. Kennedy Blvd., Philadelphia, Pa. 19103

PHOENIX, ARIZ.

Incorporated as city: 1881
Mayor: Margaret T. Hance (to Jan. 1984)
City Manager: Marvin A. Andrews (appt. Oct. 1976)
1970 population & (rank): 581,303 (20)
1980 population (1980 census) & (rank): 789,704 (9)
1970–80 population change: +35.2%
1981 land area: 324.0 sq mi.
Altitude: Highest, 2,740 ft.; lowest, 1,017
Location: In center of state, on Salt River
County: Seat of Maricopa Co.
City-owned parks: 130 (25,841 ac.)
Telephones (Jan. 1, 1979): 1,089,327
Radio stations: AM, 19; FM, 15
Television stations: 8 commercial; 1 PBS
Assessed valuation (1981–82): $2,126,254,456
City tax rate (1981–82): $15.90 per $1,000
Bonded debt (May 1982): $596,489,000
Revenues (est. 1982–83): $528,580,000
Expenditures (est. 1982–83): $502,304,000
Chamber of Commerce: Phoenix Chamber of Commerce, 805 N Second St., Phoenix, Ariz. 85004

PITTSBURGH, PA.

Incorporated as city: 1816
Mayor: Richard S. Caliguiri (to Jan. 1986)
1970 population & (rank): 520,089 (23)
1980 population (1980 census) & (rank): 423,959 (30)
1970–80 population change: −18%
1981 land area: 55.4 sq mi. (144 sq km)
Altitude: Highest, 1,240 ft; lowest, 715
Location: In southwestern part of state, at beginning of Ohio River
County: Seat of Allegheny Co.
Churches: Protestant, 348; Roman Catholic, 86; Jewish, 28; Orthodox, 26
City-owned parks and playgrounds: 88 (2,471 ac.)
Telephones (Jan. 1, 1979): 821,039
Radio stations: AM, 18; FM, 9
Television stations: 4
Assessed valuation (1982): land, $343,582,636; buildings, $1,162,089,145
City tax rate (1982): $33 per $1,000 buildings; $133 per $1,000 land
Net bonded debt (Dec. 1981): $205,552,314
Revenue (1981): $362,137,515
Expenditures (1981): $301,821,641
Chamber of Commerce: The Chamber of Commerce of Greater Pittsburgh, 411 Seventh Ave., Pittsburgh, Pa. 15222

PORTLAND, ORE.

Incorporated as city: 1851
Mayor: Francis Ivancie (to Jan. 1984)
1970 population & (rank): 379,967 (36)
1980 population (1980 census) & (rank): 366,383 (35)
1970–80 population change: −3.6%
1981 land area: 103.3 sq mi. (267.5 sq km)
Altitude: Highest, 1,073 ft; lowest, sea level
Location: In northwestern part of state, on Willamette River
County: Seat of Multnomah Co.
Churches: Protestant, 332; Roman Catholic, 27; Jewish, 4; Buddhist, 4; Vedanta Society, 1
City-owned parks: 228 (8,718 ac.)
Telephones (Jan. 1, 1979): 511,223
Radio stations: AM, 12; FM, 12
Television stations: 5
Assessed valuation (1981–82): $10,228,513,919 (at 100% of cash value)
City tax rate (1981–82): $6.48 per $1,000
Bonded debt (April 1982): $230,630,239
Revenue (est. 1982–83): $276,097,271
Expenditures (est. 1982–83): $293,327,620
Chamber of Commerce: Portland Chamber of Commerce, 824 SW Fifth Ave., Portland, Ore. 97204

ST. LOUIS, MO.

Incorporated as city: 1822
Mayor: Vincent Schoemehl, Jr. (to April 1985)
1970 population & (rank): 622,236 (18)
1980 population (1980 census) & (rank): 453,085 (26)
1970–80 population change: −27.2%
1981 land area: 61.4 sq mi. (159 sq km)
Altitude: Highest, 616 ft; lowest, 413
Location: In east central part of state, on Mississippi River
County: Independent city
Churches: 900[1]
City-owned parks: 89 (2,639 ac.)
Telephones (Jan. 1, 1979): 586,830
Radio stations: AM, 18; FM, 20[1]
Television stations: 5 commercial; 1 PBS
Assessed valuation (1981): $1,104,194,252
City tax rate (1981): $62.50 per $1,000
Bonded debt (1981–82): $37,355,865
Revenue (1981–82): $254,089,718
Expenditures (1981–82): $261,000,000
Chamber of Commerce: St. Louis Regional Commerce and Growth Association, 10 Broadway, St. Louis, Mo. 63102.

1. Metropolitan area.

SAN ANTONIO, TEX.

Incorporated as city: 1837
Mayor: Henry Cisneros (to May 1983)
City Manager: Louis J. Fox (apptd. Jan. 1982)
1970 population & (rank): 654,153 (15)
1980 population (1980 census) & (rank): 786,023 (11)
1970–80 population change: +20.1%
1981 land area: 262.7 sq mi. (680 sq km)
Altitude: 700 ft
Location: In south central part of state, on San Antonio River
County: Seat of Bexar Co.
City-owned parks: Approximately 5,881 ac.
Telephones (Jan. 1, 1979): 428,249
Radio stations: AM, 13; FM, 12
Television stations: 5
Assessed valuation (1980): $6,311,658,070
City tax rate (1981): $4.40 per $1,000[1]
Net funded debt (1981): $142,481,848
Revenue (est. 1981–82): $274,636,010
Expenditures (est. 1981–82): $282,101,395
Chamber of Commerce: Greater San Antonio Chamber of Commerce, P.O. Box 1628, 602 E Commerce, San Antonio, Tex. 78296

1. Based on 7-month tax year due to change in fiscal year.

SAN DIEGO, CALIF.

Incorporated as city: 1850
Mayor: Pete Wilson (to Dec. 1984)

City Manager: Ray T. Blair, Jr. (apptd. May 1978)
1970 population & (rank): 697,471 (14)
1980 population (1980 census) & (rank): 875,538 (8)
1970–80 population change: +25.5%
1981 land area: 320.0 sq mi. (829 sq km)
Altitude: Highest, 1,591 ft; lowest, sea level
Location: In southwesternmost part of state, on San Diego Bay
County: Seat of San Diego Co.
Churches: Roman Catholic, 80; Jewish, 8; Protestant 334; Eastern Orthodox, 7; other, 6
City park and recreation facilities: 200 (16,499 ac.)
Telephones (Jan. 1, 1979): 1,101,169[1]
Radio stations: AM, 10; FM, 19
Television stations: 4
Assessed valuation (1982): $21,948,374,383
City tax rate (1982): $10.91 per $1,000 (includes county and school district)
Bonded debt (1982): $27,765,000
Revenue (est. 1983): $410,500,680
Expenditures (est. 1983): $410,500,680
Chamber of Commerce: San Diego Chamber of Commerce, 110 W. C St., Suite 1600, San Diego, Calif. 92101

1. Metropolitan area.

SAN FRANCISCO, CALIF.

Incorporated as city: 1850
Mayor: Dianne Feinstein (to Jan. 1984)
1970 population & (rank): 715,674 (13)
1980 population (1980 census) & (rank): 678,974 (13)
1970–80 population change: −5.1%
1981 land area: 46.4 sq mi. (120 sq km)
Altitude: Highest, 925 ft; lowest, sea level
Location: In northern part of state between Pacific Ocean and San Francisco Bay
County: Coextensive with San Francisco Co.
Churches: 540 of all denominations
City-owned parks and squares: 120
Telephones (Jan. 1, 1979): 845,547
Radio stations: 22
Television stations: 7
Assessed valuation (1981–82): $21,237,461,737 (100% of valuation)
City and county tax rate (1981–82): $47.60 per $1,000
Bonded debt (April 1982): $940,600,000
Revenue (1981–82): $1,175,000,000
Expenditures (1981–82): $1,175,000,000
Chamber of Commerce: Greater San Francisco Chamber of Commerce, 465 California St., San Francisco, Calif. 94104

SAN JOSE, CALIF.

Incorporated as city: 1850
Mayor: Janet Gray Hayes (to Dec. 31, 1982)
1970 population & (rank): 459,913 (29)
1980 population (1980 census) & (rank): 629,546 (17)
1970–80 population change: +36.9%
1981 land area: 158.0 sq mi. (409 sq km)
Altitude: 80 ft
Location: In northern part of state, on south San Francisco Bay, 50 miles from San Francisco
County: Santa Clara
Churches: Protestant, 195; Roman Catholic, 29; Jewish, 4; others, 24
City-owned parks and playgrounds: 150 (2,919 ac.)[1]
Telephones (Jan. 1, 1979): 638,121
Radio stations: AM, 5; FM, 6
Television stations: 5 commercial; 1 PBS
Assessed valuation (1981–82): $14,452,841,098 (100% of valuation)
City tax rate (1981–82): $1.55 per $1,000
Bonded debt (June 1981): $34,274,000
Revenue (1981–82): $477,918,000
Expenditures (1981–82): $477,918,000
Chamber of Commerce: San Jose Chamber of Commerce, One Paseo de San Antonio, San Jose, Calif. 95113

1. Includes undeveloped sites.

SEATTLE, WASH.

Incorporated as city: 1869
Mayor: Charles Royer (to Nov. 1985)
1970 population & (rank): 530,831 (22)
1980 population (1980 census) & (rank): 493,846 (23)
1970–80 population change: −7.0%
1981 land area: 144.6 sq mi. (375 sq km)
Altitude: Highest, 540 ft; lowest, sea level
Location: In west central part of state, on Puget Sound
County: Seat of King Co.
Churches: Roman Catholic, 36; Jewish, 13; Protestant and others, 535
City-owned parks, playgrounds, etc.: 278 (4,773.4 ac.)
Telephones (Jan. 1, 1979): 660,792
Radio stations: AM, 22; FM, 26
Television stations: 3 commercial; 1 educational
Assessed valuation (1982): $18,820,532,117
City tax rate (1982): $9.44 per $1,000
Bonded debt (1981): $508,446,000
Revenue (1981): $272,495,346
Expenditures (1981): $268,803,694
Chamber of Commerce: Seattle Chamber of Commerce, 215 Columbia Street, Seattle, Wash. 98104

TOLEDO, OHIO

Incorporated as city: 1837
Mayor: Doug DeGood (to Dec. 1983)
City Manager: David Boston (apptd. Sept. 1981)
1970 population & (rank): 383,062 (34)
1980 population (1980 census) & (rank): 354,635 (40)
1970–80 population change: −7.4%
1981 land area: 84.2 sq mi. (218 sq km)
Altitude: 630 ft
Location: In northwestern part of state, on Maumee River at Lake Erie
County: Seat of Lucas Co.
Churches: Protestant, 301; Roman Catholic, 55; Jewish, 4; others, 98
City-owned parks and playgrounds: 134 (2,650.90 ac.)
Telephones (Jan. 1, 1979): 315,797
Radio stations: AM, 8; FM, 8
Television stations: 4
Assessed valuation (1981): $2,431,067,916
City tax rate (1982): $58.80 per $1,000
Bonded debt (1982): $171,233,182
Revenue (est. 1982): $162,907,686
Expenditures (est. 1982): $157,028,454
Chamber of Commerce: Toledo Area Chamber of Commerce, 218 Huron St., Toledo, Ohio 43604

TUCSON, ARIZ.

Incorporated as city: 1877
Mayor: Lewis C. Murphy (to Dec. 1983)
1970 population & (rank): 262,933 (53)
1980 population (1980 census) & (rank): 330,537 (45)
1970–80 population change: +25.7%
1981 land area: 98.8 sq mi. (256 sq km)
Altitude: 2,500 ft
Location: In southeastern part of state, on the Santa Cruz River

County: Seat of Pima Co.
Churches: Protestant, 181; Roman Catholic, 24; other, 136
City-owned parks and parkways: (2,001.75 ac.)
Telephones (Jan. 1, 1979): 335,032
Radio stations: AM, 12; FM, 6
Television stations: 3 commercial; 1 educational; 1 other
Assessed valuation (1981): $680,386,981
City tax rate (1981): $9.80 per $1,000
Net bonded debt (1982): $125,155,000
Revenue (1981): $146,548,057
Expenditures (1981): $142,341,697
Chamber of Commerce: Tucson Chamber of Commerce, P.O. Box 991, Tucson, Ariz., 85702

TULSA, OKLA.

Incorporated as city: 1898
Mayor: James Inhofe (to May 1984)
1970 population & (rank): 330,350 (43)
1980 population (1980 census) & (rank): 360,919 (38)
1970–80 population change: +9.3%
1981 land area: 185.6 sq mi. (481 sq km)
Altitude: 674 ft
Location: In northeastern part of state, on Arkansas River
County: Seat of Tulsa Co.
Churches: Protestant, 593; Roman Catholic, 32; Jewish, 2; others, 4
City parks and playgrounds: 110 (4,908 ac.)
Telephones (Jan. 1, 1979): 412,906
Radio stations: AM, 9; FM, 6
Television stations: 4 commercial; 1 PBS
Assessed valuation (1981–82): $1,166,543,929
City tax rate (1981–82): $75.39 per $1,000
Bonded debt (July 1981): $102,800,000
Revenue (1980–81): $179,683,708
Expenditures (1980–81): $179,528,431
Chamber of Commerce: Metropolitan Tulsa Chamber of Commerce, 616 S Boston, Tulsa, Okla. 74119

WASHINGTON, D.C.

Land ceded to Congress: 1788 by Maryland; 1789 by Virginia (retroceded to Virginia Sept. 7, 1846)
Seat of government transferred to D. C.: Dec. 1, 1800
Created municipal corporation: Feb. 21, 1871
Mayor: Marion S. Barry, Jr. (to Jan. 1983)
Motto: *Justitia omnibus* (Justice to all)
Flower: American beauty rose
Tree: Scarlet oak
Origin of name: In honor of Columbus
1980 population (1980 census) & (rank): 638,432 (15)
1970–80 population change: −15.6%
1981 land area: 62.7 sq mi. (162 sq km)
Geographic center: Near corner of Fourth and L Sts., NW
Altitude: Highest, 420 ft; lowest, sea level
Location: Between Virginia and Maryland, on Potomac River
Churches: Protestant, 446; Roman Catholic, 23; Jewish, 10; others, 23
City parks: 753 (7,725 ac.)
Telephones (Jan. 1, 1979): 1,056,076
Radio stations: AM, 15; FM, 16
Television stations: 6 (including 2 UHF stations)
Assessed valuation (1980): $12,400,776,662[1]
City tax rate (1981–82): $21.30 per $1,000 (commercial)
Bonded debt: None
Revenue (est. 1982): $1,175,608,000
Expenditures (est. 1982): $2,058,229,000
Chamber of Commerce: D.C. Chamber of Commerce, 1319 F St., NW, Washington, D.C. 20004

1. On taxable property only. More than 50% of all land in District of Columbia is owned by the Federal government and tax-exempt organizations, and therefore is nontaxable.

The District of Columbia—identical with the City of Washington—is the capital of the United States and the first carefully planned capital in the world.

D.C. history began in 1790 when Congress directed selection of a new capital site, 10 miles square, along the Potomac. When the site was determined, it included 30.75 square miles on the Virginia side of the river. In 1846, however, Congress returned that area to Virginia.

The city was planned and partly laid out by Major Pierre Charles L'Enfant, a French engineer. This work was perfected and completed by Major Andrew Ellicott. In 1814, during the War of 1812, a British force fired the capital, and it was from the white paint applied to cover fire damage that the President's home was called the White House.

Until Nov. 3, 1967, the District of Columbia was administered by three commissioners appointed by the President. On that day, a government consisting of a mayor-commissioner and a 9-member Council, all appointed by the President with the approval of the Senate, took office. On May 7, 1974, the citizens of the District of Columbia approved the Home Rule Charter, giving them their first form of elected government in over 100 years. The District also has one non-voting member in the House of Representatives.

On Aug. 22, 1978, the Senate passed a proposed constitutional amendment to give Washington, D.C., voting representation in the Congress. The House had approved the legislation in the spring. The amendment must be ratified by at least 38 state legislatures within the next seven years to become effective.

Tornado Fatalities

In the 1970s, there were 8,573 tornadoes in the United States resulting in the deaths of 986 people. If the previous decades are any indication of the future, the National Oceanic and Atmospheric Administration forsees that there will be at least 7,000 tornadoes during the 1980s in which up to 1,000 Americans will be killed.

1981 Saw Fewer Earthquakes

The number of major earthquakes around the world dropped sharply in 1981, with the death toll about half normal, according to the U.S. Geological Survey. There were 50 significant quakes as compared to 71 the year before. The worldwide death toll was 5,239, down from 7,139 in 1980. In the United States there were only two significant quakes and no fatalities.

Tabulated Data on City Governments

City	Mayor: Term, years	Mayor: Salary[1]	City manager's salary[2]	Council or Commission: Name	Members	Term, years	Salary[3]
Albuquerque, N.M.	4	$46,000	$47,362[4]	Council	9	4	$ 4,600
Atlanta	4	50,000	—	Council	19	4	8,800
Austin, Tex.	2	18,312	69,500	Council	6	2	16,300
Baltimore	4	47,000	—	Council	19	4	19,500
Birmingham, Ala.	4	52,500	—	Council	9	4	6,900
Boston	4	60,000	—	Council	9	2	32,500
Buffalo, N.Y.	4	41,500	—	Council	15	2[5]	22,000
Charlotte, N.C.	2	11,770	64,200	Council	11	2	6,099
Chicago	4	60,000	—	Council	50	4	27,600
Cincinnati	2	27,875	67,500	Council	9	2	24,375
Cleveland	4	60,000	—	Council	21	4	19,800
Columbus, Ohio	4	52,000	—	Council	7	4	10,000
Dallas	2	50[6]	85,800	Council	11	2	50[6]
Denver	4	50,000	—	Council	13	4	18,675
Detroit	4	75,172	—	Council	9	4	40,771
El Paso	2	9,600	—	Council	7[7]	2	4,800
Fort Worth	2	10[8]	63,690	Council	9	2	10[8]
Honolulu	4	66,409	60,372	Council	9	4	17,500[9]
Houston	2	81,560	—	Council	14	2	21,750
Indianapolis	4	43,500	—	Council	29	4	3,800[10]
Jacksonville, Fla.	4	40,000	32,000[11]	Council	19	4	10,000
Kansas City, Mo.	4	35,000	70,980	Council	13[7]	4	9,600
Long Beach, Calif.	2	674[12]	70,563	Council	9[13]	4	674[12]
Los Angeles	4	72,925	86,528	Council	15	4	43,755
Louisville, Ky.	4	47,310	—	Board of Aldermen	12	2	14,290
Memphis, Tenn.	4	40,000[14]	43,056	Council	13	4	6,000
Miami, Fla.	2	5,000[15]	82,600	Commission	4	4	5,000
Milwaukee	4	58,964	—	Council	16	4	24,880
Minneapolis	4	40,588	58,777	Council	13	2	34,881
Nashville, Tenn.	4	50,000	—	Council	41	4	5,400
Newark, N.J.	4	52,500	50,000[17]	Council	9	4	24,500
New Orleans	4	59,868	—	Council	7	4	29,500
New York	4	80,000	76,650[16]	Council	43	4	35,000
Oakland, Calif.	4	15,000	59,500	Council	9[7]	4	([18])
Oklahoma City	4	2,000	55,000	Council	8	4	20[19]
Omaha, Neb.	4	38,520	—	Council	7	4	10,272
Philadelphia	4	55,000	50,000[20]	Council	17	4	25,000
Phoenix, Ariz.	2	25,000	80,000	Council	7[7]	2	12,000
Pittsburgh	4	57,000	—	Council	9	4	([21])
Portland, Ore.	4	55,395	—	Commission	4	4	44,412
St. Louis	4	59,758	—	Board of Aldermen	29	4	12,500
San Antonio	2	3,000[22]	71,500	Council	11[7]	2	20[23]
San Diego, Calif.	4	36,625	75,000	Council	8	4	25,750
San Francisco	4	84,225	83,180	Board of Supervisors	11	4	9,600
San Jose, Calif.	4	7,200	68,619	Council	10	4	4,800
Seattle	4	75,237	—	Council	9	4	49,643
Toledo, Ohio	2	23,350	55,000	Council	9[13]	2	7,800
Tucson, Ariz.	4	14,000	45,000	Council	7	4	7,200
Tulsa, Okla.	2	45,996	—	Commission	4	2	35,496
Washington, D.C.	4	67,410	58,500	Council	13	4	41,290[24]

1. Annual salary unless otherwise indicated. 2. Annual salary. City Manager's term is indefinite and at will of Council. 3. Annual salary unless otherwise indicated. In some cities, President of Council receives a higher salary. 4. City Administrative Officer appointed by Mayor, approved by Council. 5. For 9 District Councilmen; 4 years for 5 Councilmen-at-Large. 6. Per Council meeting; not over $2,600 per year. 7. Including Mayor. 8. Per week and per Council meeting. 9. Managing Director appointed by Mayor; no Council approval required. 10. Plus $30 per meeting for three meetings a month. 11. Chief Administrative Officer appointed by Mayor; not subject to Council confirmation. 12. Per month. 13. Including Mayor and Vice-Mayor. 14. Plus $5,000 expense account. 15. Plus $2,500 expense account. 16. No City Manager; salary is for Deputy Mayor. 17. Business Administrator, appointed by Mayor and confirmed by Council. 18. Flat $500 per month, or $6,000 annually. 19. Per Council meeting; not to exceed 5 meetings a month. 20. Appointed by Mayor, with title of Managing Director. 21. 4 members at $32,500; 5 members at $27,500. 22. Plus Council pay. 23. Per Council meeting; not over $1,040 per year. 24. $10,000 additional for Chairman. *Source: Information Please* questionnaires to the cities.

The Future of Social Security —It's Up To All of Us

Barry Robinson
American Association of Retired Persons

Here is the secret of how to become the conversational center of attention at any party or gathering of people over the age of 30.

Simply let it be known quite casually that you are working on an article about the Future of Social Security, and you will quickly find yourself surrounded by men and women of all ages asking questions like these:

"All the years I've been working, money was taken out of my paycheck for Social Security. Now they tell us it may run out of funds. How come? And what happened to the money I paid in? Isn't it still in my account so I can at least get that much back?"

"I was planning to retire next year or maybe the year after that, depending on how my health is, but now I don't know. My wife and I, we have some savings, and the house is paid for, but if they take Social Security away, we won't have enough to live on even if we manage to cash everything in. How can anyone be expected to get by without Social Security?"

"Okay, I'll grant you that the system's in trouble and that Social Security has some serious problems, but it can be fixed, can't it? It'll still be there for my wife and me when we retire, and for our kids when they grow old, won't it? What's going to happen?"

These are questions which obviously demand responses and, unfortunately, there are no clear and easy answers.

At this point no one knows—and therefore no one can predict—what will eventually be done about the Social Security system and its function in our society. All that one can do is to explain how the system works, and what it's supposed to accomplish, define the problems confronting it, and debunk a few of the myths which have arisen about it over the years. That is what this article seeks to do.

Perhaps the most pervasive misunderstanding about Social Security is the myth that the system is essentially a giant piggybank into which all the money deducted from our paychecks (or, if we're self-employed, the money remitted along with our income tax return) goes to sit and collect interest until it is paid back to us in the form of retirement benefits.

In reality, our Social Security system is what economists call an intergenerational income transfer program through which active workers help support former workers who are now retired. When today's retirees were still employed, they paid into the system to assist those who had gone before, and when today's workers retire, they will in turn be supported by a future generation of workers.

Historically, the present system is essentially an institutionalized extension of the fifth biblical commandment to "honor thy father and mother." Years ago, children supported their aged parents directly—sometimes by giving them money, sometimes by taking them into their own homes, and occasionally by not leaving the family homestead until the surviving parent had died and their children, when their time came, assisted them. As the structure of our industrialized and increasingly mobile society changed, this arrangement became less and less common. Thus, Social Security evolved as an indirect means of one generation assisting another, with the government acting as intermediary.

While this approach has been working well for nearly half a century—during which its coverage was expanded to provide benefits to widows, orphans, and the disabled, and extended in 1965 to embrace the Medicare program—the system is now confronted with changing circumstances which may demand new responses to old problems.

At the root of the system's difficulties is the simple demographic fact that, in the world today (not just the United States), more people than ever before are living longer. Combined with other social and economic changes, this has resulted in two perceivable problems for the American Social Security system—an essentially short-term difficulty, and a long-range dilemma.

Although the short-term—and thus more immediate—problem is currently commanding the most public attention, it is the long-range outlook which would turn out to be the most serious problem. Since the short-term problem will have the most immediate impact, let's look at it first.

From its inception, Social Security has been operated on an essentially pay-as-you-go basis. Yet, except for its early years during the Great Depression of the 1930s, the system has generally managed to take in more money than it has paid out each year. These excess revenues have gone into a so-called trust fund to be held in reserve for use in times of crisis.

Since the mid-1970s, however, the system has frequently been paying out more money than it has been taking in, and has therefore had to draw on its reserves. According to some estimates, the trust fund could be depleted during 1983 unless there is

Barry Robinson is communication counsel for the American Association of Retired Persons which, with 13.5 million members, is the largest organization of older people in the world today. He is the author of *Options for Older Americans*, *On the Beat: Policemen at Work*, and *The Vision of Aging: Sight and Insight* in *Visual Acuity and Aging*. Founded in 1958, AARP is a nonprofit, nonpartisan organization providing older Americans with a wide range of membership programs and services, including legislative representation at both federal and state levels.

a dramatic upswing in Social Security's fiscal fortunes.

Why has the system suddenly been afflicted with a "case of the shorts?"

To begin with, there are more people living longer, resulting in there being more people to collect Social Security benefits for a longer duration than had been anticipated when the system was first conceived. By itself, this factor would not have been a serious problem, but the situation was—and still is—exacerbated by unexpected fluctuations taking place in the nation's economy.

A long period of high inflation has resulted in individual Social Security benefit payments having to be increased each year just to keep pace with the constantly rising cost of living. Thus, more and more money has had to be paid out of the system's coffers.

At the same time, the nation's working population has been afflicted with frequent—and often serious—bouts of unemployment during the past decade, thereby reducing the number of active workers paying into the system.

Inflation does not usually occur in tandem with unemployment. When it does, it confounds most economic experts who insist that rising unemployment is supposed to be accompanied by falling prices. This multiple malaise has taken a double toll on Social Security by reducing the amount of money coming into the system while making it necessary for more to be paid out in benefits.

These short-term problems are not an indication that the system isn't working or that Social Security's usefulness has come to an untimely end. The system is indeed working, and its present predicament is really nothing more than a normal reaction to an abnormal situation in our nation's overall economy.

Assuming that the nation's economic situation stabilizes in the relatively near future, it is quite possible that comparatively short-term measures will be required to keep the system solvent until the 1990s when current projections call for it to begin operating in the black again and accruing surpluses. The system's short-term difficulties, however, will not resolve themselves without assistance, and action in this direction is needed now before the situation worsens.

Unfortunately, the decision of what to do about Social Security is not one which legislators (who are, after all, politicians) are particularly anxious to make before a crucial election. This reportedly is part of the thinking behind President Reagan's decision to appoint the *ad hoc* National Commission on Social Security Reform which is not scheduled to report its recommendations until the end of 1982, a date presumably chosen to keep Social Security from becoming an issue in the 1982 Congressional Elections. As this is being written (in August 1982), there is speculation that the nonpartisan Commission might issue its findings shortly after the November elections, clearing the way for a lame duck Congress to enact legislation before its final adjournment. More likely, however, is the prospect that 1983 could become the between-elections year in which the subject of Social Security's short-term future is finally confronted—and its fiscal crisis faced up to.

The options available for dealing with Social Security's difficulties are fairly limited, and none are expected to be particularly popular. Threatened with a potentially serious deficit, those in charge of overseeing the system are faced with having to choose between increasing the revenue coming in, or decreasing the benefits being paid out, or some combination thereof. There is some flexibility in the means through which these ends might be achieved, but no matter how it is done, some segment of the population is going to be discomforted if not hurt outright.

For instance, a recent study by economist Thomas C. Borzilleri reveals that, if the annual cost-of-living benefit adjustment were to be frozen or reduced, it would force more than a million older Americans into poverty within three years. Nearly 16 percent of the nation's elderly now live in poverty, compared to about 13 percent of the total population.

The people who would be most drastically affected by any failure to increase Social Security benefits at a time when prices are rising, explains Dr. Borzilleri, are the 10 percent of those aged 65 and older who now live just above the poverty line, and who derive virtually all their income from Social Security. Any reduction in their real income would force them into poverty.

On the other hand, increasing the revenues flowing into Social Security's coffers is not without its potential drawbacks. Under legislation enacted in 1977, the last time Social Security's problems were addressed comprehensively by Congress, American workers' contributions to the system have been increasing steadily year after year, and the end is still nowhere in sight. Yet, recent polls reveal that working Americans remain consistent in their continuing support of Social Security, but there is undoubtedly a limit to what can be demanded of them.

An often-mentioned but never utilized alternative for increasing Social Security income is the use of limited amounts of general tax revenues (derived from our income tax payments and other sources) to temporarily "cushion" the system from the short-term crunch it is experiencing. Once the crisis passes, the use of general revenues would cease automatically, and there is even the possibility that Social Security could repay these sums out of the surplus it is expected to begin developing after 1990. While support is growing for this approach, there is a realization that any general revenues used for Social Security would thus be unavailable

For Additional Insight

. . . and information about Social Security's workings and prospects for the future, the best place to look is in books and other publications. The following are recommended by the staff of AARP's National Gerontology Resource Center.

Your Social Security and other pamphlets published by the Social Security Administration are available at your local Social Security office. The rest of these may be found in your local bookstore or library: *Your Rights to Social Security Benefits* by David Andrews; *Social Security: Today and Tomorrow* by Robert M. Ball, a former commissioner; *Meidinger Guide to Social Security* by Dale R. Detlefs; *Social Security* by Robert J. Myers, formerly chief actuary of the system, now staff director of the Commission studying ways to reform it; *Financing Social Security,* edited by Felicity Skidmore; and *1981 Social Security Explained Under Omnibus Budget Reconciliation Act of 1981* by the Commerce Clearing House staff. These are only a few of the many books written about Social Security, and there are surely more to come as the debate continues.

for other purposes, news which is not expected to gladden the hearts of proponents of other programs.

It has also been theorized that the salvation of Social Security might be found in the establishment of special "use" or "sin" taxes on substances which are more luxury than necessity and which, in most cases, combine pleasure with a certain amount of harm to the general well-being. Thus, it is possible that someday we might find that we are drinking a cocktail for Grandpa, smoking a cigarette for Grandma, or puffing a cigar for Uncle Elmo. Such taxation is probably the closest the American system has come to legally combining pain with pleasure.

If the recent past is any indication of the near future, we can expect to see continuing adjusting and fiddling over the years in an attempt to keep the system in sync until it is once again solvent and ready to meet its next crisis during the first third of the new century.

While the short-term crunch and its trauma may be more immediate and intense, it is the coming crisis which could have the most far-reaching impact on the relationship between work and leisure in America. This emerging dilemma has its roots not in economic fluctuations (although they may later play a role in complicating matters), but in demographic and biological trends.

With the exception of the comparatively few "baby boom" years following World War II, the American birthrate has been falling throughout the 20th century, hitting an all-time low during the early 1970s when the zero population growth (ZPG) movement was at its peak. Since the late 1970s, there has been a distinctly noticeable, but still relatively slight, rise in the birthrate among married couples in their mid-to-late 30s and early 40s. This has resulted in a return to the historically normal modern American birthrate—higher than during the ZPG years, but still much lower than the baby boom rate.

At the same time, the death rate has also been falling—first among the infants and children who eventually grew up to become today's generations of elders, and more recently among people in their mid-seventies and up—resulting in expections of an even larger elderly population by the year 2000. Thus, we have the makings of a situation in which the workers doing the supporting via Social Security and private pension plans may be outweighed by the non-workers being supported and by the burden of supporting them in a style to which they honestly deserve to become accustomed.

This phenomenon is known as the shrinking of the dependency ratio, and it may hold the key to the future of Social Security and other income support programs for retired workers. As recently as 1955, there were seven workers for each person collecting Social Security benefits. By 1960, there were four. The ratio is now in the area of three-to-one, and it has been estimated that the first three decades of the new century will see the ratio reduced to no more than two-to-one as the baby boom babies begin reaching senior citizenhood. Once the bulge has passed (sometime after the 2030s), there is the hope that the dependency ratio will become more easily manageable, but it is extremely difficult for demographers and other forecasters to make valid projections regarding birthrates that far in advance.

The only thing that is comparatively certain is that Social Security—and, for that matter, private pensions—will be facing a fiscal crunch sometime between the years 2000 and 2030. Among the possible responses already being anticipated are:

• extending the worklife in proportion to the increasing growth of the human lifespan (while this

Characteristics of Persons 65 Years Old and Over

(in percentages)

Characteristic	1980 Male	1980 Female	1979 Male	1979 Female	1975 Male	1975 Female	1970 Male	1970 Female
Marital status:[1]								
Single	5.1	5.9	5.4	6.1	4.7	5.8	7.5	7.7
Married	77.6	39.7	77.1	38.5	79.3	39.1	73.1	35.6
Spouse present	75.5	38.0	74.6	36.9	77.3	37.6	69.9	33.9
Spouse absent	2.0	1.7	2.6	1.6	2.0	1.5	3.2	1.7
Widowed	13.6	51.0	14.1	52.2	13.6	52.5	17.1	54.4
Divorced	3.7	3.4	3.3	3.3	2.5	2.6	2.3	2.3
Family status:[1]								
In families	83.0	57.0	82.3	56.5	83.3	59.3	79.2	58.5
Primary individuals	15.5	41.8	16.0	42.3	15.4	39.4	14.9	35.2
Secondary individuals	1.5	1.1	1.8	1.1	1.2	1.3	2.4	1.9
Residents of institutions[1]	n.a.	n.a.	n.a.	n.a.	n.a.	n.a.	3.6	4.4
Labor force participation:								
Employed	18.6	7.9	19.0	8.3	21.1	7.8	26.2	10.0
Unemployed	.5	.3	.9	.4	1.2	.4	1.0	.3
Not in labor force	80.9	91.8	80.1	91.3	77.7	91.8	72.8	89.7
Living arrangements:[1]								
Living in household	99.9	99.7	99.8	99.8	99.8	99.8	95.5	95.0
Living alone	14.7	40.9	15.4	41.1	14.8	38.0	14.1	33.8
Spouse present	75.5	38.0	74.6	36.9	77.3	37.6	69.9	33.9
Living with someone else	9.7	20.8	9.8	21.9	7.7	24.2	11.5	27.4
Not in household[2]	.1	.3	.2	.2	.2	.2	4.5	5.0

1. Resident population as of March of year indicated. Beginning 1975, excludes institutional population. 2. In institutions and other group quarters. NOTE: n.a. = not available. *Source:* Department of Commerce, Bureau of the Census.

would raise the so-called normal retirement age at which workers become eligible to collect benefits, it could also mean that workers would work for more years but put in less time each year as they get older);

- restructuring the system to make it more like an annuity in which benefits would be closely related to earnings and contributions, and the social welfare aspects would be achieved through a separate benefit structure specifically designed for that purpose;
- changing the formula by which benefits are computed so that Social Security would eventually replace a smaller percentage of one's pre-retirement income.

The eventual choice may be any or all of these, or perhaps a prospect which hasn't even been mentioned yet. There is no doubt, however, that the system will no longer be able to continue conducting business exactly as usual during the first third of the 21st century.

The future of Social Security is really up to us in the sense that our elected representatives must eventually be responsive to public opinion. Since Social Security is, after all, a form of social insurance designed to insure society as well as its individual members against disastrous disruption and destitution, any major change in the system could conceivably change our society for better or worse.

The present relatively unexpected shortfall caught us and our nation's leaders unaware—and we are now paying the price for this lack of foresight—but there is no excuse for letting the next crisis creep up on us. It is not only Social Security's future we are talking about determining, but our own individual and collective futures as well.

The Facts of Later Life

Income

Most economists estimate that for retirees to maintain their pre-retirement lifestyle within reasonable limits, they need a retirement income equal to 60–70% of their earnings immediately preceding retirement, plus regular adjustments for rising living costs. This is a goal generally beyond the reach of most older Americans who, on average, have half the income of their younger counterparts.

Even with annual Social Security increments, which are supposed to offset inflation, retirees continue to fall farther and farther behind. This is due primarily to the increments coming at least a year after the fact of actual increases in the cost of living, and thus never compensating fully for inflation's inroads.

One sixth of the over-65 population now lives below the poverty level—an improvement over 1970 when a full quarter of all older Americans did, but a disturbing increase over the one-seventh level maintained until 1980. Recent studies by economist Thomas C. Borzilleri indicate that this deterioration can be expected to continue if cash and in-kind (food stamps, Medicaid, etc.) benefits are reduced further.

Actually, points out Dr. Borzilleri, millions of older Americans may be considerably worse off than statistics indicate since they are not quite poor enough to fit below the official poverty line, but are, for all practical purposes, nonetheless impoverished. At the same time, there are, of course, many well-off older persons, but most tend to fall financially somewhere between poverty and affluence, and are haunted by fear of the former in their future.

Most of the aged poor did not become so until they retired, and their incomes dropped by 50–66%. These are essentially middle-class working people, and it is probably harder for them to cope with their newfound poverty than it is for people who have been poor all their lives.

Complicating the financial situations of almost all older Americans is a combination of years of continuously escalating inflation, which has steadily sapped the purchasing power of people living on relatively fixed incomes, and other economic fluctuations which have eroded their traditional income support sources. Although a growing number of retirees are now continuing to work in one way or another, the elderly do not generally possess the ability to increase their income as much as they need to. Thus, they are perenially attempting to cut back and catch up with little hope of ever breaking even again.

Health

Although generally healthier than previous generations of elders, today's older people are still more subject to chronic illness and disability than younger persons. On average, they visit physicians nearly 50% more often, and have health care and medication costs more than double those of younger individuals.

Comprising only 11% of the nation's population, older people account for 29% of total personal health care expenditures ($49.4 billion out of $167.9 billion). Yet, most older Americans regard themselves as being comparatively healthy and capable of caring for themselves well enough to continue living independently.

In a 1975 survey, 69% of the older persons questioned described their health as good or excellent in comparison with others of their own age, and 22% said their health was fair. A 1980 study, however came up with these responses: 21% excellent, 39% good, 29% fair, and 12% poor.

Those describing their health as being chronically poor reported suffering from arthritis (38%), hearing loss (29%), and vision impairment, hypertension, and heart disease (20% each). Many suffered from several of these conditions simultaneously.

A 1979 study found that 82% of the older persons polled had not been hospitalized during the previous year. And most persons entering nursing homes returned later to their own residences.

Employment

In 1900, 67% of men and 8% of women over 65 were actively working. By 1981 only 18.2% of older men remained employed, while the percentage of women in the workforce had slipped back to eight after rising to ten in 1974. In general, they are working today at part-time jobs, agricultural labor, or self-employment. There are also indications that, partially in response to economic pressures, a growing number of "retired" workers continue to work after formal retirement, but do not declare themselves officially employed.

Once unemployed, however, older workers usually experience greater difficulty finding new jobs and have longer average periods of unemployment than younger workers. This tendency begins in the mid-to-late 40s and increases with the worker's age.

Some employers have recently begun to recognize the value of older workers already in their employ, and are making efforts to encourage them to remain on the job. This is expected to increase dramatically around the coming turn of the century when fewer young adults will be entering the work force as the result of the sharp birthrate decline which followed the baby boom.

Marital Status

In 1980, 74% of all older men and 35% of all older women were married. Among older women, 54% were widows, a figure which rises to 68% after age 75. It is almost predictable: If the husband is five years younger than his wife, the chances of widowhood are 50%; if the husband and wife are the same age, the chances are two out of three; if the husband is five years older than his wife, the chances are three out of four.

Widows outnumber widowers by 5.3 to 1. Men, however, experience greater difficulty adjusting to the loss of a mate—most likely because they don't expect their wives to die before they do.

In 1977, there were 16,760 brides and 30,721 grooms over 65. For approximately 904 of these older brides and 1,438 older grooms, it was a first marriage. For the rest, remarriage came mostly after widowhood rather than divorce. Interestingly, the actual number of marriages involving people over 65 has decreased in the last few years.

Marriage rates for older men in 1977 were seven times those for older women. The number of older men entering into first marriages was 2.5 times that of older women, while the number of older men remarrying was 8.6 times greater than that of older women.

Living Arrangements

While most older persons live in a family setting —with a husband, wife or other relatives—this frequently decreases with advancing age.

More than a third of older Americans—52% of all older women, but only 21% of all older men—live alone or with non-relatives. One reason for this disparity is that women live longer than men, and thus eventually outnumber them in later life.

The majority of older women are widows or divorcees (or, in some cases, both) without adequate means of support and little, if any, preparation for living alone—a circumstance which may in time give rise to new forms of communal living.

Pensions

The newer the retiree, the greater the chances of participation in a company or union pension—and the greater the likelihood of collecting on that pension, thanks to the Employee Retirement Income Security Act (ERISA) of 1974 which regulates pension plans and insures the worker's stake in them.

Prior to that, many workers participated in plans but were unable to collect pensions upon retirement. Thus, most older retirees do not receive private pension payments, but live instead solely on Social Security and whatever savings they have managed to accumulate; some must also depend upon Supplemental Security Income (SSI) payments to assist them in making ends meet.

Of today's active workers, however, it is estimated that nearly half are covered by pension plans, but their future security may be endangered by recession-induced business failures and by efforts to amend ERISA which could result in its providing less protection for individual workers.

Transportation

Most public transportation systems are designed primarily to satisfy the needs of the commuting worker. Older people (whose needs are usually quite different) are thus forced either to rely upon automobiles—which are becoming increasingly expensive to own and maintain—or to surrender their mobility and settle for whatever is within walking distance, no matter how inferior it may be.

Some communities have attempted to provide special transportation services at reduced rates for their older residents, but many of these subsidized systems have fallen victim to their own success. The more they are utilized, the more they cost to operate, and the growing cost often exceeds a community's ability to sustain them. In this age of energy scarcity, this looms large as a major problem.

Crime

While violent crimes against the elderly have been increasing lately and have thus received the most news coverage, they are not nearly as prevalent as "bunco" offenses, in which the victim is defrauded of whatever savings he or she may have managed to accumulate over the course of a lifetime.

Older victims tend to suffer more intensely. A younger victim can recoup a monetary loss by accumulating future earnings, but older victims no longer have that opportunity. Similarly, older victims wounded in crimes of violence require longer to heal, leading to prolonged loss of mobility and the increased possibility of medical complications.

Coping

When You Need Help or Information

Whether your concern is for your own later years or for someone you know with problems, the basic approaches to seeking help or information are essentially the same. In general, your primary sources of information are your local telephone directory and your community's public library.

A good way to begin is to take stock of your resources relating to the problem. This doesn't necessarily mean financial resources, although they can be undeniably important. There are, however, other resources which you may have built up over a lifetime of activity without really being aware of them.

Did you, for instance, serve in the nation's military services? If so, check with the Veterans Administration (listed in the phonebook under "U.S. Government") to see if it can help.

Are you a union member? Then, contact your nearest local and find out if the union has any programs to help retirees with your particular problem. This also applies to any civic or fraternal organizations to which you may belong.

Don't forget the many local and national organizations for older people; being a member of one or more of them can prove helpful. These are the major national ones:

American Association of Retired Persons (AARP), 1909 K Street N.W., Washington, D.C. 20049

National Council of Senior Citizens (NCSC), 1511 K Street N.W., Washington, D.C. 20005

National Association of Retired Federal Employees (NARFE), 1533 New Hampshire Avenue N.W., Washington, D.C. 20036

Gray Panthers, 3635 Chestnut Street, Philadelphia, Pa. 19104

Older Women's League Educational Fund, 3800 Harrison Street, Oakland, Calif. 94611
For ages 50–64:

Action for Independent Maturity (AIM), 1909 K Street N.W., Washington, D.C. 20049

There are also organizations of professionals who work with and on behalf of the elderly: National Council on the Aging (NCOA), 600 Maryland Avenue, S.W., Washington, D.C. 20024; The Gerontological Society, 1835 K Street N.W., Washington, D.C. 20006; American Geriatric Society, 10 Columbus Circle, New York, N.Y. 10019.

When You Have a Problem . . .

For just about every problem today, there is a private public service organization or government program trying to solve it. The trick is for you to get in touch with the right one.

In this *Almanac (see* Index), there is a listing of U.S. Societies and Associations in which you might find the name of an organization dealing with your particular problem. Look in your telephone directory to see if there is a branch office in your area; if not, contact the organization's national headquarters at the address given.

To find government agencies that might be able to help, start with your local government (city, town, or village) and move on to county, state, and federal levels only as necessary. Often, the agency nearest home will be the most help. Again, your telephone directory can be your best source of information; if you can't find exactly what you're looking for there, try phoning the municipal or country clerk's office for more specific guidance.

Keys to Finding Help

A few of the sources of assistance or information to which you might turn when dealing with a specific problem are given below. (Unless an address is given, look in your phonebook for the key-word indicated.)

Aging. Administration on Aging, U.S. Department of Health and Human Services, Washington, D.C. 20201. Locally, try state **Offices, Commissions, Departments,** or **Bureaus** on **Aging** or **Senior Citizens Affairs;** look for county or municipal agencies with similar titles, and for regional **Area Agencies on Aging.**

Career Considerations: If you're unhappy in your present work situation, and are trying to decide whether to stick with it until you can retire gracefully or to attempt to start anew in middle age, these books might provide some helpful insights. *Overcoming Executive Mid-Life Crisis* by Homer R. Figler; *Second Chance: Blueprints for Change* by Herbert B. Livesey; *What Color Is Your Parachute?* by Richard N. Bolles; *The Three Boxes of Life and How to Get Out of Them* by Richard N. Bolles; *The Women's Guide to Re-Entry Employment* by Mary Zimmeth; *What To Do With the Rest of Your Life* by the Catalyst staff.

Federal Government. Your tie-line and guide to the federal bureaucracy is the **Federal Information Center,** listed in the phonebook under "U.S. Government." If nothing else works, try phoning your Congressional representative's local office; his or her staff can sometimes cut through a lot of red tape.

Food. The key words here are **Food Stamps, Meals on Wheels, National Nutrition Program for the Elderly.** If none of these is listed in your phonebook, check with the agencies listed under Aging.

Funerals. Helpful information and advice about this difficult and potentially expensive purchase may be found in *It's Your Choice: The Practical Guide to Planning a Funeral* by Thomas C. Nelson, Senior Coordinator of AARP's consumer affairs programs.

Health Care. Don't overlook your local **health department.** If your problem involves a hospital, there is probably a staff social worker to whom you can turn. Also, try local medical and dental societies and schools—the latter frequently provide quality care at relatively low cost. For information about health care at home, contact the National Homecaring Council, 67 Irving Place, New York, N.Y. 10003.

Housing. The key agency here is the U.S. Department of Housing and Urban Development; check your phonebook for a local office, or write to HUD, Washington, D.C. 20410. If you live in a rural area, contact your agricultural extension agent or write directly to Farmers Home Administration, U.S. Department of Agriculture, 14th Street and Independence Avenue S.W., Washington, D.C. 20250. Your local **housing authority** can also prove helpful.

Legal Problems. Many communities have special legal counseling programs for older residents. Try your local **Aging** agency, or write to National Senior Citizens Law Center, 1709 West 8th Street, Los Angeles, Calif. 90017. Information is also available from the National Resource Center for Consumers of Legal Services, 1302 18th Street N.W., Washington, D.C. 20036.

Middle Age. The processes, problems, and potentials of adult development in the middle years are explored in authoritative depth in two recent books, *The Seasons of a Man's Life* by Daniel Levinson and *Transformations* by Roger Gould. The original research and theories of both of these psychiatrists served as a basis for Gail Sheehy's best-selling *Passages*.

Money. Information about **Social Security** and **Supplemental Security Income** may be found in this *Almanac* or from the **Social Security Administration** office nearest you. Also helpful in special circumstances are the U.S. Office of Personnel Management, Compensation Group, Bureau of Retirement, 1900 E Street N.W., Washington, D.C. 20415; and the U.S. Railroad Retirement Board, Headquarters office, 844 Rush Street, Chicago, Ill. 60611.

Nursing Homes. Check with your local **health department**, hospital social worker, or the nearest branches of the American Nursing Home Association and the American Association of Homes for the Aging. Some state **Aging** agencies have a **Nursing Home Ombudsman.** Write for the free pamphlet *Thinking About a Nursing Home* to the American Health Care Association, 1200 15th Street N.W., Washington, D.C. 20005.

Parents. There is a steadily growing selection of books about aging child/elderly parent relationships. My personal favorites are *You and Your Aging Parent* by Barbara Silverstone and Helen Kandel Hyman, *When Your Parents Grow Old* by Jane Otten and Florence D. Shelley, and *Aging Parents* by Pauline K. Ragan. Also worth perusing are *Understanding Aging Parents* by Andrew D. and Judith L. Lester, *Your Aging Parents: When and How To Help* by Margaret J. Anderson, and *Caring for Your Aged Parents* by Earl A. and Sharon Hya Grollman.

Research. If you want to read more about growing older, look in your local library catalog under **aging, gerontology, geriatrics, retirement.**

Volunteering. If you're interested in working as a volunteer, check with your local **hospitals, nonprofit nursing homes, social service agencies,** and **civic organizations.** Or write to: National Center for Citizen Involvement, 1214 16th Street, N.W., Washington, D.C. 20036, ACTION, Older Americans Volunteer Programs, Washington, D.C. 20525; Service Corps of Retired Executives (SCORE), Small Business Administration, 1441 L Street N.W., Washington, D.C. 20416.

Social Security

The original Social Security Act was passed in 1935 and amended in 1939, 1946, 1950, 1952, 1954, 1956, 1958, 1960, 1961, 1965, 1967, 1969, 1972, 1974, 1977, and 1980.

The act is administered by the Social Security Administration and the Health Care Financing Administration, and other agencies within the Department of Health and Human Services.

For purposes of clarity, the explanations given below will describe the provisions of the act as amended.

Old Age, Disability, and Survivors Insurance

Practically everyone who works fairly regularly is covered by social security. Many state and local government employees are covered under voluntary agreements between states and the Secretary of Health and Human Services. Workers not covered include most federal civilian employees, career railroad workers, and a few other exceptions.

Cash tips count for social security if they amount to $20 or more in a month from employment with a single employer.

To qualify for benefits or make payments possible for your survivors, you must be in work covered by the law for a certain number of "quarters of coverage." Before 1978, a quarter of coverage was earned if a worker was paid $50 or more wages in a 3-month calendar quarter. A self-employed person got 4 "quarters of coverage" for a year in which his net earnings were $400 or more.

In 1978, a worker, whether employed or self-employed, received one quarter of coverage for each $250 of covered annual earnings up to a maximum of four for a year. The quarter of coverage measure was increased to $260 in 1979 and $290 in 1980, $310 in 1981, $340 in 1982, and will increase automatically in future years to keep pace with increases in average wages. The number of quarters needed differs for different persons and depends on the date of your birth; in general, it is related to the number of years after 1950, or after the year you reach 21, if later, and up to the year you reach 62, become disabled, or die. One "quarter of coverage" is required for each such year in order for you or your family to get benefits. No one will need more than 40 quarters. Your local social security office can tell you how long you need to work.

Who Pays for the Insurance?

Both workers and their employers pay for the workers' insurance. Self-employed persons pay

Social Security Contribution and Rate Schedule
(percent of covered earnings)

Year	Retirement, survivors, and disability insurance	Hospital insurance	Total
EMPLOYERS AND EMPLOYEES			
1978	4.95%	1.10%	6.05%
1979–80	5.08	1.05	6.13
1981	5.35	1.30	6.65
1982–84	5.40	1.30	6.70
1985	5.70	1.35	7.05
1986–89	5.70	1.45	7.15
1990 & later	6.20	1.45	7.65
SELF-EMPLOYED			
1978	7.00%	1.10%	8.10%
1979–80	7.05	1.05	8.10
1981	8.00	1.30	9.30
1982–84	8.05	1.30	9.35
1985	8.55	1.35	9.90
1986–89	8.55	1.45	10.00
1990 & later	9.30	1.45	10.75

their own social security contributions annually along with their income tax. The rates include the cost of Medicare hospital insurance. The contribution and benefit base is $32,400 for 1982, and will increase automatically in future years as earnings levels rise. The contribution rate schedules under present law are shown in a table in this section.

The separate payroll contribution to finance hospital insurance is placed in a separate trust fund in the U.S. Treasury. In addition, the medical insurance premiums, currently $12.20 a month, and the government's shares go into another separate trust fund.

How to Apply for Benefits

You apply for benefits by filing a claim either in person, by mail, or by telephone at any social security office. You can get the address either from the post office or from the phone book under the listing, United States Government—Department of Health and Human Services—Social Security Administration. You will need certain kinds of proof, depending upon the type of benefit you are claiming. If it is a retirement benefit, you should provide a birth or baptismal certificate. If you are unable to get these documents, other old documents showing your age or date of birth—such as census records, school records, early naturalization certificate, etc. —may be acceptable. A widow, or widower, 60 or older who is claiming widow's benefits based on his or her spouse's earnings should have both proof of age and a copy of the marriage certificate. If formal proof is not available, the social security office will tell you what kinds of information will be acceptable.

What Does Social Security Offer?

The social security contribution you pay gives you four different kinds of protection: (1) retirement benefits, (2) survivors' benefits, (3) disability benefits, and (4) Medicare hospital insurance benefits.

Retirement benefits A worker becomes eligible for the full amount of his retirement benefits at age 65, if he has retired under the definition in the law. A worker may retire at 62 and get 80% of his full benefit. The closer he is to age 65 when he starts collecting his benefit, the larger is the fraction of his full benefit that he will get.

The amount of the retirement benefit you are entitled to at 65 is the key to all other benefits under the program. The retirement benefit is based on covered earnings, generally those after 1950. Your covered earnings will be updated (indexed) to the second year before you reach age 62, become disabled, or die, and will reflect the increases in average wages that have occurred since the earnings were paid.

A worker who delays his retirement past age 65, or who does not receive a benefit for some months after age 65 because of high earnings will get a special credit that can mean a larger benefit. The credit adds to a worker's benefits 1% (3% for workers age 62 after 1978) for each year (1/12 of 1% for each month) from age 65 to age 72 for which he did not get benefits.

The law provides a special minimum benefit at retirement for people who worked under social security for many years. The provision will help people who had low incomes, but above a specific level, in their working years. The amount of the special minimum depends on the number of years of coverage. For a worker retiring at 65 in June 1982 with 30 or more years of coverage, the special minimum benefit would be $345.10 (effective June 1982). These benefits are reduced if a worker is under 65 and are increased automatically for increases in the cost of living.

If you retired at age 65 in June 1982 with average earnings, you would get a benefit of $575.00.

If your spouse is also 65, then he or she will get a spouse's benefit that is equal to half your benefit. So if your benefit is $575.00, your spouse gets $287.50.

If your spouse is between ages 62 and 65, he or she can draw a reduced benefit; the amount depends on the number of months before 65 that he or she starts getting checks. If he or she draws his or her benefit when he or she is 62, he or she will get about 3/8 of your basic benefit, or $215.60. (He or she will get this amount for the rest of his or her life, unless you should die first; then he or she can start getting widow's, or widower's, benefits, described below.)

If the spouse is entitled to a worker's retirement benefit on his or her own earnings, he or she can draw whichever amount is larger. If the spouse is entitled to a retirement benefit which is less than the spouse's benefit, he or she will receive his or her own retirement benefit plus the difference between the retirement benefit and the spouse's benefit.

If you have children under 18 or a child under age 19 attending elementary or secondary school or a son or daughter who became totally disabled prior to reaching age 22, when you retire they will get a benefit equal to half your full retirement benefits (subject to maximum payments that can be made to a family). If your spouse is caring for a child who is under 16 or who became disabled before 22 (and getting benefits too), he or she is eligible for benefits, even if he or she is under 62.

In general, the highest retirement check that can be paid to a worker who retired at 65 in June 1982 is about $729 a month. Maximum payment to the family of this retired worker is about $1,276 in June 1982. When your children reach age 18, their benefits will stop except for children under age 19 attending an elementary or secondary school and except for a benefit that is going to a son or daughter who became totally disabled before attaining age 22. Such a person can continue to get his benefits as long as his disability meets the definition in the law.

If you are divorced, you can get social security benefits (the same as a spouse or widow, or widower,) based on your ex-spouse's earnings record if you were married at least 10 years and if your ex-spouse has retired, become disabled, or died.

Survivor benefits. This feature of the social security program gives your family valuable life insurance protection—in some cases benefits to a family could amount to $100,000 or more over a period of years. The amount of protection is again geared to what the worker would be entitled to if he had been age 65 when he died. Your survivors could get:

1. A cash payment to help cover your burial expenses. This "lump-sum death payment" is $255.
2. A benefit for each child until he reaches 18, or 19 if the child is attending elementary or secondary school or at any age if disabled before 22. Each eligible child receives 75% of the basic benefit

(subject to reduction for the family maximum). (A disabled child can continue to collect benefits after age 22.) If certain conditions are met, dependent grandchildren of insured workers can receive survivor or dependent benefits.

3. A benefit for your widow, or widower, if she has children under 16 or disabled in her care. Her benefit is also 75% of the basic benefit. She can collect this as long as she has a child under 16 or disabled in her care. Payments stop then (they will start again upon application when she is 60 at a slightly lower amount).

Total family survivor benefits are estimated to be as high as $1,424 a month, in 1982.

4. If there are no children either under 16 or disabled, your spouse can get a widow's, or widower's, benefit starting at age 60. This would come to 71½% of the basic amount at age 60. A widow, or widower, who first becomes entitled at 65 or later may get 100% of his or her deceased spouse's basic amount (provided neither he nor she ever drew reduced benefits).

5. Dependent parents can sometimes collect survivors' benefits. They are usually eligible if: (a) they were getting at least half their support from the deceased worker at (1) the time of the worker's death if the worker did not qualify for disability benefits before death, or (2) if the worker had been entitled to disability benefits which had not been terminated before death either at the beginning of the period of disability or at the time of death; (b) they have reached 62; and (c) they are not eligible for a greater retirement benefit based on their own earnings. A single surviving parent can then get 82 ½% of the basic benefit. If two parents are eligible, each would get 75%.

Here is an example of survivors' benefits in one family situation: John Jones died at age 29 in June 1982 leaving a wife and two children aged one and three. He had average covered earnings under social security. Family survivors' benefits would include: (1) a cash lump-sum death payment of $255, and (2) a total monthly benefit of $923 for the family. When the children reach 18, their benefits stop unless they are attending an elementary or secondary school full time, in which case payments continue up to age 19. When the older child no longer collects benefits, the widow and younger child continue to get benefits until that child is 16. If he continues in school, he will still get a benefit, but Mrs. Jones' checks will stop. When Mrs. Jones becomes 60 (assuming she has not remarried), she will be able to get a reduced widow's benefit if she so chooses, or she can wait until age 65 to get a full benefit.

If in addition to your social security benefit as a wife, husband, widow, or widower you receive a pension based on your work in public employment not covered by social security, your benefit as a dependent or survivor will be reduced by the amount of that pension. Under an exception in the law, your government pension will not affect your dependent's or survivor's benefit if you became eligible for that pension before December 1982 and if, at the time you apply or become entitled to your social security benefit as a dependent or survivor, you could have qualified for that benefit if the law in effect in January 1977 had remained in effect. (At that time, men had to prove they were dependent upon their wives for support to be eligible for benefits as a dependent or survivor.) Your government pension, however, will not affect any social security benefit based on your own work covered by social security.

Disability Benefits. Disability benefits can be paid to several groups of people:

Disabled workers under 65 and their families.

Persons disabled before 22 who continue to be disabled. These benefits are payable as early as 18 when a parent (or grandparent under certain circumstances) receives social security retirement or disability benefits or when an insured parent dies.

Disabled widows and widowers and (under certain conditions) disabled surviving divorced spouses of workers who were insured at death. These benefits are payable as early as 50.

A disabled person is eligible for Medicare after being entitled to disability payments for 24 months.

If you are a worker and become severely disabled, you will be eligible for monthly benefits if you have worked under social security long enough and recently enough. The amount of work you will need depends on your age when you become disabled:

Before 24: You need credit for 1½ years of work in the 3-year period ending when your disability begins.

24 through 30: You need credit for having worked half the time between 21 and the time you become disabled.

31 or older: All workers disabled at 31 or older—except the blind—need the amount of credit shown in the chart below:

Work Credit for Disability Benefits

Born after 1929, become disabled at age	Born before 1930, become disabled before 62 in	Years of work credit you need
42 or younger	1971	5
44	1973	5½
46	1975	6
48	1977	6½
50	1979	7
51	1980	7¼
52	1981	7½
54	1983	8
56	1985	8½
58	1987	9
60	1989	9½
62 or older	1991 or later	10

NOTE: Five years of this credit must have been earned in the 10 years ending when you became disabled; years need not be continuous or in units of full years.

To be considered disabled under the social security law you must have a physical or mental condition which: (1) prevents you from doing any substantial gainful work; and (2) is expected to last (or has lasted) for at least 12 months, or is expected to result in death.

If you meet these conditions, you may be able to get payments even if your recovery from the disability is expected.

The medical evidence from your physician or other sources will show the severity of your condition and the extent to which it prevents you from doing substantial gainful work. Your age, education, training, and work experience also may be considered in deciding whether you are able to work.

If you can't do your regular work but can do other substantial gainful work, you will not be considered disabled. A person whose vision is no better than 20/200 even with glasses, or who has a limited visual field of 20 degrees or less, is considered "blind" under the social security law.

While you are receiving benefits as a disabled worker, payments can also be made to certain members of your family. These family members include:

Your unmarried children under 18.

Your children under 19 if they are unmarried and attending an elementary or secondary school full time.

Your unmarried children 18 or older who were disabled before reaching 22 and continue to be disabled.

Your wife at any age if she has in her care a child who is under 16 or disabled and who is getting benefits based on your social security record.

Your wife 62 or older even if there are no children entitled to benefits.

Your husband 62 or older.

A child may be eligible on a grandparent's social security record only if the child's parents are disabled or deceased and the child was living with and dependent upon the grandparent at the time the grandparent qualified for benefits.

Benefits begin after a waiting period of 5 full calendar months. No benefits can be paid for these first 5 months of disability; therefore, the first payment is for the 6th full month. If you are disabled more than 6 full months before you apply, back benefits may be payable, but not before the 6th full month of disability. It is important to apply soon after the disability starts because back payments are limited to the 12 months preceding the month you apply.

Certain disabled people under 65 are eligible for Medicare. They include disabled workers at any age, persons who became disabled before age 22, and disabled widows and widowers age 50 or over who have been entitled to disability checks for 2 years or more.

Medicare protection generally ends when monthly disability benefits end, and can continue an additional 3 years after benefits stop because an individual returns to gainful work.

If a person becomes entitled to disability benefits again, Medicare coverage starts at the same time if a worker becomes disabled again within 5 years after benefits end (or within 7 years for a disabled widow, widower, or person disabled before age 22).

Benefits to workers disabled after 1978 and their dependents are based, in part, on earnings that have been adjusted to take account of increases in average wages since they were earned. The adjusted earnings are averaged together and a formula is applied to the adjusted average to figure the benefit rate.

Monthly benefits in July 1982 or later can be as high as $769 for a worker and as high as $1,347 for a worker with a family. Once a person starts receiving benefits, the amount will increase automatically in future years to keep pace with the rising cost of living.

If you receive benefits as a disabled worker, an adult disabled since childhood, or a disabled widow or widower, you are not subject to the general rule under which some benefits are withheld if you have substantial earnings. There are special rules, which include medical considerations, for determining how any work you do might affect your disability payments.

If one of your dependents who is under 65 and who is not disabled works and earns more than $4,440 in 1982, some of the dependent's benefits may be withheld. In general, $1 in benefits is withheld for each $2 over $4,440. Different rules apply to your dependents who are 65 or over.

The amount a person can earn without having any benefits withheld will increase in future years as the level of average wages rises.

If you are receiving disability benefits, you are required by law to let the Social Security Administration know if your condition improves or if you return to work no matter how little you earn.

If at any time medical evidence shows that you no longer meet the requirements for entitlement to disability benefits, you will still receive benefits for a 3-month period of adjustment. Benefits will then be stopped.

Whether or not you report a return to work or that your condition has improved, social security will review your claim periodically to see if you continue to meet the requirements for benefits.

If you are a disabled worker or a person disabled in childhood and you return to work in spite of a severe condition, your benefits may continue to be paid during a trial work period of up to 9 months—not necessarily consecutive months. This will give you a chance to test your ability to work. If after 9 months it is decided that you are able to do substantial gainful work, your benefits will be paid for an adjustment period of 3 additional months.

Thus, if you go to work in spite of your disability, you may continue to receive disability benefits for up to 12 months, even though the work is substantial gainful work. If it is decided that the work you are able to do is not substantial and gainful, you may continue to receive benefits. Of course, should you no longer meet the requirements for entitlement your benefits would be stopped after a 3-month adjustment period even though your trial work period might not be over.

Disabled widows and widowers also can have a trial work period. If your benefits are stopped because you return to work and you become unable to continue working within the next 12 months, your benefits can be restarted automatically. You do not have to file a new disability application.

You Can Earn Income Without Losing Benefits

If you are 72 or over, (age 70 or over effective 1983) you can earn any amount and still get all your benefits. If you are under 72, you can receive all benefits if your earnings do not exceed the annual exempt amount. The annual amount for 1982 is $6,000 for people 65 or over and $4,440 for people under 65.

If your earnings go over the annual amount, $1 in benefits is withheld for each $2 of earnings above the limit.

The monthly measure used for 1977 and earlier years to determine whether benefits could be paid for any month during which they earned 1/12 or less of the annual exempt amount and did no substantial work in their business has been eliminated. A person can now use the monthly test only in the first year that he or she has a month in which earnings do not exceed 1/12 of the annual exempt amount or does not perform substantial services in self-employment. If such a month occurs in 1982, a benefit can be paid for any month in which you earn $500 or less (if 65 or older) or $370 (if under 65) and don't perform substantial services in self-employment even though your total yearly earnings exceed the annual amount.

The annual exempt amount will increase automatically as the level of average wages rises.

If a worker's earnings exceed the exempt amount, social security benefits to his dependents may be reduced. However, a dependent's benefits will not be reduced if another dependent has excess earnings.

Anyone earning over the annual exempt amount a year while receiving benefits (and under age 72) must report these earnings to the Social Security Administration. If you continue to work after you have applied for social security, your additional earnings may increase the amount of your monthly payment. This will be done automatically by the Social Security Administration. You need not ask for it.

Medicare

The Medicare program is administered by the Health Care Financing Administration.

Most people 65 and over and many under 65 who have been entitled to disability checks for at least 2 years have Medicare protection. So do insured people and their dependents who need a kidney transplant or dialysis treatment because of permanent kidney failure.

The hospital insurance part of Medicare helps pay the cost of inpatient hospital care and certain kinds of follow-up care. The medical insurance part helps pay for the cost of doctors' services, outpatient hospital services, and for certain other medical items and services.

A person who is eligible for monthly benefits at 65 gets hospital insurance automatically and does not have to pay a premium. He does pay a monthly premium for medical insurance.

Supplemental Security Income

The supplemental security income program started January 1974. These federal payments assure a minimum level of income for aged, blind, and disabled people who have limited income and resources.

This program is administered by the Social Security Administration, but it is financed from general revenues, not from social security contributions. Before 1974, payments to these people were made by state and local public assistance agencies.

Payments of up to $284.30 a month for an individual and up to $426.40 for a couple can be made and States may supplement the federal payments. Further information is available from any social security office.

How to Protect Your Social Security Record

Always show your social security card when you start a new job. In that way you will be sure that your earnings will be credited to *your* social security record and not someone else's. If you lose your social security card, apply for a new one at any social security office. When a woman marries, she should apply for a new card showing her married name (and the same number).

Public Assistance

The Federal government makes grants to the states to help them provide financial assistance, medical care, and social services to certain persons in need, including children dependent because of the death, absence from home, incapacity, or (in some states) unemployment of a parent. In addition, some help is provided from only state and/or local funds to some other needy persons.

Federal sharing in state cash assistance expenditures made in accordance with the Social Security Act is based on formulas which are set forth in the Act. The Social Security Act gives the states the option of using one of two formulas, whichever is to its benefit. One formula limits the amount of assistance payment in which there is federal sharing. The other formula permits federal sharing without a limit on the amount of assistance payment. Administrative costs in all the programs are shared equally by the federal and state governments.

Within these and other general patterns set by the requirements of the Social Security Act and their administrative interpretations, each state initiates and administers its own public assistance programs, including the determination of who is eligible to receive assistance, and how much can be granted and under what conditions. Assistance is in the form of cash payments made to recipients, except that direct payments are used for medical care, and restricted payments may be used in cases of mismanagement. Other social services are provided, in some instances, to help assistance recipients increase their capacity for self-care and self-support or to strengthen family life.

In the medical assistance Medicaid program, federal funds pay 50% to 83% of the costs for medical care. If it is to a state's benefit, it may use the Medicaid formula for federal sharing for its money payment programs, ignoring the maximum on dollar amounts per recipient.

Unemployment Insurance

Unemployment insurance is managed jointly by the states and the federal government. Most states began paying benefits in 1938 and 1939.

Under What Conditions Can the Worker Collect?

The laws vary from state to state. In general, a waiting period of one week is required after a claim is filed before collecting unemployment insurance; the worker must be able to work, must not have quit without good cause or have been discharged for misconduct; he must not be involved in a labor dispute; above all, he must be ready and willing to work. He may be disqualified if he refuses, without good cause, to accept a job which is suitable for him in terms of his qualifications and experience, unless the wages, hours and working conditions offered are substantially less favorable than those prevailing for similar jobs in the community.

The unemployed worker must go to the local state employment security office and register for work. If that office has a suitable opening available, he must accept it or lose his unemployment payments, unless he has good cause for the refusal. If a worker moves out of his own state, he can still collect at his new residence; the state in which he is now located will act as agent for the other state, which will pay his benefits.

Benefits are paid only to unemployed workers who have had at least a certain amount of recent past employment or earnings in a job covered by the state law. The amount of employment or earnings, and the period used to measure them, vary from state to state, but the intent of the various laws is to limit benefits to workers whose recent records indicate that they are members of the labor force. The amount of benefits an unemployed worker may receive for any week is also determined by application to his past wages of a formula specified in the law. The general objective is to provide a weekly benefit which is about half the worker's customary weekly wages, up to a maximum set by the law (see table). In a majority of states, the total benefits a worker may receive in a 12-month period is limited to a fraction of his total wages in a prior 12-month period, as well as to a stated number of weeks. Thus, not all workers in a state are entitled to benefits for the number of weeks shown in the table.

Who Pays for the Insurance?

The total cost is borne by the employer in all but three states. Each state has a sliding scale of rates. The standard rate is set at 2.7% of taxable payroll in most states. But employers with records of less unemployment (that is, with fewer unemployment benefits paid to their former workers) are rewarded with rates lower than the standard 2.7%. The estimated average rate for employers in 1980 was 2.3% of taxable wages or 1.0% of total wages. Contributions for 1982 are required on wages up to $6,000 in all states except Ala., Del., Mo., and Pa., $6,600; Ark., $6,900; Conn., Ill., $7,000; D.C., $7,500; Ky., Mont., V.I., W.Va., $8,000; N.J., $8,200; Minn., $8,300; N. Mex., $8,500; R.I., $8,600; Iowa, $8,700; N.D., $9,240; Nev., $9,300; Wash., $10,800; Or., $11,000; Utah, $12,000; Hawaii, $13,000; Idaho, $13,200; Alaska, $14,600; P.R., all wages. Employees as well as employers pay a tax in Alaska ranging from 0.3% to 1.0% in accordance with their employer's tax; in N.J., employees pay 0.5% for unemployment insurance. In Ala., employees pay contributions of 0.5% only when the fund is below a specified amount.

Employers pay an additional unemployment tax to the federal government—0.7% of the first $6,000 paid to each employee. This money is used for the federal and state costs of administering the employment security program, including both unemployment insurance and the employment service. Any amount over these costs, up to the greater of $550 million or 0.125% of total wages subject to contributions under the state unemployment compensation laws for the calendar year, is put in a special fund on which the states draw when the benefit payment funds are low. Any remaining excess is distributed to the states in proportion to their taxable payrolls. These excess funds may be used for benefit payments, or may be used for administrative expenses if so appropriated by the state legislature.

Requirements vary from state to state, but all

State Unemployment Compensation Maximums, 1982

State	Weekly benefit[1]	Maximum duration, weeks	State	Weekly benefit[1]	Maximum duration, weeks
Alabama	$90	26	Nebraska	106	26
Alaska	150–222	26	Nevada	149	26
Arizona	115	26	New Hampshire	132	26
Arkansas	136	26	New Jersey	145	26
California	136	26	New Mexico	130	26
Colorado	182	26	New York	125	26
Connecticut	156–206	26	North Carolina	152	26
Delaware	150	26	North Dakota	175	26
D. C.	206	34	Ohio	147–233	26
Florida	125	26	Oklahoma	197	26
Georgia	115	26	Oregon	175	26
Hawaii	169	26	Pennsylvania	190–198	30
Idaho	159	26	Puerto Rico	84	20
Illinois	154–206	26	Rhode Island	154–174	26
Indiana	84–141	26	South Carolina	118	26
Iowa	158–191	26	South Dakota	129	26
Kansas	163	26	Tennessee	110	26
Kentucky	140	26	Texas	147	26
Louisiana	183	28	Utah	166	26
Maine	124–186	26	Vermont	146	26
Maryland	153	26	Virgin Islands	115	26
Massachusetts	156–234	30	Virginia	138	26
Michigan	197	26	Washington	178	30
Minnesota	184	26	West Virginia	211	28
Mississippi	105	26	Wisconsin	191	34
Missouri	105	26	Wyoming	180	26
Montana	158	26			

1. Maximum amounts. When two amounts are shown, higher includes dependents' allowances. *Source:* Department of Labor, Employment and Training Administration.

states cover firms having at least one employee for 20 weeks or a quarterly payroll of $1,500 in the current or preceding calendar year. In some states, firms with one employee at any time are covered. Certain classes of workers are specifically excluded under some or all state laws—members of the employer's family, insurance agents on commission, student nurses, internes, casual labor, and the self-employed.

During periods of high unemployment on either a state or national level, federal-state extended benefits are available to workers who have exhausted their regular benefits. An unemployed worker may receive benefits equal to the weekly benefit he received under the state program for one half the weeks of his basic entitlement to benefits up to a maximum (including regular benefits) of 39 weeks.

Federal Unemployment Insurance Programs

Amendments to the Social Security Act provided unemployment insurance for Federal civilian employees (1954) and for ex-servicemen (1958). Benefits under these programs are paid by state employment security agencies as agents of the federal government under agreements with the Secretary of Labor. Eligibility for benefits and the amount of benefits paid are determined according to the terms and conditions of the applicable state unemployment insurance law. Thus, federal civilian employees and ex-servicemen are subject to the same eligibility, disqualification, and benefit payment provisions as are claimants for benefits under the state unemployment insurance system.

Railroad Workers

These are covered by the federal Railroad Retirement Act which provides retirement and survivor annuities and lump-sum death benefits for aged or disabled employees and their families. Railroad workers are also covered by the Railroad Unemployment Insurance Act, which provides unemployment and sickness benefits as well as a placement service. Both acts are administered by the U.S. Railroad Retirement Board. Those covered by the railroad retirement system also participate in the health insurance program (Medicare) provided by the Social Security Act.

Medicare Program

The Medicare program is a federal health-insurance program for persons 65 and over, disabled people under 65 who have been entitled to social security disability benefits at least 24 months, and insured workers and their dependents who need dialysis treatment or a kidney transplant because of permanent kidney failure.

Enacted under the Social Security Amendments of 1965, Medicare's official name is Title XVIII of the Social Security Act. These amendments also carried Title XIX, providing federal assistance to state medical-aid programs, which has come to be known as Medicaid.

Medicare

It will be helpful to your understanding of the Medicare program if you keep the following points in mind:

- The federal health-insurance program does not of itself offer medical services. It helps pay hospital, doctor, and other medical bills. You choose your own doctor, who prescribes your treatment and place of treatment. But, you should always make sure that health care facilities or persons who provide you with treatment or services are participating in Medicare. Usually, Medicare cannot pay for care from non-participating health care organizations.
- There are two parts of the program:
  (1) The hospital insurance part for the payment of most of the cost of covered care provided by participating hospitals, skilled nursing facilities, and home health agencies.
  (2) The medical insurance part which helps pay doctors' bills and certain other expenses.
- Another important point to remember: While Medicare pays the major share of the costs of many illnesses requiring hospitalization, it does not offer adequate protection for long-term illness or mental illness.
- Therefore, it may be advisable not to cancel any private health insurance you now carry. You may wish to cancel a policy whose benefits are duplicated by the federal program, and consider a new policy that will provide for the payment of costs not covered by the federal program. Private insurance companies offer policies supplementing the protection offered by the federal program.

If you want help in deciding whether to buy private supplemental insurance, ask at any social security office for the pamphlet, *Guide to health insurance for people with Medicare.* This free pamphlet describes the various types of supplemental insurance available.

Do You Qualify for Hospital Insurance?

If you're entitled to monthly social security or railroad retirement checks (as a worker, dependent, or survivor), you have hospital insurance protection automatically when you're 65. Disabled people will have hospital insurance automatically after they have been entitled to social security disability benefits for 24 months. (Disabled people who get railroad annuities must meet special requirements.) People 65 or older who are not entitled to monthly benefits need credit for some work under social security to get hospital insurance without paying a monthly premium. If they do not have enough work, they can buy hospital insurance. The premium is $113 a month for the 12-month period starting July 1, 1982.

To be sure your protection will start the month you reach 65, apply for Medicare insurance 3 months before reaching 65, even if you don't plan to retire.

Do You Qualify for Voluntary Medical Insurance?

The voluntary medical insurance plan is a vital supplement to the hospital plan. It helps pay for

Medicaid Services by State

(as of September 1, 1981[1])

Basic required Medicaid services: Every Medicaid program must cover at least these services for at least everyone receiving federally supported financial assistance: inpatient hospital care; outpatient hospital services; other laboratory and X-ray services; skilled nursing facility services and home health services for individuals 21 and older; early and periodic screening, diagnosis, and treatment for individuals under 21; family planning; and physician services. Federal financial participation is also available to states electing to expand their Medicaid programs by covering additional services and/or by including people eligible for medical but not for financial assistance. For the latter group, states may offer the services required for financial assistance recipients or may substitute a combination of seven services. Services provided only under the Medicare buy-in or the screening and treatment program for individuals under 21 are not shown on this chart.

NOTE: O = Offered for people receiving federally supported financial assistance. X = Offered also for people in public assistance[2] and SSI[3] categories who are financially eligible for medical but not for financial assistance. **Definitions and limitations on eligibility and services vary from state to state. Details are available from local welfare offices and state Medicaid agencies.**

		Additional services for which federal financial participation is available to states under Medicaid																	
States	Basic required Medicaid services	Clinic services	Prescribed drugs	Dental services	Prosthetic devices	Eyeglasses	Private-duty nursing	Physical therapy and/or related services[4]	Other diagnostic, screening, preventive, and rehabilitative services	Emergency hospital services	Skilled nursing facility services for patients under 21	Optometrists' services	Podiatrists' services	Chiropractors' services	Care for patients 65 or older in institutions for mental diseases[5]	Care for patients under 22 in psychiatric hospitals	Care for patients 65 or older in institutions for tuberculosis[5]	Institutional services in intermediate care facilities[6]
Alabama	0	—	0	—	0	0	—	—	—	0	0	0	—	—	0	0	0	0
Alaska	0	0	—	—	—	0	—	0	—	0	0	0	—	—	0	—	0	0
Arizona	—	—	—	—	—	—	—	—	—	—	—	—	—	—	—	—	—	—
Arkansas	X	X	X	—	X	X	—	—	—	X	0	X	—	X	0	0	X	0
California	X	X	X	X	X	X	—	X	X	X	X	X	X	X	X	X	X	X
Colorado	0	0	0	—	0	—	—	—	—	0	0	—	0	—	0	—	0	0
Connecticut	X	X	X	X	X	X	X	X	X	—	X	X	X	X	X	—	X	X
Delaware	0	0	0	—	0	—	—	—	0	0	0	—	0	—	0	—	—	0
D.C.	X	X	X	—	X	X	—	X	X	X	X	X	X	—	X	X	X	X
Florida	0	—	0	0	0	0	—	0	—	0	—	0	—	—	0	0	0	0
Georgia	0	0	0	—	0	—	—	—	—	—	0	—	0	—	0	0	—	0
Guam	X	X	X	—	—	—	—	0	—	—	—	X	—	—	—	—	—	—
Hawaii	X	X	X	X	X	X	—	X	X	X	X	X	X	—	—	—	—	X
Idaho	0	0	0	—	—	—	—	0	0	0	0	0	0	0	0	—	—	0
Illinois	X	X	X	X	X	X	X	X	X	X	X	X	X	X	X	X	X	X
Indiana	0	0	0	0	0	0	0	0	0	0	0	0	0	0	0	—	0	0
Iowa	0	0	0	0	0	0	—	0	0	0	0	0	0	0	0	—	0	0
Kansas	X	X	X	X	X	X	X	X	X	X	X	X	X	X	X	X	X	X
Kentucky	X	X	X	—	X	—	—	X	—	X	X	X	—	—	X	X	X	X
Louisiana	X	X	X	—	X	—	—	—	X	X	0	—	—	X	0	0	0	0
Maine	X	X	X	—	X	—	—	X	X	0	X	—	X	X	X	—	X	X
Maryland	X	X	X	—	X	X	—	X	—	X	X	X	X	—	X	X	—	X
Massachusetts	X	X	X	X	X	X	X	X	X	X	X	X	X	—	X	X	—	X
Michigan	X	X	X	X	X	X	—	X	X	X	X	X	X	X	X	—	X	X
Minnesota	X	X	X	X	X	X	X	X	X	X	X	X	X	X	X	X	X	X
Mississippi	0	—	0	—	—	—	—	—	—	0	0	—	—	—	0	0	0	0
Missouri	0	0	0	0	0	0	—	0	—	—	—	0	0	—	0	0	—	0
Montana	X	X	X	X	X	X	X	X	X	X	X	X	X	—	X	—	X	X
Nebraska	X	X	X	X	X	X	X	X	—	X	X	X	X	X	X	—	X	X
Nevada	0	0	0	—	0	0	0	0	0	0	0	0	0	0	0	—	—	0
New Hampshire	X	X	X	X	X	X	X	X	X	X	X	X	X	X	0	—	—	0
New Jersey	0	0	0	0	0	0	—	0	0	0	0	0	0	0	0	—	0	0
New Mexico	0	0	0	0	0	0	0	0	0	0	0	0	0	—	—	—	—	0
New York	X	X	X	X	X	X	X	X	X	X	X	X	X	—	X	X	X	X
North Carolina	X	X	X	X	—	X	—	—	X	—	X	X	X	X	X	X	X	X
North Dakota	X	X	X	X	X	X	X	X	X	X	X	X	X	X	X	—	X	X
N. Mariana Islands	X	X	X	X	X	X	—	X	—	X	X	X	—	—	X	X	X	—
Ohio	0	0	0	0	0	0	0	0	—	0	0	0	0	0	0	—	0	0
Oklahoma	X	—	X	X	X	—	—	—	X	—	—	—	X	—	X	—	X	X
Oregon	0	0	0	0	0	0	0	0	0	0	0	0	0	0	0	—	0	0
Pennsylvania	X	X	0	0	0	—	—	—	—	X	X	X	0	X	X	—	X	X

States	Basic required Medicaid services	Clinic services	Prescribed drugs	Dental services	Prosthetic devices	Eyeglasses	Private-duty nursing	Physical therapy and/or related services[4]	Other diagnostic, screening, preventive, and rehabilitative services	Emergency hospital services	Skilled nursing facility services for patients under 21	Optometrists' services	Podiatrists' services	Chiropractors' services	Care for patients 65 or older in institutions for mental diseases[5]	Care for patients 65 or older in institutions for tuberculosis[5]	Care for patients under 22 in psychiatric hospitals	Institutional services in intermediate care facilities[6]
		Additional services for which federal financial participation is available to states under Medicaid																
Puerto Rico	X	X	X	X	—	—	—	X	X	X	—	—	—	—	—	X	—	—
Rhode Island	X	—	X	X	X	X	—	—	—	—	X	X	X	—	X	—	—	0
South Carolina	0	—	0	—	0	—	—	—	—	0	0	—	0	0	0	0	0	0
South Dakota	0	0	0	0	0	—	—	0	—	0	0	—	—	0	0	—	—	0
Tennessee	X	X	X	—	0	—	—	—	—	0	—	—	—	—	X	X	X	X
Texas	0	—	0	—	0	0	—	—	0	0	—	0	0	0	—	0	—	0
Utah	X	X	X	X	X	X	X	X	—	X	X	X	X	—	X	—	X	X
Vermont	X	X	X	—	X	—	—	—	—	X	X	—	X	—	X	—	X	X
Virgin Islands	X	X	X	X	X	X	—	X	—	—	—	—	—	—	—	—	—	—
Virginia	X	X	X	—	—	X	—	X	—	X	X	X	X	—	X	X	—	X
Washington	X	X	X	—	X	X	—	X	X	X	X	X	X	—	X	X	X	X
West Virginia	X	X	X	—	X	X	X	X	—	X	X	X	X	X	—	—	—	X
Wisconsin	X	X	X	X	X	X	X	X	X	X	X	X	X	X	X	—	X	X
Wyoming	0	0	—	—	0	—	—	0	0	—	0	0	—	—	—	—	—	0

1. Data from Regional Office reports of characteristics of state programs and state plan amendments. 2. People qualifying as members of families with dependent children (usually families with at least one parent absent or incapacitated). 3. People qualifying as aged, blind, or disabled under the Supplemental Security Income program. 4. Includes therapy in speech, hearing, and language disorder. 5. In some states, services for age 65 and older may include inpatient hospital services, and/or skilled nursing facilities services, and/or intermediate care facilities services. 6. Including intermediate care facilities services in institutions for the mentally retarded. *Source:* Department of Health and Human Services, Health Care Financing Administration.

doctors' and other medical services. Many people have not been able to obtain such insurance from private companies because they could not afford it or because of their medical histories.

One difference between the hospital insurance plan and the medical insurance plan is that you do not have to be under the social security or railroad retirement systems to enroll in the medical plan. Anyone who is 65 or older or who is eligible for hospital insurance can enroll in medical insurance.

People who get social security benefits or retirement benefits under the railroad retirement system will be enrolled automatically for medical insurance—unless they say they don't want it—when they become entitled to hospital insurance. Automatic enrollment does not apply to people who plan to continue working past 65, who are disabled widows or widowers between 50 and 65 who aren't getting disability checks, who are 65 but have not worked long enough to be eligible for hospital insurance, who have permanent kidney failure, or who live in Puerto Rico or foreign countries. These people have to apply for medical insurance if they want it. People who have medical insurance pay a monthly premium covering part of the cost of this protection. The other part is paid from general federal revenues. The basic premium for enrollees is $12.20 a month for the 12-month period starting July 1, 1982.

Is Other Insurance Necessary?

As already indicated, Medicare provides only partial reimbursement. Therefore, you should know how much medical cost you can bear and perhaps arrange for other insurance.

In 1981, for the first 60 days of inpatient hospital care in each benefit period, hospital insurance pays for all covered services except for the first $260. For the 61st through 90th day of a covered inpatient hospital stay, hospital insurance pays for all covered services except for $65 a day. People who need to be in a hospital for more than 90 days in a benefit period can use their 60 inpatient hospital reserve days. Hospital insurance pays for all covered services except for $130 a day for each reserve day used. Hospital insurance also does not pay the full cost of an inpatient stay in a skilled nursing facility.

Under medical insurance, the patient must meet an annual deductible of $75. After the patient has $75 in approved amounts for covered services each year, medical insurance generally pays 80% of the approved amounts for any additional covered services the patient receives during the rest of the year.

How You Obtain Coverage

If you are receiving social security or railroad retirement monthly benefits, you will receive from the government information concerning Medicare about 3 months before you become entitled to hospital insurance.

If you are not receiving benefits or are not covered under social security, contact any social security office to find out how you can get Medicare. People who have permanent kidney failure also should contact a social security office to apply for Medicare.

EDUCATION

School Enrollment, October 1981

(in thousands)

Age	White Enrolled	White Percent	Black Enrolled	Black Percent	Spanish origin[1] Enrolled	Spanish origin[1] Percent	All races Enrolled	All races Percent
3 and 4 years	1,881	35.6	357	36.7	165	24.5	2,332	36.0
5 and 6 years	4,859	93.9	904	94.5	568	90.4	5,955	94.0
7 to 9 years	7,875	99.3	1,441	98.8	835	99.2	9,615	99.2
10 to 13 years	11,848	99.3	2,147	99.4	1,257	99.1	14,410	99.3
14 and 15 years	5,906	98.1	1,041	97.1	565	94.0	7,141	98.0
16 and 17 years	5,990	90.4	1,054	91.3	524	82.8	7,232	90.6
18 and 19 years	3,295	48.5	544	48.2	229	37.8	3,976	49.0
20 and 21 years	2,306	32.6	257	23.4	133	20.6	2,643	31.6
22 to 24 years	1,720	16.2	228	14.7	98	12.3	2,057	16.5
25 to 29 years	1,432	8.5	235	9.9	118	8.3	1,774	9.0
30 to 34 years	1,056	6.7	143	7.2	59	5.0	1,254	6.9
Total	**48,169**	**48.2**	**8,350**	**52.5**	**4,550**	**49.0**	**58,390**	**48.9**

1. Persons of Spanish origin may be of any race. NOTE: Figures include persons enrolled in nursery school, kindergarten, elementary school, high school, and college. *Source:* Department of Commerce, Bureau of the Census.

Persons Not Enrolled in School, October 1981

(in thousands)

Age	Population	Total not enrolled Number	Total not enrolled Percent	High school graduate Number	High school graduate Percent	Not high school graduate (dropouts)[1] Number	Not high school graduate (dropouts)[1] Percent
14 and 15 years	7,290	149	2.0	4	0.1	144	2.0
16 and 17 years	7,980	748	9.4	126	1.6	622	7.8
18 and 19 years	8,115	4,139	51.0	2,840	35.0	1,299	16.0
20 and 21 years	8,365	5,722	68.4	4,399	52.6	1,322	15.8
22 to 24 years	12,485	10,428	83.5	8,529	68.3	1,899	15.2

1. Persons who are not enrolled in school and who are not high school graduates are considered dropouts. *Source:* Department of Commerce, Bureau of the Census.

School Enrollment by Grade, Control, and Race

(in thousands)

Grade level and type of control	White Oct. 1981[3]	White Oct. 1980	White Oct. 1970	Black Oct. 1981[3]	Black Oct. 1980	Black Oct. 1970	All races[1] Oct. 1981[3]	All races[1] Oct. 1980	All races[1] Oct. 1970
Nursery school: Public	441	432	198	187	180	129	657	633	333
Private	1,216	1,205	695	107	115	49	1,369	1,354	763
Kindergarten: Public	2,060	2,172	2,233	415	440	374	2,540	2,690	2,674
Private	453	423	473	62	50	53	529	486	536
Grades 1–8: Public	19,390	19,743	24,923	4,072	4,058	4,668	24,083	24,398	30,001
Private	2,691	2,768	3,715	208	202	200	2,976	3,051	3,949
Grades 9–12: Public	10,849	12,056[2]	11,599	2,085	2,200[2]	1,794	13,249	14,556[2]	13,545
Private	1,013	—	1,124	65	—	41	1,100	—	1,170
College: Public	6,754	8,875[2]	5,168	857	1,007[2]	422	7,911	10,180[2]	5,699
Private	2,229	—	1,591	223	—	100	2,525	—	1,714
Total: Public	39,495	—	44,121	7,617	—	7,387	48,439	—	52,225
Private	7,603	—	7,598	665	—	443	8,499	—	8,132
Grand total	**47,098**	**47,673**	**51,719**	**8,282**	**8,251**	**7,830**	**56,938**	**57,348**	**60,357**

1. Includes persons of Spanish origin. 2. Total public and private. Breakdown not available. 3. Estimates controlled to 1970 census base. *Source:* Department of Commerce, Bureau of the Census.

State Compulsory School Attendance Laws

State	Enactment[1]	Age limits	State	Enactment[1]	Age limits
Alabama	1915	7–16	Montana	1883	7–16
Alaska	1929	7–16	Nebraska	1887	7–16
Arizona	1899	8–16	Nevada	1873	7–17
Arkansas	1909	7–15	New Hampshire	1871	6–16
California	1874	6–16	New Jersey	1875	6–16
Colorado	1889	7–16	New Mexico	1891	6–17
Connecticut	1872	7–16	New York	1874	6–16
Delaware	1907	6–16	North Carolina	1907	7–16
D. C.	1864	7–16	North Dakota	1883	7–16
Florida	1915	7–16	Ohio	1877	6–18
Georgia	1916	7–16	Oklahoma	1907	8–16
Hawaii	1896	6–18	Oregon	1889	7–18
Idaho	1887	7–16	Pennsylvania	1895	8–17
Illinois	1883	7–16	Rhode Island	1883	7–16
Indiana	1897	7–16	South Carolina	1915	7–16
Iowa	1902	7–16	South Dakota	1883	7–16
Kansas	1874	7–16	Tennessee	1905	7–16
Kentucky	1896	7–16	Texas	1915[2]	7–17
Louisiana	1910	7–15	Utah	1890	6–18
Maine	1875	7–15	Vermont	1867	7–16
Maryland	1902	6–16	Virginia	1908	6–17
Massachusetts	1852	6–16	Washington	1871	8–15
Michigan	1871	6–16	West Virginia	1897	7–16
Minnesota	1885	7–16	Wisconsin	1879	6–16
Mississippi	1918	7–13	Wyoming	1876	7–16
Missouri	1905	7–16			

1. Date of enactment of first compulsory attendance law. 2. A compulsory school attendance law was contained in a law of 1873 establishing free public schools. However, the provision was omitted in superseding legislation passed in 1876. *Source:* Department of Education, National Center for Educational Statistics.

High School and College Graduates

Year of graduation	High School			College[1]		
	Men	Women	Total	Men	Women	Total
1900	38,075	56,808	94,883	22,173	5,237	27,410
1910	63,676	92,753	156,429	28,762	8,437	37,199
1920	123,684	187,582	311,266	31,980	16,642	48,622
1929–30	300,376	366,528	666,904	73,615	48,869	122,484
1939–40	578,718	642,757	1,221,475	109,546	76,954	186,500
1949–50	570,700	629,000	1,199,700	328,841	103,217	432,058
1959–60	898,000	966,000	1,864,000	254,063	138,377	392,440
1960–61	958,000	1,013,000	1,971,000	254,215	144,495	398,710
1961–62	941,000	984,000	1,925,000	260,531	157,315	417,846
1962–63	959,000	991,000	1,950,000	273,169	174,453	447,622
1963–64	1,121,000	1,169,000	2,290,000	296,676	197,477	494,153
1964–65	1,314,000	1,351,000	2,665,000	316,286	213,717	530,003
1965–66	1,308,000	1,324,000	2,632,000	328,853	222,194	551,047
1966–67	1,332,000	1,348,000	2,679,000	353,349	237,198	590,547
1967–68	1,341,000	1,361,000	2,702,000	390,507	276,203	666,710
1968–69	1,402,000	1,427,000	2,829,000	444,380	319,805	764,185
1969–70	1,433,000	1,463,000	2,896,000	484,174	343,060	827,234
1970–71	1,456,000	1,487,000	2,943,000	511,138	366,538	877,676
1971–72	1,490,000	1,518,000	3,008,000	541,313	389,371	930,684
1972–73	1,501,000	1,536,000	3,037,000	564,680	407,700	972,380
1973–74	1,515,000	1,565,000	3,080,000	575,843	423,749	999,592
1974–75	1,541,000	1,599,000	3,140,000	533,797	425,052	978,849
1975–76	1,554,000	1,601,000	3,155,000	557,817	430,578	988,395
1976–77	1,548,000	1,606,000	3,154,000	547,919	435,989	983,908
1977–78	1,535,000	1,599,000	3,134,000	487,000	434,000	921,000
1978–79	1,531,800[2]	1,602,400[2]	3,134,200[2]	529,996	460,242	990,238

1. Includes bachelor's and first-professional degrees. 2. Preliminary data. NOTE: Includes graduates from public and private schools. Beginning in 1959–60, figures include Alaska and Hawaii. Because of rounding, details may not add to totals. Most recent data available. *Source:* Department of Education, National Center for Education Statistics.

Institutions of Higher Education—Faculty and Enrollment Characteristics and Projections to 1988

(in thousands except for institutions)

Item	1988	1985	1980	1978[2]	1977[2]	1976[2]	1975	1974	1973	1972	1971
Institutions	n.a.	n.a.	3,152	2,871	2,826	2,785	2,765	2,747	2,720	2,665	2,606
4-year	n.a.	n.a.	1,957	1,816	1,808	1,783	1,767	1,744	1,717	1,701	1,675
2-year	n.a.	n.a.	1,195	1,055	1,018	1,002	998	1,003	1,003	964	931
Resident instructional staff	n.a.	696	730	809	812	793	670	622	599	590	590
ENROLLMENT											
Degree credit	11,048	11,358	11,611	n.a.	n.a.	n.a.	9,731	9,023	8,518	8,265	8,116
Male	5,631	5,802	5,907	5,641	5,789	5,811	5,321	4,969	4,771	4,701	4,717
Female	5,417	5,556	5,704	5,619	5,497	5,201	4,410	4,055	3,747	3,564	3,399
4-year institutions	6,694	6,968	7,302	7,232	7,243	7,129	7,223	6,825	6,597	6,473	6,391
2-year institutions	4,354	4,390	4,309	4,027	4,043	3,883	2,508	2,198	1,921	1,792	1,725
Full-time	6,185	6,460	6,847	6,668	6,793	6,717	6,147	5,817	5,683	5,647	5,676
Part-time	4,863	4,898	4,764	4,592	4,493	4,295	3,584	3,206	2,835	2,618	2,440
Public	8,754	8,974	9,124	8,786	8,847	8,653	7,426	6,838	6,389	6,159	6,014
Private	2,294	2,384	2,487	2,474	2,439	2,359	2,306	2,185	2,130	2,106	2,102
Graduate	1,358	1,382	1,365	1,081	1,085	1,085	1,263	1,190	1,123	1,066	1,012
Undergraduate[1]	9,417	9,698	9,981	10,179	10,201	9,927	8,468	7,833	7,395	7,199	7,104
Male	4,713	4,870	4,996	5,057	5,193	5,209	4,621	4,306	4,124	4,074	4,102
Female	4,704	4,828	4,985	5,122	5,008	4,719	3,847	3,527	3,271	3,125	3,002
4-year institutions	5,063	5,308	5,672	6,152	6,158	6,045	5,960	5,635	5,474	5,407	5,379
Full-time	3,823	4,048	4,404	4,678	4,703	4,622	4,619	4,429	4,350	4,350	4,358
Part-time	1,240	1,260	1,262	1,474	1,456	1,423	1,341	1,206	1,124	1,057	1,021
2-year institutions	4,354	4,390	4,309	4,028	4,043	3,883	2,508	2,198	1,921	1,792	1,725
Public	7,708	7,910	8,079	8,083	8,128	7,924	6,520	5,986	5,589	5,401	5,302
Private	1,709	1,788	1,902	2,096	2,073	2,003	1,948	1,847	1,806	1,799	1,802
1st time enrolled	n.a.	n.a.	n.a.	2,422	2,432	2,377	1,910	1,854	1,757	1,740	1,766
Nondegree credit	n.a.	n.a.	n.a.	n.a.	n.a.	n.a.	1,453	1,200	1,084	950	833
Total	**11,048**	**11,104**	**11,611**	**11,260**	**11,286**	**11,012**	**11,184**	**10,223**	**9,602**	**9,215**	**8,949**

1. Includes first-professional enrollment. 2. Total enrollment, degree and nondegree credit. NOTE: As of fall. Covers universities, colleges, professional schools, junior and teachers colleges, and normal schools, both publicly and privately controlled, regular session. n.a. = not available. *Source:* Department of Education, National Center for Educational Statistics.

Major U.S. College and University Libraries

(over 1.75 million volumes)

Institution	Volumes	Microforms[1]
Harvard	10,260,571	2,387,994
Yale	7,579,121	1,389,311
U of Illinois	6,091,125	1,683,035
U of California	5,927,773	1,676,272
U of Michigan	5,345,918	2,436,039
Columbia	5,112,559	2,280,052
Stanford	4,813,393	2,257,653
U of Texas	4,702,122	2,398,405
U of Chicago	4,441,312	807,747
U of California, Los Angeles	4,346,526	2,033,831
Cornell	4,318,583	2,484,102
U of Wisconsin	4,044,136	1,940,859
U of Washington	4,024,258	3,370,411
U of Minnesota	3,870,712	1,354,831
Indiana	3,856,121	1,072,897
Ohio State	3,615,108	1,707,241
Princeton	3,363,282	1,462,882
Duke	3,006,026	798,409
U of Pennsylvania	3,000,650	1,362,969
Northwestern	2,838,187	1,094,535
North Carolina	2,722,799	1,581,639
Michigan State	2,707,779	1,174,507
U of Arizona	2,639,041	2,056,914
New York	2,613,731	1,631,238
U of Virginia	2,391,585	2,659,520
U of Iowa	2,356,096	1,618,967
Johns Hopkins	2,346,131	1,141,727
U of Pittsburgh	2,339,242	1,382,354
Rutgers	2,290,013	1,652,697
U of Florida	2,231,509	2,285,938
U of Kansas	2,214,824	1,060,979
Pennsylvania State	2,207,098	2,263,127
U of Southern California	2,105,389	1,296,695
U of Missouri	2,068,788	2,328,526
U of Georgia	2,062,499	2,056,931
SUNY, Buffalo	2,003,090	1,988,445
U of Utah	1,990,000	1,739,152
Syracuse	1,952,594	1,970,813
U of South Carolina	1,894,264	1,787,437
U of Colorado	1,888,207	2,151,777
Louisiana State	1,884,656	1,183,128
Wayne State	1,878,689	1,026,971
U of Oklahoma	1,858,658	1,360,191
MIT	1,844,451	1,028,162
Washington U, St. Louis	1,838,820	1,079,741
U of Kentucky	1,816,782	2,209,061
U of Massachusetts	1,803,647	993,566
U of Hawaii	1,786,335	1,234,329

1. Includes reels of microfilm and number of microcards, microprint sheets, and microfiches. *Source:* Association of Research Libraries.

College and University Endowments, 1980–81

(in millions)

Institution	Endowment (market value)	Voluntary support[1]	Expenditures[2]
Harvard U	$1,713.3	$91.0	$ n.a.
Yale U	799.0	58.3	268.4
Stanford U	688.4	79.5	369.0
Princeton U	685.8	35.3	110.4
Massachusetts Inst. of Tech.	629.7	47.5	311.7
Columbia U	595.0	48.4	310.2
U of Rochester	490.9	14.5	148.9
U of California	462.7	97.8	2,091.0
U of Chicago	396.1	39.2	318.9
Rice U	391.4	15.3	48.2
Cornell U	360.4	54.6	345.5
Northwestern U	341.5	33.1	211.0
New York U	276.3	28.8	310.2
Washington U	274.6	28.2	171.7
Johns Hopkins U	272.3	46.9	232.3
Rockefeller U	271.3	20.1	45.8
Dartmouth C	254.0	42.5	84.1
Emory U	252.9	12.0	100.0
U of Pennsylvania	232.7	49.0	300.1
U of Notre Dame	218.2	32.0	50.0
U of Virginia	199.5	16.4	123.7
California Inst. of Tech.	185.2	19.7	84.0
Vanderbilt U	170.6	22.6	108.3
Duke U	161.0	36.7	164.2
U of Kansas	153.3	9.6	108.6
Brown U	144.1	18.7	81.3
Case Western Reserve U	143.9	30.3	114.7
Wellesley C	142.5	12.9	32.1
U of Michigan	141.5	31.7	423.6
Wesleyan U	135.1	5.5	30.5
Carnegie–Mellon U	132.5	11.6	74.4
Smith C	130.9	15.5	30.2
U of Delaware	123.8	6.2	101.8
Williams C	120.0	11.0	20.6
Princeton Theol. Sem.	118.4	2.8	7.3
Swarthmore C	118.0	5.6	14.2
Trinity U	117.8	3.9	20.0
Southern Methodist U	116.9	12.3	56.3
U of Minnesota	114.0	49.8	499.0
U of Pittsburgh	113.5	9.1	230.1
Oberlin C	106.5	4.6	27.9
Vassar C	104.8	5.9	20.7
Rensselaer Polytech.	104.8	11.4	61.8
U of Cincinnati	103.6	10.2	194.2
Berea C	97.5	5.7	9.8
Loyola U of Chicago	96.1	15.5	74.4
Amherst C	95.0	4.2	18.7
U of Richmond	88.1	10.4	23.6
Grinnell C	86.8	4.1	11.1
Texas Christian U	83.1	13.6	33.5
Baylor U	81.6	15.6	40.1
Ohio State U	80.0	14.3	360.2
Wake Forest U	77.6	8.0	72.4
Brandeis U	76.5	15.9	45.7
Lehigh U	74.6	10.2	47.8
U of Wisconsin–Madison	73.8	33.6	378.5
Middlebury C	72.3	2.7	14.1
Tulane U	72.1	17.1	91.1
Lafayette C	71.5	6.0	16.1
Georgetown U	71.3	22.2	127.6
Harvard Law School	66.2	4.3	n.a.
Texas A & M	63.5	35.7	264.5
Carleton C	62.0	4.5	14.3
Mt. Holyoke C	61.4	6.7	18.1
Thomas Jefferson U	60.9	3.4	40.7
Loyola U	60.0	1.0	19.4
State U of NY (Buffalo)	59.7	2.8	n.a.
Bowdoin C	58.7	3.2	15.1
Syracuse U	57.7	8.8	123.2
Boston U	57.3	9.5	204.0
St. Louis U	56.7	5.1	69.6
Bryn Mawr C	56.1	8.4	18.1
Rush U	52.7	4.6	23.0
Butler U	51.5	2.7	11.6

1. Gifts from business, alumni, religious denominations, and others. 2. Figure represents about 80% of typical operating budget. Does not include auxiliary enterprises and capital outlays. NOTE: C = College; U = University; n.a. = not available. *Source:* Council for Financial Aid to Education.

Federal Grants and Loans for Education, Fiscal Year 1981

Type of support, level, and program area	Amount in millions[1]
Grants, total	$25,275
Elementary-secondary education	7,789[2]
School assistance in federally affected areas	554
Economic opportunity programs	5,187[3]
Supporting services	393
Teacher corps	15
Vocational education	461
Dependents' schools abroad	421
Public lands revenue for schools	373
Assistance in special areas	54
Emergency school assistance	227
Higher education	9,828
Basic research	3,002
Research facilities	401
Training grants, fellowships and traineeships	$1,004
Facilities and equipment	86
Other institutional support	585
Other student assistance	4,750
Vocational-technical and continuing education	7,710
Vocational-technical & work training	7,230
Veterans' education	265
General continuing education	172
Training state and local personnel	43
Loans, total (higher education)	1,496
Student loan program, National Defense Education Act	1,475
College facilities loans	21
Total grants and loans	**26,770**

1. Estimated outlay for fiscal year 1981. 2. Includes other outlays not shown separately. 3. Includes assistance for educationally deprived. NOTE. The table lists the federal funds that support education in educational institutions. Excluded are certain other federal funds for education and related activities. *Source:* Department of Education, National Center for Educational Statistics.

Community, Junior, and Technical Colleges

An asterisk indicates tuition and required fees of $600 or less for the full academic year 1981–82; where applicable, the costs are for students living within the state and within the institutional district.

ALABAMA

Publicly controlled	
Alabama Aviation and Tech. College*	Ozark
Alabama Technical College	East Gadsden
Alexander City State Junior College*	Alexander City
Atmore State Technical Institute*	Atmore
Bessemer State Technical College*	Bessemer
Brewer State Junior College*	Fayette
C. A. Fredd State Tech. Coll.*	Tuscaloosa
Carver State Technical College*	Mobile
Chattahoochee Valley State Comm. Coll.*	Phenix City
Chauncey Sparks State Tech. Coll.*	Eufaula
Community College of the Air Force	Maxwell AFB
Douglas MacArthur St. Tech. Coll.*	Opp
Enterprise State Junior College	Enterprise
Gadsden State Junior College*	East Gadsden
Gadsden State Technical Institute*	Gadsden
George C. Wallace State Comm. College*	Dothan
George C. Wallace State Comm. College*	Hanceville
George Corley Wallace St. Comm. Coll.*	Selma
Harry M. Ayers State Tech. College*	Anniston
Hobson State Technical College*	Thomasville
J. F. Drake State Technical College*	Huntsville
James H. Faulkner State Junior College*	Bay Minette
Jefferson Davis State Junior College*	Brewton
Jefferson State Junior College*	Birmingham
J. F. Ingram State Tech. Inst.*	Deatsville
John C. Calhoun State Comm. College*	Decatur
John M. Patterson State Tech. College*	Montgomery
Lawson State Community College*	Birmingham
Lurleen B. Wallace State Junior College*	Andalusia
Muscle Shoals State Tech. College*	Muscle Shoals
N.F. Nunnelley State Tech. College*	Childersburg
Northeast Alabama State Junior College*	Rainsville
Northwest Alabama State Junior College*	Phil Campbell
Northwest Alabama State Tech. College*	Hamilton
Opelika State Technical College*	Opelika
Patrick Henry State Junior College*	Monroeville
Reid State Technical College*	Evergreen
S. D. Bishop State Junior College*	Mobile
Shelton State Technical College*	Tuscaloosa
Snead State Junior College*	Boaz
Southern Union State Junior College*	Wadley
Southwest State Technical College*	Mobile
Trenholm State Technical College*	Montgomery
Walker State Technical College*	Sumiton
Privately controlled	
Concordia College	Selma
Marion Military Institute	Marion
Walker College	Jasper

ALASKA

Publicly controlled	
Univ. of Alaska Community Colleges	Fairbanks
Anchorage Community College*	Anchorage
Juneau-Douglas Community College*	Juneau
Kenai Peninsula Community College*	Soldotna
Ketchikan Community College*	Ketchikan
Kodiak Community College*	Kodiak
Kuskokwim Community College*	Bethel
Matanuska Susitna Community College*	Palmer
Northwest Community College*	Nome
Prince William Sound Comm. Coll.*	Valdez
Sitka Community College*	Sitka
Tanana Valley Community College*	Fairbanks
Privately controlled	
Sheldon Jackson College	Sitka

ARIZONA

Publicly controlled	
Arizona Western College	Yuma
Central Arizona College District*	Coolidge
Aravaipa Campus*	Winkleman
Signal Peak Campus*	Coolidge
Cochise College*	Douglas
Eastern Arizona College*	Thatcher
Maricopa County Comm. Coll. District	Phoenix
Glendale Community College*	Glendale
Maricopa Technical Community Coll.*	Phoenix
Mesa Community College*	Mesa
Phoenix College*	Phoenix
Rio Salado Community College*	Phoenix
Scottsdale Community College*	Scottsdale
South Mountain Comm. College*	Phoenix
Mohave Community College*	Kingman
Navajo Community College	Tsaile
Northland Pioneer College*	Holbrook
Pima Community College*	Tucson
Community Campus*	Tucson
Downtown Campus*	Tucson
East Campus*	Tucson
West Campus*	Tucson
Yavapai College	Prescott
Privately controlled	
Ganado, College of	Ganado

ARKANSAS

Publicly controlled	
Arkansas State Univ.—Beebe Branch*	Beebe
East Arkansas Community College*	Forrest City
Garland County Community College*	Hot Springs
Mississippi County Community College*	Blytheville
North Arkansas Community College*	Harrison
Phillips County Community College*	Helena
Southern Arkansas University	Magnolia
El Dorado Branch*	El Dorado
Technical Branch*	East Camden
Westark Community College*	Fort Smith
Privately controlled	
Shorter College	North Little Rock
Southern Baptist College	Walnut Ridge

CALIFORNIA

Publicly controlled	
Allan Hancock College*	Santa Maria
Antelope Valley College*	Lancaster
Barstow Community College	Barstow
Butte College*	Oroville
Cabrillo College*	Aptos
Canyons, College of the*	Valencia
Cerritos College	Norwalk
Chabot College	Hayward
Chaffey College*	Alta Loma
Citrus College*	Azusa
Coast Community College District	Costa Mesa
Coastline Community College	Fountain Valley
Golden West College*	Huntington Beach
Orange Coast College*	Costa Mesa
Compton Community College*	Compton
Contra Costa Community Coll. District	Martinez
Contra Costa College	San Pablo
Diablo Valley College	Pleasant Hill
Los Medanos College	Pittsburg

Cuesta College*	San Luis Obispo
Desert, College of the	Palm Desert
El Camino College	Via Torrance
Foothill-Deanza Comm. Coll. District	Los Altos Hills
De Anza College	Cupertino
Foothill College*	Los Altos Hills
Gavilan College	Gilroy
Glendale Community College*	Glendale
Grossmont Community College District	El Cajon
Cuyamaca College	El Cajon
Grossmont College	El Cajon
Hartnell College	Salinas
Imperial Valley College	Imperial
Kern Community College District	Bakersfield
Bakersfield College*	Bakersfield
Cerro Coso Community College*	Ridgecrest
Porterville College*	Porterville
Lake Tahoe Community College*	South Lake Tahoe
Lassen College*	Susanville
Long Beach City College	Long Beach
Los Angeles Community College District	Los Angeles
East Los Angeles College	Monterey Park
Los Angeles City College	Los Angeles
Los Angeles Harbor College	Wilmington
Los Angeles Metropolitan College	Los Angeles
Los Angeles Mission College	San Fernando
Los Angeles Pierce College	Woodland Hills
Los Angeles Southwest College	Los Angeles
Los Angeles Trade-Technical College	Los Angeles
Los Angeles Valley College	Van Nuys
West Los Angeles College	Culver City
Los Rios Community College District	Sacramento
American River College	Sacramento
Cosumnes River College	Sacramento
Sacramento City College	Sacramento
Marin Community College District	Kentfield
Indian Valley Colleges	Novato
Marin, College of	Kentfield
Mendocino College*	Ukiah
Merced College*	Merced
Mira Costa College*	Oceanside
Monterey Peninsula College*	Monterey
Mt. San Antonio College*	Walnut
Mt. San Jacinto College*	San Jacinto
Napa College	Napa
North Orange County Comm. Coll. District	Fullerton
Cypress College*	Cypress
Fullerton College*	Fullerton
Ohlone College*	Fremont
Palo Verde College	Blythe
Palomar College	San Marcos
Pasadena City College*	Pasadena
Peralta Community College District	Oakland
Alameda, College of	Alameda
Feather River College*	Quincy
Laney College*	Oakland
Merritt College*	Oakland
Vista College	Berkeley
Redwoods, College of the	Eureka
Rio Hondo College	Whittier
Riverside City College*	Riverside
Saddleback Community Coll. District	Mission Viejo
San Bernardino Community Coll. District	San Bernardino
Crafton Hills College*	Yucalpa
San Bernardino Valley College*	San Bernardino
San Diego Community College District	San Diego
San Diego City College	San Diego
San Diego Mesa College	San Diego
San Diego Miramar College	San Diego
San Francisco Community Coll. District	San Francisco
San Francisco, City College of	San Francisco
Community College Centers	San Francisco
San Joaquin Delta College*	Stockton
San Jose Community College District	San Jose
Evergreen Valley College	San Jose
San Jose City College	San Jose
San Mateo County Comm. Coll. District	San Mateo
Canada College*	Redwood City
San Mateo, College of*	San Mateo
Skyline College	San Bruno
Santa Ana College*	Santa Ana
Santa Barbara City College*	Santa Barbara
Santa Monica College	Santa Monica
Santa Rosa Junior College*	Santa Rosa
Shasta College*	Redding
Sequoias, College of the*	Visalia
Sierra College*	Rocklin
Siskiyous, College of the*	Weed
Solano Community College*	Suisun City
Southwestern College*	Chula Vista
State Center Community College District	Fresno
Fresno City College*	Fresno
Kings River Community College*	Reedley
Taft College	Taft
Ventura County Community Coll. District	Ventura
Moorpark College	Moorpark
Oxnard College*	Oxnard
Ventura College	Ventura
Victor Valley College	Victorville
West Hills Community College	Coalinga
West Valley Joint Comm. Coll. District	Saratoga
Mission College*	Santa Clara
West Valley College*	Saratoga
Yosemite Community College District	Modesto
Columbia College*	Columbia
Modesto Junior College*	Modesto
Yuba College*	Marysville
Privately controlled	
Brooks College	Long Beach
Don Bosco Technical Institute	Rosemead
Fashion Institute of Design/Merch.	Los Angeles
Heald Institute of Technology	Santa Clara
Humphreys College	Stockton
Marymount Palos Verdes College	Rancho Palos Verdes
Queen of the Holy Rosary College	Mission San Jose

COLORADO

Publicly controlled	
Aims Community College*	Greeley
Arapahoe Community College*	Littleton
Colorado Mountain College	Glenwood Springs
Community Education Unit*	Glenwood Springs
East Campus*	Leadville
West Campus*	Glenwood Springs
Colorado Northwestern Comm. College*	Rangely
Community College of Denver	Denver
Auraria Campus	Denver
North Campus	Westminster
Red Rocks Campus*	Golden
Lamar Community College	Lamar
Morgan Community College*	Fort Morgan
Northeastern Junior College	Sterling
Otero Junior College	La Junta
Pikes Peak Community College	Colorado Springs
Pueblo Vocational Community College*	Pueblo
Trinidad State Junior College	Trinidad

CONNECTICUT

Publicly controlled	
Asnuntuck Community College*	Enfield
Greater Hartford Community College*	Hartford
Greater New Haven State Tech. Coll.*	North Haven
Hartford State Technical College*	Hartford
Housatonic Community College*	Bridgeport
Manchester Community College*	Manchester
Mattatuck Community College*	Waterbury
Middlesex Community College*	Middletown
Mohegan Community College*	Norwich
Northwestern Connecticut Comm. College*	Winsted
Norwalk Community College*	Norwalk
Norwalk State Technical College*	Norwalk
Quinebaug Valley Community College*	Danielson
South Central Community College*	New Haven
Thames Valley State Technical College*	Norwich
Tunxis Community College*	Farmington
Waterbury State Technical College*	Waterbury
Privately controlled	
Hartford College for Women	Hartford
Mitchell College	New London

DELAWARE

Publicly controlled	
Delaware Technical and Comm. College	Dover
Southern Campus	Georgetown
Stanton/Wilmington Campuses	Wilmington
Terry Campus	Dover
Privately controlled	
Brandywine College	Wilmington

FLORIDA

Publicly controlled	
Brevard Community College*	Cocoa
Broward Community College*	Ft. Lauderdale
Central Florida Community College*	Ocala
Chipola Junior College*	Marianna
Daytona Beach Community College*	Daytona Beach
Edison Community College*	Ft. Myers
Florida Junior Coll. at Jacksonville*	Jacksonville
Downtown Campus*	Jacksonville
Fred H. Kent Campus*	Jacksonville
North Campus*	Jacksonville
South Campus*	Jacksonville
Florida Keys Community College*	Key West
Gulf Coast Community College*	Panama City
Hillsborough Community College*	Tampa
Indian River Community College*	Ft. Pierce
Lake City Community College*	Lake City
Lake-Sumter Community College*	Leesburg
Manatee Junior College*	Bradenton
Miami-Dade Community College	Miami
Medical Center Campus*	Miami
New World Center Campus*	Miami
North Campus*	Miami
South Campus*	Miami
North Florida Junior College*	Madison
Okaloosa-Walton Junior College*	Niceville
Palm Beach Junior College	Lake Worth
Pasco-Hernando Community College*	Dade City
Pensacola Junior College*	Pensacola
Polk Community College*	Winter Haven
St. Johns River Community College*	Palatka
St. Petersburg Junior College*	St. Petersburg
Santa Fe Community College*	Gainesville
Seminole Community College*	Sanford
South Florida Junior College*	Avon Park
Tallahassee Community College*	Tallahassee
Valencia Community College*	Orlando
Privately controlled	
Bauder Fashion College	Miami
Florida College	Temple Terrace
International Fine Arts College	Miami
Webber College	Babson Park

GEORGIA

Publicly controlled	
Abraham Baldwin Agriculture College*	Tifton
Albany Junior College*	Albany
Atlanta Junior College*	Atlanta
Bainbridge Junior College*	Bainbridge
Brunswick Junior College*	Brunswick
Clayton Junior College*	Morrow
Dalton Junior College*	Dalton
DeKalb Community College*	Clarkston
Emanuel County Junior College*	Swainsboro
Floyd Junior College*	Rome
Gainesville Junior College*	Gainesville
Gordon Junior College*	Barnesville
Macon Junior College*	Macon
Middle Georgia College*	Cochran
South Georgia College*	Douglas
Waycross Junior College*	Waycross
Privately controlled	
Andrew College	Cuthbert
Brewton-Parker College	Mt. Vernon
Georgia Military College	Milledgeville
Oxford College of Emory University	Oxford
Reinhardt College	Waleska
Truett-McConnell College	Cleveland
Young Harris College	Young Harris

HAWAII

Publicly controlled	
Univ. of Hawaii Community Coll. System	Honolulu
Hawaii Community College*	Hilo
Honolulu Community College*	Honolulu
Kapiolani Community College*	Honolulu
Kauai Community College*	Lihue Kauai
Leeward Community College*	Pearl City
Maui Community College*	Kahului
Windward Community College*	Kaneohe

IDAHO

Publicly controlled	
North Idaho College*	Coeur d'Alene
Southern Idaho, College of*	Twin Falls
Privately controlled	
Ricks College	Rexburg

ILLINOIS

Publicly controlled	
Belleville Area College*	Belleville
Black Hawk College	Moline
East Campus	Kewanee
Quad Cities Campus	Moline
Carl Sandburg College*	Galesburg
Chicago, City Colleges of	Chicago
Chicago City-Wide College*	Chicago
Chicago Urban Skills Institute	Chicago
Kennedy-King College*	Chicago
Loop College, The*	Chicago
Malcolm X College*	Chicago
Olive Harvey College*	Chicago
Richard J. Daley College*	Chicago
Truman College*	Chicago
Wilbur Wright College*	Chicago
Danville Area Community College*	Danville
DuPage, College of	Glen Ellyn
Dupage Open College*	Glen Ellyn
Main Campus*	Glen Ellyn
Elgin Community College*	Elgin
Highland Community College*	Freeport
Illinois Central College*	East Peoria
Illinois Eastern Community Colleges	Olney
Frontier Community College*	Fairfield

Lincoln Trail College*	Robinson
Olney Central College*	Olney
Wabash Valley College*	Mt. Carmel
Illinois Valley Community College*	Oglesby
John A. Logan College*	Carterville
John Wood Community College*	Quincy
Joliet Junior College*	Joliet
Kankakee Community College*	Kankakee
Kaskaskia College*	Centralia
Kishwaukee College*	Malta
Lake County, College of*	Grayslake
Lake Land College*	Mattoon
Lewis and Clark Community College*	Godfrey
Lincoln Land Community College*	Springfield
McHenry County College*	Crystal Lake
Moraine Valley Community College*	Palos Hills
Morton College*	Cicero
Oakton Community College*	Des Plaines
Parkland College*	Champaign
Prairie State College*	Chicago Heights
Rend Lake College*	Ina
Richland Community College*	Decatur
Rock Valley College*	Rockford
Sauk Valley College	Dixon
Shawnee Community College*	Ullin
Southeastern Illinois College*	Harrisburg
Spoon River College*	Canton
State Comm. College of East St. Louis*	East St. Louis
Thornton Community College	South Holland
Triton College*	River Grove
Waubonsee Community College*	Sugar Grove
William Rainey Harper College	Palatine
Privately controlled	
Central YMCA Community College	Chicago
Felician College	Chicago
Lincoln College	Lincoln
MacCormac College	Chicago
Mallinckrodt College	Wilmette
Springfield College in Illinois	Springfield

INDIANA

Publicly controlled	
Indiana Vocational Technical College	Indianapolis
Central Indiana Region	Indianapolis
Columbus Technical Inst.	Columbus
East Central Tech. Inst.	Muncie
Kokomo Technical Inst.	Kokomo
Lafayette Technical Inst.	Lafayette
North Central Tech. Inst.	South Bend
Northeast Technical Inst.	Fort Wayne
Northwest Region	Gary
South Central Tech. Inst.	Sellersburg
Southeast Region	Madison
Southwest Technical Inst.	Evansville
Wabash Valley Region	Terre Haute
Whitewater Technical Inst.	Richmond
Vincennes University	Vincennes
Privately controlled	
Ancilla College	Donaldson

IOWA

Publicly controlled	
Des Moines Area Community College	Ankeny
Ankeny Campus	Ankeny
Boone Campus	Boone
Eastern Iowa Community Coll. District	Davenport
Clinton Community College	Clinton
Muscatine Community College	Muscatine
Scott Community College	Bettendorf
Hawkeye Institute of Technology	Waterloo
Indian Hills Community College*	Ottumwa
Centerville Center	Ottumwa
Ottumwa Airport Center	Ottumwa
Ottumwa Heights Center	Ottumwa
Iowa Central Community College	Fort Dodge
Iowa Lakes Community College	Estherville
Iowa Valley Community Coll. District	Marshalltown
Ellsworth Community College	Iowa Falls
Marshalltown Community College	Marshalltown
Iowa Western Community College	Council Bluffs
Kirkwood Community College	Cedar Rapids
North Iowa Area Community College	Mason City
Northeast Iowa Technical Institute	Calmar
Northwest Iowa Technical College	Sheldon
Southeastern Community College*	West Burlington
North Campus	West Burlington
South Campus	Keokuk
Southwestern Community College	Creston
Western Iowa Tech. Community College	Sioux City
Privately controlled	
Sioux Empire College	Hawarden
Waldorf College	Forest City

KANSAS

Publicly controlled	
Allen County Community College*	Iola
Barton County Community Junior Coll.*	Great Bend
Butler County Community College*	El Dorado
Cloud County Community College*	Concordia
Coffeyville Community College*	Coffeyville
Colby Community Junior College*	Colby
Cowley County Community College	Arkansas City
Dodge City Community College*	Dodge City
Fort Scott Community College*	Fort Scott
Garden City Community College*	Garden City
Haskell Indian Junior College	Lawrence
Highland Community Junior College*	Highland
Hutchinson Community College*	Hutchinson
Independence Community College*	Independence
Johnson County Community College*	Overland Park
Kansas City, Kan., Community Coll.*	Kansas City
Kansas Technical Institute*	Salina
Labette Community College*	Parsons
Neosho County Community College*	Chanute
Pratt Community College*	Pratt
Seward County Community Junior Coll.*	Liberal
Privately controlled	
Brown Mackie College, The	Salina
Central College	McPherson
Donnelly College	Kansas City
Hesston College	Hesston

KENTUCKY

Publicly controlled	
Eastern Kentucky Univ.—Office of Community College Programs	Richmond
Kentucky, Univ. of, Comm. Coll. System	Lexington
Ashland Community College*	Ashland
Elizabethtown Community College*	Elizabethtown
Hazard Community College*	Hazard
Henderson Community College*	Henderson
Hopkinsville Community College*	Hopkinsville
Jefferson Community College*	Louisville
Lexington Technical Institute	Lexington
Madisonville Community College*	Madisonville
Maysville Community College*	Maysville
Paducah Community College*	Paducah
Prestonsburg Community College*	Prestonsburg
Somerset Community College*	Somerset
Southeast Community College*	Cumberland
Privately controlled	
Alice Lloyd College	Pippa Passes
Lees Junior College	Jackson
Lindsey Wilson College	Columbia
Midway College	Midway

St. Catharine College	St. Catharine
Sue Bennett College	London

LOUISIANA

Publicly controlled

Bossier Parish Community College*	Bossier City
Delgado Community College*	New Orleans
Louisiana State University	Baton Rouge
Alexandria Campus*	Alexandria
Eunice Campus*	Eunice
Southern University at Shreveport*	Shreveport

MAINE

Publicly controlled

Central Maine Vocational Tech. Inst.	Auburn
Eastern Maine Vocational Tech. Inst.	Bangor
Kennebec Valley Vocational Tech. Inst.	Waterville
Maine, University of	Bangor
Augusta Branch	Augusta
Bangor Community College	Bangor
Northern Maine Vocational Tech. Inst.	Presque Isle
Southern Maine Vocational Tech. Inst.	South Portland
Washington County Voc. Tech. Inst.	Calais

MARYLAND

Publicly controlled

Allegany Community College*	Cumberland
Anne Arundel Community College*	Arnold
Catonsville Community College*	Baltimore
Cecil Community College*	North East
Charles County Community College*	La Plata
Chesapeake College*	Wye Mills
Community College of Baltimore*	Baltimore
Dundalk Community College*	Dundalk
Essex Community College*	Baltimore Co.
Frederick Community College*	Frederick
Garrett Community College*	McHenry
Hagerstown Junior College	Hagerstown
Harford Community College*	Bel Air
Howard Community College	Columbia
Montgomery College	Rockville
Germantown Campus	Germantown
Rockville Campus	Rockville
Takoma Park Campus	Takoma Park
Prince George's Community College	Largo
Wor-Wic Tech. Community College*	Salisbury

Privately controlled

Villa Julie College	Stevenson

MASSACHUSETTS

Publicly controlled

Berkshire Community College	Pittsfield
Blue Hills Regional Tech. Institute	Canton
Bristol Community College	Fall River
Bunker Hill Community College	Boston
Cape Cod Community College	W. Barnstable
Greenfield Community College	Greenfield
Holyoke Community College*	Holyoke
Massachusetts Bay Community College*	Wellesley
Massasoit Community College	Brockton
Middlesex Community College	Bedford
Mount Wachusett Community College	Gardner
North Shore Community College	Beverly
Northern Essex Community College*	Haverhill
Quincy Junior College	Quincy
Quinsigamond Community College	Worcester
Roxbury Community College*	Roxbury
Springfield Technical Community Coll.	Springfield

Privately controlled

Aquinas Junior College	Milton
Aquinas Junior College	Newton
Bay Path Junior College	Longmeadow
Becker Junior College	Worcester
Leicester Campus	Leicester
Chamberlayne Junior College	Boston
Dean Junior College	Franklin
Endicott College	Beverly
Fisher Junior College	Boston
Franklin Institute of Boston	Boston
Laboure Junior College	Boston
Lasell Junior College	Newton
Mount Ida Junior College	Newton Centre
Newbury Junior College	Boston
Worcester Junior College	Worcester

MICHIGAN

Publicly controlled

Alpena Community College*	Alpena
Bay de Noc Community College	Escanaba
Charles Stewart Mott Community Coll.	Flint
Delta College	University Center
Glen Oaks Community College	Centreville
Gogebic Community College*	Ironwood
Grand Rapids Junior College	Grand Rapids
Henry Ford Community College	Dearborn
Highland Park Community College*	Highland Park
Jackson Community College	Jackson
Kalamazoo Valley Community College*	Kalamazoo
Kellogg Community College*	Battle Creek
Kirtland Community College*	Roscommon
Lake Michigan College*	Benton Harbor
Lansing Community College	Lansing
Macomb Community College	Warren
Center Campus*	Mt. Clemens
South Campus*	Warren
Mid Michigan Community College*	Harrison
Monroe County Community College*	Monroe
Montcalm Community College	Sidney
Muskegon Community College	Muskegon
North Central Michigan College	Petoskey
Northwestern Michigan College	Traverse City
Oakland Community College	Bloomfield Hills
Auburn Hills Campus	Auburn Heights
Highland Lakes Campus	Union Lake
Orchard Ridge Campus	Farmington
Southeast Campus	Southfield
St. Clair County Community College*	Port Huron
Schoolcraft College	Livonia
Southwestern Michigan College	Dowagiac
Washtenaw Community College*	Ann Arbor
Wayne County Community College*	Detroit
West Shore Community College	Scottville

Privately controlled

Davenport College of Business	Grand Rapids
Suomi College	Hancock

MINNESOTA

Publicly controlled

Alexandria Vocational Tech. Inst.	Alexandria
Anoka-Ramsey Community College	Coon Rapids
Arrowhead Community College	Hibbing
Hibbing Community College	Hibbing
Itasca Community College*	Grand Rapids
Mesabi Community College	Virginia
Rainy River Community College	Intl. Falls
Vermilion Community College	Ely
Austin Community College*	Austin
Brainerd Community College*	Brainerd
Fergus Falls Community College*	Fergus Falls
Inver Hills Community College*	Inver Grove Heights
Lakewood Community College	White Bear Lake
Minneapolis Community College	Minneapolis
Minnesota, Univ. of, Technical Coll.	Minneapolis
Crookston Campus	Crookston
Waseca Campus	Waseca

Normandale Community College	Bloomington
North Hennepin Community College*	Brooklyn Park
Northland Community College	Thief River Falls
Rochester Community College*	Rochester
Willmar Area Technical Institute*	Willmar
Willmar Community College	Willmar
Worthington Community College	Worthington
Privately controlled	
Bethany Lutheran College	Mankato
Crosier Seminary Junior College	Onamia
Golden Valley Lutheran College	Minneapolis
St. Mary's Junior College	Minneapolis

MISSISSIPPI

Publicly controlled	
Coahoma Junior College*	Clarksdale
Copiah-Lincoln Junior College*	Wesson
East Central Junior College*	Decatur
East Mississippi Junior College*	Scooba
Hinds Junior College*	Raymond
Holmes Junior College*	Goodman
Itawamba Junior College*	Fulton
Jones County Junior College*	Ellisville
Meridian Junior College*	Meridian
Mississippi Delta Junior College*	Moorhead
Mississippi Gulf Coast Junior College*	Perkinston
Jackson County Campus*	Gautier
Jefferson Davis Campus*	Gulfport
Perkinston Campus*	Perkinston
Northeast Mississippi Junior College*	Booneville
Northwest Mississippi Junior College	Senatobia
Pearl River Junior College*	Poplarville
Southwest Mississippi Junior College*	Summit
Utica Junior College*	Utica
Privately controlled	
Clarke College	Newton
Mary Holmes College	West Point
Wood Junior College	Mathiston

MISSOURI

Publicly controlled	
Crowder College*	Neosho
East Central College*	Union
Jefferson College*	Hillsboro
Metropolitan Community Colleges, The	Kansas City
Longview Community College*	Lee's Summit
Maple Woods Community College*	Kansas City
Penn Valley Community College*	Kansas City
Pioneer Community College*	Kansas City
Mineral Area College*	Flat River
Moberly Junior College*	Moberly
St. Louis Community College	St. Louis
St. Louis C.C.—Florissant Valley*	St. Louis
St. Louis C.C. at Forest Park*	St. Louis
St. Louis C.C.—Meramec*	St. Louis
State Fair Community College*	Sedalia
Three Rivers Community College*	Poplar Bluff
Trenton Junior College*	Trenton
Privately controlled	
Cottey College	Nevada
Kemper Military School and College	Boonville
St. Mary's College of O'Fallon	O'Fallon
St. Paul's College	Concordia
Wentworth Military Academy	Lexington

MONTANA

Publicly controlled	
Blackfeet Community College*	Browning
Dawson Community College*	Glendive
Flathead Valley Community College*	Kalispell
Miles Community College*	Miles City
Privately controlled	
Dullknife Memorial Comm. Coll.*	Lame Deer
Salish-Kootenai Comm. College*	Pablo

NEBRASKA

Publicly controlled	
Central Technical Comm. Coll. Area	Grand Island
Central Technical Community Coll.*	Hastings
Grand Island Education Center*	Grand Island
Platte Technical Community Coll.*	Columbus
Metropolitan Technical Community Coll.	Omaha
Mid-Plains Technical Comm. Coll. Area	North Platte
McCook Community College*	McCook
Mid-Plains Community College*	North Platte
Nebraska, Univ. of, Sch. of Tech. Agri.	Curtis
Northeast Technical Community College*	Norfolk
Southeast Community College*	Lincoln
Fairbury/Beatrice Campus*	Fairbury
Lincoln Campus*	Lincoln
Milford Campus*	Milford
Western Technical Comm. Coll. Area	Scottsbluff
Nebraska Western College*	Scottsbluff
Western Nebraska Technical Coll.*	Sidney
Privately controlled	
York College	York

NEVADA

Publicly controlled	
Nevada, Univ. of, Comm. Coll. System	Reno
Clark County Community College	North Las Vegas
Northern Nevada Community College*	Elko
Truckee Meadows Community College*	Sparks
Western Nevada Community College*	Carson City

NEW HAMPSHIRE

Publicly controlled	
New Hampshire Technical Institute	Concord
New Hampshire Vocational Technical Coll.	Berlin
Berlin Campus	Berlin
Claremont Campus	Claremont
Laconia Campus	Laconia
Manchester Campus	Manchester
Nashua Campus	Nashua
Portsmouth Campus	Portsmouth
Privately controlled	
White Pines College	Chester

NEW JERSEY

Publicly controlled	
Atlantic Community College*	Mays Landing
Bergen Community College	Paramus
Brookdale Community College*	Lincroft
Burlington County College*	Pemberton
Camden County College*	Blackwood
County College of Morris	Dover
Cumberland County College*	Vineland
Essex County College	Newark
Gloucester County College*	Sewell
Hudson County Community College*	Jersey City
Mercer County Community College*	Trenton
Middlesex County College	Edison
Ocean County College	Toms River
Passaic County Community College	Paterson
Salem Community College	Penns Grove
Somerset County College	Somerville
Privately controlled	
Union College	Cranford

NEW MEXICO

Publicly controlled	
Albuquerque Tech. Voc. Inst.*	Albuquerque
Eastern New Mexico University	Portales
Clovis Campus*	Clovis
Roswell Campus*	Roswell
Inst. of American Indian Arts	Santa Fe
Luna Vocational Technical Institute*	Las Vegas
New Mexico, University of	Albuquerque

Gallup Campus*	Gallup
New Mexico Junior College*	Hobbs
New Mexico Military Institute	Roswell
New Mexico State University	Las Cruces
Alamogordo Campus*	Alamogordo
Carlsbad Campus*	Carlsbad
Dona Ana Branch	Las Cruces
Grants Campus*	Grants
San Juan Campus*	Farmington
Northern New Mexico Community Coll.*	El Rito

NEW YORK

Publicly controlled

Adirondack Community College	Glens Falls
Borough of Manhattan Community Coll.	New York
Bronx Community College	Bronx
Broome Community College	Binghamton
Cayuga County Community College	Auburn
Clinton Community College	Plattsburgh
Columbia-Greene Community College	Hudson
Comm. Coll. of the Finger Lakes	Canandaigua
Corning Community College	Corning
Dutchess Community College	Poughkeepsie
Erie Community College	Buffalo
City Campus	Buffalo
North Campus	Williamsville
South Campus	Orchard Park
Fashion Institute of Technology	New York
Fulton-Montgomery Community College	Johnstown
Genesee Community College	Batavia
Herkimer County Community College	Herkimer
Hostos Community College	Bronx
Hudson Valley Community College	Troy
Jamestown Community College	Jamestown
Jefferson Community College	Watertown
Kingsborough Community College	Brooklyn
Laguardia Community College	Long Island City
Mohawk Valley Community College	Utica
Monroe Community College	Rochester
Nassau Community College	Garden City
New York City Technical College	Brooklyn
Niagara County Community College	Sanborn
North Country Community College	Saranac Lake
Onondaga Community College	Syracuse
Orange County Community College	Middletown
Queensborough Community College	Bayside
Rockland Community College	Suffern
Schenectady County Community College	Schenectady
SUNY Agricultural & Technical Colleges	
Alfred Campus	Alfred
Canton Campus	Canton
Cobleskill Campus	Cobleskill
Delhi Campus	Delhi
Farmingdale Campus	Farmingdale
Morrisville Campus	Morrisville
Suffolk County Community College	Selden
Sullivan County Community College	Loch Sheldrake
Tompkins-Cortland Community College	Dryden
Ulster County Community College	Stoneridge
Westchester Community College	Valhalla

Privately controlled

Aeronautics, Academy of	Flushing
Albany, Junior College of	Albany
Cazenovia College	Cazenovia
Elizabeth Seton College	Yonkers
Harriman College	Harriman
Hilbert College	Hamburg
Human Services, College for	New York
Lab Inst. of Merchandising	New York City
Maria College	Albany
Maria Regina College	Syracuse
Mater Dei College	Ogdensburg
Paul Smith's Coll. of Arts & Science	Paul Smiths
Trocaire College	Buffalo
Villa Maria College of Buffalo	Buffalo

NORTH CAROLINA

Publicly controlled

Albemarle, College of the*	Elizabeth City
Anson Technical College*	Ansonville
Asheville-Buncombe Technical College*	Asheville
Beaufort County Community College*	Washington
Bladen Technical College*	Dublin
Blue Ridge Technical College*	Flat Rock
Caldwell Comm. Coll. and Tech. Inst.*	Hudson
Cape Fear Technical Institute*	Wilmington
Carteret Technical College*	Morehead City
Catawba Valley Technical College*	Hickory
Central Carolina Technical College*	Sanford
Central Piedmont Community College*	Charlotte
Cleveland Technical College*	Shelby
Coastal Carolina Community College*	Jacksonville
Craven Community College*	New Bern
Davidson County Community College*	Lexington
Durham Technical Institute*	Durham
Edgecombe Technical College*	Tarboro
Fayetteville Technical Institute*	Fayetteville
Forsyth Technical Institute*	Winston Salem
Gaston College*	Dallas
Guilford Technical Institute	Jamestown
Halifax Community College*	Weldon
Haywood Technical College*	Clyde
Isothermal Community College	Spindale
James Sprunt Technical College*	Kenansville
Johnston Technical College*	Smithfield
Lenoir Community College*	Kinston
Martin Community College*	Williamston
Mayland Technical College*	Spruce Pine
McDowell Technical College*	Marion
Mitchell Community College*	Statesville
Montgomery Technical Institute*	Troy
Nash Technical Institute*	Rocky Mount
Pamlico Technical College*	Grantsboro
Piedmont Technical College*	Roxboro
Pitt Community College*	Greenville
Randolph Technical College*	Asheboro
Richmond Technical College*	Hamlet
Roanoke-Chowan Technical College*	Ahoskie
Robeson Technical College*	Lumberton
Rockingham Community College*	Wentworth
Rowan Technical College*	Salisbury
Sampson Technical College*	Clinton
Sandhills Community College*	Carthage
Southeastern Community College*	Whiteville
Southwestern Technical College*	Sylva
Stanly Technical Institute*	Albemarle
Surry Community College*	Dobson
Technical College of Alamance*	Haw River
Tri-County Community College*	Murphy
Vance-Granville Community College*	Henderson
Wake Technical College*	Raleigh
Wayne Community College*	Goldsboro
Western Piedmont Community College*	Morganton
Wilkes Community College*	Wilkesboro
Wilson County Technical Institute*	Wilson

Privately controlled

Brevard College	Brevard
Chowan College	Murfreesboro
Lees-McRae College	Banner Elk
Louisburg College	Louisburg
Montreat-Anderson College	Montreat
Mount Olive College	Mount Olive
Peace College	Raleigh
St. Mary's College	Raleigh

NORTH DAKOTA

Publicly controlled

Bismarck Junior College	Bismarck
Lake Region Junior College	Devils Lake
North Dakota, Univ. of—Williston	Williston
North Dakota State School of Science	Wahpeton
North Dakota State Univ.—Bottineau	Bottineau
Turtle Mountain Comm. College*	Belcourt

Privately controlled

Standing Rock Comm. College	Fort Yates

OHIO

Publicly controlled

Akron, Univ. of, Comm. and Tech. Coll.	Akron
Wayne General & Technical Coll.	Orrville
Belmont Technical College	St. Clairsville
Bowling Green Univ.–Firelands Campus	Huron
Central Ohio Technical College	Newark
Cincinnati, University of	Cincinnati
Clermont General & Technical Coll.	Batavia
Omi-College of Applied Science	Cincinnati
Raymond Walters Gen. & Tech. Coll.	Cincinnati
University College	Cincinnati
Cincinnati Technical College	Cincinnati
Clark Technical College	Springfield
Coll. of Applied Science & Technology	Youngstown
Columbus Technical Institute	Columbus
Cuyahoga Community College District	Cleveland
Eastern Campus	Warrensville Twnsp.
Metropolitan Campus	Cleveland
Western Campus	Parma
Edison State Community College	Piqua
Hocking Technical College	Nelsonville
Jefferson Technical College*	Steubenville
Kent State University	Kent
Ashtabula Campus	Ashtabula
East Liverpool Regional Campus	East Liverpool
Geauga Campus	Burton
Salem Campus	Salem
Stark Regional Campus	Canton
Trumbull Campus	Warren
Tuscarawas Campus	New Philadelphia
Lakeland Community College	Mentor
Lima Technical College	Lima
Lorain County Community College	Elyria
Marion Technical College	Marion
Miami University	Oxford
Hamilton Campus	Hamilton
Middletown Campus	Middletown
Muskingum Area Technical College	Zanesville
North Central Technical College	Mansfield
Northwest Technical College	Archbold
Ohio State University	Columbus
Agricultural Technical Institute	Wooster
Lima Campus	Lima
Mansfield Campus	Mansfield
Marion Campus	Marion
Newark Campus	Newark
Ohio University	Athens
Belmont County Campus	St. Clairsville
Chillicothe Campus	Chillicothe
Ironton Campus	Ironton
Lancaster Campus	Lancaster
Zanesville Campus	Zanesville
Owens Technical College	Toledo
Rio Grande Coll. & Comm. Coll.	Rio Grande
Shawnee State Community College	Portsmouth
Sinclair Community College	Dayton
Southern State Community College	Hillsboro
Stark Technical College	Canton
Terra Technical College	Fremont
Toledo, Univ. of, Comm. & Tech. Coll.	Toledo
Washington Technical College	Marietta
Wright State Univ.—Western Branch	Celina

Privately controlled

Chatfield College	St. Martin
Kettering College of Medical Arts	Kettering
Lourdes College	Sylvania

OKLAHOMA

Publicly controlled

Carl Albert Junior College	Poteau
Claremore Junior College*	Claremore
Connors State College*	Warner
Eastern Oklahoma State College*	Wilburton
El Reno Junior College*	El Reno
Murray State College*	Tishomingo
Northeastern Oklahoma A&M College*	Miami
Northern Oklahoma College*	Tonkawa
Oklahoma State U. Technical Institute*	Oklahoma City
Oscar Rose Junior College*	Midwest City
Sayre Junior College*	Sayre
Seminole Junior College*	Seminole
South Oklahoma City Junior College*	Oklahoma City
Tulsa Junior College*	Tulsa
Western Oklahoma State College*	Altus

Privately controlled

Bacone College	Muskogee
Hillsdale Free Will Baptist	Moore
St. Gregory's College	Shawnee

OREGON

Publicly controlled

Blue Mountain Community College*	Pendleton
Central Oregon Community College*	Bend
Chemeketa Community College*	Salem
Clackamas Community College*	Oregon City
Clatsop Community College*	Astoria
Lane Community College*	Eugene
Linn-Benton Community College*	Albany
Mt. Hood Community College*	Gresham
Portland Community College*	Portland
Rogue Community College*	Grants Pass
Southwestern Oregon Community Coll.*	Coos Bay
Treasure Valley Community College*	Ontario
Umpqua Community College*	Roseburg

Privately controlled

Bassist College	Portland

PENNSYLVANIA

Publicly controlled

Bucks County Community College	Newtown
Butler County Community College	Butler
Community Coll. of Allegheny County	Pittsburgh
Allegheny Campus	Pittsburgh
Boyce Campus	Monroeville
College Center—North	Pittsburgh
South Campus	West Mifflin
Community College of Beaver County	Monaca
Comm. College of Philadelphia	Philadelphia
Delaware County Community College	Media
Harrisburg Area Community College	Harrisburg
Lehigh County Community College	Schnecksville
Luzerne County Community College	Nanticoke
Montgomery County Community College	Blue Bell
Northhampton County Area Comm. Coll.	Bethlehem
Reading Area Community College	Reading
Westmoreland County Community Coll.	Youngwood
Williamsport Area Community College	Williamsport

Privately controlled

Center for Degree Studies	Scranton
Central Penn. Business School	Summerdale
Harcum Junior College	Bryn Mawr
Keystone Junior College	La Plume

Lackawanna Junior College	Scranton
Manor Junior College	Jenkintown
Mount Aloysius Junior College	Cresson
Northeastern Christian Junior College	Villanova
Peirce Junior College	Philadelphia
Pennsylvania Institute of Technology	Upper Darby
Pinebrook Junior College	Coopersburg
Valley Forge Military Junior College	Wayne
Wheeler School	Pittsburgh

PUERTO RICO

Publicly controlled

Puerto Rico, Univ. of, Regional Colleges	Rio Piedras
Aguadilla Regional College*	Aguadilla
Arecibo Regional College*	Arecibo
Bayamon U. Technological Coll.*	Bayamon
Carolina Regional College	Villa Carolina
La Montana Regional College	Utuado
Ponce Regional College*	Ponce

Privately controlled

Catholic University of Puerto Rico	Ponce
Arecibo Center	Arecibo
Guayama Center	Guayama
Mayaguez Center	Mayaguez
Ponce Center	Ponce
ICPR Junior College	Hato Rey
Interamerican University of Puerto Rico	San Juan
Aguadilla Regional College	Aguadilla
Arecibo Regional College	Arecibo
Barranquitas Regional College	Barranquitas
Fajardo Regional Campus	Fajardo
Guayama Regional College	Guayama
Ponce Regional College	Ponce
Puerto Rico Junior College	Rio Piedras
Ramirez Coll. of Business Tech.	Santurce

RHODE ISLAND

Publicly controlled

Community Coll. of Rhode Island*	Warwick
Knight Campus	Warwick
Flanagan Campus	Lincoln

SOUTH CAROLINA

Publicly controlled

State System of Technical Colleges:	Columbia
Aiken Technical College*	Aiken
Beaufort Technical College*	Beaufort
Chesterfield-Marlboro Technical Coll.*	Cheraw
Denmark Technical College*	Denmark
Florence-Darlington Technical Coll.	Florence
Greenville Technical College*	Greenville
Horry-Georgetown Technical College*	Conway
Midlands Technical College*	Columbia
Airport Campus	West Columbia
Beltline Campus	Columbia
Orangeburg-Calhoun Technical College*	Orangeburg
Piedmont Technical College*	Greenwood
South Carolina, University of	Columbia
Beaufort Regional Campus	Beaufort
Lancaster Regional Campus	Lancaster
Salkehatchie Regional Campus	Allendale
Sumter Regional Campus	Sumter
Union Campus	Union
Spartanburg Technical College*	Spartanburg
Sumter Area Technical College*	Sumter
Tri-County Technical College*	Pendleton
Trident Technical College*	Charleston
North Campus	No. Charleston
Palmer Campus	Charleston
Williamsburg Technical College*	Kingstree
York Technical College*	Rock Hill

Privately controlled

Anderson College	Anderson
North Greenville College	Tigerville
Spartanburg Methodist College	Spartanburg

SOUTH DAKOTA

Privately controlled

Oglala Sioux Community College*	Kyle
Presentation College	Aberdeen
Sinte Gleska College Center	Rosebud

TENNESSEE

Publicly controlled

Chattanooga State Tech. Comm. Coll.*	Chattanooga
Cleveland State Community College*	Cleveland
Columbia State Community College*	Columbia
Dyersburg State Community College*	Dyersburg
Jackson State Community College*	Jackson
Motlow State Community College*	Tullahoma
Nashville State Technical Institute*	Nashville
Roane State Community College*	Harriman
Shelby State Community College*	Memphis
State Technical Inst. at Memphis*	Memphis
Volunteer State Community College*	Gallatin
Walters State Community College*	Morristown

Privately controlled

Aquinas Junior College	Nashville
Cumberland College of Tennessee	Lebanon
Hiwassee College	Madisonville
John A. Gupton College	Nashville
Martin College	Pulaski
Morristown College	Morristown
State Technical Inst. at Knoxville*	Knoxville
Tomlinson College	Cleveland

TEXAS

Publicly controlled

Alvin Community College*	Alvin
Amarillo College*	Amarillo
Angelina College*	Lufkin
Austin Community College*	Austin
Bee County College*	Beeville
Blinn College*	Brenham
Brazosport College*	Lake Jackson
Central Texas College*	Killeen
Cisco Junior College*	Cisco
Clarendon College*	Clarendon
Cooke County College*	Gainesville
Dallas County Community Coll. District	Dallas
Brookhaven College*	Farmers Branch
Cedar Valley College*	Lancaster
Eastfield College*	Mesquite
El Centro College*	Dallas
Mountain View College*	Dallas
North Lake College*	Irving
Richland College*	Dallas
Del Mar College*	Corpus Christi
El Paso County Comm. Coll. District	El Paso
Rio Grande Campus*	El Paso
Transmountain Campus*	El Paso
Valle Verde Campus*	El Paso
Frank Phillips College	Borger
Galveston College*	Galveston
Grayson County Junior College*	Denison
Henderson County Junior College*	Athens
Hill Junior College*	Hillsboro
Houston Community College*	Houston
Howard County Junior Coll. District	Big Spring
Howard College*	Big Spring
SW Collegiate Inst. for Deaf*	Big Spring
Kilgore College*	Kilgore
Lamar University	Beaumont
Orange County Center*	Orange
Port Arthur Branch*	Port Arthur
Laredo Junior College*	Laredo
Lee College*	Baytown
Mainland, College of the*	Texas City
McLennan Community College*	Waco

Midland College*	Midland
Navarro College*	Corsicana
North Harris County College*	Houston
Odessa College*	Odessa
Panola Junior College*	Carthage
Paris Junior College*	Paris
Ranger Junior College*	Ranger
San Antonio Community Coll. District	San Antonio
St. Philip's College*	San Antonio
San Antonio College*	San Antonio
San Jacinto College District	Pasadena
Central Campus*	Pasadena
North Campus*	Houston
South Campus*	Houston
South Plains College*	Levelland
Southwest Texas Junior College*	Uvalde
Tarrant County Junior Coll. District	Fort Worth
Northeast Campus*	Hurst
Northwest Campus*	Fort Worth
South Campus*	Fort Worth
Temple Junior College*	Temple
Texarkana Community College*	Texarkana
Texas Southmost College*	Brownsville
Texas State Technical Institute	Waco
Harlingen Campus*	Harlingen
Mid-Continent Campus*	Amarillo
Sweetwater Campus*	Sweetwater
Waco Campus*	Waco
Tyler Junior College*	Tyler
Vernon Regional Junior College*	Vernon
Victoria College*	Victoria
Weatherford College*	Weatherford
Western Texas College*	Snyder
Wharton County Junior College	Wharton

Privately controlled

Jacksonville College	Jacksonville
Lon Morris College	Jacksonville
Schreiner College	Kerrville
Southwestern Christian College	Terrell
Southwestern Junior College	Waxahachie

JTAH

Publicly controlled

ixie College*	St. George
astern Utah, College of	Price
now College	Ephraim
tah Technical College at Provo*	Provo
tah Technical College at Salt Lake*	Salt Lake City

ERMONT

Publicly controlled

ommunity College of Vermont	Montpelier
ermont Technical College	Randolph Center

Privately controlled

amplain College	Burlington
ermont College of Norwich University	Montpelier

IRGINIA

Publicly controlled

ue Ridge Community College*	Weyers Cave
ntral Virginia Community College*	Lynchburg
bney S. Lancaster Community Coll.*	Clifton Forge
nville Community College*	Danville
stern Shore Community College*	Melfa
rmanna Community College*	Locust Grove
Sargeant Reynolds Community Coll.*	Richmond
Downtown Campus	Richmond
Parham Road Campus	Richmond
Western Campus	Richmond
n Tyler Community College*	Chester
rd Fairfax Community College*	Middletown
untain Empire Community College*	Big Stone Gap
w River Community College*	Dublin
Northern Virginia Community College*	Annandale
Alexandria Campus	Alexandria
Annandale Campus	Annandale
Loudoun Campus	Sterling
Manassas Campus	Manassas
Woodbridge Campus	Woodbridge
Patrick Henry Community College*	Martinsville
Paul D. Camp Community College*	Franklin
Piedmont Virginia Community College*	Charlottesville
Rappahannock Community College*	Glenns
North Campus	Warsaw
South Campus	Glenns
Richard Bland College	Petersburg
Southside Virginia Community College	Alberta
Christanna Campus*	Alberta
John H. Daniel Campus*	Keysville
Southwest Virginia Community College*	Richlands
Thomas Nelson Community College*	Hampton
Tidewater Community College	Portsmouth
Chesapeake Campus*	Chesapeake
Frederick Campus*	Portsmouth
Virginia Beach Campus*	Virginia Beach
Virginia Highlands Community College*	Abingdon
Virginia Western Community College*	Roanoke
Wytheville Community College*	Wytheville

Privately controlled

Southern Seminary Junior College	Buena Vista

WASHINGTON

Publicly controlled

Bellevue Community College*	Bellevue
Big Bend Community College*	Moses Lake
Clark College*	Vancouver
Columbia Basin College*	Pasco
Community College District XII	Centralia
Centralia College*	Centralia
Olympia Tech. Comm. Coll.*	Olympia
Community College District XVII	Spokane
Spokane Community College*	Spokane
Spokane Falls Comm. Coll.*	Spokane
Edmonds Community College*	Lynnwood
Everett Community College*	Everett
Fort Steilacoom Comm. Coll.*	Tacoma
Grays Harbor College*	Aberdeen
Green River Comm. College*	Auburn
Highline Community College*	Midway
Lower Columbia College*	Longview
Olympic College*	Bremerton
Peninsula College*	Port Angeles
Seattle Comm. Coll. District VI	Seattle
North Seattle Comm. Coll.*	Seattle
Seattle Central Comm. Coll.*	Seattle
South Seattle Comm. Coll.*	Seattle
Shoreline Community College*	Seattle
Skagit Valley College*	Mount Vernon
Tacoma Community College*	Tacoma
Walla Walla Community College*	Walla Walla
Wenatchee Valley College*	Wenatchee
Whatcom Community College*	Bellingham
Yakima Valley College*	Yakima

WEST VIRGINIA

Publicly controlled

Fairmont Community College*	Fairmont
Marshall Univ.—Community College*	Huntington
Parkersburg Community College*	Parkersburg
Potomac State College*	Keyser
Shepherd College—Community College Component*	Shepherdstown
Southern West Virginia Comm. College*	Logan
Logan Campus	Logan
Williamson Campus	Williamson
West Virginia Institute of Technology—Community and Technical College*	Montgomery

West Virginia Northern Comm. College*	Wheeling
West Virginia State Comm. College*	Institute
Privately controlled	
Beckley College	Beckley
Ohio Valley College	Parkersburg

WISCONSIN

Publicly controlled	
University Center System	Madison
Baraboo-Sauk County Campus	Baraboo
Barron County Campus	Rice Lake
Fond du Lac Campus	Fond du Lac
Fox Valley Campus	Menasha
Manitowoc County Campus	Manitowoc
Marathon County Campus	Wausau
Marinette County Campus	Marinette
Marshfield-Wood County Campus	Marshfield
Richland Campus	Richland Center
Rock County Campus	Janesville
Sheboygan Campus	Sheboygan
Washington County Campus	West Bend
Waukesha County Campus	Waukesha
Vocational Tech. & Adult Education Sys.	Madison
Blackhawk Technical Institute*	Janesville
Beloit Campus	
Central Campus	
District One Technical Institute*	Eau Claire
Fox Valley Technical Institute*	Appleton
Appleton Campus	Appleton
Oshkosh Campus	Oshkosh
Gateway Technical Institute*	Kenosha
Elkhorn Campus	Elkhorn
Kenosha Campus	Kenosha
Racine Campus	Racine
Lakeshore Technical Institute*	Cleveland
Madison Area Technical College*	Madison
Mid-State Technical Institute	Wisconsin Rapids
Marshfield Campus*	Marshfield
Stevens Point Campus*	Stevens Point
Wisconsin Rapids Campus*	Wisconsin Rapids
Milwaukee Area Technical College	Milwaukee
Central Campus*	Milwaukee
North Campus*	Mequon
South Campus*	Oak Creek
West Campus*	West Allis
Moraine Park Technical Institute*	Fond du Lac
Beaver Dam Campus	Beaver Dam
Fond du Lac Campus	Fond du Lac
West Bend Campus	West Bend
Nicolet College and Tech. Institute*	Rhinelander
North Central Technical Institute*	Wausau
Antigo Campus	Antigo
Wausau Campus	Wausau
Northeast Wisconsin Technical Inst.	Green Bay
Green Bay Campus*	Green Bay
Marinette Campus*	Marinette
Sturgeon Bay Campus	Sturgeon Bay
Southwest Wisconsin Technical Inst.	Fennimore
Waukesha County Technical Institute*	Pewaukee
Western Wisconsin Technical Institute*	La Crosse
Wisconsin Indianhead VTAE District	Shell Lake
Ashland Campus*	Ashland
New Richmond Campus*	New Richmond
Rice Lake Campus*	Rice Lake
Superior Campus*	Superior

WYOMING

Publicly controlled	
Casper College*	Casper
Central Wyoming College*	Riverton
Eastern Wyoming College*	Torrington
Laramie County Community College*	Cheyenne
Northern Wyoming Community College*	Sheridan
Northwest Community College*	Powell
Western Wyoming Community College*	Rock Springs

AMERICAN SAMOA

Publicly controlled	
American Samoa Community College*	Pago Pago

CANADA

Publicly controlled	
Fraser Valley College*	Mission, B.C.
Grant MacEwan Community College*	Edmonton, Alberta
Keyano College*	Alberta
Lambton College*	Sarnia, Ont.
Medicine Hat College*	Medicine Hat, Alberta
Mount Royal College*	Calgary, Albta.
Red Deer College*	Alberta

GUAM

Publicly controlled	
Guam Community College*	Guam

MICRONESIA

Publicly controlled	
Community Coll. of Micronesia	East Caroline Isl.

PANAMA

Privately controlled	
Panama Canal College*	APO Miami

OTHER COUNTRIES

Privately controlled	
American College of Switzerland	Leysin, Switz.
Schiller International Univ.	Heidelberg, W. Ger.
St. Johns College*	British Honduras

Purposes of Institutional Accreditation

Institutional accreditation of the postsecondary level is a means used by the accrediting commissio for the purposes of: fostering excellence in postsecondary education through the development of crite and guidelines for assessing educational effectiveness; encouraging institutional improvement of educ tional endeavors through continuous self-study and evaluation; assuring the educational community, t general public, and other agencies or organizations that an institution has clearly defined and appropri objectives, has established conditions under which their achievement can reasonably be expected, a pears in fact to be accomplishing them substantially, and is so organized, staffed, and supported that can be expected to continue to do so; providing counsel and assistance to established and develop institutions; protecting institutions against encroachments which might jeopardize their educational eff tiveness or academic freedom.

Accreditation is attained through a process of evaluation and periodic review of total instituti conducted by the commission in accord with policies and procedures approved by the Council Postsecondary Accreditation.

Accredited U.S. Senior Colleges and Universities, Spring 1982

Source: Information Please questionnaires to Colleges and Universities.

Schools listed are those that offer at least a Bachelor's degree, and are fully accredited by one of the institutional and professional accrediting associations recognized by the Council on Post-secondary Accreditation. The number of students is for **full-time**, matriculated, undergraduate and graduate students who are working for a degree. Actual enrollment, including part-time students, may be much higher. Number of faculty also is full-time.

Tuition, room, and board listed are average annual figures, subject to fluctuation, usually covering two semesters, two out of three trimesters, or three out of four quarters, depending on school calendar.

For further information, write to the Registrar of the school concerned.

NOTE: An asterisk (*) indicates that the college has not supplied up-to-date information. A dash (—) means the information does not apply. n.a. = information not available.

Abbreviations used for controls:

AB	American Baptist
AC	Advent Christian
AG	Assembly of God
AL	American Lutheran
AME	African Methodist Episcopal
B	Baptist
BC	Brethren in Christ
CB	Church of Brethren
CC	Church of Christ
CG	Church of God
ChC	Christian Church
CMA	Christian & Missionary Alliance
CME	Christian Methodist Episcopal
Cong	Congregationist
CP	Cumberland Presbyterian
CR	Christian Reformed
DC	Disciples of Christ
E	Episcopalian
EC	Evangelical Covenant
EF	Evangelical Friends
EFC	Evangelical Free Church
EL	Evangelical Lutheran
Fed	Federal
FG	Foursquare Gospel
FGB	Fellowship of Grace Brethren Churches
FM	Free Methodist
FWB	Free Will Baptist
GGF	Grace Gospel Fellowship
ID	Interdenominational
Ind	Independent
J	Jewish
L	Lutheran
LCA	Lutheran Church of America
LDS	Latter Day Saints
M	Methodist
MB	Mennonite Brethren
MC	Missionary Church
Men	Mennonite
Mor	Moravian
Mun	Municipal
Naz	Nazarene
ND	Non-denominational
OBS	Open Bible Standard
P	Private
PH	Pentecostal Holiness
Pres	Presbyterian
Pub	Public
PUS	Presbyterian, U.S.
RC	Roman Catholic
RCA	Reformed Church in America
RP	Reformed Presbyterian
S	State
SB	Southern Baptist
SDA	Seventh Day Adventist
SOF	Society of Friends
Sw	Swedenborgian
UCC	United Church of Christ
UM	United Methodist
UP	United Presbyterian
W	Wesleyan

	Enrollment				Tuition		
Institution and location	Male	Female	Faculty	Control	Res.	Nonres.	Rm/Bd
Abilene Christian University; Abilene, Tex. 79699	1,876[1]	1,846[1]	200	P	2,528	2,528	1,800
Academy of Art College; San Francisco, Calif. 94102	586	683	25	P	3,560	3,560	2,025
Adams State College; Alamosa, Colo. 81102	825[2]	1,059[2]	90	S	650	2,612	1,890
Adelphi University; Garden City, N.Y. 11530	1,743	3,861	385	P	4,470	4,470	2,412
Adrian College; Adrian, Mich. 49221	544[1]	517[1]	62	P	4,686	4,686	2,000
Agnes Scott College; Decatur, Ga. 30030	—	559[1]	68	P	5,100[3]	5,100[3]	1,900
Akron, The University of; Akron, Ohio 44325	13,151[1]	12,669[1]	967	S	1,250	2,722	2,130
Alabama, The University of*; University, Ala. 35486	8,699	8,220	836	S	994	2,119	1,687
Alabama, The University of, in Birmingham; Birmingham, Ala. 35294	3,703	4,199	1,387	S	1,026	1,824	—
Alabama, The University of, in Huntsville; Huntsville, Ala. 35899	2,829[1]	2,630[1]	222	S	966	1,932	2,240
Alabama A&M University; Normal, Ala. 35762	1,996[1]	1,634[1]	261	S	560	840	1,360
Alabama State University; Montgomery, Ala. 36195	1,704[1]	2,330[1]	174	S	660	1,320	1,320
Alaska, University of, Anchorage*; Anchorage, Alaska 99504	1,297	2,287	128	S	681	1,851	—
Alaska, University of, Fairbanks; Fairbanks, Alaska 99701	1,380[1]	1,110[1]	320	S	410	1,190	2,080
Albany College of Pharmacy; Albany, N.Y. 12208	246	291	29	P	2,800	2,800	2,250
Albany Law School of Union University; Albany, N.Y. 12208	399[1]	270[1]	27	P	5,400[3]	5,400[3]	—

Institution and location	Enrollment		Faculty	Control	Tuition		Rm/Bd
	Male	Female			Res.	Nonres.	
Albany Medical College; Albany, N.Y. 12084	357[1]	156[1]	350	P	12,000	12,000	2,600
Albany State College; Albany, Ga. 31705	866	1,075	127	S	726	1,776	1,875
Albertus Magnus College; New Haven, Conn. 06511	14[1]	539[1]	31	P/RC	4,700	4,700	2,900
Albion College; Albion, Mich. 49224	913	858	119	P	4,716	4,716	2,272
Albright College; Reading, Pa. 19603	655[2]	767[2]	88	P/UM	5,660[3]	5,660[3]	2,090[3]
Albuquerque, University of; Albuquerque, N.M. 87140	759	993	70	P	3,000	3,000	1,850
Alcorn State University; Lorman, Miss. 39096	1,053[1]	1,365[1]	149	S	825	1,751	1,407
Alderson–Broaddus College; Philippi, W. Va. 26416	254[1]	493[1]	52	P/AB	3,300	3,300	1,400
Alfred Adler Institute of Chicago[4]; Chicago, Ill. 60601	19[5]	57[5]	27[5]	P	1,380	1,380	—
Alfred University[6]; Alfred, N.Y. 14802	1,063[1]	947[1]	136	P	5,650	5,650	2,270
Allegheny College; Meadville, Pa. 16335	963	924	123	P	4,950	4,950	945
Allentown College of St. Francis de Sales; Center Valley, Pa. 18034	399[1]	417[1]	44	P/RC	4,060	4,060	2,420
Alliance College; Cambridge Springs, Pa. 16403	169[1]	91[1]	18	P	2,800	2,800	2,050
Alma College; Alma, Mich. 48801	543[1]	556[1]	72	P/Pres	4,899	4,899	2,201
Alvernia College; Reading, Pa. 19607	125	150	31	P/RC	2,200[3]	2,200[3]	1,900
Alverno College; Milwaukee, Wis. 53215	—	624	62	RC	3,800	3,800	1,700
American Baptist College; Nashville, Tenn. 37207	145	20	5	P/B	1,094	1,094	986
American College, The*; Bryn Mawr, Pa. 19010	14,336	2,370	31	P	220	220	—
American College in Paris, The; Paris, France 75007	203	360	22	P	4,200	4,200	3,400
American College of Switzerland; 1854 Leysin, Switzerland	100	106	19	P	10,860[7]	10,860[7]	—
American Conservatory of Music; Chicago, Ill. 60603	128		30	P	1,600	1,600	—
American Grad. School of Intl. Mgt.; Glendale, Ariz. 85306	710	374	64	P	6,745	6,745	3,200
American International College; Springfield, Mass. 01109	850[1]	649[1]	80	P	3,060	3,060	1,862
American Technological University; Killeen, Tex. 76540	416[1]	179[1]	16	P	([8])	([8])	2,154
American University, The; Washington, D.C. 20016	3,079[1]	3,376[1]	384	P/M	6,200	6,200	3,166
Americas, University of the; Puebla, Mexico 72820	1,290[9]	808[9]	76	P	1,377[5]	1,733[5]	n.a.
Amherst College*; Amherst, Mass. 01002	959	603	147	P	7,250	7,250	2,550
Ana G. Méndez Educational Foundation; Rio Piedras, P.R. 00928:							
Colegio Universitario Metropolitano; Cupey, P.R. 00928	1,066	2,118	65	P	1,200	1,200	n.a.
Turabo University College; Caguas, P.R. 00625	2,389	3,285	84	P	775	1,080	1,080
Anderson College; Anderson, Ind. 46012	808[1]	922[1]	99	P/CG	3,840	3,840	1,540
Andrews University; Berrien Springs, Mich. 49104	1,340[1]	935[1]	220	P/SDA	4,950	4,950	2,670
Angelo State University; San Angelo, Tex. 76909	2,043[1]	2,026[1]	200	S	210	750	1,940
Anna Maria College; Paxton, Mass. 01612	133	324	27	P/RC	3,600	3,600	2,360
Antillian College; Mayaguez, P.R. 00708	307	452	43	P/SDA	1,882	1,882	1,660
Antioch University; Yellow Springs, Ohio 45387	1,268[1]	2,322[1]	194	P	n.a.	n.a.	—
Appalachian Bible College; Bradley, W. Va. 25818	101	69	14	P	2,000	2,000	1,450
Appalachian State University. *See* North Carolina, University System of							
Aquinas College; Grand Rapids, Mich. 49506	1,192[1]	1,523[1]	79	P/RC	4,016	4,016	2,100
Arizona, The University of; Tucson, Ariz. 85721	15,632	13,951	1,850	S	710	3,310	1,635
Arizona State University; Tempe, Ariz. 85287	19,707	18,368	1,163	S	650	2,950	2,415
Arkansas, Univ. of, at Fayetteville; Fayetteville, Ark. 72701	7,708[1]	5,139[1]	693	S	660	1,690	1,695
Arkansas, Univ. of, at Little Rock; Little Rock, Ark. 72204	2,236[1]	2,451[1]	393	S	730	1,760	—
Arkansas, Univ. of, at Monticello; Monticello, Ark. 71655	760	767	88	S	1,056	2,384	1,810
Arkansas, Univ. of, at Pine Bluff; Pine Bluff, Ark. 71601	1,024	1,264	178	S	660	1,690	1,358
Arkansas College; Batesville, Ark. 72501	150	206	27	P/PUS	1,475	1,475	1,596
Arkansas State University; State University, Ark. 72467	3,444[1]	4,004[1]	341	S	720	1,320	1,600
Arkansas Tech. University; Russellville, Ark. 72801	1,413[1]	1,220[1]	130	S	750	1,450	600
Armstrong College; Berkeley, Calif. 94704	500[1]		30	P	2,178	2,178	—
Armstrong State College; Savannah, Ga. 31406	1,043	1,787	162	S	675	1,650	—
Art Academy of Cincinnati; Cincinnati, Ohio 45227	92[1]	87[1]	21	P	2,800	2,800	—
Art Center College of Design; Pasadena, Calif. 91103	705	526	45	P	3,920	3,920	n.a.
Arthur D. Little Management Education Institute; Cambridge, Mass. 02140	86[1]	9[1]	26[10]	P	9,075	9,075	—
Art Institute of Chicago, School of the; Chicago, Ill. 60603	382[2]	498[2]	80	P	4,950	4,950	5,500
Asbury College; Wilmore, Ky. 40390	529	617	80	P	2,960	2,960	1,965
Ashland College; Ashland, Ohio 44805	1,277	681	103	P/BC	4,626	4,626	2,030
Assemblies of God Graduate School; Springfield, Mo. 65802	233	44	11	P/AG	1,800	1,800	—
Associated Arts, School of the; St. Paul, Minn. 55102	53[1]	60[1]	3	P	2,950	2,950	4,356
Assumption College; Worcester, Mass. 01609	694[1]	784[1]	106	P/RC	4,800	4,800	n.a.
Athens State College; Athens, Ala. 35611	479	484	34	S	900	1,800	1,185
Atlanta Christian College; East Point, Ga. 30344	87	55	10	P/ChC	1,344	1,344	1,400
Atlanta College of Art; Atlanta, Ga. 30309	119[1]	131[1]	21	P	3,400	3,400	1,260
Atlanta University; Atlanta, Ga. 30314	348	376	104	P	([11])	([11])	1,000
Atlantic, College of the; Bar Harbor, Maine 04609	81	103	24	P	4,800[2]	4,800[2]	2,000

Institution and location	Enrollment		Faculty	Control	Tuition		Rm/Bd
	Male	Female			Res.	Nonres.	
Atlantic Christian College; Wilson, N.C. 27893	584[1]	980[1]	86	P/DC	2,500	2,500	1,400
Atlantic Union College; South Lancaster, Mass. 01561	240	292	56	P/SDA	4,600	4,600	3,000
Auburn University; Auburn, Ala. 36849	9,503[1]	6,915[1]	1,039	S	990	2,280	1,635
Auburn University at Montgomery; Montgomery, Ala. 36193	2,320[1]	2,749[1]	181	S	795	1,830	2,220
Augsburg College*; Minneapolis, Minn. 55454	661	801	94	P/AL	3,660	3,660	1,837
Augusta College; Augusta, Ga. 30901	1,567	2,224	145	S	750	2,040	—
Augustana College; Rock Island, Ill. 61201	1,014	1,145	117	P/LCA	4,110	4,110	1,932
Augustana College; Sioux Falls, S.D. 57197	608[1]	1,066[1]	123	P	4,680	4,680	1,755
Aurora College; Aurora, Ill. 60506	728[1]	605[1]	67	P	3,900[3]	3,900[3]	2,400[3]
Austin College; Sherman, Tex. 75090	633[1]	506[1]	99	P/PUS	4,000	4,000	1,950
Austin Peay State University; Clarksville, Tenn. 37040[12]	2,200	2,253	201	S	708	2,238	1,900
Averett College; Danville, Va. 24541	253[1]	482[1]	58	P/B	2,400	2,400	2,400
Avila College; Kansas City, Mo. 64145	192	611	59	P/RC	3,100	3,100	1,700
Azusa Pacific University; Azusa, Calif. 91702	702[1]	949[1]	100	P/ID	4,320	4,320	4,540
Babson College; Babson Park, Mass. 02157	914[1]	467[1]	92	P	5,360	5,360	2,980
Baker University; Baldwin City, Kan. 66006	368	420	61	P/UM	3,300	3,300	1,990
Baldwin–Wallace College; Berea, Ohio 44017	944[1]	964[1]	134	P/M	4,053	4,053	2,553
Ball State University; Muncie, Ind. 47306	8,218[1]	10,233[1]	862	S	1,116	2,460	1,719
Baltimore, University of; Baltimore, Md. 21201	1,186	820	134	S	990	1,990	—
Baltimore Hebrew College*; Baltimore, Md. 21215	62	142	16	P	970	970	—
Bank Street College Graduate School of Education; New York, N.Y. 10025	43	142	50	P	7,140	7,140	—
Baptist Bible College*; Springfield, Mo. 65802	995	774	59	P/B	416	416	1,200
Baptist College at Charleston; Charleston, S.C. 29411	1,222[1]	1,312[1]	70	P/SB	3,456	3,456	2,192
Barat College; Lake Forest, Ill. 60045	12[1]	690[1]	38	P	4,800	4,800	2,300
Barber–Scotia College; Concord, N.C. 28025	142[1]	205[1]	24	Pres	4,302	4,302	1,879
Bard College; Annandale-on-Hudson, N.Y. 12504	300	402	54	P	8,700	8,700	2,800
Barnard College. *See* Columbia University							
Barrington College; Barrington, R.I. 02806	180	222	2	P/ND	4,820	4,820	2,475
Barry University; Miami Shores, Fla. 33161	229	743	86	P/RC	4,400	4,400	2,250
Bartlesville Wesleyan College; Bartlesville, Okla. 74003	188	202	28	P/W	2,960	2,960	1,950
Bates College; Lewiston, Maine 04240	720[1]	710[1]	105	P	10,500[7]	10,500[7]	—
Bayamón Central University; Bayamón, P.R. 00619	529	636	26	P/RC	1,500	1,500	1,560[5]
Bayamón Technological University College. *See* Puerto Rico, Univ. of							
Baylor College of Dentistry*; Dallas, Tex. 75246	395	125	110	P	510	3,000	—
Baylor College of Medicine*; Houston, Tex. 77030	614	240	n.a.	P	n.a.	n.a.	n.a.
Baylor University; Waco, Tex. 76798	5,000	5,000	525	P/SB	2,700	2,700	2,000
Beacon College; Washington, D.C. 20009	56[1]	89[1]	n.a.	P	2,400	2,400	—
Beaver College; Glenside, Pa. 19038	146[1]	575[1]	61	P	5,400	5,400	2,400
Behrend College. *See* Pennsylvania State University							
Belhaven College; Jackson, Miss. 39202	446	589	31	P/Pres	3,000	3,000	1,640
Bellarmine College; Louisville, Ky. 40205	580[1]	576[1]	68	P/RC	2,850	2,850	1,700
Bellevue College; Bellevue, Neb. 68005	2,600		34	P	1,260	1,260	—
Belmont Abbey College; Belmont, N.C. 28012	442	323	50	P/RC	1,750	1,750	1,730
Belmont College; Nashville, Tenn. 37203	817	924	89	P/B	2,500	2,500	850
Beloit College; Beloit, Wis. 53511	569[1]	486[1]	75	P	5,730	5,730	1,920
Bemidji State Univ. *See* Minnesota State College System							
Benedict College; Columbia, S.C. 29204	493	803	101	P	2,800	2,800	1,600
Benedictine College; Atchison, Kan. 66002	462	479	67	P/RC	3,700	3,700	1,910
Benjamin Franklin University; Washington, D.C. 20036	362	206	38	P	2,700	2,700	—
Bennett College; Greensboro, N.C. 27420	600	—	48	P/UM	2,800	2,800	1,350
Bennington College; Bennington, Vt. 05201	189	418	62	P	9,620	9,620	2,520
Bentley College*; Waltham, Mass. 02154	2,249	1,191	137	P	3,970	3,970	2,320
Berea College; Berea, Ky. 40404	691[1]	843[1]	117	P	—	—	1,575
Berklee College of Music; Boston, Mass. 02215	2,252[1]	375[1]	149	P	3,390	3,390	2,490
Berkshire Christian College; Lenox, Mass. 01240	65	63	11	P/AC	2,650	2,650	2,550
Bernard M. Baruch Coll. *See* New York, City Univ. of							
Berry College; Mount Berry, Ga. 30149	572[1]	805[1]	97[5]	P	2,625	3,300	1,605
Bethany Bible College; Santa Cruz, Calif. 95066	289[1]	268[1]	29	P/AG	2,410[3]	2,410[3]	2,203
Bethany College; Bethany, W. Va. 26032	448	352	61	P/DC	5,630	5,630	1,985
Bethany College*; Lindsborg, Kan. 67456	417	403	50	P/LCA	2,740	2,740	1,655
Bethany Nazarene College; Bethany, Okla. 73008	607[1]	757[1]	71	P/Naz	2,449	2,449	1,780
Bethel College; McKenzie, Tenn. 38201	207[1]	217[1]	25	CP	1,980	1,980	1,500
Bethel College; Mishawaka, Ind. 46545	204	212	25	P/MC	3,150	3,150	1,900
Bethel College*; North Newton, Kan. 67117	314	342	55	P/Men	3,012	3,012	1,856
Bethel College; St. Paul, Minn. 55112	841	1,059	110	P/B	4,550	4,550	1,890
Bethune–Cookman College; Daytona Beach, Fla. 32015	635	939	250	P/M	3,162	3,162	1,100
Biola College; La Mirada, Calif. 90639	1,238	1,256	151	P/ID	4,082	4,082	2,390

Institution and location	Enrollment		Faculty	Control	Tuition		Rm/Bd
	Male	Female			Res.	Nonres.	
Birmingham–Southern College; Birmingham, Ala. 35254	780[1]	754[1]	90	P/M	3,990	3,990	1,800
Biscayne College; Miami, Fla. 33054	1,167	1,291	57	P/RC	3,300	3,300	2,400
Bishop College*; Dallas, Tex. 75241	654	260	52	P/B	2,400	2,400	1,580
Blackburn College*; Carlinville, Ill. 62626	201	232	37	P/UP	2,880	2,880	1,075
Black Hills State College; Spearfish, S.D. 57783	955[1]	1,218[1]	92	S	816	1,692	1,300
Bloomfield College; Bloomfield, N.J. 07003	376	665	50	P/Pres	3,960	3,960	2,200
Bloomsburg State College; Bloomsburg, Pa. 17815	1,919	2,944	332	S	1,290	2,230	1,314
Bluefield College*; Bluefield, Va. 24605	190	164	22	P/B	1,615	1,615	1,515
Bluefield State College; Bluefield, W. Va. 24701	600	500	80	S	400	1,600	—
Blue Mountain College; Blue Mountain, Miss. 38610	80[1]	217[1]	27	P/SB	1,920	1,920	1,550
Bluffton College; Bluffton, Ohio 45817	324[1]	344[1]	44	P/Men	3,960	3,960	1,660
Boise State University; Boise, Idaho 83725	3,370	2,974	400	S	—	850	1,980
Boricua College*; New York, N.Y. 10032	358	511	n.a.	P	n.a.	n.a.	n.a.
Borromeo College of Ohio*; Wickliffe, Ohio 44092	75	—	14	RC	2,375	2,375	1,200
Boston Architectural Center; Boston, Mass. 02115	562		150[13]	P	1,240	1,240	—
Boston College; Chestnut Hill, Mass. 02167	4,713[1]	6,188[1]	558	P/RC	5,180	5,180	3,000
Boston Conservatory of Music; Boston, Mass. 02215	134[1]	286[1]	35	P	3,830	3,830	2,475
Boston State College*; Boston, Mass. 02115	2,662	2,569	284	S	600	2,100	—
Boston University; Boston, Mass. 02215	9,336[1]	10,116[1]	1,454	P	7,175[3]	7,175[3]	3,400[3]
Bowdoin College; Brunswick, Maine 04011	732	574	102	P	7,600[3]	7,600[3]	10,929[3]
Bowie State College*; Bowie, Md. 20715	1,243	1,636	109	S	870	1,825	1,590
Bowling Green State University; Bowling Green, Ohio 43403	6,394	8,176	724	S	1,473	3,228	1,641
Bradford College; Bradford, Mass. 01830	120[1]	191[1]	25	P	5,800[3]	5,800[3]	3,150[3]
Bradley University; Peoria, Ill. 61625	3,171[1]	2,471[1]	270	P	4,080	4,080	1,900
Brandeis University; Waltham, Mass. 02254	1,771[1]	1,680[1]	437	P	6,700	6,700	2,975
Brenau College; Gainesville, Ga. 30501	421	989	75	P	2,688	2,688	2,562
Brescia College; Owensboro, Ky. 42301	182[1]	306[1]	50	P	2,400	2,400	1,620
Briar Cliff College; Sioux City, Iowa 51104	301	543	60	P/RC	3,300[3]	3,300[3]	1,750[3]
Bridgeport, The University of; Bridgeport, Conn. 06601	3,400	3,600	400	P	5,090	5,090	2,600
Bridgeport Engineering Institute; Bridgeport, Conn. 06606	790	29	93	P	1,600	1,600	—
Bridgewater College; Bridgewater, Va. 22812	476[1]	490[1]	60	P	3,480	3,480	1,220
Bridgewater State College; Bridgewater, Mass. 02324	1,703[1]	2,763[1]	220	S	725	2,538	1,787
Brigham Young University; Provo, Utah 84602	14,216	11,134	1,213	P/LDS	1,100[14]	1,650[15]	1,640
Hawaii Campus; Laie, Hawaii 96762	865[1]	1,080[1]	98	P/LDS	1,050[14]	1,576[15]	1,800
Brooklyn Center. *See* Long Island Univ. Center							
Brooklyn College. *See* New York, City University of							
Brooklyn Law School; Brooklyn, N.Y. 11201	680	517	39	P	5,200	5,200	—
Brooks Institute of Photography; Santa Barbara, Calif. 93108	800		32	P	1,550	1,550	4,500[16]
Brown University; Providence, R.I. 02912	3,599[1]	3,150[1]	460	P	7,120	7,120	2,915
Bryan College; Dayton, Tenn. 37321	258[1]	309[1]	37	P/ID	2,750	2,750	2,450
Bryant College; Smithfield, R.I. 01569	1,444	1,048	150	P	6,670	6,670	2,375
Bryn Mawr College; Bryn Mawr, Pa. 19010	168[1]	1,682[1]	117	P	7,725[3]	7,725[3]	3,385[3]
Bucknell University; Lewisburg, Pa. 17837	1,667	1,484	240	P	7,350[3]	7,350[3]	2,000[3]
Buena Vista College; Storm Lake, Iowa 50588	579[1]	563[1]	55	P/Pres	4,270	4,270	1,700
Butler University; Indianapolis, Ind. 46208	953[1]	1,248[1]	163	P	4,440	4,440	3,000
Cabrini College; Radnor, Pa. 19087	119[1]	461[1]	34	P/RC	3,500	3,500	2,350
Caldwell College*; Caldwell, N.J. 07006	—	555	42	P/RC	3,100	3,100	1,800
California, University of; Berkeley, Calif. 94720:							
UC, Berkeley; Berkeley, Calif. 94720	17,567[1]	12,847[1]	1,895	S	1,248	4,395	3,000
UC, Davis; Davis, Calif. 95616	9,960	9,044	2,000	S	1,200	4,350	2,205
UC, Hastings College of Law*; San Francisco, Calif. 94102	898	572	n.a.	S	n.a.	n.a.	n.a.
UC, Irvine*; Irvine, Calif. 92717	4,942	4,748	377	S	768	2,400	2,434
UC, Los Angeles; Los Angeles, Calif. 90024	17,802[1]	15,633[1]	2,140	S	1,169	4,319	2,300
UC, Riverside; Riverside, Calif. 92521	2,259[1]	2,106[1]	318	S	1,180	4,330	2,340
UC, San Diego; La Jolla, Calif. 92093	7,129	5,070	850	S	1,196	4,346	3,300
UC, San Francisco; San Francisco, Calif. 94143	1,151	1,257	800	S	1,282	4,425	5,400
UC, Santa Barbara; Santa Barbara, Calif. 93106	7,808	7,658	748	S	816	3,696	2,310
UC, Santa Cruz; Santa Cruz, Calif. 95064	3,475[1]	3,386[1]	346	S	1,261	4,141	3,058
California Baptist College; Riverside, Calif. 92504	306	294	38	P/SB	2,730	2,730	1,590
California College of Arts and Crafts; Oakland, Calif. 94618	311	626	90	P	4,810[17]	4,810[17]	3,200
California College of Podiatric Medicine; San Francisco, Calif. 94115	327	61	32	P	7,890	7,890	—
California Institute of Integral Studies*; San Francisco, Calif. 94110	49	35	n.a.	P	n.a.	n.a.	n.a.
California Institute of Technology; Pasadena, Calif. 91125	1,467	221	386	P	6,249	6,249	2,110
California Institute of the Arts; Valencia, Calif. 91355	423	318	84	P	5,000	5,000	3,000

Institution and location	Enrollment		Faculty	Control	Tuition		Rm/Bd
	Male	Female			Res.	Nonres.	
California Lutheran College; Thousand Oaks, Calif. 91360	557	668	86	P/L	4,510	4,510	2,300
California Maritime Academy*; Vallejo, Calif. 94590	470	15	30	S	645	1,290	2,100
California Polytechnic State University*; San Luis Obispo, Calif. 93407[18]	9,269	6,594	820	S	n.a.	n.a.	n.a.
California School of Professional Psychology; San Francisco, Calif. 94123	427	463	45	P	6,900	6,900	4,450
California State College; California, Pa. 15419	2,226[1]	2,184[1]	287	S	1,250	2,190	1,550
California State College, Bakersfield; Bakersfield, Calif. 93309[18]	1,046[1]	1,504[1]	132	S	350	3,500	2,400
California State College, San Bernardino; San Bernardino, Calif. 92407[18]	1,533[1]	2,120[1]	185	S	334	3,484	2,100
California State Coll., Stanislaus; Turlock, Calif. 95380[18]	1,086	1,255	177	S	312	2,958	2,125
California State Polytechnic University, Pomona; Pomona, Calif. 91768[18]	9,794[1]	6,376[1]	800	S	336	3,171	2,424
California State University and Colleges, Consortium of the*; Long Beach, Calif. 90802	170		80	S	495	495	—
California State Univ., Chico; Chico, Calif. 95929[18]	6,925[1]	7,346[1]	666	S	266	2,534	2,148
California St. Univ., Dominguez Hills; Carson, Calif. 90747[18]	1,999	2,781	280	S	330	3,350	5,600
California State Univ., Fresno; Fresno, Calif. 93740[18]	5,619[1]	5,927[1]	710	S	426	([19])	2,250
California State Univ., Fullerton; Fullerton, Calif. 92634[18]	10,295	11,512	610	S	362	567	—
California State Univ., Hayward; Hayward, Calif. 94542[18]	4,698	5,955	480	S	345	3,150	
California State University, Long Beach; Long Beach, Calif. 90840[18]	7,933	8,904	871	S	297	3,347	2,300
California State University, Los Angeles; Los Angeles, Calif. 90032[18]	4,409	5,350	501	S	342	2,610	—
California State University, Northridge; Northridge, Calif. 91330[18]	6,588	7,459	921	S	280	2,835	6,000
California State University, Sacramento; Sacramento, Calif. 95819[18]	7,155[1]	7,546[1]	839	S	400[2]	([20])	2,200
California Western School of Law; San Diego, Calif. 92101	555	197	27	P	5,200	5,200	4,200
Calumet College; Whiting, Ind. 46394	207[1]	221[1]	32	P/RC	1,883	1,883	—
Calvary Bible College; Kansas City, Mo. 64147	202	149	20	P/ND	2,000	2,000	2,860
Calvin College; Grand Rapids, Mich. 49506	1,648	1,776	205	P/CR	1,610	1,430	1,720
Cameron University; Lawton, Okla. 73505	1,268	1,344	185	S	500	1,400	1,540
Campbellsville College; Campbellsville, Ky. 42718	257	307	44	P/B	2,440	2,440	1,770
Campbell University; Buie's Creek, N.C. 27506	1,123	983	123	P/SB	3,371	3,421	1,485
Canisius College; Buffalo, N.Y. 14208	1,651	1,161	155	P	4,100	4,100	2,300
Capital University; Columbus, Ohio 43209	1,021[1]	995[1]	124	P/AL	5,350	5,350	2,240
Capitol Institute of Technology; Kensington, Md. 20895	643	62	12	P	996	996	—
Cardinal Stritch College*; Milwaukee, Wis. 53217	98	382	52	P	3,200	3,200	1,800
Caribbean Center for Advanced Studies, Santurce, P.R. 00940	100	187	9	P	2,425	2,425	—
Caribbean University College; Bayamón, P.R. 00619	749[1]	1,448[1]	39	P	1,410	1,410	—
Carleton College; Northfield, Minn. 55057	931[1]	919[1]	138	P	5,704	5,704	2,225
Carlow College; Pittsburgh, Pa. 15213	29[1]	698[1]	52	P/RC	4,140	4,140	2,280
Carnegie-Mellon University*; Pittsburgh, Pa. 15213	3,381	1,444	432	P	5,400	5,400	2,530
Carroll College; Helena, Mont. 59625	457[1]	641[1]	75	P/RC	2,420	2,420	1,756
Carroll College; Waukesha, Wis. 53186	516	530	77	P/UP	5,330[3]	5,330[3]	1,890[3]
Carson-Newman College; Jefferson City, Tenn. 37760	810[1]	852[1]	95	P/SB	2,600	2,700	1,500
Carthage College, Kenosha, Wis. 53141	509[1]	550[1]	84	P/LCA	4,135	4,135	1,790
Case Western Reserve University; Cleveland, Ohio 44106	4,085	2,063	1,200	P	6,200[3]	6,200[3]	2,650
Castleton State College*; Castleton, Vt. 05701	560	703	88	S	1,120	2,760	2,100
Catawba College; Salisbury, N.C. 28144	480	389	66	P/UCC	3,135	3,135	1,550
Cathedral College of the Immaculate Conception; Douglaston, N.Y. 11362	104	—	19	RC	3,100	3,100	2,000
Catholic University of America, The; Washington, D.C. 20064	2,175[1]	2,248[1]	385	P/RC	5,750	5,750	3,250
Catholic University of Puerto Rico*; Ponce, P.R. 00731	3,048	5,524	n.a.	P/RC	n.a.	n.a.	n.a.
Cayey University College. *See* Puerto Rico, University of							
Cedar Crest College; Allentown, Pa. 18104	41	1,061	56	P/UCC	4,500	4,500	2,100
Cedarville College; Cedarville, Ohio 45314	716	860	68	P/B	2,688	2,688	1,935
Centenary College; Hackettstown, N.J. 07840	—	635	45	P	4,000	4,000	3,250
Centenary College of Louisiana; Shreveport, La. 71104	383	371	70	P/UM	3,040	3,040	1,240
Center for Early Education, College of The; Los Angeles, Calif. 90048	15	55	20[10]	P	2,400	2,400	—
Central Arkansas, University of; Conway, Ark. 72032	2,094[1]	2,962[1]	269	S	710	1,420	1,540
Central Baptist College; Conway, Ark. 72032	107	92	16	B	720	720	1,200
Central Bible College; Springfield, Mo. 65803	627	395	35	AG	1,536	1,536	1,650
Central Connecticut State College; New Britain, Conn. 06050	3,449[1]	3,142[1]	414	S	951	1,951	2,156
Central Florida, University of; Orlando, Fla. 32807	6,779[1]	6,314[1]	469	S	876	2,766	2,098
Central Methodist College; Fayette, Mo. 65248	319	332	60	P/M	3,790	3,790	1,760

Institution and location	Enrollment: Male	Enrollment: Female	Faculty	Control	Tuition: Res.	Tuition: Nonres.	Rm/Bd
Central Michigan University; Mt. Pleasant, Mich. 48859	6,818	8,374	582	S	1,145	2,840	1,998
Central Missouri State University; Warrensburg, Mo. 64093	4,902[1]	4,985[1]	450	S	630	1,305	1,650
Central New England College of Technology; Worcester, Mass. 01610	488	159	17	P	3,300	3,300	—
Central State University; Edmond, Okla. 73034	5,243[1]	6,761[1]	336	S	500[2]	1,200[2]	1,200
Central State University; Wilberforce, Ohio 45384	1,371	1,223	133	S	3,540	4,419	789
Central University of Iowa; Pella, Iowa 50219	660	779	77	P/RCA	4,740	4,740	1,860
Central Washington University; Ellensburg, Wash. 98926	2,864	2,760	319	S	867	2,910	2,000
Central Wesleyan College; Central, S.C. 29630	178[1]	198[1]	26	P/W	3,520	3,520	1,925
Centre College of Kentucky; Danville, Ky. 40422	394[1]	292[1]	63	P	5,100	5,100	2,275
Chadron State College; Chadron, Neb. 69337	636	661	90	S	690	1,200	1,450
Chaminade University of Honolulu; Honolulu, Hawaii 96816	422	387	75	P/RC	2,600	2,600	2,360
Chapman College; Orange, Calif. 92666	569[1]	592[1]	95	P	5,570	5,570	2,500
Charleston, The College of; Charleston, S.C. 29424	1,450[1]	2,258[1]	203	S	1,120	2,020	1,850
Charleston, The University of; Charleston, W. Va. 25304	811[1]	1,311[1]	105	P	3,350	4,000[21]	2,400
Chatham College; Pittsburgh, Pa. 15232	—	676	50	P	4,975	4,975	2,425
Chestnut Hill College; Philadelphia, Pa. 19118	—	630	42	P/RC	3,100	3,100	2,300
Cheyney State College; Cheyney, Pa. 19319	1,050	850	175	S	1,450	2,400	1,550
Chicago, The University of*; Chicago, Ill. 60637	1,800	900	1,020	P	5,100	5,100	3,000
Chicago College of Osteopathic Medicine; Chicago, Ill. 60615	309	82	140	P	8,200	11,000	—
Chicago Conservatory College*; Chicago, Ill. 60605	23	25	19	P	2,380	2,380	—
Chicago State University; Chicago, Ill. 60628	1,193[1]	2,113[1]	276	S	690	2,070	—
Christ College, Irvine; Irvine, Calif. 92715	105[1]	107[1]	19	P/L	2,580	2,580	975
Christian Brothers College; Memphis, Tenn. 38104	750[1]	516[1]	72	P/RC	3,390	3,390	2,563
Christopher Newport College; Newport News, Va. 23606	847[1]	1,084[1]	112	S	1,120	1,453	—
Cincinnati, University of; Cincinnati, Ohio 45221	12,334[1]	9,913[1]	1,699	S	1,404	3,369	2,316
Circleville Bible College; Circleville, Ohio 43113	105	80	14	CC	1,093	1,093	699
Citadel, The*; Charleston, S.C. 29409	2,568	817	200	S	125	385	1,420
City College (NYC). *See* New York, City University of							
City University; Bellevue, Wash. 98008	1,421	868	240	P	n.a.	n.a.	—
Claflin College*; Orangeburg, S.C. 29115	286	580	62	P/UM	1,850	1,850	1,125
Claremont Colleges:							
Claremont Graduate School*; Claremont, Calif. 91711	433	186	58	P	4,050	4,050	—
Claremont McKenna College; Claremont, Calif. 91711[22]	594	220	70	P	6,350	6,350	2,520
Claremont Men's College. *See* Claremont McKenna College							
Harvey Mudd College; Claremont, Calif. 91711	430[1]	77[1]	56	P	6,200	6,200	2,700
Pitzer College; Claremont, Calif. 91711	367[1]	434[1]	47	P	6,330	6,330	1,022
Pomona College*; Claremont, Calif. 91711	650	650	n.a.	P	6,250	6,250	2,650
Scripps College; Claremont, Calif. 91711	—	550	65	P	6,100	6,100	2,900
Clarion State College; Clarion, Pa. 16214	2,173	2,458	294	S	1,415	2,350	1,440
Clark College; Atlanta, Ga. 30314	543	1,288	128	P	1,450	1,450	1,750
Clarke College; Dubuque, Iowa 52001	76	470	55	P/RC	4,150	4,150	1,830
Clarkson College of Technology; Potsdam, N.Y. 13676	2,965[1]	710[1]	189	P	5,100	5,100	2,415
Clark University*; Worcester, Mass. 01610	998	963	135	P	6,300	6,300	2,100
Cleary College; Ypsilanti, Mich. 48197	62	185	21	P	2,520	2,520	—
Clemson University; Clemson, S.C. 29631	6,211	4,046	870	S	1,210	2,488	1,750
Cleveland Institute of Art, The; Cleveland, Ohio 44106	246[1]	260[1]	60	P	3,575	3,575	2,500
Cleveland Institute of Music; Cleveland, Ohio 44106	111	115	40	P	5,800[3]	5,800[3]	2,650
Cleveland State University; Cleveland, Ohio 44115	9,849	7,862	533	S	1,377	2,754	540[23]
Clinch Valley College. *See* Virginia, University of							
Coe College; Cedar Rapids, Iowa 52402	686[1]	762[1]	84	P/Pres	4,600	4,600	1,650
Cogswell College; San Francisco, Calif. 94108	432[1]	79[1]	22	P	650	1,050	2,880
Coker College; Hartsville, S.C. 29550	234		38	P	3,500	3,500	1,940
Colby College; Waterville, Me. 04901	867	785	130	P	7,290[3]	7,290[3]	2,800[3]
Colby–Sawyer College; New London, N.H. 03257	5	540	54	P	5,200	5,200	2,320
Colegio Universitario Metropolitano. *See* Ana G. Méndez Educational Foundation							
Colgate University; Hamilton, N.Y. 13346	1,450[1]	1,050[1]	165	P	6,345	6,345	2,425
College Misericordia; Dallas, Pa. 18612	139	699	60	P/RC	1,582	1,582	962
Colorado, University of; Boulder, Colo. 80302:							
U. of Colorado at Boulder; Boulder, Colo. 80309	12,068[1]	10,181[1]	1,151	S	868	3,886	2,062
U. of Colorado at Colorado Springs*; Colorado Springs, Colo. 80907	2,233	2,594	117	S	600	2,600	—
U. of Colorado at Denver; Denver, Colo. 80202	2,456	2,018	263	S	666	2,930	—
Colorado College, The; Colorado Springs, Colo. 80907	983	962	137	P	6,400[3]	6,400[3]	2,100[3]
Colorado School of Mines*; Golden, Colo. 80401	2,018	377	175	S	1,282	4,564	1,800
Colorado State University; Fort Collins, Colo. 80523	9,695[1]	8,956[1]	1,126	S	978	3,496	2,160
Colorado Technical College; Colorado Springs, Colo. 80907	458	92	43	P	2,475	2,475	—
Columbia Christian College; Portland, Ore. 97220	117	151	17	P	2,452	2,452	1,785
Columbia College; Chicago, Ill. 60605	1,369[2]	1,171[2]	39	P	3,000	3,000	—
Columbia College; Columbia, Mo. 65216	324	401	65	P	3,725	3,725	1,950

Institution and location	Enrollment		Faculty	Control	Tuition		Rm/Bd
	Male	Female			Res.	Nonres.	
Columbia College; Columbia, S.C. 29203	—	922[1]	67	P/M	3,700	3,700	2,100
Columbia College–Hollywood; Los Angeles, Calif. 90038	245	80	36[10]	P	2,640	2,640	—
Columbia Union College; Takoma Park, Md. 20912	296[2]	509[2]	60	P/SDA	4,000	4,000	2,190
Columbia University in the City of New York; New York, N.Y. 10027	9,770	4,829	1,623	P	6,700	6,700	3,280
Barnard College; New York, N.Y. 10027	—	2,390[1]	150	P	7,822	7,822	3,690
Teachers College; New York, N.Y. 10027	520[1]	1,092[1]	147	P	7,040	7,040	7,200
Columbus College; Columbus, Ga. 31993	1,084	1,320	202	S	650	1,700	—
Combs College of Music; Philadelphia, Pa. 19119	57	43	11	P	3,500	3,500	2,500
Concord College; Athens, W. Va. 24712	760[1]	967[1]	66	S	452	1,452	1,902
Concordia College; Ann Arbor, Mich. 48105	260	231	45	L	2,400	2,400	1,900
Concordia College; Bronxville, N.Y. 10708	192[2]	212[2]	33	P/L	3,160	3,160	2,335
Concordia College; Milwaukee, Wis. 53208	222[1]	248[1]	34	P/L	3,300	3,300	1,900
Concordia College; Moorhead, Minn. 56560	1,116[1]	1,428[1]	148	P/AL	4,760	4,760	1,645
Concordia College; River Forest, Ill. 60305	427[1]	847[1]	69	L	3,000	3,000	2,000
Concordia College; St. Paul, Minn. 55104	361[1]	340[1]	52	P/L	3,090	3,090	1,590
Concordia Teachers College, Seward, Neb. 68434	452[1]	614[1]	85	L	3,010	3,010	1,740
Connecticut, University of; Storrs, Conn. 06250	14,175[1]	13,157[1]	1,446	S	270	615	2,210
Connecticut College; New London, Conn. 06320	633[1]	1,033[1]	154	P	8,000	8,000	2,600
Conservatory of Music of Puerto Rico; Hato Rey, P.R. 00918	186	82	17	S	210	210	—
Converse College; Spartanburg, S.C. 29301	8[1]	762[1]	85	P	6,990[7]	6,990[7]	—
Cooper Union, The; New York, N.Y. 10003	628[1]	290[1]	58	P	—	—	—
Coppin State College; Baltimore, Md. 21216	648	1,631	105	S	524	999	—
Cornell College; Mt. Vernon, Iowa 52314	466[1]	434[1]	65	P	5,112	5,112	1,866
Cornell University[24]; Ithaca, N.Y. 14853	9,759	6,892	1,850[5]	P	7,950	7,950	3,050
Cornish Institute of Allied Arts; Seattle, Wash. 98102	191	296	23	P	3,750	3,750	—
Corpus Christi State University. *See* South Texas, University System of							
Covenant College; Lookout Mountain, Tenn./Ga. 37350	244[1]	253[1]	32	RP	3,990	3,990	2,240
Cranbrook Academy of Art; Bloomfield Hills, Mich. 48013	74	71	9	P	3,750	3,750	2,150
Creative Studies, Center for; Detroit, Mich. 48202	320[1]	253[1]	41	P	3,800	3,800	—
Creighton University; Omaha, Neb. 68178	2,986[1]	2,125[1]	471	P	4,070	4,070	2,100
Criswell Bible College; Dallas, Tex. 75201	285	15	16	P/SB	([25])	([25])	—
Culver-Stockton College; Canton, Mo. 63435	279[1]	272[1]	35	P	3,620	3,620	1,780
Cumberland College; Williamsburg, Ky. 40769	842[1]	1,199[1]	100	P/B	2,380	2,380	1,576
Curry College; Milton, Mass. 02186	413	434	65	P	5,750	5,750	3,300
Curtis Institute of Music, The*; Philadelphia, Pa. 19103	77	80	69	P	—	—	—
C.W. Post Center. *See* Long Island Univ. Center							
Daemen College; Amherst, N.Y. 14226	458	794	76	P	4,090	4,090	2,200
Dakota State College; Madison, S.D. 57042	481[1]	626[1]	56	S	1,025	1,900	1,490
Dakota Wesleyan University; Mitchell, S.D. 57301	209	322	38	UM	3,065	3,065	1,743
Dallas, University of; Irving, Tex. 75061	1,811	1,004	182	P/RC	3,300	3,300	2,180
Dallas Baptist College; Dallas, Tex. 75211	680	568	59	P/B	2,160	2,160	1,900
Dallas Bible College; Dallas, Tex. 75228	88	36	10	P	2,440	2,440	1,792
Dallas Christian College; Dallas, Tex. 75234	64[1]	48[1]	12	P/ChC	1,472	1,472	1,400
Dana College; Blair, Neb. 68008	299[1]	266[1]	37	P/AL	3,300	3,300	1,505
Daniel Webster College; Nashua, N.H. 03063	674[1]	362[1]	n.a.	P	4,990	4,990	2,600
Dartmouth College; Hanover, N.H. 03755	2,777	1,448	300	P	7,050	7,050	2,983
David Lipscomb College; Nashville, Tenn. 37203	1,019	1,126	100	P/CC	2,200	2,200	1,680
Davidson College; Davidson, N.C. 28036	915	481	115	P/PUS	5,310	5,310	2,190
Davis and Elkins College; Elkins, W. Va. 26241	532[2]	543[2]	56	P/Pres	4,370	4,370	2,110
Dayton, University of; Dayton, Ohio 45469	4,151	3,012	376	P/RC	3,700	3,700	2,044
Defiance College, The; Defiance, Ohio 43512	287	310	48	P	4,090	4,090	1,870
Delaware, University of; Newark, Del. 19711	6,342[1]	7,604[1]	864	S[26]	1,160	2,900	1,073
Delaware Law School of Widener University; Wilmington, Del. 19803	595[1]	218[1]	28	P	4,100	4,100	—
Delaware State College; Dover, Del. 19901	704	894	141	S	650	1,600	1,850
Delaware Valley College of Science and Agriculture; Doylestown, Pa. 18901	928[1]	442[1]	64	P	3,680	3,680	1,770
Delta State University*; Cleveland, Miss. 38733	1,011	1,183	157	S	554	1,329	912
Denison University; Granville, Ohio 43023	1,027	1,028	148	P	6,320	6,320	2,360
Denver, University of; Denver, Colo. 80208	2,200[1]	2,200[1]	472	P	5,790	5,790	2,700
DePaul University; Chicago, Ill. 60604	4,005[1]	3,458[1]	405	P	4,260[3]	4,260[3]	2,847[3]
Goodman School of Drama*; Chicago, Ill. 60614	100	100	20	P	3,600	3,600	2,000
DePauw University; Greencastle, Ind. 46135	1,086[1]	1,344[1]	150	P/M	6,250	6,250	2,600
Detroit, University of; Detroit, Mich. 48221	3,775[1]	2,600[1]	252	P/RC	4,230	4,230	2,150
Detroit Bible College. *See* William Tyndale College							
Detroit College of Business; Dearborn, Mich. 48126	496[1]	1,089[1]	21	P	2,541	2,541	—
Detroit College of Law; Detroit, Mich. 48201	607	260	29	P	3,450	3,450	—
Dickinson College; Carlisle, Pa. 17013	805	940	145	P	5,840	5,840	2,150

Institution and location	Enrollment		Faculty	Control	Tuition		Rm/Bd
	Male	Female			Res.	Nonres.	
Dickinson School of Law; Carlisle, Pa. 17013	333	185	19	P	3,600	3,600	1,930
Dickinson State College; Dickinson, N.D. 58601	407[1]	555[1]	75	S	708	1,269	1,353
Dillard University*; New Orleans, La. 70122	306	902	92	P	2,200	2,200	1,700
District of Columbia, University of the; Washington, D.C. 20008	5,869[1]	7,587[1]	581	Pub	364	1,614	—
Divine Word College; Epworth, Iowa 52045	89	—	32	P/RC	3,000	3,000	1,200
Doane College; Crete, Neb. 68333	276	336	45	P	3,750	3,750	1,450
Dr. Martin Luther College; New Ulm, Minn. 56073	215	529	70	P/EL	1,620	1,620	1,270
Dominican College of Blauvelt; Orangeburg, N.Y. 10962	221	486	55	P	([27])	([27])	—
Dominican College of San Rafael; San Rafael, Calif. 94901	142[1]	434[1]	65	P/RC	4,450[3]	4,450[3]	3,500[3]
Dordt College; Sioux Center, Iowa 51250	503[1]	593[1]	68	P/CR	3,400	3,400	1,410
Dowling College; Oakdale, N.Y. 11769	742[1]	710[1]	70	P	3,700	3,700	2,100
Drake University; Des Moines, Iowa 50311	2,283[1]	2,171[1]	277	P/Ind	5,230	5,230	2,380
Drew University*; Madison, N.J. 07940	779	853	130	P/UM	4,700	4,700	1,820
Drexel University; Philadelphia, Pa. 19104	5,669	2,448	330	P	4,011	4,011	1,290
Dropsie College for Hebrew & Cognate Learning, The; Philadelphia, Pa. 19132	45	1	5	P	4,000	4,000	—
Drury College; Springfield, Mo. 65802	544	601	70	P	3,150	3,150	1,630
Dubuque, University of; Dubuque, Iowa 52001	580[1]	514[1]	55	P	4,200	4,200	1,700
Duke University; Durham, N.C. 27706	5,322[1]	3,737[1]	1,451	P	6,210	6,210	3,211
Duquesne University; Pittsburgh, Pa. 15282	1,921	2,237	400	P/RC	4,175	4,175	2,118
Dyke College; Cleveland, Ohio 44114	462[2]	937[2]	n.a.	P	2,200	2,200	—
D'Youville College; Buffalo, N.Y. 14201	207[1]	1,195[1]	100	P/RC	3,440	3,440	1,950
Earlham College*; Richmond, Ind. 47374	453	524	78	P/SOF	5,658	5,658	1,950
East Carolina Univ. *See* North Carolina, Univ. System of							
East Central Oklahoma State University; Ada, Okla. 74820	1,189	1,583	168	S	400	800	1,400
Eastern College; St. Davids, Pa. 19087	167	327	36	P/AB	4,470	4,470	1,880
Eastern Connecticut State College; Willimantic, Conn. 06226	1,114[1]	1,266[1]	113	S	484	1,134	2,146
Eastern Illinois University; Charleston, Ill. 61920	4,423[1]	5,593[1]	460	S	1,123	2,671	1,930
Eastern Kentucky University; Richmond, Ky. 40475	4,611[1]	5,728[1]	607	S	626	1,780	1,610
Eastern Mennonite College; Harrisonburg, Va. 22801	352	582	74	P/Men	3,831	3,831	1,785
Eastern Michigan University; Ypsilanti, Mich. 48197	8,609	11,394	624	S	1,125	2,790	2,030
Eastern Montana College; Billings, Mont. 59101	1,033[1]	1,690[1]	144	S	624	1,632	2,000
Eastern Nazarene College; Quincy, Mass. 02170	322[1]	416[1]	62	P/Naz	3,090	3,090	2,050
Eastern New Mexico University*; Portales, N.M. 88130	1,394	1,462	150	S	678	1,792	1,500
Eastern Oregon State College; La Grande, Ore. 97850	803[1]	990[1]	138	S	1,200	1,200	2,100
Eastern Virginia Medical School; Norfolk, Va. 23507	186	102	135	P	8,000	10,000	5,100
Eastern Washington University; Cheney, Wash. 99004	3,681	3,674	350	S	867	1,940	1,998
East Stroudsburg State College; East Stroudsburg, Pa. 18301	1,543[1]	1,806[1]	220	S	1,600[2]	2,710[2]	1,674
East Tennessee State University[28]; Johnson City, Tenn. 37614	2,945[1]	3,594[1]	404	S	714	2,244	1,498
East Texas Baptist College; Marshall, Tex. 75670	345	320	44	P/SB	2,310	2,310	1,922
East Texas State University; Commerce, Tex. 75428	3,794	4,081	316	S	440	1,540	1,940
East Texas State University at Texarkana; Texarkana, Tex. 75501	401	680	35	S	360	1,120	—
Eckerd College; St. Petersburg, Fla. 33733	504	486	69	P/Pres	5,495	5,495	2,360
Edgewood College; Madison, Wis. 53711	75	346	53	P/RC	3,100	3,100	1,660
Edinboro State College; Edinboro, Pa. 16444	2,010[1]	2,545[1]	353	S	1,400	2,450	1,300
Edward Waters College; Jacksonville, Fla. 32209	274[2]	593[2]	39	P/AME	2,100	2,100	7,000
Elizabeth City State University. *See* North Carolina, University System of							
Elizabethtown College; Elizabethtown, Pa. 17022	543[1]	844[1]	100	P/CB	4,740	4,740	2,300
Elmhurst College; Elmhurst, Ill. 60126	1,484	2,125	100	P/UCC	3,988	3,988	2,060
Elmira College; Elmira, N.Y. 14901	446[1]	722[1]	67	P	5,325	5,325	2,200
Elon College; Elon College, N.C. 27244	1,411[1]	1,169[1]	91	P	2,450	2,450	1,540
Embry–Riddle Aeronautical University; Daytona Beach, Fla. 32014	4,294	267	275	P	2,900	2,900	2,350
Prescott Campus; Prescott, Ariz. 86301	679	86	74	P	2,900	2,900	2,350
Emerson College; Boston, Mass. 02116	710[1]	937[1]	85	P	4,950	4,950	3,350
Emmanuel College; Boston, Mass. 02115	18[1]	1,048[1]	65	P/RC	4,700	4,700	2,844
Emory and Henry College; Emory, Va. 24327	426[1]	363[1]	60	P/UM	3,306	3,306	1,887
Emory University; Atlanta, Ga. 30322	4,528[1]	3,636[1]	940	P/M	6,200[3]	6,200[3]	2,680
Emporia State University; Emporia, Kan. 66801	1,956[1]	2,330[1]	250	S	718	1,512	2,080
Erskine College; Due West, S.C. 29639	309[1]	309[1]	48	P/RP	3,400	3,400	1,650
Eureka College; Eureka, Ill. 61530	198[1]	194[1]	30	P/DC	4,250[3]	4,250[3]	2,550[3]
Evangel College; Springfield, Mo. 65802	759[1]	1,017[1]	77	AG	2,174	2,174	1,740
Evansville, University of; Evansville, Ind. 47702	1,253[1]	1,711[1]	201	P/UM	4,188	4,188	2,127
Evergreen State College, The; Olympia, Wash. 98505	1,288[1]	1,517[1]	206	S	867	2,910	1,000[23]

Institution and location	Enrollment		Faculty	Control	Tuition		
	Male	Female			Res.	Nonres.	Rm/Bd
Fairfield University; Fairfield, Conn. 06430	1,381[1]	1,450[1]	147	P/RC	5,025[3]	5,025[3]	2,815
Fairleigh Dickinson University: Madison, N.J. 07940; Rutherford, N.J. 07070; Teaneck, N.J. 07666	3,520[1]	3,055[1]	534	P	4,576	4,576	2,633
Fairmont State College; Fairmont, W. Va. 26554	1,470[1]	1,845[1]	147	S	450	1,450	1,954
Faith Baptist Bible College, Ankeny, Iowa 50021	194	211	20	P/B	2,380	2,380	1,940
Fashion Institute of Technology[29]; New York, N.Y. 10001	593	2,971	180	S	900	1,800	2,350
Fayetteville State U. *See* North Carolina, U. System of							
Felician College; Lodi, N.J. 07644	23	653	52	P	2,250	2,250	—
Ferris State College; Big Rapids, Mich. 49307	6,665[1]	4,596[1]	500	S	1,464	3,171	2,190
Ferrum College; Ferrum, Va. 24088	871	534	75	P/M	3,440	3,440	1,550
Findlay College; Findlay, Ohio 45840	433[1]	392[1]	63	P/CG	3,992	3,992	1,800
Fisk University; Nashville, Tenn. 37203	254	532	67	P	2,275	2,275	1,042
Fitchburg State College; Fitchburg, Mass. 01420	1,396[1]	2,260[1]	225	S	725	2,538	1,928
Flagler College; St. Augustine, Fla. 32084	344	517	35	P	2,700[3]	2,700[3]	1,700[3]
Florida, University of; Gainesville, Fla. 32611	16,412[1]	11,455[1]	2,945	S	841	2,401	2,674
Florida A&M University; Tallahassee; Fla. 32307	2,435[1]	2,529[1]	389	S	787	2,347	1,440
Florida Atlantic University; Boca Raton, Fla. 33431	1,504	1,428	326	S	825	2,635	1,950
Florida Institute of Technology; Melbourne, Fla. 32901	4,767	1,589	209	P	3,519	3,519	1,905
Florida International University; Miami, Fla. 33199	1,956[1]	1,918[1]	346	S	750	1,980	—
Florida Memorial College; Miami, Fla. 33054	419	508	44	P/B	4,060	4,060	1,620
Florida Southern College; Lakeland, Fla. 33802	847	1,013	102	P/UM	2,430	2,430	1,850
Florida State University; Tallahassee, Fla. 32306	10,533[1]	11,830[1]	1,100	S	803	2,363	1,998
Fontbonne College; St. Louis, Mo. 63105	102[1]	499[1]	62	P/RC	4,100	4,100	2,100
Fordham University; Bronx, N.Y. 10458	8,000[1]	7,000[1]	480	P	4,950	4,950	3,000
Fort Hays State University; Hays, Kan. 67601	1,924[1]	1,984[1]	243	S	795	1,590	1,812
Fort Lauderdale College; Fort Lauderdale, Fla. 33301	598[1]	493[1]	28	P	1,822	1,822	4,500
Fort Lewis College; Durango, Colo. 81301	1,759[1]	1,382[1]	130	S	598	2,632	1,628
Fort Valley State College, The; Fort Valley, Ga. 31030	678[1]	790[1]	130	S	756	1,806	1,500
Fort Wayne Bible College; Fort Wayne, Ind. 46807	197	198	28	MC	2,670	2,670	1,500
Framingham State College; Framingham, Mass. 01701	1,026	2,045	161	S	845	2,792	1,743
Francis Marion College; Florence, S.C. 29501	931[1]	963[1]	103	S	805	1,570	2,100
Franklin and Marshall College; Lancaster, Pa. 17604	1,104	883	126	P	5,650	5,650	2,050
Franklin College of Indiana; Franklin, Ind. 46131	292[1]	310[1]	49	P/AB	4,730	4,730	2,120
Franklin Pierce College; Rindge, N.H. 03461	521	349	60	P	7,050	7,050	2,275
Franklin University; Columbus, Ohio 43215	879[1]	689[1]	48	P	—	—	—
Freed–Hardeman College; Henderson, Tenn. 38340	608	753	92	P	2,700	2,700	1,900
Free Will Baptist Bible College; Nashville, Tenn. 37205	220	197	29	P/FWB	1,560	1,560	1,830
Fresno Pacific College; Fresno, Calif. 93702	357[1]	464[1]	28	P/MB	3,600	3,600	2,085
Friends Bible College; Haviland, Kan. 67059	52	60	9	P/SOF	2,800	2,800	1,400
Friends University; Wichita, Kan. 67213	360	325	50	P/SOF	3,450	3,450	1,650
Frostburg State College; Frostburg, Md. 21532	1,381[1]	1,486[1]	201	S	870	1,820	1,830
Furman University; Greenville, S.C. 29613	1,260	1,225	150	SB	3,792	3,792	2,456
Gallaudet College; Washington, D.C. 20002	567	884	210	P	984	984	2,270
Gannon University; Erie, Pa. 16541	1,520[1]	1,095[1]	130	P/RC	3,400	3,400	1,750
Gardner–Webb College; Boiling Springs, N.C. 28017	765[1]	821[1]	79	SB	2,960	2,960	1,610
General Motors Institute; Flint, Mich. 48502	1,614[1]	775[1]	143	P	1,800	1,800	1,650
Geneva College; Beaver Falls, Pa. 15010	642	475	58	P/RP	2,000	2,000	1,065
George Fox College; Newberg, Ore. 97132	287[1]	420[1]	43	P/SOF	4,800	4,800	2,140
George Mason University; Fairfax, Va. 22030	2,990[1]	3,667[1]	462	S	1,176	2,232	3,292
Georgetown College; Georgetown, Ky. 40324	473	693	67	P/SB	2,960	2,960	1,950
Georgetown University; Washington, D.C. 20057	5,433[1]	4,237[1]	940	P/RC	6,830	6,830	2,800
George Washington University, The; Washington, D.C. 20052	4,931[1]	4,064[1]	1,099	P	4,900	4,900	3,400
George Williams College; Downers Grove, Ill. 60515	412	760	62	P	3,975	3,975	1,866
Georgia, University of; Athens, Ga. 30602	10,953	10,881	2,000	S	369[30]	939[30]	734[30]
Georgia College; Milledgeville, Ga. 31061	1,600[1]	1,800[1]	150	S	687	1,737	1,380
Georgia Institute of Technology; Atlanta, Ga. 30332	7,279[2]	1,883[2]	516	S	975	2,790	2,160
Southern Technical Institute*; Marietta, Ga. 30060	2,360	223	101	S	633	1,587	2,350
Georgian Court College; Lakewood, N.J. 08701	64	807	65	P/RC	2,700	2,700	1,700
Georgia Southern College; Statesboro, Ga. 30460	2,830	3,506	328	S	645	1,935	1,590
Georgia Southwestern College; Americus, Ga. 31709	638[1]	1,045[1]	110	S	693	1,743	1,515
Georgia State University; Atlanta, Ga. 30303	9,158[1]	11,811[1]	731	S	915	2,940	—
Germain School of Photography*; New York, N.Y. 10007	110	59	n.a.	P	n.a.	n.a.	n.a.
Gettysburg College; Gettysburg, Pa. 17325	963[1]	978[1]	132	P	5,300	5,300	1,900
Glassboro State College; Glassboro, N.J. 08028	2,483	3,238	400	S	1,038	1,638	1,900
Glenville State College; Glenville, W. Va. 26351	590	668	81	S	464	1,464	2,000
Goddard College[31]; Plainfield, Vt. 05667	47	67	7	P	6,700	6,700	2,000
Golden Gate University; San Francisco, Calif. 94105	1,025[1]	779[1]	55	P	2,250	2,250	—
Goldey Beacom College; Wilmington, Del. 19808	157[1]	693[1]	20	P	2,876[2]	2,876[2]	1,600
Gonzaga University; Spokane, Wash. 99258	1,711	1,047	156	P/RC	4,700[3]	4,700[3]	2,420

Institution and location	Enrollment Male	Enrollment Female	Faculty	Control	Tuition Res.	Tuition Nonres.	Rm/Bd
Goodman School of Drama. *See* DePaul University							
Gordon College; Wenham, Mass. 01984	444	562	54	P	n.a.	n.a.	7,596[3]
Goshen College; Goshen, Ind. 46526	454[1]	626[1]	75	P/Men	4,165	4,165	1,925
Goucher College; Towson, Baltimore, Md. 21204	1[1]	945[1]	74	P	6,150	6,150	3,150
Governors State University; Park Forest South, Ill. 60466	363[1]	405[1]	156	S	822[3]	2,466[3]	—
Grace Bible College; Grand Rapids, Mich. 49509	68[1]	71[1]	9	P/GGF	1,380	1,380	2,000
Grace College; Winona Lake, Ind. 46590	321	401	40	P/FGB	3,072	3,072	1,986
Grace College of the Bible; Omaha, Neb. 68108	184	171	23	P/ID	2,340	2,340	1,750
Graceland College; Lamoni, Iowa 50140	495	546	72	P	3,665	3,665	1,615
Graduate School and University Center (NYC). *See* New York, City University of							
Grambling State University; Grambling, La. 71245	1,691[1]	1,710[1]	229	S	420	420	1,664
Grand Canyon College; Phoenix, Ariz. 85017	593	634	37	P/SB	2,080	2,080	1,880
Grand Rapids Baptist College; Grand Rapids, Mich. 49505	359[1]	399[1]	40	P/B	2,850	2,850	1,950
Grand Valley State Colleges; Allendale, Mich. 49401	3,012	3,177	223	S	1,200	2,760	2,290
Grand View College; Des Moines, Iowa 50316	542[1]	754[1]	50	P/LCA	3,390	3,390	1,700
Grantham College of Engineering; Los Angeles, Calif. 90034	741	7	n.a.	P	700	700	—
Gratz College; Philadelphia, Pa. 19141	37[1]	77[1]	6	P/J	525[3]	525[3]	—
Great Falls, College of; Great Falls, Mont. 59405	226	224	35	P/RC	2,400	2,400	1,250
Great Lakes Bible College; Lansing, Mich. 48901	80	69	13	P/CC	1,680	1,680	1,990
Green Mountain College; Poultney, Vt. 05764	113	297	27	P	4,475	4,475	2,900
Greensboro College; Greensboro, N.C. 27401	203	413	32	P/M	2,750	2,750	1,800
Greenville College; Greenville, Ill. 62246	314[1]	407[1]	46	P/FM	4,290	4,290	2,060
Grinnell College; Grinnell, Iowa 50112	618	566	105	P	6,522	6,522	2,000
Grove City College; Grove City, Pa. 16127	1,156[1]	1,074[1]	98	P	2,620	2,620	1,650
Guam, University of; Mangilao, Guam 96913	666	827	183	S	450	810	2,200
Guilford College; Greensboro, N.C. 27410	708[1]	596[1]	83	P/SOF	4,320	4,320	2,030
Gulf–Coast Bible College; Houston, Tex. 77270	190	134	19	P/CG	2,054	2,054	1,656
Gustavus Adolphus College; St. Peter, Minn. 56082	999[1]	1,315[1]	174	P/LCA	535	535	1,900
Gwynedd–Mercy College; Gwynedd Valley, Pa. 19437	82	749	122	RC	3,000	3,000	2,100
Hahnemann Medical College; Philadelphia, Pa. 19102	808	1,016	392	P	2,930	2,930	2,250
Hamilton College; Clinton, N.Y. 13323	942	646	137	P	7,950	7,950	2,650
Hamline University; St. Paul, Minn. 55104	990[1]	750[1]	109	P/UM	5,350	5,350	2,140
Hampden–Sydney College; Hampden–Sydney, Va. 23943	706	1	54	P	5,040	5,040	1,575
Hampshire College; Amherst, Mass. 01002	555	600	81	P	7,450	7,450	3,315
Hampton Institute; Hampton, Va. 23668	1,328	2,058	250	P	2,900	2,900	1,500
Hannibal–LaGrange College; Hannibal, Mo. 63401	164[1]	149[1]	22	B	2,200	2,200	1,320
Hanover College; Hanover, Ind. 47243	488[1]	492[1]	71	P/Pres	3,090	3,090	1,690
Harding University; Searcy, Ark. 72143	1,249	1,369	195	P	2,475	2,475	800
Hardin–Simmons University; Abilene, Tex. 79698	654[1]	704[1]	94	P/SB	2,760[3]	2,760[3]	1,865[3]
Harris–Stowe State College; St. Louis, Mo. 63103	249[1]	535[1]	32	S	450	855	—
Hartford, University of; West Hartford, Conn. 06117	2,527	2,117	328	P	6,000	6,000	3,610
Hartford Graduate Center, The*; Hartford, Conn. 06120	1,108	264	18	P	n.a.	n.a.	—
Hartwick College; Oneonta, N.Y. 13820	569	801	102	P	5,550	5,550	2,250
Harvard University; Cambridge, Mass. 02138	10,152[1]	5,901[1]	980	P	8,195	8,195	3,905
Radcliffe College; Cambridge, Mass. 02167	—	2,377	—	P	8,195	8,195	n.a.
Harvey Mudd College. *See* Claremont Colleges							
Hastings College; Hastings, Neb. 68901	332[1]	466[1]	56	P/Pres	3,200	3,200	1,760
Haverford College; Haverford, Pa. 19041	847	216	81	P	7,150	7,150	2,510
Hawaii, University of, at Hilo; Hilo, Hawaii 96720[32]	1,248	1,243	170	S	300	900	1,440
Hawaii, University of, at Manoa; Honolulu, Hawaii 96822[32]	7,002[1]	7,764[1]	1,149	S	450	1,125	1,541
Hawaii Loa College; Kaneohe, Hawaii 96744	146	133	25	P	3,200[3]	3,200[3]	2,700
Hawaii Pacific College; Honolulu, Hawaii 96813	1,511[1]	881[1]	28	P	2,300	2,300	—
Health Sciences, University of/College of Osteopathic Medicine; Kansas City, Mo. 64124	525	95	50	P	10,500	10,500	4,500
Health Sciences, University of—The Chicago Medical School*; North Chicago, Ill. 60664	428	201	n.a.	P	n.a.	n.a.	n.a.
Hebrew College; Brookline, Mass. 02146	58[1]	87[1]	12	P	810	810	—
Heidelberg College; Tiffin, Ohio 44883	384[1]	307[1]	51	P/UCC	4,890	4,890	2,000
Henderson State University; Arkadelphia, Ark. 71923	1,100[1]	1,400[1]	180	S	720	1,440	1,400
Hendrix College; Conway, Ark. 72032	514	503	60	P	2,700	2,700	1,350
Herbert H. Lehman College. *See* New York, City University of							
High Point College; High Point, N.C. 27262	616[1]	636[1]	53	P/UM	3,000	3,000	1,507
Hillsdale College; Hillsdale, Mich. 49242	494	459	56	P	4,700	4,700	2,380
Hiram College; Hiram, Ohio 44234	506	444	77	P	5,237	5,237	1,730
Hobart and William Smith Colleges; Geneva, N.Y. 14456	1,070	711	132	P	7,200[3]	7,200[3]	2,730[3]
Hofstra University; Hempstead, N.Y. 11550	3,487[1]	2,959[1]	409	P	4,000	4,000	2,380
Hollins College; Hollins College, Va. 24020	13	824	70	P	6,100	6,100	2,650
Holy Apostles College*; Cromwell, Conn. 06416	86	2	n.a.	P/RC	1,800	1,800	2,000

Institution and location	Enrollment Male	Female	Faculty	Control	Tuition Res.	Nonres.	Rm/Bd
Holy Cross, College of the; Worcester, Mass. 01610	1,312[1]	1,182[1]	180	P/RC	5,400	5,400	2,650
Holy Family College*; Mission San Jose, Calif. 94538	—	66	n.a.	P/RC	n.a.	n.a.	n.a.
Holy Family College; Philadelphia, Pa. 19114	64	476	45	P	3,300	3,300	—
Holy Names College; Oakland, Calif. 94619	141	207	45	P/RC	1,194	1,194	1,106
Holy Redeemer College; Waterford, Wis. 53185	51[2]	1[2]	14	P/RC	2,100	2,100	1,700
Hood College; Frederick, Md. 21701	17	793	109	P	4,750	4,750	2,445
Hope College; Holland, Mich. 49423	1,077[2]	1,119[2]	140	P/RCA	4,490	4,490	2,080
Houghton College; Houghton, N.Y. 14744	524[1]	722[1]	75	P/W	3,900	3,900	1,850
Houston, University of, System:							
Central Campus; Houston, Tex. 77004	15,517[1]	12,778[1]	1,044	S	400	1,260	2,750
Downtown College; Houston, Tex. 77002	3,022	2,575	124	S	400	1,260	2,550
U. of Houston at Clear Lake City; Houston, Tex. 77058	673	990	185	S	420	1,280	—
U. of Houston at Victoria; Victoria, Tex. 77901	37	95	24	S	348	1,692	—
Houston Baptist University; Houston, Tex. 77074	664	810	116	P/SB	3,300	3,300	1,800
Howard Payne University; Brownwood, Tex. 76801	464[1]	472[1]	81	P/SB	2,100	2,100	1,820
Howard University; Washington, D.C. 20059	4,402	4,824	1,215	P	2,000	2,000	2,467
Humacao University College. *See* Puerto Rico, Univ. of							
Humboldt State University; Arcata, Calif. 95521[18]	3,700	3,700	n.a.	S	310	([33])	3,000
Hunter College. *See* New York, City University of							
Huntingdon College; Montgomery, Ala. 36106	234[1]	269[1]	36	P/UM	2,650[3]	2,650[3]	2,100[3]
Huntington College; Huntington, Ind. 46750	198[1]	225[1]	34	BC	3,600	3,600	1,850
Huron College; Huron, S.D. 57350	145	186	29	P/Pres	3,270	3,270	2,060
Husson College; Bangor, Me. 04401	346	354	34	P	3,750	3,750	2,240
Huston–Tillotson College; Austin, Tex. 78702	365	239	40	UM	2,244	2,244	2,050
Idaho, The College of; Caldwell, Idaho 83605	261[1]	264[1]	42	P	4,500	4,500	2,165
Idaho, University of; Moscow, Idaho 83843	4,417[1]	2,536[1]	390	S	701	2,501	1,850
Idaho State University; Pocatello, Idaho 83209	2,586	1,894	862	S	680	2,380	1,840
Illinois, University of; Urbana, Ill. 61801:							
Univ. of Illinois at Chicago Circle; Chicago, Ill. 60680	8,562[1]	6,635[1]	1,054	S	1,080	2,574	—
Univ. of Illinois Medical Center; Chicago, Ill. 60612	2,622	2,171	236	S	822	2,466	3,475
Univ. of Illinois at Urbana–Champaign, Urbana, Ill. 61801	20,425[1]	14,727[1]	2,940	S	1,074	2,570	2,426
Illinois Benedictine College; Lisle, Ill. 60532	551	458	66	P/RC	3,745	3,745	2,050
Illinois College; Jacksonville, Ill. 62650	407[1]	341[1]	45	P/UCC	3,075	3,075	1,915
Illinois College of Optometry; Chicago, Ill. 60616	504[2]	99[2]	33	P	5,655	5,655	2,780
Illinois College of Podiatric Medicine*; Chicago, Ill. 60610	560	63	25	P	6,600	6,600	7,500
Illinois Institute of Technology; Chicago, Ill. 60616	3,120[1]	849[1]	303	P	4,970	4,970	2,376
Illinois State University; Normal, Ill 61761	7,694[1]	9,715[1]	955	S	780[3]	2,340[3]	2,088[3]
Illinois Wesleyan University; Bloomington, Ill. 61701	729[1]	956[1]	125	P	5,295	5,295	2,280
Immaculata College; Immaculata, Pa. 19345	—	581	52	P/RC	2,950[3]	2,950[3]	2,200[3]
Incarnate Word College; San Antonio, Tex. 78209	219	816	72	P/RC	2,208	2,208	1,466
Indiana Central University; Indianapolis, Ind. 46227	414	690	105	P	4,100[3]	4,100[3]	2,050[3]
Indiana Institute of Technology; Fort Wayne, Ind. 46803	426	103	28	P	3,510	3,510	2,220
Indiana State University; Terre Haute, Ind. 47809	4,507	4,162	636	S	1,147	2,635	1,581
Evansville Campus; Evansville, Ind. 47712	1,065[1]	1,105[1]	100	S	1,116	2,404	—
Indiana University; Bloomington, Ind. 47405	13,632	13,366	1,371	S	924	2,496	1,820
Indiana Univ. at Kokomo*; Kokomo, Ind. 46901	500	554	64	Mun	780	1,770	—
Indiana Univ.–Bloomington*; Bloomington, Ind. 47401	13,776	12,635	n.a.	S	n.a.	n.a.	n.a.
Indiana Univ. at South Bend; South Bend, Ind. 46615	1,273	1,650	200	S	975	2,280	—
Indiana University Northwest*; Gary, Ind. 46408	501	904	115	S	780	1,020	—
I.U.–Purdue U. at Fort Wayne; Fort Wayne, Ind. 46805	1,899	1,714	300	S	975	2,300	—
I.U.–Purdue U. at Indianapolis; Indianapolis, Ind. 46202	7,216	6,924	1,208	S	1,207	3,172	—
Indiana University Southeast; New Albany, Ind. 47150	891[1]	1,104[1]	92	S	1,005	2,310	—
Indiana University of Pennsylvania; Indiana, Pa. 15705	4,596[1]	6,261[1]	650	S	1,250	2,190	1,520
Instituto Tecnológico*; Monterrey, Mexico	1,879	6,521	223	P	2,000	2,000	2,000
Insurance, The College of; New York, N.Y. 10038	865[1]	821[1]	25	P	4,200	4,200	3,000
Inter American University of Puerto Rico; San Juan, P.R. 00936	10,014	15,337	588	P	1,395	1,395	1,150[34]
Arecibo Regional College; Arecibo, P.R. 00612	1,454	2,049	54	P	n.a.	n.a.	—
Metropolitan Campus, Hato Rey, P.R. 00919	5,640[1]	8,778[1]	237	P	540	540	—
San Germán Campus*; San Germán, P.R. 00753	2,094	3,089	145	P	1,500	1,500	1,240
School of Law; Santurce, P.R. 00924	499	338	23	P	3,300	3,300	—
International Correspondence Institute; Brussels, Belgium	5,745		—	P	([35])	([35])	—
International Institute of the Americas*; Hato Rey, P.R. 00917	1,816	2,117	n.a.	P	n.a.	n.a.	n.a.
International Training, The School for; Brattleboro, Vt. 05301	108[1]	213[1]	34	P	5,830	5,830	3,217

Institution and location	Enrollment Male	Enrollment Female	Faculty	Control	Tuition Res.	Tuition Nonres.	Rm/Bd
Iona College; New Rochelle, N.Y. 10801	2,259[1]	1,529[1]	360	P	4,200	4,200	2,700
Iowa, University of; Iowa City, Iowa 52242	11,267[1]	9,803[1]	1,550	S	950	2,350	1,834
Iowa State University; Ames, Iowa 50011	14,814[1]	9,388[1]	1,833	S	1,040	2,580	1,762
Iowa Wesleyan College; Mount Pleasant, Iowa 52641	242[1]	327[1]	45	P/UM	4,625	4,625	1,670
Ithaca College; Ithaca, N.Y. 14850	2,127[1]	2,735[1]	306	P	5,000	5,000	2,276
Jackson College for Women. *See* Tufts University							
Jackson State University*; Jackson, Miss. 39217	1,928	2,676	307	S	750	850	1,266
Jacksonville State University; Jacksonville, Ala. 36265	2,355[2]	2,554[2]	264	S	700	1,050	1,390
Jacksonville University; Jacksonville, Fla. 32211	1,404[1]	1,192[1]	107	P	3,400	3,400	1,290
James Madison University; Harrisonburg, Va. 22807	3,561[1]	4,227[1]	444	S	1,506	2,346	2,164
Jamestown College; Jamestown, N.D. 58401	275[2]	250[2]	37	P	3,820	3,820	1,575
Jarvis Christian College; Hawkins, Tex. 75765	214	217	50	P/DC	2,250	2,250	1,750
Jersey City State College; Jersey City, N.J. 07305	2,028	2,229	275	S	1,015	1,715	—
John Brown University; Siloam Springs, Ark. 72761	383[1]	320[1]	46	P	2,500	2,500	4,400
John Carroll University; Cleveland, Ohio 44118	1,363[1]	1,193[1]	177	P/RC	4,000	4,000	2,250
John F. Kennedy University; Orinda, Calif. 94563	252[1]	357[1]	3	P	2,076	2,076	—
John Jay College of Criminal Justice. *See* New York, City University of							
John Marshall Law School, The; Chicago, Ill. 60604	665[1]	242[1]	47	P	4,500	4,500	5,000
Johns Hopkins University, The; Baltimore, Md. 21218	3,240[1]	1,768[1]	1,386	P	6,700[3]	6,700[3]	2,900[3]
Johnson and Wales College; Providence, R.I. 02903	1,700[1]	1,900[1]	135	P	3,825	3,825	2,100
Johnson Bible College; Knoxville, Tenn. 37920	212[1]	155[1]	15	P/ChC	1,440	1,440	2,140
Johnson C. Smith University; Charlotte, N.C. 28216	647	719	92	P	2,220	2,220	1,418
Johnson State College; Johnson, Vt. 05656	402	414	47	S	2,500	6,100	4,792
Johnston College, Calif. *See* Redlands, University of							
Jones College; Jacksonville, Fla. 32211	738	557	32	P	1,620	1,620	—
Jones College*; Orlando, Fla. 32803	1,288		9	P	1,093	1,093	—
Judge Advocate General's School, U.S. Army*; Charlottesville, Va. 22901	58	2	n.a.	Pub	n.a.	n.a.	n.a.
Judson College; Elgin, Ill. 60120	191[1]	207[1]	22	P/AB	4,446	4,446	3,150
Judson College; Marion, Ala. 36756	—	565	26	P/B	2,140	2,140	1,460
Juilliard School, The; New York, N.Y. 10023	670[1]	650[1]	137	P	4,000	4,000	—
Juniata College; Huntingdon, Pa. 16652	682[1]	583[1]	74	P	5,361[3]	5,361[3]	2,235[3]
Kalamazoo College; Kalamazoo, Mich. 49007	713[1]	654[1]	75	P	6,492[3]	6,492[3]	1,524
Kansas, University of; Lawrence, Kan. 66045	13,690	12,677	1,325	S	918	2,234	1,700
Kansas City Art Institute; Kansas City, Mo. 64111	263[1]	255[1]	43	P	4,740	4,740	1,030
Kansas Newman College; Wichita, Kan. 67213	204[1]	273[1]	43	P/RC	3,150	3,150	1,890
Kansas State University, Manhattan, Kan. 66506	10,633	8,021	n.a.	S	898	2,214	n.a.
Kansas Wesleyan University; Salina, Kan. 67401	167	154	34	P/UM	3,537	3,537	2,042
Kean College of New Jersey; Union, N.J. 07083	2,644[1]	3,670[1]	359	S	810	1,410	1,235
Kearney State College; Kearney, Neb. 68847	2,488[1]	3,171[1]	252	S	([36])	([37])	1,506[2]
Keene State College; Keene, N.H. 03431	1,454	2,180	161	S	1,100	3,000	967
Keller Graduate School of Management; Chicago, Ill. 60606	864	288	—	P	([38])	([38])	—
Kendall College; Evanston, Ill. 60201	130	208	24	P/M	3,710	3,710	2,788
Kendall School of Design; Grand Rapids, Mich. 49503	196	260	21	P	3,036	3,036	2,000
Kennesaw College; Marietta, Ga. 30144	1,768[1]	2,434[1]	173	S	950	2,000	1,100
Kent State University; Kent, Ohio 44242	9,210[1]	10,450[1]	800	S	747	1,347	1,682
Kentucky, University of; Lexington, Ky. 40506	10,004[1]	8,182[1]	1,524	S	846	2,470	2,220
Kentucky Christian College; Grayson, Ky. 41143	225[1]	192[1]	18	P/ChC	1,344	1,344	1,696
Kentucky State University; Frankfort, Ky. 40601	635[1]	573[1]	100	S	606	1,760	1,450
Kentucky Wesleyan College; Owensboro, Ky. 42301	308[1]	392[1]	55	P/UM	3,200	3,200	1,810
Kenyon College; Gambier, Ohio 43022	775[1]	659[1]	93	P	7,090	7,090	2,455
Keuka College; Keuka Park, N.Y. 14478	2[1]	490[1]	49	P	4,890	4,890	1,820
King College; Bristol, Tenn. 37620	159[1]	130[1]	26	P/Pres	3,360	3,360	2,030
King's College; Wilkes-Barre, Pa. 18711	958	750	100	P	3,660	3,660	1,980
King's College, The; Briarcliff Manor, N.Y. 10510	283[1]	513[1]	46	P	4,600	4,600	1,800
Kirksville College of Osteopathic Medicine; Kirksville, Mo. 63501	424	75	88	P	13,250	13,250	3,825
Knox College; Galesburg, Ill. 61401	484[1]	736[1]	91	P	5,550	5,550	2,070
Knoxville College; Knoxville, Tenn. 37921	260	167	32	UP	2,400	2,400	1,671
Kutztown State College; Kutztown, Pa. 19530	1,744	2,246	343	S	1,250	2,190	1,528
Lafayette College; Easton, Pa. 18042	1,134	856	159	P	7,025[3]	7,025[3]	2,575[3]
LaGrange College; LaGrange, Ga. 30240	400	550	53	P/M	2,145	2,145	1,545
Lake Erie College; Painesville, Ohio 44077	100[1]	405[1]	52	P	5,235	5,235	2,760
Lake Forest College; Lake Forest, Ill. 60045	502	509	96	P	6,040	6,040	2,050
Lake Forest School of Management; Lake Forest, Ill. 60045	388		—	P	([39])	([39])	—
Lakeland College; Sheboygan, Wis. 53081	213	181	28	P/UCC	4,180	4,180	2,190
Lake Superior State College; Sault Ste. Marie, Mich. 49783	1,356[1]	1,145[1]	105	S	1,403	2,283	2,085

Institution and location	Enrollment		Faculty	Control	Tuition		Rm/Bd
	Male	Female			Res.	Nonres.	
Lamar University; Beaumont, Tex. 77710	6,900	6,900	433	S	100	1,200	1,350
Lambuth College; Jackson, Tenn. 38301	211	379	48	P/UM	3,100	3,100	1,650
Lander College; Greenwood, S.C. 29646	707[1]	1,118[1]	92	S	1,050	1,650	1,520
Lane College; Jackson, Tenn. 38301	356	413	37	P/CME	2,100	2,100	1,460
Langston University; Langston, Okla. 73050	731	509	46	S	566	1,041	1,541
Laredo State Univ. *See* South Texas, Univ. System of							
La Roche College, Pittsburgh, Pa. 15237	282	409	32	P	1,585	1,585	1,160
La Salle College; Philadelphia, Pa. 19141	2,140[1]	1,672[1]	215	P/RC	4,150	4,150	2,750
La Verne, University of; La Verne, Calif. 91750	1,608[1]		92	P	4,950	4,950	2,800
Lawrence Institute of Technology*; Southfield, Mich. 48075	4,367	893	250	P	1,725	1,725	—
Lawrence University; Appleton, Wis. 54912	546	534	102	P	5,883	5,883	1,767
L.D.S. Business College*; Salt Lake City, Utah 84111	253	321	n.a.	P/LDS	n.a.	n.a.	n.a.
Lebanon Valley College; Annville, Pa. 17003	421[1]	408[1]	77	P/UM	4,790	4,790	2,185
Lee College; Cleveland, Tenn. 37311	534	527	60	P/CG	2,200	2,200	1,600
Lehigh University; Bethlehem, Pa. 18015	3,603[1]	1,326[1]	344[5]	P	6,100	6,100	2,370
Le Moyne College; Syracuse, N.Y. 13214	879	887	106	P	4,250	4,250	2,200
LeMoyne-Owen College; Memphis, Tenn. 38126	112	239	25	P	1,040[40]	1,040[40]	—
Lenoir–Rhyne College; Hickory, N.C. 28603	484[1]	709[1]	84	P/LCA	3,230	3,230	1,585
Lesley College*; Cambridge, Mass. 02238	28	1,012	45	P	4,800	4,800	2,830
LeTourneau College; Longview, Tex. 75607	838	121	65	P	3,150	3,150	1,820
Lewis and Clark College; Portland, Ore. 97219	1,553[1]	1,660[1]	151	P	5,656	5,656	2,264
Lewis–Clark State College; Lewiston, Idaho 83501	848[1]	1,103[1]	77	S	600	2,300	1,850
Lewis University; Romeoville, Ill. 60441	1,560[1]	1,216[1]	104	P/RC	4,440	4,440	2,696
Liberty Baptist College; Lynchburg, Va. 24506	1,786[1]	1,555[1]	151	P/B	2,000	2,000	2,200
L.I.F.E. Bible College; Los Angeles, Calif. 90026	284[1]	146[1]	14	P/FG	1,980	1,980	2,025
Lifelong Learning, School for, University System of New Hampshire; Durham, N.H. 03824	465[10]	564[10]	—	S	([41])	([41])	—
Limestone College; Gaffney, S.C. 29340	846[1]	669[1]	33	P	3,470	3,470	1,780
Lincoln Christian College; Lincoln, Ill. 62656	227	133	30	P/ChC	2,560	2,560	1,360
Lincoln Memorial University; Harrogate, Tenn. 37752	423	672	40	P	2,025	2,025	1,575
Lincoln University; Jefferson City, Mo. 65101	935	783	141	S	574	1,060	2,066
Lincoln University*; Lincoln University, Pa. 19352	480	462	71	P	1,430	1,930	1,650
Lindenwood Colleges, The*; St. Charles, Mo. 63301	787	1,182	50	P	4,100	4,100	3,200
Linfield College; McMinnville, Ore. 97128	542	548	80	P	2,205	2,205	1,920
Livingstone College; Salisbury, N.C. 28144	422[1]	291[1]	49	P/AME	2,610	2,610	1,696
Livingston University; Livingston, Ala. 35470	475	494	72	S	750	750	1,485
Lock Haven State College; Lock Haven, Pa. 17745	1,200[1]	1,250[1]	165	S	1,250	2,190	1,560
Logan College of Chiropractic; Chesterfield, Mo. 63017	507	131	50	P	4,050[42]	4,050[42]	7,920[42]
Loma Linda University[43]; Loma Linda, Calif. 92350	2,002[1]	1,850[1]	683	P/SDA	4,725	4,725	2,169
Long Island University Center; Greenvale, N.Y. 11548:							
Arnold and Marie Schwartz College of Pharmacy and Health Sciences. *See* Brooklyn Center							
Brooklyn Center; Brooklyn, N.Y. 11201	1,801	2,215	240	P	2,000	2,000	1,200
C.W. Post Center; Greenvale, N.Y. 11548	5,667	7,448	1,090	P	4,590	4,590	2,628
Southampton College; Southampton, N.Y. 11968	637[1]	594[1]	68	P	4,540	4,540	2,770
Longwood College; Farmville, Va. 23901	639	1,567	175	S	1,547	1,797	1,705
Loras College; Dubuque, Iowa 52001	849	620	100	P/RC	4,000	4,000	2,000
Loretto Heights College*; Denver, Colo. 80236	161	652	75	P	3,900	3,900	2,170
Los Angeles Baptist College; Newhall, Calif. 91322	190[1]	183[1]	27	P/B	3,000	3,000	3,700
Los Angeles College of Chiropractic; Glendale, Calif. 91205	501	149	43	P	5,500	5,500	—
Louise Salinger Academy of Fashion*; San Francisco, Calif. 94105	6	28	n.a.	P	n.a.	n.a.	n.a.
Louisiana College; Pineville, La. 71360	294	423	53	P/B	1,350	1,350	1,400
Louisiana State University*; Baton Rouge, La. 70803	12,651	11,157	1,069	S	281	746	670
LSU and A&M College; Baton Rouge, La. 70803	12,549[1]	10,638[1]	1,291	S	690	1,720	1,890
LSU in Shreveport; Shreveport, La. 71115	1,837[1]	2,339[1]	130	S	580	1,610	—
LSU Medical Center at New Orleans; New Orleans, La. 70112	1,349	1,111	800	S	1,600	6,350	2,500
Louisiana Tech University; Ruston, La. 71272	4,724[1]	3,199[1]	393	S	651	1,281	1,782
Louisville, University of; Louisville, Ky. 40292	6,422[1]	5,126[1]	1,038	S	746	2,324	1,672
Lowell, University of; Lowell, Mass. 01854	5,520[1]	3,295[1]	426	S	896	3,136	2,200
Loyola College; Baltimore, Md. 21210	1,337	1,154	138	P/RC	3,950	3,950	2,260
Loyola Marymount University; Los Angeles, Calif. 90045	2,529[1]	2,566[1]	214	P/RC	4,526	4,526	2,604
Loyola University, New Orleans*; New Orleans, La. 70118	2,174	2,442	196	P/RC	3,200	3,200	2,200
Loyola University of Chicago; Chicago, Ill. 60011	7,235[1]	8,905[1]	750	P/RC	4,170	4,170	2,500
Lubbock Christian College; Lubbock, Tex. 79407	613[1]	467[1]	53	P/CC	2,460	2,460	1,500
Lutheran Bible Institute of Seattle; Issaquah, Wash. 98027	103	124	11	L	1,880	1,880	2,285
Luther College; Decorah, Iowa 52101	891	1,133	129	P/AL	5,225	5,225	1,675
Lycoming College; Williamsport, Pa. 17701	671[1]	533[1]	62	P/UM	4,980[3]	4,980[3]	2,200[3]
Lynchburg College; Lynchburg, Va. 24501	716[1]	989[1]	125	P	4,900[3]	4,900[3]	2,400[3]
Lyndon State College; Lyndonville, Vt. 05851	544[1]	427[1]	59	S	1,250	3,050	2,396

Institution and location	Enrollment		Faculty	Control	Tuition		Rm/Bd
	Male	Female			Res.	Nonres.	
Macalester College; St. Paul, Minn. 55105	767	721	130	P/UP	6,225	6,225	2,180
MacMurray College; Jacksonville, Ill. 62650	213	372	60	P/UM	3,990	3,990	1,800
Madonna College; Livonia, Mich. 48150	813	2,520	83	P	2,000	2,000	2,030
Maharishi International Univ.; Fairfield, Iowa 52556	350	222	60	P	3,465	3,465	1,980[3]
Maine, Univ. of, at Farmington; Farmington, Me. 04938	406[1]	1,138[1]	85	S	1,170	3,270	2,110
Maine, Univ. of, at Fort Kent; Fort Kent, 04743	238	297	20	S	930	2,900	1,950
Maine, Univ. of, at Machias*; Machias, Me. 04654	185	235	40	S	930	2,900	1,950
Maine, Univ. of, at Orono, Me. 04469	4,799	5,610	621	S	1,240	3,570	2,430
Maine, Univ. of, at Presque Isle; Presque Isle, Maine 04769	385[1]	426[1]	56	S	1,170	3,270	2,187
Maine Maritime Academy; Castine, Me. 04421	624[1]	20[1]	60	S	4,605	6,325	2,140
Malone College; Canton, Ohio 44709	300	301	42	P/EF	3,934	3,934	1,875
Manchester College; North Manchester, Ind. 46962	529[1]	588[1]	74	CB	3,410	3,410	1,710
Manhattan Christian College; Manhattan, Kan. 66502	95	52	15	P/ChC	1,620	1,620	1,930
Manhattan College; Riverdale, Bronx, N.Y. 10471	2,509	1,010	300	P	3,900[2]	3,900[2]	2,900
Manhattan School of Music; New York, N.Y. 10027	235	280	n.a.	P	4,000	4,000	—
Manhattanville College; Purchase, N.Y. 10577	273[1]	684[1]	76	P	6,400	6,400	3,170
Mankato State University. *See* Minnesota State College System							
Mannes College of Music; New York, N.Y. 10021	201	277	180	P	4,000	4,000	4,770
Mansfield State College; Mansfield, Pa. 16933	943	1,038	168	S	1,480[3]	2,592[3]	1,764[3]
Marian College; Indianapolis, Ind. 46222	263	616	54[5]	P/RC	3,200	3,200	1,800
Marian College of Fond du Lac; Fond du Lac, Wis. 54935	77	447	46	P/RC	1,450	1,450	1,500
Marietta College; Marietta, Ohio 45750	781	413	93	P	4,500	4,500	1,650
Marion College; Marion, Ind. 46952	300[1]	481[1]	66	P/W	3,960	3,960	2,000
Marist College; Poughkeepsie, N.Y. 12601	1,569[1]	1,288[1]	82	P	4,042	4,042	2,530
Marlboro College; Marlboro, Vt. 05344	101	117	22	P	6,680	6,680	2,700
Marquette University*; Milwaukee, Wis. 53233	5,408	3,993	545	P/RC	4,010	4,010	2,100
Marshall University; Huntington, W. Va. 25701	5,866[1]	5,991[1]	367	S	415	1,405	2,027
Mars Hill College; Mars Hill, N.C. 28754	656[1]	814[1]	99	P	3,145	3,145	1,380
Mary Baldwin College; Staunton, Va. 24401	18	807	55	P/Pres	4,300	4,300	2,650
Mary College; Bismarck, N.D. 58501	258	517	44	P/RC	2,580	2,580	840
Marycrest College; Davenport, Iowa 52804	144[1]	293[1]	50	P	3,660	3,660	1,740
Marygrove College; Detroit, Mich. 48221	196	939	49	P/RC	3,712	3,712	2,100
Mary Hardin–Baylor, University of; Belton, Tex. 76513	410	685	52	P/B	2,400	2,400	1,710
Maryland, University of (System); College Park, Md. 20742:							
UM, Baltimore County (UMBC); Cantonsville, Md. 21228	3,148[1]	3,605[1]	292	S	1,028	2,953	2,280
UM University College (UMUC); College Park, Md. 20742	383[1]	326[1]	13	S	1,690	1,690	—
UM at Baltimore (UMAB); Baltimore, Md. 21201	1,752[1]	2,153[1]	746	S	870	2,835	1,409
UM–College Park (UMCP); College Park, Md. 20742	14,177	12,345	1,900	S	1,651	3,303	2,570
UM Eastern Shore (UMES); Princess Anne, Md. 21853	535	594	83	S	859	2,448	2,176
Maryland Institute College of Art; Baltimore, Md. 21217	329[1]	529[1]	50	P	4,850[3]	4,850[3]	2,400[44]
Marylhurst College for Lifelong Learning; Marylhurst, Ore. 97036	273	603	26	P	3,600	3,600	—
Marymount College*; Tarrytown, N.Y. 10591	48	971	55	P	4,250	4,250	2,860
Marymount College of Kansas; Salina, Kan. 67401	250	421	51	P/RC	2,950	2,950	1,640
Marymount College of Virginia; Arlington, Va. 22207	74	930	50	P	3,800	3,800	2,200
Marymount Manhattan College; New York, N.Y. 10021	63	757	48	P	3,450	3,450	2,590[23]
Maryville College; Maryville, Tenn. 37801	318[1]	288[1]	43	P/Pres	3,920	3,920	1,995
Maryville College; St. Louis, Mo. 63141	197	575	58	P	4,100	4,100	2,160
Mary Washington College; Fredericksburg, Va. 22401	435	1,740	133	S	958	1,804	2,124
Marywood College; Scranton, Pa. 18509	644[1]	2,547[1]	139	Ind	3,102	3,102	2,000
Massachusetts at Amherst, Univ. of; Amherst, Mass. 01003	11,546[1]	10,256[1]	1,201	S	1,081	3,389	2,150
Massachusetts at Boston, Univ. of; Boston, Mass. 02125	2,897[1]	3,131[1]	322	S	1,129[3]	1,434[3]	—
Massachusetts College of Art; Boston, Mass. 02215	411[1]	700[1]	65	S	1,100	2,500	—
Massachusetts College of Optometry. *See* New England College of Optometry							
Massachusetts College of Pharmacy & Allied Health Sciences; Boston, Mass. 02115	626[1]	479[1]	70	P	4,704	4,704	3,700
Massachusetts Institute of Technology; Cambridge, Mass. 02139	7,631[1]	1,879[1]	1,096	P	8,700[3]	8,700[3]	3,550[3]
Massachusetts Maritime Academy; Buzzards Bay, Mass. 02532	817	40	55	S	725	725	2,450
Mayo Medical School*; Rochester, Minn. 55901[45]	120	42	25	P	5,000	5,000	4,500
Mayville State College; Mayville, N.D. 58257	269[1]	345[1]	49	S	760	1,508	1,688
McKendree College; Lebanon, Ill. 62254	257[1]	206[1]	32	P/M	([46])	([46])	1,850
McMurry College; Abilene, Tex. 79697	380	393	60	P/M	2,700	2,700	1,365
McNeese State University; Lake Charles, La. 70609	2,029[1]	2,433[1]	219	S	556	1,186	1,350
McPherson College; McPherson, Kan. 67460	236	230	37	P/CB	2,950	2,950	1,800

Institution and location	Enrollment		Faculty	Control	Tuition		Rm/Bd
	Male	Female			Res.	Nonres.	
Medaille College; Buffalo, N.Y. 14214	316	417	44	P	2,990	2,990	—
Medgar Evers College. *See* New York, City College of							
Medical College of Georgia; Augusta, Ga. 30912	1,207	966	562	S	1,265	2,940	585
Medical College of Ohio at Toledo; Toledo, Ohio 43699	317	180	265	S	4,500	6,150	—
Medical College of Wisconsin, The; Milwaukee, Wis. 53005	576[1]	239[1]	545	P	6,800[3]	11,300[3]	3,483
Medical University of South Carolina; Charleston, S.C. 29425	1,311[1]	1,249[1]	700	S	1,000	1,738	2,200
Medicine and Dentistry, College of, of New Jersey; Newark, N.J. 07103	1,342[1]	754[1]	735	S	5,500	6,875	—
New Jersey Dental School; Newark, N.J. 07103	268	69	72	S	5,500	6,875	—
New Jersey Medical School*; Newark, N.J. 07103	441	150	301	S	4,500	5,625	—
New Jersey School of Osteopathic Medicine*; Camden, N.J. 08103	96	21	55	S	5,000	6,250	—
Rutgers Medical School; Piscataway, N.J. 08854	296	126	270	S	5,500	6,875	3,780
Meharry Medical College; Nashville, Tenn. 37208	489[1]	395[1]	246	P	7,500	7,500	5,000
Memphis Academy of Arts, The; Memphis, Tenn. 38117	82	92	16	P	2,700	2,700	—
Memphis State University[12]; Memphis, Tenn. 38152	9,404[1]	10,670[1]	750	S	730	2,260	800[23]
Menlo College; Menlo Park, Calif. 94025	437[1]	196[1]	40	P	5,680	5,680	3,190
Mercer University College of Liberal Arts; Macon, Ga. 31207	1,100[1]	1,100[1]	120	P/B	3,669[3]	3,669[3]	1,785[3]
Mercer University in Atlanta; Atlanta, Ga. 30341	905[1]	830[1]	56	P	2,997	2,997	—
Southern School of Pharmacy; Atlanta, Ga. 30312	222	139	35	P/B	3,750	3,750	—
Mercy College*; Dobbs Ferry, N.Y. 10522	2,684	3,219	152	P	2,550	2,550	—
Mercy College of Detroit*; Detroit, Mich. 48219	354	1,544	138	P/RC	3,000	3,000	1,400
Mercyhurst College; Erie, Pa. 16546	422[1]	669[1]	73	P/RC	3,650	3,650	1,775
Meredith College; Raleigh, N.C. 27607	25	1,538	125	P/SB	3,050	3,050	1,350
Merrimack College; North Andover, Mass. 01845	1,185	921	120	P/RC	4,260	4,260	2,700
Mesa College; Grand Junction, Colo. 81501	1,391	1,190	123	S	820	2,826	1,800
Messiah College; Grantham, Pa. 17027	520	785	64	P/BC	4,000	4,000	2,100
Methodist College*; Fayetteville, N.C. 28301	371	344	46	P/M	2,500	2,500	1,650
Metropolitan State College; Denver, Colo. 80204	3,402	2,699	340	S	716	2,595	—
Metropolitan State University, Minn. *See* Minnesota State University System							
Miami, University of*; Coral Gables, Fla. 33124	10,606	7,883	1,215	P	4,530	4,530	2,017
Miami University; Oxford, Ohio 45056	6,740	7,559	782	S	2,000	4,000	2,000
Michigan, The University of; Ann Arbor, Mich. 48109	17,972[1]	13,218[1]	2,821	S	1,962	5,382	2,497[3]
Univ. of Michigan—Dearborn; Dearborn, Mich. 48128	1,924[1]	1,597[1]	188	S	1,328	4,080	—
Univ. of Michigan—Flint; Flint, Mich. 48503	1,979	2,279	150	S	1,180	3,820	—
Michigan State University; East Lansing, Mich. 48824	18,101[1]	17,263[1]	2,493	S	1,502[3]	3,279[3]	2,112[3]
Michigan Technological University; Houghton, Mich. 49931	6,010[1]	1,769[1]	372	S	1,272	3,006	2,072
Mid-America Nazarene College; Olathe, Kan. 66061	631	644	59	P/Naz	2,142	2,142	1,884
Middlebury College; Middlebury, Vt. 05753	950	950	149	P	10,800[7]	10,800[7]	—
Middle Tennessee State Univ.[12]; Murfreesboro, Tenn. 37132	4,048[1]	4,172[1]	425	S	760[3]	2,518[3]	1,306[3]
Midland College; Fremont, Neb. 68025	477[1]	373[1]	58	P/L	3,800	3,800	1,650
Mid-South Bible College; Memphis, Tenn. 38112	40	17	8	P	2,114	2,114	1,730
Midwest Christian College; Oklahoma City, Okla. 73111	42	31	10	P	1,354	1,354	1,500
Midwest College of Engineering*; Lombard, Ill. 60148	27	1	n.a.	P	n.a.	n.a.	n.a.
Midwestern State University; Wichita Falls, Tex. 76308	951	981	138	S	400	1,225	1,110
Miles College; Birmingham, Ala. 35208	245	272	75	P/CME	2,300	2,300	600[23]
Millersville State College; Millersville, Pa. 17551	2,096[1]	2,498[1]	310	S	1,475	2,580	1,710
Milligan College; Milligan College, Tenn. 37682	301[1]	352[1]	40	P/CC	2,824	2,824	1,992
Millikin University; Decatur, Ill. 62522	731[1]	768[1]	100	P/UP	4,325	4,325	1,900
Millsaps College; Jackson, Miss. 39210	423	417	64	P/M	3,610	3,610	1,500
Mills College; Oakland, Calif. 94613	40[1]	884[1]	60	P	6,380	6,380	3,200
Milton College; Milton, Wis. 53563[31]	202[1]	96[1]	25	P	3,600	3,600	1,850
Milton S. Hershey Medical Center. *See* Pennsylvania State University							
Milwaukee School of Engineering*; Milwaukee, Wis. 53201	1,330	70	108	P	3,600	3,600	1,500
Minneapolis College of Art and Design; Minneapolis, Minn. 55404	217	287	44	P	4,070	4,070	1,040
Minnesota, The University of; Minneapolis, Minn. 55455	32,176[1]	26,727[1]	5,560	S	1,245	2,880	2,245
Univ. of Minnesota, Duluth; Duluth, Minn. 55812	3,901[1]	3,623[1]	407	S	1,044	2,847	2,148
Univ. of Minnesota, Morris; Morris, Minn. 56267	849[1]	841[1]	106	S	1,053	2,880	2,000
Minnesota Bible College; Rochester, Minn. 55901	56	47	10	P/ChC	1,800	1,800	1,500
Minnesota State University System; St. Paul, Minn. 55101:							
Bemidji State University; Bemidji, Minn. 56601	2,115[1]	1,977[1]	240	S	794	1,581	1,365
Mankato State University; Mankato, Minn. 56001	5,797	6,356	550	S	847	1,704	41,408
Metropolitan State University; St. Paul, Minn. 55101	160[1]	145[1]	20	S	800	1,600	—
Moorhead State University; Moorhead, Minn. 56560	2,694[1]	3,379[1]	297	S	794[3]	1,582[3]	1,405[3]
St. Cloud State University; St. Cloud, Minn. 56301	5,143[2]	5,380[2]	447	S	847	1,687	1,265
Southwest State University; Marshall, Minn. 56258	917	759	107	S	735	1,464	1,560

Institution and location	Enrollment		Faculty	Control	Tuition		Rm/Bd
	Male	Female			Res.	Nonres.	
Winona State University; Winona, Minn. 55987	1,729[1]	2,343[1]	200	S	655	1,303	1,323
Minot State College*; Minot, N.D. 58701	900	1,600	120	S	687	1,245	1,200
Mississippi, The University of; University, Miss. 38677	5,080[1]	4,459[1]	450	S	1,085	2,011	1,792
Medical Center; Jackson, Miss. 39216	807[1]	408[1]	436	S	2,000	2,926	—
Mississippi College; Clinton, Miss. 39058	877	818	127	P/B	2,250	2,250	4,550
Mississippi State University; Mississippi State, Miss. 39762	6,532[1]	4,182[1]	754	S	1,030	1,956	1,700
Mississippi University for Women; Columbus, Miss. 39701	1	1,808	169	S	800	1,726	1,580
Mississippi Valley State University*; Itta Benna, Miss. 38941	1,030	1,233	151	S	750	1,200	1,223
Missouri, University of; Columbia, Mo. 65201:							
Univ. of Missouri—Columbia; Columbia, Mo. 65211	12,966[1]	11,808[1]	1,500	S	1,020	3,060	1,635
Univ. of Missouri—Kansas City; Kansas City, Mo. 64110	11,066		628	Mun	1,110	3,150	1,600
Univ. of Missouri—Rolla; Rolla, Mo. 65401	5,516	1,388	340	S	1,219	3,259	2,114
Univ. of Missouri—St. Louis; St. Louis, Mo. 63121	3,252[1]	2,961[1]	442	S	510	1,020	—
Missouri Baptist College*; St. Louis, Mo. 63141	194	217	20	P/SB	2,000	2,000	1,750
Missouri Southern State College; Joplin, Mo. 64801	2,240[1]	2,090[1]	165	S	580	1,160	1,330
Missouri Valley College; Marshall, Mo. 65340	278[2]	161[2]	34	P/Pres	3,050	3,050	1,750
Missouri Western State College; St. Joseph, Mo. 64507	2,013[1]	2,258[1]	165	S	640	1,184	1,330
Mobile College; Mobile, Ala. 36613	249	474	60	P/SB	2,176	2,176	1,640
Molloy College; Rockville Centre, N.Y. 11570	30[1]	1,131[1]	113	P/RC	3,450	3,450	—
Monmouth College; West Long Branch, N.J. 07764	856	924	175	P	4,400	4,400	1,750
Monmouth College, The; Monmouth, Ill. 61462	340	305	52	P/UP	4,290	4,290	2,070
Montana, University of; Missoula, Mont. 59812	4,638[1]	4,231[1]	400	S	825	1,440	2,531
Montana College of Mineral Science and Technology; Butte, Mont. 59701	1,126	416	82	S	562	1,930	1,950
Montana State University; Bozeman, Mont. 59715	6,452[1]	4,735[1]	729	S	728	2,168	1,364
Montclair State College; Upper Montclair, N.J. 07043	5,453	8,883	583	S	432	752	3,000
Monterey Institute of International Studies; Monterey, Calif. 93940	147	193	35	P	5,450[2]	5,450[2]	—
Montevallo, University of; Montevallo, Ala. 35115	723[1]	1,299[1]	156	S	868	1,468	1,558
Moody Bible Institute; Chicago, Ill. 60610	749	537	90	P/ND	—	—	2,700
Moore College of Art; Philadelphia, Pa. 19103	—	437	40	P	4,000	4,000	1,900
Moorhead State University. *See* Minnesota State University System							
Moravian College; Bethlehem, Pa. 18018	657[1]	622[1]	87	P	5,660	5,660	2,205
Morehead State University; Morehead, Ky. 40351	2,236[1]	2,480[1]	283	S	586	1,740	1,080
Morehouse College; Atlanta, Ga. 30314	1,841[1]	—	105	P	3,256	3,256	2,060
Morgan State University; Baltimore, Md. 21239	1,623	1,985	270	S	1,111	2,146	2,490
Morningside College; Sioux City, Iowa 51106	437	571	72	P/M	4,650	4,650	1,660
Morris Brown College; Atlanta, Ga. 30314	616	769	153	P/AME	2,700	2,700	1,626
Morris College; Sumter, S.C. 29150	243	415	47	P/B	2,402	2,402	1,573
Mount Holyoke College; South Hadley, Mass. 01075	—	1,942	171[1]	P	7,750[3]	7,750[3]	2,950
Mount Marty College; Yankton, S.D. 57078	99	317	47	P/RC	3,050	3,050	1,590
Mount Mary College; Milwaukee, Wis. 53222	—	1,127	68	P/RC	3,350	3,350	700
Mount Mercy College; Cedar Rapids, Iowa 52402	189[1]	718[1]	57	P/RC	3,515	3,515	1,675
Mount Saint Clare College; Clinton, Iowa 52732	99[1]	201[1]	10	P/RC	2,450	2,450	1,870
Mount St. Joseph on the Ohio, College of; Mount St. Joseph, Ohio 45051	43[1]	875[1]	58	P	3,616	3,616	2,300
Mount Saint Mary College; Newburgh, N.Y. 12550	91[1]	682[1]	51	P	([47])	([47])	1,990
Mount Saint Mary's College; Emmitsburg, Md. 21727	792	703	91	P/RC	4,300	4,300	2,200
Mount St. Mary's College; Los Angeles, Calif. 90049	11[1]	840[1]	73	P/RC	4,420	4,420	2,625
Mount Saint Vincent, College of; Riverdale, N.Y. 10471	39[1]	815[1]	65	P	4,150	4,150	2,800
Mount Senario College; Ladysmith, Wis. 54848	169	197	30	P	3,520	3,520	1,930
Mount Sinai School of Medicine. *See* New York, City University of							
Mount Union College; Alliance, Ohio 44657	546	456	73	P	6,045[3]	6,045[3]	1.860
Mount Vernon College; Washington, D.C. 20007	—	442	24	P	4,800	4,800	3,600
Mount Vernon Nazarene College*; Mount Vernon, Ohio 43050	416	473	50	P/Naz	2,200	2,200	1,460
Muhlenberg College; Allentown, Pa. 18104	820[1]	703[1]	111	P/L	5,150	5,150	1,750
Multnomah School of the Bible; Portland, Ore. 97220	416	288	41	P	2,990	2,990	1,630
Mundelein College; Chicago, Ill. 60660	90[1]	1,280[1]	110	P	3,840	3,840	n.a.
Murray State University; Murray, Ky. 42071	2,792[1]	3,048[1]	350	S	714	2,062	1,600
Museum Art School, Portland. *See* Pacific Northwest College of Art							
Museum of Fine Arts, School of the; Boston, Mass. 02115	166	341	n.a.	P	4,500	4,500	n.a.
Muskingum College; New Concord, Ohio 43762	518[1]	474[1]	68	P/UP	4,860	4,860	1,880
Nasson College; Springvale, Me. 04083	266	151	34	P	4,680	4,680	2,220
Nathaniel Hawthorne College; Antrim, N.H. 03440	309	61	16	P	4,640	4,640	1,550
National College of Education; Evanston, Ill. 60201	1,004[1]	3,434[1]	79[5]	P	4,620	4,620	2,565

Institution and location	Enrollment: Male	Enrollment: Female	Faculty	Control	Tuition: Res.	Tuition: Nonres.	Rm/Bd
National University [31]; San Diego, Calif. 92108	3,016[1]	1,395[1]	30	P	4,080	4,080	—
Naval Postgraduate School; Monterey, Calif. 93940	1,181	68	250	Fed	—	—	—
Nazareth College at Kalamazoo; Nazareth, Mich. 49074	67[1]	343[1]	43	P/RC	4,790	4,790	2,370
Nazareth College of Rochester; Rochester, N.Y. 14610	265[1]	1,127[1]	115	P	4,200	4,200	2,500
Nebraska, University of; Lincoln, Neb. 68588	11,271[1]	7,971[1]	1,071	S	1,027	2,527	1,695
Univ. of Nebraska at Omaha; Omaha, Neb. 68182	3,612	3,056	500	S	1,000	3,000	—
Univ. of Nebraska Medical Center; Omaha, Neb. 68105	1,128[1]	1,022[1]	568	S	878	2,378	—
Nebraska Wesleyan University; Lincoln, Neb. 68504	518	629	75	P/M	3,616	3,616	1,675
Neumann College; Aston, Pa. 19014	31	309	35	P/RC	2,975	2,975	—
Nevada, University of, System; Reno, Nev. 89557							
Univ. of Nevada, Las Vegas; Las Vegas, Nev. 89154	5,131	5,545	310	S	930	2,930	2,150
Univ. of Nevada—Reno; Reno, Nev. 89557	3,460	2,904	389	S	992	2,992	2,400
Newberry College; Newberry, S.C. 29108	377	276	52	P/LCA	4,020	4,020	1,930
New Church, Academy of the; Bryn Athyn, Pa. 19009	70	60	27	P/Sw	1,359	1,359	600
New College of California; San Francisco, Calif. 94110	233	257	7	P	3,000	3,000	—
New College of the University of South Florida. *See* South Florida, University of							
Newcomb College. *See* Tulane University							
New England, University of; Biddeford, Me. 04005	155	178	23	P	4,300	4,300	2,420
College of Osteopathic Medicine; Biddeford, Me. 04005	191	39	16	P	11,000	11,000	—
New England College; Henniker, N.H. 03242	714	561	94	P	5,900[3]	5,900[3]	2,380[3]
New England College of Optometry; Boston, Mass. 02115	250	112	55	P	8,970	8,970	—
New England Conservatory of Music*; Boston, Mass. 02115	341	271	55	P	5,500	5,500	3,125
New England School of Law; Boston, Mass. 02116	703	351	25	P	4,200	4,200	—
New Hampshire, University of; Dur ham, N.H. 03824	4,684[1]	5,225[1]	532	S	1,550	4,400	2,168
New Hampshire College; Manchester, N.H. 03104	1,821[1]	1,452[1]	57	P	4,870	4,870	2,872
New Haven, University of*; West Haven, Conn. 06516	1,644	1,011	146	P	3,496	3,496	1,900
New Jersey Dental School. *See* Medicine & Dentistry, Coll. of, of New Jersey							
New Jersey Institute of Technology; Newark, N.J. 07302	3,127[1]	400[1]	26	S	1,110	2,220	2,330
New Jersey Medical School. *See* Medicine & Dentistry, Coll. of, of New Jersey							
New Jersey School of Osteopathic Medicine. *See* Medicine & Dentistry, Coll. of, of New Jersey							
New Mexico, The University of; Albuquerque, N.M. 87131	7,250	6,779	1,038	S	768[3]	2,448[3]	1,800[3]
New Mexico Highlands University*; Las Vegas, N.M. 87701	1,082	1,257	121	S	453	1,430	1,360
New Mexico Institute of Mining and Technology; Socorro, N.M. 87801	833[1]	285[1]	69	S	421	2,104	2,448
New Mexico State University; Las Cruces, N.M. 88003	6,177	5,271	683	S	744	2,256	1,488
New Orleans, University of; New Orleans, La. 70148[48]	4,260[1]	4,112[1]	548	S	624	1,654	2,300
Newport College, The—Salve Regina*; Newport, R.I. 02840	137	885	76	P/RC	3,950	3,950	2,300
New Rochelle, College of*; New Rochelle, N.Y. 10801	258	3,002	100	P	3,150	3,150	2,320
New School for Social Research; New York, N.Y. 10011	340[1]	359[1]	61	P	5,260	5,260	2,100[23]
Parsons School of Design; New York, N.Y. 10011	639[1]	1,096[1]	29	P	5,640	5,640	2,100[23]
New School of Music, The; Philadelphia, Pa. 19103	35	34	35[10]	P	3,435	3,435	2,350
New York, City University of; New York, N.Y. 10021:							
Bernard M. Baruch College; New York, N.Y. 10010	3,883[1]	4,851[1]	444	S	1,075	1,575	—
Brooklyn College; Brooklyn, N.Y. 11210	6,296	8,769	940	Mun	925	1,425	—
City College*; New York, N.Y. 10031	4,868	3,145	604	Mun	925	1,425	—
College of Staten Island; Staten Island, N.Y. 10301	5,090[1]	5,767[1]	630	S	825	1,425	—
Graduate School and University Center; New York, N.Y. 10036	1,629[1]	1,614[1]	1,351	Mun	925	1,425	—
Hebert H. Lehman College; Bronx, N.Y. 10468	1,945	3,428	423	S	925	1,425	—
Hunter College; New York, N.Y. 10021	2,332[1]	7,149[1]	612	Mun	925	1,425	—
John Jay College of Criminal Justice; New York, N.Y. 10019	1,765	1,741	257	Mun/S	925	1,425	—
Medgar Evers College; Brooklyn, N.Y. 11225	509	1,069	109	Mun	925	1,425	—
Mount Sinai School of Medicine*; New York, N:Y. 10029	309	144	968	P	7,500	7,500	3,000
Queens College; Flushing, N.Y. 11367	4,901	6,014	836	Mun/S	925	1,425	—
York College; Jamaica, N.Y. 11451	1,634	1,046	150	Mun/S	925	1,425	—
New York, State University of; Albany, N.Y. 12246:							
SUNY at Albany*; Albany, N.Y. 12222	6,025	5,847	715	S	1,050	1,750	2,020
SUNY at Binghamton; Binghamton, N.Y. 13901	4,217[1]	4,730[1]	492	S	1,050	1,750	2,340
SUNY at Buffalo*; Amherst, N.Y. 14260	11,524	7,542	1,404	S	1,050	1,750	2,282
SUNY at Stony Brook; Stony Brook, N.Y. 11794	6,814[1]	5,728[1]	1,044	S	1,050	1,750	2,340
SUNY College at Brockport; Brockport, N.Y. 14420	3,007[1]	3,040[1]	420	S	1,050	1,750	2,185
SUNY College at Buffalo; Buffalo, N.Y. 14222	3,862[1]	4,869[1]	491	S	1,050	1,650	2,200
SUNY College at Cortland; Cortland, N.Y. 13045	2,414[1]	3,656[1]	270	S	1,050	1,750	2,150

	Enrollment				Tuition		
Institution and location	**Male**	**Female**	**Faculty**	**Control**	**Res.**	**Nonres.**	**Rm/Bd**
SUNY College at Fredonia; Fredonia, N.Y. 14063	2,169[1]	2,166[1]	258	S	1,050	1,750	2,050
SUNY College at Geneseo*; Geneseo, N.Y. 14454	1,724	3,207	263	S	900	1,500	1,830
SUNY College at New Paltz; New Paltz, N.Y. 12561	3,096[1]	4,152[1]	328	S	1,050	1,750	1,085
SUNY College at Old Westbury; Old Westbury, N.Y. 11568	1,500[1]	1,945[1]	121	S	1,050	1,750	1,200
SUNY College at Oneonta; Oneonta, N.Y. 13820	2,375[1]	3,364[1]	341	S	1,158	1,858	2,088
SUNY College at Oswego; Oswego, N.Y. 13126	3,382[1]	3,407[1]	366	S	1,050	1,750	1,100
SUNY College at Plattsburgh; Plattsburgh, N.Y. 12901	2,268[1]	3,077[1]	301	S	1,050	1,750	2,164
SUNY College of Arts and Science at Potsdam; Potsdam, N.Y. 13662	1,922[1]	2,154[1]	229	S	1,050	1,750	2,000
SUNY College at Purchase; Purchase, N.Y. 10577	859	1,239	140	S	1,050	1,750	1,000
SUNY College of Environmental Science and Forestry; Syracuse, N.Y. 13210	960	309	107[5]	S	1,050	1,750	2,190
SUNY College of Optometry; New York, N.Y. 10010	158	106	40	S	4,355	6.355	3,700
SUNY College of Technology; Utica, N.Y. 13502	829[1]	602[1]	88	S	1,050	1,750	—
SUNY Downstate Medical Center*; Brooklyn, N.Y. 11203	761	547	441	S	3,100	4,500	2,800
SUNY Empire State College; Saratoga Springs, N.Y. 12866	2,845[1]	2,150[1]	114	S	1,630	2,680	—
SUNY Maritime College*; Fort Schuyler, Bronx, N.Y. 10465	845	54	66	S	1,050	1,750	2,150
SUNY Upstate Medical Center; Syracuse, N.Y. 13210	498[1]	367[1]	292	S	1,050	1,750	2,500
New York, University of the State of, Regents External Degree Program; Albany, N.Y. 12230	11,248	9,689	200	P	325[49]	325[49]	—
New York Chiropractic College; Glen Head, N.Y. 11545	571[1]	210[1]	n.a.	P	6,350	6,350	—
New York College of Podiatric Medicine*; New York, N.Y. 10035	405	48	25	P	7,095	7,095	n.a.
New York Institute of Technology; Old Westbury, N.Y. 11568	5,007	1,620	223	P	3,424	3,424	2,550
New York Law School; New York, N.Y. 10013	973	493	40	P	5,000	5,000	—
New York Medical College*; Valhalla, N.Y. 10595	578	223	527	P	9,100	9,100	—
New York University; New York, N.Y. 10003	9,196[1]	9,052[1]	n.a.	P	6,634[3]	6,634[3]	3,490[3]
Niagara University; Niagara University, N.Y. 14109	1,258	1,628	186	P	3,690	3,690	2,450
Nicholls State University; Thibodaux, La. 70301	2,099	2,221	252	S	541	1,171	1,440
Nichols College; Dudley, Mass. 01570	558[1]	231[1]	33	P	4,330[3]	4,330[3]	2,560[3]
Norfolk State University; Norfolk, Va. 23504	2,399[1]	3,442[1]	311	S	812	1,427	1,640
North Adams State College; North Adams, Mass. 01247	1,034[1]	1,208[1]	98	S	725	2,538	1,828
North Alabama, University of; Florence, Ala. 35630	1,819[1]	2,225[1]	179	S	870	1,740	1,790
North Carolina, University System of; Chapel Hill, N.C. 27514:							
Appalachian State University; Boone, N.C. 28608	4,687[1]	5,003[1]	525	S	614	2,334	1,420
East Carolina University; Greenville, N.C. 27834	5,682[1]	7,582[1]	829	S	372	2,160	1,816
Elizabeth City State University; Elizabeth City, N.C. 27909	675[1]	787[1]	102	S	318	1,900	1,580
Fayetteville State University; Fayetteville, N.C. 28301	1,061[1]	1,253[1]	155	S	350	1,135	1,550
North Carolina Agricultural and Technical State University; Greensboro, N.C. 17411	2,855	2,054	352	S	819	2,607	1,774
North Carolina Central University*; Durham, N.C. 27707	1,749	2,642	325	S	615	2,353	1,449
North Carolina School of the Arts; Winston–Salem, N.C. 27107	343[1]	383[1]	87	S	666	2,190	1,885
N.C. State Univ. at Raleigh; Raleigh, N.C. 27650	10,162[1]	4,839[1]	1,280	S	670	2,494	1,200
Pembroke State University; Pembroke, N.C. 28372	925[1]	1,262[1]	118	S	548	2,130	1,210
Univ. of N.C. at Asheville; Asheville, N.C. 28814	979[1]	1,287[1]	86	S	270	2,040	1,400
Univ. of N.C. at Chapel Hill; Chapel Hill, N.C. 27514	9,849[1]	11,726[1]	1,880	S	693	2,517	2,050
Univ. of N.C. at Charlotte; Charlotte, N.C. 28223	3,586[1]	3,121[1]	447	S	626	2,414	1,744
Univ. of N.C. at Greensboro; Greensboro, N.C. 27412	3,230[1]	6,971[1]	633	S	746	2,570	1,720
Univ. of N.C. at Wilmington; Wilmington, N.C. 28406	2,010[1]	2,064[1]	244	S	630	2,212	2,025
Western Carolina University; Cullowhee, N.C. 28723	2,592[1]	2,474[1]	325	S	673	2,461	1,540
Winston–Salem State University; Winston–Salem, N.C. 27110	734	1,068	140	S	318	1,900	1,813
North Carolina Wesleyan College; Rocky Mount, N.C. 27801	451	436	37	P/UM	3,200	3,200	1,740
North Central Bible College; Minneapolis, Minn. 55406	348	281	15	P/AG	2,070[50]	2,070[50]	1,700
North Central College; Naperville, Ill. 60566	449	430	60	P/UM	4,209	4,209	2,115
North Dakota, University of; Grand Forks, N.D. 58202	5,108	4,678	467	S	764	1,532	1,480
North Dakota, State University; Fargo, N.D. 58105	5,203[1]	3,539[1]	450	S	732	1,500	1,467
Northeastern Bible College; Essex Fells, N.J. 07021	193	128	17	P	2,800	2,800	1,900
Northeastern Illinois University; Chicago, Ill. 60625	2,065[1]	2,710[1]	350	S	843	2,440	—
Northeastern Oklahoma State University; Tahlequah, Okla. 74464	2,425[1]	3,316[1]	320	S	451	1,096	2,000
Northeastern University; Boston, Mass. 02115	11,548	6,891	830	P	4,725	4,725	3,300

Institution and location	Enrollment Male	Enrollment Female	Faculty	Control	Tuition Res.	Tuition Nonres.	Rm/Bd
Northeast Louisiana University; Monroe, La. 71209	4,833[1]	6,467[1]	367	S	527	1,157	1,544
Northeast Missouri State University; Kirksville, Mo. 63501	2,938[1]	3,711[1]	280	S	480	960	1,320
Northern Arizona University; Flagstaff, Ariz. 86011	1,602[1]	1,543[1]	550	S	710	2,750	1,850
Northern Colorado, University of; Greeley, Colo. 80631	3,827[1]	5,232[1]	464	S	1,017	3,342	1,875
Northern Illinois University; DeKalb, Ill. 60115	7,968[1]	9,415[1]	1,400	S	680	2,040	2,040
Northern Iowa, University of; Cedar Falls, Iowa 50614	3,454	4,383	559[5]	S	900	1,860	1,528
Northern Kentucky University; Highland Heights, Ky. 41076	3,972	4,318	219	S	626	1,780	1,200
Northern Michigan University; Marquette, Mich. 49855	4,643[1]	4,403[1]	320	S	1,200	2,752	2,071
Northern Montana College; Havre, Mont. 59501	758[1]	526[1]	77	S	543	1,551	1,801
Northern State College; Aberdeen, S.D. 57401	927[1]	1,192[1]	109	S	748	1,552	1,317
North Florida, University of; Jacksonville, Fla. 32216	577	954	171	S	840	2,730	2,800
North Georgia College*; Dahlonega, Ga. 30597	495	558	102	S	666	1,620	1,335
Northland College; Ashland, Wis. 54806	348	290	40	P	4,000	4,000	2,500
North Park College; Chicago, Ill. 60625	550	650	80	P/EC	4,365	4,365	2,166
Northrop University; Inglewood, Calif. 90306	1,418	187	90	P	4,725	4,725	3,210
North Texas State University; Denton, Tex. 76203	8,179	8,552	667	S	388	1,248	2,100
Northwest Bible College; Minot, N.D. 58701	124[1]	76[1]	8	P/CG	1,695	1,695	1,490
Northwest Christian College; Eugene, Ore. 97401	141	90	10	P/ChC	3,240[3]	3,240[3]	1,930[3]
Northwest College; Kirkland, Wash. 98033	386[1]	306[1]	24	P/AG	1,920	1,920	1,623
Northwestern College; Orange City, Iowa 51041	422[1]	481[1]	52	P/RCA	3,895	3,895	1,580
Northwestern College; Roseville, Minn. 55113	310	355	33	P/ID	3,450	3,450	1,770
Northwestern Coll. of Chiropractic; St. Paul, Minn. 55116	320	99	21	P	1,840	1,840	—
Northwestern Oklahoma State University; Alva, Okla. 73717	810[1]	1,106[1]	76	S	560	1,700	n.a.
Northwestern State University of Louisiana*; Natchitoches, La. 71457	1,263	1,746	n.a.	S	668	1,298	1,280
Northwestern University; Evanston, Ill. 60201	8,366[1]	7,335[1]	1,300	P	8,085	8,085	1,300
Northwest Missouri State University; Maryville, Mo. 64468	1,889	1,886	220	S	550	930	1,300
Northwest Nazarene College; Nampa, Idaho 83651	585[1]	668[1]	74	P/Naz	3,480	3,480	1,875
Northwood Institute; Midland, Mich. 48640	1,200	800	40	P	3,330	3,330	1,935
Norwich University; Northfield, Vt. 05663	1,264[2]	165[2]	111	P	8,600[7]	8,600[7]	—
Vermont College of Norwich Univ.; Montpelier, Vt. 05602	39	328	178	P	6,900[7]	6,900[7]	—
Notre Dame, College of; Belmont, Calif. 94002	308[1]	505[1]	64	P/RC	4,700	4,700	2,800
Notre Dame, University of; Notre Dame, Ind. 46556	6,564[1]	2,459[1]	630	P	6,000[3]	6,000[3]	2,110
Notre Dame College; Manchester, N.H. 03104	44[1]	344[1]	34	P/RC	2,700	2,700	1,800
Notre Dame College of Ohio; Cleveland, Ohio 44121	—	421[1]	33	P/RC	3,250	3,250	2,070
Notre Dame of Maryland, College of; Baltimore, Md. 21210	49[1]	1,583[1]	50[5]	P/RC	3,800	3,800	2,500
Nova University; Ft. Lauderdale, Fal. 33301	2,890[1]	2,394[1]	57[5]	P	2,500	2,500	3,000
Nyack College; Nyack, N.Y. 10960	298	287	47	P/CMA	3,460	3,460	2,115
Oakland City College; Oakland City, Ind. 47660	366[1]	227[1]	30	P/B	2,997	2,997	1,500
Oakland University; Rochester, Mich. 48063	4,388	6,770	376	S	1,280	3,264	2,135
Oakwood College; Huntsville, Ala. 35896	568	614	71	P/SDA	3,663	3,663	1,920
Oberlin College; Oberlin, Ohio 44074	1,219[1]	1,422[1]	226	P	6,640	6,640	2,570
Occidental College; Los Angeles, Calif. 90041	845[1]	799[1]	113	P	6,051	6,051	2,550
Oglethorpe University; Atlanta, Ga. 30319	363[1]	360[1]	35	P	3,550	3,550	1,950
Ohio College of Podiatric Medicine; Cleveland, Ohio 44106	536	61	23	P	7,800	7,800	—
Ohio Dominican College; Columbus, Ohio 43219	226[1]	397[1]	48	P/RC	3,990[3]	3,990[3]	2,280[3]
Ohio Northern University; Ada, Ohio 45810	1,628[1]	1,060[1]	168	P/UM	4,710	4,710	2,010
Ohio State University, The; Columbus, Ohio 43210	27,898	22,003	3,184	S	1,380	3,510	2,271
Columbus Campus; Columbus, Ohio 43210	21,592	16,656	2,970	S	1,305	3,350	2,514
Lima Campus; Lima, Ohio 45804	361[1]	457[1]	42	S	1,260	3,285	—
Mansfield Campus*; Mansfield, Ohio 44906	447	438	38	S	1,110	2,475	2,052
Marion Campus*; Marion, Ohio 43302	311	306	26	S	1,110	2,475	2,052
Newark Campus*; Newark, Ohio 43055	435	441	28	S	1,110	2,475	2,052
Ohio University; Athens, Ohio 45701	8,016[1]	6,588[1]	693	S	1,482	1,680	—
Ohio Wesleyan University; Delaware, Ohio 43015	1,118	1,037	155	P	5,550	5,550	2,110
Oklahoma, University of; Norman, Okla. 73019	9,844[1]	7,099[1]	821	S	643	1,712	1,670
Oklahoma, University of Science and Arts of; Chickasha, Okla. 73018	247	384	55	S	450	1,120	1,400
Oklahoma Baptist University; Shawnee, Okla. 74801	647[1]	780[1]	101	P/SB	2,100	2,100	1,505
Oklahoma Christian College; Oklahoma City, Okla. 73111	746[1]	867[1]	62	P/CC	2,250[3]	2,250[3]	1,700
Oklahoma City Southwestern Coll. *See* Southwestern Coll. of Christian Ministries							
Oklahoma City University; Oklahoma City, Okla. 73106	1,516	1,092	75	P/UM	2,640	2,640	1,475
Oklahoma College of Osteopathic Medicine and Surgery*; Tulsa, Okla. 74101	212	38	30	S	2,500	2,500	—
Oklahoma Panhandle State University; Goodwell, Okla. 73939	530	505	60	S	420	1,066	1,410
Oklahoma State University*; Stillwater, Okla. 74078	11,045	7,842	879	S	600	1,650	1,300
Old Dominion University*; Norfolk, Va. 23508	4,762	4,461	581	S	840	1,440	1,690

Institution and location	Enrollment		Faculty	Control	Tuition		
	Male	Female			Res.	Nonres.	Rm/Bd
Olivet College; Olivet, Mich. 49076	346	228	41	P	4,530	4,530	2,150
Olivet Nazarene College; Kankahee, Ill. 60901	762[1]	1,005[1]	85	P/Naz	3,210	3,210	1,916
Open Bible College; Des Moines, Iowa 50321	44	30	9	P/OBS	2,000[3]	2,000[3]	2,350[3]
Oral Roberts University; Tulsa, Okla. 74171	2,067[1]	2,041[1]	123	P	3,550	3,550	2,086
Oregon, University of; Eugene, Ore. 97403	8,515[1]	8,130[1]	679	S	1,386	3,915	1,952
Oregon, University of, Health Services Center*; Portland, Ore. 97201	738	555	n.a.	S	n.a.	n.a.	n.a.
Oregon Coll. of Education. *See* Western Oregon State College							
Oregon Graduate Center; Beaverton, Ore. 97006	36	9	23	P	6,000	6,000	—
Oregon Institute of Technology; Klamath Falls, Ore. 97601	1,816[1]	852[1]	130	S	1,252	3,781	1,995
Oregon State University; Corvallis, Ore. 97331	9,773[51]	6,473[51]	940	S	1,077[1]	3,753[1]	1,965
Osteopathic Medicine, College of, of the Pacific; Pomona, Calif. 91766	187	49	17	P	11,500	11,500	—
Osteopathic Medicine and Health Sciences, College of; Des Moines, Iowa 50312	440	116	55	P	10,500	10,500	—
Otis Art Institute of Parsons School of Design; Los Angeles, Calif. 90057	157[1]	241[1]	14	P	3,980	3,980	1,950
Ottawa University; Ottawa, Kan. 66067	258[1]	197[1]	28	P/AB	3,390	3,390	2,000
Otterbein College*; Westerville, Ohio 43081	500	657	93	P/UM	4,428	4,428	1,683
Ouachita Baptist University; Arkadelphia, Ark. 71923	727[5]	782[5]	101	P/SB	2,210	2,210	1,500
Our Lady of Angels College. *See* Neumann College							
Our Lady of Holy Cross College; New Orleans, La. 70114	199	594	35	P/RC	2,350	2,350	—
Our Lady of the Elms, College of; Chicopee, Mass. 01013	14	562	55	P/RC	3,950	3,950	2,250
Our Lady of the Lake University of San Antonio; San Antonio, Tex. 78285	258[1]	601[1]	83	P/RC	2,940	2,940	2,060
Ozarks, College of the; Clarksville, Ark. 72830	335	276	30	P/Pres	1,495	1,495	1,350
Ozarks, The School of the; Point Lookout, Mo. 65726	573	677	85	P	([52])	([52])	([52])
Pace University*; New York, N.Y. 10038	2,024	2,003	772	P	3,264	3,264	2,225
College of White Plains of Pace University; White Plains, N.Y. 10603	282	416	56	P	4,360	4,360	2,850
Pace University, Pleasantville/Briarcliff*; Pleasantville, N.Y. 10570	1,151	1,324	125	P	3,648	3,648	2,700
Pacific, University of the; Stockton, Calif. 95211	1,695	1,820	283	P	7,380[3]	7,380[3]	3,070
Pacific Christian College; Fullerton, Calif. 92631	146	182	16	P/ChC	2,570	2,570	3,000
Pacific Lutheran University; Tacoma, Wash. 98447	1,249[1]	1,585[1]	204[5]	P/L	4,950	4,950	2,370
Pacific Northwest College of Art[53]; Portland, Ore. 97205	52	99	16	P	2,980	2,980	—
Pacific Oaks College; Pasadena, Calif. 91103	7	83	3	P	([54])	([54])	—
Pacific Union College; Angwin, Calif. 94508	902	953	117	P/SDA	5,220[3]	5,220[3]	2,115
Pacific University; Forest Grove, Ore. 97116	590[1]	399[1]	77	P/UCC	4,900	4,900	2,150
Paine College*; Augusta, Ga. 30910	270	488	66	P/M	2,175	2,175	1,365
Palm Beach Atlantic College; West Palm Beach, Fla. 33401	240[1]	258[1]	30	P/SB	1,950	1,950	2,000
Pan American University; Edinburg, Tex. 78539	3,804[1]	5,297[1]	350	S	435	2,055	2,500
Paper Chemistry, The Institute of; Appleton, Wis. 54911	86	17	45	P	3,000	3,000	1,823
Park College; Parkville, Mo. 64152	250[1]	155[1]	30	P/LDS	3,290	3,290	1,700
Parks College of Saint Louis University; Cahokia, Ill. 62206	890	73	49	P/RC	2,920	2,920	1,930
Parsons School of Design. *See* New School for Social Research							
Patten College; Oakland, Calif. 94601	65	64	18	P	2,158	2,158	2,162
Paul Quinn College; Waco, Tex. 76704	211	209	28	P	1,800	1,800	1,500
Peabody Institute of the Johns Hopkins University, Conservatory of Music; Baltimore, Md. 21202	148[1]	171[1]	42	P	5,750[3]	5,750[3]	2,550
Pembroke State University. *See* North Carolina, University System of							
Pennsylvania, University of*; Philadelphia, Pa. 19104	10,575	6,875	6,298	P	6,900	6,900	3,091
Pennsylvania College of Optometry; Philadelphia, Pa. 19141	448	135	56	P	9,320[55]	9,320[55]	—
Pennsylvania College of Podiatric Medicine*; Philadelphia, Pa. 19107	409	61	35	P	6,950	6,950	6,000
Pennsylvania State University, The; University Park, Pa. 16082	31,082[1]	20,312[1]	3,004[5]	S	1,848	3,711	2,274[3]
Behrend College; Erie, Pa. 16563	1,044[2]	490[2]	104	P/S	1,677	3,711	2,037
Capitol Campus*; Middletown, Pa. 17057	1,197	520	130	S	1,233	2,748	1,566
Radnor Center for Graduate Studies*; Radnor, Pa. 19087	204	154	6	S	n.a.	n.a.	—
The Milton S. Hershey Medical Center; Hershey, Pa. 17033	270[1]	120[1]	298	S	5,829	5,829	1,950
Pepperdine University; Malibu, Calif. 90265	2,276	1,656	212	P	6,688	6,688	1,390
Peru State College; Peru, Neb. 68421	294	293	46	S	690	1,200	1,682
Pfeiffer College; Misenheimer, N.C. 28109	368[1]	327[1]	56	P/UM	2,950	2,950	1,715
Philadelphia College of Art; Philadelphia, Pa. 19102	409	569	72	P	5,800	5,800	1,900[23]

Institution and location	Enrollment Male	Enrollment Female	Faculty	Control	Tuition Res.	Tuition Nonres.	Rm/Bd
Philadelphia College of Bible; Langhorne, Pa. 19047	258	221	41	P	2,800	2,800	1,900
Philadelphia College of Osteopathic Medicine; Philadelphia, Pa. 19072	654	169	99	P	8,600	8,900	—
Philadelphia College of Pharmacy and Science; Philadelphia, Pa. 19104	551	516	71	P	4,400	4,400	1,200
Philadelphia College of Textiles and Science; Philadelphia, Pa. 19144	667	957	89	P	4,000[3]	4,000[3]	2,350
Philadelphia College of the Performing Arts; Philadelphia, Pa. 19102	147[1]	164[1]	14	P	4,560	4,560	2,350
Philander Smith College; Little Rock, Ark. 72202	263[1]	263[1]	30	P/UM	1,300	1,300	2,000
Phillips University; Enid, Okla. 73701	584	525	72	P/CC	3,000	3,000	2,000
Phoenix, University of; Phoenix, Ariz. 85024	1,272	636	165	P	3,500	3,500	7,800
Piedmont Bible College; Winston–Salem, N.C. 27101	205	129	24	P/B	1,950	1,950	1,530
Piedmont College; Demorest, Ga. 30535	197	183	22	P/Cong	1,575	1,575	1,985
Pikeville College; Pikeville, Ky. 41501	616		45	P/Pres	2,550	2,550	1,854
Pine Manor College; Chestnut Hill, Mass. 02167	—	518	40	P	6,600	6,600	3,900
Pittsburgh, University of; Pittsburgh, Pa. 15260	8,721[1]	8,519[1]	2,127	P/S	1,970	3,940	2,250
U. of Pittsburgh at Bradford, Bradford, Pa. 16701	386[1]	269[1]	51	P	1,920	3,840	2,310
U. of Pittsburgh at Johnstown; Johnstown, Pa. 15904	1,361[1]	1,030[1]	133	P/S	1,970	3,940	1,930
Pittsburgh State University; Pittsburgh, Kan. 66762	1,891[1]	1,655[1]	219	S	696	1,490	1,788
Pitzer College. *See* Claremont Colleges							
Plymouth State College; Plymouth, N.H. 03264	1,499[1]	1,423[1]	185	S	1,100	3,000	1,820
Point Loma College; San Diego, Calif. 92106	666[2]	950[2]	73	P/Naz	3,400	3,400	1,700
Point Park College; Pittsburgh, Pa. 15222	651[1]	530[1]	70	P	3,920	3,920	2,000
Polytechnic Institute of New York; Brooklyn, N.Y. 11201	2,388		220	P	5,500	5,500	3,900
Pomona College. *See* Claremont Colleges							
Portland, University of; Portland, Ore. 97203	954[1]	902[1]	110	P	3,900	3,900	2,050
Portland School of Art; Portland, Me. 04101	100	155	15	P	4,150	4,150	—
Portland State University; Portland, Ore. 97207	7,619[1]	7,852[1]	477	S	1,233	3,762	2,718
Post College; Waterbury, Conn. 06708	324[1]	543[1]	32	P	4,000	4,000	2,500
Prairie View A&M University; Prairie View, Tex. 77445	2,185[1]	2,342[1]	265	S	136	1,360	2,104
Pratt Institute; Brooklyn, N.Y. 11205	2,099[1]	1,401[1]	136	P	5,200	5,200	2,950
Presbyterian College*; Clinton, S.C. 29325	486	413	53	P/PUS	3,705	3,705	1,835
Princeton University; Princeton, N.J. 08544	3,849[1]	2,131[1]	636	P	8,380	8,380	3,090
Principia College; Elsah, Ill. 62028	347[1]	462[1]	60	P	5,666[3]	5,666[3]	3,180
Providence College; Providence, R.I. 02861	1,751[1]	1,823[1]	198	P/RC	4,628	4,628	2,900
Puerto Rico, University of; Río Piedras, P.R. 00931:							
Bayamón Technological University College; Bayamón, P.R. 00619	1,764	2,144	222	S	n.a.	n.a.	—
Cayey University College; Cayey, P.R. 00633	1,160[1]	1,995[1]	132	S	1,900	1,900	1,200
Mayaguez Campus*; Mayaguez, P.R. 00708	4,969	3,370	479	S	212	212	—
Medical Sciences Campus*; San Juan, P.R. 00936	942	1,576	702	S	150	n.a.	—
Río Piedras Campus; Río Piedras, P.R. 00931	5,287[1]	9,837[1]	1,155	S	435	2,075	902
Puget Sound, University of; Tacoma, Wash. 98416	1,357[1]	1,708[1]	162	P	5,400	5,400	2,580
Puget Sound College of the Bible; Edmonds, Wash. 98020	90	60	9	P/CC	2,025	2,025	2,025
Purdue University; West Lafayette, Ind. 47907	17,554	11,621[1]	2,033	S	1,158	3,118	2,050
Calumet Campus; Hammond, Ind. 46323	1,452[1]	1,400[1]	205	S	1,038	2,436	—
Indiana University–Purdue University at Indianapolis. *See* Indiana University							
Queens College; Charlotte, N.C. 28274	—	952[1]	48	P/Pres	4,200	4,200	2,360
Queens College (NYC). *See* New York, City University of							
Quincy College; Quincy, Ill. 62301	381	399	71	P/RC	3,950	3,950	2,000
Quinnipiac College; Hamden, Conn. 06518	799	1,427	173	P	4,500	4,500	2,260
Radcliffe College. *See* Harvard University							
Radford University*; Radford, Va. 24142	1,423	3,427	284	S	1,035	1,635	2,016
Ramapo College of New Jersey*; Mahwah, N.J. 07430	2,567		140	S	n.a.	n.a.	1,250
Rand Graduate Institute; Santa Monica, Calif. 90406	45	6	—	P	4,500	4,500	5,500
Randolph–Macon College; Ashland, Va. 23005	511	345	67	P/UM	5,000[3]	5,000[3]	2,200[3]
Randolph–Macon Woman's College; Lynchburg, Va. 24503	—	756	63	P/UM	5,900[3]	5,900[3]	2,600[3]
Redlands, University of; Redlands, Calif. 92373	1,331[1]	1,240[1]	100	P	5,650	5,650	2,350
Reed College; Portland, Ore. 97202	621[1]	448[1]	114	P	7,070	7,070	2,630
Reformed Bible College; Grand Rapids, Mich. 49507	115	87	16	P	2,120	2,120	1,750
Regis College; Denver, Colo. 80207	540	492	70	P/RC	5,160[3]	5,160[3]	3,060[3]
Regis College*; Weston, Mass. 02193	—	908	55	P/RC	4,025	4,025	2,630
Rensselaer Polytechnic Institute; Troy, N.Y. 12181	4,618[2]	1,069[2]	365	P	3,770	3,770	2,704
Rhode Island, University of; Kingston, R.I. 02881	5,449	5,289	728	S	1,028	3,552	2,598

Institution and location	Enrollment Male	Enrollment Female	Faculty	Control	Tuition Res.	Tuition Nonres.	Rm/Bd
Rhode Island College; Providence, R.I. 02908	3,025[1]	6,251[1]	376	S	854	2,838	2,206
Rhode Island School of Design; Providence, R.I. 02903	643	828	90	P	6,700[3]	6,700[3]	2,880[3]
Rice University; Houston, Tex. 77001	2,241	1,338	367	P	3,500	3,500	3,200
Richmond, University of; Richmond, Va. 23173	1,580	1,240	194	P/B	4,845	4,845	1,900
Richmond College, The American International College of London; London, England TW10 6JP	207[1]	270[1]	20	P	8,250	8,250	2,000
Rider College*; Lawrenceville, N.J. 08648	1,758	1,646	188	P	3,600	3,600	2,004
Ringling School of Art and Design; Sarasota, Fla. 33580	220[1]	250[1]	30	P	2,925	2,925	1,905
Rio Grande College; Rio Grande, Ohio 45674	526[1]	747[1]	62[5]	P/S	855	2,850	1,920
Ripon College; Ripon, Wis. 54971	536	416	71	P	6,020[3]	6,020[3]	1,845[3]
Rivier College; Nashua, N.H. 03060	36	529	42	P/RC	3,500	3,500	2,400
Roanoke Bible College; Elizabeth City, N.C. 27909	72[1]	76[1]	8	P/ChC	1,248	1,248	1,480
Roanoke College; Salem, Va. 24153	560[1]	569[1]	67	P/L	4,200	4,200	1,900
Robert Morris College; Coraopolis, Pa. 15108	1,314	1,460	95	P	2,580	2,580	1,700
Roberts Wesleyan College; Rochester, N.Y. 14624	192	399	53	P/FM	3,480	3,480	2,000
Rochester, The University of; Rochester, N.Y. 14627	4,048[1]	2,539[1]	1,056	P	5,975	5,975	2,709
Rochester Institute of Technology; Rochester, N.Y. 14623	5,094	2,539	588	P	5,064	5,064	2,904
Rockford College; Rockford, Ill. 61101	341	367	60[5]	P	3,890	3,890	1,875
Rockhurst College; Kansas City, Mo. 64110	585	627	84	P/RC	3,840	3,840	2,250
Rocky Mountain College; Billings, Mont. 59102	193	151	38	P[56]	3,124	3,124	1,950
Roger Williams College*; Bristol, R.I. 02809	1,248	642	82	P	3,100	3,100	2,000
Rollins College; Winter Park, Fla. 32789	638[1]	724[1]	105	P	5,710	5,710	2,640
Roosevelt University*; Chicago, Ill. 60605	1,767	2,385	248	P	3,000	3,000	n.a.
Rosary College; River Forest, Ill. 60305	156[1]	610[1]	75	P/RC	3,850	3,850	2,250
Rose–Hulman Institute of Technology; Terre Haute, Ind. 47803	1,213	—	85	P	4,740	4,740	2,240
Rosemont College; Rosemont, Pa. 19312	—	703	37	P	4,300	4,300	2,665
Rush University; Chicago, Ill. 60612	443[1]	729[1]	636	P	n.a.	n.a.	n.a.
Russell Sage College*; Troy, N.Y. 12180	—	1,303	133	P	4,100	4,100	2,250
Rust College; Holly Springs, Miss. 38635	328	422	40	P/UM	2,125	2,125	1,110
Rutgers Medical School. *See* Medicine & Dentistry, Coll. of, of New Jersey							
Rutgers, The State University of New Jersey; New Brunswick, N.J. 08903	16,029[1]	16,077[1]	2,602	S	1,110	2,220	2,000
Sacred Heart, Univ. of the; Santurce, P.R. 00914	2,550	4,341	131	P/RC	1,504	1,504	1,150
Sacred Heart College; Belmont, N.C. 28012	108[1]	297[1]	35	P/RC	([57])	([57])	1,793
Sacred Heart University; Bridgeport, Conn. 06606	677[1]	1,022[1]	75	P/RC	1,495	1,495	—
Saginaw Valley State College; University Center, Mich. 48710	980[1]	1,095[1]	122	S	1,519	2,790	2,126
St. Ambrose College; Davenport, Iowa 52803	655[1]	500[1]	72	P/RC	4,410	4,410	1,720
St. Andrews Presbyterian College; Laurinburg, N.C. 28352	381[1]	390[1]	50	P	4,650	4,650	2,200
St. Anselm College; Manchester, N.H. 03102	879[1]	786[1]	107	RC	4,750	4,750	2,450
St. Augustine's College; Raleigh, N.C. 27611	709[1]	918[1]	81	P/E	1,600	1,600	1,150
St. Benedict, College of; St. Joseph, Minn. 56374	2,148[1]	41[1]	88	P	4,390	4,390	n.a.
St. Bonaventure University; St. Bonaventure, N.Y. 14778	1,471[1]	1,311[1]	165	P	4,250	2,250	2,390
St. Catherine, The College of; St. Paul Minn. 55105	10[1]	1,774[1]	137	P/RC	4,480	4,480	2,200
St. Cloud State University. *See* Minnesota State University System							
St. Edward's University; Austin, Tex. 78704	1,297	1,131	71	P	2,740	2,740	2,500
St. Elizabeth, College of; Convent Station, N.J. 07961	2[1]	517[1]	47	P/RC	4,000	4,000	2,200
St. Francis, College of; Joliet, Ill. 60435	222[1]	359[1]	46	P/RC	3,560	3,560	2,364
St. Francis College; Brooklyn, N.Y. 11201	899	777	69	P	3,168	3,168	—
St. Francis College; Fort Wayne, Ind. 46808	131[1]	273[1]	36	RC	([58])	([58])	2,100
St. Francis College; Loretto, Pa. 15940	603[1]	520[1]	65	P/RC	3,520	3,520	2,000
St. John Fisher College; Rochester, N.Y. 14618	1,465	1,525	99	P	4,624[3]	4,624[3]	2,623[3]
St. John's College; Annapolis, Md. 21404	216	170	41	P	6,700	6,700	2,600
St. John's College*; Sante Fe, N.M. 87501	184	151	35	P	6,000	6,000	2,400
Saint John's College*; Camarillo, Calif. 93010	190	—	n.a.	P/RC	n.a.	n.a.	n.a.
Saint John's University; Collegeville, Minn. 56321	1,973[1]	36[1]	115	P	4,365	4,365	2,140
St. John's University; Jamaica, N.Y. 11439	7,021[1]	5,478[1]	570	P/RC	3,500[3]	3,500[3]	3,400[3]
St. Joseph College; West Hartford, Conn. 06117	—	589	65	P	4,500	4,500	2,750
St. Joseph's College; Brooklyn, N.Y. 11205	198[1]	1,047[1]	115	P	2,900[2]	2,900[2]	—
St. Joseph's College[59]; Mountain View, Calif. 94042	90	—	16	P/RC	2,750	2,750	750
St. Joseph's College; North Windham, Me. 04062	120	340	35	P/RC	3,700	3,700	2,000
St. Joseph's College; Rensselaer, Ind. 47978	565	367	50	P/RC	1,760	1,760	995
St. Joseph's University; Philadelphia, Pa. 19131	1,537[1]	1,273[1]	142	P/RC	4,110	4,110	2,700
St. Joseph the Provider, College of; Rutland, Vt. 05701	31[1]	123[1]	10	P/RC	3,330	3,330	2,390
St. Lawrence University; Canton, N.Y. 13617	1,193[1]	1,119[1]	158	P	5,745	5,745	2,165
St. Leo College; St. Leo, Fla. 33574	645[1]	520[1]	51	P/RC	3,360	3,360	1,500
St. Louis Christian College; Florissant, Mo. 63033	84	59	12	P/ChC	1,400	1,400	1,210
St. Louis College of Pharmacy; St. Louis, Mo. 63110	331[1]	316[1]	30	P	3,480	3,480	2,100
St. Louis Conservatory of Music*; St. Louis, Mo. 63130	30	25	5	P	2,700	2,700	—

Institution and location	Enrollment Male	Enrollment Female	Faculty	Control	Tuition Res.	Tuition Nonres.	Rm/Bd
St. Louis University; St. Louis, Mo. 63103	2,969	2,595	926	P	4,220	4,220	2,110
St. Martin's College*; Lacey, Wash. 98503	228	172	40	P/RC	3,422	3,422	1,800
St. Mary, College of; Omaha, Neb. 68124	203	861	58	P/RC	([60])	([60])	1,810
St. Mary College; Leavenworth, Kan. 66048	—	650[1]	45	P/RC	2,700	2,700	1,900
St. Mary of the Plains College; Dodge City, Kan. 67801	200[1]	427[1]	64	P/RC	3,000	3,000	2,100
St. Mary–of–the–Woods College; St. Mary–of–the–Woods, Ind. 47876	—	507	56	P/RC	3,900	3,900	1,890
St. Mary's College; Notre Dame, Ind. 46556	20	1,746	117	P/RC	4,930[3]	4,930[3]	2,511[3]
St. Mary's College; Orchard Lake, Mich. 48033	79	49	16	P	2,100	2,100	2,100
St. Mary's College*; Winona, Minn. 55987	634	595	72	P/RC	3,379	3,379	1,830
St. Mary's College of California; Moraga, Calif. 94575	1,258[1]	1,695[1]	120	P/RC	3,900	3,900	1,800
St. Mary's College of Maryland; St. Mary's City, Md. 20686	448	567	65	S	875	1,825	2,550
St. Mary's Dominican College; New Orleans, La. 70118	5	363	30	P/RC	3,690	3,690	2,600
St. Mary's University; San Antonio, Tex. 78284	1,816	1,452	165	P/RC	3,520	3,520	2,000
St. Michael's College; Winoski, Vt. 05404	877[1]	761[1]	100	P/RC	5,443	5,443	2,345
St. Norbert College; De Pere, Wis. 54115	759	801	95	P/RC	3,950	3,950	1,500
St. Olaf College; Northfield, Minn. 55057	1,375	1,626	210	P/AL	5,335	5,335	1,915
St. Patrick's College, Mountain View, Calif. *See* St. Joseph's College							
St. Paul Bible College; Bible College, Minn. 55375	266[1]	344[1]	36	P/CMA	n.a.	n.a.	n.a.
St. Paul's College*; Lawrenceville, Va. 23868	343	350	41	P/E	2,180	2,180	1,660
St. Peter's College; Jersey City, N.J. 07306	1,920[1]	2,287[1]	123	P/RC	3,600	3,600	—
St. Rose, The College of; Albany, N.Y. 12203	258[1]	1,024[1]	96	P	3,900[3]	3,900[3]	2,500[3]
St. Scholastica, College of; Duluth, Minn. 55811	699	183	89	RC	3,606	3,606	1,890
St. Teresa, College of; Winona, Minn. 55987	10[1]	600[1]	62	P/RC	4,500[3]	4,500[3]	1,800
St. Thomas, College of; St. Paul, Minn. 55105	3,378[1]	2,252[1]	150	P/RC	4,160	4,160	2,000
St. Thomas, University of; Houston, Tex. 77006	541	730	98	RC	2,750	2,750	1,400
St. Thomas Aquinas College; Sparkill, N.Y. 10976	577[1]	839[1]	n.a.	P	3,000	3,000	n.a.
St. Xavier College; Chicago, Ill. 60655	408	984	143	P/RC	3,630	3,630	2,454
Salem College; Salem, W. Va. 26426	330	300	60	P	3,710	3,710	2,070
Salem College; Winston–Salem, N.C. 27108	1	534	55	P/Mor	4,200	4,200	2,650
Salem State College; Salem, Mass. 01970	2,026	2,990	280	S	845	2,688	1,870
Salisbury State College; Salisbury, Md. 21801	1,308[1]	1,647[1]	184	S	960	2,000	2,270
Salve Regina College. *See* Newport College							
Samford University*; Birmingham, Ala. 35229	1,791	1,588	218	P/B	2,464	2,560	1,600
Sam Houston State University; Huntsville, Tex. 77341	4,553	4,800	392	S	404	1,264	1,904
San Diego, University of*; San Diego, Calif. 92110	1,070	1,383	175	P/RC	4,050	4,050	2,500
San Diego State University; San Diego, Calif. 92182[18]	9,270	9,831	881	S	—	2,620	3,200
San Francisco, University of; San Francisco, Calif. 94117	1,952[1]	2,110[1]	237	P/RC	4,430	4,430	2,506
San Francisco Art Institute; San Francisco, Calif. 94133	235	182	54	P	4,250[5]	4,250[5]	—
San Francisco Conservatory of Music, The; San Francisco, Calif. 94122	94[1]	80[1]	12	P	5,000	5,000	—
San Francisco State Univ.; San Francisco, Calif. 94132	5,490	7,335	1,200	S	400	2,670	2,350
Sangamon State University; Springfield, Ill. 62708	509[1]	446[1]	169	S	780	2,340	2,760
San Jose Bible College*; San Jose, Calif. 95108	87	40	7	P/ND	1,680	1,680	1,260
San Jose State University; San Jose, Calif. 95192[18]	7,136	7,140	991	S	386	386[61]	2,000
Santa Clara, University of; Santa Clara, Calif. 95053	2,501	2,193	255	P/RC	4,593	4,593	2,385
Sante Fe, College of; Santa Fe, N.M. 87501	309	430	60[5]	P/RC	2,800	2,800	2,060
Sarah Lawrence College; Bronxville, N.Y. 10708	162[2]	799[2]	69	P	8,150	8,150	3,600
Savannah State College; Savannah, Ga. 31404	991	1,112	140	S	756	1,806	2,271
Scranton, University of; Scranton, Pa. 18510	2,434	1,844	230	P/RC	3,520	3,520	2,040
Scripps College. *See* Claremont Colleges							
Seattle Pacific University; Seattle, Wash. 98119	1,132[1]	1,719[1]	133	P	4,002	4,002	2,190
Seattle University; Seattle, Wash. 98122	1,319[1]	1,429[1]	170	P	([62])	([62])	2,277
Seton Hall University*; South Orange, N.J. 07079	3,615	3,381	n.a.	P/RC	n.a.	n.a.	n.a.
Seton Hill College; Greensburg, Pa. 15601	—	727[1]	51	P	4,260[3]	4,260[3]	2,300[3]
Shaw University*; Raleigh, N.C. 27611	736	594	57	P/B	2,500	2,500	1,300
Sheldon Jackson College; Sitka, Alaska 99835	76	78	30	P/Pres	2,700	2,700	2,700
Shepherd College; Shepherdstown, W. Va. 25443	887[1]	1,117[1]	104	S	466	1,466	1,500
Sherwood Music School; Chicago, Ill. 60605	60	40	24	P	2,000	2,000	—
Shippensburg State College; Shippensburg, Pa. 17257	2,160[1]	2,507[1]	265	S	1,260	2,190	1,470
Shorter College; Rome, Ga. 30161	298[1]	475[1]	53	P	2,700[63]	2,700	1,650
Siena College; Loudonville, N.Y. 12211	1,727	1,481	131	P	3,625	3,625	2,350
Siena Heights College; Adrian, Mich. 49221	625[1]	892[1]	53	P/RC	3,330	3,330	2,000
Sierra Nevada College; Incline Village, Nev. 89402	65	62	—	P	2,000	2,000	—
Silver Lake College; Manitowoc, Wis. 54220	89[1]	311[1]	30	P/RC	3,400	3,400	2,060
Simmons College; Boston, Mass. 01940	47[1]	2,194[1]	175	P	6,464	6,464	3,170
Simon's Rock of Bard College; Great Barrington, Mass. 01230	134	154	25	P	6,400	6,400	2,300
Simpson College; Indianola, Iowa 50125	474[2]	526[2]	60	P/UM	4,535	4,535	1,785

Institution and location	Enrollment Male	Female	Faculty	Control	Tuition Res.	Nonres.	Rm/Bd
Simpson College; San Francisco, Calif. 94134	91	98	15	CMA	2,800	2,800	2,000
Sioux Falls College; Sioux Falls, S.D. 57101	244	305	42	P/B	2,900	2,900	1,500
Skidmore College; Saratoga Springs, N.Y. 12866	562[1]	1,622[1]	166	P	6,390	6,390	3,010
Slippery Rock State College; Slippery Rock, Pa. 16057	2,407[1]	2,571[1]	331	S	1,250	2,190	1,582
Smith College; Northampton, Mass. 01063	—	2,566[1]	260	P	6,800	6,800	2,700
Sojourner–Douglass College*; Baltimore, Md. 21205	170		n.a.	P	n.a.	n.a.	n.a.
Sonoma State University; Rohnert Park, Calif. 94928[18]	2,188	3,071	n.a.	S	—	2,160	3,000
South, The University of the*; Sewanee, Tenn. 37375	607	454	116	P/E	5,680	5,680	1,590
South Alabama, University of; Mobile, Ala. 36688	4,116[1]	4,509[1]	300	S	1,125	1,425	1,806
Southampton College. *See* Long Island Univ. Center							
South Carolina, University of; Columbia, S.C. 29208	6,863	6,429	976	S	1,230	2,510	1,590
USC at Aiken; Aiken, S.C. 29801	1,247		69	S	900	1,890	—
USC at Spartanburg; Spartanburg, S.C. 29303	968	1,457	75	S	425	920	—
USC–Coastal Carolina College; Conway, S.C. 29526	1,197[1]	1,182[1]	110	S	850	1,840	—
South Carolina State College; Orangeburg, S.C. 29117	1,361	1,712	232	S	810	1,620	1,640
South Dakota, University of; Vermillion, S.D. 57069	2,807[1]	2,476[1]	346	S	854	1,884	1,500
University of South Dakota at Springfield; Springfield, S.D. 57062	500	206	52	S	748	1,552	1,320
South Dakota School of Mines and Technology; Rapid City, S.D. 57701	2,100[1]	600[1]	109	S	1,010	2,000	1,500
South Dakota State University; Brookings, S.D. 57007	3,548[1]	2,896[1]	474	S	783	1,728	1,382
Southeastern Bible College; Birmingham, Ala. 35256	82	57	18	P/ND	1,200	1,200	1,920
Southeastern College of Osteopathic Medicine*; North Miami Beach, Fla. 33162	n.a.	n.a.	n.a.	P	n.a.	n.a.	n.a.
Southeastern College of the Assemblies of God; Lakeland, Fla. 33801	655[1]	505[1]	42	P/AG	1,600	1,600	1,400
Southeastern Louisiana University; Hammond, La. 70402	3,513[1]	5,476[1]	270	S	634	1,264	1,356
Southeastern Massachusetts University; North Dartmouth, Mass. 02747	2,683[1]	2,681[1]	297	S	983	2,989	2,988
Southeastern Oklahoma State Univ.; Durant, Okla. 74701	2,072	1,953	142	S	480	1,091	1,600
Southeastern University; Washington, D.C. 20024	653	467	—	P	2,000	2,000	—
Southeast Missouri State University; Cape Girardeau, Mo. 63701	3,512[1]	4,074[1]	385	S	474	1,024	1,400
Southern Arkansas University; Magnolia, Ark. 71753	891[1]	1,146[1]	140	S	720	1,110	1,330
Southern Bible College; Houston, Tex. 77213	70	51	n.a.	P/CG	1,560	1,560	1,680
Southern California, Univ. of; Los Angeles, Calif. 90007	10,430[1]	7,118[1]	1,730	P	6,300	6,300	2,822
Southern California College; Costa Mesa, Calif. 92626	325[1]	302[1]	30	P/AG	2,630	2,630	1,970
Southern California College of Optometry; Fullerton, Calif. 92631	272	110	40	P	6,000	6,000	—
Southern California Institute of Architecture; Santa Monica, Calif. 90404	262	94	35	P	3,330	3,330	—
Southern College of Optometry; Memphis, Tenn. 38104	501[1]	68[1]	38	P	5,640	9,840	n.a.
Southern College of Seventh-Day Adventists[64]; Collegedale, Tenn. 37315	656[1]	782[1]	118	SDA	3,780	3,780	1,900
Southern Colorado, University of; Pueblo, Colo. 81001	2,172	1,648	196	S	650	2,860	2,120
Southern Connecticut State College; New Haven, Conn. 06515	2,516[1]	3,853[1]	416	S	883	1,883	2,434
Southern Illinois University at Carbondale; Carbondale, Ill. 62901	12,758[1]	7,070[1]	1,454	S	810[65]	2,430[65]	2,224[2]
Southern Illinois University at Edwardsville; Edwardsville, Ill. 62026	3,392	3,393	650	S	1,068	2,664	2,000
Southern Maine, University of; Portland, Me. 04103	3,369	4,403	400	S	1,350	3,840	2,210
Southern Methodist University; Dallas, Tex. 75275	3,703[1]	3,328[1]	439	P	5,000	5,000	2,060
Southern Missionary College. *See* Southern College of Seventh-Day Adventists							
Southern Mississippi, Univ. of; Hattiesburg, Miss. 39401	4,751[1]	5,663[1]	658	S	990	1,965	1,740
Southern Oregon State College; Ashland, Ore. 97520	1,736[1]	1,706[1]	210	S	1,254	3,423	1,885
Southern School of Pharmacy. *See* Mercer Univ.							
Southern Technical Institute; Marietta, Ga. 30060	2,758	242	100	S	660	1,710	3,929
Southern University and A&M College System; Baton Rouge, La. 70813:							
Southern University and A&M College; Baton Rouge, La. 70813	4,017	4,455	499	S	269	584	1,082
Southern University of New Orleans; New Orleans, La. 70126	837	1,774	120	S	494	1,124	—
Southern Utah State College; Cedar City, Utah 84720	901[1]	778[1]	100	S	684	1,722	2,060
Southern Vermont College; Bennington, Vt. 05201	178[1]	184[1]	16	P	3,390	3,390	2,790
South Florida, The University of; Tampa, Fla. 33620	7,062[1]	6,965[1]	1,152	S	819	2,401	1,880
New College Campus; Sarasota, Fla. 33580	200	200	48	S	1,054	3,322	2,100
St. Petersburg Campus*; St. Petersburg, Fla. 33701	980	1,123	30	S	792	2,184	—
South Texas, University System of:							
Corpus Christi State Univ.; Corpus Christi, Tex. 78412	1,167	1,690	n.a.	S	328	1,188	700[23]

Institution and location	Enrollment: Male	Enrollment: Female	Faculty	Control	Tuition: Res.	Tuition: Nonres.	Rm/Bd
Laredo State University; Laredo, Tex. 78040	347	546	25	S	120	1,200	—
Texas A&I University; Kingsville, Tex. 78363	2,377	2,280	236[5]	S	492	2,031	1,954
South Texas College of Law; Houston, Tex. 77002	381	174	25	P	3,800	3,800	—
Southwest, College of the; Hobbs, N.M. 88240	93	129	10	P	1,170	1,170	720[23]
Southwest Baptist University; Bolivar, Mo. 65613	643	782	72	P/SB	2,620	2,620	1,260
Southwestern Adventist College; Keene, Tex. 76059	302[1]	342[1]	n.a.	P/SDA	4,448	4,448	2,266
Southwestern at Memphis; Memphis, Tenn. 38112	536[1]	544[1]	86	P/PUS	4,500	4,500	1,280
Southwestern Baptist Bible College; Phoenix, Ariz. 85032	101[1]	61[1]	12	P/B	2,144	2,144	1,950
Southwestern College, Winfield, Kan. 67156	274	239	42	P/UM	2,650	2,650	1,725
Southwestern College of Christian Ministries; Oklahoma City, Okla. 73127	42	18	4	P/PH	1,650	1,650	1,440
Southwestern Louisiana, University of; Lafayette, La. 70504	5,827[1]	5,173[1]	603	S	550	1,200	1,600
Southwestern Oklahoma State University; Weatherford, Okla. 73096	1,696[1]	1,911[1]	219	S	600	1,570	1,400
Southwestern University; Georgetown, Tex. 78626	435[1]	529[1]	65	P/UM	3,500[2]	3,500[2]	2,500
Southwestern University School of Law; Los Angeles, Calif. 90005	1,000	555	40	P	n.a.	n.a.	n.a.
Southwest Missouri State Univ.; Springfield, Mo. 65804	5,000[1]	5,700[1]	610	S	650	1,300	1,340
Southwest Texas State Univ.; San Marcos, Tex. 78666	7,187	7,331	494	S	848	1,504	1,750
Spalding College; Louisville, Ky. 40203	67	378	58	P/RC	2,900	2,900	1,850
Spelman College; Atlanta, Ga. 30314	—	1,447[1]	85	P	2,700	2,700	2,035
Spertus College of Judaica; Chicago, Ill. 60605	21	40	12	P	3,240	3,240	—
Spring Arbor College; Spring Arbor, Mich. 49283	302[1]	373[1]	46	P/FM	3,900	3,900	1,700
Springfield College*; Springfield, Mass. 01109	1,021	1,090	145	P	3,366	3,366	1,866
Spring Garden College; Philadelphia, Pa. 19118	1,085	258	45	P	3,550	3,550	—
Spring Hill College; Mobile, Ala. 36608	432	426	70	P/RC	4,200	4,200	2,250
Stanford University; Stanford, Calif. 94305	7,379[1]	4,227[1]	1,127	P	7,140	7,140	2,965
Staten Island, College of (NYC). *See* New York, City University of							
Stephen F. Austin State Univ.; Nacogdoches, Tex. 75962	4,800	5,500	420	S	622	1,366	3,008
Stephens College; Columbia, Mo. 65215	20[1]	1,200[1]	115	P	5,175	5,175	3,275
Sterling College; Sterling, Kan. 67579	199[1]	232[1]	36	P/UP	3,100	3,100	1,600
Stetson University; DeLand, Fla. 32720	1,452[1]	1,483[1]	120	P/B	4,200	4,200	1,850
Stetson Univ. College of Law; St. Petersburg, Fla. 33707	320	178	21	P	4,650	4,650	2,287
Steubenville, University of; Steubenville, Ohio 43952	450[1]	550[1]	50	P/RC	4,170	4,170	2,500
Stevens Institute of Technology; Hoboken, N.J. 07030	1,280	250	130	P	6,500	6,500	2,500
Stillman College; Tuscaloosa, Ala. 35401	252	388	32	P/PUS	1,800	1,800	1,758
Stockton State College; Pomona, N.J. 08240	2,093[1]	1,690[1]	156	S	1,136	1,776	2,260
Stonehill College; North Easton, Mass. 02356	815[1]	918[1]	85	P	4,750	4,750	2,700
Strayer College; Washington, D.C. 20005	665[1]	1,389[1]	50	P	([66])	([66])	—
Suffolk University; Boston, Mass. 02108	1,088	1,033	144	P	3,630[2]	3,630[2]	—
Sul Ross State University; Alpine, Tex. 79830	763[1]	575[1]	67	S	292	1,444	1,770
Susquehanna University; Selinsgrove, Pa. 17870	738	686	98	P/LCA	4,600	4,600	1,977
Swarthmore College; Swarthmore, Pa. 19081	711[1]	604[1]	135	P	7,130	7,130	3,000
Sweet Briar College; Sweet Briar, Va. 24595	1	632	66	P	6,700[3]	6,700[3]	2,250[3]
Syracuse University; Syracuse, N.Y. 13210	8,003[1]	6,897[1]	816	P	3,110	3,110	3,050
Tabor College; Hillsboro, Kan. 67063	184	200	32	P/MB	2,800	2,800	1,840
Talladega College*; Talladega, Ala. 35160	214	428	49	P	1,615	1,615	1,360
Tampa, The University of; Tampa, Fla. 33606	771	644	88	P	4,356	4,356	2,000
Tampa College; Tampa, Fla. 33607	740	900	n.a.	P	1,620	1,620	—
Tarkio College; Tarkio, Mo. 64491	175	125	30	P/UP	3,500	3,500	1,900
Tarleton State University[67]; Stephenville, Tex. 76402	1,944[1]	1,784[1]	144	S	120	1,200	1,648
Taylor University; Upland, Ind. 46989	614	766	87	P/ND	4,424	4,424	1,717
Teachers College (NYC). *See* Columbia University							
Temple University; Philadelphia, Pa. 19122	16,033[1]	15,441[1]	1,781	S	2,382	4,440	2,425
Tennessee State University[12]; Nashville, Tenn. 37203	2,246[1]	2,504[1]	406	S	—	1,530	1,826
Tennessee System, University of; Knoxville, Tenn. 37916:							
U. of Tennessee at Chattanooga; Chattanooga, Tenn. 37402	2,327[1]	2,335[1]	265	S	620	1,840	780[23]
U. of Tennessee at Knoxville; Knoxville, Tenn. 37996	15,515[1]	13,086[1]	1,245	S	852	2,611	1,800
U. of Tennessee at Martin; Martin, Tenn. 38238	2,493	2,669	225	S	750	1,530	789[68]
U. of Tennessee Center for the Health Sciences; Memphis, Tenn. 38163	1,351[1]	736[1]	n.a.	S	n.a.	n.a.	615[23]
Tennessee Technological Univ.[12]; Cookeville, Tenn. 38501	4,261	3,167	390	S	705	2,235	1,500
Tennessee Wesleyan College; Athens; Tenn. 37303	165	179	29	P/M	2,640	2,640	2,175
Texas, University of, System; Austin, Tex. 78701:							
U. of Texas at Arlington; Arlington, Tex. 76019	7,442[1]	4,964[1]	677	S	450	1,535	2,650
U. of Texas at Austin; Austin, Tex. 78712	26,269[1]	21,876[1]	1,883	S	452	1,532	2,476
U. of Texas at Dallas; Richardson, Tex. 75080	1,065	1,037	189	S	550	1,530	—
U. of Texas at El Paso; El Paso, Tex. 79968	7,871[1]	7,547[1]	430	S	150	1,440	2,670
U. of Texas at San Antonio; San Antonio, Tex. 78285	5,013[1]	5,549[1]	235	S	120	1,200	—

Institution and location	Enrollment: Male	Enrollment: Female	Faculty	Control	Tuition: Res.	Tuition: Nonres.	Rm/Bd
U. of Texas at Tyler; Tyler, Tex. 75701	798	1,244	81	S	380	1,460	—
U. of Texas Health Science Center at Dallas; Dallas, Tex. 75235	823	461	730	S	120	1,200	—
U. of Texas Health Science Center at Houston; Houston, Tex. 77025	1,255[1]	1,033[1]	700	S	400	1,200	5,000
U. of Texas Health Science Center at San Antonio; San Antonio, Tex. 78284	1,225[1]	1,047[1]	502	S	400	1,200	—
U. of Texas Medical Branch; Galveston, Tex. 77550	760[1]	839[1]	450	S	400	1,200	—
U. of Texas of the Permian Basin; Odessa, Tex. 79760	765[1]	875[1]	92	S	240	1,320	890[23]
Texas A&I Univ. *See* South Texas, Univ. System of							
Texas A&M University; College Station, Tex. 77843	20,284	12,195	2,074	S	120	1,200	2,086
Texas A&M Univ. at Galveston; Galveston, Tex. 77553	369	128	56	S	120	1,200	2,481
Texas Chiropractic College*; Pasadena, Tex. 77505	362	68	28	P	3,185	3,185	—
Texas Christian University; Fort Worth, Tex. 76129	2,919[2]	3,639[2]	303	P/DC	3,750	3,750	2,285
Texas College; Tyler, Tex. 75702	292	211	34	P	1,800	1,800	1,950
Texas College of Osteopathic Medicine; Fort Worth, Tex. 76107	259	83	130	S	400	900	—
Texas Lutheran College; Seguin, Tex. 78155	495[1]	548[1]	61	P/L	2,800	2,800	1,845
Texas Southern University; Houston, Tex. 77004	4,650[1]	3,548[1]	n.a.	S	478	1,630	970
Texas Tech University; Lubbock, Tex. 79409	9,529[1]	7,402[1]	782	S	649	1,009	3,214
Texas Wesleyan College; Fort Worth, Tex. 76105	622	826	82	P/UM	2,800	2,800	1,950
Texas Woman's University; Denton, Tex. 76204	375	5,723	460	S	128	1,280	1,224
Thiel College; Greenville, Pa. 16125	437	419	62	P/LCA	4,866[3]	4,866[3]	2,353[3]
Thomas Aquinas College; Santa Paula, Calif. 93060	57	53	14	P/RC	4,290	4,290	2,290
Thomas College; Waterville, Me. 04901	179[1]	225[1]	21	P	4,000	4,000	2,200
Thomas Jefferson University; Philadelphia, Pa. 19107	92[1]	699[1]	58	P	5,000	5,000	800[23]
Thomas M. Cooley Law School; Lansing, Mich. 48933	811	271	21	P	3,630	3,870	—
Thomas More College; Fort Mitchell, Ky. 41017	387	318	55	P/RC	3,680	3,680	2,260
Tiffin University; Tiffin, Ohio 44883	164	170	12	P	2,160	2,160	1,140
Tift College; Forsyth, Ga. 31029	107[1]	613[1]	28	P/B	2,070	2,070	1,710
Toledo, The University of; Toledo, Ohio 43606	10,801[1]	10,316[1]	654	S	1,260	2,862	2,130
Tougaloo College; Tougaloo, Miss. 39174	245	453	67	P	2,450	2,450	1,320
Touro College; New York, N.Y. 10001	735[1]	1,111[1]	123	P	3,200	3,200	1,300
Towson State University; Towson, Md. 21204	4,046	5,363	500	S	1,097	2,047	2,050
Transylvania University; Lexington, Ky. 40508	361[1]	389[1]	52	P	4,600	4,600	2,100
Trenton State College; Trenton, N.J. 08625	2,274[1]	3,493[1]	378	S	1,070	1,670	2,320
Trevecca Nazarene College; Nashville, Tenn. 37203	445[2]	424[2]	48	P/Naz	2,412	2,412	1,728
Tri-College University; Moorhead, Minn. 26260	220		4	S	([69])	([70])	—
Trinity Bible Institute; Ellendale, N.D. 58436	183	146	12	P/AG	1,568	1,568	1,500
Trinity Christian College; Palos Heights, Ill. 60463	166[1]	196[1]	25	P/CR	3,350	3,350	1,900
Trinity College; Burlington, Vt. 05401	19	411	38	P/RC	4,080	4,080	2,380
Trinity College*; Deerfield, Ill. 60015	289	351	35	P/EFC	3,900	3,900	2,000
Trinity College; Hartford, Conn. 06106	792	715	135	P	7,100	7,100	2,850
Trinity College*; Washington, D.C. 20017	50	950	50	P/RC	4,700	4,700	2,900
Trinity University; San Antonio, Tex. 78284	1,251[1]	1,358[1]	200	P/Pres	4,920[3]	4,920[3]	1,800
Tri-State University; Angola, Ind. 46703	926	242	82	P	6,908	6,908	1,950
Troy State University; Troy, Ala. 36082	2,013[1]	2,015[1]	202	S	840	1,260	1,404
Tufts University; Medford, Mass. 02155	3,436[1]	2,901[1]	445	P	7,650[3]	7,650[3]	3,830
Tulane University; New Orleans, La. 70118	6,249	3,768	444	P	5,600	5,600	2,700
Tulsa, The University of; Tulsa, Okla. 74104	2,276[1]	1,857[1]	309	P	2,700	2,700	1,515
Turabo University College. *See* Ana G. Méndez Educational Foundation							
Tusculum College; Greeneville, Tenn. 37743	143	167	25	P	2,700	2,700	1,990
Tuskegee Institute; Tuskegee Institute, Ala. 36088	1,677	1,633	306	P	2,500	2,500	1,850
Union College; Barbourville, Ky. 40906	187[1]	236[1]	n.a.	P/UM	n.a.	n.a.	n.a.
Union College; Lincoln, Neb. 68506	450[1]	490[1]	75	P/SDA	4,400	4,400	1,800
Union College; Schenectady, N.Y. 12308	1,440[1]	789[1]	150	P	6,300	6,300	2,300
Union University; Jackson, Tenn. 38301	444	659	69	SB	2,270[3]	2,270[3]	1,300[3]
U.S. Air Force Academy; USAF Academy, Colo. 80840	3,932[1]	544[1]	549	Fed	—	—	—
U.S. Army Command and General Staff College*; Fort Leavenworth, Kan. 66027	753	14	n.a.	Fed	n.a.	n.a.	n.a.
U.S. Coast Guard Academy; New London, Conn. 06320	818	108	122	Fed	—	—	—
U.S. International University; San Diego, Calif. 92131	2,087	1,252	81	P	4,770	4,770	3,000
U.S. Merchant Marine Academy; Kings Point, N.Y. 11024	1,010	89	85	Fed	—	—	—
U.S. Military Academy; West Point, N.Y. 10996	4,013	426	639	Fed	—	—	—
U.S. Naval Academy; Annapolis, Md. 21402	4,178	290	600	Fed	—	—	—
Unity College[31]; Unity, Me. 04988	180	93	25	P	4,200	4,200	2,600
Upper Iowa University; Fayette, Iowa 52142	173	112	27	P	3,700	3,700	1,860
Upsala College*; East Orange, N.J. 07019	673	423	74	P/L	4,212	4,212	2,000
Urbana College; Urbana, Ohio 43078	292	158	25	P/Sw	3,300	3,300	2,040

Institution and location	Enrollment Male	Enrollment Female	Faculty	Control	Tuition Res.	Tuition Nonres.	Rm/Bd
Ursinus College; Collegeville, Pa. 19426	601[1]	548[1]	76	P	4,950	4,950	2,300
Ursuline College; Pepper Pike, Ohio 44124	20	539	50	P/RC	6,300	6,300	1,900
Utah, University of; Salt Lake City, Utah 84112	9,903	6,614	1,000	S	831	2,211	n.a.
Utah State University; Logan, Utah 84322	5,968[1]	4,322[1]	475	S	840	2,355	1,900
Utica College of Syracuse University; Utica, N.Y. 13502	676	735	97	P	4,400	4,400	2,000
Valdosta State College*; Valdosta, Ga. 31698	2,108	2,793	250	S	663	1,620	1,200
Valley City State College; Valley City, N.D. 58072	435[1]	515[1]	55	S	572	1,132	1,500
Valley Forge Christian College; Phoenixville, Pa. 19460	255[1]	183[1]	16	P/AG	2,200	2,200	2,000
Valparaiso University; Valparaiso, Ind. 46383	1,785[1]	2,001[1]	236	P/L	4,050	4,050	2,090
Vanderbilt University; Nashville, Tenn. 37240	2,539	2,670	1,344	P	6,100	6,100	2,925
VanderCook College of Music; Chicago, Ill. 60616	75	18	14	P	3,900	3,900	2,500
Vassar College*; Poughkeepsie, N.Y. 12601	1,290	957	187	P	6,400	6,400	2,800
Vennard College; University Park, Iowa 52595	92	83	8	P/ND	1,900	1,900	1,760
Vermont, University of; Burlington, Vt. 05405	4,071[1]	5,147[1]	773	S	2,250[3]	2,250[3]	2,612[3]
Vermont College. *See* Norwich University							
Vermont Law School; South Royalton, Vt. 05068	245	124	19	P	5,700[71]	5,700[71]	—
Villa Maria College; Erie, Pa. 16505	16	623	46	P	1,920	1,920	1,020
Villanova University; Villanova, Pa. 19085	3,487[1]	2,753[1]	440	P/RC	4,362	4,362	2,774
Virginia, University of; Charlottesville, Va. 22903	8,381[1]	7,048[1]	1,436	S	1,146	2,626	2,210
Clinch Valley College; Wise, Va. 24293	326[1]	352[1]	40	S	720	1,140	1,750
Virginia Commonwealth University*; Richmond, Va. 23284	8,423	11,394	1,408	S	920	1,890	2,074
Virginia Intermont College; Bristol, Va. 24201	150[1]	527[1]	42	P/SB	3,350	3,350	2,100
Virginia Military Institute; Lexington, Va. 24450	1,309[1]	—	94	S	780	2,100	1,435
Virginia Polytechnic Institute and State University; Blacksburg, Va. 24061	12,072	7,399	1,403	S	1,281	2,526	1,503
Virginia State University; Petersburg, Va. 23803	1,803[1]	2,391[1]	218	S	1,303	2,108	2,180
Virginia Union University; Richmond, Va. 23220	635[1]	671[1]	62	P/B	2,550	2,550	1,756
Virginia Wesleyan College; Norfolk, Va. 23502	345[1]	458[1]	45	P/UM	4,100[3]	4,100[3]	2,150[3]
Virgin Islands, College of the; St. Thomas, V.I. 00801	191	441	73	S	400	1,200	1,770
Visual Arts, School of; New York, N.Y. 10010	1,232[1]	1,159[1]	15[72]	P	4,200	4,200	2,200
Viterbo College; La Crosse, Wis. 54601	218[1]	895[1]	74	P/RC	3,320	3,320	1,800
Voorhees College; Denmark, S.C. 29042	205	407	57	P	2,329	2,329	1,862
Wabash College; Crawfordsville, Ind. 47933	761	—	76	P	4,700	4,700	2,125
Wagner College; Staten Island, N.Y. 10301	1,071	1,243	80	P	4,212	4,212	2,576
Wake Forest University; Winston–Salem, N.C. 27109	2,896[1]	1,672[1]	604	P/B	4,700	4,700	1,630
Walla Walla College; College Place, Wash. 99324	901[1]	756[1]	120	P/SDA	5,115	5,115	2,250
Walsh College; Canton, Ohio 44720	335	314	36	P/RC	3,200	3,200	1,875
Walsh College of Accountancy and Business Administration; Troy, Mich. 48084	128	141	10	P	2,160	2,160	—
Warner Pacific College; Portland, Ore. 97215	261	195	32	P/CG	3,825	3,825	1,905
Warner Southern College; Lake Wales, Fla. 33853	141	133	15	P/CG	3,000	3,000	1,650
Warren Wilson College; Swannanoa, N.C. 28778	243[1]	257[1]	37	P/UP	3,950[3]	3,950[3]	1,608
Wartburg College; Waverly, Iowa 50677	451	557	71	P/AL	4,750	4,750	1,090
Washburn University of Topeka; Topeka, Kan. 66621	1,644	1,566	200	Mun	1,224	1,796	2,200
Washington, University of; Seattle, Wash. 98195	18,473[1]	16,817[1]	2,600	S	1,176	3,255	2,600
Washington and Jefferson College; Washington, Pa. 15301	654[1]	404[1]	85	P	5,900	5,900	2,190
Washington and Lee University; Lexington, Va. 24450	1,572[1]	99[1]	159	P	5,400	5,400	2,500
Washington Bible College; Lanham, Md. 20706	178	126	15	P/Ind	2,464	2,464	2,310
Washington College; Chestertown, Md. 21620	344[2]	325[2]	62	P	3,850	3,850	2,050
Washington State University; Pullman, Wash. 99164	9,750[1]	7,298[1]	1,230	S	1,060	3,048	2,004
Washington University in St. Louis; St. Louis, Mo. 63130	5,107[1]	3,347[1]	2,447	P	6,250	6,250	2,750
Wayland Baptist College*; Plainview, Tex. 79072	279	264	49	SB	1,700	1,700	1,730
Waynesburg College; Waynesburg, Pa. 15370	426	327	55	P/PUS	4,200	4,200	1,950
Wayne State College; Wayne, Neb. 68787	756[1]	1,003[1]	90	S	867	1,411	1,680
Wayne State University*; Detroit, Mich. 48202	15,108	15,688	1,400	S	1,350	2,750	1,500
Webb Institute of Naval Architecture; Glen Cove, N.Y. 11542	72	5	10	P	—	—	2,580
Weber State College; Ogden, Utah 84408	5,677[2]	4,463[2]	425	S	540	1,620	2,235
Webster College*; St. Louis, Mo. 63119	952	682	70	P	3,600	3,600	1,900
Wellesley College*; Wellesley, Mass. 02181	—	2,092	222	P	6,450	6,450	3,180
Wells College; Aurora, N.Y. 13026	—	521[1]	50	P	6,800	6,800	2,500
Wentworth Institute of Technology; Boston, Mass. 02115	2,830[1]	196[1]	164	P	3,990	3,990	3,000
Wesleyan College; Macon, Ga. 31297	2[1]	400[1]	42	P/M	2,800	3,600	2,100
Wesleyan University; Middletown, Conn. 06457	1,300	1,264	230	P	7,950	7,950	3,080
Wesley College*; Dover, Del. 19901	572	647	51	P/UM	3,850	3,850	1,930
Wesley College; Florence, Miss. 39073	38	25	7	P/M	1,090	1,090	1,400
Westbrook College; Portland, Me. 04103	174[1]	838[1]	42	P	4,400	4,400	2,370
West Chester State College; West Chester, Pa. 19380	2,773[1]	3,842[1]	469	S	1,250	2,190	1,590
West Coast Christian College; Fresno, Calif. 93710	104	78	11	P/CG	1,800	1,800	1,800
West Coast University[31]; Los Angeles, Calif. 90020	776[1]	180[1]	200	P	2,850	2,850	—

Institution and location	Enrollment		Faculty	Control	Tuition		Rm/Bd
	Male	Female			Res.	Nonres.	
Western Baptist College; Salem, Ore. 97302	197[1]	162[1]	22	P/B	3,300	3,300	2,100
Western Bible College; Morrison, Colo. 80465	116	73	12	P	2,208	2,208	1,748
Western Carolina University. *See* North Carolina, University System of							
Western Connecticut State College; Danbury, Conn. 06810	1,240[1]	1,675[1]	167	S	920	1,920	2,128
Western Illinois University; Macomb, Ill. 61455	6,752[1]	6,545[1]	617	S	798	2,394	1,950
Western Kentucky University; Bowling Green, Ky. 42101	4,612[1]	4,947[1]	664	S	714	2,062	2,120
Western Maryland College; Westminster, Md. 21157	560	660	88	P	4,500	4,500	1,925
Western Michigan University; Kalamazoo, Mich. 49007	9,761	9,002	851	S	1,200	2,800	2,011
Western Montana College; Dillon, Mont. 59725	435	445	40	S	591	n.a.	1,924
Western New England College; Springfield, Mass. 01095	1,261	784	105	P	3,588	3,588	2,130
Western New Mexico University; Silver City, N.M. 88026	710	753	68	S	530	1,816	1,600
Western Oregon State College; Monmouth, Ore. 97361	988	1,595	180[5]	S	1,235	3,405	1,995
Western State College of Colorado*; Gunnison, Colo. 81230	1,810	1,290	159	S	524	2,280	1,594
Western States Chiropractic College; Portland, Ore. 97230	320	70	18	P	4,800	4,800	800
Western State University College of Law; Fullerton, Calif. 92631	265[2]	156[2]	12	P	3,762	3,762	—
Western State University of San Diego; San Diego, Calif. 92101	171[1]	73[1]	13	P	3,762	3,762	—
Western Washington University; Bellingham, Wash. 98225	4,458	4,862	456	S	867	2,910	n.a.
Westfield State College; Westfield, Mass. 01086	1,129[1]	1,692[1]	165	S	845	2,545	1,700
West Florida, The University of; Pensacola, Fla. 32504	2,579	2,830	251	S	840	2,730	2,221
West Georgia College; Carrollton, Ga. 30118	1,708	2,133	237	S	750	1,800	1,611
West Liberty State College; West Liberty, W. Va. 26074	889	1,002	236	S	604	1,804	1,974
Westmar College; LeMars, Iowa 51031	259	221	48	P/UM	4,060	4,060	1,935
Westminster Choir College; Princeton, N.J. 08540	175[1]	211[1]	37	P	4,525	4,525	2,265
Westminster College; Fulton, Mo. 65251	565	134	46	P	3,900	3,900	1,400
Westminster College; New Wilmington, Pa. 16142	720[1]	791[1]	120	P/UP	4,900	4,900	2,006
Westminster College; Salt Lake City, Utah 84105	590[1]	745[1]	56	P[56]	3,180	3,180	2,100
Westmont College; Santa Barbara, Calif. 93108	491[1]	559[1]	59	P	4,860	4,860	2,500
West Oahu College[32]; University of Hawaii; Pearl City, Hawaii 96782	82[1]	65[1]	12	S	400	1,000	4,979
West Texas State University; Canyon, Tex. 79016	2,264	2,554	222	S	120	1,200	1,903
West Virginia College of Graduate Studies*; Institute, W. Va. 25112	1,177	2,146	60	S	250	1,270	—
West Virginia Institute of Technology; Montgomery, W. Va. 25136	1,734	692	142	S	478	1,498	1,956
West Virginia School of Osteopathic Medicine; Lewisburg, W. Va. 24901	188	45	30	S	650	1,710	—
West Virginia State College; Institute, W. Va. 25112	1,081[1]	975[1]	125	S	499	1,499	2,010
West Virginia University; Morgantown, W. Va. 26506	11,396	9,869	1,349	S	628	1,708	4,350
West Virginia Wesleyan College; Buckhannon, W. Va. 26201	688[1]	965[1]	103	P/UM	3,600	3,600	2,316
Wheaton College*; Norton, Mass. 02766	—	1,206	90	P	6,040	6,040	2,400
Wheaton College; Wheaton, Ill. 60187	1,085	1,118	150	P	4,780	4,780	2,500
Wheeling College; Wheeling, W. Va. 26003	327[1]	400[1]	68	P/RC	3,800	3,800	2,150
Wheelock College; Boston, Mass. 02215	9[1]	598[1]	56	P	4,900	4,900	2,700
Whitman College; Walla Walla, Wash. 99362	557	604	83	P	5,150	5,150	2,210
Whittier College; Whittier, Calif. 90608	544[5]	614[5]	80	P	4,950	4,950	2,255
Whitworth College; Spokane, Wash. 99251	582[1]	661[1]	69	P/UP	5,120[3]	5,120[3]	2,240[3]
Wichita State University; Wichita, Kan. 67208	3,758[1]	3,417[1]	516	S	912	2,228	1,900
Widener College*; Chester, Pa. 19013	1,275	1,000	136	P	4,475	4,475	2,400
Wilberforce University; Wilberforce, Ohio 45384	304	314	45	P/AME	2,800	2,800	1,530
Wiley College; Marshall, Tex. 75670	255[1]	311[1]	34	P/UM	2,430	2,430	1,754
Wilkes College; Wilkes-Barre, Pa. 18766	1,079[1]	1,011[1]	165	P	4,200	4,200	2,100
Willamette University; Salem, Ore. 97301	1,030[1]	783[1]	105	P	4,860	4,860	2,150
William and Mary, College of; Williamsburg, Va. 23185	2,746[1]	2,826[1]	365	S	1,334	3,368	2,123
William Carey College; Hattiesburg, Miss. 39401	497[1]	1,040[1]	73	P/SB	2,010	2,010	1,965
William Jewell College; Liberty, Mo. 64068	588	672	91	SB	3,370	3,370	1,790
William Mitchell College of Law; St. Paul, Minn. 55105	719[1]	435[1]	30	P	4,050	4,050	—
William Paterson Coll. of New Jersey; Wayne, N.J. 07470	2,838	3,217	357	S	810	1,410	1,350
William Penn College; Oskaloosa, Iowa 52577	309[1]	170[1]	35	P/SOF	5,140[2]	5,140[2]	1,640[2]
Williams College; Williamstown, Mass. 01267	1,109[1]	891[1]	154	P	6,950	6,950	2,660
William Smith College. *See* Hobart and William Smith Colleges							
William Tyndale College; Farmington Hills, Mich. 48018	92	57	14	P/ID	2,396	2,396	2,200
William Woods College; Fulton, Mo. 65251	—	821	69	P/DC	4,540	4,540	1,985
Wilmington College; New Castle, Del. 19720	147	114	12	P	1,140	1,140	1,500
Wilmington College; Wilmington, Ohio 45177	489[1]	260[1]	56	P/SOF	3,100	3,100	1,800
Wilson College; Chambersburg, Pa. 17201	—	237[1]	33	P/Pres	5,418[3]	5,418[3]	2,280
Wingate College; Wingate, N.C. 28174	740[1]	788[1]	62	P/B	2,150	2,150	1,470
Winona State Univ. *See* Minnesota State Univ. System							

Institution and location	Enrollment: Male	Female	Faculty	Control	Tuition: Res.	Nonres.	Rm/Bd
Winston–Salem State University. *See* North Carolina, University System of							
Winthrop College; Rock Hill, S.C. 29733	1,122[1]	2,645[1]	253	S	1,020	1,800	1,372
Wisconsin, University of; Madison, Wis. 53706:							
U. of Wisconsin—Eau Claire; Eau Claire, Wis. 54701	4,161[1]	5,364[1]	623	S	932	3,182	790
U. of Wisconsin—Green Bay; Green Bay, Wis. 54302	1,948[1]	2,588[1]	180	S	996	3,328	2,130
U. of Wisconsin—La Crosse; La Crosse, Wis. 54601	3,156	3,788	362	S	960	3,211	1,560
U. of Wisconsin—Madison; Madison, Wis. 53706	22,850[1]	18,841[1]	2,293	S	1,015	3,602	2,225[3]
U. of Wisconsin—Milwaukee; Milwaukee, Wis. 53201	7,268	7,118	955	S	1,046	3,633	2,466
U. of Wisconsin—Oshkosh*; Oshkosh, Wis. 54901	4,825	5,375	450	S	950	3,100	1,550
U. of Wisconsin—Parkside; Kenosha, Wis. 53141	1,597[1]	1,332[1]	175	S	921	3,172	—
U. of Wisconsin—Platteville; Platteville, Wis. 53818	3,201	1,611	304	S	650	2,342	720
U. of Wisconsin—River Falls; River Falls, Wis. 54022	2,812[1]	2,690[1]	300	S	674	2,174	2,344
U. of Wisconsin—Stevens Point; Stevens Point, Wis. 54407	4,520	4,731	488	S	989	3,240	1,806
U. of Wisconsin—Stout; Menomonie, Wis. 54751	3,574[1]	3,333[1]	341	S	964	3,215	1,858
U. of Wisconsin—Superior; Superior, Wis. 54880	1,150	1,050	145	S	969	3,222	660
U. of Wisconsin—Whitewater; Whitewater, Wis. 53190	3,982[1]	3,986[1]	400	S	984	3,236	1,530
Wittenberg University*; Springfield, Ohio 45501	1,054	1,165	136	P/LCA	5,259	5,259	2,130
Wofford College; Spartanburg, S.C. 29301	725	250	63	P/UM	3,945	3,945	2,100
Woodbury University*; Los Angeles, Calif. 90017[31]	697	512	42	P	3,048	3,048	n.a.
Wooster, The College of; Wooster, Ohio 44691	909[1]	817[1]	140	P	6,030	6,030	1,900
Worcester Art Museum, School of the*; Worcester, Mass. 01608	32	71	n.a.	P	n.a.	n.a.	n.a.
Worcester Polytechnic Institute; Worcester, Mass. 01609	2,129[1]	425[1]	190	P	5,850	5,850	2,400
Worcester State College; Worcester, Mass. 01602	1,085	1,352	174	S	885	2,688	1,790
World College West; San Rafael, Calif. 94912	30	32	9	P	3,150	3,150	2,400
Wright Institute*; Berkeley, Calif. 94704	3,135	3,092	575	S	960	1.950	n.a.
Wright State University; Dayton, Ohio 45435	4,065	3,613	640	S	1,278	2,448	1,905
Wyoming, University of; Laramie, Wyo. 82071	4,519	3,145	749	S	620	2,100	2,150
Xavier University*; Cincinnati, Ohio 45207	7,157		184	P/RC	3,400	3,400	2,000
Xavier University of Louisiana; New Orleans, La. 70125	645	1,028	153	P	1,500	1,500	1,950
Yale University*; New Haven, Conn. 06520	9,700		1,300	P	6,210	6,210	2,900
Yankton College; Yankton, S.D. 57078	143	86	25	P/UCC	3,580	3,580	1,870
Yeshiva University; New York, N.Y. 10033	3,543[1]	2,183[1]	1,221	P	5,050[2]	5,050[2]	2,825[2]
York College (NYC). *See* New York, City University of							
York College of Pennsylvania; York, Pa. 17405	930[1]	1,309[1]	103	P	2,670[3]	2,670[3]	1,828
Youngstown State Univ.; Youngstown, Ohio 44555	5,346[1]	4,649[1]	585	S	1,065	1,065	1,875

1. Fall 1981. 2. Fall 1982. 3. 1982–83. 4. Part-time school. 5. Spring 1981. 6. Includes SUNY College of Ceramics. 7. Comprehensive fee covering tuition, room, and board. 8. $60 per semester hour. 9. Fall 1980. 10. Part-time. 11. $125 per semester hour. 12. Member of State University and Community College System. 13. Volunteers. 14. LDS members. 15. Non-LDS members. 16. Off campus, 12 months. 17. Entering students 1982–83; continuing students, $4,390. 18. Member California State University and Colleges. 19. $94.50 per unit, plus registration fees. 20. $105 per unit, plus registration fees. 21. Foreign students. 22. Formerly Claremont Men's College. 23. Room only. 24. Includes SUNY statutory colleges and medical college in New York City. 25. $55 per semester hour. 26. State assisted. 27. $170 per credit. 28. Member of State University and Community College System. 29. Under SUNY supervision. 30. Per quarter. 31. Accreditation on probation. 32. Member University of Hawaii System. 33. $70 per unit. 34. Available at San Germán campus only. 35. $10 per unit. 36. $23 per credit hour, fall 1982. 37. $40 per credit hour, fall 1982. 38. $380 per course. 39. $485 per quarter course. 40. Per trimester. 41. $45 per semester hour. 42. Three trimesters. 43. Includes La Sierra Campus in Riverside. 44. Estimated living expenses; no dorms. 45. Affiliated academically with the University of Minnesota. 46. $113 per credit hour. 47. $110 per credit hour. 48. Part of Louisiana State University System. 49. Fees. 50. 1983. 51. Fall 1980. 52. Tuition, room, and board paid for by work-study program. 53. Formerly Museum Art School. 54. $160 per unit. 55. Students in certain states get financial aid from their states, which reduces tuition by an average of $4,000. 56. UM/UP/UCC. 57. $95 per semester hour. 58. $99 per semester hour. 59. Formerly St. Patrick's College; name change effective September 1982. 60. $121 per credit hour. 61. Plus $94.50 per unit. 62. $95 per credit hour. 63. Less state tuition grant. 64. Formerly Southern Missionary College. 65. Summer 1982. 66. $55 per credit. 67. Member Texas A&M System. 68. Room only, per quarter. 69. $23 per credit. 70. $44 per credit. 71. First year; second and third years, $5,500. 72. 530 part-time.

Foreign Study

Young people who want to study in Western Europe will find useful information in a guidebook published by the European Common Market. It lists school fees, entrance requirements, etc., mainly for Common Market countries. *The Handbook for Students* costs $5.00, and it can be obtained from the European Community Information Service, 2100 M Street, N.W., Suite 707, Washington, D.C. 20037.

U.S. STATISTICS

Population

Colonial Population Estimates (in round numbers)

Year	Population	Year	Population	Year	Population	Year	Population
1610	350	1660	75,100	1710	331,700	1760	1,593,600
1620	2,300	1670	111,900	1720	466,200	1770	2,148,100
1630	4,600	1680	151,500	1730	629,400	1780	2,780,400
1640	26,600	1690	210,400	1740	905,600		
1650	50,400	1700	250,900	1750	1,170,800		

National Censuses[1]

Year	Resident population[2]	Land area, sq mi.	Pop. per sq mi.	Year	Resident population[2]	Land area, sq mi.	Pop. per sq mi.
1790	3,929,214	864,746	4.5	1890	62,947,714	2,969,640	21.2
1800	5,308,483	864,746	6.1	1900	75,994,575	2,969,834	25.6
1810	7,239,881	1,681,828	4.3	1910	91,972,266	2,969,565	31.0
1820	9,638,453	1,749,462	5.5	1920	105,710,620	2,969,451	35.6
1830	12,866,020	1,749,462	7.4	1930	122,775,046	2,977,128	41.2
1840	17,069,453	1,749,462	9.8	1940	131,669,275	2,977,128	44.2
1850	23,191,876	2,940,042	7.9	1950	150,697,361	2,974,726	50.7
1860	31,443,321	2,969,640	10.6	1960	179,323,175	3,540,911	50.6
1870	39,818,449	2,969,640	13.4	1970	203,302,031	3,540,023	57.4
1880	50,155,783	2,969,640	16.9	1980	226,545,805	3,618,770	62.6

1. Beginning with 1960, figures include Alaska and Hawaii. 2. Excludes armed forces overseas. NOTE: n.a. = not available. *Source:* Department of Commerce, Bureau of the Census.

Population Distribution by Age, Race, Nativity, and Sex

	Age						Race and nativity				
							White[1]				
Year	Total	Under 5	5–19	20–44	45–64	65 and over	Total	Native born	Foreign born	Black	Other races[1]
PERCENT DISTRIBUTION											
1860[2]	100.0	15.4	35.8	35.7	10.4	2.7	85.6	72.6	13.0	14.1	0.3
1870[2]	100.0	14.3	35.4	35.4	11.9	3.0	87.1	72.9	14.2	12.7	0.2
1880[2]	100.0	13.8	34.3	35.9	12.6	3.4	86.5	73.4	13.1	13.1	0.3
1890[3]	100.0	12.2	33.9	36.9	13.1	3.9	87.5	73.0	14.5	11.9	0.3
1900	100.0	12.1	32.3	37.7	13.7	4.1	87.9	74.5	13.4	11.6	0.5
1910	100.0	11.6	30.4	39.0	14.6	4.3	88.9	74.4	14.5	10.7	0.4
1920	100.0	10.9	29.8	38.4	16.1	4.7	89.7	76.7	13.0	9.9	0.4
1930	100.0	9.3	29.5	38.3	17.4	5.4	89.8	78.4	11.4	9.7	0.5
1940	100.0	8.0	26.4	38.9	19.8	6.8	89.8	81.1	8.7	9.8	0.4
1950[4]	100.0	10.7	23.2	37.6	20.3	8.1	89.5	82.8	6.7	10.0	0.5
1960[4]	100.0	11.3	27.1	32.2	20.1	9.2	88.6	83.4	5.2	10.5	0.9
1970[2]	100.0	8.4	29.5	31.7	20.6	9.8	87.6	83.4	4.3	11.1	1.4
1980	100.0	7.2	24.8	37.1	19.6	11.3	83.2	n.a.	n.a.	11.7	5.2
MALES PER 100 FEMALES											
1860[2]	104.7	102.4	101.2	107.9	111.5	98.3	105.3	103.7	115.1	99.6	260.8
1870[2]	102.2	102.9	101.2	99.2	114.5	100.5	102.8	100.6	115.3	96.2	400.7
1880[2]	103.6	103.0	101.3	104.0	110.2	101.4	104.0	102.1	115.9	97.8	362.2
1890[3]	105.0	103.6	101.4	107.3	108.3	104.2	105.4	102.9	118.7	99.5	165.2
1900	104.4	102.1	100.9	105.8	110.7	102.0	104.9	102.8	117.4	98.6	185.2
1910	106.0	102.5	101.3	108.1	114.4	101.1	106.6	102.7	129.2	98.9	185.6
1920	104.0	102.5	100.8	102.8	115.2	101.3	104.4	101.7	121.7	99.2	156.6
1930	102.5	103.0	101.4	100.5	109.1	100.5	102.9	101.1	115.8	97.0	150.6
1940	100.7	103.2	102.0	98.1	105.2	95.5	101.2	100.1	111.1	95.0	140.5

Year	Age						Race and nativity				
							White[1]				
	Total	Under 5	5–19	20–44	45–64	65 and over	Total	Native born	Foreign born	Black	Other races[1]
1950	98.6	103.9	102.5	96.2	100.1	89.6	99.0	98.8	102.0	93.7	129.7
1960[4]	97.1	103.4	102.7	95.6	95.7	82.8	97.4	97.6	94.2	93.3	109.7
1970[2]	94.8	104.0	103.3	95.1	91.6	72.1	95.3	95.9	83.8	90.8	100.2
1980	94.5	104.7	104.0	98.1	90.7	67.6	94.8	n.a.	n.a.	89.6	100.3

1. The 1980 census data for white and other races categories are not directly comparable to those shown for the preceding years because of the changes in the way some persons reported their race, as well as changes in 1980 procedures relating to racial classification. 2. Excludes persons for whom age is not available. 3. Excludes persons enumerated in the Indian Territory and on Indian reservations. NOTES: Data exclude Armed Forces overseas. Beginning in 1960, includes Alaska and Hawaii. n.a. = not available. *Source:* Department of Commerce, Bureau of the Census.

Population and Rank of Large Metropolitan Areas, 1970–1980

(over 150,000)

Standard metropolitan statistical area	1980 Census		1970 Census		Change, 1970–80	
	Number	Rank	Number	Rank	Number	%
Akron, Ohio	660,328	57	679,239	52	−18,911	−2.7
Albany–Schenectady–Troy, N.Y.	795,019	50	777,977	43	17,042	2.2
Albuquerque, N.M.	454,499	86	333,266	102	121,233	36.4
Alexandria, La.	151,985	205	131,749	203	20,236	15.4
Allentown–Bethlehem–Easton, Pa.–N.J.	636,714	62	594,382	60	42,332	7.2
Amarillo, Tex.	173,699	188	144,396	192	29,303	20.3
Anaheim–Santa Ana–Garden Grove, Calif.	1,931,570	18	1,421,233	20	510,337	36.0
Anchorage, Alaska	173,017	191	126,385	211	46,632	36.9
Ann Arbor, Mich.	264,748	145	234,103	141	30,645	13.1
Appleton–Oshkosh, Wis.	291,325	129	276,948	121	14,377	5.2
Asheville, N.C.	177,761	184	161,059	181	16,702	10.4
Atlanta	2,029,618	16	1,595,517	18	434,101	27.3
Atlantic City, N.J.	194,119	171	175,043	168	19,076	10.9
Augusta, Ga.–S.C.	327,372	113	275,787	122	51,585	18.8
Austin, Tex.	536,450	70	360,463	93	175,987	48.9
Bakersfield, Calif.	403,089	97	330,234	104	72,855	22.1
Baltimore	2,174,023	14	2,071,016	13	103,007	5.0
Baton Rouge, La.	493,973	80	375,628	87	118,345	31.6
Battle Creek, Mich.	187,338	177	180,129	164	7,209	4.1
Beaumont–Port Arthur, Tex.	375,497	104	347,568	97	27,929	8.1
Biloxi–Gulfport, Miss.	191,918	174	160,070	183	31,848	19.9
Binghamton, N.Y.–Pa.	301,336	126	302,672	111	−1,336	−0.4
Birmingham, Ala.	847,360	45	767,230	44	80,130	10.5
Boise, Idaho	173,036	190	112,230	232	60,806	54.2
Boston	2,763,357	10	2,899,101	8	−135,744	−4.6
Bridgeport, Conn.	395,455	98	401,752	82	−6,297	−1.5
Brockton, Mass.	169, 374	196	150,416	186	18,958	12.7
Brownsville–Harlingen–San Benito, Tex.	209,680	164	140,368	194	69,312	49.4
Buffalo, N.Y.	1,242,573	31	1,349,211	24	−106,638	−7.9
Canton, Ohio	404,421	96	393,789	83	10,632	2.7
Cedar Rapids, Iowa	169,775	194	163,213	179	6,562	4.1
Champaign–Urbana–Rantoul, Ill.	168,392	197	163,281	178	5,111	3.2
Charleston–North Charleston, S.C.	430,301	91	336,036	100	94,265	28.1
Charleston, W. Va.	269,595	142	257,140	133	12,455	4.9
Charlotte–Gastonia, N.C.	637,218	61	557,785	62	79,433	14.3
Chattanooga, Tenn.–Ga.	426,540	92	370,857	90	55,683	15.1
Chicago	7,102,328	3	6,974,755	3	127,573	1.9
Cincinnati, Ohio–Ky.–Ind.	1,401,403	27	1,387,207	22	14,196	1.1
Clarksville–Hopkinsville, Tenn.–Ky.	150,220	209	118,945	220	31,275	26.3
Cleveland	1,898,720	19	2,063,729	14	−165,009	−7.9
Colorado Springs, Colo.	317,458	120	239,288	139	78,170	32.7
Columbia, S.C.	408,176	95	322,880	107	85,296	26.5
Columbus, Ga.–Ala.	239,196	154	238,584	140	612	0.3
Columbus, Ohio	1,093,293	35	1,017,847	33	75,446	7.5
Corpus Christi, Tex.	326,228	114	284,832	118	41,396	14.6

Standard metropolitan statistical area	1980 Census		1970 Census		Change, 1970–80	
	Number	Rank	Number	Rank	Number	%
Dallas–Fort Worth	2,974,878	8	2,377,623	12	597,255	25.2
Davenport–Rock Island–Moline, Iowa–Ill.	383,958	100	362,638	91	21,320	5.9
Dayton, Ohio	830,070	47	852,531	40	−22,461	−2.6
Daytona Beach, Fla.	258,762	148	169,487	174	89,275	52.7
Denver–Boulder, Colo.	1,619,921	22	1,239,545	27	380,376	30.7
Des Moines, Iowa	338,048	111	313,562	109	24,486	7.9
Detroit	4,352,762	5	4,435,051	5	−82,289	−1.8
Duluth–Superior, Minn.–Wis.	266,650	143	265,350	126	1,300	0.5
El Paso	479,899	82	359,291	94	120,608	33.6
Erie, Pa.	279,780	135	263,654	128	16,126	6.2
Eugene–Springfield, Ore.	275,226	138	215,401	151	59,825	27.8
Evansville, Ind.–Ky.	309,408	123	284,959	117	24,449	8.6
Fall River, Mass.–R.I.	176,831	185	169,549	173	7,282	4.3
Fayetteville–Springdale, Ark.	177,850	183	127,846	208	50,004	39.2
Fayetteville, N.C.	247,160	152	212,042	152	35,118	16.6
Flint, Mich.	521,589	77	508,664	69	12,925	2.6
Fort Lauderdale–Hollywood, Fla.	1,014,043	37	620,100	58	393,943	63.6
Fort Myers–Cape Coral, Fla.	205,266	166	105,216	238	100,050	95.1
Fort Smith, Ark.–Okla.	203,269	167	160,421	182	42,848	26.8
Fort Wayne, Ind.	382,961	101	361,984	92	20,977	5.8
Fresno, Calif.	515,013	78	413,329	77	101,684	24.7
Gainesville, Fla.	151,348	208	104,764	239	46,584	44.5
Galveston–Texas City, Tex.	195,940	170	169,812	172	26,128	15.4
Gary–Hammond–East Chicago, Ind.	642,781	58	633,367	54	9,414	1.5
Grand Rapids, Mich.	601,680	64	539,225	67	62,455	11.6
Green Bay, Wis.	175,280	187	158,244	185	17,036	10.8
Greensboro–Winston-Salem–High Point, N.C.	827,385	48	724,129	47	103,256	14.3
Greenville–Spartanburg, S.C.	568,758	68	473,454	71	95,304	20.2
Hamilton–Middletown, Ohio	258,787	147	226,207	145	32,580	14.5
Harrisburg, Pa.	446,072	88	410,505	80	35,567	8.7
Hartford, Conn.	726,114	54	720,581	48	5,533	0.8
Honolulu	762,874	52	630,528	55	132,346	21.0
Houston	2,905,350	9	1,999,316	16	906,034	45.4
Huntington–Ashland, W. Va.–Ky.–Ohio	311,350	122	286,935	116	24,415	8.6
Huntsville, Ala.	308,593	124	282,450	119	26,143	9.3
Indianapolis	1,166,929	34	1,111,352	29	55,577	5.1
Jackson, Mich.	151,495	207	143,274	193	8,221	5.8
Jackson, Miss.	320,425	117	258,906	130	61,519	23.8
Jacksonville, Fla.	737,519	53	621,827	57	115,692	18.7
Jersey City, N.J.	556,972	69	607,839	59	−50,867	−8.3
Johnson Cty–Kingsport–Bristol, Tenn.–Va.	433,638	90	373,591	88	60,047	16.1
Johnstown, Pa.	264,506	146	262,822	129	1,684	0.7
Kalamazoo–Portage, Mich.	279,192	137	257,723	132	21,469	8.4
Kansas City, Mo.–Kan.	1,327,020	29	1,273,926	25	53,094	4.2
Killeen–Temple, Tex.	214,656	162	159,794	184	54,862	34.4
Knoxville, Tenn.	476,517	83	409,409	81	67,108	16.4
Lafayette, La.	150,017	210	111,643	233	38,374	34.4
Lake Charles, La.	167,048	198	145,415	189	21,633	14.9
Lakeland–Winter Haven, Fla.	321,652	116	228,515	143	93,137	40.8
Lancaster, Pa.	362,346	108	320,079	108	42,267	13.3
Lansing–East Lansing, Mich.	468,482	84	424,271	75	44,211	10.5
Las Vegas, Nev.	461,816	85	273,288	123	188,528	69.0
Lawrence–Haverhill, Mass.–N.H.	281,981	133	258,564	131	23,417	9.1
Lexington–Fayette, Ky.	318,136	119	266,701	125	51,435	19.3
Lima, Ohio	218,244	160	210,074	153	8,170	3.9
Lincoln, Neb.	192,884	173	167,972	176	24,912	14.9
Little Rock–North Little Rock, Ark.	393,494	99	323,296	106	70,198	21.8
Long Branch–Asbury Park, N.J.	503,173	79	461,849	72	41,324	9.0
Longview–Marshall, Tex.	151,752	206	120,770	217	30,982	25.7
Lorain–Elyria, Ohio	274,909	139	256,843	134	18,066	7.1
Los Angeles–Long Beach, Calif.	7,477,657	2	7,041,980	2	435,677	6.2
Louisville, Ky.–Ind.	906,240	43	867,330	39	38,910	4.5
Lowell, Mass.–N.H.	233,410	155	218,268	149	15,142	7.0
Lubbock, Tex.	211,651	163	179,295	165	32,356	18.1
Lynchburg, Va.	153,260	204	134,744	198	18,516	13.8
Macon, Ga.	254,623	149	226,782	144	27,841	12.3
Madison, Wis.	323,545	115	290,272	114	33,273	11.5
Manchester, N.H.	160,767	202	132,512	201	28,255	21.4
McAllen–Pharr–Edinburg, Tex.	283,229	132	181,535	162	101,694	56.1

Standard metropolitan statistical area	1980 Census		1970 Census		Change, 1970–80	
	Number	Rank	Number	Rank	Number	%
Melbourne–Titusville–Cocoa, Fla.	272,959	140	230,006	142	42,953	18.7
Memphis, Tenn.–Ark.–Miss.	912,887	42	834,103	41	78,784	9.5
Miami, Fla.	1,625,979	21	1,267,792	26	358,187	28.3
Milwaukee	1,397,143	28	1,403,884	21	−6,741	−0.4
Minneapolis–St. Paul	2,114,256	15	1,965,391	17	148,865	7.6
Mobile, Ala.	442,819	89	376,690	86	66,129	17.6
Modesto, Calif.	265,902	144	194,506	158	71,396	36.8
Montgomery, Ala.	272,687	141	225,911	146	46,776	20.8
Muskegon–Norton Shores–Muskegon Heights, Mich.	179,591	182	175,410	166	4,181	2.4
Nashville–Davidson, Tenn.	850,505	44	699,271	50	151,234	21.7
Nassau–Suffolk, N.Y.	2,605,813	11	2,555,868	9	49,945	2.0
Newark, N.J.	1,965,304	17	2,057,468	15	−92,164	−4.4
New Bedford, Mass.	169,425	195	161,288	180	8,137	5.1
New Brunswick–Perth Amboy–Sayreville, N.J.	595,893	65	583,813	61	12,080	2.1
New Haven–West Haven, Conn.	417,592	93	411,287	79	6,305	1.6
New London–Norwich, Conn.–R.I.	248,554	151	241,862	138	6,692	2.8
New Orleans	1,186,725	33	1,046,470	32	140,255	13.5
Newport News–Hampton, Va.	364,449	107	333,140	103	31,309	9.4
New York, N.Y.–N.J.	9,119,737	1	9,973,716	1	−853,979	−8.5
Norfolk–Virginia Beach–Portsmouth, Va.–N.C.	806,691	49	732,600	46	74,091	10.2
Northeast Pennsylvania	640,396	60	621,882	56	18,514	3.0
Oklahoma City	834,088	46	699,092	51	134,996	19.4
Omaha, Neb.–Iowa	570,399	67	542,646	65	27,753	5.2
Orlando, Fla.	700,699	55	453,270	74	247,429	54.6
Oxnard–Simi Valley–Ventura, Calif.	529,899	75	378,497	85	151,402	40.1
Parkersburg–Marietta, W. Va.–Ohio	162,836	201	148,132	187	14,704	10.0
Paterson–Clifton–Passaic, N.J.	447,585	87	460,782	73	−13,197	−2.8
Pensacola, Fla.	289,782	131	243,075	137	46,707	19.3
Peoria, Ill.	365,864	106	341,979	98	23,885	7.0
Philadelphia, Pa.–N.J.	4,716,818	4	4,824,110	4	−107,292	−2.2
Phoenix, Ariz.	1,508,030	26	971,228	35	536,802	55.3
Pittsburgh	2,263,894	13	2,401,362	11	−137,468	−5.7
Portland, Me.	183,625	181	170,081	171	13,544	8.0
Portland, Ore.–Wash.	1,242,187	32	1,007,131	34	235,057	23.4
Poughkeepsie, N.Y.	245,055	153	222,295	147	22,760	10.3
Providence–Warwick–Pawtucket, R.I.–Mass.	919,216	41	908,887	37	10,329	1.2
Provo–Orem, Utah	218,106	161	137,776	196	80,330	58.4
Racine, Wis.	173,132	189	170,838	170	2,294	1.4
Raleigh–Durham, N.C.	530,673	73	419,254	76	111,419	26.6
Reading, Pa.	312,509	121	296,382	112	16,127	5.5
Reno, Nev.	193,623	172	121,068	216	72,555	60.0
Richmond, Va.	632,015	63	547,542	64	84,473	15.5
Riverside–San Bernardino–Ontario, Calif.	1,557,080	25	1,139,149	28	417,931	36.7
Roanoke, Va.	224,548	159	203,153	157	21,395	10.6
Rochester, N.Y.	971,879	39	961,516	36	10,363	1.1
Rockford, Ill.	279,514	136	272,063	124	7,451	2.8
Sacramento, Calif.	1,014,002	38	803,793	42	210,209	26.2
Saginaw, Mich.	228,059	158	219,743	148	8,316	3.8
St. Cloud, Minn.	163,256	199	134,585	199	28,671	21.4
St. Louis, Mo.–Ill.	2,355,276	12	2,410,884	10	−55,608	−2.3
Salem, Ore.	249,895	150	186,658	160	63,237	33.9
Salinas–Seaside–Monterey–Calif.	290,444	130	247,450	136	42,994	17.4
Salt Lake City–Ogden, Utah	936,255	40	705,458	49	230,797	32.8
San Antonio	1,071,954	36	888,179	38	183,775	20.7
San Diego, Calif.	1,861,846	20	1,357,854	23	503,992	37.2
San Francisco–Oakland, Calif.	3,252,721	6	3,109,249	6	143,472	4.7
San Jose, Calif.	1,295,071	30	1,065,313	31	229,758	21.6
Santa Barbara–Santa Maria–Lompoc, Calif.	298,660	128	264,324	127	34,336	13.0
Santa Cruz, Calif.	188,141	175	123,790	213	64,351	52.0
Santa Rosa, Calif.	299,827	127	204,885	156	94,942	46.4
Sarasota, Fla.	202,251	168	120,413	218	81,838	68.0
Savannah, Ga.	230,728	156	207,987	154	22,741	11.0
Seattle–Everett, Wash.	1,606,765	23	1,424,605	19	182,160	12.8
Shreveport, La.	376,646	103	336,000	101	40,646	12.1
South Bend, Ind.	280,772	134	279,813	120	959	0.4
Spokane, Wash.	341,835	110	287,487	115	54,348	19.0
Springfield, Ill.	187,789	176	171,020	169	16,769	9.9

Standard metropolitan statistical area	1980 Census		1970 Census		Change, 1970–80	
	Number	Rank	Number	Rank	Number	%
Springfield–Chicopee–Holyoke, Mass.–Conn.	530,668	74	541,752	66	−11,084	−2.0
Springfield, Mo.	207,704	165	168,053	175	39,651	23.6
Springfield, Ohio	183,885	180	187,606	159	−3,721	−1.9
Stamford, Conn.	198,854	169	206,340	155	−7,486	−3.6
Steubenville–Weirton, Ohio–W. Va.	163,099	200	166,385	177	−3,286	−1.9
Stockton, Calif.	347,342	109	291,073	113	56,269	19.4
Syracuse, N.Y.	642,375	59	636,596	53	5,779	1.0
Tacoma, Wash.	485,643	81	412,344	78	73,299	17.8
Tallahassee, Fla.	159,542	203	109,355	235	50,187	45.9
Tampa–St. Petersburg, Fla.	1,569,492	24	1,088,549	30	480,943	44.2
Terre Haute, Ind.	176,583	186	175,143	167	1,440	0.9
Toledo, Ohio–Mich.	791,599	51	762,658	45	28,941	3.8
Topeka, Kan.	185,442	179	180,619	163	4,823	2.7
Trenton, N.J.	307,863	125	304,116	110	3,747	1.3
Tucson, Ariz.	531,263	72	351,667	95	179,596	51.1
Tulsa, Okla.	689,628	56	549,154	63	140,474	25.6
Utica–Rome, N.Y.	320,180	118	340,477	99	−20,297	−5.9
Vallejo–Fairfield–Napa, Calif.	334,402	112	251,129	135	83,273	33.2
Waco, Tex.	170,755	193	147,553	188	23,202	15.8
Washington, D.C.–Md.–Va.	3,060,240	7	2,910,111	7	150,129	5.2
Waterbury, Conn.	228,178	157	216,808	150	11,370	5.3
West Palm Beach–Boca Raton, Fla.	573,125	66	348,993	96	224,132	64.3
Wheeling, W. Va.–Ohio	185,566	178	181,954	161	3,612	2.0
Wichita, Kan.	411,313	94	389,352	84	21,961	5.7
Wilmington, Del.–N.J.–Md.	524,108	76	499,493	70	24,615	5.0
Worcester, Mass.	372,940	105	372,144	89	796	0.3
Yakima, Wash.	172,508	192	145,212	191	27,296	18.8
York, Pa.	381,255	102	329,540	105	51,715	15.7
Youngstown–Warren, Ohio	531,350	71	537,124	68	−5,774	−1.0

NOTE: The general concept of a standard metropolitan statistical area (SMSA) is one of a large population nucleus together with adjacent communities that have a high degree of economic and social integration with that nucleus. *Source:* Department of Commerce, Bureau of the Census.

Population by Age, Sex, Race, and Spanish Origin, 1980

(in thousands)

Age	White		Black		Spanish origin		Other races		All persons	
	Male	Female	Male	Female	Male	Female	Male	Female	Male	Female
Under 5	6,483	6,148	1,228	1,208	848	815	650	627	8,360	7,984
5–9	6,684	6,347	1,255	1,235	783	754	598	578	8,538	8,159
10–14	7,408	7,053	1,344	1,329	747	728	563	544	9,315	8,926
15–19	8,631	8,326	1,488	1,495	826	779	632	588	10,752	10,410
20–24	8,680	8,603	1,300	1,424	819	766	680	625	10,660	10,652
25–29	8,004	7,978	1,084	1,237	697	678	615	599	9,703	9,814
30–34	7,299	7,344	871	1,017	558	570	506	521	8,676	8,882
35–39	5,830	5,929	662	795	416	438	368	378	6,860	7,103
40–44	4,849	4,976	566	684	345	367	292	300	5,708	5,961
45–49	4,638	4,818	515	627	300	321	234	255	5,388	5,701
50–54	4,918	5,239	504	624	270	294	198	226	5,620	6,089
55–59	4,852	5,385	466	570	217	237	163	178	5,481	6,133
60–64	4,173	4,801	385	486	147	174	111	130	4,669	5,416
65–69	3,481	4,330	331	445	116	148	90	104	3,902	4,879
70–74	2,552	3,542	234	329	85	109	67	72	2,853	3,944
75–79	1,650	2,659	153	235	59	77	45	52	1,847	2,945
80–84	923	1,762	75	125	27	39	21	28	1,019	1,915
85 and over	614	1,430	53	106	19	30	14	23	681	1,558
All ages	91,670	96,671	12,516	13,972	7,278	7,328	5,847	5,829	110,032	116,473
15 and over	71,095	77,124	8,689	10,200	4,901	5,030	4,035	4,080	83,819	91,404
20 and over	62,463	68,798	7,345	8,871	4,153	4,302	3,450	3,492	74,504	82,478
65 and over	9,220	13,724	846	1,240	305	404	236	277	10,302	15,242
Median age	30.0	32.6	23.6	26.2	22.7	23.8	24.1	25.7	28.8	31.1

NOTE: Figures represent resident population of the 50 states and the District of Columbia plus Armed Forces overseas.

Population by State

State	1980	Percent change, 1970–80	Pop. per sq. mi., 1980	Pop. rank, 1980	1970	1950	1900	1790
Alabama	3,893,888	+13.1	76.7	22	3,444,354	3,061,743	1,828,697	—
Alaska	401,851	+32.8	0.7	50	302,583	128,643	63,592	—
Arizona	2,718,425	+53.1	23.9	29	1,775,399	749,587	122,931	—
Arkansas	2,286,435	+18.9	43.9	33	1,923,322	1,909,511	1,311,564	—
California	23,667,565	+18.5	151.4	1	19,971,069	10,586,223	1,485,053	—
Colorado	2,889,735	+30.8	27.9	28	2,209,596	1,325,089	539,700	—
Connecticut	3,107,576	+ 2.5	637.8	25	3,032,217	2,007,280	908,420	237,946
Delaware	594,317	+ 8.4	307.6	47	548,104	318,085	184,735	59,096
D.C.	638,432	−15.6	—	—	756,668	802,178	278,718	—
Florida	9,746,324	+43.5	180.0	7	6,791,418	2,771,305	528,542	—
Georgia	5,463,105	+19.1	94.1	13	4,587,930	3,444,578	2,216,331	82,548
Hawaii	964,691	+25.3	150.1	39	769,913	499,794	154,001	—
Idaho	944,038	+32.4	11.5	41	713,015	588,637	161,772	—
Illinois	11,426,518	+ 2.8	205.3	5	11,110,285	8,712,176	4,821,550	—
Indiana	5,490,260	+ 5.7	152.8	12	5,195,392	3,934,224	2,516,462	—
Iowa	2,913,808	+ 3.1	52.1	27	2,825,368	2,621,073	2,231,853	—
Kansas	2,364,236	+ 5.1	28.9	32	2,249,071	1,905,299	1,470,495	—
Kentucky	3,660,257	+13.7	92.3	23	3,220,711	2,944,806	2,147,174	73,677
Louisiana	4,206,312	+15.4	94.5	19	3,644,637	2,683,516	1,381,625	—
Maine	1,125,027	+13.2	36.3	38	993,722	913,774	694,466	96,540
Maryland	4,216,975	+ 7.5	428.7	18	3,923,897	2,343,001	1,188,044	319,728
Massachusetts	5,737,037	+ 0.8	733.3	11	5,689,170	4,690,514	2,805,346	378,787
Michigan	9,262,078	+ 4.3	162.6	8	8,881,826	6,371,766	2,420,982	—
Minnesota	4,075,970	+ 7.1	51.2	21	3,806,103	2,982,483	1,751,394	—
Mississippi	2,520,638	+13.7	53.4	31	2,216,994	2,178,914	1,551,270	—
Missouri	4,916,759	+ 5.1	71.3	15	4,677,623	3,954,653	3,106,665	—
Montana	786,690	+13.3	5.4	44	694,409	591,024	243,329	—
Nebraska	1,569,825	+ 5.7	20.5	35	1,485,333	1,325,510	1,066,300	—
Nevada	800,493	+63.8	7.3	43	488,738	160,083	42,335	—
New Hampshire	920,610	+24.8	102.4	42	737,681	533,242	411,588	141,885
New Jersey	7,364,823	+ 2.7	986.2	9	7,171,112	4,835,329	1,883,669	184,139
New Mexico	1,302,981	+28.1	10.7	37	1,017,055	681,187	195,310	—
New York	17,558,072	− 3.7	370.6	2	18,241,391	14,830,192	7,268,894	340,120
North Carolina	5,881,813	+15.7	120.4	10	5,084,411	4,061,929	1,893,810	393,751
North Dakota	652,717	+ 5.7	9.4	46	617,792	619,636	319,146	—
Ohio	10,797,624	+ 1.3	263.3	6	10,657,423	7,946,627	4,157,545	—
Oklahoma	3,025,290	+18.2	44.1	26	2,559,463	2,233,351	790,391[1]	—
Oregon	2,633,149	+25.9	27.4	30	2,091,533	1,521,341	413,536	—
Pennsylvania	11,863,895	+ 0.5	264.3	4	11,800,766	10,498,012	6,302,115	434,373
Rhode Island	947,154	− 0.3	897.8	40	949,723	791,896	428,556	68,825
South Carolina	3,121,833	+20.5	103.4	24	2,590,713	2,117,027	1,340,316	249,073
South Dakota	690,768	+ 3.7	9.1	45	666,257	652,740	401,570	—
Tennessee	4,591,120	+16.9	111.6	17	3,926,018	3,291,718	2,020,616	35,691
Texas	14,229,288	+27.1	54.3	3	11,198,655	7,711,194	3,048,710	—
Utah	1,461,037	+37.9	17.8	36	1,059,273	688,862	276,749	—
Vermont	511,456	+15.0	55.2	48	444,732	377,747	343,641	85,425
Virginia	5,346,818	+14.9	134.7	14	4,651,448	3,318,680	1,854,184	747,610[2]
Washington	4,132,180	+21.1	62.1	20	3,413,244	2,378,963	518,103	—
West Virginia	1,950,279	+11.8	80.8	34	1,744,237	2,005,552	958,800	—
Wisconsin	4,705,521	+ 6.5	86.5	16	4,417,821	3,434,575	2,069,042	—
Wyoming	469,557	+41.3	4.8	49	332,416	290,529	92,531	—
Total U.S.	**226,545,805**	+11.4	**62.6**	—	**203,302,031**	**151,325,798**	**76,212,168**	**3,929,214**

1. Includes population of Indian Territory: 1900, 392,960. 2. Until 1863, Virginia included what is now West Virginia. *Source:* Department of Commerce, Bureau of the Census.

Measuring Earthquakes

Earthquakes are generally measured on the scale developed by Charles F. Richter in 1935. The scale is logarithmic—the release of energy increases about 10 times with each whole number of the scale. A quake whose magnitude is less than 2 will not be noticed by humans; there are thousands of such tremors per year. Earthquakes whose magnitude is more than 4.5 can cause damage; 6.5 indicates a serious and hazardous quake. At a magnitude of about 8, great damage can occur. The San Francisco earthquake of 1906 has been variously estimated at 7.8 to 8.3. The April 1979 quake in Yugoslavia was measured at magnitude 7.2; it caused heavy casualties because it occurred in a densely populated area.

Incorporated Places Over 25,000 Population

Asterisk denotes more than one ZIP code for a city and refers to Postmaster. To find the ZIP code for a particular address, consult the ZIP code directory available in every post office. For latest population figures of many cities, see listing for individual states in the United States section.

City and major ZIP code	1980 census	1970 census
Aberdeen, SD (57401)	25,851	26,476
Abilene, TX (79604*)	98,315	89,653
Addison, IL (60101)	29,759	24,482
Akron, OH (44309*)	237,177	275,425
Alameda, CA (94501)	63,852	70,968
Albany, GA (31706*)	74,550	72,623
Albany, NY (12212*)	101,727	115,781
Albany, OR (97321)	26,678	18,181
Albuquerque, NM (87101*)	331,767	244,501
Alexandria, LA (71301)	51,565	41,811
Alexandria, VA (22313*)	103,217	110,927
Alhambra, CA (91802*)	64,615	62,125
Allen Park, MI (48101)	34,196	40,747
Allentown, PA (18101*)	103,758	109,871
Alton, IL (62002)	34,171	39,700
Altoona, PA (16603*)	57,078	63,115
Amarillo, TX (79120*)	149,230	127,010
Ames, IA (50010)	45,775	39,505
Anaheim, CA (92803*)	219,311	166,408
Anchorage, AK (99502*)	174,431	48,081
Anderson, IN (46018*)	64,695	70,787
Anderson, SC (29621*)	27,965	27,556
Annapolis, MD (21401*)	31,740	30,095
Ann Arbor, MI (48106*)	107,966	100,035
Anniston, AL (36201*)	29,523	31,533
Antioch, CA (94509)	42,683	28,060
Appleton, WI (54911*)	58,913	56,377
Arcadia, CA (91006)	45,994	45,138
Arlington, TX (76010*)	160,113	90,229
Arlington Heights, IL (60004*)	66,116	65,058
Arvada, CO (80001*)	84,576	49,844
Asheville, NC (28810*)	53,583	57,820
Ashland, KY (41101)	27,064	29,245
Athens, GA (30603*)	42,549	44,342
Atlanta, GA (30304*)	425,022	495,039
Atlantic City, NJ (08401*)	40,199	47,859
Attleboro, MA (02703)	34,196	32,907
Auburn, AL (36830)	28,471	22,767
Auburn, NY (13021)	32,548	34,599
Auburn, WA (98002)	26,417	21,653
Augusta, GA (30901*)	47,532	59,864
Aurora, CO (80010*)	158,588	74,974
Aurora, IL (60507*)	81,293	74,389
Austin, TX (78710*)	345,496	253,539
Azusa, CA (91702)	29,380	25,217
Bakersfield, CA (93302*)	105,735	69,515
Baldwin Park, CA (91706)	50,554	47,285
Baltimore, MD (21233*)	786,775	905,787
Bangor, ME (04401)	31,643	33,168
Barberton, OH (44203)	29,751	33,052
Bartlesville, OK (74003)	34,568	29,683
Baton Rouge, LA (70821*)	219,419	165,921
Battle Creek, MI (49016*)	35,724	38,931
Bay City, MI (48706)	41,593	49,449
Bayonne, NJ (07002)	65,047	72,743
Baytown, TX (77520*)	56,923	43,980
Beaumont, TX (77704*)	118,102	117,548
Beavercreek, OH (45401)	31,589	—
Beaverton, OR (97005*)	30,582	18,577
Bell, CA (90201)	25,450	21,836
Belleville, IL (62220*)	41,580	41,223
Belleville, NJ (07109)	35,367	37,629
Bellevue, WA (98009*)	73,903	61,196
Bellflower, CA (90706)	53,441	52,334
Bell Gardens, CA (90201)	34,117	29,308
Bellingham, WA (98225*)	45,794	39,375
Beloit, WI (53511)	35,207	35,729
Bergenfield, NJ (07621)	25,568	29,000
Berkeley, CA (94704*)	103,328	114,091
Berwyn, IL (60402)	46,849	52,502
Bessemer, AL (35020)	31,729	33,428
Bethel Park, PA (15102)	34,755	34,758
Bethlehem, PA (18016*)	70,419	72,686
Bettendorf, IA (52722)	27,381	22,126
Beverly, MA (01915)	37,655	38,348
Beverly Hills, CA (90213*)	32,367	33,416
Billings, MT (59101*)	66,842	61,581
Biloxi, MS (39530*)	49,311	48,486
Binghamton, NY (13902*)	55,860	64,123
Birmingham, AL (35203*)	284,413	300,910
Bismarck, ND (58501)	44,485	34,703
Blacksburg, VA (24060)	30,638	9,384
Blaine, MN (55433)	28,558	20,573
Bloomfield, NJ (07003)	47,792	52,029
Bloomington, IL (61701)	44,189	39,992
Bloomington, IN (47401)	52,044	43,262
Bloomington, MN (55420)	81,831	81,970
Blue Springs, MO (64015)	25,927	6,779
Boca Raton, FL (33432*)	49,505	28,506
Boise, ID (83708*)	102,160	74,990
Bolingbrook, IL (60439)	37,261	7,651
Bossier City, LA (71111*)	50,817	43,769
Boston, MA (02109*)	562,994	641,071
Boulder, CO (80302*)	76,685	66,870
Bountiful, UT (84010)	32,877	27,751
Bowie, MD (20715)	33,695	35,028
Bowling Green, KY (42101)	40,450	36,705
Bowling Green, OH (43402)	25,728	14,656
Boynton Beach, FL (33435*)	35,624	18,115
Bradenton, FL (33506*)	30,170	21,040
Brea, CA (92621)	27,913	18,447
Bremerton, WA (98310*)	36,208	35,307
Bridgeport, CT (06602*)	142,546	156,542
Bristol, CT (06010)	57,370	55,487
Brockton, MA (02403*)	95,172	89,040
Broken Arrow, OK (74012)	35,761	11,018
Brookfield, WI (53005)	34,035	31,761
Brooklyn Center, MN (55429)	31,230	35,173
Brooklyn Park, MN (55429)	43,332	26,230
Brook Park, OH (44142)	26,195	30,774
Brownsville, TX (78520*)	84,997	52,522
Brunswick, OH (44212)	28,104	15,852
Bryan, TX (77801)	44,337	33,719
Buena Park, CA (90622*)	64,165	63,646
Buffalo, NY (14240*)	357,870	462,768
Burbank, CA (91505*)	84,625	88,871
Burbank, IL (60459)	28,462	—
Burlingame, CA (94010)	26,173	27,320
Burlington, IA (52601)	29,529	32,366
Burlington, NC (27215)	37,266	35,930
Burlington, VT (05401)	37,712	38,633
Burnsville, MN (55337)	35,674	19,940
Burton, MI (48502)	29,976	—
Butte, MT (59701)	37,205	23,368
Calumet City, IL (60409)	39,697	33,107
Camarillo, CA (93010)	37,797	19,219
Cambridge, MA (02140)	95,322	100,361
Camden, NJ (08101*)	84,910	102,551

City and major ZIP code	1980 census	1970 census
Campbell, CA (95008)	27,067	23,797
Canton, OH (44711*)	93,077	110,053
Cape Coral, FL (33904)	32,103	—
Cape Girardeau, MO (63701)	34,361	31,282
Carbondale, IL (62901)	26,414	22,816
Carlsbad, CA (92008)	35,490	14,944
Carlsbad, NM (88220)	25,496	21,297
Carrollton, TX (75006*)	40,595	13,855
Carson, CA (90749)	81,221	71,150
Carson City, NV (89701)	32,022	15,468
Casper, WY (82601*)	51,016	39,361
Cedar Falls, IA (50613)	36,322	29,597
Cedar Rapids, IA (52401*)	110,243	110,642
Cerritos, CA (90701)	53,020	15,856
Champaign, IL (61820*)	58,133	56,837
Chandler, AZ (85224)	29,673	13,763
Chapel Hill, NC (27514)	32,421	26,199
Charleston, SC (29401*)	69,510	66,945
Charleston, WV (25301*)	63,968	71,505
Charlotte, NC (28228*)	314,447	241,420
Charlottesville, VA (22906*)	39,916	38,880
Chattanooga, TN (37401*)	169,558	119,923
Chelsea, MA (02150)	25,431	30,625
Chesapeake, VA (23320*)	114,486	89,580
Chester, PA (19013*)	45,794	56,331
Cheyenne, WY (82001*)	47,283	41,254
Chicago, IL (60607*)	3,005,072	3,369,357
Chicago Heights, IL (60411)	37,026	40,900
Chico, CA (95926)	26,603	19,580
Chicopee, MA (01021*)	55,112	66,676
Chino, CA (91710)	40,165	20,411
Chula Vista, CA (92010*)	83,927	67,901
Cicero, IL (60650)	61,232	67,058
Cincinnati, OH (45234*)	385,457	453,514
Claremont, CA (91711)	30,950	24,776
Clarksville, TN (37040)	54,777	31,719
Clearwater, FL (33515*)	85,528	52,074
Cleveland, OH (44101*)	573,822	750,879
Cleveland, TN (37311)	26,415	21,446
Cleveland Heights, OH (44118)	56,438	60,767
Clifton, NJ (07015*)	74,388	82,437
Clinton, IA (52732)	32,828	34,719
Clovis, CA (93612)	33,021	13,856
Clovis, NM (88101)	31,194	28,495
College Station, TX (77840)	37,272	17,676
Colorado Springs, CO (80901*)	214,821	135,517
Columbia, MO (65201*)	62,061	58,812
Columbia, SC (29201*)	100,385	113,542
Columbia, TN (38401)	26,571	21,471
Columbus, GA (31908*)	169,441	155,028
Columbus, IN (47201)	30,614	26,457
Columbus, MS (39701)	27,383	25,795
Columbus, OH (43216*)	565,032	540,025
Compton, CA (90220*)	81,286	78,547
Concord, CA (94520*)	103,255	85,164
Concord, NH (03301*)	30,400	30,022
Coon Rapids, MN (55433)	35,826	30,505
Coral Gables, FL (33114)	43,241	42,494
Coral Springs, FL (33065)	37,349	1,489
Corona, CA (91720)	37,791	27,519
Corpus Christi, TX (78408*)	231,999	204,525
Corvallis, OR (97333*)	40,960	35,056
Costa Mesa, CA (92626*)	82,562	72,660
Council Bluffs, IA (51501)	56,449	60,348
Covina, CA (91722*)	33,751	30,395
Covington, KY (41011*)	49,563	52,535
Cranston, RI (02910)	71,992	74,287
Crystal, MN (55428)	25,543	30,925
Culver City, CA (90230)	38,139	34,451
Cumberland, MD (21502)	25,933	29,724
Cupertino, CA (95014)	34,015	17,895
Cuyahoga Falls, OH (44222*)	43,890	49,815
Cypress, CA (90630)	40,391	31,569
Dallas, TX (75260*)	904,078	844,401
Daly City, CA (94015*)	78,519	66,922
Danbury, CT (06810)	60,470	50,781
Danville, IL (61832)	38,985	42,570
Danville, VA (24541*)	45,642	46,391
Davenport, IA (52802*)	103,264	98,469
Davis, CA (95616)	36,640	23,488
Dayton, OH (45401*)	193,444	243,023
Daytona Beach, FL (32015*)	54,176	45,327
Dearborn, MI (48120*)	90,660	104,199
Dearborn Heights, MI (48127)	67,706	80,069
Decatur, AL (35602*)	42,002	38,044
Decatur, IL (62521*)	94,081	90,397
Deerfield Beach, FL (33441)	39,193	16,662
De Kalb, IL (60115)	33,099	32,949
Del City, OK (73155)	28,424	27,133
Delray Beach, FL (33444*)	34,325	19,915
Del Rio, TX (78840)	30,034	21,330
Denton, TX (76201)	48,063	39,874
Denver, CO (80202*)	492,365	514,678
Des Moines, IA (50318*)	191,003	201,404
Des Plaines, IL (60018*)	53,568	57,239
Detroit, MI (48233*)	1,203,339	1,514,063
Dothan, AL (36303*)	48,750	36,733
Downers Grove, IL (60515*)	42,572	32,544
Downey, CA (90241*)	82,602	88,573
Dubuque, IA (52001)	62,321	62,309
Duluth, MN (55806*)	92,811	100,578
Duncanville, TX (75116*)	27,781	14,105
Dunedin, FL (33528)	30,203	17,639
Durham, NC (27701*)	100,538	95,438
East Chicago, IN (46312)	39,786	49,982
East Cleveland, OH (44112)	36,957	39,660
East Detroit, MI (48021)	38,280	45,920
East Lansing, MI (48823)	51,392	47,540
Easton, PA (18042)	26,027	29,450
East Orange, NJ (07019*)	77,690	75,471
East Point, GA (30364)	37,486	39,315
East Providence, RI (02914)	50,980	48,207
East St. Louis, IL (62201*)	55,200	70,169
Eau Claire, WI (54701)	51,509	44,619
Edina, MN (55424)	46,073	44,046
Edmond, OK (73034)	34,637	16,633
Edmonds, WA (98020)	27,679	23,684
El Cajon, CA (92020*)	73,892	52,273
El Dorado, AR (71730)	25,270	25,283
Elgin, IL (60120)	63,798	55,691
Elizabeth, NJ (07207*)	106,201	112,654
Elk Grove, IL (60007)	28,907	20,346
Elkhart, IN (46515*)	41,305	43,152
Elmhurst, IL (60126)	44,276	46,392
Elmira, NY (14901*)	35,327	39,945
El Monte, CA (91734*)	79,494	69,892
El Paso, TX (79910*)	425,259	322,261
Elyria, OH (44035*)	57,538	53,427
Emporia, KS (66801)	25,287	23,327
Englewood, CO (80110*)	30,021	33,695
Enid, OK (73701)	50,363	44,986
Erie, PA (16515*)	119,123	129,265
Escondido, CA (92025*)	64,355	36,792
Euclid, OH (44117)	59,999	71,552
Eugene, OR (97401*)	105,624	79,028
Evanston, IL (60204*)	73,706	80,113
Evansville, IN (47708*)	130,496	138,764
Everett, MA (02149)	37,195	42,485
Everett, WA (98201*)	54,413	53,622
Fairborn, OH (45324)	29,702	32,267
Fairfield, CA (94533)	58,099	44,146
Fairfield, OH (45014)	30,777	14,680

City and major ZIP code	1980 census	1970 census
Fair Lawn, NJ (07410)	32,229	38,040
Fall River, MA (02722*)	92,574	96,898
Fargo, ND (58102*)	61,383	53,365
Farmington, NM (87401)	31,222	21,979
Farmington Hills, MI (48024)	58,056	—
Fayetteville, AR (72701)	36,608	30,729
Fayetteville, NC (28302*)	59,507	53,510
Ferndale, MI (48220)	26,227	30,850
Findlay, OH (45840)	35,594	35,800
Fitchburg, MA (01420)	39,580	43,343
Flagstaff, AZ (86001)	34,743	26,117
Flint, MI (48502*)	159,611	193,317
Florence, AL (35631*)	37,029	34,031
Florence, SC (29501)	29,176	25,997
Florissant, MO (63033*)	55,372	65,908
Fond du Lac, WI (54935)	35,863	35,515
Fontana, CA (92335)	37,107	20,673
Fort Collins, CO (80521*)	65,092	43,337
Fort Dodge, IA (50501)	29,423	31,263
Fort Lauderdale, FL (33310*)	153,279	139,590
Fort Lee, NJ (07024)	32,449	30,631
Fort Myers, FL (33901*)	36,638	27,351
Fort Pierce, FL (33454*)	33,802	29,721
Fort Smith, AR (72901*)	71,626	62,802
Fort Wayne, IN (46802*)	172,028	178,269
Fort Worth, TX (76101*)	385,164	393,455
Fountain Valley, CA (92708)	55,080	31,886
Frankfort, KY (40601)	25,973	21,902
Frederick, MD (21701)	28,086	23,641
Freeport, IL (61032)	26,266	27,736
Freeport, NY (11520)	38,272	40,374
Fremont, CA (94538*)	131,945	100,869
Fresno, CA (93706*)	218,202	165,655
Fridley, MN (55432)	30,228	29,233
Fullerton, CA (92631*)	102,034	85,987
Gadsden, AL (35901*)	47,565	53,928
Gainesville, FL (32602*)	81,371	64,510
Gaithersburg, MD (20877*)	26,424	8,344
Galesburg, IL (61401)	35,305	36,290
Galveston, TX (77553*)	61,902	61,809
Gardena, CA (90247*)	45,165	41,021
Garden City, MI (48135)	35,640	41,864
Garden Grove, CA (92640*)	123,307	121,155
Garfield, NJ (07026)	26,803	30,797
Garfield Heights, OH (44125)	34,938	41,417
Garland, TX (75040*)	138,857	81,437
Gary, IN (46401*)	151,953	175,415
Gastonia, NC (28052)	47,333	47,322
Glendale, AZ (85301*)	97,172	36,228
Glendale, CA (91209*)	139,060	132,664
Glendora, CA (91740)	38,500	32,143
Glenview, IL (60025)	32,060	24,880
Gloucester, MA (01930)	27,768	27,941
Goldsboro, NC (27530)	31,871	26,960
Grand Forks, ND (58201)	43,765	39,008
Grand Island, NE (68801)	33,180	32,358
Grand Junction, CO (81501*)	27,956	20,170
Grand Prairie, TX (75051*)	71,462	50,904
Grand Rapids, MI (49501*)	181,843	197,649
Granite City, IL (62040)	36,815	40,685
Great Falls, MT (59403*)	56,725	60,091
Greeley, CO (80631*)	53,006	38,902
Green Bay, WI (54305*)	87,899	87,809
Greenfield, WI (53220)	31,467	24,424
Greensboro, NC (27420*)	155,642	144,076
Greenville, MS (38701)	40,613	39,648
Greenville, NC (27834)	35,740	29,063
Greenville, SC (29602*)	58,242	61,436
Gresham, OR (97030)	33,005	10,030
Gulfport, MS (39503*)	39,676	40,791
Hackensack, NJ (07602*)	36,039	36,008
Hagerstown, MD (21740)	34,132	35,862
Hallandale, FL (33009)	36,517	23,849
Haltom City, TX (76117)	29,014	28,127
Hamilton, OH (45012*)	63,189	67,865
Hammond, IN (46320*)	93,714	107,983
Hampton, VA (23669*)	122,617	120,779
Hanover Park, IL (60103)	28,850	11,735
Harlingen, TX (78550)	43,543	33,503
Harrisburg, PA (17105*)	53,264	68,061
Hartford, CT (06101*)	136,392	158,017
Harvey, IL (60426)	35,810	34,636
Hattiesburg, MS (39401)	40,829	38,277
Haverhill, MA (01830)	46,865	46,120
Hawthorne, CA (90250)	56,447	53,304
Hayward, CA (94544*)	94,342	93,058
Hazleton, PA (18201)	27,318	30,426
Hempstead, NY (11551*)	40,404	39,411
Hendersonville, TN (37075)	26,561	412
Hialeah, FL (33010*)	145,254	102,452
Highland, IN (46322)	25,935	24,947
Highland Park, IL (60035)	30,611	32,263
Highland Park, MI (48203)	27,909	35,444
High Point, NC (27260*)	63,808	63,229
Hillsboro, OR (97123)	27,664	14,675
Hilo, HI (96720)	35,269	26,353
Hobbs, NM (88240)	29,153	26,025
Hoboken, NJ (07030)	42,460	45,380
Hoffman Estates, IL (60195)	37,272	22,238
Holland, MI (49423)	26,281	26,479
Hollywood, FL (33022*)	121,323	106,873
Holyoke, MA (01040)	44,678	50,112
Honolulu, HI (96820*)	365,048	324,871
Hopkinsville, KY (42240)	27,318	21,395
Hot Springs, AR (71901*)	35,781	35,631
Houma, LA (70360)	32,602	30,922
Houston, TX (77201*)	1,595,138	1,233,535
Huber Heights, OH (45424)	35,480	—
Huntington, WV (25704*)	63,684	74,315
Huntington Beach, CA (92647*)	170,505	115,960
Huntington Park, CA (90255)	46,223	33,744
Huntsville, AL (35804*)	142,513	139,282
Hurst, TX (76053)	31,420	27,215
Hutchinson, KS (67501)	40,284	36,885
Idaho Falls, ID (83401)	39,590	35,776
Independence, MO (64051*)	111,806	111,630
Indianapolis, IN (46206*)	700,807	736,856
Inglewood, CA (90311*)	94,245	89,985
Inkster, MI (48141)	35,190	38,595
Iowa City, IA (52240)	50,508	46,850
Irvine, CA (92713)	62,134	—
Irving, TX (75061*)	109,943	97,260
Irvington, NJ (07111)	61,493	59,743
Ithaca, NY (14850)	28,732	26,226
Jackson, MI (49201*)	39,739	45,484
Jackson, MS (39205*)	202,895	153,968
Jackson, TN (38301)	49,131	39,996
Jacksonville, AR (72076)	27,589	19,832
Jacksonville, FL (32203*)	540,920	504,265
Jamestown, NY (14701)	35,775	39,795
Janesville, WI (53545*)	51,071	46,426
Jefferson City, MO (65101)	33,619	32,407
Jersey City, NJ (07303*)	223,532	260,350
Johnson City, TN (37601)	39,753	33,770
Johnstown, PA (15901*)	35,496	42,476
Joliet, IL (60436*)	77,956	78,827
Jonesboro, AR (72401)	31,530	27,050
Joplin, MO (64801)	39,023	39,256
Kalamazoo, MI (49001*)	79,722	85,555
Kankakee, IL (60901)	30,141	30,944

City and major ZIP code	1980 census	1970 census
Kansas City, KS (66110*)	161,148	168,213
Kansas City, MO (64108*)	448,159	507,330
Kearny, NJ (07032)	35,735	37,585
Kenner, LA (70062)	66,382	29,858
Kennewick, WA (99336)	34,397	15,212
Kenosha, WI (53141*)	77,685	78,805
Kent, OH (44240)	26,164	28,183
Kentwood, MI (49508)	30,438	20,310
Kettering, OH (45429)	61,186	71,864
Killeen, TX (76541*)	46,296	35,507
Kingsport, TN (37662*)	32,027	31,938
Kingsville, TX (78363)	28,808	28,915
Kinston, NC (28501)	25,234	23,020
Kirkwood, MO (63122)	27,987	31,679
Knoxville, TN (37901*)	175,045	174,587
Kokomo, IN (46902*)	47,808	44,042
La Crosse, WI (54601)	48,347	50,286
Lafayette, IN (47901*)	43,011	44,955
Lafayette, LA (70501*)	81,961	68,908
La Habra, CA (90631)	45,232	41,350
Lake Charles, LA (70601*)	75,226	77,998
Lakeland, FL (33802*)	47,406	42,803
Lakewood, CA (90714*)	74,654	83,025
Lakewood, CO (80215)	113,808	92,743
Lakewood, OH (44107)	61,963	70,173
Lake Worth, FL (33461*)	27,048	23,714
La Mesa, CA (92041)	50,308	39,178
La Mirada, CA (90638)	40,986	30,808
Lancaster, CA (93534*)	48,027	—
Lancaster, OH (43130)	34,953	32,911
Lancaster, PA (17604*)	54,725	57,690
Lansing, IL (60438)	29,039	25,805
Lansing, MI (48924*)	130,414	131,403
La Puente, CA (91747*)	30,882	31,092
Laredo, TX (78041*)	91,449	69,024
Largo, FL (33540*)	58,977	24,230
Las Cruces, NM (88001*)	45,086	37,857
Las Vegas, NV (89114*)	164,674	125,787
Lauderdale Lakes, FL (33313)	25,426	10.577
Lauderhill, FL (33313)	37,271	8,465
Lawrence, IN (46226)	25,591	16,353
Lawrence, KS (66044)	52,738	45,698
Lawrence, MA (01842*)	63,175	66,915
Lawton, OK (73501*)	80,054	74,470
Leavenworth, KS (66048)	33,656	25,147
Lebanon, PA (17042)	25,711	28,572
Lee's Summit, MO (64063)	28,741	16,230
Leominster, MA (01453)	34,508	32,939
Lewiston, ID (83501)	27,986	26,068
Lewiston, ME (04240)	40,481	41,779
Lexington, KY (40511*)	204,165	108,137
Lima, OH (45802*)	47,381	53,734
Lincoln, NE (68501*)	171,932	149,518
Lincoln Park, MI (48146)	45,105	52,984
Linden, NJ (07036)	37,836	41,409
Lindenhurst, NY (11757)	26,919	28,359
Little Rock, AR (72231*)	158,461	132,483
Littleton, CO (80120*)	28,631	26,466
Livermore, CA (94550)	48,349	37,703
Livonia, MI (48150*)	104,814	110,109
Lodi, CA (95240)	35,221	28,691
Logan, UT (84321)	26,844	22,333
Lombard, IL (60148)	37,295	34,043
Lompoc, CA (93436)	26,267	25,284
Long Beach, CA (90809*)	361,334	358,879
Long Beach, NY (11561)	34,073	33,127
Long Branch, NJ (07740)	29,819	31,774
Longmont, CO (80501)	42,942	23,209
Longview, TX (75602*)	62,762	45,547
Longview, WA (98632)	31,052	28,373
Lorain, OH (44052*)	75,416	78,185
Los Altos, CA (94022)	25,769	25,062
Los Angeles, CA (90052*)	2,966,850	2,811,801
Los Gatos, CA (95030)	26,906	22,613
Louisville, KY (40231*)	298,840	361,706
Loveland, CO (80537)	30,244	16,220
Lowell, MA (01853*)	92,418	94,239
Lubbock, TX (79408*)	173,979	149,101
Lufkin, TX (75901)	28,562	23,049
Lynchburg, VA (24506*)	66,743	54,083
Lynn, MA (01901*)	78,471	90,294
Lynwood, CA (90262)	48,548	43,354
Macon, GA (31213*)	116,896	122,423
Madison, WI (53707*)	170,616	171,809
Madison Heights, MI (48071)	35,375	38,599
Malden, MA (02148)	53,386	56,127
Manchester, NH (03103*)	90,936	87,754
Manhattan, KS (66502)	32,644	27,575
Manhattan Beach, CA (90266)	31,542	35,352
Manitowoc, WI (54220)	32,547	33,430
Mankato, MN (56001)	28,651	30,895
Mansfield, OH (44901*)	53,927	55,047
Maple Heights, OH (44137)	29,735	34,093
Maplewood, MN (55109)	26,990	25,186
Margate, FL (33063)	35,900	8,867
Marietta, GA (30060*)	30,829	27,216
Marion, IN (46952)	35,874	39,607
Marion, OH (43302)	37,040	38,646
Marlborough, MA (01752)	30,617	27,936
Marshalltown, IA (50158)	26,938	26,219
Mason City, IA (50401)	30,144	30,279
Massillon, OH (44646)	30,557	32,539
Maywood, IL (60153)	27,998	29,019
McAllen, TX (78501)	66,281	37,636
McKeesport, PA (15134*)	31,012	37,977
Medford, MA (02155)	58,076	64,397
Medford, OR (97501)	39,603	28,973
Melbourne, FL (32901*)	46,536	40,236
Melrose, MA (02176)	30,055	33,180
Memphis, TN (38101*)	646,174	623,988
Menlo Park, CA (94025)	26,369	26,826
Menomonee Falls, WI (53051)	27,845	31,697
Mentor, OH (44060)	42,065	36,912
Merced, CA (95340)	36,499	22,670
Meriden, CT (06450)	57,118	55,959
Meridian, MS (39301)	46,577	45,083
Merrillville, IN (46410)	27,677	—
Mesa, AZ (85201*)	152,453	63,049
Mesquite, TX (75149*)	67,053	55,131
Miami, FL (33152*)	346,865	334,859
Miami Beach, FL (33139)	96,298	87,072
Michigan City, IN (46360)	36,850	39,369
Middletown, CT (06457)	39,040	36,924
Middletown, OH (45042)	43,719	48,767
Midland, MI (48640)	37,250	35,176
Midland, TX (79702*)	70,525	59,463
Midwest City, OK (73140)	49,559	48,212
Milford, CT (06460)	49,101	50,858
Milpitas, CA (95035)	37,820	26,561
Milwaukee, WI (53201*)	636,236	717,372
Minneapolis, MN (55401*)	370,951	434,400
Minnetonka, MN (55343)	38,683	35,776
Minot, ND (58701)	32,843	32,290
Miramar, FL (33023)	32,813	23,997
Mishawaka, IN (46544*)	40,201	36,060
Missoula, MT (59806*)	33,388	29,497
Mobile, AL (36601*)	200,452	190,026
Modesto, CA (95350*)	106,602	61,712
Moline, IL (61265)	45,709	46,237
Monroe, LA (71203*)	57,597	56,374
Monroeville, PA (15146)	30,977	29,011
Monrovia, CA (91016)	30,531	30,562

City and major ZIP code	1980 census	1970 census
Montclair, NJ (07042*)	38,321	44,043
Montebello, CA (90640)	52,929	42,807
Monterey, CA (93940)	27,558	26,302
Monterey Park, CA (91754)	54,338	49,166
Montgomery, AL (36116*)	177,857	133,386
Moore, OK (73153)	35,063	18,761
Moorhead, MN (56560)	29,998	29,687
Morgantown, WV (26505)	27,605	29,431
Mountain View, CA (94042*)	58,655	54,132
Mount Prospect, IL (60056)	52,634	34,995
Mount Vernon, NY (10551*)	66,713	72,778
Muncie, IN (47302*)	77,216	69,082
Murfreesboro, TN (37130)	32,845	26,360
Murray, UT (84107)	25,750	21,206
Muskegon, MI (49440*)	40,823	44,631
Muskogee, OK (74401)	40,011	37,331
Nacogdoches, TX (75961)	27,149	22,544
Nampa, ID (83651)	25,112	20,768
Napa, CA (94558*)	50,879	36,103
Naperville, IL (60566*)	42,330	22,794
Nashua, NH (03061*)	67,865	55,820
Nashville, TN (37202*)	455,651	426,029
National City, CA (92050)	48,772	43,184
Naugatuck, CT (06770)	26,456	23,034
New Albany, IN (47150)	37,103	38,402
Newark, CA (94560)	32,126	27,153
Newark, DE (19711*)	25,247	21,298
Newark, NJ (07102*)	329,248	381,930
Newark, OH (43055)	41,200	41,836
New Bedford, MA (02741*)	98,478	101,777
New Berlin, WI (53151)	30,529	26,910
New Britain, CT (06050*)	73,840	83,441
New Brunswick, NJ (08901*)	41,442	41,885
New Castle, PA (16101*)	33,621	38,559
New Haven, CT (06511*)	126,109	137,707
New Iberia, LA (70560)	32,766	30,147
New London, CT (06320)	28,842	31,630
New Orleans, LA (70113*)	557,927	593,471
Newport, RI (02840)	29,259	34,562
Newport Beach, CA (92660*)	62,556	49,582
Newport News, VA (23607*)	144,903	138,177
New Rochelle, NY (10802*)	70,794	75,385
Newton, MA (02158)	83,622	91,263
New York, NY (10001*)	7,071,639	7,895,563
Bronx borough (10451*)	1,168,972	1,471,701
Brooklyn borough (11201*)	2,230,936	2,602,012
Manhattan borough (10001*)	1,428,285	1,539,233
Queens borough[1]	1,891,325	1,987,174
Staten Island borough (10314*)	352,121	295,443
Niagara Falls, NY (14302*)	71,384	85,615
Niles, IL (60648)	30,363	31,432
Norfolk, VA (23501*)	266,979	307,951
Normal, IL (61761)	35,672	26,396
Norman, OK (73070*)	68,020	52,117
Norristown, PA (19401*)	34,684	38,169
Northampton, MA (01060)	29,286	29,664
Northbrook, IL (60062)	30,778	25,422
North Charleston, SC (29406)	62,534	—
North Chicago, IL (60064)	38,774	47,275
Northglenn, CO (80233)	29,847	27,785
North Las Vegas, NV (89030)	42,739	46,067
North Little Rock, AR (72114*)	64,288	60,040
North Miami, FL (33161)	42,566	34,767
North Miami Beach, FL (33160)	36,553	30,544
North Olmsted, OH (44070)	36,486	34,861
North Richland Hills, TX (76118)	30,592	16,514
North Tonawanda, NY (14120)	35,760	36,012
Norwalk, CA (90650)	85,286	90,164
Norwalk, CT (06856*)	77,767	79,288
Norwich, CT (06360)	38,074	41,739

City and major ZIP code	1980 census	1970 census
Norwood, OH (45212)	26,342	30,420
Novato, CA (94947)	43,916	31,006
Nutley, NJ (07110)	28,998	31,913
Oak Forest, IL (60452)	26,096	19,271
Oakland, CA (94615*)	339,337	361,561
Oak Lawn, IL (60454*)	60,590	60,305
Oak Park, IL (60301*)	54,887	62,511
Oak Park, MI (48237)	31,537	36,762
Oak Ridge, TN (37830)	27,662	28,319
Ocala, FL (32678*)	37,170	22,583
Oceanside, CA (92054*)	76,698	40,494
Odessa, TX (79760*)	90,027	78,380
Ogden, UT (84401*)	64,407	69,478
Oklahoma City, OK (73125*)	403,136	368,164
Olathe, KS (66061*)	37,258	17,917
Olympia, WA (98501*)	27,447	23,296
Omaha, NE (68108*)	313,911	346,929
Ontario, CA (91761*)	88,820	64,118
Orange, CA (92667*)	91,788	77,365
Orange, NJ (07051*)	31,136	32,566
Orem, UT (84057)	52,399	25,729
Orlando, FL (32802*)	128,291	99,006
Oshkosh, WI (54901)	49,620	53,082
Ottumwa, IA (52501)	27,381	29,610
Overland Park, KS (66204)	81,784	77,934
Owensboro, KY (42301)	54,450	50,329
Oxnard, CA (93030*)	108,195	71,225
Pacifica, CA (94044)	36,866	36,020
Paducah, KY (42001)	29,315	31,627
Palatine, IL (60067)	32,166	26,050
Palm Springs, CA (92263*)	32,366	20,936
Palo Alto, CA (94303*)	55,225	56,040
Panama City, FL (32401*)	33,346	32,096
Paramount, CA (90723)	36,407	34,734
Paramus, NJ (07652)	26,474	28,381
Paris, TX (75460)	25,498	23,441
Parkersburg, WV (26101*)	39,967	44,208
Park Forest, IL (60466)	26,222	30,638
Park Ridge, IL (60068)	38,704	42,614
Parma, OH (44129)	92,548	100,216
Pasadena, CA (91109*)	118,550	112,951
Pasadena, TX (77501*)	112,560	89,957
Pascagoula, MS (39567)	29,318	27,264
Passaic, NJ (07055)	52,463	55,124
Paterson, NJ (07510*)	137,970	144,824
Pawtucket, RI (02860*)	71,204	76,984
Peabody, MA (01960)	45,976	48,080
Pekin, IL (61554)	33,967	31,375
Pembroke Pines, FL (33024*)	35,776	15,496
Pensacola, FL (32501*)	57,619	59,507
Peoria, IL (61601*)	124,160	126,963
Perth Amboy, NJ (08861*)	38,951	38,798
Petaluma, CA (94952)	33,834	24,870
Petersburg, VA (23804*)	41,055	36,103
Phenix City, AL (36867)	26,928	25,281
Philadelphia, PA (19104*)	1,688,210	1,949,996
Phoenix, AZ (85026*)	789,704	584,303
Pico Rivera, CA (90660)	53,387	54,170
Pine Bluff, AR (71601*)	56,636	57,389
Pinellas Park, FL (33565)	32,811	22,287
Pittsburg, CA (94565)	33,034	21,423
Pittsburgh, PA (15219*)	423,959	520,089
Pittsfield, MA (01201)	51,974	57,020
Placentia, CA (92670)	35,041	21,948
Plainfield, NJ (07061*)	45,555	46,862
Plano, TX (75074*)	72,331	17,872
Plantation, FL (33318)	48,653	23,523
Pleasant Hill, CA (94523)	25,124	24,610
Pleasanton, CA (94566)	35,160	18,328
Plum, PA (15239)	25,390	21,932

City and major ZIP code	1980 census	1970 census
Plymouth, MN (55447)	31,615	18,077
Pocatello, ID (83201)	46,340	40,036
Pomona, CA (91766*)	92,742	87,384
Pompano Beach, FL (33060*)	52,618	38,587
Ponca City, OK (74601)	26,238	25,940
Pontiac, MI (48056*)	76,715	85,279
Portage, IN (46368)	27,409	19,127
Portage, MI (49081)	38,157	33,590
Port Arthur, TX (77640)	61,251	57,371
Port Huron, MI (48060)	33,981	35,794
Portland, ME (04101*)	61,572	65,116
Portland, OR (97208*)	366,383	379,967
Portsmouth, NH (03801)	26,254	25,717
Portsmouth, OH (45662)	25,943	27,633
Portsmouth, VA (23705*)	104,577	110,963
Poughkeepsie, NY (12601*)	29,757	32,029
Prichard, AL (36610)	39,541	41,578
Providence, RI (02940*)	156,804	179,116
Provo, UT (84603*)	74,108	53,131
Pueblo, CO (81003*)	101,686	97,774
Quincy, IL (62301)	42,554	45,288
Quincy, MA (02269)	84,743	87,966
Racine, WI (53401*)	85,725	95,162
Rahway, NJ (07065*)	26,723	29,114
Raleigh, NC (27611*)	150,255	122,830
Rancho Cucamonga, CA (91730)	55,250	—
Rancho Palos Verdes, CA (90274)	36,577	—
Rapid City, SD (57701)	46,492	43,836
Raytown, MO (64133)	31,759	33,306
Reading, PA (19603*)	78,686	87,643
Redding, CA (96001*)	41,995	16,659
Redlands, CA (92373)	43,619	36,355
Redondo Beach, CA (90277*)	57,102	57,451
Redwood City, CA (94064*)	54,951	55,686
Reno, NV (89510*)	100,756	72,863
Renton, WA (98057*)	30,612	25,878
Revere, MA (02151)	42,423	43,159
Rialto, CA (92376)	37,474	28,370
Richardson, TX (75080*)	72,496	48,405
Richfield, MN (55423)	37,851	47,231
Richland, WA (99352)	33,578	26,290
Richmond, CA (94802*)	74,676	79,043
Richmond, IN (47374)	41,349	43,999
Richmond, VA (23232*)	219,214	249,332
Ridgewood, NJ (07451*)	25,208	27,547
Riverside, CA (92507*)	170,591	140,089
Riviera Beach, FL (33404)	26,489	21,401
Roanoke, VA (24022*)	100,220	92,115
Rochester, MN (55901)	57,890	53,766
Rochester, NY (14692*)	241,741	295,011
Rockford, IL (61125*)	139,712	147,370
Rock Hill, SC (29730)	35,344	33,846
Rock Island, IL (61201)	47,036	50,166
Rockville, MD (20850*)	43,811	42,739
Rockville Centre, NY (11570)	25,412	27,444
Rocky Mount, NC (27801)	41,283	34,284
Rome, GA (30161)	29,654	30,759
Rome, NY (13440)	43,826	50,148
Rosemead, CA (91770)	42,604	40,972
Roseville, MI (48066)	54,311	60,529
Roseville, MN (55113)	35,820	34,438
Roswell, NM (88201)	39,676	33,908
Royal Oak, MI (48068*)	70,893	86,238
Sacramento, CA (95813*)	275,741	257,105
Saginaw, MI (48605*)	77,508	91,849
St. Charles, MO (63301)	36,087	31,834
St. Clair Shores, MI (48080*)	76,210	88,093
St. Cloud, MN (56301)	42,566	39,691
St. Joseph, MO (64501*)	76,691	72,748
St. Louis, MO (63155*)	453,085	622,236
St. Louis Park, MN (55426)	42,931	48,883
St. Paul, MN (55101*)	270,230	309,866
St. Petersburg, FL (33730*)	238,647	216,159
Salem, MA (01970)	38,220	40,556
Salem, OR (97301*)	89,233	68,725
Salina, KS (67401)	41,843	37,714
Salinas, CA (93901*)	80,479	58,896
Salt Lake City, UT (84119*)	163,697	175,885
San Angelo, TX (76902*)	73,240	63,884
San Antonio, TX (78284*)	786,023	654,153
San Bernardino, CA (92403*)	118,794	106,869
San Bruno, CA (94066)	35,417	36,254
San Buenaventura (Ventura), CA (93002*)	74,393	57,964
San Clemente, CA (92672)	27,325	17,063
San Diego, CA (92199*)	875,538	697,471
Sandusky, OH (44870)	31,360	32,674
Sandy City, UT (84070)	52,210	6,438
San Francisco, CA (94101*)	678,974	715,674
San Gabriel, CA (91776*)	30,072	29,336
San Jose, CA (95101*)	629,546	459,913
San Leandro, CA (94577*)	63,952	68,698
San Luis Obispo, CA (93401)	34,252	28,036
San Mateo, CA (94402*)	77,561	78,991
San Rafael, CA (94901*)	44,700	38,977
Santa Ana, CA (92711*)	204,023	155,710
Santa Barbara, CA (93102*)	74,414	70,215
Santa Clara, CA (95050*)	87,746	86,118
Santa Cruz, CA (95060*)	41,483	32,076
Santa Fe, NM (87501)	48,953	41,167
Santa Maria, CA (93456*)	39,685	32,749
Santa Monica, CA (90406*)	88,314	88,289
Santa Rosa, CA (95402*)	83,320	50,006
Sarasota, FL (33578*)	48,868	40,237
Saratoga, CA (95070)	29,261	26,810
Savannah, GA (31401*)	141,390	118,349
Sayreville, NJ (08872)	29,969	32,508
Schaumburg, IL (60194)	53,305	18,531
Schenectady, NY (12301*)	67,972	77,958
Scottsdale, AZ (85251*)	88,622	67,823
Scranton, PA (18505*)	88,117	102,696
Seal Beach, CA (90740)	25,975	24,441
Seaside, CA (93955)	36,567	36,883
Seattle, WA (98109*)	493,846	530,831
Selma, AL (36701)	26,684	27,379
Shaker Heights, OH (44120)	32,487	36,306
Shawnee, KS (66202*)	29,653	20,946
Shawnee, OK (74801)	26,506	25,075
Sheboygan, WI (53081)	48,085	48,484
Shelton, CT (06484)	31,314	27,165
Sherman, TX (75090)	30,413	29,061
Shreveport, LA (71102*)	205,820	182,064
Simi Valley, CA (93065*)	77,500	59,832
Sioux City, IA (51101*)	82,003	85,925
Sioux Falls, SD (57101*)	81,343	72,488
Skokie, IL (60076*)	60,278	68,322
Slidell, LA (70458)	26,718	16,101
Somerville, MA (02143)	77,372	88,779
Somerville, N.J. (18876)	29,969	32,508
South Bend, IN (46624*)	109,727	125,580
South Euclid, OH (44121)	25,713	29,579
Southfield, MI (48034*)	75,568	69,285
South Gate, CA (90280)	66,784	56,909
Southgate, MI (48195)	32,058	33,909
South San Francisco, CA (94080)	49,393	46,646
Sparks, NV (89431)	40,780	24,187
Spartanburg, SC (29301*)	43,826	44,546
Spokane, WA (99210*)	171,300	170,516
Springfield, IL (62703*)	100,054	91,753
Springfield, MA (01101*)	152,319	163,905
Springfield, MO (65801*)	133,116	120,096
Springfield, OH (45501*)	72,563	81,941

City and major ZIP code	1980 census	1970 census	City and major ZIP code	1980 census	1970 census
Springfield, OR (97477)	41,621	26,874	Vista, CA (92083)	35,834	24,688
Stamford, CT (06904*)	102,453	108,798	Waco, TX (76701*)	101,261	95,326
State College, PA (16801)	36,130	32,833	Walla Walla, WA (99362)	25,618	23,619
Sterling Heights, MI (48077)	108,999	61,365	Walnut Creek, CA (94596*)	53,643	39,844
Steubenville, OH (43952)	26,400	30,771	Waltham, MA (02154)	58,200	61,582
Stillwater, OK (74074)	38,268	31,126	Warner Robins, GA (31093)	39,893	33,491
Stockton, CA (95208*)	149,779	109,963	Warren, MI (48089*)	161,134	179,260
Stow, OH (44224)	25,303	20,061	Warren, OH (44481*)	56,629	63,494
Strongsville, OH (44136)	28,577	15,182	Warwick, RI (02887*)	87,123	83,694
Suffolk, VA (23434*)	47,621	9,858	Washington, DC (20013*)	638,432	756,668
Sunnyvale, CA (94086*)	106,618	95,976	Waterbury, CT (06701*)	103,266	108,033
Sunrise, FL (33338)	39,681	7,403	Waterloo, IA (50701*)	75,985	75,533
Superior, WI (54880)	29,571	32,237	Watertown, NY (13601)	27,861	30,787
Syracuse, NY (13220*)	170,105	197,297	Waukegan, IL (60085)	67,653	65,134
Tacoma, WA (98413*)	158,501	154,407	Waukesha, WI (53186)	50,365	39,695
Tallahassee, FL (32301*)	81,548	72,624	Wausau, WI (54401)	32,426	32,806
Tamarac, FL (33320)	29,376	5,193	Wauwatosa, WI (53213)	51,308	58,676
Tampa, FL (33602*)	271,523	277,714	Weirton, WV (26062)	25,371	27,131
Taunton, MA (02780)	45,001	43,756	West Allis, WI (53214)	63,982	71,649
Taylor, MI (48180)	77,568	70,020	West Covina, CA (91793*)	80,291	68,034
Tempe, AZ (85282*)	106,743	63,550	Westfield, MA (01085)	36,465	31,433
Temple, TX (76501*)	42,354	33,431	Westfield, N.J. (07091)	30,447	33,720
Temple City, CA (91780)	28,972	31,034	West Haven, CT (06516)	53,184	52,851
Terre Haute, IN (47808*)	61,125	70,335	West Jordan, UT (84084)	27,192	4,221
Texarkana, TX (75501*)	31,271	30,497	Westland, MI (48185)	84,603	86,749
Texas City, TX (77590*)	41,403	38,908	West Memphis, AR (72301)	28,138	26,070
Thornton, CO (80229)	40,343	13,326	West Mifflin, PA (15122)	26,279	28,070
Thousand Oaks, CA (91360*)	77,072	35,873	Westminster, CA (92683)	71,133	60,076
Tinley Park, IL (60477)	26,171	12,572	Westminster, CO (80030*)	50,211	19,512
Titusville, FL (32780)	31,910	30,515	West New York, NJ (07093)	39,194	40,627
Toledo, OH (43601*)	354,635	383,062	West Orange, NJ (07052)	39,510	43,715
Topeka, KS (66603*)	115,266	125,011	West Palm Beach, FL (33401*)	63,305	57,375
Torrance, CA (90510*)	129,881	134,968	Wheaton, IL (60187)	43,043	31,138
Torrington, CT (06790)	30,987	31,952	Wheat Ridge, CO (80033)	30,293	29,778
Trenton, NJ (08650*)	92,124	104,786	Wheeling, WV (26003)	43,070	48,188
Troy, MI (48099*)	67,102	39,419	White Plains, NY (10602*)	46,999	50,346
Troy, NY (12180*)	56,638	62,918	Whittier, CA (90605*)	69,717	72,863
Tucson, AZ (85726*)	330,537	262,933	Wichita, KS (67276*)	279,835	276,554
Tulsa, OK (74101*)	360,919	330,350	Wichita Falls, TX (76307*)	94,201	96,265
Turlock, CA (95380)	26,287	13,992	Wilkes-Barre, PA (18701*)	51,551	58,856
Tuscaloosa, AL (35403*)	75,211	65,773	Williamsport, PA (17701)	33,401	37,918
Tustin, CA (92680)	32,317	22,313	Wilmette, IL (60091)	28,229	32,134
Twin Falls, ID (83301)	26,209	21,914	Wilmington, DE (19850*)	70,195	80,386
Tyler, TX (75702*)	70,508	57,770	Wilmington, NC (28402*)	44,000	46,169
Union City, CA (94587)	39,406	14,724	Wilson, NC (27893)	34,424	29,347
Union City, NJ (07087)	55,593	57,305	Winona, MN (55987)	25,075	26,438
University City, MO (63130)	42,738	47,527	Winston-Salem, NC (27102*)	131,885	133,683
Upland, CA (91786)	47,647	32,551	Woburn, MA (01801)	36,626	37,406
Upper Arlington, OH (43221)	35,648	38,727	Woodland, CA (95695)	30,235	20,677
Urbana, IL (61801)	35,978	33,976	Woonsocket, RI (02895)	45,914	46,820
Utica, NY (13504*)	75,632	91,373	Worcester, MA (01613*)	161,799	176,572
Vacaville, CA (95688)	43,367	21,690	Wyandotte, MI (48192)	34,006	41,061
Valdosta, GA (31601)	37,596	32,303	Wyoming, MI (49509)	59,616	56,560
Vallejo, CA (94590*)	80,303	71,710	Yakima, WA (98903*)	49,826	45,588
Valley Stream, NY (11580*)	35,769	40,413	Yonkers, NY (10701*)	195,351	204,297
Vancouver, WA (98661*)	42,834	41,859	Yorba Linda, CA (92686)	28,254	11,856
Vicksburg, MS (39180)	25,434	25,478	York, PA (17405*)	44,619	50,335
Victoria, TX (77901*)	50,695	41,349	Youngstown, OH (44501*)	115,436	140,909
Vineland, NJ (08360)	53,753	47,399	Yuma, AZ (85364*)	42,481	29,007
Virginia Beach, VA (23450*)	262,199	172,106	Zanesville, OH (43701)	28,655	33,045
Visalia, CA (93277*)	49,729	27,130			

1. Queens has four major ZIP codes: 11690*—Far Rockaway; 11351*—Flushing; 11431*—Jamaica; 11101*—Long Island City. *Sources:* Department of Commerce, Bureau of the Census; *1981 National ZIP Code & Post Office Directory.*

U.S. Traditional Ethnic Stock Declining

A recent report by the Center for Continuing Study of the California Economy indicates that the proportion of Americans who are white and of European ancestry will decline at an accelerating rate in the next two decades. Americans who are white and non-Hispanic will make up 77% of the population in 1990 and 75% by 2000 compared with approximately 80% in 1980.

Territorial Expansion

Accession	Date	Area[1]
United States	—	3,618,770
Territory in 1790	—	888,685
Louisiana Purchase	1803	827,192
Florida	1819	58,560
By treaty with Spain	1819	13,443
Texas	1845	390,143
Oregon	1846	285,580
Mexican Cession	1848	529,017
Gadsden Purchase	1853	29,640
Alaska	1867	586,412
Hawaii	1898	6,450
Other territory	—	4,692
Philippines	1898	115,600[2]
Puerto Rico	1899	3,515
Guam	1899	209
American Samoa	1900	77
Canal Zone[4]	1904	553
Corn Islands[3]	1914	4
Virgin Islands of U.S.	1917	133
Trust Territory of Pacific Islands	1947	717[5]
All other	—	41
Total, 1980	—	**3,623,462**

1. Total land and water area in square miles. 2. Became independent in 1946. 3. Leased from Nicaragua for 99 years in 1914, but returned April 25, 1971. 4. Reverted to Panama. 5. Land area only; includes Northern Mariana Islands. *Source:* Department of Commerce, Bureau of the Census.

Total Population

Area	1960	1970	1980
50 states of U.S.	179,323,175	203,302,031	226,545,805
48 coterminous	178,464,236	202,229,535	225,139,344
Alaska	226,167	302,583	401,851
Hawaii	632,772	769,913	964,691
American Samoa	20,051	27,159	32,395
Canal Zone	42,122	44,198	(1)
Canton Island	320	n.a.	—
Corn Islands	1,872	(2)	—
Guam	67,044	84,996	105,821
Johnston Atoll	156	1,007	327
Midway	2,356	2,220	468
Puerto Rico	2,349,544	2,712,033	3,196,520
Swan Islands	28	22	n.a.
Trust Ter. of Pac. Is.	70,724	90,940	133,415[3]
Virgin Is. of U.S.	32,099	62,468	95,591
Wake Island	1,097	1,647	302
Population abroad	1,374,421	1,737,836	995,546
Armed forces	609,720	1,057,776	515,408
Other[4]	n.a.	n.a.	n.a.
Total	**183,285,009**	**208,066,557**	**231,106,190**

1. Granted independence on Oct. 1, 1979. 2. Returned to Nicaragua April 25, 1971. 3. Includes Northern Mariana Islands. 4. Includes Baker Island, Enderbury Island, Howland Island, and Jarvis Island, all uninhabited. NOTE: n.a. = unavailable. *Source:* Department of Commerce, Bureau of the Census.

Population by Race, 1980 Census

State	White	Black	Spanish origin	Other
Ala.	2,869,688	995,623	33,100	24,750
Alaska	308,455	13,619	9,497	78,407
Ariz.	2,240,033	75,034	440,915	402,799
Ark.	1,890,002	373,192	17,873	22,319
Calif.	18,031,689	1,819,282	4,543,770	3,817,591
Colo.	2,570,596	101,702	339,300	216,517
Conn.	2,799,420	217,433	124,499	90,723
Del.	488,543	95,971	9,671	10,711
D.C.	171,796	488,229	17,652	17,626
Fla.	8,178,387	1,342,478	857,898	219,127
Ga.	3,948,007	1,465,457	61,261	50,801
Hawaii	318,608	17,352	71,479	629,040
Idaho	901,641	2,716	36,615	39,578
Ill.	9,225,575	1,675,229	635,525	517,657
Ind.	5,004,567	414,732	87,020	70,880
Iowa	2,838,805	41,700	25,536	32,882
Kan.	2,167,752	126,127	63,333	69,329
Ky.	3,379,648	259,490	27,403	22,295
La.	2,911,243	1,237,263	99,105	55,466
Me.	1,109,850	3,128	5,005	11,682
Md.	3,158,412	958,050	64,740	99,984
Mass.	5,362,836	221,279	141,043	152,922
Mich.	7,868,956	1,198,710	162,388	190,678
Minn.	3,936,948	53,342	32,124	86,858
Miss.	1,615,190	887,206	24,731	18,242
Mo.	4,346,267	514,274	51,667	56,903
Mont.	740,148	1,786	9,974	44,756
Neb.	1,490,569	48,389	28,020	31,048
Nev.	699,377	50,791	53,786	49,016
N.H.	910,099	3,990	5,587	6,521
N.J.	6,127,090	924,786	491,867	312,282
N.M.	976,465	24,042	476,089	299,461
N.Y.	13,961,106	2,401,842	1,659,245	1,194,340
N.C.	4,453,010	1,316,050	56,607	105,369
N.D.	625,536	2,568	3,903	24,591
Ohio	9,597,266	1,076,734	119,880	123,419
Okla.	2,597,783	204,658	57,413	222,825
Ore.	2,490,192	37,059	65,833	105,412
Pa.	10,654,325	1,047,609	154,004	164,794
R.I.	896,692	27,584	19,707	22,878
S.C.	2,145,122	948,146	33,414	25,940
S.D.	638,955	2,144	4,028	49,079
Tenn.	3,835,078	725,949	34,081	29,723
Tex.	11,197,663	1,710,250	2,985,643	1,320,470
Utah	1,382,550	9,225	60,302	69,262
Vt.	506,736	1,135	3,304	3,585
Va.	4,229,734	1,008,311	79,873	108,234
Wash.	3,777,296	105,544	119,986	247,323
W. Va.	1,874,751	65,051	12,707	9,842
Wis.	4,442,598	182,593	62,981	80,144
Wyo.	447,716	3,364	24,499	19,736
Total	**188,340,790**	**26,488,218**	**14,605,883**	**11,675,817**

Source: Department of Commerce, Bureau of the Census.

One-Parent Families Increase

Families headed by one parent have doubled since 1970 according to a Census Bureau report. The number of single-parent families rose from 3.3 million to 6.6 million from 1970 to 1981. Divorce is cited as the primary cause for the increase.

Immigration to U.S. by Country of Origin

(Figures are totals, not annual averages, and were tabulated as follows: 1820–67, alien passengers arrived; 1868–91 and 1895–97, immigrant aliens arrived; 1892–94 and 1898 to present, immigrant aliens admitted. Data before 1906 relate to country whence alien came; since 1906, to country of last permanent residence.)

Countries	1979	1820–1979	1961–70	1951–60	1941–50	1931–40	1921–30	1820–1920
Europe: Albania[1]	25	2,608	98	59	85	2,040	—	
Austria[2]	507	4,315,486	20,621	67,106	24,860	3,563	32,868	3,626,110
Belgium	646	202,892	9,192	18,575	12,189	4,817	15,846	137,542
Bulgaria[3]	127	68,021	619	104	375	938	2,945	61,973
Czechoslovakia[1]	494	137,829	3,273	918	8,347	14,393	102,194	3,426
Denmark	378	364,548	9,201	10,984	5,393	2,559	32,430	300,036
Estonia[1]	9	1,148	163	185	212	506	—	—
Finland[1]	284	33,770	4,192	4,925	2,503	2,146	16,691	756
France	2,905	752,432	45,237	51,121	38,809	12,623	49,610	532,765
Germany[2]	7,166	6,984,081	190,796	477,765	226,578	114,058	412,202	5,495,691
Great Britain: England	14,336	3,189,988	174,452	156,171	112,252	21,756	157,420	2,462,015
Scotland	803	821,369	29,849	32,854	16,131	6,887	159,781	567,106
Wales	128	95,332	2,052	2,589	3,209	735	13,012	72,647
Not specified[4]	270	805,238	3,675	3,884	—	—	—	793,741
Greece	5,942	660,869	85,969	47,608	8,973	9,119	51,084	370,405
Hungary[2]	528	—	5,401	36,637	3,469	7,861	30,680	442,693
Ireland	808	4,724,609	37,461	57,332	26,967	13,167	220,591	4,358,350
Italy	5,969	5,300,770	214,111	185,491	57,661	68,028	455,315	4,195,880
Latvia[1]	13	2,604	510	352	361	1,192	—	—
Lithuania[1]	23	3,938	562	242	683	2,201	—	—
Luxembourg[1]	42	2,906	556	684	820	565	—	—
Netherlands	1,184	360,796	30,606	52,277	14,860	7,150	26,948	219,661
Norway[5]	438	856,907	15,484	22,935	10,100	4,740	68,531	731,584
Poland[6]	3,863	518,917	53,539	9,985	7,571	17,026	227,734	169,995
Portugal	7,068	452,350	76,065	19,588	7,423	3,329	29,994	222,721
Romania[7]	1,180	172,480	2,531	1,039	1,076	3,871	67,646	85,428
Spain	3,285	260,867	44,659	7,894	2,898	3,258	28,958	137,907
Sweden[5]	764	1,272,683	17,116	21,697	10,665	3,960	97,249	1,116,239
Switzerland	774	349,723	18,453	17,675	10,547	5,512	29,676	260,492
U.S.S.R.[8]	1,919	3,375,717	2,336	584	548	1,356	61,742	3,280,249
Yugoslavia[3]	1,861	115,804	20,381	8,225	1,576	5,835	49,064	1,888
Other Europe	434	56,027	4,203	8,155	3,983	2,361	22,983	10,716
Total Europe	64,173	36,264,178	1,123,363	1,325,640	621,124	347,552	2,463,194	29,658,016
Asia: China[9]	2,944	537,531	34,764	9,657	16,709	4,928	29,907	347,338
India	18,625	183,931	27,189	1,973	1,761	496	1,886	7,491
Japan[10]	4,496	410,444	39,988	46,250	1,555	1,948	33,462	242,181
Turkey	1,306	387,417	10,142	3,519	798	1,065	33,824	326,347
Other Asia	155,599	1,523,587	315,688	88,707	11,537	7,644	12,980	22,915
Total Asia[11]	182,970	3,042,910	427,771	150,106	32,360	16,081	112,059	946,272
America: Canada and Newfoundland[12]	20,181	4,118,406	413,310	377,952	171,718	108,527	924,515	1,972,686
Central America	17,709	330,244	101,330	44,751	21,665	5,861	15,769	27,524
Mexico[13]	52,479	2,175,891	453,937	299,811	60,589	22,319	459,287	296,649
South America	35,715	748,423	257,954	91,628	21,831	7,803	42,215	71,284
West Indies	71,029	1,761,474	470,213	123,091	49,725	15,502	74,899	356,570
Other America[13]	10	109,468	19,630	59,711	29,276	25	31	—
Total America	197,123	9,243,906	1,716,374	996,944	354,804	160,037	1,516,716	2,724,713
Africa	11,212	144,459	28,954	14,092	7,367	1,750	6,286	18,024
Australia and New Zealand	2,476	120,503	19,562	11,506	13,805	2,231	8,299	44,002
Pacific Islands[14]	135	24,706	1,769	4,698	5,437	780	427	9,938
Countries not specified[15]	2,259	284,651	3,884	12,493	142	—	228	253,838
Total all countries	**460,348**	**49,125,313**	**3,321,677**	**2,515,479**	**1,035,039**	**528,431**	**4,107,209**	**33,654,803**

1. Countries established since beginning of World War I are included with countries to which they belonged. 2. Data for Austria-Hungary not reported until 1861. Austria and Hungary recorded separately after 1905, Austria included with Germany 1938–45. 3. Bulgaria, Serbia, Montenegro first reported in 1899. Bulgaria reported separately since 1920. In 1920, separate enumeration for Kingdom of Serbs, Croats, Slovenes; since 1922, recorded as Yugoslavia. 4. United Kingdom not specified; for 1901–51, included in "Other Europe." 5. Norway included with Sweden 1820–68. 6. Included with Austria-Hungary, Germany, and Russia 1899–1919. 7. No record of immigration until 1880. 8. From 1931–63, the U.S.S.R. was broken down into European U.S.S.R. and Asian U.S.S.R. Since 1964, total U.S.S.R. has been reported in Europe. 9. Beginning in 1957, China includes Taiwan. 10. No record of immigration until 1861. 11. From 1952, Asia included Philippines. From 1934–51, Philippines were included in Pacific Islands; before 1934, recorded in separate tables as insular travel. 12. Includes all British North American possessions, 1820–98. 13. No record of immigration, 1886–93. 14. Included with "Countries not specified" prior to 1925. 15. Includes 32,897 persons returning in 1906 to their homes in U.S. *Source:* Department of Justice, Immigration and Naturalization Service. NOTE: Data are latest available.

Immigrant and Nonimmigrant Aliens Admitted to U.S.

Period[1]	Immigrants	Non-immigrants	Total	Period[1]	Immigrants	Non-immigrants	Total
1901–10	8,795,386	1,007,909	9,803,295	1966–70	1,871,365	16,227,660	18,099,025
1911–20	5,735,811	1,376,271	7,112,082	1971–75	1,936,281	29,545,190	31,481,471
1921–30	4,107,209	1,774,896	5,882,090	1976	398,613	7,654,491	8,053,104
1931–40	528,431	1,574,071	2,102,502	1976, TQ[2]	103,676	2,673,652	2,777,328
1941–50	1,035,039	2,461,359	3,496,398	1977[3]	462,315	8,036,916	8,499,231
1951–55	1,087,638	2,654,461	3,742,009	1978	601,442	9,343,710	9,945,152
1956–60	1,427,841	4,458,562	5,886,403	1979[4]	460,348	7,060,082	7,520,430
1961–65	1,450,312	7,879,564	9,329,876				

1. Fiscal year ending June 30, except as noted. 2. Transition Quarter, July–Sept. 3. Starting 1977, for fiscal year ending Sept. 30. 4. Figures for October 1978–June 1979. Nonimmigrant aliens include visitors for business or pleasure, students, foreign government officials, and others temporarily in the U.S. *Source:* Department of Justice, Immigration and Naturalization Service.

Persons Naturalized Since 1907

Period[1]	Civilian	Military	Total	Period[1]	Civilian	Military	Total
1907–30	2,713,389	300,506	3,013,895	1976	136,873	5,631	142,504
1931–40	1,498,573	19,891	1,518,464	1976, TQ[2]	46,705	1,513	48,218
1941–50	1,837,229	149,799	1,987,028	1977[3]	154,568	5,305	159,873
1951–60	1,148,241	41,705	1,189,946	1978	168,409	5,126	173,535
1961–70	1,084,195	36,068	1,120,263	1979	158,276	5,874	164,150
1971–75	579,672	38,882	618,554	1907–79	9,526,130	610,300	10,136,430

1. Fiscal year ending June 30, except as noted. 2. Transition Quarter, July-Sept. 1976. 3. Fiscal year, Oct. 1976–Sept. 1977. *Source:* Department of Justice, Immigration and Naturalization Service. NOTE: Data are latest available.

Population of Largest Indian Reservations, 1981

Navajo (Ariz., N.M., Utah)	160,722	Shawnee (Okla.)	11,636	Fort Apache (Ariz.)	8,010
Cherokee (Okla.)	42,992	Gila River (Ariz.)	9,592	Standing Rock (N.D., S.D.)	7,958
Creek (Okla.)	37,679	Rosebud (S.D.)	9,484	Northern Pueblos (N.M.)	7,383
Choctaw (Okla.)	19,660	Turtle Mountain (N.D.)	8,656	Pawnee (Okla.)	7,178
Papago (Ariz.)	17,651	Chickasaw (Okla.)	8,507	Zuni (N.M.)	6,999
South Pueblos (N.M.)	15,633	Yakima (Wash.)	8,502	Blackfeet (Mont.)	6,632
Pine Ridge (S.D.)	13,417	Hopi (Ariz.)	8,439	Wind River (Wyo.)	5,705

NOTE: The Bureau of Indian Affairs lists 734,895 Indians residing on or near Federal reservations as of December 1981. The total Indian population of the United States, according to the 1980 census, is 1,418,195. *Source:* Department of the Interior, Bureau of Indian Affairs.

Income of Households by Age of Head, 1980

Age of head	Households (thousands)	Income (per cent)						
		Under $5,000	$5,000 to $7,499	$7,500 to $9,999	$10,000 to $14,999	$15,000 to $24,999	$25,000 and over	Total
15–24 years	6,443	10.1	9.9	11.8	11.6	8.9	2.9	7.8
25–34 years	19,153	13.8	15.7	18.6	25.1	30.8	22.9	23.3
35–44 years	14,462	8.8	8.5	11.0	13.7	19.1	25.2	17.6
45–54 years	12,694	8.1	9.3	9.8	11.2	13.9	24.1	15.4
55–64 years	12,704	14.1	12.9	13.9	14.3	14.7	18.0	15.4
65 years and over	16,912	45.1	43.7	34.8	24.0	12.6	6.9	20.5
Total	**82,368**	**100.0**	**100.0**	**100.0**	**100.0**	**100.0**	**100.0**	**100.0**

Source: Department of Commerce, Bureau of the Census.

Marriage and Divorce

Marriages and Divorces

	Marriage		Divorce[1]			Marriage		Divorce[1]	
Year	Number	Rate[2]	Number	Rate[2]	Year	Number	Rate[2]	Number	Rate[2]
1900	709,000	9.3	55,751	.7	1958	1,451,000	8.4	368,000	2.1
1905	842,000	10.0	67,976	.8	1959	1,494,000	8.5	395,000	2.2
1910	948,166	10.3	83,045	.9	1960	1,523,000	8.5	393,000	2.2
1915	1,007,595	10.0	104,298	1.0	1961	1,548,000	8.5	414,000	2.3
1920	1,274,476	12.0	170,505	1.6	1962	1,577,000	8.5	413,000	2.2
1925	1,188,334	10.3	175,449	1.5	1963	1,654,000	8.8	428,000	2.3
1930	1,126,856	9.2	195,961	1.6	1964	1,725,000	9.0	450,000	2.4
1935	1,327,000	10.4	218,000	1.7	1965	1,800,000	9.3	479,000	2.5
1940	1,595,879	12.1	264,000	2.0	1966	1,857,000	9.5	499,000	2.5
1943	1,577,050	11.7	359,000	2.6	1967	1,927,000	9.7	523,000	2.6
1944	1,452,394	10.9	400,000	2.9	1968	2,069,258	10.4	584,000	2.9
1945	1,612,992	12.2	485,000	3.5	1969	2,145,438	10.6	639,000	3.2
1946	2,291,045	16.4	610,000	4.3	1970	2,158,802	10.6	708,000	3.5
1947	1,991,878	13.9	483,000	3.4	1971	2,190,481	10.6	773,000	3.7
1948	1,811,155	12.4	408,000	2.8	1972	2,282,154	11.0	845,000	4.1
1949	1,579,798	10.6	397,000	2.7	1973	2,284,108	10.9	915,000	4.4
1950	1,667,231	11.1	385,144	2.6	1974	2,229,667	10.5	977,000	4.6
1951	1,594,694	10.4	381,000	2.5	1975	2,152,662	10.1	1,036,000	4.9
1952	1,539,318	9.9	392,000	2.5	1976	2,154,807	10.0	1,083,000	5.0
1953	1,546,000	9.8	390,000	2.5	1977	2,178,367	10.1	1,091,000	5.0
1954	1,490,000	9.2	379,000	2.4	1978	2,282,272	10.5	1,130,000	5.2
1955	1,531,000	9.3	377,000	2.3	1979	2,341,799	10.6	1,181,000	5.4
1956	1,585,000	9.5	382,000	2.3	1980	2,406,708	10.6	1,182,000	5.2
1957	1,518,000	8.9	381,000	2.2	1981[3]	2,438,000	10.6	1,219,000	5.3

1. Includes annulments. 2. Per 1,000 population. Divorce rates for 1941–46 are based on population including armed forces overseas. Marriage rates are based on population excluding armed forces overseas. 3. Provisional. NOTE: Marriage and divorce figures for most years include some estimated data. Alaska is included beginning 1959, Hawaii beginning 1960. *Source:* Department of Health and Human Services, National Center for Health Statistics.

Percent of Population Ever Married

Age group, years[1]	1981	1980	1970	1960	1950	1940	1930	1920	1910	1900
Males: 15 to 19	2.2	2.7	2.6	3.3	2.9	1.5	1.5	1.8	1.0	0.9
20 to 24	30.5	31.2	45.3	46.9	41.0	27.8	29.0	29.1	24.7	22.2
25 to 29	66.3	67.0	80.9	79.2	76.2	64.0	63.2	60.5	57.1	54.1
30 to 34	83.6	84.1	90.6	88.1	86.8	79.3	78.8	75.8	73.9	72.3
35 to 44	91.5	92.5	93.3	91.9	90.4	86.0	85.7	83.8	83.3	83.0
45 to 54	94.9	93.9	92.5	92.6	91.5	88.9	88.6	88.0	88.8	89.7
Females: 15 to 19	8.0	8.8	9.7	13.5	14.4	10.0	10.9	10.8	9.8	9.4
20 to 24	48.1	49.8	64.2	71.6	67.7	52.8	53.9	54.4	51.5	48.4
25 to 29	78.2	79.1	89.5	89.5	86.7	77.2	78.3	76.9	75.0	72.4
30 to 34	89.6	90.5	93.8	93.1	90.7	85.3	86.8	85.1	83.8	83.4
35 to 44	94.6	94.5	94.8	93.9	91.7	89.6	90.0	88.6	88.6	88.9
45 to 54	95.3	95.3	95.1	93.0	92.2	91.3	90.9	90.4	91.4	92.2

1. 1980 and 1981: 15 years and over; previous years: 14 and older. *Source:* Department of Commerce, Bureau of the Census.

Children and Divorce

Children of divorce constitute one of the fastest-growing segments of the American population. Since 1972 more than a million additional children annually have had their homes disrupted by divorce. One third of the nation's children will undergo this experience by the time they are 18, according to a widely used estimate.

The High Cost of Rearing a Child

According to the U.S. Department of Agriculture, the cost of rearing a child to the age of 18 may be at least $100,000 more than it was for a child born in 1960, when the figure was $34,000. The department compared the cost of rearing a child born two decades ago in an urban area of the Middle West to the cost of rearing one born in 1979 in the same area.

Marriage Information by State

State	Legal minimum marriage age: With parental consent[3] M	With parental consent[3] F	Without parental consent M	Without parental consent F	Blood test required	Waiting period[1]: Before license	Waiting period[1]: After license	Marriages[2]: 1981[4]	Marriages[2]: 1980[4]
Alabama	14	14	18	18	yes	none	none	47,318	49,006
Alaska	16	16	18	18	yes	3 d	none	5,809	5,286
Arizona	18	18	18	18	yes	none	none	31,784	30,230
Arkansas	18	16	18	18	yes	3 d	none	26,724	25,197
California	18	16	18	18	yes	none	none	214,708	218,404
Colorado	16[19]	16[19]	18	18	yes[17]	none	none	36,461	34,078
Connecticut	16	16	18	18	yes	4 d	none	25,517	25,867
Delaware	18[25]	16[25]	18	18	yes[11]	none	24 h[5]	4,561	4,423
D. C.	16–17[7]	16–17[7]	18	18	yes[7]	5 d[6]	none	5,310	5,128
Florida	18	16	18	18	yes	3 d	none	111,660	110,575
Georgia	16[25]	16[25]	18	18[25]	yes[21]	3 d	none	70,486	69,416
Hawaii	16	16	18	18	yes	none	none	12,309	11,670
Idaho	18	16	18	18	yes	3 d[24]	none	14,372	13,084
Illinois	16	16	18	18	yes	none	1 d	109,449	110,667
Indiana	17	17[20]	18	18	yes	3 d	none	55,699	57,852
Iowa	16	16	18	18	yes	3 d	none	27,063	27,527
Kansas	([23])	([23])	18	18	yes	3 d	none	26,254	24,928
Kentucky	([18])	([18])	18	18	yes	3 d	none	35,201	34,291
Louisiana	18	16	18	18	no	none	72 h	44,139	41,658
Maine	16	16	18	18	no	5 d	none	12,552	14,351
Maryland	16[15]	16[15]	18	18	no	48 h	none	46,840	45,967
Massachusetts	14–17[12]	12–15[12]	18	18	yes	3 d	none	46,274	49,058
Michigan	18	16[8]	18	18	yes	3 d	none	85,814	89,606
Minnesota	18	16	21	18	no	5 d	none	37,945	37,825
Mississippi	17	15	21	21	yes	3 d	none	27,530	28,043
Missouri	15[12]	15[12]	18	18	yes	3 d	none	53,265	55,518
Montana	16[22]	16[22]	18	18	yes	5 d	3 d	8,221	8,367
Nebraska	17	17	19	19	yes	2 d	none	14,418	14,189
Nevada	16	16	18	18	no	none	none	n.a.	115,411
New Hampshire	14[12 15]	13[12 15]	18	18	no	3 d	none	9,916	9,298
New Jersey	18	16	18	18	yes	72 h	none	57,555	54,956
New Mexico	16	16	18	18	yes	none	none	17,130	16,324
New York	16	14[9]	21	18	yes	none	([10])	150,007	141,299
North Carolina	16	16	18	18	yes	none	none	48,040	46,341
North Dakota	16	16	18	18	yes	none	none	6,182	6,139
Ohio	18	16	18	18	yes	5 d	none	99,617	99,522
Oklahoma	16[19]	16[19]	18	18	yes	none[14]	none	48,127	46,509
Oregon	17	17	18	18	no	3 d	none	22,747	23,115
Pennsylvania	16	16	18	18	yes	3 d	none	92,370	95,394
Rhode Island	18	16[9]	18	18	yes	none	none	7,539	7,120
South Carolina	16	14	18	18	no	24 h	none	55,008	53,923
South Dakota	16	16	18	18	yes	none	none	8,708	8,929
Tennessee	16	16	18	18	yes	none[14]	none	59,865	58,751
Texas	16[13]	16[13]	18	18	yes	none	none	192,368	187,118
Utah	14	14	16	16	no	none	none	18,346	17,074
Vermont	14[19]	14[19]	18	18	yes	none	3 d[16]	5,207	5,187
Virginia	16	16	18	18	yes	none	none	61,460	60,193
Washington	17	17	18	18	no	3 d	none	48,901	46,617
West Virginia	18	16	18	18	yes	3 d	none	16,734	17,451
Wisconsin	16	16	18	18	no	5 d	none	40,934	40,953
Wyoming	16[19]	16[19]	19	19	yes	none	none	7,052	6,825

1. In some states, waiting period may be waived or reduced by court order. 2. By place of occurrence. 3. In most states, persons younger than the age shown may be married by court permission. 4. Provisional figures; data represent marriages reported, marriage intentions filed, or marriage licenses issued. 5. 96 hours if nonresidents. 6. Day of application and day of pickup are included in 5-day waiting period. 7. No exceptions granted under this age. 8. Consent of one parent or guardian necessary for female only. 9. Females 14 to 16 years old must also have consent of judge of Family Court. 10. Marriage may not be solemnized within 3 days from date on which specimen was taken for serological test, and not until 24 hours after issuance of marriage license. Waiting period may be waived by court order. 11. Blood test may be waived by court order. 12. Need court order. 13. Parent must appear in person or provide doctor's affidavit of his or her illness. 14. 3 days if either party is under legal age. 15. If pregnant. 16. After date on which marriage application has been filed with town clerk, excluding date of filing. 17. Blood test for rubella and RH type not required of females over 45 years or found by physician to be incapable of bearing children. 18. No age limit. 19. If under 16 need court order. 20. 15 for pregnancy or maternity. 21. Prior to issuance of license, a medical examination for rubella is required. 22. With judicial approval. 23. Under 18 with parental consent only. 24. Only for those under 18. 25. May marry at any age with proof of pregnancy signed by physician or if marrying father of child born out of wedlock. *Sources:* Legal information, *Information Please* questionnaires to states; marriage statistics, Department of Health and Human Services, National Center for Health Statistics.

Median Age at First Marriage

Year	Males	Females	Year	Males	Females	Year	Males	Females	Year	Males	Females
1890	26.1	22.0	1920	24.6	21.2	1950	22.8	20.3	1975	23.5	21.1
1900	25.9	21.9	1930	24.3	21.3	1960	22.8	20.3	1980	24.7	22.0
1910	25.1	21.6	1940	24.3	21.5	1970	23.2	20.8	1981	24.8	22.3

Source: Department of Commerce, Bureau of the Census.

Persons Living Alone, by Sex and Age
(numbers in thousands)

	1981		1980		1975		1970		1960	
Sex and age[1]	Number	Percent	Number	Percent	Number	Percent	Number	Percent	Number	Percent
BOTH SEXES										
15 to 24 years	1,651	8.7	1,726	9.4	1,111	8.0	556	5.1	234	3.3
25 to 44 years	5,138	27.1	4,729	25.8	2,744	19.7	1,604	14.8	1,212	17.2
45 to 64 years	4,663	24.6	4,514	24.7	4,076	29.2	3,622	33.4	2,720	38.5
65 years and over	7,484	39.5	7,328	40.1	6,008	43.1	5,071	46.7	2,898	41.0
Total, 15 years and over	**18,936**	**100.0**	**18,296**	**100.0**	**13,939**	**100.0**	**10,851**	**100.0**	**7,063**	**100.0**
MALE										
15 to 24 years	899	12.4	947	13.6	610	4.4	274	2.5	124	1.8
25 to 44 years	3,189	44.0	2,920	41.9	1,689	12.1	933	8.6	686	9.7
45 to 64 years	1,715	23.6	1,613	23.2	1,329	9.5	1,152	10.6	965	13.7
65 years and over	1,450	20.0	1,486	21.3	1,290	9.3	1,174	10.8	853	12.1
Total, 15 years and over	**7,253**	**100.0**	**6,966**	**100.0**	**4,918**	**35.3**	**3,532**	**32.5**	**2,628**	**37.2**
FEMALE										
15 to 24 years	752	6.4	779	6.9	501	3.6	282	2.6	110	1.6
25 to 44 years	1,949	16.7	1,809	16.0	1,055	7.6	671	6.2	526	7.4
45 to 64 years	2,948	25.2	2,901	25.6	2,747	19.7	2,470	22.8	1,755	24.8
65 years and over	6,034	51.6	5,842	51.6	4,718	33.8	3,897	35.9	2,045	29.0
Total, 15 years and over	**11,683**	**100.0**	**11,330**	**100.0**	**9,021**	**64.7**	**7,319**	**67.5**	**4,436**	**62.8**

1. Prior to 1980, data are for persons 14 years and older. *Source:* Department of Gommerce, Bureau of the Census.

Unmarried Couples, by Sex and Age of Partners, 1980
(In thousands. As of March. An "unmarried couple" is two unrelated adults of the opposite sex sharing the same household)

		Age of woman				
Age of man	All ages	Under 25 years	25–34 years	35–44 years	45–64 years	65 years and over
Under 25 years	382	312	55	4	8	2
25–34 years	637	243	368	19	5	4
35–44 years	212	33	100	46	26	7
45–64 years	230	8	41	52	98	31
65 years and over	99	2	2	3	47	47
All ages	**1,560**	**596**	**564**	**125**	**184**	**92**

Source: Statistical Abstract of the United States, 1981.

Hispanics Have Highest U.S. Birth Rate

The fastest-growing minority in the United States, Hispanics, also have the highest birth rate. It is 75% higher than that of the rest of the U.S. population. This supports the prediction of census experts that, at current rates of birth and immigration, people of Hispanic origin will outnumber American blacks before the end of the century.

Divorce Information by State

State	Residence for divorce	Period before parties may remarry		Divorce rate[1]			
		Plaintiff	Defendant	1980[3]	1979	1978	1977
Alabama	6 mo	60 d	60 d	7.1	7.0	6.7	6.4
Alaska	([24])	none	none	8.4	8.6	8.4	8.8
Arizona	90 d	none	none	7.8	8.2	7.3	7.2
Arkansas	90 d	none	none	9.9	9.3[2]	9.2	9.0[2]
California	6 mo	none	none	5.8	6.1	6.0	6.0
Colorado	90 d[19]	none	none	6.4	6.0	6.9	7.8
Connecticut	1 yr	none	none	3.8	4.5	4.1	3.9
Delaware	6 mo[19]	none[12]	none[12]	4.0	5.3	5.7	5.2
D.C.	6 mo	60 d	60	5.5	6.8	5.1	4.6
Florida	6 mo	none	none	7.8	7.9	7.6	7.4
Georgia	6 mo	none	none	6.4	6.5	6.2	6.1
Hawaii	6 mo	none	none	4.7	5.5	5.4	5.1
Idaho	6 wk	none	none	7.3	7.1	7.2	7.0
Illinois	1 yr	none	none	4.5	4.6	4.5	4.4
Indiana	6 mo[4 6]	none	none	n.a.	7.7	7.5	6.3[2]
Iowa	1 yr[11]	1 yr	1 yr	4.0	3.9	3.8	3.8
Kansas	60 d	30 d	30 d	5.6	5.4	5.4	5.4
Kentucky	6 mo[4 22]	none	none	4.8	4.5[2]	3.9[2]	4.5
Louisiana	1 yr	none[8]	none[8]	n.a.	3.8[2]	3.3	n.a.
Maine	6 mo	none	none	5.7	5.6	5.7	5.2
Maryland	1 yr[23]	none	none	3.9	4.1	4.0	4.0
Massachusetts	1 yr	none	none	2.9	3.0	2.8	2.9
Michigan	1 yr	none	none	4.4	4.8	4.9	4.7
Minnesota	180 d	6 mo	6 mo	3.7	3.7[3]	3.6	3.5
Mississippi	6 mo	([10])	([10])	5.5	5.6[3]	5.5	5.3
Missouri	90 d	none	none	5.7	5.7	5.4	5.3
Montana	1 yr	none	none	6.3	6.5	6.3	6.2
Nebraska	1 yr[5]	none	none	4.1	4.0	3.9	3.9
Nevada	6 wk	none	none	18.6	16.8	16.8	16.2
New Hampshire	1 yr	none	none	5.8	5.9	5.4	5.2
New Jersey	1 yr	none	none	3.5	3.2	3.6	2.8
New Mexico	6 mo[13]	30d	30d	8.1	8.0	7.9	7.7
New York	([14])	none	none	3.1	3.7	3.3	3.1
North Carolina	6 mo	none	none	5.0	4.9	4.8	4.5
North Dakota	1 yr	([9])	([9])	3.3	3.2	3.2	3.0
Ohio	6 mo[6]	none	none	5.4	5.5	5.5	5.4
Oklahoma	6 mo[21]	6 mo[20]	6 mo[20]	8.2	7.9	7.9	7.8
Oregon	6 mo	30 d	30 d	7.0	7.0	6.9	6.9
Pennsylvania	6 mo	none	none	3.0	3.4	3.3	3.2
Rhode Island	2 yr	none	none	3.9	3.9	3.7	3.7
South Carolina	1 yr	none	none	4.7	4.7	4.1	3.7
South Dakota	([7])	none	none	4.1	3.9	3.5	3.5
Tennessee	1 yr	none[15]	none[15]	6.8	6.8	6.6	6.4
Texas	6 mo	30 d[15]	30 d[15]	7.1	6.9	6.6	6.4
Utah	3 mo	3 mo[12]	3 mo[12]	5.6	5.6	5.4	5.5
Vermont	6 mo[18]	none	none	5.0	4.6	4.2	4.4
Virginia	6 mo	none	none	4.5	4.5	4.4	4.2
Washington	none[19]	none	none	7.0	6.9	7.0	7.3
West Virginia	1 yr[16]	([17])	([17])	5.3	5.3	5.2	5.2
Wisconsin	6 mo	6 mo	6 mo	3.7	3.6	3.4	3.1
Wyoming	60 d	none	none	8.5	7.8	7.4	7.6

1. By place of occurrence, including reported annulments. 2. Incomplete. 3. Estimated. 4. Only one party must have resided in the state for 180 days. 5. Decree not final until 6 months after trial and decision. 6. 6-month residence in state; 90-day residence in county. 7. Physical presence plus intent to make state the place of residence. 8. In case of adultery, guilty party cannot marry correspondent. 9. At discretion of court. 10. Until court that grants the divorce is adjourned. 11. No time required if both parties are residents of state and intend to make state their place of residence. 12. 30 days between first and final judgment. 13. Servicemen acquire residence by being continuously stationed at military base in state for 6 months. 14. Action for divorce may be maintained only where (1) parties were married in the state and either has been a resident for one year preceding the action; (2) parties have resided in the state as husband and wife and either has been a resident for one year preceding the action; (3) cause for divorce occurred in the state and either party has been a resident for one year preceding the action; (4) cause for divorce occurred in the state and both parties are residents at time of the action; (5) either party is a resident for at least 2 years preceding the action. 15. Parties may remarry each other at any time. 16. 2 years if residence is acquired after cause of divorce action arose. 17. Court can lengthen waiting period if desired. 18. Court must find resumption of marital relations not reasonably probable. 19. Must be domiciled in state. 20. 30 days from date of judgment of appeal. 21. 5 years if on grounds of insanity and insane spouse is in institution. 22. No decree shall be entered until parties have lived apart for 60 days. 23. When cause for divorce occurred out of state. 24. No residency requirement but action will not be heard by court until 30 days after filing for divorce. NOTE: n.a. = not available. *Sources:* Legal information, *Information Please* questionnaires to states; divorce statistics, Department of Health and Human Services, National Center for Health Statistics.

Grounds for Divorce

State	Adultery	Cruelty	Desertion	Alcoholism	Impotence	Felony conviction	Neglect to provide	Insanity	Pregnancy at marriage[1]	Bigamy	Separation	Indignities	Drug addiction	Violence	Fraudulent contract	Others
Alabama	yes	yes	yes[2]	yes	yes	yes[16]	yes[3]	yes[6]	yes[1]	—	yes[3]	—	yes	yes	—	(27 29 34)
Alaska	yes	yes	yes[2]	yes	yes	yes	—	yes[9]	—	—	—	yes	yes	yes	—	—
Arizona	—	—	—	—	—	—	—	—	—	—	—	—	—	—	—	(29)
Arkansas	yes	yes	yes[2]	yes	yes	yes	yes	yes	—	yes	yes[4]	yes	—	yes	yes	(12 31 48)
California	—	—	—	—	—	—	—	—	—	—	—	—	—	—	—	(28)
Colorado	—	—	—	—	—	—	—	—	—	—	—	—	—	—	—	(29 52)
Connecticut	yes	yes	yes[2]	yes	—	yes[20]	—	yes[6]	—	—	—	—	—	—	yes	(13 23 30 42 46)
Delaware	yes	yes	yes[2]	yes[3]	yes[61]	yes	yes	yes[6]	—	yes	yes[9]	—	yes	yes	yes	(27 68)
D.C.	yes	yes[53]	—	—	—	—	—	—	—	—	yes[2]	—	—	—	—	(63)
Florida	—	—	—	—	—	—	—	—	—	—	—	—	—	—	—	(49 52)
Georgia	yes	yes	yes[2]	yes	yes	yes[15]	yes	yes	yes	yes	yes	yes	yes	yes	yes	(27 31 44 49)
Hawaii	—	—	—	—	—	—	—	—	—	—	yes[3]	—	—	—	—	(29)
Idaho	yes	yes	yes	—	—	yes	yes	yes[4]	—	yes	—	—	—	—	—	(26 28 42)
Illinois	yes	yes	yes[2]	yes[3]	yes	yes	—	—	—	yes[51]	—	—	yes[3]	yes	—	(32 37 56)
Indiana	—	—	—	—	yes	—	—	yes[3]	—	—	—	—	—	—	—	(29 33 52)
Iowa	—	—	—	—	—	—	—	—	—	—	—	—	—	—	—	(49)
Kansas	yes	yes	yes[2]	yes	—	yes	yes	yes[6]	—	—	—	—	—	—	yes	(28 31 48 69 70)
Kentucky	—	—	—	—	—	—	—	—	—	—	—	—	—	—	—	(49)
Louisiana	yes	yes	yes	yes	—	yes	yes	—	—	yes	yes[3]	—	yes	yes	—	(37 58)
Maine	yes	yes	yes	yes	yes	yes[20]	yes	yes[36]	yes[61]	yes[61]	—	yes	yes	yes	yes[61]	(28)
Maryland[65]	yes	—	—	—	yes	yes[18]	—	yes[66]	—	—	yes[10]	—	—	—	—	(28 35 67)
Massachusetts	yes	yes	yes[2]	yes	yes	yes[19]	yes	—	—	—	—	—	yes	—	—	(29 49)
Michigan	—	—	—	—	—	—	—	—	—	—	—	—	—	—	—	(29)
Minnesota	—	—	—	—	—	—	—	—	—	—	—	—	—	—	—	(49)
Mississippi	yes	yes	yes	yes	yes	yes[22]	—	yes[47]	yes	yes	yes[2]	—	yes	yes	—	(10 28 31 49)
Missouri	yes	yes	yes	yes	yes	yes	—	—	yes	yes	—	yes		—	—	(10 30 32 52)
Montana	—	—	—	—	—	—	—	—	—	—	—	—	—	—	—	(29 52)
Nebraska	—	—	—	—	—	—	—	—	—	—	—	—	—	—	—	(49)
Nevada	—	—	—	—	—	—	—	yes[3]	—	—	yes[2]	—	—	—	—	(27)
New Hampshire	yes	yes	yes[3]	yes[3]	yes	yes[14]	yes[3]	—	—	—	—	—	—	yes	—	(25 28 40 57 60)
New Jersey	yes	yes	yes[2]	yes[2]	yes[51]	yes[44]	—	yes[3]	—	yes[51]	yes[9]	—	yes[2]	—	yes[51]	(34 49)
New Mexico	yes	yes	yes	—	—	—	—	—	—	—	—	—	—	—	—	(27)
New York	yes	yes	yes[2]	—	—	yes[17]	—	—	—	—	yes[2]	—	—	—	—	—
North Carolina	yes	—	—	—	yes	—	—	yes[6]	yes	—	yes[2]	—	—	—	—	(34)
North Dakota	yes	yes	yes[2]	yes[2]	—	yes	yes[2]	yes[6]	—	—	—	—	—	—	—	(28)
Ohio	yes	yes	yes	yes[4]	yes	yes	yes	yes[5]	—	yes	yes[2]	—	—	—	yes	(12 24 41 55)
Oklahoma	yes	yes	yes[2]	yes	yes	yes[21]	yes	yes[6]	yes	—	—	—	—	—	yes	(27 41 55)
Oregon	—	—	—	—	—	—	—	—	—	—	—	—	—	—	yes	(49)
Pennsylvania	yes	yes	yes[2]	—	yes[45]	yes[15]	—	yes	—	yes	yes[4]	yes	—	yes	yes	(29 31)
Rhode Island	yes	yes	yes[6]	yes	yes	yes[7]	yes[2]	yes[48]	—	yes	yes[3]	—	yes	yes	yes	(13 38)
South Carolina	yes	yes[39]	yes[2]	yes	—	—	—	—	—	—	yes[2]	—	yes	—	—	(50)
South Dakota	yes	yes	yes[2]	yes[2]	—	yes	yes[2]	yes[6]	—	yes[61]	—	—	—	—	yes[61]	—
Tennessee	yes	yes	yes[2]	yes[43]	yes	yes	yes	—	yes	yes	—	yes	—	—	—	(28 32 37 59)
Texas	yes	yes	yes[2]	—	—	yes[54]	—	yes[4]	—	—	yes[4]	yes	—	—	—	(28)
Utah	yes	yes	yes[2]	yes	yes	yes	yes	yes	—	—	yes[4]	—	—	—	—	—
Vermont	yes	yes	yes[7]	—	—	yes[17]	yes	yes[6]	—	—	yes[8]	—	—	—	—	(29)
Virginia	yes	yes	yes[2]	—	yes[51]	yes	—	—	yes[51]	yes[51]	yes[2]	—	—	—	yes[51]	—
Washington	—	—	—	—	—	—	—	—	—	—	—	—	—	—	—	(29)
West Virginia	yes	yes	yes[8]	yes	—	yes	yes	yes	—	—	yes[3]	—	yes	yes	—	(62)
Wisconsin	—	—	—	—	—	—	—	—	—	—	—	—	—	—	—	(29 64)
Wyoming	yes	yes	yes[2]	yes	yes	yes	yes[2]	yes[3]	yes	—	yes[3]	yes	—	—	—	(11 25 28)

1. If unknown to husband. 2. 1 year. 3. 2 years. 4. 3 years. 5. 4 years. 6. 5 years. 7. 7 years. 8. 6 months. 9. 18 months. 10. Absence of 1 year. 11. Absence of 1 year voluntarily, or under legal separation judgment. 12. Absence of 3 years. 13. Absence of one spouse; presumption of death. 14. With imprisonment of 1 year. 15. With imprisonment of 2 years. 16. With imprisonment of 2 years, sentence being for 7 years or more. 17. With imprisonment of 3 years. 18. With imprisonment of three years, or an indeterminate sentence, twelve months of which have been served. 19. With imprisonment of 5 years. 20 With imprisonment for life. 21. Imprisonment of other party in state or federal penal institution under sentence thereto fo commission of felony at time the petition is filed. 22. Unless pardoned before beginning sentence. 23. Noncohabitation for 18 months. Grounds for annulment in Maine. 24. Court of Common Pleas may grant a dissolution of marriage—6 months residency required. 25. Noncohabitation for 2 years. 26. Noncohabitation for 5 years. 27. Incompatibility. 28. Irreconcilable differences 29. Irretrievable breakdown of marriage relationship. 30. Irretrievably broken upon proof, decree of dissolution. 31. Relationshi within prohibited degree. 32. Infamous crime. 33. Infamous crime subsequent to marriage. 34. Crime against nature. 35 Excessively vicious conduct; any cause which, by laws of state, renders marriage null and void at its inception. 36. Requirin confinement in mental institution for at least 7 years prior to commencement of action. 37. Attempt by one party on life c other. 38. Any other gross misbehavior or wickedness. 39. Physical cruelty only. 40. Treatment such as to injure health c

endanger reason. 41. Gross neglect of duty. 42. Habitual intemperance. 43. Habitual drunkenness contracted after marriage. 44 With imprisonment of 18 months. 45. If at time of marriage and incurable. 46. Infamous crime involving violation of conjugal duty and punishable by imprisonment of more than 1 year. 47. Incurable, regardless when it occurs. 48. Insanity at time of marriage. 49. No-fault divorce. 50. No-fault divorce after 1 year's separation. 51. Grounds for nullity. 52. The term divorce is no longer used. The term now used is Dissolution of Marriage. 53. Limited divorce; may be enlarged into absolute divorce after separation of 1 year. 54. Suit for divorce cannot be sustained until 12 months after final judgment of conviction. Divorce cannot be obtained if plaintiff's testimony contributed toward conviction. 55. Defendant obtained divorce from plaintiff in any other state or country. 56. Infected other party with communicable venereal disease. 57. Joining a religious cult disbelieving in marriage. 58. Public defamation. 59. Wife's refusal to remove with husband to this state and willfully absenting herself for 2 years. 60. Wife gone to reside outside state and absent 10 years. 61. Annulment. 62. Abuse of a child. 63. Modified "no-fault" law enacted April 6, 1977. 64. Voluntary noncohabitation for 1 year. 65. Maryland grants two types of divorce—vinculo and mensa. The information here applies to vinculo divorce. 66. Only after confined 3 years, plus other requirements. 67. Abandonment after 12 months, or living separately for 3 years. 68. If wife was under 16 or husband was under 18 at time of marriage, unless marriage was confirmed by each after arriving at such age. 69. Failure to perform a marital duty or obligation. 70. Incompatibility by reason of mental illness or mental incapacity of one or both spouses. *Source: Information Please* questionnaires to the states.

Households, Families, and Married Couples

	Households		Families		Married couples
Date	Number	Average population per household	Number	Average population per family	Number
June 1890	12,690,000	4.93	—	—	—
April 1930	29,905,000	4.11	—	—	25,174,000
April 1940	34,949,000	3.67	32,166,000	3.76	28,517,000
April 1950	43,554,000	3.37	39,303,000	3.54	36,091,000
April 1955	47,874,000	3.33	41,951,000	3.59	37,556,000
March 1960[1]	52,799,000	3.33	45,111,000	3.67	40,200,000
March 1965	57,436,000	3.29	47,956,000	3.70	42,478,000
March 1970	63,401,000	3.14	51,586,000	3.58	45,373,000
March 1975	71,120,000	2.94	55,712,000	3.42	47,547,000
March 1978	76,030,000	2.81	57,215,000	3.33	47,920,000
March 1979	77,330,000	2.78	57,804,000	3.31	48,258,000
March 1980	80,776,000	2.76	59,550,000	3.29	49,714,000
March 1981	82,368,000	2.73	60,309,000	3.27	49,896,000

1. First year in which figures for Alaska and Hawaii are included. *Source:* Department of Commerce, Bureau of the Census.

Families Maintained by Women

(numbers in thousands)

	1981		1980		1975		1970		1960	
	Number	Percent	Number	Percent	Number	Percent	Number	Percent	Number	Percent
Age of women:										
Under 35 years	3,167	34.9	3,015	34.6	2,356	32.5	1,364	24.4	796	17.7
35 to 44 years	2,074	22.8	1,916	22.0	1,510	20.9	1,074	19.2	940	20.9
45 to 64 years	2,601	28.6	2,514	28.9	2,266	31.3	2,021	36.1	1,731	38.5
65 years and over	1,239	13.6	1,260	14.5	1,108	15.3	1,131	20.2	1,027	22.9
Median age	41.4	—	41.7	—	43.4	—	48.5	—	50.1	—
Presence of children:										
No own children under 18 years	3,448	38.0	3,260	37.4	2,838	39.2	2,665	47.7	2,397	53.3
With own children under 18 years	5,634	62.0	5,445	62.6	4,404	60.8	2,926	52.3	2,097	46.7
Total own children under 18 years	10,111	—	10,204	—	9,227	—	6,694	—	4,674	—
Average per family	1.11	—	1.17	—	1.27	—	1.20	—	1.04	—
Average per family with children	1.79	—	1.87	—	2.10	—	2.29	—	2.24	—
Race:										
White	6,266	69.0	6,052	69.5	5,212	72.0	4,165	74.5	3,547	78.9
Black[1]	2,634	29.0	2,495	28.7	1,940	26.8	1,382	24.7	947	21.1
Other	182	2.0	158	1.8	90	1.2	44	0.8	n.a.	n.a.
Marital status:										
Married, husband absent	1,865	20.5	1,769	20.3	1,647	22.7	1,326	23.7	1,099	24.5
Widowed	2,463	27.1	2,570	29.5	2,559	35.3	2,396	42.9	2,325	51.7
Divorced	3,279	36.1	3,008	34.6	2,110	29.1	1,259	22.5	694	15.4
Single	1,475	16.2	1,359	15.6	926	12.8	610	10.9	376	8.4
Total families maintained by women	**9,082**	**100.0**	**8,705**	**100.0**	**7,242**	**100.0**	**5,591**	**100.0**	**4,494**	**100.0**

1. Includes other races in 1960 and 1965. NOTE: n.a. = not available. *Source:* Department of Commerce, Bureau of the Census.

Selected Family Characteristics

Characteristics	1981 Number (thousands)	1981 Median income
ALL RACES		
All families	61,019	$22,388
Type of residence		
Nonfarm	59,421	22,554
Farm	1,598	17,082
Location of residence		
Inside metropolitan areas	40,612	24,478
1,000,000 or more	22,777	25,741
Inside central cities	8,025	20,268
Outside central cities	14,752	28,647
Under 1,000,000	17,835	22,893
Inside central cities	7,813	21,242
Outside central cities	10,022	24,286
Outside metropolitan areas	20,407	19,225
Region		
Northeast	12,924	23,706
North Central	15,718	23,118
South	20,959	20,582
West	11,417	23,873
Type of family		
Married-couple family	49,630	25,065
Wife in paid labor force	25,002	29,247
Wife not in paid labor force	24,628	20,325
Male householder, no wife present	1,986	19,889
Female householder, no husband present	9,403	10,960
Number of earners[1]	60,312	22,433
No earners	8,526	9,410
1 Earner	18,555	17,626
2 Earners	24,856	26,860
3 Earners	5,563	34,298
4 Earners or more	2,812	41,989
Size of family		
2 Persons	24,426	18,542
3 Persons	14,079	23,401
4 Persons	12,594	26,274
5 Persons	5,971	26,258
6 Persons	2,409	26,725
7 Persons or more	1,539	24,323
Occupation group of longest job of householder	47,296	25,772
White-collar workers	22,415	31,101
Professional, technical and kindred workers	7,851	34,042
Salaried	7,107	33,519
Self-employed	744	42,362
Managers and administrators, except farm	7,391	33,774
Salaried	6,200	35,610
Self-employed	1,190	23,485
Sales workers	2,766	30,421
Clerical and kindred workers	4,408	21,961
Blue-collar workers	19,001	23,417
Craft and kindred workers	9,469	25,762
Operatives, incl. transport	7,399	21,909
Operatives, except transport	5,022	21,365
Transport equip. oper.	2,377	23,262
Laborers, except farm	2,132	19,113
Service workers	4,309	17,017
Private household workers	193	7,840

Characteristics	1981 Number (thousands)	1981 Median income
Service Workers, exc. private household	4,115	17,441
Farm workers	1,571	12,992
Farmers and farm managers	1,094	13,305
Farm laborers and supervisors	478	12,494
Tenure status		
Owner occupied	45,442	25,664
Renter occupied	14,666	14,728
Occupier paid no cash rent	911	13,699
Educational attainment of householder		
Elementary	8,995	13,157
High school	28,229	21,366
College	20,173	31,331
1 to 3 years	8,783	26,873
4 years or more	11,390	35,252
4 years	6,015	32,720
5 years or more	5,375	38,575
Total, 25 years and over	57,397	23,126
WHITE		
All families	53,269	23,517
Type of residence		
Nonfarm	51,722	23,74[illegible]
Farm	1,547	17,24[illegible]
Location of residence		
Inside metropolitan areas	34,665	25,83[illegible]
1,000,000 or more	18,977	27,39[illegible]
Inside central cities	5,465	22,96[illegible]
Outside central cities	13,512	29,25[illegible]
Under 1,000,000	15,688	24,00[illegible]
Inside central cities	6,380	22,81[illegible]
Outside central cities	9,308	24,72[illegible]
Outside metropolitan areas	18,604	20,00[illegible]
Region		
Northeast	11,571	24,68[illegible]
North Central	14,270	23,88[illegible]
South	17,377	22,05[illegible]
West	10,052	24,32[illegible]
Type of family		
Married-couple families	45,007	25,47[illegible]
Wife in paid labor force	22,252	29,71[illegible]
Wife not in paid labor force	22,755	20,88[illegible]
Male householder, no wife present	1,642	20,4[illegible]
Female householder, no husband present	6,620	12,5[illegible]
Number of earners[1]	52,680	23,5[illegible]
No earners	7,062	10,6[illegible]
1 Earner	16,007	19,1[illegible]
2 Earners	22,162	27,3[illegible]
3 Earners	4,965	35,1[illegible]
4 Earners or more	2,484	42,8[illegible]
BLACK		
All families	6,413	13,2[illegible]
Type of residence		
Nonfarm	6,370	13,2[illegible]
Farm	43	n[illegible]
Location of residence		
Inside metropolitan areas	4,933	14,2[illegible]
1,000,000 or more	3,165	15,0[illegible]
Inside central cities	2,249	13,4[illegible]
Outside central cities	915	18,7[illegible]

Characteristics	1981 Number (thousands)	1981 Median income
Under 1,000,000	1,768	12,861
Inside central cities	1,248	12,058
Outside central cities	520	16,047
Outside metropolitan areas	1,480	10,965
Region		
Northeast	1,175	13,248
North Central	1,281	14,837
South	3,312	12,283
West	644	16,592
Type of family		
Married-couple families	3,535	19,624
Wife in paid labor force	2,114	25,040
Wife not in paid force	1,421	12,341
Male householder, no wife present	273	14,489
Female householder, no husband present	2,605	7,506
Number of earners[1]	6,328	13,221
No earners	1,312	4,890
1 Earner	2,190	10,968
2 Earners	2,107	22,649
3 Earners	482	25,407
4 Earners or more	238	32,319
SPANISH ORIGIN OF HOUSEHOLDER[2]		
All families	3,305	16,402
Type of residence		
Nonfarm	3,280	16,437
Farm	25	(B)
Location of residence		
Inside metropolitan areas	2,827	16,624
1,000,000 or more	1,896	16,397
Inside central cities	1,039	14,422
Outside central cities	857	19,473
Under 1,000,000	931	17,112
Inside central cities	600	16,990
Outside central cities	331	17,265
Outside metropolitan areas	478	15,368
Region		
Northeast	624	13,264
North Central	246	18,647
South	1,127	16,475
West	1,308	17,318
Type of family		
Married-couple families	2,414	19,329
Wife in paid labor force	1,162	23,641
Wife not in paid labor force	1,252	15,551
Male householder, no wife present	142	14,793
Female householder, no husband present	750	7,586
Number of earners[1]	3,281	16,412
No earners	448	5,368
1 Earner	1,111	12,586
2 Earners	1,249	20,982
3 Earners	308	25,695
4 Earners or more	165	35,881

1. Excludes families with members in Armed Forces. 2. Persons of Spanish origin may be of any race. *Source:* Department of Commerce, Bureau of the Census.

Births

Live Births and Birth Rates

Year	Births[1]	Rate[2]	Year	Births[1]	Rate[2]	Year	Births[1]	Rate[2]
1910	2,777,000	30.1	1950	3,632,000	24.1	1966[3]	3,606,274	18.4
1915	2,965,000	29.5	1951[3]	3,823,000	24.9	1967	3,520,959	17.8
1920	2,950,000	27.7	1952[3]	3,913,000	25.1	1968	3,501,564	17.5
1925	2,909,000	25.1	1953[3]	3,965,000	25.1	1969	3,600,206	17.8
1930	2,618,000	21.3	1954[3]	4,078,000	25.3	1970	3,731,386	18.4
1935	2,377,000	18.7	1955	4,104,000	25.0	1971	3,555,970	17.2
1939	2,466,000	18.8	1956[3]	4,218,000	25.2	1972	3,258,411	15.6
1940	2,559,000	19.4	1957[3]	4,308,000	25.3	1973	3,136,965	14.9
1942	2,989,000	22.2	1958[3]	4,255,000	24.5	1974	3,159,958	14.9
1943	3,104,000	22.7	1959[3]	4,295,000	24.3	1975	3,144,198	14.8
1944	2,939,000	21.2	1960[3]	4,257,850	23.7	1976	3,167,788	14.8
1945	2,858,000	20.4	1961[3]	4,268,326	23.3	1977	3,326,632	15.4
1946	3,411,000	24.1	1962[3]	4,167,362	22.4	1978	3,333,279	15.3
1947	3,817,000	26.6	1963[3]	4,098,020	21.7	1979	3,494,398	15.9
1948	3,637,000	24.9	1964[3]	4,027,490	21.0	1980[4]	3,598,000	15.8
1949	3,649,000	24.5	1965[3]	3,760,358	19.4	1981[4]	3,646,000	15.9

1. Figures through 1959 include adjustment for underregistration; beginning 1960, figures represent number registered. For comparison, the 1959 registered count was 4,245,000. 2. Rates are per 1,000 population estimated as of July 1 for each year except 1940, 1950, 1960, and 1970, which are as of April 1, the census date; for 1942–46 based on population including Armed forces overseas. 3. Based on 50% sample of births. 4. Provisional. NOTE: Alaska is included beginning 1959; Hawaii beginning 1960. Since 1972, based on 100% of births in selected states and on 50% sample in all other states. *Sources:* Department of Commerce, Bureau of the Census; and Department of Health and Human Services, National Center for Health Statistics.

Live Births by Age of Mother

Year[1] and race	Total	Age of mother: Under 15 yr	15–19 yr	20–24 yr	25–29 yr	30–34 yr	35–39 yr	40–44 yr	45 yr and over
1940	2,558,647	3,865	332,667	799,537	693,268	431,468	222,015	68,269	7,558
1945	2,858,449	4,028	298,868	832,746	785,299	554,906	296,852	78,853	6,897
1950	3,631,512	5,413	432,911	1,155,167	1,041,360	610,816	302,780	77,743	5,322
1955	4,014,112	6,181	493,770	1,290,939	1,133,155	732,540	352,320	89,777	5,430
1960	4,257,850	6,780	586,966	1,426,912	1,092,816	687,722	359,908	91,564	5,182
1965	3,760,358	7,768	590,894	1,337,350	925,732	529,376	282,908	81,716	4,614
1970	3,731,386	11,752	644,708	1,418,874	994,904	427,806	180,244	49,952	3,146
1974	3,159,958	12,529	595,449	1,108,051	923,318	372,907	118,115	27,878	1,711
1975	3,144,198	12,642	582,238	1,093,676	936,786	375,500	115,409	26,319	1,628
1976	3,167,788	11,928	558,744	1,091,602	972,130	391,896	115,662	24,383	1,443
1977	3,326,632	11,455	559,154	1,146,491	1,016,231	446,939	120,900	24,117	1,345
1978	3,333,279	10,772	543,407	1,139,524	1,015,183	474,318	126,196	22,627	1,252
1979	3,494,398	10,699	549,472	1,188,663	1,069,246	516,999	135,096	23,018	1,205
White	2,808,420	4,402	383,807	953,112	903,852	435,247	109,292	17,799	909
Black	577,855	6,139	152,805	206,006	130,145	59,136	19,264	4,136	225
Other	108,123	158	12,860	29,545	35,249	22,616	6,540	1,084	71

1. Data for 1940–55 are adjusted for underregistration. Beginning 1960, registered births only are shown. Data for 1960–70 based on a 50% sample of births. Since 1972, based on 100% of births in selected states and on 50% sample in all other states. Beginning 1960, including Alaska and Hawaii. NOTE: Data refer only to births occurring within the U.S. Figures are shown to the last digit as computed for convenience in summation. They are not assumed to be accurate to the last digit. Figures for age of mother not stated are distributed. *Sources:* Department of Commerce, Bureau of the Census; and Department of Health and Human Services, National Center for Health Statistics. NOTE: Data are latest available.

Births to Unmarried Women

(in thousands, except as indicated)

Age and race	1979	1975	1970	1965	1960	1955	1950	1945	1940
By age of mother:									
Under 15 years	9.5	11.0	9.5	6.1	4.6	3.9	3.2	2.5	2.1
15–19 years	253.2	222.5	190.4	123.1	87.1	68.9	56.0	49.2	40.5
20–24 years	210.1	134.0	126.7	90.7	68.0	55.7	43.1	39.3	27.2
25–29 years	80.6	50.2	40.6	36.8	32.1	28.0	20.9	14.1	10.5
30–34 years	31.3	19.8	19.1	19.6	18.9	16.1	10.8	7.1	5.2
35–39 years	10.6	8.1	9.4	11.4	10.6	8.3	6.0	4.0	3.0
40 years and over	2.5	2.3	3.0	3.7	3.0	2.4	1.7	1.2	1.0
By race:									
White	263.0	186.4	175.1	123.7	82.5	64.2	53.5	56.4	40.3
Black and other	334.8	261.6	223.6	167.5	141.8	119.2	88.1	60.9	49.2
Total of above births	**597.8**	**447.9**	**398.7**	**291.2**	**224.3**	**183.4**	**141.6**	**117.3**	**89.5**
Percent of all births[1]	17.1	14.2	10.7	7.7	5.3	4.5	3.9	4.1	3.5
Rate[2]	27.8	24.8	26.4	23.4	21.8	19.3	14.1	10.1	7.1

1. Through 1955, based on data adjusted for underregistration; thereafter, registered births. 2. Rate per 1,000 unmarrie (never married, widowed, and divorced) women, 15–44 years old. *Sources:* Department of Commerce, Bureau of the Census and Department of Health and Human Services, National Center for Health Statistics. NOTE: Data are latest available.

Illegitimate Births Up 50% in Decade

Over the past decade the number of births to unwed women increased 50% and now at least one ou of six births in America is illegitimate. The number of women of childbearing age has increased by 4% in the past decade while the number of births to unwed women has increased by 6.1%.

Abortions Reach Record High in 1980

About one of every four pregnancies in the United States ended in abortion in 1980 according to survey conducted by the Alan Guttmacher Institute. Some 1.55 million abortions were performed, mor than double the 744,000 legal abortions perfomed in 1973, the first year of legalized abortions. A shi from the birth control pill and intrauterine devices for health reasons was a significant factor in th increase, according to statisticians at the institute.

Live Births and Birth Rates

State	1981[1] number	1981[1] rate	1980[1] number	1980[1] rate	State	1981[1] number	1981[1] rate	1980[1] number	1980[1] rate
Alabama	61,139	15.6	62,814	16.6	Montana	13,939	17.6	13,928	17.7
Alaska	9,928	24.1	9,368	23.0	Nebraska	27,155	17.2	27,851	17.6
Arizona	51,322	18.4	50,173	19.7	Nevada	14,162	16.8	13,156	17.9
Arkansas	35,386	15.4	36,863	16.7	New Hampshire	13,501	14.4	13,647	15.2
California	422,066	17.4	401,581	17.4	New Jersey	92,049	12.4	91,047	12.4
Colorado	52,654	17.8	50,279	17.8	New Mexico	28,262	21.3	25,661	20.0
Connecticut	37,604	12.0	34,069	10.9	New York	242,873	13.8	232,491	13.2
Delaware	9,372	15.7	9,544	16.5	North Carolina	84,470	14.2	85,123	15.0
D.C.	17,801	28.2	17,835	28.0	North Dakota	13,415	20.4	12,939	19.7
Florida	138,204	13.6	131,923	14.3	Ohio	169,986	15.8	169,359	15.8
Georgia	91,991	6.5	95,980	18.4	Oklahoma	51,252	16.5	50,681	17.2
Hawaii	18,241	18.6	18,277	19.5	Oregon	44,425	16.8	43,998	17.1
Idaho	19,379	20.2	19,495	21.3	Pennsylvania	161,356	13.6	161,025	13.7
Illinois	181,560	15.8	186,576	16.7	Rhode Island	12,849	13.5	12,512	13.6
Indiana	84,634	15.5	87,906	16.2	South Carolina	49,605	15.7	49,805	16.8
Iowa	46,617	16.1	48,050	16.5	South Dakota	12,679	18.5	13,013	18.8
Kansas	40,239	16.9	39,330	16.5	Tennessee	71,696	15.5	73,500	16.5
Kentucky	58,047	15.9	60,778	17.2	Texas	287,272	19.5	268,717	19.6
Louisiana	81,995	19.0	79,202	19.3	Utah	41,973	27.7	43,708	31.0
Maine	16,482	14.5	16,095	14.6	Vermont	7,655	14.8	7,640	15.3
Maryland	54,137	12.7	52,284	12.6	Virginia	76,266	14.0	75,042	14.3
Massachusetts	76,075	13.2	73,355	12.7	Washington	70,274	16.7	67,972	16.9
Michigan	138,988	15.1	143,007	15.5	West Virginia	28,503	14.6	29,923	15.9
Minnesota	66,943	16.4	68,233	16.6	Wisconsin	73,518	15.5	74,470	15.6
Mississippi	45,842	18.1	47,538	19.5	Wyoming	10,162	20.7	9,539	20.4
Missouri	77,883	15.8	79,623	16.3	**Total**	**3,633,826**	**15.9**	**3,586,925**	**n.a.**

1. Provisional. NOTE: Based on 100% of births in selected states and 50% sample in others. Rates are per 1,000 population. *Source:* Department of Health and Human Services, National Center for Health Statistics.

Live Births and Birth Rates by Race

Race	Births 1979[1]	Rates 1979	Rates 1950	Rates 1940	Race	Births 1979[1]	Rates 1979	Rates 1950	Rates 1940
White	2,808,420	14.8	23.0	18.6	Chinese	11,732	n.a.	43.9	14.5
Black	577,855	22.3	33.1	26.5	Filipino	14,101	n.a.	n.a.	n.a.
Indian	34,269	n.a.	45.8	42.0	Other	36,264	n.a.	19.1	22.0
Japanese	8,285	n.a.	24.5	15.0	All races	3,494,398	15.9	24.1	19.4

1. Based on all births in selected states and on a 50% sample of births in all other states. NOTES: Rates per 1,000 population in each specified group. Rates for 1940 and 1950 based on births adjusted for under-registration; n.a. = not available; Data are latest available. *Source:* Department of Health and Human Services, National Center for Health Statistics.

Live Births by Sex and Sex Ratio[1]

Year	Total[2] Male	Total[2] Female	Total[2] Males per 1,000 females	White Male	White Female	White Males per 1,000 females	Black Male	Black Female	Black Males per 1,000 females
1970[3]	1,915,378	1,816,008	1,055	1,590,140	1,501,124	1,059	290,508	281,854	1,031
1972[4]	1,669,927	1,588,484	1,051	1,364,578	1,290,980	1,057	268,842	262,487	1,024
1973[4]	1,608,326	1,528,639	1,052	1,311,032	1,239,998	1,057	259,877	252,720	1,028
1974[4]	1,622,114	1,537,844	1,055	1,325,019	1,250,773	1,059	257,277	249,885	1,030
1975[4]	1,613,135	1,531,063	1,054	1,312,308	1,239,688	1,059	259,610	251,971	1,030
1976[4]	1,624,436	1,543,352	1,053	1,319,717	1,247,897	1,058	260,661	253,818	1,027
1977[4]	1,705,916	1,620,716	1,053	1,383,440	1,307,630	1,058	275,556	268,665	1,026
1978[4]	1,709,394	1,623,885	1,053	1,378,222	1,302,894	1,058	279,598	271,942	1,028
1979[4]	1,791,267	1,703,131	1,052	1,442,981	1,365,439	1,057	293,013	284,842	1,029

1. Excludes births to nonresidents of U.S. 2. Includes races other than white and black. 3. Based on 50% sample of births. 4. Based on 100% of births for selected states and 50% sample in all others. *Source:* Department of Health and Human Services, National Center for Health Statistics. NOTE: Data are latest available.

Mortality

Death Rates for Selected Causes

Cause of death	1981	1980	1950	1945–49	1940–44	1920–24	1900–04
	Death rates per 100,000						
Typhoid fever	0.0	0.0	0.1	0.2	0.6	7.3	26.7
Communicable diseases of childhood	0.0	0.0	1.3	2.3	4.6	33.8	65.2
Measles	0.0	0.0	0.3	0.6	1.1	7.3	10.0
Scarlet fever	0.0	0.0	0.2	0.1	0.4	4.0	11.8
Whooping cough	0.0	0.0	0.7	1.0	2.2	8.9	10.7
Diphtheria	0.0	0.0	0.3	0.7	1.0	13.7	32.7
Pneumonia and influenza	23.7	23.3	31.3	41.3	63.7	140.3	184.3
Influenza	1.4	1.1	4.4	5.0	13.0	34.8	22.8
Pneumonia	22.3	22.0	26.9	37.2	50.7	105.5	161.5
Tuberculosis	0.8	0.8	22.5	33.3	43.4	96.7	184.7
Cancer	184.3	182.5	139.8	134.0	123.1	86.9	67.7
Diabetes mellitus	15.1	15.0	16.2	24.1	26.2	17.1	12.2
Major cardiovascular diseases	425.1	434.5	510.8	493.1	490.4	369.9	359.5
Diseases of the heart	329.5	335.2	356.8	325.1	303.2	169.8	153.0
Cerebrovascular diseases	71.2	74.6	104.0	93.8	91.7	93.5	106.3
Nephritis and nephrosis	7.6	7.6	16.4	48.4	72.1	81.5	84.3
Syphilis	0.1	0.1	5.0	8.4	12.7	17.6	12.9
Appendicitis	0.3	0.3	2.0	3.5	7.2	14.0	9.4
Accidents, all forms	43.7	46.0	60.6	67.6	73.0	70.8	79.2
Motor vehicle accidents	22.0	23.0	23.1	22.3	22.7	12.9	n.a.
Infant mortality[1]	11.7	12.5	29.2	33.3	42.4	76.7	n.a.
Neonatal mortality[1]	7.8	8.4	20.5	22.9	26.2	39.7	n.a.
Fetal mortality[1]	n.a.	n.a.	22.9	24.3	28.5	39.2[2]	n.a.
Maternal mortality[1]	0.1	0.1	0.8	1.4	2.8	6.9	n.a.
All causes	**866.4**	**874.2**	**963.8**	**1,003.3**	**1,062.0**	**1,196.6**	**1,621.6**

1. Rates per 1,000 live births. 2. 1922–24. NOTE: Includes only deaths occurring within the registration areas. Beginning with 1940, area includes the entire United States; beginning with 1960, Alaska and Hawaii are included. Rates per 100,000 population residing in areas, enumerated as of April 1 for 1940 and 1950 and estimated as of July 1 for all other years. Due to changes in statistical methods, death rates are not strictly comparable. n.a. = not available. *Source:* Department of Health and Human Services, National Center for Health Statistics.

Transportation-Accident Death Rates

Kind of transportation	1980 Passenger miles	1980 Passenger deaths	1980 Death rate[1]	1978–80 average death rate[1]
Passenger automobiles and taxis[2]	2,200,000,000,000	29,050	1.32	1.30
Passenger automobiles on turnpikes[2]	46,100,000,000	330	0.72	0.71
Buses	85,800,000,000	130	0.15	0.15
Intercity buses	17,300,000,000	23	0.13	0.05
Railroad passenger trains	11,000,000,000	4	0.04	0.07
Scheduled air transport planes (domestic)	221,200,000,000	11	0.01	0.04

1. Per 100 million passenger miles. 2. Drivers of passenger automobiles are considered passengers. *Source:* National Safety Council. NOTE: Figures are latest available.

Accident Rates, 1980

(twelve accidental deaths every hour)

Class of accident		One every		Class of accident		One every	
All accidents	Deaths	5	minutes	Workers off-job	Deaths	13	minutes
	Injuries	3	seconds		Injuries	10	seconds
Motor-vehicle	Deaths	10	minutes	Home	Deaths	23	minutes
	Injuries	16	seconds		Injuries	9	seconds
Work	Deaths	41	minutes	Public non-motor-vehicle	Deaths	25	minutes
	Injuries	14	seconds		Injuries	12	seconds

Source: National Safety Council. NOTE: Data are latest available.

Motor-Vehicle Deaths by Type of Accident

Year	Deaths from collisions with— Pedestrians	Other motor vehicles	Railroad trains	Street cars	Pedalcycles	Animal-drawn vehicle or animal	Fixed objects	Deaths from non-collision accidents	Total deaths[1]
1941	13,550	12,500	1,840	118	910	250	1,350	9,450	39,969
1943	9,900	5,300	1,448	171	450	160	700	5,690	23,823
1945	11,000	7,150	1,703	163	500	130	800	6,600	28,076
1947	10,450	9,900	1,736	102	550	150	1,000	8,800	32,697
1949	8,800	10,500	1,452	56	550	140	1,100	9,100	31,701
1951	9,150	13,100	1,573	46	390	100	1,400	11,200	36,996
1953	8,750	13,400	1,506	26	420	120	1,500	12,200	37,955
1955	8,200	14,500	1,490	15	410	90	1,600	12,100	38,426
1957	7,850	15,400	1,376	13	460	80	1,700	11,800	38,702
1959	7,850	14,900	1,202	6	480	70	1,600	11,800	37,910
1961	7,650	14,700	1,267	5	490	80	1,700	12,200	38,091
1963	8,200	17,600	1,385	10	580	80	1,900	13,800	43,564
1965	8,900	20,800	1,556	5	680	120	2,200	14,900	49,163
1967	9,400	22,000	1,620	3	750	100	2,350	16,700	52,924
1969	10,100	23,700	1,495	2	800	100	3,900	15,700	55,791
1971	9,900	23,100	1,378	2	800	100	3,800	15,300	54,381
1973	10,200	23,600	1,194	2	1,000	100	3,800	15,600	55,511
1974	8,500	19,700	1,209	1	1,000	100	3,100	12,800	46,402
1975	8,400	19,550	979	1	1,000	100	3,130	12,700	45,853
1976	8,600	20,100	1,033	2	1,000	100	3,200	13,000	47,038
1977	9,100	21,200	902	3	1,100	100	3,400	13,700	49,510
1978	9,600	22,400	986	1	1,200	100	3,600	14,500	52,411
1979	9,700	22,200	900	—	1,200	100	3,500	15,200	52,800
1980	9,600	21,200	900	—	1,200	100	4,100	15,500	52,600

1. Yearly totals do not quite equal sums of various types because totals for most types are estimated, and these have been made to nearest 10 deaths for some types and to nearest 50 deaths for others. *Source:* National Safety Council. NOTE: Figures are latest available.

Deaths and Death Rates

State	Total deaths[1] 1980 rate	Total deaths[1] 1979 rate	Motor vehicle traffic deaths[2] 1980 number	1980 rate	1979 rate
Alabama	9.4	9.1	947	3.2	3.4
Alaska	4.1	4.0	87	3.5	3.6
Arizona	8.5	8.3	947	4.9	5.3
Arkansas	10.2	9.9	587	3.6	3.4
California	8.2	7.5	5,489	3.5	3.4
Colorado	6.9	6.9	709	3.6	3.5
Connecticut	8.5	8.4	582	3.0	3.0
Delaware	9.0	8.7	158	3.9	3.0
D.C.	14.4	13.8	46	1.4	1.5
Florida	11.6	11.4	2,879	3.9	3.5
Georgia	8.3	8.3	1,503	3.5	3.5
Hawaii	5.5	5.6	185	3.9	4.3
Idaho	7.0	6.7	329	4.4	4.4
Illinois	9.0	8.9	1,994	3.1	3.2
Indiana	8.6	8.7	1,177	3.0	3.3
Iowa	9.2	9.0	626	3.3	3.4
Kansas	9.0	8.7	595	3.5	3.0
Kentucky	9.4	9.2	825	3.0	3.3
Louisiana	8.7	8.7	1,212	5.2	5.1
Maine	9.9	9.5	260	3.7	3.4
Maryland	8.0	7.7	782	2.8	2.5
Massachusetts	9.5	9.1	881	2.5	2.6
Michigan	8.0	7.9	1,772	2.8	2.8
Minnesota	8.0	8.0	863	3.1	3.2
Mississippi	9.4	9.4	697	4.1	4.2
Missouri	10.2	10.0	1,191	3.5	3.4
Montana	8.4	8.2	325	4.9	5.0
Nebraska	9.3	9.0	396	3.5	2.9
Nevada	8.7	8.3	346	5.9	6.2
New Hampshire	8.4	8.2	194	3.1	2.9
New Jersey	8.8	8.7	1,191	2.4	2.3
New Mexico	7.1	6.9	615	5.5	5.7
New York	9.5	9.1	2,619	3.4	3.1
North Carolina	8.6	8.4	1,514	3.6	3.6
North Dakota	8.9	8.5	151	2.9	2.4
Ohio	9.1	8.7	2,033	2.8	3.1
Oklahoma	9.6	9.4	972	3.7	3.2
Oregon	8.5	8.3	646	3.3	3.5
Pennsylvania	10.5	10.0	2,114	3.0	3.1
Rhode Island	10.4	10.0	128	2.2	2.1
South Carolina	8.2	8.1	859	3.6	3.7
South Dakota	9.3	9.1	228	4.1	3.8
Tennessee	9.7	9.4	1,171	3.5	3.6
Texas	7.9	8.0	4,424	4.1	3.9
Utah	6.1	6.3	335	3.5	3.4
Vermont	8.6	8.9	134	3.7	4.4
Virginia	8.0	7.7	1,045	2.7	2.6
Washington	8.1	7.5	985	3.4	3.5
West Virginia	10.2	10.2	539	4.7	4.6
Wisconsin	8.6	8.2	985	3.0	3.0
Wyoming	6.6	6.5	244	5.2	5.1
Total U.S.	**8.7**	**8.7**	**52,600**	**3.5**	**3.5**

1. Provisional rates per 1,000 population. 2. Per 100 million vehicle-miles. *Sources:* Department of Health and Human Services, National Center for Health Statistics; National Safety Council.

Annual Death Rates

Year	Rate	Year	Rate	Year	Deaths	Rate
1900	17.2	1937	11.3	1960	1,711,982	9.5
1905	15.9	1938	10.6	1961	1,701,522	9.3
1910	14.7	1939	10.6	1962	1,756,720	9.5
1915	13.2	1940	10.8	1963	1,813,549	9.6
1918	18.1[1]	1941	10.5	1964	1,798,051	9.4
1920	13.0	1942	10.3	1965	1,828,136	9.4
1921	11.5	1943	10.9	1966	1,863,149	9.5
1922	11.7	1944	10.6	1967	1,851,323	9.4
1923	12.1	1945	10.6	1968	1,930,082	9.7
1924	11.6	1946	10.0	1969	1,921,990	9.5
1925	11.7	1947	10.1	1970[2]	1,921,031	9.5
1926	12.1	1948	9.9	1971	1,927,542	9.3
1927	11.3	1949	9.7	1972	1,963,944	9.4
1928	12.0	1950	9.6	1973	1,973,003	9.4
1929	11.9	1951	9.7	1974	1,934,388	9.2
1930	11.3	1952	9.6	1975	1,892,879	8.9
1931	11.1	1953	9.6	1976	1,909,440	8.9
1932	10.9	1954	9.2	1977	1,899,597	8.8
1933	10.7	1955	9.3	1978	1,927,788	8.8
1934	11.1	1956	9.4	1979	1,904,841	8.7
1935	10.9	1957	9.6	1980[3]	1,986,000	8.7
1936	11.6	1958	9.5	1981[3]	1,987,000	8.7

1. Year of influenza epidemic. 2. First year for which deaths of nonresidents are excluded. 3. Provisional. NOTE: Includes only deaths occurring within the registration area. Beginning with 1933, area includes entire U.S.; with 1959 includes Alaska, and with 1960 includes Hawaii. Excludes fetal deaths. Rates per 1,000 population residing in area, as of April 1 for 1940, 1950, 1960, and 1970, and estimated as of July 1 for all other years. *Sources:* Department of Commerce, Bureau of the Census; and Department of Health and Human Services, National Center for Health Statistics.

Death Rates by Age, Color, and Sex

Age	1980[1]	1975[2]	1970[2]	1960	1940	1920	1980[1]	1975[2]	1970[2]	1960	1940	1920
	White males						White females					
Under 1 year	12.5	15.9	21.1	26.9	56.7	98.1	9.7	12.2	16.1	20.1	43.6	76.1
1–4	0.7	0.7	0.8	1.0	2.8	9.8	0.5	0.6	0.8	0.9	2.4	9.0
5–14	0.4	0.4	0.5	0.5	1.1	2.7	0.3	0.3	0.3	0.3	0.8	2.3
15–24	1.7	1.7	1.7	1.4	2.0	4.2	0.6	0.6	0.6	0.5	1.4	4.3
25–34	1.8	1.7	1.8	1.6	2.8	5.9	0.7	0.7	0.8	0.9	2.2	6.5
35–44	2.6	3.0	3.4	3.3	5.1	7.7	1.3	1.6	1.9	1.9	3.7	7.3
45–54	7.2	7.9	8.8	9.3	11.4	12.0	3.7	4.1	4.6	4.6	7.5	10.9
55–64	17.5	19.5	22.0	22.3	25.2	24.2	9.0	9.4	10.1	10.8	16.8	21.7
65–74	40.2	43.6	48.1	48.5	54.0	54.2	20.4	21.5	24.7	27.8	41.5	49.9
75–84	93.6	96.1	101.0	103.0	122.0	122.5	51.5	60.3	67.0	77.0	104.8	116.4
85 and over	178.2	182.6	185.5	217.5	251.4	253.6	140.4	144.9	159.8	194.8	235.0	247.0
	All other males						All other females					
Under 1 year	23.9	30.0	40.2	51.9	101.2	167.7	20.2	25.2	31.7	40.7	77.4	131.1
1–4	1.0	1.1	1.4	2.1	5.3	15.0	0.8	0.9	1.2	1.7	4.4	14.2
5–14	0.5	0.6	0.6	0.8	1.6	3.7	0.3	0.3	0.4	0.5	1.4	3.9
15–24	2.1	2.4	3.0	2.1	5.0	9.9	0.7	0.9	1.1	1.1	5.0	10.8
25–34	3.9	4.5	5.0	3.9	8.5	12.2	1.4	1.6	2.2	2.6	7.4	13.5
35–44	6.1	7.4	8.7	7.3	13.2	14.4	2.8	3.6	4.9	5.5	11.7	16.0
45–54	12.5	14.2	16.5	15.5	24.5	20.1	7.0	7.8	9.8	11.4	21.1	23.4
55–64	27.4	28.1	30.5	31.5	37.1[3]	31.1	15.5	16.4	18.9	24.1	33.2[3]	35.8
65–74	44.7	49.7	54.7	56.6	62.8[3]	60.2	28.5	31.7	36.8	39.8	52.3[3]	60.4
75–84	97.9	86.0	89.8	86.6	108.8	116.0	68.9	59.8	63.9	67.1	84.1	106.4
85 and over	102.2	116.9	114.1	152.4	199.7	247.1	79.3	91.8	102.9	128.7	159.7	221.2

1. Provisional. 2. Excludes deaths of nonresidents of U.S. 3. Based on enumerated population adjusted for age bias in nonwhite population at ages 55–69 years. NOTE: For 1920, data are from only 10 selected states and the District of Columbia; for 1940, from D.C. and the former 48 states; for 1960, from D.C. and all 50 states. Excludes fetal deaths. Rates are per 1,000 population in each group, enumerated as of April 1 for 1940, 1950, and 1960, and estimated as of July 1 for all other years. NOTE: Data are latest available. *Sources:* Department of Commerce, Bureau of the Census; and Department of Health and Human Services, National Center for Health Statistics.

Expectation of Life

Expectation of Life in the United States

Calendar period	Age 0	10	20	30	40	50	60	70	80
WHITE MALES									
1850[1]	38.3	48.0	40.1	34.0	27.9	21.6	15.6	10.2	5.9
1890[1]	42.50	48.45	40.66	34.05	27.37	20.72	14.73	9.35	5.40
1900–1902[2]	48.23	50.59	42.19	34.88	27.74	20.76	14.35	9.03	5.10
1909–1911[2]	50.23	51.32	42.71	34.87	27.43	20.39	13.98	8.83	5.09
1919–1921[3]	56.34	54.15	45.60	37.65	29.86	22.22	15.25	9.51	5.47
1929–1931	59.12	54.96	46.02	37.54	29.22	21.51	14.72	9.20	5.26
1939–1941	62.81	57.03	47.76	38.80	30.03	21.96	15.05	9.42	5.38
1949–1951	66.31	58.98	49.52	40.29	31.17	22.83	15.76	10.07	5.88
1959–1961	67.55	59.78	50.25	40.98	31.73	23.22	16.01	10.29	5.89
1969–1971	67.94	59.69	50.22	41.07	31.87	23.34	16.07	10.38	6.18
1977	70.0	61.3	51.9	42.7	33.4	24.7	17.1	11.1	6.8
1978	70.2	61.5	52.0	42.8	33.6	24.8	17.2	11.1	6.7
1979[5]	70.6	61.8	52.3	43.2	34.0	25.2	17.5	11.4	7.0
1980[5]	70.5	61.7	52.2	43.1	33.8	25.1	17.4	11.2	6.8
WHITE FEMALES									
1850[1]	40.5	47.2	40.2	35.4	29.8	23.5	17.0	11.3	6.4
1890[1]	44.46	49.62	42.03	35.36	28.76	22.09	15.70	10.15	5.75
1900–1902[2]	51.08	52.15	43.77	36.42	29.17	21.89	15.23	9.59	5.50
1909–1911[2]	53.62	53.57	44.88	36.96	29.26	21.74	14.92	9.38	5.35
1919–1921[3]	58.53	55.17	46.46	38.72	30.94	23.12	15.93	9.94	5.70
1929–1931	62.67	57.65	48.52	39.99	31.52	23.41	16.05	9.98	5.63
1939–1941	67.29	60.85	51.38	42.21	33.25	24.72	17.00	10.50	5.88
1949–1951	72.03	64.26	54.56	45.00	35.64	26.76	18.64	11.68	6.59
1959–1961	74.19	66.05	56.29	46.63	37.13	28.08	19.69	12.38	6.67
1969–1971	75.49	66.97	57.24	47.60	38.12	29.11	20.79	13.37	7.59
1977	77.7	68.8	59.1	49.4	39.8	30.7	22.3	14.8	8.8
1978	77.8	68.9	59.1	49.5	39.9	30.7	22.3	14.8	8.8
1979[5]	78.3	69.3	59.6	49.9	40.3	31.1	22.6	15.1	9.1
1980[5]	78.1	69.1	59.4	49.7	40.1	30.9	22.4	14.9	8.8
ALL OTHER MALES[4]									
1900–1902[2]	32.54	41.90	35.11	29.25	23.12	17.34	12.62	8.33	5.12
1909–1911[2]	34.05	40.65	33.46	27.33	21.57	16.21	11.67	8.00	5.53
1919–1921[3]	47.14	45.99	38.36	32.51	26.53	20.47	14.74	9.58	5.83
1929–1931	47.55	44.27	35.95	29.45	23.36	17.92	13.15	8.78	5.42
1939–1941	52.33	48.54	39.74	32.25	25.23	19.18	14.38	10.06	6.46
1949–1951	58.91	52.96	43.73	35.31	27.29	20.25	14.91	10.74	7.07
1959–1961	61.48	55.19	45.78	37.05	28.72	21.28	15.29	10.81	6.87
1969–1971	60.98	53.67	44.37	36.20	28.29	21.24	15.35	10.68	7.57
1977	64.6	56.6	47.2	38.6	30.2	22.7	16.5	11.4	8.7
1978	65.0	57.0	47.4	38.8	30.4	22.8	16.5	11.6	8.8
1979[5]	65.5	57.4	47.8	39.3	31.0	23.3	17.1	12.0	9.7
1980[5]	65.3	57.1	47.6	39.0	30.6	22.9	16.7	11.6	8.7
ALL OTHER FEMALES[4]									
1900–1902[2]	35.04	43.02	36.89	30.70	24.37	18.67	13.60	9.62	6.48
1909–1911[2]	37.67	42.84	36.14	29.61	23.34	17.65	12.78	9.22	6.05
1919–1921[3]	46.92	44.54	37.15	31.48	25.60	19.76	14.69	10.25	6.58
1929–1931	49.51	45.33	37.22	30.67	24.30	18.60	14.22	10.38	6.90
1939–1941	55.51	50.83	42.14	34.52	27.31	21.04	16.14	11.81	8.00
1949–1951	62.70	56.17	46.77	38.02	29.82	22.67	16.95	12.29	8.15
1959–1961	66.47	59.72	50.07	40.83	32.16	24.31	17.83	12.46	7.66
1969–1971	69.05	61.49	51.85	42.61	33.87	25.97	19.02	13.30	9.01
1977	73.1	65.0	55.2	45.8	36.7	28.3	21.0	14.5	11.3
1978	73.6	65.4	55.6	46.2	37.0	28.5	21.2	14.8	11.5
1979[5]	74.5	66.2	56.4	47.0	37.7	29.2	21.7	13.2	11.8
1980[5]	74.0	65.7	55.9	46.4	37.1	28.6	21.2	14.9	11.5

1. Massachusetts only; white and nonwhite combined, the latter being about 1% of the total. 2. Original Death Registration States. 3. Death Registration States of 1920. 4. Data for periods 1900–1902 to 1929–1931 relate to blacks only. 5. Provisional. *Sources:* Metropolitan Life Insurance Company; Department of Health and Human Services, National Center for Health Statistics; Department of Commerce, Bureau of the Census. NOTE: Data are latest available.

Expectation of Life and Mortality Probabilities, 1978

Age	Expectation of life in years					Mortality probability per 1,000				
		White		All other			White		All other	
	Total persons	Male	Female	Male	Female	Total Persons	Male	Female	Male	Female
0	73.3	70.2	77.8	65.0	73.6	13.8	13.4	10.6	23.3	19.0
1	73.3	70.1	77.6	65.5	74.0	0.9	1.0	0.7	1.4	1.2
2	72.4	69.2	76.7	64.6	73.1	0.7	0.8	0.6	1.1	1.0
3	71.5	68.3	75.7	63.7	72.1	0.6	0.6	0.5	0.9	0.8
4	70.5	67.3	74.8	62.8	71.2	0.5	0.5	0.4	0.8	0.6
5	69.5	66.3	73.8	61.8	70.2	0.4	0.4	0.3	0.7	0.5
6	68.6	65.4	72.8	60.8	69.3	0.4	0.4	0.3	0.6	0.4
7	67.6	64.4	71.8	59.9	68.3	0.3	0.4	0.3	0.5	0.3
8	66.6	63.4	70.8	58.9	67.3	0.3	0.3	0.2	0.4	0.3
9	65.6	62.4	69.9	57.9	66.3	0.3	0.3	0.2	0.4	0.3
10	64.6	61.5	68.9	57.0	65.4	0.2	0.2	0.2	0.4	0.2
11	63.7	60.5	67.9	56.0	64.4	0.2	0.2	0.2	0.4	0.3
12	62.7	59.5	66.9	55.0	63.4	0.3	0.3	0.2	0.5	0.3
13	61.7	58.5	65.9	54.0	62.4	0.4	0.5	0.3	0.6	0.3
14	60.7	57.5	64.9	53.1	61.4	0.6	0.8	0.3	0.8	0.4
15	59.7	56.6	64.0	52.1	60.4	0.7	1.1	0.4	0.9	0.4
16	58.8	55.6	63.0	51.1	59.5	0.9	1.3	0.5	1.1	0.5
17	57.8	54.7	62.0	50.2	58.5	1.1	1.6	0.6	1.3	0.6
18	56.9	53.8	61.1	49.3	57.5	1.2	1.7	0.6	1.6	0.6
19	56.0	52.9	60.1	48.3	56.6	1.2	1.8	0.6	1.9	0.7
20	55.0	52.0	59.1	47.4	55.6	1.3	1.9	0.6	2.3	0.8
21	54.1	51.1	58.2	46.5	54.7	1.3	1.9	0.6	2.6	0.9
22	53.2	50.2	57.2	45.7	53.7	1.4	2.0	0.6	2.9	1.0
23	52.2	49.3	56.2	44.8	52.8	1.4	1.9	0.6	3.1	1.1
24	51.3	48.4	55.3	43.9	51.8	1.4	1.9	0.6	3.2	1.1
25	50.4	47.5	54.3	43.1	50.9	1.3	1.8	0.6	3.4	1.2
26	49.5	46.5	53.3	42.2	49.9	1.3	1.7	0.6	3.5	1.2
27	48.5	45.6	52.4	41.4	49.0	1.3	1.7	0.6	3.6	1.3
28	47.6	44.7	51.4	40.5	48.1	1.3	1.6	0.6	3.7	1.3
29	46.6	43.8	50.4	39.7	47.1	1.3	1.6	0.7	3.7	1.4
30	45.7	42.8	49.5	38.8	46.2	1.3	1.6	0.7	3.8	1.4
31	44.8	41.9	48.5	37.9	45.2	1.3	1.6	0.7	3.8	1.5
32	43.8	41.0	47.5	37.1	44.3	1.4	1.6	0.8	4.0	1.6
33	42.9	40.0	46.6	36.2	43.4	1.4	1.7	0.8	4.2	1.7
34	41.9	39.1	45.6	35.4	42.5	1.5	1.8	0.9	4.4	1.9
35	41.0	38.2	44.6	34.5	41.5	1.6	1.9	0.9	4.7	2.0
36	40.1	37.2	43.7	33.7	40.6	1.7	2.0	1.0	5.1	2.2
37	39.1	36.3	42.7	32.9	39.7	1.9	2.1	1.1	5.4	2.4
38	38.2	35.4	41.8	32.0	38.8	2.0	2.3	1.2	5.9	2.7
39	37.3	34.5	40.8	31.2	37.9	2.2	2.5	1.3	6.3	2.9
40	36.4	33.6	39.9	30.4	37.0	2.4	2.7	1.5	6.9	3.2
41	35.5	32.6	38.9	29.6	36.1	2.7	2.9	1.7	7.4	3.5
42	34.6	31.7	38.0	28.9	35.3	2.9	3.2	1.9	7.9	3.8
43	33.7	30.8	37.1	28.1	34.4	3.2	3.6	2.1	8.3	4.1
44	32.8	29.9	36.1	27.3	33.5	3.5	4.0	2.3	8.6	4.5
45	31.9	29.1	35.2	26.5	32.7	3.9	4.4	2.5	8.9	4.8
46	31.0	28.2	34.3	25.8	31.8	4.3	4.9	2.8	9.2	5.2
47	30.1	27.3	33.4	25.0	31.0	4.7	5.5	3.1	9.9	5.6
48	29.3	26.5	32.5	24.3	30.2	5.1	6.1	3.3	10.9	6.2
49	28.4	25.6	31.6	23.5	29.3	5.6	6.7	3.7	12.1	6.8
50	27.6	24.8	30.7	22.8	28.5	6.2	7.5	4.0	13.5	7.4
51	26.7	24.0	29.8	22.1	27.8	6.8	8.3	4.4	14.9	8.1
52	25.9	23.2	29.0	21.4	27.0	7.4	9.1	4.7	16.2	8.8
53	25.1	22.4	28.1	20.8	26.2	8.0	9.9	5.1	17.3	9.5
54	24.3	21.6	27.3	20.1	25.5	8.7	10.7	5.5	18.4	10.2
55	23.5	20.8	26.4	19.5	24.7	9.3	11.5	5.9	19.4	10.8
56	22.7	20.1	25.6	18.9	24.0	10.0	12.5	6.4	20.6	11.6
57	22.0	19.3	24.7	18.3	23.3	10.9	13.7	7.0	22.1	12.5
58	21.2	18.6	23.9	17.7	22.5	12.1	15.3	7.8	24.0	13.6
59	20.5	17.9	23.1	17.1	21.8	13.4	17.1	8.6	26.4	15.0
60	19.7	17.2	22.3	16.5	21.2	14.9	19.1	9.6	29.1	16.5
61	19.0	16.5	21.5	16.0	20.5	16.4	21.1	10.6	31.8	18.1
62	18.3	15.8	20.7	15.5	19.9	17.9	23.2	11.5	33.9	19.2
63	17.6	15.2	19.9	15.1	19.3	19.1	25.0	12.3	34.9	19.6
64	17.0	14.6	19.2	14.6	18.6	20.1	26.9	13.1	35.2	19.5
65	16.3	14.0	18.4	14.1	18.0	21.2	28.8	13.8	34.9	19.1

Age	Expectation of life in years					Mortality probability per 1,000				
	Total persons	White		All other		Total Persons	White		All other	
		Male	Female	Male	Female		Male	Female	Male	Female
66	15.7	13.4	17.7	13.6	17.3	22.5	30.8	14.8	34.9	19.0
67	15.0	12.8	16.9	13.1	16.7	24.1	33.2	16.0	36.1	20.0
68	14.4	12.2	16.2	12.5	16.0	26.1	36.0	17.4	39.0	22.5
69	13.7	11.6	15.5	12.0	15.4	28.5	39.2	19.1	43.3	26.2
70	13.1	11.1	14.8	11.6	14.8	31.1	42.6	20.9	48.4	30.3
71	12.5	10.6	14.1	11.1	14.2	33.9	46.3	22.9	52.5	34.4
72	12.0	10.1	13.4	10.7	13.7	37.0	50.3	25.4	59.8	39.0
73	11.4	9.6	12.7	10.4	13.2	40.6	54.8	28.2	63.9	44.0
74	10.9	9.1	12.1	10.0	12.8	44.7	59.8	32.0	68.9	49.5
75	10.4	8.6	11.5	9.8	12.5	49.2	65.3	36.0	73.9	55.0
76	9.9	8.2	10.9	9.5	12.2	54.0	71.1	40.3	79.1	60.6
77	9.4	7.8	10.3	9.3	11.9	59.0	77.4	44.9	84.4	65.7
78	9.0	7.4	9.8	9.1	11.7	64.1	84.0	49.6	89.8	70.0
79	8.5	7.1	9.3	8.9	11.6	69.5	91.0	54.7	94.8	73.1
80	8.1	6.7	8.8	8.8	11.5	75.1	98.3	60.2	98.6	74.3
81	7.8	6.4	8.3	8.7	11.3	80.9	105.9	66.3	100.0	72.8
82	7.4	6.1	7.9	8.6	11.1	86.9	113.7	73.3	97.3	67.3
83	7.1	5.8	7.5	8.5	10.9	93.1	121.3	81.3	87.9	56.8
84	6.7	5.5	7.1	8.2	10.5	99.4	128.4	90.8	68.9	40.0
85	6.4	5.3	6.7	7.8	9.9	—	—	—	—	—

Sources: Metropolitan Life Insurance Company; Department of Health and Human Services, National Center for Health Statistics. NOTE: Data are latest available.

Law Enforcement and Crime

Full-Time Law Enforcement Employees, 1980

City	Officers	Civilians	Total	Percent change 79–80
Atlanta	1,223	337	1,560	+7.8
Baltimore	3,171	555	3,726	0.0
Birmingham, Ala.	678	173	851	−2.1
Boston	2,108	420	2,528	+2.6
Buffalo, N.Y.	1,083	136	1,219	−2.2
Chicago	12,392	1,250	13,642	−10.5
Cincinnati	997	160	1,157	+5.2
Cleveland	1,877	147	2,024	+1.3
Columbus, Ohio	968	317	1,285	+6.8
Dallas	1,990	588	2,578	−0.6
Denver	1,393	297	1,690	+0.2
Detroit	4,166	590	4,756	−15.3
El Paso	665	177	842	0.0
Fort Worth	692	189	881	−6.0
Honolulu	1,484	295	1,779	−0.2
Houston	3,070	831	3,901	+13.3
Indianapolis	969	336	1,305	+1.9
Jacksonville	951	606	1,557	+2.0
Kansas City, Mo.	1,183	485	1,668	+2.3
Long Beach, Calif.	586	264	850	+0.8
Los Angeles	6,587	2,562	9,149	+1.7
Louisville, Ky.	733	219	952	+9.0
Memphis, Tenn.	1,210	451	1,661	+0.5
Miami, Fla.	688	306	994	+11.3
Milwaukee	2,039	247	2,286	+0.2
Minneapolis	713	93	806	−3.8
New Orleans	1,397	601	1,998	+0.7
New York	22,590	4,349	26,939	−3.5
Newark, N.J.	930	259	1,189	−18.2
Norfolk, Va.	581	121	702	−2.6
Oakland, Calif.	602	271	873	−4.8
Oklahoma City	725	190	915	+2.5
Omaha, Neb.	540	147	687	−3.0
Philadelphia	7,454	863	8,317	−4.9
Phoenix, Ariz.	1,622	640	2,262	+4.4
Pittsburgh	1,400	110	1,510	+7.4
Portland, Ore.	654	199	853	+2.0
Rochester, N.Y.	643	235	878	+6.0
St. Louis	1,950	591	2,541	−2.2
St. Paul	552	126	678	+0.4
San Antonio	1,137	227	1,364	−0.4
San Diego, Calif.	1,380	380	1,760	+6.0
San Francisco	1,738	510	2,248	+10.7
San Jose, Calif.	796	209	1,005	0.0
Seattle	1,036	352	1,388	+6.8
Tampa, Fla.	520	171	691	−12.0
Toledo, Ohio	553	56	609	−22.0
Tucson, Ariz.	571	202	773	+4.9
Tulsa, Okla.	667	127	794	−2.2
Washington, D.C.	3,652	486	4,138	−9.7

NOTE: As of Oct. 31, 1980. *Source:* Department of Justice, Federal Bureau of Investigation, *Uniform Crime Reports for the United States, 1980.*

Total Estimated Arrests, 1980[1]

Murder and non-negligent manslaughter	20,040	Weapons—carrying, possession, etc.	166,700
Forcible rape	31,380	Prostitution and commercial vice	88,900
Robbery	146,270	Sex offenses, except forcible rape and prostitution	67,400
Aggravated assault	277,470	Drug abuse violations	580,900
Burglary	513,300	Gambling	87,000
Larceny—theft	1;191,900	Offenses against family and children	55,400
Motor vehicle theft	138,300	Driving under the influence	1,426,700
Arson	19,800	Liquor laws	463,500
Total violent crime	475,160	Drunkenness	1,125,800
Total property crime	1,863,300	Disorderly conduct	769,700
Other assaults	488,600	Vagrancy	30,700
Forgery and counterfeiting	78,200	All other offenses, except traffic	1,775,500
Fraud	291,500	Curfew and loitering law violations	70,700
Embezzlement	8,500	Runaways	153,200
Stolen property—buying, receiving, possessing	123,200	**Total**	**10,441,000**
Vandalism	250,500		

1. Arrest totals based on all reporting agencies and estimates for unreported areas. *Source:* Department of Justice, Federal Bureau of Investigation, *Uniform Crime Reports for the United States, 1980.*

Number of Arrests by Sex and Age

	Male				Female			
	Total		Under 18		Total		Under 18	
Offense	1980	1979	1980	1979	1980	1979	1980	1979
Serious Crimes	1,750,317	1,711,465	639,351	677,345	406,330	414,367	136,897	149,389
Murder[1]	15,814	15,210	1,561	1,476	2,298	2,424	136	171
Forcible rape	28,140	28,047	4,175	4,312	254	214	76	59
Robbery	127,372	120,436	38,641	38,410	9,892	9,534	2,870	2,804
Aggravated assault	222,835	221,170	31,607	33,334	31,582	31,365	5,659	5,722
Burglary—breaking or entering	441,905	430,892	198,321	209,759	29,154	29,208	13,514	14,665
Larceny—theft	782,710	750,065	306,450	319,138	320,003	326,862	108,024	117,934
Motor vehicle theft	115,857	129,726	51,450	62,883	10,993	12,712	5,790	7,173
Arson	15,684	15,919	7,146	8,033	2,154	2,048	828	861
All Other								
Other assaults	385,537	379,577	63,221	66,176	62,363	60,040	16,924	16,932
Forgery and counterfeiting	49,211	47,743	6,404	6,914	22,285	21,357	2,769	2,875
Fraud	151,785	141,977	5,262	6,261	107,545	95,913	2,108	2,258
Embezzlement	5,573	5,830	643	762	2,217	1,990	242	229
Stolen property—buying, receiving, possessing	101,414	93,990	31,007	31,788	11,924	11,253	3,013	3,132
Vandalism	209,330	215,059	104,318	117,683	19,849	19,754	9,062	10,042
Weapons—carrying, possessing, etc.	142,318	139,380	22,093	23,157	11,009	10,948	1,341	1,456
Prostitution and commercialized vice	23,971	26,051	809	1,176	57,948	55,967	2,090	2,118
Sex offenses, except forcible rape and prostitution	58,059	57,182	10,185	10,481	4,628	4,807	767	825
Drug abuse violations	451,682	442,182	82,302	94,376	70,107	68,941	16,323	18,512
Gambling	41,726	46,559	1,649	2,057	4,711	4,876	82	87
Offenses against family and children	44,007	45,302	1,279	1,575	5,150	5,023	722	921
Driving under the influence	1,148,856	1,106,414	26,126	26,544	119,616	105,739	3,010	2,899
Liquor laws	354,728	335,942	106,989	109,511	62,685	57,664	31,131	30,275
Drunkenness	962,092	982,941	36,248	38,688	79,734	77,905	5,831	6,137
Disorderly conduct	601,023	589,165	97,006	102,936	110,691	107,334	20,893	21,215
Vagrancy	24,911	27,324	3,172	4,024	4,103	8,114	590	833
All other offenses except traffic	1,366,654	1,355,804	229,497	236,758	240,921	231,830	56,658	57,192
Curfew and loitering law violations	50,214	60,089	50,214	60,089	15,541	17,033	15,541	17,033
Runaways	58,931	62,224	58,931	62,224	82,262	87,409	82,262	87,409
Total	**7,982,339**	**7,872,200**	**1,576,706**	**1,680,525**	**1,501,619**	**1,468,264**	**408,256**	**431,769**

1. Includes non-negligent manslaughter. NOTE: 1980 figures represent arrests reported by 11,448 agencies serving a population of 203,568,711 as estimated by FBI. *Source:* Department of Justice, Federal Bureau of Investigation, *Uniform Crime Reports for the United States, 1980.*

Arrests by Race, 1980

(in thousands)

Offense	White	Black	Other	Total
Serious Crimes	1,438.1	720.7	36.9	2,195.7
Murder[1]	9.5	9.0	0.3	18.7
Forcible rape	14.9	14.0	0.4	29.4
Robbery	57.3	80.5	1.6	139.4
Aggravated assault	161.0	93.3	4.1	258.4
Burglary	333.7	139.4	6.0	479.1
Larceny—theft	758.2	342.6	21.8	1,122.7
Motor vehicle theft	89.0	38.1	2.5	129.6
Arson	14.5	3.8	0.2	18.4
All Other				
Other assaults	304.9	145.1	6.4	456.4
Forgery and counterfeiting	48.0	23.9	0.7	72.5
Fraud	183.2	80.0	2.0	265.3
Embezzlement	5.9	1.9	0.1	7.9
Stolen property—buying, receiving, possessing	77.7	36.6	1.1	115.4
Vandalism	193.6	37.1	3.0	233.6
Weapons—carrying, possessing, etc.	98.0	57.2	1.9	157.2
Prostitution and commercial vice	39.0	45.6	1.2	85.8
Sex offenses, except forcible rape and prostitution	50.0	12.6	1.0	63.4
Drug abuse violations	402.0	125.6	4.4	532.0
Gambling	14.1	31.1	1.5	46.7
Offenses against family and children	31.3	18.0	0.7	50.0
Driving under the influence	1,124.4	144.0	21.0	1,289.4
Liquor laws	392.3	27.5	8.4	428.3
Drunkenness	854.4	165.9	27.3	1,047.6
Disorderly conduct	492.4	219.4	12.0	723.8
Vagrancy	19.6	9.0	0.7	29.3
All other offenses, except traffic	1,192.7	436.7	28.4	1,657.8
Suspicion	9.4	6.6	0.1	16.1
Curfew and loitering law violations	54.5	10.8	1.1	66.4
Runaways	120.4	19.9	2.9	143.3
Total	7,145.8	2,375.2	162.7	9,683.7

1. Includes non-negligent manslaughter. NOTE: Figures represent arrests reported by 12,013 agencies serving a total 1980 population of 207,907,704 as estimated by FBI. *Source:* Department of Justice, Federal Bureau of Investigation, *Uniform Crime Reports for the United States, 1980.*

Total Arrests, by Age Groups, 1980

Age	Arrests	Age	Arrests	Age	Arrests	Age	Arrests	Age	Arrests
Under 15	603,927	18	589,996	22	447,045	30–34	905,411	50–54	257,349
15	377,972	19	575,105	23	413,528	35–39	584,122	55 and over	378,393
16	493,073	20	531,092	24	378,315	40–44	417,202		
17	550,921	21	490,597	25–29	1,392,514	45–49	316,799	Total	9,703,181

NOTE: Based on reports furnished to the FBI by 12,042 agencies covering a 1980 estimated population of 208,194,225. *Source:* Department of Justice, Federal Bureau of Investigation, *Uniform Crime Reports for the United States, 1980.*

National Crime, Rate, and Percent Change

Crime index offenses	Estimated crime 1980		Percent change over 1979		Percent change over 1976		Percent change over 1971	
	Number	Rate per 100,000 inhabitants	Number	Rate	Number	Rate	Number	Rate
Murder	23,040	10.2	+ 7.4	+ 5.2	+22.7	+15.9	+29.6	+18.6
Forcible rape	82,090	36.4	+ 8.0	+ 5.5	+44.7	+37.9	+94.2	+77.6
Robbery	548,810	243.5	+17.5	+14.8	+30.6	+24.4	+41.6	+29.5
Aggravated assault	654,960	290.6	+ 6.6	+ 4.1	+33.4	+27.1	+77.6	+62.5
Burglary	3,759,200	1,668.2	+13.9	+11.3	+21.7	+15.9	+56.7	+43.4
Larceny-theft	7,112,700	3,156.3	+ 8.1	+ 5.6	+13.4	+ 8.0	+60.8	+47.1
Motor vehicle theft	1,114,700	494.6	+ 1.6	− .8	+16.4	+10.9	+17.6	+ 7.6
Violent	1,308,900	580.8	+11.1	+ 8.5	+32.7	+26.4	+60.3	+46.7
Property	11,986,500	5,319.1	+ 9.2	+ 6.7	+16.2	+10.7	+54.2	+41.1
Total	**13,295,400**	**5,899.9**	**+ 9.4**	**+ 6.9**	**+17.6**	**+12.0**	**+54.8**	**+41.7**

Source: Department of Justice, Federal Bureau of Investigation, *Uniform Crime Reports for the United States, 1980.*

Crime Rates for Population Groups and Selected Cities, 1980

(offenses known to the police per 100,000 population)

Group and city	Violent crime: Murder	Violent crime: Forcible rape	Violent crime: Robbery	Violent crime: Aggravated assault	Violent crime: Total	Property crime: Burglary—breaking or entering	Property crime: Larceny—theft	Property crime: Motor vehicle theft	Property crime: Total	Total all crimes
Cities over 250,000	24.4	75	800	515	1,414	2,653	4,250	1,085	7,988	9,402
100,000–249,999	12.3	57	333	411	812	2,475	4,793	661	7,930	8,742
50,000–99,999	7.6	39	229	328	602	1,980	3,946	609	6,535	7,137
25,000–49,999	6.1	30	151	268	455	1,689	3,913	452	6,053	6,508
10,000–24,999	5.1	20	93	234	352	1,344	3,370	345	5,059	5,411
Under 10,000	4.5	17	55	222	298	1,131	3,172	259	4,562	4,859
Total, 8,551 cities	**11.8**	**43**	**341**	**350**	**7,238**	**1,950**	**3,913**	**629**	**6,492**	**7,238**
Suburbs	5.9	27	112	226	370	1,423	2,848	364	4,635	5,005
Rural areas	7.4	16	23	140	186	872	1,203	141	2,216	2,402
Selected cities:										
Dallas	35.4	125	554	695	1,409	3,348	6,152	869	10,369	11,778
Phoenix	13.3	63	393	439	908	3,123	6,676	746	10,545	11,454
Detroit	45.7	110	1,122	668	1,945	3,412	3,430	1,856	8,697	10,642
San Francisco	16.3	113	1,117	640	1,885	2,491	4,861	1,208	8,561	10,446
New York	25.8	53	1,429	618	2,126	2,995	3,545	1,428	7,968	10,094
Washington, D.C.	31.5	69	1,401	509	2,011	2,560	4,891	562	8,012	10,023
Los Angeles	34.2	95	868	745	1,742	2,931	3,827	1,452	8,210	9,952
Baltimore	27.5	71	1,277	736	2,112	2,251	4,697	716	7,665	9,777
Houston	39.1	89	671	176	975	3,043	3,131	1,737	7,912	8,886
San Diego	11.8	41	341	313	707	2,282	4,189	881	7,352	8,059
Memphis	23.6	122	596	327	1,070	2,912	3,173	741	6,826	7,895
San Antonio	20.8	46	221	253	541	2,256	3,963	584	6,803	7,344
Chicago	28.9	45	544	342	960	1,148	3,445	1,031	5,624	6,583
Philadelphia	25.9	56	647	300	1,029	1,483	2,433	1,070	4,987	6,016
Indianapolis	15.3	59	314	249	637	1,442	2,706	542	4,689	5,327
CRIME INDEX TRENDS										
(percent change 1980—81)										
Cities over 1,000,000 (total population 17,410,000)	−4	−3	+6	−5	+2	−1	−1	+3	0	0
Cities 500,000 to 999,999 (total population 11,594,000)	−2	−2	+9	−1	+4	+2	+1	−5	0	+1
Cities 250,000 to 499,999 (total population 11,509,000)	−3	−1	+2	+2	+2	+1	+5	−6	+2	+2
Cities 100,000 to 249,999 (total population 16,336,000)	+6	0	+6	+1	+3	+1	+2	−8	+1	+1
Cities 50,000 to 99,999 (total population 18,750,000)	−1	−1	0	−6	−3	−2	0	−6	−1	−1
Cities 25,000 to 49,000 (total population 21,012,000)	−9	0	+3	0	+1	−1	0	−6	−1	−1
Cities 10,000 to 24,999 (total population 24,299,999)	−8	+2	+2	−2	−1	−1	0	−6	−1	−1
Cities under 10,000 (total population 22,102,000)	−11	0	0	−2	−1	−1	0	−9	0	0
Suburban areas (total population 39,291,000)	−2	−1	+4	−1	0	−2	−1	−5	−2	−2
Rural areas (total population 28,716,000)	−4	−1	−2	−1	−1	−2	0	−8	−1	−1
All areas (total population 211,020,000)	−3	−1	+5	−2	+1	−1	0	−4	0	0

1. Agencies also included in other city groups. NOTE: Population in 1980 as estimated by FBI. *Sources:* Department of Justice, Federal Bureau of Investigation, *Uniform Crime Reports for the United States, 1980 and 1981 Preliminary Annual Release.*

Domestic Production and Imports of Civilian Firearms

(in thousands)

Item	1981	1980	1979	1978	1977	1976	1975	1970	1965	1960
Domestic production	5,374	5,646	5,321	4,866	5,016	5,225	5,768	n.a.	2,355	1,508
Handguns	2,537	2,371	2,124	1,889	1,868	1,833	2,024	n.a.	666	475
Rifles	1,681	1,936	1,878	1,781	1,923	2,091	2,123	n.a.	790	469
Shotguns	1,156	1,339	1,319	1,196	1,225	1,301	1,621	n.a.	899	564
Imports for consumption	690	754	886	869	782	895	1,084	826	766	655
Handguns	306	299	271	273	316	270	462	227	347	128
Rifles	200	182	257	223	170	157	166	237	245	402
Shotguns	184	273	358	373	296	468	457	363	174	125
Total	**6,064**	**6,400**	**6,207**	**5,735**	**5,798**	**6,120**	**6,852**	**n.a.**	**3,121**	**2,163**

NOTE: Beginning 1975, fiscal-year data. Include firearms sold under civilian marksmanship program of Department of Defense. n.a.=not available. *Source:* 1960–1970, Department of Commerce, Bureau of the Census; beginning 1975, Department of the Treasury, Bureau of Alcohol, Tobacco, and Firearms.

Prisoners Under Sentence of Death

Characteristic	1980	1979	1978
White	427	344	261
Black and other	287	223	184
Under 20 years	11	11	22
20–24 years	173	145	113
25–34 years	334	276	210
35–54 years	186	128	97
55 years and over	10	7	3
Schooling completed:			
7 years or less	68	55	55
8 years	74	55	46
9–11 years	204	187	158
12 years	162	121	99
More than 12 years	43	39	28
Unknown	163	110	59
Marital status:			
Never married	268	208	187
Married	229	190	136
Divorced or separated[1]	217	169	122
Time elapsed since sentencing:			
6 months or less; 7–12 months	185	158	162
1–3 years	389	309	237
4–6[2] years	102	100	46
More than 6[2] years	38	0	0
Legal status at arrest:			
Not under sentence	384	324	277
On parole or probation	115	88	60
In prison or escaped	45	38	35
Unknown	170	117	73
Total	**714**	**567**	**445**

1. Includes widows, widowers, and unknown. 2. 4-8 years, more than 8 years prior to 1980. NOTE: As of Dec. 31. Excludes prisoners under sentence of death confined in local correctional systems pending appeal or who had not been committed to prison. *Source:* Department of Justice, Law Enforcement Assistance Administration; after 1978 U.S. Bureau of Justice Statistics, *Capital Punishment,* annual.

Methods of Execution[1]

State	Method
Alabama[2]	Electrocution
Alaska	No death penalty
Arizona[2]	Lethal gas
Arkansas[2]	Electrocution
California	Lethal gas
Colorado[2]	Lethal gas
Connecticut[2]	Electrocution
Delaware	Hanging
D.C.	No death penalty
Florida	Electrocution
Georgia[2]	Electrocution
Hawaii	No death penalty
Idaho[2]	Lethal injection
Illinois	Electrocution
Indiana[2]	Electrocution
Iowa	No death penalty
Kansas	No death penalty
Kentucky[2]	Electrocution
Louisiana[2]	Electrocution
Maine	No death penalty
Maryland[2]	Lethal gas
Massachusetts	No death penalty
Michigan	No death penalty
Minnesota	No death penalty
Mississippi[2]	Lethal gas
Missouri	Lethal gas
Montana[2]	Hanging
Nebraska[2]	Electrocution
Nevada[2]	Lethal gas
New Hampshire[2]	Hanging
New Jersey[5]	No death penalty
New Mexico	Lethal injection
New York	No death penalty
North Carolina[2]	Lethal gas
North Dakota	No death penalty
Ohio[2]	Electrocution
Oklahoma	Lethal injection
Oregon	No death penalty
Pennsylvania[2]	Electrocution
Rhode Island	No death penalty([3])
South Carolina[2]	Electrocution
South Dakota	Electrocution
Tennessee[2]	Electrocution
Texas[2]	Lethal injection
Utah[2]	Firing squad
Vermont	Electrocution
Virginia	Electrocution
Washington[2]	Hanging
West Virginia	No death penalty
Wisconsin	No death penalty
Wyoming	Lethal gas
U.S. (Fed. Govt.)	([4])
American Samoa	([5])
Guam	No death penalty
Puerto Rico	No death penalty
Virgin Islands	No death penalty

1. On July 1, 1976, by a 7–2 decision, the U.S. Supreme Court upheld the death penalty as not being "cruel or unusual." However, in another ruling the same day, the Court, by a 5–4 vote, stated that states may not impose "mandatory" capital punishment on every person convicted of murder. These decisions left uncertain the fate of condemned persons throughout the U.S. On Oct. 4, the Court refused to reconsider its July ruling, which allows some states to proceed with executions of condemned prisoners. The first execution in this country since 1967 was in Utah on Jan. 17, 1977. Gary Mark Gilmore was executed by shooting. 2. Voted to restore death penalty after June 29, 1972, Supreme Court decision ruling capital punishment unconstitutional. 3. Person shall be executed by gas if he commits murder while serving a prison term. 4. Method shall be that used by state in which sentence is imposed. If state does not have death penalty, federal judge shall prescribe method for carrying out sentence. 5. New criminal code re-establishes death penalty but at this time prescribes no method. *Source: Information Please* questionnaires to the states.

Motor Vehicle Laws, 1982

State	Date new license plates can be used	Age for driver's license[1]			State gasoline tax	Percent state tax[2]	Annual saftey inspection required
		Regular	Learner's	Restrictive			
Alabama	On issue	16	15[5]	14[15]	$.11	1½	no[19]
Alaska	On issue	18		16[3]	.08	—	no[19]
Arizona	On issue	18	15 & 7 mos.[3,5]	16[3]	.10	4	no
Arkansas	On issue	18	([5])	14[3]	.095	3	yes
California	On issue	18	15[4,10]	16[4]	.09[17]	6	no[19]
Colorado	On issue	21	15½[5]	16[4]	.09	3	no
Connecticut	On issue	18		16[4]	.11	7½[6]	no
Delaware	On issue	18	([5])	16[4]	.11	2	yes
D. C.	Mar. 1	18	([5])	16[3]	.14[18]	([21])	yes
Florida	On issue	16	([5])	15[3]	.08	4	no
Georgia	Jan. 1	18	15	16[3]	.075[17]	3	no
Hawaii	On issue	18	([5])	15[3]	([8])	([9])	yes[12]
Idaho	On issue	16	([5])	14[4]	.125	3	no
Illinois	On issue	18	([5])	16[3,4]	.075[17]	4	no
Indiana	On issue	18	15[20]	16 & 1 mo.[3,4]	.111[17,18]	4	no
Iowa	Dec. 1	18	14	16[4]	.13	3	([7,19])
Kansas	On issue	16	([5])	14	.08	3	([7,19])
Kentucky	On issue	18	([5])	16[3]	.10[18]	5	no
Louisiana	On issue	17		15[11]	.08	3	yes
Maine	On issue	17	([5])	15[4]	.09	5	6 mos.
Maryland	Mar. 1	18	([5])	16	.11	5	no[22]
Massachusetts	On issue	18	([5])	16½[3,4]	.104[18]	5	6 mos.
Michigan	On issue	18		16[3,4]	.11[17]	4	no[19]
Minnesota	On issue	18	([5])	16[4]	.13	5	no[19]
Mississippi	On issue	15	([5])		.09[17]	3	yes
Missouri	On issue	16		15[4]	.07	3	yes
Montana	On issue	18	([5])	15[3,4]	.09	1½[13]	no
Nebraska	On issue	16	15[5]	14	.137[18]	3	no
Nevada	On issue	18	15½[5]	16[3]	.12	2[14]	no
New Hampshire	On issue	18		16[4]	.14	—	6 mos.
New Jersey	On issue	17		16	.08	5	2 yrs.
New Mexico	Dec. 15	16	15	15[4]	.10[18]	2	no
New York	On issue	17[4]		16[3]	.08[17,24]	4	yes
North Carolina	On issue	18		15[3,4]	.12	2[16]	yes
North Dakota	Feb. 1	16	([5])	14[3,4]	.08	3	no[19]
Ohio	1st day/mo. of exp.	18	16[3,5]	14[23]	.117[18]	5	no[19]
Oklahoma	On issue	16		15½[4]	.658	2	yes
Oregon	On issue	16	15[5]	14	.08	—	no[19]
Pennsylvania	On issue	17[4]	([5])	16[3]	.11[18]	6	yes
Rhode Island	On issue	18	([5])	16[4]	.12[18]	6	yes
South Carolina	On issue	16	15[25]	15	.13	4	yes
South Dakota	Jan. 1	16	([5])	14	.13	3[6]	no
Tennessee	On issue	16	([5])	15	.10	4½	no
Texas	On issue	16[4]	15	15	.05	4	yes
Utah	On issue	16[4]	([5])		.11	4¾	yes
Vermont	On issue	18	15[5]	16	.11	4	yes
Virginia	On issue	18	15 & 8 mos.[3,5]	16[3,4]	.11[18]	2	yes
Washington	On issue	18	15[20]	16[4]	.12[18]	5.5	no[19]
West Virginia	On issue	18	([5])	16[3]	.105	5	yes
Wisconsin	On issue	18	([5])	16[4]	.13	5	no
Wyoming	Jan. 1	18	15[3,10]	16[3]	.08	3	no

1. Full driving privileges at age given in "Regular" column. A license restricted or qualified in some manner may be obtained at age given in "Restricted" column. 2. Applicable to car sales (local and county sales taxes extra where applicable). 3. Guardian's or parent's consent required. 4. Must have completed approved Driver Education course. 5. Learner's Permit required. 6. Sales or use tax on first registration of new or used cars. 7. Prior to first registration and transfers. 8. 8.5—13.5¢ varies by county. 9. 4% on cars purchased out of state only. 10. Driver with Learner's Permit must be accompanied by locally licensed operator 18 years or older. 11. All persons under 17 are prohibited from operating vehicles between 11 p.m. and 5 a.m. 12. If car is 10 years or older, every 6 months. 13. Periodic reductions for cars purchased later in year. 14. Plus 1 1/2% school support tax and 2 1/4% city and county relief tax in selected counties. 15. Restricted to Mopeds. 16. $120 maximum. 17. Plus sales tax. 18. Variable or indexed tax rate, adjusted periodically. 19. State troopers are authorized to inspect at their discretion. 20. Must be enrolled in a Driver Education course. 21. 4–7%, depending on weight of car. 22. Upon resale or transfer. 23. Proof of hardship. 24. New York City leaded gasoline tax 1¢ extra per gallon. 25. Driver with Learner's Permit must be accompanied by locally licensed operator 21 years or older. NOTES: A driver's license is required in every state. The national speed limit is 55 miles per hour. All states have an *implied consent* Chemical Test Law for alcohol. *Source:* Amerian Automobile Association.

Law Enforcement Officers Killed in Line of Duty

(beginning 1973, includes federal officers)

Area	1980	1979	1978	1977	1976	1975	1974	1973	1970	1965	1960
New England	3	—	3	2	4	4	2	7	2	3	3
Middle Atlantic	20	13	9	12	15	24	18	21	29	10	7
East North Central	8	13	5	10	19	32	43	21	38	10	9
West North Central	7	3	5	14	11	8	8	6	6	3	3
South Atlantic	21	23	15	31	34	31	42	37	23	15	13
East South Central	9	15	13	11	14	18	12	13	5	9	2
West South Central	15	11	19	21	21	22	23	30	15	14	6
Mountain	5	8	5	3	4	14	9	16	4	7	0
Pacific	9	15	15	15	13	22	18	21	24	12	5
Puerto Rico and Virgin Islands	7	3	4	2	4	9	4	4	n.a.	n.a.	n.a.
CAUSE											
By felons	104	106[4]	93	93	111	129[1]	132	134	100	53	n.a.
In accidents	61	59	53	30[3]	29	56	47	42	46	30	n.a.
Total	**165[3]**	**165[4]**	**146**	**123[3]**	**140[2]**	**185[1]**	**179**	**176**	**146**	**83**	**48**

1. Includes one officer in Guam. 2. Includes one officer killed in Bogota, Colombia. 3. Includes one officer killed in Virgin Islands. 4. Includes two officers killed on Guam. NOTE: n.a. = not available. *Source:* Department of Justice, Federal Bureau of Investigation, *Uniform Crime Reports for the United States, 1980.*

Minimum Legal Age for Purchase of Liquor, Wine, and Beer

State	Liquor	Wine	Beer
Alabama	19	19	19
Alaska	19	19	19
Arizona	19	19	19
Arkansas	21	21	21
California	21	21	21
Colorado	21	21	21[1]
Connecticut	19	19	19
Delaware	20	20	20
D.C.	21	21[2]	18
Florida	19	19	19
Georgia	19	19	19
Hawaii	18	18	18
Idaho	19	19	19
Illinois	21	21	21
Indiana	21	21	21
Iowa	19	19	19
Kansas	21	21	21[1]
Kentucky	21	21	21
Louisiana	18	18	18
Maine	20	20	20
Maryland	21	21	21
Massachusetts	20	20	20
Michigan	21	21	21
Minnesota	19	19	19
Mississippi	21	21[2]	21[3]
Missouri	21	21	21
Montana	19	19	19
Nebraska	20	20	20
Nevada	21	21	21
New Hampshire	20	20	20
New Jersey	19	19	19
New Mexico	21	21	21
New York	19	19	19
North Carolina	21	21[2]	18
North Dakota	21	21	21
Ohio	21	21	19
Oklahoma	21	21	21[5]
Oregon	21	21	21
Pennsylvania	21	21	21
Rhode Island	19	19	19
South Carolina	21	18	18
South Dakota	21	21	21[1]
Tennessee	19	19	19
Texas	19	19	19
Utah	21	21	21
Vermont	18	18	18
Virginia	21	21	18[4]
Washington	21	21	21
West Virginia	18	18	18
Wisconsin	18	18	18
Wyoming	19	19	19

3.2 beer: 18. 2. Light wine: 18. 3. Up to 4% alcohol by weight: 18. 4. 19 for off-premises consumption. 5. 3.2 beer: 19. *ource:* Distilled Spirits Council of the United States.

Student Drug Use Declines

High school students are smoking less marijuana ese days, according to a survey conducted by the stitute for Social Research at the University of chigan. The use of illicit drugs has dropped arply since the late 1970s when it peaked. In 1978 one in every nine high school seniors said they were daily users of marijuana. By the spring of 1981 the proportion had dropped to one in 14. The use of other illicit drugs also has declined.

U.S. District Courts—Criminal Cases Commenced and Defendants Disposed of, by Nature of Offense: 1979 and 1980

[For years ending June 30]

Nature of offense	1980, cases commenced[1]	Disposition of defendants, 1980: Not convicted: Total	Not convicted: Acquitted	Convicted: Total	Convicted: Guilty plea	Convicted: Court or jury	Sentenced: Imprisonment	Sentenced: Probation	Sentenced: Fine and other	1979: Cases commenced[1]	1979: Defendants disposed of
General offenses:											
Homicide	141	62	15	108	62	46	69	15	24	148	150
Robbery	1,251	179	35	1,262	1,011	251	1,164	97	1	1,149	1,431
Assault	555	179	36	418	301	117	233	159	26	541	618
Burglary	151	42	8	134	116	18	77	57	—	198	210
Larceny—theft	3,033	745	123	3,232	2,865	367	1,290	1,612	330	3,420	4,735
Embezzlement and fraud	6,210	1,213	268	5,975	5,147	828	2,270	3,443	262	6,630	8,052
Auto theft	381	137	21	421	360	61	307	108	6	399	741
Forgery, counterfeiting	2,124	373	49	1,939	1,720	219	1,034	893	12	2,877	3,176
Sex offenses	150	39	6	98	64	34	72	20	6	139	168
Narcotics	3,130	1,594	257	4,749	3,450	1,299	3,479	1,232	38	3,277	6,609
Misc. general offenses	7,240	2,293	334	5,614	4,187	1,427	1,596	1,212	2,806	8,704	9,303
Total[2]	**27,968**	**7,962**	**1,329**	**28,598**	**23,111**	**5,487**	**13,191**	**11,053**	**4,354**	**31,536**	**41,175**

1. Excludes transfers. 2. Includes items not shown separately. *Source: Statistical Abstract of the United States.*

Murder Victims by Weapons Used

Year	Murder victims, total	Weapons used or cause of death: Guns: Total	Guns: Percent	Cutting or stabbing	Blunt object[1]	Strangulation and hands, fists, feet	Drownings, arson, etc.	All other[2]
1965	8,773	5,015	57.2	2,021	505	894	226	112
1966	9,552	5,660	59.3	2,134	516	896	203	143
1967	11,114	6,998	63.0	2,200	589	957	211	159
1968	12,503	8,105	64.8	2,317	713	936	294	138
1969	13,575	8,876	65.4	2,534	613	1,039	322	191
1970	13,649	9,039	66.2	2,424	604	1,031	353	198
1971	16,183	10,712	66.2	3,017	645	1,295	314	200
1972	15,832	10,379	65.6	2,974	672	1,291	331	185
1973	17,123	11,249	65.7	2,985	848	1,445	173[3]	423
1974	18,632	12,474	66.9	3,228	976	1,417	153[3]	384
1975	18,642	12,061	64.7	3,245	1,001	1,646	193[3]	496
1976	16,605	10,592	63.8	2,956	806	1,330	227[3]	694
1977	18,033	11,274	62.5	3,440	849	1,431	252[3]	787
1978	18,714	11,910	63.6	3,526	896	1,422	255[3]	705
1979	20,591	13,040	63.3	3,954	997	1,557	276[3]	767
1980	21,860	13,650	62.0	4,212	1,094	1,666	291[3]	947

1. Refers to club, hammer, etc. 2. Includes poison, explosives, unknown, and not stated; for 1973 to 1976, includes drowning 3. Arson only. *Source:* Department of Justice, Federal Bureau of Investigation, *Uniform Crime Reports for the United State 1980.*

South Leads in Crime

According to final 1981 Crime Index figures compiled by the Federal Bureau of Investigation, the Southern states, the most populous region, accounted for 32% of the offenses, followed by the Western states with 24%, the North Central states with 23%, and the Northeastern States with 21%. Compared to the 1980 figures, the Southern state experienced a 1% increase, the Western states n change, and the North Central and Northeaster states 1% declines.

Notable Books, 1981

This list has been compiled by the Notable Books Council of the American Library Association for use by the general reader and by librarians who work with adult readers. The titles were selected for their significant contribution to the expansion of knowledge or for the pleasure they can provide to adult readers. Criteria include wide general appeal and literary merit.

Allen, Gay Wilson, **Waldo Emerson,** Viking
Ashbery, John, **Shadow Train,** Viking
Atwood, Margaret, **Two-Headed Poems,** Simon & Schuster
Berke, Roberta, **Bounds Out of Bounds: A Compass for Recent American and British Poetry,** Oxford University Press
Bowen, Elizabeth, **The Collected Stories of Elizabeth Bowen,** Knopf
Brent, Peter, **Charles Darwin: A Man of Enlarged Curiosity,** Harper
Carpenter, Humphrey, **W.H. Auden: A Biography,** Houghton
Carver, Raymond, **What We Talk about When We Talk about Love,** Knopf
Fallows, James, **National Defense,** Random
From the Country of Eight Islands: An Anthology of Japanese Poetry, edited and translated by Hiroaki Sato and Burton Watson, University of Washington Press
Garside, Roger, **Coming Alive: China after Mao,** McGraw
Goodfield, June, **An Imagined World: A Story of Scientific Discovery,** Harper
Gordimer, Nadine, **July's People,** Viking
Gould, Stephen Jay, **The Mismeasure of Man,** Norton
Halberstam, David, **The Breaks of the Game,** Knopf
Hampl, Patricia, **A Romantic Education,** Houghton
Hughes, Robert, **The Shock of the New,** Knopf
Johanson, Donald C., and Edey, Maitland A., **Lucy: The Beginnings of Humankind,** Simon & Schuster
McCullough, David, **Mornings on Horseback,** Simon & Schuster
Malone, Dumas, **The Sage of Monticello (Jefferson and His Time, vol. 6),** Little
Mariani, Paul, **William Carlos Williams: A New World Naked,** McGraw
Mooney, Ted, **Easy Travel to Other Planets: A Novel,** Farrar
Neely, Richard, **How Courts Govern America,** Yale University Press
Nijinska, Bronislava, **Bronislava Nijinska: Early Memoirs,** translated and edited by Irina Nijinska and Jean Rawlinson, Holt
O'Connor, Frank, **Collected Stories,** Knopf
Peters, F.E., **Ours: The Making and Unmaking of a Jesuit,** Marek
Plante, David, **The Country,** Atheneum
Plath, Sylvia, **The Collected Poems,** edited by Ted Hughes, Harper
Pond, Elizabeth, **From the Yaroslavsky Station: Russia Perceived,** Universe
Robinson, Marilynne, **Housekeeping,** Farrar
Santoli, Al, **Everything We Had: An Oral History of the Vietnam War by Thirty-Three American Soldiers Who Fought It,** Random
Schwartz-Nobel, Loretta, **Starving in the Shadow of Plenty,** Putnam
Smith, Adam, **Paper Money,** Summit
Spence, Jonathan D., **The Gate of Heavenly Peace: The Chinese and Their Revolution, 1895–1980,** Viking
Spencer, Elizabeth, **The Stories of Elizabeth Spencer,** Doubleday
Stratton, Joanna L., **Pioneer Women: Voices from the Kansas Frontier,** Simon & Schuster
Timerman, Jacobo, **Prisoner without a Name, Cell without a Number,** Knopf
Totman, Conrad, **Japan before Perry: a Short History,** University of California
Tuchman, Barbara, **Practicing History: Selected Essays,** Knopf
Updike, John, **Rabbit Is Rich,** Knopf
Wilford, John Noble, **The Mapmakers,** Knopf
Woods, Donald, **Asking for Trouble: Autobiography of a Banned Journalist,** Atheneum

Source: Reprinted by permission of the American Library Association. Issued as a pamphlet by ALA, 50 E. Huron St., Chicago, Il. 60611, annually in the spring for the preceding year.

Major U.S. Symphony Orchestras and Their Music Directors

Source: American Symphony Orchestra League.

tlanta Symphony: Robert Shaw
altimore Symphony: Sergiu Comissiona
oston Symphony: Seiji Ozawa
uffalo Philharmonic: Julius Rudel
hicago Symphony: Georg Solti
incinnati Symphony: Michael Gielen
leveland Orchestra: Christoph von Dohnanyi
allas Symphony: Eduardo Mata
enver Symphony: Gaetano Delogu
etroit Symphony: Gary Bertini[2]
ouston Symphony: Sergiu Comissiona[1]
dianapolis Symphony: John Nelson
ansas City Philharmonic: Thomas Michalak[2]
os Angeles Philharmonic: Carlo Maria Giulini
ilwaukee Symphony: Lukas Foss
innesota Orchestra: Neville Marriner
ational Symphony: (Washington, D.C.): Mstislav Rostropovich
New Orleans Philharmonic Symphony Orchestra: Philippe Entremont
New York Philharmonic: Zubin Mehta
Oregon Symphony: James DePreist
Philadelphia Orchestra: Riccardo Muti
Pittsburgh Symphony: André Previn
Rochester Philharmonic: David Zinman
Saint Louis Symphony: Leonard Slatkin
Saint Paul Chamber Orchestra: Pinchas Zukerman
San Antonio Symphony: Lawrence Smith
San Diego Symphony: David Atherton
San Francisco Symphony: Edo de Waart
Seattle Symphony: Rainer Miedel
Syracuse Symphony: Christopher Keene
Utah Symphony: Varujan Kojian

Artistic Advisor. 2. Musical Advisor.

Major Public Libraries

City (branches)	Volumes	Circulation	Budget (in millions)
Akron, Ohio (18)	1,065,417	2,012,535	$ 4.8
Albuquerque, N.M. (7)	376,832	1,575,518	2.6
Annapolis, Md. (12)	1,068,247	3,605,009	4.4
Atlanta (26)	1,335,352	3,943,014	7.1
Austin, Tex. (15)	675,163	2,177,742	5.8
Baltimore (33)	2,188,901	2,318,562	10.4
Baton Rouge, La. (8)	410,041	1,260,737	2.2
Birmingham, Ala. (18)	1,100,118	2,000,158	4.3
Boston (24)	4,878,195	1,603,875	8.5
Buffalo, N.Y. (60)	3,479,650	5,781,970	13.6
Charleston, W.Va. (11)	539,444	1,101,728	1.8
Charlotte, N.C. (15)	762,250	1,975,793	4.0
Chicago (90)	6,354,072	7,811,071	41.6
Cincinnati (39)	3,312,783	6,045,487	11.1
Cleveland (32)	2,332,702	3,368,812	19.4
Columbus, Ohio (21)	1,228,969	3,652,452	8.2
Dallas (18)	1,706,262	3,714,591	9.2
Dayton, Ohio (19)	1,412,551	4,692,202	5.9
Denver (21)	1,767,159	2,838,966	8.7
Des Moines, Iowa (5)	481,000	1,245,575	2.0
Detroit (26)	2,413,462	1,719,039	15.2
D.C. (26)	1,334,289	1,528,580	10.4
El Paso (8)	472,950	1,112,448	2.5
Erie, Pa. (6)	397,826	1,250,075	1.8
Evansville, Ind. (7)	501,806	1,596,806	2.1
Fort Wayne, Ind. (12)	1,670,317	1,644,883	4.1
Fort Worth (7)	779,362	2,476,120	3.4
Grand Rapids, Mich. (5)	600,708	850,071	2.3
Greenville, S.C. (10)	484,379	1,155,055	2.3
Honolulu (21)	1,408,655	3,607,099	5.6
Houston (29)	2,556,013	5,907,226	15.6
Independence, Mo. (24)	1,179,457	3,113,132	4.4
Indianapolis (23)	1,379,124	3,945,402	7.8
Jackson, Miss. (37)	886,041	1,393,843	2.6
Jacksonville, Fla. (11)	1,307,480	2,157,906	3.3
Kansas City, Mo. (13)	1,222,644	975,000	4.5
Knoxville, Tenn. (19)	604,187	1,672,469	2.3
Lincoln, Neb. (9)	420,557	1,091,860	1.8
Long Beach, Calif. (10)	702,692	1,950,000	6.6
Los Angeles (County) (100)	4,896,134	9,677,185	29.5
Louisville, Ky. (20)	1,139,534	2,371,199	5.1
Madison, Wis. (7)	559,432	2,015,803	$ 3.5
Memphis, Tenn. (21)	1,354,005	2,572,297	6.8
Miami, Fla. (20)	3,626,395	1,827,914	16.1
Milwaukee (12)	2,335,485	3,632,727	10.3
Minneapolis (14)	1,624,196	2,623,039	9.5
Nashville, Tenn. (15)	519,717	1,821,855	3.8
Newark, N.J. (12)	1,216,335	1,726,000	5.2
New Orleans (11)	764,302	1,180,340	3.9
New York City (83)	3,386,107	7,769,193	37.1
Research	6,819,362	—	22.8
Brooklyn (58)	2,776,281	6,667,318	19.2
Queens (59)	4,402,504	6,245,766	19.9
Norfolk, Va. (11)	683,261	1,050,842	2.5
Oklahoma City (10)	620,112	1,804,693	3.2
Omaha, Neb. (9)	555,789	1,713,021	2.9
Philadelphia (52)	2,940,867	5,003,398	19.5
Phoenix, Ariz. (9)	1,186,373	3,691,745	6.0
Pittsburgh (20)	1,793,906	2,897,382	7.4
Portland, Ore. (16)	1,155,392	3,204,212	5.2
Providence, R.I. (7)	724,810	605,498	2.5
Richmond, Va. (6)	642,319	1,091,239	1.7
Rochester, N.Y. (11)	916,939	1,456,760	5.8
Sacramento, Calif. (26)	1,120,000	3,503,824	6.5
St. Louis (14)	1,372,574	1,429,294	5.4
St. Paul (10)	759,289	1,841,426	3.7
St. Petersburg, Fla. (4)	444,571	1,185,712	1.4
Salt Lake County, Utah (14)	825,138	2,866,761	5.8
San Antonio (12)	1,149,135	2,275,106	3.7
San Diego, Calif. (29)	1,684,719	4,235,888	6.2
San Francisco (26)	1,701,815	2,435,234	9.0
San Jose, Calif. (16)	1,144,840	2,565,450	4.7
Seattle (22)	1,542,440	4,605,302	10.5
Springfield, Mass. (8)	719,123	987,851	3.1
Tampa, Fla. (14)	1,111,262	2,088,708	4.5
Tucson, Ariz. (15)	750,000	3,500,000	6.0
Tulsa, Okla. (20)	854,640	1,753,570	6.3
Wichita, Kan. (11)	450,396	1,173,098	2.7
Winston–Salem, N.C. (8)	324,077	1,321,468	2.2
Worcester, Mass. (6)	991,300	805,596	2.1
Youngstown, Ohio (23)	690,460	1,441,394	3.5

Source: Information Please questionnaires to the libraries.

Glossary of Art Movements

Abstract Expressionism. American art movement of the 1940s that emphasized form and color within a nonrepresentational framework. Jackson Pollock initiated the revolutionary technique of splattering the paint directly on canvas to achieve the subconscious interpretation of the artist's inner vision of reality.

Art Deco. A 1920s style characterized by setbacks, zigzag forms, and the use of chrome and plastic ornamentation. New York's Chrysler Building is an architectural example of the style.

Art Nouveau. An 1890s style in architecture, graphic arts, and interior decoration characterized by writhing forms, curving lines, and asymmetrical organization. Some critics regard the style as the first stage of modern architecture.

Ashcan School. A group of New York realist artists, formed in 1908, who abandoned decorous subject matter and portrayed the more common as well as the sordid aspects of city life.

Assemblage (Collage). Forms of modern sculpture and painting utilizing readymades, found objects, and pasted fragments to form an abstract composition. Louise Nevelson's boxlike enclosures, each with its own composition of assembled objects, illustrate the style in sculpture. Pablo Picasso developed the technique of cutting and pasting natural or manufactured materials to a painted or unpainted surface.

Barbizon School (Landscape Painting). A group of painters who, around the middle of the 19th century, reacted against classical landscape and advocated a direct study of nature. They were influenced by English and Dutch landscape masters. Theodore Rousseau, one of the principa figures of the group, led the fight for outdoor painting. In this respect, the school was a forerunner of Impressionism.

Baroque. European art and architecture of the 17th and 18th centuries. Giovanni Bernini, a major exponent of the style, believed in the union of the arts of architecture, painting, and sculpture to overwhelm the spectator with ornate and highly dramatized themes. Although the style originated in Rome as the instrument of the Church, it spread throughout Europe in such monumental creations as the Palace of Versailles.

Beaux Arts. Elaborate and formal architectural style characterized by symmetry and an abundance of sculptured ornamentation. New York's old Custom House at Bowling Green is an example of the style.

Black or Afro-American Art. The work of American artists of African descent produced in various styles characterized by a mood of protest and a search for identity and historical roots.

Classicism. A form of art derived from the study of Greek and Roman styles characterized by harmony, balance, and serenity. In contrast, the Romantic Movement gave free rein to the artist's imagination and to the love of the exotic.

Constructivism. A form of sculpture using wood, metal, glass, and modern industrial materials expressing the technological society. The mobiles of Alexander Calder are examples of the movement.

Cubism. Early 20th-century French movement marked by a revolutionary departure from representational art. Pablo Picasso and Georges Bracque penetrated the surface of objects, stressing basic abstract geometric forms that presented the object from many angles simultaneously.

Dada. A product of the turbulent and cynical post-World War I period, this anti-art movement extolled the irrational, the absurd, the nihilistic, and the nonsensical. The reproduction of Mona Lisa adorned with a mustache is a famous example. The movement is regarded as a precursor of Surrealism. Some critics regard HAPPENINGS as a recent development of Dada. This movement incorporates environment and spectators as active and important ingredients in the production of random events.

Expressionism. A 20th-century European art movement that stresses the expression of emotion and the inner vision of the artist rather than the exact representation of nature. Distorted lines and shapes and exaggerated colors are used for emotional impact. Vincent Van Gogh is regarded as the precursor of this movement.

Fauvism. The name "wild beasts" was given to this group of early 20th-century French painters because their work was characterized by distortion and violent colors. Henri Matisse and Georges Roualt were leaders of this group.

Futurism. This early 20th-century movement originating in Italy glorified the machine age and attempted to represent machines and figures in motion. The aesthetics of Futurism affirmed the beauty of technological society.

Genre. This French word meaning "type" now refers to paintings that depict scenes of everyday life without any attempt at idealization. Genre paintings can be found in all ages, but the Dutch productions of peasant and tavern scenes are typical.

Impressionism. Late 19th-century French school dedicated to defining transitory visual impressions painted directly from nature, with light and color of primary importance. If the atmosphere changed, a totally different picture would emerge. It was not the object or event that counted but the visual impression as caught at a certain time of day under a certain light. Claude Monet and Camille Pissarro were leaders of the movement.

Mannerism. A mid-16th century movement, Italian in origin, although El Greco was a major practitioner of the style. The human figure, distorted and elongated, was the most frequent subject.

Neoclassicism. An 18th-century reaction to the excesses of Baroque and Rococo, this European art movement tried to recreate the art of Greece and Rome by imitating the ancient classics both in style and subject matter.

Op Art. The 1960s movement known as Optical Painting is characterized by geometrical forms that create an optical illusion in which the eye is required to blend the colors at a certain distance.

Pop Art. In this return to representational art, the artist returns to the world of tangible objects in a reaction against abstraction. Materials are drawn from the everyday world of popular culture—comic strips, canned goods, and science fiction.

Rococo. A French style of interior decoration developed during the reign of Louis XV consisting mainly of asymmetrical arrangements of curves in paneling, porcelain, and gold and silver objects. The characteristics of ornate curves, prettiness, and gaiety can also be found in the painting and sculpture of the period.

Surrealism. A further development of Collage, Cubism, and Dada, this 20th-century movement stresses the weird, the fantastic, and the dreamworld of the subconscious. Salvador Dali's distorted timepiece in the desert is typical.

Support for the Arts in 1982

Federal aid to the arts will decrease by 37% in 1983, from the current $143 million to $100.3 million. Since 1980, federal support for the arts has dropped by nearly $88 million.

According to the Business Committee for the Arts, corporate investment in the arts in 1982 was in excess of $500 million. This figure is vigorously contested, however, by arts administrators who claim the total includes money spent on advertising and other commercial uses of the arts.

The most generous state in arts appropriations remains New York, spending $35.5 million in 1982. At $50,155, New Hampshire spent the least.

Top 10 Classical Albums, 1981

1. **Pavarotti's Greatest Hits,** Luciano Pavarotti (London)
2. **Jean-Pierre Rampal & Claude Bolling: Suite for Flute & Jazz Piano,** Rampal & Bolling (CBS)
3. **O Sole Mio: Neapolitan Songs,** Luciano Pavarotti (London)
4. **Pachelbel: Kanon,** Paillard Chamber Orchestra (RCA)
5. **Bolling: Picnic Suite for Flute, Guitar & Jazz Piano,** Jean-Pierre Rampal, Claude Bolling, Alexandre Lagoya (CBS)
6. **Annie's Song: Galway,** James Galway, National Philharmonic Orchestra, (Gerhardt) (RCA)
7. **Hits from Lincoln Center,** Luciano Pavarotti (London)
8. **Pavarotti: Verismo Arias,** Luciano Pavarotti (London)
9. **Bravo Pavarotti,** Luciano Pavarotti (London)
10. **A Different Kind of Blues,** Itzhak Perlman & Andre Previn (Angel)

Source: Billboard. © Billboard Publications, Inc., 1981. Dec. 26, 1981. Reprinted by permission.

Artists of the Year, 1981

Based on combined singles and albums chart performance—through sales and radio play—during the year.

Single of the Year: Bette Davis Eyes, Kim Carnes
Album of the Year: Hi Infidelity, REO Speedwagon
Female Artist of the Year: Pat Benatar
Male Artist of the Year: Kenny Rogers
Group of the Year: REO Speedwagon
New Artist of the Year: Sheena Easton
Country Artist of the Year: Kenny Rogers
Disco Artist of the Year: Fantasy
Adult Contemporary Artist of the Year: Kenny Rogers
Jazz Artist of the Year: Grover Washington, Jr.
Soundtrack of the Year: The Jazz Singer (Capitol)

Source: Billboard. © Billboard Publications, Inc., 1981. Dec. 26, 1981. Reprinted by permission.

Top 10 Pop Albums, 1981

1. **Hi Infidelity,** REO Speedwagon (Epic)
2. **Double Fantasy,** John Lennon & Yoko Ono (Giffen)
3. **Greatest Hits,** Kenny Rogers (Liberty)
4. **Christopher Cross,** Christopher Cross (Warner Bros.)
5. **Crimes of Passion,** Pat Benatar (Chrysalis)
6. **Paradise Theater,** Styx (A&M)
7. **Back in Black,** AC/DC (Atlantic)
8. **Voices,** Daryl Hall & John Oates (RCA)
9. **Zenyatta Mondatta,** The Police (A&M)
10. **The River,** Bruce Springsteen (Columbia)

Source: Billboard. © Billboard Publications, Inc., 1981. Dec. 26, 1981. Reprinted by permission.

Manufacturers' Dollar Shipments of Phonograph Records
(in millions)

	Singles		Albums	
Year	Units	Dollars[1]	Units	Dollars[1]
1975	164	$212	257	$1,485
1976	190	245	273	1,663
1977	190	245	344	2,195
1978	190	260	341	2,473
1979	212	354	290	2,058
1980	157	250	308	2,200
1981	147	246	273	2,113

1. List price value. *Source:* Recording Industry Association of America, Inc.

Top 10 Country Single Recordings, 1981

1. **Fire and Smoke,** Earl Thomas Conley (Sunbird)
2. **No Gettin' Over Me,** Ronnie Milsap (RCA)
3. **Seven Year Ache,** Rosanne Cash (Columbia)
4. **I Don't Need You,** Kenny Rogers (Liberty)
5. **Party Time,** T.G. Sheppard (Warner/Curb)
6. **But You Know I Love You,** Dolly Parton (RCA)
7. **Midnight Hauler/Scratch My Back,** Razzy Bailey (RCA)
8. **Friends,** Razzy Bailey (RCA)
9. **Feels So Right,** Alabama (RCA)
10. **Too Many Lovers,** Crystal Gayle (Columbia)

Source: Billboard. © Billboard Publications, Inc., 1981. Dec. 26, 1981. Reprinted by permission.

Top 10 Pop Single Recordings, 1981

1. **Bette Davis Eyes,** Kim Carnes (EMI America)
2. **Endless Love,** Diana Ross & Lionel Richie, Jr. (Motown)
3. **Lady,** Kenny Rogers (Liberty)
4. **Starting Over,** John Lennon (Geffen)
5. **Jessie's Girl,** Rick Springfield (RCA)
6. **Celebration,** Kool & The Gang (De-Lite)
7. **Kiss on My List,** Daryl Hall & Joan Oates (RCA)
8. **I love a Rainy Night,** Eddie Rabbitt (Elektra)
9. **9 to 5,** Dolly Parton (RCA)
10. **Keep on Loving You,** REO Speedwagon (Epic)

Source: Billboard. © Billboard Publications, Inc., 1981. Dec. 26, 1981. Reprinted by permission.

Top 10 Soul Single Recordings, 1981

1. **Endless Love,** Diana Ross & Lionel Richie, Jr., Motown
2. **Master Blaster,** Stevie Wonder, Tamla
3. **Give It To Me Baby,** Rick James, Gordy
4. **Don't Stop the Music,** Yarbrough & Peoples, Mercury
5. **Being With You,** Smokey Robinson, Tamla
6. **Double Dutch Bus,** Frankie Smith, WMOT
7. **Celebration,** Kool & The Gang, De-Lite
8. **Sukiyaki,** A Taste of Honey, Capitol
9. **What Cha' Gonna Do for Me,** Chaka Khan, Warner Bros.
10. **Fantastic Voyage,** Lakeside, Solar

Source: Billboard. © Billboard Publications, Inc. 1981. Dec. 26, 1981. Reprinted by permission.

Audience Composition of Selected Prime Time Program Types

	General drama	Suspense and mystery drama	Situation comedy	Feature films	All regular network programs 7–11 p.m.
Women (18 years old and over)	12,500,000	10,650,000	11,780,000	11,510,000	11,440,000
Men (18 and over)	7,670,000	8,420,000	8,620,000	9,550,000	9,220,000
Teens (12–17)	1,390,000	1,790,000	2,510,000	2,220,000	1,940,000
Children (2–11)	2,130,000	2,130,000	4,280,000	2,270,000	2,950,000
Total	**23,920,000**	**22,990,000**	**27,190,000**	**25,550,000**	**25,550,000**

1. All figures are estimated for the period November 1981. *Source:* A. C. Nielsen Company, Nielsen Television Index Audience Estimates.

Top 15 Regular Prime Time TV Programs of 1981–82[1]

Rank	Program name (network)	Total percent of TV households
1.	60 Minutes (CBS)	28.1
2.	Dallas (CBS)	27.7
3.	Three's Company (ABC)	24.0
4.	M*A*S*H (CBS)	23.4
5.	Too Close for Comfort (ABC)	22.7
6.	One Day at a Time (CBS)	22.4
7.	ABC Sunday Night Movie	21.9
8.	NFL Monday Night Football (ABC)	21.8
9.	Archie Bunker's Place (CBS)	21.7
10.	The Dukes of Hazzard (CBS)	21.3
11.	Magnum, P.I. (CBS)	21.2
12.	Alice (CBS)	21.0
13.	The Facts of Life (NBC)	20.9
14.	Happy Days (ABC)	20.9
15.	Love Boat (ABC)	20.9
	Total U.S. TV households	**81,500,000**

1. Oct. 26, 1981, through Nov. 23, 1981. NOTE: Percentages are calculated from average audience viewings, 15 minutes or longer and 4 or more telecasts. *Source:* A. C. Nielsen Company, Nielsen Television Index Audience Estimates.

Television Network Addresses

American Broadcasting Companies (ABC)
1330 Avenue of the Americas
New York, N.Y. 10019

Canadian Broadcasting Corporation (CBC)
1500 Bronson Avenue
Ottawa, Ontario, Canada K1G 3J5

Columbia Broadcasting System (CBS)
51 W. 52nd Street
New York, N.Y. 10019

Metromedia, Inc. (WNEW)
655 3rd Avenue
New York, N.Y. 10017

National Broadcasting Company (NBC)
30 Rockefeller Plaza
New York, N.Y. 10020

Public Broadcasting Service (PBS)
475 L'Enfant Plaza West, S.W.
Washington, D.C. 20024

Westinghouse Broadcasting (Group W)
90 Park Avenue
New York, N.Y. 10016

Source of Household Viewing—Prime Time

Pay Cable, Basic Cable, and Non-Cable Households

	Nov. 1981			Nov. 1980			Nov. 1979		
	Pay cable	Basic cable	Non-cable	Pay cable	Basic cable	Non-cable	Pay cable	Basic cable	Non-cable
% TV Usage[1]	70.6	60.5	62.0	73.2	65.6	62.2	70.0	65.7	59.1
Pay Cable	12.0	—	—	10.9	—	—	10.5	—	—
Cable-originated programming	3.2	2.6	—	2.9	2.2	—	1.9	2.4	—
Other-on-air stations	13.3	10.7	9.5	12.1	11.4	8.7	9.5	10.0	6.8
Network affiliated stations	45.8	49.0	53.7	50.9	53.8	54.7	50.5	55.7	53.5
Network share[2]	(65)	(81)	(87)	(70)	(82)	(88)	(72)	(85)	(91)

1. May be less than sum of reception sources because of simultaneous viewing. 2. Percent Network/Sum of Sources. *Source:* A. C. Nielsen Company, Nielsen Television Index Estimates.

Weekly TV Viewing by Age
(in hours and minutes)

	Time per week	
	1981	1980
Women 18–34 years old	30 h 09 min	29 h 44 min
Women 35–54	32 h 37 min	33 h 31 min
Women 55 and over	39 h 20 min	38 h 26 min
Men 18–34	26 h 30 min	25 h 24 min
Men 35–54	27 h 41 min	27 h 28 min
Men 55 and over	35 h 43 min	35 h 39 min
Female Teens	18 h 19 min	22 h 19 min
Male Teens	22 h 28 min	23 h 40 min
Children 6–11	24 h 28 min	25 h 44 min
Children 2–5	27 h 04 min	29 h 14 min
Total Persons	**29 h 32 min**	**29 h 46 min**

NOTE: All figures are estimates based on National Audience Demographics Report, November 1981. *Source:* A. C. Nielsen Company, Nielsen Television Index Audience Estimates.

Persons Viewing Nightly Prime Time TV[1]
(in millions)

	Total persons[2]
Monday	94.7
Tuesday	90.5
Wednesday	90.2
Thursday	86.4
Friday	92.1
Saturday	88.5
Sunday	106.9
Total average	**92.8**

1. Average minute audiences. 2. Based on National Demographics Report (November 1981). NOTE: Prime time is 8-11 p.m. (EST), except 7-11 p.m. Sunday. *Source:* A. C. Nielsen Company, Nielsen Television Index Audience Estimates.

Top 10 Syndicated TV Programs of 1981–82

Rank	Program	Rating (% U.S.)[1]
1.	M*A*S*H	13.9
2.	Family Feud (P.M.)	13.2
3.	PM Magazine	12.7
4.	Hee Haw	9.7
5.	Happy Days Again	8.8
6.	Barney Miller	8.7
7.	Tic Tac Dough	8.7
8.	Laverne & Shirley	8.4
9.	You Asked For It	8.4
10.	Dance Fever	8.1

1. During November 1981. Ranked on the basis of average 15-minute audience ratings. *Source:* A.C. Nielsen Company, Nielsen Television Index Audience Estimates.

Average Hours of Household TV Usage
(in hours and minutes per day)

	Yearly average	February	July
1965–66	5 h 30 min	6 h 28 min	4 h 23 min
1970–71	6 h 01 min	6 h 53 min	5 h 08 min
1975–76	6 h 11 min	6 h 49 min	5 h 33 min
1976–77	6 h 13 min	6 h 55 min	5 h 13 min
1977–78	6 h 13 min	7 h 00 min	5 h 32 min
1978–79	6 h 26 min	7 h 11 min	5 h 46 min
1979–80	6 h 35 min	7 h 22 min	5 h 48 min
1980–81	6 h 44 min	7 h 32 min	6 h 08 min

NOTE: Estimates are based on total U.S. TV households, excluding unusual days. *Source:* A. C. Nielsen Company, Nielsen Television Index Audience Estimates.

Major U.S. Opera Companies

Boston Lyric Opera Company, Inc.; Gen. Dir.: John Balme
Dallas Civic Opera; Gen. Dir.: Plato S. Karayanis
Fort Worth Opera Association; Gen. Mgr.: Rudolf Kruger
Greater Miami Opera Association; Art. Dir.: Emerson Buckley
Houston Grand Opera Association; Gen. Dir.: R. David Gockley
Kentucky Opera Association; Gen. Dir.: Thomson Smillie
Lyric Opera of Chicago; Gen. Mgr.: Ardis Krainik
Lyric Opera of Kansas City; Gen. Mgr.: Russell Patterson
Metropolitan Opera Association; Gen. Mgr.: Anthony A. Bliss
Michigan Opera Theater; Gen. Dir.: David DiChiera
New Orleans Opera Association; Gen. Dir.: Arthur Cosenza
New York Opera Company; Gen. Dir.: Beverly Sills
Opera Company of Boston; Art. Dir.: Sarah Caldwell
Opera Company of Philadelphia; Mgr.: Margaret Anne Everitt
Portland (Ore.) Opera Association; Gen. Dir.: Stefan Minde
San Diego Opera Association; Gen. Dir.: Tito Capobianco
San Francisco Opera Association; Gen. Dir.: Terence A. McEwen
Santa Fe Opera; Gen. Dir.: John O. Crosby
Seattle Opera Association; Gen. Dir.: Glynn Ross
Tulsa Opera Company; Gen. Dir.: Edward C. Purrington

Major U.S. Dance Companies

Figure in parentheses is year of founding
Alvin Ailey American Dance Theatre (1958); Dir.: Alvin Ailey
American Ballet Theatre (1940); Dir.: Mikhail Baryshnikov
Boston Ballet (1964); Dir.: E. Virginia Williams
Dance Theatre of Harlem, The (1968); Dir.: Arthur Mitchell and Karel Shook
Feld Ballet, The (1974); Dir.: Eliot Feld
Houston Ballet (1968); Art. Dir.: Ben Stevenson
Joffrey Ballet, The (1954); Art. Dir.: Robert Joffrey
José Limón Dance Company (1946); Art. Dir.: Carla Maxwell
Martha Graham Dance Company (1927); Dir.: Martha Graham
Merce Cunningham Dance Group (1952); Dir.: Merce Cunningham
New York City Ballet (1948); Ballet Masters: George Balanchine, Jerome Robbins, John Taras, Peter Martins
Nikolais Dance Theatre (1948); Dir.: Alwin Nikolais
Paul Taylor Dance Company (1954); Dir.: Paul Taylor
Pennsylvania Ballet (1963); Art. Dir.: Robert Weiss
Pittsburgh Ballet Theater (1970); Art. Dir.: Patricia Wilde
San Francisco Ballet (1933); Dirs.: Lew Christensen and Michael Smuin
Twyla Tharp Dance Foundation (1965); Art. Dir.: Twyla Tharp
Washington Ballet (1962); Dir.: Mary Day

Major U.S. Fairs and Expositions

1853 Crystal Palace Exposition, New York City: modeled on similar fair held in London.

1876 Centennial Exposition, Philadelphia: celebrating 100th year of independence.

1893 World's Columbian Exposition, Chicago: commemorating 400th anniversary of Columbus' voyage to America.

1894 Midwinter International Exposition, San Francisco: promoting business revival after Depression of 1893.

1898 Trans-Mississippi and International Exposition, Omaha, Neb.: exhibiting products, resources, industries, and civilization of states and territories west of the Mississippi River.

1901 Pan-American Exposition, Buffalo, N.Y.: promoting social and commercial interest of Western Hemisphere nations.

1904 Louisiana Purchase Exposition, St. Louis: marking 100th anniversary of major land acquisition from France and opening up of the West.

1905 Lewis and Clark Centennial Exposition, Portland, Ore.: commemorating 100th anniversary of exploration of a land route to the Pacific.

1907 Jamestown Ter Centennial Exposition, Hampton Roads, Va.: marking 300th anniversary of first permanent English settlement in America.

1909 Alaska-Yukon-Pacific Exposition, Seattle: celebrating growth of the Puget Sound area.

1915–16 Panama-Pacific International Exposition, San Francisco: celebrating opening of the Panama Canal.

1915–16 Panama-California Exposition, San Diego: promoting resources and opportunities for development and commerce of the Western states.

1926 Sesquicentennial Exposition, Philadelphia: marking 150th year of independence.

1933–34 Century of Progress International Exposition, Chicago: celebrating 100th anniversary of incorporation of Chicago as a city.

1935 California Pacific International Exposition, San Diego: marking 400 years of progress since the first Spaniard landed on the West Coast.

1939–40 New York World's Fair, New York City: "The World of Tomorrow," symbolized by Trylon and Perisphere. Officially commemorating 150th anniversary of inauguration of George Washington as President in New York.

1939–40 Golden Gate International Exposition, Treasure Island, San Francisco: celebrating new Golden Gate Bridge and Oakland Bay Bridge.

1962 The Century 21 Exposition, Seattle: "Man in the Space Age," symbolized by 600-foot steel space needle.

1964–65 New York World's Fair, New York City: "Peace Through Understanding."

1974 Expo '74, Spokane: "Tomorrow's Fresh, New Environment."

1982 World's Fair, Knoxville, Tenn.: "Energy Turns the World," symbolized by the bronze-globed Sunsphere.

Motion Picture Revenues

TOP MONEY-MAKERS[1]

1. Star Wars (1977)	$185,138,000
2. The Empire Strikes Back (1980)	134,209,000
3. Jaws (1975)	133,435,000
4. Grease (1978)	96,300,000
5. Raiders of the Lost Ark (1981)	90,434,000
6. The Exorcist (1973)	88,500,000
7. The Godfather (1972)	86,275,000
8. Superman (1978)	82,500,000
9. The Sound of Music (1965)	79,748,000
10. The Sting (1973)	78,693,000
11. Close Encounters of the Third Kind (1977)	77,000,000
12. Gone With the Wind (1939)	76,700,000
13. Saturday Night Fever (1977)	74,100,000
14. National Lampoon's Animal House (1978)	74,000,000
15. Superman II (1981)	64,000,000
16. Kramer vs. Kramer (1979)	61,734,000
17. Smokey and the Bandit (1977)	61,055,000
18. One Flew Over the Cuckoo's Nest (1975)	59,166,000
19. Stir Crazy (1980)	58,408,000
20. 9 to 5 (1980)	57,850,000
21. Star Trek (1979)	56,000,000
22. Rocky (1976)	55,892,000
23. American Graffiti (1973)	55,886,000
24. Jaws II (1978)	55,608,000
25. Every Which Way but Loose (1978)	51,800,000

TOP RENTALS OF 1981[2]

1. Raiders of the Lost Ark (Paramount)	$90,434,000
2. Superman II (Warner Bros.)	64,000,000
3. Stir Crazy (Columbia)	58,408,000
4. 9 to 5 (20th Century-Fox)	57,850,000
5. Stripes (Columbia)	39,514,000
6. Any Which Way You Can (Warner Bros.)	39,500,000
7. Arthur (Orion/Warner Bros.)	37,000,000
8. The Cannonball Run (20th Century–Fox)	35,378,000
9. The Four Seasons (Universal)	26,800,000
10. For Your Eyes Only (M–G–M–United Artists)	25,439,000
11. Seems Like Old Times (Columbia)	22,068,000
12. The Fox and the Hound (Buena Vista)	18,000,000
13. Cheech and Chong's Nice Dreams (Columbia)	17,636,000
14. Excalibur (Warner Bros.)	17,000,000
15. Flash Gordon (Universal)	16,100,000
16. Time Bandits (Embassy)	16,000,000
17. The Great Muppet Caper (Universal/Associated Film Distribution)	16,000,000
18. Tarzan, the Ape Man (M–G–M–/United Artists)	15,642,000
19. Clash of the Titans (M–G–M–/United Artists)	15,632,000
20. Bustin' Loose (Universal)	15,300,000
21. Endless Love (Universal)	15,100,000
22. The Empire Strikes Back (20th Century–Fox, reissue)	14,150,000
23. History of the World—Part I (20th Century–Fox)	13,852,000
24. Fort Apache, the Bronx (20th Century–Fox)	13,653,000
25. The Jazz Singer (Associated Film Distribution)	13,000,000

NOTE: United States and Canada only. 1. Figures are total rentals collected by film distributors as of Dec. 31, 1981. 2. Figures are not to be confused with gross box-office receipts from sale of tickets. *Source: Variety.*

Museums of the United States

Source: Information Please questionnaires to museums. NOTE: Admission fees and visiting hours are subject to change.

New York City

American Academy and Institute of Arts and Letters: 633 W. 155th St., NYC 10032. Open: Tues.-Sun. 1–4 during exhibitions (closed Mon. and natl. hldys.). Free.

Annual exhibitions of work of recipients of awards and honors, and paintings eligible for purchase under Hassam and Speicher Funds. Memorial exhibition of work of deceased members.

American Museum of Natural History: Central Park West at 79th St., NYC 10024. Open: Mon., Tues., Thurs., Fri., Sun., 10–5:45; Wed., Fri., Sat., 10–9. Suggested adm.: $3.00; children, $1.50.

All branches of natural sciences with exhibits including astronomy at American Museum-Hayden Planetarium.

Brooklyn Museum, The: Eastern Pkwy., Brooklyn, N.Y. 11238. Open: Wed.-Sat. 10–5, Sun. 12–5, hldys. 1–5 (closed Jan. 1, Dec. 25). Suggested adm.: $2; students $1; under 12s and senior citizens, free.

Egyptian and classical art, American and European paintings, decorative arts and period rooms, prints, drawings, costumes, and textiles. Arts of Africa, Oceania, Orient, Middle East, Islam, and New World. Two reference libraries, sculpture garden.

Cloisters, The: Ft. Tryon Pk., NYC 10040. Open: Tues.-Sat. 10–4:45; Sun. and hldys. 1–4:45 (May-Sept., 12–4:45) (closed Mon.). Suggested adm.: $4; students and senior citizens, $2.

Cloisters, chapel, chapter house, apse. The various cloisters are reconstituted from elements of 12–15th-century French cloisters. Apse has been relocated here in its entirety. Frescoes, polychromed statues, stained glass, tapestries, paintings, ivories, precious metalwork. Medieval branch of The Metropolitan Museum of Art.

Cooper-Hewitt Museum, the Smithsonian Institution's National Museum of Design: 2 E. 91st St., NYC 10028. Open: Tues. 10–9, Wed.-Sat. 10–5, Sun. 12–5 (closed Mon.; also Jan. 1, July 4, Thanksgiving, Dec. 25). Adm.: $1.50 (free on Tues. after 5).

Regularly changing exhibitions devoted to some aspect of design.

Frick Collection: 1 E. 70th St., NYC 10021. Open: Sept.-May—Tues.-Sat. 10–6, Sun. and most hldys. 1–6 (closed Mon.; also Jan. 1, Thanksgiving, Dec. 24–25); June-Aug.—Sun. 1–6, Wed.-Sat. 10–6 (closed Mon. and Tues.; also July 4). Adm.: Tues.-Sat. $1; students and senior citizens, 50¢; Sun. $2. Children under 10 not admitted.

Paintings, prints, drawings of 14th to 19th centuries, Italian Renaissance and French sculpture and furniture. Chinese and French porcelain. Concerts, lectures.

Guggenheim Museum, The Solomon R.: 1071 Fifth Ave. at 88th St., NYC 10028. Open: Tues. 11–8; Wed.-Sun. and hldys. 11–5 (closed Mon., except hldys., and Dec. 25). Adm.: $2; under 7s, free; Tues. 5–8 free. College students with ID's, and senior citizens, $1.25; student groups of more than 10 with a teacher, 75¢.

Works of leading 20th-century foreign and American painters and sculptors.

Hayden Planetarium. *See* American Museum of Natural History.

Hispanic Society of America, The (Museum and Library): Broadway and W. 155th St., NYC 10032. Museum open: Tues.-Sat. 10–4:30, Sun. 1–4 (closed Mon.; also Jan. 1, Feb. 12, Feb. 22, Good Friday, Easter, May 30, July 4, Thanksgiving, Dec. 25). During Christmas Week, museum is open for three consecutive days from Dec. 26 through Dec. 31. Library open: Tues.-Fri. 1–4:30, Sat. 10:30–4:30 (closed Sun., Mon.; also hldys., Good Friday, month of Aug., and for two weeks beginning Tues. before Christmas Eve). Free.

Paintings, sculpture, decorative arts, manuscripts, and incunabula, representative of Hispanic culture. Works on Hispanic art, history, literature.

Jewish Museum, The: 1109 Fifth Ave. at 92nd St., NYC 10028. Open: Mon.-Thurs., 12–5, Sun. 11–6 (closed Fri. and Sat., major Jewish hldys. and certain legal hldys). Adm.: $2; 6–16s and students with ID's, $1. Members, free; senior citizens, pay what you wish.

Former Warburg mansion and adjoining Albert A. List building house most extensive collection of Jewish ceremonial objects in Western Hemisphere. Changing exhibitions of sculpture, paintings, photography and architecture illuminate Jewish experience, culture, and tradition. Also family and school programs.

Metropolitan Museum of Art, The: Fifth Ave. at 82nd St., NYC 10028. Open: Tues. 10–8:45, Wed.-Sat. 10–4:45, Sun. and hldys. 11–4:45 (closed Mon.). Discretionary admission fee.

European and American paintings, drawings, sculpture, decorative arts, prints. Egyptian, Greek, Roman, Islamic, and Near and Far Eastern art. Arts of Africa, Pacific islands and pre-Columbian and native America. Musical instruments, arms and armor. European period rooms. Costumes and textiles. See also *Cloisters.*

Museum of the American Indian, Heye Foundation: Broadway at 155th St., NYC 10032. Open: Tues.-Sat. 10–5; Sun. 1–5 (closed Mon., also Jan. 1, Easter, July 4, Thanksgiving, Dec. 25). Adm.: $1.50; students and senior citizens, 75¢; groups of 10 or more, 25¢ per person.

Archeology, ethnology, and primitive-to-20th-century arts and artifacts of North, Central, and South America.

Museum of the City of New York: 1220 Fifth Ave. at 103rd St., NYC 10029. Open: Tues.-Sat. 10–5, Sun. and hldys. 1–5 (closed Mon.; also Jan. 1, Dec. 25). Free.

History and life of New York City. Period costumes, furniture, miniature scenes, portraits, paintings, prints, manuscripts, theater and music collection, silver, dolls and doll houses.

Museum of Modern Art, The: 11 W. 53rd St., NYC 10019. Open: Mon., Tues., Fri., Sat. and Sun. 11–6, Thurs. 11–9 (closed Wed.; also Dec. 25). Adm.: $3; students with IDs, $2; under 16s and senior citizens, $1. Tuesday, pay what you wish.

Founded 1929 to help people enjoy and understand the art of our times. Changing exhibitions of contemporary painting, sculpture, drawings, prints, photography, architecture, industrial and graphic design, films, video.

National Academy of Design: 1083 Fifth Ave. at 89th St., NYC 10028. Open: Tues.-Sun. 12–5.

Exhibitions from permanent collection of American paintings, sculptures and graphics; exhibitions of contemporary art.

New-York Historical Society: 170 Central Park West at 77th St., NYC 10024. Museum open; Tues.-Fri. 11–5, Sat. 10–5, Sun. 1–5. Library open to adults: Tues.-Sat. 10–5. (Both closed Mon.; also Jan. 1, July 4, Thanksgiving, Dec. 25). Library adm.: $2; museum, $2; children, 75¢.

New York city and state historical exhibits. Early American paintings and portraits. Period rooms. Audubon watercolors. Gallery of American silver.

Pierpont Morgan Library: 29 E. 36th St. NYC 10016. Open: Tues.-Sat. 10:30–5, Sun. 1–5 (closed Mon.; also legal hldys., Sundays in July, and month of August). Suggested adm.: $2.

Medieval and Renaissance illuminated manuscripts, rare books, music and autograph manuscripts, old master drawings, bindings, early children's books, ancient written records.

Whitney Museum of American Art: 945 Madison Ave. at 75th St., NYC 10021. Open: Wed.-Sat. 11–6, Tues. 11–8 (free 5–8), Sun. and hldys. 12–6 (closed Mon.; also Dec. 25). Adm.: $2.50; senior citizens, college students with ID, and under 12s accompanied by an adult, free.

Sculpture, paintings, watercolors, drawings, and prints by 20th-century American artists. Exhibitions of contemporary and historical American art. Daily film and video showings. Downtown Branch, 384 Broadway, New York, N.Y. 10013; Fairfield County Branch, One Champion Plaza, Stamford, Conn. 06921.

Chicago

Art Institute of Chicago, The: Michigan Ave. at Adams St., Chicago, Ill. 60603. Open: Mon.-Wed. and Fri. 10:30–4:30, Thurs. 10:30–8, Sat. 10–5, Sun. and hldys. 12–5 (Closed Dec. 25). Voluntary admission fee.

Paintings, sculpture, prints, drawings, textiles, photography. Oriental arts; European, American decorative arts; primitive art. Thorne Miniature Rooms. Junior Museum. Goodman Theatre, School of Art.

Beverly Art Center: 2153 W. 111th St., Chicago, Ill. 60643. Open: daily 8–6.

Exhibitions change monthly.

Chicago Academy of Sciences, Museum of Ecology: Lincoln Park—2001 North Clark St., Chicago, Ill. 60614. Open: daily 10–5 (closed Dec. 25). Free.

Exhibits of ecology of animal and plant life, minerals and fossils of Great Lakes region. Walk-through coal forest, cave, and canyon. Lectures, field trips, movies.

Chicago Historical Society: Clark St. and North Ave., Chicago, Ill. 60614. Open: Mon.-Sat. 9:30–4:30, Sun. 12–5 (closed Jan. 1, Thanksgiving, Dec. 25). Adm.: $1; 6–17s, 50¢; senior citizens, 25¢. Free on Monday. Research collection open Tues.-Sat. 9:30–4:30.

Exhibits and collections relating to Chicago and Illinois history, Illinois pioneer crafts, American history, Lincoln, Civil War.

Field Museum of Natural History: Roosevelt Rd. at Lake Shore Dr., Chicago, Ill. 60605. Open: Daily 9–5. (closed Jan. 1, Thanksgiving, Dec. 25). Adm.: $2; families, $4; 6–17s and students with ID's, $1; senior citizens, 50¢. Free on Thurs.

Dioramas of plants, and animals; displays of fossils, rocks, and gems; anthropology exhibits from Egypt, China, Africa, Oceania, and the Americas. New exhibit, "Maritime Peoples of the Arctic and Northwest Coast."

Museum of Science and Industry: 57th St. and Lake Shore Dr., Chicago, Ill. 60637. Open: Memorial Day-Labor Day 9:30–5:30; rest of year, Mon.-Fri. 9:30–4, Sat., Sun. and hldys. 9:30–5:30 (closed Dec. 25). Free (small fee to four exhibits).

Operating coal mine, captured German submarine, giant heart, Paul Bunyan house, Colleen Moore's Fairy Castle, The Farm, the Apollo 8 spacecraft, Sears' Cinema Circus, computerized "Food for Life," historic and advanced forms of planes, ships, trains, and cars.

Oriental Institute Museum of the University of Chicago: 1155 E. 58th St., Chicago, Ill. 60637. Open: Tues.-Sat. 10–4, Sun. 12–4 (closed Mon. and hldys.). Free.

Ancient Near Eastern objects, including 40-ton human-headed winged bull from Khorsabad in Assyria, 16-ft. statue of Tutankhamen from Egypt, colossal bull's head from Persepolis; glyptic, bronze, and ivory artifacts.

Washington, D.C.

Anacostia Neighborhood Museum, Smithsonian Institution: 2405 Martin Luther King, Jr., Ave. SE, Washington, D.C. 20020. Open: Mon.-Fri. 10–6, Sat. and Sun. 1–6 (closed Dec. 25). Free.

Exhibits on Afro-American history, art shows, programs for children.

Arts and Industries Building, Smithsonian Institution: 900 Jefferson Dr. SW, Washington, D.C. 20560. Open: daily 10–5:30 (closed Dec. 25). Free.

Constructed to house exhibits from 1876 Centennial Exhibition, building has been restored as nearly as possible to original appearance.

Corcoran Gallery of Art: 17th St. and New York Ave. NW, Washington, D.C. 20006. Open: Tues.-Sun. 10–4:30, until 9 on Thurs. (closed Mon.; also Jan. 1, July 4, Thanksgiving, Dec. 25). Free.

American paintings, sculpture, graphics. European art.

Freer Gallery of Art, Smithsonian Institution: Jefferson Dr. at 12th St. SW, Washington, D.C. 20560. Open: daily 10–5:30 (closed Dec. 25). Free.

Oriental paintings, sculpture, bronzes, pottery, and metal work. Early Christian manuscripts. One of largest Whistler collections.

Hirshhorn Museum and Sculpture Garden, Smithsonian Institution: Eighth St. at Independence Ave. SW, Washington, D.C. 20560. Open: daily, 10–5:30 (closed Dec. 25). Free.

More than 7,000 works tracing development of modern painting and sculpture since 19th century. Rodin, Moore, Picasso, Calder, Miró, and Matisse among those represented.

National Air and Space Museum, Smithsonian Institution: Independence Ave. bet. 4th and 7th Sts. SW, Washington, D.C. 20560. Open: daily 10–5:30; April 1-Labor Day, 10–9 (closed Dec. 25). Free.

Exhibits on aviation and space age; Wright Brothers' Kitty Hawk Flyer, *Lindbergh's* Spirit of St. Louis.

National Gallery of Art: Constitution Ave. bet. 3rd and 7th Sts. NW, Washington, D.C. 20565. Open: Mon.-Sat. 10–5, Sun. 12–9[1] (closed Jan. 1, Dec. 25). Free.

Paintings, sculpture, drawings, prints, decorative arts Works by Raphael, Jan Van Eyck, Vermeer, Rembrandt, Van Gogh, Renoir, Monet, and Cassatt.

National Museum of African Art, Smithsonian Institution: 318 A St., N.E., Washington, D.C. 20002. Open: Mon.-Fri. 10–5; Sat. and Sun. 12–5 (closed Dec. 25). Free.

Creative heritage of Africa displayed and studied through collection of over 8,000 objects.

National Museum of American Art, Smithsonian Institution: Eighth and G Sts. NW, Washington, D.C. 20560. Open: daily 10–5:30 (closed Dec. 25). Free.
Paintings, sculptures, and graphics.

National Museum of American History, Smithsonian Institution: 14th St. and Constitution Ave. NW, Washington, D.C. 20560. Open: daily 10–5:30 (closed Dec. 25). Free.
Exhibits showing scientific, technological, and cultural development feature original Star-Spangled Banner, furnishings, gowns of First Ladies, inventions, stamps, coins, musical instruments, ceramics, and crafts.

National Museum of Natural History and National Museum of Man, Smithsonian Institution: 10th St. and Constitution Ave. NW, Washington, D.C. 20560. Open: daily 10–5:30 (closed Dec. 25). Free.
Origin, development, and physical characteristics of man. Dioramas of peoples and animals in natural settings. Land and sea mammals, birds, fish, reptiles, and gems, minerals, meteorites, volcanoes, prehistoric animals, fossils. Hope Diamond. Insect Zoo.

National Portrait Gallery, Smithsonian Institution: Eighth and F Sts. NW, Washington, D.C. 20560. Open: daily 10–5:30 (closed Dec. 25). Free.
Only major museum in hemisphere devoted exclusively to portraiture. Exhibits likenesses in all media of persons who have made significant contributions to U.S. history and culture.

Renwick Gallery, Smithsonian Institution: 17th St. and Pennsylvania Ave. NW, Washington, D.C. 20560. Open: daily 10–5:30 (closed Dec. 25). Free.
American crafts, decorative arts, and design, housed in a mid-19th-century building restored to its original appearance.

Smithsonian Institution Building: 1000 Jefferson Dr. SW, Washington, D.C. 20560. Open: daily 10–5:30 (closed Dec. 25). Free.
Information center and James Smithson's tomb are in original building. Institution maintains the museums and art galleries indicated above; also Cooper-Hewitt Museum in New York City, National Zoological Park in Washington, D.C., and research facilities elsewhere.

Philadelphia

Academy of Natural Sciences of Philadelphia: 19th St. and the Parkway, Philadelphia, Pa. 19103. Natural History Museum open: daily 10–4 (closed Jan. 1, Thanksgiving, Dec. 25). Adm.: $2.50; (students, senior citizens, $2.25; 3–12s, $2.
Exhibits on dinosaurs and extinct species; animal, bird, and gem displays. Live animal shows.

Franklin Institute, The: 20th St. and the Parkway, Philadelphia, Pa. 19103. Open: Mon.-Sat. 10–5, Sun. 12–5 (closed Jan. 1, Memorial Day, July 4, Thanksgiving, Dec. 24–25). Adm.: $3.50; students, $2.50; 4–11s, $2; senior citizens, $1.50.
Nonprofit educational and research institution operating science museum, planetarium, library, and research laboratories. "Hands-on" science and technology exhibits.

Pennsylvania Academy of the Fine Arts: Broad and Cherry Sts., Philadelphia, Pa. 19102. Open: Tues.-Sat. 10–5, Sun. 1–5 (closed Jan. 1, Dec. 25). Adm.: $1.50; students and under 12s, 50¢; senior citizens, $1.
Oldest art museum and school in U.S. Collection devoted to American art. Lectures, concerts.

Philadelphia Museum of Art: 26th St. and the Parkway, Philadelphia, Pa. 19130. Open: Tues.-Sun. 10–5 (closed major hldys.). Adm.: $2; children and senior citizens, $1. Free Sun. 10–1.
Paintings, drawings, prints, from old masters to present. Sculpture, decorative arts, period rooms and armor. Oriental collections. New American Wing open. Rodin Museum at Parkway and 22nd St. Colonial Houses in Fairmont Park. Samuel S. Fleisher Art Memorial, 715–19 Catharine St.

Museums In Other Cities

Addison Gallery of American Art: Phillips Academy, Andover, Mass. 01810. Open: Tues.-Sat. 10–5, Sun. 2:30–5 (closed Mon.; also natl. hldys.). Free.
Paintings, sculpture, graphics, photographs of 18th, 19th, and 20th centuries. Changing contemporary exhibitions.

Alabama, Museum of Natural History of: Smith Hall, on campus of U. of Alabama, Tuscaloosa, Ala. 35486. Open: Mon.-Fri. 8–5. Free.
All phases of natural history. See also *Mound State Monument Museum.*

Albright-Knox Art Gallery: 1285 Elmwood Ave., Buffalo, N.Y. 14222. Open: Tues.-Sat. 11–5; Sun. 12–5 (closed Mon.; also Jan. 1, Thanksgiving, Dec. 25). Voluntary admission fee.
Comprehensive collection of contemporary paintings; 18th-19th-century English, French, and American paintings. Sculpture since 3000 B.C.

Atomic Energy, American Museum of: *See* Science and Energy, American Museum of.

Baltimore Museum of Art: Art Museum Dr., Baltimore, Md. 21218. Open: Tues.-Sat. 11–5, Thurs. evening 7–10 (except in summer). Sun. 1–5 (closed Mon.). Free.
Paintings, sculpture, graphics, tribal arts, decorative arts, sculpture garden.

Baseball Hall of Fame and Museum, National: Main St., Cooperstown, N.Y. 13326. Open: May-Oct. 9–9, Nov.-Apr. 9–5 (closed Jan. 1, Thanksgiving, Dec. 25). Adm.: $4[2]; 7–15s, $1.50.
Memorabilia, pictures, documents of baseball history. Bronze plaques of game's immortals. Baseball movies shown daily. See also *Hall of Fame in index.*

Berkshire Museum, The: 39 South St., Pittsfield, Mass. 01201. Open: Tues.-Sat. 10–5, Sun. 1–5 (closed Mon.; also Jan. 1, July 4, Thanksgiving, Dec. 25). Open Mon. in July and Aug. Free.
Painting, sculpture, decorative arts—ancient to modern. Loan exhibits. Galleries on biology, birds, man, minerals, and American history. Live exhibits. Junior Department. Movies, lectures.

Birmingham Museum of Art: 2000 Eighth Ave. North, Birmingham, Ala. 35203. Open: Tues.-Wed., Fri. and Sat. 10–5, Thurs. 10–9, Sun. 2–6 (closed Mondays; also Jan. 1, Dec. 25). Free.
Kress Collection of Italian art; 17th-century Dutch, Flemish, and English paintings; 19th-century American paintings; Beeson Wedgwood Collection; art of Old West, including Remington bronzes; modern American paintings; silver, porcelain; Oriental art.

(Boston) Museum of Fine Arts: Huntington Ave., Boston, Mass. 02115. Open: (entire museum): Tues. and Thurs.-Sun. 10–5; Wed. 10–10; (West Wing only): Thurs. and Fri. 5–10 (closed Mon.; also Jan. 1, July 4, Labor Day, Thanksgiving, and Dec. 24–25). Adm.; $3 when entire museum is open; $2 when only West Wing is open. Members and children 16 and

under free; senior citizens $2. Free to all Sat. 10–12.
European and American paintings, sculpture, furniture, interiors, tapestries, textiles, silver, costumes, musical instruments. Prints, drawings, watercolors. Egyptian, Asiatic, contemporary collections.

Buffalo Museum of Science: Humboldt Parkway, Buffalo, N.Y. 14211. Open: Mon.-Thurs. and Sat. 10–5; Fri. 10–10; Sun. and hldys. 10–5 (Jan. 1 and July 4, 1–5) (closed Dec. 25). Free.
Exhibits of astronomy, geology, zoology, botany, anthropology. Kellogg Observatory.

California Academy of Sciences: Golden Gate Park, San Francisco, Calif. 94118. Open: daily 10–5. Adm.: $1.50; 6–11s, 50¢; 12–17s and senior citizens, 75¢. Free adm. first Wed. of month.
North American and African habitat groups. Astronomical exhibits, clocks, watches, lamps, minerals, fossils, plants. Steinhart Aquarium, Morrison Planetarium, Wattis Hall of Man.

California Palace of the Legion of Honor: 34th Ave. and Clement St., Lincoln Park, San Francisco, Calif. 94121. Open: Wed.-Sun. 10–5. Adm.: $1.50; 5–18s and senior citizens, 50¢; under 5, free. Free adm. first Wed. of month.
Devoted to arts of France: paintings, sculpture, and decorative arts; prints and drawings of all periods and nationalities.

Carnegie Institute: 4400 Forbes Ave., Pittsburgh, Pa. 15213. Open: Tues.-Sat. 10–5, Sun. 1–5 (closed Mon. and major hldys.). Suggested contributions: Adults, $1.50; children and students, 75¢. Sat. free.
Museum of Art: European and American paintings, sculpture, and decorative arts. Carnegie Museum of Natural History. Hillman Hall of Minerals and Gems. Home of the Dinosaurs.

Cincinnati Art Museum: Eden Park, Cincinnati, Ohio 45202. Open: wkdys. 10–5, Sun. 1–5 (closed Mon. and major hldys.). Adm.: $2; 12–18s and senior citizens, $1; 3–11, 25¢. Free to everyone on Sat.
European and American painting, prints, photographs, decorative arts, sculpture, costumes. Egyptian, Greco-Roman, Medieval, Near and Far Eastern arts. Ancient musical instruments.

Clark (Sterling and Francine) Art Institute: Williamstown, Mass. 01267. Open: daily except Monday, 10–5 (closed Jan. 1, Thanksgiving, Dec. 25). Free.
Paintings from 14th to 19th centuries, including works by Corot, Renoir, Degas, Toulouse-Lautrec, Homer; sculpture, antique silver, prints and drawings.

Cleveland Museum of Art: 11150 East Boulevard, Cleveland, Ohio 44106. Open: Tues. 10–6, Wed. 10–10, Thurs. and Fri. 10–6, Sat. 9–5, Sun. 1–6 (closed Mon.; also Jan. 1, July 4, Thanksgiving, Dec. 25). Free.
Paintings, sculpture, graphic arts, furniture, silver, gold, arms, armor, textiles, ceramics from all cultures and periods.

Cleveland Museum of Natural History: Wade Oval, University Circle, Cleveland, Ohio 44106. Open: Mon.-Sat. 10–5, Sun. 1–5:30 (closed Jan. 1, Memorial Day, July 4, Labor Day, Thanksgiving, Dec. 24–25). Adm.: $2; 6–18s and senior citizens, 50¢. Free Tues. after 1.
Dinosaurs, area fossils, minerals, birds, mammals, insects, reptiles, plants. American Indian and Eskimo displays. Planetarium, observatory. Hall of Man's Ecology, Hall of Earth Science.

Colonial Williamsburg: Williamsburg, Va. 23185. Open: daily. Adm.: $10 and $13; 6–12s, half price; under 6 free.
Restored 18th-century capital of Colonial Virginia; 173 acres of colonial city with more than 40 exhibition homes, craft shops, and public buildings; 90 acres of gardens; outdoor events; colonial lodging and dining.

Colorado Springs Fine Arts Center: 30 W. Dale St., Colorado Springs, Colo. 80903. Open: Tues.-Sat. 10–5; Sun. 1–5 (closed Mon.; also selected hldys.). Free.
Native American and Hispanic art; 19th- and 20th century American art; survey of world art.

Columbus Museum of Art: 480 E. Broad St., Columbus, Ohio 43215. Open: Tues., Thurs., Fri., and Sun. 11–5; Wed. 11–8:30; Sat. 10–5 (closed Mon.). Adm.: $1.50; 6–17s, students, and senior citizens, 50¢. Tues. free.
European paintings from 16th to 20th century; 19th- and 20th-century American and European paintings, sculpture, and works on paper. Chinese and Japanese ceramics. European and American decorative arts. Sculpture Park and Garden.

Corning Glass Center: Dept. IP, Corning, N.Y. 14831. Open daily 9–5 (closed Jan. 1, Thanksgiving, Dec. 24–25). Adm.: $2.50; 6–17s and senior citizens, $2; children with adult, free; family maximum, $6.
Museum of Glass, Technology Gallery, Hall of Science and Industry, Glass Factory.

Currier Gallery of Art, The: 192 Orange St., Manchester, N.H. 03104. Open: Tues., Wed., Fri., and Sat. 10–4; Sun. 2–5; Thurs. 10–10 (closed Mon. and major hldys.). Free.
European and American paintings, 13th-20th century. American decorative arts, 18th-19th century, including New England furniture, silver, pewter, and early glass.

Delaware Art Museum, The: 2301 Kentmere Pkwy., Wilmington, Del. 19806. Open: Mon.-Sat. 10–5, Sun. 1–5. Free.
English pre-Raphaelite; 19th- and 20th-century American art; paintings by Wyeth, Homer and Hooper; American photography. Art reference library.

Denver Art Museum, The: 100 W. 14th Ave. Parkway, Denver, Colo. 80204. Open: Tues.-Sat. 10–4:30 (Wed. 10–8); Sun. 1–5.
Art from nearly every culture and period.

Denver Museum of Natural History: City Park, Denver, Colo. 80205. Open: Mon.-Sat. 9–4:30, Sun. and hldys. 12–4:30 (closed Jan. 1, Thanksgiving, Dec. 24–25, Dec. 31). Adm.: $2 senior citizens, $1; 6–15s, 75¢.
Seventy life-size ecological habitat dioramas. Animals from four continents, earth-science exhibits, dinosaurs, displays of fossil mammals and historic native Americans. Planetarium (small charge).

Des Moines Art Center: Greenwood Park, 45th St. and Grand Ave., Des Moines, Iowa 50312. Open: Tues.-Sat. 11–5, Sun. 12–5. Free.
Permanent collection includes Calder, Rodin, Arp, Bellows, Johns, Hopper, Giacometti, David Smith, and Morris Louis, among others.

Detroit Historical Museum: 5401 Woodward Ave., Detroit, Mich. 48202. Open: Tues.-Sat. 9:30–5 (closed Sun., Mon. and legal hldys.).
"Streets of Old Detroit" recreates periods of 1840, 1870, and 1905; historic fashions, period rooms, automobile collection. Marine exhibits at Dossin Great Lakes Museum on Belle Isle; military history exhibits at historic Ft. Wayne.

Detroit Institute of Arts, The: 5200 Woodward Ave., Detroit, Mich. 48202. Open: Tues.-Sun. 9:30–5:30 (closed Mon.; also legal hldys.). Free.

Paintings, sculpture, decorative arts from ancient times to modern.

Dickson Mounds Museum: off Route 97–78 near Lewistown, Ill. 61542. Open: Daily 8:30–5 (closed Jan. 1, Easter, Thanksgiving, Dec. 25). Free.

Museum of anthropology with exhibits relating to prehistoric American Indian.

Farmers' Museum: Lake Rd., Route 80, Cooperstown, N.Y. 13326. Open: May 1-Oct. 31, daily. 9–5; restricted schedule for fall and winter. (closed Mon.; also Jan. 1, Thanksgiving, Dec. 25). Adm.:$4[2]; 7–15s, $1.50.

Re-created village crossroads. Early farm and handicraft tools. School house, country store, smithy, print shop, doctor's and lawyer's offices, pharmacy, tavern, church, farm unit. Cardiff Giant. Operated by New York State Historical Association.

Fenimore House: Lake Rd., Route 80, Cooperstown, N.Y. 13326. Open: summer season, daily 9–5; Nov., Dec., and April, Tues.-Sat. 9–5, Sun. 1–5 (closed Mon.; also Jan., Feb., March, Dec. 25). Adm.: $3.50[2]; 7–15s, $1.25.

American portraits, genre paintings. Browere life masks of Founding Fathers. James Fenimore Cooper memorabilia. Folk art. Library. Operated by New York State Historical Association.

Florida State Museum, University of Florida: Museum Road, Gainesville, Fla. 32611. Open: Mon.-Fri. 9–5, Sat. 9–5, Sun. 1–5 (closed Dec. 25). Free.

State and University museum with research and exhibition emphasis on natural and anthropological history of Florida, southeastern United States, and Caribbean area.

Fogg Art Museum: Harvard University, 32 Quincy St., Cambridge, Mass. 02138. Open: Mon.-Fri. 9–5, Sat. 10–5, Sun. 2–5 (closed weekends from July 1 to Labor Day; also natl. hldys.). Free.

Collections illustrate evolution of Eastern and Western art from ancient to modern times. Chinese sculpture and bronzes; Romanesque sculpture; Italian primitives; French 19th-century paintings; European drawings and prints.

Gardner (Isabella Stewart) Museum: 2 Palace Road, Boston, Mass. 02115. Open: Wed.-Sun. 12-5; Tues. 12–9 (July and Aug. 1–5:30). (closed Mon., natl. hldys.). Adm.: Suggested contribution, $1.

Paintings, 14th-20th centuries, in building of Venetian palace style. Sculpture, tapestries, furniture. Flowering courtyard. Free tours on Thursday at 2:30 p.m.

Getty (J. Paul) Museum, The: 17985 Pacific Coast Hgwy., Malibu, Calif. 90265. Open: Mon.-Fri. 10–5 (June-Sept.), Tues.-Sat. 10–5 (Oct.-May), (closed Jan. 1, Feb. 22, Memorial Day, July 4, Labor Day, Thanksgiving, Dec. 25). Free. Parking reservations for guaranteed admission are required (213 454–6541).

Re-creation of Roman seaside villa destroyed by Vesuvius in 79 A.D. Greek and Roman antiquities, Western European paintings, 18th-century French decorative arts. Research library.

Heard Museum: 22 East Monte Vista Rd., Phoenix, Ariz. 85004. Open: Mon.-Sat. 10–5, Sun. 1–5 (closed hldys.). Adm.: $1.50; senior citizens, $1; children and students, 50¢.

Anthropology and primitive arts, with emphasis on rich heritage of Southwest.

High Museum of Art, The: 1280 Peachtree St. NE, Atlanta, Ga. 30309. Open: Tues.-Sat. 10–5, Sun. 12–5 (closed Mon.; natl. hldys.). Free.

Paintings and sculpture from 14th to 18th century in Samuel H. Kress Collection. Ralph K. Uhry Print Collection; decorative arts; Richman Collection of African Art; 18th-century European porcelains; photography, contemporary art.

(Houston) Museum of Fine Arts, The: 1001 Bissonnet at Main, Houston, Tex. 77005. Open: Tues.-Sat. 10–5, Sun. 12–6 (closed Mon.; also Jan. 1, July 4, Thanksgiving, Dec. 25). Free.

American and European art through 20th century; Southwest American Indian art and artifacts; early American furniture and decorative arts; pre-Columbian and Far Eastern art; native arts from Africa, Australia, South Pacific. Impressionist and post-Impressionist paintings. 20th-century photography.

Huntington Library, Art Gallery, and Botanical Gardens: 1151 Oxford Rd., San Marino, Calif. 91108. Open: Tues.-Sun. 1–4:30; (reservations required on Sun.) (closed Mon.; Jan. 1, Easter, Memorial Day, July 4, Labor Day, Thanksgiving, Dec. 24-25). Free.

18th-century British and European paintings, including Gainsborough's "Blue Boy" and Lawrence's "Pinkie." Manuscript and rare-book exhibits include Gutenberg Bible, Franklin's Autobiography *in his handwriting. Botanical gardens. Research library.*

Illinois State Museum: Spring and Edwards Sts., Springfield, Ill. 62706. Open: Mon.-Sat. 8:30–5, Sun. 1:30–5 (closed Jan. 1, Easter, Thanksgiving, Dec. 25). Free.

Museum of natural history, anthropology, and art with emphasis on wild-life and early inhabitants of Illinois; Fine and decorative arts; works by 19th- and 20th-century Illinois artists.

Indianapolis Museum of Art: 1200 W. 38th St., Indianapolis, Ind. 46208. Krannert and Clowes Pavilions open: Tues.-Sun. 11–5 (closed Mon.; also Jan. 1, Thanksgiving, Dec. 25). Free. Lilly Pavilion of Decorative Arts open Tues.-Sun. 1–4 (closed Mon. and major hldys.). Free.

Pre-Columbian through contemporary art in all media. British and American paintings of 19th century; J.M.W. Turner collection. Dutch and Flemish paintings of 17th century; textiles, decorative arts of 18th-century Germany, England, France, and Italy. Oriental collection. Clowes Fund Collection of old masters.

Los Angeles County Museum of Art: 5905 Wilshire Blvd., Los Angeles, Calif. 90036. Open: Tues.-Fri. 10–5; Sat.-Sun. 10–6 (closed Mon.; also Jan. 1, Thanksgiving, Dec. 25). Adm.: $1; students with ID, senior citizens, and children 5–17, 50¢. Free second Tues. of month.

Permanent collection in Ahmanson Gallery; special exhibitions in Frances and Armand Hammer Wing.

(Los Angeles County) Natural History Museum: Exposition Park, 900 Exposition Blvd., Los Angeles, Calif. 90007. Open: Tues.-Sun. 10–5 (closed Mon.; also Jan. 1, Thanksgiving, Dec. 25). Adm.: $1; 5–17s, 50¢. Free first Tues. of month.

Exhibits in Pre-Columbian archeology, Pacific Islands and African ethnology, Southern California botany, evolution of life, marine biology, insects, mineralogy. Dinosaur and Cenozoic fossil reconstructions. North American and African animal habitat groups. U.S., California, Western, Plains, and West Coast Indian history. Rancho La Brea tar pits, a designated natural history landmark, are at 5801 Wilshire Blvd., Hancock Park, with satellite George C. Page Museum of La Brea. Pleistocene fossil reconstructions. Open: same as parent museum. Free to all second Tues. of month.

Milwaukee Art Museum: War Memorial Center, 750 North Lincoln Memorial Dr., Milwaukee, Wis. 53202.

Open: Tues., Wed., Fri., and Sat. 10–5; Thurs. 12–9; Sun. 1–6 (closed Mon.). Adm.: $1; students, senior citizens, 50¢; under 12s, free.

Paintings, sculpture, graphics, and decorative arts from ancient to modern; Bradley Collection of 19th- and 20th-century American art. Villa Terrace, Branch Museum for Decorative Arts, 2220 North Terrace Ave.; seasonal hours.

Milwaukee Public Museum: 800 W. Wells St., Milwaukee, Wis. 53233. Open: daily 9–5 (closed Jan. 1, July 4, Labor Day, Thanksgiving, Dec. 25). Adm.: $2; under 18s, $1; max. family rate, $5.

American Indian and West African art, pre-Columbian collections. Natural history and history displays that include Streets of Old Milwaukee, Urban Habitat, and European Village.

Minneapolis, Institute of Arts, The: 2400 Third Ave. South, Minneapolis Minn. 55404. Open: Tues., Wed., Fri., Sat. 10–5; Thurs. 10–9; Sun. 12–5 (closed Mon.; also Dec. 25). Adm.: $2 (Thurs. 5–9, free); 12–18s, $1; senior citizens and children under 12, free.

European and American paintings, sculpture, decorative arts, period rooms, prints and drawings, photography; Oriental, African, Oceanic, ancient and native North and South American arts.

Mint Museum, Art Museum: 501 Hempstead Pl., Charlotte, N.C. 28207. Open: Tues.-Fri. 10–5, Sat.-Sun. 2–5 (closed Mon. and hldys.). Free.

Paintings, sculpture, decorative arts, prints (Renaissance-20th century), pre-Columbian Collection, Delhom Gallery and Institute for Study and Research in Ceramics. Coins and artifacts from 19th-century Charlotte branch of U.S. Mint.

Mound State Monument Archaeological Museum: Rte. 69, Moundville, Ala. 35474. Open: daily 9–5 (closed Dec. 25). Adm.: $2 (children $1).

Twenty prehistoric Indian mounds, excavated artifacts, re-created temple and village of Moundville Indians. Trailer and tent campgrounds. Operated by Alabama Museum of Natural History, The University of Alabama.

Mystic Seaport: Mystic, Conn. 06355. Open: daily. May-Oct. 9–5; Nov.-April 9–4 (mid-May to mid-Sept. open until 8) (closed Dec. 25). Adm.: May-Oct. $8 (5–15s, $4); Nov.-April $7 (5–15s, $3.50). Two-day tickets and group rates available.

Maritime museum emphasizing Age of Sail. Tall ships, including Charles W. Morgan, 1841 whaling ship. Waterfront village with working craftsmen and demonstrations of maritime skills. Small boat collection and exhibits of figureheads and marine art. Working shipyard; planetarium. Summer steamboat rides at additional charge.

Nelson (William Rockhill) Gallery—Atkins Museum of Fine Arts: 4525 Oak St., Kansas City, Mo. 64111. Open: Tues.-Sat. 10–5, Sun. 2–6 (closed Mon.; also Jan. 1, Memorial Day, July 4, Thanksgiving, Dec. 25). Adm.: $1.50; 6–12s, 75¢. Free on Sun.

Egyptian, Oriental, classic, and European art. American paintings and decorative arts; five Early American rooms. Pre-Columbian and Indian art. Children's Museum, lectures, films, musical programs.

Newark Museum: 49 Washington St., Newark, N.J. 07101. Open: daily 12–5 (closed Jan. 1, July 4, Thanksgiving, Dec. 25). Free.

Collections: American painting, sculpture; Tibetan, Chinese, Japanese arts; decorative arts, ancient glass and ceramics; natural science, ethnology. Planetarium. Ballantine House restoration. Fire Museum. Sculpture garden. Junior Museum. Newark's oldest schoolhouse (1784).

New Mexico, Museum of: Admin. bldg. at 113 Lincoln St., P.O. Box 2087, Santa Fe, N.M. 87503. Museum of Fine Arts, Museum of International Folk Art, Palace of the Governors. Open: daily 9–4:45 (closed Mon. Oct. 15-March 15; also state hldys). Laboratory of Anthropology. Open: Mon.-Fri. 9–4:45 (closed Sat., Sun., and hldys.).

Exhibits of fine arts, folk arts; history of Southwest and of American Indian; archeology; ethnology.

New Orleans Museum of Art: Lelong Ave., City Park, New Orleans, La. 70179. Open: Tues.-Sun. 10–5 (closed Mon.).

Old master paintings from 14th to 19th centuries, including Kress Collection of Italian Art; 20th-century European and American art; African, Oriental and pre-Columbian collections; Latin American Colonial painting and sculpture; prints and photographs.

New York State Historical Association; Lake Rd., Rte. 80, Cooperstown, N.Y. 13326.

Administers Farmers' Museum and Fenimore House. See *those entries. Also, Cooperstown Graduate Program in history museum studies and art conservation.*

Norton Simon Museum of Art at Pasadena: Colorado Blvd. at Orange Grove, Pasadena, Calif. 91105. Open: Thurs.-Sun. 12–6. Adm.: Thurs.-Sat. $2; students and senior citizens, 75¢; under 12s, free; Sun. $3 for all.

Paintings by old masters and from Italian Renaissance; Dutch 17th-century school; paintings and sculpture by Impressionist and early 20th-century masters; Southeast Asian stone sculptures and bronzes.

Peabody Museum: East India Sq., Salem, Mass. 01970. Open: Mon.-Sat. 10–5, Sun. and hldys., 1–5 (closed Jan. 1, Thanksgiving, Dec. 25). Adm.: $2; students with IDs and senior citizens, $1.50; 6–16s, $1.

Maritime history, ethnology, and natural history. Navigational instruments, Japanese household arts and crafts.

Putnam Museum: 1717 W. 12th St., Davenport, Iowa 52804. Open: Tues.-Sat. 9–5, Sun. 1–5 (closed Mon.; also Jan. 1, Easter, Memorial Day, July 4, Labor Day, Thanksgiving, Dec. 25). Adm.: $1; 13–18s, 50¢; 5–12s, 25¢. Free Sat. 9–12.

Art, history and natural history; ethnology; archaeology; botany; paleontology; anthropology. Arts of Asia, Africa, Oceania, the American Indian and pre-Columbian era.

Ringling Museums: P.O. Box 1838, Sarasota, Fla. 33578. John and Mable Ringling Museum of Art, Asolo Theater, Ringling Residence, Museum of the Circus. Open: Mon.-Fri. 9 a.m.-10 p.m., Sat. 9–5, Sun. 11–6. Adm.: $3.50; under 12s, free; groups, $3.

Extensive collection of Rubens and Baroque art. Asolo is only 18th-century Italian theater in America. Circus Museum contains gilded wagons and memorabilia.

Rosicrucian Egyptian Museum and Art Gallery: Park and Naglee Aves., San Jose, Calif. 95191. Open: Tues.-Fri. 9–5, Sat.-Mon. 12–5 (closed Jan. 1, July 4, Aug. 2, Thanksgiving, Dec. 25). Free.

Egyptian and Oriental antiquities. Mummies, statuary, jewelry, utensils, clothing. Reproduction of Egyptian rock tomb. Babylonian collection. Art gallery.

St. Louis Art Museum, The: Forest Park, St. Louis, Mo. 63110. Open: Tues. 2:30–9:30, Wed.-Sun. 10–5 (closed Mon.; also Jan. 1, Dec. 25). Free.

American, European, and Asian painting, sculp-

ture, and decorative arts. African, Oceanic, pre-Columbian, and American Indian arts.

San Diego Museum of Art: Balboa Park, San Diego, Calif. 92101. Open: Tues.-Sun. 10–5 (closed Mon.; also Jan. 1, Thanksgiving, Dec. 25). Adm.: $2. Free on Tuesday.

European paintings, Renaissance to 20th century; American paintings and decorative arts. Oriental arts, including Indian and Persian miniatures. Contemporary sculpture.

San Diego Museum of Man: 1350 El Prado, Balboa Park, San Diego, Calif. 92101. Open: daily 10–4:30 (closed Jan. 1, Thanksgiving, Dec. 25). Adm.: $1.50; students, 50¢; 6–16s, 25¢. Free on Wed.

Exhibits on Man of the Western Americas, early man, Indians' life style, and Mayan civilization.

San Diego Society of Natural History—Natural History Museum: Balboa Park, San Diego, Calif. 92112. Open: wkdys. and Sun. 10–4:30 (closed Jan. 1, Thanksgiving, Dec. 25). Adm.: $2; (children, free).

Mammals, birds, fossils, shells, plants, insects, minerals, marine biology. Emphasis on Southwestern U.S., and Sonora and Baja California, Mexico.

San Francisco, The Fine Arts Museums of, M.H. de Young Memorial Museum: Kennedy Dr. and Eighth Ave., Golden Gate Park, San Francisco, Calif. 94118. Open: Wed.-Sun. 10–5. Adm.: $1.50; 6–18s and senior citizens, 50¢. Free first Wed. of month.

Art of Europe, America, Ancient Egypt, Greece, and Rome; traditional arts of Africa, Oceania, and the Americas. Paintings, sculpture, and decorative arts. See also *California Palace of the Legion of Honor.*

San Francisco Museum of Modern Art: Van Ness at McAllister, San Francisco, Calif. 94102. Open: Tues., Wed., and Fri. 10–6, Thurs. 10–10, Sat. and Sun. 10–5 (closed Mon.; also Jan. 1, Easter Sunday, Memorial Day, July 4, Labor Day, Nov. 11, Thanksgiving, Dec. 25). Adm.: $2; under 16s and senior citizens, $1.

Contemporary American and international paintings, sculpture, graphics, photography, and ceramics.

Science and Energy, American Museum of: 300 South Tulane St., Oak Ridge, Tenn. 37830. Open: Sept-May, Mon.-Sat. 9–5, Sun. 12:30–5; June-Aug., Mon.-Sat. 9–6, Sun. 12:30–6 (closed Jan. 1, Thanksgiving, Dec. 25). Free.

Demonstrations, exhibits, motion pictures, models, etc., relating to all forms of energy. Traveling exhibits available free to exhibitors in U.S.

Seattle Art Museum: Volunteer Park, Seattle, Wash. 98112 and the Pavilion at Seattle Center, Seattle, Wash. 98109. Both open: Tues.-Sat. 10–5 (Thurs. to 9), Sun. 12–5 (closed Mon.; also Jan. 1, Thanksgiving, Dec. 25). Adm.: $2; students and senior citizens, $1; under 6s, free. Free on Thurs.

Asian art and jade; Greek and Roman art; Samuel H. Kress Collection of 14th-18th-century European painting and sculpture. European and American modern art.

Southwest Museum: Marmion Way at Museum Dr., Highland Pk., Los Angeles, Calif. 90065. Open: Tues.-Sun. 11–4:45 (closed Mon., Jan. 1, Easter, July 4, Thanksgiving, Dec. 25). Free.

American Indian exhibits, ancient and modern. Research library. Casa de Adobe, reproduction of adobe hacienda, at 4605 N. Figueroa St.; open Tues.-Sun. 11–4:45 (closed same as Southwest Museum).

J. B. Speed Art Museum, The: 2035 S. 3rd St., Louisville, Ky. 40208. Open: Tues.-Sat. 10–4; Sun. 2–6 (closed Mon. and hldys.). Free.

Ancient relics to modern art. Sculpture court.

Toledo Museum of Art, The: Monroe St. at Scottwood Ave., Toledo, Ohio 43697. Open: Tues.-Sat. 9–5, Sun. 1–5 (closed Mon. and legal hldys.). Free.

European and American paintings and decorative arts. Ancient and medieval art; books, prints, graphics. Ancient and American glass.

Virginia Museum of Fine Arts: Boulevard and Grove Ave., Richmond, Va. 23221. Open: Tues.-Sat. 11–5, Sun. 1–5 (closed Mon.; also Jan. 1, July 4, Thanksgiving, Dec. 25). Adm.: Suggested donation of 50¢.

World art of all periods, Lillian Thomas Pratt Collection of Fabergé jewelry, Art Nouveau Gallery.

Wadsworth Atheneum: 600 Main St., Hartford, Conn. 06103. Open: Tues.-Sun. 11–5 (closed Mon.; also Jan. 1, July 4, Thanksgiving, Dec. 25). Adm.: $2; 13–18s and senior citizens, $1; under 13s, free. Free on Thurs.

European and American paintings and drawings. Sculpture. Bronzes, silver, porcelain, American period furniture, art library.

Walker Art Center: Vineland Pl., Minneapolis, Minn. 55403. Open: Tues.-Sat. 10–5 (special exhibition galleries, 5–8), Sun. 11–5 (closed Mon.; also major hldys.). Free.

Collection of major 20th-century paintings, sculpture, drawings, and prints. Music, dance, film, theater, and educational programs.

Walters Art Gallery: 600 North Charles St., Baltimore, Md. 21201. Open: Mon. 1–5, Tues.-Sat. 11–5 (July-Aug. Mon. 1–4, Tues.-Sat. 11–4), Sun. and hldys. 2–5 (closed Jan. 1, July 4, Thanksgiving, Dec. 24–25). Free.

Art from ancient empires through 19th-century Europe. Collections of paintings, sculpture, decorative arts, and manuscripts.

Wheelwright Museum of the American Indian: 704 Camino Lejo, Santa Fe, N.M. 87502. Open: May-Oct., Mon.-Sat. 10–5, Sun. 1–5; Nov.-April, same as above except closed Mon. (closed Jan. 1, Thanksgiving, Dec. 25). Free.

Baskets, textiles, pottery, jewelry. Historic and contemporary Indian art.

Worcester Art Museum: 55 Salisbury St., Worcester, Mass. 01608. Open: Tues.-Sat. 10–5, Sun. 1–5 (closed Mon.; also Jan. 1, July 4, Thanksgiving, Dec. 25). Adm.: $1.50; 10–14s and senior citizens, $1; under 10s, free. Free on Wed.

Art from Egyptian to modern times, with emphasis on painting and sculpture.

1. Summer hours (June 14-Labor Day), Mon.-Sat. 10–9, Sun. 12–9. 2. Combination rates are available for Farmers' Museum, Fenimore House, and National Baseball Hall of Fame.

Celebrating Stravinsky

To mark the centennial of Igor Stravinsky's birth, June 17, 1882, a series of tributes was held throughout the year. One of the earliest was the Metropolitan Opera's triple bill comprised of a newly choreographed version of "Le Sacre du Printemps," the opera-ballet "Le Rossignol," and the opera-oratorio "Oedipus Rex." As the year progressed, the Library for the Performing Arts in New York mounted an exhibition of materials relating to his work; the New York Philharmonic gave a Mozart & Stravinsky Festival in June; and the New York City Ballet presented a Stravinsky Festival of old and new works from June 10 to 18.

Sports Personalities

A name in parentheses is the original name or form of name. Localities are places of birth. Dates of birth appear as month/day/year. **Boldface** years in parentheses are dates of **(birth-death).**
Information has been gathered from many sources, including the individuals themselves. However, the *Information Please Almanac* cannot guarantee the accuracy of every individual item.

Aaron, Hank (Henry) (baseball); Mobile, Ala., 2/5/1934
Abdul-Jabbar, Kareem (Lewis Ferdinand Alcindor, Jr.) (basketball); New York City, 4/16/1947
Adderly, Herbert A. (football); Philadelphia, 6/8/1939
Alcindor, Lew. *See* Abdul-Jabbar
Ali, Muhammad (Cassius Clay) (boxing); Louisville, Ky., 1/18/1942
Allen, Dick (Richard Anthony) (baseball); Wampum, Pa., 3/8/1942
Allison, Bobby (Robert Arthur) (auto racing); Hueytown, Ala., 12/3/1937
Alworth, Lance (football); Houston, 8/3/1940
Anderson, Donny (Gary Donny) (football); Brooklyn, N.Y., 4/3/1949
Anderson, Ken (football); Batavia, Ill., 2/15/1949
Anderson, Sparky (George) (baseball); Bridgewater, S.D., 2/22/1934
Andretti, Mario (auto racing); Montona, Trieste, Italy, 2/28/1940
Anthony, Earl (bowling); Kent, Wash., 4/27/1938
Appling, Luke (baseball); High Point, N.C., 4/2/1907
Arcaro, Eddie (George Edward) (jockey); Cincinnati, 2/19/1916
Ashe, Arthur (tennis); Richmond, Va., 7/10/1943
Austin, Tracy (tennis); Rolling Hills, Calif., 12/2/1962
Babashoff, Shirley (swimming); Whittier, Calif., 1/31/1957
Baer, Max (boxer); Omaha, Neb. **(1909–1959)**
Bakken, Jim (James Leroy) (football); Madison, Wis., 11/2/1940
Banks, Ernie (baseball); Dallas, 1/31/1931
Bannister, Roger (runner); Harrow, England, 3/24/1929
Barry, Rick (Richard) (basketball); Elizabeth, N.J., 3/28/1944
Bauer, Hank (Henry) (baseball); East St. Louis, Ill., 7/31/1922
Baugh, Sammy (football); Temple, Tex., 3/17/1914
Bayi, Filbert (runner); Karratu, Tanganyika, 6/23/1953
Baylor, Elgin (basketball); Washington, D.C., 9/16/1934
Beamon, Bob (long jumper); New York City, 8/2/1946
Beliveau, Jean (hockey); Three Rivers, Quebec, Canada, 8/31/1931
Beman, Deane (golf); Washington, D.C., 4/22/1938
Bench, Johnny (Johnny Lee) (baseball); Oklahoma City, 12/7/1947
Berg, Patty (Patricia Jane) (golf); Minneapolis, 2/13/1918
Berning, Susie Maxwell (golf); Pasadena, Calif., 7/22/1941
Berra, Yogi (Lawrence) (baseball); St. Louis, 5/12/1925
Biletnikoff, Frederick (football); Erie, Pa., 2/23/1943
Bird, Larry (basketball); French Lick, Ind., 12/7/1956
Blaik, Earl H. (football); Detroit, 2/15/1897
Blanda, George Frederick (football); Youngwood, Pa., 9/17/1927
Blue, Vida (baseball); Mansfield, La., 7/28/1949
Borg, Björn (tennis); Stockholm, 6/6/1956
Boros, Julius (golf); Fairfield, Conn., 3/3/1920
Bossy, Mike (hockey); Montreal, 1/22/1957
Boston, Ralph (long jumper); Laurel, Miss., 5/9/1939
Bradley, Bill (William Warren) (basketball); Crystal City, Mo., 7/28/1943
Bradshaw, Terry (football); Shreveport, La., 9/2/1948
Breedlove, Craig (Norman) (speed driving); Los Angeles, 3/23/1938
Brett, George (baseball); Glendale, W. Va., 5/15/1953
Brock, Louis Clark (baseball); El Dorado, Ark., 6/18/1939
Brown, Jimmy (football); St. Simon Island, Ga., 2/17/1936
Brown, Larry (football); Clairton, Pa., 9/19/1947
Brumel, Valeri (high jumper); Tolbuzino, Siberia, 4/14/1942
Bryant, Rosalyn Evette (track); Chicago, 1/7/1956
Burton, Michael (swimming); Des Moines, Iowa, 7/3/1947
Butkus, Dick (Richard Marvin) (football); Chicago, 12/9/1942
Campanella, Roy (baseball); Homestead, Pa., 11/19/1921
Campbell, Earl (football); Tyler, Tex., 3/29/1955
Caponi, Donna Maria (golf); Detroit, 1/29/1945
Cappelletti, Gino (football); Keewatin, Minn., 3/26/1934
Carew, Rod (Rodney Cline) (baseball); Gatun, Panama, 10/1/1945
Carlos, John (sprinter); New York City, 6/5/1945
Carlton, Steven Norman (baseball); Miami, Fla., 12/22/1944
Carner, Joanne Gunderson (Mrs. Don) (golf); Kirkland, Wash., 3/4/1939
Casals, Rosemary (tennis); San Francisco, 9/16/1948
Casper, Billy (golf); San Diego, Calif., 6/24/1931
Caulkins, Tracy (swimming); Wimona, Minn., 1/11/63
Cauthen, Steve (jockey); Covington, Ky., 5/1/1960
Chamberlain, Wilt (Wilton) (basketball); Philadelphia, 8/21/1936
Chapot, Frank (equestrian); Camden, N.J., 2/24/1934
Chinaglia, Giorgio (soccer); Carrara, Italy 1/24/1947
Clarke, Bobby (Robert Earle) (hockey); Flin Flon, Manitoba, Canada, 8/13/1949
Clay, Cassius. *See* Ali, Muhammad
Clemente, Roberto Walker (baseball); Carolina, Puerto Rico **(1934–1972)**
Cobb, Tyrus Raymond (Ty) (baseball); Narrows, Ga. **(1886–1961)**
Cochran, Barbara Ann (skiing); Claremont, N.H., 1/4/1951
Cochran, Marilyn (skiing); Burlington, Vt., 2/7/1950
Cochran, Robert (skiing); Claremont, N.H., 12/11/1951
Coe, Sebastian Newbold (track); London, England, 9/29/1956
Colavito, Rocky (Rocco Domenico) (baseball); New York City, 8/10/1933
Comaneci, Nadia (gymnast); Onesti, Romania, 11/12/1961
Connors, Jimmy (James Scott) (tennis); East St. Louis, Ill., 9/2/1952
Cordero, Angel (jockey); Santurce, Puerto Rico, 5/8/1942
Cournoyer, Yvan Serge (hockey); Drummondville, Quebec, Canada, 11/22/1943
Court, Margaret Smith (tennis); Albury, New South Wales, Australia, 7/16/1942
Cousy, Bob (basketball); New York City, 8/9/1928
Crenshaw, Ben (golf); Austin, Tex., 1/11/1952
Cronin, Joe (baseball executive); San Francisco, 10/12/1906
Cruyff, Johan (soccer); Amsterdam, Netherlands, 4/25/47
Csonka, Larry (Lawrence Richard) (football); Stow, Ohio, 12/25/1946
Dancer, Stanley (harness racing); New Egypt, N.J., 7/25/1927
Dark, Alvin (baseball); Comanche, Okla., 1/7/1922
Davenport, Willie (track); Troy, Ala., 6/6/1943
Dawson, Leonard Ray (football); Alliance, Ohio, 6/20/1935
Dean, Dizzy (Jay Hanna) (baseball); Lucas, Ark. **(1911–1974)**
DeBusschere, Dave (basketball); Detroit, 10/16/1940
Delvecchio, Alex Peter (hockey); Fort William, Ontario, Canada, 12/4/1931
Demaret, Jim (golf); Houston, 5/10/1910
Dempsey, Jack (William H.) (boxing); Manassa, Colo., 6/24/1895
DeVicenzo, Roberto (golf); Buenos Aires, 4/14/1923
Dibbs, Edward George (tennis); Brooklyn, N.Y., 2/23/1951
Dietz, James W. (rowing); New York, N.Y., 1/12/1949
DiMaggio, Joe (baseball); Martinez, Calif., 11/25/1914
Dionne, Marcel (hockey); Drummondville, Quebec, Canada, 8/3/1951
Dominguín, Luis Miguel (matador); Madrid, 12/9/1926
Dorsett, Tony (football); Rochester, Pa., 4/7/1954
Dryden, Kenneth (hockey); Hamilton, Ontario, Canada, 8/4/1947
Drysdale, Don (baseball); Van Nuys, Calif., 7/23/1936
Duran, Roberto (boxing); Panama City 6/16/1951
Durocher, Leo (baseball); West Springfield, Mass., 7/27/1906
Durr, François (tennis); Algiers, Algeria, 12/25/1942
El Cordobés, (Manuel Benítez Pérez) (matador); Palma del Río, Córdoba, Spain, 5/4/1936(?)
Elder, Lee (golf); Dallas, 7/14/1934
Emerson, Roy (tennis); Kingsway, Australia, 11/3/1936
Ender, Kornelia (swimming); Plauen, East Germany, 10/25/1958
Erving, Julius (Dr. J) (basketball); Roosevelt, N.Y., 2/22/1950
Esposito, Phil (Philip Anthony) (hockey); Sault Ste. Marie, Ontario, Canada, 2/20/1942
Evans, Lee (runner); Mandena, Calif., 2/25/1947
Ewbank, Weeb (football); Richmond, Ind., 5/6/1907
Feller, Robert (Bobby) (baseball); Van Meter, Iowa, 11/3/1918
Feuerbach, Allan Dean (track); Preston, Iowa, 1/12/1948
Finley, Charles O. (sportsman); Ensley, Ala., 2/22/1918
Fischer, Bobby (chess); Chicago, 3/9/1943
Fitzsimmons, Bob (Robert Prometheus) (boxer); Cornwall, England **(1862–1917)**
Fleming, Peggy Gale (ice skating); San Jose, Calif., 7/27/1948
Ford, Whitey (Edward) (baseball); New York City, 10/21/1928
Foreman, George (boxing); Marshall, Tex., 1/10/1949
Fosbury, Richard (high jumper); Portland, Ore., 3/6/1947
Fox, Nellie (Jacob Nelson) (baseball); St. Thomas, Pa. **(1927–1975)**
Foxx, James Emory (baseball); Sudlersville, Md., **(1907–1967)**
Foyt, A. J. (auto racing); Houston, 1/16/1935
Francis, Emile (hockey); North Battleford, Sask., 9/13/1926
Fratianne, Linda (figure skating); Los Angeles, 8/2/1960
Frazier, Joe (boxing); Beauford, S.C., 1/17/1944
Frazier, Walt (basketball); Atlanta, 3/29/1945
Frick, Ford C. (baseball); Wawaka, Ind., **(1894–1978)**
Furniss, Bruce (swimming); Fresno, Calif., 5/27/1957
Gable, Dan (wrestling); Waterloo, Iowa; 10/25/1945

Gabriel, Roman (football); Wilmington, N.C., 8/5/1940
Gallagher, Michael Donald (skiing); Yonkers, N.Y., 10/3/1941
Gehrig, Lou (Henry Louis Gehrig) (baseball); New York City **(1903–1941)**
Gehringer, Charlie (baseball); Fowlerville, Mich., 5/11/1903
Geoffrion, Bernie (Boom Boom) (hockey); Montreal, 2/14/1931
Gerulaitis, Vitas (tennis); Brooklyn, N.Y., 7/26/1954
Giacomin, Ed (hockey); Sudbury, Ontario, Canada, 6/6/1939
Gibson, Bob (baseball); Omaha, Neb., 11/9/1935
Gifford, Frank (football); Santa Monica, Calif., 8/16/1930
Gilbert, Rod (Rodrique) (hockey); Montreal, 7/1/1941
Giles, Warren (baseball executive); Tiskilwa, Ill., **(1896–1979)**
Gilmore, Artis (basketball); Chipley, Fla., 9/21/1949
Glance, Harvey (track); Phenix City, Ala., 3/28/1957
Gonzalez, Pancho (tennis); Los Angeles, 5/9/1928
Goodell, Brian Stuart (swimming); Stockton, Calif., 4/2/1959
Goodrich, Gail (basketball); Los Angeles, 4/23/1943
Goolagong Cawley, Evonne (tennis); Griffith, Australia, 7/31/1951
Gottfried, Brian (tennis); Baltimore, Md., 1/27/1952
Graham, David (golf); Windson, Australia; 5/23/1946
Graham, Otto Everett (football); Waukegan, Ill., 12/6/1921
Grange, Red (Harold) (football); Forksville, Pa., 6/13/1904
Green, Hubert (golf); Birmingham, Ala., 12/28/1946
Greene, Charles E. (sprinter); Pine Bluff, Ark., 3/21/1945
Gretzky, Wayne (hockey); Brantford, Ont., 1/26/1961
Griese, Bob (Robert Allen) (football); Evansville, Ind., 2/3/1945
Grove, Lefty (Robert Moses) (baseball); Lonaconing, Md., **(1900–1975)**
Groza, Lou (football); Martins Ferry, Ohio, 1/25/1924
Guidry, Ronald Ames (baseball); Lafayette, La., 8/28/1950
Gunter, Nancy Richey (tennis); San Angelo, Tex., 8/23/1942
Halas, George (football); Chicago, 2/2/1895
Hall, Gary (swimming); Fayetteville, N.C., 8/7/1951
Hamill, Dorothy (figure skater); Chicago, 1956(?)
Hammond, Kathy (runner); Sacramento, Calif., 11/2/1951
Harris, Franco (football); Ft. Dix, N.J., 3/7/1950
Hartack, William, Jr. (jockey); Colver, Pa., 12/9/1932
Haughton, William (harness racing); Gloversville, N.Y., 11/2/1923
Havlicek, John (basketball); Martins Ferry, Ohio, 4/8/1940
Hayes, Elvin (basketball); Rayville, La., 11/17/1945
Haynie, Sandra (golf); Fort Worth, 6/4/1943
Heiden, Eric (speed skating); Madison, Wis., 6/14/1958
Hencken, John (swimming); Culver City, Calif., 5/29/1954
Henderson, Rickey (baseball); Chicago, 12/25/1958
Henie, Sonja (ice skater); Oslo **(1912–1969)**
Hernandez, Keith (baseball); San Francisco, 10/20/1953
Hickcox, Charles (swimming); Phoenix, Ariz., 2/6/1947
Hines, James (sprinter); Dumas, Ark., 9/10/1946
Hodges, Gil (baseball); Princeton, Ind. **(1924–1972)**
Hogan, Ben (golf); Dublin, Tex., 8/13/1912
Holmes, Larry (boxing); Cuthert, Ga., 11/3/1949
Hornsby, Rogers (baseball); Winters, Tex. **(1896–1963)**
Hornung, Paul (football); Louisville, Ky., 12/23/1935
Houk, Ralph (baseball); Lawrence, Kan., 8/9/1919
Howard, Elston (baseball); St. Louis **(1929–1980)**
Howe, Gordon (hockey); Floral, Sask., Canada, 3/31/1928
Howell, Jim Lee (football); Lonoke, Ark., 9/27/1914
Hubbell, Carl (baseball); Carthage, Mo., 6/22/1903
Huff, Sam (Robert Lee) (football); Morgantown, W. Va., 10/4/1934
Hull, Bobby (hockey); Point Anne, Ontario, Canada, 1/3/1939
Hunter, Jim (Catfish) (baseball); Hertford, N.C., 4/8/1946
Huntley, Joni (track); McMinnville, Ore., 8/4/1956
Hutson, Donald (football); Pine Bluff, Ark., 1/31/1913
Insko, Del (harness racing); Amboy, Minn., 7/10/1931
Irwin, Hale (golf); Joplin, Mo., 6/3/1945
Jackson, Reggie (baseball); Wyncote, Pa., 5/18/1946
Jeffries, James J. (boxer); Carroll, Ohio **(1875–1953)**
Jenkins, Ferguson Arthur (baseball); Chatham, Ontario, Canada, 12/13/1943
Jenner, (W.) Bruce (track); Mt. Kisco, N.Y., 10/28/1949
Jezek, Linda (swimming); Palo Alto, Calif., 3/10/1960
Johnson, Earvin (Magic) (basketball); E. Lansing, Mich., 8/14/1959
Johnson, Anthony (rowing); Washington, D.C., 11/16/1940
Johnson, Jack (John Arthur Johnson) (boxer); Galveston, Tex. **(1876–1946)**
Johnson, Rafer (decathlon); Hillsboro, Tex., 8/18/1935
Jones, Deacon (David) (football); Eatonville, Fla., 12/9/1938
Juantoreno, Alberto (track); Santiago, Cuba, 12/3/1951
Jurgensen, Sonny (football); Wilmington, N.C., 8/23/1934
Kaat, Jim (baseball); Zeeland, Mich., 11/7/1938
Kaline, Al (Albert) (baseball); Baltimore, 12/19/1934
Keino, Kipchoge (runner); Kapchemoiymo, Kenya, 1/?/1940
Kelly, Leroy (football); Philadelphia, 5/20/1942
Kelly, Red (Leonard Patrick) (hockey); Simcoe, Ontario, Canada, 7/9/1927
Killebrew, Harmon (baseball); Payette, Idaho, 6/29/1936
Killy, Jean-Claude (skiing); Saint-Cloud, France, 8/30/1943
Kilmer, Bill (William Orland) (football); Topeka, Kan., 9/5/1939
King, Billie Jean (Billie Jean Moffitt) (tennis); Long Beach, Calif., 11/22/1943
Kinsella, John (swimming); Oak Park, Ill., 8/26/1952
Kodes, Jan (tennis); Prague, 3/1/1946
Kolb, Claudia (swimming); Hayward, Calif., 12/19/1949
Koosman, Jerry Martin (baseball); Appleton, Minn., 12/23/1942
Korbut, Olga (gymnast); Grodno, Byelorussia, U.S.S.R., 5/16/1955
Koufax, Sandy (Sanford) (baseball); Brooklyn, N.Y., 12/30/1935
Kramer, Jack (tennis); Las Vegas, Nev., 8/1/1921
Kramer, Jerry (football); Jordan, Mont., 1/23/1936
Kuhn, Bowie Kent (baseball); Takoma Park, Md., 10/28/1926
Kwalik, Ted (Thaddeus John) (football); McKees Rocks, Pa., 4/15/1947
Lafleur, Guy Damien (hockey); Thurson, Quebec, Canada, 8/20/1951
Laird, Ronald (walker); Louisville, Ky., 5/31/1935
Lamonica, Daryle (football); Fresno, Calif., 7/17/1941
Landis, Kenesaw Mountain (1st baseball commissioner); Millville, Ohio **(1866–1944)**
Landry, Tom (football); Mission, Tex., 9/11/1924
Landy, John (runner); Australia, 4/4/1930
Larrieu, Francie (track); Palo Alto, Calif., 11/28/1952
Lasorda, Tom (baseball); Norristown, Pa., 9/22/1927
Laver, Rod (tennis); Rockhampton, Australia, 8/9/1938
Lendl, Ivan (tennis); Prague, 3/7/1960
Leonard, Benny (Benjamin Leiner) (boxer); New York City **(1896–1947)**
Leonard, Sugar Ray (boxing); Wilmington, N.C., 5/17/1956
Lewis, Carl (track); Willingboro, N.J., 7/1/1961
Linehan, Kim (swimming); Bronxville, N.Y., 12/11/1962
Liquori, Marty (runner); Montclair, N.J., 9/11/1949
Little, Floyd Douglas (football); New Haven, Conn., 7/4/1942
Little, Lou (football); Leominster, Mass., **(1893–1979)**
Littler, Gene (golf); San Diego, Calif., 11/16/1920
Lloyd, Chris Evert (Christine Marie) (tennis); Fort Lauderdale, Fla., 12/21/1954
Lombardi, Vince (football); Brooklyn, N.Y. **(1913–1970)**
Longden, Johnny (horse racing); Wakefield, England, 2/14/1907
Lopez, Al (baseball); Tampa, Fla., 8/20/1908
Lopez, Nancy (golf); Torrance, Calif., 1/6/1957
Louis, Joe (Joe Louis Barrow) (boxing); Lafayette, Ala. **(1914–1981)**
Lynn, Frederic Michael (baseball); Chicago, Ill., 2/3/1952
Lynn, Janet (figure skating); Rockford, Ill., 4/6/1953
Mack, Connie (Cornelius Alexander McGillicuddy) (baseball executive); East Brookfield, Mass. **(1862–1956)**
Mackey, John (football); New York City, 9/24/1941
Mahovlich, Frank (Francis William) (hockey); Timmins, Ontario, Canada, 1/10/1938
Mahre, Phil (skiing); White Pass, Wash., 5/10/1957
Mann, Carol (golf); Buffalo, N.Y., 2/3/1941
Manning, Madeline (runner); Cleveland, 1/11/1948
Mantle, Mickey Charles (baseball); Spavinaw, Okla., 10/20/1931
Marciano, Rocky (boxing); Brockton, Mass. **(1923–1969)**
Marichal, Juan (baseball); Laguna Verde, Montecristi, Dominican Republic, 10/20/1937
Maris, Roger (baseball); Hibbing, Minn., 9/10/1934
Martin, Billy (Alfred Manuel) (baseball); Berkeley, Calif., 5/16/1928
Martin, Rick (Richard Lionel) (hockey); Verdun, Quebec, Canada, 7/26/1951
Mathews, Ed (Edwin) (baseball); Texarkana, Tex., 10/13/1931
Matson, Randy (shot putter); Kilgore, Tex., 3/5/1945
Mays, Willie (baseball); Westfield, Ala., 5/6/1931
McAdoo, Bob (basketball); Greensboro, N.C., 9/25/1951
McCarthy, Joe (Joseph Vincent) (baseball); Philadelphia **(1887–1978)**
McCovey, Willie Lee (baseball); Mobile, Ala., 1/10/1938
McEnroe, John Patrick, Jr. (tennis); Wiesbaden, Germany, 2/16/1959
McGraw, John Joseph (baseball); Truxton, N.Y. **(1873–1934)**
McLain, Dennis (baseball); Chicago, 3/24/1944
McMillan, Kathy Laverne (track); Raeford, N.C., 11/7/1957
Merrill, Janice (track); New London, Conn., 6/18/1962
Meyer, Deborah (swimming); Haddonfield, N.J., 8/14/1952
Middlecoff, Cary (golf); Halls, Tenn., 1/6/1921
Mikita, Stan (hockey); Sokolce, Czechoslovakia, 5/20/1940
Milburn, Rodney, Jr. (hurdler); Opelousas, La., 5/18/1950
Miller, Johnny (golf); San Francisco, 4/29/1947
Montgomery, Jim (swimming); Madison, Wis., 1/24/1955
Moore, Archie (boxing); Benoit, Miss., 12/13/1916
Morgan, Joe Leonard (baseball); Bonham, Tex., 9/19/1943
Morrall, Earl (football); Muskegon, Mich., 5/17/1934
Morton, Craig L. (football); Flint, Mich., 2/5/1943
Mosconi, Willie (pocket billiards); Philadelphia, 6/27/1913
Moser, Annemarie. *See* Proell, Annemarie
Moses, Edward Corley (track); Dayton, Ohio, 8/31/1958
Munson, Thurman (baseball); Akron, Ohio, **(1947–1979)**
Murphy, Calvin (basketball); Norwalk, Conn., 5/9/1948
Musial, Stan (baseball); Donora, Pa., 11/21/1920
Myers, Linda (archery); York, Pa., 6/19/1947
Naber, John (swimming); Evanston, Ill., 1/20/1956
Namath, Joe (Joseph William) (football); Beaver Falls, Pa., 5/31/1943
Nastase, Ilie (tennis); Bucharest, 7/19/1946

Navratilova, Martina (tennis); Prague, 10/18/1956
Nehemiah, Renaldo (track); Newark, N.J., 3/24/1959
Nelson, Cindy (skiing); Lutsen, Minn. 8/19/1955
Newcombe, John (tennis); Sydney, Australia, 5/23/1943
Niekro, Phil (baseball); Lansing, Ohio, 4/1/1939
Nicklaus, Jack (golf); Columbus, Ohio, 1/21/1940
North, Lowell (yachting); Springfield, Mo., 12/2/1929
Oerter, Al (discus thrower); New York City, 9/19/1936
Okker, Tom (tennis); Amsterdam, 2/22/1944
Oldfield, Barney (racing driver); Fulton County, Ohio **(1878–1946)**
Oliva, Tony (Pedro) (baseball); Pinar Del Rio, Cuba, 7/20/1940
Olsen, Merlin Jay (football); Logan, Utah, 9/15/1940
O'Malley, Walter (baseball executive); New York City **(1903–1979)**
Orantes, Manuel (tennis); Granada, Spain, 2/6/1949
Orr, Bobby (hockey); Parry Sound, Ontario, Canada, 3/20/1948
Ovett, Steve (track); Brighton, England, 10/9/1955
Owens, Jesse (track); Decatur, Ala. **(1914–1980)**
Pace, Darrell (archery); Cincinnati, 10/23/1956
Paige, Satchel (Leroy) (baseball); Mobile, Ala., **(1906–1982)**
Palmer, Arnold (golf); Latrobe, Pa., 9/10/1929
Palmer, James Alvin (baseball); New York City, 10/15/1945
Parent, Bernard Marcel (hockey); Montreal, 4/3/1945
Park, Brad (Douglas Bradford) (hockey); Toronto, Ontario, Canada, 7/6/1948
Parseghian, Ara (football); Akron, Ohio, 5/21/1923
Pasarell, Charles (tennis); San Juan, Puerto Rico, 2/12/1944
Patterson, Floyd (boxing); Waco, N.C., 1/4/1935
Peete, Calvin (golf); Detroit, Mich., 7/18/1943
Pelé (Edson Arantes do Nascimento) (soccer); Tres Coracoes, Brazil, 10/23/1940
Perry, Gaylord (baseball); Williamston, N.C., 9/13/1938
Perry, Jim (baseball); Williamston, N.C., 9/15/1938
Pettit, Bob (basketball); Baton Rouge, La., 12/12/1932
Petty, Richard Lee (auto racing); Randleman, N.C., 7/2/1937
Pincay, Laffit, Jr. (jockey); Panama City, Panama, 12/29/1946
Plante, Jacques (hockey); Shawinigan Falls, Quebec, Canada, 1/17/1929
Player, Gary (golf); Johannesburg, South Africa, 11/1/1935
Plunkett, Jim (football); San Jose, Calif., 12/5/1947
Potvin, Denis Charles (hockey); Hull, Quebec, Canada, 10/29/1953
Powell, Boog (John) (baseball); Lakeland, Fla., 8/17/1941
Prefontaine, Steve Roland (runner); Coos Bay, Ore. **(1951–1975)**
Proell, Annemarie Moser (Alpine skier); Kleinarl, Austria, 3/27/1953
Ralston, Dennis (tennis); Bakersfield, Calif., 7/27/1942
Rankin, Judy Torluemke (golf); St. Louis, Mo., 2/18/1945
Ratelle, Jean (Joseph Gilbert Yvon Jean) (hockey); St. Jean, Quebec, Canada, 10/29/1953
Rawls, Betsy (Elizabeth Earle) (golf); Spartanburg, S.C., 5/4/1928
Reed, Willis (basketball); Hico, La., 6/25/1942
Reese, Pee Wee (Harold) (baseball); Ekron, Ky., 7/23/1919
Richard, Maurice (hockey); Montreal, 8/14/1924
Riessen, Martin (tennis); Hinsdale, Ill., 12/4/1941
Rigney, William (baseball); Alameda, Calif., 1/29/1918
Rizzuto, Phil (baseball); New York City, 9/25/1918
Roark, Helen Wills Moody (tennis); Centerville, Calif., 10/6/1906
Robertson, Oscar (basketball); Charlotte, Tenn., 11/24/1938
Robinson, Arnie (track); San Diego, Calif., 4/7/1948
Robinson, Brooks (baseball); Little Rock, Ark., 5/18/1937
Robinson, Frank (baseball); Beaumont, Tex., 8/31/1935
Robinson, Jackie (baseball); Cairo, Ga. **(1919–1972)**
Robinson, Larry Clark (hockey); Marvelville, Ontario, Canada, 6/2/1951
Robinson, (Sugar) Ray (boxing); Detroit, 5/3/1920
Rockne, Knute Kenneth (football); Voss, Norway **(1888–1931)**
Rockwell, Martha (skiing); Providence, R.I., 4/26/1944
Rono, Harry (track); Kiptaragon, Kenya, 2/12/1952
Rose, Pete (Peter Edward) (baseball); Cincinnati, 4/14/1942
Rosenbloom, Maxie (boxing); New York City **(1904–1976)**
Rosewall, Ken (tennis); Sydney, Australia, 11/2/1934
Rote, Kyle (football); San Antonio, 10/27/1928
Rozelle, Pete (Alvin Ray) (commissioner of National Football League); South Gate, Calif., 3/1/1926
Rudolph, Wilma Glodean (sprinter); St. Bethlehem, Tenn., 6/23/1940
Russell, Bill (basketball); Monroe, La., 2/12/1934
Ruth, Babe (George Herman Ruth) (baseball); Baltimore **(1895–1948)**
Rutherford, Johnny (auto racing); Fort Worth, 3/12/1938
Ryan, Nolan (Lynn Nolan, Jr.) (baseball); Refugio, Tex., 1/31/1947
Ryon, Luann (archery); Long Beach, Calif., 1/13/1953
Ryun, Jim (runner); Wichita, Kan., 4/29/1947
Salazar, Alberto (track); Havana, 8/7/1958
Santana, Manuel (Manuel Santana Martinez) (tennis); Chamartín, Spain, 5/10/1938
Sayers, Gale (football); Wichita, Kan., 5/30/1943
Schmidt, Mike (baseball); Dayton, Ohio, 9/27/1949
Schoendienst, Al (Albert) (baseball); Germantown, Ill., 2/2/1923
Schollander, Donald (swimming); Charlotte, N.C., 4/30/1946
Seagren, Bob (Robert Lloyd) (pole vaulter); Pomona, Calif., 10/17/1946
Seaver, Tom (baseball); Fresno, Calif., 11/17/1944
Seidler, Maren (track); Brooklyn, N.Y., 6/11/1962
Shoemaker, Willie (jockey); Fabens, Tex., 8/19/1931
Shorter, Frank (runner); Munich, Germany, 10/31/1947
Shula, Don (Donald Francis) (football); Grand River, Ohio, 1/4/1930
Silvester, Jay (discus thrower); Tremonton, Utah, 2/27/1937
Simpson, O. J. (Orenthal James) (football); San Francisco, 7/9/1947
Sims, Billy (football); St. Louis, 9/18/1955
Smith, Bubba (Charles Aaron) (football); Orange, Tex., 2/28/1945
Smith, Ronnie Ray (sprinter); Los Angeles, 3/28/1949
Smith, Stanley Roger (tennis); Pasadena, Calif., 12/14/1946
Smith, Tommie (sprinter); Clarksville, Tex., 6/5/1944
Smoke, Marcia Jones (canoeing); Oklahoma City, 7/18/1941
Snead, Sam (golf); Hot Springs, Va., 5/27/1912
Sneva, Tom (auto racing); Spokane, Wash., 6/1/1948
Snider, Duke (Edwin) (baseball); Los Angeles, 9/19/1926
Solomon, Harold (tennis); Washington, D.C., 9/17/1952
Spahn, Warren (baseball); Buffalo, N.Y., 4/23/1921
Speaker, Tristram (baseball); Hubbard City, Tex. **(1888–1958)**
Spinks, Leon (boxing); St. Louis, 7/11/1953
Spitz, Mark (swimming); Modesto, Calif., 2/10/1950
Stabler, Kenneth (football); Foley, Ala., 12/25/1945
Stagg, Amos Alonzo (football); West Orange, N.J. **(1862–1965)**
Stargell, Willie (Wilver Dornell) (baseball); Earlsboro, Okla., 3/6/1941
Starr, Bart (football); Montgomery, Ala., 1/9/1934
Staubach, Roger (football); Cincinnati, 2/5/1942
Steinkraus, William C. (equestrian); Cleveland, 10/12/1925
Stenerud, Jan (football); Fetsund, Norway, 11/26/1942
Stengel, Casey (Charles Dillon) (baseball); Kansas City, Mo. **(1891–1975)**
Stenmark, Ingemar (Alpine skier); Tarnaby, Sweden, 3/18/1956
Stockton, Richard LaClede (tennis); New York City, 2/18/1951
Stones, Dwight Edwin (track); Los Angeles, 12/6/1953
Sullivan, John Lawrence (boxer); Boston **(1858–1918)**
Sutton, Don (Donald Howard) (baseball); Clio, Ala., 4/2/1945
Swann, Lynn (football); Alcoa, Tenn., 3/7/1952
Tanner, Leonard Roscoe III (tennis); Chattanooga, Tenn., 10/15/1951
Tarkenton, Fran (Francis) (football); Richmond, Va., 2/3/1940
Tebbetts, Birdie (George R.) (baseball); Nashua, N.H., 11/10/1914
Thoeni, Gustavo (Alpine skier); Trafoi, Italy, 2/28/1951
Thompson, David (basketball); Shelby, N.C., 7/13/1954
Thorpe, Jim (James Francis Thorpe) (all-around athlete); nr. Prague, Okla. **(1888–1953)**
Tilden, William Tatem II (tennis); Philadelphia **(1893–1953)**
Tittle, Y. A. (Yelberton Abraham) (football); Marshall, Tex., 10/24/1926
Toomey, William (decathlon); Philadelphia, 1/10/1939
Trevino, Lee (golf); Dallas, 12/1/1939
Tunney, Gene (James J.) (boxing); New York City **(1898–1978)**
Tyus, Wyomia (runner); Griffin, Ga., 8/29/1945
Unitas, John (football); Pittsburgh, 5/7/1933
Unser, Al (auto racing); Albuquerque, N. Mex., 5/29/1939
Unser, Bobby (auto racing); Albuquerque N. Mex., 2/20/1934
Valenzuela, Fernando (baseball); Sonora, Mexico, 11/1/1960
Van Brocklin, Norm (football); Eagle Butte, S. Dak., 3/15/1926
Vilas, Guillermo (tennis); Mar del Plata, Argentina, 8/17/1952
Viren, Lasse (track); Myrskyla, Finland, 7/12/1949
Wade, Virginia (tennis); Bournemouth, England, 7/10/1945
Wagner, Honus (John Peter Honus) (baseball); Carnegie, Pa. **(1867–1955)**
Walcott, Jersey Joe (Arnold Cream) (boxing); Merchantville, N.J., 1/31/1914
Walton, Bill (basketball); La Mesa, Calif., 11/5/1952
Watson, Martha Rae (track); Long Beach, Calif., 8/19/1946
Watson, Tom (golf); Kansas City, Mo., 9/4/1949
Weaver, Earl (baseball); St. Louis, 8/14/1930
Webster, Alex (football); Kearny, N.J., 4/19/1931
Weiskopf, Tom (golf); Massillon, Ohio, 11/9/1942
Weiss, George (baseball executive); New Haven, Conn. **(1895–1972)**
Weissmuller, Johnny (swimmer and actor); Windber, Pa., 6/2/1904
West, Jerry (basketball); Cheylan, W. Va., 5/28/1938
White, Willye B. (long jumper); Money, Miss., 1/1/1936
Whitworth, Kathy (golf); Monahans, Tex., 9/27/1939
Wilkens, Mac Maurice (track); Eugene, Ore., 11/15/1950
Wilkins, Lennie (basketball); 11/25/1937
Wilkinson, Bud (football); Minneapolis, 4/23/1916
Williams, Dick (baseball); St. Louis, 5/7/1929
Williams, Ted (baseball); San Diego, Calif., 8/30/1918
Wills, Maury (baseball); Washington, D.C., 10/2/1932
Winfield, Dave (baseball); St. Paul, Minn., 10/3/1951
Wohlhuter, Richard C. (runner); Geneva, Ill. 12/23/1945
Woodhead, Cynthia (swimming); Riverside, Calif., 2/7/1964
Wottle, David James (runner); Canton, Ohio, 8/7/1950
Wright, Mickey (Mary Kathryn) (golf); San Diego, Calif., 2/14/1935
Yarborough, Cale (William Caleb) (auto racing); Timmonsville, S.C., 3/27/1939
Yastrzemski, Carl (baseball); Southampton, N.Y., 8/22/1939
Young, Cy (Denton True Young) (baseball); Gilmore, Ohio **(1867–1955)**
Young, Sheila (speed skater, bicycle racer); Detroit, 10/14/1950

THE OLYMPIC GAMES

(W)—Site of Winter Games. (S)—Site of Summer Games

1896	Athens
1900	Paris
1904	St. Louis
1906	Athens
1908	London
1912	Stockholm
1920	Antwerp
1924	Chamonix (W)
1924	Paris (S)
1928	St. Moritz (W)
1928	Amsterdam (S)
1932	Lake Placid (W)
1932	Los Angeles (S)
1936	Garmisch-Partenkirchen (W)
1936	Berlin (S)
1948	St. Moritz (W)
1948	London (S)
1952	Oslo (W)
1952	Helsinki (S)
1956	Cortina d'Ampezzo, Italy (W)
1956	Melbourne (S)
1960	Squaw Valley, Calif. (W)
1960	Rome (S)
1964	Innsbruck, Austria (W)
1964	Tokyo (S)
1968	Grenoble, France (W)
1968	Mexico City (S)
1972	Sapporo, Japan (W)
1972	Munich (S)
1976	Innsbruck, Austria (W)
1976	Montreal (S)
1980	Lake Placid (W)
1980	Moscow (S)
1984	Sarajevo, Yugoslavia (W)
1984	Los Angeles (S)
1988	Calgary, Alberta (W)
1988	Seoul, South Korea (S)

The first Olympic Games of which there is record occurred in 776 B.C. and consisted of one event, a great foot race of about 200 yards held on a plain by the River Alpheus (now the Ruphia) just outside the little town of Olympia in Greece. It was from that date that the Greeks began to keep their calendar by "Olympiads," the four-year spans between the celebrations of the famous games.

The modern Olympic Games, which started in Athens in 1896, are the result of the devotion of a French educator, Baron Pierre de Coubertin, to the idea that, since young people and athletics have gone together down the ages, education and athletics might well go hand-in-hand toward a better international understanding.

At the top of the organization responsible for the Olympic movement and the staging of the Games every four years is the International Olympic Committee (IOC). Other important roles are played by National Olympic Committees in each participating country, international sports federations, and the Organizing Committee of the host city.

In 1979, the IOC consisted of 89 members, elected by the IOC itself. Its headquarters are in Lausanne, Switzerland. The president of the IOC is Juan Antonio Samaranch of Spain.

The Olympic motto is "Citius, Altius, Fortius"—"Faster, Higher, Stronger." The Olympic symbol is five interlocking circles colored blue, yellow, black, green, and red, on a white background, representing the five continents. At least one of these colors appears in the national flag of every country.

Summer Games

TRACK AND FIELD—MEN

100-Meter Dash

1896	Thomas Burke, United States	12s
1900	Francis W. Jarvis, United States	10.8s
1904	Archie Hahn, United States	11s
1906	Archie Hahn, United States	11.2s
1908	Reginald Walker, South Africa	10.8s
1912	Ralph Craig, United States	10.8s
1920	Charles Paddock, United States	10.8s
1924	Harold Abrahams, Great Britain	10.6s
1928	Percy Williams, Canada	10.8s
1932	Eddie Tolan, United States	10.3s
1936	Jesse Owens, United States	10.3s[1]
1948	Harrison Dillard, United States	10.3s
1952	Lindy Remigino, United States	10.4s
1956	Bobby Morrow, United States	10.5s
1960	Armin Hary, Germany	10.2s
1964	Robert Hayes, United States	10s
1968	James Hines, United States	9.9s
1972	Valery Borzov, U.S.S.R.	10.14s
1976	Hasely Crawford, Trinidad and Tebago	10.06s
1980	Allan Wells, Britain	10.25s

1. Wind assisted.

200-Meter Dash

1900	John Tewksbury, United States	22.2s
1904	Archie Hahn, United States	21.6s
1908	Robert Kerr, Canada	22.6s
1912	Ralph Craig, United States	21.7s
1920	Allan Woodring, United States	22s
1924	Jackson Scholz, United States	21.6s
1928	Percy Williams, Canada	21.8s
1932	Eddie Tolan, United States	21.2s
1936	Jesse Owens, United States	20.7s
1948	Melvin E. Patton, United States	21.1s
1952	Andrew Stanfield, United States	20.7s
1956	Bobby Morrow, United States	20.6s
1960	Livio Berruti, Italy	20.5s
1964	Henry Carr, United States	20.3s
1968	Tommie Smith, United States	19.8s
1972	Valery Borzov, U.S.S.R.	20s
1976	Don Quarrie, Jamaica	20.23s
1980	Pietro Mennea, Italy	20.19s

400-Meter Dash

1896	Thomas Burke, United States	54.2s
1900	Maxwell Long, United States	49.4s
1904	Harry Hillman, United States	49.2s
1906	Paul Pilgrim, United States	53.2s
1908	Wyndham Halswelle, Great Britain (walkover)	50s
1912	Charles Reidpath, United States	48.2s
1920	Bevil Rudd, South Africa	49.6s
1924	Eric Liddell, Great Britain	47.6s
1928	Ray Barbuti, United States	47.8s
1932	William Carr, United States	46.2s
1936	Archie Williams, United States	46.5s
1948	Arthur Wint, Jamaica, B.W.I.	46.2s
1952	George Rhoden, Jamaica, B.W.I.	45.9s
1956	Charles Jenkins, United States	46.7s
1960	Otis Davis, United States	44.9s
1964	Mike Larrabee, United States	45.1s
1968	Lee Evans, United States	43.8s
1972	Vincent Matthews, United States	44.66s
1976	Alberto Juantorena, Cuba	44.26s
1980	Viktor Markin, U.S.S.R.	44.60s

800-Meter Run

1896	Edwin Flack, Australia	2m11s
1900	Alfred Tysoe, Great Britain	2m1.4s
1904	James Lightbody, United States	1m56s
1906	Paul Pilgrim, United States	2m1.2s
1908	Mel Sheppard, United States	1m52.8s
1912	Ted Meredith, United States	1m51.9s

1920	Albert Hill, Great Britain	1m53.4s
1924	Douglas Lowe, Great Britain	1m52.4s
1928	Douglas Lowe, Great Britain	1m51.8s
1932	Thomas Hampson, Great Britain	1m49.8s
1936	John Woodruff, United States	1m52.9s
1948	Malvin Whitfield, United States	1m49.2s
1952	Malvin Whitfield, United States	1m49.2s
1956	Tom Courtney, United States	1m47.7s
1960	Peter Snell, New Zealand	1m46.3s
1964	Peter Snell, New Zealand	1m45.1s
1968	Ralph Doubell, Australia	1m44.3s
1972	David Wottle, United States	1m45.9s
1976	Alberto Juantorena, Cuba	1m43.5s
1980	Steve Ovett, Britain	1m45.4s

1,500-Meter Run

1896	Edwin Flack, Australia	4m33.2s
1900	Charles Bennett, Great Britain	4m6s
1904	James Lightbody, United States	4m5.4s
1906	James Lightbody, United States	4m12s
1908	Mel Sheppard, United States	4m3.4s
1912	Arnold Jackson, Great Britain	3m56.8s
1920	Albert Hill, Great Britain	4m1.8s
1924	Paavo Nurmi, Finland	3m53.6s
1928	Harry Larva, Finland	3m53.2s
1932	Luigi Beccali, Italy	3m51.2s
1936	Jack Lovelock, New Zealand	3m47.8s
1948	Henri Eriksson, Sweden	3m49.8s
1952	Joseph Barthel, Luxembourg	3m45.2s
1956	Ron Delany, Ireland	3m41.2s
1960	Herb Elliott, Australia	3m35.6s
1964	Peter Snell, New Zealand	3m38.1s
1968	Kipchoge Keino, Kenya	3m34.9s
1972	Pekka Vasala, Finland	3m36.3s
1976	John Walker, New Zealand	3m39.17s
1980	Sebastian Coe, Britain	3m38.4s

5,000-Meter Run

1912	Hannes Kolehmainen, Finland	14m36.6s
1920	Joseph Guillemot, France	14m55.6s
1924	Paavo Nurmi, Finland	14m31.2s
1928	Willie Ritola, Finland	14m38s
1932	Lauri Lehtinen, Finland	14m30s
1936	Gunnar Hockert, Finland	14m22.2s
1948	Gaston Reiff, Belgium	14m17.6s
1952	Emil Zatopek, Czechoslovakia	14m6.6s
1956	Vladimir Kuts, U.S.S.R.	13m39.6s
1960	Murray Halberg, New Zealand	13m43.4s
1964	Bob Schul, United States	13m48.8s
1968	Mohamed Gammoudi, Tunisia	14m.05s
1972	Lasse Viren, Finland	13m26.4s
1976	Lasse Viren, Finland	13m24.76s
1980	Miruts Yifter, Ethiopia	13m21s

5-Mile Run

1906	H. Hawtrey, Great Britain	26m26.2s
1908	Emil Voigt, Great Britain	25m11.2s

10,000-Meter Run

1912	Hannes Kolehmainen, Finland	31m20.8s
1920	Paavo Nurmi, Finland	31m45.8s
1924	Willie Ritola, Finland	30m23.2s
1928	Paavo Nurmi, Finland	30m18.8s
1932	Janusz Kusocinski, Poland	30m11.4s
1936	Ilmari Salminen, Finland	30m15.4s
1948	Emil Zatopek, Czechoslovakia	29m59.6s
1952	Emil Zatopek, Czechoslovakia	29m17s
1956	Vladimir Kuts, U.S.S.R.	28m45.6s
1960	Peter Bolotnikov, U.S.S.R.	28m32.2s
1964	Billy Mills, United States	28m24.4s
1968	Naftali Temu, Kenya	29m27.4s
1972	Lasse Viren, Finland	27m38.4s
1976	Lasse Viren, Finland	27m40.38s
1980	Miruts Yifter, Ethiopia	27m42.7s

Marathon

1896	Spiridon Loues, Greece	2h58m50s
1900	Michel Teato, France	2h59m45s
1904	Thomas Hicks, United States	3h28m53s
1906	William J. Sherring, Canada	2h51m23.65s
1908	John J. Hayes, United States	2h55m18.4s
1912	Kenneth McArthur, South Africa	2h36m54.8s
1920	Hannes Kolehmainen, Finland	2h32m35.8s
1924	Albin Stenroos, Finland	2h41m22.6s
1928	A. B. El Ouafi, France	2h32m57s
1932	Juan Zabala, Argentina	2h31m36s
1936	Kitei Son, Japan	2h29m19.2s
1948	Delfo Cabrera, Argentina	2h34m51.6s
1952	Emil Zatopek, Czechoslovakia	2h23m3.2s
1956	Alain Mimoun, France	2h25m
1960	Abebe Bikila, Ethiopia	2h15m16.2s
1964	Abebe Bikila, Ethiopia	2h12m11.2s
1968	Mamo Wold, Ethiopia	2h20m26.4s
1972	Frank Shorter, United States	2h12m19.8s
1976	Walter Cierpinski, East Germany	2h09m55s
1980	Walter Cierpinski, East Germany	2h11m3s

110-Meter Hurdles

1896	Thomas Curtis, United States	17.6s
1900	Alvin Kraenzlein, United States	15.4s
1904	Frederick Schule, United States	16s
1906	R. G. Leavitt, United States	16.2s
1908	Forrest Smithson, United States	15s
1912	Frederick Kelly, United States	15.1s
1920	Earl Thomson, Canada	14.8s
1924	Daniel Kinsey, United States	15s
1928	Sydney Atkinson, South Africa	14.8s
1932	George Saling, United States	14.6s
1936	Forrest Towns, United States	14.2s
1948	William Porter, United States	13.9s
1952	Harrison Dillard, United States	13.7s
1956	Lee Calhoun, United States	13.5s
1960	Lee Calhoun, United States	13.8s
1964	Hayes Jones, United States	13.6s
1968	Willie Davenport, United States	13.3s
1972	Rodney Milburn, United States	13.24s
1976	Guy Drut, France	13.30s
1980	Thomas Munkett, East Germany	13.39s

200-Meter Hurdles

1900	Alvin Kraenzlein, United States	25.4s
1904	Harry Hillman, United States	24.6s

400-Meter Hurdles

1900	John Tewksbury, United States	57.6s
1904	Harry Hillman, United States	53s
1908	Charles Bacon, United States	55s
1920	Frank Loomis, United States	54s
1924	F. Morgan Taylor, United States	52.6s
1928	Lord David Burghley, Great Britain	53.4s
1932	Robert Tisdall, Ireland	51.8s[1]
1936	Glenn Hardin, United States	52.4s
1948	Roy Cochran, United States	51.1s
1952	Charles Moore, United States	50.8s
1956	Glenn Davis, United States	50.1s
1960	Glenn Davis, United States	49.3s
1964	Rex Cawley, United States	49.6s
1968	David Hemery, Great Britain	48.1s
1972	John Akii-Bua, Uganda	47.8s
1976	Edwin Moses, United States	47.64
1980	Volker Beck, East Germany	48.70s

1. Record not allowed.

2,500-Meter Steeplechase

1900	George Orton, United States	7m34s
1904	James Lightbody, United States	7m39.6s

3,000-Meter Steeplechase

1920	Percy Hodge, Great Britain	10m0.4s
1924	Willie Ritola, Finland	9m33.6s
1928	Toivo Loukola, Finland	9m21.8s
1932	Volmari Iso-Hollo, Finland	10m33.4s[1]
1936	Volmari Iso-Hollo, Finland	9m3.8s
1948	Thure Sjoestrand, Sweden	9m4.6s
1952	Horace Ashenfelter, United States	8m45.4s
1956	Chris Brasher, Great Britain	8m41.2s
1960	Zdzislaw Krzyskowiak, Poland	8m34.2s
1964	Gaston Roelants, Belgium	8m30.8s
1968	Amos Biwott, Kenya	8m51s
1972	Kipchoge Keino, Kenya	8m23.6s
1976	Anders Gardervd, Sweden	8m08.02s
1980	Bronislaw Malinowski, Poland	8m9.7s

1. About 3,450 meters—extra lap by error.

Cross-Country

1912	Hannes Kolehmainen, Finland (8,000 meters)	45m11.6s
1920	Paavo Nurmi, Finland (10,000 meters)	27m15s
1924	Paavo Nurmi, Finland (10,000 meters)	32m54.8s

Cross-Country Team Races

		Pts.
1912	Sweden (8,000 meters)	10
1920	Finland (10,000 meters)	10
1924	Finland (10,000 meters)	11

1,500-Meter Walk

1906	George V. Bonhag, United States	7m12.6s

3,000-Meter Walk

1920	Ugo Frigerio, Italy	13m14.2s

10,000-Meter Walk

1912	George Goulding, Canada	46m28.4s
1920	Ugo Frigerio, Italy	48m6.2s
1924	Ugo Frigerio, Italy	47m49s
1948	John Mikaelsson, Sweden	45m13.2s
1952	John Mikaelsson, Sweden	45m2.8s

20,000-Meter Walk

1956	Leonid Spirin, U.S.S.R.	1h31m27.4s
1960	Vladimir Golubnichy, U.S.S.R.	1h34m7.2s
1964	Ken Mathews, Great Britain	1h29m34s
1968	Vladimir Golubnichy, U.S.S.R.	1h33m58.4s
1972	Peter Frenkel, East Germany	1h26m42.4s
1976	Daniel Bautista, Mexico	1h24m40.6s
1980	Maurizio Damiliano, Italy	1h23m35.5s

50,000-Meter Walk

1932	Thomas W. Green, Great Britain	4h50m10s
1936	Harold Whitlock, Great Britain	4h30m41.1s
1948	John Ljunggren, Sweden	4h41m52s
1952	Giuseppe Dordoni, Italy	4h28m7.8s
1956	Norman Read, New Zealand	4h30m42.8s
1960	Donald Thompson, Great Britain	4h25m30s
1964	Abdon Pamich, Italy	4h11m12.4s
1968	Christoph Hohne, East Germany	4h20m13.6s
1972	Bern Kannernberg, West Germany	3h56m11.6s
1980	Hartwig Gauder, East Germany	3h49m24s

400-Meter Relay (4 x 100)

1912	Great Britain	42.4s
1920	United States	42.2s
1924	United States	41s
1928	United States	41s
1932	United States	40s
1936	United States	39.8s
1948	United States	40.6s
1952	United States	40.1s
1956	United States	39.5s
1960	Germany	39.5s
1964	United States	39s
1968	United States	38.2s
1972	United States	38.19s
1976	United States	38.33s
1980	U.S.S.R.	38.26s

1,600-Meter Relay (200–200–400–800)

1908	United States	3m29.4s

1,600-Meter Relay (4 x 400)

1912	United States	3m16.6s
1920	Great Britain	3m22.2s
1924	United States	3m16s
1928	United States	3m14.2s
1932	United States	3m8.2s
1936	Great Britain	3m9s
1948	United States	3m10.4s
1952	Jamaica, B.W.I.	3m3.9s
1956	United States	3m4.8s
1960	United States	3m2.2s
1964	United States	3m0.7s
1968	United States	2m56.1s
1972	Kenya	2m59.8s
1976	United States	2m58.65s
1980	U.S.S.R.	3m01.1s

Team Race

		Pts.
1900	Great Britain (5,000 meters)	26
1904	United States (4 miles)	27
1908	Great Britain (3 miles)	6
1912	United States (3,000 meters)	9
1920	United States (3,000 meters)	10
1924	Finland (3,000 meters)	9

Standing High Jump

1900	Ray Ewry, United States	5 ft 5 in.
1904	Ray Ewry, United States	4 ft 11 in.
1906	Ray Ewry, United States	5 ft 1⅝ in.
1908	Ray Ewry, United States	5 ft 2 in.
1912	Platt Adams, United States	5 ft 4⅛ in.

Running High Jump

1896	Ellery Clark, United States	5 ft 11¼ in.
1900	Irving Baxter, United States	6 ft 2¾ in.
1904	Samuel Jones, United States	5 ft 11 in.
1906	Con Leahy, Ireland	5 ft 9⅞ in.
1908	Harry Porter, United States	6 ft 3 in.
1912	Alma Richards, United States	6 ft 4 in.
1920	Richmond Landon, United States	6 ft 4¼ in.
1924	Harold Osborn, United States	6 ft 5 15/16 in.
1928	Robert W. King, United States	6 ft 4⅜ in.
1932	Duncan McNaughton, Canada	6 ft 5⅝ in.
1936	Cornelius Johnson, United States	6 ft 7 15/16 in.
1948	John Winter, Australia	6 ft 6 in.
1952	Walter Davis, United States	6 ft 8 5/16 in.
1956	Charles Dumas, United States	6 ft 11¼ in.
1960	Robert Shavlakadze, U.S.S.R.	7 ft 1 in.
1964	Valeri Brumel, U.S.S.R.	7 ft 1¾ in.
1968	Dick Fosbury, United States	7 ft 4¼ in.
1972	Yuri Tarmak, U.S.S.R.	7 ft 3¾ in.
1976	Jacek Wszola, Poland	(2.25m) 7 ft 4½ in.
1980	Gerd Wessig, East Germany	7ft 8¾ in.

Standing Long Jump

1900	Ray Ewry, United States	10 ft 6⅖ in.
1904	Ray Ewry, United States	11 ft 4⅞ in.
1906	Ray Ewry, United States	10 ft 10 in.
1908	Ray Ewry, United States	10 ft 11¼ in.
1912	Constantin Tsicilitiras, Greece	11 ft ¼ in.

Long Jump

1896	Ellery Clark, United States	20 ft 9¾ in.
1900	Alvin Kraenzlein, United States	23 ft 6⅞ in.
1904	Myer Prinstein, United States	24 ft 1 in.
1906	Myer Prinstein, United States	23 ft 7½ in.
1908	Frank Irons, United States	24 ft 6½ in.
1912	Albert Gutterson, United States	24 ft 11¼ in.
1920	William Petterssen, Sweden	23 ft 5½ in.
1924	DeHart Hubbard, United States	24 ft 5⅛ in.
1928	Edward B. Hamm, United States	25 ft 4¾ in.
1932	Edward Gordon, United States	25 ft ¾ in.
1936	Jesse Owens, United States	26 ft 5⁵⁄₁₆ in.
1948	Willie Steele, United States	25 ft 8 in.
1952	Jerome Biffle, United States	24 ft 10 in.
1956	Gregory Bell, United States	25 ft 8¼ in.
1960	Ralph Boston, United States	26 ft 7¾ in.
1964	Lynn Davies, Great Britain	26 ft 5¾ in.
1968	Bob Beamon, United States	29 ft 2½ in.
1972	Randy Williams, United States	27 ft ½ in.
1976	Arnie Robinson, United States	(8.35m) 24 ft 7¾ in.
1980	Lutz Dombrowski, Poland	28 ft ¼ in.

Standing Triple Jump

1900	Ray Ewry, United States	34 ft 8½ in.
1904	Ray Ewry, United States	34 ft 7¼ in.

Triple Jump

1896	James B. Connolly, United States	45 ft
1900	Myer Prinstein, United States	47 ft 4¼ in.
1904	Myer Prinstein, United States	47 ft
1906	P. G. O'Connor, Ireland	46 ft 2 in.
1908	Timothy Ahearne, Great Britain	48 ft 11¼ in.
1912	Gustaf Lindblom, Sweden	48 ft 5⅛ in.
1920	Vilho Tuulos, Finland	47 ft 6⅞ in.
1924	Archie Winter, Australia	50 ft 11⅛ in.
1928	Mikio Oda, Japan	49 ft 10¹³⁄₁₆ in.
1932	Chuhei Nambu, Japan	51 ft 7 in.
1936	Naoto Tajima, Japan	52 ft 5⅞ in.
1948	Arne Ahman, Sweden	50 ft 6¼ in.
1952	Adhemar da Silva, Brazil	53 ft 2½ in.
1956	Adhemar da Silva, Brazil	53 ft 7½ in.
1960	Jozef Schmidt, Poland	55 ft 1¾ in.
1964	Jozef Schmidt, Poland	55 ft 3¼ in.
1968	Viktor Saneyev, U.S.S.R.	57 ft ¾ in.
1972	Viktor Saneyev, U.S.S.R.	56 ft 11 in.
1976	Viktor Saneyev, U.S.S.R.	(17.29m) 56 ft 8¾ in.
1980	Jaak Uudmae, U.S.S.R.	56 ft 11⅛ in.

Pole Vault

1896	William Hoyt, United States	10 ft 9¾ in.
1900	Irving Baxter, United States	10 ft 9⅞ in.
1904	Charles Dvorak, United States	11 ft 6 in.
1906	Fernand Gouder, France	11 ft 6 in.
1908	Alfred Gilbert, United States, and Edward Cook, United States (tie)	12 ft 2 in.
1912	Harry Babcock, United States	12 ft 11½ in.
1920	Frank Foss, United States	13 ft 5⁹⁄₁₆ in.
1924	Lee Barnes, United States	12 ft 11½ in.
1928	Sabin W. Carr, United States	13 ft 9⅜ in.
1932	William Miller, United States	14 ft 1⅞ in.
1936	Earle Meadows, United States	14 ft 3¼ in.
1948	Guinn Smith, United States	14 ft 1¼ in.
1952	Robert Richards, United States	14 ft 11⅛ in.
1956	Robert Richards, United States	14 ft 11½ in.
1960	Don Bragg, United States	15 ft 5⅛ in.
1964	Fred Hansen, United States	16 ft 8¾ in.
1968	Bob Seagren, United States	17 ft 8½ in.
1972	Wolfgang Nordwig, East Germany	18 ft ½ in.
1976	Tadeusz Slusarski, Poland	(5.50m) 18 ft ½ in.
1980	Wladyslaw Kozakiewicz, Poland	18 ft 11½ in.

16-lb Shot-Put

1896	Robert Garrett, United States	36 ft 9¾ in.
1900	Richard Sheldon, United States	46 ft 3⅛ in.
1904	Ralph Rose, United States	48 ft 7 in.
1906	Martin Sheridan, United States	40 ft 4⅘ in.
1908	Ralph Rose, United States	46 ft 7½ in.
1912	Pat McDonald, United States	50 ft 4 in.
1920	Ville Porhola, Finland	48 ft 7⅛ in.
1924	Clarence Houser, United States	49 ft 2½ in.
1928	John Kuck, United States	52 ft 11¹¹⁄₁₆ in.
1932	Leo Sexton, United States	52 ft 6³⁄₁₆ in.
1936	Hans Woellke, Germany	53 ft 1¾ in.
1948	Wilbur Thompson, United States	56 ft 2 in.
1952	Parry O'Brien, United States	57 ft 1½ in.
1956	Parry O'Brien, United States	60 ft 11 in.
1960	Bill Nieder, United States	64 ft 6¾ in.
1964	Dallas Long, United States	66 ft 8¼ in.
1968	Randy Matson, United States	67 ft 4¾ in.
1972	Wladyslaw Komar, Poland	69 ft 6 in.
1976	Udo Beyer, East Germany	(21.05m) 69 ft ¾ in.
1980	Vladimir Kiselyov, U.S.S.R.	70 ft ½ in.

16-lb Shot-Put (Both Hands)

1912	Ralph Rose, United States	90 ft 5⅜ in.

Discus Throw

1896	Robert Garrett, United States	95 ft 7½ in.
1900	Rudolf Bauer, Hungary	118 ft 2⅞ in.
1904	Martin Sheridan, United States	128 ft 10½ in.
1906	Martin Sheridan, United States	136 ft ⅓ in.
1908	Martin Sheridan, United States	134 ft 2 in.
1912	Armas Taipale, Finland	145 ft ⁹⁄₁₆ in.
1920	Elmer Niklander, Finland	146 ft 7 in.
1924	Clarence Houser, United States	151 ft 5¼ in.
1928	Clarence Houser, United States	155 ft 2⅘ in.
1932	John Anderson, United States	162 ft 4⅞ in.
1936	Ken Carpenter, United States	165 ft 7⅜ in.
1948	Adolfo Consolini, Italy	173 ft 2 in.
1952	Simeon Iness, United States	180 ft 6½ in.
1956	Al Oerter, United States	184 ft 10½ in.
1960	Al Oerter, United States	194 ft 2 in.
1964	Al Oerter, United States	200 ft 1½ in.
1968	Al Oerter, United States	212 ft 6 in.
1972	Ludvik Danek, Czechoslovakia	211 ft 3 in.
1976	Mac Wilkins, United States	(67.5m) 221 ft 5 in.
1980	Viktor Rashchupkin, U.S.S.R.	218 ft 8 in.

Discus Throw—Greek Style

1906	Werner Jaervinen, Finland	115 ft 4 in.
1908	Martin Sheridan, United States	124 ft 8 in.

Discus Throw (Both Hands)

1912	Armas Taipale, Finland	271 ft 10⅛ in.

Javelin Throw

1906	Eric Lemming, Sweden	175 ft 6 in.
1908	Eric Lemming, Sweden	179 ft 10½ in.
1912	Eric Lemming, Sweden	198 ft 11¼ in.
1920	Jonni Myyra, Finland	215 ft 9¾ in.
1924	Jonni Myyra, Finland	206 ft 6¾ in.
1928	Eric Lundquist, Sweden	218 ft 6⅛ in.
1932	Matti Jarvinen, Finland	238 ft 7 in.
1936	Gerhard Stoeck, Germany	235 ft 8⁵⁄₁₆ in.
1948	Kaj Rautavaara, Finland	228 ft 10½ in.
1952	Cy Young, United States	242 ft ¾ in.
1956	Egil Danielsen, Norway	281 ft 2¼ in.
1960	Viktor Tsibulenko, U.S.S.R.	277 ft 8⅜ in.
1964	Pauli Nevala, Finland	271 ft 2¼ in.
1968	Janis Lusis, U.S.S.R.	295 ft 7 in.
1972	Klaus Wolfermann, West Germany	296 ft 10 in.
1976	Miklos Nemeth, Hungary	(94.58m) 310 ft 4 in.
1980	Dainis Kula, U.S.S.R.	299 ft 2⅜ in.

Javelin Throw—Free Style

1908	Eric Lemming, Sweden	178 ft 7½ in.

Javelin Throw (Both Hands)

1912	Julius Saaristo, Finland	358 ft 11½ in.

16-lb Hammer Throw

1900	John Flanagan, United States	167 ft 4 in.
1904	John Flanagan, United States	168 ft 1 in.
1908	John Flanagan, United States	170 ft 4¼ in.
1912	Matt McGrath, United States	179 ft 7⅛ in.
1920	Pat Ryan, United States	173 ft 5⅝ in.
1924	Fred Tootell, United States	174 ft 10¼ in.
1928	Patrick O'Callaghan, Ireland	168 ft 7½ in.
1932	Patrick O'Callaghan, Ireland	176 ft 11⅛ in.
1936	Karl Hein, Germany	185 ft 4 in.
1948	Imre Nemeth, Hungary	183 ft 11½ in.
1952	Jozsef Csermak, Hungary	197 ft 11⁹⁄₁₆ in.
1956	Harold Connolly, United States	207 ft 2¾ in.
1960	Vasily Rudenkov, U.S.S.R.	220 ft 1⅝ in.
1964	Romuald Klim, U.S.S.R.	228 ft 9½ in.
1968	Gyula Zsivotzky, Hungary	240 ft 8 in.
1972	Anatoly Bondarchuk, U.S.S.R.	247 ft 8½ in.
1976	Yuri Sedykh, U.S.S.R.	(77.52m) 254 ft 4 in.
1980	Yuri Sedykh, U.S.S.R.	(81.80m) 268 ft 4½ in.

Throwing the Stone (14 lbs.)

1906	Nicolas Georgantas, Greece	65 ft 4⅕ in.

56-lb Weight Throw

1904	Etienne Desmarteau, Canada	34 ft 4 in.
1920	Pat McDonald, United States	36 ft 11⅝ in.

All-Around

1904	Thomas Kiely, Great Britain	6,036 pts.

Pentathlon

1906	H. Mellander, Sweden	24 pts.
1912	Ferdinand Bie, Norway	21 pts.
1920	Eero Lehtonen, Finland	14 pts.
1924	Eero Lehtonen, Finland	16 pts.

Decathlon

1912	Hugo Wieslander, Sweden	7,724.495 pts.
1920	Helge Lovland, Norway	6,804.35 pts.
1924	Harold Osborn, United States	7,710.775 pts.
1928	Paavo Yrjola, Finland	8,053.29 pts.
1932	James Bausch, United States	8,462.23 pts.
1936	Glenn Morris, United States	7,900 pts.[1]
1948	Robert B. Mathias, United States	7,139 pts.
1952	Robert B. Mathias, United States	7,887 pts.
1956	Milton Campbell, United States	7,937 pts.
1960	Rafer Johnson, United States	8,392 pts.
1964	Willi Holdorf, Germany	7,887 pts.[1]
1968	Bill Toomey, United States	8,193 pts.
1972	Nikolai Avilov, U.S.S.R.	8,454 pts.
1976	Bruce Jenner, United States	8,618 pts.
1980	Daley Thompson, Britain	8,495 pts.

1. Point system revised.

Tug of War

1904	United States	1912	Sweden
1906	Germany	1920	Great Britain
1908	Great Britain		

TRACK AND FIELD—WOMEN

100-Meter Dash

1928	Elizabeth Robinson, United States	12.2s
1932	Stella Walsh, Poland	11.9s
1936	Helen Stephens, United States	11.5s
1948	Fanny Blankers-Koen, Netherlands	11.9s
1952	Marjorie Jackson, Australia	11.5s
1956	Betty Cuthbert, Australia	11.5s
1960	Wilma Rudolph, United States	11s
1964	Wyomia Tyus, United States	11.4s
1968	Wyomia Tyus, United States	11s
1972	Renate Stecher, East Germany	11.07s
1976	Annegret Richter, West Germany	11.08s
1980	Lyudmila Kondratyeva, U.S.S.R.	11.06s

200-Meter Dash

1948	Fanny Blankers-Koen, Netherlands	24.4s
1952	Marjorie Jackson, Australia	23.7s
1956	Betty Cuthbert, Australia	23.4s
1960	Wilma Rudolph, United States	24s
1964	Edith McGuire, United States	23s
1968	Irena Szewinska, Poland	22.5s
1972	Renate Stecher, East Germany	22.4s
1976	Baerbel Eckert, East Germany	22.37s
1980	Barbara Wockel, East Germany	22.03s

400-Meter Dash

1964	Betty Cuthbert, Australia	52s
1968	Colette Besson, France	52s
1972	Monika Zehrt, East Germany	51.08s
1976	Irena Szewinska, Poland	49.29s
1980	Marita Koch, East Germany	48.88s

800-Meter Run

1928	Lina Radke, Germany	2m16.8s
1960	Ljudmila Shevcova, U.S.S.R.	2m4.3s
1964	Ann Packer, Great Britain	2m1.1s
1968	Madeline Manning, United States	2m0.9s
1972	Hildegard Falck, West Germany	1m58.6s
1976	Tatiana Kazankina, U.S.S.R.	1m54.94s
1980	Nadezhda Olizarenko, U.S.S.R.	1m53.5s

1,500-Meter Run

1972	Ludmila Bragina, U.S.S.R.	4m01.4s
1976	Tatiana Kazankina, U.S.S.R.	4m05.48s

80-Meter Hurdles

1932	Mildred Didrikson, United States	11.7s
1936	Trebisonda Valla, Italy	11.7s
1948	Fanny Blankers-Koen, Netherlands	11.2s
1952	Shirley S. de la Hunty, Australia	10.9s
1956	Shirley S. de la Hunty, Australia	10.7s
1960	Irina Press, U.S.S.R.	10.8s
1964	Karin Balzer, Germany	10.5s[1]
1968	Maureen Caird, Australia	10.3s

1. Wind assisted.

100-Meter Hurdles

1972	Annelie Ehrhardt, East Garmany	12.59s
1976	Johanna Schaller, East Germany	12.77s
1980	Vera Komisova, U.S.S.R.	12.56s

400-Meter Relay

1928	Canada	48.4s
1932	United States	47s
1936	United States	46.9s
1948	Netherlands	47.5s
1952	United States	45.9s
1956	Australia	44.5s
1960	United States	44.5s
1964	Poland	43.6s
1968	United States	42.8s
1972	West Germany	42.81s
1976	East Germany	42.55s
1980	East Germany	41.60s

1,600-Meter Relay

1972	East Germany	3m23s
1976	East Germany	3m19.23s
1980	U.S.S.R.	3m20.2s

Running High Jump

1928	Ethel Catherwood, Canada	5 ft 3 in.
1932	Jean Shiley, United States	5 ft 5¼ in.
1936	Ibolya Csak, Hungary	5 ft 3 in.
1948	Alice Coachman, United States	5 ft 6⅛ in.
1952	Ester Brand, South Africa	5 ft 5¾ in.
1956	Mildred McDaniel, United States	5 ft 9¼ in.
1960	Iolanda Balas, Romania	6 ft ¾ in.
1964	Iolanda Balas, U.S.S.R.	6 ft 2¾ in.
1968	Miloslava Rezkova, Czechoslovakia	5 ft 11¾ in.
1972	Ulrike Meyfarth, West Germany	6 ft 3⅝ in.
1976	Rosemarie Ackerman, E. Germany	(1.93m) 6 ft 4 in.
1980	Sara Simeoni, Italy	6 ft 5½ in.

Long Jump

1948	Olga Gyarmati, Hungary	18 ft 8¼ in.
1952	Yvette Williams, New Zealand	20 ft 5¾ in.
1956	Elzbieta Krzesinska, Poland	20 ft 9¾ in.
1960	Vera Krepkina, U.S.S.R.	20 ft 10¾ in.
1964	Mary Rand, Great Britain	22 ft 2 in.
1968	Viorica Ciscopoleanu, Romania	22 ft 4½ in.
1972	Heidemarie Rosendahl, West Germany	22 ft 3 in.
1976	Angela Voigt, East Germany	(6.72m) 22 ft ½ in.
1980	Tatiana Kolpakova, U.S.S.R.	23 ft 2 in.

Shot-Put

1948	Micheline Ostermeyer, France	45 ft 1½ in.
1952	Galina Zybina, U.S.S.R.	50 ft 1½ in.
1956	Tamara Tishkyevich, U.S.S.R.	54 ft 5 in.
1960	Tamara Press, U.S.S.R.	56 ft 9⅞ in.
1964	Tamara Press, U.S.S.R.	59 ft 6 in.
1968	Margitta Gummel, East Germany	64 ft 4 in.
1972	Nadezhda Chizhova, U.S.S.R.	69 ft
1976	Ivanka Christova, Bulgaria	(21.16m) 69 ft 5 in.
1980	Ilona Sluplanek, East Germany	73 ft 6 in.

Discus Throw

1928	Helena Konopacka, Poland	129 ft 11⅞ in.
1932	Lillian Copeland, United States	133 ft 2 in.
1936	Gisela Mauermayer, Germany	156 ft 3³⁄₁₆ in.
1948	Micheline Ostermeyer, France	137 ft 6½ in.
1952	Nina Romaschkova, U.S.S.R.	168 ft 8⁷⁄₁₆ in.
1956	Olga Fikotova, Czechoslovakia	176 ft 1½ in.
1960	Nina Ponomareva, U.S.S.R.	180 ft 8¼ in.
1964	Tamara Press, U.S.S.R.	187 ft 10¾ in.
1968	Lia Manoliu, Romania	191 ft 2½ in.
1972	Faina Melnik, U.S.S.R.	218 ft 7 in.
1976	Evelin Schlaak, East Germany	(69.0m) 226 ft 4 in.
1980	Evelin Jahl, East Germany	229 ft 6½ in.

Javelin Throw

1932	Mildred Didrikson, United States	143 ft 4 in.
1936	Tilly Fleischer, Germany	148 ft 2¾ in.
1948	Herma Bauma, Austria	149 ft 6 in.
1952	Dana Zatopek, Czechoslovakia	165 ft 7 in.
1956	Inessa Janzeme, U.S.S.R.	176 ft 8 in.
1960	Elvira Ozolina, U.S.S.R.	183 ft 8 in.
1964	Mihaela Penes, Romania	198 ft 7½ in.
1968	Angela Nemeth, Hungary	198 ft 0 in.
1972	Ruth Fuchs, East Germany	209 ft 7 in.
1976	Ruth Fuchs, East Germany	(65.94m) 216 ft 4 in.
1980	Maria Colon, Cuba	224 ft 5 in.

Pentathlon

1964	Irina Press, U.S.S.R.	5,246 pts.
1968	Ingrid Becker, West Germany	5,098 pts.
1972	Mary Peters, Britain	4,801 pts.
1976	Siegrun Siegl, East Germany	4,745 pts.
1980	Nadyezhda Tkachenko, U.S.S.R.	5,083 pts.

SWIMMING—MEN

50-Yard Freestyle

1904	Zoltan de Halmay, Hungary	28s

100 Meters Freestyle

1896	Alfred Hajos, Hungary	1m22.2s
1904	Zoltan de Halmay, Hungary	1m2.8s[1]
1906	Charles Daniels, United States	1m13s
1908	Charles Daniels, United States	1m5.6s
1912	Duke P. Kahanamoku, United States	1m3.4s
1920	Duke P. Kahanamoku, United States	1m1.4s
1924	John Weissmuller, United States	59s
1928	John Weissmuller, United States	58.6s
1932	Yasuji Miyazaki, Japan	58.2s
1936	Ferenc Csik, Hungary	57.6s
1948	Walter Ris, United States	57.3s
1952	Clarke Scholes, United States	57.4s
1956	Jon Henricks, Australia	55.4s
1960	John Devitt, Australia	55.2s
1964	Don Schollander, United States	53.4s
1968	Michael Wenden, Australia	52.2s
1972	Mark Spitz, United States	51.22s
1976	Jim Montgomery, United States	49.99s
1980	Jorg Woithe, East Germany	50.40s

1. 100 yards.

200-Meter Freestyle

1900	Frederick Lane, Australia	2m25.2s
1904	Charles Daniels, United States	2m44.2s[1]
1968	Michael Wenden, Australia	1m55.2s
1972	Mark Spitz, United States	1m52.78s
1976	Bruce Furniss, United States	1m50.29s
1980	Sergei Kopliakov, U.S.S.R.	1m49.81s

1. 220 yards.

400-Meter Freestyle

1896	Paul Neumann, Austria	8m12.6s[1]
1904	Charles Daniels, United States	6m16.2s[2]
1906	Otto Sheff, Austria	6m23.8s
1908	Henry Taylor, Great Britain	5m36.8s
1912	George Hodgson, Canada	5m24.4s
1920	Norman Ross, United States	5m26.8s
1926	Jonn Weissmuller, United States	5m4.2s
1928	Albert Zorilla, Argentina	5m1.6s
1932	Clarence Crabbe, United States	4m48.4s
1936	Jack Medica, United States	4m44.5s
1948	William Smith, United States	4m41s
1952	Jean Boiteux, France	4m30.7s
1956	Murray Rose, Australia	4m27.3s
1960	Murray Rose, Australia	4m18.3s
1964	Don Schollander, United States	4m12.2s
1968	Mike Burton, United States	4m9s
1972	Bradford Cooper, Australia[3]	4m00.27s
1976	Brian Goodell, United States	3m51.93s
1980	Vladimir Salnikov, U.S.S.R.	3m51.31s

1. 500 meters. 2. 440 yards. 3. Rick DeMont, United States, won but was disqualified following day for medical reasons.

1,200-Meter Freestyle

1896	Alfred Hajos, Hungary	18m22.2s

1,500 Meters Freestyle

1904	Emil Rausch, Germany	27m18.2s[1]
1906	Henry Taylor, Great Britain	28m28s[2]
1908	Henry Taylor, Great Britain	22m48.4s
1912	George Hodgson, Canada	22m
1920	Norman Ross, United States	22m23.2s
1924	Andrew Charlton, Australia	20m6.6s
1928	Arne Borg, Sweden	19m51.8s
1932	Kusuo Kitamura, Japan	19m12.4s
1936	Noboru Terada, Japan	19m13.7s

1948	James McLane, United States	19m18.5s
1952	Ford Konno, United States	18m30s
1956	Murray Rose, Australia	17m58.9s
1960	Jon Konrads, Australia	17m19.6s
1964	Robert Windle, Australia	17m1.7s
1968	Michael Burton, United States	16m38.9s
1972	Mike Burton, United States	15m52.58s
1976	Brian Goodell, United States	15m02.4s
1980	Vladimir Salnikov, U.S.S.R.	14m58.27s

1. One mile. 2. 1,600 meters.

4,000-Meter Freestyle

1900	John Jarvis, Great Britain	58m24s

100-Meter Backstroke

1904	Walter Brack, Germany	1m16.8s[1]
1908	Arno Bieberstein, Germany	1m24.6s
1912	Harry Hebner, United States	1m21.2s
1920	Warren Kealoha, United States	1m15.2s
1924	Warren Kealoha, United States	1m13.2s
1928	George Kojac, United States	1m8.2s
1932	Masaji Kiyokawa, Japan	1m8.6s
1936	Adolph Kiefer, United States	1m5.9s
1948	Allen Stack, United States	1m6.4s
1952	Yoshinobu Oyakawa, United States	1m5.4s
1956	David Thiele, Australia	1m2.2s
1960	David Thiele, Australia	1m1.9s
1968	Roland Matthes, East Germany	58.7s
1972	Roland Matthes, East Germany	56.58s
1976	John Naber, United States	55.49s
1980	Bengt Baron, Sweden	56.53s

1. 100 yards

200-Meter Backstroke

1900	Ernst Hoppenberg, Germany	2m47s
1964	Jed Graef, United States	2m10.3s
1968	Roland Matthes, East Germany	2m9.6s
1972	Roland Matthes, East Germany	2m2.82s
1976	John Naber, United States	1m59.19s
1980	Sandor Wladar, Hungary	2:01.93s

100-Meter Breaststroke

1968	Donald McKenzie, United States	1m7.7s
1972	Nobutaka Taguchi, Japan	1m4.94s
1976	John Hencken, United States	1m03.11s
1980	Duncan Goodhew, Britain	1m03.34s

200-Meter Breaststroke

1908	Frederick Holman, Great Britain	3m9.2s
1912	Walter Bathe, Germany	3m1.8s
1920	Haken Malmroth, Sweden	3m4.4s
1924	Robert Skelton, United States	2m56.6s
1928	Yoshiyuki Tsuruta, Japan	2m48.8s
1932	Yoshiyuki Tsuruta, Japan	2m45.4s
1936	Tetsuo Hamuro, Japan	2m41.5s
1948	Joseph Verdeur, United States	2m39.3s
1952	John Davies, Australia	2m34.4s
1956	Masura Furukawa, Japan	2m34.7s
1960	Bill Mulliken, United States	2m37.4s
1964	Ian O'Brien, Australia	2m27.8s
1968	Felipe Munoz, Mexico	2m28.7s
1972	John Hencken, United States	2m21.55s
1976	David Willkie, Britain	2m15.11s
1980	Robertas Zulpa, U.S.S.R.	2m15.85s

400-Meter Breaststroke

1904	Georg Zacharias, Germany	7m23.6s[1]
1912	Walter Bathe, Germany	6m29.6s
1920	Haken Malmroth, Sweden	6m31.8s

1. 440 yards

100-Meter Butterfly

1968	Douglas Russell, United States	55.9s
1972	Mark Spitz, United States	54.27s
1976	Matt Vogel, United States	54.35s
1980	Par Arvidsson, Sweden	54.92s

200-Meter Butterfly

1956	Bill Yorzyk, United States	2m19.3s
1960	Mike Troy, United States	2m12.8s
1964	Kevin Berry, Australia	2m6.6s
1968	Carl Robie, United States	2m8.7s
1972	Mark Spitz, United States	2m00.7s
1976	Mike Bruner, United States	1m59.23s
1980	Sergei Fesenko, U.S.S.R.	1m59.76s

200-Meter Individual Medley

1968	Charles Hickcox, United States	2m12s
1972	Gunnar Larsson, Sweden	2m7.17s

400-Meter Individual Medley

1964	Dick Roth, United States	4m45.4s
1968	Charles Hickcox, United States	4m48.4s
1972	Gunnar Larsson, Sweden	4m31.98s
1976	Rod Strachan, United States	4m23.68s
1980	Aleksandr Sidorenko, U.S.S.R.	4m22.8s

60-Meter Underwater

1900	de Vaudeville, France	1m53.4s

200-Meter Obstacle

1900	Frederick Lane, Australia	2m38.4s

Relays

1900	Germany (200 meters, 5 men)	32 pts.
1904	United States (200 yards)	2m4.6s
1906	Hungary (1,000 meters)	16m52.4s

400-Meter Freestyle Relay

1964	United States	3m32.2s
1968	United States	3m31.7s
1972	United States	3m26.42s

800-Meter Freestyle Relay

1908	Great Britain	10m55.6s
1912	Australia	10m11.2s
1920	United States	10m4.4s
1924	United States	9m53.4s
1928	United States	9m36.2s
1932	Japan	8m58.4s
1936	Japan	8m51.5s
1948	United States	8m46s
1952	United States	8m31.1s
1956	Australia	8m23.6s
1960	United States	8m10.2s
1964	United States	7m52.1s
1968	United States	7m52.3s
1972	United States	7m35.78s
1976	United States	7m23.22s
1980	U.S.S.R.	7m23.50s

400-Meter Medley Relay

1960	United States	4m5.4s
1964	United States	3m58.4s
1968	United States	3m54.9s
1972	United States	3m48.16s
1976	United States	3m42.22s
1980	Australia	3m45.70s

Springboard Dive

		Points
1908	Albert Zuerner, Germany	85.5

1912	Paul Guenther, Germany	79.23
1920	Louis Kuehn, United States	675
1924	Albert White, United States	696.4
1928	Pete Desjardins, United States	185.04
1932	Michael Galitzen, United States	161.38
1936	Richard Degener, United States	163.57
1948	Bruce Harlan, United States	163.64
1952	David Browning, United States	205.59
1956	Robert Clotworthy, United States	159.56
1960	Gary Tobian, United States	170.00
1964	Ken Sitzberger, United States	159.90
1968	Bernard Wrightson, United States	170.15
1972	Vladimir Vasin, U.S.S.R.	594.09
1976	Phil Boggs, United States	619.05
1980	Alexsandr Portnov, U.S.S.R.	905.02

Platform Dive

		Points
1904	G. E. Sheldon, United States	12.75
1906	Gottlob Walz, Germany	156
1908	Hialmar Johansson, Sweden	83.75
1912	Erik Adlerz, Sweden	73.94
1920	Clarence Pinkston, United States	100.67
1924	Albert White, United States	487.3
1928	Pete Desjardins, United States	98.74
1932	Harold Smith, United States	124.80
1936	Marshall Wayne, United States	113.58
1948	Samuel Lee, United States	130.05
1952	Samuel Lee, United States	156.28
1956	Joaquin Capilla, Mexico	152.44
1960	Bob Webster, United States	165.56
1964	Bob Webster, United States	148.58
1968	Klaus Dibiasi, Italy	164.18
1972	Klaus Dibiasi, Italy	504.12
1976	Klaus Dibiasi, Italy	600.51
1980	Falk Hoffman, E. Germany	835.65

Plain High Dive

		Points
1912	Erik Adlerz, Sweden	40
1920	Arvid Wallman, Sweden	7
1924	Richard Eve, Australia	160

Plunge for Distance

1904	W. E. Dickey, United States	62 ft 6 in.

SWIMMING—WOMEN

100 Meters Freestyle

1912	Fanny Durack, Australia	1m22.2s
1920	Ethelda Bleibtrey, United States	1m13.6s
1924	Ethel Lackie, United States	1m12.4s
1928	Albina Osipowich, United States	1m11s
1932	Helene Madison, United States	1m6.8s
1936	Hendrika Mastenbroek, Netherlands	1m5.9s
1948	Greta Andersen, Denmark	1m6.3s
1952	Katalin Szoke, Hungary	1m6.8s
1956	Dawn Fraser, Australia	1m2s
1960	Dawn Fraser, Australia	1m1.2s
1964	Dawn Fraser, Australia	59.5s
1968	Marge Jan Henne, United States	1m
1972	Sandra Neilson, United States	58.59s
1976	Kornelia Ender, East Germany	55.65s
1980	Barbara Krause, East Germany	54.79s

200-Meter Freestyle

1968	Debbie Meyer, United States	2m10.5s
1972	Shane Gould, Australia	2m3.56s
1976	Kornelia Ender, East Germany	1m59.26s
1980	Barbara Krause, East Germany	1m58.33s

400-Meter Freestyle

1920	Ethelda Bleibtrey, United States	4m34s[1]
1924	Martha Norelius, United States	6m2.2s
1928	Martha Norelius, United States	5m42.8s
1932	Helene Madison, United States	5m28.5s
1936	Hendrika Mastenbroek, Netherlands	5m26.4s
1948	Ann Curtis, United States	5m17.8s
1952	Valerie Gyenge, Hungary	5m12.1s
1956	Lorraine Crapp, Australia	4m54.6s
1960	Chris von Saltza, United States	4m50.6s
1964	Ginny Duenkel, United States	4m43.3s
1968	Debbie Meyer, United States	4m31.8s
1972	Shane Gould, Australia	4m19.04s
1976	Petra Thumer, East Germany	4m09.89s
1980	Ines Diers, East Germany	4m08.76s

1. 300 meters.

800-Meter Freestyle

1968	Debbie Meyer, United States	9m24s
1972	Keena Rothhammer, United States	8m53.68s
1976	Petra Thumer, East Germany	8m37.14s
1980	Michelle Ford, Australia	8m28.90s

100-Meter Backstroke

1924	Sybil Bauer, United States	1m23.2s
1928	Marie Braun, Netherlands	1m22s
1932	Eleanor Holm, United States	1m19.4s
1936	Dina Senff, Netherlands	1m18.9s
1948	Karen Harup, Denmark	1m14.4s
1952	Joan Harrison, South Africa	1m14.3s
1956	Judy Grinham, Great Britain	1m12.9s
1960	Lynn Burke, United States	1m9.3s
1964	Cathy Ferguson, United States	1m7.7s
1968	Kaye Hall, United States	1m6.2s
1972	Melissa Belote, United States	1m5.78s
1976	Ulrike Richter, East Germany	1m01.83s
1980	Rica Reinisch, East Germany	1m00.86s

200-Meter Backstroke

1968	Pokey Watson, United States	2m24.8s
1972	Melissa Belote, United States	2m19.19s
1976	Ulrike Richter, East Germany	2m13.43s
1980	Rica Reinisch, East Germany	2m11.77s

100-Meter Breaststroke

1968	Djurdjica Bjedov, Yugoslavia	1m15.8s
1972	Catherine Carr, United States	1m13.58s
1976	Hannelore Anke, East Germany	1m11.16s
1980	Ute Geweniger, East Germany	1m10.22s

200-Meter Breaststroke

1924	Lucy Morton, Great Britain	3m33.2s
1928	Hilde Schrader, Germany	3m12.6s
1932	Clare Dennis, Australia	3m6.3s
1936	Hideko Maehata, Japan	3m3.6s
1948	Nel van Vliet, Netherlands	2m57.2s
1952	Eva Szekely, Hungary	2m51.7s
1956	Ursala Happe, Germany	2m53.1s
1960	Anita Lonsbrough, Great Britain	2m49.5s
1964	Galina Prozumenschikova, U.S.S.R.	2m46.4s
1968	Sharon Wichman, United States	2m44.4s
1972	Beverly Whitfield, Australia	2m41.71s
1976	Marina Koshevaia, U.S.S.R.	2m33.35s
1980	Lina Kachushite, U.S.S.R.	2m29.54s

100-Meter Butterfly

1956	Shelley Mann, United States	1m11s
1960	Carolyn Schuler, United States	1m9.5s
1964	Sharon Stouder, United States	1m4.7s
1968	Lynn McClements, Australia	1m5.5s
1972	Mayumi Aoki, Japan	1m3.34s
1976	Kornelia Ender, East Germany	1m00.13s
1980	Caren Metschuck, East Germany	1m00.42s

200-Meter Butterfly

1968	Ada Kok, Netherlands	2m24.7s
1972	Karen Moe, United States	2m15.57s
1976	Andrea Pollack, East Germany	2m11.41s
1980	Ines Geissler, East Germany	2m10.44s

200-Meter Individual Medley

1968	Claudia Kolb, United States	2m24.7s
1972	Shane Gould, Australia	2m23.07s

400-Meter Individual Medley

1964	Donna de Varona, United States	5m18.7s
1968	Claudia Kolb, United States	5m8.5s
1972	Gail Neall, Australia	5m2.97s
1976	Ulrike Tauber, East Germany	4m42.77s
1980	Petra Schneider, East Germany	4m36.29s

400-Meter Freestyle Relay

1912	Great Britain	5m52.8s
1920	United States	5m11.6s
1924	United States	4m58.8s
1928	United States	4m47.6s
1932	United States	4m38s
1936	Netherlands	4m36s
1948	United States	4m29.2s
1952	Hungary	4m24.4s
1956	Australia	4m17.1s
1960	United States	4m8.9s
1964	United States	4m3.8s
1968	United States	4m2.5s
1972	United States	3m55.19s
1976	United States	3m44.82s
1980	East Germany	3m42.71s

400-Meter Medley Relay

1960	United States	4m41.1s
1964	United States	4m33.9s
1968	United States	4m28.3s
1972	United States	4m20.75s
1976	East Germany	4m07.95s
1980	East Germany	4m06.67s

Springboard Dive

		Points
1920	Aileen Riggin, United States	539.90
1924	Elizabeth Becker, United States	474.5
1928	Helen Meany, United States	78.62
1932	Georgia Coleman, United States	87.52
1936	Marjorie Gestring, United States	89.27
1948	Victoria M. Draves, United States	108.74
1952	Patricia McCormick, United States	147.30
1956	Patricia McCormick, United States	142.36
1960	Ingrid Kramer, Germany	155.81
1964	Ingrid Kramer Engel, Germany	145.00
1968	Sue Gossick, United States	150.77
1972	Micki King, United States	450.03
1976	Jennifer Chandler, United States	506.19
1980	Irina Kalinina, U.S.S.R.	725.91

Platform Dive

		Points
1912	Greta Johansson, Sweden	39.9
1920	Stefani Fryland, Denmark	34.60
1924	Caroline Smith, United States	166
1928	Elizabeth B. Pinkston, United States	31.60
1932	Dorothy Poynton, United States	40.26
1936	Dorothy Poynton Hill, United States	33.92
1948	Victoria M. Draves, United States	68.87
1952	Patricia McCormick, United States	79.37
1956	Patricia McCormick, United States	84.85
1960	Ingrid Kramer, Germany	91.28
1964	Lesley Bush, United States	99.80
1968	Milena Duchkova, Czechoslovakia	109.59
1972	Ulrika Knape, Sweden	390.00
1976	Elena Vaytsekhovskaia, U.S.S.R.	406.59
1980	Martina Jaschke, East Germany	596.25

DISTRIBUTION OF MEDALS 1980 SUMMER GAMES

	Gold	Silver	Bronze	Total
Soviet Union	80	70	47	197
East Germany	47	36	43	126
Bulgaria	8	16	16	40
Hungary	7	10	15	32
Poland	3	14	14	31
Romania	6	6	13	25
Britain	5	7	9	21
Cuba	8	7	5	20
Italy	8	3	4	15
France	6	5	3	14
Czechoslovakia	2	2	9	13
Sweden	3	3	6	12
Australia	2	2	5	9
Yugoslavia	2	3	4	9
Finland	3	1	4	8
Spain	1	3	2	6
Denmark	2	1	2	5
Austria	1	3	1	5
North Korea	0	3	2	5
Brazil	2	0	2	4
Ethiopia	2	0	2	4
Mongolia	0	2	2	4
Netherlands	0	1	3	4
Mexico	0	1	3	4
Greece	1	0	2	3
Jamaica	0	0	3	3
Switzerland	2	0	0	2
Tanzania	0	2	0	2
Ireland	0	1	1	2
Belgium	1	0	0	1
India	1	0	0	1
Zimbabwe	1	0	0	1
Venezuela	1	0	0	1
Uganda	0	1	0	1
Guyana	0	0	1	1
Lebanon	0	0	1	1

BOXING

(U.S. winners only)

(U.S. boycotted Olympics in 1980)

Flyweight—112 Pounds (51 kilograms)

1904	George V. Finnegan	1952	Nate Brooks
1920	Frank De Genaro	1976	Leo Randolph
1924	Fidel La Barba		

Bantamweight—119 pounds (54 kg)

1904 O.L. Kirk

Featherweight—126 pounds (57 kg)

1904	O.L. Kirk	1924	Jackie Fields

Lightweight—132 Pounds (60 kg)

1904	H.J. Spanger	1968	Ronnie Harris
1920	Samuel Mosberg	1976	Howard Davis

Light Welterweight—140 Pounds (63.5 kg)

1952	Charles Adkins	1976	Ray Leonard
1972	Ray Seales		

Welterweight—148 Pounds (67 kg)

1904	Al Young	1932	Edward Flynn

Light Middleweight—157 Pounds (71 kg)

1960 Wilbert McClure

Middleweight—165 Pounds (75 kg)

1904	Charles Mayer	1960	Eddie Crook
1932	Carmen Barth	1976	Mike Spinks
1952	Floyd Patterson		

Light Heavyweight—179 Pounds (81 kg)

1920	Edward Eagan	1960	Cassius Clay
1952	Norvel Lee	1976	Leon Spinks
1956	James Boyd		

Heavyweight (unlimited)

1904	Sam Berger	1964	Joe Frazier
1952	Edward Sanders	1968	George Foreman
1956	Pete Rademacher		

BASKETBALL—MEN

1904	United States	1960	United States
1936	United States	1964	United States
1948	United States	1968	United States
1952	United States	1972	U.S.S.R.
1956	United States	1976	United States
		1980	Yugoslavia

BASKETBALL—WOMEN

1976 U.S.S.R.
1980 U.S.S.R.

Winter Games

FIGURE SKATING—MEN

1908	Ulrich Salchow, Sweden
1920	Gillis Grafstrom, Sweden
1924	Gillis Grafstrom, Sweden
1928	Gillis Grafstrom, Sweden
1932	Karl Schaefer, Austria
1936	Karl Schaefer, Austria
1948	Richard Button, United States
1952	Richard Button, United States
1956	Hayes Alan Jenkins, United States
1960	David Jenkins, United States
1964	Manfred Schnelldorfer, Germany
1968	Wolfgang Schwartz, Austria
1972	Ondrej Nepela, Czechoslovakia
1976	John Curry, Great Britain
1980	Robin Cousins, Great Britain

FIGURE SKATING—WOMEN

1908	Madge Syers, Britain
1920	Magda Julin-Maurey, Sweden
1924	Herma Szabo-Planck, Austria
1928	Sonja Henie, Norway
1932	Sonja Henie, Norway
1936	Sonja Henie, Norway
1948	Barbara Ann Scott, Canada
1952	Jeannette Altwegg, Great Britain
1956	Tenley Albright, United States
1960	Carol Heiss, United States
1964	Sjoukje Dijkstra, Netherlands
1968	Peggy Fleming, United States
1972	Beatrix Schuba, Austria
1976	Dorothy Hamill, United States
1980	Anett Poetzsch, East Germany

SPEED SKATING—MEN

(U.S. winners only)

500 Meters

1924	Charles Jewtraw	44.0
1932	John A. Shea	43.4
1952	Kenneth Henry	43.2
1964	Terrence McDermott	40.1
1980	Eric Heiden	38.03

1,000 Meters

1976	Peter Mueller	1:19.32
1980	Eric Heiden	1:15.18

1,500 Meters

1932	John A. Shea	2:57.5
1980	Eric Heiden	1:55.44

5,000 Meters

1932	Irving Jaffee	9:40.8
1980	Eric Heiden	7:02.29

10,000 Meters

1932	Irving Jaffee	19:13.6
1980	Eric Heiden	14:28.13

SPEED SKATING—WOMEN

500 Meters

1972	Anne Henning	43.33
1976	Sheila Young	42.76

1,500 Meters

1972	Dianne Holum	2:20.85

HEIDEN FIRST ATHLETE TO WIN 5 GOLD MEDALS IN WINTER GAMES

Eric Heiden of Madison, Wis., became the first athlete to win five gold medals in the Winter Olympics when he swept the 1980 speed skating events at Lake Placid, N.Y. The 21-year-old Heiden captured the 500-, 1,000-, 1,500-, 5,000-, and 10,000-meter events. He set an Olympic record in each event and capped his performance on Feb. 23 with a world record of 14 minutes 28.13 seconds in the 10,000-meter race, breaking the mark set in 1977 by Viktor Leskin of the Soviet Union by 16.20 seconds.

Lydia Skoblikova of the Soviet Union was the only other athlete to sweep an Olympic speed skating program. She captured all four female events in the 1964 Winter Games at Innsbruck, Austria.

The weekend after his gold-medal sweep, Heiden failed in his attempt to win a fourth straight world title, at Heerenveen, the Netherlands. He was dethroned by 22-year-old Hilbert van der Duim of the host country.

SKIING, ALPINE—MEN

Downhill

1948	Henri Oreiller, France	2m55.0s
1952	Zeno Colo, Italy	2m30.8s
1956	Anton Sailer, Austria	2m52.2s
1960	Jean Vuarnet, France	2m06.2s
1964	Egon Zimmermann, Austria	2m18.16s
1968	Jean-Claude Killy, France	1m59.85s
1972	Bernhard Russi, Switzerland	1m51.43s
1976	Franz Klammer, Austria	1m45.72s
1980	Leonhard Stock, Austria	1m45.50s

Slalom

1948	Edi Reinalter, Switzerland	2m10.3s
1952	Othmar Schneider, Austria	2m00.0s
1956	Anton Sailer, Austria	194.7 pts.
1960	Ernst Hinterseer, Austria	2m08.9s
1964	Josef Stiegler, Austria	2m10.13
1968	Jean-Claude Killy, France	1m39.73s
1972	Francisco Fernandez Ochoa, Spain	1m49.27s
1976	Piero Gros, Italy	2m03.29s
1980	Ingemar Stenmark, Sweden	1m44.26s

Giant Slalom

1952	Stein Eriksen, Norway	2m25.0s
1956	Anton Sailer, Austria	3m00.1s
1960	Roger Staub, Switzerland	1m48.3s
1964	Francois Bonlieu, France	1m46.71s
1968	Jean-Claude Killy, France	3m29.28s
1972	Gustavo Thoeni, Italy	3m09.52s
1976	Heini Hemmi, Switzerland	3m26.97s
1980	Ingemar Stenmark, Sweden	2m40.74s

SKIING, ALPINE—WOMEN

Downhill

1948	Hedi Schlunegger, Switzerland	2m28.3s
1952	Trude Jochum-Beiser, Austria	1m47.1s
1956	Madeleine Berthod, Switzerland	1m40.1s
1960	Heidi Biebl, Germany	1m37.6s
1964	Christl Haas, Austria	1m55.39s
1968	Olga Pall, Austria	1m40.87s
1972	Marie-Therese Nadig, Switzerland	1m36.68s
1976	Rosi Mittermeier, West Germany	1m46.16s
1980	Annemarie Proell Moser, Austria	1m37.52s

Slalom

1948	Gretchen Fraser, United States	1m57.2s
1952	Andrea Mead Lawrence, United States	2m10.6s
1956	Renee Colliard, Switzerland	112.3 pts.
1960	Anne Heggtveigt, Canada	1m49.6s
1964	Christine Goitschel, France	1m29.86s
1968	Marielle Goitschel, France	1m25.86s
1972	Barbara Cochran, United States	1m31.24s
1976	Rosi Mittermeier, West Germany	1m30.54s
1980	Hanni Wenzel, Liechtenstein	1m25.09s

Giant Slalom

1952	Andrea M. Lawrence, United States	2m06.8s
1956	Ossi Reichert, Germany	1m56.5s
1960	Yvonne Ruegg, Switzerland	1m39.9s
1964	Marielle Goitschel, France	1m52.24s
1968	Nancy Greene, Canada	1m51.97s
1972	Marie-Therese Nadig, Switzerland	1m29.90s
1976	Kathy Kreiner, Canada	1m29.13s
1980	Hanni Wenzel, Liechtenstein	2m41.66s

ICE HOCKEY

1920	Canada	1956	U.S.S.R.
1924	Canada	1960	United States
1928	Canada	1964	U.S.S.R.
1932	Canada	1968	U.S.S.R.
1936	Great Britain	1972	U.S.S.R.
1948	Canada	1976	U.S.S.R.
1952	Canada	1980	United States

SKIING, NORDIC, JUMPING

90-Meter Hill

		Points
1924	Jacob T. Thams, Norway	227.5
1928	Alfred Andersen, Norway	230.5
1932	Birger Ruud, Norway	228.0
1936	Birger Ruud, Norway	232.0
1948	Peter Hugsted, Norway	228.1
1952	A. Bergmann, Norway	226.0
1956	Antti Hyvarinen, Finland	227.0
1960	Helmut Recknagel, Germany	227.2
1964	Toralf Engan, Norway	230.7
1968	Vladimir Beloussov, U.S.S.R.	231.3
1972	Wojciech Fortuna, Poland	219.9
1976	Karl Schnabl, Austria	234.8
1980	Jouko Tormanen, Finland	271.0

Small Hill (70 meters)

1964	Veikko Kankkonen, Finland	229.9
1968	Jiri Raska, Czechoslovakia	216.5
1972	Yukio Kasaya, Japan	244.2
1976	Hans-Georg Aschenbach, East Germany	252.0
1980	Anton Innauer, Austria	266.3

AMERICAN HOCKEY TEAM SCORES BIGGEST UPSET IN GAMES

The United States hockey team, made up of college and minor-league players, stunned the hockey world and stirred patriotic fervor among Americans everywhere with a 4–3 upset triumph in the Winter Olympics over the Soviet Union, considered by experts as the finest hockey team in the world—amateur or professional.

The Soviet team was heavily favored to win the Olympic gold medal at Lake Placid, N.Y., for a fifth straight time. The Americans were rated seventh among the 12 national teams and were given virtually no chance of gaining the final round. The 20-man American squad was coached by Herb Brooks, the coach of the University of Minnesota team. He instituted a new style for the Americans, stressing speed and puck control, tactics generally employed by European teams. The Americans opened their unbeaten streak with a 2–2 tie against Sweden in the first round, then stormed to victories over Romania, Czechoslovakia, West Germany, and Norway. Their upset of the Russians came in the first game of the final round on a goal by Mike Eruzione, the team captain from Winthrop, Mass.

They captured the gold medal with a 4–2 victory over Finland and touched off a national celebration and a surge of patriotism seldom seen in American sports. The triumph came at a time when the Olympic movement was under fire and the United States threatened to boycott the Summer Games in Moscow because of the Soviet invasion of Afghanistan. Only once before, in 1960 at Squaw Valley, Calif., had an American team won an Olympic hockey gold medal.

HOW U.S. HOCKEY ADVANCED TO OLYMPIC TITLE

FINAL STANDING

	W	L	T	Pts	GF	GA
United States	2	0	1	5	10	7
Soviet Union	2	1	0	4	16	8
Sweden	0	2	2	2	7	14
Finland	0	2	1	1	7	11

(The top two teams in the Red Division and the two top teams in the Blue Division of the preliminary round-robin advanced to the final, where the Red Division teams played the Blue Division teams. The records of the teams who played each other in their own divisions were counted in the final standing.)

Results of Final Round Games

United States 4, Soviet Union 3
Sweden 3, Finland 3
United States 4, Finland 2
Soviet Union 9, Sweden 2

Consolation for Fifth Place

Czechoslovakia 6, Canada 1

PRELIMINARY ROUND STANDING

Red Division

	W	L	T	Pts	GF	GA
Soviet Union	5	0	0	10	51	11
Finland	3	2	0	6	26	18
Canada	3	2	0	6	28	12
Poland	2	3	0	4	15	23
Holland	1	3	1	3	16	43
Japan	0	4	1	1	7	36

Blue Division

	W	L	T	Pts	GF	GA
Sweden	4	0	1	9	26	7
United States	4	0	1	9	25	10
Czechoslovakia	3	2	0	6	34	16
Romania	1	3	1	3	13	29
West Germany	1	4	0	2	21	30
Norway	0	4	1	1	9	36

(Top two teams in each division advanced to final round. Third place teams played for fifth.)

Results of Preliminary Round Games Involving U.S.

United States 2, Sweden 2
United States 7, Czechoslovakia 3
United States 5, Norway 1
United States 7, Romania 2
United States 4, West Germany 2

DISTRIBUTION OF MEDALS 1980 WINTER GAMES

	Gold	Silver	Bronze	Total
Soviet Union	10	6	6	22
East Germany	9	7	7	23
United States	6	4	2	12
Norway	1	3	6	10
Finland	1	5	3	9
Austria	3	2	2	7
West Germany	0	2	3	5
Switzerland	1	1	3	5
Liechtenstein	2	2	0	4
Netherlands	1	2	1	4
Sweden	3	0	1	4
Italy	0	2	0	2
Canada	0	1	1	2
Britain	1	0	0	1
Hungary	0	1	0	1
Japan	0	1	0	1
Bulgaria	0	0	1	1
Czechoslovakia	0	0	1	1
France	0	0	1	1

Total countries competing: 37.

Scoring of U.S. Victory Over Soviet Union

United States	2	0	2	—	4
Soviet Union	2	1	0	—	3

FIRST PERIOD—1, Soviet Union, Krutov (Kasatonov), 9:12; 2, United States, Schneider (Pavelich), 14:03; 3, Soviet Union, Makarov (A. Golikov), 17:34; 4, United States, Johnson (Christian, Silk), 19:59
SECOND PERIOD—5, Soviet Union, Maltsev (Krutiv), power-play goal, 2:18
THIRD PERIOD—6, United States, Johnson (Silk), power-play goal, 8:39; 7, United States, Eruzione (Pavelich, Harrington), 10:00
SHOTS ON GOAL—United States on Tretiak, Myshkin, 8, 2, 6—16. Soviet Union on Craig, 18, 12, 9—39

Scoring of U.S. Gold Medal Victory Over Finland

United States	0	1	3	—	4
Finland	1	1	0	—	2

FIRST PERIOD—1, Finland, Porvari (Leinonen, Litma), 9:20
SECOND PERIOD—2, United States, Christoff (unassisted), 4:39; 3, Finland, Leinonen (Haapalainen, Kimalainen), power-play goal, 6:30
THIRD PERIOD—4, United States, Verchota (Christian), 2:25; 5, McClanahan (Johnson, Christian), 6:05; 6, United States, Johnson, (Christoff), shorthanded goal, 16:25
SHOTS ON GOAL—United States on Valtonen, 14, 8, 7—29. Finland on Craig, 7, 6, 10—23.

AMERICAN SWIMMERS RACE AGAINST OLYMPIC CLOCK

Forty-eight hours after the Olympic swimming competition in Moscow ended, United States swimmers, who had boycotted the Games, protesting the Soviet intervention in Afghanistan, took to the water at Irvine, Calif., hoping to shatter records in the United States Championships and Olympic Trials. Organizers erected a huge scoreboard showing the Olympic times in each event so swimmers and spectators could make comparisons as to how the Americans would have fared had they chosen to go to Moscow.

In a sport they usually dominated, the Americans registered three world records, and on a basis of comparative times, showed they would have won six of 11 gold medals in men's events and four of 11 in women's events had they competed in the Olympics. The world records shattered at Irvine were by Craig Beardsley of Gainesville, Fla., in the 200-meter butterfly (1:58.46); Bill Barrett of Alpharetta, Ga., in the 200 individual medley (2:03.24); and Mary T. Meagher, a 15-year-old from Cincinnati, in the 200 butterfly (2:06.37).

Other 1980 Olympic Games Champions

SUMMER

Archery
Men—Tomi Polkolainen, Finland
Women—Keto Losaberodze, U.S.S.R.

Boxing
106 lb—Shamil Sabyrov, U.S.S.R.
112 lb—Petar Lessov, U.S.S.R.
119 lb—Juan Hernandez, Cuba
126 lb—Rudi Fink, E. Ger.
132 lb—Angel Herrera, Cuba
140 lb—Patrizio Oliva, Italy
148 lb—Andres Aldama, Cuba
157 lb—Armando Martinez, Cuba
165 lb—Jose Gomez, Cuba
179 lb—Slobodan Kacar, Yugoslavia
Heavyweight—Teofilo Stevenson, Cuba

Canadian Canoeing
500 m—Sergei Postrekhin, U.S.S.R.
1,000 m—Lubomir Lubenov, Bulgaria
500–m pairs—Laszlo Foltan and Istvan Vaskutl, Hungary
1,000–m pairs—Ivan Potzalchin and Toma Simionov, Romania

Kayak—Men
500 m—Vladimir Parfenovich, U.S.S.R.
1,000 m—Rudiger Helm, E. Ger.
500–m pairs—Vladimir Parfenovich and Sergei Chukhrai, U.S.S.R.
1,000–m pairs—Vladimir Parfenovich and Sergei Chukhrai, U.S.S.R.
1,000–m fours—E. Ger.

Kayak—Women
500 m—Birgit Fischer, E. Ger.
500–m pairs—Carsta Genauss and Martina Dischof, E. Ger.

Cycling
1,000 m—Lothar Thoms, E. Ger.
Sprint—Lutz Hesslich, E. Ger.
Pursuit—Robert Dill–Bondi, Switzerland
Team pursuit—U.S.S.R.
Road Race—Sergei Soukhoroutchenkov, U.S.S.R.
Team road race—U.S.S.R.

Equestrian
Dressage—Elisabeth Theurer, Austria
Dressage team—U.S.S.R.
Jumping—Jan Kowalczky, Poland
Team jumping—U.S.S.R.
3–Day event—Federico Euro Roman, Italy
Team 3–day event—U.S.S.R. (Aleksandr Blinov, Yuri Salnikov, Valeri Volkov)

Fencing
Foil—Vladimir Smirnov, U.S.S.R.
Team foil—France
Epee—Johan Harmenberg, Sweden
Team epee—France
Saber—Viktor Krovopuskov, U.S.S.R.
Team saber—U.S.S.R.
Women's foil—Pascale Trinquet, France
Women's team foil—France

Gymnastics—Men
All–around—Aleksandr Dityatin, U.S.S.R.
Floor exercises—Roland Bruckner, E. Ger.
Horizontal bar—Stoyan Deltchev, Bulgaria
Parallel bars—Aleksandr Tkachyov, U.S.S.R.
Pommel horse—Zoltan Magyar, Hungary
Rings—Aleksandr Dityatin, U.S.S.R.
Vault—Nikolai Andrianov, U.S.S.R.
Team all–around—U.S.S.R.

Gymnastics—Women
All–around—Yelena Davydova, U.S.S.R.
Balance beam—Nadia Comaneci, Romania
Floor exercises—Nelli Kim, U.S.S.R., and Nadia Comaneci, Romania, tie
Uneven bars—Maxi Gnauck, E. Ger.
Vault—Natalya Shaposhnikova, U.S.S.R.
Team all–round—U.S.S.R.

Judo
132 lb—Thierry Rey, France
143 lb—Nikolai Solodukhin, U.S.S.R.
157 lb—Ezio Gamba, Italy
172 lb—Shota Khabarell, U.S.S.R.
190 lb—Juerg Roethilsberger, Switzerland
209 lb—Robert Van De Walle, Belgium
Over 209 lb—Angelo Parisi, France
Open—Dietmar Lorenz, East Germany

Modern Pentathlon
Individual—Anatoly Starostin, U.S.S.R.
Team—U.S.S.R.

Rowing—Men
Singles—Pertti Karppinen, Finland
Doubles—Joachim Dreifke and Klaus Kroppelien, E. Ger.
Pairs—Bernd and Jorg Landvoigt, E. Ger.
Pairs with coxswain—Harald Jahrling–Friedrich-Wilhelm Ulrich–Georg Spohr, E. Ger.
Fours—Jurgen Thiele–Andreas Decker–Stefan Semmier–Siegfried Brietzke, E. Ger.
Fours with coxswains—Dieter Wemdisch–Ullrich Diessner–Walter Diessner–Gottfried Dohn–Andreas Gregor, E. Ger.
Quadruple sculls—Frank Dunba–Karstn Bünk–Uwe Heppner–Martin Winter, E. Ger.
Eights—Bernd Krauss–Hans-Peter Koppe–Ulrich Kons–Jorg Friedrich–Jens Doberschutz–Ulrich Karnatz–Uwe Duhring–Bernd Hoing–Klaus-Dieter Ludwig, E. Ger.

Rowing—Women
Singles—Sanda Toma, Romania
Doubles—Yelena Khloptseva and Larisa Popova, U.S.S.R.
Pairs—Ute Steindorf and Cornelia Klier, E. Ger.
Fours with coxswains—Romona Kapheim–Silvia Frohlich–Angelika Noack–Romy Saalfeld–Kirsten Wenzel, E. Ger.
Quadruple sculls—Sybille Reinhardt–Jutta Ploch–Jutta Lau–Roswietha Zobelt–Liane Buhr, E. Ger.
Eights—Martina Boesler–Kersten Neisser–Christiane Kopke–Brigit Schutz–Gabriele Kuhn–Ilona Richter–Marita Sandig–Karin Metze–Marina Wilke, E. Ger.

Shooting
Free pistol—Aleksandr Melentev, U.S.S.R.
Rapid–fire pistol—Corneliu Ion, Romania
Small–bore rifle, prone—Karoly Varga, Hungary
Small–bore rifle, 3 positions—Viktor Vlasov, U.S.S.R.
Rifle, running game target—Igor Sokolov, U.S.S.R.
Trap—Luciano Giovannetti, Italy
Skeet—Hans Kjeld Rasmussen, Denmark

Weight Lifting
114 lb—Kanybek Osmonalieu, U.S.S.R.
123 lb—Daniel Nunez, Cuba
132 lb—Viktor Mazin, U.S.S.R.
149 lb—Yanko Roussev, Bulgaria
165 lb—Assen Zlatev, Bulgaria
182 lb—Yurik Vardanyan, U.S.S.R.
198 lb—Peter Baczako, Hungary
220 lb—Ata Zaremba, Czechoslovakia
242 lb—Leonid Taranenko, U.S.S.R.

Wrestling—Freestyle
106 lb—Claudio Pollio, Italy
115 lb—Anatoly Belogiazov, U.S.S.R.
126 lb—Sergei Belogiazov, U.S.S.R.
137 lb—Magomrdgasan Abushev, U.S.S.R.
149 lb—Salpulla Absaidov, U.S.S.R.
163 lb—Valentin Raitchev, Bulgaria
181 lb—Ismail Abilov, Bulgaria
198 lb—Sanasar Oganesyan, U.S.S.R.
220 lb—Ilya Mate, U.S.S.R.
Over 220 lb—Sosian Andlev, U.S.S.R.

Wrestling—Greco-Roman
106 lb—Saksylik Ushkempirov, U.S.S.R.
114 lb—Vakhtang Blagidze, U.S.S.R.
125 lb—Shamil Sherikov, U.S.S.R.
136 lb—Stillanos Migiakis, Greece
150 lb—Stefan Rusu, Romania
163 lb—Ferenc Kocsis, Hungary
180 lb—Gennady Korban, U.S.S.R.
198 lb—Norbert Nottny, Hungary
220 lb—Gheorghi Raikov, Bulgaria
Over 220 lb—Aleksandr Kolchinsky, U.S.S.R.

Yachting
Finn—Esko Rechardt, Finland
Flying Dutchman—Alesandro Abascal and Miguel Noguer, Spain
470 Class—Marcos Soares and Eduardo Penido, Brazil
Soling—Poul Richard, Erik Hansen and

Valdemar Bandolowski, Denmark
Star—Valentin Mankin and Aleksandr Muzyschenko, U.S.S.R.
Tornado—Alexandre Welter and Lars Bjorkstrom, Brazil

Team Champions
Field hockey, men—India
Field hockey, women—Zimbabwe
Handball, men—E. Ger.
Handball, women—U.S.S.R.
Soccer—Czechoslovakia
Volleyball, men—U.S.S.R.
Volleyball, women—U.S.S.R.
Water polo—U.S.S.R.

WINTER

Biathlon
Individual—(10 km): Frank Ullrich, East Germany (20 km): Anatoly Alabyev, Soviet Union
Relay—Soviet Union (Vladimir Aliken, Aleksandr Tikhonov, Vladimir Barnaschov, and Anatoly Alabyev)

Bobsledding
2-Man—Erich Schaerer and Josef Benz, Switzerland
4-Man—East Germany (Meinhard Nehmer, Bogdan Musiol, Bernhard Germeshausen, and Hans Jurgen Gerhardt)

Figure Skating
Men—Robin Cousins, Great Britain
Women—Anett Poetzsch, East Germany
Pairs—Irina Rodnina and Aleksandr Zaitsev, Soviet Union
Dance—Natalya Linichuk and Gennadi Karponosov, Soviet Union

Speed Skating—Men
500 m—Eric Heiden, Madison, Wis.
1,000 m—Eric Heiden, Madison, Wis.
1,500 m—Eric Heiden, Madison, Wis.
5,000 m—Eric Heiden, Madison, Wis.
10,000 m—Eric Heiden, Madison, Wis.

Speed Skating—Women
500 m—Karin Enke, East Germany
1,000 m—Natalya Petruseva, Soviet Union
1,500 m—Annie Borckink, Netherlands
3,000 m—Bjoerg Eva Jensen, Norway

Hockey
Team—United States

Luge
Men—Bernhard Glass, East Germany
Doubles—Hans Rinn and Norbert Hahn, East Germany
Women—Vera Zozulya, Soviet Union

Skiing, Nordic—Men
Combined—Ulrich Wehling, East Germany
70-m jump—Anton Innauer, Austria
90-m jump—Jouko Tormanen, Finland

Cross-Country Skiing—Men
15 km—Thomas Wassberg, Sweden
30 km—Nikolai Zimyatov, Soviet Union
50 km—Nikolai Zimyatov, Soviet Union
40-km relay—Soviet Union (Vasily Rochev, Nikolai Bazhukov, Yevgeny Beliaev, and Nikolai Zimyatov)

Cross-Country Skiing—Women
5 km—Raisa Smetanina, Soviet Union
10 km—Barbara Petzold, East Germany
20-km relay—East Germany (Marlies Rostock, Carola Anding, Veronika Hesse, and Barbara Petzold)

JAMES E. SULLIVAN MEMORIAL AWARD WINNERS

(Amateur Athlete of Year Chosen in Amateur Athletic Union Poll)

1930	Robert Tyre Jones, Jr.	Golf
1931	Bernard E. Berlinger	Track and field
1932	James A. Bausch	Track and field
1933	Glenn Cunningham	Track and field
1934	William R. Bonthron	Track and field
1935	W. Lawson Little, Jr.	Golf
1936	Glenn Morris	Track and field
1937	J. Donald Budge	Tennis
1938	Donald R. Lash	Track and field
1939	Joseph W. Burk	Rowing
1940	J. Gregory Rice	Track and field
1941	Leslie MacMitchell	Track and field
1942	Cornelius Warmerdam	Track and field
1943	Gilbert L. Dodds	Track and field
1944	Ann Curtis	Swimming
1945	Felix (Doc) Blanchard	Football
1946	Y. Arnold Tucker	Football
1947	John B. Kelly, Jr.	Rowing
1948	Robert B. Mathias	Track and field
1949	Richard T. Button	Figure skating
1950	Fred Wilt	Track and field
1951	Robert E. Richards	Track and field
1952	Horace Ashenfelter	Track and field
1953	Major Sammy Lee	Diving
1954	Malvin Whitfield	Track and field
1955	Harrison Dillard	Track and field
1956	Patricia McCormick	Diving
1957	Bobby Jo Morrow	Track and field
1958	Glenn Davis	Track and field
1959	Parry O'Brien	Track and field
1960	Rafer Johnson	Track and field
1961	Wilma Rudolph Ward	Track and field
1962	Jim Beatty	Track and field
1963	John Pennel	Track and field
1964	Don Schollander	Swimming
1965	Bill Bradley	Basketball
1966	Jim Ryun	Track and field
1967	Randy Matson	Track and field
1968	Debbie Meyer	Swimming
1969	Bill Toomey	Decathlon
1970	John Kinsella	Swimming
1971	Mark Spitz	Swimming
1972	Frank Shorter	Marathon
1973	Bill Walton	Basketball
1974	Rick Wohlhuter	Track
1975	Tim Shaw	Swimming
1976	Bruce Jenner	Track and field
1977	John Naber	Swimming
1978	Tracy Caulkins	Swimming
1979	Kurt Thomas	Gymnastics
1980	Eric Heiden	Speed skating
1981	Carl Lewis	Track and field

FOOTBALL

The pastime of kicking around a ball goes back beyond the limits of recorded history. Ancient savage tribes played football of a primitive kind. There was a ball-kicking game played by Athenians, Spartans, and Corinthians 2500 years ago, which the Greeks called *Episkuros.* The Romans had a somewhat similar game called *Harpastum* and are supposed to have carried the game with them when they invaded the British Isles in the First Century, B.C.

Undoubtedly the game known in the United Stated as Football traces directly to the English game of Rugby, though the modifications have been many. Informal football was played on college lawns well over a century ago, and an annual Freshman-Sophomore series of "scrimmages" began at Yale in 1840. The first formal intercollegiate football game was the Princeton-Rutgers contest at New Brunswick, N.J., on Nov. 6, 1869, with Rutgers winning by 6 goals to 4.

In those days, games were played with 25, 20, 15, or 11 men on a side. In 1880, there was a convention at which Walter Camp of Yale persuaded the delegates to agree to a rule calling for 11 players on a side. The game grew so rough that it was attacked as brutal, and some colleges abandoned the sport. Conditions were so bad in 1906 that President Theodore Roosevelt called a meeting of Yale, Harvard, and Princeton representatives at the White House in the hope of reforming and improving the game. The outcome was that the game, with the forward pass introduced and some other modifications of the rules inserted, became faster and cleaner.

The first professional game was played in 1895 at Latrobe, Pa. The National Football League was founded in 1921. The All-American Conference went into action in 1946. At the end of the 1949 season the two circuits merged, retaining the name of the older league. In 1960, the American Football League, began operations. In 1970, the leagues merged.

College Football

NATIONAL COLLEGE FOOTBALL CHAMPIONS

The "National Collegiate A. A. Football Guide" recognizes as unofficial national champion the team selected each year by press association polls. Where The Associated Press poll (of writers) does not agree with the United Press International poll (of coaches), the guide lists both teams selected.

1937	Pittsburgh
1938	Texas Christian
1939	Texas A & M
1940	Minnesota
1941	Minnesota
1942	Ohio State
1943	Notre Dame
1944	Army
1945	Army
1946	Notre Dame
1947	Notre Dame
1948	Michigan
1949	Notre Dame
1950	Oklahoma
1951	Tennessee
1952	Michigan State
1953	Maryland
1954	Ohio State and U.C.L.A.
1955	Oklahoma
1956	Oklahoma
1957	Auburn and Ohio State
1958	Louisiana State
1959	Syracuse
1960	Minnesota
1961	Alabama
1962	So. California
1963	Texas
1964	Alabama
1965	Alabama and Michigan State
1966	Notre Dame
1967	So. California
1968	Ohio State
1969	Texas
1970	Texas and Nebraska
1971	Nebraska
1972	So. California
1973	Notre Dame
1974	Oklahoma and So. California
1975	Oklahoma
1976	Pittsburgh
1977	Notre Dame
1978	Alabama and So. California
1979	Alabama
1980	Georgia
1981	Clemson

ARMY-NAVY SERIES RECORD SINCE 1962

1962	Navy 34, Army 14
1963	Navy 21, Army 15
1964	Army 11, Navy 8
1965	Army 7, Navy 7
1966	Army 20, Navy 7
1967	Navy 19, Army 14
1968	Army 21, Navy 14
1969	Army 27, Navy 0
1970	Navy 11, Army 7
1971	Army 24, Navy 23
1972	Army 23, Navy 15
1973	Navy 51, Army 0
1974	Navy 19, Army 0
1975	Navy 30, Army 6
1976	Navy 38, Army 10
1977	Army 17, Navy 14
1978	Navy 28, Army 0
1979	Navy 31, Army 7
1980	Navy 33, Army 6
1981	Army 3, Navy 3

RECORD OF ANNUAL MAJOR BOWL COLLEGE FOOTBALL GAMES

Rose Bowl

(At Pasadena, Calif.)

1902	Michigan 49, Stanford 0
1916	Washington State 14, Brown 0
1917	Oregon 14, Pennsylvania 0
1918	Mare Island Marines 19, Camp Lewis 7
1919	Great Lakes 17, Mare Island Marines 0
1920	Harvard 7, Oregon 6
1921	California 28, Ohio State 0
1922	Washington and Jefferson 0, California 0
1923	So. California 14, Penn State 3
1924	Navy 14, Washington 14
1925	Notre Dame 27, Stanford 10
1926	Alabama 20, Washington 19
1927	Alabama 7, Stanford 7
1928	Stanford 7, Pittsburgh 6
1929	Georgia Tech 8, California 7
1930	So. California 47, Pittsburgh 14
1931	Alabama 24, Washington State 0
1932	So. California 21, Tulane 12
1933	So. California 35, Pittsburgh 0
1934	Columbia 7, Stanford 0
1935	Alabama 29, Stanford 13
1936	Stanford 7, So. Methodist 0
1937	Pittsburgh 21, Washington 0
1938	California 13, Alabama 0
1939	So. California 7, Duke 3
1940	So. California 14, Tennessee 0
1941	Stanford 21, Nebraska 13
1942	Oregon State 20, Duke 16[1]
1943	Georgia 9, U.C.L.A. 0
1944	So. California 29, Washington 0
1945	So. California 25, Tennessee 0
1946	Alabama 34, So. California 14
1947	Illinois 45, U.C.L.A. 14
1948	Michigan 49, So. California 0
1949	Northwestern 20, California 14
1950	Ohio State 17, California 14
1951	Michigan 14, California 6
1952	Illinois 40, Stanford 7
1953	So. California 7, Wisconsin 0

1954 Michigan State 28, U.C.L.A. 20
1955 Ohio State 20, So. California 7
1956 Michigan State 17, U.C.L.A. 14
1957 Iowa 35, Oregon State 19
1958 Ohio State 10, Oregon 7
1959 Iowa 38, California 12
1960 Washington 44, Wisconsin 8
1961 Washington 17, Minnesota 7
1962 Minnesota 21, U.C.L.A. 3
1963 So. California 42, Wisconsin 37
1964 Illinois 17, Washington 7
1965 Michigan 34, Oregon State 7
1966 U.C.L.A. 14, Michigan State 12
1967 Purdue 14, So. California 13
1968 So. California 14, Indiana 3
1969 Ohio State 27, So. California 16
1970 So. California 10, Michigan 3
1971 Stanford 27, Ohio State 17
1972 Stanford 13, Michigan 12
1973 So. California 42, Ohio State 17
1974 Ohio State 42, So. California 21
1975 So. California 18, Ohio State 17
1976 U.C.L.A. 23, Ohio State 10
1977 So. California 14, Michigan 6
1978 Washington 27, Michigan 20
1979 So. California 17, Michigan 10
1980 So. California 17, Ohio State 16
1981 Michigan 23, Washington 6
1982 Washington 28, Iowa 0

1. Played at Durham, N.C.

Orange Bowl

(At Miami)

1933 Miami (Fla.) 7, Manhattan 0
1934 Duquesne 33, Miami (Fla.) 7
1935 Bucknell 26, Miami (Fla.) 0
1936 Catholic 20, Mississippi 19
1937 Duquesne 13, Mississippi State 12
1938 Auburn 6, Michigan State 0
1939 Tennessee 17, Oklahoma 0
1940 Georgia Tech 21, Missouri 7
1941 Mississippi State 14, Georgetown 7
1942 Georgia 40, Texas Christian 26
1943 Alabama 37, Boston College 21
1944 Louisiana State 19, Texas A&M 14
1945 Tulsa 26, Georgia Tech 12
1946 Miami (Fla.) 13, Holy Cross 6
1947 Rice 8, Tennessee 0
1948 Georgia Tech 20, Kansas 14
1949 Texas 41, Georgia 28
1950 Santa Clara 21, Kentucky 13
1951 Clemson 15, Miami (Fla.) 14
1952 Georgia Tech 17, Baylor 14
1953 Alabama 61, Syracuse 6
1954 Oklahoma 7, Maryland 0
1955 Duke 34, Nebraska 7
1956 Oklahoma 20, Maryland 6
1957 Colorado 27, Clemson 21
1958 Oklahoma 48, Duke 21
1959 Oklahoma 21, Syracuse 6
1960 Georgia 14, Missouri 0
1961 Missouri 21, Navy 14
1962 Louisiana State 25, Colorado 7
1963 Alabama 17, Oklahoma 0
1964 Nebraska 13, Auburn 7
1965 Texas 21, Alabama 17
1966 Alabama 39, Nebraska 28
1967 Florida 27, Georgia Tech 12
1968 Oklahoma 26, Tennessee 24
1969 Penn State 15, Kansas 14
1970 Penn State 10, Missouri 3
1971 Nebraska 17, Louisiana State 12
1972 Nebraska 38, Alabama 6
1973 Nebraska 40, Notre Dame 6
1974 Penn State 16, Louisiana State 9
1975 Notre Dame 13, Alabama 11
1976 Oklahoma 14, Michigan 6
1977 Ohio State 27, Colorado 10
1978 Arkansas 31, Oklahoma 6
1979 Oklahoma 31, Nebraska 24
1980 Oklahoma 24, Florida State 7
1981 Oklahoma 18, Florida State 17
1982 Clemson 22, Nebraska 15

Sugar Bowl

(At New Orleans)

1935 Tulane 20, Temple 14
1936 Texas Christian 3, Louisiana State 2
1937 Santa Clara 21, Louisiana State 14
1938 Santa Clara 6, Louisiana State 0
1939 Texas Christian 15, Carnegie Tech 7
1940 Texas A & M 14, Tulane 13
1941 Boston College 19, Tennessee 13
1942 Fordham 2, Missouri 0
1943 Tennessee 14, Tulsa 7
1944 Georgia Tech 20, Tulsa 18
1945 Duke 29, Alabama 26
1946 Oklahoma A & M 33, St. Mary's (Calif.) 13
1947 Georgia 20, North Carolina 10
1948 Texas 27, Alabama 7
1949 Oklahoma 14, North Carolina 6
1950 Oklahoma 35, Louisiana State 0
1951 Kentucky 13, Oklahoma 7
1952 Maryland 28, Tennessee 13
1953 Georgia Tech 24, Mississippi 7
1954 Georgia Tech 42, West Virginia 19
1955 Navy 21, Mississippi 0
1956 Georgia Tech 7, Pittsburgh 0
1957 Baylor 13, Tennessee 7
1958 Mississippi 39, Texas 7
1959 Louisiana State 7, Clemson 0
1960 Mississippi 21, Louisiana State 0
1961 Mississippi 14, Rice 6
1962 Alabama 10, Arkansas 3
1963 Mississippi 17, Arkansas 13
1964 Alabama 12, Mississippi 7
1965 Louisiana State 13, Syracuse 10
1966 Missouri 20, Florida 18
1967 Alabama 34, Nebraska 7
1968 Louisiana State 20, Wyoming 13
1969 Arkansas 16, Georgia 2
1970 Mississippi 27, Arkansas 22
1971 Tennessee 34, Air Force Academy 13
1972 Oklahoma 40, Auburn 22
1973 Oklahoma 14, Penn State 0
1974 Notre Dame 24, Alabama 23
1975 Nebraska 13, Florida 10
1976 Alabama 13, Penn State 6
1977 Pittsburgh 27, Georgia 3
1978 Alabama 35, Ohio State 6
1979 Alabama 14, Penn State 7
1980 Alabama 24, Arkansas 9
1981 Georgia 17, Notre Dame 10
1982 Pittsburgh 24, Georgia 20

Cotton Bowl

(At Dallas)

1937 Texas Christian 16, Marquette 6
1938 Rice 28, Colorado 14
1939 St. Mary's (Calif.) 20, Texas Tech. 13
1940 Clemson 6, Boston College 3
1941 Texas A & M 13, Fordham 12
1942 Alabama 29, Texas A & M 21
1943 Texas 14, Georgia Tech 7
1944 Randolph Field 7, Texas 7
1945 Oklahoma A & M 34, Texas Christian 0
1946 Texas 40, Missouri 27
1947 Louisiana State 0, Arkansas 0
1948 So. Methodist 13, Penn State 13
1949 So. Methodist 21, Oregon 13
1950 Rice 27, North Carolina 13
1951 Tennessee 20, Texas 14
1952 Kentucky 20, Texas Christian 7
1953 Texas 16, Tennessee 0
1954 Rice 28, Alabama 6
1955 Georgia Tech 14, Arkansas 6
1956 Mississippi 14, Texas Christian 13
1957 Texas Christian 28, Syracuse 27
1958 Navy 20, Rice 7
1959 Air Force 0, Texas Christian 0
1960 Syracuse 23, Texas 14
1961 Duke 7, Arkansas 6
1962 Texas 12, Mississippi 7
1963 Louisiana State 13, Texas 0
1964 Texas 28, Navy 6
1965 Arkansas 10, Nebraska 7
1966 Louisiana State 14, Arkansas 7
1967 Georgia 24, So. Methodist 9
1968 Texas A & M 20, Alabama 16
1969 Texas 36, Tennessee 13
1970 Texas 21, Notre Dame 17
1971 Notre Dame 24, Texas 11
1972 Penn State 30, Texas 6
1973 Texas 17, Alabama 13
1974 Nebraska 19, Texas 3
1975 Penn State 41, Baylor 20
1976 Arkansas 31, Georgia 10
1977 Houston 30, Maryland 21
1978 Notre Dame 38, Texas 10
1979 Notre Dame 35, Houston 34
1980 Houston 17, Nebraska 14
1981 Alabama 30, Baylor 2
1982 Texas 14, Alabama 12

Gator Bowl

(At Jacksonville, Fla. Played on Saturday nearest New Year's Day of year indicated)

1953 Florida 14, Tulsa 13
1954 Texas Tech 35, Auburn 13
1955 Auburn 33, Baylor 13
1956 Vanderbilt 25, Auburn 13
1957 Georgia Tech 21, Pittsburgh 14
1958 Tennessee 3, Texas A & M 0
1959 Mississippi 7, Florida 3
1960 Arkansas 14, Georgia Tech 7
1961 Florida 13, Baylor 12
1962 Penn State 30, Georgia Tech 15
1963 Florida 17, Penn State 7
1964 No. Carolina 35, Air Force 0
1965 Florida State 36, Oklahoma 19
1966 Georgia Tech 31, Texas Tech 21
1967 Tennessee 18, Syracuse 12
1968 Penn State 17, Florida State 17
1969 Missouri 35, Alabama 10
1970 Florida 14, Tennessee 13
1971 Auburn 35, Mississippi 28
1972 Georgia 7, North Carolina 3
1973 Auburn 24, Colorado 3
1974 Texas Tech 28, Tennessee 19

1975 Auburn 27, Texas 3
1976 Maryland 13, Florida 0
1977 Notre Dame 20, Penn State 9
1978 Pittsburgh 34, Clemson 3
1979 Clemson 17, Ohio State 15
1980 North Carolina 17, Michigan 15
1981 Pittsburgh 37, South Carolina 9
1982 North Carolina 31, Arkansas 27

RESULTS OF OTHER 1981 SEASON BOWL GAMES

Bluebonnet (Houston)—Michigan 33, U.C.L.A. 14
California Bowl (Fresno, Calif.)—Toledo 27, San Jose State 25
Fiesta (Tempe, Ariz.)—Penn State 26, Southern California 10
Hall of Fame (Birmingham, Ala.)—Mississippi State 10, Kansas 0
Holiday (San Diego)—Brigham Young 38, Washington State 36
Independence (Shreveport, La.)—Texas A. and M. 33, Oklahoma State 16
Liberty (Memphis)—Ohio State 31, Navy 28
Garden State (East Rutherford, N.J.)—Tennessee 28, Wisconsin 21
Peach (Atlanta)—West Virginia 26, Florida 6
Sun (El Paso)—Oklahoma 40, Houston 14
Tangerine (Orlando, Fla.)—Missouri 19, Southern Mississippi 17

HEISMAN MEMORIAL TROPHY WINNERS

The Heisman Memorial Trophy is presented annually by the Downtown Athletic Club of New York City to the nation's outstanding college football player, as determined by a poll of sportswriters and sportscasters.

1935	Jay Berwanger, Chicago
1936	Larry Kelley, Yale
1937	Clinton Frank, Yale
1938	Davey O'Brien, Texas Christian
1939	Nile Kinnick, Iowa
1940	Tom Harmon, Michigan
1941	Bruce Smith, Minnesota
1942	Frank Sinkwich, Georgia
1943	Angelo Bertelli, Notre Dame
1944	Leslie Horvath, Ohio State
1945	Felix Blanchard, Army
1946	Glenn Davis, Army
1947	Johnny Lujack, Notre Dame
1948	Doak Walker, So. Methodist
1949	Leon Hart, Notre Dame
1950	Vic Janowicz, Ohio State
1951	Dick Kazmaier, Princeton
1952	Billy Vessels, Oklahoma
1953	Johnny Lattner, Notre Dame
1954	Alan Ameche, Wisconsin
1955	Howard Cassady, Ohio State
1956	Paul Hornung, Notre Dame
1957	John Crow, Texas A & M
1958	Pete Dawkins, Army
1959	Billy Cannon, Louisiana State
1960	Joe Bellino, Navy
1961	Ernie Davis, Syracuse
1962	Terry Baker, Oregon State
1963	Roger Staubach, Navy
1964	John Huarte, Notre Dame
1965	Mike Garrett, Southern California
1966	Steve Spurrier, Florida
1967	Gary Beban, U.C.L.A.
1968	O. J. Simpson, Southern California
1969	Steve Owens, Oklahoma
1970	Jim Plunkett, Stanford
1971	Pat Sullivan, Auburn
1972	Johnny Rodgers, Nebraska
1973	John Cappelletti, Penn State
1974–75	Archie Griffin, Ohio State
1976	Tony Dorsett, Pittsburgh
1977	Earl Campbell, Texas
1978	Billy Sims, Oklahoma
1979	Charles White, Southern California
1980	George Rogers, South Carolina
1981	Marcus Allen, Southern California

COLLEGE FOOTBALL HALL OF FAME

(Kings Island, Interstate 71, Kings Mills, Ohio)
(Date given is player's last year of competition)

Players

Abell, Earl—Colgate, 1915
Agase, Alex—Purdue/Illinois, 1946
Agganis, Harry—Boston Univ., 1952
Albert, Frank—Stanford, 1941
Aldrich, Chas. (Ki)—T.C.U., 1938
Aldrich, Malcolm—Yale, 1921
Alexander, John—Syracuse, 1920
Ameche, Alan (Horse)—Wisconsin, 1954
Anderson, H. (Hunk)—Notre Dame, 1921
Bacon, C. Everett—Wesleyan, 1912
Bagnell, Francis (Reds)—Penn, 1950
Baker, Hobart (Hobey)—Princeton, 1913
Baker, Terry—Oregon State, 1962
Ballin, Harold—Princeton, 1914
Banker, Bill—Tulane, 1929
Barnes, Stanley—S. California, 1921
Barrett, Charles—Cornell, 1915
Baston, Bert—Minnesota, 1916
Battles, Cliff—W. Va. Wesleyan, 1931
Baugh, Sammy—Texas Christian U., 1936
Bausch, James—Kansas, 1930
Beckett, John—Oregon, 1913
Bednarik, Chuck—Pennsylvania, 1948
Bellini, Joe—Navy, 1960
Benbrook, A.—Michigan, 1911
Bertelli, A.—Notre Dame, 1943
Berry, Charlie—Lafayette, 1924
Berwanger, John (Jay)—Chicago, 1935
Bettencourt, Larry—St. Mary's, 1927
Blanchard, Felix (Doc)—Army, 1946
Bock, Ed—Iowa State, 1938
Bomar, Lynn—Vanderbilt, 1924
Bomeisler, Doug (Bo)—Yale, 1913
Booth, Albie—Yale, 1931
Borries, Fred—Navy, 1934
Bosely, Bruce—West Virginia, 1955
Bottari, Vic—California, 1939
Boynton, Ben—Williams, 1920
Brewer, Charles—Harvard, 1895
Brooke, George—Pennsylvania, 1895
Brown, Gordon—Yale, 1900
Brown, John, Jr.—Navy, 1913
Brown, Johnny Mack—Alabama, 1925
Brown, Raymond (Tay)—So. California, 1932
Bunker, Paul—Army, 1902
Butler, Robert—Wisconsin, 1912
Cafego, George—Tennessee, 1939
Cagle, Chris—SW La./Army, 1929
Cain, John—Alabama, 1932
Cameron, Eddie—Wash. & Lee, 1924
Campbell, David C.—Harvard, 1901
Cannon, Jack—Notre Dame, 1929
Carideo, Frank—Notre Dame, 1930
Caroline, J.C.—Illinois, 1954
Carney, Charles—Illinois, 1921
Carpenter, Bill—Army, 1959
Carpenter, C. Hunter—VPI, 1905
Carroll, Charles—Washington, 1928
Casey, Edward L.—Harvard, 1919
Cassady, Howard—Ohio State, 1955
Chamberlain, Guy—Nebraska, 1915
Christman, Paul—Missouri, 1940
Clark, Earl (Dutch)—Colo. College, 1929
Clevenger, Zora—Indiana, 1903
Cochran, Gary—Princeton, 1895
Cody, Josh—Vanderbilt, 1920
Coleman, Don—Mich. State, 1951
Conerly, Chuck—Mississippi, 1947
Connor, George—Notre Dame, 1947
Corbin, W.—Yale, 1888
Corbus, William—Stanford, 1933
Cowan, Hector—Princeton, 1889
Coy, Edward H. (Tad)—Yale, 1909
Crawford, Fred—Duke, 1933
Crow, John D.—Texas A&M, 1957
Crowley, James—Notre Dame, 1924
Cutter, Slade—Navy, 1934
Czarobski, Ziggie—Notre Dame, 1947
Dalrymple, Gerald—Tulane, 1931
Daniell, James—Ohio State, 1941
Dawkins, Pete—Army, 1958
Dalton, John—Navy, 1912
Daly, Charles—Harvard/Army, 1902
Daniell, Averell—Pittsburgh, 1936
Davies, Tom—Pittsburgh, 1921
Davis, Ernest—Syracuse, 1961
Davis, Glenn—Army, 1946
Davis, Robert T.—Georgia Tech, 1947

DesJardien, Paul—Chicago, 1914
Devine, Aubrey—Iowa, 1921
DeWitt, John—Princeton, 1903
Dobbs, Glenn—Tulsa, 1942
Dodd, Bobby—Tennessee, 1930
Donchess, Joseph—Pittsburgh, 1929
Dougherty, Nathan—Tennessee, 1909
Drahos, Nick—Cornell, 1940
Driscoll, Paddy—Northwestern, 1917
Drury, Morley—So. California, 1927
Dudley, William (Bill)—Virginia, 1941
Eckersall, Walter—Chicago, 1906
Edwards, Turk—Washington State, 1931
Edwards, William—Princeton, 1900
Eichenlaub, R.—Notre Dame, 1913
Evans, Ray—Kansas, 1947
Exendine, Albert—Carlisle, 1908
Falaschi, Nello—Santa Clara, 1937
Fears, Tom—Santa Clara/UCLA, 1947
Feathers, Beattie—Tennessee, 1933
Fenimore, Robert—Oklahoma State, 1947
Fenton, G.E. (Doc)—La. State U., 1910
Ferraro, John—So. California, 1944
Fesler, Wesley—Ohio State, 1930
Fincher, Bill—Georgia Tech, 1920
Fish, Hamilton—Harvard, 1909
Fisher, Robert—Harvard, 1911
Flowers, Abe—Georgia Tech, 1920
Fortmann, Daniel—Colgate, 1935
Francis, Sam—Nebraska, 1936
Franco, Edmund (Ed)—Fordham, 1937
Frank, Clint—Yale, 1937
Franz, Rodney—California, 1949
Friedman, Benny—Michigan, 1926
Gain, Bob—Kentucky, 1950
Gallarneau, Hugh—Stanford, 1941
Garbisch, Edgar—Army, 1924
Gelbert, Charles—Pennsylvania, 1896
Geyer, Forest—Oklahoma, 1915
Giel, Paul—Minnesota, 1953
Gifford, Frank—So. California, 1951
Gilbert, Walter—Auburn, 1936
Gipp, George—Notre Dame, 1920
Gladchuk, Chet—Boston College, 1940
Goldberg, Marshall—Pittsburgh, 1938
Goodreault, Gene—Boston College, 1940
Gordon, Walter—California, 1918
Graham, Otto—Northwestern, 1943
Grange, Harold (Red)—Illinois, 1925
Grayson, Robert—Stanford, 1935
Gulick, Merel—Hobart, 1929
Guyon, Joe—Georgia Tech, 1919
Hale, Edwin—Mississippi Col, 1921
Hamilton, Robert (Bones)—Stanford, 1935
Hamilton, Tom—Navy, 1925
Hanson, Vic—Syracuse, 1926
Hardwick, H. (Tack)—Harvard, 1914
Hare, T. Truxton—Pennsylvania, 1900
Harley, Chick—Ohio State, 1919
Harmon, Tom—Michigan, 1940
Harpster, Howard—Carnegie Tech, 1928
Hart, Edward J.—Princeton, 1911
Hart, Leon—Notre Dame, 1949
Hazel, Homer—Rutgers, 1924
Healey, Ed—Dartmouth, 1916
Heffelfinger, W. (Pudge)—Yale, 1891
Hein, Mel—Washington State, 1930
Henry, Wilber—Wash. & Jefferson, 1919
Herschberger, Clarence—Chicago, 1899
Herwig, Robert—California, 1937
Heston, Willie—Michigan, 1904
Hickman, Herman—Tennessee, 1931
Hickok, William—Yale, 1895
Hill, Dan—Duke, 1938
Hillebrand, A.R. (Doc)—Princeton, 1900
Hinkey, Frank—Yale, 1894
Hinkle, Carl—Vanderbilt, 1937
Hinkle, Clark—Bucknell, 1932
Hirsch, Elroy—Wis./Mich., 1943
Hitchcock, James—Auburn, 1932
Hoffman, Frank—Notre Dame, 1931
Hogan, James J.—Yale, 1904
Holland, Jerome (Brud)—Cornell, 1938
Hollenbeck, William—Penn., 1908
Holovak, Michael—Boston College, 1942
Horrell, Edwin—California, 1924
Horvath, Les—Ohio State, 1944
Howe, Arthur—Yale, 1911
Howell, Millard (Dixie)—Alabama, 1934
Hubbard, Cal—Centenary, 1926
Hubbard, John—Amherst, 1906
Hubert, Allison—Alabama, 1925
Huff, Robert Lee (Sam)—W. Va., 1955
Humble, Weldon G.—Rice, 1946
Hunt, Joel—Texas A&M, 1927
Huntington, Ellery—Colgate, 1914
Hutson, Don—Alabama, 1934
Ingram, James—Navy, 1906
Isbell, Cecil—Purdue, 1937
Jablonsky, Harvey—Wash. U./Army, 1933
Janowicz, Vic—Ohio State, 1951
Jenkins, Darold—Missouri, 1941
Joesting, Herbert—Minnesota, 1927
Johnson, James—Carlisle, 1903
Jones, Calvin—Iowa, 1955
Jones, Gomer—Ohio State, 1935
Juhan, Frank—Univ. of South, 1910
Justice, Charlie—North Carolina, 1949
Kaer, Mort—So. California, 1926
Kavanaugh, Kenneth—La. State U., 1939
Kaw, Edgar—Cornell, 1922
Kazmaier, Richard—Princeton, 1951
Keck, James—Princeton, 1921
Kelley, Larry—Yale, 1936
Kelly, William—Montana, 1926
Ketcham, Henry—Yale, 1913
Killinger, William—Penn State, 1922
Kimbrough, John—Texas A&M, 1940
Kinard, Frank—Mississippi, 1937
King, Phillip—Princeton, 1893
Kinnick, Nile—Iowa, 1939
Kipke, Harry—Michigan, 1923
Kirkpatrick, John Reed—Yale, 1910
Kitzmiller, John—Oregon, 1929
Koch, Barton—Baylor, 1931
Kitner, Malcolm—Texas, 1942
Kramer, Ron—Michigan, 1956
Lach, Steve—Duke, 1941
Lane, Myles—Dartmouth, 1927
Lattner, Joseph J.—Notre Dame, 1953
Lauricella, Hank—Tennessee, 1952
Lautenschlaeger—Tulane, 1925
Layden, Elmer—Notre Dame, 1924
Layne, Bobby—Texas, 1947
Lea, Langdon—Princeton, 1895
LeBaron, Eddie—Univ. of Pacific, 1949
Leech, James—Va. Mil. Inst., 1920
Lilly, Bob—Texas Christian, 1960
Lio, Augie—Georgetown, 1940
Locke, Gordon—Iowa, 1922
Lourie, Don—Princeton, 1921
Luckman, Sid—Columbia, 1938
Lujack, John—Notre Dame, 1947
Lund, J.L. (Pug)—Minnesota, 1934
Macomber, Bart—Illinois, 1915
MacLeod, Robert—Dartmouth, 1938
Maegle, Dick—Rice, 1954
Mahan, Edward W.—Harvard, 1915
Mallory, William—Yale, 1893
Mann, Gerald—So. Methodist, 1927
Markov, Vic—Washington, 1937
Marshall, Robert—Minnesota, 1907
Matson, Ollie—San Fran. U., 1952
Matthews, Ray—Texas Christ. U., 1928
Maulbetsch, John—Michigan, 1914
Mauthe, J.L. (Pete)—Penn State 1912
Maxwell, Robert—Chi./Swarthmore, 1906
McAfee, George—Duke, 1939
McColl, William F.—Stanford, 1951
McCormick, James B.—Princeton, 1907
McDowall, Jack—No. Car. State, 1927
McElhenny, Hugh—Washington, 1951
McEver, Gene—Tennessee, 1931
McEwan, John—Minn./Army, 1916
McFadden, J.B.—Clemson, 1939
McClung, Thomas L.—Yale, 1891
McGinley, Edward—Pennsylvania, 1924
McGovern, J.—Minnesota, 1910
McGraw, Thurman—Colorado State, 1949
McLaren, George—Pittsburgh, 1918
McMillan, Dan—U.S.C./Calif., 1922
McMillin, A.N. (Bo)—Centre, 1921
McWhorter, Robert—Georgia, 1913
Mercer, Leroy—Pennsylvania, 1912
Meredith, Don—Southern Methodist, 1959
Metzger, Bert—Notre Dame, 1930
Mickal, Abe—La. State U., 1935
Miller, Creighton—Notre Dame, 1943
Miller, Don—Notre Dame, 1925
Miller, Edgar (Rip)—Notre Dame, 1924
Miller, Eugene—Penn State, 1913
Milstead, Century—Wabash, Yale 1923
Minds, John—Pennsylvania, 1897
Moffatt, Alex—Princeton, 1884
Montgomery, Cliff—Columbia, 1933
Moomaw, Donn—U.C.L.A., 1952
Morley, William—Columbia, 1903
Morris, George—Georgia Tech, 1952
Morton, William—Dartmouth, 1931
Muller, Harold (Brick)—Calif., 1922
Nagurski, Bronko—Minnesota, 1929
Nevers, Ernie—Stanford, 1925
Newell, Marshall—Harvard, 1893
Newman, Harry—Michigan, 1932
Nobis, Tommy—Texas, 1965
Nomellini, Leo—Minnesota, 1949
Oberlander, Andrew—Dartmouth, 1925
O'Brien, Davey—Texas Christ. U., 1938
O'Dea, Pat—Wisconsin, 1899
O'Hearn, J.—Cornell, 1915
Oliphant, Elmer—Purdue/Army, 1917
Olsen, Merlin—Utah State, 1961
Oosterbaan, Ben—Michigan, 1927
O'Rourke, Charles—Boston College, 1940
Orsi, John—Colgate, 1931
Osgood, W.D.—Cornell/Penn, 1895
Osmanski, William—Holy Cross, 1938
Owens, Jim—Oklahoma, 1949
Parilli, Vito (Babe)—Kentucky, 1951
Parker, Clarence (Ace)—Duke, 1936
Parker, Jackie—Miss. State, 1953
Parker, James—Ohio State, 1956
Pazzetti, V.J.—Wes./Lehigh, 1912
Peabody, Endicott—Harvard, 1941
Peck, Robert—Pittsburgh, 1916
Pennock, Stanley B.—Harvard, 1914
Pfann, George—Cornell, 1923
Phillips, H.D.—U. of South, 1904

Pingel, John—Michigan State, 1938
Pihos, Pete—Indiana, 1945
Pinckert, Ernie—So. California, 1931
Poe, Arthur—Princeton, 1899
Pollard, Fritz—Brown, 1916
Poole, Barney—Miss./Army, 1947
Pregulman, Merv—Michigan, 1943
Price, Eddie—Tulane, 1949
Pund, Henry—Georgia Tech, 1928
Ramsey, Gerrard—Wm. & Mary, 1942
Reeds, Claude—Oklahoma, 1913
Reid, William—Harvard, 1900
Rentner, Ernest—Northwestern, 1932
Reynolds, Robert—Stanford, 1935
Richter, Les—California, 1951
Rinehart, Charles—Lafayette, 1897
Rodgers, Ira—West Virginia, 1919
Rogers, Edward L.—Minnesota, 1903
Rosenberg, Aaron—So. California, 1934
Rote, Kyle—So. Methodist, 1950
Routt, Joe—Texas A&M., 1937
Salmon, Louis—Notre Dame, 1904
Sauer, George—Nebraska, 1933
Sayers, Gale—Kansas, 1964
Scarlett, Hunter—Pennsylvania, 1909
Schoonover, Wear—Arkansas, 1929
Schreiner, Dave—Wisconsin, 1942
Schultz, Adolf (Germany)—Mich., 1908
Schwab, Frank—Lafayette, 1922
Schwartz, Marchmont—Notre Dame, 1931
Schwegler, Paul—Washington, 1931
Scott, Clyde—Arkansas, 1949
Scott, Tom—Virgina, 1953
Seibels, Henry—Sewanee, 1899
Shelton, Murray—Cornell, 1915
Shevlin, Tom—Yale, 1905
Shively, Bernie—Illinois, 1926
Simons, Claude—Tulane, 1934
Sington, Fred—Alabama, 1930
Sinkwich, Frank—Georgia, 1942
Skladany, Joe—Pittsburgh, 1933
Slater, F.F. (Duke)—Iowa, 1921
Smith, Bruce—Minnesota, 1941
Smith, Ernie—So. California, 1932
Smith, Harry—So. California, 1939
Smith, John (Clipper)—Notre Dame, 1927
Smith, Vernon—Georgia, 1931
Snow, Neil—Michigan, 1901
Spears, Clarence W.—Dartmouth, 1915
Spears, W.D.—Vanderbilt, 1927
Sprackling, William—Brown, 1911
Sprague, M. (Bud)—Texas/Army, 1928
Stafford, Harrison—Texas, 1932
Stagg, Amos Alonzo—Yale, 1889
Staubach, Roger—Navy, 1963
Steffen, Walter—Chicago, 1908
Stein, Herbert—Pittsburgh, 1921
Steuber, Robert—Missouri, 1943
Stevens, Mal—Yale, 1923
Stinchcomb, Gaylord—Ohio State, 1920
Stevenson, Vincent—Pennsylvania, 1905
Strong, Ken—New York Univ., 1928
Strupper, George—Georgia Tech, 1917
Stuhldreher, Harry—Notre Dame, 1924
Stydahar, Joe—West Virginia, 1935
Suffridge, Robert—Tennessee, 1940
Sundstrom, Frank—Cornell, 1923
Swanson, Clarence—Nebraska, 1921
Swiacki, Bill—Holy Cross/Colombia. 1947
Swink, Jim—Texas Christian, 1956
Taliafarro, George—Indiana, 1948
Thompson, Joe—Pittsburgh, 1907
Thorne, Samuel B.—Yale, 1906
Thorpe, Jim—Carlisle, 1912
Ticknor, Ben—Harvard, 1930
Tigert, John—Vanderbilt, 1904
Tinsley, Gaynell—La. State U., 1936
Tipton, Eric—Duke, 1938
Tonnemaker, Clayton—Minnesota, 1949
Torrey, Robert—Pennsylvania, 1906
Travis, Ed Tarkio—Missouri, 1920
Trippi, Charles—Georgia, 1946
Tryon, J. Edward—Colgate, 1925
Utay, Joe—Texas A&M, 1907
Van Brocklin, Norm—Oregon, 1948
Van Sickel, Dale—Florida, 1929
Van Surdam, Henderson—Wesleyan, 1905
Very, Dexter—Penn State, 1912
Vessels, Billy—Oklahoma, 1931
Wagner, Huber—Pittsburgh, 1913
Walker, Doak—So. Methodist, 1949
Wallace, Bill—Rice, 1935
Walsh, Adam—Notre Dame, 1924
Warburton, I. (Cotton)—So. Calif., 1934
Ward, Robert (Bob)—Maryland, 1951
Warner, William—Cornell, 1903
Washington, Ken—U.C.L.A., 1939
Wedemeyer, Herman J.—St. Mary's, 1947
Weekes, Harold—Columbia, 1902
Weir, Ed—Nebraska, 1925
Welch, Gus—Carlisle, 1914
Weller, John—Princeton, 1935
Wendell, Percy—Harvard, 1913
West, D. Belford—Colgate, 1919
Weyand, Alex—Army, 1915
Wharton, Charles—Pennsylvania, 1896
Wheeler, Arthur—Princeton, 1894
White, Byron (Whizzer)—Colorado, 1937
Whitmire, Don—Alabama/Navy, 1944
Wickhorst, Frank—Navy, 1926
Widseth, Ed—Minnesota, 1936
Wildung, Richard—Minnesota, 1942
Williams, James—Rice, 1949
Willis, William—Ohio State, 1945
Wilson, George—Washington, 1925
Wilson, Harry—Penn State/Army, 1923
Wistert, Albert A.—Michigan, 1942
Wistert, Al—Michigan, 1949
Wistert, Frank (Whitey)—Mich., 1933
Wood, Barry—Harvard, 1931
Wojciechowicz, Alex—Fordham, 1936
Wyant, Andrew—Bucknell/Chicago, 1894
Wyatt, Bowden—Tennessee, 1938
Wyckoff, Clint—Cornell, 1896
Yoder, Lloyd—Carnegie Tech, 1926
Young, Claude (Buddy)—Illinois, 1946
Young, Harry—Wash. & Lee, 1916
Zarnas, Gus—Ohio State, 1937

Coaches

Bill Alexander
Dr. Ed Anderson
Ike Armstrong
Matty Bell
Hugo Bezdek
Dana X. Bible
Bernie Bierman
Earl (Red) Blaik
Charles W. Caldwell
Walter Camp
Len Casanova
Frank Cavanaugh
Fritz Crisler
Bob Devaney
Gil Dobie
Michael Donohue
Gus Dorais
Charles (Rip) Engle
Don Faurot
Jake Gaither
Ernest Godfrey
Jack Harding
Edward K. Hall
Richard Harlow
Jesse Harper
Percy Haughton
John W. Heisman
R. A. (Bob) Higgins
Orin E. Hollingberry
William Ingram
Morley Jennings
Howard Jones
L. (Biff) Jones
Thomas (Tad) Jones
Ralph (Shug) Jordan
Andy Kerr
Frank Leahy
George E. Little
Lou Little
El (Slip) Madigan
Herbert McCracken
Daniel McGugin
DeOrmond (Tuss) McLaughry
L. R. (Dutch) Meyer
Bernie Moore
Scrappy Moore
Ray Morrison
George A. Munger
Clarence Munn
William Murray
Ed (Hooks) Mylin
Earle (Greasy) Neale
Jess Neely
Robert Neyland
Homer Norton
Frank (Buck) O'Neill
Bennie Owen
Ara Parseghian
James Phalea
E. N. Robinson
Knute Rockne
E. L. (Dick) Romney
William W. Roper
George F. Sanford
Francis A. Schmidt
Floyd (Ben) Schwartzwalder
Clark Shaughnessy
Buck Shaw
Andrew L. Smith
Carl Snavely
Amos A. Stagg
Jock Sutherland
Frank W. Thomas
John H. Vaught
Wallace Wade
Lynn Waldorf
Glenn (Pop) Warner
E. E. (Tad) Wieman
John W. Wilce
Bud Wilkinson
Henry L. Williams
George W. Woodruff
Fielding H. Yost
Robert Zuppke

MAJOR COLLEGE FOOTBALL RECORDS (1940–1981)

(Opposing teams are listed in parentheses. *Source:* National Collegiate Sports Services)

LONGEST PLAYS
Rushing

	Yards
Kelsey Finch, Tennessee (Florida) 1977	99
Ralph Thompson, W. Tex. State (Wichita State) 1970	99
Max Anderson, Arizona State (Wyoming) 1967	99
Gale Sayers, Kansas (Nebraska) 1963	99
Granville Amos, Virginia M. I. (Wm. & Mary) 1964	98
Jim Thacker, Davidson (George Washington) 1952	98
Bill Powell, California (Oregon State) 1951	98
Al Yannelli, Bucknell (Delaware) 1946	98
Meredith Warner, Iowa State (Iowa Pre-Flight) 1943	98

Stanley Howell, Miss. State (Southern Miss.) 1979	98
Mark Malone, Arizona State (Utah State) 1979	98
Steve Atkins, Maryland (Clemson) 1978	98

Punt Returns

	Yards
Jimmy Campagna, Georgia (Vanderbilt) 1952	100
Hugh McElhenny, Washington (So. Cal.) 1951	100
Frank Brady, Navy (Maryland) 1951	100
Bert Rechichar, Tennessee (Wash. & Lee) 1950	100
Eddie Macon, Pacific (Boston U.) 1950	100
Richie Luzzi, Clemson (Georgia) 1968	100[1]
Don Guest, California (Washington State) 1966	100[1]

1. Return of a field goal attempt.

Passing

	Yards
Chris Collingsworth–Derrick Gaffney, Florida (Rice) 1977	99
Terry Peel–Robert Ford, Houston (San Diego St.) 1972	99
Terry Peel–Robert Ford, Houston (Syracuse) 1970	99
Colin Clapton–Eddie Jenkins, Holy Cross (Boston U.) 1970	99
Bo Burris–Warren McVea, Houston (Wash. St.) 1966	99
Fred Owens–Jack Ford, Portland (St. Mary's) 1947	99
Jeff Martin–Mark Flaker, Drake (N.M. State) 1976	98
Pete Woods–Joe Stewart, Missouri (Nebraska) 1976	98
Dan Hagemann–Jack Steptoe, Utah (New Mexico) 1976	98
Bruce Shaw–Pat Kenny, N.C. State (Penn State) 1972	98
Jerry Rhome–Jeff Jordan, Tulsa (Wichita State) 1963	98
Bob Dean–Norman Dawson, Cornell (Navy) 1947	98

Punts

	Yards
Pat Brady, Nevada-Reno (Loyola, L. A.) 1950	99
George O'Brien, Wisconsin (Iowa) 1952	96
John Hadl, Kansas (Oklahoma) 1959	94
Carl Knox, Texas Christian (Oklahoma State) 1947	94
Preston Johnson, SMU (Pittsburgh) 1940	94

Field Goals

	Yards
Joe Williams, Wichita State (So. Illinois) 1978	67
Steve Little, Arkansas (Texas) 1977	67
Russell Erxleben, Texas (Rice) 1977	67
Tony Franklin, Texas A&M (Baylor) 1976	65
Russell Erxleben, Texas (Oklahoma) 1977	64
Tony Franklin, Texas A&M (Baylor) 1976	64
Morten Andersen, Mich. State (Ohio State) 1981	63
Clark Kemble, Colorado State (Arizona) 1975	63
Dan Christopulos, Wyoming (Colorado State) 1977	62
Iseed Khoury, North Texas State (Richmond) 1977	62
Dave Lawson, Air Force Academy (Iowa State) 1975	62
Steve Little, Arkansas (Tulsa) 1976	61
Wayne Latimer, Virginia Tech (Florida State) 1975	61
Ray Guy, Southern Mississippi (Utah State) 1972	61

CAREER LEADERS

Rushing

	Years	Plays	Yds	Avg
Tony Dorsett, Pittsburgh	1973–76	1,074[1]	6,082[1]	5.66
Charles White, So. Calif.	1976–79	1,023	5,598	5.47
Archie Griffin, Ohio State	1972–75	845	5,177	6.13
George Rogers, So. Calif.	1977–80	902	4,958	5.50
Ed Marinaro, Cornell	1969–71	918	4,715	5.14
Marcus Allen, So. Calif.	1978–81	893	4,682	5.24
Ted Brown, No. Carolina State	1975–78	860	4,602	5.35
Terry Miller, Oklahoma State	1974–77	847	4,582	5.41
Earl Campbell, Texas	1974–77	765	4,443	5.81
Amos Lawrence, North Carolina	1977–80	881	4,391	4.98
Joe Morris, Syracuse	1978–81	813	4,299	5.29
Jerome Persell, Western Mich.	1976–78	842	4,190	4.98
Stump Mitchell, Citadel	1977–80	756	4,062	5.37
Charles Alexander, L.S.U.	1975–78	855	4,035	4.72
Darrin Nelson, Stanford	1977–78 1980–81	703	4,033	5.74

1. Record.

Passing

	Years	Cmp	Pct	Yds	Td
Mark Herrmann, Purdue	1977–80	717[1]	.589	9,188	62
Jim McMahon, Brigham Young	1977–78 1980–81	653	.616	9,536[1]	84[1]
Chuck Hixson, Southern Methodist	1968–70	642	.576	7,179	40
Joe Adams, Tennessee State	1977–80	604	.549	8,649	81
John Reaves, Florida	1969–71	603	.535	7,549	54
Jack Thompson, Washington State	1975–78	601	.553	7,818	53
Ed Luther, San Jose State	1976–79	600	.537	7,190	47
Rich Campbell, California	1977–80	574	.644[1]	6,933	33
Randy Hertel, Rice	1977–80	561	.500	6,161	38
Gene Swick, Toledo	1972–75	556	.593	7,267	44
Marc Wilson, Brigham Young	1977–79	535	.571	7,637	61
Jim Plunkett, Stanford	1968–70	530	.551	7,544	52
John Elway, Stanford	1979–81	512	.609	6,107	54
Tommy Kramer, Rice	1973–76	507	.489	6,197	37

1. Record.

Total Offense

	Years	Plays	Yds	Tdr[1]
Jim McMahon, Brigham Young	1977–78 1980–81	1,325	9,723[2]	94[2]
Mark Herrmann, Purdue	1977–80	1,354	8,444	63
Gene Swick, Toledo	1972–75	1,579[2]	8,074	63
Joe Adams, Tennessee State	1977–80	1,256	7,972	86
Jim Plunkett, Stanford	1968–70	1,174	7,887	62
Art Schlicter, Ohio State	1978–81	1,316	7,869	n.a.
Jack Thompson, Washington State	1975–78	1,345	7,698	63
Marc Wilson, Brigham Young	1977–79	1,183	7,602	68
John Reaves, Florida	1969–71	1,258	7,283	58
Steve Brown, Appalachian State	1977–80	1,160	7,129	49
Ed Luther, San Jose State	1976–79	1,230	6,981	55
Chuck Hixson, Southern Methodist	1968–70	1,358	6,884	50
Pat Sullivan, Auburn	1969–71	970	6,884	71

1. Touchdowns responsible for—scored or passed for. 2. Record. n.a.—not available.

Pass Receiving

	Years	Rec	Yds	Td
Howard Twilley, Tulsa	1963–65	261[1]	3,343	32
Darren Nelson, Stanford	1977–78 1980–81	214	2,368	16
Ron Sellers, Florida State	1966–68	212	3,598[1]	23
Gerald Harp, Western Carolina	1977–80	197	3,305	26
Phil Odle, Brigham Young	1965–67	181	2,548	25
Tim Delaney, San Diego State	1968–70	180	2,535	22

1. Record.

BEST SINGLE-GAME PERFORMANCES

Most yards, rushing—356, Eddie Lee Ivery, Georgia Tech (Air Force) 1978

Most yards, total offense—599, Virgil Carter, Brigham Young (Texas–El Paso) 1966

Most yards, passing—621, Dave Wilson, Illinois (Ohio State) 1980

Most yards, pass receiving—349, Chuck Hughes, Texas–El Paso (North Texas State) 1965

Most points scored—44, Jim McMahon, Brigham Young, 1981

Most passes attempted—69, Chuck Hixson, Southern

Methodist (Ohio State) 1968 and Dave Wilson, Illinois (Ohio State) 1980

Most passes completed—43, Dave Wilson, Illinois (Ohio State) 1980 and Rich Campbell, California (Florida) 1980

Most passes caught—22, Jay Miller, Brigham Young (New Mexico) 1973

Scoring

	Years	Td	Pat	Fg	Pts
Tony Dorsett, Pittsburgh	1973–76	59[1]	2	0	356[1]
Glenn Davis, Army	1943–46	59[1]	0	0	354
Art Luppino, Arizona	1953–56	48	49	0	337
Steve Owens, Oklahoma	1967–69	56	0	0	336
Wilford White, Arizona State	1947–50	48	27	4	327
Ed Marinaro, Cornell	1969–71	52	6	0	318
Pete Johnson, Ohio State	1973–76	53	0	0	318
Ted Brown, North Carolina State	1975–78	51	6	0	312
Eddie Talboom, Wyoming	1948–50	34	99	0	303

1. Record.

N.C.A.A. DIVISION II AND III FOOTBALL RECORDS (1942–1981)

LONGEST PLAYS

Rushing

	Yards
Kevin Doherty, Mass. Maritime (New Haven) 1980	99
Fred Deutsch, Springfield (Wagner) 1977	99
Sam Hallston, Albany State, N.Y. (Norwich) 1977	99
Sammy Croom, San Diego (Azusa Pacific) 1972	99
John Stenger, Swarthmore (Widener) 1970	99
Jed Knuttila, Hamline (St. Thomas) 1968	99
Dave Lanoha, Colorado College (Texas Lutheran) 1967	99
Tom Pabst, Cal–Riverside (Cal. Tech) 1965	99
George Phillips, Concord (Davis and Elkins) 1961	99
Gerry White, Connecticut (Rhode Island) 1960	99
Leo Williams, St. Augustine's (Morris) 1960	99
George Phelps, Cornell College (Monmouth) 1959	99
Mark Lydon, Tufts (Bowdoin) 1958	99
David Wells, Tufts (Williams) 1956	99
Jack Moskal, Western Reserve (Case Tech) 1954	99
Lou Mariano, Kent State (Western Reserve) 1954	99
Ron Temple, Chico State (Southern Oregon) 1953	99
Ellis Horton, Eureka, (Rose–Hulman) 1952	99
Pat Abbruzzi, Rhode Island (New Hampshire) 1951	99

Field Goals

Joe Duren, Arkansas State (McNeese State) 1974	63
Dom Antonini, Glassboro State (Salisbury State) 1976	62
Mike Flater, Colorado Mines (Western State) 1973	62
Duane Christian, Cameron (Southwestern Oklahoma) 1976	61
Mike Wood, Southeast Missouri (Lincoln) 1975	61
Bill Shear, Cortland State (Hobart) 1966	61

Passing

	Yards
John Guercio–Tom Bennett, C.W. Post (Juniata) 1980	99
Mike Moroski–Calvin Ellison, California-Davis (Puget Sound) 1978	99
Rich Boling–Lewis Borsellino, DePauw (Valparaiso) 1976	99
John Wicinski–Donnell Lipford, John Carroll (Allegheny) 1975	99
Jack Berry–Mercer West, Washington and Lee (Hampden–Sydney) 1974	99
Gary Shope–Rick Rudolph, Juniata (Moravian) 1973	99
Gary Dusenberg–Harvey King, North Park (Illinois Wesleyan) 1970	99
Bob Janesko–Frank Stankiewicz, Emporia (Pittsburg State) 1969	99
John Williams–Bill Carter, N.M. Highlands (North Colorado) 1964	99
Carl Meyers–Roger Sayers, Nebraska-Omaha (Drake) 1963	99

Punts

Earl Hurst, Emporia State (Central Missouri) 1964	97
Gary Frens, Hope (Olivet) 1966	96
Jim Jarrett, North Dakota (South Dakota) 1957	96
Elliot Mills, Carleton (Monmouth) 1970	93
Kaspar Fitins, Taylor (Georgetown, Ky.) 1966	93
Leeroy Sweeney, Pomona (Cal–Riverside) 1960	93

CAREER LEADERS

Rushing

	Years	Plays	Yds	Avg
Chris Cobb, Eastern Illinois	1976–79	930	5,042[1]	5.42
Jerry Linton, Panhandle State	1959–62	648	4,839	7.47
John VanWagner, Mich. Tech.	1973–76	958	4,788	5.00
Rich Kowalski, Hobart	1972–75	907	4,631	5.11
Don Aleksiewicz, Hobart	1969–72	819	4,525	5.53
Dale Mills, NE Missouri	1957–60	751	4,502	5.99
Leo Lewis, Lincoln (Mo.)	1951–54	623	4,458	7.16
Bernie Peeters, Luther	1968–71	1,072[1]	4,435	4.14
Larry Schreiber, Tenn. Tech.	1966–69	878	4,421	5.04
Brad Rowland, McMurry	1947–50	683	4,347	6.36
Vincent Allen, Indiana State	1973–77	832	4,335	5.21
Bill Rhodes, Colorado Western	1953–56	506	4,294	8.49[1]
Lem Harkey, Col. of Emporia	1951–54	502	4,232	8.43

1. Record.

Scoring

	Years	Td	Pat	Fg	Pts
Walter Payton, Jackson State	1971–74	66[1]	53	5	464[1]
Dale Mills, NE Missouri	1957–60	64	23	0	407
Garney Henley, Huron	1956–59	63	16	0	394
Leo Lewis, Lincoln (Mo.)	1951–54	64	0	0	384
Billy Johnson, Widener	1971–73	62	0	0	372
Tank Younger, Grambling	1945–48	60	9	0	369

1. Record

Passing

	Years	Cmp	Pct	Yds	Td
Jim Lindsey, Abilene Chr.	1967–70	642[1]	.519	8,521[1]	61
Bob Caress, Bradley	1962–65	610	.528	7,115	64
Dan Miles, So. Oregon	1964–67	577	.662[1]	6,531	52
George Bork, N. Illinois	1960–63	577	.640	6,782	60
Mike Houston, St. Joseph's	1978–81	576	.559	6,815	57
Curt Strasheim, Southwest St.	1978–81	568	.526	5,837	29
Craig Soloman, Southwestern Tennessee	1975–78	542	.530	7,314	71
Ron Meehan, Towson State	1977–80	529	.527	6,164	31
Kim McQuilken, Lehigh	1971–73	516	.558	6,996	37
Tim Von Dulm, Portland St.	1969–70	500	.541	5,967	51
Greg Cavanaugh, St. Norbert	1977–80	489	.499	5,442	37
Doug Williams, Grambling	1974–77	484	.480	8,411	93[1]

1. Record.

Pass Receiving

	Years	Rec	Yards	Td
Bill Stromberg, Johns Hopkins	1978–81	258[1]	3,776	39
Chris Myers, Kenyon	1967–70	253	3,897	33
Bruce Cerone, Yankton–	1966–67			
Emporia St.	1968–1969	241[1]	4,354[1]	49[1]
Harold Roberts, Austin Peay	1967–70	232	3,005	31
Jerry Hendren, Idaho	1967–69	230	3,435	27
Terry Fredenberg, Wis.–Milwaukee	1965–68	206	2,789	24
Rick Fry, Occidental	1974–77	200	3,073	18
Jay True, DePauw	1977–80	195	2,567	12
Bill Wick, Carroll (Wis.)	1966–69	190	2,967	20
Don Hutt, Boise State	1971–73	187	2,716	30

1. Record.

MOST POINTS IN SEASON

	Yards	Tds	PAT	Fg	Pts
Terry Metcalf, Long Beach St.	1971	29[1]	4	0	178
Jim Switzer, Coll. Emporia	1963	28	0	0	168
Carl Herakovich, Rose Polytech	1958	25	18	0	168
Ted Scown, Sul Ross State	1948	28	0	0	168
Eddie McGovern, Rose Polytech	1942	23	27	0	165
Leon Burns, Long Beach State	1969	27	2	0	164

1. Record.

Total Offense

	Years	Plays	Yds
Jim Lindsey, Abilene Christian	1967–70	1,510[1]	8,385[1]
Doug Williams, Grambling	1974–77	1,072	8,195
Donald Smith, Langston	1958–61	998	7,376
Bruce Upstill, Coll. Emporia	1960–63	922	7,122
Mike Houston, St. Joseph's (Ind.)	1978–81	1,298	7,104
Craig Solomon, SW Tennessee	1975–78	1,261	7,055
Clay Sampson, Denison	1977–80	1,225	6,920
Kim McQuilken, Lehigh	1971–73	991	6,878
Bob Caress, Bradley	1962–65	1,361	6,757

1. Record.

N.C.A.A. 1981 CHAMPIONSHIP PLAYOFFS

DIVISION I–AA
Semifinals

Eastern Kentucky 23, Boise State 17
Idaho State 41, South Carolina State 12

Championship

Idaho State 34, Eastern Kentucky 23

DIVISION II
First Round

Shippensburg (Pa.) State 40, Virginia Union 27
Northern Michigan 55, Elizabeth City (N.C.) State 6
Southwest Texas State 38, Jacksonville State 22
North Dakota State–Fargo 24, Puget Sound 10

Semifinals

Southwest Texas State 62, Northern Michigan 0
North Dakota State 18, Shippensburg State 6

Championship

Southwest Texas State 42, North Dakota State 13

DIVISION III
Semifinals

Widener 23, Montclair State 12
Dayton 38, Lawrence Univ. 0

Championship

Widener 17, Dayton 10

NATIONAL ASSOCIATION OF INTERCOLLEGIATE ATHLETICS 1981 CHAMPIONSHIPS

DIVISION I
Semifinals

Elon (N.C.) 41, Hillsdale (Mich.) 13
Pittsburg (Kan.) State won by forfeit from Cameron, Okla.

Championship

Elon 3, Pittsburg State 0

DIVISION II
Championship

Austin College 24, Concordia (Minn.) 24

Professional Football

NATIONAL FOOTBALL LEAGUE FINAL STANDING 1981

AMERICAN CONFERENCE
Eastern Division

	W	L	T	Pct	Pts	OP
Miami	11	4	1	.719	345	275
New York Jets[1]	10	5	1	.657	355	287
Buffalo[1]	10	6	0	.625	311	276
Baltimore	2	14	0	.125	259	533
New England	2	14	0	.125	322	370
Central Division						
Cincinnati	12	4	0	.750	421	304
Pittsburgh	8	8	0	.500	356	297
Houston	7	9	0	.438	281	355
Cleveland	5	11	0	.313	276	375
Western Division						
San Diego	10	6	0	.625	478	390
Denver	10	6	0	.625	321	289
Kansas City	9	7	0	.563	343	290
Seattle	6	10	0	.375	322	388

1. Wild card qualifier for playoffs.

Playoffs: Buffalo 31, New York Jets 27; Cincinnati 28, Buffalo 21; San Diego 41, Miami 38 (overtime).
Conference championship: Cincinnati 27, San Diego 7.

NATIONAL CONFERENCE
Eastern Division

	W	L	T	Pct	Pts	OP
Dallas	12	4	0	.750	367	277
Philadelphia[1]	10	6	0	.625	368	221
New York Giants[1]	9	7	0	.563	295	257
Washington	8	8	0	.500	347	349
St. Louis	7	9	0	.438	315	408

Central Division

Tampa Bay	9	7	0	.563	315	268
Detroit	8	8	0	.500	397	322
Green Bay	8	8	0	.500	324	361
Minnesota	7	9	0	.438	325	369
Chicago	6	10	0	.375	253	324

Western Division

San Francisco	13	3	0	.813	357	250
Atlanta	7	9	0	.438	426	355
Los Angeles	6	10	0	.375	303	351
New Orleans	4	12	0	.250	207	378

1. Wild card qualifier for playoffs.

Playoffs: New York Giants 27, Philadelphia 21; San Francisco 38, New York Giants 24; Dallas 38, Tampa Bay 0.
Conference championship: San Francisco 28, Dallas 27.

LEAGUE CHAMPIONSHIP—SUPER BOWL XVI

(Jan. 24, 1982; at Silverdome, Pontiac, Mich.; Attendance 81,270)

Scoring

	1st Q	2nd Q	3rd Q	4th Q	Final
San Francisco (NFC)	7	13	0	6	26
Cincinnati (ACF)	0	0	7	14	21

Scoring—San Francisco: Touchdowns: Montana, 1–yard run; Cooper, 11–yard pass from Montana. Conversions: Wersching 2 (kicks). Field goals: Wersching 4, 22 yards, 26 yards, 40 yards, and 23 yards. Cincinnati: Touchdowns: Anderson, 4–yard run; Ross, 4–yard pass from Anderson; Ross, 3–yard pass from Anderson. Conversions: Breech 3 (kicks).

Statistics of the Game

	San Francisco	Cincinnati
First downs	20	24
Yards gained rushing	127	72
Yards gained passing	148	284
Passes completed	14	25
Passes intercepted by	2	0
Punts	4–46	3–44
Ball lost, fumbles	1	2
Yards penalized	65	57

SUPER BOWLS I–XVI[1]

Game	Date	Winner	Loser	Site	Attendance
XVI	Jan. 24, 1982	San Francisco (NFC) 26	Cincinnati (AFC) 21	Silverdome, Pontiac, Mich.	81,270
XV	Jan. 25, 1981	Oakland (AFC) 27	Philadelphia (NFC) 10	Superdome, New Orleans	75,500
XIV	Jan. 20, 1980	Pittsburgh (AFC) 31	Los Angeles (NFC) 19	Rose Bowl, Pasadena	103,985
XIII	Jan. 21, 1979	Pittsburgh (AFC) 35	Dallas (NFC) 31	Orange Bowl, Miami	79,484
XII	Jan. 15, 1978	Dallas (NFC) 27	Denver (AFC) 10	Superdome, New Orleans	75,583
XI	Jan. 9, 1977	Oakland (AFC) 32	Minnesota (NFC) 14	Rose Bowl, Pasadena	103,424
X	Jan. 18, 1976	Pittsburgh (AFC) 21	Dallas (NFC) 17	Orange Bowl, Miami	80,187
IX	Jan. 12, 1975	Pittsburgh (AFC) 16	Minnesota (NFC) 6	Tulane Stadium, New Orleans	80,997
VIII	Jan. 13, 1974	Miami (AFC) 24	Minnesota (NFC) 7	Rice Stadium, Houston	71,882
VII	Jan. 14, 1973	Miami (AFC) 14	Washington (NFC) 7	Memorial Coliseum, Los Angeles	90,182
VI	Jan. 16, 1972	Dallas (NFC) 24	Miami (AFC) 3	Tulane Stadium, New Orleans	81,591
V	Jan. 17, 1971	Baltimore (AFC) 16	Dallas (NFC) 13	Orange Bowl, Miami	79,204
IV	Jan. 11, 1970	Kansas City (AFL) 23	Minnesota (NFL) 7	Tulane Stadium, New Orleans	80,562
III	Jan. 12, 1969	New York (AFL) 16	Baltimore (NFL) 7	Orange Bowl, Miami	75,389
II	Jan. 14, 1968	Green Bay (NFL) 33	Oakland (AFL) 14	Orange Bowl, Miami	75,546
I	Jan. 15, 1967	Green Bay (NFL) 35	Kansas City (AFL) 10	Memorial Coliseum, Los Angeles	61,946

1. Super Bowls I to IV were played before the American Football League and National Football League merged into the NFL, which was divided into two conferences, the NFC and AFC.

NATIONAL LEAGUE CHAMPIONS

Year	Champion (W-L-T)
1921	Chicago Bears (Staley's) (10–1–1)
1922	Canton Bulldogs (10–0–2)
1923	Canton Bulldogs (11–0–1)
1924	Cleveland Indians (7–1–1)
1925	Chicago Cardinals (11–2–1)
1926	Frankford Yellow Jackets (14–1–1)
1927	New York Giants (11–1–1)
1928	Providence Steamrollers (8–1–2)
1929	Green Bay Packers (12–0–1)
1930	Green Bay Packers (10–3–1)
1931	Green Bay Packers (12–2–0)
1932	Chicago Bears (7–1–6)

Year	Eastern Conference winners (W-L-T)	Western Conference winners (W-L-T)	League champion playoff results
1933	New York Giants (11–3–0)	Chicago Bears (10–2–1)	Chicago Bears 23, New York 21
1934	New York Giants (8–5–0)	Chicago Bears (13–0–0)	New York 30, Chicago Bears 13
1935	New York Giants (9–3–0)	Detroit Lions (7–3–2)	Detroit 26, New York 7
1936	Boston Redskins (7–5–0)	Green Bay Packers (10–1–1)	Green Bay 21, Boston 6
1937	Washington Redskins (8–3–0)	Chicago Bears (9–1–1)	Washington 28, Chicago Bears 21
1938	New York Giants (8–2–1)	Green Bay Packers (8–3–0)	New York 23, Green Bay 17
1939	New York Giants (9–1–1)	Green Bay Packers (9–2–0)	Green Bay 27, New York 0
1940	Washington Redskins (9–2–0)	Chicago Bears (8–3–0)	Chicago Bears 73, Washington 0
1941	New York Giants (8–3–0)	Chicago Bears (10–1–1)[2]	Chicago Bears 37, New York 9

1942	Washington Redskins (10–1–1)	Chicago Bears (11–0–0)	Washington 14, Chicago Bears 6
1943	Washington Redskins (6–3–1)[2]	Chicago Bears (8–1–1)	Chicago Bears 41, Washington 21
1944	New York Giants (8–1–1)	Green Bay Packers (8–2–0)	Green Bay 14, New York 7
1945	Washington Redskins (8–2–0)	Cleveland Rams (9–1–0)	Cleveland 15, Washington 14
1946	New York Giants (7–3–1)	Chicago Bears (8–2–1)	Chicago Bears 24, New York 14
1947	Philadelphia Eagles (8–4–0)[2]	Chicago Cardinals (9–3–0)	Chicago Cardinals 28, Philadelphia 21
1948	Philadelphia Eagles (9–2–1)	Chicago Cardinals (11–1–0)	Philadelphia 7, Chicago Cardinals 0
1949	Philadelphia Eagles (11–1–0)	Los Angeles Rams (8–2–2)	Philadelphia 14, Los Angeles 0
1950[1]	Cleveland Browns (10–2–0)[2]	Los Angeles Rams (9–3–0)[2]	Cleveland 30, Los Angeles 28
1951[1]	Cleveland Browns (11–1–0)	Los Angeles Rams (8–4–0)	Los Angeles 24, Cleveland 17
1952[1]	Cleveland Browns (8–4–0)	Detroit Lions (9–3–0)[2]	Detroit 17, Cleveland 7
1953	Cleveland Browns (11–1–0)	Detroit Lions (10–2–0)	Detroit 17, Cleveland 16
1954	Cleveland Browns (9–3–0)	Detroit Lions (9–2–1)	Cleveland 56, Detroit 10
1955	Cleveland Browns (9–2–1)	Los Angeles Rams (8–3–1)	Cleveland 38, Los Angeles 14
1956	New York Giants (8–3–1)	Chicago Bears (9–2–1)	New York 47, Chicago Bears 7
1957	Cleveland Browns (9–2–1)	Detroit Lions (8–4–0)[3]	Detroit 59, Cleveland 14
1958	New York Giants (9–3–0)[2]	Baltimore Colts (9–3–0)	Baltimore 23, New York 17[3]
1959	New York Giants (10–2–0)	Baltimore Colts (9–3–0)	Baltimore 31, New York 16
1960	Philadelphia Eagles (10–2–0)	Green Bay Packers (8–4–0)	Philadelphia 17, Green Bay 13
1961	New York Giants (10–3–1)	Green Bay Packers (11–3–0)	Green Bay 37, New York 0
1962	New York Giants (12–2–0)	Green Bay Packers (13–1–0)	Green Bay 16, New York 7
1963	New York Giants (11–3–0)	Chicago Bears (11–1–2)	Chicago 14, New York 10
1964	Cleveland Browns (10–3–1)	Baltimore Colts (12–2–0)	Cleveland 27, Baltimore 0
1965	Cleveland Browns (11–3–0)	Green Bay Packers (11–3–1)[2]	Green Bay 23, Cleveland 12
1966	Dallas Cowboys (10–3–1)	Green Bay Packers (12–2–0)	Green Bay 34, Dallas 27
1967	Dallas Cowboys (9–5–0)[2]	Green Bay Packers (9–4–1)[2]	Green Bay 21, Dallas 17
1968	Cleveland Browns (10–4–0)[2]	Baltimore Colts (13–1–0)[2]	Baltimore 34, Cleveland 0
1969	Cleveland Browns (10–3–1)[2]	Minnesota Vikings (12–2–0)[2]	Minnesota 27, Cleveland 7

1. League was divided into American and National Conferences, 1950–52 and again in 1970, when leagues merged. 2. Won divisional playoff. 3. Won at 8:15 of sudden death overtime period.

NATIONAL CONFERENCE CHAMPIONS

Year	Eastern Division	Central Division	Western Division	Champion
1970	Dallas Cowboys (10–4–0)	Minnesota Vikings (12–2–0)	San Francisco 49ers (10–3–1)	Dallas
1971	Dallas Cowboys (11–3–0)	Minnesota Vikings (11–3–0)	San Francisco 49ers (9–5–0)	Dallas
1972	Washington Redskins (11–3–0)	Green Bay Packers (10–4–0)	San Francisco 49ers (8–5–1)	Washington
1973	Dallas Cowboys (10–4–0)	Minnesota Vikings (12–2–0)	Los Angeles Rams (12–2–0)	Minnesota
1974	St. Louis Cardinals (10–4–0)	Minnesota Vikings (10–4–0)	Los Angeles Rams (10–4–0)	Minnesota
1975	St. Louis Cardinals (11–3–0)	Minnesota Vikings (12–2–0)	Los Angeles Rams (10–4–0)	Dallas
1976	Dallas Cowboys (11–3–0)	Minnesota Vikings (11–2–1)	Los Angeles Rams (10–3–1)	Minnesota
1977	Dallas Cowboys (12–2–0)	Minnesota Vikings (9–5–0)	Los Angeles Rams (10–4–0)	Dallas
1978	Dallas Cowboys (12–4–0)	Minnesota Vikings (8–7–1)	Los Angeles Rams (12–4–0)	Dallas
1979	Dallas Cowboys (11–5–0)	Tampa Bay Buccaneers (10–6–0)	Los Angeles Rams (9–7–0)	Los Angeles
1980	Philadelphia Eagles (12–4–0)	Minnesota Vikings (9–7–0)	Atlanta Falcons (12–4–0)	Philadelphia
1981	Dallas Cowboys (12–4–0)	Tampa Bay Buccaneers (9–7–0)	San Francisco 49ers (13–3–0)	San Francisco

AMERICAN CONFERENCE CHAMPIONS

Year	Eastern Division	Central Division	Western Division	Champion
1970	Baltimore Colts (11–2–1)	Cincinnati Bengals (8–6–0)	Oakland Raiders (8–4–2)	Baltimore
1971	Miami Dolphins (10–3–1)	Cleveland Browns (9–5–0)	Kansas City Chiefs (10–3–1)	Miami
1972	Miami Dolphins (14–0–0)	Pittsburgh Steelers (11–3–0)	Oakland Raiders (10–3–1)	Miami
1973	Miami Dolphins (12–2–0)	Cincinnati Bengals (10–4–0)	Oakland Raiders (9–4–1)	Miami
1974	Miami Dolphins (11–3–0)	Pittsburgh Steelers (10–3–1)	Oakland Raiders (12–2–0)	Pittsburgh
1975	Baltimore Colts (10–4–0)	Pittsburgh Steelers (12–2–0)	Oakland Raiders (12–2–0)	Pittsburgh
1976	Baltimore Colts (11–3–0)	Pittsburgh Steelers (10–4–0)	Oakland Raiders (13–1–0)	Oakland
1977	Baltimore Colts (10–4–0)	Pittsburgh Steelers (9–5–0)	Denver Broncos (12–2–0)	Denver
1978	New England Patriots (11–5–0)	Pittsburgh Steelers (14–2–0)	Denver Broncos (10–6–0)	Pittsburgh
1979	Miami Dolphins (10–6–0)	Pittsburgh Steelers (12–4–0)	San Diego Chargers (12–4–0)	Pittsburgh
1980	Buffalo Bills (11–5–0)	Cleveland Browns (11–5–0)	San Diego Chargers (11–5–0)	Oakland
1981	Miami Dolphins (11–4–1)	Cincinnati Bengals (12–4–0)	San Diego Chargers (10–6–0)	Cincinnati

AMERICAN LEAGUE CHAMPIONS

Year	Eastern Division (W-L-T)	Western Division (W-L-T)	League champion, playoffs results
1960	Houston Oilers (10–4–0)	Los Angeles Chargers (10–4–0)	Houston 24, Los Angeles 16
1961	Houston Oilers (10–3–1)	San Diego Chargers (12–2–0)	Houston 10, San Diego 3
1962	Houston Oilers (11–3–0)	Dallas Texans (11–3–0)	Dallas 20, Houston 17[1]
1963	Boston Patriots (8–6–1)[2]	San Diego Chargers (11–3–0)	San Diego 51, Boston 10
1964	Buffalo Bills (12–2–0)	San Diego Chargers (8–5–1)	Buffalo 20, San Diego 7

1965	Buffalo Bills (10–3–1)	San Diego Chargers (9–2–3)	Buffalo 23, San Diego 0
1966	Buffalo Bills (9–4–1)	Kansas City Chiefs (11–2–1)	Kansas City 31, Buffalo 7
1967	Houston Oilers (9–4–1)	Oakland Raiders (13–1–0)	Oakland 40, Houston 7
1968	New York Jets (11–3–0)	Oakland Raiders (12–2–0)[2]	New York 27, Oakland 23
1969	New York Jets (10–4–0)	Oakland Raiders (12–1–1)	Kansas City 17, Oakland 7[3]

1. Won at 2:45 of second sudden death overtime period. 2. Won divisional playoff. 3. Kansas City defeated New York, 13–6, and Oakland defeated Houston, 56–7, in interdivisional playoffs.

NATIONAL FOOTBALL LEAGUE GOVERNMENT

Commissioner's Office: Pete Rozelle, commissioner; Don Weiss, executive director; Bill Ray, treasurer; Jay Moyer, counsel to commissioner; Jan Van Duser, director of operations; Jim Heffernan, director of public relations; Joe Browne, director of information; Warren Welsh, director of security; Charles R. Jackson, assistant director of security; Joel Bussert, director of personnel; Art McNally, supervisor of officials; Peter Hadhazy, administrative coordinator; Val Pinchbeck, Jr., director of broadcasting; Jim Steeg, director of special events.

American Conference: Lamar Hunt, president; Al Ward, assistant to the president; Fran Connors, director of information.

National Conference: George Halas, president; Joe Rhein, assistant to the president; Dick Maxwell, director of information.

PRO FOOTBALL HALL OF FAME

(National Football Museum, Canton, Ohio)

Teams named are those with which player is best identified; figures in parentheses indicate number of playing seasons.

Adderley, Herb, defensive back, Packers, Cowboys (12)	1961–72
Alworth, Lance, wide receiver, Chargers, Cowboys (11)	1962–72
Atkins, Doug, defensive end, Browns, Bears, Saints (17)	1953–69
Badgro, Morris, end, N.Y. Yankees, Giants, Bklyn. Dodgers (8)	1927, 1930–36
Battles, Cliff, back, Redskins (6)	1932–37
Baugh, Sammy, quarterback, Redskins (16)	1937–52
Bednarik, Chuck, center-lineback, Eagles (14)	1949–62
Bell, Bert, N.F.L. founder, owner Eagles and Steelers, N.F.L. Commissioner	1946–59
Berry, Raymond, end, Colts (13)	1955–67
Bidwell, Charles W., owner Chicago Cardinals	1933–47
Blanda, George, quarterback–kicker, Bears, Oilers, Raiders (27)	1949–75
Brown, Jim, fullback, Browns (9)	1957–65
Brown, Paul E., coach, Browns (1946–62), Bengals (1968–75)	1946–75
Brown, Roosevelt, tackle, Giants (13)	1953–65
Butkus, Dick, linebacker, Bears (19)	1965–73
Canadeo, Tony, back, Packers (11)	1941–52
Carr, Joe, president N.F.L. (18)	1921–39
Chamberlin, Guy, end 4 teams (9)	1919–27
Christiansen, Jack, defensive back, Lions (8)	1951–58
Clark, Earl (Dutch), Qback, Spartans, Lions (7)	1931–38
Connor, George, tackle, linebacker, Bears (8)	1948–55
Conzelman, Jimmy, Qback 5 teams (10), owner	1921–48
Davis, Willie, defensive end, Packers (10)	1960–69
Donovan, Art, defensive tackle, Colts (12)	1950–61
Driscoll, John (Paddy), Qback, Cards, Bears (11)	1919–29
Dudley, Bill, back, Steelers, Lions, Redskins (9)	1942–53
Edwards, Albert Glen (Turk), tackle, Redskins (9)	1932–40
Ewbank, Weeb, coach Colts, Jets (20)	1954–73
Fears, Tom, end, Rams (9); coach, Saints	1948–56
Flaherty, Ray, end, Yankees, Giants (9); coach, Redskins, Yankees (14)	1928–49
Ford, Len, end, def. end, Browns, Packers (11)	1948–58
Fortmann, Daniel J., guard, Bears (8)	1936–43
George, Bill, linebacker, Bears, Rams (15)	1952–66
Gifford, Frank, back, Giants (12)	1952–64
Graham, Otto, quarterback, Browns (10)	1946–55
Grange, Harold (Red), back, Bears, Yankees (9)	1925–34
Gregg, Forrest, tackle, Packers (15)	1956–71
Groza, Lou, place-kicker, tackle, Browns (21)	1946–67
Guyon, Joe, back, 6 teams (8)	1919–27
Halas, George, N.F.L. founder, owner and coach, Staleys and Bears, end (11)	1919–67
Healey, Ed, tackle, Bears (8)	1920–27
Hein, Mel, center, Giants (15)	1931–45
Henry, Wilbur (Pete), tackle, Bulldogs, Giants (8)	1920–28
Herber, Arnie, Qback, Packers, Giants (13)	1930–45
Hewitt, Bill, end, Bears, Eagles (9)	1932–43
Hinkle, Clarke, fullback, Packers (10)	1932–41
Hirsch, Elroy (Crazy Legs), back, end, Rams (12)	1946–57
Hubbard, R. (Cal), tackle, Giants, Packers (9)	1927–36
Huff, Sam, linebacker, Giants, Redskins (13)	1956–67, 1969
Hunt, Lamar, Founder A.F.L., owner Texans, Chiefs	1959– —
Hutson, Don, end, Packers (11)	1935–45
Jones, David (Deacon), defensive end, Rams, Chargers, Redskins (14)	1961–74
Kiesling, Walt, guard 6 teams (13)	1926–38
Kinard, Frank (Bruiser), tackle, Dodgers (9)	1938–47
Lambeau, Earl (Curly), N.F.L. founder, coach, end, back, Packers (11)	1919–53
Lane, Richard (Night Train), defensive back, Rams, Cardinals, Lions (14)	1952–65
Lary, Yale, defensive back, punter, Lions (11)	1952–64
Lavelli, Dante, end, Browns (11)	1946–56
Layne, Bobby, Qback, Bears, Lions, Steelers (15)	1948–62
Leemans, Alphonse (Tuffy), back, Giants (8)	1936–43
Lilly, Bob, defensive tackle, Cowboys (14)	1961–74
Lombardi, Vince, coach, Packers, Redskins (11)	1959–70
Luckman, Sid, quarterback, Bears (12)	1939–50
Lyman, Roy (Link), tackle, Bulldogs, Bears (11)	1922–34
Mara, Tim, N.F.L. founder, owner Giants	1925–59
Marchetti, Gino, defensive end, Colts (14)	1952–66
Marshall, George P., N.F.L. founder, owner Redskins	1932–65
Matson, Ollie, back, Cardinals, Rams, Lions, Eagles (14)	1952–66
McAfee, George, back, Bears (8)	1940–50
McElhenny, Hugh, back, 49ers, Vikings, Giants (13)	1952–64
McNally, John (Blood), back, 7 teams (15)	1925–39
Michalske, August, guard, Yankees, Packers (11)	1926–37
Millner, Wayne, end, Redskins (7)	1936–45
Mix, Ron, tackle, Chargers (11)	1960–71
Moore, Lenny, back, Colts (12)	1956–67
Motley, Marion, fullback, Browns, Steelers (9)	1946–55
Musso, George, guard-tackle, Bears (12)	1933–44
Nagurski, Bronko, fullback, Bears (9)	1930–43

Neale, Earle (Greasy), coach, Eagles 1941–50
Nevers, Ernie, fullback, Chicago Cardinals (5) 1926–31
Nitschke, Ray, linebacker, Packers (15) 1958–72
Nomellini, Leo, defensive tackle, 49ers (14) 1950–63
Olsen, Merlin, defensive tackle, Rams (15) 1962–76
Otto, Jim, center, Raiders (15) 1960–74
Owen, Steve, tackle, Giants (9), coach, Giants (13) 1924–53
Parker, Clarence (Ace), quarterback, Dodgers (7) 1937–46
Parker, Jim, guard, tackle, Colts (11) 1957–67
Perry, Joe, fullback, 49ers, Colts (16) 1948–63
Pihos, Pete, end, Eagles (9) 1947–55
Ray, Hugh, Shorty, N.F.L. advisor 1938–52
Reeves, Dan, owner Rams 1941–71
Ringo, Jim, center, Packers (15) 1953–67
Robustelli, Andy, def. end, Rams, Giants (14) 1951–64
Rooney, Art, N.F.L. founder, owner Steelers 1933– —
Sayers, Gale, back, Bears (7) 1965–71
Schmidt, Joe, linebacker, Lions (13) 1953–65
Starr, Bart, quarterback, coach, Packers (16) 1956–71
Stautner, Ernie, defensive tackle, Steelers (14) 1950–63
Strong, Ken, back, Giants, Yankees (14) 1929–47
Stydahar, Joe, tackle, Bears (9); coach, Rams, Cardinals (5) 1936–54
Taylor, Jim, fullback, Packers, Saints (10) 1958–67
Thorpe, Jim, back, 7 teams (12) 1915–28
Tittle, Y. A., Qback, Colts, 49ers, Giants (17) 1948–64
Trafton, George, center, Bears (13) 1920–32
Trippi, Charley, back, Chicago Cardinals (9) 1947–55
Tunnell, Emlen, def. back, Giants, Packers (14) 1948–61
Turner, Clyde (Bulldog), center, Bears (13) 1940–52
Unitas, John, quarterback, Colts (18) 1956–73
Van Brocklin, Norm, Qback, Rams, Eagles (12) 1949–60
Van Buren, Steve, back, Eagles (8) 1944–51
Waterfield, Bob, quarterback, Rams (8) 1945–52
Willis, Bill, Guard, Browns (8) 1946–53
Wilson, Larry, defensive back, Cardinals (13) 1960–72
Wojciechowicz, Alex, center, Lions, Eagles (13) 1938–50

N.F.L. INDIVIDUAL LIFETIME, SEASON, AND GAME RECORDS

(American Football League records were incorporated into N.F.L. records after merger of the leagues)

All-Time Leading Touchdown Scorers

	Yrs	Rush	Pass rec	Returns	TD
Jim Brown	9	106	20	0	126
Lenny Moore	12	63	48	2	113
Don Hutson	11	3	99	3	105
Jim Taylor	10	83	10	0	93
Franco Harris	10	84	7	0	91
Bobby Mitchell	11	18	65	8	91
Leroy Kelly	10	74	13	3	90
Charley Taylor	13	11	79	0	90
Don Maynard	15	0	88	0	88
Lance Alworth	11	2	85	0	85

All-Time Leading Passers

	Comp	Pct comp	Yds	TD	Int	Rating
Roger Staubach	1,685	57.0	22,700	153	109	83.5
Sonny Jurgensen	2,433	57.1	32,224	255	189	82.8
Len Dawson	2,136	57.1	28,711	239	183	82.6
Ken Anderson	2,036	57.5	25,562	160	124	80.5
Fran Tarkenton	3,686	57.0	47,003	342	266	80.5
Bart Starr	1,808	57.4	24,718	152	138	80.3
Bert Jones	1,382	56.1	17,663	122	97	79.1
Dan Fouts	1,849	57.7	24,256	145	142	78.4
Johnny Unitas	2,830	54.6	40,239	290	253	78.2
Otto Graham	872	55.7	13,499	88	94	78.1

The passing ratings are based on performance standards established for completion percentage, interception percentage, touchdown percentage, and average pass gain. Passers are allocated points according to how their marks compare with those standards. This listing is based on 1,500 or more pass attempts.

All-Time Leading Receivers

	Yrs	Pass rec	Yds	Avg
Charley Taylor	13	649	9,110	14.0
Don Maynard	15	633	11,834	18.7
Raymond Berry	13	631	9,275	14.7
Fred Biletnikoff	14	589	8,974	12.7
Harold Jackson	14	571	10,246	17.9
Lionel Taylor	10	567	7,195	12.7
Lance Alworth	11	542	10,266	18.9
Bobby Mitchell	11	521	7,954	15.3
Harold Carmichael	11	516	7,923	15.4
Billy Howton	12	503	8,459	16.8
Tommy McDonald	12	495	8,410	17.0
Charlie Joiner	13	485	8,476	17.0

All-Time Leading Scorers

	Yrs	TD	FG	PAT	Pts
George Blanda	26	9	335	943	2,002
Jim Turner	16	1	304	521	1,439
Jim Bakken	17	0	282	534	1,380
Fred Cox	15	0	282	519	1,365
Lou Groza	17	1	234	641	1,349
Jan Stenerud	15	0	304	432	1,344
Gino Cappelletti	11	42	176	350	1,130[1]
Don Cockroft	13	0	216	432	1,080
Garo Yepremian	14	0	210	444	1,074
Bruce Gossett	11	0	219	374	1,031

1. Includes four 2-point conversions.

All-Time Leading Rushers

	Yrs	Att	Yds	Avg
Jim Brown	9	2,359	12,312	5.2
O.J. Simpson	11	2,404	11,236	4.7
Franco Harris	10	2,462	10,339	4.2
Walter Payton	7	2,204	9,608	4.4
Jim Taylor	10	1,941	8,597	4.4
Joe Perry	14	1,737	8,378	4.8
Larry Csonka	11	1,891	8,081	4.3
John Riggins	10	1,861	7,536	4.0
Leroy Kelly	10	1,727	7,274	4.2
John Henry Johnson	13	1,571	6,803	4.3

Scoring

Most points scored, lifetime—2,002, George Blanda, Chicago Bears, 1949–58; Baltimore, 1950; Houston, 1960–66; Oakland, 1967–75 (9tds, 943 pat, 335 fgs).
Most points, season—176, Paul Hornung, Green Bay, 1960 (15 td, 41 pat, 15 fg).
Most points, game—40, Ernie Nevers, Chicago Cardinals, 1929 (6 td, 4 pat).
Most points, per quarter—29, Don Hutson, Green Bay, 1945 (4 td, 5 pat).
Most touchdowns, lifetime—126, Jim Brown, Cleveland, 1957–65.
Most touchdowns, season—23, O.J. Simpson, Buffalo, 1975.
Most touchdowns, game—6, Ernie Nevers, Chicago Cardinals, 1929; William Jones, Cleveland, 1951; Gale Sayers, Chicago Bears, 1965.
Most points after touchdown, lifetime—943, George Blanda, Chicago Bears, 1949–58; Baltimore, 1950; Houston, 1960–66; Oakland, 1967–75.
Most points after touchdown, game—9, Pat Harder, Chicago Cardinals, 1948; Bob Waterfield, Los Angeles, 1950; Charlie Gogolak, Washington, 1966.
Most consecutive points after touchdown—234, Tommy Davis, San Francisco, 1959–65.
Most points after touchdown, no misses, season—56, Danny Villanueva, Dallas, 1966.
Most field goals, lifetime—335, George Blanda, Chicago Bears 1949–58; Baltimore, 1950; Houston, 1960–66; Oakland 1967–75.
Most field goals, season—34, Jim Turner, New York Jets, 1968.
Most field goals, game—7, Jim Bakken, St. Louis, 1967.
Longest field goal—63 yards, Tom Dempsey, New Orleans, 1970.

Rushing

Most yards gained, lifetime—12,312, Jim Brown, Cleveland, 1957–65.
Most yards gained, season—2,003, O. J. Simpson, Buffalo, 1973.
Most yards gained, game—275, Walter Payton, Chicago, 1977.
Most touchdowns, lifetime—106, Jim Brown, Cleveland, 1957–65.
Most touchdowns, season—19, Earl Campbell, Houston, 1979; Jim Taylor, Green Bay, 1962; Chuck Muncie, San Diego, 1981.
Most touchdowns, game—6, Ernie Nevers, Chicago Cardinals, 1929.
Longest run from scrimmage—97 yards, Andy Uram, Green Bay, 1939; Bob Gage, Pittsburgh, 1949 (both for touchdowns).

Passing

Most passes completed, lifetime—3,686, Fran Tarkenton, Minnesota, 1961–66, 72–78; New York Giants, 1967–71.
Most passes completed, season—360, Dan Fouts, San Diego, 1981.
Most passes completed, game—42, Richard Todd, New York Jets, 1980.
Most consecutive passes completed—17, Bert Jones, Baltimore, 1974.
Most yards gained, lifetime—47,003, Fran Tarkenton, Minnesota, 1961–66, 72–78; New York Giants, 1967–71.
Most yards gained, season—4,802, Dan Fouts, San Diego, 1981.
Most yards gained, game—554, Norm Van Brocklin, Los Angeles, 1951
Most touchdown passes, lifetime—342, Fran Tarkenton, Minnesota, 1961–66, 72–78; New York Giants, 1967–71.
Most touchdown passes, season—36, George Blanda, Houston, 1961; Y. A. Tittle, New York Giants, 1963.
Most touchdown passes, game—7, Sid Luckman, Chicago Bears, 1943; Adrian Burk, Philadelphia, 1954; George Blanda, Houston 1961; Y.A. Tittle, New York Giants, 1963; Joe Kapp, Minnesota, 1969.
Most consecutive games, touchdown passes—47, John Unitas, Baltimore.
Most consecutive passes attempted, none intercepted—294, Bart Starr, Green Bay, 1964–65.
Longest pass completion—99 yards, Frank Filchock (to Andy Farkas), Washington, 1939; George Izo (to Bob Mitchell), Washington, 1963; Karl Sweetan (to Pat Studstill), Detroit, 1966; Sonny Jurgensen (to Gerry Allen), Washington, 1968, (all for touchdowns).
Most pass receptions, lifetime—649, Charley Taylor, Washington, 1964–75, 1977.
Most pass receptions, season—101, Charley Hennigan, Houston, 1964.
Most pass receptions, game—18, Tom Fears, Los Angeles, 1950.
Most consecutive games, pass receptions—127, Harold Carmichael, Philadelphia, 1972–80.
Most yards gained, pass receptions, lifetime—11,834, Don Maynard, New York Giants, 1958; New York Jets, 1960–72; St. Louis, 1973.
Most yards gained receptions, season—1,746, Charley Hennigan, Houston, 1961.
Most yards gained receptions, game—303, Jim Benton, Cleveland Rams, 1945.
Most touchdown pass receptions, lifetime—99, Don Hutson, Green Bay, 1935–45.
Most touchdown pass receptions, season—17, Don Hutson, Green Bay, 1942; Elroy Hirsch, Los Angeles, 1951; Bill Groman, Houston, 1961.
Most touchdown pass receptions, game—5, Bob Shaw, Chicago Cards, 1950.
Most consecutive games, touchdown pass receptions—11, Elroy Hirsch, Los Angeles, 1950–51; Buddy Dial, Pittsburgh, 1959–60.
Most pass interceptions, lifetime—81, Paul Krause, Washington, 1964–67; Minnesota, 1968–79.
Most pass interceptions, season—14, Richard (Night Train) Lane, Los Angeles, 1952.
Most pass interceptions, game—4, by 15 players.
Longest pass interception return—102 yards, Bob Smith, Chicago Bears, 1949; Erich Barnes, New York Giants, 1961; Gary Barbaro, Kansas City, 1977; Louis Breeden, Cincinnati, 1981.

Kicking

Longest punt—98 yards, Steve O'Neal, New York Jets, 1969.
Highest average punting, lifetime—45.10 yards, Sammy Baugh, Washington, 1937–52.
Longest punt return—98 yards, Gil LeFebvre, Cincinnati Reds, 1933; Charlie West, Minnesota, 1968; Dennis Morgan, Dallas, 1974.
Longest kick-off return—106 yards, Roy Green, St. Louis, 1979; Al Carmichael, Green Bay, 1956; Noland Smith, Kansas City, 1967.

TABLE TENNIS

U.S. OPEN CHAMPIONSHIPS—1982

Men's singles—Zoran Kosanovic, Canada
Women's singles—Kayoko Kawahigashi, Japan
Men's doubles—Danny and Ricky Seemiller, Pittsburgh
Women's doubles—Shin Deuk Hwa and Jung Kyung, South Korea
Mixed doubles—Koichi Kawamura and Tomoko Tamura, Japan
Men's team—Japan
Women's team—South Korea

TEAM NICKNAMES AND HOME FIELD STADIUM CAPACITIES

AMERICAN CONFERENCE

Eastern Division

Baltimore Colts	Memorial Stadium (G)	60,020
Buffalo Bills	Rich Stadium (AT)	80,020
Miami Dolphins	Orange Bowl (G)	75,449
New England Patriots	Schaefer Stadium (ST)	61,297
New York Jets	Shea Stadium (G)	60,000

Central Division

Cincinnati Bengals	Riverfront Stadium (AT)	56,200
Cleveland Browns	Cleveland Stadium (G)	80,385
Houston Oilers	Astrodome (AT)	50,000
Pittsburgh Steelers	Three Rivers Stadium (TT)	50,350

Western Division

Denver Broncos	Mile High Stadium (G)	75,087
Kansas City Chiefs	Arrowhead Stadium (TT)	78,094
Los Angeles Raiders[1]	Memorial Coliseum (G)	73,999
San Diego Chargers	San Diego Stadium (G)	52,552
Seattle Seahawks	Kingdome (AT)	64,752

1. Moved franchise to Los Angeles for 1982 season.
NOTE: Stadium playing surfaces in parentheses: AT = Astro-Turf; G = grass; ST = Super Turf; TT = TartanTurf.

NATIONAL CONFERENCE

Eastern Division

Dallas Cowboys	Texas Stadium (TT)	65,101
New York Giants	Giants Stadium (AT)[1]	76,500
Philadelphia Eagles	Veterans Stadium (AT)	66,052
St. Louis Cardinals	Busch Mem. Stadium (AT)	51,392
Washington Redskins	R. F. Kennedy Stadium (G)	55,031

1. At East Rutherford, N.J.

Central Division

Chicago Bears	Soldier Field (AT)	58,064
Detroit Lions	Pontiac Silverdome (AT)	80,638
	Lambeau Field (G)	56,267
Green Bay Packers	Milwaukee Stadium (G)	55,958
Minnesota Vikings	Metropolitan Stadium (G)	48,446
Tampa Bay Buccaneers	Tampa Stadium (G)	72,112

Western Division

Atlanta Falcons	Atlanta-Fulton Stadium (G)	60,489
Los Angeles Rams[1]	Anaheim Stadium (G)	70,000
New Orleans Saints	Louisiana Superdome (AT)	71,330
San Francisco 49ers	Candlestick Park (G)	61,246

1. Moved to Anaheim Stadium at start of 1980 season.

FISHING

WORLD ALL-TACKLE FISHING RECORDS

Caught With Rod and Reel in Fresh Water

Source: International Game Fish Association

Species	lb–oz	Length	Girth	Where caught	Year	Angler
Bass, Largemouth	22–4	32½"	28½"	Montgomery Lake, Ga.	1932	George W. Perry
Bass, Peacock	21	—	—	Orinoco River, Colombia	1981	David Orndorf
Bass, Redeye	8–3	23"	16½"	Flint River, Ga.	1977	David A. Hubbard
Bass, Rock	3	13½"	10¾"	York River, Ontario	1974	Peter Gulgin
Bass, Smallmouth	11–15	27"	21⅔"	Dale Hollow Lake, Ky.	1955	David L. Hayes
Bass, Spotted	8–15	—	—	Smith Lake, Ala.	1978	Philip C. Terry Jr.
Bass, Striped (landlocked)	59–12	—	—	Colorado River, Ariz.	1977	Frank W. Smith
Bass, White	5–9	—	—	Colorado River, Texas	1977	David S. Cordill
Bass, Whiterock	20–6	—	—	Savannah River, Ga.	1978	Danny Wood
Bass, Yellow	2–4	16¼"	12¾"	Lake Monroe, Ind.	1977	Donald L. Stalker
Bluegill	4–12	15"	18¼"	Ketona Lake, Ala.	1950	T. S. Hudson
Bowfin	21–8	—	—	Florence, N.C.	1980	Robert L. Harmon
Buffalo, Bigmouth	70–5	—	—	Bussey Brake, Bastrop, La.	1980	Delbert Sisk
Buffalo, Smallmouth	51	—	—	Lawrence, Kan.	1979	Scott Butler
Bullhead, Black	8	24"	17¾"	Lake Waccabuc, N.Y.	1951	Kani Evans
Bullhead, Brown	5–8	—	—	Veal Pond, Ga.	1975	Jimmy Andrews
Bullhead, Yellow	3	—	—	Nelson Lake, Wis.	1977	Mark Nessman
Burbot	18–4	—	—	Pickford, Mich.	1980	Thomas Courtemanche
Carp	55–5	42"	31"	Clearwater Lake, Minn.	1952	Frank J. Ledwein
Catfish, Blue	97	57"	37"	Missouri River, S.D.	1959	Edward B. Elliott
Catfish, Channel	58	47¼"	29⅛"	Santee-Cooper Res., S.C.	1964	W. B. Whaley
Catfish, Flathead	79–8	44"	27"	White River, Ind.	1966	Glenn T. Simpson
Catfish, White	10–5	25"	17½"	Raritan River, N.J.	1976	L. W. Lomerson
Char, Arctic	29–11	39¾"	26"	Arctic River, N.W.T.	1968	Jeanne P. Branson
Crappie, Black	6	—	—	Seaplane Canal, Westwego, La.	1969	Lettie Theresa Robertson
Crappie, White	5–3	21"	19"	Enid Dam, Miss.	1957	Fred L. Bright
Dolly Varden	3–13	—	—	Unalaklett River, Alaska	1980	Roy Lawson
Drum, Freshwater	54–8	31½"	29"	Nickajack Lake, Tenn.	1972	Benny E. Hull
Gar, Alligator	279	93"	—	Rio Grande River, Tex.	1951	Bill Valverde
Gar, Florida	21–3	—	—	Boca Raton, Fla.	1981	Jeff Sabol
Gar, Longnose	50–5	72¼"	22½"	Trinity River, Texas	1954	Townsend Miller
Gar, Shortnose	3–5	—	—	Lake Francis Case, S.D.	1977	J. Pawlowski
Grayling, Arctic	5–15	29⅞"	15⅛"	Katseyedie River, N.W.T.	1967	Jeanne P. Branson
Huchen	70–12	—	—	Carinthia, Austria	1980	Martin F. Esterl
Inconnu	33–9	—	—	Kobuk River, Alaska	1981	John A. Berg
Kokanee	6–9	24½"	14½"	Priest Lake, Idaho	1975	Jerry Verge

Muskellunge	69–15	64½"	31¾"	St. Lawrence River, N.Y.	1957	Arthur Lawton
Muskellunge, Tiger	51–3	—	—	Lac Vieux–Desert, Wis./Mich.	1919	John A. Knobla
Perch, White	4–12	19½"	13"	Messalonskee Lake, Me.	1949	Mrs. Earl Small
Perch, Yellow	4–3	—	—	Bordentown, N.J.	1865	Dr. C. C. Abbot
Pickerel, Eastern chain	9–6	31"	14"	Homerville, Ga.	1961	Baxley McQuaig, Jr.
Pike, Northern	62–8	—	—	Reuss-Weiher, Richenbach, Switz.	1979	Jurg Notzli
Redhorse, Northern	3–11	—	—	Missouri River, S.D.	1977	Philip Laumeyer
Redhorse, Silver	5–13	—	—	Betsie River, Frankfort, Mich.	1980	Darrell T. Hasler
	5–14	—	—	Shelbyville, Ind.	1980	Ernest Harley Jr.
Salmon, Atlantic	79–2	—	—	Tana River, Norway	1928	Henrik Henriksen
Salmon, Chinook	93	50"	39"	Kelp Bay, Alaska	1977	Howard C. Rider
Salmon, Chum	27–3	39⅜"	24½"	Raymond Cove, Alaska	1977	Robert A. Jahnke
Salmon Landlocked	22–8	36"	—	Sebago Lake, Me.	1907	Edward Blakely
Salmon, Pink	12–9	—	—	Moose and Kenai Rivers, Alaska	1974	Steven Alan Lee
Salmon, Sockeye	7–14	—	—	American River, Alaska	1981	Brooke P. Halsey Jr.
Sauger	8–12	28"	15"	Lake Sakakawea, N.D.	1971	Mike Fischer
Shad, American	9–4	—	—	Delaware River, Pa.	1979	J. Edward Whitman
	9–4	—	—	Connecticut River, Wilson, Conn.	1981	Edward William Cypus
Splake	16–12	—	—	Island Lake, Colo.	1973	Del Canty
Sturgeon	407	—	—	Sacramento River, Colusa, Calif.	1979	Raymond Pittenger
Sturgeon, White	360	111"	86"	Snake River, Idaho	1956	Willard Cravens
Sunfish, Green	2–2	14¾"	14"	Stockton Lake, Mo.	1971	Paul M. Dilley
Sunfish, Redbreast	1–8	11"	12⅝"	Suwannee River, Fla.	1977	Tommy D. Cason, Jr.
Sunfish, Redear	4–8	16¼"	17¾"	Chase City, Va.	1970	Maurice E. Ball
Trout, Brook	14–8	31½"	11½"	Nipigon River, Ontario	1916	Dr. W. J. Cook
Trout, Brown	35–15	—	—	Nahuel Haupi, Argentina	1952	Eugenio Cavaglia
Trout, Bull	32	—	—	Lake Pend Oreille, Idaho	1949	N.L. Higgins
Trout, Cutthroat	41	39"	—	Pyramid Lake, Nev.	1925	John Skimmerhorn
Trout, Golden	11	28"	16"	Cook's Lake, Wyo.	1948	Charles S. Reed
Trout, Lake	65	52"	38"	Great Bear Lake, N.W.T.	1970	Larry Daunis
Trout, Rainbow or Steelhead	42–2	43"	23½"	Bell Island, Alaska	1970	David R. White
Trout, Sunapee	11–8	33"	21"	Lake Sunapee, N.H.	1954	Ernest Theoharis
Trout, Tiger	20–13	—	—	Lake Michigan, Wis.	1978	Pete M. Friedland
Walleye	25	41"	29"	Old Hickory Lake, Tenn.	1960	Mabry Harper
Warmouth	2–2	—	—	Douglas Swamp, S.C.	1973	Willie Singletary
Whitefish, Lake	13–15	—	—	Meaford, Ontario	1981	Wayne Caswell
Whitefish, Mountain	5	19"	14"	Athabasca River, Alberta, Can.	1963	Orville Welch
Whitefish, Round	3–4	—	—	Leland Harbor, Mich.	1977	Vernon A. Bauer

Caught With Rod and Reel in Salt Water

Source: International Game Fish Association

Species	lb–oz	Length	Girth	Where caught	Year	Angler
Albacore	88–2	—	—	Canary Islands	1977	Siegfried Dickemann
Amberjack	155–10	—	—	Challenger Bank, Bermuda	1981	Joseph Dawson
Barracuda	83	72¼"	29"	Lagos, Nigeria	1952	K. J. W. Hackett
Bass, Black Sea	8–12	—	—	Oregon Inlet, N.C.	1979	Joe W. Mizelle Sr.
Bass, Giant Sea	563–8	89"	72"	Anacapa Island, Calif.	1968	J. D. McAdam, Jr.
Bass, Striped	76	—	—	Montauk, Long Island, N.Y.	1981	Robert A. Rocchetta
Blackfish (Tautog)	21–6	31½"	23½"	Cape May, N.J.	1954	R. N. Sheafer
Bluefish	31–12	47"	23"	North Carolina	1972	James M. Hussey
Bonefish	19	—	—	Zululand, S. Africa	1962	Brian W. Batchelor
Bonito, Atlantic	16–12	—	—	Canary Islands	1980	Rolf Fredderies
Bonito, Pacific	23–8	35¼"	23¼"	Victoria, Mahe	1975	Mrs. Anne Cochain
Cobia	110–5	—	—	Mombasa, Kenya	1964	Eric Tinworth
Cod	98–12	63"	41"	Isle of Shoals, N.H.	1969	Alphonse Bielevich
Conger	39–7	—	—	Pornichet–La Baule, France	1980	Jean–Claude Guilmineau
Dolphin	87	81⅔"	28"	Papagallo Gulf, Costa Rica	1976	Manual Salazar
Drum, Black	113–1	53⅛"	43½"	Lewes, Del.	1975	G. M. Townsend
Drum, Red	90	55½"	38¼"	Rodanthe, N.C.	1973	Elvin Hooper
Flounder, Summer	22–7	—	—	Montauk, N.Y.	1975	Charles Nappi
Halibut, Atlantic	250	—	—	Gloucester, Mass.	1981	Louis P. Sirard
Halibut, California	42	—	—	Santa Rosa Island, Calif.	1981	Jerry Yahiro
Halibut, Pacific	235	—	—	Juneau, Alaska	1980	Norbert U. Koch
Jack, Crevalle	51	—	—	Lake Worth, Fla.	1978	Stephen Schwenk
Jack, Horse–eye	23–2	—	—	Cancun, Mexico	1981	Norman A. Carpenter
Jewfish	680	85½"	66"	Fernandina Beach, Fla.	1961	Lynn Joyner
Kawakawa	26	—	—	Merimbula, N.S.W., Australia	1980	Wally Elfring
Mackerel, King	90	—	—	Key West, Florida	1976	Norton I. Thomton
Marlin, Black	1560	174"	81"	Cabo Blanco, Peru	1953	A. C. Glassel, Jr.
Marlin, Atlantic Blue	1282	176"	76½"	St. Thomas, Virgin Islands	1977	Larry Martin
Marlin, Pacific Blue	1153	176"	73"	Ritidian Point, Guam	1969	Greg G. Perez
Marlin, Striped	417–8	139½"	52½"	Cavalli Island, New Zealand	1977	Phillip Bryers
Marlin, White	181–14	—	—	Victoria, Brazil	1979	Evandro Luiz Coser

Permit	51–8	—	—	Lake Worth, Fla.	1978	William M. Kenney
Pollack	16–1	—	—	Plymouth, England	1978	Peter J. Peck
Pollack (virens)	46–7	50½"	30"	Brielle, N.J.	1975	John T. Holton
Pompano, African	41–8	—	—	Fort Lauderdale, Fla.	1979	Wayne Sommers
Roosterfish	114	64"	33"	La Paz, Mexico	1960	Abe Sackheim
Runner, Rainbow	33–10	55¼"	22½"	Clarion Island, Mexico	1976	R. A. Mikkelsen
Sailfish, Atlantic	128–1	106¼"	34¼"	Luanda, Angola, Africa	1974	Harm Steyn
Sailfish, Pacific	221	129"	—	Santa Cruz Is., Galapagos Is.	1947	C. W. Stewart
Seabass, White	83–12	65½"	34"	San Felipe, Mexico	1953	L. C. Baumgardner
Seatrout, Spotted	16	32½"	21¾"	Mason's Beach, Va.	1977	William G. Katko
Shark, Blue	437	—	—	Catherine Bay, Australia	1976	Peter Hyde
Shark, Hammerhead	717	—	—	Jacksonville Beach, Fla.	1980	Richard Edward Morse
Shark, Mako	1080	—	—	Montauk, N.Y.	1979	James L. Melanson
Shark, Porbeagle	465	111"	56"	Padstow, Cornwall, England	1976	Jorge Potier
Shark, Thresher	802	—	—	Tutukaka, New Zealand	1981	Dianne North
Shark, Tiger	1780	166½"	103"	Cherry Grove, S.C.	1964	Walter Maxwell
Shark, White	2664	202"	114"	South Australia	1959	Alfred Dean
Skipjack, Black	14–8	—	—	Baja, Mexico	1977	Lorraine Carlton
Snapper, Cubera	60–12	—	—	Miami Beach, Fla.	1980	Dr. Richard A. Klein
Snook	53–10	—	—	Costa Rica	1978	Gilbert Ponzi
Spearfish	90–13	—	—	Madeira Island, Portugal	1980	Joseph Larkin
Swordfish	1182	179¼"	78"	Iquique, Chile	1953	L. E. Marron
Tanguigue	85–6	—	—	Western Australia	1978	Barry Wrightson
Tarpon	283	85⅗"	—	Lake Maracaibo, Venezuela	1956	M. Salazar
Tautog (See Blackfish)						
Trevally, Giant	116	—	—	American Samoa	1978	William G. Foster
Tuna, Yellowfin	388–12	—	—	Mexico	1977	Curt Wiesenhutter
Tuna, Atlantic Bigeye	375–8	—	—	Ocean City, Md.	1977	Cecil Browne
Tuna, Blackfin	42	—	—	Bermuda	1978	Alan J. Card
Tuna, Bluefin	1496	—	—	Nova Scotia, Canada	1979	Ken Fraser
Tuna, Dog–tooth	194	—	—	Kwan-Tall Island, Korea	1980	Kim Chul
Tuna, Longtail	60	—	—	Bermagui, Australia	1975	N. Noel Webster
Tuna, Pacific Big-Eyed	435	93"	63½"	Cabo Blanco, Peru	1957	R.V. A. Lee
Tuna, Skipjack	39–15	39"	28"	Walker City, Bahamas	1952	R. Drowley
	40	38¾"	27½"	Baie du Tambeau, Mauritius	1971	Joseph R. Cabache
Tuna, Southern Bluefin	348–5	—	—	Whakatane, New Zealand	1981	Rex Wood
Tunny, Little	27	39"	22"	Key Largo, Fla.	1976	William E. Allison
Wahoo	149	—	—	Cat Cay, Bahamas	1962	John Pirovano
Weakfish	17–14	—	—	Rye, N.Y.	1980	William N. Herold
Yellowtail, California	71–15	—	—	Alijos Rocks, Mexico	1979	Michael Carpenter
Yellowtail, Southern	111	—	—	Bay of Islands, New Zealand	1961	A. F. Plim

CHESS

WORLD CHAMPIONS

1894–1921 Emanuel Lasker, Germany
1921–27 Jose R. Capablanca, Cuba
1927–35 Alexander A. Alekhine, U.S.S.R.
1935–37 Dr. Max Euwe, Netherlands
1937–46 Alexander A. Alekhine, U.S.S.R.[1]
1948–57 Mikhail Botvinnik, U.S.S.R.
1957–58 Vassily Smyslov, U.S.S.R.
1958–60 Mikhail Botvinnik, U.S.S.R.
1960–61 Mikhail Tal, U.S.S.R.
1961–63 Mikhail Botvinnik, U.S.S.R.
1963–68 Tigran Petrosian, U.S.S.R.
1969–71 Boris Spassky, U.S.S.R.
1972–74 Bobby Fischer, Los Angeles
1975 Bobby Fischer[2]; Anatoly Karpov, U.S.S.R.
1976–82 Anatoly Karpov, U.S.S.R.[3]

1. Alekhine, a French citizen, died while champion. 2. Relinquished title. 3. In 1978, Karpov defeated Viktor Korchnoi 6 games to 5.

UNITED STATES CHAMPIONS

1909–36 Frank J. Marshall, New York
1936–44 Samuel Reshevsky, New York[1]
1944–46 Arnold S. Denker, New York
1946 Samuel Reshevsky, Boston
1948 Herman Steiner, Los Angeles
1951–52 Larry Evans, New York
1954–57 Arthur Bisguier, New York
1958–61 Bobby Fischer, Brooklyn, N.Y.
1962 Larry Evans, New York
1963–67 Bobby Fischer, New York
1968 Larry Evans, New York
1969–71 Samuel Reshevsky, Spring Valley, N.Y.
1972 Robert Byrne, Ossining, N.Y.
1973 Lubomir Kavelek, Washington; John Grefe, San Francisco
1974–77 Walter Browne, Berkeley, Calif.
1978–79 Lubomir Kavalek, New York
1980 Tie, Walter Browne, Berkeley, Calif. Larry Christiansen, Modesto, Calif. Larry Evans, Reno, Nev.
1981–82[2] Tie, Walter Browne Yasser Seirawan, Seattle, Wash.

1. In 1942, Isaac I. Kashdan of New York was co-champion for a while because of a tie with Reshevsky in that year's tournament. Reshevsky won the play-off. 2. Championship not contested in 1982.

BASKETBALL

Basketball may be the one sport whose exact origin is definitely known. In the winter of 1891–92, Dr. James Naismith, an instructor in the Y.M.C.A. Training College (now Springfield College) at Springfield, Mass., deliberately invented the game of basketball in order to provide indoor exercise and competition for the students between the closing of the football season and the opening of the baseball season. He affixed peach baskets overhead on the walls at opposite ends of the gymnasium and organized teams to play his new game in which the purpose was to toss an association (soccer) ball into one basket and prevent the opponents from tossing the ball into the other basket. The game is fundamentally the same today, though there have been improvements in equipment and some changes in rules.

Because Dr. Naismith had eighteen available players when he invented the game, the first rule was: "There shall be nine players on each side." Later the number of players became optional, depending upon the size of the available court, but the five-player standard was adopted when the game spread over the country. United States soldiers brought basketball to Europe in World War I, and it soon became a world-wide sport.

College Basketball

NATIONAL COLLEGIATE A.A. CHAMPIONS

1939	Oregon	1949	Kentucky	1959	California	1975	U.C.L.A.
1940	Indiana	1950	C.C.N.Y.	1960	Ohio State	1976	Indiana
1941	Wisconsin	1951	Kentucky	1961	Cincinnati	1977	Marquette
1942	Stanford	1952	Kansas	1962	Cincinnati	1978	Kentucky
1943	Wyoming	1953	Indiana	1963	Loyola (Chicago)	1979	Michigan State
1944	Utah	1954	La Salle	1964	U.C.L.A.	1980	Louisville
1945	Oklahoma A & M	1955	San Francisco	1965	U.C.L.A.	1981	Indiana
1946	Oklahoma A & M	1956	San Francisco	1966	Texas Western	1982	North Carolina
1947	Holy Cross	1957	North Carolina	1967–73	U.C.L.A.		
1948	Kentucky	1958	Kentucky	1974	No. Carolina State		

NATIONAL INVITATION TOURNAMENT (NIT) CHAMPIONS

1939	Long Island U.	1951	Brigham Young	1962	Dayton	1973	Virginia Tech
1940	Colorado	1952	La Salle	1963	Providence	1974	Purdue
1941	Long Island U.	1953	Seton Hall	1964	Bradley	1975	Princeton
1942	West Virginia	1954	Holy Cross	1965	St. John's (Bklyn.)	1976	Kentucky
1943–44	St. John's (Bklyn.)	1955	Duquesne	1966	Brigham Young	1977	St. Bonaventure
1945	DePaul	1956	Louisville	1967	So. Illinois	1978	Texas
1946	Kentucky	1957	Bradley	1968	Dayton	1979	Indiana
1947	Utah	1958	Xavier (Cincinnati)	1969	Temple	1980	Virginia
1948	St. Louis	1959	St. John's (Bklyn.)	1970	Marquette	1981	Tulsa
1949	San Francisco	1960	Bradley	1971	North Carolina	1982	Bradley
1950	C.C.N.Y.	1961	Providence	1972	Maryland		

N.C.A.A. MAJOR COLLEGE INDIVIDUAL SCORING RECORDS

Single Season Averages

Player, Team	Year	G	FG	FT	Pts	Avg
Pete Maravich, Louisiana State	1969–70	31	522[1]	337	1381[1]	44.5[1]
Pete Maravich	1968–69	26	433	282	1148	44.2
Pete Maravich	1967–68	26	432	274	1138	43.8
Frank Selvy, Furman	1953–54	29	427	355[1]	1209	41.7
Johnny Neumann, Mississippi	1970–71	23	366	191	923	40.1
Freeman Williams, Portland State	1976–77	26	417	176	1010	38.8
Billy McGill, Utah	1961–62	26	394	221	1009	38.8
Calvin Murphy, Niagara	1967–68	24	337	242	916	38.2
Austin Carr, Notre Dame	1969–70	29	444	218	1106	38.1

1. Record.

LONGEST FIELD GOAL IN COLLEGE BASKETBALL

What was the longest field goal ever scored in a college basketball game? Would you believe 89 ft 3 in.? That's only 4 ft 9 in. short of the regulation length of a court. It happened on January 21, 1980, at Tallahassee, Fla., and the shooter was Les Henson, a 6-ft-6-in. senior forward for Virginia Tech. He took the shot with only two seconds left in the game against Florida State and gave the Gobblers a 79–77 victory. Henson had just grabbed a rebound off the Florida State boards about a foot from the baseline. The normally left-handed-shooting Henson unleashed a right-handed shot in desperation and it went in. At first the shot was reported as 93 ft, but a later measurement established it at 89–3. "It was eerie while the ball was in the air," Henson later recalled. "Everything was quiet, you couldn't hear a thing in the arena. At first, I thought it was going to hit one of the light fixtures, but it didn't, and then it just swished through the hoop." It bettered the previous longest scoring shot of 8[illegible] ft by Rudy Williams of Providence College against Rhode Island on February 17, 1979.

N.C.A.A. CAREER SCORING TOTALS

Division I

Player, Team	Last year	G	FG	FT	Pts	Avg
Pete Maravich, Louisiana State	1970	83	1387[1]	893[1]	3667[1]	44.2[1]
Austin Carr, Notre Dame	1971	74	1017	526	2560	34.6
Oscar Robertson, Cincinnati	1960	88	1052	869	2973	33.8
Calvin Murphy, Niagara	1970	77	947	654	2548	33.1
Dwight Lamar[2]	1973	57	768	326	1862	32.7
Frank Selvy, Furman	1954	78	922	694	2538	32.5
Rick Mount, Purdue	1970	72	910	503	2323	32.3
Darrel Floyd, Furman	1956	71	868	545	2281	32.1
Nick Werkman, Seton Hall	1964	71	812	649	2273	32.0

1. Record. 2. Also played two seasons in college division.

Division II

Player, Team	Last year	G	FG	FT	Pts	Avg
Travis Grant, Kentucky State	1972	121	1760[1]	525	4045[1]	33.4[1]
John Rinka, Kenyon	1970	99	1261	729	3251	32.8
Florindo Vierira, Quinnipiac	1957	69	761	741	2263	32.8
Willie Shaw, Lane	1964	76	960	459	2379	31.3
Mike Davis, Virginia Union	1969	89	1014	730	2758	31.0
Henry Logan, Western Carolina	1968	107	1263	764	3290	30.7
Willie Scott, Alabama State	1969	103	1277	601	3155	30.6
Gregg Northington, Alabama State	1972	75	894	403	2191	29.2
Bob Hopkins, Grambling	1956	126	1403	953	3759	29.8

1. Record.

TOP SINGLE-GAME SCORING MARKS

Player, Team (Opponent)	Yr	Pts	Player, Team (Opponent)	Yr	Pts
Selvy, Furman (Newberry)	1954	100[1]	Floyd, Furman (Morehead)	1955	67
Williams, Portland State (Rocky Mtn.)	1978	81	Maravich, LSU (Tulane)	1969	66
Mlkvy, Temple (Wilkes)	1951	73	Handlan, W & L (Furman)	1951	66
Williams, Portland State (So. Oregon)	1977	71	Roberts, Oral Roberts (N.C. A&T)	1977	66
Maravich, LSU (Alabama)	1970	69	Williams, Portland State (Geo. Fox Coll.)	1978	66
Murphy, Niagara (Syracuse)	1969	68	Roberts, Oral Roberts (Oregon)	1977	65

1. Record.

NATIONAL COLLEGIATE ATHLETIC ASSOCIATION (N.C.A.A.)—1982

DIVISION I

First Round—East

James Madison 55, Ohio State 48
Northeastern 63, St. Joseph's 62
St. John's 66, Pennsylvania 56
Wake Forest 74, Old Dominion 57

First Round—Mideast

Indiana 94, Robert Morris 62
Middle Tennessee 50, Kentucky 44
Tennessee 61, Southwestern Louisiana 57
Tennessee–Chattanooga 58, North Carolina State 51

First Round—Midwest

Boston College 70, San Francisco 66
Houston 94, Alcorn State 84
Kansas State 77, Northern Illinois 68
Marquette 67, Evansville 62

First Round—West

Iowa 70, Northeastern Louisiana 63
Pepperdine 99, Pittsburgh 88
West Virginia 102, North Carolina A and T 72
Wyoming 61, Southern California 58

Second Round—East

Alabama 69, St. John's 68
Memphis State 56, Wake Forest 55
North Carolina 52, James Madison 50
Villanova 76, Northeastern 72 (3 overtimes)

Second Round—Mideast

Alabama–Birmingham 80, Indiana 70
Louisville 81, Middle Tennessee 56
Minnesota 62, Tennessee–Chattanooga 61
Virginia 54, Tennessee 51

Second Round—Midwest

Boston College 82, De Paul 75
Houston 78, Tulsa 74
Kansas State 65, Arkansas 64
Missouri 73, Marquette 69

Second Round—West

Fresno State 50, West Virginia 46
Georgetown 51, Wyoming 43
Idaho 69, Iowa 67 (overtime)
Oregon State 70, Pepperdine 51

Third Round—East

Villanova 70, Memphis State 66 (overtime)
North Carolina 74, Alabama 69

Third Round—Mideast

Alabama–Birmingham 68, Virginia 66
Louisville 67, Minnesota 61

Third Round—Midwest

Boston College 69, Kansas State 65
Houston 79, Missouri 78

Third Round—West

Georgetown 58, Fresno State 40
Oregon State 60, Idaho 42

Regional Finals

East—North Carolina 70, Villanova 60
Mideast—Louisville 75, Alabama–Birmingham 68
Midwest—Houston 99, Boston College 92
West—Georgetown 69, Oregon State 45

National Semifinals

(New Orleans, March 27, 1982)
North Carolina 68, Houston 63
Georgetown 50, Louisville 46
Third Place—Not contested.

National Final

(New Orleans, March 29, 1982)
North Carolina 63, Georgetown 62

DIVISION II
Semifinals

District of Columbia 76, Bakersfield State 71
Florida Southern 90, Kentucky Wesleyan 89 (2 overtimes)

Third Place

Kentucky Wesleyan 77, Bakersfield State 66

Championship

(Springfield, Mass., March 20, 1982)
District of Columbia 73, Florida Southern 63

DIVISION III
Semifinals

Potsdam State 50, Brooklyn College 49
Wabash 68, Stanislaus State 64

Third Place

Brooklyn College 68, Stanislaus State 62 (overtime)

Championship

(Grand Rapids, Mich., March 20, 1982)
Wabash 83, Potsdam State 62

JUNIOR COLLEGES
Championship

(Hutchinson, Kan., March 20, 1982)
Midland (Tex.) College 93, Miami-Dade (Fla.) 88

ASSOCIATION FOR INTERCOLLEGIATE ATHLETICS FOR WOMEN

(A.I.A.W.—1982)

QUARTERFINALS

Texas 73, Wisconsin 61
Villanova 87, Delta State 72
Rutgers 83, Minnesota 75
Wayland Baptist 85, California 70

NATIONAL SEMIFINALS

(Philadelphia, March 26, 1982)
Texas 82, Wayland Baptist 63
Rutgers 83, Villanova 75

THIRD PLACE

Villanova 90, Wayland Baptist 81

CHAMPIONSHIP

(Philadelphia, March 28, 1982)
Rutgers 83, Texas 77

DIVISION II
Final

(Charleston, S.C., March 27, 1982)
Francis Marion College (S.C.) 92, College of Charleston (S.C.) 83

DIVISION III
Final

(Cedar Rapids, Iowa, March 27, 1982)
Concordia (Minn.) 73, Mount Mercy (Iowa) 72

WOMEN'S COLLEGE BASKETBALL—1982

N.C.A.A. CHAMPIONSHIPS*

First Round—East

Cheyney State 75, Auburn 64
Kansas State 78, Stephen F. Austin 75
North Carolina State 75, Northwestern 71
Old Dominion 75, St. Peter's 42

First Round—Mideast

Memphis State 72, Mississippi 70
Penn State 96, Clemson 75
Southern California 99, Kent State 55
Tennessee 72, Jackson State 56

First Round—Midwest

Arizona State 97, Georgia 77
Kentucky 88, Illinois 80
Louisiana Tech 114, Tennessee Tech 53
South Carolina 79, East Carolina 54

First Round—West

Drake 90, Ohio State 79
Long Beach State 95, Howard 57
Maryland 82, Stanford 48
Missouri 59, Oregon 53

Second Round—East

Cheyney State 74, North Carolina State 61
Kansas State 76, Old Dominion 67

Second Round—Mideast

Southern California 73, Penn State 70
Tennessee 78, Memphis State 63

Second Round—Midwest

Kentucky 73, South Carolina 69
Louisiana Tech 92, Arizona State 54

Second Round—West

Drake 91, Long Beach State 78
Maryland 80, Missouri 68

Regional Finals

East—Cheyney State 93, Kansas State 71
Mideast—Tennessee 91, Southern California 90 (overtime)

Midwest—Louisiana Tech 82, Kentucky 60
West—Maryland 89, Drake 78

NATIONAL SEMIFINALS

(Norfolk, Va., March 26, 1982)
Cheyney State 76, Maryland 66
Louisiana Tech 69, Tennessee 46

CHAMPIONSHIP

(Norfolk, Va., March 28, 1982)
Louisiana Tech 76, Cheyney State 62

DIVISION II
Final

(Springfield, Mass., March 20, 1982)
California State Poly-Pomona 93, Tuskegee 74

*First year of tournament.

NATIONAL INVITATION TOURNAMENT (N.I.T.)—1982

Semifinals

(March 22, 1982, Madison Square Garden, New York)
Bradley 84, Oklahoma 68
Purdue 61, Georgia 60
Third Place—Not contested

Championship

(March 24, 1982, Madison Square Garden, New York)
Bradley 67, Purdue 58

A.A.U. CHAMPIONSHIP—MEN

(Portland, Ore., March 28, 1982)

Semifinals

Brewster Packing (Seattle) 124, Houston Flyers 116
Marathon Oil (Lexington, Ky.) 116, Sports in Action (Wash.) 96

Championship

Brewster Packing 93, Marathon Oil 91

N.B.A. ALL-ROOKIE TEAM—1982

Buck Williams, New Jersey Nets; Isiah Thomas, Detroit Pistons; Kelly Tripucka, Detroit Pistons; Jay Vincent, Dallas Mavericks; Jeff Ruland, Washington Bullets

LEADING N.C.A.A. SCORERS—1981–1982

Division I

	FG	FT	Pts	Avg
Harry Kelly, Texas Southern	336	190	862	29.7
Ricky Pierce, Rice	314	177	805	26.8
Dan Callandrillo, Seton Hall	250	198	698	25.9
Kevin Magee, California-Irvine	272	188	732	25.2
Quintin Dailey, San Francisco	286	183	755	25.2
Willie Jackson, Centenary	273	147	693	23.9
Mitchell Wiggins, Florida State	223	77	523	23.8
Perry Moss, Northeastern	279	152	710	23.7
Melvin McLaughlin, Central Mich.	255	71	581	23.2
Joe Jakubick, Akron	235	124	594	22.8
Steve Barker, Samford	222	140	584	22.5
Terry Cummings, De Paul	244	136	624	22.3
Terry Teagle, Baylor	259	104	622	22.2
Steve Burtt, Iona	251	182	684	22.1
Wayne Sappleton, Loyola (Ill.)	238	162	638	22.0
Mark McNamara, California	231	131	593	22.0

NATIONAL ASSOCIATION OF INTERCOLLEGIATE ATHLETICS—1982

Round of 16

Kearney (Neb.) State 77, Hanover (Ind.) 76
Saginaw Valley (Mich.) 67, Southern Tech (Ga.) 61 (overtime)
South Carolina–Spartanburg 63, St. Mary's (Tex.) 53
Henderson State (Ark.) 70, Moorhead State (Minn.) 61
Biola (Calif.) 62, Quincy (Ill.) 56
Hampton Institute (Va.) 63, Central Washington 49
Wisconsin–Eau Claire 91, St. Thomas Aquinas (N.Y.) 77
Western Oregon 63, Briar Cliff (Iowa) 55

Quarterfinals

Biola 42, Saginaw Valley 40
Hampton Institute 70, Henderson State 66
South Carolina–Spartanburg 76, Wisconsin–Eau Claire 64
Kearney State 97, Western Oregon 95

Semifinals

South Carolina–Spartanburg 68, Hampton Institute 54
Biola 84, Kearney State 75

Third Place

Hampton Institute 98, Kearney State 94

Championship

South Carolina–Spartanburg 51, Biola 38

Professional Basketball

NATIONAL BASKETBALL ASSOCIATION CHAMPIONS

Source: Matt Winick, Director of Media Information, National Basketball Association

The National Basketball Association was originally the Basketball Association of America. It took its current name in 1949 when it merged with the National Basketball League.

Season	Eastern Conference (W-L)	Western Conference (W-L)	Playoff Champions[1]
1946–47	Washington Capitols (49–11)	Chicago Stags (39–22)	Philadelphia Warriors
1947–48	Philadelphia Warriors (27–21)	St. Louis Bombers (29–19)	Baltimore Bullets
1948–49	Washington Capitols (38–22)	Rochester Royals (45–15)	Minneapolis Lakers
1949–50	Syracuse Nationals (51–13)	Indianapolis Olympians (39–25)	Minneapolis Lakers
1950–51	Philadelphia Warriors (40–26)	Minneapolis Lakers (44–24)	Rochester Royals
1951–52	Syracuse Nationals (40–26)	Rochester Royals (41–25)	Minneapolis Lakers
1952–53	New York Knickerbockers (47–23)	Minneapolis Lakers (48–22)	Minneapolis Lakers
1953–54	New York Knickerbockers (44–28)	Minneapolis Lakers (46–26)	Minneapolis Lakers
1954–55	Syracuse Nationals (43–29)	Ft. Wayne Pistons (43–29)	Syracuse Nationals
1955–56	Philadelphia Warriors (45–27)	Ft. Wayne Pistons (37–35)	Philadelphia Warriors
1956–57	Boston Celtics (44–28)	St. Louis Hawks (34–38)	Boston Celtics

Season	Eastern Conference (W-L)	Western Conference (W-L)	Playoff Champions[1]
1957–58	Boston Celtics (48–23)	St. Louis Hawks (41–31)	St. Louis Hawks
1958–59	Boston Celtics (52–20)	St. Louis Hawks (49–23)	Boston Celtics
1959–60	Boston Celtics (59–16)	St. Louis Hawks (46–29)	Boston Celtics
1960–61	Boston Celtics (57–22)	St. Louis Hawks (51–28)	Boston Celtics
1961–62	Boston Celtics (60–20)	Los Angeles Lakers (54–26)	Boston Celtics
1962–63	Boston Celtics (58–22)	Los Angeles Lakers (53–27)	Boston Celtics
1963–64	Boston Celtics (59–21)	San Francisco Warriors (48–32)	Boston Celtics
1964–65	Boston Celtics (62–18)	Los Angeles Lakers (49–31)	Boston Celtics
1965–66	Philadelphia 76ers (55–25)	Los Angeles Lakers (45–35)	Boston Celtics
1966–67	Philadelphia 76ers (68–13)	San Francisco Warriors (44–37)	Philadelphia 76ers
1967–68	Philadelphia 76ers (62–20)	St. Louis Hawks (56–26)	Boston Celtics
1968–69	Baltimore Bullets (57–25)	Los Angeles Lakers (55–27)	Boston Celtics
1969–70	New York Knickerbockers (60–22)	Atlanta Hawks (48–34)	New York Knicks
1970–71	Baltimore Bullets (42–40)	Milwaukee Bucks (66–16)	Milwaukee Bucks
1971–72	New York Knickerbockers (48–34)	Los Angeles Lakers (69–13)	Los Angeles Lakers
1972–73	New York Knickerbockers (57–25)	Los Angeles Lakers (69–22)	New York Knicks
1973–74	Boston Celtics (56–26)	Milwaukee Bucks (59–23)	Boston Celtics
1974–75	Washington Bullets (60–22)	Golden State Warriors (48–34)	Golden State Warriors
1975–76	Boston Celtics (54–28)	Phoenix Suns (42–40)	Boston Celtics
1976–77	Philadelphia 76ers (50–32)	Portland Trail Blazers (49–33)	Portland Trail Blazers
1977–78	Washington Bullets (44–38)	Seattle Super Sonics (47–35)	Washington Bullets
1978–79	Washington Bullets (54–28)	Seattle Super Sonics (52–30)	Seattle Super Sonics
1979–80	Philadelphia 76ers (59–23)	Los Angeles Lakers (60–22)	Los Angeles Lakers
1980–81	Boston Celtics (62–20)	Phoenix Suns (57–25)	Boston Celtics
1981–82	Boston Celtics (63–19)	Los Angeles Lakers (57–25)	Los Angeles Lakers

1. Playoffs may involve teams other than conference winners.

INDIVIDUAL N.B.A. SCORING CHAMPIONS

Season	Player, Team	G	FG	FT	Pts	Avg
1953–54	Neil Johnston, Philadelphia Warriors	72	591	577	1759	24.4
1954–55	Neil Johnston, Philadelphia Warriors	72	521	589	1631	22.7
1955–56	Bob Pettit, St. Louis Hawks	72	646	557	1849	25.7
1956–57	Paul Arizin, Philadelphia Warriors	71	613	591	1817	25.6
1957–58	George Yardley, Detroit Pistons	72	673	655	2001	27.8
1958–59	Bob Pettit, St. Louis Hawks	72	719	667	2105	29.2
1959–60	Wilt Chamberlain, Philadelphia Warriors	72	1065	577	2707	37.6
1960–61	Wilt Chamberlain, Phildelphia Warriors	79	1251	531	3033	38.4
1961–62	Wilt Chamberlain, Philadelphia Warriors	80	1597	835	4029	50.4
1962–63	Wilt Chamberlain, San Francisco Warriors	80	1463	660	3586	44.8
1963–64	Wilt Chamberlain, San Francisco Warriors	80	1204	540	2948	36.9
1964–65	Wilt Chamberlain, San Francisco Warriors-Phila. 76ers	73	1063	408	2534	34.7
1965–66	Wilt Chamberlain, Philadelphia 76ers	79	1074	501	2649	33.5
1966–67	Rick Barry, San Francisco Warriors	78	1011	753	2775	35.6
1967–68	Dave Bing, Detroit Pistons	79	835	472	2142	27.1
1968–69	Elvin Hayes, San Diego Rockets	82	930	467	2327	28.4
1969–70	Jerry West, Los Angeles Lakers	74	831	647	2309	31.2
1970–71	Lew Alcindor,[1] Milwaukee Bucks	82	1063	470	2596	31.7
1971–72	Kareem Abdul-Jabbar, Milwaukee Bucks	81	1159	504	2822	34.8
1972–73	Nate Archibald, Kansas City-Omaha Kings	80	1028	663	2719	34.0
1973–74	Bob McAdoo, Buffalo Braves	74	901	459	2261	30.8
1974–75	Bob McAdoo, Buffalo Braves	82	1095	641	2831	34.5
1975–76	Bob McAdoo, Buffalo Braves	78	934	559	2427	31.1
1976–77	Pete Maravich, New Orleans Jazz	73	886	501	2273	31.1
1977–78	George Gervin, San Antonio Spurs	82	864	504	2232	27.2
1978–79	George Gervin, San Antonio	80	947	471	2365	29.6
1979–80	George Gervin, San Antonio	78	1024	505	2585	33.1
1980–81	Adrian Dantley, Utah Jazz	80	909	632	2452	30.7
1981–82	George Gervin, San Antonio	79	993	555	2551	32.3

1. (Kareem Abdul-Jabbar).

N.B.A. LIFETIME LEADERS

(Through 1981–1982 season)

Scoring

	Yrs	FG	FT	Pts
Wilt Chamberlain	14	12,681	6,057	31,419
Kareem Adbul–Jabbar	13	11,568	4,952	28,088
Oscar Robertson	14	9,508	7,694	26,710
John Havlicek	16	10,513	5,369	26,395
Elvin Hayes	14	10,394	5,074	25,8[illegible]
Rick Barry*	14	9,695	5,713	25,[illegible]
Jerry West	14	9,016	7,160	25,[illegible]
Dan Issel*	12	8,828	5,570	23,[illegible]
Elgin Baylor	14	8,693	5,763	23,[illegible]
Julius Erving*	11	9,004	4,744	22,[illegible]

Hal Greer	15	8,504	4,578	21,586
Walt Bellamy	14	7,914	5,113	20,941
Bob Pettit	11	7,349	6,182	20,880

*Includes statistics compiled in the American Basketball Association.

Scoring Average

(400 games or 10,000 points minimum)

	Games	Pts	Avg
Wilt Chamberlain	1,045	31,419	30.1
Kareem Abdul-Jabbar	1,011	28,088	27.8
Elgin Baylor	846	23,149	27.4
Jerry West	932	25,192	27.0
Bob Pettit	792	20,880	26.4
George Gervin*	752	19,736	26.2
Julius Erving*	882	22,851	25.9
Oscar Robertson	1,040	26,710	25.7
Bob McAdoo	640	16,184	25.3
David Thompson*	516	12,728	24.7
Pete Maravich	658	15,948	24.2
Rick Barry	794	18,395	23.2
Elvin Hayes	1,141	25,865	22.7

*Includes statistics compiled in the American Basketball Association.

Rebounds

Wilt Chamberlain	23,924
Bill Russell	21,620
Elvin Hayes	15,403
Nate Thurmond	14,464
Walt Bellamy	14,241
Kareem Abdul-Jabbar	13,826
Wes Unseld	13,769
Jerry Lucas	12,942
Bob Pettit	12,849
Paul Silas	12,357

N.B.A. ALL-DEFENSIVE TEAM—1982

Forwards—Bobby Jones, Philadelphia, and Dan Roundfield, Atlanta

Center—Caldwell Jones, Philadelphia

Guards—Michael Cooper, Los Angeles, and Dennis Johnson, Phoenix

Free-Throw Percentage

(1,400 free throws made minimum)

	Att	FT	Pct
Rick Barry	4,243	3,818	.900
Calvin Murphy	3,714	3,307	.890
Bill Sharman	3,557	3,143	.884
Mike Newlin	3,456	3,005	.870
Fred Brown	2,053	1,761	.858
Larry Siegfried	1,945	1,662	.854
Ricky Sobers	1,959	1,655	.845
Dolph Schayes	8,273	6,979	.844
Jack Marin	2,852	2,405	.843
Flynn Robinson	2,061	1,722	.836

Field-Goal Percentage

(2,000 field goals minimum)

	Att	FG	Pct
Artis Gilmore	5,827	3,425	.588
Kareem Abdul-Jabbar	20,741	11,568	.558
Bobby Jones	4,584	2,540	.554
Adrian Dantley	7,387	4,039	.547
Walter Davis	5,792	3,150	.544
Marques Johnson	5,875	3,177	.541
Swen Nater	4,255	2,302	.541
Wilt Chamberlain	23,497	12,681	.540
Bernard King	5,712	3,050	.534
Cliff Ray	4,450	2,333	.524
George Gervin	10,351	5,404	.522
Walt Bellamy	15,340	7,914	.516

Assists

Oscar Robertson	9,887
Lenny Wilkens	7,211
Bob Cousy	6,955
Guy Rodgers	6,917
Jerry West	6,238
John Havlicek	6,114
Nate Archibald	5,907
Dave Bing	5,397
Kevin Porter	5,268
Norm Van Lier	5,217
Walt Frazier	5,040

N.B.A. MOST VALUABLE PLAYERS

1956	Bob Pettit
1957	Bob Cousy
1958	Bill Russell
1959	Bob Pettit
1960	Wilt Chamberlain
1961–63	Bill Russell
1964	Oscar Robertson
1965	Bill Russell
1966–68	Wilt Chamberlain
1969	Wes Unseld
1970	Willis Reed
1971–72	Lew Alcindor (Kareem Abdul-Jabbar)
1973	Dave Cowens
1974	Kareem Abdul-Jabbar, Milwaukee
1975	Bob McAdoo, Buffalo
1976–77	Kareem Abdul-Jabbar, Los Angeles
1978	Bill Walton, Portland
1979	Moses Malone, Houston
1980	Kareem Abdul-Jabbar, Los Angeles
1981	Julius Erving, Philadelphia
1982	Moses Malone, Houston

N.B.A. TEAM RECORDS

Most points, game—173, Boston vs. Minneapolis, 1959
Most points, quarter—58, Buffalo vs. Boston, 1968
Most points, half—97, Atlanta vs. San Diego, 1970
Most points, overtime period—22, Detroit vs. Cleveland, 1973
Most field goals, game—72, Boston, 1959
Most field goals, quarter—23, Boston, 1959; Buffalo, 1972
Most field goals, half—40, Boston, 1959; Syracuse, 1963; Atlanta, 1979
Most assists, game—53, Milwaukee, 1978
Most rebounds, game—112, Philadelphia, 1959
Most points, both teams, game—337 (San Antonio 171, Milwaukee 166), 3 overtimes, San Antonio, March 6, 1982
Most points, both teams, quarter—96 (Boston 52, Minneapolis 44), 1959; (Detroit 53, Cincinnati 43), 1972
Most points, both teams, half—170 (Philadelphia 90, Cincinnati 80), Philadelphia, 1971
Longest winning streak—33, Los Angeles, 1971–72
Longest losing streak—20, Philadelphia, 1973
Longest winning streak at home—36, Philadelphia, 1966–67
Most games won, season—69, Los Angeles, 1971–72
Most games lost, season—73, Philadelphia, 1972–73
Highest average points per game—126.5, Denver, 1981–82

N.B.A. INDIVIDUAL RECORDS

Most points, game—100, Wilt Chamberlain, Philadelphia vs. New York at Hershey, Pa., 1962
Most points, quarter—33, George Gervin, San Antonio, 1978
Most points, half—59, Wilt Chamberlain, Philadelphia, 1962
Most free throws, game—28, Wilt Chamberlain, Philadelphia, vs. New York at Hershey, Pa. 1962
Most free throws, quarter—14, Rick Barry, San Francisco, 1966
Most free throws, half—19, Oscar Robertson, Cincinnati, 1964
Most field goals, game—28, Wilt Chamberlain, Philadelphia, 1962
Most consecutive field goals, game—18, Wilt Chamberlain, San Francisco, 1963; Wilt Chamberlain, Philadelphia, 1967
Most assists, game—29, Kevin Porter, New Jersey Nets, 1978
Most rebounds, game—55, Wilt Chamberlain, Philadelphia, 1963

NATIONAL BASKETBALL ASSOCIATION FINAL STANDING OF THE CLUBS—1981-1982

EASTERN CONFERENCE
Atlantic Division

	W	L	Pct	Scoring For	Scoring Agst
Boston Celtics	63	19	.768	112.0	105.6
Philadelphia 76ers	58	24	.707	111.2	105.5
New Jersey Nets	44	38	.537	106.7	106.0
Washington Bullets	43	39	.524	103.5	102.6
New York Knicks	33	49	.402	106.2	108.9

Central Division

	W	L	Pct	Scoring For	Scoring Agst
Milwaukee Bucks	55	27	.671	108.4	102.9
Atlanta Hawks	42	40	.512	101.0	100.5
Detroit Pistons	39	43	.476	111.1	112.0
Indiana Pacers	35	47	.427	102.2	104.0
Chicago Bulls	34	48	.415	106.6	108.6
Cleveland Cavaliers	15	67	.183	103.2	111.7

WESTERN CONFERENCE
Midwest Division

	W	L	Pct	Scoring For	Scoring Agst
San Antonio Spurs	48	34	.585	113.1	110.8
Denver Nuggets	46	36	.561	126.5	126.0
Houston Rockets	46	36	.561	105.9	105.9
Kansas City Kings	30	52	.366	107.1	110.2
Dallas Mavericks	28	54	.341	104.6	109.0
Utah Jazz	25	57	.305	110.9	116.6

Pacific Division

	W	L	Pct	Scoring For	Scoring Agst
Los Angeles Lakers	57	25	.695	114.6	109.8
Seattle SuperSonics	52	30	.634	107.3	103.1
Phoenix Suns	46	36	.561	106.2	102.7
Golden State Warriors	45	37	.549	110.9	109.8
Portland Trail Blazers	42	40	.512	109.8	109.2
San Diego Clippers	17	65	.207	108.5	115.9

N.B.A. PLAYOFFS—1982

EASTERN CONFERENCE
First Round

Washington defeated New Jersey, 2 games to 0
Philadelphia defeated Atlanta, 2 games to 0

Semifinal Round

Boston defeated Washington, 4 games to 1
Philadelphia defeated Milwaukee, 4 games to 2

Conference Finals

Philadelphia defeated Boston, 4 games to 3
May 9—Boston 121, Philadelphia 81
May 12—Philadelphia 121, Boston 113
May 15—Philadelphia 99, Boston 97
May 16—Philadelphia 119, Boston 94
May 19—Boston 114, Philadelphia 85
May 21—Boston 88, Philadelphia 75
May 23—Philadelphia 120, Boston 106

WESTERN CONFERENCE
First Round

Seattle defeated Houston, 2 games to 1
Phoenix defeated Denver, 2 games to 1

Semifinal Round

Los Angeles defeated Phoenix, 4 games to 0
San Antonio defeated Seattle, 4 games to 1

Conference Finals

Los Angeles defeated San Antonio, 4 games to 0
May 9—Los Angeles 128, San Antonio 117
May 11—Los Angeles 110, San Antonio 101
May 14—Los Angeles 118, San Antonio 108
May 15—Los Angeles 128, San Antonio 123

Championship

Los Angeles defeated Philadelphia, 4 games to 2
May 27—Los Angeles 124, Philadelphia 117[1]
May 30—Philadelphia 110, Los Angeles 94[1]
June 1—Los Angeles 129, Philadelphia 108
June 3—Los Angeles 111, Philadelphia 101
June 6—Philadelphia 135, Los Angeles 102[1]
June 8—Los Angeles 114, Philadelphia 104

1. At Philadelphia.

FIELD-GOAL LEADERS—1981-1982

(Minimum 300 FG made)

	FG	Att	Pct
Artis Gilmore, Chicago	546	837	.652
Steve Johnson, Kansas City	395	644	.613
Buck Williams, New Jersey	513	881	.582
Kareem Abdul-Jabbar, Los Angeles	753	1,301	.579
Calvin Natt, Portland	515	894	.576
Adrian Dantley, Utah	904	1,586	.570
Bernard King, Golden State	740	1,307	.566
Bobby Jones, Philadelphia	416	737	.564
Bill Cartwright, New York	390	694	.562
Jeff Ruland, Washington	420	749	.561

FREE-THROW LEADERS—1981-1982

(Minimum 125 FT made)

	FT	Att	Pct
Kyle Macy, Phoenix	152	169	.899
Charlie Criss, San Diego	141	159	.887
John Long, Detroit	238	275	.865
George Gervin, San Antonio	555	642	.864
Larry Bird, Boston	328	380	.863
James Silas, Cleveland	246	286	.860
Mike Newlin, New York	126	147	.857
Kiki Vandeweghe, Detroit	347	405	.857
Kevin Grevey, Washington	165	193	.855
Jack Sikma, Seattle	447	523	.855

LEADING SCORERS—1981–1982

	G	FG	FT	Pts	Avg
George Gervin, San Antonio	79	993	555	2,551	32.3
Moses Malone, Houston	81	945	630	2,520	31.1
Adrian Dantley, Utah	81	904	648	2,457	30.3
Alex English, Denver	82	855	372	2,082	25.4
Julius Erving, Philadelphia	81	780	411	1,974	24.4
Kareem Abdul–Jabbar, Los Angeles	76	753	312	1,818	23.9
Gus Williams, Seattle	80	773	320	1,875	23.4
Bernard King, Golden State	79	740	352	1,833	23.2
World B. Free, Golden State	78	650	479	1,789	22.9
Larry Bird, Boston	77	711	328	1,761	22.9
Dan Issel, Denver	81	651	546	1,852	22.9
John Long, Detroit	69	637	238	1,514	21.9
Kelly Tripucka, Detroit	82	636	495	1,772	21.6
Kiki Vandeweghe, Denver	82	706	347	1,760	21.5
Jay Vincent, Dallas	81	719	293	1,732	21.4
Jamaal Wilkes, Los Angeles	82	744	246	1,734	21.1
David Thompson, Portland	79	681	280	1,642	20.8

BLOCKED-SHOTS LEADERS—1981–1982

(Minimum 70 games or 100 blocked shots)

	G	No.	Avg
George Johnson, San Antonio	75	234	3.12
Wayne Rollins, Atlanta	79	224	2.84
Kareem Abdul–Jabbar, Los Angeles	76	207	2.72
Artis Gilmore, Chicago	82	221	2.70
Robert Parish, Boston	80	192	2.40
Kevin McHale, Boston	82	185	2.26
Herb Williams, Indiana	82	178	2.17
Terry Tyler, Detroit	82	160	1.95
Caldwell Jones, Philadelphia	81	146	1.80
Julius Erving, Philadelphia	81	141	1.74

ASSISTS LEADERS—1981–1982

(Minimum 70 games or 400 assists)

	G	No.	Avg.
Johnny Moore, San Antonio	79	762	9.6
Earvin Johnson, Los Angeles	78	743	9.5
Maurice Cheeks, Philadelphia	79	667	8.4
Nate Archibald, Boston	68	541	8.0
Norm Nixon, Los Angeles	82	652	8.0
Isiah Thomas, Detroit	72	565	7.8
Rickey Green, Utah	81	630	7.8
Geoff Huston, Cleveland	78	590	7.6
Kelvin Ransey, Portland	78	555	7.1
Michael Ray Richardson, New York	82	572	7.0

STEALS LEADERS—1981–1982

(Minimum 70 games or 125 steals)

	G	No.	Avg
Earvin Johnson, Los Angeles	78	208	2.67
Maurice Cheeks, Philadelphia	79	209	2.65
Michael Ray Richardson, New York	82	213	2.60
Quinn Buckner, Milwaukee	70	174	2.49
Ray Williams, New Jersey	82	199	2.43
Rickey Green, Utah	81	185	2.28
Gus Williams, Seattle	80	172	2.15
Isiah Thomas, Detroit	72	150	2.08
Johnny Moore, San Antonio	79	163	2.06
Don Buse, Indiana	82	164	2.00

3-POINT FIELD-GOAL LEADERS—1981–1982

(Minimum 25 made)

	FG	Att	Pct
Campy Russell, New York	25	57	.439
Andrew Toney, Philadelphia	25	59	.424
Kyle Macy, Phoenix	39	100	.390
Brian Winters, Milwaukee	36	93	.387
Don Buse, Indiana	73	189	.386
Mike Dunleavy, Houston	33	86	.384
Mark Aquirre, Dallas	25	71	.352
Kevin Grevey, Washington	28	82	.341
Mike Bratz, San Antonio	46	138	.333
Joey Hassett, Golden State	71	214	.332

REBOUND LEADERS—1981–1982

(Minimum 70 games or 800 rebounds)

	G	Off	Def	Total	Avg
Moses Malone, Houston	81	558	630	1,188	14.7
Jack Sikma, Seattle	82	223	815	1,038	12.7
Buck Williams, New Jersey	82	347	658	1,005	12.3
David Thompson, Portland	79	258	663	921	11.7
Maurice Lucas, New York	80	274	629	903	11.3
Phil Smith, Golden State	74	279	534	813	11.0
Larry Bird, Boston	77	200	637	837	10.9
Robert Parish, Boston	80	288	578	866	10.8
Artis Gilmore, Chicago	82	224	611	835	10.2
Leonard Robinson, Phoenix	74	202	519	721	9.7

N.B.A. ALL-STAR TEAM—1982

First Team	Pos.	Second Team
Larry Bird, Boston	F	Alex English, Denver
Julius Erving, Philadelphia	F	Bernard King, Golden State
Moses Malone, Houston	C	Robert Parish, Boston
George Gervin, San Antonio	G	Earvin (Magic) Johnson, Los Angeles
Gus Williams, Seattle	G	Sidney Moncrief, Milwaukee

ARCHERY

NATIONAL ARCHERY ASSOCIATION CHAMPIONSHIPS

(Oxford, Ohio, Aug. 2–6, 1982)

Men's Division	Pts
Richard McKinney, Glendale, Ariz.	2,616
Edwin Eliason, Seattle	2,571
Philip Hoelle, Smithtown, N.Y.	2,523
Larry Smith, Shrewsbury, Pa.	2,523
Gerry Pylypchuk, Brooklyn, N.Y.	2,514

Women's Division	Pts
Luann Ryon, Riverside, Calif.	2,541
Ruth Rowe, Gaithersburg, Md.	2,511
Nanby Myrick, Huntington Beach, Calif.	2,487
Trena King, Cutlerville, Mich.	2,487
Eileen Pylypchuck, Brooklyn, N.Y.	2,483

Other Champions	Pts
Intermediate boys—Johnny Kazak, Aurora, Ill.	2,449
Intermediate girls—Becky Liggett, Muncie, Ind.	2,466
Junior boys—James Swanson, Brighton, Mich.	2,428
Junior girls—Angela Nusz, Wrightsville, Pa.	2,314
Cadet boys—Scott Raunigk, Wilmington, Del.	2,543
Cadet girls—Lara Corya, Anderson, Ind.	2,213

Crossbow	Pts
Men's division—Ervin Myers, Dallastown, Pa.	3,361
Women's division—Carol Pelosi, Greenbelt, Md.	3,260
King's round—Ervin Myers	56
Queen's round—Carol Pelosi	36

HOCKEY

Ice hockey, by birth and upbringing a Canadian game, is an offshoot of field hockey. Some historians say that the first ice hockey game was played in Montreal in December 1879 between two teams composed almost exclusively of McGill University students, but others assert that earlier hockey games took place in Kingston, Ontario, or Halifax, Nova Scotia. In the Montreal game of 1879, there were fifteen players on a side, who used an assortment of crude sticks to keep the puck in motion. Early rules allowed nine men on a side, but the number was reduced to seven in 1886 and later to six.

The first governing body of the sport was the Amateur Hockey Association of Canada, organized in 1887. In the winter of 1894–95, a group of college students from the United States visited Canada and saw hockey played. They became enthused over the game and introduced it as a winter sport when they returned home. The first professional league was the International Hockey League, which operated in northern Michigan in 1904–06.

Until 1910, professionals and amateurs were allowed to play together on "mixed teams," but this arrangement ended with the formation of the first "big league," the National Hockey Association, in eastern Canada in 1910. The Pacific Coast League was organized in 1911 for western Canadian hockey. The league included Seattle and later other American cities. The National Hockey League replaced the National Hockey Association in 1917. Boston, in 1924, was the first American city to join that circuit. The league expanded to include western cities in 1967. The Stanley Cup was competed for by "mixed teams" from 1894 to 1910, thereafter by professionals. It was awarded to the winner of the N.H.L. playoffs from 1926–67 and now to the league champion. The World Hockey Association was organized in October 1972 and was dissolved after the 1978–79 season when the N.H.L. absorbed four of the teams.

STANLEY CUP WINNERS

Emblematic of World Professional Championship; N.H.L. Championship after 1967

1894	Montreal A.A.A.
1895	Montreal Victorias
1896	Winnipeg Victorias
1897–99	Montreal Victorias
1900	Montreal Shamrocks
1901	Winnipeg Victorias
1902	Montreal A.A.A.
1903–05	Ottawa Silver Seven
1906	Montreal Wanderers
1907	Kenora Thistles[1]
1907	Mont. Wanderers[2]
1908	Montreal Wanderers
1909	Ottawa Senators
1910	Montreal Wanderers
1911	Ottawa Senators
1912–13	Quebec Bulldogs
1914	Toronto
1915	Vancouver Millionaires
1916	Montreal Canadiens
1917	Seattle Metropolitans
1918	Toronto Arenas
1919	No champion
1920–21	Ottawa Senators
1922	Toronto St. Patricks
1923	Ottawa Senators
1924	Montreal Canadiens
1925	Victoria Cougars
1926	Montreal Maroons
1927	Ottawa Senators
1928	N.Y. Rangers
1929	Boston Bruins
1930–31	Montreal Canadiens
1932	Toronto Maple Leafs
1933	N.Y. Rangers
1934	Chicago Black Hawks
1935	Montreal Maroons
1936–37	Detroit Red Wings
1938	Chicago Black Hawks
1939	Boston Bruins
1940	N.Y. Rangers
1941	Boston Bruins
1942	Toronto Maple Leafs
1943	Detroit Red Wings
1944	Montreal Canadiens
1945	Toronto Maple Leafs
1946	Montreal Canadiens
1947–49	Toronto Maple Leafs
1950	Detroit Red Wings
1951	Toronto Maple Leafs
1952	Detroit Red Wings
1953	Montreal Canadiens
1954–55	Detroit Red Wings
1956–60	Montreal Canadiens
1961	Chicago Black Hawks
1962–64	Toronto Maple Leafs
1965–66	Montreal Canadiens
1967	Toronto Maple Leafs
1968–69	Montreal Canadiens
1970	Boston Bruins
1971	Montreal Canadiens
1972	Boston Bruins
1973	Montreal Canadiens
1974–75	Philadelphia Flyers
1976–79	Montreal Canadiens
1980–82	New York Islanders

1. January. 2. March.

NATIONAL HOCKEY LEAGUE YEARLY TROPHY WINNERS

The Hart Trophy—Most Valuable Player

1924	Frank Nighbor, Ottawa
1925	Billy Burch, Hamilton
1926	Nels Stewart, Montreal Maroons
1927	Herb Gardiner, Montreal Canadiens
1928	Howie Morenz, Montreal Canadiens
1929	Roy Worters, New York Americans
1930	Nels Stewart, Montreal Maroons
1931–32	Howie Morenz, Montreal Canadiens
1933	Eddie Shore, Boston
1934	Aurel Joliat, Montreal Canadiens
1935–36	Eddie Shore, Boston
1937	Babe Siebert, Montreal Canadiens
1938	Eddie Shore, Boston
1939	Toe Blake, Montreal Canadiens
1940	Ebbie Goodfellow, Detroit
1941	Bill Cowley, Boston
1942	Tom Anderson, New York Americans
1943	Bill Cowley, Boston
1944	Babe Pratt, Toronto
1945	Elmer Lach, Montreal Canadiens
1946	Max Bentley, Chicago
1947	Maurice Richard, Montreal Canadiens
1948	Buddy O'Connor, New York Rangers
1949	Sid Abel, Detroit
1950	Chuck Rayner, New York Rangers
1951	Milt Schmidt, Boston
1952–53	Gordon Howe, Detroit
1954	Al Rollins, Chicago
1955	Ted Kennedy, Toronto
1956	Jean Beliveau, Montreal Canadiens
1957–58	Gordon Howe, Detroit
1959	Andy Bathgate, New York Rangers
1960	Gordon Howe, Detroit
1961	Bernie Geoffrion, Montreal Canadiens
1962	Jacques Plante, Montreal Canadiens
1963	Gordon Howe, Detroit
1964	Jean Beliveau, Montreal Canadiens
1965–66	Bobby Hull, Chicago
1967–68	Stan Mikita, Chicago
1969	Phil Esposito, Boston

1970–72	Bobby Orr, Boston
1973	Bobby Clarke, Philadelphia
1974	Phil Esposito, Boston
1975–76	Bobby Clarke, Philadelphia
1977–78	Guy Lafleur, Montreal
1979	Bryan Trottier, N.Y. Islanders
1980	Wayne Gretzky, Edmonton
1981	Wayne Gretzky, Edmonton
1982	Wayne Gretzky, Edmonton

Vezina Trophy—Leading Goalkeeper

1956–60	Jacques Plante, Montreal
1961	Johnny Bower, Toronto
1962	Jacques Plante, Montreal
1963	Glenn Hall, Chicago
1964	Charlie Hodge, Montreal
1965	Terry Sawchuk–Johnny Bower, Toronto
1966	Lorne Worsley–Charlie Hodge, Montreal
1967	Glenn Hall–Denis DeJordy, Chicago
1968	Lorne Worsley–Rogatien Vachon, Montreal
1969	Glenn Hall–Jacques Plante, St. Louis
1970	Tony Esposito, Chicago
1971	Ed Giacomin–Gilles Villemure, New York
1972	Tony Esposito–Gary Smith, Chicago
1973	Ken Dryden, Montreal
1974	Bernie Parent, Philadelphia, and Tony Esposito, Chicago
1975	Bernie Parent, Philadelphia
1976	Ken Dryden, Montreal
1977–79	Ken Dryden–Michel Larocque, Montreal
1980	Bob Sauve–Don Edwards, Buffalo
1981	Richard Sevigny, Denis Herron and Michel Larocque, Montreal
1982	Billy Smith, New York Islanders

James Norris Trophy—Defenseman

1954	Red Kelly, Detroit
1955–58	Doug Harvey, Montreal
1959	Tom Johnson, Montreal
1960–62	Doug Harvey, Montreal, New York (62)
1963–65	Pierre Pilote, Chicago
1966	Jacques Laperriere, Montreal
1967	Harry Howell, New York
1968–75	Bobby Orr, Boston
1976	Denis Potvin, N.Y. Islanders
1977	Larry Robinson, Montreal
1978	Denis Potvin, N.Y. Islanders
1980	Larry Robinson, Montreal
1981	Randy Carlyle, Pittsburgh
1982	Doug Wilson, Chicago

Lady Byng Trophy—Sportsmanship

1960	Don McKenney, Boston
1961	Red Kelly, Detroit
1962–63	Dave Keon, Toronto
1964	Ken Wharram, Chicago
1965	Bobby Hull, Chicago
1966	Alex Delvecchio, Detroit
1967–68	Stan Mikita, Chicago
1969	Alex Delvecchio, Detroit
1970	Phil Goyette, St. Louis
1971	John Bucyk, Boston
1972	Jean Ratelle, New York
1973	Gil Perreault, Buffalo
1974	John Buyck, Boston
1975	Marcel Dionne, Detroit
1976	Jean Ratelle, N.Y. Rangers–Boston
1977	Marcel Dionne, Los Angeles
1978	Butch Goring, Los Angeles
1979	Bob MacMillan, Atlanta
1980	Wayne Gretzky, Edmonton
1981	Rick Kehoe, Pittsburgh
1982	Rick Middleton, Boston

Calder Trophy—Rookie

1962	Bobby Rousseau, Montreal
1963	Kent Douglas, Toronto
1964	Jacques Laperriere, Montreal
1965	Roger Crozier, Detroit
1966	Brit Selby, Toronto
1967	Bobby Orr, Boston
1968	Derek Sanderson, Boston
1969	Danny Grant, Minnesota
1970	Tony Esposito, Chicago
1971	Gilbert Perreault, Buffalo
1972	Ken Dryden, Montreal
1973	Steve Vickers, New York Rangers
1974	Denis Potvin, N.Y. Islanders
1975	Eric Vail, Atlanta
1976	Bryan Trottier, N.Y. Islanders
1977	Willi Plett, Atlanta
1978	Mike Bossy, N.Y. Islanders
1979	Bobby Smith, Minnesota
1980	Ray Bourque, Boston
1981	Peter Stastny, Quebec
1982	Dale Hawerchuk, Winnipeg

Art Ross Trophy—Leading scorer

1955	Bernie Geoffrion, Montreal
1956	Jean Beliveau, Montreal
1957	Gordie Howe, Detroit
1958–59	Dickie Moore, Montreal
1960	Bobby Hull, Chicago
1961	Bernie Geoffrion, Montreal
1962	Bobby Hull, Chicago
1963	Gordie Howe, Detroit
1964–65	Stan Mikita, Chicago
1966	Bobby Hull, Chicago
1967–68	Stan Mikita, Chicago
1969	Phil Esposito, Boston
1970	Bobby Orr, Boston
1971–74	Phil Esposito, Boston
1975	Bobby Orr, Boston
1976–78	Guy Lafleur, Montreal
1979	Bryan Trottier, N.Y. Islanders
1980	Marcel Dionne, Los Angeles
1981	Wayne Gretzky, Edmonton
1982	Wayne Gretzky, Edmonton

N.H.L. CHAMPIONS

Prince of Wales Trophy

1939	Boston
1940	Boston
1941	Boston
1942	New York
1943	Detroit
1944–47	Montreal
1948	Toronto
1948–55	Detroit
1956	Montreal
1957	Detroit
1958–62	Montreal
1963	Toronto
1964	Montreal
1965	Detroit
1966	Montreal
1967	Chicago

Eastern Division

1968–69	Montreal
1970	Chicago
1971	Boston
1972	Boston
1973	Montreal
1974	Boston

Prince of Wales Conference

1975	Buffalo
1976–79	Montreal
1980	Buffalo
1981	Montreal
1982	New York Islanders

CAMPBELL BOWL
Western Division

1968	Philadelphia
1969	St. Louis
1970	St. Louis
1971–73	Chicago
1974	Philadelphia

Clarence Campbell Conference

1975	Philadelphia
1976–77	Philadelphia
1978–79	N.Y. Islanders
1980	Philadelphia
1981	New York Islanders
1982	Edmonton

NATIONAL HOCKEY LEAGUE
Final Standing of the Clubs—1981–1982

PRINCE OF WALES CONFERENCE
Patrick Division

	W	L	T	GF	GA	Pts
New York Islanders	54	16	10	385	250	118
New York Rangers	39	27	14	316	306	92
Philadelphia Flyers	38	31	11	325	313	87
Pittsburgh Penguins	31	36	13	310	337	75
Washington Capitals	26	41	13	319	338	65

Adams Division

	W	L	T	GF	GA	Pts
Montreal Canadiens	46	17	17	360	223	109
Boston Bruins	43	27	10	323	285	96
Buffalo Sabres	39	26	15	307	273	93
Quebec Nordiques	33	31	16	356	345	82
Hartford Whalers	21	41	18	264	351	60

CLARENCE CAMPBELL CONFERENCE
Norris Division

	W	L	T	GF	GA	Pts
Minnesota North Stars	37	23	20	346	288	94
Winnipeg Jets	33	33	14	319	332	80
St. Louis Blues	32	40	8	315	349	72
Chicago Black Hawks	30	38	12	332	363	72
Toronto Maple Leafs	20	44	16	298	380	56
Detroit Red Wings	21	47	12	271	350	54

Smythe Division

	W	L	T	GF	GA	Pts
Edmonton Oilers	48	17	15	417	295	111
Vancouver Canucks	30	33	17	290	286	77
Calgary Flames	29	34	17	334	345	75
Los Angeles Kings	24	41	15	314	369	63
Colorado Rockies	18	49	13	241	362	49

Stanley Cup Playoffs—1982

Preliminary Round

New York Islanders defeated Pittsburgh Penguins, 3 games to 2
New York Rangers defeated Philadelphia Flyers, 3 games to 1
Quebec Nordiques defeated Montreal Canadiens, 3 games to 2
Boston Bruins defeated Buffalo Sabres, 3 games to 1
Vancouver Canucks defeated Calgary Flames, 3 games to 0
Chicago Black Hawks defeated Minnesota North Stars, 3 games to 1
St. Louis Blues defeated Winnipeg Jets, 3 games to 1
Los Angeles Kings defeated Edmonton Oilers, 3 games to 2

Quarterfinal Round

New York Islanders defeated New York Rangers, 4 games to 2
Chicago defeated St. Louis, 4 games to 2
Vancouver defeated Los Angeles, 4 games to 1
Quebec defeated Boston, 4 games to 3

Semifinal Round

New York Islanders defeated Quebec, 4 games to 0
April 27—New York 4, Quebec 1[1]
April 29—New York 5, Quebec 2[1]
May 1—New York 5, Quebec 4 (overtime)
May 4—New York 4, Quebec 2
1. At Nassau Coliseum, Uniondale, New York.

Vancouver defeated Chicago, 4 games to 1
April 27—Vancouver 2, Chicago 1 (2 overtimes)[1]
April 29—Chicago 4, Vancouver 1[1]
May 1—Vancouver 4, Chicago 3
May 4—Vancouver 5, Chicago 3
May 6—Vancouver 6, Chicago 2[1]
1. At Chicago.

Championship

New York Islanders defeated Vancouver, 4 games to 0
May 8—New York 6, Vancouver 5 (overtime)[1]
May 11—New York 6, Vancouver 4[1]
May 13—New York 3, Vancouver 0
May 16—New York 3, Vancouver 1
1. At Nassau Coliseum, Uniondale, New York.

N.H.L. LEADING SCORERS—1981–1982

	GP	G	A	Pts
Wayne Gretzky, Edmonton	80	92	120	212
Mike Bossy, New York Islanders	80	64	83	147
Peter Stastny, Quebec	80	46	93	139
Dennis Maruk, Washington	80	60	76	136
Bryan Trottier, N.Y. Islanders	80	50	79	129
Denis Savard, Chicago	80	32	87	119
Marcel Dionne, Los Angeles	78	50	67	117
Bobby Smith, Minnesota	80	43	71	114
Dino Ciccarelli, Minnesota	76	55	52	107
Dave Taylor, Los Angeles	78	39	67	106
Glenn Anderson, Edmonton	80	38	67	105
Dale Hawerchuk, Winnipeg	80	45	58	103
Mike Rogers, New York Rangers	80	38	65	103
Neal Broten, Minnesota	73	38	59	97
Real Cloutier, Quebec	67	37	60	97
Rick Middleton, Boston	75	51	43	94
John Tonelli, N.Y. Islanders	80	35	58	93
Barry Pederson, Boston	80	44	48	92
Ken Linseman, Philadelphia	79	24	68	92
Bernie Federko, St. Louis	74	30	62	92
Morris Lukowich, Winnipeg	77	43	49	92
Blaine Stoughton, Hartford	80	52	39	91
Brian Propp, Philadelphia	80	44	47	91

N.H.L. ALL-STAR TEAMS—1982

First Team	Pos.	Second Team
Billy Smith, New York Islanders	G	Grant Fuhr, Edmonton
Doug Wilson, Chicago	D	Paul Coffey, Edmonton
Ray Bourque, Boston	D	Brian Engblom, Montreal
Wayne Gretzky,	C	Bryan Trottier,

Edmonton		New York Islanders
Mark Messier, Edmonton	LW	John Tonelli, New York Islanders
Mike Bossy, New York Islanders	RW	Rick Middleton, Boston

OTHER N.H.L. AWARDS—1982

Selke (Best defensive forward)—Steve Kasper, Boston
Smythe (Most valuable in playoffs)—Mike Bossy, New York Islanders

N.H.L. LEADING GOALTENDERS—1981–1982

	G	Min	GA	Avg
Denis Herron, Montreal	27	1,547	68	2.64
Rick Wamsley, Montreal	38	2,206	101	2.75
Bill Smith, New York Islanders	46	2,685	133	2.97
Roland Melanson, N.Y. Islanders	36	2,115	114	3.23
Grant Fuhr, Edmonton	48	2,847	157	3.31
Richard Brodeur, Vancouver	52	3,010	168	3.35
Mario Baron, Boston	44	2,515	144	3.44
Gilles Meloche, Minnesota	51	3,026	175	3.47
Don Edwards, Buffalo	62	3,500	205	3.51
Ed Mio, New York Rangers	25	1,500	89	3.56
Rogie Vachon, Boston	38	2,165	132	3.66
Don Beaupre, Minnesota	29	1,634	101	3.71
Pete Peeters, Philadelphia	44	2,591	160	3.71
Steve Weeks, N.Y. Rangers	49	2,852	179	3.77

Top Team Averages

Montreal (Holden, Herron, Wamsley Sevigny)	80	4,800	223	2.79
New York Islanders (Smith, Melanson)	80	4,800	250	3.13

N.H.L. CAREER SCORING LEADERS

(Listed in order of total points scored; figures in parentheses indicate the top 10 in goals scored)

	Yrs	Games	G	A	Pts
Gordie Howe (1)	26	1,767	801	1,049	1,850
Phil Esposito (2)	18	1,282	717	873	1,590
Stan Mikita (6)	22	1,394	541	926	1,467
John Bucyk (4)	23	1,540	556	813	1,369
Alex Delvecchio	24	1,549	456	825	1,281
Jean Ratelle (9)	21	1,281	491	776	1,267
Norm Ullman (10)	20	1,410	490	739	1,229
Jean Beliveau (8)	20	1,125	507	712	1,219
Marcel Dionne[1]	11	857	488	692	1,180
Bobby Hull (3)	16	1,063	610	560	1,170
Frank Mahovlich (7)	18	1,181	533	570	1,103
Guy Lafleur[1]	11	794	459	636	1,095
Bobby Clarke[1]	13	991	318	747	1,065
Henri Richard	20	1,256	358	688	1,046
Rod Gilbert	18	1,065	406	615	1,021
Gil Perreault[1]	12	871	391	610	1,001
Dave Keon[1]	18	1,296	396	590	986
Andy Bathgate	17	1,069	349	624	973
Maurice Richard (5)	18	978	544	421	965
Darryl Sittler[1]	12	879	403	545	948
Bobby Orr	12	657	207	645	915

1. Still active in N.H.L.

AMATEUR LEAGUES—1982

International League—Regular season: Toledo. Playoffs: Toledo defeated Saginaw, 4 games to 1, in final.
Western League—Regular season: Eastern Division: Lethbridge; Western Division: Portland. Playoffs: Portland defeated Regina, 4 games to 1, in final.
Ontario Major League—Regular season: Leyden Division: Ottawa; Emms Division: Kitchener. Playoffs: Kitchener defeated Ottawa 9-1 in points (Kitchener won 4 games and 1 was tied in final 5–game series).
Quebec Major League—Regular season: Sherbrooke. Playoffs: Sherbrooke defeated T-Rivieres, 4 games to 0, in final.
Memorial Cup—Kitchener.

MINOR LEAGUE HOCKEY CHAMPIONS

American League—1982

	W	L	T	GF	GA	Pts
Northern Division						
New Brunswick Hawks	48	21	11	338	227	107
Maine Mariners	47	26	7	325	272	101
Nova Scotia Voyageurs	35	35	10	330	313	80
Springfield Indians	32	43	5	278	319	69
Fredericton Express	20	55	5	275	408	45
Southern Division						
Binghamton Dusters	46	28	6	329	266	98
Rochester Americans	40	31	9	325	286	89
New Haven Nighthawks	39	33	8	292	276	86
Hershey Bears	36	38	6	316	347	78
Adirondack Red Wings	34	37	9	299	285	77
Erie Blades	22	52	6	317	425	50

CALDER CUP PLAYOFFS
Quarterfinals

New Brunswick defeated Adirondack, 3 games to 2
Nova Scotia defeated Maine, 3 games to 1
Binghamton defeated Hershey, 3 games to 2
Rochester defeated New Haven, 3 games to 1

Semifinals

Binghamton defeated Rochester, 4 games to 1
New Brunswick defeated Nova Scotia, 4 games to 1

Final

New Brunswick defeated Binghamton, 4 games to 1

Central League—1981–1982

	W	L	T	GF	GA	Pts
Northern Division						
Salt Lake City Golden Eagles	47	30	3	368	329	97
Cincinnati Tigers	46	30	4	375	340	96
Indianapolis Checkers	42	33	5	319	259	89
Nashville South Stars	41	35	4	313	319	86
South Division						
Wichita Wind	44	33	3	343	289	91
Tulsa Oilers	43	36	1	355	324	87
Dallas Black Hawks	37	37	6	394	382	80
Oklahoma City Stars	25	54	1	300	397	51
Fort Worth Texans	20	57	3	273	401	43

ADAMS CUP PLAYOFFS
Semifinals

Dallas defeated Salt Lake City, 4 games to 2
Indianapolis defeated Wichita, 4 games to 0

Final

Indianapolis defeated Dallas, 4 games to 2

COLLEGE CHAMPIONS—1982

N.C.A.A. Division I (Providence, R.I.)—Final: North Dakota defeated Wisconsin, 5–2. Third place: Northeastern defeated New Hampshire, 10–4. Semifinals: North Dakota defeated Northeastern, 6–2; Wisconsin defeated New Hampshire, 5–0.

E.C.A.C. Division I—Final: Northeastern defeated Harvard, 5–2. Semifinals: Northeastern defeated New Hampshire, 4–2; Harvard defeated Clarkson, 7–1. Quarterfinals: Clarkson defeated Colgate, 7–4; Northeastern defeated St. Lawrence, 5–3; New Hampshire defeated Providence, 4–2; Harvard defeated Boston College, 2–0.

C.C.H.A.—Final: Michigan State defeated Notre Dame, 4–1. Third place: Bowling Green defeated Michigan Tech, 2–1. Semifinals: Notre Dame defeated Bowling Green, 8–5; Michigan State defeated Michigan Tech, 3–2.

W.C.H.A.—Final: Wisconsin defeated North Dakota in two-game total-goals series, 12–1.

BOWLING

AMERICAN BOWLING CONGRESS CHAMPIONS

Year	Singles	All-events	Year	Singles	All-events
1959	Ed Lubanski	Ed Lubanski	1971	Al Cohn	Al Cohn
1960	Paul Kulbaga	Vince Lucci	1972	Bill Pointer	Mac Lowry
1961	Lyle Spooner	Luke Karen	1973	Ed Thompson	Ron Woolet
1962	Andy Renaldo	Billy Young	1974	Gene Krause	Bob Hart
1963	Fred Delello	Bus Owalt	1975	Jim Setser	Bobby Meadows
1964	Jim Stefanich	Les Zikes, Jr.	1976	Mike Putzer	Jim Lindquist
1965	Ken Roeth	Tom Hathaway	1977	Frank Gadaleto	Bud Debenham
1966	Don Chapman	John Wilcox	1978	Rich Mersek	Chris Cobus
1967	Frank Perry	Gary Lewis	1979	Rick Peters	Bob Basacchi
1968	Wayne Kowalski	Vince Mazzanti	1980	Mike Eaton	Steve Fehr
1969	Greg Campbell	Eddie Jackson	1981	Rob Vital	Rod Toft
1970	Jake Yoder	Mike Berlin	1982	Bruce Bohm	Rich Wonders

PROFESSIONAL BOWLERS ASSOCIATION

National Championship Tournament

1960	Don Carter	1966	Wayne Zahn	1972	Johnny Guenther	1978	Warren Nelson
1961	Dave Soutar	1967	Dave Davis	1973	Earl Anthony	1979	Mike Aulby
1962	Carmen Salvino	1968	Wayne Zahn	1974	Earl Anthony	1980	Johnny Petraglia
1963	Billy Hardwick	1969	Mike McGrath	1975	Earl Anthony	1981	Earl Anthony
1964	Bob Strampe	1970	Mike McGrath	1976	Paul Colwell	1982	Earl Anthony
1965	Dave Davis	1971	Mike Lemongello	1977	Tommy Hudson		

BOWLING PROPRIETORS' ASSOCIATION OF AMERICA—MEN

United States Open[1]

1971	Mike Lemongello	1974	Larry Laub	1977	Johnny Petraglia	1980	Steve Martin
1972	Don Johnson	1975	Steve Neff	1978	Nelson Burton, Jr.	1981	Marshall Holman
1973	Mike McGrath	1976	Paul Moser	1979	Joe Berardi	1982	Dave Husted

1. Replaced All-Star tournament and is rolled as part of B.P.A. tour.

WOMEN'S INTERNATIONAL BOWLING CONGRESS CHAMPIONS

Year	Singles	All-events	Year	Singles	All-events
1959	Mae Bolt	Pat McBride	1971	Mary Scruggs	Lorrie Nichols
1960	Marge McDaniels	Judy Roberts	1972	D. D. Jacobson	Mildred Martorella
1961	Elaine Newton	Evelyn Teal	1973	Bobby Buffaloe	Toni Calvery
1962	Martha Hoffman	Flossie Argent	1974	Shirley Garms	Judy C. Soutar
1963	Dot Wilkinson	Helen Shablis	1975	Barbara Leicht	Virginia Norton
1964	Jean Havlish	Jean Havlish	1976	Bev Shonk	Betty Morris
1965	Doris Rudell	Donna Zimmerman	1977	Akiko Yamaga	Akiko Yamaga
1966	Gloria Bouvia	Kate Helbig	1978	Mae Bolt	Annese Kelly
1967	Gloria Paeth	Carol Miller	1979	Betty Morris	Betty Morris
1968	Norma Parks	Susie Reichley	1980	Betty Morris	Cheryl Robinson
1969	Joan Bender	Helen Duval	1981	Virginia Norton	Virginia Norton
1970	Dorothy Fothergill	Dorothy Fothergill	1982	Gracie Freeman	Aleta Rzepecki

WIBC QUEENS TOURNAMENT CHAMPIONS

1961	Janet Harman	1967	Mildred Martorella	1973	Dorothy Fothergill	1979	Donna Adamek
1962	Dorothy Wilkinson	1968	Phyllis Massey	1974	Judy Soutar	1980	Donna Adamek
1963	Irene Monterosso	1969	Ann Feigel	1975	Cindy Powell	1981	Katsuko Sugimoto
1964	D.D. Jacobson	1970	Mildred Martorella	1976	Pamela Buckner	1982	Katsuko Sugimoto
1965	Betty Kuczynski	1971	Mildred Martorella	1977	Dana Stewart		
1966	Judy Lee	1972	Dorothy Fothergill	1978	Loa Boxberger		

BOWLING PROPRIETORS' ASSOCIATION OF AMERICA—WOMEN

United States Open[1]

1971	Paula Carter	1974	Pat Costello (Calif.)	1977	Betty Morris	1980	Pat Costello (Calif.)
1972	Lorrie Nichols	1975	Paula Carter	1978	Donna Adamek	1981	Donna Adamek
1973	Mildred Martorella	1976	Patty Costello (Pa.)	1979	Diana Silva	1982	Shinobu Saitoh

1. Replaced All-Star tournament.

AMERICAN BOWLING CONGRESS TOURNAMENT—1982

(Baltimore, Md., Feb. 6-May 16, 1982)

Regular Division

Singles—Bruce Bohm, Chicago	748
Doubles—Rich Wonders, Racine, Wis., and Darold Meisel, Milwaukee	1,364
All events—Rich Wonders, Racine, Wis.	2,076
Team—Carl's Bowlers Paddock, Cincinnati	3,268
Team All events—Kender No. 1, Milwaukee	9,498
Booster Team—Charlotte B.A. No. 1, Charlotte, N.C.	2,734

MASTERS TOURNAMENT—1982

(Baltimore, Md., May 11–15, 1982)

Singles—Joe Berardi, Brooklyn, N.Y. (defeated Ted Hannahs, Zanesville, Ohio, 236–216, in final)
Third place—Sam Maccarone, Glassboro, N.J.
Fourth place—Tom Baker, Buffalo, N.Y.
Fifth place—Steve Fehr, Cincinnati

WOMEN'S INTERNATIONAL BOWLING CONGRESS—1982

(St. Louis, Mo., April 3-June 18, 1982)

Open Division

Singles—Gracie Freeman, Alexandria, Va.	652
Doubles—Tie between Pat Costello, Fremont, Calif., and Donna Adamek, Duarte, Calif., and Shirley Hintz, Merritt Island, Fla., and Lisa Wrathgeber, Palmetto, Fla.	1,264
All events—Aleta Rzepecki, Detroit, Mich.	1,905
Team—Zavakos Realtors, Dayton, Ohio	2,961

Division I

Singles—Jan Sammon, Davenport, Iowa	650
Doubles—Bridgett Basiak, Chesterton, Ind., and Donna Oldaker, Lake Station, Ind.	1,211
All events—Elmere Harrison, Chalmette, La.	1,770
Team—Century Lanes, Hampton, Va.	2,856

Division II

Singles—Sammie Gray, Martin, Tenn.	582
Doubles—Gloria Tayek, Crystal Lake, Ill., and Gayle Comerer, Elgin, Ill.	1,067
All events—Brenda Draper, Auburn, Neb.	1,672
Team—Baldwin State Bank, Baldwin City, Kan.	2,526

WIBC QUEENS TOURNAMENT—1982

Winner—Katsuko Sugimoto, Tokyo, Japan (defeated Nikki Giamulias, Vallajo, Calif., in final)

COLLEGIATE
Association of College Unions–International

(St. Louis, April 15, 1982)

Singles—Melisa Day, Ball State	575
Doubles—Melisa Day, Ball State, and Donna Kolb, Western Illinois	1,118
All events—Melisa Day, Ball State	1,698

WEIGHT LIFTING

U.S. WEIGHTLIFTING FEDERATION MEN'S NATIONAL CHAMPIONSHIPS

(Glenbrook, Ill., May 29–30, 1982)

	Snatch	C&J[1]	Total[2]
114 lb—Brian Okada, Wailuku, Hawaii	72.5	97.5	170
123 lb—Albert Hood, Los Angeles	97.5	117.5	215
132 lb—Philip Sanderson, Billings, Mont.	105	135	240
148 lb—Don Abrahamson, San Jose, Calif.	127.5	157.5	285
165 lb—Cal Schake, Butler, Pa.	147.5	167.5	315
181 lb—Curt White, Colorado Springs, Colo	150	172.5	322.5
198 lb—Kevin Winter, San Jose, Calif.	155	185	340
220 lb—Ken Clark, Pacifica, Calif.	157.5	210	367.5
242 lb—Jeff Nichels, Chicago	182.5[3]	217.5	400
Over 242 lb—Mario Martinez, San Francisco	170	210	380

1. Clean and Jerk. 2. All results in kilograms. 3. American record.

WOMEN'S NATIONAL CHAMPIONSHIPS

(St. Charles Park District, St. Charles, Ill., April 4, 1982)

	Snatch	C&J[1]	Total[2]
97 lb—Pam Bickler, Milwaukee, Wis.	32.5	42.5	75
105.8 lb—Michelle Evris, Garfield, Ohio	47.5	60	107.5
114.5 lb—Rachel Silverman, Berkeley, Calif.	52.5	65	117.5
123 lb—Mary Beth Cervenak, U.S. Air Force Base, Colo.	52.5	72.5	125
132 lb—Diane Redgate, Delaware	47.5	62.5	110
148¾ lb—Judy Glenney, Farmington, N.M.	77.5	90	167.5
165¼ lb—Karen Tarter, Harrison, N.Y.	62.5	85	147.5
181¾ lb—Mary Hyden, Jefferson City, Mo.	60	80	140
Over 181¾ lb—Lorna Griffin, Huntington Beach, Calif.	75	100	175

1. Clean and Jerk. 2. All results in kilograms.

SKIING

ALPINE WORLD CUP OVERALL WINNERS

	Men	Women	Team
1967	Jean-Claude Killy, France	Nancy Greene, Canada	France
1968	Jean-Claude Killy, France	Nancy Greene, Canada	France
1969	Karl Schranz, Austria	Gertrude Gabl, Austria	Austria
1970	Karl Schranz, Austria	Michel Jacot, France	France
1971	Gustavo Thoeni, Italy	Annemarie Proell, Austria	France
1972	Gustavo Thoeni, Italy	Annemarie Proell, Austria	France
1973	Gustavo Thoeni, Italy	Annemarie Proell Moser, Austria	Austria
1974	Piero Gros, Italy	Annemarie Proell Moser, Austria	Austria
1975	Gustavo Thoeni, Italy	Annemarie Proell Moser, Austria	Austria
1976	Ingemar Stenmark, Sweden	Rosi Mittermaier, West Germany	Austria
1977	Ingemar Stenmark, Sweden	Lise-Marie Morerod, Switzerland	Austria
1978	Ingemar Stenmark, Sweden	Hanni Wenzel, Liechtenstein	Austria
1979	Peter Luescher, Switzerland	Annemarie Proell Moser, Austria	Austria
1980	Andreas Wenzel, Liechtenstein	Hanni Wenzel, Liechtenstein	Liechtenstein
1981	Phil Mahre, United States	Marie-Theres Nadig, Switzerland	Switzerland
1982	Phil Mahre, United States	Erika Hess, Switzerland	Austria

UNITED STATES CHAMPIONSHIPS—1982

ALPINE

Men's Events

Downhill—Steve Hegg, Olympic Valley, Calif.	1:54.05
Slalom—Francois Jodoin, Ste. Adele, Quebec, Canada	1:33.90
Leading American—Felix McGrath, Norwich, Vt.	1:34.21
Giant slalom—Canceled because of bad weather	

Women's Events

Downhill—Cindy Oak, Orchard Park, N.Y.	1:15.58
Slalom—Tara McKinney, Olympic Valley, Calif.	1:29.91
Giant slalom—Canceled because of bad weather	

NORDIC

Men's Cross-Country

15 kilometers—Bill Koch, Putney, Vt.	47:11.18
30 kilometers—Stan Dunklee, Brattleboro, Vt.	1:32:38.9
50 kilometers—Tim Caldwell, Putney, Vt.	2:11:47.1
Relay—East (Bruce Likely, Dan Simoneau, Howie Bean)	1:33:23.3
Veterans 10 km—Paul Daly	30:31
Veterans 30 km—Paul Daly	1:43:28

Women's Cross-Country

5 kilometers—Lynn Spencer Galanes, Vermont	18:56.5
10 kilometers—Lynn Spencer Galanes	34:15.1
20 kilometers—Lynn Spencer Galanes	58:25.1
Relay—East (Leslie Bancroft, Beth Paxson, Lindsay Putnam)	49:18.3
Veterans 5 km—Linda Stetson, Pittsfield, Mass.	21:09
Veterans 15 km—Draha Strnad, Portchester, N.Y.	1:06.38

FREESTYLE

Men's Event

Ballet—Ian Edmondson, Grand Rapids, Mich.
Moguls—Frank Beddor III, Chanhassen, Minn.
Aerials—Wayne Hilterbrand, Salem, Ore.
Combined—Frank Beddor III

Women's Events

Ballet—Jan Bucher, Salt Lake City, Utah
Moguls—Hilary Engisch, Williston, Vt.
Aerials—Hayley Wolff, New York City
Combined—Hayley Wolff

COLLEGIATE

Men—N.C.A.A.

(Lake Placid, N.Y. March 6, 1982)

Slalom—Gale Shaw, Dartmouth
Giant Slalom—Seth Bayer, Colorado
Cross-country—Egil Nilsen, Colorado
Cross-country relay—Colorado
Team—Colorado

WORLD CHAMPIONSHIPS—1982

ALPINE

(Schladming, Austria, Jan. 31–Feb. 7, 1982)

Men's Events

Downhill—Harti Weirather, Austria	1:55.10
Slalom—Ingemar Stenmark, Sweden	1:48.48
Giant slalom—Steve Mahre, Yakima, Wash.	2:38.80
Combined—Michel Vion, France	12.64 pts

Women's Events

Downhill—Gerry Sorensen, Canada	1:37.47
Slalom—Erika Hess, Switzerland	1:41.60
Giant slalom—Erika Hess	2:37.17
Combined—Erika Hess	8.99 pts

NORDIC

(Oslo, Norway, Feb. 17–27, 1982)

Jumping

70-meter—Armin Kogler, Austria (237 ft 11 in. and 241–2)	249.3 pts
90-meter—Matti Nykanen, Finland (355–9, 336–3)	257.9 pts

Combined

70-meter jump—Hubert Schwartz, West Germany	221.7 pts
15-km cross-country—Tom Sandberg, Norway	40:06
Combined—Tom Sandberg, Norway (13th in jump, 1st in run)	426.600 pts

Men's Cross-Country

15 kilometers—Oddvar Bra, Norway	38:52.5
30 kilometers—Thomas Eriksson, Sweden	1:21:52.3
50 kilometers—Thomas Wassberg, Sweden	2:32:00.9
40-km relay—Norway and Soviet Union (tie)	1:56:27.6

Women's Cross-Country

5 kilometers—Berit Aunli, Norway	14:30.2
10 kilometers—Berit Aunli, Norway	29:25.9
20 kilometers—Raisa Smetanina, Soviet Union	1:06:16.9
20-km relay—Norway	1:02.15.9

ALPINE WORLD CUP—1982

Overall—Men

	Pts
Phil Mahre, Yakima, Wash.	309
Ingemar Stenmark, Sweden	211
Steve Mahre, Yakima, Wash.	183
Peter Mueller, Switzerland	132
8—Steve Podborski, Canada	115

Overall—Women

	Pts
Erika Hess, Switzerland	297
Irene Epple, West Germany	282
Christin Cooper, Sun Valley, Idaho	198
Maria Epple, West Germany	166
5—Cindy Nelson, Reno, Nev.	158
9—Tamara McKinney, Olympic Valley, Calif.	116

Event Leaders—Men

	Pts
Downhill—Steve Podborski,* Canada	115
2—Peter Mueller, Switzerland	115
3—Harti Weirather, Austria	97
*Won title with more finishes in top three in races.	
Slalom—Phil Mahre, Yakima, Wash.	120
2—Ingemar Stenmark, Sweden	110
3—Steve Mahre, Yakima, Wash.	92
Giant Slalom—Phil Mahre, Yakima, Wash.	105
2—Ingemar Stenmark, Sweden	101
3—Marc Girardelli, Luxembourg	77
7—Steve Mahre, Yakima, Wash.	66
Combined—Phil Mahre, Yakima, Wash.	75
2—Andreas Wenzel, Liechtenstein	60
3—Evan Hole, Norway	37

Event Leaders—Women

	Pts
Downhill—Marie Cecile Gros-Gaudenier, France	87
2—Doris de Agostini, Switzerland	84
3—Holly Flanders, Deerfield, N.H.	84
Slalom—Erika Hess, Switzerland	125
2—Ursula Konzett, Liechtenstein	100
3—Christin Cooper, Sun Valley, Idaho	88
Giant Slalom—Irene Epple, West Germany	120
2—Maria Epple, West Germany	110
3—Erika Hess, Switzerland	105
4—Tamara McKinney, Olympic Valley, Calif.	74
5—Christin Cooper, Sun Valley, Idaho	68
7—Cindy Nelson, Reno, Nev.	47
Combined—Irene Epple, West Germany	70
2—Erika Hess, Switzerland	45
3—Lea Soelkner, Austria	41

NORDIC WORLD CUP—1982

Overall-Men

	Pts
Cross-country	
1—Bill Koch, Guilford, Vt.	121
2—Thomas Wassberg, Sweden	114
3—Harri Kirvesniemi, Finland	106
Jumping	
1—Armin Kogler, Austria	189
2—Hubert Neuper, Austria	174
3—Horst Bulau, Canada	150

ALPINE NATIONS CUP—1982

	Pts
Overall—Austria	1,492
Switzerland	1,423
United States	1,196
West Germany	677
Italy	547
France	526
Liechtenstein	447
Canada	433
Sweden	362
Yugoslavia	284

WRESTLING

A.A.U. NATIONAL CHAMPIONSHIPS—1982

Freestyle

(Lincoln, Neb., April 29–May 1, 1982)

105.5 lb—Bill Rosado, Sunkist Kids
114.5 lb—Bob Weaver, New York Athletic Club
125.5 lb—Gene Mills, New York A.C.
136.5 lb—Lee Roy Smith, Cowboy Wrestling Club
149.5 lb—Andy Rein, Wisconsin Wrestling Club
163 lb—Lee Kemp, Wisconsin Wrestling Club
180.5 lb—Bruce Kinseth, Hawkeye Wrestling Club
198 lb—Bill Scherr, Nebraska Olympic Club
220 lb—Greg Gibson, United States Marines
Heavyweight—Bruce Baumgartner, New York A.C.
Team—New York A.C. (85 points)
Outstanding wrestler—Lee Roy Smith

Greco-Roman

(Cincinnati, Ohio, May 7–8, 1982)

105.5 lb—T.J. Jones, United States Navy
114.5 lb—Mark Fuller, Little C Athletic Club
125.5 lb—Dan Mello, United States Marines
136.5 lb—Frank Famiano, Adirondack 3-Style Club
149.5 lb—Doug Yeats, Canada
163 lb—John Matthews, Michigan Wrestling Club
180.5 lb—Tom Press, Minnesota Wrestling Club
198 lb—Steve Fraser, Michigan Wrestling Club
220 lb—Greg Gibson, United States Marines
Heavyweight—Pete Lee, Grand Rapids, Mich.
Team—United States Marines (58 points)
Outstanding wrestler—Dan Mello

WORLD CUP CHAMPIONSHIPS—1982

Freestyle

(Toledo, Ohio, March 27–28, 1982)

105.5 lb—Adam Cuestas, United States
114.5 lb—Joe Gonzales, United States
125.5 lb—Sergei Beloglazov, Soviet Union
136.5 lb—Viktor Alexeev, Soviet Union
149.5 lb—Makhail Kharachura, Soviet Union
163 lb—Lee Kemp, United States
180.5 lb—Mark Schultz, United States
198 lb—Clark Davis, Canada
220 lb—Magomed Magomedov, Soviet Union
Heavyweight—Salman Chasimikov, Soviet Union
Team—United States; 2. Soviet Union. 3. Canada. 4. South Korea. 5. Africa.

SPEED SKATING

U.S. OUTDOOR CHAMPIONS

Men

1959–60	Ken Bartholomew
1961	Ed Rudolph
1962	Floyd Bedbury
1963	Tom Gray
1964	Neil Blatchford
1965–66	Rich Wurster
1967	Mike Passarella
1968–70	Peter Cefalu
1971	Jack Walters
1972	Barth Levy
1973	Mike Woods
1974	Leigh Barczewski, Mike Passarella
1975	Rich Wurster
1976	John Wurster
1977	Jim Chapin
1978	Bill Heinkel
1979	Erik Henriksen
1980	Greg Oly
1981	Tom Grannes
1982	Greg Oly

Women

1960	Mary Novak
1961	Jean Ashworth
1962	Jean Omelenchuk
1963	Jean Ashworth
1964	Diane White
1965	Jean Omelenchuk
1966	Diane White
1967	Jean Ashworth
1968	Helen Lutsch
1969	Sally Blatchford
1970–71	Sheila Young
1972	Ruth Moore, Nancy Thorne
1973	Nancy Class
1974	Kris Garbe
1975	Nancy Swider
1976	Connie Carpenter
1977	Liz Crowe
1978	Paula Class, Betsy Davis
1979	Gretchen Byrnes
1980	Shari Miller
1981	Lisa Merrifield
1982	Lisa Merrifield

WORLD SPEED SKATING RECORDS

Men

Distance	Time	Skater	Place	Year
500 m	0:36.91	Yevgeny Kulikov, U.S.S.R.	Alma–Ata, U.S.S.R.	1981
1,000 m	1:13.39	Gaetan Boucher, Canada	Davos, Switzerland	1981
1,500 m	1:55.18	Jan Egil Storholt, Norway	Medeo, U.S.S.R.	1977
3,000 m	4:04.01	Eric Heiden, U.S.	Inzell, Austria	1978
5,000 m	6:54.66	Aleksandr Baranov, U.S.S.R.	Alma-Ata, U.S.S.R.	1982
10,000 m	14:23.59	Thomas Gustafsson, Sweden	Oslo, Norway	1982

Women

Distance	Time	Skater	Place	Year
500 m	0:40.18	Christa Rothenburger, E. Germany	Alma-Ata, U.S.S.R.	1981
1,000 m	1:20.81	Natalya Petruseva, U.S.S.R.	Alma-Ata, U.S.S.R.	1981
1,500 m	2:05.39	Natalya Petruseva, U.S.S.R.	Alma-Ata, U.S.S.R.	1981
3,000 m	4:21.70	Gabi Schoenbrunn, E. Germany	Alma-Ata, U.S.S.R.	1981

WORLD CHAMPIONSHIPS—1982

Men

(Assen, the Netherlands, Feb. 20–21, 1982)

Champion—Hilbert van der Duim, Netherlands	168.410 pts
500 m—Gaetan Boucher, Canada	0:38.53
1,500 m—Hilbert van der Duim	2:00.59
5,000 m—Dmitri Bochkarev, Soviet Union	7:13.64
10,000 m—Dmitri Bochkarev	14:55.2

Women

(Inzell, Germany, Feb. 13–14, 1982)

Champion—Karin Busch, East Germany	168.271 pts
500 m—Karin Busch	0:40.81
1,000 m—Karin Busch	1:20.98
1,500 m—Karin Busch	2:05.79
3,000 m—Andrea Schone, East Germany	4:24.26

WORLD SPRINT CHAMPIONSHIPS—1982

(Alkmaar, the Netherlands, Feb. 6–7, 1982)

Men's champion—Sergei Khlebnikov, Soviet Union	154.250 pts
Women's champion—Natalya Petruseva, Soviet Union	167.985 pts

U.S. OUTDOOR CHAMPIONS

(St. Paul, Minn., Feb. 6–7, 1982)

Men—Greg Oly, Minneapolis, Minn.
Women—Lisa Merrifield, Butte, Mont.
Intermediate men—Michael Ralston, Streamwood, Ill.
Intermediate women—Bonnie Blair, Champaign, Ill.
Junior boys—David Silk, Butte, Mont.
Junior girls—Ann Hills, Shoreview, Minn.

U.S. INDOOR CHAMPIONS

(St. Louis, Mo., March 13–14, 1982)

Men—Tie, Jack Mortell, Evanston, Ill., and Paul Jacobs, Park Ridge, Ill.
Women—Lydia Stephans, Northbrook, Ill.
Intermediate men—Andy Gabel, Northbrook, Ill.
Intermediate women—Lisa Parfitt, Alpena, Mich.
Junior boys—Marty Pierce, St. Francis, Wis.
Junior girls—Michelle Fang, Arlington Heights, Ill.

NORTH AMERICAN OUTDOOR CHAMPIONS

(Lake Placid, N.Y., Feb. 13–14, 1982)

Men—Kevin O'Brien, Prince Edward Island
Women—Katie Class, St. Paul, Minn.
Intermediate men—Michael Ralston, Streamwood, Ill.
Intermediate women—Rhonda Reinke, Milwaukee, Wis.
Junior boys—Tony Meibock, Fairview Park, Ohio
Junior girls—Susan Auch, Manitoba, Canada

NORTH AMERICAN INDOOR CHAMPIONS

(Sherbrooke, Quebec, March 27–28, 1982)

Men—Louis Baril, Quebec, Canada
Women—Susan Hellingwerf, Quebec, Canada
Intermediate men—Robert Tremblay, Quebec, Canada
Intermediate women—Tie, Lisa Parfitt, Alpena, Mich., and M–Josee Martin, Quebec, Canada
Junior boys—Benoit Lamarche, Quebec, Canada
Junior girls—Susan Auch, Manitoba, Canada

SPORTS ORGANIZATIONS AND INFORMATION BUREAUS

Amateur Athletic Union of the U.S. 3400 West 86th St., Indianapolis, Indiana 46862
Amateur Fencers League of America. 601 Curtis St., Albany, Calif. 94706
Amateur Hockey Association of the U.S. 10 Lake Circle, Colorado Springs, Colo. 80906
Amateur Skating Union of the U.S. 4423 West Deming Place, Chicago, Ill. 60639
Amateur Softball Association. 2801 N.E. 50th St., P.O. Box 11437, Oklahoma City, Okla. 73111
Amateur Trapshooting Association of America. Vandalia, Ohio 45377
American Amateur Baseball Congress. 212 Plaza Building, 2855 W. Market St., Akron, Ohio 44313
American Association (baseball). P.O. Box 382, Wichita, Kan. 67201
American Bowling Congress. 5301 South 76th St., Greendale, Wis. 53129
American Canoe Association. P.O. Box 248, Lorton, Va. 22079
American Hockey League. 31 Elm St., Suite 533, Springfield, Mass. 01103
American Horse Shows Association. 527 Madison Ave., New York, N.Y. 10022
American Kennel Club. 51 Madison Ave., New York, N.Y. 10010
American League (baseball). 280 Park Ave., New York, N.Y. 10017
American Motorcycle Association. 33 Collingwood Rd., Westerville, Ohio, 43081
American Power Boat Association. 17640 East 9-Mile Rd., P.O. Box 377, East Detroit, Mich. 48021
American Water Ski Association. State Route 550 at Carl Floyd Road, P.O. Box 191, Winter Haven, Fla. 33880
Association of Intercollegiate Athletics for Women. 1201 16th St. N.W., Washington, D.C.
Athletics Congress, The. 3400 West 86th St., Indianapolis, Ind. 46268
Baseball Commissioner. 75 Rockefeller Plaza, New York, N.Y. 10019
Baseball Hall of Fame. Cooperstown, N.Y.
Bowling Proprietors' Association of America. P.O. Box 5802, Arlington, Texas 76011
Central Hockey League. 5740 Oakland Ave., St. Louis, Mo. 63110
Championship Auto Racing Teams (CART). 2655 Woodward Ave., Suite 275, Bloomfield Hills, Mich. 48013
Eastern College Athletic Conference. P.O. Box 3, Centerville, Mass. 02632
Elias Sports Bureau. 500 Fifth Ave., New York, N.Y. 10036
Fish and Wildlife Service. Department of the Interior, Washington, D.C. 20240
Football Hall of Fame (college). Kings Mills, Ohio 45034
Football Hall of Fame (pro). Canton, Ohio 44708
Intercollegiate (Big Ten) Conference (1896). 1111 Plaza Dr., Schaumburg, Ill. 60195
International Amateur Athletic Federation. 62 Upper Richmond Rd., Putney, London, SW15 2 SL, England
International Game Fish Association. 3000 East Las Olas Blvd., Fort Lauderdale, Fla. 33316
International League (baseball). Box 608, Grove City, Ohio 43123
International Motor Sports Association. P.O. Box 805, Fairfield, Conn. 06430
International Olympic Committee. Chateau de Vidy, Lausanne, Switzerland
The Jockey Club. 380 Madison Ave., New York, N.Y. 10017
Ladies Professional Golf Association. 919 Third Ave., New York, N.Y. 10022
Little League Baseball. Williamsport, Pa. 17701
National Archery Association. 1951 Geraldson Drive, Lancaster, Pa. 17601
National Association for Girls and Women in Sports. 1201 16th St. N.W., Washington, D.C.
National Association of Amateur Oarsmen. 4 Boathouse Row, Philadelphia, Pa. 19130
National Association of Intercollegiate Athletics. 1221 Baltimore St., Kansas City, Mo. 64105
National Association of Professional Baseball Leagues (minors). P.O. Box A, St. Petersburg, Fla. 33731
National Association for Stock Car Auto Racing. P.O. Box K, Daytona Beach, Fla. 32015
National Baseball Congress. Wichita, Kan. 67201
National Basketball Association. Olympic Tower, 645 Fifth Ave., New York, N.Y. 10022
National Collegiate Athletic Association. P.O. Box 1906, Shawnee Mission, Kan. 66222
National Duck Pin Bowling Congress. 711–14th St. N.W., Washington, D.C. 20005
National Field Archery Association. Rt. 2, Box 514, Redlands, Calif. 92373
National Football Foundation. 201 East 42nd St., New York, N.Y. 10017. *See also:* Football Hall of Fame (college)
National Football League. 410 Park Ave., New York, N.Y. 10022
National Hockey League. 922 Sun Life Bldg., Montreal, Que., Canada
National Horseshoe Pitchers Association. Route 5, Lucasville, Ohio 45648
National Hot Rod Association. P.O. Box 150, North Hollywood, Calif. 91603
National Junior College Athletic Association. P.O. Box 1586, Hutchinson, Kan. 67501
National Lawn Tennis Hall of Fame. Newport Casino, Newport, R.I., 02840
National League (baseball). 1 Rockefeller Plaza, New York, N.Y. 10019
National Rifle Association of America. 1600 Rhode Island Ave., N.W., Washington, D.C. 20036
National Skeet Shooting Association. P.O. Box 28188, San Antonio, Tex. 78228
New York Racing Association. P.O. Box 90, Jamaica, N.Y. 11417
New York State Athletic Commission (boxing). 270 Broadway, New York, N.Y.
National Shuffleboard Association. 5612 Plattsburg Road, Springfield, Ohio, 45505
North American Yacht Racing Union. *See* United States Yacht Racing Union
North American Soccer League. 1133 Avenue of the Americas, New York, N.Y. 10036
Pacific Coast League (baseball). 2509 South Shannon Drive, Tempe, Ariz., 85282
Professional Bowlers Association. 1720 Merriman Road, Akron, Ohio 44313
Professional Golfers' Association of America. Box 12458, Lake Park, Fla. 33403
Rodeo Cowboys Association. 2929 W. 19th Ave.,

Denver, Colo. 80204

Roller Skating Rink Operators Association. P.O. Box 81846, Lincoln, Neb. 68501

Sports Car Club of America. 6750 S. Emporia St., Englewood, Colo. 80112

Thoroughbred Racing Associations of the U.S. 3000 Marcus Ave., Lake Success, N.Y. 11040

Track and Field Hall of Fame. Charleston, W. Va.

United States of America Roller Skating Confederation. 7700 "A" St., Lincoln, Neb. 68501

United States Auto Club. 4910 West 16th St., Speedway, Ind. 46224

United States Badminton Association. P.O. Box 237, Swartz Creek, Mich. 48473

U.S. Chess Federation. 186 Route 9W, New Windsor, N.Y. 12550

U.S. Cycling Federation. Box 669, Wall Street Station, New York, N.Y. 10005

U.S. Figure Skating Association. Sears Crescent Building, Suite 500, City Hall, Boston, Mass. 02108

U.S. Golf Association. Far Hills, N.J. 07931

U.S. Handball Association. 4101 Dempster St., Skokie, Ill. 60077

U.S. Men's Curling Association. 12822 Water Street, Duluth, Minn., 55008

U.S. Olympic Committee. 1750 East Boulder Street, Colorado Springs, Colo. 80909

U.S. Olympic Training Center. P.O. Box 4000, Colorado Springs, Colo. 80930

U.S. Parachute Association. 806–15th St. N.W., Washington, D.C. 20005

U.S. Polo Association. 1301 W. 22nd St., Oak Brook, Ill. 60521

U.S. Ski Association. P.O. Box 100, Park City, Utah 84060

U.S. Ski Team. P.O. Box 100, Park City, Utah 84060

U.S. Soccer Federation. 350 Fifth Ave., New York, N.Y. 10001

U.S. Squash Racquets Association. 211 Ford Road, Bala-Cynwyd, Pa., 19004

U.S. Table Tennis Association. 3466 Bridgeland Drive, Bridgeland Square Building, St. Louis, Mo. 63044

U.S. Tennis Association. 51 E. 42nd St., New York, N.Y. 10017

U.S. Touch and Flag Football Association. 2705 Normandy Drive, Youngstown, Ohio, 49511

U.S. Trotting Association. 750 Michigan Ave., Columbus, Ohio 43215

U.S. Volleyball Association. 1750 East Boulder St., Colorado Springs, Colo. 80909

U.S. Women's Curling Association. 635 Chatham Road, Glenview, Ill. 60025

U.S. Yacht Racing Union. P.O. Box 209, Goat Island, Newport, R.I. 02840

Women's International Bowling Congress. 5301 S. 76th St., Greendale, Wis. 53129

STANDARD MEASUREMENTS IN SPORTS

BASEBALL

Home plate to pitcher's box: 60 feet 6 inches.

Plate to second base: 127 feet 3⅜ inches.

Distance from base to base (home plate included): 90 feet.

Size of bases: 15 inches by 15 inches.

Pitcher's plate: 24 inches by 6 inches.

Batter's box: 4 feet by 6 feet.

Home plate: 17 inches by 12 inches by 12 inches, cut to a point at rear.

Home plate to backstop: Not less than 60 feet (recommended).

Weight of ball: Not less than 5 ounces nor more than 5¼ ounces.

Circumference of ball: Not less than 9 inches nor more than 9¼ inches.

Bat: Must be round, not over 2¾ inches in diameter at thickest part, nor more than 42 inches in length, and of solid wood in one piece or laminated wood.

FOOTBALL

(N.C.A.A.)

Length of field: 120 yards. (including 10 yards of end zone at each end).

Width of field: 53⅓ yards (160 feet).

Height of goal posts: At least 20 feet.

Height of crossbar: 10 feet.

Width of goal posts (above crossbar): 23 feet 4 inches, inside to inside, and not more than 24 feet, outside to outside.

Length of ball: 10⅞ to 11 7/16 inches (long axis).

Circumference of ball: 20¾ to 21¼ inches (middle); 27¾ to 28½ inches (long axis).

LAWN TENNIS

Size of court: Rectangle 78 feet long and 27 feet wide (singles); 78 feet long and 36 feet wide (doubles).

Height of net: 3 feet in center, gradually rising to reach 3-foot 6-inch posts at a point 3 feet outside each side of court.

Ball: Shall be more than 2½ inches and less than 2⅝ inches in diameter and weight more than 2 ounces and less than 2 1/16 ounces.

Service line: 21 feet from net.

HOCKEY

Size of rink: 200 feet long by 85 feet wide surrounded by a wooden wall not less than 40 inches and not more than 48 inches above level of ice.

Size of goal: 6 feet wide by 4 feet in height.

Puck: 1 inch thick and 3 inches in diameter; made of vulcanized rubber; weight 5½ to 6 ounces.

Length of stick: Not more than 58 inches from heel to end of shaft nor 12½ inches from heel to end of blade. Blade should not be more than 3 inches in width but not less than 2 inches, except goal keeper's stick, which shall not exceed 3½ inches in width except at the heel, where it must not exceed 4½ inches.

BOWLING

Lane dimensions: Overall length 62 feet 10 3/16 inches, measuring from foul line to pit (not including tail plank), with ½ inch tolerance permitted. Foul line to center of No. 1 pinspot 60 feet, with ½ inch tolerance permitted. Lane width, 41½ inches with a tolerance of ½ inch permitted. Approach, not less than 15 feet. Gutters, 9 5/16 inches wide with 3/16 plus or 5/16 minus tolerances permitted.

Ball: Circumference, not more than 27 inches. Weight, 16 pounds maximum.

GOLF

The ball, specifications: Broadened to require that the ball be designed to perform as if it were spherically symmetrical. The weight of the ball shall not be greater than 1.620 ounces avoirdupois, and the size shall not be less than 1.680 inches in diameter.

Velocity of ball: Not greater than 250 feet per second when tested on U.S.G.A. apparatus, with 2 percent tolerance.

Hole: 4¼ inches in diameter and at least 4 inches deep.

Clubs: 14 is the maximum number permitted.

BASKETBALL

(National Collegiate A.A. Rules)

Playing court: College: 94 feet long by 50 feet wide (ideal dimensions). High School: 84 feet long by 50 feet wide (ideal inside dimensions).

Baskets: Rings 18 inches in inside diameter, with white cord 12-mesh nets, 15 to 18 inches in length. Each ring is made of metal, is not more than ⅝ of an inch in diameter, and is bright orange in color.

Height of basket: 10 feet (upper edge).

Weight of ball: Not less than 20 ounces nor more than 22.

Circumference of ball: No greater than 30 inches and not less than 29½.

Free-throw line: 15 feet from the face of the backboard, 2 inches wide.

BOXING

Ring: Professional matches take place in an area not less than 18 nor more than 24 feet square including apron. It is enclosed by four covered ropes, each not less than one inch in diameter. The floor has a 2-inch padding of Ensolite (or equivalent) underneath ring cover that extends at least 6 inches beyond the roped area in the case of elevated rings. For U.S.A./A.B.F. boxing, not less than 16 nor more than 20 feet square within the ropes. The floor must extend beyond the ring ropes not less than 2 feet. The ring posts shall be connected to the three ring ropes with the extension not shorter than 18 inches and must be properly padded.

Gloves: In professional fights, not less than 8-ounce gloves generally are used. U.S.A./A.B.F., not less than 10 ounces for all divisions; for international competition not less than 8 ounces.

FIGURE SKATING

WORLD CHAMPIONS

Men

1960	Alain Giletti, France
1961	No competition
1962	Donald Jackson, Canada
1963	Don McPherson, Canada
1964	Manfred Schnelldorfer, West Germany
1965	Alain Calmat, France
1966–68	Emmerich Danzer, Austria
1969–70	Tim Wood, United States
1971–73	Ondrej Nepela, Czechoslovakia
1974	Jan Hoffman, East Germany
1975	Sergei Yolkov, U.S.S.R.
1976	John Curry, Britain
1977	Vladimir Kovelov, U.S.S.R.
1978	Charles Tickner, United States
1979	Vladimir Kovalev, U.S.S.R.
1980	Jan Hoffman, East Germany
1981	Scott Hamilton, United States
1982	Scott Hamilton, United States

Women

1956–60	Carol Heiss, United States
1961	No competition
1962–64	Sjoukje Dijkstra, Netherlands
1965	Petra Burka, Canada
1966–68	Peggy Fleming, United States
1969–70	Gabriele Seyfert, East Germany
1971–72	Beatrix Schuba, Austria
1973	Karen Magnusson, Canada
1974	Christine Errath, East Germany
1975	Dianne de Leeuw, Netherlands
1976	Dorothy Hamill, United States
1977	Linda Fratianne, United States
1978	Anett Poetzsch, East Germany
1979	Linda Fratianne, United States
1980	Anett Poetzsch, East Germany
1981	Denise Biellmann, Switzerland
1982	Elaine Zayak, United States

U.S. CHAMPIONS

Men

1946–52	Richard Button
1953–56	Hayes Jenkins
1957–60	David Jenkins
1961	Bradley Lord
1962	Monty Hoyt
1963	Tommy Litz
1964	Scott Allen
1965	Gary Visconti
1966	Scott Allen
1967	Gary Visconti
1968–70	Tim Wood
1971	John M. Petkevich
1972	Ken Shelley
1973–75	Gordon McKellen
1976	Terry Kubicka
1977–80	Charles Tickner
1981	Scott Hamilton
1982	Scott Hamilton

Women

1943–48	Gretchen Merrill
1949–50	Yvonne Sherman
1951	Sonya Klopfer
1952–56	Tenley Albright
1957–60	Carol Heiss
1961	Laurence Owen
1962	Barbara Roles Pursley
1963	Lorraine Hanlon
1964–68	Peggy Fleming
1969–73	Janet Lynn
1974–76	Dorothy Hamill
1977–80	Linda Fratianne
1981	Elaine Zayak
1982	Rosalynn Sumners

UNITED STATES CHAMPIONS—1982

(Indianapolis, Ind., Jan. 27–30, 1982)

Men's singles—Scott Hamilton, Denver, Colo.
Women's singles—Rosalynn Sumners, Edmonds, Wash.
Pairs—Peter and Caitlin Carruthers, Wilmington, Del.
Dance—Judy Blumberg, Colorado Springs, and Michael Seibert, Indianapolis
Junior dance—Amanda Newman, Short Hills, N.J., and Jerry Santoferrara, Syracuse, N.Y.

WORLD CHAMPIONS—1982

(Copenhagen, Denmark, March 9–13, 1982)

Men's singles—Scott Hamilton, Denver, Colo.
Women's singles—Elaine Zayak, Paramus, N.J.
Pairs—Sabine Baess and Tassilo Thierbach, East Germany
Dance—Jayne Torvill and Christopher Dean, Britain

SWIMMING

WORLD RECORDS—MEN

(Through Oct. 4, 1982)
Approved by International Swimming Federation (F.I.N.A.)
(F.I.N.A. discontinued acceptance of records in yards in 1968)

Distance	Record	Holder	Country	Where Made	Date
Freestyle					
100 Meters	0:49.36	Rowdy Gaines	U.S.	Austin, Tex.	April 3, 1981
200 Meters	1:48.93	Rowdy Gaines	U.S.	Mission Viejo, Calif.	July 20, 1982
400 Meters	3:49.57	Vladimir Salnikov	U.S.S.R.	Moscow	March 12, 1982
800 Meters	7:52.83	Vladimir Salnikov	U.S.S.R.	Moscow	Feb. 15, 1982
1,500 Meters	14:56.35	Vladimir Salnikov	U.S.S.R.	Moscow	March 13, 1982
Backstroke					
100 Meters	0:55.49	John Naber	U.S.	Montreal	July 19, 1976
200 Meters	1:59.19	John Naber	U.S.	Montreal	July 24, 1976
Breaststroke					
100 Meters	1:02.53	Steve Lundquist	U.S.	Indianapolis, Ind.	Aug. 17, 1982
200 Meters	2:14.77	Victor Davis	Canada	Guayaquil, Ecuador	Aug. 5, 1982
Butterfly					
100 Meters	0:53.81	William Paulus	U.S.	Austin, Tex.	April 3, 1981
200 Meters	1:58.01	Craig Beardsley	U.S.	Kiev, U.S.S.R.	Aug. 22, 1981
Individual Medley					
200 Meters	2:02.25	Alex Baumann	Canada	Brisbane, Australia	Oct. 3, 1982
400 Meters	4:19.78	Ricardo Prado	Brazil	Guayaquil, Ecuador	Aug. 1, 1982
Freestyle Relays					
400 Meters	3:19.26	National Team	U.S.	Guayaquil, Ecuador	Aug. 7, 1982
(Chris Cavanaugh, Robin Leamy, David McCagg, Rowdy Gaines)					
800 Meters	7:20.82	National Team	U.S.	West Berlin	Aug. 24, 1978
(Bruce Furniss, Bill Forrester, Bobby Hackett, Rowdy Gaines)					
Medley Relay					
400 Meters	3:40.84	National Team	U.S.	Guayaquil, Ecuador	Aug. 7, 1982
(Rick Carey, Steve Lundquist, Matt Gribble, Rowdy Gaines)					

WORLD RECORDS—WOMEN

Distance	Record	Holder	Country	Where made	Date
Freestyle					
100 Meters	0:54.79	Barbara Krause	East Germany	Moscow	July 21, 1980
200 Meters	1:58.23	Cynthia Woodhead	U.S.	Tokyo	Sept. 3, 1979
400 Meters	4:06.28	Tracey Wickham	Australia	West Berlin	Aug. 24, 1978
800 Meters	8:24.62	Tracey Wickham	Australia	Edmonton, Canada	Aug. 5, 1978
1,500 Meters	16:04.49	Kim Linehan	U.S.	Ft. Lauderdale, Fla.	Aug. 19, 1979
Backstroke					
100 Meters	1:00.86	Rica Reinisch	East Germany	Moscow	July 23, 1980
200 Meters	2:09.91	Cornelia Sirch	East Germany	Guayaquil, Ecuador	Aug. 7, 1982
Breaststroke					
100 Meters	1:08.60	Ute Geweniger	East Germany	Split, Yugoslavia	Sept. 8, 1981
200 Meters	2:28.36	Lina Kachushite	U.S.S.R.	Potsdam	April 6, 1979
Butterfly					
100 Meters	0:57.93	Mary T. Meagher	U.S.	Brown Deer, Wis.	Aug. 16, 1981
200 Meters	2:05.96	Mary T. Meagher	U.S.	Brown Deer, Wis.	Aug. 13, 1981
Individual Medley					
200 Meters	2:11.73	Ute Geweniger	East Germany	East Berlin	July 4, 1981
400 Meters	4:36.10	Petra Schneider	East Germany	Guayaquil, Ecuador	Aug. 1, 1982

Freestyle Relay

400 Meters	3:42.71	National Team	East Germany	Moscow	July 27, 1980
800 Meters	8:07.44	Mission Viejo A	U.S.	Milwaukee	Aug. 14, 1981

Medley Relay

400 Meters	4:05.88	National Team	East Germany	Guayaquil, Ecuador	Aug. 7, 1982
(Kristin Otto, Ute Geweniger, Ines Geissler, Birgit Meineke)					

U.S. SHORT-COURSE SWIMMING RECORDS

(Listed by Amateur Athletic Union)

MEN

Freestyle

50 yards—Robin Leamy, 1981	0:19.36
100 yards—Rowdy Gaines, 1981	0:42.38
100 yards—Rowdy Gaines, 1980	0:43.16
100 yards—Andy Coan, 1979	0:43.25
100 yards—Jonty Skinner, 1978	0:43.29[1]
100 yards—Joe Bottom, 1977	0:43.49
200 yards—Rowdy Gaines, 1981	1:33.80
200 yards—Rowdy Gaines, 1980	1:34.57
200 yards—Andy Coan, 1979	1:35.62
200 yards—Jim Montgomery, 1977	1:35.67
500 yards—Brian Goodell, 1978	4:16.40
500 yards—Brian Goodell, 1979	4:16.43
1,000 yards—Jeff Kostoff, 1982	8:49.97
1,650 yards—Brian Goodell, 1979	14:47.27
1,650 yards—Rafael Escalas, 1981	14:53.90[1]
1,650 yards—Brian Goodell, 1979	14:54.13
1,650 yards—Brian Goodell, 1978	14:54.54

Backstroke

100 yards—Dave Bottom, 1982	0:48.94
100 yards—Clay Britt, 1981	0:49.08
200 yards—Wladar Sandor, 1982	1:45.22[1]
200 yards—Rick Carey, 1982	1:45.80

Breaststroke

100 yards—Steve Lundquist, 1981	0:52.93
100 yards—Steve Lundquist, 1980	0:53.59
100 yards—Steve Lundquist, 1979	0:54.08
100 yards—Graham Smith, 1977	0:54.91[1]
100 yards—Scott Spann, 1977	0:55.19
200 yards—Steve Lundquist, 1981	1:55.01
200 yards—Bill Barrett, 1980	1:58.43
200 yards—Steve Lundquist, 1979	1:59.18
200 yards—Graham Smith, 1977	2:00.05[1]
200 yards—Nick Nevid, 1978	2:00.53

Butterfly

100 yards—Scott Spann, 1981	0:47.22
100 yards—Par Arvidsson, 1980	0:47.34[1]
100 yards—Par Arvidsson, 1979	0:47.76[1]
100 yards—Joe Bottom, 1977	0:47.77
200 yards—Craig Beardsley, 1982	1:43.81
200 yards—Craig Beardsley, 1982	1:44.10
200 yards—Craig Beardsley, 1981	1:44.15
200 yards—Par Arvidsson, 1980	1:44.43[1]

Individual Medley

200 yards—Bill Barrett, 1982	1:45.00
200 yards—Bill Barrett, 1981	1:45.01
400 yards—Ricardo Prado, 1982	3:47.97[1]
400 yards—Jesse Vassallo, 1981	3:48.16

Relays

400-yard freestyle—U.C.L.A., 1982	2:53.15
400-yard freestyle—Mission Viejo, 1981	2:53.86
400-yard freestyle—Tennessee, 1979	2:54.54
400-yard freestyle—Gatorade S.C., 1978	2:55.27
800-yard freestyle—Florida Aquatic Club, 1979	6:25.42
800-yard freestyle—Auburn, 1981	6:26.49
800-yard freestyle—Florida A.C., 1978	6:29.81
400-yard medley—Texas, 1981	3:12.93
400-yard medley—California-Berkeley, 1979	3:15.22[1]
400-yard medley—Indiana, 1977	3:17.14[1]
400-yard medley—Auburn, 1977	3:17.62

WOMEN

Freestyle

50 yards—Jill Sterkel, 1981	0:22.41
100 yards—Jill Sterkel, 1982	0:48.61
100 yards—Jill Sterkel, 1980	0:48.76
100 yards—Cynthia Woodhead, 1979	0:49.39
100 yards—Jill Sterkel, 1979	0:49.55
100 yards—Tracy Caulkins, 1978	0:49.58
200 yards—Cynthia Woodhead, 1979	1:44.10
200 yards—Marybeth Linzmeier, 1982	1:45.82
500 yards—Tracy Caulkins, 1979	4:36.25
500 yards—Cynthia Woodhead, 1978	4:39.94
1,650 yards—Kim Linehan, 1979	15:49.10
1,650 yards—Cynthia Woodhead, 1978	15:55.15

Backstroke

100 yards—Sue Walsh, 1982	0:54.81
100 yards—Linda Jezek, 1978	0:54.94
200 yards—Linda Jezek, 1978	1:57.79

Breaststroke

100 yards—Tracy Caulkins, 1979	1:01.82
100 yards—Tracy Caulkins, 1979	1:02.06
100 yards—Tracy Caulkins, 1978	1:02.20
200 yards—Tracy Caulkins, 1980	2:11.46
200 yards—Tracy Caulkins, 1978	2:14.07

Butterfly

100 yards—Jill Sterkel, 1981	0:53.10
100 yards—Mary T. Meagher, 1980	0:53.18
100 yards—Jill Sterkel, 1979	0:53.76
100 yards—Diane Johannigman, 1978	0:54.11
200 yards—Mary T. Meagher, 1980	1:53.21
200 yards—Nancy Hogshead, 1978	1:55.74

Individual Medley

200 yards—Tracy Caulkins, 1979	1:57.86
200 yards—Tracy Caulkins, 1978	1:59.33
400 yards—Tracy Caulkins, 1979	4:08.09
400 yards—Tracy Caulkins, 1978	4:11.38

Relays

200-yard freestyle—Stanford, 1981	1:31.12
400-yard freestyle—Stanford, 1981	3:19.70
400-yard freestyle—Nashville A.C., 1979	3:20.51
400-yard freestyle—Nashville A.C., 1978	3:20.69
800-yard freestyle—Mission Viejo S.C., 1979	7:15.14
800-yard freestyle—U.S. Team, 1976	7:15.64
200-yard medley—Florida, 1982	1:42.10
400-yard medley—Florida, 1982	3:40.99

1. Open American record by non-U.S. competitors.

U.S. SHORT-COURSE CHAMPIONSHIPS—1982

(Gainesville, Fla., April 7–10, 1982)

INDOORS

Men's Events

50–yd freestyle—Siong Ang, Houston	0:19.86
100–yd freestyle—Rowdy Gaines, Winter Haven, Fla.	0:43.64
200–yd freestyle—Rowdy Gaines	1:35.17
500–yd freestyle—Jeff Kostoff, Upland, Calif.	4:19.39
1,000–yd freestyle—Jeff Kostoff	8:49.97[1 2]
1,650–yd freestyle—Jeff Kostoff	14:52.39
100–yd backstroke—Dave Bottom, Danville, Calif.	0:48.94[1 2]
200–yd backstroke—Sandor Wladar, Hungary	1:45.22[2]
100–yd butterfly—David Cowell, Belpre, Ohio	0:47.89
200–yd butterfly—Craig Beardsley, Harrington Park, N.J.	1:43.81[1]
100–yd breaststroke—Steve Lundquist, Jonesboro, Ga.	0:53.84
200–yd breaststroke—John Moffett, Newport Beach, Calif.	1:59.44
200–yd individual medley—Roger Von Jouanne, Southern Illinois	1:48.41
400–yd individual medley—Ricardo Prado, Mission Viejo, Calif.	3:47.97[2]
400–yd freestyle relay—Mission Viejo (Calif.) A Team	2:55.01
800–yd freestyle relay—Florida Aquatic Swim Team A (Bill Sawchuk, John Hillencamp, Steve Wood, Geoff Gaberino)	6:27.94
400–yd medley relay—Mission Viejo Nadadores A Team (Jay Yarid, Bill Barrett, Bob Placak, Robin Leamy)	3:16.22

1. American record. 2. United States Open record.

Women's Events

50–yd freestyle—Dana Torres, Tandem Swim Club, Calif.	0:22.44
100–yd freestyle—Jill Sterkel, Austin, Tex.	0:48.94
200–yd freestyle—Cynthia Woodhead, Mission Viejo, Calif.	1:45.46
500–yd freestyle—Tiffany Cohen, Mission Viejo, Calif.	4:39.97
1,000–yd freestyle—Tiffany Cohen	9:34.61
1,650–yd freestyle—Tiffany Cohen	15:58.52
100–yd backstroke—Debbie Risen, Overland Park, Kan.	0:55.49
200–yd backstroke—Tracy Caulkins, Nashville, Tenn.	1:57.77
100–yd breaststroke—Tracy Caulkins	1:02.41
200–yd breaststroke—Kim Rhodenbaugh, Cincinnati	2:14.17
100–yd butterfly—Jill Sterkel	0:53.20
200–yd butterfly—Mary T. Meagher, Louisville, Ky.	1:53.37
200–yd individual medley—Tracy Caulkins	1:58.94
400–yd freestyle relay—Mission Viejo (Calif.) A Team	3:20.68
800–yd freestyle relay—Mission Viejo Nadadores A Team (Tiffany Cohen, Marybeth Linzmeier, Julie Williams, Cynthia Woodhead)	7:10.55[1 2]
400–yd medley relay—Nashville A Team (Amy Caulkins, Tracy Caulkins, Patty King, Libby Pruden)	3:44.01

1. American record. 2. United States Open record.

U.S. LONG-COURSE CHAMPIONSHIPS

(Indianapolis, Ind., Aug. 18–21, 1982)

Men's Events

50–m freestyle—Ping Siong Ang, Singapore and Univ. of Houston	0:22.69
100–m freestyle—Rowdy Gaines, Winter Haven, Fla.	0:50.27
200–m freestyle—Rowdy Gaines	1:49.64
400–m freestyle—Bruce Hayes, Mission Viejo, Calif.	3:54.80
800–m freestyle—Tony Corbisiero, Bayside, N.Y.	7:58.50[1]
1,500–m freestyle—Jeff Kostoff, Upland, Calif.	15:17.77
100–m breaststroke—Steve Lundquist, Jonesboro, Ga.	1:02.53[2]
200–m breaststroke—John Moffet, Costa Mesa, Calif.	2:17.88
100–m backstroke—Mark Rhodenbaugh, Cincinnati	0:56.90
200–m backstroke—Steve Barnicoat, Mission Viejo, Calif.	2:02.91
100–m butterfly—David Cowell, Belpre, Ohio	0:54.61
200–m butterfly—Craif Beardsley, Gainesville, Fla.	1:59.01
200–m ind. medley—Bill Barrett, Mission Viejo, Calif.	2:04.03
400–m ind. medley—Ricardo Prado, Mission Viejo, Calif.	4:22.54
400–m medley relay—Mission Viejo Nadadores (Jay Yarid, Bill Barrett, John Critchfield, Robin Leamy)	3:46.96
800–m freestyle relay—Mission Viejo Nadadores (Bruce Hayes, Bill Barrett, John Hillencamp, Rich Saeger)	7:29.14
400–m freestyle relay—Mission Viejo Nadadores (Rich Saeger, Bill Barrett, Stuart MacDonald, Robin Leamy)	3:21.89[1]

Women's Events

50–m freestyle—Dara Torres, Beverly Hills, Calif.	0:26.13
100–m freestyle—Paige Zemina, Fort Lauderdale, Fla.	0:57.45
200–m freestyle—Sarah Linke, Walnut Creek, Calif.	2:01.25
400–m freestyle—Tiffany Cohen, Mission Viejo, Calif.	4:11.61
800–m freestyle—Marybeth Linzmeier, Mission Viejo, Calif.	8:35.48
1,500–m freestyle—Karin LaBerge, Doylestown, Pa.	16:18.94
100–m breaststroke—Kim Rhodenbaugh, Cincinnati	1:10.79
200–m breaststroke—Beverly Acker, Richmond, Ky.	2:35.45
100–m backstroke—Sue Walsh, Hamburg, N.Y.	1:02.48[1]
200–m backstroke—Tracy Caulkins, Nashville, Tenn.	2:15.53
100–m butterfly—Mary T. Meagher, Louisville, Ky.	0:59.75
200–m butterfly—Mary T. Meagher	2:07.14
200–m ind. medley—Tracy Caulkins	2:15.66
400–m ind. medley—Tracy Caulkins	4:44.26
400–m medley relay—Cincinnati Marlins (Kim Nicholson, Kim Rhodenbaugh, Betsy Mitchell, Beth Washut)	4:15.19
800–m freestyle relay—Mission Viejo Nadadores (Marybeth Linzmeier, Cynthia Woodhead, Tiffany Cohen, Vera Barker)	8:17.00
400–m freestyle relay—Mission Viejo Nadadores (Susan Habernigg, Cynthia Woodhead, Julie Williams, Marybeth Linzmeier)	3:49.36
Combined team—Mission Viejo Nadadores	1,255 pts

1. American record. 2. World record.

U.S. INDOOR DIVING CHAMPIONSHIPS—1982

(Brown Deer, Wis., April 13–17, 1982)

INDOOR

Men's Events	Pts
1 meter—Ron Merriott, Kimball	603.57
3 meter—Ron Merriott	610.44
Platform—Dan Watson, Danvers Y	531.99
High point winner—Ron Merriott	
Team—Mission Viejo Nadadores	103

Women's Events

1 meter—Megan Neyer, Mission Viejo Nadadores	427.38
3 meter—Megan Neyer	512.40
Platform—Wendy Wyland, Mission Viejo	367.59
High point winner—Megan Neyer	
Team—Mission Viejo Nadadores	155

OUTDOOR

(Pittsburgh, Pa., Aug. 17–21, 1982)

Men's Events	**Pts**
1 meter—Greg Louganis, Mission Viejo, Calif.	626.13
3 meter—Greg Louganis	703.14
Platform—Bruce Kimball, Ann Arbor, Mich.	603.63
Team—Mission Viejo, Calif.	

Women's Events	
1 meter—Megan Neyer, Mission Viejo, Calif.	468.27
3 meter—Kelly McCormick, Columbus, Ohio	513.57
Platform—Wendy Wyland, Mission Viejo, Calif.	427.14
Team—Mission Viejo, Calif.	

NATIONAL COLLEGIATE ATHLETIC ASSOCIATION

(Brown Deer, Wis., March 25–27, 1982)

50–yd freestyle—Robin Leamy, U.C.L.A.	0:19.85
100–yd freestyle—Robin Leamy	0:43.59
200–yd freestyle—Pelle Holmertz, California	1:36.46
500–yd freestyle—Andy Astbury, Arizona State	4:18.15
1,650–yd freestyle—Arne Borgstrom, Alabama	15:02.24
100–yd backstroke—Clay Britt, Texas	0:49.09
200–yd backstroke—Rick Carey, Texas	1:46.01
100–yd breaststroke—Steve Lundquist, Southern Methodist	0:53.09
200–yd breaststroke—Steve Lundquist	1:56.84
100–yd butterfly—Matt Gribble, Miami	0:47.35
200–yd butterfly—Craig Beardsley, Florida	1:44.10[1]
200–yd individual medley—Bill Barrett, U.C.L.A.	1:45.00[1]
400–yd individual medley—Jeff Float, Southern California	3:49.00
400–yd freestyle relay—U.C.L.A. (Bill Barrett, Chris Silva, Stuart MacDonald, Robin Leamy)	2:53.15[1]
800–yd freestyle relay—California (Paolo Revelli, P.A. Magnuson, Todd Trowbridge, Pelle Holmertz)	6:28.94
400–yd medley relay—Texas (Jim Britt, Nick Nevid, Bill Paulus, Eric Finical)	3:14.24
1–m dive—Robert Bollinger, Indiana	554.95 pts
3–m dive—Ron Merriott, Michigan	600.30 pts
Team—U.C.L.A.	219 pts

1. American record.

ASSOCIATION FOR INTERCOLLEGIATE ATHLETICS FOR WOMEN—1982

(Austin, Tex., March 17–20, 1982)

50–yd freestyle—Jill Sterkel, Texas	0:22.59
100–yd freestyle—Jill Sterkel	0:48.61[1]
200–yd freestyle—Jill Sterkel	1:46.47[1]
500–yd freestyle—Kim Linehan, Texas	4:44.12
1,650–yd freestyle—Kim Linehan	16:18.50
50–yd backstroke—Marci Ballard, Ohio State	0:26.97
100–yd backstroke—Elaine Palmer, Brown	0:57.61
200–yd backstroke—Elaine Palmer	2:02.60
50–yd breaststroke—Amanda Martin, Southern Illinois	0:29.36
100–yd breaststroke—Jeanne Childs, Hawaii	1:02.08[2]
200–yd breaststroke—Jeanne Childs	2:11.90[2]
50–yd butterfly—Jill Sterkel	0:24.03[1]
100–yd butterfly—Jill Sterkel	0:53.49
200–yd butterfly—Kim Linehan	2:00.21
100–yd ind. medley—Carol Borgmann, Texas	0:57.40
200–yd ind. medley—Carol Borgmann	2:03.55
400–yd ind. medley—Sue Cahill, Michigan	4:20.86
200–yd medley relay—Florida State University	1:42.86
400–yd medley relay—Texas	3:45.37
200–yd freestyle relay—Florida State University	1:33.50
400–yd freestyle relay—Texas	3:21.46
800–yd freestyle relay—Princeton	n.a.
1–meter dive—Lona Foss, Indiana	449.55 pts[2]
3–meter dive—Kelly McCormick, Ohio State	550.20 pts[2]
Team—Texas	755 pts

1. American record. 2. A.I.A.W. record. n.a. = not available.

NATIONAL ASSOCIATION OF INTERCOLLEGIATE ATHLETICS—1982

(Burnaby, British Columbia, March 4–6, 1982)

50–m freestyle—Steve Koga, Willamette (Ore.) University	0:23.42
100–m freestyle—Steve Koga	0:50.98[1]
200–m freestyle—Dan Sullivan, Drury	1:52.78[1]
400–m freestyle—Dan Sullivan	4:00.55[1]
1,500–m freestyle—Russell Dale, Simon Fraser University	16:05.51
100–m backstroke—Sean Allison, Drury	0:58.00[1]
200–m backstroke—Bryce Fleming, Simon Fraser	2:08.30[1]
100–m breaststroke—Ray Markle, Drury	1:06.06
200–m breaststroke—Ray Markle	2:23.53[1]
100–m butterfly—Thomas Ullrich, Denver	0:56.59[1]
200–m butterfly—Roger Bird, Drury	2:09.14
200–m ind. medley—Paul Stanford, Denver	2:09.12[1]
400–m ind. medley—Paul Stanford	4:33.76
400–m medley relay—Drury College	3:53.47[1]
400–m freestyle relay—Denver	3:28.18[1]
800–m freestyle relay—Drury	7:39.81
1–meter dive—Mike Lewis, Drury	460.53 pts
3–meter dive—Mike Lewis	455.50 pts
Team—Drury College	456 pts

1. N.A.I.A. record.

PADDLE TENNIS

Source: Murray Geller, Executive-Secretary, U.S. Paddle Tennis Association

NATIONAL OPEN CHAMPIONSHIPS—1982

(Santa Monica, Calif., July 31–Aug. 1, 1982)

Men's singles—Mark Rifenbark, Los Angeles

Men's doubles—Jeff Fleitman, Brooklyn, N.Y., and Sol Hauptman, Santa Monica, Calif.

Women's singles—Carolyn Dadian, Venice, Calif.

WOMEN'S EAST COAST CHAMPIONSHIPS—1982

Singles—Mary Ellen Stewart, St. Augustine, Fla.

PLATFORM TENNIS

UNITED STATES CHAMPIONS—1982
American Platform Tennis Association

Open singles* (Apple Platform Tennis Club, New York City)—Doug Russell, New York City, defeated Gregg Brents, White Plains, N.Y., in final

Men's doubles—Stephen Baird, Harrison, N.Y., and Rich Maier, Allendale, N.J.

Women's doubles (Montclair Golf Club, West Orange, N.Y.)—Evonne Hackenberg, Kalamazoo, Mich., and Hilary Hilton Marold, Glen Ellyn, Ill.

Mixed doubles (Sleepy Hollow Country Club, Scarborough, N.Y.)—Doug Russell and Hilary Marold.

* Open is for men and women.

GYMNASTICS

WORLD CHAMPIONSHIPS—1981*

(Moscow, Soviet Union, Nov. 22–29, 1981)

Men's Events

	Pts
All–around—Yuri Kovolev, Soviet Union	118.375
Floor exercises—Yuri Kovolev	19.775
Pommel horse—Tie between Xiaopong Li, China, and Michael Nikolai, Soviet Union	19.9
Still rings—Aleksandr Dityatin, Soviet Union	19.825
Parallel bars—Tie between Aleksandr Dityatin, Soviet Union, and Koji Gushiken, Japan	19.825
Vault—Ralph Peter Heman, East Germany	19.9
Horizontal bars—Aleksandr Tkachev, Soviet Union	19.9
Team—Soviet Union	586.95

Women's Events

	Pts
All–around—Olga Bicherova, Soviet Union	78.5
Floor exercises—Natalie Menko, Soviet Union	19.85
Balance beam—Maxi Gnauck, East Germany	19.525
Uneven parallel bars—Maxi Gnauck	19.9
Vault—Maxi Gnauck	19.675
Team—Soviet Union	389.3

*World championships are held every two years, on odd-numbered years. The next competition will be held in the Fall of 1983 in Budapest, Hungary.

NATIONAL COLLEGIATE ATHLETIC ASSOCIATION

Men's Division I

(Lincoln, Neb., April 2–4, 1982)

All–around—Peter Vidmar, U.C.L.A.
Floor exercise—Steve Elliott, Nebraska
Pommel horse—Peter Vidmar and Steve Jennings, New Mexico (tie)
Still rings—Jim Hartung, Nebraska
Vault—Steve Elliott and Randy Wickstrom, California-Berkeley (tie)
Horizontal bars—Peter Vidmar
Team—Nebraska, 286.45 pts

Women's Division I

(Salt Lake City, Utah, March 25–27, 1982)

	Pts
All–around—Sue Stednitz, Utah	37.20
Balance beam—Sue Stednitz	18.7
Floor exercise—Mary Ayotte-Law, Oregon State	18.85
Vault—Elaine Alfano, Utah	18.9
Uneven parallel bars—Lisa Shirk, Pittsburgh	19.0
Team—Utah	148.6

ASSOCIATION FOR INTERCOLLEGIATE ATHLETICS FOR WOMEN

DIVISION I

(Memphis, Tenn., April 2–3, 1982)

	Pts
All–around—Ann Woods, Florida	37.05
Balance beam—Lynn McDonnell, Florida	18.65
Floor exercise—Ann Woods	18.65
Uneven parallel bars—Ann Woods	18.85
Vault—Kathy Niebel, Georgia	18.65
Team—Florida	143.90

DIVISION II

(Denver, Colo., March 26–27, 1982)

	Pts
All–around—Karen Beer, Denver	36.80
Balance beam—Karen Beer	18.70
Floor exercise—Karen Beer	18.10
Uneven parallel bars—Karen Beer	18.75
Vault—Margot Todd, Centenary College	18.40
Team—University of Denver	141.30

DIVISION III

(Keene, N.H., March 19–20, 1982)

	Pts
All–around—Tari Gould, Gustavus Adolphus	16.75
Balance beam—Patty Ritter, Pittsburgh–Johnstown	17.30
Floor exercise—Lisa Harlan, Texas Woman's University	17.45
Uneven parallel bars—Tari Gould	16.75
Vault—Gretchen Gunderson, Gustavus Adolphus	17.75
Team—Gustavus Adolphus, St. Peter, Minn.	133.55

WORLD CUP*

(Toronto, Oct. 24–26, 1980)

Men's Events

All around—Bogdan Makuz, Soviet Union
Floor exercise—Roland Brueckner, East Germany
Horizontal bar—Tie among Makuz, Koji Gushiken, Japan, and Toshiomi Nishikii, Japan
Still rings—Tie between Makuz and Yubin Huang, China
Pommel horse—Roland Brueckner, East Germany
Parallel bars—Yuejiu Li, China
Vault—Roland Brueckner, East Germany

Women's Events

All around—Stella Zakharova, U.S.S.R.
Floor exercise—Maxi Gnauck, East Germany
Balance beam—Elena Naymoushina, U.S.S.R.
Vault—Stella Zakharova, U.S.S.R.
Uneven parallel bars—Maxi Gnauck, East Germany

*The World Cup was not contested in 1981. The 1982 Cup competition was scheduled for Oct. 22–24 in Zagreb, Yugoslavia.

QUARTER HORSE RACING—1982

Kansas Futurity (Ruidoso Downs, N.M., purse: $760,000)—Chicks Etta Wind (Rudy Bustamante, jockey)
Rainbow Futurity (Ruidoso Downs, N.M., purse: $617,514)—Yankee Wind
Skoal Dash for Cash Futurity (Los Alamitos, Calif., purse: $750,000)—Sail on Bunny (Gary Sumpter, jockey)
Kindergarten (Los Alamitos, Calif., purse: $715,000)—Sail on Bunny
Champion of Champions (Los Alamitos, Calif., purse: $700,000)—Denim N Diamonds (Jerry Nicodemus, jockey)

EQUESTRIAN EVENTS—1982

World Cup jumping (Goteborg, Sweden)—Melanie Smith, United States, riding Calypso. Runnerup: Paul Schockemohle, West Germany; third: tie between Hugo Simon, Austria, and John Whitaker, Britain
World Horse Trial (Luhmuehlen, West Germany)—Lucinda Green, Britain. Team: Britain
World dressage—Team: West Germany

BOXING

Whether it be called pugilism, prize fighting or boxing, there is no tracing "the Sweet Science" to any definite source. Tales of rivals exchanging blows for fun, fame or money go back to earliest recorded history and classical legend. There was a mixture of boxing and wrestling called the "pancratium" in the ancient Olympic Games and in such contests the rivals belabored one another with hands fortified with heavy leather wrappings that were sometimes studded with metal. More than one Olympic competitor lost his life at this brutal exercise.

There was little law or order in pugilism until Jack Broughton, one of the early champions of England, drew up a set of rules for the game in 1743. Broughton, called "the father of English boxing," also is credited with having invented boxing gloves. However, these gloves—or "mufflers" as they were called—were used only in teaching "the manly art of self-defense" or in training bouts. All professional championship fights were contested with "bare knuckles" until 1892, when John L. Sullivan lost the heavyweight championship of the world to James J. Corbett in New Orleans in a bout in which both contestants wore regulation gloves.

The Broughton rules were superseded by the London Prize Ring Rules of 1838. The 8th Marquis of Queensberry, with the help of John G. Chambers, put forward the "Queensberry Rules" in 1866, a code that called for gloved contests. Amateurs took quickly to the Queensberry Rules, the professionals slowly.

HISTORY OF WORLD HEAVYWEIGHT CHAMPIONSHIP FIGHTS

(Bouts in which a new champion was crowned)

Source: Nat Fleischer's Ring Boxing Encyclopedia and Record Book, published and copyrighted by The Ring Book Shop, Inc., 120 West 31st St., New York, N.Y. 10001.

Date	Where held	Winner, weight, age	Loser, weight, age	Rounds	Referee
Sept. 7, 1892	New Orleans, La.	James J. Corbett, 178 (26)	John L. Sullivan, 212 (33)	21	Prof. John Duffy
March 17, 1897	Carson City, Nev.	Bob Fitzsimmons, 167 (34)	James J. Corbett, 183 (30)	KO 14	George Siler
June 9, 1899	Coney Island, N.Y.	James J. Jeffries, 206 (24)[1]	Bob Fitzsimmons, 167 (37)	KO 11	George Siler
Feb. 23, 1906	Los Angeles	Tommy Burns, 180 (24)[2]	Marvin Hart, 188 (29)	20	James J. Jeffries
Dec. 26, 1908	Sydney, N.S.W.	Jack Johnson, 196 (30)	Tommy Burns, 176 (27)	KO 14	Hugh McIntosh
April 5, 1915	Havana, Cuba	Jess Willard, 230 (33)	Jack Johnson, 205½ (37)	KO 26	Jack Welch
July 4, 1919	Toledo, Ohio	Jack Dempsey, 187 (24)	Jess Willard, 245 (37)	KO 3	Ollie Pecord
Sept. 23, 1926	Philadelphia	Gene Tunney, 189 (28)[3]	Jack Dempsey, 190 (31)	10	Pop Reilly
June 12, 1930	New York	Max Schmeling, 188 (24)	Jack Sharkey, 197 (27)	WF 4	Jim Crowley
June 21, 1932	Long Island City	Jack Sharkey, 205 (29)	Max Schmeling, 188 (26)	15	Gunboat Smith
June 29, 1933	Long Island City	Primo Carnera, 260½ (26)	Jack Sharkey, 201 (30)	KO 6	Arthur Donovan
June 14, 1934	Long Island City	Max Baer, 209½ (25)	Primo Carnera, 263¼ (27)	KO 11	Arthur Donovan
June 13, 1935	Long Island City	Jim Braddock, 193¾ (29)	Max Baer, 209½ (26)	15	Jack McAvoy
June 22, 1937	Chicago	Joe Louis, 197¼ (23)	Jim Braddock, 197 (31)	KO 8	Tommy Thomas
June 22, 1949	Chicago	Ezzard Charles, 181¾ (27)[4]	Joe Walcott, 195½ (35)	15	Davey Miller
Sept. 27, 1950	New York	Ezzard Charles, 184½ (29)[5]	Joe Louis, 218 (36)	15	Mark Conn
July 18, 1951	Pittsburgh	Joe Walcott, 194 (37)	Ezzard Charles, 182 (30)	KO 7	Buck McTiernan
Sept. 23, 1952	Philadelphia	Rocky Marciano, 184 (29)[6]	Joe Walcott, 196 (38)	KO 13	Charley Daggert
Nov. 30, 1956	Chicago	Floyd Patterson, 182¼ (21)	Archie Moore, 187¾ (42)	KO 5	Frank Sikora
June 26, 1959	New York	Ingemar Johansson, 196 (26)	Floyd Patterson, 182 (24)	KO 3	Ruby Goldstein
June 20, 1960	New York	Floyd Patterson, 190 (25)	Ingemar Johansson, 194¾ (27)	KO 5	Arthur Mercante
Sept. 25, 1962	Chicago	Sonny Liston, 214 (28)	Floyd Patterson, 189 (27)	KO 1	Frank Sikora
Feb. 25, 1964	Miami Beach, Fla.	Cassius Clay, 210 (22)[7]	Sonny Liston, 218 (30)	KO 7	Barney Felix
March 4, 1968	New York	Joe Frazier, 204½ (24)[8]	Buster Mathis, 243½ (23)	KO 11	Arthur Mercante
April 27, 1968	Oakland, Calif.	Jimmy Ellis, 197 (28)[9]	Jerry Quarry, 195 (22)	15	Elmer Costa
Feb. 16, 1970	New York	Joe Frazier, 205 (26)[10]	Jimmy Ellis, 201 (29)	KO 5	Tony Perez
Jan. 22, 1973	Kingston, Jamaica	George Foreman, 217½ (24)	Joe Frazier, 214 (29)	KO 2	Arthur Mercante
Oct. 30, 1974	Kinshasa, Zaire	Muhammad Ali, 216½ (32)	George Foreman, 220 (26)	KO 8	Zack Clayton
Feb. 15, 1978	Las Vegas, Nev.	Leon Spinks, 197 (25)	Muhammad Ali, 224½ (36)	15	Howard Buck
June 9, 1978	Las Vegas, Nev.	Larry Holmes, 212 (28)[11]	Ken Norton, 220 (32)	15	Mills Lans
Sept. 15, 1978	New Orleans	Muhammad Ali, 221 (36)[12]	Leon Spinks, 201 (25)	15	Lucien Joubert
Oct. 20, 1979	Pretoria, S. Africa	John Tate, 240 (24)[13]	Gerrie Coetzee, 222 (24)	15	Carlos Berrocal
March 31, 1980	Knoxville, Tenn.	Mike Weaver, 207½ (27)	John Tate, 232 (25)	KO 15	Ernesto Magana Ansorena

1. Jeffries retired as champion in March 1905. He named Marvin Hart and Jack Root as leading contenders and agreed to referee their fight in Reno, Nev., on July 3, 1905, with the stipulation that he would term the winner the champion. Hart, 190 (28), knocked out Root, 171 (29), in the 12th round. 2. Burns claimed the title after defeating Hart. 3. Tunney retired as champion after defeating Tom Heeney on July 26, 1928. 4. After Louis announced his retirement as champion on March 1, 1949, Charles won recognition from the National Boxing Association as champion by defeating Walcott. 5. Charles gained undisputed recognition as champion by defeating Louis, who came out of retirement. 6. Retired as champion April 27, 1956. 7. The World Boxing Association later withdrew its recognition of Clay as champion and declared the winner of a bout between Ernie Terrell and Eddie Machen would gain its version of the title. Terrell, 199 (25), won a 15-round decision from Machen, 192 (32), in Chicago on March 5, 1965. Clay, 212¼ (25) and Terrell, 212½ (27) met in Houston on Feb. 6, 1967, Clay winning a 15-round decision. 8. Winner recognized by New York, Massachusetts, Maine, Illinois, Texas and Pennsylvania to fill vacated title when Clay was stripped of championship for failing to accept U. S. Induction. 9. Bout was final of eight-man tournament to fill Clay's place and is recognized by World Boxing Association. 10. Bout settled controversy over title. 11. Holmes won World Boxing Council title after W.B.C. had withdrawn recognition of Spinks, March 18, 1978, and awarded its title to Norton. W.B.C. said Spinks had reneged on agreement to fight Norton 12. Ali regained World Boxing Association championship. 13. Tate won W.B.A. title after Ali retired and left it vacant.

CHAMPIONSHIP BOUTS—1982

(Through Aug. 20, 1982)

Junior Flyweight

(108 pound limit)

Amado Ursua of Mexico knocked out Hilario Zapata of Panama in the second round to win the World Boxing Council title on Feb. 6 at Panama City. Zapata was making the 9th defense of the title he won by beating Shigeo Nakajima of Japan in March of 1980. In April, Ursua lost the title on a split decision to Tadashi Tomori of Japan in a 15–rounder in Tokyo and then in July Zapata got the title back by defeating Tomori, also on a split decision, at Kanazawa, Japan.

Katsuo Tokashiki of Japan, who won the W.B.A. version of the title in December 1981, retained it in his 1st defense with an 8th–round knockout of countryman Masaharu Inami in Tokyo.

Flyweight

(112 pound limit)

There were several new champions crowned during the year and the succession was complicated. Santos Laciar of Mexico lost his W.B.A. title to Luis Ibarra of Panama in 1981. Ibarra then lost it to Juan Herrera of Mexico in December 1981. Then Laciar reclaimed it with a 13th–round knockout of Herrera in May. Shoji Uguma of Japan, who won the W.B.C. title in 1980, lost it to Antonio Avelar of Mexico in 1981. Avelar lost it in turn to Prudencio Cardona of Colombia, who was dethroned in August by Freddie Castillo of Mexico.

Junior Bantamweight

(115 pound limit)

Kim Chul Ho of South Korea, who won the crown in January 1981 with a knockout of Rafael Orono of Venezuela, made two successful defenses in the first half of the year. He scored an 8th–round knockout of Koki Ishii of Japan on Feb. 10 at Taegu, South Korea. On July 4, at Taejon, South Korea, the 21–year–old Kim battled to a 15–round draw with Raul Valdez of Mexico to retain the W.B.C. title. The 28–year–old Mexican was warned several times against holding and butting.

Jiro Wantanabe of Japan took the W.B.A. title from Rafael Pedroza of Panama with a unanimous 15–round decision at Tokyo in April, then made a successful defense in July with a 9th–round knockout of Gustavo Ballas in Osaka, Japan.

Bantamweight

(118 pound limit)

Jeff Chandler of Philadelphia remained unbeaten and retained his W.B.A. title with a 6th–round knockout of Johnny Carter, also from Philadelphia, on March 27. The two fighters had been high school classmates in Philadelphia. The 25–year–old Chandler knocked Carter down with a left hook midway in the 6th, then pummeled him before referee Frank Cappuccino stopped the fight at 2:28 of the 6th. Chandler had lost only once—as an amateur to Carter in December 1975. He raised his pro record to 28–0–2, with 15 knockouts. It was the 5th defense of the title he won in 1980 by knocking out Julian Solis in the 14th round at Miami.

Lupe Pintor, who has held the W.B.C. crown since 1979, retained it again in July. The popular Mexican champion stopped Seung Hoon Lee of Korea with an 11th–round knockout in Los Angeles.

Junior Featherweight

(122 pound limit)

Sergio Palma of Argentina successfully defended his W.B.A. crown for the fifth time, scoring a unanimous decision over Jorge Lujan of Panama at Cordoba, Argentina, on Jan. 16. Each weighed 122 pounds. Palma, who was on the offensive for most of the 15–round bout, posted his 47th victory against 4 losses and 3 draws. Lujan is a former W.B.A. bantamweight champion.

In his next defense, on June 12 at Miami Beach, Palma lost his title on a 15–round unanimous decision to Leo Cruz of the Dominican Republic. Cruz connected with a straight right hand to close Palma's left eye in the 4th round and pounded the eye the rest of the bout. Cruz lifted his record to 45 victories, 5 losses and 1 draw, with 17 knockouts.

Wilfredo Gomez, the W.B.C. champion from Puerto Rico, made two title defenses through July. He knocked out Juan (Kid) Meza at 2:28 of the 6th round at Atlantic City on March 27. On June 11, at Las Vegas, Nev., as part of the undercard to the Holmes–Cooney heavyweight title fight, he scored a 10th–round knockout over Juan Antonio Lopez of Mexico. Gomez has 36 career victories, all by knockouts, has lost only once and fought one draw. All of his 15 title defenses have ended in knockout victories—a stunning record for any weight division. Against Meza, a 26–year–old who lives in Hawthorne, Calif., Gomez was warned several times for hitting low.

Featherweight

(128 pound limit)

Eusebio Pedroza surpassed Abe Attell's record of 13 successful defenses of the title when he won a unanimous decision from Juan LaPorte of New York and retained his W.B.A. crown. The 28–year–old champion was penalized a point in the 8th round for low blows and a point in the 14th for using his elbows. But his 3–inch reach advantage was too much for his opponent and he was able to set up LaPorte for solid rights with a persistent left jab. Pedroza, whose record is 33–3, is unbeaten since July 1976. The 5′–8″ Panamanian champion received $65,000 and $150,000 from Latin American TV rights. LaPorte received $40,000 for the bout at Atlantic City on Jan. 24.

Salvador Sanchez, the W.B.C. champion, settled for a unanimous decision after throwing all he had at Jorge (Rocky) Garcia in their title bout at Dallas, May 8. The Mexican champion tried desperately to score a knockout, but Garcia weathered his best flurries. It was Sanchez's 8th title defense and the 1st title fight in Dallas in 14 years. Sanchez raised his record to 42–1–1. Sanchez, regarded by boxing experts as one of the finest ever to battle in the division, knocked out Azumah Nelson in the 15th round at Madison Square Garden in New York in July and it proved to be his last bout. Shortly after the fight, Sanchez was killed in an auto accident in Mexico.

Junior Lightweight

(130 pound limit)

Rolando Navarette of the Philippines retained the W.B.C. title by knocking out Choi Chung Il of South Korea in the 11th round at Manila on Jan. 16. The 24–year–old champion survived a 5th–round knockdown and came back to beat the 20–year–old challenger. Choi was taken to a hospital for observation. He suffered a broken nose and an injured right arm, and complained of pain in the groin.

Sammy Serrano of Puerto Rico lost his W.B.A. title at Santiago, Chile, on June 6 after a doctor ruled in the 11th round he could not continue because of a deep cut over his eye. But Serrano was reinstated as champion two weeks later by the W.B.A., which ruled that Serrano's cut was inflicted by an illegal head butt. Benedicto Villablanca of Chile was declared the winner, becoming the first Chilean to win a world title, when the bout was halted by the referee, Jesus Celis of Venezuela. Serrano had dominated the fight through 10 rounds and appeared on his way to winning the 15th defense of the title he won in 1976. The W.B.A. Championship Committee, on appeal from Serrano, voided the bout, however, and reinstated Serrano as titleholder.

Rafael Limon of Mexico, a former champion, regained the W.B.C. title in May by knocking out Navarette in the 12th round at Las Vegas.

Lightweight

(135 pound limit)

Arturo Frias, from Montebello, Calif., making his first title defense, kept the W.B.A. lightweight crown at Los Angeles on Jan. 30. The ring doctor halted the fight with Ernesto Espana of Caracas, Venezuela in the 9th round because of cuts inflicted on the champion by butts from Espana.

Frias was cut over the left eye in the 2nd round and slashed under the same eye in the 9th. Frias was ahead on all cards at the time. Frias won the title on Dec. 5, 1981, by knocking out Claude Noel of Trinidad in the 8th round. Frias lifted his record to 24–1. He had lost previously only to Espana, whose record slipped to 34–4. The 25–year–old Frias earned $125,000; Espana, 27, received $40,000.

Alexis Arguello, the W.B.C. champion, kept his title with a 6th–round knockout of Bubba Busceme at Beaumont, Tex., Busceme's hometown, on Feb. 13. Arguello, with a 74–4 record, scored his 60th knockout. He stunned Busceme with a left hook, then following with a series of punches that led to the knockout at 2:35 of the round.

At Las Vegas, on May 22, Arguello survived a 1st–round knockdown and came back to knock out Andrew Ganigan, a Hawaiian, in the 5th round. The Nicaraguan champion earned $400,000, Ganigan $130,000. The victory was the 19th straight in a title fight for Arguello, one of six fighters to win titles in three weight divisions.

The W.B.A. title changed hands on May 8 at Las Vegas, when Ray (Boom Boom) Mancini, of Youngstown, Ohio, stopped Frias with six seconds left in the 1st round. Mancini took the title in his second attempt in seven months. He suffered his only defeat in 24 bouts in October 1981 when he was knocked out in the 14th by Arguello in a W.B.C. title match. Mancini put Frias down midway in the round, then pursued the attack with 25 to 30 punches to the head before the referee Richard Green halted the action. Mancini retained the title with a 6th–round knockout of Ernesto Espana in July at Warren, Ohio.

Junior Welterweight

(140 pound limit)

Aaron Pryor, the W.B.A. champion, made two defenses and raised his unbeaten record to 31–0 through the Fourth of July. Pryor's first defense of the year came on March 21 at Atlantic City when he knocked out Miguel Montilla of the Dominican Republic at 42 seconds of the 12th round. Pryor had never been forced to go a full 10 rounds in winning 29 previous fights. The knockout was Pryor's 22nd in a row and 28th in 30 bouts. The 26–year–old Pryor scored another knockout on July 4 at Cincinnati, his hometown, stopping Akio Kameda of Japan at 1:44 of the 6th round. Kameda was knocked down twice in the 6th before the fight was halted. He was floored five times in the bout.

Leroy Haley, from Las Vegas, dethroned Saoul Mamby, from New York City, on an upset majority decision to take the W.B.C. title on June 26 at Highland Heights, Ohio. Haley, who had been the fourth–ranked contender, raised his record to 45–2–2. The 29–year–old champion outscored Mamby on the cards of two judges, 145–142 and 148–144. The third judge scored for Mamby 144–143. The defense was the sixth for Mamby, 35, who won the title on Feb. 23, 1980. His record is 33–13–5.

Welterweight

(147 pound limit)

Sugar Ray Leonard, in his first defense since he became undisputed champion by defeating Thomas Hearns in September 1981, lost the 1st round on the cards of the three judges, then swarmed back to knock out Bruce Finch at 1:50 of the 3rd round on Feb. 15 at Reno, Nev. Leonard floored Finch twice in the 2nd round. In the 3rd, a left hook buckled the challenger's knees and two left-right combinations sent him to the canvas for the last time. Leonard received $1 million for the fight. In June, Leonard underwent surgery for a detached retina and the injury left the status of his boxing future in doubt.

Junior Middleweight

(154 pound limit)

Wilfred Benitez, the 23–year–old Puerto Rican champion, kept the W.B.C. title with a unanimous decision over Roberto Duran of Panama at Las Vegas on Jan. 30. Benitez kept the 30–year–old Duran off balance with straight right–hand leads and scored with an effective jab and combinations. The loss was Duran's third in 77 pro fights. Benitez's record was raised to 43–1–1. His only loss was to Sugar Ray Leonard. He received more than $1 million for the bout. Duran, who received $750,000, won only four rounds on the cards of the three judges. Benitez weighed 152¼, Duran 152½.

Davey Moore of New York captured the W.B.A. crown on Feb. 2 at Tokyo by knocking out Tadashi Mihara of Japan in the 6th round. It was the ninth victory and sixth straight knockout for the unbeaten, 22–year–old Moore, who knocked Mihara down three times in the 6th. Under rules agreed upon before the fight, three knockdowns in one round would constitute a knockout. The defense was the first for Mihara, who won the crown in November 1981 after the division title was vacated by Sugar Ray Leonard.

Moore continued winning on April 26 at Johannesburg, South Africa, where he knocked out Charlie Weir, a South African who went down five times and was counted out at 25 seconds of the 5th round. A crowd of 45,000 saw the fight. Moore weighed 152 and Weir 151¾. Moore won again in July, stopping Ayub Kalule in the 10th round at Atlantic City.

Middleweight

(160 pound limit)

Marvelous Marvin Hagler, the undisputed champion, stopped Bill (Caveman) Lee at 67 seconds of the 1st round on March 7 at Atlantic City. It was the first one–round knockout in a world title fight in more than three and a half years, covering more than 275 bouts. Hagler scored the 45th knockout of his career that shows 54 victories, 2 defeats, and 2 draws. The previous 1st–round knockout in a title match was on June 3, 1978, when Alexis Arguello stopped Diego Alcala in a W.B.C. junior lightweight fight. It was the first 1st–round knockout in the middleweight division since Aug. 25, 1950, when Sugar Ray Robinson stopped Jose Basora in 52 seconds. The 29–year–old Hagler weighed 158, and Lee, 26, scaled 159½. Lee's record is 20–3.

Light Heavyweight

(175 pound limit)

Michael Spinks registered knockouts in title bouts in February, April, and June in retaining the W.B.A. crown. At Atlantic City on Feb. 13, he battered Mustapha Wassaja, a Ugandan, with four successive left hooks for a 6th–round knockout. He floored Murray Sutherland, from Bay City, Mich., three times in the 8th round and was declared the winner by an automatic knockout in the same Atlantic City ring on April 11. On June 12, again at the Playboy Hotel and Casino ballroom, he posted his 21st straight victory when the referee stopped the bout with Jerry Celestine at 1:58 of the 8th round.

Dwight Braxton, making his first defense since winning the W.B.C. title in December 1981 from Matthew Saad Muhammad, dominated Jerry Martin from the start. He floored Martin twice in the 2nd round and stopped him with a relentless assault in the 6th, when he opened a cut over Martin's right eye. Braxton, from Camden, N.J., weighed 175 pounds. His record is 17–1–1. Martin, from Antigua, West Indies, weighed 173½. His record is 22–4. In a rematch with Matthew Saad Muhammad at Philadelphia, Braxton was clearly superior as he scored a 6th–round knockout.

Junior Heavyweight

(190 pound limit)

In the new weight division, Ossie Ocasio of Puerto Rico used left hooks and jabs to defeat Robbie Williams of South Africa and take the W.B.A. title on a 15–round split decision. It was the W.B.A.'s first championship bout since the weight division was created. Ocasio weighed 188½, Williams 186¼. A cut under William's left eye hampered him from the 8th round on in the bout at Johannesburg, South Africa, on Feb. 13.

S.T. Gordon of Los Angeles dethroned Carlos DeLeon of Puerto Rico with a knockout at 2:51 of the 2nd round at Highland Heights, Ohio, on June 27 to win the W.B.C. crown. DeLeon, who had won his title in 1981, had made a successful defense against Marvin Camel in February at Atlantic City, scoring an 8th–round knockout.

Heavyweight

Larry Holmes, the undefeated W.B.C. champion, fought 12 dangerous rounds with Gerry Cooney on June 11 before he knocked out the previously unbeaten 25–year–old challenger at 2:52 of the 13th round at Las Vegas. It was the 40th victory, 30 by knockout, for Holmes and the 11th knockout victory in his 12 defenses of the title. The 32–year–old champion bloodied Cooney's left eye and nose from a two–fisted barrage in the 13th, putting on one of his finest performances. Cooney was penalized 2 points in the 9th and 1 point in the 11th for low blows. The fight was the richest in boxing history, grossing more than $40 million, including pay TV and other ancillary rights. Each fighter earned more than $8 million. Postponed once because of an injury to Cooney's shoulder, the fight was one of the most highly publicized in boxing history. Cooney made a game effort to stay with the champion and, surprisingly, through 12 rounds he trailed Holmes by only 2 points on the scorecards of two judges. Holmes weighed 212½ pounds, Cooney 225½. It was Cooney's only loss in 26 fights.

OTHER WORLD BOXING TITLEHOLDERS

(Through Aug. 20, 1982)

Light Heavyweight

1903	Jack Root, George Gardner
1903–05	Bob Fitzsimmons
1905–12	Philadelphia Jack O'Brien[1]
1912–16	Jack Dillon
1916–20	Battling Levinsky
1920–22	Georges Carpentier
1923	Battling Siki
1923–25	Mike McTigue
1925–26	Paul Berlenbach
1926–27	Jack Delaney[2]
1927	Mike McTigue
1927–29	Tommy Loughran
1930	Jimmy Slattery
1930–34	Maxie Rosenbloom
1934–35	Bob Olin
1935–39	John Henry Lewis
1939	Melio Bettina
1939–41	Billy Conn[2]
1941	Anton Christoforidis (NBA)
1941–48	Gus Lesnevich
1948–50	Freddie Mills
1950–52	Joey Maxim
1952–61	Archie Moore[3]
1961–63	Harold Johnson
1963–65	Willie Pastrano
1965–66	José Torres
1966–67	Dick Tiger
1968	Dick Tiger, Bob Foster
1969–70	Bob Foster
1971	Vicente Rondon (WBA), Bob Foster (WBC)
1972–73	Bob Foster (WBA, WBC)
1974	John Conteh (WBA), Bob Foster (WBC)[1 4]
1975–76	Victor Galindez (WBA), John Conteh (WBC)
1977	Victor Galindez (WBA), John Conteh (WBC)[4], Miguel Cuello (WBC)
1978	Victor Galindez (WBA), Mike Rossman (WBA), Miguel Cuello (WBC), Mate Parlov (WBC), Marvin Johnson (WBC)
1979	Mike Rossman (WBA), Victor Galindez (WBA), Marvin Johnson (WBC), Matthew (Franklin) Saad Muhammad (WBC)
1980	Matthew Saad Muhammad (WBC), Marvin Johnson (WBA), Eddie (Gregory) Mustafa Muhammad (WBA)
1981	Matthew Saad Muhammad (WBC), Eddie Mustafa Muhammad (WBA), Michael Spinks (WBA), Dwight Braxton (WBC)
1982	Dwight Braxton (WBC), Michael Spinks (WBA)

1. Retired. 2. Abandoned title. 3. NBA withdrew recognition in 1961, New York Commission in 1962; recognized thereafter only by California and Europe. 4. WBC withdrew recognition.

Middleweight

1867–72	Tom Chandler
1872–81	George Rooke
1881–82	Mike Donovan[1]
1884–91	Jack (Nonpareil) Dempsey
1891–97	Bob Fitzsimmons[2]
1908	Stanley Ketchel, Billy Papke
1908–10	Stanley Ketchel[3]
1913	Frank Klaus
1913–14	George Chip
1914–17	Al McCoy
1917–20	Mike O'Dowd
1920–23	Johnny Wilson
1923–26	Harry Greb
1926	Tiger Flowers
1926–31	Mickey Walker[2]
1931–41	Gorilla Jones, Ben Jeby, Marcel Thil, Lou Brouillard, Vince Dundee, Teddy Yarosz, Babe Risko, Freddy Steele, Al Hostak, Solly Kreiger, Fred Apostoli, Ceferino Garcia, Ken Overlin, Billy Soose, Tony Zale[4]
1941–47	Tony Zale
1947–48	Rocky Graziano
1948	Tony Zale
1948–49	Marcel Cerdan
1949–51	Jake LaMotta
1952	Ray Robinson, Randy Turpin
1951–52	Ray Robinson[1]
1953–55	Carl Olson
1955–57	Ray Robinson[5]
1957	Gene Fullmer, Ray Robinson
1957–58	Carmen Basilio
1958–60	Ray Robinson[6]
1960–61	Paul Pender[7]
1959–62	Gene Fullmer (NBA)
1961–62	Terry Downes[1]
1962	Paul Pender[1]
1962–63	Dick Tiger
1963–65	Joey Giardello
1965–66	Dick Tiger
1966	Emile Griffith
1967	Nino Benvenuti, Emile Griffith
1968	Emile Griffith, Nino Benvenuti
1969	Nino Benvenuti
1970	Nino Benvenuti, Carlos Monzon
1971–73	Carlos Monzon
1974–75	Carlos Monzon (WBA), Rodrigo Valdez (WBC)
1976	Carlos Monzon (WBA, WBC), Rodrigo Valdez (WBC)
1977	Carlos Monzon (WBA, WBC)[1], Rodrigo Valdez (WBA, WBC)
1978	Rodrigo Valdez, Hugo Corro
1979	Hugo Corro, Vito Antuofermo
1980	Vito Antuofermo, Alan Minter, Marvin Hagler
1981	Marvin Hagler
1982	Marvelous Marvin Hagler

1. Retired. 2. Abandoned title. 3. Died. 4. National Boxing Association and New York Commission disagreed on champions. Those listed were accepted by one or the other until Zale gained world-wide recognition. 5. Ended retirement in 1954. 6. NBA withdrew recognition. 7. Recognized by New York, Massachusetts, and Europe.

Welterweight

1892–94	Mysterious Billy Smith
1894–96	Tommy Ryan
1896	Kid McCoy[2]
1896–1900	Mysterious Billy Smith
1900	Rube Ferns
1900–01	Matty Matthews
1901	Ruby Ferns
1901–04	Joe Walcott
1904	Dixie Kid[2]
1904–06	Joe Walcott
1906–07	Honey Mellody
1907	Mike (Twin) Sullivan[2]
1915–19	Ted Lewis
1919–22	Jack Britton
1922–26	Mickey Walker
1926–27	Pete Latzo
1927–29	Joe Dundee
1929–30	Jackie Fields
1930	Young Jack Thompson
1930–31	Tommy Freeman
1931	Young Jack Thompson
1931–32	Lou Brouillard
1932–33	Jackie Fields
1933	Young Corbett 3rd
1933–34	Jimmy McLarnin, Barney Ross
1934–35	Jimmy McLarnin
1935–38	Barney Ross
1938–40	Henry Armstrong
1940–41	Fritzie Zivic
1941–46	Freddie Cochrane
1946	Marty Servo[1]
1946–51	Ray Robinson[2]
1951	Johnny Bratton (NBA)
1951–54	Kid Gavilan
1954–55	Johnny Saxton
1955	Tony DeMarco
1955–56	Carmen Basilio
1956	Johnny Saxton
1956–57	Carmen Basilio[2]
1958	Virgil Akins
1959–60	Don Jordan
1960–61	Benny (Kid) Paret
1961	Emile Griffith
1961–62	Benny (Kid) Paret
1962–63	Emile Griffith, Luis Rodriguez
1963–66	Emile Griffith[2]
1966–69	Curtis Cokes
1969	Curtis Cokes, José Napoles
1970	José Napoles, Billy Backus
1971	Billy Backus, José Napoles
1972–74	José Napoles
1975	José Napoles (WBA, WBC)[3], Angel Espada (WBA), John Stracey (WBC)
1976	Angel Espada (WBA), José Cuevas (WBA), John Stracey (WBC), Carlos Palomino (WBC)
1977–78	José Cuevas (WBA), Carlos Palomino (WBC)
1979	José Cuevas (WBA), Carlos Palomino (WBC), Wilfredo Benitez (WBC)
1980	Jose Cuevas (WBA), Sugar Ray Leonard (WBC), Roberto Duran (WBC), Thomas Hearns (WBA)
1981	Ray Leonard (WBC), Thomas Hearns (WBA), Ray Leonard (WBC,WBA)
1982	Ray Leonard

1. Retired. 2. Abandoned title. 3. WBA withdrew recognition.

Lightweight

1869–99	Kid Lavigne
1899–1902	Frank Erne
1902–08	Joe Gans
1908–10	Battling Nelson
1910–12	Ad Wolgast
1912–14	Willie Ritchie
1914–17	Freddy Welsh
1917–25	Benny Leonard[1]
1925	Jimmy Goodrich
1925–26	Rocky Kansas
1926–30	Sammy Mandell
1930	Al Singer
1930–33	Tony Canzoneri
1933–35	Barney Ross[2]
1935–36	Tony Canzoneri
1936–38	Lou Ambers
1938–39	Henry Armstrong
1939–40	Lou Ambers
1940–41	Lew Jenkins
1941–42	Sammy Angott[1]
1943–47	Beau Jack (N.Y.), Bob Montgomery (N.Y.), Sammy Angott (NBA), Juan Zurita (NBA), Ike Williams (NBA)
1947–51	Ike Williams
1951–52	James Carter
1952	Lauro Salas
1952–54	James Carter
1954	Paddy DeMarco
1954–55	James Carter
1955–56	Wallace Smith
1956–62	Joe Brown
1962–65	Carlos Ortiz
1965	Ismael Laguna
1965–68	Carlos Ortiz
1968	Teo Cruz
1969	Teo Cruz, Mando Ramos
1970	Mando Ramos, Ismael Laguna, Ken Buchanan
1971	Ken Buchanan (WBA), Mando Ramos (WBC), Pedro Carrasco (WBC)
1972	Ken Buchanan (WBA), Roberto Duran (WBA), Pedro Carrasco (WBC), Mando Ramos (WBC), Chango Carmona (WBC), Rodolfo Gonzalez (WBC)
1973	Roberto Duran (WBA), Rodolfo Gonzalez (WBC)
1974	Roberto Duran (WBA), Rodolfo Gonzalez (WBC), Guts Ishimatsu (WBC)
1975	Roberto Duran (WBA), Guts Ishimatsu (WBC)
1976	Roberto Duran (WBA), Guts Ishimatsu (WBC), Esteban De Jesus (WBC)
1977	Roberto Duran (WBA), Esteban De Jesus (WBC)
1978	Roberto Duran (WBA, WBC)
1979	Roberto Duran[2]; Jim Watt (WBC), Ernesto Espana (WBA)
1980	Ernesto Espana (WBA), Hilmer Kenty (WBA), Jim Watt (WBC)
1981	Hilmer Kenty (WBA), Sean O'Grady (WBA), James Watt (WBC), Alexis Arguello (WBC), Arturo Frias (WBA)
1982	Arturo Frias (WBA), Ray Mancini (WBA), Alexis Arguello (WBC)

1. Retired. 2. Abandoned title.

Featherweight

1889	Dal Hawkins[1]
1890	Billy Murphy
1892–1900	George Dixon
1900–01	Terry McGovern
1901	Young Corbett[1]
1901–12	Abe Attell
1912–23	Johnny Kilbane
1923	Eugene Criqui
1923–25	Johnny Dundee[1]
1925–27	Louis (Kid) Kaplan[1]
1927–28	Benny Bass
1928	Tony Canzoneri
1928–29	Andre Routis
1929–32	Battling Battalino[1]
1932	Tommy Paul (NBA), Kid Chocolate (N.Y.)
1933–36	Freddie Miller
1936–37	Petey Sarron
1937–38	Henry Armstrong[1]
1938–40	Joey Archibald
1940–41	Harry Jefra, Joey Archibald
1941–42	Chalky Wright
1942–48	Willie Pep
1948–49	Sandy Saddler[2]
1949–50	Willie Pep
1950–57	Sandy Saddler
1957–59	Kid Bassey
1959–63	Davey Moore
1963–64	Sugar Ramos
1964–67	Vicente Saldivar[2]
1968	Howard Winstone, José Legra,[3] Paul Rojas (WBA), Sho Saijo (WBA)
1969	Sho Saijo (WBA), Johnny Famechon[3]
1970	Sho Saijo (WBA), Johnny Famechon,[3] Vicente Salvidar,[3] Kuniaki Shibata[3]
1971	Sho Saijo (WBA), Antonio Gomez (WBA), Kuniaki Shibata (WBC)
1972	Antonio Gomez (WBA), Ernesto Marcel (WBA), Kuniaki Shibata (WBC),

	Clemente Sanchez (WBC),[2] José Legra (WBC)
1973	Ernesto Marcel (WBA), José Legra (WBC), Eder Jofre (WBC)
1974	Ernesto Marcel (WBA)[2], Ruben Olivares (WBA), Alexis Arguello (WBA), Eder Jofre (WBC), Bobby Chacon (WBC)
1975	Alexis Arguello (WBA), Bobby Chacon (WBC), Ruben Olivares (WBC), David Kotey (WBC)
1976	Alexis Arguello (WBA),[2] David Kotey (WBC), Danny Lopez (WBC)
1977	Rafael Ortega (WBA), Danny Lopez (WBC)
1978	Rafael Ortega (WBA), Cecilio Lastra (WBA), Eusebio Pedrosa (WBA), Danny Lopez (WBC)
1979	Eusebio Pedrosa (WBA), Danny Lopez (WBC)
1980	Eusebio Pedroza (WBA), Danny Lopez (WBC), Salvador Sanchez (WBC)
1981	Eusebio Pedroza (WBA), Salvador Sanchez (WBC)
1982	Eusebio Pedroza (WBA), Salvador Sanchez (WBC)[4]

1. Abandoned title. 2. Retired. 3. Recognized in Europe, Mexico, and Orient. 4. Killed in auto accident.

Bantamweight

1890–92	George Dixon[1]
1894–99	Jimmy Barry[2]
1899–1900	Terry McGovern[1]
1901	Harry Harris[1]
1902–03	Harry Forbes
1903–04	Frankie Neil
1904	Joe Bowker[1]
1905–07	Jimmy Walsh[1]
1910–14	Johnny Coulon
1914–17	Kid Williams
1917–20	Pete Herman
1920	Joe Lynch
1920–21	Joe Lynch, Pete Herman, Johnny Buff
1922	Johnny Buff, Joe Lynch
1923	Joe Lynch
1924	Joe Lynch, Abe Goldstein
1924	Abe Goldstein, Eddie (Cannonball) Martin
1925	Eddie (Cannonball) Martin, Charlie (Phil) Rosenberg[3]
1927–28	Bud Taylor (NBA)[1]
1929–34	Al Brown
1935	Al Brown, Baltazar Sangchili
1936	Baltazar Sangchili, Tony Marino, Sixto Escobar
1937	Sixto Escobar, Harry Jeffra
1938	Harry Jeffra, Sixto Escobar
1939–40	Sixto Escobar[2]
1940–42	Lou Salica
1942–46	Manuel Ortiz
1947	Manuel Ortiz, Harold Dade
1948–50	Manuel Ortiz
1950–52	Vic Toweel
1952–54	Jimmy Carruthers[2]
1954–55	Robert Cohen
1956	Robert Cohen, Mario D'Agata, Raul Macias (NBA)
1957	Mario D'Agata, Alphonse Halimi
1958–59	Alphonse Halimi
1959–60	Jose Becerra[2]
1960–61	Alphonse Halimi[4]
1961–62	Johnny Caldwell[4]
1961–65	Eder Jofre
1965–68	Masahika (Fighting) Harada
1968	Masahika (Fighting) Harada, Lionel Rose
1969	Lionel Rose, Ruben Olivares
1970	Ruben Olivares, Chucho Castillo
1971	Chucho Castillo, Ruben Olivares
1972	Ruben Olivares, Rafael Herrera, Enrique Pinder
1973	Enrique Pinder (WBA), Romeo Anaya (WBA), Arnold Taylor (WBA), Rodolfo Martinez (WBC), Rafael Herrera (WBC)
1974	Arnold Taylor (WBA), Soo Hwan Hong (WBA), Rafael Herrera (WBC), Rodolfo Martinez (WBC)
1975	Soo Hwan Hong (WBA), Alfonso Zamora (WBA), Rodolfo Martinez (WBC)
1976	Alfonso Zamora (WBA), Rodolfo Martinez (WBC), Carlos Zarate (WBC)
1977	Alfonso Zamora (WBA), Jorge Lujan (WBA), Carlos Zarate (WBC)
1978	Jorge Lujan (WBA), Carlos Zarate (WBC)
1979	Jorge Lujan (WBA), Carlos Zarate (WBC), Lupe Pintor (WBC)
1980	Jorge Lujan (WBA), Lupe Pintor (WBC), Julian Solis (WBA) Jeff Chandler (WBA)
1981	Lupe Pintor (WBC), Jeff Chandler (WBA)
1982	Lupe Pintor (WBC), Jeff Chandler (WBA)

1. Abandoned title. 2. Retired. 3. Deprived of title for failing to make weight. 4. Recognized in Europe.

Flyweight

1916–23	Jimmy Wilde
1923–25	Pancho Villa[1]
1925	Frankie Genaro
1925–27	Fidel La Barba[2]
1927–31	Corporal Izzy Schwartz, Frankie Genaro, Emile (Spider) Pladner, Midget Wolgast, Young Perez[3]
1932–35	Jackie Brown
1935–38	Bennie Lynch[4]
1939	Peter Kane[4]
1943–47	Jackie Paterson[1]
1947–50	Rinty Monaghan[2]
1950	Terry Allen
1950–52	Dado Marino
1952–54	Yoshio Shirai
1954–60	Pascual Perez
1960–62	Pone Kingpetch
1962–63	Masahika (Fighting) Harada
1963–64	Hiroyuki Ebihara
1964–65	Pone Kingpetch
1965–66	Salvatore Burrini
1966	Walter McGown, Chartchai Chionoi
1966–68	Charchai Chionoi
1969	Bernabe Villacampa, Efran Torres (WBA)
1970	Bernabe Villacampa, Chartchai Chionoi, Erbito Salavarria, Berkrerk Chartvanchai (WBA), Masao Ohba (WBA)
1971	Masao Ohba (WBA), Erbito Salavarria (WBC)
1972	Masao Ohba (WBA), Erbito Salavarria (WBC), Betulio Gonzalez (WBC), Venice Borkorsor (WBC)
1973	Masao Ohba (WBA), Chartchai Chionoi (WBA), Venice Borkorsor (WBC), Betulio Gonzalez (WBC)
1974	Chartchai Chionoi (WBA), Susumu Hanagata (WBA), Betulio Gonzalez (WBC), Shoji Oguma (WBC)
1975	Susumu Hanagata (WBA), Erbito Salavarria (WBA), Shoji Oguma (WBC), Miguel Canto (WBC)
1976	Erbito Salavarria (WBA), Alfonso Lopez (WBA), Guty Espadas (WBA), Miguel Canto (WBC)
1977	Guty Espadas (WBA), Miguel Canto (WBC)
1978	Guty Espadas (WBA), Betulio Gonzalez (WBA), Miguel Canto (WBC)
1979	Betulio Gonzalez (WBA), Miguel Canto (WBC), Park Chan-Hee (WBC)
1980	Luis Ibarra (WBA), Kim Tae Shik (WBA), Park Chan-Hee (WBC), Shoji Oguma (WBC) Peter

	Mathebula (WBA)
1981	Shoji Oguma (WBC), Peter Mathebula (WBA), Santos Laciar (WBA), Luis Ibarra (WBA), Juan Herrera (WBA), Antonio Avelar (WBC)
1982	Juan Herrera (WBA), Prudencio Cardona (WBC), Santos Laciar (WBA), Antonio Avelar (WBC), Freddie Castillo (WBC)

1. Died. 2. Retired. 3. Claimants to NBA and New York Commission titles. 4. Abandoned title.

FIGHTER OF THE YEAR

Selected by *The Ring* Magazine.

1928	Gene Tunney
1929	Tommy Loughran
1930	Max Schmeling
1931	Tommy Loughran
1932	Jack Sharkey
1933	No award
1934	Barney Ross and Tony Canzoneri
1935	Barney Ross
1936	Joe Louis
1937	Henry Armstrong
1938	Joe Louis
1939	Joe Louis
1940	Billy Conn
1941	Joe Louis
1942	Ray Robinson
1943	Fred Apostoli
1944	Beau Jack
1945	Willie Pep
1946	Tony Zale
1947	Gus Lesnevich
1948	Ike Williams
1949	Ezzard Charles
1950	Ezzard Charles
1951	Ray Robinson
1952	Rocky Marciano
1953	Bobo Olson
1954	Rocky Marciano
1955	Rocky Marciano
1956	Floyd Patterson
1957	Carmen Basilio
1958	Ingemar Johansson
1959	Ingemar Johansson
1960	Floyd Patterson
1961	Joe Brown
1962	Dick Tiger
1963	Cassius Clay
1964	Emile Griffith
1965	Dick Tiger
1966	No award
1967	Joe Frazier
1968	Nino Benvenuti
1969	Jose Napoles
1970–71	Joe Frazier
1972	Carlos Monzon and Muhammad Ali
1973	George Foreman
1974–75	Muhammad Ali
1976	George Foreman
1977	Carlos Zarate
1978	Muhammand Ali
1979	Sugar Ray Leonard
1980	Thomas Hearns
1981	Sugar Ray Leonard

BOXING—AMATEUR

U.S. AMATEUR CHAMPIONSHIPS—1982

U.S. Amateur Boxing Federation

(Charlotte, N.C., April 12–17, 1982)

106 lb—Mario Lesperance, Vallejo, Calif.
112 lb—Steve McCrory, Detroit, Mich.
119 lb—Floyd Favors, Capitol Heights, Md.
125 lb—Orlando Johnson, Chicago
132 lb—Pernell Whitaker, Norfolk, Va.
139 lb—Henry Hughes, Cleveland, Ohio
147 lb—Mark Breland, Brooklyn, N.Y.
156 lb—Dennis Milton, Bronx, N.Y.
165 lb—Michael Grogan, Atlanta
178 lb—Bennie Heard, Augusta, Ga.
201 lb—Elmer Martin, United States Navy
Over 201 lb—Tyrell Biggs, Philadelphia

WORLD CHAMPIONSHIPS—1982

(Munich, West Germany, May 15, 1982)

106 lb—Ismail Mustafov, Bulgaria
112 lb—Yuri Alexandrov, Soviet Union
119 lb—Floyd Favors, United States
125 lb—Adolfo Hortz, Cuba
132 lb—Angel Herrera, Cuba
139 lb—Carlos Garcia, Cuba
147 lb—Mark Breland, United States
156 lb—Aleksandr Koshkin, Soviet Union
165 lb—Bernardo Comas, Cuba
178 lb—Pablo Romero, Cuba
Heavyweight—Aleksandr Yagubkin, Soviet Union
Super heavyweight—Tyrone Biggs, United States

NATIONAL GOLDEN GLOVES CHAMPIONS—1982

(Kansas City, Mo., April 4, 1982)

106 lb—Jose Rosario, Jersey City, N.J.
112 lb—Jesse Benavides, Corpus Christi, Tex.
119 lb—Meldrick Taylor, Philadelphia
125 lb—Shelton LeBlanc, Lafayette, La.
139 lb—Timmy Rabon, Lafayette, La.
147 lb—Roman George, Lafayette, La.
156 lb—Sanderline Williams, Cleveland, Ohio
165 lb—Arthel Lawhorn, Detroit, Mich.
178 lb—Keith Vining, Detroit, Mich.
Heavyweight—Earl Lewis, Cleveland, Ohio
Superheavyweight—Warren Thompson, Baltimore, Md.
Team—Lafayette, La.
Outstanding boxer—Jesse Benavides

LUGE

UNITED STATES CHAMPIONSHIPS

(Lake Placid, N.Y., Feb. 16–17, 1982)

Men—Frank Masley, Newark, Del.
Women—Erica Terwillegar, Lake Placid, N.Y.
Men's doubles—Terry Morgan, Saranac Lake, N.Y., and Bo Jamieson, Hudson, Ohio
Women's junior—Erica Terwillegar
Women's youth division—Cammy Myler, Willsboro, N.Y.
Men's junior—Christian Bochniowicz, Old Forge, Pa.
Men's junior doubles—Christian Bochniowicz and Duncan Kennedy, Lake Placid, N.Y.

WORLD JUNIOR CHAMPIONS

(Lake Placid, N.Y., Jan. 23–24, 1982)

Men—Hans-Joachim Shurack, East Germany
Women—Elena Buslaeva, Soviet Union
Men's doubles—Jorg Hoffmann and Jocher Pietzsch, East Germany

WORLD CHAMPIONS*

(Hammarstrand, Sweden, Feb. 1–3, 1981)

Men—Sergei Damilin, Soviet Union
Women—Melitta Sollman, East Germany
*The world championship was not contested in 1982.

HORSE RACING

Ancient drawings on stone and bone prove that horse racing is at least 3000 years old, but Thoroughbred Racing is a modern development. Practically every thoroughbred in training today traces its registered ancestry back to one or more of three sires that arrived in England about 1728 from the Near East and became known, from the names of their owners, as the Byerly Turk, the Darley Arabian, and the Godolphin Arabian. The Jockey Club (English) was founded at Newmarket in 1750 or 1751 and became the custodian of the Stud Book as well as the court of last resort in deciding turf affairs.

Horse racing took place in this country before the Revolution, but the great lift to the breeding industry came with the importation in 1798, by Col. John Hoomes of Virginia, of Diomed, winner of the Epsom Derby of 1780. Diomed's lineal descendants included such famous stars of the American turf as American Eclipse and Lexington. From 1800 to the time of the Civil War there were race courses and breeding establishments plentifully scattered through Virginia, North Carolina, South Carolina, Tennessee, Kentucky, and Louisiana.

The oldest stake event in North America is the Queen's Plate, a Canadian fixture that was first run in the Province of Quebec in 1836. The oldest stake event in the United States is The Travers, which was first run at Saratoga in 1864. The gambling that goes with horse racing and trickery by jockeys, trainers, owners, and track officials caused attacks on the sport by reformers and a demand among horse racing enthusiasts for an honest and effective control of some kind, but nothing of lasting value to racing came of this until the formation in 1894 of The Jockey Club.

"TRIPLE CROWN" WINNERS IN THE UNITED STATES[1]

(Kentucky Derby, Preakness and Belmont Stakes)

Year	Horse	Owner
1919	Sir Barton	J. K. L. Ross
1930	Gallant Fox	William Woodward
1935	Omaha	William Woodward
1937	War Admiral	Samuel D. Riddle
1941	Whirlaway	Warren Wright
1943	Count Fleet	Mrs. John Hertz
1946	Assault	Robert J. Kleberg
1948	Citation	Warren Wright
1973	Secretariat	Meadow Stable
1977	Seattle Slew	Karen Taylor
1978	Affirmed	Louis Wolfson

1. Statistics relative to thoroughbred racing in this publication are reproduced from the *American Racing Manual,* by special permission of the copyright owners. TRIANGLE PUBLICATIONS, INC. Reproduction prohibited.

KENTUCKY DERBY

Churchill Downs; 3-year-olds; 1 1/4 miles.

Year	Winner	Jockey	Wt.	Win val.
1875	Aristides	O. Lewis	100	$2,850
1876	Vagrant	R. Swim	97	2,950
1877	Baden Baden	W. Walker	100	3,300
1878	Day Star	J. Carter	100	4,050
1879	Lord Murphy	C. Schauer	100	3,550
1880	Fonso	G. Lewis	105	3,800
1881	Hindoo	J. McLaughlin	105	4,410
1882	Apollo	B. Hurd	102	4,560
1883	Leonatus	W. Donohue	105	3,760
1884	Buchanan	I. Murphy	110	3,990
1885	Joe Cotton	E. Henderson	110	4,630
1886	Ben Ali	P. Duffy	118	4,890
1887	Montrose	I. Lewis	118	4,200
1888	Macbeth II	G. Covington	115	4,740
1889	Spokane	T. Kiley	118	4,970
1890	Riley	I. Murphy	118	5,460
1891	Kingman	I. Murphy	122	4,680
1892	Azra	A. Clayton	122	4,230
1893	Lookout	E. Kunze	122	4,090
1894	Chant	F. Goodale	122	4,020
1895	Halma	J. Perkins	122	2,970
1896	Ben Brush	W. Simms	117	4,850
1897	Typhoon II	F. Garner	117	4,850
1898	Plaudit	W. Simms	117	4,850
1899	Manuel	F. Taral	117	4,850
1900	Lieut. Gibson	J. Boland	117	4,850
1901	His Eminence	J. Winkfield	117	4,850
1902	Alan-a-Dale	J. Winkfield	117	4,850
1903	Judge Himes	H. Booker	117	4,850
1904	Elwood	F. Prior	117	4,850
1905	Agile	J. Martin	122	4,850
1906	Sir Huon	R. Troxler	117	4,850
1907	Pink Star	A. Minder	117	4,850
1908	Stone Street	A. Pickens	117	4,850
1909	Wintergreen	V. Powers	117	$ 4,850
1910	Donau	F. Herbert	117	4,850
1911	Meridian	G. Archibald	117	4,850
1912	Worth	C. H. Shilling	117	4,850
1913	Donerail	R. Goose	117	5,475
1914	Old Rosebud	J. McCabe	114	9,125
1915	Regret	J. Notter	112	11,450
1916	George Smith	J. Loftus	117	9,750
1917	Omar Khayyam	C. Borel	117	16,600
1918	Exterminator	W. Knapp	114	14,700
1919	Sir Barton	J. Loftus	112 1/2	20,825
1920	Paul Jones	T. Rice	126	30,375
1921	Behave Yourself	C. Thompson	126	38,450
1922	Morvich	A. Johnson	126	46,775
1923	Zev	E. Sande	126	53,600
1924	Black Gold	J. D. Mooney	126	52,775
1925	Flying Ebony	E. Sande	126	52,950
1926	Bubbling Over	A. Johnson	126	50,075
1927	Whiskery	L. McAtee	126	51,000
1928	Reigh Count	C. Lang	126	55,375
1929	Clyde Van Dusen	L. McAtee	126	53,950
1930	Gallant Fox	E. Sande	126	50,725
1931	Twenty Grand	C. Kurtsinger	126	48,725
1932	Burgoo King	E. James	126	52,350
1933	Brokers Tip	D. Meade	126	48,925
1934	Cavalcade	M. Garner	126	28,175
1935	Omaha	W. Saunders	126	39,525
1936	Bold Venture	I. Hanford	126	37,725
1937	War Admiral	C. Kurtsinger	126	52,050
1938	Lawrin	E. Arcaro	126	47,050
1939	Johnstown	J. Stout	126	46,350
1940	Gallahadion	C. Bierman	126	60,150
1941	Whirlaway	E. Arcaro	126	61,275
1942	Shut Out	W. D. Wright	126	64,225

Year	Winner	Jockey	Wt.	Win val.
1943	Count Fleet	J. Longden	126	$ 60,725
1944	Pensive	C. McCreary	126	64,675
1945	Hoop Jr.	E. Arcaro	126	64,850
1946	Assault	W. Mehrtens	126	96,400
1947	Jet Pilot	E. Guerin	126	92,160
1948	Citation	E. Arcaro	126	83,400
1949	Ponder	S. Brooks	126	91,600
1950	Middleground	W. Boland	126	92,650
1951	Count Turf	C. McCreary	126	98,050
1952	Hill Gail	E. Arcaro	126	96,300
1953	Dark Star	H. Moreno	126	90,050
1954	Determine	R. York	126	102,050
1955	Swaps	W. Shoemaker	126	108,400
1956	Needles	D. Erb	126	123,450
1957	Iron Liege	W. Hartack	126	107,950
1958	Tim Tam	I. Valenzuela	126	116,400
1959	Tomy Lee	W. Shoemaker	126	119,650
1960	Venetian Way	W. Hartack	126	114,850
1961	Carry Back	J. Sellers	126	120,500
1962	Decidedly	W. Hartack	126	119,650
1963	Chateauguay	B. Baeza	126	$108,900
1964	Northern Dancer	W. Hartack	126	114,300
1965	Lucky Debonair	W. Shoemaker	126	112,000
1966	Kauai King	D. Brumfield	126	120,500
1967	Proud Clarion	R. Ussery	126	119,700
1968	Forward Pass[1]	I. Valenzuela	126	122,600
1969	Majestic Prince	W. Hartack	126	113,200
1970	Dust Commander	M. Manganello	126	127,800
1971	Canonero II	G. Avila	126	145,500
1972	Riva Ridge	R. Turcotte	126	140,300
1973	Secretariat	R. Turcotte	126	155,050
1974	Cannonade	A. Cordero, Jr.	126	274,000
1975	Foolish Pleasure	J. Vasquez	126	209,600
1976	Bold Forbes	A. Cordero, Jr.	126	165,200
1977	Seattle Slew	J. Cruguet	126	214,700
1978	Affirmed	S. Cauthen	126	186,900
1979	Spectacular Bid	R. Franklin	126	228,650
1980	Genuine Risk	J. Vasquez	126	250,550
1981	Pleasant Colony	J. Velasquez	126	317,200
1982	Gato del Sol	E. Delahoussaye	126	417,600

1. Dancer's Image finished first but was disqualified after traces of drug were found in system.

PREAKNESS STAKES

Pimlico; 3-year-olds; $1\frac{3}{16}$ miles; first race 1873.

Year	Winner	Jockey	Wt.	Win Val.
1919	Sir Barton	J. Loftus	126	$ 24,500
1930	Gallant Fox	E. Sande	126	51,925
1931	Mate	G. Ellis	126	48,225
1932	Burgoo King	E. James	126	50,375
1933	Head Play	C. Kurtsinger	126	26,850
1934	High Quest	R. Jones	126	25,175
1935	Omaha	W. Saunders	126	25,325
1936	Bold Venture	G. Woolf	126	27,325
1937	War Admiral	C. Kurtsinger	126	45,600
1938	Dauber	M. Peters	126	51,875
1939	Challedon	G. Seabo	126	53,710
1940	Bimelech	F.A. Smith	126	53,230
1941	Whirlaway	E. Arcaro	126	49,365
1942	Alsab	B. James	126	58,175
1943	Count Fleet	J. Longden	126	43,190
1944	Pensive	C. McCreary	126	60,075
1945	Polynesian	W.D. Wright	126	66,170
1946	Assault	W. Mehrtens	126	96,620
1947	Faultless	D. Dodson	126	98,005
1948	Citation	E. Arcaro	126	91,870
1949	Capot	T. Atkinson	126	79,985
1950	Hill Prince	E. Arcaro	126	56,115
1951	Bold	E. Arcaro	126	83,110
1952	Blue Man	C. McCreary	126	86,135
1953	Native Dancer	E. Guerin	126	65,200
1954	Hasty Road	J. Adams	126	91,600
1955	Nashua	E. Arcaro	126	67,550
1956	Fabius	W. Hartack	126	$ 84,250
1957	Bold Ruler	E. Arcaro	126	65,250
1958	Tim Tam	I. Valenzuela	126	97,900
1959	Royal Orbit	W. Harmatz	126	136,200
1960	Bally Ache	R. Ussery	126	121,000
1961	Carry Back	J. Sellers	126	126,200
1962	Greek Money	J. Rotz	126	135,800
1963	Candy Spots	W. Shoemaker	126	127,500
1964	Northern Dancer	W. Hartack	126	124,200
1965	Tom Rolfe	R. Turcotte	126	128,100
1966	Kauai King	D. Brumfield	126	129,000
1967	Damascus	W. Shoemaker	126	141,500
1968	Forward Pass	I. Valenzuela	126	142,700
1969	Majestic Prince	W. Hartack	126	129,500
1970	Personality	E. Belmonte	126	151,300
1971	Canonero II	G. Avila	126	137,400
1972	Bee Bee Bee	E. Nelson	126	135,300
1973	Secretariat	R. Turcotte	126	129,900
1974	Little Current	M. Rivera	126	156,000
1975	Master Derby	D. McHargue	126	158,100
1976	Elocutionist	J. Lively	126	129,700
1977	Seattle Slew	J. Cruguet	126	138,600
1978	Affirmed	S. Cauthen	126	136,200
1979	Spectacular Bid	R. Franklin	126	165,300
1980	Codex	A. Cordero	126	180,600
1981	Pleasant Colony	J. Velasquez	126	270,800
1982	Aloma's Ruler	J. Kaenel	126	209,900

BELMONT STAKES

Belmont Park; 3-year-olds; $1\frac{1}{2}$ miles.

Run at Jerome Park 1867 to 1890; at Morris Park 1890–94; at Belmont Park 1905–62; at Aqueduct 1963–67. Distance $1\frac{5}{8}$ miles prior to 1874; reduced to $1\frac{1}{2}$ miles, 1874; reduced to $1\frac{1}{4}$ miles, 1890; reduced to $1\frac{1}{8}$ miles, 1893; increased to $1\frac{1}{4}$ miles, 1895; increased to $1\frac{3}{8}$ miles, 1896; reduced to $1\frac{1}{4}$ miles in 1904; increased to $1\frac{1}{2}$ miles, 1926.

Year	Winner	Jockey	Wt.	Win val.
1919	Sir Barton	J. Loftus	126	$ 11,950
1930	Gallant Fox	E. Sande	126	66,040
1931	Twenty Grand	C. Kurtsinger	126	58,770
1932	Faireno	T. Malley	126	55,120
1933	Hurryoff	M. Garner	126	49,490
1934	Peace Chance	W.D. Wright	126	43,410
1935	Omaha	W. Saunders	126	35,480
1936	Granville	J. Stout	126	29,800
1937	War Admiral	C. Kurtsinger	126	38,020
1938	Pasteurized	J. Stout	126	34,530
1939	Johnstown	J. Stout	126	37,020
1940	Bimelech	F.A. Smith	126	$ 35,030
1941	Whirlaway	E. Arcaro	126	39,770
1942	Shut Out	E. Arcaro	126	44,520
1943	Count Fleet	J. Longden	126	35,340
1944	Bounding Home	G.L. Smith	126	55,000
1945	Pavot	E. Arcaro	126	56,675
1946	Assault	W. Mehrtens	126	75,400
1947	Phalanx	R. Donoso	126	78,900
1948	Citation	E. Arcaro	126	77,700
1949	Capot	T. Atkinson	126	60,900
1950	Middleground	W. Boland	126	61,350

Year	Winner	Jockey	Wt.	Win val.
1951	Counterpoint	D. Gorman	126	82,000
1952	One Count	E. Arcaro	126	82,400
1953	Native Dancer	E. Guerin	126	82,500
1954	High Gun	E. Guerin	126	89,000
1955	Nashua	E. Arcaro	126	83,700
1956	Needles	D. Erb	126	83,600
1957	Gallant Man	W. Shoemaker	126	77,300
1958	Cavan	P. Anderson	126	73,440
1959	Sword Dancer	W. Shoemaker	126	93,525
1960	Celtic Ash	W. Hartack	126	96,785
1961	Sherluck	B. Baeza	126	104,900
1962	Jaipur	W. Shoemaker	126	109,550
1963	Chateauguay	B. Baeza	126	101,700
1964	Quadrangle	M. Ycaza	126	110,850
1965	Hail to All	J. Sellers	126	104,150
1966	Amberoid	W. Boland	126	117,700
1967	Damascus	W. Shoemaker	126	104,950
1968	Stage Door Johnny	H. Gustines	126	117,700
1969	Arts and Letters	B. Baeza	126	104,050
1970	High Echelon	J. Rotz	126	115,000
1971	Pass Catcher	R. Blum	126	97,710
1972	Riva Ridge	R. Turcotte	126	93,540
1973	Secretariat	R. Turcotte	126	90,120
1974	Little Current	M. Rivera	126	101,970
1975	Avatar	W. Shoemaker	126	116,160
1976	Bold Forbes	A. Cordero, Jr.	126	117,000
1977	Seattle Slew	J. Cruguet	126	109,080
1978	Affirmed	S. Cauthen	126	110,580
1979	Coastal	R. Hernandez	126	161,400
1980	Temperence Hill	E. Maple	126	176,220
1981	Summing	G. Martens	126	170,580
1982	Conquistador Cielo	L. Pincay, Jr.	126	159,720

TRIPLE CROWN RACES—1982

(For 3–year–olds, carrying 126 pounds; jockeys in parentheses)

Kentucky Derby (Churchill Downs, Lousiville, Ky., May 1; gross purse: $522,600; 1¼ miles)—1. Gato del Sol (Eddie Delahoussaye), owned by Arthur Hancock III and Leone J. Peters; mutuel returns: $44.40, 19.00, 9.40. 2. Laser Light (Maple) $17.00, 9.20. 3. Reinvested (MacBeth) $4.40. 4. Water Bank (Castaneda). 5. Muttering (Pincay). 6. Rockwall (Valdivieso). 7. Air Forbes Won (Cordero). 8. Star Gallant (Shoemaker). 9. Majesty Prince (Hernandez). 10. Cupecoy's Joy [1] (Santiago). 11. El Baba (Brumfield). 12. Wavering Monarch (Romero). 13. Cassaleria (McHargue). 14. Royal Roberto (Rivera). 15. Music Leader (Day). 16. Bold Style (Fell). 17. Wolfie's Rascal (Velasquez). 18. New Discovery (Bailey). 19. Real Dare (Guidry). Time: 2:02 2/5. Winner's purse: $417,600. Margin of victory: 2½ lengths. Attendance: 141,009.

1. Filly, carried 121 pounds.

Preakness Stakes (Pimlico, Baltimore, Md., May 15; gross purse: $279,900; 1³⁄₁₆ miles)—1. Aloma's Ruler (Jack Kaenel), owned by Nathan Scherr; mutuel returns: $15.80, 4.60, 3.60. 2. Linkage (Shoemaker) $2.60, 2.60. 3. Cut Away (Bailey) $6.00. 4. Bold Style (Moyers). 5. Laser Light (Maple). 6. Reinvested (MacBeth). 7. Water Bank (Castaneda). Time: 1:55 ⅖. Winner's purse: $209,900. Margin of victory: half–length. Attendance: 80,724.

Belmont Stakes (Elmont, N.Y., June 5; gross purse: $266,200; 1½ miles)—1. Conquistador Cielo (Laffit Pincay Jr.), owned by Henryk de Kwiatkowski; mutuel returns: $10.20, 7.40, 6.80. 2. Gato del Sol (Delahoussaye) $8.00, 6.40. 3. Illuminate (Velasquez) $6.40. 4. Linkage (Shoemaker). 5. High Ascent (Lovato). 6. Lejoil (Samyn). 7. Estoril (Fell). 8. Royal Roberto (Cordero). 9. Aloma's Ruler (Kaenel). 10. Anemal (Martens). 11. Cut Away (Bailey). Time: 2:28 ⅕. Winner's purse: $159,720. Margin of victory: 14½ lengths. Attendance: 45,128.

POWERBOAT RACING

BENIHANA GRAND PRIX

(Point Pleasant, N.J., July 14, 1982)

Open Class I—Benihana, Rocky Aoki, Englewood, N.J., 30–foot Active; 2 hours, 35 minutes, 33 seconds
Sports Class II—El Boss, Willie Diaz, Miami, Fla., 30–foot Shadow, 1:22:48
Modified Class III—Seahawk, Sal Magluta, Miami, Fla., 31–foot Seahawk, 1:36:56
Pro Stock IV—Fox, Gene Whipp, Sarasota, Fla., 30–foot Velocity, 1:44:05
Class V—K & K Outboard, Kenny Kalibat, Island Park, N.Y., 23–foot Ghost, 2:05:21
Bacardi Trophy (Miami, Fla.)—Jerry Jacoby, Westbury, N.Y.

ECLIPSE AWARDS—1981

The Eclipse Awards in thoroughbred racing are given on the basis of voting by three groups: the Daily Racing Form, the National Turf Writers Association, and the racing secretaries at tracks that are members of the Thoroughbred Racing Association.

Horse of the year and best older male horse	John Henry
2–year–old colt	Deputy Minister
2–year–old filly	Before Dawn
3–year–old colt	Pleasant Colony
3–year–old filly	Wayward Lass
Older filly or mare	Relaxing
Male turf horse	John Henry
Female turf horse	De La Rose
Sprinter	Guilty Conscience
Steeplechase	Zaccio

FENCING

UNITED STATES CHAMPIONS—1982
U.S. Fencing Association

Men's foil—Michael Marx, Salle Auriol, Portland, Ore.
Men's epee—Lee Shelley, Salle Orsi, Rutherford, N.J.
Men's saber—Peter Westwood, New York Fencers Club, New York City
Women's foil—Jana Angelakis, Tanner City Fencing Club, Peabody, Mass.
Women's epee—Vincent Bradford, Pentathlon Center, San Antonio, Tex.
Men's foil team—New York Fencers Club
Men's saber team—New York Athletic Club
Men's epee team—United States Modern Pentathlon, Fort Sam Houston, Tex.
Women's foil team—Tanner City Fencing Club, Peabody, Mass.

WORLD CHAMPIONSHIPS—1982

Men's foil—Aleksandr Romankov, Soviet Union
Men's epee—Jeno Pap, Hungary
Men's saber—Viktor Krovopouskov, Soviet Union
Women's foil—Naila Giliazova, Soviet Union
Men's foil team—Soviet Union
Men's epee team—France
Men's saber team—Hungary
Women's foil team—Italy

NORTH AMERICAN CUP—1982

Men's foil—Greg Massialas, United States
Men's epee—Lee Shelley, United States
Men's saber—Peter Westwood, United States
Women's foil—Jana Angelakis, United States

TRACK AND FIELD

Running, jumping, hurdling and throwing weights—track and field sports, in other words—are as natural to young people as eating, drinking and breathing. Unorganized competition in this form of sport goes back beyond the Cave Man era. Organized competition begins with the first recorded Olympic Games in Greece, 776 B.C., when Coroebus of Elis won the only event on the program, a race of approximately 200 yards. The Olympic Games, with an ever-widening program of events, continued until "the glory that was Greece" had faded and "the grandeur that was Rome" was tarnished, and finally were abolished by decree of Emperor Theodosius I of Rome in A.D. 394. The Tailteann Games of Ireland are supposed to have antedated the first Olympic Games by some centuries, but we have no records of the specific events and winners thereof.

Professional contests of speed and strength were popular at all times and in many lands, but the widespread competition of amateur athletes in track and field sports is a comparatively modern development. The first organized amateur athletic meet of record was sponsored by the Royal Military Academy at Woolwich, England, in 1849. Oxford and Cambridge track and field rivalry began in 1864, and the English amateur championships were established in 1866. In the United States such organizations as the New York Athletic Club and the Olympic Club of San Francisco conducted track and field meets in the 1870s, and a few colleges joined to sponsor a meet in 1874. The success of the college meet led to the formation of the Intercollegiate Association of Amateur Athletes of America and the holding of an annual set of championship games beginning in 1876. The Amateur Athletic Union, organized in 1888, has been the ruling body in American amateur athletics since that time. In 1980, The Athletics Congress of the U.S.A. took over the governing of track and field from the A.A.U.

WORLD RECORDS—MEN

(Through Sept. 19, 1982)
Recognized by the International Athletic Federation
The I.A.A.F. decided late in 1976 not to recognize records in yards except for the one-mile run.
The I.A.A.F. also requires automatic timing for all records for races of 400 meters or less.

Event	Record	Holder	Home Country	Where Made	Date
Running					
100 m	0:09.95	Jim Hines	U.S.	Mexico City	Oct. 14, 1968
200 m	0:19.72	Pietro Mennea	Italy	Mexico City	Sept. 17, 1979
400 m	0:43.86	Lee Evans	U.S.	Mexico City	Oct. 18, 1968
800 m	1:41.8	Sebastian Coe	England	Florence, Italy	June 10, 1981
1,000 m	2:12.40	Sebastian Coe	England	Oslo, Norway	July 11, 1981
1,500 m	3:31.36	Steve Ovett	England	Koblenz, W. Ger.	Aug. 27, 1980
1 mile	3:47.33	Sebastian Coe	England	Brussels	Aug. 28, 1981
2,000 m	4:51.4	John Walker	New Zealand	Oslo	June 30, 1976
3,000 m	7:32.1	Henry Rono	Kenya	Oslo	June 27, 1978
3,000 m steeplechase	8:05.4	Henry Rono	Kenya	Seattle, Wash.	May 13, 1978
5,000 m	13:00.42	David Moorcroft	England	Oslo	July 7, 1982
10,000 m	27:22.4	Henry Rono	Kenya	Vienna, Austria	June 11, 1978
25,000 m	1:13:55.8	Toshihiko Seko	Japan	Christchurch, N.Z.	March 22, 1981
30,000 m	1:29:18.8	Toshihiko Seko	Japan	Christchurch, N.Z.	March 22, 1981
20,000 m	57:24.2	Jos Hermans	Netherlands	Papandal, Neth.	May 1, 1976
1 hour	13 mi. 24 yd	Jos Hermans	Netherlands	Papandal, Neth.	May 1, 1976
Walking					
20,000 m	1:20.06.8	Daniel Bautista	Mexico	Montreal	Oct. 17, 1979
2 hours	17 mi. 1,092 yd	Ralph Kowalsky	East Germany	East Berlin	March 28, 1982
30,000 m	2:06.54	Ralph Kowalksy	East Germany	East Berlin	March 28, 1982
50,000 m	3:41:39	Raul Gonzales	Mexico	Bergen, Norway	May 25, 1979
Hurdles					
110 m	0:12.93	Renaldo Nehemiah	U.S.	Zurich, Switzerland	Aug. 19, 1981
400 m	0:47.13	Edwin Moses	U.S.	Milan, Italy	July 3, 1980
Relay Races					
400 m (4x100)	0:38.03	National Team	U.S.	Dusseldorf, W. Ger.	Sept. 3, 1977
800 m (4x200)	1:20.26	So. California (Joel Andrews, James Sanford, Billy Mullins, Clancy Edwards)	U.S.	Tempe, Ariz.	May 27, 1978
1,600 m (4x400)	2:56.16	National Team (Vince Matthews, Ron Freeman, Larry James, Lee Evans)	U.S.	Mexico City	Oct. 20, 1968
3,200 m (4x800)	7:03.89	National Team (Peter Elliott, Garry Cook, Steve Cram, Sebastian Coe)	Britain	London	Aug. 30, 1982
Field Events					
High jump	7 ft 8¾ in.	Gerd Wessig	East Germany	Moscow	Aug. 1, 1980

Long jump	29 ft 2½ in.	Bob Beamon	U.S.	Mexico City	Oct. 18, 1976
Triple jump	58 ft 8¼ in.	Joao Oliveira	Brazil	Mexico City	Oct. 15, 1975
Pole vault	19 ft ¾ in.	Vladimir Polyakov	U.S.S.R.	Tbilisi, U.S.S.R.	June 26, 1981
Shotput	72 ft 8 in.	Udo Beyer	East Germany	Goteborg, Sweden	July 6, 1978
Discus throw	233 ft 5 in.	Wolfgang Schmidt	East Germany	East Berlin	Aug. 9, 1978
Javelin throw	317 ft 4 in.	Ferenc Paragi	Hungary	Tata, Hungary	April 23, 1980
Hammer Throw	275 ft 6 in.	Sergei Litvinov	U.S.S.R.	Moscow	June 3, 1982
Decathlon	8,743 pts	Daley Thompson	England	Athens	Sept. 7–8, 1982

WORLD RECORDS—WOMEN

Event	Record	Holder	Home Country	Where Made	Date
Running					
100 m	0:10.88	Marlies Goehr	East Germany	Dresden, E. Ger.	July 1, 1977
200 m	0:21.71	Marita Koch	East Germany	Karl Marx Stadt	June 10, 1979
400 m	0:48.15	Marita Koch	East Germany	Athens	Sept. 8, 1982
800 m	1:53.42	Nadezhda Olizaryenko	U.S.S.R.	Moscow	June 27, 1980
1,500 m	3:52.47	Tatyana Kazankina	U.S.S.R.	Zurich, Switz.	Aug. 13, 1980
1 mile	4:17.44	Maricica Puica,	Rumania	Rieti, Italy,	Sept. 16, 1982
3,000 m	8:26.78	Svetlana Ulmasova,	U.S.S.R.	Kiev, U.S.S.R.	July 25, 1982
5,000 m	15:08.26	Mary Decker	United States	Eugene, Ore.	June 5, 1982
10,000 m	31:35.3	Mary Decker	United States	Eugene, Ore.	July 17, 1982
Hurdles					
100 m	0:12.36	Grazyna Rabsztyn	Poland	Warsaw	June 13, 1980
400 m	0:54.28	Karin Rossley	East Germany	Jena, E. Ger.	May 17, 1980
Relay Races					
400 m (4x100)	0:41.60	National Team	East Germany	Moscow	Aug. 1, 1980
		(Romy Mueller, Barbel Woeckel, Ingrid Auerwald, Marlies Goehr)			
800 m (4x200)	1:28.15	National Team	East Germany	Jena, E. Ger.	July 9, 1980
		(Marlies Goehr, Romy Mueller, Barbel Woeckel, Marita Koch)			
1,600 m (4x400)	3:19.05	National Team	East Germany	Athens	Sept. 11, 1982
		(Kirsten Siemon, Sabine Busch, Dagmar Ruebsam, Marita Koch)			
3,200 m (4x800)	7:52.3	National Team	U.S.S.R.	Podolsk, U.S.S.R.	Aug. 16, 1976
		(Tatyana Providokhina, Vera Gerasimova, Svetlana Styrkina, Tatyana Kazankina)			
Field Events					
High jump	6 ft 7½ in.	Ulrike Meyfarth	West Germany	Athens	Sept. 8, 1982
Long jump	23 ft 7½ in.	Vali Ionescu	Romania	Bucharest	Aug. 8, 1982
Shotput	73 ft 4¼ in.	Ilona Slupianek	East Germany	Celje, Yugoslavia	May 2, 1980
Discus throw	235 ft 7 in.	Maria Vergova	Bulgaria	Sofia, Bulgaria	July 13, 1980
Javelin throw	237 ft 6 in.	Tiina Lillak	Finland	Helsinki	July 29, 1982
Heptathlon	6,717 pts	Ramona Neubert	East Germany	Kiev, U.S.S.R.	June 27, 1981

AMERICAN RECORDS—MEN

Officially approved by The Athletics Congress

Event	Record	Holder	Where Made	Date
Running				
100 m	0:09.95	Jim Hines	Mexico City	Oct. 14, 1968
200 m	0:19.83	Tommie Smith	Mexico City	Oct. 16, 1968
400 m	0:43.86	Lee Evans	Mexico City	Oct. 16, 1968
800 m	1:43.9	Richard Wohlhuter	Stockholm	July 18, 1974
1,000 m	2:13.9	Richard Wohlhuter	Oslo	July 30, 1974
1,500 m	3:31.96	Steve Scott	Koblenz, W. Ger.	Aug. 26, 1981
1 mile	3:47.69	Steve Scott	Oslo, Norway	July 7, 1982
2,000 m	4:54.71	Steve Scott	Ingelheim, W. Germany	Aug. 31, 1982
3,000 m	7:36.68	Steve Scott	Ingelheim, W. Germany	Sept. 1, 1981
5,000 m	13:11.93	Alberto Salazar	Oslo	July 7, 1982
10,000 m	27:25.61	Alberto Salazar	Oslo	June 26, 1982
20,000 m	58:15.0	Bill Rodgers	Boston	Aug. 9, 1977
25,000 m	1:14:12	Bill Rodgers	Saratoga, Calif.	Feb. 21, 1979
30,000 m	1:31:50	Bill Rodgers	Saratoga, Calif.	Feb. 21, 1979
1 hour	12 mi. 997 yds	Bill Rodgers	Saratoga, Calif.	Feb. 21, 1979
3,000 m steeplechase	8:15.68	Henry Marsh	Eugene, Ore.	June 28, 1980

Hurdles				
110 m	0:12.93	Renaldo Nehemiah	Zurich, Switzerland	Aug. 19, 1981
400 m	0:47.13	Edwin Moses	Milan, Italy	July 3, 1980
Relay Races				
400 m (4x100)	0:38.03	U.S. Team (Bill Collins, Steve Riddick, Cliff Wiley, Steve Williams)	Dusseldorf, W. Ger.	Sept. 3, 1977
800 m (4x200)	1:20.26	Southern California (Joe Andrews, James Sanford, Billy Mullins, Clancy Edwards)	Tempe, Ariz.	May 27, 1978
1,600 m (4x400)	2:56.16	U.S. Team (Vince Matthews, Ron Freeman, Larry James, Lee Evans)	Mexico City	Oct. 20, 1968
3,200 m (4x800)	7:10.4	U. of Chicago T.C. (Tom Bach, Ken Sparks, Lowell Paul, Rick Wohlhuter)	Durham, N.C.	May 12, 1973
Field Events				
High jump	7 ft 7¼ in.	Dwight Stones	Philadelphia	Aug. 14, 1982
Long jump	29 ft 2½ in.	Bob Beamon	Mexico City	Oct. 18, 1968
Triple jump	57 ft 7½ in.	Willie Banks	Sacramento, Calif.	June 21, 1981
Pole vault	18 ft 10¼ in.	Dave Volz	Nice, France	Aug. 14, 1982
Shotput	72 ft 3 in.	David Laut	Koblentz, W. Germany	Aug. 25, 1982
		Brian Oldfield	Modesto, Calif.	May 16, 1981
Discus throw	237 ft 4 in.	Ben Plucknett	Stockholm	July 7, 1981
Javelin throw	314 ft 3 in.	Bob Roggy	Stuttgart, W. Germany	Aug. 29, 1982
Hammer throw	243 ft 11 in.	Dave McKenzie	Durham, N.C.	June 27, 1982

AMERICAN RECORDS—WOMEN

Event	Record	Holder	Where Made	Date
Running				
100 m	0:10.90	Evelyn Ashford	Colorado Springs	July 22, 1981
200 m	0:21.83	Evelyn Ashford	Montreal	Aug. 24, 1979
400 m	0:50.62	Rosalyn Bryant	Montreal	July 28, 1976
800 m	1:57.9	Madeline Jackson	College Park, Md.	Aug. 7, 1976
1,500 m	3:59.43	Mary Decker	Zurich, Switzerland	Aug. 13, 1980
1 mile	4:18.08	Mary Decker	Paris	July 9, 1982
3,000 m	8:29.71	Mary Decker	Oslo, Norway	July 7, 1982
5,000 m	15:08.26	Mary Decker	Eugene, Ore.	June 5, 1982
10,000 m	31:35.3	Mary Decker	Eugene, Ore.	July 17, 1982
Hurdles				
100 m	0:12.79	Stephanie Hightower	Karl–Marx–Stadt, E. Germany	July 10, 1982
400 m	0:56.16	Esther Mahr	Sittard, Netherlands	Aug. 15, 1980
Relay Races				
400 m (4x100)	0:42.29	United States Team (Alice Brown, Florence Griffith, Randy Givens, Diane Williams)	Karl–Marx–Stadt, E. Germany	July 9, 1982
800 m (4x200)	1:32.6	U.S. National Team (Wanda Hooker, Karen Hawkins, Chandra Cheeseborough, Brenda Morehead)	Bourges, France	June 23, 1979
1,600 m (4x400)	3:22.81	U.S. Team (Debra Sapenter, Sheila Ingram, Pam Jiles, Rosalyn Bryant)	Montreal	July 31, 1976
Field Events				
High jump	6 ft 6 in.	Coleen Sommer	Durham, N.C.	June 26, 1982
Long jump	22 ft 11½ in.	Jodi Anderson	Eugene, Ore.	June 28, 1980
Shotput	62 ft 7¾ in.	Maren Seidler	Walnut, Calif.	June 16, 1979
Discus throw	207 ft 5 in.	Lorna Griffin	Long Beach, Calif.	May 24, 1980
Javelin throw	227 ft 5 in.	Kathy Schmidt	Furth, W. Ger.	Sept. 11, 1977
Heptathlon	6,458 pts	Jane Frederick	Goleta, Calif.	July 17–18, 1982

HISTORY OF THE RECORD FOR THE MILE RUN

Time	Athlete	Country	Year	Location
4:36.5	Richard Webster	England	1865	England
4:29.0	William Chinnery	England	1868	England
4:28.8	Walter Gibbs	England	1868	England
4:26.0	Walter Slade	England	1874	England
4:24.5	Walter Slade	England	1875	London

4:23.2	Walter George	England	1880	London
4:21.4	Walter George	England	1882	London
4:18.4	Walter George	England	1884	Birmingham, England
4:18.2	Fred Bacon	Scotland	1894	Edinburgh, Scotland
4:17.0	Fred Bacon	Scotland	1895	London
4:15.6	Thomas Conneff	United States	1895	Travers Island, N.Y.
4:15.4	John Paul Jones	United States	1911	Cambridge, Mass.
4:14.4	John Paul Jones	United States	1913	Cambridge, Mass.
4:12.6	Norman Taber	United States	1915	Cambridge, Mass.
4:10.4	Paavo Nurmi	Finland	1923	Stockholm
4:09.2	Jules Ladoumegue	France	1931	Paris
4:07.6	Jack Lovelock	New Zealand	1933	Princeton, N.J.
4:06.8	Glenn Cunningham	United States	1934	Princeton, N.J.
4:06.4	Sydney Wooderson	England	1937	London
4:06.2	Gundar Hägg	Sweden	1942	Göteborg, Sweden
4:06.2	Arne Andersson	Sweden	1942	Stockholm
4:04.6	Gunder Hägg	Sweden	1942	Stockholm
4:02.6	Arne Andersson	Sweden	1943	Göteborg, Sweden
4:01.6	Arne Andersson	Sweden	1944	Malmö, Sweden
4:01.4	Gunder Hägg	Sweden	1945	Malmö, Sweden
3:59.4	Roger Bannister	England	1954	Oxford, England
3:58.0	John Landy	Australia	1954	Turku, Finland
3:57.2	Derek Ibbotson	England	1957	London
3:54.5	Herb Elliott	Australia	1958	Dublin
3:54.4	Peter Snell	New Zealand	1962	Wanganui, N.Z.
3:54.1	Peter Snell	New Zealand	1964	Auckland, N.Z.
3:53.6	Michel Jazy	France	1965	Rennes, France
3:51.3	Jim Ryun	United States	1966	Berkeley, Calif.
3:51.1	Jim Ryun	United States	1967	Bakersfield, Calif.
3:51.0	Filbert Bayi	Tanzania	1975	Kingston, Jamaica
3:49.4	John Walker	New Zealand	1975	Göteborg, Sweden
3:49.0	Sebastian Coe	England	1979	Oslo
3:48.8	Steve Ovett	England	1980	Oslo
3:48.53	Sebastian Coe	England	1981	Zurich, Switzerland
3:48.40	Steve Ovett	England	1981	Koblenz, W. Ger.
3:47.33	Sebastian Coe	England	1981	Brussels

WORLD'S FASTEST INDOOR MILES

Time	Athlete	Country	Date	Location
3:50.6	Eamonn Coghlan	Ireland	Feb. 20, 1981	San Diego
3:51.8	Steve Scott[1]	United States	Feb. 20, 1981	San Diego
3:52.6	Eamonn Coghlan	Ireland	Feb. 16, 1979	San Diego
3:52.8	John Walker[2]	New Zealand	Feb. 20, 1981	San Diego
3:52.8	John Walker	New Zealand	Feb. 19, 1982	San Diego
3:52.9	Eamonn Coghlan	Ireland	Feb. 15, 1980	Los Angeles
3:53.0	Steve Scott[1]	United States	Feb. 15, 1980	Los Angeles
3:53.0	Eamonn Coghlan	Ireland	Feb. 6, 1981	New York
3:53.6	Ray Flynn[3]	Ireland	Feb. 20, 1981	San Diego
3:53.6	Tom Byers[1]	United States	Feb. 19, 1982	San Diego
3:53.7	Steve Scott	United States	Jan. 30, 1981	Los Angeles
3:53.8	Ray Flynn	Ireland	Feb. 6, 1981	New York
3:54.1	Steve Scott[1]	United States	Feb. 16, 1979	San Diego
3:54.1	Ray Flynn[2]	Ireland	Feb. 19, 1982	San Diego
3:54.3	Eamonn Coghlan[1]	Ireland	Jan. 30, 1981	Los Angeles
3:54.4	Ray Flynn[2]	Ireland	Jan. 30, 1981	Los Angeles
3:54.5	Filbert Bayi[2]	Tanzania	Feb. 15, 1980	Los Angeles
3:54.7	Steve Lacy[2]	United States	Feb. 16, 1979	San Diego
3:54.7	Thomas Wessinghage[2]	West Germany	Feb. 6, 1981	New York
3:54.9	Ray Flynn	Ireland	Feb. 13, 1981	Inglewood, Calif.
3:55.0	Tony Waldrop	United States	Feb. 17, 1974	San Diego
3:55.0	Dick Buerkle	United States	Jan. 13, 1978	College Park, Md.
3:55.0	Eamonn Coghlan	Ireland	Feb. 9, 1979	New York
3:55.0	Steve Scott[3]	United States	Feb. 6, 1981	New York
3:55.0	Steve Scott[3]	United States	Feb. 19, 1982	San Diego
3:55.2	John Walker[1]	New Zealand	Feb. 13, 1981	Inglewood, Calif.
3:55.3	Steve Scott	United States	Feb. 21, 1981	Daly City, Calif.
3:55.37	Steve Scott	United States	Feb. 12, 1982	New York
3:55.4	Niall O'Shaughnessy	Ireland	Jan. 28, 1977	Columbia, Mo.
3:55.41	Tom Byers[1]	United States	Feb. 12, 1982	New York
3:55.5	Filbert Bayi	Tanzania	Feb. 22, 1980	San Diego

3:55.5	Sydney Maree[1]	South Africa	Feb. 21, 1981	Daly City, Calif.
3:55.55	Eamonn Coghlan	Ireland	Jan. 31, 1981	Dallas
3:55.62	John Walker[2]	New Zealand	Feb. 12, 1982	New York
3:55.6	Steve Lacy[3]	United States	Feb. 15, 1980	Los Angeles
3:55.63	Eamonn Coghlan	Ireland	Feb. 13, 1981	Toronto
3:55.7	Wilson Waigwa	Kenya	Feb. 18, 1977	San Diego
3:55.7	Eamonn Coghlan[1]	Ireland	Feb. 22, 1980	San Diego
3:55.8	Marty Liquori	United States	Feb. 7, 1975	Philadelphia
3:55.8	John Walker[2]	New Zealand	Feb. 22, 1980	San Diego
3:55.87	Wilson Waigwa	Kenya	Jan. 31, 1981	Dallas
3:56.0	Eamonn Coghlan	Ireland	Feb. 17, 1978	San Diego
3:56.0	Tom Byers[2]	United States	Feb. 13, 1981	Inglewood, Calif.
3:56.1	Filbert Bayi	Tanzania	Feb. 27, 1976	New York
3:56.1	Eamonn Coghlan	Ireland	Jan. 20, 1979	Los Angeles

1. Finished second. 2. Finished third. 3. Finished fourth.

WORLD'S FASTEST OUTDOOR MILES

Time	Athlete	Country	Date	Location
3:47.33	Sebastian Coe	England	Aug. 28, 1981	Brussels
3:47.69	Steve Scott	United States	July 7, 1982	Oslo
3:48.40	Steve Ovett	England	Aug. 26, 1981	Koblenz, W. Ger.
3:48.53	Sebastian Coe	England	Aug. 19, 1981	Zurich
3:48.53	Steve Scott	United States	June 26, 1982	Oslo
3:48.8	Steve Ovett	England	July 1, 1980	Oslo
3:48.83	Sydney Maree	United States	Sept. 9, 1981	Rieti, Italy
3:48.85	Sydney Maree[1]	United States	June 26, 1982	Oslo
3:48.95	Sebastian Coe	England	July 17, 1979	Oslo
3:49.08	John Walker[1]	New Zealand	July 7, 1982	Oslo
3:49.25	Steve Ovett	England	July 11, 1981	Oslo
3:49.34	David Moorcroft[2]	England	June 26, 1982	Oslo
3:49.4	John Walker	New Zealand	Aug. 12, 1975	Goteborg, Sweden
3:49.44	Sydney Maree	United States	July 13, 1982	Cork, Eire
3:49.45	Mike Boit[1]	Kenya	Aug. 28, 1981	Brussels
3:49.50	John Walker[3]	New Zealand	June 26, 1982	Oslo
3:49.57	Steve Ovett	England	Aug. 31, 1979	London
3:49.66	Steve Ovett	England	July 14, 1981	Lausanne, Switz.
3:49.67	Jose–Luis Gonzalez[1]	Spain	July 11, 1981	Oslo
3:49.68	Steve Scott[2]	United States	July 11, 1981	Oslo
3:49.72	Steve Scott	United States	Aug. 25, 1982	Koblenz, W. Ger.
3:49.74	Mike Boit[1]	Kenya	Aug. 19, 1981	Zurich
3:49.75	Sydney Maree[1]	United States	Aug. 25, 1982	Koblenz, W. Ger.
3:49.77	Ray Flynn[2]	Eire	July 7, 1982	Oslo
3:49.92	Steve Cram[1]	England	July 13, 1982	Cork, Eire
3:49.93	Sydney Maree	United States	Sept. 16, 1981	Aichach, W. Ger.
3:49.95	Steve Cram[2]	England	Aug. 19, 1981	Zurich
3:50.03	John Walker[2]	New Zealand	July 13, 1982	Cork, Eire
3:50.12	John Walker[3]	New Zealand	Aug. 19, 1981	Zurich
3:50.19	Thomas Wessinghage[2]	West Germany	Aug. 25, 1982	Koblenz, W. Ger.
3:50.23	Steve Ovett[1]	England	Sept. 9, 1981	Rieti, Italy
3:50.26	John Walker[3]	New Zealand	July 11, 1981	Oslo
3:50.34	Todd Harbour[4]	United States	July 11, 1981	Oslo
3:50.38	Steve Cram[5]	England	July 11, 1981	Oslo
3:50.38	Pierre Deleze[3]	Switzerland	Aug. 25, 1982	Koblenz, W. Ger.
3:50.51	Mike Boit[1]	Kenya	Sept. 16, 1981	Aichach, W. Ger.
3:50.54	Ray Flynn[4]	Eire	June 26, 1982	Oslo
3:50.55	Ray Flynn[4]	Eire	Aug. 25, 1982	Koblenz, W. Ger.
3:50.56	Thomas Wessinghage[1]	West Germany	Aug. 31, 1979	London
3:50.58	John Walker	New Zealand	Mar. 19, 1981	Auckland, N.Z.
3:50.65	Graham Williamson[3]	England	July 13, 1982	Cork. Eire
3:50.84	Tom Byers[5]	United States	Aug. 25, 1982	Koblenz, W. Ger.
3:50.87	Jose–Luis Gonzalez[1]	Spain	July 14, 1981	Lausanne, Switz.
3:50.91	Thomas Wessinghage[6]	West Germany	July 11, 1981	Oslo
3:50.95	Thomas Wessinghage[4]	West Germany	Aug. 19, 1981	Zurich
3:51.0	Filbert Bayi	Tanzania	May 17, 1975	Kingston, Jamaica
3:51.1	Jim Ryun	United States	June 23, 1967	Bakersfield, Calif.

1. Finished second. 2. Finished third. 3. Finished fourth. 4. Finished fifth. 5. Finished sixth. 6. Finished seventh. NOTE: Professional marks not included.

HISTORY OF THE POLE VAULT

(Some of early dates are the winning heights of A.A.U. champion for that year, used to show progression from one foot level to the next. Figures from A.A.U. records and *Track & Field News.*)

Bamboo Poles

1877	G. McNichol	9 ft 7 in.
1879	W. J. Van Houten	10 ft $4\frac{3}{4}$ in.
1883	Hugh Baxter	11 ft $0\frac{1}{2}$ in.
1904	Norman Dole	12 ft $1\frac{3}{10}$ in.
1912	Robert Gardner	13 ft 1 in.
1927	Sabin Carr	14 ft 0 in.
1940	Cornelius Warmerdam	15 ft 1 in.
1942	Cornelius Warmerdam	15 ft $7\frac{3}{4}$ in.

Metal Poles

1957	Bob Gutowski	15 ft $8\frac{1}{4}$ in.
1960	Don Bragg	15 ft $9\frac{1}{4}$ in.

Fiberglas Poles

1961	George Davis	15 ft $10\frac{1}{4}$ in.
1962	John Uelses	16 ft $0\frac{3}{4}$ in.
1962	Dave Tork	16 ft 2 in.
1962	Pentti Nikula	16 ft $2\frac{1}{2}$ in.
1963	John Pennel	16 ft 4 in.
1963	Brian Sternberg	16 ft 5 in.
1963	John Pennel	16 ft $6\frac{3}{4}$ in.
1963	Brian Sternberg	16 ft 8 in.
1963	John Pennel	16 ft 10 in.
1963	John Pennel	17 ft $0\frac{3}{4}$ in.
1964	Fred Hansen	17 ft 4 in.
1966	Bob Seagren	17 ft $5\frac{1}{2}$ in.
1966	John Pennel	17 ft $6\frac{1}{4}$ in.
1967	Bob Seagren	17 ft 7 in.
1967	Paul Wilson	17 ft $7\frac{3}{4}$ in.
1968	Bob Seagren	17 ft 9 in.
1969	John Pennel	17 ft $10\frac{1}{4}$ in.
1970	Wolfgang Norwig	17 ft $10\frac{1}{2}$ in.
1970	Chris Papanicolaou	18 ft $0\frac{1}{4}$ in.
1972	Kjell Isaksson	18 ft 1 in.
1972	Kjell Isaksson	18 ft 2 in.
1972	Kjell Isaksson, Bob Seagren	18 ft $4\frac{1}{4}$ in.
1972	Bob Seagren	18 ft $5\frac{3}{4}$ in.
1975	Dave Roberts	18 ft $6\frac{1}{2}$ in.
1976	Earl Bell	18 ft $7\frac{1}{4}$ in.
1976	Dave Roberts	18 ft $8\frac{1}{4}$ in.
1980	Thierry Vigneron	18 ft $10\frac{1}{4}$ in.
1980	Philippe Houvion	18 ft 11 in.
1980	Wladyslaw Kozakiewicz	18 ft $11\frac{1}{2}$ in.
1981	Thierry Vigneron	19 ft $\frac{1}{4}$ in.
1981	Vladimir Polyakov	19 ft $\frac{3}{4}$ in.

UNITED STATES MARATHON CHAMPIONS

(26 miles, 385 Yards)

Boston Marathon

1970	Ron Hill, England	2:10:30
1971	Alvaro Meija, Colombia	2:18:45
1972	Olavi Suomalainen, Finland	2:15:39
1973	Jon Anderson, Eugene, Ore.	2:16:03
1974	Neil Cusack, Ireland	2:13:39
1975	William H. Rodgers, Boston	2:09:55
1976	Jack Fultz, Arlington, Va.	2:20:19
1977	Jerome Drayton, Toronto	2:14:46
1978	William H. Rodgers, Melrose, Mass.	2:10:13
1979	William H. Rodgers, Melrose, Mass.	2:09.27
1980	William H. Rodgers, Melrose, Mass.	2:12:11
1981	Toshihiko Seko, Japan	2:09:26
1982	Alberto Salazar, Eugene, Ore.	2:08:51

Amateur Athletic Union

1970	Bob Fitts, Wisconsin	2:24:11
1971	Ken Moore, Portland, Ore.	2:16:49
1972	Edmund Norris, Brockton, Mass.	2:24:42.8
1973	Doug Schmenk	2:15:48
1974	Ron Wayne, Eugene, Ore.	2:18:52
1975	Gary Tuttle, Beverly Hills Strider	2:17:27
1976	Gary Tuttle, Los Angeles	2:15:15
1977	Not Held	
1978	Carl Hatfield, West Va. T.C.	2:17.20
1979	Tom Antczak, Rockford, Ill.	2:15.28

The Athletics Congress

1980	Paul Richardson, Ames, Iowa	2:13:54*

*Time not recognized because course was too short.

CROSS COUNTRY RACE CHAMPIONS

The Athletics Congress

(A.A.U. before 1980)

(10,000 Meters)

1971	Frank Shorter, Gainesville, Fla.; Florida T.C.
1972	Frank Shorter, Gainesville, Fla.; Florida T.C.
1973	Frank Shorter, Gainesville, Fla.; Florida T.C.
1974	John Ngeno, Kenya; Colorado T.C.
1975	Greg Fredericks, Philadelphia; Colorado T.C.
1976	Rick Rojas, San Diego; Jamul Toads
1977	Nick Rose, England; Colorado T.C.
1978	Greg Meyer, Boston; Mason Dixon A.C.
1979	Alberto Salazar, Boston; Greater Boston T.C.
1980	Jon Sinclair, Boulder, Colo. Victory A.C.
1981	Adrian Royle, Reno, Nev.; Athletics West

N.C.A.A. (University)

(10,000 meters)

1973	Steve Prefontaine, Oregon; Oregon
1974	Nick Rose, Western Kentucky; Oregon
1975	Craig Virgin, Illinois; Texas-El Paso
1976	Henry Rono, Wash. State; Texas-El Paso
1977	Henry Rono, Wash. State; Oregon
1978	Alberto Salazar, Oregon; Texas-El Paso
1979	Henry Rono, Washington State; Texas-El Paso
1980	Suleiman Nyambui, Texas-El Paso, Texas-El Paso
1981	Matthews Motshwaraten, Texas-El Paso; Texas-El Paso

N.C.A.A. (College)

(10,000 meters)

1975	Div. II: Ralph Serna, Calif.-Irvine; Calif.-Irvine
	Div. III: Vin Fleming, Lowell; N. Central Illinois
1976	Div. II: Ralph Serna, Calif.-Irvine; Calif.-Irvine
	Div. III: Dale Cramer, Carleton; N. Central Illinois

1977 Div. II: Michael Bollman, N.D. State; E. Illinois
Div. III: Dale Kramer, Carleton; Occidental
1978 Div. II: Jim Schankel, Cal Poly, San Luis Opisbo; Cal Poly, San Luis Opisbo
Div. III: Dan Henderson, Wheaton; N. Cent. Illinois
1979 Div. II: Jim Schankel, Cal Poly, San Luis Opisbo
Div. III: Steve Hunt, Boston State; North Central, Ill.
1980 Div. II: Gary Henry, Pembroke State; Humboldt State
Div. III: Jeff Millman, North Central; Carleton
1981 Div. II: Mark Conover, Humboldt State; Millersville State
Div. III: Mark Whalley, Principia; North Central

N.A.I.A.

(5 Miles)
1973 Tony Brien, Marymount; Eastern New Mexico
1974 Mike Boit, Eastern New Mexico; Eastern New Mexico
1975 Mike Boit, Eastern New Mexico; Edinboro State
1976 John Kebiro, Eastern New Mexico; Edinboro State
1977 Garry Henry, Pembroke State; Adams State
1978 Kelly Jensen, So. Oregon; Pembroke State
1979 Sam Montoya, Adams State; Adams State
1980 Pat Porter, Adams State; Adams State
1981 Pat Porter, Adams State; Adams State

CROSS-COUNTRY WORLD CHAMPIONSHIPS—1982

(Rome, Italy, March 21, 1982)

Men—Mohammad Kedir, Ethiopia	33:40.5
Women—Maricica Puica, Romania	14:38.9
Junior men—Zurabachew Gelaw, Ethiopia	22:45.3
Men's team—Ethiopia	98 pts
Women's team—Soviet Union	44 pts
Junior men's team—Ethiopia	12 pts

WORLD AND AMERICAN BEST PERFORMANCES IN INDOOR TRACK

The International Amateur Athletic Union does not recognize indoor records. The following best performances, often called world records, are from lists provided by The Athletics Congress of the United States and *Track and Field News*, published in Los Altos, Calif., Bert Nelson, editor and publisher.

MEN

Running

50 yards—Stanley Floyd, Los Angeles, 1982	0:05.22
60 yards—Stanley Floyd, Dallas, 1981	0:06.04
70 yards—Herb McFarland, Louisville, Ky.	0:06.7
100 yards—Don Quarrie, Pocatello, Idaho, 1971	0:09.3
Carl Lawson, Pocatello, Idaho, 1971	0:09.3
Cliff Branch, Pocatello, Idaho, 1972	0:09.3
300 yards—Terron Wright, Bloomington, Ind., 1981	0.29.26
440 yards—Tommie Smith, Louisville, Ky., 1967	0:46.2
Deon Hogan (Am.), Lincoln, Neb., 1981	0:47.20
500 yards—Lee Evans, College Park, Md., 1971	0:54.4
Pro—Larry James, Salt Lake City, Utah, 1973	0:53.9
600 yards—Martin McGrady, New York, 1970	1:07.6
880 yards—Ralph Doubell, Albuquerque N.M., 1969	1:47.9
Mark Belger (Am.), College Park, Md., 1978	1:48.1
Tom Von Ruden (Am.), College Park, Md., 1971	1:48.5
1,000 yards—Don Paige, Inglewood, Calif., 1982	2:04.7
Mile—Eamonn Coghlan, San Diego, 1981	3:50.6
Steve Scott (Am.), San Diego, 1981	3:51.8
2 miles—Emiel Puttemans, Berlin, 1973	8:13.2
Doug Padilla (Am.) San Diego, 1982	8:16.8
3 miles—Emiel Puttemans, Pentin, Belgium, 1976	12:54.6
Alberto Salazar (Am.), New York, 1981	12:56.6

Running—Metric Distances

50 meters—Manfred Koket, East Germany, 1971	0:05.4
Bill Gaines (Am.), Highland Park, N.J., 1968	0:05.4
James Sanford (Am.), San Diego, 1981	0:05.61
60 meters—Houston McTear, New York, 1978	0:06.11
70 meters—Helmut Kornig, Germany, 1932	0:07.5
Ira Murchison (Am.), United States	0:07.5
Pro—John Carlos, Pocatello, Idaho, 1974	0:07.3
100 meters—Eugen Ray, East Berlin, 1976	0:10.16
Pro—Warren Edmonson, Pocatello, Idaho, 1973	0:10.2
200 meters—Erwin Skamrahl, Dortmund, West Germany, 1982	0:20.99
Mel Lattany (Am.), Milan, Italy, 1982	0:21.25
300 meters—Pietro Mennea, Italy, 1978	0:32.83
Cliff Wiley (Am.), Saskatchewan, 1981	0:33.33
400 meters—Hartmut Weber, West Germany, 1981	0:45.96
Bill Green (Am.), Sherbrooke, Quebec, 1981	0:46.08
500 meters—Herman Frazier, Long Beach, Calif., 1979	1:01.2
Pro—Lee Evans, Pocatello, Idaho, 1973	1:02
600 meters—Coloman Trabado, Madrid, 1982	1:17.2
Fred Sowerby (Am.), Newark, Del. 1982	1:17.60
Pro—Lee Evans, Pocatello, Idaho, 1977	1:16.7
800 meters—Sabastian Coe, England, 1981	1:46.0
Ted Nelson (Am.), Berlin, 1965	1:47.4
1,000 meters—Paul-Heinz Wellmann, West Germany, 1976	2:19.1
Tom Byers (Am.), Louisville, Ky., 1982	2:19.5
Pro—Chris Fisher, Daly City, Calif., 1973	2:19.7
1,500 meters—Eamonn Coghlan, San Diego, 1981	3:35.6
Steve Smith (Am.), San Diego, 1981	3:36.0
2,000 meters—Steve Scott, Louisville, Ky., 1981	4:58.6
3,000 meters—Emiel Puttemans, Berlin, 1973	7:39.2
Steve Scott (Am.), Long Beach, Calif., 1980	7:45.2
5,000 meters—Suleiman Nyambui, New York, 1981	13:20.4
Doug Padilla (Am.), New York, 1982	13:20.55

Hurdles

50 yards—Renaldo Nehemiah, Toronto, 1982	0:05.92
60 yards—Renaldo Nehemiah, Dallas, 1982	0:06.82
50 meters—Renaldo Nehemiah, Edmonton, 1979	0:06.36
60 meters—Andre Prokofyev, Vilnius, 1979	0:07.54
Renaldo Nehemiah, (Am.), Montreal, 1979	0:07.62

Walking

1,500 meters—Jim Heiring, East Rutherford, N.J., 1982	5:27.1
Mile—Jim Heiring, Richfield, Ohio, 1982	5:47.39
3,000 meters—Yevgeny Yavsyukov, Montreal, 1979	11.31.1
2 miles—Jim Heiring, Kansas City, Mo., 1982	12:20.6
3 miles—Antoli Soloman, Toronto, 1978	19:40.0

Relays

1,600 meters—West Germany, Dortmund, West Germany, 1981	3:34.38
880 yards—Idaho State, Pocatello, Idaho, 1979	1:26.9
Mile—Pacific Coast Club, Pocatello, Idaho, 1971	3:09.4
2 miles—Univ. of Chicago, T.C., Louisville, Ky., 1974	7:20.8
4 miles—Villanova, Hanover, N.H., 1976	16:19
Sprint medley—Philadelphia T.C., New York, 1980	2:01.1
Distance medley—Villanova, Louisville, Ky., 1980	9:38.4

Field Events

High jump—Dietmar Mogenburg, West Germany, 1980	7 ft 8¾ in.
Jeff Woodard (Am.), New York, 1981	7 ft 7¾ in.
Long jump—Carl Lewis, East Rutherford, N.J., 1982	28 ft 1 in.
Triple jump—Willie Banks, San Diego, 1982	57 ft 1½ in.
Pole Vault—Billy Olson, Kansas City, Mo., 1982	18 ft 10 in.
Pro—Steve Smith, New York, 1975	18 ft 5 in.
Shotput—George Woods, Inglewood, Calif., 1974	72 ft 2¾ in.
Brian Oldfield (pro), El Paso, Tex., 1975	72 ft 6½ in.
35-pound weight throw—Yuri Syedikh, Montreal, 1979	76 ft 11¾ in.
Ed Kania (Am.), Princeton, N.J., 1981	73 ft 4 in.
Penthathlon—Daley Thompson, Canyon, Tex., 1982	4.314 pts

WOMEN

Running

50 yards—Andrea Lynch, Toronto, 1978	0:05.80
Deandra Carney (Am.), Toronto, 1978	0:05.68
Evelyn Ashford (Am.), Toronto, 1981	0:05.83
60 yards—Evelyn Ashford, New York, 1982	0:06.54
100 yards—Marita Koch, East Berling, 1979	0:10.40
Wilma Rudolph (Am.), Tennessee State, 1960	0:10.70
220 yards—Chandra Cheeseborough, New York, 1982	0:23.25
300 yards—Merlene Ottey, Cedar Falls, Neb., 1982	0:32.63
Randy Givens (Am.), Cedar Falls, Neb., 1982	0:34.07
440 yards—Rosalyn Bryant, New York, 1977	0:53.20
500 yards—Rosalyn Bryant, San Diego, 1977	1:03.30
Janine MacGregor, Inglewood, Calif., 1982	1:03.30
600 yards—Delisa Walton, Cedar Falls, Neb., 1982	1:17.38
880 yards—Mary Decker, San Diego, 1980	1:59.70
1,000 yards—Mary Decker, Inglewood, Calif., 1978	2:23.80
Mile—Mary Decker Tabb, San Diego, 1982	4:20.5
2 miles—Joan Hansen, New York, 1982	9:37.03

Running—Metric Distances

50 meters—Jeanette Bolden, Edmonton, Alberta, 1981	0:06.13
60 meters—Marlies Gohr, East Germany, 1980	0:07.10
Brenda Moorehead (Am.), Louisville, Ky., 1980	0:07.28
100 meters—Marlies Gohr, East Berlin, 1979	0:11.30
Mamie Rallins (Am.), San Diego, 1975	0:12.40
200 meters—Gesine Walther, Budapest, 1982	0:22.64
300 meters—Merlene Ottey, Lincoln, Neb., 1981	0:33.12
Janet Dodson (Am.), Morgantown, W. Va., 1982	0:37.54
400 meters—Jarmila Kratochvilova, Milan, Italy, 1982	0:49.59
Sharon Dabney (Am.), Italy, 1978	0:53.27
500 meters—Lorna Forde, Hanover, N.H., 1978	1:10.50
600 meters—Anita Weiss, East Berlin, 1980	1:26.20
Chris Muller (Am.), Columbia, Mo., 1980	1:28.80
800 meters— Olga Vakrusheva, Moscow, 1980	1:58.40
Mary Decker (Am.), San Diego, 1980	1:58.90
1,000 meters—Bridgette Kraus, West Germany 1978	2:34.80
Francie Larrieu (Am.), Los Angeles, 1975	2:40.20
1,500 meters—Mary Decker, New York, 1980	4:00.80
2,000 meters—Francie Larrieu, Edmonton, Alberta, 1981	5:55.2
3,000 meters—Mary Decker Tabb, Inglewood, Calif., 1982	8:47.3

Hurdles

50 yards—Johanna Klier, Toronto, 1978	0:06.20
Deby LaPlante (Am.), Toronto, 1978	0:06.37
60 yards—Candy Young, New York, 1982	0:07.37
Stephanie Hightower, New York, 1982	0:07.37
60 yards—Stephanie Hightower, New York, 1980	0:07.47
70 yards—Mamie Rallins, Chicago, 1970	0:08.80
Deby LaPlante, Louisville, Ky., 1976	0:08.80
50 meters—Annelie Ehrhardt, Berlin, 1973	0:06.74
Sofia Bielczyzk, Grenoble, France, 1981	0:06.74
Candy Young (Am.), Edmonton, Alberta, 1979	0:06.95
60 meters—Sofia Bielczyzk, Poland, 1980	0:07.77
Stephanie Hightower, (Am.), Milan, Italy, 1982	0:08.04
100 meters—Annelie Ehrhardt, East Germany, 1976	0:13.12
Patty van Wolvelaere (Am.), New York, 1974	0:13.20

Walking

Mile—Susan Brodock, New York, 1978	7:01.70
1,500 meters—Susan Brodock, Toronto, 1976	6:42.90

Relays

640 yards—Tennessee State, New York, 1981	1:08.99
880 yards—Tennessee State, Louisville, Ky., 1980	1:37.80
880 yard medley relay—Tennessee State, New York, 1981	1:42.17
Mile—Los Angeles Mercurettes, New York, 1981	3:40.46
2 miles—Soviet Union, 1972	8:41.60
Distance medley—Virginia, Princeton, N.J., 1982	11:19.39

Field Events

Long jump—Svyetlana Vanyushina, Vilnius, U.S.S.R., 1982	22 ft 5 in.
Veronica Bell (Am.), New York, 1982	21 ft 11¾ in.
High jump—Coleen Rienstra, Ottawa, 1982	6 ft 6¾ in.
Shotput—Helena Fibingerova, Czechoslovakia, 1977	73 ft 9¾ in.
Maren Seidler (Am.), West Germany, 1978	61 ft 2¼ in.

THE ATHLETICS CONGRESS NATIONAL CHAMPIONSHIPS

INDOOR

(Madison Square Garden, New York, Feb. 26, 1982)

Men's Events

60 yd—Ron Brown, Arizona State	0:06.14
600 yd—Fred Sowerby, D.C. International	1:09.50
1,000 yd—Don Paige, Athletic Attic	2:05.81[1]
440 yd—Walter McCoy, Athletic Attic	0:48.24
Mile—Jim Spivey, Indiana University	3:57.04
3 Miles—Paul Cummings, Pacific Coast Club	13:00.52
60-yd hurdles—Tony Campbell, Maccabi Track Club	0:07.13
2-mile walk—Jim Heiring, Athletic Attic	12:24.82[1]
Sprint medley relay—Athletic Attic (Ron Nelson, Floyd Brown, Vescoe Bradley, Terron Wright)	2:03.98
2-mile relay—University of Richmond (Ed Koech, Phil Norgate, Barnabas Kipkorior, Julian Spooner)	7:28.14[1]
Mile relay—Morgan State (Gary Goodman, Mitch Lovett, Carlton McNorton, Ed Yearwood)	3:13.46
Long jump—Carl Lewis, (Houston) unattached	28 ft ¾ in.[1]
Triple jump—Keith Connor, Southern Methodist	55 ft 11 in.[1]
High jump—Dwight Stones, Pacific Coast Club	7 ft 4½ in.
Pole vault—Billy Olson, Pacific Coast Club	18 ft 6½ in.[1]
Shotput—Jeff Baum, University of Chicago	65 ft 10½ in.
35-lb weight throw—Ed Kania, Pacific Coast Club	70 ft ½ in.
Team—Athletic Attic	38 pts
Outstanding athlete—Carl Lewis	

Women's Events

60 yd—Evelyn Ashford, Medalist Track Club 0:06.54[1]
220 yd—Chandra Cheeseborough, Tennessee State (Miss Cheeseborough set world best in heat of 0:23.25) 0:23.46
440 yd—Maxine Underwood, Boston International A.C. 0:54.55[2]
880 yd—Leann Warren, University of Oregon 2:04.61
Mile—Cathie Twomey, Athletics West 4:32.92[1]
2 miles—Joan Hansen, Athletics West 9:37.03[3]
60-yd hurdles—Stephanie Hightower, Los Angeles Naturites 0:07.38[1]
Mile walk—Susan Brodock, Southern California Road Runners 7:14
640-yd relay—Tennessee State (Chandra Cheeseborough, Wanda Fort, Sheryl Pernell, Ernestine Davis) 1:09.36
880-yd medley relay—Tennessee State (Judith Pollion, Wanda Fort, Sheryl Pernell, Chandra Cheeseborough) 1:44.26
Mile relay—Atoms Track Club (Stephanie Vega, Dorionne McClure, Lorna Forde, Diane Dixon) 3:40.54
High jump—Coleen Rienstra, Wilt's Athletic Club 6 ft 3¼ in.[1]
Long jump—Veronica Bell, Southern California 21 ft 11¾ in.[1, 4]
Shotput—Marita Walton, University of Maryland 55 ft 11¾ in.

1. Meet record. 2. National high school record. 3. World best. 4. American record.

THE ATHLETICS CONGRESS NATIONAL CHAMPIONSHIPS—1982

(Knoxville, Tenn., June 18–20, 1982)

OUTDOOR

Men's Events

100 m—Carl Lewis, Santa Monica Track Club 0:10.11
200 m—Calvin Smith, Athletic Attic 0:20.47
400 m—Cliff Wiley, unattached 0:45.05
800 m—James Robinson, Inner City Athletic Club 1:46.12
1,500 m—Steve Scott, Sub 4 Track Club 3:34.92[1]
3,000-m steeplechase—Henry Marsh, Athletics West 8:22.94
5,000 m—Matt Centrowitz, New York Athletic Club 13:31.96
10,000 m—Craig Virgin, Front Runner Track Club 28:33.02
20,000-m walk—Jim Heiring, Athletic Attic 1:30:21.8
110-m hurdles—Willie Gault, Athletic Attic 0:13.54
400-m hurdles—David Patrick, Athletics West 0:48.57
High jump—Milt Ottey, Philadelphia Pioneers 7 ft 5¾ in.
Pole vault—Tie between Dan Ripley, Pacific Coast Club, and Billy Olson, Pacific Coast Club 18 ft 9¼ in.[2]
Long jump—Carl Lewis, Santa Monica Track Club 27 ft 10 in.
Triple jump—Robert Cannon, Athletic Attic 55 ft ¾ in.
Shot-put—Kevin Akins, Ohio State 69 ft 9½ in.
Discus—Louis Delis, Cuba 225 ft 5 in.
Hammer—David McKenzie, unattached 235 ft 2 in.
Javelin—Bob Roggy, Athletics West 289 ft 9 in.[1]

1. Meet record. 2. American record.

Women's Events

100 m—Evelyn Ashford, Medalist Track Club 0:10.96[1]
200 m—Merlene Ottey, Los Angeles Naturite-Jamaica 0:22.17[1]
400 m—Denean Howard, Los Angeles Naturite 0:50.87[1]
800 m—Delisa Walton, Los Angeles Naturite 2:00.91
1,500 m—Mary Decker Tabb, Athletics West 4:03.37[1]
3,000 m—Francie Larrieu-Smith, New Balance Track Club 8:58.66
10,000 m—Kim Schurpfeil, Stanford Track Club 33:35.88
100—m hurdles—Stephanie Hightower, Los Angeles Naturite 0:12.86[2]
400-m hurdles—Tammy Etienne, Metroplex Striders 0:56.55
5,000-m walk—Susan Liers-Westerfield, Island Track Club 24:56.6
400-m relay—Wilt's Athletic Club (Brenda Morehead, Jeannette Bolden, Alice Brown, Florence Griffith) 0:43.45
800-m relay—Wilt's Athletic Club (Brenda Morehead, Jeanette Bolden, Alice Brown, Arlise Emerson) 1:36.79
1,600-m relay—Los Angeles Naturite (Sharon Dabney, Denean Howard, Sherry Howard, Rosalyn Bryant) 3:28.68
3,200-m relay—Stanford Track Club (Evonne Hannus, Regina Jacobs, June Griffith, Tami Essington) 8:22.26[1]
High jump—Debbie Brill, Pacific Coast Club 6 ft 4 in.
Long jump—Carol Lewis, Willingboro, N.J. 22 ft 4½ in.
Shot-put—Maria Sarria, Cuba 61 ft 8¼ in.
Discus—Ria Stalman, Los Angeles Naturite 203 ft 10 in.
Javelin—Lynda Huges, Oregon 202 ft 3 in.

1. Meet record. 2. Ties American record.

N.C.A.A. CHAMPIONSHIPS—1982

INDOOR

(Pontiac, Mich., March 12–13, 1982)

60 yd—Rod Richardson, Texas A. and M. 0:06.07[1]
440 yd—Anthony Ketcham, Houston 0:47.47
600 yd—Eugene Sanders, Mississippi Valley 1:08.51[1]
880 yd—David Patrick, Tennessee 1:49.94
1,000 yd—John Stephens, Arkansas 2:07.37
Mile—Suleiman Nyambui, Texas–El Paso 4:00.65
2 miles—Suleiman Nyambui 8:38.91
3 miles—Gabriel Kamau, Texas–El Paso 13:07.81[1]
60-yd hurdles—Tony Campbell, Southern California 0:07.14
Mile relay—Oklahoma (Freddie Wilson, Donald Bly, Coty Duling, Dannie Cater) 3:11.07[1]
2-mile relay—Richmond (Edwin Koech, Julian Spooner, Phil Norgate, Sosthenes Bitok) 7:24.48
Distance medley relay—Georgetown (John Padati, Patrick McCabe, Kevin King, John Gregorek) 9:45.97
Long jump—Gilbert Smith, Texas–Arlington 26 ft 1 in.
High jump—Leo Williams, Navy 7 ft 5¾ in.[1]
Pole vault—Doug Lytle, Kansas State 17 ft 9¾ in.
Triple jump—Keith Connor, Southern Methodist 55 ft 3 in.
35-lb weight throw—Tore Johnsen, Texas–El Paso 70 ft 3¼ in.
Shotput—Mike Lehmann, Illinois 67 ft 7¾ in.
Team—Texas–El Paso 67 pts

1. Meet record.

OUTDOOR

(Provo, Utah, May 31–June 5, 1982)

Men's Events

100 m—Stanley Floyd, Houston 0:10.03[1]
200 m—James Butler, Oklahoma State 0:20.07
400 m—Kashoof Hassan, Oregon State 0:45.47
800 m—David Mack, Oregon 1:48.00
1,500 m—Jim Spivey, Indiana 3:45.42

3,000 steeplechase—Richard Tuwei, Washington State	8:42.73
5,000 m—Suleiman Nyambui, Texas-El Paso	13:54.09
10,000 m—Suleiman Nyambui	29:03.54
110–m hurdles—Milan Stewart, Southern California	0:13.53
400–m hurdles—David Patrick, Tennessee	0:48.44[1]
400–m relay—Houston (Charles Young, Mark McNeil, Anthony Ketchum, Stanley Floyd)	0:38.53[2]
1,600–m relay—Mississippi State (Michael Hadley, George Washington, Michael Moore, Daryl Jones)	3:03.49
Discus—Dean Crouser, Oregon	207 ft 4 in.
Javelin—Brian Crouser, Oregon	274 ft 7 in.
Shot–Put—Dean Crouser, Oregon	68 ft 4¼ in.
Hammer—Richard Olsen, Southern Methodist	240 ft 6 in.
Pole vault—Dave Kenworthy, Southern California	18 ft 2½ in.
High jump—Milt Ottey, Texas-El Paso	7 ft 7¼ in.[3]
Triple jump—Keith Connor, Southern Methodist	57 ft 7¾ in.[2]
Long jump—Vance Johnson, Arizona	26 ft 11¼ in.
Decathlon—Trond Skramstad, Mount St. Mary's	7,770 pts
Team—Texas-El Paso	105 pts

1. Meet record. 2. Collegiate record. 3. Tied collegiate record.

Women's Events[1]

100 m—Merlene Ottey, Nebraska	0:10.97
200 m—Florence Griffith, U.C.L.A.	0:23.20
400 m—Marita Payne, Florida State	0:52.01
800 m—Delisa Walton, Tennessee	2:05.22
1,500 m—Leann Warren, Oregon	4:17.90
3,000 m—Ceci Hopp, Stanford	9:28.92
5,000 m—Kathy Bryant, Tennessee	16:10.41
10,000 m—Kim Schnurpfeil, Stanford	n.a.
100–m hurdles—Benita Fitzgerald, Tennessee	0:13.13
400–m hurdles—Tonja Brown, Florida State	0:56.46
High jump—Disa Gisladdottir, Alabama	6 ft 1¼ in.
Long jump—Jennifer Innis, California State-Los Angeles	21 ft 9½ in
Shot–Put—Meg Ritchie, Arizona	55 ft 5¼ in
Discus—Meg Ritchie	202 ft
Javelin—Karin Smith, California Poly-San Luis Obispo	206 ft 8 in.
400–m relay—Nebraska (Kristen Engle, Alicia McQueen, Rhonda Blanford, Merlene Ottey)	0:43.72
1,600–m relay—Tennessee (Cathy Rattray, Sharieffa Barksdale, Joetta Clark, Delisa Walton)	3:28.55[2]
Heptathlon—Jackie Joyner, U.C.L.A.	6,099 pts
Team—U.C.L.A.	153 pts

1. First time women's N.C.A.A. competition was held. 2. Collegiate record. n.a. = not available.

NATIONAL ATHLETIC CONGRESS RELAY CHAMPIONSHIPS

(New Brunswick, N. J., July 4, 1982)

400 meters—New York Pioneer Club (Michael McKnight, Brian Denman, Brady Crain, Elliott Quow)	0:40.6
800 meters—New York Pioneer Club (Brady Crain, Brian Denman, Derrick Peynado, Elliott Quow)	1:26.1
1,600 meters—BOHAA Club of New York (Dennis Duckworth, Nigel Gabriel, Gordon Hinds, Richard Louis)	3:09.7
3,200 meters—Fort Lee Athletic Attic (Jim McKeon, John Borgese, Ray Oglesby, Tavo Rivera)	7:36.3
Sprint medley—Alliance Track Club of Long Island (Kevin Price, Alfred Daley, Hubert Blue, Larry Brooks)	3:22.6[1]
6,000 meters—New York Athletic Club (John Malone, John Hunter, Vince Draddy, Jim DiRienzo)	15:34.6[1]
Distance medley—New York Athletic Club (Brian McNellis, Tim Hanlon, John Hunter, Ross Donoghue)	9:45.0[1]
440–meter shuttle hurdles—Shore Athletic Club (Joe Myatt, Bob Beaman, John Charniga, Leon Devero)	0:57.3
Team—Fort Lee Athletic Attic	42 pts

1. Meet record.

ASSOCIATION FOR INTERCOLLEGIATE ATHLETICS FOR WOMEN

(Cedar Falls, Iowa, March 12–13, 1982)

Indoor

60 yd—Merlene Ottey, Nebraska	0:06.61
300 yd—Merlene Ottey, Nebraska	0:32.63[1 2]
440 yd—Lori McCauley, Rutgers	0:55.12
600 yd—Delisa Walton, Tennessee	1:17.38[1 2 3]
880 yd—Doriane McClive, Cornell	2:05.34
1,000 yd—Goetta Clark, Tennessee	2:26.70
Mile—Darleen Beckford, Harvard	4:38.30
2 miles—Bernadette Badigan, Kentucky	9:58.22
3 miles—Kellie Cathy, Oklahoma	15:18.47[4]
60–yd hurdles—Benita Fitzgerald, Tennessee	0:07.54
880–yd relay—Nebraska (Ottey, Gorham, Blanford, James)	1:37.70[5]
Mile relay—Texas (Sherfield, Walker, Bean, Coleman)	3:44.66[5]
2–mile relay—Florida State (Coomber, Borovicha, Wood, Brown)	8:47.26[4]
Distance medley relay—Virginia (Nicholoson, Hatchett, Welch, Haworth)	11:21.92[4]
Long jump—Donna Thomas, North Texas State	20 ft. 8½ in.
High jump—Gale Charmaine, Arizona	6 ft. 1¾ in.
Shot–put—Rosemary Blauch, Tennessee	54 ft. 11¾ in.
Pentathlon—Julie White, Boston University	4,268 pts
Team—Nebraska	84 pts

1. World best. 2. U.S. collegiate best. 3. American best. 4. New event, record. 5. Meet record.

Outdoor

(College Station, Tex., May 27–29, 1982)

100 m—Colleen Hanna, Iowa State	0:11.73
200 m—Merry Johnson, West Texas State	0:23.57
400 m—Merry Johnson	0:52.43
800 m—Louise Romo, California–Berkeley	2:04.39[1]
1,500 m—Rose Thomson, Wisconsin–Madison	4:18.78
3,000 m—Andrea Marek, Purdue	9:16.18
5,000 m—Midde Hamrin, Lamar University	16:03.75[1]
10,000 m—Midde Hamrin	33:37.68
100–m hurdles—Lori Dinello, Florida	0:13.48
400–m hurdles—Edna Brown, Temple	0:57.17[1]
400–m relay—Texas–Austin (H. Denny, S. Bean, D. Sherfield, S. Shurr)	0:46.04
800–m relay—Texas–Austin (D. Hollie, S. Shurr, D. Sherfield, R. Coleman)	1:39.92
1,600–m relay—Texas–Austin (D. Sherfield, F. Walker, S. Bean, R. Coleman)	3:37.66
3,200–m relay—Texas–Austin (S. Neugebauer, R. Coleman, F. Walker, T. Arnold)	8:39.67[1]
Long jump—Pat Johnson, Wisconsin–Madison	21 ft 4¾ in.[1]
Javelin—Lorri Kokkola, Texas–Austin	170 ft 10 in.
Shotput—Sandy Burke, Northeastern	52 ft 2¾ in.
Discus—Penny Neer, Michigan	183 ft
High jump—Carolyn Ford, Lamar University	6 ft ½ in.[1]
Hepthathlon—Kathy Raugust, California–Berkeley	5,514 pts
Team—Texas–Austin	82 pts

1. A.I.A.W. record.

TENNIS

Lawn tennis is a comparatively modern modification of the ancient game of court tennis. Major Walter Clopton Wingfield thought that something like court tennis might be played outdoors on lawns, and in December, 1873, at Nantclwyd, Wales, he introduced his new game under the name of *Sphairistike* at a lawn party. The game was a success and spread rapidly, but the name was a total failure and almost immediately disappeared when all the players and spectators began to refer to the new game as "lawn tennis." In the early part of 1874, a young lady named Mary Ewing Outerbridge returned from Bermuda to New York, bringing with her the implements and necessary equipment of the new game, which she had obtained from a British Army supply store in Bermuda. Miss Outerbridge and friends played the first game of lawn tennis in the United States on the grounds of the Staten Island Cricket and Baseball Club in the spring of 1874.

For a few years, the new game went along in haphazard fashion until about 1880, when standard measurements for the court and standard equipment within definite limits became the rule. In 1881, the U.S. Lawn Tennis Association (whose name was changed in 1975 to U.S. Tennis Association) was formed and conducted the first national championship at Newport, R.I. The international matches for the Davis Cup began with a series between the British and United States players on the courts of the Longwood Cricket Club, Chestnut Hill, Mass., in 1900, with the home players winning.

Professional tennis, which got its start in 1926 when the French star Suzanne Lenglen was paid $50,000 for a tour, received full recognition in 1968. Staid old Wimbledon, the London home of what are considered the world championships, let the pros compete. This decision ended a long controversy over open tennis and changed the format of the competition. The United States championships were also opened to the pros and the site of the event, long held at Forest Hills, N.Y., was shifted to the National Tennis Center in Flushing Meadows, N.Y., in 1978. Pro tours for men and women became worldwide in play that continued throughout the year.

DAVIS CUP CHAMPIONSHIPS

No matches in 1901, 1910, 1915–18, and 1940–45.

1900	United States 3, British Isles 0	1930	France 4, United States 1	1960	Australia 4, Italy 1
1902	United States 3, British Isles 2	1931	France 3, Great Britain 2	1961	Australia 5, Italy 0
1903	British Isles 4, United States 1	1932	France 3, United States 2	1962	Australia 5, Mexico 0
1904	British Isles 5, Belgium 0	1933	Great Britain 3, France 2	1963	United States 3, Australia 2
1905	British Isles 5, United States 0	1934	Great Britain 4, United States 1	1964	Australia 3, United States 2
1906	British Isles 5, United States 0	1935	Great Britain 5, United States 0	1965	Australia 4, Spain 1
1907	Australasia 3, British Isles 2	1936	Great Britain 3, Australia 2	1966	Australia 4, India 1
1908	Australasia 3, United States 2	1937	United States 4, Great Britain 1	1967	Australia 4, Spain 1
1909	Australasia 5, United States 0	1938	United States 3, Australia 2	1968	United States 4, Australia 1
1911	Australasia 5, United States 0	1939	Australia 3, United States 2	1969	United States 5, Romania 0
1912	British Isles 3, Australasia 2	1946	United States 5, Australia 0	1970	United States 5, West Germany 0
1913	United States 3, British Isles 2	1947	United States 4, Australia 1	1971	United States 3, Romania 2
1914	Australasia 3, United States 2	1948	United States 5, Australia 0	1972	United States 3, Romania 2
1919	Australasia 4, British Isles 1	1949	United States 4, Australia 1	1973	Australia 5, United States 0
1920	United States 5, Australasia 0	1950	Australia 4, United States 1	1974	South Africa (Default by India)
1921	United States 5, Japan 0	1951	Australia 3, United States 2	1975	Sweden 3, Czechoslovakia 2
1922	United States 4, Australasia 1	1952	Australia 4, United States 1	1976	Italy 4, Chile 1
1923	United States 4, Australasia 1	1953	Australia 3, United States 2	1977	Australia 3, Italy 1
1924	United States 5, Australasia 0	1954	United States 3, Australia 2	1978	United States 4, Britain 1
1925	United States 5, France 0	1955	Australia 5, United States 0	1979	United States 5, Italy 0
1926	United States 4, France 1	1956	Australia 5, United States 0	1980	Czechoslovakia 3, Italy 2
1927	France 3, United States 2	1957	Australia 3, United States 2	1981	United States 3, Argentina 1
1928	France 4, United States 1	1958	United States 3, Australia 2		
1929	France 3, United States 2	1959	Australia 3, United States 2		

FEDERATION CUP CHAMPIONSHIPS

World team competition for women conducted by International Lawn Tennis Federation

1963	United States 2, Australia 1	1970	Australia 3, West Germany 0	1977	United States 2, Australia 1
1964	Australia 2, United States 1	1971	Australia 3, Britain 0	1978	United States 2, Australia 1
1965	Australia 2, United States 1	1972	South Africa 2, Britain 1	1979	United States 3, Australia 0
1966	United States 3, West Germany 0	1973	Australia 3, South Africa 0	1980	United States 3, Australia 0
1967	United States 2, Britain 0	1974	Australia 2, United States 1	1981	United States 3, Britain 0
1968	Australia 3, Netherlands 0	1975	Czechoslovakia 3, Australia 0	1982	United States 3, West Germany 0
1969	United States 2, Australia 1	1976	United States 2, Australia 1		

FOUR PLAYERS WIN GRAND SLAM OF TENNIS

Only four players, two men and two women, have won the Grand Slam of Tennis by winning the Australian, French, Wimbledon, and United States singles championships. Rod Laver of Australia did it twice, in 1962 and again in 1969 when the tourneys were opens. Don Budge, an American, was the first to complete the slam in 1938. Maureen Connolly of California in 1953 was the first woman to take the four titles. Margaret Smith Court of Australia won them all in 1970.

U.S. CHAMPIONS

Singles—Men

NATIONAL

1881–87	Richard D. Sears
1888–89	Henry Slocum, Jr.
1890–92	Oliver S. Campbell
1893–94	Robert D. Wrenn
1895	Fred H. Hovey
1896–97	Robert D. Wrenn
1898–1900	Malcolm Whitman
1901–02	William A. Larned
1903	Hugh L. Doherty
1904	Holcombe Ward
1905	Beals C. Wright
1906	William J. Clothier
1907–11	William A. Larned
1912–13	Maurice McLoughlin[1]
1914	R. N. Williams II
1915	William Johnston
1916	R. N. William II
1917–18	R. Lindley Murray[2]
1919	William Johnston
1920–25	Bill Tilden
1926–27	Jean Rene Lacoste
1928	Henri Cochet
1929	Bill Tilden
1930	John H. Doeg
1931–32	Ellsworth Vines
1933–34	Fred J. Perry
1935	Wilmer L. Allison
1936	Fred J. Perry
1937–38	Don Budge
1939	Robert L. Riggs
1940	Donald McNeill
1941	Robert L. Riggs
1942	Fred Schroeder
1943	Joseph Hunt
1944–45	Frank Parker
1946–47	Jack Kramer
1948–49	Richard Gonzales
1950	Arthur Larsen
1951–52	Frank Sedgman
1953	Tony Trabert
1954	Vic Seixas
1955	Tony Trabert
1956	Ken Rosewall
1957	Mal Anderson
1958	Ashley Cooper
1959–60	Neale Fraser
1961	Roy Emerson
1962	Rod Laver
1963	Rafael Osuna
1964	Roy Emerson
1965	Manuel Santana
1966	Fred Stolle
1967	John Newcombe
1968	Arthur Ashe[3]
1969	Stan Smith[3]

OPEN

1968	Arthur Ashe
1969	Rod Laver
1970	Ken Rosewall
1971	Stan Smith
1972	Ilie Nastase
1973	John Newcombe
1974	Jimmy Connors
1975	Manuel Orantes
1976	Jimmy Connors
1977	Guillermo Vilas
1978	Jimmy Connors
1979	John McEnroe
1980–81	John McEnroe
1982	Jimmy Connors

Singles—Women

NATIONAL

1887	Ellen F. Hansel
1888–89	Bertha Townsend
1890	Ellen C. Roosevelt
1891–92	Mabel E. Cahill
1893	Aline M. Terry
1894	Helen R. Helwig
1895	Juliette P. Atkinson
1896	Elisabeth H. Moore
1897–98	Juliette P. Atkinson
1899	Marion Jones
1900	Myrtle McAteer
1901	Elisabeth H. Moore
1902	Marion Jones
1903	Elisabeth H. Moore
1904	May Sutton
1905	Elisabeth H. Moore
1906	Helen Homans
1907	Evelyn Sears
1908	Maud Bargar-Wallach
1909–11	Hazel V. Hotchkiss
1912–14	Mary K. Browne
1915–18	Molla Bjurstedt
1919	Hazel Hotchkiss Wightman
1920–22	Molla Bjurstedt Mallory
1923–25	Helen N. Wills
1926	Molla B. Mallory
1927–29	Helen N. Wills
1930	Betty Nuthall
1931	Helen Wills Moody
1932–35	Helen Jacobs
1936	Alice Marble
1937	Anita Lizana
1938–40	Alice Marble
1941	Sarah Palfrey Cooke
1942–44	Pauline Betz
1945	Sarah Cooke
1946	Pauline Betz
1947	Louise Brough
1948–50	Margaret Osborne duPont
1951–53	Maureen Connolly
1954–55	Doris Hart
1956	Shirley Fry
1957–58	Althea Gibson
1959	Maria Bueno
1960–61	Darlene Hard
1962	Margaret Smith
1963–64	Maria Bueno
1965	Margaret Smith
1966	Maria Bueno
1967	Billie Jean King
1968–69	Margaret Smith Court[3]

OPEN

1968	Virginia Wade
1969–70	Margaret Court
1971–72	Billie Jean King
1973	Margaret Court
1974	Billie Jean King
1975–78	Chris Evert
1979	Tracy Austin
1980	Chris Evert Lloyd
1981	Tracy Austin
1982	Chris Evert Lloyd

Doubles—Men

NATIONAL

1920	Bill Johnston–C. J. Griffin
1921–22	Bill Tilden–Vincent Richards
1923	Bill Tilden–B. I. C. Norton
1924	H. O. Kinsey–R. G. Kinsey
1925–26	Vincent Richards–R. N. Williams II
1927	Bill Tilden–Frank Hunter
1928	G. M. Lott, Jr.–V. Hennessy
1929–30	G. M. Lott, Jr.–J. H. Doeg
1931	W. L. Allison–John Van Ryn
1932	E. H. Vines, Jr.–Keith Gledh
1933–34	G. M. Lott, Jr.–L. R. Stoefen
1935	W. L. Allison–John Van Ryn
1936	Don Budge–Gene Mako
1937	G. von Cramm–H. Henkel
1938	Don Budge–Gene Mako
1939	A. K. Quist–J. E. Bromwich
1940–41	Jack Kramer–F. R. Schroeder
1942	Gardnar Mulloy–Bill Talbert
1943	Jack Kramer–Frank Parker
1944	Don McNeill–Bob Falkenburg
1945	Gardnar Mulloy–Bill Talbert
1946	Gardnar Mulloy–Bill Talbert
1947	Jack Kramer–Fred Schroeder
1948	Gardnar Mulloy–Bill Talbert
1949	John Bromwich–William Sidwell
1950	John Bromwich–Frank Sedgman
1951	Frank Sedgman–Ken McGregor
1952	Vic Seixas–Mervyn Rose
1953	Mervyn Rose–Rex Hartwig
1954	Vic Seixas–Tony Trabert
1955	Kosei Kamo–Atsushi Miyagi
1956	Lewis Hoad–Ken Rosewall
1957	Ashley Cooper–Neale Fraser
1958	Ham Richardson–Alex Olmedo
1959–60	Neale Fraser–Roy Emerson
1961	Chuck McKinley–Dennis Ralston
1962	Rafael Osuna–Antonio Palafox
1963–64	Chuck McKinley–Dennis Ralston
1965–66	Fred Stolle–Roy Emerson
1967	John Newcombe–Tony Roche
1968	Stan Smith–Bob Lutz[3]
1969	Richard Crealy–Allan Stone[3]

OPEN

1968	Stan Smith–Bob Lutz
1969	Fred Stolle–Ken Rosewall
1970	Nikki Pilic–Fred Barthes

1. Challenge round abandoned in 1912. 2. Patriotic Tournament in 1917. 3. With the inaugural of the Open Tournament in 1968, the United States Lawn Tennis Association held a national championship at Longwood, Chestnut Hill, Mass. which barred contract professionals in 1968 and 1969.

1971	John Newcombe–Roger Taylor
1972	Cliff Drysdale–Roger Taylor
1973	John Newcombe–Owen Davidson
1974	Bob Lutz–Stan Smith
1975	Jimmy Connors–Ilie Nastase
1976	Marty Riessen–Tom Okker
1977	Frew McMillan–Bob Hewitt
1978	Bob Lutz–Stan Smith
1979	John McEnroe–Peter Fleming
1980	Stan Smith–Bob Lutz
1981	John McEnroe–Peter Fleming
1982	Kevin Curren–Steve Denton

Doubles—Women

NATIONAL

1924	G. W. Wightman–Helen Wills
1925	Mary K. Browne–Helen Wills
1926	Elizabeth Ryan–Eleanor Goss
1927	L. A. Godfree–Ermyntrude Harvey
1928	Hazel Hotchkiss Wightman–Helen Wills
1929	Phoebe Watson–L. R. C. Michell
1930	Betty Nuthall–Sarah Palfrey
1931	Betty Nuthall–E. B. Wittingstall
1932	Helen Jacobs–Sarah Palfrey
1933	Betty Nuthall–Freda James
1934	Helen Jacobs–Sarah Palfrey
1935	Helen Jacobs–Sarah Palfrey Fabyan
1936	Marjorie G. Van Ryn–Carolin Babcock
1937–40	Sarah Palfrey Fabyan–Alice Marble
1941	Sarah Palfrey Cooke–Margaret Osborne
1942–47	A. Louise Brough–Margaret Osborne
1948–50	A. Louise Brough–Margaret O. duPont
1951–54	Doris Hart–Shirley Fry
1955–57	A. Louise Brough–Margaret O. duPont
1958–59	Darlene Hard–Jeanne Arth
1960	Darlene Hard–Maria Bueno
1961	Darlene Hard–Lesley Turner
1962	Darlene Hard–Maria Bueno
1963	Margaret Smith–Robyn Ebbern
1964	Karen Hantze Susman–Billie Jean Moffitt
1965	Nancy Richey–Carole Caldwell Graebner
1966	Nancy Richey–Maria Bueno
1967	Billie Jean King–Rosemary Casals
1968	Margaret Court–Maria Bueno[3]
1969	Margaret Court–Virginia Wade[3]

OPEN

1968	Maria Bueno–Margaret Court
1969	Darlene Hard–Francoise Durr
1970	Margaret Court–Judy Dalton
1971	Rosemary Casals–Judy Dalton
1972	Francoise Durr–Betty Stove
1973	Margaret Court–Virginia Wade
1974	Billie Jean King–Rosemary Casals
1975	Margaret Court–Virginia Wade
1976	Linky Boshoff–Ilana Kloss
1977	Martina Navratilova–Betty Stove
1978	Billie Jean King–Martina Navratilova
1979	Betty Stove–Wendy Turnbull
1980	Billie Jean King–Martina Navratilova
1981	Kathy Jordan–Anne Smith
1982	Rosemary Casals–Wendy Turnbull

1. Challenge round abandoned in 1912. 2. Patriotic Tournament in 1917. 3. With the inaugural of the Open Tournament in 1968, the United States Lawn Tennis Association held a national championship at Longwood, Chestnut Hill, Mass. which barred contract professionals in 1968 and 1969.

U.S. INDOOR CHAMPIONS

Singles—Men

1964	Charles McKinley
1965	Erik Lundquist
1966	Charles Pasarell
1967	Charles Pasarell
1968	Cliff Richey
1969	Stan Smith
1970	Ilie Nastase
1971	Clark Graebner
1972	Stan Smith
1973–75	Jimmy Connors
1976	Ilie Nastase
1977	Bjorn Borg
1978–79	Jimmy Connors
1980	John McEnroe
1981	Gene Mayer
1982	Johan Kriek

Singles—Women

1964	Mary Ann Eisel
1965	Nancy Richey
1966	Billie Jean King
1967	Billie Jean King
1968	Billie Jean King
1969	Mary Ann Eisel
1970	Mary Ann Curtis
1971	Billie Jean King
1972	Not held
1973	Evonne Goolagong
1974	Billie Jean King
1975	Martina Navratilova
1976	Virginia Wade
1977–82	Not held

Doubles—Men

1967	Arthur Ashe–Charles Pasarell
1968	Thomas Koch–Tom Okker
1969	Stan Smith–Bob Lutz
1970	Arthur Ashe–Stan Smith
1971	Manuel Orantes–Juan Gisbert
1972	Manuel Orantes–Andres Gimeno
1973	Juan Gisbert–Jurgen Fassbender
1974	Jimmy Connors–Frew McMillan
1975	Jimmy Connors–Ilie Nastase
1976–77	Sherwood Stewart–Fred McNair
1978	Brian Gottfried–Raul Ramirez
1979	Wojtek Fibak–Tom Okker
1980	John McEnroe–Brian Gottfried
1981	Gene Mayer–Sandy Mayer
1982	Kevin Curren–Steve Denton

Doubles—Women

1967	Carol Aucamp–Mary Ann Eisel
1968	Rosemary Casals–Billie Jean King
1969	Mary Ann Eisel–Valerie Ziegenfuss
1970	Peaches Bartkowicz–Nancy Richey
1971	Billie Jean King–Rosemary Casals
1972	Not held
1973	Olga Morozova–Marina Kroshina
1974	Not held
1975	Billie Jean King–Rosemary Casals
1976	Rosemary Casals–Francoise Durr
1977–82	Not held

BRITISH (WIMBLEDON) CHAMPIONS

(Amateur from inception in 1877 through 1967)

Singles—Men

1908–09	Arthur Gore	1929	Jean Cochet	1950	Budge Patty	1964–65	Roy Emerson
1910–13	A. F. Wilding	1930	Bill Tilden	1951	Richard Savitt	1966	Manuel Santana
1914	N. E. Brookes	1931	S. B. Wood	1952	Frank Sedgman	1967	John Newcombe
1919	G. L. Patterson	1932	Ellsworth Vines	1953	Vic Siexas	1968–69	Rod Laver
1920–21	Bill Tilden	1933	J. H. Crawford	1954	Jaroslav Drobny	1970–71	John Newcombe
1922	G. L. Patterson	1934–36	Fred Perry	1955	Tony Trabert	1972	Stan Smith
1923	William Johnston	1937–38	Don Budge	1956–57	Lewis Hoad	1973	Jan Kodes
1924	Jean Borotra	1939	Robert L. Riggs	1958	Ashley Cooper	1974	Jimmy Connors
1925	Rene Lacoste	1946	Yvon Petra	1959	Alex Olmedo	1975	Arthur Ashe
1926	Jean Borotra	1947	Jack Kramer	1960	Neale Fraser	1976–80	Bjorn Borg
1927	Henri Cochet	1948	R. Falkenburg	1961–62	Rod Laver	1981	John McEnroe
1928	Rene Lacoste	1949	Fred Schroeder	1963	Chuck McKinley	1982	Jimmy Connors

Singles—Women

1919–23	Lenglen	1937	D. E. Round	1959–60	Maria Bueno	1972–73	Billie Jean King
1924	Kathleen McKane	1938	Helen Wills Moody	1961	Angela Mortimer	1974	Chris Evert
1925	Lenglen	1939	Alice Marble	1962	Karen Susman	1975	Billie Jean King
1926	Godfree	1946	Pauline M. Betz	1963	Margaret Smith	1976	Chris Evert
1927–29	Helen Wills	1947	Margaret Osborne	1964	Maria Bueno	1977	Virginia Wade
1930	Helen Wills Moody	1948–50	A. Louise Brough	1965	Margaret Smith	1978–79	Martina Navratilova
1931	Frl. C. Aussen	1951	Doris Hart	1966–67	Billie Jean King		
1932–33	Helen Wills Moody	1952–54	Maureen Connolly	1968	Billie Jean King	1980	Evonne Goolagong Cawley
1934	D. E. Round	1955	A. Louise Brough	1969	Ann Jones		
1935	Helen Wills Moody	1956	Shirley Fry	1970	Margaret Court	1981	Chris Evert Lloyd
1936	Helen Jacobs	1957–58	Althea Gibson	1971	Evonne Goolagong	1982	Martina Navratilova

Doubles—Men

1953	K. Rosewall–L. Hoad	1964	Fred Stolle–Bob Hewitt	1976	Brian Gottfried–Raul Ramirez
1954	R. Hartwig–M. Rose	1965	John Newcombe–Tony Roche	1977	Ross Case–Geoff Masters
1955	R. Hartwig–L. Hoad			1978	Frew McMillan–Bob Hewitt
1956	L. Hoad–K. Rosewall	1966	John Newcombe–Ken Fletcher	1979	Peter Fleming–John McEnroe
1957	Gardnar Mulloy–Budge Patty	1967	Bob Hewitt–Frew McMillan	1980	Peter McNamara–Paul McNamee
1958	Sven Davidson–Ulf Schmidt	1968–70	John Newcombe–Tony Roche		
1959	Roy Emerson–Neale Fraser	1971	Rod Laver–Roy Emerson	1981	John McEnroe–Peter Fleming
1960	Dennis Ralston–Rafael Osuna	1972	Bob Hewitt–Frew McMillan	1982	Paul McNamee–Peter McNamara
1961	Roy Emerson–Neale Fraser	1973	Jimmy Connors–Ilie Nastase		
1962	Fred Stolle–Bob Hewitt	1974	John Newcombe–Tony Roche		
1963	Rafael Osuna–Antonio Palafox	1975	Vitas Gerulaitis–Sandy Mayer		

Doubles—Women

1956	Althea Gibson–Angela Buxton	1965	Billie Jean Moffitt–Maria Bueno	1975	Ann Kiyomura–Kazuko Sawamatsu
1957	Althea Gibson–Darlene Hard	1966	Nancy Richey–Maria Bueno	1976	Chris Evert–Martina Navratilova
1958	Althea Gibson–Maria Bueno	1967–68	Billie Jean King–Rosemary Casals	1977	Helen Cawley–JoAnne Russell
1959	Darlene Hard–Jeanne Arth	1969	Margaret Court–Judy Tegart	1978	Wendy Turnbull–Kerry Reid
1960	Darlene Hard–Maria Bueno	1970–71	Billie Jean King–Rosemary Casals	1979	Billie Jean King–Martina Navratilova
1961	Karen Hantze–Billie Jean Moffitt	1972	Billie Jean King–Betty Stove	1980	Kathy Jordan–Anne Smith
1962	Karen Hantze Susman–Billie Jean Moffitt	1973	Billie Jean King–Rosemary Casals	1981	Martina Navratilova–Pam Shriver
1963	Darlene Hard–Maria Bueno	1974	Evonne Goolagong–Peggy Michel	1982	Pam Shriver–Martina Navratilova
1964	Margaret Smith–Les Turner-ley				

UNITED STATES CHAMPIONSHIPS—1982

Open

(Flushing Meadows, N.Y., Aug. 31–Sept. 12, 1982)

Men's singles—Final: Jimmy Connors, Miami Beach, Fla., defeated Ivan Lendl, Czechoslovakia, 6–3, 6–2, 4–6, 6–4. Semifinals: Connors defeated Guillermo Vilas, Argentina, 6–1, 3–6, 6–2, 6–3; Lendl defeated John McEnroe, Douglaston, N.Y., 6–4, 6–4, 7–6.

Women's singles—Final: Chris Evert Lloyd, Amelia Island, Fla., defeated Hana Mandlikova, Czechoslovakia, 6–3, 6–1.Seminfinals: Mrs. Lloyd defeated Andrea Jaeger, Lincolnshire, Ill., 6–1, 6–2; Miss Mandlikova defeated Pam Shriver, Lutherville, Md., 6–4, 2–6, 6–2.

Men's doubles—Final: Kevin Curren, South Africa, and Steve Denton, Driscoll, Tex., defeated Victor Amaya, Louisville, Ky., and Hank Pfister, Los Gatos, Calif., 6–2, 6–7, 5–7, 6–2, 6–4.

Women's doubles—Final: Rosemary Casals, Sausalito, Calif., and Wendy Turnbull, Australia, defeated Barbara Potter, Woodbury, Conn., and Sharon Walsh, Novato, Calif., 6–4, 6–4.

Mixed doubles—Final: Anne Smith, Dallas, Tex., and Kevin Curren defeated Barbara Potter and Ferdi Taygan, Framingham, Mass., 6–7, 7–6, 7–6.

Junior boys singles—Final: Pat Cash, Australia, defeated Guy Forget, France, 6–3, 6–3.

Junior girls singles—Final: Beth Herr, Dayton, Ohio, defeated Gretchen Rush, Pittsburgh, 6–3, 6–1.

National Clay Court
(Indianapolis, Aug. 2-8, 1982)

Men's singles final—Jose Higueras, Spain, defeated Jimmy Arias, Grand Island, N.Y., 7–5, 5–7, 6–3.

Women's singles final—Virginia Ruzici, Romania, defeated Helena Sukova, Czechoslovakia, 6–2, 6–0.

Men's doubles final—Sherwood Stewart, Houston, Tex., and Ferdy Taygan, Framingham, Mass., defeated Robbie Venter, South Africa, and Baline Willenborg, Miami Shores, Fla., 6–4, 7–5.

Women's doubles final—Ivanna Madruga-Osses, Argentina, and Katherine Tanvier, France, defeated Joanne Russell, Naples, Fla., and Virginia Ruzici, Romania, 7–5, 7–6.

World Championship Tennis
(Dallas, April 29–May 2, 1982)

Final—Ivan Lendl, Czechoslovakia, defeated John McEnroe, Douglaston, N.Y., 6–2, 3–6, 6–3.

U.S. National Indoor
(Memphis, Tenn., Feb. 8–14, 1982)

Singles final—Johan Krick, Naples, Fla., defeated John McEnroe, Douglaston, N.Y., 6–3, 3–6, 6–4. Doubles final—Kevin Curren, South Africa and Steve Denton, Driscoll., Tex., defeated McEnroe and Peter Fleming, Seabrook Island, S.C., 7–6, 4–6, 6–2.

U.S. Pro Indoor
(Philadelphia, Jan. 25–31, 1982)

Final—John McEnroe, Douglaston, N.Y., defeated Jimmy Connors, Miami Beach, Fla., 6–3, 6–3, 6–1.

U.S. Pro
(Brookline, Mass., July 12–19, 1982)

Singles final—Guillermo Vilas, Argentina, defeated Mel Purcell, Murray, Ky., 6–4, 6–0. Doubles final—Steve Meister and Craig Wittus, United States, defeated Freddie Sauer and Schalk van der Merwe, South Africa, 6–2, 6–3.

OTHER 1982 CHAMPIONSHIPS

Wimbledon Open

Men's singles—Jimmy Connors, Belleville, Ill., defeated John McEnroe, Douglaston, N.Y., 3–6, 6–3, 6–7, 7–6, 6–4.

Women's singles—Martina Navratilova, Dallas, defeated Chris Evert Lloyd, Fort Lauderdale, Fla., 6–1, 3–6, 6–2.

Men's doubles—Paul McNamee and Peter McNamara, Australia, defeated John McEnroe and Peter Fleming, United States, 6–3, 6–2.

Women's doubles—Pam Shriver and Martina Navratilova, United States, defeated Kathy Jordan and Anne Smith, United States, 6–4, 6–1.

Mixed doubles—Kevin Curren, South Africa, and Anne Smith, United States, defeated John Lloyd, Britain, and Wendy Turnbull, Australia, 2–6, 6–3, 7–5.

French Open

Men's singles—Mats Wilander, Sweden, defeated Guillermo Vilas, Argentina, 1–6, 7–6, 6–0, 6–4.

Women's singles—Martina Navratilova, Dallas, defeated Andrea Jaeger, Lincolnshire, Ill., 7–6, 6–1.

Men's doubles—Sherwood Stewart and Ferdi Taygan, United States, defeated Hans Gildemeister and Belus Prajoux, Chile, 7–5, 6–3, 1–1, retired (Gildemeister injured his back and could not continue).

Women's doubles—Martina Navratilova and Anne Smith, United States, defeated Rosemary Casals, United States, and Wendy Turnbull, Australia, 6–3, 6–4.

Australian Open
(Men's events at Melbourne, Australia, Dec. 26, 1981-Jan. 2, 1982)
(Women's events at Melbourne, Australia, Nov. 30-Dec. 5, 1981)

Men's singles—Johan Kriek, South Africa, defeated Steve Denton, Driscoll, Tex., 6–2, 7–6, 6–7, 6–4.

Women's singles—Martina Navratilova, Dallas, defeated Chris Evert Lloyd, Fort Lauderdale, Fla., 6–7, 6–4, 7–5.

Men's doubles—Mark Edmondson and Kim Warwick, Australia, defeated Hank Pfister and John Sadri, United States, 6–3, 7–6.

Women's doubles—Kathy Jordan and Anne Smith, United States, defeated Martina Navratilova and Pam Shriver, United States, 6–2, 7–5.

DAVIS CUP RESULTS—1981
Final Round (Championship Competition)

United States 3, Argentina 1 (At Cincinnati, Ohio)
John McEnroe (U.S.) defeated Guillermo Vilas (A), 6–3, 6–2, 6–2; Jose-Luis Clerc (A) defeated Roscoe Tanner (U.S.), 7–5, 6–3, 8–6; Peter Fleming and McEnroe (U.S.) defeated Clerc-Vilas, 6–3, 4–6, 6–4, 4–6, 11–9; McEnroe defeated Clerc, 7–5, 5–7, 3–6, 6–3, 6–3. Tanner vs. Vilas suspended at 11 games to 10 in the first set, Tanner.

Semifinal Round

United States 5, Australia 0 (At Portland, Ore.)
Argentina 5, Britain 0 (At Buenos Aires)

Quarterfinal Round

Argentina 3, Romania 2 (At Timisoara)
Britain 4, New Zealand 1 (At Christchurch)
Australia 3, Sweden 1 (At Baastad)
United States 4, Czechoslovakia 1 (At Flushing Meadows)

First Round

Argentina 3, Federal Republic of Germany 2 (At Munich)
Romania 3, Brazil 2 (At Timisoara)
Britain 3, Italy 2 (At Brighton)
New Zealand 5, Korea 0 (At Seoul)
Sweden 5, Japan 0 (At Yokohama)
Australia 3, France 2 (At Lyons)
Czechoslovakia 3, Switzerland 2 (At Zurich)
United States 3, Mexico 2 (At Carlsbad, Calif.)

MEN'S FINAL TENNIS EARNINGS—1981

Player	Amount
John McEnroe	$991,000
Ivan Lendl	846,037
Jimmy Connors	405,872
Guillermo Vilas	402,261
Jose-Luis Clerc	327,375
Vitas Gerulaitis	288,475
Heinz Gunthardt	278,642
Peter McNamara	273,066
Eliot Teltscher	267,630
Roscoe Tanner	245,380

WOMEN'S FINAL TENNIS EARNINGS—1981

Player	Amount
Martina Navratilova	$865,437
Chris Evert Lloyd	572,162
Tracy Austin	453,409
Andrea Jaeger	392,115
Pam Shriver	366,530
Hana Mandlikova	339,602
Wendy Turnbull	225,161
Anne Smith	192,311
Sylvia Hanika	190,898
Virginia Ruzici	179,115

ROWING

Rowing goes back so far in history that there is no possibility of tracing it to any particular aboriginal source. The oldest rowing race still on the calendar is the "Doggett's Coat and Badge" contest among professional watermen of the Thames (England) that began in 1715. The first Oxford-Cambridge race was held at Henley in 1829. Competitive rowing in the United States began with matches between boats rowed by professional oarsmen of the New York water front. They were oarsmen who rowed the small boats that plied as ferries from Manhattan Island to Brooklyn and return, or who rowed salesmen down the harbor to meet ships arriving from Europe. Since the first salesman to meet an incoming ship had some advantage over his rivals, there was keen competition in the bidding for fast boats and the best oarsmen. This gave rise to match races.

Amateur boat clubs sprang up in the United States between 1820 and 1830 and seven students of Yale joined together to purchase a four-oared lap-streak gig in 1843. The first Harvard-Yale race was held Aug. 3, 1852, on Lake Winnepesaukee, N.H. The first time an American college crew went abroad was in 1869 when Harvard challenged Oxford and was defeated on the Thames. There were early college rowing races on Lake Quinsigamond, near Worcester, Mass., and on Saratoga Lake, N.Y., but the Intercollegiate Rowing Association in 1895 settled on the Hudson, at Poughkeepsie, as the setting for the annual "Poughkeepsie Regatta." In 1950 the I.R.A. shifted its classic to Marietta, Ohio, and in 1952 it was moved to Syracuse, N.Y. The National Association of Amateur Oarsmen, organized in 1872, has conducted annual championship regattas since that time.

INTERCOLLEGIATE ROWING ASSOCIATION REGATTA

(Varsity Eight-Oared Shells)

Rowed at 4 miles, Poughkeepsie, N.Y., 1895–97, 1899–1916, 1925–32, 1934–41. Rowed at 3 miles, Saratoga, N.Y., 1898; Poughkeepsie, 1921–24, 1947–49; Syracuse, N.Y., 1952–1963, 1965–67. Rowed at 2,000 meters, Syracuse, N.Y., 1964 and from 1968 on. Rowed at 2 miles, Ithaca, N.Y., 1920; Marietta, Ohio, 1950–51. Suspended 1917–19, 1933, 1942–46.

Year	Time	First	Second
1895	21:25	Columbia	Cornell
1896	19:59	Cornell	Harvard
1897	20:47 4/5	Cornell	Columbia
1898	15:51 1/2	Pennsylvania	Cornell
1899	20:04	Pennsylvania	Wisconsin
1900	19:44 3/5	Pennsylvania	Wisconsin
1901	18:53 1/5	Cornell	Columbia
1902	19:03 3/5	Cornell	Wisconsin
1903	18:57	Cornell	Georgetown
1904	20:22 3/5	Syracuse	Cornell
1905	20:29	Cornell	Syracuse
1906	19:36 4/5	Cornell	Pennsylvania
1907	20:02 2/5	Cornell	Columbia
1908	19:24 1/5	Syracuse	Columbia
1909	19:02	Cornell	Columbia
1910	20:42 1/5	Cornell	Pennsylvania
1911	20:10 4/5	Cornell	Columbia
1912	19:31 2/5	Cornell	Wisconsin
1913	19:28 3/5	Syracuse	Cornell
1914	19:37 4/5	Columbia	Pennsylvania
1915	19:36 3/5	Cornell	Stanford
1916	20:15 2/5	Syracuse	Cornell
1920	11:02 3/5	Syracuse	Cornell
1921	14:07	Navy	California
1922	13:33 3/5	Navy	Washington
1923	14:03 1/5	Washington	Navy
1924	15:02	Washington	Wisconsin
1925	19:24 4/5	Navy	Washington
1926	19:28 3/5	Washington	Navy
1927	20:57	Columbia	Washington
1928	18:35 4/5	California	Columbia
1929	22:58	Columbia	Washington
1930	21:42	Cornell	Syracuse
1931	18:54 1/5	Navy	Cornell
1932	19:55	California	Cornell
1934	19:44	California	Washington
1935	18:52	California	Cornell
1936	19:09 3/5	Washington	California
1937	18:33 3/5	Washington	Navy
1938	18:19	Navy	California
1939	18:12 3/5	California	Washington
1940	22:42	Washington	Cornell
1941	18:53 3/10	Washington	California
1947	13:59 1/5	Navy	Cornell
1948	14:06 2/5	Washington	California
1949	14:42 3/5	California	Washington
1950	8:07.5	Washington	California
1951	7:50.5	Wisconsin	Washington
1952	15:08.1	Navy	Princeton
1953	15:29.6	Navy	Cornell
1954	16:04.4	Navy[1]	Cornell
1955	15:49.9	Cornell	Pennsylvania
1956	16:22.4	Cornell	Navy
1957	15:26.6	Cornell	Pennsylvania
1958	17:12.1	Cornell	Navy
1959	18:01.7	Wisconsin	Syracuse
1960	15:57	California	Navy
1961	16:49.2	California	Cornell
1962	17:02.9	Cornell	Washington
1963	17:24	Cornell	Navy
1964	6:31.1	California	Washington
1965	16:51.3	Navy	Cornell
1966	16:03.4	Wisconsin	Navy
1967	16:13.9	Pennsylvania	Wisconsin
1968	6:15.6	Pennsylvania	Washington
1969	6:30.4	Pennsylvania	Dartmouth
1970	6:39.3	Washington	Wisconsin
1971	6:06	Cornell	Washington
1972	6:22.6	Pennsylvania	Brown
1973	6:21	Wisconsin	Brown
1974	6:33	Wisconsin	Mass. Inst. of Technology
1975	6:08.2	Wisconsin	M.I.T.
1976	6:31	California	Princeton
1977	6:32.4	Cornell	Pennsylvania
1978	6:39.5	Syracuse	Brown
1979	6:26.4	Brown	Wisconsin
1980	6:46	Navy	Northeastern
1981	5:57.3	Cornell	Navy
1982	5:57.5	Cornell	Princeton

1. Disqualified.

COLLEGIATE—1982

Intercollegiate Rowing Association

(Lake Onondaga, Syracuse, N.Y., June 3–5, 1982)
(All races at 2,000 meters.)

Eights—1. Cornell, 5 minutes 57.5 seconds. 2. Princeton, 5:59.6; 3. Syracuse, 6:01.2; 4. Navy, 6:01.7; 5. Brown, 6:02.3; 6. Boston University, 6:03.6.

Junior varsity eights—Navy	6:01.4
Freshman eights—California	6:08.3
Pairs with coxswain—Northeastern	8:02.3
Pairs without coxswain—Wisconsin	7:26.5
Fours with coxswain—Wisconsin	6:54.1
Fours without coxswain—Pennsylvania	6:46.2
Freshman fours—Navy	7:03

U.S. MEN'S CHAMPIONSHIPS
U.S. Rowing Association

(Stony Creek Metropark, Mich., July 16–18, 1982)

Lightweight ¼-mile dash—Bill Belden, Fairmount Rowing Club	1:16.47
Intermediate doubles—Fairmount Rowing Association	6:54.40
Intermediate lightweight doubles—Woodstock, Canada	6:52.80
Intermediate fours with coxswain—Vesper Boat Club B team, Philadelphia	6:46.00
Elite Lightweight fours without coxswain—Lightweight Camp	6:23.80
Elite fours with coxswain—Vesper B.C., Philadelphia	6:36.4
Intermediate pairs without coxswain—Detroit Boat Club C team	7:14.16
Elite Lightweight singles—Paul Fuchs, Detroit Boat Club	7:05.9
Intermediate lightweight singles—D. Chandler, Durham R.A.	7:31.00
Intermediate singles—M. Totta, New York Athletic Club	7:21.19
Elite pairs without coxswain—Detroit Boat Club	6:47.9
Elite Lightweight Eight—Lightweight Camp	5:52.41
Lightweight quads—Malta Rowing Association	6:14.80
Elite singles—P. McGowan, Ridley Graduates, Canada	7:18.02
Intermediate eights—New York Athletic Club	6:07.8
Intermediate Lightweight eights—West Side Rowing Club	6:09.77
Quarter-mile singles—Jim Dietz, New York Athletic Club	1:12.9
Senior doubles—Vesper Boat Club, Philadelphia	6:50.75
Senior lightweight doubles—Malta Rowing Association	6:46.2
Senior fours with coxswain—New York Athletic Club	6:37.36
Elite fours without coxswain—Vesper Boat Club, Philadelphia	6:32.80
Senior lightweight fours without coxswain—New York Athletic Club	6:36.3
Senior quads—Vesper Boat Club, Philadelphia	6:16.77
Senior pairs without coxswain—Jablonic-Erickson	7:00.4
Elite doubles—Ridley Graduates, Canada	6:29.2
Elite pairs with coxswain—Detroit Boat Club	7:17.5
Elite lightweight doubles—St. Catherines, Canada	6:41.1
Senior singles—Sean Colgan, University of Pennsylvania	7:17.8
Senior lightweight singles—E. Lentz, Malta R.A.	7:20.7
Elite lightweight fours with coxswain—Vesper Boat Club, Phila.	6:54.99
Elite lightweight pairs without coxswain—Ecorse Boat Club, Detroit	7:17.3
Senior lightweight eight—New York Athletic Club	6:11.8
Senior eights—Vesper Boat Club, Philadelphia	6:04.5
Elite quads—Ridley/Burnaby, Canada	6:06.1
Elite eights—Lightweight Camp	5:50.68

U.S. WOMEN'S CHAMPIONSHIPS

(Lake Waramaug, Conn., June 17–21, 1982)

Senior fours—College Boat Club	3:45.1
Lightweight quads—Durham Boat Club	3:59.0
Elite singles—Judy Geer, Dartmouth Rowing Club	3:59.1
Intermediate singles—Eileen O'Rourke, New York Rowing Association	4:10.2
High School eight—Lakeside High School	3:34.7
Flyweight fours—West Side Rowing Association	4:20.8
Lightweight pairs—Potomac River Development Center	4:29.9
Elite Quads—Boston/Dartmouth/California–Irvine	3:45.6
Senior doubles—Bachelors Barge Club	4:02.0
Lightweight singles—Billie Brown, Harbor City Boat Club	4:29.5
Elite pairs—Lake Washington A team	3:58.5
Junior quads—Durham Boat Club B team	3:50.9
Lightweight eights—Lightweight Development Camp	3:30.4
Junior doubles—Durham Boat Club C team	3:44.5
Elite fours—College Boat Club	3:24.0
Lightweight singles dash—Beth Stickney, Dartmouth Rowing Club	1:55.5
High school fours—Durham Boat Club	3:34.3
Elite doubles—Dartmouth Rowing Club	3:28.2
Lightweight fours—Pioneer Valley Rowing Association	3:39.2
Senior eights—Lightweight Dev. Camp/Boston Univ.	3:14.2
Elite singles dash—Ann Marden, 1980 Rowing Club	1:43.8
Lightweight doubles—Pioneer Valley Rowing Association	3:50.2
Elite eights—College Boat Club	3:06.2
Junior points trophy—Durham Boat Club	251 pts
Lightweight points trophy—Pioneer Valley Rowing Association	59½ pts
All events trophy—Pioneer Valley Rowing Association	87 pts

WORLD CHAMPIONSHIPS—1982

Fours with coxswain—East Germany	6:19.04
Doubles sculls—Norway	6:23.66
Pairs without coxswain—Norway	6:41.98
Singles sculls—East Germany	7:00.67
Pairs with coxswain—Italy	6:59.63
Fours without coxswain—Switzerland	6:10.41
Fours without coxswain (small)—United States	6:15.19
Quads—East Germany	5:55.50
Eights—New Zealand	5:36.39

Lightweights

Men's singles—Austria	7:12.57
Men's fours without coxswain—Italy	6:17.79
Men's doubles—Italy	6:34.85
Men's eights—Italy	5:49.45
Men's eights (small)—United States	5:56.92
Women's fours with coxswain—Soviet Union	3:17.16
Women's doubles—Soviet Union	3:19.47
Women's pairs without coxswain—East Germany	n.a.
Women's pairs without coxswain (small)—United States	n.a.
Women's singles—Soviet Union	3:42.83
Women's quads—Soviet Union	3:07.58
Women's eights—Soviet Union	2:57.97

n.a. = not available.

SLED DOG RACING

INTERNATIONAL CHAMPIONSHIPS—1982

Unlimited-dog class—Peter Norberg, Tuktoyartur, N.W.T. (14.7 miles, 46 minutes, 38.02 seconds, 16 dogs)

Five-dog class—Dan Larkin, Buena Vista, Calif. (6.5 miles, 20:41.35)

Junior Iditarod—Tom Osmar, Clam Gulch, Alaska (130 miles, 12 hours, 31 minutes, 41.10 seconds)

National Sports Festival 1982 Champions

(Indianapolis, Ind., July 22–31, 1982)

Archery

Men—Rick McKinney, Glendale, Ariz.
Women—Luanne Ryon, Parker Dam, Calif.

Boxing

106 lb—Bryan Johnes, Philadelphia
112 lb—Jesse Benavides, Corpus Christi, Tex.
119 lb—Floyd Favors, Capitol Heights, Md.
125 lb—Bernard Gray, Boyton Beach, Fla.
132 lb—Pernell Whitaker, Norfolk, Va.
139 lb—Jerry Page, Columbus, Ohio
147 lb—Roman George, Lafayette, La.
156 lb—Dennis Milton, New York City
165 lb—Nathan Houser, Detroit
178 lb—Bennie Heard, Augusta, Ga.
Heavyweight—Craig Payne, Livonia, Mich.

Diving—Men

3-meter springboard—Greg Louganis, Mission Viejo, Calif.
10-meter platform—Greg Louganis

Diving—Women

3-meter springboard—Megan Neyer, Mission Viejo, Calif.
10-meter platform—Wendy Wyland, Mission Viejo, Calif.

Fencing

Men's foil—Alex Flom, Fairfax, Va.
Men's epee—Tim Glass, Houston, Tex.
Men's saber—Steve Mormando, Lakewood, N.J.
Women's foil—Stacy Johnson, San Antonio, Tex.

Figure Skating

Men—Brian Boitano, Sunnyvale, Calif.
Women—Vikki de Vries, Colorado Springs, Colo.
Pairs—Le Ann Miller, Wilmington, Del., and Billy Fauver, Claymont, Del.
Dance—Elisa Spitz, Short Hills, N.J., and Scott Gregory, Wilmington, Del.

Gymnastics—Men

All-around—Mitch Gaylord, Los Angeles
Floor exercise—Mitch Gaylord
Pommel horse—Roy Palassou, Santa Clara, Calif.
Still rings—Matt Arnot, Albuquerque, N.M.
Vault—Chris Riegel, Wyomissing, Pa.
Parallel bars—Scott Johnson, Colorado Springs, Colo.
High bar—Mitch Gaylord
Team—West

Gymnastics—Women

Vault—Barrie Muzbeck, Novi, Mich.
Parallel bars—Lucy Wener, Memphis, Tenn.
Beam—Jessica Armstrong, Allentown, Pa.
Floor exercise—Kym Fischler, Center Valley, Pa.
All-around—Kelly Garrison, Altus, Okla.
Team—South

Judo—Men

132 lb—Eddie Liddle, Union City, Ga.
143 lb—James Martin, San Gabriel, Calif.
156 lb—Steven Seck, Los Angeles
172 lb—Nicky Yonezuka, Watchung, N.J.
189 lb—Robert Berland, Wilmette, Ill.
209 lb—Leo White, Colorado Springs, Colo.
Over 209 lb—Brad Moss, Colorado Springs, Colo.
Open—Mitch Santa Maria, Roselle Park, N.J.

Judo—Women

106 lb—Janice Zakarzecki, Rockford, Mich.
114 lb—Mary Lewis, Albany, N.Y.
123 lb—Eve Aronoff, Hartsdale, N.Y.
134 lb—Robin Chapman, Rahway, N.J.
145 lb—Becky Scott, Kansas City, Mo.
158 lb—Maureen Braziel, New York City
Over 158 lb—Margaret Castro, New York City
Open—Heidi Bauersachs, New York City

Modern Pentathlon

Individual—John Helmick, Long Beach, Calif.
Team—North

Speed Skating—Men

500 meters—Steve Merrifield, Canoga Park, Calif.
1,000 meters—Steve Merrifield
1,500 meters—Steve Merrifield
5,000-meter relay—West

Speed Skating—Women

500 meters—Lydia Stephans, Northbrook, Ill.
1,000 meters—Lydia Stephans
1,500 meters—Lydia Stephans
3,000-meter relay—South

Swimming—Men

50-m freestyle—Bruce Foster, Tallahassee, Fla.
100-m freestyle—Stuart McDonald, Mission Viejo, Calif.
200-m freestyle—Geoff Gaberino, Chattanooga, Tenn.
400-m freestyle—Matt Cetlinski, Lake Worth, Fla.
1,500-m freestyle—Paul Budd, Memphis, Tenn.
100-m butterfly—Robert Placak, San Rafael, Calif.
200-m butterfly—Tie between Dennis Baker, Portland, Ore., and Roger Von Jouanne, Renton, Wash.
100-m breaststroke—Robert Lager, Mission Viejo, Calif.
200-m breaststroke—Greg Rhodenbaugh, Cincinnati
100-m backstroke—Eric Ericson, Wilmington, Del.
200-m backstroke—Rich Hughey, Atlanta
200-m ind. med.—Roger Von Jouanne
400-m ind. med.—Roger Von Jouanne
400-m freestyle relay—North A.
800-m freestyle relay—East A
400-m med. relay—East A

Swimming—Women

50-m freestyle—Dara Torres, Beverly Hills, Calif.
100-m freestyle—Heather Strang, East Lansing, Mich.
200-m freestyle—Stacy Shupe, Cerritos, Calif.
400-m freestyle—Sherri Hanna, Miami, Fla.
800-m freestyle—Michele Richardson, Memphis, Tenn.
100-m butterfly—Laurie Lehner, Fort Lauderdale, Fla.
200-m butterfly—Terrianne McGuirk, Churchville, Pa.
100-m breaststroke—Jacqueline Komenij, Rohnert Park, Calif.
200-m breaststroke—Susan Rapp, Alexandria, Va.
100-m backstroke—Theresa Andrews, Annapolis, Md.
200-m backstroke—Theresa Andrews
200-m ind. med.—Karin Werth, Austin, Tex.
400-m ind. med—Karen LaBerge, Doylestown, Pa.
400-m freestyle relay—West A
800-m freestyle relay—West A
400-m med. relay—East A
1,500-m freestyle—Karen LaBerge
Team—Men: East. Women: East.

Track and Field—Men

100-m dash—Calvin Smith, Boulton, Miss.
200-m dash—James Butler, Stillwater, Okla.
400-m run—Sunder Nix, Chicago
800-m run—James Hays, Hereford, Tex.
1,500-m run—Chuck Aragon, Las Lunas, N.M.
5,000-m run—Jim Spivey, Wood Dale, Ill.
10,000-m run—Pat Porter, Alamosa, Colo.
3,000-m steeplechase—Henry Marsh, Bountiful, Utah
Marathon—Tom Raunig, Great Falls, Mont.
20-k walk—Tie between Jim Heiring, Colorado Springs, Colo., and Ray Sharp, Colorado Springs, Colo.

(Continued on page 913)

HARNESS RACING

Oliver Wendell Holmes, the famous Autocrat of the Breakfast Table, wrote that the running horse was a gambling toy but the trotting horse was useful and, furthermore, "horse-racing is not a republican institution; horse-trotting is." Oliver Wendell Holmes was a born-and-bred New Englander, and New England was the nursery of the harness racing sport in America. Pacers and trotters were matters of local pride and prejudice in Colonial New England, and, shortly after the Revolution, the Messenger and Justin Morgan strains produced many winners in harness racing "matches" along the turnpikes of New York, Connecticut, Rhode Island, Massachusetts, Vermont, and New Hampshire.

There was English thoroughbred blood in Messenger and Justin Morgan, and, many years later, it was blended in Rysdyk's Hambletonian, foaled in 1849. Hambletonian was not particularly fast under harness but his descendants have had almost a monopoly of prizes, titles, and records in the harness racing game. Hambletonian was purchased as a foal with its dam for a total of $124 by William Rysdyk of Goshen, N.Y., and made a modest fortune for the purchaser.

Trotters and pacers often were raced under saddle in the old days, and, in fact, the custom still survives in some places in Europe. Dexter, the great trotter that lowered the mile record from 2:19¾ to 2:17¼ in 1867, was said to handle just as well under saddle as when pulling a sulky. But as sulkies were lightened in weight and improved in design, trotting under saddle became less common and finally faded out in this country.

WORLD RECORDS

Established in a Race or Against Time at One Mile
Source: Research Specialist, United States Trotting Association

Trotting on Mile Track

	Record	Holder	Driver	Where Made	Year
All Age	1:54 4/5[1]	Lindy's Crown	Howard Beissinger	DuQuoin, Ill.	1980
	1:54 4/5*	Nevele Pride	Stanley Dancer	Indianapolis	1969
2–year–old	1:56 3/5*	Star Investment, f	William Herman	Lexington, Ky.	1979
3–year–old	1:55[1]	Speedy Somolli	Howard Beissinger	DuQuoin, Ill.	1978
		Florida Pro	George Sholty	DuQuoin, Ill.	1978
4–year–old	1:54 4/5[1]	Lindy's Crown	Howard Beissinger	DuQuoin, Ill.	1980
	1:54 4/5*	Nevele Pride	Stanley Dancer	Indianapolis	1969

Trotting on Five-Eighths Mile Track

	Record	Holder	Driver	Where Made	Year
All Age	1:57 1/5[1]	Lindy's Crown	Howard Beissinger	Wilmington, Del.	1980
2–year–old	2:00 1/5[1]	Smokin Yankee	Stanley Dancer	Laurel, Md.	1980
3–year–old	1:58[1]	Keystone Sister	Delvin Miller	Meadow Lands, Pa.	1981
4–year–old	1:57 1/5[1]	Lindy's Crown	Howard Beissinger	Wilmington, Del.	1980

Trotting on Half-Mile Track

	Record	Holder	Driver	Where Made	Year
All Age	1:56 4/5[1]	Nevele Pride	Stanley Dancer	Saratoga Springs, N.Y.	1969
2–year–old	2:00[1]	Incredible Nevele	Glen Garnsey	Delaware, Ohio	1981
3–year–old	1:58[1]	Incredible Nevele	Glen Garnsey	Saratoga Springs, N.Y.	1982
4–year–old	1:56 4/5[1]	Nevele Pride	Stanley Dancer	Saratoga Springs, N.Y.	1969

Pacing on Mile Track

	Record	Holder	Driver	Where Made	Year
All Age	1:51 3/5[1]	Trenton	Tommy Haughton	Springfield, Ill.	1982
	1:49 1/5*	Niatross	Clint Galbraith	Lexington, Ky.	1980
2–year–old	1:53 4/5[1]	Merger	John Campbell	Lexington, Ky.	1981
3–year–old	1:51 3/5[1]	Trenton	Tommy Haughton	Springfield, Ill.	1982
	1:49 1/5*	Niatross	Clint Galbraith	Lexington, Ky.	1980
4–year–old	1:52*	Steady Star	Joe O'Brien	Lexington, Ky.	1971

Pacing on Five-Eighths Mile Track

	Record	Holder	Driver	Where Made	Year
All Age	1:53 2/5[1]	Storm Damage	Joe O'Brien	Meadow Lands, Pa.	1980
2–year–old	1:56 1/5[1]	French Chef	Stanley Dancer	Columbus, Ky.	1980
3–year–old	1:53 2/5[1]	Storm Damage	Joe O'Brien	Meadow Lands, Pa.	1980
4–year–old	1:54 2/5[1]	Direct Scooter	Warren Cameron	Windsor, Ontario	1980

Pacing on Half-Mile Track

	Record	Holder	Driver	Where Made	Year
All Age	1:54 3/5[1]	Temujin	Clarence Martin	Delaware, Ohio	1982
2–year–old	1:56 1/5[1]	Temujin	Clarence Martin	Louisville, Ky.	1981
3–year–old	1:54 3/5[1]	Temujin	Clarence Martin	Delaware, Ohio	1982
4–year–old	1:55 2/5[1]	Bandelier	Joe O'Brien	Delaware, Ohio	1981

1. Record set in race. *Record set in time trial. f=filly.

HARNESS RACING RECORDS FOR THE MILE

Trotters

Time	Trotter, age, driver	Year
2:00	Lou Dillon, 5, Millard Sanders	1903
1:58½	Lou Dillon, 5, Millard Sanders	1903
1:58	Uhlan, 8, Charles Tanner	1912
1:58	Peter Manning, 5, T. W. Murphy	1921
1:57¾	Peter Manning, 5, T. W. Murphy	1921
1:57	Peter Manning, 6, T. W. Murphy	1922
1:56¾	Peter Manning, 6, T. W. Murphy	1922
1:56¾	Greyhound, 5, Sep Palin	1937
1:56	Greyhound, 5, Sep Palin	1937
1:55¼	Greyhound, 6, Sep Palin	1938
1:54⅘	Nevele Pride, 4, Stanley Dancer	1969

Pacers

Time	Pacer, age, driver	Year
2:00½	John R. Gentry, 7, W.J. Andrews	1896
1:59¼	Star Pointer, 8, D. McClary	1897
1:59	Dan Patch, 7, M. E. McHenry	1903
1:56¼	Dan Patch, 7, M. E. McHenry	1903
1:56	Dan Patch, 8, H. C. Hersey	1904
1:55	Billy Direct, 4, Vic Fleming	1938
1:55	Adios Harry, 4, Luther Lyons	1955
1:54⅗	Adios Butler, 4, Paige West	1960
1:54	Bret Hanover, 4, Frank Ervin	1966
1:53⅗	Bret Hanover, 4, Frank Ervin	1966
1:52	Steady Star, 4, Joe O'Brien	1971
1:49⅕	Niatross, 3, Clint Galbraith	1980

HARNESS HORSE OF THE YEAR

Chosen in poll conducted by United States Trotting Association in conjunction with the U.S. Harness Writers Assn.

1959	Bye Bye Byrd, Pacer
1960	Adios Butler, Pacer
1961	Adios Butler, Pacer
1962	Su Mac Lad, Trotter
1963	Speedy Scot, Trotter
1964	Bret Hanover, Pacer
1965	Bret Hanover, Pacer
1966	Bret Hanover, Pacer
1967	Nevele Pride, Trotter
1968	Nevele Pride, Trotter
1969	Nevele Pride, Trotter
1970	Fresh Yankee, Trotter
1971	Albatross, Pacer
1972	Albatross, Pacer
1973	Sir Dalrae, Pacer
1974	Delmonica Hanover, Trotter
1975	Savoir, Trotter
1976	Keystone Ore, Pacer
1977	Green Speed, Trotter
1978	Abercrombie, Pacer
1979	Niatross, Pacer
1980	Niatross, Pacer
1981	Fan Hanover, Pacer

HISTORY OF TRADITIONAL HARNESS RACING STAKES

The Hambletonian

Three-year-old trotters. One mile. Guy McKinney won first race at Syracuse in 1926; held at Goshen, N.Y., 1930–1942, 1944–1956; at Yonkers, N.Y., 1943; at Du Quoin, Ill., 1957–1980. In 1981 and 1982 the race was held at the Meadowlands in East Rutherford, N.J.

Year	Winner	Driver	Best time	Total purse
1967	Speedy Streak	Del Cameron	2:00	122,650
1968	Nevele Pride	Stanley Dancer	1:59⅖	116,190
1969	Lindy's Pride	Howard Beissinger	1:57⅗	124,910
1970	Timothy T.	John Simpson, Jr.	1:58⅖[1]	143,630
1971	Speedy Crown	Howard Beissinger	1:57⅖	129,770
1972	Super Bowl	Stanley Dancer	1:56⅖	119,090
1973	Flirth	Ralph Baldwin	1:57⅕	144,710
1974	Christopher T	Billy Haughton	1:58⅗	160,150
1975	Bonefish	Stanley Dancer	1:59[2]	232,192
1976	Steve Lobell	Billy Haughton	1:56⅖	263,524
1977	Green Speed	Billy Haughton	1:55⅗	284,131
1978	Speedy Somolli	Howard Beissinger	1:55[3]	241,280
1979	Legend Hanover	George Sholty	1:56⅕	300,000
1980	Burgomeister	Billy Haughton	1:56⅗	293,570
1981	Shiaway St. Pat	Ray Remmen	2:01⅕[4]	838,000
1982	Speed Bowl	Tommy Haughton	1:56⅘	875,750

1. By Formal Notice. 2. By Yankee Bambino. 3. By Speedy Somolli and Florida Pro. 4. By Super Juan.

Little Brown Jug

Three-year-old pacers. One Mile. Raced at Delaware County Fair Grounds, Delaware, Ohio.

Year	Winner	Driver	Best time	Total purse
1967	Best of All	Jim Hackett	1:59[1]	84,778
1968	Rum Customer	Billy Haughton	1:59⅗	104,226
1969	Laverne Hanover	Billy Haughton	2:00⅖	109,731
1970	Most Happy Fella	Stanley Dancer	1:57⅕	100,110
1971	Nansemond	Herve Filion	1:57⅖	102,994
1972	Strike Out	Keith Waples	1:56⅗	104,916
1973	Melvin's Woe	Joe O'Brien	1:57⅗	120,000
1974	Ambro Omaha	Billy Haughton	1:57	132,630
1975	Seatrain	Ben Webster	1:57[2]	147,813
1976	Keystone Ore	Stanley Dancer	1:56⅘[3]	153,799
1977	Governor Skipper	John Chapman	1:56⅕	150,000
1978	Happy Escort	William Popfinger	1:55⅖[4]	186,760
1979	Hot Hitter	Herve Filion	1:55⅗	226,455
1980	Niatross	Clint Galbraith	1:54⅘	207,361
1981	Fan Hanover	Glen Garnsey	1:56[5]	243,799
1982	Merger	John Campbell	1:56⅗	328,900

1. By Nardin's Byrd. 2. By Armbro Ranger. 3. By Falcon Almahurst. 4. By Falcon Almahurst. 5. By Seahawk Hanover.

GOLF

It may be that golf originated in Holland—historians believe it did—but certainly Scotland fostered the game and is famous for it. In fact, in 1457 the Scottish Parliament, disturbed because football and golf had lured young Scots from the more soldierly exercise of archery, passed an ordinance that "futeball and golf be utterly cryit doun and nocht usit." James I and Charles I of the royal line of Stuarts were golf enthusiasts, whereby the game came to be known as "the royal and ancient game of golf."

The golf balls used in the early games were leather-covered and stuffed with feathers. Clubs of all kinds were fashioned by hand to suit individual players. The great step in spreading the game came with the change from the feather ball to the gutta-percha ball about 1850. In 1860, formal competition began with the establishment of an annual tournament for the British Open championship. There are records of "golf clubs" in the United States as far back as colonial days but no proof of actual play before John Reid and some friends laid out six holes on the Reid lawn in Yonkers, N.Y., in 1888 and played there with golf balls and clubs brought over from Scotland by Robert Lockhart. This group then formed the St. Andrews Golf Club of Yonkers, and golf was established in this country.

However, it remained a rather sedate and almost aristocratic pastime until a 20-year-old ex-caddy, Francis Ouimet of Boston, defeated two great British professionals, Harry Vardon and Ted Ray, in the United States Open championship at Brookline, Mass., in 1913. This feat put the game and Francis Ouimet on the front pages of the newspapers and stirred a wave of enthusiasm for the sport. The greatest feat so far in golf history is that of Robert Tyre Jones, Jr., of Atlanta, who won the British Open, the British Amateur, the U.S. Open, and the U.S. Amateur titles in one year, 1930.

U.S. OPEN CHAMPIONS

Year	Winner	Score	Where played
1895	Horace Rawlins	173	Newport
1896	James Foulis	152	Shinnecock Hills
1897	Joe Lloyd	162	Chicago
1898[3]	Fred Herd	328	Myopia
1899	Willie Smith	315	Baltimore
1900	Harry Vardon	313	Chicago
1901	Willie Anderson[1]	331	Myopia
1902	Laurie Auchterlonie	307	Garden City
1903	Willie Anderson[1]	307	Baltusrol
1904	Willie Anderson	303	Glen View
1905	Willie Anderson	314	Myopia
1906	Alex Smith	295	Onwentsia
1907	Alex Ross	302	Philadelphia
1908	Fred McLeod[1]	322	Myopia
1909	George Sargent	290	Englewood
1910	Alex Smith[1]	298	Philadelphia
1911	John McDermott[1]	307	Chicago
1912	John McDermott	294	Buffalo
1913	Francis Ouimet[1 2]	304	Brookline
1914	Walter Hagen	290	Midlothian
1915	Jerome D. Travers[2]	297	Baltusrol
1916	Charles Evans, Jr.[2]	286	Minikahda
1917–18	No tournaments[4]		
1919	Walter Hagen[2]	301	Brae Burn
1920	Edward Ray	295	Inverness
1921	Jim Barnes	289	Columbia
1922	Gene Sarazen	288	Skokie
1923	R. T. Jones, Jr.[1 2]	296	Inwood
1924	Cyril Walker	297	Oakland Hills
1925	Willie Macfarlane[1]	291	Worcester
1926	R. T. Jones, Jr.[2]	293	Scioto
1927	Tommy Armour[1]	301	Oakmont
1928	Johnny Farrell[1]	294	Olympia Fields
1929	R. T. Jones, Jr.[1 2]	294	Winged Foot
1930	R. T. Jones, Jr.[2]	287	Interlachen
1931	Billy Burke[1]	292	Inverness
1932	Gene Sarazen	286	Fresh Meadow
1933	John Goodman[2]	287	North Shore
1934	Olin Dutra	293	Merion
1935	Sam Parks, Jr.	299	Oakmont
1936	Tony Manero	282	Baltusrol
1937	Ralph Guldahl	281	Oakland Hills
1938	Ralph Guldahl	284	Cherry Hills
1939	Byron Nelson[1]	284	Philadelphia
1940	Lawson Little[1]	287	Canterbury
1941	Craig Wood	284	Colonial
1942–45	No tournaments[5]		
1946	Lloyd Mangrum[1]	284	Canterbury
1947	Lew Worsham[1]	282	St. Louis
1948	Ben Hogan	276	Riviera
1949	Cary Middlecoff	286	Medinah
1950	Ben Hogan[1]	287	Merion
1951	Ben Hogan	287	Oakland Hills
1952	Julius Boros	281	Northwood
1953	Ben Hogan	283	Oakmont
1954	Ed Furgol	284	Baltusrol
1955	Jack Fleck[1]	287	Olympic
1956	Cary Middlecoff	281	Oak Hill
1957	Dick Mayer[1]	298	Inverness
1958	Tommy Bolt	283	Southern Hills
1959	Bill Casper, Jr.	282	Winged Foot
1960	Arnold Palmer	280	Cherry Hills
1961	Gene Littler	281	Oakland Hills
1962	Jack Nicklaus[1]	283	Oakmont
1963	Julius Boros[1]	293	Country Club
1964	Ken Venturi	278	Congressional
1965	Gary Player[1]	282	Bellerive
1966	Bill Casper[1]	278	Olympic
1967	Jack Nicklaus	275	Baltusrol
1968	Lee Trevino	275	Oak Hill
1969	Orville Moody	281	Champions G. C.
1970	Tony Jacklin	281	Hazeltine
1971	Lee Trevino[1]	280	Merion
1972	Jack Nicklaus	290	Pebble Beach
1973	Johnny Miller	279	Oakmont
1974	Hale Irwin	287	Winged Foot
1975	Lou Graham[1]	287	Medinah
1976	Jerry Pate	277	Atlanta A.C.
1977	Hubert Green	278	Southern Hills
1978	Andy North	285	Cherry Hills
1979	Hale Irwin	284	Inverness
1980	Jack Nicklaus	272	Baltusrol
1981	David Graham	273	Merion
1982	Tom Watson	282	Pebble Beach

1. Winner in playoff. 2. Amateur. 3. In 1898, competition was extended to 72 holes. 4. In 1917, Jock Hutchison, with a 292, won an Open Patriotic Tournament for the benefit of the American Red Cross at Whitemarsh Valley Country Club. 5. In 1942, Ben Hogan, with a 271 won a Hale American National Open Tournament for the benefit of the Navy Relief Society and USO at Ridgemoor Country Club.

U.S. AMATEUR CHAMPIONS

1895	Charles B. Macdonald	1920	Charles Evans, Jr.	1946	Ted Bishop	1966	Gary Cowan[1]
1896–97	H. J. Whigham	1921	Jesse P. Guilford	1947	Robert Riegel	1967	Bob Dickson
1898	Findlay S. Douglas	1922	Jess W. Sweetser	1948	Willie Turnesa	1968	Bruce Fleisher
1899	H. M. Harriman	1923	Max R. Marston	1949	Charles Coe	1969	Steven Melnyk
1900–01	Walter J. Travis	1924–25	R. T. Jones Jr.	1950	Sam Urzetta	1970	Lanny Wadkins
1902	Louis N. James	1926	George Von Elm	1951	Billy Maxwell	1971	Gary Cowan
1903	Walter J. Travis	1927–28	R. T. Jones Jr.	1952	Jack Westland	1972	Vinny Giles 3d
1904–05	H. Chandler Egan	1929	H. R. Johnston	1953	Gene Littler	1973[3]	Craig Stadler
1906	Eben M. Byers	1930	R. T. Jones, Jr.	1954	Arnold Palmer	1974	Jerry Pate
1907–08	Jerome D. Travers	1931	Francis Ouimet	1955–56	Harvie Ward	1975	Fred Ridley
1909	Robert A. Gardner	1932	Ross Somerville	1957	Hillman Robbins	1976	Bill Sander
1910	W. C. Fownes, Jr.	1933	G. T. Dunlap, Jr.	1958	Charles Coe	1977	John Fought
1911	Harold H. Hilton	1934–35	Lawson Little	1959	Jack Nicklaus	1978	John Cook
1912–13	Jerome D. Travers	1936	John W. Fischer	1960	Deane Beman	1979	Mark O'Meara
1914	Francis Ouimet	1937	John Goodman	1961	Jack Nicklaus	1980	Hal Sutton
1915	Robert A. Gardner	1938	Willie Turnesa	1962	Labron Harris, Jr.	1981	Nathaniel Crosby
1916	Charles Evans, Jr.	1939	Marvin H. Ward	1963	Deane Beman	1982	Jay Sigel
1919	S. D. Herron	1940	R. D. Chapman	1964	Bill Campbell		
		1941	Marvin H. Ward	1965[2]	Robert Murphy, Jr.		

1. Winner in playoff. 2. Tourney switched to medal play through 1972. 3. Return to match play.

U.S. P.G.A. CHAMPIONS

1916	Jim Barnes	1939	Henry Picard	1955	Doug Ford	1970	Dave Stockton
1919	Jim Barnes	1940	Byron Nelson	1956	Jack Burke, Jr.	1971	Jack Nicklaus
1920	Jock Hutchison	1941	Victor Ghezzi	1957	Lionel Hebert	1972	Gary Player
1921	Walter Hagen	1942	Sam Snead	1958[2]	Dow Finsterwald	1973	Jack Nicklaus
1922–23	Gene Sarazen	1944	Bob Hamilton	1959	Bob Rosburg	1974	Lee Trevino
1924–27	Walter Hagen	1945	Byron Nelson	1960	Jay Hebert	1975	Jack Nicklaus
1928–29	Leo Diegel	1946	Ben Hogan	1961	Jerry Barber[1]	1976	Dave Stockton
1930	Tommy Armour	1947	Jim Ferrier	1962	Gary Player	1977	Lanny Wadkins[1]
1931	Tom Creavy	1948	Ben Hogan	1963	Jack Nicklaus	1978	John Mahaffey
1932	Olin Dutra	1949	Sam Snead	1964	Bobby Nichols	1979	David Graham[1]
1933	Gene Sarazen	1950	Chandler Harper	1965	Dave Marr	1980	Jack Nicklaus
1934	Paul Runyan	1951	Sam Snead	1966	Al Geiberger	1981	Larry Nelson
1935	Johnny Revolta	1952	Jim Turnesa	1967	Don January[1]	1982	Ray Floyd
1936–37	Denny Shute	1953	Walter Burkemo	1968	Julius Boros		
1938	Paul Runyan	1954	Chick Harbert	1969	Ray Floyd		

1. Winner in playoff. 2. Switched to medal play.

THE MASTERS TOURNAMENT WINNERS

Augusta National Golf Club, Augusta, Ga.

Year	Winner	Score	Year	Winner	Score	Year	Winner	Score
1934	Horton Smith	284	1952	Sam Snead	286	1968	Bob Goalby	277
1935	Gene Sarazen[1]	282	1953	Ben Hogan	274	1969	George Archer	281
1936	Horton Smith	285	1954	Sam Snead[1]	289	1970	Billy Casper[1]	279
1937	Byron Nelson	283	1955	Cary Middlecoff	279	1971	Charles Coody	279
1938	Henry Picard	285	1956	Jack Burke	289	1972	Jack Nicklaus	286
1939	Ralph Guldahl	279	1957	Doug Ford	283	1973	Tommy Aaron	283
1940	Jimmy Demaret	280	1958	Arnold Palmer	284	1974	Gary Player	278
1941	Craig Wood	280	1959	Art Wall, Jr.	284	1975	Jack Nicklaus	276
1942	Byron Nelson[1]	280	1960	Arnold Palmer	282	1976	Ray Floyd	271
1943–45	No Tournaments		1961	Gary Player	280	1977	Tom Watson	276
1946	Herman Keiser	282	1962	Arnold Palmer[1]	280	1978	Gary Player	277
1947	Jimmy Demaret	281	1963	Jack Nicklaus	286	1979	Fuzzy Zoeller[1]	280
1948	Claude Harmon	279	1964	Arnold Palmer	276	1980	Severiano Ballesteros	275
1949	Sam Snead	282	1965	Jack Nicklaus	271	1981	Tom Watson	280
1950	Jimmy Demaret	283	1966	Jack Nicklaus[1]	288	1982	Craig Stadler[1]	284
1951	Ben Hogan	280	1967	Gay Brewer, Jr.	280			

1. Winner in playoff.

U.S. WOMEN'S AMATEUR CHAMPIONS

1916	Alexa Stirling	1925	Glenna Collett	1935	Glenna Collett Vare	1939–40	Betty Jameson
1919–20	Alexa Stirling	1926	Helen Stetson	1936	Pamela Barton	1941	Mrs. Frank Newell
1921	Marion Hollins	1927	Mrs. M. B. Horn	1937	Mrs. J. A. Page, Jr.	1946	Mildred Zaharias
1922	Glenna Collett	1928–30	Glenna Collett	1938	Patty Berg	1947	Louise Suggs
1923	Edith Cummings	1931	Helen Hicks			1948	Grace Lenczyk
1924	Dorothy Campbell Hurd	1932–34	Virginia Van Wie			1949	Mrs. D. G. Porter

1950	Beverly Hanson	1959	Barbara McIntire	1967	Lou Dill	1976	Donna Horton
1951	Dorothy Kirby	1960	JoAnne Gunderson	1968	JoAnne G. Carner	1977	Beth Daniel
1952	Jacqueline Pung	1961	Anne Quast	1969	Catherine Lacoste	1978	Cathy Sherk
1953	Mary Lena Faulk		Decker	1970	Martha Wilkinson	1979	Carolyn Hill
1954	Barbara Romack	1962	JoAnne Gunderson	1971	Laura Baugh	1980	Juli Inkster
1955	Patricia Lesser	1963	Anne Quast Welts	1972	Mary Ann Budke	1981	Juli Inkster
1956	Marlene Stewart	1964	Barbara McIntire	1973	Carol Semple	1982	Juli Inkster
1957	JoAnne Gunderson	1965	Jean Ashley	1974	Cynthia Hill		
1958	Anne Quast	1966	JoAnne Gunderson	1975	Beth Daniel		

U.S. WOMEN'S OPEN CHAMPIONS

Year	Winner	Score	Year	Winner	Score	Year	Winner	Score
1946	Patty Berg (match play)	—	1959	Mickey Wright	287	1972	Susie Berning	299
1947	Betty Jameson	295	1960	Betsy Rawls	291	1973	Susie Berning	290
1948	Mildred D. Zaharias	300	1961	Mickey Wright	293	1974	Sandra Haynie	295
1949	Louise Suggs	291	1962	Murle Lindstrom	301	1975	Sandra Palmer	295
1950	Mildred D. Zaharias	291	1963	Mary Mills	289	1976	JoAnne Carner	292
1951	Betsy Rawls	293	1964	Mickey Wright[1]	290	1977	Hollis Stacy	292
1952	Louise Suggs	284	1965	Carol Mann	290	1978	Hollis Stacy	289
1953	Betsy Rawls[1]	302	1966	Sandra Spuzich	297	1979	Jerilyn Britz	284
1954	Mildred D. Zaharias	291	1967	Catherine LaCoste	294	1980	Amy Alcott	280
1955	Fay Crocker	299	1968	Susie Berning	289	1981	Pat Bradley	279
1956	Katherine Cornelius[1]	302	1969	Donna Caponi	294	1982	Janet Alex	283
1957	Betsy Rawls	299	1970	Donna Caponi	287			
1958	Mickey Wright	290	1971	JoAnne Carner	288			

1. Winner in playoff. 2. Amateur.

BRITISH OPEN CHAMPIONS

(First tournament, held in 1860, was won by Willie Park, Sr.)

Year	Winner	Score	Year	Winner	Score	Year	Winner	Score
1920	George Duncan	303	1939	R. Burton	290	1964	Tony Lema	279
1921	Jock Hutchison[1]	296	1946	Sam Snead	290	1965	Peter Thomson	285
1922	Walter Hagen	300	1947	Fred Daly	294	1966	Jack Nicklaus	282
1923	A. G. Havers	295	1948	Henry Cotton	283	1967	Roberto de Vicenzo	278
1924	Walter Hagen	301	1949	Bobby Locke[1]	283	1968	Gary Player	289
1925	Jim Barnes	300	1950	Bobby Locke	279	1969	Tony Jacklin	280
1926	R. T. Jones, Jr.	291	1951	Max Faulkner	285	1970	Jack Nicklaus[1]	283
1927	R. T. Jones, Jr.	285	1952	Bobby Locke	287	1971	Lee Trevino	278
1928	Walter Hagen	292	1953	Ben Hogan	282	1972	Lee Trevino	278
1929	Walter Hagen	292	1954	Peter Thomson	283	1973	Tom Weiskopf	276
1930	R. T. Jones, Jr.	291	1955	Peter Thomson	281	1974	Gary Player	282
1931	Tommy Armour	296	1956	Peter Thomson	286	1975	Tom Watson[1]	279
1932	Gene Sarazen	283	1957	Bobby Locke	279	1976	Johnny Miller	279
1933	Denny Shute[1]	292	1958	Peter Thomson[1]	278	1977	Tom Watson	268
1934	Henry Cotton	283	1959	Gary Player	284	1978	Jack Nicklaus	281
1935	A. Perry	283	1960	Kel Nagle	278	1979	Severiano Ballesteros	283
1936	A. H. Padgham	287	1961	Arnold Palmer	284	1980	Tom Watson	271
1937	Henry Cotton	290	1962	Arnold Palmer	276	1981	Bill Rogers	276
1938	R. A. Whitcombe	295	1963	Bob Charles[1]	277	1982	Tom Watson	284

1. Winner in playoff.

MEN'S U.S. OPEN—1982

[Pebble Beach (Calif.) Golf Links, June 17–20, 1982]

Tom Watson	72	72	68	70—282	$60,000
Jack Nicklaus	74	70	71	69—284	34,506
Bobby Clampett	71	73	72	70—286	14,967
Dan Pohl	72	74	70	70—286	14,967
Bill Rogers	70	73	69	74—286	14,967
Gary Koch	78	73	69	67—287	8,011
Jay Haas	75	74	70	68—287	8,011
Lanny Wadkins	73	76	67	71—287	8,011
David Graham	73	72	69	73—287	8,011
Calvin Peete	71	72	72	73—288	6,332
Bruce Devlin	70	69	75	74—288	6,332

Leaders—18 holes, Bruce Devlin and Bill Rogers, 70; 36 holes, Bruce Devlin, 139; 54 holes, Tom Watson and Bill Rogers, 212.

MASTERS TOURNAMENT—1982

(Augusta, Ga., April 8–11, 1982)

Craig Stadler*	75	69	67	73—284	$64,000
Dan Pohl	75	75	67	67—284	39,000
Severiano Ballesteros	73	73	68	71—285	21,000
Jerry Pate	74	73	67	71—285	21,000
Tom Watson	77	69	70	71—287	13,500
Tom Kite	76	69	73	69—287	13,500
Ray Floyd	74	72	69	74—289	11,067
Curtis Strange	74	70	73	72—289	11,067
Larry Nelson	79	71	70	69—289	11,067
Fuzzy Zoeller	72	76	70	72—290	8,550
Mark Hayes	74	73	73	70—290	8,550
Andy Bean	75	72	73	70—290	8,550
Tom Weiskopf	75	72	68	75—290	8,550
Bob Gilder	79	71	66	75—291	6,700

*Won playoff on first extra hole.

P.G.A. CHAMPIONSHIP—1982

(Southern Hills Country Club, Tulsa, Okla., Aug. 5–8, 1982)

Ray Floyd	63	69	68	72—272	$65,000
Lanny Wadkins	71	68	69	67—275	45,000
Fred Couples	67	71	72	66—276	25,000
Calvin Peete	69	70	68	69—276	25,000
Jerry Haas	71	66	68	72—277	16,000
Jim Simons	68	67	73	69—277	16,000
Bob Gilder	66	68	72	72—278	11,000
Tom Kite	73	70	70	67—280	7,919
Lonnie Hinkle	70	68	71	71—280	7,919
Tom Watson	72	69	71	68—280	7,919
Jerry Pate	72	69	70	69—280	7,919

BRITISH OPEN—1982

(Troon, Scotland, July 15–18, 1982)

Tom Watson	69	71	74	70—284	$57,600
Nick Price	69	69	74	73—285	34,750
Peter Oosterhuis	74	67	74	70—285	34,750
Nick Faldo	73	73	71	69—286	19,800
Des Smyth	70	69	74	73—286	19,800
Masahiro Kuramoto	71	73	71	71—286	19,800
Tom Purtzer	76	66	75	69—286	19,800
Sandy Lyle	74	66	73	74—287	15,550
Fuzzy Zoeller	73	71	73	70—287	15,550
Bobby Clampett	67	66	78	77—288	13,230
Jack Nicklaus	77	70	72	69—288	13,230

U.S. WOMEN'S OPEN—1982

(Sacramento, Calif., July 22–25, 1982)

Janet Alex	70	73	72	68—283	$27,315
JoAnne Carner	69	70	75	75—289	10,659
Beth Daniel	71	71	71	76—289	10,659
Donna White	70	74	73	72—289	10,659
Sandra Haynie	70	74	74	71—289	10,659
Susie McAllister	77	70	75	71—293	5,673
Carole Jo Callison	76	69	72	77—294	4,540
Nancy Lopez	78	73	74	69—294	4,540
Vicki Tabor	70	76	75	73—294	4,540
Beverly Cooper	73	72	76	74—295	3,637
Stephanie Farwig	75	76	72	72—295	3,637
Muffin Spencer-Devlin	76	71	76	72—295	3,637

L.P.G.A. CHAMPIONSHIP—1982

(Jack Nicklaus Sports Center, Kings Island, Ohio, June 10–13, 1982)

Jan Stephenson	69	69	70	71—279	$30,000
JoAnne Carner	71	70	71	69—281	19,600
Janet Alex	72	72	72	67—283	12,000
Pam Gietzen	72	69	71	71—283	12,000
Amy Alcott	74	68	72	70—284	7,500
Kathy Young	72	74	70	68—284	7,500
Beth Daniel	69	70	71	75—285	5,866
Hollis Stacy	73	70	69	73—285	5,866
Sandra Haynie	73	69	73	70—285	5,866
Sally Little	71	73	71	71—286	4,800
Sandra Palmer	70	70	74	72—286	4,800

1982 COLLEGIATE GOLF CHAMPIONS NATIONAL COLLEGIATE ATHLETIC ASSOCIATION

Division I—Men: Individual: Billy Ray Brown, Houston, 280; Team: Houston; 1,141. Women: Individual: Kathy Baker, Tulsa, 295; Team: Tulsa, 1,191.

Division II—Individual: Vic Wilk, California State–Northridge, 288; Team: Florida Southern, 1,181.

Division III—Individual: Cliff Smith, California State–Stanislaus, 295; Team: Ramapo, 1,200.

FINAL 1981 LEADING L.P.G.A. EARNINGS

Player	Amount	Player	Amount
Beth Daniel	$206,977	Nancy Lopez	$165,679
JoAnne Carner	206,648	Amy Alcott	149,089
Pat Bradley	197,050	Sally Little	142,251
Donna Caponi	193,916	Hollis Stacy	138,908
Jan Stephenson	180,528	Kathy Whitworth	134,937

FINAL 1981 LEADING P.G.A. EARNINGS

Player	Amount	Player	Amount
Tom Kite	$375,699	Jerry Pate	$280,627
Ray Floyd	359,360	Hale Irwin	276,499
Tom Watson	347,660	Craig Stadler	218,829
Bruce Lietzke	343,446	Curtis Strange	201,513
Bill Rogers	315,411	Larry Nelson	193,342

1982 LEADING L.P.G.A. EARNINGS

(Through Aug. 22, 1982)

Player	Amount	Player	Amount
JoAnne Carner	$248,109	Jerry Pate	$234,141
Sally Little	214,510	Bob Gilder	230,998
Sandra Haynie	212,820	Calvin Peete	223,111
Beth Daniel	201,298	Jack Nicklaus	217,645
Patty Sheehan	169,817	Bruce Lietzke	210,928

1982 LEADING P.G.A. EARNINGS

(Through Aug. 22, 1982)

Player	Amount	Player	Amount
Ray Floyd	$331,809	Hollis Stacy	$145,340
Craig Stadler	328,101	Amy Alcott	143,145
Tom Kite	308,076	Nancy Lopez	126,397
Tom Watson	296,715	Jan Stephenson	121,893
Lanny Wadkins	290,138	Kathy Whitworth	111,839

U.S.G.A. SENIORS CHAMPIONSHIP—1982

(Portland, Ore., July 8–11, 1982)
(For professionals and amateurs 50 and older)

Miller Barber	72	74	71	65—282	$28,648
Gene Littler	73	69	76	68—286	12,519
Dan Sikes	75	69	72	70—286	12,519
Bob Goalby	72	71	74	72—289	6,532
Gay Brewer	73	70	75	73—291	4,813
Arnold Palmer	73	71	73	74—291	4,813
Ken Towns	71	74	72	75—292	3,942
Charles Sifford	76	71	77	69—293	3,572
Jack Fleck	73	72	75	74—294	3,282
Bob Gajda	75	74	72	74—295	2,890
H. Johnson	74	73	72	76—295	2,890

MEN'S U.S. AMATEUR

(Brookline, Mass., Aug. 31-Sept. 5, 1982)

Final (36 holes)—Jay Sigel, Philadelphia, defeated David Tolley, Roanoke, Va., 8 and 7, in final

Semifinals—Sigel defeated Richard Fehr, Seattle, Wash., 1 up, and Tolley defeated Jim Hallet, South Yarmouth, Mass., 1 up

WOMEN'S U.S. AMATEUR

(Colorado Springs, Colo., Aug. 17–22, 1982)

Final (36 holes)—Juli Inkster, Los Altos, Calif., defeated Cathy Hanlon, Palos Verdes Estates, Calif., 4 and 3

Semifinals—Miss Inkster defeated Lisa Kluver, Alexandria, Minn., 3 and 2; Miss Hanlon defeated Lindy Goggin, Australia, 6 and 4

OTHER 1982 PGA TOUR WINNERS
(Through Aug. 22, 1982)

Tucson Open—Craig Stadler (266)	$54,000
Bob Hope Classic—Ed Fiori* (335)	50,000
Phoenix Open—Lanny Wadkins (263)	54,000
San Diego Open—Johnny Miller (270)	54,000
Crosby Pro-Am—Jim Simons (274)	54,000
Hawaii Open—Wayne Levi (277)	58,500
Los Angeles Open—Tom Watson* (271)	54,000
Doral Open—Andy Bean (278)	54,000
Bay Hill Classic—Tom Kite* (278)	54,000
Inverrary Classic—Hale Irwin (269)	72,000
Tournament Players Championship—Jerry Pate (280)	90,000
Heritage Classic—Tom Watson* (280)	54,000
Greensboro Open—Danny Edwards (285)	54,000
Tournament of Champions—Lanny Wadkins (280)	63,000
Tallahassee Open—Bob Shearer (272)	18,000
USF&G Classic—Scott Hoch (206)	54,000
Nelson Classic—Bob Gilder (266)	63,000
Houston Open—Ed Sneed* (275)	63,000
Colonial Invitational—Jack Nicklaus (273)	63,000
Atlanta Classic—Keith Fergus* (273)	54,000
Memorial Tournament—Ray Floyd (281)	63,000
Kemper Open—Craig Stadler (275)	72,000
Memphis Open—Ray Floyd (271)	72,000
Westchester Classic—Bob Gilder (261)	72,000
Western Open—Tom Weiskopf (276)	63,000
Milwaukee Open—Calvin Peete (274)	45,000
Quad Cities Open—Payne Stewart (268)	36,000
Anheuser-Busch Classic—Calvin Peete (203)	63,000
Canadian Open—Bruce Lietzke (277)	76,500
Hartford Open—Tim Norris (259)	54,000

*Won playoff.

OTHER 1982 L.P.G.A. TOUR WINNERS
(Through Aug. 22, 1982)

Whirlpool—Hollis Stacy* (282)	$18,750
Elizabeth Arden Classic—JoAnne Carner (283)	18,750
S&H Classic—Hollis Stacy (204)	18,750
Bent Tree Classic—Beth Daniel (276)	22,500
Arizona Copper—Ayako Okamoto* (281)	18,750
Sun City Classic—Beth Daniel* (278)	15,000
Olympia Gold—Sally Little (288)	22,500
J&B Scotch—Nancy Lopez (279)	30,000
Kemper—Amy Alcott (286)	26,250
Dinah Shore Classic—Sally Little (278)	45,000
CPC International—Kathy Whitworth (281)	22,500
Orlando Classic—Patty Sheehan* (209)	22,500
Birmingham Classic—Beth Daniel (203)	15,000
UVB Classic—Sally Little* (208)	18,750
Lady Michelob—Kathy Whitworth (207)	22,500
Chrysler Classic—Cathy Morse (216)	18,750
Borning Classic—Sandra Spuzich* (280)	18,750
McDonald's Kids—JoAnne Carner (276)	37,500
Lady Keystone—Jan Stephenson (211)	30,000
Rochester—Sandra Haynie (276)	30,000
Jackson Classic—Sandra Haynie (280)	30,000
West Virginia—Hollis Stacy* (209)	18,750
Mayflower—Sally Little (275)	30,000
Columbia Savings—Beth Daniel (276)	30,000
Boston Five—Sandra Palmer (281)	26,250
WUI Classic—Beth Daniel (276)	18,750

*Won playoff.

SOCCER

WORLD CUP

1930	Uruguay	1946	No competition
1934	Italy	1950	Uruguay
1938	Italy	1954	West Germany
1942	No competition	1958	Brazil
1962	Brazil	1978	Argentina
1966	England	1982	Italy
1970	Brazil		
1974	West Germany		

WORLD CUP—1982 SEMIFINALS
(Madrid, Spain, July 8, 1982)

Italy 2, Poland 0
West Germany 5, France 4 (penalty kicks)

FINAL
(Madrid, Spain, July 11, 1982)

Italy 3, West Germany 1

THIRD PLACE
(Madrid, Spain, July 10, 1982)

Poland 3, France 2

The following are the results of matches played by the four teams which reached the semifinals:

Italy (Group C)

Italy 0, Poland 0
Italy 1, Peru 1
Italy 1, Cameroon 1
Italy 2, Argentina 1
Italy 3, Brazil 2

Poland (Group A)

Poland 0, Italy 0
Poland 0, Cameroon 0
Poland 5, Peru 1
Poland 3, Belgium 0
Poland 0, Soviet Union 0

West Germany (Group B)

West Germany 1, Algeria 2
West Germany 4, Chile 1
West Germany 1, Austria 0
West Germany 0, England 0
West Germany 2, Spain 1

France (Group D)

France 1, England 3
France 4, Kuwait 1
France 1, Czechoslovakia 1
France 1, Austria 0
France 4, Northern Ireland 1

MAJOR INDOOR SOCCER LEAGUE FINAL STANDING—1982

EASTERN DIVISION

	W	L	Pct	GB
New York	36	8	.818	—
Pittsburgh	31	13	.705	5
Baltimore	27	17	.614	9
Buffalo	24	20	.545	12
New Jersey	17	27	.386	19

Cleveland	15	29	.341	21
Philadelphia	11	33	.250	25

WESTERN DIVISION

St. Louis	28	16	.636	—
Wichita	27	17	.614	1
Memphis	20	24	.455	8
Denver	19	25	.432	9
Phoenix	17	27	.386	11
Kansas City	14	30	.318	14

CHAMPIONSHIP PLAYOFFS
Quarterfinal Round

New York defeated Buffalo, 2 games to 1
Baltimore defeated Pittsburgh, 2 games to 1
St. Louis defeated Denver, 2 games to 0
Wichita defeated Memphis, 2 games to 1

Semifinal Round

New York defeated Baltimore, 2 games to 0
St. Louis defeated Wichita, 2 games to 1

Final

New York defeated St. Louis, 3 games to 2

LEADING N.A.S.L. SCORERS—1982

	GP	G	A	Pts
Giorgio Chinaglia, Cosmos	32	20	15	55
Karl–Heinz Granitza, Chicago	32	20	9	49
Peter Ward, Seattle	32	18	18	49
Ricardo Alonzo, Jacksonville	30	21	4	46
Laurie Abrahams, Tulsa	31	17	10	44
Neill Roberts, Toronto	28	17	8	42
Ace Ntsoelengoe, Toronto	32	14	12	40
Mark Peterson, Seattle	31	17	5	39
David Byrne, Toronto	32	8	23	39
Godfrey Ingram, San Jose	31	17	3	37
Alan Willey, Montreal	27	15	7	37
Branko Segota, Fort Lauderdale	29	12	13	37

OUTDOOR SOCCER
NORTH AMERICAN SOCCER LEAGUE
Final Standing—1982

	W	L	GF	GA	BP[1]	Pts
EASTERN DIVISION						
Cosmos	23	9	73	52	67	203
Montreal Manic	19	13	60	43	49	159
Toronto Blizzard	17	15	64	47	49	151
Chicago Sting	13	19	56	67	53	129
SOUTHERN DIVISION						
Fort Lauderdale Strikers	18	14	64	74	57	163
Tulsa Roughnecks	16	16	69	57	59	151
Tampa Bay Rowdies	12	20	47	77	42	112
Jacksonville Tea Men	11	21	41	71	39	105
WESTERN DIVISION						
Seattle Sounders	18	14	72	48	60	166
San Diego Sockers	19	13	71	54	54	162
Vancouver Whitecaps	20	12	58	48	46	160
Portland Timbers	14	18	49	44	42	122
San Jose Earthquake	13	19	47	62	38	114
Edmonton Drillers	11	21	38	65	33	93

1. A bonus point is awarded for each goal scored to a maximum of three a game, excluding overtimes and shootouts; teams receive 6 points for each victory in regulation time or overtime, but only 4 points for winning a game decided by a shootout.

CHAMPIONSHIP PLAYOFF—1982

(San Diego, Calif. Sept. 18, 1982)
Cosmos 1, Seattle 0
(Scoring: Chinaglia 0)

Semifinals

Cosmos defeated San Diego, 2 games to 0
Seattle defeated Ft. Lauderdale, 2 games to 1

N.A.S.L. INDOOR SOCCER—1982
FINAL STANDING

ATLANTIC CONFERENCE
Central Division

	W	L	Pct	GB
Chicago	12	6	.667	—
Tampa Bay	11	7	.611	1
Tulsa	10	8	.556	2
Eastern Division				
Montreal	9	9	.500	—
Toronto	8	10	.444	1
Jacksonville	7	11	.389	2
Cosmos	6	12	.333	3
PACIFIC CONFERENCE				
Western Division				
San Diego	10	8	.556	—
Portland	7	11	.389	3
San Jose	5	13	.278	5
Northwest Division				
Edmonton	13	5	.722	—
Vancouver	10	8	.556	3
Seattle	9	9	.500	4

CHAMPIONSHIP PLAYOFFS
Quarterfinal Round

Tulsa defeated Chicago, 2 games to 1
Tampa Bay defeated Montreal, 2 games to 1
Edmonton defeated Seattle, 2 games to 0
San Diego defeated Vancouver, 2 games to 0

Semifinal Round

Tampa Bay defeated Tulsa, 2 games to 1
San Diego defeated Edmonton, 2 games to 0

Final

San Diego 9, Tampa Bay 7
San Diego 10, Tampa Bay 5 (San Diego won series 2 games to 0)

COURT TENNIS

UNITED STATES CHAMPIONS—1982

Men's open—Wayne Davies, New York City
Men's amateur—Gene Scott, New York City
Men's seniors—Bill Vogt, Philadelphia
Men's amateur doubles—O.M. Phipps and Gene Scott, New York City
Men's open doubles—Wayne Davies and O.M. Phipps

SURFING—1982

World men's amateur—Tom Curren, Santa Barbara, Calif.
World women's amateur—Jerry Gill, Australia

NATIONAL SPORTS FESTIVAL

(Continued from page 904)

50-k walk—Ray Somers—Flemington, N.J.
110-m hurdles—Willie Gault, Knoxville, Tenn.
400-m hurdles—Andre Phillips, Los Angeles
400-m relay—South
1,600-m relay—South
Hammer throw—Dave McKenzie, Fairfield, Calif.
Javelin—Brian Crouser, Gresham, Ore.
Long jump—Carl Lewis, Willingsboro, N.J.
High jump—Dwight Stones, Irvine, Calif.
Shotput—Dean Crouser, Gresham, Ore.
Triple jump—Robert Cannon, Lake Charles, La.
Decathlon—Bob Stebbins, Reading, Pa.

Track and Field—Women

100-m dash—Evelyn Ashford, Hollywood, Calif.
200-m dash—Florence Griffith, Los Angeles
400-m run—Rosalyn Bryant, Inglewood, Calif.
800-m run—Kim Gallagher, Ambler, Pa.
1,500-m run—Francie Larrieu Smith, Lubbock, Tex.
3,000-m run—Jan Merrill, New London, Conn.
Marathon—Carol Chilcoat, Seattle, Wash.
100-m hurdles—Stephanie Hightower, Columbus, Ohio
400-m hurdles—Edna Brown, Philadelphia
400-m relay—West
1,600-m relay—East
High jump—Kym Carter, Wichita, Kan.
Javelin—Karin Smith, Venice, Calif.
Shotput—Denise Wood, Knoxville, Tenn.
Discus—Leslie Deniz, Gridley, Calif.
Long jump—Jodi Anderson, Los Angeles
Teams—Men: West, 236 pts. Women: West, 166 pts.

MOTORCYCLE RACING

WORLD CHAMPION—1982

500 c.c.—Franco Uncini, Italy (Suzuki)

TRIATHLON—1982

World Ironman championships—Scott Tinley, San Diego, Calif. (swimming 2.4 miles, 1:10.45; bicycling 112 miles, 5:05.11; marathon running 3:03.45), 9 hours, 19 minutes, 41 seconds.

LACROSSE

NATIONAL INTERCOLLEGIATE CHAMPIONS

1946	Navy
1947–48	Johns Hopkins
1949	Johns Hopkins, Navy
1950	Johns Hopkins
1951	Army, Princeton
1952	Virginia, R.P.I.
1953	Princeton
1954	Navy
1955–56	Maryland
1957	Johns Hopkins
1958	Army
1959	Army, Johns Hopkins, Maryland
1960	Navy
1961	Army, Navy
1962–66	Navy
1967	Johns Hopkins, Maryland, Navy
1968	Johns Hopkins
1969	Army, Johns Hopkins
1970	Johns Hopkins, Navy, Virginia
1971[1]	Cornell
1972	Virginia
1973	Maryland
1974	Johns Hopkins
1975	Maryland
1976–77	Cornell
1978–80	Johns Hopkins
1981	North Carolina
1982	North Carolina

1. First year of N.C.A.A. Championship Tournaments.

N.C.A.A. CHAMPIONSHIPS—1982

DIVISION I

Final

(Charlottesville, Va., May 29, 1982)
North Carolina 7, Johns Hopkins 5

Semifinals

North Carolina 15, Cornell 8
Johns Hopkins 13, Virginia 9

Quarterfinals

Cornell 11, Army 9
Johns Hopkins 14, Maryland 9
North Carolina 16, Navy 2
Virginia 15, Adelphi 9

DIVISION III

Final

(Geneva, N.Y., May 23, 1982)
Hobart 9, Washington (Md.) College 8

Semifinals

Hobart 22, Salisbury State 4
Washington College 19, Roanoke 11

WOMEN'S LACROSSE N.C.A.A. CHAMPIONSHIP—1982

Massachusetts 9, Trenton (N.J.) State 6

A.I.A.W. CHAMPIONSHIPS—1982

DIVISION I

Temple 3, Maryland 2

DIVISION II

Delaware 10, Lehigh 8

DIVISION III

Millersville (Pa.) State 10, Lynchburg (Va.) 3

LACROSSE ALL-AMERICAN TEAM DIVISION I

Attack—Mike Burnett, North Carolina; Jeff Cook, Johns Hopkins; Jim Wilkerson, Maryland
Midfield—Peter Voelkel and Jeff Homire, North Carolina; Al Ray, Rutgers; Rick Giusto, Virginia
Defense—John Haus, North Carolina; George McGeeney, Maryland-Baltimore; Mike Sotir, Virginia
Goal—Tom Sears, North Carolina

YACHTING

AMERICA'S CUP RECORD

First race in 1851 around Isle of Wight, Cowes, England. First defense and all others through 1920 held 30 miles off New York Bay. Races since 1930 held 30 miles off Newport, R.I. Conducted as one race only in 1851 and 1870; best four-of-seven basis, 1871; best two-of-three, 1876–1887; best three-of-five, 1893–1901; best four-of-seven, since 1930. Figures in parentheses indicate number of races won.

Year	Winner and owner	Loser and owner
1851	AMERICA (1), John C. Stevens, U.S.	AURORA, T. Le Marchant, England[1]
1870	MAGIC (1), Franklin Osgood, U.S.	CAMBRIA, James Ashbury, England[2]
1871	COLUMBIA (2), Franklin Osgood, U.S.[3] SAPPHO (2), William P. Douglas, U.S.	LIVONIA (1), James Ashbury, England
1876	MADELEINE (2), John S. Dickerson, U.S.	COUNTESS OF DUFFERIN, Chas. Gifford, Canada
1881	MISCHIEF (2), J. R. Busk, U.S.	ATALANTA, Alexander Cuthbert, Canada
1885	PURITAN (2), J. M. Forbes-Gen. Charles Paine, U.S.	GENESTA, Sir Richard Sutton, England
1886	MAYFLOWER (2), Gen. Charles Paine, U.S.	GALATEA, Lt. William Henn, England
1887	VOLUNTEER (2), Gen. Charles Paine, U.S.	THISTLE, James Bell et al, Scotland
1893	VIGILANT (3), C. Oliver Iselin et al., U.S.	VALKYRIE II, Lord Dunraven, England
1895	DEFENDER (3), C. O. Iselin-W. K. Vanderbilt-E. D. Morgan, U.S.	VALKYRIE III, Lord Dunraven-Lord Lonsdale-Lord Wolverton, England
1899	COLUMBIA (3), J. P. Morgan-C. O. Iselin, U.S.	SHAMROCK I, Sir Thomas Lipton, Ireland
1901	COLUMBIA (3), Edwin D. Morgan, U.S.	SHAMROCK II, Sir Thomas Lipton, Ireland
1903	RELIANCE (3), Cornelius Vanderbilt et al., U.S.	SHAMROCK III, Sir Thomas Lipton, Ireland
1920	RESOLUTE (3), Henry Walters et al., U.S.	SHAMROCK IV (2), Sir Thomas Lipton, Ireland
1930	ENTERPRISE (4), Harold S. Vanderbilt et al., U.S.	SHAMROCK V, Sir Thomas Lipton, Ireland
1934	RAINBOW (4), Harold S. Vanderbilt, U.S.	ENDEAVOUR (2), T. O. M. Sopwith, England
1937	RANGER (4), Harold S. Vanderbilt, U.S.	ENDEAVOUR II, T. O. M. Sopwith, England
1958	COLUMBIA (4), Henry Sears et al., U.S.	SCEPTRE, Hugh Goodson et al., England
1962	WEATHERLY (4), Henry D. Mercer et al., U.S.	GRETEL (1), Sir Frank Packer et al., Australia
1964	CONSTELLATION (4), New York Y.C. Syndicate, U.S.	SOVEREIGN (0), J. Anthony Bowden, England
1967	INTREPID (4), New York Y.C. Syndicate, U.S.	DAME PATTIE (0), Sydney (Aust.) Syndicate
1970	INTREPID (4), New York Y.C. Syndicate, U.S.	GRETEL II (1), Sydney (Aust.) Syndicate
1974	COURAGEOUS (4), New York, N.Y. Syndicate, U.S.	SOUTHERN CROSS (0), Sydney (Aust.) Syndicate
1977	COURAGEOUS (4), New York, N.Y. Syndicate, U.S.	AUSTRALIA (0), Sun City (Aust.) Syndicate
1980	FREEDOM (4), New York, N.Y. Syndicate, U.S.	AUSTRALIA (1), Alan Bond et al, Australia

1. Fourteen British yachts started against America; Aurora finished second. 2. Cambria sailed against 23 U.S. yachts and finished tenth. 3. Columbia was disabled in the third race, after winning the first two; Sappho substituted and won the fourth and fifth.

YACHTING—1982

Newport-to-Bermuda Race (635 miles, held every 2 years)—Corrected time winner: Brigadoon, Class B, 57-foot sloop, skippered by Robert Morton, handicapped under Measurement Handicap System, 2 days 20 hours 42 seconds. First to finish: Nirvana, Class A, 81-foot Maxi, skippered by M.H. Green, handicapped under International Offshore Rule, elapsed time: 2:14:29:16

Chicago-to-Mackinac Island (Lake Michigan, 333 miles)—Corrected time winner: Leading Edge, 40-foot sloop, skippered by Eugene Mondry, 41 hours 38 minutes 27 seconds. First to finish: Heritage, 63-foot sloop, skippered by Don Wildman, elapsed time: 48:45:18

Onion Patch National Team Series (Hamilton, Bermuda)—Canada (Ontario), 711 points

DUCKPIN BOWLING

NATIONAL CHAMPIONSHIPS—1982

(Providence, R.I.)

National Duckpin Bowling Congress

Men's singles—Bart Matteson, East Taunton, Mass.	568
Women's singles—Pat Smith, Warwick, R.I.	523
Men's doubles—Thomas Bohara Sr. and Len Gdula, Norwich, Conn.	1,037
Women's doubles—Carol Deshong, Riverside, R.I., and Anne Mello, Rehoboth, R.I.	913
Championship Team—Legion Major No. 3, Cranston, R.I.	2,200
Class A Teams—Walko Five, Fall River, Mass.	2,164
Class B Teams—Rhode Island Paper Box, Cranston, R.I.	2,065
Class C Teams—Samor Funeral Home, Bridgeport, Conn.	1,897
Class D Teams—Moss Trucking, Charlotte, N.C.	1,763

KARATE

AMATEUR ATHLETIC UNION NATIONAL CHAMPIONSHIPS

(Palatine, Ill., July 25, 1982)

Open heavyweight class—Bob Allen, New Orleans, La.
80–kilogram class—Terrance Tokey Hill, Chillicothe, Ohio
75–kilogram class—John DiPasquale, Chicago
70–kilogram class—Michael Sledge, New York City
60–kilogram–and–under class—George Gino, Cleveland, Ohio

SHUFFLEBOARD

U.S.-INTERNATIONAL PRO WORLD CHAMPIONSHIP

(Lakeland, Fla., Jan. 28–30, 1982)

Men—Jason Baade and Len deBoer, Lakeland, Fla.
Women—Therese Charbonneau, St. Petersburg, Fla., and Thea Harris, Fort Myers, Fla.

AUTO RACING

INDIANAPOLIS 500

Year	Winner	Car	Time	mph	Second place
1911	Ray Harroun	Marmon	6:42:08	74.59	Ralph Mulford
1912	Joe Dawson	National	6:21:06	78.72	Teddy Tetzloff
1913	Jules Goux	Peugeot	6:35:05	75.93	Spencer Wishart
1914	René Thomas	Delage	6:03:45	82.47	Arthur Duray
1915	Ralph DePalma	Mercedes	5:33:55.51	89.84	Dario Resta
1916[1]	Dario Resta	Peugeot	3:34:17	84.00	Wilbur D'Alene
1919	Howard Wilcox	Peugeot	5:40:42.87	88.05	Eddie Hearne
1920	Gaston Chevrolet	Monroe	5:38:32	88.62	René Thomas
1921	Tommy Milton	Frontenac	5:34:44.65	89.62	Roscoe Sarles
1922	Jimmy Murphy	Murphy Special	5:17:30.79	94.48	Harry Hartz
1923	Tommy Milton	H. C. S. Special	5:29.50.17	90.95	Harry Hartz
1924	L. L. Corum–Joe Boyer	Dusenberg Special	5:05:23.51	98.23	Earl Cooper
1925	Peter DePaolo	Dusenberg Special	4:56:39.45	101.13	Dave Lewis
1926[2]	Frank Lockhart	Miller Special	4:10:14.95	95.904	Harry Hartz
1927	George Souders	Dusenberg Special	5:07:33.08	97.54	Earl DeVore
1928	Louis Meyer	Miller Special	5:01:33.75	99.48	Lou Moore
1929	Ray Keech	Simplex Special	5:07:25.42	97.58	Louis Meyer
1930	Billy Arnold	Miller–Hartz Special	4:58:39.72	100.448	Shorty Cantlon
1931	Louis Schneider	Bowes Special	5:10:27.93	96.629	Fred Frame
1932	Fred Frame	Miller–Hartz Special	4:48:03.79	104.144	Howard Wilcox
1933	Louis Meyer	Tydol Special	4:48:00.75	104.162	Wilbur Shaw
1934	Bill Cummings	Boyle Products Special	4:46:05.20	104.863	Mauri Rose
1935	Kelly Petillo	Gilmore Special	4:42:22.71	106.240	Wilbur Shaw
1936	Louis Meyer	Ring Free Special	4:35:03.39	109.069	Ted Horn
1937	Wilbur Shaw	Shaw–Gilmore Special	4:24:07.80	113.580	Ralph Hepburn
1938	Floyd Roberts	Burd Piston Ring Special	4:15:58.40	117.200	Wilbur Shaw
1939	Wilbur Shaw	Boyle Special	4:20:47.39	115.035	Jimmy Snyder
1940	Wilbur Shaw	Boyle Special	4:22:31.17	114.277	Rex Mays
1941	Floyd Davis–Mauri Rose	Noc–Out Hose Clamp Special	4:20:36.24	115.117	Rex Mays
1946	George Robson	Thorne Engineering Special	4:21:26.71	114.820	Jimmy Jackson
1947	Mauri Rose	Blue Crown Special	4:17:52.17	116.338	Bill Holland
1948	Mauri Rose	Blue Crown Special	4:10:23.33	119.814	Bill Holland
1949	Bill Holland	Blue Crown Special	4:07:15.97	121.327	Johnny Parsons
1950[3]	Johnnie Parsons	Wynn's Friction Proof Special	2:46:55.97	124.002	Bill Holland
1951	Lee Wallard	Belanger Special	3:57:38.05	126.244	Mike Nazaruk
1952	Troy Ruttman	Agajanian Special	3:52:41.88	128.922	Jim Rathmann
1953	Bill Vukovich	Fuel Injection Special	3:53:01.69	128.740	Art Cross
1954	Bill Vukovich	Fuel Injection Special	3:49:17.27	130.840	Jim Bryan
1955	Bob Sweikert	John Zink Special	3:53:59.13	128.209	Tony Bettenhausen
1956	Pat Flaherty	John Zink Special	3:53:28.84	128.490	Sam Hanks
1957	Sam Hanks	Belond Exhaust Special	3:41:14.25	135.601	Jim Rathmann
1958	Jimmy Bryan	Belond A–P Special	3:44:13.80	133.791	George Amick
1959	Rodger Ward	Leader Card 500 Roadster	3:40:49.20	135.857	Jim Rathmann
1960	Jim Rathmann	Ken–Paul Special	3:36:11.36	138.767	Rodger Ward
1961	A. J. Foyt	Bowes Special	3:35:37.49	139.130	Eddie Sachs
1962	Rodger Ward	Leader Card Special	3:33:50.33	140.293	Len Sutton
1963	Parnelli Jones	Agajanian Special	3:29:35.40	143.137	Jim Clark
1964	A. J. Foyt	Offenhauser Special	3:23:35.83	147.350	Rodger Ward
1965	Jim Clark	Lotus–Ford	3:19:05.34	150.686	Parnelli Jones
1966	Graham Hill	Lola–Ford	3:27:52.53	144.317	Jim Clark
1967[4]	A. J. Foyt	Coyote–Ford	3:18:24.22	151.207	Al Unser
1968	Bobby Unser	Eagle–Offenhauser	3:16:13.76	152.882	Dan Gurney
1969	Mario Andretti	STP Hawk–Ford	3:11:14.71	156.867	Dan Gurney
1970	Al Unser	P. J. Colt–Ford	3:12:37.04	155.749	Mark Donohue
1971	Al Unser	P. J. Colt–Ford	3:10:11.56	157.735	Peter Revson
1972	Mark Donohue	McLaren–Offenhauser	3:04:05.54	162.962	Al Unser
1973[5]	Gordon Johncock	Eagle–Offenhauser	2:05:26.59	159.036	Bill Vukovich
1974	Johnny Rutherford	McLaren–Offenhauser	3:09:10.06	158.589	Bobby Unser
1975[6]	Bobby Unser	Eagle–Offenhauser	2:54:55.08	149.213	Johnny Rutherford
1976[7]	Johnny Rutherford	McLaren–Offenhauser	1:42:52.48	148.725	A. J. Foyt
1977	A. J. Foyt	Coyote–Foyt	3:05:57.16	161.331	Tom Sneva
1978	Al Unser	Lola–Cosworth	3:05:54.99	161.363	Tom Sneva
1979	Rick Mears	Penske–Cosworth	3:08:27.97	158.899	A. J. Foyt
1980	Johnny Rutherford	Chaparral–Cosworth	3:29:59.56	142.862	Tom Sneva
1981[8]	Bobby Unser	Eagle–Offenhauser	3:35:41.78	139.029	Mario Andretti

1982	Gordon Johncock	Wildcat–Cosworth	3:05:09.14	162.029	Rick Mears

1. 300 miles. 2. Race ended at 400 miles because of rain. 3. Race ended at 345 miles because of rain. 4. Race, postponed after 18 laps because of rain on May 30, was finished on May 31. 5. Race postponed May 28 and 29 was cut to 332.5 miles because of rain, May 30. 6. Race ended at 435 miles because of rain. 7. Race ended at 255 miles because of rain. 8. Andretti was awarded the victory the day after the race after Bobby Unser, whose car finished first, was penalized one lap and dropped from first place to second for passing other cars illegally under a yellow caution flag. Unser appealed the decision to the U.S. Auto Club and was upheld. A panel ruled the penalty was too severe and instead fined Unser $40,000, but restored the victory to him.

U.S. AUTO CLUB NATIONAL CHAMPIONS

1910	Ray Harroun	1926	Harry Hartz	1950	Henry Banks	1968	Bobby Unser
1911	Ralph Mulford	1927	Peter DePaolo	1951	Tony Bettenhausen	1969	Mario Andretti
1912	Ralph DePalma	1928–29	Louis Meyer	1952	Chuck Stevenson	1970	Al Unser
1913	Earl Cooper	1930	Billy Arnold	1953	Sam Hanks	1971–72	Joe Leonard
1914	Ralph DePalma	1931	Louis Schneider	1954	Jimmy Bryan	1973	Roger McCluskey
1915	Earl Cooper	1932	Bob Carey	1955	Bob Sweikert	1974	Bobby Unser
1916	Dario Resta	1933	Louis Meyer	1956–57	Jimmy Bryan	1975	A. J. Foyt
1917	Earl Cooper	1934	Bill Cummings	1958	Tony Bettenhausen	1976	Gordon Johncock
1918	Ralph Mulford	1935	Kelly Petillo	1959	Rodger Ward	1977–78	Tom Sneva
1919	Howard Wilcox	1936	Mauri Rose	1960–61	A. J. Foyt	1979	A. J. Foyt
1920	Gaston Chevrolet	1937	Wilbur Shaw	1962	Rodger Ward	1980	Johnny Rutherford
1921	Tommy Milton	1938	Floyd Roberts	1963–64	A. J. Foyt	1981–82	George Snider
1922	James Murphy	1939	Wilbur Shaw	1965–66	Mario Andretti		
1923	Eddie Hearne	1940–41	Rex Mays	1967	A. J. Foyt		
1924	James Murphy	1946–48	Ted Horn				
1925	Peter DePaolo	1949	Johnnie Parsons				

NATIONAL ASSOCIATION FOR STOCK CAR AUTO RACING (NASCAR) GRAND NATIONAL CHAMPIONS

1949	Red Byron	1956–57	Buck Baker	1966	David Pearson	1976–78	Cale Yarborough
1950	Bill Rexford	1958–59	Lee Petty	1967	Richard Petty	1979	Richard Petty
1951	Herb Thomas	1960	Rex White	1968–69	David Pearson	1980	Dale Earnhardt
1952	Tim Flock	1961	Ned Jarrett	1970	Bobby Isaac	1981	Darrell Waltrip
1953	Herb Thomas	1962–63	Joe Weatherly	1971–72	Richard Petty		
1954	Lee Petty	1964	Richard Petty	1973	Benny Parsons		
1955	Tim Flock	1965	Ned Jarrett	1974–75	Richard Petty		

WORLD GRAND PRIX DRIVER CHAMPIONS

1950	Giuseppe Farina, Italy, Alfa Romeo
1951	Juan Fangio, Argentina, Alfa Romeo
1952	Alberto Ascari, Italy, Ferrari
1953	Alberto Ascari, Italy, Ferrari
1955	Juan Fangio, Argentina, Maserati, Mercedes-Benz
1955	Juan Fangio, Argentina, Mercedes-Benz
1956	Juan Fangio, Argentina, Lancia-Ferrari
1957	Juan Fangio, Argentina, Masserati
1958	Mike Hawthorn, England, Ferrari
1959	Jack Brabham, Australia, Cooper
1960	Jack Brabham, Australia, Cooper
1961	Phil Hill, United States, Ferrari
1962	Graham Hill, England, BRM
1963	Jim Clark, Scotland, Lotus-Ford
1964	John Surtees, England, Ferrari
1965	Jim Clark, Scotland, Lotus-Ford
1966	Jack Brabham, Australia, Brabham-Repco
1967	Denis Hulme, New Zealand, Brabham-Repco
1968	Graham Hill, England, Lotus-Ford
1969	Jackie Stewart, Scotland, Matra-Ford
1970	Jochen Rindt, Austria, Lotus-Ford
1971	Jackie Stewart, Scotland, Tyrrell-Ford
1972	Emerson Fittipaldi, Brazil, Lotus-Ford
1973	Jackie Stewart, Scotland, Tyrrell-Ford
1974	Emerson Fittipaldi, Brazil, McLaren-Ford
1975	Niki Lauda, Austria, Ferrari
1976	James Hunt, Britain, McLaren-Ford
1977	Niki Lauda, Austria, Ferrari
1978	Mario Andretti, Nazareth, Pa., Lotus
1979	Jody Scheckter, South Africa
1980	Alan Jones, Australia
1981	Nelson Piquet, Brazil
1982	Kiki Rosberg, Finland

GRAND PRIX RACING EVENTS—1982

(Through Aug. 29, 1982)

Formula One Competition

South Africa (Kyalami, South Africa, Jan. 23)—Alain Prost, France; driving a Renault–turbo; 1 hour 32 minutes 8.4 seconds; 128.59 miles per hour

Brazil (Rio de Janiero, March 21)—Nelson Piquet, Brazil; Brabham; 1:43:54.760; 114.086 mph

Long Beach (Long Beach, Calif., April 4)—Niki Lauda, Austria; McLaren; 81.4 mph

San Marino (Imola, Italy, April 25)—Didier Pironi, France; Ferrari; 1:36:38.887; 116.9 mph

Belgium (Zolder, Belgium, May 9)—John Watson, Britain; McLaren–Cosworth; 1:35:41.995; 116.19 mph

Monaco (Monte Carlo, Monaco, May 23)—Riccardo Patrese, Italy; Brabham–Ford; 1:54:11.259; 82.21 mph

Detroit (Detroit, Mich., June 6)—John Watson, Britain; McLaren–Cosworth; 1:58:4.043; 78.2 mph

Canada (Montreal, June 13)—Nelson Piquet, Brazil; Brabham BT–50; 104.22 mph

Dutch (Zandvoort, The Netherlands, July 3)—Didier Pironi, France; Ferrari; 1:38:03.25; 116.386 mph

Britain (Brands Hatch, England, July 18)—Niki Lauda, Austria; McLaren; 1:35:33.812; 124.7 mph

France (LeCastellet, France, July 25)—Rene Arnoux, France; Renault; 1:33:33.217; 125.0 mph

Germany (Hockenheim, West Germany, Aug. 8)—Patrick Tambay, France; Ferrari; 1:27:25.17; 130.42 mph
Austria (Zeltwig, Austria, Aug. 15)—Elio de Angelis, Italy; Lotus; 1:25:02.212; 138.1 mph
Switzerland (Dijon, France, Aug. 29)—Keke Rosberg, Finland; Williams; 1:33:50.32; 122.286 mph

U.S. AUTO CLUB

1982 Triple Crown Races

Indianapolis 500 (Indianapolis Motor Speedway, May 30, 500 miles)—1. Gordon Johncock, Coldwater, Mich.; STP Wildcat–Cosworth; 200 laps; 3:05:9.14; 162.029 mph; first-place prize; $290,609. 2. Rick Mears, Bakersfield, Calif.; Penske–Ford; 200 laps. 3. Pancho Carter, Brownsburg, Ind.; March–Cosworth; 199 laps. 4. Tom Sneva, Spokane, Wash., Texaco Star March; 197 laps. 5. Al Unser, Albuquerque, N.M., Longworth–Cosworth, 197 laps.

Pocono 500 (Pocono International Raceway, Long Pond, Pa., Aug. 15, 500 miles)—Rick Mears, Bakersfield, Calif., Penske PC–10 Ford; 3:25:39; 145.879 mph; 200 laps; $66,435. 2. Kevin Cogan, Redondo Beach, Calif.; Penske PC–10 Ford; 200 laps. 3. Bobby Rahal, Columbus, Ohio; 82C Cosworth; 197 laps. 4. Geoff Brabham, San Clemente, Calif.; March–Cosworth, 197 laps. 5. Tony Bettenhausen, Speedway, Ind.; March–Cosworth.

FINAL 1981 WINSTON CUP GRAND NATIONAL POINT LEADERS

Darrell Waltrip	4,880
Bobby Allison	4,827
Harry Gant	4,210
Terry Labonte	4,052
Jody Ridley	4,002
Ricky Rudd	3,988
Dale Earnhardt	3,975
Richard Petty	3,880
Dave Marcis	3,507
Benny Parsons	3,449

FINAL 1981 NASCAR LEADING MONEY-WINNERS

Darrell Waltrip	$693,342
Bobby Allison	644,311
Richard Petty	389,214
Ricky Rudd	381,968
Dale Earnhardt	347,113
Terry Labonte	334,987
Benny Parsons	287,949
Harry Gant	280,047
Jody Ridley	257,318
Neil Bonnett	181,670

OTHER 1982 CHAMPIONSHIP AUTO RACES

Championship Auto Racing Team (CART) Events

Kraco Phoenix 150 (Phoenix, Ariz., March 28, 150 miles)—Rick Mears, Bakersfield, Calif.; Penske P-C 10 Ford; 1 hour 15 minutes 48.231 seconds; 118.727 mph; $19,415
Stroh's 200 (Atlanta, Ga., March 1, 200 miles)—Rick Mears; Penske P–C 10 Ford; 1:13:10; 164,750 mph; $22,974
Gould Rex Mays 150 (Milwaukee, Wis., June 13, 150 miles)—Gordon Johncock, Coldwater, Mich.; ST Wildcat; 1:10:52.79; 126.978 mph; $19,979
Budweiser 500 kilometers (Cleveland, Ohio, July 4)—Bobby Rahal, Columbus, Ohio; Red Roof March; 3:03:44; 101.234 mph; $42,341
Norton 500 (Norton, Mich., July 18, 500 miles)—Gordon Johncock; ST Wildcat; 3:14:54; 153.925 mph; $89,303
Tony Bettenhaunsen 200 (Milwaukee, Wis., Aug. 1, 200 miles)—Tom Sneva, Paradise Valley, Ariz.; Texaco Star March; 1:49:57.54; 109.132 mph; $23,079
Domino's Pizza Pocono 500 (Pocono, Pa., Aug. 15, 500 miles)—Rick Mears, Penske P–C 10 Ford; 3:25:39; 145.879 mph; $66,435
Aircal 500 kilometers (Riverside, Calif., Aug. 29)—Rick Mears; Penske P–C 10 Ford; 2:42:14; 115.955 mph; $33,391

NATIONAL ASSOCIATION FOR STOCK CAR RACING (NASCAR)—1982

(Through races of Aug. 22, 1982)

Daytona 500 (Daytona Beach, Fla., Feb. 14, 500 miles)—Bobby Allison, Hueytown, Ala., Buick, 3 hours 14 minutes 49 seconds; average speed: 153.991 mph; total purse: $927,625; winner's purse: $120,630
Richmond 400 (Richmond, Va., Feb. 21, 216.8 miles)—Dave Marcis, Averys Creek, N.C.; Chevrolet; 1:51:30; 72.914 mph; $187,655; $19,145
Valleydale 500 (Bristol, Tenn., March 14, 266.5 miles)—Darrell Waltrip, Franklin, Tenn.; Buick; 2:49:52; 94.025 mph; $179,-175; $26,520
Coca–Cola 500 (Atlanta, Ga., March 21, 500 miles)—Darrell Waltrip; Buick; 3:29:58; 124.824 mph; $300,775; $49,615
Hodgdon Carolina 500 (Rockingham, N.C., March 28, 500 miles)—Cale Yarborough, Timmonsville, S.C.; Buick; 4:35:27; 108.992 mph; $232,665; $17,360
CRC Chemicals Rebel 500 (Darlington, S.C., April 4, 500 miles)—Dale Earnhardt, Kannapolis, N.C.; Ford; 4:03:27; 123.554 mph; $267,025; $31,450
Northwestern Bank 400 (North Wilkesboro, N.C., April 18, 250 miles)—Darrell Waltrip; Buick; 2:33:37; 97.646 mph; $181,-390; $32,300
Virginia National Bank 500 (Martinsville, Va., April 25, 262.5 miles)—Harry Gant, Taylorsville, N.C.; Buick; 3:30:01; 75.073 mph; $203,750; $26,795
Winston 500 (Talladega, Ala., May 2, 500 miles)—Darrell Waltrip; Buick; 3:11:19; 156.697 mph; $398,575; $44,250
Cracker Barrel 420 (Nashville, Tenn., May 8, 250.3 miles)—Darrell Waltrip; Buick; 2:59:52; 83.502 mph; $159,225; $24,-025
Mason–Dixon 500 (Dover, Del., May 16, 500 miles)—Bobby Allison; Chevrolet; 4:09:43; 120.136 mph; $224,300; $25,350
World 600 (Harrisburg, N.C., May 30, 600 miles)—Neil Bonnett, Hueytown, Ala.; Ford; 4:36:48; 130.058 mph; $430,325; $50,650
Van Scoy Diamond Mine 500 (Pocono, Pa., June 6, 500 miles)—Bobby Allison; Buick; 4:24:08; 113.579 mph; $250,525; $25,500
Budweiser 400 (Riverside, Calif., June 13, 400 kilometers)—Tim Richmond, Ashland, Ohio; Buick; 2:23:51; 103.816 mph; $217,400; $21,530
Gabriel 400 (Brooklyn, Mich., June 20, 400 miles)—Cale Yarborough; Buick; 3:23:13; 118.101 mph; $295,325; $24,700
Firecracker 400 (Daytona Beach, Fla., July 4, 400 miles)—Bobby Allison; Buick; 2:27:09; 163.099 mph; $318,675; $42,-100
Busch Nashville 420 (Nashville, Tenn., July 10, 250 miles)—Darrell Waltrip; Buick; 2:53:35; 86.524 mph; $158,575; $22,-025
Mountain Dew 500 (Mt. Pocono, Pa., July 25, 500 miles)—Bobby Allison; Buick; 4:19:45; 115.496 mph; $261.075; $24,-200
Talladega 500 (Talladega, Ala., Aug. 1, 500 miles)—Darrell Waltrip; Buick; 2:58:26; 168.157 mph; $351,725; $58,770
Champion Spark Plug 400 (Brooklyn, Mich., Aug. 22, 400 miles)—Bobby Allison; Buick; 2:45:53; 136.454 mph; $267,905; $26,900

RACQUETBALL

AMERICAN AMATEUR RACQUETBALL ASSOCIATION—1982

(Buffalo, N.Y., May 31, 1982)

Men's open champion—Jack Newman, Morton Grove, Ill. (defeated Larry Fox, Cincinnati, 21–14, 21–10, in final)
Men's Class B champion—Dan Gordon, Fargo, N.D. (defeated Warren Searles, Madison, N.J., 21–7, 21–8, in final)
Men's 30's champion—Joe Wirkus, Madison, Wis. (defeated Ed Remen, Sterling, Va., 21–5, 8–21, 15–13, in final)
Men's 35's champion—John Hennen, Chattanooga, Tenn. (defeated Bud Stange, Amherst, N.Y., 21–6, 21–0, in final)
Men's 40's champion—Charlie Garfinkle, Buffalo, N.Y. (defeated Ron Galbreath, Sharon, Pa., 11–21, 21–20, 15–9, in final)
Men's 45's champion—Charlie Solomon, Indianapolis (defeated Pete Talbot, Green Brook, N.J., 10–21, 21–4, 15–4, in final)
Men's 50's champion—Chuck Lake, Virginia Beach, Va. (defeated Harvey Clar, Oakland, Calif., 21–19, 21–18, in final)
Men's 55's champion—Finton Kilbride, Toronto, (defeated Rich Caretti, St. Paul, Minn., 21–2, 21–3, in final)
Men's 60's champion—Art Payne, Columbus, Ohio (defeated Marv Simikins, York, Pa., 21–19, 21–11, in final)
Men's 65's champion—Ike Gumer, Louisville, Ky. (defeated Lou Getlin, St. Louis, 21–7, 21–15, in final)
Women's open champion—Diane Bullard, Gainesville, Fla. (defeated Cindy Baxter, Lewiston, Pa., 21–14, 21–14, in final)
Women's Class B champion—Debbie Weber, Sterling, Va. (defeated Jan Peterson, Meadville, Pa., 14–21, 21–14, 15–5, in final)
Women's 30's champion—Carol Frenck, Virginia Beach, Va. (defeated Holly Ferris, Napa, Calif., 8–21, 21–15, 15–5, in final)
Women's 35's champion—Barb Smith, Boise, Idaho (defeated Rene Hebert, New Orleans, 20–21, 21–14, 15–14, in final)
Women's 40's champion—Mildred Gwinn, Charlotte, N.C. (defeated Kathy Mueller, St. Cloud, Minn., 21–17, 21–17, in final)
Women's 45's champion—Kathy Mueller, St. Cloud, Minn. (defeated Colleen Sloan, Los Gatos, Calif., 21–11, 21–20, in final)
Women's 50's champion—Sippy Hayman, Columbus, Ohio (defeated Mary Lou Acuff, Indianapolis, 21–6, 21–15, in final)
Men's Pro—Marty Hogan, San Diego, Calif. (defeated Dave Peck, El Paso, Tex., 11–9, 6–11, 11–5, 11–4, in final)
Women's Pro—Lynn Adams (defeated Shannon Wright, 2–3, 3–2, 15–14, in final)

ROLLER SKATING

NATIONAL CHAMPIONSHIPS

Speed—1982

Senior men—Robb Dunn, Farmington Hills, Mich.
Senior women—Elaine Coley Lemmons, Davey, Fla.
Senior two–man relay—Santa Ana, Calif.
Senior two–women relay—Irving, Tex.
Senior four–man relay—Santa Ana, Calif.
Senior four–women relay—Farmington Hills, Mich.
Mixed couples relay—Farmington Hills, Mich.
Mixed four relay—Irving, Tex.

Artistic—1981

Men's singles—Tim McGuire, Flint, Mich.
Women's singles—Tina Kneisley, Marion, Ohio
Men's figures—Tony St. Jacques, Virginia Beach, Va.
Women's figures—Rita Drogo, Landisville, N.J.
World class dance—Holly Valente and Bill Richardson, Waltham, Mass.
World class pairs—Tina Kneisley, Marion, Ohio, and Paul Price, Howell, Mich.
American dance—Dana Miner and Rick Garrett, Indianapolis, Ind.
Free dance—James Lemma and Barbara Meyers, Levittown, Pa.

SQUASH RACQUETS

1982 U.S. SQUASH RACQUETS CHAMPIONSHIPS

Men's Events

Singles—John Nimick, Narberth, Pa.
Singles, 35 and over—Thomas Poor, Boston
Singles, 40 and over—Ian Dowdswell, Indianapolis
Singles, 45 and over—Gerry Shugar, Toronto
Singles, 50 and over—Neil Desaulniers, Montreal
Singles, 55 and over—Henri Salaun, Needham, Mass.
Singles, 60 and over—F. Hastings Griffin, Jr., Philadelphia
Singles, 65 and over—Paul Norton, Amherst, Mass.
Singles, 70 and over—John A. Weissenfluh, Rockville, Md.
Class B singles—Alan Horowitz, Whitestone, N.Y.
Class C singles—Allen Davis, Bronxville, N.Y.
Class D singles—Charles Stebbins, New York City
Doubles—Lawrence S. Heath III, Cos Cob, Conn., and John R. Reese, Cold Spring Harbor, N.Y.
Veterans doubles—Edward D. Simmons III, St. Louis, and Mel Sokolow, New York City
Seniors doubles—James Bentley and William Bewley, Canada
College A singles—Victor Wagner, Yale
College B singles—Thomas Shepherd, Princeton
College C singles—Charles Duffy, Harvard
United States 5–man team—Mexico A
College 6–man team—Harvard
Lapham Cup (singles)—Canada 11, United States 4
Grant Trophy (doubles)—Canada 6, United States 5
North American Open singles—Michael Desaulniers, New York City

Women's Events

Singles—Alicia McConnell, Brooklyn, N.Y.
Singles, 35 and over—Mariann Greenberg, Mamaroneck, N.Y.
Singles, 40 and over—Marigold Edwards, Pittsburgh
Class B singles—Margaret McQuown, New York City
Class C singles—Martha Ashley
Doubles—Joyce Davenport, King of Prussia, Pa., and Carol Thesieres, Broomall, Pa.
Senior doubles—Carol Thesieres and Irma Brogan, Wynnewood, Pa.
Mixed doubles—Gail Ramsey, Brooklyn, N.Y., and William Ramsey, Bala Cynwyd, Pa.
College singles—Alicia McConnell, Brooklyn, N.Y.

Junior Events

Girls, 18 and under singles—Alicia McConnell, Brooklyn, N.Y.
Girls, 16 and under singles—Ingrid Boyum, Brooklyn, N.Y.
Boys, 18 and under singles—Kenton Jernigan, Newport, R.I.
Boys, 16 and under singles—Russell D. Ball III, Malvern, Pa.

BASEBALL—MINOR LEAGUES—1982

CLASS AAA

AMERICAN ASSOCIATION

Eastern Division

	W	L	Pct
Indianapolis (Reds)	75	61	.551
Iowa (Cubs)	73	62	.541
Louisville (Cardinals)	73	62	.541
Evansville (Tigers)	68	65	.511

Western Division

	W	L	Pct
*Omaha (Royals)	71	66	.518
Wichita (Expos)	70	67	.511
Denver (Rangers)	68	67	.504
Oklahoma City (Phillies)	43	91	.321

*Qualified by beating Wichita in one-game playoff.

Playoffs

League championship—Indianapolis defeated Omaha, 4 games to 2

INTERNATIONAL LEAGUE

	W	L	Pct
Richmond (Braves)	82	57	.590
Columbus (Yankees)	79	61	.564
Tidewater (Mets)	74	63	.540
Rochester (Orioles)	72	68	.514
Pawtucket (Red Sox)	67	71	.486
Syracuse (Blue Jays)	65	75	.464
Charleston (Indians)	59	81	.421
Toledo (Twins)	59	81	.421

Playoffs

Semifinals—Tidewater defeated Columbus, 3 games to 0. Rochester defeated Richmond, 3 games to 0

Final—Tidewater defeated Rochester, 3 games to 0

PACIFIC COAST LEAGUE

North Division

First half winner—Tacoma (A's)
Second half winner—Spokane (Angels)
Playoff—Spokane defeated Tacoma, 2 games to 1

South Division

First half winner—Albuquerque (Dodgers)
Second half winner—Salt Lake City (Mariners)
Playoff—Albuquerque defeated Salt Lake City, 2 games to 0
Championship playoff—Albuquerque defeated Spokane, 4 games to 2

CLASS AA

Eastern League—North Division, first half: Glen Falls (White Sox); second half: Lynn (Mariners); playoff: Lynn. South Division, first half: West Haven (A's); second half: West Haven (A's). League championship: West Haven defeated Lynn, 3 games to 0

Southern League—East Division, first half: Jacksonville (Royals); second half: Jacksonville (Royals). West Division, first half: Knoxville (Blue Jays); second half: Nashville (Yankees); playoff: Nashville. League championship: Nashville defeated Jacksonville, 3 games to 1

Texas League—East Division, first half: Jackson (Mets); second half: Tulsa; playoff: Tulsa. West Division, first half: El Paso (Brewers); second half: Midland (Cubs); playoff: El Paso. League championship: Tulsa defeated El Paso, 3 games to 0

CLASS A

California League—North Division, first half: Modesto (A's); second half: Modesto (A's). South Division; first half: Visalia (Twins); second half: Visalia (Twins). League championship: Modesto defeated Visalia, 4 games to 2

Midwest League—North Division: Madison (A's); Central Division: Springfield (Cardinals); South Division: Quad City (Cubs). Playoff: Semifinals: *Appleton defeated Springfield, 2 games to 0; Madison defeated Quad City, 2 games to 1. League Championship: Appleton defeated Madison, 2 games to 1

Carolina League—North Division, first half: Alexandria (Pirates); second half: Lynchburg (Mets); playoff: Alexandria. South Division, first half: Durham (Braves); second half: Peninsula (Phillies); playoff: Durham. League championship: Alexandria defeated Durham, 3 games to 0

Florida State League—North Division, first half: Tampa (Reds); second half: Tampa (Reds). South Division, first half: Fort Lauderdale (Yankees); second half: Vero Beach (Dodgers); playoff: Fort Lauderdale. League championship: Fort Lauderdale defeated Tampa, 3 games to 2

South Atlantic League—North Division, first half: Greensboro (Yankees); second half: Greensboro (Yankees). South Division, first half: Charleston (Royals); second half: Florence (Blue Jays); playoff: Florence. League championship: Greensboro defeated Florence, 3 games to 2

New York–Penn League—Yawkey Division: Oneonta (Yankees); Wrigley Division: Niagara Falls (White Sox). League championship: Niagara Falls defeated Oneonta, 2 games to 1

Northwest League—North Division: Salem (Angels); South Division: Medford (A's). League championship: Salem defeated Medford, 2 games to 0

*Wild-card team.

ROOKIE LEAGUES

Appalachian—North Division: *Bluefield (Orioles). South Division: Johnson City (Cardinals).

Gulf Coast—Yankees

Pioneer—North Division: Medicine Hat (Blue Jays); South Division: Idaho Falls (Angels). League championship: Medicine Hat defeated Idaho Falls, 3 games to 1

*Bluefield declared league champion on basis of best over-all record.

HYDROPLANE RACING

UNLIMITED CLASS—1982

Gold Cup (Detroit River)—Chip Hanauer, Atlas Van Lines, 122.566 mph

Champion Spark Plug (Miami Marine Stadium)—Dean Chenoweth*, Miss Budweiser, 109.656 mph

Columbia Cup (Columbia River, Pasco, Wash.)—Tom D'Eath, Squire Shop

Emerald Cup (Seattle)—Chip Hanauer, Atlas Van Lines

Bill Muncey Memorial (Evansville, Ind.)—Chip Hanauer, Atlas Van Lines, 116.580 mph

Indiana Governor's Cup (Ohio River, Madison, Ind.)—Tom D'Eath, Squire Shop, 114.242 mph

*Chenoweth was killed in a qualifying race on July 31 at Pasco, Wash.

LITTLE LEAGUE WORLD SERIES

1947	Williamsport, Pa.	1959	Hamtramck, Mich.	1971	Taiwan (Nationalist China)
1948	Lock Haven, Pa.	1960	Levittown, Pa.	1972	Taiwan (Nationalist China)
1949	Hammonton, N.J.	1961	El Cajon, Calif.	1973	Taiwan (Nationalist China)
1950	Houston, Tex.	1962	San Jose, Calif.	1974	Taiwan (Nationalist China)
1951	Stamford, Conn.	1963	Granada Hills, Calif.	1975	Lakewood Township, N.J.
1952	Norwalk, Conn.	1964	Staten Island, N.Y.	1976	Tokyo, Japan
1953	Birmingham, Ala.	1965	Windsor Locks, Conn.	1977	Tapei, Taiwan
1954	Schenectady, N.Y.	1966	Houston, Tex.	1978–79	Pintung, Taiwan
1955	Morrisville, Pa.	1967	West Tokyo, Japan	1980	Hua Lian, Taiwan
1956	Roswell, N.M.	1968	Wakayama, Japan	1981	Taiwan
1957	Monterrey, Mexico	1969	Taiwan (Nationalist China)	1982	Kirkland, Wash.
1958	Monterrey, Mexico	1970	Wayne, N.J.		

SOFTBALL

Source: Amateur Softball Association.

Amateur Champions

1959	Aurora (Ill.) Sealmasters	1969	Raybestos Cardinals, Stratford, Conn.	1977	Billard Barbell, Reading, Pa.
1960	Clearwater (Fla.) Bombers	1971	Welty Way, Cedar Rapids, Iowa	1978	Reading, Pa.
1961	Aurora (Ill.) Sealmasters	1972	Raybestos Cardinals, Stratford, Conn.	1979	Midland, Mich.
1962–63	Clearwater (Fla.) Bombers	1973	Clearwater (Fla.) Bombers	1980	Peterbilt Western, Seattle
1964	Burch Gage & Tool, Detroit	1974	Santa Rosa (Calif.)	1981	Archer Daniels Midland, Decatur, Ill.
1965	Aurora (Ill.) Sealmasters	1975	Rising Sun Hotel, Reading, Pa.	1982	Peterbilt Western, Seattle
1966	Clearwater (Fla.) Bombers	1976	Raybestos Cardinals, Stratford, Conn.		
1967	Aurora (Ill.) Sealmasters				
1968	Clearwater (Fla.) Bombers				

YOUTH TOURNAMENTS—1982

Boys 16–18 fast pitch—Prescott Merchants, Prescott, Ariz.
Boys 18 and under slow pitch—Turner's, Franklin, Ohio
Boys 13–15 fast pitch—Ludd's Team and Trophy House, Peoria, Ill.
Boys 13–15 slow pitch—The Swampfrogs, Pembrook Pines, Fla.
Boys 12 and under fast pitch—Baton Rouge, La.
Boys 12 and under slow pitch—East Denison, Cleveland, Ohio
Girls 16–18 fast pitch—Santa Monica Raiders, Santa Monica, Calif.
Girls 16–18 slow pitch—PDS Sunshiners, Jacksonville, Fla.
Girls 13–15 fast pitch—Tri-Valley Shilos, Sylmer, Calif.
Girls 13–15 slow pitch—The Mets, Satellite Beach, Fla.
Girls 12 and under fast pitch—Gordon's, Buena Park, Calif.
Girls 12 and under slow pitch—River City Rebels, Jacksonville, Fla.

WORLD CHAMPION—1982*

Women's fast pitch—New Zealand

*Men's world championship not contested in 1982.

AMATEUR SOFTBALL ASSOCIATION CHAMPIONS—1982

Men's major fast pitch—Peterbilt Western, Seattle
Women's major fast pitch—Raybestos Brakettes, Stamford, Conn.
Women's Class A fast pitch—San Diego Astros, San Diego, Calif.
Men's Class A fast pitch—Tee House, Stockton, Calif.
Men's major slow pitch—Triangle, Minneapolis, Minn.
Women's major slow pitch—Stompers, Richmond, Va.
Men's major industrial slow pitch—Sikorsky Aircraft, Shelton, Conn.
Women's industrial slow pitch—Provident Vets, Chattanooga, Tenn.
Men's Class A slow pitch—Lawson Auto Parts, Altamonte Springs, Fla.
Women's Class A slow pitch—Circle K Roadrunners, Phoenix, Ariz.
Men's Class A industrial slow pitch—General Dynamics, Detroit, Mich.
Men's modified slow pitch—Sylvestro's, Staten Island, N.Y.
Men's church slow pitch—Grace Methodist Black, Oklahoma City, Okla.
Women's church slow pitch—First Baptist Church, Tallahassee, Fla.

VOLLEYBALL

U.S. VOLLEYBALL ASSOCIATION CHAMPIONSHIPS

(Hilo, Hawaii, May 11–15, 1982)

National Champions

Men—Chuck's Steak House National, Los Angeles; runnerup: Olympic Club, San Francisco.
Women—Monarch, Honolulu; runnerup: Gym Master, Logan, Utah.
Senior men—Outrigger Canoe Club, Honolulu; runnerup: Legends Restaurant, Long Beach, Calif.
Senior women—South Bay Spoilers, Hermosa Beach, Calif.; runnerup: Alumnae, San Francisco.
Golden masters—Outrigger Canoe Club, Honolulu; runnerup, Virginia Beach, Va.

N.C.A.A. CHAMPIONSHIPS

(Muncie, Ind., May 7–8, 1982)

Men

Final—U.C.L.A. defeated Penn State.
Third place—Southern California defeated Ohio State.

Women

Division I—Southern California
Division II—Sacramento State
Division III—University of California–San Diego

A.I.A.W. CHAMPIONSHIPS

Division I—Texas–Austin
Division II—Hawaii–Hilo
Division III—LaVerne

BASEBALL

The popular tradition that baseball was invented by Abner Doubleday at Cooperstown, N.Y., in 1839 has been enshrined in the Hall of Fame and National Museum of Baseball erected in that town, but research has proved that a game called "Base Ball" was played in this country and England before 1839. The first team baseball as we know it was played at the Elysian Fields, Hoboken, N.J., on June 19, 1846, between the Knickerbockers and the New York Nine. The next fifty years saw a gradual growth of baseball and an improvement of equipment and playing skill.

Historians have it that the first pitcher to throw a curve was William A. (Candy) Cummings in 1867. The Cincinnati Red Stockings were the first all-professional team, and in 1869 they played 64 games without a loss. The standard ball of the same size and weight, still the rule, was adopted in 1872. The first catcher's mask was worn in 1875. The National League was organized in 1876. The first chest protector was worn in 1885. The three-strike rule was put on the books in 1887, and the four-ball ticket to first base was instituted in 1889. The pitching distance was lengthened to 60 feet 6 inches in 1893, and the rules have been modified only slightly since that time.

The American League, under the vigorous leadership of B. B. Johnson, became a major league in 1901. Judge Kenesaw Mountain Landis, by action of the two major leagues, became Commissioner of Baseball in 1921, and upon his death (1944), Albert B. Chandler, former United States Senator from Kentucky, was elected to that office (1945). Chandler failed to obtain a new contract and was succeeded by Ford C. Frick (1951), the National League president. Frick retired after the 1965 season, and William D. Eckert, a retired Air Force lieutenant general, was named to succeed him. Eckert resigned under pressure in December, 1968. Bowie Kuhn, a New York attorney, became interim commissioner for one year in February. His appointment was made permanent with two seven-year contracts until August 1983.

BASEBALL PLAYERS' STRIKE HALTED 1981 SEASON FOR 7 WEEKS

A seven-week strike by major league players began on June 12 and disrupted the 1981 baseball season, canceled 713 games, caused heavy financial losses in all 26 big-league cities, and created confusion and ill-feelings among fans, players, and officials.

The major issue stemmed from a disagreement between the players and the club owners over compensation for the signing of free agents. The two sides finally worked out an agreement and the strike ended on Aug. 1. A pool arrangement under which teams losing a ranking free agent would receive a professional player as compensation as well as a selection in the amateur free-agent draft was the key to the accord. It also resolved a service credit issue for the players for the time lost during the strike. Service credit is used to determine eligibility for free agency and salary arbitration.

The players were allowed a week to get into condition and the season resumed on Aug. 10. The All-Star Game at Cleveland, postponed from its original date of July 14 because of the strike, was played on Aug. 9. Rescheduling the championship season became a problem. Normally the regular-season winners in the two divisions—Eastern and Western—in the National and American leagues meet in a best-of-five-game playoff series for their respective league pennants.

Because the 162-game regular season was shortened, officials decided to split the season into two halves. The four leaders in the two leagues when the strike began were declared champions of the first half. The four leaders in the second half were also declared champions. Those teams played off in a preliminary, or miniseries, playoff round. The survivors played off for their respective league pennants and the right to move on to the World Series, which started on Oct. 20, much later than usual.

AMERICAN LEAGUE*
(Final Standing—1981)

EASTERN DIVISION
FIRST-HALF SEASON

Team	W	L	Pct	GB
New York Yankees*	34	22	.607	—
Baltimore Orioles	31	23	.574	2
Milwaukee Brewers	31	25	.554	3
Detroit Tigers	31	26	.544	3½
Boston Red Sox	30	26	.536	4
Cleveland Indians	26	24	.520	5
Toronto Blue Jays	16	42	.276	19

WESTERN DIVISION

Team	W	L	Pct	GB
Oakland A's*	37	23	.617	—
Texas Rangers	33	22	.600	1½
Chicago White Sox	31	22	.585	2½
California Angels	31	29	.517	6
Kansas City Royals	20	30	.400	12
Seattle Mariners	21	36	.368	14½
Minnesota Twins	17	39	.304	28

SECOND-HALF SEASON
EASTERN DIVISION

Team	W	L	Pct	GB
Milwaukee Brewers*	31	22	.585	—
Boston Red Sox	29	23	.558	1½
Detroit Tigers	29	23	.558	1½
Baltimore Orioles	28	23	.549	2
Cleveland Indians	26	27	.491	5
New York Yankees	25	26	.490	5
Toronto Blue Jays	21	27	.438	7½

WESTERN DIVISION

Team	W	L	Pct	GB
Kansas City Royals*	30	23	.566	—
Oakland A's	27	22	.551	1
Texas Rangers	24	26	.480	4½
Minnesota Twins	24	29	.453	6
Seattle Mariners	23	29	.442	6½
Chicago White Sox	23	30	.434	7
California Angels	20	30	.400	8½

*Qualified for postseason playoffs.

AMERICAN LEAGUE PLAYOFFS
EASTERN DIVISION—Preliminary Round
1st game, Milwaukee, Oct. 7

New York	000	400	001—5	13	1
Milwaukee	011	010	000—3	8	3

Guidry, Davis (5), Gossage (8); Haas, Bernard (4), McClure (5), Slaton (6), Fingers (8). Winner: Davis; Loser: Haas. Home run: New York: Gamble. Attendance: 35,064.

2nd game, Milwaukee, Oct. 8

New York	000	100	002—3	7	0
Milwaukee	000	000	000—0	7	0

Righetti, Davis (7), Gossage (7); Caldwell, Slaton (9). Winner: Righetti; Loser: Caldwell. Home runs: New York: Piniella, Jackson. Attendance: 26,395.

3rd game, New York, Oct. 9

Milwaukee	000	000	320—5	9	0
New York	000	100	200—3	8	2

Lerch, Fingers (7); John, May (8). Winner: Fingers; Loser: John. Home runs: Milwaukee: Simmons, Molitor. Attendance: 54,171.

4th game, New York, Oct. 10

Milwaukee	000	200	000—2	4	2
New York	000	001	000—1	5	0

Vuckovich, Easterly (6), Slaton (7), McClure (8), Fingers (9); Reuschel, R. Davis (7). Winner: Vuckovich; Loser: Reuschel. Attendance: 52,077.

5th game, New York, Oct. 11

Milwaukee	011	000	100—3	8	0
New York	000	400	12x—7	13	0

Haas, Caldwell (4), Bernard (4), McClure (6), Slaton (7), Easterly (8), Vuckovich (8); Guidry, Righetti (5), Gossage (8). Winner: Righetti; Loser: Haas. Home runs: Milwaukee: Thomas; New York: Jackson, Gamble, Cerone. Attendance: 47,505.

WESTERN DIVISION—Preliminary Round
1st game, Kansas City, Oct. 6

Oakland	000	300	010—4	8	2
Kansas City	000	000	000—0	4	1

Norris; Leonard, Martin (9). Winner: Norris; Loser: Leonard. Home runs: Oakland: Gross, Murphy. Attendance: 40,592.

2nd game, Kansas City, Oct. 7

Oakland	100	000	010—2	10	1
Kansas City	000	010	000—1	6	0

McCatty; Jones, Quisenberry (9). Winner: McCatty; Loser: Jones. Attendance: 40,274.

3rd game, Oakland, Oct. 9

Kansas City	000	100	000—1	10	3
Oakland	101	200	00X—4	7	0

Gura, Martin (4); Langford, Underwood (8), Beard (8). Winner: Langford; Loser: Gura. Home run: Oakland: McKay. Attendance: 40,002.

CHAMPIONSHIP ROUND
1st game, New York, Oct. 13

Oakland	000	010	000—1	6	1
New York	300	000	00X—3	7	1

Norris, Underwood (8); John, Davis (7), Gossage (8). Winner: John; Loser: Norris. Attendance: 55,740.

2nd game, New York, Oct. 14

Oakland	001	200	000—3	11	1
New York	100	701	40x—13	19	0

McCatty, Beard (4), Jones (5), Kingman (7), Owchinko (7); May, Frazier (4). Winner: Frazier; Loser: McCatty. Home runs: New York: Piniella, Nettles. Attendance: 48,497.

3rd game, Oakland, Oct. 15

New York	000	001	003—4	10	2
Oakland	000	000	000—0	5	0

Righetti, Davis (7), Gossage (9); Keough, Underwood (9). Winner: Righetti; Loser: Keough. Home run: New York: Randolph. Attendance: 47,302.

NATIONAL LEAGUE* (Final Standing—1981)

EASTERN DIVISION
FIRST-HALF SEASON

Team	W	L	Pct	GB
Philadelphia Phillies*	34	21	.618	—
St. Louis Cardinals	30	20	.600	1½
Montreal Expos	30	25	.545	4
Pittsburgh Pirates	25	23	.521	5½
New York Mets	17	34	.333	15
Chicago Cubs	15	37	.288	17½

WESTERN DIVISION

Team	W	L	Pct	GB
Los Angeles Dodgers*	36	21	.632	—
Cincinnati Reds	35	21	.625	½
Houston Astros	28	29	.491	8
Atlanta Braves	25	29	.463	9½
San Francisco Giants	27	32	.458	10
San Diego Padres	23	33	.411	12½

SECOND-HALF SEASON
EASTERN DIVISION

	W	L	Pct	GB
Montreal Expos*	30	23	.566	—
St. Louis Cardinals	29	23	.558	½
Philadelphia Phillies	25	27	.481	4½
New York Mets	24	28	.462	5½
Chicago Cubs	23	28	.451	6
Pittsburgh Pirates	21	33	.389	9½

WESTERN DIVISION

	W	L	Pct	GB
Houston Astros*	33	20	.623	—
Cincinnati Reds	31	21	.596	1½
San Francisco Giants	29	23	.558	3½
Los Angeles Dodgers	27	26	.509	6
Atlanta Braves	25	27	.481	7½
San Diego Padres	18	36	.333	15½

*Qualified for postseason playoffs.

NATIONAL LEAGUE PLAYOFFS
EASTERN DIVISION—Preliminary Round
1st game, Montreal, Oct. 7

Philadelphia	010	000	000—1	10	1
Montreal	110	100	00X—3	8	0

Carlton, R. Reed (7); Rogers, Reardon (9). Winner: Rogers; Loser: Carlton. Home run: Philadelphia: Moreland. Attendance: 34,327.

2nd game, Montreal, Oct. 8

Philadelphia	000	000	010—1	6	2
Montreal	012	000	00X—3	7	0

Ruthven, Brusstar (5), Lyle (7), McGraw (8); Gullickson, Reardon (8). Winner: Gullickson; Loser: Ruthven. Home run:

Montreal: Carter. Attendance: 45,896.

3rd game, Philadelphia, Oct. 9

Montreal	010	000	010—2	8	4
Philadelphia	020	002	20X—6	13	0

Burris, Lee (6), Sosa (7); Christenson, Lyle (7), R. Reed (8). Winner: Christenson; Loser: Burris. Attendance: 36,835.

4th game, Philadelphia, Oct. 10 (10 innings)

Montreal	000	112	100	0—5	10	1
Philadelphia	202	001	000	1—6	9	0

Sanderson, Bahnsen (3), Sosa (5), Fryman (6), Reardon (7); Noles, Brusstar (5), Lyle (6), R. Reed (7), McGraw (8). Winner: McGraw; Loser: Reardon. Home runs: Montreal: Carter. Philadelphia: Schmidt, Matthews, G. Vukovich. Attendance: 38,818.

5th game, Philadelphia, Oct. 11

Montreal	000	021	000—3	8	1
Philadelphia	000	000	000—0	6	0

Rogers; Carlton, R. Reed (9). Winner: Rogers; Loser: Carlton. Attendance: 47,384.

WESTERN DIVISION—Preliminary Round
1st game, Houston, Oct. 6

Los Angeles	000	000	1000—1	2	0
Houston	000	001	002—3	8	0

Valenzuela, Stewart (9); Ryan. Winner: Ryan; Loser: Stewart. Home runs: Los Angeles: Garvey; Houston: Ashby. Attendance: 44,836

2nd game, Houston, Oct. 7 (11 innings)

Los Angeles	000	000	000	00—0	9	1
Houston	000	000	000	01—1	9	0

Reuss, S. Howe (10), Stewart (11), Forster (11), Niedenfuer (11); Niekro, D. Smith (10), Sambito (11). Winner: Sambito; Loser: Stewart. Attendance: 42,398

3rd game, Los Angeles, Oct. 9

Houston	001	000	000—1	3	2
Los Angeles	300	000	03X—6	10	0

Knepper, LaCorte (6), Sambito (8), B. Smith (8); Hooton, S. Howe (8), Welch (8). Winner: Hooton; Loser: Knepper. Home runs: Houston: A. Howe; Los Angeles: Garvey. Attendance: 46,820.

4th game, Los Angeles, Oct. 10

Houston	000	000	001—1	4	0
Los Angeles	000	010	10X—2	4	0

Ruhle: Valenzuela. Winner: Valenzuela; Loser: Ruhle. Home run: Los Angeles: Guerrero. Attendance: 55,983.

5th game, Los Angeles, Oct. 11

Houston	000	000	000—0	5	3
Los Angeles	000	003	10X—4	7	2

Ryan, D. Smith (7), LaCorte (7); Reuss. Winner: Reuss; Loser: Ryan. Attendance: 55,979.

CHAMPIONSHIP ROUND
1st game, Los Angeles, Oct. 13

Montreal	000	000	001—1	9	0
Los Angeles	020	000	03X—5	8	0

Gullickson, Reardon (8); Hooton, Welch (8), Howe (9). Winner: Hooton; Loser: Gullickson. Home runs: Los Angeles: Guerrero, Scioscia. Attendance: 51,273.

2nd game, Los Angeles, Oct. 14

Montreal	020	001	000—3	10	1
Los Angeles	000	000	000—0	5	1

Burris; Valenzuela, Niedenfuer (7), Forster (7), Pena (7), Castillo (9). Winner: Burris; Loser: Valenzuela. Attendance: 53,463.

3rd game, Montreal, Oct. 16

Los Angeles	000	100	000—1	7	0
Montreal	000	004	00X—4	7	1

Ruess, Pena (8); Rogers. Winner: Rogers; Loser: Reuss. Home run: Montreal: White. Attendance: 54,372.

4th game, Montreal, Oct. 17

Los Angeles	001	000	024—7	12	1
Montreal	000	100	000—1	5	1

Hooton, Welch (8), Howe (9); Gullickson, Fryman (8), Sosa (9), Lee (9). Winner: Hooton; Loser: Gullickson. Home run: Los Angeles: Garvey. Attendence: 54,499.

5th game, Montreal, Oct. 19

Los Angeles	000	010	001—2	6	0
Montreal	100	000	000—1	3	1

Valenzuela, Welch (9); Burris, Rogers (9). Winner: Valenzuela; Loser: Rogers. Home runs: Los Angeles: Monday. Attendance: 36,491.

AMERICAN LEAGUE LEADERS—1981

Batting—Carney Lansford, Boston	.336
Runs—Rickey Henderson, Oakland	89
Hits—Rickey Henderson, Oakland	135
Runs batted in—Eddie Murray, Baltimore	78
Doubles—Cecil Cooper, Milwaukee	35
Triples—John Castino, Minnesota	9
Home runs—Eddie Murray, Baltimore	22
Dwight Evans, Boston	22
Bobby Grich, California	22
Tony Armas, Oakland	22
Stolen Bases—Rickey Henderson, Oakland	56
Pitching	
Victories—Jack Morris, Detroit	14
Dennis Martinez, Baltimore	14
Bill Vuckovich, Milwaukee	14
Steve McCatty, Oakland	14
Earned-run average—Steve McCatty, Oakland	2.32
Strikeouts—Len Barker, Cleveland	127
Shutouts—Steve McCatty, Oakland	4
Ken Forsch, California	4
Richard Dotson, Chicago	4
Doc Medich, Texas	4

NATIONAL LEAGUE LEADERS—1981

Batting—Bill Madlock, Pittsburgh	.341
Runs—Mike Schmidt, Philadelphia	78
Hits—Pete Rose, Philadelphia	140
Runs batted in—Mike Schmidt, Philadelphia	91
Doubles—Bill Buckner, Chicago	35
Triples—Craig Reynolds, Houston	12
Gene Richards, San Diego	12
Home runs—Mike Schmidt, Philadelphia	31
Stolen bases—Tim Raines, Montreal	71
Pitching—	
Victories—Tom Seaver, Cincinnati	14
Earned-run average—Nolan Ryan, Houston	1.69
Strikeouts—Fernando Valenzuela, Los Angeles	180
Shutouts—Fernando Valenzuela, Los Angeles	8

AMERICAN LEAGUE AVERAGES—1981
(Unofficial)

Batting—Club

	AB	R	H	HR	RBI	PCT
Boston	3,820	519	1,052	90	493	.275
Chicago	3,615	476	982	76	435	.272
Texas	3,582	452	968	49	418	.270
Kansas City	3,562	397	952	61	381	.267
Cleveland	3,507	431	922	38	397	.263
Milwaukee	3,743	493	961	97	477	.257
Detroit	3,599	427	922	65	403	.256
California	3,688	476	944	97	439	.256
New York	3,528	421	889	100	403	.252
Seattle	3,780	426	950	89	405	.251
Baltimore	3,516	429	883	88	408	.251
Oakland	3,678	458	910	104	429	.247
Minnesota	3,776	378	884	48	358	.234
Toronto	3,521	329	797	61	315	.226

Batting Leaders

Player/team	AB	R	H	HR	RBI	PCT
Lansford, Boston	399	61	134	4	52	.336
Gibson, Detroit	290	41	95	9	40	.329
Paciorek, Seattle	405	50	132	14	66	.326
C. Cooper, Milwaukee	416	70	133	12	60	.320
R. Henderson, Oakland	423	89	135	6	35	.319
Hargrove, Cleveland	322	44	102	2	49	.317
G. Brett, Kansas City	347	42	109	6	43	.314
Zisk, Seattle	357	42	111	16	43	.311
Oliver, Texas	421	53	130	4	55	.309
Remy, Boston	358	55	110	0	31	.307
Murphy, New York	320	44	98	6	32	.306
Carew, California	364	57	111	2	21	.305
Murray, Baltimore	378	57	115	22	78	.304
Grich, California	352	56	107	22	61	.304
Wilson, Kansas City	439	54	133	1	32	.303
Lemon, Chicago	328	51	99	9	50	.302
Almon, Chicago	349	46	105	4	40	.301
Evans, Boston	412	84	122	22	71	.296
B. Bell, Texas	360	44	106	10	64	.294
Winfield, New York	388	52	114	13	68	.294
Burleson, California	431	53	126	5	33	.292
Miller, Boston	316	38	92	2	33	.291
Harrah, Cleveland	361	64	105	5	44	.291
Baines, Chicago	280	43	80	10	41	.286
Rivers, Texas	399	62	114	3	26	.286
Stapleton, Boston	355	45	101	10	42	.285

Leading Pitchers
(110 or more innings)

Player/team	IP	H	BB	SO	W	L	ERA
McCatty, Oakland	186	140	61	91	14	7	2.32
Stewart, Baltimore	112	89	57	57	4	8	2.33
Lamp, Chicago	127	103	43	71	7	6	2.41
John, New York	140	135	39	50	9	8	2.64
Burns, Chicago	157	139	49	108	10	6	2.64
Gura, Kansas City	172	139	35	61	11	8	2.72
Guidry, New York	127	101	26	104	11	5	2.76
Blyleven, Cleveland	159	145	40	107	11	7	2.89
Forsch, California	153	143	27	55	11	7	2.94
Leonard, Kansas City	202	202	41	107	13	11	2.99
Langford, Oakland	195	190	58	84	12	10	3.00
Petry, Detroit	141	115	57	79	10	9	3.00

FIELD HOCKEY—1982

World Cup men—Pakistan
International Cup women—Netherlands

NATIONAL LEAGUE AVERAGES—1981
(Unofficial)

Batting—Club

	AB	R	H	HR	RBI	PCT
Philadelphia	3,665	491	1,002	69	453	.273
Cincinnati	3,637	464	972	64	429	.267
St. Louis	3,538	464	936	50	431	.265
Los Angeles	3,751	450	984	82	427	.262
Pittsburgh	3,576	407	920	55	384	.257
Houston	3,693	394	948	45	369	.257
San Diego	3,758	382	963	32	350	.256
San Francisco	3,765	427	941	63	399	.250
New York	3,493	348	868	57	323	.249
Montreal	3,591	443	883	81	407	.246
Atlanta	3,642	395	886	64	366	.243
Chicago	3,546	370	838	57	348	.236

Batting Leaders

Player/team	AB	R	H	HR	RBI	PCT
Madlock, Pittsburgh	279	35	95	6	45	.341
Rose, Philadelphia	431	73	140	0	33	.325
Baker, Los Angeles	400	48	128	9	49	.320
Schmidt, Philadelphia	354	78	112	31	91	.316
Buckner, Chicago	421	45	131	10	75	.311
Griffey, Cincinnati	396	64	123	2	34	.311
May, San Francisco	316	20	98	2	33	.310
Brooks, New York	358	34	110	4	38	.307
Concepcion, Cincinnati	421	57	129	5	67	.306
Hernandez, St. Louis	376	65	115	8	48	.306
Cromartie, Montreal	358	41	109	6	42	.304
Raines, Montreal	313	61	95	5	37	.304
Salazar, San Diego	400	37	121	3	38	.303
Dawson, Montreal	394	71	119	24	64	.302
T. Kennedy, San Diego	382	32	115	2	41	.301
Matthews, Philadelphia	359	62	108	8	67	.301
Guerrero, Los Angeles	347	46	104	12	48	.300
A. Howe, Houston	361	43	107	3	36	.296
Foster, Cincinnati	414	64	122	22	90	.295
Henderson, Chicago	287	32	84	5	35	.293
Oberkfell, St. Louis	376	43	110	2	45	.293
Washington, Atlanta	320	37	93	5	37	.291
Bonilla, San Diego	369	30	107	1	25	.290
Durham, Chicago	328	42	95	10	35	.290
Cey, Los Angeles	312	42	90	13	50	.288
Herndon, San Francisco	364	48	105	5	41	.288
Templeton, St. Louis	333	47	96	1	33	.288
Richards, San Diego	393	47	113	3	42	.288

Leading Pitchers
(110 or More Innings)

Player/team	IP	H	BB	SO	W	L	ERA
Ryan, Houston	149	99	68	140	11	5	1.69
Knepper, Houston	157	128	38	75	9	5	2.18
Hooton, Los Angeles	142	124	33	74	11	6	2.28
Reuss, Los Angeles	153	138	27	51	10	4	2.29
Carlton, Philadelphia	190	152	62	179	13	4	2.42
Blue, San Francisco	125	97	54	63	8	6	2.45
Valenzuela, Los Angeles	192	140	61	180	13	7	2.48
Seaver, Cincinnati	166	120	66	87	14	2	2.55
Sutton, Houston	159	132	29	104	11	9	2.60

BIATHLON

WORLD CHAMPIONSHIPS—1982

Men's 10 kilometers—Erik Kvalfoss, Norway
Men's 20 kilometers—Frank Ullrich, East Germany
World Cup—Frank Ullrich

WORLD SERIES—1981

Los Angeles Dodgers (NL) defeated New York Yankees (AL), 4 games to 2

1st Game—New York, Oct. 20

LOS ANGELES (NL)

	AB	R	H	BI
Lopes, 2b	3	1	0	0
Russell, ss	3	0	0	0
Johnstone, ph	1	0	1	1
Stewart, p	0	0	0	0
Baker, lf	2	0	1	1
Garvey, 1b	4	0	1	0
Cey, 3b	4	0	1	0
Guerrero, cf	3	0	0	0
Monday, rf	4	0	0	0
Yeager, c	3	1	1	1
Landreaux, ph	1	0	0	0
Reuss, p	1	0	0	0
Castillo, p	0	0	0	0
Goltz, p	0	0	0	0
Sax, ph	1	0	0	0
Niedenfuer, p	0	0	0	0
Thomas, ss	0	1	0	0
Total	30	3	5	3

NEW YORK (AL)

	AB	R	H	BI
Randolph, 2b	3	0	0	0
Mumphrey, cf	3	2	2	0
Winfield, lf	3	0	0	1
Piniella, rf	4	1	2	1
Watson, 1b	3	1	2	3
Nettles, 3b	3	0	0	0
Cerone, c	3	0	0	0
Milbourne, ss	4	1	0	0
Guidry, p	2	0	0	0
Davis, p	0	0	0	0
Gossage, p	0	0	0	0
Total	28	5	6	5

Los Angeles	000 010 020—3
New York	301 100 00X—5

DP—Los Angeles. LOB—Los Angeles 5, New York 6. 2B—Piniella. HR—Watson, Yeager. SB—Mumphrey, Piniella. S—Guidry. SF—Baker.

	IP	H	R	ER	BB	SO
Los Angeles						
Reuss (L)	2⅔	5	4	4	0	2
Castillo	1	0	1	1	5	0
Goltz	⅓	0	0	0	0	0
Niedenfuer	3	1	0	0	0	0
Stewart	1	0	0	0	1	0
New York						
Guidry (W)	7	4	1	1	2	6
Davis	0	0	2	2	2	0
Gossage (S)	2	1	0	0	0	2

PB—Cerone. Time of game—2:32. Attendance—56,470.

2nd Game—New York. Oct. 21

LOS ANGELES (NL)

	AB	R	H	BI
Lopes, 2b	3	0	0	0
Monday, ph	1	0	0	0
Howe, p	0	0	0	0
Stewart, p	0	0	0	0
Russell, ss	4	0	1	0
Baker, lf	4	0	0	0
Garvey, 1b	3	0	2	0
Cey, 3b	4	0	0	0
Guerrero, rf	4	0	0	0
Landreaux, cf	3	0	0	0
Yeager, c	2	0	0	0
Johnstone, ph	1	0	0	0
Scioscia, c	0	0	0	0
Hooton, p	2	0	0	0
Forster, p	0	0	0	0
Smith, ph	1	0	1	0
Sax, 2b	0	0	0	0
Total	32	0	4	0

NEW YORK (AL)

	AB	R	H	BI
Mumphrey, cf	2	0	0	0
Milbourne, ss	4	0	1	1
Winfield, lf	4	0	0	0
Gamble, rf	2	0	0	0
Piniella, ph	1	0	1	0
Brown, rf	0	1	0	0
Nettles, 3b	4	1	2	0
Watson, 1b	4	0	2	1
Cerone, c	2	0	0	0
Randolph, 2b	2	1	0	1
John, p	1	0	0	0
Murcer, ph	0	0	0	0
Gossage, p	1	0	0	0
Total	27	3	6	3

Los Angeles	000 000 000—0
New York	000 010 02X—3

E—Milbourne, Lopes, Stewart. DR—Los Angeles. LOB—Los Angeles 6, New York 9. 2B—Milbourne. S—John, Murcer. SF—Randolph.

	IP	H	R	ER	BB	SO
Los Angeles						
Hooton (L)	6	3	1	0	4	1
Forster	1	0	0	0	1	0
Howe	⅓	2	2	2	0	0
Stewart	⅔	1	0	0	1	1
New York						
John (W)	7	3	0	0	0	4
Gossage (S)	2	1	0	0	1	3

Hooton pitched to 2 batters in the seventh. Time of game—2:29. Attendance—56,505

3rd Game—Los Angeles, Oct. 23

NEW YORK (AL)

	AB	R	H	BI
Randolph, 2b	2	0	0	0
Mumphrey, cf	5	0	0	0
Winfield, lf	3	0	0	0
Piniella, rf	5	1	1	0
Watson, 1b	4	1	2	1
Cerone, c	4	2	2	1
Rodriguez, 3b	4	0	2	0
Milbourne, ss	2	0	2	1
Righetti, p	1	0	0	0
Frazier, p	1	0	0	0
May, p	0	0	0	0
Murcer, ph	1	0	0	0
Davis, p	0	0	0	0
Total	32	4	9	3

LOS ANGELES (NL)

	AB	R	H	BI
Lopes, 2b	4	1	2	0
Russell, ss	5	1	2	0
Baker, lf	4	0	0	0
Garvey, 1b	4	1	2	0
Cey, 3b	2	2	2	3
Guerrero, cf	3	0	1	1
Monday, rf	2	0	1	0
Thomas, rf	1	0	0	0
Yeager, c	1	0	0	0
Scioscia, c	3	0	1	0
Valenzuela, p	3	0	0	0
Total	32	5	11	4

New York	022 000 000—4
Los Angeles	300 020 00X—5

E—Lopes. DP—New York 2, Los Angeles 3. LOB—New York 9, Los Angeles 9. 2B—Lopes, Cerone, Watson, Guerrero. HR—Cey, Watson, Cerone. S—Righetti, Lopes.

	IP	H	R	ER	BB	SO
New York						
Righetti	2	5	3	3	2	1
Frazier (L)	2	3	2	2	2	1
May	3	2	0	0	0	2
Davis	1	1	0	0	0	1
Los Angeles						
Valenzuela (W)	9	9	4	4	7	6

HBP—by Righetti (Guerrero). Time of game—3:04. Attendance—56,236.

COLLEGE BASEBALL

1982 CHAMPIONS

N.C.A.A. Division I—Miami (Fla.) defeated Wichita State, 9–3, in title game

N.A.I.A.—Grand Canyon (Ariz.) College defeated Lewis & Clark (Idaho) State, 10–6, in title game

4th Game—Los Angeles, Oct. 24

NEW YORK (AL)	AB	R	H	BI	LOS ANGELES (NL)	AB	R	H	BI
Randolph, 2b	5	3	2	1	Lopes, 2b	5	2	2	2
Milbourne, ss	4	1	1	1	Russell, ss	5	0	1	1
Winfield, lf, cf	4	0	0	0	Garvey, 1b	5	1	3	0
Jackson, rf	3	2	3	1	Cey, 3b	5	0	2	2
Gamble, lf	4	1	2	1	Baker, lf	5	1	1	0
Brown, cf	0	0	0	0	Monday, rf	3	1	1	0
Piniella, lf	1	0	0	0	Thomas, cf	1	0	0	0
Watson, 1b	3	0	1	2	Guerrero, rf	3	0	2	0
Cerone, c	5	0	2	1	Scioscia, c	1	1	0	0
Robertson, ph	0	0	0	0	Yeager, c	0	0	0	1
Rodriguez, 3b	4	0	2	0	Welch, p	0	0	0	0
Foote, ph	1	0	0	0	Goltz, p	0	0	0	0
Reuschel, p	2	0	0	0	Landreaux, ph	1	1	1	0
May, p	1	0	0	0	Forster, p	0	0	0	0
Davis, p	0	0	0	0	Smith, ph	1	0	0	0
Frazier, p	1	0	0	0	Niedenfuer, p	0	0	0	0
John, p	0	0	0	0	Johnstone, ph	1	1	1	2
Murcer, ph	1	0	0	0	Howe, p	0	0	0	0
Total	**39**	**7**	**13**	**7**	**Total**	**36**	**8**	**14**	**8**

New York	211 002 010—7
Los Angeles	002 013 20X—8

E—Russell, Jackson, Howe. LOB—New York 12, Los Angeles 10. 2B—Milbourne, Landreaux, Garvey, Monday. 3B—Randolph. HR—Randolph, Johnstone, Jackson. SB—Winfield, Lopes 2. S—Milbourne, Scioscia, Howe. SF—Watson, Yeager.

	IP	H	R	ER	BB	SO
New York						
Reuschel	3	6	2	2	1	2
May	1⅓	2	1	1	0	1
Davis	1	2	3	2	1	2
Frazier (L)	⅔	2	2	2	1	0
John	2	2	0	0	0	2
Los Angeles						
Welch	0	3	2	2	1	0
Goltz	3	4	2	2	1	2
Forster	1	1	0	0	2	0
Niedenfuer	2	2	2	0	1	0
Howe (W)	3	3	1	1	0	1

Time of game—3:32. Attendance—56,242.

5th Game—Los Angeles, Oct. 25

NEW YORK (AL)	AB	R	H	BI	LOS ANGELES (NL)	AB	R	H	BI
Randolph, 2b	3	0	0	0	Lopes, 2b	3	0	0	0
Milbourne, ss	4	0	1	0	Russell, ss	4	0	0	0
Winfield, cf	4	0	1	0	Garvey, 1b	4	0	1	0
Jackson, rf	4	1	1	0	Cey, 3b	2	0	0	0
Gossage, p	0	0	0	0	Landreaux, cf	0	0	0	0
Watson, 1b	3	0	0	0	Baker, lf	4	0	0	0
Piniella, lf	4	0	2	1	Guerrero, rf	3	1	1	1
Brown, pr	0	0	0	0	Yeager, c	3	1	2	1
Cerone, c	4	0	0	0	Thomas, cf	3	0	0	0
Rodriguez, 3b	3	0	0	0	Reuss, p	2	0	0	0
Guidry, p	3	0	0	0	**Total**	**28**	**2**	**4**	**2**
Mumphrey, cf	0	0	0	0					
Total	**32**	**1**	**5**	**1**					

New York	010 000 000—1
Los Angeles	000 000 20X—2

E—Lopes 3. DP—Los Angeles 2. LOB—New York 7, Los Angeles 6. 2B—Jackson, Yeager. HR—Guerrero, Yeager. SB—Lopes, Landreaux.

	IP	H	R	ER	BB	SO
New York						
Guidry (L)	7	4	2	2	2	9
Gossage	1	0	0	0	1	0
Los Angeles						
Reuss (W)	9	5	1	1	3	6

HBP—by Gossage (Cey). Time of game—2:19. Attendance—56,115.

6th Game—New York, Oct. 28

LOS ANGELES (NL)	AB	R	H	BI	NEW YORK (AL)	AB	R	H	BI
Lopes, 2b	4	2	1	0	Randolph, 2b	3	1	2	1
Russell, ss	4	0	2	1	Mumphrey, cf	5	0	1	0
Garvey, 1b	4	1	1	0	Winfield, lf	4	0	0	0
Cey, 3b	3	1	2	1	Jackson, rf	5	0	0	0
Thomas, 3b	2	1	0	1	Watson, 1b	5	0	0	0
Baker, lf	5	2	2	0	Nettles, 3b	3	0	2	0
Guerrero, cf	5	1	3	5	Rodriguez, 3b	1	1	1	0
Monday, rf	3	0	1	0	Cerone, c	3	0	0	0
Landreaux, cf	1	0	0	0	Milbourne, ss	2	0	0	0
Yeager, c	5	0	1	1	John, p	1	0	0	0
Hooton, p	2	1	0	0	Murcer, ph	1	0	0	0
Howe, p	2	0	0	0	Frazier, p	0	0	0	0
Total	**40**	**9**	**13**	**9**	Davis, p	0	0	0	0
					Reuschel, p	0	0	0	0
					Gamble, ph	0	0	0	0
					Piniella, ph	1	0	1	1
					May, p	0	0	0	0
					Brown, ph	1	0	0	0
					LaRoche, p	0	0	0	0
					Total	**35**	**2**	**7**	**2**

Los Angeles	000 134 010—9
New York	001 001 000—2

E—Milbourne, Nettles, Lopes. LOB—Los Angeles 10, New York 12. 2B—Nettles, Randolph. 3B—Guerrero. HR—Randolph, Guerrero. SB—Lopes, Russell, Randolph. S—Russell.

	IP	H	R	ER	BB	SO
Los Angeles						
Hooton (W)	5⅓	5	2	2	5	2
Howe (S)	3⅔	2	0	0	1	3
New York						
John	4	6	1	1	0	2
Frazier (L)	1	4	3	3	0	1
Davis	⅓	1	3	2	2	1
Reuschel	⅔	1	1	0	2	0
May	2	1	1	1	1	2
LaRoche	1	0	0	0	0	2

Time of game—3:09. Attendance—56,513.

RUGBY—1982

Five Nations—Ireland
United States champion—Old Blues, Berkeley, Calif.
United States college—California

SQUASH TENNIS

UNITED STATES OPEN CHAMPION—1982

Men's open singles—Gary Squires, New Haven, Conn., defeated Stuart MacFarlane, New York City, 15–12, 15–6, 15–9, in final. Semifinals: MacFarlane defeated David Stafford, Bronxville, N.Y., and Squires defeated Bill Rubin, White Plains, N.Y.

MAJOR LEAGUE ALL-STAR GAME

Year	Date	Winning league and manager	Runs	Losing league and manager	Runs	Winning pitcher	Losing pitcher	Site	Paid attendance
1933	July 6	A.L. (Mack)	4	N.L. (McGraw)	2	Gomez	Hallahan	Chicago A.L.	47,595
1934	July 10	A.L. (Cronin)	9	N.L. (Terry)	7	Harder	Mungo	New York N.L.	48,363
1935	July 8	A.L. (Cochrane)	4	N.L. (Frisch)	1	Gomez	Walker	Cleveland A.L.	69,831
1936	July 7	N.L. (Grimm)	4	A.L. (McCarthy)	3	J. Dean	Grove	Boston N.L.	25,556
1937	July 7	A.L. (McCarthy)	8	N.L. (Terry)	3	Gomez	J. Dean	Washington A.L.	31,391
1938	July 6	N.L. (Terry)	4	A.L. (McCarthy)	1	Vander Meer	Gomez	Cincinnati N.L.	27,067
1939	July 11	A.L. (McCarthy)	3	N.L. (Hartnett)	1	Bridges	Lee	New York A.L.	62,892
1940	July 9	N.L. (McKechnie)	4	A.L. (Cronin)	0	Derringer	Ruffing	St. Louis N.L.	32,373
1941	July 8	A.L. (Baker)	7	N.L. (McKechnie)	5	E. Smith	Passeau	Detroit A.L.	54,674
1942	July 6	A.L. (McCarthy)	3	N.L. (Durocher)	1	Chandler	Cooper	New York N.L.	34,178
1943	July 13[1]	A.L. (McCarthy)	5	N.L. (Southworth)	3	Leonard	Cooper	Philadelphia A.L.	31,938
1944	July 11[1]	N.L. (Southworth)	7	A.L. (McCarthy)	1	Raffensberger	Hughson	Pittsburgh N.L.	29,589
1946	July 9	A.L. (O'Neill)	12	N.L. (Grimm)	0	Feller	Passeau	Boston A.L.	34,906
1947	July 8	A.L. (Cronin)	2	N.L. (Dyer)	1	Shea	Sain	Chicago N.L.	41,123
1948	July 13	A.L. (Harris)	5	N.L. (Durocher)	2	Raschi	Schmitz	St. Louis A.L.	34,009
1949	July 12	A.L. (Boudreau)	11	N.L. (Southworth)	7	Trucks	Newcombe	Brooklyn N.L.	32,577
1950	July 11	N.L. (Shotton)	4	A.L. (Stengel)	3[3]	Blackwell	Gray	Chicago A.L.	46,127
1951	July 10	N.L. (Sawyer)	8	A.L. (Stengel)	3	Maglie	Lopat	Detroit A.L.	52,075
1952	July 8	N.L. (Durocher)	3	A.L. (Stengel)	2[4]	Rush	Lemon	Philadelphia N.L.	32,785
1953	July 14	N.L. (Dressen)	5	A.L. (Stengel)	1	Spahn	Reynolds	Cincinnati N.L.	30,846
1954	July 13	A.L. (Stengel)	11	N.L. (Alston)	9	Stone	Conley	Cleveland A.L.	68,751
1955	July 12	N.L. (Durocher)	6	A.L. (Lopez)	5[5]	Conley	Sullivan	Milwaukee N.L.	45,643
1956	July 10	N.L. (Alston)	7	A.L. (Stengel)	3	Friend	Pierce	Washington A.L.	28,843
1957	July 9	A.L. (Stengel)	6	N.L. (Alston)	5	Bunning	Simmons	St. Louis N.L.	30,693
1958	July 8	A.L. (Stengel)	4	N.L. (Haney)	3	Wynn	Friend	Baltimore A.L.	48,829
1959[2]	July 7	N.L. (Haney)	5	A.L. (Stengel)	4	Antonelli	Ford	Pittsburgh N.L.	35,277
	Aug. 3	A.L. (Stengel)	5	N.L. (Haney)	3	Walker	Drysdale	Los Angeles N.L.	55,105
1960[2]	July 11	N.L. (Alston)	5	A.L. (Lopez)	3	Friend	Monbouquette	Kansas City A.L.	30,619
	July 13	N.L. (Alston)	6	A.L. (Lopez)	0	Law	Ford	New York A.L.	38,362
1961[2]	July 11	N.L. (Murtaugh)	5	A.L. (Richards)	4[6]	Miller	Wilhelm	San Francisco N.L.	44,115
	July 31	N.L. (Murtaugh)	1	A.L. (Richards)	1[7]	—	—	Boston A.L.	31,851
1962[2]	July 10	N.L. (Hutchinson)	3	A.L. (Houk)	1	Marichal	Pascual	Washington A.L.	45,480
	July 30	A.L. (Houk)	9	N.L. (Hutchinson)	4	Herbert	Mahaffey	Chicago N.L.	38,359
1963	July 9	N.L. (Dark)	5	A.L. (Houk)	3	Jackson	Bunning	Cleveland A.L.	44,160
1964	July 7	N.L. (Alston)	7	A.L. (Lopez)	4	Marichal	Radatz	New York N.L.	50,850
1965	July 13	N.L. (March)	6	A.L. (Lopez)	5	Koufax	McDowell	Minnesota A.L.	46,706
1966	July 12	N.L. (Alston)	2	A.L. (Mele)	1[6]	Perry	Richert	St. Louis N.L.	49,926
1967	July 11	N.L. (Alston)	2	A.L. (Bauer)	1[8]	Drysdale	Hunter	Anaheim A.L.	46,309
1968	July 9	N.L. (Schoendienst)	1	A.L. (Williams)	0	Drysdale	Tiant	Houston N.L.	48,321
1969	July 23	N.L. (Schoendienst)	9	A.L. (M. Smith)	3	Carlton	Stottlemyre	Washington A.L.	45,259
1970	July 14	N.L. (Hodges)	5	A.L. (Weaver)	4[5]	Osteen	Wright	Cincinnati N.L.	51,838
1971	July 13	A.L. (Weaver)	6	N.L. (Anderson)	4	Blue	Ellis	Detroit A.L.	53,559
1972	July 25	N.L. (Murtaugh)	4	A.L. (Weaver)	3[6]	McGraw	McNally	Atlanta N.L.	53,107
1973	July 24[1]	N.L. (Anderson)	7	A.L. (Williams)	1	Wise	Blyleven	Kansas City A.L.	40,849
1974	July 23[1]	N.L. (Berra)	7	A.L. (Williams)	2	Brett	Tiant	Pittsburgh N.L.	50,706
1975	July 15[1]	N.L. (Alston)	6	A.L. (Dark)	3	Matlack	Hunter	Milwaukee A.L.	51,540
1976	July 13	N.L. (Anderson)	7	A.L. (D. Johnson)	1	R. Jones	Fidrych	Philadelphia N.L.	63,974
1977	July 19[1]	N.L. (Anderson)	7	A.L. (Martin)	5	Sutton	Palmer	New York A.L.	56,683
1978	July 11[1]	N.L. (Lasorda)	7	A.L. (Martin)	3	Sutter	Gossage	San Diego N.L.	51,549
1979	July 17[1]	N.L. (Lasorda)	7	A.L. (Lemon)	6	Sutter	Kern	Seattle A.L.	58,905
1980	July 8[1]	N.L. (Tanner)	4	A.L. (Weaver)	2	Reuss	John	Los Angeles N.L.	56,088
1981	Aug. 9[1]	N.L. (Green)	5	A.L. (Frey)	4	Blue	Fingers	Cleveland* A.L.	72,086
1982	July 13[1]	N.L. (Lasorda)	4	A.L. (Martin)	1	Rogers	Eckersley	Montreal N.L.	59,057

1. Night game. 2. Two games. 3. Fourteen innings. 4. Five innings, rain. 5. Twelve innings. 6. Ten innings. 7. Called because of rain after nine innings. 8. Fifteen innings. NOTE: No game in 1945. *Game was originally scheduled for July 14, but was put off because of players' strike.

PAWTUCKET WINS LONGEST GAME IN 33RD INNING

The Pawtucket Red Sox and the Rochester Red Wings of the International League played one of the most bizarre games and the longest in baseball history during 1981. Pawtucket won it, 3–2, after 33 innings, 67 days after it had begun. The teams made 39 hits in the marathon that lasted 8 hours 25 minutes of actual playing time. The Class AAA game started on April 18 at McCoy Stadium in Pawtucket, R.I., and was tied at 2–2 when it was called at 4:07 in the morning by order of the league president. On Rochester's next visit to Pawtucket, June 23, the teams resumed the game and took only 18 minutes to decide the outcome. Miami and St. Petersburg of the Florida State League had played 29 innings on June 14, 1966, the previous longest game. Miami won, 4–3. In the major leagues the longest game was played on May 2, 1920, between the Brooklyn Dodgers and Boston Braves. It went 26 innings and was called with the teams tied at 1–1.

NATIONAL BASEBALL HALL OF FAME

Cooperstown, N.Y.

Fielders

Member	Active years
Aaron, Henry (Hank)	1954–1976
Anson, Adrian (Cap)	1876–1897
Appling, Lucius (Luke)	1930–1950
Averill, H. Earl	1929–1941
Baker, J. Frank (Home Run)	1908–1922
Bancroft, David	1915–1930
Banks, Ernest	1953–1971
Beckley, Jacob	1888–1907
Bell, James (Cool Papa)[1]	1920–1947
Berra, Lawrence (Yogi)	1946–1965
Bottomley, James	1922–1937
Boudreau, Louis	1938–1952
Bresnahan, Roger	1897–1915
Brouthers, Dennis	1879–1896
Burkett, Jesse	1890–1905
Campanella, Roy	1948–1957
Carey, Max	1910–1929
Chance, Frank	1898–1914
Charleston, Oscar[1]	1915–1954
Clarke, Fred	1894–1915
Clemente, Roberto	1955–1972
Cobb, Tyrus	1905–1928
Cochrane, Gordon (Mickey)	1925–1937
Collins, Edward	1906–1930
Collins, James	1895–1908
Comiskey, Charles	1882–1894
Combs, Earle	1924–1935
Connor, Roger	1880–1897
Crawford, Samuel	1899–1917
Cronin, Joseph	1926–1945
Cuyler, Hazen (Kiki)	1921–1938
Delahanty, Edward	1888–1903
Dickey, William	1928–1946
Dihigo, Martin[1]	1923–1945
DiMaggio, Joseph	1936–1951
Duffy, Hugh	1888–1906
Evers, John	1902–1919
Ewing, William	1880–1897
Flick, Elmer	1898–1910
Foxx, James	1925–1945
Frisch, Frank	1919–1937
Gehrig, H. Louis (Lou)	1923–1939
Gehringer, Charles	1924–1942
Gibson, Josh[1]	1929–1946
Goslin, Leon (Goose)	1921–1938
Greenberg, Henry (Hank)	1933–1947
Hafey, Charles (Chick)	1924–1937
Hamilton, William	1888–1901
Hartnett, Charles (Gabby)	1922–1941
Heilmann, Harry	1914–1932
Herman, William	1931–1947
Hooper, Harry	1909–1925
Hornsby, Rogers	1915–1937
Irvin, Monford (Monte)[1]	1939–1956
Jackson, Travis	1922–1936
Jennings, Hugh	1891–1918
Johnson, William (Judy)[1]	1921–1937
Kaline, Albert W.	1953–1974
Keeler, William (Wee Willie)	1892–1910
Kelley, Joseph	1891–1908
Kelly, George	1915–1932
Kelly, Michael (King)	1878–1893
Kiner, Ralph	1946–1955
Klein, Charles H. (Chuck)	1928–1944
Lajoie, Napoleon	1896–1916
Leonard, Walter (Buck)[1]	1933–1955
Lindstrom, Frederick	1924–1936
Lloyd, John Henry[1]	1905–1931
Mantle, Mickey	1951–1968
Manush, Henry (Heinie)	1923–1939
Maranville, Walter (Rabbit)	1912–1935
Mathews, Edwin	1952–1968
Mays, Willie	1951–1973
McCarthy, Thomas	1884–1896
McGraw, John J.	1891–1906
Medwick, Joseph (Ducky)	1932–1948
Mize, John (The Big Cat)	1936–1953
Musial, Stanley	1941–1963
O'Rourke, James	1876–1894
Ott, Melvin	1926–1947
Rice, Edgar (Sam)	1915–1934
Robinson, Frank	1956–1976
Robinson, Jack	1947–1956
Robinson, Wilbert	1886–1902
Roush, Edd	1913–1931
Ruth, George (Babe)	1914–1935
Schalk, Raymond	1912–1929
Sewell, Joseph	1920–1933
Simmons, Al	1924–1944
Sisler, George	1915–1930
Snider, Edwin D. (Duke)	1947–1964
Speaker, Tristram	1907–1928
Terry, William	1923–1936
Thompson, Samuel	1885–1906
Tinker, Joseph	1902–1916
Traynor, Harold (Pie)	1920–1937
Wagner, John (Honus)	1897–1917
Wallace, Roderick (Bobby)	1894–1918
Waner, Lloyd	1927–1945
Waner, Paul	1926–1945
Ward, John (Monte)	1878–1894
Wheat, Zachariah	1909–1927
Williams, Theodore	1939–1960
Wilson, Lewis R. (Hack)	1923–1934
Youngs, Ross (Pep)	1917–1926

Pitchers

Member	Active years
Alexander, Grover	1911–1930
Bender, Charles (Chief)	1903–1925
Brown, Mordecai (3-Finger)	1903–1916
Chesbro, John	1899–1909
Clarkson, John	1882–1894
Coveleski, Stanley	1912–1928
Dean, Jerome (Dizzy)	1930–1947
Faber, Urban (Red)	1914–1933
Feller, Robert	1936–1956
Ford, Edward (Whitey)	1950–1967
Foster, Andrew (Rube)	1897–1926
Galvin, James (Pud)	1876–1892
Gibson, Bob	1959–1975
Gomez, Vernon (Lefty)	1930–1943
Griffith, Clark	1891–1914
Grimes, Burleigh	1916–1934
Grove, Robert (Lefty)	1925–1941
Haines, Jesse	1918–1937
Hoyt, Waite	1918–1938
Hubbell, Carl	1928–1943
Johnson, Walter	1907–1927
Joss, Adrian	1902–1910
Keefe, Timothy	1880–1893
Koufax, Sanford (Sandy)	1955–1966
Lemon, Robert	1946–1958
Lyons, Theodore	1923–1946
Marquard, Richard (Rube)	1908–1925
Mathewson, Christopher	1900–1916
McGinnity, Joseph	1899–1908
Nichols, Charles (Kid)	1890–1906
Paige, LeRoy (Satchel)[1]	1926–1965
Pennock, Herbert	1912–1934
Plank, Edward	1901–1917
Radbourn, Charles (Hoss)	1880–1891
Rixey, Eppa	1912–1933
Roberts, Robert (Robin)	1948–1966
Ruffing, Charles (Red)	1924–1947
Rusie, Amos	1889–1901
Spahn, Warren	1942–1965
Vance, Arthur (Dazzy)	1915–1935
Waddell, George	1897–1910
Walsh, Edward	1904–1917
Welch, Michael (Mickey)	1880–1892
Wynn, Early	1939–1963
Young, Denton (Cy)	1890–1911

Officials and Others

Barrow, Edward[2,3]
Bulkeley, Morgan G.[3]
Cartwright, Alexander[3]
Chadwick, Henry[4]
Chandler, A.B.[7]
Conlan, John[5]
Connolly, Thomas[5]
Cummings, William A.[6]
Evans, William G.[5,3]
Frick, Ford C.[7,3]
Giles, Warren C.[3]
Harridge, William[3]
Harris, Stanley R.[8]
Hubbard, R. Calvin[5]
Higgins, Miller J.[2]
Johnson, B. Bancroft[3]
Klem, William[5]
Landis, Kenesaw M.[7]
Lopez, Alfonso R.[8]
Mack, Connie[2,3]
MacPhail, Leland S.[3]
McCarthy, Joseph V.[2]
McKechnie, William B.[2]
Rickey, W. Branch[2,3]
Spalding, Albert G.[6]
Stengel, Charles D.
Weiss, George M.[3]
Wright, George[6]
Wright, Harry[6,2]
Yawkey, Thomas[3]

1. Negro league player selected by special committee. 2. Manager. 3. Executive. 4. Writer-statistician. 5. Umpire. 6. Early player 7. Commissioner. 8. Player-manager

OTHER LIFETIME BATTING, PITCHING, AND BASE-RUNNING RECORDS

Sources: Baseball Record Book, published and copyrighted by The Sporting News, St. Louis, Mo. 63166, and *The Book of Baseball Records,* published and copyrighted by Seymour Siwoff, New York, N.Y. 10036

Hits (3,000 or More)

Ty Cobb	4,191
Pete Rose	3,869
Henry Aaron	3,771
Stan Musial	3,630
Tris Speaker	3,515
Honus Wagner	3,430
Carl Yastrzemski	3,318
Eddie Collins	3,311
Willie Mays	3,283
Nap Lajoie	3,251
Paul Waner	3,152
Cap Anson	3,081
Lou Brock	3,023
Al Kaline	3,007
Roberto Clemente	3,000

Earned-Run Average[1]

Walter Johnson	2.37
Grover Alexander	2.56
Tom Seaver*	2.60
Whitey Ford	2.74
Jim Palmer*	2.78
Stanley Coveleski	2.88
Juan Marichal	2.89
Wilbur Cooper	2.89
Bob Gibson	2.91
Carl Mays	2.92
Don Drysdale	2.95
Bert Blyleven*	2.95
Carl Hubbell	2.98
Gaylord Perry*	2.99
Steve Carlton*	3.00

Runs Scored

Ty Cobb	2,245
Henry Aaron	2,174
Babe Ruth	2,174
Willie Mays	2,062
Pete Rose*	1,995
Stan Musial	1,949
Lou Gehrig	1,888
Tris Speaker	1,881
Mel Ott	1,859
Frank Robinson	1,829
Eddie Collins	1,816
Ted Williams	1,798
Carl Yastrzemski*	1,778
Charlie Gehringer	1,774
Jimmie Foxx	1,751
Honus Wagner	1,740
Willie Keeler	1,720
Cap Anson	1,712
Jesse Burkett	1,708
Billy Hamilton	1,690
Mickey Mantle	1,677
John McPhee	1,674
George Van Haltren	1,650

Strikeouts, Pitching

Walter Johnson	3,508
Nolan Ryan*	3,494
Gaylord Perry*	3,452
Steve Carlton*	3,434
Tom Seaver*	3,163
Bob Gibson	3,117
Ferguson Jenkins*	3,096
Jim Bunning	2,855
Mickey Lolich	2,832
Cy Young	2,819
Don Sutton*	2,792
Phil Niekro*	2,784
Warren Spahn	2,583
Bob Feller	2,581
Tim Keefe	2,538
Christy Mathewson	2,505

Home Runs (350 or More)

Henry Aaron	755
Babe Ruth	714
Willie Mays	660
Frank Robinson	586
Harmon Killebrew	573
Mickey Mantle	536
Jimmie Foxx	534
Ted Williams	521
Willie McCovey	521
Eddie Mathews	512
Ernie Banks	512
Mel Ott	511
Lou Gehrig	493
Stan Musial	475
Willie Stargell*	475
Reggie Jackson*	464
Carl Yastrzemski*	442
Billy Williams	426
Duke Snider	407
Al Kaline	399
Frank Howard	382
Orlando Cepeda	379
Norm Cash	377
Johnny Bench*	377
Rocky Colavito	374
Gil Hodges	370
Ralph Kiner	369
Tony Perez*	363
Joe DiMaggio	361
Lee May*	360
Johnny Mize	359
Yogi Berra	358
Dick Allen	351

Shutouts

Walter Johnson	110
Grover Alexander	90
Christy Mathewson	83
Cy Young	77
Ed Plank	64
Warren Spahn	63
Ed Walsh	58
James Galvin	57
Bob Gibson	56
Don Sutton*	56
Tom Seaver*	54
Jim Palmer*	53
Gaylord Perry*	52
Steve Carlton*	52
Juan Marichal	52

Strikeouts, Batting[1]

Willie Stargell*	1,912
Reggie Jackson*	1,810
Bobby Bonds	1,757
Lou Brock	1,730
Mickey Mantle	1,710
Harmon Killebrew	1,699
Tony Perez*	1,694
Dick Allen	1,556
Lee May*	1,552
Willie McCovey	1,550
Frank Robinson	1,532
Willie Mays	1,526
Eddie Mathews	1,487
Frank Howard	1,460
Jim Wynn	1,427

Bases on Balls[1]

Babe Ruth	2,056
Ted Williams	2,019
Mickey Mantle	1,734
Carl Yastrzemski*	1,732
Mel Ott	1,708
Joe Morgan*	1,625
Eddie Yost	1,614
Stan Musial	1,599
Harmon Killebrew	1,559
Lou Gehrig	1,508
Willie Mays	1,464
Jimmie Foxx	1,452
Eddie Mathews	1,444
Frank Robinson	1,420
Henry Aaron	1,402

Stolen Bases

Lou Brock	938
Billy Hamilton	937
Ty Cobb	892
Walter Latham	791
Harry Stovey	744
Eddie Collins	743
Max Carey	738
Honus Wagner	720
Tom Brown	697
Joe Morgan*	663
Bert Campaneris	643

*Active player through 1982. 1. Through 1981 season.

RECORD OF WORLD SERIES GAMES

Source: The Book of Baseball Records, published by Seymour Siwoff, New York City.

Figures in parentheses for winning pitchers (WP) and losing pitchers (LP) indicate the game number in the series

1903—Boston A.L. 5 (Jimmy Collins); Pittsburgh N.L. 3 (Fred Clarke). WP—Bos.: Dinneen (2, 6, 8), Young (5, 7); Pitts.: Phillippe (1, 3, 4). LP—Bos.: Young (1), Hughes (3), Dinneen (4); Pitts.: Leever (2, 6), Kennedy (5), Phillippe (7, 8).

1904—No series.

1905—New York N.L. 4 (John J. McGraw); Philadelphia A.L. 1 (Connie Mack). WP—N.Y.: Mathewson (1, 3, 5); McGinnity (4); Phila.: Bender (2). LP—N.Y.: McGinnity (2); Phila.: Plank (1, 4), Coakley (3), Bender (5).

1906—Chicago A.L. 4 (Fielder Jones); Chicago N.L. 2 (Frank Chance). WP—Chi.: A.L.: Altrock (1), Walsh (3, 5), White (6); Chi.: N.L.: Reulbach (2), Brown (4). LP—Chi. A.L.: White (2), Altrock (4); Chi.: N.L.: Brown (1, 6), Pfeister (3, 5).

1907—Chicago N.L. 4 (Frank Chance); Detroit A.L. 0 (Hugh Jennings). First game tied 3–3, 12 innings. WP—Pfeister (2), Reulbach (3), Overall (4), Brown (5). LP—Mullin (2, 5), Siever (3), Donovan (4).

1908—Chicago N.L. 4 (Frank Chance); Detroit A.L. 1 (Hugh Jennings). WP—Chi.: Brown (1, 4), Overall (2, 5); Det.: Mullin (3). LP—Chi.: Pfeister (3); Det.: Summers (1, 4), Donovan (2, 5).

1909—Pittsburgh N.L. 4 (Fred Clarke); Detroit A.L. 3 (Hugh Jennings). WP—Pitts.: Adams (1, 5, 7), Maddox (3); Det.: Donovan (2), Mullin (4, 6). LP—Pitts.: Camnitz (2), Leifield (4), Willis (6); Det.: Mullin (1), Summers (3, 5), Donovan (7).

1910—Philadelphia A.L. 4 (Connie Mack); Chicago N.L. 1 (Frank Chance). WP—Phila.: Bender (1), Coombs (2, 3, 5); Chi.: Brown (4). LP—Phila.: Bender (4); Chi.: Overall (1), Brown (2, 5), McIntyre (3).

1911—Philadelphia A.L. 4 (Connie Mack); New York N.L. 2 (John J. McGraw). WP—Phila.: Plank (2), Coombs (3), Bender (4, 6); N.Y.: Mathewson (1), Crandall (5). LP—Phila.: Bender (1), Plank (5); N.Y.: Marquard (2), Mathewson (3, 4), Ames (6).

1912—Boston A.L. 4 (J. Garland Stahl); New York N.L. 3 (John J. McGraw). Second game tied, 6–6, 11 innings. WP—Bos.:

Wood (1, 4, 8), Bedient (5); N.Y.: Marquard (3, 6), Tesreau (7). LP—Bos.: O'Brien (3, 6), Wood (7); N.Y.: Tesreau (1, 4), Mathewson (5, 8).

1913—Philadelphia A.L. 4 (Connie Mack); New York N.L. 1 (John J. McGraw). WP—Phila.: Bender (1, 4), Bush (3), Plank (5); N.Y.: Mathewson (2); LP—Phila.: Plank (2); N.Y.: Marquard (1), Tesreau (3), Demaree (4), Mathewson (5).

1914—Boston N.L. 4 (George Stallings); Philadelphia A.L. 0 (Connie Mack). WP—Rudolph (1, 4), James (2, 3). LP—Bender (1), Plank (2), Bush (3), Shawkey (4).

1915—Boston A.L. 4 (Bill Carrigan); Philadelphia N.L. 1 (Pat Moran). WP—Bos.: Foster (2, 5), Leonard (3), Shore (4); Phila.: Alexander (1). LP—Bos.: Shore (1); Phila.: Mayer (2), Alexander (3), Chalmers (4), Rixey (5).

1916—Boston A.L. 4 (Bill Carrigan); Brooklyn N.L. 1 (Wilbert Robinson). WP—Bos.: Shore (1, 5), Ruth (2), Leonard (4); Bklyn.: Coombs (3). LP—Bos.: Mays (3); Bklyn.: Marquard (1, 4), Smith (2), Pfeffer (5).

1917—Chicago A.L. 4 (Clarence Rowland); New York N.L. 2 (John J. McGraw). WP—Chi.: Cicotte (1), Faber (2, 5, 6); N.Y.: Benton (3), Schupp (4). LP—Chi.: Cicotte (3), Faber (4); N.Y.: Sallee (1, 5), Anderson (2), Benton (6).

1918—Boston A.L. 4 (Ed Barrow); Chicago N.L. 2 (Fred Mitchell). WP—Bos.: Ruth (1, 4), Mays (3, 6); Chi.: Tyler (2), Vaughn (5). LP—Bos.: Bush (2), Jones (5); Chi.: Vaughn (1, 3), Douglas (4), Tyler (6).

1919—Cincinnati N.L. 5 (Pat Moran); Chicago A.L. 3 (William Gleason). WP—Cin.: Ruether (1), Sallee (2), Ring (4), Eller (5, 8); Chi.: Kerr (3, 6), Cicotte (7). LP—Cin.: Fisher (3), Ring (6), Sallee (7); Chi.: Cicotte (1, 4), Williams (2, 5, 8).

1920—Cleveland A.L. 5 (Tris Speaker); Brooklyn N.L. 2 (Wilbert Robinson). WP—Cleve.: Coveleski (1, 4, 7), Bagby (5), Mails (6); Bklyn.: Grimes (2), Smith (3). LP—Cleve.: Bagby (2), Caldwell (3). Bklyn.: Marquard (1), Cadore (4), Grimes (5, 7), Smith (6).

1921—New York N.L. 5 (John J. McGraw); New York A.L. 3 (Miller Huggins). WP—N.Y. N.L.: Barnes (3, 6), Douglas (4, 7), Nehf (8); N.Y. A.L.: Mays (1), Hoyt (2, 5). LP—N.Y. N.L.: Nehf (2, 5), Douglas (1). N.Y. A.L.: Quinn (3), Mays (4, 7), Shawkey (6), Hoyt (8).

1922—New York N.L. 4 (John J. McGraw); New York A.L. 0 (Miller Huggins). Second game tied 3–3, 10 innings. WP—Ryan (1), Scott (3), McQuillan (4), Nehf (5); LP—Bush (1, 5), Hoyt (3), Mays (4).

1923—New York A.L. 4 (Miller Huggins); New York N.L. 2 (John J. McGraw). WP—N.Y. A.L.: Pennock (2, 6), Shawkey (4), Bush (5); N.Y. N.L.:Ryan (1), Nehf (3). LP—N.Y. A.L.: Bush (1), Jones (3); N.Y. N.L.: McQuillan (2), Scott (4), Bentley (5), Nehf (6).

1924—Washington A.L. 4 (Bucky Harris); New York N.L. 3 (John J. McGraw). WP—Wash.: Zachary (2, 6), Mogridge (4), Johnson (7); N.Y.: Nehf (1), McQuillan (3), Bentley (5). LP—Wash.: Johnson (1, 5), Marberry (3); N.Y.: Bentley (2, 7), Barnes (4), Nehf (6).

1925—Pittsburgh N.L. 4 (Bill McKechnie); Washington A.L. 3 (Bucky Harris). WP—Pitts.: Aldridge (2, 5), Kremer (6, 7); Wash.: Johnson (1, 4), Ferguson (3). LP—Pitts.: Meadows (1), Kremer (3), Yde (4); Wash.: Coveleski (2, 5), Ferguson (6), Johnson (7).

1926—St. Louis N.L. 4 (Rogers Hornsby); New York A.L. 3 (Miller Huggins). WP—St. L.: Alexander (2, 6), Haines (3, 7); N.Y.: Pennock (1, 5), Hoyt (4). LP—St. L.: Sherdel (1, 5), Reinhart (4); N.Y.: Shocker (2), Ruether (3), Shawkey (6), Hoyt (7).

1927—New York A.L. 4 (Miller Huggins); Pittsburgh N.L. 0 (Donie Bush). WP—Hoyt (1), Pipgras (2), Pennock (3), Moore (4). LP—Kremer (1), Aldridge (2), Meadows (3), Miljus (4).

1928—New York A.L. 4 (Miller Huggins); St. Louis N.L. 0 (Bill McKechnie). WP—Hoyt (1, 4), Pipgras (2), Zachary (3). LP—Sherdel (1, 4), Alexander (2), Haines (3).

1929—Philadelphia A.L. 4 (Connie Mack); Chicago N.L. 1 (Joe McCarthy). WP—Phila.: Ehmke (1), Earnshaw (2), Rommel (4), Walberg (5); Chi.: Bush (3). LP—Phila.: Earnshaw (3); Chi.: Root (1), Malone (2, 5), Blake (4).

1930—Philadelphia A.L. 4 (Connie Mack); St. Louis N.L. 2 (Gabby Street). WP—Phila.: Grove (1, 5), Earnshaw (2, 6); St. L.: Hallahan (3), Haines (4). LP—Phila.: Walberg (3), Grove (4); St. L.: Grimes (1, 5), Rhem (2), Hallahan (6).

1931—St. Louis N.L. 4 (Gabby Street); Philadelphia A.L. 3 (Connie Mack). WP—St. L.: Hallahan (2, 5), Grimes (3, 7); Phila.: Grove (1, 6), Earnshaw (4). LP—St. L.: Derringer (1, 6), Johnson (4); Phila.: Earnshaw (2, 7), Grove (3), Hoyt (5).

1932—New York A.L. (Joe McCarthy); Chicago N.L. 0 (Charles Grimm). WP—Ruffing (1), Gomez (2), Pipgras (3), Moore (4). LP—Bush (1), Warneke (2), Root (3), May (4).

1933—New York N.L. 4 (Bill Terry); Washington A.L. 1 (Joe Cronin.). WP—N.Y.: Hubbell (1, 4), Schumacher (2), Luque (5); Wash.: Whitehill (3). LP—N.Y.: Fitzsimmons (3); Wash.: Stewart (1), Crowder (2), Weaver (4), Russell (5).

1934—St. Louis N.L. 4 (Frank Frisch); Detroit A.L. 3 (Mickey Cochrane). WP—St. L.: J. Dean (1, 7), P. Dean (3, 6); Det.: Rowe (2), Auker (4), Bridges (5). LP—St. L.: W. Walker (2, 4), J. Dean (5); Det.: Crowder (1), Bridges (3), Rowe (6), Auker (7).

1935—Detroit A.L. 4 (Mickey Cochrane); Chicago N.L. 2 (Charles Grimm). WP—Det.: Bridges (2, 6), Rowe (3), Crowder (4); Chi.: Warneke (1, 5); LP—Det.: Rowe (1, 5); Chi.: Root (2), French (3, 6), Carleton (4).

1936—New York A.L. 4 (Joe McCarthy); New York N.L. 2 (Bill Terry). WP—N.Y. A.L.: Gomez (2, 6), Hadley (3), Pearson (4); N.Y. N.L.: Hubbell (1), Schumacher (5); LP—N.Y. A.L.: Ruffing (1), Malone (5); N.Y. N.L.: Schumacher (2), Fitzsimmons (3, 6), Hubbell (4).

1937—New York A.L. 4 (Joe McCarthy); New York N.L. 1 (Bill Terry). WP—N.Y. A.L.: Gomez (1, 5), Ruffing (2), Pearson (3); N.Y. N.L.: Hubbell (4). LP—N.Y. A.L.: Hadley (4); N.Y. N.L.: Hubbell (1), Melton (2, 5), Schumacher (3).

1938—New York A.L. 4 (Joe McCarthy); Chicago N.L. 0 (Gabby Hartnett). WP—Ruffing (1, 4), Gomez (2), Pearson (3). LP—Lee (1, 4), Dean (2), Bryant (3).

1939—New York A.L. 4 (Joe McCarthy); Cincinnati N.L. 0 (Bill McKechnie). WP—Ruffing (1), Pearson (2), Hadley (3), Murphy (4). LP—Derringer (1), Walters (2, 4), Thompson (3).

1940—Cincinnati N.L. 4 (Bill McKechnie); Detroit A.L. 3 (Del Baker). WP—Cin.: Walters (2, 6), Derringer (4, 7); Det.: Newsom (1, 5), Bridges (3). LP—Cin.: Derringer (1), Turner (3), Thompson (5); Det.: Rowe (2, 6), Trout (4), Newsom (7).

1941—New York A.L. 4 (Joe McCarthy); Brooklyn N.L. 1 (Leo Durocher). WP—N.Y.: Ruffing (1), Russo (3), Murphy (4), Bonham (5); Bklyn: Wyatt (2). LP—N.Y.: Chandler (2); Bklyn: Davis (1), Casey (3, 4), Wyatt (5).

1942—St. Louis N.L. 4 (Billy Southworth); New York A.L. 1 (Joe McCarthy). WP—St. L.: Beazley (2, 5), White (3), Lanier (4); N.Y.: Ruffing (1). LP—St. L.: Cooper (1); N.Y.: Bonham (2), Chandler (3), Donald (4), Ruffing (5).

1943—New York A.L. 4 (Joe McCarthy); St. Louis N.L. 1 (Billy Southworth). WP—N.Y.: Chandler (1, 5), Borowy (3), Russo (4); St. L.: Cooper (2). LP—N.Y.: Bonham (2); St. L.: Lanier (1), Brazle (3), Brecheen (4), Cooper (5).

1944—St. Louis N.L. 4 (Billy Southworth); St. Louis A.L. 2 (Luke Sewell). WP—St. L. N.L.: Donnelly (2), Brecheen (4), Cooper (5), Lanier (6); St. L. A.L.: Galehouse (1), Kramer (3). LP—St. L. N.L.: Cooper (1), Wilks (3); St. L. A.L.: Muncrief (2), Jakucki (4), Galehouse (5), Potter (6).

1945—Detroit A.L. 4 (Steve O'Neill); Chicago N.L. 3 (Charles Grimm). WP—Det.: Trucks (2), Trout (4), Newhouser (5, 7); Chi.: Borowy (1, 6), Passeau (3). LP—Det.: Newhouser (1), Overmire (3), Trout (6); Chi.: Wyse (2), Prim (4), Borowy (5, 7).

1946—St. Louis N.L. 4 (Eddie Dyer); Boston A.L. 3 (Joe Cronin). WP—St. L.: Brecheen (2, 6, 7), Munger (4); Bos.: Johnson (1), Ferriss (3), Dobson (5). LP—St. L.: Pollet (1), Dickson (3), Brazle (5); Bos.: Harris (2, 6), Hughson (4), Klinger (7).

1947—New York A.L. 4 (Bucky Harris); Brooklyn N.L. 3 (Burt Shotton). WP—N.Y.: Shea (1, 5), Reynolds (2), Page (7);

Bklyn.: Casey (3, 4), Branca (6). LP—N.Y.: Newsom (3), Bevens (4), Page (6); Bklyn.: Branca (1), Lombardi (2), Barney (5), Gregg (7).

1948—Cleveland A.L. 4 (Lou Boudreau); Boston N.L. 2 (Billy Southworth). WP—Cleve.: Lemon (2, 6), Bearden (3), Gromek (4); Bos.: Sain (1), Spahn (5). LP—Cleve.: Feller (1, 5); Bos.: Spahn (2), Bickford (3), Sain (4), Voiselle (6).

1949—New York A.L. 4 (Casey Stengel); Brooklyn N.L. 1 (Burt Shotton). WP—N.Y.: Reynolds (1), Page (3), Lopat (4), Raschi (5); Bklyn.: Roe (2). LP—N.Y.: Raschi (2); Bklyn.: Newcombe (1, 4), Branca (3), Barney (5).

1950—New York A.L. 4 (Casey Stengel); Philadelphia N.L. 0 (Eddie Sawyer). WP—Raschi (1), Reynolds (2), Ferrick (3), Ford (4). LP—Konstanty (1), Roberts (2), Meyer (3), Miller (4).

1951—New York A.L. 4 (Casey Stengel); New York N.L. 2 (Leo Durocher). WP—N.Y. A.L.: Lopat (2, 5), Reynolds (4), Raschi (6); N.Y. N.L.: Koslo (1), Hearn (3). LP—N.Y. A.L.: Reynolds (1), Raschi (3); N.Y. N.L.: Jansen (2, 5), Maglie (4), Koslo (6).

1952—New York A.L. 4 (Casey Stengel); Brooklyn N.L. 3 (Chuck Dressen). WP—N.Y.: Raschi (2, 6), Reynolds (4, 7); Bklyn.: Black (1), Roe (3), Erskine (5). LP—N.Y.: Reynolds (1), Lopat (3), Sain (5); Bklyn.: Erskine (2), Black (4, 7), Loes (6).

1953—New York A.L. 4 (Casey Stengel); Brooklyn N.L. 2 (Chuck Dressen). WP—N.Y.: Sain (1), Lopat (2), McDonald (5), Reynolds (6); Bklyn.: Erskine (3), Loes (4). LP—N.Y.: Raschi (3), Ford (4); Bklyn.: Labine (1, 6), Roe (2), Podres (5).

1954—New York N.L. 4 (Leo Durocher); Cleveland A.L. 0 (Al Lopez). WP—Grissom (1), Antonelli (2), Gomez (3), Liddle (4). LP—Lemon (1, 4), Wynn (2), Garcia (3).

1955—Brooklyn N.L. 4 (Walter Alston); New York A.L. 3 (Casey Stengel). WP—Bklyn.: Podres (3, 7), Labine (4), Craig (5); N.Y.: Ford (1, 6), Byrne (2). LP—Bklyn.: Newcombe (1), Loes (2), Spooner (6); N.Y.: Turley (3), Larsen (4), Grim (5), Byrne (7).

1956—New York A.L. 4 (Casey Stengel); Brooklyn N.L. 3 (Walter Alston). WP—N.Y.: Ford (3), Sturdivant (4), Larsen (5), Kucks (7); Bklyn.: Maglie (1), Bessent (2), Labine (6). LP—N.Y.: Ford (1), Morgan (2), Turley (6); Bklyn.: Craig (3), Erskine (4), Maglie (5), Newcombe (7).

1957—Milwaukee N.L. 4 (Fred Haney); New York A.L. 3 (Casey Stengel). WP—Mil.: Burdette (2, 5, 7), Spahn (4); N.Y.: Ford (1), Larsen (3), Turley (6). LP—Mil.: Spahn (1), Buhl (3), Johnson (6); N.Y.: Shantz (2), Grim (4), Ford (5), Larsen (7).

1958—New York A.L. 4 (Casey Stengel); Milwaukee N.L. 3 (Fred Haney). WP—N.Y.: Larsen (3), Turley (5, 7), Duren (6); Mil.: Spahn (1, 4), Burdette (2). LP—N.Y.: Duren (1), Turley (2), Ford (4); Mil.: Rush (3), Burdette (5, 7), Spahn (6).

1959—Los Angeles N.L. 4 (Walter Alston); Chicago A.L. 2 (Al Lopez). WP—L.A.: Podres (2), Drysdale (3), Sherry (4, 6); Chi.: Wynn (1), Shaw (5). LP—L.A.: Craig (1), Koufax (5); Chi.: Shaw (2), Donovan (3), Staley (4), Wynn (6).

1960—Pittsburgh N.L. 4 (Danny Murtaugh); New York A.L. 3 (Casey Stengel). WP—Pitts.: Law (1, 4), Haddix (5, 7); N.Y.: Turley (2), Ford (3, 6). LP—Pitts.: Friend (2, 6), Mizell (3); N.Y.: Ditmar (1, 5), Terry (4, 7).

1961—New York A.L. 4 (Ralph Houk); Cincinnati N.L. 1 (Fred Hutchinson). WP—N.Y.: Ford (1, 4), Arroyo (3), Daley (5); Cin.: Jay (2). LP—N.Y.: Terry (2); Cin.: O'Toole (1, 4), Purkey (3), Jay (5).

1962—New York A.L. 4 (Ralph Houk); San Francisco N.L. 3 (Al Dark). WP—N.Y.: Ford (1), Stafford (3), Terry (5, 7); S.F.: Sanford (2), Larsen (4), Pierce (6). LP—N.Y.: Terry (2), Coates (4), Ford (6); S.F.: O'Dell (1), Pierce (3), Sanford (5, 7).

1963—Los Angeles N.L. 4 (Walter Alston); New York A.L. 0 (Ralph Houk). WP—Koufax (1, 4), Podres (2), Drysdale (3). LP—Ford (1, 4), Downing (2), Bouton (3).

1964—St. Louis N.L. 4 (Johnny Keane); New York A.L. 3 (Yogi Berra). WP—St. L.: Sadecki (1), Craig (4), Gibson (5, 7); N.Y.: Stottlemyre (2), Bouton (3, 6). LP—St. L.: Gibson (2), Schultz (3), Simmons (6); N.Y.: Ford (1), Downing (4), Mikkelsen (5), Stottlemyre (7).

1965—Los Angeles N.L. 4 (Walter Alston); Minnesota A.L. 3 (Sam Mele). WP—L.A.: Osteen (3), Drysdale (4), Koufax (5, 7); Minn.: Grant (1, 6), Kaat (2). LP—L.A.: Drysdale (1), Koufax (2), Osteen (6); Minn.: Pascual (3), Grant (4), Kaat (5, 7).

1966—Baltimore A.L. 4 (Hank Bauer); Los Angeles N.L. 0 (Walter Alston). WP—Drabowsky (1), Palmer (2), Bunker (3), McNally (4). LP—Drysdale (1, 4), Koufax (2), Osteen (3).

1967—St. Louis N.L. 4 (Red Schoendienst); Boston A.L. 3 (Dick Williams). WP—St. L.: Gibson (1, 4, 7), Briles (3); Bos.: Lonborg (2, 5); Wyatt (6). LP—St. L.: Hughes (2), Carlton (5), Lamabe (6); Bos.: Santiago (1, 4), Bell (3), Lonborg (7).

1968—Detroit A.L. 4 (Mayo Smith); St. Louis N.L. 3 (Red Schoendienst). WP—Det.: Lolich (2, 5, 7), McLain (6); St. L.: Gibson (1, 4), Washburn (3), LP—Det.: McLain (1, 4), Wilson (3); St. L.: Briles (2), Hoerner (5), Washburn (6), Gibson (7).

1969—New York N.L. 4 (Gil Hodges); Baltimore A.L. 1 (Earl Weaver). WP—N.Y.: Koosman (2, 5), Gentry (3), Seaver (4); Balt.: Cuellar (1). LP—N.Y.: Seaver (1); Balt.: McNally (2), Palmer (3), Hall (4), Watt (5).

1970—Baltimore A.L. 4 (Earl Weaver); Cincinnati N.L. 1 (Sparky Anderson) 1. WP— Balt.: Palmer (1), Phoebus (2), McNally (3), Cuellar (5); Cin.: Carroll (4). LP—Cin.: Nolan (1), Wilcox (2), Cloninger (3), Merritt (5); Balt.: Watt (4).

1971—Pittsburgh N.L. 4 (Danny Murtaugh); Baltimore A.L. 3 (Earl Weaver). WP—Pitts.: Blass (3, 7), Kison (4), Briles (5); Balt.: McNally (1, 6), Palmer (2). LP—Pitts.: Ellis (1), R. Johnson (2), Miller (6); Balt.: Cuellar (3, 7), Watt (4) McNally (5).

1972—Oakland A.L. 4 (Dick Williams); Cincinnati N.L. (Sparky Anderson) 3. WP—Oakland: Holtzman (1), Hunter (2, 7), Fingers (4); Cincinnati: Billingham (3), Grimsley (5, 6). LP—Oakland: Odom (3), Fingers (5), Blue (6); Cincinnati: Nolan (1), Grimsley (2), Carroll (4), Borbon (7).

1973—Oakland A.L. 4 (Dick Williams): New York N.L. 3 (Yogi Berra). WP—Oakland: Holtzman (1, 7), Lindblad (3), Hunter (6). New York: McGraw (2), Matlack (4), Koosman (5). LP—Oakland: Fingers (2), Holtzman (4), Blue (5). New York: Matlack (1, 7) Parker (3), Seaver (6).

1974—Oakland A.L. 4 (Al Dark); Los Angeles N.L. 1 (Walter Alston). WP—Oakland: Fingers (1), Hunter (3), Holtzman (4), Odom (5). Los Angeles: Sutton (2). LP—Oakland: Blue (2), Los Angeles: Messersmith (1, 4), Downing (3), Marshall (5).

1975—Cincinnati N.L. 4 (Sparky Anderson); Boston A.L. 3 (Darrell Johnson). WP—Cincinnati: Eastwick (2-3), Gullett (5), Carroll (7); Boston: Tiant (1–4), Wise (6). LP—Cincinnati: Gullett (1), Norman (4), Darcy (6); Boston: Drago (2), Willoughby (3), Cleveland (5), Burton (7).

1976—Cincinnati N.L. 4 (Sparky Anderson); New York A.L. 0 (Billy Martin). WP—Gullett (1), Billingham (2), Zachry (3), Nolan (4). LP—Alexander (1), Hunter (2), Ellis (3), Figueroa (4).

1977—New York A.L. 4 (Billy Martin); Los Angeles N.L. 2 (Tom Lasorda). WP—New York: Lyle (1), Torrez (3,6), Guidry (4); Los Angeles: Hooton (2), Sutton (5). LP—New York: Hunter (2), Gullett (5); Los Angeles: Rhoden (1), John (3), Rau (4), Hooton (6).

1978—New York A.L. 4 (Bob Lemon), Los Angeles N.L. 2 (Tom Lasorda); WP—New York: Guidry (3), Gossage (4); Beattie (5), Hunter (6); Los Angeles: John (1), Hooton (2). LP—New York: Figuero (1), Hunter (2); Los Angeles: Sutton (3-6), Welch (4), Hooton (5).

1979—Pittsburgh N.L. 4 (Chuck Tanner), Baltimore A.L. 3 (Earl Weaver); WP—Pittsburgh: D. Robinson (2), Blyleven (5), Candelaria (6), Jackson (7); Baltimore: Flanagan (1), McGregor (3), Stoddard (4). LP—Pittsburgh: Kison (1), Candelaria (3), Tekulve (4); Baltimore: Stanhouse (2), Flanagan (5), Palmer (6), McGregor (7).

1980—Philadelphia N.L. 4 (Dallas Green), Kansas City A.L. 2 (Jim Frey); WP—Philadelphia: Walk (1), Carlton (2), McGraw (5), Carlton (6); Kansas City: Quisenberry (3), Leonard (4). LP—Philadelphia: McGraw (3), Christenson (4); Kansas City: Leonard (1), Quisenberry (2), Quisenberry (5), Gale (6).

1981—Los Angeles N.L. 4 (Tom Lasorda), New York A.L. 2 (Bob Lemon); WP—Los Angeles: Valenzuela (3), Howe (4), Reuss (5), Hooton (6); New York: Guidry (1), John (2). LP—Los Angeles: Reuss (1), Hooton (2); New York: Frazier (3), Frazier (4), Guidry (5), Frazier (6).

1982—St. Louis N.L. 4 (Whitey Herzog), Milwaukee A.L. (Harvey Kuenn); WP—St. Louis: Sutter (2), Andujar (3), Stuper (6), Andujar (7). Milwaukee: Caldwell (1), Slaton (4), Caldwell (5). LP—St. Louis: Forsch (1), Bair (4), Forsch (5). Milwaukee: McClure (2), Vuckovich (3), Sutton (6), McClure (7).

WORLD SERIES CLUB STANDING (THROUGH 1982)

	Series	Won	Lost	Pct.
Oakland (A)	3	3	0	1.000
Pittsburgh (N)	7	5	2	.714
St. Louis (N)	13	9	4	.692
New York (A)	33	22	11	.667
Cleveland (A)	3	2	1	.667
Boston (A)	8	5	3	.625
Philadelphia (A)	8	5	3	.625
Los Angeles (N)	8	4	4	.500
New York (N-Mets)	2	1	1	.500
Milwaukee (N)	2	1	1	.500
Boston (N)	2	1	1	.500
Chicago (A)	4	2	2	.500
Cincinnati (N)	8	4	4	.500
Baltimore (A)	5	2	3	.400
Detroit (A)	8	3	5	.375
New York (N-Giants)	14	5	9	.357
Washington (A)	3	1	2	.333
Philadelphia (N)	3	1	2	.333
Chicago (N)	10	2	8	.200
Brooklyn (N)	9	1	8	.111
St. Louis (A)	1	0	1	.000
San Francisco (N)	1	0	1	.000
Minnesota (A)	1	0	1	.000
Kansas City (A)	1	0	1	.000
Milwaukee (A)	1	0	1	.000

Recapitulation

	Won
American League	45
National League	34

SINGLE GAME AND SINGLE SERIES RECORDS

Most hits game—5, Paul Molitor, Milwaukee A.L., first game vs. St. Louis, N.L., 1982.

Most 4-hit games, series—2, Robin Yount, Milwaukee A.L., first and fifth games vs. St. Louis N.L., 1982.

Most hits inning—2, held by many players.

Most hits series—13 (7 games) Bobby Richardson, New York A.L., 1964; Lou Brock, St. Louis N.L., 1968; 12 (6 games) Billy Martin, New York A.L., 1953; 12 (8 games) Buck Herzog, New York N.L., 1912; Joe Jackson, Chicago A.L., 1919; 10 (4 games) Babe Ruth, New York A.L., 1928; 9 (5 games) held by 7 players.

Most home runs, series—5 (6 games) Reggie Jackson, New York A.L., 1977; 4 (7 games) Babe Ruth, New York A.L., 1926; Duke Snider, Brooklyn N.L., 1952, 1955; Hank Bauer, New York A.L., 1958; Gene Tenace, Oakland A.L., 1972; 4 (4 games) Lou Gehrig, New York A.L., 1928; 3 (6 games) Babe Ruth, New York A.L., 1923; Ted Kluszewski, Chicago A.L., 1959; 3 (5 games) Donn Clendenon, New York Mets N.L., 1969.

Most home runs, game—3, Babe Ruth, New York A.L., 1926 and 1928; Reggie Jackson, New York A.L., 1977.

Most strikeouts, series—12 (6 games) Willie Wilson, Kansas City A.L., 1980; 11 (7 games) Ed Mathews, Milwaukee N.L., 1958; Wayne Garrett, New York N.L., 1973; 10 (8 games) George Kelly, New York N.L., 1921; 9 (6 games) Jim Bottomley, St. Louis N.L., 1930; 8 (5 games) Rogers Hornsby, Chicago N.L., 1924; Duke Snider, Brooklyn N.L., 1949; 7 (4 games) Bob Muesel, New York A.L., 1927.

Most stolen bases, game—3, Honus Wagner, Pittsburgh N.L., 1909; Willie Davis, Los Angeles N.L., 1965; Lou Brock, St. Louis N.L., 1967 and 1968.

Most strikeouts by pitcher, game—17, Bob Gibson, St. Louis N.L. 1968.

Most strikeouts by pitcher in succession—6, Horace Eller, Cincinnati N.L., 1919; Moe Drabowsky, Baltimore A.L., 1966.

Most strikeouts by pitcher, series—35 (7 games) Bob Gibson, St. Louis N.L., 1968; 28 (8 games) Bill Dinneen, Boston A.L., 1903; 23 (4 games) Sandy Koufax, Los Angeles, 1963; 20 (6 games) Chief Bender, Philadelphia A.L., 1911; 18 (5 games) Christy Mathewson, New York N.L., 1905.

Most bases on balls, series—11 (7 games) Babe Ruth, New York A.L., 1926; Gene Tenace, Oakland A.L., 1973; 9 (6 games) Willie Randolph, New York A.L., 1981; 7 (5 games) James Sheckard, Chicago N.L., 1910; Mickey Cochrane, Philadelphia A.L., 1929; Joe Gordon, New York A.L., 1941; 7 (4 games) Hank Thompson, New York N.L., 1954.

Most consecutive scoreless innings, one series—27, Christy Mathewson, New York N.L., 1905.

LIFETIME WORLD SERIES RECORDS

Most hits—71, Yogi Berra, New York A.L., 1947, 1949–53, 1955–58, 1960–63.

Most runs—42, Mickey Mantle, New York A.L., 1951–53, 1955–58, 1960–64.

Most runs batted in—40, Mickey Mantle, New York A.L., 1951–53, 1955–58, 1960–64.

Most home runs—18, Mickey Mantle, New York A.L., 1951–53, 1955–58, 1960–64.

Most bases on balls—43, Mickey Mantle, New York A.L., 1951–53, 1955–58, 1960–64.

Most strikeouts—54, Mickey Mantle, New York A.L., 1951–53, 1955–58, 1960–64.

Most stolen bases—14, Eddie Collins, Philadelphia A.L. 1910–11, 13–14; Chicago A.L., 1917, 1919. Lou Brock, St. Louis N.L., 1964, 67–68.

Most victories, pitcher—10, Whitey Ford, New York A.L., 1950, 1953, 1955–58, 1960–64.

Most times member of winning team—10, Yogi Berra, New York A.L., 1947, 1949–53, 1956, 1958, 1961–62.

Most victories, no defeats—6, Vernon Gomez, New York A.L., 1932, 1936(2), 1937(2), 1938.

Most shutouts—4, Christy Mathewson, New York N.L., 1905 (3), 1913.

Most innings pitched—146, Whitey Ford, New York A.L., 1950, 1953, 1955–58, 1960–1964.

Most consecutive scoreless innings—33⅔, Whitey Ford, New York A.L., 1960 (18), 1961 (14), 1962 (1⅔).

Most strikeouts by pitcher—94, Whitey Ford, New York A.L., 1950, 1953, 1955–58, 1960–64.

AMERICAN LEAGUE HOME RUN CHAMPIONS

Year	Player, team	No.
1901	Nap Lajoie, Phila.	13
1902	Ralph Seybold, Phila.	16
1903	Buck Freeman, Bost.	13
1904	Harry Davis, Phila.	10
1905	Harry Davis, Phila.	8
1906	Harry Davis, Phila.	12
1907	Harry Davis, Phila.	8
1908	Sam Crawford, Det.	7
1909	Ty Cobb, Det.	9
1910	J. Garland Stahl, Bost.	10
1911	Franklin Baker, Phila.	9
1912	Franklin Baker, Phila.	10
1913	Franklin Baker, Phila.	12
1914	Franklin Baker, Phila., and Sam Crawford, Det.	8
1915	Robert Roth, Chi.-Cleve.	7
1916	Wally Pipp, N.Y.	12
1917	Wally Pipp, N.Y.	9
1918	Babe Ruth, Bost., and Clarence Walker, Phila.	11
1919	Babe Ruth, Bost.	29
1920	Babe Ruth, N.Y.	54
1921	Babe Ruth, N.Y.	59
1922	Ken Williams, St. L.	39
1923	Babe Ruth, N.Y.	41
1924	Babe Ruth, N.Y.	46
1925	Bob Meusel, N.Y.	33
1926	Babe Ruth, N.Y.	47
1927	Babe Ruth, N.Y.	60
1928	Babe Ruth, N.Y.	54
1929	Babe Ruth, N.Y.	46
1930	Babe Ruth, N.Y.	49
1931	Lou Gehrig, N.Y., and Babe Ruth, N.Y.	46
1932	Jimmy Foxx, Phila.	58
1933	Jimmy Foxx, Phila.	48
1934	Lou Gehrig, N.Y.	49
1935	Jimmy Foxx, Phila., and Hank Greenberg, Det.	36
1936	Lou Gehrig, N.Y.	49
1937	Joe DiMaggio, N.Y.	46
1938	Hank Greenberg, Det.	58
1939	Jimmy Foxx, Bost.	35
1940	Hank Greenberg, Det.	41
1941	Ted Williams, Bost.	37
1942	Ted Williams, Bost.	36
1943	Rudy York, Det.	34
1944	Nick Etten, N.Y.	22
1945	Vern Stephens, St. L.	24
1946	Hank Greenberg, Det.	44
1947	Ted Williams, Bost.	32
1948	Joe DiMaggio, N.Y.	39
1949	Ted Williams, Bost.	43
1950	Al Rosen, Cleve.	37
1951	Gus Zernial, Chi.-Phila.	33
1952	Larry Doby, Cleve.	32
1953	Al Rosen, Cleve.	43
1954	Larry Doby, Cleve.	32
1955	Mickey Mantle, N.Y.	37
1956	Mickey Mantle, N.Y.	52
1957	Roy Sievers, Wash.	42
1958	Mickey Mantle, N.Y.	42
1959	Rocky Colavito, Cleve., and Harmon Killebrew, Wash.	42
1960	Mickey Mantle, N.Y.	40
1961	Roger Maris, N.Y.	61
1962	Harmon Killebrew, Minn.	48
1963	Harmon Killebrew, Minn.	45
1964	Harmon Killebrew, Minn.	49
1965	Tony Conigliaro, Bost.	32
1966	Frank Robinson, Balt.	49
1967	Carl Yastrzemski, Bost., and Harmon Killebrew, Minn.	44
1968	Frank Howard, Wash.	44
1969	Harmon Killebrew, Minn.	49
1970	Frank Howard, Wash.	44
1971	Bill Melton, Chicago	33
1972	Dick Allen, Chicago	37
1973	Reggie Jackson, Oak.	32
1974	Dick Allen, Chicago	32
1975	Reggie Jackson, Oak., and George Scott, Mil.	36
1976	Graig Nettles, N.Y.	32
1977	Jim Rice, Boston	39
1978	Jim Rice, Boston	46
1979	Gorman Thomas, Milwaukee	45
1980	Reggie Jackson, N.Y., and Ben Oglivie, Mil.	41
1981*	Tony Armas, Oak., Dwight Evans, Bost., Bobby Grich, Calif., and Eddie Murray, Balt. (tie)	22
1982	Gorman Thomas, Mil., and Reggie Jackson, Calif.	39

*Split season because of player strike.

AMERICAN LEAGUE BATTING CHAMPIONS

Year	Player, team	Avg
1901	Nap Lajoie, Phila.	.422
1902	Ed Delahanty, Wash.	.376
1903	Nap Lajoie, Cleve.	.355
1904	Nap Lajoie, Cleve.	.381
1905	Elmer Flick, Cleve.	.306
1906	George Stone, St. L.	.358
1907	Ty Cobb, Det.	.350
1908	Ty Cobb, Det.	.324
1909	Ty Cobb, Det.	.377
1910	Ty Cobb, Det.	.385
1911	Ty Cobb, Det.	.420
1912	Ty Cobb, Det.	.410
1913	Ty Cobb, Det.	.390
1914	Ty Cobb, Det.	.368
1915	Ty Cobb, Det.	.369
1916	Tris Speaker, Cleve.	.386
1917	Ty Cobb, Det.	.383
1918	Ty Cobb, Det.	.382
1919	Ty Cobb, Det.	.384
1920	George Sisler, St. L.	.407
1921	Harry Heilmann, Det.	.394
1922	George Sisler, St. L.	.420
1923	Harry Heilmann, Det.	.403
1924	Babe Ruth, N.Y.	.378
1925	Harry Heilmann, Det.	.393
1926	Heinie Manush, Det.	.378
1927	Harry Heilmann, Det.	.398
1928	Goose Goslin, Wash.	.379
1929	Lew Fonseca, Cleve.	.369
1930	Al Simmons, Phila.	.381
1931	Al Simmons, Phila.	.390
1932	Dale Alexander, Det.-Bost.	.367
1933	Jimmy Foxx, Phila.	.356
1934	Lou Gehrig, N.Y.	.363
1935	Buddy Myer, Wash.	.349
1936	Luke Appling, Chi.	.388
1937	Charley Gehringer, Det.	.371
1938	Jimmy Foxx, Bost.	.349
1939	Joe DiMaggio, N.Y.	.381
1940	Joe DiMaggio, N.Y.	.352
1941	Ted Williams, Bost.	.406
1942	Ted Williams, Bost.	.356
1943	Luke Appling, Chi.	.328
1944	Lou Boudreau, Cleve.	.327
1945	George Sternweiss, N.Y.	.309
1946	Mickey Vernon, Wash.	.353
1947	Ted Williams, Bost.	.343
1948	Ted Williams, Bost.	.369
1949	George Kell, Det.	.343
1950	Billy Goodman, Bost.	.354
1951	Ferris Fain, Phila.	.344
1952	Ferris Fain, Phila.	.327
1953	Mickey Vernon, Wash.	.337
1954	Bobby Avila, Cleve.	.341
1955	Al Kaline, Det.	.340
1956	Mickey Mantle, N.Y.	.353
1957	Ted Williams, Bost.	.388
1958	Ted Williams, Bost.	.328
1959	Harvey Kuenn, Det.	.353
1960	Pete Runnels, Bost.	.320
1961	Norman Cash, Det.	.361
1962	Pete Runnels, Bost.	.326
1963	Carl Yastrzemski, Bost.	.321
1964	Tony Oliva, Minn.	.323
1965	Tony Oliva, Minn.	.321
1966	Frank Robinson, Balt.	.316
1967	Carl Yastrzemski, Bost.	.326
1968	Carl Yastrzemski, Bost.	.301
1969	Rod Carew, Minn.	.332
1970	Alex Johnson, Calif.	.329
1971	Tony Oliva, Minn.	.337
1972	Rod Carew, Minn.	.318
1973	Rod Carew, Minn.	.350
1974	Rod Carew, Minn.	.364
1975	Rod Carew, Minn.	.359
1976	George Brett, Kansas City	.333
1977	Rod Carew, Minn.	.388
1978	Rod Carew, Minn.	.333
1979	Fred Lynn, Boston	.333
1980	George Brett, Kansas City	.390
1981*	Carney Lansford, Bost.	.336
1982	Willie Wilson, Kansas City	.332

*Split season because of player strike.

NATIONAL LEAGUE HOME RUN CHAMPIONS

Year	Player, team	No.
1876	George Hall, Phila. Athletics	5
1877	George Shaffer, Louisville	3
1878	Paul Hines, Providence	4
1879	Charles Jones, Bost.	9
1880	James O'Rourke, Bost., and Harry Stovey, Worcester	6
1881	Dan Brouthers, Buffalo	8
1882	George Wood, Det.	7
1883	William Ewing, N.Y.	10
1884	Ed Williamson, Chi.	27
1885	Abner Dalrymple, Chi.	11
1886	Arthur Richardson, Det.	11
1887	Roger Connor, N.Y., and Wm. O'Brien, Wash.	17
1888	Roger Connor, N.Y.	14
1889	Sam Thompson, Phila.	20
1890	Tom Burns, Bklyn., and Mike Tiernan, N.Y.	13
1891	Harry Stovey, Bost., and Mike Tiernan, N.Y.	16
1892	Jim Holliday, Cin.	13
1893	Ed Delahanty, Phila.	19
1894	Hugh Duffy, Bost., and Robert Lowe, Bost.	18
1895	Bill Joyce, Wash.	17
1896	Ed Delahanty, Phila., and Sam Thompson, Phila.	13
1897	Nap Lajoie, Phila.	10
1898	James Collins, Bost.	14
1899	John Freeman, Wash.	25
1900	Herman Long, Bost.	12
1901	Sam Crawford, Cin.	16
1902	Tom Leach, Pitts.	6
1903	James Sheckard, Bklyn.	9
1904	Harry Lumley, Bklyn.	9
1905	Fred Odwell, Cin.	9
1906	Tim Jordan, Bklyn.	12
1907	David Brain, Bost.	10
1908	Tim Jordan, Bklyn.	12
1909	John Murray, N.Y.	7
1910	Fred Beck, Bost., and Frank Schulte, Chi.	10

Year	Player, team	No.
1911	Frank Schulte, Chi.	21
1912	Henry Zimmerman, Chi.	14
1913	Cliff Cravath, Phila.	19
1914	Cliff Cravath, Phila.	19
1915	Cliff Cravath, Phila.	24
1916	Davis Robertson, N.Y., and Fred Williams, Chi.	12
1917	Davis Robertson, N.Y., and Cliff Cravath, Phila.	12
1918	Cliff Cravath, Phila.	8
1919	Cliff Cravath, Phila.	12
1920	Cy Williams, Phila.	15
1921	George Kelly, N.Y.	23
1922	Rogers Hornsby, St. L.	42
1923	Cy Williams, Phila.	41
1924	Jacques Fournier, Bklyn.	27
1925	Rogers Hornsby, St. L.	39
1926	Hack Wilson, Chi.	21
1927	Hack Wilson, Chi., and Cy Williams, Phila.	30
1928	Hack Wilson, Chi., and Jim Bottomley, St. L.	31
1929	Chuck Klein, Phila.	43
1930	Hack Wilson, Chi.	56
1931	Chuck Klein, Phila.	31
1932	Chuck Klein, Phila., and Mel Ott, N.Y.	38
1933	Chuck Klein, Phila.	28
1934	Mel Ott, N.Y., and Rip Collins, St. L.	35
1935	Wally Berger, Bost.	34
1936	Mel Ott, N.Y.	33
1937	Mel Ott, N.Y., and Joe Medwick, St. L.	31
1938	Mel Ott, N.Y.	36
1939	John Mize, St. L.	28
1940	John Mize, St. L.	43
1941	Dolph Camilli, Bklyn.	34
1942	Mel Ott, N.Y.	30
1943	Bill Nicholson, Chi.	29
1944	Bill Nicholson, Chi.	33
1945	Tommy Holmes, Bost.	28

Year	Player, team	No.
1946	Ralph Kiner, Pitts.	23
1947	Ralph Kiner, Pitts., and John Mize, N.Y.	51
1948	Ralph Kiner, Pitts., and John Mize, N.Y.	40
1949	Ralph Kiner, Pitts.	54
1950	Ralph Kiner, Pitts.	47
1951	Ralph Kiner, Pitts.	42
1952	Ralph Kiner, Pitts., and Hank Sauer, Chi.	37
1953	Ed Mathews, Mil.	47
1954	Ted Kluszewski, Cin.	49
1955	Willie Mays, N.Y.	51
1956	Duke Snider, Bklyn.	43
1957	Henry Aaron, Mil.	44
1958	Ernie Banks, Chi.	47
1959	Ed Mathews, Mil.	46
1960	Ernie Banks, Chi.	41
1961	Orlando Cepeda, San Fran.	46
1962	Willie Mays, San Fran.	49
1963	Henry Aaron, Mil., and Willie McCovey, San Fran.	44
1964	Willie Mays, San Fran.	47
1965	Willie Mays, San Fran.	52
1966	Henry Aaron, Atlanta	44
1967	Henry Aaron, Atlanta	39
1968	Willie McCovey, San Fran.	36
1969	Willie McCovey, San Fran.	45
1970	Johnny Bench, Cin.	45
1971	Willie Stargell, Pitts.	48
1972	Johnny Bench, Cin.	40
1973	Willie Stargell, Pitts.	44
1974	Mike Schmidt, Phila.	36
1975	Mike Schmidt, Phila.	38
1976	Mike Schmidt, Phila.	38
1977	George Foster, Cin.	52
1978	George Foster, Cin.	40
1979	Dave Kingman, Chicago	48
1980	Mike Schmidt, Phila.	48
1981*	Mike Schmidt, Phila.	31
1982	Dave Kingman, N.Y.	37

*Split season because of player strike.

NATIONAL LEAGUE BATTING CHAMPIONS

Year	Player, Team	Avg
1876	Roscoe Barnes, Chicago	.404
1877	Jim White, Boston	.385
1878	Abner Dalrymple, Mil.	.356
1879	Cap Anson, Chicago	.407
1880	George Gore, Chicago	.365
1881	Cap Anson, Chicago	.399
1882	Dan Brouthers, Buffalo	.367
1883	Dan Brouthers, Buffalo	.371
1884	James O'Rourke, Buffalo	.350
1885	Roger Connor, N. Y.	.371
1886	King Kelly, Chicago	.388
1887	Cap Anson, Chicago	.421
1888	Cap Anson, Chicago	.343
1889	Dan Brouthers, Boston	.373
1890	John Glasscock, N. Y.	.336
1891	William Hamilton, Phila.	.338
1892	Dan Brouthers, Bklyn., and Clarence Childs, Cleve.	.335
1893	Hugh Duffy, Boston	.378

Year	Player, Team	Avg
1894	Hugh Duffy, Boston	.438
1895	Jesse Burkett, Cleveland	.423
1896	Jesse Burkett, Cleveland	.410
1897	Willie Keeler, Baltimore	.432
1898	Willie Keeler, Baltimore	.379
1899	Ed Delahanty, Phila.	.408
1900	Honus Wagner, Pittsburgh	.381
1901	Jesse Burkett, St. Louis	.382
1902	Clarence Beaumont, Pitts.	.357
1903	Honus Wagner, Pittsburgh	.355
1904	Honus Wagner, Pittsburgh	.349
1905	Cy Seymour, Cincinnati	.377
1906	Honus Wagner, Pittsburgh	.339
1907	Honus Wagner, Pittsburgh	.350
1908	Honus Wagner, Pittsburgh	.354
1909	Honus Wagner, Pittsburgh	.339
1910	Sherwood Magee, Philadelphia	.331
1911	Honus Wagner, Pittsburgh	.334

Year	Player, Team	Avg
1912	Henry Zimmerman, Chicago	.372
1913	Jake Daubert, Brooklyn	.350
1914	Jake Daubert, Brooklyn	.329
1915	Larry Doyle, New York	.320
1916	Hal Chase, Cincinnati	.339
1917	Edd Roush, Cincinnati	.341
1918	Zack Wheat, Brooklyn	.335
1919	Edd Roush, Cincinnati	.321
1920	Rogers Hornsby, St. Louis	.370
1921	Rogers Hornsby, St. Louis	.397
1922	Rogers Hornsby, St. Louis	.401
1923	Rogers Hornsby, St. Louis	.384
1924	Rogers Hornsby, St. Louis	.424
1925	Rogers Hornsby, St. Louis	.403
1926	Gene Hargrave, Cincinnati	.353
1927	Paul Waner, Pittsburgh	.380
1928	Rogers Hornsby, Boston	.387
1929	Lefty O'Doul, Phila.	.398
1930	Bill Terry, N. Y.	.401

Year	Player, Team	Avg	Year	Player, Team	Avg	Year	Player, Team	Avg
1931	Chick Hafey, St. Louis	.349	1949	Jackie Robinson, Brooklyn	.342	1967	Roberto Clemente, Pitts.	.357
1932	Lefty O'Doul, Brooklyn	.368	1950	Stan Musial, St. Louis	.346	1968	Pete Rose, Cincinnati	.335
1933	Chuck Klein, Phila.	.368	1951	Stan Musial, St. Louis	.355	1969	Pete Rose, Cincinnati	.348
1934	Paul Waner, Pittsburgh	.362	1952	Stan Musial, St. Louis	.336	1970	Rico Carty, Atlanta	.366
1935	Arky Vaughan, Pittsburgh	.385	1953	Carl Furillo, Brooklyn	.344	1971	Joe Torre, St. Louis	.363
1936	Paul Waner, Pittsburgh	.373	1954	Willie Mays, N. Y.	.345	1972	Billy Williams, Chicago	.333
1937	Joe Medwick, St. Louis	.374	1955	Richie Ashburn, Phila.	.338	1973	Pete Rose, Cincinnati	.338
1938	Ernie Lombardi, Cin.	.342	1956	Henry Aaron, Mil.	.328	1974	Ralph Garr, Atlanta	.353
1939	John Mize, St. Louis	.349	1957	Stan Musial, St. Louis	.351	1975	Bill Madlock, Chicago	.354
1940	Debs Garms, Pittsburgh	.355	1958	Richie Ashburn, Phila.	.350	1976	Bill Madlock, Chicago	.339
1941	Pete Reiser, Brooklyn	.343	1959	Henry Aaron, Mil.	.355	1977	Dave Parker, Pittsburgh	.338
1942	Ernie Lombardi, Boston	.330	1960	Dick Groat, Pittsburgh	.325	1978	Dave Parker, Pittsburgh	.334
1943	Stan Musial, St. Louis	.357	1961	Roberto Clemente, Pitts.	.351	1979	Keith Hernandez, St. Louis	.344
1944	Dixie Walker, Brooklyn	.357	1962	Tommy Davis, L. A.	.346	1980	Bill Buckner, Chicago	.324
1945	Phil Cavarretta, Chicago	.355	1963	Tommy Davis, L. A.	.326	1981*	Bill Madlock, Pittsburgh	.341
1946	Stan Musial, St. Louis	.365	1964	Roberto Clemente, Pitts.	.339	1982	Al Oliver, Montreal	.331
1947	Harry Walker, St. L.-Phila.	.363	1965	Roberto Clemente, Pitts.	.329			
1948	Stan Musial, St. Louis	.376	1966	Matty Alou, Pittsburgh	.342			

*Split season because of player strike.

AMERICAN LEAGUE PENNANT WINNERS

Year	Club	Manager	Won	Lost	Pct	Year	Club	Manager	Won	Lost	Pct
1901	Chicago	Clark C. Griffith	83	53	.610	1943[1]	New York	Joseph V. McCarthy	98	56	.636
1902	Philadelphia	Connie Mack	83	53	.610	1944	St. Louis	Luke Sewell	89	65	.578
1903[1]	Boston	Jimmy Collins	91	47	.659	1945[1]	Detroit	Steve O'Neill	88	65	.575
1904[2]	Boston	Jimmy Collins	95	59	.617	1946	Boston	Joseph E. Cronin	104	50	.675
1905	Philadelphia	Connie Mack	92	56	.622	1947[1]	New York	Stanley R. Harris	97	57	.630
1906[1]	Chicago	Fielder A. Jones	93	58	.616	1948[1]	Cleveland	Lou Boudreau	97	58	.626
1907	Detroit	Hugh A. Jennings	92	58	.613	1949[1]	New York	Casey Stengel	97	57	.630
1908	Detroit	Hugh A. Jennings	90	63	.588	1950[1]	New York	Casey Stengel	98	56	.636
1909	Detroit	Hugh A. Jennings	98	54	.645	1951[1]	New York	Casey Stengel	98	56	.636
1910[1]	Philadelphia	Connie Mack	102	48	.680	1952[1]	New York	Casey Stengel	95	59	.617
1911[1]	Philadelphia	Connie Mack	101	50	.669	1953[1]	New York	Casey Stengel	99	52	.656
1912[1]	Boston	J. Garland Stahl	105	47	.691	1954	Cleveland	Al Lopez	111	43	.721
1913[1]	Philadelphia	Connie Mack	96	57	.627	1955	New York	Casey Stengel	96	58	.623
1914	Philadelphia	Connie Mack	99	53	.651	1956[1]	New York	Casey Stengel	97	57	.630
1915[1]	Boston	William F. Carrigan	101	50	.669	1957	New York	Casey Stengel	98	56	.636
1916[1]	Boston	William F. Carrigan	91	63	.591	1958[1]	New York	Casey Stengel	92	62	.597
1917[1]	Chicago	Clarence H. Rowland	100	54	.649	1959	Chicago	Al Lopez	94	60	.610
1918[1]	Boston	Ed Barrow	75	51	.595	1960	New York	Casey Stengel	97	57	.630
1919	Chicago	William Gleason	88	52	.629	1961[1]	New York	Ralph Houk	109	53	.673
1920[1]	Cleveland	Tris Speaker	98	56	.636	1962[1]	New York	Ralph Houk	96	66	.593
1921	New York	Miller J. Huggins	98	55	.641	1963	New York	Ralph Houk	104	57	.646
1922	New York	Miller J. Huggins	94	60	.610	1964	New York	Yogi Berra	99	63	.611
1923[1]	New York	Miller J. Huggins	98	54	.645	1965	Minnesota	Sam Mele	102	60	.630
1924[1]	Washington	Stanley R. Harris	92	62	.597	1966[1]	Baltimore	Hank Bauer	97	63	.606
1925	Washington	Stanley R. Harris	96	55	.636	1967	Boston	Dick Williams	92	70	.568
1926	New York	Miller J. Huggins	91	63	.591	1968[1]	Detroit	Mayo Smith	103	59	.636
1927[1]	New York	Miller J. Huggins	110	44	.714	1969	Baltimore[3]	Earl Weaver	109	53	.673
1928[1]	New York	Miller J. Huggins	101	53	.656	1970[1]	Baltimore[3]	Earl Weaver	108	54	.667
1929[1]	Philadelphia	Connie Mack	104	46	.693	1971	Baltimore[4]	Earl Weaver	101	57	.639
1930[1]	Philadelphia	Connie Mack	102	52	.662	1972[1]	Oakland[5]	Dick Williams	93	62	.600
1931	Philadelphia	Connie Mack	107	45	.704	1973[1]	Oakland[6]	Dick Williams	94	68	.580
1932[1]	New York	Joseph V. McCarthy	107	47	.695	1974[1]	Oakland[6]	Alvin Dark	90	72	.556
1933	Washington	Joseph E. Cronin	99	53	.651	1975	Boston[4]	Darrell Johnson	95	65	.594
1934	Detroit	Gordon Cochrane	101	53	.656	1976	New York[7]	Billy Martin	97	62	.610
1935[1]	Detroit	Gordon Cochrane	93	58	.616	1977[1]	New York[7]	Billy Martin	100	62	.617
1936[1]	New York	Joseph V. McCarthy	102	51	.667	1978[1]	New York[7]	Billy Martin			
1937[1]	New York	Joseph V. McCarthy	102	52	.662			and Bob Lemon	100	63	.613
1938[1]	New York	Joseph V. McCarthy	99	53	.651	1979	Baltimore[8]	Earl Weaver	102	57	.642
1939[1]	New York	Joseph V. McCarthy	106	45	.702	1980	Kansas City[9]	Jim Frey	97	65	.599
1940	Detroit	Delmar D. Baker	90	64	.584	1981	New York[10]	Gene Michael–Bob			
1941[1]	New York	Joseph V. McCarthy	101	53	.656			Lemon	59	48	.551*
1942	New York	Joseph V. McCarthy	103	51	.669	1982	Milwaukee[11]	Harvey Kuenn	95	67	.586

*Split season because of player strike. 1. World Series winner. 2. No World Series. 3. Defeated Minnesota, Western Division winner, in playoff. 4. Defeated Oakland, Western Division Leader, in playoff. 5. Defeated Detroit, Eastern Division winner, in playoff. 6. Defeated Baltimore, Eastern Division winner, in playoff. 7. Defeated Kansas City, Western Division winner, in playoff. 8. Defeated California, Western Division winner, in playoff. 9. Defeated New York, Eastern Division winner, in playoff. 10. Defeated Oakland, Western Division winner, in playoff. 11. Defeated California, Western Division winner, in playoff.

NATIONAL LEAGUE PENNANT WINNERS

Year	Club	Manager	Won	Lost	Pct
1876	Chicago	Albert G. Spalding	52	14	.788
1877	Boston	Harry Wright	31	17	.646
1878	Boston	Harry Wright	41	19	.683
1879	Providence	George Wright	55	23	.705
1880	Chicago	Adrian C. Anson	67	17	.798
1881	Chicago	Adrian C. Anson	56	28	.667
1882	Chicago	Adrian C. Anson	55	29	.655
1883	Boston	John F. Morrill	63	35	.643
1884	Providence	Frank C. Bancroft	84	28	.750
1885	Chicago	Adrian C. Anson	87	25	.777
1886	Chicago	Adrian C. Anson	90	34	.726
1887	Detroit	W. H. Watkins	79	45	.637
1888	New York	James J. Mutrie	84	47	.641
1889	New York	James J. Mutrie	83	43	.659
1890	Brooklyn	William H. McGunnigle	86	43	.667
1891	Boston	Frank G. Selee	87	51	.630
1892	Boston	Frank G. Selee	102	48	.680
1893	Boston	Frank G. Selee	86	44	.662
1894	Baltimore	Edward H. Hanlon	89	39	.695
1895	Baltimore	Edward H. Hanlon	87	43	.669
1896	Baltimore	Edward H. Hanlon	90	39	.698
1897	Boston	Frank G. Selee	93	39	.705
1898	Boston	Frank G. Selee	102	47	.685
1899	Brooklyn	Edward H. Hanlon	88	42	.677
1900	Brooklyn	Edward H. Hanlon	82	54	.603
1901	Pittsburgh	Fred C. Clarke	90	49	.647
1902	Pittsburgh	Fred C. Clarke	103	36	.741
1903	Pittsburgh	Fred C. Clarke	91	49	.650
1904	New York[2]	John J. McGraw	106	47	.693
1905	New York[1]	John J. McGraw	105	48	.686
1906	Chicago	Frank L. Chance	116	36	.763
1907	Chicago[1]	Frank L. Chance	107	45	.704
1908	Chicago[1]	Frank L. Chance	99	55	.643
1909	Pittsburgh[1]	Fred C. Clarke	110	42	.724
1910	Chicago	Frank L. Chance	104	50	.675
1911	New York	John J. McGraw	99	54	.647
1912	New York	John J. McGraw	103	48	.682
1913	New York	John J. McGraw	101	51	.664
1914	Boston[1]	George T. Stallings	94	59	.614
1915	Philadelphia	Patrick J. Moran	90	62	.592
1916	Brooklyn	Wilbert Robinson	94	60	.610
1917	New York	John J. McGraw	98	56	.636
1918	Chicago	Fred L. Mitchell	84	45	.651
1919	Cincinnati[1]	Patrick J. Moran	96	44	.686
1920	Brooklyn	Wilbert Robinson	93	61	.604
1921	New York[1]	John J. McGraw	94	59	.614
1922	New York[1]	John J. McGraw	93	61	.604
1923	New York	John J. McGraw	95	58	.621
1924	New York	John J. McGraw	93	60	.608
1925	Pittsburgh[1]	William B. McKechnie	95	58	.621
1926	St. Louis[1]	Rogers Hornsby	89	65	.578
1927	Pittsburgh	Donie Bush	94	60	.610
1928	St. Louis	William B. McKechnie	95	59	.617
1929	Chicago	Joseph V. McCarthy	98	54	.645
1930	St. Louis	Gabby Street	92	62	.597
1931	St. Louis[1]	Gabby Street	101	53	.656
1932	Chicago	Charles J. Grimm	90	64	.584
1933	New York[1]	William H. Terry	91	61	.599
1934	St. Louis[1]	Frank F. Frisch	95	58	.621
1935	Chicago	Charles J. Grimm	100	54	.649
1936	New York	William H. Terry	92	62	.597
1937	New York	William H. Terry	95	57	.625
1938	Chicago	Gabby Hartnett	89	63	.586
1939	Cincinnati	William B. McKechnie	97	57	.630
1940	Cincinnati[1]	William B. McKechnie	100	53	.654
1941	Brooklyn	Leo E. Durocher	100	54	.649
1942	St. Louis[1]	William H. Southworth	106	48	.688
1943	St. Louis	William H. Southworth	105	49	.682
1944	St. Louis[1]	William H. Southworth	105	49	.682
1945	Chicago	Charles J. Grimm	98	56	.636
1946	St. Louis[1]	Edwin H. Dyer	98	58	.628
1947	Brooklyn	Burton E. Shotton	94	60	.610
1948	Boston	William H. Southworth	91	62	.595
1949	Brooklyn	Burton E. Shotton	97	57	.630
1950	Philadelphia	Edwin M. Sawyer	91	63	.591
1951	New York	Leo E. Durocher	98	59	.624
1952	Brooklyn	Charles W. Dressen	96	57	.630
1953	Brooklyn	Charles W. Dressen	105	49	.682
1954	New York[1]	Leo E. Durocher	97	57	.630
1955	Brooklyn[1]	Walter Alston	98	55	.641
1956	Brooklyn	Walter Alston	93	61	.604
1957	Milwaukee[1]	Fred Haney	95	59	.617
1958	Milwaukee	Fred Haney	92	62	.597
1959	Los Angeles[1]	Walter Alston	88	68	.564
1960	Pittsburgh[1]	Danny Murtaugh	95	59	.617
1961	Cincinnati	Fred Hutchinson	93	61	.604
1962	San Francisco	Alvin Dark	103	62	.624
1963	Los Angeles[1]	Walter Alston	99	63	.611
1964	St. Louis[1]	Johnny Keane	93	69	.574
1965	Los Angeles[1]	Walter Alston	97	65	.599
1966	Los Angeles	Walter Alston	95	67	.586
1967	St. Louis[1]	Red Schoendienst	101	60	.627
1968	St. Louis	Red Schoendienst	97	65	.599
1969	New York[1,3]	Gil Hodges	100	62	.617
1970	Cincinnati[4]	Sparky Anderson	102	60	.630
1971	Pittsburgh[1,5]	Danny Murtaugh	97	65	.599
1972	Cincinnati[4]	Sparky Anderson	95	59	.617
1973	New York[6]	Yogi Berra	82	79	.509
1974	Los Angeles[6]	Walter Alston	102	60	.630
1975	Cincinnati[1,4]	Sparky Anderson	108	54	.667
1976	Cincinnati[7,1]	Sparky Anderson	102	60	.630
1977	Los Angeles[7]	Tom Lasorda	98	64	.605
1978	Los Angeles[7]	Tom Lasorda	95	67	.586
1979[1]	Pittsburgh[6]	Chuck Tanner	98	64	.605
1980[1]	Philadelphia[8]	Dallas Green	91	71	.562
1981	Los Angeles[1,9]	Tom Lasorda	63	47	.573*
1982[1]	St. Louis[10]	Whitey Herzog	92	70	.568

*Split season because of player strike. 1. World Series winner. 2. No World Series. 3. Defeated Atlanta, Western Division winner, in playoff. 4. Defeated Pittsburgh, Eastern Division winner, in playoff. 5. Defeated San Francisco, Western Division winner, in playoff. 6. Defeated Cincinnati, Western Division winner, in playoff. 7. Defeated Philadelphia, Eastern Division winner, in playoff. 8. Defeated Houston, Western Division winner, in playoff. 9. Defeated Montreal, Eastern Division winner, in playoff. 10. Defeated Atlanta, Western Division winner, in playoff.

GAYLORD PERRY JOINS 300-VICTORY CLUB

Gaylord Perry, the 44-year-old right-hander for the Seattle Mariners, became only the 15th pitcher in baseball history to record 300 victories in 1982. Perry, who pitched for seven teams in both major leagues over 21 years, won his 300th on May 6. He is the only pitcher to win the Cy Young Award, for best pitcher of the year, in both major leagues. He finished the 1982 season with a 10–12 won-lost record and 307 career victories. He is also third in career strikeouts, with 3,452, behind Walter Johnson, the leader with 3,508, and Nolan Ryan of Houston, who is second with 3,494.

MOST VALUABLE PLAYERS

(Baseball Writers Association selections)

American League

1931 Lefty Grove, Philadelphia
1932–33 Jimmy Foxx, Philadelphia
1934 Mickey Cochrane, Detroit
1935 Hank Greenberg, Detroit
1936 Lou Gehrig, New York
1937 Charlie Gehringer, Detroit
1938 Jimmy Foxx, Boston
1939 Joe DiMaggio, New York
1940 Hank Greenberg, Detroit
1941 Joe DiMaggio, New York
1942 Joe Gordon, New York
1943 Spurgeon Chandler, New York
1944–45 Hal Newhouser, Detroit
1946 Ted Williams, Boston
1947 Joe DiMaggio, New York
1948 Lou Boudreau, Cleveland
1949 Ted Williams, Boston
1950 Phil Rizzuto, New York
1951 Yogi Berra, New York
1952 Bobby Shantz, Philadelphia
1953 Al Rosen, Cleveland
1954–55 Yogi Berra, New York
1956–57 Mickey Mantle, New York
1958 Jackie Jensen, Boston
1959 Nellie Fox, Chicago
1960–61 Roger Maris, New York
1962 Mickey Mantle, New York
1963 Elston Howard, New York
1964 Brooks Robinson, Baltimore
1965 Zoilo Versalles, Minnesota
1966 Frank Robinson, Baltimore
1967 Carl Yastrzemski, Boston
1968 Dennis McLain, Detroit
1969 Harmon Killebrew, Minnesota
1970 John (Boog) Powell, Baltimore
1971 Vida Blue, Oakland
1972 Dick Allen, Chicago
1973 Reggie Jackson, Oakland
1974 Jeff Burroughs, Texas
1975 Fred Lynn, Boston
1976 Thurman Munson, New York
1977 Rod Carew, Minnesota
1978 Jim Rice, Boston
1979 Don Baylor, California
1980 George Brett, Kansas City
1981 Rollie Fingers, Milwaukee

National League

1931 Frank Frisch, St. Louis
1932 Chuck Klein, Philadelphia
1933 Carl Hubbell, New York
1934 Dizzy Dean, St. Louis
1935 Gabby Hartnett, Chicago
1936 Carl Hubbell, New York
1937 Joe Medwick, St. Louis
1938 Ernie Lombardi, Cincinnati
1939 Bucky Walters, Cincinnati
1940 Frank McCormick, Cincinnati
1941 Dolph Camilli, Brooklyn
1942 Mort Cooper, St. Louis
1943 Stan Musial, St. Louis
1944 Marty Marion, St. Louis
1945 Phil Cavarretta, Chicago
1946 Stan Musial, St. Louis
1947 Bob Elliott, Boston
1948 Stan Musial, St. Louis
1949 Jackie Robinson, Brooklyn
1950 Jim Konstanty, Philadelphia
1951 Roy Campanella, Brooklyn
1952 Hank Sauer, Chicago
1953 Roy Campanella, Brooklyn
1954 Willie Mays, New York
1955 Roy Campanella, Brooklyn
1956 Don Newcombe, Brooklyn
1957 Henry Aaron, Milwaukee
1958–59 Ernie Banks, Chicago
1960 Dick Groat, Pittsburgh
1961 Frank Robinson, Cincinnati
1962 Maury Wills, Los Angeles
1963 Sandy Koufax, Los Angeles
1964 Ken Boyer, St. Louis
1965 Willie Mays, San Francisco
1966 Roberto Clemente, Pittsburgh
1967 Orlando Cepeda, St. Louis
1968 Bob Gibson, St. Louis
1969 Willie McCovey, San Francisco
1970 Johnny Bench, Cincinnati
1971 Joe Torre, St. Louis
1972 Johnny Bench, Cincinnati
1973 Pete Rose, Cincinnati
1974 Steve Garvey, Los Angeles
1975–76 Joe Morgan, Cincinnati
1977 George Foster, Cincinnati
1978 Dave Parker, Pittsburgh
1979 Willie Stargell, Pittsburgh
1979 Keith Hernandez, St. Louis
1980 Mike Schmidt, Philadelphia
1981 Mike Schmidt, Philadelphia

CY YOUNG AWARD

1956 Don Newcombe, Brooklyn N.L.
1957 Warren Spahn, Milwaukee N.L.
1958 Bob Turley, New York A.L.
1959 Early Wynn, Chicago A.L.
1960 Vernon Law, Pittsburgh, N.L.
1961 Whitey Ford, New York A.L.
1962 Don Drysdale, Los Angeles N.L.
1963 Sandy Koufax, Los Angeles N.L.
1964 Dean Chance, Los Angeles A.L.
1965 Sandy Koufax, Los Angeles N.L.
1966 Sandy Koufax, Los Angeles N.L.
1967 Jim Lonborg, Boston A.L.; Mike McCormick, San Francisco N.L.
1968 Dennis McLain, Detroit A.L.; Bob Gibson, St. Louis N.L.
1969 Mike Cuellar, Baltimore, and Dennis McLain, Detroit, tied in A.L.; Tom Seaver, N.Y. N.L.
1970 Jim Perry, Minnesota A.L.; Bob Gibson, St. Louis N.L.
1971 Vida Blue, Oakland A.L.; Ferguson Jenkins, Chicago N.L.
1972 Gaylord Perry, Cleveland A.L.; Steve Carlton, Phila. N.L.
1973 Jim Palmer, Baltimore A.L.; Tom Seaver, New York N.L.
1974 Catfish Hunter, Oakland A.L.; Mike Marshall, Los Angeles N.L.
1975 Jim Palmer, Baltimore A.L.; Tom Seaver, New York N.L.
1976 Jim Palmer, Baltimore A.L.; Randy Jones, San Diego N.L.
1977 Sparky Lyle, N.Y., A.L.; Steve Carlton, Philadelphia N.L.
1978 Ron Guidry, N.Y., A.L.; Gaylord Perry, San Diego N.L.
1979 Mike Flanagan, Baltimore, A.L.; Bruce Sutter, Chicago, N.L.
1980 Steve Stone, Baltimore, A.L.; Steve Carlton, Philadelphia, N.L.
1981 Rollie Fingers, Milwaukee, A.L.; Fernando Valenzuela, Los Angeles, N.L.

ROOKIE OF THE YEAR

(Baseball Writers Association selections)

American League

1949 Roy Sievers, St. Louis
1950 Walt Dropo, Boston
1951 Gil McDougald, New York
1952 Harry Byrd, Philadelphia
1953 Harvey Kuenn, Detroit
1954 Bob Grim, New York
1955 Herb Score, Cleveland
1956 Luis Aparicio, Chicago
1957 Tony Kubek, New York
1958 Albie Pearson, Washington
1959 Bob Allison, Washington
1960 Ron Hansen, Baltimore
1961 Don Schwall, Boston
1962 Tom Tresh, New York
1963 Gary Peters, Chicago
1964 Tony Oliva, Minnesota
1965 Curt Blefary, Baltimore
1966 Tommy Agee, Chicago
1967 Rod Carew, Minnesota
1968 Stan Bahnsen, New York
1969 Lou Piniella, Kansas City
1970 Thurman Munson, New York
1971 Chris Chambliss, Cleveland
1972 Carlton Fisk, Boston
1973 Alonzo Bumbry, Baltimore
1974 Mike Hargrove, Texas
1975 Fred Lynn, Boston
1976 Mark Fidrych, Detroit
1977 Eddie Murray, Baltimore
1978 Lou Whitaker, Detroit
1979 Alfredo Griffin, Toronto
1979 John Castino, Minnesota
1980 Joe Charboneau, Cleveland
1981 Dave Righetti, New York

National League

1949 Don Newcombe, Brooklyn
1950 Sam Jethroe, Boston
1951 Willie Mays, New York
1952 Joe Black, Brooklyn
1953 Jim Gilliam, Brooklyn
1954 Wally Moon, St. Louis
1955 Bill Virdon, St. Louis
1956 Frank Robinson, Cincinnati

1957	Jack Sanford, Philadelphia	1966	Tommy Helms, Cincinnati	1975	John Montefusco, San Francisco
1958	Orlando Cepeda, San Francisco	1967	Tom Seaver, New York	1976	Pat Zachry, Cincinnati
1959	Willie McCovey, San Francisco	1968	Johnny Bench, Cincinnati	1977	Andre Dawson, Montreal
1960	Frank Howard, Los Angeles	1969	Ted Sizemore, Los Angeles	1978	Bob Horner, Atlanta
1961	Billy Williams, Chicago	1970	Carl Morton, Montreal	1979	Rick Sutcliffe, Los Angeles
1962	Ken Hubbs, Chicago	1971	Earl Williams, Atlanta	1980	Steve Howe, Los Angeles
1963	Pete Rose, Cincinnati	1972	Jon Matlack, New York	1981	Fernando Valenzuela, Los Angeles
1964	Richie Allen, Philadelphia	1973	Gary Matthews, San Francisco		
1965	Jim Lefebvre, Los Angeles	1974	Bake McBride, St. Louis		

MAJOR LEAGUE LIFETIME RECORDS

Source: The Book of Baseball Records, published and copyrighted by Seymour Siwoff, New York, N.Y. 10036.

Leading Batters, by Average

(Over 2,000 Hits)

	Years	At Bats	Hits	Avg
Ty Cobb	24	11,429	4,191	.367
Rogers Hornsby	23	8,173	2,930	.358
Dan Brouthers	19	6,725	2,349	.349
Ed Delahanty	16	7,493	2,593	.346
Tris Speaker	22	10,196	3,515	.345
Willie Keeler	19	8,564	2,955	.345
Ted Williams	19	7,706	2,654	.345
Billy Hamilton	14	6,262	2,157	.344
Harry Heilmann	17	7,787	2,660	.342
Babe Ruth	22	8,399	2,873	.342
Jesse Burkett	16	8,389	2,872	.342
Bill Terry	14	6,428	2,193	.341
Lou Gehrig	17	8,001	2,721	.340
George Sisler	15	8,267	2,812	.340
Nap Lajoie	21	9,589	3,251	.339
Cap Anson	22	9,084	3,081	.339
Sam Thompson	15	6,004	2,016	.336
Al Simmons	20	8,761	2,927	.334
Eddie Collins	25	9,949	3,311	.333
Paul Waner	20	9,459	3,152	.333
Stan Musial	22	10,972	3,630	.331
Rod Carew*	16	8,071	2,672	.331
Heinie Manush	17	7,653	2,524	.330
Hugh Duffy	17	6,999	2,307	.330
Honus Wagner	21	10,427	3,430	.329
Joe DiMaggio	13	6,821	2,214	.325
Jimmie Foxx	20	8,134	2,646	.325

*Active player.

Leading Pitchers

(Over 250 Victories)

	Years	W	L	Pct
Cy Young	22	511	315	.619
Walter Johnson	21	416	279	.599
Grover Alexander	20	373	208	.642
Christy Mathewson	17	373	188	.665
James Galvin	15	365	309	.542
Warren Spahn	21	363	245	.597
Charles Nichols	15	360	202	.641
Tim Keefe	14	346	225	.606
John Clarkson	12	328	175	.652
Eddie Plank	17	325	190	.631
Mickey Welch	13	316	214	.596
Hoss Radbourne	11	308	191	.617
Gaylord Perry*	21	307	251	.550
Lefty Grove	20	300	141	.680
Early Wynn	23	300	244	.551
Steve Carlton*	18	285	184	.608
Robin Roberts	19	286	245	.539
Tony Mullane	14	282	221	.561
Jim Kaat*	24	283	236	.545
Ferguson Jenkins*	18	278	217	.561
Red Ruffing	22	273	225	.548
Burleigh Grimes	19	270	212	.560
Bob Feller	18	266	162	.621
Eppa Rixey	21	266	251	.515
Gus Weyhing	14	265	236	.529
Jim McCormick	10	264	217	.549
Tom Seaver*	16	264	156	.628
Jim Palmer*	17	263	145	.645
Ted Lyons	21	260	230	.531
Phil Niekro*	19	257	220	.539
Red Faber	20	254	212	.545
Carl Hubbell	16	253	154	.622
Bob Gibson	17	251	174	.591

*Active player.

BASEBALL'S PERFECTLY PITCHED GAMES[1]

(no opposing runner reached base)

John Richmond—Worcester vs. Cleveland (NL) June 12, 1880	1–0
John M. Ward—Providence vs. Buffalo (NL) June 17, 1880	5–0
Cy Young—Boston vs. Philadelphia (AL) May 5, 1904	3–0
Addie Joss—Cleveland vs. Chicago (AL) Oct. 2, 1908	1–0
Ernest Shore[2]—Boston vs. Washington (AL) June 23, 1917	4–0
Charles Robertson—Chicago vs. Detroit (AL) April 30, 1922	2–0
Don Larsen[3]—New York (AL) vs. Brooklyn (NL) Oct. 8, 1956	2–0
Jim Bunning—Philadelphia vs. New York (NL) June 21, 1964	6–0
Sandy Koufax—Los Angeles vs. Chicago (NL) Sept. 9, 1965	1–0
Jim Hunter—Oakland vs. Minnesota (AL) May 8, 1968	4–0
Len Barker—Cleveland vs. Toronto (AL) May 15, 1981	3–0

1. Harvey Haddix, of Pittsburgh, pitched 12 perfect innings against Milwaukee (NL), May 26, 1959 but lost game in 13th on error and hit. 2. Shore, relief pitcher for Babe Ruth who walked first batter before being ejected by umpire, retired 26 batters who faced him and baserunner was out stealing. 3. World Series.

MAJOR LEAGUE INDIVIDUAL ALL-TIME RECORDS

Highest Batting Average—.442, James O'Neill, St. Louis, A.A., 1887; .438, Hugh Duffy, Boston, N.L., 1894 (Since 1900—.424, Rogers Hornsby, St. Louis, N.L., 1924; .422, Nap Lajoie, Phil., A.L., 1901)
Most Times at Bat—12,364, Henry Aaron, Milwaukee N.L., 1954–65; Atlanta N.L., 1966–74; Milwaukee A.L., 1975–76.
Most Years Batted .300 or Better—23, Ty Cobb, Detroit A.L., 1906–26, Philadelphia A.L., 1927–28.
Most hits—4,191, Ty Cobb, Detroit A.L., 1905–26, Philadelphia A.L., 1927–28.
Most Hits, Season—257, George Sisler, St. Louis A.L., 1920.
Most Hits, Game (9 innings)—7, Wilbert Robinson, Baltimore N.L., 6 singles, 1 double, 1892. Rennie Stennett, Pittsburgh N.L., 4 singles, 2 doubles, 1 triple, 1975.
Most Hits, Game (extra innings)—9, John Burnett, Cleveland A.L., 18 innings, 7 singles, 2 doubles, 1932.
Most Hits in Succession—12, Mike Higgins, Boston A.L., in four games, 1938; Walt Dropo, Detroit A.L., in three games, 1952.
Most Consecutive Games Batted Safely—56, Joe DiMaggio, New York A.L., 1941.
Most Runs—2,244, Ty Cobb, Detroit A.L., 1905–26, Philadelphia A.L., 1927–28.
Most Runs, Season—196, William Hamilton, Philadelphia N.L., 1894. (Since 1900—177, Babe Ruth, New York A.L., 1921.)
Most Runs, Game—7, Guy Hecker, Louisville A.A., 1886. (Since 1900—6, by Mel Ott, New York N.L., 1934, 1944; Johnny Pesky, Boston A.L., 1946; Frank Torre, Milwaukee N.L., 1957.)
Most Runs Batted In—2,297, Henry Aaron, Milwaukee N.L., 1954–1965; Atlanta N.L., 1966–74; Milwaukee A.L., 1975–76.
Most Runs Batted in, Season—190, Hack Wilson, Chicago N.L., 1930.
Most Runs Batted In, Game—12, Jim Bottomley, St. Louis N.L., 1924.
Most Home Runs—755, Henry Aaron, Milwaukee N.L., 1954–1965; Atlanta N.L., 1966–74; Milwaukee A.L., 1975–76.
Most Home Runs, Season—61, Roger Maris, New York A.L., 1961 (162-game season); 60, Babe Ruth, New York A.L., 1927 (154-game season)
Most Home Runs with Bases Filled—23, Lou Gehrig, New York A.L., 1927–39.
Most 2-Base Hits—793, Tris Speaker, Boston A.L., 1907–15, Cleveland A.L., 1916–26, Washington A.L., 1927, Philadelphia A.L., 1928.
Most 2-Base Hits, Season—67, Earl Webb, Boston A.L., 1931.
Most 2-base Hits, Game—4, by many.
Most 3-Base Hits—312, Sam Crawford, Cincinnati N.L., 1899–1902, Detroit A.L., 1903–17.
Most 3-Base Hits, Season—36, Owen Wilson, Pittsburgh N.L., 1912.
Most 3-Base Hits, Game—4, George Strief, Philadelphia A.A., 1885; William Joyce, New York N.L., 1897. (Since 1900—3, by many.)
Most Games Played—3,298, Henry Aaron, Milwaukee N.L., 1954–1965; Atlanta, N.L., 1966–74; Milwaukee A.L., 1975–76.
Most Consecutive Games Played—2,130, Lou Gehrig, New York A.L., 1925–39.
Most Bases on Balls—2,056, Babe Ruth, Boston A.L., 1914–19; New York A.L., 1920–34, Boston N.L., 1935.
Most Bases on Balls, Season—170, Babe Ruth, New York A.L., 1923.
Most Bases on Balls, Game—6, Jimmy Foxx, Boston A.L., 1938.
Most Strikeouts, Season—189, Bobby Bonds, San Francisco N.L., 1970.
Most Strikeouts, Game (9 innings)—5, by many.
Most Strikeouts, Game (extra innings)—6, Carl Weilman, St. Louis A.L., 15 innings, 1913; Don Hoak, Chicago N.L., 17 innings, 1956; Fred Reichardt, California A.L., 17, innings, 1966; Billy Cowan, California A.L., 20, 1971; Cecil Cooper, Boston A.L., 15, 1974.
Most pinch-hits, lifetime—150, Manny Mota, S.F., 1962; Pitt., 1963–68; Montreal, 1969; L.A., 1969–80, N.L.
Most Pinch-hits, season—25, Jose Morales, Montreal N.L., 1976.
Most consecutive pinch-hits—9, Dave Philley, Phil., N.L., 1958 (8), 1959 (1).
Most pinch-hit home runs, lifetime—18, Gerald Lynch, Pitt.-Cin. N.L., 1957–66.
Most pinch-hit home runs, season—6, Johnny Frederick, Brooklyn, N.L., 1932.
Most stolen bases, lifetime (since 1900)—938, Lou Brock, Chicago N.L. 1961–64; St. Louis, N.L. 1964–79.
Most stolen bases, season—156, Harry Stovey, Phil., A.A., 1888. Since 1900: 130, Rickey Henderson, Oak., A.L., 1982; 118, Lou Brock, St. Lou., 1974.
Most stolen bases, game—7, George Gore, Chicago N.L. 1881; William Hamilton, Philadelphia N.L. 1894. (Since 1900—6, Eddie Collins, Philadelphia A.L., 1912.)
Most times stealing home, lifetime—35, Ty Cobb, Detroit-Phil. A.L., 1905–28.

MAJOR LEAGUE ALL-TIME PITCHING RECORDS

Most Games Won—511, Cy Young, Cleveland N.L., 1890–98, St. Louis N.L., 1899–1900, Boston A.L., 1901–08, Cleveland A.L., 1909–11, Boston N.L., 1911.
Most Games Won, Season—60, Hoss Radbourne, Providence N.L., 1884. (Since 1900—41, Jack Chesbro, New York A.L., 1904.)
Most Consecutive Games Won—24, Carl Hubbell, New York N.L., 1936 (16) and 1937 (8).
Most Consecutive Games Won, Season—19, Tim Keefe, New York N.L., 1888; Rube Marquard, New York N.L., 1912.
Most Years Won 20 or More Games—16, Cy Young, Cleveland N.L., 1891–98, St. Louis N.L., 1899–1900, Boston A.L., 1901–04, 1907–08.
Most Shutouts—113, Walter Johnson, Wash. A.L., 1907–27.
Most Shutouts, Season—16, Grover Alexander, Philadelphia N.L., 1916.
Most Consecutive Shutouts—6, Don Drysdale, Los Angeles, N.L., 1968.
Most Consecutive Scoreless Innings—58, Don Drysdale, Los Angeles, N.L., 1968.
Most Strikeouts—3,508, Walter Johnson, Washington A.L. 1907–27.
Most Strikeouts, Season—505, Matthew Kilroy, Baltimore A.A., 1886. (Since 1900—383, Nolan Ryan, California, A.L., 1973.)
Most Strikeouts, Game—21, Tom Cheney, Washington A.L. 1962, 16 innings. Nine innings: 19, Charles McSweeney, Providence N.L., 1884; Hugh Dailey, Chicago U.A., 1884. (Since 1900—19, Steve Carlton, St. Louis N.L. vs. New York, Sept. 15, 1969; Tom Seaver, New York N.L. vs. San Diego, April 22, 1970; Nolan Ryan, California A.L. vs. Boston, Aug. 12, 1974.)
Most Consecutive Strikeouts—10, Tom Seaver, New York N.L. vs. San Diego, April 22, 1970.
Most Games, Season—106, Mike Marshall, Los Angeles, N.L., 1974.
Most Complete Games, Season—74, William White, Cincinnati N.L., 1879. (Since 1900—48, Jack Chesbro, New York A.L., 1904.)

MAJOR LEAGUE ATTENDANCE RECORDS

Single game—78,672, San Francisco at Los Angeles (N.L.), April 18, 1958. (At Memorial Coliseum.)
Doubleheader—84,587, New York at Cleveland (A.L.), Sept. 12, 1954.
Night—78,382, Chicago at Cleveland (A.L.), Aug. 20, 1948.
Season, home—3,608,881, Los Angeles (N.L.), 1982.
Season, road—2,461,240, New York (A.L.), 1980.
Season, league—23,080,449, American League, 1982.
Season, both leagues—44,584,943, 1982.
World Series, single game—92,706, Chicago (A.L.) at Los Angeles (N.L.), Oct. 6, 1959.
World Series, all games (6)—420,784, Chicago (A.L.) and Los Angeles (N.L.), 1959.

MOST HOME RUNS IN ONE SEASON

(45 or More)

HR	Player/Team	Year
61	Roger Maris, New York (AL)	1961
60	Babe Ruth, New York (AL)	1927
59	Babe Ruth, New York (AL)	1921
58	Jimmy Foxx, Philadelphia (AL)	1932
58	Hank Greenberg, Detroit (AL)	1938
56	Hack Wilson, Chicago (NL)	1930
54	Babe Ruth, New York (AL)	1920
54	Babe Ruth, New York (AL)	1928
54	Ralph Kiner, Pittsburgh (NL)	1949
54	Mickey Mantle, New York (AL)	1961
52	Mickey Mantle, New York (AL)	1956
52	Willie Mays, San Francisco (NL)	1965
52	George Foster, Cincinnati (NL)	1977
51	Ralph Kiner, Pittsburgh (NL)	1947
51	John Mize, New York (NL)	1947
51	Willie Mays, New York (NL)	1955
50	Jimmy Foxx, Boston (AL)	1938
49	Babe Ruth, New York (AL)	1930
49	Lou Gehrig, New York (AL)	1934
49	Lou Gehrig, New York (AL)	1936
49	Ted Kluszewski, Cincinnati (NL)	1954
49	Willie Mays, San Francisco (NL)	1962
49	Harmon Killebrew, Minnesota (AL)	1964
49	Frank Robinson, Baltimore (AL)	1966
49	Harmon Killebrew, Minnesota (AL)	1969
48	Jimmy Foxx, Philadelphia (AL)	1933
48	Harmon Killebrew, Minnesota (AL)	1962
48	Willie Stargell, Pittsburgh (NL)	1971
48	Dave Kingman, Chicago (NL)	1979
48	Mike Schmidt, Philadelphia (NL)	1980
47	Babe Ruth, New York (AL)	1926
47	Ralph Kiner, Pittsburgh (NL)	1950
47	Ed Mathews, Milwaukee (NL)	1953
47	Ernie Banks, Chicago (NL)	1958
47	Willie Mays, San Francisco (NL)	1964
47	Henry Aaron, Atlanta (NL)	1971
47	Reggie Jackson, Oakland (AL)	1969
46	Babe Ruth, New York (AL)	1924
46	Babe Ruth, New York, (AL)	1929
46	Babe Ruth, New York (AL)	1931
46	Lou Gehrig, New York (AL)	1931
46	Joe DiMaggio, New York (AL)	1937
46	Ed Mathews, Milwaukee (NL)	1959
46	Orlando Cepeda, San Francisco (NL)	1961
46	Jim Rice, Boston (AL)	1978
45	Harmon Killebrew, Minnesota (AL)	1963
45	Willie McCovey, San Francisco (NL)	1969
45	Johnny Bench, Cincinnati (NL)	1970
45	Gorman Thomas, Milwaukee (AL)	1979
45	Henry Aaron, Milwaukee (NL)	1962

RODEO

PROFESSIONAL RODEO COWBOY ASSOCIATION, ALL AROUND COWBOY

1953	Bill Linderman
1954	Buck Rutherford
1955	Casey Tibbs
1956–59	Jim Shoulders
1960	Harry Tompkins
1961	Benny Reynolds
1962	Tom Nesmith
1963–65	Dean Oliver
1966–70	Larry Mahan
1971–72	Phil Lyne
1973	Larry Mahan
1974	Tom Ferguson
1975	Leo Camarillo and Tom Ferguson
1976–79	Tom Ferguson
1980	Paul Tierney
1981	Jimmie Cooper

CURLING

WORLD CHAMPIONSHIPS—1982

Men (Garmisch-Partenkirchen, West Germany, March 29–April 4, 1982)—Canada, Al Hackner, skip (defeated Switzerland, 9–7, in final)
Women (Geneva, Switzerland, March 21–27, 1982)—Denmark, Helena Blach, skip (defeated Sweden, 8–7, in final)

UNITED STATES CHAMPIONSHIPS—1982

Men (Brookline, Mass., Feb. 28–March 6, 1982)—Madison, Wis., Steve Brown, skip
Women (Bowling Green, Ohio)—Illinois, Ruth Schwenker, skip (defeated North Dakota, 11–3, in final)
Mixed (Madison, Wis., March 15–19, 1982)—Minnesota, Bemidji, Mark Haluptzak, skip (defeated Illinois, Willamette, 8–2, in final)
Junior—Seattle, Wash., Dale Risling, skip (defeated Minnesota in final)

TUMBLING—1982

World men's champion—Steve Elliott, Amarillo, Tex.
Women's champion—Jill Hollenbeck, Rockford, Ill.
World men's trampoline champion—Carl Furrer, Britain
World women's trampoline champion—Ruth Keller, Switzerland

MAJOR LEAGUE BALL PARK STATISTICS*

lf—Left-field foul line; cf—center field; rf—right-field foul line

Club, nickname, and grounds	Distance, feet			Seating capacity	Record Attendance[4]		
	lf	cf	rf		Day game	Double-header[3]	Night game
American League							
Baltimore Orioles—Memorial Stadium	309	405	309	53,208	51,798	46,796	51,649
Boston Red Sox—Fenway Park	315	390	302	33,536	36,350	41,766	36,228
California Angels—Anaheim Stadium	333	404	370	67,335	42,655	37,768	53,591
Chicago White Sox—Comiskey Park	352	402	375	44,492	51,560	55,555	53,940
Cleveland Indians—Municipal Stadium	320	400	320	74,208	74,420	84,587	78,382
Detroit Tigers—Tiger Stadium	340	440	325	52,687	57,888	58,369	56,586
Kansas City Royals—Royals Stadium	330	410	330	40,635	41,329	40,525	41,860
Milwaukee Brewers—County Stadium	362	402	362	53,192	55,120	49,054	52,968
Minnesota Twins—Metropolitan Stadium[5]	385	407	367	54,711	46,963	43,419	45,890
New York Yankees—Yankee Stadium[1]	387	417	353	57,545	73,205	81,841	74,747
Oakland A's—Oakland Coliseum	330	397	330	50,255	48,758	48,592	47,741
Seattle Mariners—Kingdome	316	410	316	59,438	47,353	25,344	57,762
Texas Rangers—Arlington Stadium	330	400	330	41,284	40,078	24,241	41,097
Toronto Blue Jays—Exhibition Stadium	330	400	330	43,737	44,649	41,308	39,347
National League							
Atlanta Braves—Atlanta Stadium	330	402	330	52,785	51,275	46,489	53,775
Chicago Cubs—Wrigley Field	355	400	353	37,272	46,572	46,965	No lights
Cincinnati Reds—Riverfront Stadium	330	404	330	52,392	53,390	52,147	52,315
Houston Astros—Astrodome	340	406	340	45,000	49,442	42,648	50,908
Los Angeles Dodgers—Dodger Stadium[2]	330	400	330	56,000	78,672	53,856	67,550
Montreal Expos—Olympic Stadium	325	404	325	58,838	57,592	59,282	57,121
New York Mets—Shea Stadium	338	410	338	55,300	56,738	57,175	56,658
Philadelphia Phillies—Veterans Stadium	330	408	330	65,454	60,120	40,720	63,283
Pittsburgh Pirates—Three Rivers Stadium	335	400	335	54,499	51,726	49,412	48,846
St. Louis Cardinals—Busch Memorial Stadium	330	414	330	50,222	50,548	49,743	50,340
San Diego Padres—Jack Murphy Stadium	330	420	330	51,362	42,142	43,373	50,569
San Francisco Giants—Candlestick Park	335	400	335	58,000	56,196	50,924	55,920

*At end of 1981 season. 1. Distance and capacity after rebuilding; attendance records prior to rebuilding. 2. Played also in Los Angeles Coliseum. 3. Two day games. 4. Through 1981 season. 5. Moved into Hubert H. Humphrey Metrodome for 1982 season; distance for 1982, attendance figures through 1981.

MAJOR LEAGUE FRANCHISE SHIFTS AND ADDITIONS

1953—Boston Braves (N.L.) became Milwaukee Braves. Home attendance, last season in Boston (1952), 281,278; first season in Milwaukee (1953), 1,826,397.

1954—St. Louis Browns (A.L.) became Baltimore Orioles. Home attendance, last season in St. Louis (1953), 297,238; first season in Baltimore (1954), 1,060,910.

1955—Philadelphia Athletics (A.L.) became Kansas City Athletics. Home attendance, last season in Phila. (1954), 627,-100; first season in K.C. (1955), 1,393,054.

1958—New York Giants (N.L.) became San Francisco Giants. Home attendance, last season in New York (1957), 653,923; first season in San Francisco (1958), 1,272,625.

1958—Brooklyn Dodgers (N.L.) became Los Angeles Dodgers. Home attendance, last season in Brooklyn (1957), 1,028,258; first season in Los Angeles (1958), 1,845,556.

1961—Washington Senators (A.L.) became Minnesota Twins. Home attendance, last season in Washington (1960), 743,-404; first season in Minneapolis-St. Paul (1961), 1,256,722.

1961—Los Angeles Angels (later renamed the California Angels) enfranchised by the American League.

1961—Washington Senators enfranchised by the American League (a new team, replacing the former Washington club, whose franchise was moved to Minneapolis-St. Paul).

1962—Houston Colt .45's (later renamed the Houston Astros) enfranchised by the National League.

1962—New York Mets enfranchised by the National League. Home attendance, first season (1962), 922,530.

1966—Milwaukee Braves (N.L.) became Atlanta Braves. Home attendance, last season in Milwaukee (1965), 555,584; first season in Atlanta (1966), 1,539,801.

1968—Kansas City Athletics (A.L.) became Oakland Athletics.

1969—Two major leagues each added two teams for totals of 12 and split into two divisions. American League additions: Kansas City Royals and Seattle Pilots; National League additions: Montreal Expos and San Diego Padres. The Division leaders met for the league championship and the two league winners met in the World Series.

1970—Seattle franchise was shifted to Milwaukee, with final court approval coming on March 31. Club was renamed Milwaukee Brewers.

1971—Washington franchise shifted at end of season to Dallas-Fort Worth Texas Rangers with field at Arlington, Tex.

1977—Seattle and Toronto began play in American League.

MAJOR LEAGUE BASEBALL BREAKS ATTENDANCE RECORD IN 1982

Major league baseball attendance rose to 44,584,943 in 1982, breaking a record set in 1979 when the 26 teams drew 43,550,398 fans to the ball parks. The American League also broke a mark it set in 1979, drawing 23,080,440 in 1982 compared with the previous record of 22,371,979. The Los Angeles Dodgers broke their own home attendance record by drawing 3,608,881 fans, bettering the figure of 3,347,845 of 1978, which was the previous record for a major league team.

MAJOR LEAGUE BASEBALL—1982

AMERICAN LEAGUE (Final Standing—1982)

EASTERN DIVISION

Team	W	L	Pct	GB
Milwaukee Brewers	95	67	.586	—
Baltimore Orioles	94	68	.580	1
Boston Red Sox	89	73	.549	6
Detroit Tigers	83	79	.512	12
New York Yankees	79	83	.488	16
Cleveland Indians	78	84	.481	17
Toronto Blue Jays	78	84	.481	17

WESTERN DIVISION

Team	W	L	Pct	GB
California Angels	93	69	.574	—
Kansas City Royals	90	72	.556	3
Chicago White Sox	87	75	.537	6
Seattle Mariners	76	86	.469	17
Oakland A's	68	94	.420	25
Texas Rangers	64	98	.395	29
Minnesota Twins	60	102	.370	33

AMERICAN LEAGUE PLAYOFFS—1982

1st game, Anaheim, Calif., Oct. 5

Milwaukee	021	000	000	—	3	7	2
California	104	210	00X	—	8	10	0

Caldwell, Slaton (4), Ladd (7), Bernard (8); John. Winner: John. Loser: Caldwell. Home Runs: Milwaukee: Thomas. California: Lynn. Attendance: 64,406.

2nd game, Anaheim, Calif., Oct. 6

Milwaukee	000	020	000	—	2	5	0
California	021	100	00X	—	4	6	0

Vuckovich; Kison. Winner: Kison. Loser: Vuckovich. Home Runs: Milwaukee: Molitor. California: Reggie Jackson. Attendance: 64,179.

3rd game, Milwaukee, Oct. 8

California	000	000	030	—	3	8	0
Milwaukee	000	300	20X	—	5	6	0

Zahn, Witt (4), Hassler (7); Sutton, Ladd (8). Winner: Sutton. Loser: Zahn. Home Runs: California: Boone. Milwaukee: Molitor. Attendance: 50,135.

4th game, Milwaukee, Oct. 9

California	000	001	040	—	5	5	3
Milwaukee	030	301	02X	—	9	9	2

John, Goltz (4), Sanchez (8); Haas, Slaton (8). Winner: Haas. Loser: John. Home Runs: California: Baylor. Milwaukee: Brouhard. Attendance: 51,003.

5th game, Milwaukee, Oct. 10

California	101	100	000	—	3	11	1
Milwaukee	100	100	20X	—	4	6	4

Kison, Sanchez (6), Hassler (7); Vuckovich, McClure (7), Ladd (9). Winner: McClure. Loser: Sanchez. Home Runs: Milwaukee: Oglivie. Attendance: 54,968.

AMERICAN LEAGUE LEADERS—1982

Batting—Willie Wilson, Kansas City	.332
Runs—Paul Molitor, Milwaukee	136
Hits—Robin Yount, Milwaukee	210
Runs batted in—Hal McRae, Kansas City	133
Doubles—Robin Yount, Milwaukee	46
Triples—Willie Wilson, Kansas City	15
Home runs—Gorman Thomas, Milwaukee, and Reggie Jackson, California	39
Stolen bases—Rickey Henderson, Oakland	130

Pitching

Victories—LaMarr Hoyt, Chicago	19
Earned run average—Rick Sutcliffe, Cleveland	2.96
Strikeouts—Floyd Bannister, Seattle	209
Shutouts—Dave Stieb, Toronto	5

NATIONAL LEAGUE (Final Standing—1982)

EASTERN DIVISION

Team	W	L	Pct	GB
St. Louis Cardinals	92	70	.568	—
Philadelphia Phillies	89	73	.549	3
Montreal Expos	86	76	.531	6
Pittsburgh Pirates	84	78	.519	8
Chicago Cubs	73	89	.451	19
New York Mets	65	97	.401	27

WESTERN DIVISION

Team	W	L	Pct	GB
Atlanta Braves	89	73	.549	—
Los Angeles Dodgers	88	74	.543	1
San Francisco Giants	87	75	.537	2
San Diego Padres	81	81	.500	8
Houston Astros	77	85	.475	12
Cincinnati Reds	61	101	.377	28

NATIONAL LEAGUE PLAYOFFS—1982

1st game, St. Louis, Oct. 6

Atlanta	000	000	000	—	0	3	0
St. Louis	001	005	01X	—	7	14	1

Perez, Bedrosian (6), Moore (6), Walk (9); Forsch. Winner: Forsch. Loser: Perez. Attendance: 53,008.

2nd game, St. Louis, Oct. 9

Atlanta	002	010	000	—	3	6	0
St. Louis	100	001	011	—	4	9	1

P. Niekro, Garber (7); Stuper, Bair (7), Sutter (8). Winner: Sutter. Loser: Garber. Attendance: 53,408.

3rd game, Atlanta, Oct. 10

St. Louis	040	010	001	—	6	12	0
Atlanta	000	000	200	—	2	6	1

Andujar, Sutter (7); Camp, Perez (2), Moore (5), Mahler (7), Bedrosian (8), Garber (9). Winner: Andujar. Loser: Camp. Home Runs: St. Louis: McGee. Attendance: 52,173.

NATIONAL LEAGUE LEADERS—1982

Batting—Al Oliver, Montreal	.331
Runs—Lonnie Smith, St. Louis	120
Hits—Al Oliver, Montreal	204
Runs batted in—Al Oliver, Montreal	109
Doubles—Al Oliver, Montreal	43
Triples—Dick Thon, Houston	10
Home runs—Dave Kingman, New York	37
Stolen bases—Tim Raines, Montreal	78

Pitching

Victories—Steve Carlton, Philadelphia	23
Earned run average—Steve Rogers, Montreal	2.40
Strikeouts—Steve Carlton, Philadelphia	286
Shutouts—Steve Carlton, Philadelphia	6

AMERICAN LEAGUE AVERAGES—1982

(Unofficial)

Batting—Club

	AB	R	H	HR	RBI	PCT
Kansas City	5,629	784	1,603	132	746	.285
Milwaukee	5,733	891	1,599	216	843	.279
Boston	5,596	753	1,536	136	705	.274
California	5,532	814	1,518	186	760	.274
Chicago	5,575	786	1,523	136	747	.273
Detroit	5,590	729	1,489	177	684	.266
Baltimore	5,557	774	1,478	179	735	.266
Cleveland	5,559	683	1,458	109	639	.262
Toronto	5,526	651	1,447	106	605	.262
Minnesota	5,545	657	1,427	148	623	.257
New York	5,526	709	1,417	161	666	.256
Seattle	5,626	651	1,431	130	613	.254
Texas	5,445	590	1,354	115	558	.249
Oakland	5,448	691	1,287	149	659	.236

Batting Leaders

Player/Team	AB	R	H	HR	RBI	PCT
Wilson, Kansas City	585	87	194	3	46	.332
Yount, Milwaukee	635	129	210	29	114	.331
Carew, California	523	88	167	3	44	.319
Murray, Baltimore	550	87	174	32	110	.316
Cooper, Milwaukee	654	104	205	32	121	.313
Paciorek, Chicago	382	49	119	11	55	.312
Garcia, Toronto	597	89	185	5	42	.310
Rice, Boston	573	86	177	24	97	.309
McRae, Kansas City	613	91	189	27	133	.308
Harrah, Cleveland	602	100	183	25	78	.304
Molitor, Milwaukee	666	136	201	19	71	.302
DeCinces, California	575	94	173	30	97	.301
Lansford, Boston	482	65	145	11	63	.301
Hrbek, Minnesota	532	82	160	23	92	.301
Brett, Kansas City	552	101	166	21	82	.301
Mumphrey, New York	477	76	143	9	68	.300
Lynn, California	472	89	141	21	86	.299
White, Kansas City	524	71	156	11	56	.298
Bochte, Seattle	509	58	151	12	70	.297
Bell, Texas	537	62	159	13	67	.296
Gantner, Milwaukee	447	48	132	4	43	.295
Bonnell, Toronto	437	59	128	6	49	.293
Evans, Boston	609	122	178	32	98	.292
Zisk, Seattle	503	61	147	21	61	.292
Luzinski, Chicago	583	87	170	18	102	.292
Herndon, Detroit	614	92	179	23	88	.292

Leading Pitchers

(15 or more decisions)

Player/Team	IP	H	BB	SO	W	L	ERA
Spillner, Cleveland	133	117	45	90	12	10	2.49
Quisenberry, Kansas City	136	126	12	46	9	7	2.57
Sutcliffe, Cleveland	216	174	98	142	14	8	2.96
Stanley, Boston	168	161	50	83	12	7	3.10
Palmer, Baltimore	227	195	63	103	15	5	3.13
Kison, California	142	120	44	86	10	5	3.17
Petry, Detroit	246	220	100	132	15	9	3.22
Stieb, Toronto	288	271	75	141	17	14	3.25
Underwood, Oakland	153	136	68	79	10	6	3.29
Vuckovich, Milwaukee	223	234	102	105	18	6	3.34
Beattie, Seattle	172	149	65	140	8	12	3.34
Bannister, Seattle	247	225	77	209	12	13	3.33
Hoyt, Chicago	239	248	48	124	19	15	3.53
Wilcox, Detroit	193	187	85	112	12	10	3.62
Tudor, Boston	195	215	59	146	13	10	3.63
Castillo, Minnesota	218	194	85	124	13	11	3.66
Udjur, Detroit	178	150	69	86	10	10	3.69
John, California (N.Y.)	221	239	39	68	14	12	3.69
Clancy, Toronto	266	251	77	139	16	14	3.71
Zahn, California	229	225	65	81	18	8	3.73
Eckersley, Boston	224	228	43	127	13	13	3.73
Blue, Kansas City	181	163	80	103	13	12	3.78
Righetti, New York	183	155	108	163	11	10	3.79
Guidry, New York	222	216	69	162	14	8	3.81
Koosman, Chicago	173	194	38	88	11	7	3.84

NATIONAL LEAGUE AVERAGES—1982

(Unofficial)

Batting—Club

	AB	R	H	HR	RBI	PCT
Pittsburgh	5,614	724	1,535	134	688	.273
St. Louis	5,455	685	1,439	67	632	.264
Los Angeles	5,642	691	1,487	138	661	.264
Montreal	5,557	697	1,454	133	656	.262
Philadelphia	5,454	664	1,417	112	624	.260
Chicago	5,531	676	1,436	102	647	.260
San Diego	5,575	675	1,435	81	611	.257
Atlanta	5,507	739	1,411	146	687	.256
San Francisco	5,499	673	1,393	133	631	.253
Cincinnati	5,479	545	1,375	82	496	.251
New York	5,510	609	1,361	97	568	.247
Houston	5,440	569	1,342	74	533	.247

Batting Leaders

Player/Team	AB	R	H	HR	RBI	PCT
Oliver, Montreal	617	90	204	22	109	.331
Madlock, Pittsburgh	566	92	181	19	95	.319
Durham, Chicago	539	84	168	22	90	.312
L. Smith, St. Louis	592	120	182	8	69	.307
Buckner, Chicago	657	93	201	15	105	.306
Guerrero, Los Angeles	575	87	175	32	100	.304
Dawson, Montreal	608	107	183	23	83	.301
Baker, Los Angeles	570	80	171	23	88	.300
Hernandez, St. Louis	579	79	173	7	94	.299
McGee, St. Louis	422	43	125	4	56	.296
Pena, Pittsburgh	497	53	147	11	63	.296
Kennedy, San Diego	562	75	166	21	97	.295
Knight, Houston	609	72	179	6	70	.294
Carter, Montreal	557	91	163	29	97	.293
Morgan, San Francisco	463	68	134	14	61	.289
Lezcano, San Diego	470	73	136	16	84	.289
Oberkfell, St. Louis	470	55	136	2	34	.289
Cedeno, Cincinnati	492	52	142	8	57	.289
Diaz, Philadelphia	525	69	151	18	85	.288
Concepcion, Cincinnati	572	48	164	5	53	.287
Richards, San Diego	521	63	149	3	28	.286
Landreaux, Los Angeles	461	71	131	7	50	.284
Maddox, Philadelphia	412	39	117	8	61	.284
Thompson, Pittsburgh	550	87	156	31	101	.284
Jones, San Diego	424	69	120	12	61	.283

Leading Pitchers

(15 or more decisions)

	IP	H	BB	SO	W	L	ERA
Rogers, Montreal	277	245	65	179	19	8	2.40
J. Niekro, Houston	270	224	64	130	17	12	2.47
Andujar, St. Louis	265	237	50	137	15	10	2.47
Show, San Diego	150	117	48	88	10	6	2.64
Soto, Cincinnati	257	202	71	274	14	13	2.79
Tekulve, Pittsburgh	128	113	46	66	12	8	2.87
Valenzuela, Los Angeles	285	247	83	199	19	13	2.87
Candelaria, Pittsburgh	174	166	37	133	12	7	2.94
Breining, San Francisco	143	146	52	98	11	6	3.08
Carlton, Philadelphia	295	253	86	286	23	11	3.10
Reuss, Los Angeles	254	232	50	138	18	11	3.11
Krukow, Philadelphia	208	211	82	138	13	11	3.12
Lollar, San Diego	232	192	87	150	16	9	3.13
Laskey, San Francisco	189	186	43	88	13	12	3.14

Jenkins, Chicago	217	221	68	134	14	15	3.15
Ryan, Houston	250	196	109	245	16	12	3.16
Lea, Montreal	177	145	56	115	12	10	3.24
Swan, New York	166	165	37	67	11	7	3.35
Stuper, St. Louis	136	137	55	53	9	7	3.36
Berenyi, Cincinnati	222	208	96	157	9	18	3.36
Welch, Los Angeles	235	199	81	176	16	11	3.36
Sanderson, Montreal	224	213	58	158	12	12	3.46
Christenson, Philadelphia	223	212	53	145	9	10	3.47
Forsch, St. Louis	233	238	54	69	15	9	3.48
Gullickson, Montreal	236	231	61	155	12	14	3.57

WORLD SERIES—1982

St. Louis Cardinals (NL) defeated Milwaukee Brewers (AL), 4 games to 3

1st Game—St. Louis, Oct. 12

MILWAUKEE (A)	AB	R	H	BI	ST. LOUIS (N)	AB	R	H	BI
Molitor, 3b	6	1	5	2	Herr, 2b	3	0	0	0
Yount, ss	6	1	4	2	L. Smith, lf	4	0	0	0
Cooper, 1b	4	1	0	0	Hernandez, 1b	4	0	0	0
Simmons, c	5	1	2	1	Hendrick, rf	4	0	0	0
Oglivie, lf	4	1	0	0	Tenace, dh	3	0	0	0
Thomas, cf	4	0	1	1	Porter, c	3	0	2	0
Howell, dh	2	0	0	0	Green, cf	3	0	0	0
Money, dh	2	1	1	1	Oberkfell, 3b	3	0	1	0
Moore, rf	5	2	2	0	O. Smith, ss	3	0	0	0
Gantner, 2b	4	2	2	2	**Total**	**30**	**0**	**3**	**0**
Total	**42**	**10**	**17**	**9**					

Milwaukee	**200**	**112**	**004**	**—**	**10**
St. Louis	**000**	**000**	**000**	**—**	**0**

E—Hernandez. DP—St. Louis. LOB—Milwaukee 10, St. Louis 4. 2B—Porter, Moore, Yount. 3B—Gantner. HR—Simmons. S—Gantner.

	IP	H	R	ER	BB	SO
Milwaukee						
Caldwell (W)	9	3	0	0	1	3
St. Louis						
Forsch (L)	5⅔	10	6	4	1	1
Kaat	1⅓	1	0	0	1	1
LaPoint	1⅔	3	2	2	1	0
Lahti	⅓	3	2	2	0	1

HBP—by Forsch (Howell). Time of game—2:30. Attendance—53,723.

2nd Game—St. Louis, Oct. 13

MILWAUKEE (A)	AB	R	H	BI	ST. LOUIS (N)	AB	R	H	BI
Molitor, 3b	5	1	2	0	Herr, 2b	3	1	1	1
Yount, ss	4	1	1	1	Oberkfell, 3b	3	1	2	1
Cooper, 1b	5	0	3	1	Tenace, ph	1	0	0	0
Simmons, c	3	1	1	1	Ramsey, 3b	0	0	0	0
Oglivie, lf	4	0	1	0	Hernandez, 1b	3	0	0	0
Thomas, cf	3	0	0	0	Hendrick, rf	3	2	0	0
Howell, dh	4	1	0	0	Porter, c	4	0	2	2
Moore, rf	4	0	2	1	L. Smith, lf	3	0	0	0
Gantner, 2b	3	0	0	0	Iorg, dh	2	0	1	0
Total	**35**	**4**	**10**	**4**	Green, ph	1	0	0	0
					Braun, ph	0	0	0	1
					McGee, cf	4	1	0	0
					O. Smith, ss	4	0	2	0
					Total	**31**	**5**	**8**	**5**

Milwaukee	**012**	**010**	**000**	**—**	**4**
St. Louis	**002**	**002**	**01X**	**—**	**5**

E—Oglivie. DP—St. Louis. LOB—Milwaukee 8, St. Louis 7. 2B—Moore, Herr, Yount, Porter, Cooper. HR—Simmons. SB—Molitor, McGee, Oberkfell, O. Smith.

	IP	H	R	ER	BB	SO
Milwaukee						
Sutton	6	5	4	4	1	3
McClure (L)	1⅓	2	1	1	2	2
Ladd	⅔	1	0	0	2	0
St. Louis						
Stuper	4	6	4	4	3	3
Kaat	⅔	1	0	0	0	0
Bair	2	1	0	0	0	3
Sutter (W)	2⅓	2	0	0	1	1

WP—Stuper, 2. Time of game—2:54. Attendance—53,723.

3rd Game—Milwaukee, Oct. 15

ST. LOUIS (N)	AB	R	H	BI	MILWAUKEE (A)	AB	R	H	BI
Herr, 2b	5	0	0	0	Molitor, 3b	4	0	0	0
Oberkfell, 3b	4	0	0	0	Yount, ss	3	1	0	0
Hernandez, 1b	4	0	0	0	Cooper, 1b	4	1	1	2
Hendrick, rf	2	1	1	0	Simmons, c	4	0	1	0
Porter, c	4	0	0	0	Oglivie, lf	4	0	0	0
L. Smith, lf	4	2	2	0	Thomas, cf	4	0	1	0
Green, lf	0	0	0	0	Howell, dh	2	0	0	0
Iorg, dh	4	1	1	0	Money, dh	1	0	0	0
McGee, cf	3	2	2	4	Moore, rf	3	0	0	0
O. Smith, ss	3	0	0	1	Gantner, 2b	3	0	2	0
Total	**33**	**6**	**6**	**5**	**Total**	**32**	**2**	**5**	**2**

St. Louis	**000**	**030**	**201**	**—**	**6**
Milwaukee	**000**	**000**	**020**	**—**	**2**

E—Cooper, Gantner, Simmons, Hernandez. DP—St. Louis. LOB—St. Louis 4, Milwaukee 6. 2B—Gantner, L. Smith, Iorg. 3B—L. Smith. HRs—McGee 2; Cooper.

	IP	H	R	ER	BB	SO
St. Louis						
Andujar (W)	6⅓	3	0	0	1	3
Kaat	⅓	1	0	0	0	1
Bair	0	0	0	0	1	0
Sutter	2⅓	1	2	2	1	1
Milwaukee						
Vuckovich (L)	8⅔	6	6	4	3	1
McClure	⅓	0	0	0	0	0

Time of game—2:53. Attendance—56,556.

HENDERSON OF A'S SETS STOLEN-BASES RECORD

Rickey Henderson of the Oakland A's broke the major league record for stolen bases in one season on Aug. 27, 1982, at Milwaukee when he stole his 119th base in the third inning. The previous record of 118 was held by Lou Brock of St. Louis and was set in 1974. Henderson had broken the American League stolen-bases mark in 1980 when he surpassed Ty Cobb's record of 96, set in 1915. Henderson finished the 1980 season with 100 stolen bases. In 1982 he completed the season with 130. The major league record for career stolen bases is held by Brock with 938.

4th Game—Milwaukee, Oct. 16

ST. LOUIS (N)

	AB	R	H	BI
Herr, 2b	4	0	0	2
Oberkfell, 3b	2	2	1	0
Tenace, ph	1	0	0	0
Hernandez, 1b	4	0	0	0
Hendrick, rf	4	0	1	1
Porter, c	3	0	1	0
L. Smith, lf	4	1	1	0
Iorg, dh	4	0	2	1
Green, pr	0	0	0	0
McGee, cf	4	1	1	0
O. Smith, ss	3	1	1	0
Total	33	5	8	4

MILWAUKEE (A)

	AB	R	H	BI
Molitor, 3b	4	1	0	0
Yount, ss	4	1	2	2
Cooper, 1b	4	1	2	1
Simmons, c	2	0	0	0
Thomas, cf	4	0	1	2
Oglivie, lf	3	1	1	0
Money, dh	4	2	2	0
Moore, rf	4	0	1	0
Gantner, 2b	4	1	1	1
Total	33	7	10	6

St. Louis	130	001	000	—	5
Milwaukee	000	010	60X	—	7

E—Gantner, Yount, LaPoint. DP—St. Louis 2; Milwaukee 2. LOB—St. Louis 6, Milwaukee 6. 2B—Oberkfell, Money, L. Smith, Iorg, Gantner, 3B—Oglivie. SB—McGee, Oberkfell. SF—Herr.

	IP	H	R	ER	BB	SO
St. Louis						
LaPoint	6⅔	7	4	1	1	3
Bair (L)	0	1	2	0	1	0
Kaat	0	1	1	0	1	0
Lahti	1⅓	1	0	0	1	0
Milwaukee						
Haas	5⅓	7	5	4	2	3
Slaton (W)	2	1	0	0	2	1
McClure	1⅔	0	0	0	0	2

WP—Hass, Kaat. Time of game—3:04. Attendance—56,560.

5th Game—Milwaukee, Oct. 17

ST. LOUIS (N)

	AB	R	H	BI
L. Smith, dh	5	0	2	0
Green, lf	5	2	2	0
Hernandez, 1b	4	1	3	2
Hendrick, rf	5	0	3	2
Porter, c	5	0	1	0
Ramsey, pr	0	0	0	0
McGee, cf	5	0	1	0
Oberkfell, 3b	4	0	3	0
Tenace, ph	1	0	0	0
Herr, 2b	4	0	0	0
O. Smith, ss	3	1	0	0
Total	41	4	15	4

MILWAUKEE (A)

	AB	R	H	BI
Molitor, 3b	4	1	1	1
Yount, ss	4	2	4	1
Cooper, 1b	4	0	1	1
Simmons, c	3	0	0	1
Oglivie, lf	4	1	2	0
Thomas, cf	4	0	0	0
Money, dh	3	1	0	0
Moore, rf	4	1	2	1
Gantner, 2b	4	0	1	1
Total	34	6	11	6

St. Louis	001	000	102	—	4
Milwaukee	101	010	12X	—	6

E—Forsch, Gantner, Herr. DP—St. Louis 2; Milwaukee. LOB—St. Louis 12, Milwaukee 7. 2B—Hernandez 2, Yount, Moore, Green. 3B—Green. HR—Yount. SB—L. Smith.

	IP	H	R	ER	BB	SO
St. Louis						
Forsch (L)	7	8	4	3	2	3
Sutter	1	3	2	2	1	2
Milwaukee						
Caldwell (W)	8⅓	14	4	4	2	3
McClure	⅔	1	0	0	0	1

Time of game—3:02. Attendance—56,562.

6th Game—St. Louis, Oct. 19

MILWAUKEE (A)

	AB	R	H	BI
Molitor, 3b	4	0	1	0
Yount, ss	4	0	0	0
Cooper, 1b	4	0	0	0
Simmons, c	2	0	0	0
Yost, c	0	0	0	0
Oglivie, lf	4	0	1	0
Thomas, cf	3	0	0	0
Edwards, cf	0	0	0	0
Money, dh	3	0	0	0
Moore, rf	3	0	1	0
Gantner, 2b	3	1	1	0
Total	30	1	4	0

ST. LOUIS (N)

	AB	R	H	BI
L. Smith, lf	3	1	1	0
Green, lf	1	1	0	0
Oberkfell, 3b	5	1	0	0
Hernandez, 1b	5	2	2	4
Hendrick, rf	5	2	2	1
Porter, c	4	1	1	2
Brummer, c	0	0	0	0
Iorg, dh	4	3	3	0
McGee, cf	4	1	1	1
Herr, 2b	3	1	2	2
O. Smith, ss	4	0	0	0
Total	38	13	12	10

Milwaukee	000	000	001	—	1
St. Louis	020	326	00X	—	13

E—Yount 2, Gantner 2, Oberkfell. DP—St. Louis 2. LOB—Milwaukee 4, St. Louis 3. 2B—Iorg 2, Herr, Gantner. 3B—Iorg. HR—Porter, Hernandez. SB—L. Smith. S—Herr.

	IP	H	R	ER	BB	SO
Milwaukee						
Sutton (L)	4⅓	7	7	5	0	2
Slaton	⅔	0	0	0	0	0
Medich	2	5	6	4	1	0
Bernard	1	0	0	0	0	1
St. Louis						
Stuper (W)	9	4	1	1	2	2

WP—Medich 2, Stuper. Balk—Sutton. Time of game—2:21. Attendance—53,723.

7th Game—St. Louis, Oct. 20

MILWAUKEE (A)

	AB	R	H	BI
Molitor, 3b	4	1	2	0
Yount, ss	4	0	1	0
Cooper, 1b	3	0	1	1
Simmons, c	4	0	0	0
Oglivie, lf	4	1	1	1
Thomas, cf	4	0	0	0
Howell, dh	3	0	0	0
Moore, rf	3	0	1	0
Gantner, 2b	3	1	1	0
Total	32	3	7	2

ST. LOUIS (N)

	AB	R	H	BI
L. Smith, lf	5	2	3	1
Oberkfell, 3b	3	0	0	0
Tenace, ph	0	0	0	0
Ramsey, 3b	1	1	0	0
Hernandez, 1b	3	1	2	2
Hendrick, rf	5	0	2	1
Porter, c	5	0	1	1
Iorg, dh	3	0	2	0
Green, ph	0	0	0	0
Brauen, dh	2	0	1	1
McGee, cf	5	1	1	0
Herr, 2b	3	0	1	0
O. Smith, ss	4	1	2	0
Total	39	6	15	6

Milwaukee	000	012	000	—	3
St. Louis	000	103	02X	—	6

E—Andujar. LOB—Milwaukee 3, St. Louis 13. 2B—Gantner, L. Smith 2. HR—Oglivie. SF—Cooper.

	IP	H	R	ER	BB	SO
Milwaukee						
Vuckovich	5⅓	10	3	3	2	3
McClure (L)	⅓	2	1	1	1	0
Haas	2	1	2	2	1	1
Caldwell	⅓	2	0	0	0	0
St. Louis						
Andujar (W)	7	7	3	2	0	1
Sutter	2	0	0	0	0	2

Time of game—2:50. Attendance—53,723.

HANDBALL

U.S.H.A. NATIONAL FOUR-WALL CHAMPIONS

Singles

1960	Jimmy Jacobs
1961	John Sloan
1962–63	Oscar Obert
1964–65	Jimmy Jacobs
1966–67	Paul Haber
1968	Simon (Stuffy) Singer
1969–71	Paul Haber
1972	Fred Lewis
1973	Terry Muck
1974	Fred Lewis
1975	Jay Bilyeu
1976	Vern Roberts, Jr.
1977	Naty Alvarado
1978	Fred Lewis
1979	Naty Alvarado
1980	Naty Alvarado
1981	Fred Lewis
1982	Naty Alvarado

Doubles

1960	Jimmy Jacobs-Dick Weisman
1961	John Sloan-Vic Hershkowitz
1962–63	Jimmy Jacobs-Marty Decatur
1964	John Sloan-Phil Elbert
1965	Jimmy Jacobs-Marty Decatur
1966	Pete Tyson-Bob Lindsay
1967–68	Jimmy Jacobs-Marty Decatur
1969	Lou Kramberg-Lou Russo
1970	Karl and Ruby Obert
1971	Ray Neveau-Simie Fein
1972	Kent Fusselman-Al Drews
1973–74	Ray Neveau-Simie Fein
1975	Marty Decatur-Steve Lott
1976	Gary Rohrer-Dan O'Connor
1977	Skip McDowell-Matt Kelly
1978	Stuffy Singer-Marty Decatur
1979	Stuffy Singer-Marty Decatur
1980	Skip McDowell-Harry Robertson
1981	Tom Kopatich-Jack Roberts
1982	Naty Alvarado-Vern Roberts

U.S. HANDBALL ASSOCIATION FOUR-WALL CHAMPIONS

(Tucson, Ariz., June 5–12, 1982)

Men's open singles—Naty Alvarado, Hesperia, Calif. (defeated Fred Lewis, Tucson, Ariz., 21–5, 21–9, in final)
Men's open doubles—Naty Alvarado and Vern Roberts, Chicago (defeated Jack Roberts and Tom Kopatich, Chicago, 21–10, 21–8, in final)
Women's open singles—Rosemary Bellini, New York (defeated Rossanna Ettinger, Long Beach, Calif., 21–12, 21–12, in final)
Women's doubles—Allison Roberts, Ohio, and Glorian Motal, Houston (defeated Rosemary Bellini, New York, and Sue Oakleaf, Texas, 13–21, 21–18, 11–2, in final)
23 and under singles—Alfonse Monreal, Texas (defeated Todd Worrell, Texas, 21–17, 21–14, in final)
35 and over singles—Larry Bookman, Colorado (defeated Larry Aguilar, California, 21–17, 21–12, in final)
40 and over singles—Pat Kirby, Tucson, Ariz. (defeated Ed Bellochio, Texas, 21–13, 21–6, in final)
40 and over doubles—Pat Kirby and Fred Munsch, New York, (defeated Jeff Capell and Joe McDonald, California, 21–14, 21–12, in final)

BADMINTON

WORLD CHAMPIONS—1982*

Men's singles—Rudy Hartono, Indonesia
Women's singles—Wiharjo Verawaty, Indonesia
Men's doubles—Ade Chandra and Christian Hadinata, Indonesia
Women's doubles—Nora Perry and Jane Webster, England
Mixed doubles—Christian Hadinata and Imelda Wigoeno, Indonesia

*World championships were not contested in 1981 and 1982. The 1983 championships are scheduled for May in Copenhagen, Denmark.

UNITED STATES CHAMPIONSHIPS

(Countryside, Ill., April 7–10, 1982)

Open

Men's singles—Gary Higgins, Alhambra, Calif.
Women's singles—Cheryl Carton, San Diego, Calif.
Men's doubles—Don Paup, Washington, D.C., and Bruce Pontow, Chicago
Women's doubles—Pam Brady, Flint, Mich., and Judianne Kelly, Costa Mesa, Calif.
Mixed doubles—Pam Brady and Danny Brady, Flint, Mich.

Seniors

(San Diego, Calif., Jan. 21–23, 1982)

Men's singles—Tom Carmichael, Ortonville, Mich.
Men's doubles—Tom Carmichael and Jim Poole, Westminster, Calif.
Women's doubles—Helen Tibbetts, Torrance, Calif., and Vicky Toutz, Las Alamitos, Calif.
Mixed doubles—Jim Poole and Vicky Toutz

Masters

Men's singles—Jim Bell, Ypsilanti, Mich.
Men's doubles—Tom Carmody, Freeport, La., and Dick Witte, St. Louis
Women's singles—Carlene Starkey, San Diego, Calif.
Women's doubles—Ruth Hoffman and Carlene Starkey, San Diego, Calif.
Mixed doubles—Bill Berry and Carlene Starkey, San Diego, Calif.

Grand Masters

Men's singles—Ed Phillips, Warwick, R.I.
Men's doubles—John Forsythe, Canada, and Tom Graham, Canada
Women's singles—Mary Ann Wolfe, Seattle, Wash.
Women's doubles—Dorothy Tinline, Canada, and Ruth Hoffman, San Diego
Mixed doubles—Ed Phillips and Ruth Hoffman

Juniors

Men's singles—Rodney Barton, Palo Alto, Calif.
Women's singles—Fran Hughes, Miller Place, N.Y.
Men's doubles—Rodney Barton and Marty French, Elmhurst, Ill.
Mixed doubles—Rodney Barton and Barb Morrison, DeKalb, Ill.

ALL-ENGLAND CHAMPIONSHIPS

(Wembley, England, March 20–23, 1982)

Men's singles—Morton Frost, Denmark
Women's singles—Zhang Ailing, China
Men's doubles—R. Sidek and J. Sidek, Malaysia
Women's doubles—Liu Ying and Wu Dixi, China
Mixed doubles—M. Dew and Gillian Gilks, England

BILLIARDS—1982

Men's world pocket billiards champion—Steve Mizerak, Fords, N.J.
Women's world pocket billiards champion—Jean Balukas, Brooklyn, N.Y.

COMPREHENSIVE INDEX

A

B

D

E

F

G

H

I

J

K

L

M

N

O

P

Q

R

S

T

U

V

W

X

Y

Z